Continued on back

HANDBOOK OF CLINICAL
CHILD PSYCHOLOGY

HANDBOOK OF CLINICAL CHILD PSYCHOLOGY

Editors

C. EUGENE WALKER
University of Oklahoma Medical School

MICHAEL C. ROBERTS
University of Alabama

A WILEY-INTERSCIENCE PUBLICATION

JOHN WILEY & SONS
New York   Chichester   Brisbane   Toronto   Singapore

Copyright © 1983 by John Wiley & Sons, Inc.

All rights reserved. Published simultaneously in Canada.

Reproduction or translation of any part of this work
beyond that permitted by Section 107 or 10% of the
1976 United States Copyright Act without the permission
of the copyright owner is unlawful. Requests for
permission or further information should be addressed to
the Permissions Department, John Wiley & Sons, Inc.

Library of Congress Cataloging in Publication Data:
Main entry under title:

Handbook of clinical child psychology.

(Wiley series on personality processes, ISSN 0195-
4008)
Includes index.
1. Clinical child psychology—Handbooks, manuals,
etc. 2. Child psychopathology—Handbooks, manuals, etc.
3. Child psychotherapy—Handbooks, manuals, etc.
I. Walker, C. Eugene (Clarence Eugene), 1939–
II. Roberts, Michael C. III. Series. [DNLM: 1. Child
psychology. WS 105 H2355]

RJ503.3.H36 1983   618.92'89   83-1386
ISBN 0-471-09036-0

Printed in the United States of America

10 9 8 7 6 5 4 3 2 1

This book is dedicated with admiration and affection to our parents Olga Thresa Brioli and Lewis G. Walker (C.E.W.); Winona Clark and J. Kent Roberts (M.C.R.).

Preface

The purpose of the present volume is to provide a text and reference work dealing in a comprehensive manner with the range of children's psychological problems that confront clinical child psychologists, pediatric psychologists, child psychiatrists, and other mental health professionals. The chapters in this volume have been prepared with a view toward active professionals charged with the care of children. Thus intervention and management have been emphasized. However, research in the relevant areas has not been slighted. In the majority of cases, the author of the chapter is both a scholar and a clinician in the area in question. The general format of each of the chapters is to provide the reader with a scholarly review of research in the area, followed by practical suggestions and advice for high quality clinical practice. The goal has been to bridge the gap between research and practice.

The order of the sections follows from the logical progression of providing a basic background in child development, through diagnosis and treatment, to consideration of more specific disorders and topics. This book is based on the concept that psychological disorders of childhood are best understood in the context of human development. Thus, the chapters in Section I provide a background for conceptualizing both normal and abnormal development in children and their families. Section II provides basic information for the application of a wide range of assessment procedures available to the child psychologist in his or her armamentarium.

Sections III, IV, and V are organized around the three general developmental stages of early life, childhood, and adolescence respectively. These sections examine in detail the particular disorders most commonly confronting the clinical child psychologist working with children of that age. Some of the chapters in these sections contain only information about the age group under discussion (e.g., "Clinical Problems of Birth, the Neonate, and Infant"). Others (e.g., "Psychosomatic Problems of Children") contain some references to such problems in older and/or younger groups but have been placed in the section where they reside because most of the *unique* information needed by the clinical child psychologist pertains to the age group under discussion. However, this unique body of information is placed in context with respect to other information for the other age groups.

Section VI elaborates intervention strategies generally used in clinical child practice. The coverage of these procedures is broad and reflects a wide variety of practices. Finally, Section VII, on special topics, is an attempt to reflect the more interesting and developing areas of clinical child psychology. Chapter topics were chosen to reflect the new and innovative issues of social, ethical, clinical, and practical importance to the child, family, and clinician.

The present volume is written on the level

of the advanced graduate student and professional. It is hoped that it will find use as a primary text for the clinical child and child practicum portions of training received by advanced graduate students. Additionally, it is hoped that it will prove useful as a reference for all clinical child psychologists as well as for related professionals dealing with children and families in a variety of settings (e.g., medicine, social work, education, nursing, and other areas). This compendium represents in wealth and diversity, the problems and excitement of research and practice in clinical child psychology.

C. EUGENE WALKER
MICHAEL C. ROBERTS

Oklahoma City, Oklahoma
University, Alabama
January 1983

Contents

Contributors

Lowell T. Anderson, Ph.D.
Associate Professor of Psychiatry
New York University Medical Center
New York, New York

Paul G. Banikiotes, Ph.D.
Vice President
ARD Corporation
Columbia, Maryland

Willis E. Bartlett, Ph.D.
Associate Professor
Psychology Department
University of Notre Dame
Notre Dame, Indiana

Joy Bengfort, B.A.
Graduate Student in Psychology
Texas Women's University
Denton, Texas

Stefanie F.A. Bergey, Ph.D.
Assistant Professor in Pediatrics
University of Maryland School of Medicine
Baltimore, Maryland

Teresa Bolick, Ph.D.
Assistant Professor
Department of Psychology
University of Kentucky
Lexington, Kentucky

Thomas J. Boll, Ph.D.
Professor of Psychology,
   Pediatrics and Neurological Surgery and
Director of the Medical Psychology Program
University of Alabama
University, Alabama

Magda Campbell, M.D.
Professor of Psychiatry
Director, Children's
   Psychopharmacology Unit
New York University Medical Center
New York, New York

Pamela Cantor, Ph.D.
Board of Directors for American
   Association of Suicidiology
Chestnut Hill, Massachusetts

Edward R. Christopherson, Ph.D.
Professor and Chief, Behavioral Sciences
Department of Pediatrics
College of Health Sciences and Hospital
The University of Kansas Medical Center
Kansas City, Kansas

Charles Carr Cleland, Ph.D.
Professor, Special Education and
   Educational Psychology
University of Texas at Austin
Austin, Texas

Geraldine Dawson, Ph.D.
Assistant Professor of Psychology
Department of Psychology
University of North Carolina
Chapel Hill, North Carolina

Stephen J. Dollinger, Ph.D.
Associate Professor
Clinical Center and Department
   of Psychology
Southern Illinois University at Carbondale
Carbondale, Illinois

Joseph A. Durlak, Ph.D.
Associate Professor
Loyola University in Chicago
Chicago, Illinois

Nancy S. Ehrenreich, LL.M.
Instructor of Law
University of Virginia School of Law
Charlottesville, Virginia

Michele Eliason, Ed.D.
Pediatric Psychologist
Department of Pediatrics
Division of Pediatric Psychology
The University of Iowa Hospitals and Clinics
Iowa City, Iowa

Pauline D. Elkins, M.A.
Graduate Student
Department of Psychology
University of Alabama
University, Alabama

Charles Elliott, Ph.D.
Director, Consultation-Liaison Division
Mental Health Services
Oklahoma Children's Memorial Hospital
and Assistant Professor
University of Oklahoma Health
   Sciences Center
Oklahoma City, Oklahoma

Sheila M. Eyberg, Ph.D.
Associate Professor
Department of Medical Psychology
Oregon Health Sciences University
Portland, Oregon

Eileen B. Fennell, Ph.D.
Assistant Professor
Department of Psychology
University of Florida
Gainesville, Florida

William W. Finley, Ph.D.
Research Psychologist & Director,
Department of Electrophysiological Studies
Children's Medical Center of Tulsa
Tulsa, Oklahoma

Donald K. Freedheim, Ph.D.
Associate Professor
Department of Psychology

Case Western Reserve University
Cleveland, Ohio

Jacqueline French, Ph.D.
Chief Psychologist, Riley Child Guidance
   Clinic Outpatient and Consultation
   Services
Indiana University School of Medicine
Indianapolis, Indiana

Kathleen M. Gerrity, Ph.D.
Assistant Professor
Department of Pediatrics
University of Oklahoma Health
   Sciences Center
Oklahoma City, Oklahoma

Betty N. Gordon, Ph.D.
Staff Psychologist
Division for Disorders of Development
   and Learning
Clinical Assistant Professor
Department of Psychiatry
University of North Carolina
Chapel Hill, North Carolina

Robert Gordon, J.D., Ph.D.
Forensic and Clinical Psychologist
Private Practice
Dallas, Texas

Sol Gordon, Ph.D.
Professor, Child and Family
   Study Department
Director, the Institute for Family Research
   and Education
Syracuse University
Syracuse, New York

Paula D. Graves, Ph.D.
Postdoctoral Child Fellow
Indiana University School of Medicine
Indianapolis, Indiana

Wayne H. Green, M.D.
Assistant Professor of Psychiatry
New York University Medical Center
New York, New York

Gerald E. Gruen, Ph.D.
Professor
Department of Psychological Sciences
Purdue University
West Lafayette, Indiana

Robert Habenstein, Ph.D.
Professor Emeritus
University of Missouri
Columbia, Missouri

Loretta Mason Haroian, Ph.D.
Dean of Professional Studies
Institute for Advanced Study of
 Human Sexuality
San Francisco, California

Barbara Hawk, M.S.
Research Associate
Biological Sciences Research Center
University of North Carolina
Chapel Hill, North Carolina

Deborah Young-Hyman, Ph.D.
Instructor in Pediatrics
University of Maryland School of Medicine
Baltimore, Maryland

Russell H. Jackson, Ph.D.
Associate Professor of Medical Psychology
Oregon Health Sciences University
Portland, Oregon

James H. Johnson, Ph.D.
Associate Professor
Department of Clinical Psychology
University of Florida
Gainesville, Florida

Robyn Ridley-Johnson, M.S.
Advanced Clinical Graduate Student
Department of Psychology
University of Missouri-Columbia
Columbia, Missouri

Freda A. Jones, Ph.D.
Associate Professor
Department of Pediatrics
University of Oklahoma Health
 Sciences Center
Oklahoma City, Oklahoma

Anthony P. Jurich, Ph.D.
Professor of Family and Child Development
Kansas State University
Manhatten, Kansas

Ruth Kanfer, Ph.D.
Post-Doctoral Fellow
Department of Psychology

University of Illinois
Champaign, Illinois

Thomas J. Kenny, Ph.D.
Director of Pediatric Psychology
Associate Professor
Department of Pediatrics
Walter P. Carter Center
University of Maryland School of Medicine
Baltimore, Maryland

Dean Kerasotes, Ph.D.
Post-Doctoral Fellow, Pediatric Psychology
Department of Psychiatry and
 Behavioral Sciences
University of Oklahoma Health Sciences
 Center
Oklahoma City, Oklahoma

H. Elizabeth King, Ph.D.
Clinical Associate Professor
Department of Psychiatry
Emory University School of Medicine
Tucker, Georgia

Carol P. Kleemeier, Ph.D.
Assistant Professor in Psychiatry
 (Psychology)
Emory University School of Medicine
Tucker, Georgia

Gerald P. Koocher, Ph.D.
Director of Training in Psychology
Children's Hospital Medical Center
Assistant Professor of Psychology
Harvard Medical School
Boston, Massachusetts

Gloria L. Krahn, Ph.D.
Resident in Medical Psychology
Department of Medical Psychology
Oregon Health Sciences University
Portland, Oregon

Ronald S. Krug, Ph.D.
Professor/Director of Undergraduate
 Education
Department of Psychiatry and Behavioral
 Sciences
University of Oklahoma Health
 Sciences Center
Oklahoma City, Oklahoma

Annette M. La Greca, Ph.D.
Associate Professor of Psychology and
   Pediatrics
Department of Psychology
University of Miami
Coral Gables, Florida

Benjamin B. Lahey, Ph.D.
Professor of Psychology
University of Georgia
Athens, Georgia

Julie Larrieu, M.S.
Graduate Student (Developmental
   Psychology)
Department of Psychological Sciences
Purdue University
West Lafayette, Indiana

Eugene E. Levitt, Ph.D.
Director, Section of Psychology
Indiana University School of Medicine
Indianapolis, Indiana

J. Michael Liebowitz, Ph.D.
Associate Director, Clinical Services
Meyer Children's Rehabilitation Institute
Omaha, Nebraska

Thomas R. Linscheid, Ph.D.
Associate Professor of Pediatric Division
Director of Psychology
Georgetown University
Child Development Center
Washington, D.C.

Robert D. Lyman, Ph.D.
Executive Director
Brewer Porch Children Center
Assistant Professor of Psychology
University of Alabama
University, Alabama

Phyllis R. Magrab, Ph.D.
Professor of Psychology
Director, Child Development Center
Georgetown University Hospital
Washington, D.C.

Janet R. Matthews, Ph.D.
Associate Professor of Psychology
Creighton University
Omaha, Nebraska

Lee H. Matthews, Ph.D.
Assistant Professor of Medical Psychology
University of Nebraska Medical Center
Omaha, Nebraska

Gary B. Melton, Ph.D.
Associate Professor of Psychology and
Director, Law/Psychology Program
Department of Psychology
University of Nebraska-Lincoln
Lincoln, Nebraska

Gary B. Mesibov, Ph.D.
Associate Professor of Psychiatry
Department of Psychiatry
University of North Carolina, School
   of Medicine
Chapel Hill, North Carolina

Lovick Miller, Ph.D.
Professor
Department of Psychiatry and Behavioral
   Science
University of Louisville
Louisville, Kentucky

Ronald Neeper, M.S.
Doctoral Candidate in Clinical Psychology
University of Georgia
Athens, Georgia

Cynthia A. Noble, M.A.
Doctoral Candidate
Department of Psychology
University of Oklahoma
Norman, Oklahoma

Stephen Nowicki, Jr., Ph.D.
Professor of Psychology
Emory University
Atlanta, Georgia

Roberta Olson, Ph.D.
Assistant Professor
Department of Psychiatry and Behavioral
   Sciences
Consultation-Liaison Division
University of Oklahoma Health
   Sciences Center
Oklahoma City, Oklahoma

William C. Orr, Ph.D.
Director, Sleep Disorders Center

Presbyterian Hospital
Oklahoma City, Oklahoma

Mickey S. Ozolins, M.Ed.
Staff Psychologist
Mental Health Services
Oklahoma Children's Memorial Hospital
Oklahoma City, Oklahoma

Richard Perry, M.D.
Clinical Assistant Professor of Psychiatry
New York University Medical Center
New York, New York

Lizette Peterson, Ph.D.
Assistant Professor
Department of Psychology
University of Missouri-Columbia
Columbia, Missouri

Beeman N. Phillips, Ed.D.
Professor/Educational Psychology
Director, School Psychology
  (doctoral) Program
Department of Educational Psychology
University of Texas
Austin, Texas

William A. Rae, Ph.D.
Assistant Professor
Department of Psychiatry of Behavioral
  Sciences and Department of Pediatrics
Texas A & M University
College of Medicine and Scott and
  White Clinic
Temple, Texas

Michael A. Rapoff, Ph.D.
Clinical Instructor, Department of Pediatrics
University of Kansas Medical Center
Kansas City, Kansas

George A. Rekers, Ph.D.
Professor of Family and Child Development
Kansas State University
Manhattan, Kansas

Lynn C. Richman, Ph.D.
Associate Professor
Department of Pediatrics
Division of Pediatric Psychology
The University of Iowa Hospitals and Clinics
Iowa City, Iowa

Henry C. Rickard, Ph.D.
Department of Psychology
University of Alabama
University, Alabama

Sandra R. Russ, Ph.D.
Assistant Professor
Department of Psychology
Case Western Reserve University
Cleveland, Ohio

Jerome M. Sattler, Ph.D.
Professor of Psychology
Department of Psychology
San Diego State University
San Diego, California

Carolyn S. Schroeder, Ph.D.
Biological Sciences Research Center
University of North Carolina
Chapel Hill, North Carolina

Patricia A. Self, Ph.D.
Director/Associate Professor
School of Human Development
University of Oklahoma
Norman, Oklahoma

William James Shaw, Psy.D.
Assistant Professor
Psychology and Behavior Sciences
Clinical Assistant Professor of Pediatrics
University of Oklahoma Health Sciences
  Center
Division of Adolescent Medicine
Oklahoma City, Oklahoma

Peter L. Sheras, Ph.D.
Associate Professor of Education and
Associate Professor of the Institute of
  Clinical Psychology
University of Virginia
Charlottesville, Virginia

Jeffrey Siegel, Ph.D.
Forensic and Clinical Psychologist
Private Practice
Dallas, Texas

Lawrence J. Siegel, Ph.D.
J. Hillis Miller Health Center
University of Florida
Gainesville, Florida

Rune J. Simeonsson, Ph.D.
Frank Porter Graham Child Development
    Center
University of North Carolina
Chapel Hill, North Carolina

Diana Sims, M.Ed.
Research Assistant
Psychiatry and Behavioral Sciences
University of Oklahoma Health Sciences
    Center
Oklahoma City, Oklahoma

Susan Untener Snyder, M.A.
Graduate Assistant
Child and Family Study Department
The Institute for Family Research
    and Education
Syracuse University
Syracuse, New York

Anita Miller Sostek, Ph.D.
Assistant Professor
Georgetown University Hospital
Washington, D.C.

Elton Stetson, Ph.D.
Assistant Professor
Department of Curriculum and Instruction
College of Education
University of Houston
Houston, Texas

Theodore D. Wachs, Ph.D.
Professor
Department of Psychological Sciences
Purdue University
West Lafayette, Indiana

Alexis J. Walker, Ph.D.
Assistant Professor Home Economics
School of Human Development
University of Oklahoma
Norman, Oklahoma

C. Eugene Walker, Ph.D.
Professor and Director of Pediatric
    Psychology
University of Oklahoma Medical School
Oklahoma City, Oklahoma

J. Catesby Ware, Ph.D.
Director, Sleep Disorders Center
San Antonio, Texas

Alan S. Weiner, Ph.D.
Department of Psychiatry
The New York Hospital—
    Cornell Medical Center
Westchester Division
White Plains, New York

Paul Weisberg, Ph.D.
Professor of Psychology and Director
Early Childhood Day Care Center
University of Alabama
University, Alabama

Gertrude J. Rubin Williams, Ph.D.,
Private Practice
St. Louis, Missouri

David R. Wilson, Ph.D.
Coordinator of Psychological Services
    and Research and Evaluation
Brewer-Porch Children's Center
University of Alabama
University, Alabama

Jeffrey Zimmerman, Ph.D.
Assistant Professor
Department of Psychiatry and Behavioral
    Sciences
University of Oklahoma Health
    Sciences Center
Oklahoma City, Oklahoma

SECTION ONE
Child Development

CHAPTER 1

Families and Children in History

ROBERTA OLSON AND ROBERT HABENSTEIN

The American family has experienced profound changes in both structure and function during the past three centuries. Throughout history, the family has changed in response to changes in society, and, in turn, has influenced society's perceptions of and demands upon the family. The unique role of the family as a social unit results from many factors. The modern family evolved from earlier forms of the family developed under previous economic and social conditions. The existing social and economic conditions and the prevailing culture and evolving ideology also influence the family continuously (Burgess, 1948). In American society today, there are many different types of families (Mindel & Habenstein, 1981). Families differ in geographic location, ethnic norms, religious orientation, economic status, vocational skills, and social class. Moreover, family structures vary greatly in size, lines of authority, degree of inclusion of extended kin, roles of family members, childrearing techniques, and lifestyle. The traditional family unit provides its members with economic status, religious orientation, educational level, sense of identity, and affectional bonds. Although American families are quite diverse, it is still possible to examine the concept of the family and to explore the distinctive characteristics of American families to gain an understanding of how general patterns of family functions and structures have emerged and changed since the early days of the American colonies.

This chapter will first trace major changes in the structure and function of the American family during the past three centuries and discuss the effects of these changes on the family unit and the changing concepts of children. The second section of the chapter will examine the effects on the family of rapid changes in American society during the past 25 years and the assumption that family isolation and mobility have led to increased child abuse and child neglect, higher divorce rates, and childhood pathology. The final section will examine possible types of future family organizations and their probable effects on the family unit. Before considering colonial families, let us look briefly to their European roots.

European Families

The origins of family ideology and institutional practice stretch back to the ancient Greek, Roman, and Judeo-Christian cultures with their systems of patrilineage, patriarchy, extended kinship, and other forms of affiliative bonds. Father-centered families have dominated Western society for several thousand years. The paterfamilias of the ancient Romans stands as an extreme example of authority vested in the male parent. While the role of the father as absolute head of the family is no longer prevalent in American society, it is still a recognizable cultural model among many ethnic groups (Mindel & Habenstein, 1981).

A pervasive, counterbalancing alternative to the ancient patriarchal, patrilineal family has always existed but has received little historical attention. Trumbach, in his comprehensive and anthropologically sophisticated

3

The Rise of the Egalitarian Family (1978), has delineated a constant, dialectical opposition in Western society between the *patriarchal* and *kindred* forms of kinship and family organization. In Western societies, writes Trumbach:

The patriarchal household was one of ancient provenance. It was enshrined in the Odyssey and in the law codes of Exodus and Deuteronomy. Its basic presumption was that at the head of each household stood a man who in his role as master, father, and husband owned his wife, his children, his slaves, his animals, and his land. The authority of master over his household was the model for all dependent relationships, including that of king and subject. (p. 3)

In contrast to the system of patrilineage, particularly but not exclusively, barbarian peoples associated with the "Dark Ages" organized their relations into systems of cognatic kindred:

Each individual...stood at the center of a unique circle of kinsmen connected to him through both mother and father and through his spouse. Inheritances were equally divided among all children; the position of women with regard to property and divorce was relatively high; and friendship was a stronger bond than kinship. (p. 14)

Through the later centuries of feudalism, the kindred form of family structure declined and was gradually eclipsed by a growth in the ideal of continuity in family lines and the transfer of property through patrilineal inheritance. Primogeniture and other special rights accorded to the eldest son, the loss of property rights of women, and the turn to paternal relatives instead of friends relegated kindreds to a secondary status (Trumbach, 1978).

However, as feudalism gave way to mercantilism, colonization, urbanization, and neoindustrialism, the system of kindred organization with its nonpatriarchal mode of kinship reckoning reemerged in European society. Consequently, today both the mother's and the father's family line is recognized. However, the patronymic (the naming of children through the father's line) remains established

for all but the very rich and aristocratic and, since the mid-eighteenth century, family and kinship organization has been oriented more toward males than females. The alternation between kindred and patrilineal family structures, as Trumbach (1978) notes, remains part of the social dynamics of traditional European society.

Whichever family system was currently dominant, it did not operate to the exclusion of the other. Nor did these opposing forms exist in a social vacuum. The simplicity of a patriarchal, patrilineal, primogeniture system of relations and affiliation, which operated to keep property and blood lines intact, commended it to property-based and agricultural pursuits because it could easily become a building block in larger forms of kinship organization such as sibs, clans, and even larger societal divisions.

Kindreds, however, were idiosyncratic and difficult to weld into systems of social organization. They began with individuals, not classes of individuals, and consequently each person had his or her unique constellation of kindred. Roughly stated, the principle of kindreds was "to each his own."

Whether the dominant family form of the times was patriarchal or kindred, the ideal of the large household prevailed from ancient to relatively recent times. It is hardly necessary to point out that some modern religious and ethnic groups still hold tenaciously to the ideal of a large family. Large households might contain not only many children but also servants, boarders, children from other primary relatives, and members of elder generations. The large household could thus function as an economic and protective unit with a ramified division of labor and the potential for survival in troubled and perilous times. The extended family was thus a microcosm of the larger society.

Within the large households (and among them when they were physically close), kinship bonds extended between and across generations. For example, the mother's sister would be available to take charge of the family during the birth of children or during periods of family crisis such as sickness or separation.

The maternal aunt has always been a favorite category of kin in Western society. The father's brother, by the same token, could assist in matters of authority and discipline. Parental siblings have played various roles in the family throughout history, but their role has always been important. The same is true of grandparents.

While the ideal of large kindreds and households was often approximated, these larger family units always contained a nucleus of husband, wife, and children. This nucleus, when shorn of other kin to form a distinct family unit, has come to be known as the "nuclear" family. The concept of the nuclear family has caused considerable confusion and argument among those who study the family. Nevertheless, in Western society, this small, tightly knit nucleus of husband, wife, and children has always existed within any larger family unity. The larger family unity, with its variety of ascending or cross-generational relatives operating under a set of unifying rules and expectations, has come to be called the "extended" family.

Family researchers and scholars have failed to recognize the enduring historical character of the nuclear family. Instead, they have argued that the nuclear family is a product and foundation of capitalism and the Protestant ethic. Without elaboration, a strong argument can be made that capitalism and Protestantism, in conjunction with the Industrial Revolution of late eighteenth- and early nineteenth-century industrialism did not "produce" the nuclear family. On the other hand, it can also be reasonably argued that these major social institutions (and others) have to some degree changed the size and functions of the European and, later, the American family.

Max Weber (1958), for example, contends that the nuclear family originated in the decline of Catholicism and the influences of the Protestant Reformation. The change from a primary focus on religion and the rewards to be gained in heaven to a focus on the earthly rewards of economic gain in the present world profoundly affected the family. The Protestant ethic stressed the need for stronger personal and societal concentration of thought and energy on economic production and consumption. Action in the service of the Lord would replace contemplation. Initially, this change of focus reduced the power of the Church to dictate the actions of family members in their daily lives. Patriarchal power and the importance of family lineage were reduced by the desire for individual achievement. Also important were the mass emigrations to the New World and the later movement westward.

Another argument comes from Shorter (1975), who has suggested that the striving for personal gain and emotional satisfaction which increased during the Industrial Revolution eventually led to the active pursuit of individual gain and reduced the influence of extended kin on the nuclear family.

HISTORY OF THE AMERICAN FAMILY

The history of the American family can best be traced through the changes in structure and function that the family unit underwent from the period of colonization through the later westward movement, industrialization, and urbanization. During each of these periods, the family changed and adapted to the demands of society (Ogburn, 1953). At the same time, to a lesser extent, the family contributed to changes in society as a whole (Parsons, 1949; Sennett, 1970). Society's conception of the proper family structure and function can be seen clearly in the type of childrearing practices advocated during each period. Childrearing literature provides an insight into the qualities considered desirable in children and the ways in which society socialized children during a specific period.

Colonial Families: New England (1620–1780)

During the colonial period, the ideal family unit would have provided the setting for economic, educational, social, recreational, and religious functions (Ogburn, 1953). Most early settlers in the New World were either members of nuclear families or single males. However, a resemblance to the nuclear family structure then and now does not necessarily imply an identification with its values or functions (Albin & Cavallo, 1981). Although most grandparents and older parents did not travel to the New World during its early stages of settlement, the ideal of the extended family was not forgotten. This was true even though the forces for disorder and declension in England, particularly in rural areas in the seventeenth century, along with the beginnings of an urbanization that would transfer attention away from land ownership and toward the production and marketing of industrial goods, disrupted the traditional patriarchal extended family organization (Greven, 1970).

Early colonists did not necessarily come from extended families. Even those who did found it difficult to transport such families intact to the New World. If the extended family ideal included cousins, aunts, uncles, affinals, and older generations, such an assemblage would almost never be found living under one roof in colonial New England (Demos, 1970). However, a number of close relatives, including married children, might live very near each other. Usually a male colonist would acquire a modest holding and, with his wife and children, develop it. The typical colonial home was neither large nor small, but it was not designed to accommodate a large household with many kin (Demos, 1970).

The husband/father would assume a patriarchal role, but kindred, including close and supportive friends, were not forgotten. Male children grew up with the expectation that they would some day acquire the entire family homestead or would receive part of the original holding upon which to settle and start a new homestead. In earlier colonial New England, family structure was not clear cut; it incorporated, in order of importance, patriarchal authority, utilization of both family lines to aid in surviving the hardships of settling, friendships, indentured servants, other primary and nonprimary relatives, primogeniture, and the settling of grown children on nearby family land. Generally, families were large only to the extent that there were many children born into them who survived. Through generations the nuclear family thus remained dominant but was both buttressed and intruded upon by close kin living nearby.

The utility of the large family to rural agricultural pursuits is obvious. The many tasks required in farming can be accomplished through a division of labor with important roles for all members regardless of age or sex. But the physical environment adds a limiting factor. Goldschmidt (1976) points out that the New England colonists in their farming developed a Northern tradition

adapted to the relatively hilly lands of the North; the land was held by the farmer himself who was independent in his operation.... Hard work, ingenuity, and independence were critical features of the morality that developed in this area, a pattern we have come to know as the "Protestant Ethic." (Weber, 1958, p. 4)

Incorporated into the new ethic was a dour and somewhat anxiety-ridden religious ideology called Puritanism that emphasized hard work, prudence, avoidance of ritual and display, rigorous caste lines, and repression of emotional display.

The Puritan religion considered the birth of children to be a "divine obligation" (Bell, 1971), but children were also considered to be an economic asset. The typical family of the 1790s had eight children (Kephart, 1977). In both the isolated southern farms and the small New England colonies, large families were able to function as quasi-independent economic units. Children provided economic services for the family by helping to build the family home, farming the land, learning the family trade, and making and storing the food. The struggle for existence in early colonial days did not allow for an extended childhood at home.

Play and amusement were considered sinful pursuits; education in the home often began at 3 or 4 years of age (Calhoun, 1960). Children's books usually consisted of Bible stories or verses such as "The Prodigal Daughter" or "The Disobedient Lady Reclaimed." By 1649, some degree of classroom education was required for boys in every New England colony except for Rhode Island. Schools of this period, in session seven or eight hours a day, were equally strict in discipline and in their reliance on religious psalms and scriptures as major teaching tools. Basic knowledge such as reading and mathematics was supplemented by the teaching of a practical skill. Boys were taught farming or were trained in their father's trade. Girls were taught domestic skills.

Religious teaching and worship were home centered. The early Puritan ideology emphasized the role of the family as guardian of the public as well as the private good (Shorter, 1975). Not only did religion specify the approved relationships among family members and their duties and responsibilities to each other, but it also made it a sacred duty of the patriarch to see that the edicts of the church were carried out in the home and community (Calhoun, 1917).

The patriarch was responsible for reading daily scriptures in the home and modeling the ethical and moral standards of the community. He was responsible for setting and enforcing the religious and ethical standards of all family members. The patriarch's role of supreme authority in the home was sanctioned and encouraged by the Church (Goodsell, 1934). As the Puritan religion waned in favor of less restrictive religious practices, the Church's support of patriarchal dominance lessened.

Childrearing

The structure of the family and childrearing practices during the colonial period were influenced by Puritan society's view of children. Obedience to parents, the importance of work, the evils of idleness, and strict adherence to church doctrine were stressed. The father, as the sole guardian of his family, determined the education, religious training, work apprenticeship, distribution of land, and marriage of his children. Children were viewed as easy prey for the devil. Idleness and play were the "devil's playground." The Puritans viewed children as basically depraved and this perception made it necessary to seek infantile conversions. Children were confronted from their earliest years with the terrors of hell,

which they could escape only by following what they were taught and avoiding all pleasures of childhood (Calhoun, 1917). Strict discipline and the use of corporal punishment to "break the child's will" were encouraged (Miller & Swanson, 1958). John Robinson, a Pilgrim teacher, advised parents:

Surely, there is in all children (though not alike) a stubberness and stoutness of mind arising from naturall pride which must in the first place be broken and beaten down that so the foundations of their education being layd in humilitie and tractableness other virtues may in their time be build theron. (quoted in Earle, 1895, p. 192)

Children had no legal rights and parents had almost unlimited authority in childrearing and discipline. Children were expected to obey their parents without question. A book of etiquette for children entitled *A Pretty Little Pocket Book* instructed children never to speak unless spoken to, never to sit at the dinner table until grace had been spoken, and never to dispute with parents or other adults (Goodsell, 1934). Parents had the legal right to punish children severely. Massachusetts and Connecticut had laws that permitted the killing of an "unrully child." The Piscataqua colony passed a law stating, "if any child or children above 16 years of competent understanding, shall curse or smite their natural father or mother, he or they shall be put to death unless it can be sufficiently testified that the parents have been unchristianly negligent of the education of such child" (Calhoun, 1960, p. 120). Although no record exists of such punishment actually being carried out, parents did use beatings and denial of food as punishment for acts of disobedience (Bell, 1971).

During the colonial period, marriage was considered by the Puritans to be both a spiritual and contractual union. The patriarch of the family arranged the marriages of his children, although the daughter did have the right to refuse the marital agreement. Consensus for marriage was based primarily on the financial ability of the man to support his wife. Love, attraction, and affection were not

considered adequate reasons for the arrangement of a marriage.

During the period from colonization to
after the American Revolution, the importance of the extended family network increased. The nuclear family of the early colonial days was to some extent replaced or
strongly reinforced by the extended family kin
network. The extended family provided a
strong patriarchal system that encouraged
stability, financial interdependence, and the
importance of family lineage (Leslie, 1976;
Winch, 1952). The status of the extended
family stemmed from its land holdings or
family enterprise. Membership in a family
traditionally defined each member's place in
the community. Family membership also defined how far the child would go in school,
what trade he or she would learn, whom the
child could marry, and where the child would
live.

Colonial Family: Southern
Plantation (1620–1780)

Before dealing with the movement west, it is
necessary to add a few paragraphs on the
structure and function of the colonial family
of the South. Again physical environment was
a major factor in the development during that
time of a family type quite different from that
of New England. Goldschmidt (1976) has
sketched the parameters of the Southern
plantation tradition, but Queen and Habenstein (1974) have described the Southern
colonial household in some detail:

There were many Cavaliers and few Puritans.
Many of the earliest settlers were detached males
seeking their fortunes instead of families seeking
homes. There was marked stratification which
involved social distance between first families,
yeomen, a pioneer fringe of poor whites, indentured servants, and Negro slaves. Gradually there
was built up a social system reminiscent of feudalism and chivalry, though actually very different
from anything ever developed in Europe. (p. 315)

On the large plantations each household
was a relatively self-sufficient group that
produced a large part of its own food, cloth-

ing, and other necessities, erected buildings,
made tools, trained its children, cared for its
sick, dispensed homemade justice, and provided amusement. Southern households were
often much larger and more isolated than
those of New England (Queen & Habenstein,
1974).

Women, who through chivalry were put on
a pedestal, nevertheless usually occupied an
inferior social position. Through the years
primogeniture had come to prevail, and females were limited in inheritance of land and
property. The eldest son would almost always
inherit the manor house and principal lands.
Thus lands were kept in the same male line for
many generations (Queen & Habenstein,
1974). The *Virginia Gazette* in 1737 advised
women for the "advancement of matrimonial
felicity" never to dispute with their husbands
under any circumstances. Generally it was
believed that the husband should guide, defend, and provide for the wife, while she was
expected to serve him in subjection, be modest
in speech and dress, and be a good housewife.
It was held that "while marriage was for man a
pleasant duty, it was woman's reason for
existence" (Spruill, 1938, p. 318). Women
were expected to be chaste before marriage
and observe marital fidelity afterwards. Males
were relatively free to exploit both black and
white females sexually.

As in New England, marital selection involved both romantic and practical considerations. Both men and women married at an
early age. Courtship with parental consent
preceded marriage, but considerations of economic and social status were more important
than romantic love as ·the chief bases for
marriage (Queen & Habenstein, 1974).

Childrearing

Children in the southern colonies grew up
under varying circumstances, depending on
the social class into which they were born
(Morgan, 1952). The children of the well-to-
do enjoyed comforts provided by nurses,
tutors, and governesses; farmers' children
were cared for chiefly by their own mothers,
but very early they began to assume responsibilities and to share the work of house, barn,

and field. Finally, children of indentured servants and slaves received haphazard attention and were soon incorporated into the work force (Queen & Habenstein, 1974).

Birth and death rates were both consistently high. Formal education for children who survived, with the exception of those in upper classes, was limited. There were far fewer schools in the South than in New England, and it is said that only three white men out of five could spell their own names (Morgan, 1952). Again, in matters of religion, the New England family was more active than the Southern. But in both the North and South, marriages were encouraged or almost demanded of single persons, and the expectation of a large family was universal in all the colonies. The affectional function would be underplayed publicly, whether involving children, juveniles, or adults. Queen and Habenstein summarize:

In general it is correct to say that the [colonial] family was a much more important *institution* in colonial times than today. Its functions were much more inclusive, almost everyone was a member of some family group, and there were fewer agencies to threaten the family's hold on its members. (p. 327)

Movement West: 1780–1880

The mass movement of the population westward across the Appalachian mountains to the Mississippi and later to the Pacific Ocean created a major shift in the function and structure of the family. Again, nuclear families and single men moved while the elderly were left behind. Migration created major structural changes in the family system. Throughout history, patriarchal societies are associated with nonmobile extended family units and usually with large households. As young families broke economic and sentimental ties to their parental families, patriarchal control declined.

Children growing up on the frontier never experienced the direct authority of a grandparent and therefore did not learn to expect great control over their own grandchildren. The father continued to be the final authority

in the frontier family, but the isolation of the family and the struggle for survival led to the wife's sharing more of the responsibility and authority in the family. This relationship led to an increased democratization of the family. Changes were made in the laws of inheritance of land and transmission of the family business. No longer were the family lands held intact for future generations. When young adults left the families of the east coast, the landholdings to which extended and nuclear patriarchal families traditionally had been tied were often sold. The democratic ideology of the new nation demanded an equal distribution of the land among all children, including the females. The loss of patriarchal power and the break-up of family land holdings led to basic changes in the family structure. Family functions also changed, and family status no longer defined the economic, educational, or social limits of the children. Young adults were less restricted in their choice of education, schooling, trade, landholdings, or marriage. Marriages were no longer arranged by the fathers, although parental approval of a fiancee's economic abilities might still be a major factor in a marriage. The patriarchal family embedded in a cluster of extended kin living neolocally changed and in its place emerged a conjugal family system without strong tradition or economic and sentimental ties to the extended kin. Kin were not abandoned, but they were often left behind.

Although the westward movement of young families created a period of loss of kinship and extended family networks, the following generations of pioneers often settled down in small agricultural communities to create a new, perhaps modified, extended kinship network. The new network of kin functioned primarily as a support system. The tradition of powerful patriarchal dominance did not exist even though the patriarchal role might have had strong appeal to males. Another consequence of the pioneer movement westward was the loss of formal education in schools and a return to education in the family homes. The education of children continued to be in the home or in small schools over which parents retained considerable control.

The religious practices also remained in the home or small community church.

Childrearing

Relatively few books on childrearing were written before 1825. Most books advising parents about childrearing were written in England (Seymour, 1754; Appleton, 1821). Apparently little advice about toilet training, thumbsucking, or behavior problems was discussed. Instead, these books contained numerous "moral homilies" (Demos & Demos, 1969) that provided little concrete advice to parents about childrearing problems.

The movement westward did change childrearing practices. There was a decline in the practice of "breaking the child's will" (Miller & Swanson, 1958). Use of corporal punishment began to lessen. Etiquette on the frontier changed; children no longer stood during meals; they talked more freely with parents and had more freedom to express their opinions. In general, arbitrary patriarchal or parental authority diminished. Children were expected to be working members of the family. Work and home life were one and the same. Adolescence was not a unique stage of development during this period. Young adults contributed to the family work. When they married, the new couple usually moved onto land of their own or onto a nearby piece of parental land. With the loss of patriarchal authority and the emergence of the conjugal, more democratic families, independence and self-reliance were most often stressed as important qualities to instill in children on the frontier.

Industrial Revolution (Nineteenth Century)

One of the most dramatic changes in the American family's structure and function occurred during the Industrial Revolution. Prior to the 1800s, the largest "immigration" was 10–20 million black slaves primarily in the Southern states. The ethnic composition of the immigrants changed after 1882, as did the character of the country's economy. The great influx of Southern, Eastern, and Central European immigrants, mostly of peasant stock, coincided with the rapid surge of industrial and urban growth in America. No longer needed to build the railroads or settle the virgin land of the Western states, the new arrivals—Bohemians, Slovaks, Poles, Russians and Russian/Polish Jews, Czechs, and Italians—were directed to the factories and sweatshops of America's slum-ridden cities (Feldstein & Costello, 1974). This large population influx into the cities of America created one of the most dramatic periods of change in the society as well as the family.

Prior to the early 1800s, the economy was primarily agricultural. The agricultural family was a fairly self-sufficient unit. The development of an industrial society dramatically altered many of the traditional family functions. Production of goods and services, for example, was removed from the home. Children no longer participated in the family economy of farming or a family trade. Business and industry became structural units outside the home. There was a continual reduction in homemaking activities. The home became increasingly separate from the workplace. Movement to the cities created a family in which children, for the first time, became an economic liability instead of an asset. Many children did not have a significant economic function within the family. Poor children working in the factories provided some economic contribution to the family, but their work was often separated from the previous family work system. A new extension of the kindred principle appeared for the first time when children and adolescents had the opportunity to form numerous contacts with other children their age. This was the beginning of age separate functions for adolescents.

The protective functions of the agricultural family included the promise of economic security from childhood to old age. Movement to the cities again was a movement of the young or the nuclear families; the older generations were usually left behind. The industrialization of the country lessened the protective functions of the family, and the movement of nuclear families to the cities lessened the responsibility and commitment to care for previous generations.

The religious functions of the family during the period of industrialization also witnessed a shift in emphasis. Religious dicta of the agricultural family stressed the family as a religious unit with the father as the head of the family. The family was primarily responsible for the ethical standards of its members. Family prayers and Bible readings were common customs. The advent of the movement to the cities reduced the family's religious functions as large churches and Sunday schools began to assume primary responsibility for religious training of the children and the setting of ethical standards for the community.

This period of rapid change affected the status-conferring functions of the family. In an agricultural community the family directly participated in defining each member's role in the community. Boys usually followed in their father's occupational footsteps, and girls were expected to become housewives and mothers. Children grew up and usually married within their social class; often they stayed within the same town as their parents. Industrialization changed the traditions of the family and the family's ability to define the child's occupation within the community. Industrialization not only brought young adults to urban areas but offered them the opportunity to "further or better their parents' place in society" (Mead, 1976). Worth began to be defined in terms of the amount of money a person made.

Women, for the first time, entered the marketplace in large numbers. The previous roles of mother or housewife were expanded. The added cost of child care and the crowding of families into tenement houses created conditions in which the limiting of the number of children in a family was desirable. Women gained the right to own their own property and to enter into contracts. Unmarried women were now able to leave home and live independently. As noted previously, Shorter (1975) has suggested that the most dramatic changes in the family had their seeds in the period of industrialization and the emergence of capitalism. Previously, unmarried women

stayed in the family home and were able to move out only at the time of marriage. Now, the ability to obtain a job for the first time freed women from the family and allowed them an increased opportunity to choose a marriage partner on the basis of emotional needs instead of financial ability (Shorter, 1975). Shorter further suggests that the shift from economical to emotional needs as a basis for marriage initially led to the decrease in extended kinship control and eventually to the increases in the divorce rate of the twentieth century.

The increased wealth of families, accompanied by improved health care, allowed more children to live and allowed mothers to spend more time in childrearing and building emotional attachments to children within the family. The strengthened attachment of mother and child led to an increased sense of nuclear family solidarity and the beginning withdrawal of the family unit from the community.

Education prior to industrialization took place in the home or small school. The advent of large urban areas created two major changes. First, children of lower income families were often forced to work in factories. Previously these children had learned a trade within the family or worked the family farm. Now children from poor families were separated from family production and interaction with other family members. Second, public education in large cities further diluted parental involvement in the teaching of their children. This function was increasingly assumed by state and federal government agencies.

Childrearing

During the industrial revolution, childhood and later adolescence began to be viewed as distinctly different periods of development. Children were, for the first time, no longer considered to be miniature adults. Demos and Demos (1969) identify the early industrial period as the beginning of the "child centered families." After 1825, childrearing books by American authors began to appear and many sold thousands of copies. Magazines such as *Mother's Magazine* and *Mother's Assistant* were specifically addressed to child care and childrearing issues (Demos & Demos, 1969). The popularity of these magazines and books indicated society's increased interest in the child and recognition of the importance of child rearing. Changes in the family structure during the nineteenth century were met with considerable anxiety about the quality of American family life (Wishy, 1968). Child-rearing books stressed the importance of parental authority, the need for strict discipline in early childhood, and the maintenance of this authority throughout the formative years. As late as mid-century Bulkeley (1858) advised parents that even the smallest infant reveals a "willfullness that springs from a depraved nature and is intensely selfish." Parents were warned that if strict discipline was not instituted and maintained the child would quickly become uncontrollable and would suffer permanent damage. The author appeared to believe that parents were rapidly losing all control and authority over their children and predicted dire consequences if this trend continued. Parents were strongly advised not to "show off" their children to guests because this would create a conceited and selfish child (Child, 1835).

The concept of adolescence began to emerge during this period. The separation of generations, as seen in the "new custom" of holding parties exclusively for young people, was viewed as an alarming development that would endanger the unity of the family if it were to continue (Child, 1835). By 1900, writings on youth gangs, juvenile delinquency, and vocational guidance indicated that society was beginning to recognize and attempt to deal with adolescence as a special period of child development (Demos & Demos, 1969). G. Stanley Hall, a leader in the child study movement in the late nineteenth century, was the first to write about adolescence as a separate stage of child development. Hall (1882) published a paper entitled "The Moral and Religious Training of Children" and later *Adolescence: Its Psychology, and its Relations to Physiology, Anthropology, Sociology, Sex, Crime, Religion, and Education* (1904). These works were the first to describe

the "storm and stress" of adolescence. Hall's theory postulated that each individual "lives through each of the major steps in the evolution of the race as a whole." Adolescence was viewed as a time of great change and confusion. Hall's writings had a profound effect on psychology (Angell, 1904), education (Betts, 1906), childrearing (McKeever, 1913), child labor laws, vocational guidance (Mangold, 1910), and religious training. Adolescence as a separate stage of development was accepted, and the rudimentary beginnings of a youth culture were beginning to be recognized. After 1925, Hall's theories of adolescence were discarded. Thorndike (1908), Judd (1915), King (1903), and Mead (1928) claimed that Hall's theories were too tied to set stages, overemphasized physiological functions, and ignored cultural determinants. Nevertheless, adolescence continued to be recognized and studied as a stage in child development.

Childrearing: Early Twentieth Century

Perhaps a milestone in the changing attitude toward child care occurred in 1914 when the federal government first published *Infant Care,* a booklet on childrearing for parents. This booklet has been repeatedly revised over the years and provides an interesting indication of the changes in childrearing from 1914 to the present. From 1914 to 1921, parents were warned of the great potential harm in allowing children to act on their autoerotic impulses. Thumbsucking and masturbation were to be promptly and rigorously stopped; otherwise, it was suggested, these behaviors would "grow" beyond control and permanently damage the child. The child was to be bound both hand and foot while in the crib so that he or she would not be able to thumbsuck, masturbate, or rub his or her thighs together.

During the period from 1929 to 1938 there was a shift in emphasis. Autoeroticism was considered less a problem. Regularity in daily living was most important and strict, and early toilet training was stressed. Children were to be fed, weaned, toilet trained, and put to bed on a strict schedule and with firmness. Parents were warned not to yield to the "baby's resistance." A major danger in childrearing was allowing the child to dominate the parents.

Between 1942 and 1945, the watchword was noninterference. Children were viewed as devoid of sexual impulses. Parents were to be "mild" and not to interfere with children's thumbsucking or masturbation. Weaning and toilet training were started later, and punishment for failure was less severe than suggested in earlier editions.

By 1951 there was still the suggestion of mildness in the role of parents. Yet concerns that had been expressed in 1929 that the child would dominate the parents were once again expressed. Parents were cautioned not to pick up the baby every time it cried because this could eventually lead to the child's becoming a tyrant.

Present suggestions in childrearing books continue to stress understanding and leniency in matters such as thumbsucking, weaning, toilet training, and masturbation. Meanwhile, an enormous popular literature on child care has come into existence, and parents can pick and choose the philosophy and prescriptions for child care that suit their own preconceptions.

The role of social scientists, in the field of child development, is assumed to be one of leadership and guidance in childrearing issues. Brief historical review of childrearing literature indicates that, on the contrary, social scientists have often mirrored or fostered society's current beliefs and perceptions concerning children's roles and functions in the family.

Urbanization: The Twentieth-Century Family

In the past 25 years, the family has experienced increasing stress as a result of the structural and functional changes demanded of it and its members. Social scientists have identified these stresses, including the disintegration or attenuation of extended kinship, increased mobility, the increasing number of working mothers, rising divorce rates, loss of parental power, and changes in childrearing practices, all of which are considered to be directly or partly responsible for the increase

in child abuse and neglect, lower school achievement of children, increased dissonance within the family, and challenges to family unity. The relationship between changes in the family and the prediction of family stress and disorganization are critically examined in this section to ascertain if this relationship provides an adequate explanation of current familial and societal dysfunction.

Theories of Family Change

Changes in the structure of the American family have led to changes in the functions of families. One of the most important alleged changes in family structure is the further isolation of the nuclear family. There continues to be disagreement, however, over the concept of the nuclear family. Parsons (1949) first described the isolated nuclear family. Litwak (1965) has more recently suggested the term "modified extended family." Sussman and Burchinal (1962) have supported the Litwakian notion of a modified extended family. It is clear that few real systems of kinship in the anthropological sense exist in mainstream American society. But while few people spend time counting kin, it is still evident that kin count. A larger debate has examined the question of the functions, problems, and advantages encountered by the changing American family structure.

Three divergent views of changes in the American family and the ensuing changes in family functions can be identified. Ogburn (1953) and Bronfenbrenner (1958) are leading proponents of the view that the loss of what they conceive to be the extended family has led to major functional changes that are detrimental to the family unit and the development of children. The family unit's loss of function is viewed as a major cause of present social disorganization.

Ogburn (1953) suggested that prior to the industrial period the power and prestige of the traditional family unit were due to seven functions it performed. These seven functions included economic, religious, educational, protective, status giving, recreational, and affectional functions that bound the family members together. Family cohesiveness was based on the ability of the family to provide these needed functions. Changes in some of society's attitudes, values, and customs often result in a lag of time in changes in other aspects of society. During this lag period there is social disorganization. Changes produced by industrialization included the lessening of the functions previously controlled by the family. Ogburn suggested that the family is no longer the site of business, religious activities, education, or recreational activities, nor does the family take primary responsibility for the protection of family members. In modern society, institutions such as large public schools, nationwide church organizations, social service agencies, and police forces have now taken over functions previously performed by the family.

The dilemma of the modern family is caused by the loss of many of these functions in recent times.... At least six of the seven family functions have been reduced as family activities, and it may be claimed that only one remains as vigorous and extensive as in prior eras. (p. 139)

Ogburn has further noted that the affectional function and the emotional relationship of family members have increased since the Industrial Revolution. Prior to the industrial period, marriage partnerships were primarily based on economic and status-conferring qualities. Today, emotional satisfaction of partners is considered an adequate reason for marriage or divorce. Families are now free from the added responsibility of being the sole unit of production. As a result, parents have more time to devote to the social and emotional growth of their children. The concept of emotional adjustment and happiness of children has increased in importance, and the emotional well being of children is now a primary function of the family.

Bronfenbrenner (1972) has also identified the loss of family functions and the creation of the isolated nuclear family as a major cause of social disorganization. He further suggests that the nuclear family is responsible for the increased rates of divorce, child abuse, drug addiction, lowered educational achievement of children, and increased pathology of family members.

An alternative view of the creation of the nuclear family was first suggested by Talcott Parsons (1949). Parsons views the shift from the "extended" to the "nuclear" family as a positive outgrowth of industrial society. The nuclear family is viewed as the most efficient unit of socialization and preparation of children for a technologically advanced society. The traditional society allowed little mobility and provided an extended family unit that wielded control over children's choices of educational, religious, vocational, marital, and social status. An industrial society demands increased mobility and urbanization. These demands are best met by nuclear families in which vocational training, public education, status in the community, and upward mobility are possible.

The loss of the extended family is viewed as a potentially positive cultural change in which the control of the head of the family kinship network is weakened, family lineage and status are no longer inexorably linked to jobs, and the individual's improved position in the community and upward mobility are possible and desirable. Marriage is now based on affectional qualities of the partner instead of decisions strongly influenced by the family and social status. The family has assumed a more specialized task of socializing children and stabilizing adult personalities. The nuclear family has taken on increased significance for the personal identity and emotional gratification of each member. Winch (1952) has taken Parsons's view of the nuclear family one step further. He suggests that the family not only has lost all its functions, but also that society no longer needs the familial system to survive.

Litwak (1965), in an attempt properly to characterize the present family system, suggests that a more accurate term is the "modified extended family." This type of family relationship provides positive identification of family membership without the interference and rigid adherence to patriarchal authority found in the traditional extended family.

The reduction of the traditional family functions is viewed as allowing for the intensification of the emotional aspects of the family relationship. Litwak's theory of family structure is supported by Laslett's (1978) review of the history of family structure in America, which indicates that the membership of most households was and is composed of primarily nuclear family members (Anderson, 1971; Demos, 1970; Greven, 1970). In the preindustrial and early industrial periods, households had more people in a conjugal unit, including boarders, lodgers, servants, and apprentices or employees (Blumin, 1975; Laslett, 1978). About 15–20 percent of preindustrial households contained individuals other than the nuclear family. Today only 3 percent of American families contain more than nuclear family members (U.S. Bureau of the Census, 1975). The changing composition of the family is viewed as a reduction in the number of nonkin relations contained within the household. Laslett suggests that nonkin in a family household may have led to a diffusion of family identity. The reduction of nonkin in the family is seen as leading to the strengthening of the family unit and family identity. In fact, the number of family members remaining in the household is suggested to have increased with the urbanization of families.

During the pre- and early industrial period many adolescents left the family home for work, apprenticeship, or education (Bloomberg, 1974; Dublin, 1975; Little & Laslett, 1977). Transportation allowed only infrequent visits back to the family. In the late nineteenth century, however, adolescents attended work or school while remaining within the family unit. A structural change in the number and age of children living in the home is suggested to have allowed adolescents increased identity with the family unit and greater clarity of family/nonfamily membership.

Gray (1977) examined the mortality, fertility, and age of marriage rates in the pre- and postindustrial periods. In 1970 there were more living kin relationships than in the pre- and early industrial period, which allowed children an increased opportunity for contact with extended family members and increased socialization of children within the family unit. The increased speed of communication and transportation allows for continued contact with family members living outside the home or city (Potter, 1970).

Migration of the nuclear family has been identified as a major cause of the decimation of the extended family unit. Early westward migration did have this effect on extended families. Yet in the late nineteenth and early twentieth centuries, evidence indicates that because families chose to migrate to a particular destination, in part because of the presence of an established kin group in the new area (Hareven, 1971), migration during the late industrial period did not necessarily terminate kinship contacts.

Litwak (1960a) suggests that the modified extended family is a coalition of nuclear families in a state of "partial dependence." That is, the nuclear families exchange significant services with each other, thus differing from the isolated nuclear family, as well as retaining considerable autonomy not found in the classical extended family. Exchanges of services may include parents paying for their children's college education, giving money and providing emotional support to their grown children, or providing child care services to their grandchildren. A distinguishing feature of modified extended family support is that contact and limited support are offered, but dominance or restriction of the nuclear family activities is excluded. Litwak described the tacit norm of the modified extended family in which support is available but noninterference in nuclear family job or geographical location is the expected mode. Almost one-half of the families studied by Litwak visit with kin relations at least once a week.

Today three-fourths of the population live in urban centers. The concentration of populations in urban settings now has reduced the past need for migration of nuclear families that migrated to the cities in the early industrial period. Litwak (1960b) also found in his research that the relationships of modified extended families did not impede geographical mobility of the nuclear family members. Movement of the nuclear family members and geographical distance of relations did not entail a loss of family identity. The communication and support of extended family members continued after the nuclear family move.

Family Stress

The preceding discussion of the state of the family indicates that there is little agreement concerning the structure, function, and adaptability of the modern American family. There is also disagreement concerning the effects of the changing society and family on the social problems present in the society today. The breakdown of the traditional large families and extended kinship systems, the stress of highly mobile and isolated nuclear families, and the two-working-parent families have been identified as major contributing factors to social problems. These problems include child abuse, incest, soaring divorce rates, and inappropriate alternative child care, which in turn have led to increased behavior problems and lower academic achievement of school-aged children (Pardeck, 1979). The relationship between these stresses and family pathology will be examined in this section.

Mobility and Support System

Each year 300,000–500,000 employees are transferred (Associated Press, 1981). Approximately one family in five moves each year. Mobility is highest for the young adult and families at the middle income level (Pedersen, 1965). An extremely mobile society allows young families to move to better paying or higher status jobs. The traditional, highly structured, more extended family offered financial and emotional support but at the cost of the individual's freedom of upward mobility. In the industrial society, movement of employees to different jobs became an expected aspect of movement up the corporate ladder.

Yet the cost for high mobility is frequent moves from city to city, causing increased isolation from extended kin and social support mechanisms. More mothers are working outside the home, extended family support is less available, and divorce and single parenting are becoming commonplace. Families are increasingly vulnerable to isolation from one another as well as from extended kin (Bronfenbrenner, 1980). Children are particularly affected by social isolation. Socially isolated children are more likely to become physically ill or emotionally disturbed than children from intact families with kin and support systems (Berle, Pinsky, & Wolf, 1952; Cobb, 1976; Eisenberg, 1979). Children without adequate family support systems cope with life stresses less effectively (Patterson, 1977). Children at "special risk" include those whose families are disrupted by marital and family discord and those whose parents lack adequate childrearing skills, extended family, or social support systems (Tableman, 1979). Eisenberg (1979) and Wallerstein (1974) have documented increased rates of psychiatric disorder, medical disability, and mortality among children who are experiencing this type of social isolation.

Working Mothers

During the past 20 years a larger percentage of mothers have been entering the labor force (U.S. Department of Labor, 1975). The proportion of married women in the labor force more than doubled between 1950 and 1978, increasing from 22.2 percent to 55.4 percent (Bernard, 1981). Smith (1979) estimates that the proportion of working mothers by 1990 will be 66.7 percent. The increase in maternal employment has led to an increase in the demand for child care services. The President's Advisory Committee on Child Development (1976) estimated that more than one million children do not have formal care from the time school closes until parents return from work, and 10 percent of the children from lower socioeconomic homes are unsupervised for large portions of their days. One of the major concerns is whether or not alternative child care services can meet the child's need for socialization and psychological support, functions now considered to be the primary functions of the modern family.

The traditional belief in American society has been that a good mother stayed in the home at least until her children reached primary school age (Russo, 1976; Howrigan, 1973). Early researchers in child development have helped to foster the belief that only mothers who stayed in the home could provide appropriate cognitive, social, and emotional experiences. Early researchers examined the effects of long term maternal deprivation experienced by institutionalized children. Long term separation from the mother had subsequent detrimental effects on the child's intellectual, social, and emotional development (Bowlby, 1952; Pringle, 1965; Spitz, 1945). However, Yarrow (1961) and Swift (1964) have emphasized the differential effects between residential or institutional care settings and the consistent, briefer separations of a working mother. Reviews by Etaugh (1974) and Hoffman (1974) of more current literature indicate that maternal employment is not necessarily harmful to the preschool child.

Some tentative conclusions have been drawn regarding the effects of nonmaternal care on children. Etaugh (1980), Belsky and Steinberg (1978), and Kagan, Kearsley, and Zelazo (1978) have suggested that high quality nonmaternal care does not appear to have harmful effects on the preschool child's maternal attachment, intellectual development, socioemotional behavior, or physical health. Studies of elementary school children also indicate no consistent differences in children's psychological or social adjustment due to maternal employment. The effects of maternal absence depend on a number of mediating variables including age and sex of the child, socioeconomic status, intactness of the family, ethnic and racial background, attitudes of both parents toward maternal employment, the length of time and consistency of time absent from the home, and the kind and quality of child care setting (Etaugh, 1980).

Divorce and Reconstituted Families

The long term trend in the American divorce rate is upward, and prospects are that this trend will continue (Kephart, 1977). Divorce rates have been affected by both wars and depressions. After a war, divorce rates accelerate and then return to the prewar level. During the Great Depression, divorce rates decreased, but with economic recovery divorce rates again rose. In 1940, before World War II, there was one divorce for every six marriages. By 1946 there was one divorce for every 3.8 marriages, and in 1970 one out of every three marriages ended in divorce (Leslie, 1976). Increases in the divorce rate have also accompanied urbanization, industrialization, and the shift to a conjugal family unit. Approximately 900,000 children are involved in divorce cases each year (U.S. Bureau of the Census, 1975). Children's reactions to divorce and psychological adjustment after the divorce have been the focus of many researchers. Divorce has been cited as a major deterrent to optimal family functions of socializing and meeting the psychological needs of its members (Adams, 1971). Pardeck (1979) suggests that both the socialization process and the psychological satisfaction gained from the family are disrupted through personal conflicts between family members and the conflict over new roles thrust upon family members after a divorce. Presently there are no comprehensive social services which offer support or help to families affected by divorce or remarriage.

Landis (1960) found in a retrospective study of children's reactions to divorce that the child's evaluation of the parent's marriage and the child's feelings of security in its familiy were the major factors in adjustment to the divorce. Children from unhappy homes reported greater happiness and security after the divorce, while children from homes perceived as happy reported either no change or a shift to feeling less happy and less secure. These findings suggest that children who perceived the family as unhappy viewed divorce with some relief, while children who perceived their homes as happy were more likely to experience trauma at the point of divorce. A consistent effect for children was their increased feelings of closeness to their mothers and increased emotional distance from their fathers. Since mothers traditionally gain custody of the children, this is an expected finding.

Most children reported feeling "used" or having to take one parent's side during and after the divorce. Children of divorce in Landis's study reported feeling shame and perceiving themselves as inferior to other children. One out of ten children lied about the absence of his or her parent.

Goode's (1956) interviews with divorced mothers found that 55 percent of the mothers reported no increase in behavioral problems of their children. Eighteen percent reported that their children were more difficult to handle during the divorce or immediately afterwards. Only 14 percent reported that their children continued to be more difficult to handle one year after the divorce, while 13 percent of the mothers reported improved behavior after the divorce.

Landis (1960, 1953) found no difference between children from happy unbroken, broken, and reconstituted families on measures of personality adjustment, social relationships, school grades, and friendships. Burchinal's (1964) investigation of broken, unbroken, and reconstituted families indicates that unhappy, unbroken homes may have a more deleterious effect on children than broken homes. Children in intact happy homes experience the best adjustment.

A series of studies by the Gluecks (1951) has reported that broken homes may contribute to problems of delinquency. Using matched samples of delinquents and nondelinquents, they found that 9 percent of the delinquents and only 6 percent of the nondelinquents had divorced parents. Yet children from homes in which a parent had died or separated without divorce exhibited a higher rate of delinquency. This finding has led Browning (1960) to suggest that the findings "support the hypothesis that delinquents are as likely to come from disorganized but structurally unbroken homes as they are from broken homes" (p. 43).

Most divorced parents remarry and the reconstituted family again must struggle to define each member's role in this new family. Reconstituted families are a growing phenomenon (Glick, 1976). The reconstituted family is confronted with an expanded number of social roles and relationships for which our society has not adequately developed a set of social roles and expectations. Several studies have found that the levels of satisfaction and happiness are lower for reconstituted family members. Glenn and Weaver (1977) and Renne (1971) found that family members rated levels of satisfaction and happiness lower in the reconstituted family than in the original families. Providing the psychological and social needs of family members is more difficult under these conditions of role confusion, stress, and lack of societal expectations for and definitions of roles for members of a reconstituted family.

Child Abuse, Neglect, and Incest

Child abuse and neglect have occurred since the beginning of recorded time (Starr, 1979). The American Humane Association (1979) reported over 600,000 documented child abuse/neglect cases. Gelles (1978) estimated that child abuse ranges from 1.4 million to 1.9 million cases a year. Differences in reporting procedures and definitions of abuse and the reluctance of private physicians to report abuse or neglect have compounded the problems of accurately estimating the rate of abuse or neglect. It cannot be ascertained with any assurance that child abuse or neglect has increased or decreased from any prior historical period.

Child abuse is committed by parents of all social classes, educational levels, religious affiliations, and geographical locations (Young, 1964). Belsky (1980) suggested that child maltreatment should be viewed as multiply determined by factors within the individual, the family, and the community. Characteristics of abusive parents include a past history of maltreatment in their own family (Steele & Pollack, 1968) or the more general experience of parental rejection (Rohner, 1975). As a result of parental rejection, role reversal by abusive parents is often observed (Spinetta & Rigler, 1972). A parent's experiences as a child do not appear to be sufficient, by themselves, to account for later abusive or neglectful behavior as adults.

Factors within the child and those within the family system interact with parental developmental history to increase the likelihood of abuse or neglect. Child factors include: premature birth (Klein & Stern, 1971), hyperactivity (Parke & Collmer, 1975), or lethargy (Belsky, 1980). Factors within the family system include parents' unsuccessful adaptation to a new role (Elder, 1977), parents' inaccurate perceptions of child development, or parents' inappropriate expectations for their child (Blumberg, 1974). Burgess and Conger (1978) have shown that abusive parents had 40 percent less positive interactions and 60 percent more negative interactions with family members than did nonabusive parents. Marital tension (Clark, 1976), joblessness (Newberger & Bourne, 1978), and drug or alcohol abuse are factors which appear to predispose the family to violence and possible child abuse.

A third set of factors identified as contributing to child abuse and neglect includes the isolation of the nuclear family, increased mobility, and the inability of the family to deal with the myriad stresses in today's complex society. Characteristics of abusive parents appear to offer support for the view held by Bronfenbrenner (1976) that the isolated nuclear family is a greater risk for child abuse than the extended family model. Gelles (1973) and Newberger and Bourne (1978) have suggested that family isolation, unemployment, and stress are major contributing factors in child abuse. Starr (1979) reported in his investigation of low income families that "abuse is essentially a problem in parent-child interactions and is fostered by such social factors as isolation, stress and cultural acceptance of violence as a disciplinary technique" (p. 874). Garbarino (1977) found that abuse stemmed from the combination of social stress (excessive change) and a low level of skill of the caretaker. Garbarino and Sherman (1980) identified high and low risk neighborhoods, which they matched for social economic characteristics. Social impoverishment, isolation, and individual or family pathology were found to be characteristics of high risk families for child maltreatment.

Child abuse appears to be correlated with many factors, including stress, isolation, and family mobility. These correlations appear to indicate that certain social stresses place some families at a higher risk of abusing their children.

Isolation from the community and extended kinship networks are also thought to be related to incestuous behavior. The incestuous family is typically a culturally isolated social unit whose individual members are both less responsive and less accessible to cultural rewards and norms than are members of a functional family (Jackson, 1957; Kaufman, Peck, & Tagiuri, 1954; Lidz, 1958).

Lustig et al.'s (1966) study of incestuous families found that the relationship of the family to the larger society was tenuous. These families were physically or culturally isolated and unable to obtain gratification from the larger society. This finding suggests that isolation allows role reversal or role confusion to be more likely. The evidence from incestuous families appears to suggest that social isolation is related to incest. But, as in child abuse, the evidence cannot directly identify isolation or high rates of mobility as the sole cause of incest. The isolated nuclear family may be at higher risk, but isolation alone is not a sufficient factor to produce child abuse, neglect, or incest.

FUTURE FAMILIES

Alternative family organizations have been attempted at various times in America during the past three centuries. Most of these attempts have been short lived. During the 1960s and early 1970s, there were movements to form communal living groups, multilateral or group marriages, and open marriages. During this period of American history there was great turbulence: civil rights issues, women's liberation, gay liberation, the Vietnam War protests, urban riots, and the increased use of drugs all played major roles in the social upheaval. Changes in the birth rates were in part responsible for this period in which relatively larger proportions of the population were adolescents and young adults. The large number of young adults came at a period of the postindustrial period in which the requirements for labor intensive jobs were decreasing and the discretionary income of families of young adults was high.

A common cliché of this period was that American society was in need of major reorganization; the conventional marriage and the middle class nuclear family were no longer relevant in contemporary society. Trial marriages, group marriages, open marriages, and communal living arrangements were touted as the counterculture's answer to the nonfunctional traditional family lifestyle.

The National Institute of Mental Health funded research to examine nontraditional marriages. Kafka and Ryder (1973) found that open marriages, over time, tended either to end in divorce or a return to more conventional marriage. Pomeroy (1973), of the Kinsey Institute for Sex Research, estimated that there were only a few thousand group marriages. The Constantines (1973) could locate only 31 true group marriages in three years of research. Within this small sample, breakup of the group marriage was very high. The median length of the group marriage was 16 months.

Communal living arrangements appear to have been the most popular alternative to nuclear or extended family structures. Accurate statistics on the number of communes in the United States are not readily available. Otto (1971) estimated that there were 3,000 communes in the United States. Typically, commune membership is unstable and most communes are short lived. The failure of communes is usually attributable to financial pressures and sexual and personal rivalries, as well as hostility from the larger community. Although alternative family systems have frequently been discussed, relatively few nontraditional family systems have been identified. Most have not remained active long enough to enable in-depth study.

The families of the 1980s are faced with both old and new issues. Economic and demographic changes are already having a profound effect on the modern family. The "baby boom" children are now in their thirties and forties. Couples with alternative lifestyles and marriages have become more conventional with the birth of children and the couple's entrance into traditional career choices. But changes are being seen in traditional male/female roles: women are entering the job market in increasing numbers and are making noticeable inroads into the corporate and professional ranks, while males, on the other hand, are increasingly becoming involved in childrearing and sharing household tasks.

Meanwhile the birthrate remains comparatively low, and the average family consists of husband, wife, and two children. The large discretionary income that adolescents of the 1960s enjoyed seems less available in a downturned economy with high youth unemployment. Also, the rate of marital dissolution has increased to the point that currently one divorce is granted for every two marriages performed. Remarriage, however, remains high, and those most likely to be without a spouse for a lengthy period are elderly females whose husbands have died. And, while there is a substantial gain in number and percentage of church attenders, there does not seem to be a correlative decrease in marital disruption or other social problems.

The litany of family and childhood problems seems unending. Many have been noted and discussed earlier. Some may be amenable to improvement if not solution; others seem to emanate from deep fissures in the basic structure of society or from the friction of opposing large scale systems of values and beliefs. In looking to the future, it is necessary to reassess the present in light of major social dynamics, in particular to get beyond description to analysis, interpretation, and, within limits, to prediction of future outcomes.

One cautious proposition, based in part on the earlier portion of this chapter, would be that any theory of personal and social disorganization or deviance will be an oversimplification if causation is attributed to a faltering "nuclear" family or even to the decline of the "extended" family. The family, whatever its size, parameters, or functions, has never in the past three centuries been a free standing, totally self-sufficient social unit. Families will, however, thrive in and contribute heavily to integrated communities. Perhaps the two are reciprocally related. The community may accept or arrogate to itself functions previously performed by the family, but nurturance, succor, intimacy, and the provision of a setting in which a limited number of persons may live in and through each others' lives is a family function *sui generis*. Given a supportive and relatively continuous social milieu, the family will extend, create, or activate kinship and affiliative bonds. But, and this may be the most important "but" in this essay, family members today, subject to the ideology of egalitarianism and personal freedom, will be *selective* in their affiliations, in their extension of kinship, and in their incorporation of a limited number of persons into their personal life space. Attempts to restructure the American family along traditional lines will not be successful if by traditional we mean the large, father dominated, and partially kin-controlled family in which options to accept or reject affiliations are minimal. What must be accepted is the large amount of indeterminancy that will exist in present and future families. Indeterminancy may be the bane of the scientist, but it is part of the price to be paid for egalitarianism, freedom, and democracy in the relationships of American people. Since, however, indeterminancy and the principle of kindred organization have a certain consonance, clinicians and practitioners should be aware that what is happening in the cases they are dealing with is not necessarily rejection of social and personal bonds or of authority per se, but perhaps rather a rejection of the claims, expectations, and authority of persons not acceptable to and incorporated within their personally assembled kindred. Both socially and personally, there is a world of difference between (1) total alienation from and rejection of family and kin, (2) selective rejection of some family and kin with acceptance of others into a personal kindred, and (3) total or a high degree of integration into the nucleus of the modified extended family. It is the second possibility that can be easily overlooked or only partially uncovered in the clinician's routine search for peer group affiliation.

Another form of oversimplification is seen in attempts to project a single type or form of family emerging in the 1980s. On the basis of the above argument and past and current social, economic, and religious developments, we envision a number of possibilities. We assume that there is some validity to the argument that alternative orientations to family and kinship organization exist now as through previous centuries and millenia. To this we add a modern phenomenon: with a continuing energy crisis and little chance of a prosperous and expanding economy, with the continuing growth of conservative and politically active religious groups, with continued high divorce and remarriage rates, and with the increasing number of young persons building private worlds of their own with self-conscious attention to a distinctive lifestyle, one can easily project not one but several alternative future family forms. Briefly, these might be first a traditional family, nuclear centered with supporting extended kin, institutionalized around dominance in the father's role and subordination and acquiescence in the female's and children's roles. Such a traditional patriarchal family will come back as the model for the traditional and the conservative minded.

Second, we project that a liberal and science-oriented family with concern for the latest findings of social and behavioral sciences will be identifiable, particularly among the great numbers of bureaucrats, technicians, and professionals who make up a third or more of the work force. This family type will exhibit both patrilineage and kindred-building aspects but will also have a high degree of interpersonal interaction carried on under the guise of rational management of the family's own affairs.

A third family type may emerge out of earlier youth protest movements and the yearning of the younger, and some older, generation members to work out alternative styles of intimate and presumably lasting male/female relationships. Formal marriage may eventuate, but other types of mating and bonding may initiate other alternatives. Lastly, we project that another family form of the present and future decades may well result from two seemingly strong but opposing motivations: to marry and to divorce. The divorced persons who remarry and bring children into the second or third marriage will constitute the "recombined" family.

This recombined family would be one in which couples, each with children from previous marriages, combine. Joint custody, more frequent awarding of custody to the father, and variations in visitation rights provide a setting in which the stable traditional family unit is no longer viewed as the only normal or expected functional unit. Establishing new roles and identities for biological and stepparents and children will become a more common function of families. Children and parents may be able to view themselves as members of more than one family and gain emotional support and socialization from different parents, stepchildren, and extended kin relations.

In the past as well as the present, the family unit has attempted to accommodate and assimilate family structures and functions to adapt to the economic, religious, and social changes within the society. The role of the clinical psychologist and other practicing social scientists is first to understand the demands placed on the family and the types of family structures that may emerge from this society. Whether the structure adopted by the family is traditional, kindred, or recombined, the primary aim of the psychologist should be to aid families in dealing more effectively with the changing family structures, functions, and roles.

REFERENCES

Adams, B.N. *The American family; A sociological interpretation.* Chicago: Markham, 1971.

Albin, M., & Cavallo, D. *Family life in America, 1620–2000.* New York: Revisionary Press, 1981.

American Humane Association. *Annual statistical report: National analysis of official child neglect and abuse reporting.* Englewood, Col.: American Humane Association, 1979.

Anderson, M. *Family structure in nineteenth-century Lancashire.* Cambridge: Cambridge University Press, 1971.

Angell, J.R. *Psychology,* New York: Holt, 1904.

Appleton, Miss. *Early education.* London: 1821.

Associated Press, August 12, 1981.

Bell, R. *Marriage and family interaction* (3rd ed.). Homewood, Ill.: Irwin-Dorsey, 1971.

Belsky, J. Child maltreatment: An ecological integration. *American Psychologist,* 1980, **35,** (4), 320–335.

Belsky, J., & Steinberg, L. The effects of day care: A critical review. *Child Development,* 1978, **49,** 929–949.

Berle, B., Pinsky, R., & Wolf, S. Berle index: A clinical guide to prognosis in stress disease. *Journal of American Medical Association,* 1952, **149,** 1624–1628.

Bernard, J. The good provider role. *American Psychologist,* 1981, **36**(1), 1–12.

Betts, G.H. *The mind and its education.* New York: Appleton, 1906.

Bloomberg, S. The household and the family: The effects of industrialization on skilled workers in Newark, 1840–1860. Paper presented at the meeting of the Organization of American Historians, Denver, 1974.

Blumberg, M. Psychopathology of the abusing. *American Journal of Psychotherapy,* 1974, **28,** 21–29.

Blumin, S.M. Rip Van Winkle's grandchildren: Family and household in the Hudson Valley, 1800–1860. *Journal of Urban History,* May 1975, **1,** 293–315.

Bowlby, J. *Maternal care and mental health.* Geneva: World Health Organization, 1952.

Bronfenbrenner, U. Socialization and social class through time and space. In E. MacCoby, T.M. Newcomb, & E. Hurtley (Eds.), *Readings in social psychology.* New York: Holt, 1958.

Bronfenbrenner, U. *Influences on human development.* Hinsdale, Ill.: Dryden, 1972.

Bronfenbrenner, U. The comparative ecology of human development: A research proposal. Unpublished manuscript, Cornell University, 1976.

Bronfenbrenner, U. On making human beings human. *Character,* 1980, **2** (2), 1–7.

Browning, C.J. Differential impact of family disorganization upon male adolescents. *Social Problems,* 1960, **8,** 43.

Bulkeley, H.W. *A word to parents.* Philadelphia: Presbyterian Board of Publication, 1858.

Burchinal, L. Characteristics of adolescents from unbroken, broken, and reconstituted families. *Journal of Marriage and the Family,* 1964, **26,** 44–51.

Burgess, E. The family in a changing society. *The American Journal of Sociology,* 1948, **53,** 417–422.

Burgess, R., & Conger, R. Family interaction in abusive, neglectful, and normal families. *Child Development,* 1978, **49,** 1163–1173.

Calhoun, A. *A social history of the American family from colonial times to the present* (Vol. 1). Cleveland: Arthur Clark, 1917.

Calhoun, A.Q. *A social history of the American family: Colonial period.* New York: Barnes & Noble, 1960.

Child, L. *The mother's book.* Boston: Carter, Hendee, & Babcock, 1835.

Clark, J. *The incidence of child abuse and neglect in the population at the Utah State University Industrial School.* Unpublished master's thesis, Utah State University, 1976.

Cobb, S. Social support as a moderator of life stress. *Psychosomatic Medicine,* 1976, **38**(6), 300–314.

Constantine, L., & Constantine, J. *Group marriage: A study of contemporary multilateral marriage.* New York: MacMillian, 1973.

Demos, J. *A little commonwealth: Family life in Plymouth colony.* New York: Oxford, 1970.

Demos, J., & Demos, V. Adolescence in historical perspective. *Journal of Marriage and the Family,* 1969, **31** (Nov.), 632–638.

Dublin, T. Women, work, and the family: Women operatives in the Lowell Mills, 1830–1860. *Feminist Studies,* Summer 1975, **3,** 30–39.

Earle, A.M. *Colonial dames and goodwives.* MacMillian, 1895.

Eisenberg, L. A friend not an apple a day will help keep the doctor away. *The American Journal of Medicine,* 1979, **66,** 551–553.

Elder, G. Family history and the life course. *Journal of Family History,* 1977, **2,** 279–304.

Etaugh, C. Effects of maternal employment on children: A review of recent research. *Merrill Palmer Quarterly of Behavior and Development,* 1974, **20,** 71–98.

Etaugh, C. Effects of nonmaternal care on children. *American Psychologist,* 1980, **35**(4), 309–319.

Feldstein, S., & Costello, L. (Eds.). *The ordeal of assimilation.* New York: Anchor Press/Doubleday, 1974.

Garbarino, J. The human ecology of child maltreatment; A conceptual model for research. *Journal of Marriage and the Family,* 1977, **39,** 721–735.

Garbarino, J., & Sherman, D. High-risk neighborhoods and high-risk families; The human ecology of child maltreatment. *Child Development,* 1980, **51,** 188–198.

Gelles, R.J. Child abuse as psychopathology: A sociological critique and reformation. *American Journal of Orthopsychiatry,* 1973, **43,** 611–621.

Gelles, R.J. Violence toward child in the United States. *American Journal of Orthopsychiatry,* 1978, **48,** 580–592.

Glenn, N., & Weaver, C. The marital happiness of remarried divorced persons. *Journal of Marriage and the Family.* 1977, **39,** 331–337.

Glick, P.C. *Some recent changes in American families.* U.S. Public Health Service Publication No. 52. Washington, D.C.: U.S. Government Printing Office, 1976.

Glueck, S., & Glueck, E. *Unravelling juvenile delinquency.* New York: The Commonwealth Fund, 1951.

Goldschmidt, G. Cecil Gregory Memorial Lecture. University of Missouri, Columbia, Mo., October 1976.

Goode, W.J. *After divorce.* Glencoe, Ill.: The Free Press, 1956.

Goodsell, W. *A history of marriage and the family.* New York: MacMillian, 1934.

Gray, J. Prediction and prevention of child abuse and neglect. Paper presented at the Biennial Meeting of the Society for Research in Child Development, New Orleans, March 17–20, 1977.

Greven, P. *Four generations: Population, land and family in colonial Andover, Massachusetts.* Ithaca: Cornell University Press, 1970.

Hall, G.S. The moral and religious training of children. *Princeton Review,* January 1882, 26–48.

Hall, G.S. *Adolescence: Its psychology, and its relations to physiology, anthropology, sociol-*

ogy, sex, crime, religion, and education. New York: Appleton, 1904.

Hareven, T.K. The history of the family as an interdisciplinary field. In T.K. Rabb & R. Rotberg (Eds.), *The family in history: Interdisciplinary essays.* New York: Harper & Row, 1971.

Hoffman, L.W. Effects of maternal employment on the child: A review of the research. *Developmental Psychology,* 1974, **10**, 204–228.

Howrigan, G. Effects of working mothers on children. Unpublished manuscript, Center for the Study of Public Policy. Cambridge, Mass.: 1973.

Jackson, D. The question of family homeostatis: Part I. *Psychiatric Quarterly,* 1957, **31**, 1979.

Judd, C.H. *The psychology of high school subjects.* Boston: Ginn, 1915.

Kafka, J., & Ryder, R. Notes on marriages in the counterculture. *Journal of Applied Behavioral Science,* 1973, **9**, 323.

Kagan, J., Kearsley, R., & Zelazo, P. *Infancy: Its place in human development.* Cambridge: Harvard University Press, 1978.

Kaufman, I., Peck, A.L., & Tagiuri, C. The family constellation and overt incestuous relations between a father and daughter. *American Journal of Orthopsychiatry,* **24**, 226–279, 1954.

Kephart, W. *The family society and the individual* (4th ed.). Boston: Houghton Mifflin, 1977.

King, I. *The psychology of child development.* Chicago: University of Chicago Press, 1903.

Klein, M., & Stern, L. Low birth weight and the battered child syndrome. *American Journal of Diseases of Childhood,* 1971, **122**, 15–18.

Landis, P. The broken home in teenage adjustment. Agricultural Experiment Station Bulletin, No. 542. Washington: Pullman, June 1953.

Landis, J. The trauma of children when parents divorce. *Marriage and Family Living,* 1960, **22**, 7–13.

Laslett, B. Family membership, past and present. *Social Problems,* 1978, **25**(5), 476–490.

Leslie, G.R. *The family in social context.* New York: Oxford, 1976.

Lidz, R. The intrafamilial environment of the schizophrenic patient: Parental personalities and family interaction, *American Journal of Orthopsychiatry,* 1958, **28**, 766–770.

Little, M., & Laslett, B. Adolescence in historical perspective: The decline of boarding in 19th-century Los Angeles. Paper presented at the Annual Meeting of the American Sociological Association, Chicago, 1977.

Litwak, E. Geographic mobility and extended family cohesion. *American Sociological Review,* 1960, **25** (3), 385–394.

Litwak, E. The use of extended family groups in the achievement of social goals: Some policy implications. *Social Problems,* 1960, **7**, 177–186.

Litwak, E. Extended kin relations in an industrial democratic society. In E. Shanas & F. Streib, (Eds.), *Social structure and the family: Gerontological relations.* Englewood Cliffs, New Jersey: Prentice-Hall, 1965.

Lustig, N., Dresser, J., Spellman, S., & Murray, T. Incest: A family group survival pattern. *Archives of General Psychiatry,* January 1966, **14**, 21–30.

Mangold, G.B. *Child problems.* New York: MacMillian, 1910.

McKeever, W. *Training the boy.* New York: MacMillian, 1913.

Mead, M. *Coming of age in Samoa.* New York: Morrow, 1928.

Mead, M. The development of Western family organization. In G.R. Leslie (Ed.), *The family in social context.* New York: Oxford Press, 1976.

Miller, D., & Swanson, G. *The changing American parent.* New York: Wiley, 1958.

Mindel, C., & Habenstein, R. *Ethnic families in America* (2nd ed.). New York: Elsevier, 1981.

Morgan, E.S. *Virginians at home: Family life in the eighteenth century.* Williamsburg, Va.: Colonial Williamsburg, Inc., 1952.

Newberger, E.H., & Bourne, R. The medicalization and legalization of child abuse. *American Journal of Orthopsychiatry,* 1968, **48**, 593–607.

Ogburn, W.F. *The changing functions of the family: Selected studies in marriage and the family.* New York: Holt, 1953.

Otto, H. Communes: The alternative life style. *Saturday Review,* April 24, 1971.

Pardeck, J.T. Supporting American families through a national social policy. *Family Therapy,* 1979, **6** (1), 11–20.

Parke, R.D., & Collmer, C. Child abuse: An interdisciplinary review. In E.M. Hetherington (Ed.), *Review of child development research*

(Vol. 5). Chicago: University of Chicago Press, 1975.

Parsons, T. The social structure of the family. In R.N. Ashen (Ed.), *The family: Its functions and destiny*. New York: Harper, 1949.

Patterson, S. Toward a conceptualization of natural helping. *Arete*, 1977, **4**(3), 1–11.

Pedersen, H.A. (Ed.). Family mobility rural and urban. In *Family mobility in our dynamic society*. Ames, Iowa: Iowa State University Press, 1965.

Pomeroy, W. Playboy panel: New sexual lifestyles. *Playboy*, September 1973, p. 86.

Potter, J. Demography: The missing link in American history. Paper presented at the meeting of the Organization of American Historians, Denver, 1970.

President's Advisory Committee on Child Development. Toward a national policy for children and families. Washington, D.C.: National Academy of Sciences, 1976.

Pringle, M.L. *Deprivation and education*. London: Longmans, 1965.

Queen, S., & Habenstein, R. *The family in various cultures* (4th ed.). Philadelphia: Lippincott, 1974.

Renne, K.S. Health and experience in an urban population. *Journal of Marriage and the Family*, 1971, **33**, 338–350.

Rohner, R. Parental acceptance-rejection and personality: A universalistic approach to behavioral science. In R. Brislin et al. (Eds.), *Cross-cultural perspectives on learning*. New York: Halstead, 1975.

Russo, N.F. The motherhood mandate. *Journal of Social Issues*, 1976, **32**, 143–154.

Sennett, R. *Families against the city: Middle class homes of industrial Chicago, 1872–1890*. Cambridge: Harvard, 1970.

Seymour, J. *On the management and education of children*. London: 1754.

Shorter, F. *The making of the modern family*. New York: Basic Books, 1975.

Smith, R.E. (Ed.). *The subtle revolution*. Washington, D.C.: Urban Institute, 1979.

Spinetta, J., & Rigler, D. The child-abusing parent: A psychological review. *Psychological Bulletin*, 1972, **77**, 296–304.

Spitz, R.A. Hospitalism. In *The psychoanalytic study of the child* (Vol. 1). New York: International Universities Press, 1945.

Spruill, J.C. *Women's life and work in the Southern colonies*. Chapel Hill: University of North Carolina Press, 1938.

Starr, R. Child abuse. *American Psychologist*, 1979, **34**(10), 872–878.

Steele, B.F., & C.B. Pollack. A psychiatric study of parents who abuse infants and small children. In R.E. Helfer & C.H. Kempe (Eds.), *The battered child*. Chicago: University of Chicago Press, 1974.

Sussman, M., & Burchinal, L. Kin family network: Unheralded structure in current conceptualizations of family functioning. *Marriage and Family Living*, 1962, **24**, 231–240.

Swift, J.W. Effects of early groups experience: The nursery school and day nursery. In M.L. Hoffman & L.W. Hoffman (Eds.), *Review of child development research* (Vol. 1). New York: Russell Sage Foundation, 1964.

Talbeman, B. Commonalities in prevention programming to reduce alcohol, drug abuse and mental health problems among children and youth. Paper presented at the First Annual Alcohol, Drug Abuse, and Mental Health Administration Conference on Prevention, Silver Spring, Maryland, September 1979.

Thorndike, E.L. Notes on child-study. *Columbia University Contributions to Philosophy, Psychology, and Education*, 1908, **3**(4), 143.

Trumbach, R. *The rise of the egalitarian family*. New York: Academic Press, 1978.

U.S. Bureau of the Census. *Statistical abstract of the United States* (96th ed.). Washington, D.C.: U.S. Government Printing Office, 1975.

U.S. Department of Labor. Child care arrangement of the nation's working mothers. Washington, D.C.: United States Government Printing Office, 1975.

U.S. Government Printing Office. *Infant care*. Washington, D.C.: 1914.

Wallerstein, J. *A nation of strangers*. New York: Pocket Books, 1974.

Weber, M. *The Protestant ethic*. New York: Scribner's, 1958.

Winch, R.F. *The modern family*. New York: Holt, 1952.

Wishy, B. *The child and the republic*. Philadelphia: University of Pennsylvania Press, 1968.

Yarrow, M.R. Maternal employment and child rearing. *Children*, 1961, **8**, 223–228.

Young, L. *Wednesday's children*. New York: McGraw-Hill, 1964.

CHAPTER 2

Theories of Child Development

RUNE J. SIMEONSSON

In contrast to the provision of psychological services to adults, every facet of clinical work with children is influenced by the variables of age and stage of development. The identification of presenting problems, the selection of assessment instruments, and the implementation of interventions will differ significantly if the client is an infant, a preschooler, or a young adolescent. Yet, in clinical practice, the activities of assessment, diagnosis, and intervention are usually not carried out in isolation but are linked in conceptual frameworks that recognize, implicitly or explicitly, the role of development through continuity and change. While the formality and explicitness of conceptual frameworks may vary from clinician to clinician, it seems clear that such frameworks do form the basis for clinical activities. Some clinicians adopt a well-established theory as a framework, whereas others operate out of a commonsense theory based on subjective insights and personal experiences. For many clinicians, the framework is eclectic, drawing on various theories to match presenting problems. Traditionally, conceptual frameworks for clinical services to children have been derived from learning and psychoanalytic theories. In recent years, however, the applicability of other theories to clinical service, particularly Piaget's theory (Weiner, 1975; Schmid-Kitsikis, 1973), has been considered.

An expanded consideration of various child development theories seems appropriate given the increased diversity of settings, clients, and clinical problems. Children are being seen not only in mental health and psychiatric settings but also in schools, in correctional facilities, in pediatric wards and clinics, and in residential and community settings for the handicapped. Client populations range from infants to handicapped adolescents and involve methods ranging from conditioning strategies (Sajwaj, Libet, & Agras, 1974) to psychotherapy (Brier & Demb, 1980). To meet the increased variety of clinical needs of children, it is important to extend the range of theoretical frameworks available for consideration. Freeman's (1976) stress on the value of conceptual frameworks in services for families seems equally appropriate in the consideration of services for children. Not only does the framework adopted influence the understanding of child functioning, but it may determine the effectiveness of the goals and strategies that are implemented.

The purpose of this chapter is to review theories of child behavior and development from which frameworks for clinical practice can be considered. In developing the chapter, two guidelines were followed. The first pertains to the nature of the review. Emphasis is placed on the identification and analysis of selected dimensions of various theories of relevance to clinical concerns. This approach seems consistent with the applied focus of the volume and seeks to synthesize, rather than duplicate, more comprehensive, detailed presentations available elsewhere (Baldwin, 1967; Maier, 1965; Rutter & Hersov, 1977; Bemporad, 1980; Salkind, 1981). A second guideline is that the scope of the review should extend beyond theories typically considered in volumes of this nature. Thus in addition to representative psychoanalytic, learning, and cognitive-developmental theories, the review also encompasses the theories of Ausubel, Sullivan, and Ives (1980), Werner (1957), Loevinger (1966), and Erikson (Baldwin, 1967). The goal of this chapter is thus to present information from which inferences for clinical service can be derived. While the potential contribution of one individual theory may be greater than that of another, general benefits may accrue from an eclectic approach. Such eclecticism does not imply mixture of models, as Reese and Overton (1970) have pointed out, but the specification of conditions under which they can be applied. Reese and Overton suggest that "at our present state of knowledge,...eclectic theories seem to be necessary to account for the whole range of human behaviors throughout the lifespan" (p. 123). Along this same line, Baldwin (1967) has suggested that an eclectic integration should result from the fact that theories often focus on different behaviors rather than different explanations of similar behaviors. To this end, selected dimensions have been chosen by which theories can be reviewed.

A DIMENSIONAL APPROACH TO THEORIES OF DEVELOPMENT

The dimensions along which theories could be reviewed are numerous and vary from basic assumptions to methodological details. In selecting specific dimensions for this chapter, a large number of dimensions identified in earlier contributions were considered. Reese and Overton (1970) and Looft (1973), for example, have examined broad issues pertaining to models and theories of development. Baldwin (1967) and Maier (1965), on the other hand, have each proposed specific dimensions along which to compare the contributions of several theories. The dimensions selected for this review were designed to identify features of each theory of particular relevance for child clinical applications. To this end, eight some-

what arbitrary dimensions were specified: model of development, nature of development, explanation of normal and abnormal or atypical development, role of early experience, role of environment, basis for behavior change, and clinical implications. Prior to the review and comparison of theories, a brief explanation of these dimensions in terms of the issues each will address follows:

1. *Model of development:* This dimension will focus on the general philosophical model on which the theory is built. For the purpose of this review, theories will be considered in the context of the models of organismic and mechanistic world views discussed by Reese and Overton (1970). The former represents the individual as an active, organized entity, whereas in the latter the individual is seen as passive, reactive, and empty.

2. *Nature of development:* This dimension combines several issues raised by Looft (1973) and Reese and Overton (1970). In general, these issues deal with the manner in which the theory represents development and change. In regard to development, is it assumed to be continuous or discontinuous, and in regard to change, quantitative or qualitative?

3. *Explanation of normal development:* This and the following dimension are essentially self-explanatory; how does the theory explain or account for normal development?

4. *Explanation of abnormal/atypical development:* How does the theory explain or account for nonnormal development?

5. *Role of early experience:* What importance, if any, is attached by the theory to early experience as an influence on behavior and development?

6. *Role of the environment:* In what manner does the environment influence a child's behavior in development?

7. *Basis for behavior change:* This dimension is concerned with the manner in which a theory proposes to account for novel behavior in the child.

8. *Clinical implications:* What are the clinical implications of the theory in terms of assessment, diagnosis, and/or treatment?

THEORIES

Review of Child Development Theories

Each of the theories selected for review in this chapter may singly or in combination contribute information useful in the provision of clinical services to children. While the theories may resemble each other in one or more ways, each also has some unique features. By reviewing the theories through the dimensions described above, similarities and differences among them should become evident and facilitate the derivation of conceptual frameworks for clinical work.

Psychoanalytic Theories

It should be readily obvious from a review of psychoanalytic theories that the original formulations of Freud have been extended into a number of revisions and formulations, many with unique and distinct perspectives on child development. For the purpose of this review, the approaches of Anna Freud (1963) and Klein (1958) will be considered as representative of two different orientations of the psychoanalytic school. Erikson's epigenetic theory will be considered separately. Additional Freudian and non-Freudian psychoanalytic approaches to child development have been reviewed by Dare (1977), Lesser (1972), Bryt (1972), and Ekstein (1979).

Anna Freud's Theory of Developmental Lines

Model of Development

A central assumption of Freud's (1963) theory is that the child's development represents the interaction of maturation, adaptation, and structuralization. She maintains that developmental outcomes are included in the constitutional makeup of each child, subject to environmental influences. A substantial role is assigned to the ego in terms of innate tenden-

cies toward organization. Thus the psychoanalytic school appears to adhere to an organismic rather than mechanistic view of the child. Langer (1969), however, has suggested that psychoanalytic orientations actually constitute yet a third model of the child, which he has labeled "mechanical mirror" or the "organic lamp."

Nature of Development

Building on the original formulations of psychosexual development, Freud (1963) proposed the concept of developmental lines as sequences of gradated steps applicable to most areas of the child's personality. These developmental lines trace the child's gradual outgrowing of dependent, irrational, id- and object-determined attitudes to an increasing ego mastery of his or her "internal and external world" (p. 246). The prototypic developmental lines consist of eight steps or phases covering the period from infancy to adolescence:

1. Biological mother-infant tie.
2. Part object, anaclitic relationship phase.
3. Object constancy phase.
4. Preoedipal ambivalent phase.
5. Object-centered phallic-oedipal phase.
6. Latency period.
7. Preadolescent prelude to "adolescent revolt."
8. Adolescent struggle and stabilization.

Role of Early Experience

Early experience is given substantial emphasis in Freud's concept of developmental lines. From early infancy, it is postulated that the mother's interest and predilection serve as a source of stimulation for the infant. The infant is assumed to concentrate on those developmental lines that evoke maternal response and to ignore or neglect those where maternal attention is minimal. Growth and development thus reflect approved activities, which are repeated by the infant. Lack of maternal interest or approval may result in delayed or atypical development in a corresponding developmental line. The importance of early experience is evident in that "tendencies, inclinations, predilections (including the tendency to depression, to masochistic attitudes, etc.) which are present in all human beings, can be eroticized and stimulated toward growth through forming emotional links between the child and his first object" (Freud, 1963, p. 264).

Role of the Environment

An important issue to be considered when imbalance is found between developmental lines is a determination of the role of innate and environmental factors. The developmental level achieved by a given child is seen as a result of interaction of ego, superego development, and drive in reaction to environmental influences. Thus, to account for the unique development of a child, "that is, for what singles out individual lines for special promotion in development, we have to look to accidental environmental influences" (Freud, 1963, p. 263). For the infant and young child, these environmental influences are tied closely to the mother, whereas for the older child, the range is broader, encompassing the family and the cultural setting as well.

Basis for Behavior Change

New behavior appears to be acquired as a function of maturation as well as adaptation to environmental influences and demands. The child's biological endowment in terms of the id is assumed to account for maturation, and in terms of the ego, for organizational tendencies. New behaviors are acquired as the environment influences and interacts with these endowments.

Clinical Implications

In working with children, it is possible for the clinician to trace developmental lines by examining them progressively through observation and longitudinal analysis or by reconstructing adult recollections.

The clinical relevance of the concept of developmental lines has been proposed, for example, to explain preoedipal ambivalence (phase 4) as the basis for clinging behavior in the toddler rather than spoiling by the mother and the necessity of phase 6 functioning for adequate integration into school. Disturbances in development of specific phases have been causally linked with separation anxiety (phase 1), anaclitic depression (phase 2), and aggressive/destructive behavior (phase 4) (Freud, 1963).

Klein's English School of Psychoanalytic Theory

Model of Development

Klein's (1958) view of the child seems consistent with those of psychoanalytic theory in general; that is, the child is active in his or her own development, but primarily on a mental plane. Internally produced, unconscious fantasies are present in infancy and are responded to with defenses as well as projections to external reality (Dare, 1977).

Nature of Development

Klein's theory is, in her own words, an extension of Freud's original formulation, and she appears to incorporate the concept of qualitative psychosexual stages as a major feature. A review of her theory, however, does not indicate a detailed treatment of qualitative differences between stages, nor is there evidence for the fact that development is seen as a discontinuous process.

Explanation of Normal Development

A central feature of Klein's theory is the presence of self-destructive and self-preserving instincts in early infancy and the emergence of defensive techniques of projection, introjection, and splitting to deal with anxieties and conflicts. For normal development to occur, "a division between the good and the bad object, between love and hate, should take place in early infancy. When such a division is not too severe and yet sufficient to differentiate between good and bad, it forms in my view one of the basic elements for stability and mental health" (Klein, 1958, pp. 87–88).

Explanation of Abnormal/Atypical Development

The resolution of the two conflicting instincts in normal development is achieved in part by splitting, that is, the differentiation of the role of the id, the ego, and the superego in dealing with conscious and unconscious material. From this perspective, abnormal development is seen as the failure of the ego to develop adequately in terms of its conscious and unconscious parts. "When however, there is a very rigid barrier produced by splitting, the implication is that development has not proceeded normally. The conclusion would be that the death instinct is dominant" (Klein, 1958, p. 88). Inadequate ego development may result in subsequent problems of integration and object synthesis.

Role of Early Experience

The first years of life are crucial for subsequent development according to Klein. As Lesser (1972) has noted, the attribution of defenses to the infant to deal with psychoticlike conflicts (paranoia and depression) represents a significant revision of traditional Freudian concepts. The presence of the superego within the first year of life represents a collapsing of all libidinal stages into the oral stage. "To what extent the strength of the ego can be maintained and increased is in part affected by external factors, in particular the mother's attitude towards the infant" (Klein, 1958, p. 85).

Role of the Environment

The orientation of Klein's theory places primary emphasis on the parents, particularly the mother, as the important element of the infant's environment. Relationships with the mother in terms of internal and external objects become prototypic of relationships with all subsequent internalized objects.

Basis for Behavior Change

In the context of Klein's theory, it would seem that the acquisition of new behavior is tied to the function of the ego's "need and capacity not only to split but also to integrate itself....

The more the ego can integrate its destructive impulses and synthesize the different aspects of its objects, the richer it becomes" (Klein, 1958, p. 89).

Clinical Implications

The importance attached to early mother-child interactions for subsequent development and elaboration of the nature of the functions of the ego in the very young child are two aspects of Klein's theory that may have potential clinical significance. As Lesser (1972) has noted, however, acceptance of the theory by clinicians has been primarily in England rather than in this country.

The Cognitive Developmental Theory of Piaget

Model of Development

A basic premise of Piaget's theory is that development is more than simply maturational unfolding or the accumulation of experiences. Development is the expression of the child's active, progressive construction of reality. "To present an adequate notion of learning, one first must explain how the subject manages to construct and invent, not merely how he repeats and copies" (Piaget, 1970, p. 704). This constructivist approach to development is clearly consistent with an organismic view of the child and posits that reality is, in fact, the product of the interaction between the child and the environment. The role of action in development is essential since "there can be no experience without action as its source, whether real or imagined, because its absence would mean that there would be no contact with the external world"(Piaget, 1970, p. 721).

Nature of Development

Piaget's theory assumes an adaptive process with common biological as well as cognitive aspects. Adaptation to the environment involves the active construction of reality in which the child both influences and is influenced by experiences. Development is seen as a process in which successive adaptations result in qualitatively different stages of reality construction. Thus, although common adaptive processes are found across development, structural change produces four successively different stages of thought:

1. The sensorimotor period of infancy encompasses six distinct stages of practical intelligence. Reality construction in this period is dependent upon and governed by actions initially in the form of reflex activity ending in new mental combinations to achieve goals.
2. The period of preoperational thought is characterized by perceptual and intuitive qualities.
3. Transition to the concrete operations stage involves the acquisition of internalized mental operation in which construction of reality is no longer subject to the distortions of perception.
4. Entry to the formal operations stage, in late childhood, is characterized by the ability to engage in hypothetical, abstract, and propositional thinking. Development is thus represented in Piaget's theory in discontinuous qualitative units that may vary in rate, but not in sequence, of emergence.

Explanation of Normal Development

The nature of adaptation by the child to physical and psychological reality is a function of the complementary processes of assimilation and accommodation. The process of assimilation is one in which environmental stimuli are changed or modified to conform to the child's existing cognitive structures. Accommodation is the process whereby encounters with environmental elements or events result in change of cognitive structure. Hunt (1961) has suggested that these processes correspond respectively to inner organization and outward coping. Piaget (1970) has indicated that the pure or essential forms of these processes correspond to play and imitation. Effective adaptation is the relative balance or equilibrium between these processes. Although the specific ratio of assimilation/accommodation may vary across activities, the resultant equilibrium/disequilibrium con-

tributes to progressive qualitative transitions of cognition.

Explanation of Abnormal/Atypical Development

A disproportionate imbalance between assimilation and accommodation may result in lack of adaptation and cognitive development. If assimilation predominates over accommodation, that is, organization over coping, extreme results may take the form of egocentric or autisticlike thought and behavior in which the environment is incorporated into, or interpreted to conform to, existing mental structures. "If assimilation alone were involved in development, there would be no variation in the child's structures. Therefore, he would not acquire new content and would not develop further" (Piaget, 1970, p. 707). Reciprocally, accommodation predominates over assimilation when environmental demands require coping in excess of organization, with the result that imitative, rote behavior is expressed. In addition to explaining abnormal development in terms of adaptive processes, Piaget and his colleagues (Inhelder, 1966; Schmid-Kitsikis, 1973) have proposed that aberrations of stage transitions also reflect disorders of development. More specifically, aberrations such as stage fixation, false equilibrium, and oscillations between stages have been proposed to explain the development of retarded and emotionally disturbed children (Inhelder, 1966).

Role of Early Experience

While the sequence of a child's development is seen as invariant, the rate of development may differ, reflecting genetic endowment as well as the range and intensity of available environmental stimulation. Although an assumption of the invariant sequence is that earlier structures form the building blocks for subsequent structures, there is no stress on one stage of development being uniquely important compared to the others. Each stage requires opportunities for the child to act upon, structure, and restructure reality to facilitate transitions to the next stage of development.

Role of the Environment

The environment provides the child with physical and nonphysical stimuli essential for developmental progress. The importance of the object world for development is evident in that "to know objects, the subject must act upon them, and therefore transform them. He must displace, connect, combine, take apart and re-assemble them" (Piaget, 1970, p. 704). While the nature and extent of the correspondence between cognition about the physical and social world have been questioned (Damon, 1979), it is clear that social as well as physical objects provide the basis for reality construction.

Bases for Behavior Change

The notion of disequilibrium, as advanced by Piaget, implies an imbalance between the adaptive processes of assimilation and accommodation. Acquisition of new behavior can thus be seen as a disequilibrium in which accommodation predominates, requiring a restructuring or modification of the child's cognitive framework to fit new experiences. As noted earlier, Piaget maintains that, without accommodation, there would be no acquisition of new content. In this context, accommodation is a repeated process that results in developmental change within and across qualitative stages.

Clinical Implications

At least two broad areas of clinical significance derive from Piaget's theory. The first pertains to the use of the qualitative cognitive structural framework in which to view clinical populations. The assumptions of an invariant sequence of structural development and active reality construction across children provide alternative means by which to assess and classify children with varying cognitive and affective disorders (e.g., disturbed, mentally retarded, autistic children, etc.). Second, the importance assigned to experience in adaptation supports the value of deliberate enrichment and variation of the environment to promote accommodation and developmental structural change.

Learning Theory

While there are various learning theorists, many hold common positions regarding models of development and the role of the environment in the acquisition of normal and abnormal behavior. While recognizing that theorists may differ on selected aspects, this review will draw collectively on the work of Sears, Rau, and Alpert (1961), Bijou and Baer (1961), and Eysenck (1967) as representative of the learning theory position.

Model of Development

Learning theories generally adopt a mechanistic view in which the child produces responses to external forces or stimuli as a machine would. The passive and reactive role of the child is paralleled by the assumption that life is begun as a blank slate on which experiences are accumulated. Reality is grasped on the basis of a copying theory of knowledge (Reese & Overton, 1970).

Nature of Development

A derivation of the reactive/passive nature of the child is that development is characterized by quantitative change. The mechanistic emphasis further implies that complex behavior is reducible to simpler elements that can be related functionally to specific external forces or stimuli. Development from a learning theory standpoint is thus seen as quantitative and continuous in nature. Reese and Overton (1970) have indicated, however, that the assumption of qualitatively different operations is possible in the theory. Maier (1965), in fact, infers three developmental phases from the learning theory of Sears. Maier is careful to qualify the fact that these phases are his own interpretive efforts rather than Sears' stated position.

Explanation of Normal Development

A central assumption of learning theories is that behavior is learned, whether learning takes place by imitation, association, conditioning, or observation. Given the elementary components of stimulus and response (s-r) in behavior acquisition, a variety of s-r combinations or change can be specified to account for complex behaviors. Normal development thus represents the acquisition of an appropriate response repertoire to environmental demands.

Explanation of Abnormal/Atypical Development

Given the emphases upon learning in normal development, abnormal/atypical development is, by extension, an exaggerated form of learned behavior (Berger, 1977). Abnormal or atypical development may be characterized by inappropriate or deficient behavior repertoires. In the context of mental (developmental) retardation, Bijou (1967) has proposed that environmental variables can account for atypical development through specific reinforcement histories. Intermittent reinforcement, extinction, and severe punishment may each operate to suppress, distort, or eliminate behavioral development. With a recognition of the role of biological factors on development, Eysenck (1967) has proposed individual differences in conditionability as an aspect of abnormal development. Differences in conditionability may predispose individuals to disorders associated with learning aberrations. The generalizability of this conception, however, seems limited (Berger, 1977).

The Role of Early Experience

While recognizing that behavior is learned and reinforcement history is an important determinant of behavioral development, learning theories generally focus on current conditions. Since learning theories assume that behavior is a function of environmental conditions, analysis is made of those stimuli (antecedent or consequent) that influence current behavior and that can be manipulated for behavior change.

Role of the Environment

The passive and reactive model assumed by learning theories serves to emphasize the critical role of the environment in behavioral development. The environment consists of the range of stimuli that serve to elicit behavior, as in respondant conditioning, or reinforce behavior, as in operant conditioning. Bijou (1967) has posed that "when the environment is dull, routine, unvaried, and limited in range, interactions are restricted" (p. 266). Inadequate reinforcement histories viewed in this context may thus result in a retarded or aberrant behavioral repertoire.

Basis for Behavior Change

The central role attributed to the environment in learning theories implies that behavioral development is largely a function of environmental events. Since behavior is assumed to be under stimulus control, new behaviors can be developed and strengthened through the use of behavioral techniques such as shaping and chaining.

Clinical Implications

Given the assumption that all behaviors are learned, the acquisition of appropriate behaviors and inappropriate behaviors can be achieved through variations of learning such as new learning, relearning, or unlearning (Berger, 1977).

Loevinger's Model of Ego Development

Model of Development

Loevinger has proposed that ego development is one of four major lines of development. Along with development of the physical, psychosexual, and intellectual lines, ego development is seen as an integrative process, a "framework of meaning which one subjectively imposes on experience" (Hauser, 1976, p. 930). Since an essential function of the ego is to master and make sense of experience (Loevinger, 1966), the successive stages of ego development seem consistent with an organismic, active view of the child (Looft, 1973).

Nature of Development

The integrative process of ego development and the imposition of meaning on experience are assumed to occur in successive stages of differentiation and complexity. These stages of qualitative change are assessed on the basis of responses to a sentence completion test developed by Loevinger. Ego development is represented in seven invariant, sequential stages and three transitional phases. Although correlated with age, the stages are not defined by age. The first stage has three social and symbiotic phases, the second is characterized by impulsivity, the third by self-protection, and the fourth by conformism. The fifth stage is identified as the conscientious stage, the sixth as autonomous, and the highest as integrated. It should be noted that the three transitional phases come between the third and the fourth, the fourth and the fifth, and the fifth and the sixth stages.

Explanation of Normal Development

In a review of Loevinger's model, Holt (1974) has commented on the lack of detail regarding normal development. It appears, however, that one important aspect of normal ego development is that progress in one area should be accompanied by corresponding progress in other areas such as cognitive complexity and emotional differentiation. In general, normal development may be seen as satisfactory progression through the stages.

Explanation of Abnormal/Atypical Development

The issue of abnormal development has not been addressed by Loevinger in any detail. In keeping with the central theme of the model, however, it seems reasonable to assume that abnormal development is the fixation of ego development at early levels. In regard to rigidity of behavior patterns, Loevinger suggests that selective inattention may contribute to a recognition of what is uniquely a part of the self system (Holt, 1974).

Role of Early Experience

No systematic emphasis on early experience appears in Loevinger's theory on ego development. This lack of emphasis may be due to the fact that the method used to assess ego development is a 36-item sentence completion test. Since the first stages of ego development, consisting of the presocial and symbiotic phases, cover the period prior to language

acquisition, it is not sensible to study them by means of verbal techniques. The verbally laden method for assessing ego development may thus contribute to a lack of emphasis on early experience.

Role of the Environment

Social processes appear to constitute significant factors in ego development. The relationship between social variables and ego development is complex and includes variables such as social role, social class, and technological development in socialization practices (Hauser, 1976). The manner in which social variables influence ego development may further be a function of intellectual status, since intelligence may be a necessary, but not sufficient, condition for attainment of various stages of ego development (Hauser, 1976).

Basis for Behavior Change

Loevinger's explanation for the acquisition of new behavior is tied to the assumption that exposure to features of a level immediately above the person's present functioning will promote developmental growth. This conceptualization of developmental change is similar to that of Kohlberg's model of moral development, on which Loevinger drew for her model of ego development. While the precise mechanism for behavior change is unclear, stimulation designs have been developed to facilitate change in ego development.

Clinical Implications

The theory of ego development provides a framework in which to view a master trait that is inclusive of the major lines of development. One important clinical implication is that, since stages are assessed through the use of a specific measurement instrument, the theory is amenable to empirical validation. A second implication pertains to the fact that stages of ego development are reflective of qualitative personality traits. Fixation or interruption of ego development will thus be evidenced by the characteristic of personality corresponding to a particular stage.

Werner's Organismic Developmental Theory

Model of Development

Werner's theory has been labeled as organismic, indicative of the emphasis placed upon the active, structuring role of the child in development. While Werner drew substantively on developmental concepts derived from biology, he also recognized the fact that behavior and developmental change involved the organism as an integrated whole (Baldwin, 1967).

Nature of Development

Developmental change is defined in terms of the orthogenetic principle, in which the changes from childhood thinking to adult thinking are paralleled by the changes differentiating a primitive society from a technologically advanced society. "Wherever development occurs it proceeds from a state of relative globality and lack of differentiation to a state of increasing differentiation, articulation and hierarchical integration" (Werner, 1957, p. 126). Five aspects of developmental process are indicated from undifferentiated, syncretic, diffuse, rigid, unstable organization to differentiated, articulated, flexible, and hierarchically organized symptoms.

Explanation of Normal Development

Mental functioning is seen as a result of many processes. Adaptation to environmental demands is represented by stabilization at a given level.

Explanation of Abnormal/Atypical Development

Developmental regression or arrest is suggested as a basis for abnormal development. Mature organisms have available the processes that are differentiated in hierarchical organization. Younger or less mature organisms are limited to functioning corresponding to primitive processes. Cognitive pathology as seen in schizophrenia, for example, is viewed as functioning at a primitive level.

Role of Early Experience

In a critique of Werner's theory, Baldwin (1967) has concluded that the theory is limited in scope and explanatory power. One important limitation in this regard is that it fails to deal with the relationship of childhood experiences with subsequent adult characteristics. The role of early experience, therefore, appears to be undefined.

Role of the Environment

Werner's theory places emphasis upon the individual's reaction to total stimuli similar to that of the Gestalt school (Baldwin, 1967). Werner elaborated this concept of total stimulus response in the sensoritonic theory of perception. The sensoritonic theory posits that perceptual experiences are a relationship between organism state and object characteristics.

Basis for Behavior Change

The introduction of a situation involving a problem or crisis places a demand on available adaptive functions and may require new functions. Reorganization of functioning usually involves some regression or redifferentiation to a lower level of functioning with subsequent subordination of lower levels to higher levels.

Clinical Implications

Several concepts of Werner's theory appear to have implications for clinical work with children. These concepts are the orthogenetic principle, analogous processes, microgenesis, and the sensoritonic theory of perception. In the most general sense, Werner's statement of the orthogenetic principle provides a definition of development in terms of direction and qualitative changes from globality and vagueness to differentiation and articulation. In microgenesis, Werner extended broad concepts of developmental change to specific change processes that occur in thought and perception. Such an approach has been found to be effective in differentiating the pathology of thought associated with schizophrenia. Finally, an aspect of the sensoritonic theory of perception is that there is a tendency of the organism to seek to balance sensory input that is imbalanced or asymmetrical (Baldwin, 1967). In terms of the concept of analogous processes, Werner proposed that different mental functions could result in the same mental achievement. The above are illustrative of the contribution of Werner's theory to an understanding of the nature of development and adaptation.

Erikson's Theory of Epigenetic Development

Model of Development

Freud's original formulation of the ego as a structure of a personality was extended by Erikson (1946, 1956, 1962) to synthesize and coordinate responses to the environment. The ego as a process is assumed to provide direction and control in adaptation to personal and environmental stimuli. The child is further assumed to have an active role in development that is both influencing and being influenced by the family (Maier, 1965). To this extent, Erikson's theory seems consistent with an organismic, active orientation to development.

Nature of Development

Development is conceptualized in terms of eight qualitative, differentiated stages of ego development and redevelopment. Each stage is characterized by a crisis or dilemma that needs to be resolved for normal development. The eight stages or phases encompass five of those originally proposed by Freud and three additional stages dealing with adult development. As Maier (1965) has suggested, each phase involves both a "vertical crisis culminating in an individual psychosocial solution and a horizontal crisis calling for a personally and socially satisfactory solution to the problem of motivational forces" (p. 30). The eight developmental phases, each represented by a specific psychosocial crisis, are:

1. Trust versus mistrust
2. Autonomy versus shame and doubt
3. Initiative versus guilt
4. Industry versus interiority
5. Identity and repudiation versus identity diffusion
6. Intimacy and solidarity versus isolation
7. Generativity versus self-absorption
8. Integrity versus despair

Explanation of Abnormal/Atypical Development

Normal development is tied to the mastery of successive crises across the eight phases. Psychological well-being and developmental maturity involve meeting the needs of the ego in the social context.

Explanation of Abnormal Development

Abnormal or atypical development is characterized by the failure to solve a crisis or conflict at a certain phase of development. As such it may be due to physical as well as psychological factors. "Retardation or failure in the development will rob the individual of his potential supremacy and endanger his whole hierarchy of development" (Maier, 1965, p. 30). Since normal development involves a balance of three affective processes (id, ego, and superego), disturbances of interpersonal relationships reflect imbalances between these processes. Abnormal or atypical development, however, is not viewed as a fixed outcome or as an irreversible condition, but rather as a variation of normal processes (Maier, 1965).

Role of Early Experience

Consistent with Freud's theory on which Erikson's views are based, significance is attached to early experience. "The first two years of life, the formative years, provide the foundation for all later motivation and personal disposition" (Maier, 1965, p. 25). In the early development of the ego, play serves a major function in adaptation to demands through organization of experience. The dynamic and developmental significance of play as a form of ego expression is emphasized by Erikson: "The child uses play to make up for the defeats, sufferings and frustrations, especially those resulting from a technically and culturally limited use of language" (Erikson, 1940, p. 567).

Role of the Environment

The environment is seen as the dynamic interchange between family members in a sociocultural context. The totality of environment in physical, social, and cultural aspects contributes, along with innate processes, to development. While the specific manner in which the environment influences a given child may be due to chance, the family and society provide direction for development. Of particular importance for development are cultural forces, guiding and selecting experiences for the child (Maier, 1965).

Basis for Behavior Change

Erikson accepts the psychodynamic position that libido is a basic force energizing development. There are two opposing drives of this basic force that contribute to an ongoing struggle between progressive and reactionary facets of the personality across stages of development (Maier, 1965). The recurrent struggle between these polar opposites forms the basis for change in development.

Clinical Implications

The major clinical implications of Erikson's theory pertain to its lifespan approach (Erikson, 1959) and to the role it assigns to the ego in the integration and adaptation to various life crises. The eight stages of development provide a useful framework in which to identify the level and direction of psychological functioning in the childhood years as well as into adolescence and adulthood.

Ausubel's Theory of Development

Model of Development

Ausubel's theory of ego development defines the ego as an abstraction: "At any given stage of development it constitutes the conceptual essence of the person's notions of himself or herself as a functioning individual endowed with certain attributes related to role and status" (Ausubel et al., 1980, p. 170). Ego development is assumed to occur as a result of ongoing interactions between social experiences and individual characteristics such as personality and capacity. These interactions, however, are mediated by perceptual variables; that is, the manner in which reality affects ego development is a function of what is perceived. The significance attached to the role of perception in ego development seems consistent with an organismic, active model of development.

Nature of Development

Ausubel et al. (1980) have proposed a normative sequence of ego development, although they qualify it in terms of its speculative and theoretical derivation. Based on naturalistic developmental data, sequential phases of development from infancy through adolescence are proposed. Each developmental phase is characterized by differences in ego structure. Although psychosocial, cultural, and idiosyncratic differences may influence the rate of ego development, the sequence of stages is assumed to be common to all individuals. The proposed stages and approximate age norms are as follows:

1. Emergence of functional self concept (0–6 months).
2. Omnipotent phase (6–30 months).
3. Ego devaluation crisis—satellizing stage (3–8 years).
4. Ego maturation crisis—desatellization (middle/late childhood to late adolescence).

Explanation of Normal Development

Normal development occurs when the child successfully negotiates changes in ego valuation engendered by parents and significant others at different stages of development. Following the initial stage of omnipotence, normal ego development involves satellization to the ego devaluation crisis that occurs in early childhood. "The solution chosen by nearly all children is to reconceive (that is, reorganize) their ego structure by satellizing (identifying) with their parents" (Wyne & O'Connor, 1979, p. 302). Resolution of the subsequent crisis of desatellization in adolescence is also essential for normal ego development.

Explanation of Abnormal/Atypical Development

If the crisis of ego devaluation is not met through satellization, use of alternative strategies often results in abnormal or atypical ego development. "Children who fail to satellize generally also fail to undergo ego devaluation. Infantile personality structures that are not presented with the prerequisite conditions for reorganization tend to persist despite various shifts in bio-social status" (Ausubel et al., 1980, p. 184). At the subsequent stage of desatellization, other factors may facilitate or retard ego development.

Role of Early Experience

Given the centrality of satellization in normal ego development, importance of early experience is shifted from infancy to early childhood. The process of satellization is of profound significance for the future development of personality. "Satisfactory resolution of the ego devaluation crisis by satellization in this period means that the children avoid both unfavorable alternatives and maintain the maximum degree of self-esteem realistically compatible with the cultural status of children everywhere" (Ausubel et al., 1980, p. 181).

Role of the Environment

Given the interactional nature of ego development, Ausubel et al. (1980) have proposed that social environments involving parents, teachers, siblings, and peers influence not only the pattern and range of individual development, but also the characteristics of stages themselves. As an organizing framework, culture gives the direction and guidance for normative ego growth.

Basis for Behavior Change

Biosocial status is an abstraction that Ausubel uses to refer to the role and status of a person's ego at a certain stage of development. Biosocial status can either be derived or earned. In the former, identification-acceptance occurs on the basis of vicarious or ordered status, that is, status that is intrinsically valued. In earned status, on the other hand, functional competence forms the basis for biosocial status. The child's progression through stages of ego development is influenced to a substantial degree by the parents' manner of assigning earned or derived status to the child through parental attitudes and behaviors.

Clinical Implications

A major feature of Ausubel's theory is that it is directed toward affective development and affective deviance. The interactional emphasis provides a framework for viewing normality and pathology of development in terms of child characteristics as well as parent attitude and behavior. Furthermore, the concepts of satellization and desatellization appear applicable as clinical elements for therapeutic change.

SUMMARY AND IMPLICATIONS

After having reviewed eight different theoretical approaches to child development in some detail, their salient features are summarized to provide a basis for considering clinical implications. In carrying out this task, it should be emphasized that the identification of key features reflects the author's personal interpretation. While the interpretations are derived from the reviewed materials pertaining to each theory, alternate interpretations can obviously be derived by others.

Table 2.1 summarizes the theories according to the dimensions specified previously in this chapter. An overview of the table reveals that the eight approaches to child development are characterized by commonalities as well as differences. Although it is beyond the scope of this chapter to carry out a detailed critique of the theories, a comparative analysis along each of the dimensions will facilitate a consideration of implication for clinical service.

In terms of models of development, it is not surprising that all but learning theory attribute an active (organismic) role to the child. The manner in which the nature of development is portrayed as qualitative and discontinuous, however, varies substantially, with Piaget, Erikson, Loevinger, Ausubel, and Freud specifying well-defined stages and Werner and Klein providing less detail in this regard.

Explanations by theories for normal and atypical development appear to fall into three clusters. Although the nature of the mechanism may differ for each, the theories of Klein, Piaget, Werner, Erikson, and Ausubel appear to share a common approach in which development is seen as the resolution of conflict or imbalance. Correspondence across developmental areas constitutes a second approach, reflective of Loevinger's and Anna Freud's theories. Learning theory constitutes the third approach, in which development is represented by the adequacy of acquired behavioral repertoires.

The importance attached to early experience in the infancy period on subsequent development differs substantially across theories. The three theories with psychoanalytic roots—Freud, Klein, and Erikson—all assign significant value to the formative period of infancy. For Ausubel, significance is shifted from infancy to experience in early childhood. While experience is an important factor for Piaget, Loevinger, Werner, and the learning theorists, no unique importance appears to be attached to infancy since experience is important throughout development.

A review of the role of the environment in these theories reveals linkages with the importance attached to early experience. For Freud, Klein, and Erikson, the immediate family, particularly the mother, constitutes a major environmental force for development. Loevinger, Werner, and Ausubel also emphasize social relationships but also extend the sphere to include other social agents and the culture in general. While the environment is central to Piaget's theory and learning theory, its role is radically different for each. For Piaget, the environment, both physical and social, provides the basis for active structuring experiences by the child. Learning theory, on the other hand, sees the child in a more passive and reactive role, with experience determining the nature of environmental contingencies for behavior.

Considering the basis for behavior change, grouping of the theories parallels those pertaining to the dimension of explanations of development. Theories with psychoanalytic derivations assume innate energizing forces that contribute to change and development (Freud, Klein, Erikson). For Piaget, Loevinger, Werner, and Ausubel, behavioral and developmental change can be seen as reorganization or restructuring resulting from exposure to environmental novelty or discrepancy. For learning theories, behavior change is a function of stimulating and/or reinforcing properties of the environment.

While the theories have a variety of implications, salient features with clinical relevance were selected from each for consideration. From this perspective, the theories of Freud, Piaget, Loevinger, Erikson, and Ausubel share an important feature of specifying developmental sequences. Such sequences can be of value in determining the qualitative nature, level, and direction of a child's functioning. While several theories have stressed the importance of significant others on the child's development, Klein's contribution may be the most emphatic regarding the role of the mother. Similarly, several theories have dealt with adaptation and the context of environmental demands; Werner's theory has this as a central contribution. A major clinical implication of learning theory is its contribution of techniques specifying the basis for behavioral change.

The above comparisons reveal substantial differences in the extent to which reviewed theories address the issues considered under each dimension. Rather than making an overall evaluation of the merits of each theory, all appear to have features of relevance to some issue. Consideration of each theory may thus proceed on the basis of its unique features and selected applicability. Some theories may then be applicable in certain contexts but not others. From this perspective, the theories of Freud, Klein, Erikson, and perhaps the learning theories may be appropriate to consider if

Table 2.1 A Dimensional Approach to Theories of Development

Developmental Model Theory	Model of Development	Nature of Development	Explanation of Normal Development	Explanation of Atypical Development
Freud, A.	Organismic	Qualitative steps of developmental lines	Correspondence of developmental lines	Excessive imbalance of developmental lines
Klein	Organismic	Assumed to be qualitative but not detailed	Resolution of conflicting instincts	Failure or inadequacy to resolve conflicting instincts
Piaget	Organismic	Qualitative stages of thought	Successive balance of assimilation-accommodation	Relative imbalance of assimilation-accommodation
Learning Theory	Mechanistic	Quantitative continuous behavior development	Acquisition of appropriate response repertoire	Inappropriate deficient behavior repertoire
Loevinger	Organismic	Qualitative stages of ego development	Ego as master trait assumes corresponding development of other areas	Fixation of ego development at lower levels
Werner	Organismic	Qualitative change from globality, undifferentiation to articulation, hierarchial organization	Progressive stabilization of mental functioning	Developmental regression or arrest
Erikson	Organismic	Eight qualitative stages across lifespan	Mastery of crises in successive stages	Imbalance of affective processes and failure to master stage crises
Ausubel	Organismic	Qualitative sequential phases of ego structures	Successful ego restructuring to changing valuation status	Failure to solve ego devaluation crises

early infant experience is of concern, whereas Loevinger, Werner, and Ausubel would have little to offer in this regard. If clinical efforts are directed toward older children and adolescents, on the other hand, the theories of Piaget, Loevinger, Ausubel, and Erikson could make important contributions. From yet another perspective, if change in behavior or development is of concern, learning theory could provide very specific techniques, whereas the theories of Piaget, Loevinger, Werner, and Ausubel would have more generalized implications. From these examples, it should be evident that the contributions of theories for clinical practice vary as a function of several factors such as the nature of the problem, developmental level of the child, and strategy for therapeutic intervention.

In the preceding summary and comparative review of theories, we have emphasized that a theory should not be evaluated on an overall basis but considered in terms of the specific contributions it may have for clinical concerns. This is in keeping with the advocacy for eclecticism recommended by Reese and Overton (1970). Yet it is clear that the individual cinician does not typically adopt frameworks for diagnostic therapeutic efforts in a totally neutral, objective, and eclectic manner. The adoption of a theoretical framework involves

Role of Early Experience	Role of the Environment	Basis for Behavior Change	Clinical Implications
Mother-infant relationship	Progressive role of mother, family, culture	Maturation and adaptation	Tracing of developmental lines
Infancy crucial in ego development	Relationship with mother prototypic of environmental influence	Ego functions	Value of mother-infant relationships
Each stage requires structuring/restructuring	Environment must be acted upon	Disequilibrium leading to structural change	Qualitative stages—construction of reality
Reinforcement history recognized but emphasis on current stimuli	Behavior a function of environmental contingencies	Nature and/or rate of antecedent & consequent stimuli	Techniques for behavior change
Limited emphasis on early experience due to verbal nature of assessing ego development	Social environment and processes significant relationship of organism reaction to total stimulus situation	Exposure to next level above present promotes change	Stages of ego development correspond to personality structures
No importance specified for early experience	Importance of family and culture in guiding, selecting experience	Problem demands result in reorganization	Adaptive nature of organism's response to environment
Ego function in early years formative for later development	Parent, siblings, peers, teachers, and culture reflect	Energizing force assumed, struggle between progressive-reactionary drives	Lifespan approach
Emphasis placed on early childhood rather than infancy	Role of social environment	Influence of earned and derived status	Interactional emphasis of child/significant others in developmental stages

evaluation along implicit or explicit criteria such as practicality, inclusiveness, and degree of fit with the clinician's personal philosophy. Given the reality that evaluation is involved in the adoption of theoretical frameworks, it seems fitting, as we conclude this chapter, to propose some elements that should be present in good, useful, and inclusive theories of child development.

The proposal of elements that should characterize useful and inclusive theories draws on findings of comparative analyses summarized above as well as recent theoretical contributions in the literature. An assessment of relevant literature reveals that substantial

efforts have been made to elaborate clinical implications of child development theories in recent years. On this basis, there are at least five elements that could be proposed:

1. *Commonsense basis.* An important element of a theory in terms of its usefulness should be the extent to which it is consistent with commonsense notions about child development. Theories with greater reliance on abstraction and symbolism to explain developmental phenomena are likely to be viewed as less applicable to clinical problems with more practial bases. The "naive psychology" of Heider (Baldwin, 1967), for example, is

representative of a theory that seeks to explain development with minimal recourse to abstract constructs. Thus, to the extent that a theory is able to present developmental characteristics with greater parsimony in terms of concepts and abstracts, it is likely to be seen as having greater utility.

2. *Empirical base.* A second element of importance focuses on the amenability of the theory to empirical validation. There are two aspects to be considered in this regard. The first pertains to the data base from which the theory was derived. Was it prospective or retrospective, anecdotal or systematic, clinical or empirical? Second, is the theory operationalized in such a manner as to permit empirical tests of hypotheses generated from it? Among the theories reviewed in this chapter, those of Ausubel and Loevinger are representative approaches that were derived empirically and amenable to validation.

3. *Inclusiveness of normality-pathology.* The manner and extent to which a theory can encompass normal as well as abnormal or atypical development constitutes a third element of importance. The comparative review made earlier suggested that some theories primarily address normality, where others primarily address pathology. Still others appear to be applicable only to certain kinds of pathology but lack breadth to account for variations in type or severity of atypical development. With the trend of educational and clinical programs to serve younger children with multiple problems or handicaps, quite often of a severe nature, comprehensiveness constitutes an element highly desirable for child development theories. Inhelder's (1966) presentation of cognitive developmental theory illustrates its inclusiveness by encompassing such diverse developmental problems as mental retardation, emotional disturbance, senile dementia, and dyspraxia in terms of central concepts of that theory. The applicability of Inhelder's proposals has been validated in empirical research with various special populations (Chandler, Greenspan, & Barenboim, 1974; Simeonsson, 1973; Simeonsson, Monson, & Blacher-Dixon, 1979).

4. *Developmental comprehensiveness.* An element related to the normality-pathology dimension is that of developmental comprehensiveness. In this regard, comprehensiveness involves both vertical and horizontal dimensions. Comprehensiveness in a vertical sense implies that the theory encompasses a broad, rather than a narrow, segment of the lifespan. From this perspective, Erikson's (1959) theory of eight life stages is representative of vertical comprehensiveness, whereas the focus on infancy and early childhood in Klein's (1958) psychoanalytic theory deals with a very limited developmental segment. Horizontal comprehensiveness, on the other hand, refers to the breadth of the theory to account for development in a variety of domains. Theories with limited horizontal comprehensiveness focus on a single developmental process such as affective states with minimal attention to other processes such as language, cognition, or perception. Klein's (1958) psychoanalytic theory would also seem illustrative of limited comprehensiveness in this regard. Theories with greater horizontal comprehensiveness address, or have the potential to address, correspondences of development across domains. The cognitive developmental theory of Piaget, particularly as elaborated by others, exemplifies an approach with horizontal comprehensiveness. Not only were Piaget's own efforts relevant to cognitive, perceptual, and linguistic processes of development, but others have demonstrated the comprehensiveness of the theory in application to academic skills such as reading (Elkind, 1976a) to interpersonal concept development and psychopathology (Elkind, 1976b). Further evidence of the comprehensiveness of cognitive developmental theory is found in the area of social cognition (Shantz, 1975), with developmental implications elaborated for clinical aspects of interpersonal awareness (Selman, Jaquette, & Lavin, 1977) as well as educational applications (Enwright, 1980).

5. *Applied relevance.* A final element to consider pertains to the applicability of a theory to practical and clinical realities. While the clinical needs of children are not likely to

change, the manner and extent of meeting these needs may change in the future as a function of legal, legislative, and/or political realities. Recent years have witnessed societal changes with significant clinical implications for habilitative and educational settings. Policies and mandates such as deinstitutionalization, primary prevention, early intervention, and mainstreaming of handicapped children are requiring reformulation of the logic and methods of providing clinical services. The return of institutionalized disturbed and retarded children to the community and the integration and mainstreaming of special children with normal peers has not occurred without controversy. While commendable on a philosophical basis, these policies often have pragmatic rather than theoretical foundations and are susceptible to a confusion of means and ends in implementation. The absence of a theoretical framework of development in policies and mandates may result in erratic and/or inappropriate clinical applications. Theoretical frameworks are needed to insure that means such as deinstitutionalization and mainstreaming lead to goals of behavioral adaptation and developmental maturity for children. The framework of a developmental theory can contribute direction and sequence for clinical efforts by specifying conditions and characteristics of developmental change. This approach has been illustrated by Simeonsson, Grunewald, and Scheiner (1976), who juxtaposed the policy of normalization to habilitate retarded persons with the cognitive developmental theory of Piaget. By juxtaposing habilitation policy and developmental theory, the means of clinical strategies and environments can be conceptualized in terms of their contributory roles to goals of successive stages of personal independence and developmental maturity.

While it is acknowledged that evaluative elements such as those presented above are not exclusive and may vary from one professional to another in importance, they can be used on an informal level to evaluate theories. Drawing on the review, an evaluation of the theories presented in this chapter is made in Table 2.2.

As an exploratory exercise, this evaluation provides a means of comparing the relative status of theories in terms of the proposed elements of utility and inclusiveness. A specific theory may thus be seen to have strength in terms of one element, or on an overall basis, or both. In reference to the summary in Table 2.2, the strength of Freud's theory seems to be in one area, whereas learning theory and the

Table 2.2   Evaluation of Theories in Terms of Proposed Elements of Utility and Inclusiveness

	Parsimony	Empirical Base	Definitional Inclusiveness Normality/Pathology		Developmental Comprehensiveness	Applied Relevance
Freud, A.	0	0	1	1	2	0
Klein	0	0	0	1	0	0
Piaget	1	2	2	2	2	2
Learning theory	2	2	2	2	1	2
Werner	1	2	1	1	1	1
Loevinger	2	2	2	0	1	1
Erikson	1	1	1	1	1	2
Ausubel	1	2	2	1	1	2

Note:

0 = Minimal feature
1 = Moderate feature
2 = Strong feature

theory of Piaget appear to have strengths on an overall basis. The evaluative summary presented above assumes that each element is of equal importance. In actual clinical practice they may be weighted differentially, yielding a different evaluation of theories.

Although the specific elements considered above may not be found equally useful by all clinicians, systematic evaluation by some specified set of criteria is recommended as a productive means of identifying the relative contributions of different theories to clinical problems. This approach is consistent with Goldfried's (1980) position on the status of competing orientations on psychotherapy: "We have all 'taken up sides' and have placed far too much emphasis on *who* is correct not *what* is correct" (p. 991). Further support for the value of systematically considering the contributions of a variety of theories is evident in Goldfried's reference to the therapy field.

More than 50 percent of clinical psychologists saw themselves as adhering to an eclectic rather than single therapy orientation. Analogous to Goldfried's focus on therapy approaches, there is a shared emphasis on the consideration of the difficult but essential task to "set aside our well-established, if not time honored, practice of setting one approach against another and, instead, to work toward a rapprochement" (1980, p. 996).

One step toward the goal of rapprochement has been the review and evaluation of selected theories in this chapter. Among additional steps that could be taken is the systematic review of other theories not considered here. Candidates that may be appropriate for such a review include the approaches of Lewin (Baldwin, 1967), Kohlberg (1969), Mahler (1975), Bruner (1965), Bandura and Walters (1963), and Wallon (de Aguriaguerra, 1980), among others. A second step involves the consideration of efforts to synthesize similar or different approaches. The similarity of the cognitive theories of Piaget, Bruner, and Ausubel, for example, has been reviewed for implications by Lawton, Saunder, and Muhs (1980). Representative contributions in regard to different approaches have been the synthesis of psychoanalytic and learning theory (Alexander,

1963; Wachtel, 1977) and psychoanalytic and cognitive-developmental theory (Greenspan, 1980). Although these synthesizing efforts have been restricted to certain theories, they illustrate the value of identifying commonalities that go beyond the contribution of single theories in isolation.

To reiterate the original premise, recent trends toward growing diversity of clinical problems, clients, and settings for children dictate the need for expansion of theoretical frameworks and eclecticism in identifying commonalities with clinical implications. "In breaking set and looking for commonalities, we might even find ourselves more willing to acknowledge the unique contributions that other orientations have to offer" (Goldfried, 1980, p. 997). The benefits that derive from such action are likely to result in the provision of more precise and more effective clinical services for children.

REFERENCES

Alexander, F. The dynamics of psychotherapy in light of learning theory. *American Journal of Psychiatry,* 1963, **120,** 440–448.

Ausubel, D.P., Sullivan, E.V., & Ives, S.W. *Theory and problems of child development* (3rd ed.). New York: Grune & Stratton, 1980.

Baldwin, A.L. *Theories of child development.* New York: Wiley, 1967.

Bandura, A., & Walters, R.H. *Social learning and personality development.* New York: Holt, Rinehart & Winston, 1963.

Bemporad, J.R. Theories of development. In J.R. Bemporad (Ed.), *Child development in normality and psychopathology.* New York: Brunner-Mazel, 1980.

Berger, M. Learning theories. In M. Rutter & L. Hersov (Eds.), *Child psychiatry: Modern approaches.* Oxford: Blackwell Scientific, 1977.

Bijou, S.W. Theory and research in mental (developmental) retardation. In S.W. Bijou & D.M. Baer (Eds.), *Child development: Readings in experimental analysis.* New York: Appleton-Century-Crofts, 1967.

Bijou, S.W., & Baer, D.M. *Child development: A systematic and empirical theory.* New York: Appleton-Century-Crofts, 1961.

Brier, N.M., & Demb, H.B. Psychotherapy with a developmentally disabled adolescent. *Journal of Developmental Behavioral Pediatrics,* 1980, **1,** 19–23.

Bruner, J.S. The growth of mind. *American Psychology,* 1965, **20,** 1007–1017.

Bryt, A. Non-Freudian methods of psychoanalysis with children and adolescents. In B.B. Wolman (Ed.), *Manual of child psychopathology.* New York: McGraw-Hill, 1972.

Chandler, M.J., Greenspan, S., & Barenboim, C. Assessment and training of roletaking and referential communication skills in institutionalized emotionally disturbed children. *Developmental Psychology,* 1974, **10,** 546–553.

Damon, W. Why study social-cognitive development? *Human Development,* 1979, **22,** 206–211.

de Aguriaguerra, J. *Handbook of child psychiatry and psychology.* R.P. Lorion (Ed. and trans.). New York: Masson, 1980.

Dare, C. Psychoanalytic theories. In M. Rutter & L. Hersov (Eds.), *Child psychiatry: Modern approaches.* Oxford, Blackwell Scientific, 1977.

Ekstein, R. Psychoanalysis. In S.I. Harrison (Ed.), *Basic handbook of child psychiatry: Therapeutic intervention* (Vol. 3). New York: Basic Books, 1979.

Elkind, D. Cognitive development and reading. In H. Singer & R.B. Ruddell (Eds.), *Theoretical models and processes of reading* (2nd ed.). Newark, Del.: International Reading Assoc., 1976.(a)

Elkind, D. Cognitive development and psychopathology: Observations on egocentrism and ego defense. In E. Schopler & R.J. Reichler (Eds.), *Psychopathology and child development.* New York: Plenum, 1976.(b)

Enwright, R.D. An integration of social cognitive development and cognitive processing: Educational applications. *American Education Research Journal,* 1980, **17,** 21–41.

Erikson, E. Studies in the interpretation of play; PL 1. Clinical observations of play disruption in young children. *Genel. Psychology Monograph,* 1940, **22,** 557–671.

Erikson, E. Ego development and historical change. In P. Greenacre et al. (Eds.), *The psychoanalytic study of the child.* (Vol. 2) New York: International University Press, 1946, pp. 359–396.

Erikson, E. The problem of ego identity. *Journal of the American Psychoanalists Association,* 1956, **4,** 56–121.

Erikson, E. Identity and the life cycle: Selected papers. *Psychological Issues* (Monograph). New York: International University Press, 1959, **I**:1.

Erikson, E. Reality and actuality. *Journal of the American Psychoanalists Association,* 1962, **10,** 451–473.

Eysenck, H.J. *The biological basis of personality.* Springfield, Ill.: Thomas, 1967.

Freeman, D.S. The family as a system: Fact or fancy. *Comprehensive Psychiatry,* 1976, **17,** 735–749.

Freud, A. The concept of developmental lines. *Psychoanalytic Study of the Child,* 1963, **18,** 245–265.

Goldfried, M.R. Toward the delineation of therapeutic change principles. *American Psychologist,* 1980, **35,** 991–999.

Greenspan, S.I. Intelligence and adaptation: An integration of psychoanalytic and Piagetian developmental psychology. *Psychological Issues.* 1979, **12,** 1–108.

Hauser, S.T. Loevinger's model and measure of ego development: A critical review. *Psychological Bulletin.* 1976, **83,** 928–955.

Holt, R.R. Review of measuring ego development, (Vols. 1 & 2). *Journal of Nervous Mental Disease.* 1974, **158,** 310,316.

Hunt, J. McV. *Intelligence and experience.* New York: Ronald, 1961.

Inhelder, B. Cognitive development and its contribution to the diagnosis of some phenomena of mental deficiency. *Merrill–Palmer Quarterly,* 1966, **12,** 299–321.

Klein, M. On the development of mental functioning. *International Journal of Psychoanalysis,* 1958, **39,** 84–90.

Kohlberg, L. Stage and sequence: The cognitive-developmental approach to socialization. In D. Goslin (Ed.), *Handbook of socialization theory and research.* New York: Rand McNally, 1969.

Langer, J. *Theories of development.* New York: Holt, Rinehart & Winston, 1969.

Lawton, J.T., Saunders, R.A., & Muhs, P. Theories of Piaget, Bruner, and Ausubel: Explications and implications. *Journal of Genetic Psychology,* 1980, **136,** 121–136.

Lesser, S.R. Psychoanalysis with children. In B.B. Wolman (Ed.), *Manual of child psychopathology.* New York: McGraw-Hill, 1972.

Loevinger, J. The meaning and measurement of ego development. *American Psychologist,* 1966, **21,** 195–206.

Looft, W.R. Socialization and personality throughout the life span: An examination of contemporary psychological approaches. In P.B. Baltes & K.W. Schaie (Eds.), *Life-span developmental psychology: Personality and socialization.* New York: Academic Press, 1973.

Mahler, M.S., Pine, F., & Bergman, A. *The psychological birth of the human infant.* New York: Basic Books, 1975.

Maier, H.W. *Three theories of child development.* New York: Harper & Row, 1965.

Piaget, J. Piaget's theory. In P.H. Mussen (Ed.), *Carmichael's manual of child psychology* (Vol. I, 3rd ed.). New York: Wiley, 1970.

Reese, H.W., & Overton, W.F. Models and theories of development. In L.R. Goulet & P.B. Baltes (Eds.), *Life-span developmental psychology: Research and theory.* New York: Academic Press, 1970.

Rutter, M., & Hersov, L. *Child psychiatry: Modern approaches.* Oxford: Blackwell Scientific, 1977.

Sajwaj, T., Libet, E., & Agras S. Lemon juice therapy: The control of life threatening rumination in a six-month-old infant. *Journal of Applied Behavior Analysis,* 1974, **7,** 557–563.

Salkind, N. *Theories of human development.* New York: Van Nostrand, 1981.

Schmid-Kitsikis, E. Piagetian theory and its approach to psychopathology. *American Journal of Mental Deficiency,* 1973, **77,** 694–705.

Sears, R.R., Rau, L., & Alpert R. *Identification and child rearing.* Stanford: Stanford University Press, 1965.

Selman, R.L., Jaquette, D., & Lavin, D.R. Interpersonal awareness in children: Toward an integration of developmental and clinical child psychology. *American Journal of Orthopsychiatry,* 1977, **47,** 264–274.

Shantz, C.V. The development of social cognition. In M. Hetherington (Ed.), *Review of child development research* (Vol. 5). Chicago: University of Chicago Press, 1975.

Simeonsson, R.J. Egocentric responses of normal and emotionally disturbed children in different treatment settings. *Child Psychiatry & Human Development,* 1973, **3,** 179–186.

Simeonsson, R.J., Grunewald, K., & Scheiner, A.P. Piaget and normalization: Developmental humanism. *Research Exchange and Practice,* 1976, **2,** 229–242.

Simeonsson, R.J., Monson, L.B., & Blacher-Dixon, J. Promoting social competence in exceptional children through perspective taking and sociodramatic activities. *Psychodrama and Sociometry,* 1979, **32,** 156–163.

Wachtel, P.L. *Psychoanalysis and behavior therapy.* New York: Basic Books, 1977.

Weiner, J. The concept of development from a comparative and organismic point of view. In D. Harris (Ed.), *The concept of development. An issue in the study of human behavior.* Minneapolis: University of Minnesota Press, 1957.

Weiner, M.L. *Cognitive unconscious: A Piagetian approach to psychotherapy.* Davis, Calif.: International Psychological Press, 1975.

Werner, H. The concept of development from a comparative and organismic point of view. In D. Harris, (Ed.), *The concept of development: An issue in the study of human behavior.* Minneapolis: University of Minnesota Press, 1957.

Wyne, M.D., & O'Connor, P.D. *Exceptional children: A developmental view.* Lexington, Mass.: Heath, 1979.

CHAPTER 3

Developmental Psychology for the Clinical Child Psychologist

KATHLEEN M. GERRITY, FREDA A. JONES, AND PATRICIA A. SELF

Common roots and interests are shared by clinical child and developmental psychologists. The task of the developmental psychologist is to describe developmental change and to explain processes that regulate that change across the lifespan. The task of the clinical child psychologist is to facilitate development in children whose normal developmental trajectories are at risk for delay or aberration due to wide varieties of possibly deleterious factors. Because of these common efforts at understanding and manipulating developmental processes, dialogue among developmentalists and clinicians is essential for arriving at the optimal "how to" of intervention in a child's psychological growth.

The purpose of this chapter is to present the product of such a dialogue. It consists of five sections. The first section provides a conceptual framework that emphasizes critical issues in development. Such issues include the roles of age, stability and change, continuity and discontinuity, and interactional processes in development within the framework of different models of development. The next three sections contain discussions of development within three specific behavioral areas selected as representative from the many that are of concern to clinicians. These areas are play, communication/language, and attachment. The particular organizational approach used here is not the traditional separation of developmental realms, but rather one that emphasizes the interactive processes of various dimensions of development. Therefore, each of the three sections will present one aspect of development in childhood and describe how its outcome is codetermined by the interactive effects of psychological, biological, cultural, and outerphysical factors. The final section includes a summary of clinical implications.

CONCEPTUAL FRAMEWORK

A logical first step in providing a conceptual framework is to define the term "development." However, it has been argued that a definition of development is determined by the particular conceptual framework to which one subscribes (Overton & Reese, 1973; Reese & Overton, 1970). Therefore, we will first consider factors that influence development and how these factors are involved in the developmental process. Next we will discuss definitions of development, and finally we will look at the implications that developmental principles have for particular areas of development.

Factors Influencing Development

Riegel (1975, 1976, 1977) has described four dimensions that are integral to developmental processes. These are biological, psychological, cultural, and outerphysical factors. These four sets of determinants are illustrative of the importance of context for individual development, where context involves all of the factors that continually interweave in the developmental process. Every developmental context includes parameters of individual functioning, as well as cultural and outerphysical events. The final dimension, outerphysical events, refers to earthquakes, floods, climatic changes, etc., which present a society with the challenge of protecting its members from catastrophe. Examples of other specific developmental influences will be given in further sections of this chapter.

A notable exception to the developmental codeterminants listed above is age. This variable is helpful as an organizer of information, rather than as an explanation of development, during life periods involving numerous age-graded experiences. Therefore, age is most useful during infancy and childhood, least useful during adulthood, and slightly more useful again during the final years when age-related events show a small increase (Baltes et al., 1980). Indeed, age accounts for a wide variety of behaviors. However, it has sometimes been a conceptual obstacle to the identification of mechanisms that actually determine development (Reese & Overton, 1970; Wohlwill, 1973). Age per se does not cause development. Rather, the important variables to examine are the multiple factors mentioned above (biological, psychological, cultural, and outerphysical) and the resulting effects of their interactions across time.

The idea that age is a useful organizational tool during some periods of development but not others leads to the task of differentiating non-age-related from age-related influences during any life period. In addressing this issue, Baltes and associates (1980) have developed a three-category model of normative age graded, normative history graded, and non-normative events, which can be applied to the basic determinants of development described by Riegel. Table 3.1 gives examples of biological, psychological, cultural, and outerphysical events falling in each category. Normative age-graded events are biological, psychological, or environmental phenomena that have a strong relationship to chronological age in terms of onset and duration. Examples of this are puberty, infant develop-

ment of attachment to his or her primary caretaker, or school attendance (the cell for normative, age graded, outerphysical events is blank because these two categories have no overlap). Child developmentalists and clinicians are perhaps most accustomed to thinking in terms of such age-related factors, where much of the child's experience and development is understood as linked to maturation. Such perspectives rely heavily on "mean age" information. However, it should be remembered that there is a great deal of individual variation in the accomplishment of tasks that have been conceptualized as age related. This variation occurs even within a normal population. For example, on the Mental Scale of the Bayley Scales of Infant Development (Bayley, 1969) one is provided with the mean age of passing, as well as with the age range within which 90 percent of the normal infants tested passed each item. Mean age for expressive jabbering is 12 months, while the range for onset in normal infants is from 9 to 18 months. The mean age for placing two round and two square pieces in a puzzle board is 19.3 months, with a range of 14–30+ months. These ranges indicate that functioning at a mean age level cannot be assumed even in a normally developing child. Such wide age variation in developmental accomplishments drastically reduces the utility of age, as opposed to functional level, as a clinical tool for both normal and exceptional populations.

The second category of time-related developmental events are normative history-graded phenomena. These are factors associated with the historical events and contexts that are experienced by a majority of a given generational group. General examples of normative history-graded events might be wars, epidemics, economic depressions, or events associated with modernization of a society, all of which take place against the general sociocultural background. Examples of normative history-graded developmental determinants in Riegel's (1975) scheme would be specific factors derived from historical contexts. For example, "consciousness raising" among minorities, childhood exposure to recreational drug use, and rearing in single-parent families are socie-

Table 3.1. Examples of Biological, Psychological, Cultural, and Outerphysical Events that Occur in Normative Age Graded, Normative History Graded, and Nonnormative Fashions

Developmental Determinants	Relationships to Age and History		
	Normative Age Graded	Normative History Graded	Nonnormative
Biological	Puberty	Amenorrhea due to war-related malnutrition	Illness
Psychological	Mother-infant attachment	Consciousness raising among minority group members	Death of significant other
Cultural	School attendance	Early exposure to recreational drug use	Born into power
Outerphysical		Exposure to environmental pollution	Tornado

tal changes which influence the nature of contemporary childhood.

The final category of Baltes et al.'s (1980) model is that of nonnormative life events, that is, those events that do not occur in any normative age- or history-graded fashion. Such events can occur at any age and in many or all generations. The impact of such an event depends on developmental level at time of onset and the cultural context within which it occurs. For example, the death of a significant other will be understood differently by a child than an adult (Dunton, 1970) and will be understood differently from Judaic, Christian, or Eastern religious perspectives. Additionally, illness can occur during any developmental period, but its effects will vary. For instance, chronic illness during childhood would be expected to affect autonomy and parent-child and sibling relationships. During adolescence, chronic illness might affect the establishment of intimate relationships outside the family (Willis, Elliot, & Jay, 1982). There are also nonnormative outerphysical events. For instance, in 1979 a tornado killed several people and caused much destruction in Wichita Falls, Texas. For an extended period of time following that disaster, special psychological services were offered by the school system because of the high anxiety level aroused among the children by even mild signs of bad weather. The perception of the physical environment as unpredictable, mov-

ing from benign to catastrophic without warning, can be expected to have far-reaching effects even after the resolution of trauma. For example, feelings of vulnerability, risk-taking behavior, attitudes toward life and property, and awareness of natural forces might be different than if the experience had never occurred.

Thus far we have described four sets of factors which contribute to ontogeny: biological, psychological, cultural, and outerphysical. Further, these factors may influence development in normative age graded, normative history graded, or nonnormative ways. However, understanding development requires more than knowing what factors are involved. It also requires the use of conceptual tools to understand how these factors are involved in the developmental process. Such tools are provided by theoretical models and are the principles thought to regulate developmental change at various ages and across specific behavioral areas.

Models of Development

Models that provide the conceptual tools for understanding how development might proceed have been divided into three categories: mechanistic, organismic, and contextualistic. The mechanistic and organismic models involve differing philosophical presuppositions regarding the relationship between person and environment. The primary emphasis of mechanistic theories lies in the environment acting on the individual (Reese & Overton, 1970), and the primary emphasis of the organismic model lies in the individual acting on his or her surroundings (Lerner, Skinner, & Sorrell, 1980; Reese & Overton, 1970; Riegel, 1975). There is some discussion as to whether the current expression of contextualism (i.e., dialecticism described by Riegel, 1975, 1976, 1977) involves yet a third set of presuppositions (Riegel, 1975; Lerner et al., 1980) or a combination of those of the other two models (Tolman, 1981). In dialecticism the active interaction of the individual with the environment, and the environment with the individual, is stressed. Although no attempt will be made to resolve philosophical issues here, each model will be described and its contributions emphasized.

Mechanistic and Organismic Models

The mechanistic and organismic models of development and their corollary issues have been extensively treated in a series of essays by Overton and Reese (1973, 1981; Reese & Overton, 1970). The basic metaphor for the mechanistic model is that a person functions "as if" he or she were a machine. This viewpoint is derived from a metaphysics of stability in which objects are inert until acted upon. Thus the individual is seen as reactive with no spontaneous means for action at birth (hence the tabula rasa notion). The organismic perspective relies upon current conceptions of biological organisms for its metaphor, with the individual understood as inherently active, and spontaneously interacting, rather than reacting, from birth. It is based upon a metaphysics that sees not stability but activity as primary. This perspective is also held by dialectic developmentalists who focus on "a changing individual in a changing world" (Riegel, 1976, p. 690). From the dialectic perspective, the interaction of basic determinants of development must be considered with all of the determinants in states of perpetual change.

The assumption that either stability or change is primary leads to studying develop-

ment in different ways. A mechanist is interested in static traits and abilities (Riegel, 1976) and their predictability or stability across ages. Change is conceptualized in terms of quantitative increments over time in learned traits. Thus development is continuous, with no truly novel (Overton & Reese, 1981) or qualitative changes in functioning occurring. Any behavior is understandable through reduction to its component parts, and any change is predictable through addition of its component behaviors. This model is preferred by learning theorists, who see reinforcement as the mechanism through which development proceeds. The implication of this model is that any behavior is changeable by changing response contingencies because all behavior is controlled by response contingencies.

Organismic models allow for the emergence of novelty in functioning. This novelty is not reducible to precursor structures or behaviors. It is emergent from, although discontinuous with, preceding development. In contrast to the mechanistic model, a given level of functioning is considered to be more than the sum of the parts of the preceding level. Overton and Reese (1981, p. 24) have provided an example of such emergence from the work of Piaget. During the period of 6–8 years, the operations of addition and subtraction initially function independently. The operation of taking away objects is not integrated with the operation of putting objects together. When these skills are integrated, new systemic properties emerge. The most important property, and one that is possessed by neither addition nor subtraction independently, is reversibility. It emerges as a property of the higher level system, and with its emergence thought becomes logical. Reversibility is not directly predictable from or reducible to the precursor operations. In the same sense that wetness emerges as a quality of integrated hydrogen and oxygen, levels of organization emerge in human development that cannot be accounted for from a purely reductionist perspective. This is a discontinuity model, which characterizes development as proceeding in an invariant sequence of stages, each one qualitatively different from the next, and proceeding toward a final end state. An example of the organismic model is Piaget's theory of cognitive development.

One implication of this type of theory is that all aspects of behavior or understanding would not be mutable through reinforcement. For example, a child's ability to understand illness seems to coincide roughly with Piagetian stages of cognitive development (Willis et al., 1982), and reinforcement would not be expected to increase understanding beyond one's cognitive limitations.

Dialectic Model

As mentioned above, the dialectic model combines perspectives held by organismic and mechanistic theorists. Combining these two perspectives, however, has more than an additive effect. One might say that a new level of analysis emerges in the same sense that we see emergents in cognitive development. Rather than simply looking at the effect of the environment on man and man on the environment, dialectic developmental psychology is concerned with the relationships among changes. The changes of concern are the simultaneous progressions among the four interdependent dimensions (psychological, biological, cultural, and outerphysical). Development occurs as a function of the relationships among these progressions, and the relationships of concern are synchrony and dysynchrony.

The relationship of synchrony occurs when two or more of the biological, psychological, cultural, or outerphysical dimensions progress in a mutually facilitative fashion. An example of synchronous progressions might be found in parent-child interaction. Sameroff (1974) suggests that from the low levels of social cognition found in parts of society one might expect greater numbers of children whose development is limited by inadequate caretaking. He attributes a lower than expected level to "self-righting tendencies" arising from the transactional nature of parent-child interaction. His example, which follows, can also be viewed as synchronous progression in two developmental dimensions that results from the interaction of those dimensions.

The mother has little difficulty viewing the infant from a sensori-motor level of cognition while the infant is in the sensori-motor period. However, as the child progresses through his own development, his caretakers are forced to view him from different perspectives potentially causing a restructuring in their view of the child. At each new level the child makes interactional demands at higher levels of of complexity, frequently surprising parents by this emerging precocity. (Sameroff, 1974, p. 33)

Breakdowns in synchrony give rise to conflicts or crises, which generate dialectic tension from which further development derives. An example of crises arising from dysynchronous progressions is apparent in teenage pregnancy. Although biological factors enable adolescents to conceive and bear offspring, this capacity conflicts with the existing moral climate and economic system. The simultaneous occurrence of bearing a child, straining family support systems, interrupting routine educational processes, and facing limited economic resources requires extensive adaptation, which doubtless subserves the progression of individual psychological development. This progression may not be of the nature we are accustomed to observing. In Eriksonian terms (Erikson, 1950), instead of resolving identity versus role confusion followed by intimacy versus isolation, these adolescents are facing both conflicts simultaneously. The individual psychological outcome will necessarily be different than in those individuals that resolve these crises sequentially.

Such synchrony and dysynchrony may occur internally (i.e., between various psychological factors), externally (between the cultural and outerphysical dimensions), or between the internal and external dimensions (psychological and cultural). Thus dialectic developmental psychology is concerned with changes not only in the individual but also among individuals and in society at large. The influences of one upon the other are reciprocal and inseparable. "In this dynamic interaction of inner and outer dialectics, man not only transforms the outer world in which he lives, but is himself transformed by the world which he and others have created" (Riegel, 1975, p. 694).

In summary, three models have been described: the mechanistic, the organismic, and the dialectic. Since different models have been used with varying success in different behavioral areas and in different age groups, an eclectic (Reese & Overton, 1970) or pluralistic (Baltes et al., 1980) approach to human development has evolved. Thus multiple models are used to explain the progressions of human behavior.

Definitions of Development

Having described the three major developmental models, we return to the tasks of defining development. The authors support the view that one's conceptual framework determines one's definition, and that each model has different criteria for determining which behavioral changes are considered developmental in nature. From an organismic perspective, change is developmental only if it reflects sequential, qualitatively different stages, is irreversible, is directed toward a mature end state, and is universal (Baltes et al., 1980; Overton & Reese, 1981; Wohlwill, 1973). Other models have fewer criteria for defining change as developmental. Mechanistic theorists would describe, explain, or modify intra- and interindividual developmental changes through reference to the concept of reinforcement (Baltes, Reese, & Nesselroade, 1977; Langer, 1969). Lifespan dialectic developmentalists, on the other hand, see development not only as the acquisition of behavior, but also as the maintenance and transformation of useful skills and the extinction of formerly adaptive behaviors. As in other models, time of onset and duration are considered important features of behavior, but variations in time of termination are also emphasized (Baltes et al., 1980). In addition, a dialectic approach can incorporate both continuous and discontinuous development. However, because of ongoing change in all developmental dimensions and the impact this has on the nature of maturity, no particular end state is predicted. In fact, Riegel (1973) has suggested a period of cognitive development beyond Piaget's final stage of formal operational thought, which he calls dialectic operations.

The remainder of this chapter will be presented within a dialectic framework. This framework was chosen because it is comprehensive in its capacity to include critical aspects of various models of development in a manner that is not conceptually contradictory. For example, the role played by discontinuous cognitive development in understanding illness can be considered simultaneously with behavioral interventions based on reinforcement programs. Thus both mechanistic and organismic concepts can be drawn upon where relevant. In addition, this framework makes explicit the importance of considering all contextual factors in the process of development. Outerphysical and cultural events must be included in attempts either to understand or to influence a developmental pathway. Reflection on the age-graded, history-graded, or nonnormative nature of these factors is also of use.

For example, the impact of being the first generation to experience a particular cultural/ psychological dysynchrony is not to be ignored. Exposure to drug abuse during the elementary school years is a high-risk, contemporary cultural phenomenon. Few models exist either for children or parents in handling the situation itself, or for the emotional response to the situation. A parent might be inclined to ask, "What is wrong with my child? I never took drugs at that age, nor did my parents." The focus here is on the "fault" of the child for ingesting drugs. A lessening of that focus might be accomplished through realization of the uniqueness of this generation of children compared with prior generations in even experiencing exposure to dangerous substances before reasoning capacities are well developed. A child of this generation may be disobeying parental orders in accepting a Quaalude, whereas a child of the last generation might have ignored parental guidelines in accepting a piece of bubblegum.

The dialectic framework, therefore, was chosen as the perspective within which to present the information on behavioral development because it best structures the consideration of the multiple factors that influence development and the multiple points at which clinical intervention is possible.

BEHAVIORAL DEVELOPMENT

In this section, the development of play, communication/language, and parent-child attachment will be discussed within a dialectic framework. Examples of the interactive impact of psychological, cultural, and biological factors on each behavioral area will be drawn primarily from infancy and early childhood. Because of the rarity of occasions calling for extensive survival-oriented adjustments by a culture, specific examples of the impact of outerphysical events on development will not be addressed.

Play

Play has been described as both multiply determined and multiply functional (Drucker, 1979). No specific activity is necessarily play, but almost any activity can be done playfully. As such, it is a phenomenon rich in examples of the developmental interactions of psychological, biological, and cultural dimensions.

Psychological Determinants

Examples of relationships between play and psychological variables are abundant. A developmental theory of play with primary emphasis on cognitive influences and implications is that of Piaget (1962) and Piaget and Inhelder (1969). From this perspective, play is understood as integrally involved in the development of representational thought, that is, the ability to use symbols, and is also seen as the primary "language" of the child from about 2–4 years. It is important, however, to look at forms of play that are precursors to symbolic play. Lack of stimulation and encouragement of the precursor behaviors would be expected to affect the time of onset of symbolic play. Therefore, awareness and encouragement of rudimentary forms of play are desirable in cases of developmental delay.

During the early part of the sensorimotor stage, play involves the exercise of simple motor schemata performed for the pleasure of functioning, for the pleasure of causing an effect, or both. Sucking in the absence of feeding, play coughing, or batting bells on a mobile are examples of such exercise play.

This sort of play stays with us through adulthood in the pleasurable confirmation of new skills.

A further step in the development of symbolic play is the ritualization of particular schemata. Piaget (1962, p. 95) gives the example of his 1-year-old daughter rocking an orange peel from side to side but before doing so looking playfully underneath it each time. Looking underneath was not necessary to setting the peel in motion, but this ritual was performed at least 20 times repeating both instrumental (rocking) and noninstrumental (looking under) elements. With the creation of playful rituals, action moves for the first time outside the realm of adaptation or exercise. It is no longer tied functionally to the situation and therefore is moving toward actualizing the potential for symbolic expression.

Parallel changes that occur in imitation skills toward the end of the sensorimotor period set the stage for the beginnings of symbolic play, an activity which is central to the self-expression of the young child. As with play, imitation is gradually dissociated from the immediate context in which the imitated act was observed. With the onset of deferred imitation (e.g., imitating another child's antics the day after seeing them) comes evidence of the use of internal representation. The child imitates images drawn from memory. Thus the child demonstrates attainment of object permanence, that is, the ability to hold within memory objects that are outside immediate perception. It is at this juncture in the developmental sequence that we encounter the emergence of symbolic play.

The synchronous development of symbolic play and deferred imitation provides evidence at approximately 18 months of age of a new skill with sweeping developmental implications: the ability to use symbols. Cognitively, representational thought opens up all the potential of integrating past with present experience. Language development, with all it implies for the transmission of knowledge and culture, will also make great gains, and synchronous advancements in ego development have been noted. Drucker (1979) indicates that just as Piaget discusses the gradual differentiation between self and object, psychoanalytic workers write of the differentiation of self from other. She suggests that both (1) the common emphasis of cognitive and psychoanalytic theorists on differentiation, distancing, and object concept in the development of separate representations of self and object and self and other and (2) the chronological overlap of the emergence of these differentiations imply crucial relationships among them.

Symbolic play is, therefore, an expression of representational thinking, the developmental influence of which is also seen in other areas of functioning: imitation, language, and ego development. In addition, during the period from about 2–7 years symbolic play has a special role in furthering the development of the child. It has been considered a special form of language (Drucker, 1979; Furth, 1969; Piaget, 1962), which is used to express everything in the child's experience that cannot be integrated by means of the child's limited language skills. Thus it provides the most direct access for clinicians to the subjective experience of the child. The content of play is primarily affective. It is in this sense that play is comparable to adult dreams, which express content without benefit of language or the logic of mature intelligence (Piaget & Inhelder, 1969).

Types of symbolic games range from projection of earliest schemata to new objects (making the teddy bear sleep), through the use of the body as a symbol (walking fingers for a person), to enactment of long scenes sustained over periods of time. Observers of children are also familiar with compensatory play (doing in make believe what is forbidden in reality) and cathartic play (lessening of emotion through imaginary rehearsal of trying events).

In addition to cognition, separation-individuation, and affective content, levels of play have been found to be synchronously related to the development of social interaction skills. Parten's (1932) early work in this area defined six categories of play participation behavior: unoccupied, solitary, onlooker, parallel, associative, and cooperative play. Her cross-sectional findings indicated that play was predominantly solitary at 2–2.5 years, parallel from 2.5–3.5 years, and group

(associative and cooperative) between 3.5–4.5 years. This resulted in an understanding of solitary play as the most immature form of play, which was often interpreted as indicative of poor social adjustment (Moore, Everton, & Brophy, 1974). It also resulted in the view that parallel play (proximal play with similar materials but minimal interaction between children) is a transitional stage between solitary and group play. Recent research, however, has called these views into question. A longitudinal study by Smith (1978) found that only six of 48 preschool age children showed transitions from solitary to parallel to group play during a 9-month observation period. Other children showed various amounts and patterns of shifting among some or all of Parten's categories. Most 3- to 4-year-olds in Smith's study moved directly from solitary to group play; parallel play in children between two and three years of age was found often to precede a period of group play.

In 1980 Bakeman and Brownlee suggested that "movement from parallel play to group play may be more a matter of minutes than months," (p. 873) and reported that parallel play often served as a bridge to group behavior in the ongoing activities of 32- to 42-month-old children observed by them. In addition, findings from a study of Howes (1980) showed that functioning at the higher levels of play is related to amount of experience with peers and not to chronological age. Thus the assumption that parallel play is a step between solitary and group functioning in an age-related developmental sequence has been discarded. Also, the interpretation of solitary play as immature has been questioned. Moore et al. (1974) report that the majority of solitary play of 116 kindergarten children involved independent, goal-directed activities that were indicative of maturity rather than immaturity.

Cultural Determinants

As would be predicted from a dialectic perspective, cultural factors have also been found to influence the development of play. Representational play as observed in Western societies has not been found to be a universal phenomenon either in type or quantity. Feitelson (1977) has summarized cross-cultural observations in terms of degree of discrepancy from Western behaviors. In small, homogeneous agricultural communities of India and Africa there is a very close link between children's play and adult activities, so much so that work and play eventually fuse. In Sutton-Smith's (1972) terms, play in these cultures is ascriptive, that is, basically copy imitation with no transformations. Feitelson (1977) has herself observed Middle Eastern and African communities where even ascriptive play is all but absent. In these cultures (e.g., among people of the Kurdish Mountains of Iraq), children are very quiet, passive observers of adult activity and do not initiate either individual or group play. In 12 months of data collection in 75 households in this region, not a single case of toy ownership was observed. It has also been reported that in rural Egypt and Kenya adults actively prevent play among children. Thus the kind and extent of representational play described by cognitive and psychoanalytic theorists in Western society are largely dependent upon cultural context. Factors synchronous with the development of symbolic play exist only in cultures where such activity is valued.

Feitelson (1977) has related play behavior to four cultural factors: space, time, objects, and conducive atmosphere. Space is available for play only if adult attitudes permit it to be. Free time is necessary for the unfolding themes of make believe. This may be compromised by the necessity for work such as tending to younger siblings from a very young age or by the attitude that play is frivolous. Play objects are also necessary for elaborate representational play, and these objects are not always available. Not all settings contain abundant natural materials facilitative to play, nor are all societies wealthy enough that household objects can be used for play without interfering with ongoing domestic work. In addition, some North African and Middle Eastern cultures regard playthings as trash. Feitelson (1977) reports that mothers of children participating in a research project that provided toys disposed of them regularly, even though they were proud of the impact of the intervention on the language and cognitive development of their children. Finally, a play-conducive atmosphere is most important in producing the potential for representative play. If play is valued as an important activity of childhood, it will be not only allowed but stimulated by adults. If not, it will be restricted. Feitelson (1977) provides examples of adults throwing missiles to break up play or correcting children who pretend that one thing is another, for example, act as if clay balls were oranges. These types of determinants are clearly dysynchronous with the development of symbolic play as Western cultures know it.

One can also look closer to home and find cultural differences in play across socioeconomic groups in this country. Disadvantaged children have been shown to participate in lower level and less sociodramatic play than more advantaged children (Rubin, Maion, & Hornung, 1976; Similansky, 1968). Such cross-cultural and class differences as those described above in a skill considered to be so important to the cognitive and affective growth of a child would be expected to have some impact on developmental outcome. Will mature use of symbols be different without its early exercise in symbolic play? Will patterns of emotional adjustment develop in synchrony with the exercise of compensatory and cathartic play that might not develop in its absence? Will rate of cognitive development differ among populations that do and do not show symbolic play? It is likely that the answer to all of these questions is yes. The specifics of the impact of little or no symbolic play on development remain as yet unknown. It is interesting to note, however, that intervention studies that tutor disadvantaged children in symbolic play have found improvement not only in play skills but also in creativity (Feitelson & Ross, 1973), problem solving, role taking (Rosen, 1974), and impulse control (Saltz, Dixon, & Johnson, 1977). Thus synchronous relationships between changes in play and other behavioral areas are evident.

Biological Determinants

Sensory, motor, and cognitive handicaps related to biological functioning also have immediate implications for the development of play and related faculties. Mogford (1977) has discussed the developmental impact of not being able to access stimulating environments due to handicap as equivalent to environmental deprivation. Children with severe handicaps and those who have experienced severe environmental deprivation may show the same symptoms of self-stimulating behaviors (rocking, hand flapping, teeth grinding), which eventually act as a barrier to active, outward exploration. Caretakers are depended upon longer by handicapped children than by normal infants for help in interacting, exploring, and playing, that is, for help in accessing the normal contingencies present in the environment that stimulate play and other forms of development. Therefore, in some cases, developmental dysynchronies exist for handicapped children between their needs for affective and cognitive stimulation and their ability to seek stimulation at the appropriate level.

Among the biologically based mental handicaps that have been examined through play are autism and Down's Syndrome. The symbolic play of children with Down's Syndrome has been found to exhibit the same developmental sequences as that of normal children and to be more strongly related to mental age than chronological age (Hill & McCune-Nicholich, 1981). This study confirmed earlier findings with a severely retarded population of mixed etiologies, which included Down's Syndrome (Whittaker, 1980).

In a study of the symbolic play of autistic children, it was found that although a wide range of play behaviors were observed, they were distributed differently than in a normal sample. Equal amounts of time were spent in object manipulation, relational play, pretend functional use of objects, and self-stimulation. Normal children of the same developmental level spend the majority of their time in functional play (Ungerer & Sigman, 1981). In the same study, autistic children spent much more of the functional playtime in self-directed activities (pretending to drink from cup) than in doll-directed play (pretending doll drinks from cup). The reverse pattern would be

expected for children over 21 months of age. Such behaviors reveal impaired ability to differentiate object from action. In addition, it was observed that the ability not only to differentiate action and object, but also to perform multischeme sequences (pretending to drink, stir with spoon, drink again) appeared in synchrony with the possession of greater language comprehension in autistic children. Children with lower abilities showed neither of these play skills. It was therefore concluded that the impairment of symbolic functioning in autistic children generalized across both play and language.

In her overview of research on play of handicapped children, Mogford (1977) points to special conditions created by specific handicaps that clearly influence the nature of play. For example, there is a need for caretakers to behave synchronously with the altered attention patterns, slow movement, and positional and mobility limitations of children with cerebral palsy. Blind children will be expected to be delayed in reaching and manual exploration. In addition to the difficulty of locating objects, the motivation to reach is decreased by lack of awareness of the object's visual appeal. The blind child may also appear unresponsive while listening to, as opposed to watching, attempts at play by parents, a response pattern that is somewhat dysynchronous with maintaining parental interest. In addition, imitation and eventually role playing will differ from that of sighted children. The blind preschooler may rehearse verbal exchanges (assuming different roles) and show delays in doll play.

Mogford (1977) makes several suggestions for helping to avoid the dysynchrony of expectations of normal play from handicapped children. Caretakers need sensitization to rudimentary forms of play and the role that they have in the developmental sequence leading to more commonly recognized forms of play. Demonstration of this capacity with toys that give obvious sensory rewards for the smallest responses can encourage more positive attitudes in discouraged parents. Such demonstration and discussion can also help them to realize their special importance in making play accessible, attractive, and meaningful and in ensuring success so that the urge to explore is maintained.

Communication/Language

According to Nelson (1979), recent research on language development has tended to follow one of two directions: either the documentation of the acquisition of adult grammar or the study of the roots of linguistic competence in prelanguage development. The latter direction is of interest to this discussion; indeed, considerable research has begun to focus on the communicative skills of the preverbal child (Lewis & Rosenblum, 1977). This research suggests considerable communicative competence in the young infant; it further suggests that these preverbal skills may be the basis for later language learning. Since language and communication problems form the basis of so many clinical anomalies, it seems appropriate to examine language/communication development and the possible effects of specific language abnormalities. As noted above, the framework provided by Riegel (1976) will provide the organizing theme for our discussion.

Psychological Determinants

Variables that might be placed in the psychological realm in Riegel's framework have been found to influence significantly communication/language development. Variables in this realm include cognitive development, age, and individual differences in temperament and personality. Research with normal infants and children has demonstrated the usefulness of considering cognitive level in social communication. Snow (1972) has noted that adult language to children changes depending upon the perceived cognitive level (in this case, age) of the child; that is, both adult and child characteristics show synchronous changes during the development of communication skills. Similarly, Crawley et al. (1978) have noted the complexity of mother-infant communications changes with the increasing cognitive level of the child. In their investigations of 4-, 6-, and 8-month-old infants, they found

mothers actively stimulated their 4-month-old infants (as in peek-a-boo), whereas mothers of 8-month-olds incorporated motoric roles into their games such that the infants were more actively involved (as in pat-a-cake). Similarly, Elliott et al. (1980) found that both mental and chronological age were important variables in the examination of mother-infant communication when the infants had a variety of congenital-environmental problems associated with developmental delay. Elliott et al. found that mothers of younger, less delayed infants played more visual stimulation games, whereas the greatest number of different games were played by the mothers of the younger, more delayed infants. In the group of older infants (9–21 months of age) the mothers of the least-delayed infants (greater than 6 months mental age) played more tactile stimulation games. Thus mothers differentiated among both chronological and mental age determinants of infant interactive behaviors, allowing for more synchronous stimulation of infants by mothers.

Individual differences associated with temperament and personality have also contributed to differences in communication/language development as well as to the overall development of the young child. Goldberg (1977) delineated several aspects of early behavior that would facilitate parental communication. Among these were the clarity of the infant's signals and the predictability of the infant's behaviors. Campbell (1977), in turn, has documented the impact of various infant types (normal, at risk, and difficult) upon maternal perceptions and their enduring impact across time. Campbell suggests that negative maternal perceptions may have long term consequences for the mother-child relationship. Similarly, Robinson and Robinson (1976) note the importance of individual characteristics in their discussion of the mentally retarded child. As a group, retarded children tend to be more anxious, defensive, and passively conforming and to have more negative self-concepts.

As one moves from an example of what Riegel considers an individual determinant (i.e., psychological or biological), the interactive variables are considered. Probably the most important interactive variable to include relates to the synchrony of caregiver-infant interaction.

When one considers the maternal and infant/child characteristics as they influence language/communication development, the influence of synchrony of interaction styles cannot be overlooked. Several investigators have suggested that both maternal and infant characteristics can influence the synchrony of the interaction and thus possibly affect the development of communication. For instance, Osofsky and Connors (1979) suggest that an appropriate "match" of maternal and infant characteristics is necessary to develop an adaptive relationship and that this development of synchrony is of great importance. The literature is just beginning to document the importance of both maternal and infant characteristics in this process. The early work of Ainsworth (Ainsworth, Bell, & Stayton, 1971; Bell & Ainsworth, 1972) noted the importance of maternal sensitivity and responsiveness in secure infant attachment. Likewise, Thoman (1976) and Goldberg (1977) have suggested that the infant's ability to signal clearly her or his needs is important in establishing an appropriate relationship, as noted earlier. The link between early social synchrony and later language development is not yet clear, although the data of Klaus and Kennell (1976) and their colleagues certainly proffer such a relationship. Ringler, Trause, and Klaus (1976) reported that infants given extended contact with their mothers at birth had mothers who used different language styles when the infants were 2 years of age (e.g., more adjectives and questions, fewer commands) and that the infants had more advanced scores on two language tests at 5 years of age.

Cultural Determinants

The cultural factors are among the best documented as they relate to communication/ language development. These factors illustrate the importance of their consideration in the examination of communication/language development. For instance, we have moved from a conceptualization that various subcul-

tures possessed language deficits to a realization that their language behaviors may only be *different* and not deficient (Baratz, 1969). Super (1981) has recently summarized the differences in social communication among various cultures, particularly the Japanese and American. Societal differences appear very early in the parent-infant relationship and seem to characterize differences in both infants and parents, in this case, mothers. The Japanese mother is described as soothing, pacifying, and calming; the infant is quiet and accepting. The American mother is much more verbal and stimulating; her infant is described as active and irritable in comparison to a Japanese infant. Cultural/sociological factors not only affect the child-rearing expectations, but also appear to regulate the individual behaviors of the mother and infant.

Biological Determinants

The contextual framework suggests that the biological realm may be important in the development of communication/language. Three examples help to clarify the importance. Included in this discussion are timing mechanisms, congenital anomalies, and injuries or illnesses.

Researchers have recently noted that there may be inborn timing mechanisms that underlie even mother-neonate interaction (Self et al., 1981). These biological mechanisms have already been noted in the behavioral stereotypes of infant motor responses. Numerous investigators have documented the dialogue-like interactions that occur in preverbal games of infants and their caregivers (Schaffer & Crook, 1978); these possible endogenous dialogues are felt to be the prototypes of later language-based interactions. For instance, Schaffer, Collis, and Parson (1977) described turn-taking episodes in the vocal behavior of both 1- and 2-year-old infants and their mothers. These investigators commented upon the smoothness of the partners' vocal turns.

Congenital anomalies certainly alter the development of these dialogues. Perhaps the best-documented change in such patterns is that provided by Fraiberg (1974). Her description of blind infants and their interaction with their caregivers demonstrated that if a caregiver expects a normal interaction from a child who is blind (a clearly dysynchronous expectation), then social communication skills will not develop normally. However, if the caregivers are taught to observe differential communicative behaviors, in this case hand behaviors, then much more usual patterns are observed. Similarly, Fulwiler and Fouts (1976) have suggested that the teaching of sign language to autistic children may result in much greater language facility among such children. In their report, these investigators found that by teaching a young autistic child to use American Sign Language they could get this child to attend to usual linguistic signals (words).

Injuries may also contribute to the loss of communicative skills. Brain damage (Robinson & Robinson, 1976), premature birth (Ehrlich et al., 1977), and multiple births may all contribute to lessened communicative ability. It is important to note, however, the self-righting tendencies of many minor deviations, whether illnesses or accidents. For instance, short term acute illness (e.g., otitis media) that may cause significant alterations in behavioral development is also short-lived in its effects on communication development. Thus many factors that Riegel might place in the biological realm of development have significant impact on the development of communication/ language skills.

This brief exploration into the development of language and communication demonstrates the utility of Riegel's framework. His scheme provides an organizational basis for categorizing variables that significantly influence both normal and aberrant development of communication/language skills.

Attachment

Under normal conditions the behavioral repertoires of young infants and their parents appear to be well adapted for the development of harmonious, reciprocal interaction from which, in turn, optimal attachment patterns emerge (Goldberg, 1977; Stern 1974, 1977).

Further, investigators have examined the relationship between early social interactions and competence in normal full-term infants and have found caregiver/infant interaction to be significantly associated with cognitive-motivational variables. Such variables include curiosity, exploration, language acquisition, and mental test performance, and relationships among these variables appear when assessed both concurrently and at later ages (Ainsworth & Bell, 1973; Bradley & Caldwell, 1976; Clarke-Stewart, 1973; Elardo, Bradley, & Caldwell, 1975; Nelson, 1973; Yarrow, Rubenstein, & Pedersen, 1975). These findings indicate that mother-infant interaction, attachment, and bonding perhaps represent the area of development that most easily lends itself to a dialectic framework. From a dialectic perspective, one aspect of development during this most primitive period takes place as the result of synchronous interaction between two individuals (i.e., mother and infant). This development is observed in concrete changes in common activities and everyday situations (Riegel, 1976) and is comprised of the growth of attachment.

Several definitions of attachment have been offered. According to Ainsworth (1964), attachment is an observable phenomenon, implying affection, discrimination, active participation by both partners, and reciprocal response; that is, attachment is a two-way interactional process. Kennell (Klaus & Kennell, 1976) defines attachment as a unique emotional relationship between two individuals that is specific and endures through time. Emphasis is on the synchrony of the interaction. As summarized by Sroufe and Waters (1977):

Attachment is not reducible to the interaction between infant and caregiver, though it is a product of that interaction (as it is shaped by species general characteristics, cognitive development, and characteristics of the individual baby and caregiver). Rather, attachment refers to an affective tie between infant and caregiver, and to a behavioral system, flexibly operating in terms of set goals, mediated by feeling and in interaction with other behavioral systems. (p. 1185)

Thus a dialectic view of attachment as the product of relationships among changes (i.e., in infant, in caretaker, and in other behavioral systems) has been developed by several authors.

With the set goal of the attachment behavioral system viewed as "felt security," attachment behavior is measured by the infants' proximity seeking, and proximity seeking is determined by the infants' evaluation of a variety of internal and external parameters contributing to security and insecurity (Bichof, 1975). Anxiety is one of these factors and sharply differentiates attachment from other forms of social interaction; whereas social play is inhibited by anxiety, attachment is intensified (Lamb, 1977). Thus, when a child is with his or her parents, the entrance of a stranger inhibits playful interactions but intensifies attachment behavior.

Also of importance is the quality of the relationship between the mother/infant pair. Ainsworth (1973) suggests that sensitive responsiveness seems to be the one quality in any interaction most likely to foster personal bonding. Sensitive responsiveness reflects the general shift of view that parenting is doing things with, rather than for, the baby. It is a process of reciprocal interaction, an active dialogue between parent and child (Lewis & Rosenblum, 1974). Bonding implies selective attachment that persists over time, even during a period of no contact with the person with whom the bond exists. However, bonding may be secure or insecure, despite its apparent "purpose," which is to give the child security of relationships so that it may stop clinging and following. In that way he or she becomes detached. From this point, the child can develop a more generalized attitude of trust in the benevolence of the world and proceed with confidence beyond the safe mother-child tie into the external world of people and objects. Indeed, Crawley et al. (1978) and Beckwith (1971) have found dyadic interaction patterns to have a developmental course of their own, with mothers shifting from "proximal" (touching) to "distal" (looking) behaviors with increasing infant age. The complexity and fluidity of such a dynamic organizational system can be most easily encompassed using a dialectic model of development.

Psychological Determinants

Attachment is often viewed primarily as a psychological phenomenon. However, it is closely intertwined with sociocultural and biological or maturational dimensions of development. Indeed, to understand the importance of attachment as an integrative, developmental construct is to uncover the roles that infant, caregiver, context, and interaction play in the development and maintenance of a relationship (Waters, Wippman, & Sroufe, 1979).

Establishing a secure adaptive attachment relationship may be viewed as a major developmental task during the first year of life. According to Stone, Smith, and Murphy (1973), this is accomplished in three stages. In the first stage (birth–4 months), the baby is "addicted" to social objects. The early indicators of attachment are generally considered to be visual following and concentration on the human face, especially the eyes, alerting to the human voice, and social smiling. During the second stage of infant attachment, which occurs during the second trimester of the first year, the infant selectively distinguishes mother from others. Mother is not only the most responsive partner but also the preferred source of varied and multiple pleasures. Stranger anxiety develops in the third period of attachment, which takes place the last trimester of the first year. At this time mother becomes a "safe base" from which the infant gains emotional refueling.

Mahler and Pine (1975) have described the process of infant separation and individuation, which occurs synchronously with the development of attachment. They regard infant development, beginning in the second stage of attachment (fourth to fifth month of age) and continuing until mother and child relate to each other as individuals (thirtieth to thirty-sixth months of age), as "the psychological birth" of the human infant. The purpose of this phase of development (the separation-individuation process) is to achieve emotional object constancy.

Included in the separation-individuation process are four overlapping subphases: differentiation, practicing, rapprochement, and object constancy. It has been emphasized that separation and individuation are intertwined developmental processes that may proceed divergently as a result of a developmental lag of one or the other. Thus the interaction between the mother and child during the child's maturation may be on the one hand reciprocal and synchronous or on the other hand dysynchronous. For example, in the third trimester of the infant's first year, stranger anxiety develops, marking the beginning of the differentiation subphase. According to Mahler, he or she ventures away from his or her mother but remains nearby. With the spurt in autonomous functions, such as cognition and upright locomotion, the toddler changes perspectives. Now walking freely in upright posture, his or her plane of vision changes; there is more to hear, to see, to touch. In this practicing subphase of separation he or she ventures further away but still returns to mother, needing her proximity from time to time. Children who achieve premature locomotion and are therefore able to separate physically from their mothers may prematurely become aware of their own separateness much before their reality testing, cognition, etc. have given them the means to cope with this awareness. On the other hand, infants with overprotective and infantilizing mothers may have their readiness to separate thwarted, resulting in undue anxiety.

By the middle of the second year, the toddler's awareness of separateness grows. Stimulated by the toddler's maturationally acquired ability to move physically away from his or her mother and by his or her cognitive growth, he or she now seems to have an increased need and wish for his or her mother to share every new acquisition of skill and experience. This phase is called the period of rapprochement. Finding obstacles that lie in the way of his or her "conquest" of the world, the toddler becomes aware of his or her own helplessness and vulnerability. In the rap-

prochement subphase, the toddler is noted to demonstrate a wooing behavior toward the mother in an attempt to establish a state of cordial relations.

According to Mahler, it is in this rapprochement subphase that the foundation for subsequent psychological health is laid. Incompatibilities and misunderstandings between even the normal mother and her normal toddler occur during this period. During this subphase, relationships may become dysynchronous due to a mother's inability either to accept her child's demanding behavior or to accept gradual separation, that is, not facing the fact that the child is becoming increasingly independent and separate from her. Depending on her own adjustment, the mother may react either by continued emotional availability and playful participation in the child's world or by becoming unavailable. If the mother is "quietly available" and shares the toddler's adventuresome exploits, the relationship between the mother and child is able to progress to where verbal communication takes over. This is the point of emotional object constancy in which the child and mother relate as individuals. This event occurs during the course of the child's third year.

Thus, according to Erikson (1950), if parents allow the child to function with some autonomy and if they are supportive without being overprotective, the child gains a certain confidence by age 3. The child feels a balance of love over hate, of cooperation over willfulness, of self-expression over suppression. Autonomy overbalances shame and doubt, and the child feels not only a capacity for self-control, but also a sense of control over his or her world. This achievement signifies the emergence of a sense of ego or individuality, a development that is synchronous with the healthy resolution of the separation-individuation process.

However, a dysynchronous system of interaction may exist between toddler and parent during this very important period of attachment-separation-individuation or formation of a sense of self. Under dysynchronous conditions, the child is likely to develop feelings of helplessness, fearfulness, or insecurity. Such maladaptive attachment ultimately may bring the child and/or family into a clinical setting.

The concept of the adaptive attachment versus maladaptive attachment has been behaviorally defined by Ainsworth in her widely used Stranger Situation Experiments (Ainsworth et al., 1977). One-year-old infants are observed in a standardized laboratory setting consisting of the following eight episodes: (1) mother and infant enter an unfamiliar room, (2) infant at play with mother present, (3) stranger and mother present, (4) infant left with stranger, (5) mother returns (stranger leaves), (6) infant left alone, (7) stranger returns, (8) mother returns. Within the laboratory setting three groups of infants have been defined: (1) securely attached, (2) ambivalent and (3) avoidant. The first is considered to represent infants who have adaptive maternal attachment behavior, while the other two groups are considered to be maladaptive.

In stress situations, securely attached infants seek maternal proximity on reunion, maintain contact, are comforted by contact, and return to play; they are unlikely to seek contact during preseparation. Ambivalent babies, who resist as well as seek contact upon reunion, are not comforted, tend to cry during preseparation, are wary of a stranger, are generally apprehensive, and show impoverished exploration. Babies who are avoidant ignore the caregiver upon reunion, do not seek proximity in preseparation, are not distressed by separation (unless left alone), and interact and are comforted as readily by a stranger as by the mother. They may also show an affectless, superficial quality in play.

Such behavioral description of adaptive versus maladaptive behavior in toddlers is useful to the clinician. Attachment ratings by Ainsworth et al. (1978) of 1-year-old children raised in traditional two-parent homes were: (1) most securely attached, 66 percent; (2) ambivalent or anxious-insecure, 12 percent; and (3) avoidant behavior, 22 percent.

Cultural Determinants

Cultural as well as psychological and biological factors intertwine in the formation of mother-infant attachment patterns. In general population studies, the particular strains of childrearing for women of low social status have been well documented by Brown et al. (1975). Rather long-lasting changes in mother-infant interaction were found by Klaus and Kennell (1976) in their groups of socially disadvantaged mothers. On the other hand, the effects were much more transitory in the studies by Leiderman and Seashore (1975) and Whiten (1977). According to Rutter (1979), it seems unlikely that stressful events in the neonatal period have an inevitable lasting impact on mother-child relationships; but if early stresses are combined with persisting disadvantage, the damage may be enduring. It is known that under adverse home environments the quality of the mother-infant interaction is often identified by the physical condition of the infant. Extreme disturbances in the mother-to-infant interactions are evident in the mother of the child who is battered and in the mother of the infant with no organic disease who fails to thrive at home but gains weight easily when his or her needs are met by another caretaker.

Perinatal events produced as a side effect of contemporary medical culture may also affect the mother-infant relationship. Disturbances of mother-to-infant attachment are often evident after prolonged separations in the neonatal period due to prematurity, low birth weight, or illness (Kennell, Vous, & Klaus, 1979). These mothers are observed to be less confident and less competent in some aspects of mothering during the subsequent months. Further, longstanding developmental problems experienced by infants reared in institutions, who in the absence of their mother or a designated primary caretaker are provided an aberrant attachment experience, are well documented by Spitz (1945). Comprehensive recent studies by Tizard (1971, 1975) of institutional children show that at 2 years of age institution-reared children were both more clinging and diffuse in their attachment than children brought up in ordinary families. At 4 years, the institutional children were still more clinging and less likely to have deep attachments and they now tended to be overly friendly with strangers and attention seeking.

Tizard's studies further showed impaired relationships with adults and other children in middle childhood. In follow-through studies of these children to age 8 (Tizard, 1977; Tizard & Hodges, 1978), less than half of these institutional children were said to be closely attached to their housemothers and they still sought affection more often than other children. At school, the differences were more striking, with institutional children more attention seeking, restless, disobedient, and unpopular. Although all the children were of normal intelligence, those with disturbed relationships were found to have associated problems in task involvement of assigned work.

In a currently changing culture that provides increased autonomy for American women as well as an economic condition that places increased demands on the American family for a two-parent income, a growing number of young mothers are employed outside the home, and more children are placed in daycare facilities. Cognizant of the findings of problems in social and emotional development in institutional children, Kagan (1978, 1980) questioned whether infants who attend daycare centers on a regular basis develop in a different way from children of the same family background who are raised entirely at home. Kagan's findings showed that if a caretaker has responsibility for no more than three or four infants, and if the young children have an opportunity to explore their environments, their psychological growth does not deviate seriously from norms of children not in daycare.

The changing culture has also provided more opportunity as well as responsibility for the father to interact with his child, and the question arises, "How do mother-infant and father-infant attachments differ?" Parke and Sawin (1975) conducted a series of observational studies to describe the nature of the father's interaction with his newborn infant. With one exception, all fathers had been present during delivery of the child. The results, in a context where participation was voluntary, indicated that fathers were just as involved as mothers in interaction with their infants. The study further suggests that pos-sibly paternal behavior or involvement with a newborn can be facilitated by the fathers being present at the infant's birth. Other findings by Lamb (1977a, 1977b) and Clarke-Stewart (1977) indicate that play is an important ingredient of the father-infant relationship. Consistent with Lamb's observations, Clarke-Stewart found that 20-month-old children were significantly more responsive to playful social interaction initiated by the father than by the mother.

Often, however, the father's attitude and interaction with his infant may become a codeterminant of the mother's interaction with the baby. As Pedersen et al. (1975) note:

If the father feels positively towards the infant, it is likely that the mother's positive feelings and behavior may be enhanced. But at the pathological extreme a mother may be jealous of the father's affection for the child and may be more harsh and demanding of the infant. (p. 3)

Thus development of the infant emerges from intertwining environmental factors, which are readily conceptualized using a dialectic framework.

Finally, Bernstein, Zimmerman, and Eidison (1981) investigated maternal-infant attachment in both traditional families (married parents) and families with alternative lifestyles. Their findings showed that most 1-year-olds were characterized by secure attachment regardless of the lifestyle of the family. Alternative lifestyles included: (1) social contract or unwed parents living together; (2) the unwed mother living alone with her child; and (3) the living-group family that had significantly more people living in the household, both adults and children. The proportion of securely attached 1-year-olds in the Bernstein study, regardless of lifestyle, is consistent with Ainsworth's (1978) proportion of securely attached 1-year-olds found in traditional families. However, Bernstein found that by the time the 1-year-old child becomes 3, a different pattern of attachment behavior emerges, unaltered by lifestyle. Three-year-olds become progressively detached from their mothers, with attachment rated "avoidant" as often as "secure." According to Bernstein, this shows an increasingly age appropriate independence, which coincides with the child's entry into nursery school. Culturally, the 3-year-old child beginning nursery school is expected to be sufficiently secure in his or her mother's absence to be able to relate to peers and adults and to explore, manipulate, and learn in a new environment.

Biological Determinants

A mushrooming of infant literature during the past 10 to 20 years reveals that biologically the human infant has remarkable cognitive and perceptual abilities and is an active and competent contributor to developing social relationships with caretakers (Goldberg, 1977). In turn, Klaus and Kennell (1976) have recently observed "species-specific" behavior common to mothers at the first postnatal contact with their unclothed infants as they establish affectional ties. This behavior involves an orderly, progressive transaction by the mother with the infant, such as seeking eye contact, touching (first with the fingertips on the infant's extremities, followed by palm encompassing contact of the trunk), along with smiling and vocalization. Such "species-specific" behavior in the female is interesting in view of the acknowledged diversity of factors that provide her inheritance for a mother role, such as her native endowment, culture, and long history of personal relationships within her own family. Thus a biological substrate for an attachment to form between an infant and its mother is provided at birth at the same time that forming this attachment is the infant's developmental task. Further, from a dialectical point of reference, attachment as a developmental process is enhanced in psychological dimensions through biological counterparts.

The "species-specific" behavior in human females is consistent with Bowlby's (1958) ethological concept of development. Bowlby theorized that in the early life of the human infant there matures a complex array of instinctual repsonses (crying, smiling, sucking, clinging, and following), the function of

which is to ensure that he or she obtains parental care sufficient for survival. Bowlby subsequently grouped the specific forms of behavior into two main classes and emphasized maternal as well as child behavior:

1. Signaling behavior, the effect of which is to bring mother to child.
2. Approach behavior, the effect of which is to bring child to mother.

It is Ainsworth (1972, 1974) who broadened Bowlby's concept of attachment from that of a survival mechanism to that of a secure base with preferential treatment under stress. Other than the biological competence of the newborn to develop a relationship and the instinctual "species-specific" response of the mother to establish affective ties to her newborn, Lozoff et al. (1977) found that hormonal levels of the mother prior to term delivery tend to foster maternal behavior. Thus, in a premature birth, the mother's hormonal level, as well as hospital practices that separate infant and mother, may interfere with the attachment process. Additionally, Jones, Green, and Kraus (1980) found that mother's age, unconfounded by socioeconomic status, race or marital status, may determine the amount and nature of the interaction between the mother and her newborn.

It is through a dialectic model of development that one is able to grasp most comprehensively the impact that biological deficits have on the attachment process. According to Goldberg (1977):

It is important to note that the predictable, readable, responsive infant has the potential for "capturing" the initially unresponsive parent into cycles of effective interactions by generating parental feelings of effectiveness. Similarly, the unpredictable, unreadable, unresponsive infant has the potential for "trapping" an initially unresponsive parent in cycles of ineffective interaction by generating parental feelings of failure and helplessness. This suggests that whenever parents are confronted with an infant of limited competence the potential risks of interactive failures are high. (p. 174)

The importance of harmonious interaction is that it provides the basis for learning social contingencies. Interestingly, McCall (1972) has reported that performance on social contingency tasks during early infancy is correlated with school age IQ. Recently several researchers following the development of medically at-risk infants and children have noted interaction patterns that are different from those of normal mother-infant pairs and have speculated that there may be a circular relationship between disturbances in early interaction and developmental problems. Caputo and Mandell (1970) have found preterm infants as a class to be at increased statistical risk for deficits in cognitive functioning, but the fact of prematurity alone is insufficient to allow prediction of developmental disturbance.

These findings are important in an at-risk group, where the preterm infant is probably a less active, less capable social partner (Field, 1977) whose parents have experienced multiple stresses, which may include grief, anxiety, guilt, lowered self-esteem, increased isolation, and lessened emotional support as the infant's survival and psychological outcome remain in jeopardy. Drotar et al. (1975) identify five stages of parental reactions (shock, denial, sadness, anger, and adaptive reorganization) to the birth of a child with a congenital malformation. McMichael (1971) has documented that over 50 percent of mothers of physically handicapped school children experienced moderate or severe depression and degrees of overanxiety and failure to adjust. Such parental responses might be viewed as elicited by the infant's lack of social competence and may be dysynchronous in that healthy attachment is not fostered.

Excessive stress and anxiety are also evident in parents of the critically ill child, for example, a child cancer patient. Parents do not know whether to prepare to mourn the loss of their child, a state that has been labeled "anticipatory grief," or to dare to hope for a sustained remission or "elusive" cure (Kellerman, 1980).

Additionally, it is assumed that a mother's perceptions and feelings about her child can affect her behavior toward him or her. Green and Solnit (1964) found that children who undergo serious illness may afterwards be considered by the parents to be vulnerable, subject to further serious illness or accident, and destined to die during childhood. The parents have the feeling that these children are not completely theirs but only on tenuous loan. Parents tend to treat these children differently than their other children. Similar perceptions of mothers' alienation from their handicapped children were found by Jones (1980). Mothers seemed to think they had a different "species" on their hands and had difficulty perceiving their child as becoming a person in the way we recognize "personness." Finally, in any family, parents can be in different places in terms of their individual parent-child relationship, which in itself may produce tension and dysynchrony within the family environment.

Other investigators are discovering the need for altered styles of maternal behavior to facilitate their interaction with various subgroups of handicapped infants. As mentioned earlier, Fraiberg's (1974) work with blind infants best exemplifies this need. Only 2 of 10 mothers in Fraiberg's study of blind infant–sighted mother pairs were able to interpret their infant's altered and alien hand gesturing signals without assistance. Additionally, a study by Jones (1980) comparing normal and Down's syndrome children at a prelinguistic stage of development showed a dysynchronous pattern of maternal interaction. Although Down's syndrome children could and did participate in interaction, they lacked referential eye contact, did not demonstrate full understanding of their actions as signals, and did not seem to appreciate the role of "the other" in social dialogue. Mother's verbal interactions with her Down's syndrome versus normal child were equally active, but she tended to "instruct" her Down's syndrome child, while mother "conversed" with her normal child.

Jones and Francis (1981) investigated the interactive behaviors of mothers and handicapped infants in a nontoy setting. They found that with increasing cognitive or mental age, infants generally exhibited more tactile (touching) and vocal behaviors. This corroborates the findings of Uzgiris and Hunt (1975) that vocal imitation tends to increase as infants cognitively advance. However, maternal behaviors did not change with an increase in the infant's cognitive level. These findings are contradictory to predictions based on findings by Crawley et al. (1978) and Elliott et al. (1980). While Elliott's mothers of delayed infants did tend to interact using more "distal" interactive behavior, with an increase in the infant's mental age, it was a toy play rather than a nontoy setting. These findings suggest that in a nontoy setting mothers of handicapped infants have more difficulty reading their infants' cues. Similarly, Jones (1981) compared interaction patterns of mothers and handicapped infants according to subgroups of handicap (auditory or visual deficit, motoric involvement, or comprehensive delay in all areas) and found very little evidence that mothers respond differentially to types of infant disability. As with interaction patterns between mothers and handicapped infants in a nontoy setting, mothers interacting with particular subgroups of handicapped infants seemed insensitive or unable to cue into their infants' specific deficits.

Further, Field's (1980) study investigating groups of normal and high risk premature Respiratory Distress Syndrome infant-mother pairs found the spontaneous interactions of normal and high risk dyads dramatically different. High risk groups interacted significantly less than healthy, normal infants, and high risk babies were classified by observers in a "worrisome" interaction category and rated by their mothers as difficult babies. Field's study suggests that experienced nurses are able to interpret the cues of high risk infants but new mothers are not. The mothers stimulate their infants more and are less sensitive to their infants' subtle signals than are the nurses who perceive the cues and contingently respond to them. Thus interaction with a newborn having distinct limitations or handicaps may be effective when complemented by an unusually sensitive and responsive caretaker (Goldberg, 1977).

Numerous studies now point to the higher incidence of emotional difficulties among children with developmental disabilities than among normal children (Mordock, 1978), while other studies (Hardy, 1968) suggest that the magnitude of the handicap is not the sole determinant of the degree of disturbance. In reviewing programs for handicapped children and their families, Mordock found that the majority of infant stimulation programs focused on the deficit of the child and, additionally, provided support and instructions for parents. Very few programs made an effort to assess the degree of maternal-infant bonding that existed or to enhance the ability of the dyad to relate when maternal infant interaction appeared dysfunctional.

According to Goldberg (1977), the mother-infant dyad can be helped toward effective interactions under conditions that: (1) facilitate infant development (i.e., develop predictability, readability, and responsiveness) and (2) develop parental skills in predicting and reading infant behavior and (3) foster parental sensitivity to the contingency experiences provided by the infant. Both types of intervention, which are aimed at increasing mutual contingency experiences, should be broadly applicable to infants of limited competence regardless of the specific nature of the handicap.

IMPLICATIONS FOR CLINICAL CHILD PSYCHOLOGY

Developmental principles have important implications for clinical child psychology. Santostephano (1980) has suggested that the most basic principle involves the nosological diagnostic model. If a child is placed in a diagnostic category (hyperactive, anxiety neurosis, etc.), perception of that child's behavior is altered in a way that not only biases but sometimes precludes consideration of other issues. Using a developmental framework provides a more "mobile" model of treatment by virtue of its emphasis on multiply determined progression through levels and stages of behavioral organization. It allows the therapists to focus on where the child is developmentally, how the developmental level would affect the child across behavioral areas, and what the impediments might be to further development. For instance, a young child referred for severe anxiety upon separation from his or her mother might be observed for levels of subject-object differentiation demonstrated in play and language. If the child appears to have attained differentiation between self and object but is not yet certain of object constancy, this would have implications for his or her progress through the separation-individuation process. Until constancy is attained the rapprochement crisis cannot be successfully resolved. Therefore, cognitive as well as affective intervention would be expected to hasten a child's resolution of this crisis.

Developmental level and progress become the primary considerations, with the particular diagnostic category being less salient. From dialectic perspective, the diagnostic "label" would involve one or more of the dimensions in the system of interdependent developmental variables. For example, hyperactivity might be largely biological; however, diagnosis and treatment from a dialectic perspective would include psychological, cultural, and outerphysical events (where relevant) as well. In the same sense that a presenting problem is multiply determined, its solution is multiply determined. Any definition of either exceptionality or treatment that is made exclusive of context is of limited usefulness. On the other hand, the dialectic developmental framework (1) allows the clinician to work with the same basic contextual principles and issues for each child treated and (2) can help prevent specific labeling and its sequelae.

Another implication of dialectic developmental principles lies in the interpretation of the importance of early experience. In order to understand its significance, early experience must be studied in relation to later behavior, where later refers not only to later childhood but also to adolescence, adulthood, and aging. If early experience is a primary determinant of all further development, its effects would be expected to appear at every phase of the lifespan. However, continuity between the first two years of life and later periods has been difficult to demonstrate. Studies looking for linear relationships between a single precursor (prematurity, IQ) and later development will miss the impact of other experiences on development. For instance, we know that not all severely at-risk children have poor outcomes. We even know that some, the "invulnerables" (children from disadvantageous backgrounds who develop normally), do extremely well (Rutter, 1979). In addition, we know that good early experience does not protect one from the effects of later disadvantage. Studies indicate that early educational intervention leads to limited or temporary benefits if the child's general context remains disadvantaged and that children whose families' socioeconomic status drops during middle school years show a corresponding decrease in IQ (Rutter, 1979). In addition, Sameroff (1974) failed to find a linear causal chain between reproductive casualty and later developmental aberrations, concluding that the importance of pre- and perinatal complications for development pales in comparison to the massive influence of socioeconomic factors.

All of these findings point to the overriding importance of interaction among developmental dimensions in determining functioning during any developmental period and lead to a modification of the assumption regarding the primacy of early experience. The results of early experience, good or bad, are not isolated from the effects of all later experience, good or bad. Such continued plasticity is necessarily potentiated by existing synchrony or dysynchrony in developmental dimensions, and this occurs without consideration of what is better or worse for the child.

The primacy accorded the consideration of relationships among changes in psychological, biological, and cultural developmental determinants in the dialectic model emphasizes the necessity of anticipating the multiple effects of any intervention. What types of synchrony or dysynchrony will be caused across behavioral systems by alleviating problematic behavior or psychological distress in a single target area? Many children may need assistance in adjusting to such indirectly mediated changes, and a dialectic framework assists in anticipating what those changes might be.

In summary, Riegel's dialectic model of development was selected as the most useful organizational framework for clinical child psychologists. Its relevance to the understanding of both normal and exceptional development was demonstrated through discussions of the impact of psychological, biological, and cultural determinants in the areas of play, communication/language, and parent-child attachment. In addition, the implications of the model for definitions of exceptionality, "labeling," intervention, and the primacy of early experience were discussed.

REFERENCES

Ainsworth, M.D. Patterns of attachment behavior shown by the infant in interaction with its mother. *Merrill-Palmer Quarterly,* 1964, **10,** 51–58.

Ainsworth, M.D. Attachment and dependency: A comparison. In J. Gewirtz (Ed.), *Attachment and dependency.* Washington, D.C.: Winston, 1972.

Ainsworth, M.D. The development of mother-infant attachment. In B. Caldwell & H. Ricciuti (Eds.), *Review of child development research* (Vol. 3). Chicago: University of Chicago Press, 1973.

Ainsworth, M.D. Infant-mother attachment and social development: Socialization as a product of reciprocal responsiveness to signals. In M. Richards (Ed.), *The integration of the child into the social world.* Cambridge: Cambridge University Press, 1974.

Ainsworth, M.D., & Bell, S.M. Mother-infant interaction and the development of competence. In K.S. Connolly & J.S. Bruner (Eds.), *The growth of competence.* New York: Academic Press, 1973.

Ainsworth, M.D., Bell, S., & Stayton, D.J. Individual differences in strange situation behavior of one-year-olds. In H.R. Schaffer (Ed.), *The origins of human social relations.* London: Academic Press, 1971.

Ainsworth, M.D., Blehar, M., Waters, E., & Wall, S. *Patterns of attachment: Observations in the strange situation and at home.* Hillsdale, N.J.: Erlbaum, 1977.

Ainsworth, M.D., Blehar, M., Waters, E., & Wall, S. *Patterns of attachment: A psychological study of the strange situation.* Hillsdale, N.J.: Erlbaum, 1978.

Bakeman, R., & Brownlee, J.R. The strategic use of parallel play: A sequential analysis. *Child Development,* 1980, **51,** 873–878.

Baltes, P.B., Reese, H.W., & Lipsitt, L.P. Life-span developmental psychology. *Annual Review of Psychology,* 1980, **31,** 65–110.

Baltes, P.B., Reese, H.W., & Nesselroade, J.R. *Life-span developmental psychology: Introduction to research methods.* Monterey, Calif.: Brooks-Cole, 1977.

Baratz, J. A bi-dialectical task for determining language proficiency in economically disadvantaged Negro children. *Child Development,* 1969, **30,** 889–901.

Bayley, N. *Manual for the Bayley scales of infant development.* New York: The Psychological Corporation, 1969.

Beckwith, L. Relationships between attributes of mothers and their infants' I.Q. scores. *Child Development,* 1971, **42,** 1083–1097.

Bell, S., & Ainsworth, M.D. Infant crying and maternal responsiveness. *Child Development,* 1972, **43,** 1171–1190.

Bernstein, M., Zimmerman, I.L., & Eidison, B.T. Attachment of infants reared in alternative lifestyles. Paper presented at the 89th Annual Meeting of the American Psychological Association, Los Angeles, August 24–28th, 1981.

Bichof, N. A systems approach toward the functional connections of fear and attachment. *Child Development,* 1975, **46,** 801–817.

Bowlby, J. The nature of a child's tie to his mother. *International Journal of Psychoanalysis,* 1958, **39,** 350–373.

Bradley, R.H., & Caldwell, B.M. Early home environment and changes in mental test performance in children from 6 to 36 months. *Developmental Psychology,* 1976, **12,** 93–97.

Brown, J.V., Blakeman, R., Snyder, P.A., Frederickson, W.T., Morgan, S.T., & Hepler, R. Interactions of black inter-city mothers with their newborn infants. *Child Development,* 1975, **46,** 677–686.

Campbell, S.B. Maternal and infant behavior in normal, "high risk," and difficult infants. Paper presented at the meetings of the Society for Research in Child Development, New Orleans, March 1977.

Caputo, D.V., & Mandell, W. Consequences of low birth weight. *Developmental Psychology,* 1970, **3,** 363–383.

Clarke-Stewart, K. Interactions between mothers and their young children: Characteristics and consequences. *Monographs for the Society for Research in Child Development,* 1977, **38**(6–7, Serial No. 153).

Crawley, S.B., Rogers, P.P., Friedman, S., Iacobbo, M., Criticos, A., Richardson, L., & Thompson, M.A. Developmental changes in the structure of other-infant play. *Developmental Psychology,* 1978, **14,** 37–43.

Drotar, D., Baskiewicz, A., Ivin, N., Kennell, J., & Klaus, M. The adaptation of parents to the birth of an infant with a congenital malformation: A hypothetical model. *Pediatrics,* 1975, **56**(5), 710–717.

Drucker, J. The affective context and psychodynamics of first symbolization. In N.R. Smith & M.B. Franklin (Eds.), *Symbolic functioning in childhood.* New York: Wiley, 1979.

Dunton, M.D. The child's concept of death. In B. Schoenberg, A.C. Carr, D. Peretz, & A.H. Kutscher (Eds.), *Loss and grief: Psychological management in medical practice.* New York: Columbia University Press, 1970.

Ehrlich, C.H., Shapiro, E., Kimball, B.D., & Huttner, M. Communication skills in five-year-old children with high-risk neonatal histories. In J.L. Schwartz & L.H. Schwartz (Eds.), *Vulnerable infants: A psychosocial dilemma.* New York: McGraw-Hill, 1977.

Elardo, R., Bradley, R.H., & Caldwell, B.M. The relation of infants' home environments to mental test performance from 6–36 months: A longitudinal analysis. *Child Development,* 1975, **46,** 71–76.

Elliott, J., Self, P.A., Francis, P.L., & Jones, F. The effects of chronological and estimated mental age of infants on caregiver play behavior. Paper presented at the annual meeting of the Oklahoma Psychological Association, 1980.

Erikson, E. *Childhood and society.* New York: Norton, 1950.

Feitelson, A. Cross-cultural studies of representational play. In B. Tizard & D. Harvey (Eds.), *Biology of play* (*Clinics in Developmental Medicine,* No. 62). Philadelphia: Lippincott, 1977.

Feitelson, D., & Ross, G.S. The neglected factor—Play. *Human Development,* 1973, **16,** 202–223.

Field, T.M. Effects of early separation, interactive deficits, and experimental manipulations on infant-mother face-to-face interaction. *Child Development,* 1977, **348,** 763–771.

Field, T.M., Goldberg, S., Stern, D., & Foster, A.M. (Eds.), *High risk infants and children.* New York: Academic Press, 1980.

Fraiberg, S. Blind infants and their mothers: An examination of the sign system. In M. Lewis & L.A. Rosenblum (Eds.), *The effect of the infant on its caregivers.* New York: Wiley, 1974.

Fulwiler, R., & Fouts, R. Acquisition of sign language by a non-communicating autistic child. *Journal of Autism and Childhood Schizophrenia,* 1976, **6,** 43–51.

Furth, H. *Piaget and knowledge: Theoretical foundations.* Englewood Cliffs, N.J.: Prentice-Hall, 1969.

Goldberg, S. Social competence in infancy: A model of parent-infant interaction. *Merrill-Palmer Quarterly,* 1977, **23,** 163–178.

Green, M., & Solnit, A.J. Reactions to the threatened loss of a child: A vulnerable child syndrome. *Pediatrics,* 1964, **34,** 58–66.

Hardy, R.E. A study of manifest anxiety among blind residential school students. *New Outlook for the Blind,* 1968, **62,** 173–180.

Hill, P.M., & McCune-Nicolich, L. Pretend play and patterns of cognition in Down's syndrome children. *Child Development,* 1981, **52,** 611–617.

Howes, C. Peer play scales as an index of complexity of peer interaction. *Developmental Psychology,* 1980, **16**(4), 371–372.

Jones, F.A. Maternal attachment to infants during the postnatal period. Paper presented at the annual meeting of the American Psychological Association, Washington, D.C., 1976.

Jones, F.A. Maternal interaction with developmentally handicapped infants. Paper presented at the annual meeting of the American Psychological Association, Los Angeles, 1981.

Jones, F.A., & Francis, P.L. Aspects of maternal

interaction with developmentally delayed infants. Paper presented at the annual meeting of the American Psychological Association, Los Angeles, 1981.

Jones, F.A., Green, V., & Krauss, D.R. Maternal responsiveness of primiparous mothers during the postpartum period: Age differences. *Pediatrics*, 1980, **65**(3), 579–584.

Jones, O.H.M. Prelinguistic communication skills in Down's syndrome and normal infants. In T.M. Field, S. Goldberg, D. Stern, & A.M. Miller (Eds.), *High-risk infants and children*. New York: Academic Press, 1980.

Kagan, J. Kearsley, R.B., & Zelago, P.R. *Infancy: Its place in human development*. Cambridge: Harvard University Press, 1980.

Karger, R.H. Synchrony in mother-infant interaction. *Child Development*, 1979, **50**(3), 882–885.

Kellerman, J. *Psychological aspects of childhood cancer*. Springfield, Ill.: Thomas, 1980.

Kennell, J., Voos, D., & Klaus, M. Parent-infant bonding. In J. Isofsky (Ed.), *Handbook of infant development*. New York: Wiley, 1979.

Klaus, M.H., & Kennell, J.H. *Maternal-infant bonding*. St. Louis: Mosby, 1976.

Lamb, M.E. The development of mother-infant and father-infant attachments in the second year of life. *Developmental Psychology*, 1977, **13**, 637–648. (a)

Lamb, M.E. Father-infant and mother-infant interaction in the first year of life. *Child Development*, 1977, **48**, 167–181. (b)

Langer, J. *Theories of development*. New York: Holt, Rinehart & Winston, 1969.

Leiderman, P.H., & Seashore, M.J. Mother-infant neonatal separation: Some delayed consequences. In R. Porter & M. O'Conner (Eds.), *Parent-infant interaction* (CIBA Foundation Symposium 33, new series). Amsterdam: Associated Scientific Publishers, 1975.

Lerner, R.M., Skinner, E.A., & Sorrell, G.T. Methodological implications of contextual/dialectic theories of development. *Human Development*, 1980, **23**, 225–235.

Lewis, M., & Rosenblum, L.A. *The effect of the infant on its caregiver*. New York: Wiley, 1974.

Lewis, M., & Rosenblum. L.A. *Interaction, conversation and the development of language*. New York: Wiley, 1977.

Lozoff, B., Brittenham, G.M., Trause, M.A., Kennell, J.H., & Klaus, M.H. The mother-newborn relationship: Limits to adaptability. *Pediatrics*, 1977, **91**, 1–12.

Mahler, M. *Separation-individuation*. The selected papers of Margaret S. Mahler, M.D. (Vol. II). New York: Aronson, 1979.

Mahler, M., & Pine, F. *The psychological birth of the human infant*. New York: Basic Books, 1975.

McCall, R.B., Hogarty, P.S., & Hurlburt, N. Transitions in infant sensorimotor development and the prediction of I.Q. *American Psychologist*, 1972, **27**(8), 728–748.

McMichael, J. *Handicap: A study of physically handicapped children and their families*. London: Samples Press, 1971.

Mogford, K. The play of handicapped children. In B. Tizard & D. Harvey (Eds.), *Biology of play* (Clinics in Developmental Medicine, No. 62). Philadelphia: Lippincott, 1977.

Moore, N.V., Everton, C.M., & Brophy, J.E. Solitary play: Some functional reconsiderations. *Developmental Psychology*, 1974, **10** (6), 830–834.

Mordock, J.B. The separation–individuation process and developmental disabilities. *Exceptional Children*, 1978, pp. 176–184.

Nelson, K. Structure and strategy in learning to talk. *Monographs of the Society for Research in Child Development*, 1973, 149.

Nelson, K. The role of language in infant development. In M. Bornstein & W. Kessen (Eds.), *Psychological development from infancy: Image to intention*. New York: Wiley, 1979.

Osofsky, J., & Connors, K. Mother-infant interaction: An integrative view of a complex system. In J. Osofsky (Ed.), *Handbook of infant development*. New York: Wiley, 1979.

Overton, W.F., & Reese, H.W. Models of development: Methodological implications. In J.R. Nesselroade & H.W. Reese (Eds.), *Life-span developmental psychology: Methodological issues*. New York: Academic Press, 1973.

Overton, W.F., & Reese, H.W. Conceptual prerequisites for an understanding of stability-change and continuity-discontinuity. *International Journal of Behavior Development*, 1981, **4**, 99–123.

Parke, R.D., & Sawin, D.B. Father-infant interaction in the newborn period: A reevaluation of some current myths. Paper presented at a meeting of the American Psychological Association, Chicago, September 1975.

Parten, M.D. Social participation among preschool children. *Journal of Abnormal and Social Psychology*, 1932, **27**, 243–269.

Pedersen, F.A. Mother, father, and infants as an interactive system. Paper presented at the annual convention of the American Psychological Association, Chicago, September 1975.

Piaget, J. *Play, dreams, and imitation in childhood.* New York: Norton, 1962.

Piaget, J., & Inhelder, B. *The psychology of the child.* New York: Basic Books, 1969.

Reese, H.W., & Overton, W.F. Models of development and theories of development. In L.R. Goulet & P.B. Baltes (Eds.), *Life-span developmental psychology: Research and theory.* New York: Academic Press, 1970.

Riegel, K. Dialectic operations: The final period of cognitive development. *Human Development,* 1973, **16**, 346–370.

Riegel, K. Dialectic operations: The final period of cognitive development. *Human Development,* 1975, **18**, 50–64.

Riegel, K. The dialectics of human development. *American Psychologist,* 1976, **10**, 689–700.

Riegel, K. The dialectics of time. In N. Datan & H. Reese (Eds.), *Life-span developmental psychology: Dialectical perspective on experimental research.* New York: Academic Press, 1977.

Ringler, N.M., Trause, M.A., & Klaus, M.H. Mother's speech to her two-year-old: Its effect on speech and language comprehension at five years. *Pediatric Research,* 1976, **10**, 307.

Robinson, N.M., & Robinson, H.B. *The mentally retarded child.* New York: McGraw-Hill, 1976.

Rosen, C.E. The effects of sociodramatic play on problem-solving behavior among culturally disadvantaged preschool children. *Child Development,* 1974, **45**, 920–927.

Rubin, K.H., Maion, T.L., & Hornung, M. Free play behaviors in middle- and lower-class preschoolers: Parten and Piaget revisited. *Child Development,* 1976, **47**, 414–419.

Rutter, M. Maternal deprivation, 1972–1978: New findings, new concepts, new approaches. *Child Development,* 1979, **50**, 283–305.

Saltz, E., Dixon, D., & Johnson, J. Training disadvantaged preschoolers on various fantasy activities: Effects on cognitive functioning and impulse control. *Child Development,* 1977, **48**, 367–380.

Sameroff, A.J. Early influences on development: Fact or fancy? Paper presented at the Merrill-Palmer Conference on Infancy, Detroit, 1974.

Santostephano, S. Clinical psychology: The need for developmental principles. *New Directions for Child Development,* 1980, **7**, 1–19.

Schaffer, H.R., Colis, G.M., & Parson, G. Vocal interchange and visual regard in verbal and pre-verbal children. In H.R. Schaffer (Ed.), *Studies in mother-infant interaction.* London: Academic Press, 1977.

Schaffer, H.R., & Crook, C.K. The role of the mother in early social development. In McGurk, H. (Ed.), *Issues in childhood social development.* London: Methuen, 1978.

Self, P.A., Noble, C.A., Francis, P.L., Schafaie, M.S., Guillory, A.W., Biscoe, B., & Cole, C.A. Mother-infant interaction: Who adjusts to whom? Paper presented at the meeting of the International Society for the Study of Behavioral Development, Toronto, Canada, 1981.

Similansky, S. *The effects of sociodramatic play on disadvantaged preschool children.* New York: Wiley, 1968.

Smith, P.K. A longitudinal study of social participation in preschool children: Solitary and parallel play reexamined. *Developmental Psychology,* 1978, **14**(5), 517–523.

Snow, C. Mother's speech to children learning language. *Child Development,* 1972, **43**, 549–565.

Spitz, R.A. Hospitalism. *The Psychoanalytic Study of the Child,* 1945, **1**, 53.

Stern, D.N. Mother and infant at play: The dyadic interaction involving facial, vocal, and gaze behaviors. In M. Lewis & L.A. Rosenblum (Eds.), *The effect of the infant on its caregiver.* New York: Wiley, 1974, 187–213.

Stern, D.N. *The first relationship: Infant and mother.* Cambridge: Harvard University Press, 1977.

Stone, L.J., Smith, H.T., & Murphy, L.B. (Eds.), *The competent infant.* New York: Basic Books, 1973.

Sroufe, L.A. The coherence of individual development: Early care, attachment, and subsequent developmental issues. *American Psychologist,* 1979, **34**(10), 834–841.

Sroufe, L.A., & Waters, E. Attachment as an organizational construct. *Child Development,* 1977, **48**, 1184–1199.

Super, C.M. Cross-cultural research on infancy. In H.C. Triandis & A. Heron (Eds.), *Handbook of cross-cultural psychology: Developmental psychology* (Vol. 4). Boston: Allyn & Bacon, 1981.

Sutton-Smith, B. *Play and learning.* New York: Gardner, 1972.

Tizard, B. *Adoption: A second chance.* London: Open Books, 1977.

Tizard, B., & Hodges, J. The effect of early institutional rearing on the development of eight-year-old children. *Journal of Child Psychology and Psychiatry,* 1978, **19**, 99–118.

Tizard, B., & Rees, J. The effect of early institutional rearing on the behavior problems and affectional relationships of four-year-old children. *Journal of Child Psychology and Psychiatry,* 1975, **16**, 61–74.

Tizard, J., & Tizard, B. The social development of two-year-old children in residential nurseries. In H.E. Schaffer (Ed.), *The origins of human social relations.* London: Academic Press, 1971.

Thoman, E.B. Development of synchrony in mother-infant interaction in feeding and other situations. Federation of American Societies for Experimental Biology, 1975, **34**, 1587–1592.

Tolman, C. The metaphysics of relations in Klaus Riegel's "dialectics" of human development. *Human Development,* 1981, **24**, 33–51.

Ungerer, J.A., & Sigman, M. Symbolic play and language comprehension in autistic children. *Journal of the American Academy of Child Psychiatry,* 1981, **20**, 318–337.

Uzgiris, I.C., & Hunt, J. McV. *Toward ordinal scales of psychological development in infancy.* Champaign, Ill.: University of Illinois, 1975.

Waters, E., Wippman, J., & Sroufe, L.A. Attachment, positive affect, and competence in the peer group: Two studies in construct validation. *Child Development,* 1979, **50**, 821–829.

Whiten, A. Assessing the effects of perinatal events on the success of the mother-infant relationship. In H.R. Schaffer (Ed.), *Studies in mother-infant interaction.* London: Academic Press, 1977.

Whittaker, C.H. A note on developmental trends in the symbolic play of hospitalized profoundly retarded children. *Journal of Child Psychology and Psychiatry,* 1980, **21**, 253–261.

Willis, D.J., Elliott, C.H., & Jay, S. Psychological effects of physical illness and its concomitants. In J. Tuma (Ed.), *The practice of pediatric psychology.* New York: Wiley, 1982.

Wohlwill, J. *The study of behavioral development.* New York: Academic Press, 1973.

Yarrow, L.J., Rubenstein, J.L., & Pedersen, F.A. *Infant and environment: Early cognitive and motivational development.* Washington, D.C.: Hemisphere (distributed by Wiley), 1975.

CHAPTER 4

Cross-Cultural Research with Children and Families

ALEXIS J. WALKER, CYNTHIA A. NOBLE, AND PATRICIA A. SELF

The premise of this chapter is that the primary value of cross-cultural research lies in its ability to bring to our attention the factors influencing behavior and development in our own society that we are likely to ignore due to cultural absolutism or ethnocentrism. For example, in our culture, we share an empirically supported point of view that even young infants are capable of learning. Thus brightly colored mobiles, decorated walls, and parental vocalization are not uncommon in an American infant's experience. In China, on the other hand, where the Cultural Revolution perpetuated the ideology that infants are incapable of learning, parents are observed primarily keeping their babies comfortable (Kessen, 1975). Chinese infants, as a result, may be doing much of their learning through stimulation of an indirect nature. Subtle influences may therefore be easier to study and isolate in China than in our own culture with its many varieties of indirect infant stimuli. Thus research in another culture can increase the awareness of the complexity of factors influencing development here as well as elsewhere.

The cross-cultural literature pertaining to children and families, however, has been lacking a conceptual framework by which to organize the research. The contextual scheme (Riegel, 1976) seems particularly suited to provide such a framework. In the contextual (dialectic) approach, development is viewed as simultaneous change across multiple dimensions. For example, as the individual develops cognitively, the family unit may be in transition; the family may be changing during a period of ideological change in the culture. Development occurs, then, across several levels or realms; each of these levels is in constant interaction with the other levels at any point in time. The individual and development are viewed in constant flux; the individual is in constant dialogue with the other levels of development. To date, the literature would suggest seven levels of influence in the development of the child: individual, dyadic, familial, network, subcultural, cultural, and setting.

Each of these levels is a distinct system with which the child has direct interaction. At the same time, these levels directly affect each other. The outcome of interlevel interaction probably has an indirect influence on the child. The child, an active organism, is also likely to have direct and indirect influences on these realms. In effect, each level of influence comprises a multitude of variables, both independent and dependent, that directly and indirectly affect and respond to each other and that affect and respond to the multitude of variables in other realms.

Some of these levels of development, especially the individual and the dyadic, have received more empirical attention than others. At the network level, for instance, research and theory have not gone much beyond structural characteristics or macrolevel influences such as size and density. In the individual realm, on the other hand, a great number of relevant factors or variables have been isolated as influencing development. It would be unreasonable to expect cross-cultural researchers to include all possible influential variables in their work. Yet studies in which scant or no attention is given to one or more of these systems are severely limited in their ability to further our understanding of developmental processes. It may be fruitful to group a number of factors in such a way as to index a variety of microlevel influences, thereby broadening the scope of individual projects. Though this method lacks precision, it provides a means of coping with multidimensional influences.

The remainder of this chapter explicates the issues involved in this kind of formulation. Following this is an application of the model to issues in therapeutic techniques and an application of the model to an exemplary case. Conclusions appear at the end of the chapter.

LEVELS OF INFLUENCE

Individual

Among the individual variables that seem to have the greatest impact upon development, and certainly among those subject to cultural influence, are the effect of sex of the individual, the developmental level or age of the child, and possibly the temperamental characteristics of the child. Regardless of the realm of development of which one speaks, whether social, physiological, emotional, or cognitive, the individual variables above—sex, cognitive level, and temperament—significantly influence the development of the child.

Distinctive development in accordance with one's sex has long been noted; physical dimorphism in the direction of greater body weight and height for males has been documented across a variety of cultures (Hoyenga & Hoyenga, 1979). Of more interest, cross-culturally and clinically, are the behaviors that are responded to differentially, based upon the child's sex. Rubin, Provenzano, and Luria (1974) and Will, Self, and Datan (1976) are among those who have documented that this differential treatment by caregivers begins shortly after birth; this may be stereotypic based upon the prevailing belief system. In a single culture, such as American culture, the importance of the infant's or child's sex is subject to considerable variability, depending upon the particular ethnic groups involved. Williamson (1976) suggests that Jewish and Catholic ethnic groups in American culture prefer to have male rather than female children, whereas Protestant families prefer a child of each sex.

At older ages, societies further differentiate appropriate behaviors by sex. Initiation rites are prevalent for both males and females as they enter puberty. However, these rites denote fertility for the female and adult role status for the male (Radcliffe-Brown, 1922). Throughout the childhood and adolescent periods, parents and/or the peer group structure the behaviors of the child in accordance with the prevailing view of the sex-appropriateness of the behavior.

Another equally significant determinant of behavior toward a child is the concept of age or developmental level. While most researchers differentiate children's behaviors and those of adults to the child in terms of the child's chronological age, generally these behaviors are determined by the child's cognitive status, not by age. We would not teach an 8-year-old higher mathematics, but this is a function of the child's cognitive level, rather than age. During at least the period of childhood, then, it tends to be the cognitive level, rather than age, that distinguishes behavior.

Recent work by Kagan et al. (1979) highlights this perspective. These investigators studied improvements in children's recall memory cross-culturally and noted that improvements in memory varied as much as four to six years, but that all children improved across time. Chronological age would not be a useful indicator for memory ability; a more useful index would be the cognitive level of the child. As their data indicate, there is little doubt that the culture has significant impact upon cognitive development. The wealth of research clearly supports this interpretation, although multiple hypotheses accounting for the differences have been suggested (Pick, 1980).

Differing definitions for children's cognitive processing have been suggested by LeVine (1970). These have included modes of thought, developmental structures (such as those suggested by Piaget in 1952), representations of experience (the learning view, or that of Bruner proposed in 1979), and the psychometric representation of cognition. All of these definitions of cognition have been studied cross-culturally, and variations by culture have been noted.

The study of the individual differences in temperament has made significant gains in American culture in the last decade. Measurement of differences has been fostered by the development of various devices such as the Brazelton Neonatal Behavioral Scale (Brazelton, 1973) or the Carey Infant Temperament Scale (Carey, 1970). In addition, clinical work such as that by Campbell (1977) has emphasized the possibly long term effects of maternal perceptions of infant temperament. In her study, she found that if mothers perceive an infant to be difficult, this perception may have more effects on the infant's development than birth complications.

Aspects of temperamental differences among infants and children have been examined in the cross-cultural literature. The data suggest that such differences may be largely a function of differing responsiveness by the caregiver. For example, Brazelton (1977) describes how Zincanteco Indian mothers respond to their infants before the infant ever makes a demand; even minimal motor activity by the infant elicits a feeding situation by the mother. Quiet passivity and low motor activity are the rule in the early behaviors of these infants.

Future cross-cultural research must articulate the nature of the culture's impact on temperamental characteristics. It is equally important to note, however, as does Goldberg (1977), that even when rearing conditions are very different across cultures, there should still be a range of individual characteristics that need to be scrutinized in terms of their impact on development.

Obviously, other individual characteristics can influence the developing organism in its interaction both within the various realms of individual development and in its interaction with the other levels. Sex of the child, cog-

nitive level, and temperament, however, seem among the most pervasive in their effects at the individual level. In addition to the consideration of the characteristics of the child, at any time when the child interacts with another person, such as the caregiver, the individual characteristics of that person must be considered as well. An example of such considerations is included in the discussion of child abuse at the end of this chapter.

Dyadic

At the dyadic level, it is the interaction of the child with another person that is the focus of interest. In contrast to those espousing the salience of cognitive processes in determining development, proponents of this dyadic perspective suggest that social relationships are crucial to development (Bowlby, 1969). Following this point of view, numerous investigators (e.g., Ainsworth, 1977) have suggested that, at the very least, early relationships serve as the model for all later interpersonal relationships. Others (e.g., Bowlby, 1969) suggest that the formation of interpersonal relationships, or attachments, are crucial to the survival of the species.

There seems to be little doubt that adequate attachment of infants or children to their caregiver(s) does indeed foster subsequent behavioral development in realms other than social development. Securely attached infants are more compliant (Stayton, Hogan, & Ainsworth, 1971), exploratory (Ainsworth & Bell, 1970), and cognitively advanced (Bell, 1970). Recent reports by Klaus and Kennell (1976) have examined the possible enhancement of this attachment bond through early and extended contact in the neonatal period. Their follow-up data across a 6-year period indicate increased development status (increased language facility and intellectual development) in children who have been afforded early and extended contact (Klaus & Kennell, 1976).

The development of specific social relationships, or attachments, has been the subject of considerable cross-cultural research. In general, these data suggest that while there may be fairly dramatic differences in caregiver-child behavior patterns, significant social relationships are formed almost inevitably. For example, Ainsworth has noted the difference in physical contact between mother-infant pairs in Ghana and America, but both groups showed similar attachment characteristics (Ainsworth, 1977). Unfortunately, cross-cultural studies have not yet systematically examined attachment bonds of infants/young children to individuals other than the primary caregiver. Bonds formed to extended-family members or friends have not yet been examined cross-culturally.

Familial

The family is the small social group or basic unit of society within which much early development takes place. Its ubiquity renders its examination imperative in cross-cultural work. Though families are widely variant in structure and function, they seem to differ in degree along several basic dimensions.

Kantor and Lehr (1975) developed a typology of families to reflect the way in which family members regulate intrafamily and interfamily interaction. According to their classification scheme, families vary in the degree to which they allow themselves to be actively influenced by the external environment; they operationalize this phenomenon as openness. Closed families are markedly restrictive in their degree of openness to the broader environment. They emphasize group solidarity relative to individual autonomy of members and tend to have well defined and institutionalized rules for the conduct of intragroup behavior. In closed families, power is distributed hierarchically, with adults exercising legitimate control over children. Decisions are made and enforced by parents, and children are not consulted. Behavior indicative of obedience, punctuality, and neatness is encouraged and expected. Family members may care deeply about one another, but emotional outbursts are discouraged. Rubin (1976) identified similar characteristics in her study of workingclass families in the United States. She suggested that families expect their children to behave in ways that will be reinforced in the work world (Bowles & Gintis, 1976; Kohn, 1969).

Open families are similar to the American ideal of a family type. They strive to maintain an equal balance between group cohesiveness and individual autonomy and do this by allowing more freedom for members than is acceptable in the closed family. Open families have rules for interaction and behavior, but they tend to use them as guidelines rather than laws. In this family type, consensus is the usual decision-making tool. Children participate in the resolution of problems or issues, though parents can, and on occasion do, exercise legitimate power. Children in open families are encouraged to exhibit self-reliance, take responsibility, and show initiative. This pattern, too, seems to parallel a particular socioeconomic group, the United States' middle class. And again, behavior valued in the children is similar to what might be expected in whitecollar or professional occupations (Bowles & Gintis, 1976; Kohn, 1969).

Random families, a relatively unusual type, emphasize individual autonomy over a sense of group solidarity. They are so markedly open to external influence that it is often difficult to find the boundary between the external system and the family itself. Such families have very few rules since rules are perceived as interfering with the development of individual growth. Power in random families is almost totally lateral, that is, attempts to reach a group consensus are marked by persuasion, compromise, and conflict, although each person frequently makes unilateral decisions. Children are encouraged to develop whatever interests and talents they may have, even if this occasionally interferes with some family goal. Behavior relatively unusual in the other family types, for example, intense emotional outbursts, is common in the random family. Though research has not definitively described this pattern as representative of a particular socioeconomic group, one might expect this style to be possible in the nonpatriarchal upper class.

These family types are probably correlated

with socioeconomic status for a number of reasons. First, there are value differences across socioeconomic levels, and values can and do influence the ways people choose to structure their interpersonal behavior and interactions. In addition, income and prestige act to set limits on the structural possibilities within families. For example, large families of low income are likely to be housed in crowded conditions. Many people in a small space render the development and enforcement of rules essential to smooth and stable interaction.

The family's location on this continuum of openness no doubt is reflective of its direct and indirect influences on its child members. Parents' conscious socialization of their offspring will differ in predictable ways with family type. In addition, the unplanned influences resulting from their patterns of small group interaction (LeVine, 1969), though less rigidly conforming to the family model, will also be correlated with family type.

Several theorists have attempted to typologize the marital dyad in a way that is reflective of spousal interaction. The broadest scheme is that of Bernard (1964), who identified two basic types: *interactional,* in which the spouses value and share companionship; and *parallel,* in which roles and interaction are relatively segregated and complementary. Cuber and Harroff (1965), using an unrepresentative sample, developed a similar system of *intrinsic* and *utilitarian* marriages and created subdivisions within each type. *Intrinsic* marriages emphasize the relationship and are of two types: (1) vital and (2) total. Vital marriages are those in which the relationship is characterized by high levels of satisfaction and companionship; total marriages follow the same patterns but are more intense. *Utilitarian* marriages allow the partners to pursue their own individual goals since the focus is not on the relationship. They are of three types: (1) devitalized, in which the partners formerly shared companionship norms but now perceive themselves as just "going through the motions"; (2) passive-congenial, in which the couple has always felt the relationship was secondary to individual interests and goals; and (3) conflict-habituated, in which the relationship is characterized by an atmosphere of tension. For Cuber and Haroff (1965), each of these types is a stable pattern reflecting styles of interaction and not satisfaction with or stability of the marriage.

One can only speculate on the influence of the marriage type on childrearing practices or on the development of children. It is clear, however, that utilitarian and parallel types facilitate parental involvement with children in a way that interactional and intrinsic types do not. Cuber and Harroff (1965) suggest that partners in utilitarian patterns have the children, not the marriage, as a central concern.

Although families may be similar in terms of values, goals, and interactional styles, they, too, are changing systems. Each family has its own history and anticipated future. Its location at a particular stage of the family life cycle will affect the way it relates to the environment and the way the environment will affect it (Brim, 1959). For instance, closed families, of necessity, will become somewhat more open in their interactions with external systems as their children grow older. Basically, the family can be seen as a system which acts to "filter, order, distort, and interpret" the external environment to the child, while the child's interaction with the broader context becomes more and more direct with age (Hess, 1970, p. 473). This increasingly direct interaction with the environment on the part of the child, at least in some respects, will force the family to be more open.

Network

One's social network, or those persons with whom one interacts directly and their interconnection, is another changing system influencing development. Over time, individuals develop a pattern of exchanging goods and services with their social network members. Thus networks facilitate the achievement of personal goals (Boissevain, 1974).

Networks can be examined according to their structural and interactional properties (Ridley & Avery, 1979). The two principal structural properties are size and density. Size is the number of persons in the network; density is the degree to which individuals in the network are connected with network members other than the central figure. The interactional properties of a network are:

1. Diversity of linkages—whether the individual comes into contact with network members through a single role (uniplex) or through many roles (multiplex).
2. Exchange content—the nature of the elements exchanged between the individual and network members when in interaction.
3. Directional flow—whether elements are exchanged in one direction or mutually, and whether exchanges are equal, unequal, or complementary.
4. Frequency and duration of interaction.

Sex, age, and appearance seem to influence network properties. For example, children and the elderly tend to have small networks; young adults have large networks with high density and multiplexity. Through middle age, networks seem to increase in size and decrease in density and multiplexity (Boissevain, 1974).

Kin or relatives tend to be a prominent group in an individual's network (Shulman, 1975) though cultural and subcultural expectations for kinship ties are influential in the degree to which kin are incorporated into the network (Nye & Berardo, 1973; Tulkin, 1977). Bott's (1957) study of kinship patterns in London found that workingclass families tended to have close relationships with kin, residential proximity to parents, and more traditional marital role structure as contrasted with middle class families. The latter were characterized by loosely knit family ties, neolocal residence patterns, and a tendency toward egalitarianism in marital dyads (Bott, 1957). Using Boissevain's (1974) model, workingclass networks are small and dense, with multiplex linkages, varied and mutual exchange patterns, and long, frequent interactions. Such networks will have homogeneous value patterns and will be more successful at enforcing behavioral standards because of the degree of agreement and consistency among members (Ridley & Avery, 1979).

How all of this affects the development of children is difficult to assess. For the child in the workingclass family, however, one might expect the degree of congruence between home and the network to be high (Hess, 1970). This no doubt will mean a more limited variety of experiences available to the child than would be the case in larger, uniplex networks and probably greater homogeneity of intraclass behavior.

The social network is likely to have greater influence on development in those cultures in which substitute parental care is available and encouraged. The daycare centers in the United States, for example, result in children having larger networks at earlier ages than may have occurred in the past and suggest a greater diversity of influence on developmental processes as well as on the parent-child relationship.

Community/Subcultural

A more remote, yet still influential, system is that of the community or subculture in which the child and family are embedded. It includes local educational, industrial, medical, political, religious, and social institutions, and its members may be seen as similar or different according to their socioeconomic status and ethnic background.

The degree to which socialization practices are institutionalized would be visible at this level (LeVine, 1969). For example, if schools, medical personnel, and religious leaders treat children in a similar manner, this would be indicative of both shared values regarding childrearing and institutionalized childrearing practices. In such cases, the degree of homogeneity between the child's home and environmental experience would be great (Hess, 1970).

The degree to which kinship systems are central in the subculture seems to be related to broad sociocultural values. Farber (1975) suggests that cultures may sometimes rely on families and their networks to dominate social institutions. This type of culture is characterized by centripetal or formalized kinship patterns in which the tendency is to maintain very strong, centralized kin ties. Systems following this model exhibit a high degree of intrasystem loyalty and stable obligation patterns. In these cases, children's external experiences would be relatively similar to family experience.

The alternative, according to Farber (1975), is a culture reflecting a centrifugal or communal ideology in which the tendency is to have diffuse kin patterns. Though families in this cultural type may exhibit strong affective ties, neolocal residence patterns and reduced kin obligations are likely to be the norm. The result is the existence of cross-pressures exerted on the family, and a reduction of the power of kin to act collectively. In such societies, family problems or crises such as violence or delinquency become matters of public concern. That is, the community, rather than the network, is the social support system and the child is likely to have frequent and variant interaction with institutions from a rather early age.

The degree of subcultural heterogeneity appears to be an important influence on children's development. A child who differs from the dominant social pattern is reminded of that difference in most extrafamilial interactions. Children are aware of their uniqueness, perhaps as a result of this constant reminding, in terms of race, ethnicity, and status. This awareness appears sometime during school age and is positively related to feelings of helplessness and negatively related to feelings of self-esteem (Hess, 1970).

Cultural

The broader sociocultural system, though perhaps the farthest removed from direct child contact, has a pervasive influence on the other systems. Cultural ideologies, beliefs, and practices place structural constraints on individuals, families, networks, and communities, which, in turn, directly influence children.

The culture has well-established norms of marriage and family organization (Whiting & Child, 1953) in terms of sexual behavior, reproduction, inheritance, and residence patterns (Mogey, 1964). It also sets the dominant social norms for parental behavior (LeVine, 1969), helping to define what caregivers actually believe they are doing in childrearing activities (Tulkin, 1977). It is the culture that delineates the standard social character, that is, those positively valued traits and personality characteristics that will be, for any particular society, facilitative of successful conformity and social interaction (LeVine, 1969). Not only are the models established at this level, but the beliefs about the methods deemed to be successful in achieving these ideals are also culturally determined. In fact, the culture influences the degree to which deliberate socialization is believed to be possible; childrearing practices are culture specific within the limits established by the universal characteristics of infants and children and by ubiquitous social needs (LeVine, 1969). At the same time, the culture has pervasive influences on social networks and communities through its structuring of education and through pressures toward either centripetal or centrifugal kinship systems (Farber, 1975).

LeVine (1977) identified two cultural factors which directly influence socialization practices:

1. The degree to which there is a threat to the physical survival and health of infants and young children.
2. The scarcity of resources in the culture.

From this perspective, the goals of parents in the socialization of their children will be determined largely by these two factors. If there is a high infant mortality rate in a particular culture, parents will direct their efforts toward keeping their children alive. If resources are scarce, however, parents will exert much effort toward developing in their children the capacity for self-maintenance as adults. If neither of these issues is critical, parents can focus on maximizing cultural values in their children.

Setting

In addition to these interpersonal or social levels of influence, there is a myriad of influences inherent in a particular setting. Basically, setting conditions may sustain, enhance, or impair processes of interaction and development such that they may not be the same across contexts (Bronfenbrenner, 1979). Cultures, subcultures, networks, families, and individuals have differential access to media, comfort, labor-saving devices, and aesthetic beauty. Poverty illustrates well the impact of a fundamental contextual characteristic. Families living in poverty are more vulnerable to disease, have lower prestige, and experience a great deal of daily strain with regard to material resources when compared with moderate and high income families (Hess, 1970). The effects of such circumstances are probably pervasive, though it would be difficult to be precise about how these effects are played out. Bronfenbrenner (1979) recently addressed this problem:

We still lack a specific taxonomy for analyzing settings in terms of developmentally relevant parameters or for assessing development in terms of environmentally relevant outcomes. (p. 844)

An attempt has been made, however, to identify environmental dimensions for the purpose of quantifying environmental properties. Insel and Moos (1974) believe that focusing on the objective, physical characteristics of an environment, such as pollution; temperature; noise level; rainfall; and buildings and their shapes, sizes, and placement, without focusing on the interaction of these elements with social systems, is short sighted. They say the "climate" of the environment can be studied and assessed through these dimensions:

1. Relationship—the degree and type of affiliation, spontaneity, and involvement of members in the setting.

2. Personal development—the degree to which the environment permits and encourages personal growth as represented by autonomy, degree of competition, and degree of practicality of orientation.

3. System maintenance and change—the degree of order, clarity of rules, degree of control, and responsiveness to change in the setting.

Insel and Moos (1974) believe that this climate will influence the mood, self-esteem, satisfaction, and personal growth of its participant members. Attempts to classify environments in this way have been limited, but Insel and Moos (1974) have sucessfully categorized certain institutions according to their ratings on these three dimensions.

Probably the most important setting factor is the change in developmental influences associated with sociohistorical time. Inherent in the contextual model is the notion that every culture has a changing gestalt of development; that is, over time or with development variables and the realms in which they operate cannot be assumed to be morphostatic. Witness in American culture the change in ideology regarding infant care. Rigid feeding schedules and accelerated toilet training were advocated in the 1920s and 1930s, but parents were advised to be a bit more indulgent in the 1940s (Melville, 1980). As a result, the explication of the variables affecting developmental processes would require constant and frequent revision. Recognition of, and attention to, the changing *Zeitgeist* is essential to the understanding of setting.

The interplay among these levels, in direct and indirect contact with each other, is assumed. The complexity of causes, effects, and interactions resulting from such interplay leads to the conclusion that cultures differing significantly in only one of these areas are likely to achieve different developmental effects. Thus, to understand thoroughly the way in which a particular interpersonal or social phenomenon is spawned and developed in any particular culture, one would need information at all of these levels.

This is equally true in clinical practice, that is, individuals manifesting particular behavioral difficulties are subject to the same range of influences. One will best understand a clinical case by familiarity with the contextual issues involved. The following section is an application of the model to issues in therapeutic techniques designed to acquaint readers with these issues.

ISSUES IN THERAPEUTIC TECHNIQUES

Riegel's framework is useful when one examines the possible obstacles to therapeutic success with children. Numerous authors (e.g., Draguns, 1976; Stewart, 1976) have noted the multiplicity of problems when one attempts to counsel persons from another culture or subculture. Few researchers, however, have tried to organize these variables so that one can easily systematize the issues involved. Each of the levels of influence that Riegel describes is dealt with briefly below and is summarized in Table 4.1.

Individual

One of the most troublesome problems to the clinician is the inability to assess adequately a child's ability. When a child from another culture or subculture is the client, assessment is even more difficult. Both psychometrician and clinician may be unsure of the adequacy of the assessment and the demands that another culture may place upon a child in a testing situation. Lonner (1976) suggests that caution is necessary whether the test is used for intelligence or personality assessment or for projective purposes.

Lonner also suggests that the controversy involving testing across cultures revolves around three central issues. First, psychological phenomena are seldom invariant across cultures. Shyness, for example, is defined differently in differing cultures. So even though a test can be used in cultures other than Western cultures, it probably should not be. Second, in spite of the prevailing assump-

Table 4.1.   Contexts of Development

Levels of Influence	Selected Variables
Individual	Age
	Developmental level
	Sex
	Temperament
Dyadic	Attachment to caregiver
Familial	Degree of openness
	Socioeconomic status
	Type of marriage
Network	Density
	Diversity of linkages
	Size
Subcultural	Degree of heterogeneity of members
	Institutionalization of socialization practices
	Role of the kinship system
Cultural	Degree of threat to survival
	Norms of childrearing
	Scarcity of resources
Setting	Change over sociohistorical time
	Organizational climate
	Poverty

tion that nonverbal tests are more culture free, neither verbal nor nonverbal stimuli transcend cultural differences. If any test is used, one must be aware of its biases. Finally, Lonner notes that the norms of a test are especially culture bound. Since most techniques have been standardized in Western (predominantly American and European) cultures, the norms used for evaluation cannot be transposed easily for use in another culture.

Likewise, individual characteristics such as temperament, age, or sex have differential impact on therapies. Broverman et al. (1970) have noted the "double standard" for mental health applied to males and females. A stereotypically "healthy" female is more submissive, less independent, less adventurous, more easily influenced, less aggressive, and less objective than the male counterpart, according to a group of practicing clinicians. Female versus male children similarly have different values placed upon their behavior. Females are expected to be more dependent upon the teacher or authority figure, while males are expected to function at a further distance. Indeed, recent research (Fagot, 1980) has substantiated these expectations.

Dyadic

In the use of therapeutic techniques, the dyadic realm is particularly important. The development of rapport with the child client and her/his parents is crucial, yet it may be very difficult if the individual is from another culture/subculture. In order to counsel effectively those from another culture/subculture, some clinicians argue that one must live in another culture (Wintrob, 1976).

The emphasis upon the clinician as the person who must provide the behavioral and communicative flexibility for the therapeutic relationship is an important one. Similar to parental attachment, the nature of the relationship determines the success of the counseling situation. Thus Draguns (1976) suggests that the clinician be prepared to accept the client in her or his cultural frame of reference, adjust communicative style to the cultural background of the client, and be willing to adjust intervention techniques to the cultural frame of reference that the client chooses.

Familial

Several familial variables affect the success of therapeutic techniques. Researchers have noted the importance of socioeconomic status and family structure as mediating therapeutic success. Pedersen (1976) summarized the effects of social class. He noted that low income persons are less likely to be in therapy, or, if they are, they remain in therapy for shorter periods. On the clinician's side, low income individuals are treated by less experienced staff and with possibly less valuable short term therapies. Pedersen notes that clinicians who are most similar to their clients in sex, race, and social class have the greatest likelihood of success.

Vontress (1976) has described several examples of familial structure and the corresponding impact upon the clinical relationship.

Japanese-American families, for instance, attribute total authority to the father in the family. This respect of authority may transfer as well to the therapeutic relationship in the form of hesitancy to become involved. Similarly, Vontress describes a school counselor who insists that a Puerto Rican girl with high aptitude scores apply for admission to college without consulting her father, who believes that a Puerto Rican girl should get married, have children, and obey her husband. Further, in some families individual decisions are rarely made; thus family therapy may be the only way to make progress with a particular child.

Network

Vontress (1976) also provides examples of network influences upon therapeutic processes. As noted above, network influences include the persons external to the immediate family with whom an individual interacts. The network may include relatives or kin and other persons in the immediate social milieu. Vontress describes the black youngster from the ghetto who may be reluctant to accept a scholarship to a predominantly Caucasian university because he fears losing the "blackness" that his friends consider important.

Vontress also describes the Appalachian white who derives self-identification from relationships with others and from being neighborly. As such, it is much more important to pass the time of day with a friend than to keep an appointment punctually.

The density, size, and diversity of the network all interact to describe the impact of these influences upon the individual. In turn, these influences may determine the impact of the therapy upon the individual.

Community/Subcultural

Similarly, the subculture of an individual affects therapeutic success. The subcultural effects are somewhat better documented than those of the network system. Numerous investigators have documented the differences in language behavior of American blacks (Baratz, 1969). Achievement differences have been noted in various subcultures of American children such as Mexican-Americans (Price-Williams, 1975).

As in the network considerations, the mobility or integration of the subculture may determine the differences between the subcultural group and the larger population. The study on elevations in intelligence of American blacks as they were assimilated into white adoptive homes is a prime example of this phenomenon (Scarr-Salapatek & Weinberg, 1981). Vontress (1976) describes examples of outsiders entering either barrios of the Southwest or areas in Appalachia and receiving not only curiosity of the natives of the area but also outright hostility. These factors will undoubtedly enter into any clinical relationship.

Cultural

Many of the cultural influences in the success of therapeutic techniques have already been mentioned in the other portions of this section. These include the influences of culture on assessment, development of rapport with the clinician, objectives of the therapy, and the type of therapy.

B.F. Skinner (1966), in "The Design of Culture," has presented both an optimistic and pessimistic view of the impact of cultures upon human development. Skinner believes that we will soon reach the point where the intentional design of cultures may be possible based upon the knowledge of social contingency systems. He also notes, however, that cultures often have been exploitive of human behavior and have used dubious social practices for the maintenance of cultural norms. Regardless of one's belief in the possibility of the intentional shaping of cultures, one cannot help but note the impact of culture on a child's development. Likewise, the success of clinical treatment may rest solely with the transmission of cultural values upon the child and his or her family.

The utility of clinical treatment is a good example of culture's impact. In some cultures, where even health treatment is lacking, a child's access to clinical service may be nil. Clinical services for children are much more available in Western countries than in any other part of the world.

Setting

The final realm of influence that Riegel (1976) describes is the setting. Included in setting effects are such influences as sociohistorical time and poverty. As noted above, access to clinical services may be a function of sociohistorical time. The recognition of children as appropriate clinical patients has been a recent development. Earlier views of children and knowledge of therapeutic techniques have been replaced by an acknowledgment of the value of early intervention with specialized techniques appropriate for children of different ages.

Riegel also would include phenomena that do not fit easily into the other categories in this classification. This would include natural disasters such as wars, earthquakes, and famine, as well as the devastation caused by poverty. Spitz (1945) has described eloquently the clinical problems that ensue as a result of the loss of both parents in times of war. These may include not only depression and growth retardation, but also severe sequelae such as increased susceptibility to disease and death.

Perhaps the best way to elucidate the importance to development of contextual influences is through the use of an exemplary case. The following section is an application of the model to the problem of child abuse.

AN EXEMPLARY CASE

A number of authors have addressed the need to use a multisystem approach to the issue of child abuse (e.g., Belsky, 1980; Vietze et al., 1980). In no case, however, do we find consideration of the seven influences outlined in this chapter as being important in a discussion of any social phenomenon, particularly one as complex as child abuse. In the remainder of this chapter, we will illustrate the necessity of considering each of these factors independently, as well as in complex interaction with one another, through a presentation of child abuse data within the context of American culture.

Perhaps Belsky (1980) comes closest to considering the multiple influences on the ecological integration of child maltreatment. In doing so, however, Belsky has subsumed under four categories an enormous body of data and theoretical literature, thus prohibiting finer discriminations in terms of influence. For example, his discussion includes the following influences on the development of child abuse: ontogenetic development, microsystems, exosystems, and macrosystems, roughly equivalent to our individual, familial, subcultural, and cultural factors respectively. Consequently, dyadic influences have been incorporated under the heading of familial factors; network influences are included in exosystems; and the various setting influences virtually are ignored except where these fit into other categories. We contend that the finer discriminations allowed by the seven-factor approach are crucial to an understanding of the total context of child abuse or any other complex social phenomenon.

Individual

At the level of the individual, Frodi and Lamb (1980) point out, "Infants can be 'at risk' for abuse because they are born with physical or behavioral abnormalities which render them vulnerable to abuse or because they have developed characteristics (perhaps through interaction with their parents) which affect the likelihood of abuse" (p. 241). For example, a number of studies have demonstrated a relationship between abuse and factors such as prematurity or, more specifically, birthweight (Elmer & Gregg, 1967; Klein & Stern, 1971; Frodi & Lamb, 1980; Vietze et al., 1980), physical or mental handicaps (Morse, Sahler, & Friedman, 1970; Sandgrund et al., 1974), unattractiveness (Dion, 1974), and passivity and the presence of developmental delays (Knutson, 1978). Two additional areas of concern have been those of infant sex and individual differences in infant temperament. According to Gil (1970) and Maden and Wrench (1977), male infants are more likely to

be abused than female infants. In a less direct association, it appears that the infant's temperament also has important implications for the quality of infant-caregiver interaction (Thomas et al., 1963; Campbell, 1977) and that such infant characteristics as fussiness, soothability, and cuddliness may be related to the occurrence of child abuse (Thomas, Chess, & Birch, 1968).

It is also important to note characteristics of the caregiver which may play a role in precipitating the occurrence of abuse. Knutson (1978) has postulated that abusers may be more prone to react in an abusive manner to aggression-eliciting stimuli. Certainly supportive of this notion is the work of Passman and Mulhern (1977). These researchers experimentally manipulated maternal stess and found a relationship between stress, the child's behavior, and the intensity of punishment administered. Additionally, individuals who were themselves abused or rejected as children (Gelles, 1980) or who were vicariously exposed to violence as children (Gelles & Straus, 1979) are more likely to be aggressive as children (George & Main, 1979) and to grow up to be abusive parents. Furthermore, Disbrow, Doerr, and Caulfield (1977) and Frodi and Lamb (1980) obtained results that indicated that there may be more pronounced levels of physiological arousal in abusers than nonabusers. Finally, in regard to individual characteristics, Spinetta and Rigler (1972) have summarized the attributes that have been associated with abusive parents. Typically, these parents are less intelligent, more aggressive, more impulsive, more immature, more egocentric, and more self-criticizing than nonabusive parents. Thus it appears that a number of individual characteristics on the part of parent and child can be identified as concomitant with abusive situations.

Dyadic

As Belsky (1980) has stressed, however, it is absolutely necessary to recognize the interactional nature of abuse. At the most basic level, the child indeed may play a role in eliciting abuse, but there must be an abuser as well.

Consequently, the individual characteristics discussed previously can be elaborated within the context of the dyadic interaction between abuser and abused. As an illustration, we know that parents-to-be often have certain expectations of what their child will be like. If these expectations are violated, for example, by disability, temperament difficulties, or the "wrong" sex, the infant may become at-risk for abuse (Frodi & Lamb, 1980). Thus characteristics such as a lack of social responsiveness or cuddliness on the part of a premature infant, coupled with a parent who "expects" a cuddly infant, may result in abuse via some sort of "mismatching" phenomenon (Frodi & Lamb, 1980). This matching of parent to child has been postulated to have implications for future interaction in regard to Knutson's notion of hyperreactivity (1978). For example, Frodi and Lamb (1980) have suggested that rather than being an innate trait, the tendency on the part of the caregiver to react aggressively may actually be a dyadic phenomenon developing as a result of interacting with an atypical child.

Certainly important in this regard are the data of Kennell and his colleagues. Their studies (Klaus & Kennell, 1976; Kennell, Voos, & Klaus, 1976) have indicated that neonatal separation or any separation during the first 6 months of life that interferes with parent-infant bonding places the child at-risk for maltreatment. Consequently, a number of intervention programs have been aimed at enhancing this early bonding process.

These are only a few of the possible examples of how dyadic interactions may influence child abuse. In light of these, abuse cannot be viewed simply as the result of particular characteristics of either the infant or the caregiver. Rather, at its most basic level, abuse is a complex dyadic phenomenon.

Familial

Since the child-caregiver dyad is often embedded within a spouse-spouse and/or a larger family unit, we can carry our discussion one step further. That is, the family interaction patterns also become important in understanding abuse and, in fact, may be crucial given the increasingly prevalent belief among researchers that recurrent abuse is typically acquiesced to by persons other than the abused-abuser dyad (Garbarino & Gilliam, 1980).

A number of investigators have examined family interaction patterns in abusive and nonabusive households. The results have indicated that abuse and neglect vary as a function of factors such as social isolationism of the family (Garbarino & Sherman, 1980; Parke, 1977; Polansky et al., 1979), degree of interaction among family members (Burgess & Conger, 1978), marital conflict/discord (Clark, 1976), number and temporal spacing of children (Gil, 1970), household disorganization (Elmer, 1967), and family stress (Elmer, 1979). To illustrate, Elmer (1979) has discussed how infants themselves may be the source of enough stress to result in abuse. For example, parents of abused chidren are often found to have unrealistic expectations of their children, even in the case of infants. According to Elmer (1979), where these expectations are coupled with a commonly held practice such as physical punishment, the results may easily be abuse.

Thus, within the context of the family, there may also be multiple interacting factors contributing to the total context within which child abuse occurs. Therefore, it may not be possible to isolate one particular dyadic relationship as faulty. Rather, in many cases, the most frequently used approach is to view the family as the "faulty unit."

Network

Despite their apparent isolation as distinct units, families are in fact socially defined institutions. Thus the broader personal-social network within which the child and family exist may also exert a powerful influence on the probability of child abuse. For example, Parke and Collmer (1975) found that abusing families tended to be isolated from their extended families. Again, we can note the more general social isolationism which is often seen in abusive families and expand this notion somewhat. It appears that these families may be lacking personal support systems and that this factor may be crucial to the abusive situation. As Garbarino (1980) stated, "When families are divorced from personal support systems, they are divorced from those sets of relationships that provide nurturance and feedback, that tell the individual what is expected of him and guide him in what to do, and that provide access to a variety of resources, both social and material" (p. 272). Thus Powell (1980) suggests that personal-social networks may facilitate parental adaptation to stress that in turn lowers the likelihood of abusive parent-child interaction. Equally critical may be the fact that the abused child, in this instance, literally has no one to turn to for help or protection.

Increasingly, then, we see the futility of attempting to isolate single factors as "the cause" of child abuse. Instead, we recognize the interaction of multiple systems and, even at the current level of discussion, the interaction of the extended family and personal-social network in the development of child abuse. We must look beyond to the subcultural level to understand additional influences upon the network itself.

Community/Subcultural

As Gordon (1979) has pointed out, "We know that families and children are influenced by a host of forces—local, national, and international in nature" (p. 2). That the goals and values of the community and, in fact, the larger culture have an impact on the nature of the child's social network is also a well-accepted view (Lewis, 1980). Furthermore, research on unemployment (Gil, 1971; Light, 1973) and job satisfaction (McKinley, 1964) has linked both of these community-defined variables to maltreatment. It seems crucial, then, that we admit the influence of subcultural variables into our discussion of child abuse. Also at this level we can again introduce the notion of isolationism. For example, we observe the lack of formal support systems (i.e., daycare centers and other social services) for abusive families that parallels the lack of

informal support systems in terms of neighbors and extended families. Thus undue pressures or stresses exerted on the family may not be alleviated when these formal support services are absent. Further, if intrafamilial stress is already high, such as with spousal conflict or a fussy baby, these community influences may increase the likelihood of maltreatment (Belsky, 1980).

Cultural

It is crucial to remember, however, that all of the aforementioned factors may be indicative of occurrences at the macrolevel of the culture, for example, the case of widespread unemployment resulting from economic crises. In the past, these macrolevel influences such as inequality, poverty, or drug abuse were ignored in regard to the issue of abuse (Steele & Pollock, 1974). More recently, however, the data have suported a mutual relationship between child abuse and other social problems such as running away and substance abuse (Chibucos, 1980). As further evidence for this new cultural emphasis, many investigators have cited the "violence orientation" of American culture and, more specifically, our general attitudes toward childrearing and family relations. As Gelles and Straus (1979) stated so succinctly, "Any theory purporting to explain human violence must take into account such cultural rules or norms, that specify the conditions under which violence is and is not appropriate, and the nature of the violent acts which are legitimate" (p. 34). Society has, in essence, provided parents with the right to employ violence against their children. Support for this societal view of child abuse also comes from cross-cultural studies that show the importance of the social environment in controlling child abuse (Garbarino, 1980).

Thus, even in our limited presentation of the child abuse literature, we see the interrelationships of levels of influence as causal factors. It is simply unrealistic to assume that any one factor at any one level can be targeted as "the factor" in child abuse. Rather, it is necessary to examine a hierarchy of factors, all in complex, simultaneous interaction with one another.

Setting

Having reached the highest social system of interest in the current paper, we are nonetheless left with one additional factor of importance. Research has indicated that almost no one is immune to the role of child abuser (Garbarino & Gilliam, 1980). In effect, we can all be broken, given the "right" situation (Passman & Mulhern, 1977). Thus the final factor to consider is one that will often overlap with the six factors already presented—in other words, the setting or context within which abuse is likely to occur. Included here would be factors already discussed under familial influences, such as crowding (Gil, 1970) or household disorganization (Elmer, 1967). We can also discuss research that has revealed a relationship between socioeconomic status and child abuse (Gil, 1970; Garbarino & Crouter, 1978) and a variety of demographic factors such as percentages of families headed by females (Garbarino & Crouter, 1978).

Additional influences that have not received attention in the child abuse literature but whose relevance may be demonstrated by other related literature should be considered. Specifically, heat, noise (Geen & O'Neal, 1969), and pressure from others (Milgram, 1964) are situational/environmental factors that have been related to the occurrence of aggression at a general level. Thus we might ask how each of these factors influences the occurrence of child abuse and, further, how each interacts with the factors previously discussed. Several researchers, for example, have questioned what the environmental factors (sufficient conditions) are that may result in parental abuse rather than discipline of the child (Gil, 1970; Garbarino & Gilliam, 1980).

More directly, Green (1980) discusses how the changing pattern of childrearing practices may also be important in this respect. Essentially, he argues that although the child-rearing function has spread from the parents to more diverse areas (e.g., the courts), the parents are still the ultimate source of governance. Nevertheless, many of their rights and wishes as caretakers have been denied in the push for children's "rights." As Green asserts, how a family setting constrained in this manner may function in family violence awaits investigation.

CONCLUSION

It should be apparent that attempts to isolate singular causal factors in child abuse are doomed to failure. It is simply not the case that we can take a complex social phenomenon such as child abuse and explain it unidimensionally. Rather, even under the constraints of a limited presentation of the data, we become aware of the necessity of viewing child abuse as a multidimensinal situation influenced by a variety of complex, interacting, hierarchically arranged factors.

Similarly, it is obvious that any aspect of child development which is viewed from a single perspective is also lacking. Each level of influence that we have described is composed of multiple variables that must be considered whether we are looking at normal or abnormal development. We have attempted to describe the more salient variables at each level rather than simply listing the multitude of variables involved. Table 4.1 summarizes the important variables of each level.

In summary, the dialectic-contextual approach highlights the impact of a variety of levels on child and family development. Each child and each family are subject to the unique influences of the interplay of their own multi-level systems; therefore, their behavior is best understood within the context of that particular culture.

REFERENCES

Ainsworth, M.D.S. Infant development and mother-infant interaction among Ganda and American families. In P.H. Leiderman, S.R. Tulkin, & A. Rosenfeld (Eds.), *Culture and infancy: Variations in the human experience.* New York: Academic Press, 1977.

Ainsworth, M.D.S., & Bell, S.M. Attachment, exploration, and separation: Illustrated by the behavior of one-year-olds in a strange situation. *Child Development,* 1970, **41,** 49–67.

Baratz, J.A. Bi-directional task for determining language proficiency in economically disadvantaged Negro children. *Child Development,* 1969, **30,** 889–901.

Bell, S.M. The development of the concept of object as related to infant-mother attachment. *Child Development,* 1970, **41,** 291–311.

Belsky, J. Child maltreatment: An ecological integration. *American Psychologist,* 1980, **35,** 320–335.

Bernard, J. The adjustments of married mates. In H.T. Christensen (Ed.), *Handbook of marriage and the family.* Chicago: Rand McNally, 1964.

Boissevain, J. *Friends of friends.* Oxford: Blackwell, 1974.

Bott, E. *Family and social networks.* London: Tavistock, 1957.

Bowlby, J. *Attachment and loss, I: Attachment.* New York: Basic Books, 1969.

Bowles, S., & Gintis, H. *Schooling in capitalist America: Educational reform and the contradictions of economic life.* New York: Basic Books, 1976.

Brazelton, T.B. *The neonatal behavioral assessment scale.* Philadelphia: Lippincott, 1973.

Brazelton, T.B. Implications of infant development among the Mayan Indians of Mexico. In P.H. Leiderman, S.R. Tulkin, & A. Rosenfeld (Eds.), *Culture and infancy: Variations in the human experience.* New York: Academic Press, 1977.

Brim, O.G., Jr. *Education for child rearing.* New York: Sage, 1959.

Bronfenbrenner, U. Contexts of child rearing: Problems and prospects. *American Psychologist,* 1979, **34,** 844–850.

Broverman, I.K., Broverman, D.M., Clarkson, F.E., Rosenkrantz, P.S., & Vogel, S.R. Sex role stereotypes and clinical judgments of mental health. *Journal of Consulting and Clinical Psychology,* 1970, **34,** 1–7.

Bruner, J.S. Eye, hand and mind. In D. Elkind & J.H. Flavell (Eds.), *Studies in cognitive devel-*
opment. New York: Oxford University Press, 1969.

Burgess, R., & Conger, R. Family interaction in abusive, neglectful, and normal families. *Child Development,* 1978, **49,** 1163–1173.

Campbell, S. Maternal and infant behavior in normal, high risk, and "difficult" infants. Paper presented at the meetings of the Society for Research in Child Development, New Orleans, March 1977.

Carey, W.B. A simplified method of measuring infant temperament. *Journal of Pediatrics,* 1970, **77,** 188–194.

Chibucos, T.R. A perspective on the mistreatment of children. *Infant Mental Health Journal,* 1980, **1,** 212–223.

Clark, J. The incidence of child abuse and neglect in the population at the Utah State University Industrial School. Unpublished master's thesis, Utah State University, 1976.

Cuber, J.F., & Haroff, P.B. *The significant Americans.* New York: Appleton-Century, 1965.

Dion, K. Children's physical attractiveness and sex as determinants of adult punitiveness. *Developmental Psychology,* 1974, **10,** 772–778.

Disbrow, M., Doerr, H., & Caulfield, C. Measures to predict child abuse. Final project report, University of Washington, Seattle, 1977. Taken from Chibucos, T.R. A perspective on the mistreatment of children. *Infant Mental Health Journal,* 1980, **1,** 212–223.

Draguns, J. Counseling across cultures: Common themes and distinct approaches. In P. Pedersen, W.J. Lonner, & J.G. Draguns (Eds.), *Counseling across cultures.* Honolulu: University Press of Hawaii, 1976.

Elmer, E. *Children in jeopardy: A study of abused minors and their families.* Pittsburgh: University of Pittsburgh Press, 1967.

Elmer, E. Child abuse and family stress. *Journal of Social Issues,* 1979, **35,** 60–71.

Elmer, E., & Gregg, G. Developmental characteristics of abused children. *Pediatrics,* 1967, **40,** 596–602.

Fagot, B.I. The maintenance of aggression in toddlers. Paper presented at the International Conference on Infant Studies, New Haven, Conn., 1980.

Farber, B. Bilateral kinship: Centripetal and centrifugal types of organization. *Journal of Marriage and the Family,* 1975, **37,** 871–888.

Frodi, A., & Lamb, M. Infants at risk for child

abuse. *Infant Mental Health Journal*, 1980, **1**, 240–247.

Garbarino, J. What kind of society permits child abuse? *Infant Mental Health Journal*, 1980, **1**, 270–280.

Garbarino, J., & Crouter, A. Defining the community context for parent-child relations: The correlates of child maltreatment. *Child Development*, 1978, **49**, 604–616.

Garbarino, J., & Gilliam, G. *Understanding abusive families.* Lexington, Mass.: Lexington, 1980.

Garbarino, J., & Sherman, D. High-risk families and high-risk neighbors: Studying the ecology of child maltreatment. *Child Development*, 1980, **51**, 188–198.

Geen, R.G., & O'Neal, E.C. Activation of cue elicited aggression by general arousal. *Journal of Personality & Social Psychology*, 1969, **11**, 289–292.

Gelles, R.J. Violence in the family: A review of research in the seventies. *Journal of Marriage and the Family*, 1980, **42**, 873–885.

Gelles, R.J., & Straus, M.A. Violence in the American family. *Journal of Social Issues*, 1979, **35**, 15–39.

George, C., & Main, M. Social interactions of young abused children: Approach, avoidance and aggression. *Child Development*, 1979, **50**, 306–318.

Gil, D.S. *Violence against children: Physical child abuse in the United States.* Cambridge: Harvard University Press, 1970.

Gil, D.S. Violence against children. *Journal of Marriage and the Family*, 1971, **33**, 639–648.

Goldberg, S. Infant development and mother-infant interaction in urban Zambia. In P.H. Leiderman, S.R. Tulkin, & A. Rosenfeld (Eds.), *Culture and infancy: Variations in the human experience.* New York: Academic Press, 1977.

Gordon, I.J. Seek continuity in social policy concerning child achievement. *Young Children*, 1979, **34**, 2–3.

Green, M.R. Introduction. In M.R. Green (Ed.), *Violence and the family.* Boulder, Colo.: Westview, 1980.

Hess, R.D. Social class and ethnic influences on socialization. In P.H. Mussen (Ed.), *Carmichael's manual of child psychology* (3rd ed.). New York: Wiley, 1970.

Hoyenga, K.B., & Hoyenga, K.T. *The question of sex differences: Psychological, cultural, and biological issues.* Boston: Little, Brown, 1979.

Insel, P.M., & Moos, R.H. Psychological environments: Expanding the scope of human ecology. *American Psychologist*, 1974, **29**, 179–188.

Kagan, J., Klein, R.E., Finley, G.E., Rogoff, B., & Nolan, E. A cross-cultural study of cognitive development. *Monographs of the Society for Research in Child Development*, 1979, **44**(5, Serial No. 180).

Kantor, D., & Lehr, W. *Inside the family: Toward a theory of family process.* New York: Harper Colophon, 1975.

Kennell, J.H., Voos, D., & Klaus, M.H. Parent infant bonding. In R. Helfer & C.H. Kempe (Eds.), *Child abuse and neglect: The family and the community.* Cambridge, Mass.: Ballinger, 1976.

Kessen, W. (Ed.), *Childhood in China.* New Haven, Conn.: Yale University, 1975.

Klaus, M.H., & Kennell, J.H. Parent-to-infant attachment. In D. Hull (Ed.), *Recent advances in pediatrics.* New York: Churchill-Livingstone, 1976.

Klein, M., & Stern, L. Low birthweight and the battered child syndrome. *American Journal of Diseases of Childhood*, 1971, **122**, 15–18.

Knutson, J.F. Child abuse as an area of aggression research. *Journal of Pediatric Psychology*, 1978, **3**, 20–27.

Kohn, M. *Class and conformity.* Homewood, Ill.: Dorsey, 1969.

LeVine, R.A. Culture, personality, and socialization: An evolutionary view. In D.A. Goslin (Ed.), *Handbook of socialization theory and research.* Chicago: Rand McNally, 1969.

LeVine, R.A. Cross-cultural study in child psychology. In P.H. Mussen (Ed.), *Carmichael's manual of child psychology* (Vol. 2). New York: Wiley, 1970.

LeVine, R.A. Child rearing as cultural adaption. In P.H. Leiderman, S.R. Tulkin, & A. Rosenfeld (Eds.), *Culture and infancy: Variations in the human experience.* New York: Academic Press, 1977.

Lewis, M. Peer interaction and maltreated children: Social network and epigenetic models. *Infant Mental Health Journal*, 1980, **1**, 224–231.

Light, R. Abused and neglected children in America: A study of alternative policies. *Harvard Educational Review*, 1973, **43**, 556–598.

Lonner, Walter J. The use of Western-based tests in intercultural counseling. In P. Pedersen, W.J. Lonner, & J.G. Draguns (Eds.), *Counseling across cultures.* Honolulu: University Press of Hawaii, 1976.

Maden, M.F., & Wrench, D.F. Significant findings in child abuse research. *Victimology,* 1977, **2,** 196–224.

McKinley, D. *Social class and family life.* New York: Glencoe, 1964.

Melville, K. *Marriage and family today* (2nd ed.). New York: Random House, 1980.

Milgram, S. Group pressure and action against a person. *Journal of Abnormal and Social Psychology,* 1964, **69,** 137–143.

Mogey, J. Family and community in urban-industrial societies. In H.T. Christensen (Ed.), *Handbook of marriage and the family.* Chicago: Rand McNally, 1964.

Morse, C.W., Sahler, O.J.Z., & Friedman, S.B. A three-year follow-up study of abused and neglected children. *American Journal of Disabled Children,* 1970, **120,** 439–446.

Nye, F.I., & Berardo, F.M. *The family: Its structure and interaction.* New York: Macmillan, 1973.

Parke, R. Socialization into child abuse: A social interactional perspective. In J. Tapp & F. Levine (Eds.), *Law, justice and the individual in society: Psychological and legal issues.* New York: Holt, Rinehart & Winston, 1977.

Parke, R., & Collmer, C. Child abuse: An interdisciplinary review. In E.M. Hetherington (Ed.), *Review of child development research* (Vol. 5). Chicago: University of Chicago Press, 1975.

Passman, R.H., & Mulhern, R.K., Jr. Maternal punitiveness as affected by situational stress: An experimental analogue of child abuse. *Journal of Abnormal Psychology,* 1977, **86,** 565–569.

Pedersen, P. The field of intercultural counseling. In P. Pedersen, W.J. Lonner, & J.G. Draguns (Eds.), *Counseling across cultures.* Honolulu: University Press of Hawaii, 1976.

Piaget, J. *The origins of intelligence in children.* New York: Norton, 1952.

Pick, A.D. Cognition: Psychological perspectives. In H. Triandis & W. Lonner (Eds.), *Handbook of cross-cultural psychology: Basic processes* (Vol. 3). Boston: Allyn & Bacon, 1980.

Polansky, N., Chalmers, M., Buttenweiser, R., & Williams, P. Isolation of the neglectful family. *American Journal of Orthopsychiatry,* 1979, **49,** 149–152.

Powell, D.R. Personal social networks as a focus for primary prevention of child mistreatment. *Infant Mental Health Journal,* 1980, **1,** 232–239.

Price-Williams, D.R. *Achievement explorations in cross-cultural psychology.* San Francisco: Chandler & Sharp, 1975.

Radcliffe-Brown, A.R. *The Andaman Islanders.* Cambridge, England: Cambridge University Press, 1922.

Ridley, C.A., & Avery, A.W. Social network influence on the dyadic relationship. In R.L. Burgess & T.L. Huston (Eds.), *Social exchange in developing relationships.* New York: Academic Press, 1979.

Riegel, K. The dialectics of human development. *American Psychologist,* 1976, **31,** 689–700.

Rubin, L.B. *Worlds of pain: Life in the working-class family.* New York: Basic Books, 1976.

Rubin, J.Z., Provenzano, F.J., & Luria, Z. The eye of the beholder: Parents' views on sex of newborns. *American Journal of Orthopsychiatry,* 1974, **44,** 512–519.

Sandgrund, A., Gaines, R., & Green, A. Child abuse and mental retardation: A problem of cause and effect. *American Journal of Mental Deficiency,* 1974, **79,** 327–330.

Scarr-Salapatek, S., & Weinberg, R.A. The war over race and IQ: When black children grow up in white homes. In E.M. Hetherington & R.D. Parke (Eds.), *Contemporary readings in child psychology* (2nd Ed.). New York: McGraw-Hill, 1981.

Shulman, N. Life-cycle variations in patterns of close relationships. *Journal of Marriage and the Family.* 1975, **37,** 813–821.

Skinner, B.F. The design of cultures. In R. Ulrich, T. Stachnik, & J. Mabry, (Eds.), *Control of human behavior.* Glenview, Ill.: Scott, Foresman, 1966.

Spinetta, J., & Rigler, D. The child-abusing parent: A psychological review. *Psychological Bulletin,* 1972, **77,** 296–304.

Spitz, R.A. Hospitalism: An inquiry into the genesis of psychiatric conditions in early childhood. *Psychoanalytic study of the child,* 1945, **1,** 53–74.

Stayton, D., Hogan, R., & Ainsworth, M.D.S. Infant obedience and maternal behavior: The origins of socialization reconsidered. *Child Development,* 1971, **42,** 1057–1069.

Steele, B.F., & Pollock, C.B. A psychiatric study of parents who abuse infants and small children. In R. Helfer & C.H. Kempe (Eds.), *The battered child* (2nd Ed). Chicago: University of Chicago Press, 1974.

Stewart, E.C. Cultural sensitivities in counseling. In P. Pedersen, W.J. Lonner, & J.G. Draguns, (Eds.), *Counseling across cultures.* Honolulu: University Press of Hawaii, 1976.

Thomas, A., Chess, S., & Birch, H.G. *Temperament and behavior disorders in children.* New York: New York University Press, 1968.

Thomas, A., Chess, S., Birch, H.G., Hertzig, M.E., & Korn, S. *Behavioral individuality in early childhood.* New York: New York University Press, 1963.

Tulkin, S.R. Dimensions of multicultural research in infancy and early childhood. In P.H. Leiderman, S.R. Tulkin, & A. Rosenfeld (Eds.), *Culture and infancy: Variations in the human experience.* New York: Academic Press, 1977.

Vietze, P., Falsey, S., Sandler, H., O'Conner, S., & Altemeier, W.A. Transactional approach to prediction of child maltreatment. *Infant Mental Health Journal,* 1980, **1,** 248–261.

Vontress, C.E. Racial and ethnic barriers in counseling. In P. Pedersen, W.J. Lonner, & J.G. Draguns (Eds.), *Counseling across cultures.* Honolulu: University Press of Hawaii, 1976.

Whiting, J.W.M., & Child, I.L. *Child training and personality: A cross-cultural study.* New Haven, Conn.: Yale University, 1953.

Will, J.A., Self, P.A., & Datan, N. Maternal behavior and sex of infants. *American Journal of Orthopsychiatry,* 1976, **46,** 135–139.

Williamson, N.E. *Sons or daughters: A cross-cultural survey of parental preferences.* Beverly Hills, Calif.: Sage, 1976.

Wintrob, R.M. Psychotherapy in intercultural perspective: Some personal reflections. In P. Pedersen, W.J. Lonner, & J.G. Draguns (Eds.), *Counseling across cultures.* Honolulu: University Press of Hawaii, 1976.

SECTION TWO

Diagnostic Assessment of Children

CHAPTER 5

Interviewing Strategies In Child Assessment

RUTH KANFER, SHEILA M. EYBERG, AND GLORIA L. KRAHN

Interviewing children has long been an integral part of traditional approaches to the treatment of childhood disorders. The important role that the clinician-child relationship played in such forms of treatment placed great emphasis on the initial interaction with the child. As McDonald (1965) noted in her review of the early child psychiatry literature, traditional approaches frequently did not distinguish between evaluation and treatment with respect to therapist interactions with the child. Because treatment gains were postulated to occur as a direct result of the relationship, strong emphasis was placed on the clinician's ability to develop a therapeutic alliance with the child and to facilitate resolution of personal conflicts through an interpretive/interactive process. More recently, there has been increasing emphasis on differentiating the diagnostic interview from the treatment process.

Within behavioral approaches to assessment and treatment, advocating use of an interview with the child as a means of gathering information has been relatively recent. Before the late 1960s, the prevailing attitude regarding the child interview as an assessment tool was aptly depicted in O'Leary's (1972) statement:

Interviews with children—particularly young children—are often difficult and provide little information about the target problems. Nonetheless, some time should generally be spent with the child or with the child and his parent(s) together.... Most importantly, the therapist can make some assessment of the child's physical appearance, his general interview demeanor, and his relations with his parent(s). However, one should be cautious in drawing conclusions based on the interview with the child. The child may be delightful in one interview yet be a hellion in school or at home. (p. 260)

O'Leary's comments illustrate a number of important points regarding recent trends and continuing concerns about interviewing children. First, because of concerns about the validity and reliability of the specific information obtained during the child interview, interviewers have tended to restrict the use of the interview to making global observations of appearance and demeanor. Recent research on the development and use of standardized interview formats, however, has demonstrated at least preliminary validity and reliability with these interviews (e.g., Herjanic & Campbell, 1977; see La Greca, chap. 6 of this book). This suggests that some relevant content information may be obtained in interviews with children ages 6 years and older.

Second, O'Leary's comments reflect the generally held assumption that some direct interaction with the child is desirable. While the rationale for this assumption is not always apparent, several explanations can be offered. As already mentioned, the clinician-child relationship based on direct interaction has been a central focus in traditional therapies. Anna Freud (1946) wrote extensively on the establishment of a therapeutic alliance with the child. In addition, therapists with a nondirective and relationship-oriented approach (Allen, 1942; Axline, 1947; Freidheim & Russ, chap. 40 of this book; Moustakas, 1959) have placed even greater emphasis on the development of a positive relationship between therapist and child as a precondition for successful treatment. Rapport with the child obviously has long been recognized as a crucial aspect of treatment. In addition to providing an opportunity to build rapport with the child, direct interactions between the clinician and child may also improve rapport with the parent(s) who have brought the child to the clinic. Most parents expect and want the clinician to interact directly with their child, and failure to do so may in the eyes of the parents jeopardize the face validity of the assessment conclusions and treatment recommendations (see also Goodman, 1972; La Greca, chap. 6 of this book; Reisman, 1973).

As noted by O'Leary, the kinds of information that can be obtained during the child interview include the child's perceptions and observations of the child's physical appearance and general interview demeanor, which may provide a relevant context for understanding the presenting problems of the child. In addition, the child interview allows the clinician to sample the "flavor" of the child and match this perception to that obtained from parental description. At times these two perceptions can be widely discrepant, with the parents over- or underestimating the pathology of the child, or perhaps the child's behavior being situationally specific. During a period of direct interaction with the child, the interviewer can also assess how well the child engages with the interviewer and whether or not individual relationship therapy would be recommended.

The final major point made by O'Leary pertains to the difficulties inherent in conducting a child interview. While an extensive body of literature exists on research into those interviewer and therapist behaviors and skills which facilitate adult interactions (Goldstein, 1980; Hackney & Cormier, 1979; Parloff, Waskow, & Wolfe, 1978), less attention has been directed toward process skills which are effective in communication with children. Process skills here refer to the "soft clinical skills" which guide and direct the interview sequence, build and maintain rapport, and facilitate resolution of conflicts that may arise during the initial interview.

Direct application of research findings in adult interactions to the realm of child interviewing is generally limited by consideration of the child's developmental level, cognitive-verbal abilities, and previous experience with the environment. For example, research findings with adults suggesting that interviewer warmth and empathy are central ingredients in rapport building may also be true of interactions with children; however, findings which suggest that relationships can be enhanced by therapist characteristics of expertness and status are not as clearly applicable to the child interaction.

Although process skills related to interactions with children are frequently discussed without regard to a distinction between assessment and treatment, important differences between the goals of the clinician in each of these situations may directly influence the selection of particular strategies. Within the assessment context, the clinician's goals are not to promote treatment change, but rather to obtain information and ease the child's possible apprehension about subsequent sessions. As a result, interviewer skills in demonstrating warmth and acceptance must be integrated with interviewer behaviors directed toward obtaining specific information. Similarly, play activities that are frequently employed in a treatment context to facilitate therapy goals may also be used in the initial child interview as a means of obtaining information. In the assessment interview, play activities most frequently serve as an effective means of building rapport, reducing the verbal demands made upon the child, and as a medium for sampling the content of a child's cognitions.

The problem of identifying specific interviewer skills which facilitate communication with children has encouraged several clinicians (Greenspan & Greenspan, 1981; Goodman & Sours, 1967; Goodman, 1973; Riesman, 1973; Rich, 1968) to delineate both specific clinician characteristics and clinic situations that uniquely characterize interactions with the child in assessment and treatment. In most cases, discussion of process skills and effective interviewer/therapist strategies has developed from a review of clinical experiences.

In accord with Goodman's (1973) reflection that "talking with children in an attempt to gain information is a practiced act," there has been little emphasis in the literature on training beginning clinicians in relationship-building skills specifically involved in the child assessment interview. As a result, the beginning child clinician frequently comes into the clinical setting knowing what information is needed from the child assessment interview but at a loss as to how to get there. Effective child interviewers often develop their expertise through supervision, via anecdotal information, or as the result of trial-and-error experiences in the interview situation.

The purpose of this chapter is to provide both the novice child clinician and the experienced adult clinician beginning to work with children with a repertoire of specific interview skills and strategies to facilitate communication with the preschool to preadolescent child during the assessment interview. To simplify discussion of the many types of interviewer behaviors that will be considered, these process skills are divided into two types. General communication skills that can be implemented throughout the interview and serve to build and maintain rapport are described first. Process skills that guide the interview sequence and facilitate resolution of frequently occurring interview problems are discussed within a chronological model of the child interview in the final section.

GENERAL COMMUNICATION SKILLS

Two continuous process goals throughout the interview are (1) establishing rapport and (2) maintaining the child's cooperation. We have identified five basic communication techniques which are helpful in obtaining these goals. The use of these skills is not limited to interviewing; they are frequently implemented in therapy as well. Rather than explicating their use in therapy, however, we will limit our current scope to their use in the assessment interview. No single technique is usually sufficient; rather, they are most successfully used in combination and as the situation demands.

Description

A descriptive statement is a verbal picture of the ongoing behavior of the child. The interviewer's descriptions typically include objective comments on the child's appearance, nonnegative behavior, and demeanor. Examples:

"I see you are holding a teddybear." (behavior)
"That's a very bright red dress." (appearance)
"You look very happy today." (demeanor)

Descriptive statements are a simple way to give attention to the child and to focus on those aspects of the situation that are likely to be interesting to the child. Children are generally egocentric; descriptions of their behavior let them know that you can share their perspective. Descriptive statements can also point out and "teach" the child what it is that you want him or her to do. They provide an easy way to encourage the child to continue in ongoing behavior. Perhaps of most importance to the novice interviewer is that when one is uncertain about where to proceed next, descriptive statements can provide a means for maintaining communication while planning the next step.

Reflection

Reflective statements "echo" or mirror what the child says. They may be literally the same words or they may provide some elaboration or interpretation of what the child said, but they always retain the essential meaning of the child's expression through reflecting the content and/or the emotion of the child's expression. Examples:

CHILD: "The train is coming to the station."

INTERVIEWER: "The train is coming to the station." (literal)

INTERVIEWER: "The silver train is chugging up slowly to the train station." (elaboration)

CHILD: (throwing toys) "I don't like it here."

INTERVIEWER: "You seem angry today." (interpretation of emotion)

Reflective statements, like descriptive statements, provide clarity and help to organize the child's behavior (descriptions) and thoughts and feelings (reflections). Reflective statements generally result in increased verbal interchange between the interviewer and child.

Praise

A "labeled praise" is a statement that indicates approval and specifies exactly what act or event the interviewer is encouraging. Examples:

"You're doing a good job of telling me what happened."

"That's hard to remember, but I like how you keep trying."

Labeled praise serves to guide and encourage the child in the direction the clinician desires. These statements let the child know what he or she can do to continue to please the clinician. The initial contact is frequently anticipated as negative by the child; labeled praise helps to minimize the child's trepidation and thereby facilitates continued interaction. The type of labeled praise that the interviewer would use changes as a function of the child's age. One would be less effusive in praising older children.

Avoid Critical Statements

Critical statements are verbal statements which indicate disapproval, such as negative "stop" commands and insults to the child. Critical statements may also be verbalizations which imply that what the child says, thinks,

or does is in some way wrong or bad. Examples:

"You should know better than that."

"Stop climbing out of your chair."

"You don't try very hard to remember."

Critical statements foster negative emotional reactions such as anger, resentment, and frustration, and can lead to counterattack which is unproductive. These statements are particularly detrimental to rapport and may lead the child to act negatively for the remainder of the interview. For example, a child who is told that he or she is not trying hard enough may lose the motivation to respond further. Although blatant criticism is rarely a problem, the interviewer should be vigilant to avoid subtle criticism such as "I know you could have done better." As an alternative, the interviewer might choose to acknowledge the effort that was made by saying, "It's a hard task and I'm glad you're still trying."

Often children's negative, aggressive, or destructive behavior is avoided in the playroom by the clinician's initial structuring of the situation (see "Getting Started" later in this chapter), but occasionally negative behavior will be presented that is too harmful or damaging to be continued. If the rules of the playroom have been previously stated, rule-based correction can be used to avoid direct critical statements. For example, a reiteration such as, "One of the rules of the playroom is that things cannot be broken," is preferable to "Don't break the doll." In other instances, a critical statement intended to change a child's inappropriate behavior might be restated as a direction for an incompatible behavior. Examples:

CHILD: (hitting head against wall)

INTERVIEWER: "Stop hitting your head." (poor)

INTERVIEWER: "Come and play at the table." (better)

CHILD: (throwing blocks at interviewer)

INTERVIEWER: "I don't like it when you throw blocks at me." (poor)

INTERVIEWER: "The blocks belong in the box." (better)

CHILD: (drawing on table)

INTERVIEWER: "Don't draw on the table." (poor)

INTERVIEWER: "Please draw your picture on this paper." (better)

There may also be many situations in which an inappropriate behavior can simply be ignored. Rather than criticizing, the clinician can make a mental note to watch for positive behaviors and reinforce them when they occur. Examples:

CHILD: (climbs on table)

INTERVIEWER: (ignores climbing)

CHILD: (gets off table)

INTERVIEWER: "I like it when you stand on the floor."

INTERVIEWER: "Tell me a story about this picture."

CHILD: "I can't think of anything."

INTERVIEWER: (ignores)

INTERVIEWER: "What is this girl doing?"

CHILD: "She's sitting."

INTERVIEWER: "She is sitting. I'm glad you told me about part of this picture."

Open-Ended Questions

An open-ended, in contrast to a closed-ended question, is any question which cannot be answered with a simple "yes" or "no." Open-ended questions are generally preferable. Examples:

"Do you like Etch-a-Sketch?" (closed-ended)

"What toys do you like best?" (open-ended)

"Do you remember anything else about that?" (close-ended)

"What can you remember about that?" (open-ended)

"Was it bad?" (closed-ended)

"What was it like for you?" (open-ended)

Asking open-ended questions leads to more information per question, and minimizes the possibility that the interviewer will lead the child to conclusions that are the interviewer's rather than the child's. They are especially useful in opening up new areas of discussion and facilitate spontaneous, continued conversation.

A note of caution: One type of open-ended question to be avoided is one which begins with "why." "Why" questions tend to increase the child's defensiveness. Most children referred to a clinician have already heard "why" many times in the areas surrounding their difficulties. If anything, their responses are likely to be post hoc rationalizations rather than the desired information which would describe the steps actually leading to the problem behavior. For example, the question "Why did you skip school?" would be rephrased better as "What things about school don't you like?" or "What things do you do instead of going to school?" It is the interviewer's responsibility to determine motivation; it is unproductive to ask the child to make these interpretations.

Age Appropriate Communication

We have identified three major areas in which an interviewer may alter his style depending on the age of the child. The first and perhaps most obvious is the vocabulary and sentence structure that is used in talking with a child. It is frequently difficult for a novice interviewer to translate sophisticated concepts into the simple terminology that a young child can understand. For example, in attempting to determine possible reinforcers for use in a token program with a fourth-grader, the child would have difficulty understanding "What kinds of activities are reinforcing for you?"

Instead, one might ask, "What things do you like to do?"

Children can become particularly confused with the adult use of "feeling words" such as "depressed," "anxious," "disappointed," or "guilty." Typically, young children understand few feeling descriptions other than "mad," "sad," "glad" or "scared." To obtain more information about the affective experience of the child, the clinician would do better to work toward having the child describe specific examples behaviorally. Rather than saying "What is it about your mother that angers you?," the clinician can more profitably ask the child "What things does your mother do that make you mad?"

At other times the child may incorrectly use words or phrases to describe feelings. When a child uses sophisticated words to describe feelings, it is advisable that the interviewer explore the child's understanding of the words. This point was made apparent to the authors recently when a 6-year-old child said, "Can I leave here? I'm really nervous to go to Susie's house." In this case, it became obvious that she meant she was anxious or eager to go.

In addition to using clear and simple vocabulary, the clinician should limit the information conveyed in each sentence. As a general rule, each statement or question should be short and simple and should contain only one idea. For example, the interviewer would not want to say, "When is it that you feel bad and what do you do then?" but instead, "When do you feel bad?" and then follow obtained leads with subsequent questions.

Another source of confusion for the child is the overuse of qualifying phrases. Although the clinician's intent is to increase accuracy when using a statement such as "Where are you most likely to be when you cry?," that information is more apt to be obtained by asking "Where do you cry?"

A second major style issue in age appropriate communication concerns the use of silences. While the therapeutic use of silence with adults is sometimes valuable (Hackney & Cormier, 1979), we believe that a silence of more than a few seconds is aversive to children when the primary mode of interaction is verbal. In particular, we have found that an extended silence following an interviewer's question tends to be nonproductive and may lead to resistance. In some cases the child may perceive the "pregnant silence" as being a challenge or an indication of disapproval from the interviewer. In contrast to the strictly verbal exchange interview often used with the older child, the silences which occur spontaneously during play interactions with younger children can be used productively to allow nonverbal communications.

The third major stylistic variable related to age is what we term reference points of interest. Different age groups of children relate to different media heroes, games, clothing fads, and hobbies. Conversation about topics that are current can be very effective in establishing rapport. This means that the clinician needs to be familiar with what is current in the child's world and not rely on recollection of his or her own childhood to determine what activities the child is likely to be interested in. For interviewers who have daily contact with children, this may not be difficult. For others, deliberate efforts to learn more about the child's world may be necessary. Browsing in the children's section of toy, book, or clothing stores, or leafing through toy or clothes catalogues can familiarize the clinician with the trade names of popular items (e.g., dolls) or current trends in collectables (e.g., trading cards). Watching the Saturday morning cartoons and the after-school-to-early-evening television programs can serve as an introduction to the media heroes of different age groups. Knowing the traits of the characters a child identifies with can be revealing about the child's values. Simply talking with friends who are parents can provide a wealth of information about popular interests and activities of children of various ages.

Physical Contact and Nurturance

The use of physical contact and nurturance in interviewing children appears to be primarily regulated by personal preferences, with few clear guidelines and no known empirical research. The reasons for possibly using physical contact are varied: you might wish to gain a child's attention, to encourage a child to continue in an activity (often used in conjunction with praise), to calm a child, or to demonstrate affection. A touch on the child's hand might be used to redirect the child's attention to the task, while a pat on the shoulder might accompany verbal praise. In general, physical contact is used judiciously. Paralleling general societal norms, the interviewer will provide relatively less physical contact to older children. In rare cases where a child exhibits acute emotional distress (such as crying, sobbing, or intense fear), the interviewer may feel it important to provide additional physical comforting. In most cases, however, the role of the interviewer is not to provide nurturance. The interviewer can typically minimize emotional distress by using one of the following strategies: (1) verbal reassurance, (2) distracting the child toward a pleasant activity, or (3) redirecting the topic into more neutral areas. For example, with younger children, the introduction of toys or a game immediately following a stressful interchange may reduce emotional distress without need for physical comforting. Older children may benefit from having conversation redirected toward areas in which they have personal strengths.

Another way in which clinicians may sometimes demonstrate nurturance is by sharing food or drink with the child. Opinions on this as a practice in child therapy vary considerably (e.g., Greenspan & Greenspan, 1981). Some clinicians argue that it is critical to respond concretely to the unmet dependency needs of some children, or that use of such primary reinforcers can enhance the therapist's reinforcement valence. Others argue that this is an unnecessary procedure which distracts from the impact of the verbal therapy. In the initial diagnostic interview, however, this issue of "supping together" may be less salient than in later therapy.

Although it may be tempting to do so, we believe it is advisable to avoid assuming a parental role with the child during the interview. That is, the interviewer would avoid becoming overly physical or nurturant with a child despite indication of distress. This will both provide information about how the child handles his or her emotion and help to prevent alienating parents who may feel defensive about their ability to provide nurturance in comparison to the interviewer. Excessive interviewer nurturance may also preclude later opportunities to teach the parent how to provide the needed care. Sometimes it is necessary to remind yourself that you cannot be the child's savior and that you cannot provide for all of the dependency needs of the child. Overnurturance in the evaluation can lead to potential treatment difficulties in parental compliance and may jeopardize parental follow-through with your recommendations.

CONDUCTING THE INTERVIEW

For heuristic purposes we have divided the child interview process into five successive stages. We present each stage in terms of the way in which the interviewer typically wishes to conduct the session. In describing each stage we also present (1) problems arising from child behaviors that may interrupt or interfere with forward progress through the stages and (2) ways that the interviewer can handle these disruptions.

Getting Started

In most instances the interviewer will meet the family in the waiting room. Prior to approaching the parent and child, the interviewer can make valuable observations about the child's physical appearance, coordination, mood, activity level, location, and responses to parents and others. The interviewer can also observe parent-child activities. This may be the most naturalistic observation period available.

There are several suggested ways to introduce yourself to the parents and child (e.g., Greenspan & Greenspan, 1981; Reisman, 1973). Opinions vary widely as to whether to introduce yourself to the parents or child first, and as to the degree of formality desirable in these initial introductions. Our particular bias is to introduce ourselves to the parents first, using a formal title (e.g., Dr., Mr., Ms.), and to address the parents using their surname. Although some clinicians prefer to avoid using a formal title, we agree with the view expressed by Reisman (1973) that such a procedure clearly establishes the nature of the relationship as a helping relationship and different from a casual friendship.

Following your introduction to the parents, you may wait briefly for the parents to introduce the child or you may choose to immediately introduce yourself to the child. The first approach might be preferable when the child appears frightened, when the interviewer desires to observe a brief sample of how the parents gain the child's cooperation, or when the interviewer wishes to acknowledge the parents' authority. Introducing yourself immediately to the child may be the preferred strategy when you wish to communicate an immediate interest in the child or when it seems important to avoid appearing allied with the parents. This latter approach seems most advantageous with an older child. Of course, if you prefer that the parents make the introduction but they fail to do so, you would turn to the child and introduce yourself.

When introducing yourself to the child you might say, for example, "Hello Susie, I'm Dr. Jones." Immediately following the introduction, we have found it extremely useful to make a comment to the child about something important to the child, such as something he or she is wearing, doing, or has brought along. Comments such as "What a neat cowboy on your teeshirt," or "That's a cute little bunny you're holding," let children know that you are interested in them. These comments should be positive, brief, and enthusiastic in nature.

Next you will want to provide information to the child and family about the plan for the session. Stating the plan while in the waiting room can help to decrease the child's initial apprehension. The plan should clearly tell the child what he or she will be doing, where he or she will be doing it, and where his or her parents will be. There are a number of ways in which the interviews can be sequenced. For example, you might say to the younger child:

1.   "I brought a special picture book that you can look at while I talk to your mom and dad. We will be talking in a room down the hall for a little while. Then we'll come back, and you and I will get a chance to play and talk." (Parent interview first)

2.   "I have some special toys and pictures for us. Your mom and dad will be working on some papers right here while we play and talk. I want you to come with me, and I will show you where the toys are." (Child interview first)

3.   "The three of us will go to the play room so that we can have a chance to talk, and I have some special toys for you to play with." (Family interview first)

A typical procedure we use is to ask the parents to fill out standardized assessment questionnaires about the child's behavior (e.g., Achenbach, 1979; Cassel, 1962; Eyberg, 1980; Miller, 1977; Quay & Peterson, 1975) while waiting for the child. Giving this task to the parents at this time can set the stage for asking the child to come with you while the parents are filling out the forms. Also, if the assessment session will include standardized parent-child observations (e.g., Robinson & Eyberg, 1981; see also LaGreca, chap. 6 of this book), you can, for example, explain to the child that after the two of you play (talk), he or she will have an opportunity to play (talk) with his or her parents in the playroom.

While walking to the room with the child, you may use this time to begin establishing rapport. It is useful to chat with the child about interesting and nonthreatening topics (e.g., "It's raining hard today"; "It looks like you have new tennis shoes"; "I have a brand new puppet in my office").

Potential Problems in Getting Started

Since beginning clinicians often find it more comfortable to deal with adults, it may be tempting to ignore the child and to focus on the parent. The ideas outlined above will help to prevent this from happening. Second, it is important to prevent the parents from beginning to describe the child's problems too soon. Often parents wish to "begin treatment" when they first meet the interviewer. For example, one of the parents may start by saying, "Something new has happened." This often occurs because of their lack of knowledge about the interview structure. In general, the premature offering of information can be curtailed by assuring the parents that there will be an opportunity to talk in detail at a later point in the session.

Another potential problem arises when the clinician is surprised by finding a different set of persons waiting than was expected. Some examples which we have encountered are: a different parent than was expected, more parents than expected, additional children, absence of parents, or even absence of the target child. The interviewer will need to be flexible in dealing with these kinds of unanticipated situations. It is most important to remain calm and to convey to the family a sense of your being relaxed and in control. Remaining calm allows you to think through your alternative strategies more clearly and to maintain your credibility with the family. To do this, you can remind yourself of what the overall goal for the interview is and consider the options that are available to you. Unexpected problems do not need to be resolved immediately. You may feel most comfortable by taking an extra few minutes to revise your plan. You might, for example, tell the family that before you begin you need to check on the availability of the room. You may decide to call on a colleague for babysitting extra children or you may prepare additional seating for unexpected adults.

A fourth potential problem in getting started occurs when the child you intend to interview is screaming and crying in the waiting room. The first option available is to wait a few minutes before entering the waiting area. The child's distress may be situation-specific. Allowing the parent to calm the child may prevent a circumscribed outburst from setting up a negative interaction between clinician and child which could persist throughout the session. If the child continues to cry or begins crying after you have entered the waiting room, then there are a number of strategies you can attempt. You may ignore the crying and attend to the parents or may attempt to distract the child by offering him or her a toy or engaging in parallel play. In parallel play, the interviewer essentially plays alongside the child in a way that does not require mutual participation or cooperation by the child. Typically, parallel play is imitative play where the interviewer might, for example, build separate structures from the same set of blocks used by the child. Parallel play can serve to redirect verbal interaction toward pleasant topics and often provides a means of establishing rapport. Alternatively, you may decide to interview the parents first and leave the child in the waiting room, or you may suggest a joint interview with the parents. In general, parents know their children well and may have some valuable suggestions for how to comfort the child.

A fifth problem encountered occasionally in the initial greeting involves difficulties in separation. As a first consideration, most children under the age of 3 or 3½ years can be expected to resist separating. Unless seeing the child alone is important, it might be wise to avoid unnecessary separation. Separation problems with children aged 4 years and older can often be prevented by the interviewer's careful and clear structuring of the situation. In implementing the separation, the interviewer typically would not *ask* the child if he or she would like to come. This question may inaccurately imply a choice. Instead, it will more likely be effective to tell the child that you would like him or her to come with you, offering your hand to the young child as you do so. By having provided the directive and having taken the initiative as if you expect compliance, you will frequently minimize potential separation problems. Alternatively, at times you may be able to provide the child with two or more possible options, any of which is acceptable to you. For example, you could ask the child, "Would you like to leave your dolly here with your mother, or would you like to bring it with you?" In this way you can provide the child with some semblance of choice and control in the situation, which may allow the child to feel more comfortable. Sometimes carrying a particularly enticing toy (e.g., a bubble-blowing bear), demonstrating it, and then offering that the child can play with it but only in the special playroom, allows you to coax a hesitant child into the playroom.

When separation problems persist, one strategy would be to have the parents accompany you and the child to the interview room and encourage the child to explore the toys. Typically the child will calm down, and, as this occurs, the interviewer can increase the one-to-one involvement with the child while he or she remains focused on play materials. When the child becomes more subdued and engaged in play, the interviewer could give the parent explicit verbal permission to leave the room. We have found that parents also may be ambivalent about separating if the child begins to protest or remains unresponsive to the interviewer. If this is the case, you could give the parents brief verbal assurance, such as, "Things will be fine" and the directive "Please wait in the waiting room." If this is not enough to reassure the parents and/or child, your best alternative may be to redirect the parents to stay. At this point, any further attempts at separation are likely to be unproductive and possibly to have deleterious effects.

Setting the Stage

The initial few minutes with the child in the interview room can be awkward and anxiety-inducing for both the child and the novice interviewer. The child typically looks toward the adult for guidance regarding appropriate behavior in this new setting. By providing structure at the outset in both an explicit and implicit manner, the clinician can ease the child's anxiety and can set the stage for conduct during the session.

The goals for the session may determine the degree of structure the clinician will choose to employ. If the intent is to evaluate the child formally by use of standardized assessment instruments, such as those described by Sattler (chap. 7 of this book), a high degree of initial structure is recommended. On the other hand, if the intent is only to interview the child (clinically), less structure may be needed or even desired.

The presence and placement of objects in the room are initial means of structuring. Structure is decreased as the number of play objects is increased. By limiting the number of choices, the interviewer guides the child toward playing with the specific toys that may have the most clinical relevance. If the interviewer wishes, for example, to assess the child's perception of his or her family through houseplay, then only those materials relating to houseplay should be made available. Additional materials visible to the child during testing or interviewing are likely to be a distraction.

The degree of structure is also influenced by the explicitness and immediacy with which the child is directed to a seat. If you wish to have the child remain seated throughout most of the session, it is advisable to direct him or her to a seat shortly after entering the room. One way of saying this is, "I have a special chair just for you (pointing to chair). Sit right here." If it is necessary for the child to remain seated for an extended period of time or if you suspect that he or she is highly active, plan your placement of the chair carefully. We have found it helpful to contain the child by placing the chair in a corner with exits blocked on the remaining two sides by a table and the interviewer's chair. Gentle physical constraint, along with explicit directions, may be necessary and usually is not upsetting to the child. For example, we have held the child's hands while setting out objects and extended an arm to the child's shoulder whenever the child started to get up. Of course, as described previously, frequent praise of the child for appropriate behavior is likely to maintain the child's attention on the tasks of the interview. Initial comments like "Thank you for sitting in the chair" as well as comments throughout the interview such as "I like playing this game with you" (young child) or "You're doing a nice job of describing what happened" (older child) serve to reinforce the ongoing behavior. Additionally, and particularly if you are aware that the child presents conduct problems in other settings, you may wish initially to point out to the child what he cannot do, as well as what he can do. You might add something like, "The only rules of the playroom are that you cannot break anything and that you cannot do anything that will hurt you or me." By setting the behavioral limits at the outset, occurrences of rule breaking provide information about how the child responds to rules, as well as providing a means of avoiding direct personal criticism to the child. Instead, rule-based corrections are possible.

Particularly for the preteen or more verbally oriented child, an important consideration of setting the stage will be indicating to the child who you are and some idea about what you will be talking about. There are a number of ways to broach this topic. It may be that the child will provide initial verbal or nonverbal cues such as a look of apprehension or a direct question like, "Are you going to give me a needle?" At other times you may need to broach the topic directly with a statement like, "I wonder whether you know what kind of a doctor I am." Your explanation then might vary according to the age of the child. Your preference may be to introduce yourself as "a doctor for feelings, someone who talks with boys and girls who sometimes feel bad and helps them feel happier." Another introduction might be as "a psychologist, someone who works with kids and their families when there are some problems and helps them learn better ways of getting along." It is then usually sufficient to indicate that you would like to spend some time playing and talking with the child to get to know him or her better.

An area often anticipated by the novice interviewer as being a potential problem is that of confidentiality. With children in the preschool to preadolescent age range, this is rarely an issue and can perhaps best be dealt with by ignoring it (Pearson, 1968). When the interviewer has not raised the issue of confidentiality, and often even when he or she has, young children generally assume that parents will be informed about what they have said. Introducing such concepts as "the limits of confidentiality" with a preadolescent child may serve to confuse and intimidate the child. The development of trust is fostered more by the warmth and empathy conveyed by the clinician than by verbal assurances of limited confidentiality. With teenagers the issue of confidentiality is much more salient.

Gathering Information

As soon as the process of establishing rapport has been initiated, the gathering of relevant information can begin. The basic information usually desired for effective diagnosis and treatment planning with children includes assessment of (1) intellectual and academic functioning, (2) developmental level, (3) personality functioning, (4) family functioning, (5) social functioning, and (6) temperament and affect. Not all of this information is sought in the child interview; formal psychometric assessment, structured behavioral observations, parent interviews, and agency contacts serve as important additional sources of this information.

Given the large number of topics which could be covered in a child interview, it is important that the clinician pay careful attention to the selection of areas. A careful review of all background information and presenting problem(s) of the particular child you are interviewing can guide the selection of those areas. It is often a good idea then to prepare in advance a brief outline of the information you wish to obtain during the interview. In order to maintain your rapport with the child in the face of unanticipated events, it is important to realize the need to remain flexible and not follow your outline rigidly. Once the interview has begun, you will likely find that you can remember the basic information needed. Periodic reference to your notes can provide reassurance and help to guarantee that important topic areas are not forgotten.

An organizational format which we have found to be helpful begins with the assumption of the child's world as consisting of three major areas: (1) the child's perception of his environment, (2) his or her perception of himself or herself, and (3) his or her perception of the presenting problem(s). Included in "environment" would be peer relations, school, and family; included in "self" might be wishes, interests, and fears. The presenting problem consists of the specific complaint which led to the referral. It may stem from either the environment or the self. Movement of the interview might best proceed from discussion of the environment, to the self, to the problem. Addressing the presenting problem last allows the interviewer to have the opportunity to establish a degree of rapport and trust before addressing the most difficult issues. A second important feature is that you have already developed a more comprehensive understanding of the child's perceptions and the context within which he or she views the problem.

Often it is useful to employ "selective reflection" to structure the direction of the child's talk during the interview. This involves listening to the total content but reflecting only that portion of the verbalization which leads into the area you wish to explore further. For example, a child might say, "Sometimes I get really mad at my sister, but Mom always takes her side." Here you have at least two choices of content area to follow. If you wish to explore the child's relationship with his or her sister, you might focus on the first part of the statement by reflecting, "Your sister does some things that make you mad." If, on the other hand, you wish at this point to focus on the child's relationship with the mother, you might reflect something like, "Your mother doesn't always seem to understand how you feel." Another technique useful in providing transitions between topic areas is to use a summary statement of the content areas just covered, placing last in the summary the area you wish to pursue further. Then you can easily say something like, "I'd like to talk to you more about (the last point)." Summary statements can also be used to provide closure to a topic area, and then new topic areas can be introduced simply by asking new questions.

An approach which can be used within each of the content areas is to move from positive, nonthreatening topics toward more threatening topics. The problem topic is generally avoided until the broader contexts are understood. Younger children can be made to feel more comfortable at the beginning by talking about subjects they know and like. Aspects of the child such as age, nursery school, birthday, pets, favorite games, and TV shows are good topics. Questions about parents and why the child is at the session do not generally put the child at ease. Older children, who have had more social contacts, may be relaxed by allowing discussion to focus on friends, school, sports, or social activities.

In exploring self-perceptions, one may initially ask children such things as what they like best about themselves or what they are most proud of. Discussion of strengths is in most cases nonthreatening and eases the transition into more threatening topics. For example, asking a child to list three positive things about himself or herself leads logically to asking the child to describe three negative things about himself or herself. The pairing of positives and negatives in this way minimizes the child's reactivity to discussion of threatening topics.

Another procedure one may use for shifting into more direct discussion of a threatening topic area is to acknowledge your source of information before asking the questions. For example, "Your mother said you cry a lot; what things make you feel bad?," or "You told me before that you don't like school; what things about school don't you like?" These introductions help to legitimize your shift into a threatening area.

Once a threatening topic area has been opened, the child will frequently display resistance. The child may give cues such as becoming silent, changing the subject, saying, "I don't know," changing affect, or changing activity. Often this resistance is an internally imposed protection against embarrassment or fear of disapproval. There are several strategies we have found helpful in reducing the child's anxiety. One is to allow the child to play simultaneously with a toy (e.g., blocks) while talking to you. This provides an opportunity to fall back on description of play activities as a means of reducing the child's anxiety withut having to enter into a new area of discussion. The interviewer can describe the play briefly and then ease the conversation back to the clinical issue. This general strategy is advantageous in that it can be used repeatedly without disrupting the natural flow of conversation. A variant of this approach is the use of puppet play. Some children may find it easier to express themselves by talking through or to a puppet rather than directly to the clinician. A second strategy for reducing the child's anxiety when dealing with threatening material is to explicitly acknowledge his discomfort. By saying, "It's alright if you don't feel like talking about that yet," the clinician not only gives permission for hesitancy in discussion but also establishes the expectation that the child will be ready to discuss the topic again and that the clinician may ask again. A third strategy to employ when encountering resistance is to follow or immediately to direct the child back to a nonthreatening topic, and gradually approach the threatening topic again, in a different way.

At times the interviewer may suspect that the child's resistance to talking is more externally imposed; that is, he or she may have been directed not to talk about certain things. This is perhaps most frequently encountered with children who have been abused. In these instances, gentle questioning needs to convey support and acceptance. One approach might be to say, "I know that sometimes kids are told not to talk with me about things that have happened. Were you told not to say anything about this to me?" Here, a closed-ended question may provide the child the safety of responding with a simple head nod or shake. Further support and careful probing can then be undertaken.

It is during discussion of these most sensitive topics that the issue of confidentiality with the young child may need to be directly addressed. For example, the child may tell you that he or she is afraid that his or her parent might find out what is said, or the child may ask you if you are going to tell anyone what he or she says. We believe it is important for the interviewer to be honest with the child in telling him or her that the primary goal is to protect him or her from being hurt and that this might mean that others would have to be informed about what he or she says. The interviewer might explain that he or she will use his or her best judgment in deciding whether to tell another person this and express the hope that the child would trust this judgment. Ultimately, most clinicians agree that the child should know that he or she has the right to withhold information and that the interviewer will understand and respect the child's decision and will still do everything he or she can to help and protect the child.

Wrapping Up

After the relevant topic areas have been explored, it is important to acknowledge any efforts the child has made during the interview in helping you to get to know him or her. Summarizing for the child your perception of what he or she has shared with you will enable you to demonstrate that you have listened to and understood his or her perspective. It is useful at this point, especially with the older child, to ask for any additional information the child might want to offer, or for any suggestions the child might have for solving identified problems. You might then convey your desire to help the child with these problems. A final step in wrapping up is to provide for the child as much information as possible about what you intend to do. In keeping with the notion of protecting the child's rights, we believe the child should be informed about what information will be communicated to the parents or others as well as any plans or recommendations regarding intervention. One example of the concluding comments to an assessment interview with a child, where the referring problem is enuresis, might be:

I really enjoyed talking with you today. You did a nice job of helping me to understand you and what's going on. It sounds like you have quite a lot of friends to play with and that school is going very well for you in second grade. But it seems like things haven't been as good for you at home with your mom. I guess she, and you too, have been unhappy because you sometimes wet the bed. There are some ways that I can help you learn how to stay dry at night. What I'd like to do now is to have your parents come in so we can all talk together about some of these ways and see if they would like to help us. How does that sound to you?

These final comments exemplify several of the basic interviewer skills discussed in this chapter. These comments include acknowledging and praising the child's efforts in the interview, reflecting and summarizing some of the major content areas addressed, and leading from the discussion of the child's strengths into more threatening problem areas. The problems are stated in a way that does not criticize the child, and an open-ended question is used to elicit the child's responses to the plan. The words used are simple and appropriate to the age of the child interviewed. Deliberate use of the process skills described in this chapter will hopefully enable the beginning clinician to achieve this "practiced art" more rapidly and painlessly.

REFERENCES

Achenbach, T.M. The Child behavior profile: An empirically based system for assessing children's behavioral problems and competencies. *International Journal of Mental Health,* 1979, **7,** 24–42.

Allen, F.H. *Psychotherapy with children.* New York: Norton, 1942.

Axline, V.M. *Play therapy.* Boston: Houghton Mifflin, 1947.

Cassell, R.N. *The Child behavior rating scale manual.* Los Angeles: Western Psychological Services, 1962.

Eyberg, S. Eyberg child behavior inventory, *Journal of Clinical Child Psychology,* 1980, **9** (1), 29.

Freud, A. *The psychoanalytic treatment of children.* London: Imago, 1946.

Goldstein, A.P. Relationship-enhancement methods. In F.H. Kanfer & A.P. Goldstein (Eds.), *Helping people change* (2nd ed.). New York: Pergamon Press, 1980.

Goodman, J.D. The psychiatric interview. In B.B. Wolman (Ed.), *Manual of child psychopathology.* New York: McGraw-Hill, 1972.

Goodman, J., & Sours, J. *The Child mental status examination.* New York: Basic Books, 1967.

Greenspan, S.I., & Greenspan, N.I. *The clinical interview with children.* New York: McGraw-Hill, 1981.

Hackney, H., & Cormier, S. *Counseling strategies and objectives* (2nd ed.). Englewood Cliffs, N.J.: Prentice-Hall, 1979.

Herjanic, B., & Campbell, W. Differentiating psychiatrically disturbed children on the basis of a structured interview. *Journal of Abnormal Child Psychology,* 1977, **5,** 127–134.

McDonald, M. The psychiatric evaluation of children. *Journal of the American Academy of Child Psychiatry,* 1965, **4,** 569–612.

Miller, L.M. *Louisville behavior checklist manual.* Los Angeles: Western Psychological Service, 1977.

Moustakas, C.E. *Psychotherapy with children.* New York: Harper & Row, 1959.

O'Leary, D.K. The assessment of psychopathology in children. In H.C. Quay & J.S. Werry (Eds.), *Psychopathological disorders of childhood.* New York: Wiley, 1972.

Parloff, M.B., Waskow, I.E., & Wolfe, B.E. Research on therapist variables in relation to process and outcome. In S. Garfield & A. Bergen (Eds.), *Handbook of psychotherapy and behavior change: An empirical analysis* (2nd ed.). New York: Wiley, 1978.

Pearson, G.H.J. (Ed.) *A Handbook of child psychoanalysis.* New York: Basic Books, 1968.

Quay, H.C., & Peterson, D.R. Manual for the Behavior problem checklist. Unpublished manuscript, University of Miami, 1975. Available from D.R. Peterson, 59 North Fifth Avenue, Highland Park, New Jersey, 08914.

Reisman, J.M. *Principles of psychotherapy with children.* New York: Wiley, 1973.

Rich, J. *Interviewing children and adolescents.* London: Macmillan, 1968.

Robinson, E.A., & Eyberg, S.M. The dyadic parent-child interaction coding system: Standardization and validation. *Journal of Consulting and Clinical Psychology,* 1981, **49,** (2), 245–250.

CHAPTER 6

Interviewing and Behavioral Observations

ANNETTE M. LA GRECA

Assessment represents the initial step in all clinical work with children and families. It is the process by which the clinician and clients identify the problems of concern and develop treatment strategies to deal effectively with the defined problems. Beyond initial problem identification, assessment should be a continuing area of importance, in order to tailor the treatment plan more effectively to the needs of the child and family and to evaluate the impact of intervention efforts.

Perhaps the two most commonly employed methods of assessment with children and their families are those of interviews and behavioral observations. These assessment methods are shared by clinicians of all orientations, even though the exact format of the methods may differ considerably. The present chapter will attempt to delineate some of the basic elements of these two assessment methods while noting some of the diversity within each procedure. The focus will be on the uses of interviewing and behavioral observations for the purposes of (1) initial problem determination and selection of treatment strategies and (2) evaluation of treatment outcome. The approach to the two assessment methods will be largely empirical in orientation. Where possible, the discussion will be restricted to the examples of interviews and behavioral observations which have the most empirical suport and/or promise to be clinically useful in a variety of settings. However, prior to a discussion of assessment strategies, some general comments regarding the child assessment process are in order.

CHARACTERISTICS OF CHILD ASSESSMENT

Several authors have noted important differences between the assessment process for children and adults (Evans & Nelson, 1977; Roberts & La Greca, 1981). These differences may influence the type of assessment procedure selected. For instance, objective personality measures (e.g., MMPI) are more likely to be used with adult clients, whereas parent-completed behavioral checklists (e.g., Behavior Problem Checklist, Quay & Peterson, 1975) are more likely to be found in a child assessment battery. Differences between the child and adult assessment processes may also affect the manner in which any one assessment procedure is employed, as evidenced by differences in the interview process for children and adults. Therefore, as a framework for understanding the child assessment process, some general rules and guidelines will be discussed.

The first basic characteristic of child assessment is that the assessment process usually involves *multiple persons in the child's environment,* including the child. This feature contrasts sharply with the adult assessment process, which often involves only the adult client. However, there are several reasons for the multiple person assessment process employed with child cases. For one, children are generally not self-referred for treatment. More typically, referral is initiated by the significant others in the child's life (parents, teachers, pediatricians). In many cases, the referral may bear little relationship to the child's feelings of distress (Evans & Nelson, 1977), suggesting that input from the child *and* significant others will be important in order to obtain an accurate picture of the problem. Second, a child's behavior is often situation specific, and a child who is rather mild mannered in school may be a tyrant at home (or vice versa). Here again, input from a number of persons (parents, teachers) will be needed. Finally, it will be important to assess how the adults in the child's life behave toward the child and how their behavior may contribute to the child's problem. As others have noted (Ciminero & Drabman, 1977; Evans & Nelson, 1977; Roberts & La Greca, 1981), the behaviors of parents, teachers, and other significant persons (including peers) will have an important impact on the child. Since intervention efforts will often involve multiple persons, the assessment process must take this factor into account as well.

The second basic characteristic of child assessment (and assessment in general) is that *multiple methods* of assessment are desirable. Although the present chapter will cover only interviews and behavioral observations, skilled clinicians will certainly not limit themselves to one or two assessment tools. Multiple assessment methods are desirable due to the limitations inherent in any one method. Interviews, for instance, may provide valuable information about the parents' and child's behavior, yet parents' retrospective accounts have shown little stability over time and tend to distort the child's behavior in the direction of precocity (Hetherington & Martin, 1979). On the other hand, while behavioral observations may appear to provide more objective information, problems with reliability and reactivity of observers are common (Kent & Foster, 1977). In order to minimize the limitations of any one procedure, a multimethod approach to assessment is needed.

A third aspect of child assessment involves evaluating the child from a developmental perspective. An understanding of "age appropriate" functioning is critical to the identification and understanding of many childhood problems. For instance, hyperactivity has been defined as "a child's frequent failure to comply in an *age appropriate* fashion with situational demands for restrained activity, sustained attention, resistance to distracting influences, and inhibition of impulsive responses" (Routh, 1980, p. 56). An understanding of developmental norms will be an important prerequisite to the identification of hyperactivity problems in a child. As another example, nocturnal bed wetting may be a common occurrence for a 3-year-old, yet represent a problem of concern for a 6-year-old. Thus developmental information and evaluation may play a significant role in the child assessment process.

Finally, the *evaluation of a child's cognitive skills* is often an important aspect of the child assessment process. Certainly, this is not true for every child; however, a cognitive/intellectual evaluation is much more typically a part of the assessment battery for children than for adults (Evans & Nelson, 1977; Roberts & La Greca, in press). Considering that many childhood problems are, at least in part, school related (e.g., learning disabilities, mental retardation, hyperactivity), it is often necessary to obtain information on the child's cognitive and academic level in order to understand adequately the child's behavior problems. Even in cases with no apparent relation to a school setting—such as the parent's physical abuse of a 5-year-old child—the child's cognitive affects may contribute to (Burgess, 1979) and have implications for treatment.

In summary, there are several characteristics of the child assessment process which may guide the clinician in his or her selection of appropriate assessment procedures. These include: (1) involving the child *and* significant others in the assessment process, (2) using multiple methods of assessment, (3) evaluating the child's behavior relative to developmental norms, and, in many cases, (4) obtaining information on the child's level and pattern of cognitive functioning. Now we will turn our attention to two specific assessment methods that are commonly employed with children and families—interviews and behavioral observations.

INTERVIEWS

Interviews have become an important part of the assessment process, regardless of the theoretical orientation of the clinician. Interviews are especially important for obtaining initial information about the child and the family and for establishing rapport with clients. Thus a clinician may be chiefly concerned about the *content* of the interview (i.e., what specific information should be gathered) as well as the *process* of the interview (i.e., how to conduct the interview in a relationship-enhancing manner). Each of these considerations will be addressed in the ensuing discussion.

Interviews with Children

Far more attention has been devoted to the interview process with adults than children, though there has been a recent surge of interest in developing successful interview formats for children (e.g., Chambers, Puig-Antich, & Tabrize, 1978; Herjanic et al., 1975; Hodges et al., 1981; Webb & Van Devere, 1980). The relative paucity of information on child interviews may be related to reported difficulties in obtaining reliable and valid information from children (Yarrow, 1960) compounded by the cognitive and verbal demands an interview assessment necessarily imposes on a child. Despite these problems, interviews with children have been widely used in clinical settings to obtain a better understanding of the child's perspective and to establish a positive therapeutic relationship with the child.

Information on child interviews may be derived from two main sources: the literature on empirically oriented interview formats and traditional (psychodynamic) approaches to child treatment. Several interview formats have been developed for use with children in clinical research (e.g., Chambers et al., 1978; Herjanic et al., 1975; Hodges et al., 1981; Rutter & Graham, 1968). These investigators have been especially concerned with the issues of reliability and validity of child reports. Consequently, these interview formats provide a heuristic means for obtaining clinically

relevant information from a child. On the other hand, the literature on psychodynamic approaches to child treatment has generated a wealth of information that may be particularly valuable in developing clinical skill in the *process* of interviewing children (e.g., Axline, 1947; Gardner, 1971, 1975; Rich, 1968; Simmons, 1974). This latter point is not surprising, given that a major focus of traditional treatment has been on developing a positive therapeutic relationship between the therapist and child. The ensuing discussion of child interviews will be drawn primarily from these two informative sources.

Structured Observations

The interview formats that have been most successful in obtaining reliable and valid information from children are those that employ a structured format. A structured format generally refers to an organized list of specific questions to which the child is asked to respond. The semistructured interview format developed by Rutter and Graham (1968) for the Isle of Wight studies of childhood psychopathology has paved the way for more recent works in this area. Current examples of structured child interviews include the Structured Pediatric Psychosocial Interview (Webb & Van Devere, 1980), the Child Assessment Schedule (Hodges et al., 1981, 1982), and the Diagnostic Interview for Children and Adolescents developed by Herjanic (Herjanic et al., 1975; Herjanic & Campbell, 1977).

Most of the structured interviews have been developed for children in the 6–12-year or 6–18-year age range; investigators generally agree that it is difficult to obtain reliable information from preschool children (Ciminero & Drabman, 1977; Hodges et al., 1981; O'Leary & Johnson, 1979). In addition to providing support for the reliability and validity of the child's report, these structured interviews have a number of other assets. Most of the interviews require minimal verbal responses from the child and thus do not overtax the child's verbal expressive skills. The interview questions tend to be child oriented, that is, geared toward the child's language skills so that the questions are readily understandable to children of elementary school age and older. Also, the standard format and scoring procedures permit the use of these interviews in treatment evaluation and clinical research.

The two structured child interviews that have been designed for use in a wide variety of clinical settings and that appear to have received the most empirical support are the Diagnostic Interview for Children and Adolescents (Herjanic et al., 1975; Herjanic & Campbell, 1977) and the Child Assessment Schedule (Hodges et al., 1981, 1982).

The Diagnostic Interview for Children and Adolescents (DICA) was developed for use with children in the 6–16-year age range (Herjanic et al., 1975). This structured interview consists of 207 questions, many of which require a simple "yes" or "no" response from the child. The interview takes approximately 1½ hours to administer, and covers four main content areas: factual information (e.g., age, address, reason for referral), behavior (e.g., at home, at school, with peers), psychiatric symptoms (e.g., phobias, obsessions, compulsions, suicidal thoughts), and mental status (e.g., orientation, insight, impulse control, judgment).

Two evaluation studies of this interview format have been conducted (Herjanic et al., 1975; Herjanic & Campbell, 1977). Herjanic and her associates compared the responses of 50 children (6–16 years) with maternal reports on a similar structured interview to assess the reliability of the children's self-reports. Overall, there was an 80 percent agreement between the child and parent reports, with the highest agreement for questions relating to factual information (84 percent) and lowest for questions concerning the child's mental status (69 percent). In addition, girls were found to be more reliable reporters than boys in terms of their self-reports of behavior (78 percent vs. 72 percent) and mental status (76 percent vs. 64 percent). In a second study (Herjanic & Campbell, 1977), 50 pediatric outpatients were compared with 50 psychiatric outpatients, who were matched in terms of sex, age, race, and socioeconomic status. As in the first study, all children were in the 6–16-year age range. The child interview responses distinguished the two groups, with the reports of behavior problems and school symptoms providing the sharpest distinction between the pediatric and psychiatric groups. These data provide support for the validity of this interview schedule with children in the 6–16-year age range.

While the DICA has some promising empirical support, this interview schedule is not without some difficulties. The list of questions asked of a child is very lengthy (207 items) and may prove to be counterproductive in terms of establishing rapport with the child. In addition, some of the items are grouped by symptomatology (e.g., obsessions, compulsions, somatic concerns) rather than by conversational topics, and the items within a section focus almost exclusively on negative behaviors (e.g., "Do you: Sass your parents? Tell lies to them? Take things at home that don't belong to you? Throw or break things up when you are mad?"). Again, this may impede the natural flow of conversation and limit rapport.

The Child Assessment Schedule (CAS) was developed with these specific concerns in mind (Hodges et al., 1981, 1982). The CAS was designed to enhance rapport with the child, as well as obtain information needed for DSM-III childhood diagnoses (Hodges et al., 1982). The interview takes about 45 minutes to administer and consists of approximately 75 questions which cover the following content areas: friends, school, family, activities, fears, worries, self-image, mood, somatic concerns, expression of anger, and thought disorder symptomatology. Many questions are open ended, so that several items can be scored from one question. This interview format is conversationally oriented, and with an experienced clinician the child may experience the interview as an informal discussion (Hodges et al., 1982). Examples of the questions asked in this interview appear in Table 6.1.

The second part of the CAS consists of 53 items which are scored by the examiner after the interview has been completed. These items cover such areas as: insight, grooming, motor

Table 6.1.   Excerpts from the Child Assessment Schedule

Questions	Scoring		
School			
What grade are you in? Where do you go to school?			
How do you get along with your teachers?	Reports significant difficulty in getting along with teachers (e.g., most of the time; most teachers; is a definite problem).	Y	N
What do you like best about school?	Cannot report on anything he or she likes best about school (e.g., "leaving school at the end of day" would not be scored).	Y	N
Do you like to (the best liked activity mentioned in the previous question) as much lately as you used to?	Reports significant decrease in enjoyment of "best liked thing" lately.	Y	N
Friends			
How many friends do you have in school or in your neighborhood? (NOTE: friends is to refer to peers).	Does not have at least three or more friends and cannot give names.	Y	N
How many are good friends?	Does not have at least one.	Y	N
Activities			
What do you do for fun? (in spare or extra time) (What are your hobbies?)	Cannot give an activity he or she does for fun.	Y	N

Note: Taken from *The Child Assessment Schedule: A Diagnostic Interview for Research and Clinical Use.* K. Hodges et al., *Catalogue of Selected Documents in Psychology,* 1981, **11,** 56. Copyright © 1981 by Dr. Kay Hodges. Used with permission of Dr. Kay Hodges.

coordination, activity level, quality of verbal communications, quality of emotional expressions, and so on.

With a sample of 87 children (32 child outpatients, 18 inpatients, and 37 normal controls), the CAS was shown to have good discriminant validity and test-retest reliability (Hodges et al., 1982). In addition, the total CAS score was found to correlate with mothers' reports of the number and severity of child problems as assessed by the Child Behavior Checklist (Achenbach, 1978; Achenbach & Edelbrock, 1979). In addition, scores on two of the CAS symptom complexes (Depression and Overanxious, respectively) correlated with children's scores on self-report measures of these affective states (Child Depression Inventory and State-Trait Anxiety Inventory for Children, respectively). Thus the initial data on the reliability and validity of this measure are very promising. Further investigation of the psychometric properties of this scale and compilation of normative data will additionally enhance the utility of this interview assessment.

Although these structured interviews have some very appealing aspects, they do pose some limitations, perhaps due to the "newness" of their development. Most notably, there are no normative data available as yet for any of the structured interviews. With the exception of the CAS, many of the interview schedules may not be designed in such a way as to facilitate rapport with the child. In addition,

Table 6.2.   Content Areas Frequently Assessed in Child Interviews

Area	Examples of Specific Content
All Ages	
Referral problem	What does the child think the main problem is? Does the child see the referral problem as a problem? What does the child think will help?
Interests	What does the child like to do (in spare time)? What does the child like to do alone? with friends? with family members?
School	What does the child like best about school? Least? How does the child feel about his or her teachers? What kinds of grades does the child get in school?
Peers	Who does the child like to play with? Who are the child's friends? What do they like to do together? Who does the child dislike?
Family	How does the child get along with his or her parents? What do they do that the child likes? That makes the child angry? How does the child get along with his or her brothers and sisters? What do they do that the child likes/dislikes?
Fears/Worries	What kinds of things is the child afraid of? What kinds of things make the child nervous, jumpy? What kinds of things does the child worry about?
Self-Image	What does the child like/dislike about himself or herself? What can the child do well, relative to peers? How would the child describe himself or herself?
Mood/Feelings	What kinds of things make the child feel sad? happy? How often do these feelings happen? What kinds of things make the child feel mad? What does he or she do when mad?

some clinical situations may call for a more flexible interview format than the structured interview allows. In some instances, the clinician may need to adapt the structured format to the needs of a particular child. Despite these limitations, structured interviews represent a very useful tool for clinical practice and clinical research.

One way in which the structured interviews are valuable is in terms of providing a list of very specific content areas that could be assessed during a child interview, along with specific types of questions that could be asked. Table 6.2 contains a list of topical areas commonly assessed in child interviews and a *sample* of the types of information that may be useful to inquire about. This list is based on a summary of a number of sources, to which the reader is referred for additional details

(Herjanic et al., 1975; Hodges et al., 1981, 1982; Roberts & La Greca, 1981; Simmons, 1974).

The list of areas for assessment, though suggestive, is not comprehensive. There may be other areas that a clinician may wish to include, depending on the particular child. For example, some behavior therapists have suggested that a child interview may be useful for obtaining information regarding potential reinforcers (child's specific likes and dislikes), which can then be instrumental in planning an effective behavioral intervention (Ciminero & Drabman, 1977; Evans & Nelson, 1977). Similarly, some of the areas listed in Table 6.2 may be excluded in some cases. Questions regarding thought disorder symptomatology, for instance, will not be appropriate for many children who are basically normal in function-

Table 6.2. *(continued)*

Area	Examples of Specific Content
Somatic concerns	Does the child have any headaches or stomachaches? Or other kinds of body pains? How often does this happen? What does the child usually do?
Thought disorder	Does the child hear things or see things that seem funny or unusual? Describe them.
Aspirations	What would the child like to do for a living when he or she gets older? What are other things the child would like to do when older?
Fantasy	What kinds of things does the child daydream about? What kinds of things does the child dream about? If the child could have any three wishes, what would they be?
Adolescents	
Heterosexual relations	Is the adolescent involved in any dating activities? What kinds of dating activities? Are there any restrictions on the adolescent's dating activities? How does he or she feel about them?
Sex	What kinds of sexual concerns does the adolescent have? What are his or her attitudes toward premarital sex? Do these conflict at all with parents' views? Is the adolescent adequately informed about contraception?
Drug/Alcohol use	What kinds of things has the adolescent ever used to get "high" (e.g. pills, alcohol, pot, glue)? Are other friends involved in these activities?

ing but who have problems in a specific area (e.g., learning disabilities, child management problems). The clinician should use judgment and discretion in selecting the content areas that will be most productive in terms of understanding the child's perspective and formulating an effective treatment approach.

Interview Process

The importance of the therapeutic relationship has been stressed by traditional therapists (Axline, 1947; Gardner, 1971, 1975; Rich, 1968) as well as more behaviorally oriented clinicians (Evans & Nelson, 1977; Morganstern, 1976; Rimm & Masters, 1974; Roberts & La Greca, 1981). Some of the process considerations involved in interviewing children can be very complex and may depend to a certain extent on the particular child being interviewed (e.g., learning disabled, mentally retarded, conduct disordered), as well as the age of the child (e.g., preschooler vs. adolescent). The focus here will be on some basic considerations for the child interview process; the reader is referred to alternative sources for a more detailed discussion of these issues (Conn, 1939; Erickson, 1958; Gardner, 1971, 1975; Rich, 1968; Simmons, 1974).

Therapist warmth and acceptance have been emphasized as important considerations for interviews with children as well as with adults (Rich, 1968; Rimm & Masters, 1974). In addition, children should be encouraged to express their thoughts and feelings freely, and this can be accomplished by adopting a neutral and permissive attitude toward the child's self-expression (Rich, 1968). Here perhaps a distinction should be made between the child's *behavior* and *verbal reports*. Limits can and should (in many cases) be set on a child's behavior, as when a child attempts physically to assault the therapist or destroy property. However, more freedom should be allowed in terms of the child's verbal expression of thoughts and feelings. In behavioral terms, this would translate into encouraging the child to talk (reinforcing verbal expression) rather than selectively attending to the kinds of things the child reports (e.g., reinforcing positive statements about others but ignoring negative statements). Bear in mind, when assessment is the goal of the interview, the clinician usually wants to obtain an accurate understanding of the child's perspective. Approval or disapproval of certain types of information on the therapist's part may create a biased impression of the child. Once the treatment program has been initiated this focus may change, but, at least for the initial data gathering, a permissive and neutral attitude may be most instrumental in obtaining an accurate picture of the child.

Other factors which may contribute in a positive way to the child-interviewing process include: gearing the interview questions to the child's level of cognitive understanding; asking questions which do not overtax the child's verbal expression skills; having the clinician take an active role in guiding the interview process; and establishing that the interview has some relevance to the child and his or her problems.

In terms of the child's level of cognitive understanding and verbal expression skills, it will be important for the clinician to use vocabulary that can be readily understood by the child and to keep sentence length relatively brief. It may also be useful to ask more specific questions than one normally would with an adult. For instance, asking "What do you like best about your mom? What do you like least about her?" are likely to be more productive than "Describe your mother," or "How do you feel about your mom?" Rather than asking very broad questions, such as "What is school like for you?," the clinician may find it more useful to ask questions about specific school-related areas (e.g., "What is your teacher like? What are your favorite subjects? Least-liked subjects? What area do you do best

in? Have the most trouble with?"). Especially with younger children (8 years of age or less) and those with cognitive difficulties, even more concrete types of questions may be needed (e.g., "What do you do in the afternoons after school?" rather than "What are your interests and hobbies?").

With children, the clinician will usually need to play a more active role in the interview process than with adults; he or she will need to guide and direct the interview discussion more carefully. Children are more likely to get "off-task" or to provide shorter responses to questions, and the interviewer should be sensitive to and prepared for these occurrences. In addition, the interviewer may need to be prepared to change the topic of conversation when a child becomes distressed, as many children do not have the conversational skills to do so effectively (Rich, 1968).

Finally, it will be important to establish, from the beginning, that the interview will have relevance to the child. Many children are not given adequate preparation for clinical contacts (Simmons, 1974). Thus, in order to enlist the attention and cooperation of the child, it is advisable to discuss the reasons for the interview with the child, relating it as much as possible to the child's own concerns.

Interviews with Parents and Significant Others

In keeping with the multiperson nature of child assessment, interviews are likely to be conducted with parents and teachers as well as with the child. These interviews will provide valuable information about the child and family and provide directions for further assessment and treatment. Establishing rapport is also essential here, as parents and others will play an instrumental role in the treatment program.

The initial parent interview will cover many of the same content areas that are included in child interviews (see Table 6.2) though more detailed information may be obtained from parents. In addition, information regarding the reasons for referral should be obtained, including a complete description of the presenting problem and possible controlling factors and a history of previous attempts to remedy the problem. Special areas to inquire about with parents include: parents' methods of discipline (Which methods are used? What is the child disciplined for? In what ways do the parents agree/disagree about child management?); developmental history of the child (e.g., problems with pregnancy, birth, perinatal development; when the child achieved developmental milestones); and medical history of the child (e.g., any severe or unusual illnesses or injuries). For additional suggestions concerning the content of parent interviews, see Kanfer and Saslow (1969), O'Leary and Johnson (1979), Roberts and La Greca (in press), and Simmons (1974).

As with children, some structured interview formats have been developed for use with parents (Herjanic et al., 1975; Holland, 1970). For example, the Diagnostic Interview for Children and Adolescents developed by Herjanic and colleagues has a parental counterpart, which closely parallels the child's version. However, several additional areas are assessed in the parent form, including questions about: birth and pregnancy (e.g., age of mother at time of birth, type of delivery, complications during pregnancy); developmental history of the child (age appropriate attainment of developmental milestones such as crawling, walking, speaking), and family history (problems experienced by the parents such as hospitalization for psychiatric or medical reasons, alcoholism, history of suicide attempts, etc.).

Although structured parent interviews exist, there has been little attempt to evaluate their reliability and validity except to note their correspondence to child versions of the interview (Herjanic et al., 1975). Thus structured parent interviews have very limited utility as treatment outcome measures or for clinical research. Most likely, the paucity of attention devoted to parent interviews is the result of the significant development of behavioral checklists for obtaining information on child behavior problems from parents and others. (See chap. 9 of this book.) Behavioral checklists are frequently administered to parents in conjunction with initial interviews and

do provide a reliable and valid means of obtaining information about the child. Although the discussion of behavior checklists is beyond the scope of this chapter, there are a number of resources available which discuss this assessment method more fully (Achenbach, 1978, 1979; Conners, 1970; Evans & Nelson, 1977; Goyette, Conners, & Ulrich, 1978; Humphries & Ciminero, 1979; O'Leary & Johnson, 1979; Quay, 1977; Roberts & La Greca, 1981).

Little direct information is available on interviewing the significant adults in the child's life other than the parents. In clinical practice, such interviews are generally problem focused, that is, geared toward obtaining information about the specific referral problem. Interviews with teachers and other adults may also provide useful information about the child's functioning in areas outside of the home setting (e.g., school, scouts) and offer still another perspective on the child and family. In terms of obtaining information which has demonstrated reliability and validity, many of the parent-completed behavioral checklists referred to above (e.g., Quay, 1977) can also be administered to teachers or other significant adults.

Aside from obtaining information about the child and family, initial interviews with parents and other adults are especially important for establishing a positive working relationship and often set the tone for future intervention efforts. For these reasons, the interview process merits close attention. For the most part, the process of interviewing parents and other adults will be very similar to the process of interviewing adult clients. To this end, the considerable literature on interviewing processes and methods will be very useful. The reader is referred to a number of excellent sources, among many others (Bernstein, Bernstein, & Dane, 1974; Hackney & Nye, 1973; Kanfer & Phillips, 1970; Meyer, Liddell & Lyons, 1977; Morganstern, 1976; Pope, 1979; Sullivan, 1954). Several additional considerations for parent interviews will be discussed.

During assessment interviews with parents, the clinician should be very sensitive to the stress and anxiety that the parents may be experiencing in discussing their child's referred problems with a professional (Evans & Nelson, 1977). Special care should be taken to convey respect for the parents' feelings and to avoid any suggestion that they are fully to blame for the child's difficulties. This sensitive and nonjudgmental approach to parents may seem obvious; yet, unfortunately, this often is not the case (Mesibov & La Greca, 1981). In addition, other rapport-enhancing skills (e.g., warmth, empathy) will assist in laying the groundwork for a positive working relationship—usually essential for successful therapy outcome. Finally, the importance of including both parents in the interview process has often been stressed (O'Leary & Johnson, 1979); this increases the accuracy of the information obtained and may help to enlist the cooperation of both parents in the treatment process.

In sum, interviews with parents and significant adults are most valuable for establishing rapport and obtaining a detailed, comprehensive picture of child and family functioning that will provide directions for further assessment and the formulation of treatment plans. Despite the utility of interviews, clinicians should be aware of some of the biases inherent in this assessment method.

Several authors (Evans & Nelson, 1977; Hetherington & Martin, 1979; Macfarlane, 1938; O'Leary & Johnson, 1979; Yarrow, 1963) have discussed the limitations of parents' retrospective accounts of child behaviors and childrearing practices. Common problems that are cited include: low reliability, poor accuracy of recall (especially for subjective impressions), overemphasis on cultural stereotypes, and a bias toward describing the child in a positive and precocious manner. In addition, fathers may be less reliable reporters than mothers (Evans & Nelson, 1977).

Although these limitations clearly underscore the need for multiple methods of assessment, it is possible to minimize some of these difficulties. Problems with parent interviews are less apparent when the parents are questioned about *current* behaviors and *current* child management practices and when the questions are objective and easily quantified (O'Leary & Johnson, 1979). Additionally,

Evans and Nelson (1977) suggest obtaining independent reports from both parents and then checking for areas of agreement. The clinician may have greater confidence in the validity of the information for which there is high agreement.

In keeping with the multimethod assessment process, we will now turn our attention to another important assessment tool—behavioral observations.

BEHAVIORAL OBSERVATION

The observation of behavior has been an especially important assessment tool for child and family problems. Children are generally more accessible for observations than adult clients, and, given the degree of social control evident in a child's environment and the situation specificity of child behavior, behavioral observations play a critical role in the child assessment and treatment process.

While much of the empirical development of behavioral observation as an assessment procedure can be credited to behaviorally oriented therapists and researchers, clinicians of varying orientations have employed informal observations of children and parents for many years. Psychodynamically oriented clinicians, such as Simmons (1974), have noted areas of parent-child interactions that could be observed in a clinic waiting room or during an interview. However, given the concern for assessment procedures having empirical support and psychometric properties, the present section will focus on observational assessment from a behavioral perspective. Adaptations of these procedures, consonant with other theoretical approaches, are left to the discretion of the individual clinician.

The following section will be organized according to the type of observation format employed. Discussion of the problems and limitations inherent in these procedures will then be addressed.

Naturalistic Observations

Observations in natural settings represent the hallmark of behavioral assessment (Ciminero,

1977; Gelfand & Hartman, 1975) and consequently have received considerable attention. Naturalistic observations of children have been conducted in family settings (Patterson, 1977; Patterson & Reid, 1970), classrooms (Abikoff, et al., 1977; O'Leary et al., 1976), and during naturally occurring peer interactions (Hartup, Glazer, & Charlesworth, 1967; Strain, Shores, & Kerr, 1976), to name just a few.

To a certain extent, the utility of behavioral observations is determined by the reliability and validity of the coding systems employed for organizing the observations. Many advantages of employing well-validated observational codes have been cited (Abikoff et al., 1977; Evans & Nelson, 1977; Kent & Foster, 1977). For one, objective behavioral definitions minimize bias due to halo effects and rater expectations (Abikoff et al., 1977; Kent et al., 1974). This is especially important when evaluating the effects of an intervention program. Change agents (e.g., teacher, parents) are very likely to report information consonant with behavior change; objective behavioral measures reduce such bias and provide a more accurate view of behavior change. A well-defined and validated observation code is additionally advantageous for providing reliable diagnostic information. Two examples of well-validated coding methodologies will be presented here.

Patterson and colleagues (Patterson, Cobb, & Ray, 1973; Patterson & Reid, 1970) have developed a format for observing family interactions in a home setting. Family members are generally observed for an hour, prior to dinner, and are asked to limit their activities to two adjacent rooms to facilitate the observations. Each family member is observed for two 5-minute observation periods, each comprised of ten 30-second intervals.[1] Family interaction behaviors are coded in 29 categories, including both positive (attention, approval, etc.) and negative behaviors (destructiveness, ignoring, disapproval, noncompliance, etc.).

The available data on the reliability and validity of this observation system have been quite impressive. Both interobserver agreement and test-retest reliability have been demonstrated (Jones, Reid, & Patterson, 1975). Thus information obtained from this observation system can be used effectively to pinpoint family interaction difficulties, design treatment programs to remedy these difficulties, and evaluate intervention outcome. (For a further discussion and description of this coding system, the reader is referred to several sources: Patterson, 1977; Patterson et al., 1969; Patterson et al., 1973; Patterson & Reid, 1970).

Naturalistic observations in the classroom setting may also facilitate the identification and treatment of child behavior problems. Children who have difficulty with hyperactivity provide a good example. Abikoff and colleagues (Abikoff et al., 1977) developed a behavioral coding system for identifying hyperactive children, which also has implications for treatment. This system is a revision of the Stony Brook Observation Code designed for use with "problem children" in a school setting (Tonick, Friehling, & Warhit, 1973); it can be used with children between 6 and 12 years of age. Children are observed in the classroom during didactic teaching and independent work activities for four 4-minute periods (comprised of 15-second intervals). Fourteen behavioral categories are coded: interference, solicitation, off task, minor motor movements, gross motor movement (all), gross motor movement (standing), gross motor movement (vigorous), noncompliance, out-of-chair, physical aggression, verbal threat of aggression (to children and to teacher), extended verbalization, and daydreaming.

Evidence on the reliability and validity of this coding system has been very promising. Abikoff et al. compared 60 identified hyperactive children with 60 normal children matched for sex and age. All children were in the 6–12-year age range and were observed in their classrooms. Interobserver agreement for the behavioral categories was noted to be high. Although there was overlap in the range of scores, in all 14 categories, the hyperactive children displayed the observed behaviors at a higher rate than the normal children. Twelve of the 14 behaviors (all except extended verbalizations and daydreaming) significantly discriminated the two groups, and five of these were noted to have especially high reliability and relevance to hyperactivity (interference, off task, minor motor movements, gross motor movement [all], and solicitation).

To address the issue of clinical utility, Abikoff et al. developed a screening procedure for differentiating the hyperactive and nonhyperactive children. Using the combined categories of interference and off-task behavior, cut-off scores correctly classified 58 percent of the hyperactive children and 100 percent of the normal children. While promising, this procedure does underidentify hyperactivity problems. The advantage of this observation method is that it allows the clinician to compare a child's behavior normatively, in a systematic manner, with the behavior of hyperactive and nonhyperactive children of similar age. However, as the authors aptly note, the identification of hyperactivity should not be based solely on this observation code. In keeping with the multiperson, multimethod approach to child assessment, this point should be underscored. Additional input from parents and teachers will be critical for proper identification, though this observational system can facilitate the process. (See chap. 20 of this book; Safer & Allen, 1976; and Wender, 1971, for a more complete discussion of diagnostic issues in hyperactivity.) When considered with other assessment methods, this observational system can be utilized to identify activity problems in children, pinpoint relevant classroom behaviors which interfere with successful academic work, and assist in evaluating the impact of treatment efforts (Gittleman-Klein et al., 1976).

Although the two behavioral observation systems described are relevant for several clinical problems, many clinicians will be faced with the task of identifying and defining target behaviors for observation that are particular to a specific child or family. Several guides may be useful here (Bijou & Baer, 1961; Bijou & Peterson, 1971; Gelfand & Hartman, 1975).

Generally, the first step in selecting an appropriate target behavior for observation involves clearly defining the behavior(s) of interest, so that it may be readily observable and independent observers can agree on the behavior's occurrence. Target behaviors which have implications for treatment are mainly of interest (e.g., Does the behavior represent some deficit or excess that will be involved in the intervention process?). Further, it is good practice to select behaviors for which desired goals can be specified. For instance, in targeting a child's temper tantrums for observation, the parents and clinician should have in mind what a desirable level of tantrumming would be (None? Once per day? Once per week?). If behavioral goals cannot be specified, this may not be a target behavior amenable to intervention.

Once the target behaviors of interest have been selected, the observation should include a situational or functional analysis of the behaviors. This means including observations of the antecedent events and consequences of the behaviors. In order to determine the kinds of actions and events that contribute to maintaining (or inhibiting) the target behavior, the observer/clinician should record the events immediately preceding the behavior under observation (antecedents) as well as the immediate consequences. Information on the antecedents and consequences of the target behavior should lead to the formulation of a treatment plan.

To illustrate these points, consider the example of a mother who is extremely concerned about her 4-year-old's aggressive behavior. Initially, it will be important to establish a clear definition of the child's reported aggressive behavior: (1) *What is meant* by aggressive? (e.g., hitting, kicking, throwing objects, etc.), (2) *When and where* does this occur? (e.g., at home, in the preschool, during peer play activities, etc.), and (3) *With whom?* (e.g., parents, siblings, teachers, peers). Once the aggressive behavior has been defined—say, in this case, throwing toys at a younger sibling— observations of the antecedent events and consequences would be obtained. Antecedent events might be the mother telling the child to "play nicely" or giving attention to the younger sibling, or the younger child pulling the older child's hair. Consequences might be the mother moving the younger child to another room (leaving the older child with all the toys) or a brief verbal reprimand. This functional analysis will provide information needed for establishing an intervention plan; antecedent events and/or consequences may be changed in an effort to eliminate the "aggressive" behavior. Continued observation of the target behavior (throwing toys at the younger sibling) will help to evaluate the outcome of these intervention efforts.

In addition to conducting behavioral observations, clinicians are frequently involved in teaching others (parents, teachers, etc.) how to observe behavior systematically. Several helpful guides are available here (Becker, 1971; Patterson, 1971, among others).

In sum, naturalistic observations of the child and/or family can provide important information useful for problem identification, treatment planning, and evaluation of treatment outcome. Although there are several cautions and limitations in their use (to be discussed in a later section), they offer the advantages of providing objective information on behaviors of interest, while minimizing some of the biases inherent in more traditional self-report assessment procedures.

Now we will turn our attention to another type of observational format—structured observations.

Structured Observation Formats

In some instances, it will not be practical or feasible for the clinician to observe the child and family in a naturalistic setting; yet, observation of the target behaviors may be important to the treatment process. Such instances are especially conducive to structured observation formats.

Structured observations involve observing the child and/or parents in a standard situation which has been designed to elicit the behavior(s) of interest. Despite some problems with generalization to the natural environment, structured observations have been widely used in behaviorally oriented clinical-child settings (Hughes & Haynes, 1978; Roberts & Forehand, 1978) and offer a number of distinct advantages. For instance, they promote an efficient use of the clinician's and clients' time, while affording the clinician an opportunity to observe the child and/or family in a seminaturalistic manner. One serious drawback to naturalistic observation is that the behaviors of interest may not occur during the observation period; structured observations attempt to circumvent this difficulty. In addition to practicality, the frequent use of standard structured situations for observational assessment would allow the clinician to establish a normative base for clinical observations, which would further enhance the utility and validity of this assessment procedure.

Structured observation formats have been designed to assess a variety of behaviors, including parent-child interactions (Hughes & Haynes, 1978; Lytton, 1971), activity level (Routh & Schroeder, 1976; Routh, Schroeder, & O'Tuama, 1974), medical anxiety (Burnstein & Meichenbaum, 1979) and peer interaction skills (Gottman, Gonso, & Rasmussen, 1975; Stark & La Greca, 1981), to list a few. In addition to assessing different kinds of behaviors, the formats developed have also differed in the extent to which they are structured or contrived. Roleplay assessments, for instance, fall at the "high structure" end of the continuum. In a roleplay assessment, the client (child, parent) is asked to respond to a "pretend" situation as if the situation were really occurring. An example of a roleplay designed to assess conversational skills might consist of asking a child to pretend the clinician is a friend at school and to converse with the friend (i.e., clinician) as he or she normally would. Observations of behavior during roleplay assessments may be even further removed from naturalistic observations than with some of the less contrived structured formats, and problems concerning the external validity of roleplay assessments have been noted (Bellack, Hersen, & Turner, 1978; Higgins, Alonso, & Pendleton, 1979). Despite these difficulties, roleplay assessments and other structured observations will have definite clinical utility when it is not feasible to observe the behaviors of interest in a natural setting. Several examples of structured observational formats that have implications for clinical practice with children and families will be noted.

In the area of parent-child interactions, a number of observational formats have been developed (Campbell, 1973, 1975; Cunningham & Barkley, 1979; Lytton, 1971). Although studies of structured parent-child interactions during the preschool and early elementary school years have focused almost exclusively on child management behaviors, such as child compliance or parental discipline methods, family problem solving (O'Rourke, 1963; Straus & Tallman, 1971) and general rapport among family members (Kogan & Wimberger, 1969; Wahler & Nordquist, 1973) have received some attention. (See Hughes & Haynes, 1978, for a critical review of this literature.)

Structured parent-child observations might be typified by the work of Forehand and associates (Forehand, Cheney, & Yoder, 1974; Forehand & King, 1974; Forehand, 1975; Forehand et al., 1979; Forehand, Wells, & Sturgis, 1978). A typical procedure has been to observe a mother and child in a clinic playroom, instructing the mother to spend the first 10 minutes engaged in whatever activity the child chooses ("free play") and the subsequent 10 minutes engaged in a mother-determined activity ("command situation"). The child's behavior is scored for compliance/noncompliance, and the mother's behavior is scored for commands, criticism, and rewards.

Comparisons between children referred to a psychological clinic and nonreferred children (all ages 4–6) disclosed that clinic children exhibited lower rates of compliant behavior and the mothers of these children employed more commands and criticisms of their child (Forehand et al., 1975). This observational system has also been found to be responsive to treatment effects (Forehand & King, 1974; Forehand et al., 1979). Parents of 3- to 8-year-old children who received intensive training in child management skills were found to display lower rates of commands and higher rates of rewards at postintervention assessments; children's noncompliant behaviors were also observed to decrease.

The results of these studies suggest that this structured parent-child observation format could be adopted readily in a clinic setting with pre-school-aged children and their par-

ents. The procedure would involve a minimal amount of time to administer (20 minutes) yet would yield clinically useful information.

Another similar parent-child observation format, designed for use with hyperactive children and their mothers, has been reported by Cunningham and Barkley (1979). Children are observed with their mothers in a playroom for 15 minutes of free play followed by 15 minutes of mother-directed structured-task activity (e.g., have the child put away the toys used in free play, complete a set of math problems, etc.). Based on the observation system developed by Mash and colleagues (Mash, Terdal, & Anderson, 1973), sequences of mother-child and child-mother behaviors are coded. (See Cunningham & Barkley, 1979, for a detailed description.)

Comparisons of 20 normal and 20 hyperactive males (5–12 years of age) and their mothers disclosed a number of interesting behavioral differences between the two groups. Hyperactive children were less compliant and more active than the nonhyperactive children. The mothers of hyperactive males displayed management techniques described as "controlling" and "intrusive"; they provided fewer positive responses to the child and devoted more time to controlling and directing the child's activities. By contrast, the mothers of the nonhyperactive children attended to their children in an interested and positive manner, more frequently praising, talking to, and questioning the child about activities. In other studies (Barkley & Cunningham, in press; Cunningham & Barkley, in press) this parent-child interaction task was found to be sensitive to treatment effects. Hyperactive children receiving stimulant drug therapy were observed to increase on-task behavior, compliance, and sustained independent play and to decrease activity level. Concomitantly, mothers of these children were observed to interact in a less controlling and more responsive manner. These data suggest that this assessment procedure can be a useful tool for identifying management problems in hyperactive children and, further, can be instrumental in evaluating treatment progress. As with the procedure developed by Forehand

and associates, this parent-child interaction task could easily be employed in a clinic setting with children and families.

Although the literature on structured parent-child interactions provides heuristic models for clinical assessment procedures, some limitations within this area do exist. Most glaringly, there has been a paucity of studies that focus on father-child and mother-father-child interactions or that deal with behaviors unrelated to child management problems (Hughes & Haynes, 1978). In extending assessment procedures beyond existing limitations, it would be of value to develop additional formats for structured observations that would include both parents and possibly all immediate family members. It would also be of interest to broaden the types of family behaviors being assessed and to establish some developmental guidelines for "normal" behavior.

While parent-child interactions have been a major area of focus, structured observations have not been limited to assessments of these behaviors. Children's interpersonal skills, such as friendship making and assertive behaviors, have been assessed using roleplay formats. Roleplays, again, tend to be very structured and ask the individual to respond to a "pretend" situation as if it were occurring. While roleplays have been used predominantly with adults, several examples of child-oriented roleplays can be found.

Gottman and colleagues (Gottman et al., 1975) describe a roleplay situation which can be used in the assessment of children's friendship-making skills. Children are asked to pretend they are "making friends with a new child in school." Four areas of social behavior are observed in this roleplay: (1) whether the child *greets* the new peer, (2) whether the child *asks for information* (e.g., "What's your name?"), (3) whether the child *offers information about him or herself* (e.g., "My name is John. I really like this school"), and (4) whether the child *extends inclusion* to the new peer to engage in a mutual activity (e.g., "Would you like to play ball with me today?"). This roleplay sequence was administered to a sample of third- and fourth-graders who were further categorized by their level of peer acceptance. It was found that the children who exhibited high levels of peer acceptance (i.e., were well liked by other children) were much more likely to display the four social behaviors than those who were low on peer acceptance (i.e., had very few friends). Another study (La Greca & Santogrossi, 1980), which focused on social skills training with low-accepted elementary school students (grades 3, 4, and 5), found that children who originally displayed peer interaction problems demonstrated marked improvements on this roleplay assessment of social skills after their participation in a treatment program.

These data provide evidence for the validity of this roleplay assessment and suggest that it may be a useful tool for pinpointing peer interaction difficulties in elementary-school-aged children. Recently, a more extended roleplay format for comprehensively assessing children's peer interaction skills has been developed (Stark & La Greca, 1981); it obtained promising results with regard to reliability and validity. Roleplay assessments of children's assertive behaviors have also received some attention (Reardon et al., 1979).

In summary, structured observational formats (including roleplay assessments) have been developed to assess a variety of child and family behaviors. They are particularly advantageous in providing information on behaviors of interest in a cost efficient manner, though concerns regarding their external validity have been noted.

In the next section, attention will be directed toward several issues which affect the use of observational assessments in general.

Issues in Observational Assessment

While there are many benefits to be gained from the inclusion of behavioral observations in the child assessment process, several issues affecting their utility emerge that warrant careful consideration. Concerns about the reliability, validity, and reactivity of this form of assessment have been noted. Although more extensive treatment of these issues can be found (Johnson & Bolstad, 1973; Kazdin,

1979; Kent & Foster, 1977), some discussion is in order. The following section will consider some of the psychometric and methodological issues involved in observational assessment.

Reliability

Reliability generally refers to the extent to which observers' recordings of behaviors correspond to the actual behavioral events. Although reliability has often been confused with observer agreement (i.e., the extent to which independent observers agree on the occurrence or nonoccurrence of behaviors), these really represent two separate issues (Johnson & Bolstad, 1973). (For more detailed discussions concerning the reliability of behavioral observations, see Johnson & Bolstad, 1973; Kent & Foster, 1977; Reid, 1970.)

The reliability of behavioral observations has been found to be affected by several factors. First, characteristics of the recording procedures, such as the complexity of the category definitions or the number of behaviors coded simultaneously, can adversely influence the accuracy of the observations (Johnson & Bolstad, 1973; Mash & McElwee, 1974). For clinical practice, this suggests that it would be advisable to limit the number of behaviors being observed (keeping just the essentials) in order to optimize the accuracy of the observations. Clearly defined behavioral categories are also very important.

A second factor influencing reliability involves the characteristics of the observer (i.e., clinician, parent, teacher, trained observers). Most notably, the expectancies of the observers (Johnson & Bolstad, 1973; Kent & Foster, 1977) and their prior training and experiences (Mash & McElwee, 1974; Reid, 1970) have been found to influence accuracy. Kent and Foster (1977) reviewed studies designed to assess the effects of observer expectancy and concluded, at least with trained observers, that expectancies for change had little effect on the behavioral recordings but had a significant effect on global or subjective ratings of behavior. Generally, observers who were led to expect behavioral change subjectively reported "improvement," even

though the behavioral coding data appeared to be relatively immune from bias. While this appears very encouraging, it should be noted that studies of observer bias that employed untrained observers have obtained different results (Johnson & Bolstad, 1973). They have found greater evidence for bias in behavioral recording. This would suggest that relatively untrained observers (parents, teachers, clinicians) should be trained to whatever extent is possible, especially since these persons are likely to have clear expectations for behavioral change. Moreover, it would be helpful to include observations conducted by impartial or nonbiased observers and/or to obtain observations from a number of different persons. Johnson and Bolstad (1973) note that when interobserver agreement is high, it is less likely that observer bias is a concern.

There is one additional note concerning observer bias. Studies on the effects of experimenter feedback suggest that observers can be "shaped" into giving biased behavioral recordings (Kent & Foster, 1977). O'Leary, Kent and Kanowitz (1975) led observers to expect behavioral change for several coding categories and coupled this with daily feedback on how well or poorly the data conformed to expectations. This "bias plus feedback" was found to have a significant effect on behavioral coding; the observational data changed in line with the bias and feedback, even though no actual behavior change had occurred. Such findings highlight the need for caution in clinical settings. Clinicians should be wary of providing evaluative feedback to parents, teachers, or other observers that may bias the results of observational efforts.

Finally, as already indicated, the prior experience of the observers can affect accuracy of behavioral recording (Mash & McElwee, 1974). Generally, trained raters perform more accurately than those lacking in experience. This suggests that clinicians, in addition to sharpening their own observational skills, should be prepared to teach observational recording to others who may be observing the child (e.g., parents, teachers). Several guides may be useful here (Becker,

1971; Gelfand & Hartman, 1975; Patterson, 1971).

Reactivity

With respect to observational assessment, reactivity generally refers to the extent to which the method of observation influences the behaviors of those being observed. The presence of observers in the home or classroom may have an effect on the behavior of children, parents, and/or teachers. For instance, Johnson, Christensen, and Bellamy (1976) found that different results were obtained when parent-child interactions were recorded in an obtrusive versus an unobtrusive manner. Patterson (1977) noted that older children tend to reduce their deviancy when they are aware of being observed relative to a situation in which their behavior is observed covertly. Similar results have been reported in other studies (Mercatoris & Craighead, 1974; Roberts & Renzaglia, 1965).

The potential reactivity of observational assessment is of particular concern in clinical settings. Generally, as Kazdin (1979) has observed, clinical intervention

is designed to produce behavior change in a person's everyday life, usually in situations when the person does not believe that his or her behavior is assessed. For example, one would like assurances that a parent is responding appropriately to a child when observers are not in the home or when tape recordings are not made. Showing appropriate behavior only when the observer is present runs the risk that changes in behavior are restricted to reactive assessment periods. (p. 715)

In view of these concerns, it is generally desirable to minimize the reactivity of the assessment procedure in order to obtain a more realistic picture of behavior.

One way of limiting the reactivity of observational assessment may be to minimize the obtrusiveness of the assessment. Observations conducted behind one-way mirrors or using concealed video equipment may be preferable to employing *in vivo* observers. Kazdin (1979) offers additional suggestions for conducting unobtrusive assessments and is a good re-

source here. When observers must be present, it will be helpful to allow some time for the child (family, class members, etc.) to become acclimated to the presence of others until the observers are largely ignored. Still another method for minimizing reactivity is to have the observations conducted by persons who are usually present in the child's daily environment (e.g., parent, teacher).

Some situations may arise where reactivity is a benefit rather than hindrance to the assessment. This occurs when the process of observation changes the behavior in the desired direction (provided it is a lasting change). Most often this occurs when the individual is observing his or her own behavior, a process also referred to as self-monitoring. For instance, a parent who is monitoring his or her own praising and nagging behaviors may find that praising increases and nagging decreases as a result of keeping track of these behaviors. Self-monitoring has been employed both as an assessment and as an intervention procedure. When assessment is the goal, it is desirable to minimize reactivity; however, when intervention is the goal, reactivity can be maximized to enhance the effectiveness of this procedure. Nelson (1977) provides a thorough discussion of self-monitoring as both an assessment and intervention method.

Validity

The validity of observational assessment is an often neglected issue in behavioral research (Johnson & Bolstad, 1973; Kazdin, 1979). For the most part, behaviors are selected for observation based on "face validity" and content validity. If a behavior seems to be relevant to the problem at hand, it is considered to be a valid behavior for observation. Unfortunately, this approach has not always led to the selection of behaviors that are valid indicators of the problem in question. For instance, several investigators have selected children who evidenced low frequencies of peer interactions as candidates for social skills intervention (Keller & Carlson, 1974; O'Connor, 1969, 1972) and demonstrated that intervention effectively increased these children's rates of peer interactions. However, "frequency of peer interaction" has not been found to be a valid indicator of peer problems (Asher, Markell, & Hymel, 1981). Children exhibiting low frequencies of peer interactions are not necessarily disliked by peers, and many children with high rates of interactions may actually be very problematic. Thus, whenever possible, care should be taken to select behaviors for assessment and intervention that have demonstrated validity. (Several of the behavioral codes discussed earlier in this chapter provide data to substantiate the validity of the selected behaviors.) Moreover, as stressed previously, it is important not to rely on only one main method of assessment. By taking a multimethod approach to the assessment process the validity of the assessment may be enhanced.

Other Issues

In this section, several issues affecting the utility of behavioral observations have been discussed, namely, reliability, reactivity, and validity. In addition to these issues, other concerns emerge that have implications for observational assessment. For instance, to the extent possible, it is desirable to obtain information on behavioral norms so that problems of an extreme nature can be more readily recognized and so that those that fall within normal limits will not receive undue attention. When behavioral norms are not available, it would be advisable to compare observations of the target child with those of other children who are not experiencing similar problems.

Another issue relevant to conducting behavioral observations concerns the level of agreement obtained among observers (i.e., interobserver agreement). This is a complex issue that can be affected by a number of factors, such as the nature of training and the method of checking accuracy. Here the reader is referred to several sources for more complete treatment of this topic (Johnson & Bolstad, 1973; Kazdin, 1977; Kent & Foster, 1977; O'Leary & Kent, 1973).

SUMMARY

In the present chapter we have focused on two main methods of assessment employed with children and families—interviews and behavioral observations. Both types of assessments yield information that can be invaluable for treatment planning and evaluation. However, both methods of assessment present problems and limitations and are not intended to be employed as the sole means of assessment. In keeping with the multiperson, multimethod approach to child assessment, the use of interviews, observations, *and* other methods of assessment will be most productive in obtaining a comprehensive evaluation of the child and family.

NOTE

1. This method of coding observational data is often referred to as time sampling. With a time-sampling procedure, the total observation period is divided into a number of smaller time intervals (e.g., 10 seconds, 30 seconds, etc.) of equal length, and the behaviors of interest are observed and coded for each designated interval. Frequency counts of the behaviors may then be obtained by summing across all time intervals. Further discussion of time sampling and other measurement procedures may be found elsewhere (Doke, 1976; Mann, 1976; Roberts & Forehand, 1978).

REFERENCES

Abikoff, H., Gittelman-Klein, R., & Klein, D.F. Validation of a classroom observation code for hyperactive children. *Journal of Consulting and Clinical Psychology,* 1977, **45**(5), 772–783.

Achenbach, T.M. The Child behavior profile: I. Boys aged 6–11. *Journal of Consulting and Clinical Psychology,* 1978, **46,** 478–488.

Achenbach, T.M. The Child behavior profile: An empirically based system for assessing children's behavioral problems and competencies. *International Journal of Mental Health,* 1979, **7,** 24–42.

Achenbach, T.M., & Edelbrock, C.S. The Child behavior profile: II. Boys aged 12–16 and girls 6–11 and 12–16. *Journal of Consulting and Clinical Psychology,* 1979, **47,** 223–233.

Asher, S.R., Markell, R.A., & Hymel, S. Identifying children at risk in peer relations: A critique of the rate-of-interaction approach to assessment. *Child Development,* 1981, **52,** pp. 1239–1245.

Axline, V. *Play therapy.* New York: Balantine Books, 1947.

Barkley, R., & Cunningham, C.E. The effects of Ritalin on the mother-child interactions of hyperactive children. *Archives of General Psychiatry,* in press.

Becker, W.C. *Parents are teachers: A child management program.* Champaign, Ill.: Research Press, 1971.

Bellack, A.S., Hersen, M., & Turner, S.M. Role-play tests for assessing social skills: Are they valid? *Behavior Therapy, 1978,* **9,** 448–461.

Bernstein, L., Bernstein, R.S., & Dana, R.H. *Interviewing: A guide for health professionals* (2nd ed.). New York: Appleton-Century-Crofts, 1974.

Bijou, S.W., & Baer, D.M. *Child development: A systematic and empirical theory* (Vol. 1). New York: Appleton-Century-Crofts, 1961.

Bijou, S.W., & Peterson, R.F. The psychological assessment of children: A functional analysis. In P. McReynolds (Ed.), *Advances in psychological assessment* (Vol. 2). Palo Alto, Calif.: Science and Behavior Books, 1971, pp. 63–78.

Burgess, R.L. Child abuse: A social interactional analysis. In B.B. Lahey & A.E. Kazdin (Eds.), *Advances in clinical child psychology* (Vol. 2). New York: Plenum Press, 1979.

Burnstein, S., & Meichenbaum, D. The work of worrying in children undergoing surgery. *Journal of Abnormal Child Psychology,* 1979, **7**(2), 121–132.

Campbell, S. Mother-child interaction in reflective, impulsive, and hyperactive children. *Developmental Psychology,* 1973, **8,** 341–347.

Campbell, S. Mother-child interaction: A comparison of hyperactive, learning disabled, and normal boys. *American Journal of Orthopsychiatry,* 1975, **45,** 51–57.

Chambers, W., Puig-Antich, J., & Tabrize, M.A. *The ongoing development of the KIDDIE-SADS.* Paper presented at the meeting of the American Academy of Child Psychiatry, San Diego, October, 1978.

Ciminero, A.R. Behavioral assessment: An overview. In A.R. Ciminero, K.S. Calhoun, & H.E. Adams (Eds.), *Handbook of behavioral assessment.* New York: Wiley, 1977.

Ciminero, A.R., & Drabman, R.S. Current developments in the behavioral assessment of children. In B.B. Lahey & A.E. Kazdin (Eds.), *Advances in clinical child psychology* (Vol. 1). New York: Plenum Press, 1977.

Conn, J.H. The child reveals himself through play: The method of the play interview. *Mental Hygiene,* 1939, **23,** 46–49.

Conners, C.K. Symptom patterns in hyperkinetic, neurotic, and normal children. *Child Development,* 1970, **41,** 667–680.

Cunningham, C.E. & Barkley, R. The interactions of normal and hyperactive children with their mothers in free play and structured tasks. *Child Development,* 1979, **50,** 217–224.

Cunningham, C., & Barkley, R. The effects of Ritalin on the mother-child interactions of hyperactive identical twins. *Developmental Medicine and Neurology,* in press.

Doke, L.A. Assessment of children's behavior deficits. In M. Hersen & A.S. Bellack (Eds.), *Behavioral assessment: A practical handbook.* Oxford: Pergamon Press, 1976.

Erickson, E.H. Play interview for four-year-old hospitalized children. *Monographs of the Society for Research in Child Development,* 1958, No. 23.

Evans, I.M., & Nelson, R.O. Assessment of child behavior problems. In A.R. Ciminero, K.S. Calhoun, & H.E. Adams (Eds.), *Handbook of behavioral assessment.* New York: Wiley, 1977.

Forehand, R., Cheney, T., & Yoder, P. Parent behavior training: Effects of the noncompliance of a deaf child. *Journal of Behavior Therapy and Experimental Psychiatry,* 1974, **5,** 281–283.

Forehand, R., & King, H.E. Pre-school children's noncompliance: Effects of short-term behavior therapy. *Journal of Community Psychology,* 1974, **2.** 42–44.

Forehand, R., & King, H.E. Noncompliant children: Effects of parent training on behavior and attitude change. *Behavior Modification,* 1977, **1,** 93–108.

Forehand, R., King, E., Peed, S., & Yoder, P. Mother-child interactions: Comparison of a non-compliant clinic group and a non-clinic group. *Behavior Research and Therapy,* 1975, **13,** 79–84.

Forehand, R., Sturgis, E.T., McMahon, R.J., Aguar, D., Green, K., Wells, K.C., & Breiner, J. Parent behavioral training to modify child noncompliance: Treatment generalization across time and from home to school. *Behavior Modification,* 1979, **3**(1), 3–25.

Forehand, R., Wells, K.C., & Sturgis, E.T. predictors of child noncompliant behavior in the home. *Journal of Consulting and Clinical Psychology,* 1978, **46**(1), 179.

Gardner, R. *Therapeutic communication with children: The mutual story telling technique.* New York: Science House, 1971.

Gardner, R. Techniques for involving the child with MBD in meaningful psychotherapy. *Journal of Learning Disabilities,* 1975, **8**(5), 16–26.

Gelfand, D.M., & Hartman, D.P. *Child behavior: Analysis and therapy.* New York: Pergamon Press, 1975.

Gittelman-Klein, R., Klein, D.F., Abikoff, H., Katz, S., Gloisten, A., & Kates, W. Relative efficacy of methylphenidate and behavior modification in hyperkinetic children: An interim report. *Journal of Abnormal Child Psychology,* 1976, **4,** 361–379.

Gottman, J., Gonso, J., & Rasmussen, B. Friendships in children. *Child Development,* 1975, **46,** 709–718.

Goyette, C., Conners, C., & Ulrich, R. Normative data on Revised Conners parent and teacher rating scales. *Journal of Abnormal Child Psychology,* 1978, **6,** 221–236.

Hackney, H., & Nye, S. *Counseling strategies and objectives.* Englewood Cliffs, N.J.: Prentice-Hall, 1973.

Hartup, W.W., Glazer, J.A., & Charlesworth, R. Peer reinforcement and sociometric status. *Child Development,* 1967, **38,** 1017–1024.

Herjanic, B., & Campbell, W. Differentiating psychiatrically disturbed children on the basis of a structured interview. *Journal of Abnormal Child Psychology,* 1977, **5,** 127–134.

Herjanic, B., Herjanic, M., Brown, F., & Wheatt, J. Are children reliable reporters? *Journal of Abnormal Child Psychology,* 1975, **3,** 41–48.

Hetherington, E.M., & Martin, B. Family inter-

action. In H.C. Quay & J.S. Werry (Eds.), *Psychopathological disorders of chldhood* (2nd ed). New York: Wiley, 1979.

Higgins, R.L., Alonso, R.R., & Pendleton, M.G. The validity of role-play assessments of assertiveness. *Behavior Therapy,* 1979, **10,** 655–662.

Hodges, K., Kline, J., Fitch, P., McKnew, D., & Cytryn, L. The Child assessment schedule: A diagnostic interview for research and clinical use. *Catalogue of Selected Documents in Psychology,* 1981, **11,** 56.

Hodges, K., Kline, J., Stern, L., Cytryn, L., & McKnew, D. The development of a child assessment interview for research and clinical use. *Journal of Abnormal Child Psychology,* 1982, **10,** 173–189.

Holland, C.J. An interview guide for behavioral counseling with parents. *Behavior Therapy,* 1970, **1,** 70–79.

Hughes, H.M., & Haynes, S.N. Structured laboratory observation in the behavioral assessment of parent-child interactions: A methodological critique. *Behavior Therapy,* 1978, **9,** 428–447.

Humphreys, L.E., & Ciminero, A.R. Parent report measures of child behavior: A review. *Journal of Clinical Child Psychology,* 1979, **8,** 56–63.

Johnson, S.M., & Bolstad, O.D. Methodological issues in naturalistic observations: Some problems and solutions for field research. In L.A. Hamerlynck, L.C. Handy, & E.J. Mash (Eds.), *Behavior change: Methodology, concepts and practice.* The Fourth Banff International Conference on Behavior Modification. Champaign, Ill.: Research Press, 1973.

Johnson, S.M., Christensen, A., & Bellamy, G.T. Evaluation of family intervention through unobtrusive audio recordings: Experiences in "bugging" children. *Journal of Applied Behavior Analysis,* 1976, **9,** 213–219.

Jones, R.R., Reid, J.B., & Patterson, G.R. Naturalistic observations in clinical assessment. In P. McReynolds (Ed.), *Advances in psychological assessment* (Vol. 3). San Francisco: Jossey-Bass, 1975.

Kanfer, F.H., & Phillips, J.S. *Learning foundations of behavior therapy.* New York: Wiley, 1970.

Kanfer, F.H., & Saslow, G. Behavioral diagnosis. In C.M. Franks (Ed.), *Behavior therapy: Appraisal and status.* New York: McGraw-Hill, 1969.

Kazdin, A.E. Artifact, bias, and complexity of assessment: The ABC's of reliability. *Journal of Applied Behavior Analysis,* 1977, **10,** 141–150.

Kazdin, A.E. Unobtrusive measures in behavioral assessment. *Journal of Applied Behavior Analysis,* 1979, **12,** 713–724.

Keller, M.F., & Carlson, P.M. The use of symbolic modeling to promote social skills in preschool children with low levels of social responsiveness. *Child Development,* 1974, **45,** 912–919.

Kent, R.N., & Foster, S.L. Direct observation procedures: Methodological issues in naturalistic settings. In A.R. Ciminero, K.S. Calhoun, & H.E. Adams (Eds.), *Handbook of behavioral assessment.* New York: Wiley-Interscience, 1977.

Kent, R.N., & O'Leary, K.D. A controlled evaluation of behavior modification with conduct problem children. *Journal of Consulting and Clinical Psychology,* 1976, **44,** 586–596.

Kent, R.N., O'Leary, D.K., Diament, C., & Dietz, A. Expectation biases in observational evaluation of therapeutic change. *Journal of Consulting and Clinical Psychology,* 1974, **42,** 774–780.

Kogan, K.L., & Wimberger, H.C. Interaction patterns in disadvantaged families. *Journal of Clinical Psychology,* 1969, **25,** 247–352.

La Greca, A.M., & Santogrossi, D.A. Social skills training: A behavioral group approach. *Journal of Consulting and Clinical Psychology,* 1980, **48,** 220–228.

Lytton, H. Observation studies of parent-child interaction: A methodological review. *Child Development,* 1971, **42,** 651–684.

Macfarlane, J.W. Studies in child guidance. I. Methodology of data collection and organization. *Monograph of the Society for Research in Child Development,* 1938, 3(6).

Mann, R.A. Assessment of behavioral excesses in children. In M. Hersen & A.S. Bellack (Eds.), *Behavioral assessment: A practical handbook.* Oxford: Pergamon Press, 1976.

Mash, E.J., & McElwee, J.D. Situational effects on observer accuracy: Behavioral predictability, prior experience, and complexity of coding categories. *Child Development,* 1974, **45,** 367–377.

Mash, E.J., Terdal, L., & Anderson, K. The response class matrix: A procedure for recording parent-child interactions. *Journal of Consulting and Clinical Psychology,* 1973, **40,** 163.

Mercatoris, M., & Craighead, W.E. Effects of nonparticipant observation on teacher and pupil classroom behavior. *Journal of Educational Psychology,* 1974, **66,** 512–519.

Mesibov, G.B., & La Greca, A.M. Ethical issues in parent-professional service interaction. In J.L. Paul (Ed.), *Understanding and working with parents of children with special needs.* New York: Holt, Rinehart & Winston, 1981.

Meyer, V., Liddell, A., & Lyons, M. Behavioral interviewing. In A.R. Ciminero, K.S. Calhoun, & H.E. Adams (Eds.), *Handbook of behavioral assessment.* New York: Wiley, 1977.

Morganstern, K.P. Behavioral interviewing: The initial steps of assessment. In M. Hersen & A.S. Bellack (Eds.), *Behavioral assessment: A practical handbook.* New York: Pergamon Press, 1976.

Nelson, R.O. Assessment and therapeutic functions of self-monitoring. In M. Hersen, R.M. Eisler, & P.M. Miller (Eds.), *Progress in behavior modification,* Vol. 5. New York: Academic Press, 1977.

O'Connor, R.D. Modification of social withdrawal through symbolic modeling. *Journal of Applied Behavior Analysis,* 1969, **2,** 15–22.

O'Connor, R.D. The relative efficacy of modeling, shaping, and the combined procedure for the modification of social withdrawal. *Journal of Abnormal Psychology,* 1972, **79,** 327–334.

O'Leary, K.D., & Johnson, S.B. Psychological assessment. In H.C. Quay & J.S. Werry (Eds.), *Psychopathological disorders of childhood* (2nd ed.). New York: Wiley, 1979.

O'Leary, K.D., & Kent, R. Behavior modification for social action: Research tactics and problems. In L.A. Hamerlynck, L.C. Handy, & E.J. Mash (Eds.), *Behavior change: Methodology, concepts and practice.* Champaign, Ill.: Research Press, 1973.

O'Leary, K.D., Kent, R.N., & Kanowitz, J. Shaping data collection congruent with experimental hypothesis. *Journal of Applied Behavior Analysis,* 1975, **8,** 43–51.

O'Leary, K.D., Pelham, W.E., Rosenbaum, A., & Price, G.H. Behavioral treatment of hyperkinetic children: An experimental evaluation of its usefulness. *Clinical Pediatrics,* 1976, **15,** 274–279.

O'Rourke, J.F. Field and laboratory: The decision-making behavior of family groups in two experimental conditions. *Sociometry*, 1963, **26**, 422–435.

Patterson, G.R. *Living with children* (rev. ed.). Champaign, Ill.: Research Press, 1971.

Patterson, G.R. Naturalistic observation in clinical assessment. *Journal of Abnormal Child Psychology*, 1977, **5**(3), 309–322.

Patterson, G.R., Cobb, J.A., & Ray, R.S. Direct intervention in the classroom: A set of procedures for the aggressive child. In F.W. Clark, D.R. Evans, & L.A. Hamerlynck (Eds.), *Implementing behavioral programs in educational and clinical settings*. Champaign, Ill.: Research Press, 1972.

Patterson, G.R., Cobb, J.A., & Ray, R.S. A social engineering technology for retaining the families of aggressive boys. In H.E. Adams & I.P. Unikel (Eds.), *Issues and trends in behavior therapy*. Springfield, Ill.: Thomas, 1973.

Patterson, G.R., Ray, R.S., Shaw, D.A., & Cobb, J.A. *Manual for coding family interactions* (6th rev. ed.), 1969. Available from ASIS National Auxiliary Publications Service, c/o CCM Information Services, Inc., 909 Third Av., New York, N.Y. 10022. Document No. 01234.

Patterson, G.R., & Reid, J.B. Reciprocity and coercion: Two facets of social systems. In C. Neuringer & J.L. Michael (Eds.), *Behavior modification in clinical psychology*. New York: Appleton-Century-Crofts, 1970.

Pope, B. *The mental health interview: Research and application*. New York: Pergamon, 1979.

Quay, H.C. Measuring dimensions of deviant behavior: The Behavior problem checklist. Journal of Abnormal Child Psychology, 1977, **5**(3), 277–287.

Quay, H.C., & Peterson, D.R. *Manual for the Behavior problem checklist*. Unpublished manuscript, University of Miami, 1975. Available from D.R. Peterson, 59 North Fifth Avenue, Highland Park, New Jersey, 08914.

Reardon, R.C., Hersen, M., Bellack, A.S., & Foley, J.M. Measuring social skills in grade school boys. *Journal of Behavioral Assessment*, 1979, **1**(1), 87–105.

Reid, J.B. Reliability assessment of observation data: A possible methodological problem. *Child Development*, 1970, **41**, 1143–1150.

Rich, J. *Interviewing children and adolescents*. London: Macmillan, 1968.

Rimm, D., & Masters, J. *Behavior therapy*. New York: Academic Press, 1974.

Roberts, M.W., & Forehand, R. The assessment of maladaptive parent-child interaction by direct observation: An analysis of methods. *Journal of Abnormal Child Psychology*, 1978, **6**(2), 257–270.

Roberts, M.C., & LaGreca, A.M. Behavioral assessment. In C.E. Walker (Ed.), *Clinical practice of psychology: A practical guide for mental health professionals*. New York: Pergamon Press, 1981.

Roberts, R.R., & Renzaglia, G.A. The influence of tape recording on counseling. *Journal of Counseling Psychology*, 1965, **12**, 10–16.

Routh, D.K. Developmental and social aspects of hyperactivity. In C.K. Whalen & B. Henker (Eds.), *Hyperactive children: The social ecology of identification and treatment*. New York: Academic Press, 1980.

Routh, D.K., & Schroeder, C.S. Standardized playroom measures as indices of hyperactivity. *Journal of Abnormal Child Psychology*, 1976, **4**, 199–207.

Routh, D.K., Schroeder, C.S., & O'Tuama, L.A. Development of activity level in children. *Developmental Psychology*, 1974, **10**, 163–168.

Rutter, M., & Graham, P. The reliability and validity of psychiatric assessment of the child: I. Interview with the child. *British Journal of Psychiatry*, 1968, **114**, 563.

Safer, D.J., & Allen, R.P. *Hyperactive children: Diagnosis and management*. Baltimore, Md.: University Park Press, 1976.

Simmons, J.E. *Psychiatric examination of children* (2nd ed.). Philadelphia: Lea & Febiger, 1974.

Stark, P., & La Greca, A.M. *Assessing children's social behavior: The social skills role play test*. Paper presented at the annual meeting of the Southeastern Psychological Association, Atlanta, 1981.

Strain, P.S., Shores, R.E., & Kerr, M.M. An experimental analysis of "spillover" effects on the social interaction of behaviorally handicapped preschool children. *Journal of Applied Behavior Analysis*, 1976, **9**, 31–40.

Straus, M.A., & Tallman, I. SIMFAM: A technique for observational measurement and experiment study of families. In J. Aldous et al. (Eds.), *Family problem solving*. Hinsdale, Ill.: Dryden Press, 1971.

Sullivan, H.S. *The psychiatric interview.* New York: Norton, 1954.

Tonick, I., Friehling, J., & Warhit, J. *Classroom observational code.* Unpublished manuscript, Point of Woods Laboratory School, State University of New York at Stony Brook, 1973.

Wahler, R.G., & Nordquist, K.M. Adult discipline as a factor in childhood imitation. *Journal of Abnormal Child Psychology,* 1973, **1,** 40–56.

Webb, T.E., & Van Devere, C.A. *Interviewing methodology for psychosocial factors in pediatrics: A search for attributes.* Paper presented at the meeting of the Association for Care of Children in Hospitals, Dallas, Texas, July 1980.

Wender, P.H. *Minimal brain dysfunction in children.* New York: Wiley, 1971.

Yarrow, L.J. Interviewing children. In P.H. Mussen (Ed.), *Handbook of research methods in child development.* New York: Wiley, 1960.

Yarrow, M.R. Problems of methods in parent-child research. *Child Development,* 1963, **34,** 215–226.

CHAPTER 7

Assessment of Children's Intelligence

JEROME M. SATTLER

In the field of clinical child psychology, the assessment of intelligence constitutes an important part of the diagnostic process. Although intelligence testing provides valuable diagnostic information, an intelligence test can never serve by itself as the sole vehicle for diagnostic purposes. It complements other assessment devices and must be used in conjunction with all available sources of data.

DEFINITIONS OF INTELLIGENCE

Anyone involved in the study of intelligence must eventually confront the problem of definition. Humphreys' (1979) definition appears to synthesize the major components of intelligence: *"Intelligence is the resultant of the processes of acquiring, storing in memory, retrieving, combining, comparing, and using in new contexts information and conceptual skills; it is an abstraction"* (p. 115). While there is no universal consensus as to one definition, a common thread appears to exist in the many definitions that have been offered over the years. Whatever else intelligence might be, it likely involves the cognitive (or thinking) domain as contrasted with the affective (or feeling) domain. Judgment, reasoning, and adaptation form the foundation of intellectual processes.

The material covered in this chapter is based on *Assessment of Children's Intelligence and Special Abilities* (2nd ed.) by J.M. Sattler. Copyright © 1982 by Allyn & Bacon. Used with the permission of Allyn & Bacon.

Three relatively recent contributions to our understanding of intelligence have been offered by Cattell and Horn, Jensen, and Das. Let us briefly examine these positions.

Cattell and Horn

Raymond B. Cattell and John Horn (Cattell, 1963; Horn, 1967, 1968, 1978a, 1978b; Horn & Cattell, 1967) have provided an innovative theory on the structure of intelligence. Their theory holds that there are two types of intelligence: fluid and crystallized. Fluid intelligence refers to essentially nonverbal, relatively culture free mental efficiency, while crystallized intelligence refers to acquired skills and knowledge that are strongly dependent for their development on exposure to culture.

Examples of tasks that measure fluid intelligence are figure classifications, figural analyses, number and letter series, matrices (e.g., Progressive Matrices), and paired associates. Crystallized intelligence is measured by such tests as vocabulary, general information, abstract word analogies, and mechanics of language. Tests that load equally on both factors include arithmetic reasoning, inductive verbal reasoning, and syllogistic reasoning. The Stanford-Binet, Wechsler Intelligence Scale for Children—Revised (WISC-R), Wechsler Preschool and Primary Scale of Intelligence (WPPSI), and Wechsler Adult Intelligence Scale—Revised (WAIS-R) contain measures of both fluid and crystallized intelligence. Tasks that measure fluid intelligence may require more concentration and problem solving than crystallized tasks, which tap retrieval and application of general knowledge abilities.

Fluid intelligence, in comparison with crystallized intelligence, is more dependent on the physiological structures (e.g., cortical and lower cortical regions) that support intellectual behavior. It increases until sometime during adolescence and then declines thereafter because of the gradual degeneration of physiological structures. Fluid intelligence is also more sensitive to the effects of brain injury. Crystallized intelligence reflects cultural assimilation, being highly influenced by formal and informal educational factors throughout the lifespan. It is only through the exercise of fluid intelligence that crystallized intelligence develops.

Jensen

Arthur Jensen (1970, 1980) has proposed that mental abilities fall into two major classes: associative (or level I) and cognitive (or level II). Associative ability involves rote learning and short term memory, and is measured by tasks involving digit span memory, free recall, serial learning, and paired-associate learning. Cognitive ability involves reasoning and problem solving and is measured by most tests of general intelligence, particularly those with tasks involving reasoning, problem solving, use of concepts, verbal and figural analogies, number series, and progressive matrices. Many tests of intelligence are likely to measure both levels, but different tests measure the abilities to different degrees.

The major difference between level I and level II is that in level I tasks there is little transformation of the input; a high degree of correspondence exists between the form of the stimulus input and the form of the response output. On the other hand, level II processes involve a transformation of the stimulus input; the input must be consciously manipulated in order to arrive at the correct output. The crucial distinction between levels I and II, according to Jensen (1980), involves a difference in the complexity of the transformation and mental manipulations that occur between the presentation of a given mental task and the response.

Das

An information-processing model, based in part on Aleksandr Luria's (1966a, 1966b) work, has been proposed by Jagannath Das and his colleagues as a way of categorizing cognitive ability (Das, 1972, 1973; Das, Kirby, & Jarman, 1975; Das & Molloy, 1975; Jarman & Das, 1977). The model has two primary modes. In one mode, termed *simultaneous processing* (or *simultaneous synthesis*), stimuli are arranged in a simultaneous manner in order to make a decision. Processing is in an integrated, usually semispatial form. Examples of tasks measuring simultaneous processing are the Progressive Matrices, Figure Copying, and Memory for Designs. In the other mode, termed *successive processing* (or *successive synthesis*), stimuli are arranged in a sequence in order to make a decision. Processing is in a sequence dependent, temporal based series. Examples of successive processing tasks are auditory short term memory, visual short term memory, word reading, color naming, and Digit Span.

The two modes of processing are available to individuals for their use according to the demands of the task and their past experiences. No hierarchy is implied, so that equal status is given to simultaneous and successive modes. Complexity, too, is not tied to either mode. The model also assumes that a given task can be solved by more than one method (or mode). The occipitoparietal region of the cortex is probably involved in simultaneous processing, whereas the frontotemporal region may be responsible for successive processing. It also may be that simultaneous processing of nonverbal information is carried out in the right hemisphere, whereas successive processing of both verbal and nonverbal information as well as verbal simultaneous information is carried out in the left hemisphere. Intelligence is viewed as the ability to use information obtained through the simultaneous and successive transformation procedures in order to plan and structure behavior effectively for goal attainment.

Comment on Definitions of Intelligence

A common trend emerging from contemporary views of intelligence is that both innate and developmental influences are seen to play important roles (Shouksmith, 1970). A "fluid" kind of genetically determined mental ability is seen as always being modified by experience. Measures of intelligence sample only a limited spectrum of intellectual ability, and the test responses given by individuals are related to their unique learning history. Contemporary views suggest that intelligence is a more global concept than was earlier imagined. Whatever position one adopts toward definitions of intelligence, it is still important to recognize that the unique learning history of individuals determines the ways in which they use their intelligence.

INTELLECTUAL FUNCTIONING: HEREDITARY AND ENVIRONMENTAL INFLUENCES

Heritability of Intelligence

An estimate of the heritability of a trait describes the proportion of the variation of a trait in a given population that is attributable to genetic differences in that population. The degree of heritability can range from 0 to 100 percent. If we say that the heritability of the Intelligence Quotient (IQ) is .60 in a given population, we mean that 60 percent of the variation in IQs in that population is attributable to genetic differences among the members of the population and that 40 percent of the observed variation is attributable to other sources. A heritability estimate refers only to population variance in a trait; it is not applicable to individuals.

A polygenic model is useful for understanding the heritability of intelligence. This model assumes that intelligence is the result of the combined action and influence of many genes. Techniques of biometrical genetics clearly indicate that intelligence is under polygenic control (Jinks & Fulker, 1970).

Heritability estimates for human intelligence are obtained using the correlations between groups of individuals of different degrees of kinship, such as between monozygotic and dizygotic twins. Heritability estimates must remain as *estimates* because experimental manipulations of human matings cannot be performed. Studies of European and North American Caucasian populations suggest that the heritability of intelligence varies from .40 to .80. As the genetic component between persons becomes more similar, their IQs also become more highly related.

A high heritability index does not mean that the environment is not important or necessary for the expression of a trait. Furthermore, a heritability index does not provide answers "to such questions as the etiology of an individual's handicaps, the origin of ethnic differences in test performance, or the anticipated benefits of compensatory education or other programs of environmental intervention" (Anastasi, 1971, p. 1037).

Environmental Influences on Intelligence

There are numerous environmental factors that may affect the development of intelligence. These factors include perinatal influences, birth weight, malnutrition, and familial influences. These factors not only interact with each other but also with genetic factors.

Perinatal Influences

Rubin and Balow's (1977) review of the literature suggests that perinatal anomalies do not provide a firm ground for making adequate predictions about school achievement or emotional status. Therefore, any attempts that are made to develop programs for early screening of potentially handicapped children based on perinatal anomalies cannot be justified on the basis of the available evidence.

Birth Weight

While low birth weight is associated with increased neonatal mortality as well as with relative mental and educational impairment in surviving infants (Wiener & Milton, 1970), there appears to be a demarcation between infants who weigh below 2,000 grams and those who weigh between 2,000 and 2,500 grams. Intellectual impairment is much more frequent in those below 2,000 grams (Caputo & Mandell, 1970). Improved care for premature infants appears to be leading to better levels of intellectual development (Francis-Williams & Davies, 1974).

Malnutrition

Although research into the effects of malnutrition on intelligence is difficult to conduct because of ethical problems, there is sufficient evidence, from both human and animal studies, to lead to the conclusion that early malnutrition contributes to the incidence of mental retardation (Birch, 1972; Kaplan, 1972; Lester, 1976; Lloyd-Still, 1976; Loehlin, Lindzey, & Spuhler, 1975). Vulnerability to malnutrition is greatest during the nine months of gestation and the first few years of life, the most critical periods in the growth of brain tissue. Nutritional stress can lead to learning difficulties by (1) affecting the central nervous system and (2) creating disturbances in social experiences. Malnutrition is thus linked to both organic changes (preventing the expression of the full genetic potential for mental development) and social learning factors (interfering with learning time, concentration, motivation, and social interaction). Nutritional inadequacy also increases the risk of infection and interferes with immune mechanisms. Much remains to be learned about the effects of malnutrition on learning, personality, and motor performance.

Familial Factors

The familial environment appears to play a significant role in affecting the growth of intellectual skills. While it is difficult to generalize on the basis of rather limited evidence, the following trends have been observed (Sattler, 1982). Children tend to acquire higher IQs with (1) higher socioeconomic status of parents; (2) superior play facilities; (3) parental concern that children get a good education; (4) parental harmony; (5) mothers who appear worrisome, tense, highly active, and energetic; and (6) a familial environment that fosters freedom to engage in verbal expression, direct teaching of language behavior, and parental involvement with child. Verbal, number, and reasoning skills are more susceptible to familial influences than are spatial skills (Marjoribanks, 1972).

Comment on Hereditary and Environmental Influences

The score on an intelligence test does not permit us to draw inferences about either genetic influences (or the biological substrate) or environmental influences (or the psychosocial substrate) (Humphreys, 1971). The independent contribution of these two components is extremely difficult to assess. Intelligence tests measure acquired behavior and yield an estimate of the child's current level of performance (or observed behavior). It is dangerous to make inferences from this level of behavior to another level, termed "innate potential." We cannot observe potential—all we can observe is actual behavior. Furthermore, performance on a test reflects the complex and pervasive cumulative effects of education and upbringing. It has not been possible to arrive at an index or estimate of innate potential by abstracting it from the child's interactions with the environment and from something measurable in the child's behavior. In the assessment situation, the focus should be on what the child can or cannot do and not on the child's innate potential.

A BRIEF SURVEY OF INDIVIDUAL INTELLIGENCE TESTS

There is a variety of individual intelligence tests available to clinical child psychologists. Some are omnibus tests—like the Stanford-Binet, WISC-R, WPPSI, and McCarthy Scales of Children's Abilities—that cover both verbal and nonverbal areas. The Slosson Intelligence Test is a crude screening measure of intelligence using verbal stimuli. Still other tests focus on nonverbal reasoning, such as the Progressive Matrices, Goodenough-Harris Drawing Test, Leiter International Performance Scale, Pictorial Test of Intelligence, and Columbia Mental Maturity Scale. Tests that focus exclusively on preschool children include the Extended Merrill-Palmer Scale, the Merrill-Palmer Scale of Mental Tests, the Bayley Scales of Infant Development, and the Infant Psychological Developmental Scale. The Bayley Scales provide Developmental Quotients rather than Intelligence Quotients. Other tests that purport to measure intelligence, but should be considered primarily as measures of receptive vocabulary, are the Peabody Picture Vocabulary Test—Revised and the Quick Test. Table 7.1 presents some of the major highlights for each of the tests cited above. We now consider some additional material for the Stanford-Binet and WISC-R.

Stanford-Binet Intelligence Scale

The Stanford-Binet Intelligence Scale provides both an IQ and a mental age. With the restandardization of the Stanford-Binet norms in 1972, mental age lost its meaning as a score that reflects children's ability to do things that children of a given age normally do. This is because the average mental age for a particular chronological age no longer numerically corresponds to that chronological age. For example, a 5-year-old child needs a mental age score of 5-6, not 5-0, in order to obtain an IQ of 100. Thus, "average" 5-year-old children have a mental age that is six months higher than their chronological age.

The changes in the relationship between chronological age and mental age for the 1972 norms indicate that the mental age is an MA in name only. The MA on the test is simply a raw score (Goodman, 1978). However, a conversion table can be used to obtain a true mental age (see Sattler, 1982).

Obtaining a profile of the child's strengths and weaknesses on the Stanford-Binet is a difficult task because the age level format of the scale does not permit a simple way of calculating significant differences between

those tests that are passed and those that are failed. However, some guideposts can be obtained by use of the standard deviation technique (SD) in connection with the examinee's CA and MA.

The SD technique is needed because differences between successive year levels do not mean the same thing throughout the scale. For example, the difference between year level II and year level III represents approximately a 50-percent increase in mental development, whereas the difference between year level X and year level XI represents approximately a 10-percent increase in mental development. Thus a 2-year-old child who obtains an MA of 3–0 receives an IQ of 147, whereas a 10-year-old child who obtains an MA of 11–0 receives an IQ of 107. The statement in a test report that "tests were passed on a year level one above the examinee's chronological age," while literally accurate, does not describe the level of mental functioning represented by the successes. For a 2-year-old, passing tests "one year above" may indicate superior functioning, while for a 10-year-old, passing tests "one year above" may indicate normal functioning. Therefore, such a statement needs elaboration by the examiner.

The use of the SD technique guards against overinterpretation of minor fluctuations or unwarranted interpretations of chance deviations in a child's performance. The SD technique is based on the premise that tests passed within 1 SD of the child's chronological age or mental age represent normal (i.e., expected) fluctuations in ability. Tests passed or failed within these boundaries, therefore, should not be considered as indicative of strengths or weaknesses.

Two different reference points can be used for the SD technique. The CA reference point is used for comparing the child's performance with that of children of similar chronological age. This is an *intergroup comparison* or normative group comparison. The MA reference point is an *intraindividual comparison* and is used for interpreting strengths and weaknesses in relation to the child's own level of performance. In the psychological report it is important to indicate clearly which refer-

Table 7.1 Highlights of Some Major Individual Intelligence Tests

Title, Author, and Publisher	Description	Norms Reliability Validity	Comment
Bayley Scales of Infant Development (Bayley, 1969) Psychological Corporation	Provides a Mental Developmental Index and a Psychomotor Developmental Index. Both Indexes are standard scores ($M = 100$, $SD = 16$). For ages 2 months to 2–6 years. Takes 45–75 minutes to administer.	Norms are excellent. Reliability and validity are satisfactory.	The best measure of infant development available.
Columbia Mental Maturity Scale (CMMS) (Burgemeister, Blum, & Lorge, 1972) Psychological Corporation	Child selects one drawing that is different from the others. Contains 92 cards. Measures general reasoning ability. Deviation scores are provided ($M = 100$, $SD = 16$). For ages 3–6 to 9–11 years. Takes 15–20 minutes to administer.	Norms are excellent. Reliability and validity are satisfactory.	Serves as a supplementary nonverbal measure of intelligence. May be less culturally loaded than other intelligence tests.
Extended Merrill-Palmer Scale (Ball, Merrifield, & Stott, 1978) Stoelting Co.	16 verbal and nonverbal tests grouped into 4 dimensions: Semantic Production, Figural Production, Semantic Evaluation, and Figural Evaluation. Provides percentile bands. For ages 3–0 to 5–11 years. Takes approximately 1 hour to administer.	Norms not representative of the country. Reliability data and validity data are inadequate.	Test has a unique way of organizing abilities. However, it does not provide an overall score or a precise way of evaluating a child's performance. Further research is needed to evaluate its usefulness.
Goodenough-Harris Drawing Test (Draw-A-Man) (Harris, 1963) Psychological Corporation	Child is asked to draw a man, woman, and self. Provides a Deviation IQ ($M = 100$, $SD = 15$). For ages 3–0 to 15–11 years. Takes approximately 5–15 minutes to administer.	Norms are excellent. Reliability somewhat poor, but validity is satisfactory.	A useful supplementary instrument for measuring cognitive ability. Can be used as a screening instrument. May be less culturally loaded than other intelligence tests.
Infant Psychological Developmental Scale (Uzgiris & Hunt, 1975) All information needed to administer test contained in text by Uzgiris and Hunt.	Contains 8 subscales based on Piagetian theory. Score is the highest number on each scale. For ages 2 weeks to 2 years. Takes approximately 40–60 minutes to administer.	Norm group limited. Reliability is satisfactory. More information needed about validity.	A useful addition to the area of infant assessment.
Leiter International Performance Scale (LIPS) (Leiter, 1948) Stoelting Co.	Age scale format. Measures intelligence by means of nonverbal items. Ratio method used to compute IQs. For ages 2 years to adult. Takes approximately 30–45 minutes to administer.	Norm group poorly described. Reliability and validity satisfactory.	Norms are outdated and standardization is inadequate. It serves as a supplementary measure of intelligence. May be less culturally loaded than other intelligence tests.

Table 7.1 *(continued)*

Title, Author, and Publisher	Description	Norms Reliability Validity	Comment
McCarthy Scales of Children's Abilities (McCarthy, 1972) Psychological Corporation	18 tests grouped into 6 scales: Verbal, Perceptual-Performance, Quantitative, Memory, Motor, and General Cognitive. Provides a General Cognitive Index (GCI) ($M = 100$, $SD = 16$). For ages 2–6 to 8–6 years. Takes about 1 hour to administer.	Excellent norms, reliability, and validity.	A useful test. Profile of abilities is an advantage. CGIs may not be interchangeable with Stanford-Binet or WISC-R IQs.
Merrill-Palmer Scale of Mental Tests (Stutsman, 1931) Stoelting Co.	38 verbal and nonverbal tests in 6-month intervals. Ratio method used to compute IQs. For ages 1–6 to 5–11 years. Takes approximately 30–40 minutes to administer.	Norms are seriously outdated. Reliability is poor, but validity is satisfactory.	Test provides some information about the cognitive ability of preschool children.
Peabody Picture Vocabulary Test—Revised (PPVT-R) (Dunn & Dunn, 1981) American Guidance Service	A nonverbal, multiple choice test that measures receptive vocabulary. Standard scores ($M = 100$, $SD = 15$) are available. For ages 2–6 through adult. Takes 10–15 minutes to administer.	Norm group is excellent. Reliability is marginally satisfactory. Validity is likely to be satisfactory, based on prior edition.	This is a vocabulary test, and should not be used to measure intelligence. Useful as a screening device for measuring extensiveness of vocabulary, particularly for children with expressive difficulties.
Pictorial Test of Intelligence (PTI) (French, 1964) Riverside Press	Contains 6 subtests: Picture Vocabulary, Form Discrimination, Information and Comprehension, Similarities, Size and Number, and Immediate Recall. Deviation IQs are available ($M = 100$, $SD = 16$). For ages 3–0 to 8–0 years. Takes approximately 45 minutes to administer.	Norms are excellent. Reliability and validity are satisfactory.	Serves as a supplementary nonverbal measure of learning aptitude for young children with motor and speech handicaps.
Progressive Matrices (Raven, 1938, 1947a, 1947b) Psychological Corporation	3 different forms measuring nonverbal reasoning ability. Task is to discover the missing symbol from matrices that are arranged in increasing order of difficulty. Percentiles are available. For ages 6 years to adult. Takes 15–30 minutes to administer.	No norms for U.S. children. Reliability and validity are satisfactory.	Main limitation is that it measures cognitive ability through one process—figural reasoning. Norms are needed for U.S. children (and adults). A useful supplementary measure of nonverbal reasoning ability. It may be less culturally loaded than other intelligence tests.

Test	Description	Norms/Reliability	Comments
Quick Test (Ammons & Ammons, 1962) Psychological Test Specialists	A nonverbal multiple choice test that measures receptive vocabulary. Provides mental age scores. Ratio method used to compute IQs. For ages 2-0 years to adult. Takes 3–10 minutes to administer.	Norm group is limited. Reliability and validity are satisfactory.	This is a vocabulary test, and should not be used to measure intelligence. Useful as a screening device for measuring extensiveness of vocabulary, particularly for children with expressive difficulties.
Slosson Intelligence Test (SIT) (Slosson, 1963) Slosson Educational Publications, Inc.	Age scale format. Items are similar to those on the Gessell and Stanford-Binet. Ratio method used to compute IQs. For ages .5 months to 27 years. Takes 10–30 minutes to administer.	No norms are described. Reliability and validity are satisfactory.	Test is poorly standardized and does not use a satisfactory method of computing IQs. It may serve as a screening device.
Stanford-Binet Intelligence Scale (SB) (Terman & Merrill, 1960) Riverside Publishing Co.	Primarily a global measure of intelligence. Provides a mental age and a Deviation IQ ($M = 100$, $SD = 16$). For ages 2 years through adult. Takes approximately 1 hour to administer.	Excellent norms, reliability, and validity.	One of the best intelligence tests available.
Wechsler Intelligence Scale for Children—Revised (WISC-R) (Wechsler, 1974) Psychological Corporation	12 subtests grouped into a Verbal Scale and a Performance Scale. Provides subtest standard scores ($M = 10$, $SD = 3$) and Deviation IQs ($M = 100$, $SD = 15$). For ages 6-0 through 16-11 years. Takes approximately 1 hour to administer.	Excellent norms, reliability, and validity.	One of the best intelligence tests available.
Wechsler Preschool and Primary Scale of Intelligence (WPPSI) (Wechsler, 1967) Psychological Corporation	11 subtests grouped into a Verbal Scale and a Performance Scale. Provides subtest standard scores ($M = 10$, $SD = 3$) and Deviation IQs ($M = 100$, $SD = 15$). For ages 4-0 to 6-6 years. Takes approximately 1 hour to administer.	Excellent norms, reliability, and validity.	One of the best intelligence tests available.

Note. Adapted from Sattler (1982).

ence point is being discussed; however, both reference points are potentially useful. Sattler (1982) provides a table that allows for a quick and convenient way of determining the band of year levels surrounding the child's chronological age and mental age that reflects normal variability.

WISC-R

Table 7.2 summarizes the results of studies that have compared the WISC-R with a variety of ability and achievement tests and grades. The studies indicate that when intelligence tests, receptive vocabulary tests, achievement tests, and school grades are used as criteria, the WISC-R has satisfactory concurrent validity. Median correlations range from the upper .30s to low .80s.

An evaluation of the IQs provided by the WISC-R and other tests indicates that, for group purposes, IQs on the Stanford-Binet and WISC-R are generally similar. The Slosson Intelligence Test, on the average, yields IQs that are about 5 points higher than those

of the WISC-R. The McCarthy Scales of Children's Abilities, on the average, yields GCIs (General Cognitive Indexes) that are lowered by 6 points. There are no trends evident with respect to whether or not group tests yield higher or lower IQs than the WISC-R does. The Peabody Picture Vocabulary Test generally yields higher scores than the WISC-R by about 3 points. The Quick Test has been found to be about 9 points lower than the WISC-R with a low ability group and 5 points higher with a normal ability group. Although many studies report small mean differences between the WISC-R and other intelligence tests, IQs should not be considered interchangeable for a particular child. Furthermore, one would not want to say that a child has problems simply because he or she shows fluctuations in IQ when tested by different scales over time.

A Successive-Level Approach to Test Interpretation

Many different kinds of information are obtained from a child's performance on the

Table 7.2   Concurrent Validity Studies for the WISC-R

Criterion	Median Correlations		
	Verbal Scale	Performance Scale	Full Scale
Stanford-Binet	.75	.68	.82
Slosson Intelligence Test	.81	.50	.61
McCarthy Scales of Children's Abilities	—	—	.68
Group intelligence tests[a]	.61	.59	.66
Peabody Picture Vocabulary Test	.66	.32	.58
Quick Test	.73	.74	.76
Wide Range Achievement Test			
Reading	.61	.35	.60
Spelling	.60	.26	.56
Arithmetic	.64	.48	.58
Peabody Individual Achievement Test	—	—	.60
Other achievement tests[b]			
Reading	.66	.47	.65
Arithmetic	.56	.48	.58
School grades	—	—	.39

[a]Group intelligence tests include Lorge-Thorndike, Otis-Lennon, Pintner Cunningham, Revised Beta, and Culture Fair Intelligence Test.

[b]Other achievement tests include California Achievement Test and Metropolitan Achievement Tests.

Note. Sattler (1982). Copyright © 1982 by Allyn & Bacon. Used with permission of Allyn & Bacon.

WISC-R and other Wechsler scales. In order to place the information in perspective, it is useful to follow a successive-level approach to test interpretation. This approach is valuable, especially for the development of hypotheses that are useful for clinical and psychoeducational purposes. This approach, formulated by Rabin and McKinney (1972), is presented in a modified fashion below. The five levels of analysis are as follows:

LEVEL I. THE FULL SCALE IQ.   The Full Scale IQ forms the basis for the entire evaluation. In most cases, it is the most reliable and valid estimate of intellectual ability provided by the scale. The Full Scale IQ is the primary or major numerical and quantitative index. It gives us information about the child's relative standing in the general population, as represented by the standardization group. The Full Scale IQ is a global estimate of the child's level of cognitive ability.

LEVEL II. VERBAL AND PERFORMANCE IQs. The second level focuses on the Verbal and Performance IQs and the extent to which there are significant differences between the two scales. The Verbal Scale provides information about verbal comprehension skills, while the Performance Scale covers perceptual organization skills.

LEVEL III. INTERSUBTEST SCATTER.   The third level focuses on deviations of the various subtests from the *mean* of the Verbal Scale or Performance Scale *and* comparisons between subtests. Hypotheses about strengths and weaknesses can be developed from these analyses.

LEVEL IV. INTRASUBTEST SCATTER.   The fourth level focuses on the pattern of performance within each individual subtest. Since the items are arranged in order of difficulty, deviations of successes and failures from the prearranged order of difficulty need to be evaluated carefully. For example, a child who passes the first item, fails the next four, passes the next one, fails the next four, and overall passes a total of four items is showing a different pattern from one who passes the first

four items and fails the remainder. In these two cases, each child receives 4 raw score points, even though the 4 points were obtained in different ways. The child with the markedly uneven pattern may have cognitive or attentional inefficiencies that should be explored further.

LEVEL V. QUALITATIVE ANALYSIS.   The last level focuses on the content of the responses, or qualitative analysis. Careful attention to unique or highly personal responses may be especially informative. Both verbal and nonverbal responses should be evaluated. For example, a child with paranoid tendencies may give querulous, distrustful, or legalistic responses, while one who is depressed may give slow, hesitant, and blocked responses, interspersed with self-deprecatory remarks.

Profile (or Scatter) Analysis

The cardinal rule for use of profile analysis on the Wechsler scales is that *profile analysis is dependent upon the presence of statistically significant differences between Verbal and Performance Scale IQs and between subtest scaled scores.* Thus, before any statements are made about whether the examinee obtained higher (or lower) IQs (or scaled scores) on one scale (or subtest) than on another scale (or subtest), significant differences between IQs (or scaled scores) should be present. Sattler (1982) provides a number of tables that indicate the critical values necessary to determine significant differences between various scores on the WISC-R and WPPSI.

The WISC-R has an advantage over the Stanford-Binet for the purposes of profile analysis. The items on the WISC-R are already grouped into subtests that might reveal specific mental operations. The subtest scaled scores permit ready comparisons and preparation of profiles. Scatter, the pattern or configuration formed by the child's subtest scaled scores, is not fortuitous. Several possible factors may account for the performance. Ideally it would be necessary to consider to what extent age, sex, racial or ethnic group membership, socioeconomic status, occupation, education, special training, social and physical environment, family background, and nationality have affected the examinee's performance on the scale. Only after the above factors have been considered should diagnostic interpretive hypotheses be sought to account for the examinee's performance (Ogdon, 1967).

The intent of profile analysis is to determine whether a child is more adept in one area or skill than in another. Such information is used by psychologists and educators to evaluate a child's strengths and weaknesses and to plan programs of instruction most suitable for the child's needs. If a child's profile on an intelligence or special ability test is flat and significantly above average, it likely indicates that the child is gifted and would profit from instruction that capitalizes on these exceptional skills. Conversely, a profile that is flat and significantly below average may be indicative of limited intellectual ability. Special instructional programs might best meet the needs of children with this type of profile. Profiles with peaks and valleys may be indicative of special strengths and weaknesses and may provide cues about the child's cognitive style and possible remediation efforts.

It is important to reiterate that, before any statements are made about cognitive strengths and weaknesses, it must be determined that:

1. The IQs on the Verbal and Performance Scales are significantly different from each other.
2. Subtest scaled scores are significantly different from the mean of their respective scales.
3. Subtest scaled scores (of interest) are significantly different from one another.
4. Cultural factors are taken into account.
5. Other important factors (e.g., sex, age, special training, and socioeconomic status) are considered in evaluating the test scores.

The possibility must be considered that scatter is simply a reflection of the unreliability of the individual subtest scores, examiner variability, or situational variability, rather than a reflection of cognitive strengths and weaknesses.

While profile analysis has difficulties, it is still useful to evaluate routinely the pattern of scores obtained by the examinee. The goal of profile analysis is not to classify or categorize children; rather, it is to seek clues about their abilities. Ideas generated from profile analysis must be viewed simply as hypotheses to be checked against other information about the examinee. Profile analysis may assist the examiner in arriving at recommendations for clinical treatment, educational programs, or vocational placement. For example, the functional nature of the child's learning problems can be better understood by use of profile analysis.

Many different patterns are, of course, possible. Some configurations have all subtest scaled scores within 3 or 4 points of each other, while other configurations have greater variability, with subtest scaled scores differing from each other by many points. Marked intersubtest variability may be due to temporary inefficiencies, permanent incapacity, or disturbed school experiences (Blatt & Allison, 1968). Psychologists believe that profiles showing much scatter may reflect more potential than profiles showing limited scatter (Sattler & Kuncik, 1976). However, research is needed to support this belief. You will, in each case, have to seek out the best explanation of the child's profile by using all of the test data and the case history material.

When a child's profile of subtest scores is within normal limits, it should not be considered diagnostic of any exceptionality. However, even when scatter is outside of "normal limits," it does not necessarily indicate the presence of pathology. It may simply be a reflection of the child's cognitive style. There is no evidence to support the assumption that pathology and scatter are necessarily linked.

INTELLECTUAL ASSESSMENT OF LEARNING DISABILITIES

Intelligence tests play an important role in the assessment of children with learning disabilities. Establishing whether or not a child has a learning disability is not a simple task. A significant discrepancy between ability (as defined by an intelligence test) and achievement (as defined by an achievement test) is currently one major part of the identification process (Department of Health, Education, & Welfare, *Federal Register,* December 29, 1977, p. 65083, 121a. 541). Another part in the identification of learning disabilities is an exclusionary process—absence of visual, hearing, or motor handicap; mental retardation; emotional disturbances; or environmental, cultural, or economic disadvantage.

On the Stanford-Binet, learning-disabled children may demonstrate difficulty with verbal materials, perceptual difficulty, poor recall of visual patterns, poor copying and reproduction of forms, and short memory span. Studying the child's pattern of successes and failures may provide clues to various kinds of cognitive difficulties.

Attempts have been made to determine whether or not various WISC-R (or WISC) patterns—such as Verbal-Performance discrepancy, pattern of subtest scores, and range of scatter—can distinguish learning-disabled children from normal children, behavior problem children, and mentally retarded children. The evidence indicates that these attempts have not been successful (Sattler, 1982). There is no one particular WISC-R (or WISC) pattern that is reliably diagnostic of learning disability. The WISC-R should be used to assess the child's intelligence and patterns of cognitive efficiency; it should not be used in the absence of other tests and information to make a differential diagnosis. Additional tests useful in the assessment of learning disabilities include the Auditory Discrimination Test, Bender Visual Motor Gestalt Test, Bruininks-Oseretsky Test of Motor Proficiency, Token Test for Children, KeyMath Diagnostic Test, Peabody Individual Assessment Test, and Wide Range Achievement Test. (See Sattler, 1982, for a discussion of these and other special ability tests. Also see Stetson on educational assessment, chap. 8 of this book, and Routh on learning disabilities, chap. 28 of this book.)

An inspection of 30 studies does indicate, however, some trends in the difficulty level of WISC and WISC-R subtests in heterogeneous groups of reading-disabled children. The average subtest ranks of inadequate readers, from easiest to most difficult, are as follows (Sattler, 1982): (1) Picture Completion, (2) Picture Arrangement, (3) Block Design, (4) Object Assembly, (5) Similarities, (6) Comprehension, (7) Vocabulary, (8) Coding, (9) Digit Span, (10) Arithmetic, (11) Information. The four most difficult subtests form the acronym ACID (Arithmetic, Coding, Information, and Digit Span). In addition, Verbal Scale IQs were lower than Performance Scale IQs. This discrepancy could be expected from the rank order data, which showed that the four easiest subtests were Performance Scale subtests. The low Coding score may reflect the failure to use an effective labeling strategy as a memory aid, thereby increasing the time needed to complete the task (Lyle & Goyen, 1969).

Investigators have been interested in determining the correlates of Verbal-Performance discrepancies in learning-disabled children. First, three groups usually are established, namely, (1) those whose Performance Scale is greater than their Verbal Scale by a specific number of points (e.g., 9 or more points) (P>V), (2) those whose Verbal and Performance Scales are similar (e.g., within ±5 points) (V = P), and (3) those whose Verbal Scale is greater than their Performance Scale (e.g., 9 or more points) (V>P). The three groups usually are matched on Full Scale IQ.

The findings of a number of different studies are by no means clear cut, although some trends appear to exist (Sattler, 1982).

1.   Learning-disabled children with P>V tend to do better on visual-perceptual tasks, complex motor and psychomotor tasks, and tactual performance tasks than those with V>P. However, they perform more poorly on reading tasks and tasks requiring language expression.

2.   Learning-disabled children with V>P tend to do better on verbal and auditory-perceptual tasks than those with P>V. However, they tend to be more impaired neurologically and have impaired finger differentia-

tion, constructional ability, and left-right orientation.

The above trends must be tempered by a number of other findings. First, they are more likely to hold for older learning-disabled children (e.g., 9–14 years) than for younger ones (e.g., 5–8 years). Second, not all investigators have been able to replicate these trends. For example, in two studies of learning-disabled children most of the neuropsychological measures failed to discriminate between the P>V and V>P groups (Larsen et al., 1973; Wener & Templer, 1976).

INTELLECTUAL ASSESSMENT OF BEHAVIOR DISORDERS

The WISC-R (and the WISC) appears to be a reliable and stable instrument for evaluating the intelligence of children who have behavior disorders. However, there are no WISC-R (or WISC) patterns that have been found that can reliably distinguish between various groups of emotionally disturbed children, although there may be greater variability of scores in some emotionally disturbed children (Sattler, 1982). There appears to be no qualitative difference in the structure of intellectual abilities of normal children and those with behavior disorders, as indicated by factor analytic studies of the WISC-R (DeHorn & Klinge, 1978; Petersen & Hart, 1979).

However, there is conclusive evidence that delinquents, on the average, obtain higher Wechsler Performance IQs than Verbal IQs (Sattler, 1982). Thus, on the average, the perceptual organization abilities of delinquents are better developed than their verbal comprehension abilities. But the fact that a Verbal-Performance discrepancy is likely to appear in samples of delinquent children does not mean that this pattern can be used as a diagnostic sign of delinquency. Many different types of normal and exceptional children may show this same type of discrepancy. The discrepancy may have no diagnostic significance, especially when it is not statistically

significant, or it may be a reflection of poor education, reading disability, bilingualism, cognitive style, or some other factor. Perhaps the Performance>Verbal pattern is a reflection of the learning handicaps that are a relatively frequent concomitant of delinquency rather than of delinquency itself.

INTELLECTUAL ASSESSMENT OF MENTAL RETARDATION

The term "mental retardation" describes a heterogeneous group of conditions characterized by low or very low intelligence and deficits in adaptive behavior. (See also chap. 26 in this book on mental retardation by Cleland.) The most widely used definition of mental retardation is the one proposed by the American Association on Mental Deficiency (AAMD) (Grossman, 1973): "Mental retardation refers to significantly subaverage general intellectual functioning existing concurrently with deficits in adaptive behavior, and manifested during the developmental period" (p. 11). This definition refers to a level of behavioral performance without reference to etiology. The key terms in the definition bear closer inspection.

1. *Significantly subaverage* refers to overall test performance that is two or more standard deviations below the population mean on a standard intelligence test.

2. *General intellectual functioning* refers to performance on a standardized intelligence test that measures, as far as is possible, general cognitive ability rather than one limited facet of ability, such as receptive vocabulary only or spatial-analytic skills only.

3. *Adaptive behavior* refers to the effectiveness with which individuals meet the standards of personal independence and social responsibility expected of individuals of their age and cultural group. Deficits in adaptive behavior are evaluated according to developmental age. During *infancy and early childhood,* adaptive behavior deficits are evaluated in relationship to sensory-motor skills, com-

munication skills, self-help skills, and socialization skills. During *childhood and early adolescence,* the focus is on the application of (1) basic academic skills in daily life activities, (2) appropriate reasoning and judgment in interacting with the environment, and (3) social skills. During *late adolescence and adult life,* adaptive behavior centers on vocational and social responsibilities and performances.

4. *The developmental period* is regarded as the period between birth and about 18 years of age.

The AAMD definition indicates that two criteria—level of intelligence and level of adaptive behavior—must be evaluated in making classifications. The classification of mental retardation is appropriate only when an individual falls into the retarded category in both intellectual functioning *and* adaptive behavior functioning. Intelligence is assessed through objective measurement, whereas adaptive behavior can be assessed clinically or by means of an objective scale (e.g., AAMD Adaptive Behavior Scale, Adaptive Behavior Inventory for Children, or Vineland Social Maturity Scale).

The AAMD definition has several implications. First, the assessment must focus on a description of *present behavior;* prediction of later intelligence is a separate process and fraught with many difficulties. Second, the contribution of individually administered intelligence tests is specifically recognized. Third, diagnosis is tied to a developmental process, with behavioral descriptions anchored to the individual's own age level. Fourth, it is recognized that mental retardation can exist together with other forms of childhood disorders: the definition "*avoids specific differentiations of mental retardation from other childhood disorders* such as childhood schizophrenia or brain damage" (Robinson & Robinson, 1976, p. 31). Fifth, the definition avoids the implication that mental retardation is irreversible. Finally, a diagnosis of mental retardation is not given when individuals are adequately meeting the demands of their environment.

Classification of Mental Retardation

The AAMD classification of mental retardation contains four categories—mild, moderate, severe, and profound—based on levels of intelligence used in conjunction with the classification of adaptive behavior. In using the AAMD classification system, it is important to recognize that the level of retardation arrived at by an intelligence test is dependent upon the standard deviation *(SD)* of the test. For example, if the $-2\ SD$ criterion is used, then the IQ just below the $-2\ SD$ point is 69 for the WISC-R (or WPPSI or WAIS-R), but 67 for the Stanford-Binet. These different IQs meet the criterion because the WISC-R (and the other Wechsler tests) has an SD of 15, whereas the Stanford-Binet has an SD of 16. Still other cut-off points may be appropriate depending on the SD of the test. While the WISC-R (and the other Wechsler tests) and the Stanford-Binet have been standardized so that the SDs are the same throughout the ages covered by the scales, such may not be the case for other instruments. It is therefore important that the examiner study test manuals carefully in order to become knowledgeable about the psychometric properties of each test.

Prevalence Rates of Mental Retardation as a Function of the Relationship Between Measured Intelligence and Adaptive Behavior

We have seen that the AAMD's definition of mental retardation requires that a child be below the population average by at least two standard deviations on (1) a measure of intelligence and (2) a measure of adaptive behavior. Because intelligence and adaptive behavior are not perfectly correlated, children who fall below $-2\ SD$ on an intelligence test may have adaptive behavior skills that do not fall into this range. Silverstein (1973) and Mastenbrook (1978) have reported how the application of both criteria affects the number of children classified as mentally retarded. Silverstein estimated various hypothetical prevalence rates as a function of the correlation between measures of intelligence and adaptive behavior. As can be seen in Table 7.3, rates increase markedly as one moves from a correlation of .00 to a correlation of 1.00. Nationwide prevalence rates, using −2 SD as the cutting score on each measure, range from 104,000 to over 4,500,000, depending on the correlation between the two measures.

Table 7.3   Hypothetical Prevalence Rates of Mental Retardation

Correlation	Hypothetical Prevalence Rate per 1,000	Hypothetical Nationwide Prevalence
.00	.5	104,000
.20	1.4	274,000
.40	2.9	584,000
.60	5.5	1,100,000
.80	9.8	1,965,000
1.00	22.8	4,550,000

Note. Per 1,000 population and hypothetical nationwide prevalence using −2 standard deviation cutting score for estimates of the population correlation between measured intelligence and adaptive behavior. These data are based on an assumed population of 200,000,000.

Adapted from Silverstein (1973).

Mastenbrook (1978) administered both the WISC-R and an adaptive behavior scale to a large number of children. Of those 300 children who obtained an IQ between 50 and 70, less than 35 percent had adaptive behavior scores that also were lower than two standard deviations below the mean. Consequently, the joint use of the two criteria—IQ and adaptive behavior—for the classification of mental retardation eliminated 65 percent of those who would be so classified by the exclusive use of the IQ criterion.

Using the Stanford-Binet for the Assessment of Mental Retardation

One of the Stanford-Binet's principal missions since its inception has been to be of aid to examiners in determining whether children should be placed in mentally retarded classes in the school. Over the years this purpose has been served remarkably well. The latest revision of the Stanford-Binet (Form L-M), like its predecessors, has been found to have substantial relationships with scholastic achievement, social maturity measures, and developmental schedules for mentally retarded children, thus indicating that Form L-M is a good predictor of learning and other facets of intelligence (Himelstein, 1968). Also, the internal consistency of Form L-M with retarded individuals appears to be satisfactory (Silverstein, 1969).

Stanford-Binet patterns that can reliably differentiate brain-injured from non-brain-injured mentally retarded children generally have not been found (Sattler, 1982). Similarities between the two groups are much greater than their differences. Overall, there is no single test pattern that clearly differentiates non-brain-injured mentally retarded children from other groups (cf. Sarason, 1953). Although the Stanford-Binet is not sensitive to factors that differentiate brain-injured from non-brain-injured mentally retarded children (cf. Himelstein, 1968), qualitative observations of the child's test performance and behavior may provide clues useful in making a differential diagnosis.

Using the WISC-R for the Assessment of Mental Retardation

The WISC-R is a reliable and valid instrument for use in the assessment of mental retardation. Factor analytic studies indicate that the factor structure of the WISC-R for mentally retarded children is similar to that for normal children, although some minor differences emerge (Sattler, 1982). It appears that the Freedom from Distractibility factor (Arithmetic, Digit Span, and Coding) is less stable for retarded children than for normal children. In general, however, the factor analytic studies suggest that there may be no qualitative differences in the structure of intelligence for normal and mentally retarded children.

The relative difficulty of WISC-R subtests for mentally retarded children, from easiest to hardest, is as follows (Sattler, 1982): (1) Object Assembly, (2) Picture Completion, (3)

Block Design, (4) Coding, (5) Similarities, (6) Comprehension, (7) Picture Arrangement, (8) Information, (9) Arithmetic, (10) Vocabulary. These ranks indicate that both Verbal and Performance Scale subtests are about equally placed in the distribution.

There is no evidence that the WISC-R can reliably differentiate brain-injured from non-brain-injured mentally retarded children. What is still needed, however, is a careful description of the child's performance. The results of the evaluation, in conjunction with other test results and qualitative data and case history information, are likely to be very useful in assessing the child's abilities.

INTELLECTUAL ASSESSMENT OF BRAIN-DAMAGED CHILDREN

Intelligence tests provide a standardized series of tasks that can be used to evaluate the cognitive and visual-motor skills of brain-injured children. Brain-injured children may show extreme variability in their subtest scores (Rudel, Teuber, & Twitchell, 1974). In some cases, there may be as much as a 30-point difference between WISC-R Verbal and Performance Scale IQs, while in others there is little difference. Subtest scores may range from considerably above average to below average or even retarded levels. Consequently, there is no single pattern of scores that reveals brain damage. Even though brain-damaged children may perform in the average range, they may have difficulties in sustaining attention and in filtering salient stimuli from their background (Hutt, 1976).

Intelligence tests permit the study not only of patterns of test performance but also of numerous qualitative indices that reveal difficulties with cognitive efficiency and control, such as perseveration, confusion, conceptual and reasoning difficulties, attention difficulties, memory difficulties, and visual-motor difficulties. Some of these difficulties may reflect compensatory adjustments associated with brain damage, while others are a more direct expression of the injury. Illustrations of how these indices appear on the Stanford-Binet and WISC-R are shown in the text by Sattler (1982). It is important to reiterate that on these and other tests the child's entire performance must be evaluated along with other available life history data.

Intelligence tests (and also other ability tests) can be varied in order to evaluate the adequacy of performance using different sensory modalities (Smith, 1975). For example, on the Digit Span subtest of the WISC-R or Stanford-Binet, the child's spoken responses can be compared with those that are written in order to examine the adequacy of different response modalities to the same stimulus (or test of mental function—short term auditory memory). A child might also be asked to copy a circle from a stimulus figure or to draw a circle from an oral request only.

The psychological evaluation that follows illustrates how an assessment of intellectual functioning contributes to the assessment of brain injury that resulted from an automobile accident. In this case, the psychologist used a variety of cognitive procedures to estimate the client's level of functioning, including both verbal and nonverbal measures. While the various measures yielded scores that were considerably different from one another, all scores were significantly below average. The case illustrates (1) that brain injury often does not produce a uniform pattern of deficit and (2) that objective measures of cognitive ability can be used to compare an individual's present level of performance with that which existed prior to the injury (i.e., the premorbid level).

Psychological Evaluation: An Automobile Accident Results in Brain Damage

Name: John

Birth date: May 3, 1964

Age: 13 years, 2 months

Date of examination: August 23, 1977

Date of report: August 30, 1977

Grade: 7th

Reason for Referral

John was referred for psychological evaluation by his attorney to determine if any mental impairment existed and how this impairment, if present, might manifest itself in John's future development.

Tests Administered

Wechsler Intelligence Scale for Children—Revised (WISC-R):

Verbal Scale

Information	2
Similarities	4
Arithmetic	4
Vocabulary	1
Comprehension	3
(Digit Span)	4

Performance Scale

Picture Completion	4
Picture Arrangement	9
Block Design	2
Object Assembly	6
Coding	1

Verbal Scale IQ = 55
Performance Scale IQ = 64
Full Scale IQ = 55 ± 5
Coloured Progressive Matrices
Peabody Picture Vocabulary Test, Form B (PPVT)
Bender Visual Motor Gestalt Test

Background Information

John was struck by a car in February of 1973 when he was 9 years old. After pulling through a rather stormy hospital stay, he was observed to be aphasic and hemiparetic on the right side. When he was well enough, John received intensive physical, occupational, and speech therapy at a rehabilitation center. Four months after the accident, a psychological evaluation was attempted. However, the evaluation was difficult to perform. John tired quickly, and his attention was inconsistent. It appeared at that time that his verbal abilities were well below average, with some performance skills closer to the average. He had an abnormal gait and his right hand was practically nonfunctional. On a second evaluation two years later, there was virtually no change

in his performance. John is currently attending school. His school records indicated that he was functioning at a high normal level prior to the accident.

Behavioral Observations

John did not remember me initially, but as rapport built he began to recognize me and remember that I was connected somehow with the rehabilitation center. He looked very much the same as when I saw him two years ago, although somewhat taller. John seemed more alert, attentive, and coordinated than in the past. The test results appear to be valid, as John was quite cooperative and patient.

John did not talk much, tending to give one-word responses to questions. Pencil-and-paper activities were executed with his right hand. Most visual-motor tasks were done slowly. When assembling multicolored blocks into designs, several rotations of designs were observed. Yet he never became frustrated and kept at the tasks. Many times John would surprise me with the sudden capability of solving complex problems. This was especially evident when arranging cut-up cartoon pictures into meaningful stories.

Test Results

John, whose chronological age is 13–2, earned a Verbal Scale IQ of 55, a Performance Scale IQ of 64, and a Full Scale IQ of 55 ± 5 on the Wechsler Intelligence Scale for Children—Revised. The latter score places him in the 1st percentile rank and is descriptively classified as Mentally Deficient. The chances that the range of scores from 50 to 60 includes his true IQ are about 90 out of 100.

The majority of John's subtest scores on the WISC-R are extremely below average. Only in one area, ability to arrange pictures into a meaningful arrangement, was his performance at an average level. Psychomotor speed was especially poor, as was his ability to define words.

He also performed poorly on the Coloured Progressive Matrices, Peabody Picture Vocabulary Test, and Bender Visual Motor Gestalt Test. John's performance on the Coloured Progressive Matrices was similar to that of an average 8-year-old and slightly better than his WISC-R performance. This test measures nonverbal or nonlanguage abilities and is closely related to some of the WISC-R Performance subtests, but it requires only pointing and eliminates almost completely the demand for a motor output.

His Peabody Picture Vocabulary performance was somewhat better, with a mental age level of 9–4 and a receptive vocabulary score of 78 (5th percentile). The PPVT does not require expressive language; only a pointing response is needed. The test measures receptive language ability and is sensitive to cultural factors and school learning experiences. Slightly better performance on this test magnified the expressive language deficit displayed by John.

His Bender-Gestalt performance revealed poor visual-motor skills. His performance was similar to that of 6-year-olds. The designs were drawn slowly and he had difficulty with curvature, angulation, and closure.

Impressions

John is a 13-year-old boy who is functioning at a mentally retarded level. He displays an expressive language disorder and visual-motor deficits. It appears that his deficits are a result of the damage sustained in the automobile accident. Improvement has been minimal since the initial evaluation four years ago.

The prognosis in my opinion is guarded to poor as to whether John can be a self-sufficient adult. Probably extensive rehabilitative procedures and care will be needed in the future. Certainly, special education will be necessary. Reevaluations are recommended every two years to determine his degree of progress.

INTELLECTUAL ASSESSMENT OF PSYCHOTIC CHILDREN

Intelligence Level in Childhood Psychosis

Level of intelligence plays an important role in the prognosis of psychotic children. It is a measure of the psychotic child's current overall level of organization and integration and is the best single measure of integrative functioning (Goldfarb, 1970). Frequently, psychotic children do not perform well on intelligence tests. Between one-third and one-half obtain IQs lower than 70, and less than one-quarter obtain IQs above 90 (Pollack, 1967). The critical variable determining the level of intelligence of psychotic children seems to be their age when they first come to the attention of mental health professionals: *the younger they are when first seen, the lower their obtained IQ.* Thus preschool children diagnosed as psychotic usually have lower IQs than those so diagnosed in preadolescent years. No doubt the more severe cases are seen earlier. (Also see Dawson & Mesibov, chap. 22 in this book, on psychosis in children.)

Level of intelligence is related to childhood psychosis in a number of different ways. First, there is some evidence that in a family predisposed to schizophrenia, the child with the lowest IQ is most vulnerable (Offord & Cross, 1971). Second, level of intelligence may be related to etiology: those psychotic children with nonorganic etiologies tend to obtain higher IQs than those with organic etiologies (Gittleman & Birch, 1967; Goldfarb, 1961). Third, level of intelligence may be related to symptom content, with the more intelligent psychotic children demonstrating more complex and involved rituals and compulsions than those with less intelligence (Rutter & Lockyer, 1967). Finally, the higher the intelligence, the better the prognosis.

On intelligence tests, there is no one pattern of test performance that is diagnostic of childhood psychosis. Some children differ little in performance from normal children, while others show considerable unevenness in functioning. In some cases, performance tests may be the only way to obtain an estimate of the psychotic child's intelligence level. The Merrill-Palmer test, the Block Design and Object Assembly subtests of the WISC-R, or some of the WPPSI performance subtests are likely choices. On the Stanford-Binet and Wechsler tests (and on other assessment instruments) illogical reasoning may appear in the child's response. Scatter on the WISC has not been shown to be a useful index in differentiating childhood psychosis from other conditions (e.g., Kissel, 1966).

Intelligence and Infantile Autism

In the past, IQs obtained from autistic children were often considered to be invalid. The hope was that with the right treatment, intellectual ability could develop to a normal level. Unfortunately, however, therapy with autistic children has not resulted in significantly improved levels of intellectual performance.

Research on autistic children's intellectual functioning points to several important findings (Sattler, 1982).

1. As many as three-fourths of autistic children obtain IQs that are in the mentally retarded range of functioning.

2. IQs obtained by autistic children have the same properties as do those obtained by other children. Thus, for example, (1) IQs show moderate stability throughout childhood and adolescence (correlations between IQs obtained over periods of 2–15 years have been found to range from .63 to .90), especially if the children are tested after 5 years of age, and (2) IQs provide a reasonable predictor of later educational attainments.

3. IQs fail to change markedly even after autistic children's social responsiveness greatly improves. Poor motivation, consequently, does not appear to be an explanation for autistic children's below average performance on intelligence tests.

4. Initially untestable autistic children later have been found to perform in a manner similar to that of severely retarded children. In addition, those who appear to be untestable may be testable when given items representing sufficiently low mental age levels.

5. IQs obtained by autistic children are higher when they have adequate conversational speech or adequate social relationships.

6. The cognitive skills shown by autistic children suggest a specific cognitive defect involving the use of language—namely, they have relatively good visual-spatial and memory abilities coupled with poor sequencing and language abilities.

On the basis of the above findings, it is important to recognize that autistic children with low IQs are as retarded as any other children having low IQs. The intellectual level obtained by autistic children, therefore, should not be dismissed simply as a result of some temporary impairment that is easily reversible.

The effectiveness of treatment, as determined by increases in IQs, also is related to the autistic child's IQ at the beginning of treatment (DeMyer et al., 1974). Treated children with IQs equal to or over 50 had a better chance of improving their IQs than untreated children in the same IQ range. However, treatment did not improve the intelligence level of children who had IQs at or below 40. The brighter autistic children who received treatment improved their (1) Performance IQ by about 13 points (70–83), (2) Verbal IQ by about 23 points (42–65), and (3) general IQ by about 17 points (57–74). No such changes were evident in the children with IQs below 40. If the research design had not separated the children according to IQ level (over 50 and below 40), treatment would have been found to have no effect at follow-up in the total group.

Comparison of autistic children who were functioning in the mentally retarded range with those functioning at higher levels has shown that both groups had (1) serious impairment in the development of social relationships; (2) delayed speech and marked impairment in imaginative or pretended play in early childhood; (3) some form of stereotyped, ritualistic, or compulsive behavior; and (4) disruptive or socially embarrassing behavior in public situations or in the company of other people (Bartak & Rutter, 1976). However, differences between the two groups also emerged. The autistic children who functioned in the mentally retarded range, when compared with the other autistic children, were more likely to show impaired physical responsiveness in infancy, delayed motor development, neurological dysfunctions (including epileptic seizures during adolescence), retarded language development, poor educational progress (including poor reading ability), difficulties in sequencing, impaired social behavior with adults, inappropriate behavior when in shops and when in buses and trains, resistance to environmental change, minimal concern with rituals, self-injurious behavior (such as head banging or wrist biting), hand and finger gestural stereotypes, and poor adjustment and limited gainful employment in adult life.

Thus mentally retarded autistic children showed greater language difficulties, more severely disturbed interpersonal relationships, and more disruptive behavior than autistic children of higher intelligence, who showed more sensitivity to noise and exhibited more rituals. Overall, the findings suggest (1) that different etiological factors may be present in autism, depending on the presence or absence of mental retardation, and (2) that level of intelligence is associated with autistic children's scholastic progress, social competence, work opportunities, neurological intactness, and symptom formation.

THE TESTING OF INTELLIGENCE: PRO AND CON

The decade of the seventies has seen the profession of applied clinical and school psychology attacked from both within and without. Accusations arose from ethnic minority groups that those "standardized tests" used to allocate limited educational resources penalized children whose familial, socioeconomic, and cultural experiences were different from those of white, middle class, normative groups. The very foundations of the profession have been questioned, including the tools that are used and the situations in which they are administered. Some members of minority groups maintain that intelligence tests and achievement tests are culturally biased and harmful to black children and other ethnic minority children. Others, such as Bersoff (1971), believe that many of the activities of clinical child psychologists and school psychologists are not in the best interests of the child. These include (1) labeling children, (2) testing children without their permission and without giving them full knowledge of the possible consequences of testing, and (3) removing children from regular classrooms and referring them to potentially damaging special classes. These criticisms have little merit, I believe, because they are not based on any foundation of research and merely skim the surface of clinical activities.

Critics fail to consider that tests have valid uses. Tests allow for accountability, for measurement of change, and for evaluating the effectiveness of programs. Assessment efforts help children obtain special programs that can contribute to their educational experiences, growth, and development. We must recognize that it is crucial for children of all ethnic groups to learn the basic cognitive and academic skills necessary for survival in our culture. Few of the critics have yet to propose reasonable alternatives to supplant present methods.

Clinical and school psychologists have reeled under the numerous attacks of the past decade. (Also see Ehrenreich & Melton, chap. 55 in this book, for further discussion of ethical and legal issues in the treatment of children.) Courts have issued subpoenas limiting the freedom of psychologists to use and select tests for evaluation and placement decisions. In the *Larry P. v. Wilson Riles* case, a federal court ruled that intelligence tests were culturally biased and could not be used for the placement of black children in educable mentally retarded classes. In contrast, another federal court ruled in the *PASE v. Joseph P. Hannon* case that intelligence tests were not culturally biased. These attacks have uncovered some real shortcomings. To label a Spanish-speaking child who does not speak English as mentally retarded, based on the administration of an English-language verbal intelligence test, is unconscionable and unforgivable. To keep poor records of the parental permission that acknowledged and authorized an evaluation is shoddy practice. To give tests to children without explanation and discussion is inconsiderate. These and other such practices must not continue.

It is important to recognize that intelligence tests, as presently constituted, cannot be divorced from the social order of our society, which values academic excellence over other kinds of excellence. Our intelligence tests, which measure success in school quite effectively, are value laden. They represent primarily such societal values as schooling, verbal abilities, and abstraction and concept formation skills. These are important skills in Western society, but they are not the only ones. Attempts are being made to find ways to measure and reward different kinds of skills (e.g., creativity) from those currently associated with intelligence tests (cf. Resnick, 1975). Such efforts are needed because our tests tap only part of the spectrum of human ability. Still, our current intelligence tests do their job

well. They predict success in school, and they measure some of the important skills needed in our industrialized society. Table 7.4 summarizes some of the major assets and limitations of intelligence tests, and Table 7.5 presents some important misconceptions about intelligence tests and testing.

The real importance of the IQ, as Jensen (1974) points out, is the fact that it has something of a threshold character—below some very low point on the IQ distribution people do not function well in society nor can any of their other possible latent talents ever be manifested.

There seems to be no other human defect...as severely limiting as a very low intelligence. Deafness, blindness, physical deformity, paralysis—all

Table 7.4   Intelligence Testing: Pro and Con

Pro	Con
1. The IQ has a larger collection of correlates that are predictive of success in a wide variety of human endeavors than any other variable.	1. Intelligence tests limit our understanding of intelligence.
2. Intelligence testing is the primary leveler preventing the classes from hardening into castes.	2. IQs are used to sort children into stereotyped categories, thereby limiting their freedom to choose fields of study.
3. Intelligence testing has revealed unsuspected talents in many individuals and has improved educational opportunity.	3. Knowledge of their IQs may inhibit children's level of aspiration and affect their self-concept.
4. Intelligence tests provide standardized ways of comparing a child's performance with that of other children observed in the same situations represented by the test items.	4. Intelligence tests fail to measure the processes underlying the child's responses.
5. IQs may be regarded as a measure of the child's ability to compete in our society in ways that have economic and social consequences.	5. Intelligence tests are culturally biased against ethnic minorities.
6. Intelligence tests provide a profile of strengths and weaknesses.	6. The single IQ does not do justice to the multidimensional nature of intelligence.
7. IQs are excellent predictors of scholastic achievement.	7. IQs are limited in predicting occupational success.
8. IQs measure the effects of changes associated with special programs, treatment, and training.	8. IQs are limited in predicting nontest or nonacademic intellectual activity.
9. Intelligence tests assess individual differences and provide useful reflections of cultural and biological differences among individuals.	9. IQs are misused as measures of innate capacity.
10. Intelligence tests are valuable tools in working with handicapped children.	10. Nonconventional, original, or novel responses are penalized on intelligence tests.

Note. Adapted from Sattler (1982).

Table 7.5   Some Misconceptions About Intelligence Tests and Testing

Misconception	Comment
1. Intelligence tests measure innate intelligence.	1. IQs always are based on the individual's interactions with the environment; they never measure innate intelligence exclusively.
2. IQs are fixed and immutable and never change.	2. IQs change in the course of development, especially from birth through 6 years of age. Even after 6 years of age, significant changes can occur.
3. Intelligence tests provide perfectly reliable scores.	3. Test scores are only estimates. Every test score should be reported as a statement of probability (or odds): "There is a 90% chance that the child's IQ falls between ___ and ___."
4. Intelligence tests measure all we need to know about a person's intelligence.	4. Most intelligence tests do not measure the entire spectrum of abilities that are related to intellectual behavior. Some stress verbal and nonverbal intelligence, but do not adequately measure other areas, such as mechanical skills, creativity, and social intelligence.
5. IQs obtained from a variety of tests are interchangeable.	5. While there is some degree of overlap among intelligence tests, IQs are not always interchangeable, especially when the standard deviations of the tests are different.
6. A battery of tests can tell us everything that we need to know in making judgments about a person's competence.	6. No battery of tests can give us a complete picture of any person. A battery can only illuminate various areas of functioning.

Note. Sattler (1982). Copyright © 1982 by Allyn & Bacon. Used with permission of Allyn & Bacon.

are not incompatible with achievement, athletic enjoyment, and self-realization. Very low intelligence, on the other hand, seems a different order of misfortune. (p. 434)

A central criticism, perhaps at the heart of many other criticisms, is that tests are used to allocate the limited resources of our society (Lewis, 1973). Intelligence test results are used to provide rewards or privileges, such as special classes for the gifted, admission to college or advanced study, and jobs. Those who do not qualify for these programs may readily direct their anger at the tests, because they see the tests as denying opportunity for success. Hudson (1972) points out that, for reasons that are still unclear, the IQ has come to be associated not only with an individual's ability to perform certain tasks, but with his or her essential worth as well: "To have a low IQ is seen as the equivalent of having low caste" (p. 15). This mystique surrounding the IQ must be squelched. It has no place in our society.

The IQ obtained from standardized intelligence tests can be extremely helpful in work with handicapped and severely handicapped children. Because the IQ is the best available long range predictor of outcome and adjustment, it provides teachers and parents with a helpful timetable for planning the child's progress. Furthermore, because intelligence tests provide some measure of the child's developmental limitations or impairments, teachers and parents can develop individualized curriculums within the limits of the child's level of development and developmental expectations.

We are accountable, as a profession, to the children we serve, to their parents, to the schools, and to the larger community. We must not ignore the many valid criticisms of the tests and test practices simply because we do not like them. We must continue to develop procedures and instruments that will best serve our clients. Procedures now available to protect our clients must be adhered to scrupulously. While none of us like our short-comings to be pointed out in private, much less in public, we must listen to our critics and make sure that we are following the best scientific and clinical practices. I believe that the discord of the seventies has had a cleansing and beneficial effect.

CONCLUDING COMMENT

The clinical child psychologist should be aware of the issues raised in this chapter. Obviously, one would not consider testing intelligence in children without adequate training and preparation. Thorough familiar-ity with test manuals and kits is necessary before any attempt is made to test children. Practice in testing both normal and clinical populations is highly recommended. The reader is referred to Sattler (1982) for special considerations in testing the intelligence of ethnic minority children, young children, learning-disabled children, mentally retarded children, brain-damaged children, and autis-tic and schizophrenic children.

In using intelligence tests (as well as other tests), the following guidelines are important to consider:

1. Tests are samples of behavior.
2. Tests do not reveal traits or capacities directly.
3. Tests purporting to measure a particu-lar ability or skill should have adequate reliability and validity.
4. Test results should be interpreted in light of the child's cultural background, primary language, and handicapping conditions.
5. Test scores and other test performances may be affected by temporary states of fatigue, anxiety, or stress; by basic disturbances in personality; or by brain damage.
6. Tests purporting to measure the same ability may provide different scores for that ability.
7. Test results should be interpreted in relation to other behavioral data, prior

test results, and case history informa-tion.
8. Test results are dependent on the child's cooperation and motivation.

Intelligence tests are part of the domain of norm-referenced measurement. They are use-ful in evaluating developmental changes, the effects of psychopathology, and the effects of various treatment and remediation ap-proaches. At present, however, our tests pro-vide limited information about the ways chil-dren learn or about ways to ameliorate their handicaps. Much has yet to be learned about tailoring remediation strategies to individual test patterns and profiles. Standardized intel-ligence tests need to be supplemented with assessment procedures and techniques that are designed to provide guidelines for treat-ment and remediation.

REFERENCES

Ammons, R.B., & Ammons, C.H. The Quick test (QT): Provisional manual. *Psychological Re-ports,* 1962, **11,** 111–161.

Anastasi, A. More on heritability: Addendum to the Hebb and Jensen interchange. *American Psychologist,* 1971, **26,** 1036–1037.

Ball, R.S., Merrifield, P., & Stott, L.H. *Extended Merrill-Palmer scale.* Chicago: Stoelting, 1978.

Bartak, L., & Rutter, M. Differences between mentally retarded and normally intelligent autistic children. *Journal of Autism and Child-hood Schizophrenia,* 1976, **6,** 109–120.

Bayley, N. *Bayley scales of infant development: Birth to two years.* New York: Psychological Corporation, 1969.

Bersoff, D.N. School psychology as "institutional psychiatry." *Professional Psychology,* 1971, **2,** 266–270.

Birch, H.G. Malnutrition, learning, and intelli-gence. *American Journal of Public Health,* 1972, **62,** 773–784.

Blatt, S.J., & Allison, J. The intelligence test in personality assessment. In A.I. Rabin (Ed.), *Projective techniques in personality assess-ment.* New York: Springer, 1968.

Burgemeister, B.B., Blum, L.H., & Lorge, I. *Colum-bia mental maturity scale* (3rd ed.). New York: Harcourt Brace Jovanovich, 1972.

Caputo, D.V., & Mandell, W. Consequences of low birth weight. *Developmental Psychology,* 1970, **3,** 363–383.

Cattell, R.B. Theory of fluid and crystallized intelligence: A critical experiment. *Journal of Educational Psychology,* 1963, **54,** 1–22.

Das, J.P. Patterns of cognitive ability in nonretarded and retarded children. *American Journal of Mental Deficiency,* 1972, **77,** 6–12.

Das, J.P. Cultural deprivation and cognitive competence. In N.R. Ellis (Ed.), *International review of research in mental retardation* (Vol. 6). New York: Academic Press, 1973.

Das, J.P., Kirby, J., & Jarman, R.F. Simultaneous and successive syntheses: An alternative model for cognitive abilities. *Psychological Bulletin,* 1975, **82,** 87–103.

Das, J.P., & Molloy, G.N. Varieties of simultaneous and successive processing in children. *Journal of Educational Psychology,* 1975, **67,** 213–220.

DeHorn, A., & Klinge, V. Correlations and factor analysis of the WISC-R and the Peabody picture vocabulary test for an adolescent psychiatric sample. *Journal of Consulting and Clinical Psychology,* 1978, **46,** 1160–1161.

Department of Health, Education, and Welfare. Assistance to states for education of handicapped children: Procedures for evaluating specific learning disabilities. *Federal Register,* December 29, 1977, Part III, pp. 65082–65085.

DeMyer, M.K., Barton, S., Alpern, G.D., Kimberlin, C., Allen, J., Yange, E., & Steele, R. The measured intelligence of autistic children. *Journal of Autism and Childhood Schizophrenia,* 1974, **4,** 42–60.

Dunn, L.M., & Dunn, L.M. *Peabody picture vocabulary test—revised.* Circle Pines, Minn.: American Guidance Service, 1981.

Francis-Williams, J., & Davies, P.A. Very low birthweight and later intelligence. *Developmental Medicine and Child Neurology,* 1974, **16,** 709–728.

French, J.L. *Manual: Pictorial test of intelligence.* Boston: Houghton Mifflin, 1964.

Gittleman, M., & Birch, H.G. Childhood schizophrenia: Intellect, neurologic status, perinatal risk, prognosis, and family pathology. *Archives of General Psychiatry,* 1967, **17,** 16–25.

Goldfarb, W. *Childhood schizophrenia.* Cambridge, Mass.: Harvard University Press, 1961.

Goldfarb, W. Childhood psychosis. In P.H. Mussen (Ed.), *Carmichael's manual of child psychology* (3rd ed.). New York: Wiley, 1970.

Goodman, J.F. Wanted: Restoration of the mental age in the 1972 revised Stanford-Binet. *Journal of Special Education,* 1978, **12,** 45–49.

Grossman, H.J. *Manual on terminology and classification in mental retardation* (Rev. ed.). Washington, D.C.: American Association on Mental Deficiency, 1973.

Harris, D.B. *Children's drawings as measures of intellectual maturity: A revision and extension of the Goodenough draw-a-man test.* New York: Harcourt, Brace & World, 1963.

Himelstein, P. Use of the Stanford-Binet, form L-M, with retardates: A review of recent research. *American Journal of Mental Deficiency,* 1968, **72,** 691–699.

Horn, J.L. Intelligence—Why it grows, why it declines. *Trans-action,* 1967, **5,** 23–31.

Horn, J.L. Organization of abilities and the development of intelligence. *Psychological Review,* 1968, **75,** 242–259.

Horn, J.L. Human ability systems. In P.B. Baltes (Ed.), *Life-span development and behavior* (Vol. 1). New York: Academic Press, 1978. (a)

Horn, J.L. The nature and development of intellectual abilities. In R.T. Osborn, C.E. Noble, & N. Weyl (Eds.), *Human variation: The biopsychology of age, race, and sex.* New York: Academic Press, 1978. (b)

Horn, J.L., & Cattell, R.B. Age differences in fluid and crystallized intelligence. *Acta Psychologica,* 1967, **26,** 107–129.

Hudson, L. The context of the debate. In K. Richardson, D. Spears, & M. Richards (Eds.), *Race and intelligence: The fallacies behind the race-IQ controversy.* Baltimore, Md.: Penguin Books, 1972.

Humphreys, L.G. Theory of intelligence. In R. Cancro (Ed.), *Intelligence: Genetic and environmental influences.* New York: Grune & Stratton, 1971.

Humphreys, L.G. The construct of general intelligence. *Intelligence,* 1979, **3,** 105–120.

Hutt, S.J. *Cognitive development and cerebral dysfunction.* In V. Hamilton & M.D. Vernon (Eds.), *The development of cognitive processes.* New York: Academic Press, 1976.

Jarman, R.F., & Das, J.P. Simultaneous and successive syntheses and intelligence. *Intelligence,* 1977, **1,** 151–169.

Jensen, A.R. A theory of primary and secondary familial mental retardation. In N.R. Ellis

(Ed.), *International review of research in mental retardation* (Vol. 4). New York: Academic Press, 1970.

Jensen, A.R. Review of T. Dobzhansky, *Genetic diversity and human equality. Perspectives in Biology and Medicine,* 1974, **17**, 430–434.

Jensen, A.R. The nature of intelligence and its relation to learning. *Journal of Research and Development in Education,* 1979, **12**(2), 79–95.

Jensen, A.R. *Bias in mental testing.* New York: The Free Press, 1980.

Jinks, J.L., & Fulker, D.W. Comparison of the biometrical genetical, MAVA, and classical approaches to the analysis of human behavior. *Psychological Bulletin,* 1970, **73**, 311–349.

Kaplan, B.J. Malnutrition and mental deficiency. *Psychological Bulletin,* 1972, **78**, 321–334.

Kissel, S. Schizophrenic patterns on the WISC: A missing control. *Journal of Clinical Psychology,* 1966, **22**, 201.

Larsen, J.J., Tillman, C.E., Ross, J.J., Satz, P., Cassin, B., & Wolking, W.D. Factors in reading achievement: An interdisciplinary approach. *Journal of Learning Disabilities,* 1973, **6**, 636–644.

Leiter, R.G. *Leiter international performance scale.* Chicago: Stoelting Co., 1948.

Lester, B.M. Psychological and central nervous system consequences of protein-calorie malnutrition: A review of research findings and some implications. *Revista Interamericana de Psicologia,* 1976, **10**, 17–31.

Lewis, M. Infant intelligence tests: Their use and misuse. *Human Development,* 1973, **16**, 108–118.

Lloyd-Still, J.D. *Malnutrition and intellectual development.* Littleton, Mass.: Publishing Sciences Group, 1976.

Loehlin, J.C., Lindzey, G., & Spuhler, J.N. *Race differences in intelligence.* San Francisco: W.H. Freeman, 1975.

Luria, A.R. *Higher cortical functions in man.* New York: Basic Books, 1966. (a)

Luria, A.R. *Human brain and psychological processes.* New York: Harper & Row, 1966. (b)

Lyle, J.G., & Goyen, J. Performance of retarded readers on the WISC and educational tests. *Journal of Abnormal Psychology,* 1969, **74**, 105–112.

Marjoribanks, K. Environment, social class, and mental abilities. *Journal of Educational Psychology,* 1972, **63**, 103–109.

Mastenbrook, J. Future directions in adaptive behavior assessment: Environmental adaptation measure. In A.T. Fisher (Chair), *Impact of adaptive behavior: ABIC and the environmental adaptation measure.* Symposium presented at the meeting of the American Psychological Association, Toronto, Canada, 1978.

McCarthy, D.A. *Manual for the McCarthy scales of children's abilities.* New York: Psychological Corporation, 1972.

Offord, D.R., & Cross, L.A. Adult schizophrenia with scholastic failure or low IQ in childhood: A preliminary report. *Archives of General Psychiatry,* 1971, **24**, 431–436.

Ogdon, D.P. *Psychodiagnostics and personality assessment: A handbook.* Los Angeles: Western Psychological Services, 1967.

Petersen, C.R., & Hart, D.H. Factor structure of the WISC-R for a clinic-referred population and specific subgroups. *Journal of Consulting and Clinical Psychology,* 1979, **47**, 643–645.

Pollack, M. Mental subnormality and childhood schizophrenia. In J. Zubin & G.A. Jervis (Eds.), *Psychopathology in mental development.* New York: Grune & Stratton, 1967.

Rabin, A.I., & McKinney, J.P. Intelligence tests and childhood psychopathology. In B.B. Wolman (Ed.), *Manual of child psychopathology.* New York: McGraw-Hill, 1972.

Raven, J.C. *Progressive matrices.* London: Lewis, 1938.

Raven, J.C. *Advanced progressive matrices.* London: Lewis, 1947. (a)

Raven, J.C. *Coloured progressive matrices.* London: Lewis, 1947. (b)

Resnick, L.B. Social and scientific conceptions of intelligence. *International Review of Applied Psychology,* 1975, **24**, 131–138.

Robinson, N.M., & Robinson, H.B. *The mentally retarded child: A psychological approach* (2nd ed.). New York: McGraw-Hill, 1976.

Rubin, R.A., & Balow, B. Perinatal influences on the behavior and learning problems of children. In B.B. Lahey & A.E. Kazdin (Eds.), *Advances in clinical child psychology* (Vol. 1). New York: Plenum, 1977.

Rudel, R.G., Teuber, H.L., & Twitchell, T.E. Levels of impairment of sensori-motor functions in children with early brain damage. (Swed) *Neuropsychologia,* 1974, **12**, 95–108.

Rutter, M., & Lockyer, L. A five to fifteen year follow-up study of infantile psychosis: I. Description of sample. *British Journal of Psychiatry,* 1967, **113,** 1169–1182.

Sarason, S.B. *Psychological problems in mental deficiency* (2nd ed.). New York: Harper, 1953.

Sattler, J.M. *Assessment of children's intelligence and special abilities* (2nd ed.). Boston: Allyn & Bacon, 1982.

Sattler, J.M., & Kuncik, T.M. Ethnicity, socio-economic status, and pattern of WISC scores as variables that affect psychologists' estimates of "effective intelligence." *Journal of Clinical Psychology,* 1976, **32,** 362–366.

Shouksmith, G. *Intelligence, creativity and cognitive style.* New York: Wiley, 1970.

Silverstein, A.B. The internal consistency of the Stanford-Binet. *American Journal of Mental Deficiency,* 1969, **73,** 753–754.

Silverstein, A.B. Note on prevalence. *American Journal of Mental Deficiency,* 1973, **77,** 380–382.

Slosson, R.L. *Slosson intelligence test (SIT) for children and adults.* New York: Slosson Educational Publications, 1963.

Smith, A. Neuropsychological testing in neurological disorders. In W.J. Friedlander (Ed.), *Advances in neurology* (Vol. 7). *Current reviews of higher nervous system dysfunction.* New York: Raven Press, 1975.

Stutsman, R. *Mental measurement of preschool children.* Yonkers-on-Hudson, N.Y.: World Books, 1931.

Terman, L.M., & Merrill, M.A. *Stanford-Binet intelligence scale.* Boston: Houghton Mifflin, 1960.

Uzgiris, I.C., & Hunt, J. McV. *Assessment in infancy: Ordinal scales of psychological development.* Urbana: University of Illinois Press, 1975.

Wechsler, D. *Manual for the Wechsler preschool and primary scale of intelligence.* New York: Psychological Corporation, 1967.

Wechsler, D. *Manual for the Wechsler intelligence scale for children—revised.* New York: Psychological Corporation, 1974.

Wener, B.D., & Templer, D.I. Relationship between WISC Verbal-Performance discrepancies and motor and psychomotor abilities of children with learning disabilities. *Perceptual and Motor Skills,* 1976, **42,** 125–126.

Wiener, G., & Milton, T. Demographic correlates of low birth weight. *American Journal of Epidemiology,* 1970, **91,** 260–272.

Wilson, T.S. Twins: Patterns of cognitive development as measured on the Wechsler preschool and primary scale of intelligence. *Developmental Psychology,* 1975, **11,** 126–134.

CHAPTER 8

Educational Assessment of the Child

ELTON STETSON

It is fitting that this chapter on educational assessment is included since frustrated parents are constantly seeking the aid of nonschool specialists for school-related problems. When a child fails in school, the agency most able to offer assessment—the school—is often rejected in favor of the physician or psychologist who may not be familiar with the practices of the school. The end result is that the information obtained by the nonschool specialist and forwarded to the school is often rejected, and the child is subjected to another procedure, more testing, conflicting diagnoses, and a delay in services.

The Education For All Handicapped Children Act Of 1975, better known as Public Law 94-142, has elevated educational assessment to a significantly higher level of sophistication than ever before. If the nonschool specialist is to be welcomed into the school family, he or she should possess adequate knowledge in at least four areas:

1. Current theory and practice in educational assessment.

2. The complex decision-making process schools must use in considering students for placement in special classes, usually referred to as the admission, retention, and dismissal process (ARD).

3. Specific assessment instruments, procedures, and interpretation patterns.

4. Procedures for reporting assessment

information back to the schools using appropriate scores and language that will be welcomed, understood, and used to the benefit of the student.

The purpose of this chapter is to acquaint the physician, psychologist, and other nonschool specialists with: (1) components and instruments utilized in the *ideal* education assessment battery; (2) a basic Level I assessment battery, usually referred to as a "screening;" (3) an in-depth Level II assessment battery known as a "diagnostic evaluation;" (4) interpretation of a Level II assessment; and (5) controversies and procedures surrounding the the determination of remediation strategies in education.

For the serious clinician who intends the active pursuit of education assessment, there are three additional references to consider. First, a copy of PL 94-142 would provide a full explanation of the law and can be obtained through most local school districts. Second, the article by Ballard and Zettel (1977) will aid in the interpretation of the law. Finally, the exceptional work of Salvia and Ysseldyke (1981), which evaluates and summarizes the research on most of the assessment instruments identified in this chapter, will be a valuable addition and will provide information that could not be included here. Their work is even more appropriate than that of Buros (1972) since it is more recent and contains many of the instruments not identified in Buros.

SCHOOL-ADMINISTERED EDUCATIONAL BATTERIES

Since one of the provisions of PL94-142 states that each state must create its own version of the Education Act of 1975, there is a variety of approaches to establishing educational batteries. It would be wise for the private clinician to contact the state department of education, local school district, or a local chapter of the Association for Children with Learning Disabilities (ACLD), all of whom have copies of the national and state versions of PL 94-142. For the sake of discussion, however, the intent of educational assessment is to evaluate some or all of the following general domains: academic achievement, intelligence, language facility, cognitive learning style, and adaptive behavior. Each of the domains is discussed separately here.

Academic Achievement

Achievement tests are devices that assess students' skill development in academic content areas (Salvia & Ysseldyke, 1981, p. 131). For the most part, educators are interested in measuring achievement in reading, mathematics, and spelling. Achievement tests are of two types: screening tests that convey global or general measures of achievement and diagnostic achievement tests that attempt to identify specific subskills within a content area so that strengths and weaknesses can be delineated.

Screening Tests of Achievement

There are relatively few screening tests available that are individually administered. The most often used include the Wide Range Achievement Test (WRAT) (Jastak & Jastak, 1978), the Peabody Individual Achievement Test (PIAT) (Dunn & Markwardt, 1970), and the Woodcock-Johnson Psychoeducational Battery (W-J) (Woodcock & Johnson, 1977). Table 8.1 identifies the subtests for each screening test as well as the specific content areas measured by each.

The WRAT is the oldest of the three tests and requires the least time for administration (15–20 minutes). It includes a word-calling reading test, a written spelling test, and a 10-minute paper-and-pencil math computation test. Like most new tests, the PIAT enjoyed wide use when it first appeared. However, many now consider the PIAT to be the least desirable and least reliable of the tests currently in use. The Woodcock-Johnson is the most recent test to gain popularity and appears to have avoided many of the negative features of the other tests.

Diagnostic Tests in Achievement

Since most screening tests predict achievement in reading, spelling, and mathematics, diagnostic tests are always needed when the screening indicates possible deficiencies. Diagnostic tests break a content area into small components, examine each separately, and assist the clinician in determining the specific components that might be causing low achievement.

The primary diagnostic test used in reading is the Woodcock Reading Mastery Test (WRMT) (Woodcock, 1973). There are two diagnostic math tests frequently used. The most popular is the KeyMath Diagnostic Arithmetic Test (KeyMath) (Connolly, Nachtman, & Pritchett, 1971), while the Kraner Pre-School Math Inventory (KPMI) (Kraner, 1976) is often used with children at the preschool through second grade level. The Test of Written Spelling-TWS (Larsen & Hammill, 1976) and the Reading-Spelling Vocabulary Proficiency Test-RSVPT (Stetson, 1981) provide different approaches to spelling diagnosis. Table 8.2 illustrates each of these instruments along with age ranges and subtest titles.

All of the diagnostic tests are administered individually except for the two spelling tests that can be given individually or in groups. While both spelling tests employ written spelling, only the RSVPT measures the individual's competence in spelling the most frequently used words in the English language. From the results of the RSVPT, students can be placed into one of the 60 lessons of the 900-word Reading-Spelling Vocabulary Program for direct instruction.

Table 8.1   Three Achievement Screening Tests, Age Range, Substest Recommended, and Description

Screening Test	Subtests Recommended	Specific Content Measured	Age Range
Wide Range Achievement Test (WRAT) (Jastak & Jastak, 1978)	Reading	Reading words in isolation	5–64
	Math	Oral and written computation	
	Spelling	Written from dictation	
Peabody Individual Achievement Test (PIAT) (Dunn & Markwardt, 1970)	Reading Recognition	Pronouncing letters and words in isolation	5–18
	Reading Comprehension	Silent reading with multiple choice pictures to select	
	Math	Multiple choice, all verbal; no computation	
	Spelling	Selecting 1 of 4 spellings that is correct	
Woodcock-Johnson Psycho-educational Battery (W-J) (Woodcock & Johnson, 1977)	#13 Letter/word identification	Naming letters and words in isolation	3–adult
	#15 Passage comprehension	Silent reading comprehension	
	#Calculation	Computation in math	
	#17 Applied problems	Multiple choice verbal math problems	
	#18 Dictation	Written from dictation	

Intelligence Tests

While no other area of assessment has created as much controversy as intelligence testing, there remains one observation that leaves little room for debate: students who score low on tests of intelligence tend to score comparatively low on tests of achievement. That relationship between performance on IQ tests and on achievement tests is significantly high and difficult to deny. Whether IQ tests actually measure "intelligence" or whether they merely predict academic aptitude or potential for success in an academic setting is a controversy that continues.

At the University of Houston Diagnostic Learning Center where hundreds of children are evaluated annually, parents are told that children possess a variety of intelligences. However, the kind of intelligence measured by the Wechsler series or other intelligence tests is the type that seems to predict how the child will function in an academic setting. From the obtained scores it is possible to predict the chances for success or failure by comparing scores with other students of the same age who have succeeded or failed. It is also possible to compare *potential* achievement (using scores on IQ tests) with *actual* achievement (using scores on achievement tests) to determine whether the student is achieving up to potential and whether remediation would benefit the student.

Table 8.3 illustrates some of the intelligence tests that are typically used by diagnosticians. The Slosson Intelligence Test (Slos-

Table 8.2   Diagnostic Achievement Tests Most Often Used in Educational Diagnosing in the Content Areas of Reading, Mathematics, and Spelling

Diagnostic Achievement Tests	Age Range	Specific Subtests
Reading		
Woodcock Reading Mastery Test (WRMT) (Woodcock, 1973)	Grade 6–12	*5 Subtests* Letter Identification, Word Identification, Word Attack, Word Comprehension, Passage Comprehension
Mathematics		
Key Math Diagnostic Arithmetic Tests (Connolly et al., 1976)	Grade K–8	*3 Content Tests* numeration, fractions, geometry & symbols *6 Operations Tests* addition, subtraction, division, multiplication, mental computation, numerical reasoning *5 Application Tests* word problems, missing elements, money, measurement, and time
Kraner Preschool Math Inventory (Kraner, 1976)	Ages 3–6	*7 Tests* counting, cardinal numbers, quantities, sequence, position, direction, and geometry/measurement
Spelling		
Test of Written Spelling (Larsen & Hammill, 1976)	Grade 1–12	Tests ability with predictable spelling (regular spellings) and unpredictable spelling (nonregular spelling)
Reading-Spelling Vocabulary Proficiency Test (RSVPT) (Stetson, 1981)	Grade 1–14	Measures ability to spell the 900 most often written words in the English language

son, 1971) is used primarily as a "screening" test of intelligence. The WPPSI, WISC-R, and WAIS (Wechsler, 1955; 1967; 1974;) are the popular IQ tests for most special placement purposes. The Stanford-Binet (Terman & Merrill, 1973) is used primarily as a backup and as a means to corroborate findings with other tests. An emerging IQ test for the young child is the McCarthy Scales (McCarthy, 1972). It is predicted by many to become more widely used than the WPPSI. For students with possible language problems, several non-verbal measures of intelligence are available. The Columbia Mental Maturity Scale (Burgemeister, Blum, & Lorge, 1972), the Arthur Adaptation of the Leiter International Performance Scale (Arthur, 1950), and the Peabody Picture Vocabulary Test—Revised (Dunn, 1981) are often used in cases where the verbal IQ might be depressed because of language problems.

Most of the discussion in this section will be limited to the use and interpretation of the Slosson Intelligence Test (SIT) and the

Table 8.3   Intelligence Tests Used Most Often by Educational Diagnosticians—Listed by Type, Age Range, and Description

Type and Title of Test	Age Range	Description
Screening IQ Tests		
Slosson Intelligence Test (SIT) (Slosson, 1971)	Infancy to adult	Measure of verbal or expressive language
General IQ Tests		
Wechsler Intelligence Scale For Children—Revised (WISC-R) (Wechsler, 1974)	6–16	12 tests measuring verbal, performance, and full scale IQ
Wechsler Preschool and Primary Scale of Intelligence (WPPSI) (Wechsler, 1967)	4–6½	11 tests measuring verbal, performance, and full scale IQ
Wechsler Adult Intelligence Scale (WAIS) (Wechsler, 1955)	16 & over	11 tests measuring verbal, performance, and full scale IQ
McCarthy Scales of Children's Abilities (MSCA) (McCarthy, 1972)	2½–8½	18 tests measuring verbal, perceptual-performance, quantitative, motor, memory, & general cognitive
Stanford-Binet Intelligence Scales (Terman & Merrill, 1973)	Preschool to Adult	Verbal IQ
Tests for Special Populations		
Peabody Picture Vocabulary Test (PPVT) (Dunn, 1981)	2½–18	Receptive or nonverbal abilities
Leiter International Performance Scale—Arthur Adaptation Version (AALIPS) (Arthur, 1950)	2–12	Nonverbal IQ
Columbia Mental Maturity Scale (Burgemeister et al., 1972)	3½–10	Nonverbal IQ

Wechsler Intelligence Scale For Children—Revised (WISC-R) because they are used most often with school age children by educational diagnosticians and other school personnel. It is imperative that users of intelligence tests review Sattler's chapter on Intellectual Assessment of the Child. In this chapter, I intend to limit my discussion to the use of IQ scores to: (1) predict academic potential, (2) determine elegibility for placement into special classes, and (3) analyze factors of intelligence associated with cognitive skills that are essential in an academic environment.

Using IQ Scores to Predict Potential Achievement

Many schools use IQ scores to determine the potential achievement level of students. Bond and Tinker (1967) suggested a formula to calculate such a prediction.

$$\text{Potential Achievement (PA)} = \left[\frac{\text{IQ}}{100} \times \text{Yrs. in School}\right] + 1$$

For example, Joseph has a measured IQ of 87 and is in grade 5.5. Since he has completed four years of school plus five months of the fifth year, his "years in school" is 4.5 (kindergarten does not count). A simple substitution of scores will deterimine PA.

$$PA = \left[\frac{87}{100} \times 4.5 \right] + 1 = \left[.87 \times 4.5 \right]$$

$$+ 1 = 3.9 + 1 = 4.9$$

While Joseph is in grade 5.5, his potential achievement, based solely on IQ, is grade 4.9 or six months below his actual grade placement (GP).

The Stetson formula for determining potential achievement is presented as well because of its simplicity:

$$PA = \frac{IQ}{100} \times \text{Grade Placement (GP)}$$

$$PA = \frac{87}{100} \times 5.5 = .87 \times 5.5 = 4.8$$

The variance in PA between the two formulae is only one month in the above example. Whether one uses the Bond and Tinker or the Stetson formula is a matter of personal choice since there will be no more than one or two months variance in most cases. The primary purpose for determining potential is to assist the clinician, family, and school in comparing actual achievement scores with the grade level of the student and to compare actual achievement with potential achievement. While teachers tend to compare students' work with the work of others in their classes and against the expectations for that grade level, the most logical comparison is between a student's *actual* achievement and his or her *potential* achievement.

If the SIT is used to determine PA, there is only one IQ score available to use. However, when the WISC-R is used, it is advisable to use either the Verbal IQ (minus the Digit Span score) or the Full Scale IQ (minus the Digit Span and Coding scores), whichever is higher. There is little question that achievement in school is associated more with verbal than with performance intelligence. Using the Performance IQ only is questionable, particularly when the Performance IQ is significantly lower than the Verbal IQ (15 points or more). A large P>V difference may indicate language deficits which are severe enough that a student may not be able to compete successfully in an academic setting even though the difference is attributed to cultural, psychological, or genetic problems. The interpretation of differences between V and P is also controversial. Chapter 2 in Kaufman (1975) and chapter 14 in Sattler (1974) will provide the reader with a wealth of knowledge concerning these issues.

Using IQ Scores in Reporting

Although an IQ score is necessary to determine PA, IQ "range" is far more meaningful and honest when reporting data in case studies or during conferences with parents and school personnel. Sattler (1974, pp. 554–556) reports error variance or "band of error" at various confidence intervals. Listed in Table 8.4 are the bands of error for various confidence intervals for the Full-Scale WISC-R only.

Educational diagnosticians and others tend to report IQ ranges at the 68 percent confidence (±3). This is a rather narrow window that raises many questions of validity when retesting occurs using the same instrument. A more reasonable confidence level is 85 to 90 percent intervals where the error band is ±5 points. Reporting an IQ score of 85 using a band of error of ±5 means that the IQ range is 80<85<90. This manner of reporting helps the reader understand that, in the majority of cases, the IQ should range between 80 (below average) and 90 (average). The lower range is more than one standard deviation below the

Table 8.4 Bands of Error at Various Confidence Levels for Wechsler Intelligence Scale for Children—Revised

Confidence Interval	Band of Error
68%	±3
85%	±5
90%	±5
95%	±6
99%	±8

Table 8.5   Combination and Modification of IQ Classifications

IQ	Classification	Range of Percentile Rank	Percent in Sample
135 +	Very superior	98–99	2
120–134	Superior	91–98	8
110–119	High average	75–90	16
90–109	Average	25–74	50
80– 89	Low average	9–24	16
70– 79	Borderline	2– 8	6
69 & below	Mentally retarded	.1– 1	2

mean while the upper range is less than one s.d. below the mean.

Interpreting an IQ score is very important. Joseph's family probably knows little about the concept of IQ, what an "87" means, or what to expect from their child in an academic setting. Wechsler (1974, p. 26) and Slosson (1971, p. i) have grouped IQ scores into categories. Because there is some disagreement in the highest and lowest categories, Table 8.5 represents a combination and slight modification of their classification systems.

Using the classification system above, one can easily identify the category, percentile range, and the percentage of students in the sample population who scored in the same IQ range. However, while 92 percent of the population obtained an IQ of 80 or higher and are classified as "low average" or better, it is not reasonable to believe that 92 percent of children perform low average or better in school. In fact, present day curricula have been stepped up, more pressure is placed on schools to increase achievement, and the majority of textbooks are written from one-and-a-half to three grade levels above the grade for which they were prepared, particularly in social and natural science textbooks. These problems, along with crowded classrooms that cut down on individual teacher-student interaction, place the "average" student at a disadvantage. The average classroom now has a "high average" curriculum. One of the great mistakes in counseling families and teachers is to evaluate the child as "average" and predict that the student is capable of "A" work without evaluating the curriculum that the student is

expected to master. Making such judgments places pressure on the child to produce at a level that may be unreasonable when the problem lies with the program.

Table 8.6 is an attempt to adjust for these problems by regrouping IQ scores into a more realistic classification system for interpreting IQ scores and for developing prediction or prognosis statements about the child's chances for success in the school in which he or she is enrolled—private or public, average or accelerated.

Using IQ Scores For Special Placement

In addition to the use of IQ scores to determine potential achievement and reporting predictions for success, IQ scores are often used to determine whether or not a student will qualify for placement into special classes. Generally, a student must (1) have an IQ of below 70 or (2) function two academic years or more below his or her potential achievement before special placement is considered. In Joseph's case, his IQ of 87 is too high to qualify him for special classes for the mentally retarded, and his actual achievement will need to be at a grade equivalent of 2.9 or lower in order to place him into classes for the learning disabled or other special help classes.

Complete details for using the combination of IQ and achievement scores in determining special placement are included later in this chapter and will not be pursued here.

Using Subtest Scores For Factor Analysis

Another advantage of intelligence tests like the Wechsler tests is the factor analysis that

Table 8.6   A Classification System for Interpreting IQ Scores

IQ Range	Prediction Statements
130 + (Superior)	Normally have little difficulty competing in average or accelerated programs; usually achieve above grade placement; often qualify for classes for the gifted; respond rapidly to remediation when needed.
115–129 (Above average)	Usually compete comfortably in an accelerated program; capable of earning As in average programs; respond well to remediation when needed.
105–114 (High average)	Desired intellectual development for most average programs; questionable for accelerated programs; capable of earning Bs and some As.
95–104 (Average)	Average intelligence and ability to achieve Bs and Cs in average programs; accelerated programs should be avoided; prone to fail as much as succeed, often leading to poor self-concept; response to remediation is guarded.
85–94 (Low average)	Usually experience difficulty in average programs because of inflexible curriculum demands; achievement is often two years or more below average; often qualify for special programs such as learning resource and reading labs; large amount of supervision always needed; possible candidates for distributive education or other work-study type programs; high drop-out rate; not typically college bound.
70–84 (Below average)	Experience great difficulty with academic tasks—seldom qualify for special education because of low potential and low achievement; normally gain only 4–5 months of achievement for 9 months of instruction; respond poorly to remedial procedures; high drop-out rate.
Below 70 (Mentally retarded)	Should not be placed in regular classes; normally qualified for classes for the educable or trainable mentally handicapped; emphasis should be placed on survival skills and on training in semiskilled labor professions.

can be completed using the scaled scores of the various subtests. Many authorities support the theory that the results obtained on the subtests can be regrouped into "factors" that provide meaningful insight into different aspects of intelligence. Kaufman (1975) suggested that the 12 subtest scaled scores can be regrouped into three factors: verbal comprehension, perceptual organization, and freedom from distractibility. Bannatyne (1971, 1974) identified four factors of intelligence: verbal conceptualization ability, spatial ability, sequencing ability, and acquired knowledge. Guilford (1967) developed a three-dimensional model for labeling the abilities that are measured by the WISC. The first of the three dimensions (operations) contains four factors: cognition, memory, evaluation, and convergent production. Table 8.7 illustrates how subtest scores have been grouped into factors according to models established by Kaufman, Bannatyne, Guilford, and Stetson.

There are two reasons for establishing the

Stetson model. First, there is a need to identify factors which epitomize those characteristics most closely associated with academics. Second, there is a need to attach names to those factors so that the language is acceptable and clearly understood by the educational community. Comparing expressive and receptive language factors allows the evaluator to make some decisions as to whether language is adequate, delayed, or disordered. For example, a high expressive and a low receptive language suggests possible problems with nonverbal comprehension, while a high receptive and low expressive language could indicate an expressive delay that hides academic potential and deserves special attention as well. Analytical thinking factors provide insight into mental alertness which a Verbal, Performance, or Full Scale IQ might not identify.

Cognitive processing in the Stetson model has other synonyms such as "learning style" and "learning modalities." Its history is long,

Table 8.7 Factor Analysis Worksheet for the WISC-R Scaled Scores Based on Models of Kaufman, Bannatyne, Guilford, and Stetson

Factors	Verbal Subtests						Performance Subtests					
	I	S	A	V	C	DS	PC	PA	BD	OA	CD	M
Kaufman												
Verbal comprehension	x	x		x	x							
Perceptual organization							x	x	x	x		x
Freedom from distractibility			x			x						
Bannatyne												
Verbal conceptualizing		x		x	x							
Spatial ability							x		x	x		
Sequencing ability			x			x					x	
Acquired knowledge	x		x	x								
Guilford[a]												
Cognition	x	x	x	x			x		x	x		x
Memory	x		x			x						
Evaluation					x		x	x	x	x	x	
Convergent production	x							x			x	
Stetson												
Language Facility	—	—	—	—	—	—	—	—	—	—	—	—
Expressive language	x	x		x								
Receptive language							x	x		x		
Analytical thinking		x	x		x			x		x		x
Cognitive processing	—	—	—	—	—	—	—	—	—	—	—	—
Auditory processing			x			x						
Visual processing							x	x	x			
Visual-motor integration										x	x	

[a]This display represents only the operations (intellectual processes) component of Guilford's three-dimensional theoretical model. Refer to Guilford (1967) for complete details.

but it is currently experiencing a revival not only in educational circles but in counseling practices as well, which are often referred to as neurolinguist communications. The three factors of cognitive processing are explained in detail later in this chapter. For now it is sufficient to mention that an emerging thought in education is that the learning of skills is tied to one or more cognitive processes. Therefore, the inability to learn a skill may indicate a possible deficiency in the specific processing factor upon which the learning of that skill is most dependent. The presence of the three factors in cognitive processing in the Stetson model will aid the clinician in planning for remedial strategies which depend on the strongest processing factors of the child. Each of the six factors is listed in Table 8.8 with some of the associated abilities.

Dangers in Using Factor Analysis

One of the problems of many professionals is to administer a minimum test battery (e.g., WISC-R, Wide Range Achievement Test, and Bender Gestalt) and depend on the obtained scores and a factor analysis of the WISC-R to generate an educational diagnosis and remedial plan. Most of us abhor such practices, and schools are slowly realizing that test batteries must be more comprehensive. Factor

Table 8.8   Learning Processing Factors and Associated Abilities

Factor	Associated Abilities
Expressive language	Verbal comprehension, acquired knowledge, long term memory, verbalization, abstract thinking, word knowledge.
Receptive language	Nonverbal comprehension, evaluation, distinguishing essential from nonessential holistic processing (closure), perceptual organization, convergent production, common sense synthesis.
Analytical thinking	Abstract thinking, verbal and numerical reasoning, conceptualization; mental alertness, common sense, cause and effect relationships, determining essential from nonessential, synthesizing.
Auditory processing	Sequencing, concentration ability, short term memory, mental alertness with verbal stimuli.
Visual processing	Spatial awareness, visual perception of meaningful and nonessential stimuli, visual sequencing, visual organization, visual memory.
Visual-motor integration	Perceptual organization, visual/motor coordination, visual memory, paper-and-pencil skills, reproduction of models, learning ability.

analysis using only WISC-R subtests could never replace the value of factor analysis when scores from a variety of measures are blended into the factoring process. The Psychometric Data profile illustrated later in this chapter represents an example of a comprehensive factor analysis procedure involving the rearrangement of scores from nine different evaluation instruments onto a factor analysis or data profile sheet. Rather than using tests as individual entities, test scores are disenfranchised from their identity with test titles and are placed into appropriate factor categories so that a diagnosis can be completed.

Measures of Language Facility

Educational diagnosticians normally view language facility as the ability to understand and express language. In this sense, language facility is defined as listening and speaking proficiency. Its components include word knowledge, information acquired, ability to analyze and synthesize, and reasoning ability. According to our definition, language facility can be measured with several of the instruments already mentioned as intelligence tests: the Slosson Intelligence Test, verbal portions of the three Wechsler Scales, the Stanford-Binet, and the verbal scale of the McCarthy.

Excluded from this definition is grammatical competence, which deals with the order and relationships among words; phonology, which involves sounds; articulation; and discrimination. All of these aspects of language concern the proficiency and accuracy with which language is articulated. Language facility is at the center of communications, meaning, comprehension, and learning. A student with poor language may decode print beautifully and sound like a fluent reader but may not remember what was read or understand the passage. The excellent language user, on the other hand, can have poor decoding skills and sound like a sloppy reader and still get the main idea from a passage. Table 8.9 lists several instruments currently used by diagnosticians in estimating language facility.

One of the tests highly regarded by many is missing from Table 8.9—the Illinois Test of Psycholinguistic Abilities (ITPA) (Kirk, McCarthy, & Kirk, 1968). It has been excluded because of its limited age range (3–10), standardization based on a narrowly defined population, test-retest reliabilities much lower than is normally desired, and a total absence of validity data. In its place is the Detroit Test of Learning Aptitude (DTLA) (Baker & Leland, 1967). The DTLA can be administered to individuals age three to adult and contains tests of language facility, cognitive

Table 8.9   Assessment Areas in Language Facility Arranged by Type of Language, Instruments, Age Ranges, and Subtests

Language Type and Instrument	Age Range	Subtest(s)
Receptive Language Tests		
Peabody Picture Vocabulary Test—Revised (Dunn, 1980)	2½–18	Entire battery
Columbia Mental Maturity Scales (Burgemeister et al., 1972)	3½–10	Entire battery
Wechsler Intelligence Scales WPPSI (1967), WISC-R (1974) WAIS (1955)	4–16+	Picture arrangement
Expressive Language Tests		
Slosson Intelligence Test-SIT (Slosson, 1971)	Preschool to adult	Entire battery
Stanford-Binet (Terman & Merrill, 1973)	Preschool to adult	Entire battery
McCarthy Scales (McCarthy, 1972)	2½–8½	Verbal tests only
Wechsler Scales	4–16+	Information, similarities, & vocabulary
Vocabulary Tests		
Wechsler Intelligence Scales	4–16+	Vocabulary
Woodcock Reading Mastery Test (Woodcock, 1973)	Gd. K–12	Subtest on word meaning
Detroit Test of Learning Aptitude (Baker & Leland, 1967)	3– adult	# 1-Picture absurdities #11-Free association
Language Association Tests		
Wechsler Intelligence Scales	4–16+	Similarities
Detroit Test of Learning Aptitude	3– adult	# 2-Verbal absurdities # 4-Verbal opposites #19-Likenesses & differences

processing, perceptual-motor abilities, and social adjustment.

Cognitive Processing

Cognitive processing is one of several terms that describe the manner or style that one uses to receive and remember information. Other terms include "cognitive learning style" and "learning modalities." One often hears educators talking about visual learning, auditory learning, kinesthetic learning, and many combinations of the three. While much of what is written remains at the theoretical level, the majority of learners have nevertheless preferred learning modalities. The purpose for determining an individual's preferred learning style is to offer possible explanations or causes for the inability to learn certain tasks.

What happens between the time one receives information and then expresses that knowledge is difficult to explain. It is generally accepted, however, that one can receive stimuli through the visual, auditory, or tactile channels or a combination of the three. During the early years of schooling, teaching is thought to be heavily involved in combining these modalities to maximize the stimulation. As the learner progresses through the grades, learning becomes more dependent upon the single modality—particularly the auditory mode, as demonstrated by a learner's comprehension of a lecture. Since most individuals claim that they learn best through visual and kinesthetic channels, the school system tends to operate more and more in the least effective modality of the majority of learners.

This section on cognitive processing will address itself to the three most important in the school setting: auditory processing, visual processing, and visual-motor integration.

Auditory Processing

It is possible to isolate and predict the efficiency of auditory processing by measuring the individual's ability to hear, receive, remember, and retell what is presented auditorily. Some of the factors that constitute auditory processing are identified in Table 8.10 along with instruments designed to measure each factor.

Processing itself cannot be observed or measured; only the effects or results can be evaluated. Tests used to estimate auditory processing usually involve memory. Unfortunately, users of these tests often conclude that memory and processing are one and the same and that, therefore, the training of memory through exercises will improve processing. Nothing is further from the truth. However, observing the effects of processing will allow predictions to be made about the individual's ability to learn those skills that require a pro-

Table 8.10 Specific Components of Auditory Processing, Assessment Instruments, and Specific Subtests

Area of Auditory Processing	Assessment Instrument	Specific Subtest(s)
Auditory acuity	Pure-tone audiometer	Pure-tone air conduction threshold test
Auditory discrimination	Auditory Discrimination Test (ADT) (Wepman, 1958)	Administer all 40 items
	Stetson Auditory Discrimination Test (SADT) (Stetson, 1978)	Administer all 45 items
Memory for digits	Wechsler Scales, (WPPSI, WISC-R, and WAIS)	Digit span
Memory for words	Detroit Test of Learning Aptitudes (DTLA) (Baker & Leland, 1967)	# 6 Auditory attention span for unrelated words
Memory for sentences	Detroit Test of Learning Aptitudes	#13 auditory attention span for related syllables
Following oral directions	Detroit Test of Learning Aptitudes	# 7 Oral commissions

ficient auditory processing system. For example, there are several behaviors associated with students who score low on auditory processing tasks. Some of these academic difficulties are identified here:

1. Learning and using phonic analysis skills during reading is often difficult or ineffective.
2. Spelling is poor when taught with an emphasis on learning phonic rules for spelling.
3. Remembering information presented in lecture form is most difficult unless visual or kinesthetic reinforcement is included.
4. Note taking is frustrating because the student cannot write down information without losing both the thought and the information being presented during the writing act.
5. Staying on-task and remaining free from distractions is most difficult and attention span becomes shorter.
6. Working independently results in nonproduction after short periods unless there is contact and intervention by the teacher.
7. Remembering literal or factual information obtained through reading or listening is difficult, particularly when answering questions dealing with who, what, where, when, and how.
8. Remembering basic duties and responsibilities at school or home is almost always a problem regardless of the amount of reminding that may be done.
9. Some school environments, such as "open schools," can often become ineffective learning environments for such students.

In other words, the student with auditory processing difficulties is very likely to be disadvantaged in an academic setting simply because such a setting expects the highest amount of efficiency with auditory processing.

Visual Processing

Visual processing is defined in a manner similar to auditory processing: the efficiency with which one receives visual stimuli, remembers, and recalls that information. While visual processing includes acuity and binocularity (using both eyes together), the major emphases are visual perception, visual closure, visual comprehension, and visual memory. Table 8.11 presents individual components of visual processing along with test instruments appropriate for each.

High achievers normally score acceptably on both auditory and visual processing tests. However, the overwhelming majority of students experiencing difficulty in school, particularly those exhibiting behaviors associated with learning disabilities, will normally perform considerably higher on tests of visual processing than on tests of auditory processing. Listed below are some of the learning patterns associated with the high visual processor. Typically this student will:

1. Learn word recognition more readily through a visual, sight, or whole word approach than through a phonic analysis approach.
2. Spell more effectively when taught by a visual-memory process rather than a rule-based (phonics) approach.
3. Respond to and use structural analysis more effectively than phonic analysis when decoding print.
4. Follow directions better when such directions are written.
5. Usually benefit from a language experience approach when learning how to read.
6. Retain more knowledge through reading than through lecture.
7. Need good note-taking skills for use during lectures.
8. Remember duties more successfully when duties are written on a chart for easy reminder.
9. Tend to have the ability to increase attention ability when auditory information is reinforced visually.

Table 8.11 Specific Components of Visual Processing, Assessment Instruments, and Specific Subtests

Area of Visual Processing	Assessment Instrument	Specific Subtest(s)
Visual acuity	Keystone Visual Survey Tests	All 14 subtests
	Titmus School Vision Tester	Entire battery
Visual perception	Motor-Free Visual Perception Test (MVPT) (Colarusso & Hammill, 1972)	Entire battery
	Wechsler Scales (WPPSI, WISC-R, & WAIS)	Picture completion, block design
Visual comprehension	Wechsler Scales (WPPSI, WISC-R, & WAIS)	Picture arrangement, object assembly
Visual memory	Detroit Test of Learning Aptitude (DTLA) (Baker & Leland, 1967)	# 9 Visual attention span for objects #16 Visual attention span for letters
Visual-auditory integration[a]	Detroit Test of Learning Aptitude (DTLA)	#18 Oral directions

[a]This last component is not a pure measure of visual processing. Rather, it is a measure of visual and auditory processing combined. Therefore, it should be considered separate from the others.

Visual-Motor Integration

Visual-motor integration (VMI) is a subset of the broader area of perceptual-motor development, one of the most controversial subjects in education. According to the review of literature reported by Salvia and Ysseldyke (1978), not only is perceptual-motor training ineffective in improving academic performance, but instruments designed to assess perceptual-motor ability are equally questionable (p. 303).

In this chapter, visual-motor integration refers primarily to handwriting, one of the slowest forms of communication. Copying is an incredibly difficult and arduous task that is far from a natural act. To copy effectively from a chalkboard, a student must possess adequate acuity, perceive the stimulus accurately, read the words and sentences correctly, form the letters correctly, utilize visual memory to retain what is read, and locate the appropriate place on the board each time a new fixation is needed. A breakdown of any one of these skills can easily affect efficiency. Handwriting is reported by teachers as a problem more often than problems with math, spelling, or behavior; handwriting problems are second only to reading problems. Table 8.12 identifies some of the components of visual-motor integration along with recommended assessment instruments.

In the event that handwriting is a problem area, each of the components can be evaluated to determine possible causes. In the majority of cases, scores on timed tests of visual-motor integration are considerably lower than on untimed tests. However, the breakdown in neatness usually occurs when the student is expected to simultaneously use the many skills in the VMI system in rapid fire fashion, particularly during note taking and copying tasks. As the amount of writing increases and the time allotted lessens, the problem will

Table 8.12 Specific Components of Visual-Motor Integration, Assessment Instruments, and Specific Subtests

Area of Visual-Motor Integration	Assessment Instrument	Specific Subtest(s)
Visual-motor integration (untimed)	Developmental Test of Visual-Motor Integration (VMI) (Beery & Buktenica, 1967)	Entire battery
	Detroit Test of Learning Aptitude (DTLA) (Baker & Leland, 1967)	#12 Designs
	Bender Visual-Motor Gestalt Test (BVMGT) (Bender, 1938; Koppitz, 1963)	Entire test
Visual-motor integration (timed)	Detroit Test of Learning Aptitude (DTLA)	# 4 Motor speed and precision
	Wechsler Scales (WPPSI, WISC-R, & WAIS)	Coding
	Informal Copy Test (ICT) (Stetson, 1980)	Near point copying —Words per fixation —Words per minute
		Far point copying —Words per fixation —Words per minute

Table 8.13 Assessment Instruments Used by Educational Diagnosticians to Identify Adaptive Behavior, Personality and Emotional Development, and Self-Concept

Specific Area	Assessment Instrument	Specific Subtest(s)
Adaptive behavior	Vineland Social Maturity Scale VSMS (Doll, 1953)	Entire battery
	AAMD Adaptive Behavior Scale, Public School Version (1974 revision) (Lambert et al., 1975)	Entire battery
Personality & emotional development	Bender Visual-Motor Gestalt Test BVMGT (Bender, 1938; Koppitz, 1963)	Entire battery
	Draw-a-Person (DAP) (Urban, 1963)	Entire battery
	House-Tree-Person HTP (Buck & Jolles, 1966)	Entire battery
Self-concept	Piers-Harris Children's Self Concept Scale (Piers & Harris, 1969)	Entire battery
	Tennessee Self Concept Inventory (Fitts, 1965)	Entire battery

intensify, and it is not likely that the student will improve his or her neatness.

Adaptive Behavior, Personality, and Self-Concept

Because this text provides ample information pertaining to behavior and personality, the space taken here is used only to identify those assessment instruments typically used in the school setting. It should be noted that most of the instruments listed in Table 8.13 are less sophisticated than many used by psychologists and psychiatrists to evaluate behavior and personality. The primary reason is that diagnosticians are not usually trained in projective testing.

Although the Bender Visual Motor Gestalt Test is listed (Bender, 1938), it continues to fall under increased criticism by those who claim that the BVMGT is little more than a measure to copy designs. In spite of the updated scoring systems offered by Koppitz (1963, 1975), who claims that the test predicts IQ, achievement, and visual perception, many educators favor the Developmental Test of Visual-Motor Integration (Beery & Buktenica, 1967), which has a high reliability compared to other tests of perceptual-motor ability.

LEVEL I ASSESSMENT—SCREENING

Because the manuals of the various tests provide complete information on administration and scoring, space will not be alloted to such details. Interpretation, on the other hand, is a matter deserving of some attention. Professionals are known to interpret test data in a variety of ways depending on their training. Schools have been forced to attempt some sort of "standardized" approach to interpretation simply because there are many more children in need of services than there are openings. This has led to the Level I and the Level II assessment strategy. The Level I assessment is often called the screening level since it is used primarily to determine whether the student qualifies in any way for special services. In most cases an achievement test and an intelligence test are administered, the scores are converted to grade scores and standard scores, the student's "potential achievement" is calculated, and the difference between the student's potential and actual achievements is used to determine eligibility. The criterion for admission to many special classes is that the student must be functioning two years or more below potential achievement. Other schools compare standard scores and require at least one standard deviation (15 standard score points) between potential and actual achievements. The Level II assessment, which is far more diagnostic, is used to determine specific strengths and weaknesses within the five areas of assessment.

Categories of Special Classes

As would be expected, the larger urban school districts will have the largest number of special classes and trained teachers, while the smaller districts in rural settings tend to have more limited services. Private schools rarely have special classes, mainly because the law does not currently require private schools to comply with the requirements that public schools must fulfill. While every state and district has its own selection of classes, Table 8.14 illustrates some of the more readily available classes and examples of criteria normally used for placement.

The primary basis for placement in classes for the mentally handicapped is IQ scores. On the other hand, placement in classes for the learning disabled or reading disabled employs two criteria: IQ and achievement. In these cases the student must be certified as having "normal intelligence, interpreted to mean IQ of 70 or higher, and a two-year deficiency in achievement. Close evaluation of the categories in Table 8.14 will show that there is a very large group of students whose IQ is 70 or higher (normal), but whose achievement scores are not two full years below their potential levels. Unless the school breaks the rules, most of these students are classified as "corrective" and are sent back to the regular classroom under the assumption that their needs can be accommodated within the regular classroom. It is estimated that approximately one-third of the students in an average classroom will fall into the "corrective" category

Table 8.14 Nonregular Classes Available in Most School Districts along with Accepted Criteria for Placement, Including Intelligence, Achievement, and Cognitive Deficiencies

Special Class[a]	IQ Criterion	Achievement Criterion	Cognitive Learning Deficiencies
Reading classes	Normal and above (70+)	2 years or more below	No requirement
Resource room	Normal and above (70+)	1+ standard deviation below potential	No requirement
Learning-disabled class	Normal and above (70+)	1 or more standard deviation below potential	Deficiency in one or more area
EMR classes; Educable mentally retarded	50–70	No requirement	No requirement
TMR classes; Trainable mentally retarded	Below 50	No requirement	No requirement
Gifted	135 and above	2 years or more above grade placement	No requirement

[a]Not included are classes for the emotionally disturbed, physically handicapped, and multiply handicapped.

and will receive no special help other than what the regular teacher can provide.

Determining Eligibility Using Grade Scores

Based on Table 8.14 many special classes require a two-year difference between potential and achievement. For example, suppose Joseph T. has been referred for testing because of low grades. The diagnostician administers a screening (Level I) battery to determine whether Joseph will qualify for any of the classes based on achievement and IQ. The battery includes the Slossen Intelligence Test (SIT) and the Wide Range Achievement Test (WRAT). After testing, the raw scores are converted to grade scores and standard scores as illustrated in Table 8.15.

Now that all raw scores have been converted to grade and standard scores and the IQ score has been translated into a grade equivalent score, a profile can be completed for purposes of analysis. Grade scores can be used to make two different types of comparisons: (1) the comparison of actual achievement with that achievement expected in the classroom and (2) the comparison of actual achievement with the potential achievement. A form similar to the one in Table 8.16 could easily be established for use with all students for whom grade comparisons will be made.

Columns b, c, and d should be filled in directly from the grade scores obtained from the tests. The grade score in column b will always be the same, that is, the actual grade placement of the student, in this case grade 5.5. Column c contains the three scores obtained from the WRAT. Column d is the grade equivalent for the IQ score of 87 and is always repeated on each line of the column. By comparing columns b and c, it is easy to calculate differences between actual and expected achievement. According to column a,

Table 8.15   Conversion of Raw Scores on SIT and WRAT Intelligence Tests to Grade Scores and Standard Scores (Joseph T., Age: 11-1, Grade 5.5)

Area Tested	Raw Scores	Grade Scores	Standard Scores (SS)
IQ (SIT)	M.A. 9-8	4.9[a]	87 (IQ Score)
Reading (WRAT)	56	4.0	85
Spelling (WRAT)	34	3.5	79
Math (WRAT)	36	5.1	94

[a]Determined by using the Bond and Tinker (1967) formula for converting IQ to an eqivalent potential.

$$\frac{IQ}{100} \times \text{Years in School} + 1.0$$

Joseph is functioning one-and-a-half to two years below expected levels in reading and spelling, but only 4 months below in math. In this case if the district requires a two-year difference between actual and expected scores to qualify for placement in resource rooms or reading labs, he will barely qualify based on the spelling score. On the other hand, column e can be completed by comparing columns c and d. It is easy to determine that when Joseph's intelligence (IQ=87) is used to determine potential (grade level 4.9), the differences between actual and potential are only nine months in reading and 1.4 years in spelling. Using this criterion for placement, Joseph will not qualify for special assistance and will be sent back to the regular classroom.

This type of analysis provides a great deal of insight into the reasons for low grades and aids in making some comparisons about stronger and weaker achievement areas. It also gives the diagnostician a glimpse of a student's scores to determine whether there is any reason to complete a full diagnosis that could take many hours to finish. Incidentally, using grade scores to interpret performance can be very meaningful when talking with parents or most professionals who are not familiar with educational nomenclature.

Determining Eligibility Using Standard Scores

Since the trend in education is to compare standard scores (SS) rather than grade scores, it is important to know that most schools use the criterion that a student must score more than one standard deviation (SD) below his or her potential to qualify for special placement. In most cases, 15 SS points is equal to one SD. For example, an IQ score of 100 represents the mean or average score. A score of 85, however, is exactly one SD below the mean. Table

Table 8.16   Comparing Actual Grade Scores, Expected Grade Scores, and Potential Grade Scores in Determining Eligibility for Special Placement

Actual vs. Expected		Grade Score Analysis	Actual vs. Potential	
(a)	(b) Expected Present Grade Level	(c) Actual Achievement Grade Scores	(d) Potential IQ Grade Equivalents	(e)
Difference				Difference
−1.5	5.5	4.0 (reading)	4.9	− .9[a]
−2.0	5.5	3.5 (spelling)	4.9	−1.4[a]
− .4	5.5	5.1 (math)	4.9	+ .2[a]

[a]Although this student is 1.5 and 2.0 years below grade level in reading and spelling (column a), he does not qualify for special help outside of this classroom because there is not at least a two-year difference in grade scores between actual (column c) and potential achievement (column d).

Table 8.17 A Method of Comparing Standard Scores Calculated for Actual Achievement, Expected Achievement, and Potential Achievement to Determine Eligibility for Placement in Special Classes

Actual vs. Expected		Standard Score Analysis	Actual vs. Potential	
(a)	(b)	(c)	(d)	(e)
Difference	Expected Present Grade Level	Actual Achievement Grade Scores	Potential IQ Grade Equivalents	Difference
-15^a	100	85 (reading)	87	-2^b
-21	100	79 (spelling)	87	-8
-6	100	94 (math)	87	$+7$

[a]Student is 15 or more standard score points below actual grade placement.

[b]When actual achievement is compared with potential achievement based on IQ (column d), the student does not qualify for special placement since there is less than a 15-point difference between actual and potential achievement.

8.17 is provided to illustrate the use of SSs rather than grade scores.

Column b is always 100, no matter what grade level the student may be attending. This figure is based on the fact that if a student in grade 7.6 scores grade equivalents of 7.6 on achievement tests, the SS will be 100. Therefore, the SS for the expected achievement will be 100. Column c is taken directly from the table of SSs in the test manuals. The SS in column d will always be the student IQ score. Column a shows a 15 and 21 SS difference in reading and spelling, both being one standard deviation (SD) or more below the expected SS for the grade placement, which is 100. On the right side of the chart (column e), the differences are considerably less than one SD below the student's potential. In other words, the effect of the IQ score (87) is to reduce the potential achievement, resulting in two and eight point deficiencies in reading and spelling respectively. Since the difference must be at least 15 points or one SD, this student does not qualify for special assistance.

In most systems, Joseph would not qualify for any type of help, whether the decision is based on grade scores or standard scores. His IQ is too high for mentally handicapped classes, achievement is too high for resource or learning disability classes, and he is neither physically handicapped nor emotionally disturbed. Joseph stays in the regular classroom and functions two years below his average peers; the gap between him and his peers will continue to widen.

Is the Current System Fair?

Two illustrations are presented here to shed light on the fairness of such decision making. The first is a student with above average intelligence who is also achieving above her grade placement and who will qualify for special classes based on the criteria identified here. In Table 8.18, the diagnostician selects the

Table 8.18 Conversion of Raw Scores on WISC-R and WRAT Intelligence Tests to Grade Scores and Standard Scores (Evelyn, Age: 12-4, Grade 7.3)

Areas Tested	Raw Scores	Grade Scores	Standard Scores
Verbal IQ (WISC-R)	SS=71	8.9	125
Performance IQ (WISC-R)	SS=64	8.6	120
Full Scale IQ (WISC-R)	SS=135	8.9	126
Reading (WRAT)	52	8.0	110
Spelling (WRAT)	26	7.7	106
Math (WRAT)	27	7.8	109

WISC-R and the WRAT to complete the screening.

When comparing grade scores it is easy to see that this student is achieving from four to seven months above present grade placement. Even so, a comparison of grade scores on the WRAT against her potential achievement levels of 8.9 (using the verbal or full scale IQ scores) shows that she is performing from 9 to 12 months below her potential. When comparing SSs, Evelyn is functioning between 15 and 19 SS points below her potential SS of 126. Because there is more than a 15 point (one SD) difference between actual and potential, Evelyn would qualify for placement in a resource room for additional help in all three areas of achievement.

A second example would be to compare students at various grade levels, all of whom have identical IQs of 100. The first grader with an IQ of 100 would need to score 1.2 years below his or her grade placement before qualifying for special classes. The sixth-grader would have to be two-and-a-half years behind to qualify, and a tenth-grader would have to be four years below grade level to qualify if standard scores are used.

Is the system fair? Of course not. The net result of decision making based on a minimum of two-years or 15-points difference between actual and potential achievement is that fewer students are placed for special help, while significantly larger numbers of students remain in the regular classes. This creates a widening of academic differences within each room, places additional strain on the regular teacher who is often not trained to accommodate individual differences, and lowers the overall mean achievement for most classes. The use of this system also means that a significantly larger number of families will be turning to the nonschool specialist for help.

LEVEL II ASSESSMENT—DIAGNOSTIC EVALUATION

In addition to an intelligence and achievement test included in a Level I screening, a Level II assessment battery will add diagnostic instruments to assess specific areas of reading, arithmetic, language facility, and cognitive processing. Properly selected instruments will provide the examiner with specific details about the strengths and weaknesses within the area for which the test is designed. This diagnostic information will not only give clues to possible causes for academic difficulties but will also lead to specific remediation strategies.

One of the frustrating experiences in diagnosis is the interpretation of data. While most individuals can administer and score all of the instruments identified in this chapter with minimum instruction, translating a group of scores into a meaningful diagnosis is quite another matter. For example, many teachers refer children for testing because they have observed that the student experiences difficulty in comprehension. The diagnostician administers a reading test and, as predicted, the results verify that the student has a comprehension problem. If one is not aware that several possible variables contribute to the skill called comprehension, the recommendation might suggest that the student needs comprehension training when, in fact, the comprehension problem was caused by a lack of concentration, low language facility, or exposure to printed materials written at a readability level considerably above the reading level of the student. In other cases, it is determined that the student has not learned phonic analysis skills adequately. If the teacher does not realize that poor auditory processing ability creates an inability to learn phonics, the teacher might continue to make the assumption that the student must learn phonics.

What is suggested here is that test interpretation is extremely important in the design of remedial strategies. To aid educational diagnosticians in training at the University of Houston Diagnostic Learning Center, a Psychometric Data Profile was designed to assist clinicians in displaying scores in a manner that would form an objective picture of the student's performance (Stetson, 1978). The Psychometric Data Profile illustrated in Table 8.19 represents about 90 percent of the assessment profiles completed on several hundred students each year at the DLC. From the example of the profile, it is hoped that readers will learn what a good educational assessment

Table 8.19   Psychometric Data Profile

Name: Tom B.   Age 7-4 Years   Grade: 1.6
School: Private School of High Academic Expectations
Purpose of Testing: To determine possible causes for
                                 failure and frustration in the school
                                 setting.

I.   TESTS ADMINISTERED

Wechsler Intelligence Scale For Children—Revised (WISC-R)

Wide Range Achievement Test (WRAT), Level I

Woodcock Reading Mastery Tests (WRMT)

KeyMath Diagnostic Arithmetic Test (K-M)

Detroit Test of Learning Aptitude (DTLA)
    Subtest #5, #6, #9, #12, #13, and #16

Developmental Test of Visual-Motor Integration (VMI)

Motor Free Visual Perception Test (MVPT)

Stetson Auditory Discrimination Test (SADT)

Reading-Spelling Vocabulary Proficiency Test (RSVPT), Form A

ABBREVIATIONS USED

RS — raw score
SS — standard score
BA — below average (inadequate)
A — average (adequate)
AA — above average
g.e. — grade equivalent
a.e. — age equivalent

II.   SUMMARY OF DIAGNOSTIC DATA

A.   *Intelligence (WISC-R)*

Verbal IQ	RS	SS	BA	A	AA
Information	11	13			X
Similarities	10	12		X	
Arithmetic	7	9		X	
Vocabulary...........................	23	12		X	
Comprehension	11	10		X	
Digit span	[5]	[6]	X		
Performance IQ					
Picture Completion....................	14	10		X	
Picture Arrangement	17	10		X	
Block Design	6	8		X	
Object Assembly	11	8		X	
Coding	13	3	X		
Mazes	—	—			
VERBAL IQ _____	56	107		X	
PERFORMANCE IQ _____	39	85	X	XX	
FULL SCALE IQ_____	95	96		X	

Table 8.19 *(continued)*

B. *Achievement Test (WRAT)*

Subtests	RS	SS	g.e.	RATING BA	A	AA
Reading	41	115	2.6			XX
Spelling...........................	31	121	2.9			XX
Arithmetic	24	116	2.7			XX
OVERALL RATING						XX

C. *Achievement Potential*

$$\left(\frac{IQ}{100} \times \text{Years in School}\right) + 1.0$$

$$\left(\frac{107}{100} \times 0.6\right) \qquad + 1.0 =$$

$$\left(1.07 \times 0.6\right) \qquad + 1.0 = 1.6^a \text{ (Achievement potential)}$$

[a]Note: In this case achievement potential and actual grade placement are the same: 1.6.

D. *Language Facility*

Area	RS	SS	a.e. g.e.	RATING BA	A	AA
Information (WISC-R)	11	13	8-6			XX
Similarities (WISC-R)	10	12	8-6			XX
Vocabulary (WISC-R)	23	12	8-2		XX	
Word Meaning (WRMT).............			1.5		XX	
OVERALL RATING					XX	XX

E. *Diagnostic Reading*

Subtest Area	RS	SS	g.e.	RATING BA	A	AA
Letter Identification (WRMT)			2.3			XX
Word Identification (WRMT).........			2.4			XX
Sight Vocabulary (RSVPT)...........			2.5			XX
Word Attack (WRMT)			1.0	XX		
Word Meaning (WRMT).............			1.5		XX	
Passage Meaning (WRMT)...........			1.2	XX		
Total Reading (WRMT)			1.4	XX	XX	
ESTIMATED INSTRUCTIONAL LEVEL	Primer			XX		

Table 8.19 *(continued)*

F. *Diagnostic Mathematics (K-M)*

Numeration	RS	g.e.	BA	A	AA
			RATING		
Numeration	12	2.5			XX
Fractions	2	2.3			XX
Geometry/Symbols....................	7	1.2	XX		

Operations

	RS	g.e.	BA	A	AA
Addition	6	2.0		XX	
Subtraction	3	2.0		XX	
Multiplication	0	.5-	XX		
Division	1	1.2	XX		
Mental Computation	2	2.0		XX	
Numerical Reasoning	4	2.3			XX

Application

	RS	g.e.	BA	A	AA
Word Problems	5	2.4		XX	
Missing Elements	0	.5-	XX		
Money	4	2.1		XX	
Measurement	3	.8	XX		
Time	4	1.4	XX		
TOTAL KEYMATH—ALL TESTS	53	2.0		XX	

G. *Cognitive Processing*

Auditory Processing	RS	SS	a.e.	BA	A	AA
				RATING		
Auditory Acuity (Beltone 10-D)					OK	
Auditory Discrimination (SADT)	41/45				OK	
Memory for Digits (WISC-R).........	5	6.	6-2	XX		
Memory for Words (DTLA)..........	35		5-2	XX		
Memory for Sentences (DTLA)	30		4-3	XX		
AVERAGE AUDITORY PROCESSING AGE		5-2 Years		XX		

Visual Processing	RS	SS	a.e.	BA	A	AA
				RATING		
Visual Perception (MVPT)	28		7-4		XX	
Block Design (WISC-R)	6	8	6-2	XX		
Memory for Designs (DTLA)	15		7-5		XX	
Memory for Letters (DTLA)..........	4-1		706		XX	
AVERAGE VISUAL PROCESSING AGE		7-1 Years		XX		

Table 8.19   *(continued)*

Visual-Motor Integration	RS	SS	a.e.	RATING		
				BA	A	AA
Copying Designs-Untimed (DTLA)	14		7-3		XX	
Copying Designs-Untimed (VMI)	14		7-4		XX	
Motor Speed-Timed (DTLA)	68		6-9	XX		
Coding-Timed (WISC-R)	13	3	-(6-2)	XX		
AVERAGE VMI—UNTIMED		7-3 Years			XX	
AVERAGE VMI—TIMED		6-5 Years		XX		

battery might look like and see how scores from a variety of assessment instruments can be grouped together to form a diagnosis.

INTERPRETING A PSYCHOMETRIC DATA PROFILE

Once a profile has been filled in, interpretation is half completed. All the raw scores, standard scores, age equivalents, and grade equivalents are clearly displayed. Each subtest is rated as below average (BA), average (A), or above average (AA) by comparing the obtained scores with the student's age and/or grade. Subtests which measure the same skill area are clustered together regardless of the test in which the subtest appeared. This regrouping procedure facilitates the evaluation of individual components (e.g., auditory memory for digits) as well as the overall skill area (e.g., auditory processing). Finally, each skill area is given a general rating by either (1) averaging age or grade scores within an area or (2) a general impression of the examiner.

Summary statements can now be formulated by examining the profile. The well-trained diagnostician might summarize the diagnosis and generate the following statements:

1. Overall intelligence is within the "average" range. Specific areas of intelligence that might enhance or hinder academic achievement are listed from the most efficient to the least efficient along with estimated IQ equivalent.

Area of Intelligence	*IQ Equivalent*
1. Verbal comprehension (I, S, V, C)	109
2. Long term memory (I, A, V)	107
3. Reasoning ability (S, A, C, PA)	102
4. Common sense (C, PA)	100
5. Visual perception—meaningful (PC, PA, OA)	97
6. Working under pressure (A, PC, PA, BD, OA, CD)	90
7. Mental alertness—distractibility (A, DS)	87
8. Visual-motor integration (BD, OA, CD)	82
9. Visual perception—abstract (BD, CD)	77
10. Short term memory (DS, CD)	72

2. Potential achievement based on IQ is grade level 1.6, identical to present grade placement.

3. Screening for actual achievement (WRAT) indicates grade equivalent scores of 2.6 in reading, 2.9 in spelling, and 2.7 in arithmetic—at least one year above present grade placement and potential achievement.

4. Expressive language facility is average to above average.

5. Overall reading is estimated to be low-

to mid-first-grade level which is: (1) slightly below present grade level; (2) considerably below the expected achievement levels of the private school setting; and (3) significantly lower than the readability levels of most of the textbooks used in first-grade classes. Strengths in reading include an above average sight vocabulary (instant recognition and pronunciation without need for analysis) and average to above average language skills that facilitate meaningful understanding. A pronounced weakness in reading is the ineffective use of decoding skills, particularly phonics analysis, which appears to be nonfunctional at this time.

6.   Overall math ability, while estimated to be grade level 2.0, is inadequate because (1) the deficiencies involve computational and application skills, and (2) the expectations of the private school are somewhat higher than the test results indicate.

7.   Severe deficiencies exist in the auditory processing area, predicting many or all of the academic and social problems identified in the section of this chapter on auditory processing, including:

1.   Poor short term memory
2.   Incompatibility with phonics instruction
3.   Easily distracted
4.   Difficulty remembering factual information
5.   Poor memory for basic number facts
6.   Problems working independently and for long periods of time
7.   Forgets directions in school and in the home

8.   The significant variance between the verbal and the performance sections of the WISC-R (22 points) and the two-year deficiency in auditory processing will classify the student as "learning disabled" in many school districts, provided that actual achievement is also deficient.

9.   The scores on processing favoring the visual over the auditory modalities for learning suggest that learning styles favor the following, in order of preference:

1.   Visual-kinesthetic-auditory
2.   Visual-kinesthetic
3.   Visual-auditory
4.   Visual

10.   Handwriting and copying can be accurate when the assignments are short in duration and when time pressures are not imposed. Otherwise, the prognosis for efficient handwriting is poor. It is likely that handwriting will be poor and prove a continual source of frustration and failure with any teacher who places importance on neatness.

11.   The prognosis for success in the present private school accelerated environment is extremely guarded without constant supervision, intervention, and special assistance in and out of the school. Chances for success will increase dramatically as the academic expectations are matched with the student's capabilities.

REMEDIATION IN EDUCATION

The intent of this section is to draw attention to some of the major issues surrounding proposed remedial strategies, all of which are controversial. The suggestions here are reinforced by 12 years of clinical work with reading/learning disabled students as well as research findings among the foremost authorities in the field. It is understood that the reader will use the statements here as a guide to additional reading and inquiry. Chapters 27, 28, 34, and 48 of this book also supply valuable information to be considered in generating remedial objectives.

1.   *Remediating versus tutoring.* Most special education is designed to remediate deficient skills. While important, remediating usually is a long term program that does little to assist the student in passing weekly spelling tests, preparing for a social studies test over a textbook chapter, or completing a math assignment. This is tutoring! A good special program will consider the importance of both approaches, and make provisions for spend-

ing time in remediation and in tutoring. Unfortunately, this circumstance rarely happens and the result is continued low grades in school except in the special class.

2. *Inefficient phonics usage.* Teachers often claim that a student has not learned phonics and insist it must be mastered for reading to improve. This is not always the case, particularly for the low auditory processor. One should be assured that if a student has not mastered phonics analysis after the second grade there is a good likelihood it will never be mastered. A shift to a structural analysis approach, heavily dependent upon visual processing, usually proves to be far more profitable.

3. *Sight vocabulary training.* Since the vast majority of disabled learners are more proficient visual processors, teaching vocabulary by sight or through a "whole word method" usually produces immediate improvement. This terribly overlooked procedure has taken a back seat to the use of phonics. An effective way to systematically teach sight vocabulary is through the use of a high frequency word list. The most recently produced list is the 900-word Reading-Spelling Vocabulary Program (RSVP) (Stetson, 1981), which contains words most frequently used in print and in writing among students in grades 1–9.

4. *Poor comprehension.* When the readability of the printed material is equal to or lower than the capability of the reader, comprehension *will* occur. However, when comprehension does not occur, the materials must be altered (see item 5), or the student's ability to comprehend can be improved by increasing (1) decoding efficiency, (2) sight vocabulary, and/or (3) language facility, particularly vocabulary knowledge. Programming students into graded reading passages containing comprehension questions may be the least effective way to improve comprehension.

5. *Comprehending difficult textbooks.* Teachers can employ two simple techniques to assist the poor reader in preparing for a test taken from a textbook. First, be sure to include oral discussion of the text, particularly those areas to be covered by the test.

Second, take time to ask the class what specific information from the chapter should be recorded in order to study for the test. Of course, the teacher makes sure that all essential items are identified and that students take notes from such a discussion. Another more formal aid for students is for teachers and/or parents to use a guided study technique such as S4R, which means SURVEY, READ, RECITE, RECORD, and REVIEW. First, the parent and child SURVEY the chapter by reading the introduction, the first sentence of each paragraph, major and minor headings, and the final paragraph. Second, the student and parent READ the first paragraph completely, orally or silently. At the end of the paragraph the student RECITES what was learned in the paragraph. Some believe that recitation is the most important factor in remembering. Once the facts are recited, the parent and student determine the specific information in the paragraph that should be RECORDED (i.e., information important to remember for a test). Finally, the recorded information is REVIEWED for the test. This simple system exposes the student to information several times and in several ways, which increases the chances for recall on a test.

6. *Poor spelling.* Contrary to the methods proposed by most spelling programs, the best spelling methods employ strong emphasis on visual processing, visual imagery, writing words from dictation, analyzing words structurally rather than phonetically, and providing immediate feedback and self-correction.

7. *Auditory/visual memory problems.* As stated earlier, low scores on tests of auditory or visual memory imply difficulties in the cognitive processing. A prevalent theory among many special educators is that remediation in memory will improve concentration, on-task behavior, and cognitive processing. Research continues to cast doubt on such theories. Unfortunately, thousands of students assigned to resource rooms during the 1970s have been involved in memory games to accomplish this unsupported objective. Just as training in perceptual-motor skills fails to produce academic achievement, auditory and visual memory games fail to improve or

change cognitive processes. Enrollment in such programs should be questioned carefully.

8. *Poor handwriting.* Students who have spatial problems or difficulty in forming letter shapes obviously need help. The majority of complaints, however, relate to sloppiness or poor quality of writing. Until teachers give shorter assignments, provide ample time for completion, and emphasize the content or thought of the passage, the problem remains. In the meantime, it is wise to provide typing lessons and to help students to understand that the penalty for sloppy work will be lower grades. As a student moves from lower to upper grades, the amount of writing increases and the probability for improved quality decreases.

9. *Best overall reading approach.* For the poor reader, the leanguage experience approach (LEA) is considered by many to be the most personalized and productive method for improving reading ability. The LEA begins with oral language as the student tells a story or engages in conversation with the teacher who writes down that story or conversation using the language expressed by the student. Then the teacher begins to assist the student in reading his or her own language through a series of oral reading activities which emphasize the "whole word" or "sight" approach, shown to be most effective for the visual learner. The LEA is appropriate for students at any level of development and can be used with individuals or groups. Additional information on LEA can be obtained through most of the written work of Roach Van Allen (1973), one of the great authorities in the field.

CONCLUSIONS

The purpose of this chapter is to provide some insight into the theory and practice of quality educational assessment. Not many school districts will operate at the level of sophistication presented here, but most are continually improving. If the nonschool clinician is to work effectively with schools, it will be important for the school to feel that he or she has credibility. This aim can be accomplished by understanding their language, communicating with them in their terms, and even using some of their assessment instruments.

REFERENCES

Allen, R.V. The language experience approach. In Robert Karlin (Ed.), *Perspectives on elementary reading: Principles and strategies.* New York: Harcourt Brace Jovanovich, 1973.

Arthur, G. *The Arthur adaptation of the Leiter international performance scale.* Chicago: Stoelting, 1950.

Baker, H.J., & Leland, B. *Detroit test of learning aptitude.* Indianapolis: Bobbs-Merrill, 1967.

Ballard, J., & Zettel, J. Fiscal arrangements for Public Law 94–142. *Exceptional Children,* 1977, **44** (No. 5), 333–337.

Bannatyne, A. *Language, reading, and learning disabilities.* Springfield, Ill.: Thomas, 1971.

Bannatyne, A. Diagnosis: A note on recategorization of the WISC scaled scores. *Journal of Learning Disabilities,* 1974, **7,** 272–274.

Beery, K.E., & Buktenica, N.A. *Developmental test of visual-motor integration.* Chicago: Follett, 1967.

Bender, L. A visual motor gestalt test and its clinical use. *Research Monograph of the American Orthopsychiatric Association,* 1938 (No. 3).

Bond, G.L., & Tinker, M.A. *Reading difficulties: Their diagnosis and correction* (2nd ed.). New York: Appleton-Century Crofts, 1967.

Buck, J., & Jolles, I. *House-tree-person.* Los Angeles: Western Psychological Services, 1966.

Burgemeister, B.B., Blum, L.H., & Lorge, I. *Columbia mental maturity scale* (3rd ed.). New York: Harcourt Brace Jovanovich, 1972.

Buros, O.K. *Seventh mental measurement yearbook.* Highland Park, N. J.: Gryphon, 1972.

Colarusso, R.P., & Hammill, D.D. *Motor-free visual perception test.* Novato, Calif.: Academic Therapy Publications, 1972.

Connolly, A.J., Nachtman, W., & Pritchett, E.M. *Key Math diagnostic arithmetic test—manual.* Circle Pines, Minn.: American Guidance Services, 1976.

Doll, E. *Vineland social maturity scale.* Circle Pines, Minn.: American Guidance Services, Inc., 1953 & 1965.

Dunn, L.M., & Markwardt, F.C. *Peabody individual achievement test manual.* Circle Pines, Minn.: American Guidance Services, 1970.

Dunn, L.M. *Peabody picture vocabulary test—revised.* Circle Pines, Minn.: American Guidance Services, 1981.

The education for all handicapped children act (PL 94-142). 1975. 20 U.S.C. 1401.

Fitts, W. *Tennessee self concept inventory.* Nashville, Tennessee: Counselor Recordings and Tests, 1965.

Guilford, J.P. *The nature of human intelligence.* New York: McGraw-Hill, 1967.

Jastak, J.E., & Jastak, S.R. *The wide range achievement test.* Wilmington, Delaware: Guidance Associates, 1978.

Kaufman, A.S. Factor analysis of the WISC-R at eleven age levels between 6½ and 16½ years. *Journal of Consulting and Clinical Psychology,* 1975, **43,** 135–147.

Keystone View Company. Keystone visual survey tests. Davenport, Iowa: Keystone View, n.d.

Kirk, S., McCarthy, J., & Kirk, W. *Illinois test of psycholinguistic abilities.* Urbana: University of Illinois Press, 1968.

Koppitz, E.M. *The Bender gestalt test for young children.* New York: Grune & Stratton, 1963.

Koppitz, E.M. *The Bender gestalt test for young children. Volume II: Research and application, 1963-1973.* New York: Grune & Stratton, 1975.

Kraner, R.E. *Kraner preschool math inventory.* Austin: Learning Concepts, 1976.

Lambert, N., Windmiller, M., Cole, L., & Figueroa, R. *Manual for AAMD adaptive behavior scale—public school version* (Rev. 1974). Washington, D.C.: The Association, 1975.

Larsen, S.C., & Hammill, D.D. *The test of written spelling.* Austin: Empire, 1976.

McCarthy, D. *Manual for the McCarthy scales of children's abilities.* New York: Psychological Corp., 1972.

Piers, E., & Harris, D. *The Piers-Harris children's self concept scale.* Nashville, Tennessee: Counselor Recordings & Tests, 1969.

Salvia, J., & Ysseldyke, J.E. *Assessment in special and remedial education* (2nd ed.). Boston: Houghton Mifflin, 1981.

Sattler, J.M. *Assessment of child's intelligence* (rev. ed.). Philadelphia: Saunders, 1974.

Slosson, R.L. *Slosson intelligence test (SIT) for children and adults.* East Aurora, N. Y.: Slosson Educational Publications, 1963 & 1971.

Stetson, E.G., *The psychometric data profile.* Houston: University of Houston Diagnostic Learning Center, 1978.

Stetson, E.G. *Stetson auditory discrimination test (SADT).* Houston: Educational Services, 1978.

Stetson, E.G. *Informal copy test (ICT).* Houston: Educational Services, 1980.

Stetson, E.G. *Reading-spelling vocabulary proficiency test.* Houston: Educational Services, 1981.

Stetson, E.G. *Reading-spelling vocabulary program (RSVP).* Houston: Educational Services, 1981.

Terman, L., & Merrill, M. *Stanford-Binet intelligence scale* (1972 norms edition). Boston: Houghton Mifflin, 1973.

Titmus Optical Vision Testers. *Titmus school vision tester.* Piscataway, N. J.: Titmus Optical Vision Testers, n.d.

Urban, W. *Draw-a-person.* Los Angeles: Western Psychological Services, 1963.

Wechsler, D. *Manual for the Wechsler adult intelligence scale.* New York: Psychological Corporation, 1955.

Wechsler, D. *Manual for the Wechsler preschool and primary scale of intelligence.* New York: Psychological Corp., 1967.

Wechsler, D. *Manual for the Wechsler intelligence scale for children—revised.* New York: Psychological Corp., 1974.

Wepman, J.M. *Auditory discrimination test (ADT).* Chicago: Language Research Associates, 1958.

Woodcock, R.W. *Woodcock reading mastery tests.* Circle Pines, Minn.: American Guidance Services, 1973.

Woodcock, R.W., & Johnson. *Woodcock-Johnson psychoeducational battery.* Boston: Teaching Resources Corp., 1977.

CHAPTER 9

Neuropsychological Assessment of the Child: Myths, Current Status, and Future Prospects

THOMAS J. BOLL

Myth: An ill-founded belief held uncritically by an interested group. A story whose origin is forgotten or obscure, which is used to explain some belief or practice (Webster, 1970).

There are a multitude of myths about the behavioral effects of brain damage and dysfunction. Some are widely accepted, predate clinical neuropsychology as an identified discipline, and, in fact, have served to aid its past growth and current popularity. Other myths have developed because of the necessary but potentially misleading developmental process that provides the scientific underpinnings of the practice of neuropsychology. Before we can discuss neuropsychology and the role of neuropsychologists, several of these myths must be identified and some current understandings of their implications for practice must be expanded.

Myth I: People with brain damage[1] can be identified due to certain predictable characteristics of their behavior. These behavioral characteristics involve motor, cognitive, and emotional aspects of their psychological functioning. Bakwin (1966) declared that "the behavioral manifestations of cerebral damage, whatever the etiology, are fairly uniform and characteristic" (p. 567). Wender (1971) stated that "the behavioral pattern associated with minimal brain dysfunction is rather distinct and is easily identified" (p. 3). Wender went on to suggest that no identifiable neurological abnormality was necessary for classification of a child with minimal brain dysfunction.

The problem with such statements goes well beyond the fact that they represent a significant oversimplification of clinical experience. Little in the experience of clinicians who actually deal with persons with brain damage would confirm such claims—just the opposite in fact. In addition to clinical experience, a glance at almost any journal article comparing patients with and without brain damage would suggest quite the opposite finding as well. It is true that in the typical group study the central tendency or level of performance of the brain-damaged group is significantly inferior to that of matched non-brain-damaged subjects. Examination of the data reflecting variability (standard deviations), however, will reveal even wider differences between the groups. Clinical and experimental empirical data indicate that if there were one single overriding effect of brain damage upon human psychological functioning (and most certainly there is not), it would be an increase in behavioral variability and not one unvarying picture of behavioral deficit (Head, 1926).

The problem with pronouncements regarding the uniform behavioral effects of brain damage is their tendency to produce an orientation among practitioners toward identification of presence or absence of the impairment while failing to focus at all upon the normal brain as the organ of the mind and human behavior. The focus on identification or diagnosis as an end in itself is indefensible unless some value is gained from the diagnosis. If all persons with brain damage could, by that diagnosis, be understood to possess certain behavioral characteristics, such information would be useful to overall clinical management. It is not only clinically obvious but has been scientifically well documented recently (Boll, 1978, 1981; Boll & Barth, 1981; Lezak, 1976; Smith, 1975, 1981) and long ago (Jackson, 1898; Lashley cited by Cobb, 1960) that brain damage is not a unitary phenomenon. The diversity of brain damage includes its size, rate of growth, location within the brain, lateralization, age at onset, chronicity, origin (external trauma or internal disease), histopathological characteristics, and significance for improvement or decline of the patient's physical state. Early references to the relationship between differing aspects of brain impairment and human behavior are available: "It should be a fundamental principle of neural interpretation of psychological factors that the nervous activities are as complex as psychological activities which they constitute" (Lashley quoted by Cobb, 1960, p. xx).

The very existence of this discussion after over 100 years of formal research in the field of brain behavior relationships suggests that the myths about brain damage and the understandings surrounding them are well ingrained in our professional culture. It is necessary then to discuss various aspects of the relationship between brain damage and human behavior before other issues can be taken up. Three general areas of sequelae of brain damage, that is, motor, cognitive, and emotional, will be discussed as representative of neuropsychological evidence on the topic of behavioral correlates of brain damage.

MOTOR FUNCTIONS

Myth 2: Brain damage causes a characteristic change in motor behavior: Hyperactivity. Changes in motoric behavior following brain damage divide into issues of deficit and excess. *The first question is:* Does brain damage cause a change in motor ability and, if so, how much, what kind, and in whom? Boll (1974) demonstrated that children of school age, with various types of cerebral pathology, showed, as a group, a significantly reduced level of motor speed, strength, psychomotor coordination, and problem-solving ability. Reitan (1974), in a similar study, found the same results for a somewhat younger patient group. Klonoff and Low (1974), found that following head injury general motor ability was reduced. Each of these investigators pointed out, however, that within their groups patients existed whose motor skills were entirely normal despite the presence of well-documented brain damage.

A finer type of motor behavior is referred to as persistence. Such behaviors as protruding the tongue, keeping the eyes closed, fixing the gaze, saying "ahh" for 20–30 seconds are included in this category of behavior. Benton and his colleagues, pursuing yet another innovative line of research from his productive laboratory, found that brain-damaged children had significantly greater difficulty with such tasks than did normals (Benton, Garfield, & Chiorini, 1964; Garfield, 1964). Knights studied tasks somewhat intermediate between gross speed, strength, and coordination on the one hand and persistence on the other. Measures of tremor and fine motor steadiness again revealed deficits in samples of brain-damaged children (Knights & Moule, 1968; Knights, 1973).

Three studies examined the issues of lateralization of brain damage upon motor deficit and lateralization of motor deficits reflecting lateralized brain damage and its effect on other psychological functions. Atkinson (1970) reported that, among children with lateralized brain damage, those with right cerebral hemisphere lesions experienced greatest motor difficulties on the left side of the body and those with left cerebral hemisphere damage showed right-sided motor deficits. Garfield (1964) found that children, unlike adults, with left cerebral hemisphere impairment showed greater motor impersistence than children with comparable right cerebral hemisphere damage.

A comparison of the relative degree of motor deficit compared to four other ability areas following brain damage was performed by Boll using brain-damaged patients who were, as a group, worse than matched normals on all psychological functions examined (Boll, 1972). This study demonstrated that conceptual, visual-perceptual deficits were greater among brain-damaged children than were motor deficits. Motor impairment exceeded only tactile perceptual deficits in severity among the abilities measured. Even here, however, it is easy to identify exceptions to this order of relative deficit. Children with several very different types of brain impairment (e.g., cerebral palsy, muscular dystrophy, posterior fossa tumors) will demonstrate greater problems on motor tasks than on other pyschological functions (Knights, Hinton, & Drader, 1973; Knights & Hinton, 1973) while other types of damage (e.g., closed head injury) appear to affect nonmotor functions more strongly (Klonoff, Low, & Clark, 1977).

The second question is: Does brain damage cause hyperactivity, or, conversely, are hyperactive children brain damaged? Review of the relevant literature reveals not only that the majority of articles on hyperactivity discuss children without documented brain impairment but also that few articles on children with proven brain impairment of any type describe hyperactivity. In fact, the previously cited studies of motor performance indicate that of the three possible outcomes following a wide variety of types of brain damage (normoactivity, hypoactivity, hyperactivity) the former is the most frequent and the latter the least.

The most careful and comprehensive investigation of the relationship between brain damage and hyperactivity was included in the Isle of Wight study (Rutter, Graham, & Yule, 1970). They found hyperkinesis very rare among their brain-damaged children and more strongly associated with mental retardation than brain damage. Shaffer, Chadwick, and Rutter (1975) found few hyperactive children among their head injury patients and Seidel, Chadwick, and Rutter (1975) found this behavioral characteristic equally uncommon in a population of children with cerebral palsy. Rutter et al. (1970) concluded: There may be a slight tendency for disorders of attention and of activity level (both an increase and

a decrease of activity) to be minimally more frequent in brain damaged children but the differences are slight and of little, if any, practical importance.

In fact, out of 2,000 children included in this study, Rutter was only able to identify one with a "true" hyperactive syndrome. Graham et al. (1962) also concluded that hyperactivity was not a prominent feature of children with brain damage due to fetal anoxia. Indeed, this series of excellent investigations found that impulsiveness was somewhat more common among children with psychiatrically labeled conduct disorders but showed no association with neurologic abnormality. Rutter et al. concluded: "It seems that most of the features, such as impulsiveness and overactivity, which are reputed to be indicators of brain damage, are in fact merely very common features of psychiatric disorder regardless of the presence of neurologic abnormality." What are the implications of this data for the correctness of the reflexlike connection by clinicians of hyperactivity with brain damage? Rutter concludes that "it is not a syndrome of brain damage, although biological factors probably often play an important part in its etiology" (Rutter, 1977, p. 11). Obviously, myths not only require little support for their continued existence but can thrive in the face of significant evidence denying them.

In response to question 1, brain damage frequently does result in motor changes. These changes occur in simple and complex skills, with greatest motor deficit contralateral to the site of brain damage in lateralized cases. Some types of brain damage (posterior fossa tumors) produce motor deficits greater than cognitive changes, while other disorders (closed head injury) produce the opposite pattern. With regard to the frequently assumed relationship between brain damage and hyperactivity, the data indicate that, despite its popularity as support for certain diagnoses, hyperactivity is not a common or likely result of brain injury. It may represent a separate and possibly physiological syndrome whose frequency is actually far lower than the amount of interest in it would suggest—a situation quite similar to that of early infantile autism of a decade ago.

COGNITIVE FUNCTIONS

Myth 3: Perceptual deficits are the major higher psychological function difficulty produced by brain damage. Issues of cognitive function following brain damage can be addressed with two questions in a fashion similar to that used to discuss motor deficit. These questions are: (1) *Does brain damage cause cognitive impairment?* and (2) *Is there a single invariant pattern of cognitive sequelae following brain damage, and, if so, is it best appreciated by examination of children using tasks requiring visuospatial perception?*

An early and excellent attempt to address both of these questions was published by Graham and Ernhart and their colleagues (Graham et al., 1963; Ernhart et al., 1963). In answer to question 1 (Does brain damage cause cognitive impairment in children?), they found in the affirmative. Their results indicated that all areas of cognitive functioning tapped were impaired in the diffusely brain-damaged children considered as a group. A study using an even more extensive battery of behavioral measures tapping areas of memory, language, perception, and learning was employed by Reed, Reitan, and Kløve (1965). They, too, found impairment across this inclusive sample of cognitive functions. Like Graham et al., they concluded that heterogeneously brain-damaged groups of children showed relatively greater impairment in language skill than in other cognitive areas but found no single function always deficient in each child considered individually. No single pattern emerged as characteristic of the "brain-damaged child." This finding occurred despite their reliance upon patients with well-documented brain impairment. Support for these general findings, for the globally impaired cognitive functioning of groups of heterogeneously brain-damaged children and for the absence of a most characteristic cognitive profile has been consistently repeated (Boll, 1974; Klonoff & Low, 1974; Klonoff & Paris, 1974; Reitan, 1974).

The question of whether a particular type or pattern of cognitive compromise characteristic of children with brain damage exists continues to be asked despite overwhelming evidence that such is not the case. Implicit in this question is the expectation that one particular type of impairment within an individual's cognitive repertoire will emerge as preeminent. The most frequently anticipated deficit is in the area of visuospatial perceptual performance. A direct examination of the comparative degree of compromise in various cognitive abilities following brain damage in children was conducted by Boll (1972). Patients with brain damage were compared in areas of concept formation ability, visuospatial perception, auditory-nonverbal perception, tactile form perception, and motor functioning. The brain-damaged children as a group were found to be significantly poorer in each of these important behavioral areas than were non-brain-damaged controls. Conceptual ability was found to be more impaired than visuospatial skill. It was more impaired than any of the other perception or motor areas. Visual perception was more impaired than tactile and motor skills but not more than auditory perception. This general ordering of cognitive functions with most complex activities being most vulnerable was predicted by Vigotsky (1962) and described most eloquently by Dreifuss (1975):

Central processing and the quality of communication in man is such a high adornment of his culture and requires such cortical sophistication that lesions will interfere with these highly developed functions, although they may yet be too slight to affect less specialized activities, as it were, truncating the apex of man's ability, the capacity to communicate abstract thought. (p. 390)

That language rather than visuoperceptual ability emerges consistently as the preeminent area of cognitive deficit in no way suggests that a one-to-one relationship exists and we need only switch allegiance from "perceptual handicap" to "language handicap." Factors such as age at onset (Boll, 1973; Teuber & Rudel, 1962), type of lesion (Knights et al., 1973), and lateralization of lesion (Atkinson, 1970) in many cases play a role in enhancing or diminishing the applicability of this general finding.

An example of the need for caution in adopting general understandings for clinical practice is the experience with the Verbal and Performance IQ scores as postulated indicators of left (verbal) or right (performance) cerebral hemisphere impairment in children. The validity of the VIQ-PIQ split and the critical qualifications and exceptions to the general findings with adults have been recently reviewed (Boll, 1978). With children, due in part to the different neuropathological characteristics of children's versus adults' brain damage, the findings require even further qualifications. No study of children's lateralized brain damage has yet to be reported comparing VIQ and PIQ. Studies using indications of lateralizations, such as EEG, focus in what are likely generalized conditions such as epilepsy, have been equivocal. With one major exception (Fedio & Mirsky, 1969), the behavioral association with indications of lateralized epilepsy in children has not been found to hold for the predicted patterns of verbal and nonverbal functioning on the Wechsler Scale (Black, 1976; Boll & Berent, 1977; Pennington, Galliani, & Voegle, 1965). Reed and Reitan (1969) found that damage to motor skills (not necessarily due to strictly cortical damage), on the left side of the body opposite to the cerebral hemisphere usually responsible for perceptual functions, produced a Verbal-Performance split on the Wechsler Scale in favor of the Verbal IQ. Children with motor deficit on the right side of the body across from the cerebral hemisphere usually thought of as responsible for language skills, however, also showed Verbal IQs significantly greater than Performance IQs. This tendency toward higher VIQ than PIQ in brain-damaged children regardless of whether the impairment was assessed as primarily right lateralized, left lateralized, or nonlateralized has been confirmed by Black (1976) and Boll and Berent (1977). Among children in our study (Boll & Berent, 1977) with evidence for lateralization of brain impairment provided by seizure manifestations and unilateral physical-neurological, and electroencephalographic abnormalities (but who may well have generalized brain impairment despite these indications of lateralization), 40 percent produced VIQ-PIQ splits of 14 points or more. There was no correspondence found, however, between indications of the right or left or generalized nature of the disorder and presence or absence of a VIQ-PIQ split or its direction. In fact, fully 85 percent of the children with 14 points or greater VIQ-PIQ splits had VIQ greater than PIQ. This was equally true for the right hemisphere, left hemisphere, and generalized damage groups.

With regard to cognitive effects of brain damage, the answer to question 1 is affirmative. Brain damage does, as a rule in most children, produce general reduction in cognitive functions. This reduction varies from very mild to severe and, in any single child, while certain skills may be obviously affected, others may demonstrate high levels of excellence. As for question 2, no single pattern of cognitive functioning is specifically suggestive of brain damage, nor is brain damage always productive of any single cognitive style or disability. While certain areas of cognitive functioning may be somewhat more subject to impairment, when comparing groups of children, the myth of visuospatial perception as the area particularly vulnerable to the effects of brain impairment is not supported by available evidence when patients are considered individually or in groups.

EMOTIONAL FUNCTIONING

Myth 4: Brain damage produces serious emotional disturbance. The two questions addressed to the effects of brain damage on motor and cognitive functioning are appropriate for emotional correlates as well. (1) *Does brain damage produce an increased or general incidence of emotional disturbance:* If so, (2) *Is there a particular psychiatric category or behavioral pattern that is typical of the effects of brain damage?*

There seems little doubt that brain damage during childhood places one at greater risk for difficulties in life adjustment, including diagnosed psychiatric disorder. Estimates of children with brain damage who experience identifiable emotional disorder tend to cluster around 30–35 percent or five to six times that of non-chronically-ill, non-mentally-retarded and non-brain-damaged children (Boll & Berent, 1977; Rutter, 1977; Shaffer, 1974). Factors that contribute to this increased incidence have been reviewed by Boll and Barth (1981) and Rutter (1977). Some of these factors include presence of physical handicap, lowered intellectual ability, abnormal electrical activity in the brain, and occurrence of seizures.

Despite the increased frequency of emotional disturbance, however, no characteristic behavior or syndrome has been demonstrated. Ernhart et al. (1963) stated that "there is little evidence for the generalization...that there is a unique personality syndrome characteristic of the young brain injured child" (p. 32). Rutter (1977) found that the brain-impaired children showed the typical mixture of emotional and conduct disorders seen in non-brain-damaged children but no stereotyped psychiatric syndrome. He concluded:

Brain damaged children show an excess of most types of symptomatology, but that, if like is compared with like, there is nothing characteristic about the symptoms. In other words, the symptoms of brain damaged children without psychiatric disorder are similar to those of children in the general population. The symptoms of brain damaged children with psychiatric disorder are similar to those non-brain damaged children with psychiatric disorder. (p. 10)

He identified six factors which can be seen as contributing to emotional difficulties. These are: (1) abnormal brain activity; (2) cognitive defects critical to the patient's subjective self-awareness and socioeconomic coping; (3) direct effects of brain damage on such personality related variables as frustration tolerance, mental-emotional resilience, or temporary lethargy or irritability; (4) secondary effects of treatment including drug side effects, physical restriction, repeated hospitalization; (5) responses of others to their own myths and understandings leading to avoidance, scapegoating, or overprotection; and (6) the indi-

vidual's own response to a damaging event, ranging from unrealistic bravado and denial of difficulties to unnecessary reliance upon mild deficits as excuses for reduced participation in some aspect of one's previous life activities. Often-noted clinical pictures include difficulty with impulse control, temper outbursts, irritability, depression, reduced social interest, isolation, and boredom. Impairment in social judgment, reduced initiative, immaturity, vacillating affect, and blunted affect, along with unusual anxiety and denial of emotional problems and change, have been seen repeatedly as the short term and frequently persisting sequelae of acquired brain damage in later childhood and adolescence. Some of these difficulties are secondary to or at least connected with reduced cognitive capacity and reduced stress tolerance that in turn make successful coping with school, friends, family, and even self-imposed demands difficult or impossible in new, unpredictable, and unsettling, even frightening ways. Such consequences following mild head injury and infections or toxicities involving the CNS frequently go undiagnosed and are, therefore, misunderstood as resulting from patients' poor motivation or wrong-headedness. Such misunderstanding leads to anger and confusion from parents and teachers and misguided psychotherapeutic efforts aimed at remedying problem behavior without appreciating its cause and its nature, that is, the actual personal deficits leading to the behavior and their neurologically mediated changes with time.

The incompleteness of our neuropsychological knowledge of psychiatric disorders in children is obvious and considerable. Certainly the scientific study of the emotional correlates of neurological disorder can be added to the list of research-clinical needs and opportunities presented as the final section of this chapter. Such is frequently the case in this rapidly developing field.

Myth 5: The primary activity of clinical neuropsychology is diagnosis of brain damage.

Myth 5 is based on the following assumption: Given that there is an entity or condition called "brain damage" that can be identified through behavioral examination, the primary role of clinical neuropsychology is to discover that human behavior, the measurement of which provides the most accurate hit rate for presence or absence of that condition. Leaving the neuroanatomic and neuropathological inadequacy of this myth to our previous discussion and recent reviews (Boll, 1978; Lezak, 1976; Smith, 1975, 1981), some discussion from a purely behavioral viewpoint is still in order.

The first four myths produced a tendency to look at the brain and the behavior it subserves as a unitary entity. The fifth myth produces an even greater difficulty for clinical practice. This myth suggests that a legitimate clinical task is to identify something as defective either because such identification is possible or because such identification conveys sufficient information to suggest further activities that will be of use to the clinician. The idea that there can be a behavioral test for brain damage demands that a single behavior will always be affected by such damage; this implies, in turn, that all brain damage produces an identical behavioral effect. We have spent considerable time demonstrating that despite some reasonable group generalizations, no single, simple or complex, cognitive, motor, or affective deficit or alteration is a dependable result of brain damage in a single patient. No behavior has been found that is produced solely by brain damage and no other human condition or situation. We are in a situation, then, where brain damage may result in one or a few or many psychological changes. It may also leave major areas of human functioning apparently untouched. The factors that influence which behaviors will and will not be affected by brain impairment in an individual case are fully as numerous as the human abilities available to such alteration. Failure to attend to other than a restricted sample of human behavior allowed Dandy (1928) to report that an entire cerebral hemisphere could be removed without psychological consequences. Much more recently, a similar removal produced no abnormality in the most widely used test of "organicity" (Bruell & Albee, 1962), and Russell (1976) reported no deficits on several well-validated procedures. This was true despite the fact that the patient had obvious behavioral deficits in areas of functioning not tapped by these procedures. Even when correct identification of deficits is made, however, simply knowing of the presence of brain damage cannot be assumed to contribute to understanding the patient's complaints, and such assumption may, in fact, hinder or prevent appropriate treatment (Boll, 1978).

For many clinicians, even those who were trained recently, the focus remains on finding something wrong. It is as though the normal brain, far from being the organ of the human mind, is so much inert matter used to provide proper spacing between the ears. This organ, like none other in the body, seems to become of clinical interest and functional significance only following damage. Such damage causes the brain to bring under its control one or several behaviors that were, prior to that damage, considered to be the product of psychosituational factors without biological referent. In other words, the area of interest for clinical neuropsychologists is mistakenly thought to be brain damage and not brain function and organization.

Such a one-sided notion is incorrect on two counts. First, there is considerable and mounting evidence that the differential, normal organization of the brain is inseparable from the differential conglomeration of psychological-behavioral strengths and weaknesses that describe normal individual differences. Knowledge of the biological basis of behavior, while in no way discounting the importance of psychosituational factors, provides information by itself or in a broader context of considerable relevance to many usual life activities such as education and occupation.

Second, it is not possible to appreciate the significance of brain damage either neuropathologically or psychologically by focusing exclusively upon the deficit area. Hughlings Jackson (1898) states: "We are obliged in each case to deal with the diseased part as a flow in the whole nervous system; we thus have to take into account the undamaged remainder. ... A great part of symptomatology in nervous maladies with negative lesions is the outcome of activities of undamaged healthy structures" (p. 79). Jackson's statement applies directly to neuropsychology. We cannot assume that aberrant behavior is produced by the damaged area. It is more likely the product of the rest of the brain expressing its reaction to a damaged part. A careful pursuit of behavioral deficiency in a limited area of neurological (temporal lobe) or psychological (language) functioning, no matter how important or interesting, is deficient clinically and scientifically. Scientifically, a deficit which occurs in the presence of damage to one area cannot be assumed to be due to damage there until it has been demonstrated that damage elsewhere does not produce the same effect. Clinically, knowledge of a language or motor deficit allows for little description and recommendation without an appreciation of the perceptual, learning, tactile, and emotional capacities of the patient in question. Only after the whole patient is understood can the significance of the deficient parts be properly understood and treated.

The goal of clinical neuropsychology, then, is description of the relationship between brain function and human behavior. If the brain and damage to it do not represent unitary entities and conditions, then simple identification of presence or absence of brain damage can be seen as an impossible and meaningless task. If the functioning of normals and normal functioning of brain-damaged individuals are of equal interest to the identification of deficit, then diagnosis can be seen as only one part of the much larger role of clinical neuropsychology. The clinical purpose is to provide a unique area of understanding of the effect of neurological development and disorder on the human behavioral repertoire.

The rest of this chapter will describe a series of procedures for obtaining such information and will discuss the range of conditions in which current and future neuropsychological evaluations will aid in description, management, and treatment.

SELECTION OF EXAMINATION PROCEDURES

Assuming, as we must, that identification of presence or absence of brain damage is not the sole purpose of the examination, what will guide the selection of neuropsychological procedures? Factors to be considered can be grouped into five broad and somewhat overlapping areas: (1) purposes of the evaluation, (2) behavioral coverage, (3) availability to efficient interpretation, (4) practical and technical psychometric issues, and (5) validity for the purpose.

Purposes of Evaluation

The two most common purposes for neuropsychological evaluation are clinical service and research. It is fortunate that these two purposes, far from posing a point of conflict, represent the essence of professional synergism. Without clinical questions, research would lose its meaning. Without constant attempts to add evaluation of current practice and efforts to learn from current activities, best services cannot be provided. Procedures must be designed to obtain information that can be compared across individuals and groups. This allows clinicians to benefit from individual uniqueness rather than be defeated by it. Identification of the critical individual and group variants is the essence of clinical understanding and can only be obtained through comparisons made with a common referent.

The two main types of clinical service within clinical neuropsychology are identification and description. There are many situations in which identification of neurological impairments through neuropsychological examination is not only acceptable but essential. Conditions of neurological impairment following head injury are, in many instances, not subject to identification through any other set of procedures. Without recognition of the cause of a behavioral deficit as coming from brain injury, the description of the behavior may do little more than confirm the obvious or open additional questions. Knowledge that a certain behavioral profile is produced by head injury not only aids in understanding the source of the behavior (the patient is brain damaged, not crazy or ill willed) but provides a structure of knowledge about prognosis that can only come from identification of etiology. It may be common knowledge that a person had a head injury. Frequently, however, the patient looks, talks, and feels normal and appears normal on standard physical-neurological tests as well. If such a patient begins to encounter significant behavioral difficulty at work or school, what is the relationship of this difficulty to the head injury? Not all head injuries produce significant cognitive deficits. How can one be sure the deficits seen on behavioral examination are due to the head injury and not one of several other causes such as anxiety, preexisting deficits, and so on? If independent evaluation of the examination data suggests the cause without prior reference to the patient's history, one's confidence in the association between the behavior and the head injury rises considerably.

Many conditions exist that (unlike head injury) do not lead to immediate suspicion of cerebral deficit. Certain chronic physical disorders may produce not only eventual secondary central nervous system effects but also measurable behavior changes. Such changes have been demonstrated to precede other, more explicit medical indicators of such conditions as decreased adequacy of kidney function (Wright, Schaefer, & Solomons, 1979).

The accuracy and validity of neuropsychological procedures in identifying the relationship between behavior and brain functions provide the basis for description, which, in turn, is the largest portion of clinical neuropsychological practice. Knowledge of the presence of brain damage, even including considerable detail about its type, location, and so on, gives no information about the conse-

quences of the condition for human functioning. Careful clinical neurological examination provides very useful general clues and areas for further investigation. It is the role of the neuropsychologist to delineate the details of the psychological consequences of the brain damage and from that data influence the overall management, treatment, and particularly the chronic or long range as opposed to acute medical crisis aspects of that treatment. Particularly in children whose neurological disorders are more commonly long term, nonprogressive, and generalized, behavioral consequences are likely to emerge as the largest factor in the day-to-day lives of the children and their families.

The behavioral aspects of recovering, fluctuating, and deteriorating neurologic disorders are not perfectly correlated with the findings of physical examinations. Following head injury, the recovery course for abnormalities on the physical exam and electroencephalogram are typically complete many months before full return of highest skills. Cognitive sequelae of conditions with variable courses cannot be assumed to be absent in times of physical remission and, in instances of deterioration, neuropsychological compromise may lead or follow changes in physical symptomatology. The effectiveness of medical-neurological interventions is measurable in neuropsychological terms. Hammock, Milhorat, and Baron (1976) state that "psychological testing has proven to be of particular significance not only in the diagnosis of normal pressure hydrocephalus in the child, but also in the estimation of success or failure of its treatment"(p. 62). Neuropsychological procedures have documented the remarkable ability of children to recover from significant neurological damage (Boll & Barth, 1981). Such clinical documentation also provides the patient and family with a detailed and periodically updated behavioral profile from which strategies for coping, adaptation, and rehabilitation can be developed and modified during the entire course of the patient's recovery and eventual stabilization of psychological capabilities. One of the major sources of significant behavioral difficulties in a patient and family after the period of health crisis is failure to realize the consequences of the damage upon the patient's behavioral repertoire. Provision of an understanding of the patient's abilities and deficits, and aid in modification of the environment to prevent undue failure resulting from transient as well as permanent deficits while rehabilitation and other long term adjustments are being accomplished are activities central to clinical neuropsychology.

Behavioral Coverage

Recognition that the brain is the organ of the mind leads to a discussion of mind or psychological behavioral functions or abilities as the entities to be examined and removes us from the tendency to think of tests for "organicity." What human abilities and functions are of interest? Among those some must be chosen for examination while others must, unfortunately, be passed over. The areas of function to be covered can be varied depending upon the interest and priorities of the neuropsychologist, but there is little argument that sufficient breadth to cover the most obvious and major areas must be provided. These areas can be considered arbitrarily as reflecting *content* and *process*. *Content* areas include language, perception, and motor and sensory functions. Within these major content areas, variations of modality (auditory or visual), and material (figure or symbol), and subareas (visual, auditory, tactile modes of perception) must be considered. Mental *processes* such as memory, attention, problem solving, and learning are central to human day-to-day competence and interact with content to define the core human repertoire of behaviors whose relationship to normal and impaired states of brain function is the focus of neuropsychological evaluation. More intensive investigation into subsets of language or memory, for example, guided by the clinical requirements of the patient or the special skills of the neuropsychological clinician, represents an appropriate and necessary degree of flexibility once the basic requirements have been

met. It is common for the naive or fledgling neuropsychologist to express an interest in brief, short term, streamlined examinations. This interest turns, with experience, toward a wish for ever greater amounts of clinical information as the complexity of human-brain-behavior-relationships becomes more fully understood.

Interpretation of Neuropsychological Procedures

The behavioral consequences of brain damage, like the damage to the brain itself, are complex and variable. Just as no single psychological content or process can be found that is always affected (let alone a single psychometric test), so, too, no single expression of deficit, that is, reduced ability, absent ability, increased variability, and so on, can be said to characterize universally the effect of brain damage on the human behavioral repertoire. For that reason, several ways of evaluating the patient's performance across the various content and process areas must be identified to maximize the likelihood of appreciating the existence and significance of behavioral changes resulting from the many conditions of neurological damage and impairment. Of the many possible inferential-interpretive strategies identified within neuropsychology and described in detail recently along with clinical investigational examples, four emerge as being of particular relevance (Boll, 1978, 1981). These are relevant not only for interpretation of a group of neuropsychological tests once administered, but also provide an important guide in initial task selection.

Behavioral Level

The most frequently identified correlate of brain impairment is reduced ability in one or a number of areas. Most psychometric procedures provide information about the level of the person's performance relevant to some reference group. Most of these groups are normal and become individually useful due to age, education, sex, geographic location, or other specifying characteristics. Other groups are chosen for their possession of a documented deviation from normality due to such characteristics as brain damage, mental deficiency, criminality, attempted suicide, and so on. When related to the normal groups, performance characteristics are usually couched in terms of the amount of particular ability or tendency a person possesses that places him or her below or above the reference group to a specific degree. No indication is provided as to whether the person has ever possessed more or less than this ability or style or whether he or she is gaining or losing some of it. Neither does such data provide much information about the many possible reasons for the currently obtained level.

Reference to nonnormal populations is usually made in terms of closeness to a particular group. Performance above or below a certain level, found to characterize many members of a known group (the brain damaged), is then used to characterize similar performers as likely members of the same group. Here, too, no data is provided on whether performance is rising or falling, better or worse than was previously the case, nor is the reason for such performance provided. Naming a range of scores for a group likely to perform in that range is no assurance that all (or even most) persons in that range are also in that group. The syllogism of cars and Fords applies here.

A battery of behavioral measures must, and almost inevitably will, include some procedures for which good information about levels is available. Just as one must be alert to avoid restriction of inquiry to one behavioral content or process, however, one must also recognize that a single manifestation of ability or deficit, no matter how many times or following what provocation it is seen, possesses only the strength, and is subject to all of the limitations, of that content or process or inferential strategy. It is far more efficient and productive for patient care to maximize variety in each of these measurement categories than to depend upon exhaustive coverage in one to the exclusion of the rest. Obviously an approach that provides both breadth and depth is ideal. So much for the quickie test!

Behavioral Pattern

Analysis of the patient's performance, whether by means of clinical or actuarial procedures, has advantages well beyond a sequential procedure in which each test is reported by itself following a multiple t-test model. Interactions, patterns, and groupings receive at least as much attention as any single score or sum of scores. There is abundant evidence that the combination of clinical and actuarial approach produces the best clinical information both diagnostically and descriptively (Filskov & Goldstein, 1974; Goldstein, Deysach, & Kleinknecht, 1973; Matthews, Shaw, & Kløve, 1966; Reitan, 1964; Reitan & Boll, 1973; Selz & Reitan, 1979).

Behavioral pattern as a strategy of inference leads to explicit attention to comparisons of areas of strength and weakness. This has the advantage of making explicit a clinical process that is commonly employed, albeit implicitly. It also allows comparison of patients with themselves. In order to take advantage of this strategy, the neuropsychological examination must measure more than one psychological content or process. If its only influence were to cause neuropsychologists to attend more broadly to the human behavioral repertoire in instrument choice, its value would be clear. In comparing people with themselves, a second view of one's patients' psychological functioning is provided. Even for the patient with very good general skill, or for one who is generally very limited, expectances have been developed for intraindividual ability relationships (Boll & Reitan, 1972; Knights, 1973; Matarazzo, 1972; Selz & Reitan, 1979). If these expectations are not met, information beyond level is obtained about possibilities for cognitive disruption, change from previous levels in certain areas and, in some instances, existence of impairment of brain functions. No single inferential strategy, like no area of psychological content or processes, is sufficient to provide this information by itself but must be considered in the total context of examination of psychological content, process, and expression to provide description of function and, where appropriate, identification of disorder.

Specific Behavioral Deficit

The urge to quantify, ubiquitous in American psychometric tradition, has produced, with its rigor, a respect for and use of psychological assessment unlikely to have emerged in its absence. Few specialty areas have reaped greater benefit from the movement from subjective to objective data than has clinical neuropsychology. For this reason, it may seem remarkable that neuropsychologists have consistently defended the inclusion of procedures neither easily nor necessarily subject to quantitative analysis. Certain behaviors can be recognized as incompatible with normality in a particular dimension of functioning and can be so classified without recourse to other than dichotomous scaling techniques. Within the field of neurology, certain signs such as paralysis, reflex absence, or reflex deviation such as toe flaring instead of curling as a reaction to stimulation to the sole of the foot are simply recorded, when found, as abnormalities. These are not tests for or signs of brain damage but are indications of abnormality to be considered in the context of the complete examination. More complex behaviors such as severe distortion of the spatial configurations of shapes, inability to perform or abnormal performance of common acts (inability to demonstrate use of a key or hammer or use of comb to brush teeth) are incompatible with normality and are recorded as having occurred. Such specific signs must be designed to exclude their occurrence due to anxiety, limited intelligence, or other difficulties not of the type being examined for. There is, of course, well-recognized variability within and across the ability of totally normal persons to accomplish any task or perform any task at a selected time. The behaviors chosen and the identification criterion established, in order to avoid categorization of manifestations of normal variability as impaired, will necessarily also fail to identify certain instances of actual impairment. This bias shift away from false positives toward false negatives is necessary to allow high confidence in interpretation when the sign is present. It is possible to include such procedures because they are not used alone or in isolation. In the context of other expressions of deficit, that is, level and pattern, specific behavioral deficits can be modified for purposes of diagnosis and enriched for purposes of description without compromising the sign test as part of the neurological evaluation. The not-so-secret additional advantage of inclusion of this mode of expression of deficit is the requirement for inclusion of still other behavioral samples not routinely employed in traditional psychological assessments.

Behavior of the Right versus the Left Side of the Body

Two of the major psychological content areas, motor and sensory functions, while subject to analysis by means of the three inferential schemes outlined above, are also available for at least one more type of evaluation. Motor and sensory tests can be presented to or performed by one side of the body at a time. Comparisons of the two sides can then be obtained. For certain tasks, such as those of a tactile perceptual nature, equivalence is expected. Evidence of difficulty experienced on one side of the body but not the other is quite different from generalized, bilateral incapacity. Unilateral deficit reveals the ability and willingness to perform and suggests that that deficit is particular to the modality tested, limited to one side of the body and possibly referable to the contralateral side of the brain. Such data are helpful in situations where information from other inferential strategies is equivocal. Such factors as cultural deprivation and poor motivation are not prone to produce unilateral motor or sensory deficit and the presence of such deficits or their absence provides fuller context for the understanding of higher level psychological functions. Because the "correct" level for an individual cannot be known, only relative statements can be made. Independent of level, however, discrepancies in such expressions of behavior as pattern and right/left relationships can be identified. We do know that on motor tasks not subject to learning (strength, speed), the preferred hand performs about 10 percent better than the nonpreferred hand. Such information, coupled with careful measurement of these psychological content areas, can identify even such subtle findings as bilateral equivalence in strength. This is a deviation from expectation in need of explanation (sprained wrist—brain damage) and allows its incorporation into the total understanding of the patient's behavioral repertoire.

This last inferential strategy and the psychological contents (motor and sensory) it measures are of particular usefulness in the examination of children. Children are in the process of rapid development. Development in this era of life is naturally uneven, even erratic, within the most normal and well-functioning child. Development can be significantly influenced temporarily by emotional trauma; physical, nonneurological illness; and, of course, neurological impairment. Following recovery from a medical, neurological, or emotional difficulty, development frequently not only returns to normal rate but provides a catch-up spurt as well. Neurological impairment produces different results in children depending upon when, within a range of a very few years, the damage occurs. It is also the case that damage occurring at one time may be the cause of biological deficits not manifest until several years afterwards, at the time when the damaged structures or connections were normally scheduled to express themselves. Because these issues are more complex in children than adults, because children are subject to greater influence from normal behavioral change due to development than are adults, and because we know less about brain behavior relationships in children than in adults, it would seem proper to proceed with greater rather than less caution in attributing to brain damage any set of behavioral expressions. Obviously, just the opposite has occurred.

Technical Considerations and Test Selection

The preceding discussion has dealt with broad and more conceptual than practical-technical issues of test selection for a neuropsychological examination battery. It appears so far that many individual tasks would fit into a neuropsychological battery, and such is the case. There are only two sets of factors that would steer one toward a particular procedure or away from another. The first set consists of practical-technical factors to be discussed in this section. It provides more specific focus in the decision process, but still suggests that many task combinations could emerge as effective brain behavior relationship evaluation batteries. The second, that of demonstrated validity, to be discussed in the next section, narrows the choices for current clinical use considerably but in no way reduces the options for future development through clinical investigation.

There are many issues that can be considered. Most of these apply to all areas of clinical psychological examination including, but not limited to, neuropsychology. Depending upon one's purposes and preferences, tests chosen may be: (1) portable and not dependent upon bulky equipment or equipment requiring special sound proofing, wiring, or lighting; (2) available in alternate forms that, with proper validation, would be of considerable utility where testing before and after brief procedures is indicated (surgery, ECT, etc.); (3) narrow band, that is, able to measure a single skill so that the source of poor performance can be clearly identified; (4) broad band, that is, requiring several skills (visual, perceptual, speed, coordination, learning), thus maximizing the likelihood of sensitivity to subtle difficulty; (5) appropriate for patients across the entire age range either through normatively based differences in requirements or alterations in forms for each age group; (6) possessed of independent normative and/or standardization data; (7) subject to objective scoring; (8) designed to minimize false positives; (9) designed to minimize false negatives; and (10) subject to qualitative analysis of the performances obtained. These characteristics pertain to individual tasks rather than to the entire battery, which may contain some tasks possessing each of these characteristics.

An example of one such set or battery of procedures is that developed by Halstead and modified and expanded by Reitan to be appropriate for children. This continually evolving evaluation procedure contains many general clinical psychometric measures as well as those with more specialized purpose. As will be demonstrated in the next section, this general set of procedures is the most commonly used and currently well-validated neuropsychological battery. This is not to imply that other modifications and new approaches will possess lesser clinical or scientific utility. The Halstead-Reitan procedures, because of their established familiarity and documented validity and utility, serve as an example of an examination of human adaptive ability sensitive to brain behavior relationships in children beginning at age 5. Many of these procedures such as the Wechsler Intelligence Scale for Children—Form R and the Wide Range Achievement Test are generally familiar. The Wechsler Scale is in fact more sensitive to the kinds of deficits produced by neurological deficit in children than is the comparable Wechsler Scale in assessing neurologically induced impairment in adults (Boll, 1978; Boll & Barth, 1981). The Wide Range Achievement Test, while far from a comprehensive academic skills battery, provides a sample of production ability (as opposed to multiple choice recognition) in three major areas, which is useful in comparing current skills with past levels of acquisition. The rest of the intermediate and young children's neuropsychology battery tests have been discussed in detail elsewhere (Boll, 1978, 1981) and will be described briefly here.

Neuropsychology Battery for Children

CATEGORY TEST. Ages 5–8, 80 items in 5 subtests; ages 9–14, 168 items in 6 subtests; no time limit; score is total errors. Requires no motor or verbal response. Measures learning, problem solving, grasp of cause and effect relationships. Poor performances often reflect poor judgment, inconsistencies in learning, and impaired memory.

TACTUAL PERFORMANCE TEST. Motor component. Three trials (one with each hand and final trial using both hands); score is time to completion; 5- to 8-year version requires 6

blocks to be placed in a rectangular board standing horizontal in a stand; 9- to 14-year version uses same blocks and board, but board is turned 90° to be held vertical in the stand. The patient is blindfolded before board and blocks are presented and remains so until all materials are removed. Requires motor speed, tactile form perception, and learning. Measures ability to utilize tactile and kinesthetic cues in the absence of visual feedback to solve a psychomotor problem. Also measures learning in trials 1–3 and provides comparison of right- versus left-sided upper extremity performance.

TACTUAL PERFORMANCE TASK. Memory and Localization component. Same for ages 5–14; score is number of blocks correctly remembered and located. The patient is required to draw from memory as many of the blocks as possible and locate them correctly inside the drawn outline of the board. Measures ability to benefit from situations when attention has not been directed toward remembering—a form of incidental memory.

FINGER OSCILLATION TEST. Manual tapping recommended for all ages (5–14)—electric tapper not recommended. Score is number of taps in a 10-second period; score is obtained for each hand. Requires motor speed. Measures speed and effort, and compares right and left sides of the body.

STRENGTH OF GRIP TEST. Plunger type and hand dynamometer; same apparatus for age 5–14. Score is strength recorded in pounds or kilograms for each side of the body.

SPEECH SOUNDS PERCEPTION TEST. Ages 9–14; 60 items; not timed, but patient is required to keep pace with tape-recorded presentation. Score is total errors. Requirement is to listen to nonsense words and identify each from three words on a printed page. Test measures sustained attention and concentration and auditory verbal perception.

SEASHORE RHYTHM TEST. Ages 9–14; 30 items; not timed, but patient is required to keep pace with a tape-recorded presentation.

Scaled score based on a number of correct ranges from 1 (best) to 10 (worst). Requirement is to identify two sets of rhythmic beats as same or different. Measures attention, concentration, and auditory nonverbal perception.

TRAIL-MAKING TEST, PARTS A AND B. Ages 9–14. Score is time to completion. Part A requires connection of circles numbered 1–15 distributed on blank page. Part B requires connection of numbers 1–8 and letters A–G in alternation, that is, 1,A,2,B, and so on.

TACTILE, AUDITORY, AND VISUAL SUPPRESSION. Ages 5–14. Score is number of failures to identify bilateral, simultaneous stimulation. Stimuli initially presented unilaterally on each side of the body then presented in bilateral simultaneous fashion and patients should respond "both." Requires simultaneous recognition of stimuli to each side of the body. Compares two sides of the body.

TACTILE FINGER LOCALIZATION. Ages 5–14. Score is number of errors for each hand. Without visual cues (blindfold, eyes closed, or hands through screen), patient must identify which finger was touched. Measures body awareness and localization through tactile perception. Compares two sides of the body.

FINGERTIP SYMBOL WRITING PERCEPTION. Ages 5–8. Same as Fingertip Number Writing Perception except x's and o's are substituted for numbers.

TACTILE FORM RECOGNITION TEST. Ages 5–14. Score is number of errors and total response time per hand. Requires tactile perception of shapes and visual perception and identification of same shape. Shape naming and verbal response not required. Tests tactile skill cross-modal transfer and compares two sides of the body.

APHASIA SCREENING TEST. Separate forms for ages 5–8 and 9–14. Responses are evaluated for presence or absence of several types of expressive and language disorder. Also provides sample of visuospatial reproductive tasks.

INDIVIDUAL PERFORMANCE TESTS. Ages 5–8. Color Form, Marching, Progressive Figures, Matching Figures, Matching Vs, Picture Matching, Target Tests. Despite reports of statistical validity with group data (Reitan, 1974) and individual description (Reitan & Boll, 1973) these tests have not been routinely utilized in the majority of clinical child neuropsychology laboratories and cannot be recommended until additional information about their clinical validity becomes available.

Administration time for these batteries is approximately 5 hours and is routinely accomplished in a single day. Details about administrative issues have been recently reported (Boll, 1981; Heaton & Heaton, 1981). Discussion about professional training requirements has also been published (Boll, 1978; Matthews, 1976; Reed, 1976; Rourke, 1976).

Validity of Psychological Tests as Measures of Brain Behavior Relationships

The questions of whether brain damage in children has behavioral correlates and, if so, whether they can be measured by psychological-behavioral assessment procedures have been answered repeatedly in the affirmative (Reitan & Davison, 1974; Filskov & Boll, 1981). Several challenges face clinical child neuropsychologists. Questions about relationships between such neurological variables as type of lesion, age at onset, duration, and even lateralization have received far less attention and produced information with far less certainty than have similar questions about adult brain behavior relationships. Despite our need for increased specificity in all areas, the time for argument about the high risk for psychological sequelae following primary central nervous system disorders of all types has long past. Careful documentation and discussion of type of disorder and course of deterioration or recovery have been provided for several important areas such as head injury (Klonoff, Clark, & Low, 1977; Levin & Eisenberg, 1979; Boll, 1982), anoxia (Graham et al., 1963), muscular dystrophy (Knights, Hinton, & Drader, 1973), posterior fossa tumors (Knights & Hinton, 1973), and epilepsy (Seidenberg et al., 1981).

Clinically acceptable levels of identification of differences between patients with real, questionable, and no brain damage have been demonstrated (Reitan & Boll, 1973; Selz & Reitan, 1971a; Tshushima & Towne, 1977). Initial rule making for clinical interpretation with children has been attempted (Selz & Reitan, 1979b), and the review of experimental and clinical status of knowledge of behavioral effects of children's brain damage has been recently published (Boll & Barth, 1981). Such documentation amply supports the position that children with known brain impairment cannot be considered to have received the best care if the behavioral correlates of their disorder have not been carefully and explicitly addressed in a manner integral to the overall management of the patient. That such care is not routinely provided in many medical settings identifies the current clinical need and future investigational opportunity, which cannot be properly responded to until the ranks of trained clinical child neuropsychologists have significantly expanded.

An area of even vaster need and opportunity is that of serious, especially chronic, physical disorders of childhood not traditionally associated with compromise of brain functions and/or psychological functions. Data on the brain behavior relationship implications of disorders such as kidney disease, asthma, diabetes, cystic fibrosis, and leukemia, to name only a few, are sparse. What behavioral data do exist are often either subjective, extremely skimpy, or gathered in such a manner as to suggest few conclusions. Meanwhile, excellent data on adult patients do exist for some conditions such as kidney disorder (Ryan, Souheaver, & DeWolfe, 1981), and asthma (Dunleavy, 1981; Dunleavy & Baade, 1980; Suess & Chai, 1981). The generalization to children without explicit study is not clinically or scientifically acceptable. Despite the difficulties with quality and quantity of current information, a review of what is known cannot help but suggest that, when more is discovered, a much-expanded role for clinical neuropsychology in describing, monitoring, and aiding in management of many impaired children without primary neurological disorder will have been established.

Diabetes

Neurological dysfunction as a complication of diabetes is well recognized. Neuropathy in adult diabetics has a reported incidence of up to 90 percent (Kohrman & Weil, 1971). Eeg-Olofsson and Petersen (1966) found pathologic EEGs in 35 percent of diabetic patients whereas controls had 13-percent EEG abnormalities. The association of repeated states of ketoacidosis with severe behavioral and emotional deficits has been reported by Drash (1971), but the decline in patient's ability to solve problems, think clearly, and deal effectively with life situations has not been investigated. Investigations of select aspects of mental ability and development of children with diabetes have been carried out. With the exception of one report dealing with psychomotor performance (Dashiell, 1930) studies have been limited to psychometric intelligence. Ack, Miller, and Weil (1961) found IQ decrements in children with diabetes of onset before 5 years of age while Swift, Seidman, and Stein (1967) found higher IQs among diabetics in good control as compared with those in poor control of their disease. In addition to the apparent risk and the need to document further the natural history of this disorder, an understanding of psychological function also has treatment implications. A patient's participation in treatment regimes and desire to obtain and maintain independence require sufficient mental and motor ability (Garner & Thompson, 1974), yet such patient data and documented monitoring are yet to be routinely provided in this common childhood disorder.

In the areas of investigation of causes for psychological/behavioral problems of childhood, a term referring to a type of brain impairment as the cause of this behavior has swept the field. This term is "minimal brain dysfunction." Despite the reference to the brain, however, this diagnosis is frequently arrived at from patient performance not related to and sometimes contrary to that seen in patients with definite evidence of impaired brain functions. In fact, logic has been strained beyond the breaking point by claims such as those by Wender (1971) that 50 percent of children with emotional problems have minimal brain dysfunction although "neurologically intact" and with "total absence of neurological signs or symptoms or EEG abnormalities." If Wender is trying to assert that the brain is the organ of the mind and, therefore, must be involved in all types of psychological considerations, certainly such could have been said without invoking a diagnostic label expressly lacking confirmatory criteria.

What is equally unfortunate, although in light of earlier discussion in this chapter not surprising, is that the term carefully chosen to suggest something less serious than brain damage, that is, brain dysfunction, may in fact suggest a type of neurological impairment that, if present, would have more behaviorally disabling implications than actual damage. Many children with severe, focal, destructive damage to brain tissue suffer fewer and less severe behavioral sequelae than do children with diffuse and generalized cerebral dysfunction (Kinsbourne, 1974; Dreifuss, 1975). During the developmental process of childhood, complete absence or total destruction of an area originally slated to subserve a particular function may not prevent the emergence of that ability. The brain is capable of providing the child with a full repertoire of functions even when as much as half the brain has been removed. If, however, an area of abnormality exists short of destruction or absence, its continued functional presence, albeit in deficient quality, may prevent more normal brain areas from taking up activities usually referable to the impaired area. Such impairment may in fact result in propagation of abnormality (electrical discharges) throughout the brain and in this way, too, wreak greater havoc than would total absence of that part of the brain. Thus, a child with a clear focal area of brain loss due to severe illness such as tumor may be found clinically less impaired than a child with a structurally unimpaired but generally dysfunctional brain due to various forms of epilepsy. For example, a child whose left cerebral hemisphere has been totally removed before age 2 may develop language without aphasia or even developmental delay and enjoy language quality commensurate with overall intelligence. Similar loss of brain mass between ages 2 and 5 results in cessation of speech but redevelopment with little or no aphasia while loss of the entire left cerebral hemisphere after age 12 results in aphasic language and generally incomplete recovery. Certainly, many destructive lesions produce significant impairment and some general dysfunctions do not. Nevertheless, to choose as particularly descriptive of a group of children with mild problems a term which might, particularly for children, be invoked to raise suspicion of considerable general psychological-behavioral risk reflects, if nothing else, the distance between common and carelessly used terms such as "minimal brain dysfunction" and our knowledge of actual brain behavior relationships.

Kidney Disorder

Clinical impressions of intellectual impairment resulting from kidney disease have been reported (Merkel et al., 1974). No quantification of this impression was provided. Behavior such as memory impairment and confusion may result from transient systemic reaction to kidney malfunction, drug effect, or permanent central nervous system disorder. Poor perceptual motor performance has been observed before other symptoms of kidney insufficiency were detectable in children requiring dialysis (Wright et al., 1979). No implication of permanent damage is required to make obvious the need for psychological-behavioral evaluation of the status of children in various stages of renal disease, treatment, and transplantation. Monitoring of psychological status seems long overdue not only to plot natural history, educational and life-functioning concerns, and treatment efficacy but also to assess initial and continuing ability to participate in complex home care procedures.

Heart Disease—Congenital and Acquired

Congenital heart disorders result from malformation of the cardiovascular system occurring early in fetal development. Abnormal behavior and developmental problems of varying degrees of severity and duration have been reported frequently. These signs include restlessness, lethargy, and failure to grow. Delay in motor developmental milestones have been reported by Linde, Rasof, and Dunn (1967). Children with cyanotic forms of this disorder perform more poorly than acyanotic groups. Below average verbal as well as nonverbal and motor findings have been excused as due to stimulus restriction (DeTraubenberg, 1967). The fact that cyanotic children do consistently worse than acyanotic children on a broad range of behaviors and the finding that surgical intervention resulting in more adequate general circulation produces intellectual improvement (Stevenson et al., 1974) certainly point to the likelihood of factors within as well as outside of the child. An examination of such children with validated neuropsychological procedures to assess comparative areas of normality and impairment and to evaluate intervention beyond IQ measures has yet to be accomplished. Until such examination has been done, questions embedded in the instruments themselves (culture and IQ) will obscure the meaning of the data obtained. Certainly information about motor, perceptual, sensory, linguistic, memory, and conceptual abilities would be of great clinical aid in management with or without surgical intervention. Czerwenka-Wenkstetten and Wimmer (1973) reported improved academic competence one year after surgery, but no data on the mental mechanisms that improved to support the increased achievement were identified. Even this much-studied area provides more questions than answers.

While congenital heart disease is a relatively infrequent chronic illness, acquired heart disease (rheumatic fever and rheumatic heart disease) is considered the most prevalent and disabling of childhood diseases (Levitt & Taran, 1963). The same investigators (Levitt & Taran, 1963; Taran, 1967) report over 50 percent of children with rheumatic heart disease showed academic difficulties. They indicated that 97 percent of these patients have IQs in the average range, a fact that by no means contraindicates significant problems in other psychological content areas and resultant academic deficits (Boll, Berent, & Richards, 1977; Boll, Richards, & Berent, 1978). Nevertheless, due to the perceived importance of the emotional concomitants of this disorder and/or to the absence of facilities for more frequent and complete ability examinations Wright et al. (1979) were able to find only a single study investigating psychological ability and this one focused exclusively upon IQ. Without additional information, even the context of the frequently identified affective component remains unexplored. Is it fear of death or physical disability, reaction to reduction in ability to cope with life tasks due to alterations in cognitive process or content, or all of the above (to various degrees) that produce this emotional reaction? Taran (1967) felt psychological sequelae may outweigh the cardiac damage in its impact on life functioning. Yet, over a decade later, no more data on the nature of the consequences of this relatively frequently occurring severe chronic childhood disorder have been forthcoming.

Asthma

As is the case with many disorders that fall within the framework of psychosomatics, most if not all psychological effort in early investigation was directed toward overlapping questions: (1) is there a particular personality style that characterizes asthmatics and (2) what are the psychological precipitants of asthma or asthmatic attacks? Later investigations have leaped over the middle ground of natural history and descriptive investigation and sought to develop treatment strategies for the observed behaviors. These may well have considerable merit but are likely to do little for those aspects of asthma not yet documented at present let alone understood as to their independent and contributing significance. EEG abnormalities have been reported among asthmatics (DiGruttola, Raganati, & Fanuel, 1962). While average IQs have been reported for asthmatics in general, an incomplete and conflicting literature was pointed out by Graham and associates (1967). Most noticeable by its absence is any comprehensive evaluation of psychological ability structure in this socially and often physically restricting and even disabling condition. Missing also were data on short and long term effects of varying degrees of respiratory distress and crisis such as status asthmaticus on psychological functioning and development. Wright et al. (1979) point to the difficulty in teasing out cause and effect in explaining why so little is understood of the mental content and process correlates of asthma. A series of studies has dealt well with one specific aspect of the management of asthma: medication and its influence on human ability. While the definitive answer may not be available, it seems supportable to say that asthma itself does result in psychological-behavioral difficulties involving several cognitive areas taped by careful neuropsychological evaluation, which would otherwise go unnoted or, worse, be misunderstood. That medication variables (amount, type) produce their own effects and that variable interactions occur with patient variables (age, size, sensitivity) suggest the high need for more routine consideration of the overall higher and lower level (motor skill to abstract reasoning) psychological sequelae of the disorder and its management (Dunleavy & Baade, 1980; Suess & Chai, 1981; Dunleavy, 1981).

Turner's Syndrome

There are many long term biopsychosocial disorders of childhood that could be pointed to as an area in need of much further, and in some instances, initial neuropsychological understanding. Others have fared much better, and Turner's syndrome is representative of such a condition. Initial arguments as to whether Turner's syndrome resulted in mental retardation gave way to careful investiga-

tion and improved understanding about the complexity of cognitive patterns in need of attention along with all other management issues dealing with patients with this disorder. Somewhat reduced verbal ability (Waber, 1979) has been consistently found to be less a factor in cognitive development than is visuospatial expressive and receptive ability (Kolb & Heaton, 1975; Money, 1973; Silbert, Wolff, & Lilienthal, 1977). By attending to psychological process as well as content, Waber (1979) in a careful neuropsychological analysis based upon her own and others' examinations of performance of Turner's syndrome patients, found motor coordination and memory deficits that could account for many visual as well as nonvisual perceptual, that is, auditory processing, deficits. In so doing, the hypothesis of a generalized rather than localized or lateralized cerebral referent is generated that not only fits much past data, but signals the need for clinical identification and educational monitoring across the entire repertoire of neurocognitive activities. Wright et al. (1979), after an excellent description of the advanced state of neuropsychological awareness and the utility of these findings, conclude: "Neuropsychological assessment of individuals with Turner's Syndrome would permit the best educational planning, and would shed more light on the specific cognitional patterns involved in the disorder. Systematic investigation of psychological response to hormone therapy is needed" (p. 661).

Clinical child neuropsychologists are in a position to contribute to the understanding and significance for the patient and patient's families of a wide range of neurological disorders. This is also the case for many ostensibly nonneurological conditions in which patient care issues may be strongly affected by psychological consequences that can only be identified by careful examination and are not likely to be understood by reliance upon IQ alone. At the same time, the investigational opportunities range from issues of basic natural history description to treatment effectiveness evaluation at a time when such issues are a high priority in a strictly clinical as well as in a more overtly research-oriented setting.

The fact that clinical neuropsychological examinations and neuropsychological investigational efforts are synonymous when systematically approached may be a large reason for the rapid growth of this field as in integral part of the overall child health care effort.

NOTES

1. Because the term "brain damage" is frequently used to refer to all types of cerebral pathology and because most studies of children have included subjects with a heterogenous mixture of types (most typically the diffuse, the early occurring, the static) of brain damage, the term "brain damaged" will be used when referring to children in the many studies cited unless a more specific or more homogenous group was employed.

REFERENCES

Ack, M., Miller, I., & Weil, W.B. Intelligence of children with diabetes mellitus. *Pediatrics,* 1961, **28,** 764–770.

Annett, M. Laterality of childhood hemiplegia and the growth of speech and intelligence. *Cortex,* 1973, **9,** 4–33.

Atkinson, B.R. *The effect of activity level and social stimulation on attending behavior in children.* Ph.D. thesis, University of Western Ontario, 1970.

Bakwin, H., & Bakwin, R.M. *Clinical management of behavior disorders in children.* Philadelphia: Saunders, 1966.

Benton, A.L., Garfield, J.C., & Chiorini, J.C. Motor impersistence in mental defectives. International Copenhagen Congress on Scientific Study of Mental Retardation, 1964.

Black, F.W. Learning problems and seizure disorders. *Journal of Pediatric Psychology,* 1976, **1,** 32–35.

Boll, T.J. Behavioral sequelae of head injury. In P.R. Cooper (Ed.), *Management of head injuries.* New York: Williams & Wilkins, 1982.

Boll, T.J. Conceptual vs. perceptual vs. motor deficits in brain-damaged children. *Journal of Clinical Psychology,* 1972, **28,** 157–159.

Boll, T.J. The effect of age at onset of brain damage on adaptive abilities in children. Paper presented at American Psychological Association, Montreal, 1973.

Boll, T.J. Behavioral correlates of cerebral damage in children aged 9–14. In R.M. Reitan & L.A. Davison (Eds.), *Clinical neuropsychology: Current status and applications.* Washington, D.C.: Winston, 1974.

Boll, T.J. Diagnosing brain impairment. In B.B. Wolman (Ed.), *Clinical diagnosis of mental disorders.* Plenum, 1978.

Boll, T.J. The Halstead-Reitan neuropsychology battery. In S.B. Filskov & T.J. Boll (Eds.), *Handbook of Clinical Neuropsychology.* New York: Wiley, 1981.

Boll, T.J., & Barth, J. Neuropsychology of brain damage in children. In S.B. Filskov & T.J. Boll (Eds.), *Handbook of clinical neuropsychology.* New York: Wiley, 1981.

Boll, T.J., Berent, S., & Richards, H. Tactile-perceptual functioning as a factor in general psychological abilities. *Perceptual and Motor Skills,* 1977, **44,** 535–539.

Boll, T.J., & Reitan, R.M. Motor and tactile-perceptual deficits in brain-damaged children. *Perceptual and Motor Skills,* 1972, **34,** 353–350.

Boll, T.J., Richards, H., & Berent, S. Tactile perceptual functioning and academic performance in brain-impaired and unimpaired children. *Perceptual and Motor Skills,* 1978, **47,** 491–495.

Bruel, J.H., & Albee, G.W. Higher intellectual functions in a patient with hemispherectomy for tumors. *Journal of Consulting Psychology,* 1962, **15,** 281–285.

Cobb, S. A salute from neurologists. In F.A. Beach, D.O. Hebb, C.T. Morgan, & H.W. Nissen (Eds.), *The neuropsychology of Lashley,* New York: McGraw-Hill, 1960.

Czerwenka-Wenkstetten, G., & Gilmer, M. Prae und postoperativer Vergleich der Persönlichkeits und Intelligenzentwicklung von Kindern mit angeborenen Herzfehlern. *Pediatric und Padologie,* 1973, **8,** 430–432.

Dandy, W.E. Removal of right cerebral hemisphere for certain tumors with hemoplegia. *Journal of the American Medical Association,* 1928, **90,** 823.

DiGruttola, G., Raganati, M., & Fanule, G. Electroencephalographic in children with bronchial asthma. *Pediatria* (Napoli), 1962, **7**, 1025–1031.

Drash, A. Diabetes mellitus in childhood: A review. *Journal of Pediatrics,* 1971, **78,** 919.

Dreifuss, F.P. The pathology of central communicative disorders in children. In D.B. Tower (Ed.), *The nervous system: Human communication and its disorders* (Vol. 3). New York: Raven, 1975.

DeTraubenberg, N. Psychological implications of congenital cardiopathies in the child. *Revue de Neuropsychiatrie Infantile et d'Hygiene Mentale de l'Enfance,* 1967, **15,** 695–706.

Eeg-Olofsson, O., & Petersen, I. Childhood diabetic neuropathy: A clinical and neurophysiological study. *Acta Paedeatrica Scandinavida,* 1966, **55,** 163.

Ernhart, C.B., Graham, F.K., Eichman, P.L., Marshall, J.M., & Thurston, D. Brain injury in the preschool child: Some developmental considerations: II. Comparison of brain-injured and normal children. *Psychological Monographs,* 1963, **77** (Whole No. 574), 17–33.

Fedio, P., & Mirsky, A.F. Selective intellectual deficits in children with temporal lobe or centrancephalic epilepsy. *Neuropsychologia,* 1969, **7,** 287–300.

Filskov, S.B., & Boll, T.J. *Handbook of clinical neuropsychology.* New York: Wiley, 1981.

Filskov, S.B., & Goldstein, S.G. Diagnostic validity of the Halstead-Reitan neuropsychological battery. *Journal of Consulting and Clinical Psychology,* 1974, **42,** 383–388.

Garfield, J.C. Motor impersistence in normal and brain damaged children. *Neurology,* 1964, **14,** 623–630.

Gardner, A.M., & Thompson, C.W. Facts in management of juvenile diabetes. *Pediatric Psychology,* 1974, **2,** 6–7.

Goldstein, S.G., Deysach, R.E., & Kleinknecht, R.A. Effect of experience and amount of information on identification of cerebral impairment. *Journal of Consulting and Clinical Psychology,* 1973, **41,** 30–34.

Graham, F.K., Ernhart, C.B., Craft, M., & Berman, P.W. Brain injury in the preschool child: Some developmental considerations. I. Performance of normal children. *Psychological Monographs,* 1963, **77** (Whole No. 573), 1–16.

Graham, F.K., Ernhart, C.B., Thurston, D., & Craft, M. Development three years after perinatal anoxia and other potentially damaging new born experiences. *Psychological Monographs,* 1962, **76,** (Whole No. 522).

Graham, P., Rutter, M.L., Yule, W., & Pless, I.B. Childhood asthma: A psychosomatic disorder: Some hypodemological considerations. *British Journal of Preventative and Social Medicine,* 1967, **21,** 78–85.

Hammock, M.K., Milhorat, T.H., & Baron, I.S. Normal pressure hydrocephalus in patients with myelomeningocele. *Developmental Medicine in Child Neurology,* 1976, **18** (Supplement 37), 55–68.

Head, H. *Aphasia and kindred disorders of speech.* Cambridge: Cambridge University Press, 1926.

Heaton, S.R., & Heaton, R.R. Testing the impaired patient. In S.B. Filskov & T.J. Boll (Eds.), *Handbook of clinical neuropsychology.* New York: Wiley, Inc., 1981.

Jackson, J.H. Relations of different divisions of the central nervous system to one another and to parts of the body. *Lancet,* 1898 (1), 79–87.

Kinsbourne, M. Mechanisms of hemispheric interaction in man. In M. Kinsbourne & W.L. Smith (Eds.), *Hemispheric disconnection and cerebral function.* Springfield, Ill.: Thomas, 1974.

Klonoff, H., & Low, M. Disordered brain function in young children and early adolescents: Neuropsychological and electroencephalographic correlates. In R.M. Reitan & L.A. Davison (Eds.), *Clinical neuropsychology: Current status and applications.* Washington, D.C.: Winston, 1974.

Klonoff, H., Low, M.D., & Clark, C. Head injuries in children: A prospective 5-year follow-up. *Journal of Neurology, Neurosurgery and Psychiatry,* 1977, **40**.

Klonoff, H., & Paris, R. Immediate, short-term and residual effects of acute head injuries in children: Neuropsychological and neurological correlates. In R.M. Reitan & L.A. Davison (Eds.), *Clinical neuropsychology: Current status and applications.* Washington, D.C.: Winston, 1974.

Knights, R.M. Problems of criteria and diagnosis: A profile similarity approach. *Annals of the New York Academy of Sciences,* 1973, **205,** 124–131.

Knights, R.M., & Hinton, G.G. Neuropsychological test results in children of posterior fossa tumors. Research Bulletin No. 8, Department of Psychology, Carleton University, Ottawa, Canada, 1973.

Knights, R.M., Hinton, G.G., & Drader, D. Changes in intellectual ability with Duchene Muscular Dystrophy. Research Bulletin No. 8, Department of Psychology, Carleton University, Ottawa, Canada, 1973.

Knights, R.M., & Moule, A.D. Normative data on the Motor Steadiness Battery for Children. *Perceptual and Motor Skills,* 1968, **26,** 643-650.

Kohrman, A.F., & Weil, W.J. Juvenile diabetes mellitus. *Advances in Pediatrics,* 1971, **18,** 123.

Kolb, J.E., & Heaton, R.K. Lateralized neurologic deficits and psychopathology in a Turner syndrome patient. *Archives of General Psychiatry,* 1975, **32,** 1198-1200.

Levin, H.S., & Eisenberg, H.M. Neuropsychological outcome of closed head injury in children and adolescence. *Child's Brain,* 1979, **5,** 281-289.

Levitt, J., & Taran, L.M. Some of the problems in the education of rheumatic children. *Journal of Pediatrics,* 1963, **32,** 553-557.

Lezak, M.D. *Neuropsychological assessment.* New York: Oxford Press, 1976.

Linde, L.M., Rasof, B., & Dunn, O.J. Mental development in congenital heart disease. *Journal of Pediatrics,* 1967, **71,** 198-203.

Matarazzo, J.D. *Wechsler's measurement and appraisal of adult intelligence, fifth and enlarged edition.* Baltimore: Williams & Wilkins, 1972.

Matthews, C.G. Problems in the training of neuropsychologists. *The Clinical Psychologist,* 1976, **20,** 11-13.

Matthews, C.G., Shaw, D.J., & Kløve, H. Psychological test performances in neurologic and "pseudoneurologic" subjects. *Cortex,* 1966, **2,** 244-253.

Merkel, F.K., Ing, T.S., Ahmadian, Y., Lewy, P., Ambruster, K., Oyama, J., Sulieman, J.S., Belman, A.B., & King, L.R. Transplantation and of the young. *The Journal of Urology,* 1974, **111,** 679-686.

Money, J. Turner Syndrome and parietal lobe functions. *Cortex,* 1973, **9,** 385-393.

O'Leary, D.S., Seidenberg, M., Berent, S., & Boll, T.J. The effects of age on onset of tonic-clonic seizures on neuropsychological performance in children. *Epilepsia,* 1981, **22,** 197-204.

Pennington, H., Galliani, C., & Voegele, G. Unilateral EEG dysrhythmia and children's intelligence. *Child Development,* 1965, **35,** 539-546.

Reed, H.B.C. Pediatric neuropsychology. *Journal of Pediatric Psychology,* 1976, **1,** 5-7.

Reed, H.B.C., Reitan, R.M., & Kløve, H. Influence of cerebral lesions on psychological test performances of older children. *Journal of Consulting Psychology,* 1965, **29,** 247-251.

Reed, J.C., & Reitan, R.M. Verbal and performance differences among brain-injured children with lateralized motor deficits. *Perceptual and Motor Skills,* 1969, **29,** 747-752.

Reitan, R.M. Psychological deficits resulting from cerebral lesions in man. In J.M. Warren & K. Akert (Eds.), *The frontal granular cortex and behavior.* New York: McGraw-Hill, 1964.

Reitan, R.M. Psychological effects of cerebral lesions in children of early school age. In R.M. Reitan & L.A. Davison (Eds.), *Clinical neuropsychology: Current status and applications.* Washington, D.C.: Winston, 1974.

Reitan, R.M., & Boll, T.J. Neuropsychological correlates of minimal brain dysfunction. *Annals of the New York Academy of Sciences,* 1973, **205,** 65-88.

Reitan, R.M., & Davison, L. *Clinical neuropsychology: Current status and applications.* Washington, D.C.: Winston, 1974.

Rourke, B.P. Issues in the neuropsychological assessment of children with learning disabilities. *Canadian Psychological Review,* 1976, **17,** 89-102.

Russell, E.W. The Bender-Gestalt and the Halstead-Reitan battery: A case study. *Journal of Clinical Psychology,* 1976, **32,** 355-361.

Rutter, M. Brain damage syndromes in childhood: Concepts and findings. *Journal of Child Psychology and Psychiatry,* 1977, **18,** 1-21.

Rutter, M., Graham, P., & Yule, W. A neuropsychiatric study in childhood. *Clinics in Developmental Medicine.* Nos. 35 and 36. London: Simp/Seineman, 1970.

Ryan, J.J., Souheaver, G.T., & DeWolfe, A.A. Halstead-Reitan test results in chronic hemodialysis. *The Journal of Nervous and Mental Disease,* 1981, **169,** 5.

Seidel, U.P., Chadwick, O.F.D., & Rutter, M. Psychological disorders in crippled children.

A comparative study of children with and without brain damage. *Developmental Medicine and Child Neurology,* 1975, **17,** 563–573.

Seidenberg, M., O'Leary, D.S., Berent, S., & Boll, T.J. Changes in seizure frequency and test-retest scores on the WAIS. *Epilepsia,* 1981, **22,** 75–84.

Seidenberg, M., O'Leary, D.S., Giordani, B., Berent, S., & Boll, T.J. Test retest IQ changes of epilepsy patients: Assessing the influence of practice effects. *Journal of Clinical Neuropsychology,* 1981, **3,** 237–255.

Selz, M., & Reitan, R.M. Neuropsychological test performance of normal, learning-disabled, and brain-damaged older children. *Journal of Nervous and Mental Disease,* 1979, **167,** 298–302. (a)

Selz, M., & Reitan, R.M. Rules for neuropsychological diagnosis: Classification of brain function in older children. *Journal of Consulting and Clinical Psychology,* 1979, **47,** 258–264. (b)

Shaffer, D. Psychiatric aspects of brain injury in childhood: A review. In S. Chess & A. Thomas (Eds.), *Annual progress in child psychiatry and child development.* New York: Brunner Mazel, 1974.

Shaffer, D., Chadwick, O., & Rutter, M. Psychiatric outcome of localized head injuries in children. In R. Porter & D. FitzSimons (Eds.), *Outcome of severe damage to the central nervous system.* SIBA Foundation Symposium, 34. Amsterdam: Elsevier, Excerpta Medica, N. Holland, 1975.

Silbert, A.R., Wolff, P.H., & Lilienthal, J. Spatial and temporal processing in patients with Turner Syndrome. *Behavior Genetics,* 1977, **7,** 11–21.

Smith, A. Neuropsychological testing in neurological disorders. In W.J. Friedlander (Ed.), *Advances in Neurology,* (Vol. 7). New York: Raven, 1975.

Smith, A. Principles underlying human brain functions in neuropsychological sequelae of different neuropathological processes. In S.B. Filskov & T.J. Boll (Eds.), *Handbook of Clinical Neuropsychology.* New York: Wiley, 1981.

Stevenson, J.G., Stone, E.F., Dillard, D.H., & Morgan, B.C. Intellectual development of children subjected to prolonged circulatory rest during hypothermic open heart surgery in infancy. *Circulation,* 1974, **50,** 54–59.

Swift, C.R., Seidman, F., & Stein, H. Adjustment problems in juvenile diabetes. *Psychosomatic Medicine,* 1967, **20,** 555–571.

Taran, L.M. Problems in management of rheumatic diseases in children. In L.M. Taran (Ed.), *Collected works on rheumatic fever.* New York: International Professional Publications, 1967.

Teuber, H.L., & Rudel, R.G. Behavior after cerebral in children and adults. *Developmental Medicine and Child Neurology,* 1962, **4,** 3–20.

Tshushima, W.T., & Towne, W.S. Neuropsychological abilities of young children with questionable brain disorders. *Journal of Consulting and Clinical Psychology,* 1977, **45,** 757–762.

Vigotsky, L.S. *Thought and language.* Cambridge: Massachusetts Institute of Technology Press, 1962.

Waber, D.P. Neuropsychological aspects of Turner Syndrome. *Developmental Medicine and Child Neurology,* 1979, **21,** 58–70.

Wender, P.H. *Minimal brain dysfunction in children.* New York: Wiley, 1971.

Wright, L., Schaefer, A.B., & Solomons, G. *Encyclopedia of Pediatric Psychology.* Baltimore: University Park Press, 1979.

CHAPTER 10

Objective and Projective Testing of Children

JACQUELINE FRENCH, PAULA D. GRAVES, AND EUGENE E. LEVITT

Assessment is the broadest topic in clinical psychology. The area is not appreciably reduced by eliminating intellectual and neuropsychological evaluation. When space is limited, it becomes a necessary expedient to restrict the exposition to formal instruments in clinical use and to eliminate those measures that have been employed primarily in research. Even then, it is hardly possible to cover the full range of assessment techniques.

Our approach in this chapter has been to deal with those instruments that are in common use and also, in our opinion, have the maximum utility in clinical assessment. This explains the absence of attention to drawing techniques like the DAP, HTP, and the Bender-Gestalt, which are often used in child guidance clinics but which we feel are ineffective assessment tools of personality. Sentence completion techniques are also not covered primarily because they are less frequently employed with the youthful patient. Also missing from the chapter are two anxiety scales that have been accorded considerable research employment but are seldom found in the clinician's battery: the Children's Manifest Anxiety Scale (Castaneda, McCandless, & Palermo, 1956) and its contemporary counterpart, the State-Trait Anxiety Inventory for Children (Spielberger et al., 1973). Considerations of space permit us to deal, among projective tests, with the Rorschach, the TAT and several other picture thematic tests, and the Rosenzweig Picture-Frustration Study, and with the MMPI among objective tests. Among them, the instruments that we will discuss in this chapter probably represent

about 90 percent of all of the instances of formal personality evaluation in clinical settings for children.

RORSCHACH

The Rorschach competes perennially with the MMPI and the Wechsler tests as the most widely used formal evaluation instrument in the clinician's battery. Exner (1974) points out that it "has a long history of usefulness with younger clients" (p. 460). An early survey of its employment clinically (Anderson & Higham, 1956) suggested that the Rorschach was administered to about one of every two child patients. In 20 percent of clinics in the United States, a Rorschach was obtained from almost every child. On the average, responding clinics in the Anderson-Higham survey believed that 8 years was the minimum age for employment of the Rorschach, but 20 percent of the clinics felt that it was equally useful with preschoolers.

Despite its utility, Rorschach training and research with younger respondents has been proportionately neglected. Teaching of the Rorschach technique in graduate departments in psychology deals almost entirely with adults (Jackson & Wohl, 1966). Less than one of every 10 Rorschach investigations examined child subjects (Levitt & Truumaa, 1972). Among the standard Rorschach "bibles," only one (Klopfer, 1956) devotes any reasonable amount of space to the child respondent. Among the more recent general works in the field, Exner's Volume I (1974) makes scant mention of children. His Volume II (1978) has six pages of tabled norms for children in the age range from 5–16 years and a section on treatment planning for younger patients, which is essentially a presentation of three cases.

A small number of books deal entirely with the child respondent. Most of these are presentations of normative data (Ames et al., 1952; Ames, Metraux, & Walker, 1959; Davidson, 1943; Ford, 1946; Ledwith, 1959, 1960; Levitt & Truumaa, 1972). Except for the Levitt-Truumaa data, all are derived from special populations that seriously limit their application. The Ames, Davidson, and Ford samples are composed entirely of children of superior intelligence from upper socio-economic classes. Ledwith administered repeated Rorschachs personally, thereby creating an unusual testing situation that has been shown to have significantly increased the productivity of her subjects (Levitt & Truumaa, 1972). Two other child books in the field (Halpern, 1953; Francis-Williams, 1968) are essentially collections of case studies.

The relative paucity of Rorschach studies of children is further complicated by their poor quality. The reviewer of Rorschach research in general is invariably struck by this unfortunate characteristic (for example, Megargee, 1966; Suinn & Oskamp, 1969; Levitt & Truumaa, 1972). Naive methodological errors abound, especially in the earlier reports. The most recent efforts are somewhat more sophisticated methodologically but unfortunately constitute only a small proportion of the published literature. This modest improvement in methodology is reflected to a notably lesser degree in studies of children, which tend to be poorer than the adult reports.

It is not at all unusual to find no mention of the entitlements of the Rorschach examiner, the circumstances under which the data were obtained, the style of adminstration, or the method of scoring. It might be noted that the test was administered by social work students (Lifshitz, 1975) or by different examiners at different age levels (Schinek, 1968), circumstances that hardly inspire confidence in the findings.

A common practice in Rorschach research is to extract protocols from clinic or hospital files. Such a retrospective sample is highly likely to be contaminated by variations in administration and scoring. Unfortunately, candor on the part of the experimenter is rare. The outstanding example is a report by Lessing (1960) in which she describes her samples as follows:

The 49 Rorschachs in the original sample were adminstered and scored by 17 psychologists of varying levels of experience: 14 Rorschachs were given and interpreted by trainees, 24 by staff members with 2–5 years of experience, 11 by staff members with over 5 years of experience. The Rorschachs were administered as part of a battery of diagnostic tests which might include other projective techniques and/or intelligence tests (page 313).... The 53 Rorschachs in the cross-validation sample were administered by 20 psychologists of varying levels of experience: 13 Rorschachs were given and interpreted by trainees, 28 by staff members with 2–5 years of experience, and 12 by staff members with over 5 years of experience. (p. 318)

One should not be amazed to learn that Lessing's findings were essentially negative.

In some investigations that contrast child groups, it is clear that the Rorschach examiner could not be blind, as he or she ought to have been. In others, the examiner's awareness of the contrasting groups is unknown and unreported.

In general, details of administration and scoring of protocols are neglected in the published reports except to indicate deviations from normal administration procedure, such as requiring a specified number of responses per card.

The use of multiple scorers and the reporting of interscorer reliability are rare. Scoring systems are ordinarily not noted, though of course one may draw inferences from the symbols that are used. But how does one reconcile scoring "after Klopfer and Kelley, generally" (Siegel, 1954, p. 410)?

Individual administration is probably most prevalent but group administration is occasionally noted. One is left to wonder how movement is scored in group administration (Baker, 1978). It may be reported that one group of subjects received individual administration while another group had group administration, without recognition that this variation could have affected the study's outcome (Liebetrau & Pienaar, 1974).

A review of the literature for substantive content thus becomes a slippery undertaking. It certainly seems necessary to pick one's way carefully through the published reports, maintaining a wary eye for serious methodological shortcomings. On the other hand, if the reviewer is too demanding, he or she may be left with very little to review. Some compromise position is evidently necessary. In this review, we have depended on the more recent investigations and on those in which methodological flaws were not patent. No attempt has been made to review the literature comprehensively and therefore, of necessity, uncritically.

Norms

Clinical application of the Rorschach has been perennially plagued by a scarcity of normative data. For children, the work of Ames and her associates (Ames et al., 1952, 1959) is well known. It is not as well known that the samples on which these norms are based represent upper socioeconomic strata with a reported median IQ of 125. Ledwith's research (1959, 1960) is also fairly well known. Again, it is not usually realized that Ledwith personally administered consecutive Rorschachs to her longitudinal sample, thereby creating an unusual testing situation that has been shown to have significantly increased the productivity of her subjects (see Levitt & Truumaa, 1972). Norms presented by Davidson (1943) and Ford (1946) are also derived from special populations that seriously limit their clinical application.

Levitt and Truumaa (1972), after an intensive survey of the literature, selected 15 reports of Rorschach children's norms, and aggregated them carefully, keeping separate those based on children of average intelligence from those of bright children. The data were then submitted to analysis by a polynomial regression formula to provide norms over the age range 5–16 years. With the exception of the F+%, which is based on Beck scoring, all of the Levitt-Truumaa norms are based on Klopfer scoring.

Tables 10.1 and 10.2 have been adapted from the original source by Levitt (1980). Table 10.1 illustrates F+% as a function of age and Table 10.2 provides norms at ages 6, 10 and 16 for some 14 factors, either for children of average intelligence, or for bright children, or for the two groups combined if the factor was found to be unrelated to intelligence.

Table 10.1. Form Quality Percent as a Function of Age

Age	F+%[a]
5	60
6	62
8	66
11	72
14	78
16	82

[a]Correlation between age and F+% for all ages 5–16 =0.99
Note: From E.E. Levitt, *Primer on the Rorschach Technique,* 1980. Courtesy of Charles C. Thomas, Publisher, Springfield, Illinois.

Mention should be made at this point of the Hertz tables for scoring form quality (Hertz, 1970). The responses are derived entirely from the records of adolescents, and the form quality ratings are based on frequencies of responses in those records. Thus the Hertz tables are actually calculated to provide F+% norms for teenagers though they are probably used widely for respondents of all ages.

Reliability

A primary consideration in assessing the validity of the Rorschach in general is that careful studies of adults over time have shown that the test has as high a reliability as objective tests (Levitt, 1980). Reliabilities for the child respondent tend to be lower as, for example, testings at 6 and 9 years of age and retestings at 8 and 11. However, even at these age levels, F+% and populars (P) have been reported to have reliabilities ranging from

Table 10.2.   Child and Adolescent Norms for Various Rorschach Factors

Factor	Group[a]	Age		
		6	10	16
R	a+b	16.0	17.9	20.8
W%	a	48.6	37.9	21.9
	b	52.4	49.2	44.4
D%	b	46.5	44.4	41.2
d%	a	1.3	12.0	28.0
	b	1.1	6.4	14.4
F+%	a	61.6	69.7	81.7
M	a	0.62	1.32	2.36
	b	1.34	1.91	2.77
AM	a+b	1.91	2.71	2.44
C	a+b	0.34	0.22	0.03
CF	a+b	1.02	0.67	0.76
Sum C	a	2.08	1.39	1.60
	b	1.85	1.36	1.02
	a+b	1.97	1.39	1.03
H%	b	12.2	18.0	20.6
A%	a+b	47.9	51.3	51.2
An	b	0.45	0.69	0.63
P	a+b	2.86	4.21	5.33

[a]a   =average group
 b   =bright group
 a+b=average and bright groups do not differ and are combined
Note. From E.E. Levitt, *Primer on the Rorschach Technique,* 1980. Courtesy of Charles C. Thomas, Publisher, Springfield, Illinois.

.74–.84 (Exner, 1980). Age trends in reliability are clear in Schinek's (1968) data: from age 14 on, all scoring categories show great stability.

Administration

Most of the writing on administration to the child respondent derives from clinical impressions. Investigations by McCraw and Tuma (1977) and Tuma and McCraw (1978) are among the infrequent experimental studies. Unfortunately, both are inconclusive, the former suggesting that failure to control for the response total may yield spurious results. The latter also does no more than hint at the possibility that there may be meaningful interactions between sex of the Rorschach examiner and sex and age of the subject.

Magnussen (1967) found that other tests in the battery may influence Rorschach responses. Those children to whom the CAT or the Draw-An-Animal test was administered before the Rorschach gave almost 10 percent more animal responses than those who received the Rorschach first.

Administration is treated in some detail by Levitt and Truumaa (1972) and by Levitt (1980). The positions of Klopfer, Hertz, Beck, Piotrowski, and Halpern are summarized. Briefly, it is concluded that (1) the use of a trial blot is unnecessary; (2) if reaction time of responses is recorded, it should be done surreptitiously (see Sarason, 1975); (3) immediate inquiry should be used only when absolutely necessary, occasionally with very young children or hyperactive children; (4) testing the limits should be used only with children who give very impoverished records; (5) the examiner should take time to attempt to establish rapport with the child but it is unwise for the examiner to be well known to the child; (6) the Rorschach should be administered before other tests in a battery or on a different day.

Genetic Studies of Validity

Rorschach researchers have occasionally found access to a number of pairs of twins and have exploited the experimental situation to examine the validity of the Rorschach as a measure of personality. In each instance, the working hypothesis, which seems to stand on a firm base, states that the Rorschach patterns of identical twins ought to be significantly more alike than those of fraternal twins.

Hamilton, Blewett and Sydiahia (1971) reported on data from 26 pairs of identical twins and 26 pairs of fraternal twins between the ages of 12 and 15, equally divided as to sex. Correlations between pairs of twins were computed for 10 conventional Rorschach factors and two special indices based on word counts. A total of four of these measures including the two word counts were found to be significantly correlated for the identical twins with a range from .42 to .94, with the exception of populars (P) which had a low negative coefficient. (It was also negative for the fraternal twins.)

Murawski (1971) administered Rorschachs to 20 pairs of identical twins and 10 pairs of fraternal twins. Of the total of 15 factors, there are four significant coefficients for the identical twins compared to only one for the fraternal twins. Ten of the coefficients for the fraternal twins are exactly zero, but only three for the identical twins. Two other coefficients for the identical twins approach significance (.28 and .29). The rather unusual results may be an artifact of the method of computation—intraclass correlation based on one-way analysis of variance.

The findings of the Hamilton and Murawski studies are clearly in accord with the hypothesis. The test protocols definitely reflect the greater personality similarities to be expected among identical twins. Unfortunately, both studies are subject to a damaging methodological flaw. With a few exceptions in the Hamilton study, all of the records were obtained by a single examiner who quite obviously could not have been blind with respect to the research design. This defect is not found in a similar investigation by Basit (1972). Rorschachs were administered to seven pairs of identical twins and eight pairs of fraternal twins by a group of graduate students, presumably under the direction of a faculty member who scored all of the protocols while being unaware of the identities of the subjects. The findings are strikingly similar to those of Hamilton. For the identical twins, there were only two coefficients below .5 among 11 factors. No significant coefficients were found among the fraternal twins. As in the Hamilton study, an exception was P, which had a low negative relationship for the identical twins.

Similarities between the results obtained by Basit and by Hamilton suggest that the latter's data were not contaminated by the study's methodological defects. Overall, the twin studies suggest that formal factors derived from the Rorschach are indeed measuring personality dimensions of some sort. Of course, the data do not support interpretations of specific factors except to suggest that the scoring of P in the Klopfer system is invalid.

The hypothesis of the relationship between the personalities of parents and their children is less tenable than the twins hypothesis but is certainly not unreasonable. Fisher and Fisher (1976) bravely paid a fee to 119 families so that a Rorschach could be administered to the father, mother and at least two children in each family. On the average, the children tested were adolescents. Three inventory instruments were also used in the study. The results are a melange of positive and negative correlations between parents' scores and those of the oldest male and female child in each family. Various methodological shortcomings add to the inconclusiveness of the results.

Psychopathology and Differential Diagnosis

The investigations in this critical area of Rorschach application appear to be most plagued by methodological shortcomings. Even the reviews manage to be shabby. Dudek (1975) reviewed studies of regression in children without ever defining the expression "primary process thinking" in Rorschach terms. Bergman and Schubert (1974) have assembled a totally uncritical review of some of the literature on emotionally disturbed children. All of the results are cited without a word of criticism. Gittelman (1980) concludes that the Rorschach, like other tests, fails as a differential diagnostic aid. While Gittelman is properly critical of many of the studies that she reviewed, she shows a tendency to select reports that support her conclusion, like the aforementioned Lessing (1960) study, and to misconstrue some positive results.

In her review, Gittelman appears to have trouble with a number of reports that manifest poor hypothesis construction, a deficiency that is indigenous to this area. For example, Kodemen and Waters (1961) obtained Rorschach records from eight children diagnosed as cases of psychogenic deafness and contrasted them with a matched group of eight children with actual serious hearing losses. The results suggest that the psychogenically deaf group are considerably more normal and less hysterical than the hard-of-hearing group, that is, higher form quality percent, more FC and less CF- and C. The authors, however, are so concerned with the hypothesis of hysterical features in the psychogenic group that they ignore the obvious inference that an actual serious hearing difficulty is very likely to cause emotional disturbance. A similar investigation (Fiedler & Stone, 1956) found no differences between the two groups, but the authors realize at any rate that both of the groups, drawn as they are from lower socioeconomic strata, manifest poorer form level and more blunted affect than children from higher socioeconomic strata. Williams (1961) contrasted children who became emotionally disturbed in group homes with those who did not, the (unwarranted) implication being that there is something special about a child who becomes emotionally disturbed in a group home and that this will be reflected in the test results.

If one does not ask impossible tasks of the Rorschach, like differentiating between functional and organic psychosis or between socialized and unsocialized conduct disorders, the Rorschach does fairly well in discerning psychopathology, especially in the more recent investigations. Weiner and Exner (1978) reviewed more than 1,500 Rorschach records for indicators of thought disorder such as contaminations and peculiar verbalization. They found that the frequency of these indicators among the records varied from most to least in the following order: adult patients, adolescent patients, adolescent nonpatients, adult nonpatients. This supports an early report that perseveration, confabulation, and poor form quality occurred significantly more often among the records of emotionally disturbed, hospitalized children than among outpatient children with only minor physical ailments (Taterka & Katz, 1955).

Conflicting findings between an earlier and a more recent report suggest the necessity for sophisticated assessment of results. Townsend (1967) found few differences in aggressive content on the Rorschach between boys who were rated as high in aggression and those rated low in aggression. Crain and Smoke (1981) also found that the frequency of aggressive content did not distinguish between a group of children referred for psychological treatment and a group considered to be well adjusted. However, they did note significant differences in the *quality* of responses. For example, the normal children tended to give fighting responses in which the combatants were of equal power. The disturbed children identified overpowering monsters or individuals who were the victims of violence. The authors suggest that these types of responses "seem to project a greater feeling of hopelessness in a hostile world."

There have been a number of investigations of children removed from the home of the biological parents and placed in foster homes or institutions. Most are of poor quality methodologically. One of the sounder investigations (Cohen & Weiner, 1977) found significant differences in the use of color and on qualititative indicators of thinking disorder between a group of adolescents that had been placed in an institution prior to age 9 and those who were separated from a home environment at an earlier age. These findings are not supported by the results of a similar study of separation using the Rorschach Prognostic Rating Scale (Greenberg, 1969). The RPRS is an arbitrary method of assigning numerical values to each response (Klopfer et al., 1954). A group of male adolescents separated from the home before age 3 could not be distinguished from a group separated after age 4, though both did more poorly on the RPRS than a control group of unseparated adolescents.

The aforementioned study by Williams is questionable methodologically, primarily because little attention is paid to the administration and scoring of the Rorschach as opposed to the CAT, for which interrater reliability as well as the scoring system is reported. It is not known whether the Rorschach examiner or examiners were blind. Nonetheless, the results are of sufficient interest to report.

Essentially, the study is a cross-sectional contrast of emotionally disturbed and nondisturbed (or perhaps very disturbed and minimally disturbed) children at various ages. Between the ages of 5 and 8, the disturbed children gave significantly more chromatic and achromatic responses. This changes sharply in the 9–11-year-old group in which the nondisturbed group gave more color responses and there was no difference in the achromatic responses. Unfortunately, the IQ matching, which is fairly satisfactory in the 5–6-year-old group, begins to break down in the 7–8-year-old group where there is a significant difference in the verbal and total IQs on the WISC which is carried on into a significant difference in verbal IQs in the 9–11-year-old group. The overall general trend with age is for color responses to diminish from a high in the youngest group to a low in the lowest group among the emotionally disturbed, while the controls hold fairly steady, beginning with less color and ending with more. Dark color responses show similar decreases for the emotionally disturbed group and the hold-steady pattern for the nondisturbed group. No age trends were found for response total or for any kind of movement response.

Robbertse (1955) did an excellent job of selecting and matching contrasting samples of maladjusted and well-adjusted early adolescents. The administration instructions and the method of scoring are mentioned. Unfortunately, it is not noted whether the examiner was blind, and there is no report of the reliability of scoring. The data indicate that the maladjusted children had more card rejections, fewer human movement responses, less FC and more CF and C, lower F+% and more anatomy responses. There were no differences in the response total, on other movement responses, on achromatic color, and on P.

Fisher (1966) reports significantly higher "barrier" (Fisher & Cleveland, 1958) scores for normal children compared to a group of children rated as "disturbed impulsive." He concluded that boundary definiteness seems to be less well developed in acting-out children.

Schlesinger (1978) attempted to distinguish between human movement responses given by hospitalized acting-out adolescents and those who were classified as severely withdrawn though not psychotic. He found that the two groups did not differ in mean frequency of M. However, the behavior disorder children produced more than twice as much extensor M.

There is a perennial consensus among Rorschach clinicians that the tendency to use the whole response (W) is related to intellectual function. The experimental results in general, summarized by Exner (1974) and Marsden (1970), are conflicting and ambiguous. Evidently, the *quality* of the W response must also be considered. This has led to the development of several methods for rating W responses among which Friedman's Developmental Level (DL) (Friedman, 1952) is most often employed. A recent study by Marsden (1970) using the DL typifies the confusion. A positive correlation was found between WISC scores and good whole responses but not with *very good* whole responses. The expected significant *negative* correlation with vague, amorphous, and otherwise poor W responses was also not found.

Related investigations by O'Neill, O'Neill and Quinlan (1976) and Weisz et al., (1978) examined the relationship between the DL and intelligence. The main findings of this methodologically sound research is that the DL is related to mental age independent of chronological age but not to intelligence. The same conclusion applies to form level quality scored on a 7-point scale and a special index of complexities of the W response.

Russ (1980) looked at the relationship between development in young children as measured by Holt's primary process integration method and intellectual factors. She found that the PPI was positively related to reading, academic grades, and intelligence in second grade children and also to reading and academic grades with intelligence held constant. These results are essentially in accord with the DL findings previously cited.

Miscellaneous Studies

The concepts of the "father card" (IV) and "mother card" (VII) are commonly considered by clinicians to apply most clearly to the child respondent, if at all. The research evidence, however, is largely clinical except for an investigation by Beck and Herron (1969). They asked more than 500 elementary school children which cards "look like" mother and father and which ones they liked the best and the least. The findings support the notion of Card IV as representing the father but Cards II and III were more often selected as looking like the mother. Card X was best liked and Cards IV(!) and VI were least liked. There are differences between boys and girls at various levels, but no age correlations.

The affective ratio (the number of responses to the first seven cards divided by the number of responses to the last three cards) is usually interpreted to reflect emotional reactivity and impulsivity. If this interpretation is correct, one would expect a significant negative relationship with age over the formal school years. This hypothesis was not supported in a recent study by Loucks et al. (1980). A reasonable inference is that the affective ratio is probably a function of stimulus pull of the cards and response tendencies of the individual that have nothing to do with affectivity.

Rychlak and Maier (1964) looked at Rorschach content of eighth graders identified as

isolates and populars by a sociometric technique. They found that unpopular boys and girls tended to give more responses that were classified as "absurd fantasy"(caricatures and cartoon characters) and "general tension" (physical attack, blood, frustration). Differences between the two groups, however, were not statistically significant for boys alone. The total amount of morbid content—which was found to average about 10 percent of responses—is unrelated to either popularity with peers or psychological adjustment (Rychlak & O'Leary, 1966). It is related to socioeconomic status, with high level adolescents producing 5–10 percent morbid content compared with 25–30% for lower level teenagers (Rychlak & Boland, 1973). These relatively high percentages are in accord with the general view of adolescence as a time of unusual emotional stress.

Moelis, Wright, and Fisher (1977) developed a "symbiosis scale" based on Rorschach content of children. (Symbiosis is apparently used in the same sense as close-binding, tending to perpetuate childhood dependency.) The scale is exceedingly complex and is obviously related both to dependency and to psychological adjustment. Findings bearing positively on the scale's validity were found in two of three small scale investigations in children ages 8–11.

THE THEMATIC APPERCEPTION TEST

The Thematic Apperception Test as we now know it is the third revision of an original set of pictures distributed by the Harvard Psychological Clinic in 1936. According to Henry Murray, the test's developer, it was designed to bring out "some of the dominant drives, emotions, sentiments, complexes and conflicts of a personality" (Murray, 1943, p. 1). He did not see the TAT as an objective measure. From the very first he observed that the tester's clinical intuition played a vital part in the interpretation of the results. Furthermore, he visualized his instrument being used to generate tentative hypotheses that should then be confirmed by data from other sources.

The TAT consists of 30 black-and-white pictures and one blank card. Eleven of these cards are to be used with all subjects. From the remaining 20 cards, nine are to be selected based on the subject's sex and age. The first 10 cards depict males and females in fairly routine, even nondescript, situations. By design, the remaining cards involve more unusual scenes or no scene at all. The manual instructs the examiner to give 20 cards to each subject, the first 10 on one day, the remaining 10 on a subsequent day. The subject is requested to make up a story about each picture, telling what happened before the pictured scene, what is happening now, what will happen, and how the depicted people are thinking and feeling. Clinical experience suggests that most subjects feel tricked by the blank card and respond defensively or humorously if given the standard instructions. A way to avoid this is to say to the subject before showing the card, "This card has no picture on it. What I want you to do is to make up a story of your own. Some people find that it helps to make believe there's a picture on the card. You do whatever is easier for you; just tell me a story of your own."

An interesting variation in administration is the negative TAT proposed by Jones (1956), using the Freudian concept of negation as a substitute for repression. Following the completion of all the TAT stories using the standard instructions, the subject is shown some or all of the same cards as before with such questions as "What is the most unlikely theme this picture might represent?" or "What is the one thing that could *not* be happening in this picture?" Jones found that the stories told to the negation instructions were rated as more lucidly suggestive of repressed psychic content than those stories told under standard instructions. While his sample was composed of adults, it seems likely that the negation TAT could also be used effectively with children.

Murray (1943) cited 150 words as the average length for stories expected from 10-year-olds. Friedman (1972) found it to be much less, with children 8–11 and those 12–15 years producing stories whose mean length

ranged from 40 to 114 words, with most stories averaging less than 100 words. Children 5–7 years told even shorter stories, ranging from 12 to 55 words.

Standardization

The 1943 TAT *Manual* did not list any validity or reliability statistics. Murray and his colleagues did try to determine the "stimulating power of the picture" (Murray, 1943, p. 2). Each picture was rated for the amount of information the stories told about it contributed to the final diagnosis of the subject. The ratings were then averaged for each picture to determine its stimulating power. The subjects tested were between the ages of 14 and 40.

Perhaps one of the reasons Murray did not look systematically into reliability of his instrument was because he did not expect it to be high. Acknowledging that the TAT could discern ongoing tendencies and traits, he felt that transient moods were also identified, moods which might not be in existence at a subsequent retesting. Murray did propose a system of content analysis. First, the hero was to be identified; then the inner motives and feelings (needs), along with the forces from the environment (press), were categorized. Story outcomes, interactions (themas) of needs and press, and interests and sentiments expressed were also to be identified. From a thorough study of all of these factors the interpreter could then formulate the hypotheses to be added to other pertinent data about the subject.

As is evident, the TAT in its infancy had little of the complex standardization expected of current new tests. Indeed, even after 10 years, Rosenzweig (1948) noted the extraordinary lack of TAT normative research in existence. This state of events changed. Reviews of the literature (e.g., Harrison, 1965; Murstein, 1963, 1965) have generally studied TAT research without regard to age of subject. A more recent review (Gittelman, 1980) focused on projective testing for the differential diagnosis of children and adolescents, and cites a goodly number of TAT studies.

Card Selection

Murray's proposal that all 20 TAT cards be given to each subject has not had universal acceptance. Both in research and in clinical practice, many psychologists give only those cards that pull for specific dynamics. It is not unusual to find psychologists intermingling cards from several thematic apperception instruments. Clinicians have their favorite cards. Hartman (1970) canvassed 80 experienced psychologists and obtained a list of the 10 most universally applicable cards for use with children under the age of 17. In rank order these were: 1, 3BM, 6BM, 7BM, 13MF, 2, 7GF, 8BM, 4, 10, 12M, 16, and 18GF (the last four cards being tied for tenth place).

Weisskopf (1950) recognized that clinicians frequently give abbreviated TATs. She sought a way of aiding in the selection of cards most likely to elicit useful diagnostic information. She designed the Transcendence Index, a measure of the number of comments made for TAT pictures that were not merely pure description. She theorized that pictures with high transcendence indices (those pictures shown to draw the most nondescriptive responses) would provide more valuable clinical material than those with low transcendence indices (those pictures evoking mainly pure descriptive responses). While the members of her original sample were college students, the Transcendence Index has been used with younger subjects as well.

Kalter (1970) proposed allowing uncooperative children to do their own card selection. While recognizing that such deviation from the standardized procedure has its dangers, Kalter felt it also has merit in certain cases, particularly where a battle for control interferes with the child's willingness to cooperate. It is one way to obtain data when a child simply refuses to respond under the usual instructions.

Codification of Responses

In the main, researchers have used a small number of TAT cards in their studies, often 10 or less. Typically the cards are selected for the stimulus pull they evoke. Numerous techniques for codifying TAT respnses have evolved. Some are based on the thematic content of the responses of the child or adolescent, such as hostility or aggression (Hafner & Kaplan, 1960; Mussen & Naylor, 1954; Skolnick, 1966), alienation (Davids & Rosenblatt, 1958), achievement (McClelland et al., 1953), depression (Aaron, 1967), power (Wolowitz & Shorkey, 1969), and adaptive ego functioning (Whiteley, 1966). Other methods involve the child's or adolescent's verbalisms or approaches in responding, such as the degree of plot elaboration (Slemon et al., 1976), specific sentence components and verb and adverbial decriptions (Kempler & Scott, 1970), and number of words used and initial response latency (Schaible, 1975).

Two ambitious studies were undertaken by the Institute of Behavioral Research (Neman, Brown, & Sells, 1973; Neman, Neman, & Sells, 1974). Their aim was the construction of an objective scoring system and scaling procedure for assessing psychological development and normal behavior on the TAT. Factors measured were verbal fluency, conceptual maturity, dysphoric mood, emotionality, and narrative fluency. Subjects represented a national cross-section of children and adolescents. The 1974 publication warns, however, that "as a clinical instrument the objectively scored TAT appears to be inappropriate for assessing personal adjustment" (Neman et al., 1974, p. 31).

Validity Studies

How well *does* the TAT measure dynamics and diagnoses? Some research is positive, some negative. Based on his research with 150 male veterans of World War II, Eron (1965) disagrees with those who would use the TAT to differentiate clinical groups. With his adult subjects he found that the fantasy productions of the various clinical groups were not significantly distinct from each other. He deduced that there is a commonality in fantasies among all adults. Normal adults may be better at correcting their fantasies by comparing them with reality than are maladjusted individuals.

Thus he concludes: "A technique such as the TAT cannot be used as a diagnostic instrument in the sense of pigeonholing people into different Kraepelian categories" (1965, p. 504).

Eron's admonition did not deter attempts to differentiate psychiatric groups. Wolowitz and Shorkey (1969) searched for differences in the expression of power themes on eight TAT cards. They compared a group of normal boys with 10- and 11-year-old male psychiatric patients having diagnoses of paranoid schizophrenia, nonparanoid schizophrenia, passive-aggressive (aggressive), passive-aggressive (passive), anxiety neurosis, and psychoneurosis. Unfortunately no criteria were given for determining the original diagnoses. Only one significant difference was found. The paranoid schizophrenic boys gave significantly more power themes in their TAT stories than did any of the other psychiatric groups or the controls. The power theme as measured in this study did not distinguish one psychiatric group from another.

Silver (1963) attempted to differentiate reform school male adolescents having characteristics associated with psychopathology from matched groups of reform school mild offenders, orphan home residents, and high school students. Six TAT pictures and the MMPI were given each subject. Only in their expression of more need sex and press reduction did the psychopathic subjects differ significantly from other reform school subjects.

Kempler and Scott (1970) studied the thematic stories of boys between the ages of 11 and 18 years in an attempt to distinguish between an antisocial group and a normal group. Nine TAT cards plus eight other thematic picture cards were used, and the stories scored by the authors' own system. Significant differences were found. The antisocial boys were less likely to attribute themes of conformity or remorse to their story characteristics. Their characters were seen as less nurturant or protective.

Aggression Studies

Davids (1973) was interested in aggression as reflected in the TAT. Boys 7–12 years with IQs ranging from 70 to 110 were given a battery of tests, including the TAT. All the boys were institutionalized for emotional disturbances, and most were diagnosed as having severe difficulties coping with aggression. Only one of the four scoring methods for aggression used in analyzing the TAT stories yielded significant findings. The Davids and Rosenblatt (1958) scale did reveal a significant correlation between TAT aggression scores and ratings of overt aggressive behavior. A very high correlation was found between the behavioral ratings and the psychologists' clinical evaluations gleaned from the entire battery of tests. This supports Murray's basic premise that hypotheses generated from the TAT should be verified by use of other methods (Murray, 1943).

Matranga (1976) used the Hafner and Kaplan (1960) scoring system for hostility as Davids did, and was more successful with its use. He tested delinquent male adolescents committed to a training school by giving them six TAT cards. Results indicated that the type of defense mechanism was significantly and positively correlated with the amount of fantasied aggression on the TAT.

Aggressive characteristics of abused and neglected children were the focus of Reidy's (1977) study. She compared physically abused children with nonabused-neglected children and normal children. Each child was given six TAT cards. The stories were rated for aggression by the Hafner and Kaplan (1960) method. Results showed that abused children showed significantly more fantasy aggression on the TAT than did either of the other groups. Abused children and neglected children were rated significantly higher in aggression by their teachers than were the normal subjects. The abused children also used much more aggressive behavior in their play than did either normal or neglected children.

Research by Mussen and Naylor (1954) gives an added dimension to the TAT study of aggression. The subjects were institutionalized lower class boys between 9 and 15 years of age. Results showed that lower class children having a greater amount of fantasy aggression showed significantly more overt aggression than those with less fantasy aggression. Those having high levels of fantasy aggression but relatively little fear of punishment tended to express a great deal of overt aggression. Those with less fantasy aggression but with high fear of punishment showed less overt aggression.

Schaefer and Norman (1967), using children judged antisocial but not institutionalized, found a trend for these subjects to give more external punishment themes following an aggression theme on the TAT and other thematic cards than did a control group. The authors chose to measure the presence rather than the frequency of themes of aggression on the thematic cards because of the brevity of the stories of the control group.

From all these studies, then, it would seem that aggressive fantasy of children can be measured in an objective way in TAT stories. Other themes investigated in children via the TAT include control of aggression (Shore, Massimo, & Mack, 1965), death and departure (North & Keiffer, 1966), and future time perspective (Klineberg, 1967).

Samples

The TAT has been used on a wide variety of subjects, including kibbutz children (Lifshitz, 1974), allergic children (Long et al., 1958; Aaron, 1967; Rawls, Rawls, & Harrison,, 1971), fatally ill children (McCully, 1963), early- and late-maturing boys (Mussen & Jones, 1957), educationally handicapped, emotionally disturbed boys (Bachtold, 1975), and retarded children (Rourke & Quinlan, 1973).

Reliability

The question of rater reliability is obviously of importance and has been found to be high, depending upon the scoring system used. Almost all of the studies have been careful to report the interrater reliability for the study. What can be said about the test reliability itself? One way this question has been addressed is by longitudinal studies.

Kagan and Moss (1959) investigated the stability of fantasy measures of achievement striving over time. They used records of 86

children at the Fels Research Institute, studied at ages 8-9, 11-6, and 14-6. Stories told to seven TAT cards were analyzed for achievement themes. The average number of achievement themes per protocol was only one, and this was generally elicited by either card 1 or card 17BM. The occurrence of achievement fantasy at age 8 was significantly correlated to its occurrence at ages 11 and 14.

In a separate publication based on the same data, Kagan (1959) reported that the achievement themes showed a significant increase with age for both sexes. Overall, however, he found that the content dimensions of the TAT in these studies were not very stable over time, except for physical aggression by the hero and by need achievement. The amount of theme stability seemed to be tied in with the pull of the card for that theme. Kagan theorized that the long term stability of a fantasy theme tends to be very low when the stimulus of the card itself does not suggest that content.

Longitudinal data from the Fels Research Institute was also studied by Schaible (1975) but with an emphasis on the noncontent aspects of TAT stories. TAT protocols of 50 males and 50 females studied at ages 11–6, 14–6, and 17–6, were analyzed for verbal frequency (word count), response latency between presentation of the TAT card and the subject's first verbalization, and need achievement. She found a significant main effect for age on latency, word count, and need achievement. There was a difference between ages 11-6 and 17-6 on the three variables, but it was a gradual one, since the differences between ages 11-6 and 14-6, and between 14-6 and 17-6 were not significant. Since the stability over time was greater for word count than for the other dependent variables, she noted the importance of examining how the subject verbalizes the stories and not merely the content of the stories.

Skolnick (1966) analyzed the TAT protocols of 91 males and females given first at ages 17-18, and then 20 years later. Recognizing that the methodology of the study was limited by the available data, the author did attempt to correlate themes of achievement, affiliation, power, and aggression with behavioral measures. Relatively few significant correlations were found. McClelland (1966), in reviewing the study, noted that the TAT adolescent scores related significantly less often to the other measures than the adult TAT scores. Sholnick viewed her results as suggesting that no relationship can be identified between TAT fantasy and behavior that holds true for all motives, ages, and for both sexes.

Overall, research on the TAT does support its ability to tap a variety of underlying personality dynamics in children and youth. In and of itself, it is not useful as a tool to differentiate between specific psychiatric syndromes or diagnoses or to predict whether or not covert themes will become overt. We strongly endorse Murray's statement: "The conclusions that are reached by an analysis of TAT stories must be regarded as good 'leads' or working hypotheses to be verified by other methods, rather than as proved facts" (Murray, 1943, p. 14). The TAT can provide themes or leads that are not verbalized openly and directly and as such is an important part of any mental status assessment.

The use of any of the large variety of scoring systems is important in research projects but is admittedly tedious. It is safe to venture that most clinicians do not take the time to score TAT protocols. Instead, they develop their own inner norms for the pull of the cards and the expected responses. Deviant responses and the patterning of responses take on significance. In this way the clinician evaluates the content much as one would a mental status interview. If this is the case, the need for validation of the interpretations by other tests or interview responses is crucial.

SYMONDS PICTURE-STORY TEST

Impressed by the TAT and the picture-story technique, Symonds (1948) developed a set of pictures specifically for use with adolescents (SPST). From a pool of 42 pictures given to 40 "normal" teenage boys and girls in junior and senior high schools, 20 were eventually chosen. Criteria used for the final selection were: (1) pictures yielding the largest number of themes,

(2) pictures producing stories with the most important themes, (3) pictures judged best by the examiners in the study, and (4) pictures whose stories were cited most frequently for illustrative purposes in Symonds' (1949) report on the instrument, *Adolescent Fantasy*.

The pictures are divided into A and B sets, 10 cards in each. The examiner is urged to give all 20 cards, Set A the first day, Set B at the next session. If only 10 cards can be given, Set B is the author's recommended choice since it contains the cards rated highest by the four criteria. In giving the 42 pictures to his original sample group, Symonds noted that stories told to the first cards incorporated fewer and less significant themes than those told to later cards. He theorized that, late in the series, the subject's resistance is lessened, allowing fuller and more meaningful fantasies to be revealed. For this reason, when both sets are administered, Set B, comprising the most effective cards, is given second.

Directions for administering the Picture-Story Test differ somewhat from the TAT. The respondent is instructed: "Imagine yourself a story writer and tell a story in which the picture could be used as an illustration.... Please do not feel that you must make your story commonplace and conventional. It can be as absurd, as wild, or as silly as you wish" (Symonds, 1948, p. 6). Following completion of the first story, the examiner may question about action, outcome, or feelings if the story has been mainly descriptive or too brief. When all the stories are told, there is an association period. The examiner reads back each story to the subject, showing the picture involved, and asks where the story came from.

Analysis

Symonds' system of content analysis is compatible with Murray's TAT analysis, but not identical. The principal hero is to be identified for each story, along with additional heroes if present. The character of the hero should be noted, as well as the principal psychological forces that correspond to factors in dynamic psychology. Such factors include hostility and aggression, love and eroticism, ambivalence, punishment, anxiety, conflicts, guilt, ambition, depression, happiness, and sublimation. Interpersonal relationships should be looked for. Interest, attitudes, and outcomes should be examined.

Factors such as reaction time, card rejection, and attitude toward the testing are also important. Labeled as formal factors, they also include spontaneous comments by the subject, adequacy of the story, constriction or freedom in story production, close adherence to the details of the picture, emotional tone, language, and consistency. Study of these and other factors would enable the examiner to derive hypotheses about the adolescent.

Symonds stressed that interpretations of material from the Picture-Story Test must be considered as hypotheses, not as facts. He warned against interpretation from a blind analysis, feeling the hypotheses need verification from other sources such as case history.

Norms

Symond's norms were based on stories told to the 42 cards by the 40 adolescents in the original sample. Presented briefly in the *Manual* (Symonds, 1948) and in more detail in his book (Symonds, 1949), medians and upper and lower quartiles are given for story themes. The assumption is made that a theme occurring with greater frequency than the upper quartile has special significance to the individual. Themes found less frequently than the lower quartile are judged by Symonds as insignificant to the person, or as themes that are inhibited or blocked.

Validity and Reliability

While the SPST has been used in many unpublished doctoral dissertations, it has never enjoyed the research popularity of the TAT or CAT. One reason could be Symonds's initial study itself. His rationale for his norms is questionable, particularly in his interpretation of themes occurring below the lower quartile in frequency. Kass (1959), in his review of the test, wisely points out that it is often the rare story or the rare variation of a

theme that provides insight into unique aspects of the subject's personality.

Symonds's 1949 study was a definite contribution to the evolution of the SPST, but its criteria were often arbitrary. His aim was to select normal or typical children, yet the sample was composed of volunteers, and at least one known "problem" boy was included. Analysis of the themes was done by Symonds and an associate with rather vague guidelines. Symonds stated that no system for identifying themes was completely satisfactory, and no interrater reliability statistics were attempted. Separation of themes into categories of psychological, environmental, and stylistic was deemed arbitrary even by the author. It must be said that Symonds was aware of many of the flaws to his research and called attention to them himself.

In 1958, Symonds and Jensen published results of a longitudinal study of the SPST. Of the 40 adolescents used in the original norming study (Symonds, 1949), 28 were willing to be retested 13 years later. One subject did not complete all the retesting, but the 27 others were given the 20-card SPST in two sessions. The authors' finding of persistence of fantasy over a 13-year period is based on the large number of themes that appeared with the same frequency in 1940 and in 1953, both for the individual subject and for the sample as a whole. No statistics for level of significance were given. Some differences did occur, such as an increase in themes of depression in the 1953 stories. Decreases were found in themes of violent aggression or punishment for aggression, mystery and trick or magic, and in stories with happy or favorable ending. Again, no levels of statistical significance were offered. The authors theorized that changes in fantasy take place as a result of life changes, such as leaving home and marriage. As with his earlier work on the test, the lack of rigorous research methodology takes away from the applicability of his findings.

Gorlow, Zimet, and Fine (1952) unsuccessfully attempted to use the Elizur (1949) method to score the SPST for anxiety and hostility. A group of 13 adolescent delinquents and a control group of nondelinquent adolescents were given a Rorschach and the SPST. Responses were scored for unveiled anxiety and less overt anxiety or hostility. Interrater agreement was 83 percent. While a significant difference was found between the Anxiety Content Scores on the Rorschach for the delinquent and nondelinquent samples, no similar differences were found for responses to the SPST. In trying to explain the lack of significant differences, the authors observed that the negative structure of the pictures possibly limited positive projections to them.

The dearth of adequate research studies on the SPST need not make this instrument worthless to the clinician. As with the TAT, scoring systems are frequently of more use to the researcher than to the clinician seeking to evaluate individual patients. The scenes depicted are pertinent to adolescents and can be useful to elicit projective material about certain types of situations. The Gorlow et al. (1952) study suggests that there is a great pull for stories with a negative flavor. The pictures do frequently seem stark and dreary. However, when a clinician wants to explore areas of depression with a teenager, perhaps the SPST cards are the stimuli of choice.

CHILDREN'S APPERCEPTION TEST

The Children's Apperception Test (CAT) is an offspring of the Thematic Apperception Test (TAT) and the Symonds Picture-Story Test. Since the TAT was developed with subjects 14 years and older, and the SPST was designed for adolescents, no set of thematic pictures existed specifically for younger children. Bellak and Bellak sought to fill that gap. Following Ernst Kris's (Bellak & Bellak, 1952a) premise that children tend to identify themselves more easily with animals than with people, a set of pictures showing animals in various life situations was designed. In 1949, the 10 most useful of these cards became the CAT.

The CAT cards depict scenes designed to elicit material on feeding and oral problems,

sibling rivalry, attitude toward parental figures, Oedipal feelings, aggression, acceptance by the adult world, nighttime loneliness, and toilet behavior. According to the revised manual (Bellak & Bellak, 1952a), the CAT is most useful for boys and girls between 3 and 10 years old. Children older than 10 may not respond as well. The instructions for administration require the child to tell a story about the picture, to tell what is going on and what the animals are doing now. As the story is told, the examiner may ask what happened before and what will happen later. In contrast to the TAT, the child is *not* instructed to tell what the story figures are feeling and thinking.

The authors suggest that the cards be given in numerical order. They do not insist that all 10 cards be given if the child becomes restless or if only certain problems are to be investigated. To aid in card selection, the manual gives card-by-card descriptions of expected themes.

To interpret the stories, the Bellaks suggest 10 variables to be analyzed: main theme; main hero; the way figures are seen; identification; figures, objects, or external circumstances introduced; objects or figures omitted; nature of anxieties; significant conflicts; punishment for crime; and outcome of stories. The authors believe in looking for trends or commonality of themes rather than making judgments from a single isolated story. This is similar to Murray's (1943) advice to verify TAT hypotheses with other diagnostic methods.

CAT Supplement

The CAT Supplement (CAT-S) consists of 10 additional pictures showing situations that are not necessarily universal problems and therefore are not needed for all children. As the manual (Bellak & Bellak, 1952b) indicates, those supplementary scenes pertinent to the specific child can be given along with the standard CAT. Instructions for the CAT and the CAT-S are identical. The pictures depict a play situation, a classroom scene, children playing "house," a parent-child scene, an injured animal, a race, an animal looking at itself in a mirror, a doctor-patient scene, a bathing scene, and a pregnant animal. Stories to these pictures are to be analyzed in the same way as are CAT stories.

The Animal-Human Figure Controversy

In the late 1940s, Bills (1950) presented 10 colored pictures of rabbits along with 10 TAT cards to 48 school children, ages 5–10 years. He found that the total word count was significantly higher for stories about the animal cards than for the TAT stories. Only one animal card elicited no story, while 18 of the TAT cards were rejected. Thus it appeared easier for the children to tell stories to the animal cards than to the TAT. However, Bills did not control for the fact that the rabbit pictures were in color while the TAT was in black and white.

A second study with colleagues (Bills, Leiman, & Thomas, 1950) involved the reuse of the rabbit pictures and the TAT. Eight third-grade children were given six individual nondirective play therapy interviews as well as the 10 rabbit pictures and the first 10 TAT cards. The four boys and four girls were deemed well adjusted by teacher report as well as by their responses to the Rorschach and to the California Test of Personality. All of the material obtained for the study was scored by 26 of Murray's manifest needs. Of the eight subjects, only one child had a significant correlation between the needs revealed from interview and those revealed from the animal pictures; one child had a significant correlation between the needs obtained from interview and those obtained from the TAT; three children had significant correlations of the needs expressed on the animal pictures and on the TAT. Obviously the amount of agreement of manifest needs that was found among the instruments was not strikingly high. The small size of the sample obviously lessens the usefulness of any findings, but nevertheless it was one of the first animal-versus-human-figure studies involving manifest needs instead of word count, response time, and the like.

With the introduction of the CAT, research proliferated contrasting it with the TAT.

Attempts were made to validate the Bellaks' theory that children relate better to pictures of animals than to those of humans. Biersdorf and Marcuse (1953) compared six drawings of CAT cards with six drawings of human figures in CAT scenes. Subjects were 30 "normal" first graders whose mean age was 7 years. No significant differences were found between instruments on any of their seven criteria. No attempt was made to compare the types of themes elicited by each set of cards.

Armstrong's (1954) study used five CAT cards and five similar CAT scenes with human figures. Her sample was composed of 60 bright, upper socioeconomic level school children, grades one through three. She found no consistent tendency for longer responses to the animal pictures. However, at a significant level, children did have a higher Transcendence Index for the human figure cards; that is, there were more nondescriptive comments for the human figure cards than for the animal cards. The potential for more psychologically useful material was therefore greater for the human stimulus than for the animal stimulus.

In general, the results of subsequent studies remained consistent. The research comparing the CAT cards with similar scenes using human figures continued to find human figure cards to be either superior or equal to the CAT in evoking expression of feelings, conflicts, and clinically useful information (Light, 1954; Mainord & Marcuse, 1954; Furuya, 1957; Budoff, 1960; Butler, 1961; Weisskopf-Joelson & Foster, 1962; Budoff, 1963). The lack of superiority of the CAT held across various populations: preschool children; children in grades one through six; children considered well adjusted, as well as those emotionally disturbed; retarded children as well as intellectually gifted children; males and females; and even Japanese children.

The CAT-H

The Bellaks were attentive to the animal versus human figures controversy. They hypothesized that a significant cause for the conflicting results lay in the specific human figure cards used for comparison with the original CAT cards. As Bellak and Hurvich (1965) noted, "Very few investigators maintained the ambiguity of age or sex in the human drawings that is inherent in the animal figures" (p. 3). The Bellaks then published their own human modification of the CAT, the CAT-H. While they still suggested that the CAT should be the preferred choice for use with children, they acknowledged that the CAT-H might be more useful with children between 7 and 10 and those of higher IQ. No special scoring procedures were offered for the CAT-H.

Haworth carried out an unpublished study cited at length in Bellak and Hurvich (1966) and briefly in her own book (1966). She gave the CAT and the CAT-H to 22 children, ages 6–10, whose psychiatric problems ranged from neurotic difficulties and behavior problems to borderline psychoses. Haworth's Analysis Schedule of defense mechanisms (Haworth, 1963) was used to score the responses. Though a trend appeared for more projection-introjection to be used on the animal cards, no significant differences were found on the total number of defense categories for either form.

Lawton (1966) used the CAT and CAT-H with kindergarten children and second graders in an upper-middle-class school and scored them by Haworth's Analysis Schedule. No significant similarities were found in the defense mechanisms used for cards on either form, except for projection. A significant agreement between stories involving projection on the CAT and CAT-H was reported. A child who had a critical score for projection on the CAT-H most likely also had a critical score for projection on the CAT.

Fourth-grade children of varying levels of anxiety were studied by Neuringer and Livesay (1970). Using the Children's Manifest Anxiety Scale (Castaneda, McCandless, & Palermo, 1956) to differentiate, those children scoring in the top, middle, and lowest deciles were given the CAT and the CAT-H. The thematic stories were analyzed for word count, number of emotional words, and number of expressed negative emotions. The Haworth Adaptive Mechanism scoring system and the Transcendence Index were applied. There was only one significant finding. Higher mean Transcendence Index scores were found for the CAT, a measure that was consistent no matter which anxiety group was measured. On the CAT, then, children made more comments about the picture beyond mere description than they did on the CAT-H cards. Other than this, the CAT was no more effective with the children than the CAT-H.

Myler, Rosenkrantz, and Holmes (1972) designed an ambitious study comparing the CAT, CAT-H, and the TAT. Subjects were 60 second-grade girls of average intelligence. Stories were analyzed for initial word count (responses based on the first question, "What's happening?"), interim word count (total remaining responses to further questioning), the Transcendence Index, creativity, and organization of responses. No differences were found on any measures when contrasting the CAT with the CAT-H. This is consistent with most of the studies comparing human figures in CAT-like scenes with the CAT itself. Unlike previous research, the TAT was less effective than the CAT on every measure used, but the level only reached statistical significance for the Transcendence Index and the initial word count. The CAT-H stories also had a statistically higher mean Transcendence Index than the TAT. The authors suggest that the CAT and CAT-H appear more suitable for the second- and third-grade child in eliciting clinically relevant stories, while the TAT may be more effective with the fourth- and fifth-grader, as seen in Light's (1954) study. Another unmentioned factor may be the sex of the child. Light's subjects were both boys and girls while Myler et al. tested only girls.

Much time and effort have been spent on the animal versus human figure controversy. Most studies fail to support the Bellaks' hypothesis that children identify more easily with animal figures. The more important question, however, is whether or not children produce clinically useful information on the CAT.

Scoring Systems for the CAT

In order to evaluate children's responses to the CAT statistically, scoring systems had to be developed. A popular one has been Haworth's Adaptive Mechanism scoring method, consisting of 10 categories of defenses, identification, and other adaptive mechanisms. It was first used in her 1962 study and later presented in greater detail (Haworth, 1963). Weisskopf's (1950) Transcendence Index has been successfully applied to the CAT and CAT-H as well as to the TAT it was designed for.

Byrd and Witherspoon (1954) classified each CAT response as enumerative (naming of objects), descriptive (description of objective features of the picture), and apperceptive (interpretation beyond the objective features of the picture). Witherspoon (1968) later attempted to analyze the CAT for psychoanalytic personality dynamics by way of nine scoring categories. He concluded that his instrument needed further refining. Scroth (1977) felt his study showed that Slemon et al.'s (1976) Associative Elaboration and Integration Scales could be used successfully for the CAT. Scheffler (1975) attempted to construct scales for rating personality dimensions on Cards 2 and 6 of the CAT but found those cards too weak in eliciting consistent, clear identification of characters to do so. Many studies use such mechanistic features as word count, response time, response latency, and so on. The CAT was even used as a way to elicit children's verbalizations in speech research (Winitz, 1959; Siegel, 1962).

Validity Studies

Can the CAT measure dynamics and defenses of use to the clinician? The Bellaks (1952a) contended that validation and establishment of norms as would be done for intelligence tests are unnecessary for projective tests if the concept of projective phenomena itself is accepted. Haworth (1966), in her extensive review of the CAT literature, decries the imprecise evaluation measures and the small samples in most of the validity studies she cited. She felt the results often failed to be impressive. In the years since her review, the intensity of CAT research has decreased. A handful of studies have appeared, mostly in foreign journals.

A symposium on the CAT was held in 1967 calling for the establishment of baselines from normative data. Introducing the panel, Haworth (1968) stressed the symposium's concern with the assessment of ego functions in the personality evaluation of normal children. In general, however, the panelists did not provide such norms. Witherspoon (1968) offered beginning data on scoring CAT stories for psychoanalytic personality dynamics. Moriarty (1968) reported fairly generally on her research with bright, preschool age children, stressing that the uniqueness and pattern of each child's responses should be viewed in relation to "standard expectations, feelings, conflicts, and resolutions" (p. 418). The need for more provision of such "standard" responses continues, however.

Reliability Studies

Haworth (1966) reviewed reliability studies with the CAT. Test-retest reliability figures in the few available studies were not high, but the changing maturation level of the child must be taken into consideration for any prolonged longitudinal study. Rater reliability for various CAT scoring systems is sometimes high, suggesting that rating systems can be devised with enough clarity to be used successfully in analyzing records. Not all scoring systems reach this goal, of course.

Additional CAT Variations

An interesting attempt to involve children more deeply in the CAT task was reported by Hoar and Faust (1973). Eighteen children 3 and 4 years of age were given a set of regular CAT pictures to respond to, as well as a set of CAT cards in jigsaw puzzle form that the child had to put together. The two sets were given at least a month apart in counterbalanced order within the sample. More descriptive responses and interpretive responses were given to the puzzle CAT than to the regular CAT before any additional questioning for further information. The authors concluded that the puzzle form of the CAT was a better instrument for very young children.

Cain (1961) proposed a way to elicit additional fantasy from CAT responses. At the end of a story in whch any of the characters is portrayed as sleeping, the examiner asks, "What did X dream?" Cain has found that this technique works well with children 6 years and older, with children of borderline and dull average intelligence being particularly receptive. Of his sample, 80 percent responded with a dream.

Conclusions

The introduction of the CAT was designed to encourage children to reveal more about themselves than they would on the TAT. The literature, however, fails to support the overall superiority of the CAT. This does not mean that the CAT is useless. Research studies deal, perforce, with numbers of children, with means and chi-squares. Clinicians deal with individuals. As with the TAT, the usefulness of a specific thematic card often lies in the "pull of the card," that is, the storyline it typically brings forth. Thus investigators with children who have specific problems may find certain CAT cards particularly helpful. Some children definitely do react better to animal pictures even if the majority do not. It is in the clinician's best interest, therefore, to have the CAT readily available for use with that child who can use it.

MICHIGAN PICTURE TEST—REVISED

During the period in which the CAT was being developed, the Michigan Picture Test (MPT) was in preparation for children from 8 to 14 years of age. This test filled the remaining gap in thematic apperception tests between the CAT for younger children and the Symonds Picture-Story Test for adolescents. The major purpose of the MPT from its inception was to differentiate the emotionally maladjusted child from a well-adjusted classmate. It was based on almost three years of preliminary studies, plus later validation with children from nine public school systems and 11 child guidance clinics. First published in 1953, the test was in use for well over 10 years

but then became unavailable. Happily, in 1978 a revision was undertaken and the Michigan Picture Test—Revised (MPT-R) appeared in 1980.

The MPT-R consists of 15 cards, including one blank card. There is a basic Core Series of four cards to be used mainly for screening purposes. Children receiving the Full Series are given 11 cards, four of which are designed for boys and four others for girls. One of the original MPT cards showing pupils and a teacher in a very old fashioned classroom is no longer included.

Because a suitable card showing a mother-daughter relationship could not be found, Card 7GF from the TAT was used (Hartwell et al., 1951). Test instructions are similar in content to those of the TAT. The examiner may make an inquiry for clarification or for obtaining additional information, but the inquiry responses are not scored.

Normative Data

The MPT has not been the subject of many published studies. However, the test's authors strongly believed that the MPT should be based on good normative data, and they did extensive testing to accomplish this. Results of these studies appear in the original manual (Michigan Department of Mental Health, 1953) and in the new manual (Hutt, 1980). Additional reports on the normative process (Hartwell et al., 1951; Andrew, Walton, & Hartwell, 1951; Walton, Andrew, & Hartwell, 1951) emphasized the MPT authors' intention to make this instrument more objective than some of the other projective measures. Hutt regards these studies as only the beginning of the standardization process.

In evaluating the subject's responses, objective test variables are offered in both manuals along with normative statistics for comparison purposes. The quantative scoring involves a Tension Index, the use of tense, and Direction of Forces. Critical scores on all three of these indices are used to derive the Combined Maladjustment Index. All of these scores can be obtained by giving only the four Core Cards.

The Tension Index is composed of verbally expressed needs of love, extrapunitiveness, submission, and personal adequacy. Walton et al. (1951) studied fifth-graders, 15 of whom were judged well adjusted and 15 poorly adjusted by teachers' evaluations of their objective behavior in the classroom. A third group was made up of 15 children of similar age who were in treatment at child guidance clinics. The Tension Index was defined as the index of psychic tension that assesses the degree of adjustment on the basis of verbal expressions of unresolved psychological needs. It has two factors: expression of needs and intensity of needs. Comparison of the well adjusted and poorly adjusted school children's responses to the Core Cards revealed a significant difference between the means on expression of needs, and between the means on intensity of needs. Cross-validation with a new sample of 15 well adjusted and 15 poorly adjusted fifth-graders also revealed significant differences in the Tension Index. They then compared their well adjusted sample with 15 clinic cases of the same age. The difference in means was again significant. The Tension Index does discriminate between well adjusted and poorly adjusted children.

The use of tense was defined by Hartwell et al. (1951) as all references to past, present, and future tense verbs within each story for each picture. At issue was not the total number of references to tense but the much greater use of one tense as compared to the others. Of the 116 school children tested in grades 3, 5, and 7–9, the poorly adjusted group significantly used more past tense references than the well adjusted at all grade levels. It was also found that third-graders in general tended to use the present tense almost exclusively and that the higher grade children used both past and future tense more frequently.

In the same study Hartwell et al. also investigated the index of Direction of Forces, that is, the forces impinging upon the central character. The action in the story was classified as (1) *centrifugal* in which forces emanate from the central figure in the story, (2) *centripetal* in which forces are directed upon the central figure, (3) *ambivalent* in which the central figure is involved with both centrifugal and centripetal forces, and (4) *ambiguous* where there is more than one central figure and some show centrifugal forces and others show centripetal ones. Great differences were found in the stimulus values of the Core Cards' Direction of Forces, but no final conclusions were drawn.

To aid the clinician in scoring and interpreting cases, the MPT and MPT-R manuals offer weighted scores for the Tension Index, tense, and Direction of Forces, broken down by grade and age and with the critical score best discriminating between good and poor adjustment. The Combined Maladjustment Index is obtained by summing up the number of times the child had scores at or above the critical level for each factor.

The test authors acknowledge that the scoring procedure is time consuming but hope that it is simple enough that the psychologist can train a staff person to do it. A record form is available to aid in the scoring. It is also recognized that clinicians will also want to evaluate the test content qualitatively, and suggestions for this are offered in the 1980 manual. Such qualitative analysis is championed by Hutt, who feels such interpretive data "may not easily be available in any other form" (Hutt, 1980, p. 52). The typical caution is made to consider such test interpretations only in context with developmental and physical history, current circumstances, the nature of the diagnostic setting, and other sources. With the renewed availability of the MPT in its revised form, opportunities for new research on this instrument abound.

TASKS OF EMOTIONAL DEVELOPMENT (TED)

Brief mention should be made of the TED, a thematic test created by Cohen and Weil (1971a, 1971b) for children between 6 and 18 years. Photographic scenes are based on a "task" of emotional development. There are 13 tasks: socialization within the peer group, establishment of trust in people, acceptance and control of aggressive feelings toward peers, establishment of positive attitudes toward academic learning, establishment of a conscience with respect to the property of others, separation from the mother figure, identification with the same sex parent, acceptance of siblings, acceptance of limits from adults, acceptance of affection between parents, establishment of positive attitudes toward orderliness and cleanliness, establishment of a positive self-concept, and establishment of positive heterosexual socialization. While only Erikson's (1950) trust versus basic mistrust concept was included in the selection of the pictures, the authors readily acknowledge that his theories played a large part in the development of the TED, as did the work of Gardner (Cohen & Weil, 1971a).

The photographs are divided into sets for boys 6–11, girls 6–11, boys 12–18, and girls 12–18. The unique aspect of the test is that each set is roughly parallel to the other, differing chiefly in the age of the pictured child. However, some subtle differences do exist, such as facial expressions of the adult figures. Only the adolescent sets include a heterosexual, possible "dating" card.

Reviews of the TED as an instrument ("Reviews," 1972; Levitt, 1975; Wise, 1975) have been critical, particularly regarding the methodology of test development. The validity of the TED is questionable, despite a favorable review of investigations employing the TED (Pollak, Cohen, & Weil, unpublished). It is mentioned in this chapter because it includes a variety of everyday situations that often involve conflict for young people. Many clinicians prefer to assess specific problem areas by selecting pictures from among available thematic tests rather than using only a single test series. The TED offers an additional resource to select from.

MAKE A PICTURE STORY TEST (MAPS)

The MAPS introduces a new aspect into the thematic apperception technique. Cut-out story figures are placed on a series of background pictures, enabling the respondent to "people" the story situation with an individualized cast of characters. Sixty-seven figures are provided in varying poses: male and female children and adults, minority group figures, animals, figures of indeterminate sex, legendary and fictitious characters, silhouettes, and figures with blank faces. There are 22 black and white background scenes, generally devoid of any human faces. Some backgrounds are unstructured or ambiguous, some are semistructured, and some are definitely structured. In selecting the scenes, Shneidman (1948) attempted to use those reflecting clinically important problem areas and dynamics.

The test is presented with the instructions to take one or more of the figures and put them on the background picture as they might be in real life. A story about the scene is then requested. The examiner notes the subject's choice and placement of the figures and records the story told. A MAPS Figure Location Sheet showing all scenes aids this process. At the end of the story the examiner may question for omitted information, for clarification, for age, sex, or personality of the characters, and for the title of the story.

Initially, Shneidman (1948) suggested 11 pictures should usually be presented to adults in the following order: livingroom, street scene, medical scene, bathroom, dream, bridge, bedroom, blank, forest, closet, and the eleventh picture chosen by the subject from the 12 remaining cards. Later he suggested that 10 pictures are usually given (Shneidman, 1949). No instructions were given in the manual specifically for use with children although its potential use with children and adolescents was noted.

The MAPS has not had the same popularity as the TAT or the CAT with children, but it offers an intriguing aspect in the separation of figure from background picture. Spiegelman (1955) observed that "Shneidman's MAPS test is the most productive of thematic material which can be used in a typically Jungian manner" (p. 261).

Advantages of the MAPS listed by Shneidman (1949) include exceptional subject appeal of the test situation, latitude for demonstration of thought and feeling as well as moral support for the timorous subject via the manipulable figures, and the choice and placement of figures allowing for analysis of the characters of fantasy and for objective scoring of diagnostic signs.

Scoring

Shneidman's (1948) original research with the MAPS involved normal and schizophrenic hospitalized adults, all male veterans. From this study, he constructed statistically significant lists of schizophrenic signs and normal signs involving the selection of figures for the stories. Bindon (1957) used Shneidman's sign categories in her MAPS study of rubella deaf, nonrubella deaf, and hearing adolescents. Because of the deafness factor, the study focused primarily on comparison of figures chosen rather than on stories elicited. Eleven pictures were shown along with the complete set of cut-out figures. Results confirmed her hypothesis that rubella deaf children and nonrubella deaf children do not differ significantly in the number of normal and schizophrenic signs. Rubella deaf children gave significantly fewer normal signs and significantly more schizophrenic signs, however, than did the hearing group. It was also noted that the deaf children characteristically gave themes involving interpersonal relationships.

Fine (1955) offered a detailed method for scoring feelings, outcomes, and interpersonal relationships for verbal projective techniques such as the TAT and the MAPS. The sensitivity of Fine's scoring system for use with all populations was questioned by Spiegelman (1956), citing the negative findings of the latter's study with 64 children seen in an outpatient child guidance clinic. A paucity in scorable feelings and relationships was noted. Of the outcomes of the stories, 68 percent were indeterminate, 24 percent were favorable, and 8 percent were unfavorable. However, the sample was perhaps too broad. There were 41 boys and 23 girls ranging in age from 3 years, 6 months to 16 years. All but seven children were between 6 and 13 years. The variety of referring problems was extensive, comprising 12 symptom categories. The children used

between 2 and 12 pictures, with an average of 8. Moreover, the tests were given by 12 different examiners. Spiegelman noted that a larger sample given a standard set of MAPS cards might produce statistically significant results and suggested the need for normative research.

The MAPS as a Diagnostic Technique

Joel (1948) studied the MAPS responses of disturbed inpatient and outpatient adolescents ranging in age from 11 to 18 years. All were described as having a "personality disturbance" severe enough to warrant psychiatric consultation. Between one and 21 pictures were given to the subjects. Results are provided for card rejections, number of figures used per story and per picture, choice of figures, and choice of figures in relation to the background picture. Joel observed that the MAPS allows the subject to structure the social situation from the very beginning, in contrast to the TAT pictures, which suggest either interpersonal relationships or solitude as a starting point for each story. Minor drawbacks to the MAPS were listed as the rather structured and narrow range of facial expression.

Smith and Coleman (1956) investigated the relationship between overt hostility in the classroom and hostile content produced on the Rorschach and the MAPS. The predicted positive linear relationship between the hostile content on the MAPS and overt hostility was only partially supported. Subjects were 30 white male schoolchildren between 9 and 15 years. Their responses to eight background pictures were analyzed by three measures of hostility and compared to teacher-rated measures of classroom hostility. The correlation between the hostility control score on the MAPS and physical hostility in the classroom was the only significant statistic found involving the MAPS.

Tolor and Orange (1969) used the MAPS to study psychological distance in 20 advantaged (family income above $7,000) and 20 disadvantaged (family income less than $4,000) children. There were 10 boys and 10 girls in each group, ranging in age from 5 to 14. The livingroom scene and the shanty scene were given to each child, the former representing an advantaged setting, the latter a disadvantaged one. Two series of figures were used, six advantaged and six disadvantaged. Placement of each figure on the card was measured exactly and the stories were recorded. For both background pictures, disadvantaged children significantly placed disadvantaged figures farther apart than did the advantaged children. The disadvantaged children expressed far more themes in which the characters were engaged in a pleasurable or constructive associational act than did the advantaged children and far fewer themes involving harmful or destructive relationships.

A review of MAPS research by Shneidman (1960) includes unpublished studies and details about the use of MAPS with children.

THE ROSENZWEIG PICTURE-FRUSTRATION STUDY, CHILDREN'S FORM

The Children's Form of the Rosenzweig Picture-Frustration Study, designed for the age range 4–13, was first published in 1948. It was initially constructed as a research instrument, but interest in its clinical applications soon became apparent. The P-F consists of 24 cartoonlike pictures, presenting two persons engaged in frustrating situations. One figure is depicted making a statement describing the frustration of the other figure, who is shown with a blank caption box above. The subject is instructed to write in the box the first repsonse that occurs to him or her that the character might reply. It is assumed that "the subject will 'project' himself into the stimulus situation and possibly 'identify' with the central figure of it, i.e., the frustrated character in each of the test items" and will "respond in some sense more or less unconsciously for himself" (Rosenzweig, 1960, p. 151). While in all 24 captions the frustrated figure is portrayed as a child, approximately half of the items depict a child inflicting the frustration and the remaining half present an adult as the

frustrater. The sex of both figures is varied. A variety of needs commonly frustrated in a child's life (e.g., approval) and several forms of frustration (e.g., privation) are included.

Each response is scored under two major categories: Direction of Aggression and Type of Aggression. Direction of Aggression comprises extrapunitive (E), in which aggression is directed onto the environment, intropunitive (I), in which the subject turns aggression upon himself or herself; and impunitive (M), in which the subject attempts to avoid expression of aggression by minimizing or denying the presence of frustration. Type of Aggression comprises obstacle-dominance (O-D), in which the barrier creating the frustration is emphasized in the response; ego-defense (E-D), which emphasizes the subject defending himself or herself; and need-persistence (N-P), in which resolution of the frustrating situation predominates in the response. Nine possible scoring factors result for each test item from the combination of these six categories. In addition to these scoring categories and factors are the Group Conformity Rating (GCR) and Trends. The GCR, an index of social adjustment, measures a subject's tendency to perceive and respond to frustration in a manner that is generally acceptable to the majority of society. Trends reflect a shift from a predominant manner of response in the first half of the record form to another predominant mode in the latter half. The reader may refer to the manual (Rosenzweig, Fleming, & Rosenzweig, 1948), which provides a more detailed discussion of the description and scoring of the Children's Form of the P-F.

Norms

A dearth of normative data exists regarding the Children's Form of the P-F. Children's norms (Rosenzweig et al., 1948) were initially derived from a group of 256 children (131 males, 125 females), ranging in age from 4 through 13 years. The 4- through 7-year-old subjects were enrolled in private school; the 8-through 13-year-olds attended public school. The younger group was administered the P-F individually; the older sample was examined by the group administration method. Perusal of the original standardization study triggers several questions regarding the soundness of its methodology. A major question concerns whether biases in selection of the sample exist. There is no mention that variables such as race, socioeconomic level, and intelligence were controlled. Furthermore, there is no apparent recognition that the variation in administration methods or in public versus private school status may have affected the normative study's outcome. Notwithstanding these limitations, findings revealed changes in the Direction of Aggression and GCR, which are consistent with child developmental theory. The data demonstrated steady decreases in E and increases in I and M as the children increased in age. The GCR tended to increase over the age span of 4–11. No notable age differences were discerned regarding the Type of Aggression. Norms are also available for special populations such as child guidance patients (Rosenzweig & Rosenzweig, 1952) and mentally retarded children (Angelino & Shedd, 1956).

Reliability Studies

Very little research regarding the reliability of the Children's Form of the P-F has been conducted. The reliability literature (Rosenzweig, 1978; Rosenzweig, Ludwig, & Adelman, 1975) that is available has typically employed brief intervening periods between test administrations. Nevertheless, the research has shown moderate stability over time regarding the Direction of Aggression categories. Moderate reliability has also been demonstrated for E-D and N-P while the reliability findings for O-D and GCR have been ambiguous.

Validity Studies

A major question in P-F research, as in other personality research, concerns whether the P-F can accurately predict behavior. Research findings pertinent to this question are equivocal but skewed in the negative direction.

Concerning research that has indicated

positive correspondence between the Children's P-F and behavior, in one study (Rosenzweig & Rosenzweig, 1952), child guidance patients were shown to differ from the normative sample, although the differences were not significant at every age level. In comparison to the normative group, they demonstrated a higher E and a lower I and GCR, reflecting that maladjusted children have less fully assimilated ways of coping with frustrating situations. A study conducted by Levitt and Lyle (1955) reflected positively on the validity of the Children's P-F. Fifth-grade children, 24 with high scores and 28 with low scores on the Problem Situation Test (PST), a verbal measure of punitiveness, were compared on their performances on the P-F. The data revealed that punitive subjects (high scorers) gave significantly more extrapunitive and ego defensive responses than the nonpunitive subjects (low scorers), while the nonpunitive subjects responded significantly more often in intropunitive and need persistive modes than the punitive subjects. The GCR did not differ for the two groups and its variablity was limited, resulting in the authors raising questions regarding the utility of the GCR as an index of social adjustment.

Several studies have indicated a lack of correspondence between the Children's P-F and behavior. In an attempt to assess the relationship between overt aggressive behavior and aggressive fantasy, Coleman (1967) conducted a study composed of 72 10- and 13-year-old boys primarily from lower and lower-middle-class families and having average to above average verbal intellectual functioning. Aggressive behavior was assessed by a peer-rating technique that delineates aggression into five subcategories: (1) provoked physical aggression, (2) unprovoked physical aggression, (3) outburst aggression, (4) indirect aggression, and (5) verbal aggression. Aggressive fantasy was elicited by three projective techniques: (1) Children's Form of the P-F, (2) TAT, and (3) Rorschach. Only the extrapunitive category of the P-F was scored. No significant correlations were noted between E and the rating scale. Coleman suggested that highly structured tests such as the

P-F have limited predictive value because responses are considerably influenced by the stimulus factors. In another study (Lipman, 1959), two groups, matched for sex, age, race, socioeconomic level, and intelligence, were selected from a mentally retarded population, one group designated as "behavior problems" and the other labelled as "behavior models," that is, manifesting no discernible signs of behavioral problems. The data revealed no significant differences on the P-F between the two groups. Mitchell (1967) has contended that the P-F lacks clinical utility because it is limited by the influence of extrinsic and intrinsic variables that contribute to the tendency to provide censored responses. In a study of 245 sixth-grade boys divided into 3 adjustment groups (well adjusted, average adjusted, and poorly adjusted), Smith (1958) investigated the concurrent validity of the Children's P-F and five additional children's personality and adjustment tests. Although the findings reflected some degree of validity for the P-F, particularly regarding the GCR, the distributions of the three adjustment groups evidenced marked overlap. Smith contended that the overlap of the distributions would contribute to a high percentage of false positives and, consequently, concluded that the use of the P-F "alone for individual prediction, or...as a screening device, is extremely hazardous" (p. 20).

In a study of 272 4- through 13-year-old children (141 boys, 131 girls), Rosenzweig and Mirmow (1949) investigated the validity of trends as an index of conflict in reacting to frustration. A significant increase in trends was noted after age 5. A trend toward O-D predominated at every age level. Trends toward extrapunitiveness predominated only in the 4-through 5-year age group, while trends toward intropunitiveness and away from extrapunitiveness occurred in the older children. In addition, subjects whose records showed trends demonstrated a significantly lower percentage of E and higher percentages of I and O-D than those whose records showed no trends. These findings were interpreted as depicting the "process of socialization, involving the progressive inhibition of

infantile aggression and the development of more indirect reactions to frustration" (p. 308).

Gender Differences

The relationship between sex of subject and responses on the P-F has also been explored. In general, data have revealed no consistent sex differences (Spache, 1951; Stoltz & Smith, 1959). However, when Spache scored separately the child-versus-child (C-C) and the adult-versus-child (A-C) P-F items, sex differences appeared. In Spache's study, both the boys and girls displayed a heightened tendency to direct their aggression toward children rather than toward adults and were noted more often to accept responsibility and pursue resolutions when dealing with adults. In addition, the boys were found more often to direct their aggression against the environment when in conflict with adults but against the other individual when in conflict with children. In contrast to the Spache study, Stoltz and Smith did not find any significant sex-of-subject differences when the P-F was separated into A-C and C-C conditions.

Miscellaneous Studies

The P-F has also been employed to investigate differences in reaction to frustration among handicapped children (Lynch & Arndt, 1953; Johannsen & Bennett, 1955), in children of various sociometric statuses (Coons, 1957; Krieger & Schwartz, 1965), and in family interactions (Reck, McCary, & Weatherly, 1969). The relationship between direction and type of aggression and achievement has also been examined (Roth & Puri, 1967; Zimet, Rose, & Camp, 1973).

Conclusion

Unlike the Rorschach, the thematic tests, and the MMPI, the Children's P-F is not an instrument commonly included in psychological test batteries. The literature raises serious questions regarding its clinical utility and indicates that, when used for clinical purposes, it should be used along with other data.

VERBAL INVENTORIES

Projective tests have been, and will doubtlessly continue to be, the procedures of choice with the child patient, Gittleman's (1980) gloomy review notwithstanding, in good part because the employment of verbal inventories is frequently contraindicated by the youthful respondent's incomplete reading skill and reading comprehension and limited worldly experience. Even with adolescent patients, Hirsch (1970) elected to exclude verbal inventories from his extensive clinical battery. Yet, a variety of verbal instruments designed for the youthful respondent is actually available, some requiring reading by pupils at the fourth grade level (Johnson & Bommarito, 1971). Clinical use of these measures is uncommon; even research reports appear infrequently. There are a few exceptions, notably the MMPI. The MMPI literature clearly indicates that its application with youth has been restricted to adolescents. Its developers (Hathaway & McKinley, 1967) cautioned that the test should not be used with individuals under the age of 16 or with less than 6 years of formal education. Graham (1977) suggests that the MMPI may be reasonably administered to a bright 13-year-old and, Dahlstrom, Welsh, and Dahlstrom (1972) add, "on occasion," even to a bright 12-year-old. This emendation seems in accord with clinical experience. However, no one has suggested that the MMPI should be employed with preteenagers, and published reports of its use deal almost entirely with samples in age range 13–18 years. Finally, a recent study by Ward and Ward (1980) suggests that a reading grade level of 6.7 is required for the average MMPI scale.

MMPI

Norms

It has been known for the past 20 years that the adult MMPI norms are likely to yield somewhat distorted interpretations when applied to adolescents. Data for the latter group published by Hathaway and Monachesi (1961, 1963) indicate that, compared to adult records, K-corrected adolescent records are higher on Scales 6, 7, and 9 and especially on Scales 4 and 8. This pattern of distortion was recently verified with psychiatric patients with a further indication that the use of adult K-corrected norms produced more false classifications and code type changes among males (Klinge & Strauss, 1976).

Dahlstrom, Welsh, and Dahlstrom (1972) and Marks, Seeman, and Haller (1974) provide T-score norms for respondents aged 15, 16, 17, and 14 and younger based on a sample of 1,800 teenagers furnished by the latter. The tables in Marks et al. (1974) are somewhat easier to read. These norms are not corrected by K but the discrepancies with adult T-scores are hardly affected.

Hathaway and Monachesi (1961, 1963) and Marks, Seeman, and Haller (1974) present high point code types for adolescents in each source based on the T-scores contained therein.

There is some question whether norms obtained from adolescents in Minnesota two and three decades ago remain applicable. A contrast of reports by McDonald and Gynther (1962) and Moore and Handal (1980) indicate that norms may be significantly affected by such variables as race, location of residence, and time. The latter factor is clearly delineated in a study by Schubert and Wagner (1975). Data for freshman college students obtained in 1958 and 1969 show significant changes on Scales 2, 6, 7, 8, 9, 0, and F and K. Of course, MMPI adult norms suffer from the same potential shortcomings.

Delinquency

The cornerstone MMPI research on delinquency is the aforementioned statewide study by Hathaway and Monachesi (1963) in which 15,000 ninth-grade pupils in Minnesota schools were tested between 1947 and 1954. A number of other studies conducted between 1945 and 1965 are summarized by Lanyon (1968). Much of the recent literature, especially dealing with delinquent female samples, has been summarized by Haymond (1981).

In general, the findings support those of Hathaway and Monachesi in finding a primary high point on Scale 4 and secondary elevations on Scales 6, 7, 8, and 9. Scores on Scale 4 alone have been employed as a criterion of success in the treatment of delinquency (Caditz, 1961). For the most part, special delinquency scales composed of MMPI items (Gough & Peterson, 1952; Hathaway & Monachesi, 1957; Kanun & Monachesi, 1960; Abe, 1969; Tsubouchi & Jenkins, 1969) have been ignored, as Haymond points out.

An item analysis of the F Scale by McKegney (1965) disclosed that delinquent boys normally score much higher than normals so that a high score should not invalidate the delinquent's profile. An investigation by Gynther and Shinkunas (1965) suggests that the inflated F is likely to be a function of low intelligence—a characteristic of institutionalized delinquents—rather than of delinquency itself. At almost every age level beginning with 14, those with IQs below 90 had the highest F scores.

Several MMPI investigations (e.g., Randolph, Richardson, & Johnson, 1961) suggested that the so-called solitary delinquent— one who acts out alone and in a totally unacceptable manner—is more intelligent and more emotionally disturbed than the "social" delinquent whose crimes are relatively acceptable and who employs accomplices. However, when the incidence of delinquent behaviors in noninstitutionalized adolescents is used as a criterion, the MMPI differences disappear (Hindelang, 1973).

Thorne (1971) reported that scores on Zuckerman's Sensation Seeking Scale were significantly correlated with scores on Scale 9 for delinquent females but not for males.

Psychiatric Disturbance

The general finding is that adolescents hospitalized with emotional problems tend to have a peak on Scale 8, and frequently are 8–4 code types (e.g., McCormick et al., 1971; Archer, White, & Orvin, 1979). However, the 8–4 code type has also been reported for adolescent outpatients (Lauterbach, Vogel, & Hart, 1962), for teenage medical patients (Colligan & Osborne, 1977), as well as for some of the drug abuser groups described later in this chapter. It has also been reported that two-thirds of the adolescent patients with 8–6 and 8–7 code types are clinically diagnosed as psychotic (Chase, Chaffin, & Morrison, 1975). On the basis of a long term follow-up study, Hathaway, Monachesi, and Salasin (1970) have described the young persons who peak on Scale 8 as "unfortunate social outcomes...associated with the high 8 condition which has a clear positive relation to low school achievement and low socioeconomic origins and outcomes" (p. 184).

Mezzich and Mezzich (1979a) developed a 35-item MMPI depression scale for adolescents using expert judgment as a basis. Using this Face Valid Depression Scale for Adolescents as a criterion, they found that a little more than 20 percent of a group of adolescent psychiatric patients could be characterized as primarily depressed (Mezzich & Mezzich, 1979b).

Manifest Aggression

A reasonable inference from the studies of delinquency is that at least some of the five discriminating scales should also distinguish the aggressive teenager. Huesmann, Lefkowitz, and Eron (1978) found that 19-year-old males rated as aggressive by peers did score higher on Scales 4, 9, and F and females rated as aggressive rated higher on Scale 4 and F. Butcher (1965) found that aggressive eighth-grade boys scored slightly higher on Scales 3, 4, and 9. Spellacy (1977) reported significant elevations on Scales 3, 6, 8, and F. However, multivariate prediction based on all scales did not yield a significant result. Furthermore, superior prediction was accomplished with a special neuropsychological battery.

Drug Abusers

Greaves (1971) found that hospitalized adolescent drug users scored higher on Scales 2, 4, and 8 than a reference group of nonhospitalized adolescents. However, when compared with a matched sample of hospitalized non-drug-users, no significant differences were found. A report that only Scale 0 differentiated hospitalized adolescent drug users from nonusers (nonusers higher) (Klinge et al., 1978) is more or less in accord with the earlier study. Notably, Kling et al. also found that study. Notably, Klinge et al. also found that several special scales were more effective in scored higher on the McAndrew Alcoholism Scale (McAndrew, 1965) and lower on Wiggins' Depression, Poor Morale, and Social Maladjustment scales (Wiggins, 1966) and on the Welsh Anxiety Scale (Welsh, 1965).

Burke and Eichberg (1972) discovered that the MMPI was more discriminating if the drug user group was broken down into hospitalized and nonhospitalized drug users and narcotics addicts. All groups tended to be 4–9 types with much lower-ranging profiles in general. Adolescent amphetamine users have also been reported to run to high scores on Scale 8 and to 8–4 code types (Brook, Kaplun, & Whitehead, 1974).

Special Groups

An investigation of teenagers with IQs above 135 found the usual elevations when adult norms are applied. Males scored unusually high on Scales 3 and 5 (Kennedy, 1962). Ball (1962), however, reported no difference between high-, average-, and low-achieving boys while the high-achieving girls were lower on Scales 5, 6, 8, and 0.

Obese teenage females showed evidence of psychopathology on Scales 2, 4, 6, 7, and 8 (Held & Snow, 1972; Snow & Held, 1973).

Kane, Moan, and Bolling (1974) were able to separate adolescents who had become pregnant out of wedlock into an emotionally normal group (about 60 percent) and a group that was an elevated 4–8 code type (40 percent). The latter group was characterized as "acting-out character disorders of the antisocial type." Perez-Reyes and Falk (1973), on the other hand, found that a similar group was higher using adolescent norms on all scales except 5 and 0. They were, however, also 4–8

code types. All scale scores were lowered following a therapeutic abortion, but the code type was unchanged. Adolescent boys who had been reported to have fathered a child out of wedlock were significantly higher than a control group on Scales 8, 9, and F, but differences were small.

Among emotionally disturbed adolescents, those with insomnia as a serious complaint were elevated on Scales 1, 2, 3, and 0, and lower on 9, than emotionally disturbed children without this complaint (Monroe & Marks, 1977). Adolescents terminating prematurely from therapy at a youth-counseling service manifested significant elevations on Scales 6, 8, 9, and F compared to continuers in therapy, suggesting that the former were more seriously disturbed and more often psychotic.

The MMPI scales failed to distinguish between a group of adolescents determined to have voice quality abnormalities and a control group (Muma, Laeder, & Webb, 1968).

The Mini-Mult

Two investigations of the Mini-Mult (Kincannon, 1968) with adolescents yielded contrasting results. Mlott (1973) found that scores on this instrument agreed closely with those obtained from the full MMPI in nine out of ten inpatients. A similar scale-by-scale close correspondence between the Mini-Mult and the MMPI was also reported with psychiatric outpatients (Gayton & Wilson, 1971). However, the Mini-Mult misclassified a full third of the male patients.

Finally, a computerized narrative program was found to be more accurate for adolescents than adults as measured by clinical ratings (Lachar, Klinge, & Grisell, 1976).

ADDITIONAL INVENTORIES

Although space does not allow a full description of other inventories, mention should be made of some of them. The California Personality Inventory (CPI) is an offshoot of the MMPI, and is designed for "normal" people ages 13 and older. Although it has been frequently researched, there is a dearth of studies focusing on its use with adolescents. Other comprehensive inventories include the ESPQ which measures personality factors for children ages 6–8, the CPQ designed for children 8–12, and the HSPQ for junior high and senior high school students. Interpretation of these instruments, like the CPI and the MMPI, is complex. All three inventories are described in Buros' *Eight Mental Measurements Yearbook* (1978). No literature reviews of these inventories have appeared since that time, and research involving their use with children and adolescents since the mid-1970s has been sparse.

Brief mention should also be made of two other measures: figure drawings and sentence completion tests. Burns and Kaufman (1972) may be consulted for a review of the use of children's drawings as a psychological tool. The interpretive use of drawings of human figures, either as separate individuals, as family units, or in conjunction with drawings of houses and trees, has its strong proponents and opponents.

A variety of sentence completion tests have appeared, such as the Rotter Incomplete Sentences Blank, which is reviewed in Buros (1978). However, a search of the literature failed to produce any other reviews on the use of sentence completion tests with children, and few studies have been reported. An advantage of the use of sentence completion instruments is that the child's responses can often be used as springboards for more in-depth interview material.

Two personality instruments pertaining to children and adolescents were introduced within the last ten years, both designed to be given to the *parents* rather than to the child. The Personality Inventory for Children (PIC) (Wirt et al., 1977), standardized on normal children ages 3–16, employed the same general methodological approach used in the development of the MMPI. There are 600 true-false statements to be answered by a parent or by anyone who has known the youngster since early childhood. Although there has not been extensive published research involving the PIC, it has been used in many unpublished doctoral dissertations. A

quick response by Lachar and Wirt (1981) followed Achenbach's (1981) critical review of the PIC.

The Child Behavior Profile (CBP) (Achenbach, 1978, 1979; Achenbach & Edelbrock, 1979, 1981; Edelbrock & Achenbach, 1980) is scored from the Child Behavior Checklist (CBCL) (Achenbach, 1978, 1979) given to the child's parents. Giving the CBCL to teachers, clinicians, or other observers is discouraged for the authors feel parents' reports are generally more reliable and comprehensive. A teachers' version has been developed, however, that omits behavior beyond their observation, such as bedwetting, but includes items on classroom behavior and achievement. The CBCL is scored by scales of the CBP. Norms are standardized separately for each sex and for age ranges of 4–5, 6–11, and 12–16 years. Norming data were obtained from parents of children in outpatient mental health settings and in randomly selected homes of children who had not received mental health services in the preceding year. Weaknesses of the standardization process include the selection of a "normal" sample based on only one year free of mental health care, the fact that the whole norming process seems to have been carried out on the East Coast instead of a broader geographical base, and a rather small n in their reliability statistics. However, the CBCL and the CBP do have value in providing a structured base for evaluating children's behavioral problems and competencies from parental observations.

CONCLUSION

The popularity of researching personality instruments has waned in the last two decades. Some graduate schools now teach these techniques quite begrudgingly and with the clear message that they are a waste of the clinician's time. This is particularly true of the projective technique, but even the hallowed MMPI has lost its sparkle in some quarters. What a tragedy! It is true that the clinical psychologist has increasingly become more adept at providing mental status evaluations based on interview material alone. However, clinicians still do have to face clients who cannot or will not reveal their emotions, impulses, or thought processes. Children and adolescents can be refreshingly open, but they also can be frustratingly secretive. The use of personality instruments is often the best way to circumvent the child's defensiveness or the developmental inability to describe inner feelings. Test data often enrich and explain interview impressions.

Research indicates that certain personality tests are superior to others. However, even the best of these provides only one sample of the client's dynamics, feelings, behavior, or whatever. Murray's (1943) advice to consider test data merely as working hypotheses in need of further verification from other sources continues to have merit. Test information has much more validity when convalidated by other data such as similar themes obtained from other tests, background information, and interview. Test information can be misused, misinterpreted. When this happens, the tests are *worse* than nothing at all. Clinicians have the duty both to know the limits of the tests and to seek validation of their test response deductions.

REFERENCES

Aaron, N.S. Some personality differences between asthmatic, allergic and normal children. *Journal of Clinical Psychology,* 1967, **23**, 336–340.

Abe, M. The Japanese MMPI and its delinquency scale. *Tohoku Psycholigica Folia,* 1969, **28**, 54–68.

Achenbach, T.M. The Child behavior profile: I. Boys aged 6–11. *Journal of Consulting and Clinical Psychology,* 1978, **46**, 478–488.

Achenbach, T.M. The Child behavior profile: An empirically based system for assessing children's behavioral problems and competencies. *International Journal of Mental Health,* 1979, **7**, 24–42.

Achenbach, T.M. A junior MMPI? *Journal of Personality Assessment,* 1981, **45**, 332–333.

Achenbach, T.M., & Edelbrock, C.S. The Child behavior profile: II. Boys aged 12–16 and girls aged 6–11 and 12–16. *Journal of Consulting and Clinical Psychology,* 1979, **47**, 223–233.

Achenbach, T.M., & Edelbrock, C.S. Behavioral problems and competencies reported by parents of normal and disturbed children aged four through sixteen. *Monographs of the Society for Research in Child Development,* 1981, **46**, (Whole No. 1, 188).

Ames, L.B., Learned, J., Métraux, R.W., & Walker, R.N. *Child Rorschach responses.* New York: Hoeber-Harper, 1952.

Ames, L.B., Métraux, R.W., & Walker, R.N. *Adolescent Rorschach responses.* New York: Hoeber, 1959.

Ames, L.B., Métraux, R.W., Rodell, J.L., & Walker, R.N. *Child Rorschach responses.* New York: Bruner-Mazel, 1974.

Anderson, D.V., & Higham, E. The use of the Rorschach technique in child guidance clinics. In B. Klopfer, (Ed.), *Developments in the Rorschach technique,* Vol. II. Yonkers-on-Hudson, N.Y.: World Book, 1956.

Andrew, G., Walton, R.E., & Hartwell, S.W. The Michigan picture test: The stimulus values of the cards. *Journal of Consulting Psychology,* 1951, **15**, 51–54.

Angelino, H.R., & Shedd, C.L. A study of the reactions to "frustration" of a group of mentally retarded children as measured by the Rosenzweig picture-frustration study. *Psychology Newsletter,* 1956, **8**, 49–54.

Archer, R.P., White, J.L., & Orvin, G.H. MMPI characteristics and correlates among adolescent psychiatric inpatients. *Journal of Clinical Psychology,* 1979, **35**, 498–504.

Armstrong, M.A.S. Children's responses to animal and human figures in thematic pictures. *Journal of Consulting Psychology,* 1954, **18**, 67–70.

Bachtold, L.M. Perceptions of emotionally disturbed male adolescents on the Thematic apperception test. *Perceptual and Motor Skills,* 1975, **40**, 867–871.

Baker, M. The Torrance tests of creative thinking and the Rorschach inkblot test: Relationships between two measures of creativity. *Perceptual & Motor Skills,* 1978, **46**, 539–547.

Ball, J.C. *Social deviancy and adolescent personality,* Lexington, Ky.: University of Kentucky Press, 1962.

Basit, A. A Rorschach study of personality development in identical and fraternal twins. *Journal of Personality Assessment,* 1972, **36**, 23–27.

Beck, N., & Herron, W.G. The meaning of the Rorschach cards for children. *Journal of*

Projective Techniques and Personality Assessment, 1969, **33,** 150–53.

Bellak, L., & Bellak, S.S. *Children's apperception test* (2nd Rev. ed.). New York: C.P.S., 1952a.

Bellak, L., & Bellak, S.S. *Manual for the supplement to the Children's apperception test.* New York: C.P.S., 1952b.

Bellak, L., & Hurvich, M.S. *Manual for the C.A.T.-H, Children's apperception test (human figures).* Larchmont, N.Y.: C.P.S., 1965.

Bellak, L., & Hurvich, M.S. A human modification of the Children's apperception test (CAT-H). *Journal of Projective Techniques and Personality Assessment,* 1966, **30,** 228–242.

Bergman, A., & Schubert, J. The Rorschach of normal and emotionally disturbed children: A review of the literature. *British Journal of Projective Psychology & Personality Study,* 1974, **19,** 7–13.

Biersdorf, K.R., & Marcuse, F.L. Responses of children to human and to animal pictures. *Journal of Projective Techniques,* 1953, **17,** 455–459.

Bills, R.E. Animal pictures for obtaining children's projections. *Journal of Clinical Psychology,* 1950, **6,** 291–293.

Bills, R.E., Leihman, C.J., & Thomas, R.W. A study of the validity of the TAT and a set of animal pictures. *Journal of Clinical Psychology,* 1950, **6,** 293–295.

Bindon, D.M. Make-a-picture story (MAPS) test findings for rubella deaf children. *Journal of Abnormal and Social Psychology,* 1957, **55,** 38–42.

Brook, R., Kaplun, J., & Whitehead, P.C. Personality characteristics of adolescent amphetamine users as measured by the MMPI. *British Journal of Addictions,* 1974, **69,** 60–66.

Budoff, M. The relative utility of animal and human figures in a picture-story test for young children. *Journal of Projective Techniques,* 1960, **24,** 347–352.

Budoff, M. Animal vs. human figures in a picture story test for young, mentally backward children. *American Journal of Mental Deficiency,* 1963, **68,** 245–250.

Burke, E.L., & Eichberg, R.H. Personality characteristics of adolescent users of dangerous drugs as indicated by the Minnesota multiphasic personality inventory. *Journal of Nervous and Mental Disease,* 1972, **154,** 291–298.

Burns, R.C., & Kaufman, S.H. *Actions, styles and symbols in kinetic family drawings (K-F-D): An interpretive manual.* New York: Brunner-Mazel, 1972.

Buros, O.K. (Ed.). *The eighth mental measurements yearbook.* Highland Park, New Jersey: Gryphon, 1978.

Butcher, J.N. Manifest aggression: MMPI correlates in normal boys. *Journal of Consulting Psychology,* 1965, **29,** 446–454.

Butler, R.L. Responses of institutionalized mentally retarded children to human and to animal pictures. *American Journal of Mental Deficiency,* 1961, **65,** 620–622.

Byrd, E. & Witherspoon, R.L. The responses of preschool children to the Children's apperception test. *Child Development,* 1954, **25,** 35–44.

Caditz, S.B. Effects of a forestry camp experience on the personality of delinquent boys. *Journal of Clinical Psychology,* 1961, **17,** 78–81.

Cain, A.C. A supplementary dream technique with Children's apperception test. *Journal of Clinical Psychology,* 1961, **17,** 181–183.

Castaneda, A., McCandless, B.R., & Palerno, D.S. The children's form of the Manifest anxiety scale. *Child Development,* 1956, **27,** 317–326.

Chase, T.V., Chaffin, S.J., & Morrison, S.D. False positive adolescent MMPI profiles. *Adolescence,* 1975, **10,** 507–519.

Cohen, H., & Weil, G.R. *Tasks of emotional development: A projective test for children and adolescents.* Lexington, Mass.: Heath, 1971a.

Cohen, H., & Weil, G.R. *Tasks of emotional development test manual.* Lexington, Mass.: Heath, 1971b.

Cohen, L., & Weiner, F.J. Adolescent Rorschach responses as a function of age at first institutionalization. *Journal of Personality Assessment,* 1977, **41,** 227–229.

Cole, S. Symbolic meaning of card II. *Perceptual & Motor Skills,* 1967, **24,** 66.

Cole, S., & Williams, R. Age as a determinant of parental interpretation of Rorschach cards IV and VII. *Perceptual & Motor Skills,* 1968, **26,** 55–58.

Coleman, J.C. Stimulus factors in the relation between fantasy and behavior. *Journal of Projective Techniques and Personality Assessment,* 1967, **31,** 68–73.

Colligan, R.C. &, Osborne, D. MMPI profiles from adolescent medical patients. *Journal of Clinical Psychology,* 1977, **33,** 186–189.

Coons, M.O. Rosenzweig differences in reaction to frustration in children of high, low, and middle sociometric status. *Group Psychotherapy,* 1957, **10**, 60–63.

Crain, W.C., & Smoke, L. Rorschach aggressive content in normal and problematic children. *Journal of Personality Assessment,* 1981, **45**, 2–4.

Dahlstrom, W.G., Welsh, G.S., & Dahlstrom, L.E. *An MMPI handbook: Clinical interpretation* (Vol. 1). University of Minnesota Press, 1972.

Davids, A. Aggression in thought and action of emotionally disturbed boys. *Journal of Consulting and Clinical Psychology,* 1973, **40**, 322–327.

Davids, A., & Rosenblatt, D. Use of the TAT in assessment of the personality syndrome of alienation. *Journal of Projective Techniques,* 1958, **22**, 145–152.

Davidson, H.H. *Personality and economic background: A study of highly intelligent children.* New York: King's Crown, 1943.

Dudek, S. Regression in the service of the ego in young children. *Journal of Personality Assessment,* 1975, **39**, 369–376.

Edelbrock, C., & Achenbach, T.M. A typology of Child behavior profile patterns: Distribution and correlates for disturbed children aged 6–16. *Journal of Abnormal Child Psychology,* 1980, **8**, 441–470.

Elizur, A. Content analysis of the Rorschach with regard to anxiety and hostility. *Rorschach Research Exchange and Journal of Projective Techniques,* 1949, **13**, 247–284.

Erikson, E.H. *Childhood and society.* New York: Norton, 1950.

Eron, L.D. A normative study of the Thematic apperception test. In B.I. Murstein (Ed.), *Handbook of projective techniques.* New York: Basic Books, 1965.

Exner, J.E. *The Rorschach: A comprehensive system.* (Vol. 1). New York: Wiley, 1974.

Exner, J.E. *The Rorschach: A comprehensive system* (Vol. 2). New York: Wiley, 1978.

Exner, J.E. But it's only an inkblot. *Journal of Personality Assessment,* 1980, **44**, 563–576.

Fiedler, M.F., & Stone, J.L. The Rorschachs of selected groups of children in comparison with published norms. *Journal of Projective Techniques,* 1956, **20**, 273–279.

Fine, R. Manual for a scoring scheme for verbal

projective techniques (TAT, MAPS, stories and the like). *Journal of Projective Techniques,* 1955, **19**, 310–316.

Fisher, R.L. Failure of the conceptual styles test to discriminate normal and highly impulsive children. *Journal of Abnormal Psychology,* 1966, **71**, 429–431.

Fisher, S., & Cleveland, S. *Body image and personality.* New York: Van Nostrand, 1958.

Fisher, S., & Fisher, R. Parental correlation of Rorschach human movement responses in children. *Perceptual & Motor Skills,* 1976, **42**, 31–34.

Ford, M. *The application of the Rorschach test to young children.* Institute of Child Welfare, University of Minnesota, Monograph Series No. 23, Minneapolis: University of Minnesota Press, 1946.

Francis-Williams, J. *Rorschach with children.* London: Pergamon, 1968.

Friedman, H. Perceptual regression in schizophrenia: An hypothesis suggested by the use of the Rorschach test. *Journal of Genetic Psychology,* 1952, **81**, 39–63.

Friedman, R.J. TAT story length in children. *Psychology in the Schools,* 1972, **9**, 411–412.

Furuya, K. Responses of school-children to human and animal pictures. *Journal of Projective Techniques,* 1957, **21**, 248–252.

Gayton, W.F., & Wilson, W.T. Utility of the Mini-Mult in a child guidance setting. *Journal of Personality Assessment,* 1971, **35**, 569–575.

Gittelman, R. The role of psychological tests for differential diagnosis in child psychiatry. *Journal of the American Academy of Child Psychiatry,* 1980, **19**, 413–438.

Gorlow, L., Zimet, C.N., & Fine, H.J. The validity of anxiety and hostility Rorschach content scores among adolescents. *Journal of Consulting Psychology,* 1952, **16**, 73–75.

Gough, H.G., & Peterson, D.R. The identification and measurement of predispositional factors in crime and delinquency. *Journal of Consulting Psychology,* 1952, **16**, 207–212.

Graham, J.R. *The MMPI: A practical guide.* New York: Oxford Press, 1977.

Greaves, G. MMPI correlates of chronic drug abuse in hospitalized adolescents. *Psychological Reports,* 1971, **29**, 1222.

Greenberg, N. The use of the Rorschach prognostic rating scale with foster-home children.

Journal of Projective Techniques and Personality Assessment, 1969, **33**, 451–453.

Gynther, M.D., & Shimkunas, A.M. Age, intelligence, and MMPI F scores. *Journal of Consulting Psychology,* 1965, **29**, 383–388.

Hafner, A.J., & Kaplan, A.M. Hostility content analysis of the Rorschach and TAT. *Journal of Projective Techniques,* 1960, **24**, 137–143.

Halpern, F. *A clinical approach to children's Rorschachs.* New York: Grune & Stratton, 1953.

Hamilton, J., Blewett, D., & Sydiahia, D. Inkblot responses of identical and fraternal twins. *Journal of Genetic Psychology,* 1971, **119**, 37–41.

Harrison, R. Thematic apperceptive methods. In B.B. Wolman (Ed.), *Handbook of clinical psychology.* New York: McGraw-Hill, 1965.

Hartman, A.A. A basic TAT set. *Journal of Projective Techniques and Personality Assessment,* 1970, **34**, 391–396.

Hartwell, S.W., Hutt, M.L., Andrew, G., & Walton, R.E. The Michigan picture test: Diagnostic and therapeutic possibilities of a new projective test in child guidance. *American Journal of Orthopsychiatry,* 1951, **21**, 124–137.

Hathaway, S.R. & McKinley, J.C. *The Minnesota multiphasic personality inventory manual.* New York: Psychological Corporation, 1967.

Hathaway, S.R., & Monachesi, E.D. The personalities of predelinquent boys. *Journal of Criminal Law, Criminology and Police Science,* 1957, **48**, 149–163.

Hathaway, S.R., & Monachesi, E.D. *An atlas of juvenile MMPI profiles.* University of Minnesota Press, 1961.

Hathaway, S.R., & Monachesi, E.D. *Adolescent personality and behavior.* University of Minnesota Press, 1963.

Hathaway, S.R., Monachesi, E. & Salasin, S. A follow-up study of MMPI high 8 schizoid, children. In M. Roff & D.F. Ricks (Eds.), *Life history research in psychopathology,* Minneapolis: University of Minnesota Press, 1970.

Haworth, M.R. Responses of children to a group projective film and to the Rorschach, CAT, Despert fables and D-A-P. *Journal of Projective Techniques,* 1962, **26**, 47–60.

Haworth, M.R. A schedule for the analysis of CAT responses. *Journal of Projective Techniques and Personality Assessment,* 1963, **27**, 181–184.

Haworth, M.R. *The CAT: Facts about fantasy.* New York: Grune & Stratton, 1966.

Haworth, M.R. Symposium: The Children's apperception test: Its use in developmental assessments of normal children. Introduction. *Journal of Projective Techniques and Personality Assessment,* 1968, **32**, 405.

Hayden, B.C. Rorschach cards IV and VII revisited. *Journal of Personality Assessment,* 1981, **45**, 226–229.

Haymond, P.J. *A new look at an old team: A correlational study of the Rorschach and the MMPI with adolescent female delinquents.* Unpublished doctoral dissertation, Indiana University, 1981.

Held, M.L., & Snow, D.L. MMPI, internal-external control and problem check list scores of obese adolescent females. *Journal of Clinical Psychology,* 1972, **28**, 523–525.

Hertz, M.R. *Frequency tables for scoring Rorschach responses* (5th ed.). Cleveland: Press of Case Western Reserve University, 1970.

Hindelang, M.J. Variations in personality attributes of social and solitary self-reported delinquents. *Journal of Consulting and Clinical psychology,* 1973, **40**, 452–454.

Hirsch, E.A. *The troubled adolescent.* New York: International University Press, 1970.

Hoar, M.W., & Faust, W.L. The Children's apperception test: Puzzle and regular form. *Journal of Personality Assessment,* 1973, **37**, 244–247.

Horton, M., & Kriauciunas, R. Minnesota multiphasic personality inventory differences between terminators and continuers in youth counseling. *Journal of Counseling Psychology,* 1970, **17**, 98–101.

Huesmann, L.R., Lefkowitz, M.M. & Eron, L.D. Sum of MMPI scales F, 4, 9 as a measure of aggression. *Journal of Consulting and Clinical Psychology,* 1978, **46**, 1071–1078.

Hutt, M.L. *The Michigan picture test—revised.* New York: Grune & Stratton, 1980.

Jackson, C.W., & Wohl, J. A survey of Rorschach teaching in the university. *Journal of Projective Techniques and Personality Assessment,* 1966, **30**, 115–134.

Joel, W. The use of the Make-a-picture-story (MAPS) test with disturbed adolescents. *Ror-*

schach *Research Exchange and Journal of Projective Techniques,* 1948, **12,** 155–164.

Johannsen, D.E., & Bennett, E.M. The personality of diabetic children. *Journal of Genetic Psychology,* 1955, **87,** 175–185.

Johnson, O.G., & Bommarito, J.W. *Tests and measurements in child development: A handbook.* San Francisco: Jossey-Bass, 1971.

Jones, R.M. The negation TAT; a projective method for eliciting repressed thought content. *Journal of Projective Techniques,* 1956, **20,** 297–303.

Kagan, J. The stability of TAT fantasy and stimulus ambiguity. *Journal of Consulting Psychology,* 1959, **23,** 266–271.

Kagan, J., & Moss, H.A. Stability and validity of achievement fantasy. *Journal of Abnormal and Social Psychology,* 1959, **58,** 357–364.

Kalter, N. Self-selection of TAT cards: A technique for assessing test-resistant children. *Journal of Projective Techniques and Personality Assessment,* 1970, **34,** 324–327.

Kane, F.J., Moan, C.A., & Bolling, B. Motivational factors in pregnant adolescents. *Diseases of the Nervous System,* 1974, **35,** 131–134.

Kanun, C., & Monachesi, E.D. Delinquency and the validating scales of the MMPI. *Journal of Criminal Law and Criminology,* 1960, **50,** 525–534.

Kass, W. Symonds picture-story test. In O.K. Buros (Ed.), *The fifth mental measurements yearbook.* Highland Park, N.J.: Gryphon, 1959.

Kempler, H.L., & Scott, V. Can systematically scored thematic stories reflect the attributes of the antisocial child syndrome? *Journal of Projective Techniques and Personality Assessment,* 1970, **34,** 204–211.

Kennedy, W.A. MMPI profiles of gifted adolescents. *Journal of Clinical Psychology,* 1962, **18,** 148–149.

Kincannon, J.C. Prediction of the standard MMPI scales scores from 71 items: the Mini-Mult. *Journal of Clinical and Consulting Psychology,* 1968, **32,** 319–325.

Klineberg, S.L. Changes in outlook on the future between childhood and adolescence. *Journal of Personality and Social Psychology,* 1967, **7,** 185–193.

Klinge, V., & Strauss, M.E. Effects of scoring norms on adolescent psychiatric patients'

MMPI profiles. *Personality Assessment,* 1976, **40,** 13–17.

Klinge, V., & Strauss, M.E. Effects of scoring norms on adolescent psychiatric patients' MMPI profiles. *Personality Assessment,* 1976, **40,** 13–17.

Klopfer, B. (Ed.), *Developments in the Rorschach technique* (Vol. II). New York: World Book, 1956.

Klopfer, B., Ainsworth, M.D., Klopfer, W.G., & Holt, R.R. *Developments in the Rorschach technique* (Vol. I). Yonkers-on-Hudson, N.Y.: World Book, 1954.

Kodman, F., & Waters, J.E. Rorschach responses of children exhibiting psychogenic auditory symptoms. *Journal of Clinical Psychology,* 1961, **17,** 305–306.

Kreiger, L., & Schwartz, M.M. The relationship between sociometric measures of popularity among children and their reactions to frustration. *Journal of Social Psychology,* 1965, **66,** 291–296.

Lachar, D., Klinge, V., & Grisell, J.L. Relative accuracy of automated MMPI narratives generated from adult norm and adolescent norm profiles. *Journal of Counseling & Clinical Psychology,* 1976, **44,** 20–24.

Lachar, D., & Wirt, R.D. A data-based analysis of the psychometric performance of the Personality inventory for children (PIC): An alternative to the Achenbach review. *Journal of Personality Assessment,* 1981, **45,** 614–616.

Lanyon, R.I. *A handbook of MMPI group profiles.* Univ. of Minnesota Press, 1968.

Lauterbach, C.G., Vogel, W., & Hart, J. Comparison of the MMPI's of male problem adolescents and their parents. *Journal of Clinical Psychology,* 1962, **18,** 485–487.

Lawton, M.J. Animal and human CATs with a school sample. *Journal of Projective Techniques and Personality Assessment,* 1966, **30,** 243–246.

Ledwith, N.H. *Rorschach responses of elementary school children.* Pittsburgh: University of Pittsburgh Press, 1959.

Ledwith, N.H. *A Rorschach study of child development.* Pittsburgh: University of Pittsburgh Press, 1960.

Lessing, E.E. Prognostic value of the Rorschach in a child guidance clinic. *Journal of Projective Techniques,* 1960, **24,** 310–321.

Levitt, E.E. A diagnostic test for children and

adolescents: A methodological review. *Professional Psychology*, 1975, **6**, 101–102.

Levitt, E.E. *Primer on the Rorschach technique: A method of administration, scoring and interpretation.* Springfield, Ill.: Thomas, 1981.

Levitt, E.E., & Lyle, W.H. Evidence for the validity of the children's form of the Picture-frustration study. *Journal of Consulting Psychology,* 1955, **19**, 381–386.

Levitt, E.E., & Truumaa, A. *The Rorschach technique with children and adolescents: Application and norms.* New York: Grune & Stratton, 1972.

Liebetrau, C.E., & Pienaar, W.D. The relation between adjustment and body image at various age levels. *Journal of Personality Assessment,* 1974, **38**, 230–233.

Lifshitz, M. Achievement motivation and coping behavior of normal and problematic preadolescent kibbutz children. *Journal of Personality Assessment,* 1974, **38**, 138–143.

Lifshitz, M. Social differentiation and organization of the Rorschach in fatherless and two-parented children. *Journal of Clinical Psychology,* 1975, **31**, 126–130.

Light, B.H. Comparative study of a series of TAT and CAT cards. *Journal of Clinical Psychology,* 1954, **10**, 179–181.

Lipman, R.S. Some test correlates of behavioral aggression in institutionalized retardates with particular reference to the Rosenzweig picture-frustration study. *American Journal of Mental Deficiency,* 1959, **63**, 1038–1045.

Long, R.T., Lamont, J.H., Whipple, B., Bandler, L., Blom, G.E., Burgin, L., & Jessner, L. A psychosomatic study of allergic and emotional factors in children with asthma. *American Journal of Psychiatry,* 1958, **114**, 890–899.

Loucks, S., Burstein, A.G., Boros, T., & Kregor, E. The affective ration in Rorschach's test as a function of age. *Journal of Personality Assessment,* 1980, **44**, 590–591.

Lynch, D.J., & Arndt, C. Developmental changes in response to frustration among physically handicapped children. *Journal of Personality Assessment,* 1973, **37**, 130–135.

Magnussen, M.G. Effect of test order upon children's Rorschach animal content. *Journal of Projective Techniques and Personality Assessment,* 1967, **31**, 41–43.

Mainord, F.R., & Marcuse, F.L. Responses of disturbed children to human and to animal pictures. *Journal of Projective Techniques,* 1954, **18**, 474–477.

Marks, P.A., Seeman, W., & Haller, D.L. *The actuarial use of the MMPI with adolescents and adults.* Baltimore: Williams & Wilkins, 1974.

Marsden, G. Intelligence and the Rorschach whole response. *Journal of Projective Techniques and Personality Assessment,* 1970, **34**, 470–476.

Matranga, J.T. The relationship between behavioral indices of aggression and hostile content on the TAT. *Journal of Personality Assessment,* 1976, **40**, 130–134.

MacAndrew, C. The differentiation of male alcoholic outpatients from nonalcoholic psychiatric patients by means of the MMPI. *Quarterly Journal of Studies on Alcohol,* 1965, **26**, 238–246.

McClelland, D.C. Longitudinal trends in the relation of thought to action. *Journal of Consulting Psychology,* 1966, **30**, 479–483.

McClelland, D.C., Atkinson, J.W., Clark, R.A. & Lowell, E.L. *The achievement motive.* New York: Appleton-Century-Crofts, 1953.

McCormick, C.C., Klappauf, J., Schnobrich, J.N., & Harvey, J. Relationships among Arrow-Dot IES scores and Wechsler IQs and MMPI scales for hospitalized, disturbed adolescents. *Perceptual and Motor Skills,* 1971, **33**, 1227–1234.

McCraw, R.K., & Tuma, J.M. Rorschach content categories of juvenile diabetics. *Psychological Reports,* 1977, **40**, 818.

McCully, R.S. Fantasy productions of children with a progressively crippling and fatal illness. *Journal of Genetic Psychology,* 1963, **102**, 203–216.

McDonald, R.L., & Gynther, M.D. MMPI norms for southern adolescent negroes. *Journal of Social Psychology,* 1962, **58**, 277–282.

McKegney, F.P. An item analysis of the MMPI F scale in juvenile delinquents. *Journal of Clinical Psychology,* 1965, **21**, 201–205.

Megargee, E.I. Validation of inkblot techniques. In E.I. Megargee (Ed.), *Research in clinical assessment.* New York: Harper & Row, 1966.

Mezzich, A.C., & Mezzich, J.E. A data-based typology of depressed adolescents. *Journal of Personality Assessment,* 1979, **43**, 238–246.(a)

Mezzich, A.C., & Mezzich, J.E. Symptomatology

of depression in adolescence. *Journal of Personality Assessment,* 1979b, **43,** 267–275.

Michigan Department of Mental Health. *The Michigan picture test: An introductory symposium, a research report, and a manual.* Chicago: Science Research Associates, 1953.

Mitchell, K.M. The Rosenzweig picture-frustration study as a measure of reaction to personal evaluation. *Journal of Projective Techniques and Personality Assessment,* 1967, **31,** 65–68.

Mlott, S.R. The Mini-Mult and its use with adolescents. *Journal of Clinical Psychology,* 1973, **29,** 376–377.

Moelis, I., Wright, D.M., & Fisher, S. The Symbiosis scale: Inkblot responses of children from symbiotically and non-symbiotically oriented families. *Journal of Personality Assessment,* 1977, **41,** 238–247.

Monroe, L.J., & Marks, P.A. MMPI differences between adolescent poor and good sleepers. *Journal of Consulting and Clinical Psychology,* 1977, **45,** 151–152.

Moore, C.D., & Handal, P.J. Adolescents' MMPI performance, cynicism, estrangement, and personal adjustment as a function of race and sex. *Journal of Clinical Psychology,* 1980, **36,** 932–936.

Moriarty, A.E. Normal preschoolers' reactions to the CAT: Some implications for later development. *Journal of Projective Techniques and Personality Assessment,* 1968, **32,** 413–419.

Muma, J.R., Laeder, R.L., & Webb, C.E. Adolescent voice quality aberrations: Personality and social status. *Journal of Speech and Hearing Research,* 1968, **11,** 576–582.

Murawski, B.J. Genetic factors in tests of perception and the Rorschach. *Journal of Genetic Psychology,* 1971, **119,** 43–52.

Murray, H.A. *Thematic apperception test manual.* Cambridge: Harvard University Press, 1943.

Murstein, B.I. *Theory and research in projective techniques (emphasizing the TAT).* New York: Wiley, 1963.

Murstein, B.I. The stimulus. In B.I. Murstein (Ed.), *Handbook of projective techniques.* New York: Basic Books, 1965.

Mussen, P.H., & Jones, M.C. Self-conceptions, motivations, and interpersonal attitudes of late- and early-maturing boys. *Child Development,* 1957, **28,** 243–256.

Mussen, P.H., & Naylor, H.K. The relationship between overt and fantasy aggression. *Journal*

of *Abnormal and Social Psychology,* 1954, **49,** 235–240.

Myler, B., Rosenkrantz, A., & Holmes, G. A comparison of the TAT, CAT and CAT-H among second grade girls. *Journal of Personality Assessment,* 1972, **36,** 440–444.

Neman, R.S., Brown, T.S., & Sells, S.B. Language and adjustment scales for the Thematic apperception test for children 6–11 years. *Vital and Health Statistics, Series 2,* 1973, **58,** 1–70.

Neman, R.S., Neman, J.F., & Sells, S.B. Language and adjustment scales for the Thematic apperception test for youths 12–17 years. *Vital and Health Statistics, Series 2,* 1974, **62,** 1–84.

Neuringer, C., & Livesay, R.C. Projective fantasy on the CAT and CAT-H. *Journal of Projective Techniques and Personality Assessment,* 1970, **34,** 487–491.

North, G.E., & Keiffer, R.S. Thematic productions of children in foster homes. *Psychological Reports,* 1966, **19,** 43–46.

O'Neill, P., O'Neill, P.C., & Quinlan, M. Perceptual development on the Rorschach. *Journal of Personality Assessment,* 1976, **40,** 115–121.

Pauker, J.D. Fathers of children conceived out of wedlock: Prepregnancy, high school, psychological test results. *Developmental Psychology,* 1971, **4,** 215–218.

Perez-Reyes, M.G., & Falk, R. Follow-up after therapeutic abortion in early adolescence. *Archives of General Psychiatry,* 1973, **28,** 120–126.

Pollak, J., Cohen, H., & Weil, G. *The Tasks of emotional development test: A survey of research applications.* Unpublished manuscript, 1981. (Available from Department of Psychiatry, Children's Hospital Medical Center, Boston, Mass.).

Randolph, M.H., Richardson, H., & Johnson, R.C. A comparison of social and solitary male delinquents. *Journal of Consulting Psychology,* 1961, **25,** 293–295.

Rawls, D., Rawls, J.R. & Harrison, C.W. An investigation of six- to eleven-year-old children with allergic disorders. *Journal of Consulting and Clinical Psychology,* 1971, **36,** 260–264.

Reck, J.J., McCary, J.L., & Weatherly, J.K. Intrafamilial comparisons of frustration-aggression patterns. *Psychological Reports,* 1969, **25,** 356.

Reidy, T.J. The aggressive characteristics of

abused and neglected children. *Journal of Clinical Psychology*, 1977, **33**, 1140–1145.

Reviews. *Psychological Reports*, 1972, **31**, 679.

Robbertse, P.M. Personality structure of socially adjusted and socially maladjusted children, according to the Rorschach test. *Psychological Monographs*, 1955, **69** (Whole No. 404).

Rosenzweig, S. Apperceptive norms for the Thematic apperception test. I. The problem of norms in projective methods. *Journal of Personality*, 1948, **17**, 475–482.

Rosenzweig, S. The Rosenzweig picture-frustration study, children's form. In Rabin, A.I. & Haworth, M.R. (Eds.), *Projective techniques with children*. New York: Grune & Stratton, 1960, 149–176.

Rosenzweig, S. An investigation of the reliability of the Rosenzweig picture-frustration (P-F) study, children's form. *Journal of Personality Assessment*, 1978, **42**, 483–488.

Rosenzweig, S., Fleming, E.E., & Rosenzweig, L. *The children's form of the Rosenzweig picture-frustration study*. St. Louis: Rosenzweig, 1948.

Rosenzweig, S., Ludwig, D.J., & Adelman, S. Retest reliability of the Rosenzweig picture-frustration study and similar semiprojective techniques. *Journal of Personality Assessment*, 1975, **39**, 3–12.

Rosenzweig, S., & Mirmow, E.L. The validation of trends in the children's form of the Rosenzweig picture-frustration study. *Journal of Personality*, 1949, **18**, 306–314.

Rosenzweig, S., & Rosenzweig, L. Aggression in problem children and normals as evaluated by the Rosenzweig P-F study. *Journal of Abnormal and Social Psychology*, 1952, **47**, 683–687.

Roth, R.M., & Puri, P. Direction of aggression and the achievement syndrome. *Journal of Counseling Psychology*, 1967, **14**, 277–281.

Rourke, P.G., & Quinlan, D.M. Psychological characteristics of problem children at the borderline of mental retardation. *Journal of Consulting and Clinical Psychology*, 1973, **40**, 59–68.

Russ, S.W. Primary process integration on the Rorschach and achievement in children. *Journal of Personality Assessment*, 1980, **44**, 338–344.

Rychlak, J.F. & Boland, G.C. Socioeconomic status and the diagnostic significance of healthy and unhealthy group Rorschach content. *Journal of Personality Assessment*, 1973, **37**, 411–419.

Rychlak, J.F., & Maier, L.R. Rorschach content responses of popular and unpopular junior high school students. *Journal of Clinical Psychology*, 1964, **20**, 381–384.

Rychlak, J.F., & O'Leary, L.R. Unhealthy content in the Rorschach responses of children and adolescents. *Journal of Projective Techniques and Personality Assessment*, 1966, **30**, 354–368.

Sarason, I.G. Test anxiety, attention, and the general problem of anxiety. In C.D. Spielberger & I.G. Sarason (Eds.), *Stress and anxiety* (Vol. 1). New York: Halsted Press/Wiley, 1975.

Schaefer, J.B., & Norman, M. Punishment and aggression in fantasy responses of boys with antisocial character traits. *Journal of Personality and Social Psychology*, 1967, **6**, 237–240.

Schaible, M. An analysis of noncontent TAT variables in a longitudinal sample. *Journal of Personality Assessment*, 1975, **39**, 480–485.

Scheffler, R.Z. The child from five to six: A longitudinal study of fantasy change. *Genetic Psychology Monographs*, 1975, **92**, 19–56.

Schinek, J.G. A note on the long range stability of selected Rorschach scores. *Journal of Projective Techniques and Personality Assessment*, 1968, **32**, 63–65.

Schlessinger, L.B. Rorschach human movement responses of acting-out and withdrawn adolescents. *Perceptual & Motor Skills*, 1978, **47**, 68–70.

Schubert, D.S.P., & Wagner, M.E. A subcultural change of MMPI norms in the 1960s due to adolescent role confusion and glamorization of alienation. *Journal of Abnormal Psychology*, 1975, **84**, 406–411.

Scroth, M.L. The use of the associative elaboration and integration scales for evaluating CAT protocols. *Journal of Psychology*, 1977, **97**, 29–35.

Shneidman, E.S. *Manual: Make a picture story test*. New York: The Psychological Corporation, 1948.

Shneidman, E.S. Some comparisons among the Four picture test, Thematic apperception test, and Make a picture story test. *Rorschach Research Exchange and Journal of Projective Techniques*, 1949, **13**, 150–154.

Shneidman, E.S. The MAPS test with children. In

A.I. Rabin & M.R. Haworth (Eds.), *Projective techniques with children*. New York: Grune & Stratton, 1960.

Shore, M.F., Massimo, J.L., & Mack, R. Changes in the perception of interpersonal relationships in successfully treated adolescent delinquent boys. *Journal of Consulting Psychology*, 1965, **29**, 213–217.

Siegel, G.M. Interexaminer reliability for mean length of response. *Journal of Speech and Hearing Research*, 1962, **5**, 91–95.

Siegel, M. The personality structure of children with reading disabilities as compared with children presenting other clinical problems. *Nervous Child*, 1954, **10**, 409–414.

Silver, A.W. TAT and MMPI psychopath deviant scale differences between delinquent and non-delinquent adolescents. *Journal of Consulting Psychology*, 1963, **27**, 370.

Skolnick, A. Motivational imagery and behavior over twenty years. *Journal of Consulting Psychology*, 1966, **30**, 463–478.

Slemon, A.G., Holzwarth, E.J., Lewis, J., & Sitko, M. Associative elaboration and integration for evaluating TAT protocols. *Journal of Personality Assessment*, 1976, **40**, 365–369.

Smith, J.R., & Coleman, J.C. The relationship between manifestations of hostility in projective tests and overt behavior. *Journal of Projective Techniques*, 1956, **20**, 326–334.

Smith, L.M. The concurrent validity of six personality and adjustment tests for children. *Psychological Monographs: General and Applied*, 1958, **72** (457), 1–30.

Snow, D.L., & Held, M.L. Relation between locus of control and the MMPI in obese female adolescents. *Journal of Clinical Psychology*, 1973, **29**, 24–25.

Spache, G. Sex differences in the Rosenzweig P-F study, children's form. *Journal of Clinical Psychology*, 1951, **7**, 235–238.

Spellacy, F. Neuropsychological differences between violent and nonviolent adolescents. *Journal of Clinical Psychology*, 1977, **33**, 966–969.

Spiegelman, M. Jungian theory and the analysis of thematic tests. *Journal of Projective Techniques*, 1955, **19**, 253–263.

Spiegelman, M. A note on the use of Fine's scoring system with the MAPS tests of children. *Journal of Projective Techniques*, 1956, **20**, 442–444.

Spielberger, C.D., Edwards, C.D., Lushene, R.E.,

Montuori, J., & Platzek, D. *Preliminary test manual for the State-trait anxiety inventory for children*. Palo Alto, California: Consulting Psychologists Press, Inc., 1973.

Stoltz, R.E., & Smith, M.D. Some effects of socio-economic, age and sex factors on children's responses to the Rosenzweig picture-frustration study. *Journal of Clinical Psychology*, 1959, **15**, 200–203.

Suinn, R.M., & Oskamp, S. *The predictive validity of projective measures: A fifteen-year evaluative review*. Springfield, Ill.: Thomas, 1969.

Symonds, P.M. *Manual for Symonds picture-story test*. New York: Teachers College Press, 1948.

Symonds, P.M. *Adolescent fantasy: An investigation of the picture-story method of personality study*. New York: Columbia University Press, 1949.

Symonds, P.M., & Jensen, A.R. Psychoanalytic concepts and principles discernible in projective personality tests; Workshop, 1956: 6. The predictive significance of fantasy. *American Journal of Orthopsychiatry*, 1958, **28**, 73–84.

Taterka, J.H., & Katz, J. Study of correlations between encephalographic and psychological patterns in emotionally disturbed children. *Psychosomatic Medicine*, 1955, **17**, 62–72.

Thorne, G.L. Sensation seeking scale with deviant populations. *Journal of Consulting and Clinical Psychology*, 1971, **37**, 106–110.

Tolor, A., & Orange, S. An attempt to measure psychological distance in advantaged and disadvantaged children. *Child Development*, 1969, **40**, 407–420.

Townsend, J.K. The relations between Rorschach signs of aggression and behavioral aggression in emotionally disturbed boys. *Journal of Projective Techniques and Personality Assessment*, 1967, **31**, 13–21.

Tsubouchi, K., & Jenkins, R.L. Three types of delinquents: Their performance on the MMPI and the PRC. *Journal of Clinical Psychology*, 1969, **25**, 353–358.

Tuma, J.M., & McCraw, R.K. Influence of examiner difference on Rorschach productivity in children. *Journal of Personality Assessment*, 1975, **39**, 362–368.

Walton, R.E., Andrew, G., & Hartwell, S.W. A tension index of adjustment based on picture stories elicited by the Michigan picture test. *Journal of Abnormal and Social Psychology*,

1951, **46**, 438–441.

Ward, L.C., & Ward, J.W. MMPI readability reconsidered. *Journal of Personality Assessment,* 1980, **44**, 387–389.

Weiner, I.B., & Exner, J.E. Rorschach indices of disordered thinking in patient and nonpatient adolescents and adults. *Journal of Personality Assessment,* 1978, **42**, 339–343.

Weisskopf, E.A. A transcendence index as a proposed measure in the TAT. *Journal of Psychology,* 1950, **29**, 379–390.

Weisskopf-Joelson, E., & Foster, H. An experimental study of the effect of stimulus variation upon projection. *Journal of Projective Techniques,* 1962, **26**, 366–370.

Welsh, G.S. MMPI profiles and factor scales A and R. *Journal of Clinical Psychology,* 1965, **21**, 43–47.

Whiteley, J.M. A method for assessing adaptive ego functioning using the Thematic apperception test. *Journal of Experimental Education,* 1966, **34**, 1–21.

Wiesz, J.R., Quinlan, D.M., O'Neill, P., & O'Neill, P.C. The Rorschach and structured tests of perception as indices of intellectual development in mentally retarded and nonretarded children. *Journal of Experimental Child Psychology,* 1978, **25**, 326–336.

Wiggins, J.S. Substantive dimensions of self-report in the MMPI item pool. *Psychological Monographs:* 1966, **80**(22), 42.

Williams, J.M. Children who break down in foster homes. *Journal of Child Psychology and Psychiatry,* 1961, **2**, 5–20.

Winitz, H. Language skills of male and female kindergarten children. *Journal of Speech and Hearing Research,* 1959, **2**, 377–386.

Wirt, R.D., Lachar, D., Klinedinst, J.K., & Seat, P.D. *Multidimensional description of child personality: A manual for the Personality inventory for children.* Los Angeles: Western Psychological Services, 1977.

Wise, J. A diagnostic test for children and adolescents: Clinical review. *Professional Psychology,* 1975, **6**, 102–103.

Witherspoon, R.L. Development of objective scoring methods for longitudinal CAT data. *Journal of Projective Techniques and Personality Assessment,* 1968, **32**, 406–412.

Wolowitz, H.M., & Shorkey, C. Power motivation in male paranoid children. *Psychiatry,* 1969, **32**, 459–466.

Zimet, S.G., Rose, C., & Camp, B. Relationship between reading achievement and Rosenzweig picture-frustration study in early grades. *Psychology in the Schools,* 1973, **10**, 433–436.

SECTION THREE

Problems of Early Life

CHAPTER 11

Prenatal and Genetic Influences Upon Behavior and Development

THEODORE D. WACHS AND FREDRIC WEIZMANN

INTRODUCTION

Genetic influence is currently viewed as one of gene-environment transaction[1] rather than a genetic-environmental dichotomy (Ehrlen-meyer-Kimling, 1972). Transaction refers to the interaction between parameters that change over time. Over the course of development of the organism, there is a continual transaction between genetic and environmental influences; the end product of this interaction is observed behavior at a specific point in time. Rather than asking how much of behavior is due to heredity versus how much is due to environment, the critical question is how heredity and environment work together to produce an observed pattern of behavior (Allen, 1961; Hanson, Gottesman, & Meehl, 1977).

A similar developmental transactional model is also emerging in the study of prenatal influences. Until recently it was thought the placenta constituted a barrier that provided almost absolute protection for the fetus (Wilson, 1977a). Concern for intrauterine influences increased markedly after the thalidomide tragedy of the early 1960s, when it was discovered that an apparently harmless sedative given to mothers could cause severe malformations in infants. It is now, in fact, realized that there are a number of environ-mental agents that can act on the fetus through the placenta.

There are a number of implications that follow from the acceptance of the transactional approach. First, it becomes impossible to understand the long term impact of prenatal and genetic influences upon behavior without some knowledge of subsequent environmental influences. Available evidence clearly indicates the inadequacy of causal explanations based solely either on initial genotype (Scarr-Salapatek, 1976), or prenatal injury (e.g., Hunt, 1976).

A second implication is that it becomes difficult to understand the impact of the environment on behavior without some knowledge of the biological history of the organism upon which the environment is imping-ing. Environment-development relationships found for one class of individuals may not occur when individuals with a different biological background are studied. For example, many teratogenic agents only have their effects on individuals with certain genotypes, and this perhaps only in certain environments (Fraser, 1976b).

An additional implication that comes from acceptance of a transactional model is the necessity of adopting a developmental frame-work. Gene-environment transactions that produce a result at one age may be quite irrelevant at earlier or later ages. This com-plexity is not due only to changes in the nature of the child's environment as the child devel-

We wish to thank Sandra Scarr and Richard Schreiner for their reading and comments.

ops. Evidence from the field of molecular genetics indicates the existence of "regulator" genes whose functions appear to be turning on or off the structural genes that regulate enzyme production (McClearn, 1970). The process of differential genetic activation appears to be influenced by environmental factors (Oppenheimer, 1980, p. 24) and even organ functioning itself (Gottlieb, 1976; Wilson, 1977a). Given the fact that both effective genotype and environment change over the lifespan, it becomes obvious that the study of their transaction must be considered within a developmental framework.

A similar case occurs with the study of prenatal influences. The concept of critical period, in fact, comes from the study of prenatal development (Stockard, 1921). Insults occurring at one point during prenatal development may have a different impact than if they occur at a slightly different time.

The major implication of what has been discussed is that to understand fully the nature of behavioral development, neither biological predeterminism nor radical environmentalism will suffice. Rather it seems necessary to utilize a transactional-developmental perspective. Given this state of affairs, it would seem foolish simply to devote the present chapter to a listing of genetic or prenatal influences. Such a listing would suggest a one-to-one correspondence between these influences and behavior that would not reflect the true nature of prenatal or genetic influences. Rather than listing, our aim in writing this chapter is to illustrate the nature of this transactional process.

THE STUDY OF GENETIC INFLUENCES

Methodology

In this section we will discuss assumptions and methodological strategies underlying behavior genetic research in order to provide a perspective by which to evaluate this research.

Assumptions

Although not commonly recognized, the basic model of genetic influences at the human level shares the same assumptions as models used to study genetic influences in plant and animal breeding (Feldman & Lewontin, 1975). One major assumption utilized by plant and animal breeders is no gene-environment correlation (no correlation between genotype and environment). In human studies, where biological families raise their own offspring, this assumption is quite difficult, if not impossible, to meet (Wachs & Mariotto, 1978). Accurate estimates of genetic influence may be particularly difficult to establish in the presence of gene-environment correlation (Plomin, DeFries, & Loehlin, 1977), even when this correlation exists at low levels (Linn, 1974). Simply reassigning the variance associated with gene-environment correlation to genes or environment does not reflect the fact that the former is a unique source of variance not easily subsumed under genetic or environmental influences (Plomin et al., 1977; Wachs & Mariotto, 1978).

A second assumption often made is that the impact of heredity upon human development can be summarized by use of a single term, namely heritability (h^2). At the human level, available research clearly suggests that estimates of h^2 may change as a function of instrument changes, population changes, age changes, or changes in nongenetic influences (DeFries, 1972; Feldman & Lowontin, 1975; Dworkin et al. 1976).

One implication of the above is that a high level of h^2 for a trait essentially means that there is a high level of genetic influence on a trait, *given current conditions* (Scarr-Salapatek, 1975). Changing any one of the above parameters may well result in a dramatic drop in the h^2 estimate for the trait.

Twin Studies

Since monozygotic (MZ) twins share both common genes and common environment while dizygotic twins (DZ) mainly share the latter, greater similarity of MZ twins on a trait can be taken as evidence for genetic influence upon that trait.

The most common criticism of twin studies is that greater MZ similarity may be due to the environment of MZ twins being more similar than that of DZ twins. In general, this criticism has not been supported by available research (Lytton, 1977; Plomin, Willerman, & Loehlin, 1976; Scarr & Carter-Saltzman, 1979).

A more serious limitation of results derived from twin studies has to do with their generalizability outside of a twin population. Estimates of h^2 are population specific, and there clearly are many factors that are unique to twin populations, such as a unique placental environment. Interestingly, Melnick, Myrcanthopoulos, and Christian (1978) report significantly more concordance in seven-year IQ scores for MZ twins who share a common placenta than for those who do not. This suggests that placental type may be more critical for MZ concordance than zygosity. In addition to placental factors, twins also have a high incidence of prenatal and perinatal medical problems (Cohen, 1974) and unique interaction patterns with parents (Lytton, Conway, & Sauve, 1977). These unique factors may explain why we see notably higher estimates of genetic influence when these estimates are based upon twin populations as opposed to nontwin populations (Scarr-Salapatek, 1976; Plomin, 1976).

Family Studies

Where we suspect the influence of a single gene, one approach is to determine whether the observed distribution of a trait across generations fits one of the expected Mendelian distributions (Bodmer & Cavalli-Sforza, 1976). However, the retrospective nature of pedigree studies often leads to a certain amount of guesswork in terms of whether a specific disorder was really manifest in earlier generations. Further, the rarity of certain disorders often means that pedigree studies are based on a small number of families (Hanson & Gottesman, 1976).

For a variety of human traits, particularly those that are normally distributed, genetic effects may be due more to the influence of multiple genes with each gene involved having a small effect on the trait in question (polygenic inheritance). In this situation, the classic family pedigree study is of limited utility. However, family studies may still be useful, based on the hypothesis that since relatives share common genes there should be some degree of correlation between relatives in terms of the trait under study.

The major methodological problem associated with family studies is that relatives share not only genes but also environments. Thus in these studies we are continually faced with the problem of whether observed correlations are due to shared genes, shared environments, or a combination of the two (gene–environment correlation) (Plomin et al., 1977; Wachs & Mariotto, 1978).

Adoption Studies

The basic logic of adoption studies is that a child who is adopted at a very early age receives only its genes from its biological parents and only its environment from its adoptive parents. Thus the degree to which the child resembles the adoptive or the biological parent may indicate the degree of environmental or genetic influence respectively.

The degree to which conclusions drawn from adoption studies are valid depends on the degree to which certain assumptions are met (i.e., no selection in terms of who is placed or with whom the child is placed). However, few if any adoption studies meet all necessary assumptions (Munsinger, 1975), many of which are mutually exclusive.

Further, as Plomin, DeFries, and Loehlin (1977) have noted, the presence of gene–environment correlation can inflate child–biological-parent correlations and either inflate or deflate child–foster-parent correlations depending upon the family structure and the design of the study.

One final problem with adoptive studies concerns the fact that correlational statistics are insensitive to mean differences (Weizmann, 1971). Thus while there may be a significant correlation between child's and biological parent's intelligence scores, the child's intelligence score may be well above the level of the biological parent, suggesting simultaneous environmental influences. Unless both correlations and means are reported, erroneous conclusions may be drawn from adoptive studies.

High Risk Studies

High risk studies typically involve the follow-up of children at risk for a particular disorder, such as schizophrenia, due to one or both parents having the disorder. If the child is living with the biological parents, we again have the obvious problem of gene-environment correlation. In addition, there is also a critical problem of accurately diagnosing parental disorders. Inaccurate diagnosis of parental disorder may severely limit interpretation of offspring breakdown rates (Hanson, Gottesman, & Meehl, 1977).

For high risk studies where the child has been adopted, the same constraints noted above for adoptive studies also apply.

Inbreeding Studies

Inbreeding increases the probability that recessive gene effects will become manifest, since common recessives are more likely among relatives. Since recessive genes are more likely to be deleterious to the organism (Bodmer & Cavalli-Sforza, 1976), an association is predicted between degree of loss of function and degree of inbreeding (inbreeding depression). However, since most inbred unions tend to be between parents of lower IQ or lower social class, it is difficult to know whether observed results are due to inbreeding depression or deleterious environmental factors associated with inbreeding (Kamin, 1980).

Biomedical Studies

For many disorders, physical evidence such as chromosome breakage or metabolic disorder can be shown to be associated with behavioral disorders. Two constraints must be noted here. First, in many cases there is no clear pathway between the physical evidence and the behavior; the two are associated but causal relationships may not be clear (Belmont, 1971). Second, even when causality can be established, such cases are extremely rare; thus generalizability is often quite limited.

Summary

Based on the above review, it seems clear that no single approach to the study of genetic influences is sufficient to give an unambiguous answer concerning the nature of these influences. In order to come to a satisfatory conclusion concerning the nature of genetic influences, it is necessary to look for congruencies in results across studies using a variety of methodological strategies. The greater the degree of congruence across studies using different methods, the greater confidence we have in conclusions about genetic influences upon behavior.

It should also be noted that although the preferred model is one of gene-environment transaction, most behavior-genetic studies are designed to isolate genetic influences and not to illustrate the process by which genes transact with environment. Hence, in our discussion of genetic influences it will often be necessary to use nongenetic studies as a means of illustrating the nature of gene-environment transaction.

SCOPE OF THE REVIEW ON GENETIC INFLUENCES

In our review of genetic influences, we will restrict our discussion to two areas of behavior: intelligence and behavior disorders. There are two reasons for our choice of these areas. First, these are the areas in which most behavior genetic research has been done. Second, these are the areas that are likely to be of most interest to the practicing clinician.

This is not to say that there is not evidence for genetic influences in other areas of behavior. Based on studies of infant twins, available evidence suggests significant genetic influence in the area of early temperament (Plomin & Rowe, 1977; Torgerson & Kringlen, 1978; Goldsmith & Gottesman, 1981). There is also the possibility of genetic influences on the quality of infant social interaction with strangers though not on the quality of interaction with parents (Lytton, Martin, & Eaves, 1977; Plomin & Rowe, 1979). Any difference may be mediated by the infant's ability to adapt to new situations, which has also been shown to be influenced by genetic factors (Matheney &

Dolan, 1975). Such adaptability would be more critical in reaction to strangers than in reaction to parents.

For older children, available evidence indicates the existence of genetic influences upon temperament (Goldsmith & Gottesman, 1981), reflectivity-impulsivity (Plomin & Willerman, 1975), and personality (Loehlin & Nichols, 1976; Carey et al., 1978). There is also evidence from an adoption study indicating the existence of genetic influences upon vocational interests (Grottevant, Scarr, & Weinberg, 1977). The authors of this latter study suggest that vocational choices may be mediated by inherent personality orientations.

In addition to the above, evidence is also available suggesting patterns of indirect genetic influence, that is, situations wherein a genetically based physical disorder predisposes to the development of specific behavioral or personality patterns (Reed, 1975). Examples of indirect genetic influences would include milk-drinking patterns associated with lactose intolerance (Gottesman & Heston, 1972) or the development of fears associated with hemophilia (Reed, 1975).

GENETICS AND INTELLIGENCE

Chromosomal Influences on Intelligence

Epidemiological studies suggest that approximately one-third of all severe mental retardation is caused by chromosomal accidents (Hanson, Belmont, & Stein, 1980). In terms of intellectual retardation, the most common of the chromosomal accidents is Trisomy 21 Down's Syndrome. In this disorder the child has 47 rather than the normal 46 chromosomes (Koch & De La Cruz, 1975). Although the exact causal pathway is still unclear (Belmont, 1971), one of the characteristic features of Down's Syndrome is moderate levels of mental retardation (Koch & De La Cruz, 1975). Children with Trisomy 21 typically show normal developmental levels until about six months of age when they begin to fall progressively further and further behind their normal counterparts (Share, 1975; Fishler, Koch, &

Donnell, 1976); deficits starting earlier than six months have also been reported (Dicks-Mireaux, 1972). Trisomy 21 is also associated with a variety of other cognitive deficits, particularly in the area of expressive language (Dodd, 1975; Katz, 1978) and social competence (Katz, 1978). Social stereotypes of Down's Syndrome children having good rote imitative skills or unusual musical aptitude have not been supported by available research evidence (Belmont, 1971).

In addition to Trisomy 21, there are several other extremely rare forms of this syndrome such as Translocation (46 chromosomes but one of the 21 chromosome pair is found with the 14 pair) and Mosaic (Trisomy 21 in some cell lines and a normal chromosome complement in the remainder) (Koch & De La Cruz, 1975). In general, the evidence relating type of chromosomal disorder to IQ is highly variable and inconclusive (Belmont, 1971); existing studies are plagued by a variety of methodological problems (Gibson, 1973). At least for Mosaics, the most comprehensive study with this population revealed no relationship between percent of normal cells and IQ score (Fishler et al., 1976).

Besides Down's Syndrome, a variety of other chromosomal disorders associated with mental retardation have also been identified. Most are extremely rare, involving situations where the child has one or more extra X chromosomes. Examples would be Kleinfelter's Syndrome for males (XXY—mild retardation) and the XXX Syndrome for females (severe mental retardation). In general, available evidence seems to suggest that the greater the number of *extra* X chromosomes, the more severe the associated retardation (Trunca, 1980). For a detailed review of these types of disorders, see Rubenstein (1980) and Trunca (1980).

One particularly interesting disorder is Turner's Syndrome, in which for females there is deletion of an X chromosome (XO). While most women with Turner's Syndrome have normal verbal intelligence (Garron, 1970), they also have a specific deficit in spatial skills (Garron, 1970; McGee, 1979; Trunca, 1980). This deficit clearly seems due to the loss of the X chromosome and not to the physical characteristics associated with Turner's Syndrome (Nyborg & Neilson, 1977). The fact that males also have only one X chromosome and do not show the loss in spatial skills associated with Turner's Syndrome has led some researchers to suggest that the spatial deficit may be due to an interaction between genotype and hormonal factors (Garron, 1970; McGee, 1979).

Under a model of genetic predeterminism, it would be predicted that little could be done for individuals with any of the chromosomal disorders described above. With a transactional model, we start with the fact of biological damage and look at the degree to which the resulting developmental course may be modified by later environmental factors. Most work here has been done with Down's Syndrome children.

Consistent with a transactional position, available evidence indicates that intellectual gains or losses by Down's Syndrome children are related to type of rearing environment, such as home versus institution (Stedman & Eichorn, 1964) and the quality of the child's home environment (Piper & Ramsay, 1980). Reviews of early cognitive intervention projects with Down's Syndrome babies clearly support the hypothesis that significant gains in cognitive functioning occur as a result of intensive early intervention (Caldwell, Bradley, & Elardo, 1975). Childhood IQ scores in the 80s and evidence for reading ability have been reported by some projects (Hayden & Dmitriev, 1975), though gains may decline when intervention is discontinued (Aronson & Fallstrom, 1977). This data illustrates the importance of a developmental-transactional model, which assumes a continuing transaction between the organism and its environment.

Two conclusions can be drawn from the above pattern of evidence. First, there appear to be clear chromosomal influences upon intelligence. Second, eventual outcomes are not rigidly fixed but will vary according to the experiences encountered by the individual with a particular chromosomal disorder.

Genes and Intelligence: Single Gene Influences

At the human level, single gene effects upon intelligence are typically manifested through some form of recessive gene-based metabolic disorder. Epidemiological estimates indicate that such disorders account for about 7–8 percent of all severe mental retardation (Hansen, Belmont, & Stein, 1980).

The classic disorder in this category is phenylketonuria (PKU). PKU results from the inactivity of a gene-coded enzyme responsible for governing the conversion of phenylalanine to tyrosine. The resulting buildup of unmetabolized phenylalanine results in an excess of certain biochemical substances such as phenylpyruvic acid, which are thought to be neurotoxic (Koch, Acosta, & Dobson, 1971).

In general, *untreated* PKU children show a rapid decline in IQ; the rate of decline slows somewhat after 10 months of age (Katz, 1978). One study (Pitts, 1971) suggests a continuing, slow intellectual decline through adulthood for individuals with untreated PKU. However, when the appropriate controls for institutionalization are utilized, available evidence indicates that the intellectual decline associated with PKU seems to stop somewhere around 4 years of age (Partington & Laverty, 1978). Most untreated PKU children show moderate-severe levels of mental retardation, though there is a wide range of intellectual level seen in this population (Dobson et al., 1976; Katz, 1978). Deficits in manual dexterity and attention have also been reported (Anderson, 1972).

In addition to PKU, there is a variety of other rare, recessive gene-based metabolic disorders associated with mental retardation. These include disorders of amino acids, carbohydrates, and mucopolysacheride metabolism. For a more detailed description of these disorders and their effects, see the review by Snyderman (1975).

Based on patterns of family correlations, a number of researchers have suggested the possibility that spatial abilities are influenced by a single, *sex-linked* gene (Stafford, 1961;

Bock & Kolakowski, 1973). However, more recent evidence has not supported this hypothesis (McGee, 1979). Data from one recent study (Ashton, Polovina, & Vandenberg, 1979) have lent support to the possibility that a single, *autosomal* gene may influence spatial abilities.

The above pattern of data clearly indicates the relevance of single genes for intelligence. Again, this does not suggest a predeterministic model. Nowhere is the gene-environment transaction model better illustrated than in the case of PKU. The fact that one of the characteristic features of this disorder is a buildup of unmetabolized phenylalanine suggested that a diet low in phenylalanine might be an effective treatment. Evidence indicates that PKU children on such a diet typically score in the low-average to average range of intelligence (Dobson et al., 1968, 1976, 1977; Katz, 1978; Berry et al., 1979). Similar effects of the diet are seen using measures of neurological functioning (Johnson et al., 1978) and school performance (Berry et al., 1979). In general, the earlier the diet is begun, the greater degree of recovery (Dobson et al., 1968; Berry et al., 1979). Further, with increasing age, there is a cumulatively higher negative correlation between the level of serum phenylalanine for the individual (a measure of degree of dietary control) and the individual's level of IQ (Berry et al., 1979). This correlational pattern suggests that the degree of recovery from PKU may be governed by the *effectiveness* of subsequent environmental (dietary) interventions.

Given the rarity of other gene-based metabolic disorders, few attempts at remediation similar to that done for PKU have been attempted. However, a pattern of results similar to that found for PKU has also been reported for single gene recessive disorders such as galactosemia (Kamrower & Lee, 1970; Koch et al., 1971; Fishler et al., 1972) and maple syrup urine disease (Snyderman, 1975).

The above pattern of evidence leads to conclusions similar to those drawn for chromosomal influences. There appear to be clear-cut single gene influences upon intelligence. The fact that intellectual retardation associated with certain single gene recessive disorders can be ameliorated by dietary treatment nicely illustrates the importance of the transactional model.

Genes and Intelligence: Polygenic Effects

As noted earlier, polygenic inheritance refers to the cumulative influence of a number of genes, each making a small contribution to the development of a specific trait. Looking across studies utilizing divergent methods clearly indicates evidence for polygenic influences upon intelligence.

For twin studies, available reviews indicate consistently greater MZ than DZ concordance for IQ (Scarr-Salapatek, 1975; Wilson, 1978). Reviews of adoptive studies generally indicate that the IQ correlation between biological parent/adopted child is consistently higher than the correlation between foster parent/adopted child (Munsinger, 1975). Natural family studies typically yield correlational patterns among relatives that are consistent with expected correlations derived from genetic models (Scarr-Salapatek, 1975). High risk studies indicate a greater risk for lower intelligence in families where one or more members has mental retardation that is not associated with genetic disorders or chromosomal accidents (Anderson, 1974). In terms of inbreeding, several studies do indicate modest and, in some cases, significant amounts of inbreeding depression in IQ when societal factors are either statistically controlled (Schull & Neel, 1965) or do not bias against inbred unions (Bashi, 1977).

Notwithstanding the consistency of results, available evidence also suggests that polygenic influences upon intelligence cannot be conceptualized through use of a simple *additive hypothesis* of genetic influence, that is, an hypothesis that intelligence is determined *primarily* by the number of "smart" genes the individual possesses (McAskie & Clarke, 1976). The inadequacy of a simple additive hypothesis as an explanatory device has been shown for family studies (McAskie & Clarke,

Horn, Loehlin, & Willerman, 1979), and adoptive studies (McAskie & Clarke, 1976; Kamin, 1978).

Until now we have been discussing intelligence as if it were represented solely by a global IQ score. It is now generally accepted that the term *intelligence* connotes a variety of distinct abilities. Available evidence indicates that some of these abilities may be more influenced by genetic factors than others. Evidence suggests significant polygenic influence on verbal abilities (Vandenberg, 1968, p. 521; Williams, 1975; DeFries et al., 1976; Wilson, 1977), spatial abilities (Vandenberg, 1968, p. 521; DeFries et al., 1976), and certain components of performance abilities including block design (Vandenberg, 1968; Williams, 1975; Rose et al., 1979), and coding (Vandenberg, 1968; Williams, 1975). Overall, there appears to be less polygenic influence on performance abilities as compared to verbal abilities (Williams, 1975; Wilson, 1977). Polygenic influences appear to be limited in the case of numerical abilities (Vandenberg, 1968, p. 521), reasoning (Vandenberg, 1968), and perceptual speed (DeFries et al., 1976). A significant genetic component for memory has not been demonstrated at this time (Vandenberg, 1968, p. 521; DeFries et al., 1976). The possibility has also been raised that the influence of genes upon specific cognitive abilties may vary as a function of the age of the child (Ho, Foch, & Plomin, 1980).

Again, postulating a polygenic influence upon intelligence in no way implies predeterminism. The process of gene-environment transaction is illustrated here by intervention studies with the mildly retarded and by adoption studies.

Haywood and Wachs (1981) have hypothesized that children who fall in the mildly retarded range do so because they inherit both an unfavorable genotype and unfavorable environment from their parents (i.e., gene-environment correlation). Within this framework, two predictions can be made. First, it would be predicted that the risk of mild mental retardation could be lowered through interventions that enhance unfavorable environments. In general, reviews of early inter-

vention research with children at risk for mild mental retardation have supported this prediction (Caldwell et al., 1975; Hunt, 1979). Second, based on unfavorable genotypes, limitations on the degree of expected gains following intervention would be hypothesized. As predicted, most intervention projects show significant but modest gains in intellectual functioning for children in these programs (Williams, 1977).

For adoption studies, the process of gene-environment transaction is most clearly seen when the child's adoptive environment is dramatically different from the child's biological family environment. In studies of lower class black children adopted in to upper-middle-class white homes (Scarr & Weinberg, 1976) or lower class children adopted into upper class homes (Schiff et al., 1978), the adopted children's intellectual level was significantly higher than both the level that would be expected if the children were raised with their biological parents and the mean population intelligence level. Biological limitations on environmental effects are seen in evidence indicating that the adopted children's intellectual level rarely reached the intellectual level attained by the natural children of their adoptive parents (Scarr & Weinberg, 1976). Multiple regression techniques, employed to predict the adopted children's intellectual level, indicated that maximal prediction was attained with a combination of genetic and environmental parameters rather than either genetic or environmental predictors (Scarr & Weinberg, 1976).

Thus as with single gene and chromosomal influences, an analysis of polygenic factors indicates that such factors do exercise a differential effect on intelligence. This analysis also reveals that, once again, genetic and environmental factors transact to influence the process of intellectual development.

Summary of Genetic Influences Upon Intelligence

Our review suggests the operation of two classes of genetic influence upon intellectual development.[2] For the normal range of intelligence (50–150) polygenes, combined with prenatal and subsequent environmental factors, continually transact to influence the individual's level of general and specific cognitive functioning. For those individuals functioning in the moderately and severely retarded range of intelligence, chromosomal damage or single recessive genes lead to an impaired level of intellectual functioning. However, the degree to which the individual varies from this level appears to be, in good part, a function of subsequent environmental influences.

GENETICS AND BEHAVIOR DISORDERS

Chromosomal Influences

In contrast to intelligence, remarkably little attention has been paid to the possibility of a relationship between chromosomes and behavior disorders. Much of what evidence is available in this area has been collected on individuals with Kleinfelter's Syndrome (XXY). Available data suggest an elevated rate of antisocial behavior (Reed, 1975) and poor impulse control (Campbell et al., 1972) for affected individuals. These behavioral patterns may not be due to the extra X chromosome per se but rather to the lower levels of intelligence found in chromosomal disorders such as Kleinfelter's (Witkin et al., 1976). (A similar explanation also appears to hold for individuals with the XYY syndrome as well; see Witkin et al., 1976). In addition to antisocial behavior, psychoticlike behaviors have also been noted for some children with Kleinfelter's, starting as early as 3 years of age (Campbell et al., 1972). Similar symptom patterns have also been noted in the XXX syndrome (Trunca, 1980).

The above pattern of results, although fragmentary, does at least suggest the potential influence of chromosomal accidents upon disordered behavioral patterns. Such an association appears to be more likely when chromosomal disorders are characterized by extra chromosomes rather than by chromosomal breakage and recombination (Walzer et al., 1978). As with intelligence, the presence of extra chromosomes does not lead to a predetermined course of development. Many of the behaviors associated with disorders such as Kleinfelter's have been shown to be treatable by various behavioral strategies (Hamilton, Stephens, & Allen, 1976).

Genetics and Behavior Disorders: Single Gene Influences

As with chromosomal disorders, there has been remarkably little research on single gene influences on behavioral disorders. Disturbed behavioral patterns have been noted for children with PKU (Koch et al., 1971; Reed, 1975; Katz, 1978), galactosemia (Fishler et al., 1972), and other gene-based metabolic deficiencies (Rosenberg, 1974; Coleman, 1978). However, it is unclear whether these abnormal behaviors are due to the gene-mediated disorder, to disturbances in parent-child interactions (Kamrower & Lee, 1970), or to institutional effects (Pitts, 1971).

Given the general lack of evidence in this area, the existence of the Lesch-Nyhan Syndrome proves to be of particular interest. Lesch-Nyhan Syndrome is a rare (1 per 50,000 births) sex-linked genetic disorder of purine metabolism, which leads to an overproduction of uric acid (Nyhan, 1976). The classic feature of Lesch-Nyhan Syndrome is extreme self-mutilative behavior. The exact pathway from abnormal metabolism to self-mutilative behavior has not yet been established. Biochemical approaches to treatment, on the whole, have not been successful (Anderson et al., 1977).

Given the bizarre nature of Lesch-Nyhan Syndrome, it might be predicted that this disorder is one that does not easily fit our gene-environment transaction model. However, a recent report by Anderson et al. (1977) suggests that providing either increased attention for nonmutilative behavior or loss of attention following mutilation may be effective in altering the behavioral patterns of these children. These results not only illustrate the impact of environment upon a single gene behavior disorder, but also the impact of genotype upon the environment. Specifically, even though responsive to pain, children with Lesch-Nyhan Syndrome were unable to learn to control their behavior under conditions of aversive stimulation (Anderson et al., 1977).

Genes and Behavior: Polygenic Effects[3]

Most of the evidence on polygenic influences on behavior disorders has come in the area of schizophrenia. However, some data also exist for other areas of psychopathology as well. For example, results indicate that there appears to be a clear-cut shift in degree of genetic influence on MMPI psychoneurosis scores at different ages (Dworkin et al., 1976). The nature of this shift suggests a greater degree of genetic control on adolescent than on adult MMPI scores (Dworkin et al., 1977, p. 509).

An argument for genetic influences upon hyperactivity in childhood was made by Morrison and Stewart (1971; 1973; 1974). However, methodological flaws, including the use of nonblind interviews (Dubey, 1976) and retrospective parent reports, severely limit the confidence that can be placed in this data. Thus, contrary to Morrison and Stewart, we must conclude that, at present, there is no compelling evidence to support a hypothesis of genetic influences on hyperactivity.

Given recent concerns over teenage alcoholism, it is also worth noting the review of genetic influences on this disorder by Schulsinger (1980). Based on high risk studies, Schulsinger concludes that, for males, having an alcoholic father clearly predisposes the offspring to alcoholism. This influence occurs regardless of whom the male child is actually reared with in childhood. For females, the Schulsinger (1980) review indicates little consistent evidence supporting a hypothesis of genetic influences upon alcoholism. Schulsinger (1980) also notes the existence of evidence suggesting the possibility of genetic influences upon antisocial behavior.

As noted above, most genetic research on psychopathology has been concerned with schizophrenia. Based on a large number of studies with diverse methodologies, there seems little doubt that there is at least some degree of genetic influence on *adult* schizo-

phrenia. (For reviews of this area, see Gottesman & Shields, 1972, 1976.) The degree to which we can generalize from this adult data to either early (beginning in infancy) or late onset (beginning in childhood or adolescence) childhood schizophrenia depends directly on whether we wish to assume continuity between the adult and childhood forms of this disorder. (For a discussion on this issue, see chap. 22 by Dawson and Mesibov in this book.) Given the lack of conclusive evidence, we will adopt a conservative strategy and look at the early and late onset forms of childhood schizophrenia separately.

The strongest argument against genetic influences in early onset schizophrenia has been made by Hanson and Gottesman (1976). They note that early onset schizophrenia does not follow any of the classic Mendelian inheritance patterns, nor is there consistent evidence for chromosomal damage. The low risk rate for sibs of autistic children also seems to rule out polygenic inheritance.

The strongest argument in favor of genetic influences on early onset schizophrenia has been made by Rutter. Rutter and Bartak (1971) note that the actual risk rate for sibs of autistic chidlren, although low (2 percent), is still above the risk rate for the general population (1/10,000 births = .01 percent). As further evidence for genetic influences, Folstein and Rutter (1977) have reported that 4 of 11 MZ twins pairs were concordant for early onset schizophrenia, as compared to 0 of 10 DZ pairs. Folstein and Rutter (1977) hypothesize that what is inherited may not be early onset schizophrenia per se. Rather, what is inherited is a predisposition to certain cognitive or linguistic deficits, which may manifest themselves as early onset schizophrenia under conditions of biological trauma. As evidence for this viewpoint, Folstein and Rutter (1977) report that 9 of the 11 MZ twins were concordant *either* for early onset schizophrenia *or* for specific cognitive/linguistic deficits, as compared to 1 in 10 of the DZ twins.

This interpretation by Folstein-Rutter is confounded by the fact that MZ twins share a very similar prenatal environment. Concordance for cognitive/linguistic impairment may reflect not so much genetic influences as the influence of shared intrauterine trauma (Eshkevan, 1979). It is worth noting, however, that August and Stewart (1981) have recently reported significant concordance for autism using a family study approach in which the possibility of prenatal confounding was minimized.

Given the variability of evidence, it seems clear that no strong conclusion can be drawn regarding the influence of genetic factors upon *early onset* schizophrenia. Several researchers have suggested the possibility of subclasses of early onset schizophrenia, where some cases may be due to biological trauma per se, while others may be caused by a combination of genetic predisposition and biological trauma (Folstein & Rutter, 1977; Coleman, 1978; August & Stewart, 1981).

For late onset child schizophrenia (particularly in the adolescent years), the evidence for genetic influences is much more clear-cut. The congruent symptom patterns found between the late onset and adult forms of schizophrenia at least suggest the possibility of a common genetic influence (Hanson & Gottesman, 1976). Twin studies, studies of adopted offspring of schizophrenic parents, and studies of the risk rates in biological and adoptive families of late onset child schizophrenics all yield data congruent with a hypothesis of genetic influences (Schulsinger, 1980). Family stress or the effects of parental hospitalization do not seem to be viable alternative explanations (Worland, Landes, & Hesselbrock, 1979).

The evidence for genetic influence in late onset child schizophrenia does not mean genetic predeterminism (Hanson et al., 1977). A variety of factors support the validity of a gene-environment transaction position. They include the following. First, a majority of children at risk for schizophrenia, due to parental psychosis, show essentially normal development (Hanson et al., 1977; Schulsinger, 1980). Even children reared at home by two schizophrenic parents have only a 60 percent risk rate (Zubin & Spring, 1977). A second factor is the wide variability in behavior (from normal to schizophrenic) shown by relatives of the offspring of schizophrenics

(Zubin & Spring, 1977). A third fact is that a significant number of MZ twin pairs are discordant for schizophrenia (Wahl, 1976; Zubin & Spring, 1977). This variability of outcomes is clearly inconsistent with a pre-deterministic genetic model of late onset schizophrenia.

The preferred etiological model, adopted by most active researchers in the area of schizophrenia, is one encompassing the idea of genetically based predisposition or vulnerability, combined with environmental stressors (Hanson et al., 1977; Zubin & Spring, 1977; Schulsinger, 1980). The environmental contribution is seen by the fact that specific environmental stressors are necessary to actualize the genetic predisposition. The genetic influence is seen in the fact that the same environmental stressors that cause anxiety for some or ulcers in others may be the trigger for late onset schizophrenia for those individuals with a particular genotype. Thus, to understand this disorder it becomes necessary to understand the transaction of both environmental and genetic influences rather than either genetics or environment.

Summary: Genes and Behavior Disorders

The strongest evidence for genetic influences upon behavior disorders is found for late onset schizophrenia, the single-gene disorder of Lesch-Nyhan Syndrome, and for male alcoholism. Less clear-cut evidence is found for possible chromosomal influences, psychoneurosis, and early onset schizophrenia. There appears to be little consistent evidence for a genetic influence on hyperactivity. None of the available evidence is inconsistent with a gene-environment transaction model as an approach to understanding the development of childhood behavior disorders.

PRENATAL INFLUENCES: INTRODUCTION

Historically, concern regarding prenatal conditions centered around their effects on infant survival. More recently, the emphasis has 1976), twin studies (Scarr-Salapatek, 1976;

shifted from simple viability to encompass milder or more delayed impacts of prenatal factors. Hagberg (1975) has recently estimated that prenatal factors are responsible for 85–95 percent of severe neurological and intellectual problems. Although this estimate may be somewhat high, it does illustrate the potential severity of the problem.

It is worth noting that the risk of severe intellectual disability in premature infants has declined in recent years (Fitzhardinge & Ramsay, 1973). It is not clear, however, if premature infants born recently will show an increased incidence of milder deficits at older ages (Hunt, 1979). Further, the fact that perinatal medicine is cutting down on mortality means that infants are surviving who previously would have died, particularly those whose weight at birth is under 1,000 grams. As Hunt (1979) points out, the intellectual outcomes for these children are as yet unknown.

On the other hand, many children with prenatal difficulties appear to develop normally. There is also evidence, consistent with what one would expect from a transactional perspective, that postnatal environmental factors (e.g., Sameroff & Chandler, 1975; Werner, Bierman, & French, 1971) may mediate eventual outcome.

The possible impact of prenatal events has been investigated employing both retrospective and prospective methodologies. Perhaps the best known example of the former is the studies of Pasamanick and Knobloch (e.g., 1961, 1966) and their colleagues, in which they concluded that a number of behavioral, cognitive-intellectual, and neurological problems were related to pregnancy complications.

Their conclusions have been severely criticized on a variety of grounds (e.g., Joffe, 1969; Sameroff & Chandler, 1975). Chief among them is the problem that postdictive probabilities relating outcome to putative causes are poor guides to the predictive probabilities that are obtained between cause and effect (Gottfried, 1973). Further, there is no guarantee that historical descriptions (chiefly clinical records) are accurate or that they will describe the actual causes of later problems as opposed to correlates of the causes. Finally, other factors (e.g., death rates, mobility) may interact with outcome and distort the results of an investigation.

In fairness to these early studies, it should be remembered that teratogenic agents such as prenatal rubella and thalidomide were identified retrospectively.

In terms of prospective studies, perhaps the best known is the National Collaborative Project, which involved following up more than 50,000 pregnancies. By necessity, there was a reliance on relatively gross and easily administered instruments, which make intensive investigations of particular conditions difficult. Studies of specific populations "at risk" for various problems may be needed as well as large scale studies to remedy these problems.

While they have a number of virtues, prospective studies are time consuming and expensive. Often the appropriate control groups may be difficult to obtain.

Both prospective and retrospective studies share the common problem that prenatal conditions must be inferred indirectly. Further, some conditions (malnutrition, drugs) affect the mother as well as the fetus. Thus it may be difficult to separate these effects. Where the conditions continue past birth, it may be difficult to separate prenatal from postnatal effects.

THE COURSE OF PRENATAL DEVELOPMENT: SOME CONSIDERATIONS

Although space limitations preclude a detailed account of prenatal development, we will present a summary of some of its major features and their implications for later development.

The first trimester of pregnancy is the one in which the most rapid growth occurs. By 120 days gestational age, the organs have assumed their gross shape. Since organs and organ systems are most susceptible to external influences during the time they are growing most rapidly, this period of organogenesis is the one in which the fetus is most susceptible to gross anatomical defects (Wilson, 1977a). It is during the first trimester that major gene effects have their impact, and where all sorts of insults can distort the arrangement of cells (Laroche, Amiel-Tison, & Dreyfus-Brisac, 1980). In the case of the central nervous system, this can lead to such gross anatomical disorders as anencephaly and spina bifida.

There are several periods of rapid brain growth, but one must distinguish between periods of rapid cell multiplication and periods in which growth is mainly in terms of cell size. For neurons, the former occurs primarily in the second trimester, while cell size increases occur chiefly during the third trimester and postnatally. Glial cells, which form the basis for later myelinization, develop most rapidly during the first year of life (Dobbing, 1974).

Beyond the first trimester, the adequacy of prenatal development depends increasingly upon the adequacy of the intrauterine environment, and especially the placenta, which by the end of the third month has become fully operational. Although the placenta plays a much more active role in development than was previously thought (Beaconsfield, Birdwood, & Beaconsfield, 1980), the placental protection provided against infection and teratogenic agents (such as radiation or chemicals) is only partial. In addition, there are conditions that can reduce the flow of nutrients or oxygen to the fetus. If these conditions are chronic and occur prior to birth, they can cause death or fetal growth retardation. If they are acute and occur during labor, they can cause fetal distress or anoxia (Botelli-Llusia, 1980). These two are not totally independent, insofar as fetal distress and anoxia are more likely to occur where a chronic problem already exists (Esteban-Altirriba, Cabero, & Calaf, 1980). The blood supply to the fetus is interrupted by uterine contractions during labor. While this has little effect on a well nourished infant, it can result in a reduction of oxygen to the nervous system in a fetus whose reserves are already low. This also illustrates an additional point: namely, that difficulties in the prenatal period make difficulties during and after birth more likely.

SOME PRENATAL FACTORS AND OUTCOMES

In this section we will survey some selected prenatal factors which may have a significant impact on later development. These are not simply independent influences and conditions. As mentioned above, many prenatal complications are apt to covary and interrelate with one another. In addition, many diverse etiological agents may have some final common pathway such as their effect on fetal growth. Consequently, what follows is not simply a survey of a group of independent, sharply defined entities but rather a discussion of factors or conditions that overlap and interweave to some extent.

Unlike the studies in the section dealing with genetic effects, we have not organized this section in terms of simple outcomes. This is because, to a large extent, the ultimate effects of many prenatal conditions have not been established, and such conditions may have more than one outcome.

Intrauterine Growth Retardation

It has become customary, beginning with the work of Grunewald (1963), to distinguish between infants who are premature and those who are growth retarded (i.e., small-for-date or small-for-gestational-age). This replaces the older convention under which all infants whose birth weight was less than 2,500 grams were grouped together.

Several different fetal growth curves, inferred from infants born prematurely, have been proposed as indices of appropriate fetal size at various points in prenatal development (e.g., Lubchenko et al., 1963). Unfortunately, in addition to problems regarding the representativeness of norms derived from premature infants, factors such as ethnicity and geography may affect birth weight (Aubrey et al., 1977). Some investigations have begun using a ponderal index (PI), a weight-length ratio that seems to avoid many of the ambiguities associated with birth weight alone (Lester, 1979).

Placental and circulatory adequacy are two

of the major determinants of fetal growth (Gluck et al., 1977), since the ability to transfer oxygen, nutrients, and waste products between mother and fetus sets an upper limit to fetal growth. Toxemia, or pregnancy-induced hypertension (to use a more accurate description), is probably the leading cause of placental insufficiency (Botelli-Llusia, 1980). In this condition, abnormalities in maternal peripheral blood vessels restrict adequate blood flow to the fetus. There are many theories about the causes of toxemia, including psychogenic ones (see below), but its etiology remains controversial.

Toxemia is not the only cause of placental difficulties. As Kopp and Parmalee (1979) note, infections, heart disease, structural problems of the uterus, and various fetal conditions can also cause intrauterine growth retardation. Maternal smoking is often also included in this list of etiological agents (Rush, 1976) (see below).

Often intrauterine growth retardation and prenatal malnutrition are viewed as being virtually coextensive with one another. Lester (1979), for example, has noted that the number of infants whose birth weight is affected by infections or congenital anomalies is small (Lubchenko, 1976). He argues that once such intrinsic abnormalities are taken into account, restrictions on nutritional adequacy represent the common denominator of growth-retarded infants. Further, malnutrition and other fetal-maternal diseases and conditions that can cause growth retardation are not independent of one another. For example, severe food deprivation may lead to placental insufficiency (Winick, 1977; Shanklin & Hodin, 1979), and both maternal disease and malnutrition are related to poverty (Lester, 1979). Hence, separating nutritional from other causes of growth retardation may not be practical or desirable.

In evaluating the impact of fetal malnutrition, a distinction must be made between severe and moderate or mild fetal malnutrition. Conditions of severe nutritional deprivation are only likely to be obtained under conditions of famine or in experimental work with infrahuman organisms. As Lester (1979)

has contended, it may be unwise to generalize from such extreme cases to the more frequent forms of prenatal malnutrition/intrauterine growth retardation usually encountered at least in Western societies. Winick (1977) has also argued that milder and more severe forms of malnutrition may be quite different in their effects.

Much of the research into the effects of severe prenatal dietary deficiency has been inconsistent (Brozek, 1978). Studies of extreme food deprivation have largely been retrospective studies that, it has been charged (Shanklin & Hodin, 1979), underestimate the effects of very severe malnutrition. In a widely cited study of the effects of prenatal malnutrition during the Dutch famine of World War II (Stein et al., 1972), for example, the authors reported that despite effects on birth weight, prematurity, and the number of stillbirths, there were no intellectual effects on the survivors at age nineteen. This conclusion ignores the fact that extra food was available for many people and there were, in fact, serious neurological consequences for many of those deprived of adequate nutrition prenatally (see Shanklin & Hodin, 1979).

Research on the effects of maternal diet during pregnancy on offspring's birth weight *per se* has also yielded inconsistent results (Haas, 1981). As noted by several commentators (Lester, 1979; Rush, Stein & Susser, 1980; Haas, 1981), however, many of the studies reporting no relationship between the two can be challenged because the range of nutritional adequacy sampled in these studies was relatively narrow and there is reason to believe that they did not include mothers whose diet was truly inadequate.

Research on the effects of intrauterine growth retardation on future development and functioning, apart from the studies of extreme malnutrition referred to above, has been more consistent and has involved prospective as well as retrospective studies. Small-for-date infants generally score lower in IQ than normal sized infants (e.g., Lester, 1976; Zeskind & Ramey, 1978; Kopp & Parmalee, 1979) and are more likely to encounter school difficulties (Fitzhardinge & Steven, 1972a, 1972b). Kopp and Parmalee (1979) suggest that these children score about 10 points lower in IQ than normal children but still fall within the normal range. Below normal scores are more likely to be found for fetally malnourished, low SES infants, but the gap between these infants and matched controls remains about the same as for higher SES infants (Zeskind & Ramey, 1978).

There is general agreement (Drillien, 1970, 1972; Zeskind & Ramey, 1978; Kopp & Parmalee, 1979) that social environmental variables are related to intellectual outcome in fetally malnourished infants. These data argue against a fixed impact model of fetal malnutrition; rather, they support a transactional position such as the one advocated by both Zeskind and Ramey (1979) and Lester (1979).

Further support for a transactional position in humans comes from the work of Zeskind and Ramey (1978, 1981). They found that not only did a special daycare program for small-for-date, low SES infants begun shortly after birth eliminate IQ differences between these children and normal controls, but it also appeared to change the home environment for infants (followed up to 36 months of age) through increasing maternal involvement with the infants.

Preterm Birth

Since prematurity is covered in more detail in chapter 12, we will confine ourselves to a few general comments. The first is that although in many cases the causes of preterm birth are not known, they do appear to be associated with prenatal problems or complications of pregnancy. Specifically, conditions such as prenatal maternal infection or malnutrition are thought to result in prematurity, in addition to their other effects (e.g., Barden, 1977).

The second point is that prematurity does appear to carry some risk of intellectual impairment and later school problems (Sameroff & Chandler, 1975; Caputo, Goldstein, & Taub, 1979) even apart from SES factors alone, although this conclusion is not unanimous (Kopp & Parmalee, 1979). Given recent improvements in perinatal care, however, the degree of impairment appears to be small unless there are other prenatal complications (e.g., Sostek, Quinn, & Davitt, 1979).

This does not mean that environmental interaction plays no role in determining outcome. There is evidence (e.g., Sostek et al., 1979; Field, 1979) that preterm infants behave differently than normal infants and that early parental interaction with infants may be affected by preterm birth.

Maternal Infections

There are a number of maternal infections that can be transmitted to the fetus. The effects of these infections can vary from mild to serious and can include prematurity, malformations, and stillbirths (Alford, Stagnio, & Reynolds, 1980). Even usually mild diseases can have a devastating effect on the fetus. Some of the more common infectious diseases to which women in the childbearing years are susceptible include rubella, cytomegalovirus, herpes simplex, toxoplasmosis, hepatitis-B, and syphilis (Alford et al., 1980).

The effects of prenatal rubella perhaps can serve as a model for such diseases (Chess, 1979). Chess and her colleagues have conducted a longitudinal study of 243 children infected as a result of the rubella epidemic of 1964–1965 (Chess, 1971, 1977, 1978; Chess, Korn, & Fernandez, 1971; Chess, Fernandez, & Korn, 1980; Chess & Fernandez, 1980). In rubella, if the virus is passed to the fetus, the organ systems then forming may fail to develop properly. The virus may continue to do damage until after birth. Those children who survive may be born with various handicaps including hearing, visual, or cardiac deficits or neuromuscular damage (Chess et al., 1971). Chess (1971) reports that approximately one-fifth of the preschool sample were retarded to one degree or another, although only one-fourth were still so diagnosed at 8–9 years of age.

One of the more interesting findings was the high rate of autism among these children, with 10 displaying some and eight displaying all the symptoms of autism. The high incidence of autism coupled with a relatively high (40–50 percent) rate of recovery (despite, in some cases, severe environmental stresses) resembles the pattern found in infectious diseases and has led Chess (1977) to propose that rubella may be one cause of autism.

Although Chess and her colleagues have demonstrated the serious effects of prenatal rubella on development, she has emphasized that outcomes are not fixed (Chess, 1978). The affected children manifest a wide range of coping skills, and there are alternative developmental pathways available to children whose handicaps interfere with the usual route to developmental achievement. The extent to which the child's family, teachers, and others can adapt the way they interact with the child to take account of the child's disabilities as well as needs, abilities, and temperament (Chess et al., 1980) appears to be critical in determining outcome. (It should be kept in mind, however, that within a transactional framework outcome is not a static terminal state; as Chess and Fernandez (1980) point out, outcomes may change as new developmental situations arise, demanding new forms of coping.)

Perinatal Anoxia

Despite its name, perinatal anoxia is employed as a generic term to include oxygen deficiency during the pre- or neonatal periods (Hunt, 1976). The possible effects of anoxia were first observed by William Little in 1862. The neuromuscular difficulties he described were, in fact, called Little's Disease until the 1940s, when the disorder was renamed cerebral palsy.

Anoxia can occur prior to, during, or after delivery, but its occurrence prenatally can make later anoxia more likely (Cohen & Schifrin, 1977). There are many factors associated with the development of anoxia: toxemia or other maternal illness, infection, kernictrus (a complication of infant jaundice), hemorrhaging, birth complications, and prematurity are some of the more important

(Botelli-Llusai, 1980). The nature and extent of the neurological damage and associated effects may vary depending upon the timing and duration of the insult. In addition, the occurrence of anoxia is strongly associated with parental poverty (Niswander & Gordon, 1972).

Overall, there is some diversity in research findings (Gottfried, 1973; Sameroff & Chandler, 1975) on the effect of anoxia, perhaps reflecting differences in the methodology, criteria, and types of control employed by various investigators (Gottfried, 1973). In spite of this, Gottfried (1973) has been able to make some tentative generalizations from this research. The first is that the relation between prenatal anoxia and cognitive functioning is more apparent at younger than at older ages. This may reflect the fact that IQ tests at younger ages tap sensorimotor abilities rather than verbal ones, and it is the former that may be more affected by anoxia. The second is that while anoxic children were not on the whole retarded, anoxia did increase the probability of mental retardation.

In studies based on data from the Collaborative Project, Broman (Broman & Nichols, 1975; Broman, Nichols & Kennedy, 1979) reports findings generally consonant with Gottfried's. Small IQ differences existed at early ages but decreased between 7 months and 8 years of age. While on the whole the anoxic children were not retarded, anoxia increased the risk of retardation twelvefold in infancy and sixfold at 7 years of age.

When the IQ scores of children with major neurological disorders were removed from the analysis, however, the differences in the frequency of perinatal anoxia between normal and retarded children were dramatically reduced. Hence, while anoxia does appear to be an intellectual risk factor to some extent, by itself it does not appear to be a major one.

DRUGS AND CHEMICALS

In general, relatively few drugs have been shown to be embryotoxic in humans, at least not in the usual dosages (Wilson, 1977b). Teratogenicity in animals is not a perfectly reliable guide to the effects of drugs in humans. Of the hundreds of drugs studied in animals, only 3 percent of those producing congenital defects in animals have been demonstrated to have similar effects in humans (Evans et al., 1975), and preliminary reports on many drugs (e.g., LSD) have tended to exaggerate the danger to humans. Similarly, relatively few environmental chemicals have been demonstrated to be harmful (Wilson, 1977c). Occasionally, however, a compound that causes little reaction in test species may be dangerous to humans (Wilson, 1977b), with thalidomide being the most prominent example, although even here genotypes vary considerably in their sensitivity to its effects (Wilson, 1977b).

Even where an individual drug or chemical may be harmless by itself it may interact with other substances to cause problems. Estimates (Wilson, 1977b) indicate that the causes of over 60 percent of all birth defects are unknown, and drug and/or chemical interactions may account for a significant proportion of them.

In general, the aim of most studies in the area has been to screen those drugs and chemicals that cause death or major malformations. Perhaps partly because of the large number of substances in need of screening, there have been few attempts to develop and use indicators of behavioral functioning and development apart from IQ tests, although there is a widening interest in what is coming to be called "behavioral teratology," which is leading to an increased interest in the behavioral effects of teratogens (e.g., Lefkowitz, 1981; Abel 1980b).

One reason for this change is that drugs and chemicals may cause behavioral abnormalities (see below) even where they do not cause physical ones (Vorhees, Brunner, & Butcher, 1979). Furthermore, traditional evaluations of toxicity may be insensitive to these effects. Brackbill (1979) has charged, for example, that the effects of obstetric medication on the child have been underestimated for this

reason. Dosages that are too low to have structural effects may have behavioral effects, and the period of susceptibility for such effects may be broader than those for structural ones and may go undetected (Vorhees et al., 1979).

Ironically, the publicity that often surrounds findings from preliminary animal or clinical studies may lead to overestimating some of the dangers from drugs or chemicals, while the lack of knowledge regarding behavioral and developmental consequences may lead to underestimating others.

In the following sections we will examine a few of the more prominent substances mentioned as possible causes of prenatal damage. (See Wilson, 1977a & 1977b for a more complete review.)

Narcotic and Psychotropic Drugs

Keeping the above qualifications in mind, generally the evidence linking marijuana and narcotic usage to prenatal damage is not strong (Wilson, 1977b; Abel, 1980a). Many of the effects sometimes claimed for these substances are probably due to the parallel deleterious health, stress, nutritional, and social conditions associated with heavy drug usage during pregnancy. The evidence with regard to the harmful effects of some tranquilizers (particulary diazepam, meprobromate, and chlordiazepoxide), in humans as well as animals, is somewhat stronger (Wilson, 1977b; Vorhees et al., 1979) but is not conclusive.

Smoking

Smoking is commonly regarded as a cause of intrauterine growth retardation, and there are a number of studies (U.S. Department of Health, Education, and Welfare, 1979) that suggest an inverse relationship between the amount smoked by mothers during pregnancy and birth weight. On the average, women who smoked during pregnancy had infants whose birth weight was 200 grams less than infants born to nonsmoking mothers (U.S. Department of HEW, 1979; Lefkowitz, 1981).

On the other hand, Yerushalmy's research,

as both Joffe (1969) and Sameroff and Chandler (1975) point out, raises some doubts about the apparently straightforward relationship between smoking and birth weight. Yerushalmy (1962, 1964, 1972, 1974) has reported that paternal smoking predicts the prenatal effects of smoking even better than maternal smoking and that the rate of low birth weight infants is similar both for mothers who smoke throughout pregnancy and for those who start smoking only after the termination of pregnancy. The rate of such births is also as low for women who smoke throughout pregnancy and then quit, as it is for those who never smoke. It is difficult to explain these results, but they suggest that caution should be exercised in assuming that the relationship between smoking and birth weight is a simple inverse one.

Beyond the issue of the relationship between smoking and birth weight, however, is the fact that while the long term effects of maternal smoking on offspring are not clear, they may be less than often thought. As Lefkowitz (1981) points out, the research is inconsistent. Many of the studies reporting positive findings are statistically biased, since they rely on separate bivariate analyses comparing smokers and nonsmokers on a number of dimensions, a procedure that can produce spurious positive findings by chance. This is compounded by the tendency of many investigators to resist drawing negative conclusions (see Lefkowitz, 1981).

Lefkowitz (1981), in a multivariate study of a large, predominantly middle class sample of 11-year-olds, found no relationship between maternal smoking during pregnancy and a number of measures of physical status and intellectual, affective, and personal-social functioning. As Lefkowitz (1981) notes, these findings lend support to the hypothesis that, beyond the perinatal period, maternal smoking during pregnancy has no long term harmful effects on offspring.

Alcohol

In the early 1970s, the publication in English of descriptions of what has come to be called Fetal Alcohol Syndrome (FAS) (Jones &

Smith, 1973) renewed a longstanding concern about the effects of alcohol on unborn children. FAS is characterized by pre- and postnatal growth retardation, mild-to-moderate mental retardation, and a number of physical characteristics including microcephaly and short palpebral fissures (i.e., the size of the eye opening).

The prevalence of FAS is difficult to gauge. The accepted estimate of the frequency of the syndrome is between .1 percent and .2 percent of all live births for its full expression and between .3 percent and .5 percent for its partial expression (Abel, 1980b). Abel (1980b), among others, has argued that these estimates may be too low. Alcohol may cause a number of undiagnosed behavioral and intellectual problems, and no safe dosage has been established for these effects. On the other hand, Hansen et al. (1980) suggest that the extent of retardation due to alcohol usage may be overstated due to biased sample selection; that is, those children who are evaluated are those who have been clinically identified as "suspect."

Both Hansen et al. (1980) and Abel (1980b) also point out that alcohol usage correlates or may interact with many other factors, including poverty, stress, maternal health, and metabolic functioning, whose effects have yet to be evaluated. Studies of infrahuman organisms are inconsistent, inconclusive, and often methodologically flawed (Abel, 1980b). Clearly, more research, including well-controlled prospective studies in humans (several of which are underway), is necessary before the nature and extent of the prenatal effects of alcohol become clear.

Maternal Biochemical Influences

It should be noted that substances harmful to the fetus may be produced by the mother as well as by the external environment. In phenylketonuria, for example, both clinical (e.g., Howell & Stevenson, 1971; Macready & Levy, 1972) and animal (Wapner, Moak, & Lifschitz, 1977) evidence suggests that high maternal phenylalanine levels are associated with intrauterine growth retardation and severe mental retardation in offspring. Fetal damage does not occur if the mother is on a low phenyl-alanine diet (Macready & Levy, 1972), although there are some questions as to whether the diet should be initiated prior to pregnancy (Howell & Stevenson, 1971).

STRESS AND MATERNAL EMOTIONALITY

While maternal health, diet, and drug use during pregnancy have been a focus of much research attention, much less emphasis has been put on the role of maternal emotional reactions. As Ferreira (1969) has noted, many investigators are loathe to assume that maternal emotional state during pregnancy is part of the fetal environment, perhaps because it is too close to the idea that maternal experiences during pregnancy can influence the fetus (e.g., Barrow, 1971).

Nonetheless, interest in the topic has appeared to have grown recently, and there have been several reviews of the area that have appeared in the past decade or so (e.g., Ferreira, 1969; Joffe, 1969; Sameroff & Chandler, 1975; Carlson & La Barba, 1979).

Although Joffe's review was published in 1969, it still provides one of the best discussions of the issues involved in research on the topic. Joffe (1969) concludes that although research in the human area is methodologically flawed, evidence from infrahuman studies suggests strongly that stress and maternal emotionality affect the development of offspring. Since the animal studies are typically much better controlled than the human studies, they argue against the view that similar findings at the human level are necessarily artifacts, due to sloppy methodology.

Carlson and La Barba's (1979) conclusions a decade later are similar to Joffe's (1969). They find tentative support for the view that maternal emotionality contributes to habitual abortions, toxemia, deviant infant behavior, and pronounced vomiting during pregnancy. Anxiety appears to bear the most consistent relationship to pregnancy complications, while the relationship of complications of labor and delivery, stillbirth, and physical or verbal handicaps is much less clear.

SEX HORMONES

The major effect of prenatal hormones is to be seen in sexual development. Evidence (e.g., Peterson, 1979) indicates that the Y chromosome in males initiates the development of the testes. Androgen secreted from the testes leads to the degeneration of potential female sexual structures and to the further sexual differentiation of male sex organs. The lack of androgen in females, on the other hand, leads to the degeneration of potential male sexual organs, and the development of female sexual organs.

There is also evidence (e.g., Peterson, 1979) that such exposure exerts an effect on the hypothalamus, which, through its influence on the pituitary, controls the flow of sex hormones from the gonads after puberty. Whether the hormonal pattern is male or female depends upon this prenatal adrenergic exposure.

Goy and his colleagues at the Oregon Primate Research Center (Young, Goy, & Phoenix, 1964; Phoenix, 1974) have proposed that masculinity and feminity are basically organized, both psychologically and biologically, through the prenatal exposure or lack of exposure to androgen. For example, prenatal exposure to large amounts of testosterone in female rhesus monkeys leads to their behaving more as typical males than females. Although postnatal exposure has physical effects, it has no such behavioral effects.

The clearest evidence regarding the effects of prenatal androgens in humans comes from the study of androgenized females; these are genetic females born with a clitoris resembling a penis as a result of prenatal exposure to androgen. Money and Ehrhardt (1972) reported on a group of androgenized females who had been surgically feminized shortly after birth. Compared to a matched control group, the female subjects were more tomboyish, and showed a more masculine pattern of interests. However, both parents and children were aware of the latter's status, and it is possible that this affected the socialization of these children and/or biased parental reports regarding sex-typed behavior. Notwithstanding their tomboyishness, however, the androgenized females were not more physically aggressive than the controls, nor did they reject their feminine identity. As Money (1975) notes, the effect of the prenatal androgenic exposure was to add a "special tint" to a basically feminine identity.

In other studies, Reinisch (1977) reported that both males and females exposed to synthetic progesterone prenatally were more independent, individualistic, and self-reliant than untreated siblings. Analogous findings have emerged from studies of the prenatal effects of female hormones, although the effects are somewhat weaker and more equivocal. (See the review by Ehrhardt & Meyer-Bahlberg, 1979.)

Generally, this evidence suggests that prenatal hormones may influence later behavior but that these influences are not categorical and do not by themselves determine sexual identity in humans. This conclusion is compatible with an interactional-transactional model and is, in fact, one that has been advocated variously by Money (1975), Ehrhardt (1979), Beach (1976a, 1976b), and Peterson (1979) among others.

Unfortunately, the issue of prenatal determination of sexuality, including identity as well as behavior, is still somewhat controversial. Imperato-McGinley et al. (1974) reported on a group of males reared in an isolated village in the Dominican Republic. Because of an endocrine disturbance, these males appeared to be female and were reared as such until adolescence when they were masculinized by pubertal hormones. At that time, these "females" were apparently able to change to a male sexual identity rather easily. The researchers conclude that sex of rearing is less important than the combination of testosterone exposure *in utero* and at puberty. It has been argued, however, that these "females" were different from ordinary girls even as young children and were treated differently. (See the discussion in Sachar, 1979, pp. 50–68).

There has also been a recent revival of claims that disturbances in the prenatal hormone balance lead to homosexuality (Dorner, 1976). This latter hypothesis represents a minority view (Meyer-Bahlberg, 1980; Beach,

1976a), and despite criticisms (e.g., Zuger, 1970) the bulk of the evidence cited above suggests that the development of human sexuality is not simply hormonally determined.

In addition to hormonal influences on sex role behavior, there is also considerable interest in sex differences in cognition. While a general discussion of this topic is beyond the scope of this chapter (see Wittig & Peterson, 1979, for a detailed review), some of this interest has focused on prenatal factors. In their review of the literature, Reinisch, Gandelman, and Spiegel (1979) report that no firm conclusions can be drawn regarding the relationships of prenatal hormonal factors to male-female differences in cognitive ability. The possible interactive influences of genotype and hormones on cognitive performance by females with Turner's Syndrome have been noted earlier in this chapter.

At one time, it was thought that the androgenital syndrome produced elevated IQ, but this finding appears to have been an artifact due to inadequate controls (Reinisch et al., 1979). Reinisch et al. (1979) suggest that insofar as sex differences in particular abilities are hormonally related, the effect may be indirect. For example, hormones may affect brain plasticity, physical activity, and/or perception and sensory perceiving, all of which may affect environmental interaction giving rise to characteristic sex differences.

Perhaps the general point to be taken from this discussion is that the interrelationships among the endocrine system, the environment, and behavior are enormously complex. A reliance on isolated correlations between prenatal hormone levels and later behaviors is misleading, since the interactive pathways between the two are long and involved.

IMPLICATIONS OF GENETIC AND PRENATAL FACTORS FOR THE CHILD CLINICIAN

Even a predeterministic model allows some scope for clinical-child psychologists. One can deal with the familial stresses and feelings that surround having a disabled child as well as dealing with the child's own fears and feelings. These activities are very important for such genetically related disorders as cystic fibrosis or hemophilia and will even probably expand as psychologists become more involved with general medicine.

Nonetheless, interactional and transactional models offer wider views of concepts such as "disorder," "cause," and "cure" than do more traditional ones. The traditional view assumes that each disorder is the result of a single primary cause and that cure involves reversing its direct effect.

This view is one stemming originally from the nineteenth-century study of infectious diseases (Dubos, 1962), but it is not even applicable to these disorders themselves. The threat of the infectious plague that used to sweep over Europe was removed largely through sanitation measures, not vaccines or agents that destroyed germs directly (Dubos, 1962).

Viewed transactionally, although disturbances may arise at one level of an interactive system, their effects depend on the interaction among all levels of the system. These may act to maintain, augment, or diminish the disturbance, as some of the examples cited earlier in the review illustrate. The issue then becomes one not so much of searching for the cure but rather in seeking points of intervention, chosen in terms of the tools and opportunities available, and the potential impact of such interventions.

In some disorders, as in gene-based metabolic disorders such as PKU or galactosemia, psychologists may be able to influence their developmental outcomes. As noted earlier, the consequences of these disorders can be minimized through strict, long term dietary control (Kamrorer & Lee, 1970; Berry, 1979). Here, psychologists may work with the family to develop practical dietary programs and to deal with the problems such restrictive diets entail.

More generally, clinical child psychologists may develop early intervention strategies. For example, they may design and implement programs that provide support and help to parents of growth-retarded infants, who are apt to be difficult and unresponsive, in order to diminish the effects that unresponsive environments play in augmenting the effects of the prenatal insult. In a number of cases, such as some sensory handicaps or cerebral palsy, these interventions can make the difference between normal and retarded functioning. In other cases, such as Down's Syndrome, early intervention may allow handicapped children to develop their cognitive capacities to the fullest and to become more self-reliant and independent.

As the range of above examples suggests, from a transactional perspective biological factors channel, potentiate, and constrain the potential impact of environmental interaction, just as the environment channels, constrains, and potentiates biological factors. In some cases, biological factors may place strong limits on the scope of possible interventions. These constraints do not challenge a transactional perspective—both environment and biological conditions can place severe limits on development when they are extreme—but they do call attention to the fact that transaction is a two-way street. Even where strong biological constraints exist, within a transactional perspective they are limiting cases, not prototypes.

Perhaps one final comment about the direction of future research in this area needs to be made. The development of effective and efficient intervention strategies, and ultimately the test of the transactional perspective itself, depends upon knowledge of how disabilities develop in risk populations and how this development is mediated by environmental interaction. Most of the research to date, however, has not focused on the social or perceptual-cognitive development of high risk and at-risk children, as Kopp and Parmalee (1979) have pointed out. Instead, research has relied chiefly on outcome measures, such as IQ or demographic information such as SES. Such measures may provide clues to cognitive functioning or the effects of environmental interaction, but they are too far removed from these processes to provide the knowledge we need about the nature of specific organism-environment transactions (Wachs, 1972).

What we need are longitudinal investigations, of high risk and at-risk children, that can address such questions directly. Such research (which can also incorporate carefully described remediation procedures) will provide the best basis for both understanding and action.

NOTES

1. In a general sense, much of what we call transaction could more accurately refer to the process of interaction. However, given the fact that the term interaction has a highly specific meaning in genetics, we are using the word transaction to avoid confusion.

2. At present there does not appear to be any consistent evidence for a major gene influence on the production of extremely high levels of intelligence (Anderson, 1974), though this is still clearly an open question.

3. In the present section, we are making an assumption that the behavior disorders described are influenced by polygenes rather than by single genes. Particularly for schizophrenia, this assumption is still very much an open question (Morton et al., 1979). We have made the assumption of polygenic inheritance due to a slightly better fit of the data by current poylgenic models (Hanson et al., 1977).

REFERENCES

Abel, E.L. Fetal alcohol syndrome: Behavioral teratology. *Psychology Bulletin,* 1980, **87,** 29–50. (a)

Abel, E.L. Prenatal exposure to cannabis: A critical review of effects on growth, development, and behavior. *Behavioral and Neural Biology,* 1980, **29,** 137–156. (b)

Alford, C.P., Stagnio, S., & Reynolds, D.W. Perinatal infections caused by viruses, toxoplasma, and treponema pallidum. In S. Aladjem, S.K. Brown & C. Sureau (Eds.), *Clinical Perinatology* (2nd ed.). St. Louis: Mosby, 1980.

Allen, G. Intellectual potential and heredity. *Science,* 1961, **133,** 378–379.

Anderson, L., Dancis, J., Alpert, M., & Herrman, L. Punishment, learning, and self-mutilation in Lesch-Nyhan disease. *Nature,* 1977, **265,** 461–463.

Anderson, V. Discussion of Omenn and Motulsky paper. In L. Ehrman, G. Omenn, & E. Caspari (Eds.), *Genetics, environments, and behavior.* New York: Academic Press, 1972.

Anderson, V. Genetics and intelligence. In J. Wortis (Ed.), *Mental retardation and development disabilities III.* New York: Brunner-Mazel, 1974.

Aronson, M., & Fallstrom, K. Immediate and long term effects of developmental training in children with Downs Syndrome. *Developmental Medicine and Child Neurology,* 1977, **19,** 489–494.

Ashton, G., Polovina, J., & Vandenberg, S. Segregation analysis of family data for IQ tests of cognitive ability. *Behavior Genetics,* 1979, **9,** 329–343.

Aubrey, R.H., Beydoun, S., Cabalum, M.T., & Williams, M.L. Fetal growth retardation. In R.J. Bolognese & R.H. Schwartz (Eds.), *Perinatal medicine,* Baltimore: Williams & Wilkins, 1977.

August, G., & Stewart, M. Autistic spectrum disorder: A genetic study. Paper presented to the Society for Research in Child Development, Boston, April 1981.

Barden, T.P. Prematurity. In R.J. Bolognese & R.H. Schwartz (Eds.), *Perinatal medicine.* Baltimore: Williams & Wilkins, 1977.

Barrow, M.V. A brief history of teratology to the early 20th century. *Teratology,* 1971, **4,** 119–130.

Bashi, J. Effects of inbreeding on cognitive performance. *Nature,* 1977, **266,** 440–442.

Beach, F.A. Human sexuality in four perspectives. In F.A. Beach (Ed.), *Human sexuality in four perspectives.* Baltimore: Johns Hopkins University Press, 1976. (a)

Beach, F.A. Hormonal control of sex-related behavior. In F.A. Beach (Ed.), *Human sexuality in four perspectives.* Baltimore: Johns Hopkins University Press, 1976. (b)

Beaconsfield, P., Birdwood, G., & Beaconsfield, R. The placenta. *Scientific American,* 1980, **243,** 122–138.

Belmont, J. Medical-behavioral research in retardation. In N. Ellis (Ed.), *International review of research in mental retardation V.* New York: Academic Press, 1971.

Berry, H., O'Grady, D., Perlmutter, L., & Bofinger,

M. Intellectual and academic achievement of children treated early for phenylketonuria. *Developmental Medicine and Child Neurology*, 1979, **21**, 311–320.

Bock, R., & Kolakowski, D. Further evidence of sex-linked major gene influences on human spatial visualizing abilities. *American Journal of Human Genetics*, 1973, **25**, 1–14.

Bodmer, W., & Cavalli-Sforza, L. *Genetics, evolution, and men*. San Francisco: Freeman, 1976.

Botelli-Llusia, T. Placental insufficiency syndrome. In S. Aladjem, A.K. Brown, & C. Sureau (Eds.), *Clinical perinatology* (2nd ed.). St. Louis: Mosby, 1980.

Brackbill, Y. Obstetrical medication and infant behavior. In J. Osofsky (Ed.), *Handbook of infant development*. New York: Wiley, 1979.

Broman, S.H. Prenatal anoxia and cognitive development. In T.M. Field, S.M. Sostek, S. Goldberg, & H.H. Shuman (Eds.), *Infants born at risk*. New York: Spectrum, 1979.

Broman, S., & Nichols, P.L. Early mental development, social class, and school age IQ. Paper presented at the Annual Meeting of the American Psychological Association, Chicago, 1975.

Broman, S., Nichols, P., & Kennedy, W. *Preschool IQ: Prenatal and early developmental correlates*. New York: Wiley, 1979.

Brozek, J. Nutrition, malnutrition, and behavior. *Annual Review of Psychology* 1978, **29**, 157–178.

Caldwell, B., Bradley, R., & Elardo, R. Early stimulation. In J. Wortis (Ed.), *Mental retardation and developmental disabilities VII*. New York: Brunner-Mazel, 1975.

Campbell, M., Wolman, S., Breuer, S., Muller, F., & Perlman, B. Klinefelter's Syndrome in a three year old severely disturbed child. *Journal of Autism and Childhood Schizophrenia*, 1972, **2**, 34–48.

Caputo, D.V., Goldstein, K.M., & Taub, H.B. The development of prematurely born children through middle childhood. In T.M. Field, A.M. Sostek, S. Goldberg, & H.H. Shuman (Eds.), *Infants born at risk*. New York: Spectrum, 1979.

Carey, C., Goldsmith, H., Tellegin, A., & Gottesman, I. Genetics and personality inventories. *Behavior Genetics*, 1978, **8**, 299–313.

Carlson, P., & LaBarba, R. Maternal emotionality during pregnancy and reproductive outcome:

A review of the literature. *International Journal of Behavioral Development*. 1979, **2**, 343–377.

Chess, S. Autism in children with congenital rubella. *Journal of Autism and Childhood Schizophrenia*, 1971, **1**, 33–47.

Chess, S. Follow-up report on autism in congenital rubella. *Journal of Autism and Childhood Schizophrenia*, 1977, **7**, 70–81.

Chess, S. The plasticity of human development. *Journal of the American Academy of Child Psychiatry*, 1978, **17**, 80–91.

Chess, S., & Fernandez, P. Do deaf children have a typical personality? *Journal of the American Academy of Child Psychiatry*, 1980, **17**, 654–665.

Chess, S., Fernandez, P., & Korn, S.J. The handicapped child and his family: Consonance and dissonance. *Journal of the American Academy of Child Psychiatry*, 1980, **19**, 56–67.

Chess, S., Korn, S.J., & Fernandez, P. *Psychiatric disorders of children with congenital rubella*. New York: Brunner-Mazel, 1971.

Cohen, D. Competence and biology. In E. Anthony & C. Koupernik (Eds.), *The child in his family IV*. New York: Wiley, 1974.

Cohen, W.R., & Schifrin, B.S. Diagnosis and treatment of fetal distress. In R.J. Bolognese & R.H. Schwartz (Eds.), *Perinatal medicine*. Baltimore: Williams & Wilkins, 1977.

Coleman, M. The autistic syndrome. In J. Wortis (Ed.), *Mental retardation and developmental disabilities X*. New York: Brunner-Mazel, 1978.

DeFries, J. Quantitative aspects of genetics and environment in the determination of behavior. In C. Ehrman, G. Omenn, & E. Caspari (Eds.), *Genetics, environment, and behavior*. New York: Academic Press, 1972.

DeFries, J., Ashton, G., Johnson, R., Kuse, A., McClearn, G., Mu, N., Rashad, N., Vandenberg, S., & Wilson, J. Parent-offspring resemblance for specific cognitive abilities in two ethnic groups. *Nature*, 1976, **261**, 131–133.

Dicks-Mireaux, M. Mental development of infants with Downs Syndrome. *American Journal of Mental Deficiency*, 1972, **77**, 26–32.

Dobbing, J. Prenatal nutrition and neurological development. In J. Cravioto, L. Hambraeus, & B. Vahlquist (Eds.), *Early malnutrition and mental development.* Symposia of the Swedish

Nutrition Foundation (No. XII). Stockholm: Almquist & Wiksell, 1974.

Dobson, J., Koch, R., Williamson, M., Spector, R., Frankenburg, W., O'Flynn, M., Warner, R., & Hudson, F. Cognitive development and dietary therapy in phenylketonuric children. *New England Journal of Medicine*, 1968, **270**, 1142–1144.

Dobson, J., Kushida, E., Williamson, N., & Friedman, E. Intellectual performance of 36 phenylketonuric patients and their nonaffected siblings. *Pediatrics*, 1976, **58**, 53–58.

Dobson, J., Williamson, M., Azen, C., & Koch, R. Intellectual assessment of 111 four year old children with phenylketonuria. *Pediatrics*, 1977, **60**, 822–827.

Dodd, B. Recognition and reproduction of words by Downs Syndrome and non-Downs Syndrome retarded children. *American Journal of Mental Deficiency*, 1975, **80**, 306–311.

Dorner, G. *Hormones and brain differentiation.* Amsterdam: Elsevier, 1976.

Drillien, C.M. The small-for-dates infant: Etiology and prognosis. *Pediatric Clinics of North American*, 1970, **17**, 19-23.

Drillien, C.M. Aetiology and outcome in low-birth-weight infants. *Developmental Medicine and Child Neurology*, 1972, **14**, 563–574.

Dubey, D. Organic factors in hyperkinesis. *American Journal of Orthopsychiatry*, 1976, **46**, 353–366.

Dubos, R. *The mirage of health.* New York: Anchor, 1962.

Dworkin, R., Burke, B., Maher, B., & Gottesman, I. A longitudinal study of the genetics of personality. *Journal of Personality and Social Psychology*, 1976, **34**, 510–518.

Dworkin, R., Burke, B., Maher, B., & Gottesman, I. Genetic influences on the organization and development of personality. *Developmental Psychology*, 1977, **13**, 164–165.

Ehrhardt, A.A. The interactional model of sex hormones and behavior. In H.A. Katchadourian (Ed.), *Human Sexuality.* Berkeley: University of California Press, 1979.

Ehrhardt, A.A., & Meyer-Bahlberg. Psychosexual development: An examination of the role of prenatal hormones. In E.J. Sachar (Ed.), *Sex, hormones, and behaviour.* Ciba Foundation symposium 62 (New Series). New York: Excerpta Medica, 1979.

Erlenmeyer-Kinling, L. Gene-environment inter-

action and the variability of behavior. In L. Ehrman, G. Omenn, & I. Caspari (Eds.), *Genetics, environment, and behavior.* New York: Academic Press, 1972.

Eshkevan, H. Early infantile autism in two twins. *Journal of Autism and Developmental Disorders*, 1979, **9**, 101–109.

Esteban-Altirriba, L., Cabero, L., & Calaf, J. Correction of fetal homeostatic disturbances. In S. Aladjem, S.K. Brown, & C. Sureau (Eds.), *Clinical perinatology* (2nd ed.). St. Louis: Mosby, 1980.

Evans, M.P., Stevens, B., Mantilla-Plata, J., & Harbison, R.D. Drugs of abuse: Teratogenic and mutagenic considerations. In R.D. Harbison (Ed.), *Perinatal addiction.* New York: Spectrum, 1975.

Feldman, M., & Lewontin, R. The heritability hang-up. *Science*, 1975, **190**, 1163–1168.

Ferreira, S.J. *Prenatal environment.* Springfield, Ill.: Thomas, 1969.

Field, T.M. Interaction patterns of preterm and term infants. In T.M. Field, A.M. Sostek, S. Goldberg, & H.H. Shuman (Eds.), *Infants born at risk.* New York: Spectrum, 1979.

Fishler, K., Donnell, G., Bergren, W., & Koch, R. Intellectual and personality development in children with galactosemia. *Pediatrics*, 1972, **50**, 412–419.

Fishler, K., Koch, R., & Donnell, G. Comparison of mental development in individuals with mosaic and trisomy 21 Downs Syndrome. *Pediatrics*, 1976, **58**, 744–748.

Fitzhardinge, P., & Ramsay, M. The improving outlook for the prematurely born infant. *Developmental Medicine and Child Neurology*, 1973, **15**, 447–459.

Fitzhardinge, P.M., & Steven, E.M. The small-for-date infant. I: Later growth patterns. *Pediatrics*, 1972, **16**, 180–185. (a)

Fitzhardinge, P.M., & Steven, E.M. The small-for-date infant II: Neurological and intellectual sequelae. *Pediatrics*, 1972, **50**, 50–57. (b)

Folstein, S., & Rutter, M. Infantile autism: A genetic study of 21 twin pairs. *Journal of Child Psychology and Psychiatry*, 1977, **18**, 297–321.

Fraser, F.C. Interactions and multiple causes. In J.G. Wilson & F.C. Fraser (Eds.), *Handbook of teratology* (Vol. 1). New York: Plenum, 1977.

Garron, D. Sex-linked recessive inheritance of spatial-numerical abilities and Turner's Syndrome. *Psychological Review,* 1970, **77,** 147–152.

Gluck, L., Warshaw, D.C., Abramson, K., & Benirschke, K. Fetal and placental physiology and biochemistry: Present and future. In R.L. Brent & M.I. Harris (Eds.), *Prevention of embryonic, fetal, and perinatal disease.* Bethesda, Md.: National Institutes of Health, DHEW Publication No. (NIH) 76–853, 1977.

Gibson, D. Karyotype variation and behavior in Downs Syndrome. *American Journal of Mental Deficiency,* 1973, **78,** 128–133.

Goldsmith, H., & Gottesman, I. Origins of variation in behavioral style: A longitudinal study of temperament in young twins. *Child Development,* 1981, **52,** 91–103.

Gottesman, I., & Heston, L. Human behavioral adaptations: Speculation on their genesis. In L. Ehrman, G. Omenn, & E. Caspari (Eds.), *Genetics, environment, and behavior.* New York: Academic Press, 1972.

Gottesman, I., & Shields, J. *Schizophrenia and genetics.* New York: Academic Press, 1972.

Gottesman, I., & Shields, J. A critical review of recent adoption, twin, and family studies of schizophrenia. *Schizophrenia Bulletin,* 1976, **2,** 360–402.

Gottfried, A.W. Intellectual consequences of perinatal anoxia. *Psychological Bulletin,* 1973, **80,** 321–242.

Gottlieb, G. Conceptions of prenatal development: Behavioral embryology. *Psychological Review,* 1976, **83,** 215–234.

Grottevant, H., Scarr, S., & Weinberg, R. Patterns of interest similarity in adoptive and biological families. *Journal of Personality and Social Psychology,* 1977, **35,** 667–676.

Grunewald, P. Chronic fetal distress and placental insufficiency. *Biologia Neuratorum,* 1963, **5,** 215–265.

Haas, J.D. Nutrition during pregnancy. *Science,* 1981, **212,** 804–805.

Hagberg, B. Pre-, peri-, and postnatal prevention of major neuropediatric handicaps. *Neuropaediatrie,* 1975, **6,** 331–338.

Hamilton, J., Stephens, L., & Allen, P. Controlling aggressive and destructive behavior in severely retarded institutionalized residents. In D. Gibson & R. Brown (Eds.), *Managing the severely retarded.* Springfield, Ill.: Thomas, 1976.

Hansen, H., Belmont, L., & Stein, Z. Epidemiology. In J. Wortis (Ed.), *Mental retardation and developmental disabilities XI.* New York: Brunner-Mazel, 1980.

Hanson, D., & Gottesman, I. The genetics, if any, of infantile autism and childhood schizophrenia. *Journal of Autism and Childhood Schizophrenia,* 1976, **6,** 209–233.

Hanson, D., Gottesman, I., & Meehl, P. Genetic theories and the validation of psychiatric diagnosis: Implications for the study of children of schizophrenics. *Journal of Abnormal Psychology,* 1977, **86,** 575–588.

Hayden, A., & Dmitriev, V. The multidisciplinary preschool program for Down's Syndrome children at the University of Washington Model Preschool Center. In B. Friedlander, G. Sterritt, & G. Kirk (Eds.), *Exceptional infant 3.* New York: Brunner-Mazel, 1975.

Haywood, H.C., & Wachs, T.D. Intelligence, cognition, and individual differences. In M. Begab, H.C. Haywood, & H. Garber (Eds.), *Psychosocial influences in retarded performance I.* Baltimore: University Park Press, 1981.

Ho, H., Foch, T., & Plomin, R. Developmental stability of the relative influence of genes and environment on specific cognitive abilites during childhood. *Developmental Psychology,* 1980, **16,** 340–346.

Horn, J., Loehlin, J., & Willerman, L. Intellectual resemblance among adoptive and biological relatives. *Behavior Genetics,* 1979, **9,** 177–201.

Howell, R., & Stevenson, P. The offspring of phenylketonuric women. *Journal of Biology Supplement,* 1971, **18,** 519–529.

Hunt, J.V. Environmental risk in fetal and neonatal life and measured infant intelligence. In M. Lewis (Ed.), *Origins of intelligence.* New York: Plenum, 1976.

Hunt, J. McV. Psychological development: Early experience. *Annual Review of Psychology,* 1979, **80,** 103–144.

Imperato-McGinley, J. Guerrero, L., Gautier, J., & Peterson, R.E. Steroid 5-reductase in man: An inherited form of male pseudohermaphroditism. *Science,* 1974, **186,** 1213–1215.

Joffe, J.M. *Prenatal determinants of behavior.* Oxford: Pergamon, 1969.

Johnson, L., Koch, R., Peterson, R., & Friedman, E. Congenital and neurological abnormalities in infants with phenylketonuria. *American*

Journal of Mental Deficiency, 1978, **82,** 375–379.

Jones, K.L., & Smith, D.W. Recognition of the fetal alcohol syndrome in early infancy. *The Lancet,* 1973, **2,** 999–1001.

Kamin, L. Comment on Munsinger's adoption studies. *Psychological Bulletin,* 1978, **81,** 194–201.

Kamin, L. Inbreeding, depression, and IQ. *Psychological Bulletin,* 1980, **87,** 469–478.

Kamrower, G., & Lee, D. Long term follow-up of galactosemia. *Archives of Disease in Childhood,* 1970, **45,** 367–373.

Katz, K. Inherited disorders. In P. Magrab (Ed.), *Psychological management of pediatric problems I.* Baltimore: University Park Press, 1978.

Koch, R., Acosta, P., & Dobson, J. Two metabolic factors in causation. In R. Koch & J. Dobson (Eds.), *The mentally retarded child and his family.* New York: Brunner-Mazel, 1971.

Koch, R., & De La Cruz, F. *Down's Syndrome.* New York: Brunner-Mazel, 1975.

Kopp, C.B., & Parmalee, S.H. Prenatal and perinatal influences on infant behavior. In J. Osofsky (Ed.), *Handbook of infant development.* New York: Wiley, 1979.

Laroche, J.C., Amiel-Tison, C., & Dreyfus-Brisac, V. Fetal and neonatal brain. In S. Aladjem, A.K. Brown, & C. Sureau (Eds.), *Clinical perinatology,* (2nd ed.). St. Louis: Mosby, 1980.

Lefkowitz, M.M. Smoking during pregnancy: Long-term effects on offspring. *Developmental Psychology,* 1981, **17,** 192–194.

Lester, B.M. The consequences of infantile malnutrition. In H.E. Fitzgerald & J.P. McKinney (Eds.), *Developmental psychology: Studies in human development* (Rev. ed.). Homewood, Ill.: Dorsey, 1976.

Lester, B.M. A synergistic process approach to the study of prenatal malnutrition. *International Journal of Behavioral Development,* 1979, **2,** 377–395.

Linn, R. Unsquared genetic correlations. *Psychological Bulletin,* 1974, **81,** 203–206.

Loehlin, J., & Nichols, P. *Heredity, environment, and personality.* Austin: University of Texas Press, 1976.

Lubchenko, L.O. *The high risk infant.* Philadelphia: Saunders, 1976.

Lubchenko, L.O., Hansman, C., Bresser, M., &

Boyd, E. Intrauterine growth as estimates from live born birth data at 24–42 weeks of gestation. *Pediatrics,* 1963, **32,** 793.

Lytton, H. Do parents create or respond to differences in twins? *Developmental Psychology,* 1977, **13,** 456–459.

Lytton, H., Conway, D., & Sauve, R. The impact of twinship on parent-child interaction. *Journal of Personality and Social Psychology,* 1977, **35,** 97–107.

Lytton, H., Martin, N., & Eaves, C. Environmental and genetical causes of variation in ethological aspects of behavior in two year old boys. *Social Biology,* 1977, **24,** 200–211.

Macready, R., & Levy, H. The problem of maternal phenylketonuria. *American Journal of Obstetrics and Gynecology,* 1972, **113,** 113, 121–128.

Matheney, A., & Dolan, A. Persons, situations, and time: A genetic view of behavioral change in children. *Journal of Personality and Social Psychology,* 1975, **32,** 1106–1110.

McAskie, M., & Clarke, A. Parent-offspring resemblance in intelligence: Theories and evidence. *British Journal of Psychology,* 1976, **67,** 243–273.

McGee, M. Human spatial abilities. *Psychological Bulletin,* 1979, **86,** 889–918.

McClearn, G. Genetic influences on behavior and development. In P. Mussen, (Ed.), *Carmichael's manual of child psychology.* New York: Wiley, 1970.

Melnick, M., Myrcanthopoulos, N., & Christian, J. The effects of chorion type on variation in IQ in the NCPP twin population. *American Journal of Human Genetics,* 1978, **30,** 420–433.

Meyer-Bahlberg, H.F.L. Homosexual orientation in women and men: A hormonal basis? In J.E. Parsons (Ed.), *The psychobiology of sex differences and sex roles.* Washington, D.C.: Hemisphere, 1980.

Money, J. Nativism versus culturalism in gender-identity differentiation. In E. Adelson (Ed.), *Sexuality and psychoanalysis.* New York: Brunner-Mazel, 1975.

Money, J., & Ehrhardt, A.S. *Man and woman, boy and girl: The differentiation and dimorphism from conception to maturity.* Baltimore: Johns Hopkins University Press, 1972.

Morrison, J., & Stewart, M. A family study of the hyperactive child syndrome. *Biological Psychiatry,* 1971, **3,** 189–195.

Morrison, J., & Stewart, M. The psychiatric status of the legal families of hyperactive adopted children. *Archives of General Psychiatry,* 1973, **28,** 888–891.

Morrison, J., & Stewart, M. Bilateral inheritance as evidence for polygenicity in the hyperactive child syndrome. *Journal of Nervous and Mental Diseases,* 1974, **158,** 226–228.

Morton, L., Kidd, K., Matthysse, S., & Richards, P. Recurrence rates in schizophrenia. *Behavior Genetics,* 1979, **9,** 389–406.

Munsinger, H. The adopted child's IQ: A critical review. *Psychological Bulletin,* 1975, **82,** 623–659.

Niswander, K.R., & Gordon, M. (Eds.). *The collaborative perinatal study of the National Institute of Neurological Diseases and Stroke: The women and their pregnancies.* Philadelphia: Saunders, 1972.

Nyborg, H., & Nielson, J. Sex chromosome abnormalities and cognitive performance. *Journal of Psychology,* 1977, **96,** 205–211.

Nyhan, W. Behavior in the Lesch-Nyhan Syndrome. *Journal of Autism and Childhood Schizophrenia,* 1976, **6,** 235–252.

Oppenheimer, S.B. *Introduction to embryonic development.* Boston: Allyn & Bacon, 1980.

Partington, M., & Laverty, T. Long term studies of untreated phenylketonuria I. *Neuropediatric,* 1978, **9,** 245–254.

Pasamanick, B., & Knobloch, H. Epidemiological studies on the complications of pregnancy and the birth process. In G. Caplan (Ed.), *Prevention of mental disorders in children.* New York: Basic Books, 1961.

Pasamanick, B., & Knobloch, H. Retrospective studies on the epidemiology of reproductive casualty: Old and new. *Merrill-Palmer Quarterly,* 1966, **12,** 7–26.

Peterson, A.C. Hormones and cognitive functioning in normal development. In M.P. Wittig & A.C. Peterson (Eds.), *Sex-related differences in cognitive functioning.* New York: Academic Press, 1979.

Phoenix, C.H. Prenatal testerone in the nonhuman primate and its consequences for behavior. In R.C. Friedman, R.M. Richart, & R.L. Van de Wiele (Eds.), *Sex differences in behavior.* New York: Wiley, 1974.

Piper, M., & Ramsay, M. Effects of early home environment on the mental development of Down's Syndrome infants. *American Journal of Mental Deficiency,* 1980, **85,** 39–44.

Pitts, D. The natural history of untreated phenylketonuria. *Medical Journal of Australia,* 1971, **1,** 378–383.

Plomin, R. A twin and family study of personality in young children. *Journal of Psychology,* 1976, **94,** 233–235.

Plomin, R., DeFries, J., & Loehlin, J. Genotype-environment interaction and correlation in the analysis of human behavior. *Psychological Bulletin,* 1977, **84,** 309–322.

Plomin, R., & Rowe, D. A twin study of temperament in young children. *Journal of Psychology,* 1977, **97,** 107–113.

Plomin, R., & Rowe, D. Genetic and environmental etiology of social behavior in infancy. *Developmental Psychology,* 1979, **15,** 62–72.

Plomin, R., & Willerman, L. A co-twin-control study and a twin study of reflection-impulsivity in children. *Journal of Education Psychology,* 1975, **67,** 537–543.

Plomin, R., Willerman, L., & Loehlin, J. Resemblance in appearance and the equal environment assumption in twin studies of personality traits. *Behavior Genetics,* 1976, **6,** 43–52.

Reed, E. Genetic anomalies in development. In F. Horowitz (Ed.), *Review of child development research IV.* Chicago: University of Chicago Press, 1975.

Reinisch, J.M. Prenatal exposure of human foetuses to synthetic progestin and oestrogen affects personality. *Nature,* 1977, **266,** 561–562.

Reinisch, J.M., Gandelman, R., & Spiegel, F.S. Prenatal influences on cognitive abilities: Data from experimental animals and human and endocrine syndromes. In M.A. Wittig & A.C. Peterson (Eds.), *Sex-related differences in cognitive functioning.* New York: Academic Press, 1979.

Rose, P., Harris, E., Christian, T., & Nance, W. Genetic variance in nonverbal intelligence. *Science,* 1979, **205,** 1153–1154.

Rosenberg, L. A geneticist's approach to the vulnerable child. In E.J. Anthony & K. Koupernik (Eds.), *The child and his family III.* New York: Wiley, 1974.

Rubenstein, J. Congenital malformations. In J. Wortis (Ed.), *Mental retardation and developmental disabilities XI.* New York: Brunner-Mazel, 1980.

Rush, D. Cigarette smoking during pregnancy: The relationship with depressed weight gain and birthweight. An updated report. In S.

Kelly, E.B. Hook, D.T. Janerick, & I.H. Porter (Eds.), *Birth defects, risks, and consequences.* New York: Academic Press, 1976.

Rush, D., Stein, Z., & Susser, M. *Diet in pregnancy: A randomized controlled trial of nutritional supplements.* New York: Liss, 1980.

Rutter, M., & Bartak, L. Causes of infantile autism. *Journal of Autism and Childhood Schizophrenia,* 1971, **1,** 20–32.

Sachar, E.J. (Ed.), *Sex, hormones, and behaviour.* Ciba Foundation Symposium 62 (New Series). New York: Excerpta Medica, 1979.

Sameroff, A., & Chandler, M. Reproductive risk and the continuum of caretaking casualty. In F.D. Horowitz, M. Heatherington, S. Scarr-Salapatek, & G. Siegel (Eds.), *Review of child development research* (Vol. 4). Chicago: University of Chicago Press, 1975.

Scarr-Salapatek, S. Genetic determinants of infant development: An overstated case. In L. Lipsitt (Ed.), *Developmental psychobiology.* Hillsdale, N.J.: Erlbaum, 1976.

Scarr, S., & Carter-Saltzman, L. Twin method: Defense of a critical assumption. *Behavior Genetics,* 1979, **9,** 527–542.

Scarr, S., & Weinberg, R. IQ test performance of black children adopted by white families. *American Psychologists,* 1976, **31,** 726–739.

Scarr-Salapatek, S. Genetics and the development of intelligence. In F.D. Horowitz (Ed.), *Review of child development research IV.* Chicago: University of Chicago Press, 1975.

Schiff, M., Duyme, M., Dumaret, A., Stewart, J., Tomkiewicz, S., & Feingold, J. Intellectual status of working class families adopted early into upper middle class families. *Science,* 1978, **200,** 1503–1504.

Schull, W., & Neel, J. *The effects of inbreeding on Japanese children.* New York: Harper & Row, 1965.

Schulsinger, F. Biological psychopathology. *Annual Review of Psychology,* 1980, **31,** 583–606.

Shanklin, D., & Hodin, J. *Maternal nutrition and child health.* Springfield, Ill.: Thomas, 1979.

Share, J. Developmental progress in Downs Syndrome. In R. Koch & F. De La Cruz (Eds.), *Downs Syndrome: Research, prevention and management.* New York: Bruner-Mazel, 1975.

Snyderman, S. Metabolism. In J. Wortis (Ed.), *Mental retardation and developmental disabilities VIII.* New York: Brunner-Mazel, 1975.

Sostek, S.M., Quinn, P.O., & Davitt, M.K.

Behavior, development, and neurological status of premature and full-term infants with varying medical complications. In T.M. Field, S.M. Sostek, S. Goldberg, & H.H. Shuman (Eds.), *Infants born at risk.* New York: Spectrum, 1979.

Stafford, R. Sex differences in spatial visualization as evidence of sex-linked inheritance. *Perceptual Motor Skills,* 1961, **13,** 428.

Stedman, D., & Eichorn, D. A comparison of the growth and development of institutionalized and home-reared mongoloids during infancy and early childhood. *American Journal of Mental Deficiency,* 1964, **69,** 391–401.

Stein, Z., Susser, M., Saengar, G., & Moralla, F. Nutrition and mental performance. *Science,* 1972, **178,** 708.

Stockard, C.R. Developmental rate and structural expression: An experimental study of twins, "double monsters," and single deformities and the interaction among embryonic organs during their origin and development. *American Journal of Anatomy,* 1921, **28,** 115–227.

Torgerson, A., & Kringlen, E. Genetic aspects of temperamental differences in infants. *Journal of the American Academy of Child Psychiatry,* 1978, **17,** 433–444.

Trunca, C. The chromosome syndromes. In J. Wortis (Ed.), *Mental retardation and developmental disabilities XI.* New York: Brunner-Mazel, 1980.

U.S. Department of Health, Education and Welfare. *Smoking and health: A report of the Surgeon General.* Washington, D.C.: DHEW Publication No. (PHS) 79-5066, 1979.

Vandenberg, S. The nature and nurture of intelligence. In D. Glass (Ed.), *Genetics.* New York: Rockefeller University Press, 1968.

Vorhees, C.V., Brunner, R.L., & Butcher, R.E. Psychotropic drugs as behavioral teratogens. *Science,* 1979, **205,** 1220–1225.

Wachs, T.D. Similarity in developmental profiles among related pairs of human infants. *Science,* 1972, **178,** 1005–1006.

Wachs, T.D., & Mariotto, M. Criteria for the assessment of organism environment correlation in human developmental studies. *Human Development,* 1978, **21,** 268–288.

Wahl, O. Monozygotic twins discordant for schizophrenia: A review. *Psychological Bulletin,* 1976, **83,** 91–106.

Walzer, S., Wolff, P., Bowen, D., Gilbert, A.,

Bashir, A., Gerald, P., & Richmond, J. A method for the longitudinal study of behavioral development of infants and children: The early development of XXY children. *Journal of Child Psychology and Psychiatry*, 1978, **19**, 213–229.

Wapner, R., Moak, S., & Lifshitz, F. Decreased foetal amino acid uptake, brain pyruvate, and intrauterine damage in maternal PKU. *Nature*, 1977, **265**, 647–649.

Weizmann, F. Correlational statistics and the nature-nuture problem. *Science*, 1971, **171**, 589.

Werner, E., Bierman, J., & French, F. *The children of Kauai: A longitudinal study from the prenatal period to age ten.* Honolulu: University of Hawaii Press, 1971.

Williams, T. Family resemblance in intelligence: The Wechsler scale. *Behavior Genetics*, 1975, **5**, 405–409.

Williams, T. Infant development and supplemental care. *Human Development*, 1977, **20**, 1–30.

Wilson, J.G. Current status of teratology—General principles and mechanisms derived from animal studies. In J.G. Wilson & F.C. Fraser (Eds.), *Handbook of teratology* (Vol. 1). New York: Plenum, 1977. (b)

Wilson, J.G. Embryotoxicity of drugs in man. In J.G. Wilson & F.C. Fraser (Eds.), *Handbook of teratology* (Vol. 1). New York: Plenum, 1977. (b)

Wilson, J.G. Environmental chemicals. In J.G. Wilson & F.C. Fraser (Eds.), *Handbook of teratology* (Vol. 1). New York: Plenum, 1977. (c)

Wilson, R. Twins and siblings: Concordance for school age mental development. *Child Development*, 1977, **48**, 211–216.

Wilson, R. Synchronies in mental development. *Science*, 1978, **202**, 939–948.

Winick, M. Maternal nutrition. In R. Brent & M. Harris (Eds.), *Prevention of embryonic, fetal, and perinatal disease.* Bethesda, Md.: National Institute of Health, DHEW Publication No. (NIH) 76-853, 1977.

Witkin, H., Mednick, S., Schulsinger, F., Bakke-strom, E., Christiansen, K., Goodenough, D., Hirschhorn, K., Lundsteen, C., Owen, D., Phillips, J., Rubin, D., & Stocking, M. Criminality in XYY and XXY men. *Science*, 1976, **193**, 547–555.

Wittig, M.A., & Peterson, S.C. (Eds.), *Sex-related differences in cognitive functioning.* New York: Academic Press, 1979.

Worland, J., Landes, H., & Hesselbrock, V. Psychological evaluation of clinical disturbances in children at risk for psychopathology. *Journal of Abnormal Psychology*, 1979, **88**, 13–26.

Yerushalmy, J. Statistical considerations and evaluations of epidemiological evidence. In G. James & T. Rosenthal (Eds.), *Tobacco and health.* Springfield, Ill.: Thomas, 1962.

Yerushalmy, J. Mother's cigarette smoking and survival of infant. *American Journal of Obstetrics and Gynecology*, 1964, **88**, 501–518.

Yerushalmy, J. The relationship of parents' smoking to outcome of pregnancy: Implications as to the problem of inferring causation from observed effects. *American Journal of Epidemiology*, 1971, **93**, 443–456.

Yerushalmy, J. Infants with low birthweight born before their mothers started to smoke cigarettes. *American Journal of Obstetrics and Gynecology*, 1972, **112**, 277–284.

Young, W., Goy, R., & Phoenix, C. Hormones and sexual behavior. *Science*, 1964, **143**, 212–218.

Zeskind, P.S., & Ramey, C.T. Fetal malnutrition: An experimental study of its consequences on infant development in two care-giving environments. *Child Development*, 1978, **49**, 1158–1162.

Zeskind, P.S., & Ramey, C.T. Preventing intellectual and interactional sequelae of fetal malnutrition: A longitudinal transactional and synergistic approach to development. *Child Development*, 1981, **52**, 213–218.

Zubin, J., & Spring, B. Vulnerability: A new view of schizophrenia. *Journal of Abnormal Psychology*, 1977, **86**, 103–126.

Zuger, B. Gender role differentiation: A critical review of the evidence from hermaphroditism. *Psychosomatic Medicine*, 1970, **32**, 449–463.

CHAPTER 12

Clinical Problems of Birth, the Neonate, and Infant

PHYLLIS R. MAGRAB AND ANITA MILLER SOSTEK

While the birth of a normal newborn presents demands on the organization of any family, infants born with medical or developmental problems require additional services and supports. Many of the needs of their families are similar, regardless of the nature of the infants' problems. Some problems are identifiable at birth, others during infancy. After briefly reviewing the most common neonatal difficulties and their implications, we will discuss other psychological problems that emerge during the period of infancy. Both the needs of the child and of the family will be considered.

PROBLEMS OF THE NEONATE

The most prevalent condition that puts an infant at risk for mortality and morbidity and that also requires mother-infant separation is preterm birth. Prematurity is defined as birth before term or 37-weeks gestation. Typically, preterm infants weigh less than 5 pounds. However, birth weight alone cannot be used as a criterion for shortened gestation because intrauterine growth retardation can produce infants as small as 3 or 4 pounds at full term. Prematurity can be caused by obstetric difficulties, maternal health factors, placental abnormalities, or fetal problems.

Preterm births account for 10 percent of white infants and 20 percent of black infants, with increasing risk at lower socioeconomic levels. Not many years ago, it was felt that infants could not survive if they were born before the seventh month (27–31 weeks) or

weighed less than 2 pounds (Babson & Benson, 1971). Because of continuing advances in obstetrical and pediatric practices, in 1980 approximately 30 percent of infants between 1 and 1½ pounds and 70 percent of infants between 1½ and 2 pounds survived.

The current medical philosophy of aggressive care for preterm infants contrasts sharply with the practice 20 or more years ago of leaving them warm, but without special respiratory support, for the first 24 hours, and then treating them only if they survived that period. This change is attributable in large part to improvements in respiratory, nutritional, and other medical techniques; the growing knowledge about their applications; and appreciation of our ignorance about the lower limits of viability or survival. Even with improved care, however, the preterm infant was born too soon and too small to sustain life independently. The baby was not yet meant to be breathing, digesting, and regulating body temperature on his or her own.

Several aspects of physical functioning may jeopardize the infant's brain development. First or foremost, immaturity of the lungs frequently causes respiratory distress and reduced oxygenation of the brain and body organs. Preterm infants have difficulties regulating breathing rate as well as efficiency, and they tend to have episodes of apnea or pauses in respiration. Adequate nutrition is problematic because the intestines are often too immature to absorb nutrients and the sucking reflex is weak or absent before the eighth or ninth month of gestation. Temperature regulation is ineffective in the preterm infant because the amount of fat under the skin is too limited to maintain warmth. Finally, the immaturity of various metabolic and organ systems may lead to problems that can impede brain functioning or development. The most devastating damage to the central nervous system of the preterm infant is hemorrhage into the ventricles of the brain (Volpe, 1980). Intraventricular hemorrhage results from trauma at delivery or poor oxygenation of the brain as a consequence of asphyxia or respiratory distress. The major consequences of the hemorrhage are direct damage to parts of the brain and/or a buildup of fluid pressure from the hydrocephalus that can result.

While preterm infants are clearly at greater risk for long term developmental and/or neurological problems than are normal full terms (Caputo & Mandell, 1970), after a period of catch-up, the majority function within the normal range without any serious difficulties. Assessing risk for any individual poses a number of problems. First, rapidly changing technology and understanding of many neonatal disorders has affected treatment to the extent that published studies from ten years ago may not reflect current risk. Second, risk tends to be multiplicative, with problems clustering in the most compromised infants (e.g., the 1,000 g infant is more likely to have severe respiratory distress with complications than is the 2,000 g infant).

Several studies have examined particular aspects of prematurity that might contribute to the risk status of individual infants (Fisch et al., 1975; Fitzhardinge, 1980; Fitzhardinge et al., 1976; Marriage & Davies, 1977). The factors associated with the highest risk are severe asphyxia reflected by 5-minute Apgar scores of 0–3, meningitis, severe intrauterine growth retardation indicative of prenatal asphyxia, intraventricular hemorrhage, and gestation less than 28 weeks.

Behaviorally, preterm infants have been described as more difficult in temperament than fullterms of similar background (Field et al., 1978). They are less rewarding initially because it takes them longer to show alerting, to regulate their sleep-waking patterns, and to respond socially. It is difficult for the parents of preterm infants to know what to expect of them because their development is often variable with transient abnormalities, prolonged delays, and uneven spurts of progress. The popular literature on childrearing provides little help although books for parents of preterms are beginning to appear (Brazelton, 1981; Nance, 1982).

Even with normal development, parents of preterms have to wait for longer than usual to see progress in their infants. Through the first months, their interactive abilities are limited as well. Field (1979) found high risk infants at 4 months old to be less attentive, more fussy, and more restless during face-to-face interactions. In feedings, face-to-face play, or object play, the adult partner appears to exert more effort with preterms than with fullterms (DiVitto & Goldberg, 1979). All these factors probably contribute to the fact that preterms are at higher risk for child abuse (Klein & Stern, 1971). Early separation of mother and infant necessitated by the special care hospitalization of the preterm may also interfere with early attachment and make it more difficult for parents to tolerate the periods of trying behavior common to all infants (Klaus & Kennell, 1976).

Postmaturity

Approximately 3 percent of infants are born after 42 weeks gestation. In some of these cases, pregnancy is accompanied by placental aging or dysfunction which deprives the fetus of adequate nutrients and oxygenation. Placental insufficiency is particularly risky during labor and delivery because the stress of contractions further diminishes the oxygen received by the fetus. Increased chances of asphyxiation at the time of birth almost double the mortality rate of postmature infants (Babson & Benson, 1971). Those infants who have experienced chronic placental insufficiency for some weeks after their expected dates of birth typically have the characteristic appearance of postmaturity which Clifford (1954) describes as dry, parchmentlike skin, a long, thin body, and a wizened appearance.

They may also be more alert and hungry than the average fullterm.

The risk status of postmatures without asphyxiation is far less pronounced than that of preterms. In comparison to fullterms, they show higher risks of developmental and neurological problems, and their temperament in infancy tends to be more difficult (Field et al., 1977).

Intrauterine Growth Retardation

Birthweight and gestational age do not correspond invariably, Intrauterine growth retardation can be diagnosed at any gestational age when birthweight is less than the tenth percentile for the infant's stage of maturation. Growth retardation can be caused by prenatal infection, extremely poor nutrition, substance abuse, or placental insufficiency. When intrauterine growth retardation is accompanied by adequate head growth in relation to body size, outcome tends to be favorable. Compared to appropriate-sized preterms, infants who were small-for-dates had approximately the same rate of neurological abnormalities at each gestation age (Drillien, 1967; Lubchenco, 1974). Fitzhardinge and Steven's (1972) study of small-for-date infants also showed similar incidences of minimal brain dysfunction in varying sized groups at different gestational ages.

Congenital Malformations

Genetic Disorders

Congenital malformations can be grossly categorized as deriving from these sources: genetics, teratogens, or unknown causes. There are numerous known genetic syndromes, but most are rare and do not correspond to identifiable chromosomal abnormalities. The most common disorders that do correspond to chromosomal abnormalities include Trisomy 21 (Down's syndrome), Trisomy 13 (Trisomy E), Trisomy 18 (Trisomy D), and the sex chromosome disorders of Turner's syndrome and Klinefelter's syndrome. Increasing maternal age has been implicated in Down's syndrome

and Trisomy 18 but appears unrelated to the other abnormalities.

Although Turner's and Klinefelter's syndromes produce characteristic physical and cognitive features and may have implications for fertility, functioning in most areas is typically normal. These patients tend to require emotional support and education about their problem rather than remedial therapies and occupational assistance (see Wachs & Weizmann, chap. 11 of this book).

Infants with Trisomy 13 or 18, as well as some of the more unusual chromosomal aberrations, have life expectancies of less than one year. From the standpoint of the infant, therefore, the needs are basically for medical care and comfort. Trisomy 21 is associated with unusual facies, cardiac abnormalities, hypotonia, and mental retardation. The hypotonicity creates further difficulties for motor development, and milestones after 6 months of age are delayed (Carr, 1970; Share, 1975). Outcome in Down's syndrome depends on institutional versus home placement and may relate to parental intelligence (Katz, 1978). The majority of home-reared Down's syndrome children fall into the moderately retarded range with some performing at mildly retarded to borderline levels.

Informing parents of the diagnosis of Down's syndrome is recommended as early as possible (Gayton & Walker, 1974). If a definite diagnosis requires chromosomal analysis, the physician's suspicions should be related at once (Pueschel & Murphy, 1975). Parents should be made to understand that the child will develop in a normal sequence although more slowly and with lower limits of capabilities than other children. Difficulties with predicting the range of functioning of Down's syndrome children and the benefits of a nurturant, stimulating environment should be discussed. The positive features of emotional rewards and available support services in the areas of assessment, stimulation, and counseling should also be emphasized.

Effects of Teratogens

Any agent or factor that produces physical defects in the embryo or fetus is called a teratogen, and this category includes chemical agents including prescribed and over-the-counter medications, substance abuse, maternal illness, radiation, and environmental factors such as altitude and pollutants. The period of maximal vulnerability occurs during the embryonic stage from the fourth to twelfth weeks of pregnancy when all major organ systems are forming. The effects of teratogens range from fetal death to physical defects in the central nervous system, sense organs, limb, or heart, to functional defects of various organ systems and/or intrauterine growth retardation (Vaughan & McKay, 1975).

Substance abuse of nicotine, addictive drugs, or alcohol also produces physical and behavioral abnormalities (Harbison, 1975). Smoking has been associated with intrauterine growth retardation and obstetrical complications. Heroin or morphine addiction in the mother produces addicted newborns who have to withdraw after birth and risk seizure disorders. Recently, fetal alcohol syndrome has been identified in the offspring of alcoholic women. The major features are head and face deformities; limb, joint, and heart abnormalities; growth retardation; poor fine motor coordination; and developmental delay. In some cases, the newborn has difficulty breathing, and heart murmur is noted. Head size tends to be small, and birth length is limited. Frequently, poor growth continues into infancy and childhood even if the child is in foster care (Jones, 1975). Mental retardation typically results with mean IQ scores in the low 80s.

Clearly, there is enormous potential for guilt in any parent whose infant is malformed as a result of a teratogen. Although it may not be possible to be certain of the etiology of a malformation, suspicion may be strong, particularly in cases of substance abuse. Where the mother could not avoid the agent, such as a virus or systemic illness, adjustment would be expected to be easier. If medications were essential to the mother's health and continuation of the pregnancy, one would hope the parents received enough information during the pregnancy as to risks and benefits to have made an informed decision about treatment.

Malformations of Unknown Origin

Many malformations have no identifiable cause. Among other problems, these include dysmorphic syndromes with no apparent chromosomal basis and the neural tube defects of spina bifida, myelomeningocele, hydrocephaly, microcephaly, and anencephaly. Anencephaly is the lack of a cerebral cortex and is incompatible with long term survival. Microcephaly refers to a cerebral cortex reduced in size and is associated with serious mental retardation and neurological abnormalities. Microcephalic infants should receive periodic developmental assessments to determine rate of progress and potential skills. Physical and/or occupational therapy is typically advised and intervention is often necessary to develop feeding skills and coordination. Parents generally require extensive supports both emotionally and for the physical maintenance of the child, and at times long term or respite institutional care is advised.

Spina bifida and myelomeningocele are lesions of the spinal cord which produce paralysis of the lower limbs. The specific extent of the paralysis depends on the specific location of the lesion (Brocklehurst, 1976). A lesion high in the spinal column involves a greater portion of the lower body than a lesion located at the lower level of the spine. In the higher lesions, bowel and bladder control are usually affected. Repair of the spinal lesion typically causes increased fluid pressure on the brain (or hydrocephalus), which often remains a long term management problem. Although gross motor development in the lower limbs is obviously impaired as a result of the spinal lesion, intelligence can be normal if the hydrocephalus is controlled.

Needs of the Infant

In addition to basic medical care, infants with neonatal difficulties associated with poor outcome or early diseases with developmental implications (such as meningitis) require periodic developmental follow-up and possible therapeutic intervention. Customarily, infants are seen at 3- or 4-month intervals through the first year and yearly thereafter (Field et al.,

1979). Developmental assessments typically involve an infant evaluation such as the Bayley Scales of Infant Development (mental and motor), a neurologic examination, and growth measurements.

For prematures, there is some controversy about the need to adjust the evaluations to expected date of birth rather than chronologic age (Hunt & Rhodes, 1977; Sostek, Quinn, & Davitt, 1979; Tilford, 1976). While some investigators feel that there should be full allowance for shortened gestation, others maintain that this procedure overinflates developmental scores. Whatever procedure is used by a particular follow-up service, it is important that the approach is consistent and that results are interpreted adequately.

Whether preterms or infants with other problems are evaluated, developmental progress should always be measured against the infant's own previous performance and the wide range of normality should be emphasized. At each visit there should be discussion of general home stimulation techniques and developmental expectations for the next few months. Because of the paucity of popular developmental information about prematurity and other problems such as spina bifida or early illness, this approach aids the parents in anticipating and facilitating appropriate skills at each developmental point.

In cases where development is not proceeding adequately, neurological difficulties are interfering with acquisition of skills, or long term deficits are expected, therapeutic interventions may be required. This can range from language or motor stimulation that can be carried out at home (with some professional input) to regular physical therapy sessions or full infant stimulation programs. Multidisciplinary follow-up services including psychology, physical or occupational therapy, pediatrics, and social work are typically most capable of making appropriate diagnoses and referrals for these infants and their families. In every case, it is critical to weigh the benefits of the therapy for that individual infant against the anxiety the referral may produce in the parents and the effort required to carry it out.

Parents of preterms, postterms, or malformed infants may also require assistance in optimizing the interaction potential of their infants. Field (1977) has evaluated interventions such as teaching mothers how to stimulate feeding around the pause-burst suck rhythm of the infant and how to direct social interactions to the infant's receptive periods. She found that such simple techniques can be very effective in terms of both the mother's and the infant's behavioral and psychophysiological responses. It is tempting to speculate that such interventions might reduce the incidence of abuse or neglect among infants with early difficulties.

Needs of the Family

The parents of the sick or malformed newborn have several important and difficult emotional tasks to accomplish during their infant's illness and after his or her recovery. Although they are described in sequence, they may occur in varying orders. First, after being confronted with the reality of their ill newborn, the parents must grieve for the anticipated normal baby. This grief can be just as deep and painful as if that normal baby had actually lived and then died. The parents must come to accept the existing infant as their own and then cope with the emotional stress that comes with having a loved one critically ill. Finally, if the infant survives, they must still face the uncertainty of the future.

Drotar et al. (1975) have described the adaptation of parents of malformed newborns in five stages: shock, denial, sadness and anger, equilibrium, and reorganization. Frequently, the parents of very premature, ill infants experience much the same feelings.

Initially, shock or disbelief occur, often accompanied by a feeling of numbness or immobility. For the mother of the premature, it may begin when she realizes that she is going to deliver prematurely, or it may not occur until after the fact. For parents of malformed infants, it may begin when they receive the news of their infant's deformity. Numbness and immobility are quickly followed by denial or disbelief and possibly avoidance of the infant. Very soon, the predominant feelings are sadness and often anger that may be rooted in guilt. For example, the mother of the premature feels as though she was unable to nurture her developing fetus adequately, that she is biologically unable to bear a normal baby. Parents of infants with genetic problems may feel that they are unfit. The questions of medications taken, physician's advice not followed, smoking, alcohol or drug abuse, may arise to augment this guilt. Religious convictions of parents frequently surface and the affected infant may be seen as punishment. During this time, parents may have difficulty becoming attached to their infant and may hold back emotionally or even feel anger at the ordeal the infant has caused them. This can be intensified by the fear that the child may die.

During the period of time that the parents are working through these first three stages, there are a number of helpful things that hospital staff can do. First, it is important that the parents be encouraged to express their feelings both to one another and to the staff, that the feelings be recognized as normal, and that an attitude of permissiveness about these feelings be maintained. Second, as soon as possible, the parents should be encouraged to see and touch their infant and to care for him or her as soon as it is medically and emotionally possible. What they imagine their child to be like is often far worse than the reality (Klaus & Kennell, 1976).

In addition to explaining what is wrong with the infant, what is normal, healthy, and appealing can also be pointed out at this time. This is not an attempt to minimize problems or deny grief but to help reassure the parents that their infant is one that they can grow to love. During this time, parents are frequently not ready to cope with a great deal of factual information. The physician should be as optimistic as honestly possible, even though the situation may be grave. If the infant does die, the parents' attachment does not make mourning more difficult; in fact, it may even facilitate the parents' grieving (Kennell, Slyter, & Klaus, 1970).

Once these processes are underway, the parents will soon be able to move into the final stages of equilibrium and then reorganization. Feelings of fear and sadness may reappear particularly as new crises arise. When a child is permanently handicapped, sadness may never be completely gone but will resurface periodically or remain low key but chronic. During this time of equilibrium, the parents begin to cope with their infant, to accept and process information, and to start assuming responsibility for the infant's care. The parents will benefit greatly from assurances that their presence is as important for their infant as it is for themselves (Kennell & Klaus, 1976).

At the time of discharge, the parents should be given an accurate idea of what to expect and clear instructions on how to proceed should a problem arise. After discharge, the process of reorganization continues as the parents get to know their infant better. However, should developmental problems arise, the feelings of disbelief and sadness may recur and need to be dealt with again.

Prognosis raises serious questions, and there is considerable disagreement about the usefulness of discussing the possibility of retardation or brain damage with parents before it is evident to them. If there is strong medical certainty that this has occurred (as in Down's syndrome or severe intraventricular hemorrhage), it is generally agreed that the parents should know as soon as possible what the future holds for them and their baby. When, however, there is uncertainty, care must be exercised. It is probably best in these circumstances to be as optimistic as honesty permits and to emphasize the need for continued developmental evaluation and a general idea of available services. This recommendation will be stronger if there is a continuity of care from the nursery to the follow-up program. The question of retardation frequently comes from the parents who should be made aware of the difficulty of early prediction and of the variety of factors that contribute to outcome. The importance of measuring the infant's progress against himself or herself is particularly crucial where developmental norms are not available.

Finally, in families where the adaptation does not seem to be proceeding well, professional help (from psychiatric, social work, or other mental health professionals) should be encouraged. Attention should be paid to the reactions of siblings who may serve as an additional stress to the parents if their adaptation is poor. Their need for adequate information may go unrecognized, and their fears may be worse than the actual situation. There is a higher incidence of marital dissolution in families with a retarded or chronically ill child, and parenting disorders are more frequent following neonatal separation and early medical difficulties. The continued availability of support personnel is critical and may be provided by the infant follow-up or therapy services utilized by the family.

The Normal Newborn

For parents of the vast majority of infants who are normal, there are challenges in the first weeks after birth that may form the basis of future interactions. Most fundamentally, the parents intensify whatever attachment to the infant they had prenatally. Attachment can be defined as a unique, long term, positive relationship between two people (Klaus & Kennell, 1976). Behaviors from which attachment can be inferred include kissing, fondling, cuddling, and prolonged gaze. Each is affectionate and serves to maintain contact between individuals.

Early attachment occurs during the postpartum hospitalization and may be influenced by the attitudes and policies of the hospital staff. Modern practices of normal postnatal care generally provide extensive opportunities for mother-infant contact. Mothers are no longer encouraged to remain inactive after childbirth and to have contact with their newborns only for feedings. Most hospitals allow mothers to spend as much time as they desire with their babies and to assume responsibility for the basic care of their babies at a time when the nursing staff is available to answer questions. The mothers become acquainted with their babies physically; learn how the baby reacts to hunger, fatigue, and satiation; and experience his or her periods of alertness and responsivity. Pacing interactions around the infant's active and quiet times can establish the basis for reciprocity later in infancy. The importance of such synchrony and rhythmic patterning has been emphasized by Stern et al. (1975).

Opportunities for mother-infant contact are particularly beneficial for those women who are having first babies and who have not had previous caregiving experience (Greenberg, Rosenberg, & Lind, 1973).

Sostek, Scanlon, and Abramson (1982) have found increased maternal confidence and decreased anxiety shortly after birth when first mothers had extensive contact with their babies during the days immediately following delivery.

Part of the impetus for the change in philosophy in postnatal care comes from the recent emphasis on the emotional attachment (or bonding) between the mother and newborn. Klaus and Kennell (1976) are among the earliest proponents of extensive mother-infant contact. They argue that skin-to-skin contact and an opportunity to nurse the baby should be allowed immediately after birth. The first 90–120 minutes of life typically find babies remarkably alert and responsive, while the following days they sleep most of the time. The immediate newborn period may, therefore, be a particularly sensitive time for intiating a pattern of mother-infant responsivity. Whether it is a unique, critical period with irreversible effects is highly doubtful, however (Svejda, Compos, & Elnde, 1980).

Most of the principles of attachment between mothers and infants apply to fathers as well. The majority of hospitals today do not consider fathers to be visitors, and they are allowed to spend as many hours as they desire with the mother and baby. Given ample opportunity to interact with their infants, fathers have been found to behave toward their newborns very much as mothers do (Parke & O'Leary, 1976). Previous opinions about the uniqueness of the attachment between mothers and infants may have been the result of limited interaction opportunities for fathers.

Interactional difficulties in the newborn period might be indicated by lack of interest; consistent negative affect; poor responsiveness in the mother, father, or newborn; or insensitivity of the parents to cues. Counseling about the needs and capabilities of the newborn as well as caregiving and interaction demonstrations may be helpful in the postpartum period. To parents, it is often helpful to provide an opportunity to observe the Brazelton Neonatal Assessment Scale (Brazelton, 1973), which demonstrates the sensory, social, motoric, and state regulation capabilities of the infant. Techniques for comforting and alerting the infant are also included. Optimally, continuity of this type of care should be available long term if necessary through the infant's pediatrician. If it is not, the counseling services of a therapist specializing in infant development and family interaction might be required.

PROBLEMS IN INFANCY

During infancy, serious and enduring psychological problems can emerge that will require ongoing clinical management. There is a variety of handicapping conditions that may not be identifiable at birth such as retardation, affect disturbance, motor problems, hearing loss, chronic disease, and other, more subtle, problems that can have long term developmental consequences. Informing parents, planning diagnostic-intervention strategies, and identifying community resources are essential in all of these instances. Continuity of care over the course of a condition, which is frequently the full lifespan of the individual, must begin in infancy for these children. In all instances, the child must be viewed in the context of the family. The reaction and adjustment of parents and siblings to the early onset of a serious and/or potentially chronic problem is an important determinant in planning care. The expected feelings of grief, fear,

anger, and guilt of family members call for recognition, respect, and support.

Failure to Thrive

Failure to thrive is an example of a serious condition that usually becomes evident during the period of infancy. It is a perplexing syndrome of growth failure that can occur on an organic or nonorganic basis. Those who characterize the nonorganic or environmental causes of failure to thrive, look toward characteristics of the mother, family, and child.

For mothers of failure-to-thrive infants, there may be significant maternal events that correlate with the condition. Barbero (1974) identifies past events, such as loss of parent figures early in life of the mother and illness during the mother's childhood; pregnancy events, such as protracted emotional problems, physical illness, and deaths or major illness of key family figures; perinatal events, such as prematurity, congenital defects, or diseases; and current life events, such as marital strains, mental illness, alcoholism, drugs, and financial crises.

The families of failure-to-thrive infants usually are overwhelmed by financial and marital problems. The family is unable to use the support of their extended famly and lack a network of close friends. The family income may be lower than in families where there is not an affected child and there may be an increase in household density with a larger number of children born close together (Cupoli, Hallock, & Barnes, 1980).

The characteristics of the failure-to-thrive children include prematurity or small size for gestational age and poor feeding behavior. Their early temperament is usually described by parents as difficult, irritable, hyperactive, overly sensitive, or passive and unresponsive. The overall picture presents a potentially maladaptive transaction between the infant and the environment.

In planning for treatment of a failure-to-thrive child, an initial step must be made to distinguish between nonorganic and organic etiology. Nonorganic causes are reported to account for more cases of failure to thrive than organic causes (Barnes, 1972; Sills, 1978). The organic causes may be related to genetic, nutritional, metabolic, constitutional, or external variables. A systematic approach to care should begin with a medical examination and social-medical history. Whether the diagnostic and treatment process can continue on an outpatient basis or whether the child will require hospitalization will be determined by the suspected etiology and the coping patterns of the family. Failure to thrive usually represents a multifaceted problem that requires comprehensive clinical management.

Rumination represents a special instance of failure to thrive in infancy. It has been defined as "bringing up food without nausea, retching, or disgust. The food is then ejected from the mouth or reswallowed" (Kanner, 1972, p. 463). Rumination is a voluntary process with a usual onset of 3–8 months of age. It occurs during self-stimulation activity, not while the infant is asleep or actively engaged. Most mothers of ruminating infants seem to have a poor sense of what comforts the infants, and other maladaptive family patterns are often noted (Fleisher, 1979). A variety of treatments has been used to inhibit ruminating behaviors, including surgery, drugs, mechanical devices, and thickening the food with farina. One effective treatment has been to provide extended and massive attention to the infant for the main part of the day (Kanner, 1972). When the problem is chronic and, in effect, life threatening, intensified behavioral procedures can be employed (see Linscheid, chap. 25 of this book).

Child Abuse and Neglect

Abused and neglected infants represent another group of children who will require clinical intervention. Because the scope of the problem is so broad and to a large extent involves parental propensity and psychological variables, this discussion is confined to findings related to characteristics of infants that place them at a greater risk for abuse or neglect. There have been a number of reports

that show a significantly greater incidence of abuse in low birthweight (Klein & Stern, 1971; Martin & Beezley, 1974; Mitchell, 1977) and premature infants (Martin, 1976; Newberger & Hyde, 1975; Stern, 1973). Some suggest that this is related to the separation of mother and neonate during the hospital stay (Klein & Stern, 1971). Others point to prenatal variables, such as early negative reaction to the pregnancy, that may have caused undernutrition during the prenatal period, Williams (1978) summarizes preabusive characteristics to include congenital defects, mild neurological dysfunctions, developmental deviations, atypical response patterns, and infant irritability/difficulties. All these infants are at greater risk for abuse. (For diagnostic and treatment approaches to be utilized when abuse is suspected, see Williams, chap. 52 of this book.)

Medical Conditions

Illness and the emergence of a chronic medical condition during infancy may have little or no effect on psychological development (transient or long term effect) or be immediately life threatening. Assisting families to cope in all of these circumstances is an important role for the health professional.

Infants with chronic medical conditions constitute a risk population for psychological problems because of the loss of stimulation through prolonged hospitalization, restricted physical activity (related to either illness or treatment), and delayed or interrupted parent/child attachment. The disruption of the bonding and attachment process through separation can have prolonged effects. The youngest infant (0–6 months) is particularly affected by the type of care given in the hospital and may evidence a range of signs of distress (Prugh & Eckhardt, 1975). Repeated separations increase the potential for later problems.

Cognitive development may also be adversely affected, particularly in the short term. Research on cognitive assessment of chronically ill infants is limited, but reports on the most thoroughly studied group—those infants diagnosed with congenital heart disease—support this premise. The delayed motor milestones of these infants, especially those who are cyanotic, lower their performance on infant scales such as the Bayley and Cattell (Feldt et al., 1969); however, on follow-up assessments, subsequent to cardiac surgery, using scales such as the Stanford-Binet, there is no difference between cyanotic and normal children (Linde, Rasof, & Dunn, 1967). Surgical correction of congenital heart defects is associated with either a maintenance of prior average functioning or a postoperative increase of IQ (Landtman et al., 1960; Stevenson et al., 1974; Whitman et al., 1973).

Infections that affect the central nervous system represent a serious threat to the developmental integrity of the infant. The effects of meningitis and encephalitis during this period are particularly startling. The risk of neurological involvement in meningitis and encephalitis has been found to be particularly handicapping when onset occurs during the first two years of life (Boll, 1973; Finley et al., 1967; Ford, 1944; Vernon, 1967). If meningitis occurs in the first year of life, there is a 4-5 times greater chance that the child's IQ will be below average (Wolff & Smallwood, 1952). Neurological sequelae are usually found in 55 percent of these same infants (Kresky, Buchbiner, & Greenberg, 1962). The longer the delay in treatment, the greater the interim consequences.

The sudden onset of central nervous system infections and the dramatic changes that result usually have a profound effect on families. Helping families to accept the long term changes is a difficult task for the clinician. These infants will require continuous medical management and developmental stimulation because of the long term and pervasive effects of the illness.

Sudden Infant Death Syndrome

Sudden infant death syndrome (SIDS) is an example of a condition that arises in infancy that represents a very significant clinical management problem in terms of the enduring psychological effects on the family. The incidence of SIDS is 2-3 deaths per 1,000 live births, and it is the leading cause of death of infants one week to one year of age. It has been estimated that 8,000 infants die of SIDS each year in the United States (Mandell & Belk, 1977). The death of the infant is sudden, mysterious, and bewildering to families. The cause of death is not understood by professionals and over 70 different theories of etiology have been catalogued (Beckworth, 1975). The death occurs unaccompanied by outcry and at times with another person asleep in the room. Studies seem to indicate that the incidence of SIDS is higher in the winter, with a higher frequency in males and an increased risk among low birthweight infants (Bergman, Ray, & Pomeroy, 1972; Froggatt, Lynas, & MacKenzie, 1971).

The grief reaction to the loss of a child to SIDS is often very acute and intense for parents. Feelings of guilt and blame often endure after the initial shock. The effect on siblings can also be devastating. Fear of its happening to them and guilt are typical responses. At times, they will associate the death with something they did to the infant that day. Siblings should be actively included in the grieving process and in any supportive treatment that is offered to the family. Also, the family should be encouraged to work through their grief feelings before planning a next pregnancy (Defrain & Ernst, 1978). In working with all family members around their grief, it is important to assure them that they did *not* cause the death, that SIDS is not preventable or predictable, and that it is the most prevalent cause of death in young infants.

A four-point management program has been proposed to alleviate the long term psychological effects of SIDS on a family:

1. Prompt identification of SIDS as a preliminary cause of death within 24-28 hours.
2. Correct use of diagnostic terminology on the death certificate.
3. Notification of the diagnosis to the family as soon as it is made.
4. Provision of facts on SIDS and grief

counseling by a qualified professional (Nikolaisen & Williams, 1980).

Neurological and Sensory/Motor Problems

There is a range of neurological and sensory/motor conditions that presents in infancy that will require long term management. The impact of these conditions on cognitive, language, motor, and adaptive functions often will require an interdisciplinary approach to ongoing care.

When a sensory defect, either visual or auditory, presents during infancy, there is not only the issue of the adaptation of the family and child to the disability, but also the possibility of accompanying deficits in intellectual and cognitive functioning. The severity and prognosis of the sensory loss will have a direct relationship to the intensity of parental reaction. For example, profound bilateral deafness will be more difficult for parents to accept than a mild hearing loss. Often it is the parent, and not the professional, who identifies the problem, particularly with hearing loss. This creates an additional stress when it is coupled with a loss of confidence in professionals.

Following infants with sensory problems requires ongoing assessment of psychological and development functioning. In determining the extent to which intellectual functioning is also affected, the clinician must be aware of the cautions in evaluating this population.

Assessing the cognitive status of multiply or sensorily impaired infants presents special problems since most infant tests have not been standardized for this population. Whether to adapt tests specially to the sensory handicap of the infant has been a controversial issue. Most psychologists agree that adaptation of these tests to accommodate the specific handicaps of the infant offers a better understanding of the infant's skills and learning potential; but there are some who argue the other way. Criticos (in press), in an extensive discussion of the applicability and adaptability of infant tests for the multiply and sensorily impaired infant, suggests that the Bayley Infant Scales have more cognitive items than most other

infant scales and leave the most room for adaptation. She stresses the need for adapting to the handicap through item omissions, substitution, and alternative scoring. Visually handicapped infants require kinesthetic and physical guidance to compensate for visual clues. For the auditorily impaired infant, language items are more difficult to adapt and greater examiner judgment is required. (See Richman, chap. 29 of this book.)

There will be a group of infants who will be diagnosed during infancy to have moderate to severe impairment of neurological and cognitive functioning. Their deficits will be pronounced, suggesting life cycle problems in intellectual development. Care of these infants will require coordinated diagnostic and intervention programs along with support to the family.

Retardation

A number of factors can contribute to the presence of significant retardation. The American Association of Mental Deficiencies divides these into ten broad areas of classification: (1) infection and intoxication, (2) trauma or physical agents, (3) metabolism or nutrition, (4) postnatal gross brain disease, (5) unknown prenatal influences, (6) chromosome abnormalities, (7) gestational disorders, (8) psychiatric disorders, (9) environmental influences, and (10) other conditions. It is beyond the scope of this chapter to discuss each of these categories, but it is imperative that professionals working with infants be aware of the potential etiologies of retardation and the accompanying implications. (See Cleland, chap. 26 of this book.)

In providing care to infants suspected of retardation, there are several important clinical issues. First of all, since the course of infant development is not predictably smooth, rapid developmental gains or long plateaus must not be overinterpreted. Careful monitoring of the infant's developmental progress should occur. Assessments should take place in an interdisciplinary context to provide for in-depth observations of motor, language, and adaptive gains. A decade ago, most of the moderately and severely retarded infants were institutionalized for care as early as possible to reduce the burden to the family. Today, families are encouraged to keep these infants at home, which requires providing the family with an adequate health, educational, and social support system. The developmental benefit to the infant of remaining in the home for variety of physical and emotional stimulation will be great but only if the stress on the family is appropriately supported. Clinicians must work towards helping families identify community resources where continuity of care and comprehensive services are available. This is not always easy because of the still fragmented nature of our service delivery system. Assisting families of infants suspected of retardation in advocacy for services and ongoing care management is critical.

Problems of the Normal Infant

During the period of infancy, even for the normal infant, there is an array of clinical problems that may arise during early development. Transient problems specific to the developmental tasks of this period usually represent a shared concern of health care professionals working with the families of infants. Differentiating mild disturbances from more complex and involved problems is an important task in intervention planning.

During the early months, disturbances in feeding and sleep patterns represent typical clinical concerns that may affect infant temperament and arouse parental anxiety. In this general category, infantile colic is one of the most distressing and perplexing behavioral problems occurring to otherwise normal infants. Typically, it involves a complex set of behaviors including crying, drawing up of the legs, passing of flatus and occasional straining with passage of stool (Wright, Schaefer, & Solomons, 1979). These infants frequently are wakeful and irritable during the day and restless sleepers during the night. Feeding problems, including the rejection of nursing and vomiting, often occur.

The etiology of infant colic is not well understood and how maternal anxiety contributes to its occurrence is controversial. Some studies have demonstrated a connection between maternal anxiety and colic; others have not (Carey, 1968; Paradise, 1966). The differential diagnosis and treatment of colic is an ongoing process that is based on observing irritability, fussing, and crying lasting more than 3 hours a day, occurring at least 4 days a week, usually at night, beginning at 2 weeks of age and lasting 3 months in an infant who is well fed, burped, and in dry clothes (Palumbo et al., 1978). Colic does appear to be more prevalent in firstborn children and occurs more often at times of family stress (Barbero, 1964). The most successful of the numerous methods to treat infant colics include rocking, drug therapy, changes in diet, and use of a pacifier. At times, parents will need supportive counseling to cope with their feelings about their difficult infant or to be guided in more effective caretaking techniques.

Nightwaking is another common problem in infancy. Reports of early predictors of later sleep problems implicate variables such as length of labor and latency to first cry (Bernal, 1973), as well as prematurity, neonatal asphyxia, and insufficient nursing time (Moore & Ucko, 1957). Interestingly, contrary to popular belief, there appears to be no clearcut relationship between nightwaking and feeding patterns, either time of feeding or caloric intake (Bernal, 1973). An association has been reported between maternal anxiety and sleep problems with an emphasis on parental mishandling (Goldfarb, Lagercrant, & Lagerdahl, 1961; Ragins & Schachter, 1971). These findings point to the need to work with parents to examine their interactions with their infants, especially with respect to the parents' inadvertent reinforcement of sleep avoidance in the infant. Sostek and Anders (1981) point out that the serious study of the complexity of infant sleep behaviors has been a neglected and underrated area of infant research.

Helping families to recognize that infant development does not proceed at a uniform rate in all infants is another important clinical issue of the infancy period. Within the range of normality, there will be variation in the development of motor, language, and adaptive skills. Sometimes parents have unrealistic expectations and become anxious in the face of normal developmental deviations of their infant. Comparisons with other children and some of the normative popular literature on infant development can lead parents to underestimate the broad range of normal infants. Parents do not always realize that each child may have specific areas of strength and weakness and that development of various abilities may proceed at different paces. It is often helpful simply to point out facts such as the average age range for walking (9–18 months). Sometimes experiential factors in the environment contribute to developmental lags and families can profit from guidance around providing increased stimulation in the home. Supportive counseling and recommendation of literature that emphasizes developmental progression and individual differences can be useful.

Obviously, the professionals in contact with the family have to strike a balance between not overlooking developmental problems and minimizing parental anxiety. The "late talkers" can represent a significant clinical concern. Making a differential diagnosis of those infants who may be more permanently involved is a difficult task and requires excellent clinical judgment. Screening tools such as the Denver Developmental Screening Test can point up potential deficits but these must be viewed in a context of cautious interpretation. It is well known that assessment of infant development has a low correlation with later measure of intelligence. It is important that clinicians be well trained in assessing developmental delays and evaluating both the implications of the delays for potential longer term problems and their emotional impact on the family.

In the period of infancy, there must be close collaboration among all health professionals. The early identification of problems coupled with comprehensive intervention is the best "head start" we can give to both the child and the family. To assure the optimum development of all infants, clinicians must be alert to the wide array of potential difficulties discussed in the chapter and be willing to help families gain access to appropriate programs and resources.

REFERENCES

Babson, S.G., & Benson, R.C. *Management of high-risk pregnancy and intensive care of the neonate* (2nd ed.). St. Louis: Mosby, 1971.

Barbero, G.B. *Failure to thrive. Maternal attachment and mothering disorders.* A round table. Sausalito, Calif., October 18–19, 1974.

Barbero, G.J. Etiology and treatment of infantile colic. *Feelings and their medical significance.* 1964, **6**, 1–4.

Barnes, L.A. Failure to thrive. *Dallas Medical Journal,* 1972, **58**, 325.

Beckworth, J.B. *The sudden infant death syndrome.* DHEW publication No. HSA 75-5137. Washington, D.C.: U.S. Government Printing Office, 1975.

Bergman, A.B., Ray, C.G., & Pomeroy, M.A. Studies of the sudden infant death syndrome in King County, Washington. Part III, Epidemiology. *Pediatrics,* 1972 **49**, 860.

Bernal, J.F. Night waking in infants during the first 14 months. *Developmental Medicine and Child Neurology,* 1973, **15**, 760–769.

Boll, T.J. *The effect of age at onset of brain damage on adaptive abilities in children.* Paper presented at American Psychological Association Convention, Montreal, August 25–September 1, 1973.

Brazelton, T.B. *Neonatal behavioral assessment scale.* London: Heinemann, 1973.

Brazelton, T.B. On becoming a family: The growth of attachment. New York: Delacorte, 1981.

Brocklehurst, G. *Spina bifida for the clinician.* London: Heinemann, 1976.

Caputo, D.V., & Mandell, W. Consequences of low birth weight. *Developmental Psychology,* 1970, **3**, 363–383.

Carey, W.B. Maternal anxiety and infantile colic, is there a relationship? *Clinical Pediatrics,* 1968, **7**(10), 590–595.

Carr, J. Mental and motor development in young mongol children. *Journal of Mental Deficiency Research,* 1970, **14**, 205–220.

Clifford, S.H. Postmaturity—with placental dysfunction: Clinical syndrome and pathologic findings. *Journal of Pediatrics,* 1954, **44,** 1–13.

Criticos, A.K. Psychological assessment of multi-handicapped children. *Diagnosis and management of the multi-handicapped child.* New York: Dekker, in press.

Cupoli, J.M., Hallock, J.A., & Barnes, L.A. Failure to thrive. *Current Problems in Pediatrics,* September, 1980, **10, 11,** 43.

Defrain, J.D., & Ernst, L. The psychological effects of sudden infant death syndrome on surviving family members. *Journal of Family Practice,* May, 1978, **6,** 985–989.

DiVitto, B., & Goldberg, S. The effects of newborn medical status on early parent-infant interaction. In T.M. Field, A.M. Sostek, S. Goldberg, & H.H. Shuman (Eds.), *Infants born at risk: Behavior and development.* New York: Spectrum, 1979.

Drillien, C.M. The incidence of mental and physical handicaps in school age children of very low birthweight. *Pediatrics,* 1967, **39,** 238–247.

Drotar, D., Baskieivicz, A., Irwin, N., Kennell, J., & Klaus, M. The adaptation of parents to the birth of an infant with a congenital malformation: A hypothetical model. *Pediatrics,* 1975, **56,** 710–721.

Feldt, R.H., Ervert, J.C., Stickler, G.B., & Weidman, W.H. Children with congenital heart disease. *American Journal of Diseases of Childhood,* 1969, **117,** 281–284.

Field, T.M. Maternal stimulation during infant feeding. *Developmental Psychology,* 1977, **13,** 539–540.

Field, T.M. Interaction patterns of preterm and term infants. In T.M. Field, A.M. Sostek, S. Goldberg, & H.H. Shuman. *Infants born at risk: Behavior and development.* New York: Spectrum, 1979.

Field, T., Dabiri, C., Hallock, N., & Shuman, H.H. Developmental effects of prolonged pregnancy and the postmaturity syndrome. *Journal of Pediatrics,* 1977, **90,** 836–839.

Field, T., Hallock, N., Dempsey, J., & Shuman, H.H. Mother's assessments of term infants with respiratory distress syndrome: Reliability and predictive validity. *Child Psychiatry and Human Development,* 1978, **9,** 75–85.

Field, T.M., Sostek, A.M., Goldberg, S., & Shuman, H.H. *Infants born at risk: Behavior and development.* New York: Spectrum, 1979.

Finley, K.H. Fitzgerald, L.H., Pichter, R.W.,

Riggs, N., & Shelton, J.T. Western encephalitis and cerebral ontogenesis. *Archives of Neurology,* 1967, **16,** 140–164.

Fisch, R.O., Bilek, M.K., Millen, L.D., & Engel, R.R. Physical and mental status at 4 years of survivors of the respiratory distress syndrome. *Journal of Pediatrics,* 1975, **86,** 497–503.

Fitzhardinge, P. Current outcome. ICU populations. In A.W. Brann & J.J. Volpe (Eds.), *Neonatal neurological assessment and outcome.* Report of the 77th Ross Conference in Pediatric Research, Columbus, Ohio: Ross Laboratories, 1980.

Fitzhardinge, P.M., Pape, K., Arstikaitis, M., Boyle, M., Ashby, S., Rawley, A., Netley, C., & Sawyer, P.R. Mechanical ventilation of infants of less than 1501 grams birthweight. Health, growth and neurologic sequelae. *Journal of Pediatrics,* 1976, **88,** 531–541.

Fitzhardinge, P.M., & Stevens, E.M. The small-for-date infant: Neurologic and intellectual sequelae. *Pediatrics,* 1972, **50,** 50–57.

Fleisher, D.R. Infant rumination syndrome. *American Journal of the Disabled Child,* 1979, **133,** 266.

Ford, F.R. *Diseases of the nervous system.* Springfield, Ill.: Thomas, 1944.

Froggatt, P., Lynas, M.A., & MacKenzie, G. Epidemiology of sudden unexpected death in infants (cot death) in Northern Ireland. *British Journal of Preventive Social Medicine,* 1971, **25,** 119–134.

Gayton, W., & Walker, L. Down's Syndrome: Informing parents. *American Journal of Disease of Children,* 1974, **127,** 510–512.

Goldfarb, L., Lagercrant, R., & Lagerdahl, A. Sleep disturbances in infancy and early childhood. *Acta Paediatrica,* 1961, **50,** 212.

Greenberg, M., Rosenberg, I., & Lind, J. First mothers rooming-in with their newborns: Its impact on the mother. *American Journal of Orthopsychiatry,* 1973, **43,** 783–788.

Harbison, R.D. *Perinatal addiction.* New York: Spectrum, 1975.

Hunt, J., & Rhodes, L. Mental development of preterm infants during the first year. *Child Development,* 1977, **8,** 204–210.

Jones, K.L. The fetal alcohol syndrome. *Addictive Diseases: An International Journal,* 1975, **2,** 79–88.

Kanner, L. *Child psychiatry.* Springfield, Ill.: Thomas, 1972.

Katz, K.S. Inherited disorders: Down's Syndrome and phenylketonuria. In P.R. Magrab (Ed.), *Psychological management of pediatric problems, Volume I: Early life conditions and chronic diseases.* Baltimore: University Park Press, 1978.

Kennell, J.H., Slyter, H., & Klaus, M.H. The mourning response of parents to the death of a newborn infant. *New England Journal of Medicine,* 1970, **283**, 344–349.

Klaus, M.H., & Kennell, J.H. Maternal-infant bonding. In M.H. Klaus & J.H. Kennell (Eds.), *Maternal-infant bonding.* St. Louis, Mo.: Mosby, 1976.

Klein, M., & Stern, L. Low birthweight and the battered child syndrome. *American Journal of Diseases of Children,* 1971, **122**, 15–18.

Kresky, B., Buchbiner, S., & Greenberg, I.M. The incidence of neurologic residua in children after recovery from bacterial meningitis. *Archives of Pediatrics,* 1962, **79**, 63–71.

Landtman, B., Valanne, E., Pentti, R., & Aukee, M. Psychosomatic behavior of children with congenital heart disease. Pre- and postoperative studies of eighty-four cases. *Annales Paediatrial Fennial,* 1960, **6**, 1–78.

Linde, L.M., Rasof, B., & Dunn, O.J. Mental development in congenital heart disease. *Journal of Pediatrics,* 1967, **71**, 198–203.

Lubchenco, L.O., Bard, H., Goldman, A.L., Coyer, W.E., McIntyre, C., & Smith, D.M. Newborn intensive care and long-term prognosis. *Developmental Medicine and Child Neurology,* 1974, **16**, 421–431.

Mandell, F., & Belk, B. Special aspects of primary care, pediatrics, sudden infant death syndrome: The disease and its survivors. *Postgraduate Medicine,* October, 1977, **62**, 193–197.

Marriage, K.J., & Davies, D.A. Neurological sequelae in children surviving mechanical ventilation in the neonatal period. *Archives of Diseases in Childhood,* 1977, **52**, 176–182.

Martin, H.P. *The abused child: A multidisciplinary approach to developmental issues and treatment.* Cambridge, Mass.: Ballinger, 1976.

Martin, H.P., & Beezley, P. Prevention and the consequences of child abuse. *Journal of Operational Psychiatry,* 1974, **6**, 68–77.

Mitchell, R.G. *Child health in the community: A handbook of social and community pedia-*

trics. Edinburgh, Scotland: Churchill Livingstone, 1977.

Moore, T., & Ucko, L.E. Night waking in early infancy: Part 1. *Archives of Diseases in Childhood,* 1957, **32**, 333–342.

Nance, S. *Premature babies: A handbook for parents.* New York: Arbor House, 1982.

Newberger, E.H., & Hyde, J.N. Child abuse: Principles and implications of current pediatric practice. *Pediatric Clinics in North America,* 1975, **22**, 695–715.

Nikolaisen, S.M., & Williams, R.A. Parent's view of support following the loss of their infant to sudden death syndrome. *Journal of Nursing Research,* 1980, **2**, 593–601.

Palumbo, F.M., Licamele, W.L., Quinn, P.Q., & Zuckerman, A.E. *Colic: A pediatric, psychiatric review & survey.* American Academy of Child Pediatricians, San Diego, October, 1978.

Paradise, J.L. Maternal and other factors in the etiology of infantile colic. *Journal of the American Medical Association,* 1966, **197**, 191.

Parke, R.D., & O'Leary, S. Father-mother-infant interaction in the newborn period: Some findings, some observations, and some unresolved issues. In M.K. Riegel & J. Meacham (Eds.), *The developing individual in a changing world (Vol. II.): Social and environmental issues.* The Hague: Mouton, 1976.

Prugh, D., & Eckhardt, L.O. Children's reactions to illness, hospitalization and surgery. In A.M. Friedman, H.I. Kaplan, & B.J. Sadock (Eds.), *Comprehensive textbook of psychiatry* (2nd ed.). Baltimore: Williams & Wilkins Co., 1975.

Pueschel, S., & Murphy, A. Counseling parents of infants with Down's syndrome. *Postgraduate Medicine,* 1975, **58**, 90–95.

Ragins, N., & Schachter, J. A study of sleep behavior in two-year old children. *Journal of the American Academy of Child Psychiatry,* 1971, **10**, 464.

Share, J. Developmental progress in Down's syndrome. In R. Koch, & F. de la Cruz (Eds.), *Down's syndrome (mongolism) research: Prevention and management.* New York: Brunner/Mazel, 1975.

Sills, R.H. Failure to thrive. The role of clinical and

laboratory evaluation. *American Journal of the Disabled Child,* 1978, **10,** 967–969.

Sostek, A.M., Quinn, P.O., & Davitt, M.K. Behavior, development, and neurologic status of premature and full-term infants with varying medical complications. In T.M. Field, A.M. Sostek, S. Goldberg, & H.H. Shuman (Eds.), *Infants born at risk: Behavior and development.* New York: Spectrum, 1979.

Sostek, A.M., & Anders, T.F. The biosocial importance and environmental sensitivity of infant sleep-wake behavior. In K. Bloom (Ed.), *Prospective issues in infancy research.* Hillsdale, N.J.: Ehrlbaum, 1981.

Sostek, A.M., Scanlon, J.W., & Abramson, D.C. Postpartum contact and maternal cnfidence and anxiety: A confirmation of short-term effects. *Infant Behavior and Development,* 1980.

Stern, L. Prematurity as a factor in child abuse. *Hosptial Practices,* 1973, **8,** 117–123.

Stern, D.N., Jaffe, J., Beebe, B., & Bennett, S.L. Vocalizing in unison and in alternation: Two modes of communication within the mother-infant dyad. *Annals of the New York Academy of Science,* 1975, **283,** 89–100.

Stevenson, J.G., Stone, E.F., Dillard, D.H., & Morgan, B.C. Intellectual development of children subjected to prolonged circulatory arrest during hypothermic open heart surgery in infancy. *Circulation,* 1974, **50,** 54–59.

Svejda, M.J., Campos, J.J., & Elnde, R.N. Mother-infant bonding: Failure to generalize. *Child Development,* 1980, **51,** 775–779.

Tilford, J.A. The relationship between gestational age and adaptive behavior. *Merrill-Palmer Quarterly of Behavior and Development,* 1976, **22,** 319–326.

Vaughan, V.C., & McKay, R.J. *Nelson textbook of pediatrics* (10th ed.). Philadelphia: Saunders, 1975.

Vernon, M. Characteristics associated with post-rubella deaf children: Psychological, educational and physical. *Volta Review,* 1967, **69,** 176–185.

Volpe, J.J. Intraventricular hemorrhage—Major neurologic complications of prematurity. In A.W. Brann & J.J. Volpe (Eds.), *Neonatal neurological assessment and outcome.* Report of the 77th Ross Conference on Pediatric Research. Columbus, Ohio: Ross Laboratories, 1980.

Whitman, V., Drotar, D., Lambert, S., Van Heeckeren, D.W., Borkat, G., Ankeney, J., & Liebman, J. Effects of cardiac surgery with extracorporeal circulation on intellectual function in children. *Circulation,* 1973, **48,** 160–163.

Williams, G.J. Child abuse. *Psychological management of pediatric problems.* Baltimore: University Park Press, 1978.

Wolff, O.H., & Smallwood, W.C. Effects of meningococcal meningitis on intelligence and hearing. *Archives of Disease in Childhood,* 1952, **27,** 302.

Wright, L., Schaefer, A., & Solomons, G. *Encyclopedia of pediatric psychology.* Baltimore, University Park Press, 1979.

CHAPTER 13

Clinical Problems of the Preschool Child

CAROLYN S. SCHROEDER, BETTY N. GORDON, AND BARBARA HAWK

The preschool years, ages 2–5, are considered by child psychologists to be one of the most important developmental periods since it is during this time that the foundations for many complex behaviors are laid. The emergence of language, peer relationships, gender identity, emotional behavior, the growth of play, increased locomotion, and the development of cognitive skills all set the stage for increased and often intense interaction between the child and the environment. As a child's capabilities of interacting with the environment increase, so do the problems and concerns of parents. Studies have shown, however, that developmental status and behavior problems during these years do not necessarily predict future behavior of the child (Chess, 1970; Bijou, 1974; Furman, 1980). Sandra Scarr (1979), in the introduction to the special issue of the *American Psychologist* on children, points out that no theory of infancy and preschool development can adequately explain the later course of children's lives. Children are ever-developing organisms. The interaction of hereditary-constitutional factors, current physiological status, current environmental conditions, and past learning determine the child's behavior at any given point in time (Ross, 1980).

This chapter will focus on clinical problems in the preschool years. The first part of the chapter will cover developmental milestones, important assessment issues for this age, and the prevalence of preschool problems. This will be followed by more in-depth but brief reviews of specific problem areas as related to the preschool years including the exceptional child, separation problems, child maltreatment, and common but troublesome behavior problems. Finally, prevention of such problems through parent education and early stimulation programs will be discussed.

DEVELOPMENTAL MILESTONES

The importance given to the various developmental characteristics of the preschool years has depended to a great extent on the theoretical approach taken to this period. Psychoanalytic theory emphasizes the emergence of independence and the resolution of the Oedipus complex. Social learning theory focuses on decreasing dependency, the development of self control, the development of the conscience, and the beginnings of social habits and social drives. Cognitive theory views the child as becoming increasingly able to reason and therefore less dependent on sensorimotor actions for directing behavior. Bijou (1974) gives a functional analysis of the preschool years, which he terms the "basic stage." In a functional or behavioral analysis approach the child's observable behavior is analyzed with reference to the environment, and the environment is analyzed with reference to the child. The two are seen as inseparable, and their continuous interaction results in changes in both the child and the environment. These theoretical approaches vary from viewing the child's behavior as the result of internal forces to describing the observable behavioral-environmental interactions as shaping the child's behavior. While the limitations of this chapter do not permit a critical evaluation of the merits of each approach, the review of specific milestones and their importance to the preschool child's development will reflect information gathered from each of these theoretical approaches.

In reviewing developmental milestones, inter- and intraindividual differences should be kept in mind. Individual differences in rate of development are nowhere more apparent than during the preschool years. Some children, for example, have extensive language before the age of 2 while other "normal" children don't acquire speech until the age of 3. An individual child's rate of development within various areas such as language, motor abilities, or perceptual abilities can vary as much as the rate of development between children. Some of these inter- and intraindividual differences are primarily the result of genetic-organic factors while other variations seem to be more the result of environmental factors. It is, of course, the unique interaction of these two factors—the child and the environment—that ultimately determine a child's developmental level.

Physical and Motor Development

There is a steady growth of both height and weight during the preschool years; by age 5 weight is double that of 1 year and height has doubled birth length by age 4. Most remarkably, by age 5 the brain has reached 90 percent of its adult weight (Rutter, 1975). The relevant brain maturation, along with adequate stimulation, sets the stage for learning.

Most children have accomplished the gross motor skills of climbing, balancing, jumping, running, pushing, and pulling by 5 years of age. Hopping and proper throwing are usually not yet possible. Locomotor activity in an unfamiliar laboratory setting was found to reach a peak around 18–23 months with a steady decline after age 3 (Routh, Schroeder, & O'Tuama, 1974). Fine motor skills move from scribbling at age 2 to copying a circle by 3, a square by 4, a triangle by 5, and by 5.5 years most children are able to print their own names (Rand, 1973). While still crude and

with little detail, the drawings of 5-year-old children are usually recognizable as pictures of houses or people (Rutter, 1975). Drawing rules such as "start at the left," "start at the top," and "draw horizontal lines from left to right," seem to occur in a developmental sequence (Goodnow & Levine, 1973), and preschoolers can improve their reproduction of geometric shapes by learning rules (Rand, 1973).

Toilet training, including bowel and urine control, has been found to be most successful when started at 24–25 months (Butler, 1976). To be toilet trained, a child must have voluntary control of the sphincter muscles, the ability to communicate needs either verbally or by other means, and the desire to control the impulses to defecate and urinate (Leventhal, 1981). Although there are large individual differences in the age at which complete toilet training is accomplished, it is mastered by most children by the age of 4 years. Bedwetting, particularly for boys, often continues well into the school age years (Routh, 1980).

Cognitive Development

The area of cognitive development is so complex that only a brief discussion is possible. The simplest operational definition of cognitive behavior is given by Skinner (1968) who says it is: (1) knowing how to do things, that is, abilities, and (2) knowing about things, that is, knowledge. Assessment of cognitive repertoires is most often done through the use of intelligence tests that are related to academic achievement and based on normative data. While there are wide individual differences in predictability, IQ test scores do tend to become more stable by the end of the preschool years.

The work of Piaget has greatly influenced the study of cognitive development. Piaget views the preschool child as moving from sensorimotor actions to a conceptual-symbolic mode of interaction that involves symbolic thinking. During the preschool years the child changes from someone with action structures to someone with thought structures (Piaget &

Inhelder, 1969). The preschooler is said to lack the concrete operational reasoning that is involved in conservation of mass, weight, volume, and number (Flavell, 1977) because the child is too preoccupied with one aspect of a perceptual display. For example, a preschooler is likely to focus on the level of liquid in two jars and ignore the width of the jars in determining if one jar has more liquid than the other jar. Egocentrism is also a characteristic of preschool thinking with the child unable to view the world from another person's perspective.

Perceptual development as reflected in a child's ability to recognize a particular visual form lags behind the ability to draw the forms accurately. Gibson's (1969) early work indicated that most 4-year-olds can differentiate according to closure (O versus C), but they still have trouble with line to curve transformation (V to U) and rotational transformations (b to d). Caldwell and Hall's (1970) work, however, indicates that, while preschoolers are visually able to discriminate letters or letterlike forms differing in orientation (b and d, m and w), they have trouble remembering what names and more important what sounds go with each one. Development in this area is an important prerequisite to reading.

Language Development

The period between 2 and 6 years of age represents a time of enormous growth in children's language abilities. Accomplishments of the average child during this time are: (1) speech comes to be clearly understood by persons outside the family, (2) the child becomes increasingly aware of the power of speech as a means of communication, (3) vocabulary increases from 100–200 words to several thousand words, and (4) syntax and sentence structure reach complex, adultlike levels (Lillywhite, Young, & Olmsted, 1970). Recognizing the importance of the preschool years for language development, the notion of a *critical period* for learning language has been popular in the past although the evidence for this idea is not conclusive. It is now more generally accepted that, while learning a language may be more difficult and perhaps less complete the older one gets, it is certainly not impossible (deVilliers & deVilliers, 1979).

Questions are an important part of the preschoolers' language development with the sequence usually going from "what," "where," and "who" questions to "why" questions. Children seem to like to hear how the adult responds as much as to want specific information. Likewise, they like to talk to themselves and try out different word combinations and ways of saying things (Rutter, 1975).

Social and Personality Development

In contrast to the view that development of later social relationships is dependent upon the early attachment relationships between mother and infant (Bowlby, 1969), Lewis and Schaeffer (1981) have proposed a social network model that describes social development as involving a number of independent relationships. Children are seen as having multiple needs that are independently satisfied by multiple social objects, that is, the parents and peers. Research suggests that parents (adults) are associated with security and dependency while peers are associated with play and teaching (Edwards & Lewis, 1979; Whiting & Whiting, 1975). The mother-infant attachment relationship may indirectly affect peer relationships, but peer relationships are not determined by mother-infant relationships. Lewis and Schaeffer (1981) discuss two negative indirect effects of the mother-infant relationship: (1) the mother may not provide the opportunity for the child to socialize with peers, or (2) a poor attachment relationship might produce fearfulness that would inhibit the child's approach to peers. This social network system views the social network of *both* the child and the family as important in social development. The importance of this work for the use of peer therapy groups and the importance of peer groups in general is obvious.

Children probably learn new age appropriate social behavior more easily in new stimulus settings than more familiar ones and societal pressures probably increase parental desire for control in public settings. Parents and children have been found to respond to each other differently depending on whether they are at home or in public. Four-year-old children are more obedient to strangers than to their mothers (Landauer, Carlsmith, & Lepper, 1970). Parents of 2–5-year-olds use more positive and encouraging statements with other children and more negative and controlling statements with their own children (Halverson & Waldrop, 1970).

As the child moves out into the world, solitary play decreases. Parallel play begins to occur around age 2, and gradually play becomes increasingly more cooperative for short periods of time. By age 3 children play cooperatively with one child, and by age 5 engage in cooperative play in groups (Parten, 1932). This increased peer interaction often brings an increase in temper tantrums and aggression as the child gradually learns to share and cooperate. The desire for peer interaction is great, however, and in its absence children often develop imaginary playmates (Manosevitz, Prentice, & Wilson, 1973).

Play is an extremely important part of development in the preschool years, and Rutter (1975) points out that pretend play serves many purposes. He summarizes a statement by Susanna Miller:

[In pretend play] the child may be exploring his feelings, lessening his fears, increasing his excitement, trying to understand a puzzling event by graphic representations, seeking confirmation of a hazy memory or altering an event to make it pleasant to himself in fantasy. (p. 75)

Observation of the preschool child's play can give much information about the child's intellectual development, language development, feelings, thoughts, and social relationships; fantasy play may reflect current concerns and anxieties. Play is thus important in the assessment and treatment of the preschool child.

A number of studies have focused on the attachment of a special, soft object that some preschoolers especially like to hold or carry with them in times of stress or at bedtime.

Winnicott (1953) described these as "transitional objects" that bridge the gap between the comforting relationship of the mother and greater independence. The number of preschoolers reported engaging in this behavior and the importance given to it have varied. Boniface and Graham (1979), however, found that only about 16 percent of a survey of 702 3-year-old children were using such an object. While no relationship was found between object usage and sex, social class or sleeping arrangements, object usage was significantly related to the child's level of independence, tendency to suck fingers and other objects, and ease of going to sleep. There was a tendency for children described as disturbed to use such objects less!

Identification

During the preschool years, children begin to identify with one or both parents and at times with people outside the home. Bandura (1969a) found that children imitate those who appear powerful and competent and who share a warm, loving relationship with them. The importance of the identification process in terms of action and prohibition has often been viewed (although with limited evidence) as the beginning of moral development, that is, how a child manages the conflict between his or her personal needs and his or her obligation to societal expectations. In the preschool years we might call this "resisting temptation." The parents' method of enforcing the family moral code plus the child's interaction with family members are probably the most important factors in this process for preschoolers.

The 2–4-year-old child demonstrates some empathetic behavior, that is, a vicarious emotional response to others in stress, but the child often fails to do anything to help the other person or acts inappropriately (Zahn-Waxler, Radke-Yarrow, & King, 1979). Children respond more empathetically to others of the same sex or race. Cognitive development increases the ability to perceive others as similar in abstract terms (Hoffman, 1979).

Guilt, a person's ability to be aware that he

or she is the cause of distress and to feel badly as a result is thought to be related to the development of empathy (Hoffman, 1965). There is evidence that some 2-year-olds have the beginnings of this response, and a definite guilt response appears in children as young as age 6 (Thompson & Hoffman, in press; Zahn-Waxler, Radke-Yarrow & King, 1979).

Psychosexual Development

Children's psychosexual development during the preschool years involves three sequential levels of knowledge according to Slaby and Frey (1975): (1) gender identity (knowing own sex and that of dolls); (2) gender stability (you always stay the same sex); and (3) gender consistency (sex does not change regardless of actions and clothes). Same sex preferences are usually reflected in children's behavior (choice of games, clothing) by the age of 4 or 5, but there is great variation in this (Rutter, 1971). It is interesting that boys develop a same sex preference earlier and more consistently than girls (Rutter, 1975). Societal attitudes undoubtedly greatly influence sex role preferences.

Curiosity about sex and sexual exploration via "playing doctor," "bathroom" talk, and masturbation are all common occurrences between 4 and 6 years (Routh & Schroeder, 1981). While psychoanalytic theory places much emphasis on castration anxiety and sexual rivalry with the same-sexed parent (the Oedipus complex), there is little evidence regarding their significance in the developmental process.

Emotional Behavior

The expression of emotional responses such as anger, fear, love, and joy is usually both intense and labile during the preschool years. These emotional responses, like other behaviors, are the result of an interaction between genetic-constitutional factors, environmental influences, past learning, and the developmental level of the child.

The temperament or behavioral style of a child's interaction with the environment is important to consider in the development of emotions. The work of Thomas and Chess (1977) demonstrates individual differences as early as the first few weeks of life. While they emphasize that temperament cannot predict the development of behavior problems, certain temperamental characteristics can increase the child's vulnerability. Chess and colleagues (Thomas, Chess, & Birch, 1968) assessed temperament in terms of nine categories of reactivity: mood, activity level, rhythmicity of biological functions, initial approach-withdrawal response to a new stimulus, speed and ease of adapting to altered environments, intensity or energy level of reaction, sensory threshold necessary to evoke a response, persistence, and distractibility. From these categories they derived three clinically significant clusters of traits: (1) the difficult child (arhythmic, low on approach and adaptability, intense and predominantly negative in mood); (2) the easy child (rhythmic, approaching, adaptable, mild and positive); (3) slow-to-warm-up child (low in activity, approach and adaptability, and negative mood, but variable in rhythmicity and mild in intensity). McDevitt and Carey (1978) in a sample of 350 3–5-year-old children from a pediatric practice found almost 19 percent to be difficult, 16 percent slow-to-warm-up, and 33 percent easy with 32 percent not fitting in any of these groups. About 35 percent of the New York Longitudinal Study (NYLS) (Thomas, Chess, & Birch, 1968) sample also did not fit into these diagnostic clusters. In general, the NYLS found the difficult and slow-to-warm-up children harder to parent and to have a greater risk of developing behavior problems than other children. When easy children developed behavior problems, it was more likely due to situational stress. Excessive persistence, excessive distractibility, and markedly low or high activity levels also were found to be more frequently associated with behavior disorders (Chess, 1970). Carey and McDevitt (in press) found that temperament characteristics regarded by parents as difficult to handle changed with age: at ages 1–3 the difficult child syndrome was the most troublesome while at ages 3–7 years rhythmicity decreased in importance as low persistence and high activity assumed greater significance. Cameron (1978) reports that parental intolerance, inconsistency, and conflict were associated with negative temperament changes over time.

The expression of emotion during the preschool years is usually uninhibited because the child is in the process of learning how to express emotions in a socially acceptable way. Anger is often expressed physically by biting, scratching, or kicking, and boys are commonly more physical than girls (Rutter, 1975). Anger is usually in response to an immediate stimulus and shortlived. The increased interaction with peers and family also increases negative behavior and temper outbursts which occur most often around 2–3 years and then gradually diminish during the later preschool years (Mesibov, Schroeder, & Wesson, 1977). Fears increase and change during the preschool years with fears of animals at 2–3 years changing to fears of darkness, nightmares, and imaginary creatures at ages 4–5 (Jersild & Holmes, 1935; Bauer, 1976).

ASSESSMENT

General Considerations

Children are developing organisms, changing over time as does their impact on the environment and the environment's impact on them. Targeting behavior for intervention and selection of intervention techniques must be done within the social context and the developmental framework of a particular child. Preschool children do not refer themselves for treatment; rather, referral to a professional is usually made because a parent, teacher or some other adult is concerned about annoying behavior or the absence of desired behavior (Ross, 1980). This does not necessarily mean that there is anything wrong with the behavior. In determining whether a behavior should be targeted for intervention, Furman (1980) outlines three approaches that can be taken: a *normative approach* that compares the frequency of the behavior to the behavior of other children the same age; a *social validity approach* where targeting and programming

for a behavior are based on experts' rating of the social significance of the behavioral goal and appropriate treatment (Wolf, 1978); and *current-future adjustment* factors that determine if the targeted behavior is associated with current and/or future adjustment. Each of these areas should be taken into account when evaluating the behavior of the preschool child.

Normative data can tell us whether a child's behavior is occurring at a deviant rate as compared to some accepted norm but it cannot tell us whether it is a problem. Some behaviors can occur at an atypical rate but are of little consequence for the child (Furman, 1980).

Also, the accepted or common behavior in one social setting might be considered deviant or atypical in another social setting. A case example given by Routh and Schroeder (1981) illustrates this point. A mother of a 3-year-old frantically asked for help in stopping her child's occasional masturbation while watching TV in the afternoons. When asked why she was concerned now as opposed to some other time, she blurted out, "My mother-in-law is coming to visit next week!" This mother did not view this behavior as deviant, but she viewed its occurrence in an upcoming social context (grandmother's visit) as inappropriate.

The frequency of almost all problem behaviors changes developmentally (Hartup, 1970; Mussen & Eisenberg-Berg, 1977). Thus some behaviors can change in the appropriate or desired direction without any intervention. For example, physical aggression reaches an asymptote during the preschool years and then declines. Other behaviors increase with age, such as verbal aggression (Feshbach, 1970). Thus the time when a behavior occurs in a child's life is as important as the behavior itself.

The *social validity* approach has value because the problem behaviors are viewed in the wider context of societal attitudes and values that vary by culture and with time. In some cultures, for example, aggression is sanctioned for survival purposes. The goal for a child from this culture would be to discriminate inappropriate and appropriate settings for aggression rather than to decrease the level of aggression. Traditionally, the social validity approach has required that a group of experts determine the importance of a behavior (Furman, 1980).

Current and future adjustment approaches try to target behaviors that are highly associated with other facets of current social adjustment or development and that would predict trouble for future adjustment. It must be remembered, however, that prediction of later adjustment changes developmentally. What is predictive at one age is not necessarily predictive at another age. Early childhood intelligence, for example, is not predictive of later childhood intelligence, but later childhood intelligence is predictive of adult intelligence. Also, many behaviors such as sleep disturbance, timidity, overdependence, and anxiety are often considered to be significant problems in the preschool years but are not predictive of later emotional disturbance or social adjustment (Kohlberg, LaCrosse, & Ricks, 1972). On the other hand, antisocial behaviors such as lying and the quality of peer relations are important predictors for later social behaviors (Furman, 1980). As Furman points out, this does not mean we should not treat behaviors that are interfering with a child's current adjustment but do not happen to be predictive of future problems. Priority, however, should be given to determining the cause of and effective treatment for behavior known to have predictive validity. It is interesting to note that the best childhood predictor of adult adjustment is intelligence (Furman, 1980). Furman says its strong predictive validity should lead us to foster learning and intellectual development as a means of promoting social development. As we will see later in the chapter, however, early intervention programs have indeed focused on this aspect of development but with little long term effect. This is probably because many intervention programs assume a causal relationship between social and cognitive development. It should be remembered that the correlation of behaviors does not give us information on causal relationships, so the

modification of one behavior (e.g., cognitive) may not affect a correlate (e.g., social behavior).

Areas to Assess

In assessing the preschool child, four general areas should be covered: (1) the *presenting behavior* including an objective description of the type of behavior, the severity and frequency of the behavior, the situation specificity of the behavior, the persistence of the behavior, the change from previous behavior, and the extent of the disturbance of the behavior, that is, an isolated behavior or a cluster of behaviors; (2) the *developmental* status of a child's physical, cognitive, emotional, and social behavior; (3) *environmental* factors such as the sociocultural setting including parental attitudes and expectations as well as life circumstances; and (4) the *consequences* of the behavior for the child, his or her family and his community (Rutter, 1975; Schroeder et al., 1981).

Methods that can be used to assess these variables could include standardized developmental instruments such as intelligence tests, parent interviews (Holland, 1970), parent questionnaires (Wahler & Cormier, 1970; Eyberg & Ross, 1978), and observation of the behavior in the clinic, home, school, or any other setting in which the behavior primarily occurs (Peed, Roberts, & Forehand, 1977). Direct observation of the child's interaction with his or her environment is important for all children and especially for preschool children because an adult's description is not always a valid reflection of the child's actual behavior (Ross, 1980). Forehand and associates (1975) in a study using parent questionnaires and home and clinic observations of clinic and nonclinic populations found that factors other than the child's behavior contributed to the parents' labeling a child as deviant and seeking clinic help. Low parental tolerance, high expectations for child behavior, marital distress, and other family problems played a major role in the parents' perceptions of their child's behavior. Thus setting conditions in the environment can affect the perception of a child's behavior and may be the more appropriate target of intervention. Assessment of these variables is imperative before embarking on a program to change the child's behavior.

At the conclusion of a thorough assessment, hypotheses should be generated about the behavior: Is it a developmental problem? Is the expected behavior absent or occurring at a rate that is too high or too low? Are parental expectations, attitudes, or beliefs appropriate for the social situation, the age, and developmental level of the child? Are there environmental conditions contributing to the perception of the behavior or setting conditions for the behavior? Will the behavior cause the child, parents, or environment to suffer now or in the future? Should a referral for a physical evaluation be made to determine a possible organic problem? The data gathered should answer these questions, giving information on the nature of the behavior problem, the target of intervention, and the selection of an appropriate intervention strategy (Schroeder & Schroeder, in press).

Prevalence of Problems

It should be clear at this point that the child's behavior is ever changing and evolving through interaction with the environment. As Chess and Thomas (1978) state, "No single aspect of the child or environment—whether it be intellectual level, temperament, parental characteristics, relationships to sibs or peers, etc.—no matter how important in general, is necessarily a significant etiological factor in every instance of problem behavior development" (p. 229). So we can make statements about prevalence of behavior problems, but only in rare cases can we make predictions about their significance for future adjustment. Prevalence studies on problems during the preschool years are sparse. Richman, Stevenson, and Graham (1974), interviewing mothers of 800 randomly selected 3-year-old children in London, estimated 7 percent to have moderate-to-severe problems, and 15 percent to have mild problems. In this study, there were no sex differences although a similar study found

significantly more boys having problems (Behar & Stringfield, 1974). Language delay in 3-year-old children was associated with behavior problems, and this was also found in a study by Jenkins, Bax, and Hart (1980). As the latter study points out, there is evidence to indicate that these same children are likely to have difficulty learning to read and write. In a follow-up of the children from the Richman et al. (1974) study, two-thirds of the problem children continued to present problems a year later as compared to 15 percent of the control group (Richman, 1977).

In a follow-up of children from the New York Longitudinal Study (NYLS), Thomas and Chess (1972) found in 34 out of 47 children with behavior disorders onset was before the age of 6. Only one new case developed between the ages of 9 and 12 years. In contrast, the incidence of behavior disorders in a population of workingclass Puerto Rican children was higher during the early school years than the preschool years. They concluded that the preschool years presented more stress to the middle class children of the NYLS study because of the emphasis on routinization and socialization while for the Puerto Rican youngsters it was only at age 5 or 6, with the start of school, that demands for regularity of sleep, discipline, learning and obedience were made (Thomas et al., 1974). In the NYLS the behavior problems in the younger children were sleep disturbances, temper tantrums, and maladaptation to the rules of social living. By school age, the problems centered on peer relationships and learning.

Jenkins, Bax, and Hart (1980) studied 412 preschoolers and found that the percentage of parents worried about their children was highest at 3 years (23 percent). The problems included difficulty in management, the child demanding too much attention, and the occurrence of temper tantrums. While food fads and poor appetite also were more common at age 3, the parents did not view them as significant problems. Mesibov, Schroeder, and Wessen (1977) found similar results in 672 parent concerns reported to a consultation service in a pediatric office. The greatest number of concerns were among the 2- and 3-year-old age range with negative behavior, toileting, and developmental delays being the most frequent concerns. Rolf and Harig (1975) surveyed risk studies and follow-up studies and concluded that the most vulnerable children at any age are: (1) children with deviant parents, such as schizophrenics; (2) children with unsocialized, aggressive behavior; (3) children with severe social, cultural, economic, and nutritional deprivation in their environment; and (4) children with physical and intellectual handicaps.

The next sections of this chapter will focus on a review of problem areas that are often brought to the attention of the clinical child psychologist during the preschool years: the exceptional child, separation, child maltreatment, and some common behavior problems.

EXCEPTIONAL CHILDREN

Because the preschool years are a time of enormous developmental progress, the period of 2 years through 5 years is a critical time for the exceptional child. It is during this period that many exceptional children are first identified, often because they fail to achieve the expected developmental progress in one or many areas. This section will cover developmental disorders that are often diagnosed during the preschool years or have special impact on the preschool child: mental retardation, language disorders, autism, and childhood schizophrenia. The gifted child and the chronically ill child with their exceptional needs are included in this section.

Mentally Retarded Children

Approximately 75 percent of the cases of mental retardation have no known cause (Zigler, 1978). Increasing numbers of these children, called "cultural-familial" or "sociocultural" mentally retarded persons, are being identified during the preschool years (Edgerton, 1979). Most often these children are referred for evaluation because of slow or atypical language development, behavior

problems such as noncompliance, short attention span or distractibility, because a preschool teacher or daycare worker senses that "something is not quite right," or because parents become concerned that the child will not be ready to start school.

While our knowledge of the causes of this form of retardation is sorely lacking, we do know that it reflects a complex interaction between genetic factors and environmental circumstances (Zigler 1978). Children born into impoverished environments are 15 times more likely to be retarded than those born into enriched environments, and of these children boys are more likely to be retarded than girls (Edgerton, 1979). Environmental features that have been identified as being important in understanding cultural/familial retardation are maternal IQ and education (Golden & Birns, 1976), family size (Zajonc, 1976), maternal health and nutrition during pregnancy, child health and nutrition (Robinson & Robinson, 1976; Winick, Meyer, & Harris, 1975), and the quality of life in the home, including such variables as parental language, parent-child interaction, parental aspirations for the child, and the toys and games available (Edgerton, 1979). Clearly all these factors are interwoven into the context of a poverty-stricken environment, and no one factor is thought to be sufficient to cause retardation by itself. Malnutrition, for example, probably plays only a minor role in causing irreversible central nervous system damage and mental retardation, but it does dramatically depress alertness, curiosity, motivation, and attention—all critical to learning (Robinson & Robinson, 1976; Winick et al., 1975).

Other causes of mental retardation in preschool children are head injuries, either accidental or as a result of abuse, brain tumors, or infections such as meningitis or encephalitis. The incidence of retardation, however, resulting from each of these factors is relatively small (Robinson & Robinson, 1976).

Families of mentally retarded children often experience the preschool years as a time of particular stress. Because normal children are making such rapid progress during these years, changing, and learning new skills almost daily, the contrast of their own slower child is often striking. Also parents may realize the impact of having a handicapped child for the first time during these years. Each developmental change necessitates a new adjustment for parents of these children. Toilet training is likely to be slower and more difficult; the child may be slower to learn to dress and eat independently; retarded children continue to need constant supervision at a time when most children are becoming independent, helpful family members. Parents may find their own social activities and career aspirations drastically curtailed because of difficulties in obtaining adequate child care. In addition, parents are faced with the frustrations of obtaining appropriate services in a society where these are sorely lacking despite the passage of PL 94–142, the Education for All Handicapped Children's Act (1974).

Intervention programs during this period (to be discussed in a later section) must not only focus on the child's particular physical or cognitive needs but must also provide the parents with support in understanding and caring for their child. Assessment and clear, accurate interpretation of the child's current functioning helps parents understand their child's developmental status. Putting parents in touch with groups such as the American Association for Retarded Citizens, mobilizing family and community resources, and teaching parents to become advocates for their child are also important.

Gifted Preschool Children

At the opposite end of the spectrum from the retarded child, but no less exceptional, is the gifted child. Gifted children are also most often identified during the preschool years because they go beyond our developmental expectations (Roedell, Jackson, & Robinson, 1980). Gifted preschool children have not yet had the opportunity to realize their full potential and thus one of the goals of early identification is to nurture their exceptional talent. Current definitions of giftedness have been broadened from a unitary concept of general intelligence to include measures of intellectual, scholastic, and psychomotor ability, as well as creativity, leadership, and artistic talent (Roedell et al., 1980).

Gifted children have variously been described as possessing a variety of desirable characteristics including independence, persistence in the face of difficulty, broad attention span, industriousness, forcefulness, and competitiveness (Chess & Hassibi, 1978). It is generally accepted, however, that it is foolish to attempt to characterize them as a group since they differ in all areas as much as average or handicapped children differ from one another. Gifted children also differ amongst themselves in the areas in which they demonstrate precocity. One child might be gifted in mathematical reasoning and another in spatial reasoning. Even within the same child, the variation in different skill areas can be tremendous. It is not uncommon to find children gifted in one area and average or even below average in another.

Gifted children can come from families of any culture or socioeconomic class although problems have been noted in identifying gifted children from low income or minority group families (Roedell et al., 1980). In general, parents have been found to be the best source for identifying gifted young children (Ciha et al., 1974), whereas teachers may tend to overestimate intelligence in cooperative, verbal children and to bias their nominations on the basis of social class, race, and sex (Jacobs, 1971). Parents are in the best position to observe and report their child's everyday behavior and, in general, have been found to do so reliably enough to predict their child's performance on standardized tests (Roedell et al., 1980). Objective questionnaires that focus on specific behaviors have been developed to circumvent parental biases in interpreting child behavior (Roedell et al., 1980).

Programs for gifted children are not widespread although there appears to be an increasing awareness of the need for early educational opportunities for these children as well as a need to prevent adjustment problems. Extremely gifted children are "at risk" for adjustment problems, in part because of the wide gaps between level of intellectual and physical and social or emotional development (Getzels & Dillon, 1973; Terman & Oden, 1947). In addition, gifted children must cope with being isolated from peers or being seen as different or peculiar because of their extraordinary abilities. In general, programs for gifted preschoolers should take into account the tremendous diversity among these children, focusing on cognitive, physical, and social skill development. While several different program models have been developed, there is little data on their relative effectiveness at this time (Roedell et al., 1980).

Early Infantile Autism

While it is generally accepted that autism is present at birth (DeMeyer, 1979; Newsom, 1980), most autistic children are first evaluated and diagnosed during the preschool years (Ornitz & Ritvo, 1976). Particularly sensitive parents may become concerned while their child is still in infancy, noticing that the child seems different from their other children, is less responsive, cries less, overreacts, or is either limp or rigid when held. It is more common, however, that these subtle signs are overlooked until 2–3 years of age when the child has failed to develop language or other symptoms are so obvious that parents become seriously worried (Kolvin, 1971).

DeMeyer (1979) studied 58 autistic children through in-depth parent interviews as well as extensive testing and retesting of the children. She found that parents considered the preschool years to be the most difficult time for them and their children. Seventy-eight percent of the children were reported to be most severely disturbed in the areas of speech, social relatedness, and general disposition between 2 and 4 years of age. DeMeyer suggests two reasons for the particular difficulties of the preschool years. First, parental fears, anxieties, and feelings of helplessness are at a peak during this time. Secondly, the years from 2–4 are a time of enormous developmental progress in normal children while autistic children have difficulties in almost all developmental areas. For example, speech fails to develop or develops atypically; autistic children's play lacks all the features of normal preschool play; toilet training is delayed and often accompanied by significant problems such as frequent smearing of feces and chronic constipation or diarrhea; feeding and sleeping problems are more common; and parents report that their discipline techniques are not effective (DeMeyer, 1979).

Incidence of autism is estimated to range from .7/10,000 to 4.5/10,000. Current research indicates that autism is found in children of all social classes, races, and cultures (Ornitz & Ritvo, 1976). Two-thirds to three-fourths of all autistic children are also retarded (Rutter, 1970), and many later develop seizure disorders (Schopler & Rutter, 1978).

While some disagreement about what constitutes the essential features of autism remains despite considerable efforts to clarify the diagnostic criteria, Ornitz and Ritvo (1976) propose the following six distinguishing characteristics that seem to encompass the most essential features: (1) present at birth with the appearance of obvious symptoms by 30 months; (2) disturbance of perception—faulty modulation of external sensory input; (3) disturbance of developmental rate—uneven profiles or development that is out of sequence; (4) disturbance of relating—possibly secondary to perceptual disturbances; (5) disturbance of speech and language—mutism, echolalia, pronoun reversal; and (6) disturbance of motility—peculiar mannerisms and stereotypies.

Current research and clinical experience indicate that autism is not an either/or disease; rather it exists on a continuum of severity ranging from high functioning, mildly impaired to extremely low functioning, severely impaired (DeMeyer, 1977). DeMeyer (1979) suggests that autism is the outward manifestation of a continuum of neurological impairment similar to that which causes severe learning disability. While much research remains to be done before we understand the etiology of this disorder, it is important to note that current work is focusing on neurological or biochemical factors rather than on environmental variables such as parental characteristics or behavior.

Overall, the prognosis for children with autism is poor, and those who have not developed communicative language by age 5 have the poorest prognosis of all (Ornitz & Ritvo, 1976). Treatment approaches have ranged from prefrontal lobotomy to megavitamins to psychoanalytic therapy (Newsom, 1980). Behavior therapy focusing on decreasing inappropriate behaviors, increasing attending skills, and language development (e.g., Lovaas, 1978) has been demonstrated to be the most effective approach to date, especially when parents are trained along with their children (Newsom, 1980). Treatment for the majority of autistic children, however, consists of a special education approach. This approach views the child from a developmental perspective and focuses on stimulating development of cognitive, perceptual-motor, language, and social skills (Lansing & Schopler, 1978; Rutter & Sussenwein, 1971). Research comparing the special education and behavioral approaches or a combination of the two is still needed.

DeMyer (1979) suggests that it is critical for treatment to begin during the preschool years when the family is under the most stress and points to the pros and cons of inpatient versus outpatient placement. In either case, she states that autistic children learn best when their environment is familiar and remains stable and where material can be repeated daily throughout the year. Realistic and continual appraisal of the child's developmental level is cited as critical to any program.

Childhood Schizophrenia

Rutter (1972, 1974) indicates that there are so many differences between infantile autism and childhood schizophrenia that they should be regarded as separate conditions. He distinguishes between psychosis that begins in the first three years of life (autism) and psychosis that begins during or after puberty (schizo-

phrenia). Schizophrenic children are said to differ from autistic children in developing normal language, having remissions and relapses, and developing delusions and hallucinations in adulthood (Rutter, 1970).

This bimodal distribution (early versus later onset) ignores preschool children. Anthony (1958, 1962) identifies three groups of psychotic children that include cases with an acute onset between the ages of 3 and 5 years. The rarity of these children who develop normally up to about 3 years and then deteriorate rapidly may have caused them to be overlooked. Char and Lubetsky (1979) report on six such children seen over a two-year period in a mental health center. The course of the disorder in these children was remarkably similar and with treatment, three made significant improvement. This suggests that identification of these children early in the course of their deterioration is critical since their prognosis is likely to be more positive than that of autistic children or children with later onset schizophrenia.

Language Disorders

Because language develops so rapidly during the preschool years, it is not surprising that many speech and communication disorders are identified during this period. Any of the major categories of speech and language disorders can be seen in preschool youngsters. Briefly, there are disorders of speech (articulation, voice quality, and fluency); disorders of language (understanding the symbol system, and production of words, meanings, and grammar); and disorders of communication or pragmatics (social uses of language as a communication system) (Vetter, 1980a).

In the absence of mental retardation, deafness, or emotional disorder, the term "childhood aphasia" or "developmental aphasia" has been used to describe the failure of some children to develop or the tendency to have extreme difficulty using language and speech (Cohen, Caparulo, & Shaywitz, 1976). Others feel this is a confusing label that should be reserved for those children who have acquired language and lost it through some trauma (Vetter, 1980a). The etiology of childhood aphasia is not clear although Cohen et al. (1976) cite some evidence for subtle, diffuse neurological dysfunction in the higher order associative areas of the brain and in the specific speech areas.

Speech and language disorders are often associated with other disabilities. In fact, it is often because parents are concerned that their preschool child is not developing language that they seek professional help and evaluation, resulting in a primary diagnosis of mental retardation, hearing loss, autism, or other disorder. For example, articulation problems, comprehension and production delays, and difficulties in understanding the communication function are associated with mental retardation (Lassman et al., 1980). General language delays and problems with articulation and intelligibility are associated with hearing impairment. In addition, many of the social factors that place children at increased risk for mental retardation are also associated with language disorders: low socioeconomic status, mothers under 18 years of age, number of children in the family, and maternal IQ and education are all cited (Vetter, 1980b).

Of course, any language problem must always be assessed relative to the child's developmental status and environmental circumstances. Stuttering, for example, which can be a major problem for older children, is not uncommon in preschoolers who hesitate and stutter because they do not yet have the vocabulary to express all that they know. Pressure by anxious parents only creates more difficulty. In fact, most serious cases of dysfluency in older children have their origins between the ages of 2–5 (Lillywhite, Young, & Olmsted, 1970). Similarly, articulation errors are common in preschool children whose vocabulary increases at such a rapid pace. In addition, there is a great deal of variability in the rate with which individual children meet the developmental milestones for language (see Vetter, 1980a, for a table of milestones). Lillywhite et al. (1970) have compiled a list of twenty guidelines useful for determining when a child has a significant problem needing

Table 13.1   Guidelines for Referral to Communication Specialist

Refer if any of the following conditions exist:

1. Child is not talking at all by age 2.
2. Speech is largely unintelligible after age 3.
3. There are many omissions of initial consonants after age 3.
4. There are no sentences by age 3.
5. Sounds are more than a year late in appearing according to development sequence.
6. There is an excessive amount of indiscriminate, irrelevant verbalizing after 18 months.
7. There is consistent and frequent omission of initial consonants.
8. There are many substitutions of easy sounds for difficult ones after age 5.
9. The amount of vocalizing decreases rather than steadily increases at any period up to age 7.
10. The child uses mostly vowel sounds in his speech at any age after 1 year.
11. Word endings are consistently dropped after age 5.
12. Sentence structure is consistently faulty after age 5.
13. The child is embarrassed or disturbed by his speech at any age.
14. The child is noticeably nonfluent (stuttering) after age 5.
15. The child is distorting, omitting, or substituting any sounds after age 7.
16. The voice is a monotone, extremely loud, largely inaudible, or of poor quality.
17. The pitch is not appropriate to the child's age and sex.
18. There is noticeable hypernasality or lack of nasal resonance.
19. There are unusual confusions, reversals, or telescoping in connected speech.
20. There is abnormal rhythm, rate, and inflection after age 5.

Note: Taken from *Pediatricians Handbook of Communication Disorders* by H.S. Lillywhite, N.B. Young, and R.W. Olmsted. Used with the permission of Lea & Febiger. Copyright © 1970 by Lea & Febiger.

referral or when he or she is developing normally, albeit at his or her own pace, and is best left alone (Table 13.1).

Treatment of speech and language disorders has two goals: helping the child to communicate his or her thoughts and needs to others and helping the child understand the communication of others (Vetter, 1980a). In a recent review of the pragmatics of language development, Hart (1980) suggests that the clinician should first understand the environment in which a child will use language. Training should take place in that or a similar context and should focus on the function that language will have for the child in the environment in which he or she lives. An increased rate of a child's use of communication should be established before correct usage and form are trained.

For a variety of reasons, some children never acquire adequate language for communication even when extensive efforts at remediation are made. The necessity of communication is no less important for these children, and they should be evaluated for the appropriateness of an augmentative system of communication (Vanderheiden & Grilley, 1975; Wilbur, 1976).

Chronic Illness

There is not much written specifically about the chronically ill preschool child. It seems apparent, however, that the onset of serious illness in the preschool years has the potential seriously to compromise the child's rapid development and the parent-child relationship, which is still in the formative stages. The chronically ill preschool child must not only cope with developmental issues such as mastery over bowels, dressing, eating, language, and an increasing need for independence, but also with the physical and emotional effects of the disease that may conflict with or inhibit the child's sense of competence and undermine a growing sense of self-esteem (Friedrich, 1977). Parents, in turn, must accept the disease and its often unpredictable cause and outcome and balance their own anxieties and desire to protect the child with the child's need to grow and become independent. Some parents find themselves fearful of overindulging the child and become overly strict. Others (more commonly) suspend all discipline (Freud, 1952).

While the chronically ill preschool child is vulnerable to behavioral and adjustment problems, it is a mistake to assume that all chronically ill children develop problems. One study (Tavormina et al., 1976) of 132 children with a variety of chronic illnesses found that the children's strengths and coping abilities outweighed their personality weaknesses. In a review of the literature on congenital heart disease, Kitchen (1978) found that children's emotional adjustment was related to their mothers' level of anxiety about the disease. Maternal anxiety was in turn related to the *presence* of congenital heart disease rather than its severity. Others have found, however, that a mild illness in a child may mobilize a family's strengths, make them more aware of various aspects of childrearing and thus more effective, while severe illness in children may have an immobilizing effect on the family (Markova, MacDonald, & Forbes, 1980). A certain amount of anxiety is to be expected when one is parenting a chronically ill child. The critical factor seems to be the extent to which parents can meet their child's needs while at the same time coping with their own emotional distress (Tropauer, Franz, & Dilgard, 1970).

In order to know how best to help chronically ill preschool children continue along a relatively smooth developmental course, one must remember that children's understanding of illness is dependent on their level of cognitive development (Schroeder, Teplin, & Schroeder, 1981). Children under 3 years are likely to view their illness as punishment for misbehavior and are not able to understand the reasons given for the illness (Blos, 1978). Simple statements of fact or warning, such as "You did nothing to cause your illness" or "This will hurt" can be understood and help the child build a sense of trust (Blos, 1978). Older preschool children, because of their excellent verbal skills, often mislead adults into thinking they understand more than they do. These children can distort explanations through visual imagery and fantasy to produce their own theories of causality.

A major intervention focus for chronically ill preschool children has been on play therapy to help them express their fears and anxiety and regain a sense of mastery (Tavormina et al., 1976). Parents have been helped through supportive parent groups (Bardach, 1976; Knapp & Hansen, 1973) and workshops (David & Donovan, 1975). Additionally, family therapy has been found to be especially effective in modifying the family's functioning so that its tasks of support, nurturance, regulation and socialization can continue to be performed adequately (Minuchin, 1974). However, as Johnson (1979) points out, little is known about the relative effectiveness of different strategies for children of different ages and with different illnesses.

SEPARATION ISSUES

Largely because of their developmental status, preschool children are thought to be particularly vulnerable to adverse effects of separation from important people in their lives. Preschool children are not cognitively capable of understanding all aspects of the events that cause separation and have not yet established adequate coping mechanisms. They are still very dependent on adult caregivers and yet are in the process of becoming increasingly independent. A stable base of emotional support and nurturance is very important for this process to continue. It should therefore not surprise us that events such as hospitalization, parental divorce, death of a loved person or entry into daycare are separation issues from the preschool child's point of view. Rutter (1979), however, states that separation, for whatever reason, is not in itself necessarily harmful. He believes that the adverse effects of separation on the preschool child documented in the literature are due to other accompanying factors such as discord and disharmony in the home, lack of adequate stimulation, or a failure to form affectional bonds in infancy. This section will briefly

discuss the concept of childhood depression, a disorder that has been thought to result from separation. This will be followed by a brief literature review on effects of several common types of separation: divorce, daycare, death, and hospitalization.

Childhood Depression

Early work (Goldfarb, 1943; Spitz, 1946) first identified childhood depression in institutionalized or severely deprived children. "Anaclitic depression," as this syndrome was called, is now thought to represent the effects of deprivation rather than the result of maternal separation as was originally proposed. Current work has focused primarily on the question of whether childhood depression can even be identified as a distinct clinical syndrome.

Kovacs and Beck (1977) suggest that childhood depression is a condition similar to that which can be delineated and measured in adults but add that preschool children, because of their level of cognitive development, cannot be labeled "depressed." Those who take the opposing view suggest that the symptoms of childhood depression are characteristic of normal development in children and dissipate with time and, for the most part, without intervention. In a recent review, Lefkowitz and Burton (1978) state that the presence of depressive symptoms is fairly common in any population of children (both clinic and normal) and that the symptoms are age related, decreasing in deviance with increasing age. Lefkowitz and Burton (1978) suggest that parental thresholds for deviance may determine which children are referred for treatment. Once the child is referred, "depression" is inferred from the presenting symptoms, and then the symptoms are said to be caused by the depressive disorder. Gittleman-Klein (1977) suggests that many young children exposed to stressful situations (particularly those involving separation) or to extreme deprivation manifest depressive symptoms. These symptoms generally disappear with time or when the environmental conditions are improved. Other children are described as being chronically sad or withdrawn even when no specific stressful event can be identified and the environment adequately meets the child's needs.

Seligman (1975) has proposed a model of "learned helplessness" as a way of understanding depression in very young children and its relationship to adult depression. According to this model the child learns that significant events (such as loss of the mother figure) occur that are outside the child's control; that no response or behavior on the part of the child is successful in alleviating the trauma or stress. Thus the child begins to perceive himself or herself as being helpless. Watson (1977) has extended this model by suggesting that perceived control over environmental events leads to a sense of mastery or competence that is inconsistent with depression. Children may learn early in life, through excessive noncontingent reinforcement experiences, to perceive themselves as having no control even when this is not the case. Watson suggests that this "interference effect" or misperception of contingencies based on previous experience may cause one to be more vulnerable to depression later in life. Dweck (1977), however, indicates that learned helplessness may not cause childhood depression because young children have no expectancy for control. Rather, as the expectancy for control increases with age so does the risk of depression.

In summary, there seems to be moderate agreement that some young children do experience something like adult depression. It is important, however, to determine if the depressive behavior is endogenous or situational depression, that is, characteristic of the child's affective state in an adequate environment or due to current environmental conditions. The questions which need to be addressed in diagnosis are: (1) How is the depression expressed or manifested in the child? and (2) How pervasive, intense, and long lasting are these behaviors and feelings? Differential diagnosis is particularly important in light of the fact that considerable numbers of young children are currently being treated with antidepressant medications (Rapoport, 1977) despite the lack of demonstrated effectiveness of these drugs for children and the considerable

controversy surrounding the validity of the concept of childhood depression.

Effects of Divorce

Until recently there has been little research on the effects of divorce on young children. The present alarming rise in the incidence of divorce and the increasing numbers of children who are experiencing parental separation has led to an increased interest in this area. Most notably, the work of Wallerstein and Kelly (1980) has been instrumental in surveying the issues in this area from a developmental perspective.

Wallerstein and Kelly (1975) state clearly that, from the point of view of the preschool child, the central issue in the divorce experience is the loss of a parent and the resulting fear of disruption of nurturance and abandonment by both parents. The preschool child is thought to be particularly vulnerable to detrimental effects of parental divorce because of their relative dependence, their cognitive confusion about the causes and implications of the divorce, and their lack of adequate coping strategies (Wallerstein & Kelly, 1975). In addition, because the stress and disequilibrium experienced by families of divorce has been found to extend over 2 or more years (Hetherington, Cox, & Cox, 1975), the preschool child is exposed to considerable environmental instability and stress at the same time that significant normal developmental changes are occurring. Others (e.g., Gardner, 1977) cite the Oedipal period as contributing to the preschool child's increased vulnerability, particularly when the lost parent is of the opposite sex. Thus it is not surprising that 44 percent of the preschool children studied by Wallerstein and Kelly were in "significantly deteriorated psychological condition" at their one year follow-up (Wallerstein & Kelly, 1975).

The immediate response of the preschool child to parental divorce is similar to that seen by others who have studied the effects of maternal separation (e.g., Bowlby, 1969) although it is the father-child relationship that is most often disrupted in divorce. Wallerstein and Kelly (1975) found that younger preschoolers are likely to display regression in self-help areas recently mastered (particularly toileting), acute separation anxiety, increased irritability, and sleep problems, as well as increased aggression and tantrums. Older preschoolers show less regression but more cognitive confusion such as self-blame, fears about the dependability of relationships, and increased aggression and separation anxiety. Longfellow (1979) suggests that these reactions reflect the older preschool child's level of social-cognitive development, which is characterized by egocentric and concrete reasoning. Preschool children put two unrelated events together in a causal fashion and assume that their parents have separated because the child has been bad. Their concept of family is concrete: a family consists of those who live together in the same house.

Several variables have been identified that may influence outcome for children of divorce, regardless of age (Wallerstein & Kelly, 1975). These include continued disorganization in the family, undiminished anger or psychological illness in the custodial parent, and insufficient contact with the noncustodial parent. For the preschool child, the critical variable for adjustment seems to be the quality of the custodial parent-child relationship, specifically the extent to which this parent, who is experiencing considerable stress, is able to meet the child's emotional needs. Unfortunately, mothers of children under 5 years of age are most likely to experience depression following marital separation (Longfellow, 1979). Factors that are not directly related to the preschool child's adjustment are the level of initial turmoil, the intensity of the child's immediate symptoms, the mother's employment status, and the existence of external support systems although these are all related to maternal depression.

Many of the intervention techniques reported in the literature have been geared toward older children (e.g., Gardner, 1976; Kessler & Bostwick, 1977) and little is known of the most effective strategies for helping preschool children. Sang (1979) suggests that preschool children understand more than they can express and that professionals need to teach parents to supply the language to help the child express feelings of loss and pain. In view of Wallerstein and Kelly's findings, it would seem that intervention focused on alleviating the economic and emotional stress of the custodial parent, enabling that parent to better meet the child's needs, might be an effective approach for helping the preschool child. Woody (1978) proposes a preventive approach focused on collaboration with the legal community, divorce counseling and mediation, and developing community resources.

Effects of Daycare

Fears that the psychological development of children in daycare would be seriously impaired arose from early research on the effects of institutionalization. Because of these fears and because increasing numbers of children under 6 years of age are being placed in daycare, research in this area has burgeoned. Review of this research suggests that many of the old fears can be laid to rest, but new ones have arisen, and, as Belsky and Steinberg (1978) concluded, we still know alarmingly little about the effects of daycare on young children. What is known can be summarized briefly.

Belsky and Steinberg (1978) state in a recent paper that, although the most common type of daycare (other than a relative) is a sitter in one's own home or in someone else's home, most of the research is on the effects of center-based group care. In addition, while research has focused on relatively high quality, demonstration daycare centers, most of the centers in one survey were rated only fair or poor (Keyserling, 1972). There are also no studies of long term effects beyond the preschool years.

Daycare in general appears to have little effect on the cognitive development of most preschool children. Group daycare, however, appears to be beneficial in preventing a decline in the test scores of high risk children from inadequate home environments (Golden & Birns, 1976). It also seems that the effects of daycare on cognitive development vary as a function of the type of program, the type of activities offered, and family characteristics (Belsky & Steinberg, 1978).

There is contradictory evidence that the mother-child attachment bond is adversely affected by placing a child in daycare. Some studies have found that daycare children are less securely attached to their mothers (Blehar, 1974; Cochran, 1977) while others find that home-reared children are less secure (Moskowitz, Schwarz, & Corsini, 1977). When the quality of the caretaker-child relationship is taken into account, however, it appears that significant disruption of the mother-child bond is unlikely (Belsky & Steinberg, 1978). Anderson (1980) supports this conclusion. She states that the quality and stability of caregiving relationships predict healthy social and emotional development in preschool children. Quality is defined as caregiver sensitivity and responsivity. Stability is the extent to which the child can predict the availability and responsiveness of the caregiver. Anderson asserts that the effects of any parent-child separations, including hospitalization, death, divorce, and daycare, are mediated by these two variables (stability and quality of the caregiver-child relationship). This finding is particularly disturbing in light of a recent survey of the characteristics of federally funded (Title XX) daycare programs (Sheehan & Abbott, 1979). This study found that, while all the classrooms were pleasant and well equipped, the caregiver-child interaction could best be described as custodial. The caregivers were involved with the children most of the time, but their involvement was neutral or management oriented in quality, focusing on maintenance of functions.

Many parents expect that group care will help their children get along better with peers. Belsky and Steinberg (1978), however, state that, while most studies find daycare children are more peer oriented and are rated higher in sociability than home-reared children, daycare children are also more aggressive and less cooperative with adults. They are also more impulsive and egocentric than home-reared children. Belsky and Steinberg suggest that these characteristics may reflect the values held by the program sponsors and, indirectly,

the community at large. Lewis and Schaeffer's (1981) work on the development of peer relationships, however, indicates the value of well-organized programs staffed by sensitive people for high risk children, such as maltreated preschoolers.

Effects of Death

For the preschool child, death is also a separation issue, whether it is their own impending death or that of a loved person. Cognitively, preschool children are not capable of understanding the abstract concept of death (Spinetta, 1974). Studies of normal preschool children indicate that they believe death is completely reversible and is something that happens only to others (Easson, 1968; Koocher, 1974). In the child's experience, television actors die on one show and reappear on another, deceased pets are quickly replaced, and children are protected by all-powerful adults. Thus it is not surprising that many parents feel it is better to shield young children from knowledge that they or a loved person is dying. On the other hand, current research has indicated that most preschool children are aware of the seriousness of a life-threatening illness even though this is not discussed with them. In addition, most preschool children, when faced with death, have fears and anxieties that need to be expressed and dealt with (Grogan, O'Malley, & Foster, 1977; Kellerman et al., 1977).

In their attempts to understand death, preschool children often develop their own theories about what happened and why. These theories at the preschool level are usually related to the child's own responsibility in causing the death and reflect the child's omnipotent thinking (Weston & Irwin, 1963). Thus importance of honesty and factual information is stressed in helping young children deal with death. Reassurance that the child will be cared for and did nothing to cause the death is critical, as well as a willingness to answer any and all questions raised by the child.

Spinetta (1977) suggests that dying children can adjust reasonably well to their situation. Children who are coping well maintain their sense of self-worth, maintain rewarding interpersonal relationships, and can tolerate most of the stressful procedures necessitated by their illness. When a young child is dying, intervention should focus on maintaining the quality of the child's life, encouraging open communication about the child's fears and anxieties, preparation for painful procedures, and reassurance that someone will be there (Spinetta, 1977). It is often the case, particularly when the child has been ill for some time, that parents are unable to meet their child's needs for emotional support, either because of the intensity of their own grief or because they have finished the mourning process long before the child dies and have isolated themselves from the child (Easson, 1968).

Young children cannot be expected to feel the same intensity of sadness that adults feel and may experience some confusion in witnessing the grief of others (Harrison, Davenport, & McDermott, 1967). On the other hand, parents are often upset by seeing their child continue in day-to-day activities as if nothing has happened following the death of a family member.

Effects of Hospitalization

With increasing recognition of the potential adverse effects of hospitalization on children, considerable work is being devoted to understanding the psychological aspects of hospital care. A basic assumption is made that the stress and trauma of hospitalization can lead to transitory or long term psychological disturbance in young children (Siegel, 1976). Intervention strategies are being designed to alleviate this assumed stress (Johnson, 1979).

Prugh and his colleagues (Prugh et al., 1953) studied the emotional reactions of children to hospitalization without intervention and found that all children showed at least some distress. The extent of the distress was age related, with children under 3 years of age having the most severe reactions. As in the findings of studies on divorce, young preschool children (ages 2–4) most often demonstrated separation anxiety that was manifested by sadness, withdrawal, regression in toileting and feeding, and sleep disturbances. Older preschool children (4–6 years) showed less separation anxiety and less regression but had more difficulty accepting the dependent state necessitated by their illness. Somatic complaints and obsessivelike fears were more common in this group. At a 3-month follow-up, Prugh et al. (1953) found that half the children still showing signs of disturbance were under 4 years of age. Posthospital behaviors observed included demanding behavior, greater dependence, fear of strangers, separation anxiety, nightmares, and hyperactivity.

Siegel (1976) suggests that one variable that may mediate the potential adverse effects of hospitalization on the child is the age of the child. He states that while the necessity for preparation and/or intervention is generally agreed upon for all children, the type and timing relative to the child's developmental level are not. A wide variety of intervention strategies have been tried and are reviewed by Johnson (1979). Research that evaluates the effectiveness of intervention procedures, however, has been limited and severely hampered by methodological problems. Play therapy programs have been found somewhat effective with preschool children, particularly when they are accompanied by substitute mothers and transitional objects such as familiar toys, blankets, and parental clothing (Prugh et al., 1955; Tisza, Hurwitz, & Angoff, 1970). Clearly, more work is needed in this area, particularly with respect to the preschool child.

CHILD MALTREATMENT

Child maltreatment is regarded as a leading cause of children's death, with estimates of 1.6 million children being abused or neglected each year and 2,000–4,000 deaths a year (Green, 1978; Wright, Schaefer, & Solomons, 1979). One-half to two-thirds of the reported cases of abuse and neglect involve children under 6 with the most severe cases involving children under 3 years of age (Blumberg, 1974; Gil, 1970; Green, 1978). The definition of child abuse given by the Department of

Health, Education and Welfare is "any crisis situation in which nonaccidental, physical, or mental harm resulting from abuse, exploitation, or neglect requires immediate intervention or removal of the child from the home" (Nazzaro, 1974). Broader definitions include the deprivation of children's rights and opportunities to develop to their optimal level (Gil, 1973). Regardless of the current definition of child maltreatment, it is obvious that it should be a major concern of all clinical psychologists.

Characteristics of abused children and their families differ from the general population in the United States. Abusing parents are younger, less educated, have greater unemployment rates, and were often maltreated themselves as children. Abusing parents are also described as less verbal, less positive, and directing substantially more negative behavior toward the maltreated child than nonabusing parents (Green, 1978). Abused children are more likely to be unplanned or unwanted, premature, or physically defective (Blumberg, 1974; Elmer, 1977; Lewis & Schaeffer, 1981). Martin (1972) reported a study in which he found one-third of the abused children to be mentally retarded, 43 percent neurologically damaged, and 38 percent exhibiting language delays. Kempe and Kempe (1978) estimate that 20–50 percent of abused children are significantly neurologically damaged so as to have delayed language and physical skills. Abused children also have been characterized negatively as fussy, listless, chronically crying, demanding, stubborn, resistive, unresponsive, pallid, sickly, emaciated, panicky, fearful, and unsmiling (Johnson & Morse, 1968). Johnson and Morse (1968) also report that active, restless, aggressive children are more vulnerable to abuse, with boys being the target for more abuse than girls in the younger years.

In a study examining the behavior of abused children in contact with nursery school caregivers, George and Main (1979) found that abused children, 1–3 years of age, assaulted or threatened to assault caregivers at a high rate. Many were also found to avoid friendly overtures by the caregivers although they were uninhibited in their spontaneous approach to caregivers. Manning, Heron, and Marshall (in press) found that preschool children who characteristically harassed other people had poor school adjustments by age 7 and 8. Academic problems also appear to be a result of child abuse with many of these children placed in special education classes and institutions at school age (Green, 1978).

Child maltreatment appears to result from the interaction of environmental stress, parent characteristics, and child characteristics with no single factor necessary or sufficient for maltreatment. Unfortunately, the treatment of these families and children has not kept pace with increased reporting and awareness of the problem. It is difficult to involve these families in traditional counseling or psychotherapy. Often the parents are viewed as too difficult to treat or beyond help, resulting in foster home or institutional placement for the children (Green, 1978). The treatment approach for these families must be multifaceted, including: (1) teaching parents more effective, less punitive management techniques and coping strategies; (2) focusing on those characteristics of the child that may elicit abuse; (3) supporting parents in finding ways to get reinforcement; and (4) helping to change the precipitators of environmental stress. Lewis and Schaeffer's (1981) social network approach to socialization points to the value of day care centers for these children where they can experience and develop closer interpersonal relationships and friendships with peers. Likewise, increasing the parents' social network system would seem crucial to treatment (Bronfenbrenner, 1975b; Wahler, 1980).

Long term successful treatment approaches for child abuse cases are rare, but a case study reported by DeBortali-Tregerthan (1979) demonstrated the success of a multifaceted approach. In 16 sessions carried over a three-month period she decreased physical abuse to 0 with an 18 month follow-up. Treatment included teaching the mother behavior incompatible with abuse, child management techniques and cognitive control of negative thoughts and helping the mother increase her sources of reinforcement. Daycare and a brief period of foster placement were also used.

It should be noted that while child abuse and child neglect are often discussed as a collective group, most of the literature focuses on abused children and does not necessarily hold true for neglected children. The failure of investigators to differentiate these two groups has been a drawback to research and program development for neglected children and their families (Polansky, Holly, & Polansky, 1975). Martin (1978) estimates that child neglect is about five times greater than child abuse, and its emotional and physical sequelae can be as serious (Aragona & Eyberg, in press; Friedman & Morse, 1974). Burgess and Conger (1977, 1978) found that both abusive and neglectful families were negative, demanding, less positive, and less verbally and physically interactive than control groups.

Aragona and Eyberg (in press) studied parental report of behavior problems and observed verbal behavior in groups of neglected, behavior problem, and nonproblem children. Both neglectful mothers and mothers with behavior problem children described high levels of conduct problems with their children. They also found that while mothers of both the neglect and problem behavior groups were negative and controlling, they used these modes of interaction in different situations. The neglectful mothers were more negative and controlling during child-directed play than the problem behavior mothers, who were more negative and controlling during parent-directed play. It appears that neglectful mothers have more difficulty giving positive attention to their children in unstructured situations while problem behavior mothers have more difficulty directing their child's behavior. More studies such as this are needed to determine the appropriate treatment focus of the neglected child and his family.

COMMON BEHAVIOR PROBLEMS

In the normal course of the preschool years, children are sure to exhibit some behavior problems at one time or another. In our experience the questions and concerns of parents of preschool children are most often about fears, sleeping, bad habits, noncompliance, and aggression. Toilet training is also often a concern of parents but is briefly covered in the Developmental Milestones section of this chapter and is discussed in depth in another chapter in this book.

Fears

Almost all children develop specific fears at some time during their development. In a parent survey done through a pediatrician's office, fears were perceived by parents as a "problem" most often at 2 years, while dropping off at 3–5 years (Schroeder, 1979). Two-year-olds tend to develop fears of concrete objects (large dogs, trains) or loud noises (thunder, vacuum cleaners), while 3–5 year olds increasingly develop fears of imaginary creatures, being alone in the dark, and bad dreams (Ilg & Ames, 1955; Jersild & Holmes, 1935). This seems to parallel the increasing development of cognitive skills and imagination. Although 4 and 5 year olds may have the imagination and cognitive sophistication to conceive of Batman or men from outer space, they usually do not have the formal reasoning powers to judge those thoughts and images against reality. Thus fears are an almost inevitable occurrence. They are considered more normal in young children than in older children or adults; however, if these fears persist into latency age or reach an intensity that causes additional and/or chronic problems (refusal to go certain places, refusal to sleep alone, uncontrollable fear reactions), professional intervention may be indicated.

Regardless of the etiology of a specific fear, behavioral techniques appear to be most successful in treating intense fears in preschool children. The literature suggests that, for preschool age children, the most effective treatment strategies are modelling and/or *in vivo* desensitization. As early as 1924, Jones treated a phobia in a 2-year-old using eating as an incompatible response in a reciprocal inhibition paradigm. Parents have also been trained to conduct *in vivo* desensitization programs in the home (Pomerantz et al., 1977; Stableford, 1979). Pomerantz et al. (1977) included participant modelling (e.g., observing someone else gradually approach the feared object) in their design, as well as using toys as reciprocal inhibitors. Stableford (1979) emphasized the pairing of the desensitization program with selective inattention to attention-getting fear reactions. It appears that 2–5-year-olds often have difficulty learning to use relaxation as a reciprocal inhibitor in desensitization programs although it can be considered in individual cases, especially among 4- and 5-year-olds. Four and 5-year olds generally can only imagine simple images like "fun" or "sad," so the use of imagery versus *in vivo* techniques is difficult (Rosenstiel & Scott, 1977). Bandura (1969b) advocates the use of modelling in eliminating phobias or fears. Modelling works best when the model has high status for the child, when the model gradually increases contact with the feared object, and when the child is in a state of arousal (e.g., fear, excitement) during the modelling.

Therapists should carefully evaluate the word preferences a child uses in describing his or her fear through a forced word choice task (Ryall & Dietiker, 1978). Word choice varies from age to age, and this knowledge will ensure better tailoring of a program to each individual child. When confronted by a child's fear, parents need to be encouraged to remain grounded in reality while still showing concern for the child. For example, giving in to a child's demands to "chase the bears out of the closet" merely confirms for the child that there *are* bears in the closet. Instead, a parent might reflect that sometimes it can be scary to be alone in the dark, and that when the child feels afraid he or she might turn on his light, look at a book, and so on.

Sleep Problems

The sleeping patterns of children change with age and, consequently, sleep problems vary with age. Frequently the problems are transitory with parental patience and consistency helping the process. They can, however, become so severe (and exhausting for parents) that professional consultation and/or inter-

vention is required. The sleep problems during the preschool years most often include fear of the dark and/or of sleeping alone (discussed under fears), nightmares, night terrors, nightwaking, and occasionally sleepwalking.

By 2 years of age the total sleep time is about 14 hours. This gradually decreases to nine hours in school children. Normal sleep is composed of (1) REM (rapid-eye-movement) sleep, which is characterized by irregular pulse and respiration rate, body movements, rapid eye movements and dreams, and (2) NREM (non-REM) sleep, which is divided into four stages varying from drowsiness to deep sleep, slow regular pulse and respiratory rates, and absence of body movements (Zuckerman & Blitzer, 1981). NREM deep sleep is thought to restore physical strength while REM sleep is thought to restore adaptive abilities and learning abilities (Kales, 1969). Kales reports that the sleep cycle of a period of NREM followed by REM sleep usually lasts about 90–100 minutes in adults. Children have more REM sleep which gradually decreases by age 8 until it is more like an adult's cycle.

Nightmares that occur during REM sleep are vivid, elaborate and usually clearly remembered. Monsters and strangers are often the content, and since they exist as reality in the preschool years it is sometimes difficult to comfort the child. Calming and comforting the child in his or her room, however, is recommended. Chronic nightmares are generally thought to result from emotional strain, either ongoing or from a specific traumatic event (Bakwin & Bakwin, 1953; Roberts & Gordon, 1979). If a specific nightmare is repeated, systematic desensitization to the feared object may eliminate the nightmares (Geer & Silverman, 1967). Kellerman (1980) stresses the importance of specifying stimuli (if known) that elicit, maintain, and follow the nightmare and consequent anxiety in designing an intervention. An incompatible response was used in a 5-year-old, teaching him to be angry at Dracula instead of afraid of him. In addition, the boy's parents were instructed not to protect him from fearful stimuli such as television characters, since this tended to confirm his fears. Counteranxious, more appro-

318 Clinical Problems of the Preschool Child

priate nighttime behavior was also taught and positively reinforced, such as looking at a book and turning on a light, but not going to his parents' bedroom (Kellerman, 1980).

Night terrors, while infrequent, are more prevalent in the preschool years, are very different from nightmares, and are far more terrifying to the parent than to the child. Unlike nightmares, which a child can vividly describe, night terrors are rarely remembered. They are thought to be the result of an abrupt transition from deep sleep (stage 4 NREM) to REM sleep and usually occur 15–90 minutes after sleep onset (Zuckerman & Blitzer, 1981). The child sits up in bed or cowers in a corner, has a glassy stare, screams or cries inconsolably, and cannot be awakened for 10–20 minutes. Some children never seem to awaken. Night terrors can occur at frequent or infrequent intervals, may or may not be associated with stress, are not correlated with psychiatric disturbance, and produce no harmful aftereffects (Zuckerman & Blitzer, 1981). The only treatment recommended is reassuring the parents!

Resistance to sleeping and waking up during the night are common for 2- to 3-year-olds. Bedtime rituals are at a peak during this age and along with a quiet period help the child make the transition to sleep. When the child resists sleep, firmness and consistency in not responding to cries are usually all that is needed. If the restrictive behavior persists, using a storytelling framework to let the child know what is expected and what the parent is going to do (ignore) plus a star in the morning for good nighttime behavior can be helpful. A related problem is the child who leaves his or her bedroom to sleep in the parents' bed. Again, consistency and firmness in returning the child to his or her room is important with the storytelling and reward interventions reserved for the persistent child.

Sleepwalking and sleeptalking are common during the late preschool years and early school years. They can occur for 5–30 minutes and the only danger is the child hurting himself or herself during the walk (Zukerman & Blitzer, 1981). Safety precautions and locking the bedroom door are recommended interventions (Wright, Schaefer, & Solomons, 1979).

Bad Habits

Children display a number of "bad habits" throughout the preschool years. However, most of these habits seem to appear in the normal sequence of development and only become problems under certain circumstances, that is, (1) the behavior continues longer than is typical (into school age, for example); (2) the behavior becomes severe or chronic enough to cause physical damage; (3) the behavior is engaged in so frequently that it interferes with ongoing physical, social, and/or cognitive development.

Thumbsucking usually peaks before 2 years but may continue through the preschool years: 47 percent of all 2-year-olds, 42 percent of all 3-year-olds, 36 percent of all 4-year-olds, and 30 percent of all 5-year-olds suck their thumbs (Klackenberg, 1949). Most children gradually decrease thumbsucking during the day while continuing this habit at night and when under stress. Hargett and associates (1967) studied children using dental cribs (a "hayrake" that deters inserting a thumb in one's mouth) and found that the group that did not receive concurrent "psychological support" showed a good deal of symptom substitution while the group receiving such support did not. Popovich and Thompson (1973) found that the incidence of malocclusion did not increase if thumbsucking was stopped by age 6. Nagging, admonitions, and bad-tasting substances placed on the fingers have not proven to be very effective. Behavioral approaches including token systems, positive reinforcement, and time out have had mixed results (Schaefer & Millman, 1977). Wright, Schaefer, and Solomons (1979) state that the palatal crib (dental crib) appears to be the most effective treatment approach at present. Parent consultation and reassurance are probably the most viable treatment options.

Body rocking and head banging are common behaviors in children under 3 years but are quite likely to be distressing to parents (Sallustro & Atwell, 1978). Head banging, which occurs three times more often in boys, rarely results in serious injury although parents are cautioned to pad and anchor the crib (Yancy, 1981). Ilg and Ames (1955) advocate comforting and/or distracting the child who engages in head banging. Wright, Schaefer, and Solomons (1979) point out that this probably reinforces the head banging. They list three areas of important information when considering an intervention: (1) parents' typical response to the head banging and how they might inadvertently be reinforcing it; (2) other psychogenic tendencies; and (3) parents' ability to follow through on recommendations.

Padding the child's crib, tightening the screws to eliminate squeaking, and placing a soft rug under the crib may sufficiently reduce noise and movement to cause the child to "lose interest" in rocking, at least in the crib. More direct approaches to body rocking, if its severity has been determined to be a significant problem for the child and/or parents, include reassurance, support, consultation with the parents, alternate activities, and positive attention (thereby providing physical, social, and/or cognitive enrichment) (Greenberg, 1964; Lourie, 1949).

Although pulling hair out, or trichtillomania, is rare and occurs most frequently during adolescence, some preschool children do engage in this behavior (Mannino & Delgado, 1969). It should be differentiated from simply playing with a single strand of hair, pulling due to tight braids, and scalp problems (Telzrow, 1981). Pulling hair out is often seen along with other behavior disorders, but its manipulative potential is great due to the child's unsightly appearance. Sanchez (1979) described a behavioral intervention involving differential reinforcement and response chain interruption procedures that successfully eliminated chronic hair pulling in a 27-month-old boy. Gray (1979) presents a case where positive reinforcement (using marbles to be exchanged for a toy) successfully reduced hair-pulling in two 5-year-old girls, but punishment (four handslaps on the hand) was required to eliminate it. Massong et al. (1980) trained a 3-year-old boy's mother to reinforce appropriate play behavior and ignore hair pulling.

Intervention was successful until the mother terminated the contingencies. She later agreed to a "response prevention procedure," a haircut, which successfully eliminated the hair pulling. The authors comment that "this case provides evidence that professionals familiar with relatively complex multielement treatment strategies may overlook the simplest and least restrictive intervention" (p. 233).

Azrin and Nunn (1973) describe a treatment method called "habit reversal" for eliminating nervous habits such as nail biting, thumbsucking, eyelash picking, and tics. It has been used successfully with preschool children as well as adults and is based on the rationale that nervous habits persist because of response chaining, limited awareness of doing the behavior, excessive practice, and social tolerance. To counteract these influences the child practices physical movements that are the reverse of the bad habit, is taught to be aware of each time he or she engages in the behavior, as well as when the behavior is likely to occur, and is given social approval for inhibiting the behavior. For example, hair pullers may be taught to squeeze a portion of their clothing and then relax, rather than pulling the hair or thumbsuckers may be taught to clench their fists rather than suck their thumbs. By recording each incidence of the inappropriate behavior, or in the case of the preschool child, having someone else record the behavior, one is able to track the conditions under which the behavior occurs and practice the competing response during those times. We have also found that rewarding the child with stickers or pennies for not engaging in the inappropriate behavior for gradually increasing periods of time is a necessary part of this treatment technique. The consistency with which parents are able to record, reward, and encourage the competing response is crucial in the success of this method with the preschooler.

Noncompliance

One of the most frequent complaints from parents of preschool children is that of noncompliance. This behavior includes not following directions, disregarding adults, not attending to requests or doing the opposite, and can also involve behaviors such as tantrums, breath holding, and physical and verbal aggression. Bernal (Bernal, et al., 1968) referred to it as "the bratty child syndrome." These types of behaviors seem to peak between 2 and 4 years in part because of the pressures of socialization and routinization. However, there appear to be differences between "normal" noncompliance and noncompliance that is viewed as a "problem," leading parents to seek professional help. Studies that have compared clinic and nonclinic populations provide some normative data on both child and parent behaviors (Forehand, Gardner, & Roberts, 1978; Forehand et al., 1975). "Normal" child compliance to maternal commands ranges from 51 percent to 74 percent (Forehand et al., 1978; Johnson et al., 1973) while children referred to clinics for treatment of noncompliance exhibit compliance to only 41 percent of parental commands. Mothers of clinic children also tend to issue more commands and use more criticism than do mothers of nonclinic children (Forehand et al., 1975). Clinic parents frequently interrupt the behavioral sequence by repeating the command, giving help, retrieving the command, and so on, so that compliance is not possible. Clinic mothers also differ from nonclinic mothers in their perception of their child, viewing him or her as more deviant or maladjusted than other children (Forehand et al., 1975).

Little research has been done on the development of compliance versus noncompliance in children. Common sense seems congruent with Milgram's (1974) behavioral explanation that being rewarded for compliance and punished for noncompliance significantly affects the development of compliant behavior. The converse of this also seems logical. For example, parent tells the child to pick up the toys, the child whines and cries, and parent withdraws the request. Removing the aversive stimulus (a command to pick up the toys) could be accomplished by either compliance or noncompliance, and in this example noncompliance was successful and reinforced.

Parent-child training programs involving both the parent and the child are the most frequent and successful treatment cited for noncompliance in the literature. One highly effective program is that developed by Hanf (1969) and used extensively with preschoolers by Rex Forehand (Forehand, 1977; Forehand, Wells, & Griest, 1980; Hobbs & Forehand, 1977; Roberts et al., 1978). This is a two-part program which first trains parents in praising and attending to their child's appropriate behavior. Once this skill is polished (indeed, overlearned), parents are taught to give simple, clear commands, followed by a five-second pause; if compliance is not initiated, a warning is given. After another five seconds, if compliance is not initiated, the child is placed in a time-out chair or in his or her room. Other important parameters are duration of time-out (one to four minutes appears to be an effective length) and contingent release from time-out (terminating time-out only after a period of nondisruptive behavior) (Hobbs & Forehand, 1977). Although the combined attention and time-out procedures are thought to be the most effective approach to noncompliant behavior, Roberts, Hatzenbuehler, and Bean (1981) found that only time-out contributed to compliance acquisition. Working with 32 noncompliant, clinic-referred preschool children they used four experimental conditions: attention, time-out, attention plus time-out, and control. The potential positive effects of appropriate positive attention in parent-child relationships, however, should not be overlooked.

Despite the fact that many professionals find compliance training an effective approach, recent studies (Patterson & Fleischmann, 1979; Wahler, 1980) have found a lack of long term effectiveness for some families, particularly low income socially isolated, multiproblem families.

Aggression

The data on the developmental course of aggression are sparse, particularly in clarifying the form of aggressive acts (physical or verbal), the context in which aggression originates (child-child relationships or adult-child relationships), the circumstances that trigger aggressive episodes (being blocked in getting a desired object or derogatory remarks), and stability in an individual to respond aggressively over time and circumstances (Hartup, 1974). Temper tantrums in response to habit training are probably the first real expression of aggression. As Goodenough (1931) states, temper tantrums produce both negative and positive feedback to the child (gets what is wanted or punished) and probably serve as opportunities for the young child to learn the efficacy of aggressive actions as well as the efficacy of aggressive inhibitors.

There is evidence that it is in early peer relationships that children learn to master their aggressive behavior. Work by Harlow and Harlow (1965) on nonhuman primates demonstrates the importance of the early rough and tumble play that escalates into aggression and then deescalates into playful interaction. This affords, according to Hartup (1974), the opportunity to develop: (1) a variety of aggressive behaviors, *and* (2) ways of coping with the affective and other outcomes of aggressive interaction. Hartup (1976) suggests that the unique egalitarian relationship with age mates permits aggressive acts to be successful at some times and unsuccessful at other times. This balance has the effect of neither allowing the child to become excessively aggressive or excessively permissive.

Goodenough's (1931) and Darve's (1934) early work and Hartup's (1976) more recent work document the changes in aggressive behavior during the years from 2–6:

1. The form of aggression changes from more physical acts to increased verbal attacks.
2. The frequency of "after reaction" including sulking, whining and brooding increases markedly after 4 years even though there is little change in the duration of angry outbursts.
3. The stimuli eliciting aggression change from habit training to peers and while instrumental aggression (for posses-

sion or loss of object) predominates, there is an increase in person-oriented retaliatory hostile outbursts.
4. The frequency of aggression decreases after 6 years primarily due to a decrease in instrumental aggression.
5. When younger children are insulted they are more likely to retaliate with hitting than older children who reciprocate with insults.
6. Boys engage in more hostile (person-oriented) aggression than girls with no sex difference in rate of instrumental aggression.
7. The levels of aggression appear to stabilize earlier for boys than for girls.
8. Aggressive behavior in preschool children is initially positively reinforced, that is, child gets what he or she wants, but if this aggression continues unchecked it is negatively reinforced; that is, others use aggressive behavior to stop the aggressor, and this operates to increase the aggressive behavior (Patterson, 1976).

Spivack and Shure's (1974) work sheds light on the social cognitive skills that develop in the preschool years and are associated with increased social adjustment in later years. Alternative solutions thinking, that is, the generation of alternative solutions to a social problem such as conflict over a toy, and consequential thinking, that is, accurate recognition of the likely results of different social behaviors such as hitting, increase with age. This reflects changes in the cognitive abilities of the child and differences in the skills required for effective social interaction at different developmental levels. Spivack and Shure (1974) found that both aggressive children and more withdrawn children have marked deficits in alternative solution thinking in comparison to other children. Socially withdrawn children also have deficits in consequential thinking. Their training program (Spivack, Platt, & Shure, 1976) focuses on "how" to think about social problems rather than "what" to do when presented with a particular social problem. They initially teach prerequisite language skills (concepts such as if-then) with later sessions consisting of group discussions where children are taught to generate many solutions, to anticipate consequences, and finally to pair different solutions with different likely consequences. Their data show that improvement in social behavior was correlated with the degree of change in cognitive social skills, leading to the conclusion that social cognitive skills mediate social behavior.

Furman (1980) reviews a number of other factors that must be considered in designing programs for aggressive behavior of preschool children and are applicable to the treatment of any behavior problem:

1. Social praise from women is more effective for preschool children than for older children, who respond best to praise from opposite sex adults.

2. Small rewards work better for preschool children than large rewards.

3. Approval is more important for preschool children than pointing out the appropriateness or inappropriateness of the behavior.

4. The preschool child perceives punishment as disapproval and is not yet able to understand the rules behind the behavior.

5. Age mates are the best models for demonstration of age appropriate social behavior for preschool children.

6. Preschoolers do not yet have the cognitive ability to evaluate their own behaviors or to understand a rationale for a behavior, skills which are prerequisites to self-control.

Determining the antecedents and consequences of the aggressive behavior is as important in treating aggression as is the developmental level of the child. Aggression is maintained by its consequences and, therefore, identification and manipulation of these consequences can decrease the aggressive behavior. Likewise, the environmental conditions can set the stage for increased aggression, such as having only one tricycle for 10 4-year-olds to ride or asking children to perform behavior beyond their ability. It should be remembered that the preschool child is in the process of learning prosocial behaviors and, therefore, teaching appropriate social skills is as important as decreasing the aggressive behavior.

Since the peer group is often the setting for aggressive behavior, it can serve as an important reinforcer for this behavior. Firestone (1976) demonstrated that the removal of a 4.5-year-old to a chair in a nursery school classroom for two minutes contingent on physical aggression (striking, hitting, kicking and pulling, and destruction of property) significantly decreased not only the physical aggression but also the verbal aggression. Teacher attention has also been shown to be a powerful reinforcer for aggressive behavior (Slaby & Crowly, 1977). The techniques of ignoring aggressive behavior while simultaneously reinforcing socially desirable behavior have also been successful in decreasing aggressive behavior in the preschool child (Pinkston et al., 1973).

PREVENTION

An ideal prevention program according to Tarjan (1980) would "assure every child of being born with a healthy central nervous system, of having a set of early experiences supportive of intellectual, emotional, and social growth, and of being protected from damaging physical and psychological traumas" (p. 449). We can strive to reach the ideal, but our real task would seem to be to strengthen children and their families to cope more effectively with the stresses of life.

There is little in the literature that sheds light on the primary prevention of specific behavior disorders in children, only suggestions or theoretical discussions (Rolf & Harig, 1975). Work with parents is often viewed as primary prevention. The role and expectation of parents, however, have changed dramatically over the years. Abramovitz (1976) traces parenthood in America from the "Break the

Will" era (1600–1775) to the current "The Competent Healthy Child Era." He points out that despite a great deal of studying and theorizing we have yet to find one simple plan to guide all of the child's complex growth and development. In fact, we have become more aware that there are numerous ways to raise healthy children and that the environment and the child continuously interact to determine a child's future. Assumptions about the family, childrearing practices, and appropriate intervention techniques are constantly being challenged. For example, the two-parent nuclear family has long been thought to be the optimal milieu for a child's growth and development, yet work by Eiduson (1981) indicates that alternative family groups do not necessarily have any negative effect on the infant and young child's development.

Bronfenbrenner (1975a) points to the need to make our research more "ecologically valid" in terms of studying the child where he or she actually lives and develops: the family, the daycare center, the preschool, play groups, school classroom, and neighborhood. Perhaps prevention should focus as much on the environment in which people live as on the child or the parent.

Our society has taken several approaches to the prevention of childhood problems. The education of parents and early intervention programs for children at risk for sociocultural retardation are two currently popular approaches for the preschool child.

Parent Education

Parent education in the United States is not new, dating back to the 1800s. Since the early 1960s with the publication of Kempe's (1962) article on child abuse, government and private agencies have devoted increasingly more time and money to parent education programs. The goal has been to improve parenting skills as well as to change societal attitudes about childrearing (Sherrets, Authier, & Tramontana, 1980). Primary prevention through effecting changes in parenting skills leading to enhancement of competency in children is the major goal of parent education programs. The

focus has been on families at risk, such as pregnant teenagers and parents of handicapped children, as well as on promoting normal development in children through pre-parent groups at the high school level and work with parents and teachers in general. Sherrets et al. (1980) summarize the reasons for the current interest in parent education:

1. Teenage pregnancies are on the increase with one girl in ten a mother before 18 years and more pregnancies occurring at a younger age (14–16 years).
2. The increase in single-parent families with increased divorce rates and one child in eight born to an unwed mother.
3. Abusive and neglectful parents often lack appropriate information on child development.
4. Traditional training and support systems are not as available with increased mobility, decreased emphasis on the nuclear family, and the fact that families have become smaller.
5. Professionals think parenting skills can be taught.
6. Increased importance attached to the first years of life.
7. Abnormal parenting tends to be cyclic; that is, we parent as we were parented.
8. To increase quality of life and enhance children's development.

Parents get their childrearing information from books, physicians, friends, social agencies, and educational classes, with socioeconomic level, parental age, and type and severity of their child's problem determining the source of help (Clarke-Stewart, 1978). Parent education classes have received increased attention with the models varying as much as the imagination. Time frames range from single sessions to ongoing programs as part of daycare settings, curriculum focuses on narrow topics (toilet training) to all-inclusive parenting information, and the sponsors of the education vary from schools to private individuals (Authier, Sherrets, & Tramontana, 1980). The theoretical views taken in these programs are as varied as the qualifications of the persons who do the educating. Programs are generally based on what professionals think parents should know rather than on what parents would like to know. Likewise, Clarke-Stewart (1978) found popular parenting books are most often based on the author's opinions about child development and management rather than on substantial evidence. A national survey by Sparling (1980) provides data on the focus that parent education should take. Parents with at least one child under 3 were asked their information needs as revealed through interests, problems, attitudes, and preferences. Parents wanted comprehensive rather than narrowly defined information in the following hierarchy: (1) promoting health, (2) family coping/community resources, and (3) promoting learning and development. The more educated the parents, the more information on learning and development was wanted.

Tramontana, Sherrets, and Authier's (1980) evaluation of current parent education programs concludes that the rationale for the proliferation of these programs is based more on belief in the efficacy of parent education than any demonstration of effectiveness. The few evaluation studies that have been done give little information on the goal of parent education: the improvement of parent-child interactions leading to a healthier adjustment of the child. Tramontana et al. (1980) report that none of the studies addressing the effect of parent education in *both* the parent and child showed any significant positive effects on the child. Only those studies focusing on the child alone were reported to demonstrate any significant positive effects on the child as a result of parent education. One is left to wonder about the possible negative effects parent education could have on parents and children. It is evident that, without careful evaluation, parent education groups cannot be justified as a means of intervention.

While parent education is one target in the prevention of childhood disorders, the other target has been children themselves. Just as direct work with the child is usually excluded from parent education, so are the personal strengths and weaknesses of the parents often ignored in intervention and treatment done with children. Early Headstart programs were a prime example of excluding parents. When parents are included in the child's intervention program they are usually taught or given information about childrearing. Naylor's (1980) work at the Yale Child Study Center gives striking data supporting the need for a greater focus on parent needs and characteristics in planning education and treatment programs. Naylor (1980) reports that two-thirds of the 189 parents of 100 children under 5 treated at their center were moderately to severely disturbed. Forty of the parents had been neglected as children, and 25 had been physically abused. Naylor (1980) states that the parents' capacity to parent was severely impaired by their own pathology. This work indicates the need for careful consideration of the strengths and weaknesses not only of the child and his or her environment but also of the parents if prevention methods are to have any long term effect.

Providers of parent education as well as early child intervention programs (which will be discussed next) should be cautioned not to offer too much or oversell themselves. "No matter how excellent and effective [they are] at one stage of a child's life, there are no assurances against future problems. New developmental tasks, new stresses upon the child and his family, can bring adaptation beyond coping capacity" (Naylor, 1980, p. 470).

Early Intervention Programs

Efforts to deal with the problem of sociocultural retardation have resulted in the establishment of a variety of intervention programs for preschool children. These programs are designed to counter the effects of growing up in a poverty-stricken environment. They are based on: (1) early studies of the effects of early stimulation on animals and humans, (2) the work of Hunt (1961) on early childhood education, and (3) an oft-quoted statement by Bloom (1965) that 50 percent of intellectual development occurs in the first five years of life. The first experimental programs (e.g., Gray & Klaus, 1965; Kirk, 1958) did in fact demonstrate substantial short term gains in IQ scores for children from disadvantaged backgrounds. The long term effects and the differential effectiveness of various types of programs for different kinds of children, however, have only recently been evaluated (Bronfenbrenner, 1975b).

It is generally agreed that children of mothers with IQs of less than 80 who live in poverty are at the greatest risk for sociocultural retardation (Haskins, Finkelstein, & Stedman, 1978). While these children may begin life on an equal intellectual footing with other children, it is thought that the environment in which they live adequately fails to support intellectual development (Haskins et al., 1978). Recent work has shown that one aspect of the environment that is critical to cognitive as well as social development is the quality and extent of maternal stimulation of the infant and young child (Bradley & Caldwell, 1976a, 1976b).

While early intervention of any type is generally effective in preventing the decline in cognitive functioning seen in these children, it is not surprising that different types of programs are differentially effective. Those that intervene in the parent-child interaction and that do not take primary responsibility for childrearing away from parents are most effective in increasing IQ scores and in maintaining the gains after the program is terminated (Bronfenbrenner, 1975b). Benefits of this type of program are inversely related to age at entry and extent of maternal involvement in the program.

Center-based programs with little parental involvement, on the other hand, demonstrate substantial initial gains in IQ that are *not* maintained after the program is terminated. Factors in the child's home environment are seen as critical in contributing to this decline (Bronfenbrenner, 1975b).

Neither of these two types of programs has been effective for the most severely deprived children. Bronfenbrenner (1975b) suggests that radical changes in these families' imme-

diate environment are necessary so that the family can function as an effective "child-rearing system"; he calls this ecological intervention and includes meeting basic needs such as health care, nutrition, housing, and employment opportunities.

While IQ continues to be a primary means of measuring early stimulation program effectiveness, current efforts are shifting more toward the broader measure of "competence" in these high risk children. The rationale for this is that poor social adjustment impedes a child's success in school and in society as much as low intelligence (Bronfenbrenner, 1967). In reviewing the research on the effects of early intervention programs on social and adaptive behavior, Haskins et al. (1978) conclude that intellectual gains may be mediated by changes in other behaviors such as motivation, curiosity, task persistence, and the like. In addition, it seems that social and adaptive behaviors are much more sensitive to program differences, such as teacher-child ratio or age of the children. Social behavior of children in their homes and schools will need study if intervention programs are to fully address the needs of preschool children in this area.

REFERENCES

Abramovitz, R. Parenthood in America. *Journal of Clinical Child Psychology*, 1976, **4**, 43–50.

Anderson, C.W. Attachment in daily separations: Reconceptualizing daycare and maternal employment issues. *Child Development*, 1980, **51**, 242–245.

Anthony, E.J. An etiological approach to the diagnosis of psychosis in childhood. *Revue de Psychiatrie Infantile*, 1958, **25**, 89–96.

Anthony, E.J. Low grade psychosis in childhood. In B.W. Richards (Ed.), *Proceedings of London conference on scientific study of mental deficiency*. London: May & Baker, 1962.

Aragona, J.A., & Eyberg, S.M. Neglected children: Mothers' report of child behavior problems and observed verbal behavior. *Child Development*, in press.

Authier, K.J., Sherretts, S.D., & Tramontana, M.G. Methods and models of parent education. *Journal of Clinical Child Psychology,* 1980, **9,** 38–40.

Azrin, N.H., & Nunn, R.G. Habit-reversal: A method of eliminating nervous habits and tics. *Behavior, Research and Therapy,* 1973, **11,** 619–628.

Bakwin, H., & Bakwin, R.M. *Clinical management of behavior disorders.* Philadelphia: Saunders, 1953.

Bandura, A. Social-learning theory of identificatory processes. In D.A. Goslin (Ed.), *Handbook of socialization theory and research.* Chicago: Rand McNally, 1969.(a)

Bandura, A. *Principles of behavior modification.* New York: Holt, Rinehart & Winston, 1969.(b)

Bauer, D. An exploratory study of developmental changes in children's fears. *Journal of Child Psychology and Psychiatry,* 1976, **17,** 69–74.

Bardach, J.L. Psychological adjustment of handicapped children and their families. *White House conference on handicapped individuals.* 1976.

Behar, L., & Stringfield, S. A behavior rating scale for the pre-school child. *Developmental Psychology,* 1974, **10,** 601–610.

Belsky, J., & Steinberg, L.D. The effects of day care: A critical review. *Child Development,* 1978, **49,** 929–949.

Bernal, M.E., Duryee, J.S., Pruett, H.L., & Burns, B.J. Behavior modification and the brat syndrome. *Journal of Consulting and Clinical Psychology,* 1968, **32,** 447–455.

Bijou, S.W. Development in the preschool years: A functional analysis. *American Psychological Association Annual Meeting,* New Orleans, 1974.

Blehar, B. Anxious attachment and defensive reactions associated with day care. *Child Development,* 1974, **45,** 683–692.

Bloom, B.S. *Compensatory education for cultural deprivation.* New York: Holt, Rinehart & Winston, 1965.

Blos, P., Jr. Children think about illness: Their concepts and beliefs. In E. Gellert (Ed.), *Psychosocial aspects of pediatric care.* New York: Grune & Stratton, 1978.

Blumberg, M.L. Psychopathology of the abusing parent. *American Journal of Psychotherapy,* 1974, **28,** 21–29.

Boniface, D., & Graham, P. The three-year-old and his attachment to a special soft object. *Journal of Child Psychology and Psychiatry,* 1979, **20,** 217–224.

Bowlby, J. *Attachment and loss: Attachment* (Vol. 1). New York: Basic Books, 1969.

Bradley, R., & Caldwell, B. Early home environment and changes in mental test performance in children from 6 to 36 months. *Developmental psychology,* 1976, **12,** 93–97.(a)

Bradley, R., & Caldwell, B. The relation of infants' home environments to mental test performance at fifty-four months: A follow-up study. *Child Development,* 1976, **47,** 1172–1174.(b)

Bronfenbrenner, U. The psychological costs of quality and equality of education. *Child Development,* 1967, **38,** 909–925.

Bronfenbrenner, U. Developmental research, public policy, and the ecology of childhood. In S. Chess & A. Thomas (Eds.), *Annual progress in child psychiatry and child development.* New York: Brunner-Mazel, 1975.(a)

Bronfenbrenner, U. Is early intervention effective? In M. Guttentag & E.L. Struening (Eds.), *Handbook of evaluation research* (Vol. 2). Beverly Hills: Sage, 1975.(b)

Burgess, R.L., & Conger, R.D. Family interaction patterns related to child abuse and neglect: Some preliminary findings. *Child Abuse and Neglect,* 1977, **1,** 269–277.

Burgess, R.L., & Conger, R.D. Family interaction in abusive, neglectful and normal families. *Child Development,* 1978, **49,** 1163–1173.

Butler, J.F. The toilet training success of parents after reading 'Toilet training in less than a day.' *Behavior Therapy,* 1976, **7,** 185–191.

Caldwell, E.C., & Hall, V.C. Concept learning in discrimination tasks. *Developmental Psychology,* 1970, **2,** 41–48.

Cameron, J.R. Parental treatment, children's temperament, and the risk of childhood behavior problems: 1. Relationships between parental characteristics and changes in children's temperament over time. In S. Chess & A. Thomas (Eds.), *Annual progress in child psychology and child development.* New York: Brunner-Mazel, 1978.

Carey, W.B., & McDevitt, S.C. Stability and change in individual temperament diagnoses from infancy to early childhood. *Journal of American Academy of Child Psychiatry,* in press.

Char, J., & Lubetsky, S. Childhood psychosis in the preschool child. *Journal of Autism and Developmental Disorders,* 1979, **3,** 271–277.

Chess, S. Temperament and children at risk. In E.J. Anthony & C. Koupernik (Eds.), *The child in his family* (Vol. 1). New York: Wiley-Interscience, 1970.

Chess, S., & Hassibi, M. *Principles and practice of child psychology.* New York: Plenum, 1978.

Chess, S., & Thomas, A. *Annual progress in child psychiatry and child development.* New York: Brunner/Mazel, 1978.

Ciha, T.E., Harris, T.E., Hoffman, C., & Potter, M.W. Parents as identifiers of giftedness, ignored but accurate. *The Gifted Child Quarterly,* 1974, **18,** 191–195.

Clarke-Stewart, A.K. Popular primers for parents. *American Psychologist,* 1978, **33,** 359–369.

Cochran, M.A. A comparison of group day and family child-rearing patterns in Sweden. *Child Development,* 1977, **48,** 702–707.

Cohen, D.J., Caparulo, B., & Shaywitz, B. Primary childhood aphasia and childhood autism: Clinical, biological, and conceptual observations. *Journal American Academy Child Psychiatry,* 1976, **15,** 604–645.

Darve, H.C. An analysis of two hundred quarrels of preschool children. *Child Development,* 1934, **5,** 139–157.

David, A.C., & Donovan, E.H. Initiating group process with parents of multi-handicapped children. *Social Work in Health Care,* 1975, **1,** 177–183.

De Bortali-Tregerthan, G.J. A behavioral treatment of child abuse: A case report. *Child Behavior Therapy,* 1979, **3,** 287–293.

De Myer, M.K. *Parents and children in autism.* Washington, D.C.: Winston, 1979.

de Villiers, P.A., & de Villiers, J.G. *Early language.* Cambridge, Harvard University Press, 1979.

Dweck, C.S. Learned helplessness: A developmental approach. In J.G. Schulterbrandt & A. Raskin (Eds.), *Depression in childhood: Diagnosis, treatment, and conceptual models.* New York: Raven, 1977.

Easson, W.M. Care of the young patient who is dying. *Journal of the American Medical Association,* 1968, **205,** 63–67.

Edgerton, R.B. *Mental retardation.* Cambridge: Harvard University Press, 1979.

Edwards, C.P., & Lewis, M. Young children's concepts of social relations: Social functions and social objects. In M. Lewis & L. Rosenblum (Eds.), *The child and its family: The genesis of behavior* (Vol. 2). New York: Plenum, 1979.

Eiduson, B.T. The child in the nonconventional family. In M. Lewis & L.A. Rosenblum (Eds.), *The uncommon child.* New York: Plenum, 1981.

Elmer, E. Follow-up study of traumatized children. *Child Abuse and Neglect,* 1977, **1,** 105–109.

Eyberg, S.M., & Ross, A.W. Assessment of child behavior problems: The validation of a new inventory. *Journal of Clinical Child Psychology,* 1978, **7,** 113–116.

Feshback, S. Aggression. In P.H. Mussén (Ed.), *Carmichael's manual of child psychology* (Vol. 2). New York: Wiley, 1970.

Firestone, P. The effects and side effects of timeout on an aggressive nursery school child. *Journal of Behavior Therapy and Experimental Psychiatry,* 1976, **7,** 79–81.

Flavell, J. *Cognitive development.* Englewood Cliffs, N.J.: Prentice-Hall, 1977.

Forehand, R. Child non-compliance to parental requests: Behavioral analysis and treatment. In M. Hersen, R.M. Eisler, & P.M. Miller (Eds.), *Progress in behavior modification* (Vol. 5). New York: Academic Press, 1977, 111–147.

Forehand, R., Gardner, H., & Roberts, M. Maternal response to child compliance and noncompliance: Some normative data. *Journal of Clinical Child Psychology,* 1978, **7,** 121–124.

Forehand, R., King, H.E., Peed, S., & Yoder, P. Mother-child interactions: Comparisons of a non-compliant clinic group and non-clinic group. *Behavior, Research and Therapy,* 1975, **13,** 79–84.

Forehand, R., Wells, K., & Griest, D. An examination of the social validity of a parent training program. *Behavior Therapy,* 1980, **11,** 488–502.

Freud, A. The role of bodily illness in the mental life of children. *Psychoanalytic Study of the Child,* 1952, **7,** 69–81.

Friedman, S.B., & Morse, C.W. Child abuse: A five-year followup of early case findings in the emergency department. *Pediatrics,* 1974, **54,** 404–440.

Friedrich, W.N. Ameliorating the psychological impact of chronic physical disease on the child and family. *Journal of Pediatric Psychology,* 1977, **2,** 26–31.

Furman, W. Promoting social development: Developmental implications for treatment. In B.B. Lahey, & A.E. Kazdin (Eds.), *Advances in clinical child psychology* (Vol. 3). New York: Plenum, 1980.

Gardner, R.A. *Psychotherapy with children of divorce.* New York: Aronson, 1976.

Gardner, R.A. Children of divorce: Some legal and psychological considerations. *Journal of Clinical Child Psychology,* 1977, **6,** 3–7.

Geer, J.H., & Silverman, I. Treatment of a recurrent nightmare by behavior modification procedures. *Journal of Abnormal Psychology,* 1967, **72,** 188–190.

George, C., & Main, M. Social interaction of young abused children: Approach, avoidance, and aggression. *Child Development,* 1979, **50,** 306–318.

Getzels, W., & Dillon, J.T. The nature of giftedness and the education of the gifted child. In R.W.M. Travers (Ed.), *Second handbook of research on children.* Chicago: Rand McNally, 1973.

Gibson, E.J. *Principles of perceptual learning and development.* Englewood Cliffs, N.J.: Prentice-Hall, 1969.

Gil, D.G. *Violence against children.* Cambridge: Harvard University Press, 1970.

Gil, D.G. Hearings before the U.S. Senate Subcommittee on Children and Youth on the "Child Abuse Prevention Act," S. 1911, 93rd Congress, 1st Session. Washington, D.C., March, 1973. Reprinted in *Journal of Child Psychology,* 1973, **2,** 7–10.

Gittleman-Klein, R. Definitional and methodological issues concerning depressive illness in children. In J.G. Schulterbrandt & A. Raskin (Eds.), *Depression in childhood: Diagnosis, treatment, and conceptual models.* New York: Raven, 1977.

Golden, M., & Birns, B. Social class and infant intelligence. In M. Lewis (Ed.), *Origins of intelligence.* New York: Plenum, 1976.

Goldfarb, W. Infant rearing and problem behavior. *American Journal of Orthopsychiatry,* 1943, **13,** 249–265.

Goodenough, F.L. *Anger in young children.* Minneapolis: University of Minnesota Press, 1931.

Goodnow, J.J., & Levine, R.A. "The grammar of action": Sequence and syntax in children's copying. *Cognitive Psychology,* 1973, **4,** 82–98.

Gray, J. Positive reinforcement and punishment in the treatment of childhood trichotillomania. *Journal of Behavior Therapy and Experimental Psychiatry,* 1979, **10,** 125–129.

Gray, S.W., & Klaus, R.A. Experimental preschool program for culturally deprived children. *Child Development,* 1965, **36,** 887–898.

Green, A.H. Child abuse. In B.B. Wolman, J. Egan, & A.O. Ross (Eds.), *Handbook of treatment of mental disorders in childhood and adolescence.* Englewood Cliffs, N.J.: Prentice-Hall, 1978.

Greenberg, N.H. Origins of head-rolling (spasmus mutans) during early infancy: Clinical observations and theoretical implications. *Psychosomatic Medicine,* 1964, **26,** 162–171.

Grogan, J.L., O'Malley, J.E., & Foster, D.J. Treating the pediatric cancer patient: A review. *Journal of Pediatric Psychology,* 1977, **2,** 42–48.

Halverson, C.F., Jr., & Waldrop, M.F. Nocturnal behavior towards own and other preschool children: The problem of "owners." *Child Development,* 1970, **41,** 839–845.

Hanf, C. A two-stage program for modifying maternal controlling during mother-child (M-C) interaction. Paper presented at the Western Psychological Association Meeting, Vancouver, 1969.

Hargett, R.D., Hansen, F.C., Davidson, P.O., & Sandilands, M.L. Chronic thumbsucking: The psychological effects and the relative effectiveness of various methods of treatment. *American Journal of Orthodontics,* 1967, **53,** 569–585.

Harlow, H.F., & Harlow, M.K. The affectional systems. In A.M. Schrier, H.F. Harlow, & F. Stollnitz (Eds.), *Behavior of nonhuman primates* (Vol. 2). New York: Academic Press, 1965.

Harrison, S.I., Davenport, C.W., & McDermott, J.F. Children's reactions to bereavement: Adult confusions and misperceptions. *Archives of General Psychiatry,* 1967, **17,** 593–597.

Hart, B. Pragmatics and language development. In B.B. Lahey & A.E. Kazdin (Eds.), *Advances in clinical child psychology* (Vol. 3). New York: Plenum, 1980.

Hartup, W.W. Peer interaction and social organization. In P.H. Mussen (Ed.), *Carmichael's manual of child psychology* (3rd ed.) (Vol. 2). New York: Wiley, 1970.

Hartup, W.W. Aggression in childhood: Developmental perspectives. *American Psychologist,* 1974, **29,** 336–341.

Hartup, W.W. Peer reactions and the behavioral

development of the individual child. In E. Schopler & R.J. Reichler (Eds.), *Psychopathology and child development*. New York: Plenum, 1976.

Haskins, R., Finkelstein, N.W., & Stedman, D.J. Infant stimulation programs and their effects. *Pediatric Annals*, 1978, **7**, 123–128.

Hetherington, E.M., Cox, M., & Cox, R. Beyond father absence: Conceptualization of effects of divorce. Paper presented at meetings of the Society for Research in Child Development, Denver, 1975.

Hobbs, S., & Forehand, R. Important parameters in the use of time out with children: A reexamination. *Journal of Behavior Therapy and Experimental Psychiatry*, 1977, **8**, 365–370.

Hoffman, M.L. Empathy, its development and prosocial implications. In B. Keasy (Ed.), *Nebraska symposium on motivation* (Vol. 26). Lincoln: University of Nebraska Press, 1965.

Hoffman, M.L. Development of moral thought, feeling, and behavior. *American Psychologist*, 1979, **10**, 958–966.

Holland, C.J. An interview guide for behavioral counseling with parents. *Behavior Therapy*, 1970, **1**, 70–79.

Hunt, J.McV. *Intelligence and experience*. New York: Ronald, 1961.

Ilg, F.L., & Ames, L.B. *Child behavior*. New York: Harper & Row, 1955.

Jacobs, J.C. Effectiveness of teacher and parent identification of gifted children as a function of school level. *Psychology in the Schools*, 1971, **8**, 140–142.

Jenkins, S., Bax, M., & Hart, H. Behaviour problems in preschool children. *Journal of Child Psychology and Psychiatry*, 1980, **1**, 5–18.

Jersild, A.T., & Holmes, F.B. *Children's fears*. New York: Teachers College, Columbia University, 1935.

Johnson, B., & Morse, H. Injured children and their parents. *Children*, 1968, **15**, 147–152.

Johnson, M.R. Mental health interventions with medically ill children: A review of the literature 1970–1977. *Journal of Pediatric Psychology*, 1979, **4**, 147–164.

Johnson, S.M., Wahl, G., Martin, S., & Johansson, S. How deviant is the normal child? A behavioral analysis of the preschool child and his family. In R.D. Rubin, J.P. Brady, & J.D.

Henderson (Eds.), *Advances in behavior therapy* (Vol. 4). New York: Academic Press, 1973.

Jones, M.C. A laboratory study of fear: The case of Peter. *Journal of Genetic Psychology*, 1924, **31**, 308–315.

Kales, A. (Ed.), *Sleep: Physiology and pathology*. Philadelphia: Lippincott, 1969.

Kellerman, J. Rapid treatment of nocturnal anxiety in children. *Journal of Behavior Therapy and Experimental Psychiatry*, 1980, **11**, 9–11.

Kellerman, J., Rigler, D., Siegel, S.E., & Katz, E.R. Disease related communication and depression in pediatric cancer patients. *Journal of Pediatric Psychology*, 1977, **2**, 52–53.

Kempe, R.E. The battered child. *The Journal of the American Medical Association*, 1962, **181**, 17–20.

Kempe, R.S., & Kempe, C.H. *Child abuse*. Cambridge: Harvard University Press, 1978.

Kessler, S., & Bostwick, S.H. Beyond divorce: Coping skills for children. *Journal of Clinical Child Psychology*, 1977, **6**, 38–41.

Keyserling, M.D. *Windows on day care*. New York: National Council of Jewish Women, 1972.

Kirk, S.A. *Early education of the mentally retarded*. Urbana: University of Illinois Press, 1958.

Kitchen, L.W. Psychological factors in congenital heart disease in children. *Journal of Family Practice*, 1978, **6**, 777–783.

Klackenberg, G. Thumbsucking: Frequency and etiology. *Pediatrics*, 1949, **4**, 418–423.

Knapp, V.S., & Hansen, H. Helping parents of children with leukemia. *Social Work*, 1973, **18**, 70–75.

Kohlberg, L., La Crosse, J., & Ricks, D. The predictability of adult mental health from childhood behavior. In B. Wolman (Ed.), *Manual of child psychopathology*. New York: McGraw-Hill, 1972.

Kolvin, I., Ounsted, C., Humphrey, M., & McNay, A. The phenomenology of childhood psychosis. *British Journal of Psychiatry*, 1971, **118**, 381–419.

Koocher, G.P. Talking with children about death. *American Journal of Orthopsychiatry*, 1974, **44**, 404–411.

Kovacs, M., & Beck, A.T. An empirical-clinical approach toward a definition of childhood depression. In J.G. Schulterbrandt & A. Raskin (Eds.), *Depression in childhood: Diagnosis, treatment, and conceptual models.* New York: Raven, 1977.

Landauer, T.K., Carlsmith, J.M., & Lepper, M. Experimental analysis of the factors determining obedience of four-year-old children to adult females. *Child Development,* 1970, **41,** 601–611.

Lansing, M.D., & Schopler, E. Individualized education: A public school model. In E. Schopler & M. Rutter (Eds.), *Autism: A reappraisal of concepts and treatment.* New York: Plenum, 1978.

Lassman, F.M., Fisch, R.O., Vetter, D.K., & La Benz, E.S. *Early correlates of speech, language and hearing.* Acton, Mass.: Publishing Sciences Group, 1980.

Lefkowitz, M.M., & Burton, N. Childhood depression: A critique of the concept. *Psychological Bulletin,* 1978, **85,** 716–726.

Leventhal, J.M. Enuresis. In S. Gabel (Ed.), *Behavior problems of childhood.* New York: Grune & Stratton, 1981.

Lewis, M., & Schaeffer, S. Peer behavior and mother-infant interaction in maltreated children. In M. Lewis & I.A. Rosenblum (Eds.), *The uncommon child.* New York: Plenum, 1981.

Lillywhite, H.S., Young, N.B., & Olmsted, R.W. *Pediatrician's handbook of communication disorders.* Philadelphia: Lea & Febiger, 1970.

Longfellow, C. Divorce in context: Its impact on children. In G. Levinger & O.I.C. Moles (Eds.), *Divorce and separation: Context, causes and consequences.* New York: Basic Books, 1979.

Lourie, R.S. The role of rhythmic patterns in childhood. *American Journal of Psychiatry,* 1949, **109,** 653–680.

Lovaas, O.I. Parents as therapists. In E. Schpolee & M. Rutter (Eds.), *Autism: A reappraisal of concepts and treatment.* New York: Plenum, 1978.

Manning, M., Heron, J., & Marshall, T. Styles of hostility and social interactions at nursery, at home and at school. An extended study of children. In L. Hersov & M. Berger (Eds.), *Aggression and conduct disorder in childhood and adolescence.* New York: Pergamon, in press.

Mannino, F.V., & Delgado, R.A. Trichotillomania

in children: A review. *American Journal of Psychiatry,* 1969, **126,** 87–93.

Manosevitz, M., Prentice, N.M., & Wilson, F. Individual and family correlates of imaginary companions in preschool children. *Developmental Psychology,* 1973, **8,** 72–79.

Markova, I., MacDonald, K., & Forbes, C. Impact of haemophilia on childrearing practices and parental cooperation. *Journal of Child Psychology and Psychiatry,* 1980, **21,** 153–162.

Martin, H. The child and his development. In C.H. Kempe & R.E. Helfer (Eds.), *Helping the battered child and his family.* Philadelphia: Lippincott, 1972.

Martin, M.P. *1977 analysis of child abuse and neglect research.* Report submitted to National Center on Child Abuse and Neglect, DHEW, 1978.

Massong, S.R., Edwards, R.P., Sitton, L.R., & Hailey, B.J. A case of trichotillomania in a three year old treated by response prevention. *Journal of Behavior Therapy and Experimental Psychiatry,* 1980, **11,** 223–225.

McDevitt, S.C., & Carey, W.B. The measurement of temperament in 3–7 year old children. *Journal of Child Psychology and Psychiatry,* 1978, **19,** 245–253.

Mesibov, G.B., Schroeder, C.S., & Wesson, L. Parental concerns about their children. *Journal of Pediatric Psychology,* 1977, **2,** 13–17.

Milgram, S. *Obedience to authority.* New York: Harper, 1974.

Minuchin, S. *Families and family therapy.* Cambridge: Harvard University Press, 1974.

Moskowitz, D., Schwartz, J., & Corsini, D. Initiating day care at three years of age: Effects of attachment. *Child Development,* 1977, **48,** 1271–1276.

Mussen, P., & Eisenberg-Berg, N. *Roots of caring, sharing and help: The development of prosocial behavior in children.* San Francisco: Freeman, 1977.

Naylor, A.K. Early intervention: Panacea or challenge: Characteristics of parents in a mental health clinic for young children. In E.J. Anthony & C. Chiland (Eds.), *The child in his family: Preventive child psychiatry in an age of transition.* New York: Wiley, 1980.

Nazzaro, J. Child abuse and neglect. *Exceptional Children,* February 1974, 351–359.

Newsom, C.D. Childhood psychosis. In S. Gabel & M.T. Erickson (Eds.), *Child development and developmental disabilities.* Boston: Little, Brown, 1980.

Ornitz, E.M., & Ritvo, E.R. The syndrome of autism: A critical review. *American Journal of Psychiatry,* 1976, **133,** 609–622.

Parten, M.B. Social participation among preschool children. *Journal of Abnormal and Social Psychology,* 1932, **27,** 243–269.

Patterson, G.R., & Fleischmann, M.J. Maintenance of treatment effects: Some considerations concerning family systems and follow-up data. *Behavior Therapy,* 1979, **10,** 168–185.

Peed, S., Roberts, M., & Forehand, R. Evaluation of the effectiveness of a standardized parent training program in altering the interactions of mothers and their non-compliant children. *Behavior Modification,* 1977, **1,** 323–350.

Piaget, J., & Inhelder, B. *The psychology of the child.* New York: Basic Books, 1969.

Pinkston, E.M., Reese, N.M., Le Blanc, J.M., & Baer, D.M. Independent control of a preschool child's aggression and peer interaction by contingent teacher attention. *Journal of Applied Behavior Analysis,* 1973, **6,** 115–124.

Polansky, N.A., Hally, C., & Polansky, N.F. *Profile of neglect. A survey of knowledge of child neglect.* Washington, D.C.: Community Services Administration, Social and Rehabilitation Services, DHEW, 1975.

Pomerantz, P.B., Peterson, N.T., Marholin, D., & Stern, S.. The *in vivo* elimination of a child's water phobia by a paraprofessional at home. *Journal of Behavior Therapy and Experimental Psychiatry,* 1977, **8,** 417–421.

Popovich, F., & Thompson, G.W. Thumb-and-finger sucking: Its relation to malocclusion. *American Journal of Orthodontics,* 1973, **63,** 148–155.

Prugh, D.G., Staub, E.M., Sands, H.H., Kirschbaum, R.M., & Lenihan, E.A. A study of the emotional reactions of children and families to hospitalization and illness. *American Journal of Orthopsychiatry,* 1953, **23,** 70–106.

Public Law 94–142. The education for all handicapped children's act. November 1974.

Rand, C.W. Copying in drawing: The importance of adequate visual analysis versus the ability to utilize drawing rules. *Child Development,* 1973, **44,** 47–53.

Rapoport, J.L. Pediatric psychopharmacology and childhood depression. In J.G. Schulterbrandt & A. Raskin (Eds.), *Depression in childhood: Diagnosis, Treatment, and Conceptual Models.* New York: Raven, 1977.

Richman, N. Is a behaviour check list for preschool children really useful? In P.J. Graham (Ed.), *Epidemiological approaches in child psychiatry.* New York: Academic Press, 1977.

Richman, N., Stevenson, J.E., & Graham, P.J. Prevalence of behaviour problems in three-year-old children: An epidemiological study in a London borough. *Journal of Child Psychology and Psychiatry,* 1974, **6,** 272–287.

Robert, M.W., Hatzenbuehler, L.C., & Bean, A.W. The effects of differential attention and time out on child noncompliance. *Behavior Therapy,* 1981, **12,** 93–99.

Roberts, M.W., McMahon, R.J., Forehand, R., & Humphreys, L. The effect of parental instruction-giving on child compliance. *Behavior Therapy,* 1978, **9,** 793–798.

Roberts, R.N., & Gordon, S.B. Reducing childhood nightmares subsequent to a burn trauma. *Child Behavior Therapy,* 1979, **1,** 373–381.

Robinson, N.M., & Robinson, H.B. *The mentally retarded child.* New York: McGraw-Hill, 1976.

Roedell, W.C., Jackson, N.E., & Robinson, H.B. *Gifted young children.* New York: Teachers College Press, 1980.

Rolf, J.E., & Harig, P.T. Etiological research in schizophrenia and the rationale for primary prevention. In S. Chess & A. Thomas (Eds.), *Annual progress in child psychiatry and child development.* New York: Brunner/Mazel, 1975.

Rosensthal, A.K., & Scott, D.S. Four considerations in using imagery techniques with children. *Journal of Behavior Therapy and Experimental Psychiatry,* 1977, **8,** 287–290.

Ross, A.O. *Child behavior therapy.* New York: Wiley, 1980.

Routh, D.K. The preschool child. In S. Gabel & M.T. Erickson (Eds.), *Child development and developmental disabilities.* Boston: Little, Brown, 1980.

Routh, D.K., & Schroeder, C.S. Masturbation and other sexual behaviors. In S. Gabel (Ed.), *Behavior problems of childhood.* New York: Grune & Stratton, 1981.

Routh, D.K., Schroeder, C.S., & O'Tuama, L.A. Development of activity level in children. *Developmental Psychology,* 1974, **10,** 163–168.

Rutter, M. Autistic children: Infancy to adulthood.

Seminars in Psychiatry, 1970, **2**, 435–450.

Rutter, M. Normal psychosexual development. *Journal of Child Psychology and Psychiatry and Allied Professions,* 1971, **11**, 259–283.

Rutter, M. Childhood schizophrenia reconsidered. *Journal of Autism and Childhood Schizophrenia,* 1972, **2**, 315–337.

Rutter, M. The development of infantile autism. *Psychological Medicine,* 1974, **4**, 147–163.

Rutter, M. *Helping troubled children.* New York: Plenum, 1975.

Rutter, M. Maternal deprivation, 1972–1978: New findings, new concepts, new approaches. *Child Development,* 1979, **80**, 283–305.

Rutter, M., & Sussenwein, F. A developmental and behavioral approach to the treatment of preschool autistic children. *Journal of Autism and Childhood Schizophrenia,* 1971, **1**, 376–397.

Ryall, M.R., & Dietiker, E. Fear word choice in preschoolers. *Journal of Behavior Therapy and Experimental Psychiatry,* 1978, **9**, 189–190.

Sallustro, F., & Atwell, C.W. Body rocking, head banging, and head rolling. *Journal of Pediatrics,* 1978, **93**, 704–708.

Sanchez, V. Behavioral treatment of chronic hairpulling in a two year old. *Journal of Behavior Therapy and Experimental Psychiatry,* 1979, **10**, 241–245.

Sang, D.M. Re-establishing communication between parents and their young children following a disruptive life crisis. *Journal of Clinical Child Psychology,* 1979, **8**, 52–55.

Scarr, S. Introduction to the special issue. *American Psychologist,* 1979, **10**, 809–811.

Schopler, E., & Rutter, M. (Eds.), *Autism: A reappraisal of concepts and treatment.* New York: Plenum, 1978.

Schroeder, C.S. Psychologist in a private pediatric office. *Journal of Pediatric Psychology,* 1979, **1**, 5–18.

Schroeder, C.S., Mesibov, G., Eastman, J., & Goolsby, E. Preventive services for children: A model. In A.W. Burgess & B.A. Baldwin (Eds.), *Crisis intervention theory and practice: A clinical handbook.* Englewood Cliffs, N.J.: Prentice-Hall, 1981.

Schroeder, C.S., & Schroeder, S.R. Behavior theory and practices. In J. Paul & J. Epanchin (Eds.), *Educating emotionally disturbed children.* Columbus, O.: Merrill, in press.

Schroeder, C.S., Teplin, S., & Schroeder, S.R. Common medical problems in the classroom. In C.R. Reynolds & T.B. Gutkin (Eds.), *Handbook of school psychology.* New York: Wiley, 1981.

Seligman, M.E.P. *Helplessness: On depression, development and death.* San Francisco: Freeman, 1975.

Sheehan, A.M., & Abbott, M.S. A descriptive study of day care characteristics. *Child Care Quarterly,* 1979, **8**, 206–219.

Sherretts, S.D., Authier, K.J., & Tramontana, M.G. Parent education: Rationale, history, and funding sources. *Journal of Clinical Child Psychology,* 1980, **9**, 35–37.

Siegel, L.J. Preparation of children for hospitalization: A selected review of the research literature. *Journal of Pediatric Psychology,* 1976, **1**, 26–30.

Skinner, B.R. *The technology of teaching.* New York: Appleton-Century-Crofts, 1968.

Slaby, R.G., & Crowly, C.G. Modification of cooperation and aggression through teacher attention to children's speech. *Journal of Experimental Child Psychology,* 1977, **23**, 442–458.

Slaby, R.G., & Frey, K.S. Development of gender constancy and selective attention to same-sex models. *Child Development,* 1975, **46**, 849–856.

Sparling, J. (Ed.), *Information needs of parents with young children.* Chapel Hill: Frank Porter Graham Center, 1980.

Spinetta, J.J. The dying child's awareness of death: A review. *Psychological Bulletin,* 1974, **81**, 256–260.

Spinetta, J.J. Adjustment in children with cancer. *Journal of Pediatric Psychology,* 1977, **2**, 49–51.

Spitz, R. Anaclitic depression. *Psychoanalytical Study of the Child,* 1946, **2**, 113–117.

Spivack, G., Platt, J.J., & Shure, M.B. *The problem-solving approach to adjustment.* San Francisco: Jossey-Bass, 1976.

Spivack, G., & Shure, M.B. *Social adjustment of young children: A cognitive approach to solving real-life problems.* San Francisco: Jossey-Bass, 1974.

Stableford, W. Parental treatment of a child's noise phobia. *Journal of Behavior Therapy and Experimental Psychiatry,* 1979, **10**, 159–160.

Tarjan, C. The prevention of psychosocial retardation. In E.J. Anthony & C. Chiland (Eds.), *The child in his family: Preventive child psychiatry in an age of transition.* New York: Wiley, 1980.

Tavormina, J.B., Kastner, L.S., Slater, P.M., & Watt, S.L. Chronically ill children: A psychologically and emotionally deviant population? *Journal of Abnormal Child Psychology,* 1976, **4,** 99–110.

Telzrow, R.W. Habit patterns. In S. Gabel (Ed.), *Behavior problems of childhood.* New York: Brunner/Mazel, 1981.

Terman, M., & Oden, M.N. *Genetic studies of genius. The gifted group at mid-life: Thirty-five years follow-up of the superior child* (Vol. 5). Stanford: Stanford University Press, 1959.

Thomas, A., & Chess, S. Development in middle childhood. *Seminars in Psychiatry,* 1972, **4,** 331–341.

Thomas, A., & Chess, S. *Temperament and development.* New York: Brunner/Mazel, 1977.

Thomas, A., Chess, S., & Birch, H.G. *Temperament and behavior disorders in children.* New York: New York University Press, 1968.

Thomas, A., Chess, S., Sillen, J., & Mendez, O. Crosscultural study of behavior in children with special vulnerabilities to stress. In D.F. Ricks, A. Thomas, & M. Roff (Eds.), *Life history research in psychopathology* (Vol. 3). Minneapolis: University of Minnesota Press, 1974.

Thompson, R., & Hoffman, M.L. Empathic arousal and guilt feelings in children. *Developmental Psychology,* in press.

Tisza, V.B., Hurwitz, I., & Angoff, K. The use of a play program by hospitalized children. *Journal of the American Academy of Child Psychiatry,* 1970, **9,** 515–531.

Tramontana, M.G., Sherretts, S.D., & Authier, K.J. Evaluation of parent education programs. *Journal of Clinical Child Psychology,* 1980, **9,** 40–43.

Tropaner, A., Franz, M.N., & Dilgard, V.W. Psychological aspects of the case of children with cystic fibrosis. *American Journal of Disabled Children,* 1970, **119,** 424–432.

Vanderheiden, G., & Grilley, K. (Eds.), *Nonvocal communication techniques and aids for the severely physically handicapped.* Baltimore: University Park Press, 1975.

Vetter, D.K. Speech and language disorders. In S. Gabel & M.T. Erickson (Eds.), *Child development and developmental disabilities.* Boston: Little, Brown, 1980a.

Vetter, D.K. Overview: Psychosocial factors. In F.M. Lassman, R.O. Fisch, D.K. Vetter, & E.S. LaBenz (Eds.). *Early correlates of speech, language, and hearing.* Acton, Mass.: Publishing Sciences Group, 1980b.

Wahler, R.G. The insular mother: Her problems in parent-child treatment. *Journal of Applied Behavior Analysis,* 1980, **13,** 207–219.

Wahler, R.G., & Cormier, W.H. The ecological interview: A first step in out-patient child behavior therapy. *Journal of Behavior Therapy and Experimental Psychiatry,* 1970, **1,** 279–289.

Wallerstein, J.S., & Kelly, J.B. The effects of parental divorce: Experiences of the preschool child. *Journal of the American Academy of Child Psychiatry,* 1975, **14,** 600–616.

Wallerstein, J.S., & Kelly, J.B. *Surviving the breakup: How children and parents cope with divorce.* New York: Basic Books, 1980.

Watson, J.S. Depression and the perception of control in early childhood. In J.G. Schulterbrandt & A. Raskin (Eds.), *Depression in childhood: Diagnosis, treatment, and conceptual models.* New York: Raven, 1977.

Weston, D.L., & Irwin, R.C. Preschool child's response to death of an infant sibling. *American Journal of Disabled Children,* 1963, **106,** 74–77.

Whiting, B.B., & Whiting, J.W.M. *Children of six cultures: A psychocultural analysis.* Cambridge: Harvard University Press, 1975.

Wilbur, R.B. The linguistics of manual language and manual systems. In L.L. Lloyd (Ed.), *Communication, assessment and intervention strategies,* Baltimore: University Park Press, 1976.

Winick, M., Meyer, K.K., & Harris, R.C. Malnutrition and environmental enrichment by early adoption. *Science,* 1975, **190,** 1173–1175.

Winnicott, D.W. Transitional objects and transitional phenomena. *International Journal of Psychoanalysis,* 1953, **34,** 89–97.

Wolf, M. Social validity: The case for subjective measurement of how applied behavior analysis is finding a heart. *Journal of Applied Behavior Analysis,* 1978, **11,** 203–214.

Woody, J.D. Preventive intervention for children of divorce. *Social Casework,* 1978, **59,** 537–544.

Wright, L., Schaefer, A.B., & Solomons, G. *Encyclopedia of pediatric psychology.* Baltimore: University Park Press, 1979.

Yancy, W.S. Repetitive movements. In S. Gabel (Ed.), *Behavior problems of childhood.* New York: Brunner/Mazel, 1981.

Zahn-Waxler, C., Radke-Yarrow, M., & King, R.M. Childrearing and children's prosocial imitations toward victims of distress. *Child Development,* 1979, **50,** 319–330.

Zajonc, R.B. Family configuration and intelligence. *Science,* 1976, **192,** 227–229.

Zigler, E. National crisis in mental retardation research. *American Journal of Mental Deficiency,* 1978, **83,** 1–8.

Zuckerman, B.S., & Blitzer, E.C. Sleep disorders. In S. Gabel (Ed.), *Behavior problems of childhood.* New York: Grune & Stratton, 1981.

Problems of Childhood

CHAPTER 14

Fears and Anxiety in Children

LOVICK C. MILLER

Fear and anxiety have been universal experiences of man throughout recorded history in every culture and at every age and stage of ontological development. Hippocrates, in 420 B.C., described two adults, one with a fear of the notes of a flute and the other with a fear of heights. Since these experiences exist universally, they are presumed to be necessary for the survival of the species as well as important ingredients in the socialization process of the individual and the efficient functioning of social groups. Without anxiety, there would be little incentive to work, to learn, to organize, to plan, to individuate, or to separate. Even though fear can be necessary for survival and socialization of the species, individuals of all ages can become incapacitated by an excess of anxiety.

Despite the fact that anxiety has been known to incapacitate people since the earliest of times and has been studied extensively since the turn of this century, the phenomenon remains a mystery. We know that it exists at every age, that it can be extremely painful and can severely interrupt and cripple a person's life, and yet we lack an adequate theory to explain it, have few reliable instruments to measure its presence or progress, little sophisticated research on it, and no generally agreed-upon definition. Berecz (1968, pp. 704–705) concluded a review of the literature in 1968 as follows: "There is presently little empirical evidence in the area of childhood phobias to allow many meaningful generalizations." Graziano and DeGiovanni (1979) note that, "despite some sixty years of psychological research in children's fears, little is known in any systematic way about the development,

response characteristics, maintenance and reduction of children's fears and phobias" (p. 161). The same state of affairs exists in 1981, although we are beginning to clarify the major issues upon which research and theory can be built. This chapter will attempt to specify the critical issues and to cite some of the relevant literature on childhood anxiety as well as the experiences of workers who have attempted to help children and parents to ameliorate the crippling effects of anxiety during the childhood years.

DEFINITION

When we attempt to define "anxiety," the complexity of our subject becomes readily apparent. The issue that emerges immediately is the distinction between fear, anxiety, and phobia. Both fear and anxiety are subjectively experienced as dysphoric, aversive feelings with a heightened sense of uncertainty. Fear is commonly thought of as the normal physiological reaction to a genuine threat and disappears with the withdrawal of the dangerous object. Anxiety, on the other hand, is a response to an internal cue without an obvious external threatening cause precipitating the reaction. Anxiety also may become attached to an external nondangerous object or situation, in which case the person acts "as if" afraid for no apparent reason. Such a condition is considered to be a phobia.

In this chapter we will define fear as a normal physiological response to a threatening stimulus. It involves outer behavioral expressions, inner subjective feelings, and accompanying physiological changes. The subjective experience is described as a sense of being frozen and an inability to think clearly; the victim's response to the environment appears irrational, automatic, and hypersuggestible. Both parts of the autonomic nervous system normally come into play: the parasympathetic, which controls the life-sustaining organs of the body, and the sympathetic, which prepares the body for "fight or flight."

Anxiety is defined as a dysphoric, aversive feeling similar to fear that arises *without* an obvious external threat. It may be transitory or be present throughout the life of the individual, and it may be a primary psychological state or a symptom of an underlying somatic disease or toxic condition. It may occur after a trauma, but more frequently no precipitating event can be identified. The main characteristic is a constant feeling of tension that persists in the absence of threat. Stress may increase the feelings of anxiety to intolerable or panic levels. The autonomic responses and biochemical changes are similar to those of fear, except that they are not limited to specific situations. Since the main distinction between anxiety and fear is the degree of threat of the stimulus, it is difficult to tell in most situations which label is appropriate. When a mother leaves a 9-month-old with a stranger, the situation is not actually life threatening; but it is a frightening situation for the child, and whether we call the child's response anxiety or fear is an arbitrary and meaningless distinction. We will use the terms interchangeably in this chapter, since we will not be concerned with fear generated by life-threatening events.

A phobia is a subtype of anxiety attached to a specific object. There is debate in the literature as to whether a phobia must have an unconscious conflict associated with the manifest behavior. We will discuss this aspect of the definition at greater length in the section on manifest versus latent anxiety, but we have decided not to include the presence of an unconscious conflict as part of the definition of phobia. This is due primarily to the problem of identifying and measuring such conflicts in

children. We define a phobia (Miller, Barrett, & Hampe, 1974) as anxiety which:

1. Is attached to a specific nonthreatening stimulus
2. Is out of proportion to the demands of the situation
3. Cannot be explained or reasoned away
4. Is beyond voluntary control
5. Leads to avoidance of the feared situation
6. Persists over an extended period of time
7. Is unadaptive
8. Is not age or stage specific

In the research cited above, Miller et al. (1974) found that many child phobias spontaneously remitted. Based on this and other research, Graziano, DeGiovanni, and Garcia (1979) proposed that clinical level fears be defined as those with a duration of over two years or an intensity that is debilitating to the patient's routine lifestyle. There is merit in this proposal, particularly for research, but when a child is suffering, two years is a long time to wait. We found that many phobias remitted after three months when the child was placed on a waiting list. Our experience would suggest that if a child with an anxiety condition is helped on a bi-weekly basis with a supportive regime, the three-month waiting period is a more realistic and tolerable length of time. If the problem remits, then further treatment would be unnecessary.

FEAR AND ANXIETY AS CONSTRUCTS

Fear and anxiety are hypothetical constructs; they cannot be seen, heard, smelled, or felt by an external observer. Rather, they are inferred from multiple cues including self-reports, behavioral signs, avoidance responses, physiological responses, and so on. A discussion of a number of issues related to this fact should help to clarify certain confusing aspects of fear and anxiety in childhood.

Manifest-Latent Issue

We have defined anxiety as a condition that is manifested overtly and can be readily inferred, particularly if the inference includes the subjective report of the person experiencing the anxiety. The question arises if anxiety is also covert and not manifested by signs typically used to identify anxiety. Many diverse types of psychopathology in childhood are thought to have underlying anxiety "causing" the manifest behavior. Such conditions as hyperactivity, enuresis, encopresis, learning disabilities, aggressive behavior, and social withdrawal are often thought to arise from anxiety, and yet many children manifesting these symptoms do not appear overtly anxious. The anxiety is thought to be latent and is used as an independent variable to "explain" the manifest behavior. From the clinical literature, it is difficult to know on what basis latent anxiety is inferred when the child does not appear frightened or anxious. There is no measure of latent anxiety and no research has determined if latent and manifest anxiety are the same or different phenomena, if they arise from the same source, or if they are ameliorated by identical procedures.

Another aspect of the latent-manifest issue is the psychoanalytic contention that phobias are external representations of internal conflicts. Sperling (1961) reports a case to illustrate that anxiety represents unconscious conflicts and that diminution of anxiety is impossible without a resolution of the conflict:

No matter how difficult the cases may appear clinically, the basic conflict underlying the symptoms is the same and the phobia demands prompt treatment based on psychological understanding.... The precipitating events that touch off the acute anxiety, manifested in school phobia, are always events that unconsciously are interpreted by the child as a danger to his mother's life and his own life...a phobia is not amenable to reason, persuasion, or punishment.... I also do not believe in "self cures" of phobics.... I recommend...exposing to the patient as soon as possible the basic conflict underlying the phobia. (pp. 507–508)

Psychoanalysts have studied phobias too extensively for us to brush aside their contention, yet we see no way to assess unconscious conflicts. Case examples (Arieti, 1961; Bornstein, 1935; Freud, 1962; Renik, 1972; Sperling, 1961; Waugh, 1967) of child phobias are subject to so many divergent interpretations (Rachman & Costello, 1961; Wolpe & Rachman, 1960) that answers are not forthcoming. Therefore, until measurements of unconscious conflicts can be made, we have chosen to table the analytic contention and to assess phobias in terms of behavioral, subjective, physiological components.

For clinicians, the concept of latent anxiety has considerable utility because it helps to explain how children with many diverse symptoms get better as they gain self-confidence and are more at ease with themselves and their world. It is also known that many children who at first deny fears and anxieties in a "macho" way will later admit to them within the context of a trusting relationship. Nonetheless, it is a difficult construct to discuss when it cannot be measured and studied directly. Therefore, in this chapter, we will limit our remarks to the manifest fears and anxieties of childhood. We will be using anxiety as a dependent variable that needs explanation rather than as an independent variable that explains other behaviors.

Developmental Aspects

The question arises as to whether anxiety is the same across all age groups. Is the manifest anxiety of a 6-month-old infant the same as that of a 2-, 4-, 13-, 16-, 20-, 50-, 85-year-old? Most likely not, for although the evidence is not definitive, it appears that the subjective experience may be similar but the causes and consequences are quite different. For example, fear or anxiety in the newborn appears to be a reflexive, instinctual reaction to the sudden loss of support or to excessive or unexpected sensory stimuli. By 6 months, infants begin to manifest anxiety associated with novel stimuli (Rutter & Hersov, 1976a; Spitz et al., 1946), and male children with an overdeveloped fear of novelty have been shown to maintain a heightened fearfulness into the early child-hood years (Bronson, 1970). This suggests that, for males, experiences before 6 months of age form a base for anxiety which may emerge well into the latency years. A number of other fears begin to emerge around 6 months, such as fear of masks, heights, dogs, jacks-in-the-box. These fears tend to increase until 18–24 months and then decrease. Children rated high at one point in time on these fears tend to be high at a later date, indicating that fears are stable (Scarr & Salapatek, 1970). By 9 months of age, crying (anxiety) can be precipitated by the mother's leaving a male or female child for too long a period or in a strange environment, suggesting that *separation* from the mother produces anxiety by this age (Weinraub & Lewis, 1977). Separation anxiety usually reaches its most acute phase at the end of the second year of life. Many authorities believe that when mastery of separation does not occur, separation anxiety becomes the core problem in school phobia (Rodriguez, Rodriguez, & Eisenberg, 1959; Johnson et al., 1941; Eisenberg, 1958).

Separation anxiety presupposes the emergence of another process, namely the ability of the child to formulate an abstract image and to attach this image to a significant figure such as the mother. The mother's presence produces security and her absence, anxiety. This newfound ability is known as *object constancy* and signals the beginning of the child's cognitive development as an important component of anxiety. The symbolic aspect of anxiety has been discussed most extensively by psychoanalytic writers but has been most carefully studied by Piaget (1970), who has demonstrated the emergence of a number of cognitive processes such as reversals, conservation of mass, egocentricity, and concrete and abstract thinking, all of which form a conceptual and perceptual base from which the child perceives and processes information coming from his or her immediate environment.

Many studies have demonstrated the maturational aspects of anxiety and the presumed underlying cognitive factors. For example, Jones and Jones (1928) found that children up to 2 years of age showed no fear of a large, harmless mask, while children aged 3 were cautious, and, by 4, definite signs of fear were displayed. However, the relation of cognitive processes to anxiety has not as yet been experimentally demonstrated beyond doubt. In a study by Scarr and Salapatek (1970), stranger anxiety was found to correlate with measures of object permanence, but, when age was partialed out, the correlation became nonsignificant, suggesting that some factor other than object permanence was underlying the development of anxiety. With fear of a visual cliff (depth perception anxiety), the emergence of anxiety was clearly associated with locomotion. Even though a child could clearly perceive depth, no fear was shown unless he was able to locomote. So although the emergence of anxiety associated with many different stimuli can be clearly demonstrated to be a natural developmental phenomenon, it is not at all clear as to the exact variables precipitating the reactions.

Around age 2, when toilet training begins for most children, fear of the toilet is not uncommon. Fears of imaginary creatures, death, robbers, and being alone begin around 15 months of age, tend to increase up to age 4, and then show a steady decrease until age 11 when there is again an upsurge of fear (Macfarlane, Allen, & Honzik, 1954). Dogs are the predominant fear at age 3, while by the fourth year the fear of the dark predominates. At age 6, fear of school becomes a problem and declines in frequency until age 11 when there is an acceleration of school-associated anxiety (Smith, 1970). By age 12, there appears to be a decrease in fears of natural events, and at some point between 12 and adulthood a cluster of fears emerges, centering around sexuality, abortion, suicide, defective children, and such. Fears of injury and social anxieties stay throughout the lifespan from the time they originate in early childhood. In an interesting factor analytic study of self-reported fears at ages 11, 17, and 70, Russell (1967) found three clusters of fears that were found at all three age levels, which he labeled Disability and Cold War, Macabre, and Social Alienation. For the 17- and 70-year-olds, the factor structure became more complex, with moral and religious fears, among others, emerging as main factors. Russell found that categories differed quantitatively and qualitatively between sexes and between age levels. Females admitted to more fears than males. In a recent factor analytic study of the Louisville Fear Survey, Staley and O'Donnell (1981) found five primary factors: physical injury, animals, schoolrelated, night, and public places. The content of these factors was similar across the age range from 6 to 16. While these factors carry names which are different from those used in other factorial studies, the authors conclude that the extracted factors appeared in some form in previous studies. Thus systematic studies of children's fears using factor analyses of parent ratings reveal a basic dimensional structure which remains constant after 6 years of age, with the emergence of moral and religious fears beginning in the adolescent years. Table 14.1 summarizes the major sources of anxiety emerging through the childhood years.

In summary, the clinical and experimental evidence clearly demonstrates that source and content of anxiety and fears change with age but begin to stabilize around age 6. In general, the number of stimuli capable of eliciting fears increases with age. This increase seems to be associated with an increased cognitive capacity to abstract and generalize, but one study has questioned whether the development of abstract abilities is directly related to the emergence of an abstract capacity for conceptualizing a permanent object. Other studies have demonstrated that variables causing anxiety are quite complex. Cognitive variables may be necessary but not sufficient explanations for the emergence of anxiety in the developing child. Since there is a developmental component to anxiety, it is important to recognize a normal developmental process in which anxiety is expected to arise at certain ages around specific situations and objects and then gradually to diminish. This delineation helps to differentiate normal from pathological anxiety. The presence of such anxiety is not pathological, whereas its absence can denote serious developmental abnormalities.

State versus Trait

When a clinician notes that a child is anxious, the statement may mean that the individual is anxious at the moment or that he or she is an anxious person. The term refers to quite different states, the former to a temporary state and the latter to a constant condition. Clinically, the terms are differentiated with the adjectives "acute" and "chronic." "Acute" means high intensity of relatively short duration while "chronic" refers to a relatively low intensity of indefinite duration. "Acute" applies reasonably well to pathological anxiety

Table 14.1 Main Sources of Anxiety at Different Age Levels

Age	Sources of Anxiety
0–6 months	Excessive or unexpected sensory stimuli, loss of support, loud noises
6–9 months	Strangers, novel stimuli (masks, heights, etc.)
1st year	Separation, injury, toilet
2nd year	Imaginary creatures, death, robbers
3rd year	Dogs, being alone
4th year	Dark
6–12 years	School, injury, natural events, social anxiety
13–18 years	Injury, social alienation, the macabre
19+ years	Injury; natural events; sexual, moral and religious issues

states; however, "chronic" does not, since the person is not in a continuing state of low anxiety but rather is prone or predisposed to experience anxiety on a relatively large number of occasions and in a large number of different situations. Experimental workers such as Cattell and Scheier (1961), Lazarus (1966), and Spielberger (1966) prefer the terms *state* and *trait*. *Situational anxiety* is a transitory state which occurs in response to a stimulus and is likely to vary in intensity as a function of the stimulus. *Trait anxiety* is a relatively unfluctuating condition which exerts a constant influence on the person's behavior, resulting in a high level of anxiety more frequently but not necessarily more intensively than others.

The distinction between State and Trait is helpful, but in childhood the terms must be further delineated to encompass developmental stages. We have already noted, for example, that separation anxiety originates around 9 months and generally peaks around the second year of life. Separation anxiety during this period might be considered a trait because of its duration, yet since it has an expected termination point and the stimulus is relatively specific, it would perhaps be better classed as state. However, a condition that lasts for a year and a half is quite different from a transitory state that lasts for a week or two. Therefore, the concept of state in childhood may have a variable duration period. Trait anxiety in childhood should refer to a condition characterized by a high frequency of manifest anxiety to a variety of stimuli that are not age specific. The necessity to differentiate age specific stimuli once again points to the difference between anxiety during the childhood and the adult years.

Primary versus Secondary

A major issue in the diagnosis of anxiety in childhood is whether anxiety will be considered the primary or secondary diagnosis. As we have already noted, manifest anxiety arises from many sources, but it also accompanies many types of psychopathology. Psychotic or autistic children frequently exhibit much generalized or focalized anxiety, but the primary diagnosis is psychosis. Illnesses and drug overdoses can produce intense anxiety reactions in children as can certain types of central nervous system insults. Almost every type of childhood psychopathology may be associated with manifest anxiety, although in general there is less manifest anxiety in the aggressive disorders than in the inhibition disorders. Chess (1973) illustrates the necessity of determining whether anxiety is primary or secondary by showing the function and underlying causes of anxiety in four types of emotional disorders: developmental delays, organic brain dysfunction, and neurotic and psychotic problems.

In a recent survey of 218 Louisville Behavior Checklist (Miller, 1977) protocols of children applying to the Child Psychiatric Services of the University of Louisville School of Medicine, we found that 37 percent of the children between ages 3 and 18 had elevated scores on the Anxiety scale in the mild to moderate pathological range, and 33 percent in the severe range. This indicates that one-third of the children applying for service presented with manifest anxiety symptoms at a clinical level of severity. Another survey of 1,568 patients referred to the service over a two-year period showed that 42 percent were given diagnoses of anxiety as the primary disability. These surveys indicate that anxiety is used as the primary diagnosis in 30–40 percent of the children referred to the Child Psychiatric Services. In contrast, a recent survey by Graziano and DeGiovanni (1979) found that only 6.8 percent of children referred to behavior therapists carried the primary diagnosis of anxiety, a percentage that is considerably below the level of the Louisville service. It appears evident that a distinction should be drawn between the primary and secondary aspects of anxiety in clinical cases. However, the literature does not clearly specify the rules to be used for classifying anxiety as primary or secondary. Also, it is not clear whether secondary anxiety is an independent phenomenon or an aspect of a more general problem. Such questions are important in terms of treatment and prognosis, but considerable research needs to be done before the answers will be forthcoming. In the meantime, it is important to note that the clinical literature will at times refer to anxiety as a primary condition and at other times as a secondary condition.

Anxiety versus Depression

Like anxiety, depression is a nebulous concept in child psychopathology. It is used as both a dependent and an independent variable and refers to both latent and manifest states. Depression is thought to be masked by other behaviors, and it can contain symptoms of manifest anxiety in the same way that manifest anxiety may contain symptoms of depression. It can be state or trait and is thought to arise from both endogenous and exogenous factors.

Unlike anxiety, clinical symptoms of depression in childhood are generally thought to be quite different from symptoms of adult depression, except during the first 18 months of life. Spitz (1946) noted a condition of extreme withdrawal, called anaclitic depression, which occurred in the first year of life when children were kept in a foundling home without proper stimulation and "mothering." Many of these children became totally unresponsive to their environment and died; others were severely retarded for life. Other researchers such as Provence and Lipton (1962) and Dennis (1960, 1973) and Dennis and Najarian (1957) have also shown the debilitating effects of institutional care upon the developing infant. Bowlby (1961a, 1961b, 1973) has studied depression that follows separation from and loss of a significant caretaking person during the early years of childhood. Removal of young children from their mothers initiates successive psychological phases: numbness, protest, despair, and detachment. Each phase has an accompanying parallel response of separation anxiety, grief, and mourning, and together they act as a unitary process. Depression arising from separation or environmental deprivation is similar to anxiety arising from separation and the development of object constancy, which is one of the reasons for the two concepts being

so closely linked, both conceptually and operationally.

However, after the early childhood years, clinicians seldom report adultlike symptoms of depression, whereas anxiety is manifested in similar ways throughout the lifespan. This arises in part from the belief of psychoanalytic writers (Rado, 1968; Freud, 1968; Abraham, 1968, pp. 26–49) that the basic cause of depression is the dependence upon love objects for maintenance of self-esteem and the belief that self-punishment (atonement) is a way to win this love. In adults, this process depends upon a strong ego and superego that displaces the punitive parent. The child is still dependent upon the adult and does not have the well-differentiated ego or superego necessary to produce adult symptoms of depression. This view had dominated theory, resulting in the belief that depression does not exist between the ages of 4 to midadolescence. As an example, the recently released DSM III (1980) does not have a specific category for childhood depression, although the manual specifies that children may be diagnosed as depressed when they match adult criteria.

Aaron Beck (1967) and his colleagues have noticed for years that many adult depressive patients attest to the continuity of their depression from the childhood years. Beck became convinced that depression did exist in childhood and with Marion Kovacs (Schulterbrandt & Raskin, 1977) set out to describe childhood depression. In reviewing the literature they became convinced that not only did depression exist (Ling, Oftedal, & Weinberg, 1970; Weinberg et al., 1973; McConville, Boag, & Purohit, 1973; Frommer, 1968) but in all the adult aspects: affective, cognitive, motivational, vegetative, and psychomotor. The main difference is that dysphoric mood per se is not a primary symptom. However, in all other respects, child and adult depression are similar, and it is not necessary to use a term such as "masked" (latent) depression. Kovacs and Beck constructed the Child Depression Inventory to test out their belief and are currently involved in a research program to describe and understand childhood depression. Kovacs (1980–81) reports that the inventory has adequate reliability in general population studies of children and that research is currently under way to assess the validity of the instrument by comparing clinical judgment to self-reports.

In addition to the Kovacs and Beck studies, a number of investigators (Achenbach, 1978) have applied multivariant statistical techniques to ratings of child behavior based primarily on parent or teacher ratings. It is clear from these studies that depression and anxiety are closely associated and are statistically linked through a broad band Inhibition or Overcontrolled factor. Only one study (Miller, 1967) out of 25 isolated a manifest anxiety factor and two (Achenbach, 1978; Achenbach & Edelbrock, 1979) described a depression factor. This would suggest that anxiety and depression are not clear entities when parents and teachers are used as raters. Other factors reported in Achenbach's review strongly suggest the presence of both anxiety and depression, but the symptoms are so intermixed that no simple anxiety or depression factors emerge. It is premature to draw definite conclusions from these studies because there are many sources of variation that affect results, such as population sampled, raters and items used, type of statistical analyses, and so on. However, we might conclude that neither depression nor anxiety is a unitary phenomenon and therefore each needs to be subdivided, or that on the basis of the three studies, both anxiety and depression exist as unitary dimensions but are also found in other types of child psychopathology. Much more extensive research, which would include clinical raters and other statistical techniques, needs to be carried out before answers to these questions are discovered.

Since both anxiety and depression in childhood are so poorly understood and so closely linked conceptually as well as operationally, it is difficult to make a clear distinction between the two at this time. However, it appears that they both exist at a manifest level. Further, they appear to be components of a general inhibition syndrome. This inhibition affects affective, behavioral, and cognitive processes and includes social withdrawal and oversensitivity as well as anxiety and depression. Conceptually, anxiety appears to be related to an inhibition of impulses based on fear of need satisfaction while the inhibition connected with depression is based upon fear of object loss.

To clarify the distinction between symptoms of anxiety and depression, we asked the staff of the Child Psychiatric Services of the University of Louisville School of Medicine to rate a pool of items for both anxiety and depression. The items were rated on a 5-point scale for the degree to which they indicated the presence of anxiety and depression. Twenty-one professionals rated 68 items. Fifty-two items significantly differentiated anxiety from depression at the .01 level of confidence, 26 for anxiety and 26 for depression. Table 14.2 provides the items found to be significant for anxiety and depression as well as those which appear to indicate both conditions. It is clear that the staff believes that there are two distinct conditions and that anxiety is represented by indicators of the child's fear while depression is indicated by signs of withdrawal, self-deprecation, and generalized inhibition. Further research will need to determine if clinicians can distinguish these phenomena in actual children or if the distinctions are basically conceptual.

THEORY

We stated at the beginning of this chapter that no adequate theory explains the etiology or the maintenance of anxiety. Theories have been advanced, yet all fail to account for some aspects of the phenomenon. In this section, we discuss briefly the major theories which purport to account for anxiety. Since our discussion of theory is brief, we urge readers to turn to original sources for a more comprehensive view of this complex subject.

There are two major theories and five minor but significant theories that compete for professional attention. Psychoanalytic theory was advanced in the early 1900s and

Table 14.2 Symptoms of Anxiety, Depression, and Mixed Indicators

Anxiety	Mixed	Depression
Worries constantly	Being scapegoated	Suicidal ideation
Fearful, constantly afraid	Sleep disturbance	Withdrawn, unresponsive
Afraid of taking tests	Often cries	Feelings of helplessness and
Often terrified	Disturbance in concentration	hopelessness
Jumpy—frequent stress reaction	Distractible	Preoccupied with death or suicidal
Afraid of social events	Poor concentration	thoughts
Afraid of school	Somaticizes—headaches,	Complaint of depression
Afraid at night	abdominal pain	Retreats, loses interest in objects or
Separation problem	Unspecified feelings of being bad	situations previously interested in
Demands sleeping companion	Restless sleeper	Feels rejected or unloved
Nervous	Tends to give up when losing	Worries parents may die
Panicky	Appears desperate	Feelings of worthlessness
Obsessive-compulsive behavior	Often says can't do things	Seems tired, listless
Fear of death	Lacks self-confidence	Often looks lonely
Tense	Reassurance accepted as his	Self-deprecation
Worries parents may die	due—remaining dissatisfied	Withdrawn, unresponsive
Fear of war, injury	Low frustration tolerance	Recent weight loss
Frequent nightmares	Beliefs of persecution	Increasingly poor performance in
Fear of dark	Talks in sleep	school
Ritual behavior	Blatant denial of helplessness	Feels unlikable
Overreacts to pain	and hopelessness	Negative self-concept
Fidgety, small muscle activity		Excessive self-criticism
Refuses shots		Readiness to condemn self for
Enuresis		failure, tending to be harsh and
Encopresis		self-critical
		Low self-esteem
		Anorexia
		Lack of spontaneous activity
		Negative self-concept
		Believes others don't like him
		Passivity—wanting others to
		anticipate needs

Note: Symptoms ranked in decreasing order of probability of representing disorder as judged by 20 clinicians.

became the dominant theory during the first half of the twentieth century. Behavior theory followed a few years later, but did not gain much support outside of the academic community until recently. Cognitive-developmental theory has contributed important insights, but no total explanation of anxiety has been advanced by its adherents or by those advocating either transactional or existential approaches. Differential emotional theory based upon experimental findings in a number of areas has been developed recently and holds considerable promise for advancing our knowledge in this area.

Psychoanalytic Theory

Sigmund Freud first regarded anxiety as a purely physiological reaction to a chronic inability to reach orgasm in sexual relations. The process was thought to occur on a neurophysiological level and was not thought to be a psychological problem. Much later, he revised his thinking and published "The Problem of Anxiety" (1936) and "Inhibitions, Symptoms, and Anxiety" (1936), in which he developed the idea that anxiety was a signal designed to alert the person to danger. This formulation was possible after he had developed his structural concept of personality that assumes three interacting groupings of function: the id, ego, and superego. When an instinctual impulse arises which clashes with realistic, self-preservative, or conscious-directed interests, a slight degree of anxiety is used as a signal to warn of impending danger. The anxiety signal mobilizes defensive maneuvers aimed at keeping the instinct under control while simultaneously permitting the person to continue to function.

Freud believed that all anxiety originated from libidinal (sexual) conflicts, but other theorists assumed that aggression and dependence also played an important role. Freud, however, distinguished different varieties of anxiety based upon the specific threat. Thus he explained the fear of the dark, of being left alone, and of strangers as deriving from the need for the presence of the mother. He postulated that libido was mobilized as tension increased (longing), and, when discharge was not possible, "separation anxiety" occurred as a signal of danger of loss of mother. The next level of fear was fear of castration arising from the Oedipus conflict in which the child's affection for the parent of the opposite sex created a fear of damage to the genitals because of the same sex parent's jealousy. Superego anxiety, together with social anxiety, represented the next stage of anxiety development. What was formerly experienced as castration anxiety now became internalized as the disapproval of conscience. The ensuing guilt dominated the personality and regulated the person's actions. In brief, the conscious anxiety experienced by the person was the result of unconscious anxiety produced by a conflict between id, ego, and superego.

Freud's theory of phobia was first formulated around the case of Little Hans (1962). Little Hans was 5 years of age when treated by Freud. He had developed a sexual attraction to his mother and greatly feared his father. Out of this case came much of Freud's original theorizing regarding the Oepidal Complex.

Childhood phobia has been elaborated upon by a number of psychoanalytic investigators (Arieti, 1961; Bornstein, 1935; Klein,

1945; Renik, 1972; Sperling, 1961; Waugh, 1967). The primary distinction of phobia from anxiety is that the unconscious anxiety was displaced to an external concrete object, which permitted the child to function except in the presence of the phobic object. The object was a symbol of the unconscious wish; thus, by avoiding the object, one avoided expressing the forbidden wish. Further, since the instinctual danger was internal and inescapable, externalization transferred the danger to an external object that then could be avoided while displacement removed the danger from within the intimate family relationships to neutral objects, usually outside the home.

Psychoanalytic theorists recognize that the analytic theory of anxiety is incomplete, and current workers are proposing revisions to the theory (Compton, 1980, pp. 6–35). However, most of the changes are refinements of Freud's basic theory and do not essentially enhance our understanding of childhood anxiety.

Social Learning Theory

Social learning theory has evolved as a strong competitor to psychoanalysis. While psychoanalytic theory was based primarily on clinical data, social learning theory emerged from the experimental laboratory. Within social learning, there are three divergent theories of behavior: Respondent Conditioning, Operant Conditioning, and the Two Factor Theory of Conditioning. Each of these assumes that anxiety is learned. Respondent theory assumes that any neutral stimulus that happens to make an impact on an individual at the time that a fear reaction occurs will subsequently evoke the fear reaction. If the original conditioning situation is of high intensity or if repeated some number of times, the conditioned fear will then tend to persist without obvious reinforcement. Anxiety persists paradoxically, since it is unpleasant. Having acquired an unpleasant association and reaction to a particular stimulus or situation, the person will tend to avoid exposure to this noxious stimulus. The tendency to avoid the noxious situation impedes spontaneous recovery, since learned patterns of behavior can only be extinguished by repeated, nonreinforced behavior. Anxiety responses are also subject to generalization so that the response may generalize to a range of stimuli similar to the original noxious stimulus. The essentials of the theory are most clearly worked out for phobias and are summarized by Rachman and Costello (1961, p. 101):

1. Phobias are learned responses.
2. Phobic stimuli, simple or complex, develop when they are associated temporally and spatially with a fear-producing state of affairs.
3. Neutral stimuli that are of relevance in the fear-producing situation and/or make an impact on the person in the situation are more likely to develop phobic qualities than weak or irrelevant stimuli.
4. Repetition of the association between the fear situation and the new phobic stimuli will strengthen the phobia.
5. Associations between high intensity fear situations and neutral stimuli are more likely to produce phobic reactions.
6. Generalization from the original phobic stimulus to stimuli of a similar nature will occur.

Operant theory postulates that behavior that is rewarded will tend to reoccur while behavior that is not rewarded will extinguish. This theory would assume that avoidance behavior observed in anxiety as well as many of the accompanying behaviors such as temper tantrums are positively and systematically reinforced. The primary reinforcers are social rewards dispensed by significant persons in the immediate environment, primarily members of the family. Attention, whether affectionate or punitive, apparently serves equally well as a reinforcer. Parents and other significant persons teach children to be afraid by selectively attending and rewarding fearful and avoidant behaviors. Thus children are taught fear of the dark, death, dogs, separation, school, and such by parents and age mates responding with affection, anger, or reassurance to the child's fear, cautious approaches, and avoidance of these situations. The child, in turn, learns that parents are sensitive to such behaviors and respond with much attention and preoccupation so that a little fear evokes intense and frequent responses from significant others. Thus the more fear and avoidance behavior that a child evokes, the more attention he or she will receive from significant others. Since fear and avoidance rather than coping responses are consistently rewarded by significant others, the child fails to develop adaptive responses to aversive stimuli. This lack increases his potential to feel afraid and to try to manipulate others to help him avoid the noxious situation. This theory helps to account for the frequent observation of the tyrannical, manipulative, and narcissistic behavior of phobic children (Greenacre, 1952; Hersov, 1960a, 1960b; Leventhal & Sills, 1964) and the problems of distinguishing between "brat" behavior and anxiety (Williams, 1959).

Two Factor Theory recognizes the validity of both Respondent and Operant social learning explanations and increases the sophistication of the theory. Mowrer (1956) was the first to recognize the need for a combined theory and speculated that anxiety originated according to the Respondent conditioning paradigm. Anxiety reduction associated with the noxious stimulus became a secondary reinforcer. Since anxiety is most unpleasant, any behavior that reduces anxiety, such as avoidance of the noxious stimulus, is rewarding. Thus anxiety reduction associated with elimination of the noxious stimulus becomes the operant reward for avoiding the noxious stimulus created by associative conditioning. This theory assumes that phobias are mediated through the autonomic nervous system. However, Soloman and Turner (1962) have shown experimentally that behavior is in large part regulated by the central nervous system. Based on Soloman's work and a series of their own studies, Bandura, Blanchard, and Ritter (1969) have advanced a dual process theory that recognizes that threatening stimuli evoke emotional arousal that has both autonomic and central nervous system components, but that the *arousal process* operates primarily at the central level, exercising some degree of control over instrumental avoidance. It follows that if the arousal capacity of subjective threatening events is extinguished, then both the motivation and one set of controlling stimuli for avoidance behavior are removed. This theory has led to a series of studies aimed at eliminating fear behavior, based on the assumptions that extinction of fear arousal will reduce anxiety behavior, that fear arousal can be eliminated on a vicarious level (Modeling), and that the absence of anticipated negative consequences is a requisite condition for fear extinction.

Cognitive Development Theory

Cognitive development theory is concerned primarily with the interaction between the developing organism and the increasing complexity of his or her world. While there is no developmental theory of anxiety as such, we have previously noted that certain anxieties are more prevalent at specific ages than at others and that anxieties in children tend to disappear more rapidly than in adults. When we discuss treatment, we also note that a crucial ingredient in overcoming anxiety is the patient's willingness to confront the stimulus. Developmental theory postulates that maturation affects the way a person perceives and reacts to his or her environment. We have seen that fear of snakes is absent below the age of 2, apparently because the infant has not yet developed a concept of a snake. We can postulate that the central nervous system has to be sufficiently mature before the person is capable of developing anxiety. Furthermore, the transient quality of anxiety in childhood probably reflects a different condition of the organism rather than a difference in the conditioning history or the maintenance reinforcements. Surwillo (1971) has found, for example, that somewhere around the age of 12, the alpha rhythm of the central nervous system matures to an adult level. This phenomenon coincides with the age at which school anxieties become a more serious prob-

lem. It may be that child anxieties are actually quite different phenomena from adult anxieties even though there is behavioral similarity.

Developmental Theory

Developmental theory addresses a point that learning theories tend to minimize: the differential effect of stimuli on subjects. Social learning theories explain an individual's stimulus perceptions on the basis of his or her unique conditioning history, but clinical evidence suggests that conditioning does not occur on the basis of a simple stimulus-response model. Very seldom does a clinician obtain a history of a uniquely painful situation associated with the onset of the anxiety. More typically, the child reports events at onset that have no deleterious effects on many other children who are equally exposed. But the anxious child sees as dangerous a stimulus that most children disregard even though there may be some potential unpleasantness or a low probability of danger (e.g., wind noise and thunderstorms). Such interpretation of the stimulus does not seem to occur in laboratory conditions that, as a rule, take a universally noxious stimulus as the unconditioned one.

The role of the subject's interpretation of the feared stimulus has had little attention in the etiology of anxieties. We will not undertake a discussion of the evolution of meaning. However, we suggest that some examples from Piaget may have analogs in the development of childhood anxieties.

Piaget (1970) has demonstrated that a child's sense perceptions are based on constructions arising from interaction of subject and object. An example is the construction which enables a 9- to 12-month-old child to discover the permanence of objects. Initially, the child relies on the position of the object in his perceptual field, and later permanence occurs independent of any actual perception. During the early months, there are no permanent objects, only perceptual pictures that appear, dissolve, and sometimes reappear. The "permanence" of an object to a child is first demonstrated when the child searches for the object after it has disappeared.

Thus a child is not a passive receiver who ingests the adult's view of the world. Input undergoes significant transformation, the nature of which depends on the child's age. Another example of the child's age-related conception of reality involves the perception of the conservation of quantity of matter across changes in shape. A 5-year-old who has witnessed milk being poured from a short, broad glass into a tall, narrow glass will state that the quantity of milk has increased ("The milk is higher in this glass"). An 8-year-old, though, will state promptly that the amount of milk has not changed across pourings. The 8-year-old's conception of reality includes the notion that quantity is conserved across transformations; the 5-year-old's world view does not include this concept.

Thus, according to developmental theory, objects as perceived by children are age and state dependent as the child's constructions and schema about the nature of reality evolve. Although we have no empirical evidence, we would postulate that a precondition for anxiety is a construction of the object as dangerous and that anxieties that occur frequently at certain ages reflect the structuring process typical for that stage in development. Far from being pathognomonic, such fears would be considered a necessary and desirable aspect of development. This line of reasoning suggests that preconditions for treatment are desire on the part of patients to be rid of the anxiety and a willingness to consider the treatment appropriate to their schema of their personal world.

Transactional Approaches

Transactional approaches incorporate elements of the psychoanalytic, developmental, and social learning theories, but to date represent no integrated theory. The primary thesis is that social intercourse is critical in the generation and maintenance of pathognomic behavior. Individuals consciously and unconsciously construct social contracts with one another that form the matrix within which business is "transacted." The social contracts that are set up and the methods used to transact interpersonal business are a function of individuals' present experience, their past experience, and their hopes and expectations for the future. These experiences are processed in terms of three cognitive constructs: the individual as child, as parent, and as adult. Thus personality, interpersonal relationships, and psychopathology are viewed as an interaction among these constructs, the social contracts, and the methods for transacting business.

The primary contribution of this theory to understanding anxiety lies in the importance accorded the mutually influencing relationships of an anxious child and the significant persons in his or her environment, particularly the mother. We have already noted the explanation advanced by operant theory that emphasizes the reward function of social reinforcers. Transactional approaches incorporate operant principles, assuming that the anticipatory anxiety of parents, the anxious response of the child, and the protective or punitive response of parents are all mutually reinforcing. But it is further postulated that to change the contingencies, some member of the relationship has to decide to renegotiate the social contract and develop other transactional methods. To do this, an internal adjustment within all subsystems would have to occur. Transactionalists postulate that persons involved in an anxiety process believe that the anxiety contract "makes sense" and resist attempts to change it. It makes sense to them not only in terms of the immediate transactions but also in terms of the balance among their child, adult, and parent subsystems. Thus when parents of a school phobic are asked how they decide to permit a child to stay out of school in defiance of the law, they will explain that the child is "sick" and they do not wish to precipitate a "nervous breakdown." This makes sense to all parties and is the basis of their social contract with one another. The directive from a therapist to return the child to school will usually be resisted unless a new contract can be negotiated that "makes more sense." According to this theory, a therapist's job is not one of simply reconditioning a child to a noxious situation but also entails the renegotiation of a social contract between parent, child, and school.

Differentiated Emotions Theory

Differentiated emotions theory is relatively new (Izard, 1977, 1979; Buechler & Izard, 1980, chap. 16, pp. 285–298) but holds considerable promise for advancing our knowledge of anxiety. The theory holds that emotions constitute the primary motivational system in the human being. Emotions and drives interact with perceptions and cognitions, resulting in the great variety of human motivations. When an affect interacts frequently with an image or cognition, a pattern results that assumes the stability of an affective-cognitive structure to form complex personality traits such as passivity, skepticism or egotism. The theory describes eleven fundamental emotions, and when two or more are experienced simultaneously they form a pattern of emotions. Anxiety, depression, social affection, and hostility are four such patterns. If an emotion pattern is a frequent experience, it may emerge as a stable emotion trait which would increase the probability of that emotion when similar conditions recur.

This theory differs from others in that anxiety is not defined as a unidimensional experience but a pattern of emotions and affective-cognitive structures. An anxiety pattern always includes fear as the key component with two or more of the emotions of sadness, anger, shame, shyness, guilt, or interest. Anxiety patterns will differ, say, between an individual's early experience resulting in fear/shame/guilt rather than fear/anger/sadness.

Developmentally, the theory holds that the capacity for experiencing and expressing fear results primarily from maturation; from the point of emergence, it has characteristic, identifiable, unchanging neurological, expressive, and experiential components. The invariance of fear as a quality of consciousness contributes to the development of the sense of continuity and the concept of self. The facial expression of fear in an infant is essentially the same as its adult expression, and fear emerges when its experience and expression can serve adaptive purposes in promoting learning and social attachment. Fear adds to the complexity of the infant's conscious experience. The theory also assumes that the emergence of an emotion is not necessarily preceded by any particular cognitive attainment.

The emergence of fear and anxiety problems fosters a new awareness of the vulnerability of the self and strengthens the social bond to the caregiver. The motivating experience of fear is distinctly different from that of sadness. Fear motivates urgent defensive strategies geared toward escape and avoidance of the situation while sadness elicits less crisis-oriented strategies, such as time-consuming cognitive efforts.

The theory postulates a number of anxiety patterns. For example, fear may become coupled with shame and guilt as the infant develops a capacity for these emotions. Parents begin to evoke shame and guilt when they begin to assume that the infant deliberately behaves wrong. One of the most pervasive methods of regulating an emotion is by using another emotion. In the process of regulating fear, parents often use shame. The frequent message that one ought to feel shame for being afraid will result in a fear-shame anxiety problem that in turn could interfere with the development of the concept of self as an adequate individual.

The promising feature of this theory is the relationship between the child's anxiety and child-rearing practices. As yet, research has not demonstrated a systematic connection but theoretically there is the possibility of establishing this connection. For example, Tomkins (Izard & Tomkins, 1966) has differentiated left wing socialization of fear from right wing socialization. Left wing parents tend to minimize fear experiences that right wing parents do not, and the child is encouraged to be unafraid of fear. One particular combination is thought to be particularly pathogenic and that is when sadness is strongly linked to fear. Thus, whenever the individual faces a distressing problem, he or she tends to become afraid and attempts to escape rather than cope with the source of sadness. By focusing attention on the emotions that form different anxiety problems, differential emotional theory suggests the clinical and theoretical importance of future work to elucidate the antecedents and the adaptive and maladaptive consequences of each pattern.

Existential Theory

Existential theory is built upon the conflicts that flow from the individual's confrontation with the givens of human existence: the ultimate concerns, certain intrinsic properties that are an inescapable part of the human being's existence in the world such as death, freedom, isolation, and meaninglessness. A cause of existential tension is the conflict between the awareness of the inevitability of death and the wish to continue to exist. Freedom refers to the absence of external structure, which means that the individual is responsible for his or her own world and that, beneath, there is no ground, only a void. A key dynamic is the clash between groundlessness and the wish for structure. Isolation refers to the realization that no matter how close we come to another, there remains an unbridgeable gap. The existential tension is the conflict between the awareness of absolute isolation and the wish for contact, protection, and unification with a larger whole. The fourth concern arises from the first three: If we must die, if we create our own world, if we are ultimately alone in an indifferent universe, what is the meaning of life? The existential dynamic stems from the dilemma of a meaning-seeking creature who is thrown into a universe that has no meaning.

Existential theorists believe that psychopathology springs from these basic concerns in the following way:

Awareness of
Ultimate concern – – → Anxiety – – → Defense mechanism

Figure 14.1.

The key words for children are "awareness" and "anxiety." Employed in this formula, anxiety refers to latent anxiety or anxiety used as an independent variable which previously has not been the concern of this chapter. Manifest anxiety is a defense mechanism erected against latent anxiety arising from an awareness of ultimate concerns. However, since manifest anxiety cannot arise until the child has developed a capacity for cognitive awareness, the primary question is, "When do children become aware of ultimate concerns?" We have already discussed the possibility that children must have a concept of object permanence before they develop separation anxiety. However, separation anxiety is far different from the existential concept of absolute isolation, which the 9-month-old would be incapable of conceptualizing. Perhaps separation anxiety is the initial awareness of absolute isolation that continues to evolve as a concept until it emerges fully developed later in life. Yalom (1980) argues that children, contrary to the child development literature, are extraordinarily preoccupied with death, a fear which exerts far-reaching influence on their experiential worlds. Yalom further believes that concern about death begins earlier than generally thought and goes through progressive stages of awareness of death and that children use coping strategies that are invariably denial based. Citing some empirical research and some anecdotes, Yalom believes children as young as 18 months are aware of life and death. More importantly for this discussion, the existentialists argue that studies of children's fears have completely neglected the underlying meaning of these fears. For example, when we note that a child is afraid of the dark, we neglect to investigate the significance to children of darkness. May (1977) noted that Jersild's study indicated that children's fears are often unpredictable and unrelated to reality. For example, the child is more likely to fear remote animals, like gorillas and bears, than familiar ones. But what is unpredictable on the surface, May argues, is consistent at a deeper level when one realizes that anxiety (about ultimate concerns) is converted into fear. May says the child's fears are "objectivated forms of underlying anxiety" (pp. 105–109).

These thoughts are provocative and deserve considerable attention and research. However, the existentialists have not developed a uniform developmental theory of psychopathology of childhood. We do not know when death becomes a reality to children, what the effect is of this knowledge on their experience, or why some children develop a manifest fear of death of self or loved ones while others do not. Further, we do not know when children develop a sense of freedom, isolation, or meaninglessness in the existential sense. Yet this theory asks fundamental questions which cry for investigation, for understanding of not only the source of children's fears and anxiety, but also their amelioration. At some point in life, each child becomes aware of the ultimate concerns. Psychology needs to know how this comes about and how to help children face the inescapable dilemmas of being human.

CLASSIFICATION

In view of the dearth of knowledge about the nature and origin of anxiety in childhood, the classification of anxiety disorders is perhaps premature. However, classification is an attempt to bring order out of chaos. Each attempt, no matter how imperfect, should advance understanding since it provides a base for clarification by future scholars. In this section, we will present a tentative classification schema based upon a summary of the issues and research in the field. This is a very sketchy outline of a complex issue, so the reader is referred to the work of others in this field.

Thus far, we have noted that a workable definition of anxiety is required before a classification schema can be possible: we need to know what is to be classified before we attempt to classify. The latent-manifest issues need to be resolved as well as the state-trait and primary-secondary dilemmas. We need a clear distinction, both theoretical and empirical, between depression and anxiety as well as

a clear outline of developmental changes in order to differentiate normal from pathological anxiety. While it may not be wise to wait for clarification of all the nuances of the issues, it would be prudent to state the premises upon which a schema is to be built. Based on these premises, future empirical research or scholarship could reconcile many of the conflicting issues generated by a classification system.

Central to any classification is whether types of disorder should be built upon dimensional or categorical constructs. This issue currently differentiates the main approaches to classification. The official Diagnostic and Statistical Manual of Mental Disorders of the American Psychiatric Association (1980) classifies along categorical lines while most systematic research in childhood disorders uses dimensional constructs. DSM III distinguishes five types of psychopathology which usually arise and are first evident in childhood. One of these describes the anxiety disorders, of which there are four subtypes: separation anxiety, avoidant disorder, overanxious disorder, and adjustment disorder with anxious mood. The authors of DSM III believe that the essential features of the Affective Disorders are the same in children and adults and, therefore, that no special category for children is necessary. Symptoms indicating each disorder are presented with a specific number of symptoms needing to be present for the diagnosis to be established. In addition to the symptom complex, information is provided for the age of onset, course, impairment, complications, predisposing factors, prevalence, sex ratio, and familial pattern. Differential diagnosis is made by noting distinguishing features when symptoms overlap. For example, extreme anxiety may occur in schizophrenic children upon separation, but other symptoms that are present distinguish this disorder from a separation anxiety disorder.

This method of classification has intrinsic heuristic value, for it describes and differentiates many of the major behavioral deviances of childhood. However, it assumes that categories of behavior are discrete entities in which the correlation among category symptoms is greater than the correlation of symptoms in other categories (within versus between). This is an empirical question that has never been examined and should be tested before the system can be considered valid. The system also needs to establish a hierarchical relationship among categories since children usually manifest more than one type of disorder.

Systematic studies of psychopathology assume that behavior is dimensional rather than categorical and that types of disorder would constitute a pattern of basic dimensions of psychopathology. Symptoms such as enuresis that do not correlate with a basic dimension, or symptoms such as anorexia nervosa that demand special remedial or custodial actions would also constitute a specific type of disorder. A task force of the American Psychological Association on Descriptive Classification of Children's Behavior (Achenbach, Conners, & Quay, 1980) has recommended a dimensional approach to the classification of childhood disorders. The task force found six syndromes for which there was strong empirical support and five others that warranted consideration. Anxious and depressed behaviors emerged as a single syndrome separate from Somatic, Withdrawn, and Obsessive-Compulsive disorders. Achenbach (1978) has reviewed over 90 studies of parent and teacher ratings of child psychopathology and has concluded that there are two broad dimensions of pathological behavior: overcontrolled and undercontrolled syndromes. Within the overcontrolled syndrome, most studies have isolated subdimensions of anxiety, depression, social withdrawal, and somaticization. Many of these dimensions are roughly equivalent to the categories of DSM III but systematic studies of child psychopathology indicate that individual children often have elevations on a number of pathological dimensions. Dimensional analysis diverges from the categorical approach at this point since a configuration of elevations constitutes a pathological type rather than the manifestation of a particular cluster of similar symptoms. Multivariant statistical techniques such as cluster analysis are used to obtain dimensional syndromes.

Achenbach (1979) has developed a typology based upon dimensional analysis that shows considerable promise. Thus far, the systematic studies have not, like DSM III, linked their typology to such variables as age of onset, course, impairment, and so on.

The dimensional and categorical approaches are actually not too divergent. Both describe and include manifest anxiety, social withdrawal, and depression. Separation Anxiety of DSM III is generally a subtype of manifest anxiety within the systematic studies. DSM III has a category of Adjustment Disorder for which there is no equivalent dimension in the systematic studies, probably because the systematic studies have not included time and etiological factors in their investigations. Also, there is no somaticization category in DSM III since these symptoms are seen as indicators of other disorders, such as depression and anxiety.

Within the anxiety disorders, it is possible to make further differentiations within both systems. Adams (1979) has summarized the various anxiety disorders that have been described and observed in children over the past 100 years, among which are anxiety reaction, phobia, obsessive-compulsive neurosis, hysterical neurosis, and traumatic reactions. Although each of these disorders has been described in single case studies, no systematic studies have been done, so we do not know the link between them and the other anxiety or inhibition disorders. However, several systematic studies of phobia (Scherer & Nakamura, 1968; Miller et al., 1972a; Russell, 1967; Bamber, 1977; Staley & O'Donnell, 1981) have been carried out using factor analysis to obtain the basic dimensions of fears. These studies have found that three or four dimensions adequately describe the major fears of childhood and adolescence. Three basic dimensions have been described and labeled by Miller et al. (1972a) as Physical Injury, Natural Events, and Social Anxiety. These studies are based on parent ratings of anxiety in children. When the child's self-reports are factored, a different structure emerges. Finch, Kendall, and Montgomery (1974) factored the Children's Manifest Anxiety Scale and found three dimensions: Worry and Oversensitivity, Physiological, and Concentration. In addition, the three dimensions have been shown to serve different psychological functions within the child. This research suggests that we need to consider whether classification will be based upon child or parent perceptions of anxiety.

There is still considerable argument in the literature as to whether school phobia should be classed as a true phobia, a separation anxiety, or a special type of disorder designated as "school avoidance." There are a number of theoretical and empirical reasons to support the idea of a special subtype, the primary one being that school avoidance characterizes a large percentage of phobic children referred for treatment. For example, Miller et al. (1972b) found that 69 percent of children referred to a phobia study had school avoidance problems, despite much effort to recruit every type of phobia. School avoidance has been studied extensively and found not to correlate highly with other types of phobias (Miller, Barrett, & Hampe, 1974), and remedial techniques have been specifically developed for that disorder. Furthermore, it appears that there are two distinct types of school avoidance problems, with age being a decisive variable (Kennedy, 1965). Type I (ages 3–10) school avoiders are very treatable, while Type II (ages 11–22) are quite recalcitrant with current treatment methods. This by no means exhausts the possible classification categories for school phobia. Waldron et al.

(1975) believe there are three major types of school phobia in children below age 13: (1) Family Interaction, with emphasis on Separation Anxiety and a mutually hostile dependent relationship; (2) Situational-Characterological type in which the child employs strong defenses of displacement, projection, and externalization; (3) Classical type of phobia in which the child, separated from the parent, becomes overwhelmingly concerned that the parent will die. While this typology has some research backing by Waldron's group, it has not had independent verification, nor have the categories been shown to differ functionally.

It appears, then, that anxiety disorders constitute a subtype of the Inhibition Disorders, along with depression, social withdrawal, and somaticization. Within anxiety, there is the possibility of further differentiation into generalized anxiety, phobia, obsessive-compulsive, hysteria, traumatic, and school avoidance. Phobias can be subdivided into at least three major dimensions: physical injury, natural events, and social anxiety. Table 14.3 shows a possible way of organizing the major Inhibition disorders of childhood.

ASSESSMENT

Determining the presence and intensity of an anxiety reaction is a difficult undertaking if one goes beyond a verbal report. The classical literature on anxiety is misleading because it gives the impression that anxiety is such an

Table 14.3 Classification Schema for the Inhibition Disorders

Anxiety		Depression		Social Withdrawal	Somaticization	
1. Anxiety reaction		a. Manifest		1. Social withdrawal	1.	Headaches
2. Obsessive-compulsive		b. Masked			2.	Stomach aches
3. Hysterical					3.	Other
a. Conversion						
b. Disassociation						
4. Traumatic						
5. School avoidance						
a. Type I						
b. Type II						
6. Phobic						
a. Physical injury						
b. Natural events						
c. Social anxiety						

obvious phenomenon that measurement is unnecessary. Thus, when Freud (1962) studied Little Hans, it apparently did not occur to him to determine whether the child was, in fact, afraid of horses. Acceptance of a parent's report is suspect in view of the Lapousse and Monk (1959) evidence that mothers report 41 percent fewer fears for their children than do the children themselves. More significant is the Jersild and Holmes (1935) finding that a fear stimulus is often quite complex. A child, for example, may be afraid of the dark only when alone. He or she may not be afraid of being alone during the day or in the dark when with someone else. It is the combination of aloneness and dark that evokes the fear. This problem of stimulus complexity is also illustrated by the fact that Jersild and Holmes found, in an experimental situation, that a small, energetic dog evoked more fear than a large, lethargic one. This suggests that energy level is a more important variable than size in children's fear of dogs. Also, we found (Miller et al., 1972b) that phobias were often unpredictable, that monophobias were rare, and that phobic stimuli were complex. This is consistent with the finding by Lang (1966) in adult phobics of a positive but low correlation of subjective reports of phobia, behavior ratings, and physiological measurements. These observations all point to the fact that anxiety is often a variable response to multiple stimuli and that assessment of anxiety is a complex problem. Reliability and validity are as difficult to establish for anxiety as for other manifestations of psychopathology. Thus it is important to discuss ways in which investigators have attempted to measure and evaluate anxiety in childhood.

Anxiety is expressed through three modalities: behavior, subjective experience, and physiological responses. Direct observation of anxious behavior can be made in the laboratory when the controlling stimulus is available for presentation. Such a situational test was first reported by Watson and Rayner (1920) in their study of infant startle responses. Since then, other investigators have employed similar techniques. Holmes (Jersild & Holmes, 1935) studied children experimentally from ages 2–6 using the following stimuli: being left alone, noise, a falling board, the dark, a stranger, walking on a high board, a snake, and a large dog. Interest in situational tests was renewed by Lang and Lasovik's (1963) work with snakes. Their model uses a room containing a box in which a large snake is placed. Floor stripes placed one foot apart extend from the door to the snake. The subject is asked to enter the room and to go as close to the snake as possible. The distance between the farthest approach and the snake becomes a quantitative measure of the phobia. Many studies with adults, but only a few with children, have used the situational test. The work of Bandura, Grusec, and Menlove (1967) with children who feared dogs is a notable exception.

When the anxiety-arousing stimulus is not available for direct laboratory study, behavior can be evaluated in the field by trained or nontrained observers such as parents or teachers. Such observations are often the only alternative to the child's report of his or her anxious behavior. Only parents or a participant observer can observe bedtime behaviors, reactions to certain foods, illnesses in the family, and such. Teachers are the obvious observers of behavior on academic tests or while speaking in front of the class. Trained field observers are generally more reliable than either parents or teachers, but they are expensive and alter the situation that they are observing. Also, Patterson, Ray, and Shaw (1968) reported that even highly trained observers tend to be affected by the situation they are observing so that, within a month of field observations, correlations between observers drop from the mid-90s to mid-60s. Thus observers, whether parents, teachers, or participant observers who record observations of children's behavior directly, require training and frequent retraining to ensure collection of good data. Fortunately, Patterson et al. (1968) and Caldwell and Honig (1971) provided some of the complex technology needed in such efforts.

When direct observations are not available, indirect methods have to be used. Retrospective ratings of fear behavior are probably even less reliable than concurrent observations, but they are quicker and less expensive to obtain. In our study of phobia (Miller, 1972b), we had parents rate the intensity and extensity (i.e., the extent to which the fear affected the child's life), on a 7-point scale. The geometric mean of these two ratings was used as an indication of the severity of a given phobia. We found that parents tended to overestimate severity at intake but that in time parents' and clinicians' ratings were highly correlated. This suggests that ratings could be used as a criterion measure for follow-up. In addition to ratings of specific fears, four inventories are available: Bamber, 1977; Miller et al., 1972a; Russell, 1967; Scherer and Nakamura, 1968. For school anxiety, Sarason and Gordon (1953) have developed quite an extensive inventory. A fear scale, consisting of parent ratings, that provides an overall fear index in relation to other types of deviant behaviors (Miller et al. 1971b), is available in the Louisville Behavior Checklist. Miller (1972) has developed an anxiety scale for the School Behavior Checklist. Miller (1972) has developed an anxiety scale for the School Behavior Checklist that provides evidence of fear behavior in the school. Berg and McGuire (1971) used the Highlands Dependency Inventory to study the extent of dependent behavior in school phobias. All of these inventories are useful for some purposes, and all are subject to the problems inherent in ratings.

Perhaps the most widely used method for obtaining indirect information is the interview. The interview has been studied extensively as an information source, and many biases and distortions are known to occur. Despite these limitations, the interview remains the central clinical tool, probably because a relationship is being built and maintained while information is gathered.

To illustrate how the interview is used to gain information, as well as how the interviewer's theoretical orientation shapes the information obtained. we quote from two case studies.

Smith and Sharpe (1970) noted that a standard interviewing technique failed to identify the stimuli associated with a 13-year-old boy's school phobia. Using a behaviorally oriented technique, they asked him to visual-

ize and minutely describe a school day. They noted at which stages of his description behavioral indications of anxiety occurred. These indications included flushing of skin, increased body movements, vocal tremors, and muscular tension. This procedure indicated that he became highly anxious at the prospect of being called on to speak in mathematics and literature classes and of having to answer teachers' questions. Visualization of neither home nor his mother evoked manifest anxiety. Here the use of visual imagery and nonverbal cues helped to clarify the noxious stimuli. This information was then used to set up a hierarchy for implosive therapy, which in this instance was successful.

Sperling (1961), beginning from a psychoanalytic frame of reference, discussed a case of a 12-year-old female, whose school phobia began when she became upset with a teacher who took her music book away in class. Instead of eating lunch at school that day, she went home and found her mother gone. Upon telephoning her father, she learned that her mother had gone to the doctor to get an allergy shot. Next morning, the child did not feel well, but went to school.

For several days, the child was upset until one day she became panicky and her mother had to go to school and take her home. The mother was asked if the patient had any reason to be concerned about her visit to the doctor. The mother related that on the Sunday before the first incident in school, she had fainted during a church ceremony while sitting next to the child. The mother had also fainted five years before in her presence due to a gall bladder disease for which she received a injection and an operation. When the child was interviewed, she described the story of the music teacher and going home to find her mother missing; she did not relate the previous history. The child was reminded of the earlier fainting episode, which she remembered. Sperling writes,

I suggested to her that her mother's recent fainting had brought back fears which she must have had when her mother fainted and was operated upon... Without realizing it, she had been worried about her mother since the incident in church, and that she came home for lunch because the incident in school had in some way increased her worry.... Not finding mother home and then learning that she was at the doctor's office had intensified and confirmed her fear about mother's being in danger, a fear of which she had not been consciously aware. I told her that children sometimes have angry feelings toward their mothers, and, because they also believe in the magic power of their thoughts, they are afraid that something terrible may happen to mother. I assured her that thoughts and wishes are not dangerous and cannot kill anyone, but added that such thoughts can cause much fear in the child who has them and does not want to acknowledge them.... I pointed out that this was really a conflict within herself which had to do with her feelings about mother and not a conflict with the teacher at school..... My patient, too, went back to school the day after her interview. (pp. 510–511)

These two cases illustrate how different frames of reference shape the inquiry process to elicit information necessary to fulfill the applied aspect of the theory. Smith and Sharpe needed information on the stimuli currently arousing anxiety in order to implode the child, while Sperling wanted information to clarify the preconscious conflict that could then be made conscious. Each approach adds to the interviewing process a dimension that should be considered when attempting to understand a child's anxiety.

It is also possible to assess anxiety through subjective measurements of fear made by the person who experiences it. Individuals may rate the intensity of their feelings either in the presence of the stimulus or from their memories of past events. Such ratings can be made on single fears or on an inventory of fears. The inventories give an estimate of the total amount of focalized anxiety experienced by the person. However, children's subjective reports are difficult to appraise. We found some children who seemed to glory in describing their fears, while other children were very reticent. Some even refused to communicate at all. One child objected strongly to using fear as an explanation of his refusal to attend school. He simply maintained that he did not like school. We suspected that "fear" was a very unpleasant word for him to associate

with himself. Thus subjective ratings pose very special problems when obtained from children, especially young children. Walk (1956) reports a method for obtaining subjective reports of fear by asking the subject to estimate his or her anxiety on a fear thermometer in which zero (0) represents no fear and the top of the scale represents extreme fear. We used a fear thermometer with children but did not analyze the data since our clinical observer thought that many of the estimates were random guesses by children. We have come to believe that the interview allows an adult to judge the child's emotional responses, which, when added to all other data, provide important qualitative information about the phobia. However, we question the value of a quantified estimate of subjective fears by children as an independent estimate of phobia. Much research needs to be done in this area before confidence can be placed in children's subjective reports. Perhaps a more valid assessment is a fear scale. Casteneda, McCandless, and Palermo (1956) have adapted the Taylor Manifest Anxiety Scale for children. Reynolds and Richmond (1978) have recently revised the Taylor for children from 6–18, making it shorter and more psychometrically sound. Their 37-item questionnaire, named "What I Think and Feel," indicates no variance across age or race, but girls admitted to more anxiety than boys. The scale contains a 9-item lie scale which appears to indicate a personality characteristic of defensiveness rather than an indication of an invalid score. The scale holds considerable promise for the study of anxiety in children.

Physiological measures of anxiety have an extensive research history and can be obtained from most autonomic channels: blood pressure, heart rate, muscular tension, or sweating. Instruments are available for obtaining measures of autonomic responses when the subject is presented with the phobic stimulus or its verbal equivalent.

A number of investigators have studied the psychophysiological aspects of adult phobias (Lacey, 1958; Leitenberg et al., 1971; Lader, 1967; Wilson, 1966; Marks, 1969; Lang, Melamed, & Hart, 1970) but we have found little work on children. This is, perhaps, a promising area but technical and equipment problems are so enormous that this psychophysiological aspect of phobias must be considered a highly specialized and complex area of research. The primary problem lies in the well-established fact that each individual has his or her own idiosyncratic way of reacting to stress so that intragroup measures are difficult to establish. For the moment, then, physiological measures of childhood anxiety are promising tools of the future but have little clinical utility.

A final assessment issue concerns the distinction in behavior theory between respondent and operant conditioning. In theory, anxiety arising from respondent conditioning should be reduced through extinction while contingency management would be necessary for operant anxiety. We find this an impossible distinction to make with child anxiety and point out that Mowrer would have predicted our difficulty. But if we accept the respondent operant distinction, clinical histories often point to both types of conditioning. Furthermore, anxiety is so commanding once it emerges that reinforcement schedules are always established within the family. It is then impossible to determine, with current methods, whether they played a part in its etiology. In brief, we find the distinction between operant and respondent conditioning to be of little practical value. Therefore, we have omitted the distinction both in the definition and in the assessment procedures.

There are advantages and disadvantages associated with measurements from each expressive modality. Direct behavior ratings have the advantage of reliable quantification and of openness to multiple observers. This is particularly true when the stimulus is presented in an experimental situation where the measure is a function of the subject's approach behavior. Laboratory control can only occur, however, with a limited number of simple and concrete objects and has the disadvantage of selecting only subjects who invariably respond with fear to the stimulus. Such subjects probably have little in common with others who present themselves in clinical situations. Also direct behavior ratings do not elicit

subjective feelings and do not distinguish low motivation from anxiety. That is, failure to approach could reflect either immobilization or lack of interest. For research on specific stimuli, however, direct behavior ratings are probably the most objective measure of anxiety.

Field observations have the advantage of access to the child's exposure to many stimuli that would otherwise go unobserved, but of course observer error is introduced. Parents and teachers are often "members of the problem," so that they do not give unbiased observations, but trained observers are very expensive and, as previously noted, are subject to the influence of the situation. Furthermore, we have found that anxiety, even of long standing, often disappears during the process of evaluation. One example occurred when the authors observed a child with an elevator/escalator phobia making three unsuccessful attempts to ride the escalator before her mother got on and left her. At that moment another child stepped on the escalator and our patient watched his every move, imitated his behavior, and successfully rode away. She spent the rest of the morning riding both the escalator and the elevator. The mother could not believe that this had occurred because her child had previously made shopping an impossible undertaking. This case illustrates not only the effects of modeling, but also the effects of the assessment procedures themselves. The situational test that we had employed for measurement served as a therapeutic procedure. We noted enough of these variable responses to become convinced that anxiety, as reported by parents, is subject to many effects that can be sorted out only by time and extended case study.

In view of the complex problems associated with the assessment of anxiety and the lack of consensus as to the best assessment method, we recommend an intensive clinical case study, followed by a rating of the anxiety's intensity and extensity. After evaluating a number of procedures, including field observers and situational tests, we believe that clinical behavior ratings based on all material are the best indicator of anxiety. To obtain these ratings, the parents need to be interviewed intensively to establish the child's specific fear reactions as well as the context in which the events take place. In addition, one needs to establish how much of the child's life is affected by the anxiety. Parents should also complete an inventory such as the Louisville Behavior Checklist (Miller et al., 1971a) so that one can determine whether other problem areas exist in the child's life, and the Louisville Fear Survey Schedule (Miller et al., 1972a) to determine the total number of fears. Generally, children do have other behavioral problems and anxieties that are not reported in the interviews. It would also be wise to include a test such as "What I Think and Feel," as well as an interview with children, to obtain views and reactions to their world and their problems. In addition, when feasible, a situational test should be run, particularly if there is a phobia. Following these procedures, it is important to check with the mother for five days, by telephone, to establish frequency counts of anxiety. When the child has multiple fears, the most disabling of them should be selected as the target problem and the intensity and extensity of that anxiety rated on a 7-point scale. The geometric mean for each rating provides an index of the severity of the anxiety. Children whose anxiety is rated 3.0 or higher are considered to have a clinical level anxiety.

To recapitulate, anxiety is seldom an invariant response to simple, discrete stimuli. Rather, anxiety responses range from highly variable and episodic to invariant while stimuli range from simple to complex. There are instances of monophobias, but these are rare, for generally several stimuli elicit a child's anxiety. In the case of multiple phobias or general anxiety, a single target should be selected for a treatment focus. Factor analysis suggests that the multiple fear stimuli are organized into dimensions that perhaps reflect response gradients so that reduction of anxiety associated with one stimulus would be followed by a reduction of anxiety toward all stimuli in that dimension. We prefer an intense clinical case study to assess anxiety except in instances where an investigator needs a homogeneous population based upon one dependent measure. There is still much to

learn about assessment procedures and, in turn, the phenomenon of anxiety itself. Graziano and his co-workers have quite cogently summarized current knowledge of assessment of anxiety in children in the following quote:

The identification of fear stimuli touches on only a small part of what must be a complex fear process. It seems reasonable to assume that children's fears, like other human reactions, proceed through complex paradigms from fear stimuli that vary in number, type, and intensity and that may be internal, external, or both; through emotional and cognitive operations within the child; through overt fear responses that may act upon and modify both the social and physical environment and that themselves, by means of feedback loops and chaining, may occasion variations in any part of the process. The processes themselves may further vary with developmental factors.... Remaining unasked are questions concerning the operation of mediating cognitions in children's fear experiences, the degree to which fears are externally or selfgenerated and maintained, and the effects of fear behavior on the child's social environment and the effects' feedback influence on the child. One must investigate how children in their natural environments typically deal with fearful events and how their strategies vary with developmental level, sex, and so on. One must study the conditions under which natural coping processes fail and fear processes become debilitating, and one must determine the optimum conditions for fear reduction intervention. (Graziano, DeGiovanni, & Garcia, 1979, p. 813)

CHARACTERISTICS

Frequency

In this section, we will examine the overall frequency of fear to be expected in the general population. Jersild and Holmes (1935) noted that children aged 2–6 had an average of 4.64 fears per child and manifested fear once every four and one half days. They concluded that overt fears were relatively infrequent at this age compared to other types of deviant behavior. Hagman (1932) found in a comparable group of children that there was an average of 2.7 fears per child. Macfarlane, Allen, and

Honzik (1954) reported that at least 90 percent of the children in their study had a specific fear at least once during the first 14 years of their lives and that up until the age of 12 at least 35 percent showed some fear. Lapousse and Monk (1959), in a general population sample of 482 children aged 6–12, found that 43 percent had seven or more fears and worries. They concluded that fears are quite common in children of this age. Each of these studies differs in the method of establishing and rating fears and each sampled from different sections of the country, so that findings are not absolutely comparable. However, it would appear that children aged 2–6 have about three fears on the average, and that 40 percent of the children aged 6–12 show some fears, perhaps as many as seven.

In a recent study of a general population sample of 249 children aged 7–12, using the Louisville Fear Survey Schedule, the authors found that the number of excessive reactions was small. Moreover, while some stimuli evoked considerable fear, the child's family felt such strong reactions were normal. Table 14.4 shows parent rating of the percentage of fears at three intensity levels: no fear, normal or expected fear, and excessive or unrealistic fear. With a few exceptions, stimuli evoke extreme fear in less that 5 percent of the general population. The most typical response pattern approximates a J-curve in which 84 percent or more of the children show no fear of the stimuli, while 5 to 15 percent show what parents consider to be normal fear and 0 to 5 percent show excessive fears. Stimuli eliciting the J-curve pattern include dirt, furry toys, masks or puppets, old people, and toilets, as well as many others. Responses to a smaller group of stimuli more closely approximate a normal curve, in which 25 to 45 percent show no fear, 50 to 60 percent show normal fear, and 4 to 6 percent show excessive fear. This group includes snakes, rats, lightning, fire, and tornadoes, along with being wounded, getting shots, or being seen naked. The third group falls somewhere in between the first two with an approximately equal split between no fear and normal fear. This group includes stimuli such as insects, sight of blood, dark,

ghosts, and war, along with fear of being locked up and of being kidnapped, and many more. These different reaction patterns suggest that extreme fears (phobias) are rare in 7–12 age group. Fear behavior is observed quite frequently by parents, but it is considered normal. Also, Table 14.4 indicates that the intensity and frequency of fear reactions are a function of the stimulus object.

Table 14.4 also shows that snakes evoked the most extreme fear in girls in this age group (13 percent), followed by rats and mice (11 percent), and then by dark (8 percent), war (8 percent), being kidnapped (8 percent), and being seen naked (8 percent). Boys, on the other hand, showed less overall fear than girls and reacted most to criticism (7 percent) and shots (7 percent), followed by snakes (6 percent) and deep water (5 percent). In our study of child phobia (Miller et al., 1972b), we found that 69 percent of our referrals were for school phobia, which occurred in less than 1 percent of the general population. The next highest referral was for sleeping alone (9 percent) which occurs in 1 percent of the boys in the general population and in 2 percent of the girls. The third referral fear was of the dark (6 percent) which approximates the percentage found in the general population (M = 3 percent, F = 8 percent). However, quite a number of other fears which were not referred for treatment occurred as frequently as fear of the dark: snakes, rats/mice, death, deep water, tornadoes, space creatures, war, being seen naked, being criticized, and being kidnapped. This suggests that the existence of excessive fear is not by itself cause for referral. The fear of school has such major secondary effects that, even though it is rare, help is sought when it occurs. Fears of the dark and sleeping alone probably are sufficiently noxious to parents to cause them to seek help. We can postulate, then, that as long as a child's excessive fear does not seriously impede the socialization process or interfere with the parents' lives, children's anxieties will not be brought to the attention of health professionals. When fears are merely passing episodes in the developmental process, their neglect is of no consequence, but when they

Table 14.4 Frequency of Fears at Three Intensity Levels[b]

Fears	Male			Female			Fears	Male			Female		
	1	2	3	1	2	3		1	2	3	1	2	3
1. Dirt	93	7	0	86	14	0	47. Being separated from parents	67	32	1	44	52	4
2. Furry toys	98	2	0	98	2	0	48. Parents getting divorce	76	21	3	62	33	5
3. Masks/puppets	95	5	0	90	10	0	49. Reciting in class	58	41	1	45	52	3
4. Sirens	87	13	0	69	30	1	50. Attending social events due to worries of rejection embarrassment	76	23	1	71	29	0
5. Insects or spiders	53	45	2	14	81	5	51. Breaking religious law (sin)	57	41	2	51	48	1
6. Frogs or lizards	72	28	0	24	71	5	52. War, enemy invasion, bombing	52	45	3	51	41	8
7. Horses/cows	85	15	0	71	29	0	53. Making another person angry	52	46	2	53	47	0
8. Dogs/cats	86	12	2	79	20	1	54. Entering a strange room	65	34	1	56	43	1
9. Snakes	28	66	6	5	82	13	55. Being confined or locked up	49	50	1	37	56	7
10. Rats/mice	46	52	2	11	78	11	56. Going to sleep at night	88	11	1	84	14	2
11. Storms	53	44	3	33	63	4	57. Being touched by others	89	11	0	78	22	0
12. Lightning	46	51	3	24	73	3	58. People with deformities	74	26	0	59	40	1
13. Thunder	55	43	2	30	66	4	59. Uniformed people, policemen, etc.	90	10	0	83	15	2
14. Fire	39	59	2	17	79	4	60. High places	61	35	4	53	44	3
15. Old people	95	5	0	87	12	1	61. Opposite sex	90	9	1	85	15	0
16. Crossing street	84	16	0	71	29	0	62. Enclosed places	77	23	0	63	35	2
17. Sight of blood	57	41	2	40	57	3	63. Elevators	89	11	0	78	20	2
18. People who are ugly	84	16	0	82	17	1	64. Certain part of house (attic, etc.)	83	15	2	68	31	1
19. Faces at windows	56	42	2	38	57	5	65. Being ill	67	32	1	63	36	1
20. Being kidnapped	55	43	2	38	54	8	66. Family member becoming ill	61	37	2	55	44	1
21. Specific foods	90	10	0	79	20	1	67. Going crazy (insane)	80	18	2	79	20	1
22. Being alone	63	36	1	40	56	4	68. Getting lost	57	41	2	51	47	2
23. Being criticized	51	42	7	39	57	4	69. Seeing someone wounded	29	67	4	24	72	4
24. Being in the dark	51	46	3	34	58	8	70. Being wounded	29	68	3	29	67	4
25. Crowds	89	11	0	83	17	0	71. Being seen naked	38	59	3	26	66	8
26. Strangers	60	39	1	45	53	2	72. Having bowel movements	92	7	1	89	10	1
27. Hospitals	57	41	2	60	39	1	73. Receiving shots	36	57	7	33	64	3
28. Bathrooms	95	5	0	91	9	0	74. Doctors or dentists	49	48	3	38	60	2
29. Closets	94	6	0	77	22	1	75. Having operation	38	60	2	39	56	5
30. Toilets	96	4	0	91	9	0	76. Family member dying	45	51	4	37	56	7
31. Ghosts	51	46	3	38	59	3	77. Members of another race	85	15	0	76	22	2
32. The devil	54	44	2	34	63	3							
33. Hell	53	45	2	39	56	5							
34. School	93	6	1	90	10	0							
35. Germs	77	22	1	67	32	1							
36. Choking	67	32	1	61	37	2							
37. Nightmares	63	35	2	54	40	6							
38. Riots	63	36	1	54	44	2							
39. Dying	54	45	1	48	49	3							
40. Deep water	56	39	5	40	53	7							
41. Tornadoes, floods, earthquakes	40	56	4	29	65	6							
42. Space creatures, monsters	57	39	4	41	54	5							
43. Food that might be poisoned	56	42	2	49	47	4							
44. Riding in bus or car	93	7	0	87	13	0							
45. Flying in airplane	73	26	1	60	38	2							
46. Loud sounds, as caps, firecrackers, explosions	76	24	0	50	48	2							

Table 14.4 *(continued)*

Fears	Male			Female			Fears	Male			Female		
	1	2	3	1	2	3		1	2	3	1	2	3
78. Making mistakes, doing something wrong	44	53	3	37	60	3	80. Tests, examinations	58	41	1	41	57	2
79. Frightening thoughts or daydreams	76	24	0	69	29	2	81. Being adopted	84	14	2	73	23	4

Note: Data taken in a general population of 123 boys and 126 girls between the ages of 7–12.
[a]Reproduced from "Phobias of Childhood in a Prescientific Era," L.C. Miller, C.L. Barrett and E. Hampe, in *Child Personality and Psychopathology: Current Topics* (Vol. I). A. Davids, ed. Copyright © 1974 by John Wiley & Sons, Inc. Used with the permission of John Wiley & Sons, Inc.
[b]Intensity levels: 1. no fear observed; 2. normal or reasonable fear; 3. unreasonable or excessive fear.

represent a stable condition, they can cause considerable distress throughout the lifespan.

In a replication study of the Louisville Fear Survey, Staley and O'Donnell (1981) found that the mode for fear was zero in a general population of 868 children ranging in age from 6–16. However, unlike Miller et al., these investigators found that 10–20 percent of children evidenced extreme fears, indicating that excessive anxiety is not at all rare in the general population. This is even more striking in view of the consistent finding that parents tend to underestimate anxiety in their children. These findings tend to corroborate the conclusions of Lapousse and Monk (1959), who concluded that fears are quite common in children.

Data on clinical disorders are not readily available. We surveyed the cases of the Child Psychiatric Service of the University of Louisville School of Medicine and found that over the two years of 1979–80, 42 percent of 1,568 children referred were diagnosed as having some type of anxiety disorder. Graziano and DeGiovanni (1979) surveyed the case load of 26 behavioral therapists for six months, and found that only 7 percent of the 547 child referrals were treated for phobias. Neither of these findings reflects the number of clinical level cases to be found in the general population. The wide discrepancy in the frequency of anxiety in these two clinical settings most likely reflects differences in diagnostic techniques and definitions rather than variations in the frequency of anxiety in clinical populations. It is clear that there is a need for a definitive method of diagnosing anxiety disorders and determining their frequency within both general and clinical populations.

Prognosis and Natural History

Data on age-related fears do not reflect changes that take place over time for individual subjects. Hagman (1932), for example, found that 6 percent of the fears noted in his study disappeared within one week, 54 percent were gone in three months, and 100 percent had disappeared in three years. However, Scarr and Salapatek (1970) found fears to be stable over the first 18 months of life and Bronson (1970) found that 6-month-old male children with an overdeveloped fear of novelty maintained a heightened fearfulness into the early childhood years.

Eme and Schmidt (1978), using an interviewing technique, studied the stability of fears over a one-year span in a group of 27 fourth-grade children. They found that the number and type of fears were stable over the year and that 83 percent of the fears initially expressed were admitted to the following year. However, the stability of the relative rank in the group was low ($r = .38$). Berganza and Anders (1978) traced the school attendance of 114 children over an eight-year span. Children in the upper quartile of school absentees in the seventh grade were found to have manifested a high degree of absenteeism in the first grade, which had continued and accelerated in the fourth grade, until absenteeism had reached a peak in the seventh grade and continued through the eighth. The lowest quartile children, on the other hand, started with a lower absentee record in the first grade and gradually diminished their absenteeism through the eighth grade. The authors also found that three years' attendance records were necessary to establish a trend and that there was no greater frequency of absenteeism on Mondays or during September and January than at other times, contrary to the expectations of students of school phobia. This is a very valuable type of study to show the frequency and pattern of absenteeism in the general population against which clinical data can be compared and suggests the possibility that absenteeism is a habit which is reinforced each year with accelerating frequency. By adolescence, absenteeism is a highly reinforced habit, which might help to account for the intractability of school phobia during the adolescent years.

In an interesting study in Japan, Abe (1972) had mothers of 3-year-olds describe their own fears and the fears of their children. He also asked the maternal grandmothers to describe the fears the mothers had at age 3. He found that the mothers' current phobias dated from their childhood but that 65 percent of the mothers who had phobias as children had no symptoms in adult life. Marks (1971) partially confirmed Abe's findings in his retrospective study of adult phobics. He found animal phobias tended to arise in early childhood while most situational and social phobias began after puberty. Agoraphobia began at any age, but the peak onset age was adolescence.

Hellman (1962) gives a clinical description of the dissipation of a child's phobia. A 2.5-year-old female child developed an acute and overwhelming separation reaction when she was left on the spur of the moment by her mother at the Hampstead Nursery during World War II. At first, there was continuous and incessant crying followed by gradual and almost complete social withdrawal and loss of interaction with surroundings. She made and maintained an extremely close and exclusive relationship with her nurse to whom she clung with desperation. This condition lasted for six months before it began to abate. As an adult, a follow-up study revealed an extroverted, competent person with a satisfactory career, good social relationships, and opportunities for gratification in work and leisure. Hellman noted that she had survived the separation trauma with less negative effect than expected by the original caretakers and predicted by analytic theory. Hampe et al. (1973) found that when 62 phobic children 6–15 years old were followed up by two years after termination of treatment, only 7 percent still had a severe phobia, and 80 percent were symptom free. Bandura, Grusec, and Menlove (1967) found that untreated children with a fear of dogs did not improve over a one-week period, while treated children lost their fear. Agras (1972) found in a five-year follow-up of 30 phobics that 100 percent of persons under 20 were free of their symptoms, while only 43 percent of the adults had shown significant improvement and 37 percent were worse.

These studies suggest that, in general, childhood phobias are self-limiting disorders and dissipate within a two-year span. While this outcome may be generally true, it is not universal. This author has in his case files three children referred for manifest anxiety during their latency years who subsequently developed serious problems in late adolescence. One committed suicide, one had a serious psychotic break diagnosed as paranoid schizophrenia at age 19, and the third died after being diagnosed as a paranoid character with antisocial behavior and drug abuse. A postmortem on their files did not reveal differences in their personalities or families which distinguished them from other latency age cases with manifest anxiety. However, they stand as testimony that manifest anxiety can indicate serious psychopathology and should not be discounted even though the majority of these disorders are self-limiting.

A number of follow-up studies have been done with school phobias. Coolidge, Brodie, and Feeney (1964) followed up 56 children 10 years after initial intake. Of the 56 children, 54 had returned to and remained in school, and two-thirds were performing up to IQ expectations. One of the two who did not return was psychotic. Most of the group were described as passive and compliant in their school behavior, as having many problems in making friends, and as being slow and cautious in their dating pattern. One-third of the group were still experiencing moderate-to-serious difficulties. Hersov (1960a), 12 months after termination of treatment, evaluated 50 school phobics, 28 of whom had been hospitalized, and found that 68 percent had returned to school. Recovery was not related to age, sex, IQ, duration of symptoms, or quality of family relationships. Rodriguez, Rodriguez, and Eisenberg (1959) followed 41 cases of school phobia three years after termination of treatment and found that 71 percent were attending school regularly and that 89 percent of children below 11 years of age were free of fear, as contrasted to 64 percent of children 11 years and older. Berg (1970) found that 59 percent of adolescent school phobics admitted to an inpatient service had recovered one year after discharge and 41 percent had not. Weiss and Burke (1970) found in a five-to-ten-year follow-up that 16 school-phobic children 8–16 years old who were treated in a hospital had little problem returning to school after hospitalization. All but one graduated from high school and achieved up to IQ level. About one-half had good social adjustments, but one-half remained shy and hesitant to date and had few friends. With a few exceptions, all were found to maintain good performance at work and in school and were economically independent. The exceptions to these general findings were two boys, originally diagnosed as psychotic, who remained completely dependent and unproductive at follow-up.

Phobias in adults have a different history. Tucker (1956) followed up a group of 100 adult phobics and found that only 28 percent had recovered, 53 percent had improved, and 19 percent were unchanged. Marks (1971) found in a four-year follow-up that only 26 percent had much improved, 32 percent improved, and 42 percent showed no change. Glick (1970) reported a 37 percent success rate with 48 adult phobics. Errera and Coleman (1963) found at a 23-year follow-up of 19 adult phobics that 79 percent had remained essentialy unchanged, while only 21 percent were improved. Contrary to these findings, Terhune (1949) reported that 67 percent of his 86 adult phobic patients recovered and 24 percent improved while only 9 percent showed no change.

In summary, it appears that fears and phobias in children under 10 years of age generally arise and dissipate rapidly. In the Miller and Bandura studies this process was hastened with psychotherapy. There is little information on the natural history of phobias during adolescence, except for school phobia, which has a poorer prognosis during adolescence than during preadolescence. However, the long range prognosis appears quite good for most adolescent school phobics unless they show psychotic symptoms. Phobias in adults appear to be much more intractable since full recovery is somewhere between 20 and 30 percent. The new behavior therapies hold promise, but firm evidence of therapeutic efficacy is far from clear at this writing. However, despite the generally good prognosis for manifest anxiety in childhood, the author warns that there are dramatic exceptions to the general rule and that clinicians should take seriously the anguish and potential seriousness of manifest anxiety in childhood.

Personality Characteristics

Many investigators attribute various types of personality characteristics to anxious children. Unfortunately, there is very little systematic research upon which to draw conclusions. The best documentation comes from two areas: (1) studies using behavioral checklists for parent and teacher ratings of deviant behavior and (2) studies using childhood anxiety scales. The checklists have clearly shown that manifest anxiety can be identified as an independent dimension in child psychopathology (Achenbach, 1966; Cattell & Coan, 1957; Dreger et al., 1964; Miller, 1967, 1971a, 1971b; Peterson, 1961). Miller (1967) showed that manifest anxiety was one aspect of a behavioral triad making up an inhibition dimension. The other two aspects were social withdrawal and sensitivity. That anxiety may be an independent dimension has been confirmed by investigators using other methods. Lapousse and Monk (1959), for example, found no correlation between child fears and other forms of deviant behavior. Jersild and Holmes (1935) found a correlation of .58 between children's fears observed by parents and those observed in experimental situations. Macfarlane et al. (1954) found low correlations with irritability ($r = .28$) and temper ($r = .21$), but high correlation with the inhibition behaviors such as timidity ($r = .64$), overdependence ($r = .35$), and mood swings ($r = .31$). Contrary to other research, Joshi (1974) found no relation between anxiety and Witkin's tests of field dependence. Scherer and Nakamura (1968) found a correlation of .49 between total number of fears and the children's manifest anxiety scale. This was affirmed by L'Abate (1960) for girls but not for boys. L'Abate felt that different anxiety scales needed to be constructed for boys and girls. There is little doubt, then, that anxious behavior forms a specific dimension that can be recognized both at home and in school.

Similar studies of children's self reports of fears have shown that the Children's Manifest Anxiety Scale is made up of three factors (Reynolds & Richmond, 1978; Finch, Kendall, & Montgomery, 1974), which react differentially to independent variables. Spielberger (1973) also introduced the State-Trait Anxiety Inventory for children, which has stimulated research to confirm the existence and differential effects of these two dimensions (Finch & Kendall, 1976). Sarason also developed a scale to measure trait anxiety in children (Sarason et al., 1960), as did Cattell (Cattell, Shrader, & Barton, 1974).

To what extent anxious children possess specific personality characteristics beyond the presenting behavior is still a moot question. Anna Freud (1977) states that it is very difficult to distinguish true phobias from other manifestations of anxiety in children but believes that true phobics use a mechanism of condensation to a much greater degree than other children and that they do not investigate or are not curious about the phobic stimulus: "Out of sight, out of mind." Greenacre (1952) thought that anxious subjects had a predisposition to anxiety related to the prenatal or postnatal period of life that left an organic stamp on the child that heightened the anxiety potential. This tension in early infancy led to an increased and prolonged narcissism and later to an ineffective sense of reality. Leventhal and Sills (1964) have formulated this narcissistic characteristic in reference to school phobia. They noted that these children overvalue themselves and their achievements and then try to hold onto their unrealistic self-image. When they are threatened in the school situation, they suffer anxiety and retreat to another situation where they can maintain their narcissistic self-image. Nichols and Berg (1970) attempted to test Leventhal's contention by comparing the self-concepts of school-phobics to other types of disturbed children and found no support for Leventhal's thesis. We suspect that Leventhal did not formulate the proposition correctly and that Nichols and Berg's study is not an adequate test.

The research on the state-trait dimension generally confirms the existence of two dimensions. In addition to the factor studies, stress has been shown to increase state anxiety but not trait (Biddle & Roitsch, 1976; Finch et al., 1978). However, when anxiety is measured as a general trait, differentiated effects are often not found. For example, Verma and Nijhawan (1975) found that anxiety interfered with performance of children of low intelligence but not high, whereas anxiety interfered with the performance of middle IQ children only when the reinforcement was negative. Prytula and Hiland (1975) found no relationship between anxiety level and measures of pathology on human figure drawings; Kendall et al. (1976) found that high anxious subjects required no greater personal space with strangers than low anxious children; Kumar et al. (1976) found no difference between normally healthy black children and those with sickle cell anemia on many personality variables, but sickle cell patients did manifest more state anxiety than those of normal health.

The Judge Baker group of investigators (Coolidge et al., 1960; Waldfogel, Coolidge, & Hahn, 1957) separated school phobias into two types, neurotic and characterological. The neurotic group tended to be younger, had acute and traumatic onset, and generally functioned well in other areas (Kennedy Type I). The characterological group were older and more disturbed. Symptoms in this second group had a more gradual onset and were the culmination of a lengthy process. These children had a generalized fear of the outside world, were basically mistrusting, used projection and externalization, and refused to take responsibility for their feelings and actions. The central conflict in the characterological group revolved around the symbiotic relationship with the mother.

Other investigators believe the key conflict in school phobia to be separation anxiety. Johnson et al. (1941) were the first to suggest that the basic difficulty lay in leaving home rather than in going to school. Eisenberg (1958) supported the contention and suggested that the problem was bilateral; that is, the involved parent (usually the mother) intensified and reciprocated the child's anxiety. Gittelman-Klein and Klein (1971), who found that children treated with imipramine returned to school while a no-drug control group did not, challenged this argument. They argued that there could be no difference in reduction of communicated parental anxiety in the two groups, which separation theory would postulate, since each group received identical parental counseling. The difficulty with all of these ideas is that there is little systematic research and the one test of Leventhal's thesis

was not adequate. Since there are common themes running through many of the clinical studies, we cannot discount the possibility of their validity, but as yet we cannot draw any conclusions.

The available systematic studies on personality attributes of anxious children suggest that manifest anxiety, even school phobia, occurs at all intelligence levels (Hampe et al., 1973; Hersov, 1960a, 1960b), although some studies with biased samples contradict this conclusion (Eisenberg, 1958). Miller et al. (1972b) in contrast to Lapousse and Monk (1959) found that anxiety in children was generally associated with an increase in many forms of deviant behavior as reported by parents and teachers although the primary increase was in inhibition.

Table 14.5 shows standard scores ($M = 50$, $SD = 10$) at intake on the Louisville Behavior Checklist, School Behavior Checklist, and Louisville Fear Survey of 67 phobic children accepted for a psychotherapy project. It can be seen from Table 14.5 that all deviant scales were elevated above a matched general population sample except Aggression (Item 13) and Physical Injury (Item 18) while the nondeviant scales, Prosocial Behavior and Extraversion, were depressed. It appears that disturbance in one area tends to create disturbance in other areas.

Hersov (1960b) found that 74 percent of school phobics were timid and fearful away from home, but willful and dominating at home (e.g., Leventhal). He also found that 25 percent were passive and obedient at home. Hersov further found that, as young children, school-phobics had had less experience in coping with parental absence, tended to be overprotected, and had high standards of work performance. Berg and McGuire (1971) also found school-phobics overly dependent, using a high immaturity score and a low sociability score on the Highland Dependency Inventory as a measure. Waldron et al. (1975) compared school phobics to other neurotic children and found that they manifested more separation anxiety, depression, unrealistic high expectations and were more preoccupied with mistreatment at the hands of others. Thus, while anxiety is an independent dimen-

Table 14.5 Scores on Louisville Behavior Check List and Louisville Fear Survey

	Phobic		General		F^b
	M	*SD*	*M*	*SD*	
Louisville Behavior Check List					
1. Infantile aggression	60.95	15.01	49.11	7.7	31.43
2. Hyperactivity	57.30	13.14	49.20	8.19	17.48
3. Antisocial behavior	55.48	16.28	48.94	8.06	8.31
4. Social withdrawal	62.92	13.39	48.52	9.42	49.54
5. Sensitivity	64.63	17.12	49.50	9.78	37.65
6. Fear	73.08	21.22	49.91	7.67	67.50
7. Academic disability	55.14	10.97	49.63	10.98	8.08
8. Immaturity	58.75	15.10	49.17	9.63	18.31
9. Normal irritability	56.61	10.31	48.16	9.61	23.02
10. Rare deviance	1.84	1.45	0.08	0.27	91.72
11. Prosocial	43.09	14.54	55.27	14.08	23.14
School Behavior Check List					
12. Low need achievement	58.75	9.55	48.84	9.11	36.06
13. Aggression	54.14	11.49	51.44	10.37	1.95
14. Anxiety	71.52	13.59	49.59	10.07	107.48
15. Academic disability	51.93	10.18	48.28	8.67	4.78
16. Extraversion	39.73	15.52	49.31	11.28	15.94
Louisville Fear Survey for Children					
17. Natural events	57.49	14.47	47.28	9.60	22.57
18. Physical injury	48.94	11.17	47.31	9.26	0.80
19. Social stress	63.06	15.58	49.19	8.97	38.10

[a]Reproduced from "Phobias of Childhood in a Prescientific Era," L.C. Miller; C.L. Barrett & E. Hampe, in *Child Personality and Psychopathology: Current Topics* (Vol. 1) A. Davids, ed. Copyright © 1974 by John Wiley & Sons. Used with permission of John Wiley & Sons.
[b]$F = 2.11$, $df = 19/108$, $p < .01$

sion, there is some evidence that personality characteristics are associated with specific types of anxiety problems.

In regard to mother-child relationships, Hersov (1960b) found that 50 percent of the mothers of school-phobics were overindulgent and dominated by the child while 28 percent were demanding, severe, and overcontrolling. Fifty-four percent of the fathers were described as inadequate, passive, but good providers, while 28 percent were severe and dominating. Hersov (1960a) also noted a high incidence of neurosis in the families of school-phobic children.

These sketchy findings certainly point to no single type of personality or parent-child relationship that is associated with or that is specific to anxiety. There is some indication that there are subtypes, the most frequent being the child who is inhibited outside the home but who is a tyrant within the home. However, this is by no means the only pattern associated with anxiety, and we have no idea

how frequently such personalities and relationships develop with no consequent symptom. Also, this pattern has been noted in other forms of psychopathology. A most promising line of inquiry is the state-trait issue as well as the multidimensional structure of children's self-reports. Research thus suggests that a global concept of manifest anxiety has limited utility but the more specific dimensions are associated with many independent variables that can begin to provide the information needed for a general theory of childhood anxiety. At this point, then, we must conclude that investigations have raised some interesting suppositions, but as yet there are no compelling answers.

TREATMENT

In spite of the lack of a generally accepted definition and theory of phobia, a plethora of remedial techniques have been developed in recent years. Advocates of most of these techniques, however, have based their claims upon single cases or uncontrolled studies. Hersen (1971) reviewed the literature on school phobia and found that the new behavioral therapies held promise, but he noted a dearth of well-controlled studies upon which to base generalizations. With a few exceptions the same state of affairs exists at this writing. Thus we are still forced to use the conventional wisdom of clinical experience.

Techniques developed over the past 75 years include interpretation, clarification, catharsis, abreaction, transactional analysis, reciprocal inhibition, hierarchy construction, systematic desensitization, implosion, positive and negative reinforcement, modeling, functional analysis, and contingency management. While each of these techniques involves different processes and each has been associated with the alleviation of phobias, the treatment process can be reduced to four basic essentials: establishment of a relationship, clarification of the stimulus, desensitization to the stimulus, and confrontation of the stimulus. This section on the treatment of anxiety is organized around these basic processes.

Establishment of a Relationship

Strupp (1973) has stated that one basic condition for therapeutic change is that the "therapist creates and maintains a helping relationship (patterned in significant respects after the parent-child relationship) characterized by respect, interest, understanding, tact, maturity, and a firm belief in his ability to help" (p. 1). Precisely how the therapist creates this relationship varies with the therapist, but most experts believe that a relationship begins and is maintained through interviews with parents and children. Some professionals prefer a family group interview. These decisions, however, appear to be more stylistic than crucial in forming a helping relationship.

An eclectic approach that attempts to draw the best from all systems would use the initial interview to establish as clearly as possible the history of the presenting symptoms, precipitating conditions, previous efforts made by child

and parents to reduce the anxiety, stimuli controlling the anxiety, events within the family that might be related to the symptom (e.g., deaths, changes in locations of home, or a serious illness), and practical questions such as family and community resources, sleeping arrangements, and neighborhood conditions. If the anxiety occurs outside the home, an eclectic therapist would need to know the context in which the noxious stimulus evokes fear. In the case of a school phobia, for example, one needs to know what has previously been done at school to help the child, the nature of the relationship of parents with school personnel, and what school resources may be available when the child reenters. Some of this information will have to be gathered from the school, but some information can be obtained from the child and parent. During the interview, the therapist would also try to determine which parent is most involved with the child as well as who is most capable of helping the child through the difficult confrontation stage. Also, an assessment of the family transactions at this stage would help the therapist to know how parents reinforce the child's avoidance and dependence behaviors and what might be done to encourage a different type of transactional system.

Information gathering is not only important for treatment planning, but it is also a necessary aspect of Strupp's definition of a helping relationship. The opportunity for parents to be able to relate their problems and express their anxieties and frustrations to an empathetic listener seems to reduce much of their anxiety. By the time parents reach a therapist, they have tried many techniques to help their child and have received much outside aid and advice from well-meaning friends and relatives that has not improved the situation but has often created even greater guilt and frustration. Feeling trust and confidence in a therapist goes a long way toward restoring parents' confidence in themselves and in their child. This sense of trust is often further facilitated if parents can voice their own guilt and anxiety arising from the contribution they believe they have made to the child's problems. Often the guilt stems from their own problems, which they try not to pass on to their children. This guilt gives rise to compensatory child-rearing practices by which the parents attempt to make up to the child unfulfilled needs from their own childhood. As these concerns are voiced and clarified, parents not only separate the present from the past but also gain greater confidence in the therapist's capacity to help. It is within the context of a helping relationship that the three remaining treatment processes take place.

Stimulus Clarification

The first step in treatment planning is to determine the stimuli controlling the anxiety. This is usually done within the context of the theory to which the therapist subscribes. For example, we have already noted that Sperling (1961) was interested in revealing the unconscious connection between the mother's operation and the child's school refusal, while Smith and Sharpe (1970) used nonverbal cues to obtain content areas to desensitize. The theoretical orientation of these therapists guided them to the discriminative stimuli they wished to work with in therapy. While theory can be helpful as a guide, the literature abounds with case histories which illustrate that the controlling stimuli turn up in the most unexpected places. Pittman (1970) reports a case of a 13-year-old girl who refused to go to school and all efforts to understand or remediate the case failed. A hospital team was sent to take the child forcibly to school and quite accidentally discovered that her refusal was a way of resisting the parents' decision to place her grandmother in a nursing home. With this information, a plan was worked out to keep the grandmother in the home, and the child went back to school with no further problems. This case involved neither an unconscious conflict nor a conditioned response that needed desensitization but a deliberate maneuver to keep the grandmother out of a nursing home. Messer (1964) reports a case in which an 8-year-old school-phobic returned to school after a complex family relationship was aired in a family therapy session. Following the revelation, parents returned the child

to school with no further problems. In each of these examples of successfully treated school phobics, therapists used a wide range of theoretical orientations and interviewing techniques to ascertain the discriminative stimuli. This suggests caution about becoming too attached to a single theoretical position that demands an automatic and rigid application of technique. This point is supported by our controlled study of treatment effectiveness (Miller et al., 1972b) in which we concluded that the basic therapeutic ingredients alleviating phobic behavior had not as yet been identified and isolated but probably were not to be found in any one type of therapy. Furthermore, when a clinician must depend upon a child's or parent's words to determine the discriminative stimuli, further caution is required since words mean different things to different people. Not only are children's self-observations often unreliable, but frequently they say what they believe adults want to hear rather than what they personally experience. It surprised us that children, asked if they wanted to be free of their fears, often said no. We finally realized that the children thought we were asking if they wanted to confront the feared object. Of course, they did not want to confront the noxious stimulus as long as it produced anxiety. Our words simply meant something different to the children than they meant to us. In view of these considerations, we believe that clinicians should remain open-minded and should bring to bear all theoretical notions and assessment techniques when determining the stimuli controlling anxiety. This belief does not imply that all possible dynamics and contingencies should be investigated before a treatment plan is formulated, but it does assert that therapists should avoid automatically applying a procedure or technique without thought to the individual characterisitics of each case. The determination of the discriminative stimuli and the formulation of the treatment plan demand creative talent from the therapist and the use of the full repertoire of theoretical ideas and technological innovations. Remember, in our study (Miller et al., 1972b), there was often a relief of anxiety during the assessment period, as if the clarification process itself was at times sufficient to relieve the child and family from the crippling anxiety.

Desensitization to the Stimulus

Desensitization occurs in many ways. Dr. Lucie Jessner, a child analyst in Boston, told of a child with a school phobia who went back to school after an initial visit. Upon inquiry, the mother reported that the child agreed to go back to school if she did not have "to see that woman again."

Wolpe (1958) has developed the most elaborate approach, known as systematic desensitization. This method has been so extensively described in the literature that we mention only the main elements. The basic idea is that a person cannot experience incompatible stimuli (e.g., anxiety and relaxation) simultaneously and that relaxation can be used to inhibit an anxiety response. In the classical use of the procedure, the approach to the stimulus is first made through the imagination; however, *in vivo* desensitization is also possible. Wolpe adapted a method of muscular relaxation to offset the anxiety associated with the noxious stimulus. After constructing a stimulus hierarchy, graded from least to most anxiety-provoking, and after the subject has learned muscular relaxation, the therapist presents the least threatening stimulus, asking the child to imagine the stimulus while remaining relaxed. This process continues step-by-step until the most anxiety-provoking stimulus can be imagined in a relaxed state. Systematic desensitization (SDT) has been successfully applied to children (Miller et al., 1972a; Tasto, 1969; Obler & Terwilliger, 1969; Miller, 1972b; Lazarus, 1959). However, many behavior therapists prefer to use *in vivo* desensitization procedures, especially with children (e.g., Walker et al., 1981). More will be said of this later in connection with our discussion of confronting the stimulus.

Perhaps the most intensive research on anxiety reduction in children over the past ten years has been the procedure known as modeling. Graziano, DeGiovanni, and Garcia (1979) found 20 studies of fear reduction in children published in the past ten years, stimulated in large part by Bandura's research (Bandura et al., 1967; Bandura et al., 1969). An extension of operant conditioning, modeling assumes that behavior can be changed through the various experiences of rewards for new behavior and through the information value of the modeled behavior. The technique consists of having fearful subjects first observe models who demonstrate an approach to the fearful stimuli. The subject then attempts to perform the approach behavior. The models can be live or symbolic, such as on video tape. Sometimes, single models are used, and at other times multiple models are employed. Many components of the modeling procedures have been examined experimentally, and some have been shown to aid fear reduction while others do not. However, the bulk of the research evidence supports modeling as an effective set of techniques and a rich area for further research. This technique has been particularly effective with common, everyday fears such as fear of the dark, animals, water in baths and with anxiety associated with dental and surgical procedures.

Other procedures have individual case support. Lazarus and Abramovitz (1962) used a doll play technique called "emotive imagery" to stimulate fantasy rehearsal of assertive behaviors in school. Conn (1941) describes a more elaborate play technique in which dolls are used to act out fearful fantasies. Conn's case was a 9-year-old who was afraid of being kidnapped and through doll-play became desensitized.

Other techniques, such as implosive therapy or flooding have a theoretical base similar to systematic desensitization, but instead of a gradual introduction to the stimulus, the subject is exposed in imagery and sometimes *in vivo* to the most intense stimulus from the start. We could find no systematic studies of implosion with children, although Marks (1969) reports that when used with adults this technique achieves the best results of all desensitization procedures. We have already mentioned Smith and Sharpe's (1970) study of a successful implosion of a 13-year-old, and Hersen (1968) reports a case of a periodic school-phobic with a compulsion ritual against disease that was successfully imploded.

In an unreported study, a research group of the University of Louisville School of Medicine imploded three adolescent school-phobics with one succcess, one partial success, and one failure. For reasons other than the outcome of these efforts, the program was discontinued, but these results do not point to implosion as a panacea. While systematic desensitization is dull, implosive therapy is nerve-wracking when it works well. Once, during the implosion of a case, the therapist broke off the procedure and recommended to observing colleagues that the implosion be stopped and the child hospitalized. He was urged to continue, however, and did so with a successful outcome. Some researchers (Morganstern, 1973), however, are skeptical about the rationale and effectiveness of implosive therapies and, in particular, some child clinicians (Walker, 1981) are concerned that implosive therapy may be misunderstood by children, resulting in an increase in their fear: that is, the session might turn out to be a learning trial rather than an extinction trial as often occurs in other contexts, such as "scary" movies and so forth.

Another desensitization technique that bears mentioning is an operant procedure. Ayllon, Smith, and Rogers (1970) discuss the case of an 8-year-old school-phobic girl who was successfully treated by contingency management. A behavioral assessment revealed that Valerie slept one hour later than her siblings and then went to a neighbor's who provided a pleasant and compatible reinforcer to remaining out of school. No particularly unpleasant experiences had occurred at school. Treatment first involved bringing Valerie to school the last one-and-a-half hours of the day, accompanied by an attendant who had established a relationship, then prompting and shaping school attendance through use of primary and secondary reinforcers, and finally withdrawing positive reinforcers and using aversive consequences when she was not attending. Valerie was back in school in 45 days. One wonders why the elaborate procedures of Ayllon et al. (1970) were necessary with this age child when our success rate was 96 percent with a much less complex procedure. Yet, since the mother was working

and there was little adult pressure, an operant technique may have been the therapy of choice. Again, it is a procedure to keep in mind, but it appears very inefficient with young phobics. Lazarus, Davison, and Polefka (1965) also used a combination of token reinforcement and emotive imagery after an unsuccessful treatment of a 9-year-old with systematic desensitization, and Patterson (1965) reports a successful treatment of school phobia by operant methods. Once again, single case studies make generalizations difficult.

Group therapy has not received much attention as a treatment procedure in recent years. In the University of Louisville Medical School Partial Hospitalization Program, the staff has been particularly impressed with the beneficial effects of group therapy with the overly anxious and socially inhibited child. Children referred for phobia and social anxiety have been observed initially to retreat in panic from all social interaction in the group. Gradually, in response to the group process, they begin to interact verbally and behaviorally. After a month or two, they gain confidence in asserting themselves and participating in the social give-and-take. A few of these children have made such remarkable changes it is often difficult for the staff to remember the anxious, retiring child who originally entered the unit. Invariably, these findings generalize to the home and neighborhood settings, but we do not have sufficient follow-up data to know the degree of permanence. Since this setting is a multi-therapeutic program, it is impossible to partial out the singular effects of group therapy, but we are sufficiently impressed to believe that group therapy should be considered a powerful therapeutic agent in the treatment of anxious children.

A final desensitization method is the use of drugs. Gittelman-Klein and Klein (1971) reported a double blind study of the effects of imipramine (Tofranil) on 35 school phobics, ages 6–14. Children, stratified by age and sex, were randomly assigned to imipramine or placebo pills. Evaluation after six weeks of treatment revealed that 47 percent of the subjects with placebo returned, but 80 percent with imipramine returned. This difference was not established until after six weeks of treatment, for during the first three weeks there was no difference between drug and placebo groups. These investigators also found that there were no age effects, and that the drug group reported much less subjective anxiety than the placebo group. This study needs to be replicated, but the evidence suggests that Tofranil is a powerful desensitizer and may be the most effective method for desensitizing adolescent phobias.

It is often necessary in working with children's anxiety to disengage the parents from the phobic process, perhaps even to desensitize them. Almost all writers have noted the close involvement of at least one parent in the child's problem. Very little therapy with parents has been reported although an operant theory of anxiety would suggest that the involved parent would be the most advantageous person with whom to work. Also, several studies (Abe, 1972; Hagman, 1932; Hersov, 1960a) have found that many parents have phobias which could serve as models for their children. Bandura et al.'s (1967) work on modeling and vicarious learning lends credence to the idea that phobic children may be imitating phobic parents.

We had one case of an 8-year-old girl who periodically refused to go to school, manifesting the usual signs of terror that baffled the mother and school personnel. This was the only child of an older couple. The mother had worked for years but was delighted at the birth of her daughter, not only because she had always wanted children, which many miscarriages had prevented, but also because she had always wanted to give to her child many of the things that she had missed in growing up. The mother felt close to her parents but also exploited by them because of the illness of her own mother and the selfishness of her father and brothers. Even as an adult, she was the only child who took care of her parents, but still she felt they favored her brothers. Despite the family conflict, her only real problems had occurred in adolescence when she felt unappreciated by her teachers despite the fact that she worked hard at her studies. Several instances in which teachers had embarrassed her

were recalled with a vividness as if they had occurred yesterday. She was determined that her daughter was not going to have to repeat her experiences. To avoid this, she made sure that her daughter had all the material advantages and was never exploited at home, although she did not spoil her in the usual sense of the word. The daughter was the center of parental interest and affection and every slight by peers or teachers was deeply felt by mother. The mother also went to school with some regularity to ensure that her daughter was not abused as she felt she had been.

In the course of 12 hours of therapy, this mother painfully reexperienced those events of her past and connected them to her current inability to let her daughter work out her own relationships with her peers and teachers. Behind it all was a conflict between the ideal mother of her dreams and the woman and mother she now realized she must be to help her child. The dream mother that she had tried to be was the all-giving, self-sacrificing, fiercely protective mother: the opposite of her own self-pitying, sickly, and exploitive mother. The real mother had been an efficient and highly respected career woman, who, now as a housewife, was resentful when her husband and child went into the exciting world. Moreover, she was afraid to stay alone in the house. She usually finished her work by 10:00 A.M. and then had nothing to do with her energy and talents except to worry about her daughter and mull over her past rejections. As she faced this conflict and released the past, she decided to go back to work and let her daughter fight her own battles. Almost like magic, when mother decided she no longer needed the daughter, the daughter decided she no longer needed mother. It was, however, with the ambivalence of pride and fear that she related in the last therapeutic session, with a smile and a tear, the sight of her only child going out on Halloween night with her friends, "tricking and treating."

This case, of course, argues for the thesis that separation anxiety is the basis of this school phobia, but the point here is that the child's fear of school was diminished partially by desensitizing the mother to the hurts of her own past. It was the child's resistance to school that was the stimulus for mother to recall her own past and face the major conflict in her current life. However, as the mother did this, she was able to help her daughter master the anxiety associated with school and her relationships with her peers. Even though the child was never seen in therapy, the mother was helping the child to confront and desensitize the school as a noxious stimulus.

In brief, there appear to be a number of techniques available to help a child desensitize noxious stimuli, including systematic desensitization, implosion, emotive imagery, doll-play, interpretation, operant conditioning, family therapy, group therapy, modeling, tranquilizing drugs, and parent therapy. Each of these methods must be applied within the context of a relationship, and each must be associated with a continuous and eventually successful confrontation of the stimulus by the child.

Confrontation of the Stimulus

The last essential element in the treatment of anxiety is stimulus confrontation. All research and clinical experience suggests that confrontation is an absolutely necessary aspect of treatment as well as a measure of its success. In the presence of the stimulus, the child learns how not to be afraid or learns that he is no longer anxious. All investigators believe that anxiety and phobias in particular will not dissipate through time alone but rather by a process of direct confrontation with the noxious stimulus. Differences arise only as to when and how the confrontation should take place.

Central to confrontation is attitude. In our experience, parents are usually ambivalent about a confrontation. Consciously, they recognize that the child needs to sleep in his own bed, to go to school, or to be comfortable during a thunderstorm, but they will also have many reasons why the child should not be forced to confront any of these stimuli. In our experience, there comes a point in all successful treatment when at least one parent resolves this ambivalence and decides that no matter what happens, the child will confront the stimuli and that they will not feel sorry or

guilty at having forced the confrontation. This resolution of ambivalence is true of parents of both young and older children and is a critical ingredient in arranging a confrontation. We seldom see such dramatic attitude changes in children. Generally, children are initially opposed to all confrontation, and only gradually and incidentally do they mention that they now do with ease what a few weeks previously had been done with such anguish.

It is generally unwise to expect children to confront voluntarily a noxious experience early in treatment because they do not recognize the long range advantages. As desensitization proceeds and as parents become less and less involved, we find that, with skill and planning, the children will make the effort to confront. Therapists need to realize that not all efforts succeed immediately, and, in cases where continuous confrontation is not possible, further desensitization will be necessary. It is a creative act on the part of the therapist to judge when a child and his or her parents are ready for confrontation and to employ the necessary supports to help at the critical time. In the case of school phobia, advance planning with school personnel is usually helpful. We like to secure the service of someone at school who will receive the child when the parents arrive so that separation is swift and sure. This person can also help the child into the classroom. Occasionally, a room near the principal's office can be provided for the child if the panic in the classroom gets too severe. Our experience, however, suggests that all of these auxiliary supports should be used sparingly since the main message is that the schoolroom is a safe place and that the child is expected to stay and do his work just like everyone else. We seek to provide the school personnel with professional support through the initial crisis and to guide them so that they treat the child matter-of-factly; remain calm in face of the child's fear, temper, or tears; and give the child time to master his or her anxiety without becoming the focus of either special privileges or animosity. Once parent and school personnel realize that confrontation is necessary and will not provoke disastrous effects and that a caring but calm attitude helps the child gain control, then the phobic reaction usually dissipates. If it does not, then the therapist has to weigh the possible advantage of continuing the confrontation against the ability of others to tolerate the child's anxiety reaction. In older children, one often has to resort to hospitalization or to tranquilizing drugs. As mentioned earlier, hospitalization is reported in the literature as being a successful method of confronting parents and children with their separation anxiety, but, in our experience, we have seen no better results with hospitalization than with outpatient treatment. We want to stress, however, that there is little research upon which to base these judgments.

Kennedy (1965) prefers a management approach with Type I school-phobics in which the therapist maximizes influence variables by leading the interview, being optimistic, emphasizing success, and presenting a formula. This formula includes a moratorium on all topics related to school, a deemphasis on somatic complaints, a forced reentry of the child on the following Monday morning with the least involved parent taking the child to school, matter-of-fact approval, compliments to the child on the first night for attending school, and a party on Wednesday for successful attendance.

Kennedy seems to be saying that if the parents' confidence can be restored by these simple techniques, then the therapist does not have to deal with all the other complicated issues. On the other hand, techniques such as Sperling's interpretation or Jessner's single interview resulted in the child's returning to school without Kennedy's management techniques. Thus many methods seem to work, and we again urge a selection of the method to fit the case.

Some professionals advocate the use of the juvenile court as a means for forcing confrontation. Our experience argues against this procedure for many reasons, but basically it is cumbersome, has many undesirable side effects, and we know of no instances when it has been effective. Even the threat is of no value because phobics do not anticipate logical consequences. Therefore, we urge that this solution be dropped, as well as all threats, because they seem to increase anxiety and withdrawal behavior. Even hospitalization should not be used as a threat but rather presented when all other alternatives have been exhausted. In brief, we find that threats and punishment are ineffective methods to help a child become desensitized to a noxious stimulus. If desensitization cannot be accomplished by means discussed in this chapter, then resorting to punishment represents the final failure and becomes an outlet for therapist resentment and frustration.

Orchestrating a confrontation requires the full range of therapeutic imagination and creativity. We have already seen how Sperling used interpretation and suggestion to get the child to go back to school, while in Messer's case the suggestion was made in the context of a discussion of family dynamics. In the Allyon et al. case an elaborate reward system was worked out, combined with aversive stimuli, while Smith and Sharpe imploded their child with verbal imagery until he was willing to confront the stimuli *in vivo*.

In our own study we used virtually every conceivable procedure to prepare the child for a confrontation with the feared stimulus. A partial list of procedures would include systematic desensitization, interpretations, and ensuring that the consequences of avoidance were as noxious as possible (e.g., removing television and insisting the child stay in bed if he or she was not in school). We found that all of these procedures worked and all of them failed to work. Hence, we would respond with skepticism to any statement linking a specific technique to a successful outcome. A clinician has to discover, often by trial and error, the appropriate technique for the specific case.

In brief, confrontation is a necessary step in the treatment of anxiety. It can be done only when parents have resolved their ambivalence and when other persons in the situation can receive the child without getting involved in the child's manipulative and anxious reactions. The therapist must continuously judge whether child, parent, and environment are ready for the confrontation, and, once it is begun, every effort should be made to bring it to a successful conclusion lest the child's avoidance be reestablished.

REFERENCES

Abe, K. Phobias and nervous symptoms in childhood and maturity: Persistence and associations. *British Journal of Psychiatry,* 1972, **120,** 275–283.

Abraham, K. Notes on the psychoanalytical investigation and treatment of manic-depressive insanity and allied conditions. In W. Gaylin (Ed.), *The meaning of despair.* New York: Science House, 1968.

Achenbach, T.M. The Child behavior profile: An empirically based system for assessing children's behavior problems and competencies. *International Journal of Mental Health,* 1979, **7,** 24–42.

Achenbach, T.M. The Child behavior profile: I. Boys ages 6–11. *Journal of Consulting and Clinical Psychology,* 1978, **46,** 478–488.

Achenbach, T.M. The classification of children's psychiatric symptoms: A factor analytic study. *Psychological Monograph,* 1966, **80**(6, Whole No. 615).

Achenbach, T.M., Conners, C., & Quay, H.C. Report of the task force on descriptive classification of children's behavior. *American Psychological Association Report to the Board of Directors,* Unpublished, September 1980.

Achenbach, T.M., & Edelbrock, C.S. The Child behavior profile: II. Boys aged 12–16 and girls aged 6–11 and 12–16. *Journal of Consulting and Clinical Psychology,* 1979, **47** (2), 223–233.

Achenbach, T.M., & Edelbrock, C.S. The classification of child psychopathology: A review and analysis of empirical efforts. *Psychological Bulletin,* 1978, **85,** 1275–1301.

Adams, P.L. Psychoneuroses. In Joseph Noshpitz (Ed.), *Basic handbook of child psychiatry: Disturbances in development* (Vol. 2). New York: Basic Books, 1979.

Agras, W.S., Chapin, H.N., & Oliveau, D.C. The natural history of phobia. *Archives of General Psychiatry,* 1972, **26,** 315–317.

Arieti, S. A re-examination of the phobic symptom and of symbolism in psychopathology. *American Journal of Psychiatry,* 1961, **118,** 106–110.

Ayllon, T., Smith, D., & Rogers, M. Behavioral management of school phobia. *Journal of Behavioral Therapy and Experimental Psychiatry,* 1970, **1,** 125–138.

Bamber, J.H. The factorial structure of adolescent responses to the fear survey schedule. *Journal of Genetic Psychology,* 1977, **130,** 229–238.

Bandura, A., Blanchard, E.B., & Ritter, B. Relative efficacy of desensitization and modeling approaches for inducing behavioral, affective, and attitudinal changes. *Journal of Desensitization and Modeling,* 1969, **13,** 173–199.

Bandura, A., Grusec, J.E., & Menlove, F.L. Vicarious extinction of avoidance behavior. *Journal of Personality and Social Psychology,* 1967, **5,** 16–23.

Beck, Aaron T. *Depression: Causes and treatment.* Philadelphia: University of Pennsylvania Press, 1967.

Berecz, John M. Phobias of childhood: Etiology and treatment. *Psychological Bulletin,* 1968, **70**(6), 694–720.

Berg, I. A follow-up study of school phobic adolescents admitted to an in-patient unit. *Journal of Child Psychology and Psychiatry,* 1970, **2,** 37–47.

Berg, I., & McGuire, R. Are school phobic adolescents overdependent? *British Journal of Psychiatry,* 1971, **119,** 167–168.

Berganza, C.E., & Anders, T.F. An epidemiologic approach to school absenteeism. *Journal of the American Academy of Child Psychiatry,* 1978, **17**(1), 117–125.

Biddle, J.R., & Rotisch, J. The effects of stress on state and trait anxiety in emotionally disturbed, normal, and delinquent children. *Journal of Abnormal Child Psychology,* 1976, **4**(2), 173–177.

Bornstein, B. Phobia in a two-and-a-half year old child. *Psychoanalytic Quarterly,* 1935, **4,** 93–119.

Bowlby, J. Childhood mourning and its implication for psychiatry. *American Journal of Psychiatry,* 1961, **118,** 481–498. (a)

Bowlby, J. Processes of mourning. *International Journal of Psychoanalysis,* 1961, **42,** 317–340.(b)

Bowlby, J. *Attachment and loss* (Vol. 2). New York: Basic Books, 1973.

Bronson, G.W. Fear of visual novelty: Developmental patterns in males and females. *Developmental Psychology,* 1970, **2,** 33–40.

Buechler, S., & Izard, C. Anxiety in childhood and adolescence. In Kutash, I.L., Schlesinger, L.B., & Associates (Eds.), *Handbook on stress and anxiety.* San Francisco: Jossey-Bass, 1980.

Caldwell, B.M., & Honig, A. Approach: A procedure for patterning responses of adults and children. *JSAS Catalog of Selected Documents in Psychology,* 1971, **1** (Ms. No. 2).

Castaneda, A., McCandless, B.R., & Palermo, D.S. The children's form of the Manifest anxiety scale, *Child Development,* 1956, **16,** 1317–1326.

Cattell, R.B., & Coan, R.W. Child personality structure as revealed in teachers' behavior ratings. *Journal of Clinical Psychology,* 1957, **13,** 315–327.

Cattell, R.B., & Scheier, I.H. *The meaning and measurement of neuroticism and anxiety.* New York: Ronald, 1961.

Cattell, R.B., Shrader, R.R., & Barton, K. The definition and measurement of anxiety as a trait and a state in the 12- to 17-year range. *British Journal of Social and Clinical Psychology,* 1974, **13**(Pt. 2), 173–182.

Chess, S. Marked anxiety in children. *American Journal of Psychotherapy,* 1973, **17**(3), 390–395.

Compton, A. Psychoanalytic theories. In Kutash, Schlesinger, & Associates (Eds.), *Handbook on stress and anxiety,* 1980.

Conn, J.H. The treatment of fearful children. *The American Journal of Orthopsychiatry,* 1941, **2,** 744–751.

Coolidge, J.C., Brodie, R.D., & Feeney, B. A 10-year follow-up study of 66 school phobic children. *American Journal of Orthopsychiatry,* 1964, **34,** 675–695.

Coolidge, J.C., Tessman, E., Waldfogel, S., & Miller, M.L. School phobia in adolescence: A manifestation of severe character disturbance. *American Journal of Orthopsychiatry,* 1960, **30,** 483–494.

Dennis, W. Causes of retardation among institutional children: Iran. *Journal of Genetic Psychology,* 1960, **96,** 47–59.

Dennis, W. *Children of the creche.* New York: Appleton-Century-Crofts, 1973.

Dennis, W., & Najarian, P. Infant development under environmental handicap. *Psychological Monographs,* 1957, **71** (Whole No. 436).

Dreger, R.M., Lewis, P.M., Rich, T.A., Miller, K.S., Reid, M.P., Overlade, D.C., Taffel, C., & Flemming, E.L. Behavioral classification project. *Journal of Consulting Psychology,* 1964, **28,** 1–13.

Eisenberg, L. School phobia: Diagnosis, genesis, and clinical management. *Pediatric Clinics of North America,* 1958, (Vol. 5).

Eme, R., & Schmidt, D. The stability of children's fears. *Child Development,* 1978, **49**(4), 1277–1279.

Errera, P., & Coleman, J.V. A long-term follow-up study of neurotic phobia patients in a psychiatric clinic. *Journal of Nervous and Mental Disease,* 1963, **136,** 267.

Finch, A.J., Jr., Kendall, P.C., Dannenburg, M.A., & Morgan, J.R. Effects of task difficulty on state-trait anxiety in emotionally disturbed children. *Journal of Genetic Psychology,* 1978, **133,** Second half, 253–259.

Finch, A.J., Jr., Kendall, P.C., & Montgomery, L.E. Multidimensionality of anxiety in children: Factor structure of the Children's manifest anxiety scale. *Journal of Abnormal Child Psychology,* 1974, **2,** 331–336.

Finch, A.J., Jr., Kendall, P.C., Montgomery, L.E. Qualitative differences in the experience of state-trait anxiety in emotionally disturbed and normal children. *Journal of Personality Assessment,* 1976, **40**(5), 522–530.

Freud, A. Fears, anxieties, and phobic phenomena. *The Psychoanalytic Study of the Child,* 1977, **32,** 85–90.

Freud, S. Analysis of a phobia in a five-year-old boy. In *Complete psychological works* (Vol. 10). London: Hogarth Press, 1962.

Freud, S. *Inhibitions, symptoms and anxiety:* London: Hogarth, 1936.

Freud, S. Mourning and melancholia. In W. Gaylin (Ed.), *The meaning of despair.* New York: Science House, 1968.

Freud, S. *The problem of anxiety.* New York: Psychoanalytic Quarterly & Norton, 1936.

Frommer, E. Depressive illness in childhood. *British Journal of Psychiatry,* 1968, **2,** 117–123.

Gittelman-Klein, R., & Klein, D. Controlled imipramine treatment of school phobia. *Archives of General Psychiatry,* 1971, **25,** 204–207.

Glick, B.S. Conditioning therapy with phobic patients: Success and failure. *American Journal of Psychotherapy,* 1970, **24,** 92–101.

Graziano, A.M., DeGiovanni, I.S., & Garcia, K.A. Behavioral treatment of children's fears: A review. *Psychological Bulletin,* 1979, **86**(4), 804–830.

Graziano, A.M., & DeGiovanni, I.S. Case histories and shorter communications: The clinical significance of childhood phobias: A note on the proportion of child-clinical referrals for the treatment of children's fears. *Behavioral Research and Therapy,* 1979, **17**(2), 161–162.

Greenacre, P. *Trauma, growth and personality.* New York: Norton, 1952.

Hagman, E.R. A study of fears of children of preschool age. *Journal of Experimental Education,* 1932, **1,** 110–130.

Hampe, E., Noble, H., Miller, L.C., & Barrett, C.L. Phobic children one and two years posttreatment. *Journal of Abnormal Psychology,* 1973, **82**(3), 446–453.

Hellman, I. Hampstead nursery follow-up studies: Sudden separation and its effect followed over twenty years. *Psychoanalytic Study of the Child,* 1962, **17,** 159–174.

Hersen, M. Treatment of a compulsive and phobic disorder through a total behavior therapy program: A case study. *Psychotherapy: Theory, Research and Practice,* 1968, **5,** 220–224.

Hersen, M. The behavioral treatment of school phobia. *The Journal of Nervous and Mental Disease,* 1971, **153,** 2.

Hersov, L.A. Persistent non-attendance at school. *Journal of Child Psychology and Psychiatry,* 1960, **1,** 130–136. (a)

Hersov, L.A. Refusal to go to school. *Journal of Child Psychology and Psychiatry,* 1960, **1,** 137–145. (b)

Izard, C.E. (Ed.) *Emotions in personality and psychopathology.* New York: Plenum, 1979.

Izard, C.E. *Human emotions.* New York: Plenum, 1977.

Izard, C.E., & Tomkins, S.S. Affect and behavior: Anxiety as a negative affect. In C.D. Spielberger (Ed.), *Anxiety and behavior,* New York: Academic Press, 1966.

Jersild, A.T., & Holmes, F.B. Children's fears. *Child Development,* (Monograph 20.) N.Y.: Teachers' College, Columbia University, 1935.

Jessner, L. Personal communication. 1951.

Johnson, A.M., Falstein, E.J., Szurek, S.A., & Svendsen, M. School phobia. *American Journal of Orthopsychiatry,* 1941, **11,** 702–722.

Jones, H.E., & Jones, M.C. A study of fear. *Childhood Education,* 1928, **5,** 136–143.

Joshi, R.T. Field-dependence, anxiety and personality, *Perceptual and Motor Skills,* 1974, **38**(3, Pt. 2) 1328.

Kendall, P.C., Deardorff, P.A., Finch, A.J., Jr., & Graham, L. Proxemics, locus of control, anxiety and type of movement in emotionally disturbed and normal boys. *Journal of Abnormal Child Psychology,* 1976, **4**(1), 9–16.

Kennedy, W.A. School phobia: Rapid treatment of fifty cases. *Journal of Abnormal Psychology,* 1965, **70,** 285–289.

Klein, E. The reluctance to go to school. *The Psychoanalytic Study of the Child,* 1945, **1,** 263–281.

Kovacs, M. Rating scales to assess depression in school-aged children. *Acta Paedopsychiatrica,* **46,** 305–35, 1980/1981.

Kovacs, M. & Beck, A.T. An empirical-clinical approach toward a definition of childhood depression. In J.G. Schulterbrandt & A. Raskin (Eds.), *Depression in childhood: Diagnosis, treatment, and conceptual models.* New York: Raven, 1977.

Kumar, S., Powars, D., Allen, J., & Haywood, L.J. Anxiety, self-concept, and personal and social adjustments in children with sickle cell anemia. *Journal of Pediatrics,* 1976, **88**(5), 859–863.

L'Abate, L. Personality correlates of manifest anxiety in children. *Journal of Consulting Psychology,* 1960, **24,** 342–348.

Lacey, J.I. Psychophysiological approaches to the evaluation of psychotherapeutic process and outcome. In F. Rubenstein & M.B. Perloff (Eds.), *Research in psychology.* Washington, D.C.: American Psychological Assocation, 1958.

Lader, M.H. Palmar skin conductance measures in anxiety and phobic states. *Journal of Psychosomatic Research,* 1967, **2,** 271–281.

Lang, P.J. Fear reduction and fear behavior, patterns in treating a construct. Presented in 3rd Conference in Research in Psychotherapy, Chicago, Ill.: June 1966.

Lang, P.J., & Lasovik, A.D. Experimental desensitization of phobia. *Journal of Abnormal and Social Psychology,* 1963, **66,** 519–525.

Lang, P.J., Melamed, B.G., & Hart, J. A psychophysiological analysis of fear modification using an automated desensitization procedure. *Journal of Abnormal Psychology,* 1970, **76,** 220–234.

Lapousse, R., & Monk, M.A. Fears and worries in a representative sample of children. *American Journal of Orthopsychiatry,* 1959, **29,** 223–248.

Lazarus, A.A. The elimination of children's phobias by deconditioning. In H.J. Eysenck (Ed.), *Behavior therapy and the neuroses,* Oxford: Pergamon, 1959.

Lazarus, A.A., & Abramovitz, A. The use of "emotive imagery" in the treatment of children's phobias. *Journal of Mental Science,* 1962, **108,** 191–195.

Lazarus, A.A., Davison, G.C., & Polefka, D.A. Classical and operant factors in the treatment of school phobia. *Journal of Abnormal Psychology,* 1965, **70,** 225–229.

Lazarus, R.S. *Psychological stress and the coping process.* New York: McGraw-Hill, 1966.

Leitenberg, H., Agras, S., Butz, R., & Wincze, J. Relationship between heart rate and behavioral change during the treatment of phobias. *Journal of Abnormal Psychology,* 1971, **78**(1), 59–68.

Leventhal, T., & Sills, M. Self-image in school phobia. *American Journal of Orthopsychiatry,* 1964, **34,** 685–695.

Ling, W., Oftedal, G., & Weinberg, W. Depressive illness in childhood presenting as severe headache. *American Journal of Diseases in Children,* 1970, **120,** 122–124.

Macfarlane, J.W., Allen, L., & Honzik, M.P. *A developmental study of the behavior problems of normal children between twenty-one months and fourteen years.* University of California Press, 1954.

Marks, I.M. *Fears and phobias.* New York: American Press, 1969.

Marks, I.M. Phobic disorders four years after treatment: A prospective follow-up. *British Journal of Psychiatry,* 1971, **118,** 683–688.

May, Rollo. *The meaning of anxiety.* N.Y.: Norton, 1977.

McConville, B.J., Boag, L.C., & Purohit, A.P. Three types of childhood depression. *Canadian Psychiatric Association Journal,* 1973, **18,** 133–138.

Messer, A.A. Family treatment of a school phobic child. *Archives of General Psychology,* 1964, **2,** 548.

Miller, L.C. Louisville behavior check list for males 6–12 years of age. *Psychological Reports,* 1967, **21,** 885–896.

Miller, L.C. Evaluation of Southfields: A short-term inpatient treatment center for delinquents. *Crime and Delinquency,* 1970, **16**(3), 305–36.

Miller, L.C. *Louisville behavior check list manual.* Los Angeles: Western Psychological Services, 1977.

Miller, L.C. School behavior checklist: An inventory of deviant behavior for elementary school children. *Journal of Consulting and Clinical Psychology,* 1972, **38**(1), 134–144.

Miller, L.C., Barrett, C.L., Hampe, E., & Noble, H. Comparison of reciprocal inhibition, psychotherapy, and waiting list control for phobic children. *Journal of Abnormal Psychology,* 1972, **79**(3), 269–279. (b)

Miller, L.C., Barrett, C.L., & Hampe, E. Phobias of childhood in a prescientific era. In A. Davids, (Eds.), *Child personality and psychopathology: Current topics* (Vol. I). New York: Wiley, 1974.

Miller, L.C., Hampe, E., Barrett, C.L., & Noble, H. Children's deviant behavior within the general population. *Journal of Consulting and Clinical Psychology,* 1971, **34,** 16–22. (a)

Miller, L.C., Barrett, C.L., Hampe, E., & Noble, H. Revised anxiety scales for the Louisville behavior check list. *Psychological Reports,* 1971, **29,** 503–511. (b)

Miller, L.C., Barrett, C.L., Hampe, E., & Noble, H. Factor structure of childhood fears. *Journal of Consulting and Clinical Psychology,* 1972, **39**(2), 264–268. (a)

Morganstern, K.P. Implosive therapy and flooding procedures: A critical review. *Psychological Bulletin,* 1973, **79** (5), 318–334.

Mowrer, O.H. Two-factor learning theory reconsidered, with special reference to secondary reinforcement and the concept of habit. *Psychological Review,* 1956, **63,** 114–128.

Nichols, K.A., & Berg, I. School phobia and self-evaluation. *Journal of Child Psychology and Psychiatry,* 1970, **2,** 133–141.

Obler, M., & Terwilliger, R.F. Pilot study on the effectiveness of systematic desensitization among children with phobic disorders. 1969 APA presentation.

Patterson, G.R. A learning theory approach to the treatment of the school phobic child. In L.P. Ullmann & L. Krasner (Eds.), *Case studies in behavior modification.* New York: Holt, Rinehart & Winston, 1965.

Patterson, G.R., Ray, R.S., & Shaw, D.A. Direct intervention in families of deviant children. *Oregon Research Institute Research Bulletin,* 1968, **8**(9), 1–62.

Peterson, D.R. Behavior problems of middle childhood. *Journal of Consulting Psychology,* 1961, **25,** 205–209.

Piaget, J. Piaget's theory. In P.H. Mussen (Ed.), *Manual of child psychology* (3rd ed.). New

York: Wiley, 1970.

Pittman, F.S., III. Critical incident No. 7. *International Psychiatric Clinic*, 1970, **7,** 335–341.

Provence, S., & Lipton, R.C. *Infants in institutions.* New York: International Universities Press, 1962.

Prytula, R.E., & Hiland, D.N. Analysis of General anxiety scale for children and Draw-a-person measures of general anxiety level of elementary school children. *Perceptual and motor skills,* 1975, **41**(3), 995–1007.

Rachman, A., & Costell, C.B. The aetiology and treatment of children's phobias: A review. *American Journal of Psychiatry,* 1961, **118,** 97–105.

Rado, S. Psychodynamics of depression from the etiologic point of view. In W. Gaylin (Ed.): *The meaning of despair.* New York: Science House, 1968.

Renik, O. Cognitive ego function in the phobic symptom. *Psychoanalytic Quarterly,* 1972, **41,** 537–555.

Reynolds, C.R., & Richmond, B.O. What I think and feel: A revised measure of children's manifest anxiety. *Journal of Abnormal Child Psychology,* 1978, **6**(2), 271–280.

Rodriguez, A., Rodriguez, M., & Eisenberg, L. The outcome of school phobia: A follow-up study based on 41 cases. *American Journal of Psychiatry,* 1959, **116,** 540–544.

Russell, G.W. Human fears: A factor analytic study of three age levels. *Genetic Psychology Monographs,* 1967, **76,** 141–162.

Rutter, M., & Hersov, L. Separation, loss and family relationships. In M. Rutter & L. Hersov (Eds.), *Child psychiatry—Modern approaches.* Blackwell: Oxford, 1976. (a)

Sarason, S.B., Davidson, K.S., Lighthall, F.F., Waite, R.R., & Ruebush, B.K. *Anxiety in elementary school children.* New York: Wiley, 1960.

Sarason, S.B., & Gordon, E.M. The Test anxiety questionnaire: Scoring norms. *Journal of Abnormal and Social Psychology,* 1953, **48,** 447–448.

Scarr, S., & Salapatek, P. Patterns of fear development during infancy. *Merrill-Palmer Quarterly,* 1970, **16,** 53–90.

Scherer, M.W., & Nakamura, C.Y. A Fear survey schedule for children (FSS-FC): A factor analytic comparison with manifest anxiety (CMAS). *Behavior Research and Therapy,*

1968, **6,** 173–182.

Smith, R.E., & Sharpe, T.M. Treatment of a school phobia with implosive therapy. *Journal of Consulting and Clinical Psychology,* 1970, **35,** 239–243.

Smith, S.L. School refusal with anxiety: A review of sixty-three cases. *Canadian Psychiatric Association Journal,* 1970, **15,** 257–264.

Soloman, R.L., & Turner, L.H. Discriminative classical conditioning in dogs paralyzed by curare can later control discriminative avoidance responses in the normal state. *Psychology Review,* 1962, **69,** 202–219.

Sperling, M. Analytic first aid in school phobias. *Psychoanalytic Quarterly,* 1961, **30,** 504–518.

Spielberger, C.D. Theory and research on anxiety. In C.D. Spielberger (Ed.), *Anxiety and behavior.* New York: Academic Press, 1966.

Spielberger, C.D. *Manual for the State-trait anxiety inventory of children.* Palo Alto: Consulting Psychologists Press, 1973.

Spitz, R.A. Anaclitic depression. In *The psychoanalytic study of the child* (Vol. 2). New York: International Universities Press, 1946.

Spitz, R.A., & Wolff, K.M. Anaclitic depression: An inquiry into the genesis of psychiatric conditions in early childhood, II. In A. Freud et al. (Eds.), *The psychoanalytic study of the child* (Vol. II). New York: International Universities Press, 1946, pp. 313–342.

Staley, A., & O'Donnell, J.P. *A Developmental analysis of normal children's fears.* Manuscript submitted for publication, 1981.

Stern, D.N. Mother and infant at play: The dyadic interaction involving facial, vocal, and gaze behaviors. In M. Lewis & L.A. Rosenblum (Eds.), *The effect of the infant on its caregiver.* New York: Wiley, 1974, 187–213.

Stern, D.N. *The first relationship: Infant and mother.* Cambridge: Harvard University Press, 1977.

Stone, L.J., Smith, H.T., & Murphy, I.B. (Eds.), *The competent infant.* New York: Basic Books, 1973.

Strupp, H.H. On the basic ingredients of psychotherapy. *Journal of Consulting and Clinical Psychology,* 1973, **41,** 1–8.

Surwillo, W.W. Human reaction time and period of the EGG in relation to development. *Psychophysiology,* 1971, **8,** 468–481.

Tasto, D. Case histories and shorter communications: Systematic desensitization, muscle relaxation and visual imagery in the counterconditioning of four-year-old phobic child. *Behavior Research and Therapy,* 1969, **7,** 409–411.

Terhune, W.B. The phobic syndrome. *Archives of Neurology and Psychiatry,* 1949, **62,** 162–172.

Tucker, W.I. Diagnosis and treatment of the phobic reaction. *American Journal of Psychiatry,* 1956, **12,** 825–830.

Verma, P., & Nijhawan, H.K. The effect of anxiety, reinforcement, and intelligence on the learning of a difficult task. *Journal of Experimental Child Psychology,* 1975, **22**(2), 302–308.

Wardfogel, S., Coolidge, J.C., & Hahn, P.B. The development, meaning and management of school phobia. *American Journal of Orthopsychiatry,* 1957, **27,** 754–780.

Waldron, S., Jr., Shrier, D.K., Stone, B., & Tobin, F. School phobia and other childhood neuroses: A systematic study of the children and their families. *American Journal of psychiatry,* 1975, **8**(132), 802–808.

Walk, R.D. Self ratings of fear in a fear invoking situation. *Journal of Abnormal and Social Psychology,* 1956, **52,** 171–178.

Walker, C.E. Personal communication, October, 1981.

Walker, C.E., Hedberg, A.G., Clement, P.W., & Wright, L. *Clinical procedures for behavior therapy.* Englewood Cliffs, N.J.: Prentice Hall, 1981.

Watson, J., & Rayner, R. Conditioned emotional reactions. *Journal of Experimental Psychology,* 1920, **3,** 1–14.

Waugh, M. Psychoanalytic thought on phobia: Its evolution and its relevance for therapy. *American Journal of Psychiatry,* 1967, **123,** 1075–1080.

Weinberg, W.A., Rutman, J., Sullivan, L., Penick, E.C., & Dietz, S.G. Depression in children referred to an educational diagnostic center: Diagnosis and treatment. *Journal of Pediatrics,* 1973, **83,** 1065–1072.

Weinraub, M., & Lewis, M. The determinants of children's responses to separation. *Monographs of the Society for Research in Child Development,* **42**(4, Serial No. 172) 1977.

Weiss, M., & Burke, A. A 5 to 10 year follow-up of hospitalized school phobic children and adolescents. *American Journal of Orthopsychiatry,* 1970, **40,** 672–676.

Williams, C.D. The elimination of tantrum behavior by extinction procedures. *The Journal of Abnormal and Social Psychology,* 1959, **2,** 269.

Wilson, G.D. An electrodermal technique for the study of phobias. *New Zealand Medical Journal,* 1966, **65,** 696–698.

Wolpe, J. *Psychotherapy by reciprocal inhibition.* Stanford: Stanford University Press, 1958.

Wolpe, J., & Rachman, S. Psychoanalytic "evidence": A critique based on Freud's case of Little Hans. *Journal of Nervous and Mental Disorders,* 1960, **131,** 135–148.

Yalom, Irvin D. *Existential psychotherapy.* New York: Basic Books, 1980.

CHAPTER 15

Sleep Disorders in Children

J. CATESBY WARE AND WILLIAM C. ORR

Most new parents quickly learn that "sleeping like a baby" means more than they thought it did. Walking the floor at night with an infant who is not inclined to go to sleep, getting up periodically to feed, diaper, and calm an infant who is not inclined to stay asleep, and arising early in the morning are disconcerting to even the most prepared parent. To make matters worse, knowledge of the sudden infant death syndrome (SIDS) may create anxiety even during quiet periods of the night.

Parents of infants and children are now more likely to present their concerns over their child's sleep to a health care professional. Because of the potential seriousness of some sleep problems, it is no longer appropriate to treat a complaint casually. While many sleep difficulties are transient and developmentally related, early signs of psychopathology or organic pathology may be manifested in a sleep disturbance. Present technological, scientific, and clinical advances in the understanding of sleep and sleep disorders mandate a very systematic approach in the evaluation of a possible sleep problem.

Four basic questions need to be dealt with whenever there is a complaint of a sleep disturbance: (1) Does the complaint reflect a lack of parental experience rather than a true sleep problem, or are the parents misattributing another problem to sleep—as was the case with a mother who insisted her daughter had a sleep problem because of slow swim lap times? (2) Is the child normal but creating a stress that the parents are not dealing with adequately, or are the parents actually complaining about their own problem rather than

the child's? For example, a mother who was awake much of the night herself following her separation from her husband sought consultation for her son's frequent awakenings at night rather than her own. In a recent French survey, 44 percent of the mothers of children who awakened had a sleep problem themselves, and 50 percent of the mothers of sleep talkers or sleep rockers had a sleep problem or had nightmares (Salzarulo et al., 1980). (3) Are the parents creating a sleep disturbance? Common, but not trivial, examples of this would be letting the child drink caffeinated beverages in the evening while watching TV or using going to bed as a punishment. (4) Are the parents describing a problem that possibly has a physiological basis? All too often in the past this possibility has been overlooked when in fact current data suggest that sleep problems often have an organic etiology.

NORMAL STRUCTURE OF SLEEP

To begin to deal effectively with sleep complaints, the clinician must know what to expect from normal sleep and how sleep changes with age. Behaviorally, sleep is relatively homogenous to the casual observer, seasoned only here and there with jerks, twitches, and larger body movements. A closer inspection, though, reveals that under the calm exterior of a sleeping person there is a rich complexity of physiological variability that has unfolded in thousands of miles of closely inspected polygraphic tracings of brain waves, eye movements, muscle tension, and other physiological systems. In-phase physiological cycles of quiescence and activation compose the dominant motif of sleep. With the exception of a few counterpunctual systems and with certain predictable modifications, this motif and its repetitions make up each sleep period from birth to death.

In the normal adult sleep pattern, the period of relative quiescence is broken down into four stages (1–4) and referred to collectively as non-rapid-eye-movement (NREM) sleep. The period of activation is characterized by the occurrence of rapid, typically conjugate, eye movements and is termed rapid-eye-movement (REM) sleep. Stage REM sleep is broken down into tonic and phasic components. The phasic events (e.g., bursts of eye movements) occur within a background of fairly stable activity (such as the EEG pattern). Stages 1–4 sleep signify changes from very light to very deep sleep respectively. The terms light and deep sleep are behavioral terms indicating the ease of awakening a sleeper. A child in stage 1 sleep is likely to be awakened by a peeking parent. But, in stage 4 sleep, a child may roll off the bed onto the floor without waking up. Humans are awakened from REM sleep about as easily as they are from stage 2 (Rechtschaffen, Hauri, & Zeitlin, 1966).

A typical child in a sleep laboratory will fall asleep in 15–20 minutes and reach stage 4 via stages 1–3 in 15–20 minutes after falling asleep (Williams, Karacan, & Hursch, 1974). One to two hours after sleep onset the first REM period will begin. Though the first REM period may last only five minutes, other REM sleep periods are usually 15–20 minutes long. Following this REM period, NREM sleep will begin again with the cycle repeating itself approximately every hour and a half. A sleep histogram of a 12-year-old girl showing the normal progression of sleep stages throughout the night can be seen in Figure 15.1. Interestingly, it is during the NREM sleep, particularly in the first half of the night where the most stage 4 is concentrated, that "all hell may break loose" behaviorally with the occurrence of night terrors, sleeptalking, and sleepwalking. Paradoxically, during REM sleep,

one's heart and respiration rate increase and become irregular, blood flow to the brain dramatically increases (Meyer, Sakai, & Naritomi, 1979), and dreams and nightmares occur, but little occurs behaviorally.

Brain Waves, Eye Movements, and Muscle Tension

Early research determined that during sleep a variety of brainwave patterns occur (Loomis, Harvey, & Hobart, 1935). When awake or relaxed with eyes closed, alpha waves (regular 8–12 Hz waves of moderate amplitude) occur, and subjects will easily respond to the clicks, flashes, and bells of a laboratory setting. However, as the subject becomes drowsy, alpha waves disappear along with any consistent responding to a stimulus. This is referred to as stage 1 (or transition) sleep. The stage 1 electroencephalogram (EEG) is a low voltage, mixed frequency brainwave pattern that quickly (in about five minutes) changes into stage 2 sleep, a sleep characterized by one-second bursts of 14 Hz waves called sleep spindles. In addition, large amplitude biphasic waves called K-complexes appear. In most cases, these K-complexes can also be elicited by an external stimulus. In the progression from stage 2 sleep to stages 3 and 4, delta waves begin to appear that are slow in frequency (<4 Hz) with high amplitudes (>75 microvolts). More than 20 percent in the EEG tracing characterizes stage 3 sleep; stage 4 sleep is identified when the percentage of delta waves reaches 50 or more. As with any NREM stage of sleep, it may be possible to awaken the sleeper only to hear the claim that he or she was not asleep but lying peacefully thinking. This interesting phenomenon is most common when the sleeper is awakened from stage 1 sleep and least common when awakened from stages 3 and 4 sleep.

Aserinsky, while studying an infant, noticed that during some stage 1 sleep the baby's eyes moved very rapidly under the closed lids (Aserinsky & Kleitman, 1953). Further work clearly established that there was a period of sleep (stage REM) with stage-1-like EEG accompanied by a host of previously thought

VARIABLE	PATIENT VALUES	EXPECTED FOR 12 YEAR OLD FEMALES
SLEEP LAT (mins)	17	7– 27
SLEEP LAT 2 (mins)	22	10– 36
PERCENT 0	1	0– 3
PERCENT 1	3	1– 4
PERCENT 2	49	44– 54
PERCENT 3	5	2– 5
PERCENT 4	17	13– 20
PERCENT 3 & 4	22	16– 24
PERCENT REM	24	24– 31
REM LAT (mins)	103	92–164
# REM PERIODS	5	5– 6
REM CYCLE (mins)	98	94–123
TIME IN BED (mins)	549	542–610
SLEEP PERIOD (mins)	532	525–590
TOTAL SLEEP (mins)	525	517–585
NUMBER STAGES	31	27– 39
# AWAKENINGS > 30 SECS	2	0– 3
# MVMNTS/ARSLS < 30 SECS	22	20– 40
SLEEP EFFICIENCY	.96	.93–.98
STAGE 2 SPINDLES/min	3	2– 4

```
                  RR              RRR      RRRRRRRR         RRRRRRRR       RRRR
sleep  00012222223444444444221 22RR23444444 2222222222442RRR0222222222RRRRRRRRR222344 2222222222RRRRRRRRRR122223302RRRR222
       1222222234444444442212 2RR23444444 2222222222442RRR0222222222RRRRRRRRR22234 42222222222RRRRRRRRRR1222233 2RRRR222
stages 2222223444444444221 22RR234444442222222222442RRR0222222222RRRRRRRRR2223442222222222RRRRRRRRRR1222233 2RRRR222
       344444444        3444444          44                   344              33
       44444444         444444           44                   44
_____100_____200_____300_____400_____500_____600
```

                              minutes

                           SLEEP-STAGE

Figure 15.1 Polysomnographic summary of sleep of 12-year-old female. The abscissa indicates the time in bed as well as the average sleep stage for that time period (1 dash equals 5 minutes). The ordinate indicates the relative depth of sleep, i.e., the further down a stage goes toward the abscissa, the deeper the stage of sleep. Stage REM (R) extends above, indicating that it is qualitatively different from the other stages of sleep. Normative data are derived from Williams et al. (1974).

to be non-sleep-like activities (Aserinsky & Kleitman, 1955); but because antigravity muscles were paralyzed during this phase of sleep, behavioral responding was prevented. Though typically muscle tension is reduced at onset and may get very low during deep sleep, the actual inhibition that occurs in REM sleep is not present in any other stage. When this stage REM paralysis is not well buffered from consciousness by other sleep stages, symptoms characteristic of certain sleep disorders may occur.

Other Physiological Systems

Almost any physiological system monitored will reveal circadian or ultradian rhythms associated with sleep and waking cycles. Hormonal cycles are often ultradian (shorter than 24 hours), following the NREM-REM cycle of sleep. During NREM sleep, particularly during stage 4 sleep, growth hormone is secreted (Takahashi, Kipnis, & Daughaday, 1968). Also, prolactin secretion is more likely to peak during NREM sleep (Parker, Rossman, & Vanderlaan, 1974). In both infants as well as adult males, REM sleep is associated with penile erections despite the fact that mental content may be devoid of sexual thoughts (Karacan et al., 1976).

Heart rate and respiratory rate typically slow during NREM sleep. In a well-conditioned athlete, a heart rate in the forties is not unusual. During REM sleep, heart and respiratory rate generally increase while at the same time becoming more irregular. During an eye movement burst in REM sleep, respiration may halt for several seconds, particularly in infants. A momentary slowing of the heart (or an asystole) is also not uncommon.

Core body temperature also fluctuates in relation to sleep and wakefulness. Throughout the 24-hour day, body temperature may fluctuate 1.5 to 2 degrees with the low point in the late phase of sleep around awakening time and the peak body temperature in the late afternoon. Though at times body temperature and the sleep-wake cycle may get out of phase and cause sleep problems, they typically are closely related. Systematic investigation of the relationship of body temperature to sleep has shown that bed selection times, self-rated alertness, the amount of time after sleep onset to REM onset (REM latency), and the duration of the sleep period are related to body temperature (Czeisler et al., 1980). For example, in an experimental environment devoid of time cues, going to sleep near the body temperature minimum results in a sleep period approximately six hours shorter than if sleep onset occurs at the maximum of the temperature cycle.

Ontogeny of Sleep

Though the same basic (NREM-REM) patterns occur throughout one's life, there are very significant changes that occur as one ages that must be used as the background within which sleep complaints are understood. During the first few days of life, an infant sleeps on the average of 16–17 hours, broken into periods of sleep typically less than four in duration (Parmelee, Schulz, & Disbrow, 1961). By the sixth month of life, total sleep per 24-hour period (on the average) is 13–14 hours (Kleitman & Engelmann, 1953). However, there is considerable variability among infants. Soon after birth, a maturation occurs and the infant starts to become responsive to certain time cues or *Zeitgebers*, bodily functions begin to establish a circadian rhythm, and sleep becomes more consolidated. By the first year, 90 percent of infants are able to sleep for at least a five-hour period during the night. Seventy percent of infants settle (are quiet for a five-hour stretch at night) by the age of 3 months, and 83 percent by 6 months (Moore & Ucko, 1957). However, less than half actually sleep throughout the night since many "settled" children will awaken during the night without crying or calling their parents (Anders, 1979).

Infants spend approximately half of their sleep time in REM sleep, and their REM-NREM cycles are much shorter than the 90-minute cycle seen in adults (Roffwarg, Muzio, & Dement, 1966). Because their sleep is fragmented and because they have a higher percentage of REM sleep, an observer is more likely to notice an early or sudden onset of REM sleep; that is, REM sleep occurs almost immediately after sleep onset rather than being buffered from waking by 90-minutes of NREM sleep as in adults, particularly in premature infants. The term "indeterminate sleep" is used to describe about 10–15 percent of sleep in infants under three months (Anders, Emde, & Parmelee, 1971).

An early sleep milestone occurs around the age of 3 months. At this time, sleep spindles begin to appear (Lenard, 1970; Metcalf, 1970), making sleep stages more easily classifiable and, therefore, reducing or eliminating periods of indeterminate sleep. At about the same time, other indices of nervous system maturation occur during sleep. Normally, during sleep, bursts of autonomic activity can be detected by recording electrodermal activity (EDA) (Johnson & Lubin, 1966). In adults, these bursts of EDA activity occur primarily in NREM sleep. However, in newborn infants, EDA occurs more in REM sleep than in NREM sleep; and, concurrent with sleep spindle appearance, EDA changes to the adult pattern of occurring predominately in NREM sleep (Curzi-Dascalova & Dreyfus-Brisac, 1976). In certain pathological conditions of adults, sleep spindles may disappear or EDA may again predominate in REM sleep (Hachinski, Mamelak, & Norris, 1977; Ware et al., 1980).

One of the most striking sleep changes that occurs as one ages is the decrease in sleep EEG amplitude and the overall reduction in the delta waves. Even an untrained observer knowing this would be able to distinguish among the sleep records of the preschooler, the young adult, and the retiree. While these marked changes in sleep EEG patterns with age have been the focus of much academic interest, the changes in respiratory patterns of infants have attracted the clinician's interest as a result of their possible relationship to sudden infant death syndrome.

All infants breathe irregularly. Measured continuously across states, respiratory rate and variability in infants is greatest when awake, lowest when in NREM sleep, and intermediate when in REM sleep (Carskadon et al., 1978; Hoppenbrouwers et al., 1978). Both respiration rate and variability decline up to 3 months of age, when they tend to stabilize (Hoppenbrouwers et al., 1978). Respiratory pauses (or apnea periods if longer than 10 seconds) contribute to the variability in respiratory rate in normal infants. These pauses are primarily a result of lack of respiratory effort rather than a blockage of air flow. They occur maximally beween 6 and 12 weeks of age, and by the end of the first year are clustered primarily in REM sleep (Guilleminault, 1980). Typically, their duration is less than 15 seconds (Hoppenbrouwers et al., 1977).

* * *

The first attempt by the Association of Sleep Disorders Centers (ASDC) and the Association for the Psychophysiological Study of Sleep (APSS) to develop a Diagnostic Classification of sleep and arousal disorders (Association of Sleep Disorders Centers, 1979) has produced a much-needed aid in the accurate classification of sleep disorders. One of the earlier difficulties was the ambiguity even in the terms used to describe sleep problems. Though the classification system was developed primarily from experience with adults, many descriptions are applicable to sleep problems of children, and the terms used here will be compatible with the ASDC classification system.

SLEEP-WAKE SCHEDULE DISORDERS

All infants have a schedule disorder since initially their sleeping pattern is sporadic. Therefore, a true schedule disorder cannot be diagnosed until after the child is well into the age at which sleep and waking periods should be synchronized with clock time. As indicated earlier, most infants (90 percent) will settle within the first year. Infants who suffer from certain perinatal problems—for example, anoxia—will typically settle later (Moore & Ucko, 1957). Parents may affect settling by the type of response the child is given when he or she does awaken and by the daily consistency in the child's schedule. Once an infant has settled, waking at night may reappear as a result of a variety of factors, including illness, environmental changes, or emotional trauma (Guilleminault & Anders, 1976). Of patients seen in a pediatric sleep disorders clinic in Boston, 9 percent received a primary diagnosis of a schedule disorder (Ferber, Boyle, & Belfer, 1981).

A common schedule disorder is the Delayed Sleep Phase Syndrome. Particularly adolescents will complain that it is difficult for them to fall asleep at night and equally difficult to wake up on time in the morning. However, the total sleep time is not outside of the expected range; they sleep well once asleep and they function well once awake though they may complain of some fatigue. Since most circadian rhythms are somewhat greater than the 24-hour-day, there may be a normal tendency to go to bed and wake up later each day. Uncontrolled, this may produce the delayed sleep phase syndrome indicated by sleep and wake times that are consistently later than desired (Weitzman et al., 1979). However, for most children, a strict bed and arising schedule keeps the sleep period from drifting. Perhaps in adolescence a circadian rhythm disturbance may be more prevalent than once thought since of the 10–20 percent of adolescents complaining of a sleep disturbance, a large percentage reported problems of falling asleep and feeling tired during the day (Anders, Carskadon, & Dement, 1980; Price et al., 1978). These are prime clues to the existence of a circadian rhythm disturbance. For the most part, circadian rhythm disturbances in children should be relatively transient. A shift in time zones and other sleep disturbances as a result of medical or psychological problems, may additionally result in a schedule disturbance that will be self-correcting once the cause has been eliminated and regular bed and arising times can be established.

By having a patient suspected of such a disorder record body temperature every three hours (while awake) for several days, a temperature-by-time graph can be plotted and inspected to determine whether the peak body temperature is shifted forward in time. If such is the case, successful behavioral treatment may be employed (Czeisler et al., 1981). This entails having the patient delay his or her bedtime three hours each day until the desired bedtime is reached. At that point, the bed schedule is stabilized. Since the patient is staying up later each day, falling asleep is typically not a problem. Following the stabilization of bedtime, patients then over a period of days gradually shift their bedtime across the final hour. Though this technique is easily described, it takes careful planning and help of the family members to work successfully.

THE PARASOMNIAS

In terms of frequency of complaints, the parasomnias are the most common (Anders & Weinstein, 1972) and often the most misunderstood. They are attention getters in children's sleep disorders, though they generally are benign in the sense that they are not signs of more serious pathology. Perhaps 20 percent of all children experience a parasomnia at least once though it is more likely to occur in males. In most cases, there is no clear etiological factor, the frequency of occurrence on a nightly basis is relatively rare, and the problem disappears with maturation. Treatment consists of providing information and support and treating any secondary problem that may arise, for example, the enuretic child's self-image. Nevertheless, in some situations the complaint of a parasomnia may indicate a more serious problem.

Sleepwalking (Somnambulism)

Sleepwalking is a NREM phenomenon usually occurring in the first third of the sleep period. It occurs out of stage 4 sleep (Kales et al., 1966b), and the behavioral arousal may last a few seconds to several minutes. In the sleep laboratory at the beginning of the first movements, the EEG is still indicative of deep sleep. In patients predisposed to sleepwalking, a sharp noise or standing them on their feet may precipitate an episode (Broughton, 1968; Kales et al., 1966a). The fact that sleepwalking usually disappears by adulthood suggests involvement of a maturational factor. Kales et al. (1980) have documented the mean age of onset to be 5.8 years in a group of patients with a history of childhood sleepwalking. They also found a high incidence of other parasomnias (ie., night terrors and enuresis) in this group, suggesting a common pathophysiological substrate. Often there is a family history of sleepwalking (Kales et al., 1980). In isolated occurrences, one should consider the possibility that it was precipitated by a febrile illness (Kales et al., 1979). Injuries during these episodes are not unusual, and parents should remove objects that may injure the child. Recollection of the episodes and purposeful speech or actions are unusual and suggest the possibility of a psychological problem rather than a parasomnia. Sleepwalking in the early morning hours when stage 4 is less concentrated is also suggestive of a problem other than true somnambulism, for example, a seizure disorder.

We have seen two recent examples of sleepwalking associated with seizure disorders in young females. One patient had infrequent periods of sleepwalking but was referred for evaluation after an episode where she drove 5 miles out of town before "awakening." Because of its occurrence in the early morning hours, an all-night clinical EEG was performed (in conjunction with other polysomnographic variables) that indicated abnormal EEG activity from the temporal lobe area. The second case, however, presented as a typical sleepwalker; she would sleepwalk two to four nights per week and had been a sleepwalker and talker for most of her life. These events were restricted to the first part of the night, and she did not remember them the next morning. While sleepwalking, she had a blank expression and was moderately uncoordinated. She had frequent traumas during these episodes, including two teeth-breaking accidents and one coccyx fracture after falling downstairs. Her father had been a sleepwalker his entire life. Her family's solution had been to tie her in bed at night. Though routine laboratory tests, a general physical, a CT scan, and a

waking EEG were normal, the polysomnogram, which included a clinical EEG montage, indicated significant EEG abnormalities. The patient was then put on an anticonvulsant medication that eliminated her sleepwalking (Dervent et al., 1978).

Sleep Terrors (Pavor Nocturnus)

Usually within the first two hours of going to bed, perhaps while parents are still awake and can fully appreciate its sudden and frightening occurrence, the preschool child sits up and lets out a loud, panic-stricken scream followed by several minutes when he or she is quite inconsolable. There is considerable autonomic activation with pulse rates well above 100 beats per minute. Subsequently, the child is totally amnesic for the event.

A sleep terror, like sleepwalking, is a NREM phenomenon occurring out of stage 4 sleep. This and other stage 4 parasomnias may be related since more than one often occurs within the same child. Sleep terrors as a rule do not appear to be associated with any particular pathology though as in sleepwalking they may be precipitated by a febrile illness (Kales et al., 1979). They generally occur infrequently, and any treatment initiated is more likely to be for the benefit of the parents and other household members rather than the child. In cases that occur frequently, diazepam (Valium) is reported to be helpful in attenuating the problem for reasons that are unclear (Fisher et al., 1973). Diazepam does tend to reduce stage 4, which may be one mechanism of its action. Another possible mode of action is that it decreases the arousability or response of the child to some precipitating event. However, before any drug treatment is instituted, the beneficial effects must be carefully considered against the known side effects (daytime sedation, alteration of normal sleep) and the possible unknown effects of a sedative on a developing nervous system. Education and reassurance are typically the best treatments. A case seen by one of the authors (WCO) was successfully treated by having the parents awaken the child just prior to their going to bed (which was usually before the sleep terror attack) to have the child urinate. This completely eliminated the attacks and suggested that the sleep terror was triggered by the internal stimulus of a distended bladder.

Nightmares

Nightmares are often confused with, but are considerably different from, sleep terrors. Nightmares are a REM-related phenomenon and, therefore, unlike the sleep terror, a considerable amount of dream content can be recalled; and, because of the suppression of muscle tonus in REM sleep, there is no pronounced behavioral component. Virtually all children have nightmares at one time or another. Nightmares per se are not pathological but may create a disturbance in the child's sleep and concern over going to bed. For reoccurring nightmares, the suggestion by Moore (1945) to have the patient tell and retell the nightmare may act as an effective desensitization method. Nightmares may also be a symptom of some significant psychopathology that may need more in-depth psychotherapy. However, when such is the case there are often other psychological symptoms.

Sleep Enuresis

One of the most common parasomnias, enuresis, is estimated to occur in 5–17 percent of the population between the ages of 3 and 15 (Lovibond, 1964; Martin, 1966; Tapia, Jekel, & Domke, 1960), and it is more likely to occur in males (Rutter, Yule, & Graham, 1973). Enuresis can be primary (the child has never had a significant dry period), or secondary, where control of bladder function is learned, and then the child begins having problems with incontinence. Although primary enuresis is often thought to be a developmental delay (Edvardson, 1972), it may occur in response to some pathophysiology such as sleep apnea, diabetes, urinary tract infection, or epilepsy, or in response to emotional problems. Likewise, though secondary enuresis is often assumed to be in response to psychological factors, it may have an organic etiology (Guilleminault &

Anders, 1976). An interesting historical account of the problem is given by Salmon (1975). Though there was little understanding of the cause, there was no lack of treatment, which varied from eating boiled mice and wood lice to strychnine injections into the perineum and cauterization of the urinary meatus with silver nitrate.

Unlike many other parasomnias, enuresis does not appear to be specifically sleep-stage–related and may even occur when the child is awake at night (Broughton & Gastaut, 1975; Finley, 1971; Gastaut & Broughton, 1964; Kales et al., 1977; Weinmann, 1968). Enuretic children are similar in that they often have a family history of the problem (Frary, 1935; Hallgren, 1957); and their sleep, based on parental reports and experimental data, is deeper than that of nonenuretics (Finley, 1971; Hallgren, 1957). Etiological theories have focused on physical or psychological immaturity, psychopathology, and arousal problems (Werry & Cohrssen, 1965).

If a thorough evaluation (including urologic) is compatible with an idiopathic condition, treatment usually falls into one of three categories: (1) no treatment, (2) behavioral treatment, and (3) drug treatment with imipramine. When giving no specific treatment other than support to the patient and family in dealing with the problem, the underlying assumption is that the problem is primarily developmental. This, however, is much easier to do with a 3- to 5-year-old than a 13- to 15-year-old. If there is a family history of enuresis, the age at which enuresis corrected itself in the parent may be helpful in predicting when the episodes will end.

Behavioral treatment with a bell that rings when the child urinates assumes that the underlying etiology is either a disorder of arousal (Broughton, 1968; Finley, 1971) or failure to attend and respond to the appropriate cues for another reason. With its use the child wakes up sooner and sooner after a micturation episode has begun, resulting in smaller and smaller wet spots that eventually disappear altogether (Crosby, 1950; Finley et al., 1973; Mowrer & Mowrer, 1938). Another behavioral method has been aimed at increasing bladder capacity since the enuretic child's bladder capacity may be smaller than that of a nonenuretic (Starfield, 1972).

The decision to treat with imipramine is an easy one to make on a purely pragmatic basis since it works effectively in terms of reducing the number of episodes by about half (Kales et al., 1977; MacLean, 1960; Ritvo et al., 1967), even though not all children are responders (Mikkelsen & Rapoport, 1980). However, the mechanism of its actions is unclear along with what effect it may have on the developing nervous system. An overdose problem is also present since a child may reason "if two pills help, twenty should stop it altogether," particularly when he or she plans to spend a night away from home. Thus a rational approach might be to initiate treatment with behavioral techniques and reserve the drugs as adjuncts to these approaches or in unsuccessful cases.

Sleep Rocking or Head Banging (Jactatio Capitus Nocturnal)

Sleep rocking is a relatively rare phenomenon that has infrequently been studied in the sleep laboratory. The phenomenon consists of rhythmical movements of the patient's head or body during sleep and initially occurs around the age of 6 months (Evans, 1961). It may begin just prior to sleep. Like enuresis, sleep rocking episodes have been observed in all stages of sleep (Baldy-Moulinier, Levy & Passouant, 1970; Gastaut & Broughton, 1964; Oswald, 1959). Also, like some cases of enuresis, sleep rocking may be maturational and, therefore, self-limiting. Besides maturational processes, it has also been attributed to a variety of factors ranging from relief of sleep-associated anxiety to epilepsy.

How vigorously treatment is pursued depends on the severity of the problem. Parents of otherwise healthy children who have merely observed the occurrence of the behavior and incidentally reported it, merely need to be told what is known about the phenomenon. At the other extreme, patients who have injured themselves as a result of the phenomenon should have evaluations for psychological and physiological pathology as well as instituting protective measures against injury.

Familial Sleep Paralysis

As described in the ASDC diagnostic classification manual (1979, p. 110), "familial sleep paralysis is characterized by a sudden inability to execute voluntary movements either just at the onset of sleep or on awakening during the night or in the morning."

As is easily imagined, waking up and being unable to move would be a terrifying experience either for a child or an adult. It sounds so bizarre that parents may not take a child's complaint seriously, attributing it to a dream; and adults will often not complain if it happens to them for fear of being labeled as "crazy." This phenomenon is even more unusual and frightening when it is accompanied by hallucinations. We have seen adults who have had these "terrifying" experiences off and on since childhood who had never previously told anyone but their most trusted friend. Sleep paralysis is explained as a dissociation of the REM-sleep phenomenon. The person actually awakens but the loss of muscle tonus that accompanies REM sleep remains. Some patients try to return to sleep and wake up again; others have found that by moving their eyes back and forth quickly an arousal momentum is initialized that breaks the paralysis. Also, if the patient is touched by someone, the paralysis will often disappear (Williams & Karacan, 1975).

Sleep paralysis often occurs in association with narcolepsy (discussed later), and the clinician must be careful not to overlook the possible existence of this condition. For true familial sleep paralysis, there is no cure, though there is no real danger except for the anxiety produced by its occurrence. Just having the clinician recognize the problem rather than shake his or her head in disbelief is enough for most patients.

Sleep Bruxism

Sleep bruxism is often a problem that "only your dentist knows for sure," though any bed partner may run the dentist a close race since a distinct teeth grinding noise may be produced as the masseter muscle contracts rhythmically (Reding, Zepelin, & Robinson, 1968). Sleep bruxism, though it can occur in all ages, has its maximum incidence in children and adolescents. Fifteen percent of those 3–17 years of age have a history of bruxism (Reding et al., 1966). Bruxism, though rarely awakening the person, does cause a distinct EEG change (Reding et al., 1968; Satoh & Harada, 1971). In some severe cases, the patient may complain of fatigue or sleepiness during the day, perhaps as a result of the disturbance in the sleep EEG.

Generally, psychological trait factors are not thought to be related (Reding, Zepelin, & Monroe, 1968) though some evidence (Clark, Rugh, & Handelman, 1980; Rugh & Solberg, 1975) suggests that anxiety may be a factor. Since the etiology in children is unknown and the condition tends to alleviate with time, treatment in severe cases consists of the fitting of a tooth-protecting prosthesis. Though behavioral treatments have been used successfully in adults, there is little evidence to suggest that these are beneficial in children.

DISORDERS OF EXCESSIVE SLEEPINESS (DOES)

The symptoms of sleepiness in children may be less clear cut than in adults. Besides the fact that adults are more likely to say "I'm sleepy," adults spend more time in sedentary activities (e.g., reading, driving) that are compatible with the onset of sleepiness or sleep. In children, the first sign of sleepiness may be behavior changes such as a shorter attention span, reduced coordination, or fussiness. Though a variety of disorders may result in excessive sleepiness, including the parasomnias if they sufficiently disturb sleep, as well as a variety of medical, toxic, and environmental conditions (ASDC, 1979), we will limit our discussion to narcolepsy and sleep-related respiratory disorders.

Narcolepsy

Narcolepsy is generally diagnosed in adults. However, one-third date the onset of their sleepiness to adolescence or perhaps earlier (Anders et al., 1980). Narcolepsy is not a form of epilepsy. Narcoleptic symptoms are best understood as the result of an uncontrolled REM-sleep-system producing (in addition to inappropriate sleepiness) perhaps cataplexy, hypnagogic hallucinations, and sleep paralysis. The narcoleptic has periods of sleepiness that may be virtually uncontrollable. Sixty-eight to eighty-eight percent of narcoleptics have episodes of muscle weakness (cataplexy) most often associated with emotion-evoking events (Anders et al., 1980; Yoss & Daly, 1957). However, cataplexy may not develop until after the sleepiness has first become a problem. Particularly in adolescents, the narcoleptic's sleepiness is very likely to be thought of as laziness or interpreted as a sign of psychopathology. The sleep of a narcoleptic is often characterized by the appearance of REM sleep within 15 minutes of sleep onset. Narcoleptics are also more likely to have disturbed sleep than normals. Diagnostic evaluation for narcolepsy should: (1) rule out other possible problems that may cause sleepiness; (2) document the sleepiness; and (3) document the appearance of REM sleep soon after sleep onset. A multiple sleep latency test (MSLT) is usually performed, consisting of five naps at two-hour intervals during the day. Narcoleptics will fall asleep within five minutes, often with the appearance of REM sleep immediately or within a few minutes after sleep onset. The sleep latency of normal subjects is typically 10 minutes or longer (Richardson, Carskaden, & Flagg, 1978), and REM sleep appears only in rare instances at sleep onset.

Hypnagogic hallucinations occur in 19–30 percent of narcoleptics (Roth & Bruhova, 1969; Yoss & Daly, 1957) and may be either auditory or visual. Most patients find them to be disturbing if not frightening but typically are able to differentiate between reality and the hallucinations. These may be vivid, dreamlike experiences that occur as the patient is falling asleep and are thought to be secondary to the occurrence of sleep onset REM periods. The sleep paralysis of narcolepsy is essentially no different from the familial sleep paralysis discussed earlier except for its association with narcoleptic sleepiness and perhaps the other symptoms. It occurs in approximately 24 percent of narcoleptics (Yoss & Daly, 1957). Yoss and Daly also reported that from a sample of approximately 300 patients, 11 percent had the complete set of narcoleptic symptoms.

Dement and colleagues (Dement, Carskadon, & Ley, 1973) estimated the prevalence of narcolepsy to be .07 percent. In teenagers in Japan, the prevalence has been estimated at .16 percent (Honda, 1979). Narcolepsy is more likely to occur in families with an incidence of about 60 times that of the normal population (Kessler, 1976). In certain species of dogs, an autosomal, recessive gene appears to transmit narcolepsy (Foutz et al., 1979).

Narcolepsy cannot be cured, but it may be managed so that the symptoms are sufficiently suppressed by medications so that the child's performance can be improved. We have seen some narcoleptic children excel in school. Though narcoleptics may do poorly in school, it is most likely a result of their sleepiness resulting in inattentiveness. Most commonly, a short-acting stimulant, methylphenidate hydrochloride, is given to combat the sleepiness. However, it must be used with caution since continued use will not only produce tolerance but may result in a sleep disturbance that further increases the daytime sleepiness. Often a small dose one-half hour before the maximum period of sleepiness (e.g., school period right after lunch) and none on the weekend will be sufficient to overcome the major episodes of sleepiness and retard the development of tolerance. Short naps (10–15 minutes) can often be used in place of the stimulant since narcoleptics characteristically experience considerable relief of sleepiness after a short nap.

If cataplexy is a problem, imipramine, a trycyclic antidepressant that is an effective REM suppressant, usually will reduce or eliminate the episodes. However, one of the most important treatments is to give the child, the parents, and the teachers a thorough explanation of the problem. Once there is a clear understanding of the problem, most patients can effectively organize their lives, in conjunction with medical help, in order to cope with narcolepsy.

Sleep-Related Breathing Disorders

Sleep-related breathing disorders have become increasingly recognized as substantial medical problems that may produce both a sleep disturbance and daytime sleepiness. Though an airway obstruction has long been known to occur in upper airway anomalies such as the Pierre-Robin syndrome and hypertrophied tonsils, it is now recognized that sleep may result in a marked exacerbation of the airway obstruction. In many instances, repeated complete occlusions of the upper airway during sleep produce hundreds of apneic periods. Sleep-related breathing disorders are now identified in a wide variety of conditions ranging from cystic fibrosis to the sudden and unexplained death of a newborn infant. Though once thought to be rare, 14 percent of the patients evaluated in a pediatric sleep disorders clinic in Boston received a primary diagnosis of sleep apnea (Ferber et al., 1981).

Upper Airway Obstruction During Sleep

Of the sleep-related breathing disorders, perhaps the most common is that associated with adenotonsillar hypertrophy. Studies have documented that children with markedly enlarged tonsils can obstruct their upper airway during sleep as many as 200 times (Eliaschar et al., 1980; Manget, Orr, & Smith, 1977; Richardson et al., 1980). In some cases, a partially obstructed airway may exist the entire night with interspersed, but less frequent, episodes of complete occlusion (Manget et al., 1977). Tonsillectomy on these children markedly improved the sleep-related breathing disturbance in all cases. Though an airway obstruction during sleep in the child with hypertrophied tonsils is an indication for consideration of a tonsillectomy, the decision to intervene surgically is difficult since these children are not always hypersomnolent during the day. There is no clear-cut relationship beween tonsillar hypertrophy and the number of upper airway obstructive episodes that need to be present to be considered clinically significant. In fact well over 100 episodes of upper airway obstruction have been identified in asymptomatic adults with loud snoring (Orr, Imes, & Martin, 1979). Thus the treatment decision must take account of a complex set of parameters that should include (in addition to the evaluation in a sleep-related breathing disorder) its sequelae, that is, hypoxemia and cardiac arhythmias.

Other upper airway anomalies that have been identified as potential causes of obstructive sleep apnea include Pierre Robin syndrome (a congenital defect in the normal prenatal development of the mandible), repaired cleft palate, and other congenital anomalies that may constrict the normal diameter of the upper airway. The profound retrognathia associated with Pierre-Robin syndrome results in a posterior displacement of the base of the tongue that produces a very constricted upper airway. This greatly increases the probability of airway occlusion during sleep that is associated with upper airway muscular hypotonia. The latter makes it quite likely that inspiratory efforts will result in sufficient negative pressure to "suck" the structures of the upper airway into apposition, thereby completely occluding the airway. Through a similar mechanism, a cleft palate that is sometimes repaired by rotating a pharyngeal flap to close the palate, oftentimes results in a constriction of the upper airway, making it more susceptible to airway occlusion during sleep. We have documented one such case (WCO) that was not diagnosed until after a respiratory arrest resulted in an emergency tracheostomy. We subsequently studied the patient approximately two years after the permanent tracheostomy was in place; with the tracheostomy plugged, over 400 episodes of airway obstruction were noted. The child was studied over the next two years intermittently and a rather marked decrease in the incidence of airway obstruction during sleep was noted. On the basis of these data, one may assume that airway obstruction secondary to anatomic anomalies of the upper airway may resolve as the child develops.

Sleep apneic children may present to the clinician in a variety of ways. Most frequently, the parent or physician has noted extremely restless sleep associated with loud snoring and sternal retractions. The parent may have even noted episodes of cyanosis associated with a cessation of breathing. Profound hypersomnolence has been well documented in association with obstructive sleep apnea in adults, but in our experience, it is a somewhat less consistent finding in children. It is more likely that the child will present with complaints of lethargy, daytime fatigue, and extreme difficulty awakening in the morning. In addition, it has been our experience that, although a premorbid diagnosis of failure to thrive is rare, such children will experience an appreciable increase in activity level and food intake, as well as growth, subsequent to treatment of this condition. Thus the clinician should be quite aware that a variety of behavioral manifestations may underlie this potentially lethal condition.

Other Sleep-Related Breathing Disorders in Children

Abnormal breathing patterns as well as episodes of spontaneous oxygen desaturation have been shown to be associated with chronic obstructive lung disease in adults (Wynne et al., 1979). Similar observations have been made in children with chronic lung disease such as cystic fibrosis (Muller et al., 1980; Stokes et al., 1980). These investigators have identified sleep-related breathing disorders associated with mild-to-moderate oxygen desaturation in patients with cystic fibrosis. They have concluded that this sleep-related breathing disorder accelerates the cardiopulmonary complications of this condition. A recent study has evaluated the occurrence of similar disorders in children with asthma, the most common obstructive lung disease in children. Although small and statistically significant decreases in arterial oxygen saturation during sleep were identified in the asthmatic group, these were not felt to be clinically significant (Chipps et al., 1980). It should be noted that these patients were maintained on relatively high doses of Theophylline during the study. It is reasonable to assume that sleep-related drops in arterial oxygen saturation might be found to be considerably greater without respiratory stimulant medication.

Lastly, a relatively rare condition has been identified in infants associated with extreme aveolar hypoventilation and apnea during sleep. This has been referred to as the Ondine's Curse Syndrome (Mellins et al., 1970). This condition has been associated with a marked decrease in carbon dioxide sensitivity (Mellins et al., 1970), and treatment is generally via ventilator or electrophrenic stimulation (Hunt et al., 1978; Langou et al., 1978). A recent case report has postulated that the absence of the external arcuate nucleus plays an important role in the pathogenesis of this syndrome (Folgering, Kuyper, & Killie, 1979).

The Sudden Infant Death Syndrome (SIDS)

As has been previously noted, short respiratory pauses (no respiratory effort or central apnea) are normal in the newborn infant. However, repeated or prolonged episodes of apnea constitute cause for concern. Breathing abnormalities in the newborn can be a sign of a multiplicity of medical disorders such as congestive heart failure, patent ductus arteriosus, and central nervous system abnormalities. In addition, unexplained apneic episodes may occur and are felt to place an infant at high risk for SIDS. Currently, pathologic apnea (central and/or obstructive) is the most popular hypothesis used to explain the mechanism in SIDS.

The sudden and unexplained demise of an ostensibly healthy infant is the sine qua non of SIDS. Death in nearly all instances has been associated wih a presumably sleeping infant. There are considerable data available now to indicate that, although there is no consistent abnormality that has been noted common to all infants who have succumbed to SIDS, they are not completely normal infants (Valdes-Depena, 1978). A recent study has indicated rather consistent, albeit subtle, neurological abnormalities in a group of infants considered to be at high risk for SIDS (Korobkin & Guilleminault, 1979). Undoubtedly, the most common event occurring across all infants identified as being at risk for SIDS is the

occurrence of sleep-related breathing abnormalities. These have been noted anecdotally by parents, as well as documented in the sleep laboratory (Valdes-Depena, 1978).

Tonkin published an important and provocative paper concerning the pathogenesis of SIDS implicating the vulnerable upper airway in predisposing the infant to upper airway obstruction during sleep. Tonkin (1975) proposed that a combination of both anatomical and physiological factors converge during the first few months of life that place the infant at considerable risk for sudden death due to airway occlusion during sleep. More specifically, it was postulated that the anatomical configuration of the newborn upper airway places the base of the tongue, the posterior pharyngeal wall, and the soft palate in close proximity to one another; this allows relatively easy collapse of the upper airway in association with the muscular hypotonicity that exists during sleep. This situation is acutely exacerbated during the skeletal muscle inhibition of REM sleep. These factors make it particularly easy for the airway to become completely occluded during a relatively brisk inspiratory effort. However, a mechanism of airway occlusion alone does not account for SIDS since most children and adults will wake up or arouse to a lighter stage of sleep where breathing resumes.

Although the medical literature is replete with hypotheses concerning the etiology of SIDS, there are considerable data supporting the notion of airway obstruction during sleep as an important factor in the pathogenesis of SIDS. Guilleminault et al. (1975) identified the presence of upper airway obstruction in premature infants as well as in infants who had been resuscitated and were considered "near miss" for SIDS. In these infants, upper airway obstruction is associated with more profound hypoxemia and bradycardia. In contrast to the Tonkin (1975) hypothesis, the longest episodes of obstruction were associated with quiet or indeterminate sleep. In a subsequent publication comparing "high risk infants" for SIDS with a group of normal controls, Guilleminault and his colleagues identified the occurrence of upper airway occlusions during sleep as the single parameter that distinguished the two groups (Guilleminault et al., 1979).

A number of investigators have addressed the issue of autonomic lability during sleep as a risk factor in SIDS. Hoppenbrouwers et al. (1980) compared respiratory rates and apneic events in a group of subsequent siblings of SIDS infants with a group of matched controls. Their results indicated that respiratory pauses of 2–5 seconds were decreased at 1 week of age and the respiratory rates were increased at 1 week and 6 months of age in the subsequent sibling group. No differences were noted beween these two groups in terms of mixed or obstructive apneic episodes. In a related study, Thoman, Miano, and Freeze, (1977) found two deviant infants in a group of normals. One died of SIDS, and the other had numerous episodes of prolonged apnea with resuscitation. Both of these infants had higher and more variable respiratory rates as newborns as well as fewer identifiable periods of short apnea. In addition, Harper et al. (in press) have described similar findings in a subsequent sibling (of SIDS victims) group. They also described decreased heart rate variability in the high risk group. Also of interest is a study by Katona and Egbert (1978) showing higher heart rates and respiratory rates during the first 6 months of life in preterm compared to fullterm infants. This difference was particularly great at 10 weeks of age, which is the period of highest risk for SIDS. In addition, prematurity itself is considered a risk factor for SIDS. Although these data were not sufficiently convincing to specifically identify a "high risk" infant simply on the basis of an autonomic pattern, they clearly suggest some disregulation of the autonomic nervous system in certain groups that have been considered at high risk for SIDS.

There are data available that strongly suggest that SIDS infants have been exposed to chronic hypoxemia (Naeye, 1973; Naeye, 1974). The data reported above of rapid respiratory rates in high risk infants would be quite consistent with this hypothesis. This notion clearly points to an abnormality in chemosensitivity in infants succumbing to SIDS. In a study of infants with recurrent apnea and aborted SIDS, Brady et al. (1978) found that induction of transient mild hypoxemia resulted in increased frequency and duration of apneic spells. No change in the parameters was noted in the control group. In addition, Shannon, Kelly, and O'Connell (1977) have demonstrated decreased carbon dioxide sensitivity in a group of aborted SIDS infants. They conclude that at least in some cases, SIDS may be related to aberrant chemical control of breathing.

Abnormalities of breathing during REM sleep would seem of particular importance in newborn infants since it has been well documented that they spend approximately 50 percent of their sleeping time in REM sleep. Although the studies cited above concerning the chemical control of breathing during sleep were conducted during NREM sleep, numerous studies have shown alterations in respiratory control during REM sleep in infants. There are studies indicating a greater degree of hypoxemia during REM sleep, and it has been suggested that this is secondary to decreases in lung volume and/or ventilation/perfusion inequalities (Brooks et al., 1978; Henderson-Smart & Read, 1978). In addition, Knill et al. (1976) have demonstrated paradoxical chest wall/abdominal movements during breathing in REM sleep as well as poor responses to an inspiratory load.

Although there are clearly other highly plausible notions concerning the etiology of SIDS that are related to behavioral development in the neonatal period (Lipsitt, 1979), it seems clear that the alterations in the control of breathing during sleep must be given extremely high priority as factors important in identifying not only the etiology of SIDS but also in identifying the high risk infant.

DISORDERS IN INITIATING AND MAINTAINING SLEEP (DIMS): INSOMNIA

Insomnia used to be the catch-all category of a variety of undifferentiated disorders that resulted in complaints of a sleep disturbance. As our knowledge of sleep increases, along with our ability to diagnose specific sleep-related disorders such as sleep apnea, the problems remaining in the "insomnia bin" become less heterogeneous but still numerous. A survey by Bixler, Kales, and Soldatos (1979) reported that over the various medical specialities, physicians estimated approximately 30 percent of their patients had a sleep complaint. When broken down according to specialities, the obstetrician-gynecologists estimated 19 percent of their patients complained of sleep disturbances while the child psychiatrists estimated that 60 percent of their patients had a sleep complaint, with insomnia and nightmares the two most common complaints.

DIMS Complaint without an Objective Sleep Disturbance

One important aspect that sleep clinicians become aware of early in their careers is that the complaint of too little sleep often does not correspond to the amount of sleep a patient actually obtains. Not only may judgments of time be poor while lying awake in bed, but the cues that one may use to judge the quality or quantity of sleep (e.g., aches, fatigue, bags under eyes) may be entirely unrelated to sleep. Guilleminault and Anders (1976) give an example of a 12-year-old boy who from the age of 6 months had been considered a poor sleeper. He had received a variety of treatments, including prescriptions for phenobarbital and dextroamphetamine. When they initially saw him at 12 years of age, parents and patient indicated that he was sleeping no more than 4 hours per night. However, polysomnographic monitoring revealed a normal sleep pattern of 448 minutes in duration. Therefore, careful documentation should be obtained, either through polysomnography or reliable observation of an actual sleep disturbance, before remedial methods are undertaken.

Psychological Problems

Any psychological problem may disturb sleep, and most patients with sleep complaints have elevated MMPI profiles (Beutler, Thronby, & Karacan, 1978; Monroe, 1967). However, determining the cause-effect relationship between daytime behavior disturbance and an insomnia problem is difficult. When a child presents with a sleep disturbance and has diagnosable depression, one cannot automatically assume that the sleep disturbance is a result of depression. It may be that the patient's sleep disturbance contributes to the depression and by treating a sleep pathology the depression is reduced or eliminated. In evaluating a group of 129 children (1–19 years) presenting with sleep complaints, Ferber et al. (1981) gave a psychiatric diagnosis of 14 percent but noted that "significant psychological overlay in patients and/or parents was common in most diagnostic groups."

Typically, patients who are depressed have reduced total sleep time and longer sleep latencies, awaken more often, and stay awake longer (Diaz-Guerrero, Gottlieb, & Knott, 1946; Gresham, Agnew, & Williams, 1965; Kupfer & Foster, 1978). However, the variability among patients is large, and, in some cases, it may be that depressed patients have more sleep (Detre et al., 1972; Kupfer et al., 1972). This may be particularly true in adolescents who have an apparent normal tendency for increased sleepiness (Carskadon et al., 1980). A reliable sleep marker for primary unipolar depression is a decreased amount of time from sleep onset to REM onset (REM latency) (Kupfer & Foster, 1972; Kupfer, 1976). Interestingly, in these patients, suppression of REM sleep either medically or behaviorally improves the depression (Vogel et al., 1975). Contrary to some earlier beliefs, research has not demonstrated that stage REM deprivation will produce psychopathology (Albert, 1975; Dement, 1969; Vogel, 1972).

In adults without clearly diagnosable or treatable causes of insomnia, a number of behavioral treatments have been applied; however, when applied to unselected groups of poor sleepers, they have produced little sleep. Progressive relaxation and stimulus control techniques are two that have shown promise with adults and would perhaps have beneficial effects in some children.

Progressive relaxation involves tension-release of various muscle groups and focused attention on the resulting sensations. Of the variety of behavioral techniques, this method has perhaps the best experimental support (Borkovec & Weerts, 1976; Freedman & Papsdorf, 1976). The stimulus control technique assumes that sleep is, in part, a response to environmental stimuli. Therefore, by carefully controlling the environment, the desired response of sleep will occur (Bootzin & Nicassio, 1978). Review of other behavioral techniques with adults can be found in Hauri, 1978.

Physiological/Medical Problems

Like psychological problems, almost any medical problem (e.g., ear infections) may result in a sleep disturbance. For the most part, the cause-effect relationship is not occult and is easily picked up by the parent or pediatrician. However, there are several problems that are often missed or occur only during sleep that will be discussed here.

DIMS as a Result of Drug Use

An iatrogenic sleep problem may occur in anyone chronically using some stimulant *or* sedative/hypnotic medications (Kales, 1971). We have seen even narcoleptics whose use of daytime stimulants so disturbed their normal sleep pattern that the end result was increased rather than decreased daytime sleepiness (Ware, 1979). Though a sleep disturbance secondary to stimulant use is not unexpected, a problem that is surprising is the fact that sedative hypnotics may produce insomnia and daytime sleepiness. Hypnotics do not act by restoring normal sleep patterns. In general, hypnotics will suppress REM sleep, deep sleep, and wakefulness. (See Kay et al., 1976, for a review.) As use of a hypnotic continues, tolerance develops, and a higher dose is required for the same effect. Also, because most hypnotics have a relatively long half-life (Breimer, 1979; Mendelson, 1980), the intended beneficial effect of producing sleepiness becomes the unwanted side effect when

these patients need to remain awake for school. Though fortunately most children are not given hypnotics, they may be given hypnoticlike drugs in another context, for example, that of the epileptic child. Lairy and associates (Lairy et al., 1980) report on five children from 2.5 to 10.5 years old who were referred to them for behavioral or school problems and were on barbiturates for epilepsy. Typical complaints were school retardation, passivity, sleep disturbances, sleep attacks during the day, and frequent awakenings at night. Careful withdrawal produced a consistent increase of deep sleep (stages 3 and 4), and improvement or elimination of the sleep disturbances along with improvement of the behavioral problems.

The above study is cited to illustrate that hypnoticlike drugs used in any context may produce a significant sleep and behavioral disturbance. There are few, if any, indications for hypnotic administration in children and infants. When hypnotics are prescribed for a sleep disturbance, they should be used for only a few days at a time rather than for weeks. In addition to the hypnotic drugs, several other medications may result in disturbed sleep. The sympathomimetic amines used for allergic disorders and Theophylline and its derivatives used as an antiasthmatic agent may disturb sleep because of their stimulant properties.

Childhood Onset DIMS

Though this is a term used to describe certain types of adult insomnia patients, it also implies that a particular type of insomnia occurs in children, perhaps as a result of a dysfunction of the CNS sleep system (ASDC, 1979; Hauri, 1977). Adults with childhood onset insomnia seem to have their sleep less affected by emotional fluctuations than other insomniacs and are more likely to show "soft" neurological signs (Hauri & Olmstead, 1980). At the present time, the number of possible causes for an improperly functioning sleep system is unknown; but in addition to neurological problems, food allergies may also be a factor (Salzmann, 1976).

Sleep Hygiene Problems

Important and subtle factors that may improve or disturb sleep are grouped under the heading of sleep hygiene (Hauri, 1977; Kleitman, 1963). These are usually behaviors or routines that may disturb sleep but often go unrecognized. Many children with sleep disturbances have poor sleep hygiene. Whether these factors are the major cause of the disturbance or not, the correction at best may cure the problem and at worst may greatly increase the rate at which proper sleep is restored in conjunction with other treatments.

Prebed Routine

In addition to the predictable physiological patterns of development, certain presleep behavioral patterns develop in most children (Anders & Weinstein, 1972; Nagera, 1966). These patterns are usually developed and refined from the ages of 2–5 and consist of ritualistic behaviors (e.g., saying prayers, being read stories, putting toy animals to bed) that serve the purpose of avoiding sleep-related anxiety and calming the child from his or her active state. A certain amount of anxiety associated with sleep at this age is not unusual since the child may equate going to sleep with leaving his or her parents and a relatively predictable environment to contend with the possibly strange places and frightening characters of dreams. These anxieties, if not dealt with effectively, may lead to a true sleep problem.

Bedtime Demands

The demands being placed on the child at bedtime may be unrealistic and contribute to a problem. We often see adults in the sleep laboratory who, despite numerous sensors and a strange environment, fall asleep more easily than they typically do at home. One explanation for this is that at home they "try hard" to go to sleep, generally unsuccessfully. Once in the laboratory, they are pleased to be able to demonstrate to others what they suffer through each night and thus do not try to go to sleep. However, lying quietly with eyes closed in a darkened, sound-attenuated room is more compatible with sleep than the arousal produced by "trying hard" at home. We expect the same situation occurs in some children. The child is told all during his or her prebed routine, "It's time to go to sleep." The lights are turned off with instructions to "go to sleep." Unfortunately, the harder an obedient child tries, the less likely he or she will be successful, and the more likely he or she will associate the bed and bedroom with failure and anxiety.

Bed Schedule

Regular bed and arising times prevent schedule disorders by resulting in well-entrained circadian rhythms. Therefore, sleep latency tends to be shorter and wakenings fewer.

Meals

A light snack will improve sleep while a heavy meal will tend to disturb sleep. Milk and cereals are typically good foods to use, while caffeinated beverages, chocolate (with its caffeinelike properties), and perhaps foods with many additives are best avoided.

Naps

As a child's total daily sleep requirements decrease from over 15 hours in the infant to less than 10 in the adolescent, insistence on the daytime nap, particularly if late, will produce delayed and perhaps disturbed sleep. Data from 6-month- to 5-year-old Swiss children show that a negative correlation exists between the length of day sleep and night sleep (Basler, Largo, & Molinari, 1980). Typically, the three-nap 3-month-old becomes a one-nap 1-year old, then a no-nap 3-year-old, though the child may still lie down without actually going to sleep (Ilg & Ames, 1955).

Environment

Environmental disturbances may be present for the child but not the parents, in part depending on the location of the bedroom. Traffic noise, lights, pets, the television, room temperature, and the bed may be sleep-disturbing factors overlooked.

Exercise

Regular exercise probably benefits sleep. However, a calm down transition period between hard play and bed is important.

EVALUATION OF SLEEP DISORDERS

Many clinicians dislike being confronted with a complaint of a sleep disturbance due to the frustration that results from a lack of information on both sleep and evaluation techniques that would allow a systematic approach to the problem. The following information should help in the initial approach to a sleep complaint.

Description of the Problem

Though a thorough description of the problem seems obvious, it is seldom obtained. If possible, both the parents and the child should be interviewed separately. Besides the standard, worthwhile information obtained when different people describe the supposedly same event, sleep problems add another dimension. Many times the child is not aware of the occurrence of the events (e.g., sleepwalking). However, the child may be aware of the aftermath of some events, particularly some of the more embarrassing ones that were hidden from (or not reported to) the parents (e.g., the bedwetters who change their own bed).

In addition to interviewing parents and child separately, essential elements for a complete description of the problem are described below.

The First Occurrence

The initial date of occurrence is valuable in helping to separate developmental from pathological problems, as well as helping to discern any associated events. What was happening in the child's environment? Had there been changes in the bedroom, family members, or daytime activities? Had any stressful events occurred such as loss of friends, divorce, or a death in the family? Had the child been healthy? Had he or she been on, or recently removed from, any medications? Often we will see sleep problems that were started by a particular event that has long vanished, but the sleep problem remains. However, knowing the precipitating event makes finding the source presently feeding the sleep disturbance easier.

The Frequency of Occurrence

What is the frequency of occurrence? Is the problem occurring with increasing frequency? If nightly, how many times per night?

The Time of Occurrence

If the problem is reported to occur only in the first part of the night, is that because the parents are only awake then to notice it? If the problem is one of inability to sleep, is it more likely to be a problem initiating sleep, maintaining sleep, or waking up too early in the morning?

Description of the Behavior

What does the child do while awake during the night? In parasomniacs, are the movements repetitive? Are they purposeful? Has the child ever been injured? Can he or she remember any of the events or thought content at the time of occurrence?

The Other Sleep Parameters

Is the present problem an isolated sleep event, or are there other sleep problems? Did the child settle normally? Is his or her total bedtime within the normal range for his or her age? How easily awakened is the child in the morning? From a nap?

Assessment of Sleep Hygiene

Assessment of sleep hygiene is discussed in the previous section.

Medical History

Sleep complaints, like waking complaints, are often not confined to either the physical or psychological domains but typically are the result of an interaction of the two. In order to be effective, the evaluation must be multidimensional. A particularly important part of the evaluation is a careful history of medication use.

Child's Daytime Performance

Has there been a change in the child's attention span, fussiness, school performance, etc.? Significant daytime psychopathology does not rule out the possibility that the performance change, the psychopathology, and the sleep disturbance are all precipitated by a sleep disturbance such as sleep apnea.

Family Sleep History

Did the parents have a similar sleep problem? If so, was its course similar to that of their child's? How was it treated? How did the parents react to their own sleep problem? It may be the case that the parents' own experience is not helpful in dealing with the child's problem. For example, with an enuretic, the parent may want the child to excel when he failed. Or the parent may believe (incorrectly) that his or her problem was due to laziness and project the same cause onto the child's enuresis.

Reaction of Family to Sleep Problems

How anxious is the family concerning the problem? Has the child's problem significantly increased the amount of attention he or she is getting? Does the child's anxiety over the problem match that of his or her parents? What was the actual event that caused the parents to seek help?

Referral to a Sleep Disorder Center

Every time the clinician is faced with a sleep problem, it should not be necessary to do an overnight evaluation. However, when in doubt, it is much more economical to refer the child to a Sleep Disorders Center for evaluation first in order to treat the child correctly than not to evaluate and mistreat. Generally,

(1) when narcolepsy or sleep apnea is suspected; or (2) with any problem affecting sleep sufficiently to impair daytime performance; or (3) when the problem is longstanding (more than a month) and severe enough for the child to have an unsuccessful treatment history, consultation with a Sleep Disorders Center is warranted. Though a variety of laboratories perform "sleep studies," only a relatively small number have been judged to have properly trained technical and professional personnel and the equipment necessary to perform adequate evaluations. A list of the presently accredited centers may be obtained by writing to the: Sleep Disorders Program, Stanford University Medical Center, Stanford, California, 94305.

CONCLUSION

Most complaints of sleep problems are not occult and have causative factors that can be discovered when one uses current knowledge and evaluation techniques appropriately. Undoubtedly the key to successful treatment is in an accurate evaluation. Because a combination of factors may contribute to a sleep disorder, the evaluation needs to be comprehensive and the treatment often eclectic, keeping in mind, however, that some childhood sleep disorders are best treated by time and reassurance. However, the fact that significant medical problems may be reflected in or caused by certain sleep disturbances has contributed to the current interest in and concern over sleep disorders. The seriousness of problems such as sleep apnea and possible risk of SIDS has also increased the burden of the clinician, particularly in terms of the need for an accurate diagnosis. The option of waiting to see whether it will go away may no longer be available.

REFERENCES

Albert, I.B. REM sleep deprivation. *Biological Psychiatry,* 1975, **10**, 341–351.

Anders, T. Night waking in infants during the first year of life. *Pediatrics,* 1979, **63,** 860–864.

Anders, T.F., Carskadon, M.A., & Dement, W.C. Sleep and sleepiness in children and adolescents. *Pediatric Clinics of North America,* 1980, **27,** 29–42.

Anders, T., Emde, R., & Parmelee, A., Jr., (Eds.). *A manual of standardized terminology, techniques and criteria for scoring states of sleep and wakefulness in newborn infants.* Los Angeles, UCLA Brain Information Service, NINDS, Neurological Information Network, 1971.

Anders, T., & Weinstein, P. Sleep and its disorders in infants and children: A review. *Pediatrics,* 1972, **50,** 312–324.

Aserinksy, E., & Kleitman, N. Regularly occurring periods of eye motility, and concomitant phenomena during sleep. *Science,* 1953, **118,** 273–274.

Aserinksy, E., & Kleitman, N. A motility cycle in sleeping infants as manifested by ocular and gross bodily activity. *Journal of Applied Physiology,* 1955, **8,** 11–18.

Association of Sleep Disorders Centers. *Diagnostic classification of sleep and arousal disorders* (1st ed.). Prepared by the Sleep Disorders Classification Committee, H.P. Roffwarg, Chairman, *Sleep,* 1979, **2,** 1–37.

Baldy-Moulinier, M., Levy, M., & Passouant, P. A study of jactatio capitis during night sleep. *Electroencephalography and Clinical Neurophysiology,* 1970, **23,** 87.

Basler, K., Largo, R.H., & Molinari, L. Die Entwicklung des Schlafverhaltens in den ersten funf Lebensjarhren. *Helvetica Paediatrica Acta,* 1980, **35,** 211–223.

Beutler, L., Thronby, J., & Karacan, I. Psychological variables in the diagnosis of insomnia. In R.L. Williams & I. Karacan (Eds.), *Sleep disorders: Diagnosis and treatment.* New York: Wiley, 1978, pp. 61–100.

Bixler, E.O., Kales, A., & Soldatos, C.R. Sleep disorders encountered in medical practice: A national survey of physicians. *Behavioral Medicine,* November 1979, 13–21.

Bootzin, R.R., & Nicassio, P.M. Behavioral treatments for insomnia. In M. Hersen, R. Eisler, & P. Miller (Eds.), *Progress in behavior modification.* New York: Academic Press, 1978, **6,** 1–45.

Borkovec, T.D., & Weerts, T.C. Effects of progres-

sive relaxation on sleep disturbance: An electroencephalographic evaluation. *Psychosomatic Medicine,* 1976, **38,** 173–180.

Brady, J., Chir, B., Ariagno, R., Watts, J., Goldman, S., & Dumpit, F. Apnea, hypoxemia, and aborted sudden infant death syndrome. *Pediatrics,* 1978, **62,** 686–691.

Breimer, D.D. Pharmacokinetics and metabolism of various benzodiazepines used as hypnotics. *British Journal of Clinical Pharmacology,* 1979, **8,** 7S–13S.

Brooks, J., Schlueter, M., Navelet, Y., & Tooley, W. Sleep state and arterial blood gases and pH, in human newborn and young infants. *Journal of Perinatal Medicine,* 1978, **6,** 280–286.

Broughton, R. Sleep disorders: Disorders of arousal. *Science,* 1968, **159,** 1070–1078.

Broughton, R., & Gaustaut, H. Recent sleep research on enuresis nocturna, sleep walking, sleep terrors and confusional arousals. In P. Levin & W. Loella, (Eds.), *Sleep 1974.* Basel: Kargen, 1975, 82–91.

Carskadon, M.A., Harvey, K., Dement, W.C., Guilleminault, C., Simmons, F.B., & Anders, T. Respiration during sleep in children. *Western Journal of Medicine,* 1978, **128,** 477–481.

Carskadon, M.A., Harvey, K., Duke, P., Anders, T.F., Litt, I.F., & Dement, W.C. Pubertal changes in daytime sleepiness. *Sleep,* 1980, **2,** 453–460.

Chipps, B., Max, H., Schuberth, K., Talamo, J., Menkes, H., & Scherr, M. Nocturnal oxygen saturation in normal and asthmatic children. *Pediatrics,* 1980, **65,** 1157–1159.

Clark, G. T., Rugh, J.D., & Handelman, S.L. Nocturnal masseter muscle activity and urinary catecholamine levels in bruxers. *Journal of Dental Research,* 1980, **59,** 1571–1576.

Crosby, N. Essential enuresis: Successful treatment based on physiological concepts. *Medical Journal of Australia,* 1950, **2,** 533–543.

Curzi-Dascalova, L., & Dreyfus-Brisac, C. Distribution of skin potential responses according to state of sleep during the first month of life in human babies. *Electroencephalography and Clinical Neurophysiology,* 1976, **41,** 399–407.

Czeisler, C.A., Richardson, G.S., Coleman, R.M., Zimmerman, J.C., Moore-Ede, M.C., Dement, W.C., & Weitzman, E.D. Chronotherapy: Resetting the circadian clocks of patients with delayed sleep phase insomnia. *Sleep,* 1981, **4,** 1–21.

Czeisler, C.A. Weitzman, E.D., Moore-EDE, M.C., Zimmerman, J.C., & Knauer, R.S. Human sleep: Its duration and organization dependent on its circadian phase. *Science,* 1980, **210,** 1264–1267.

Dement, W.C. The biological role of REM sleep (circa 1968). In A. Kales (Ed.), *Sleep: Physiology and pathology.* Philadelphia: Lippincott, 1969.

Dement, W.C., Carskadon, M., & Ley, R. The prevalence of narcolepsy. II. *Sleep Research,* 1973, **2,** 147.

Dervent, A., Karacan, I., Ware, J.C., & Williams, R.L. Somnambulism: A case report. *Sleep Research,* 1978, **7,** 220.

Detre, T. Himmelhoch, J., Swartzburg, M., Anderson, C.M., Byck, R., & Kupfer, D.J. Hypersomnia and manic-depressive disease. *American Journal of Psychiatry,* 1972, **128,** 1303–1305.

Diaz-Guerrero, R.J., Gottlieb, J.S., & Knott, J.R. The sleep of patients with manic-depressive psychosis, depressive type: An electroencephalographic study. *Psychosomatic Medicine,* 1946, **8,** 399–404.

Edvardson, P. Neurophysiological aspects of enuresis. *Acta Neurologica Scandinavica,* 1972, **48,** 222–230.

Eliaschar, I., Lavie, P., Halperin, E., Gordon, C., & Alroy, G. Sleep apneic episodes as indications for adenotonsillectomy. *Archives of Otolaryngology,* 1980, **106,** 492–496.

Evans, J. Rocking at night. *Journal of Child Psychology,* 1961, **2,** 71–85.

Ferber, R., Boyle M.P., & Belfer, M. Initial experience of a pediatric sleep disorders clinic. Paper presented at the 21st Annual Meeting of the Association for the Psychophysiological Study of Sleep. Hyannis, Massachusetts, June 1981.

Finley, W.W. An EEG study of the sleep of enuretics at three age levels. *Clinical Electroencephalography,* 1971, **2,** 35–39.

Finley, W.W., Besserman, R.L., Bennett, L.F., Clapp, R.K., & Finley, P.M. The effect of continuous, intermittent, and "placebo" reinforcement on the effectiveness of conditioning treatment for enuresis nocturna. *Behavior Research and Therapy,* 1973, **11,** 289–297.

Fisher, C., Kahn, E., Edwards, A. & Davis, N. A psychophysiological study of nightmares and night terrors: The suppression of stage 4 night terrors with diazepam. *Archives of General Psychiatry,* 1973, **28,** 252–259.

Folgering, H., Kuyper, F., & Kille, J. Primary alveolar hypoventilation (Ondine's curse syndrome) in an infant without external arcuate nucleus. Case report. *Bulletin European Physiopathology Respiratory,* 1979, **15,** 659–665.

Foutz, A.S., Mitler, M.M., Cavalli-Sforza, L.L., & Dement, W.C. Genetic factors in canine narcolepsy. *Sleep,* 1979, **1,** 413–422.

Frary, L. G. Enuresis: A genetic study. *American Journal of Diseases of Children,* 1935, **49,** 557–578.

Freedman, R., & Papsdorf, J. Biofeedback and progressive relaxation treatment of insomnia: A controlled, all-night investigation. *Biofeedback and Self-Regulation,* 1976, **1,** 253–271.

Gastaut, H., & Broughton, R. A clinical and polygraphic study of episodic phenomena during sleep. *Recent Advances in Biological Psychiatry,* 1964, **7,** 197–221.

Gresham, S.C., Agnew, H.W., Jr., & Williams, R.L. The sleep of depressed patients: An EEG and eye movement study. *Archives of General Psychiatry,* 1965, **13,** 503–507.

Guilleminault, C. Sleep and respiration in infants. In L. Popoviciu, B. Asgian, & G. Badiu (Eds.), *Sleep 1978.* Basel: Karger, 1980, pp. 133–137.

Guilleminault, C., & Anders, T. Sleep disorders in children, Part II. *Advances in Pediatrics,* 1976, **22,** 151–174.

Guilleminault, C., Ariagno, R., Korobkin, R., Nagel, L., Baldwin, R., Coons, S., & Owen, M. Mixed and obstructive sleep apnea and near miss for sudden infant death syndrome: 2. Comparison of near miss and normal control infants by age. *Pediatrics,* 1979, **64,** 882–891.

Guilleminault, C., Peraita, R., Souquet, M., & Dement, W.C. Apneas during sleep in infants: Possible relationship with sudden infant death syndrome. *Science,* 1975, **190,** 677–679.

Hachinski, V., Mamelak, M., & Norris, J.W. Sleep morphology and prognosis in acute cerebrovascular lesions. In J.S. Meyer, H. Lechner, & M. Reivich (Eds.), *Cerebral vascular disease: Proceedings of the Eighth International Salzburg Conference,* Amsterdam, Excerpta Medica, 1977, pp. 69–71.

Hallgren, B. Enuresis: A clinical and genetic study. *Neurologica Scandinavica and Acta Psychiatrica Neurologica*, 1957, 1–159.

Harper, R.M., Leake, B., Hodgman, J., Hoppenbrouwers, T., & Sterman, M. Developmental patterns of heart rate variability in normal infants and infants at risk for the sudden infant death syndrome. *Pediatrics*, in press.

Hauri, P. *The sleep disorders*. Kalamazoo: UpJohn, 1977.

Hauri, P. Biofeedback techniques in the treatment of insomnia. In R.L. Williams & I. Karacan (Eds.), *Sleep disorders: Diagnosis and treatment*. New York: Wiley, 1978, pp. 145–159.

Hauri, P., & Olmstead, E. Childhood-onset insomnia. *Sleep*, 1980, **3**, 59–65.

Henderson-Smart, D., & Read, D. Depression of intercostal and abdominal muscle activity and vulnerability to asphyxia during active sleep in the newborn. In C. Guilleminault & W. Dement (Eds.), *Sleep apnea syndromes*. New York: Liss, Inc., 1978, pp. 93–118.

Honda, Y. Census of narcolepsy, cataplexy and sleep life among teenagers in Fujisawa City. *Sleep Research*, 1979, **8**, 191.

Hoppenbrouwers, T., Harper, R.M., Hodgman, J.E., Sterman, M.B., & McGinty, D.J. Polygraphic studies of normal infants during the first six months of life. II. Respiratory rate and variability as a function of state. *Pediatric Research*, 1978, **12**, 120–125.

Hoppenbrouwers, T., Hodgman, J.E., Harper, R.M., Hofman, E., Sterman, M.B., & McGinty, D.J. Polygraphic studies of normal infants during the first six months of life. III. Incidence of apnea and periodic breathing. *Pediatrics*, 1977, **60**, 418–425.

Hoppenbrouwers, T., Hodgman, J.E., McGinty, D., Harper, R., & Sterman, M. Sudden infant death syndrome: Sleep apnea and respiration in subsequent siblings. *Pediatrics*, 1980, **66**, 205–213.

Hunt, C., Madalon, S., Thompson, T., DeMuth, S., Loew, J., Liu, H., Mastri, A., & Burke, B. Central hypoventilation syndrome: Experience with bilateral phrenic nerve pacing in 3 neonates. *American Review of Respiratory Diseases*, 1978, **118**, 23–28.

Ilg, F.L., & Ames, L.B. Child behavior. New York: Harper, 1955.

Johnson, L.C., & Lubin, A. Spontaneous electrodermal activity during waking and sleeping. *Psychophysiology*, 1966, **3**, 8–17.

Kales, A. Hypnotic drug abuse: Clinical and experimental aspects. *Medical Counterpoint*, 1971, **3**, 13–23.

Kales, A., Jacobson, A., Kun, T., Klein, J., Heuser, G., & Paulson, M. Somnambulism: Further all-night EEG studies. *Electroencephalography and Clinical Neurophysiology*, 1966, **21**, 410. (a)

Kales, A., Jacobson, A., Paulson, M., Kales, J., & Walter, R. Somnambulism: Psychophysiological correlates. I. *Archives of General Psychiatry*, 1966, **14**, 586–594. (b)

Kales, A., Kales, J., Jacobson, A., Humphrey, F.J., & Soldatos, G.R. Effects of imipramine on enuretic frequency and sleep stages. *Pediatrics*, 1977, **60**, 431–436.

Kales, A., Soldatos, C., Bixler, E., Ladda, R., Charney, D., Weber, G., & Schweitzer, P. Hereditary factors in sleepwalking and night terrors. *British Journal of Psychiatry*, 1980, **137**, 111–118.

Kales, J.D., Kales, A., Soldatos, C.R., Chamberlin, K., & Martin, E.D. Sleepwalking and night terrors related to febrile illness. *American Journal of Psychiatry*, 1979, **136**, 1214–1215.

Kales, A., Soldatos, C., Caldwell, A., Kales, J., Humphrey II, F., Charney, D., & Schweitzer, P. Somnambulism. *Archives of General Psychiatry*, 1980, **37**, 1406–1410.

Karacan, I., Salis, P., Thornby, J., & Williams, R.L. The ontogeny of nocturnal penile tumescence. *Waking and Sleeping*, 1976, **1**, 27–44.

Katona, P., & Egbert, J. Heart rate and respiratory rate differences beween preterm and full-term infants during quiet sleep: Possible implications for sudden infant death syndrome. *Pediatrics*, 1978, **62**, 91–95.

Kay, D.C., Blackburn, A.B., Buckingham, J.A., & Karacan, I. Human pharmacology of sleep. In R.L. Williams & I. Karacan (Eds.), *Pharmacology of sleep*. New York: Wiley, 1976, pp. 82–210.

Kessler, S. Genetic factors in narcolepsy. In C. Guilleminault, W. Dement, & P. Passouant (Eds.), *Narcolepsy*. New York: Spectrum, 1976, pp. 285–302.

Kleitman, N. *Sleep and wakefulness*. Chicago: University of Chicago Press, 1963.

Kleitman, N., & Englemann, T.G. Sleep characteristics of infants. *Journal of Applied Physiology*, 1953, **6**, 269–282.

Knill, R., Andrews, W., Bryan, A., & Bryan, H. Respiratory load compensation in infants. *Journal of Applied Physiology*, 1976, **40**, 357–361.

Korobkin, R., & Guilleminault, C. Neurological abnormalities in near miss for sudden infant death syndrome infants. *Pediatrics*, 1979, **64**, 369–374.

Kupfer, D.J. REM latency: A psychobiologic marker for primary depressive disease. *Biological Psychiatry*, 1976, **11**, 159–174.

Kupfer, D.J., & Foster, G.F. Interval between onset of sleep and rapid-eye-movement sleep as an indication of depression. *Lancet*, 1972, **2**, 684–686.

Kupfer, D.J., & Foster, F.G. EEG sleep and depression. In R.L. Williams & I. Karacan (Eds.) *Sleep disorders: Diagnosis and treatment*. New York: Wiley, 1978, pp. 163–204.

Kupfer, D.J., Himmelhoch, G.R., Swarzburg, M., Anderson, C.M., Byck, R., & Detre, T.P. Hypersomnia in manic-depressive disease (a preliminary report). *Diseases of the Nervous System*, 1972, **33**, 720–724.

Lairy, C.G., Catani, P., Findjii, F., & Laird, C. Contribution of sleep recordings to the control of anticonvulsant withdrawal. In L. Popoviciu, B. Asyian, & G. Badiu (Eds.), *Sleep 1978*. Basel: Karger, 1980, pp. 87–103.

Langou, R., Cohen, L, Sheps, D., Wolfson, S., & Glenn, W. Ondine's curse: Hemodynamic response to diaphragm pacing electrophrenic respiration. *American Heart Journal*, 1978, **95**, 295–300.

Lenard, H.G. The development of sleep spindles in the EEG during the first two years of life. *Neuropaediatrie*, 1970, **1**, 264–276.

Lipsitt, L. Infants at risk: Perinatal and neonatal factors. *International Journal of Behavioral Development*, 1979, **2**, 23–42.

Loomis, A.L., Harvey, E.N., & Hobart, G. Further observations on the potential rhythms of the cerebral cortex during sleep. *Science*, 1935, **82**, 198–200.

Lovibond, S. *Conditioning and enuresis*. New York: Macmillan, 1964.

MacLean, R. Imipramine hydrochloride and enuresis. *American Journal of Psychiatry*, 1960, **117**, 551.

Manget, D., Orr, W.C., & Smith, R.O. Sleep apnea, hypersomnolence and upper airway obstruction secondary to adenotonsillar enlargement. *Archives of Otolaryngology*, 1977, **103**, 383–386.

Martin, C. *A new approach to nocturnal enuresis.* London: Lewis, 1966.

Mellins, R., Balfour, H., Turinao, G., & Winters, R. Failure of automatic control of ventilation (Ondine's curse). *Medicine*, 1970, **49**, 487–504.

Mendelson, W.B. *The use and misuse of sleeping pills.* New York: Plenum, 1980.

Metcalf, D.R. EEG sleep spindle ontogenesis. *Neuropaediatrie*, 1970, **1**, 428–433.

Meyer, J.S., Sakai, F., & Naritomi, H. Regional cerebral blood flow in man during different stages of wakefulness and sleep. In B.B. Mrsulja et al. (Eds.), *Pathophysiology of cerebral energy metabolism*. New York: Plenum, 1979, pp. 433–440.

Mikkelsen, E.J., & Rapoport, T.L. Enuresis: Psychopathology, sleep stage, and drug response. *Urologic Clinics of North America*, 1980, **7**, 361–377.

Monroe, L.J. Psychological and physiological differences beween good and poor sleepers. *Journal of Abnormal Psychology*, 1967, **72**, 255–264.

Moore, M. Recurrent nightmares: A simple procedure for psychotherapy. *Military Surgeon*, 1945, **97**, 281–285.

Moore, T., & Ucko, C. Night waking in early infancy: Part I. *Archives of Diseases of Children*, 1957, **33**, 333–342.

Mowrer, O.H., & Mowrer, W.M. Enuresis—A method for its study and treatment. *American Journal of Orthopsychiatry*, 1938, **8**, 436–459.

Muller, N., Francis, P., Gurwitz, D., Levison, H., & Bryan, C. Mechanism of hemoglobin desaturation during rapid-eye-movement sleep in normal subjects and in patients with cystic fibrosis. *American Review of Respiratory Diseases*, 1980, **121**, 463–469.

Nagera, H. Sleep and its disturbances approached developmentally. *Psychoanalytic Study of the Child*, 196, **21**, 393–447.

Naeye, R. Pulmonary arterial abnormalities in the sudden infant death syndrome. *New England Journal of Medicine*, 1973, **289**, 1167–1170.

Naeye, R. Hypoxemia and the sudden infant death syndrome. *Science*, 1974, **186**, 837–838.

Orr, W.C., Imes, N.K., & Martin, R.J. Hypersomnolent and nonhypersomnolent patients with upper airway obstruction during sleep. *Chest*, 1979, **75**, 418–422.

Oswald, I. Experimental studies of rhythm, anxiety and cerebral vigilance. *Journal of Mental Sciences*, 1959, **105**, 269–294.

Parker, D.C., Rossman, L.G., & Vanderlaan, E. F. Relation of sleep-enhanced human prolactin release to REM-nonREM cycles. *Journal of Clinical Endocrinological Metabolism*, 1974, **38**, 646–651.

Parmelee, A.H., Schulz, H.R., & Disbrow, M.A. Sleep patterns of newborn. *Journal of Pediatrics*, 1961, **58**, 241–250.

Price, V., Coates, T., Thoresen, C., & Grinstead, O.A. Prevalence and correlates of poor sleep among adolescents. *American Journal of Diseases of Children*, 1978, **132**, 583–586.

Rechtschaffen, A., Hauri, P., & Zeitlin, M. Auditory awakening thresholds in REM and NREM sleep stages. *Perceptual and Motor Skills*, 1966, **22**, 927–942.

Reding, G.R., Rubright, L., & Zimmerman, W.C. Incidence of bruxism. *Journal of Dental Research*, 1966, **45**, 1198–1204.

Reding, G.R., Zepelin, H., & Monroe, L.J. Personality study of nocturnal teeth grinders. *Perceptual and Motor Skills*, 1968, **26**, 523–532.

Reding, G.R., Zepelin, H., Robinson, J.E., Zimmerman, S.O., & Smith, V.H. Nocturnal teeth grinding: All-night psychophysiologic studies. *Journal of Dental Research*, 1968, **47**, 786–797.

Richardson, G., Carskadon, M., & Flagg, W., van Den Hoed, J., Dement, W.C., Mitler, M.M. Excessive daytime sleepiness in man: Multiple sleep latency measurement in narcoleptic and control subjects. *Electroencephalography and Clinical Neurophysiology*, 1978, **45**, 621–627.

Richardson, M., Seid, A., Cotton, R., Benton, C., & Kramer, M. Evaluation of tonsils and adenoids in sleep apnea syndrome. *The Laryngoscope*, 1980, **90**, 1106–1110.

Ritvo, E., Ornitz, E., LaFranchi, S., & Walter, R. Effects of imipramine on the sleep-dream cycle: An EEG study in boys. *Electroencephalography and Clinical Neurophysiology*, 1967, **22**, 465–468.

Roffwarg, H., Muzio, J., & Dement, W. Ontogenetic development of the human sleep-dream cycle. *Science*, 1966, **152**, 604.

Roth, B., & Bruhova, S. Dreams in narcolepsy, hypersomnia and dissociated sleep disorders. *Experimental Medicine and Surgery*, 1969, **27**, 187–209.

Rugh, J.D., & Solberg, W.K. Electromyographic studies of bruxist behavior before and during treatment. *Journal of the California Dental Association*, 1975, **43**, 56–59.

Rutter, M., Yule, W., & Graham, P. Enuresis and behavioral deviance: Some epidemiological considerations. In I. Kolvin, R. MacKeith, & R. Meadows (Eds.), *Bladder control and enuresis*. Philadelphia: Lippincott, 1973, pp. 137–147.

Salmon, M.A. An historical account of nocturnal enuresis and its treatment. *Proceedings of the Royal Society of Medicine*, 1975, **68**, 443–445.

Salzarulo, P., Chevalier, A., Colvez, A., Brunel, M., Sender, C., Kastler, B., & Roc, M. Child sleep problems: Parental attitude and recourse: An approach by survey. *Sleep 1978*. Basel: Karger, 1980, pp. 595–598.

Salzman, L.K. Allergy testing, psychological assessment and dietary treatment of the hyperactive child syndrome. *Medical Journal of Australia*, 1976, **2**, 248–251.

Satoh, T., & Harada, Y. Tooth grinding during sleep and arousal reaction. *Experientia*, 1971, **27**, 785–786.

Shannon, D., Kelly, D., & O'Connell, K. Abnormal regulation of ventilation in infants at risk for sudden infant death syndrome. *New England Journal of Medicine*, 1977, **297**, 747–784.

Starfield, B. Enuresis: Its pathogenesis and management. *Clinical Pediatrics*, 1972, **11**, 343–350.

Stokes, D., McBride, T., Wall, M., Erba, G., & Strieder, D. Sleep hypoxemia in young adults with cystic fibrosis. *American Journal of Diseases of Childhood*, 1980, **134**, 741–743.

Takahashi, Y., Kipnis, D.M., & Daughaday, W.H. Growth hormone secretion during sleep. *Journal of Clinical Investigations*, 1968, **47**, 2079–2090.

Tapia, F., Jekel, J., & Domke, H. Enuresis: An emotional symptom? *Journal of Nervous and Mental Diseases*, 1960, **130**, 61–66.

Thoman, E., Miano, V., & Freese, M. The role of respiratory instability in the sudden infant death syndrome. *Developmental Medical Child Neurology*, 1977, **19**, 729–738.

Tonkin, S. Sudden infant death syndrome: Hypothesis of causation. *Pediatrics*, 1975, **55**, 650–661.

Valdes-Depena, M.A. Sudden unexplained infant death, 1970 through 1975: An evolution in understanding. 1978, Washington: DHEW Publication No. 78-5255.

Vogel, G.W. Review of REM sleep deprivation. *Archives of General Psychiatry,* 1972, **26,** 449–455.

Vogel, G.W., Thurmond, A., Gibbons, P., Sloan, K., Boyd, M., & Walker, M. REM sleep reduction effects on depression syndromes. *Archives of General Psychiatry,* 1975, **32,** 765–777.

Ware, J.C. The symptom of insomnia: Causes and cures. *Psychiatric Annals,* 1979, **9,** 27–49.

Ware, J.C., Karacan, I., Salis, P., Hirshkowitz, M., & Thornby, J.I. Patterning of electrodermal activity during sleep: Relation to impotence. *Sleep Research,* 1980, **1,** 296.

Weinmann, H.M. Telemetric recordings of sleep rhythms in enuretic children. *Electroencephalography and Clinical Neurophysiology,* 1968, **24,** 391.

Weitzman, E.D., Czeisler, C.A., Coleman, C., Dement, W., & Richardson, G. Delayed sleep phase syndrome: A biological rhythm disorder. *Sleep Research,* 1979, **8,** 221.

Werry, J.S., & Cohrssen, J. Enuresis—An etiologic and therapeutic study. *Journal of Pediatrics,* 1965, **67,** 423–431.

Williams, R.L., Karacan, I., & Hursch, C.J. *EEG of human sleep: Clinical applications.* Wiley, 1974.

Williams, R.L., & Karacan, I. Sleep disorders and disordered sleep. In S. Arieti (Ed.), *American handbook of psychiatry* (Vol. 4). New York: Basic Books, 1975, pp. 854–904.

Wynne, J., Block, A., Hemenway, J., Hunt, L., & Flick, M. Disordered breathing and oxygen desaturation during sleep in patients with chronic obstructive lung disease (COLD). *The American Journal of Medicine,* 1979, **66,** 573–579.

Yoss, R., & Daly, D. Criteria for the diagnosis of the narcoleptic syndrome. *Proceedings of the Staff Meetings of the Mayo Clinic,* 1957, **32,** 320–328.

CHAPTER 16

Tics, Habits, and Mannerisms

LEE H. MATTHEWS, J. MICHAEL LEIBOWITZ, AND JANET R. MATTHEWS

The turn of this century marked the beginning of interest in childhood behavior disorders. Prior to that time, little account was made of the special characteristics of psychopathology in children, especially those that occurred during various developmental periods and that were not present by the time the individual reached adulthood. This chapter will focus on tics (stereotyped movement disorders), habits, and mannerisms commonly seen during a child's developing years. However, this chapter will not include topics such as sleep disorders, toileting problems, or eating problems, all of which are covered elsewhere in this book. Specific habits and mannerisms that apply to special subgroups, such as in childhood neurosis, childhood psychosis, or those seen to a greater extent in individuals with mental retardation, also will not be covered in detail in this section (but they will be covered when necessary). Additional information will be found in the appropriate chapters dealing with these conditions.

The format that is used throughout this chapter consists of a brief definition of the disorder, incidence rates, and specific diagnostic criteria used in its differential diagnosis. Following this material, information regarding etiology, including behavioral formulations; traditional psychoanalytic and psychodynamic theory; and organic, environmental, genetic or familial hypotheses, is presented. Each section includes treatment recommendations based on behavioral, traditional psychotherapeutic, and organic (or pharmacologic) treatments, depending on the specific disorder.

Because of the difference in length of time in which the two major theoretical approaches have investigated these habits, the majority of the articles and books are within a psychodynamic framework. However, most of these reports are case studies with little or no experimental control. In contrast, the behavioral literature, while not as extensive, has better methodological controls and provides evidence of rapid, reliable treatment effects.

STEREOTYPED MOVEMENT DISORDERS

Disorders covered within this section relate to the Diagnostic and Statistical Manual of Mental Disorders 1980 classification of "Stereotyped Movement Disorders." The major defining characteristic is abnormality in the child's gross motor movement. All disorders within this DSM-III classification include tics. Specific subclassifications include transient tic disorder, chronic motor tic disorder, Tourette's disorder, atypical tic disorder, and atypical stereotyped movement disorder. Conclusive evidence is lacking whether these classifications represent distinct problems or a continuum of severity of the same problem.

A tic is defined as any rapid, involuntary movement of a functionally related group of skeletal muscles or the involuntary production of noises or words. These are considered different from those movement problems that

Supported in part by Project 405, awarded to C. Louis Meyer Children's Rehabilitation Institute, by the Bureau of Maternal and Child Health Services, Department of Health and Human Services.

are associated with excessive muscle tension, as well as those problems that affect only part of a particular muscle group. Although the most obvious facet of the stereotyped movement disorder is the observable external movement, consideration also must be given to the emotional reactions that are frequently associated with this behavior. Tics are likely to contribute to feelings such as shame and self-consciousness on the part of the child. Depending on the severity of the tic, the child may be excluded from certain social activities and thus lag behind the peer group in social experiences and development.

The "atypical tic disorder" is reserved for those tics that are considered to fall within the diagnostic category "tic" but do not meet any of the more common classifications of these problems.

The "atypical stereotyped movement disorder" includes a number of behaviors that are considered voluntary. They are not spasmodic in nature and include head banging, rocking, repetitive hand movements, and repetitive movements of the fingers or arms. While most children who suffer from one of the tic type behaviors tend to be distressed about their problem, that is not true of those with the atypical stereotyped movement disorder. Children in the latter category may seem to be enjoying their idiosyncratic behavior. Although these behaviors are found in adults, the majority of reported cases involve children. Many of those children who exhibit these behaviors have also been found to have some form of developmental disorder or are suffering from a major lack of social stimulation. It is possible, however, to find atypical stereotyped movement disorders in the absence of any other form of mental disorder.

Because the differential diagnosis among the tic disorders (with the exception of Tourette's and atypical stereotyped movement disorder) is based on the duration of symptomatology, they will be described in one section entitled "Tics."

Tics

Sudden, brisk, intermittent, nonpurposeful, (but recurrent) muscle spasms may be considered as tics. With some notable exceptions, tics appear to be functional in origin and tend to increase during stress. Tics never appear to occur in sleep. In some instances, the individual is aware of the mannerism, but in most cases it is automatic and unconscious (Goldenson, 1970). Tics may involve almost any part of the body, especially the head and neck. Common tics include blinking, grimacing, shaking or nodding the head, pouting, grinning, clearing the throat, swallowing, coughing, or shrugging the shoulders. (Barrett, 1962; Coleman, Butcher, & Carson, 1980; Corbett et al., 1969; Rafi, 1962; Walton, 1961).

Incidence

Due to the transitory nature of tics, no accurate incidence rates appear to be available. Azrin and Nunn (1977) indicate 1–5 percent of the population. Tics are most common in the 8–12-year age range (Ilg & Ames, 1955; Holvey & Talbott, 1972) with onset at 5–7 years (Corbett et al., 1969). The male/female ratio is 3:1 and is greatest in children of Jewish and other eastern European ancestry. Retrospective studies (Corbett et al., 1969) suggest a spontaneous recovery rate of at least 50 percent after 2–15 years.

Diagnosis

The child with a "transient tic disorder" has the ability to suppress the tic for as short as a few minutes to as long as a few hours. Variability of symptoms can be expected over time. While the most common form appears to be the eye blink or other facial tic, the entire head or even torso may be involved. Vocal tics may occur. In children with a prior history of tics, stress may precipitate a return to this behavior.

In the "chronic motor tic," usually no more than three muscle groups are involved at any one time. Voluntary suppression of the tic is possible. To be a chronic tic, it must be present for one year. Vocal tics are quite rare, and, if present, are usually a grunt or noise. The category of "atypical tic disorder" is used when tics cannot be adequately classified in either of the above categories or as Tourette's disorder.

Tics must be differentiated from facial

spasms and chorea. Tics are most frequently confused with chorea, although patients with tics usually have a longer asymptomatic period between movements and always perform the movements in the same stereotyped manner (Holvey & Talbott, 1972).

Etiology

There is disagreement as to the causes and conditions associated with ticing behavior. Corbett et al. (1969) state that tics do not appear to result from any specific precipitating factor, but Bakwin and Bakwin (1972) state that in only about one-third of the cases is the precipitating factor unknown.

BEHAVIORAL.   Coleman et al. (1980) have suggested that unwitting reinforcement by increased attention or stress by significant others may serve to maintain the ticing behavior. Other authors (Holvey & Talbott, 1972) suggest that tics begin as purposeful movements in response to definite stimuli, but eventually similar movements are carried out automatically in a purposeless fashion. For example, a neck tic may have its origin in a collar that was too tight or otherwise annoying.

TRADITIONAL.   Psychodynamic theories stress that tics represent repressed feelings or conflicts expressed in a symbolic manner (Cavenar, Spaulding, & Sullivan, 1979). As such, they are often viewed as hysterical reactions in which the tics may represent an attempt to ward off danger—for instance, blinking the eye or repeatedly turning the head—or angry feelings, revealed by tics resembling a hitting motion (Gerard, 1946; Moldofsky, 1971).

Mahler (1949) suggested that tics are of various categories: systematic tics, such as transient tics that indicate tension phenomena; tics as a sign of primarily reactive behavior disorders on the verge of internalization; or the tic as a symptom of psychoneurosis or a psychosis. Mahler said that in some cases the unconscious fantasies producing the tics concern the movement or paralysis. Cavenar et al. (1979) cited unresolved Oedipal conflicts as the etiology of such disorders.

Gerard (1946), in a review, concluded that tics as an ego defense mechanism developed when the ego was confronted with the task of integrating two opposing impulses striving toward opposing goals. The ego then became fixated, and the tic was a partial substitute for the impulse expression.

ORGANIC.   Genetic or other familial factors may play a role in the onset of tics. A family history of tics is found in about 10–30% of all cases (Abe & Oda, 1978; Corbett et al., 1969). Missildine (1964) reported that over 85 percent of his study children were either the only child, the youngest child, or the oldest child currently in the family because of the death, miscarriage, or abortion of an older sibling. He concluded that birth order was a critical factor.

Golden (1977b) discussed the genetic aspects of tics. He noted that soft neurological signs were present in 87 percent of the children and that the children with a family history of simple tics had many affected relatives, all but two on the maternal side of the family, suggestive of an autosomal, dominant, genetic transmission of the tics.

ENVIRONMENTAL.   Tics are sometimes acquired by imitating other tiqueurs. Other factors include: a background of emotional tension (Bakwin & Bakwin, 1972); serious home conflicts (Corbett et al., 1969; Feldman & Werry, 1966; Miller, 1970); and psychiatrically ill parents (Bruch & Thum, 1968).

Treatment

BEHAVIORAL.   A variety of behavioral techniques have been successfully employed in the treatment of nervous tics, including operant conditioning (Barrett, 1962; Schulman, 1974), negative or massed practice (Feldman & Werry, 1966; Rafi, 1962), self-monitoring (Maletzky, 1974; Thomas, Abrams, & Johnson, 1971), and habit reversal (Azrin & Nunn, 1973, 1977; Beck & Fedoravicius, 1977). Self-monitoring procedures have been observed to be tic inhibiting with rates of 50–100 percent reduction and associated with long-lasting remission of symptoms

(Haidar & Clancy, 1973; Ollendick, 1981). Negative practice and reactive inhibition (Rafi, 1962; Walton, 1961) have been used successfully. Feedback has also been used successfully (Bernhardt, Hetsen, & Barlow, 1972). Uchiyama (1976) used reciprocal inhibition techniques through autogenic training, while Schulman (1974) successfully removed multiple tics by reducing parental attention.

Azrin and Nunn (1973) indicated that tics persist because of limited awareness on the part of the patient to the tics, the response chaining of the specific tic, and excessive practice and social tolerance for the tic. Their treatment consisted of having the patient first practice movements that provide muscle opposition to the tic; for example, in a neck tic, the patient practices tensing his or her neck muscles. The patient also self-monitors the behavior. These articles suggest that the longer the follow-up after treatment, the better the recovery rate.

Aversive techniques have included the use of electric shock (Brierly, 1967); avoidance of a loud noise (Rafi, 1962) by a response incompatible with a tic; and response cost (Barrett, 1962). These techniques led to marked reductions or elimination of the tics but should be used only after all other procedures have been attempted.

TRADITIONAL. Tiller (1978) used brief analytic outpatient family therapy. Other therapies include: dream analysis (Voth, 1979), Oedipal conflict resolution (Cavenar et al., 1979), psychoanalysis and play therapy (Gerard, 1946), and hypnosis (Goldenson, 1970). DeAjuriaguerra (1980) says if the tic is hysterical, due to a traumatic experience, hypnosis may eliminate the tics, but they may return or take a different form if the individual remains tense. In contrast, for obsessive patients, tics often are cured spontaneously.

ORGANIC. Blau (1978) and White (1976) reviewed psychotropic drugs in the treatment of tic disorders in children. Tapia (1969) reported a 50–90 percent reduction in the frequency of tics, although the drugs did not eliminate the tics completely. Good treatment results with haloperidol in tiqueurs have been reported by Barker (1975) and Bixby (1970). Other drugs used to decrease tics have included chlorpromazine (Lucas, 1964) and diazepam (Tapia, 1969).

Conclusions

A review of the literature indicates that there are few psychoanalytic studies in which the data were collected in a systematic manner. The recent increase in behavioral articles points to the interest in this area by such practitioners and has also demonstrated more effective and more data-based cure rates, while pharmacologic intervention may facilitate early reduction in rates of ticing.

Tourette's Disorder

Tourette's Disorder falls under the DSM-III classification of "Stereotyped Movement Disorders." Variously called Tourette's Syndrome or Gilles de la Tourette Syndrome, it has been recognized for well over 100 years since Gilles de la Tourette, a pupil of Charcot, first described a chronic tic of the face and body accompanied by speech aberrations in one of his patients. This disorder includes the use of shouted obscenities (copralalia) or other vocal disturbances in about 60 percent of the patients. Early cases were described by Itard (1825), Beard (1880), and several others prior to the turn of the century. Although one of the rarer of the movement disorders, its unusual and oftentimes bizarre presentation has resulted in a considerable interest in its etiology and treatment.

One of the earliest apparent victims of this disorder was Prince de Conde, who served in the seventeenth-century French court of Louis XIV. He was seized by barking attacks at royal receptions and so made it a practice to stand next to a window so he could stuff curtains in his mouth. Studies suggest that Samuel Johnson, the noted English writer, also exhibited a number of the signs of this disorder including tics of the mouth, torso, and feet. He was also noted for making unusual vocalizations ("Medical Mystery," 1981).

Additional symptoms include mimicking the movements of others, compulsively touching persons or objects, and periodic displays of jumping or aggressive behavior (Martin, 1977). Compulsive thought patterns occur in some patients, and about 50 percent of these children suffer from diagnosable learning disabilities.

Incidence

Estimates on incidence vary greatly from 20,000 to more than 100,000 cases. Lucas (1970) reported only seven cases in 1.5 million clinic visits while Woodrow (1974) suggests prevalence rates from 4/1,000,000 to a high of 1/1,000 in psychiatric patients. The disorder is much more common in males than in females, with Kelman (1965) reporting 77 percent of an identified patient population as male. Corbett et al. (1969) suggest approximately a 3.6:1 ratio of males to females.

Diagnosis

"Tourette's Disorder" has several characteristic symptoms. Muscularly, there are recurrent, involuntary, repetitive, rapid, and apparently purposeless motor movements (American Psychiatric Association, 1980). These movements affect multiple muscle groups. Voluntary suppression is possible for a period of time. While these tics usually include head movements, other parts of the body are also involved in many cases. In 50 percent of the cases, it starts with a single tic such as the eyes, head, or face, but that may include sniffling, hacking, throat clearing, tongue protrusion, snorting, barking, or other noises. Some patients present with two to eight of these signs initially, but all eventually have involuntary movements and some vocal tics (Bruun & Shapiro, 1972). Symptoms appear between the ages of 2 and 15, typically around 7 or 8 years of age. In order to satisfy the diagnostic criteria for this category, the problem must have been present for at least one year.

This disorder is often misdiagnosed due to its erratic course or because transient tics, which occur in approximately 5 percent of all children, may be diagnosed as Tourette's Disorder. Several authors (Golden, 1977b; Shapiro et al., 1972) have noted the difficulty with accurate diagnosis of this disorder and the frequent long delay between onset of the symptoms and effective diagnosis. Many patients suffer the affliction for 10 years before the illness is properly diagnosed ("Medical Mystery," 1981), and it is not unusual for periods of three to four years to elapse between onset and diagnosis (Golden, 1977b). Diagnosis is also complicated by the fact that, at times, new symptoms replace previous ones. Symptoms become more pronounced under periods of high emotional stress such as anger, highly positive emotional excitement, or when excessively tired or physically exhausted, but diminish with sleep, rest or relaxation (Sweet et al., 1973; Woodrow, 1974).

The diagnosis can also be overlooked as a transient tic, but, unlike a transient tic, the tic changes in intensity or in type. Medical literature ("Medical Mystery," 1981) suggests that the throat-clearing grunts frequently seen with the disorder are often mistaken for allergic rhinitis, and Golden (1977b) says that the presence of such noises in a child with facial tics increases the diagnostic certainty of Tourette's Disorder. A 1981 medical census of school age children in Monroe County, New York, should give us our first detailed analysis of the incidence of Tourette's Syndrome.

Etiology

A variety of etiologies have been cited as "the cause" for Tourette's Syndrome. Medical texts, as recently as five years ago, frequently listed Tourette's as a psychoneurotic disorder; however, it is now believed to be caused by abnormal catecholamine metabolism and some suspect that a genetic link is involved ("Medical Mystery," 1981).

BEHAVIORAL. Conceptualizations have stressed the importance of reinforcement through increased attention and focused on tics as a learned habit or response (Logue et al., 1973). Coleman et al. (1980) suggest that tics serve to release tension; thus the response is reinforced and learned. Because the tic itself generates reactions from others that increase tension, there is a chronic need to reduce tension that increases the ticing behavior that increases the anxiety and produces a recurrent cycle.

TRADITIONAL.   Based on patients relating perinatal experiences through the use of LSD-25, Lake (1978) suggested that perinatal recall of birth trauma may point to the origin of Tourette's Syndrome. Kim (1971) says that the child's relationship with the parents is the significant factor. Sperling and Sperling (1978) placed emphasis on the genital phases of the pre-Oedipal years. Fernando (1976) hypothesized that the onset of coprolalia indicated a disturbance in normal balance between tension release by swearing and a capacity to control such a balance. Psychoanalytic theory suggests that the various tics and explosive verbalizations represent symbolic expressions of repressed emotional states such as obsessional symptomatology (Singer, 1963) and hostility (Ascher, 1948).

ORGANIC.   Many studies have found aberrant physiological findings in Tourette's patients (Shapiro et al., 1973). Lucas and Rodin (1973) found that over half of the Tourette patients studied showed abnormal EEGs, including bilateral sharp waves, defused background disorganization and, infrequently, unilateral temporal shifts and sharp waves. Children with Tourette's Syndrome show a disproportionate tendency toward minimal brain dysfunction (Golden, 1977a) and are three times more likely than control subjects to yield other organic findings on psychological assessments. Golden (1977a) and Shapiro, Shapiro, and Clarkin, (1974) found evidence of organicity in 50 percent of their subjects on psychiatric assessment, 76 percent on psychological assessment, and 50 percent on neurological evaluation. Thompson, O'Quinn, and Logue (1979) presented neuropsychological data on four cases, two of them a father and son, and reported that the data were consistent with longstanding, nonprogressive organic dysfunction of the left or right cerebral hemispheres. They concluded that there is not yet sufficient data in all these studies from neuropsychological assessment to indicate a specific locus for Tourette's. Sand (1972), however, found no significant cerebral deficits.

Within the past few years, there have been increased investigations of a biochemical basis for Tourette's. Studies on the neurochemical or organic basis for this disorder have increased markedly, especially in the past eight years. Boshes (1976) reported that some postmortem examinations have revealed changes in the basal ganglium of the brain, while other reports support an organic involvement of the central nervous system (Lucas & Rodin, 1973; Martin, 1977). These findings were consistent with the work of Shapiro and Shapiro and their colleagues (Shapiro et al., 1974; Shapiro et al., 1972; Shapiro et al., 1973) where 50 percent or more of their patients had histories of delayed development associated with perceptual deficits and hyperactivity. Abuzzahae and Ehlen (1971) stressed the need for early diagnosis because those patients with the more severe cases showed no improvement, while those with no evidence of organic CNS changes had markedly improved responses to medication. Koranyi (1977) reported a case of a 16-year-old who, since the age of 10, had inhaled gasoline up to ten times per day. The child developed facial tics along with grunting sounds and coprolalia. Abnormal cortical and subcortical EEG findings were evident.

GENETIC.   Corbett et al. (1969) stated that there is a family history of tics in 10 percent of all the cases reported (which is twice the usual frequency). Golden (1977a, 1978) noted that a comparison of the number of Tourette patients with family members with tics or Tourette's suggests that an autosomal, dominant transmission of the tic syndrome is possible and he differentiated two groups, one in which a full-blown Tourette's Syndrome rarely develops, with another group at high risk for Tourette's.

ENVIRONMENTAL.   Ascher (1948) has suggested that both a hereditary disposition and an emotional stress must be present for the disorder to manifest itself. Specific environmental stressors have been associated with the onset of symptoms (Boshes, 1976; Rosenthal, Nicholson, & Coller, 1975; Shapiro et al., 1972) such as removal of teeth, tonsillectomies, birth of siblings, starting school, automobile accidents, parental illness, parental quarreling, stopping thumbsucking, attack by a dog, and separation from parents or siblings. Diseases that have been considered of etiological importance include mumps, measles, chicken pox, whooping cough, scarlet fever, encephalopathy, and cholera.

Pharmacological

Bremness and Sverd (1979) reported a case of apparent drug-related onset in which a boy referred for behavioral problems was treated using a combination of behavior therapy and methylphenidate. After ten weeks, the child developed multiple tics and vocal tics progressing to a fully developed Tourette's Syndrome. Medication was discontinued with rapid symptom reduction; however, the disorder reappeared approximately five weeks later.

Treatment

BEHAVIORAL.   Haidar and Clancy (1973) and Thomas, Abrams, and Johnson (1971) found that self-monitoring with the use of a wrist counter was effective. The application of behavioral techniques to "verbal tics" was first reported by Clark (1966) who produced complete elimination of obscenities in two of three subjects by instructing them to repeat the obscenities until they could no longer do so. This procedure was also used by Lahey, McNees, and McNees (1973). This procedure, referred to as "negative" or "massed practice," has been successfully applied by several authors to reduce many high frequency motor behaviors (Feldman & Werry, 1966; Rosen & Wesner, 1973), including facial and head jerking tics (Varni, Boyd, & Cataldo, 1978).

Schulman (1974) utilized removal of maternal attention to eliminate tics, while Lahey et al. (1973), although obtaining some control of coprolalia with massed practice, produced even more striking results with the use of a time-out procedure. The child's parents reported that for the first time in two years, he had gone an entire weekend without saying an obscene word. As a result, he was taken out into the public for the first time in many years. Hutzell, Platzek, and Logue (1974) utilized self-monitoring and eliminated verbal tics in both the therapeutic setting and the patient's natural environment.

Miller (1970) eliminated verbal and facial tics in a 5-year-old boy by utilizing his parents and school teachers as therapists. Treatment involved the reinforcement of incompatible behaviors in the classroom. This study, as well as several others, indicates that nonprofessionals can effectively treat Tourette's (with professional supervision) using operant and other behavioral techniques (Doleys & Kurtz, 1974; Rosen & Wesner, 1973; Shapiro et al., 1980).

Although behavioral techniques are successful, concerns have been raised recently over the possibility of unwanted side effects. Several of these articles appear to be concerned with the theoretical application and the possibility of "symptom substitution"; however, some studies do indicate that, under certain circumstances, behavior applications are not effective with certain patients. Savicki and Carlin (1972) reported an unsuccessful attempt to teach self-monitoring and self-regulation methods. Failure was attributed to the lack of appropriate behavior cueing within the family and lack of support from these family members for reducing the rate of tics. Shapiro et al. (1978) concluded that the success rate is within the 20–25 percent range and similar to that found for other forms of psychological intervention.

TRADITIONAL.   The bizarre symptoms of Tourette's disorder have in turn resulted in some equally unusual treatment procedures, primarily because of the perceived etiology of this disorder. Exorcism has been used in an attempt to rid individuals of a supposed possession by the devil. Other more "enlightened treatments" have included hot and cold hydrotherapy, hot mustard plasters, tonsillectomies, chiropractic adjustment for extra nerves in the spine, and slowly sipping water for an hour at a time, 12 hours a day (Wright, Schaefer, & Solomons, 1979).

Because of the earlier focus on this disorder as a manifestation of repressed emotions, id-ego conflict resolution treatments such as psychoanalysis, hypnotherapy, sleep therapy, insulin coma, carbon dioxide inhalation, and electroconvulsive therapy have been utilized. Psychosurgical procedures, including ligature of various prefrontal nerves (leukotomy) as well as lobotomies, have also been prescribed as "treatment" in the past (Coleman et al., 1980).

A variety of therapeutic procedures have been used, including paraverbal psychother-apy (MacKay & Heimlich, 1972) and psycho-analytic family therapy (Tiller, 1978). Abuzzahae, Anderson, and Sekhon (1975) sug-gest that psychoanalytic psychotherapy in conjunction with the use of haloperidol, is the most effective treatment procedure.

ORGANIC.   The interest in psychopharma-cological agents since the early 1960s has seen the use of almost every stimulant, anticonvul-sant, vitamin, anti-Parkinsonian, and antide-pressant drug with Tourette's patients. One review ("Medical Mystery," 1981) mentions over 100 major chemicals used with varying success. Kelman (1965) reported only one of six patients being helped by amphetamines. Chorpromazine (Lucas, 1964), diazepam, and phenothiazine have all been reported as some-what helpful (Bixby, 1970) in that these drugs often reduce, but may not completely elimi-nate, the frequency of some tics.

The role of dopamine as the neurotrans-mitter mediator for stereotypic behaviors has received increased attention in recent years (Cohen et al., 1979; Klawans et al., 1978). Fras and Karlavage (1977) reported three cases of children with Tourette's whose symptoms increased when they were treated with methyl-phenidate. Golden (1974, 1977a) reported similar findings. In the first study, these children were also briefly treated with imipra-mine with similar results. Fras and Karlavage concluded that the increase in symptoms lends support to the catecholamine hypothesis as an etiological factor in the onset of Tourette's.

Dr. Sheldon Norvick, Medical Director of the Tourette's Syndrome Association, ("Medi-cal Mystery," 1981) reports about half of the patients enjoy a good-to-fair result with haloperidol. Others (Bixby, 1970; Golden, 1977a) suggest that of these successful cases, about 90 percent control of the symptoms is obtained. However, it should be remembered that this only applies to approximately 50 percent of the individuals treated (Martin, 1977; Shapiro et al., 1973).

Surwillo, Shafii, and Barrett (1978) fol-lowed a 10-year-old boy over a period of 20 months during which he was treated with haloperidol. Although there was marked reduc-tion in the rate of ticing, stressful life events were found markedly to affect the rate at which tics occurred. These authors suggest that medication alone should not be used, but that parental counseling should be involved, in-cluding informing the family that the presence of stressful life events may produce an increase in the symptoms. This latter finding is con-sistent with Shapiro et al. (1973) who noted a spontaneous increase and decrease in symp-toms. Sand (1972) obtained neuropsychologi-cal assessment of a child prior to and during treatment with haloperidol and found little or no disruption in intellectual performance as a function of the drug.

Frequently, high levels of haloperidol are necessary to maintain good therapeutic dos-ages. Inability to tolerate high levels is a chief cause of therapeutic failure, and side effects may include cognitive impairment, hyper-somnia, extreme anxiety, and depression. Parkinsonlike effects such as drooling, tremors, rigidity, and loss of associated movements have been reported. Although these reactions are often temporary, usually disappearing after three or four months, addi-tional use of anti-Parkinsonian agents is usu-ally suggested.

Conclusions

Significant advances are being made in under-standing the etiology, diagnosis, and treat-ment of Tourette's. Psychological counseling to help patients adjust to the social stresses associated with manifestations of this disorder is frequently used. Special clinics devoted to Tourette's research and treatment are maintained at a variety of medical centers around the United States, and there are many state associations for these children and their parents. A national clearinghouse for information is maintained by the Tourette's Syndrome Association, Bayside, New York. The use of medication (especially haloperidol) along with behavioral techniques, appears to be an effective treatment plan that eliminates many of the manifestations of Tourette's.

Atypical Stereotyped Movement Disorders

Voluntary, rhythmic motor movements such as head banging, rocking, and repetitive hand movements (consisting of small, quick, rhythmic hand rotations or repetitive, voluntary movements that typically involve the fingers or arms) are considered atypical stereotyped movement disorders. These behaviors are distinguishable from tics in that they consist of purely voluntary movements and are not spasmodic.

The occurrence of head banging and body rocking is frequently described in the literature as examples of "self-injurious behavior" (Tate & Baroff, 1966) or "self-mutilation" (Phillips & Muzaffer, 1961). Although such forms of self-injurious behavior (SIB) do occur in association with a number of psychiatric disorders (Green, 1967) such as schizophrenia or autism, developmental delay, mental retardation or organic disabilities, the primary focus of this section will be on the occurrence of such behaviors as a habit disorder in essentially normal children.

Incidence

Motor habits such as head rolling, head banging, and bed rocking are common in infants and children, both during the day and night, and are observed in 15–20 percent of pediatric clinic patients. Although usually transitory, about 5 percent of children have symptoms for months or even years, usually disappearing at 2.5–3 years of age. Such habits are three-and-a-half times more common in boys than in girls (Bakwin & Bakwin, 1972).

Head rolling or head rocking may begin as early as 2–3 months of age. Incidence increases up to 6 or 7 months and rocking of the body and head banging usually first appear after 8 months of age. Body rocking is often a repetitive movement in a seated position and frequently begins or becomes more intense when a child goes from the sitting to the standing stage, although the rocking may occur when the child is passing from one developmental phase to another (Brody, 1960).

Several investigators (Green, 1967; DeLissovoy, 1961) report that in normal children from the ages of 9 months to 6 years of age, self-injurious behavior of various unspecified forms is frequently observed. It occurs in 11–17 percent at ages 9–18 months, and in 9 percent at 2 years of age. By 5 years of age it is virtually absent (Williams, 1974).

Head banging occurs in approximately 3.5 percent of infants of normal intellect and is about three-and-a-half times as common in boys as in girls (Kravitz et al., 1960). Onset is between 5 and 11 months and lasts about 17 months. About 67 percent of head bangers also rock. The usual duration is approximately 15 minutes but may continue for an hour or more. The frontal-parietal region is most frequently struck, and the most common position is for the child to be on his or her knees with hands in the crib. DeLissovoy (1961) found an incidence rate as high as 15.2 percent in the normal population between 19 and 32 months, with a 22.3 percent rate in boys as opposed to 7.4 percent in girls.

Diagnosis

Body rocking and head banging are both monotonous, repetitive movements that occur with a set rhythm. Information should be obtained regarding onset, duration, the situations in which it occurs, a precise behavioral description, parental responses, associated behaviors, and some measure of whether the child's functioning has been impaired or whether the behavior is an indication of severe emotional disturbance or deprivation. Wright et al. (1979) state that head banging and other SIB behavior is more likely to be an indication of severe disturbance than body rocking or other compulsive habits.

Etiology

BEHAVIORAL. Bachman (1972) and others (Bandura, 1969; Skinner, 1953) suggested that self-injurious behavior (SIB) may be developed if the behavior leads to the avoidance of even more aversive consequences (avoidance hypothesis) or an aversive event might be paired with a positive reinforcer that maintains a given activity (discriminative stimulus–conditioned reinforcer hypothesis). Since SIB often appears to occur only in the presence or absence of specific stimuli and is maintained by social reinforcement that follows it (Lane & Dormath, 1970), it appears that SIB may be a learned operant under the control of environmental stimuli. Green (1967) postulated that self-stimulatory patterns were adaptive responses to a reduction of environmental stimulation as they serve to increase sensory input. Thus the child who is waving his or her hands may accidentally bang or hit his or her head. Random head banging then develops in association with this increased stimulation.

Green (1978) cites a case where an abused child developed SIB as an avoidance response to parental attack until the parents stopped the abuse. Money, Wolff, and Annecillo (1972) report higher rates of SIB in abused children than in neglected or normal children as support for the avoidance hypothesis that SIB is a learned pattern originating in early traumatic experiences with hostile, aversive, primary caretakers. An alternative explanation might be that the behavior is due to mild organic dysfunction, often associated with abuse. Paskal (1969) used modeling of stereotyped behaviors in a classical conditioning paradigm and produced increases in such behavior among normal first-grade female students.

TRADITIONAL. Spitz (1945) attributed rocking to maternal deprivation, and Greenberg (1964) feels that it is a symptom associated with deprivation. Other hypotheses include: an anxiety-reducing response (Clerk, 1972); repression of hostility (Saul, 1976); disturbed narcissism (Kohut, 1972); an inability to detach libidinal ties or displaced genital damage (Friedman et al., 1972); and antecedents of aggression directed toward the self as a result of oral fixation (Clerk, 1972).

ORGANIC. The increased rates of body rocking and head banging in mental retardation and childhood psychoses suggest some central nervous system involvement in the etiology of these behaviors. Supporting this view, Cantwell and Baker (1980) reported that stereotypic behavior occurred with significantly greater frequency in language-delayed subjects, while Hutt and Hutt (1968) found an association between high levels of arousal and stereotyped movement, with stereotyped behavior occurring most frequently in the presence of desynchronized EEG activity.

Thelen (1980) suggested that the amount of vestibular stimulation was critical (although such activities were also associated with being in close proximity with a caregiver). Thelen found an inverse relationship between the amount of holding, moving, and touching of the child, and the amount of stereotyped behavior.

Two medical conditions, Lesch-Nyhan Syndrome (Dizmang & Cheatham, 1970) and Cornelia de Lange Syndrome (Shear et al., 1971), are associated with head banging and other SIB. Although the de Lange Syndrome has an unknown etiology, Smith (1970) suggests it may be transmitted by a single recessive gene. Lesch-Nyhan Syndrome is a heritable disorder of metabolism of uric acid that is determined by a mutant gene on the X chromosome. It is associated with developmental delays and severe self-injurious behavior (Partington & Hennen, 1967).

Treatment

BEHAVIORAL. A variety of behavioral techniques have been used for the elimination of self-stimulatory and self-injurious behavior (Bachman, 1972; Johnson & Baumeister, 1978). Intervention procedures can be classified as extinction (Lovaas & Simmons, 1969); reinforcement of incompatible responses through positive reinforcement (Carr & McDowell, 1980; Peterson & Peterson, 1968); time-out procedures (Tate & Baroff, 1966; Solnick, Rincover, & Peterson, 1977); punishment techniques, including the use of electric shock (Baroff & Tate, 1968; Browning & Stover, 1971); and overcorrection (Foxx & Azrin, 1973; Harris & Romanczyk, 1976; Shapiro, Barrett, & Ollendick, 1980).

Although many of the above studies involved children with severe self-injurious or self-stimulatory behaviors, the use of many of these techniques can be successfully applied to habit disorders in normal children. Martin and Conway (1976) used bright light as an aversive stimulus to eliminate nocturnal rocking in a normal 25-month-old. Dougherty and Lane (1976), using a 2-year-old's parents as therapists, had them remove the child's pacifier immediately upon head banging and to return it after a specified length of time had elapsed without head banging.

Overcorrection has been successfully used by Barnard, Christopherson, and Wolf (1976) who trained parents in the use of overcorrection procedures and produced zero or near zero rates of SIB, with follow-up indicating durable treatment effects. Linscheid et al. (1981), in a report of treatment of nighttime self-injurious behavior, emphasized the intensive practice of correct forms of the relevant behavior (within the overcorrection procedure) by telling their subjects to roll over and to lie still on their stomachs for 15 seconds. The sequence of cue, rolling, and being still was repeated 15 times following each occurrence of head rocking or banging and produced rapid and durable decreases in the rate of these behaviors. Frazier and Williams (1973) eliminated long term rocking by the use of a point contract system, time-out, and stimulus control procedures.

TRADITIONAL. Several authors (Greenberg, 1964; Ilg & Ames, 1955; Jorgenson, 1974) have suggested sensory stimulation, such as reading to the child or playing music, as a means of disrupting body or head rocking. Harris (1968) used psychoanalytic play therapy to resolve the conflict that was producing the head banging. Kohut (1972) investigated the relationship of narcissism and aggression and suggested that psychoanalysis was of value in taming narcissistic rage manifested by self-mutilation.

ORGANIC.   Sprague (1977), in a review of psychopharmacology in children, indicated that neuroleptic medication reduces bizarre or stereotypical behavior but also suppresses learning performance. However, Kravitz et al. (1960) suggested the use of tranquilizing or sedative drugs for chronic head bangers.

Conclusions

Although there are a variety of etiological factors associated with the occurrence of body rocking and head banging, including some genetically determined diseases, the most effective methods of controlling these behaviors in normal children have been the use of operant conditioning techniques. The increase in the literature on intervention techniques for normal children and the ease with which many parents can successfully apply behavioral procedures, suggest that the focus on these procedures will increase in the future.

HABITS AND MANNERISMS

Childhood development normally proceeds through a succession of phases. Almost all children, at some point, experience stress that comes from difficulties of adjusting to their changing roles and interactions with their environment. This section considers the major developmental or habit disorders that are not covered under the chapters on Communication, Eating, Toileting, Sleep, or Sexual Problems. The focus of this section will be on the habit disorders that occur primarily in normal children although reference will be made to other childhood populations when necessary. The habit disorders to be covered include: breath holding, bruxism (teeth grinding), nail biting, thumbsucking, and trichotillomania (hair pulling).

Breath Holding

Breath holding can occur in very young children and consists of holding the breath (apnea) for approximately 30 seconds. For parents, this is often very frightening, especially if their child turns blue. Yet, "this common condition is probably more alarming than dangerous" (Wittkower & White, 1959).

Incidence

Breath holding may begin as early as 6 months of age, and is a common disorder before the age of 4. The majority of attacks usually start within the first 2 years of life and generally disappear spontaneously when the period of violent crying ends, between the ages of 4 and 6. The behavioral pattern tends to occur in children who are tense and overly active, and it affects both males and females in approximately equal percentages (Simmons, 1977; Warme, 1977). In most instances, it is benign and self-limiting. Frequency of occurrence varies widely from several times daily to once per month. The most common frequency is once a week.

Diagnosis

Breath holding generally follows some disturbing or frustrating event, often minor in character, that precipitates disproportional and violent crying. The breath is held, and after approximately 30 seconds the child shows signs of apneic distress, cyanosis, and, in a few cases, the breath may be held until some tetanic twitches occur or unconsciousness intervenes to end the attack.

Etiology

BEHAVIORAL. According to Simmons (1977), breath holding appears to be a learned response that is inadvertently shaped by parents. The initial behavior is reinforced by increasing amounts of differential attention on the part of the parents as they attempt to direct the child. The child engages in this behavior as a conscious attempt to manipulate the environment.

TRADITIONAL. Breath holding episodes are assumed to be a manifestation of an attempt to control parents or adults. When unable to do so, the child experiences overwhelming rage. Often the child succeeds in frightening his or her parents into compliance with his or her demands. Psychoanalytically, this disorder occurs during the anal stage when the child is attempting to gain mastery or control of his or her environment (Brown, 1978) and is assumed to be a sign of disturbance in parent-child relationships. Goldenson (1970) says that the parents are usually overprotective and, at the same time, tense in their insistence upon a rigid feeding schedule or premature toilet training.

ORGANIC. Breath holding spells during the newborn period suggest the influence of a constitutional factor. This hypothesis is supported by the frequency in which a family history of breath-holding episodes is obtained (Simmons, 1977). A significant positive correlation has been found between breath holding and red-blood-cell anemia (Holowach & Thurston, 1963).

Treatment

BEHAVIORAL. Treatment generally focuses on the removal of positive reinforcement for breath-holding episodes and usually is accomplished by teaching parents to ignore the breath holding, while giving attention for more appropriate compliant behaviors. Techniques may include having the parent leave the room or, if the child does hold his or her breath long enough to become unconscious, remaining out of the room until the child recovers and he or she realizes that additional attention has not been provided for such behavior (Warme, 1977).

TRADITIONAL. Several authors (Brown, 1978; Simmons, 1977; Warme, 1977) suggest that the parents need therapy in helping the child develop greater frustration tolerance and that the parents need to learn the difference between permissiveness and firm limits. Therapy directed toward improving the parents' own emotional adjustment is frequently recommended.

ORGANIC. No specific medical treatments were found in the literature concerning this frequent but harmless habit. In our experience, minor tranquilizers have been used occasionally, but most pediatricians seem to recommend "tincture of time" and parental reassurance.

Conclusions

Although often frightening to parents when episodes initially occur, breath holding appears to have few long term consequences for the parents and child. Ignoring the behavior while reinforcing more compliant behaviors is an easy and effective method of eliminating breath holding. The common "household remedy" of sprinkling water on the child does not appear to be effective.

Bruxism

Bruxism refers to any habitual gnashing, grinding, clicking, or clenching of the teeth and may occur either nocturnally or in the daytime. This habit has been listed under a variety of terms throughout the centuries. As Wright et al. (1979) have noted, it is mentioned in the Bible and was described as "Bruxomania" by Marie and Pietkiewicz in 1907 to indicate neurotic grinding. Frohman originally called it "occlusal neurosis"; however, he first suggested the term bruxism (Frohman, 1932) to describe nonneurotic nocturnal grinding. Today the term bruxism is used to describe all forms of teeth-gnashing behavior.

Incidence

Reding, Rubright, and Zimmerman (1966) report rates of between 5 and 15 percent. The rates seem to be based upon dental articulation, with up to 18 percent of males and 12 percent of females with poor dental alignment being bruxists, while only 2 percent for females and 7 percent for males with good dental articulation. The incidence rates in males is 2–3 times that of females in most reports. The onset of bruxism most commonly occurs prior to the age of 3 years, usually is nocturnal, is more frequent in older children and adolescents and persists into adult life in about 35 percent of the cases (Abe, 1976; Moore, 1956).

Diagnosis

The initial diagnosis of the condition should be made by a dentist. The recurrent gnashing of the teeth may at times be so loud that parents or others around the child can hear it, and any grinding that is said to occur for over one hour per day should be considered as bruxism (Gottlieb, 1947). Psychological evaluation to determine any significant degree of psychopathology may be made (Holvey & Talbott, 1972) and should include both the child and his or her parents, with specific information to be elicited with regard to whether the bruxism only occurs at night or during the day, and whether any environmental stresses increase or decrease the frequency of the behavior.

Etiology

BEHAVIORAL. Several authors (Moore, 1956; Shaffer, 1936; Wilder, 1946) have suggested that bruxism is a learned behavior associated with a response to excessive stress.

TRADITIONAL. These viewpoints generally conclude that bruxism is a manifestation of a fixation at the oral-aggressive stage of psychosexual development or that it is the result of repression or self-aggression (Strother & Mitchell, 1953; Walsh, 1965). Although assumed to be a symptom of aggression and hostility, Vernallis's (1955) appears to be the only report in the literature indicating a significant correlation between these behaviors. Several other studies (Frisch, Katz, & Ferreira, 1960; Reding, Zepelin, & Monroe, 1968; Thaller, Rosen, & Saltzman, 1967) found no correlation between bruxism and aggression. However, several researchers (Miller, Thaller, & Soberman, 1956; Thaller, 1960; Vernallis, 1955) found significant correlations between anxiety states and bruxism. Two studies (Clarke & Kardachi, 1977; Sheppard & Sheppard, 1977) suggest that in the majority of patients the etiology is on a psychophysiological basis.

ORGANIC. A variety of dental problems or other medical conditions may be significant factors in bruxism. Included may be malocclusion, missing or rough teeth, oral or systemic infections, or malnutrition (Brauer et al.,

1947; Frohman, 1932). In recent years, bruxism has been associated with the presence of allergies, and Marks (1980) says that allergic reactions may be a causative factor.

Genetic and familial aspects have been postulated as being associated with the occurrence of bruxism. Several authors have noted higher incidence rates in parents and siblings of bruxists than in the normal population (Abe, 1976; Reding et al., 1966) and higher incidence rates when both parents exhibited the behavior.

Treatment

BEHAVIORAL.   A biofeedback procedure in which a tiny ear piece and three electrodes are attached to the jaw, allowing a tone to be sounded when the patient begins to grind his or her teeth, has been used by Clarke and Kardachi (1977) in reducing facial pains experienced as a result of bruxism. This procedure was also used by Kardachi, Bailey, and Ash (1978) who compared such biofeedback with occlusal adjustment on bruxist patients. They found (based on the assumption that EMG activity is related to bruxism) that the effects of biofeedback in reducing EMG activity are more consistent than an occlusal adjustment. It should be noted that Wright et al. (1979) feel that the biofeedback technique seems to constitute the single most productive area for future behavioral research on bruxism. Since bruxism appears to be associated with increased anxiety, it might be treated with relaxation techniques or through the used of massed practice.

TRADITIONAL.   Treatment approaches are based on the conceptualization that the behavior results from an oral-aggressive or oral-sadistic personality and that the individual has ungratified oral and dependency needs (Ewen, 1967; Shapiro & Shannon, 1966). These oral needs have been treated by brief psychotherapy aimed at verbally releasing hostility or other pent-up feelings (Goldenson, 1970). Several authors (Gelberd, 1958; Goldenson, 1970) have suggested the use of autosuggestion or hypnosis as an appropriate method of treating bruxism.

ORGANIC.   Medical and dental treatment of bruxism has focused on improvements of malocclusion when it exists or on the use of a bite block to reduce the possibility of damage to the teeth (Holvey & Talbott, 1972; Zarcone & Dement, 1979). The use of drugs has included diazepam and methocarbamol, with some reduction in the frequency and severity of teeth grinding (Zarcone & Dement, 1979).

Conclusions

Medical research is being undertaken into conditions associated with bruxism (such as allergies) as a way of identifying and eliminating the habit disorder. At the same time, the cost of dental injury resulting from bruxism continues to increase. Several behavioral techniques, especially biofeedback, have the potential to rapidly reduce the incidence of this disorder. Increased emphasis should be placed on further research in this area.

Nail Biting (Onychophagy)

Nail biting (or onychophagy) is one of the most common habit disturbances among children and is no longer classified as a "special symptom reaction." This behavior consists of biting on or chewing the nails of the hand.

Incidence

This behavior rarely occurs before 4 years of age. At around 6 years there is a marked increase, and the incidence rate seems to remain constant from 6 years until puberty when the highest incidence occurs (Birch, 1955; Ilg & Ames, 1955). It is occasionally associated with biting of the toenails and with picking at the nails with the fingers. Massler and Malone (1950) suggest that it occurs about 1.5 times as frequently in girls as in boys. Coleman and McCalley (1948) say that nail biting is more common in males than females. The difference in reports may be developmental as girls and boys seem equally prone to this habit during the early years, but males outnumber females at a later age (Coleman et al., 1980).

Warme (1977) indicates that 40 percent of

children between the ages of 5 and 18 bite one or more nails and 18 percent bite all 10 nails severely and persistently. In contrast to the other authors, he states the incidence peaks in boys at age 12–13 and in girls at 8–9. However, other studies of nail-biting rates in preadolescent children range from 33 percent to 50 percent, dropping to around 24 percent by 17–18 years of age (McCandless, 1954), and progressively declining after age 40.

Diagnosis

Diagnosis and measurement of nail biting can be accomplished based on reports by the patient or parent and by visual inspection of the nails. The length of the nail can be measured over a period of time, and severity of biting can be determined in this way (Billig, 1941).

Etiology

Nail biting has changed from a disorder that primarily had been seen as an indicator of extreme pathology to a more normally accepted habit. Although it was initially assumed that nail biting was of psychopathic proportion, the data do not fit the assumption, in that large numbers of nail-biting children are neither psychopaths nor victims of unresolved complexes.

BEHAVIORAL.   Coleman et al. (1980) note that several explanations have been advanced about nail biting, but the most widely accepted is tension reduction. They indicate that the behavior is a learned habit that provides a physical outlet; thus it relieves anxiety, most pronounced during periods of stress. Several other authors (Pierce, 1972; Valentine, 1955; and Warme, 1977) agree that nail biting is a simple tension-reducing mechanism that occurs in fidgety, somewhat anxious, children.

TRADITIONAL.   Goldenson (1970) states that studies have suggested that nail biters as a group are more anxious than other children. Other psychodynamic explanations have considered it as a substitute for masturbation, a fixation at the oral-aggressive stage of develop-

ment, or as an outlet for hostile or sexual impulses. Goldenson also indicated that nail biters are usually "intropunitive", that is, they tend to blame or punish themselves instead of directing their hostility against others. Sunanda (1972) stated that nail biting was an indication that the child was unsure of himself or herself and lacked self-confidence.

Deardoff, Finch, and Royall (1974) administered the Children's Anxiety Scale to 90 students in the seventh and eighth grade. The percentage of nail biters was 12.2 percent, lower than that indicated by other studies (Pierce, 1972). Although nail biters reported more anxiety than non-nail-biters, the difference was not found to be significant. Tupin, Mahar, and Smith (1973) compared three groups of male offenders and reported that a variety of childhood behavior symptoms, including nail biting, was found in the habitually violent groups more than in the other groups. They suggest a classification system based on overt behavior as a means of identifying groups of convicts.

ORGANIC.   Studies suggest both a strong familial as well as a genetic component, in that monozygotic twins were found to have rates of nail biting four times that of dizygotic twins (Bakwin, 1971a). Up to two-thirds of monozygotic twins and one-third of dizygotic twins were found to be concordant for nail biting in a number of other studies (Bakwin & Bakwin, 1972; Billig, 1941; Massler & Malone, 1950; McCandless, 1954).

Treatment

BEHAVIORAL.   Coleman et al. (1980) suggest that physical restraint and the use of bitter-tasting materials are ineffective and indicate behavior therapy is more effective. Smith (1957) used a massed practice technique and helped 50 percent of the subjects in his study. Aversive consequences for nail biting, including the use of overcorrection (Stephen & Koenig, 1970; Vargas & Adesso, 1976), have been used with some success. Vargas and Adesso (1976) evaluated the effectiveness of three modes of aversive therapy, with and without self-monitoring, in the suppression of nail biting. The treatments reduced nail biting, with self-monitoring subjects exhibiting significantly greater increases in nail growth than non–self-monitored subjects. Adesso, Vargas, and Siddall (1979) used self-monitoring, positive incentive, negative incentive, nail measurement alone, and a minimal contact control group. While all treatment conditions resulted in a decrease in biting frequency and increase in nail lengths, subjects receiving a treatment package consisting of self-monitoring plus regularly scheduled nail measurements were most effective in increasing awareness of and reduction in nail biting. Many of these authors note that aversive procedures will reduce the frequency of nail biting but do not seem adequate for total suppression of the behavior.

Mulick et al. (1978) reduced finger picking and nail biting in an institutionalized male by increasing the occurrence of independent toy play, an example of reinforcing alternative behaviors. Recent studies and books (Azrin & Nunn, 1973; Nunn & Azrin, 1976) have used a "Habit Reversal Procedure," including awareness training and competing activity procedures, with excellent results.

TRADITIONAL.   Birch (1955) and Warme (1977) suggest that generally no intervention is indicated, and that the behavior should be ignored if infrequent, but that severe nail biting is a symptom of some underlying disorder for which the child and the family may need to receive treatment. Goldenson (1970) suggests that persistent nail biting be treated by reducing stressful family situations, having the child talk over tensions, and using tranquilizing drugs as an adjunct to these approaches during periods of special strain and tension. Bakwin and Bakwin (1972) note that other treatment procedures include softening of the cuticles with olive oil, wearing white cotton mittens at night as a reminder not to bite the nails, and using a bitter substance or adhesive tape on the nails. They further recommend gum chewing during activities such as watching television as a substitute for nail biting. Goldenson (1970) says that

the use of punishment, such as forcing the child to wear gloves or applying a bitter tasting substance to the nails, is not recommended as it produces few positive results.

Bakwin and Bakwin (1972) indicate that rewards are of value in some instances, but recommend that they be used very sparingly; instead, they recommend that an appeal to the child's vanity has good results, especially in older girls. The child should be taught to trim and file the nails and provided with a manicure set. It is recommended that the nail biter always carry a nail file since a rough nail is an invitation to biting behavior. Several authors (Bakwin, 1971a; Spock, 1968) have suggested that parental nagging as punishment may increase the frequency of this behavior rather than remove it.

ORGANIC.   No specific drugs have been recommended for the treatment of nail biting. However, when the nail-biting behavior is assumed, from a psychodynamic point of view, to be a symptom of an underlying disorder such as obsessive-compulsive neurosis or acute anxiety, the drug of choice for each of these disorders has been used. Examples include: chlorpromazine for obsessive-compulsive neurosis (Grimshaw, 1965) and imipramine hydrochloride for acute anxiety (Mendel & Klein, 1969). In a novel approach, Wright et al. (1979) suggest the possibility of providing minor tranquilizers to parents who are unable to ignore nail biting in their child.

Conclusions

Nail biting or onychophagy is a common habit disturbance in children. The use of behavioral techniques, especially a shaping program for growing first a single nail, then the others, seems to be the best approach if the habit is distressful to the child or his or her parents.

Thumbsucking

Thumbsucking may on occasion include not only the sucking of one or both thumbs, but also may include fingers and fist sucking.

According to Klackenberg (1949), this behavior is one that has shifted in the past century from being interpreted as a sign of placidity to a symptom of infant sexuality and possible neurosis or at least a habit disturbance.

Wolfenstein (1972), in a study of trends of severity in handling children's impulse disorders, noted that between 1914 and 1951 the severity in handling thumbsucking showed a consistently declining curve, even though thumbsucking became a diagnosed psychiatric condition.

Incidence

Thumbsucking commonly has its onset between 3 and 4 months of age (Ilg & Ames, 1955) and most often occurs immediately after feeding. By the time the child is 6 months of age, it occurs during the day and for much of the night. After a reduction in the amount of sucking, there is an increase around 18 months of age. By 2.5–3 years of age, thumbsucking in many children occurs less during the day and at night may be associated with the child holding some other object, such as a favorite blanket. By 3.5, most daytime sucking is stimulated by activities such as watching television. In the majority of children by age 5, some sucking will be associated only with sleep. About 20 percent of thumbsuckers began between 3 and 5 months of age while 15 percent start between 6 and 9 months of age. Only 10 percent of children began after 9 months of age. Studies suggest that approximately 45 percent of all 2-year-olds, 42 percent of all 3-year-olds, 36 percent of all 4-year-olds, 20–30 percent of all 5-year-olds, 21 percent of all 6-year-olds, but only approximately 5 percent of all 11-year-olds, engage in these behaviors (Klackenberg, 1949; Lichstein & Kackmarik, 1980). Traisman and Traisman (1958) indicated that 46 percent of children from birth to 16 years are reported thumbsuckers. Specific data concerning the ratio of males to females are lacking. Some authors say the habit is slightly more frequent in males than in females (Palermo, 1956), while Bakwin and Bakwin (1972) report more girls than boys.

Several studies have indicated that the incidence of emotional disturbance is no higher among thumbsuckers than nonthumbsuckers (Lapouse & Monk, 1959; Traisman & Traisman, 1958), and other authors indicate there may be some positive effects in that the child may cry less, be less distractible, get through teething easier, and sleep much better (Ilg & Ames, 1955; Lester et al., 1976).

Diagnosis

The diagnosis of this disorder is relatively simple, involving the observation of the child with his or her thumb or fingers in his or her mouth. Since it is often impractical to do continuous observations of children, a "time-sampling" procedure may be utilized at appropriate intervals. Studies suggest that the behavior often occurs when the child is hungry, sleepy, frustrated, or fatigued and that associated movements frequently accompany thumbsucking. The child may pull an ear, pat the head, twist or pull the hair, suck a blanket or diaper, rub his or her cheek with a pillow, or pull a blanket in front of his or her face (Bakwin & Bakwin, 1972; Ilg & Ames, 1955).

Etiology

BEHAVIORAL.   Bakwin and Bakwin (1972) noted that the choice of the thumb as a sucking object is probably accidental, the thumb coming in contact with the mouth in the course of random movements that young infants make. Because of its pleasurable associations with feeding and alleviation of hunger, it then continues to be pleasurable as a result of such pairings (Benjamin, 1967). Lichstein (1978), Palermo (1956), and Pierce (1972), view thumbsucking as a conditioned response based on a stress-related need for tension reduction.

TRADITIONAL.   The psychoanalytic viewpoint holds that thumbsucking and other activities performed with the lips are expressions of the oral stage of psychosexual development (Fenichel, 1945; Freud, 1965). The mouth is viewed as an erotic zone and adequate stimulation is considered essential if the child's sexual and character development is to proceed normally. The individual who successfully goes through this stage has the capacity for oral satisfaction and continues getting "sucking satisfaction" not only from thumbsucking but in later life from activities such as gnawing on pencils, biting the lips, and sucking on a pipe or cigar (the latter, a highly frequent behavior with Freud himself). Johnson and Johnson (1975) report that later-born children exhibit more thumbsucking than firstborn and suggest that mothers provide more consolation and comfort to firstborns, forcing the later-borns to turn to themselves for comfort.

Although psychodynamic hypotheses are often stated, it should be noted that there is little direct evidence for these conclusions and several authors (Davidson et al., 1967; Haryett, Hansen, & Davidson, 1970; Palermo, 1956) indicate that the data available do not warrant these assumptions, especially those adult behaviors related to inadequate sucking in infancy. Sears and Wise (1950) compared the reactions of babies during the first ten days of life to feeding by cup, bottle, or breast and present data which suggest that excessive breast- or bottle-sucking leads to thumbsucking.

Thumbsucking has been associated with psychiatric illness, family disruption, or medical/dental disorders (Klackenberg, 1949; Lewis, 1937; Money, 1967). Thumbsucking, at times, has been looked upon as a habit related to masturbation, in that the behavior can serve as an erotic gratification or as a means of reducing tension or anxiety. Although such assumptions or myths frequently exist, there are no data to indicate that children who suck their thumbs will, at a later age, masturbate more often than others who do not suck their thumbs (Bakwin & Bakwin, 1972). Tryon (1968) found that thumbsucking is not related to anxiety, as measured by the Children's Manifest Anxiety Scale. Nor is it related to personality disturbances, as measured on the Children's Apperception Test, California Test of Personality, or the Family Relations Test (Davidson et al., 1967).

Other authors (Levy, 1928; Ribble, 1944; Roberts, 1944) believe that these activities are the result of inadequate sucking in infancy or that they stem from a biological need to exercise the sucking mechanism. They support this contention by pointing out that many children who do not get enough sucking satisfaction at the breast or bottle suck their thumbs and that it apparently serves as a soothing device when the child wants to go to sleep or when he or she is frustrated and upset. Levy points out that many children who have ample sucking satisfaction during infancy revert to some sucking as a means of relieving irritation on gums during the teething process and indicates that this is why older children and even adults revert to thumbsucking during periods of stress or emotional strain.

ORGANIC.   Traisman and Traisman (1958) reported malocclusion in 10 percent of thumbsuckers and in 7 percent of nonthumbsuckers, while Murray and Anderson (1969) indicated the rates were 30 percent in the thumbsuckers and only 9 percent for the nonthumbsuckers. Other studies have suggested other jaw and dental problems can result from excessive thumbsucking (Lewis, 1937; Ruttle et al., 1953). Perhaps the clearest description of orthodontic problems associated with thumbsucking was provided by Haryett et al. (1970), who noted in a review of the literature that the incidence rate of malocclusion for thumbsuckers ranged from a low of 14 percent to a high of 87 percent. This review also noted that there is likely to be little permanent damage to the dentition, providing that the habit is discontinued prior to the age of 4 years. These authors also noted that the relationship between thumbsucking and malocclusion is a matter of concern to dentists, but many hesitate to treat the habit because of the possibility of psychological trauma to the child. However, several authors feel that thumbsucking is much less often the cause for dental irregularities than is generally believed (Bakwin & Bakwin, 1972; Sillman, 1940).

Minimal research has been undertaken into the genetic or familial aspects of thumbsucking. Sillman (1940) suggests that heredity rather than thumbsucking is critical for dental alignment, while Bakwin (1971b), in a study of twins, failed to find a genetic predisposition to thumbsucking persisting after 3 years of age.

Treatment

BEHAVIORAL.   A variety of behavioral techniques have been successfully applied to reduce or eliminate thumbsucking. Cohen, Monty, and Williams (1980) had a 10-year-old self-record thumbsucking. This procedure reduced the frequency of the behavior, although never completely eliminated it. Daniels (1974) presented a therapy package for use at home and in the school, while Martin (1975) taught a 6-year-old to treat her 4-year-old sibling, a chronic thumbsucker, using modeling, shaping techniques, and a token economy. This case indicates that behavior programs can be used, even by very small children, to control the behavior of others in the family.

Differential reinforcement of other behavior (DRO) has been successfully employed as a treatment procedure for thumbsucking in the home by Kauffman and Scranton (1974) and in the classroom (Ross, 1974; Ross & Levine, 1972; Skiba, Pettigrew, & Alden 1971). The use of a DRO procedure has also been successfully applied by Lichstein and Kachmarik (1980) in both the home and at school, with stickers that could be used as tokens to exchange for rewards. Lowitz and Suib (1978) used pennies and access to television to reinforce nonthumbsucking through the use of a DRO schedule. The behavior was eliminated in three months and was not reported during any of the 12-month follow-ups. Home-based programs have been successful using specific reinforcers such as reading stories at bedtime (Knight & McKenzie, 1974), access to television programs (Ross, 1975), or the use of edible reinforcers such as hard candy (Hughes, Hughes, & Dial, 1978, 1979). The potential for dental problems, however, is present using the latter approach. All of these procedures were effective in markedly reducing the frequency of thumbsucking. In addition, the Hughes et al. (1979) study used a "behavioral seal" in which a small amount of litmus paper was affixed to the finger or thumbnail as a means

of obtaining a reliable measure of the presence or absence of thumbsucking over longer periods of time. These authors suggest that this procedure eliminates the possibility of overlooking and/ or inadvertently reinforcing the occurrence of the target behavior between observations. It also enjoys the advantage of being an economic, highly reliable, observation technique. Azrin, Nunn, and Frantz (1980) applied differential reinforcement using competing response training, parental support, and stimulus identification during a single session. Thumbsucking was reduced 92 percent in the first week and by 89 percent in a 20-month follow-up. A controlled comparison with a bitter-tasting substance on the finger produced a reduction of only 35 percent. In all of the above studies, use of DRO proved to be an effective means of producing substantial reductions in thumbsucking although treatment effects were relatively short lived in some studies.

Behavioral intervention using overcorrection and time-out has been used effectively in a number of studies (Azrin & Nunn, 1973; Bishop & Stumphauzer, 1973; Foxx & Azrin, 1973; Knight & McKenzie, 1974; Ross, 1975). Of special interest are Doke and Epstein (1975) who used an overcorrection procedure in which tooth brushing with an oral antiseptic was used on each occurrence of the behavior. The treatment rapidly suppressed the thumbsucking of this child and also that of another child who was not treated but who witnessed the procedure. Contingent threats were found to suppress thumbsucking behavior in the second child.

Baer (1962) used a response cost procedure in which access to watching cartoons was contingent upon the absence of thumbsucking. He produced a rapid decrease in the rate of thumbsucking behavior using this technique. Bishop and Stumphauzer (1973) in a procedure similar to Baer (1962) used removal of cartoon watching contingent upon thumbsucking. They used an instructional procedure to tell the subjects why they were stopping the cartoons. Results indicated generalization was highest in the instructed subjects. Ross (1975) used this procedure and applied medication to inhibit thumbsucking and produce a marked reduction in the frequency of the behavior although he did not eliminate it. Kauffman and Scranton (1974) used interruption of reading time effectively to reduce thumbsucking and produce generalization to other situations.

TRADITIONAL.   In the early 1900s, a number of devices to halt thumbsucking were developed. Duke and Nowicki (1979) remarked that foul-tasting preparations that were smeared on children's fingers were used in an attempt to make the behavior "distasteful," but many of the children soon liked the taste because of its association with the pleasurable act of thumbsucking.

Thom (1927) pointed out that thumbsucking can sometimes distract parents from concentrating on more important child development behaviors. A number of authors (Bakwin & Bakwin, 1972; Goldenson, 1970) have suggested ignoring the behavior, especially in preschool-age children. Ignoring the behavior, however, is often difficult in a world where everyone from the milkman to grandparents may comment, in tones ranging from mild disapproval to horror, about the child's thumbsucking. One consequence has been the use of threats, nagging, and restrictive devices such as mittens, cages for the thumbs, elbow braces so the child could not bend his arms, or bandages (Benjamin, 1967; Lassen & Flubt, 1978; Watson, 1969). The result of attempts to reduce thumbsucking by making the thumb or finger taste unpleasant with substances such as quinine, mustard, vinegar, and commercial preparations (such as Red Hot and Finger Tip), has generally been poor (Klackenberg, 1949).

DENTAL.   Dentists have advocated the use of unattractive oral devices or the palatal crib, which has spurs. The latter device is one in which thumb insertion in the mouth produces a painful sensation. Positive results have been reported with this device by a number of authors (Graber, 1961; Haryett et al., 1970; Moyers, 1963; Norton & Gellin, 1968; Watson, 1969). However, while producing a reduction in the rate of thumbsucking, especially in those who had the appliance in for more than

six months, sucking did recur in some of these children following removal of the device.

Conclusions

Thumbsucking is a habit disorder that often produces ridicule from others around the child. Of all the habit disorders, it may be the most misunderstood as well as the disorder for which everyone, from the mailman to the president, has an opinion as to its cause and cure. Behavioral procedures often produce immediate and lasting results, while foul-tasting liquids placed on the thumb are often ineffective.

Trichotillomania (Hair Pulling)

Hair pulling or trichotillomania is used to describe alopecia (baldness) produced by an individual pulling his or her own hair. Although the disorder manifests itself in the pulling of hair from the head, there are also individuals who pluck their eyelids, eyebrows, pubic region, and other axillary hair (Berg, 1978; Delgado & Mannino, 1969).

The disorder was first described by Hallopeau in 1889 and few references can be found in the literature. It is a rare condition, although fiddling with the hair is quite common and may be considered to be a normal activity.

Incidence

The incidence rate for hair pulling is difficult to ascertain, partly because cases are divided between dermatologists and psychotherapists (McLaughlin & Nay, 1975). One dermatology clinic reported seeing 24 cases in a 2-year period (Muller & Winkelmann, 1972) while a psychological service reported 19 cases in a 3-year period (Greenberg & Sarner, 1965). Studies limited to patients referred to mental health centers (Mannino & Delgado, 1969) suggest that the incidence rates of trichotillomania within a psychiatric population is less than 1 percent.

This disorder generally appears between 1.5 and 5 years of age and may persist until, or start in, adolescence. It appears to be a sex-linked trait, with 80–85 percent of all patients being female. The behavior is often episodic, occurring only during periods of stress (Bakwin & Bakwin, 1972; Wright et al., 1979). Trichotillomania has been associated with mentally retarded, autistic, and normal individuals, and research by Greenberg and Sarner (1965) indicated that the intellectual level of 65 percent of the cases was either average or above average.

Diagnosis

This disorder primarily involves hair pulling from the head, although other body areas are occasionally involved. The hair loss from the head is divided about 50 percent between the parietal-occipital area and the top of the head. The area in which hair is missing is frequently oblong and vertical to the ground. This area will consist of missing hair, broken hair, and hair that is intact with normal hair follicles. Differential diagnosis concerning other diseases of the hair and scalp is frequently made on the basis of the lack of inflammation, plus numerous broken hairs of varying size. Trichotillomania should be distinguished from alopecia areata, which occurs commonly in children and is manifested by noninflammatory alopecia. This disorder has lesions that are approximately the size of a nickel, smooth and completely without hair. It frequently develops a few weeks after severe emotional insult (Owen & Fliegelman, 1978).

Etiology

BEHAVIORAL. Little has been written on the specific behaviorally based etiological factors in hair pulling. Although it has been suggested (deL. Horne, 1977; McLaughlin & Nay, 1975) that the behavior is related to tension and anxiety, regardless of the initial etiology, there is a strong habitual component by the time the individual presents for treatment. Because the person may no longer attend to the hair pulling, feedback to enhance awareness of the maladaptive habit appears to be critical in the treatment.

TREATMENT. Twisting, stroking, or pulling the hair traditionally has been interpreted as reflecting the child's attempt to regain the positive feelings associated with his or her contact with the mother's body and clothes or as a conflict-resolving type of habit (Spock, 1968). It has been described as a normal autoerotic pattern in developing children. Other researchers have felt that, in cases of severe encephalopathy or schizophrenia, this behavior reflects aggression both toward oneself and toward others, with greater hair loss asociated with more severe psychopathology (Toback & Rajkumar, 1979).

The psychopathology of this disorder is assumed by many authors to be multiply determined. It may be the result of fixation at any level of psychosexual development; a response to deprivation or neglect (Abel & Mastriana, 1976); or a desire to incorporate mother and identify with her in order to reassure oneself against her loss. Or it may imply a masochistic response to the treatment of a sadistic parent (Oguchi & Miura, 1977); the denial of femininity (Davenport & Finch, 1973); or a recurrence of the Oedipal conflict (Monroe & Abse, 1963). Hair pulling has also been attributed to serious psychiatric illness as a form of fetish or as a form of masturbation (Buxbaum, 1960; Delgado & Mannino, 1969; Monroe & Abse, 1963). It has also been considered a manifestation of castration anxiety or castration complex (Berg, 1978).

The onset of this disorder in approximately 50 percent of the cases is at the time of an emotional precipitating event in the family, such as a death, divorce, illness, or the birth of a sibling (Litt, 1980). Irwin (1953) sees hair pulling as grief or rage turned inward. This description is often used as a definition for depression and is supported by Greenberg and Sarner's study (1965), which reported 65–70 percent of the patients were suffering episodic depression.

ORGANIC. The disorder is assumed to be a neurotic habit tic. It should not be confused with toxic alopecias, which result from severe illnesses, drug overdoses (especially Vitamin A), or hypopituitarism (Holvey & Talbott, 1972).

Treatment

BEHAVIORAL. A variety of behavioral techniques have been used to reduce or eliminate trichotillomania in children, including the use of self-monitoring procedures (Anthony, 1978; Stabler & Warren, 1974; Wulfsohn & Barling, 1978); operant conditioning using positive reinforcement and punishment (Gray, 1979; Saper, 1971); and the use of DRO or response cost techniques (Sanchez, 1979). McLaughlin and Nay (1975) used a treatment program that involved relaxation training, positive cognitive images of having long hair, a response cost component for pulling hair, and more assertive ways of interacting with family members to eliminate hair pulling in an adolescent girl.

Although the behavioral programs described often used components of other treatment procedures, at times the naturalistic environment provides quick alternatives to hair-pulling behavior. Wolff (1977) presented a case in which intervention by a ward aide was implemented while the psychologist was obtaining a list of appropriate references to research a treatment procedure. The aide's procedure consisted of cutting off all of the child's hair. The study was reported because once the child's hair grew back in, no further episodes of trichotillomania were observed. It could be hypothesized that, because the onset of this disorder is often associated with emotional stress, the specific environmental stressor was no longer present or that the ward aide's behavior acted as a severe punisher, suppressing further episodes of hair pulling. However, some children do not have hair regrowth, so this is not an appropriate treatment. One of the most promising behavioral treatments appears to be an adaptation of the habit reversal procedures developed by Azrin and Nunn (1973) for treatment of tics. This procedure is described in detail in a recent article by Rosenbaum and Ayllon (1981).

TRADITIONAL. A number of reports have stressed the necessity for psychodynamic intervention in cases of hair pulling (Abel & Mastriana, 1976; Davenport & Finch, 1973). Successful analytic treatment has been reported by a number of authors (Buxbaum, 1960; Delgado & Mannino, 1969; Lester, 1968). The assumed necessity in psychoanalytic theory for an "underlying disorder" can be seen in a study by Nagaraja (1976), who

presented three cases of hair pulling; however, he indicated that because one of the children was grossly retarded, this case could not be labeled as trichotillomania unless there was an emotional psychopathology not associated with decreased intelligence or brain damage. Lester (1968) used brief, dynamic psychotherapy with the parents and play therapy sessions with the child, producing successful results after four separate weekly appointments.

ORGANIC. Trichotillomania needs to be differentially diagnosed from a variety of other diseases of the hair and scalp, including alopecia areata. A variety of differential diagnostic tests, including microscopic examination of the scalp, and culturing for fungi may need to be obtained to rule out other conditions. A number of different treatments have been used, including systemic corticosteroids and triamcinolone acetonide, which is injected intradermally in the affected area (Holvey & Talbott, 1972; Owen & Fliegelman, 1978).

Conclusions

A variety of approaches, both behavioral and traditional, have been used in the treatment of trichotillomania. The bulk of the evidence suggests that the most effective treatment procedures at this time, in terms of rapid disruption of the behavior and long term results, appear to be combination behavioral programs, using feedback to improve awareness of the response, and positive reinforcement, in combination with an aversive component and perhaps some form of cognitive imagery, once organic etiology has been ruled out. Short term psychodynamic treatment has also been successful.

REFERENCES

Abe, K. Persistence of some behavior characteristics from childhood to maturity. *American Journal of Psychoanalysis,* 1976, **36,** 273–276.

Abe, K., & Oda, N. Follow-up study of children of childhood tiquers. *Biological Psychiatry,* 1978, **13,** 629–630.

Abel, J.A., & Mastriana, L. Children with alocepia

need psychiatric help. *Journal of the American Medical Association,* 1976, **235,** 698–699.

Abuzzahae, F.S., Anderson, F.O., & Sekhon, S.M. Multiple tic disorder: Gilles de la Tourette's syndrome. *Practical Psychology for Physicians,* 1975, **3,** 58–61.

Abuzzahae, F.S., & Ehlen, K.J. The clinical picture and management of Gilles de la Tourette's syndrome. *Child Psychiatry and Human Development,* 1971 **2,** 41–25.

Adesso, V.J., Vargas, J.M., & Siddall, J.W. The role of awareness in reducing nail-biting behavior. *Behavior Therapy,* 1979, **10,** 148–154.

American Psychiatric Association. Diagnostic and statistical manual of mental disorders (3rd ed.). Washington, D.C.: Author, 1980.

Anthony, W.Z. Brief intervention in a case of childhood trichotillomania by self-monitoring. *Journal of Behavior Therapy and Experimental Psychiatry,* 1978, **9,** 173–175.

Ascher, E. Psychodynamic considerations in Gilles de la Tourette's disease with a report of five cases and discussion of the literature. *American Journal of Psychiatry,* 1948, **105,** 267–275.

Azrin, N.H., & Nunn, R.G. Habit reversal: A method of eliminating nervous habits and tics. *Behaviour Research and Therapy,* 1973, **11,** 619–628.

Azrin, N.H., & Nunn, R.G. *Habit control in a day.* New York: Simon & Schuster, 1977.

Azrin, N.H., Nunn, R.G., & Frantz, R.S. Habit reversal treatment of thumbsucking. *Behaviour Research and Therapy,* 1980, **18,** 395–399.

Bachman, J.A. Self-injurious behavior: A behavioral analysis. *Journal of Abnormal Psychology,* 1972, **80,** 211–224.

Baer, D.M. Laboratory control of thumbsucking in three young children by withdrawal and re-presentation of positive reinforcement. *Journal of the Experimental Analysis of Behavior,* 1962, **5,** 525–528.

Bakwin, H. Nail-biting in twins. *Developmental Medicine and Child Neurology,* 1971, **13,** 304–307. (a)

Bakwin, H. Persistent finger-sucking in twins. *Developmental Medicine and Child Neurology,* 1971, **13,** 307–309. (b)

Bakwin, H. & Bakwin, R.M. *Behavior disorders in children* (4th ed.). Philadelphia: Saunders, 1972.

Bandura, A. *Principles of behavior modification.*

New York: Holt, Rinehart & Winston, 1969.

Barker, P. Haloperidol. *Journal of Child Psychology and Psychiatry,* 1975, **16,** 169–172.

Barnard, J.D., Christopherson, E.R., & Wolf, M.M. Parent-mediated treatment of children's self-injurious behavior using overcorrection. *Journal of Pediatric Psychology,* 1976, **1,** 56–61.

Baroff, G.S., & Tate, B.G. The use of aversive stimulation in the treatment of chronic self-injurious behavior. *Journal of American Academy of Child Psychiatry,* 1968, **7,** 454–470.

Barrett, B.H. Reduction in rate of multiple tics by free operant conditioning methods. *Journal of Nervous and Mental Diseases,* 1962, **135,** 187–195.

Beard, G. Experiments with the "jumpers" or "jumping Frenchmen" of Maine. *Journal of Nervous and Mental Diseases,* 1880, **7,** 487.

Beck, S., & Fedoravicius, A. Self-control treatment of an eye blink tic. *Behavior Therapy,* 1977, **8,** 277–279.

Benjamin, L.S. The beginning of thumbsucking. *Child Development,* 1967, **38,** 1065–1078.

Berg, B.O. Disorders of sleep. In S.S. Gellis & B.K. Kagan (Eds.), *Current pediatric therapy* (Vol. 8). Philadelphia: Saunders, 1978.

Bernhardt, A.J., Hersen, M., & Barlow, D.H. Measurement and modification of spasmodic torticollis: An experimental analysis. *Behavior Therapy,* 1972, **3,** 294–297.

Billig, A.L. Fingernail biting: The incipiency, incidence and amelioration. *Genetic Psychology Monographs,* 1941, **24,** 123–218.

Birch, L.B. The incidence of nailbiting among school children. *British Journal of Educational Psychology,* 1955, **25,** 123–128.

Bishop, B.R., & Stumphauzer, J.S. Behavior therapy of thumbsucking in children: A punishment (time-out) and generalization effect—What's a mother to do. *Psychological Reports,* 1973, **33,** 939–944.

Bixby, E.W. Haloperidol for the Gilles de la Tourette syndrome. *Journal of the American Medical Association,* 1970, **211,** 633.

Blau, S. A guide to the use of psychotropic medication in children and adolescents. *Journal of Clinical Psychiatry,* 1978, **39,** 766–772.

Boshes, L.D. Gilles de la Tourette's syndrome.

American Journal of Nursing, 1976, **76,** 1637–1638.

Brauer, J.C., Higley, L.B., Massler, M., & Schour, I. *Dentistry for children* (2nd ed.). Philadelphia: Blakiston, 1947.

Bremness, A.B., & Sverd, J. Methylphenidate-induced Tourette syndrome: Case report. *American Journal of Psychiatry,* 1979, **136,** 1334–1335.

Brierly, H. The treatment of hysterical spasmodic torticollis by behavior therapy. *Behaviour Research and Therapy,* 1967, **5,** 139–142.

Brody, S. Self-rocking in infancy. *Journal of the American Psychoanalytic Association,* 1960, **7,** 464–491.

Brown, S. Emotional disorders. In S. Gellis & B. Kagan (Eds.), *Current pediatric therapy* (8th ed.). Philadelphia: Saunders, 1978.

Browning, R.M., & Stover, D.O. *Behavior modification in child treatment.* Chicago: Aldine-Atherton, 1971.

Bruch, H., & Thum, L.C. Maladie des tics and maternal psychosis. *Journal of Nervous and Mental Disease,* 1968, **146,** 446–456.

Bruun, R.D., & Shapiro, A.K. Differential diagnosis of Gilles de la Tourette's syndrome. *Journal of Nervous and Mental Disorders,* 1972, **155,** 328–334.

Buxbaum, E. Hair pulling and fetishism. *Psychoanalytic Study of the Child,* 1960, **15,** 243–249.

Cantwell, D.P., & Baker, L. Psychiatric and behavioral characteristics of children with communication disorders. *Journal of Pediatric Psychology,* 1980, **5,** 161–178.

Carr, E.G., & McDowell, J.J. Social control of self-injurious behavior of organic etiology. *Behavior Therapy,* 1980, **11,** 402–409.

Cavenar, J.O., Spaulding, J.G., & Sullivan, J.L. Child's reaction to mother's abortion: Case report. *Military Medicine,* 1979, **144,** 412–413.

Clark, D.F. Behavior therapy of Gilles de la Tourette's syndrome. *British Journal of Psychiatry,* 1966, **112,** 771–778.

Clark, D.F. Behavior therapy of Gilles de la Tourette's syndrome. *New York State Journal of Medicine,* 1970, **70,** 2205–2210.

Clarke, N.G., & Kardachi, B.J. The treatment of myofascial pain-dysfunction syndrome using the biofeedback principle. *Journal of Periodontology,* 1977, **48,** 643–645.

Clerk, G. An ego-psychological approach to the problem of oral aggression. *International Journal of Psychoanalysis,* 1972, **53,** 77–82.

Cohen, D.J., Monty, H., & Williams, D. Management of thumbsucking using self-recording with parent as observer and experimenter. *Perceptual and Motor Skills,* 1980, **50,** 136.

Cohen, D.J., Nathanson, J.A., Young, J.G., & Shaywitz, B.A. Clonidine in Tourette's syndrome. *Lancet,* 1979, **8142,** 551–553.

Coleman, J.C., Butcher, J.N., & Carson, R.C. *Abnormal psychology and modern life* (6th ed.). Glenview, Ill.: Scott, Foresman, 1980.

Coleman, J.C., & McCalley, J.E. Nailbiting among college students. *Journal of Abnormal Psychology,* 1948, **43,** 517–525.

Corbett, J.A., Matthews, A.M., Connell, P.H., & Shapiro, D.A. Tics and Gilles de la Tourette's syndrome: A follow-up study and critical reviews. *British Journal of Psychiatry,* 1969, **115,** 1229–1241.

Daniels, L.K. *The management of childhood behavior problems in school and at home.* Springfield, Ill.: Thomas, 1974.

Davenport, C.W., & Finch, S.M. Compulsive hair pulling. *Medical Insight,* 1973, **5,** 23–25.

Davidson, P.O., Haryett, R.D., Sandilands, M., & Hansen, F.C. Thumbsucking: Habit or symptom? *Journal of Dentistry for Children,* 1967, **34,** 252–259.

deAjuriaguerra, J. *Handbook of child psychiatry and psychology.* New York: Masson, 1980.

Deardoff, P.A., Finch, A.J., & Royall, L.R. Manifest anxiety and nail-biting. *Journal of Clinical Psychology,* 1974, **30,** 378.

deL. Horne, D.J. Behavior therapy for trichotillomania. *Behaviour Research and Therapy,* 1977, **15,** 192–196.

Delgado, R.A., & Mannino, F.V. Some observations on trichotillomania in children. *Journal of the American Academy of Child Psychiatry,* 1969, **8,** 229–246.

DeLissovoy, V. Head-banging in early childhood: A study of incidence. *Journal of Pediatrics,* 1961, **58,** 803–805.

Dizmang, L.H., & Cheatham, C.F. The Lesch-Nyhan syndrome. *American Journal of Psychiatry,* 1970, **127,** 671–677.

Doke, L.A., & Epstein, L.H. Oral overcorrection: Side effects and extended applications. *Journal of Experimental Child Psychology,* 1975, **20,** 496–511.

Doleys, D.M., & Kurtz, P.S. A behavioral treatment program for the Gilles de la Tourette syndrome. *Psychological Reports,* 1974, **35,** 43–48.

Dougherty, E.H., & Lane, J.R. Naturalistic alternatives to extinction: An application to self-injurious bedtime behavior. *Journal of Behavior Therapy and Experimental Psychiatry,* 1976, **7,** 373–375.

Duke, M., & Nowicki, S.Jr. *Abnormal psychology: Perspectives on being different.* Belmont, Calif.: Wadsworth, 1979.

Evans, B. A case of trichotillomania in a child treated in a home token program. *Journal of Behavior Therapy and Experimental Psychiatry,* 1976, **7,** 197–198.

Ewen, S.J. Psychiatry and dentistry. In A.M. Freedman & H.J. Kaplan (Eds.), *Comprehensive textbook of psychiatry.* Baltimore: Williams & Wilkins, 1967.

Feldman, R.B., & Werry, J.S. An unsuccessful attempt to treat a tiqueur by massed practice. *Behavior Research and Therapy,* 1966, **4,** 111–117.

Fenichel, O. *The psychoanalytic theory of neurosis.* New York: Norton, 1945.

Fernando, S.J. Six cases of Gilles de la Tourette's syndrome. *British Journal of Psychiatry,* 1976, **128,** 436–441.

Foxx, R.M., & Azrin, N.H. The elimination of autistic self-stimulatory behavior by overcorrection. *Journal of Applied Behavior Analysis,* 1973, **6,** 1–14.

Fras, I., & Karlavage, J. The use of methylphenidate and imipramine in Gilles de la Tourette's disease in children. *American Journal of Psychiatry,* 1977, **134,** 195–197.

Frazier, J.R., & Williams, B.R. The application of multiple contingencies to rocking behavior in a nonretarded child. *Journal of Behavior Therapy and Experimental Psychiatry,* 1973, **4,** 289–291.

Freud, A. *Normality and pathology in childhood.* New York: International Universities Press, 1965.

Friedman, M., Glasser, M., Laufer, E., Laufer, M., & Wohl, M. Attempted suicide and self-mutilation in adolescence: Some observations from a psychoanalytic research project. *International Journal of Psycho-Analysis,* 1972, **53,** 179–183.

Frisch, J., Katz, L., & Ferreira, A.J. A study of the relationship between bruxism and aggression. *Journal of Periodontics,* 1960, **31,** 409–412.

Frohman, B.S. Occlusal neuroses. *Psychoanalytic Review,* 1932, **19,** 297–309.

Gelberd, M.W. Treatment of bruxism: A case report. *Journal of Hypnosis and Psychology in Dentistry,* 1958, **1,** 18.

Gerard, M.W. The psychogenic tic in ego development. *Psychoanalytic Study of the Child,* 1946, **2,** 133–141.

Golden, G.S. Gilles de la Tourette's syndrome following methylphenidate administration. *Developmental Medicine and Child Neurology,* 1974, **16,** 76–78.

Golden, G.S. The effect of central nervous system stimulants on Tourette's syndrome. *Annals of Neurology,* 1977, **2,** 69–70. (a)

Golden, G.S. Genetic aspects of Tourette syndrome. *Neurology,* 1977, **27,** 400. (b)

Golden, G.S. Tics and Tourette's: A continuum of symptoms. *Annals of Neurology,* 1978, **4,** 145–148.

Goldenson, R.M. *The encyclopedia of human behavior: Psychology, psychiatry and mental health* (Vol. 2). Garden City, N.Y.: Doubleday, 1970.

Gottlieb, B. Traumatic occlusion and the rest position of the mandible. *Journal of Periodontology,* 1947, **18,** 7–21.

Graber, T.M. *Orthodontics.* Philadelphia: Saunders, 1961.

Gray, J.J. Positive reinforcement and punishment in the treatment of childhood trichotillomania. *Journal of Behavior Therapy and Experimental Psychiatry,* 1979, **10,** 125–129.

Green, A.H. Self-mutilation in schizophrenic children. *Archives of General Psychiatry,* 1967, **17,** 234–244.

Green, A.H. Self-destructive behavior in battered children. *American Journal of Psychiatry,* 1978, **135,** 579–582.

Greenberg, H.R., & Sarner, C.A. Trichotillomania. *Archives of General Psychiatry,* 1965, **12,** 482–489.

Greenberg, N.H. Origins of head-rolling (spasmus mutans) during early infancy. *Psychosomatic Medicine,* 1964, **26,** 162–171.

Grimshaw, L. The outcome of obsessional disorder: A follow-up study of 100 cases. *British Journal of Psychiatry,* 1965, **111,** 1051–1056.

Haidar, A., & Clancy, J. Case report of successful

treatment of a reflex trigeminal nerve blepharospasm by behavior modification. *American Journal of Opthalmology,* 1973, **75,** 148–149.

Harris, M. The child psychotherapist and the patient's family. *Journal of Child Psychotherapy,* 1968, **2,** 50–63.

Harris, S.L., & Romanczyk, R.G. Treating self-injurious behavior of a retarded child by overcorrection. *Behavior Therapy,* 1976, **7,** 235–239.

Haryett, R.D., Hansen, F.C., & Davidson, P.O. Chronic thumbsucking: A second report on treatment and its psychological effects. *American Journal of Orthodontics,* 1970, **57,** 164–177.

Holowach, J., & Thurston, D.L. Breath-holding spells and anemia. *New England Journal of Medicine,* 1963, **268,** 21–23.

Holvey, D.N., & Talbott, J.H. *The Merck manual of diagnosis and therapy.* Rahway, N.J.: Merck, Sharp, & Dohme Research Laboratories, 1972.

Hughes, H., Hughes, A., & Dial, H. A behavioral seal: An apparatus alternative to behavioral observation of thumbsucking. *Behavior Research Methods and Instrumentation,* 1978, **10,** 460–461.

Hughes, H., Hughes, A., & Dial, H. Homebased treatment of thumbsucking: Omission training with edible reinforcers and a behavioral seal. *Behavior Modification,* 1979, **3,** 179–186.

Hutt, S.J., & Hutt, C. Stereotypy, arousal, and autism. *Human Development,* 1968, **11,** 277–286.

Hutzell, R.R., Platzek, D., & Logue, P.E. Control of symptoms of Gilles de la Tourette's syndrome by self-monitoring. *Journal of Behavior Therapy and Experimental Psychiatry,* 1974, **5,** 71–76.

Ilg, F.L., & Ames, L.B. *Child behavior.* New York: Harper, 1955.

Irwin, D. Alopecia. In B.G. Russell & E.D. Wittkower (Eds.), *Emotional factors in skin disease.* New York: Paul Hoeber, 1953.

Itard, J.M.G. Memories of some involuntary functions of the appearance of movement, grasp, and voice. *Archives of General Medicine,* 1825, **8,** 358.

Johnson, P.B., & Johnson, H.L. Birth order and thumbsucking. *Psychological Reports,* 1975, **36,** 598.

Johnson, W.L., & Baumeister, A.A. Self-injurious

behavior: A review and analysis of methodological details of published studies. *Behavior Modification,* 1978, **2,** 456–487.

Jorgenson, H. The use of a contingent music activity to modify behaviors which interfere with learning. *Journal of Music Therapy,* 1974, **11,** 41–44.

Kardachi, B.J., Bailey, J.O., & Ash, M.M. A comparison of biofeedback and occlusal adjustment on bruxism. *Journal of Periodontology,* 1978, **49,** 367–372.

Kauffman, J.M., & Scranton, T.R. Parent control of thumbsucking in the home. *Child Study Journal,* 1974, **4,** 1–10.

Kelman, D.H. Gilles de la Tourette's disease: A review of the literature. *Journal of Child Psychology and Psychiatry,* 1965, **6,** 219–226.

Kim, K.I. A case of Gilles de la Tourette's disease— A psychodynamic study. *Neuropsychiatry,* 1971, **10,** 35–41.

Klackenberg, G. Thumbsucking: Frequency and etiology. *Pediatrics,* 1949, **4,** 418–424.

Klawans, H.L., Falk, D.K., Navsieda, P.A., & Weiner, W.K. Gilles de la Tourette's syndrome after long-term chlorpromazine therapy. *Neurology,* 1978, **28,** 1064–1068.

Knight, M.F., & McKenzie, H.S. Elimination of bedtime thumbsucking in home settings through contingent reading. *Journal of Applied Behavior Analysis,* 1974, **7,** 33–38.

Kohut, H. Thoughts on narcissism and narcissistic rage. *Psychoanalytic Study of the Child,* 1972, **27,** 360–400.

Koranyi, B.K. Remarkable etiology in Gilles de la Tourette's disease. *Journal of the University of Ottawa,* 1977, **1,** 507.

Kravitz, H., Rosenthal, V., Teplitz, Z., Murphy, J., & Lesser, R. A study of head banging in infants and children. *Diseases of the Nervous System,* 1960, **21,** 203–208.

Lahey, B.B., McNees, M.P., & McNees, M.C. Control of an obscene "verbal tic" through timeout in an elementary school classroom. *Journal of Applied Behavior Analysis,* 1973, **6,** 101–104.

Lake, F. Treating psychosomatic disorders related to birth trauma. *Journal of Psychosomatic Research,* 1978, **22,** 227–238.

Lane, R.G., & Dormath, R.P. Behavior therapy: A case history. *Hospital and Community Psychiatry,* 1970, **21,** 150–153.

Lapouse, R., & Monk, M.A. Fears and worries in a

representative sample of children. *American Journal of Orthopsychiatry*, 1959, **29**, 803–818.

Lassen, M.K., & Flubt, N.R. Elimination of nocturnal thumbsucking by glove wearing. *Journal of Behavior Therapy and Experimental Psychiatry*, 1978, **9**, 85.

Lester, E.P. Brief psychotherapies in child psychiatry. *Canadian Psychiatric Association Journal*, 1968, **13**, 301–309.

Lester, G., Bierbrauer, B., Selfridge, B., & Gomeringer, D. Distractibility, intensity of reaction, and non-nutritive sucking. *Psychological Reports*, 1976, **39**, 1212–1214.

Levy, D.M. Finger-sucking an accessory movements in early infancy: Etiologic study. *American Journal of Psychiatry*, 1928, **7**, 881–887.

Lewis, S.J. The effect of thumb and finger sucking on the primary teeth and dental arches. *Child Development*, 1937, **8**, 93–98.

Lichstein, K.L. Thumbsucking: A review of dental and psychological variables and their implications for treatment. *JSAS Catalog of Selected Documents in Psychology*, 1978, **8**, 13.

Lichstein, K.L., & Kachmarik, G. A non-aversive intervention for thumbsucking: Analysis across settings and time in the natural environment. *Journal of Pediatric Psychology*, 1980, **5**, 405–414.

Linscheid, T.R., Copeland, A.P. Jacobstein, D.M., & Smith, J.L. Overcorrection treatment for nighttime self-injurious behavior in two normal children. *Journal of Pediatric Psychology*, 1981, **6**, 29–35.

Litt, C.J. Trichotillomania in childhood: A case of successful short-term treatment. *Journal of Pediatric Psychology*, 1980, **5**, 37–42.

Logue, P.B., Platzek, D., Hutzell, R., & Robinson, B. Neurological, neuropsychological and behavioral aspects of Gilles de la Tourette's syndrome: A case. *Perceptual and Motor Skills*, 1973, **37**, 855–861.

Lovaas, O., & Simmons, J.Q. Manipulation of self-destruction in three retarded children. *Journal of Applied Behavior Analysis*, 1969, **2**, 143–152.

Lowitz, G.H., & Suib, M.R. Generalized control of persistent thumbsucking by differential reinforcement of other behaviors. *Journal of Behavior Therapy and Experimental Psychiatry*, 1978, **9**, 343–346.

Lucas, A.R. Gilles de la Tourette's disease in children: Treatment with phenothiazine drugs. *American Journal of Psychiatry*, 1964, **121**, 606–608.

Lucas, A.R. Gilles de la Tourette's disease: An overview. *New York State Journal of Medicine*, 1970, **70**, 2197–2200.

Lucas, A.R., & Rodin, E.A. Electroencephalogram in Gilles de la Tourette's disease. *Diseases of the Nervous System*, 1973, **34**, 85–89.

MacKay, M.C., & Heimlich, E.P. Case report: Psychotherapy with paraverbal therapy in a case of Gilles de la Tourette syndrome. *American Journal of Psychotherapy*, 1972, **26**, 571–577.

Mahler, M.S. A psychoanalytic evaluation of tic in psychopathology of children: Symptomatic and the syndrome. *Psychoanalytic Study of the Child*, 1949, **3**, 279–285.

Maletzky, B.M. Behavior recording as treatment: A brief note. *Behavior Therapy*, 1974, **5**, 107–111.

Mannino, F.V., & Delgado, R.A. Trichotillomania in children: A review. *American Journal of Psychiatry*, 1969, **126**, 505–511.

Marks, M.B. Bruxism in allergic children. *American Journal of Orthodontics*, 1980, **77**, 48–59.

Martin, A. Tourette's syndrome. *Children Today*, 1977, **6**, 26–27.

Martin, D. A six-year-old "behaviorist" solves her sibling's chronic thumb-sucking problem. *Corrective and Social Psychiatry and Journal of Applied Behavior Technology*, 1975, **21**, 19–21.

Martin, R.D., & Conway, J.B. Aversive stimulation to eliminate infant nocturnal rocking. *Journal of Behavior Therapy and Experimental Psychiatry*, 1976, **7**, 200–201.

Massler, M., & Malone, A.J. Nail-biting: A review. *Journal of Pediatrics*, 1950, **36**, 523–531.

McCandless, B.R. Problems of childhood and adolescence. In L.A. Pennington & I.A. Berg (Eds.), *An introduction to clinical psychology* (2nd ed.). New York: Ronald, 1954.

McLaughlin, J.G., & Nay, W.R. Treatment of trichotillomania using positive coverants and response cost: A case report. *Behavior Therapy*, 1975, **6**, 87–91.

Medical mystery: Tourette's. *MD*, January, 1981, **25**(1), 62–64.

Mendel, J.G.C., & Klein, D.F. Anxiety attacks

with subsequent agoraphobia. *Comprehensive Psychiatry,* 1969, **10,** 190–195.

Miller, A.L. Treatment of a child with Gilles de la Tourette's syndrome using behavior modification techniques. *Journal of Behavior Therapy and Experimental Psychiatry,* 1970, **1,** 319–321.

Miller, S.C., Thaller, J.L., & Soberman, A. The use of the Minnesota multiphasic personality inventory in peridontal disease. *Journal of Peridontology,* 1956, **27,** 44–46.

Missildine, W.H. Intrafamilial relationships of children with tics. *Feelings and Their Medical Significance,* 1964, **6,** 1–4.

Moldofsky, H. A psychophysiological study of multiple tics. *Archives of General Psychiatry,* 1971, **25,** 79–87.

Money, J. Dwarfism: Questions and answers in counseling. *Rehabilitation Literature,* 1967, **28,** 134–138.

Money, J., Wolff, G., & Annecillo, C. Pain agnosia and self-injury in the syndrome of reversible somatotropin deficiency (psychosocial dwarfism). *Journal of Autism and Childhood Schizophrenia,* 1972, **2,** 127–139.

Monroe, J.T., & Abse, D.W. The psychopathology of trichotillomania and trichophagy. *Psychiatry,* 1963, **26,** 95–103.

Moore, D.S. Bruxism, diagnosis and treatment. *Journal of Periodontology,* 1956, **27,** 277–283.

Moyers, R.E. *Handbook of orthodontics* (2nd ed.). Chicago: Year Book Medical Publishers, 1963.

Mulick, J.A., Hoyt, P., Rojahn, J., & Schroeder, S.R. Reduction of a nervous habit in a profoundly retarded youth by increasing toy play. *Journal of Behavior Therapy and Experimental Psychiatry,* 1978, **9,** 381–385.

Muller, S.A., & Winkelmann, R.K. Trichotillomania: A clinicopathologic study of twenty-four cases. *Archives of Dermatology,* 1972, **105,** 535–540.

Murray, A.B., & Anderson, D.O. The association of incisor protrusion with digit sucking and allergic nasal itching. *Journal of Allergy,* 1969, **44,** 239–247.

Nagaraja, J. Tricomania. *Child Psychiatry Quarterly,* 1976, **9,** 6–9.

Norton, L.A., & Gellin, M.E. Management of digital sucking and tongue thrusting in children. *Dental Clinics of North America,* 1968, **12,** 363–382.

Nunn, R.G., & Azrin, N.H. Eliminating nail-biting by the habit reversal procedure. *Behavior Research and Therapy,* 1976, **14,** 65–67.

Oguchi, T., & Miura, S. Trichotillomania: Its psychopathological aspect. *Comprehensive Psychiatry,* 1977, **18,** 177–182.

Ollendick, T.H. Self-monitoring and self-administered overcorrection: The modification of nervous tics in children. *Behavior Modification,* 1981, **5,** 75–84.

Owen, L.G., & Fliegelman, M.T. Diseases of the hair and scalp. In S.S. Gellis & B.K. Kagan (Eds.), *Current pediatric therapy* (Vol. 8). Philadelphia: Saunders, 1978.

Palermo, D.S. Thumbsucking: A learned response. *Pediatrics,* 1956, **17,** 392–399.

Partington, M.W., & Hennen, B.K. The Lesch-Nyhan syndrome: Self-destructive biting, mental retardation, neurological disorder and hyperuricacemia. *Developmental Medicine and Child Neurology,* 1967, **9,** 563–572.

Paskal, V. The value of imitative behavior. *Developmental Psychology,* 1969, **1,** 463–469.

Peterson, R.F, & Peterson, L.R. The use of positive reinforcement in the control of self-destructive behavior in a retarded boy. *Journal of Experimental Child Psychology,* 1968, **6,** 351–360.

Phillips, R.H., & Muzaffer, A. Some aspects of self-mutilation in the general population of a large psychiatric hospital. *Psychiatric Quarterly,* 1961, **35,** 421–423.

Pierce, C.M. Nail-biting and thumb-sucking. In A.M. Freedman & H.I. Kaplan (Eds.), *The child: His psychological and cultural development: I. Normal development and psychological assessment.* New York: Atheneum, 1972.

Rafi, A.A. Learning theory and the treatment of tics. *Journal of Psychosomatic Research,* 1962, **6,** 71–76.

Reding, G.R., Rubright, W.C., & Zimmerman, S.O. Incidence of bruxism. *Journal of Dental Research,* 1966, **45,** 1198–1204.

Reding, G.R., Zepelin, H., & Monroe, L.J. Personality study of nocturnal teeth-grinders. *Perceptual and Motor Skills,* 1968, **26,** 523–531.

Ribble, M.A. Infantile experience in relation to personality development. In J.McV. Hunt (Ed.), *Personality and the behavior disorders* (Vol. 2). New York: Ronald, 1944.

Roberts, E. Thumb and finger sucking in relation to feeding in early infancy. *American Journal of Diseases in Children,* 1944, **68,** 7–8.

Rosen, M., & Wesner, C. A behavioral approach to Tourette's syndrome. *Journal of Consulting and Clinical Psychology,* 1973, **41,** 308–312.

Rosenbaum, M.S., & Ayllon, T. The habit-reversal technique in treating trichotillomania. *Behavior Therapy,* 1981, **12,** 473–481.

Rosenthal, J.H., Nicholson, R., & Coller, E. The syndrome of Gilles de la Tourette. *Journal of Learning Disabilities,* 1975, **8,** 95–97.

Ross, J.A. Use of teacher and peers to control classroom thumbsucking. *Psychological Reports,* 1974, **34,** 327–330.

Ross, J.A. Parents modify thumbsucking: A case study. *Journal of Behavior Therapy and Experimental Psychiatry,* 1975, **6,** 248–249.

Ross, J.A., & Levine, B.A. Control of thumbsucking in the classroom: Case study. *Perceptual and Motor Skills,* 1972, **34,** 584–586.

Ruttle, A.T., Quigley, W., Crouch, J.T., & Ewan, G.E. A serial study of the effects of finger sucking. *Journal of Dental Research,* 1953, **32,** 739–748.

Sanchez, V. Behavioral treatment of chronic hair pulling in a two-year-old. *Journal of Behavior Therapy and Experimental Psychiatry,* 1979, **10,** 241–245.

Sand, P. Neuropsychological test performance before and after symptom removal in a child with Gilles de la Tourette's syndrome. *Journal of Clinical Psychology,* 1972, **28,** 596–600.

Saper, B. A report on behavior therapy with outpatient clinic patients. *Psychiatric Quarterly,* 1971, **45,** 209–215.

Saul, L.J. A psychoanalytic view of hostility: Its genesis, treatment, and implications for society. *Humanitas,* 1976, **12,** 171–182.

Savicki, V., & Carlin, A.S. Behavioral treatment of Gilles de la Tourette syndrome. *International Journal of Child Psychotherapy,* 1972, **1,** 97–109.

Schulman, M. Control of tics by maternal reinforcement. *Journal of Behavior Therapy and Experimental Psychiatry,* 1974, **5,** 95–96.

Sears, R.R., & Wise, G.W. Relation of cup feeding to thumbsucking and the oral drive. *American Journal of Orthopsychiatry.* 1950, **20,** 123–128.

Shaffer, L.F. *Psychology of adjustment: An objective approach to mental hygiene.* Boston: Houghton Mifflin, 1936.

Shapiro, A.K., Shapiro, E., Wayne, H., & Clarkin, J. The psychopathology of Gilles de la Tourette's syndrome. *American Journal of Psychiatry,* 1972, **129,** 427–434.

Shapiro, A.K., Shapiro, E., Wayne, H., Clarkin, J., & Bruun, R. Tourette's syndrome: Summary of data on 34 patients. *Psychosomatic Medicine,* 1973, **35,** 419–433.

Shapiro, A.K., Shapiro, E.S., Bruun, R.D., & Sweet, R.D. *Gilles de la Tourette's syndrome.* New York: Raven, 1978.

Shapiro, E., Shapiro, A.K., & Clarkin, J. Clinical psychological testing in Tourette's syndrome. *Journal of Personality Assessment,* 1974, **38,** 464–478.

Shapiro, E.S., Barrett, R.P., & Ollendick, T.H. A comparison of physical restraint and positive practice overcorrection in treating stereotypic behavior. *Behavior Therapy,* 1980, **11,** 227–233.

Shapiro, S., & Shannon, J. Bruxism as an emotional reactive disturbance. *Psychosomatics,* 1966, **6,** 427–430.

Shear, C.S., Nyhan, W.L., Kirman, B.H., & Stern, J. Self-mutilative behavior as a feature of the deLange syndrome. *Journal of Pediatrics,* 1971, **78,** 506–509.

Sheppard, I.M., & Sheppard, S.M. Characteristics of temporomandibular joint problems. *Journal of Prosthetic Dentistry,* 1977, **38,** 180–191.

Sillman, J.H. Serial study of occlusion from birth to three years. *American Journal of Orthodontics,* 1940, **26,** 207–301.

Simmons, R. Psychophysiological disorders in childhood and adolescenc.e In P.D. Steinhauer & Q. Rae-Grant (Eds.), *Psychological problems of the child and his family.* Toronto: Macmillan, 1977.

Singer, K. Gilles de la Tourette's disease. *American Journal of Psychiatry,* 1963, **120,** 80–81.

Skiba, E.A., Pettigrew, E., & Alden, S.E. A behavioral approach to the control of thumbsucking in the classroom. *Journal of Applied Behavior Analysis,* 1971, **4,** 121–125.

Skinner, B.F. *Science and human behavior.* New York: Macmillan, 1953.

Smith, D.W. *Recognizable patterns of human malformation.* Philadelphia: Saunders, 1970.

Smith, M. Effectiveness of symptomatic treatment

of nailbiting in college students. *Psychological Newsletter,* 1957, **8,** 219–231.

Solnick, J.V., Rincover, A., & Peterson, C.R. Some determinants of the reinforcing and punishing effects of timeout. *Journal of Applied Behavior Analysis,* 1977, **10,** 415–424.

Sperling, M., & Sperling, O.E. *Psychosomatic disorders in childhood.* New York: Aronson, 1978.

Spitz, R.A. Hospitalism: An inquiry into the genesis of psychiatric conditions in early childhood. *Psychoanalytic Study of the Child,* 1945, **1,** 53–74.

Spock, B. *Baby and child care.* New York: Pocket Books, 1968.

Sprague, R.L. Psychopharmacotherapy in children. In M. McMillan (Ed.), *Child psychiatry: Treatment and research.* New York: Brunner/Mazel, 1977.

Stabler, B., & Warren, A.B. Behavioral contracting in treating trichotillomania: Case note. *Psychological Reports,* 1974, **34,** 401–402.

Stephen, L.S., & Koenig, K.P. Habit modification through threatened loss of money. *Behaviour Research and Therapy,* 1970, **8,** 211–212.

Strother, E.W., & Mitchell, E. Bruxism: A review and a case report. *Journal of Dental Medicine,* 1953, **8,** 189–202.

Sunanda, A. Some childhood aberrations. *Social Welfare,* 1972, **18,** 29–30.

Surwillo, W.W., Shafii, M., & Barrett, C.L. Gilles de la Tourette syndrome: A 20-month study of the effects of stressful life events and haloperidol on symptom frequency. *Journal of Nervous and Mental Disease,* 1978, **166,** 812–816.

Sweet, R.D., Solomon, G.E., Wayne, H., Shapiro, E., & Shapiro, A.K. Neurological features of Gilles Tourette's syndrome. *Journal of Neurology, Neurosurgery, and Psychiatry,* 1973, **36,** 1–9.

Tapia, F. Haldol in the treatment of children with tics and stutters and an incidental finding. *Psychiatric Quarterly,* 1969, **43,** 646–649.

Tate, B.G., & Baroff, G.S. Aversive control of self-injurious behavior in a psychotic boy. *Behaviour Research and Therapy,* 1966, **4,** 281–287.

Thaller, J.L. The use of the Cornell Index to determine the correlation between bruxism and the anxiety state: A preliminary report. *Journal of Periodontics,* 1960, **31,** 138–140.

Thaller, J.L., Rosen, G., & Saltzman, S. Study of the relationship of frustration and anxiety to bruxism. *Journal of Periodontology,* 1967, **38,** 193–197.

Thelen, E. Determinants of amounts of stereotyped behavior in normal human infants. *Ethology and Sociobiology,* 1980, **1,** 141–150.

Thom, D.A. *Everyday problems of the everyday child.* New York: Appleton-Century-Crofts, 1927.

Thomas, E.J., Abrams, K.S., & Johnson, J.B. Self-monitoring and reciprocal inhibition in the modification of multiple tics of Gilles de la Tourette's syndrome. *Journal of Behavior Therapy and Experimental Psychiatry,* 1971, **2,** 159–171.

Thompson, R.J., O'Quinn, A.N., & Logue, P.E. Gilles de la Tourette's syndrome: A review and neuropsychological aspects of four cases. *Journal of Pediatric Psychology,* 1979, **4,** 371–387.

Tiller, J.W.G. Brief family therapy for childhood tic syndrome. *Family Process,* 1978, **17,** 217–223.

Toback, C., & Rajkumar, S. The emotional disturbance underlying alopecia areata, alopecia totalis, and trichotillomania. *Child Psychiatry and Human Development,* 1979, **10,** 114–117.

Traisman, A.S., & Traisman, H.S. Thumb and finger-sucking: A study of 2,650 infants and children. *Journal of Pediatrics,* 1958, **52,** 566–572.

Tryon, A.F. Thumb-sucking and manifest anxiety: A note. *Child Development,* 1968, **39,** 1159–1163.

Tupin, J.P., Mahar, D., & Smith, D. Two types of violent offenders with psychosocial descriptors. *Diseases of the Nervous System,* 1973, **34,** 356–363.

Uchiyama, K. Effects of reciprocal inhibition through autogenic training relaxation on psychogenic tics. *Bulletin of Clinical and Consulting Psychology,* 1976, **15,** 1–10.

Valentine, C.W. *The normal child and some of his abnormalities.* Santa Fe: Gannon, 1955.

Vargas, J.M., & Adesso, V.J. A comparison of aversion therapies for nailbiting behavior. *Behavior Therapy,* 1976, **7,** 322–329.

Varni, J.W., Boyd, E.F., & Cataldo, M.F. Self-monitoring, external reinforcement, and time-out procedures in the control of high rate tic behaviors in a hyperactive child. *Journal of*

Behavior Therapy and Experimental Psychiatry, 1978, **9,** 353–358.

Vernallis, F.F. Teeth-grinding: Some relationships to anxiety, hostility, and hyperactivity. *Journal of Clinical Psychology,* 1955, **11,** 389–391.

Voth, H.M. Dream analysis in the treatment of an eleven-year-old boy. *International Journal of Psychoanalytic Psychotherapy,* 1979, **7,** 254–274.

Walsh, J.P. The psychogenesis of bruxism. *Journal of Periodontology,* 1965, **36,** 417–420.

Walton, D. Experimental psychology and the treatment of a tiqueur. *Journal of Child Psychology and Psychiatry,* 1961, **2,** 148–155.

Warme, G. Childhood developmental problems. In P.D. Steinhauer & Q. Rae-Grant (Eds.), *Psychological problems of the child and his family.* Toronto: Macmillan, 1977.

Watson, D.H. Orthodontics and the growing child problems encountered in the primary dentition. *International Journal of Orthodontics,* 1969, **7,** 68–75.

White, J.H. The use and misuse of psychotropic drugs in children. *Psychiatric Digest,* 1976, **37,** 13–16.

Wilder, J. Tic convulsive as a psychosomatic problem. *Nervous Children,* 1946, **5,** 365–371.

Williams, C. Self-injury in children. *Developmental Medicine and Child Neurology,* 1974, **16,** 88–90.

Wittkower, E.D., & White, K.L. Psychophysiologic aspects of respiratory disorders. In S. Arieti (Ed.), *American handbook of psychiatry* (Vol. 1). New York: Basic Books, 1959.

Wolfenstein, M. Trends in infant care. In S. Harrison (Ed.), *Childhood psychopathology.* New York: International Universities Press, 1972.

Wolff, R. Trichotillamania: Harriet's treatment. *Psychological Reports,* 1977, **40,** 50.

Woodrow, K.M. Gilles de la Tourette's disease: A review. *American Journal of Psychiatry,* 1974, **131,** 1000–1003.

Wright, L., Schaefer, A.B., & Solomons, G. *Encyclopedia of pediatric psychology.* Baltimore: University Park Press, 1979.

Wulfsohn, D., & Barling, J. From external to self-control: Behavioral treatment of trichotillomania in an eleven-year-old girl. *Psychological Reports,* 1978, **42,** 1171–1174.

Zarcone, V., & Dement, W. Diagnosis and treatment of sleep disorders. In A.M. Freeman III, R.L. Sack, & P.A. Berger (Eds.), *Psychiatry for the primary care physician.* Baltimore: Williams & Wilkins, 1979.

CHAPTER 17

Psychosomatic Problems of Children

THOMAS J. KENNY, STEFANIE F.A. BERGEY, AND DEBORAH YOUNG-HYMAN

Psychologists are reactivating their relationships with medical colleagues in the area of primary health care and are expanding beyond the role of a mental health subspecialist who relates primarily to the psychiatrist. Nowhere is this change more apparent and more productive than in the area called "psychosomatic illness," especially as the concept of psychosomatic illness applies to children. However, if the skills of psychology and medicine are to focus effectively on health maintenance or facilitation, we must discard the concept of mind-body separation, especially in the area of psychosomatic illness.

The idea presented in contrast to the mind-body thesis is one that places psychosomatic problems on a continuum, ranging from those that are overwhelmingly psychological, with a lesser physical component, to those that are primarily physical, with a lesser psychological component. This concept has significant implications for the understanding and management of psychosomatic illness.

The aim of this chapter will be: (1) to examine the concepts and theories underlying the field of psychosomatic illness; (2) to trace the development of changes in the concept of psychosomatic illness; and (3) to project the optimal contributions of psychology to the treatment of psychosomatic problems in children and discuss the issues of training, research, and service as they relate to this expanded role.

The major premise of this chapter is that the mind/body dichotomy has held back the effective understanding of psychosomatic illness in children and has outlived any pretense of usefulness. By abandoning the either/or associated with mind-body, we may view illness (and illness behavior in children) as a continuum. This concept allows for evaluation of the complex interactions between the organism and environment and the consequent effect of such interactions on the manifestation of illness or the suppression of illness.

CONCEPTUALIZATION OF PSYCHOSOMATIC ILLNESS

This section will examine the historical origins of the field of psychosomatics, trace its evolution, and propose an expanded concept that will include chronic illness. In this conceptual view of the field, psychosomatics is part of a continuum ranging from conversion reaction, to psychosomatic illness, to somatopsychic illness, to chronic illness.

The traditional hysterical conversion reactions signify an extreme point in the psychological end of the continuum of psychosomatic disorders, with disorders such as ulcers, migraine, or chronic, recurring abdominal pain; problems with a large emotional component and a vague physical basis are the next point on the continuum. Somatopsychic problems have an identifiable physical base, but the severity and management of the problem are greatly influenced by psychological variables, as in the case of asthma or diabetes. Chronic illness is a physically handicapping condition that requires an effective psychological adaption to facilitate optimal adjustment.

The roots of the theories of psychosomatic illness are strongly bound to psychoanalytic thought and the mind-body dualism. Freud's early success in treating "hysteria," an illness that had no identifiable physical basis, produced several results. First, it thrust Freud to the forefront of the emerging field of psychiatry, but, in an associative manner, it also set the theory of psychosomatic illness in a position where the illness was a manifestation of the mind. This tenet was so strong as to suggest that the body had little or no part in the illness. The psychoanalytic concept of conversion reaction has been founded in the belief that the physical symptoms were functional manifestations of "converted" mental processes. In defining the conversion reaction, Engle (1970) states that it is a "psychic mechanism whereby an idea, fantasy, or wish is expressed in bodily rather than verbal terms and is experienced by the patient as a physical rather than a mental symptom" (p. 650). Engle goes on to describe conversion symptoms and states that they "derive from stored mental representations (memories) of bodily activities or functioning which are utilized to express symbolically unconscious wishes or impulses as a means of coping with psychological conflict" (p. 651).

The impact on medicine and the public of these psychoanalytic theories of conversion was to treat the patients as mentally and not physically ill. As a result, persons with "psychosomatic illness" were not really sick; they "imagined" they were sick while they were really emotionally ill. Perhaps if this had led to enlightened or even humane treatment of the patient, this would still be the operative theory in psychosomatic illness. However, in practice this concept produced a situation where persons—adults and children—who presented with vague, unusual, persistent, or unexplainable physical symptoms were first evaluated by the usual medical diagnostic procedures and, if no clear diagnostic explanation resulted, the patient was considered to be "psychosomatic."

There are several detrimental consequences that have been a major part of the "all in the mind" approach to unexplained illness. First is the negative attitude engendered by the patient from the professional and the general public. The term "crock" has long been associated with patients who have recurrent, unexplained illnesses. When seen by the physician, the vague symptoms or inconsistent patterns of dysfunction cause frustration to the physician, who sees himself or herself as trying to cure the patient and is thwarted by the "poor" picture given by the patient. When all of the usual medical test procedures provide no help in explaining the problem, the physician's frustration increases and all too frequently is projected onto the patient. After all, the patient's symptoms and the test findings do not make sense; ergo, it is the patient's fault. Hollender (1972) talks of psychosomatic symptoms as a code concealed from the sender as well as the receiver. This is a cogent explanation of the situation, but usually the examining physician is not thinking in these terms and so experiences the frustration that produces a negative response to the patient.

A second consequence of the mind-body approach to psychosomatic illness is the process of excluding one before considering the other. When a child presents with a complaint of illness or pain, the first approach is to "rule out" all reasonable physical explanations for the problem. To an extent, this is as it should be. The complication comes with the consequence of the "either-or" process. Too often the medical evaluation starts with a physical model for the problem; for example, abdominal pain—rule out appendicitis. As these hypotheses fail to produce an explanation, the physician, as a last resort, turns to the alternate explanation—the mind. When the switch in focus comes, the patient and/or parents have often been poorly prepared for the shift. From the CAT scan to the "shrink" is an abrupt turnabout. In the case of children's illness, the parent who has been led to look for a physical answer sees the shift as a failure by the professional to be able to unravel the problem. The additional effect of the mind-body approach when the parents and patient have not been well prepared is their resentment and resistance to the alternate hypothesis.

A third negative effect of this approach is the excessive cost, the invasiveness of the procedures, and the consequent discomfort to the patient.

A final problem associated with the mind-body concept is the strong implication that the patient was not really physically ill—all of the problems are imaginary and therefore the patient could stop the whole business anytime he or she wished. This concept had the corollary that there was no pain in those problems considered to be conversion reactions or psychosomatic illness, and this led to a lesser regard for the patient and the patient's problem.

The first major change in the theory of conversion and psychosomatics came about as a result of the original focus in the studies by Alexander and Engel—the ulcer. In investigating the emotional factors that were associated with this illness, the researchers began to look at stress as a major cause of the problem. Studies were looking for links between stress and increased gastric secretions producing an ulcer. The original focus of the theories was one of organ specificity; that is, certain effects of stress or other emotional experiences were directly expressed by consequent changes in receptor organ systems. The lack of support for this theory began the shift to the integrative approach of the interaction of physical and environmental factors as an explanation for psychosomatic illness. In their research on the cause of ulcers, Weiner et al. (1957) clearly moved the state of the art to an interactive model of causation, stating that:

The study indicates that neither a high rate of gastric secretions nor a specific psychodynamic constellation is independently responsible for the development of peptic ulcers. Together, however, these two parameters contribute the essential determinants in the precipitation of peptic ulcers on exposure to social situations noxious to the specific individual. (p. 9)

This shift in theory development and research had a two-tiered impact on the field.

First, it expanded the dualism of mind-body and brought in social stresses, the environment, and the multiple-tiered impact of these factors. Second, it expanded the focus beyond conversion reactions and psychosomatic illness to include chronic illness and illness vulnerability. The role of emotional health and the personal/social environment of the patient were examined in numerous studies covering a wide range of illnesses and an equally broad set of environmental/emotional parameters. Jacobs et al. (1969) compared a group of college students reporting to the college health service with upper respiratory infections and a group of college students without illness. On the basis of psychological testing, they found that the group who had upper respiratory infections showed greater evidence of problems involving role crisis, personal failure, hostility, depression, and anxiety than the control group.

Vallant (1979) reports on a 40-year prospective study of 200 males in which he found that of 59 men in the best mental health, only 2 became chronically ill or died by age 53. In a group of 48 men with the poorest mental health, 18 became chronically ill or died. The data, as interpreted by Vallant, suggest that good mental health retards midlife deterioration of physical health.

The work of Holmes (Petrich & Holmes, 1977) and Rahe (1972) emphasized the effect of "life change" experiences on the expression of illness. These studies led to the development of the Schedule of Recent Experiences (SRE) as a means of assessing life change and relating this factor to illness behavior.

Heisel (Heisel et al., 1973) used a children's version of the SRE with 5 groups of children with specific medical problems including (1) victims of juvenile rheumatoid arthritis, (2) hemophiliacs, (3) general pediatric patients, (4) surgical patients, and (5) psychiatric patients. In four of the groups (all except the group of hemophiliacs) they found "2 to 3 times as many [children] experienced more frequent and/or more severe life events prior to the onset of their illness than did their healthy peers." Meyer and Haggerty (1962) reported a strong relationship between patterns of streptococcal illness and the degree of chronic family stress. After studying the influence of life events on childhood respiratory tract illness, Boyce et al. (1977) found that "the magnitude of life change was strongly related to the average duration and illness experienced" and concluded that:

Relationships exist between social factors and respiratory disease that deserve further consideration. The true complexity of childhood respiratory illness is only partially explained by the microbiologic model of disease causation. By studying the social context in which respiratory disease occurs, a new model may evolve that is both richer and more useful in interpreting patterns of pediatric disease. (p. 614)

With these studies of general pediatric illness, streptococcal infection, and respiratory tract infections, psychosomatic illness not only moved to an interactive, causative model but expanded the scope of the model to include the broadest variety of problems, including diseases that had very specific pathophysiologic bases.

Logan Wright further extended the interactive theory of psychosomatic illness by bringing attention to the effects of experience on the expression of physical problems and at the same time further expanded the range of problems that had psychosomatic relationships (Wright 1977, 1978; Wright, Schaeffer, & Solomons, 1979). The Encyclopedia of Pediatric Psychology (Wright et al., 1979) lists 114 medical/psychological problems and, more importantly, points out that many of these problems are experienced by large numbers of children. In this conceptualization, psychosomatic disorders are classified into three general categories:

1. Medical difficulties caused by problems of learning or development rather than by stress.

2. Behavioral problems caused indirectly by an illness that may interfere with management or control of the disease.

3. Problems of behavior or development

caused directly by disease (psychological sequelae).

An example of a problem relating to Wright's first category would be instances of encopresis where the initial difficulty began as a problem in toilet training and then produced a behavioral response—the retention of feces. This behavior subsequently produces a physical change, megacolon, which is an enlargement of the colon as it adapts to the retention of feces. This behaviorally produced physical change has as its consequence the problem, encopresis, in which the megacolon regularly seeps feces that produce soiling by the child.

The so-called "brittle diabetic" is an example of the second of Wright's categories where behaviors consequent to the disease interfere with management of the disease. The literature is replete with studies showing that diabetic patients, especially adolescents, react to and act out their feelings about their illness by noncompliance to medical regimen. Some diabetics will "forget" to take insulin or to test the urine for sugar level or will go on sprees of eating "junk" food, with the result that they become ketotic and may put themselves into coma.

An example of Wright's third category would be the behaviors associated with the Lesch Nyhan syndrome. In this genetically related syndrome, the child engages in self-mutilation, including biting and chewing, that can cause the loss of fingers.

Wright's conceptualization of psychosomatic disorders is of great significance because of the focus on behavior, which stems from psychologic theories of reinforcement. This expansion of the theory emphasizes the potential contributions of psychologists, as behavioral scientists, to the field of psychosomatic disorders. The shift in Wright's theory moves the role of psychology from a secondary or subspecialist role to the position of an active associate or at times the primary care provider. In effect, Wright's work is clearly a part of the progression of psychological expertise from a more limited mental illness focus to a broader involvement in health maintenance.

THE CONTINUUM OF PSYCHOSOMATIC ILLNESS

The "what" and "who" of psychosomatic illness is now in such a state of flux that the decision of which illnesses are psychosomatic and how big a population is involved in psychosomatic illness depends on who does the counting. Rae (1977) cites these difficulties in establishing incidence of childhood conversion reactions in a pediatric population. Although he used a narrower concept—conversion reaction—rather than the broader field of psychosomatics, he still found the task complicated by definitional issues. However, by using hospital records and by comparing the experience across several hospitals, he was able to estimate that between 5 and 24 percent of patient referrals to these facilities involved conversion symptoms. His data also indicate that the occurrence rate is higher in females than males. On a more practical level, Apley (1959) investigated the problem of children with abdominal pain and found that the majority were probably examples of conversion reaction or psychosomatic problems. In a study of 100 children who received extensive medical evaluations, in only eight children did he establish an organic cause. Abdominal pain, as a presenting complaint, is one of the most common pediatric problems. Taking Apley's data, one would conclude that 92% of this population represents psychosomatic illness and that the incidence of psychosomatic problems is a major aspect of pediatric medical practice.

Wright et al. (1979) not only make the case, in *The Encyclopedia of Pediatric Psychology,* for many types of problems that are psychosomatic, they also stress that many of these problems are so pervasive that there are not enough mental health professionals available to provide services to any one population. As an example, Wright et al. refer to the problem of bruxism—the grinding of teeth, especially in children. Statistics indicate that there are between 20 and 30 million bruxists in the country. If one then adds in the number of enuretic children, diabetics, and asthmatics, it is very clear that psychosomatics is an area of vast proportions that deserves the broadest measure of professional resources and attention.

Additionally, epidemiological investigation has shown that between 10 and 20 percent of children under 18 years suffer from a chronic illness or handicapping condition. Thirty percent of these children are expected to have identifiable psychological problems as measured by poor school performance, poor peer relationships, social isolation, and troublesome or truant behavior (Pless & Roghmann, 1971). This increase in psychopathology over the general pediatric population is inversely related to such variables as the income and educational status of the family as well as the emotional adjustment of the mother. These factors are also associated with an increased incidence of life stress events, the number of stress events being positively correlated with the increased evidence of acute illness. Although socioeconomic status and family problems appear unrelated to compliance to medical regimen, the presence of a supportive family who provide supervision and a positive attitude toward the medical regimen increased the likelihood of adherence to prescribed treatment (Litt & Cuskey, 1980).

Thus those chronically ill children who have a good psychosocial support system will experience less acute illness and less psychopathology; those from more marginal environments are more likely to be maladjusted themselves and exhibit more psychosomatic symptomatology in relation to their longstanding illness.

The expansion of the focus of psychosomatics from the early psychoanalytic concepts to the broader spectrum of today's definition has been accompanied by a concurrent shift in the research reported in the professional literature. The early literature began with attention to "conversion reaction" problems and ulcers. A recent review of a National Institute of Mental Health computer-generated list of articles on "psychosomatic illness in children" produced graphic evidence in the shift in research focus. Table 17.1 lists the topics

Table 17.1 The Major Problem/Illness Cited in a List of 138 Articles Relating to Psychosomatic Problems in Children

Problem	Number of Articles	% of Total	Rank
Asthma	55	40	1
General review	21	15	2
Migraine	10	7	3
Encopresis	6	4	4
Enuresis	5	3.6	5
Ulcers	5	3.6	5
Vomiting	3	2	7
Conversion reaction	2	1.5	8
Diabetes	2	1.5	8
Persistent pain	2	1.5	8
Arthritis	2	1.5	8
Abdominal pain	2	1.5	8
School phobia	2	1.5	8
Heart disease	2	1.5	8
Obesity	2	1.5	8
Renal problems	2	1.5	8
Gastrointestinal disorders	1	.7	16
Walking disorders	1	.7	16
Respiratory illness	1	.7	16
Depression	1	.7	16
Neurological (general) disorders	1	.7	16
Subdural hematoma	1	.7	16
Crohn's disease	1	.7	16
Fainting	1	.7	16
Hemophilia	1	.7	16
Prematurity	1	.7	16
Child abuse	1	.7	16
Hypertension	1	.7	16
Fetishism	1	.7	16
Trauma	1	.7	16
Bacteriuria	1	.7	16
Blindness	1	.7	16
Epilepsy	1	.7	16
Rheumatic disease	1	.7	16
Sudden infant death syndrome	1	.7	16
Inflammatory bowel	1	.7	16
Total =	143		

covered in 138 articles comprised by the computer search. By far, the most prevalent topic in the literature dealt with asthma in children. This was followed by articles that were a general review of the field and, in third place on the list, were migraine headaches, followed by encopresis. Ulcers wound up in a

tie with enuresis for fifth place. While this survey does not use a rigorous scientific method, it does indicate an interesting shift in the focus of research activity. The prevalence of articles on asthma represents the "fit" of that disease to the interactive model and to other major issues in psychosomatics—mainly, the influence of family factors on illness behavior and/or management. Asthma, along with diabetes has received great attention because of the family factors and behavior problems associated with those diseases. While diabetes had only two articles on the list generated by the computer search, a review of the literature in the area indicates in excess of 140 articles dealing with the psychosomatic aspect of diabetes. Asthma captured the attention of the professional community with the advent of "parentectomies" as a means of treating asthma in children. This practice found that separating children with asthma from their families led to a better management of the disease. From this beginning came a flood of studies considering the role of the family, family dynamics, life events, and mother-child relations as factors in the management of disease processes.

In the realm of chronic disease processes, juvenile onset diabetes mellitus has been among those illnesses most frequently receiving attention regarding psychogenic/psychosomatic components. Thomas Willis in 1684 connected diabetes with "prolonged sorrow" and thus began the attribution of diabetes to psychogenic causes. Looking at a psychiatric population, William Menninger (1935a, 1935b) concluded that in some instances psychological factors may be etiologically significant as well as affect the course of the illness. Analytic writers have suggested that the precondition necessary in a physiologically predisposed individual was one of longstanding unconscious conflict (Benedeck, 1948; Daniels, 1939; Falstein & Judas, 1955) and that studying these individuals as children would show "unresolved infantile neurosis" (Mirsky, 1948) to which they respond physiologically with a "starvation reaction." Turning her attention to the issue of psychic causality, Bruch (1949) found that the onset of diabetes in 10 out of 37 of her subjects was preceded by an infection or accident causing physiological and psychological stress. Since that time, antecedent stress—in the form of physiological trauma or infection, loss (change of schools, loss of parent through death, divorce, or separation), and family pathology—and its relation to onset of juvenile diabetes have been well studied. Diabetic children have been found to have significantly more of all of the above life changes when compared to nondiabetic controls (Danowski, 1963; Hinkle & Wolf, 1952a, 1952b; Leaverton et al., 1980; Stein & Charles, 1971; Treuting, 1962). It has been reiterated, however, that trauma, life change, and/or prolonged psychosocial stress must be accompanied by a physiological predisposition. The "stress" converts "prediabetes" to actual diabetes.

The actual mechanism by which this occurs has also been well documented. In their work, Hinkle and Wolfe (1952a, 1952b) noted that the standard response to stress of a nondiabetic individual is a decrease in blood glucose and concomitant rise in ketones. Diuresis was also shown to be a typical stress response in the nondiabetic. The diabetics' response is different in that their regulatory mechanisms are not able to return glucose and ketone levels to normal ranges even after the stress is removed, resulting in further dehydration and ketoacidosis. Epinephrine and insulin-inhibiting hormones are identified as causing an increase in lipolysis (free fatty acid production) without either the usual lag period associated with this phenomenon, or the ability of the individual to turn off catecholamine and insulin-inhibiting hormone production (Baker et al., 1969a; Baker, Kaye, & Hague, 1969b; Baker & Barcai, 1970; Baker et al., 1975). Thus diabetic decompensation can be defined as the underutilization of glucose concomitant with excessive mobilization of free fatty acids (and subsequent conversion to ketones). This is due to the increased production of insulin-inhibiting substances triggered by the autonomic nervous system's response to stress (Tarnow & Silverman, 1981).

The sources of this stress, as with any chronic illness, may be external (i.e., psycho-

pathology). For example, dietary restrictions, the need for insulin injections and urinalysis, bodily changes due to complications and fear of "reactions" have all been identified as sources of heightened anxiety for the child. The "stigma" of being diabetic may complicate long term social adaptation and the child's perception of his or her social adequacy. Bedwetting, initially caused by polyuria and polydypsia, may cause enough anxiety in the child or adolescent to perpetuate itself even when the physiologically based cause is removed (Fischer, 1948). In the same vein, hypoglycemia, which causes irritability, confusion, bizarre behavior, and anxiety, as well as hyperglycemia, which causes lethargy, confusion, and diffuse feelings of anxiety, may be misinterpreted by the patient as "going crazy." A physiological response to both the real and imagined stress is created, ultimately causing long term physical complications that contribute to the overall pattern of decompensation (Tomm, McArthur, & Leahey, 1977).

The most important information emerging out of this area is that diabetics can be grouped into those with good and poor control, and various extrinsic factors can be identified as contributing to poor psychological and medical adjustment. Also evident is that just as psychological stress may precipitate diabetes in a physiologically vulnerable child, so may the concomitant of a long term disease process produce emotional problems in a child who is predisposed to this type of difficulty (Simonds, 1976, 1977). Factors most frequently associated with good control have been a supportive family environment characterized by (1) stability; (2) intact intergenerational boundaries; (3) realistic and relaxed attitude towards treatment and diet regimen; (4) positive self-esteem on the part of the parents (mothers in particular); and (5) the ability to maintain a balance between the child's needs for growth and independence versus the dependency fostered by the illness. Deterioration of control is strongly associated with familial loss and/or the decompensation of family life (Bennett & Johannsen, 1954; LaHood, 1970; Katz, 1957; Koski, 1969;

Koski, Ahlas, & Kumento, 1972; Tarnow & Tomlinson, 1978).

Additionally, the child and family's premorbid psychosocial adjustment has been shown to correlate with measures of control and later psychopathology (Stein & Charles, 1971, 1975). Duration of illness and the adolescent years have also consistently been associated with poor control (Garner & Thompson, 1975; Swift & Seidman, 1964; Tietz & Vidmar, 1972). Correlations between socioeconomic status, family composition, and control have been equivocal; however, age of onset, degree of self-care, and knowledge about the illness and medical regimen are positively correlated with good control (La-Hood, 1970; Garner & Thompson, 1975).

In reviewing the 138 articles on the computer list on psychosomatic research and very roughly classifying the focus of the article, it is easy to discern the major area of interest—the role of the family. Twenty-five articles dealt with the mother–child relationship as a factor in the illness while another 21 articles focused on the role of the family in the course of the disease and its management. There were 10 articles that had a psychiatric construct or interest as an identifiable theme, while only two articles were solely concerned with the physical parameters of the illness.

Given this strong family orientation and the broadening of the original concept of conversion reaction to psychosomatic and somatopsychic illnesses, it is a bit surprising to find that the major therapeutic orientation in the list of articles is still psychoanalytically based (Table 17.2). This may reflect the long-established pattern of conceptualization and the inclusion of European literature in the survey. The older ideas of conversion seem still to persist in the foreign literature but are being overtaken by the current focus on family issues.

Equally interesting in the list of therapeutic approaches is the diversity of the field. No less than 14 therapeutic systems are represented in this survey. This finding suggests two important premises—first, that psychology and the behavioral sciences have a broad armamentarium to bring to bear on the problem of

Table 17.2 Therapeutic Approaches Mentioned in Articles Related to Psychosomatic Problems in Children

Type of Therapy	Frequency Cited
Psychoanalytic	14
Family therapy	12
Behavior modification	6
Biofeedback	5
Relaxation training	3
Psychodynamic	3
Operant conditioning	2
Psychomotor retraining	2
Chemotherapy	2
Hypnotherapy	2
Nondirective therapy	1
Group therapy	1
Play therapy	1
Assertiveness training	1

psychosomatic illness; and, second, it suggests that issues related to psychosomatic problems are interesting and/or challenging a broad spectrum of the practitioners in the behavioral sciences. The reciprocal attraction/interest evidenced by the data from the literature promises to be mutually reinforcing and beneficial. The problems of the child/patient, his or her family, and society will benefit, to requote Boyce et al. (1977), by producing "a new model...that is both richer and more useful in interpreting patterns of pediatric disease" (p. 614). At the same time, the skills, training, and functions of the psychologist will be expanded to areas where they will be able to make increased contributions to science and society.

It is especially heartening to note that areas of psychology particularly concerned with children are most actively carrying psychology's skills and interest into the realm of psychosomatic problems. A review of the last five years of publication of the *Journal of Pediatric Psychology* and the *Journal of Clinical Child Psychology* showed numerous articles on psychosomatic and/or health-related problems in children. In the last 20 issues of the *Journal of Pediatric Psychology* there are 18 articles related to these issues, which is by itself a significant number. Additionally, during this same period, three entire issues were devoted to topics of health or psychosomatics. In the last 15 issues of the *Journal of Clinical Child Psychology,* there were 13 articles related to health or psychosomatics and one whole issue devoted to the topic of "Primary Health Care Providers."

TREATMENT/INTERVENTION STRATEGIES

The list of therapeutic interventions reported in the literature on psychosomatic problems highlights the difficulty of this section. Any attempt to deal with the literature of all of these areas would be too cumbersome and would surely omit some therapeutic approach. Similarly, attempts to provide in-depth coverage of approaches would require a fair-sized book to do reasonable justice to the topic. As a practical attempt to manage the issue of intervention, this section will present a general overview of some representative approaches to intervention and will use one approach, family therapy, as a "model" or example of intervention strategies. Family therapy was selected as a model for several reasons. First, it relates well to the current theoretical construct of psychosomatics which emphasizes an interaction between several factors—physical, psychological, and environmental—and especially the family. Second, the current trend in the literature reflects a heavy interest in this area. And third, the family therapy approach incorporates aspects of several other intervention strategies.

In examining major treatment strategies, it is important to look at the application of behavior modification techniques to psychosomatic illness or health care problems. Behavioral approaches are a central focus of Wright's conceptualization of psychosomatic illness. The expansion of the concept of psychosomatics to deal with acquired problems that result from behavioral experience (e.g., encopresis) suggests behavior modification as a means of manipulating these same behaviors to relieve the problem.

Behavior techniques, including classic conditioning, desensitization, behavior modification, counterconditioning, and other variants of the technique have been applied, usually with a reasonable degree of effectiveness for a variety of psychosomatic problems. The management of enuresis and encopresis is one area where behavioral techniques have been utilized. Obesity, anorexia nervosa, bruxism, tracheotomy addiction, diabetes, and a wide variety of other problems have all been involved in studies using behavior strategies as an intervention approach. Rather than making a cursory survey of the extensive literature in the field, the reader is referred to the *Encyclopedia of Pediatric Psychology* (Wright et al., 1979) for an extensive reference list.

Behavior modification as a treatment approach usually works at the symptom level and attempts to produce change by symptom modification, including extinction or establishing alternative behaviors. Attacking symptoms is a legitimate intervention approach if one accepts the interactive theory of the problem. Where behavior modification is effective, the change in behaviors/symptoms acts in a reciprocal manner on both the physical and emotional systems involved in the psychosomatic problem. This treatment approach is much favored because of the direct, positive, short term nature of the technique.

A related intervention technique of relatively recent origin that has had a central focus on the area of psychosomatic, somatopsychic, and chronic illness, is biofeedback. This system, with its laboratory origins, has been used in numerous studies as an intervention or change agent for a variety of health problems. Basically, biofeedback is a learning experience where the patient is provided with a means of learning to use self-management to regulate physiological functions. The system has had successful application with coronary problems, including tachycardia and hypertension. It has also been used with respiratory problems, including asthma, migraine headaches, and the management of pain. Extension of the applications and improvement of the techniques are proceeding at a rapid pace. A most interesting and encouraging use of biofeedback is in its application to the prevention of illness. There are clinics using this approach, where the aim is to "teach" subjects to use the technique to facilitate better health rather than to "cure" existing problems.

There are many variants of biofeedback that use similar principles in a less formal, extensive, or laboratory-oriented manner. Foremost among these approaches is relaxation training. Walker (1979) refers to relaxation training as "the poor man's biofeedback." In his review of the utility of relaxation training, Walker finds this method effective in helping children prevent asthmatic attacks, avert epileptic seizures, reduce hyperactivity, relieve skin disorders, and avoid ulcers. As with biofeedback, relaxation training stresses teaching the subject self-control that results in change on the physical expression of problems.

As mentioned at the beginning of this section, family therapy and/or family intervention approaches are fast becoming the "treatment of choice" in psychosomatic problems. Family therapy serves as a "model" for intervention strategies because it incorporates many other approaches in its application and its theoretical structure is derived from an interactive framework.

In the 1970s, a research treatment project was begun at the Philadelphia Child Guidance Clinic and the Children's Hospital that embodied the multidisciplinary, multifactoral approach to psychosomatics. Three specific disorders—intractable asthma, juvenile diabetes with frequent episodes of ketoacidosis, and anorexia nervosa—were studied to determine if common family characteristics existed. Minuchin and his group (Baker et al., 1975; Minuchin et al., 1975; Minuchin, Rosman, & Baker, 1978) discovered that the development of severe psychosomatic symptoms in a child *was* associated with certain patterns of family organization and functioning with the following characteristics:

1. Enmeshment. Family members are overinvolved with one another and have little regard for individual autonomy, independence, and privacy.

2. Overprotectiveness. Family members exhibit a high degree of concern for each other, with considerable nurturant and protective response.

3. Rigidity. Such families are heavily committed to maintaining the status quo and experience difficulty when change and growth are necessary; family members deny any problems but the child's medical problems.

4. Lack of conflict resolution. There is a low threshold for overt conflict and direct confrontations are avoided or diffused; consequently, such families live in a chronic state of submerged conflict with associated stress and tension.

5. Use of the patient's symptoms as a conflict-detouring mechanism. The patient is involved in parental and family conflict.

The sick child is involved in parental conflict in three regularly observed patterns: (1) triangulation—the child is put into a position where he or she cannot express himself or herself without siding with one parent against the other, as each parent attempts to ally with the child; (2) parent-child coalition—the child moves into a stable coalition, joining with one parent against the other; (3) detouring—both parents submerge their differences in a gesture of protecting or blaming their sick child, who is seen as the only family problem.

Minuchin's group (Minuchin et al., 1975) indicates that these three parent-child patterns do not represent a classification schema. They describe interactional sequences that occur in response to family conflict and may also be observed in effectively functioning families. As such, the patterns are within the wide range of coping behaviors for dealing with conflict. Families in the normal range of adjustment can shift into other modes of conflict confrontation and negotiation while psychosomatic families are constricted in their use of alternative patterns. In addition to identifying a family profile associated with psychosomatic illness in children, the Philadelphia group developed a therapeutic approach designed to change these patterns (Hodas & Liebman, 1978; Liebman, Minuchin, & Baker, 1974a, 1974b; Minuchin et al., 1978; Minuchin & Fishman, 1979).

As an example of this group's approach, Liebman et al. (1974b) treated a group of children with intractable asthma. They contend that intractable asthma represents a psychosomatic disorder in which the primary allergic disorder has been profoundly complicated by emotional factors, especially chronic, unresolved conflicts in the family. These conflicts contribute to a state of chronic family stress that precipitates acute attacks and perpetuates the severity of the asthma. Children with intractable asthma—a chronic, severe relapsing form of asthma—constitute 10–12 percent of children with asthma. Liebman et al., (1974b) believe that the success of parentectomy (separating child from family) in alleviating the symptoms indicates the effect of the family on the clinical course of intractable asthma.

Therapeutic success is reported by this team in treatment consisting of weekly outpatient family sessions. The family therapy sessions are organized into three stages: Stage 1—focus is on the alleviation of the asthmatic symptoms in order to decrease the use of the child-patient as a means of detouring family conflicts; Stage 2—consists of identifying and changing patterns in the family and extrafamilial environment that tend to exacerbate and maintain the severe symptoms; and Stage 3—consists of interventions to change the structure and functioning of the family system to secure a lasting disengagement of the patient from his/her central detouring role in order to prevent recurrence of symptoms. Behavior modification techniques and breathing exercises are effectively used with the patient in order to decrease the intensity and frequency of attacks (Liebman et al., 1974b). Several other general treatment goals listed by the authors include:

1. Helping parents terminate special treatment of the child and returning him/ her to equal status with his or her siblings.

2. Enlisting parental encouragement of the child in his or her development of autonomy, age appropriate peer relations, sibling relations, and extrafamilial activities.

Ultimate goals for the asthmatic child include termination of acute asthmatic attacks requiring hospitalization, reduced dependency on the use of steroids, Intermittent Positive Pressure Breathing treatments or desensitization programs to control symptoms, and a return to a lifestyle associated with regular school attendance, increased peer group involvement, and increased physical activities.

Another psychosomatic disorder to which the structural family therapy approach has been applied is anorexia nervosa. Anorexia nervosa is defined as a clinical syndrome characterized by a voluntary refusal to eat and a weight loss of 20 percent or more of average body weight without an underlying organic etiology. This disorder occurs more frequently in females and is generally manifest in adolescence or young adulthood. Associated symptoms include amenorrhea, generally reversible, and clinical characteristics described by Bruch (1973, 1978) such as disturbance of body image, misperception of internal physiological stimuli, a sense of ineffectiveness, and hyperactivity.

Liebman et al. (1974a) proposed an integrated pediatic and psychiatric program for the treatment of anorexia nervosa. There was an inpatient and outpatient phase to the program. During the inpatient phase of the program, individual therapy sessions and an operant behavior paradigm were used to encourage weight gain. The behavioral protocol made access to physical activity completely contingent on weight gain. Weigh-ins occurred daily for each patient before breakfast. If the requisite one-half pound was not gained, the patient was not allowed out of bed for the day. With a weight gain of at least one-half pound, the patient was allowed out of bed to eat, watch TV, use the bathroom, and have visitors. Other privileges include a four- to six-hour period of unrestricted activity on the ward or in the hospital. The pediatrician, nursing staff, and patient were exclusively involved with his or her eating behavior while in the hospital. The general goals were progressive weight gain and returning control of his or her eating behavior to the patient. The individual therapy sessions aimed at the establishment of a trusting therapeutic relationship between child and therapist and did not focus on his or her eating behavior per se.

As progress was achieved with the beginning of weight gain, family lunch sessions were scheduled. These were used for diagnostic and therapeutic purposes (Rosman, Minuchin, & Liebman, 1975). The goals for the sessions were: (1) to begin to change the status and role of the identified patient within the family; (2) to begin the translation of an eating problem into a problem of interpersonal relationships; and (3) disengagement of the parents from using the child's eating behavior as a conflict-detouring mechanism. Rosman et al. (1975) indicated that an important focus of the lunch sessions was to change or inhibit the typical pattern of parental interactions around the symptomatic behavior in such a way as to bring about a separation, an increase in distance, between parents and child. Successful lunch sessions facilitated remission of the symptom and initiated a therapeutic process of change in family functioning. When the pediatrician's requisite weight gain was attained, family therapy commenced on an outpatient basis.

The outpatient treatment phase continued with an initial focus on the behavioral paradigm and the use of family tasks to support progressive weight gain and to disengage the anorectic from the arena of submerged parental conflicts and family tensions. Structured family goals included the resolution of intrafamilial and interpersonal issues. With the emergence of constructive changes in the family, the emphasis shifted to the patient's peer group relations and school and community activities. Concomitantly there was a shifting focus to the parental dyad, who were then seen separately, with gradual disengagement of the children from parental conflicts.

Structural family therapy has proven effective in severe childhood and adolescent psychosomatic disorders often unresponsive to medical management or other forms of psychotherapy. Hodas and Liebman (1978) contend that as a child-oriented approach, structural family therapy provides a nonthreatening quality as the therapist initially joins the family system by focusing on the child and his or her physical symptom, thus accepting the family's orientation and view of the problem. Given the gravity of the psychosomatic symptoms, the illness itself does not permit the family to deny its significance or the ultimate life-threatening aspects of medical crisis in disorders such as asthma, diabetes, and anorexia nervosa. Thus the family can be more readily engaged in the treatment process for the sake of their child.

In treating families with a psychosomatic child, structural family therapy generally lasts from six to twelve months, with weekly sessions or more frequent sessions as indicated. Outcome studies revealed a low drop-out rate and improvements generally above the 80 percent range for all three disorders studied (anorexia, asthma, and diabetes) with regard to both overt psychosomatic symptomatology and the overall psychosocial functioning of the child (Hodas & Liebman, 1978; Liebman et al., 1974a; Minuchin et al., 1978).

ISSUES OF TRAINING, RESEARCH, AND SERVICE

Psychology's initial contribution to psychosomatic research was generally restricted to diagnostic testing to "define" the problem. The major theoretical and treatment role rested with medicine, either a medical subspecialty such as endocrinology in the area of diabetes or psychiatry for those problems that were seen as "conversion reactions." When psychology was involved in service, it was usually in the model of psychiatry, that is, managing those patients diagnosed as having a conversion reaction.

The interactive concept of psychosomatics has raised new challenges to psychology and broadened the area for the use of psychological expertise. As a social and behavioral science, psychology has a major role to play in investigating and managing the social and environmental factors that are operative in psychosomatics. To meet this new opportunity and responsibility effectively, psychology must more fully deal with issues of academic preparation of psychologists. This section will focus on several of these issues:

1. Academic preparation
2. Postacademic training, that is, internships
3. The psychologist's role in a multidisciplinary setting
4. Psychology as a medically based versus mental health based discipline
5. Psychologist as primary health care provider
6. Psychology and the maintenance of health

Academic preparation of professionals, including psychologists, has a strong tendency to be traditional and conservative by the very nature of the educational process. The area of psychosomatics requires new interests and skills in psychologists, but equally it requires that training institutions interest students in pursuing this field. The system works to constrain this process in that academic institutions are not usually or easily involved in the implementation of new service models. By definition, academicians teach, and clinicians or researchers are in the settings where new role models are developed. This is an overstatement, but it is unfortunate that the types of activities that are promoted in an academic setting are different from those that are encouraged in a service setting. Graduate level training programs do not provide the groundwork for the "tracking" of students into "subspecialty" areas such as health care. This is much the same as medical schools where "doctors" are produced, while the medical internship and residency provide a structure

within which they then learn to be pediatricians or surgeons, and so on, after their basic academic preparation. The need to increase or emphasize an academic track to prepare psychologists to work in "health care" or even clinical child psychology has been an issue in professional circles for quite some time. There are only scattered programs that include a focus on these issues. In an article on research training in pediatric psychology, Routh (1980) discussed the issue and concluded:

My own advice to students interested in this field has been to seek out a graduate program in *clinical* psychology which is APA approved and has a known child emphasis, such as University of California at Los Angeles; Case Western Reserve, Denver, Iowa, Miami (Coral Gables); Minnesota, Purdue, or Washington (Seattle), and then an internship known to emphasize Pediatric Psychology such as those in the medical schools at Maryland, North Carolina, or Oklahoma. (p. 288)

This is a small portion of the facilities offering academic training in psychology and suggests that limited resources are available in this area and the major focus of preparation rests elsewhere.

The situation for postacademic training is no better. If one checks the listing of internship training programs approved by the American Psychological Association, between two-thirds and three-fourths are in what would seem to be settings dealing with adult mental health. There is a lesser emphasis on children's programs and an even smaller availability of nonpsychiatric training experiences. Two factors play a part in this situation: first, the longstanding record of inattention to children's needs (Kenny, 1977); second, lack of "official" categories to recognize such training.

In order to prepare psychologists to work in the area of psychosomatics, it would be beneficial to have experience working in a health care setting and an opportunity to relate to an interdisciplinary team that deals with health issues as a primary emphasis. The reciprocal benefits of such an experience are central to the educational process. Psychologists need to learn the strengths and limitations of medical care, and, at the same time, it is important to acquaint physicians with the potential services of the psychologist. Health care psychology and pediatric psychology provide a means for psychologists to work in a "primary care" setting as part of the primary care team and develop skills in working at health facilitation and the prevention of illness. On a practical level, this type of experience should lead to an increase in the number of psychologists working with nonpsychiatric physicians in hospitals, medical schools, and even in private practice settings. There is obviously a need for psychologists in these settings, but insufficient opportunities for academic preparation and practice experience limit the growth of the field.

At the same time Cummings (1977) has provided data to document the cost effectiveness of the services that psychologists can provide to a medical population. The availability of counseling, psychotherapy, and behavioral techniques can lead to a significant reduction in patient visits for general health problems. The expanded definition of pediatric health care as well as psychosomatic illness suggests that this is an area that psychologists must address in the future as teachers, researchers, and care providers.

REFERENCES

Alexander, F. *Psychosomatic medicine.* New York: Norton, 1950.

Apley, J. *The child with abdominal pain.* Oxford: Blackwell, 1959.

Baker, L., & Barcai, A. Psychosomatic aspects of diabetes mellitus. In Hill, D.W. (Ed.), *Modern trends in psychosomatic medicine* (Vol. 2). New York: Appleton-Century, 1970.

Baker, L., Barcai, A., Kaye, R., & Hague, N. Beta adrenergic blockade and juvenile diabetes: Acute studies and long term therapeutic trial. *Journal of Pediatrics,* 1969, **75**, 19–29.

Baker, L., Kaye, R., & Hague, N. Metabolic homeostatis in juvenile diabetes II: Increased ketone responsiveness to epinephrine. *Diabetes,* 1969, **18**, 421–427.

Baker, L., Minuchin, S., Milman, L., Liebman, R. & Todd, T. Psychosomatic aspects of juvenile diabetes mellitus: A progress report. *Modern Problems in Pediatrics,* 1975, **12**, 332–343.

Baker, L., Minuchin, S., & Rosman, B. The use of Beta-adrenergic blockage in the treatment of psychosomatic aspects of juvenile diabetes mellitus. In Snart, A. (Ed.), *Advances in beta-adrenergic blocking therapy* (Vol. V). Princeton: Excerpta Medica, 1974, 67–80.

Benedeck, T. An approach to the study of the diabetic. *Psychosomatic Medicine,* 1948, **10**, 284–287.

Bennett, A.M., & Johannsen, D.E. Psychodynamics of the diabetic child. *Psychological Monographs,* 1954, **68**(11), 1–23.

Boyce, W.T., Cassel, J.C., Collier, A.M., Jensen, E.W., Romez, C.T., & Smith, A.H. Influences of life events and family routines on childhood respiratory tract illness. *Pediatrics,* 1977, **60**, 609–615.

Bruch, H. Physiologic and psychologic interrelationships in diabetes in children. *Psychosomatic Medicine,* 1949, **11**, 200–210.

Bruch, H. *Eating disorders: Obesity and anorexia nervosa.* New York: Basic Books, 1973.

Bruch, H. Obesity and anorexia nervosa. *Psychosomatics,* 1978, **19**, 208–212.

Cummings, N. Prolonged (ideal) versus short-term (realistic) psychotherapy. *Professional Psychology,* 1977, **8**, 491–501.

Daniels, G.E. Present trends in the evaluation of psychic factors in diabetes mellitus: A critical review of the experimental, general medical and psychiatric literature of the last five years. *Psychosomatic Medicine,* 1939, **1**, 527–552.

Danowski, T.S. Emotional stress as a cause of diabetes mellitus. *Diabetes,* 1963, **12**, 183–188.

Engel, G. Conversion symptoms. In C.M. Mac Bryde & R.S. Blacklow (Eds.), *Signs and symptoms: Applied physiology and clinical interpretations.* Philadelphia: Lippincott, 1970.

Falstein, E.I., & Judas, I. Juvenile diabetes and its psychiatric implications. *American Journal of Orthopsychiatry,* 1955, **25**, 330–342.

Fischer, A.E. Factors responsible for emotional disturbances in diabetic children. *Nervous Child,* 1948, **17**, 78–83.

Garner, A.M., & Thompson, G.W. Psychological factors in the management of juvenile diabetes. *Journal of Clinical Child Psychology,* 1975, **4**, 43–45.

Heisel, J.S., Coddington, R.D., Raity, R., & Reams, S. The significance of life events as contributing factors in the disease of children. *Journal of Pediatrics,* 1973, **83,** 119–123.

Hinkle, L., & Wolfe, S. A summary of experimental evidence relating life stress to diabetes mellitus. *Journal of American Medical Association,* 1952, **148,** 513–520. (a)

Hinkle, L., & Wolfe, S. Importance of life stress in the course of management of diabetes mellitus. *Journal of the American Medical Association,* 1952, **148,** 513–520. (b)

Hodas, G.R., & Liebman, R. Psychosomatic disorders in children: Structural family therapy. *Psychosomatics,* 1978, **19,** 709–719.

Hollender, M. Conversion hysteria—A post-Freudian reinterpretation of nineteenth century psychosocial data. *Archives of General Psychiatry,* 1972, **26,** 311–319.

Jacobs, M.A., Norman, M., & Spiklen, A. Relationship of life change, maladaptive aggression, and upper respiratory infections in male college students. *Psychosomatic Medicine,* 1969, **31,** 31–34.

Katz, P. Behavior problems in juvenile diabetics. *Canadian Medical Association Journal,* 1957, **76,** 738–743.

Kenny, T. Should the six-year-old have the vote? *Journal of Pediatric Psychology,* 1977, **2,** 4–8.

Koski, M.L. The coping processes in childhood diabetes. *Acta Paediatrica Scandinavica,* 1969 (supplement), **198,** 1–56.

Koski, M.L., Ahlas, A., & Kumento, A. A psychosomatic follow-up study of childhood diabetics. *Acta Paedopsychiatrica,* 1976, **42,** 12–26.

LaHood, B.J. Parental attitudes and their influence on the medical management of diabetic adolescents. *Clinical Pediatrics,* 1970, **9,** 468–471.

Laron, Z. More on diabetic control. *Journal of Pediatrics,* 1978, **92,** 340–341.

Leaverton, D., White, C., McCormick, C.R., Smith, P., & Sheikholislam, B. Parental loss antecedent to childhood diabetes mellitus. *Journal of the American Academy of Child Psychiatry,* 1980, **19,** 678–689.

Liebman, R., Minuchin, S., & Baker, L. An integrated treatment program for anorexia nervosa. *American Journal of Psychiatry,* 1974, **131,** 432–436. (a)

Liebman, R., Minuchin, S., & Baker, L. The use of structural family therapy in the treatment of intractable asthma. *American Journal of Psychiatry,* 1974, **131,** 535–540. (b)

Litt, I.F., & Cuskey, W.F. Compliance with medical regimens during adolescence. *Pediatric Clinics of North America,* 1980, **127,** 3–15.

Menninger, W.C. Psychological factors in the etiology of diabetes. *The Journal of Nervous and Mental Diseases,* 1935, **81,** 1–13. (a)

Menninger, W.C. The interrelationships of mental disorders and diabetes mellitus. *Journal of Mental Science,* 1935, **81,** 332–357. (b)

Meyer, R.J., & Haggerty, R.J. Streptococcal infections in families, altering individual susceptibility. *Pediatrics,* 1962, **29,** 539–549.

Minuchin, S., Baker, L., Rosman, B.L., Liebman, R., Milman, L., & Todd, T.C. A conceptual model of psychosomatic illness in children. *Archives of General Psychiatry,* 1975, **32,** 1031–1038.

Minuchin, S., & Fishman, H.C. The psychosomatic family in child psychiatry. *Journal of American Academy of Child Psychiatry,* 1979, **18,** 76–90.

Minuchin, S., Rosman, B., & Baker, L. *Psychosomatic families: Anorexia nervosa in context.* Cambridge: Harvard University Press, 1978.

Mirsky, I.A. Emotional factors in the patient with diabetes mellitus. *Bulletin of the Menninger Clinic,* 1948, **12,** 148–194.

Petrih, J., & Holmes, T.H. Life change and onset of illness. *Medical Clinics of North America,* 1977, **61,** 825–838.

Pless, I.B., & Roghmann, K.J. Chronic illness and its consequences: Observation based on three epidemiologic surveys. *Journal of Pediatrics,* 1971, **79,** 351–359.

Rae, W. Childhood conversion reactions: A review of the incidence in pediatric settings. *Journal of Clinical Child Psychology,* 1977, **6,** 69–72.

Rahe, R.H. Subjects' recent life changes and their near-future illness susceptibility. *Advances in Psychosomatic Medicine,* 1972, **8,** 2–19.

Rosman, B.L., Minuchin, S., & Liebman, R. Family lunch session: An introduction to family therapy in anorexia nervosa. *American Journal of Orthopsychiatry,* 1975, **45,** 847–853.

Routh, D. Research training in pediatric psychology. *Journal of Pediatric Psychology,* 1980, **3,** 287–294.

Simonds, J.F. Psychiatric status of diabetic youth

in good and poor control. *International Journal of Psychiatry in Medicine,* 1976, **7,** 133–151.

Simonds, J.F. Psychiatric status of diabetic youth matched with a control group. *Diabetes,* 1977, **26,** 921–925.

Stein, S.P., & Charles, M.A. Emotional factors in juvenile diabetes mellitus: A study of early life experience of adolescent diabetics. *American Journal of Psychiatry,* 1971, **128,** 56–60.

Stein, S.P., & Charles, M.A. Emotional factors in juvenile diabetes mellitus: A study of the early life experiences of eight diabetic children. *Psychosomatic Medicine,* 1975, **37,** 237–241.

Swift, C.R., & Seidman, F.L. Adjustment problems of juvenile diabetes. *Journal of the American Academy of Child Psychiatry,* 1964, **3,** 500–515.

Tarnow, J.D., & Silverman, S.W. The psychophysiologic aspects of stress in juvenile diabetes mellitus. Manuscript submitted for publication, 1981.

Tarnow, J.D., & Tomlinson, N. Juvenile diabetes: Impact on the child and family. *Psychosomatics,* 1978, **19,** 487–491.

Tomm, K.M., McArthur, R.G., & Leahey, M.D. Psychologic management of children with diabetes mellitus. *Clinical Pediatrics,* 1977, **16,** 1151–1155.

Tietz, W., & Vidmar, J.T. The impact of coping styles on the control of juvenile diabetes. *Psychiatry in Medicine,* 1972, **3,** 67–74.

Treuting, T.F. The role of emotional factors in the etiology and course of diabetes mellitus: A review of the recent literature. *American Journal of Medical Science,* 1962, **244,** 93–109.

Vallant, G. Natural history of male psychologic health. *New England Journal of Medicine,* 1979, **301,** 1244–1254.

Walker, C.E. Treatment of children's disorders by relaxation training: The poor man's biofeedback. *Journal of Clinical Child Psychology,* 1979, **8,** 22–25.

Weiner, H., Thaler, M., Reiser, M., & Mirsky, I. Etiology of duodenal ulcer: I. Relation of specific psychological characteristics to rate of gastric secretion (serum pepsinogen). *Psychosomatic Medicine,* 1957, **19,** 1–10.

Willis, T. Practice of physik; Treatise II. *Pharmaceutic rationalis.* London: Dring, Hayer & Leight, 1684.

Wright, L. Conceptualizing and defining psychosomatic disorders. *American Psychologist,* 1977, **32,** 625–628.

Wright, L. Assessing the psychosomatic status of children. *Journal of Clinical Child Psychology,* 1978, **7,** 94–112.

Wright, L., Schaeffer, A.B. & Solomons, G. *The Encyclopedia of Pediatric Psychology.* Baltimore: University Park Press, 1979.

CHAPTER 18

Depression and Suicide in Children

PAMELA CANTOR

INTRODUCTION

Suicide and attempted suicide disturb us all because self-destruction rejects the deeply held belief that life must be worth living. It particularly disturbs those of us in the health professions because we dedicate our professional lives to sustaining physical life and maintaining emotional well being. We applaud individuals who struggle to survive, often under conditions which appear intolerable. Yet in the United States alone it is conservatively estimated that 20,000 persons choose to die by their own hands each year. Of these deaths, the most tragic and disturbing are the deaths of children. Most of us can at least comprehend the deaths of the old or the incurably ill. But the thought that a child, just beginning life, should be devoid of any desire to live, is anathema to us (Seiden, 1969).

The question of adolescent suicide has received a good deal of attention. The question of childhood suicide has not. What has been written is inconclusive as most of the research has focused on issues of a demographic nature. This paper attempts to review the available information regarding the incidence of childhood suicide, to review the literature on depression and suicide in children, to discuss the psychological and social correlates of youthful suicidal behavior, to outline the treatment of suicidal children, and finally to discuss the effects of childhood suicide on the family.

INCIDENCE OF SUICIDE

According to the U.S. Office of Vital Statistics, suicides are rare before the age of 10, with their frequency rising during the later part of the latency period and increasing sharply after age 14. More specifically, suicide is statistically nonexistent before age 5, virtually nonexistent at 5–9 years of age, and still rare at ages 10–14 (approximately one case in every 100,000 children). The low recorded rate of completed suicide among children is in large part due to the policy of the Division of Vital Statistics which does not allow deaths of children under 8 years of age to be recorded as suicide regardless of the information entered on the death certificate. The deaths have to be coded as if they had occurred from unknown or unspecified causes. This policy, which has been in effect since 1962, has spuriously decreased the already low rate of suicide in the 5–9 year age group.

Suicide while statistically nonexistent, is not actually nonexistent before age five. The youngest suicide attempt reported in the literature involved a 3-year-old child who was found along with his 18-month-old sibling in a room with the gas jet turned on. The child reported that he was angry with his parents for not taking him for a walk that day and had therefore attempted to kill himself. The father had discussed in front of the child the manner in which an acquaintance committed suicide by turning on the gas (Bakwin & Bakwin, 1972).

A 4-year-old child this author once treated was an abused child who preferred to jump out of a hospital window rather than admit to others, and to himself, that his mother had frequently used his and his younger sister's bare hands as her ashtray and a place for extinguishing her cigarettes. He was more frightened of her disapproval and of having to admit that his loved mother was fallible than he was of ending his life. For all practical and statistical purposes, however, suicide is rare before age 10.

Suicide thus appears to be negligible as a ranking cause of death up to age 14. The accidental death rate at these ages, however, is so extraordinarily high that some researchers regard it with suspicion and conclude that many accidental deaths are probably suicides that are not tabulated as such. Particularly suspect are the accidental deaths of very young children who do not have access to lethal weapons such as firearms or drugs and who die from falls and drowning (Seiden, 1969).

Suicide among adolescents, however, is a problem of serious proportions, claiming an increasing number of lives each year. Completed suicide is the third cause of death among adolescents, following accidents and homicides, some of which may be victim-precipitated or thinly disguished suicides (Fredericks, 1979). Four thousand young people between the ages of 15 and 24 kill themselves every year, and an estimated 400,000–500,000 adolescents attempt suicide every year in the United States alone. That means that approximately 57 adolescents attempt suicide every hour (Cantor, 1982).

The increase in the rates of suicide during recent years is also alarming. Statistics available for the time period of 1955–1978 state that the rate of suicide in 1955 for children in the age range of 10–14, rose from 0.3 per 100,000 population annually to 0.8. This is a 166 percent increase. During this same period, the rates for 15–19 and 20–24-year-olds have increased 200 percent. The 0.8 persons per 100,000 10–14-year-olds who committed suicide during the year 1978 is expected to rise to 1.64 per 100,000 by the year 2000. This would mean a projected increase of 105 percent during the 12-year period. The projected increase for the 15–19-year-old range during the same 12 years is 94 percent and the increase for the 20–24-year-old age range is 114 percent (Fredericks, 1974). Thus, while the absolute number of suicides is small in

children below the age of 15, and certainly smaller than the actual numbers of older adolescents who commit suicide, the increase and projected increase in the incidence of suicide among children and young adolescents is equal to that of older adolescents and certainly is equally distressing.

THEORIES OF SUICIDE

Why has the suicide rate increased so drastically, and why can we expect it to increase beyond the already alarming rate? The answers are not readily apparent.

What follows is an attempt to answer those questions by a review of the exhaustive material on suicide and attempted suicide among children. Although the number of references is prodigious, the writings vary greatly in quality. Even the best studies contain some problems that impede the literature survey and lend a cautionary tone to the conclusions. There are four major cautions which should be noted.

First, surveys of the literature on suicide in children are handicapped by the unreliability of the statistical data. The problem of suicide cannot be entirely subject to statistical evaluation since suicide as a cause of death is underreported for a variety of reasons. Childhood deaths are often concealed to protect the family's name or to protect the survivors. Suicide always leaves the survivors with feelings of guilt and failure at having been part of an environment that proved so intolerable as to offer no alternative. Parents, family, and friends feel helpless at having been unable to rectify the situation while the young person was alive. Thus many suicides are denied by the victims' family and are classified as accidents.

Suicide notes, most often regarded as the only proof of suicidal intent, are less likely to be left by children who may be either too young to write or may not give thought to written communication. Not infrequently, psychological autopsies reveal overt attempts at communication that were ignored by significant others. Many parents are unaware of their children's emotional distress and are unable to comprehend their subtle cries for help (Farberow et al., 1963). Western culture in general tends to underestimate the strength of children's emotions. Suicidal motives in children are unthinkable—and therefore uninvestigated—in a majority of cases.

Authorities agree that a large number of suicides go unreported because of legal, social, and religious taboos. Suicide for many centuries has been considered a crime, a sin, or both.

It is obvious that under these circumstances the data cover the smallest and possibly least representative number of suicides. The figure may be underreported by as much as one-fourth (Dublin, 1963) to one-half (National Institute of Mental Health, 1969). It seems fair to say that the statistics, divorced from the study of the etiology of suicide, are more likely to lead to misconception than to an understanding of the problem.

The second caution is that most all of the studies suffer from the lack of a uniform definition of "suicide." Often studies of partial, threatened, attempted, or completed suicide are categorized together under the term "suicide." Recent studies have demonstrated the necessity for distinctions between types of suicidal behavior (Peck & Shrut, 1967; Cantor, 1972a). Many of the earlier studies in this review did not make the distinction between types of suicidal behavior. Most of the studies were based on attempted suicides and generalized to completed suicides.

A third deficiency is that much of the literature consists of anecdotal observations and case histories. These data usually are not representative of the population and obviously lack any statistical treatment. Of those studies that more closely approximate good research design, only a few utilize control groups.

The fourth major deficiency in the literature of child suicides is the absence of a theoretical orientation where hypotheses may be tested and verified. This is not surprising as there are no theories of suicide that are directly based upon child cases. The one exception is that of psychoanalytic theory, which emphasizes the importance of renewed libidinal impulses at puberty. Otherwise, the theories are largely derived from adult cases. With these four cautions in mind, let us review the literature relating to the etiology of attempted and completed suicide among children.

PSYCHOLOGICAL DETERMINANTS OF SUICIDE

The Question of Depression in Children

A depressed child is one who is characteristically sad, unhappy, often without interest in the outside world. He feels rejected and unloved, is not easily comforted, nor can his interest be readily engaged. He frequently suffers from insomnia or other sleep disturbance. He prefers autoerotic or other self-comforting activities to play. If he has any complaint at all, it may be of a stomachache or headache, rarely of depression per se. (Frisch, 1979, p. 115)

After these concise statements, we enter into areas of disagreement regarding the diagnosis and treatment of childhood depression. It is only within recent years that the psychiatric literature has even acknowledged the presence of depression in children. There is no category "Depression: Childhood Type" in DSM II. In most textbooks of childhood psychopathology, there are few, if any, references to childhood depression.

Pediatric, psychoanalytic, and primate literature offers a greater discussion of the presence of depression in children and in infants. The work of Bakwin (1942), Spitz (1946), Bowlby (1953), and Harlow (1958) has confirmed the possibly lethal and surely devastating effects of severe maternal deprivation, especially the deprivation of physical contact. Their work has left little doubt that infants who suffer insufficient body contact and inadequate response from their caretakers suffer serious psychological and physical damage.

Bakwin (1942) noted that infants and children who were admitted to the pediatric unit of a large hospital developed an unusually large incidence of infections and failed to thrive. He concluded that separation from their families had produced these effects and instituted a care program in which volunteers were responsible for "loving" specific children. The

456 Depression and Suicide in Children

program produced remarkable results in the decreased incidence of morbidity.

Spitz (1946) observed children who differed in the amount of affection that was offered to them. In the "nursery group," mothers took care of their infants. In the "foundling home group," overworked nurses cared for the children. The development of the "foundling home group" was severely retarded, and the incidence of death among the group was close to 40 percent, while the incidence of death among the "nursery children" was zero. Spitz subsequently coined the term *anaclitic depression* to characterize a syndrome that consists of a progressive reaction to separation from the mother. It begins with increased demandingness and weepiness and rapidly moves to weight loss, an arrest in developmental progress, refusal to make contact with other human beings, assumption of the fetal position (with an averted face), insomnia, recurrent physical ailments, and rigidity of emotions and facial expressions. It culminates in retardation, lethargy, and—not infrequently—death. If, within a critical period of three to five months, the mother is returned to the child or an adequate substitute is found, the condition can be corrected with surprising rapidity.

Bowlby (1953, 1960a, 1960b) has noted that even brief mother-child separations leave their damage, although it is reversible in most instances. He described the anxiety the infant or child experiences with separation as encompassing three stages of progressive destruction protest, despair, and finally detachment. The infants and children in this last stage could only be described as depressed. Bowlby named this syndrome *merasmus,* a wasting away of infants as a result of an inadequate amount of loving attention.

Harlow's (1958) work with monkeys confirmed what Spitz, Bowlby, and Bakwin observed with infants. When a monkey is brought up without feeling contact comfort and without the formation of the infant-maternal love bond, indiscriminate violent behavior, bizarre sexual behavior, and, ultimately, self-destructive behavior, damage the monkey's emotional and physical health.

Klein (1948) postulates the *depressive position* that occurs among all infants during the first six months of life. Klein states that the infant sees the world as a dichotomy of good and bad, according to whether someone or something is need satisfying or frustrating. He or she splits his or her ego into good/loving and bad/hating parts during the first three months of life. During the second three months, the mother is perceived as a whole, and, because both good and bad now stem from the same source, the child feels ambivalence and establishes a depressive position. He or she now has feelings of wishing to destroy his or her love object (mother), and needs to work through the longings for his or her mother and to develop defenses against these longings and subsequent sense of loss. Klein ascribes complex psychological mechanisms to the earliest period of life.

Bibring (1953) defines depression as the state of helplessness. Frustration of a child's needs results in anxiety followed by anger. When his or her signals of pain and distress are not met, he or she becomes exhausted, helpless, and subsequently depressed. According to Bibring, anxiety and depression are diametrically opposed basic ego responses. Anxiety is a reaction to external or internal perceived danger and is the ego's effort to survive. When the ego is unable to meet the danger, depression ensues.

Mahler (1961) states that depression may originate in the *symbiotic phase* of normal development, which is characterized by the anxiety the infant exhibits around the eighth month. She states that during this stage the infant behaves as if he or she and his or her mother were symbiotically attached. Later the infant achieves physical autonomy when he or she begins to walk, but emotional autonomy lags behind. "In infant autistic psychosis the central disturbance is the child's inability to perceive the mother and her functioning on his or her behalf. In symbiotic psychosis there is regression to a secondary undifferentiated stage of mother-child unity and a psychotic fusion with the need-satisfying object" (Frisch, 1979, p. 118). Mahler clearly states that the immature ego of the child is not capable of producing a state of depression such as that seen in the adult. She states that a child's grief is short lived because the ego cannot sustain itself without taking rapid defensive actions against loss. Instead of long term depression, as one might see in an adult, children employ the defenses of denial and repression.

One of the factors that has hampered the classification of depression among children is the difficulty of distinguishing between clinical depression as a pathological state and depression as a basic affect. Clinical depression can be defined as a prolonged state during which there exists a pervading feeling

of worthlessness and low self-esteem, often accompanied by varying kinds of ideation which may include guilt, pessimism, self-deprecation, self-destructive thoughts, distrust and general agitation. Thinking and physical activity are often impaired and the ability to function in daily activities is usually reduced. (Dizmang, 1969, p. 187.

Depressive affect is of shorter duration and is not pathological in nature. Depression and anxiety are basic affects and are a normal part of living (Bibring, 1953). Few clinicians would deny that children experience depressive affect, an emotional state of a helpless and powerless ego. The confusion in discussing depression in children stems largely from the division of opinion as to whether children can experience depression as a pathological state and whether the child's ego can sustain depressive affect to the point of clinical pathology.

Clearly the ego does have the ability to defend against feelings of depression just as it does against other painful experiences. The defenses that are most often employed result in hyperactivity, weepiness, or psychosomatic complaints, and these behaviors are often referred to as *depressive equivalents.* Just as hypomanic behavior and extreme lethargy are considered symptomatic of underlying depression in adults, hyperactive behavior is often symptomatic of underlying depression in children.

The question is—Is this underlying pathological depression or underlying depressive affect? In fact, in neither child nor adult is the symptom actually a depressive equivalent but rather is an indication of the defense mechanisms at work (Dizmang, 1969).

Much of the confusion surrounding past attempts to discuss depression and "depressive equivalents" has resulted from the failure to distinguish clinical depression from depressive affect. Object loss, a state of hopeless helplessness or a loss of self-esteem essentially are different ways of describing the same state. The affect basic to this existential position is depression. In children this depressive reaction is usually short lived; in adults it may become intense and self-perpetuating (Dizmang, 1969).

There appears to be some agreement regarding the symptoms of overt depression. The following behaviors are most frequently described: apprehension, sadness, rejection of the environment (stemming from a lack of contact and leading to emotional and physical withdrawal), retardation in development, loss of appetite, excessive sleeping or insomnia, poor school performance, helplessness, loss of self-esteem, feelings of being bad, feelings of not being liked, weepiness, moodiness, suicidal thoughts or actions, self-criticism, and psychosomatic symptoms. Beck (1972) has developed an inventory of depression for adults and has modified it for use with older children and adolescents, ages 10–15. Depressive equivalents were eliminated due to the difficulty in agreement of symptoms. The Subcommittee on Clinical Criteria for Diagnosis of Depression in Children of the American Psychiatric Association, in 1977 recommended their own criteria for the diagnosis of depression to include two factors: dysphoria and impairment in response, and decrease of interest in pleasurable behaviors. If both criteria are met, the diagnosis of childhood depression can be made.

In sum, it is clear that from birth the infant's behavior is focused on a primary love object. Psychological and physical development, of an optimal nature, are dependent upon the consistent presence of this primary object. Initial identification is with this object. This process continues into adolescence while the child develops numerous secondary sources of identification and gratification. Initially the child is totally symbiotic and then grows towards increased autonomy. The successful completion of the developmental sequence gives the child a sense of self-esteem.

It is also clear that when self-esteem is seriously threatened in the child, it is likely that as an adult he or she will be subject to depressive episodes. What is in question is whether a child is capable of pathological depression before he or she has developed to the point of accrued ego identity which occurs at adolescence. No one would argue that a child can and does react to loss; the dissension regards the nature of the depression and its causal connection to suicidal ideation and behaviors.

In spite of this confusion, there is little doubt among current researchers and clinicians that a significant factor in infant and child depressions is the loss of the significant love object.

The most common cause of neurotic depression in children is thought to be the feeling of being unloved. In the school age child, this is expressed as self-reproach, feelings of unworthiness, frequent accidents, and even frank suicidal attempts. The accidents are often really an expression of a wish to die (Teicher, 1970, p. 47). Children are sensitive to subtle or overt rejection and react with anxiety and rage that can be expressed in psychosomatic disturbances or in disruptive classroom behavior or delinquency. Children who feel rejected by their parents often react with hostility, anger, and unconscious death wishes towards parents, and with sadistic or suicidal behavior. The children are seeking attention and affection through behavior that drives the adults further away. The child wants and needs affection yet is forced to be hostile and reject those adults from whom he or she most wants love.

Depression in young people is usually associated with the loss of the love object either through death or a separation. Spitz's (1946) research on anaclitic depression offers evidence for the assumption that the equivalent of a depression can be observed even during the first year of life. The clinical picture of a depression due to loss of a love object may be almost as varied in the infant as it is in the adult. Spitz describes the consequences of the loss of the love object as varying in degree of severity from temporary, observable phenomena of withdrawal, dejection, anxiety, and turning away from the environment to complete self-deprivation resulting in affect-impoverished expression; stuporous, deteriorated catatonia; great susceptibility to recurrent sickness; and finally death.

Depression in children whose psychic structure more completely resembles that of the adult follows more closely the dynamic structure of the adult reaction. A significant difference between the adult and the child is the extreme dependence of the child on his or her love object. "Thus, whenever children feel the loss of a love object, they not only develop feelings of rage toward the frustrating object, but feelings of helplessness and worthlessness as well. This results in, and is equivalent to, a depression" (Schechter, 1957, p. 132). Actually these states of tension occur rather frequently during childhood. Schecter feels that it is when the degree of tension is extremely high or when the defense mechanisms become ineffective that suicide or suicidal equivalents may appear. Faigel (1966) and Toolan (1962, 1978), as well as Schechter, have observed feelings of helplessness, worthlessness, and impairment of ego functioning after the death of a parent. These investigators feel that this combination of symptoms may lead to a serious suicide attempt as a means of regaining contact with the lost love object.

Studies by Lawler, Nakielny, and Wright (1963), Cerny and Cerna (1962), Teicher (1970), Toolan (1962, 1978), and Goldberg (1981) have also found depression to be characteristic of young people who have attempted suicide, but there are investigators who do not feel that depression is characteristic of children making suicide attempts (Lourie, 1966; Balser & Masterson, 1959; Winn & Halla, 1966). Lourie suggests that it is not until late adolescence that the clinical picture of depression can appear as a factor in suicide. Balser and Masterson conclude that depression is not an important factor in children making suicide attempts. Winn and Halla voice similar skepticism as to the importance of depression in children who threaten suicide.

Psychoanalytic Theory—Puberty and Suicide

The one other area of psychoanalytic literature that is directly related to suicide among older children and adolescents is the area that deals with renewed libidinal impulses at puberty. The data reveal that at puberty there is a sudden increase in suicide and suicide attempts. This increase has most often been explained by conflicts over sexuality combined with increased strains of the onset of adolescence.

Schneer, Kay, and Brozovsky (1961) and Bigras et al. (1966) view a failure in sexual identification and concerns about possible homosexual tendencies as leading to attempted or completed suicides in early adolescence. Peck (1967), in a study of suicide attempters, found that in families where the father placed a high premium on his son's masculinity the concern had the opposite effect, leading to a weakening of the son's sense of masculine identity. Stearns (1953) studied a group of boys between the ages of 11 and 13 who hanged themselves in a twelve year period between 1941 and 1953. The majority of these boys were dressed in female clothing. Similar cases of young men hanging themselves while engaged in transvestite activities were reported by Ford (1957), Litman et al. (1963), and Shankel and Carr (1956).

Zilboorg (1937) reported 926 suicides of adolescents between the ages of 15 and 19 as opposed to 81 suicides under the age of 15. The inference he draws from this data is that the age of puberty is a crucial period in the balance of self-destruction.

At puberty the characteristic distinction between the sexes with regard to suicidal behavior becomes apparent. There is an increase in the female rate of attempted suicide and the male rate of completed suicide. Just before puberty, the number of suicides among boys is usually smaller than or equal to the number of suicides among girls. After puberty, the number is higher among boys. Mulcock (1955) did a study of suicide in England and Wales. By breaking the data into age groups, he was able to show the increase of suicide at puberty. He cited 112 deaths by hanging in children ages 10–15 during the years 1935–1949. Of these deaths, 110 were males; only two were females.

Leonard (1967) notes that suicide from puberty on is the prerogative of the male in Western cultures but is monopolized by the female in primitive cultures. She offers an explanation of this fact.

The puberty rites in many primitive cultures which seem abrupt and often cruel may have provided an outlet for the adolescent boy to define himself and his role as a male with privilege for full use of his maturing drives and physical strength. Symbolically the feminine identification carried over from childhood is stripped from him and the culture helps him define his position and take his place among men....This role is defined by society for him and for them. (Leonard, 1967, p. 244)

In Western society there is no such culturally defined and accepted method of publicly proving masculinity and the successful passage into manhood. Boys must attempt this task alone. They play out the struggle with experimentation, often with accompanying guilt anxiety. Leonard feels that:

Death probably occurs when there is miscalculation or when situational frustrations coupled with unconscious impulses momentarily overwhelm his ability to control the situation....Does the boy know the chances he is taking? Probably. There is sufficient gratification that he takes the risk. Occasionally the boy loses. Is it suicide? It is probably best labeled a "sub-intentioned" death which is the term Shneidman (1963) has given to those instances in which the individual plays an indirect, partial or unconscious role in his own interruption or cessation of life's processes. (Leonard, 1967, p. 245)

Suggestion, Imitation, and Identification

A child's capacity for responding to suggestion is given important consideration in the literature. Shaw and Schelkun (1965) propose that suicides that seem to be without cause are often reminiscent of compulsive responses to posthypnotic suggestion. They cite a case of suicide by hanging in which the suicide took place shortly after suggestive influences (such as reading a book in which a similar hanging took place). Winn and Hall (1966) report a large percentage of the children in their study had experienced hallucinations that directed them to kill themselves. Lawler et al. (1963) also reported that the youngsters in their study had experienced auditory hallucinations telling them to kill themselves. Ellis and Allen (1961) describe a situation in which strong death wishes toward the child by those closest to him or her make him or her aware of the "wish or command" implying that he or she must die. Children who are openly rejected by their parents, who are told that they are unwanted and that their parents would be better off without them, may respond to these death wishes with a suicide attempt.

Reports of suicidal epidemics among adolescents of various cultures, such as the wave of suicides in India after exam results are published (Funkenstein, 1959; Temby, 1961) and reports of anniversary suicides in which the chosen date matches that of another's death, point to the presence of imitation.

Mechanisms of identification with parental objects are known to be crucial in personality development. Identification with absent or dead parents has been cited as a factor in the transistion from normal thoughts of death to abnormal suicidal thoughts and ultimately to suicidal behavior (Adam, 1967). Keeler (1954) reported that suicide attempts seemed to represent an identification with the dead parent and a wish to be reunited for six of the 11 children in his study. He reported fantasies of reunion with the dead parent in eight of the children. Lourie (1966) cited identification as an important factor for children in his study. He believes a suicide or suicide attempt in the family may lead a child to copy the example, even to the point of choosing the identical weapon. Bender and Schilder (1937) suggest that a deep attachment to a parent who is suicidal may foster suicidal thoughts in the child. Schrut (1964) suggests that if a young child does not clearly differentiate himself or herself from his or her mother, and if the mother harbors feelings of hatred and worthlessness about herself, the child is likely to harbor these same feelings.

Aggression

All types of suicidal behaviors in the young have been explained as aggression that becomes displaced and self-directed. The frequency of this explanation is due to the influence of Freudian theory (1925). Freud stated that the love object becomes incorporated within the ego through narcissistic identification. When the individual feels hostility against the love object, the hostility is turned against the individual himself. The motive for suicide would therefore involve the unconscious death wish against the introjected object that is normally held in check by the individual's self-love. In sum, the theory states that the suicide is a victim of strong aggressive impulses that he or she failed to express outwardly and as a result turned inward.

Moss and Hamilton (1956) see the relationship between aggression and suicide as stemming from the belief that direct expressions of hostility, which are usually provoked by disappointments in love, are thwarted and turned inward. They feel that the reason for this is that the child becomes so overwhelmed by guilt or fear about his or her feelings of hostility that he or she directs this aggression inward.

Bender and Schilder (1937) studied children under 13 years of age and concluded that suicide in young children is an effort to escape an unbearable situation that usually means a deprivation of love. Aggression tendencies are provoked against the depriving figure but are turned against the self. The stronger the identification with the depriving figure, the stronger the aggressions.

Stengel (1964) modifies these theories and argues that aggression directed toward others, not toward oneself, is characteristic of the suicide attempter. He agrees, however, that aggression turned toward oneself is characteristic of the suicide completer. He believes this means of directing aggression is an important difference that distinguishes attempted suicide from completed suicide.

Manipulation and Revenge

An almost universal fantasy among children is the admonition, "If I die, my parents will be sorry." Faigel (1966) stated that the desire to punish parents who will grieve at their death was one of the most frequent suicidal motivations in young children. Research by Hall (1904, pp. 374–385), Lourie (1966), and Bender and Schilder (1937) supports this conclusion. Lourie states that the ultimate goal children hope to achieve as a result of suicidal behavior is the love and attention of their parents. Bender and Schilder believe that suicide threats are frequently used by young children who need to assert their independence. According to Lawler et al. (1963), attempts with revenge as a motive are manipulative and are not likely to end in death except by miscalculation.

Impulsivity

Suicide and suicide attempts among the young are often attributed to impulsivity. Bakwin (1957) proposes that most suicides under the age of 10 are impulsive acts to punish parents for refusal to grant the child's wishes. Despert (1952) reviewed 400 cases, ages 2–16, and concluded that child suicides are impulsive acts that usually escape the attention of a mental health professional.

Winn and Halla (1966) define impulsivity as an important feature in the personality of two-thirds of the children in their study of attempted suicide. Lourie (1966) supports this finding and concludes that most of the children in his study of attempted suicide had problems of impulse control. Jacobziner (1960) believes that the high incidence of attempts in girls is due to the greater impulsivity of the young female. In a study of attempted suicide in Sweden, Bergstrand and Otto (1962) also conclude that suicidal attempts in girls are impulsive acts connected with immediate problems.

Teicher and Jacobs (1966) are in strong disagreement with these studies. They refute the theory that suicide attempts are impulsive or precipitated by some trivial or immediate problem. They see suicide attempts as the result of a person's total life history. They believe that suicide attempts are considered in advance and are weighed rationally against the other alternatives in the individual's life. They do not see the suicide attempt as an impulsive act but rather as the end of a long history of problems of adjustment.

According to Menninger (1938) suicide should not be seen as a simple, isolated act of impulsion. Instead, it should be viewed as a continuum of self-destructive acts that began long before the final act was realized. Schneer, Kay, and Brogovsky (1961), in agreement with Menninger, see the suicidal gesture as a phase in the continuum of self-destructive behavior that may or may not end in death.

Concept of Death

Integrally related to suicide is an individual's concept of death. To understand why a child takes his or her own life, we should understand what death means to the child. Suicide among the young is particularly tragic because young people frequently seem to be unaware of their own mortality. As a result, any type of threat by children is particularly dangerous. Children who don't understand that they may indeed kill themselves, may choose a method that will leave little room for rescue. The thought of death for the child may involve the denial of death as an irreversible act or a lack of understanding of the finality of death.

Winn and Halla (1966) found that young children attach as much significance to stealing petty amounts as they do to the threat of killing themselves. The children equate death, in severity and permanence, to running away from home in order to escape an unhappy situation. They conclude that while children do have a concept of death, it is qualitatively different from that of an adult. Schilder and Wechsler (1934), in the earliest investigation of this topic, found that children who talked about violence and death really did not believe in the possibility of their own destruction. Similarly, Bender and Schilder (1937) believe that children conceive of death as temporary and reversible.

Nagy (1959) devised an analytic framework for the developmental sequence of a child's concept of death. On the basis of drawings, compositions, and stories collected from children ages 3–10 she was able to distinguish a developmental sequence that corresponds to chronological age. In the first stage, children do not understand death as an irreversible act. In their egocentric ways they imagine the outside world after their own fashion, lifeless things and dead people alike, as living. At this stage, death is denied. This is usually characteristic of children under 5 years of age. For children between the ages of 5 and 9, death is personified. If in general death exists, it is a person, the death-man, who "does it." At this stage, death is accepted but averted. Finally, in the third stage, which becomes prominent in children in their ninth and tenth years, death is recognized as a process that takes place in all of us, the perceptible result of which is the dissolution of bodily life.

Lourie (1966) confirmed this developmental sequence. He points out that an awareness of and concern with death is quite common among school age children. Rochlin (1965) also agrees that an awareness of death is common at this age. However, he disagrees with the developmental sequence and states that children are aware of their own mortality by age 3 or 4. If children state that death is temporary, Rochlin explains that they are defending themselves against fears of their death. Ackerly (1967) also interprets children's view of death as reversible as a defensive tactic.

Alexander and Alderstein (1958) measured emotional responses to death (using word association techniques) with different age groups. They found that death had the greatest emotional impact on children ages 5–8 and adolescents ages 13–16 as compared to the latency age child, 9–12. They attribute this finding to the fact that there are fewer areas of conflict for the child to deal with during latency, thus allowing for less anxiety in this sphere. Kastenbaum (1959) studied attitudes toward death among adolescents. He concluded that adolescents live in the present and pay little attention to the future, which they regard as both unpleasant and devoid of significance. This finding, like that of Alexander and Alderstein, seems to indicate that the concept of death achieves emotional importance during adolescence but that it is

handled by denial that is similar to that of young children.

PSYCHOSOCIAL DETERMINANTS

Family Disorganization and Loss

Family relationships are given important consideration in the literature because of the significance of the family in the life of the young. Most studies have emphasized family disorganization and loss as the prime examples of destructive parent-child relationships. The investigator who focuses on family relationships will have a different viewpoint on the origins of self-destructive behavior than will the investigator who focuses on areas such as impulsive or imitative behavior. These divergent areas of focus raise an important question. Is suicide the result of environmental circumstances acting on a normal psychological mechanism, or is the suicidal individual particularly sensitized to suicide by the pathological altering of the normal mechanism earlier in life? Investigators of family relationships will favor the latter explanation.

A significant number of young people who attempt or commit suicide have a history of broken or disorganized homes. Zilboorg (1937) was the first to note the relationship between family disorganization and suicide. Walton (1958) found the incidence of broken homes in patients who committed suicide to be much greater than in those who did not. Bruhn (1962) found a history of family disorganization to be very high among attempted suicides. Dorpat, Jackson, and Ripley, (1965) compared an attempt population with a completed population and found that 50 percent of the completed suicides and 64 percent of the attempted suicides had a definite history of separation from one or both of the parents. Jacobziner (1964) studied 100 persons under the age of 18 who attempted suicide. Parental neglect, cruelty, and even abandonment were frequent occurrences. In 29 percent of the families, the home situation was so poor that intervention by the Society for the Prevention of Cruelty to Children was necessary. Almost one-half of the children were from homes broken by divorce, separation, or death of one or both of the parents. Recent studies reiterate these findings (Stack, 1980; Goldberg, 1981; and Richman, 1980).

There is a great deal of discrepancy among various investigators with regard to the definition of family disorganization. Family disorganization may be defined as any of the following: severe quarreling between parents or between parent and child, sibling conflict, illegitimate children, parental absence, rejection, cruelty or abandonment, loss of a parent or sibling through death, institutionalization of a family member, a history of suicide or suicide attempts in the family, or disruption of the family by other means (such as alcoholism). Palmer (1941), Reitman (1942), and Robbins, Schmidt, and O'Neal (1957) define family disorganization simply as the loss of a parent through death. Simon (1950) and Batchelor and Napier (1953) define it broadly as absence due to separation, divorce, desertion, illegitimacy, parental rejection, emotional deprivation, quarreling, or alcoholism. However, regardless of the definition, the findings are highly consistent. The investigators found family disorganization and emotional deprivation to be characteristic of young persons attempting suicide.

Loss appears to be the major aspect of family disorganization that traumatically alters the child's environment. Moss and Hamilton (1956), in examining 50 adult suicide attempters, found that 95 percent had suffered the loss of a parent, sibling, or mate under traumatic circumstances. In addition 40 percent had lost their fathers and 20 percent had lost their mothers in infancy, and 75 percent—a very high proportion—had incurred such a loss before completing adolescence. In a control population of 50 nonsuicidal adults the death of a parent or sibling had occurred only one-fourth as frequently. Palmer (1941) reviewed developmental histories of 25 cases of attempted suicide among adults and found that 84 percent had experienced the death or absence of a parent

or sibling, and 68 percent had lost a parent before the age of 14. Palmer concludes that an arrest in psychosexual development, due to the loss or unavailability of parents, is the basic mechanism in the majority of these attempts.

Bruhn (1962) compared a group of adolescents who attempted suicide with a control group who were nonsuicidal. The adolescents who had attempted suicide had experienced either a loss of both parental figures or the absence or death of a family member. Greer (1964) found similar results. His study showed that the incidence of parental loss was higher in suicidal than in nonsuicidal persons. Paffenbarger and Asnes (1966) found that death or absence of the father was the major precursor of suicide among adolescent college males.

Dorpat et al. (1965) studied 114 cases of completed suicide and 121 cases of attempted suicide. They found that those individuals who had committed suicide had the highest incidence of loss of a parent through death, whereas attempted suicides had the highest incidence through divorce or separation. They concluded that an unresolved loss in childhood leads to an inability to sustain object loss in later life.

These studies point to the theory that parental loss early in a child's life may result in a definite predisposition to suicide. Shaw and Schelkun (1965) summarize the consequences of such a loss.

1. The loss may condition the suggestible child who identifies with the lost love object. As a result of this identification, the child may attempt suicide in order to rejoin or copy his or her dead parent or sibling and yet not wish to die permanently.

2. The loss may precipitate anxiety or depression through a sense of guilt. The child will feel guilty if he or she suspects that in some way he or she has been responsible for the desertion. The guilt that the child feels may drive him or her to attempt suicide.

3. The death of a parent may decrease the child's sense of worth. The child may view the death as an abandonment and suffer a loss of status when the parent is lost.
4. The death of a parent or near relative may disrupt the interpersonal relations that the child had previously established.

Despite the general agreement that family disruption is causally related to suicidal behaviors among the young, a note of caution is injected by Jacobs and Teicher (1967). They warn against the simple relationship between loss and suicide. In their study of adolescent suicide attempts, they found that both suicidal and nonsuicidal control groups demonstrated similarly high percentages of disorganized homes. The important distinction, however, was that the control group had experienced a stable life during the preceding five years while the suicide group had not. They suggest that particular attention be paid not merely to the absence of a parent or sibling, but to when and how the loss occurred.

Social Isolation and Communication

Of all the psychodynamic attributes associated with suicidal behavior, the factor of human isolation and withdrawal appears to be the most effective in distinguishing those who kill themselves and those who will not. While withdrawal and alienation can be important determinants of many types of suicidal behavior, they seem to characterize cases of completed suicides rather than suicide attempts or threats. (Seiden, 1969, pp. 34–35)

Reese (1967) investigated suicides in children and found severe social isolation to be the single most characteristic feature of these children. The children had an almost total lack of involvement with members of their school class and with their teachers. Jan-Tausch (n.d.) also studied school age children who committed suicide. He found that in every case the children were without friends from whom they might receive any psycho-

logical support or with whom they might talk. He states that the major difference between those children whose attempts fail and those whose attempts succeed is that those who failed had one relationship with someone with whom they could feel close. He concludes that the child suicide is an individual who has withdrawn so completely that he or she can no longer identify with any person, sees himself or herself rejected by all he or she knows, and is therefore unable to establish a close relationship with any individual.

What factors can explain this state of social isolation? Stengel (1964, p. 47) writes that

the lack of a secure relationship to a parent figure early in childhood may have lasting consequences for a person's ability to establish relationships with other people. Such individuals are likely to find themselves socially isolated in adult life, and social isolation is one of the most important factors in the causation of suicidal acts.

Schrut (1967) states that the young female attempter in his study saw herself as being chronically and unjustly isolated from her peers as well as experiencing a chronic decrease in intrafamilial communications. He found social isolation to be a long term, progressive phenomenon that is always associated with family conflict.

Difficulty in communicating with others is closely related to social isolation. In some instances the suicide attempt can be seen as an attempt at communication: a cry for help. In these cases, self-destruction is not the real purpose of the suicide attempt. These attempts are directed toward human contact, not toward self-destruction. Often children who are using the attempt as a means of communication give warning of their intentions and allow for probable intervention when making an attempt.

Why do young people resort to this dangerous method of getting attention? Speculating on this question, Louire (1966) states that the answer lies in problems of earlier development, problems dealing with the handling of aggressive impulses as well as with methods of getting attention. Peck (1967) feels that young-sters who attempt suicide are not simply attention seeking or manipulative but are unhappy and hopeless to the point that they are unable to change things in any other way. The attempt is their sole means of obtaining attention. If the attempt results in a confronta-tion of the underlying problem, the suicidal behavior is likely to disappear. If the commu-nication goes unheeded or if the conditions do not improve, these children become more lethal, and the consequences, regardless of the original intentions, may become tragic. Teicher and Jacobs (1966) have commented that more often than not the person who resorts to an attempt as a means of getting attention finds that this too fails. The child is then convinced that death is the only solution to the problems of living.

Sibling Position

Kallman et al. (1949) examined 296 cases of completed suicide, ranging in age from 15–65. However, only 7 percent, or approximately 21 individuals, were in the adolescent age range. Kallman observed that the suicide rate of only children did not differ significantly from that of the general population. Several recent investigators, however, have suggested that a child's sibling position may be related to his or her suicidal behavior.

Toolan (1962) reported on 102 children and adolescents admitted to Bellevue Hospital in New York City for suicide attempts in 1960. Toolan found that 49 of the 102 adolescent suicide attempters were firstborn children. Lester (1966) compared Toolan's statistics on sibling positions with data from the New York City population. He confirmed that the distribution of sibling positions in Toolan's sample—especially the high number of first-borns—differed significantly from the ex-pected distribution.

Other investigators, Lawler et al. (1963), studied 22 children and adolescents who had been admitted to Winnipeg Children's Hos-pital in Canada during the two year period of 1960–1962. The investigators concluded from their study that a disproportionate number of

suicidal children occupy special sibling posi-tions. Of the 22 children, 14 occupied special positions (3 only, 7 firstborn, 4 youngest), but the sample was too small for adequately reliable conclusions.

Lester (1966) reexamined the relationship between sibling position and suicidal behav-ior. He reasoned that suicide attempts might express an affiliative tendency to communi-cate with others. Noting that such affiliative tendencies are strongest in firstborn and only children, Lester predicted an overrepresenta-tion of firstborn and only children attempting suicide. He did not carry out an investigation to confirm the hypothesis.

Data from 17 adolescents who attempted suicide and came to the attention of the Cornell University Payne Whitney Suicide Prevention in New York were analyzed for information regarding sex, birth order, sex of siblings, and family constellation. The results indicated that there was a significant trend for firstborn females to be overrepresented among adolescent suicide attempters (Cantor, 1972).

Subsequent studies conducted in Boston (Cantor 1975, 1976) analyzed data on females ranging in age from 18–25 years. A 31-item questionnaire designed by the investigator was given to 199 students, 20 of whom were found to have histories of one or more previous suicide attempts. Again, the first-born females were significantly present among the 20 attempters.

Discussion

During the past ten years the number of writings on suicide has increased sharply. It is therefore surprising that there are only four comprehensive reviews of the literature of suicide in childhood and adolescence (Bakwin, 1957; Shaw & Schelkun, 1965; Seiden, 1969; and Cantor, 1972). This discussion presents a critical review of the literature that was written during the twentieth century on the topic of suicide and attempted suicide among the young. It conveys the present state of our knowledge, analyzes current research, and indicates the most important areas for future research.

Although this review is comprehensive, the quality of the studies that contribute to it is not consistent. Bakwin (1957), in reviewing the literature up to 1957, was able to cite only five studies that he considered to be important in the literature. At present, the picture is not quite so dismal. However, Bakwin's pessimistic statement still has justification. A large number of articles consist of simple anecdotal accounts or uncritical reports of previous findings, and most do not contain any theoretical orientation. Many lack a uniform criterion for the definition of suicide, failing to differentiate between threatened, attempted, and completed suicide. There is often a lack of any statistical treatment and of a control or comparison group in research design. In addition, the field is handicapped by its interdisciplinary nature. Psychoanalysts, psychologists, sociologists, and public health workers each come to the problem with their own particular tools and their own particular bias. The interdisciplinary nature of suicidology has contributed greatly to its recent growth but it has also handicapped it in its efforts to develop a unified approach to the question of suicide.

Such complicated material presents numerous problems in the arrangement and categorization of data. These problems are exacerbated by two considerations: the methodological defects and the noncomparability of many of the studies, and the enormous volume of literature written on this subject. The major obstacle to neat organization was introduced by the prodigious number of psychodynamic characteristics that have been linked to youthful suicide.

In spite of the difficult nature of the task, it has been possible to draw conclusions about the character and extent of childhood suicide, as well as to indicate which areas appear to be most promising for future research. In brief, we may list these conclusions as they relate to the epidemiology and etiology of suicide as follows:

Epidemiology

(1) In recent years, there has been an increase in suicide among young people, an increase which it appears will continue indefinitely. (2) Suicide is statistically nonexistent under age 5, virtually nonexistent at 5–9, rare at 10–14, increases in frequency about eight- to tenfold at ages 15–19, and again doubles in frequency in the 20–24 age group. (3) There are no official statistics on suicide attempts. However, we know that attempted suicides outnumber completed suicides by estimates of 7:1 (Dublin, 1963) to 50:1 (Jacobziner, 1960). Of all suicide attempts in the United States, 12 percent are made by adolescents and about 90 percent of these attempts are made by adolescent girls (Balser & Masterson, 1959).

Etiology

PSYCHOLOGICAL DETERMINANTS. (1) Depression is the single sign most often observed by those reporting on suicidal behavior. Depression in young people is usually associated with the loss of the love object either through death or separation. (2) Puberty appears to be a crucial period in the balance of self-destruction. (3) Studies of suicidal behavior have found that children may imitate the actions or follow the suggestions of people close to them who have died, attempted suicide or who openly reveal suicidal wishes toward them. (4) All types of suicidal behaviors among the young have been explained as aggression that becomes displaced and self-directed. Most investigators feel that the child becomes so overwhelmed by guilt or fear about his or her feelings of hostility that he or she directs aggression inward. (5) Manipulative attempts that are aimed at achieving love and attention are frequently used by young people. Few of these are likely to end in death except by miscalculation. (6) There is much disagreement among theorists with regard to the importance of impulsivity. A few investigators state that most suicides under the age of ten are impulsive acts to punish parents for refusal to grant the child's wishes. Other investigators refute the theory that suicide attempts are impulsive or precipitated by trivial or immediate problems. (7) Integrally related to suicide is an individual's concept of death. Young children do not appear to understand the possibility of their own destruction. Most investigators have concluded that the child views death as temporary and reversible and that the concept of death achieves emotional importance during adolescence but that it is handled by denial which is similar to that of young children.

PSYCHOSOCIAL DETERMINANTS.   (1) A significant number of young people who attempt suicide have a history of broken or disorganized homes. Although there is great discrepancy among various investigators with regard to the definition of family disorganization, the findings are consistent. Family disorganization and emotional deprivation appear to be characteristic of youngsters attempting suicide. Loss is the major aspect of family disorganization that traumatically alters the child's environment. Several studies point to the theory that parental loss early in a child's life may result in a definite predisposition to suicide. (2) Of all the psychodynamic factors associated with suicide, the factors of human isolation and withdrawal appear to be most effective in distinguishing those who attempt from those who complete suicide. Suicide attempts often result from failures in communication. These attempts are directed toward human contact not toward self-destruction. (3) Several recent investigators have suggested that a child's sibling position may be related to his or her suicidal behavior.

TREATMENT AND MANAGEMENT OF SUICIDAL CHILDREN

The treatment of the depressed and suicidal child necessitates that the therapist acknowledge that he or she is the tie to life for the child from the moment he or she engages with the patient. The child has already experienced rejection, even if only subjectively, and is probably depressed and insecure and probably expects rejection from other authority figures. Most importantly, the child is feeling alone. The fear and loneliness are probably more painful than the depression. Feelings of aloneness and fears of abandonment seem to

be the pervasive factors. Parents are often angry and hostile toward the child and toward the therapist who is seen as both a potential lifesaver and potential recipient of the child's affections. They often react with an exaggeration of the problem and pain that the child is causing them (narcissistic and symbiotic) or with massive denial. Frequently, the fathers are largely physically or emotionally absent or seen as punitive and the mothers, despite a long history of problems, are described in idealized terms (Cantor, 1976).

While a suicide attempt is the result of diverse factors and it is difficult to generalize, in this author's experience there is one cornerstone of successful work with suicidal children. The therapist must offer himself or herself as a warm, caring, potentially loving person who can always be reached and who will try to be available when needed. The goal is to make the child feel wanted and to establish the possibility of the therapist becoming the stable person in the child's life. The child who has attempted suicide or who is contemplating suicide is trying to communicate his or her needs. If these needs are not heard or are ignored, as they probably have been in the past, a suicide attempt may well be carried out. Paying attention implies both concern and respect for the child rather than a dismissal of the act as a gesture for attention. Attention may be just what the child wants; but if it is necessary to go to these lengths to achieve it, then it is the desperation and the inability to cope with stress that must be noticed rather than the manipulative aspects of the act (Gould, 1965). Caring and concern must be conveyed. This necessitates the lifting of the Freudian veil of analytic anonymity. Work with suicidal young people requires a deep and often personal involvement (Cantor, 1979). The aim of the first meeting is to establish a beginning trust, to discuss the parents' and the child's most critical concerns, and to enlist the parents' cooperation in the treatment plan.

The function of the therapist is to help the child to develop the capacity for understanding. The therapist is constantly aware of the child's insatiable need for love, which may be expressed directly or indirectly through unending needs for oral gratification (to be fed by the therapist) or the child's needs for exclusivity (to be the only child the therapist sees). The therapist's task in working with suicidal children is, in one respect, somewhat more difficult than in working with suicidal adolescents. The major development task of the adolescent is that of detaching from parental authority, which, while it may be particularly painful for the adolescent with impaired object relations and minimal social contacts, can be facilitated by the therapist. The child is not able to use the therapist as a bridge from family to peers in the same way that the adolescent might. The child must remain within the womb of the family for many years to come. The therapist must, therefore, encourage the therapeutic relations but not at the expense of the parental relationship. Depressed children have lost the feeling of parental omnipotence. The parents whom the child looked up to or loved are no longer available to provide the dependent child with loved feelings. He or she feels lost and helpless and does not know where to turn and thus is predisposed to depression. Thus while individual work is imperative, the family must be intimately involved. In my opinion, this is best effected with the child's therapist also serving as the therapist for regular and frequent parent and family meetings, rather than embracing the more traditional model of a therapist for the child and a separate therapist for the parents, or allowing only one parent to be involved. The initial diagnostic session, as well as subsequent family sessions, should include both of the child's parents. Too often therapists underestimate the contribution their presence can make to the progress of therapy.

The mother, by herself usually cannot provide all the necessary information, let alone a sample of the father's personality style. By excusing the father from the evaluation, furthermore, the therapist may be sanctioning his alienation from family affairs and from the youngster who is having psychological difficulty. (Weiner, 1970, p. 374)

Direct support is essential for the child to cope with current difficulties that involve parents, siblings, peers, and school, and this is more efficiently accomplished if one person is closely involved in all spheres. If possible, a dinner with the family or, at least, a home visit and school visit should be planned. The time involvement and commitment are enormous at the beginning. The initial complete involvement is later followed by the development of a network of sustaining relationships outside the therapy setting that allow for the reduction of the intensity of treatment (Motto, 1975).

It is important to note that although the therapist must be all-involved, she or he must not present herself or himself as all-powerful. Many youngsters do not succeed in killing themselves when they really intended to do so. Many, however, miscalculate and die when what they really wanted was to get help in order to live. It is important for the therapist to make his or her limitations known. In most suicide attempts, the child really wants and expects to be saved by the "omnipotent" therapist or parent—and this is not always possible (Cantor, 1977).

In sum, the optimal sequence of treatment would be (1) the establishment of a warm caring relationship which the child and family can accept, (2) fostering emotional growth and self-sufficiency, and (3) gradually reducing the dependency on the therapist with the establishment of better parent and peer relationships.

Some practical guidelines can be offered to facilitate this sequence. It is generally not wise to reassure the child that "everything will be all right" without understanding the problem. Words such as these offer empty reassurance, are superficial, and may even be deadly. All that will result is that the child will feel a lowered sense of self-esteem and perhaps even anger at not having been understood. The child might interpret this as follows: "If things are so rosy and I am so unhappy, then why bother? And if you don't understand me, then nobody will."

Suicide attempts among children, adolescents, and adults are most likely to occur at precisely the time when it appears that the depression is lifting. This apparently contradictory event may mean that when the child is no longer depressed he or she will have the psychic energy available to carry out a suicidal act, or, more likely, the decision to do something about his or her unhappiness is the very factor which causes a lift in the depression. It is always best to avoid any diminution of the child's self-esteem as through criticism or ridicule of his or her apparently foolish behaviors. The therapist should ask the child directly if he or she was considering suicide. Much more damage can be done to the child who feels ashamed of his or her thoughts or frightened to speak about them than can ever be done by mentioning the word "suicide." The child needs to know that he or she has an ally who can accept his or her feelings, even his or her darkest thoughts. Understanding, acceptance, and concern constitute strong, immediate lifesaving measures (Cantor, 1977).

Whenever possible, it is best to utilize a wide range of supports—pediatrician, teachers, guidance counselors. Any caring adult could be in this role. The family and other caring adults can also assist with practical matters such as removing lethal agents from the home—guns, poisons, or chemical agents (Meeks, 1971). The therapist should be very careful about accepting the child's reassurances about future self-destructive behaviors. Children live in the present and rarely conceptualize any further into the future than when Christmas will come. This is not a question of truthfulness; it is a question of unpredictability. The therapist should be prepared for a good deal of anger. The child's conflicts and hurt may be turned into anger at the therapist so that the child appears more intent on making the therapist miserable than on using her or his help (Meeks, 1971).

Fears of dependency may make it difficult for the child to express feelings of warmth towards the therapist, just as he or she has had difficulty expressing feelings of tenderness towards his or her parents. The child may become demanding and irritating and the therapist runs the risk of becoming defensive and withdrawing affection from the child. This evokes feelings of abandonment and is often the prelude to intensified depression and suicidal behaviors. Or the child may idealize the therapist who is seen as the only person in the world who really cares, and the parents become jealous and find some excuse to sabotage or terminate therapy just at the point when the child most desperately needs the alliance. Suicidal behaviors are provoked in this manner. This is exhausting work, and to keep pressures from becoming excessive only a few cases of suicidal children should be handled at one time. The necessity for constant availability and flexibility is in itself demanding. But the results are rewarding, as it is primarily the development of the caring relationship that relieves the pain and places the child willingly on this side of life.

THE EFFECTS OF CHILDHOOD SUICIDE ON THE FAMILY

It is by now well understood that children can and do kill themselves, that the death of a child is tragic for the survivors, and that the literature regarding suicide is prodigious. There are, however, only two articles that deal with parental response to youthful suicide (Herzog & Resnick, 1969; Cantor, 1975). This important area is essentially ignored.

It is possible, however, to make some observations regarding the problems that are involved in approaching the family, the particular problems the family encounters in trying to cope with a loss due to suicide, and to discuss the therapeutic goals for the family which has suffered such a loss.

One of the problems the therapist encounters is the professional's attitude toward both the victim and the survivors. Bloom and Litman (1967) report that psychiatrists exhibit extreme defensiveness when questioned about patients who commit suicide while under their care, and Ansel and McGee (1971) state the patient's suicide may be taken as an indication of the therapist's incompetence. If the attitude of the therapist toward the victim is a defensive one, it is possible that this attitude may be generalized toward the survivors.

The family, on the other hand, often blames the therapist for the death of the child. As previously noted, the child and the family of the child may have seen the therapist as omnipotent and able to stop the child from suicide. It may be beyond the comprehension of the family to accept the thought that it may be beyond the capability of even the most competent therapist to prevent the death of someone hell-bent on suicide. This resentment may be generalized to all professionals, even those who were not involved prior to the suicide.

An additional aspect of the family's unwillingness to accept help from a professional may be what the family assumes is the attitude of the professional towards the parents. A suicide often creates negative or condemnatory attitudes in others, and thus the family may expect the professional to respond to the suicide victim or the surviving family members with an attitude of hostility and rejection. (Cantor, 1975, p. 8)

The family, too, is burdened with problems while trying to work through the feelings of grief which invariably accompany a death. It is generally accepted that there are three stages of nonsuicidal mourning that need to be completed if a person is to regain equilibrium after a loss (Martin, 1970). The first stage is an initial denial of the loss, often expressed through shock or disbelief, followed by an absorption of the shock. The second stage of mourning is the open expression of sorrow. The third stage brings an acceptance of the finality of death, the beginning of healing, and the conscious effort to regain emotional stability.

It is this author's opinion that the psychological effects of a suicide alter the grief reaction of those close to the victim. The first stage of the grief process involving a suicide is characterized by shock and denial of the suicide—the death is accepted but the suicide is denied. The second stage does not bring sorrow, but rather anger, strong anger at what the child has done. This anger is followed by a sense of guilt for not having loved the child enough, for not having done enough for him or her, for not having stopped the suicide, and the regret that it is now too late. The guilt and self-reproach are now combined with pity for the child, an upsurge of posthumous love and tenderness and shame for the anger previously expressed. The third stage is characterized by self-pity and long-lasting depression. Acceptance, if it comes at all, takes a long time to appear.

The parents of children who die in accidents usually resolve their guilt feelings within one year following the accident (Herzog & Resnick, 1969). The parents of children who commit suicide appear far less able to resolve their guilt and suffer from prolonged self-accusations. There appears to be no closure on the grief process for parents of children who kill themselves. Due to the stigma attached to the idea of suicide, the parents are unable to depend upon the usual avenues of support in working out their grief. In fact, parents are rarely able to talk even to each other about the death of their child (Herzog & Resnick, 1969).

The death of a child is the hardest loss for a parent to sustain. When a parent loses a child he must not only cope with his own despair but also help the other children and family members to express their feelings. This, too, is almost impossible when the parent is unable to derive any support from others in the environment. (Cantor, 1975, p. 9)

In many ways, for the family, the tragedy is just beginning. In what ways, then, can a professional be of assistance to those who face the tragedy of self-inflicted death of a child? The availability of a mental health professional immediately after the death, during the first stage of the grief process, would maximize the family's initial need to express their confusion and minimize their subsequent unwillingness to talk with anyone. "It is the task of the professional at this point to provide a large measure of reality testing by aiding the family in accepting the death as a death by suicide" (Cantor, 1975, p. 10).

The survivors should be encouraged to work through their guilt in order to be able to progress to an expression of their sorrow. The survivors, during the second stage, are often obsessed with self-blame for the things left unsaid or undone that might have prevented the suicide. It is important for the professional to allow the survivors to express their self-recriminations and hostilities, and to indicate that minor omissions or commissions that now appear to be of monumental importance probably would not have made the difference and saved the life. The sooner the survivors can express their hostilities and anger, the sooner they will be able to express their sorrow.

The third stage of the suicidal grief process is characterized by self-pity and long-lasting depression. The parents of a suicide often do not achieve acceptance; the grief is without end. It is carried in their hearts forever. The survivors may suffer distress that is characterized by pathological reactions as a result of self-perpetuating rather than self-limiting grief. Extreme forms of grief are termed pathological because of the intensity of the reaction and because prolonged depression is potentially self-destructive for the survivor. Severe depression, extreme anxiety, and somatic manifestations need treatment. Healthy defenses can be encouraged, while denial that increases anxiety can be reduced.

A mourning process that is to benefit the survivors must begin with a sense of honesty regarding the circumstances of the death. And it must begin with an honesty about death itself. When the finality of death is replaced with fantasy, the mourning process is extended and distorted. This is particularly crucial when the death is by suicide and when the survivors of the suicide include children. The loss a child endures of another child, particularly a brother or sister, is always premature and untimely and complex. The trauma involved, the hatred for the abandonment, the fears that their omnipotent thinking of death wishes toward the sibling caused the death, the fears that their parents think that the wrong child had died, the fears that violence will befall them, or that mental illness is inherited, must be expressed before the child can achieve some degree of freedom from anxiety and utilize his or her capacity to mourn.

The most common procedure in helping a family to cope has been to work with the parents and to exclude other members of the family. This is particularly true when siblings are young. It is this author's opinion that the treatment of the survivors of a suicide is the one area in which the entire family should be included, as children are at least equally affected by the traumatic nature of the loss.

If it is true that the disturbed suicidal child was a member of a disturbed or destructive family, it is particularly crucial to take advantage of the grief process as an opportunity to initiate therapeutic contact with all members of the family. "Since children learn by example, to focus therapeutic efforts on the survivors is to reduce the risk of their subsequent suicidal behavior" (Cantor, 1975, p. 10).

REFERENCES

Ackerly, W.C. Latency age children who threaten or attempt to kill themselves. *Journal of the American Academy of Child Psychiatry,* 1967, **6**, 242–261.

Adam K. Suicide. A critical review of the literature. *Canadian Psychiatric Association Journal,* 1967, **12**(4), 413–420.

Alexander, I.E., & Alderstein, A.M. Affective responses to the concept of death in a population of children and early adolescents. *Journal of Genetic Psychology,* 1958, **93**, 167–177.

Ansel, L., & McGee, R.N. Attitudes towards suicide attempters. *Bulletin of Suicidology,* 1971, **8**(27).

Bakwin, H. Loneliness in infants. *American Journal of the Disturbed Child,* 1942, **63**, 30–40.

Bakwin, H. Suicide in children and adolescents. *Journal of Pediatrics,* 1957, **50**(6), 749–769.

Bakwin, H., & Bakwin, R.M. *Behavior disorders in children.* Philadelphia: Saunders, 1972.

Balser, B.H., & Masterson, J.F. Suicide in adolescents. *American Journal of Psychiatry,* 1959, **116**(5), 400–404.

Batchelor, I.R.C., & Napier, M.B. Broken homes and attempted suicide. *British Journal of Delinquency,* 1953, **4,** 99–108.

Beck, A. Measuring depression: The depressive inventory. In T. Williams, M. Katz, & J. Shields (Eds.), *Recent advances in the psychobiology of the depressive illness.* Government Printing Office, 1972.

Bender, L., & Schilder, P. Suicidal preoccupations and attempts in children. *American Journal of Orthopsychiatry,* 1937, **7,** 225–243.

Bergstrand, C.G., & Otto, U. Suicidal attempts in adolescence and childhood. *Acta paediatrica,* 1962, **51**(1), 17–26.

Bibring, E. The mechanism of depression. In P. Greenacre (Ed.), *Affective disorders.* New York: International Universities Press, 1953.

Bigras, J., Gauthier, Y., Bouchard, C., & Tasse, Y. Suicidal attempt in adolescent girls: A preliminary study. *Canadian Psychiatric Association Journal,* 1966, **11,** (Supplement), 275–282.

Bloom, V., & Litman, R. An analysis of suicide at a training center. *American Journal of Psychiatry,* 967, **123,** 918–925.

Bowlby, J. Some pathological processes engendered by early mother-child separation. *Journal of Mental Science,* 1953, **99,** 265–272.

Bowlby, J. Grief and mourning in infancy and early childhood. *Psychoanalytic Study of the Child,* 1960, **15,** 9–52.

Bowlby, J. Separation anxiety. *Journal of Child Psychology and Psychiatry,* 1960, **1,** 251–269.

Bruhn, J.G. Broken homes among attempted suicides and psychiatric outpatients: A comparative study. *Journal of Mental Science,* 1962, **108**(457), 772–779.

Cantor, P. *Personality and status characteristics of the female youthful suicide attempter.* Doctoral dissertation, Columbia University, 1972.(a)

Cantor, P. The adolescent Attempter: sex, sibling position and family constellation. *Life-Threatening Behavior,* **2**(4), 252–261, 1972. (b)

Cantor, P.C. Personality characteristics found among youthful female suicide attempters. *Journal of Abnormal Psychology,* 1976, **85**(3), 324–239.

Cantor, P.C. Birth order and paternal absence as predisposing factors in suicide attempts among youthful females. Address presented to the American Association of Suicidology, Los Angeles, 1976.

Cantor, P.C. Suicide and attempted suicide among students: Problem, prediction and prevention. In P.C. Cantor (Ed.), *Understanding a child's world: Readings in infancy through adolescence.* New York: Random House, 1977.

Cantor, P. Student suicides: Outlook detection and intervention. Keynote address, presented at the 23rd Annual Conference of the Pennsylvania School Counselors Association, Pittsburgh, March 17, 1979.

Cantor, P.C. Suicide and depression. In M. Schwarz (Ed.), *TV and teens: Experts look at the issues.* Boston: Addison-Wesley, 1982.

Cerny, L., & Cerna, M. Depressive syndrome in adolescents with regard to suicidal tendencies. *Ceskoslovenska Psychiatrie,* 1962, **58**(3), 162–169.

Despert, J.L. Suicide and depression in children. *Nervous Children,* 1952, **9**(4), 389.

Dizmang, L. Loss, bereavement and depression in childhood. in *International Psychiatry Clinics,* 1969, **6,** 175–195.

Dorpat, T.L., Jackson, J.K., & Ripley, H.S. Broken homes and attempted and committed suicide. *Archives of General Psychiatry,* 1965, **12**(2), 213–216.

Dublin, L.I. *Suicide: A sociological and statistical study.* New York: Ronald, 1963.

Ellis, E.R., & Allen, G.N. *Traitor within: Our suicide problem.* New York: Doubleday, 1961.

Faigel, H.C. Suicide among young persons. A review for its incidence and causes, and methods of its prevention. *Clinical Pediatrics,* 1966, **5,** 87–190.

Farberow, N., Shneidman, E., Litman, R., & Wold, C. The suicidal patient and the physician. *Mind,* 1963, **1,** pp. 69–74.

Ford, R. Death by hanging of adolescent and young adult males. *Journal of Forensic Sciences,* 1957, **2**(2), 171–176.

Fredericks, C. Percentage of increase in suicide rate among younger age groups both sexes, all races 1955–1978. Portion of paper read at American Association of Suicidology conference, New Orleans, 1979.

Freud, S. Mourning and Melancholia. In *Collected Papers* (Vol. IV). London: Hogarth, 1925.

Frisch, A.J. Depressions. In M.M. Josephson & R.T. Porter (Eds.), *Clinicians' handbook of childhood psychopathology.* New York: Aronson, 1979.

Funkenstein, D. (Ed.). The student and mental health: An international view. London: *World Federation for Mental Health,* 1959.

Goldberg, E.R. Depression and suicide ideation in the young adult. *American Journal of Psychiatry,* 1981, **138**(1), 35–40.

Gould, R. Suicide problems in children and adolescents. *American Journal of Psychotherapy,* 1965, **19**, 228–246.

Greer, S. The relationship between parental loss and attempted suicide: A control study. *British Journal of Psychiatry,* 1964, **110**(468), 698–705.

Hall, G.S. *Adolescence* (Vol. I). New York: Appleton, 1904.

Harlow, H. The nature of love. *The American Psychologist.* 1958, **13**, 673–685.

Herzog, A. & Resnick, H.L.P. A clinical study of parental response to adolescent death by suicide with recommendations for approaching the survivors. *British Journal of Social Psychiatry,* 1969, **3**(3), 144–152.

Jacobs, J., & Teicher, J.D. Broken homes and social isolation in attempted suicide of adolescents. *International Journal of Social Psychiatry,* 1967, **13**(2), 139–149.

Jacobziner, H. Accidents and attempted suicide in children and adolescents. *Feelings,* 1964, **6**(1), 1–4.

Jan-Tausch, J. *Suicide of children 1960–1963: New Jersey public school students.* Trenton, N.J.: State of New Jersey Department of Education, (n.d.).

Kallman, F.J., DePorte, J., DePorte, E., & Feingold, L. Suicide in twins and only children. *American Journal of Human Genetics,* 1949, **1**, 113–126.

Kastenbaum, R. Time and death in adolescence. In H. Feifel (Ed.), *The meaning of death.* New York: McGraw-Hill, 1959.

Keeler, W.R. Children's reactions to the death of a parent. In P.H. Hoch & J. Zubin (Eds.), *Depression.* New York: Grune & Stratton, 1954.

Klein, M. *Contributions to psychoanalysis.* London: Hogarth, 1948.

Lawler, R.H., Nakielny, W., & Wright, N. Suicidal attempts in children. *Canadian Medical Association Journal,* 1963, **89**, 751–754.

Leonard, C. *Understanding and preventing suicide.* Springfield, Ill.: Thomas, 1967.

Lester, D. Sibling position and suicidal behavior. *Journal of Individual Psychology,* 1966, **22**(2), 204–207.

Litman, R.E., Curphey, T., Shneidman, E., Farberow, N., & Tabachnik, N. Investigations of equivocal suicides. *Journal of the American Medical Association,* 1963, **184**, 924–929.

Litman, R.E. When patients commit suicide. *American Journal of Psychotherapy,* 1965, **12,** 570–576.

Lourie, R.S. Clinical studies of attempted suicide in childhood. *Clinical Proceedings of Children's Hospital of the District of Columbia,* 1966, **22,** 173.

Mahler, M. On sadness and grief in infancy and childhood. *Psychoanalytic Study of the Child,* 1961, **16**, 332–351.

Martin, M. Helping children cope with sorrow. *Parents Magazine,* **42,** August 1970, 42–43, 61.

Meeks, J. *The fragile alliance.* Baltimore: Williams & Wilkins, 1971.

Menninger, K. *Man against himself.* New York: Harcourt, Brace, 1938.

Motto, Jerome A. Treatment and management of suicidal adolescents. *Psychiatric Opinion,* 1975, **12**(6), 14–20.

Moss, L., & Hamilton, D. The psychotherapy of the suicidal patient. *American Journal of Psychiatry,* 1956, **112,** 814–820.

Mulcock, D. Juvenile suicide. A study of suicide and attempted suicide over a 16 year period. *Medical Officer,* 1955, **94,** 155–160.

Nagy, M. The child's view of death. In H. Feifel (Ed.), *The meaning of death.* New York: McGraw-Hill, 1959.

National Institute of Mental Health. Personal communication while at Johns Hopkins Fellowship Program in Suicidology, 1969.

Paffenbarger, R., & Asnes, D. Chronic disease in former college students. III. Precursors of suicide in early and middle life. *American Journal of Public Health,* 1966, **56,** 1026–1036.

Palmer, D. Factors in suicidal attempts: A review of 25 consecutive cases. *Journal of Nervous and Mental Disease,* 1941, **93,** 421–442.

Peck, M.L. Optimism and despair among suicidal adolescents. Paper read at "Optimism and Suicide" seminar, San Diego, January 1967.

Peck, M.L., & Schrut, A. Statistical data on college

student suicide: Los Angeles County. Unpublished manuscript, Suicide Prevention Center, Los Angeles, 1967.

Reese, R.D. School-age suicide: The educational parameters. *Dissertation Abstracts International,* 1967, **27**(9–A), 2895–2896.

Reitman, F. On the predictability of suicide. *Journal of Mental Science,* 942, **88**, 580–582.

Richman, Joseph. Suicide and infantile fixations. *Suicide and life-threatening behavior,* 1980, **10**(1), 3–9.

Robbins, E., Schmidt, E.H., & O'Neal, P. Some interrelations of social factors and clinical diagnosis in attempted suicide: A study of 109 patients. *American Journal of Psychiatry,* 1957, **114**, 221–231.

Rochlin, C. *Griefs and discontents.* Boston: Little Brown, 1965.

Schechter, M.D. The recognition and treatment of suicide in children. In E.S. Shneidman & N.L. Farberow (Eds.), *Clues to suicide.* New York: McGraw-Hill, 1957.

Schilder, P., & Wechsler, D. The attitudes of children toward death. *Journal of Genetic Psychology,* 1934, **45**, 406–451.

Schneer, H.I., Kay, P., & Brozovsky, M. Events and conscious ideation leading to suicidal behavior in adolescence. *Psychiatric Quarterly,* **35**(3), 507–515.

Schrut, A. Suicidal adolescents and children. *Journal of the American Medical Association,* 1964, **188**(13), 1103–1107.

Schrut, A. Some typical patterns in the behavior and background of female adolescents who attempt suicide. Paper read at American Psychiatric Association, Detroit, May, 1967.

Seiden, R.H. Campus tragedy: A study of student suicide. *Journal of Abnormal Psychology,* 1966, **71**(6), 389–399.

Seiden, R.H. Suicide among youth. *Bulletin of Suicidology,* **6**, (Supplement), 1969.

Shankel, L.W., & Carr, A.C. Transvestism and hanging episodes in a male adolescent. *Psychiatric Quarterly,* 1956, **30**(1) 478–493.

Shaw, C.R., & Schelkun, R.F. Suicidal behavior in children. *Psychiatry,* 1965, **28**(2), 157–168.

Shneidman, E.S. Orientations toward death. In R.W. White (Ed.), *The study of lives.* New York: Prentice-Hall, 1963.

Simon, W. Attempted suicide among veterans: A comparative study of 50 cases. *Journal of Nervous and Mental Disease,* 1950, **3**, 451–468.

Spitz, R. Anaclitic depression: An inquiry into the genesis of psychiatric conditions in early childhood. *Psychoanalytic Study of the Child,* 1946, **2**, 313–342.

Stack, Steven. The effects of marital dissolution on suicide. *Journal of Marriage and the Family,* 1980, **42**(1), 83–91.

Stearns, A.W. Cases of probable suicide in young persons without obvious motivation. *Journal of the Maine Medical Association,* 1953, **44**(91), 16–23.

Stengel, E. *Suicide and attempted suicide.* Baltimore: Penguin, 1964.

Teicher, J. Why do adolescents kill themselves? *National Health Program Reports,* 1970.

Teicher, J.D., & Jacobs, J. Adolescents who attempt suicide: Preliminary findings. *American Journal of Psychiatry,* 1966, **122**(11), 1248–1257.

Temby, W.D. Suicide. In G.B. Blaire & C.C. McArthur (Eds.), *Emotional problems of the student.* New York: Appleton-Century-Crofts, 1961.

Toolan, J.M. Suicide and suicidal attempts in children and adolescents. *American Journal of Psychiatry,* 1962, **118**(8), 719–724.

Toolan, James M. Therapy of depressed and suicidal children. *American Journal of Psychotherapy,* 1978, **32**, 243–251.

Walton, H. Suicidal behavior in depressive illness: A study of etiological factors in suicide. *Journal of Mental Science,* 1958, **104**, 884–891.

Weiner, Irving B. *Psychological disturbance in adolescence:* New York: Wiley-Interscience, 1970.

Winn, D., & Halla, R. Observation of children who threaten to kill themselves. *Canadian Psychiatric Association Journal,* 1966, **2**(Supplement), 283–294.

Zilboorg, G. Considerations of suicide with particular reference to that of the young. *American Journal of Orthopsychiatry,* 1937, **7**, 15–31.

CHAPTER 19

Aggressive and Delinquent Behavior in Childhood and Adolescence

JAMES H. JOHNSON AND EILEEN B. FENNELL

Children who come to the attention of mental health professionals display a range of problematic behaviors that may create difficulties for themselves, their parents, or those around them. Some show evidence of mental retardation, others of neurological impairment, and still others display problems of relatedness, cognition, and behavior to such a degree that they are judged psychotic. As has been suggested by Achenbach (1980), a range of other childhood problems can be subsumed under the headings of *Internalizing* and *Externalizing* syndromes (see also Achenbach, 1966; Achenbach & Edelbrock, 1978).

Under the heading of *Internalizing* syndromes are a variety of problems reflective of depression, withdrawal, anxiety, obsessions, somatic complaints, and so-called schizoid features. Generally, children with such problems seem to suffer more than others in their environment as a result of their difficulties. These problems are most closely associated with the traditional categories of neurotic and psychophysiological (psychosomatic) disorders and are considered elsewhere in this book (see chaps. 21 by Dollinger and 17 by Kenny, Bergey, & Young-Hyman, respectively).

Under *Externalizing* syndromes (also referred to as conduct disorders) are included several other types of behavior problems. These difficulties can be distinguished from the ones listed above by the fact that they are *primarily* reflected in conflict with the environment rather than childhood distress.

Among the problems most commonly listed under this heading are aggressiveness and delinquency, although hyperactivity (discussed in this book in chap. 20 by Kerasotes & Walker) is sometimes considered under this heading as well. In the present chapter, we will focus on two of these problems: childhood aggression and delinquency. (We will also briefly allude to the issue of hyperactivity as it relates to delinquency.) While it is clear that aggressive behavior and delinquency are sometimes related, they often are not, and separate sets of literature related to these two areas have developed. For these reasons, they will be considered separately here.

In the case of both aggression and delinquency, we will attempt to comment on the general nature of the problem, factors related to etiology, the correlates of each, and intervention procedures designed to deal with these problems.

CHILDHOOD AGGRESSION

Although aggressive behavior is more frequently seen in males than females (Eme, 1979), almost all children display aggressive behavior to some degree at some point in their development. They may show physical aggression in the form of hitting, shoving, biting, scratching, kicking, or taking objects away from other children. Or they may display nonphysical aggression by being verbally abusive toward adults or other children. The high frequency of aggressive behavior in childhood is suggested by Lapouse and Monk (1959) who found that, of 482 children age 6–12, 80 percent were reported to show evidence of a loss of temper once a month or more while 48 percent were reported to lose their temper at least twice a week. Fortunately, in the case of most children, aggressive behaviors are of relatively low intensity and frequency and do not constitute a serious problem (although even low levels of aggression may cause concern to their parents). In other cases, however, children may display aggressive behaviors that are of high intensity/high frequency and that demand a response from parents, teachers, or sometimes mental health professionals. Related to the seriousness issue, it is of interest to note some recent findings published by Crowther, Bond, and Rolf (1981). These investigators obtained teacher ratings on a large sample of preschoolers who ranged in age from 2 through 5 years. At age 5, over 75 percent of the sample of boys were judged to struggle with, or pick fights with, another child or adult on at least some occasions (low severity). Approximately 18 percent showed this behavior at a moderate level of severity (once per day to several times per week). Only about 7 percent of the children displayed this behavior at the level judged to be reflective of high severity (almost all the time to several times per day). Clearly, while most children show some evidence of aggressive behavior, it is displayed to a marked degree in only a relatively small proportion of the child population.

The potential implications of marked aggressiveness in childhood are suggested by the fact that aggressive behavior has been found to be reasonably stable over time (Eron et al., 1974; Olweus, 1979) and by findings that early aggressiveness is related to later indices of delinquency (Eron et al., 1974). Also of note are other research findings reviewed by Kohlberg, LaCrosse, and Ricks (1972) that have indicated that the severity of antisocial behavior in childhood is a strong predictor of adult maladjustment. Thus aggressive behavior seems to constitute both a common and

sometimes serious problem of childhood that may have important implications for later adjustment.

The Causes of Aggressive Behavior: Theoretical Formulations

A variety of theoretical points of view have been presented to account for aggressive behaviors. As these views have been reviewed in detail by Bandura (1973), only a brief discussion of these positions will be presented here.

From a psychoanalytic perspective, aggressive behavior is seen as an inevitable part of being human. In attempting to account for a range of complex human behaviors, Freud originally postulated the existence of the so-called life instincts that function to preserve and enhance life, as well as a death instinct that is directed toward self-destruction. It is suggested that the actual behavior of the individual results from an active interplay of these two types of instincts. From this perspective then, aggressive behavior results from an inborn drive and is seen as an outerdirected manifestation of the death instinct. As Bandura (1973) has noted, contemporary psychoanalytically oriented writers (see Gillespie, 1971) have to some extent rejected Freud's notion of the death instinct but have retained the view that aggression results from an instinctual drive. A focus on the instinctual basis for aggression is also apparent in the writings of ethologists such as Lorenz (1966). Here, aggression is seen as resulting from a self-perpetuating instinct toward aggressive behavior that is elicited by "releasing stimuli" from the environment.

A second major theoretical formulation is the frustration-aggression hypothesis. Originally proposed by Dollard et al. (1939), this position suggests that aggressive behavior results from an aggressive drive that is elicited by frustration when the person's access to a goal is blocked. Thus thwarted goals lead to frustration, and frustration leads to aggressive behavior. The strong version of this theory, which was originally proposed, argued that frustration invariably results in aggression. This view was subsequently modified to suggest that, while aggression is a usual response to frustration, the probability of aggression would be modified if the person had previously been punished for engaging in aggressive behavior or had a learning history in which aggression had not been rewarded. Although the frustration-aggression view has achieved a fair amount of popularity and has served to generate much research, even the modified version of this position has not received widespread support.

The available research suggests that aggressive behavior cannot be accounted for simply on the basis of frustration. As Bandura (1973) has indicated, "Frustration or anger arousal is a facilitative but not a necessary condition for aggression" (p. 58).

The point of view that, as we will see later, has received most empirical support that seems to account most adequately for the performance of aggressive acts is the social learning position, which proposes that aggressive behaviors are largely learned behaviors. It is assumed that such learning results from observing models such as parents, peers, or others in the environment who engage in aggressive behavior. Such learning may be especially likely to occur and be reflected in behavior if models who display aggressive behavior are reinforced for their behaviors. The learning of aggressive behaviors might result also from direct experience whereby the child is reinforced for responding in an aggressive manner when frustrated or provoked. Such reinforcement might result from the attention paid to the behavior by parents, teachers, or others or because such behaviors result in the child's obtaining something from another child he or she would not have obtained unless he or she had been aggressive. Once acquired, either vicariously or directly, aggressive behaviors are said to be maintained through contingent reinforcement.

The Development and Maintenance of Aggressive Behavior: Research Findings

In support of a social-learning formulation, a number of research studies have provided data that suggest that aggressive behavior results largely from the individual's learning experiences. For example, in an early study by Bandura, Ross, and Ross (1961), nursery school children were assigned either to an experimental condition, in which they observed a model displaying novel aggressive responses toward an inflated plastic doll, or to a control group in which the model behaved in a nonaggressive manner. Children in the aggressive modeling condition were found to display more aggressive behavior in a subsequent test session with the doll than did control children. More important than the finding that there were overall group differences in aggressive behavior was the fact that children who observed aggressive models were later found to display more *novel* aggressive behaviors displayed by the model (specific aggressive verbalizations while hitting the doll, for example) than did controls. This finding suggests that modeling experiences can result in the learning of specific aggressive behaviors rather than simply the facilitation of already learned aggressive behaviors, although modeling may be important in this respect as well.

In a second study, Bandura, Ross, and Ross (1963) assigned nursery school children to one of three experimental conditions where they observed models behaving aggressively toward an inflatable Bobo doll. Models were presented live, on film, or by a filmed model dressed as a cartoon character. Control children either observed a nonaggressive model or were not exposed to modeling stimuli. As in the previous study, subjects who observed aggressive models were found later to display significantly higher levels of aggressive behavior than did children in the control conditions.

That modeling experiences resulted in the learning of *new* aggressive behaviors was again suggested by the fact that experimental subjects were found to display a range of novel aggressive behaviors displayed by the models that were unlikely to have been learned previously. These studies, along with the results of several more recent investigations, provide strong evidence for the fact that aggressive behaviors may be learned by observing aggressive behavior displayed by others.

As Bandura (1973) has noted, however, the

fact that aggressive behavior may be learned vicariously does not necessarily mean that such behaviors will be performed. That it is essential to distinguish between the acquisition and performance of aggressive behaviors is nicely illustrated in a study by Bandura (1965). Here children were presented with a model who displayed a range of novel aggressive behaviors that were rewarded, punished, or neither rewarded nor punished. In a later test session, children who observed the punished model showed the least aggressive behavior while the other two groups showed significantly higher levels.

While it might be tempting to conclude that the performance of these groups reflected differences in learning, this interpretation does not seem justified since the subjects in all three groups displayed similar levels of aggressive behavior when offered incentives for enacting those aggressive behaviors that had been modeled. These results, like others cited earlier, suggest that aggressive behaviors can be acquired vicariously. It seems that the performance of aggressive behaviors may, however, be importantly related to the consequences that are later made contingent on these behaviors.

It might be pointed out that the relationship beween modeling experiences and aggressive behaviors has not only been demonstrated in laboratory investigations but in more naturalistic situations as well. In a 10-year longitudinal study, Eron et al. (1974) have studied the relationship among a number of variables, assessed during the third grade, and aggressive behavior at age 19. In line with the results presented here, the amount of violent TV watched by males at age 9 was found to be a significant predictor of aggressive behavior 10 years later. Of particular note is the fact that the study was longitudinal and was analyzed in such a way (by applying path-analytic procedures) that it is possible to infer a causal relationship between modeling (viewing aggressive TV) and later behavior.

Several studies have also demonstrated a relationship between contingent reinforcement and continued aggressive responding. Geen (1976), for example, has noted that

several laboratory studies have demonstrated increased aggressive behavior when such behaviors are followed by verbal approval. Walters and Brown (1963) have shown that it is possible, by reinforcing children for displaying aggressive responses toward a plastic Bobo doll, to increase aggressive behavior even when assessed several days later. The effects of reinforcement on aggression have also been demonstrated in an observational study by Patterson, Littman, and Bricker (1967). Here children were observed over time to assess aggressive behavior and the naturally occurring consequences that followed such behaviors. Children whose aggressive behaviors were usually followed by reinforcement (submission, crying, etc., on the part of the child) were found to display the highest levels of aggression.

Findings such as these provide support for the notion that, once learned, aggressive behavior can be viewed as an operant that is maintained by its consequences (Ross, 1981). Taken together, the findings concerning the learning and maintenance of aggressive behavior are quite in line with the social-learning position presented earlier.

The Modification of Aggressive Behavior

Several approaches have been successfully employed in attempting to modify aggressive child behavior. Given that aggression seems importantly related to one's learning history and prevailing environmental factors, it is not surprising that these approaches have often been behavioral in nature. As behavioral approaches to the modification of behavioral excesses (such as aggressiveness) are discussed elsewhere in this book (see Rickard & Elkins, chap. 40) only an overview of research related to ways of modifying aggressive child behavior will be presented here.

Taking an observational learning approach, several studies have found that it is possible to reduce aggressive behavior by exposing the child to nonaggressive models or models whose aggressive behaviors are disapproved of or punished (see Bandura, 1973; Kirkland

& Thelen, 1977). Brown and Elliot (1965) have demonstrated how a reduction in aggressive behavior displayed by an entire preschool class was brought about by ignoring aggressive behavior and rewarding cooperative behaviors displayed by the children. It might be noted that while each of these procedures was shown to be effective, these two approaches may be limited in certain respects. It is likely, for example, that attempting to reduce aggressive behavior through vicarious punishment would have only short term effects unless other contingencies designed to reduce aggressive responding were implemented in the natural environment. Also, procedures designed to reduce aggressive behavior by ignoring it may be limited to dealing with only mild forms of aggressivity. High frequency/high intensity aggression often cannot be ignored and other procedures must be used.

An additional procedure that has been shown to be quite effective in dealing with aggressive behavior is *time-out*. This procedure is based on the notion that if the child is removed from a reinforcing situation as soon as aggressive behavior occurs and before it can be reinforced, the frequency of the behavior will be reduced. For example, in a classroom where aggressive behavior might be followed by teacher or peer attention or other reinforcers, a time-out procedure might involve removing the child from the room as soon as the aggressive behavior occurs. The child would then be placed in a time-out room for a short period of time, usually only five to ten minutes. The time-out room should be essentially bare and devoid of reinforcers. Once aggressive behavior is no longer followed by reinforcement but instead by brief isolation (where no reinforcement can occur), a decrease in aggressive behavior would be expected. It would seem likely that the decrease in aggressive behavior resulting from time-out can be accounted for largely in terms of extinction. However, the fact that time-out not only eliminates the reinforcers that are contingent upon aggressive behavior but also the opportunity to obtain any type of positive reinforcement while in time-out has resulted in most writers considering it as a type of

punishment procedure (Gelfand & Hartmann, 1975).

As there are several excellent discussions of time-out procedures in the published literature (Gelfand & Hartmann, 1975; Hobbs & Forehand, 1977; Ross, 1981), research findings related to this procedure will not be reviewed here. Suffice it to state that a range of studies has suggested the usefulness of time-out in dealing with aggressive child behavior. It should be noted that time-out procedures can often be combined with other procedures in such a way as to further enhance effectiveness. For example, time-out procedures can be combined with DRO (direct reinforcement of other behavior) procedures where the child is not only placed in time-out contingent on aggressive behavior but is also rewarded for going varying periods of time without displaying aggressive behavior. Rather than simply making reward contingent on not being aggressive, one might alternately choose to combine time-out with reward for some specific behavior that is incompatible with aggression. Through the use of such a combined approach, it is possible not only to teach the child what behaviors are undesirable (through time-out) but also which behaviors are judged to be more appropriate (through positive reinforcement). Such an approach is judged to be preferable to the use of time-out alone in most instances (Ross, 1981).

An additional point might be made regarding the use of physical punishment in dealing with childhood aggression. It might seem that the application of aversive consequences contingent on aggressive behavior would serve to reduce aggressivity, and certainly this approach is employed by many parents. Contrary to this view, there is evidence that physical punishment for aggression may actually serve to increase rather than decrease aggressive behavior (Bandura & Walters, 1959). One reason may be that the person who uses such an approach to control child behavior may be in actuality serving as a model of aggressive behavior for the child. Ideally, it would seem that aggressive behavior in children might best be dealt with in a preventive manner if children, during the process of development, were provided with ample opportunities to observe a wide range of models who display prosocial rather than aggressive behavior and were consistently rewarded for handling situations in a nonaggressive rather than an aggressive manner.

To summarize, aggressive behavior is frequently found in children. Its development is probably dependent on direct learning experiences and the observation of models who display aggressive modes of responding, and its maintenance seems to be a function of the consequences resulting from such behaviors. It would seem that aggressive behavior, of the type displayed by most children, can be dealt with through the procedures described here. More serious examples of aggressive behavior can also occur as part of the larger problem of delinquency. This problem will be considered in the following sections.

JUVENILE DELINQUENCY

Delinquency is a legal term referring to a juvenile (usually under 18 years of age) who is brought to the attention of the justice system by virtue of committing a criminal act or displaying a variety of other behaviors not specified under criminal law (e.g., truancy, curfew violations). Considered within the framework of DSM III, delinquency represents a subset of the broader spectrum of behavioral problems classified as conduct disorders (American Psychiatric Assocation, 1980). Herbert (1978) has noted that the concept of conduct disorder is imprecise but generally refers to three major problem areas: aggression, serious antisocial behavior, and overactivity. Here, one might note the similarity between this concept of conduct disorder and the category of externalizing disorders (Achenbach, 1980) that was discussed earlier. Herbert (1978) has described this heterogeneous group of children as follows:

Youngsters with conduct and delinquent disorders demonstrate a fundamental inability or unwillingness to adhere to the rules and codes of conduct prescribed by society at its various levels. Such

failures may be related to the temporary lapse of poorly established learned controls, to the failure to learn these controls in the first place, or to the fact that the behavioral standards a child has absorbed do not coincide with the norms of that section of society which enacts and enforces the rules. (p. 11)

The seriousness of problems such as these is suggested by national statistics that document the persistent problem of juvenile crime and a growing body of evidence from longitudinal studies on the poor outcomes of children identified as "at risk" for conduct disorders or already identified by the mental health or judicial systems as antisocial. As Robins (1974) notes:

Almost every study has confirmed the high prevalence rate of these disorders, their early onset, their association with maleness and severe school retardation, their persistence into adulthood, the fact that they come to treatment only under duress, that they run in families and that they do not yield to conventional psychotherapeutic techniques. (pp. 457–458)

As we have previously considered the issue of childhood aggression, the remainder of this chapter will be devoted to an overview of current views and research on juvenile delinquency and antisocial behavior. (For further consideration of the topic of delinquency, see chap. 37 in this book.) Topics to be considered here include: classification criteria, findings regarding incidence and prevalence, etiological views, variables associated with delinquency, prognosis, and approaches to treatment.

The Classification of Delinquency

Given that juvenile delinquency is essentially a legal category used to designate those who have committed any of numerous offenses, one might expect children or adolescents labeled as delinquent to represent a very heterogeneous group. In spite of this, researchers have often sought to study the causes, correlates, and treatment of delinquency without taking this variability into account. This tendency to treat delinquency as a unitary construct has often led to unreplicated findings and inconclusive results.

As a result of this observed variability within the delinquent population, researchers have focused attention on investigating the possibility that various dimensions of delinquency may exist. Most prominent in this regard is the work of Quay (1964, 1972, 1979).

Quay (1964) is generally credited with developing the most widely cited, empirically based, classification scheme for delineating dimensions of delinquent behavior. In this early study, factor analyses of ratings of behavioral traits obtained from the case histories of institutionalized male delinquents yielded four independent groupings: socialized-subcultural delinquency, unsocialized-psychopathic delinquency, disturbed-neurotic delinquency, and inadequate-immature delinquency.

Delinquents who scored high on the socialized-subcultural dimension were defined by such traits as having strong allegiance to selected peers, being accepted by delinquent subgroup, having bad companions, staying out late at night, and having low ratings on shyness and seclusiveness. Unsocialized-psychopathic delinquents, in contrast, were described as solitary rather than group-oriented delinquents who rated high on such traits as inability to profit from praise or punishment, defiance of authority, quarrelsomeness, irritability, verbal aggression, impudence, and assaultiveness. Disturbed-neurotic delinquents were described as unhappy, shy, timid and withdrawn, and prone to anxiety, worry, and guilt over their behavior. Quay (1972) has further described this subtype as less aggressive, more amenable to change, and less likely to repeat delinquent behavior than the first two subtypes. The final group, the inadequate-immature group, was described as not usually accepted by delinquent peers, passive and preoccupied, picked on by others, and easily frustrated. Quay (1979) has later characterized these youngsters as being relatively inadequate in their functioning and often unable to cope with environmental demands because of a poorly developed behavioral repertoire.

In summarizing the essential features of the first three major dimensions Achenbach (1974) has suggested:

Taken together the evidence on personality and behavioral characteristics of different types of delinquents suggests that the socialized-subcultural delinquent is a relatively normal person who happens to live in a family and community environment that enhances the learning of delinquent rather than non-delinquent norms, values, and ways of having fun. The unsocialized-psychopathic delinquent, by contrast, appears to be a relatively abnormal person who does not have good social relations even with delinquent peers and who actively seeks out trouble rather than seeking to make adaptive adjustments to his community (delinquent or otherwise). The third syndrome, disturbed-neurotic delinquency... may represent a heterogeneous class of individuals who have personality or organic problems that happen to lead to delinquency, but who differ from unsocialized-psychopathic delinquents in having high rather than unusually low anxiety. (pp. 481–482)

In contrast to these three major dimensions, it would appear that the dimensions of inadequate-immature delinquency most clearly reflect delinquents who are seriously lacking in adaptive social skills.

These four dimensions have been replicated in a number of other factor analytic studies of delinquent behavior, and variables associated with these subtypes have been examined. As research related to the correlates of these dimensions has been recently reviewed by Quay (1979) and will be alluded to at later points in this chapter, it will not be considered in detail here. It may be noted, however, that the results of this research strongly argue for the distinction between these subgroups. Unfortunately, studies that attempt to determine antecedents of delinquency, correlates of delinquency, or that attempt to develop treatments of delinquency, considering delinquency as a unitary construct, are still prominent in the research literature (Schwartz & Johnson, 1981).

Incidence and Prevalence Estimates

The true incidence and prevalence of delinquent behavior are unclear as not all offenders are detected and apprehended. Nevertheless, official statistics, based on arrest records and court appearances, provide some index of the problem of juvenile crime. For example, it would appear that delinquency as indexed by arrest rates is on the rise. Between 1960 and 1973, juvenile arrests increased a dramatic 138 percent, as compared to an increase of only 16 percent in arrest rates of those persons 18 or older. Since 1973, juvenile arrest rates have continued to increase although less dramatically (Federal Bureau of Investigation, 1978). This increasing problem of delinquency is also reflected in juvenile court statistics. Here it may be noted that the proportion of the total juvenile population (age 10–17) seen in Juvenile Court was 2 percent in 1960. This figure had increased to 4 percent by 1975 (U.S. Department of Justice, 1978).

While delinquency has often been characterized as a male problem, it is of interest to note that female arrest rates are on the rise and the sex ratio of male to female delinquents is changing. Statistics provided by the FBI (1978) suggest that between 1968 and 1977 the increase in female arrests was 3 time greater than the corresponding increase in male arrests. Offenses committed by females under the age of 18 account for over 30 percent of all female arrests (FBI, 1978). Despite the fact that female delinquency is also on the rise, there do seem to be sex differences regarding type of delinquent behavior displayed. More males than females are arrested for serious crimes such as murder, aggravated assault, and larceny. More females than males are charged with offenses such as drug abuse violations, sex offenses (excluding forcible rape and prostitution), and violation of liquor laws.

Estimates of the delinquency problem based on arrest rates and juvenile court statistics are difficult to interpret as they are biasd to some unknown degree by prevailing law enforcement practices. These official statistics, however, suggest that juvenile delinquency is indeed a significant social problem.

Information concerning the problem of delinquency within a clinic population has been provided by Rutter, Tizard, and Whit-

more (1970). These investigators found antisocial behaviors to be among the most common psychiatric problems (treated and untreated) displayed by clinic children in their study. Antisocial behaviors were found in 32 percent of the psychiatrically disturbed girls and 68 percent of the psychiatrically disturbed boys in their sample.

Studies of "normal" individuals responding to anonymous questionnaires suggest that much antisocial and delinquent behavior goes undetected, the so-called "hidden delinquency." For example, an early study by Offer, Sabshin, and Marcus (1965) found that as many as 75 percent of their respondents admitted to acts that would be labeled delinquent if detected. Similarly, Herbert (1978) cites a survey conducted in London of a population of 1,425 youths between the ages of 13 and 16. Ninety-eight percent of the youths admitted having kept something they had "found" and 70 percent had shoplifted. A recent survey of drug use among adolescents (Jalali et al., 1981) found that among the 2,131 youths surveyed (ages 12–18), 51 percent had tried marijuana at some time, about 90 percent had tried beer or wine, 21.6 percent used marijuana more than once a week, and 34 percent reported alcohol use starting at age 8 or younger. Thus, whether one selects crime statistics, clinic data, or surveys of normal individuals, an alarming percentage of young people admit to, or are charged with, antisocial and/or delinquent acts.

Theories of Delinquency

A number of different theories have been proposed to explain delinquent behavior, each emphasizing, to varying degrees, the effect of biological/genetic, sociological, and psychological variables. Detailed reviews of these theories have recently been presented (Empey, 1978; Gibbons, 1976); therefore, this section will highlight only briefly the major theoretical viewpoints.

Biological Theories

Biological views of delinquency generally attribute major weight to the influence of genetic factors (e.g., heritability studies), chromosomal abnormalities (e.g., XYY syndrome), or to physiological variations in the individual that lead to problems such as stimulus seeking.

Rosenthal (1975), for example, reviewed nine twin studies and concluded that the concordance rates for psychopathy and criminal behavior was two-and-a-half times higher in monozygotic than dizygotic twins. Eysenck (1975) also examined these studies of over 300 pairs of monozygotic twins and over 500 pairs of dizygotic twins and found concordance rates for delinquent behavior to be four times greater in identical than nonidentical twins. More recently, Crowe (1974) and Cadonet (1978) found that adoptees separated at birth from their parents who displayed antisocial behavior had higher rates of antisocial behavior than control subjects whose parents were not judged antisocial. Compelling though these findings may be, Rutter (1972) suggests that delinquent behavior is not inherited as such but rather that inherited temperamental differences, in association with family discord and disruption, are of greater influence in the development of antisocial problems in childhood.

Evidence of an unusually high incidence of males institutionalized for aggressive, antisocial behavior who have an extra Y chromosome has led some (e.g., Owen, 1972) to consider the possible role of chromosomal abnormalities in the development of criminal behavior. Individuals with this characteristic frequently show a constellation of problems, including below-average IQ, greater-than-average height, and other physical anomalies, along with behavioral problems, including social withdrawal and aggressiveness. This chromosomal abnormality, which normally occurs once in every 1000 male births, has been found to occur at a rate in excess of four times the expected rate among inmates of penal institutions. However, Nielsen and Christenson (1974) concluded that chromosomal abnormalities are not present in most children with conduct disorders nor is unusually aggressive behavior always a feature of the XYY male (cited by Herbert, 1978). As Schwartz and Johnson (1981) point out, even

if one accepts the view that the XYY individuals do show antisocial behavior, this does not necessarily allow one to invoke genetic over environmental mechanisms. The presence of temperamental differences at birth affecting parent-child interactions (Thomas & Chess, 1977) as well as distress caused by the presence of physical anomalies or lowered intelligence and/or school achievement (Rutter et al., 1970) may be more potent than genetic variations per se.

Farley's (1973) notion that an inherited defect in CNS arousal leads individuals to seek out novel stimulating experiences to increase physiological arousal represents another variant of a biological theory of delinquency. This formulation is somewhat similar to Quay's (1965) proposal that the psychopath should be viewed as a pathological stimulation seeker. The assumption underlying both proposals is that, given a less-than-optimal state of physiological arousal and an environment lacking a sufficient number of socially acceptable opportunities for stimulation, individuals may seek out exciting, novel, and challenging situations that may include antisocial activity. Evidence pertaining to this view will be considered later.

Sociological Theories

Sociological theories have placed an emphasis on a wide range of social factors in the development of delinquency (Gibbons, 1976). For example, specific theories have dealt with the cultural transmission of delinquency (Shaw & McKay, 1969), group delinquency (Thrasher, 1963), and middle class delinquency (Vaz, 1967), among other factors. The inability of an individual to obtain socially valued goals (property, status) through legitimate means has been proposed by some as a major variable in the development of antisocial behavior. Merton (1957), for instance, has suggested that when social constraints do not permit members of the lower socioeconomic classes to obtain desired goals, they often resort to delinquent behavior to reach them. A somewhat similar formulation is presented by the "opportunity structure theory" (Cloward & Ohlin, 1969). They suggest that lower socioeconomic class youths blame society for their lack of opportunity to reach desired goals and become disenchanted and alienated by society's failure to meet their needs. By affiliating with a delinquent subculture, their needs for status and material gains are met along with the opportunity to act on their feelings of frustration and alienation. Recognition of the role of limited education and job opportunities among the lower income groups in the United States has led to the development of such federally subsidized training programs as the Cooperative Education and Training Act Programs (CETA).

Psychological Theories

Two broad classes of psychological theories are evident: those that emphasize intrapsychic conflict and those that stress the effects of learning. Psychodynamic theories often emphasize the role of individual intraspychic factors or family conflicts in the development of delinquency. From this point of view, antisocial behavior is seen as a form of psychopathology, frequently symptomatic of an underlying defect in personality, conflict, or characterological disorder. In general, dynamic theories have tended to view inadequate or faulty early life interpersonal relations between the child and parent as crucial to the development of antisocial behaviors. These behaviors are seen as developing out of the neurotic need to assuage guilt through punishment or out of displaced hostility or anxiety that results in the individual's acting out against society.

In contrast, learning theories generally view antisocial behavior as resulting largely from environmental influences. For example, Bandura (1973) outlined a social-learning theory of delinquency based on two learning principles: (1) delinquent behavior can be learned either through direct experience or through the observation of others who display such behaviors, and (2) delinquent behavior, like all behavior, is influenced and maintained by environmental factors that include both the opportunity for delinquent behavior and the consequences that follow the behavior. In a similar fashion, Ross (1974) conceptualizes delinquent behavior as reflecting the failure to have learned essential controls, typically acquired during the course of childhood:

[The delinquent is] one who has either not learned to discriminate beween acceptable and unacceptable behavior or who, having learned the discrimination, has not acquired adequate controls so that his behavior is not guided by this discrimination. (p. 137)

He also proposes that delinquent behavior can be conceptualized as reflecting, in part, an absence or weakness in the ability to delay gratification, that is, to maintain a response despite delayed reinforcement. Focusing primarily on the so-called unsocialized delinquent, Ross (1974) suggests that good role models, consistent consequence for a child's behavior, and development of social approval as a secondary reinforcer for appropriate behavior are target goals to prevent the development of delinquent behavior. Based on assumptions such as these, a number of behavioral programs have been developed for treatment of juvenile offenders. These efforts will be reviewed later in this chapter.

Variables Associated with Juvenile Delinquency

A number of variables have been hypothesized to be associated with an increased incidence of delinquency and/or conduct disorders. These include socioeconomic status, a range of family variables, as well as specific personality characteristics.

Delinquency and Social Class

The apparent relationship between juvenile delinquency and lower socioeconomic classes has gained credence from official delinquency statistics that show delinquency rates to be somewhat higher among youth from lower social classes (Schwartz & Johnson, 1981). However, this relationship seems to hold only for urban areas. Studies from rural areas, small towns, and cities have generally not shown greater delinquency rates among youth from the lower socioeconomic classes (Clarizio & McCoy, 1976). Furthermore, when one examines the rates of so-called hidden or undetected delinquency among young people, the relationship between social class and antisocial behavior is even less clear. Employing anonymous self-report surveys, a number of investigators have shown that a high proportion of children from all social classes admit to antisocial behavior. Empey (1978), after reviewing a number of these studies, has concluded that the relationship between social class and delinquent behavior is small to nonexistent. He suggested that the types and extent of delinquent behavior can better be predicted from the prevailing social environment (e.g., neighborhood) than from social class per se: "The greatest differences, therefore, may be between neighborhoods, or school districts, not broad social classes" (p. 157). Thus social environment rather than social class per se seems to be related to the likelihood of committing an antisocial act. Unfortunately, the relative weightings of factors within that social environment (e.g., presence of delinquency models) remain unclear.

Family Variables

Beginning with the predictive studies of Glueck and Glueck (1950, 1968) and the retrospective data obtained from longitudinal research on delinquency (Robins, 1974, 1978), family factors have been repeatedly linked to delinquent behavior. Glueck and Glueck (1950) developed a series of predictive tables based on differences between a large sample of male delinquents and nondelinquents from the Boston area. Several familial-social factors were found to separate the delinquent from nondelinquent boys: discipline by the father, affection by the mother, affection by the father, supervision by the mother, and family cohesiveness. Parents of delinquents had more separations, divorces, or prolonged absences from the home than nondelinquents. Furthermore, parents of delinquents more often suffered from alcoholism, physical disorders, and intellectual or behavioral disturbances. Fathers of delinquents tended to use physical discipline more often while mothers were described as more permissive. Finally, both parents were more likely to be inconsistent in the application of discipline.

In a series of longitudinal studies of adult life consequences of early childhood behavior problems, Robins (1966, 1974, 1978) has investigated a number of relevant family background variables including: antisocial or alcoholic father or mother, broken home, divorce or separation of parents, living arrangements separate from both parents, and occupation of guardian. Concluding that the child's own behavior was a better predictor of his or her adult behavior than were these characteristics of the family, Robins (1978) noted that family variables were more important in moderately antisocial rather than severely antisocial children.

Other studies have described differences between families of delinquent children and families of nondelinquents in levels of moral judgment of the parents, types and extremes of discipline employed by the parents, amount of covert and overt parental conflict, and types and extent of parental antisocial behavior (see reviews by Hetherington & Martin, 1979; Trojanowicz, 1973).

Unfortunately, most studies that have found differences in the family of delinquent versus nondelinquent children have treated delinquents as a homogeneous group, failing to consider the relationship between the various subtypes of delinquency and different childrearing practices or family interactions. Hetherington and Martin (1979) suggest that these dimensions of delinquency may, in fact, be differentially related to family variables. In support of this, they cite the early studies of Hewitt and Jenkins (1946) and Lewis (1954) that seem to relate the disturbed-neurotic delinquent to an overcontrolling approach to discipline, the socialized-subcultural delinquent to neglect or permissiveness, and the unsocialized-psychopathic delinquent to parental rejection. Obviously, further research along these lines is needed.

Personality Characteristics

A number of studies have compared delinquents to nondelinquents on a variety of personality measures including interviews, protective tests (e.g., Rorschach Ink Blot Test), and objective personality measures (e.g., Minnesota Multiphasic Personality Inventory—MMPI). Only rarely, however, have the delinquents under study been classified into the subtypes cited earlier. When subtypes have been utilized, some personality differences have emerged. For example, Genshaft (1980) compared the MMPI profiles of a group of juvenile delinquents classified as belonging to one of Quay's (1964) groups. When these groups were compared with regard to profile characteristics, the mean two-point code type for the neurotic-delinquent group was 4–8/8–4 (Pd, Sc) while the predominant two-point code for the psychopathic-delinquent group was 8–9/9–8 (Sc, Ma). The mean code type for the socialized-delinquent group was 4–5/5–4 (Pd, MF). These results were replicated in a cross-validation study. Future efforts directed at describing differences among delinquent subtypes, such as Genshaft's study (1980), may delineate a relationship between personality variables and delinquent behaviors. At present, however, the bulk of the existing evidence fails to support the notion of a delinquent personality per se. In reviewing this literature, Gibbons (1976) compared the rates of psychopathology in delinquents and nondelinquents and concluded that "it appears that delinquents are no more or less ridden with personality pathology than are nonoffenders" (p. 87). Other personality traits, such as sensation seeking and moral development, have also been examined.

Sensation seeking may be defined as the tendency to engage in a variety of exciting, stimulating, and novel behaviors that may be assumed to result in an increased arousal level (e.g., race car driving, sky diving, and so forth). It has been suggested that tendencies toward sensation seeking may result from having a biologically determined deficit whereby the person displays a less-than-optimal level of arousal. Sensation seekers are thus seen as engaging in behaviors that will raise their level of stimulation to some more optimal state.

Regarding such behaviors, it may be pointed out that there are numerous antisocial acts that may be quite stimulating when engaged in (e.g., trying to get away with stealing a car, experimenting with certain drugs). It seems reasonable to assume that if socially acceptable ways of increasing stimulation are not readily available, the high sensation seeker may engage in delinquent behavior that does provide stimulation. (For a review of this construct, see Zuckerman, 1974.) The exact relationship between sensation seeking and delinquent behavior is unclear. However, Farley and Sewell (1976) found higher scores on a self-report measure of sensation seeking among adjudicated delinquents compared to nondelinquents matched for age, sex, and socioeconomic level. Earlier, Farley and Farley (1972) found that female delinquents scoring high in sensation seeking showed more aggressive behavior, attempted escape more often, and disobeyed supervisors more often than low-scoring delinquent females. Indices of sensation seeking have also been found to relate to drug usage and to extent and variety of sexual behavior (Zuckerman, 1974). It is possible, however, that the sensation-seeking dimension is only importantly related to the unsocialized psychopathic subtype of delinquency. This view is supported by findings of laboratory studies that have found unsocialized-psychopathic delinquents to differ from other delinquent subgroups in terms of stimulation-seeking behaviors (Quay, 1979). These findings are consistent with Quay's (1965) formulation of psychopathy as "pathological stimulation seeking."

A second variable that has been frequently examined is moral development. Although much has been made of the purported relationship between lower levels of moral reasoning and delinquent behavior (Kohlberg, 1964), a recent review by Jurkovic (1980) suggests that the hypothesized immaturity of moral judgments in juvenile delinquents has not received consistent empirical support. While a simple tally of studies comparing the moral reasoning of delinquents versus that of nondelinquents generally shows delinquents to reason morally at lower levels (preconventional versus conventional orientations), some differences have been found within subtypes of delinquents and by types of offense committed. Fodor (1973), for example, found that psychopathic delinquents usually scored at the preconventional level on moral reasoning tasks while the scores of nonpsychopathic delinquents ranged across both preconventional and conventional levels. Similarly, Jurkovic and Prentice (1977) studied the moral reasoning of groups of unsocialized-psychopathic, disturbed-neurotic, and socialized-subcultural delinquents. They found that the group of unsocialized-psychopathic delinquents made moral judgments at stages 1 and 2 of preconventional reasoning (in which moral and self-serving values are not differentiated). The average scores of the neurotic-disturbed group and the socialized-subcultural delinquents, in contrast, approached stage 3 in which moral reasoning is guided by stereotypes of good behavior and emphasis is on meeting others' expectations or gaining approval. Jurkovic (1980) notes that the tendency to treat the juvenile delinquent's reasoning on moral dilemmas as an enduring cross-situational characteristic fails to take into account the differences in functional judgments made by most disturbed neurotic and socialized-subcultural offenders in response to environmental variables. He proposes that the subjective values, attitudes, and preferences of the child may have stronger functional ties to his or her behavior than moral structure, as shown by reasoning on moral dilemma tasks. Taken together, studies relating personality characteristics to delinquent behavior suggest few strong and consistent relationships except perhaps when delinquent subtypes are taken into account.

Delinquency and Other Childhood Behavioral Problems

Learning Disabilities

Since the mid-1970s, a number of authors have noted the increased incidence of severe learning problems in youths charged with antisocial behavior (Satz, 1977). Critical evaluation of the empirical data supporting the role of learning problems in the development of antisocial behavior, however, leaves the exact nature of the linkage unclear. Murray (1976),

in a major review of the literature, concluded that the evidence showing a causal relationship between learning disabilities and delinquency was weak.

More recently, however, several well-designed studies suggest at least some association between persistent problems in academic achievement and delinquent behavior. For example, Jerse and Fakouri (1978) found that many delinquents could be classified as academically deficient whether one examined school performance records or scores on standardized achievement tests. Similarly, the United States Government's 1977 General Accounting Office report on learning disabilities found that the majority of a selected sample of 129 delinquents housed in institutions in Virginia and Connecticut had significant learning problems (cited in Lane, 1980). Twenty-six percent of the juveniles examined were found to have primary learning problems, defined as deficits in verbal or nonverbal skills that produced performance far below that expected (given average or near average cognitive abilities). Secondary learning problems, defined as failure to make adequate school progress because of poor attendance, serious family or social problems, or emotional disturbances were found in 51 percent of the juveniles examined. Other investigators have reported that the incidence of learning problems among adjudicated delinquents ranged from about one-third (Zimmerman et al., cited by Lane, 1980) to one-half (Offord et al., 1979), to a high of over 90 percent (Zinkus & Gottleib, 1977).

If recent empirical data provide some support for a relationship between learning handicaps and antisocial behavior, many questions remain unanswered. For example, do the learning problems drive the child to delinquency or antisocial acts because of frustration and anger over failure, or are the learning problems a consequence of associated problems of poor attendance, disruptive classroom behavior, and lack of basic study skills? Different treatment models result from these different etiologic emphases. In the former case, primary efforts in treating juvenile offenders would address improving self-esteem through improving school performance while, in the latter, specific behavioral interventions could be employed to reduce problem behaviors that impede normal learning. A second question is whether there are different relative rates of school failure between subtypes of delinquents? And finally, might there be an underlying biological/neuropsychological dysfunction among delinquents that is manifested at school age by impairments in learning? Several recent studies have begun to address these questions.

For example, Berman (1975) and Berman and Siegel (1976) found significant deficits in perception, problem solving, and concept utilization among a large group of institutionalized delinquent males despite adequate intellectual resources. Similarly, Zinkus and Gottleib (1977) found that 79 percent of their sample of male delinquents had neuropsychological deficits on formal testing that involved either auditory memory, visual-motor coordination, visuospatial orientation, or a combination of these problems. They concluded that it was the severity of these neuropsychological deficits that contributed to academic problems rather than delinquency itself.

Underlying central nervous system abnormalities may account for the neuropsychological deficits found in some delinquent offenders. Electroencephalographic abnormalities and neurological soft signs have been found in children manifesting antisocial and aggressive behavior (Denhoff, 1973; Tarnopol, 1970). Frontal lobe brain system immaturity has also been implicated (Pontius & Ruttinger, 1976). A positive response of some delinquents to amphetamine medication, particularly among those with a history of hyperkinesis, has also been reported (Satterfield, 1978).

Unfortunately, little attention has as yet been paid to the question of delinquency subtype and school failure. Future research designed to examine the role of learning disabilities in the development of delinquent behavior should avoid treating delinquency as a unitary construct. These investigations should also consider recent evidence that there are different clinical subtypes of learning problems (Mattis, French, & Rapin, 1975; Benton, 1975; Denckla, 1977; Satz & Morris,

1981). Different relative emphases on the role of central nervous system dysfunction are found in these learning disability subtypes. Careful cross-classification of subjects according to both delinquency subtype and learning disability subtype, in future empirical studies, would more precisely define the causative link, if any, between subtle neurologic dysfunction, school achievement, and delinquent behavior.

Hyperkinesis

There is much evidence concerning an association between hyperactivity and antisocial behavior. Indeed, Cantwell (1978), in a recent review, has concluded that "the data...from a variety of clinical, follow-up, family, laboratory and treatment studies all indicate... there is a relationship between the presence of the hyperkinetic syndrome in children and the likelihood of the development of an antisocial disorder later in life" (p. 260). In contrast to the incidence of hyperkinesis in the general population, where estimates range from 5 to 10 percent (Wender, 1971), among juvenile offenders estimates of incidence have ranged to over 30 percent (Taylor & Watt, 1977). Symptoms of restlessness, distractibility, irritability, and learning problems have been found in the case histories of adult criminals, in the early developmental histories of children brought before the juvenile court system, and in the parents and siblings of children displaying sociopathic behavior in adulthood (Cantwell, 1978; Ross & Ross, 1976).

The possible link between juvenile delinquency and hyperkinesis has also gained credence through follow-up studies of later life outcomes for hyperactive children and through studies of the therapeutic effectiveness of central nervous system stimulants in some delinquents. Follow-up studies of children diagnosed hyperkinetic have demonstrated that many of these children have multiple police and court contacts (Stewart, Mendelson, & Johnson, 1973), are institutionalized for antisocial behavior (Huessy, Metayer, & Townsend, 1974), and are diagnosed as sociopathic or as suffering from manifest alcohol problems as adults (Borland & Heckman, 1976). Offord et al. (1979) recently compared the birth, development, and social histories of two groups of delinquents who differed in the presence of hyperactivity in early childhood. They concluded that the subgroup of hyperactive delinquents were those most likely to show severe antisocial activities and probable poor adult outcome.

The second line of evidence comes from the positive response of some delinquents to stimulant drugs frequently employed in the treatment of hyperkinesis (Eisenberg et al., 1963; Maletsky, 1974). Reasoning that such delinquents may suffer from an abnormally low level of arousal that stimulant drugs may raise—not unlike the condition seen in hyperkinetic children (Satterfield, 1978)—Cantwell (1978) proposed that organically based defects in physiological arousal account for the frequent continuity between hyperkinesis and later delinquency. Unfortunately, the exact mechanism of action of such drugs is still unclear. The critical role of the frontal-subcortical systems in attention and arousal is well known (Heilman & Valenstein, 1978). These same higher brain systems have been implicated in the capacity to attend, to anticipate, to plan, and to execute complex behavioral sequences (Luria, 1973). It follows that less-than-optimal arousal could be manifested in behavioral symptoms such as distractibility, poor planning, impulsivity, and failure to profit from feedback—all descriptions applied to the behavior of antisocial and hyperkinetic children. Stimulant drugs may simply increase arousal level to some more optimal point, thus decreasing behavioral symptoms.

Whatever the degree to which psychophysiological variables account for the behavioral problems of antisocial children, it is clear that many hyperkinetic children do not engage in serious antisocial behavior and that many delinquents do not manifest hyperactive symptoms. Current research suggests that these variables may operate most potently among unsocialized delinquent subtypes who are hyperactive in childhood and, as adults, are described as "stimulus seekers" (Quay, 1965). Other variables would more likely need to be invoked, either alone or in combination, to account for the other delinquency subtypes.

Later Life Outcomes and Prognosis

In a major study related to the prognosis of delinquency, Glueck and Glueck (1968) conducted an extensive follow-up of 500 delinquent and 500 nondelinquent males who had participated in their earlier study (Glueck & Glueck, 1950) who were then (at follow-up) in their midtwenties and early thirties. The overall outcome for the delinquents was much worse than the nondelinquents on almost all measures considered. For example, 84 percent of the former delinquents had had court convictions. While the number of serious offenses committed did decline with increasing age, frequent arrests involving vagrancy, drunk and disorderly conduct, assault, and desertion of family persisted into adult life. In contrast, the nondelinquents generally remained out of the court systems, had more stable marriages and better educational and employment records.

Similar later life outcomes for children displaying early antisocial behavior have been reported by Robins (1966) who found that, at follow-up, 82 percent of her male subjects had been arrested for a nontraffic offense, 70 percent of female subjects had been married early to men with high rates of criminal arrests and had been divorced, and both groups had higher rates of unemployment and poor work records. About 25 percent had been on public assistance and had a very high rate of alcohol abuse.

More recently, Robins (1978) replicated these results in a study of four cohorts composed of the original child guidance sample group, a group of young black men, and a group of veterans and nonveterans of all races. The groups varied in geographical location, generation, and racial/ethnic background. Despite these differences, Robins concluded that childhood antisocial behavior best predicts adult antisocial behavior but that most antisocial children do not become antisocial adults.

A recent study by Henn, Bordwell, and

Jenkins (1980) addressed the issue of different adult life outcome for different subtypes of delinquents. Case records of a large sample of delinquents treated in the Iowa State Training School for Boys were examined, and three subgroups were identified: undersocialized aggressive, undersocialized unaggressive, and socialized delinquents. The groups differed significantly in the number of subsequent adult arrests for violent crime as well as in the number of convictions and incarcerations for crime. They concluded that there was a tendency for the juvenile behavior patterns of hostile, confrontive behavior of the undersocialized aggressive males and the runaway, sneaky activity noted for the undersocialized unaggressive males to continue into adult life. Again, it is important to note that many of the boys successfully negotiated return to their homes and had no further contact with the criminal justice system. Nevertheless, the fact that almost 53 percent of the undersocialized aggressives were subsequently jailed for crimes, including crimes of violence, suggests that the continual search for effective treatment is necessary. Specific approaches to treatment of antisocial behaviors will be reviewed in the following section.

The Modification of Delinquent Behavior

Given the seriousness of the problem, it is not surprising that a variety of treatment approaches have been developed to deal with children and adolescents who display delinquent behaviors. These approaches have ranged from probation, to institutionalization, to the development of community-based programs of various sorts.

Probably the most popular approach for dealing with delinquency has been institutionalization. This is especially true when juveniles with extensive histories of lawbreaking are considered. Most states have one or more institutions referred to as detention centers, training schools, or reform schools that are designed for the treatment of delinquents. These institutions vary widely along the custodial-rehabilitative dimension. While some have active treatment programs, others

serve primarily a custodial role of keeping the juvenile offender apart from society. Unfortunately, institutions that are adequate to meet the rehabilitation needs of residents are probably in the minority. As Gross and Brigham (1980) have pointed out:

When a youth is institutionalized it is expected that she/he will be rehabilitated through a program which consists of educational and vocational training, casework and counseling, and psychological services. More often, however, the youth is placed in an overcrowded and understaffed facility in which rehabilitative programs play a subordinate role to everyday control and maintenance. (p. 98)

They go on to cite the views of other workers in the area, e.g., Stumphauser (1976), who suggests: "Rather than being a place where youths are rehabilitated, juvenile correctional institutions provide an environment where youths learn new antisocial behaviors" (p. 98).

That institutional treatment is generally not highly successful is suggested by the high recidivism (rearrest) rates of those who have been incarcerated. Studies have shown that, at least among males, as many as 70–80 percent of juveniles who are institutionalized are likely to be rearrested within a year or so following their release (Cohen & Filipczak, 1971; Gibbons, 1976).

Because of the lack of success resulting from traditional institutional treatment, several innovative treatment programs have been developed that have been carried out both within and outside of the institutional setting. Of those programs that have been carried out within correctional institutions, two are the most notable. These are the CASE (Contingencies Applicable to Special Education) project, conducted by Cohen and Filipczak (1971) and the Cascadia project conducted by Sarason and Ganzer (1971).

In the CASE program, the focus was on developing academic skills, since a lack of such skills was assumed to preclude the individual from finishing school and finding meaningful employment and indirectly increasing the likelihood of future delinquency. The program essentially involved developing a token economy program within the institution whereby residents were reinforced with points for engaging in a range of desirable academic behaviors and for improved academic performance. Points earned could be cashed in for a range of backup reinforcers: special meals, private room, better room furnishings, noninstitutional clothing, etc. Participants in this program were found to make rapid improvement in terms of both academic and social behaviors. During the two-year period after release from the program, participants were also found to have a recidivism rate much below that of juveniles who received the usual institutional treatment. These changes were not, however, found to be maintained at a three-year follow-up. Thus, while the program effected significant change, these effects were less durable than one would wish. To bring about more long-lasting change, it may be necessary to modify contingencies, not only within the institution, but within the natural environment as well.

Sarason and his colleagues (Sarason, 1968; 1978; Sarason & Ganzer, 1971) have taken a somewhat different approach to treatment. In a large scale study conducted at the Cascadia Juvenile Reception and Diagnostic Center in Tacoma, Washington, these investigators had residents observe models who depicted behaviors appropriate to a wide range of situations that they might encounter in the future: how to apply for a job, how to resist temptation from peers, how to delay gratification, and so forth. They were asked to summarize and explain the contents of these scenes and then took turns role playing what they had observed. The program, which lasted for 16 sessions, was based on the assumption that juvenile offenders are deficient in many of the skills necessary for functioning in a socially acceptable manner and that such skills can be learned through modeling and role-playing procedures.

Residents receiving this modeling treatment were compared with others who participated in a discussion group (in which they discussed similar topics but did not observe models or engage in role playing) and with a no treatment control group who received the usual institutional treatment. While both treatments were found to result in a number of significant changes, data on recidivism rates were particularly impressive. Even after a five-year time period, residents who had participated in treatment (modeling, discussion group) were shown to have a recidivism rate less than half that of the control group receiving institutional treatment (Sarason, 1978). These findings strongly suggest that such an approach is likely to be useful in teaching adaptive prosocial behaviors to juvenile offenders and that the learning of such behaviors may relate to a decreased likelihood of repeat offenses. (For a more general discussion of issues related to residential treatment, see in this book chap. 45 by Wilson & Lyman.)

Along with those treatment programs conducted within institutions, there have been others that have been based in community settings. An early example is the Highfields program, which was conducted in the 1950s in New Jersey. Unlike more behaviorally oriented programs, the Highfields program relied heavily on intensive group therapy (guided group interaction) as the major treatment approach. The goals of this group therapy were to change delinquent attitudes, modify self-concept, and deal with defenses displayed by residents that hindered rehabilitation. In addition to group therapy, residents also were involved in work programs, were responsible for performing various duties, and participated in recreational activities. Average duration in the program was about four months. While evaluations of the effectiveness of this program are difficult, as it is not clear that a comparable control group was obtained, Weeks (1958) found that recidivism rates for those in the Highfields program were significantly lower than for juveniles treated in state training schools.

It might be noted that programs patterned after the Highfields project have achieved a fair degree of popularity within the juvenile correctional system. In some states, juveniles are not just treated within the context of larger institutions. Within some programs, after an initial evaluation at a reception-diagnostic center, those who represent less of a security risk may be staffed to camps where treatment is carried out. These camps are usually run by several trained staff members and houseparents and are frequently located in an out-of-the-way area. Residents are usually required to attend school and typically have assigned work responsibilities. As in the Highfields program, the focus of treatment is often on group interaction. Here an emphasis is not only on group therapy sessions, which may be conducted on a daily basis, but on group work that allows for dealing with problems within the group as they may arise at any time. While such programs may differ from the Highfields approach in certain respects, they often retain many of the essential elements. The actual effectiveness of such programs in these settings, however, has not been well evaluated.

A second community-based program that has received widespread attention in the literature is the Achievement Place project. This program, which has been conducted in conjunction with the Department of Human Development at the University of Kansas, probably represents the most sophisticated community-based application of behavioral principles to the treatment of delinquency. The program has been described in detail in a number of publications (Fixsen, Wolf, & Phillips, 1973; Fixsen, Phillips, & Wolf, 1978; Hoefler & Bornstein, 1975; Phillips, 1968; Phillips et al., 1973).

Like the CASE project discussed earlier, Achievement Place is based on a token economy. Rather than being carried out within the institution, however, the Achievement Place program is run by a pair of trained houseparents within a homelike residence suitable for housing up to eight juveniles at any one time. Residents in the program all attend school, have assigned work responsibilities, and are generally allowed home visits on weekends and holilldays. Within the token economy program, which serves as the basic focus of treatment, residents are rewarded with points for engaging in appropriate behaviors (or fined for displaying inappropriate behaviors), and these points can be cashed in for a wide variety of backup reinforcers.

As Fixsen et al. (1978) have noted, the program is based largely on a behavioral deficiency model of deviant behavior in which the juveniles' problems are seen as resulting from a lack of skills necessary for adaptive prosocial behavior. Thus the targets for modification have been behaviors leading to a development of more adaptive skills and to a decrease in inappropriate behaviors. Examples include completing homework assignments, increased academic performance, improving conversational skills with adults, developing negotiation skills with parents, modifying aggressive statements, as well as other behaviors related to improved social skills. Points earned for engaging in such behaviors can be cashed in for a wide variety of backup reinforcers such as an allowance, snacks, permission to watch TV, go to town by themselves, stay up later than usual, use the telephone, use tools, and so forth.

As a major problem with token economies has been that changed behavior often does not generalize to the natural environment (Kazdin, 1977), attempts have been made within the Achievement Place program to enhance the generalization and maintenance of behavior change. For example, within the program, residents are moved from a program that involves a highly structured token economy (where points are earned or lost daily) to one where points are earned or lost on a weekly basis and finally to a merit system. On the merit system, privileges residents once had to earn through obtaining points are freely available and backup reinforcers, which had once been given to maintain desirable behaviors, are replaced by social reinforcers such as approval and praise. From the merit system, residents are gradually moved back into their home environment.

A number of studies have been conducted to assess the effectiveness of Achievement Place in dealing with the behavior of juvenile offenders. As these have been reviewed in several publications (see Fixsen et al., 1978; Gross & Brigham, 1980; Hoefler & Bornstein, 1975), they will not be considered in detail here. Suffice it to say that a number of well-controlled studies have shown that this program is indeed effective in modifying a wide range of desirable and undesirable behaviors. Further, larger scale studies, comparing juveniles treated at Achievement Place with those treated elsewhere (but who were judged to have been acceptable for treatment within the Achievement Place program), have indicated that at two-year follow-up, those treated at Achievement Place had recidivism rates roughly half that of juveniles receiving institutional treatment (Fixsen et al., 1978). It may be noted that, although the duration of follow-up is less, these figures related to recidivism rates compare favorably with those reported by Sarason (1978) in his follow-up of residents treated in the Cascadia project. Given the apparent success of both modeling–role playing and operant-reinforcement approaches in the treatment of juvenile offenders, as indicated by these two programs, it would be of interest to determine whether a combination of such approaches might not be superior to either treatment program by itself. Research along these lines would seem to be particularly worthwhile.

REFERENCES

Achenbach, T.M. The classification of children's psychiatric symptoms: A factor analytic study. *Psychological Monographs,* 1966, **80** (Whole No. 615).

Achenbach, T.M. *Developmental psychopathology.* New York: Ronald, 1974.

Achenbach, T.M. DSM III in light of empirical research on the classification of child psychopathology. *Journal of the American Academy of Child Psychiatry,* 1980, **19**, 395–412.

Achenbach, T.M., & Edelbrock, C.G. The classification of child psychopathology: A review and analysis of empirical efforts. *Psychological Bulletin,* 1978, **85**, 1275–1301.

American Psychiatric Association, *Diagnostic and statistical manual of mental disorders* (3rd ed.). Washington, D.C.: American Psychiatric Association, 1980.

Bandura, A. Influence of models' reinforcement contingencies on the acquisition of imitative responses. *Journal of Personality and Social Psychology,* 1965, **11**, 589–595.

Bandura, A. *Aggression: A social learning analysis.* Englewood Cliffs, N.J.: Prentice-Hall, 1973.

Bandura, A., Ross, D., & Ross, S.A. Transmission of aggression through limitation of aggressive models. *Journal of Abnormal and Social Psychology,* 1961, **63**, 525–582.

Bandura, A., Ross, D., & Ross, S. Imitation of film-mediated aggressive models, *Journal of Abnormal and Social Psychology,* 1963, **66**, 3–11.

Bandura, A., & Walters, R.H. *Adolescent aggression,* New York: Ronald, 1959.

Benton, A.L. Developmental dyslexia: Neurological aspects. In W.J. Friedlander (Ed.), *Advances in neurology* (Vol. 7). New York: Raven, 1975.

Berman, A. Learning disabilities in juvenile delinquents. Paper presented at Association of Children's Learning Disabilities, Dallas, 1974. Reprinted in: *Youth in trouble.* New York: Academic Therapy Press, 1975.

Berman, A., & Siegal, A. A neuropsychological approach to the etiology, prevention and treatment of juvenile delinquency. In A. Davids (Ed.), *Child personality and psychopathology* (Vol. 3). New York: Wiley, 1976.

Borland, B.L., & Heckman, H.K. Hyperactive boys and their brothers. *Archives of General Psychiatry,* 1976, **33**, 669–675.

Brown, P., & Elliot, R. Control of aggression in a nursery school class. *Journal of Experimental Child Psychology,* 1965, **2**, 103–107.

Butler, E.W. Personality dimensions of delinquent girls. *Criminologica,* 1965, **3**, 7–10.

Cadonet, R.J. Psychopathology in adopted-away offspring of biologic parents with antisocial behavior. *Archives of General Psychiatry,* 1978, **35**, 176–184.

Cadonet, R.J., & Cain, C. Sex differences in predictors of antisocial behavior in adoptees. *Archives of General Psychiatry,* 1980, **37**, 1171–1175.

Cantwell, D.P. Hyperactivity and antisocial behavior. *Journal of American Academy of Child Psychiatry,* 1978, **17**, 252–262.

Chiles, J.A., Miller, M.L., & Cox, G.B. Depression in an adolescent population. *Archives of General Psychiatry,* 1980, **37**, 1179–1184.

Clarizio, H.F., & McCoy, G.F. *Behavior disorders in children.* New York: Crowell, 1976.

Cloward, R., & Ohlin, L. *Delinquency and opportunity.* Glencoe, Ill.: Free Press, 1969.

Cohen, H., & Filipczak, J. *A new learning environment.* San Francisco, Jossey Bass, 1971.

Crowe, R. An adoption study of antisocial personality. *Archives of General Psychiatry,* 1974, **31,** 785–791.

Crowther, J.H., Bond, L.A., & Rolf, J.E. The incidence, prevalence and severity of behavior disorders among preschool-aged children in day care. *Journal of Abnormal Child Psychology* 1981, **9,** 23–42.

Denckla, M.B. Minimal brain dysfunction and dyslexia: Beyond diagnosis by exclusion. In M.E. Blaw, I. Rapin, & M. Kinsbourne (Eds.), *Topics in child neurology.* New York: Spectrum, 1977.

Denhoff, E. The natural life history of children with minimal brain dysfunction. *Annals of the New York Academy of Science,* 1973, **208,** 188–205.

Dollard, J., Doob, L.W., Miller, N.E., Mower, O.H., & Sears, R.R. *Frustration and aggression.* New Haven: Yale University Press, 1939.

Eisenberg, L., Lachman, R., Mollins, P., Lockner, A., Mizelle, J. & Connors, C. A psychopharmacologic experiment in a training school for delinquent boys. *American Journal of Orthopsychiatry,* 1963, **33,** 431–447.

Eme, R.F. Sex differences in childhood psychopathology: A review. *Psychological Bulletin,* 1979, **86,** 574–595.

Empey, L.T. *American delinquency: Its meaning and construction.* Homewood, Ill.: Dorsey, 1978.

Eron, L.D., Lefkowitz, M.M., Walder, L.O., & Huesmann, L.R. Relation of learning in childhood to psychopathology and aggression in young adulthood. In A. Davids (Ed.), *Child personality and psychopathology,* (Vol. 1). New York: Wiley, 1974.

Eysenck, H.J. Crime as destiny. *New Behavior,* 1975 (October), 46–49.

Farley, F.A. A theory of delinquency. Paper presented at the annual convention of the American Psychological Association. Montreal, August, 1973.

Farley, F., & Farley, S.V. Stimulus seeking motivation and delinquent behavior among institu-

tionalized delinquent girls. *Journal of Consulting and Clinical Psychology,* 1972, **39,** 94–97.

Farley, F., & Sewell, T. Test of an arousal theory of delinquency: Stimulation seeking in delinquent and non-delinquent black adolescents. *Criminal Justice and Behavior,* 1976, **3,** 315–320.

Federal Bureau of Investigation. *Uniform crime reports.* U.S. Department of Justice, Washington, D.C., 1978.

Fixsen, D.L., Phillips, E.L., & Wolf, M.M. The teaching family model: An example of mission-oriented research. In A.C. Catania & T.A. Brigham (Eds.), *Handbook of applied behavior analysis: Social and instructional process.* New York: Irvington, 1978.

Fixsen, D.L., Wolf, M.M., & Phillips, E.L. Achievement Place: A teaching family model of community based group homes for youth in trouble. In L. Hammer & E. Mash (Eds.), *Behavior change: Methodology, concepts, and practice.* Champaign, Ill.: Research Press, 1973.

Fodor, E.M. Moral development and parent behavior antecedents in adolescent psychopaths. *Journal of Genetic Psychology,* 1973, **122,** 37–43.

Geen, R.G. *Personality: The skein of behavior.* St. Louis: Mosby, 1976.

Gelfand, D.M., & Hartmann, D.P. *Child behavior analysis and therapy.* New York: Pergamon, 1975.

Genshaft, J.L. Personality characteristics of delinquent subtypes. *Journal of Abnormal Child Psychology,* 1980, **8,** 279–283.

Gibbons, D.C. *Delinquent behavior* (2nd ed.) Englewood Cliffs, N.J.: Prentice-Hall, 1976.

Gillespie, W.H. Aggression and instinct theory. *International Journal of Psychoanalysis,* 1971, **52,** 155–160.

Glueck, S., & Glueck, E. *Unraveling juvenile delinquency.* New York: Commonwealth Fund, 1950.

Glueck, S., & Glueck, E. *Delinquents and nondelinquents in perspective.* Cambridge: Harvard University Press, 1968.

Gross, A.M., & Brigham, T.A. Behavior modification and the treatment of juvenile delinquency: A review and proposal for future research. *Corrective and Social Psychiatry,* 1980, **26,** 98–106.

Heilman, K., & Valenstein, E. *Clinical neuropsy-

chology. New York: Oxford University Press, 1978.

Henn, F., Bordwell, R., & Jenkins, R.L. Juvenile delinquents revisited. *Archives of General Psychiatry,* 1980, **37,** 1160–1163.

Herbert, M. *Conduct disorders of childhood and adolescence.* New York: Wiley, 1978.

Hetherington, E.M., & Martin, B. Family interaction. In H.C. Quay & J.S. Werry (Eds.), *Psychopathological disorders of childhood* (2nd ed.). New York: Wiley, 1979.

Hetherington, E.M., Strouwie, R., & Ridberg, E.H. Patterns of family interaction and child rearing attitudes related to three dimensions of juvenile delinquency. *Journal of Abnormal Psychology,* 1979, **77,** 160–176.

Hewitt, L.E., & Jenkins, R.L. *Fundamental patterns of maladjustment: The dynamics of their origin.* Springfield, Ill.: State of Illinois, 1946.

Hobbs, S.A., & Forehand, R. Important parameters in the use of timeout with children: A re-examination. *Journal of Behavior Therapy and Experimental Psychiatry,* 1977, **8,** 365–370.

Hoefler, S.A., & Bornstein, P.H. Achievement Place: An evaluative review. *Criminal Justice and Behavior,* 1975, **2,** 146–167.

Huessy, H., Metayer, M., & Townsend, M. 8–10 year follow-up of 84 children treated for behavior disorders of rural Vermont. *Acta Paedopsychiatrica,* 1974, **10,** 230–235.

Jalali, B., Jalali, M., Crocetti, G., & Turner, F. Adolescents and drug use: Toward a more comprehensive approach. *American Journal of Psychiatry,* 1981, **51,** 120–130.

Jerse, F.W., & Fakouri, M.E. Juvenile delinquency and academic deficiency. *Contemporary Education,* 1978, **49,** 106–109.

Jurkovic, G.J. The juvenile delinquent as a moral philosopher: A structural-developmental perspective. *Psychological Bulletin,* 1980, **88,** 709–727.

Jurkovic, G.J., & Prentice, N.M. Relation of moral and cognitive development to dimensions of juvenile delinquency. *Journal of Abnormal Psychology,* 1977, **86,** 414–420.

Kazdin, A.E. *The token economy: A review and evaluation.* New York: Plenum, 1977.

Kirkland, K.D., & Thelen, M.H. Uses of modeling in child treatment. In B. Lahey & A. Kazdin (Eds.), *Advances in clinical child psychology*

(Vol. 1). New York: Plenum, 1977.

Kohlberg, L. Development of moral character and moral ideology. In M. Hoffman & L. Hoffman (Eds.), *Review of child development research* (Vol. 1). New York: Russell Sage Foundation, 1964.

Kohlberg, L., LaCrosse, J., & Ricks, D. The predictability of adult mental health from childhood behavior. In B. Wolman (Ed.), *Manual of child psychopathology.* New York: McGraw-Hill, 1972.

Lane, B.A. The relationship of learning disabilities to juvenile delinquency: Current status. *Journal of Learning Disabilities,* 1980, **13,** 20–30.

Lapouse, R.A., & Monk, M. Fears and worries in a representative sample of children. *American Journal of Orthopsychiatry,* 1959, **29,** 803–818.

Lewis, H. *Deprived children.* London: Oxford University Press, 1954.

Lorenz, K. *On aggression.* New York: Harcourt, 1966.

Luria, A. *The working brain.* New York: Basic Books, 1973.

Maletsky, B.M. D-amphetamine and delinquency. *Diseases of the Nervous System,* 1974, **35,** 543–547.

Mattis, S., French, J.H., & Rapin, I. Dyslexia in children and young adults: Three independent neuropsychological syndromes. *Developmental Medicine and Child Neurology,* 1975, **17,** 150–163.

Mattes, J.A. The role of frontal lobe dysfunction in childhood hyperkinesis. *Comprehensive Psychiatry,* 1980, **21,** 358–369.

Merton, R.K. Social structure and anomie. In R.K. Merton (Ed.), *Social theory and social structure.* New York: Free Press, 1957.

Murray, C.A. *The link between learning disabilities and juvenile delinquency: Current theory and knowledge.* Washington, D.C.: U.S. Government Printing Offices, 1976.

Nielson, J., & Christenson, A.L. Thirty-five male and double-Y chromosomes. *Psychological Medicine,* 1974, **4,** 28–37.

Offer, D., Sabshin, M., & Marcus, D. Clinical evaluation in normal adolescents. *American Journal of Psychiatry,* 1965, **121,** 864–872.

Offord, D.R., Sullivan, K., Allen, N., & Abrams, N. Delinquency and hyperactivity. *Journal of Nervous and Mental Diseases,* 1979, **167,** 734–741.

Olweus, D. Stability of aggressive reaction patterns in males: A review. *Psychological Bulletin,* 1979, **86,** 852–875.

Owen, D.R. The 47, XYY male: A review. *Psychological Bulletin,* 1972, **78,** 209–233.

Patterson, G.R., Littman, R.A., & Bricker, W. Assertive behavior in children: A step toward a theory of aggression. *Monographs of the Society for Research in Child Development,* 1967, **32**(No. 113).

Phillips, E.L. Achievement Place: Token reinforcement procedures in a homestyle rehabilitation setting for "pre-delinquent" boys. *Journal of Applied Behavior Analysis,* 1968, **1,** 213–223.

Phillips, E.L., Phillips, E.A., Fixsen, D.L., & Wolf, M.M. Behavior shaping for delinquents. *Psychology Today,* 1973, **7,** 74–79.

Pontius, A.A., & Ruttinger, R.F. Frontal lobe maturational lag in juvenile delinquents shown in narrative tests. *Adolescence,* 1976, **11,** 509–518.

Quay, H.C. Dimensions of personality in delinquent boys as inferred from factor analysis of case history data. *Child Development,* 1964, **35,** 479–484.

Quay, H.C. Patterns of aggression, withdrawal and immaturity. In H.C. Quay & J.S. Werry (Eds.), *Psychopathological disorders of childhood.* New York: Wiley, 1972.

Quay, H.C. Classification. In H.C. Quay & J.S. Werry (Eds.), *Psychopathological disorders of childhood* (2nd ed.). New York: Wiley, 1979.

Robins, L.N. *Deviant children grown up: A sociological and psychiatric study of sociopathic personality.* Baltimore: Williams & Wilkins, 1966.

Robins, L.N. Antisocial behavior disturbances of childhood: Prevalence, prognosis and prospects. In E.J. Anthony & C. Koupernik (Eds.), *The child in his family: Children at psychiatric risk.* New York: Wiley, 1974.

Robins, L.N. Sturdy childhood predictors of adult antisocial behavior: Replications from longitudinal studies. *Psychological Medicine,* 1978, **8,** 611–622.

Rosenthal, D. Heredity in criminality. *Criminal Justice and Behavior,* 1975, **2,** 3–21.

Ross, A.O. *Psychological disorders of children: A behavioral approach to theory, research and therapy.* New York: McGraw-Hill, 1974.

Ross, A.O. *Psychological aspects of learning disabilities and reading disorders.* New York: McGraw-Hill, 1976.

Ross, A.O. *Child behavior therapy,* New York: Wiley, 1981.

Ross, D.M., & Ross, S.A. *Hyperactivity: Theory, research and action.* New York: Wiley, 1976.

Rutter, M. Parent-child separation: Psychological effects on the children. *Journal of Child Psychology and Psychiatry,* 1972, **12,** 233–260.

Rutter, M., Tizard, J., & Whitmore, K. *Education, health and behavior.* London: Longmann, 1970.

Sarason, I.G. Verbal learning modeling and juvenile delinquency. *American Psychologist,* 1968, **23,** 245–266.

Sarson, I.G. A cognitive social learning approach to juvenile delinquency. In R.D. Hare & D. Schalling (Eds.), *Psychopathic behavior: Approaches to research.* New York: Wiley, 1978.

Sarason, I.G., & Ganzer, V.J. Modeling: An approach to the rehabilitation of juvenile offenders. Report to the Social and Rehabilitation Service of the U.S. Department of Health, Education and Welfare, Washington, D.C., 1971.

Satterfield, J.H. The hyperactive child syndrome: A precursor of adult psychopathy. In R.D. Hare & D. Schalling (Eds.), *Psychopathic behavior: Approaches to research.* New York: Wiley, 1978.

Satz, P. Reading problems in perspective. In W. Otto, N. Peters, & C.W. Peters (Eds.), *Reading problems: A multidisciplinary perspective.* Reading, Mass.: Addison-Wesley, 1977.

Satz, P., & Morris, R.D. Learning disabilities subtypes: A review. In F. Pirrozollo & J. Witrock (Eds.), *Neuropsychological and cognitive processes in reading.* New York: Academic Press, 1981.

Schonhaut, S., & Satz, P. Prognosis of the learning disabled child. In M. Rutter (Ed.), *Behavioral syndromes of brain dysfunction in childhood.* New York: Guilford, 1983.

Schwartz, S., & Johnson, J.H. *Psychopathology of childhood.* New York: Pergamon, 1981.

Shanok, P.S., & Lewis, D.O. Medical histories of female delinquents. *Archives of General Psychiatry,* 1981, **38,** 211–213.

Shaw, C.R., & McKay, H.D. *Juvenile delinquency*

in urban areas. Chicago, Ill.: The University of Chicago Press, 1969.

Stewart, M.A., Mendelson, W.B., & Johnson, N.E. Hyperactive children as adolescents: How they describe themselves. *Child Psychiatry and Human Development,* 1973, **4,** 3–11.

Stumphauser, J.S. Modifying delinquent behavior: Beginnings and current practices. *Adolescence,* 1976, **11,** 13–28.

Tarnopol, L. Delinquency in minimal brain dysfunction. *Journal of Learning Disabilities,* 1970, **3,** 200–206.

Taylor, T., & Watt, D.C. The relation of deviant symptoms and behavior in a normal population to subsequent delinquency and maladjustment. *Psychological Medicine,* 1977, **7,** 163–169.

Thomas, A., & Chess, S. *Temperament and development,* London: University of London Press, 1977.

Thrasher, F.M. *The gang* (Rev. ed.). Chicago, Illinois: The University of Chicago Press, 1963.

Trojanowicz, R.S. *Juvenile delinquency: Concepts and controls.* Englewood Cliffs, N.J.: Prentice-Hall, 1973.

U.S. Department of Justice. *Sourcebook for criminal justice statistics—1977.* Washington, D.C., 1978.

Vaz, E.W. *Middle class delinquency.* New York: Harper & Row, 1967.

Walters, R.H., & Brown, M. Studies of reinforcement of aggression, III: Transfer of responses to an interpersonal situation. *Child Development,* 1963, **34,** 563–571.

Weeks, H. *Youthful offenders at Highfields.* Ann Arbor: University of Michigan Press, 1958.

Wender, P.H. *Minimal brain dysfunction in children.* New York: Wiley, 1971.

Zinkus, P.W., & Gottlieb, M.I. Learning disabilities and juvenile delinquency. *Clinical Pediatrics,* 1977, **17,** 775–780.

Zuckerman, M. The sensation seeking motive. In B. Maher (Ed.), *Progress in experimental personality research* (Vol. 7), New York: Academic Press, 1974.

CHAPTER 20

Hyperactive Behavior in Children

DEAN KERASOTES AND C. EUGENE WALKER

Hyperactive is a term frequently used to describe children referred for psychological evaluation and treatment. When these children are examined individually, a wide variety of medical and psychological disorders may be identified (Kenny et al., 1971). Some are reacting to environmental stresses such as changes in family relationships or the demands of new social situations. Such children may be confused, anxious, or seeking attention. Poor parenting skills may also be the source of uncontrolled child behavior. In other cases, children may even be perceived as hyperactive by adults intolerant of age appropriate activity levels and behavior. On the other hand, careful assessment may reveal children who exhibit signs of neurological pathology, suffer from sensory impairments, manifest language delays, experience significant learning disabilities, or are severely emotionally disturbed. Thus, as a reported symptom, hyperactivity is a diffuse and global label often overused and loosely applied. Hyperactive tends to be a "wastebasket" designation applied to any child who annoys adults charged with his or her care. Yet there does exist a group of children who manifest hyperactivity, in addition to a cluster of other cardinal symptoms, that together may be considered a distinct and diagnosable developmental disorder. However, due to the looseness with which the term is often used, one must perform a careful assessment of the child to ascertain the actual nature of the problem involved for a given child and the wisest treatment strategy. Current research suggests that there may be several distinguishable

subcategories of this disorder that should be taken into account; however, exactly how many such categories exist and how they can be identified is not yet clear in the literature. It is the purpose of this chapter to describe the nature and treatment of the hyperactive behavior syndrome, selectively reviewing the literature regarding characteristics of hyperactive children, methods of assessment, and effective treatment.

HISTORY AND DEFINITION

Historically, current conceptualizations of hyperactivity emerged from research examining the broad diagnostic category of Minimal Brain Dysfunction (MBD). Ross and Ross (1976) trace the origin of MBD to the early 1900s in which observations were made of brain-damaged adults and children who exhibited hyperactive, distractible, and unmanageable behavior patterns. Similar behaviors observed in children without demonstrable brain damage were assumed to reflect underlying neuropathology, thus the term minimal brain damage or dysfunction.

After World War II, the neurologically based interpretation of hyperactivity as one of many behaviors indicative of brain damage was elaborated. Special education programs that were developed to deal with the "brain-injured" child, in addition to being accepted by educators, brought public attention to children with learning and behavioral difficulties (Strauss & Lehtinen, 1947; Strauss & Kephart, 1955). As part of a government-sponsored task force, Clements (1966) defined minimal brain dysfunction as learning and behavioral disabilities associated with deviations of functions of the central nervous system in children with normal intelligence. He cited the most commonly noted characteristics of the child with MBD as: hyperactivity, perceptual-motor impairment, emotional lability, general coordination deficits, disorders of attention, impulsivity, disorders of speech and hearing, and equivocal neurologic signs and/or electroencephalographic irregularities. While subsequent research has not provided empirical support for the validity of MBD as a medical syndrome, researchers have focused on establishing the validity of hyperactivity as a behavioral syndrome by specifying the nature of behavioral problems shared by hyperactive children (Ross & Ross, 1976; Routh, 1978).

Hyperactivity is offically referred to as *Attention Deficit Disorder* (ADD) *with hyperactivity* by the American Psychiatric Association. As defined in the *Diagnostic and Statistical Manual of Mental Disorders III* (DSM III), (American Psychiatric Association, 1980), ADD with hyperactivity is a disorder in which the "child displays, for his or her mental or chronological age, signs of developmentally inappropriate inattention, impulsivity, and hyperactivity" (p. 43). The manual specifies the criteria for the disorder (see Table 20.1) and notes that symptomology varies with age. More severe symptoms are said to be present in younger children. Since these symptoms may vary across situations, they may not be observed during examination; therefore, parental and especially teacher reports of the behavior often must be used to confirm the presence of the behaviors. Reports from teachers are valuable because they have wider experience with larger numbers of children to use as a frame of reference. Symptomatic behaviors are more likely to be noted in situations where the child is required to display self-control, sustained attention, and inhibition.

Although the search for an adequate definition of hyperactivity has been elusive, researchers attempting to delineate its nature

Table 20.1   DSM-III   Diagnostic Criteria for Attention Deficit Disorder with Hyperactivity

A.   Inattention, including three of the following:

    (1)   Often fails to complete tasks
    (2)   Often does not listen
    (3)   Is easily distracted
    (4)   Has difficulty maintaining sustained attention

B.   Impulsivity, including three of the following:

    (1)   Does not think before acting
    (2)   Changes from one activity to another excessively
    (3)   Has work habits characterized by poor organization
    (4)   Requires much supervision
    (5)   Frequently interrupts class verbally
    (6)   Has difficulty waiting turn in group activity

C.   Hyperactivity, including two of the following:

    (1)   Runs around or climbs excessively
    (2)   Exhibits restlessness, difficulty sitting without fidgeting
    (3)   Has difficulty remaining in seat
    (4)   Moves in sleep excessively
    (5)   Exhibits driven motor behavior

D.   Early onset:

    Symptoms appear prior to 7 years of age.

E.   Symptoms are present for at least 6 months

F.   Symptoms not due to other disorders:

    Child has not been diagnosed as having schizophrenia, affective disorder, severe or profound mental retardation

Note. Criteria derived from the *Diagnostic and Statistical Manual of Mental Diseases III.* (American Psychiatric Association, 1980)

cite overactivity, inattention, and impulsivity as core symptoms that are apparent early in life to such an extent that the child is consistently unable to comply with situational demands in an age appropriate manner (Cantwell, 1975; Ross & Ross, 1976; Routh, 1978; and Safer & Allen, 1976). These researchers also note that secondary problems in personal adjustment, interpersonal relations, conduct, and learning are frequently associated with hyperactivity.

Early definitions of hyperactivity stressed excessive levels of activity as one of the more obvious symptoms of the disorder. In their now classic description of the *hyperkinetic behavior syndrome,* Laufer and Denhoff (1957) colorfully pictured the hyperactive child as displaying involuntary and constant motor activity. As infants, hyperactive children were said to display advanced motor development, frequently climbing out of their cribs and later unable to be contained in a playpen. As older children, they were described as always running, unable to sit still for anything, including meals, television, or schoolwork. Some clinicians have noted that hyperactive children were even more active in terms of kicking and movement prior to birth than other children. Ten years later, Werry (1968) defined hyperactivity as a "level of daily motor activity which is clearly greater (ideally by more than two standard deviations from the mean) than that occurring in children of similar sex, mental age, socioeconomic status, and cultural background" (p. 487). These early descriptions led many clinicians to believe hyperactivity could unmistakably be discerned by observing the child. However, as noted in the DSM III definition of ADD with hyperactivity, the overactivity may not be demonstrated in all situations at all times.

Despite notions that hyperactivity decreased with age (Laufer & Denhoff, 1957; Wender, 1971), hyperactive children appear to be at risk for emotional, academic, and societal difficulties in adolescence, particularly when aggression is an associated problem (Milich & Loney, 1979). Increasing recognition of hyperactivity as a prevalent disorder that results in a wide variety of socially defined problems has clearly shifted the focus of research from examining children's deficits to a broader study of the interaction of hyperactive children with their social ecology (Whalen & Henker, 1980).

PREVALENCE

While a variety of prevalence estimates have been reported, most investigators accept an overall rate in the population of 4–5 percent as a reasonable and conservative estimate. In their extensive review, Safer and Allen (1976) indicated that hyperactivity is the most common childhood psychiatric disability, accounting for 30–40 percent of the children evaluated in child guidance clinics and approximately 10 percent of children seen in pediatric clinics. Trites et al. (1979) recently compared data from teachers in the U.S., Canada, and New Zealand, using the Conners Teacher Rating Scale, and found the percentage of school children from different populations labeled hyperactive ranged from 7–22 percent if the standard cut-off score of 15 was employed. Lambert, Sandoval, and Sassone (1978) demonstrated that the prevalence of hyperactive children varied from 1.19 percent to 13 percent as function of the social system (medical, educational, or family) defining the disorder. In this study, from a representative sample of over 5,000 school children, hyperactive children were identified based on the following criteria: (1) diagnosed by a physician, (2) considered hyperactive by parents, and (3) judged hyperactive by school authorities. Additionally, all children in the sample were rated by their teachers on a scale measuring hyperactive behaviors. Only 1.19 percent of the children were found to be hyperactive by agreement of home, school authorities, and physician. If identification by any one of the three sources mentioned above were accepted as the criterion for hyperactivity, the estimate would rise to 4.92 percent. Of children not identified as hyperactive by any of the three sources above, 7.75 percent received teacher ratings equivalent to the hyperactive children identified by all three sources. Therefore, it was concluded that the *maximum* prevalence rate is about 13 percent when all possible means to define hyperactivity are employed.

Lambert et al. (1978) were also able to examine prevalence of hyperactivity as a function of sex, grade level, socioeconomic status, and ethnic status. Their research, as well as other studies, consistently shows that boys are six to eight times more frequently identified as hyperactive than girls (Ross & Ross, 1976; Routh, 1978). The number of medically diagnosed hyperactive children remained relatively constant across grade levels.

It should be noted that most of the measures used to define hyperactivity decreased in absolute value with age, though in terms of comparison with their peers a similar proportion of children at each age and grade level were considered to be hyperactive. Interestingly, children considered hyperactive by the schools was highest (6.3 percent) in third grade. The authors suggest that academic difficulties may become particularly evident at the third-grade level. Prevalence of hyperactivity was roughly proportional to the distribution of socioeconomic status in the population. However, there was a tendency for there to be slightly more low socioeconomic hyperactive children and slightly fewer middle income hyperactive children than would have been expected. With regard to ethnic status, children considered hyperactive by agreement of *all* defining sources were primarily white. On the other hand, the proportion of black children considered hyperactive by *only* the school was higher than the proportion of black children in the population.

CHARACTERISTICS

Pattern of Activity

There are often very strong situation variables in hyperactive children's behavior. Thus some children are hyperactive in group situations but are relatively calm and easy to control in one-to-one situations while other children demonstrate exactly the opposite pattern. Many hyperactive children display a great deal of overactivity in novel situations while others appear to be more active in situations that are familiar to them. This fact has led to much misunderstanding and breakdown in communication between clinicians and others, such as school teachers. Often, the child who is completely unmanageable in a group situation that he or she is familiar with, such as a school classroom, will be extremely docile, cooperative, and definitely not hyperactive in a one-to-one situation with a pediatrician or psychologist in his or her office. This leads the unwary clinician to deny that the child is hyperactive. However, if that clinician continues to see this youngster on a weekly basis for a period of time, the hyperactive behavior may begin to manifest itself, or, if the clinician troubles himself or herself to observe the child in the school setting, he or she will readily become aware of what the teacher is describing. Studies of hyperactive children in the classroom indicate that they do engage in more gross motor activity than other youngsters; however, even more impressive in their being defined as hyperactive children is the fact that much of their behavior takes place at inappropriate times (Abikoff, Gittelman-Klein, & Klein, 1980; Schleifer et al., 1975). In addition, some research has pointed to the fact that the hyperactive child engages in much more purposeless and random activity than other children (Barkley & Ullman, 1975). Many children who show similar energy and activity levels but who are engaged in purposeful activity do not become labeled as hyperactive.

Attention Span

Hyperactive children, when they are highly motivated or engrossed in a situation, can frequently demonstrate a much longer attention span and greater on-task behavior than is customary for them under other conditions. However, they appear less able to sustain this kind of involvement than other children. In recent years, there has been a shift in emphasis and interest from the gross motor activity level of hyperactive children to their problems with inattention or the inability to attend to relevant stimuli for sustained periods of time. For example, Douglas (1980) summarizes a program of research studying attentional deficits in hyperactive children. On tasks such as experimental measures of sustained attention, hyperactive children are found to respond more slowly and make more errors of commission than normal children. Hyperactives also perform poorly on tasks that require inhibiting their responses, such as measures of cognitive impulsivity, reaction time tests, and mazes. The response of hyperactive children to these experimental tasks seems to differentiate them from normals as well as children from other clinical populations (Firestone & Martin, 1979).

Immaturity

Hyperactive children are often described as being immature and having poor judgment. Kinsbourne (1973) has suggested that many of the characteristics associated with hyperactivity may indicate a delay in, or slowing of, neurological maturation. Numerous studies have, in fact, confirmed that, in terms of measures of impulsivity (as well as activity level and performance on tasks measuring attention), while these children's behavior is deviant for their age group, they are within normal limits for children three or four years younger than their age (Routh, Schroeder, & O'Tuama, 1974; Routh & Schroeder, 1976).

Self-Concept Problems

As a result of their frequent conflicts with others and the consequences of their behavior, many hyperactive children develop what might be termed a poor self-concept. They begin to think of themselves as "bad" kids who are not liked by others, have few friends, and are regarded as children who are troublemakers. They are also the first suspects when any kind of misbehavior or damage to property or similar situations are discovered. Studies examining ratings by their peers as well as adults do indicate a significant negative bias when rating hyperactive children (Campbell & Paulaukas, 1979). Development of a poor self-concept might be regarded as a very poor prognostic sign. A significant part of therapy with these children generally involves changing their self-concept in more positive directions as a prerequisite to bringing their behavior successfully under control.

Aggression

Numerous studies have investigated the presence or absence of hostile and aggressive behavior in hyperactive children. Indeed, some researchers indicate that differentiating conduct disorders from hyperactivity in children is extremely difficult (Lahey, Green, & Forehand, 1980; Sandberg, Wieselberg, & Shaffer, 1980). Certainly, the characteristics that hyperactive children exhibit (overactivity, impulsivity, inattention, poor judgment, etc.) predispose them to numerous conflicts with authority and peers. These conflicts and the resulting consequences would be expected to prove frustrating for these youngsters and predispose them to anger and hostile outbursts. Investigations by Loney, Langhorne, and Paternite (1978) have identified patterns of aggression and hostility in hyperactive children. When these factors are present, this has been found to be an indicator of a very poor prognosis. These children will tend to have increasing difficulties as they grow older and will suffer much more maladjustment from their overactive behavior than children who do not develop aggressive behavior along with the hyperactivity.

Sleep Disturbances

Studies of hyperactive children in infancy indicate that they sleep relatively little and are fussy babies (Ross & Ross, 1976). Later in life, they appear to be poor sleepers and often have difficulty settling down sufficiently to go to sleep at night. They are frequently reported to wake up in the middle of the night and prowl through the house, often damaging furniture or items in the house, setting fires, and so forth. Numerous theories regarding the etiology of hyperactive behavior posit some sort of dysfunction of arousal mechanism, with these children being regarded as overaroused or underaroused (see Rosenthal & Allen, 1978). Overarousal usually refers to their tendency to be over-active and lacking in inhibition, which often carries over into the night, preventing them from going to sleep and/or sleeping soundly. The underarousal theories generally posit that the child, due to some defect in the arousal mechanism, is constantly in danger of falling asleep and must maintain his or her activity level just to remain awake.

Anecdotal evidence for this is often provided by parents who state that their hyperactive children are on the go all day but as soon as they sit down in front of the TV at night, they fall asleep. The high incidence of sleep disturbances in hyperactive children might be seen as supportive of these notions. However, as in most areas having to do with etiology of hyperactivity, the results are neither sufficiently consistent nor impressive at present to demonstrate any causative mechanism (Hastings & Barkley, 1978).

Intelligence

The relationship between intelligence and hyperactivity remains a controversial issue. Some researchers report lower intellectual performance among hyperactive children while others find no differences. Loney (1974) has pointed out that studies done with younger children fail to find differences in intellectual ability while studies done with children in the upper grades and at older ages find significant differences, with hyperactive children scoring lower. This would suggest that the hyperactive children may be performing lower on the tests as a result of their failure to profit from educational experiences, no doubt as an effect of the hyperactive behavior rather than a cause of it. Similar results have been found by other authors indicating especially inferior scores on group IQ tests as well as an uneven cognitive pattern and a higher incidence of verbal difficulties including speech defects (Minde et al., 1971). Some studies have indicated discrepancies between verbal and performance scores for hyperactive children, usually with hyperactive children scoring higher on performance subtests of intellectual measures than on the verbal portions. For example, Lambert and Sandoval (1980) found significant differences between verbal and performance IQ scores occurring in over 50 percent of a group of hyperactive children; however, the occurrence of a significant verbal/performance IQ difference was also found in 30 percent of children in a random control group.

Academic Achievement

Hyperactive children are consistently found to be low achievers. However, this is most likely due to their inattention to classroom activities and general disruptive behavior that interferes with their learning and, in many cases, the learning of others. In elementary school, hyperactive children as a group repeat more grades and have lower levels of achievement in all academic subjects than their nonhyperactive peers (Minde et al., 1971). For example, Lambert and Sandoval (1980), in an identified group of hyperactive children, found only 24.8 percent scoring above grade level in mathematics, 18.2 percent scoring above average in reading recognition, and 25.6 percent scoring above average in reading comprehension.

Learning Disabilities

Learning disability is a feature commonly associated with hyperactivity. Since both learning disabilities and hyperactivity are terms applied to heterogeneous groups of children, estimates of the proportion of hyperactives who also have a learning disability vary. Safer and Allen (1976) stated that 70–80 percent of hyperactive children are learning disabled and 30–45 percent of learning-disabled children are hyperactive. However, Ross (1976) has pointed out that the relationship often noted between hyperactivity and learning disability may be spurious due to the fact that hyperactive children are more frequently referred for psychological testing. This results in a higher rate of detection of learning disability than would occur if they were not tested so frequently. Using an objective set of decision rules to define learning disabilities, Lambert and Sandoval (1980) found 42.6 percent of a sample of hyperactive students achieving sufficiently below grade level that they could be classified as learning disabled. Among a random control group, 11.3 percent were classified as learning disabled according to the same criteria. Students were identified by Lambert and Sandoval as learning disabled if significant discrepancies were noted in three of five areas:

1. Significant differences between Verbal IQ and Performance IQ measured by the WISC-R.

2. Ability (Verbal or Performance IQ) significantly greater than reading achievement (Peabody Individual Achievement Test—Reading Recognition or Comprehension).

3. Ability (Verbal or Performance IQ) significantly greater than mathematics achievement (PIAT mathematics).

4. Significant difference between reading (PIAT Reading Recognition or Comprehension) and mathematics (PIAT Mathematics).

5. Ability (Verbal IQ or Performance IQ) greater than teacher ratings of classroom adaptation (Pupil Behavior Rating Scale).

Socioeconomic Factors

In a recent study, Paternite and Loney (1980) noted that socioeconomic status (SES) was not useful in predicting presence of primary hyperactive symptoms such as overactivity and inattention. However, SES appears to be related to the severity of *secondary* symptoms associated with hyperactivity. Higher frequencies of aggression, low self-esteem, and delinquency differentiate low SES hyperactive children from high SES hyperactives (Paternite, Loney, & Langhorne, 1976). It may be that a lack of parenting skills in low SES families results in overreaction to and poor management of the hyperactive child in such families. For example, parental disturbance was found to be the best predictor of aggression at referral for hyperactive children (Paternite & Loney, 1980).

Birth Order

While some early authors (Laufer & Denhoff, 1957) commented on the tendency for hyperactive children to be firstborns, there have been very few studies that have examined data having to do with birth order. Most researchers who have included this variable have failed to find any significant relationship between birth order and hyperactivity. Paternite and Loney (1980) included birth order in a multiple regression study of hyperactivity. Birth order was not found to be a significant contributing variable. Thus, while it is plausible to expect a relationship between birth order and hyperactivity, and while some clinicians seem to note a tendency for firstborns to be more involved, data to support this are lacking.

Genetics

Given the characteristics of the behavior of hyperactive children as well as many of the theories that are proposed regarding etiology, it would be natural to assume some genetic or inherited basis for the disorder. Cantwell (1975), reviewing the admittedly limited research on familial-genetic factors and hyperactivity, suggested that the evidence for genetic factors was "tentative but strong" (p. 100). Evidence lending some support for a genetic basis for hyperactivity is found in the fact that parents of hyperactive children have a higher prevalence of psychiatric disorders than those of nonhyperactive children. Specifically, parents of hyperactive children manifest higher rates of alcoholism, sociopathy, hysteria, and hyperactivity as children (Morrison & Stewart, 1971; Cantwell, 1972). Furthermore, Morrison and Stewart (1973a) found higher rates of these psychiatric disorders in the biologic parents and relatives of hyperactive children adopted at a very young age. On the other hand, the high prevalence of these disorders was not found in the adoptive parents and relatives. Early interpretations of the data favored a polygenic mode of transmission for hyperactivity in which appearance of the disorder was influenced by an interaction between the genetic predisposition and environmental conditions (Morrison & Stewart, 1973a, 1973b, 1974; Cantwell, 1975; and Ross & Ross, 1976).

Importantly, recent research has demonstrated that the adult psychiatric disorders associated with hyperactivity are also found in parents of children with other psychiatric disorders. In studies of children attending psychiatric clinics, parental pathology does not differentiate the parents of hyperactive children from those of conduct-disordered children. (Sandberg, Rutter, & Taylor, 1978; Stewart, DeBlois, & Cummings 1980). Sandberg and his associates (Sandberg et al., 1980) have replicated these findings with a sample of children experiencing hyperactivity and conduct disorders in school but not referred to a psychiatric clinic. Therefore, while genetic transmission may play a role in childhood psychiatric disorders, researchers now generally conclude that evidence supporting a genetic explanation specifically for hyperactivity is lacking (Stewart et al., 1980; Rutter, 1982).

Organic Factors

Common among early theories regarding the etiology of hyperactivity was the notion that it was primarily an organic disorder. As noted earlier in the present chapter, this view was popularized by Clements (1966), who felt that "minimal brain dysfunction" was the underlying cause of such behavior. Following this line of reasoning, extensive studies were conducted, examining everything from prenatal factors to electroencephalographic recordings of children who were hyperactive. Unfortunately, much of the research conducted in this area suffered from inadequate research design, and few studies employed appropriate control groups. In many instances, the frequency of the symptom or sign under consideration had been greatly underestimated in the normal population. The results of most studies to date have generally indicated that no single organic sign, or pattern of signs, is adequate to account for the incidence of hyperactivity in children. While some signs seem to be statistically slightly more prevalent among hyperactive children, none have been found to be present in an overwhelming majority of the cases and all are found in other children who are not hyperactive. In addition, the majority of the studies were not double

blind in design, and there appears to be a strong tendency for the researcher to find the sign he or she expects to find in a slightly higher proportion of hyperactive children than normals. Thus, while numerous studies have seemingly reported a higher incidence of various organic signs in hyperactive children, on closer evaluation most of these are found not to be replicable, and they do not appear to suggest any underlying mechanism that accounts for the behavior manifested by such children. As a result, organic theories are on the decline and may be thought, at best, to provide a partial explanation for hyperactive behavior in some children. Dubey (1976), in a recent review of the literature in this area, examined electroencephalographic, neurological, biochemical, genetic, and pregnancy studies of hyperactive children and concluded that there is but minimal evidence of organic dysfunction in the majority of hyperkinetic children. In a recent study in England (Sandberg et al., 1980), it was found that the presence of prenatal complications, high neurodevelopmental scores, and high physical anomaly scores did not differentiate hyperactive children from either normal or conduct-disordered children.

On the other hand, it is interesting to note that minor physical anomalies (including such physical deviations as large head circumference, malformation of the ears, abnormalities of the fingers and toes) have frequently been noted to occur in hyperactive children. Some researchers in this area (e.g., Waldrop, Pederson, & Bell, 1968; Rapoport, Quinn, & Lamprecht, 1974) speculate that certain abnormal prenatal conditions may have produced these abnormalities as well as the hyperactive behavior. Thus the possibility of an organic etiology for hyperactive behavior remains tantalizing though it has not been convincingly demonstrated. The fact that findings regarding organic etiology continually crop up in the literature but either fail to replicate or produce equivocal results in the long run may point to the fact that certain subsets of hyperactive children may suffer from one or more organic etiologies while other subsets do not. As was noted earlier in this chapter, hyperactivity tends to be a "wastebasket" diagnosis. More research in this area is definitely warranted. Should it become possible to specify a clear organic etiology for certain hyperactive children, along with a convincing underlying mechanism to account for the behavior, appropriate medication and other medical treatments might become more feasible.

Dietary Factors

Many clinicians and researchers, assuming some sort of organic etiology for hyperactivity, have proposed various dietary factors related to hyperactivity. One common notion in this area is that hyperactivity is related to blood sugar level. Those who subscribe to this notion recommend restricting or eliminating refined sugars in the diet of hyperactive children. While there is much clinical anecdotal evidence from parents to support this idea, there is as yet no sound scientific evidence to support it. In fact, only one research article has appeared to date that examines this hypothesis (Prinze, Roberts, & Hantman, 1980). Another popular notion in this area has to do with what has come to be called the Feingold diet. Feingold (1975) has proposed that presence of food additives, specifically certain food colorings and natural salicylates, may stimulate hyperactivity in some children. He initially reported good results with a diet that restricted intake of these substances. Most studies have failed to find support for the efficacy of this dietary regime (Conners, 1980; Harley & Matthews, 1980). What positive results have been reported have generally reported improvement rates typical of those found in placebo studies. Thus a modest improvement will be found in some children on this diet. But it appears unlikely that the particular dietary factors are the key element since keeping the child on the diet results in a great deal of extra attention for the child. Also, parents who are willing to modify diets so drastically are also likely to change their parenting behaviors as well. On the other hand, at least a couple of studies have shown

results that seemed more promising than the majority of the studies (Rose, 1978; Swanson & Kinsbourne, 1980). It would appear that much more research is needed before a final conclusion may be reached, but at present any application of this diet clinically would have to be thought of as experimental and approached very cautiously. Other studies (e.g., Trites, Tryphonas, & Ferguson, 1980) investigating the possibility that food allergies may produce hyperactivity have shown equivocal results. In the long run, it may turn out that the dietary factor relates to only a small proportion of hyperactive children, if any.

PROGNOSIS

A common assumption regarding hyperactivity, in the older literature, was that as these children approached puberty, the hyperactivity would decrease. In fact, some speculated hormonal changes in the body at puberty might result in hyperactivity disappearing. However, more recent studies suggest that this is not the case for many hyperactive children. It does appear that as some of these children advance in age they learn to *control* their behavior better and are, therefore, not in constant conflict because of their overactivity. However, for a large number of them, attentional difficulties and impulsivity remain prominent characteristics and they continue to experience difficulty throughout their lifespan (Hoy et al., 1978; Weiss et al., 1979). Hyperactivity does not magically or mercifully disappear at puberty. Particularly those who have developed aggressiveness with their hyperactivity and who suffer from poor self-concept tend to suffer numerous social consequences such as failure in school, excessive school dropout rates, increased delinquency, underemployment, and marital/interpersonal difficulties. On the other hand, those youngsters who do increase their self-control, develop a relatively adequate self-concept and do not develop hostile or aggressive behavior, appear to self-select occupations that permit a great deal of activity and manage to adapt to social situations in a much more adequate manner.

ASSESSMENT

Hyperactive children are probably the most tested children in American today. Their general behavior results in a high rate of referral for medical and psychological intervention. The puzzling and seemingly unmanageable nature of their behavior invariably results in the physician or psychologist performing an extensive study of the case involving numerous medical and/or psychological tests. The purpose of this testing appears to be to uncover some clues as to the cause of the behavior. As suggested earlier in this chapter, most of these tests produce, at best, equivocal results.

Sandoval (1977) reviews the measurement of hyperactivity. Consistently, the most reliable and valid measures of hyperactive behavior appear to be obtained by means of observational behavior rating scales (Roberts & LaGreca, 1981). The Teacher Rating Scale (TRS) and Parent Symptom Questionnaire (PSQ), developed by Conners (1969, 1970, 1973) to aid in identification of hyperactive children, have been used extensively. The teacher form consists of 39 items. Descriptions of symptoms are rated on a 4-point scale (scored 0–3 points) that denotes whether the symptom is present "not at all," "just a little," "pretty much," or "very much." Factor analysis of the scale yielded five factors, which are the basis for the following scales: conduct disorder, inattentiveness, anxiety, hyperactivity, and sociability. Recently, Conners and his associates have presented a revised teacher form (see Figure 20.1) that is a slightly shortened (28 items) and reworded version of the original (Goyette, Conners, & Ulrich, 1978). The revised form excludes the anxiety and sociability factors but otherwise is considered to have an identical factor structure as the longer version (see Table 20.2). Normative data are available for the TRS (Sprague et al., 1974) and the revised TRS (Goyette et al.,

Table 20.2 Factors and Items for the Revised Teacher Questionnaire

Factor	Items
I. Conduct problems	4, 5, 6, 10, 11, 12, 13, 27
II. Hyperactivity	1, 2, 3, 8, 14, 15, 16
III. Inattention-passivity	7, 9, 18, 20, 21, 22, 26, 28
Hyperactivity Index	1, 5, 7, 8, 10, 11, 14, 15, 21, 26

Note. Adapted from "Normative Data on the Revised Conners Parent and Teacher Rating Scales" by C.H. Goyette, C.K. Conners, and R.F. Ulrich. *Journal of Abnormal Child Psychology,* 1978, **6,** 221–236.

1978). Initial normative data on the revised TRS are presented in Table 20.3.

An additional form, the Abbreviated Teacher Rating Scale (ATRS) (or Hyperactivity Index) composed of 10 items from the conduct disorder, inattentiveness, and hyperactivity factors is also available (see Figure 20.2). On the ATRS, a cutoff score of 15 is commonly used to discriminate between hyperactive and nonhyperactive children. Cut-off scores should be used cautiously due to the limited nature of the normative data (Trites et al., 1979) and the significant effect of age on score distributions (Goyette et al., 1978). These various forms of the Teacher Rating Scale, which are frequently used as one criterion for subject selection for research, have been shown to differentiate hyperactives from normals and appear to be sensitive to both drug and behavioral treatment effects.

The parent form, PSQ, utilizes a format similar to the teacher scale. It originally consisted of 93 items covering a broad range of symptom categories yielding eight factors: conduct problem, anxiety, impulsive-hyperactive, learning problem, psychosomatic, perfectionism, antisocial, and muscular tension. As with the TRS, a revised 48-item form has been adapted from the original (see Figure 20.3) and normative data (Table 20.4) provided (Goyette et al., 1978). This shorter version assesses five factors that are grouped into conduct problem, learning problem, psychosomatic, impulsive-hyperactive, and anxiety scales (Table 20.5). An Abbreviated Parent Symptom Questionnaire (APSQ), identical to

Figure 20.1. The Conners Teacher Rating Scale. (Reprinted by permission of C.K. Conners.)

Teacher's Questionnaire

Name of Child _____

Date of Evaluation _____

Grade _____

Please answer all questions. Beside *each* item, indicate the degree of the problem by a check mark (√)

	Not at all	Just a little	Pretty much	Very much
1. Restless in the "squirmy" sense.				
2. Makes inappropriate noises when he shouldn't.				
3. Demands must be met immediately.				
4. Acts "smart" (impudent or sassy).				
5. Temper outbursts and unpredictable behavior.				
6. Overly sensitive to criticism.				
7. Distractibility or attention span a problem.				
8. Disturbs other children.				
9. Daydreams.				
10. Pouts and sulks.				
11. Mood changes quickly and drastically.				
12. Quarrelsome.				
13. Submissive attitude toward authority.				
14. Restless, always "up and on the go."				

15.	Excitable, impulsive.			
16.	Excessive demands for teacher's attention.			
17.	Appears to be unaccepted by group.			
18.	Appears to be easily led by other children.			
19.	No sense of fair play.			
20.	Appears to lack leadership.			
21.	Fails to finish things that he starts.			

22.	Childish and immature.			
23.	Denies mistakes or blames others.			
24.	Does not get along well with other children.			
25.	Uncooperative with classmates.			
26.	Easily frustrated in efforts.			
27.	Uncooperative with teacher.			
28.	Difficulty in learning.			

Figure 20.2. Abbreviated Parent-Teacher Questionnaire from Conners, C.K. Rating scales for use in drug studies with children. *Psychopharmacology Bulletin* (Special issue. Pharmacotherapy of Children), 1973, 24-29. Reprinted by permission of C.K. Conners.

Abbreviated Parent-Teacher Questionnaire

Patient Name _____   Patient Number _____

                                                  Study Number _____

Parent's Observations

Information obtained _____ by _____

                    Month   Day   Year

Observation	Degree of Activity			
	Not at all	Just a little	Pretty much	Very much
1. Restless or overactive				
2. Excitable, Impulsive				
3. Disturbs other children				
4. Fails to finish things he starts—short attention span				
5. Constantly fidgeting				
6. Inattentive, easily distracted				
7. Demands must be met immediately—easily frustrated				
8. Cries often and easily				
9. Mood changes quickly and drastically				
10. Temper outbursts, explosive and unpredictable behavior				

Teacher's Observations

Information obtained _____ by _____

Month   Day   Year

Observation	Degree of Activity			
	Not at all	Just a little	Pretty much	Very much
1. Restless or overactive				
2. Excitable, impulsive				
3. Disturbs other children				
4. Fails to finish things he starts—short attention span				
5. Constantly fidgeting				
6. Inattentive, easily distracted				
7. Demands must be met immediately—easily frustrated				
8. Cries often and easily				
9. Mood changes quickly and drastically				
10. Temper outbursts, explosive and unpredictable behavior				

Other Observations of Parent or Teacher (Use reverse side if more space is required)

_____

_____

_____

_____

_____

Figure 20.3. The 48-item version of the Conners Parent Symptom Questionnaire. (Reprinted by permission of C. K. Conners.)

Parent's Questionnaire

Name of Child _____ Date _____

Please answer all questions. Beside *each* item, indicate the degree
of the problem by a check mark (√)

	Not at all	Just a little	Pretty much	Very much
1. Picks at things (nails, fingers, hair, clothing).				
2. Sassy to grown-ups.				
3. Problems with making or keeping friends.				
4. Excitable, impulsive.				
5. Wants to run things.				
6. Sucks or chews (thumb; clothing; blankets).				
7. Cries easily or often.				
8. Carries a chip on his shoulder.				
9. Daydreams.				
10. Difficulty in learning.				
11. Restless in the "squirmy" sense.				
12. Fearful (of new situations; new people or places; going to school).				
13. Restless, always up and on the go.				
14. Destructive.				
15. Tells lies or stories that aren't true.				
16. Shy.				
17. Gets into more trouble than others same age.				
18. Speaks differently from others same age (baby talk; stuttering; hard to understand).				
19. Denies mistakes or blames others.				
20. Quarrelsome.				
21. Pouts and sulks.				
22. Steals.				
23. Disobedient or obeys but resentfully.				
24. Worries more than others (about being alone; illness or death).				

25. Fails to finish things.
26. Feelings easily hurt.
27. Bullies others.
28. Unable to stop a repetitive activity.
29. Cruel.
30. Childish or immature (wants help he shouldn't need; clings; needs constant reassurance).

31. Distractibility or attention span a problem.
32. Headaches.
33. Mood changes quickly and drastically.
34. Doesn't like or doesn't follow rules or restrictions.
35. Fights constantly.
36. Doesn't get along well with brothers or sisters.

37. Easily frustrated in efforts.
38. Disturbs other children.
39. Basically an unhappy child.
40. Problems with eating (poor appetite; up between bites).
41. Stomach aches.
42. Problems with sleep (can't fall asleep; up too early; up in the night).

43. Other aches and pains.
44. Vomiting or nausea.
45. Feels cheated in family circle.
46. Boasts and brags.
47. Lets self be pushed around.
48. Bowel problems (frequently loose; irregular habits; constipation).

513

Table 20.3 Normative Data on the Revised Conners Teacher Rating Scale (TRS)

Age Category	(N)	I. Conduct Problem		II. Hyperactivity		III. Inattentive-passive		Index	
		X	(SD)	X	(SD)	X	(SD)	X	(SD)
Both sexes by age									
3–5	(24)	.49	(.74)	.74	(.74)	.83	(.87)	.78	(.82)
6–8	(102)	.30	(.41)	.46	(.57)	.64	(.71)	.49	(.56)
9–11	(108)	.40	(.60)	.56	(.60)	.69	(.67)	.54	(.59)
12–14	(94)	.19	(.31)	.30	(.41)	.51	(.75)	.31	(.37)
15–17	(55)	.27	(.53)	.33	(.53)	.58	(.59)	.39	(.53)
By sex									
Males	(208)	.34	(.53)	.56	(.66)	.77	(.72)	.56	(.60)
Females	(175)	.27	(.46)	.32	(.46)	.45	(.54)	.34	(.47)
Males by age									
3–5	(13)	.45	(.80)	.79	(.89)	.92	(1.00)	.81	(.96)
6–8	(60)	.32	(.43)	.60	(.65)	.76	(.74)	.58	(.61)
9–11	(59)	.50	(.66)	.70	(.78)	.85	(.73)	.67	(.65)
12–14	(46)	.23	(.38)	.41	(.49)	.71	(.63)	.44	(.43)
15–17	(30)	.22	(.37)	.34	(.44)	.68	(.67)	.41	(.45)
Females by age									
3–5	(11)	.53	(.68)	.69	(.56)	.72	(.71)	.74	(.67)
6–8	(42)	.28	(.37)	.28	.47	(.64)	.36	(.45)	
9–11	(49)	.28	(.49)	.38	(.51)	.49	(.53)	.38	(.48)
12–14	(48)	.15	(.23)	.19	(.27)	.32	(.42)	.18	(.24)
15–17	(25)	.33	(.68)	.32	(.63)	.45	(.47)	.36	(.62)

Note. From "Normative Data on the Revised Conners Parent and Teacher Rating Scales" by C.H. Goyette, C.K. Conners, and R.F. Ulrich. *Journal of Abnormal Child Psychology,* 1978, **6**, 221–236. Used with the permission of Plenum Publishing Corp. Copyright © 1978 by Plenum Publishing Corp.

The cumulative percent distributions of parent and teacher mean scores may be obtained by writing to the authors.

the ATRS (see Figure 20.2), is often used to monitor treatment effects at weekly intervals.

Several other rating scales are also available. The Werry-Weiss-Peters Activity Rating Scale (Werry, 1968) consists of 31 items describing overactive behaviors in various situations at home, at school, and in public. This scale produces behavioral descriptions specific to the situations the child is involved in (meals, play, sleep, watching television, doing homework, behavior away from home, and school behavior). Some researchers and clinicians find this instrument more useful than other rating scales that are available for planning specific intervention strategies. Routh, Schroeder, and O'Tuama (1974) have presented a revised version of this scale with preliminary normative data. Recently Zukow, Zukow, and Bentler (1978) have reported on the development of a parent's rating scale and a teacher's rating scale for hyperactivity that consists of 25 and 15 items respectively. Factor analysis of the parent's scale revealed three factors: excitability, motor coordination, and directed attention. The teacher's scale was found to have two factors: attention/excitability and motor coordination. This instrument is relatively new and is in need of further research and refinement; however, it seems to show promise of usefulness in the future. A variety of measures have been employed in research but appear to be sufficiently unwieldy and cumbersome that they are not suitable for routine clinical applica-

Table 20.4   Normative Data on the Revised Conners Parent Symptom Questionnaire (PSQ)

Age Category	(N)	I. Conduct problem X	(SD)	II. Learning problem X	(SD)	III. Psychosomatic X	(SD)	IV. Impulsive-hyperactive X	(SD)	V. Anxiety X	(SD)	Index X	(SD)
Both sexes by age													
3–5	(74)	.51	(.37)	.55	(.44)	.08	(.16)	1.06	(.70)	.61	(.60)	.74	(.46)
6–8	(133)	.46	(.36)	.56	(.43)	.16	(.25)	.94	(.59)	.54	(.58)	.65	(.42)
9–11	(128)	.48	(.37)	.55	(.48)	.17	(.27)	.87	(.59)	.45	(.52)	.60	(.40)
12–14	(122)	.44	(.41)	.55	(.52)	.22	(.37)	.77	(.54)	.56	(.56)	.55	(.40)
15–17	(72)	.43	(.39)	.49	(.49)	.16	(.26)	.65	(.53)	.56	(.55)	.47	(.38)
By sex													
M	(291)	.51	(.40)	.62	(.49)	.15	(.29)	.89	(.59)	.54	(.55)	.65	(.44)
F	(238)	.41	(.35)	.45	(.43)	.18	(.26)	.83	(.61)	.53	(.58)	.55	(.39)
Males by age													
3–5	(45)	.53	(.39)	.50	(.33)	.07	(.15)	1.01	(.65)	.67	(.61)	.72	(.40)
6–8	(76)	.50	(.40)	.64	(.45)	.13	(.23)	.93	(.60)	.51	(.51)	.69	(.46)
9–11	(73)	.53	(.38)	.64	(.52)	.18	(.26)	.92	(.60)	.42	(.47)	.66	(.44)
12–14	(59)	.49	(.41)	.66	(.57)	.22	(.44)	.82	(.54)	.58	(.59)	.62	(.45)
15–17	(38)	.47	(.44)	.62	(.55)	.13	(.26)	.70	(.51)	.59	(.58)	.51	(.41)
Females by age													
3–5	(29)	.49	(.35)	.62	(.57)	.10	(.17)	1.15	(.77)	.51	(.59)	.78	(.56)
6–8	(57)	.41	(.28)	.45	(.38)	.19	(.27)	.95	(.59)	.57	(.66)	.59	(.35)
9–11	(55)	.40	(.36)	.43	(.38)	.17	(.28)	.80	(.59)	.49	(.57)	.52	(.34)
12–14	(63)	.39	(.40)	.44	(.45)	.23	(.28)	.72	(.55)	.54	(.53)	.49	(.34)
15–17	(34)	.37	(.33)	.35	(.38)	.19	(.25)	.60	(.55)	.51	(.53)	.42	(.34)

Note. From "Normative Data on the Revised Conners Parent and Teacher Rating Scales" by C. H. Goyette, C. K. Conners, & R. F. Ulrich. *Journal of Abnormal Child Psychology*, 1978, **6**, 221–236. Used with the permission of Plenum Publishing Corp. Copyright © 1978 by Plenum Publishing Corp.

The cumulative percent distributions of parent and teacher mean factor scores may be obtained by writing to the authors.

Table 20.5   Factors and Items for the Revised
Parent Symptom Questionnaire

Factor	Items
I. Conduct Problem	2, 8, 14, 19, 20, 21, 22, 23, 27, 33, 34, 39
II. Learning Problem	10, 25, 31, 37
III. Psychosomatic	32, 41, 43, 44, 48
IV. Impulsive-hyperactive	4, 5, 11, 13
V. Anxiety	12, 16, 24, 47
Hyperactivity Index	4, 7, 11, 13, 14, 25, 31, 33, 38

Note. Adapted from "Normative Data on the Revised
Conners Parent and Teacher Rating Scales" by C.H.
Goyette, C.K. Conners, and R.F. Ulrich. *Journal of
Abnormal Child Psychology,* 1978, **6**, 221–236.

tion. For example, the actometer (Schulman
& Reisman, 1959) is a self-winding, wrist-
watchlike device that measures movement;
the activity recorder (Victor et al., 1973) is a
pedometer type device that is attached to the
child's shirt on the back and measures movement; and the stablimetric cushion (Sprague,
Christiansen, & Werry, 1974) measures movement of the child sitting on it. Foshee (1958)
placed the child's desk on a suspended plat-
form while others have divided a room into
grids (Routh & Schroeder, 1976) or fitted it
with photoelectric cells (Ellis & Pryer, 1959)
or ultrasonic sensors (McFarland, Peacock, &
Watson, 1966). Davis and his colleagues, as
well as others (Davis, Sprague, & Werry,
1969; Herron & Ramsden, 1967), even placed
a radio transmitter in a helmet worn by the
child. In addition, numerous behavioral observation systems have been developed to assess
velocity of movement (Ellis et al., 1974),
restlessness (Blunden, Spring, & Greenberg,
1974), number of times up and out of seat
(Schleifer et al., 1975), vigor of play (Victor et
al., 1973), and length of time with play
equipment (Ellis et al., 1974).

TREATMENT

While there have been few carefully controlled
studies, there is general consensus that play
therapy and relationship therapy relying on
verbal interaction have minimal impact on
hyperactive behavior in children. This may be

due in part to the fact that their behavior is so
disruptive during the therapy session that
little of substance can be accomplished unless
their behavior is brought under better control
to begin with.

From the standpoint of many who are in
charge of managing children's behavior, medication is the treatment of choice for hyperactive children. Virtually every type of medication available has been prescribed for these
children at one time or another. Studying the
prevalence of treatment regimens for children
identified as hyperactive by consensus of
physician, school authorities, and parents,
Lambert, Sandoval, and Sassone (1979) found
that 86 percent of these children had been
given medication at some time. Currently the
most popular medications are the stimulants:
amphetamines (Dexedrine), methylphenidate
(Ritalin), and pemoline (Cylert). Cantwell
and Carlson (1978) provide a thorough review
of the pharmacology and clinical use of stimulant medications. As summarized by these
authors, stimulants are usually prescribed at
the lowest possible dose and titrated upward
until a positive response is obtained or until
side effects are noted. Methylphenidate and
the amphetamines are usually given one to
three times a day in dosages ranging from
.3–1.0 mg/kg and .15–.50 mg/kg respectively.
For pemoline (a longer-acting drug) a dosage
of .5–2.0 mg/kg is administered once a day.
Major tranquilizers such as chlorpromazine
(Thorazine) and thioridazine (Mellaril), tricyclic antidepressants such as imiprimine (Tofranil), and sedatives such as diphenhydram-
ine (Benadryl) have been prescribed for hyperactive children who do not respond to stimulants (Fish, 1975; Gittelman-Klein, Spitzer, &
Cantwell, 1978).

Research on stimulant medications and
hyperactivity has generated a voluminous
body of literature. A number of authors have
reviewed this research (Barkley, 1977; Cantwell & Carlson, 1978; Ross & Ross, 1976;
Safer & Allen, 1976; Whalen & Henker, 1980).
There is general agreement on several points
regarding the treatment of hyperactive children with stimulant medications. First, a
proportion of hyperactive children respond

positively to the medications. Barkley (1977) reported that approximately 75 percent of these children are judged improved when treated with medications. Second, however, while some studies show improved performance on experimental learning tasks, such as learning paired associates, there is no evidence to indicate that actual academic achievement or performance increases with these medications. Thus the child becomes more manageable but does not appear to profit educationally beyond that. Third, numerous researchers have expressed concern about the management of this behavior over a long period of time using medication because of possible unfavorable side effects. Using such medications over long periods of time during the developmental years may have serious consequences that are not yet recognized or fully understood. Many clinicians use "drug holidays" in which the child is removed from the drug on weekends, school vacations, summers, etc., to counteract this effect partially. Side effects most commonly noted are insomnia and decreased appetite. Safer, Allen, and Barr (1972) reported that these medications appeared to result in growth deficits in children taking them regularly. However, later results failed to support this, and the general conclusion at present is that no serious height or weight deficits occur, particularly if drug holidays are employed (Roche et al., 1979).

One final point has to do with the mechanism of activity of the stimulant drugs. These drugs are often described as having a paradoxical effect in hyperactive children since the medication is a stimulant but reduces activity level—possibly because inhibitory centers of the central nervous system are more affected than other centers (though this is purely speculative and the actual mechanism of action is unknown). Recent studies indicate that these medications affect normal children in essentially the same way as they do hyperactive children (Weingartner et al., 1980; Ludlow et al., 1980). Physiologically, both hyperactive and normal children are more aroused. Behaviorally, they demonstrate increased attention span.

In sum, medications have been demonstrated to reduce activity level, making the children more manageable; however, since they do not appear to have equally salutory effects on the learning or performance of these children in other areas and may have side effects when used on a long term basis, there is considerable skepticism about whether or not these medications are the treatment of choice and the final answer to the problem of hyperactivity. In fact, it appears that they are not.

Considerable research has been done on the behavioral management of hyperactive children. Behavioral interventions are regarded as the principal alternatives to treatment with stimulant medications. Also, the complementary use of behavioral and stimulant treatments has recently been emphasized in the literature. Behavioral techniques studied with hyperactive children include contingency management, cognitive-behavior modification, and relaxation/biofeedback. Several comprehensive literature reviews are available on this topic (Mash & Dalby, 1979; O'Leary & O'Leary, 1980).

A review of classroom interventions based on behavioral principles may be found in Ayllon and Rosenbaum (1977). Barkley (1981a, 1981b) has presented a behavioral analysis of parent-child interactions with hyperactive children. He presents a guide for training parents to utilize behavioral techniques that focus on improving compliance and rule-governed behavior. Ayllon, Layman, and Kandel (1975) compared the classroom behavior and academic performance of three hyperactive children while on medication, off medication, and under a token reinforcement program. The token reinforcement system consisted of checks given for correct responses in math and reading. The checks could be exchanged for a variety of back-up reinforcers. Medication and reinforcement of academic performance suppressed hyperactivity to comparable levels. Academic gains were produced by the behavioral program but were not by medication. O'Leary et al. (1976) examined the effect of a home-based reinforcement program on teacher ratings of hyperactivity measured by the Abbreviated Conners Teacher Rating Scale. The program utilized a daily report card noting the child's progress on specified classroom goals. Parents were responsible for rewarding the child's daily behavior at school. After a 10-week treatment period, children treated with the reward program were significantly more improved than those in a control group. The authors noted that ratings of hyperactivity were decreased to a level comparable in magnitude to changes reported with stimulant drugs.

Another interesting approach involves the concept of cognitive self-control. Meichenbaum and Goodman (1971) have accomplished this by teaching the child to maintain a steady stream of self-instructions that serve to bring his behavior under internal control and keep the behavior task-oriented. Others, for example, such as Palkes, Stewart, and Kahana (1968) have taught the child a behavioral formula to use, such as self-directed commands to *stop, look, listen,* and *think* before answering while solving a problem. This, of course, closely resembles the age old approach of "stop, look, and listen" that is used to teach normal children to control their impulsive behavior with regard to street crossing. These cognitively oriented behavioral techniques appear to represent useful and exciting approaches to the management of hyperactivity in children. Meichenbaum (1979) provides a useful review and discussion of the recent literature in this area. Much more research is needed to refine these techniques.

Another interesting behavioral treatment for hyperactivity is the employment of relaxation training or biofeedback. Several studies have demonstrated that, with training in deep muscle relaxation, either using standard relaxation procedures or relaxation training assisted by biofeedback, hyperactive children can develop sufficient control over their behavior to reduce greatly their hyperactivity (e.g., Braud, 1978). The present authors have employed intensive biofeedback with severely hyperactive children with good results in a clinical situation. In this clinical regime, the child was brought to the clinic for three successive days and maintained in the clinic from 8:00 in the morning until 5:00 at night.

Every hour, the child was given 15 minutes of biofeedback training employing tangible rewards and reinforcers for meeting criteria set and revised during the three days of training. The remaining time of each hour was devoted to free play and other relatively unstructured activities. In the cases where this was employed, children were able to learn, through this massed practice biofeedback, sufficient self-control that they were able to return to their classrooms and perform successfully. Currently, more careful research is in the planning stages to further investigate this protocol.

While behavioral treatments are still in the exploratory stages, there is ample evidence that reinforcement programs in other contexts are able to produce significant increments in academic achievement. Thus a secondary benefit from such programs in contrast to medications might well be increased academic achievement. This, however, remains to be demonstrated.

Questions regarding the relative efficacy of the complementary use of behavioral and drug treatments have just begun to be systematically investigated. Wolraich et al. (1978) examined the effects of relatively low dosages of Ritalin alone, behavior modification alone, and the combination of both. In this study, drug treatment was more effective during individual classwork, while behavior modification was more effective during group work. Academic achievement also significantly improved with behavior modification. Lack of any significant interactions between the drug and behavior modification treatment conditions indicated that the treatments did not enhance or detract from one another. However, the authors noted that in some situations a combination of the two might prove more effective than either separately. Gittelman et al. (1980) compared the effects of Ritalin, Ritalin plus behavior modification, and behavior modification with placebo pills on Conners TRS ratings, direct classroom observations, and global ratings of improvements. All three treatments resulted in significant improvement. The combination of Ritalin and behavior modification produced the greatest improvement. Similar results were reported by Pelham et al. (1980).

In terms of the present state of the art, it would appear that a multifaceted treatment package is most likely to result in the greatest amount of success for these youngsters. It would appear that medication might profitably be employed in the early stages of treatment in order to bring the activity level under control and make the child more manageable for other programs. The medication might then be reduced as the child progresses in the treatment program. Along with the medication, behavioral treatments involving training in cognitive self-control as well as relaxation or biofeedback training, along with reinforcement for on-task behavior, would be important components of the treatment regime. Likewise, coaching and training of school teachers and parents in appropriate child management techniques that would be consistent with the behavioral program would be advisable. It appears that this type of treatment package, along with some discussion and modeling for the young person that would lead to improvements in self-concept and reduction of hostile and aggressive behavior, would provide the highest probability of overall success. The present authors do not know of any comprehensive program that has functioned in this manner that has been reported in the literature to date. However, some of the most impressive results have been reported by researchers who have used various combinations of treatment. Development of a multifaceted program as described here would be a very ambitious undertaking but might well prove to be highly successful.

REFERENCES

Abikoff, H., Gittelman-Klein, R., & Klein, D.F. Classroom observation code for hyperactive children: A replication of validity. *Journal of Consulting and Clinical Psychology,* 1980, **48,** 555–565.

American Psychiatric Association. *DSM-III: Diagnostic and statistical manual of mental disorders* (3rd ed.). Washington, D.C.: American Psychiatric Association, 1980.

Ayllon, T., Layman, D., & Kandel, H.J. A behavioral-educational alternative to drug control of hyperactive children. *Journal of Applied Behavioral Analysis,* 1975, **8,** 137–146.

Ayllon, T., & Rosenbaum, M. The behavioral treatment of disruption and hyperactivity in school settings. In B. Lahey & A. Kazdin (Eds.), *Advances in clinical child psychology* (Vol. 1). New York: Plenum, 1977.

Barkley, R.A. A review of stimulant drug research with hyperactive children. *Journal of Child Psychology and Psychiatry,* 1977, **18,** 137–165.

Barkley, R.A. Hyperactivity. In E.J. Mash & L.G. Terdal (Eds.), *Behavioral assessment of childhood disorders.* New York: Guilford, 1981. (a)

Barkley, R.A. *Hyperactive children: A handbook for diagnosis and treatment.* New York: Guilford, 1981. (b)

Barkley, R.A., & Ullman, D.C. A comparison of objective measures of activity and distractibility in hyperactive and nonhyperactive children. *Journal of Abnormal Child Psychology,* 1975, **3,** 231–244.

Blunden, D., Spring, C., & Greenberg, L.M. Validation of the classroom behavior inventory. *Journal of Consulting and Clinical Psychology,* 1974, **42,** 84–88.

Braud, L.W. The effects of frontal EMG biofeedback and progressive relaxation upon hyperactivity and its behavioral concomitants. *Biofeedback and Self-Regulation,* 1978, **3,** 69–89.

Campbell, S.B., & Paulaukas, S. Peer relations in hyperactive children. *Journal of Child Psychology and Psychiatry,* 1979, **20,** 233–246.

Cantwell, D.P. Psychiatric illness in the families of hyperactive children. *Archives of General Psychiatry,* 1972, **27,** 414–417.

Cantwell, D.P. *The hyperactive child.* New York: Spectrum, 1975.

Cantwell, D.P., & Carlson, G.A. Stimulants. In J.S. Werry (Ed.), *Pediatric psychopharmacology: The use of behavior modifying drugs in children.* New York: Brunner Mazel, 1978.

Clements, S.D. *Minimal brain dysfunction in children—Terminology and identification* (USPHS Publication No. 1415). Washington, D.C.: U.S. Government Printing Office, 1966.

Conners, C.K. A teacher rating scale for use in drug studies with children. *American Journal of Psychiatry,* 1969, **126,** 884–888.

Conners, C.K. Symptom patterns in hyperkinetic,

neurotic, and normal children. *Child Development,* 1970, **41**, 667–682.

Conners, C.K. Rating scales for use in drug studies with children. *Psychopharmacology Bulletin* 1973, (Special issue: Pharmacotherapy of children), 24–84.

Conners, C.K. *Food additives and hyperactive children.* New York: Plenum, 1980.

Davis, K.U., Sprague, R.L., & Werry, J.S. Stereotyped behavior and activity level in severe retardates: The effects of drugs. *American Journal of Mental Deficiency,* 1969, **72**, 721–727.

Douglas, V.I. Higher mental processes in hyperactive children. In R.M. Knights & D.J. Bakker (Eds.), *Treatment of hyperactive and learning disordered children.* Baltimore: University Park Press, 1980.

Dubey, D.R. Organic factors in hyperkinesis: A critical review. *American Journal of Orthopsychiatry,* 1976, **46**, 353–366.

Ellis, M.J., Witt, P.A., Reynolds, R., & Sprague, R.L. Methylphenidate and the activity of hyperactives in the informal setting. *Child Development,* 1974, **45**, 217–220.

Ellis, N.R., & Pryer, R. Quantification of gross bodily activity in children with severe neuropathology. *American Journal of Mental Deficiency,* 1959, **63**, 1034–1037.

Feingold, B.F. *Why your child is hyperactive.* New York: Random House, 1975.

Ferguson, H.B., & Trites, R.L. Predicting response of hyperactive children to Ritalin. In R.M. Knights & D.J. Bakker (Eds.), *Treatment of hyperactive and learning disabled children.* Baltimore: University Park Press, 1980.

Firestone, P., & Martin, J.E. An analysis of the hyperactive syndrome: A comparison of hyperactive, behavior problem, asthmatic and normal children. *Journal of Abnormal Child Psychology,* 1979, **7**, 261–273.

Fish, B. Stimulant drug treatment of hyperactive children. In D.P. Cantwell (Ed.), *The hyperactive child.* New York: Spectrum, 1975.

Foshee, J. Studies in activity level: I. Simple and complex task performance in defectives. *American Journal of Mental Deficiency,* 1958, **62**, 882–886.

Gittelman, R., Abikoff, H., Pollack, E., Klein, D.F., Datz, S., & Mattes, J. A controlled trial of behavior modification and methylphenidate in hyperactive children. In C.K. Whalen

& B. Henker (Eds.), *Hyperactive children: The social ecology of identification and treatment.* New York: Academic Press, 1980.

Gittelman-Klein, R., Spitzer, R.L., & Cantwell, D.P. Diagnostic classifications and psychopharmacological indications. In J.S. Werry (Eds.), *Pediatric psychopharmacology: The use of behavior modifying drugs in children.* New York: Brunner Mazel, 1978.

Goyette, C.H., Conners, C.K., & Ulrich, R.F. Normative data on revised parents and teacher rating scales. *Journal of Abnormal Child Psychology,* 1978, **6**, 221–236.

Harley, J.P., & Matthews, C.G. Food additives and hyperactivity in children: Experimental investigations. In R.M. Knights & D.J. Bakker (Eds.), *Treatment of hyperactive and learning disabled children.* Baltimore: University Park Press, 1980.

Hastings, J.E., & Barkley, R.A. A review of psychophysiological research with hyperactive children. *Journal of Abnormal Child Psychology,* 1978, **6**, 413–447.

Herron, R., & Ramsden, R. Continuous monitoring of overt human body movement by radio telemetry: A brief review. *Perceptual and Motor Skills,* 1967, **24**, 1303–1308.

Hoy, E., Weiss, G., Minde, K., & Cohen, N. The hyperactive child at adolescence: Cognitive emotional, and social functioning. *Journal of Abnormal Child Psychology,* 1978, **6**, 311–324.

Kenny, T.J., Clemmons, R.L., Hudson, B.W., Lentz, G.A., Cilli, R., & Nair, P. Characteristics of children referred because of hyperactivity. *Journal of Pediatrics,* 1971, **79**, 618–622.

Kinsbourne, M. Minimal brain dysfunction as a neurodevelopmental lag. *Annals of the New York Academy of Sciences,* 1973, **205**, 268–273.

Lahey, B.J., Green, K.D., & Forehand, R. On the independence of ratings of hyperactivity conduct problems, and attention deficits in children: A multiple regression analysis. *Journal of Consulting and Clinical Psychology* 1980, **48**, 566–574.

Lambert, N., & Sandoval, J. The prevalence of learning disabilities in a sample of children considered hyperactive. *Journal of Abnormal Child Psychology,* 1980, **8**, 33–50.

Lambert, N.M., Sandoval, J., & Sassone, D. Prevalence of hyperactivity in elementary school children as a function of social system definers. *American Journal of Orthopsychiatry,* 1978, **48,** 446–463.

Lambert, N.M., Sandoval, J., & Sassone, D. Prevalence of treatment regimens for children considered to be hyperactive. *American Journal of Orthopsychiatry,* 1979, **49,** 482–494.

Laufer, M.W., & Denhoff, E. Hyperkinetic behavior syndrome in children. *Journal of Pediatrics,* 1957, **50,** 463–473.

Loney, J. The intellectual functioning of hyperactive elementary school boys: A cross-sectional investigation. *American Journal of Orthopsychiatry,* 1974, **44,** 754–762.

Loney, J., Langhorne, J.E., & Paternite, C.E. An empirical basis for subgrouping the hyperkinetic/minimal brain dysfunction syndrome. *Journal of Abnormal Psychology,* 1978, **87,** 431–441.

Ludlow, C.L., Rappoport, J., Bassich, C.J., & Mikkelsen, E.G. Differential effects of dextroamphetamine on language performance in hyperactive and normal children. In R.M. Knights & D.J. Bakker (Eds.), *Treatment of hyperactive and learning disabled children.* Baltimore: University Park Press, 1980.

Mash, E.J., & Dalby, J.T. Behavior interventions for hyperactivity. In R.L. Trites (Ed.), *Hyperactivity in children.* Baltimore: University Park Press, 1979.

McFarland, N.J., Peacock, L.J., & Watson, J.A. Mental retardation and activity levels in rats and children. *American Journal of Mental Deficiency,* 1966, **71,** 381–386.

Meichenbaum, D.H. Teaching children self-control. In B. Taley & A. Kazden (Eds.), *Advances in child clinical psychology.* New York: Plenum, 1979.

Meichenbaum, D.H., & Goodman, J. Training impulsive children to talk to themselves: A means of developing self-control. *Journal of Abnormal Psychology,* 1971, **77,** 115–126.

Milich, R., & Loney, J. The role of hyperactive and aggressive symptomatology in predicting adolescent outcome among hyperactive children. *Journal of Pediatric Psychology,* 1979, **4,** 93–112.

Minde, K., Lewis, D., Weiss, G., Lavigueur, H., Douglas, V., & Sykes, E. The hyperactive child in elementary school: A 5 year controlled followup. *Exceptional Children,* 1971, **38,** 215–221.

Morrison, J.R., & Stewart, M.A. A family study of the hyperactive child syndrome. *Biological Psychiatry,* 1971, **3,** 189–195.

Morrison, J.R., & Stewart, M.A. The psychiatric status of legal families of adopted hyperactive children. *Archives of General Psychiatry,* 1973, **28,** 888–891. (a)

Morrison, J.R., & Stewart, M.A. Evidence for polygenetic inheritance in the hyperactive child syndrome. *American Journal of Psychiatry,* 1973, **130,** 791–792. (b)

Morrison, J.R., & Stewart, M.A. Bilateral inheritance as evidence for polygenicity in the hyperactive child syndrome. *Journal of Nervous and Mental Disease,* 1974, **158,** 226–228.

O'Leary, K.D., Pelham, W.E., Rosenbaum, A., & Price, G.H. Behavioral treatment of hyperkinetic children. *Clinical Pediatrics,* 1976, **15,** 510–515.

O'Leary, S.G., & O'Leary, K.D. Behavioral treatment for hyperactive children. In R.M. Knights & D.J. Bakker (Eds.), *Treatment of hyperactive and learning disabled children.* Baltimore: University Park Press, 1980.

Palkes, H., Stewart, M., & Kahana, B. Maze performance of hyperactive boys after training in self-directed verbal commands. *Child Development,* 1968, **39,** 817–826.

Paternite, C.E., & Loney, J. Childhood hyperkinesis: Relationships between symptomatology and home environment. In C.K. Whalen & B. Henker (Eds.), *Hyperactive children: The social ecology of identification and treatment.* New York: Academic Press, 1980.

Paternite, C.E., Loney, J., & Langhorne, J.E. Relationships between symptomatology and SES-related factors in hyperkinetic/MBD boys. *American Journal of Orthospsychiatry,* 1976, **46,** 291–301.

Pelham, W.E., Schnedler, R.W., Bologna, N.C., & Contreras, J.A. Behavioral and stimulant treatment of hyperactive children: A therapy study with methylphenidate probes in a within-subject design. *Journal of Applied Behavioral Analysis,* 1980, **13,** 221–236.

Prinze, R.J., Roberts, W.A., & Hantman, E. Dietary correlates of hyperactive behavior in children. *Journal of Consulting and Clinical Psychology,* 1980, **48,** 760–769.

Rapoport, J.L., Quinn, P.O., & Lamprecht, F. Minor physical anomalies and plasma dopamine-beta-hydroxylose activity in hyperactivity boys. *American Journal of Psychiatry,* 1974, **131,** 386–390.

Roberts, M., & LaGreca, A.M. Behavioral assessment. In C.E. Walker (Ed.), *Clinical practice of psychology.* New York: Pergamon, 1981.

Roche, A.F., Lipman, R.S., Overall, J.E., & Hung, W. The effects of stimulant medication on the growth of hyperactive children. *Pediatrics,* 1979, **63,** 847–850.

Rose, T.L. The functional relationship between artificial food colors and hyperactivity. *Journal of Applied Behavioral Analysis,* 1978, **11,** 439–449.

Rosenthal, R.H., & Allen, T.W. An examination of attention, arousal, and learning dysfunctions of hyperactive children. *Psychological Bulletin,* 1978, **85,** 689–715.

Ross, A.O. *Psychological aspects of learning disorders and reading disabilities.* New York: McGraw-Hill, 1976.

Ross, D.M., & Ross, S.A. *Hyperactivity: Research, theory, and action.* New York: Wiley, 1976.

Routh, D. Hyperactivity. In P. Magrab (Eds.), *Psychological management of pediatric problems* (Vol. 2). Baltimore: University Park Press, 1978.

Routh, D.K., & Schroeder, C.S. Standardized playroom measures as indices of hyperactivity in children. *Developmental Psychology,* 1976, **10,** 163–168.

Routh, D.K., Schroeder, C.S., & O'Tuama, L. Development of activity level in children. *Developmental Psychology,* 1974, **10,** 163–168.

Rutter, M. Syndromes attributed to minimal brain dysfunction in childhood. *American Journal of Psychiatry,* 1982, **139,** 21–33.

Safer, D.J., & Allen, R.P. *Hyperactive children: Diagnosis and management.* Baltimore: University Park Press, 1976.

Safer, D.J., Allen, R.P., & Barr, E. Depression of growth in hyperactive children on stimulant drugs. *New England Journal of Medicine,* 1972, **287,** 217–220.

Sandberg, S.T., Rutter, M., & Taylor, E. Hyperkinetic disorder in psychiatric clinic attenders. *Developmental Medicine and Child Neurology,* 1978, **20,** 279–299.

Sandberg, S.T., Wieselberg, M., & Shaffer, D. Hyperkinetic and conduct problem children in a primary school population: Some epidemio-

logical considerations. *Journal of Child Psychology and Psychiatry,* 1980, **21,** 293–311.

Sandoval, J. The measurement of the hyperactive syndrome in children. *Review of Education Research,* 977, **47,** 293–318.

Schleifer, M., Weiss, G., Cohen, N., Elman, M., Cvejil, H., & Kruger, E. Hyperactivity in preschoolers and the effect of methylphenidate. *American Journal of Orthopsychiatry,* 1975, **45,** 38–50.

Schulman, J., & Reisman, J. An objective measure of hyperactivity. *American Journal of Mental Deficiency,* 1959, **64,** 455–464.

Sprague, R.L., Christensen, D.E., & Werry, J.S. Experimental psychology and stimulant drugs. In C. Conners (Ed.), *Clinical use of stimulant drugs in children.* Amsterdam: Excerpta Medica, 1974.

Stewart, M.A., DeBlois, C.S., & Cummings, C. Psychiatric disorder in the parents of hyperactive boys and those with conduct disorder. *Journal of Child Psychology and Psychiatry,* 1980, **21,** 283–292.

Strauss, A.A., & Kephart, N.C. *Psychopathology and education of the brain injured child* (Vol. 2). New York: Grune & Stratton, 1955.

Strauss, A.A., & Lehtinen, L.E. *Psychopathology and education of the brain-injured child.* New York: Grune & Stratton, 1947.

Swanson, J.M., & Kinsbourne, M. Artificial color and hyperactive behavior. In R.M. Knights & D.J. Bakker (Eds.), *Treatment of hyperactive and learning disabled children.* Baltimore: University Park Press, 1980.

Trites, R.L., Dugas, E., Lynch, G., & Ferguson, H.B. Prevalence of hyperactivity. *Journal of Pediatric Psychology,* 1979, **4,** 179–188.

Trites, R.L., Tryphonas, H., & Ferguson, H.B. Diet treatment for hyperactive children with food allergies. In R.M. Knights & D.J. Bakker (Eds.), *Treatment of hyperactive and learning disabled children.* Baltimore: University Park Press, 1980.

Victor, J.B., Halverson, C.F., Inoff, G., & Buczkowski, H.J. Objective behavior measures of first and second grade boys' free play and teachers' ratings on a behavior problem checklist. *Psychology in the Schools,* 1973, **10,** 439–443.

Waldrop, M.F., Pederson, F.A., & Bell, R.O. Minor physical anomalies in preschool children. *Child Development,* 1968, **39,** 391–400.

Weingartner, H., Rapoport, J.L., Buchsbaum, M.S., Bunney, W.E., Ebert, M.H., Mikkelson, E.J., & Caine, E.D. Cognitive processes in normal and hyperactive children and their response to amphetamine treatment. *Journal of Abnormal Psychology,* 1980, **89,** 25–37.

Weiss, G., Hechtman, L., Perlman, T., Hopkins, J., & Wener, A. Hyperactives as young adults. *Archives of General Psychiatry,* 1979, **36,** 675–681.

Wender, P.H. *Minimal brain dysfunction in children.* New York: Wiley-Interscience, 1971.

Werry, J.S. Developmental hyperactivity. *Pediatric Clinics of North America,* 1968, **15,** 581–599.

Whalen, C.K., & Henker, B. (Eds.). *Hyperactive children: The social ecology of identification and treatment.* New York: Academic Press, 1980.

Wolraich, M., Drummond, T., Solomon, M.K., O'Brien, M.L., & Sivage, C. Effects of methylphenidate alone and in combination with behavior modification procedures on the behavior and academic performance of hyperactive children. *Journal of Abnormal Child Psychology,* 1978, **6,** 149–161.

Zukow, P.G., Zukow, A.H.K. & Bentler, P.J. Rating scales for the identification and treatment of hyperkinesis. *Journal of Consulting and Clinical Psychology,* 1978, **46,** 213–222.

CHAPTER 21

Childhood Neuroses

STEPHEN J. DOLLINGER

How one chooses to define childhood neurosis is usually very diagnostic of one's overall approach to personality and psychotherapy. Those whose definition involves unconscious, internalized conflict view neuroses as inherently part of the individual's total personality organization. The symptom, then, is merely a surface manifestation of underlying conflict, defense, and anxiety. Such is the view of psychodynamic formulations. Alternatively, one can dispense with concepts such as anxiety and personality and emphasize overt behavioral excesses or deficits acquired through learning processes (e.g., classical or operant conditioning). Within such a framework—the behavioral or social-learning model—the symptom and the contingencies maintaining it constitute the problem. A less dogmatic and more cognitive social-learning viewpoint would allow that the symptom is also interdependent upon functionally related behaviors and self-perceptions, the sum of which constitutes personality. Within this framework, nonsymptomatic behaviors (e.g., orderliness) might be seen as correlating with, and perhaps contributing to, a neurotic symptom such as obsessive rituals.

Other viewpoints have been offered for defining and conceptualizing the etiology of neurosis. For example, most practicing clinicians would agree that constitutional factors such as temperament (Thomas & Chess, 1977) contribute to the development of neurotic disorders. In addition, some authors have taken a more extreme position in viewing neurosis within a medical model. For example, Elkins, Rapoport, and Lipsky (1980) view a number of twin studies, psychopharmacological studies, and other areas as supporting a neurobiological hypothesis for etiology of obsessive-compulsive disorder. It is also possible to reject the view that psychopathology is to be found in individuals in favor of exploring systemic issues and interactions (e.g., child within family, family within community) for the source of a particular disorder (e.g., Haley, 1977; Madanes, 1981).

Given the multitude of viewpoints, it is appropriate that the most recent *Diagnostic and Statistical Manual of Mental Disorders* or *DSM-III* (American Psychiatric Association, 1980) takes an atheoretical position. Thus, within *DSM-III,* neurotic disorder (as distinguished from neurotic process) is defined descriptively as a disorder in which symptoms are distressing and unacceptable to an individual whose reality testing is basically intact.

In keeping with a descriptive definition, we will take up the several clusters of problems traditionally viewed under the rubric of childhood neurosis, at the same time highlighting aspects of the major viewpoints on each disorder.

OBSESSIVE-COMPULSIVE DISORDER OF CHILDHOOD

Suppose we wished to develop a "compulsive" adjective checklist to identify the child with an obsessive personality style. Such a checklist probably would look something like this:

Absolutistic	Moralistic
Belittling others	Obstinate
Boringly literal	Orderly
Constricted	Overly cautious
Deliberate	Overly serious
Egocentric	Perfectionistic
Fussy	Pseudomature
Frugal	Rigidly guarded
Humorless	Ruminative
Inflexible	Sarcastic
Introspective	Scrupulous
Lacking	Self-doubting
spontaneity	Stubborn
Meticulous	Timid

No doubt we could add to this list. Nevertheless, this cluster of adjectives drawn from throughout the literature conveys a sense of the major stylistic features of the obsessive personality. According to traditional wisdom, it is just such a child who is likely to develop the symptoms of obsessive-compulsive disorder: intrusive ideas or impulses combined with a sense of compulsion to give in to the impulse and the feeling that the compulsion must be resisted. This is the dilemma of the child who seeks or is brought for treatment of obsessive-compulsive hand washing, counting, checking, or other repetitive, irrational, and unwanted rituals.

The Disorder

Obsessive-compulsive disorder is relatively infrequent in childhood. One classic report estimated the incidence of this disorder at 1.2 percent in child psychiatric populations (Judd, 1965). However, a later study covering a wider time interval for the same psychiatric setting provided an estimated incidence of .2 percent (Hollingsworth et al., 1980). Typically, the obsessive child demonstrates above average intellectual functioning, although some authors believe intelligence to be a correlate rather than a prerequisite of the obsessive-compulsive symptom complex (Adams, 1973). The disorder appears to occur most frequently among children of middle socioeconomic class backgrounds (Adams, 1973).

In his 1965 report, Judd noted that religion played an important role in three of his five families. The common element seemed to be a strict adherence to religious principle. Similarly, Weisner and Riffel (1960) reported on their experience with a number of obsessive children of a Catholic background who exhibited scrupulosity. For such children, the notion of sin became so generalized as to be totally constricting. For example, some of these children came to believe that eating, breathing, coughing, and bathing with the lights on were sinful. Weisner and Riffel noted that, while their mothers were upset by the children's obsessive-compulsive behavior, they felt privileged to have such religious children.

As with other neurotic disorders, it is important to distinguish between those aspects of the symptom picture that might be considered normal and those that fall outside the range of normal limits. Judd (1965) highlights this issue by citing the common observation of the child who meticulously walks down a sidewalk stepping on or avoiding certain cracks. Similarly, the rituals surrounding bedtime (e.g., repetitiously saying goodnight) occur less frequently as children mature.

Likewise, the obsessive intellectuality shown by some *normal* teenagers may reflect their way of handling the anxiety associated with heightened sexual drive during adolescence (A. Freud, 1937/1966; Kessler, 1972). At the opposite extreme, several authors have commented that obsessive-compulsive reactions are often implicated in the development of *psychotic* disorder (Judd, 1965; Hollingsworth et al., 1980).

Other noteworthy distinctions within the symptom complex have been offered. Judd (1965) and others have commented on the distinction between thought and action as characterizing the difference between obsession and compulsion. Kessler (1972) has offered the important observation that therapists should distinguish between compulsions that resist temptation and those that yield to it (e.g., fetishes). Presumably compulsive masturbation (Janzen & Peacock, 1978; Wagner, 1968) falls into the latter category—that is, a behavior that more centrally involves a primary gratification rather than the gratification of reduced anxiety characteristic of neurosis.

Based on his extensive psychotherapeutic work with obsessive children, Adams (1973) has abstracted a number of common values held by the children. Included in Adams' list are: respect for thought or thinking (internalization); respect for fog or murkiness (obscurantism); respect for intellect ("loving one's IQ"); a view of life as "a power struggle" and one-upmanship; a preoccupation with death; and a striving to guarantee self-preservation and safety (avoiding risks, particularly in relationships).

These values bear a close resemblance to the characteristic defensive maneuvers of the obsessive child. Commonly used defenses against unwanted impulses include isolation of affect, ceremonialism, displacement, undoing, and reaction formation (Adams, 1973; Karush, 1979; Kessler, 1972). Such defenses can be seen in the child's symptomatic behavior, in the child's characteristic ways of approaching interpersonal relations, and often in his or her schoolwork. Recognition of the child's defensive style serves a useful diagnostic function within a psychodynamic framework. In particular, the child's defensive style can aid in distinguishing the obsessive-compulsive disorder from other diagnostic pictures that are occasionally quite similar, including phobia, depression, and schizophrenia. A similar understanding of the child's defensive style is less useful in behavioral therapies focusing directly on the child's symptom. (However, they can be relevant if defenses are conceptualized as covert operants functionally related to and supporting the presenting problems.)

Before considering more interpersonal and familial issues, the child's cognitive style deserves mention. The obsessive child is ostensibly quite mature: he or she shows advanced intellectual competencies, is likely to show a very reflective style on tests of conceptual tempo (Kagan, 1971), and sets high standards for his or her own performance. Nevertheless, the obsessive child seems to retain a number of immature forms in his or her thought processes. Adams (1973) considers the child's obsessions to be *ipso facto* evidence of cognitive pathology. Other immature cognitive processes are seen in the child's use of "magical thinking" (e.g., seen in superstitious "undoing" rituals) and in the obsessive's "black and white" manner of categorizing reality— what Zetzel (1966) calls "inexorable either-or categories." While many obsessive children may seem to value their obsessions (and are often subtly reinforced by parents for their obsessive style), such children are typically bright enough to recognize some of the cognitive immaturity involved. This self-reflexive capacity may give rise to an obsessive "worrying about worrying" (cf. Kanner, 1972).

Family Characteristics

Several authors have commented on the degree of psychological disorder in the families of obsessive children (Hollingsworth et al., 1980; Judd, 1965). In particular, the parents of such children frequently show obsessive-compulsive neurosis themselves. Hollingsworth et al. (1980) also found marital discord, depression, schizophrenia, and a high frequency of serious medical illness among parents in their sample. Pollak's (1979) review also suggests a relationship between obsessive-compulsive personality in parents and in offspring.

At a more dynamic level, Adams (1973) commented on the ambivalent, sadomasochistic attachment of the obsessive child and his or her mother. While experiencing an intense separation anxiety, the child nevertheless is locked in a battle for autonomy and control with the mother. Adams also offered several prescriptions for childrearing designed to produce an obsessive child: try to cover brutality with sweet "undoing" talk; try to "talk away" feelings instead of accepting them; encourage the frightened child to "pray again"; and tell the child with nightmares to think good thoughts instead. The latter pre-

prescription is similar to a strategy encountered by the author in the case of an obsessive adolescent—during his childhood, the mother would tell the boy that she had not given permission for him to have nightmares.

Little has been written about obsessive disorders in children from a family-systems viewpoint. Given that obsessive thinking is commonly involved in the clinical picture of anorexia nervosa, the work of Minuchin, Rosman, and Baker (1978) with anorectic families provides a framework that will surely have heuristic value for future work with families presenting an obsessive child. Minuchin has observed a number of common themes in the family structure of anorectic families that seem to contribute to the development and maintenance of the disorder. Briefly, these qualities are:

1. *Enmeshment.* The highly diffuse boundaries around family subsystems and family members are such that changes within one family member reverberate throughout the system. Boundaries are so weak and easily crossed that, for example, a child can intrude on (or take over) the parental functions toward his or her siblings.

2. *Overprotectiveness.* This is shown in family members' high degree of concern for each others' welfare, retarding the child's development of competence, autonomy, and extrafamilial interests.

3. *Rigidity.* This is seen in the inability of a family to develop new and more adaptive rules and roles as the family goes through the stages of its own life cycle.

4. *Failures in conflict resolution.* Conflict is detoured through the interventions of the identified patient. (Conflicts are frequently suppressed under the guise of a strong religious or ethical code.)

While Minuchin and his colleagues have focused their attention on psychosomatic (e.g., anorectic) families, these characteristics seem applicable to many neurotic families as well.

Such characteristics are especially noticeable within families whose identified patient is an obsessive school phobic boy.

Peer Relations

Since the "obsessive child's life *is usually the mother*" (Adams, 1973, p. 72), it is not surprising to find that peer interactions are unsatisfying. Such a child often prefers to play alone and when forced to be with other children, as at school, will frequently make sarcastic and belittling comments toward peers. Moreover, the "obsessive child" is a favored target of such comments or labels as "weirdo," "queer," or "sissy" by other children. Occasionally, a friendship will develop on the basis of a common interest, especially one in which the peer is a novice and the obsessive child an expert. Such friendships prove short lived when the obsessive child fails to accommodate to, or tries to take advantage of, a new friend. For example, one such child established a friendship based on his interest in World War II. After several weeks of pleasant and increasing interaction, the friendship dissolved when the new friend refused to join a war book club from which the obsessive child hoped to receive several free books.

Treatment

As is true throughout the child therapy literature, there are distinct and diametrically opposing viewpoints on the appropriate treatment for obsessive-compulsive neurosis. It is perhaps of some interest that the psychodynamic/behavioral paradigm clash is quite abrasive when it comes to the treatment of obsessive-compulsive disorders in children. Parenthetically, we might note that abrasive commentary also appears frequently in the literatures on elective mutism and anorexia nervosa. This commonality gives us a clue to the significance of such paradigmatic clashes since obsessives, elective mutes, and anorectics are among the most frustrating and stubborn children seen by child therapists. Perhaps the paradigmatic clash itself reflects a kind of defensive projection. In any case, the literature contains some specific suggestions for therapists of both orientations.

From a more or less traditional psychodynamic framework, Adams (1973) employs a variety of therapeutic stategies in individual therapy. These strategies directly follow from and challenge the obsessive child's values (noted above). Specifically, Adams encourages the child to: (1) give examples and communicate clearly (countering the "fog" value); (2) focus on day-to-day concerns; (3) participate in a relationship—with the therapist—that "can be talked about, discussed and questioned....[and] will end" (p. 214); (4) experience and label affects—the "feelings are in" strategy; (5) be frank and truthful; (6) "keep it clean," that is, state his or her thoughts simply and directly. (When necessary, Adams restates "simply" what the child has said "obsessively."); (7) take a chance, take risks; and (8) use language that describes what the child needs "to be cured"—phrases like "at ease," "natural," and "letting loose."

While not presenting results quantitatively, Adams (1973) noted a number of qualitative changes across his 49 patients including reduction in the obsessive-compulsive symptom, changes in other related behaviors indicative of greater spontaneity, increased self-esteem and ego strength, superego changes (in the direction of more personalized values), and improved interpersonal relations. Other useful expositions on psychodynamic therapy of the obsessive child have been presented by Cass (1967) and Chethik (1969).

Within a traditional framework such as Adams's, play therapy is particularly appropriate because, quite simply, the child needs to learn *how* to play. Adams (1973) and others (e.g., Karush, 1979) contend that what the child does *not* need is a symptom-oriented behavioral treatment that, in their view, is itself obsessive. This issue was addressed in a humorous way by Wikler, Green, and Wikler (1979) in a fictional case study of a behavior modifier who began to suffer from the too systematic application of behavioral principles to his own behavior—he developed the paradoxical problem of compulsive self-monitoring (see also Dollinger, 1979a). While this

argument may have an intuitive appeal, the limited data available tend to suggest that behavioral approaches can eliminate childhood obsessive-compulsive disorder w .hout symptom substitution. In one of the first papers in this area, Weiner (1967) treated an adolescent male with multiple rituals (washing, dressing, locker checking, and others). Initially, simple self-monitoring of rituals seemed to exacerbate the symptoms. However, the pervasive rituals were replaced with delimited ones (combined with positive rationales for engaging in rituals), and this reduced or eliminated the original, more disruptive rituals. This approach, which Adams (1973) incorrectly criticizes as an operant approach, seems more appropriately labeled a strategic therapy approach utilizing reframing and symptom prescription (Rabkin, 1977; Watzlawick, Weakland, & Fisch, 1974). Hersen (1968) used an implosive therapy approach with a 12-year-old boy presenting various dressing and cleaning rituals in addition to school phobia. The behavioral strategies were used after only limited success was obtained with weekly psychodynamic therapy utilizing free association, catharsis, and interpretation. (The major gain from this therapy was elimination of pain in the genitals.) Hersen instructed this boy to visualize the settings for his rituals but with critical elements of the rituals eliminated or changed. This procedure elicited considerable anxiety even for the least anxiety-provoking situation (i.e., that connected with the lowest item on a ritual hierarchy). Repeated presentations resulted in dissipation of the anxiety. By the tenth such session, rituals had been given up, and related anxiety dreams (dreams of physical injury and dismemberment) had also decreased in frequency. Further therapy efforts addressed the boy's school phobia and other family issues.

Procedurally dissimilar but conceptually similar to the Hersen report was a case presented recently by Stanley (1980). Stanley employed contingency management and response prevention in the treatment of an 8-year-old girl who engaged in singing, counting, and physical arrangement rituals. Family members attempted to change their own behaviors that accommodated to and inadvertently reinforced the girl's rituals. Additionally, her parents prevented her from engaging in rituals by verbal means (physical restraint was not used). The child was quite anxious for two days but soon began to relax and give up her symptoms and had done so completely within two weeks. No symptom substitution was reported.

Another recent case utilized contingency management and a self-control procedure with a 9-year-old boy presenting contamination fears, hand washing, and touching compulsions (DiNardo & DiNardo, 1981). One important aspect of this case was resolution of family members' cooperation with rituals (e.g., mother's cooperation by changing the boy's bedsheets 2–4 times per night). Additionally, the boy was trained in self-relaxation/ desensitization combined with coping imagery. The combination of these procedures eliminated the boy's problems and follow-ups showed no recurrence at six months or one year after treatment.

Other clinical studies have suggested the utility of behavioral procedures when combined with other therapies. Fine (1973) treated 2 boys, ages 11 and 9, for a variety of rituals and compulsions, using symptom interruption within a broader framework of family therapy. More recently, Kellerman (1981) employed thought stopping and covert reinforcement in combination with hypnosis and a variant of "prescribing the symptom" for a 12-year-old boy with homicidal obsessions. During two years following successful treatment, the boy was seen occasionally for brief consultations about minor adjustment issues. During this time, a homicidal obsessive thought was noted only once.

In addition to these reports, several papers have presented positive findings on behavioral procedures for treating fascination with electrical devices and compulsive light-switching rituals (Ayllon, Garber, & Allison, 1977; Rincover, Newsom, & Carr, 1979). However, as noted by Rincover et al. (1979) such behavior may be more appropriately conceptualized as under direct reinforcement control rather than reinforcement through anxiety reduction. As such, the behavior may be associated with other nonneurotic childhood disorders (e.g., developmental delay, conduct disorder).

In general, then, it appears that the behavioral approach can be effective in treating obsessive-compulsive disorders of childhood. By implication, an obsessive therapy approach can help an obsessive. While perhaps counterintuitive, acceptance of this possibility may open the door to a variety of paradoxical but promising treatment strategies. As noted above, Weiner (1967) actually prescribed variations of the child's rituals as part of treatment. More recently, the successful symptom prescription of rituals has been presented by therapists treating adult obsessions (Rabavilas, Boulougouris, & Stefanis, 1977) and the eating rituals of adolescent anorectics (Rosen, 1980). Finally, it should be noted that ritual can be used effectively in the family therapy of various neurotic and other problems (Palazzoli et al., 1977, 1978).

Other Symptom Pictures

On occasion, the obsessive disorder will be manifested in nervous habits such as ticlike behaviors or chronic trichotillomania (hairpulling). Such behaviors may also be associated with other nonneurotic disorders. (For a greater exposition on such habitual disorders, see Matthews, chap. 16 of this book.)

PHOBIC DISORDERS OF CHILDHOOD

The brevity of the present comments on phobia will not reflect the importance and clinical incidence of such conditions. In part, this neglect reflects the overlap between childhood phobia and obsession (Adams, 1973; Ajuriaguerra, 1977/1980). And, in part, phobias will be given less attention here because of the excellent companion chapter devoted exclusively to childhood fears (chap. 14 by Miller).

Definition and Theory

Phobias are severe and unreasonable fears of specific persons, objects, or situations. Relatively minor and transient fears are extremely common in childhood and can be regarded as universal and not inherently pathological. To be considered phobic, the child's fears must be both severe and irrational (or unreasonable) to the circumstances and thereby produce major inconvenience or distress for the child and his or her family. Graziano, De Giovanni, and Garcia (1979) suggest the definition of a clinical fear as one of two years duration and/or sufficiently intense as to disrupt the child's routine lifestyle.

While such features will always be relevant diagnostic considerations, others include the child's temperament (Thomas & Chess, 1977) and the presence or absence of related features in the child's behavioral style (sensitivity, timidity in verbal and motor behavior with strangers and with peers). Occasionally, one will encounter fearful children who are, nevertheless, quite tyrannical and controlling of their families (Barcai & Rosenthal, 1974).

While there is an extensive literature concerning childhood fears, many studies are of a survey nature that does not afford an easy or unquestionable distinction between fear and phobia (Kessler, 1972). Nevertheless, it is interesting that mothers report fewer fears in their children than the children report about themselves (Lapouse & Monk, 1959). A similar difference exists in children's and mothers' reports of children sleeping problems (Csikszentmihalyi & Graef, 1975). Not surprisingly, mother-child correspondence in fear reports increases with age (Staley, 1979). In a clinical setting, then, we might well question the severity of a fear reported only by the child unless there is good reason to doubt the veracity of parent-reported data.

Kessler (1972) suggests that phobias may develop in any of five ways. First, a parent's warnings about something may create a fear of that object. Second, phobias can develop through classical conditioning in which a neutral object comes to elicit fear by its association with another, feared object. Third, according to Kessler, is the child's own imagination giving rise to misunderstandings. Fourth, a child might develop a phobic reaction by modeling his or her behavior on that of someone with whom a positive identification exists. Finally, Kessler points to the classical psychoanalytic view of phobias as a defense against unconscious impulses striving for expression. To this list perhaps a sixth could be added: some children's phobic reactions seem to be related to issues of family conflict or stress (cf. Haley, 1977; Madanes, 1981; Malmquist, 1965).

The classical analytic view derives from Freud's treatment of Little Hans, a 5-year-old who developed an intense fear of horses (S. Freud, 1909/1963). Hans was, according to Freud, embroiled in the Oedipal issues of desiring sexual gratification with his mother and hating (as well as fearing) his father. The mechanisms whereby Hans's unconscious conflict created a phobia were: (1) repression of the conflictual wishes; (2) projection of his aggressive impulses onto the father; and (3) displacement from the father onto an external object (the horse). Proponents of the conditioning viewpoint (Wolpe & Rachman, 1960) take issue with this theory, claiming that Freud's evidence is primarily speculation. Wolpe and Rachman suggest that Hans's cure may be attributable to the normal developmental course of childhood fears. They also suggest that the psychoanalytic interpretations may have contributed to extinction of Hans's fear "for phobic stimuli were again and again presented to the child in a variety of emotional contexts that may have inhibited the anxiety and in consequence diminished its habit strength" (p. 146).

Treatment

In part, the position one takes on theoretical issues determines the kind of treatment recommended. If the phobia is viewed as a learned behavior, then treatment might involve systematic desensitization (Firestone, Waters, & Goodman, 1978; Hatzenbuehler & Schroeder, 1978), a vicarious- or participant-modeling strategy (Kirkland & Thelen, 1977), or a variety of other procedures, including contingency management, stimulus fading, and self-control (Richards & Siegel, 1978). With the possible exception of modeling strategies, the efficacy of behavioral treatments for childhood phobias has not yet been adequately documented (Graziano et al., 1979; see also Firestone et al., 1978; Hatzenbuehler & Schroeder, 1978).

Therapists of a more traditional orientation seem to take a flexible approach to treatment, opting for a strategy commensurate with the hypothesized severity of the phobia. Thus Kessler (1972) recommends educating the child about the reality of the danger (or lack of danger), attempting a gradual desensitizing process, presenting nonphobic models, and eliminating secondary gains (e.g., social benefits) of the symptom. More dynamic processes should be considered if these strategies do not prove effective. Neider (1979) also prefers to try short term directive procedures initially (with the caution that personality traits supporting the symptom may not change) and use more exploratory, insight-oriented therapy thereafter.

The author's strategy in many cases is to combine elements of symbolic modeling and imagery (cf. Lazarus & Abramovitz, 1962) in such a way as to enhance the child's ego strength or sense of competence, mastery, and self-efficacy. This will involve directive or subtle strategies for eliciting competencies of which the child is unaware (Erickson, Rossi, & Rossi, 1976). The following case provides an example:

Katie was a girl of 7-years referred for a fear of sleeping in the dark when she visited at her father's home. Her parents being divorced, this problem occurred infrequently since she lived with her mother and younger brother. Nevertheless it was sufficiently upsetting that Katie's mother sought help. Three features of the case were immediately problematic: the symptom had a part in her parents' postdivorce disputes since her father refused to allow such "nonsense" as a nightlight, which was her mother's custom. Second, Katie's father lived some distance from her family. Third, Katie's family would be moving within two months. This meant that: (1) the fear of sleeping in the dark at the father's could not be addressed directly and (b) treatment would have to be short and aimed at the child's competencies rather than family system issues. A further implication was that the efficacy of treatment would not be known until well after termination. Therefore, the treatment objective was changed: Katie agreed that she would like to learn to tolerate the dark without a nightlight and with the door closed *at her own home*. Over and above "relationship" elements that received attention, the basic procedures centered on (1) treatment in the clinic, (2) a "competence-eliciting" procedure at home, and (3) a generalization strategy. (1) In the clinic, Katie was taught to relax in a reclining position under increasingly anxiety-arousing, but playfully presented, conditions. For example, Katie relaxed in the darkened playroom, imagining herself in bed, and the therapist "manufactured" stimuli which metaphorically related to her fears (e.g., noises were produced via tape-recorder feedback). (2) At home, Katie's mother provided her with a small flashlight. Katie was instructed to use the light whenever she became afraid; but she was more subtly challenged to be afraid only twice each night. After two nights of much flashlight use, she met this challenge. (3) Before termination Katie felt comfortable sleeping in the dark at home, but she feared the next visit to her father's. She was assured that the therapist felt confident in her abilities so much so that he was awarding her a badge (or symbolic reward) "for bravery at bedtime" that she might hang over her bed. A letter received one month posttermination from Katie and her mother indicated that treatment had been successful.

It is clear that despite the clinical referral in this case, a relatively minor problem existed against a background of more serious family conflicts. Nevertheless, the methods sufficiently enhanced Katie's sense of competence in this area that perhaps her fearfulness no longer served as the focal point of parental conflicts.

Anna Freud (1937/1966) has similarly commented on the importance of children's sense of mastery in coping with underlying problems such as Oedipal issues (which, it can be speculated, were involved in Katie's case). Freud contrasted one of her cases to that of Little Hans (S. Freud, 1909/1963). The major similarity involved displacement onto an animal. In this case, however, the boy used an imaginary lion who terrified everyone and was controllable *only by the boy himself.*

School Phobia

Perhaps the most clinically interesting childhood phobia is presented by the child who refuses to attend school, often becoming "ill" in the struggle. Aside from those cases of children who are primarily truants (see Kennedy, 1965; Malmquist, 1965; see also Durlak, chap. 27 in this book), the school phobic is really seeking to remain home with the mother. As such, school phobia often will be more accurately described as involving separation anxiety.

Considerable attention has been directed to the family characteristics—especially maternal characteristics—in school phobia (Crumley, 1974; Davidson, 1960; Malmquist, 1965; Takagi, 1973). Mothers of school phobic children have been described as highly overprotective and ambivalent in their feelings toward the child and involved in a conflict-ridden dependency relationship with their own mothers. Thus issues of separation anxiety and dependency arise repeatedly and are transmitted from generation to generation. Related to the notion of maternal dependency is the hypothesis that the mother unconsciously acts in a manner that is contrary to her stated desire of having her child return to school. An example of such undermining comes from the treatment of Jack, an 8-year-old school phobic boy seen by the author.

Jack's mother had expressed exasperation with his behavior and a clear desire for his entrance into third grade. She ostensibly was quite familiar with the behavioral concepts of reinforcement and time-out, having read several parent-training books to deal with other problems. On the second consecutive day of therapy (at school), Jack's mother requested that·he go to his assigned classroom. His procrastinative efforts elicited more pleading from his mother, at which point the therapist reminded her of her desire to not reinforce aspects of the problem behavior. Several minutes later, Jack again began to whine as he approached his mother. This time, she refused to comment or make eye contact, "determined" not to reinforce him. Jack

then persisted, and still without commenting or making eye contact she allowed him to sit on her lap and placed her arm around him. Further work kept such sabotaging maneuvers to a minimum and Jack was attending for a full day within one week.

Malmquist (1965) has argued for greater attention to family issues, pointing to the neglect of fathers and siblings in the development of school phobia. For example, previous commentators on this problem have noted that fathers of some school phobics suffer "character problems." Such information has too often been considered secondary, however. Malmquist argues that the father should be seen as having contributed—by his behavior or behavioral omission—to the salient mother-child dependency. Malmquist highlighted this argument for a family viewpoint by a case of a boy who developed "mutual separation anxiety" with his "neurotic dog!"

Shapiro and Jegede (1973) have presented a four-dimensional approach to considering school phobia. Their first dimension concerns age or developmental stage. Obviously, separation anxiety is more inappropriate and probably more pathological in older children (cf. Smith, 1970). Second are external forces that might contribute to or account for a school phobia, including parents' attitudes to the school system, peer behavior, educational philosophy of the principal, punitive discipline of teachers, and social-cultural values. The third dimension noted by Shapiro and Jegede is the child's intrapsychic organization (conflicts and defenses). And fourth is the issue of how the child perceives his or her anxiety: Is it alien or syntonic? Anxious children who do not like the experience of anxiety are considered neurotic, while those for whom the avoidance is ego syntonic are truants. Between these extremes are possible admixtures of ego alienness and syntonicity.

The behavioral and psychodynamic treatment approaches mentioned earlier in this section have been applied to school phobia with some success. Most authors recommend that the child be returned to school as soon as possible. A more thorough exposition of the treatment of school phobia is beyond the scope of this chapter. However, several literature reviews can be recommended: Gordon and Young (1976); Kelly (1973); Miller, Barrett, and Hampe (1974); Shapiro and Jegede (1973); and the Rickard and Elkins contribution to this book (chap. 40).

CHILDHOOD HYSTERIA

While hysterical conversion and dissociative reactions have enjoyed a special place in the history of medical psychology (Veith, 1977), there has been considerably more attention devoted to adult disorders in the literature. This fact, in part, reflects the very low incidence and prevalence of childhood hysterical reactions (Ajuriaguerra, 1977/1980; see also Proctor, 1958; and Rae, 1977, for other views). Additionally, some clinicians may believe that such disorders do not occur or that the descriptor "hysterical personality" is inappropriate before adolescence. Such issues were a major focus on a 1978 conference on "the hysterical child" (Anthony & Gilpin, 1981).

Hysteria can be viewed as the language of the unconscious expressed through the body (Ajuriaguerra, 1977/1980). Descriptively, hysterical reactions are nonorganically produced losses in motor or sensory function. They include such problems as seizures; loss of hearing, vision, or speech; anesthesias; motor unsteadiness (e.g., astasia-abasia); and generalized or specific pain and are often associated with symptoms of vomiting, headache, abdominal pain, nausea, and dizziness. Dissociative reactions in children may take the form of feelings of depersonalization, hallucinations, and seizurelike absences or "spells." Sleepwalking has been considered a more innocuous form of a dissociative reaction (Kessler, 1972). In some cases, tics may represent a hysterical neurosis. (See also chap. 16 of this book.)

From a psychodynamic viewpoint, hysterical symptoms have the important function of symbolically expressing the core, intrapsychic conflict—the forbidden sexual or aggressive impulse and the defense against this impulse.

Within this framework, the symptom serves multiple purposes: primary gain is achieved by the controlling or binding of anxiety associated with the conflict; secondary gain is achieved in the attention directed by family members and others to the child's physical ailment.

Hysterical Personality

Historically associated with this psychodynamic viewpoint is the concept of "hysterical personality." Prominent among the features of individuals described as hysterical personalities are suggestibility; a vivid and imaginative fantasy life; and the tendencies to mimic, to be histrionic or dramatically expressive, egocentric, vivacious, emotionally labile, and needing attention or admiration (cf. Ajuriaguerra, 1977/1980; Jones, 1980; Shapiro, 1965).

Horowitz (1977, Introduction) classifies the hysteric's style into short, medium, and long order patterns dealing with information-processing styles, personality traits, and major themes in interpersonal relations, respectively. A common short order pattern is the hysteric's global deployment of attention. The descriptions listed above characterize Horowitz's medium order pattern. Among the more typical long order patterns are impulsive, stereotyped interpersonal relationships characterized by victim-aggressor, child-parent, rescue, and rape themes. In connection with such themes are caricaturelike roles for self and others, often with an existential sense that reality "is not really real," and that the self is helpless and not responsible (cf. Shapiro, 1965).

While such descriptions are obviously drawn from the concept of hysterical personality in adulthood, a number of such features fit those of the child as well. For example, Gilpin (1981) reported on a study of 26 girls with diagnoses of hysterical neurosis or hysterical personality style. Three main features stood out in this sample—the child's histrionicity, themes of "wanting nurturance from father," and seductiveness. Interestingly, Gilpin noted that the children's behavior varied as a function of the sex of the examining psychologist: during their evaluations, these children were perceived as competitive by female examiners and as seductive by male examiners. Also, during their evaluations, these children showed a tendency to give impulsive whole responses on the Rorschach test, again characteristic of global attention deployment.

While many authors have viewed hysterical personality as an antecedent of, or diagnostic criterion for, hysterical neurosis (e.g., Friedman, 1973; Looff, 1970), there has been considerable debate around this issue (Chodoff, 1974; Goodyer, 1981; Rada, Meyer, & Krill, 1969; Rada et al., 1973). The recently published *DSM-III* avoids reference to personality type as an antecedent to conversion reactions (see the review by Jones, 1980). With children, such issues become much more complex because many of the features of hysterical personality may be normal for children (Kessler, 1972). Moreover, Simonds (1973) has conducted a study showing that children exhibiting conversion and dissociative symptoms may fall into several diagnostic categories. Several dramatic fits of personality style and symptom picture (as in the author's experience) can be misleading, as they may arise from an illusory correlation or availability bias effect (cf. Nisbett & Ross, 1980). It simply is easier to recall cases of a dramatic fit than cases with a poor or mediocre fit, and this ease of recall may account for hypotheses held by many clinicians for which there are no solid data.

Family Characteristics

The available clinical literature does not point conclusively to any consistent general picture of the families of children exhibiting hysterical disorders. However, there are references in the psychodynamic literature to various kinds of psychopathology in the parents (e.g., Dawes, 1953; Starr, 1953; Wolpe, 1953). Gilpin (1981) suggested that mothers of such children tend to be strictly religious and to exhibit narcissistic and hysterical traits. In Gilpin's study, the most important character-

istic about fathers seemed to be the extent to which they maintained an inappropriately physically close relationship with their daughters. Gilpin also found that marital infidelity was common among these fathers. Rock (1971) suggested that mothers of hysterical children are overprotective, while fathers are ineffectual. While Rock felt that the parents had insight into their child's problem, he also noted (as have others) the parents' unwillingness to view their child's problem in psychological terms (Dollinger & Cotter, 1980; Friedman, 1973). Yates and Steward (1976) commented on the generalized inhibition of anger within the family and considered this to be an important clue for differential diagnosis when combined with discrepancies in the child's history. Laitman (1981) has commented that the family systems of children with hysterical disorders tend to have enmeshed boundaries between parent and child and that the children are commonly "triangulated" by the parents —that is, forced into cross-generational alliances as a function of parent or spouse subsystem problems.

Diagnosis

Friedman (1973) has emphasized an important diagnostic rule in possible cases of conversion reactions—base the diagnosis on positive criteria rather than the mere absence of physical or laboratory findings. As already noted, some clinicians have attempted to assess elements of the hysterical personality in making a positive diagnosis, although this rule of thumb may not be valid. Another consideration sometimes used is the child's apparent lack of concern about his or her illness—the classic *la belle indifference*. However, some authors have failed to find evidence of this attitude in their patient samples (Dubowitz & Hersov, 1976; Gold, 1965; Goodyer, 1981). Extrapolating from the adult literature, Rock (1971) suggests three criteria: (1) a prominent somatic symptom lacking anatomic or physiologic basis; (2) onset with or exacerbated by a significant emotional event; and (3) evidence that the symptom serves an emotional need. Jones (1980; citing Engel) has similar guidelines, but she also emphasizes the possible determinants of symptom choice: that the symptom expresses an unconscious wish or fantasy and was previously experienced by the patient, observed in another, or "wished on someone else." Robins and O'Neal (1953) emphasize *how not to make the diagnosis.* They believe that: (1) the presence of life stress does not afford a basis for differential diagnosis; (2) that the child is nervous or sensitive is not particularly diagnostic; and (3) impressions that the symptom does not follow "known anatomic or physiologic boundaries" can also be misleading. Finally, it should be noted that the diagnosis of hysterical conversion reaction is sometimes resisted by physicians (Dubowitz & Hersov, 1976; Rock, 1971). Such a diagnosis may be tantamount to admitting failure or admitting that one has been tricked by a child. Rock noted that this may lead to anger directed toward the child or premature release from the hospital. Another serious risk is that additional, more intensive diagnostic (medical) procedures will be attempted, resulting in reinforcement for or "consolidation" of the symptom (Dubowitz & Hersov, 1976; Leaverton, Rupp, & Poff, 1977).

Treatment

Treatment from the psychodynamic viewpoint involves uncovering, interpretation, and working through of the conflictual material, thereby eliminating the need for the symptom. An extensive and engrossing presentation of the psychoanalytic treatment of an adolescent with the "Grand Hysteria of Charcot" was published by Dawes (1953) in a special issue of the journal, *The Nervous Child,* devoted to childhood hysteria. Other useful material from a psychodynamic perspective has been presented by Gilpin and Mattes (1981); Proctor (1967); Metcalf (1977); Rock (1971); and Rosner (1975). Guidelines for the short term management and therapy of conversion reactions have also been offered (Dubowitz & Hersov, 1976; Leaverton et al., 1977).

What has been said to this point on the basis for conversion reactions and their treatment derives from a traditional psychodynamic viewpoint. A social learning or behavioral framework starts with similar observations but construes these observations differently (cf. Davis, 1953). Thus it is noted that the child presenting conversion type symptomatology frequently has important models for sick role behavior and receives considerable reinforcement from multiple sources while actively engaged in the sick role. Therefore, within this framework, the clinician attends to the observable elements of the clinical picture. Rather than ascribing a tendency to mimic or imitate, the therapist's attention is focused on behavioral models; rather than focusing on unconscious secondary gain, attention is given to changing the contingencies of reinforcement for sick role behavior. A focus on such observable and manipulable components leads to treatment strategies involving differential reinforcement of nonsick role behavior, combined with efforts to change the reinforcing patterns of family members. Useful adjuncts can include relaxation training and self-control strategies. Such methods were successfully employed in the treatment of children with hysterical contracture (Gold, 1965; Hendrix, Thompson, & Rau, 1978), paralysis and anesthesia (McKinlay, Kelly, & Collum, 1977), eructation (Munford & Chan, 1980), and motor unsteadiness following a minor gym accident (Dollinger & Cotter, 1980). Such procedures have as their major advantage that the presenting symptom is resolved fairly quickly. A major disadvantage in rapid symptomatic relief may be a tendency of the child's family to resist the working through recognized as important for maintenance of therapeutic gains—that is, correction of familial contingencies that contributed to the problem in the first place. Thus several authors have noted a tendency of families to drop out after the symptom is removed (Dollinger & Cotter, 1980; Hendrix et al., 1978). This problem is *not* specific to behavioral therapies, as others have noted this tendency for parents to challenge psychological interpretations of their child's problem or continually ask if an organic basis of the problem had been discovered (Friedman, 1973). Indeed,

Dawes' (1953) psychoanalysis of a teenage hysteric was repeatedly threatened with termination by interference from the patient's mother surrogates. In this regard, it may be most appropriate to view the problem early on in diagnostic and therapeutic work in family systems terms (see Liebman, Honig, & Berger, 1976).

Dissociative Reactions

The essential feature of dissociative disorders is an alteration of the normally integrative functions of consciousness, identity, or motor behavior (American Psychiatric Association, 1980). Examples of this disorder include psychogenic amnesia and fugue states, multiple personality, and depersonalization problems. Such problems are extremely rare in children, although sleepwalking seems to represent a mild example of this type of problem (cf. *DSM-III;* Kessler, 1972).

In contrast to the pattern in adults, children who experience hallucinations are typically showing a hysterical rather than a psychotic disorder (Bender & Lipkowitz, 1940; Despert, 1948; Kessler, 1972; Weiner, 1961; see also Egdell & Kolvin, 1972, for a slightly different view). Kessler (1972) summarizes one of her own cases in which an adolescent girl experienced an auditory hallucination of a whistling sound, called the "warning signal." Therapy revealed that the signal expressed the girl's conflicting wish to be sexually attractive (hence, receive "wolf" whistles) and a warning about the dangers of sexuality.

Egdell and Kolvin (1972) have suggested that at least some childhood hallucinations are related to stress. For example, a fourth-grade girl seen by the author reported that the devil "put a stew in her mind" shortly after her parents divorced. This bizarre bedtime-associated experience developed into visual and auditory hallucinations of the devil during the daytime. Thus it appeared that the child experienced hypnagogic and hypnopompic hallucinations at a time of family stress; partly as a function of her active imagination and fantasy-oriented reading interests, she construed her experience in demonic terms. Brief strategic treatment eliminated the hallucination. Equally of interest is the fact that this girl, who closely fit the picture of hysterical personality, was easily hypnotizable, and in a hypnotic session months after the last hallucination, she recalled reading a comic book about the devil given to her by a family friend around the time of her parents' separation.

A similar case of comic-book-mediated delusions was reported by Waye (1979). In this case, the child's Sunday School teacher had emphasized "spiritual shrinking" as a consequence of not being good. After seeing comics about a shrinking man, this 5-year-old girl reported that her own body parts were shrinking. Treatment with behavioral procedures eliminated the child's difficulties.

Saffer, Sansone, and Gentry (1979) reported several cases of children who presented bizarre and ostensibly psychotic symptoms including hallucinations. Clinical study revealed that these children's symptoms were a function of protecting family secrets often involving sexual behavior or abuse by adults in the family.

Hysterical Seizures

One set of hysterical disorders—seizures—are occasionally classified as conversion reactions and occasionally as dissociative reactions. Apparently this variation in diagnostic practice is a function of whether the disorder mimics a grand mal seizure or resembles the absences of a petit mal disorder. The latter is more likely to be diagnosed as a dissociative reaction and the former as a conversion reaction.

Hysterical seizures have been most frequently reported in adolescent girls, often in association with sexual pressure or exploitation (Bernstein, 1969; Dollinger, 1980; LaBarbera & Dozier, 1980), rape or incestuous rape (Dawes, 1953; Goodwin, Simms, & Bergman, 1979; Gross, 1979), and attempted homosexual rape (Caldwell & Stewart, 1981). Indeed, Anthony (1981) has noted with some surprise that the two psychoanalytic reports of childhood hysteria provide evidence of actual seduction in the social history, "almost as if they had set out to confirm Freud's older theory" (p. 8). At this point, the clinical literature is certainly highly suggestive if not definitive: the clinician should seriously consider the possibility of exploitation or similar dynamics in adolescent girls who present hysterical seizures. It should be noted, however, that such dynamics have not been mentioned in the case reports of younger children with psychogenic seizures. Additionally, Lindner (1973) presented the case of an adolescent (and of one adult) in which the need to cope with aggressive feelings seemed to be the predominant dynamic factor. Finally, we might note that seizures have been evidenced in cases of mass hysteria (Faigel, 1968) as seen in a novel report by Armstrong and Patterson (1975) who studied a community of Canadian Indian children.

Successful treatment approaches have included psychoanalysis (Dawes, 1953), hypnotherapy (Caldwell & Stewart, 1981; Gardner, 1973; Glenn & Simonds, 1977; Gross & Huerta, 1980; Williams & Singh, 1976), behavior modification (Gardner, 1967), behavioral strategies incorporated within family therapy (Dollinger, 1980), and behavioral procedures combined with hypnotherapy (Williams, Spiegel, & Mostofsky, 1978).

OTHER CHILDHOOD NEUROSES

Often grouped within the category of neurosis is the problem of elective mutism (also known as speech shyness, speech avoidance or phobia, selective mutism, and reluctant speech). Children presenting this problem are described as abnormally silent outside all but a small group of relatives or, occasionally, peers. Kratochwill, Brody, and Piersel (1979) recently presented a comprehensive review of the English language literature on this problem. These authors summarized several major themes found in the psychodynamically oriented reports. For example, electively mute children seem to be constitutionally hypersensitive to instinctual drives, are extremely dependent on their mothers, are fearful of strange persons and situations and show separation anxiety on entering school, and often have "disturbed" parents. Hayden (1980) has recently offered a clinically derived classification of elective mutism. Hayden's first group consists of children whose mutism is part of a symbiotic relationship with a caretaker (usually mother). Such children use their silence to control their environments. Next were "speech phobic" mutes who feared hearing their own voices, and reactive mutes whose silence seemed precipitated by trauma. Last were passive-aggressive mute children for whom silence was a kind of weapon. This thought-provoking classification, based on a sample of 68 children, deserves further empirical study.

While traditional, dynamically oriented therapies have shown little success in treating the mutism, behavioral therapies have been more promising in this regard (see reviews by Dollinger, 1979b; Kratochwill et al., 1979; Sanok & Ascione, 1979). Readers interested in examining some of the better psychodynamic presentations would do well to examine the Pustrom and Speers (1964) and Ruzicka and Sackin (1974) reports. Finally, the family-oriented presentations by Goll (1979) and Rosenberg and Lindblad (1978) are quite useful.

The clinical picture of childhood neurosis is often multisymptomatic and not amenable to simple nominal or undimensional classifications. Moreover, it is not uncommon to find that, in practice, the obvious or ostensible symptom masks other difficulties. Thus so-called neurotic depression may not seem to be obviously present at first glance. As another example, childhood sleep disturbances are often thought to reflect other underlying problems. Given the complexity and scope of problems falling under the rubric of neurosis, a brief chapter does not do justice to the area. Again, the reader is referred to companion chapters in this volume, particularly those on fears, sleep disorders, tics and habit problems, psychosomatic problems, and childhood depression.

SOME CLOSING REMARKS

In the introduction, it was noted that neurotic disorders, descriptively defined, involve problems that are distressing or ego alien to the symptom bearer. In other words, the child is not particularly pleased with the obsessive ritual, school phobia, or whatever and feels trapped by it. Thus the child's sense of competence or effectiveness is undermined by a neurotic disorder, and this feature is all too often overlooked by many therapists. To the extent that such issues as low ego strength or self-efficacy are addressed, they typically are seen as antecedent and contributing to the symptom development. However, they have not been viewed as a target for part of the intervention. Kessler (1972) implies a similar notion in criticizing behavior therapies for failing to teach children generalizable coping strategies. This point seems less true today than a decade ago because we can see now a remarkable growth in cognitive-behavioral methodologies such as self-control and problem-solving training. Nevertheless, little has been done with problems traditionally viewed under the rubric of neurosis.

The exceptions to this rule can be cited as possible guides for future clinical and research studies. The case presented by DiNardo and DiNardo (1981) illustrates self-control procedures used as part of the treatment of a boy with contamination fears and rituals. The studies by Graziano and Mooney (1980); Kanfer, Karoly, and Newman (1975); and Lazarus and Abramovitz (1962) are useful models for enhancing the child's sense of competence over fearful stimuli. Similarly, the nighttime fears case presented above illustrates a method for focusing on self-efficacy, particularly to enhance maintenance and generalization. Other examples have been offered for modifying the child's causal attributions in an ego-strengthening fashion in childhood hysteria (Dollinger, 1980; Dollinger & Cotter, 1980). Finally, it is noteworthy that most of these interventions took place in the context of family-oriented treatment. In short, as we survey the field of childhood neurosis, a number of promising directions are appearing that, if followed, may add much to the treatment of childhood neuroses.

REFERENCES

Adams, P.L. *Obsessive children: A sociopsychiatric study.* New York: Brunner/Mazel, 1973.

de Ajuriaguerra, J. *Handbook of child psychiatry and psychology* (R.P. Lorion, Ed. & trans.). New York: Masson, 1980. (Originally published, 1977.)

American Psychiatric Association. *Diagnostic and statistical manual of mental disorders (DSM-III).* Washington, D.C.: American Psychiatric Association, 1980.

Anthony, E.J. The flowers of mankind. In E.J. Anthony & D.C. Gilpin (Eds.), *Three further clinical faces of childhood.* New York: Spectrum, 1981.

Anthony, E.J., & Gilpin, D.C. *Three further clinical faces of childhood.* New York: Spectrum, 1981.

Armstrong, H., & Patterson, P. Seizures in Canadian Indian children: Individual, family and community approaches. *Canadian Psychiatric Association Journal,* 1975, **20,** 247–255.

Ayllon, T., Garber, S.W., & Allison, M.G. Behavioral treatment of childhood neurosis. *Psychiatry,* 1977, **40,** 315–322.

Barcai, A., & Rosenthal, M.K. Fears and tyranny: Observations on the tyrannical child. *Archives of General Psychiatry,* 1974, **30,** 392–395.

Bender, L., & Lipkowitz, H.H. Hallucinations in children. *American Journal of Orthopsychiatry,* 1940, **10,** 471–490.

Bernstein, N.R. Psychogenic seizures in adolescent girls. *Behavioral Neuropsychiatry,* 1969, **1,** 31–34.

Caldwell, T.A., & Stewart, R.S. Hysterical seizures and hypnotherapy. *American Journal of Clinical Hypnosis,* 1981, **23,** 294–298.

Cass, L. Psychotherapy with the obsessive-compulsive child. In M. Hammer & A.M. Kaplan (Eds.), *The practice of psychotherapy with children.* Homewood, Ill.: Dorsey, 1967.

Chethik, M. The therapy of an obsessive-compulsive boy: Some treatment considerations. *Journal of the American Academy of Child Psychiatry,* 1969, **8,** 465–484.

Chodoff, P. The diagnosis of hysteria: An overview. *American Journal of Psychiatry,* 1974, **131,** 1073–1078.

Crumley, F.E. A school phobia in a three-generational family conflict. *Journal of the American Academy of Child Psychiatry,* 1974, **13,** 536–550.

Csikszentmihalyi, M., & Graef, R. Socialization into sleep: Exploratory findings. *Merrill-Palmer Quarterly,* 1975, **21,** 3–18.

Davidson, S. School phobia as a manifestation of family disturbance: Its structure and treatment. *Journal of Child Psychology and Psychiatry,* 1960, **1,** 270–287.

Davis, D.R. Some psychological mechanisms concerned in the disorders of childhood. *The Nervous Child,* 1953, **10,** 238–245.

Dawes, L.G. The psychoanalysis of a case of "Grand Hysteria of Charcot" in a girl of fifteen. *The Nervous Child,* 1953, **10,** 272–305.

Despert, J.L. Delusional and hallucinatory experiences in children. *American Journal of Psychiatry,* 1948, **104,** 528–537.

DiNardo, P.A., & DiNardo, P.G. Self-control desensitization in the treatment of a childhood phobia. *the Behavior Therapist,* 1981, **4**(1), 15–16.

Dollinger, S.J. Dr. R.'s dilemma. *the Behavior Therapist,* 1979, **2**(3), 3–4. (a)

Dollinger, S.J. Elective mutism: A brief comparative review of behavioral and psychodynamic approaches. Paper presented in the symposium on pediatric psychology, M.C. Roberts (chair), meetings of the Midwestern Psychological Association, Chicago, May, 1979. (b)

Dollinger, S.J. Family systems/behavioral treatment for psychogenic blackouts in an adolescent girl. Paper presented in the symposium on pediatric psychology, M.C. Roberts (chair), meetings of the Southeastern Psychological Association, Washington, D.C., March, 1980.

Dollinger, S.J., & Cotter, P.D. Behavioral and cognitive-control strategies in the elimination of an 11-year-old boy's psychogenic pain. *Behavioral Disorders,* 1980, **6,** 36–40.

Dubowitz, V., & Hersov, L. Management of children with non-organic (hysterical) disorders of motor function. *Developmental Medicine and Child Neurology,* 1976, **18,** 358–368.

Egdell, H.G., & Kolvin, I. Childhood hallucinations. *Journal of Child Psychology and Psychiatry,* 1972, **13,** 279–287.

Elkins, R., Rapoport, J.L., & Lipsky, A. Obsessive-compulsive disorder of childhood and adolescence: A neurobiological viewpoint. *Journal of the American Academy of Child Psychiatry,* 1980, **19,** 511–524.

Erickson, M.H., Rossi, E.L., & Rossi, S.I. *Hypnotic realities.* New York: Irvington, 1976.

Faigel, H.C. "The wandering womb": Mass hysteria in school girls. *Clinical Pediatrics,* 1968, **7,** 377–378.

Fine, S. Family therapy and a behavioral approach to childhood obsessive-compulsive neurosis. *Archives of General Psychiatry,* 1973, **28,** 695–697.

Firestone, P., Waters, B.C.H., & Goodman, J.T. Desensitization in children and adolescents: A review. *Journal of Clinical Child Psychology,* 1978, **7,** 142–148.

Freud, A. *The ego and the mechanisms of defense* (Rev. ed.). New York: International Universities Press, 1966. (Originally published, 1937.)

Freud, S. Analysis of a phobia in a five-year-old boy. In S. Freud, *The sexual enlightenment of children.* New York: Macmillan, 1963. (Originally published, 1909.)

Friedman, S.B. Conversion symptoms in adolescents. *Pediatric Clinics of North America,* 1973, **20,** 873–882.

Gardner, J.E. Behavior therapy treatment approach to a psychogenic seizure case. *Journal of Consulting Psychology,* 1967, **31,** 209–212.

Gardner, G.G. Use of hypnosis for psychogenic epilepsy in a child. *American Journal of Clinical Hypnosis,* 1973, **15,** 166–169.

Gilpin, D.C. Hysterical disorders observed in a university child guidance clinic. In E.J. Anthony & D.C. Gilpin (Eds.), *Three further clinical faces of childhood.* New York: Spectrum, 1981.

Gilpin, D.C., & Mattes, K. Psychotherapy of the hysterical child. In E.J. Anthony & D.C. Gilpin (Eds.), *Three further clinical faces of childhood.* New York: Spectrum, 1981.

Glenn, T.J., & Simonds, J.F. Hypnotherapy of a psychogenic seizure disorder in an adolescent. *American Journal of Clinical Hypnosis,* 1977, **19,** 245–250.

Gold, S. Diagnosis and management of hysterical contracture in children. *British Medical Journal,* 1965, **1,** 21–23.

Goll, K. Role structure and subculture in families of elective mutists. *Family Process,* 1979, **18,** 55–68.

Goodwin, J., Simms, M., & Bergman, R. Hysterical seizures: A sequel to incest. *American Journal of Orthopsychiatry,* 1979, **49,** 698–703.

Goodyer, I. Hysterical conversion reactions in childhood. *Journal of Child Psychology and Psychiatry,* 1981, **22,** 179–188.

Gordon, D.A., & Young, R.D. School phobia: A discussion of etiology, treatment, and evaluation. *Psychological Reports,* 1976, **39,** 783–804.

Graziano, A.M., DeGiovanni, I.S., & Garcia, K.A. Behavioral treatment of children's fears: A review. *Psychological Bulletin,* 1979, **86**, 804–830.

Graziano, A.M., & Mooney, K.C. Family self-control instruction for children's nighttime fear reduction. *Journal of Consulting and Clinical Psychology,* 1980, **48**, 206–213.

Gross, M. Incestuous rape: A cause of hysterical seizures in four adolescent girls. *American Journal of Orthopsychiatry,* 1979, **49**, 704–708.

Gross, M., & Huerta, E. Functional convulsions masked as epileptic disorders. *Journal of Pediatric Psychology,* 1980, **5**, 71–79.

Haley, J. *Problem-solving therapy.* San Francisco: Jossey-Bass, 1977.

Hatzenbuehler, L.C., & Schroeder, H.E. Desensitization procedures in the treatment of childhood disorders. *Psychological Bulletin,* 1978, **85**, 831–844.

Hayden, T.L. Classification of elective mutism. *Journal of the American Academy of Child Psychiatry,* 1980, **19**, 118–133.

Hendrix, E.M., Thompson, L.M., & Rau, B.W. Behavioral treatment of an "hysterically" clenched fist. *Journal of Behavior Therapy and Experimental Psychiatry,* 1978, **9**, 273–276.

Hersen, M. Treatment of a compulsive and phobic disorder through a total behavior therapy program: A case study. *Psychotherapy: Theory, Research, and Practice,* 1968, **5**, 220–225.

Hollingsworth, C.E., Tanguay, P.E., Grossman, L., & Pabst, P. Long-term outcome of obsessive-compulsive disorder in childhood. *Journal of the American Academy of Child Psychiatry,* 1980, **19**, 134–144.

Horowitz, M.J. (Ed.). *Hysterical personality.* New York: Aronson, 1977.

Janzen, W.B., & Peacock, R. Treatment of public masturbation by behavioral management. *American Journal of Psychotherapy,* 1978, **32**, 300–306.

Jones, M.M. Conversion reaction: Anachronism or evolutionary form? A review of the neurologic, behavioral, and psychoanalytic literature. *Psychological Bulletin,* 1980, **87**, 427–441.

Judd, L.L. Obsessive compulsive neurosis in children. *Archives of General Psychiatry,* 1965, **12**, 136–143.

Kagan, J. *Understanding children: Behavior, motives, and thought.* New York: Harcourt Brace Jovanovich, 1971.

Kanfer, F.H., Karoly, P., & Newman, A. Reduction of children's fear of the dark by competence-related and situational threat-related verbal cues. *Journal of Consulting and Clinical Psychology,* 1975, **43**, 251–258.

Kanner, L. *Child psychiatry* (4th ed.). Springfield, Ill.: Thomas, 1972.

Karush, R.K. Obsessive-compulsive syndromes. In M.M. Josephson & R.T. Porter (Eds.), *Clinician's handbook of childhood psychopathology.* New York: Aronson, 1979.

Kellerman, J. Hypnosis as an adjunct to thought-stopping and covert reinforcement in the treatment of homicidal obsessions in a twelve-year-old boy. *International Journal of Clinical and Experimental Hypnosis,* 1981, **29**, 128–135.

Kelly, E.W. School phobia: A review of theory and treatment. *Psychology in the Schools,* 1973, **10**, 33–42.

Kennedy, W.A. School phobia: Rapid treatment of fifty cases. *Journal of Abnormal Psychology,* 1965, **70**, 285–289.

Kessler, J.W. Neurosis in childhood. In B.B. Wolman (Ed.), *Manual of child psychopathology.* New York: McGraw-Hill, 1972.

Kirkland, K.D., & Thelen, M.H. Uses of modeling in child treatment. In B.B. Lahey & A.E. Kazdin (Eds.), *Advances in clinical child psychology* (Vol. 1). New York: Plenum, 1977.

Kratochwill, T.R., Brody, G.H., & Piersel, W.C. Elective mutism in children. In B.B. Lahey & A.E. Kazdin (Eds.), *Advances in clinical child psychology* (Vol. 2). New York: Plenum, 1979.

LaBarbera, J.D., & Dozier, J.E. Hysterical seizures: The role of sexual exploitation. *Psychosomatics,* 1980, **21**, 897–903.

Laitman, R.J. A family therapy perspective on hysterical dynamics in childhood. In E.J. Anthony & D.C. Gilpin (Eds.), *Three further clinical faces of childhood.* New York: Spectrum, 1981.

Lapouse, R., & Monk, M.A. Fears and worries in a representative sample of children. *American Journal of Orthopsychiatry,* 1959, **29**, 803–818.

Lazarus, A.A., & Abramovitz, A. The use of "emotive imagery" in the treatment of children's phobias. *Journal of Mental Science,* 1962, **108,** 191–195.

Leaverton, D.R., Rupp, J.W., & Poff, M.G. Brief therapy for monocular hysterical blindness in childhood. *Child Psychiatry and Human Development,* 1977, **7,** 254–263.

Liebman, R., Honig, P., & Berger, H. An integrated treatment program for psychogenic pain. *Family Process,* 1976, **15,** 397–405.

Lindner, H. Psychogenic seizure states: A psychodynamic study. *International Journal of Clinical and Experimental Hypnosis,* 1973, **21,** 261–271.

Looff, D.H. Psychophysiologic and conversion reactions in children: Selective incidence in verbal and nonverbal families. *Journal of the American Academy of Child Psychiatry,* 1970, **9,** 318–331.

Madanes, C. *Strategic family therapy.* San Francisco: Jossey Bass, 1981.

Malmquist, C.P. School phobia: A problem in family neurosis. *Journal of the American Academy of Child Psychiatry,* 1965, **4,** 293–319.

McKinlay, T., Kelly, J.A., & Collum, J.M. The multi-modal treatment of conversion reactions in adolescence: A case study. *Journal of Clinical Child Psychology,* 1977, **6,** 66–68.

Metcalf, A. Childhood: From process to structure. In M.J. Horowitz (Ed.), *Hysterical personality.* New York: Aronson, 1977.

Miller, L.C., Barrett, C.L., & Hampe, E. Phobias of childhood in a prescientific era. In A. Davids (Ed.), *Child personality and psychopathology: Current topics* (Vol. 1). New York: Wiley, 1974.

Minuchin, S., Rosman, B.L., & Baker, L. *Psychosomatic families: Anorexia nervosa in context.* Cambridge: Harvard University Press, 1978.

Munford, P.R., & Chan, S.Q. Family therapy for the treatment of a conversion reaction: A case study. *Psychotherapy: Theory, Research, and Practice.* 1980, **17,** 214–219.

Neider, J.M. Phobias. In M.M. Josephson & R.T. Porter (Eds.), *Clinician's handbook of childhood psychopathology.* New York: Aronson, 1979.

Nisbett, R., & Ross, L. *Human inference: Strategies and shortcomings of social judgment.*

Englewood Cliffs, N.J.: Prentice-Hall, 1980.

Palazzoli, M.S., Boscolo, L., Cecchin, G., & Prata, G. A ritualized prescription in family therapy: Odd days and even days. *Journal of Marriage and Family Counseling,* 1978, **4,** 3–9.

Palazzoli, M.S., Boscolo, L., Cecchin, G., & Prata, G. Family rituals: A powerful tool in family therapy. *Family Process,* 1977, **16,** 445–453.

Pollak, J.M. Obsessive compulsive personality: A review. *Psychological Bulletin,* 1979, **86,** 225–241.

Proctor, J.T. Hysteria in childhood. *American Journal of Orthopsychiatry,* 1958, **28,** 394–407.

Proctor, J.T. The treatment of hysteria in childhood. In M. Hammer & A.M. Kaplan (Eds.), *The practice of psychotherapy with children.* Homewood, Ill.: Dorsey, 1967.

Pustrom, E., & Speers, R.W. Elective mutism in children. *Journal of the American Academy of Child Psychiatry,* 1964, **3,** 287–297.

Rabavilas, A.D., Boulougouris, J.C., & Stefanis, C. Compulsive checking diminished when over-checking instructions were disobeyed. *Journal of Behavior Therapy and Experimental Psychiatry,* 1977, **8,** 111–112.

Rabkin, R. *Strategic psychotherapy: Brief and symptomatic treatment.* New York: Basic Books, 1977.

Rada, R.T., Krill, A.E., Meyer, G.G., & Armstrong, D. Visual conversion reaction in children. II. Follow-up. *Psychosomatics,* 1973, **14,** 271–276.

Rada, R.T., Meyer, G.G., & Krill, A.E. Visual conversion reaction in children. I. Diagnosis. *Psychosomatics,* 1969, **10,** 23–28.

Rae, W.A. Childhood conversion reactions: A review of incidence in pediatric settings. *Journal of Clinical Child Psychology,* 1977, **6,** 69–72.

Richards, C.S., & Siegel, L.J. Behavioral treatment of anxiety states and avoidance behaviors in children. In D. Marholin II (Ed.), *Child behavior therapy.* New York: Wiley, 1978.

Rincover, A., Newsom, C.D., & Carr, E.G. Using sensory extinction procedures in the treatment of compulsivelike behavior of developmentally disabled children. *Journal of Consulting and Clinical Psychology,* 1979, **47,** 695–701.

Robins, E., & O'Neal, P. Clinical features of

hysteria in children. *The Nervous Child,* 1953, **10,** 246–271.

Rock, N.L. Conversion reactions in childhood: A clinical study on childhood neuroses. *Journal of the American Academy of Child Psychiatry,* 1971, **10,** 65–93.

Rosen, L.W. Modification of secretive or ritualized eating behavior in anorexia nervosa. *Journal of Behavior Therapy and Experimental Psychiatry,* 1980, **11,** 101–104.

Rosenberg, J.B., & Lindblad, M.B. Behavior therapy in a family context: Treating elective mutism. *Family Process,* 1978, **17,** 77–82.

Rosner, H. Clinical and prognostic considerations in the analysis of a five-year-old hysteric. *Journal of the American Psychoanalytic Association,* 1975, **23,** 507–534.

Ruzicka, B.B., & Sackin, H.D. Elective mutism: The impact of the patient's silent detachment upon the therapist. *Journal of the American Academy of Child Psychiatry,* 1974, **13,** 551–561.

Saffer, J.B., Sansone, P., & Gentry, J. The awesome burden upon the child who must keep a family secret. *Child Psychiatry and Human Development,* 1979, **10,** 35–40.

Sanok, R.L., & Ascione, F.R. Behavioral interventions for childhood elective mutism: An evaluative review. *Child Behavior Therapy,* 1979, **1,** 49–68.

Shapiro, D. *Neurotic styles.* New York: Basic Books, 1965.

Shapiro, T., & Jegede, R.O. School phobia: A babel of tongues. *Journal of Autism and Childhood Schizophrenia,* 1973, **3,** 168–186.

Simonds, J.F. Conversion-hypochondriacal dissociative symptoms in children. *Journal of Operational Psychiatry,* 1973, **5,** 38–41.

Smith, S.L. School refusal with anxiety: A review of sixty-three cases. *Canadian Psychiatric Association Journal,* 1970, **15,** 257–264.

Staley, A.A. *Fears and worries of normal children.* Unpublished MA thesis, Southern Illinois University at Carbondale, 1979.

Stanley, L. Treatment of ritualistic behaviour in an eight-year-old girl by response prevention: A case report. *Journal of Child Psychology and Psychiatry,* 1980, **21,** 85–90.

Starr, P.H. Some observations on the diagnostic aspects of childhood hysteria. *The Nervous Child,* 1953, **10,** 214–231.

Takagi, R. The family structure of school phobics. *Acta Paedopsychiatrica,* 1973, **39,** 131–146.

Thomas, A., & Chess, S. *Temperament and development.* New York: Brunner/Mazel, 1977.

Veith, I. Four thousand years of hysteria. In M.J. Horowitz (Ed.), *Hysterical personality.* New York: Aronson, 1977.

Wagner, M.K. A case of public masturbation treated by operant conditioning. *Journal of Child Psychology and Psychiatry,* 1968, **9,** 61–65.

Watzlawick, P., Weakland, J.H., & Fisch, R. *Change: Principles of problem formation and problem resolution.* New York: Norton, 1974.

Waye, M.F. Behavioral treatment of a child displaying comic-book mediated fear of hand shrinking: A case study. *Journal of Pediatric Psychology,* 1979, **4,** 43–47.

Weiner, I.B. Behavior therapy in obsessive-compulsive neurosis: Treatment of an adolescent boy. *Psychotherapy: Theory, Research, and Practice,* 1967, **4,** 27–29.

Weiner, M.F. Hallucinations in children. *Archives of General Psychiatry,* 1961, **5,** 544–553.

Weisner, W.M., & Riffel, P.A. Scrupulosity: Religion and obsessive-compulsive behavior in children. *American Journal of Psychiatry,* 1960, **117,** 314–318.

Wikler, D.I., Green, M., & Wikler, L. Formal limits of behavior therapy. *the Behavior Therapist,* 1979, **2**(1), 19–20.

Williams, D.T., & Singh, M. Hypnosis as a facilitating adjunct in child psychiatry. *Journal of the American Academy of Child Psychiatry,* 976, **15,** 326–342.

Williams, D.T., Spiegel, H., & Mostofsky, D.I. Neurogenic and hysterical seizures in children and adolescents: Differential diagnostic and therapeutic considerations. *American Journal of Psychiatry,* 1978, **135,** 82–86.

Wolpe, J., & Rachman, S. Psychoanalytic "evidence": A critique based on Freud's case of Little Hans. *Journal of Nervous and Mental Disease,* 1960, **131,** 135–148.

Wolpe, Z.S. Psychogenic visual disturbance in a four year old girl. *The Nervous Child,* 1953, **10,** 314–325.

Yates, A., & Steward, M. Conversion hysteria in childhood: A case report and a reminder. *Clinical Pediatrics,* 1976, **15,** 379–382.

Zetzel, E.R. 1965: Additional notes upon a case of obsessional neurosis: Freud 1909. *International Journal of Psycho-analysis,* 1966, **47,** 123–130.

CHAPTER 22

Childhood Psychoses

GERALDINE DAWSON AND GARY B. MESIBOV

HISTORICAL OVERVIEW

The existence of psychosis in childhood was documented as early as 1896 by Kraeplin who noted that a small percentage of his patients with "dementia praecox" developed this disorder in early childhood. Bleuler (1911/1950), who later coined the term schizophrenia, also wrote that in at least five percent of the cases the illness could be traced back to childhood and occasionally to the first five years of life. At this point, it was believed that there were few, if any, differences between the infantile and later forms of the disorder. Potter (1933), who was one of the first systematically to study and write about childhood psychosis, also based his work on this assumption.

It was Kanner (1943) who first argued that there exists a unique and qualitatively different syndrome of childhood psychosis that should be differentiated from schizophrenia. In particular, he noted that schizophrenia involves a *withdrawal* from interpersonal relationships in contrast with the children he was describing who actually *failed to develop* social relationships. Kanner's detailed descriptions of these 11 children included the following characteristics: an inability to relate to people that he called "extreme autistic aloneness"; language deviance that included delayed acquisition, echolalia, occasional mutism, pronoun reversals, and literalness; excellent rote memory; repetitive and stereotyped play activities, and an obsessive desire for maintenance of sameness in the environment. In addition, unlike all previously described forms of childhood psychosis that appear much later in life, Kanner noted that his

children began experiencing difficulties during infancy. The children's lack of physical stigmata and often good rote memory led Kanner to conclude that they were endowed with normal cognitive potential.

Disagreement and semantic confusion continued to exist with regard to the diagnostic classification of Kanner's syndrome as a form of childhood schizophrenia. This confusion was partly due to Kanner's use of the term "autism," which many investigators confused with Bleuler's descriptions of "autistic withdrawal from reality" found in schizophrenic patients. Furthermore, several investigators (e.g., Bender, 1947) postulated that autism and childhood schizophrenia were part of a continuum of one disease process, based mainly on the fact that both conditions involve severely disturbed relationships with people.

Verification of significant differences between Kanner's syndrome (now termed "early infantile autism") and childhood schizophrenia came from several sources. To begin with, studies (e.g., Kolvin, 1971a; Makita, 1966) began to show that the age distribution for the onset of psychosis in childhood is markedly bipolar, falling most frequently either before 3 years of age *or* in early adolescence. Psychosis with onset in middle childhood is rare. These data suggest two separate disease processes. In addition, several other important distinctions were being made. Kolvin (1971b) found significant differences between early and late onset psychosis in parental social class, family history of schizophrenia, frequency of cerebral dysfunction, speech patterns, and intelligence quotient (IQ) level. Rutter (1970) also noted that autistic persons rarely developed delusions and hallucinations, which are characteristic of schizophrenia.

Thus, for the remainder of this chapter, childhood psychosis will be considered in terms of two distinct syndromes: early infantile autism and childhood schizophrenia. It is recognized that even this distinction remains an oversimplification of the classification of many diverse forms of childhood psychosis that have yet to be systematically described and delineated. For example, several investigators recognize a disorder often termed "disintegrative psychosis of childhood" that is considered to be different from autism and childhood schizophrenia. However, due to the relative lack of research on this and other such descriptions, these will not be included in this chapter.

EARLY INFANTILE AUTISM

Characteristics

The prevalence of early infantile autism has been estimated as 4–5 cases per 10,000 population (Brask, 1967; Lotter, 1966; Rutter, 1978a) and this figure seems roughly equivalent for samples all over the world (Ritvo & Freeman, 1977). Although the syndrome is relatively rare, the number of autistic children is not inconsequential and represents a significant social problem. In comparison, the prevalence of legal blindness in children has been estimated as 5.5 per 10,000[1] and of childhood deafness as 6.5 per 10,000[2].

Although Kanner's (1943) original emphasis on peak skills led many to believe that these children have the potential for normal intellectual functioning, current estimates are quite different. Most investigators agree that approximately 70 percent of autistic people are functioning intellectually within the mentally retarded range (DeMyer et al., 1974). These IQ scores are as stable in autistic children as in nonhandicapped children (DeMyer et al., 1974; Lockyer & Rutter, 1969) and seem to be a relatively accurate predictor of later educational performance (Bartak & Rutter, 1971; Lockyer & Rutter, 1969).

As with IQ, the distribution of social class among families of autistic children has been misunderstood until recently. Kanner's original sample consisted primarily of professional families with 4 out of the 11 having a physician as one of the parents. More recent research has shown that the social class distribution of autistic children's families is quite similar to that of the population in general (Schopler, Andrews, & Strupp, 1979).

Several investigators have noted that autism occurs more frequently in males than in females. The ratio is generally reported as 3 or 4 to 1 (Gittelman & Birch, 1967; Kanner, 1957; Kolvin, 1971b; Rutter & Lockyer, 1967), which is similar to the data on sex ratios reported for the other developmental disabilities (Robinson & Robinson, 1976).

Diagnostic Criteria

Following Kanner's original description, Eisenberg and Kanner (1956) reduced the number of essential symptoms to only two: extreme aloneness and preoccupation with the preservation of sameness. Although a more clear and concise definition of the autistic syndrome was needed, the Eisenberg and Kanner attempt unfortunately left out important defining characteristics—the abnormalities of language and communication.

Several later attempts at clarification met with mixed results (Ornitz & Ritvo, 1968; Rendle-Short, 1969; Schain & Yannet, 1960; Tinbergen & Tinbergen, 1972; Wing & Ricks, 1976). The most influential of these was the definition by Creak (1963) emphasizing the following nine major points: gross impairment of emotional relationships with people; apparent unawareness of one's own identity; preoccupation with particular objects; sustained resistance to change; abnormal perceptual experiences; acute and seemingly illogical anxiety; lost or never acquired speech; distortion in motility patterns; and a background of serious retardation in which islets of normal, or near normal (or even exceptional) skills may appear. The importance of the Creak criteria is that they were the first ones to be empirically tested to determine how effective they were in differentiating autism from other conditions. Although the results of these validity checks were somewhat disappointing, they still represented a major advance over other, totally descriptive classification systems.

More recently, a consensus is emerging on the diagnostic criteria of autism. Rutter's (1978b) paper, identifying the major characteristics as early onset, impaired language and prelinguistic skills, impaired social relationships, and insistence on sameness, has been especially influential. Early onset (before 30 months) is thought by Rutter to be a major defining characteristic of autism because of the extreme differences in brain pathology, symptoms, recommended treatments, and outcomes for the psychoses evident before 30 months and those developing later on.

Delayed and markedly different speech and language patterns are another defining characteristic of autism and, in most cases, represent the most significant problem (Bartak, Rutter, & Cox, 1975; Ricks & Wing, 1975; Rutter, 1966). In addition to these severe speech and language difficulties, autistic people are deficient in a variety of prelinguistic skills including social imitation, appropriate use of objects, and ability to participate in simple and imaginative games. Their babbling is frequently abnormal as well, as is their ability to understand the language of others.

Rutter's third characteristic of autism, impaired social relationships, can manifest itself in a variety of ways. These include a lack of attachments to others, unusual eye-to-eye gaze, and numerous interpersonal difficulties including lack of cooperative group play, failure to make friends, and a lack of empathy.

Rutter's final characteristic is an insistence on sameness. In early childhood, this is manifested in rigid and limited play patterns; intense attachments to specific objects; unusual preoccupations, rituals, and compulsions; and a marked resistance to any changes in the environment.

In 1977, the National Society for Autistic Children approved a definition that was similar to Rutter's but with several small modifications (Ritvo & Freeman, 1977). Although the Society's definition included onset prior to 30 months of age, impaired speech and language, and impaired social relationships, it did not include insistence on sameness and, instead, substituted disturbances of developmental rates or sequences and disturbances of responses to sensory stimuli. Disturbances of developmental rates, according to the Society, can occur in any of three developmental pathways: motor, social-adaptive, or cognitive. Disturbances of responses to sensory stimuli can be either hyper- or hyporeactivity and can be to visual, auditory, tactile, vestibular, or olfactory stimulation.

In summary, after a history of disagreements, the syndrome described as childhood autism now has several generally agreed upon characteristics, including onset prior to 30 months of age, disturbances of speech and language, and impaired social relationships. There is still some disagreement about insistence on sameness, disturbances of developmental rates in sequence, and disturbances of responses to sensory stimuli and whether these are central or peripheral to the disorder.

Autism and Mental Retardation

After establishing the characteristics of autism, the other main diagnostic question concerns differential diagnosis, which is most difficult between autism and mental retardation, between autism and developmental language disability, and between autism and schizophrenia. Differentiating autism from mental retardation without autism is difficult because of the significant overlap in symptoms for the two conditions. Most investigators estimate that 70 percent of autistic people are also mentally retarded (Rutter, 1978b; Ritvo & Freeman, 1977; Schopler & Olley, 1981). However, autism appears to represent a more specific cognitive defect than mental retardation, involving specific language and central coding processes (Rutter et al., 1967; Schopler, 1966).

Several studies have made systematic comparisons between autistic and mentally retarded children matched for age, sex, and level of intelligence. For example, Hermelin and O'Conner (1970) found that autistic children generally have better rote verbal memory but make less use of semantic information and are more impaired in the use of concepts and categorization than retarded children. DeMyer and her co-workers (DeMyer et al., 1972a) found that autistic children are significantly more impaired in the use of motor imitation when compared to matched mentally retarded children. A follow-up study by Lockyer and Rutter (1970) demonstrated that autistic children exhibit a WISC subtest pattern that is different from retarded children's, consisting of high scores on the Block Design, Object Assembly, and Digit Span subtests combined with a very low score on Comprehension. Moreover, Rutter (1974) notes that about 25 percent of autistic children are not generally retarded (despite specific cognitive deficits), so that level of intelligence cannot account for the presence of autism. Finally, even when equated for IQ level, the prognosis for autistic children in terms of persistence of language impairment and employment prospects tends to be worse than for mentally retarded children. Thus it is generally agreed that autism and mental retardation constitute two different (though overlapping) syndromes and, furthermore, that this differentiation is of practical utility in terms of prognosis and treatment.

Autism and Developmental Language Disability

Given that autism involves a profound and persisting language deficit that appears to be developmental in nature, it is necessary to distinguish between autism and other developmental language disorders. A comparative study by Bartak et al. (1975) suggests there are marked differences between children with autism and those with severe developmental receptive dysphasia. Autistic children have more deviant language, including more frequent occurrence of pronoun reversal, echolalia, stereotyped utterances, metaphorical language, and inappropriate remarks. In addition, they make less use of language for social purposes, tend not to understand or use gestures, and show less symbolic play. On the other hand, the autistic and dysphasic groups did not differ in mean utterance length, grammatical complexity of speech, acquisition of single words or phrase speech, and most nonlinguistic skills, and autistic children were actually superior in verbal articulation and

visual word recognition. Other studies (Bartak et al., 1975; Cantwell, Howlin, & Rutter, 1977) have also supported the conclusion that language deviance is a necessary, but not sufficient, condition in autism.

Autism and Schizophrenia

There are also several factors differentiating autism from schizophrenia. First is the early onset of autism as compared with schizophrenia, which rarely develops before 10 (Ross, 1980). Second, there are family history and intellectual differences, with autism less commonly occurring in families and generally accompanied by lower IQs (Kolvin, Humphrey, & McNay, 1971a). Third, remissions and relapses are much more characteristic of schizophrenia than autism (Rutter, 1968), and autistic individuals rarely develop delusions and hallucinations during adulthood (Rutter, 1970). Fourth, there is greater evidence of cerebral dysfunction in autistic as compared with schizophrenic clients, including seizures and the association of autism with known neurological conditions such as tuberous sclerosis and phenylketonuria (Dalldorf & Schopler, 1981). Finally, whereas schizophrenia frequently represents a withdrawal from social relationships, autistic people generally are unable to form these relationships in the first place.

Theories of Causation

Kanner made the observation that the parents of autistic children were usually highly intelligent and that many seemed to be obsessive individuals who lacked warmth. Along with other researchers, he concluded that autism was due to an interaction between an innate organic defect and the specific family environment (Eisenberg, 1957; Eisenberg & Kanner, 1956; Kanner, 1949).

From these initial observations, many theories arose postulating that autism has, in part, a psychogenic basis. Some theories have stressed unusual personality traits in parents including emotional coldness, obsessiveness, introversion, intellectuality, and schizophrenic features and have posited that autism results from either genetic transmission of these traits (Ounsted, 1970; van Krevelen, 1963, 1971) or from the child's response to the personalities of the parents (Bosch, 1953/ 1970; Meyers & Goldfarb, 1961; Rank, 1949). Others have suggested that autism is the result of a pathological parent-child interaction consisting of either poor maternal communication (Clerk, 1961; Goldfarb, Levy, & Meyers, 1966), too much or too little stimulation (Anthony, 1958; Tinbergen & Tinbergen, 1972; Ward, 1970; Zaslow & Breger, 1969), or early parental rejection or separation (Bettelheim, 1967; Despert, 1951; O'Gorman, 1970).

The research investigating the psychogenic hypotheses has yielded conflicting results. Several studies (Allen et al., 1971; Creak & Ini, 1960; DeMyer et al., 1972b; Klebanoff, 1959; Kolvin, Garside, & Kidd, 1971c; Pitfield & Oppenheim, 1964) have found no support for abnormal parental characteristics or parent-child interactions. Rutter (1974) points out that those studies yielding positive results have used projective tests (Meyer & Karon, 1967; Ogdom et al., 1968; Singer & Wynne, 1963) and selected family observations (Goldfarb et al., 1966; Meyers & Goldfarb, 1961) as measures and that other studies using similar measures have produced negative results (Anthony, 1958; Bene, 1958; Block, 1969; Donnelly, 1960).

The only consistent finding with regard to parental characteristics is the high prevalence of parents with significantly higher educational and occupational levels than controls (Cox et al., 1975; Kolvin et al., 1971d; Lotter, 1966, 1967; Lowe, 1966; Rutter & Lockyer, 1967; Treffert, 1970). Yet even this finding has been disputed. Schopler et al. (1979b) have recently demonstrated that the upperclass distribution is a function of various selection factors. In light of these results, most investigators have concluded that autism does not develop as a consequence of parental personality attributes.

The theory that autism is the result of early parental rejection or separation has also been refuted. Ornitz and Ritvo (1976) have argued against the separation hypothesis because

infants who have experienced early separations from parents present a different clinical picture. Such infants become weepy and demanding. If the separation lasts for a significant length of time, retardation, delay in language development, weight loss, and persistent crying are likely to occur. These children do not show the same pattern of cognitive abilities as autistic children, nor do they show disturbances in motility but instead become apathetic and withdrawn (Ornitz & Ritvo, 1976).

Similarly, children who experience long term deprivation from birth are different from autistic children. Although some abnormal motility patterns may be present, they are of a different nature from those of autistic children and they are easily interrupted or totally eliminated (Ornitz & Ritvo, 1976). Unlike autistic children, deprived children may intensely gaze at adults. Retardation of language and other cognitive skills may be present but does not follow similar patterns to that of autistic children. Most importantly, these children are often able to catch up when their deprivation is abated.

In conclusion, there is little evidence to support a psychogenic origin of autism. However, studies have demonstrated that the extreme emotional stress of being a parent of an autistic child can precipitate emotional problems in many parents (Creak & Ini, 1960; Schopler, 1971).

Neurological Correlates

The decreasing emphasis on psychogenic theories of autism in the last two decades has been accompanied by increasing research on the possible role of brain dysfunction. Several studies of birth histories of autistic children have found an increased incidence of prenatal and perinatal complications as compared to control groups (Knobloch & Pasamanick, 1962; Kolvin, Ounsted, & Roth, 1971b; Lobascher, Kingerlee, & Gubbay, 1970; Taft & Goldfarb, 1964), including maternal rubella, prematurity, caesarean section, difficult labor, encephalitis, seizures, respiratory distress, and Rh incompatibility, among others.

used to decrease antisocial aggression and While neurological examinations of most autistic children reveal no major disturbances, the presence of "soft" neurological signs (e.g., hypotonia, hyperactive knee jerks, poor coordination, generalized hyperflexia) has been reported in 40–100 percent of autistic children, depending on the sample studied (DeMyer et al., 1973; Goldfarb, 1961; Gubbay, Lobascher, & Kingerlee, 1970; Hinton, 1963; Knoblock & Pasamanick, 1975).

Autism and autisticlike behavior have been found to occur in association with central nervous system viral infection (Chess, 1971), neonatal conditions related to brain damage such as retrolental fibroplasia (Keeler, 1958), tuberous sclerosis (Lotter, 1974), congenital syphillis (Rutter & Lockyer, 1967), infantile seizures (Creak, 1963; Kolvin et al., 1971b; Taft & Cohen, 1971), metabolic disturbances (e.g., phenylketonuria) (Knobloch & Pasamanick, 1975; Sorosky et al., 1968; Wing, 1966), and widespread neurolipidosis (Creak, 1963).

Autistic children are often reported to have seizure disorders (Creak, 1963). Kolvin et al. (1971b) found histories of grand mal seizures in five cases and of psychomotor seizures in another five cases from a group of 46 autistic children. In a follow-up study, Rutter and his colleagues (Rutter et al., 1967) found that 25 percent of their sample developed seizures in adolescence despite a lack of previous neurological signs. Rutter (1970) has suggested that this feature may be part of the natural course of the disorder in many lower functioning (IQ<50) children.

Electroencephalograms (EEG) have been abnormal for autistic children in 20–30 percent of the cases in some studies (Gubbay et al., 1970; Kolvin et al., 1971b) and in 60–80 percent of the cases in other studies (Creak & Pampiglione, 1969; White et al., 1964). These abnormal EEGs are characterized by focal slowing, spiking, or paroxysmal spike-wave discharges. Kolvin et al. (1971b) found that approximately one-third of the 46 autistic children they studied showed abnormal EEG records. Two studies reporting the presence of a low voltage EEG record (indicative of an unusually high level of cortical arousal) (Hutt et al., 1964; Kolvin et al., 1971b) have not been replicated (Creak & Pampiglione, 1969; Hermelin & O'Connor, 1968).

Ornitz and Ritvo (Ornitz, 1972; Ornitz, Ritvo, & Walter, 1965; Ritvo, Ornitz, & Eviator, 1969) have conducted a number of neurophysiological studies with autistic children. They showed that although these children have a normal sleep cycle with normal amounts of rapid eye movement (REM) sleep, the REM activity (i.e., rate of eye movements) of REM sleep is reduced, making their pattern of sleep activity similar to that of a normal infant. This finding suggests that autism might be related to a maturational defect. In addition, these authors and others (Colbert, Koegler, & Markham, 1959; Pollack & Krieger, 1958; Ritvo et al., 1969) have demonstrated that vestibularly induced nystagmus is suppressed in autistic children and that vestibular stimulation does not influence the REMs of REM sleep in autistic children as it does in normal children (Ornitz et al., 1965).

Neuropsychological Theories

The diversity of neurological and etiological findings in autistic children suggests that underlying structural and neurophysiological abnormalities are manifold. However, one must still account for how such diverse types of pathology could lead to the relatively consistent syndrome of cognitive, social, and behavioral aberrations seen in autism. Rutter (1978a) has argued that autism may be without a single cause but nevertheless have a common biological defect (similar to the case of cerebral palsy). One possibility is that while the diversity of neurological deficits may imply multiple etiologies, the deficits may have two factors in common: (1) a relatively specifically localized defect in the brain and (2) the fact that the defect is congenital (or at least present) very early in life.

Based on these assumptions, a number of hypotheses have been advanced to relate autistic behaviors to specific neurological dysfunctions. These may be grouped into four categories:

1.   Overarousal associated with dysfunction of the reticular system.

2. Perceptual inconstancy associated with dysfunction of the vestibular nuclei in the brain stem.

3. Stereotyped behaviors and learning deficits associated with dysfunction of the limbic system.

4. Specific cognitive deficits associated with left hemisphere dysfunction.

Hutt et al. (1964) hypothesized that the nonspecific activity of the reticular system is chronically high in autistic children, resulting in a constant high state of arousal. These authors reported evidence of high levels of low voltage irregular activity (indicative of a high level of arousal) in the resting EEGs of autistic children. Given that behavioral withdrawal and stereotypic behavior have been associated with high arousal levels in experimental animals, Hutt and his colleagues theorized that the stereotypic behaviors of autistic children may be an attempt to maintain sameness in their environments as a defense against overarousal. Several carefully controlled studies have tested the overarousal hypothesis. Hermelin and O'Connor (1968) found that autistic and matched mentally retarded children did not show differences in cortical arousal nor was any relationship between arousal as measured by EEG and observable behavioral arousal found. These results and those from similar studies (Churchill, 1971; Ornitz et al., 1970) have led to the conclusion that it is unlikely that autistic behaviors are a defense against overarousal.

The theory of perceptual inconstancy was advanced by Ornitz and Ritvo (1968). In this account, the inability to regulate sensory input is postulated to underlie the deficits of these children. The authors argue that an inability to maintain stable percepts over time precludes the establishment of a coherent, meaningful external reality. Their theory is based upon the observations of behaviors that have been interpreted to reflect fluctuating over- and underarousal and also on research indicating that vestibularly induced nystagmus is suppressed in autistic children (Colbert et al., 1959; Pollack & Krieger, 1958; Ritvo et al., 1969). It has also been shown that vestib-

ular stimulation does not influence the rapid eye movements or REM sleep in autistic children as it does in normal children (Ornitz, 1972; Ornitz et al., 1965). These data have been interpreted to imply a defect in the homeostatic regulation of sensory input and motor output. One weakness of Ornitz and Ritvo's theory is that the precise nature of the proposed "instability of perception" and its effect on development are not clearly delineated. Their theory does not appear to explain why autistic children do not have deficits in selective areas, such as visual-motor skills. It seems that the impairment proposed by Ornitz and Ritvo should affect perceptual processing in all spheres, and yet there are areas of functioning in which autistic children are relatively unimpaired.

A third neuropsychological explanation for autism has been proposed by Boucher and Warrington (1976) and DeLong (1978). They have suggested that autism may be similar to the amnesic syndrome arising from a lesion of the limbic system. Boucher and Warrington based their hypothesis on the fact that animals with hippocampal lesions show motor stereotypy associated with increased general activity, reduced exploration, and an inability to learn from errors. In humans, this syndrome involves specific memory deficits characterized by global deficits in long term memory with cued recall remaining intact. Therefore, to test the autism-amnesia hypothesis, Boucher and Warrington (1976) administered a series of carefully designed verbal and nonverbal memory experiments to autistic and ability-matched children. The results indicated some similarity between the memory functions of autistic children and amnesic adults. Verbal and nonverbal memory was generally impaired whereas cued recall was consistently normal. However, two major findings contradicted the autism-amnesia hypothesis. First, only some of the autistic children tested exhibited impairments in recall. Second, autistic children were found to have normal learning of unrelated word pairs, a finding that directly contradicts the data obtained from amnesic adults. While the Boucher and Warrington data are not fully supportive of a parallel between autism and amnesia, this discrepancy may be due to the lesions in autism being congenital and thus producing somewhat different clinical symptoms from amnesia.

Several investigators (Blackstock, 1978; Dawson, 1979; Prior & Bradshaw, 1979; Tanguay, 1976) have pointed out that the specific cognitive and language impairments found in autism are typical of those functions for which the left cerebral hemisphere is specialized. In contrast, many autistic children show normal or superior abilities in right hemisphere functions, such as visual-spatial skills and music (Lockyer & Rutter, 1970). Tanguay (1976) found that autistic children show larger evoked responses over the right than left hemisphere during REM sleep. Using different methods, Prior and Bradshaw (1979) and Dawson (1982) found a high percentage of autistic children to have an atypical pattern of hemispheric specialization that is often associated with early left hemisphere damage. Blackstock (1978) found that autistic children attend more readily to a story that is sung rather than spoken to them and, furthermore, do so predominantly with the left ear. Based on these findings, Blackstock suggests that autistic children prefer to process information in a "right hemisphere mode."

Two anatomical studies are also relevant to the left hemisphere theory. Hauser, DeLong, and Rosman (1975) reported pneumoencephalographic (PEG) findings for a group of 18 children who had a history of retarded language development and autistic behaviors without any specific neurological disease or gross motor disturbances. PEG findings included, most prominently, pathological enlargement of the left temporal horn in 15 cases. While this study suffers from lack of blind judgment and lack of a control group, it did serve as an impetus for further research in this area. In one such study, which utilized computerized brain tomography, Hier, LeMay, and Rosenberger (1979) measured left-right anatomical asymmetries of the parieto-occipital region in autistic, mentally retarded, and miscellaneous neurological patients. In 57 percent of the autistic patients, the right parieto-occipital region was wider than the left (a pattern reverse of that which is typically

found in normal subjects). This pattern of cerebral asymmetry was found in only 23 percent of the mentally retarded patients and 25 percent of the neurological patients.

Rutter (1974) has argued that a selective dysfunction of the left hemisphere in autism is implausible since the plasticity of the infant brain would make right hemisphere compensation for such dysfunction very likely. This apparent lack of right hemisphere compensation for left-sided dysfunction in autism is puzzling and suggests the possibility of bilateral dysfunction, at least in some cases.

Genetic Contribution

Kanner (1943) was the first to suggest that hereditary influences may play a part in the etiology of autism. A family history of speech delay is found in about one-fourth of the families with autistic children (Bartak et al., 1975), and the 2 percent rate of autism in siblings is 50 times that of the general population (Rutter, 1967b). A hereditary influence is also supported by a study carried out by Folstein and Rutter (1977). They examined 21 same-sex twins in which at least one twin was diagnosed as autistic. They found 4 of the 11 monozygotic (MZ) pairs but none of the 10 dizygotic (DZ) pairs were concordant for autism. In addition, six nonautistic co-twins (5 MZ and 1 DZ) showed a cognitive abnormality in the form of severe speech delay, learning disabilities, or mental retardation. Furthermore, in 12 of the 17 pairs of twins discordant for autism, there was evidence that the autistic member had suffered brain injury, whereas in none of the discordant pairs did this occur. Folstein and Rutter conclude that autism probably has multiple etiologies, including brain damage and genetic abnormalities.

Biochemical Studies

Studies of blood levels of the neurotransmitter serotonin have received the most attention thus far. Schain and Freedman (1961) compared 23 autistic children to those whose primary diagnosis was mental retardation and found abnormally high levels of blood serotonin in association with autism and severe mental retardation. These authors did not find a relationship between elevated serotonin levels and presenting symptoms in the children. In a series of studies, Ritvo and his colleagues (Ritvo et al., 1971; Ritvo et al., 1970) have found that while mean serotonin levels and platelet counts were significantly higher than age-matched controls, mean serotonin per platelet levels were not significantly different. Also, the blood serotonin levels appear to be an age-related phenomenon; serotonin levels decrease with age, which suggests a possible maturational basis for elevated serotonin levels in autism. Other studies (Campbell et al., 1976) have indicated that higher serotonin levels are most clearly related to low intellectual functioning. The administration of L-Dopa, which lowers blood serotonin, does not appear to produce behavioral changes in autistic children (Campbell et al., 1976; Ritvo et al., 1971).

Cohen and his colleagues (Cohen et al., 1977; Cohen, Johnson, & Bowers, 1974; Cohen, Caparulo, & Shaywitz, 1978) have postulated that autism is related to dopaminergic overactivity and furthermore that there exists a reciprocal relationship between dopaminergic and serotonergic functioning. Another promising lead is Coleman's (1978) report of zinc deficiencies in autistic children.

Thus far, autism has not been specifically and consistently related to any particular biochemical abnormality. This is due, in part, to the lack of careful diagnostic classification and control groups in most studies. Given the emerging consensus on diagnostic classification and the current emphasis on more carefully controlled studies, this approach may potentially be fruitful in our understanding and, perhaps, treatment of autism.

Fundamental Deficit

Parents of autistic children often report that the behaviors that normally elicit social responses in others, such as smiling, eye contact, cuddling, reaching out, and gesturing were lacking in their autistic infants. Experiments by Hermelin and O'Connor (1970) suggest that the social unresponsiveness of autistic children is not due to active *avoidance* of social contact. Instead, it is now generally agreed that poor communication skills due to underlying perceptual and cognitive deficiencies contribute greatly to the appearance of social indifference in autistic children. The nature of these perceptual and/or cognitive deficits is a subject of current investigation. The autistic child's severe verbal language impairment, per se, undoubtedly interferes with social interaction. Abnormalities in prelinguistic skills, such as babbling and using sounds to express desires (Ricks, 1972), are known to exist. Research has shown that autistic children have a number of verbal processing deficits including difficulties in sequential information processing (Frith, 1969; O'Connor & Hermelin, 1972); in perception of the rhythmic, intonational, and stress patterns of speech (Simmons & Baltaxe, 1975); in making auditory-visual associations (Churchill, 1972; Cowan et al., 1965; Walker & Birch, 1970); and in the use of semantic information (O'Connor & Hermelin, 19767a; O'Connor & Hermelin, 1967b; Simmons & Baltaxe, 1975). Yet based on careful comparisons of language-impaired and autistic children (Bartak et al., 1975), it is clear that the autistic child's communication disability extends beyond spoken language to include both gesture and "inner language." It is likely that a more fundamental cognitive and/or perceptual deficit is responsible for the autistic child's abnormalities in social behavior.

Based on a series of experiments involving comparisons between autistic children and children with sensory (blind, deaf) and cognitive (mentally retarded) impairments (Hermelin & O'Connor, 1970, 1971, 1975; O'Connor & Hermelin, 1973, 1975), Hermelin (1978) has concluded that autism is related to an inability to form internal representations of external events. Based on Piagetian theory, Hermelin argues that the lack of internal representation affects several realms of development, including language, play, and the formation of stable emotional relationships, all of which depend on symbolic functioning.

DeMyer and her co-workers (DeMyer et al., 1972a) believe that the autistic child's difficulty with motor imitation underlies his or her social withdrawal or ineptness. She postulates that autistic children are lacking either in the ability to remember visually their own or others' motor actions, or the ability to make the necessary cross-modal transfer from visual stimulus to their own motor system, which leads to a condition akin to motor imitative dyspraxia. DeMyer points out that when a child suffers from both an auditory processing deficit and perceptual visual-motor deficit of this kind, he or she is unable to communicate in either the verbal or nonverbal modalities.

Treatment

Treatments of autism to date can be grouped under three categories: psychodynamic, biological, and behavioral. Most of the psychodynamically oriented therapies have been based on the assumption that autism is an emotional disorder and have emphasized intensive psychotherapy for the parents and play therapy for the children. Biological interventions have explored the full range of drug treatments, while the behavioral therapies have utilized the principles of learning from experimental psychology to teach autistic people a variety of behavioral and educational skills.

Psychodynamically Oriented Therapies

One of the most influential of the psychodynamically oriented therapists has been Bruno Bettelheim (1974), who argues that cold and rejecting parents are the primary cause of the children's autism. His treatment begins with the removal of the children from their parents' home and their placement in a residential setting. Once removed from the home environment, the autistic child can let down his or her psychotic defenses and trust can be established. The combination of a separate therapeutic milieu removed from parental control plus individual, psychodynamically oriented therapy has also been advocated by Ruttenberg (1971) and Goldfarb, Mintz, and Strook (1969).

The individual therapy in these psychodynamically oriented approaches generally focuses on establishing some form of positive relationship with the child. Because most psychodynamic theories postulate the cause of the autism as residing in the parents, the establishment of this relationship is generally done by someone outside of the family who is either the therapist or a housemanager in a residential program. Play and interview techniques are utilized and interpretation of symbolic meanings is stressed. In addition to attempts at establishing relationships, attempts are made to reactivate the delayed psychosexual stages.

Although DesLauriers (1978) views autism as a sensory impairment instead of the outgrowth of inadequate parenting, he will be described under the psychodynamic approaches because of treatment similarities. DesLauriers argues for pheraplay, a form of play therapy, as the best way to provide sensory stimulating experiences that are intense enough to overcome the child's basic sensory deficit. Pheraplay is somewhat different from traditional play therapy in that the child is not taught anything specifically. Instead, the child learns to enjoy interpersonal interactions because they are of a highly stimulating nature.

In general, the psychodynamically oriented therapies are infrequently used by most clinicians working with autistic children today. One reason for this is that the cumulative evidence now refutes the assumptions upon which these theories are based. Autism is not seen as a result of inadequate parenting but rather of some nonspecific brain abnormalities (DeMyer, 1979; Ross, 1980; Rutter & Schopler, 1978). Because there is little evidence that autism is an emotional problem, there is little reason to believe that treatments based on this assumption will be effective. Moreover, the few studies done on the effectiveness of psychodynamically oriented psychotherapy with psychotic youngsters have shown no differences in children treated this way as compared with a group of untreated controls (Brown, 1960, 1963).

Biological Interventions

With the recent recognition of autism as more a biological than an emotional condition, there has been an increased emphasis on the use of drugs as a treatment strategy. The drugs that have been most frequently used with autistic clients have been the anticonvulsants, amphetamines, phenothiazines, and, more recently, the megavitamins.

Anticonvulsant drugs are used to control seizures in autistic people in much the same way that they are used with the general population and will therefore not be discussed further in this context. (See chap. 47 by Campbell, Perry, & Green in this book for information on this subject.) However, the high incidence of seizures among autistic people (Deykin & MacMahon, 1979) makes anticonvulsant medications part of many treatment regimes. The amphetamines are sometimes helpful in reducing the hyperactivity that often accompanies autism. Although these drugs do not produce recovery from autism, they can improve the attention spans and activity levels of these children and make them more susceptible to other forms of learning. Although there are many clinical reports of the effectiveness of the amphetamines, the only published studies with autistic children show worsening of behavior when treated with these drugs (Campbell et al., 1972).

The phenothiazines and haloperidol have been useful, though unpredictable, in reducing severe aggressive and self-injurious behaviors (Dalldorf & Schopler, 1981). These can also increase the learning deficits in autistic children and must be carefully monitored for side effects, including excessive weight gain, reduced seizure threshold, and tardive dyskinesia (Schiele et al., 1973).

Lithium, generally used with manic-depressive patients, has more recently been used with some autistic clients, especially those exhibiting aggressive or self-injurious behaviors, who have not been responsive to other forms of drug treatment. Campbell et al. (1972) found that, in general, lithium produced very small and relatively insignificant improvement in a sample of preschool children with the exception of one child whose self-mutilation behaviors were reduced "dramatically." Lithium is probably most appropriate for autistic children who show a cyclical behavior pattern and/or family history of cyclical affective illness. Lithium is especially difficult to monitor, and there is a very narrow range between therapeutic and toxic levels.

The use of megavitamins has been another recent addition to the available biological treatments. This approach involves the use of large doses of various standard vitamins. Although rigorous research studies have not yet demonstrated the effectiveness of megavitamin therapy for groups of autistic people (Greembaum, 1970), it is being widely used and reports of improvement for individual children are common (Rimland, 1973).

In summary, biological interventions are probably less effective with autistic children than with other populations because of their unpredictable and idiosyncratic responses. However, when responsibly administered and carefully monitored, these can, at times, represent an important adjunct to other treatment efforts.

Behavioral Interventions

It has frequently been argued that the dramatic progress in working with autistic people over the past fifteen years has been the direct result of the behavioral interventions replacing the more psychodynamically oriented treatment approaches (Ross, 1980; Rutter & Schopler, 1978). These have, in fact, become the most commonly used treatment techniques. For the purposes of this discussion, the behavioral approaches will be divided into two major categories, as outlined by Schopler and Dalldorf (1980): behavior management and special education. Although there is some overlap between the categories, behavior management is primarily concerned with social and interpersonal behaviors and special education concerns more conventional school-related skills such as lanuage.

Behavior Management

Behavior management techniques have been used to train a wide variety of social and interpersonal behaviors, including imitation skills and eye contact. They have also been self-injurious behaviors. In addition, this approach has been the crucial ingredient in a number of parent-training programs.

Behavioral techniques have been utilized in developing appropriate social skills in several ways. Although most of the socialization research has focused on improving social skills by decreasing inappropriate behaviors, there have been several attempts specifically to increase appropriate behaviors.

The early investigations of social behavior assumed the main problem to be nonresponsiveness to social rewards. Lovaas et al. (1966b) developed responsiveness to social rewards by giving food to autistic children for attending and responding to social stimuli. Later, they were able to use these social stimuli without food to reinforce other behaviors. These operant techniques have also been used gradually to shape social behaviors, such as showing affection and giving friendly greetings (Lovaas, Schreibman, & Koegel, 1974).

Another early approach to developing social behaviors through operant techniques involved the teaching of imitation skills (Metz, 1965), suggesting that these represent the foundation upon which appropriate social interactions are built. Using food, tokens that could be traded for food, and the word "good," Metz taught imitative responses like kicking a beanbag, putting a blanket on a doll, and blowing a whistle. He also demonstrated that these imitative behaviors could be generalized to new tasks.

A more recent study is one of the few to teach interactive social behaviors directly (Romancyzk et al., 1975). Using food as reward, they were able to increase the cooperative toy play of autistic children with other children in a group setting. If this reinforcement was gradually faded out instead of abruptly withdrawn, the appropriate play continued.

The severe behavioral difficulties presented by autistic children have led to considerably more effort being put into decreasing these behaviors than increasing some more appropriate alternatives. Risley and Wolf (1967) first demonstrated the effectiveness of behavioral techniques in bringing mildly disruptive

behaviors under control by looking away from a child until he sat quietly in his chair. When more severe behaviors occurred, they responded with a more severe time-out procedure consisting of leaving the room. Lovaas and Simmons (1969) used a similar time-out procedure in withdrawing attention for self-injurious behaviors. This procedure was also effective in reducing the incidence of these behaviors.

Although time-out can sometimes be an effective intervention technique, there are several drawbacks. First, as Solnick, Rincover, and Peterson (1977) demonstrated, it is important to be sure that the time-out procedure is more negative than the task the child is being asked to complete. In their study, they found that tantrums increased when the teacher left the room during a work period. Their conclusion was that time-out allowed the child to work on self-stimulatory behaviors, which were more reinforcing than the required task and the teacher's presence. In this situation, physical restraint was a more effective deterrent than time-out.

Time-out is also less effective when the behaviors in question are extremely severe and potentially dangerous. In these situations, several investigators have successfully used electric shock to suppress these potentially life-threatening behaviors (Lovaas, Schaeffer, & Simmons, 1965; Risley, 1968). These investigators are all quick to point out that shock should only be used for extremely dangerous behaviors requiring immediate suppression and when less intrusive techniques have proven ineffective. In addition to the serious ethical issues involved with the use of shock, there is also the problem that it only eliminates certain behaviors and must be used in conjunction with positive techniques designed to build more positive behaviors (Lovaas & Newsom, 1976).

Several other behavioral techniques have also proven effective with aggressive and self-injurious behaviors. Carr, Newsom, and Binkoff (1976) noted a mildly retarded child hit his head whenever the teacher made a specific request of him. This behavior was decreased by making the requests less aversive and more entertaining for the child. Carr (1977) suggests that substituting more stimulating behaviors might be a way of eliminating some of the self-injurious and destructive behaviors. Other investigators (Allen & Harris, 1966) have established competing behaviors that, once established, are incompatible with the destructive behaviors and thereby prevent them from occurring. In a recent study, Jones, Simmons, and Frankel (1974) have demonstrated the effectiveness of a noncontingent social isolation program. Working with a girl who had not responded to electroshock, the investigators placed her in an isolated room for two-hour sessions twice each day. The use of this program resulted in a significant decrease in both hitting and jabbing behaviors.

Overall, the research on reducing aggressive and self-injurious behaviors suggests that a number of techniques have been effective in specific instances. However, most of these results have only indicated suppression of specific behaviors in single, short term instances. What is now needed are more comprehensive approaches to the total child that can be applied in a variety of situations. Favell (in press) suggests such an approach by outlining six necessary conditions for any behavioral intervention to be effective. These include a careful analysis of both biological and environmental conditions that might be maintaining the behavior, environmental arrangements that insure the safety of the client while the behavior is being worked on, strengthening of appropriate alternative behaviors, reduction of reinforcement for aggression, changing the environmental conditions that are associated with aggression, and, in severe cases, including a punishment for the aggressive behavior itself. More comprehensive treatment approaches, along these lines, should be helpful in producing long term changes that generalize across situations.

In addition to the already described uses of behavioral techniques to manage specific behaviors of autistic children, behavioral approaches have also been the main component of parent-training programs. Although there is an extensive literature on behavioral techniques for parent training (Baker & Heifetz,

1976; Berkowitz & Graziano, 1972), most of this work has not involved autistic children and their families. Even though the use of these training techniques has been more limited with autistic people, the impact has been quite significant.

Schopler and Reichler (1971) have used parent collaboration and training as the major component of their statewide program. In their initial study, they demonstrated that parents were not only the victims (rather than the cause) of their children's autism, but also that they could be trained as effective teachers of their children, using behavioral techniques. Marcus et al. (1978) and Short (1980) have demonstrated specific improvement in parent-child interaction as a result of participation in the North Carolina TEACCH program. In addition to helping parents learn behavioral techniques, the TEACCH program emphasizes collaboration of parents and professionals toward meeting parent-identified needs.

Hemsley et al. (1978) have used a similar parent-training model after noting that gains produced in hospital settings did not generalize to the home. However, their technique differs from the North Carolina program in that they work directly with parents in their homes rather than at the clinic. Their rationale is that autistic children behave very differently in the clinic and the home and that certain behaviors of importance can be observed only in the home setting.

The specifics of the Hemsley et al. (1978) behavioral intervention approach are described elsewhere (Rutter & Sussenwein, 1971). In general, the parents are trained in using behavioral techniques, including identifying appropriate objectives, identifying conditions that maintain behaviors, using appropriate reinforcement and punishment techniques, and being consistent in the interactions with their autistic children. As a result of the families' participation in this program, notable progress was observed in the autistic children.

As with the England group, Lovaas (1978) began training parents when he became concerned about the lack of improvement for children discharged from his center. His parent-training model relies heavily upon the parents working as apprentices with senior therapists to learn the behavioral treatment techniques. The Lovaas model also involves some reading about behavior management and parent-therapist discussions. As a result of these interventions, Lovaas believes that institutionalization is no longer required for most of his children because effective instruction can now be carried out in the home.

In summary, most of the efforts at social and interpersonal skills training for autistic people have been placed on reducing inappropriate behaviors and parent training. The area of specific social skills training has been somewhat neglected because the severity of these inappropriate behaviors and the needs of families to deal with them more effectively have made them the major priority. Howlin (1978) accurately describes the current state of affairs in stating that "investigations of the ways in which autistic children can be helped more adequately in social situations are badly needed" (Rutter & Schopler, 1978, p. 66).

Special Education

Behavioral interventions have also been important components of the special education programs offered to autistic children. These techniques have influenced the overall organization of educational services as well as the teaching of specific skills such as language.

Until recently, it has been very difficult to assess the effectiveness of any special education services for autistic children because of the lack of controlled studies (Bartak, 1978). The few reported studies suffer from major methodological shortcomings that make them hard to evaluate (Yule & Berger, 1972). More recently, Bartak and Rutter (1973) have assessed the effectiveness of the behaviorally oriented special education component in their Maudsley study. Their preliminary results suggest that autistic children can make progress in an intensive, behaviorally oriented, individualized educational program. It also appears that the degree of organization and structure correlates positively with the amount of progress.

Lansing and Schopler (1978) also argue

that behaviorally oriented special education techniques must be adapted for individualized use if autistic children are to learn and that the involvement of parents in the learning process is essential for promoting transfer of learning from the classroom to the home. In the North Carolina statewide program, they have developed organizational structures to try to maximize individualization and generalization. Individualization is facilitated by the direct assessment of children using the Psychoeducational Profile (Schopler & Reichler, 1979a), which was developed by the program to be responsive to the needs and skills of autistic children. Generalization is brought about by the involvement of parents as cotherapists for their autistic children (Schopler & Reichler, 1971). There are five treatment centers around the state of North Carolina where parents can be trained in behavioral techniques to work individually with their autistic children. This assures the transfer of skills developed in other parts of the program to the home environment.

The major issues in the education of autistic people seem to be their need for structure and also for specialized educational programs. Many investigators have advocated the need for a structured, behavioral approach (Bartak & Pickering, 1976; Rutter, 1970; Wing, 1976); however, there are differing opinions as to what that means. Some refer to the structuring of the entire school day, including planning, organization, and regularly scheduled activities, while others talk about specific learning tasks. It appears that structure on both levels is probably optimal for this population of children who seem unable to structure adaptively and organize experiences on their own.

Because autism is above all a language and communication disorder, many of the educational intervention efforts have focused on this central problem. The earliest intervention strategy designed to improve the language skills of autistic children was the operant-conditioning approach. In one of the original studies, Lovaas et al. (1966a) trained speech word-by-word using food as a reinforcement for successive approximations of adult speech.

They began by reinforcing any sound that the child could produce and then gradually required these sounds to approximate adult speech. Similar training techniques were employed by Schell, Stark, and Giddan (1967) to increase verbal and nonverbal responses to visual and verbal stimulation and by Long and Rasmussen (1974) to teach autistic children to use simple and compound sentences and to describe a set of pictures.

The operant approach has led to significant advances in the teaching of language to autistic people. It has also helped to increase our understanding of language, thereby leading to the development of other techniques. In utilizing the operant approach, Risley and Wolf (1967) noted that it was easier to teach echolalic children than children with no language at all. This suggests that echolalia represents an early phase of language learning for autistic children, even though echolalia appears to be simple imitation. Carr, Schreibman, and Lovaas (1975) have argued that echolalic speech represents a response strategy that autistic children employ in situations where they are unable to make an appropriate response. They taught children a series of nonsense sentences and then taught appropriate responses to some of them but not to others. The children in this study tended to evidence echolalic speech when they had no appropriate responses to the nonsense syllables but were less likely to do this once appropriate responses had been taught.

The most recent approach to language training with autistic children has been the use of sign language. De Villiers and Naughton (1974) used sign language with two autistic children having very limited expressive language. By pairing signs with words, they found improvement in communication skills, even though they only used two sessions of 15 minutes per week. Fulwiler and Fouts (1976) used signs with a 5-year-old autistic boy. After 20 sessions, this child had learned to use several signs appropriately, and this seemed to increase his verbal output. The training seemed to generalize to other situations where the child was observed to be more attentive and more easily manageable as well. Offir

(1976) taught 30 autistic children to use sign language to label objects, make requests, and express feelings. A total communication approach was used in which signs and spoken English were presented simultaneously. As a result of this approach, Offir noted improvement in her most severely retarded children as well as some of the more advanced children.

In summary, behavioral interventions have been influential in improving a wide variety of behavioral and educational skills. Although the emphasis has been on using these techniques to reduce the many inappropriate behaviors that autistic children evidence, more recent applications have included the teaching of more appropriate skills as well as the integration of specific techniques into comprehensive intervention programs.

CHILDHOOD SCHIZOPHRENIA

Characteristics

In his original description of adult schizophrenia, Bleuler (1911/1950) noted that this disorder could appear as early as the seventh year. Kanner (1957) stated that the older the child at the onset of psychosis, the more closely the clinical picture resembled adult schizophrenia. Since these preliminary observations, there have been a number of studies of the children who develop Bleuler type symptoms relatively early in life. These symptoms include disturbances in thought processes and affect (e.g., thought insertion and thought broadcast), hallucinations (e.g., hallucinatory voices in the form of running commentary, visual, and bodily hallucinations), and well-formed delusions (e.g., delusions of persecution or grandeur). While auditory hallucinations are common in both children and adults (Kolvin, 1971b), the occurrence of visual hallucinations is somewhat higher in children (Eggers, 1978; Kolvin, 1971b). Kolvin (1971b) documented a number of mood abnormalities in association with childhood schizophrenia, including inappropriate giggling, incongruity, blunting of affect, perplexity, rages, self-directed aggression, and ambivalence. However, only blunting and incongruity of affect were reliable discriminators between childhood schizophrenia and autism.

Other characteristics of childhood schizophrenia include movement abnormalities (present in 18 percent of Kolvin's sample) and impaired relationships. Kolvin (1971b) stresses, however, that while poor relational ability is an important feature of schizophrenia it is not a central characteristic (as in autism). In his sample, only half of the children diagnosed as schizophrenic mixed poorly or avoided contact with adults or other children.

The prevalence of childhood schizophrenia is unknown, although it is thought to be rarer than autism (Kolvin, 1971a). Kolvin (1971b) found a predominance of boys with this disorder; the sex ratio in his sample was 2.6:1, which is somewhat lower than is typically found in autism. This ratio is similar to that reported by Loew (1966) and Kallmann and Roth (1956). Age of onset for the disorder is not well established. Most children in Kolvin's (1971b) sample were not clearly recognized as schizophrenic until 7 years of age or older. Eggers (1978) found that children who manifested the disorder below 10 years of age were more likely to have a chronic rather than acute course and were less likely to have an eventual remission. Kolvin (1971b) and Eggers (1978) both reported that at early ages the onset is usually insidious rather than acute.

Kolvin et al. (1971a) found clear evidence of a depression in IQ scores in his sample of schizophrenic children amounting to almost one standard deviation below the mean. Only half of the children scored in the normal range. However, these children scored markedly superior to a comparison group of autistic children; IQs greater than 70 were four times more prevalent in the schizophrenic group. In addition, the schizophrenic children were found to fare better than the autistic children in school and were more responsive, in general, to therapy and educational programs. Eggers (1978) found that schizophrenic children with above average IQs were more likely to show a favorable outcome; the reverse was true for children of below average intelligence.

While most investigators agree that schizophrenia is, in part, organically based, no consistent organic deficit has yet been found in childhood schizophrenia. Epilepsy is found in only a minority of cases (Kolvin et al., 1971b). Temporal lobe epilepsy is the most common, as is the case with adult schizophrenia (Slater, Beard, & Glithero, 1963; Davison & Bagley, 1969). Pregnancy and birth complications were documented in 12 percent of Kolvin's cases. Biochemical studies of schizophrenic children are generally lacking. Unfortunately, the few studies that exist suffer from unclear diagnostic criteria. A number of studies have reported that bufotenin (the N-dimethylated derivative of serotonin) is present in the urine of schizophrenic adults (Himwich et al., 1972; Narasimachari & Himwich, 1975). However, studies of schizophrenic children have found no differences in the uptake rates of serotonin by platelets of normal, autistic, or schizophrenic children (Lucas, Krause, & Domino, 1971; Siva-Sankar, 1970).

Genetic and Environmental Factors

The increased incidence of schizophrenia in families of schizophrenic patients—estimated to occur in about 11 percent of parents and siblings of schizophrenic individuals (Essen-Moller, 1955)—has led investigators to search for a genetic cause for the disorder. The concordance rate for monozygotic twins, in which at least one twin was affected, is significantly higher than that for dizygotic twins, ranging from 50 to 80 percent concordance (Gottesman & Shields, 1966; Kallmann, 1946; Kringlen, 1967; Rosenthal, 1959; Slater, 1953). The most compelling evidence for a genetic basis comes from a series of Scandinavian studies in which children of schizophrenic mothers who were adopted at an early age continued to show an increased rate of schizophrenia or other personality disorders (Rosenthal & Kety, 1968).

It is now generally agreed that in most cases a genetic predisposition is a necessary (but not sufficient) prerequisite for the development of overt schizophrenia. The fact that only approximately one-half of the monozygotic twins are concordant for the disorder indicates that other factors, such as prenatal or perinatal complications and/or environmental stresses during childhood, contribute to the development of schizophrenia. In support of environmental influences, Kringlen (1967) found that concordant twins tend to be raised in more similar environments that are characterized by less social contact with other children, closer relationships between the twins, and more overprotection by the parents than the environments of discordant twins. MacSweeney (1970), Pollin and Stabenau (1968), and Mednick et al. (1971) found that, in discordant pairs, the affected twin tended to weigh less at birth and was more likely to have feeding, sleeping, and other physiological problems during early infancy. However, these findings have not been substantiated in other studies (Kringlen, 1967; Shields, 1968). Several studies of disconcordant twins have reported that personality differences between the twins were apparent from early childhood (Kringlen, 1967; Pollin & Stabenau, 1968; Tienari, 1968). Typically, the affected twin was found to be more submissive, fearful, and dependent than the nonaffected co-twin.

The question of to what degree, if any, the family environment is a factor in the development of schizophrenia is a difficult one to resolve. The incidence of psychiatric illness is higher in parents of schizophrenic children, which could influence the quality of child rearing the child receives. Kolvin et al. (1971c) found that mothers of schizophrenic children tend to be more introverted, sensitive, and suspicious than the average. A "disturbed family atmosphere" was reported in 33 of the 57 schizophrenic children studied by Eggers (1978). However, family environment did not prove to be of prognostic value and in 24 cases, the environment was assessed as normal. While certain investigators (Singer & Wynne, 1965; Waxler & Mishler, 1970; Wynne, 1968) have documented disturbed communication patterns in families of schizophrenic children, attempts to replicate these findings have failed (Hirsch & Leff, 1971). Also, it is possible that these faulty communication patterns could have developed *in response* to the disturbed child, a conclusion that is supported by the tendency for the poor communication style to be directed toward the affected child only and not his or her siblings.

While it is likely that schizophrenia is the result of a complex interaction between genetic, interuterine, and possibly family factors, a clear understanding of the etiology of schizophrenia has not been established. There is good evidence, however, that when a strong predisposition for schizophrenia exists, environmental factors can play a significant role in the precipitation of schizophrenia. The onset of the original florid symptoms and subsequent relapses are often related to significant emotional stresses a person has recently experienced (Brown & Birley, 1968; Birley & Brown, 1970; Brown, 1972; Eggers, 1978; Kolvin, 1971b).

Early Identification

Bleuler (1911/1950) noted that early character anomalies were evident in more than half of the individuals who later became schizophrenic. These include a tendency toward seclusion, withdrawal, and irritability. Research (Garmezy, 1974; Waring & Rick, 1965; Watt, 1978) has generally supported Bleuler's observations. More recently, MacCrimmon et al. (1980) found that children who had been placed in foster homes at an early age showed increased social isolation and student role difficulties if their biological mothers were schizophrenic as compared with foster children whose biological parents have no record of psychiatric illness. In addition, half of these high risk children showed significant impairments on a battery of attention tasks. Attention deficits in offspring of schizophrenic parents have been reported in several additional studies (e.g., Asarnow et al., 1978; Grunebaum et al., 1974). These deficits are usually evident in about half of each group studied. It is not yet known whether these attentional deficits contribute to the development of schizophrenia or whether they result from it.

Kolvin (1971b) defined a number of atypical premorbid characteristics in his sample of 33 schizophrenic children. Half of the subjects showed a delay in developing speech, and 87 percent of the children were reported as being "odd or unusual" before the onset of the disorder. Most commonly, shyness, diffidence, withdrawal, timidity, and sensitivity were observed.

By studying infants born to schizophrenic mothers, Barbara Fish has identified a number of atypical features of central nervous system functioning that manifest themselves in early infancy and that are predictive of later development of schizophrenia in childhood. In a series of studies (Fish, 1957, 1959, 1971, 1975; Fish & Alpert, 1962; Fish et al., 1965, 1966b; Fish & Hagin, 1973), she and her colleagues report that young infants who eventually developed schizophrenia or severe personality disturbances showed disturbances in alertness, activity level, muscle tone, and autonomic stability. Moreover, deviations in the temporal organization of maturation that include regressions, accelerations, and/or retardation of selected areas of functioning were highly predictive of later vulnerability to psychosis. By two years of age, highly vulnerable infants were showing postural and visual-motor disturbances, physical growth irregularities, and problems of control over autonomic functions. These observations led Fish to conclude that a congenital neurointegrative deficit combined with a nonsupportive environment (e.g., pathological mothering) are highly related to the development of schizophrenia in childhood. Additional support for Fish's findings has recently been reported by Marcus et al. (1981). These authors have identified a subgroup of infants (born to a schizophrenic parent) who repeatedly perform poorly in motor and sensorimotor functioning during the first year. These infants were also particularly vulnerable to external insults and tended to have lower-than-normal birth weights.

Fish and Hagin (1973) propose that early deviations in development often cause the infant to feel incompetent and anxious in his or her strivings for mastery. Moreover, they hypothesize that visual-motor difficulties related to dyspraxia may stem from a lack of response to proprioceptive stimuli that may be indicative of an early form of impaired self-awareness.

Prognosis and Treatment

Most authors agree that the prognosis for complete recovery from childhood schizophrenia is generally poor (e.g., Fish, 1971; Rutter, 1967a). In a long term follow-up study of 57 cases of childhood schizophrenia, Eggers (1978) found that 20 percent had complete remission, 30 percent reached a relatively good social adjustment, and 50 percent had a moderate-to-poor outcome. Early age of onset (below 10 years), personality disturbances such as shyness and introversion, as well as below average intelligence were predictive of a poor outcome. Interestingly, family environment and family incidence of schizophrenia were not related to prognosis.

Treatment of childhood schizophrenia has generally consisted of a combined approach, involving behavioral management, special education, social skills training, individual and family psychotherapy, and drug therapy. Kolvin (1972) and others (Campbell et al., 1970; Engelhardt et al., 1973) have found prenothiazines to be helpful in some cases of childhood schizophrenia. However, carefully controlled drug outcome studies are lacking.

Fish (1976) advocates a preventive approach to the treatment of childhood schizophrenia. In her formulation, a multidisciplinary approach to prevention would include the following:

1. Early identification of preschizophrenic or vulnerable infants.

2. Stimulation or compensation for development in the areas in which the infant is lacking.

3. Remedial help for language and perceptual-motor problems.

4. Supervision and support to families.

Fish and her co-workers (Fish & Shapiro, 1965; Fish et al., 1966b, 1968) have found that response to treatment and long term outcome are both a function of the severity of the initial developmental impairments. In their clinical work with preschizophrenic infants, they have found that even the most severely disturbed children can be helped to develop without overt psychosis if treatment is comprehensive and begins at an early age.

CONCLUSIONS

The childhood psychoses are considered in terms of two distinct syndromes: early infantile autism and childhood schizophrenia. Significant differences between these two disorders include age of onset, symptomology, family history of schizophrenia, frequency of cerebral dysfunction, speech development, and IQ level.

It is now generally agreed that the major characteristics of early infantile autism are onset prior to 30 months of age, disturbances of speech and language, and impaired social relationships. Autistic children do share some characteristics with other developmental disabilities, such as mental retardation and developmental language disorders. However, research has now identified several significant differences between autism and each of these disorders, and, furthermore, these differences appear to be of practical utility in terms of prognosis and treatment.

The question of what the fundamental deficit is that accounts for autistic behavior has not been resolved. It is now generally agreed that the poor social and communication skills of autistic children are due to underlying perceptual and cognitive deficiencies. Careful comparisons of language impaired and autistic children suggest that the disability extends beyond spoken language to include difficulties in the use of gesture, motor imitation, and possibly in forming internal representations.

Several decades of research exploring the cause of autism have provided little evidence to support early psychogenic theories. Therefore, current research is focusing on the role of brain dysfunction in the etiology of autism. Neurological and etiological findings have included increased incidence of prenatal and perinatal complications and the presence of soft neurological signs, seizures, abnormal EEGs, and vestibular abnormalities. Autism has also been found to occur in association with a number of disease processes that affect the central nervous system.

The diversity of the neurological findings in autistic children suggests that autism is without a single cause. However, multiple etiologies may be contributing to a single biological defect, thus accounting for the relatively consistent syndrome of social and cognitive disturbances. Theories with regard to where this defect might be localized in the brain have included the reticular system, the vestibular nuclei in the brain stem, the limbic system, and the left hemisphere.

Other studies have investigated possible genetic and biochemical bases for autism. Evidence for a hereditary influence includes family history of speech delay, the 2 percent rate of autism in siblings, and the significantly higher concordance rate for autism in monozygotic as compared to dizygotic twins. Thus far, autism has not been specifically and consistently related to any particular biological abnormality. Some studies have indicated elevated serotonin levels. However, the elevation appears to be related to maturational delay rather than autism per se.

With the recent recognition of autism as a biologically based disorder, there has been increased use of drugs as a treatment method. Most frequently, these drugs have been the anticonvulsants, amphetamines, phenothiazines, and, more recently, the megavitamins. Generally, it has been found that biological interventions are less effective with autistic children than other populations because of their unpredictable and idiosyncratic responses. However, they have been found to be helpful in some cases when they are carefully monitored and used in conjunction with other treatment methods. The most commonly used treatment approach for autistic children is behavior management combined with special education programs. These techniques have been used to develop a wide variety of social skills, as well as to reduce aggressive and self-injurious behaviors. Behavioral approaches have also been a main component of parent-training programs. Effective special education for autistic children usually involves an intensive, behaviorally oriented, highly structured, individualized program that emphasizes language, social, and self-help skills.

In contrast to the abundant research in the area of autism, there exist relatively few well-controlled studies on childhood schizophrenia. This is due, in part, to the tendency of researchers in the past to fail to make careful diagnostic distinction between autism and childhood schizophrenia. Childhood schizophrenia is very similar to adult schizophrenia. The age of onset has been documented to occur as early as 7 years but more commonly occurs in early adolescence. Symptoms include disturbances in thought processes and affect, hallucinations, and delusions. Early age of onset and low intelligence are associated with poor prognosis.

Although most investigators agree that childhood schizophrenia is, in part, organically based, no consistent organic deficit has yet been found. The increased incidence of schizophrenia in families of schizophrenic patients has led to a search for a genetic cause for the disorder. Research suggests that, in most cases, a genetic predisposition is a necessary, but not sufficient, prerequisite for the development of schizophrenia. It is likely that the disorder is the result of a complex interaction between genetic, interuterine, and environmental factors.

A number of early characteristics have been identified in young infants and children who later become schizophrenic. These include personality traits, attentional deficits, visual-motor disturbances, and other maturational deviations.

Treatment of childhood schizophrenia has relied on a combined approach involving behavioral management, special education, family and individual psychotherapy, and drug therapy. Early identification of infants vulnerable to schizophrenia has allowed some clinicians to utilize a preventive approach with some success.

Our understanding of the childhood psy-choses in terms of their diagnostic criteria, causation, nature, and treatment has increased dramatically during the last several decades. Current research efforts are utilizing more consistent diagnostic criteria and carefully selected control groups. Studies that can clarify the etiology, nature, and development of the childhood psychoses will hopefully lead to better methods of early identification and more effective treatment approaches for psychotic children.

NOTES

1. Estimated Statistics on Blindness and Vision Problems. National Society for the Prevention of Blindness, New York, 1966, p. 33.

2. Human Communication and Its Disorders—An Overview. Subcommittee on Human Communication and Its Disorders, NINDS, Public Health Service, Bethesda, Maryland, 1969, p. 11.

REFERENCES

Allen, J.A., DeMyer, M.K., Norton, J.A., Pontius, W., & Yang, E. Intellectuality in parents of psychotic, subnormal and normal children. *Journal of Autism and Childhood Schizophrenia,* 1971, **1,** 311–326.

Allen, K.E., & Harris, F.R. Elimination of a child's excessive scratching by training the mother in reinforcement procedures. *Behaviour Research and Therapy,* 1966, **4,** 79–84.

Anthony, J. An experimental approach to the psychopathology of childhood: Autism. *British Journal of Medical Psychology,* 1958, **31,** 211–215.

Asarnow, R.F., Steffy, R.A., MacCrimmon, D.J., & Cleghorn, J.M. The McMaster-Waterloo project: An attentional and clinical assessment of foster children at risk for schizophrenia. In L.C. Wynne, R.L. Cromwell, & S. Matthysse (Eds.), *The nature of schizophrenia: Approaches to research and treatment.* New York: Wiley, 1978.

Baker, B.L., & Heifetz, L.J. The read project: Teaching manuals for parents of retarded children. In T.D. Tjossen (Ed.), *Early inter-*

vention with high risk infants and young children. Baltimore: University Park Press, 1976.

Bartak, L. Educational approaches. In M. Rutter & E. Schopler (Eds.), *Autism: A reappraisal of concepts and treatment.* New York: Plenum, 1978.

Bartak, L., & Pickering, C. Aims and methods of teaching. In M.P. Everard (Ed.), *Some approaches to teaching autistic children.* Oxford: Pergamon, 1976.

Bartak, L., & Rutter, M. Educational treatment of autistic children. In M. Rutter (Ed.), *Infantile autism: Concepts, characteristics and treatment.* London: Churchill, 1971.

Bartak, L., & Rutter, M. Special educational treatment of autistic children: A comparative study. I. Design of study and characteristics of units. *Journal of Child Psychology and Psychiatrics,* 1973, **14,** 161–179.

Bartak, L., Rutter, M., & Cox, A. A comparative study of infantile autism and specific developmental receptive language disorder. I. The children. *British Journal of Psychiatry,* 1975, **126,** 127–145.

Bartak, L., Rutter, M., & Cox, A. A comparative study of infantile autism and specific developmental receptive language disorder. III. Discriminant functions analysis. *Journal of Autism and Childhood Schizophrenia,* 1977, **7,** 383–396.

Bender, L. Childhood schizophrenia: Clinical study of one hundred schizophrenic children. *American Journal of Orthopsychiatry,* 1947, **17,** 40–55.

Bene, E. A Rorschach investigation into the mothers of autistic children. *British Journal of Medical Psychology,* 1958, **38,** 226–227.

Berkowitz, B.P., & Graziano, A.M. Training parents as behavior therapists: A review. *Behaviour Research and Therapy,* 1972, **10,** 297–317.

Bettelheim, B. *The empty fortress: Infantile autism and the birth of the self.* New York: The Free Press, 1967.

Bettelheim, B. *A home for the heart.* New York: Knopf, 1974.

Birley, J.L.T., & Brown, G.W. Crisis and life changes preceding the onset or relapse of acute schizophrenia: Clinical aspects. *British Journal of Psychiatry,* 1970, **116,** 327–333.

Blackstock, E.G. Cerebral asymmetry and the development of infantile autism. *Journal of*

Autism and Childhood Schizophrenia, 1978, **8,** 339–353.

Bleuler, E. *Dementia praecox or the group of schizophrenias.* New York: International Universities Press, 1950. (Originally published, 1911.)

Block, J. Parents of schizophrenic, neurotic, asthmatic and congenitally ill children. *Archives of General Psychiatry,* 1969, **20,** 659–674.

Bosch, G. Über primaren Autismus im Kindersalter. Unpublished lecture, 1953. Cited by G. Bosch. In *Infantile autism.* Berlin: Springer, 1970.

Boucher, J., & Warrington, E.K. Memory deficits in early infantile autism: Some similarities to the amnesic syndrome. *British Journal of Psychology,* 1976, **67,** 73–87.

Brask, B.H. The need for hospital beds for psychotic children. *Ugerkr Laeg,* 1967, **129,** 1559–1570.

Brown, G.W. Life-events and psychiatric illness: Some thoughts on methodology and causality. *Journal of Psychosomatic Research,* 1972, **16,** 311–320.

Brown, G.W., & Birley, J.L.T. Crisis and life changes and the onset of schizophrenia. *Journal of Health and Social Behavior,* 1968, **9,** 203–214.

Brown, J.L. Prognosis from presenting symptoms of preschool children with atypical development. *American Journal of Orthospychiatry,* 1960, **30,** 382–390.

Brown, J.L. Follow-up of children with atypical development. *American Journal of Orthopsychiatry,* 1963, **33,** 855–861.

Campbell, M., Fish, B., Shapiro, T., & Floyd, A. Thiothixene in young disturbed children. *Archives of General Psychiatry,* 1970, **23,** 70–72.

Campbell, M., Fish, B., David, R., Shapiro, T., Collins, P., & Koh, C. Response to triiodothyronine and dextroamphetamine: A study of preschool schizophrenic children. *Journal of Autism and Childhood Schizophrenia,* 1972, **2,** 343–358.

Campbell, M., Fish, B., David, R., Shapiro, T., Collins, P., & Koh, C. Liothyronine treatment in psychotic and nonpsychotic children under 6 years. *Archives of General Psychiatry,* 1973, **29,** 602–608.

Campbell, M., Small, A., Collins, P., Friedman, E., David, R., & Genieser, N. Levodopa and levoamphetamine: A crossover study in young schizophrenic children. *Current Therapeutic Research,* 1976, **19,** 70–86.

Cantwell, D., Howlin, P., & Rutter, M. The analysis of language level and language function: A methodological study. *British Journal of Disorders of Communication,* 1977, **12,** 119–135.

Carr, E.G. The motivation of self-impressions behavior: A review of some hypotheses. *Psychological Bulletin,* 1977, **84,** 800–816.

Carr, E.G., Schreibman, L., & Lovaas, O.I. Control of echolalic speech in psychotic children. *Journal of Abnormal Child Psychology,* 1975, **3,** 331–351.

Carr, E.G., Newsom, C.D., & Binkoff, J.A. Stimulus control of self-destructive behavior in a psychotic child. *Journal of Abnormal Child Psychology,* 1976, **4,** 139–153.

Chess, S. Autism in children with congenital rubella. *Journal of Autism and Childhood Schizophrenia,* 1971, **1,** 33–47.

Churchill, D.W. Effects of success and failure in psychotic children. *Archives of General Psychiatry,* 1971, **25,** 208–214.

Churchill, D.W. The relation of infantile autism and early childhood schizophrenia to developmental language disorders of childhood. *Journal of Autism and Childhood Schizophrenia,* 1972, **2,** 182–197.

Clerk, G. Reflections on the role of the mother in the development of language in the schizophrenic child. *Canadian Psychiatric Association Journal,* 1961, **6,** 252–256.

Cohen, D.J., Johnson, W.T., & Bowers, M.B., Jr. Biogenic amines in autistic and atypical children: Cerebrospinal fluid measures of homovanillic acid and 5-hydroxyindoleacetic acid. *Archives of General Psychiatry,* 1974, **31,** 845–853.

Cohen, D.J., Caparulo, B.K., Shaywitz, B.A., & Bowers, M.B., Jr. Dopamine and serotonin in neuropsychiatrically disturbed children: Cerobrospinal fluid homovanillic acid and 5-hydroxyindoleacetic acid. *Archives of General Psychiatry,* 1977, **34,** 561–567.

Cohen, D.J., Caparulo, B.K., & Shaywitz, B.A. Neurochemical and developmental models of childhood autism. In G. Serban (Ed.), *Cognitive defects in the development of mental illness.* New York: Brunner/Mazel, 1978.

Colbert, E.G., Koegler, R.R., & Markham, C.H. Vestibular dysfunction in childhood schizo-phrenia. *Archives of General Psychiatry,* 1959, **1,** 600–617.

Coleman, M. A report on the autistic syndromes. In M. Rutter & E. Schopler (Eds.), *Autism: A reappraisal of concepts and treatment.* New York: Plenum, 1978.

Cowan, P.A., Hoddinott, B.A., & Wright, B.A. Compliance and resistance in the conditioning of autistic children: An exploratory study. *Child Development,* 1965, **36,** 913–923.

Cox, A., Rutter, M., Newman, S., & Bartak, L. A comparative study of infantile autism and specific developmental receptive language disorder: II. Parental characteristics. *British Journal of Psychiatry,* 1975, **126,** 146–159.

Creak, E.M. Childhood psychosis: A review of 100 cases. *British Journal of Psychiatry,* 1963, **109,** 84–89.

Creak, M. Schizophrenic syndrome in childhood: Progress report of a working party. *Cerebral Palsy Bulletin,* 1963, **3,** 501–503.

Creak, M., & Ini, S. Families of psychotic children. *Journal of Child Psychology and Psychiatry,* 1960, **1,** 156–175.

Creak, M., & Pampiglione, G. Clinical and EEG studies on a group of 35 psychotic children. *Developmental Medicine and Child Neurology,* 1969, **11,** 218–227.

Dalldorf, J.S., & Schopler, E. Diagnosis and management of autism. *Comprehensive Therapy,* 1981, **7,** 67–73.

Davison, K., & Bagley, C. Schizophrenia-like psychoses associated with organic disorders of the central nervous system. In R.N. Herrington (Ed.), *Current Problems in Neuropsychiatry.* British Journal of Psychiatry, 1969 (Special Publication).

Dawson, G.D. *Early infantile autism and hemispheric specialization.* Unpublished doctoral dissertation, University of Washington, 1979.

Dawson, G.D. Cerebral lateralization in individuals diagnosed as autistic in early childhood. *Brain and Language,* 1982, **15,** 353–368.

DeLong, G.R. A neuropsychological interpretation of infantile autism. In M. Rutter & E. Schopler (Eds.), *Autism: A reappraisal of concepts and treatment.* New York: Plenum, 1978.

DeMyer, M.K. *Parents and children in autism.* Washington, D.C.: Winston, 1979.

DeMyer, M.K., Alpern, G.D., Barton, S., DeMyer, W.E., Churchill, D.W., Hingtgen, N.J., Bryson, C.Q., Pontius, W., & Kimberlin, C.

Imitation in autistic, early schizophrenic and non-psychotic subnormal children. *Journal of Autism and Childhood Schizophrenia,* 1972, **2,** 264–287. (a)

DeMyer, M.K., Pontius, W., Norton, J.A., Barton, S., Allen, J., & Steele, R. Parental practices and innate activity in autistic and brain-damaged infants. *Journal of Autism and Childhood Schizophrenia,* 1972, **2,** 49–66. (b)

DeMyer, M.K., Barton, S., DeMyer, W.E., Norton, J.A., Allen, J., & Steele, R. Prognosis in autism: A follow-up study. *Journal of Autism and Childhood Schizophrenia,* 1973, **3,** 199–246.

DeMyer, M.K., Barton, S., Alpern, G.D., Kimberlin, C., Allen, J., Yang, E., & Steele, R. The measured intelligence of autistic children: A follow-up study. *Journal of Autism and Childhood Schizophrenia,* 1974, **4,** 42–60.

DesLauriers, A.M. Play, symbols, and the development of language. In M. Rutter & E. Schopler (Eds.), *Autism: A reappraisal of concepts and treatment.* New York: Plenum, 1978.

Despert, J.L. Some considerations relating to the genesis of autistic behavior in children. *American Journal of Orthopsychiatry,* 1951, **21,** 335–350.

De Villiers, J.G., & Naughton, J.M. Teaching a symbol language to autistic children. *Journal of Consulting and Clinical Psychology,* 1974, **42,** 111–117.

Deykin, E.Y., & MacMahon, B. The incidence of seizures among children with autistic symptoms. *American Journal of Psychiatry,* 1979, **136,** 1310–1312.

Donnelly, E.M. The quantitative analysis of parent behavior towards psychotic children and their sibs. *Genetic Psychology Monographs,* 1960, **62,** 331–376.

Eggers, C. Course and prognosis of childhood schizophrenia. *Journal of Autism and Childhood Schizophrenia,* 1978, **8,** 21–36.

Eisenberg, L. The fathers of autistic children. *American Journal of Orthopsychiatry,* 1957, **27,** 715–724.

Eisenberg, L., & Kanner, L. Early infantile autism. *American Journal of Orthopsychiatry,* 1956, **26,** 556–566.

Engelhardt, D.M., Polizos, P., Waizer, J., & Hoffman, S.P. A double-blind comparison of fluphenazine and haloperidol in out-patient

schizophrenic children. *Journal of Autism and Childhood Schizophrenia,* 1973, **3,** 128–137.

Essen-Moller, E. The calculation of morbid risk in parents of index cases, as applied to a family sample of schizophrenics. *Acta Genetica et Statistica Medica (Basel),* 1955, **5,** 334–342.

Favell, J.E. The management of aggressive behavior. In E. Schopler & G.B. Mesibov (Eds.), *The autistic child in adolescence and adulthood.* New York: Plenum, in press.

Fish, B. The detection of schizophrenia in infancy. *Journal of Nervous and Mental Disease,* 1957, **125,** 1–24.

Fish, B. Longitudinal observations of biological deviations in a schizophrenic infant. *American Journal of Psychiatry,* 1959, **116,** 25–31.

Fish, B. Contributions of developmental research to a theory of schizophrenia. In J. Wellmath (Ed.), *Exceptional Infant* (Vol. 2). New York: Brunner/Mazel, 1971.

Fish, B. Biologic antecedents of psychosis in children. In D.X. Freeman (Ed.), *The biology of the major psychoses, Association for Research in Nervous and Mental Diseases* (Publication no. 54). New York: Raven, 1975.

Fish, B. An approach to prevention in infants at risk for schizophrenia. *Journal of Child Psychiatry,* 1976, **15,** 62–82.

Fish, B., & Alpert, M. Abnormal states of consciousness and muscle tone in infants born to schizophrenic mothers. *American Journal of Psychiatry,* 1962, **119,** 439–445.

Fish, B., & Hagin, R. Visual-motor disorders in infants at risk for schizophrenia. *Archives of General Psychiatry,* 1973, **28,** 900–904.

Fish, B., & Shapiro, T. A typology of children's psychiatric disorders. *Journal of Child Psychiatry,* 1965, **4,** 32–52.

Fish, B., Shapiro, T., Halpern, F., & Wile, R. The prediction of schizophrenia in infancy: III. A ten-year follow-up report of neurological and psychological development. *American Journal of Psychiatry,* 1965, **121,** 768–775.

Fish, B., Shapiro, T. & Campbell, M. Long-term prognosis and the response of schizophrenic children to drug therapy: A controlled study of trifluoperazine. *American Journal of Psychiatry,* 1966, **123,** 32–39. (a)

Fish, B., Wile, R., Shapiro, T. & Halpern, F. The prediction of schizophrenia in infancy: II. A ten-year follow-up report of predictions made at one month of age. In P.H. Hoch & J. Zubin (Eds.), *Psychopathology of schizophrenia,* New York: Grune & Stratton, 1966. (b)

Fish, B., Shapiro, T., Campbell, M. & Wile, R. A classification of schizophrenic children under five years. *American Journal of Psychiatry,* 1968, **124,** 1415–1423.

Folstein, S., & Rutter, M. Genetic influences and infantile autism. *Nature,* 1977, **265,** 726–728.

Frith, U. Emphasis and meaning in recall in normal and autistic children. *Language and Speech,* 1969, **12,** 29–38.

Fulwiler, R.L., & Fouts, R.S. Acquisition of American Sign Language by a non-communicating autistic child. *Journal of Autism and Childhood Schizophrenia,* 1976, **6,** 43–51.

Garmezy, N. Children at risk: The search for the antecedents of schizophrenia. *Schizophrenia Bulletin,* 1974, **9,** 55–125.

Gittelman, M., & Birch, H.G. Childhood schizophrenia: Intellect, neurological status, perinatal risk, prognosis and family pathology. *Archives of General Psychiatry,* 1967, **17,** 16–25.

Goldfarb, W. *Childhood schizophrenia.* Cambridge, Mass.: Harvard University Press, 1961.

Goldfarb, W., Levy, D.M., & Myers, D.I. The verbal encounter between the schizophrenic child and his mother. In G. Goldman & D. Shapiro (Eds.), *Developments in psychoanalysis at Columbia University.* New York: Hefner, 1966.

Goldfarb, W., Mintz, I., & Strook, K. *A time to heal.* New York: International Universities Press, 1969.

Gottesman, I.I., & Shields, J. Contributions of twin studies to perspectives on schizophrenia. In B.A. Maher (Ed.), *Progress in experimental personality* (Vol. 3). New York: Academic Press, 1966.

Greenbaum, G.H. An evaluation of niacinamide in the treatment of childhood schizophrenia. *American Journal of Psychiatry,* 1970, **127,** 129–132.

Grunebaum, H., Weiss, J.L., Gallant, D., & Cohler, B. Attention in young children of psychotic mothers. *American Journal of Psychiatry,* 1974, **131,** 887–891.

Gubbay, S.S., Lobaschen, M., & Kingerlee, P. A neurological appraisal of autistic children: Results of a Western Australian survey. *Developmental Medicine and Child Neurology,* 1970, **12,** 422–429.

Hauser, S.B., DeLong, G.R., & Rosman, N.P. Pneumographic findings in the infantile autism syndrome. *Brain,* 1975, **98,** 667–688.

Hemsley, R., Howlin, P., Berger, M., Hersov, L., Holbrook, D., Rutter, M., & Yule, W. Treating autistic children in a family context. In M. Rutter & E. Schopler (Eds.), *Autism: A reappraisal of concepts and treatment.* New York: Plenum, 1978.

Hermelin, B. Images and language. In M. Rutter & E. Schopler (Eds.), *Autism: A reappraisal of concepts and treatment.* New York: Plenum, 1978.

Hermelin, B., & O'Connor, N. Measures of the occipital alpha rhythm in normal, subnormal and autistic children. *British Journal of Psychiatry,* 1968, **114,** 603–610.

Hermelin, B., & O'Connor, N. *Psychological experiments with autistic children.* Oxford: Pergamon, 1970.

Hermelin, B., & O'Connor, N. Spatial coding in normal, autistic and blind children. *Perceptual Motor Skills,* 1971, **33,** 127–132.

Hermelin, B., & O'Connor, N. Location and distance estimates of blind and sighted children. *Quarterly Journal of Experimental Psychology,* 1975, **27,** 295–301.

Hier, D.B., LeMay, M., & Rosenberger, P.B. Autism and unfavorable left-right asymmetrics of the brain. *Journal of Autism and Developmental Disorders,* 1979, **9,** 153–159.

Himwich, H., Jenkins, R., Fujimori, M., & Narasimachari, A biochemical study of early infantile autism. *Journal of Autism and Childhood Schizophrenia,* 1972, **2,** 114–126.

Hinton, G.G. Childhood psychosis or mental retardation: A diagnostic dilemma. II. Pediatrics and neurological aspects. *Canadian Medical Association Journal,* 1963, **87,** 1020–1024.

Hirsch, S.R., & Leff, J.P. Parental abnormalities of verbal communication in the transmission of schizophrenia. *Psychological Medicine,* 1971, **1,** 118–127.

Howlin, P. The assessment of social behavior. In M. Rutter & E. Schopler (Eds.), *Autism: A reappraisal of concepts and treatment.* New York: Plenum, 1978.

Hutt, S.J., Hutt, C., Lee, D., & Ounsted, C. Arousal and childhood autism. *Nature*, 1964, **204**, 908–909.

Jones, F.H., Simmons, J.Q., & Frankel, F. An extinction procedure for eliminating self-destructive behavior in a 9-year-old autistic girl. *Journal of Autism and Childhood Schizophrenia*, 1974, **4**, 241–250.

Kallmann, F.J. The genetic theory of schizophrenia: An analysis of 691 schizophrenic twin index families. *American Journal of Psychiatry*, 1946, **103**, 309–322.

Kallmann, F.J., & Roth, B. Genetic aspects of pre-adolescent schizophrenia. *American Journal of Psychiatry*, 1956, **112**, 599–606.

Kanner, L. Autistic disturbances of affective contact. *Nervous Child*, 1943, **2**, 217–250.

Kanner, L. Problems of nosology and psychodynamics of early infantile autism. *American Journal of Orthopsychiatry*, 1949, **19**, 416–426.

Kanner, L. *Child psychiatry* (3rd ed.). Springfield, Ill.: Thomas, 1957.

Kanner, L. General concept of schizophrenia at different ages. In R. McIntosh & C. Hare (Eds.), *Proceedings of the Association for Research in Nervous and Mental Diseases. Neurology and psychiatry in childhood.* Springfield, Ill.: Thomas, 1958.

Kanner, L. *Childhood psychosis: Initial studies and new insights.* Washington: Winston, 1973.

Kanner, L., & Eisenberg, L. Notes on the follow-up studies of autistic children. In P.H. Hock & J. Zubin (Eds.), *Psychopathology of childhood.* New York: Grune & Stratton, 1955.

Kanner, L., & Eisenberg, L. Early infantile autism, 1943-1955. *American Journal of Orthopsychiatry*, 1956, **26**, 55–65.

Keeler, W.R. Autistic patterns and defective communication in blind children with retrolental fibroplasia. In P.H. Hoch & J. Zubin (Eds.), *Psychopathology of communication.* New York: Grune & Stratton, 1958.

Klebanoff, L.B. Parental attitudes of mothers of schizophrenic, brain injured and retarded, and normal children. *American Journal of Orthopsychiatry*, 1959, **29**, 445–454.

Kolvin, I. Psychoses in childhood—A comparative study. In M. Rutter (Ed.), *Infantile autism: Concepts, characteristics and treatment.* Edinburgh: Churchill Livingstone, 1971. (a)

Kolvin, I. Studies in childhood psychoses. I. Diagnostic criteria and classification. *British Journal of Psychiatry*, 1971, **118**, 381–384. (b)

Kolvin, I. Late onset psychoses. *British Medical Journal*, 1972, **3**, 816–817.

Kolvin, I., Humphrey, M., & McNay, A. Studies in childhood psychoses. VI. Cognitive factors in childhood psychoses. *British Journal of Psychiatry*, 1971, **118**, 415–419. (a)

Kolvin, I., Ounsted, C., & Roth, A. Studies in childhood psychoses. V. Cerebral dysfunction and childhood psychoses. *British Journal of Psychiatry*, 1971, **118**, 407–414. (b)

Kolvin, I., Garside, R.F., & Kidd, J.S. Studies in childhood psychoses. IV. Parental personality and attitude and childhood psychoses. *British Journal of Psychiatry*, 1971, **118**, 403–406. (c)

Kolvin, I., Ounsted, C., Richardson, I.M., & Garside, R.F. Studies in the childhood psychoses. III. The family and social background in childhood psychosis. *British Journal of Psychiatry*, 1971, **118**, 396–402. (d)

Knobloch, H., & Pasamanick, B. Etiologic factors in "early infantile autism" and "childhood schizophrenia." Presented at the 10th International Congress of Pediatrics. Lisbon, September, 1962.

Knobloch, H., & Pasamanick, B. Some etiological and prognostic factors in early infantile autism and psychosis. *Pediatrics*, 1975, **55**, 182–191.

Kringlen, E. *Hereditary and environment in the functional psychoses.* London: Heinemann, 1967.

Lansing, M.D., & Schopler, E. Individualized education: A public school model. In M. Rutter & E. Schopler (Eds.), *Autism: A reappraisal of concepts and treatment.* New York: Plenum, 1978.

Lobascher, M.E., Kingerlee, P.E., & Gubbay, S.D. Childhood autism: Aetiological factors in 25 cases. *British Journal of Psychiatry*, 1970, **117**, 525–529.

Lockyer, L., & Rutter, M. A five to fifteen year follow-up study of infantile psychosis. III. Psychological aspects. *British Journal of Psychiatry*, 1969, **115**, 865–882.

Lockyer, L., & Rutter, M. A five to fifteen year follow-up study of infantile psychosis: IV. Patterns of cognitive ability. *British Journal of Social and Clinical Psychology*, 1970, **9**, 1952–163.

Loew, L.H. Families of children with early childhood schizophrenia. *Archives of General Psychiatry,* 1966, **14,** 26–30.

Long, J.S., & Rasmussen, M. The acquisition of simple and compound sentence structure in an autistic child. *Journal of Applied Behavior Analysis,* 1974, **7,** 473–479.

Lotter, V. Epidemiology of autistic conditions in young children. I. Prevalence. *Social Psychiatry,* 1966, **1,** 124–137.

Lotter, V. Epidemiology of autistic conditions in young children. II. Some characteristics of parents and children. *Social Psychiatry,* 1967, **1,** 163–173.

Lotter, V. Factors related to outcome in autistic children. *Journal of Autism and Childhood Schizophrenia,* 1974, **4,** 263–277.

Lovaas, O.I. Parents as therapists. In M. Rutter & E. Schopler (Eds.), *Autism: A reappraisal of concepts and treatment.* New York: Plenum, 1978.

Lovaas, O.I., & Newsom, C.D. Behavior modification with psychotic children. In H. Leitenberg (Ed.), *Handbook of behavior modification and behavior therapy.* Englewood Cliffs, N.J.: Prentice-Hall, 1976.

Lovaas, O.I., & Simmons, J.Q. Manipulation of self-destruction in three retarded children. *Journal of Applied Behavior Analysis,* 1969, **2,** 143–157.

Lovaas, O.I., Schaeffer, B., & Simmons, J.Q. Experimental studies in childhood schizophrenia: Building social behavior in autistic children by use of electric shock. *Journal of Experimental Research in Personality,* 1965, **1,** 99–109.

Lovaas, O.I., Berberich, J.P., Perloff, B.F., & Schaeffer, B. Acquisition of imitative speech by schizophrenic children. *Science,* 1966, **151,** 705–707. (a)

Lovaas, O.I., Freitag, G., Kinder, M.I., Rubenstein, B.D., Schaeffer, B., & Simmons, J.O. Establishment of social reinforcers in two schizophrenic children on the basis of food. *Journal of Experimental Child Psychology,* 1966, **4,** 109–125. (b)

Lovaas, O.I., Schreibman, L., & Koegel, R.L. A behavior modification approach to the treatment of autistic children. *Journal of Autism and Childhood Schizophrenia,* 1974, **4,** 111–129.

Lowe, L.H. Families of children with early childhood schizophrenia. *Archives of General Psychiatry,* 1966, **14,** 26–30.

Lucas, A., Krause, R., & Domino, E. Biological studies in childhood schizophrenia: Plasma and RBC cholinesterase activity. *Journal of Autism and Childhood Schizophrenia,* 1971, **1,** 172–181.

MacCrimmon, D.J., Cleghorn, J.M., Asarnow, R.F., & Steffy, R.A. Children at risk for schizophrenia: Clinical and attentional characteristics. *Archives of General Psychiatry,* 1980, **37,** 671–674.

MacSweeney, D.A. A report on a pair of male MZ twins discordant for schizophrenia. *British Journal of Psychiatry,* 1970, **116,** 315–322.

Makita, K. The age of onset of childhood schizophrenia. *Folia Psychiatrica et Neurologica Japonica,* 1966, **20,** 111–121.

Marcus, J., Auerbach, J., Wilkinson, L., & Burack, C.M. Infants at risk for schizophrenia. *Archives of General Psychiatry,* 1981, **38,** 703–713.

Marcus, L.M., Lansing, M.D., Andrews, C.E., & Schopler, E. Improvement of teaching effectiveness in parents of autistic children. *Journal of Child Psychiatry,* 1978, **17,** 625–629.

Mednick, S.A., Mura, M., Schulzinger, F., & Mednick, B. Perinatal conditions and infant development in children with schizophrenic parents. *Social Biology,* 1971, **18,** 5103–5113.

Metz, J.R. Conditioning generalized imitation in autistic children. *Journal of Experimental Child Psychology,* 1965, **2,** 389–399.

Meyers, D., & Goldfarb, W. Studies of perplexity in mothers of schizophrenic children. *American Journal of Orthopsychiatry,* 1961, **31,** 551–561.

Meyer, R.B., & Karon, B.P. The schizophrenic mother concept and the T.A.T. *Psychiatry,* 1967, **30,** 173–179.

Narasimachari, N., & Himwich, H. Biochemical study in early infantile autism. *Biological Psychiatry,* 1975, **10,** 425–432.

O'Connor, N., & Hermelin, B. Auditory and visual memory in autistic and normal children. *Journal of Mental Deficiency Research,* 1967, **11,** 126–131. (a)

O'Connor, N., & Hermelin, B. The selective visual attention of psychotic children. *Journal of Child Psychology and Psychiatry,* 1967, **8,** 167–179. (b)

O'Connor, N., & Hermelin, B. Seeing and hearing in space and time. *Perception and Psychophysics,* 1972, **11,** 46–48.

O'Connor, N., & Hermelin, B. The spatial or temporal organization of short-term memory. *Quarterly Journal of Experimental Psychology,* 1973, **25,** 335–343.

O'Connor, N., & Hermelin, B. Modality specific spatial coordinates. *Perception and Psychophysics,* 1975, **17,** 213–216.

Offir, C.W. Visual speech: Their fingers do the talking. *Psychology Today,* June 1976, 72–78.

Ogdom, D.P., Bass, C.L., Thomas, E.R., & Lordi, W. Parents of autistic children. *American Journal of Orthopsychiatry,* 1968, **38,** 653–658.

O'Gorman, C. *The nature of childhood autism.* London: Butterworths, 1970.

Ornitz, E.M. Development of sleep patterns in autistic children. In C.D. Clemente, E. Purpura, & F. Mayer (Eds.), *Sleep and the maturing nervous system.* New York: Academic Press, 1972.

Ornitz, E.M., & Ritvo, E.R. Perceptual inconstancy in early infantile autism. *Archives of General Psychiatry,* 1968, **18,** 76–98.

Ornitz, E.M., & Ritvo, E.R. The syndrome of autism: A critical review. *American Journal of Psychiatry,* 1976, **133,** 609–621.

Ornitz, E.M., Ritvo, E.R., & Walter, R.D. Dreaming sleep in autistic and schizophrenic children. *American Journal of Psychiatry,* 1965, **122,** 419–424.

Ornitz, E.M., Brown, M.B., Sorosky, A.D., Ritvo, E.R., & Dietrich, L. Environmental modification of autistic behavior. *Archives of General Psychiatry,* 1970, **22,** 560–565.

Ornitz, E.M., Forsythe, A.B., & de la Pena, A. The effect of vestibular and auditory stimulation on the rapid eye movements of REM sleep in autistic children. *Archives of General Psychiatry,* 1973, **29,** 786–791.

Ounsted, C. A biological approach to autistic and hyperkinetic syndromes. In J. Apley (Ed.), *Modern trends in paediatrics.* London: Butterworths, 1970.

Pitfield, M., & Oppenheim, A.N. Child rearing attitudes of mothers of psychotic children. *Journal of Child Psychology and Psychiatry,* 1964, **5,** 51–57.

Pollack, M., & Krieger, H.P. Oculomotor and postural patterns in schizophrenic children. *Archives of Neurology and Psychiatry,* 1958, **79,** 729–726.

Pollin, W., & Stabenau, J.R. Biological, psychological, and historical differences in a series of MZ twins discordant for schizophrenia. In D.

Rosenthal & S.S. Kefy (Eds.), *The transmission of schizophrenia.* New York: Pergamon, 1968.

Potter, H. Schizophrenia in children. *American Journal of Psychiatry,* 1933, **12,** 1253–1268.

Prior, M.R., & Bradshaw, J.L. Hemisphere functioning in autistic children. *Cortex,* 1979, **15,** 73–81.

Rank, B. Adaptation of the psychoanalytic technique for the treatment of young children with atypical development. *American Journal of Orthopsychiatry,* 1949, **19,** 130–139.

Rendle-Short, J. Infantile autism in Australia. *Medical Journal of Australia,* 1969, **2,** 245–249.

Ricks, D.M. Vocal communication in pre-verbal normal and autistic children. In N. O'Connor (Ed.), *Language, cognitive deficits and retardation.* London: Butterworth, 1972.

Ricks, D.M., & Wing, L. Language, communication, and the use of symbols in normal and autistic children. *Journal of Autism and Childhood Schizophrenia,* 1975, **5,** 191–221.

Rimland, B. High dosage levels of certain vitamins in the treatment of children with severe mental disorders. In D. Hawkins & L. Pauling (Eds.), *Orthomolecular psychiatry.* San Francisco: Freeman, 1973.

Risley, T.R. The effects and side effects of punishing autistic behaviors of a deviant child. *Journal of Applied Behavior Analysis,* 1968, **1,** 20–34.

Risley, T.R., & Wolf, M. Establishing functional speech in echolalic children. *Behaviour Research and Therapy,* 1967, **5,** 73–88.

Ritvo, E.R., & Freeman, B.J. National Society for Autistic Children definition of the syndrome of autism. *Journal of Pediatric Psychology,* 1977, **2,** 146–148.

Ritvo, E.R., Ornitz, E.M., & Eviator, A. Decreased post-rotatory nystagmus in early infantile autism. *Neurology,* 1969, **19,** 653–658.

Ritvo, E.R., Yuwiler, A., Geller, E., Ornitz, E.M., Saeger, K., & Plotkin, S. Increased blood serotonin and platelets in early infantile autism. *Archives of General Psychiatry,* 1970, **23,** 566–572.

Ritvo, E.R., Yuwiler, A., Geller, E., Kales, A., Rashkis, S., Schicor, A., Plotkin, A., Axelrod, R., & Howard, C. Effects of L-dopa on autism. *Journal of Autism and Childhood Schizophrenia,* 1971, **1,** 190–205.

Robinson, N.M., & Robinson, H.B. *The mentally*

retarded child: A psychological approach (2nd ed.). New York: McGraw-Hill, 1976.

Romancyzk, R.G., Diament, C., Coren, E.R., Trunell, G., & Harris, S.L. Increasing isolate and social play in severely disturbed children: Intervention and post-intervention effectiveness. *Journal of Autism and Childhood Schizophrenia*, 1975, **5**, 57–70.

Rosenthal, D. Some factors associated with concordance and discordance with respect to schizophrenia in MZ twins. *Journal of Nervous and Mental Disease*, 1959, **129**, 1–10.

Rosenthal, D., & Kety, S.S. (Eds.), *The transmission of schizophrenia*. New York: Pergamon, 1968.

Ross, A.O. *Psychological disorders of children*. New York: McGraw-Hill, 1980.

Ruttenberg, B. A psychoanalytic understanding of infantile autism and its treatment. In D. Churchill, G. Alpern, & M. DeMyer (Eds.), *Infantile autism: Proceedings, Indiana University Colloquium*. Springfield, Ill.: Thomas, 1971.

Rutter, M. Behavioural and cognitive characteristics of a series of psychotic children. In J. Wing (Ed.), *Early childhood autism*. Oxford: Pergamon, 1966.

Rutter, M. Prognosis of infantile neuroses and psychoses. *Proceedings of the IVth World Congress of Psychiatry, Madrid, 1966*. New York: Excerpta Medica. International Congress Series No. 150, 1967. (a)

Rutter, M. Psychotic disorders in early childhood. In A. Coppen & A. Walk (Eds.), *Recent Developments in Schizophrenia* (*British Journal of Psychiatry*, special publication). Ashford, Kent: Headley, 1967. (b)

Rutter, M. Concepts of autism: A review of research. *Journal of Child Psychology and Psychiatry*, 1968, **9**, 1–25.

Rutter, M. Autistic children: Infancy to adulthood. *Seminars in Psychiatry*, 1970, **2**, 435–450.

Rutter, M. The description and classification of infantile autism. In D.W. Churchill, G.D. Alpern, & M.K. DeMyer (Eds.), *Infantile autism*. Springfield, Ill.: Thomas, 1971.

Rutter, M. The assessment and treatment of preschool autistic children. *Early Child Development and Care*, 1973, **3**, 13–29.

Rutter, M. The development of infantile autism. *Psychological Medicine*, 1974, **4**, 147–163.

Rutter, M. Diagnosis and definition. In M. Rutter

& E. Schopler (Eds.), *Autism: A reappraisal of concepts and treatment*. New York: Plenum, 1978. (a)

Rutter, M. On confusion in the diagnosis of autism. *Journal of Autism and Childhood Schizophrenia*, 1978, **8**, 137–161. (b)

Rutter, M., & Lockyer, L. A five to fifteen year follow-up study of infantile psychosis. I. Description of sample. *British Journal of Psychiatry*, 1967, **113**, 1169–1182.

Rutter, M., & Schopler, E. (Eds.), *Autism: A reappraisal of concepts and treatment*. New York: Plenum, 1978.

Rutter, M., & Sussenwein, F.A. A developmental and behavioral approach to the treatment of preschool autistic children. *Journal of Autism and Childhood Schizophrenia*, 1971, **1**, 376–397.

Rutter, M., Greenfeld, D., & Lockyer, L. A five to fifteen year follow-up study of infantile psychosis. II. Social and behavioral outcome. *British Journal of Psychiatry*, 1967, **113**, 1183–1199.

Schain, R.J., & Freedman, D. Studies on 5-hydroxyindole metabolism in autistic and other mentally retarded children. *Journal of Pediatrics*, 1961, **58**, 315–320.

Schain, R.J., & Yannet, H. Infantile autism: An analysis of 50 cases and a consideration of certain relevant neurophysiologic concepts. *Journal of Pediatrics*, 1960, **57**, 560–567.

Schell, R.E., Stark, J., & Giddan, J.J. Development of language behavior in an autistic child. *Journal of Speech and Hearing Disorders*, 1967, **32**, 51–64.

Schiele, B.C., Gallant, D., Simpson, G., Gardner, E.A., & Cole, J.O. Tardine dyskinesia. *American Journal of Orthopsychiatry*, 1973, **43**, 506, 888.

Schopler, E. Visual versus tactual receptor preference in normal and schizophrenic children. *Journal of Abnormal Psychology*, 1966, **71**, 108–114.

Schopler, E. Parents of psychotic children as scapegoats. *Journal of Contemporary Psychotherapy*, 1971, **4**, 17–22.

Schopler, E., & Dalldorf, J. Autism: Definition, diagnosis, and management. *Hospital Practice*, June 1980, 64–73.

Schopler, E., & Olley, J.G. Comprehensive educational services for autistic children: the TEACCH model. In T.B. Gutkin & C.R. Reynolds

(Eds.), *A handbook for the practice of school psychology*. New York: Wiley, 1981.

Schopler, E., & Reichler, R.J. Parents as co-therapists in the treatment of psychotic children. *Journal of Autism and Childhood Schizophrenia,* 1971, **1**, 87–102.

Schopler, E., & Reichler, R.J. *Individualized assessment and treatment of autistic and developmentally disabled children: Psychoeducational profile* (Vol. I). Baltimore: University Park Press, 1979. (a)

Schopler, E., Andrews, C.E., & Strupp, K. Do autistic children come from upper middle-class parents? *Journal of Autism and Developmental Disorders,* 1979, **9**, 139–152. (b)

Shields, J. Summary of the genetic evidence. In D. Rosenthal & S.S. Kety (Eds.), *The transmission of schizophrenia*. New York: Pergamon, 1968.

Short, A. *Evaluation of short-term outcome using parents as co-therapists for their own psychotic children*. Unpublished doctoral dissertation, University of North Carolina at Chapel Hill, 1980.

Simmons, J.Q., & Baltaxe, C. Language patterns of adolescent autistics. *Journal of Autism and Childhood Schizophrenia,* 1975, **5**, 333–351.

Singer, M.T., & Wynne, L.C. Differentiating characteristics of parents of childhood schizophrenics, childhood neurotics and young adult schizophrenics. *American Journal of Psychiatry,* 1963, **120**, 234–243.

Singer, M., & Wynne, L. Thought disorders and family relations of schizophrenics. *Archives of General Psychiatry,* 1965, **12**, 201–212.

Siva-Sankar, D. Biogenic amine uptake by blood platelets and RBC in childhood schizophrenia. *Acta Paedopsychiatra,* 1970, **37**, 174–182.

Slater, E. *Psychotic and neurotic illnesses in twins*. London: Her Majesty's Stationery Office, 1953.

Slater, E., Beard, A., & Glithero, E. The schizophrenia-like psychoses of epilepsy. *British Journal of Psychiatry,* 1963, **109**, 95–150.

Solnick, J.V., Rincover, A., & Peterson, C.R. Some determinants of the reinforcing and punishing effects of timeout. *Journal of Applied Behavior Analysis,* 1977, **10**, 415–424.

Sorosky, A.D., Ornitz, E.M., Brown, N.B., & Ritvo, E.R. Systematic observations of autistic behavior. *Archives of General Psychiatry,* 1968, **18**, 439–449.

Taft, L., & Cohen, H.J. Hypsar-rhythmia and infantile autism: A clinical report. *Journal of Autism and Childhood Schizophrenia,* 1971, **1**, 327–336.

Taft, L., & Goldfarb, W. Prenatal and perinatal factors and childhood schizophrenia. *Developmental Medicine and Child Neurology,* 1964, **6**, 32–43.

Tanguay, P.E. Clinical and electro-physiological research. In E.R. Ritvo (Ed.), *Autism: Diagnosis, current research and management*. New York: Spectrum, 1976.

Tate, B.G., & Baroff, G.S. Aversive control of self-injurious behavior in a psychotic boy. *Behavioral Research and Therapy,* 1966, **4**, 281–287.

Tiernari, P. Schizophrenia in monozygotic male twins. In D. Rosenthal & S.S. Kety (Eds.), *The transmission of schizophrenia*. New York: Pergamon, 1968.

Tinbergen, E.A., & Tinbergen, N. Early childhood autism: An ethological approach. In *Advances in ethology,* **10**, supplement to *Journal of Comparative Ethology*. Berlin & Hamburg: Verlag Paul Pany, 1972.

Treffert, D.A. Epidemiology of infantile autism. *Archives of General Psychiatry,* 1970, **22**, 431–438.

van Krevelen, D.A. On the relationship between early infantile autism and autistic psychopathy. *Acta Paedopsychiatric,* 1963, **30**, 303–323.

van Krevelen, D.A. Early infantile autism and autistic psychopathy. *Journal of Autism and Childhood Schizophrenia,* 1971, **1**, 82–86.

Ward, A.J. Early infantile autism: Diagnosis, etiology and treatment. *Psychological Bulletin,* 1970, **73**, 350–362.

Walker, H.A., & Birch, H.G. Neurointegrative deficiency in schizophrenic children. *Journal of Nervous and Mental Disease,* 1970, **151**, 104–113.

Waring, M., & Rick, D.F. Family patterns of children who became adult schizophrenics. *Journal of Nervous and Mental Disease,* 1965, **140**, 351–364.

Watt, N.F. Patterns of childhood social development in adult schizophrenics. *Archives of General Psychiatry,* 1978, **35**, 160–165.

Waxler, N.E., & Mishler, E.G. Experimental studies of families. In L. Berkowitz (Ed.), *Advances in experimental social psychology* (Vol.

5). New York: Academic Press, 1970.

White, P.T., DeMyer, W., & DeMyer, M. EEG abnormalities in early childhood schizophrenia: A double-blind study of psychiatrically-disturbed and normal children during promazine sedation. *American Journal of Psychiatry,* 1964, **120,** 950–958.

Wing, J.K. Diagnosis, epidemiology, aetiology. In J.K. Wing (Ed.), *Childhood autism: Clinical, educational, and social aspects.* London: Pergamon, 1966.

Wing, L. Perceptual and language development in autistic children: A comparative study. In M. Rutter (Ed.), *Infantile autism: Concepts, characteristics and treatment.* London: Churchill-Livingstone, 1971.

Wing, L. (Ed.). *Early childhood autism.* (2nd ed.). Oxford: Pergamon, 1976.

Wing, L. Social behavioral, and cognitive characteristics: An epidemic-logical approach. In M.

Rutter & E. Schopler (Eds.), *Autism: A Reappraisal of concepts and treatment.* New York: Plenum, 1978.

Wing, L., & Ricks, D.M. The aetiology of childhood autism: A criticism of the Tinbergens' ethological theory. *Psychological Medicine,* 1976, **6,** 533–544.

Wynne, L.C. Methodologic and conceptual issues in the study of schizophrenics and their families. In D. Rosenthal & S. Kety (Eds.), *The transmission of schizophrenics.* New York: Pergamon, 1968.

Yule, W., & Berger, M. Behavior modification principles and speed delay. In M. Rutter & J.A.M. Martin (Eds.), *The child with delayed speed.* London: Simp/Heinemann, 1972.

Zaslow, R.W., & Breger, L. A theory and treatment of autism. In L. Breger (Ed.), *Clinical-cognitive psychology.* Englewood Cliffs, N.J.: Prentice-Hall, 1969.

CHAPTER 23

Sexual Problems of Children

LORETTA MASON HAROIAN

The structure, gender, and function of the human body is the foundation of identity. The image of self, measured against the modes of the culture and society, provides for or denies feelings of normalcy and self-acceptance. As the structure or the function of the body departs from cultural norms and societal expectations, the individual must adapt and accommodate to the anatomical and/or physiological differences and also must cope with the perceptions and attitudes of others.

Sexual health includes anatomically normal genitalia, a functional sexual response cycle, positive sexual attitudes (including body image and sexual self-esteem), and sociosexual skills (including the desire for and the ability to tolerate intimacy). Although children are not sexual in the adult sense, the development of the erotic response begins in childhood. The awareness of the sexual self as an integrated aspect of identity begins with attitudes about the physical body communicated by the mother or the primary caretaker.

The first diagnosable sexual problems of children are birth defects of the external genitalia. They may be discrete malformations or stigmata of complex syndromes and may be medically or surgically correctable or irreversible. Genital surgeries, whether functional or cosmetic, are a major trauma for the child and need concomitant crisis intervention therapy to deal with the loss of body integrity, and the changing body image and to deter the development of compensatory pathological character structure (i.e., learned helplessness).

The problem of gender dysphoria, or hermaphroditic genitalia, is no longer considered a simple genital structural error but is an intensely complicated total body syndrome requiring a multilevel determination of gender reassignment. The pioneering work of John Money and his students at Johns Hopkins University has made this a specialty field. (The reader is referred to Dr. Money's publications as a review of his formidable contribution is beyond the scope of this chapter.) Suffice it to say that gender dysphoria is a total psychosoma phenomenon that necessitates surgical, medical (hormonal), and psychological diagnosis and treatment. Other chronic syndromes or conditions that affect sexuality (e.g., Klinefelter's, Turner's, cerebral palsy, muscular dystrophy, paraplegia, etc.) may not be ameliorated or improved by surgery or medicine but rather are seen as inveterate conditions to which psychological adjustment must be made. Sexual health in this instance includes adjustment to the physical limitations of the syndrome and adaptation of the erotic response to the sexual options left available. Consideration of the sexual implications of every accident, injury, and disease should be an integral part of rehabilitation programs.

The narrow religious and societal attitudes about sexual propriety have doomed scores of people to an existence devoid of satisfying sexual expression and have branded as aberrant, deviant, sick, or criminal those who did not conform to the accepted sexual fashions and standards of a particular time and place in history.

Sexologists who study sex in history, anthropology, sociology, psychology, medicine, religion, law, and art, understand the broad range of human sexual behavior and the changing and discrepant nature of what is considered acceptable sexual expression at any given time. Attitudes and behaviors that are considered sex problems or sex crimes in one instance may be accepted as normal in other societies or religions, other geographical locations, or in other eras (Haeberle, 1978).

Sexual problems of children, as seen on an outpatient basis by mental or physical health care professionals, usually are public or semi-public behaviors that cause adults (usually the parents) embarrassment and concern because they are a departure from society's expectations. It is not uncommon to find that parents' unresolved sex guilt or sexual ignorance is causing them to overvalue the significance of the child's sexual behavior. Often a pediatrician, a sex education course, a lecture, or an article on sex can reassure an anxious parent, helping him or her to understand and accept the sexual nature of his or her progeny.

Although there is only one sexual disorder of childhood included in the Diagnostic and Statistical Manual, Third Revision (DSM III), there are many sexual events and/or behaviors that cause children to be referred for psychological evaluation. The parents' decision to seek professional consultation is the solution to their feelings of worry that the child is not normal, fear that if they don't intervene the child will grow up to be a sexually deviant adult, doubt that they have the knowledge or skill to change the behavior pattern, and guilt that they have caused or contributed to the undesirable behavior. In some cases, behavior that is acceptable to the parent is identified as problematic by auxiliary caretakers or school personnel, and the parents may have little emotional investment until they are convinced there is a problem. Some children are referred by physicians and/or the legal system due to confirmed or suspected sexual events or experiences with adults. Some children exhibit nonsexual symptoms that on examination are found to have a sexual referent, and some children in therapy for other reasons use their relationship with the therapist to resolve their age appropriate sexual concerns as they arise.

The traditional mode of psychotherapy was to seek the sexual referent in nonsexual symptomatology and to attribute sexual symptomatology to unresolved conflicts with primary and secondary love objects. Sex was rarely dealt with directly in history taking or therapy with adults and even less often with children until the rise of clinical sexology. The clinical sexologist sees few children, and few clinical sexologists are experts with children. Despite the history of childhood sexuality, Freud's declaration that sexual interests and behaviors are manifest in children, and documented evidence that the sexual response cycle is operative from birth, we have failed as a culture to acknowledge the lifelong development of the erotic response and to study the importance of a person's sexuality in the quality of his or her life as a whole.

The sexual response cycle is present at birth in both males and females and finds expression developmentally as the child matures. Although sexual ages and stages have not been systematically observed and documented by developmentalists, we can assume that normative sexual behavior exists throughout childhood and that it reflects the innate aspects of the individual child interacting with the socialization of the culture. Negative and hypocritical attitudes of Western society toward sex repress and obscure the evolution of sexual interest and activity of well-supervised children. Some counterculture groups with positive attitudes toward sex well-meaningly obscure the natural evolution of their children's sexual interests and activity by encouraging early sexual awareness and behavior in the name of children's rights and sexual freedom. It would be optimally beneficial to the sex field in particular and people in general if we could observe even one generation of children who are not sexually inhibited and repressed or sexually stimulated and exploited. Because the development of the erotic response is so poorly understood, and because as a culture we eschew the concept of childhood sexuality, there is a dearth of definitive data, no chronological or developmental milestones except pubescence, and little interest in research to help professionals or parents differentiate between normative and nonnormative sexual behavior. Children's sexual interest seems to reflect a normal distribution, with some children being intensely interested, some apparently uninterested, and most whose expressed interest is reflective of the cultural mores and the family expectations and/or restrictions. Until we have data to the contrary, it would appear reasonable to hypothesize a normal curve as representative of the sexuality of children.

GENDER IDENTITY DISORDER IN CHILDREN WITH NORMAL GENITALIA

Gender Identity Disorder (GID) of childhood is described in the DSM-III as a strong and persistently stated desire to be, or belief that one is, of the opposite gender and a persistent repudiation of one's assigned anatomical structure, preoccupation with stereotypical opposite gender activities (dressing, games, pastimes, etc.) occurring before pubescence.

GID in children is often confused with homosexuality. Parents will seek diagnosis and treatment for their child in response to symptoms of opposite gender mannerisms and behavior. Their concerns include embarrassment of the family members, stigmatizing of the child, and fear of potential homosexuality. Actually, the adult manifestation of GID is transsexualism expressed as the feeling of being trapped in the body of the opposite gender. The concern over whether their sexual preference or lifestyle will be homosexual or heterosexual is a moot point. An anatomical male who experiences himself as a female, choosing a male as a primary partner, is quite different psychologically from two males who experience themselves as male and choose each other as primary partners. Although this distinction is difficult or impossible for a casual observer to make, it is crucial to the well being of the child that the differential diagnosis be made by the therapist and understood by the child and the family. The parents of a GID child need to know that such children do not grow up to be gay.

Rekers (1978) has suggested that Sexual (Gender) Identity Disorder be differentiated from Sexual (Gender) Behavior Disorder (GBD) to account for children whose cross-gender or androgynous behavior is learned and reinforced by the environment rather than linked to a persistent belief that they are in fact of the opposite sex. The adult manifestation of GBD is transvestism and effeminate behavior. It is an interesting concept and a meaningful distinction; however, its gender specific nature weakens it as a diagnostic construct of intrapsychic conflict. In our society, a tomboy girl is well accepted by many to be superior to and more versatile than an ultrafeminine girl. The tomboy girl commands attention and respect as a person as she departs from the female stereotype. An effeminate boy is less fortunate. His behavior is labeled pathological and he is teased as a "sissy." He is stigmatized as being less than he should be, and there is a consistent demand for him to meet the male stereotype. It is easy to see that if GBD were a diagnostic category, it would be almost exclusively assigned to male children exhibiting effeminate or androgynous behavior and would perpetuate our current sociobiological and legal structures that stigmatize and/or punish men for exhibitionism and cross-dressing and ignore or endorse similar behavior in women.

It is important to differentiate GID from GBD in the diagnostic process. The child who believes he or she is wrongly assigned suffers from chronic and severe cognitive dissonance, where the child who knows what his or her anatomical gender is, but who enjoys androgynous behavior, will suffer only if the environment is punitive and nonsupportive. Sexual reassignment of children is considered only in cases of gender dysphoria or nonspecific amorphous genital structure. A GID adult with normal genitalia might request gender reassignment surgery as a matter of choice.

The GID child with gender specific and normal genitalia is a candidate for psychotherapy. The treatment of choice is nonaversive behavior modification. A token reward system coordinating the home, school, and treatment facility has proved to be a non-traumatic, highly successful regime (Rekers, 1978). Education and support of the primary caretakers are essential, and it is not uncommon for parents to need some special group or individual sessions to deal with their own sexual attitudes. It is always interesting to see how the unresolved sexual concerns of the parents have shaped the behavior of the child and how attitudinal changes in the parents facilitate the progress of the child in treatment. Despite dedicated research and clinical work, the causes and cures of GID are not yet fully understood (Money & Erhardt, 1973; Stoller, 1968; Green, 1974).

EXCESSIVE OR COMPULSIVE MASTURBATION

Discovery and manipulation of the genitals is to be expected in early childhood. Spitz (1949) suggested a positive correlation between infant masturbation and the quality of the maternal relationship. There was an absence of masturbation in institutionalized children who were deprived of nurturing mothers or mother surrogates.

Although the sexual response cycle is available to both boys and girls from birth, boys tend to find their genitals earlier than girls do. This is in part because of their visibility, accessibility, and the sensation of erection and movement. The caretakers' handling and naming of the genitals, their attention to toilet training, and their acceptance of the boy's handling of his penis, help boys develop organ constancy, with their penis and testes becoming a solid part of their identity. Girls do not develop genital organ constancy as reliably as boys do, although they experience pleasurable genital sensations and smile when urinating as early as forty weeks of age. Their masturbation may or may not include manual stimulation characteristic of boys. Girls may or may not find and identify their vulva, let alone their clitoris, as an organ of genital pleasure. It is not very big, not easily visible, and it is not necessary to handle for functional purposes. It is not

named, differentiated, or attended to by caretakers, nor does its discovery and manipulation usually meet with the benign or positive endorsement by adults that is characteristic of similar discovery in boys.

Girls may masturbate to orgasm by rhythmic pelvic thrusting against multiple thicknesses of their diapers, a pillow, or a soft toy between their legs, or other ingenuous methods, without actually realizing that the genitalia are the site of excitation and orgasm. Boys may also use the nondirect humping method for genital pleasure as children, and 15 percent of adult men report that they carry this behavior into adulthood (Hite, 1981). Most childhood genital play is not orgasm seeking and may be employed as a tension reduction activity, both in private and in public (Gesell, 1974). Masturbation frequency is highly variable in an individual child as well as between children. Although normative frequency data for specific ages are not available, children are often referred to clinicians for excessive or compulsive masturbation. This is a subjective quantification taken to mean that the child is preoccupied with masturbatory activity to the exclusion of other age appropriate pursuits and/or that the scope of the masturbation activity is resulting in stigmatizing censure from others that may create secondary adjustment problems for the child. Excessive masturbation in the presence of others is successfully treated in young children by short term, nonaversive behavior modification therapy or by play therapy. Concurrent exploration of the anxieties and tensions that are being alleviated by the self-assuring mantra of masturbation is helpful to children who are capable of understanding those connections. It is important to emphasize that *excessive* is a judgment not related to specific norms or acceptable frequency ranges.

The question of appropriateness of self-stimulation has been ubiquitous throughout history. The major myth originating in Jewish law was augmented by the misinterpretation of the Biblical story of Onan. Firmly entrenched as a Judeo-Christian sin, self-abuse was later proclaimed by medical science to be the forerunner of the dread disease spermatorea. This progressive affliction deteriorated into insanity, epilepsy, consumption, and death. At the turn of this century, the United States conducted a White House conference on masturbation, and there are a number of United States patents for torturous inventions to prevent masturbation and nocturnal erection in boys. In the mid-20th century, the Spock era of childrearing, progressive parents partially endorsed masturbation but cautioned against excess. How much is too much became the unanswerable question. Even today, adolescents and adults report feelings of guilt and remorse after masturbation despite its inclusion as a regular part of their sex pattern.

Sexologists believe that masturbation is a viable sexual activity throughout the lifespan and that it need not be considered a poor postpubescent substitute for sex with a partner. Research in female sexuality (Hite, 1978) and the treatment of anorgasmia in adult women (Barbach, 1975; Dodson, 1974; Chapman, 1977) suggest that masturbation to orgasm is an important developmental step and possibly a prerequisite to becoming reliably orgasmic in adult partner sex. It is often a treatment of choice for male and female sexual dysfunction (Kaplan, 1979) and is reported as a childhood activity of some importance by most adults (Kinsey et al., 1948, 1953; Hite, 1976, 1981; Hass, 1979).

Sexologists suggest that young boys be encouraged to prolong the arousal stage of their masturbation so as not to condition a rapid stimulus-response bond between erection and ejaculation. Young girls should be encouraged to look at and identify their external genitalia and to connect their erotic feelings and sexual response cycle to the appropriate body parts.

Children manipulating their genitalia in the presence of adults is usually not well tolerated. It produces a significant level of discomfort for most adults who expect that, like other sexual activity, it should take place in private. If the activity itself is endorsed as normal, good, acceptable, etc., the request that it be done privately is reasonable and not traumatic for the child. The tasks of childhood include learning to manage personal needs, desires, and behaviors in socially acceptable ways. Children who, with a little training, cannot limit masturbation activity to appropriate circumstances are often children who are of limited mental capacity or who suffer from poor reality testing and/or deficient object relationships. Behavior modification is still the treatment of choice; however, success is less predictable, even with mildly aversive conditioning. The public masturbation of children of diminished mental capacity or severe emotional disorder is clearly the link between masturbation and insanity that children have been warned about for centuries. Unfortunately, cause and effect were reversed (masturbation caused insanity rather than insanity caused public masturbation) in an attempt to frighten normal children out of normal masturbation activity. Parents need to understand that childhood masturbation is a normal and beneficial behavior that needs to be managed to coincide with social etiquette.

PRECOCIOUS OR DELAYED PUBERTY

The psychological impact of precocious or delayed puberty is a significant trauma of childhood and adolescence. Either condition separates the child from his or her peers, undermines the security of relative sameness, and may produce tension and alienation with the family if parents overestimate or underestimate the importance of the condition. The negative impact of precocious or delayed puberty increases with (1) degree of earliness or lateness, (2) the gender of the child, and (3) the direction of the discrepancy. An 8-year-old girl who has breast development and is menstruating has a more difficult social adjustment than an early-developing boy (and is also more common); whereas a prepubescent 14-year-old boy is more subject to peer ridicule than the undeveloped girl of the same age. The troublesome feaures of these conditions have less to do with sex per se than with social adjustment. The pubescent female third-grader must restrict her childish abandon and attend prematurely to the social and hygienic rituals of menstruation. Breast development, the wearing of a bra and a sanitary pad, the inevitable blood stains on panties or skirts, and the associated odor and possible premenstrual distress and menstrual cramps are all noticeable events that mark her as different from girls her own age and may even make her the subject of teasing, social ostracism, and ridicule. Her increased self-awareness and self-concerns set her apart in her own mind, and she may try desperately to compensate. She may ignore and deny her physiological condition, or she may withdraw from age appropriate social interaction. She may or may not be sexually precocious in association with premature hormonal activity, but she may be targeted by older boys and exploited through her need of acceptance. Others may assume that she is sexually active or interested and respond accordingly, even if that is not the case.

A psychological dilemma of similar magnitude occurs for the boy who experiences delayed pubescence. The rites of passage for boys in our culture are a combination of physical development and skill, competition, and sociosexual skills. Young, small, underdeveloped boys are the scapegoats of the locker room, fare poorly in the dating scene, and restrict their options and activities in order to minimimize their vulnerability. They develop compensatory patterns to their chronic lack of self-esteem and may become the class clown or the overachiever or may simply withdraw from appropriate peer interaction. Their sexuality is usually normal, and masturbation patterns are consistent unless depression becomes a feature of the psychological profile. Girls with delayed pubescence experience a similar, but much less traumatic, situation. The condition is less obvious, more easily absorbed into the social aspects of the peer group, and of less concern to families. Their worry about inadequate breast development is shared by many pubescent female peers, and the absence of menstruation can be considered convenient (if not a blessing) by a teenage girl. Treatment for precocious or delayed pubescence is a thorough medical examination to rule out endocrine pathology followed by supportive psychotherapy.

PRECOCIOUS SEXUAL INTEREST AND BEHAVIOR

Clinicians are often consulted by parents anxious about their child's interest in sexual topics, masturbation, or sex play with siblings and peers. Despite the cultural mandate that children should be sexually innocent through programmed ignorance, many are curious and will seek knowledge if they are not intimidated, punished, or ridiculed for their sexual curiosity. There is a developmental sequence to their interest and activity that suggests that there are periods of intense interest and involvement and periods of less interest and involvement. There are children, however, who maintain a consistently high interest and some who are predominantly uninterested throughout childhood. The environment is probably the more crucial variable in how sexual interest is translated into behavior. If the child's basic interest is complemented by unsupervised opportunity to engage in trial-and-error learning with a partner, sexual rehearsal play is predictable. Some sexologists suggest that not only is sexual rehearsal play quite predictable in children but that it is advisable and should be encouraged in order to forestall adult sexual problems (Money, 1973; Yates, 1979).

Kinsey suggested that if a parent wanted to be the one to tell his or her child about the facts of life, he or she should do it before the child reaches the age of 9. With today's proliferation of sexual topics, information, and misinformation in the media, that age should probably be revised downward to about 5. Children have basic questions about sexual differences—beween boys and girls, men and women, children and adults—from the time they can formulate them verbally and may ask questions about babies, especially if their environment includes expectant mothers and/or infants. At about age 4, children develop a consuming interest in family, including the interrelatedness of family members (e.g., grandmother is mother's mother, aunt is father's sister, etc.), their own babyhood, their projected adulthood, weddings, babies of their own, how babies get in and out of mother's abdomen, and so forth. It is a good time to endorse this academic interest in sex with proper information because children at this age do not process sexual information emotionally or personally. They do, however, willingly pronounce their intellectual acquisitions to anyone who will listen, and they may ask for public confirmation from a parent or credit the parent as their source of sexual information. They may ask personal questions about a parent's sex life and suggest the possibility of a sexual encounter with a parent, and they may engage in sexual rehearsal play with peers. Their humor includes bathroom words and sounds and is actually more scatological than sexual.

Intense and continued or intermittent sexual interest in children should be accommodated as any other interest would be. Age appropriate books and conversations with parents endorse the child's curiosity about this important part of life and encourage an open and unashamed quest for sexual knowledge. In contrast, a child who shows little interest or curiosity about sex should not be overwhelmed with sex information by overzealous parents. Some children personalize their sexuality very early and are uncomfortable with candid sex conversations. They appreciate sex materials to be used in private and occasional one-on-one talks with a parent to clear up any troublesome sexual idea or feelings.

Some parents may worry about a child with low sex interest, but lack of sex interest is more often considered normal in children. Of greater concern is the child who is very public with sex talk and sex play, masturbatory or with peers. Parents are concerned that this kind of child is abnormal genetically or hormonally; that he or she will be censured by other adults and children; that his or her sexual behavior will reflect badly on siblings and family; that he or she will be a target for sexual abuse or exploitation by adults; or that he or she will grow up to be promiscuous or perverted. Nonaversive behavior modification is the treatment of choice, with the acknowledgment of the child's interest in sex, supervision of play with other children, distraction from sexually stimulating situations, and spe-

cified acceptable times and ways to experience sexual gratification or satisfy sexual interest. If parents can accept and endorse the child's interest in sex and encourage the academic acquisition of sex information, trial-and-error learning will become less necessary and the negative responses of most other adults and most children to sexual subjects will direct the child back to the parent for information, discussion, and support.

As might be expected, there is more parental and societal acceptance of sexual interest in talk and/or behavior in boy children than in girls. Young fathers often take pride in their sons' interest and awareness of sexuality, and mothers accept it as a masculine attribute, especially if their husband is more interested in sex or has a higher frequency of need for sexual intercourse than they do.

Little girls are expected to demonstrate awareness and interest in the reproductive aspects of sex rather than the pleasure or recreational aspects. Even enlightened parents respond to little girls' concerns about not having or wanting to have a penis with reassurance that she has an equally desirable vagina that will allow her to have babies when she grows up. Not only are penis and vagina not anatomically analogous organs, but she does not want to wait until she grows up and what she really wants is to be able to urinate standing up, make designs on the wall, and have something to play with or to show off to others. The information that her clitoris feels just as good as her brother's penis is rarely offered, and therapeutic water play (e.g., hoses, sprinklers, squirt guns, water balloons, etc.) is not usually prescribed or arranged.

Children who are pseudomature in any sense are special children with special needs. They demand more from parents and may be considered a blessing or a curse, depending on the value system and resources of the parents. Intellectual genius, superior athletic potential, and exceptional musical talent are all considered valuable gifts that should not be wasted. Children who are sexually precocious in development or interest are, in contrast, shunned and pitied. The parents of these children need help, not only in the management of their children's behavior, but also in considering that precocity in this area need not be thought of as an affliction.

CHILDREN WHO REPORT SEXUAL CONTACT WITH AN ADULT THAT CANNOT BE SUBSTANTIATED

Psychological literature and the popular press report and often sensationalize the plight of the traumatized child whose story of sexual activity with an adult is not believed and, conversely, of the victimized adult who steadfastly denies the sexual accusations of a child. In cases like these, psychological consultation is usually delayed until other means of determination are exhausted and everyone is thoroughly confused. A concentrated effort is first made to ascertain whether or not a prosecutable crime has been committed during which time some intervention in the family lifestyle may have already occurred (e.g., the child assigned to relatives or a foster home, the adult put in jail or, if a family member, legally restrained from going home or being in the presence of the child).

Children who report sexual contact with an adult that cannot be substantiated pose a special problem for the therapist because he or she is expected to produce information that either confirms or negates the child's original report to parents and/or authorities. The most commonly reported pedophilic situation is that of the adult male and the prepubescent female. This is not to say that sex between an adult female and a prepubescent male does not occur, but it would probably not be reported and, if it were, it would probably not be considered a traumatic experience for the child.

In Western culture, the male's need to acquire sexual knowledge is accepted. The sexually adept man is valued by society, envied by men, and sought after by women. There is a time-honored tradition of young boys being sexually initiated by an experienced, older woman (sometimes a friend or former lover of his father). Girls, in contrast, are considered permanently damaged by early

sexual initiation by an adult male. The loss of innocence, interest in sex, sexual skill, and sexual knowledge are all negative attributes in young girls who are expected to be sexually naive, pure, and possibly virginal. The society's attitude that the child has been damaged by sexual experience is extended to boys only if the sexual encounter is homosexual or if residual physical damage is sustained. Sex between an adult female and a female child is the least reported pedophilic possibility and is of least interest to law enforcement and the community at large. The lack of interest in sex between females is documented throughout history and, although politically interesting, it is beyond the scope of this chapter.

It is difficult to generalize about adult/child sex because of the variability of age and gender in any individual case. However, in all cases, a meticulous history of both parties (and the family, if it is incestuous) is the essential first step for the therapist. The possibility of a deepseated psychic conflict in either alleged participant precludes the viability of the concept of a simple lie. Details of the sexual encounter or encounters are important and are cathartic and nontraumatic for the child if the therapist has a low personal level of sexual guilt and does not project negative attitudes toward sex into the situation. It is important to note that if the sexual encounter occurred and if it was traumatic for the child, the diagnostic process with a clinical child sexologist is therapeutic. Psychotherapy consists of talking about traumatic situations in order to bring the experience into cognitive awareness and to work though the feelings engendered by the event. Properly handled, a sexual trauma is no exception to this process. A client is ill served by a therapist who feels that the child has been permanently damaged by the experience and relates to him or her as a victim.

The determination of actual events may be rapid or tediously slow. The therapist needs to be alert for a flattened affect and a rote recounting of the event from the child, because, as transference develops, details of the actual happenings should be remembered and added, and insight should allow cognitive connections to surface. If the accusation is a fantasy, the secondary gain will eventually reveal itself, and if the therapist's purpose is to separate fantasy from reality, the child will comfortably explain the reasons for the false accusation. If the child has resorted to grand scale deception to try to get his or her needs met, or if he or she is psychotic, ongoing therapy is advisable. However, it is usually not done unless required by the court.

If the sexual experience is determined to have taken place, the legal sanctions invoked take the adult out of the child's environment for a while. If the adult is a family member, the loss of integrity of the family unit may be more troublesome than the sexual event, especially if the child is held accountable by other family members for the loss of the father or father figure.

The myth of childhood sexual innocence is so intrinsic to our culture that it is difficult to acknowledge that genital stimulation at any age is a pleasurable sensation. If a trusted adult approaches the child in a loving and caring fashion and persuades him or her that genital fondling is appropriate behavior between them, the activity itself may be reported by the child as pleasurable. The admonition not to tell others may be the child's first clue that there is something wrong with the exchange. Even so, the gratification of being special, of having a secret, of genital pleasure, and of intimacy with and power over an adult, have helped to perpetuate consensual, incestuous relationships over periods of years. It is common for lengthy incestuous relationships to be revealed when the girl's wish to date peers after pubescence threatens the adult male's need for sexual exclusivity. Many adult women have reported satisfying, nontraumatic prepubescent incestuous relationships, from which they graduated to postpubescent sex with peers, without undue incident (Farrell, in press).

In contrast, many patients in psychotherapy report unresolved conflicts in association with childhood sexual experiences, and there is some evidence to suggest that the greater the age differential between participants, the greater the potential for trauma. This would imply that it is a power rather than a sexual phenomenon in that as the age difference increases the child feels less capable of resisting seduction, bribery, or coercion. When safety, security, and a sense of well being are invested in the benevolence of a caretaking adult, there is little opportunity to oppose the wishes of the caretaker. The suggestion of some pedophiles and pedophilic groups that the legality of consensual sex be expanded to include minors is ludicrous when you consider the concept of inherent power.

INCEST

Although frequency data on pedophilic sex are woefully inadequate, the reports that are available indicate that father/daughter incest is most frequent (including stepfathers, father surrogates, mothers' boyfriends, etc.). Heterosexual sibling incest is next, and all other categories (e.g., father/son, mother/son, homosexual/sibling, extended family member/child, family friend/child, caretaker/child, stranger/child) are less clearly ranked. The effects of each situation are differential, but once again the data are sparse and we must deal with the clinical impressions rather than the scientific conclusions. Reported incestuous sex and sex with persons known to the family are less apt to be believed when revealed by the child than sex with a stranger. The struggle to convince the unbelieving parent is a major stress added to the experience itself and the decision to tell. The vulnerability of the child in this situation is awesome if the trusted parent ignores or punishes him/or her, and it is not uncommon for the child to withdraw the accusation. Some variation of this situation is often reported by child and/or adult prostitutes.

Another common incest scenario is one that includes the covert awareness of the mother. She may never be present or acknowledge the event but may seemingly engineer it all by withdrawing sexually or withholding sex from her partner and leaving the father or father surrogate and the usually pubescent daughter conveniently alone for adequate periods of time. She may be shocked and horrified when the liaison is revealed, but her unconscious collusion is apparent to the skilled therapist. She may express a feeling of betrayal by both her partner and her child and is rarely emotionally supportive to her daughter. Often the mother-daughter relationship is competitive, and if the male is removed from the family unit, the whole pattern may be re-enacted with a new male.

Less common is the ménage-à-trois in which the mother is a participant in or an observer of the sexual activity. However, some women service their husbands' sexual desires by including their daughters as potential partners and again the girls are usually at least nearing pubescence. The psychological impact on the child is one of helplessness and abandonment. The decision to report the situation is often made when a younger sibling is introduced into the pattern. A trusted teacher is the most frequent confidant. Teachers are ill prepared to deal with personal matters of this magnitude, and the trauma for the child may increase significantly before things are rectified. For example, the child is placed in a juvenile facility and the momentary relief experienced after telling others is followed by a growing anxiety about what's going on at home. Parents may call or visit and their anger or anguish causes the child to doubt that she did the right thing. She fears what will happen to her if she returns home and where she will be sent if she doesn't return home. She has little or no emotional support and may agree to withdraw her complaint rather than perpetuate the adversarial situation with her parents.

Father/daughter sex is often initiated when the girl begins developing secondary sex characteristics at about age 9 or 10. Her maturing body then becomes a constant reminder of sexuality to the adult male, although she is still a child. Three- to five-year-old girls are also chosen by some fathers, more often in fact, than the 6- to 8-year-olds. This age factor is not as strange as it may appear on the surface if you consider the normative stages of child development. The 3- to 5-year-old is open, curious about bodies (her own and other people's), uninhibited, and quite often "daddy's girl." They are over the stubborn obstructionism of the terrible twos, are anxious to please, and are intensely interested in genitalia differentiation, function, etc. They are coquettish and provocative and quite amenable to sex games, sex talk, and sex rehearsal play.

Ages 6 and 7 are characterized by an intense need for privacy and a growing need to experience dominion over their own bodies. Children at this age may, at any time, not want to be looked at or touched by others without first granting permission. Their control over their own body functions, coordination, and skills, bequeaths a sense of identity and differentiation from others, and they express feelings of exploitation if they are coerced into certain behaviors. Their mental organization is capable of judgments and they may not approve of their own behavior and may feel badly for having done things that are not congruent with their values.

Sibling sex, heterosexual and homosexual, is probably the least traumatic, especially if the ages are approximate (the potential for the trauma of exploitation increases as the power of one child over the other increases through age, size, family favoritism, etc.). The exploration of anatomical differences, fondling, sex talk, mutual masturbation (common among many sibs), and sexual rehearsal, play, and intercourse (somewhat less common), are all reported frequently in adult sex histories as beginning events. They sometimes have traumatic correlates in association with being discovered by a disapproving adult, but the events themselves, unless force or coercion was used, are recalled as childhood adventures.

PEDOPHILIC SEX WITH A STRANGER

Probably one of the most psychologically traumatic pedophilic situations, for both boys and girls at any age, is reporting sex with a stranger. Even if the sexual encounter was as simple as observing a flasher, parental hysteria and the inevitable witch hunt that follows are usually beyond the child's ability to process adequately. If there was sexual contact, the child may be subjected to a secondary physical trauma in the form of a medical exam and the endless questioning by parents and police that indelibly mark and exacerbate the event. The attitude that loss of innocence is a personal devaluation held by most adults insidiously undermines the child's self-esteem. Parental fears often translate into child phobias. Separation, anxiety and regression, sleep disturbance, depression, loss of concentration, and school phobia are all possible residuals from the total network of events surrounding sex with a stranger.

Last but not least are the physical possibilities—pregnancy, venereal disease, injury, mutilation, and death. It is important to note that despite the sensationalism of the cases of sexual psychopaths, they are few in number and their victims are few in comparison to the multitude of less dramatic cases of sexual exploitation. When physical injury occurs and hospitalization or medical attention is needed, psychological services should be immediately integrated into the total treatment plan. It is sometimes forgotten by adults (who see medical treatment as positive) that children experience it as a negative, intrusive, traumatic loss of control. An experienced pediatric therapist can help the patient resolve the effects of both traumas. As a society, we have seen fit to legislate against the exploitation of children in the labor force, and it is reasonable to expect that we would protect children from sexual exploitation as well. It is important to note that most reported pedophilic sex is incestuous, and that incest is a family rather than an individual pathology. The treatment of choice is a combination of family and individual psychotherapy.

POSTPUBESCENT SEX WITH A PARTNER, HETEROSEXUAL

Sexual development and sexual awareness are occurring at a younger age than ever before in Western history. While every parent expects and hopes that his or her child will have a loving heterosexual relationship, few are ready for it when it occurs. There is pervasive feeling among parents that "they are too young," but the concept of sexual readiness is poorly understood by all. Many child experts agree that children are encouraged to be sexual too soon and that they are abandoned by frightened parents who feel unprepared to help them make that important decision. Actually, few adolescents discuss the decision with either parent, and probably few make a rational decision about activating their sex life with a partner. Most have sex in response to their feelings of the moment and request birth control as an afterthought. Mothers of girls as young as 12 facilitate birth control through planned parenthood, public clinics, or private physicians, feeling that they have no choice but to endorse their daughters' decision to be sexual with their boyfriends. Sexologists have attempted to deal with the question of sexual readiness in terms of chronological age, and there is a reasonable consensus that around the age of 16 adolescents are physiologically and psychologically ready. The late adolescent is interested in forming primary relationships outside the nuclear family, and sexual sharing is an integral part of these relationships. Sex of the early adolescent is quite different in quality. It is usually curiosity seeking and exploitive and is often an intensely negative experience for girls. Parents who consider their daughter's loss of virginity as the definitive onset of her continuing sex life with a partner make it difficult for her to change her mind. It is not uncommon for girls who begin partner sex early to have a lengthy period of celibacy in the midteens (often after a pregnancy). Adolescent girls tend to be dismayed by the frequency needs of their partner and the impersonality of the sexual encounter. Many report that they have sex because "he wants it and they want him." Most girls are responsible for birth control by default. They use the pill which in addition to preventing pregnancy, has a good record of decreasing libido, clearing up acne, eliminating menstrual cramps and irregularity, and causing a 10- to 15-pound weight gain.

Boys are encouraged from an early age to equate sexuality with manhood, and postpubescent heterosexual behavior in boys is often endorsed by adults as a hedge against homosexuality. Insensitivity, exploitation, and domination of women are still considered sure signs of masculinity to the point that gentle, caring boys who like and respect girls often see themselves as less manly than "the guys who just go for it."

Sexuality is a major concern of adolescents, and in that regard they are poorly served by the professional community, the family, the school, and the culture (Hass, 1979). The professional mental health worker sees a small fraction of adolescents and may or may not address sexual issues. Family members have little credibility in sexuality if the foundation was not accomplished in childhood. The school is still concentrating on reproductive biology and venereal disease while the adolescent needs help with sociosexual issues. At the same time, the culture stimulates and misinforms, encourages and prohibits, punishes and rewards the adolescent for sexual interest and behavior.

The revered notion that sex is natural, happening with style, sensitivity, and spirituality when two people love each other is a myth that departs significantly from most reported first encounters. It does, however, perpetuate a rationale for those who oppose real sex education and dooms the teenager, misinformed by the exploitive messages of the marketplace, to a facade of informed bravado. Despite the proliferation of monolithic audiovisual departments in secondary school districts, colleges, and universities, and audiovisual materials produced for every area of instruction, there is a firm ban on the sexual pattern films (explicit sexual activity documentaries). These films, many produced by the National Sex Forum, have been judged as helpful by over 70,000 adults. Because of their nonexploitive, true-to-life depictions of the actual sexual activity, they are viable audiovisual materials for beginners, but sexually curious or sexually active adolescents are relegated to trial-and-error learning until they reach their legal majority. It may be unrealistic to expect more than bare bones reproductive biology and venereal disease instruction from public secondary schools. The few teachers who might have the knowledge and sensitivity to teach human sexuality effectively are hampered by laws, rules, regulations, administration dicta, and hostile factions in the community.

The mental health profession has an opportunity to make a significant contribution in this area by helping adolescents directly and all children indirectly through programs for teens, parents, and child care workers. Direct mental health service to teens is in response to an identified problem and is usually too intense, too focused, and too short to accomplish broad-based educational objectives. Many concerned and responsible parents are willing to admit that they are unprepared to offer the quality and scope of sex education they want their children to have, and they are delighted to find a qualified sexologist to provide this educational experience. Parents are accustomed to augmenting the offerings of the public or private school system with lessons of all kinds and welcome the ability to pass on the sex education responsibility to an expert. Parents of young children who want to build a firm foundation for sex communication within the family unit are anxious to know more about sex in general and how to relate to their children's sexual behavior, interest, and curiosity at every age of child development. Ongoing sex education classes taught by a professional are a welcome addition to the community's adult education offerings.

For the parents who have acknowledged their adolescent's right to be sexual with a partner, there are a myriad of questions and problems that occur. In keeping with cultural mores, heterosexually active boys pose less of a problem to parents than girls do. There is some residual of premature marriages, but with the ready availability of abortion, a boy's decision to marry at a young age is usually based on more than impending fatherhood. Boys are typically given more freedom to stay out late, to not come home at night, and generally to come and go as they please. Girls are still expected to be the guardians of morality and to use their sexual potential for secondary gain. If they enjoy their sexuality as an expression of their own desire and as an acceptable interpersonal exchange, they are thought to be misusing or dissipating a valuable negotiable commodity. This attitude, pervasive among parents, becomes an internalized tenet of self-doubt that plagues girls when at any point they contemplate their dissatisfaction with their life situation. The insidious, ubiquitous message that equates female sexual skill, interest, knowledge, and behavior with sin, evil, misfortune, and a lack of value is perpetuated by loving parents, responsible adults, benevolent professionals, male and female peers, and the girl herself. It is a task of major proportion to raise a girl with the same degree of sexual self-acceptance that is common among boys. The double standard exists, often without recognition, in families of male and female children.

The permission to have sex at home in the privacy of one's own room is significant parental endorsement of the importance of sex in a person's life and communicates parental respect for the sexual aspects of their child. This decision is complicated if the parents disagree and/or there are younger children in the family the parents wish to keep uninformed. Most young people do not receive this endorsement from their parents, but because of difficult logistics and lack of funds, do end up having sex at home with the constant threat of discovery. Discovery may bring some member of the family to a therapist as the emerging sexuality of the adolescent stresses the family unit. Family structures that were tenuous before may not withstand the shifting balance created by the emerging needs of the young adult living at home. The therapist may have difficulty refocusing the treatment from the adolescent to the family unit. The adolescent may emancipate prematurely or may get caught up in the marital conflict. A combination of individual and family therapy is the treatment of choice.

POSTPUBESCENT SEX WITH A PARTNER, HOMOSEXUAL

Increasingly, counselors and therapists are consulted when parents suspect or know that their adolescent is in love with a person of the same gender. Even though societal attitudes are relaxing and homosexuality is no longer a disease category in the APA DSM-III, for the individual family it is a trauma of major stress. Revelation or conclusive evidence of the relationship elicits a plethora of paradoxical parental emotions. Shock and disbelief are offset by the satisfaction of understanding previously unexplainable reactions and events. Professional consultation is sought by the parent with the initial purpose of curing the errant child, but the family system is the actual patient or client. After the diagnostic interviews, the identified patient is benefited by information about gender preference and the lifestyle implications of homosexuality and bisexuality and also on how to survive the family crisis he or she has caused. The parents and siblings need information about homosexuality and opportunities to work through their homophobia and the potential lifestyle alteration a gay offspring sets in motion (e.g., possible stigma by family, friends, and business associates, acceptance of the gay couple in the family milieu, possibility of no grandchildren, and/or the end of the perpetuation of the family name, etc.).

Both parents and child need to know that a same sex love affair does not automatically mean that either participant is a homosexual. In times past and in some instances today, a same sex experience is considered a fall from grace from which one could never recover. Actually, it may be that the love object happens to be of the same sex but the love feelings are unique to that individual and may not be generalized to others of the same sex; or it may be that a bisexual resolution may occur with either or both genders being available as primary partners throughout a specific life phase or across the lifespan; or the first same sex love may be the expression of an exclusively homosexual life pattern to come.

The anger, disappointment, and guilt experienced by the parent need to be expressed, but it is not in the best interest of the child to hear those lamentations. It is well to keep in mind that the child is doing what comes naturally. Children experience their erotic and love feelings in association with certain people and events and not in association with other people and events. There are other romantic combinations that concern or are unacceptable to parents such as significant differences of age, socioeconomic class, race, religion, and/or highly discrepant values and lifestyles.

Occasionally, adolescents will seek consultation about homosexual feelings or experiences without parental knowledge. They may request information and some help in reconciling feelings and behavior and may subsequently resolve to homosexual, bisexual, or heterosexual lifestyles. A few adolescents are totally unaccepting of homosexuality and are repulsed by any same sex attraction they might feel. They are traumatized by a same sex approach or experience even though they may have been a willing participant. They seek professional help to get rid of whatever is causing their attraction to and by members of the same sex. Information, clarification of feelings and values, self-acceptance work, and homophobia desensitization may not significantly alter their need to disown their feelings and reject that part of themselves. If they are adamant in their need to be heterosexual, behavior modification techniques may be initiated. Homosexuality is not altered by behavior modification therapy. However, joining the resistance (e.g., allowing that same sex attraction need not be behavioralized) is effective in helping adolescents decrease their cognitive dissonance and come to know and accept themselves. It soon becomes apparent, if love and erotic feelings are felt exclusively for members of the same sex, that the choice is not between homosexuality and heterosexuality, but it is between having and not having a love life.

It should be noted that for many homosexuals and bisexuals the facade of a heterosexual lifestyle that may include marriage and children is still viable. This partial repudiation is less popular today than in times past, but it can be an emotionally healthy compromise between learned values and personal needs. "Coming out" is a personal and individual decision. Especially for adolescents, who have little knowledge of the history of homosexual repression and harassment, the therapist can play a critical role in weighing the consequences of a public declaration. It is probably best delayed until the family can function as a support system or an auxiliary support system can be provided. Most parents fervently hope that their child's same sex preference is a phase he or she is passing through and are unwilling to disown a homosexual child. Adjustment is gradual and may be facilitated by one of several new books written especially for the situation (Fairchild & Hayward, 1979; Silverstein, 1978).

Some families or individual family members may be unwilling or incapable of accepting homosexuality, thus precipitating the gay adolescent's premature emancipation from family and the need for a new support group. The gay subculture, especially in urban areas, has a network of individuals and groups who do not discriminate against homosexuals. There are hotlines, newspapers, church and social groups, and so forth, organized by and for gays. There are medical, paramedical, and psychological professionals who are either gay or not homophobic that serve the gay community without prejudice.

Fearful parents may ask the therapist for support in prohibiting an underaged adolescent from seeing the object of his or her affection. They may send their child away to school, on vacation, or may even move the entire family to break up the homosexual relationship. It is, of course, their right to make decisions concerning their underaged child, and they may need to do something dramatic in order to feel that they have done all they could to prevent the inevitable. Such thinking, however, is based on the false premise that a person can be lured into a homosexual lifestyle by others and that homosexuality can be prevented if the lovers are separated. This Romeo and Juliet situation may successfully preclude the relationship in question and may or may not precipitate serious conflict within the family. But it will not deter future same sex attraction if the child is gay.

SEXUAL CONCERNS OF THE PHYSICALLY AND MENTALLY HANDICAPPED

The myth of the sexual innocence of childhood is most secure in the homes of the handicapped child. Close parental supervision, limited autonomy with peers, identity as a physically handicapped child or child with special needs, and rejection by peers as potential sex partner all contribute to the negation of sexuality of the physically or mentally handicapped child. Not only are the sexual needs of these children not acknowledged or addressed by most parents, they are also ignored by most custodial caretakers, institutions, medical personnel, and the national societies that offer programs and services for individual disease categories (e.g., muscular dystrophy, cerebral palsy, epilepsy, etc.). Handicapped children have sexual curiosity and sexual feelings despite the conspiracy of silence, and they need not only basic sexual knowledge but also information about how they can be sexual given their specific limitations. As adolescents, they need opportunities to experience their sexual response cycle, to learn what their individual sexual limitations and abilities are and, perhaps more importantly, how to negotiate for sex with a partner. Especially the orthopedically handicapped are assumed to be incapable of sex by most able-bodied people. Adolescents need opportunity for ongoing sex education and young adults can benefit greatly by working with a sexual surrogate who is specifically trained to help people get in touch with their bodies and explore their sexual potential.

Mentally retarded, physically healthy children pose another type of problem. They may be quite normal in physical and sexual development, and as adolescents may be attractive enough to be selected as potential sex partners by peers or adults. Impaired mental function may disallow, however, good judgment in sexual situations. Their own sexual desire coupled with this lack of discrimination make them an easy target for sexual exploitation. The mentally retarded child needs explicit sex education; reinforced, plainly stated rules about sociosexual conduct; adequate supervision; and effective birth control for girls at the appropriate age.

Families of handicapped adolescents who live at home and caretakers of institutionlized teens need to facilitate the sexual opportunities of their charges. Even if they can acquire potential partners, the handicapped adoles-cent needs a safe place, privacy, and perhaps some physical assistance to have a successful sex experience. The issues of birth control and paid partners are complicated for adolescents or young adults in institutions or on public assistance, as charges for these services are not reimbursable by third-party payers. As a society, we have by default decided that the handicapped shall not have sex lives. The advocacy groups for special syndromes have not provided or demanded sexual equality and sexual rights that for many are as important as access to public buildings or the Special Olympics.

SEXUAL GUILT AS A FACTOR IN THE TREAMENT OF THE HOSPITALIZED CHILD: ACCIDENT, ILLNESS, SURGERY

Psychological services for the child hospitalized in the medical or surgical ward have become standard practice in many hospitals. Hospitalization itself is a moderate-to-severe life trauma for children in that they are displaced from familiar surroundings and the integrity of the body is violated. Hospital procedures constitute a lack of control over what happens to their bodies, and even if parents are present, they have relinquished control to the medical team. It is vulnerability in the extreme for the child. The situation is further magnified if the admission is of an emergency nature and if unconsciousness, anesthesia, or coma interrupt the time-space continuum. Psychological consultation for the hospitalized child, if not routine, may be requested in response to the child's depression, failure to adjust to hospital procedure, fears and phobias, psychosomatic symptoms, and/ or the request of the child. In both routine ward service and psychological referrals, the alleviation of sex (masturbation) guilt is often a significant factor in the understanding and treatment of the physical illness. From the concrete thinking of the young child to the maturing moralism of the teenager, the cause-and-effect rationale is predominant. Bad consequences result from bad deeds. Careful interviewing will reveal the questioning search for why the accident or illness happened. The simplistic link from bad thoughts to bad deeds usually includes the forbidden sexual behaviors. A frank discussion about masturbation (what it is and what it isn't) allows the therapist to (1) assuage the child's masturbation guilt; (2) demythologize and disconnect sexual behavior as the cause of the injury or illness; (3) impart accurate information, and (4) give permission for continued masturbatory behavior in the hospital. It also facilitates trust in the therapist about other personal concerns (e.g., recovery, abandonment, death, etc.).

The unresolved sexual guilt of hospitalized children is compounded by the secondary gain phenomenon of accident and illness. Some children are puzzled by, and unaccepting of, the gifts and favors that are a ritualized part of sickness in our culture. If they are feeling that their condition is the consequence of bad behavior, the presentation of gifts is confusing. For a gift to be offered means that the giver is not aware of the patient's culpability. Not to accept the gift would feel right for the child but would necessitate an explanation or an admission of guilt. To accept the gift would compound the guilt feeling because the child is accepting something he or she feels he or she doesn't deserve. If the feeling of the guilt is significant, the gift will be received without interest or enthusiasm. This ennui is often mistaken for a purely physiological lethargy, and the psychological determinants are left unexplored. Once the sexual guilt is resolved, gifts can be accepted and enjoyed as the diversion they are intended to be.

Most adults are ambivalent about children's masturbation. Medical and hospital personnel may need some help in understanding the purpose of dealing with masturbation when health concerns are primary. It is not helpful for the child to be endorsed by one member of the health team and censured by others for the same behavior. Masturbation is an effective tension and anxiety reducer in children and adults, and it is self-affirming. It is a physically pleasant sensation, especially important in the hospital situation in which physical pain and discomfort are predominant. It is an activity

that reclaims the body and offsets the intrusive hospital procedures. The cessation of a regular masturbation pattern constitutes an unnecessary deprivation and added stress to an already stressful situation.

The suggestion that they will get well faster by keeping as many things as possible the same as they were at home, as well as making arrangements for privacy, is all that is usually needed to get children back to their regular masturbation patterns and psychologically involved in the healing process. They begin to request favorite toys, books, and games to be brought from home. They recall and facilitate parts of their home routine and lose the feeling of helpless alienation that so often accompanies hospitalization. Their depression abates, and if their stay is lengthy and therapy is ongoing, questions about death, complications about their specific illness or injury, as well as additional questions about sex, are usually forthcoming.

Sexual guilt is a general syndrome that is found with individual variation in most hospitalized children. It should be noted that it is invariable in both children and adults who are hospitalized for burns. There seems to be a consistent association between sexual guilt and death or punishment by fire. It is common for sexual activity and interest in adults and children to wane as an aftermath of severe burns, even though the genitals are rarely included in the burnsite. Although concerns over physical unattractiveness are easily voiced by most patients, the feeling that the burn was punishment for sexual thoughts or deeds is a significant part of their depression.

CHILD PROSTITUTION AND KIDDIE PORN

The exploitation of children is anathema in our humanitarian society. We have laws to protect children from unscrupulous adults. The idealization of the innocence and vulnerability of childhood is, however, of fairly recent historical origin (DeMause, 1980). An artifact of Victorianism, society's protection of children challenged, at least in theory, parents' dominion over their offspring. The history of childhood is replete with the abuse and exploitation of children by their parents and other adults. Children were given away, abandoned, sold, beaten, maimed, starved, killed, enslaved, taught to beg and steal, and used for adults' sexual gratification, with little or no concern for their well being. They were considered the property of their parents or any adult who claimed them. The designation of childhood and adolescence as developmental stages with specific needs and tasks is of recent origin, and child labor laws and other protective legislation, compulsory education, and so forth, are still not uniformly enforced. There is a societal reluctance to intrude on the autonomy of the nuclear family. The campaign for the recognition of the battered child as a syndrome of ongoing abuse was hard fought in the 1960s. No one wanted to believe or admit that it was a widespread phenomenon that had crossed all educational, socioeconomic, racial, ethnic and religious lines.

Child prostitution and kiddie porn are similarly societal problems that adults are trying hard not to address. Runaways who become street children with no job skills (and many too young to work legally), no money, no shelter, and so forth, quickly learn that they have only one negotiable commodity: their sexuality. Male or female, they can sell their bodies to adult men. For the most part, by pleasing their client, they get attention (sometimes equated with love), food, clothing, a bath, a bed, warmth, a momentary feeling of importance, and money. They may also get drugs, sexual abuse, venereal disease, pregnant, physically injured, frightened, and/or killed. They may find a friend and a protector, or they may be arrested.

Although the ranks of street children relegated to prostitution and other forms of sexual exploitation grow consistently, some children are encouraged by a parent into prostitution to augment the family income and upgrade the standard of living of mother and siblings. These children are usually female and living with a mother as a single parent. The mother is unemployed or in a low-paying job and offers her daughter to a man or men who will pay for her services. The girl may have been used sexually by adult men in the family or may be having sex with male peers, so for many the sex issue is of little consequence. Secondarily, the power and status she receives as the female consort and as an income-producing family member may adequately offset any reluctance or displeasure she might have about the sex. The girl in this situation is more apt to come to the attention of authorities and be referred for evaluation and therapy than street children who are rarely seen professionally.

Any individual can be psychologically evaluated and can benefit from the self-knowledge gained in psychotherapy. Child prostitution and kiddie porn, however, are broad spectrum societal problems that will not be alleviated by individual psychotherapy. Society needs to address itself to the question of why 10- to 15-year-olds find life on the street preferable to life at home. That answer will not be found by concentrating on the sexual behavior of the children or the motivations of the men who buy their services. Prostitution means survival for most street children, and they have few (if any) other viable options. The old avenues for early emancipation from home and family are gone, and with the exception of welfare eligibility of a pregnant teen, society has not replaced them.

CLINICAL TECHNIQUES FOR HANDLING SEXUAL PROBLEMS OF CHILDREN

The public sentiment against children's sexuality, the vilification of the pedophile, and the absence of sexology in traditional mental health education and training combine to make the treatment of sex problems of children a difficult situation for the otherwise well-trained clinician. It goes without saying that the interview with the child should be scheduled with a professional experienced in working with children. Understanding the symbolic language of childhood is especially valuable in dealing with sexual issues, and a playroom or doll house diagnostic session often provides valuable information that is otherwise unavailable. If the child is old enough and is willing to verbalize details of the experience, he or she will be anticipating the characteristic overreaction from adults (e.g., intense interest, horror, or pity, etc.). It is imperative that the therapist not service his or her own sexual curiosity by moving into an interrogative stance. Even if there are outside pressures to obtain evidence, the child must be allowed to move at his or her own pace, and the focus of the session must remain on the child, not on the sex. If, as is often the case, the child refuses to talk, his or her need to protect his or her internal integrity should be supported as evidence of ego strength, and the focus of the session should be shifted to rapport-building and transference-generating activities. The child may at that point desperately need a safe place that does not expect or demand him or her to focus on the sexual events. As trust in the therapist ensues, the child will confide, first, his or her feelings about how the situation has been handled, and second, the actual events in question.

Working with parents and families around child sex issues is as difficult as, if not more difficult than, working with the child. Parents may be so distraught that they are unable to provide any emotional support or base of security for the child and may induce or exacerbate guilt in the child who then accepts responsibility for causing the parents' upset. If the family is seen in a clinic situtation in which another therapist is working with the child, it is helpful if occasional joint meetings with the child therapist are held. Parents are benefited by continual reassurance that sexual trauma is not beyond psychological remediation and they are encouraged to avoid secondary trauma caused by overreacting to their fears of long term effects. Sexual fears have a uniquely inflammatory nature, so it is well to have at least a brief telephone conversation with parents daily at the outset of a case. It is wise to follow closely any legal procedures that the family is involved in and to attempt to humanize the process if possible. The judicial system, while acting in the name of the child, often proceeds at the expense of the child and/or the family. Simple suggestions, like tape recording the child's first official police interview, are major steps in decreasing secondary trauma. The family is well served to have an objective professional navigator through the confusion of the sexual trauma and its aftermath. Family and extended family sessions should be held at some point as the child is affected by the unspoken attitudes and judgments of other family members.

A therapist who is not experienced in handling sexual cases is benefited greatly by requesting regular supervision by an experienced colleague to insure that he or she maintains objectivity and does not serve his or her own sexual needs at the expense of the child. Therapists who wish to acquire expertise in handling sexual situations should avail themselves of good in-service training programs in sexology. Although they are few in number, they are available, and many, like those at the Institute for Advanced Study of Human Sexuality in San Francisco, attempt specifically to accommodate the in-service needs of professionals.

OTHER SYMPTOMS OF SEXUAL SIGNIFICANCE

Peeping tomism, underwear stealing, and sex with animals are antisocial and illegal activities that may be transient attempts to satisfy child or adolescent sexual curiosity, or they may be the development of aberrant patterns of voyeurism, fetishism, and bestiality. If the behavior is found to be a response to lack of knowledge, brief cognitive therapy with sex information, endorsement of the right to be sexual, and encouragement to be sexual in socially acceptable ways are the treatment of choice. If the behavior is determined to be an expression of underlying psychopathology, behavior modification and insight therapy are indicated. It is helpful to the child if the differential diagnosis is made by a therapist that doesn't overreact to the symptoms. These symptoms are a shock to parents, who, like law enforcement personnel, tend to think the worst and compound the trauma for the troubled child. It is well to remember that society's messages about sex are contradictory and confusing to children and adolescents.

Whether the resultant dissonance is expressed as private worry, fear, and doubt, or erupts into public behavior, they are well served by accurate information, endorsement of the normalcy of sexual feelings and desires and their right to be sexual, and an opportunity to learn culturally acceptable sociosexual skills. The task of the sexologist is formidable.

THE CLINICAL SEXOLOGIST AS A NEW MEMBER OF THE MENTAL HEALTH TEAM

A specialist trained in human sexuality adds dimension to the helping professions in dealing with both adults and children. Taking a sex history, which is omitted by many therapists, reveals the basic value structure of an individual. Sexual myths and misconceptions are the basis of anxiety, tension, and depression. Parents' response to a child's sexual interest, curiosity, and behavior is a significant factor in the development of self-acceptance and worth. Fear of failure and humiliation, anxiety about the esteem of others, and depression over real and imagined incompetencies all relate to early parent-child relationships (specifically, the attitudes about the body and its functions). Especially in working with the pubescent and postpubescent child, the therapist, by example, must endorse sexuality as a necessary and legitimate topic of discussion. Like the well health check-up, sexual attitudes and behaviors can be explored as a preventive measure as well as a treatment of existing conflicts. The therapist with a low burden of personal sexual guilt, who is nonjudgmental about human sexual behavior, offers an opportunity for the client to consider his or her sexual attitudes...and to coordinate them with his or her sexual behaviors.

At present, there are few clinical sexologists and even fewer that have specialized education and training with children. Much like a speciality in pediatric gynecology or psychohormonology, the clinical child sexol-

ogist's time is yet to come. For now, child psychologists, child psychiatrists, and child protection workers can benefit by using a clinical sexologist as a consultant and by incorporating the sexological information with their own expertise in children. Continuing education in human sexuality for physicians and mental health workers is imperative if they are to keep abreast of the reemerging field of sexology. The clinical sexologist, with an extensive background of knowledge of human sexuality, focuses on sexual health care delivery to individuals and rounds out the physical and mental health care delivery services of traditional medicine and psychology.

REFERENCES

Barbach, L. *For yourself.* New York: Doubleday, 1975.

Chapman, D. *The sexual equation.* New York: Philosophica Library, 1977.

DeMause, L. (Ed.). *History of childhood.* New York: Psychohistory Press, 1980.

Dodson, B. *Liberating masturbation.* New York: Dodson, 1974.

Fairchild, B. & Hayward, N. *Now that you know.* New York: Harcourt Brace, 1979.

Farrell, W. [Untitled]. Bantam: New York, in press.

Gebhard, P.H., Gagnon, J.H., Pomeroy, W.B., Christenson, C.V. *Sex offenders.* New York: Harper & Row, 1965.

Gesell, A., Ilg, F., Ames, L.B., & Rodell, J.L. *Infant and child in the culture of today.* (Rev. ed.). New York: Harper & Row, 1974.

Green, R. *Sexual identity conflict in children and adults.* New York: Basic Books, 1974.

Haeberle, E. *The sex atlas.* New York: Seabury, 1978.

Hamilton, E. *Sex with love.* Boston: Beacon, 1978.

Haroian, L. *Childhood and adolescent sexuality* (Video tape lecture series). San Francisco: The Institute for Advanced Study of Human Sexuality, 1980.

Hass, A. *Teenage sexuality.* New York: Macmillan, 1979.

Hite, S. *The Hite report on female sexuality.* New York: Macmillan, 1976.

Hite, S. *The Hite report on male sexuality.* New

York: Knopf, 1981.

Kaplan, H.S. *The new sex therapy, Vol. II, disorders of sexual desire.* New York: Bruner/Mazel, 1979.

Kinsey, A.C., Pomeroy, W.B., Martin, C.E., & Gebhard, P.H. *Sexual behavior in the human female.* Philadelphia and London: Saunders, 1953.

Kinsey, A.C., Pomeroy, W.B., & Martin, C.E. *Sexual behavior in the human male.* Philadelphia and London: Saunders, 1948.

Marcus, I.M., & Francis, J.J. *Masturbation from infancy to senescence.* New York: Universities Press, 1975.

McIlevenna, T. *When you don't make it.* San Francisco: Multi-media Resource Center, 1972.

McIlevenna, T., & Vandervoort, H. *You can last longer.* San Francisco: Multi-media Resource Center, 1972.

Money, J., & Ehrhardt, A. *Man and woman, boy and girl.* Baltimore: Johns Hopkins, 1973.

National Sex Forum. *S.A.R. Guide for a better sex life.* San Francisco: National Sex Forum, 1975.

Rekers, G.A. *Handbook of treatment of mental disorders in childhood and adolescence.* Englewood Cliffs: Prentice-Hall, 1978.

Silverstein, C. *A family matter: A parent guide to homosexuality.* New York: McGraw-Hill, 1978.

Smith, C., Ayres, T., & Rubentein, M. *Getting in touch.* San Francisco: Multi-media Resource Center, 1972.

Spitz, R. Auto eroticism. *The Psychoanalytic Study of the Child,* 1949, **19,** 55–120.

Stoller, R.J. *Sex and gender.* New York: Science House, 1968.

Stoller, R.J. *Perversion.* New York: Pantheon, 1975.

Tannahill, R. *Sex in history.* New York: Stein & Day, 1980.

Yates, A. *Sex without shame.* New York: Morrow, 1979.

CHAPTER 24

Toileting Problems of Children

EDWARD R. CHRISTOPHERSEN AND MICHAEL A. RAPOFF

Most parents have the almost universal experience of deciding when and how to toilet train their offspring. The section of this chapter that deals with toilet training discusses the current state of the art for reducing or minimizing difficulties that stem from toilet training. Not too long after parents face the issue of toilet training, it will be found that a lesser number have children who are enuretics (approximately 25 percent of all 4-year-olds; Cohen, 1975), encopretics (approximately 3 percent of the general pediatric population; Levine, 1975) and/or constipated (no reliable estimates of occurrence available). Within each section, the available literature on etiology, developmental concerns, history and physical examination, and treatment will be discussed. General recommendations to clinicians who see children with toileting problems will also be presented.

TOILET TRAINING

The mastery of bowel and bladder control is considered to be a major milestone in the physical and social development of children. By the age of 36 months, most children have achieved diurnal bowel and bladder control although occasional accidents may occur through 5 years of age (Simonds, 1977). Coercive toilet training has been implicated in the development of problems such as enco-

presis and enuresis (Brazelton, 1962). Although much importance has been attached to this developmental task, little evaluative research has been done to date. Several reasons for the paucity of research have been suggested: (1) toilet training has been viewed as a taboo subject for study; (2) data collection on children under 3 years of age is difficult, as they are usually at home and not as accessible as children in preschools; and (3) the amount of time necessary to study the toilet training process can be prohibitive (Pumroy & Pumroy, 1965). Another possible deterrent to research may be the lack of established procedures available for systematic evaluation.

Surveys have shown that parents may have unrealistic expectations about when toilet training is to be initiated and when it can be completed (Carlson & Asnes, 1974). Of a sample of 69 mothers of firstborn children surveyed, 50 percent of them planned to initiate toilet training before their children were 16 months of age and 55 percent expected to have their children trained by 24 months of age (Stephens & Silber, 1971). A follow-up questionnaire was sent to this same sample of mothers several years later. Of the 57 mothers who responded, 58 percent reported initiating toilet training prior to their child's second birthday (Stephens & Silber, 1974). These mothers also reported whom they sought for advice about toilet training. The majority of mothers (51 percent) sought advice from a friend or relative, 30 percent consulted *Baby and Child Care* (Spock, 1976), 26 percent sought advice from their physicians, and 21 percent consulted with their husbands.

Preparation of this manuscript was partially supported by a grant (HD 03144) from NICHD to the Bureau of Child Research, University of Kansas.

Central to the task of toilet training children is the concept of readiness. Brazelton (1962) has suggested several physiological and psychological readiness criteria. Physiological readiness criteria include: (1) reflex sphincter control, which can be elicited as early as 9 months; and (b) myelinization of pyramidal tracts, which is completed between 12 and 18 months. Psychological readiness criteria include: (1) established motor milestones of sitting and walking; (2) some verbal understanding; (3) positive relationships with figures evident in the desire to please; (4) identification with and imitation of parents and significant others; and (5) the desire to be autonomous and master primitive impulses. Brazelton suggests that readiness appears to peak for most children between 18 and 30 months of age.

Azrin and Foxx (1974), in their popular book on toilet training, have suggested several specific readiness criteria that would be useful for parents. These include:

1. *Bladder Control*: The child should empty his or her bladder completely when voiding, stay dry for several hours, and indicate he or she is about to urinate or defecate by facial expressions or posturing. If the child consistently empties his or her blader completely and stays dry for several hours, then bladder control can be considered adequate for training.

2. *Physical Readiness*: The child should exhibit sufficient fine and gross motor coordination to be able to pick up objects easily and walk well without assistance.

3. *Instructional Readiness*: This criterion is important and is often left out in books about toilet training. The child should have enough receptive language to enable him or her to follow one-stage and two-stage directions (e.g., "Show me your nose. Put the dolly on the wagon."). Instructional readiness assumes that the child is also reasonably compliant with parental instructions.

Azrin and Foxx suggest that most children over 20 months can usually meet these criteria. Christophersen (1977) has suggested that parents wait 3 months after their children have

met the Azrin and Foxx readiness criteria before they actually begin training. This means that training with most children will be initiated when the child is between 24 and 30 months of age.

Until recently, a major source of information about toilet training has been childrearing books written for lay audiences (e.g., Spock's *Baby and Child Care*). Several direct attempts to expedite the toilet training process have been reported in the literature, based on operant conditioning principles such as reinforcement and stimulus control. These studies have been done with normal (Brown & Brown, 1974; Pumroy & Pumroy, 1965) and handicapped children (Giles & Wolf, 1966; Lancioni, 1980; VanWagenen et al., 1969) and both normal and handicapped children (Mahoney, VanWagenen, & Meyerson, 1971). These studies have all yielded positive results; however, the sample sizes were small and this limits the generality of the findings. One group study has been reported that compared several training procedures with a no-treatment control group (Madsen et al., 1969). The study was designed to compare the effectiveness of different techniques over a six-week period including one week of baseline, four weeks of training, and one week of posttraining follow-up. Therefore, it was expected that the children would not be completely trained. The investigators found that children treated in the reinforcement and reinforcement-plus-buzzer-pants group were trained more successfully as compared to the parent method, control, and buzzer-pants-alone groups. Although the reinforcement and the reinforcement-plus-buzzer group did not differ significantly, the addition of the buzzer apparatus did decrease the number of accidents. The investigators concluded that reinforcement procedures combined with scheduling and a buzzer apparatus (which alerts trainers to accidents) can enhance toilet training in normal children.

Brazelton (1962), a pediatrician, has outlined a more indirect method of toilet training that is often cited in the pediatric literature. This child-oriented approach emphasizes minimal guidance by the parent as the child is allowed to proceed through several phases at his or her own pace. During the first phase (sometime after 18 months of age), the child is introduced to the potty chair and invited to sit on it while fully clothed. After a week or two, the child is taken to the potty chair to sit with his or her diapers off, although no results are expected. Next, the child is taken to the chair once daily to empty soiled diapers with the intent of establishing the potty chair as a convenient receptacle for waste. The next phase involves placing the potty in the child's room or play area. The child does not wear diapers and the parent explains that the child may use the potty if he or she wishes. After cooperation has been achieved through these preceding phases, the child is dressed in training pants and encouraged to use the potty. Of the 1,170 primarily upper middle class children in 10 years of pediatric practice for whom Brazelton suggested this protocol, 80.3 percent were completely trained (daytime and nighttime) by 3 years of age. The average age for day training was 28.5 months and for day and night training, 33.3 months. Among this group of children, Brazelton reports a lower incidence of residual symptoms such as enuresis and encopresis. Although there is much surface appeal for this approach, Brazelton failed to specify how the data he reports were obtained. In addition, it would be important to compare this approach with a control group to determine if maturation combined with general methods used by parents (such as scheduling) would be as effective within the same time period.

Foxx and Azrin (1973a) reported on a rapid and effective program for toilet training normal children that has been popularized in book form for parents (Azrin & Foxx, 1974). This method was first tested with retarded children (Azrin & Foxx, 1971; Foxx & Azrin, 1973b) and later extended to normal children. There are at least 16 major characteristics of this training program that include practice and reinforcement in dressing skills, immediacy of reinforcement for correct toileting, required pratice in toilet approach after accidents, and learning by imitation. The original study with normal children (Foxx & Azrin,

1973a) included a sample of 34 children with a mean age of 25 months. The training was conducted in the natural home or in the home of the trainer with family members absent. All 34 children were trained in an average of 3.9 hours, with a range of one-half to 14 hours. Accidents within the first posttraining week had decreased by 97 percent to 0.2 accidents per day per child (about one a week). Accidents remained at a near zero level during four months of follow-up. Foxx and Azrin suggest that the results of their study indicate virtually all healthy children 20 months and older can be trained within a few hours. They do caution that because the program relies heavily on verbal, instructional, and symbolic procedures, rapid training may not be possible with the less verbal child. Although these results are the most impressive published to date, replications by other investigators are important to establish the generality of the effectiveness of the program.

Two studies have been published which involve the use of the Azrin and Foxx program. Butler (1976) reported on a group training effort based on the Azrin and Foxx book, *Toilet Training in Less Than a Day* (1974). Following a three-session training program involving lectures, written instructions, and reading the Azrin and Foxx book, there was a significant reduction in the frequency of accidents among the children as compared to pretraining levels. Butler reported that the parents experienced problems with some aspects of the training program. The parents found it difficult to deal with their children's negative reactions to the positive practice trials that involve having the child go back and forth to the bathroom 10 times from various locations in the house following an accident. Some parents also found it difficult to avoid prompting their child to go to the toilet after their child began to self-initiate going to the toilet. The other study utilizing the Azrin and Foxx program sought to determine if parents could successfully train their children without professional assistance (Matson & Ollendick, 1977). Mothers of 10 normal children were randomly assigned to a book-only group or book-plus-supervision group, with five mothers in each group. Mothers in the book-only group were given a copy of *Toilet Training in Less Than a Day* and trained their children without supervision. The mothers in the book-plus-supervision group were given the book and an experienced trainer was available during the actual training to supervise the mothers' efforts. Only one child of the mothers in the book-only group was successfully trained. In contrast, four of the five children of mothers in the book-plus-supervision group were successfully trained. Knowledge of the program was assessed by questionnaire and was found to be comparable between the two groups. All of the mothers in this study reported emotional side effects with their children, including tantrums and avoidance behaviors. Matson and Ollendick noted that their study questions the usefulness of the program when conducted by parents without professional supervision. Matson (1975) has noted that parents may experience problems with the Azrin and Foxx method, including negative reactions of their children (such as tantrums). In addition, parents may not have the necessary self-control to manage the program and may become frustrated when training is not accomplished as quickly as has been suggested by the title of the Azrin and Foxx book (Kimmel, 1974).

In terms of suggesting a particular approach to training, the clinician from either an empirical or clinical perspective has few options. The child-oriented approach suggested by Brazelton is appealing in that it involves little intensive effort for parents. However, the components of the program are not as clearly specified as with the Azrin and Foxx method. In addition, some children may not possess sufficient motivation to enable them to progress at a reasonable pace. This may lead to impatience and coercive attempts by the parents to accelerate the pace of training.

The Azrin and Foxx method has been more systematically studied, but the few replications that have been done suggest that parent-mediated training may be problematic. The program is quite intensive and may be too demanding for some parents. If a child is generally noncompliant, compliance training may be indicated before training is begun. In the authors' experience, the Azrin and Foxx method has been successful with professional supervision. Children 24 months and older can realistically be trained within three days to one week and be accident free within three to four months. Parents frequently need specific instructions on how to deal with avoidance and tantrumming behaviors exhibited by their children during training (e.g., using time-out).

The practitioner can save valuable time by providing parents with written handouts to serve as supplements to whatever verbal instructions may be provided in the office. The following is a handout that addresses several guidelines to be followed regarding toilet training.

Toilet Training: General Guidelines

1.   Long before training is begun, parents can teach readiness skills in a graduated fashion, such as dressing. Children can also be taught to follow one- and two-stage directions and to use appropriate language about toileting. The understanding and expression of language greatly facilitate the training process.

2.   Training should probably not begin before a child is 24 months of age. Children over 24 months of age are more easily and quickly trained than children under 24 months. The efforts necessary to train a younger child cancel out any potential benefit and may create unnecessary conflict.

3.   Children learn much by observing and imitating their parents. Children can occasionally accompany their parents to the bathroom. Parents can use their own preferred toileting vocabulary to describe the elimination process. The child will begin to associate his or her own elimination process with the appropriate location for that process to occur.

4.   Children should not be required to sit on the potty for extended periods of time. Five to ten minutes is sufficient. Adults do not eliminate on command and this should not be expected of children.

5.   Children can be placed on the potty at times when elimination is likely to occur, such as after a meal.

6. As much as possible, the training process needs to be pleasant for both children and parents. Physical punishment definitely has no place in the training process. Punishment does not teach, and the resulting negative side effects can create unnecesary parent-child conflicts. Praise for appropriate toileting can help to motivate the child.*

In the experience of the authors, many parents find the Azrin and Foxx "Dry Pants Training" procedures to be very complex. The following sequential outline has been used in addition to liberal phone consultation and support with parents who are trying the dry pants training procedures for the first time.

"Dry Pants" Toilet Training Procedures: Sequential Outline

1. Remove child's diaper (child sits on floor); guide legs through pants; child pulls up own pants; pin up child's shirt with safety pins.

2. Begin encouraging fluids; model by giving doll drinks; mother drinks; child drinks; variety of preferred fluids available—child should consume two cups per hour (caffeine helpful).

3. Prompted potty trial—Doll (imitation trial): "Dolly has to pee-pee."

   a. Help doll to chair, pants down; sit down; inform child about audible signal (music).

   b. Doll wets in potty—child feels stream of "pretend" urine (water).

   c. Doll praised (clap, hugs, etc.). "Dolly's a big girl—pee-peed in potty," and so forth.

   d. Candy or treat to Dolly (child consumes this).

   e. Doll wipes with toilet tissue; stands up; pants up, etc. (with help from child).

   f. Doll picks up potty container;

holds with both hands; takes to bathroom; dumps contents in toilet; flushes toilet (with help from child).

   g. Returns potty container to potty chair (with help from child).

4. Dry pants check—Doll

   "Does Dolly have dry pants?" (Child prompted to feel Dolly's pants.)

   "Dolly a big girl," and so forth. Reward doll with snack/food.

5. Dry pants check—Child

   Repeat same; child feels training pants to check for dryness; praise socials; rewards from parent.

   Dry pants checks (child) run continuously every 5 minutes until pottying self-initiated; every 15 minutes after self-initiation has occurred.

6. Accident—Doll (Imitation trial)

   a. Doll taken to "scene of accident" (child assists).

   b. Doll verbally reprimanded. ("No, Dolly can't pee-pee in pants—big Dollies don't pee-pee in pants; Mommy loves Dolly, but not wet pants.")

   c. Doll cleans up mess (child assists).

   d. Positive practice—10 times (2 from scene of accident; 8 from different parts of house); practice quickly (doll to potty; pull down pants; sit down; stand up; pull up pants; back to scene of accident): child assists.

   e. Wet pants checks—10 times— verbal disapproval (child assists).

   f. Change doll into dry pants (child assists).

7. Verbal rehearsal

   All toileting skills rehearsed verbally with child; step-by-step sequences for correct toileting; verbal rehearsal performed throughout entire training day.

---

*©Michael A. Rapoff and Edward R. Christophersen, 1980.

8. Prompted potty—Child
   a. Instruct child to toilet; instruct each skill (go to chair; pants down; sit quietly, etc.).
   b. Child remains "on" five minutes; after one to two urinations on potty chair, needs remain "on" only one minute; no tantrums when getting off chair.
   c. If urinates, much positive reinforcements (hugs, kisses, cheers, clapping, smiles, "friends who care," etc.), stands up; pulls up pants; dumps potty in bathroom; flushes toilet, etc.
   d. If no urination, no consequences; allow to get up from potty.
   e. Dry pants check; praise and treats if dry; verbal rehearsal (big boy—dry pants because just went pee-pee in potty chair).

9. Prompted potty—Doll (second time—see number 3).

10. Prompted potty—Child (See number 8).

11. Accident—Doll (second time—see number 6).

12. Prompted potty—Doll (third time).

13. Accident—Doll (third time).
    Doll put aside (may be used as is necessary).

14. Monitor child carefully.
    a. Maintain increased fluid intake.
    b. Dry pants checks occurring every 5 minutes until self-initiations (then decreased to every 15 minutes).
    c. Prompted potty—Child—every 15 minutes until self-initiation occurs several times, then discontinue—use general suggestions (rather than direct instructions) for prompted potty trial increasingly.

15. Accidents—Child
    a. Immediate verbal reprimand. (Firm "No! Big boys don't wet their pants! Mommy loves you, but not wet pants.")
    b. Child cleans up mess (in wet pants).
    c. Positive practice ten times (in wet pants).
    d. Ten wet pants checks; mild disapproval.
    e. Change into dry pants.

Material suggested for training: six pairs loose-fitting training pants; variety of fluids and edible snack treats; potty chair; doll that wets; kitchen timer; friends-who-care list; data sheet.

Surveys suggest that parents obtain advice about toilet training from relatives or friends or by reading books (Carlson & Asnes, 1974; Stephens & Silber, 1971). Parents generally do not seek professional assistance, but, when they do, they are likely to consult with their pediatrician (Stephens & Silber, 1974). Psychologists working outside of pediatric settings are not likely to be consulted very often about normal toilet training. Psychologists who are working with pediatric health care providers can assist them in offering sound advice to parents regarding toilet training.

Toilet training can create unnecessary conflicts between parents and children. Clinicians can minimize potential conflicts by giving parents advice about when to begin training and how to conduct training. The rapidity with which training is accomplished may not be as important to parents as how smoothly training proceeds. Like walking, it is fortunate that most children have been able to master toileting with minimal prompts and social reinforcement.

Both Brazelton (1962) and Azrin and Foxx (1974) tend to sidestep the issue of bowel versus bladder training. Whereas Brazelton seems to assume that the training will occur simultaneously, Azrin and Foxx state that the parent should concentrate on the bladder training since, in their experience, formal bowel training is usually not necessary. The recommendations of the present authors, as detailed above, are intended to apply to both bowel and bladder training.

Constipation and Encopresis

Approximately 80 percent of children brought to pediatricians for encopresis (fecal incontinence) present with a history of fecal retention and/or constipation. The etiology and treatment of constipation will be discussed first, followed by a brief discussion of additional considerations for the management of encopresis.

A basic working knowledge of the physiology of the colon or large intestine is an important first step in any discussion of constipation. The colon serves two major functions, which may be interrelated. One is the storage of feces until expulsion through defecation is completed. The purpose of toilet training is to acquaint the child with the proprioceptive feedback from the colon and to coordinate the relaxing of the external anal sphincter with the appropriate positioning over a potty chair or a toilet. The internal anal sphincter is stretched or distended by the presence and pressure of feces from the sigmoid colon. Afferent neural pathways signal the brain when the sigmoid colon is distended and that defecation can now occur volitionally. While the final products of digestion (primarily waste) pass through the colon, the second major function is the absorption of water back into the body through the lumen of the colon (cf. Wright, Schaeffer, & Solomons, 1979). In this way, the contents of the colon are gradually dehydrated until they assume the consistency of normal feces or can even become quite hard. If the motility of the colon is reduced, either involuntarily due to insufficient bulk or roughage or too many bland foods in the diet, or voluntarily due to the individual's retention of feces in the colon for abnormal lengths of time, then excess quantities of water can be drawn off, the feces become dryer than normal, and colonic motility is reduced or slowed down. It is this pattern, the retention of feces, which then has more water extracted than is optimal with a resulting decrease in motility, that can and does result in constipation and fecal incontinence.

Although the etiology for this cycle can rarely be accurately identified, there are several factors that have a known causative role. These include: (1) insufficient roughage or bulk, which means that the contents of the colon do not mechanically help to stimulate a normal pattern of motility; (2) a bland diet, too high in dairy products, cheeses, and so forth without enough counteracting bulk, which also results in reduced colonic motility; and (3) insufficient oral intake of fluids, which allows the normal reabsorption of water from the colon to dehydrate the feces too much. Any of these factors, singly or in some combination, can result in constipationlike symptoms or actual constipation. If a child recognizes these symptoms, he or she may associate them with similar symptoms at some earlier date that were followed by a painful or uncomfortable bowel movement. In an attempt to prevent a recurrence of the painful bowel movement, the child may voluntarily retain the feces, thinking the discomfort can be avoided when, in actuality, the retention or withholding is only going to exacerbate the condition.

If constipation results from one of the above-described factors, then the child may become lethargic, which in turn reduces activity level with a resultant decrease in colonic motility, and the constipation is perpetuated. Also, constipation frequently results in decreased appetite, which, through a decrease in the gastrocolic reflex, acts to decrease gastric motility.

If a child with constipation continues to consume a diet that is compatible with constipation, then the whole symptom complex can be exacerbated. Not infrequently, these children will experience seepage around the fecal impaction that results from prolonged constipation, producing what has been termed "paradoxical diarrhea"; that is, although the child is actually constipated or impacted, symptomatically, he or she acts as though he or she has diarrhea, producing numerous watery, foul-smelling stools each day. Occasionally, these bouts of paradoxical diarrhea will result in the passage of huge amounts of feces, enough, oftentimes, to cause problems with the plumbing in the child's domicile. A period of inactivity follows during which there is no fecal soiling until the colon gets distended again and the constipation returns, followed by the paradoxical diarrhea. Some parents will attempt to treat this type of diarrhea with over-the-counter antidiarrheal agents, an approach which, though well intentioned, will only further exacerbate the condition.

In order to rule out any of the above-described patterns, the provider needs to take a thorough dietary history (and must be aware of what effects various foods have on the colon and a thorough bowel history), that includes an abdominal examination (by a physician or a trained nurse) to check for the presence of large amounts of feces and a rectal examination, to check for either large amounts of stool or very dry stool in the rectal vault. If any of these conditions exist, then a behavior management protocol or psychotherapy will probably not only be unsuccessful but may actually further contribute to the child's problem by ignoring the reestablishment of healthy, normal colonic functioning.

If the history and physical examination clearly point to a pattern similar to that described above, the child, at the discretion of the child's physician, will probably have to be given medication—orally, rectally, or both—that will deal directly with the constipation.

The physical examination can be done by any nurse, medical student, resident, or physician who is familiar with encopresis and constipation. Although the actual examination (which usually includes palpation of the abdomen, with a rectal exam where indicated) takes only a few minutes, the provider who is inexperienced in such an exam is unlikely to be able to perform it properly.

Davidson (1958) and Davidson, Kugler, and Bauer (1963) described what has come to be called the pediatric approach to constipation or encopresis. Davidson recommends starting a child on a daily dose of mineral oil (which acts both as a stool softener and as a lubricant) and increasing the dosage until regular bowel functioning is established. To aid in the establishment of bowel functioning, Davidson also recommends cutting back (when indicated) on the amount of milk and milk products ingested and increasing the ingestion of fruits. Davidson et al. (1963) reported a high success rate (90 percent) with 119 pediatric age patients placed on this regimen.

Levine (1975) reported on the results of an analysis of 102 children with encopresis who were seen in a general pediatric outpatient clinic. Of these children, 81 were found to have stool impaction at the time of the first visit. Of these 81 children, 39 were treated for constipation in infancy. This fact by itself, if replicated by other investigators, seriously questions any general discussion of a psychosocial etiology for encopresis.

Levine and Bakow (1976) followed 110 encopretic children for one year. At first, the authors described normal intestinal function to the parents in an attempt to demystify the child's presenting problem. The parents were then instructed to use enemas and Dulcolax™ suppositories in order to get the child's bowel well cleaned out. Then the children started a daily mineral oil regimen that was to last for at least six months. In addition, the children were asked to sit on the toilet for at least 10 minutes, twice each day. Seventy-eight percent of the patients fell into the two most successful outcome groups (either marked improvement or some improvement).

Wright (1973) and Wright and Walker (1977) described a slightly different approach designed to accomplish the same purpose: to establish normal bowel functioning. Wright recommends initially cleaning out any constipated or impacted stool, then begining the child on a daily rectal suppository to stimulate daily bowel movements. Wright also recommends the use of simple social praise or reinforcement for bowel movements in the toilet or potty chair and mild forms of punishment (for example, loss of TV privileges) for any soiling episodes.

Christophersen and Rainey (1976) and Christophersen and Berman (1978) offer variations of Wright's (1973) procedure with more emphasis on dietary intake, increased fluid intake, and no punishment for soiling episodes beyond having the child clean out his or her own pants and cleaning off his or her own buttocks. In more recalcitrant cases, positive practice (cf. Azrin & Foxx, 1974) is recommended for soiling accidents. Recently, the present authors have added even more emphasis on dietary intake by using a handout for the parents that lists by brand name a number of high roughage foods and foods that have either a natural laxative effect (honey, prunes) or a lubricating effect (butter, fried foods, margarine). They also now recommend encouraging the child to ingest six to eight glasses of fluid daily (other than milk) and encourage activity for those children who prefer just to sit and read or watch TV.

The following handouts are an example of the written instructions that are provided to parents in the authors' practice.

Encopretic Treatment Instructions for Parents

Need to buy:

Pediatric Fleets Enema (3)
Adult Glycerine Suppositories (Jar of 50)
K-Y Jelly or Lubrafax

First Night Routine (one night only)

1. Begin after dinner and about two hours before your child goes to bed.
2. Give one (1) Pediatric Fleets Enema, lukewarm in temperature. It should be administered with the child lying on his or her left side. Squeeze the bottle slowly and constantly until empty. This should take two to three minutes. Do not let go of the bottle while squeezing, as this acts as a suction force in the rectum. Squeeze the buttocks together while removing the enema tip. Have the child retain the enema *at least* five (5) minutes before expelling it and fecal contents.
3. Administer a second Pediatric Fleets Enema one (1) hour after the first, whether or not the child had a bowel movement. Again, have the child retain the enema at least five (5) minutes.

Morning Routine

1. Awaken the child at least one hour before he or she has to leave the house.
2. Instruct your child to try to defecate when he or she arises in the morning. Do not have him or her sit on the toilet

for more than five (5) minutes. Make this as pleasant as possible. Don't nag. His or her feet should firmly touch the floor while sitting on the toilet. If they don't, use a footstool under his or her feet.

3. If he or she cannot defecate at least one-fourth to one-half cup after five minutes, insert a glycerin suppository. If the suppository is expelled at breakfast, insert a second one. Then allow your child to eat a high fiber breakfast and get dressed.
4. After breakfast and dressing, instruct him or her again to go to the bathroom. If he or she cannot defecate at least one-fourth to one-half cup after five minutes, give him or her a Pediatric Fleets Enema before going to school (this will not usually be necessary).
5. If an enema is needed three consecutive days to produce a bowel movement, please contact _____ at _____ .

What To Do When Proper Elimination Has Occurred

Proper elimination means any bowel movement of appropriate size (regardless of whether or not suppositories or enemas were utilized), which occurred while the child was on the toilet.

1. Check the toilet for stool, and record the amount and consistency before the child flushes the toilet.
2. Praise your child (this is *very* important).
3. Decide how you will spend your 15 minutes together for his or her Special Time (Child's Time). The Special Time should be used daily to enhance the reward for proper elimination.

Monitoring

1. Check frequently, and verbally praise not soiling. Be tactful so as not to embarrass your child when doing so.
2. *Be aware.* It is important that you

catch soiled pants as soon as possible after the soiling has occurred.

What To Do When He or She Soils His or Her Pants

1. After soiling has occurred, instruct your child to:
   a. Rinse and wash out his or her own underwear and pants.
   b. Bathe quickly (just enough time to clean himself or herself). Use a bathtub with only one or two inches of water in it.
   c. Put on clean clothes.
2. Use only enough verbal prompts to keep him or her going—no nagging. Do not mention the soiling episode *during* or *after* any of these procedures.

Cleanliness Training

Make sure the child knows how to wipe himself or herself properly by checking to see if any fecal material is still present after the child reportedly has wiped. If your child needs instruction, use the following procedure:

1. Have your child wipe once and then have him or her look at the tissue. If any fecal matter or coloration is present on the tissue, have him wipe again. Repeat this procedure until the used tissue is clean. Note: Use of a premoistened towelette initially (e.g., "Wet Ones," "Dab-a-Ways") will make this procedure easier. Praise the child and give him or her feedback after he or she has finished wiping correctly.
2. Most children require more than one day of cleanliness training. Check his or her underwear each day for evidence of coloration. Repeat number 1 above until your child has learned to wipe himself or herself properly.

Instructions for Fading Out the Suppositories

1. Begin only after two weeks without soiling.

2. Stop the use of suppositories for one day (e.g., Monday).
3. If he or she does not soil for the next week, another day's suppositories are discontinued (e.g., Thursday). (Your child does not receive any suppositories on either Monday or Thursday morning.)
4. If another week is completed without any soiling, another day's suppositories are discontinued. (This totals three days when suppositories are not used—Monday, Thursday, Saturday.)
5. If no soiling occurs, drop one day of suppositories for each week that soiling does not occur. Continue until he or she is not receiving any suppositories.
6. If soiling occurs, add one day's suppositories for each soiling episode until the child is receiving suppositories every day or until he or she again goes a week without soiling.
7. After one week with no soiling, go back to number 2 above and begin again.
8. This program is terminated if the child can function for two weeks without soiling after all suppositories are discontinued.

Since many parents are simply not prepared to work out the suggestion for a high fiber diet, the authors prepared and regularly use the following handout on the high fiber diet.

High Fiber Diet Instructions

Recommendations

1. At least one serving of high fiber foods should be eaten at each meal (see food list below).
2. Snacks should be restricted to enhance the gastrocolic reflex (emptying and filling of the stomach).
3. Fresh vegetables and fruits are better than cooked.
4. Six to eight (6–8) glasses of water or

juices should be drunk daily to help keep stools from becoming hard and dry (see drinks list below).

5. Honey, prunes have a chemical laxative effect and should be encouraged.

6. Fats (butter, margarine, fried foods) aid the intestines in evacuation of stool.

7. Protein (meats, poultry, fish, and eggs) should be included in the daily diet.

8. Milk and milk products should be restricted or eliminated. No more than one glass of milk or the equivalent per day should be drunk. (Milk products include cheese, cottage cheese, ice cream, ice milk, sherbet, yogurt, milk shake.)

9. If mineral oil has been recommended, mix it in orange juice in a blender, then add soda water or 7-Up to it. May also be mixed with any juice to make it more palatable or mix it with canned fruit in heavy syrup.

High Fiber Foods

Vegetables. 1 serving 1/2 cup: lettuce, spinach, cabbage, cauliflower, broccoli, asparagus, tomatoes, onions, peas, celery, green peppers, carrots, corn, green beans.

Fruits. 1 serving 1/2 cup or 1 whole fruit: apples, pears, oranges, grapefruit, grapes, peaches, dried figs, dried apricots, prunes, raisins, pineapple, plums.

Breads. 1 serving 1 slice bread or 1/4 to 1 cup cereal (see cereal box for equivalent of one serving): Fresh Horizon Bread™; bran cereal such as 100% Bran™, Honey Bran™, Cracklin' Bran™, Bran Chex™, 40% Bran Flakes™, Raisin Bran™, Corn Bran™, Most™; Butternut Light, White, Wheat Bread™; any whole grain bread, graham crackers.

Drinks. Juices (6–8 glasses per day): prune, water, pruneapple (Sunsweet™), any fruit juice, Kool-aide™, Hi-C™, soda pop.

Food Preparation Ideas

Julienne salad (tossed salad with strips of meat, poultry, and/or hard-boiled eggs).

Tossed salads.

Carrot, celery, green pepper sticks, raw cauliflower. May be dipped into salad dressing.

Celery with chunky peanut butter.

Stewed prunes with honey.

Stewed dried fruit with honey.

Bran muffins with prunes or raisins served with honey.

Homemade whole wheat bread with bran.

Glass of warm liquid with breakfast (example, apple juice wih a cinnamon stick).

Fresh Horizon Bread™ with butter and honey.

Add soda water or 7-Up to any juice.

Substitute whole wheat flour for white flour in baking cookies.

Add 1/4 to 1/2 cup of bran, cracked wheat, or wheat germ to cookies when baking. Add diced, dried fruit, such as prunes.

Cole slaw.

Popcorn.

To pancake or waffle mix: Add one cup 100% bran cereal to 1/2 cup milk. Let soak five to ten minutes. Then add to mix.

French toast made with Fresh Horizon Bread™ or Butternut Light Bread™.

To date, no research studies have been done that compare the mineral oil regimens with the suppository regimens. The mineral oil has the advantage that the parents do not have to administer the suppository. The suppository regimen appears to offer the advantage that the parents are better able to time the child's bowel movement and, since the colon is usually evacuated in the morning prior to departure for school, there is less likelihood of the child soiling at school.

In all the regimens reviewed above, the basic strategy is to stimulate regular bowel functioning for a long enough period of time to reestablish regularity without the use of any medications. Each of the regimens includes some form of fading in order to withdraw the medications gradually rather than abruptly discontinuing them. In the Wright and Christophersen regimens, there are also components included in order to improve the parents' compliance wih the behavorial/medical regimen. Wright has the parents mail in recording forms periodically. Chrisophersen has the parents fill out a recording form daily, with the parent and therapist maintaining phone contact until the formal fading procedure is completed.

By definition, constipation always includes episodic retention of feces. However, approximately 20 percent of encopretics do not have a history of constipation or fecal impaction. For these children, complete reduction of the soiling episodes is usually much more difficult to achieve. In the child who presents with encopresis yet has no history of constipation, several distinct possibilities exist. One is that the child has been incompletely toilet trained. These children usually have a normal stool on a regular basis, but they have it in their pants rather than in the toilet. Frequently, either a positive practice regimen for soilings or a brief trial with daily glycerine suppositories or a combination of both will yield rather rapid results. If the child has no history of constipation but does not have normal bowel functioning, then a complete medical examination is probably in order. The presence of frequent, foul-smelling stools, little or no weight gain, or abdominal cramping may be an indication of one of the variety of malabsorption syndromes that are known to be present in a small percentage of children (cf. Barr, Levine, & Watkins, 1979).

Before any intervention approach is attempted in the child with constipation or encopresis, several steps are mandatory:

1. A complete physical examination including palpation of the abdomen for stool and a rectal examination.

2. A complete diet history, including preferred and nonpreferred foods. The amount and variety of dairy products should be ascertained and an attempt made to rule out any food allergies that may be causing at least some of the problems.

3. A history should be obtained on the amount and kinds of fluids consumed by the child on a regular basis.

4. The child's growth pattern for both height and weight should be established to help assess whether the child has a malabsorption syndrome.

After this initial history taking and physical examination, several steps are common to each of the programs discussed above.

1. For the child who is found to be impacted or constipated, a thorough cleaning of the bowel is probably indicated prior to any intervention attempts. The cleaning out should be done by a professional with a wide range of experience with childhood colon dysfunctioning, since there are some conditions (e.g., severe impaction) where the vigorous use of powerful enemas is contraindicated and can actually be dangerous.

2. The child's diet should be modified so as to include more bulk and roughage in order to naturally stimulate gastric motility.

3. The child's intake of milk and dairy products should be reduced to the minimum daily requirement for calcium. Both the increase in roughage and the decrease in dairy products can probably best be handled by a registered dietician.

4. The child's daily intake of nonconstipating fluids (e.g., fruit juices, water) can usually be increased with no or very little risk of any side effects other than more frequent urination.

5. For sedentary or lethargic children, higher levels of activity will probably result in increased gastric motility.

6. A variety of oral or rectal medications (e.g., mineral oil or glycerine suppositories) can then be started in order to aid gastric functioning until normal motility is either established or recovered. With long term use of mineral oil, the patient should probably be started on a vitamin supplement due to the

decreased absorption of fat soluble vitamins (cf. Davidson, 1958).

7. The use of procedures to insure parental compliance with any regimen will probably lead to a higher success rate. This can take the form of frequent phone calls, weekly or biweekly returns to the office, or completion and mailing of recording sheets.

8. The institution of either a traditional psychodynamic treatment approach or a reward system for appropriate bowel movements in the toilet should generally not be attempted until normal gastric functioning is achieved.

Although numerous case studies have been published that anecdotally report successes with both traditional and behavioral approaches, a child who is impacted or severely constipated deserves to have this medical condition treated prior to, or in addition to, attempts to address either the child's underlying problem or his or her lack of adequate reinforcement for appropriate toileting.

Since the publication of the Davidson (1958) paper on the pediatric management of constipation and encopresis, much less emphasis has been placed on the psychodynamic view of these clinical entities. However, as more pediatric health care providers elect to treat the typical cases of constipation and encopresis, mental health professionals have become increasingly more likely to receive referrals that do present with problems amenable to intervention by a mental health worker. In the opinion of the present authors, no child with constipation and/or encopresis should be seen exclusively by a mental health professional. A physician trained in dealing with bowel dysfunction should manage the child from a medical standpoint *while* the psychologist, psychiatrist, or social worker intervenes with the presenting psychosocial problems.

Numerous case studies have appeared in the social science literature describing the outcomes of intervention programs utilizing token economies, single incentive systems, and a wide variety of psychotherapeutic techniques. However, since none of these has been subjected to scientific scrutiny, the individual practitioner is free to utilize practically whatever treatment procedures he or she chooses.

One issue that has been discussed in the psychodynamic literature on encopresis concerns the hypothesis that treatment of the mere symptom of encopresis can have undesirable results. This has come to be called *symptom substitution*. A recent study by Levine, Mazonson, and Bakow (1980) demonstrated that, while encopresis may have psychological implications, encopresis is a specific disease entity that can be treated without fear of symptom substitution. Levine et al. (1980) used a behavioral inventory to compare a group of encopretic children who were cured and a group who were not cured at the begining of treatment and at follow-up (three years later) to determine whether any significant symptom subtitution occurred in children cured of encopresis. He concluded that:

There was no consistent trend toward acquisition of any specific symptom or cluster in the cured group. In no case did a child's condition deteriorate to the point where he or she was hospitalized for emotional difficulties, arrested by the police, suspended from school, or said to have developed highly troublesome new symptoms such as fire setting, school phobia, or stealing. (p. 667)

Levine (1981) provides an excellent tabular comparison for the clinician to use in differentiating encopresis from Hirschsprung's Disease (the most common organic etiology for fecal soiling that is present from birth on). See Table 24.1.

Nocturnal Enuresis

Enuresis can be defined as persistent, uncontrolled passage of urine in the day or night in the absence of urological, neurological, and psychological pathology and beyond the age when most children are continent (McKendry et al., 1975). This discussion will be limited to nocturnal enuresis or bedwetting.

Approximately 40 percent of children wet

Table 24.1   Comparison of Encopresis and Hirschsprung's Disease

Parameter	Encopresis	Hirschsprung's Disease
Fecal incontinence	Always	Rare
Constipation	Common, sometimes intermittent	Always
Symptoms as newborn	Rare	Almost always
Infant constipation	Sometimes	Common
Late onset (after 3)	Common	Rare
Difficult bowel training	Common	Rare
Avoidance of toilet	Common	Rare
Failure to thrive	Rare	Common
Anemia	None	Common
Obstructive symptoms	Rare	Common
Stool in ampula	Common	Rare
Tight sphincter	Rare	Common
Large caliber stools	Common	Never
Preponderance of males	86%	90%
Incidence	1.5% at age 7–8	1:25,000 births
Anal manometry	Sometimes abnormal	Always abnormal

Note. Levine, M.D. The Schoolchild with Encopresis. *Pediatrics in Review,* 1981, **2**(9), 285–290. Used with the permission of John Wiley and Sons Publishers. Copyright © 1981 by John Wiley and Sons.

the bed at 3 years of age, 22 percent at 5 years, 10 percent at 10 years, and 3 percent at 15 years (Bindelglas, 1975). A positive history of enureis among family members of enuretic children has been frequently noted. When both parents were enuretic, 77 percent of children are enuretic; when one parent was enuretic, 42 percent of children are enuretic; and when neither parent had a history of enuresis, only 15 percent of children are enuretic (Cohen, 1975). Enuresis is generally a self-limiting condition with a spontaneous cure rate of 12–15 percent per year (Bindelglas, 1975).

A number of factors have been proposed as causative of enuresis, including food allergies, deep sleep, small bladder capacity, developmental delays, and faulty training habits (Cohen, 1975; McKendry & Stewart, 1974; Simonds, 1977). However, no definitive cause of enuresis has been identified. There is general agreement that enureis is *not* primarily a psychopathologic disorder (Olness, 1975; Perimutter, 1976; Werry & Cohrssen, 1965). However, secondary emotional and behavioral problems may develop as a result of having to cope with being enuretic.

Numerous treatments for enuresis have been suggested, including diet restrictions, psychotherapy, retention control training, drugs, and behavioral methods. Assuming that enuretics have a smaller bladder capacity than nonenuretic children, it has been suggested that small bladder capacity may be due to spasms of the smooth muscle in the bladder wall. This spasm may have an allergic basis and, therefore, removal of subtances that irritate the bladder wall may arrest enuresis. Esperanca and Gerrard (1968) recommend the elimination of milk and dairy products, eggs, citrus fruits and juices, tomatoes and tomato products, cocoa and chocolate, carbonated beverages containing coloring agents, and other soft drinks for 50 enuretic children. Defining a cure as no more than one wet bed in two weeks, they found dietary restrictions to be effective in 15 percent of the cases. However, it is impossible to separate the effects of imipramine (drug treatment) and dietary restrictions as both treatments were used in the study. In general, dietary restrictions have been found to be effective with only a small percentage of enuretic children and have been suggested only for children with a history of allergies (McKendry & Stewart, 1974; McKendry et al., 1975; Perimutter, 1976).

Short term psychotherapy has been recommended by some clinicians for the treatment of enuresis (Sperling, 1965). However, the few comparative studies that have been done have shown that short term psychotherapy is not more effective than no treatment, and that more direct methods (such as use of a urine alarm) are more effective (DeLeon & Mandell, 1966; Werry & Cohrssen, 1965). Psychotherapy may be indicated in those few cases where significant psychopathology is suspected in addition to the fact that the child is enuretic (Cohen, 1975; Lovibond, 1964).

It has been suggested that enuretic children have smaller functional bladder capacities as compared to nonenuretic children (Cohen, 1975; Muellner, 1960). Based on this assumption, urine retention training has been recommended as a treatment for enuresis (cf. Starfield & Mellits, 1968). Retention control training generally involves having the child delay urination (when he or she feels the urge) for increasingly longer time intervals throughout the day up to a maximum duration of 30 minutes (cf. Doleys et al., 1977). In addition, the child is instructed to stop and start his or her urine stream when voiding. With repeated practice, it is expected that the enuretic child will increase his or her bladder capacity and be able to sleep through the night without the need to void. Some clinicians have reported success in reducing the frequency of bedwetting by retention contol training (Kimmel & Kimmel, 1970; Paschalis, Kimmel, & Kimmel, 1972; Starfield & Mellits, 1968). However,

well-controlled studies have failed to demonstrate both the efficacy of retention control training for enuresis and the relationship between bedwetting frequency and bladder capacity (Doleys et al., 1977; Harris & Purohit, 1977).

The drug most commonly used to treat enuresis is imipramine (Tofranil™), a tricyclic antidepressant. In general, this drug stops enuresis completely in 40–50 percent of enuretic children while another 10–20 percent show considerable improvement (Perimutter, 1976). However, the relapse rate is high, with about two-thirds of enuretics resuming wetting after the drug is discontinued, frequently enough to warrant further treatment (Bindelglas, 1975; Marshall & Marshall, 1973; McKendry & Stewart, 1974). The FDA has recommended that imipramine be used only as "temporary adjunctive therapy" for enuretic children 6 years of age and older (Physicians' Desk Reference, 1976). Like any other powerful pharmacological agent, imipramine has potentially serious side effects and should be reserved for those cases where more conventional therapies are not practical or effective (Gaultieri, 1977).

For over four decades, the standard behavioral treatment for enuresis has been the urine alarm or bell-and-pad procedure originally suggested by Mowrer and Mowrer (1938). This procedure involves placing an apparatus on the child's bed that has a sensing mechanism that activates an alarm when urine passes into the bed. When the alarm sounds, the child is awakened, turns off the alarm, finishes voiding in the toilet, and changes his or her bedding. For a more detailed description of this procedure, the reader is referred to Turner (1973) and Dische (1973). In general, studies have shown that the urine alarm treatment initially eliminates enuresis in approximately 75 percent of enuretics, with treatment duration ranging from a mean of 5 weeks to 12 weeks (Doleys, 1977). Relapse rates are generally high and occur on the average in 46 percent of cases, although reinstatement of the procedures usually results in a complete cure (Taylor & Turner, 1975). The urine alarm treatment has also been shown to be superior to no treatment, short term psychotherapy, and imipramine (DeLeon & Mandell, 1966; McKendry et al., 1975; Werry & Cohrssen, 1965). Possible disadvantages of this treatment include the length of treatment necessary to effect a cure, the inconvenience of awakening during the night, and malfunctions of the urine alarm (Doleys, 1977; Christophersen & Rapoff, 1978).

The most promising treatment—both in terms of effectiveness and the rapidity with which enuresis is arrested—is the "dry bed training" program developed by Azrin and his colleagues. The dry bed training combines a number of behavioral procedures, including cleanliness training, positive practice, nighttime awakening, retention control training, and positive reinforcement. (See Azrin, Sneed, & Foxx, 1974, for the original program description.)

The present authors have developed a sequential outline of the "Dry Bed Training" procedures for parents. This outline gives the parents specific directions to follow during the stages of the treatment program.

Sequential Outline: Dry Bed Training

Introductory Remarks

You are about to begin a training program to help your child master nighttime toileting. Your therapist will carefully explain the procedures to you and your child. This outline is a summary of those procedures that will be left with you to refer to. A chart is also provided to record your child's progress. If possible, your child should be responsible for this chart. You will need the following materials:

1. Variety of fluids, especially tea or cola
2. Sheets
3. Pajamas or other sleeping attire
4. Washcloths

Table 24.2   Progress Chart

Name _____

Fill in card each morning. D for a dry night, W for a weight night.

	Mon	Tues	Wed	Thur	Fri	Sat	Sun
1st Week							
2nd Week							
3rd Week							
4th Week							
5th Week							
6th Week							
7th Week							
8th Week							

5. Urine alarm (We supply this for the family's use until treatment is terminated.)

Intensive Training Phase

1. First night only (therapist arrives about one hour before bedtime).
   a. The child should be offered a lot of fluids and should drink about two cups per hour beginning approximately three hours prior to bedtime.
   b. The child is informed of all aspects of training as described in this outline.
2. Bedtime
   a. Review all aspects of the treatment, again eliciting responses from the child to check his or her understanding.
   b. The alarm is placed on the bed, unconnected.
   c. Twenty positive practice trials are given.
      (1) The child lies on the bed.
      (2) Counts to 50.
      (3) Arises, goes to the bathroom, pulls pants down, sits on the toilet, counts "one thousand one, one thousand two, one thousand three," pulls pants up, and returns to the bed.
      (4) Steps 1 through 3 are repeated 20 times.
   d. Child drinks additional fluids and repeats procedures for hourly checks, self-initiations, and reports accidents to the therapist.
   e. Child given opportunity to urinate prior to retiring.
   f. Alarm connected, turned on, and child retires for the night.
3. Hourly checks: Once every hour until intensive training is discontinued (between 4:00 and 6:00 a.m.).
   a. Awaken the child with as little effort as needed. Have the child feel clothes and sheets. If dry, praise the child. If wet, follow the accident procedure in the next section.
   b. Direct the child to the toilet. At the bathroom door, ask the child if he or she can hold it for one hour.
      (1) If the child indicates he or she cannot inhibit urination, he or she urinates in the toilet, is praised for correct toileting, and returns to bed.
      (2) If the child indicates he or she can inhibit urination, he or she is praised for urinary control and is returned to bed.
   c. At bedside, sleeping clothes and sheet inspection—both of which are dry—result in praise.
   d. The child is given fluids to drink and returns to sleep until the next hourly check, accident, or self-initiation. Fluids are discontinued after about 3:00 a.m.
4. Accidents: What to do.
   a. Turn off the alarm and awaken the child with minimal prompting.
   b. Verbally reprimand the child as he or she feels the wet sheets and wet clothes. "Your bed is wet; you shouldn't wet the bed." (Said sternly but not with anger.)
   c. Send the child to the toilet in wet clothes. Two minutes on the toilet to finish urinating.
   d. Return to the bed. Second reprimand given as child inspects the bed and his or her clothing.
   e. Cleanliness training (to be done by child).
      Bed: (1) Remove and take sheets to appropriate place.

(2) Wipe the mattress.

(3) Remake the bed.

Self: (4) To the bathroom, remove clothes, and dispose of appropriately.

(5) Two-minute shower or quick bath, washing from waist down.

(6) Puts on clean clothes.

f. Twenty "positive-practice" trials given as described previously.

g. The alarm is connected and turned on, and the child retires.

h. The next hourly check is set for one hour from the completion of these steps.

5. Self-Initiations: The child arises and toilets unprompted.

a. Allow the child to finish urinating.

b. Lavish praise for adultlike behavior.

c. Have child inspect dry bed and clothing again; congratulate the child.

d. Child returns to bed without having taken fluids. Hourly check reset for one hour from this time.

Monitored-Maintenance Phase

This begins after the night of intensive training and continues until 14 consecutive dry nights are achieved.

1. Continuing alarm on the bed. Check each night to make sure it works properly.

2. Discontinue increased fluids and hourly awakenings.

3. Bedtime

a. Alarm placed on the bed and turned on.

b. If accident occurs, cleanliness training and positive practice (20 trials) given immediately. Positive practice is *also* required the following night before bedtime.

c. If dry in the morning and/or when self-initiations occur, child is praised.

Normal Routine

1. Alarm taken off the bed.

2. Child inspected each morning.

a. If wet, cleanliness training given immediately and positive practice (20 trials) given before next bedtime.

b. If dry, praise.

3. If two accidents occur within a week, reinstate monitored-maintenance phase.

Details about studies evaluating the effects of the dry bed program are presented in Table 24.3. Several procedural changes have been suggested since the original study, including omission of the use of a urine alarm and having parents conduct the training with minimal direct supervision. Dry bed training has been shown to be superior to the urine alarm treatment, retention control training, and no treatment controls (Azrin et al., 1974; Azrin & Thienes, 1978; Bollard & Woodroffe, 1977; Doleys et al., 1977). As can be seen from Table 24.3, relapse rates with dry bed training range from 7–29 percent with a mean of 18 percent. However, as with urine alarm treatment, relapsed children were cured when the training procedures were reinstated. The original dry bed program as described in Azrin et al. (1974) has been used by the authors with enuretic children treated through a pediatric outpatient clinic. When possible, the dry bed training procedures would be, in the opinion of the authors, the treatment of choice. The training procedures have been recently described in a self-help book written for parents (Azrin & Besalel, 1979).

Considering degree of effectiveness, relapse rates, rapidity of cures, and potential side-effects, the clinician may want to consider the dry bed training program as the first treatment of choice. If this is not possible, the standard urine alarm procedures may be

Table 24.3 Outcome Studies: Dry Bed Training for Nocturnal Enuresis

Reference	Dry Bed Sample	Comparison Group	Dry Bed Training Features	Outcome: Dry Bed Training	Relapse	Dropouts
Azrin et al., 1974	$N=24$ Mean age= 8 years	Urine alarm	Original study with all night intensive training done by professional in child's home. Urine alarm used.	All 24 children "cured." The average child had 2 accidents before reaching 14 consecutive dry nights.	29%	None
Bollard & Woodroffe, 1977	$N=24$ Mean age= 8 years	No treatment control	Group I dry bed training with parents doing intensive training night ($N=14$). Group II dry bed training with parents doing intensive training plus urine alarm omitted ($N=10$).	Group I children all cured within a median time of 12 days. Group II children showed substantial reductions in wetting but no child cured within the first 13 weeks of treatment.	With group I=14%	None
Doleys et al., 1977	$N=13$	Retention control training	All night intensive training done by professional in child's home. Urine alarm used.	Two-factor ANOVA with one repeated measure showed significant difference between treatment groups in favor of dry bed training. 5 of the 13 children receiving dry bed training were cured by the end of 6 weeks of treatment.	Not reported	At 3-month follow-up, 2 of 13 drop-outs (15%)
Azrin & Thienes, 1978	$N=51$ Mean age= 7 years	Urine alarm	One day intensive training conducted in late afternoon and early evening. Urine alarm omitted.	All children who continued treatment were cured. The average child had 4 accidents before reaching 14 consecutive dry nights.	20%	Four of 51 children (8%)
Azrin, Hontos, & Besalel-Azrin, 1979	$N=44$ Mean age= 6.8 years	None	Dry bed training role played and rehearsed with parent and child during a single office visit. Parent read manual and conducted training in the home without direct supervision. Urine alarm omitted.	All children cured. The average child had 4 accidents before achieving 14 consecutive dry nights.	7%	None

considered. Drug treatment and retention control training might be reserved for those cases where dry bed or urine alarm procedures are not practical or available. Regardless of the treatment approach chosen, several general recommendations can be made.

1. A thorough physical exam should be obtained before beginning treatment, including urinalysis and urine culture, to rule out the possibility of urinary tract infections and other urological problems (Moffet, 1974). This is particularly important with female patients who most often present with urinary tract infections and any patient who wets during the day, urinates frequently, feels a strong urge to urinate, and has an interrupted voiding pattern with a staccato or burst type urine stream (Noe, 1980). This recommendation for a good physical exam should *not* be taken lightly as untreated urological problems can result in permanent renal damage. The fact that a child has been referred by a physician does not mean that an adequate urological work-up has been completed. The professional who institutes any enuresis intervention program is responsible for ascertaining whether an adequate work-up has been done.

2. In addition to ruling out organicity, the authors routinely recommend that clinicians wait until a child is 7 years old or older to treat nocturnal enuresis. Treatment of enuresis should be initiated only when the problem interrupts the normal sequence of social, emotional, or cognitive development (Cohen, 1975). This does not often occur before children are of school age, when they begin to be prevented from participating in some social activities (e.g., staying overnight with a friend) because of the possibility that they might wet the bed. Another reason for waiting is that the cooperation of children who are older is easier to secure, as they have more to gain by remaining continent at night.

3. Verbal or physical punishment is counterproductive in treating enuresis. This should be explained to parents, since punishment is commonly resorted to and frequently results in higher relapses (even when it is temporarily effective). It also creates unnecessary conflicts within the family (Tough et al., 1971). The embarrassment and discouragement felt by enuretic children is enough punishment without adding to the discomfort of having this condition.

4. Parents should receive a standard explanation that bedwetting is generally not caused by emotional problems. There is ample literature to support this notion, and parents are relieved to hear this from professionals. We explain to parents that most bedwetters are deep sleepers and are not aroused by the cues associated with a full bladder.

5. In general, limiting fluids excessively and frequent nightly awakenings are not effective in treating enuresis (Perlmutter, 1976). However, copious amounts of fluids close to bedtime should be avoided. Children can be asked to change their own wet bedding and clothes in order to take some responsibility for wetting episodes. However, they should be required to do this without punitive responses on the part of the parents.

6. Generally, enuresis can be managed on an outpatient basis without the necessity for an expensive and disruptive hospital stay. Although the practice of admitting enuretics for weeks of inpatient therapy is fairly common, there are no published data to support this approach.

There have been promising trends in the treatment of nocturnal enuresis with the development of such treatments as the dry bed training program. With the increasing recognition that enuresis is not primarily a psychopathological disorder, enuretic children and their families are benefiting from direct, clinically tested treatments.

Recommendations

Toilet training, enuresis, constipation, and encopresis (i.e., most toileting problems) frequently or usually involve a complex interplay of the child's gastrointestinal and/or genital urinary system with a variety of environmental inputs. The practitioner interested in treating these conditions would be well advised to acquaint himself with some of the details of normal physiological functioning prior to embarking on a vigorous treatment program. In the majority of toileting problems, the child deserves to have organic etiology ruled out through history, physical examination, and laboratory or radiographic analysis prior to any attempt to treat the condition.

Obviously, the child's developmental status also plays an important part in determining whether or not to institute a treatment approach. For a parent to begin toilet training before a child has matured sufficiently is inviting failure and disappointment. If a parent insists on having a child treated for a toileting problem (e.g., enuresis) when the child is too young (e.g., below 3 years of age) the clinician might consider persuading the parent to wait until the child is maturationally ready. A discussion with parents about developmental norms would be helpful in pointing out to parents that toileting problems can resolve spontaneously with age or that these problems are not considered problems (abnormal) until a child reaches an age when most of his or her peers do not have the problem.

Since toileting problems are often a source of enormous frustration for parents, a carefully prepared and supervised treatment program can be a very rewarding experience for clinicians. Clinicians who seem to have the best success rates and who are most capable of dealing with occasional treatment failures are the ones who are trained to recognize possible organic cause, refer to appropriate medical staff when organicity is suspected, and to use experimentally validated procedures to treat children for whom organicity has been ruled out.

REFERENCES

Azrin, N.H., & Besalel, V.A. *A parent's guide to bedwetting control: A step-by-step method.* New York: Simon & Schuster, 1979.

Azrin, N.H., & Foxx, R.M. A rapid method of toilet training the institutionalized retarded. *Journal of Applied Behavior Analysis,* 1971, **4**, 89–99.

Azrin, N.H., & Foxx, R.M. *Toilet training in less than a day.* New York: Simon & Schuster, 1974.

Azrin, N.H., Hontos, P.T., & Besalel-Azrin, V. Elimination of enuresis without a conditioning apparatus: An extension by office instruction of the child and parents. *Behavior Therapy,* 1979, **10**, 14–19.

Azrin, N.H., Sneed, T.J., & Foxx, R.M. Dry-bed training: Rapid elimination of childhood enuresis. *Behaviour Research and Therapy,* 1974, **12**, 147–156.

Azrin, N.H., & Thienes, P.M. Rapid elimination of enuresis by intensive learning without a conditioning apparatus. *Behavior Therapy,* 1978, **9**, 342–354.

Barr, R.G., Levine, M.D., & Watkins, J.B. Recurrent abdominal pain due to lactose intolerance. *New England Journal of Medicine,* 1979, **300**, 1449.

Besalel, V.A., Azrin, N.H., Thienes-Hontos, P., & McMorrow, M. Evaluation of a parent's manual for training enuretic children. *Behaviour Research and Therapy,* 1980, **18**, 358–360.

Bindelglas, P.M. The enuretic child. *The Journal of Family Practice,* October 1975, 375–380.

Bollard, R.J., & Woodroffe, P. The effect of parent-administered dry-bed training on nocturnal enuresis in children. *Behaviour Research and Therapy,* 1977, **15**, 159–165.

Brazelton, T.B. A child-oriented approach to toilet training. *Pediatrics,* 1962, **29**, 121–128.

Brown, R.M., & Brown, N.L. The increase and control of verbal signals in the bladder training of a seventeen month old child—A case study. *Journal of Child Psychology and Psychiatry,* 1974, **15**, 105–109.

Butler, J.F. The toilet training success of parents after reading Toilet training in less than a day. *Behavior Therapy,* 1976, **7**, 185–191.

Carlson, S.S., & Asnes, R.S. Maternal expectations and attitudes toward toilet training: A comparison between clinic mothers and private practice mothers. *Journal of Pediatrics,* 1974, **84**, 148–151.

Christophersen, E.R. *Little people: Guidelines for common sense child rearing.* Lawrence, Kan.: H & H Enterprises, 1977.

Christophersen, E.R., & Berman, R. Encopresis

treatment. *Issues in Comprehensive Pediatric Nursing,* 1978, **3**(4), 51–66.

Christophersen, E.R., & Rainey, S. Management of encopresis through a pediatric outpatient clinic. *Journal of Pediatric Psychology,* 1976, **1**, 38–41.

Christophersen, E.R., & Rapoff, M.A. Enuresis treatment. *Issues in Comprehensive Pediatric Nursing,* 1978, **2**, 35–52.

Cohen, M.W. Enuresis. *Pediatric Clinics of North America,* 1975, **22**, 545–560.

Davidson, M. Constipation and fecal incontinence. *Pediatric Clinics of North America,* 1958, **5**, 749–757.

Davidson, M., Kugler, M.M., & Bauer, C.H. Diagnosis and management in children with severe and protracted constipation and obstipation. *Journal of Pediatrics,* 1963, **62**, 261–275.

DeLeon, G., & Mandell, W. A comparison of conditioning and psychotherapy in the treatment of functional enuresis. *Journal of Clinical Psychology,* 1966, **22**, 326–330.

Dische, S. Treatment of enuresis with an enuresis alarm. In I. Kolvin, R.C. MacKeith, & S.R. Meadow (Eds.), *Bladder control and enuresis.* Philadelphia: Lippincott, 1973.

Doleys, D.M. Behavioral treatments for nocturnal enuresis in children: A review of the recent literature. *Psychological Bulletin,* 1977, **84**, 30–54.

Doleys, D.M., Ciminero, A.R., Tollison, J.W., Williams, D.L., & Wells, K.C. Dry-bed training and retention control training: A comparison. *Behavior Therapy,* 1977, **8**, 541–548.

Esperanca, M., & Gerrard, J.W. Nocturnal enuresis: Comparison of the effect of imipramine and dietary restriction on bladder capacity. *Canadian Medical Association Journal,* 1968, **101**, 721–724.

Foxx, R.M., & Azrin, N.H. Dry pants: A rapid method of toilet training children. *Behaviour Research and Therapy,* 1973, **11**, 435–442. (a)

Foxx, R.M., & Azrin, N.H. *Toilet training the retarded.* Champaign, Ill.: Research Press, 1973. (b)

Gaultieri, C.T. Imipramine and children: A review and some speculations about the mechanism of drug action. *Diseases of the Nervous System,* 1977, **38**, 368–375.

Giles, D.K., & Wolf, M.M. Toilet training institutionalized, severe retardates: An application of operant behavior modification techniques.

American Journal of Mental Deficiency, 1966, **70**, 766–780.

Harris, L.S., & Purohit, A.P. Bladder training and enuresis: A controlled trial. *Behaviour Research and Therapy,* 1977, **15**, 485–490.

Kimmel, H.D. Book review: "Toilet training in less than a day: How to do it." *Journal of Behaviour Therapy and Experimental Psychiatry,* 1974, **5**, 113.

Kimmel, H.D., & Kimmel, E. An instrumental conditioning method for the treatment of enuresis. *Journal of Behaviour Therapy and Experimental Psychiatry,* 1970, **1**, 121–123.

Lancioni, G.E. Teaching independent toileting to profoundly retarded deaf-blind children. *Behavior Therapy,* 1980, **11**, 234–244.

Levine, M.D. Children with encopresis: A descriptive analysis. *Pediatrics,* 1975, **56**, 412–416.

Levine, M.D. The schoolchild with encopresis. *Pediatrics in Review,* 1981, **2**(9), 285–290.

Levine, M.D., & Bakow, H. Children with encopresis: A treatment outcome study. *Pediatrics,* 1976, **58**, 845–852.

Levine, M.D., Mazonson, P., & Bakow, H. Behavioral symptom substitution in children cured of encopresis. *American Journal of Diseases of Children,* 1980, **134**, 663–667.

Lovibond, S.H. *Conditioning and enuresis.* Oxford: Pergamon, 1964.

Madsen, C.H., Hoffman, M., Thomas, D.R., Koropsat, E., & Madsen, D.K. Comparisons of toilet training procedures. In D.M. Gelfand (Ed.), *Social learning in childhood.* Belmont, Calif.: Brooks/Cole, 1969.

Mahoney, K., VanWagenen, R.K., & Meyerson, L. Toilet training of normal and retarded children. *Journal of Applied Behavior Analysis,* 1971, **4**, 173–181.

Marshall, S., & Marshall, H.H. A practical approach to nonorganic enuresis. *Medical Times,* 1973, **101**, 58–61.

Matson, J.L. Some practical considerations for using the Foxx and Azrin rapid method of toilet training. *Psychological Reports,* 1975, **37**, 350.

Matson, J.L., & Ollendick, T.H. Issues in toilet training normal children. *Behavior Therapy,* 1977, **8**, 549–553.

McKendry, J.B., & Stewart, D.A. Enuresis. *Pediatric Clinics of North America,* 1974, **21**, 1019–1020.

McKendry, J.B., Stewart, D.A., Khana, F., & Netteg, C. Primary enuresis: Relative success of three methods of treatment. *Canadian Medical Association Journal,* 1975, **113,** 953–955.

Moffet, H.L. Urinalysis and urine cultures in children. *Urologic Clinics of North America,* 1974, **1,** 387–396.

Mowrer, O.H., & Mowrer, W.M. Enuresis: A method for its study and treatment. *American Journal of Orthopsychiatry,* 1938, **8,** 436–459.

Muellner, S.R. Development of urinary control in children: A new concept in cause, prevention, and treatment of primary enuresis. *Journal of Urology,* 1960, **84,** 714–716.

Noe, N.H. Voiding dysfunction in the child with problem "wetting." *Developmental and Behavioral Pediatrics,* 1980, **1,** 29–33.

Olness, K. The use of self-hypnosis in the treatment of childhood nocturnal enuresis. *Clinical Pediatrics,* 1975, **14,** 273–279.

Paschalis, A., Kimmel, H.D., & Kimmel, E. Further study of diurnal instrumental conditioning in the treatment of enuresis nocturna. *Journal of Behaviour Therapy and Experimental Psychiatry,* 1972, **3,** 253–256.

Perimutter, A.D. Enuresis. In T.P. Kelalis & L.R. King (Eds.), *Clinical pediatric urology.* Philadelphia: Saunders, 1976.

Physicians' desk reference. (30th ed.). Oradell, N.J.: Medical Economics, 1976.

Pumroy, D.K., & Pumroy, S.S. Systematic observation and reinforcement technique in toilet training. *Psychological Reports,* 1965, **16,** 467–471.

Simonds, J.D. Enuresis: A brief survey of current thinking with respect to pathogenesis and management. *Clinical Pediatrics,* 1977, **16,** 79–82.

Sperling, M. Dynamic considerations and treatment of enuresis. *Journal of the American Academy of Child Psychiatry,* 1965, **4,** 19–31.

Spock, B. *Baby and child care* (Rev. ed.). New York: Pocket Books, 1976.

Starfield, B. & Mellits, E.D. Increase in functional bladder capacity and improvements in enuresis. *The Journal of Pediatrics,* 1968, **72,** 483–487.

Stephens, J.A., & Silber, D.L. Parental expectations in toilet training. *Pediatrics,* 1971, **48,** 451–454.

Stephens, J.A., & Silber, D.L. Parental expectations versus outcome in toilet training. *Pediatrics,* 1974, **54,** 493–495.

Taylor, P.D., & Turner, R.K. A clinical trial of continuous, intermittent and overlearning "bell and pad" treatments for nocturnal enuresis. *Behaviour Research and Therapy,* 1975, **3,** 281–293.

Tough, J.H., Hawkins, R.P., MacArthur, M.M., & Ravensway, S.V. Modification of enuretic behaviour by punishment: A new use of an old device. *Behavior Therapy,* 1971, **2,** 567–574.

Turner, R.K. Conditioning treatment of nocturnal enuresis. In I. Kolvin, R.C. MacKeith, & S.R. Meadow (Eds.), *Bladder control and enuresis.* Philadelphia: Lippincott, 1973.

VanWagenen, R.K., Meyerson, L., Kerr, M.J., & Mahoney, K. Field trials of a new procedure for toilet training. *Journal of Experimental Child Psychology,* 1969, **8,** 147–159.

Werry, J.S., & Cohrssen, J. Enuresis—An etiologic and therapeutic study. *The Journal of Pediatrics,* 1965, **67,** 423–431.

Wright, L. Handling the encopretic child. *Professional Psychology,* 1973, **4,** 137–144.

Wright, L., Schaeffer, A.B., & Solomons, G. (Eds.), *Encyclopedia of pediatric psychology.* Baltimore: University Park Press, 1979.

Wright, L., & Walker, E. Treatment of the child with psychogenic encopresis. *Clinical Pediatrics,* 1977, **16,** 1042–1045.

CHAPTER 25

Eating Problems in Children

THOMAS R. LINSCHEID

The first area of parent-child interaction in which the child's cooperation is required is feeding. While initially the child's responses are reflexive in nature, very quickly the unique natures of both feeder (usually parent) and infant begin to affect each other's behavior within the feeding situation and help to set the stage for adaptive or maladaptive interactional patterns outside of feeding as well.

In this chapter, I will describe the incidence and nature of children's eating problems, the development of normal feeding skills and patterns in children, and a framework for diagnosis and remediation of eating problems in children. Physical and developmental factors will be stressed to an extent that may not have been anticipated in a volume designed for clinical psychologists. This is done for two reasons. First, eating problems in children have their origin during a period of very rapid physical and developmental change in the child. These factors must be well understood by the clinician in determining a realistic treatment strategy. Second, by the time most children are referred for psychological treatment of eating problems, they and their parents have had a significant amount of contact with professionals who have been schooled more in physical and developmental areas, namely pediatricians and nurses, and it is crucial to be familiar with the attitudes and knowledge imparted to parents by these individuals.

This chapter will outline a functional approach to the treatment of eating problems. This is not meant to suggest that eating problems cannot or should not be viewed as symptomatic of more complex emotional problems within either parent or child. It is more reflective of an overall attitude that I perceive in clinical child and adult psychology recently: that even if one is a true believer in the traditional psychoanalytic approach, treating the symptom has not proven harmful and in many cases has been helpful to the overall therapeutic relationship.

INCIDENCE AND NATURE OF CHILDREN'S EATING PROBLEMS

It has been pointed out (Palmer, Thompson, & Linscheid, 1975) that a standard classification system for childhood feeding disorders does not exist and that this is in part due to the wide variety of such problems and the wide variety of disciplines that may be called upon to deal with those problems. This lack of commonality in diagnostic criteria and professional involvement make the attempt to relate incidence figures somewhat futile. A best guess estimate based on reports from a variety of settings would suggest that 25–35 percent of children have recognized or reportable eating problems (Kessler, 1966; Palmer & Horn, 1978). It is likely, however, that the incidence is significantly higher for several reasons.

First, the incidence reported can only be based on cases where help was sought by parents or guardians. From clinical experience, many parents whose children are having problems in other areas will fail to report eating problems. A good example of this is the mother of a hearing-impaired child who, on initial questioning, reported that feeding was not a problem but later related that in order to induce her child to eat a sufficient quantity and variety, she had to feed her in the bathtub. A second problem arises from incidence figures reported from mental health settings where the true incidence of eating problems may be hidden by the tendency to report general diagnostic labels, such as Adjustment Reaction to Childhood (the adoption of DSM III may help to alleviate this problem).

While it may be a long time before accurate estimates of eating problems in children are available, it is certainly safe to say that any problem that may occur in as many as 25–35 percent of a population is a significant problem and knowledge of its nature, diagnosis, and treatment should be an important part of the background of the clinical child psychologist.

Eating problems of children have been classified in a variety of schemes, ranging from descriptive to causal. Kessler (1966) suggested a three-way classification based on symptoms. A child may have a problem based on eating too little, too much, or the wrong things (e.g., pica). Anna Freud (1946/1964) suggests categorization based on underlying sources of conflict. Her first level is organic changes or defects in the individual that cause a reduced drive to survive (e.g., brain damage). The second level of conflict describes a reduced drive to survive leading to reduced intake but caused by emotional factors rather than organic factors. According to Freud, these factors lead to a view of feeding as an unpleasant activity, a worklike activity rather than a pleasurable activity providing opportunity for wish fulfillment. Her third level is neurotic feeding disturbances, which she feels are a more serious and pervasive extension of the second level. While at the second level a child may use the interactions with the feeder (mother) to attempt to satisfy unmet needs at the third level, difficulties with food and eating become internalized and are present even in the absence of the feeder (mother).

Neither of these classification systems or types is sufficient. Kessler's system, while having the advantage of being descriptive, does not allow for enough specificity. For example, for a child classified as having a disorder of insufficient intake, the reasons could range from such diverse factors as cerebral palsy to chronic refusal to eat anything that is not red in color. Despite including organic interferences with eating, Freud's system is inadequate in that it ascribes all other feeding disturbances to emotional conflict between child and feeder.

Palmer et al. (1975) have proposed a classification system that classifies by the specific nature of the problems and the probable cause. Under their system the major problems are:

1.   Mealtime tantrums
2.   Bizarre food habits
3.   Multiple food dislikes
4.   Prolonged subsistence on pureed foods
5.   Delay or difficulty in sucking, chewing, or swallowing
6.   Delay in self-feeding

Possible causes for these problems are (1) behavioral mismanagement, (2) neuromotor dysfunction, and (3) mechanical obstructions. Several of the major problems may have one or more of the primary causes: for example, delays in self-feeding may be due to behavioral mismanagement, neuromotor dysfunction, or mechanical obstruction. While the Palmer et al. (1975) system was a good start, it needs expansion to include more problems and another category of possible causes. I would suggest an expansion of the classification system as shown in Table 25.1.

The major problems that have been added to the original system are pica, overeating, undereating, and rumination. These will be addressed later. To the list of possible causes have been added medical and genetic abnormalities so that allergies, rare but important disturbances in taste, smell, and genetically related disturbances in appetite (e.g., Prader-Willi Syndrome), could be included.

The term *behavioral mismanagement* was chosen to suggest that the behaviors in question are the result of a failure to train the child

Table 25.1 An Expansion of the Palmer, Thompson, and Linscheid Classification System for Childhood Feeding Problems

Major Problems	Possible Causes			
	Behavioral Mismanagement	Neuromotor Dysfunction	Mechanical Obstruction	Medical or Genetic Abnormalities
Mealtime tantrums	X			
Bizarre food habits	X			X
Multiple food dislikes	X			X
Prolonged subsistence on pureed foods	X	X	X	
Delay or difficulty in chewing, sucking, or swallowing		X	X	
Delay in self-feeding	X	X	X	
Pica	X			X
Excessive overeating	X			X
Excessive underintake of food	X	X	X	X
Rumination	X	X		X

Note. X's indicate possible causes for each major problem.

in more appropriate and productive feeding patterns. It suggests that the feeding problem is modifiable and remediable through the manipulation of environmental contingencies as opposed to medical or surgical treatment. The clinical child psychologist most often will be involved with those problems that have behavioral mismanagement as their cause. It is very important to note, however, that of the problems listed in Table 25.1 that have behavioral mismanagement as a possible cause, eight have other possible causes as well. This emphasizes the important need to consult other specialists (e.g., nutritionists, physicians) before embarking on a psychological or behavioral treatment.

Development of Normal Feeding Patterns

Anyone who works with children is acutely aware that knowledge of normal development is crucial to understanding a particular child's problem (cf. Gerrity, Jones, & Self, chap. 3, "Developmental Psychology for Clinicians,"

in this book.) This is especially true in diagnosing and treating eating problems in children because there are almost always physical, emotional, developmental, and nutritional factors that must be considered. It is also important to understand the current and historical views of childhood feeding that are put forth by the child's pediatrician or family doctor. It would be a serious error, for example, to put the blame for a feeding disorder on a mother whose strict and inflexible feeding schedule was based on the advice of a trusted family doctor and not on her own intuition.

Infants double their weight in the first five months and triple it by the end of the first year (Hoekelman et al, 1978). This is a period in which growth and intake of food are among the primary concerns of the child's parents and the pediatrician. At each well child visit, the infant will be weighed and measured and his or her growth compared to normative charts. How feeding is going and preparation for changes in feeding schedules or types of food are the most common topics of discussion during these visits. Parents come to rely a great deal on these visits for feedback on how both they and their infant are doing.

Initially, the child's feeding behavior will be controlled exclusively by reflexes and the physiological distress induced by hunger. For this reason, current pediatric practice suggests allowing the child to feed on demand for the first few months, with gradual structuring of a feeding schedule by the middle of the first year of life (Hoekelman et al., 1978; Schwartz, 1958). Nighttime feedings are the rule during the first month but usually will be eliminated by the infant himself or herself during the second month.

It is important to mention infant colic at this point. While technically not a problem of intake, colic is often included in feeding disorders because its effects typically follow feedings, especially the evening feeding. Colic is manifested as a generalized state of distress in the infant with intermittent abdominal pain, cramping, drawing up of the legs, and screaming. The cause is unknown and the symptoms spontaneously disappear abruptly at 3–4 months of age (Moss & Moss, 1980). There is little evidence that colic is directly related to specific eating problems later in life (Bakwin & Bakwin, 1972); however, it is important to be aware of the frustrations, self-doubts, and guilt feelings of new parents who are unable to comfort their infant.

Breast feeding is enjoying a new popularity, and most pediatricians and nutritionists presently recommend it as a first choice provided the mother is fully convinced that she wants to breast feed. The advantages of breast feeding are that the infant will receive a balanced and nutritionally adequate diet and will have a reduced incidence of gastrointestinal problems, at least through the first six months of life. Also, mother-child interaction and bonding will be enhanced (but not guaranteed) because of the close physical contact required in breast feeding. Recent evidence suggests, however, that bottle-fed babies grow just as well as breast-fed babies given proper vitamin and mineral supplements (AAP Committee on Nutrition, 1976; Jackson et al., 1964). A major concern in bottle feeding is that parents

will not hold their infants during feedings. This may lead to problems in mother-infant bonding because the opportunity to associate physical contact and need fulfillment is reduced. Also, dental problems, ear infections, and difficulty in weaning have been traced to the practice of putting a baby to bed with a bottle (Bernick, 1971).

Solid foods in the form of infant cereal and pureed foods are started between 4 and 6 months of age with chopped or table foods added around 8 months of age or when teeth begin to appear (Christophersen & Hall, 1978; Moss & Moss, 1980). Weaning from the breast or bottle usually occurs between 6 and 18 months. Some infants can go to cup drinking directly from the breast and do not need the intermediate step of bottle feeding.

By the end of the first year, the infant is eating three meals a day with one or two light snacks interspersed. Finger feeding, which begins sometime in the sixth or seventh month, is still occurring, and self-feeding with a spoon is often possible by the twelfth month. By 15 months, the infant should be totally capable of self-feeding (Christophersen & Hall, 1978).

After 1 year of age, an infant's appetite and interest in food will decrease dramatically. While the infant has gained 12–18 pounds in the first year, he or she will experience weight gains of only about five pounds per year over the next three to four years (Schwartz, 1958; Smith, 1977). This is an especially crucial time for the development of eating problems because parents are *quantity* oriented as a result of their experiences in the first year of the infant's life and because the child's appetite now becomes erratic with changing interests, food likes and dislikes, and an increasing willingness to assert his or her independence and will (Schwartz, 1958). Parental anxiety over their child's eating is greatest during this stage.

When the child becomes school age, appetite returns and dietary habits are now the result of patterns learned during the years 1–6 and the modeling of the family's eating habits. The main concerns during the period arise from the likely increase in nonnutritious food as a result of peer pressure and the family's decreased ability to supervise the child's consumption (Christophersen & Hall, 1978).

Relationship between Infant Feeding Practices and Later Development

Past and Present Approaches

Classic psychodynamic theorists such as Sigmund Freud placed a great deal of emphasis upon early stages of development and their relationships to adult personality and adjustment. Freud felt that failure to pass through and resolve the early psychosexual stages—namely, oral, anal, and genital—would have lasting and major effects on adjustment in adult life. For a time, much emphasis was placed on the role of early feeding events as a guide to understanding later personality traits and adjustment difficulties. Researchers attempted to relate specific variables, such as breast feeding versus bottle feeding or age of weaning, to known personality traits. In reviewing the results of these studies, Kessler (1966) concludes that this approach was naive for two reasons. First, the reasons why two mothers might decide to wean their children late may be totally different. One may do so out of an overriding need to nurture and overprotect while the other may be motivated by a desperate financial situation. Second, it assumed that as a person passed through the psychosexual stages his or her fate was sealed and whatever other life experiences might occur would have little or no effect on personality development. Needless to say, the results of this line of research were of little help in understanding or predicting later behavior (Kessler, 1966).

Despite the lack of evidence to suggest a direct relationship between specific early events in feeding, the theories are still widely circulated and are popular with the lay public. In my experience, I have frequently had mothers ask questions such as, "Is my child's problem due to my having weaned her at three months?" This type of belief is counterproductive for two reasons. First, it lays all the blame on the mother or parent who made the decision and, second, it leads parents to fear

that the treatment of any specific problem, if indeed possible at all, will be beyond their abilities and will be of a longstanding nature.

Kessler (1966), however, warns against totally negating the impact of infant experiences on later behavior. She feels that there is a continuity in child development and a child's readiness for more advanced developmental tasks is in part due to the nature of the interaction he or she has established with his or her parents, primarily his mother. Kessler was anticipating the present day emphasis on viewing the mother(parent)-child relationship not as a one-way street but rather as an interaction in which each party influences the other's behavior. Moss (1967) has done outstanding work in this area. In one study, he demonstrated that the major determinant of the amount of time spent with an infant by his or her mother was directly related to how much the infant cried or fussed. The suggestion here is that the mother's behavior may be more controlled by the idiosyncratic nature of her infant than by her feelings of nurturance, overprotection, or disinterest. In other words, the degree to which she cares for her infant is more a function of the infant than her internal motives and conflicts. The sex of the infant also elicits different responses from parents; for example, Rothbart and Maccoby (1966) found that fathers were more permissive toward girls while mothers were more permissive toward boys.

Another factor that is an integral component of this line of thinking is the recognition that infants can and do have different temperaments and response styles that can be identified very early. Brazelton (1969) has been a major exponent of the notion of infant responsivity and has described these types of infants—active, average, and quiet—and the differing demands on mothers inherent in these styles.

The purpose of the preceding discussion is twofold. First, it suggests that the answer to problems of eating in children lies in a careful analysis not only of the child's early feeding history but of the present interaction between the child and the individual(s) responsible for his or her eating, all in the context of his or her present developmental level. Second, it suggests that treatment of eating disorders is possible through reassessment of developmental expectations and direct changes in the behavior of one of the parties to the interaction. The second point is very important in that it suggests that eating disorders are directly treatable through manipulation of present day contingencies. This is in contrast to the psychodynamically based view that anxiety produced by a specific event during the oral stage is the underlying cause and the specific eating problem is merely a symptom of the underlying anxiety. Thomas, Chess, and Birch (1968) speak to this point in summarizing a series of longitudinal studies:

As has been demonstrated in the case histories, in the young child anxiety has not been evident as an initial factor preceding and determining symptom development. Where anxiety has arisen, it has been more a consequence than a cause, though it then affects the symptoms and the expression. Similarly the removal of symptoms has had positive consequences for the child's functioning and has not resulted in the appearance of overt anxiety or of new substantive symptoms. (p. 186)

With the preceding rationale as a basis, the remainder of this chapter will be devoted to descriptions of eating disorders in children and functional and direct treatment strategies for remediation of these disorders.

Prevention of Eating Disorders

It is rare to find a section on the prevention of psychological or behavioral problems in volumes of child psychology or psychiatry. These works are devoted almost exclusively to etiology, diagnoses, and treatment of existing problems. Why, then, is such a section included in this chapter? Over the past 10–15 years, there has been a closer working relationship between the fields of medical and behavioral science, as evidenced by the establishment and growth of groups such as the Society of Pediatric Psychology and the Society for Behavioral Medicine. One result has been the increase in psychologists working

in medical settings, especially those working outside of departments of psychiatry (McNett, 1981). In the medical specialty of pediatrics, a great deal of the physician's (or nurse's) time is spent in educating and advising parents in the physical and behavioral development of their children. Psychologists have been playing an increasing role in the psychological management of pediatric problems (Magrab, 1978) and in advising parents, either directly or through consultation to pediatrician and nurse, in the prevention or early remediation of behavioral or emotional problems, many of which are related to eating (cf. Peterson & Ridley-Johnson, chap. 50, of this book).

There are two major avenues to prevention of eating problems in children. The first is to ensure that the child is exposed to the type of foods that are developmentally appropriate, thereby ensuring the child the opportunity to experience different textures and quantities and to practice self-feeding if appropriate. As noted earlier, a child is primarily fed by liquids (breast milk or bottle formula) until 6 months of age, with pureed foods introduced between 4 and 6 months. More textured foods are introduced between 7 and 10 months. Illingworth and Lister (1964) have suggested that this age, 7–10 months, constitutes a critical period for the introduction of solids and children who are not introduced to solids during this time will have a great deal of difficulty with chewing later on. It is important to stress to parents the importance of successful introduction of textured foods at this age, as many parents are inclined to revert to pureed foods when their child initially rejects or gags on a new, more textured food.

Once introduction of solid food is completed, the parents need to be counseled in the need to provide their child with the full range of textures and food groups so that learning to eat a balanced diet will be possible.

The second major avenue to prevention of eating problems is to ensure that parents have sufficient knowledge and techniques to deal with feeding-related behaviors in their child. This is especially important during the ages 1–5. This is the time when the child's need for food diminishes dramatically relative to the first year, he or she experiences natural variability in appetite, and developmentally he or she is in a period of increasing independence, often demonstrating this through resistance to parental authority (Bakwin & Bakwin, 1972).

Christophersen and Hall (1978) have written an excellent article in which they spell out specific guidelines for handling mealtime problems. They propose a set of guidelines for pediatric health care providers and for parents. To summarize briefly, these guidelines provide information on proper diet, the establishment of rules governing mealtime behavior, the use of contingent parental attention, and the means to insure that mealtimes are seen as pleasant times rather than sources of stress. The reader is encouraged to obtain and use these guidelines.

Assessment of Eating Disorders in Children

The proper assessment of eating disorders requires information from three main areas: (1) medical history and status, (2) nutritional history and status, and (3) behavioral assessment. As can be seen, two of the three areas are outside of the expertise of the clinical psychologist: however, medical and nutritional assessment is extremely important, and the psychologist who works with eating disorders must be prepared and willing to develop close working relationships with the other disciplines involved.

Medical Assessment

There are several important reasons for medical assessment of the child with an eating disorder. Medical conditions that can affect diet or reduce weight gain must be ruled out. These include such conditions as food allergies, thyroid or other endocrine function anomalies, and congenital anomalies of the gastrointestinal tract (e.g., hiatal hernia). Any medical condition affecting central nervous system functioning must be assessed as well. Most frequently, these conditions affect neuromotor functioning and thereby may interfere with responses needed for proper eating. Such problems include difficulty in control of

tongue or lip closure, inability or decreased ability to chew, or interference with self-feeding caused by impaired use of the extremities, especially the arms and hands.

Medical history can also reveal past medical conditions that, even though no longer contributory, may have had a significant effect on the development of the present problem. Children who were seriously ill as infants, especially those who spent a great deal of time in hospitals, were prevented from progressing through the normal feeding stages. Often it is not the medical complication itself that prevented the succession of normal stages but the fact that the development of proper eating in the infant or child was considered of much less importance in light of his or her medical condition.

Nutritional Assessment

The nutritional assessment of a child includes assessment of the adequacy of his or her intake in relation to age, height, and weight. In a nutritional assessment, specific deficiencies or excesses in either nutrients, vitamins, or calories are established, and laboratory tests or biochemical analyses are conducted as needed. Nutritionists are also skilled at assessing oral motor function as it applies to eating (Ekvall, 1978). Nutritional assessment is extremely important in treatment planning for two reasons. First, the seriousness of a child's nutritional status is used in determining the intensity of treatment that may be needed. Some authors (Linscheid et al., 1978) have advised that nutritional status be considered a major decision criterion when deciding to treat on an outpatient or inpatient basis. Second, nutritional deficits are used to establish treatment goals. For example, if a child who had a limited diet was seriously deficient in Vitamin A, then a major treatment goal would be to increase his or her acceptance of foods containing adequate amounts of that vitamin.

Behavioral Assessment

Behavioral assessment has three major purposes: (1) assessment of preferences, (2) assessment of current intake, and (3) assessment of eating-related behaviors.

The assumption underlying behavioral assessment is that feeding and eating involve a series of behaviors on the part of the child who is eating (or not eating) and on the part of the individual who is responsible for that child's eating. These eating behaviors can be defined in objective terms, and they can be measured using common behavior assessment techniques and strategies.

A behavioral assessment is conducted in order to provide an objective and reliable description of the child's present eating behaviors and the behaviors of those who feed him or her at the time of feeding and an analysis of the interaction between feeder and child. The assessment is conducted also to document present food likes and dislikes, defined by their acceptance or rejection, and to provide a baseline against which to assess treatment progress.

Assessment of Preference

Nutritionists often use food records to assess nutritional status (Ekvall, 1978). These records usually cover a 3–7 day period and are kept by the child's mother or caretaker. The mother simply writes down what and how much the child ate at each meal. Food records can be used in the determination of a child's preferred and nonpreferred foods; however, they may be misleading in that the range of foods offered by the mother may be limited to those she knows her child will likely accept. This is especially true if the record is kept for only three days.

Birch (1979, 1980) has recently made the point that children as young as 3 years of age can reliably rate their own food preferences. In one study (Birch, 1979), children were first asked to taste small pieces of fruit. When all the fruit had been tasted, they were asked to point out their favorite. That fruit was removed, and the child was again asked to point out his or her favorite fruit and so on until all fruit had been rated. This resulted in a complete rank ordering of the fruits based on the child's stated preferences. In another study

(Birch, 1980), children were offered bites of food and then were asked to place the remainder of the food beside one of three faces. The three faces were designed so that one depicted someone who had just eaten something he or she liked, one depicted someone who had just eaten something he or she did not like, and the third face depicted a neutral expression. The reliability of rankings that Birch found in these two studies suggests that children can rate their own food preferences. The method is presently limited to children who are willing to taste the foods in question; however, a useful adaptation might be simply to have the child point to one of two foods that he or she liked the least. Through a series of paired comparisons, one might arrive at a ranking of the intensity of dislike.

To test whether reported likes or dislikes are accurate, several authors have reported placing a variety of foods in front of the child during baseline sessions and allowing the child to eat what he or she pleased (Linscheid et al., 1978; Riordan et al., 1980). No direct attempt to influence food choice via contingent approval or disapproval or other procedures is used during these baseline sessions. This is especially important if a child is to be treated outside the home or by someone other than his or her usual feeder. It is not at all uncommon in my experience to have a child readily eat a food that had been reported by a parent as being disliked.

Assessment of Present Intake

As in the assessment of preference, food records kept by the child's mother or caregiver can be helpful in determining a child's intake. Quantity is usually listed as an estimate: a half a cup of juice or a glass of milk. It is seldom the case that the food consumed is actually weighed or measured. While the food record kept by parents can supply a general estimate of intake, it should not be considered a highly reliable estimate of actual intake. Lack of reliability of parents' reports usually occurs because of variability in the accuracy of quantity estimates, parental motivation to either underrepresent or overrepresent their child's problem, and the practice of recording intake at the end of the day when it may be difficult to remember exactly what a child had for breakfast.

Published reports of feeding treatments have used several methods for assessing intake. The most simple and straightforward method, of course, is to weigh the food before and after feeding (Linscheid et al., 1978; Palmer et al., 1975; and Riordan et al., 1980). This method seems highly reliable on the surface. Any sources of error in estimates would occur as a result of food or liquid spilled that could not be retrieved for reweighing. Other authors have used number of bites of food or sips of liquid as a measure of intake (Martin & McLaughlin, 1975; Riordan et al., 1980; and Thompson & Palmer, 1974). The drawback to using bites or sips as a measure of intake lies in the variability of the amount of food or liquid that could be taken in on any single bite or sip. One can easily see that ingestion of one heaping spoonful may constitute more actual food consumed than the placing of the spoon in the mouth ten times with only minimal quantities of food on the spoon on each occasion. Riordan et al. (1980) tried to reduce this problem by defining an amount that had to be consumed before a bite was counted. A bite was recorded if "the child moved a piece of food from the tray/container so that at least ½ tsp. or ¼ in. square piece of food was deposited in the mouth" (p. 99). Thompson and Palmer (1974) defined bites simply as teaspoons of food consumed and drinks as the act of bringing the glass to the mouth, taking some liquid, and then removing the glass.

An indirect measure of intake is the child's weight. Increases in consumption should be reflected in weight gain; decreases in consumption should reflect weight loss, and consistency of intake should result in little or no weight change. This indirect method of assessing intake has been used most extensively when the presenting problem is obesity or anorexia (Cohen et al., 1980; Epstein et al., 1980; Martin & McLaughlin, 1975).

Of the three methods described for the assessment of intake, weighing of the actual food consumed is obviously the most accurate. All three methods, however, have their place and the decision to use one or the other is best made with the nature of the presenting problem and treatment goals in mind.

Assessment of Eating-Related Behaviors

The actual consumption of food itself is often a small part of a child's eating problems. This behavior during the feeding session or his or her reluctance or inability to feed himself or herself may be of more concern than the amount he or she consumed. These behaviors fall into two categories: those that are disruptive to or interfere with the consumption of food and those that need to be learned in order for self-feeding to be possible. Examples of behaviors in the first category are mealtime tantrums, excessive crying, and the spitting out of food. Examples of behaviors in the second category would be the absence of spoon use or the inability to drink from a cup.

Behaviors that interfere with eating have been defined and assessed in various ways. Thompson, Iwata, and Poynter (1979) assessed tongue thrusting in a severely mentally retarded youngster by defining two separate behaviors that interfered with feeding—"tongue out" and "food expulsion." Tongue out was defined as "the tongue protruding from the mouth enough to touch the middle of the lower lip" (p. 327) and food expulsion was described as "food and/or saliva falling from the boy's face onto the catch tray positioned beneath his chin" (p. 327).

The subject was then observed during meals and the presence or absence of "tongue out" or "food expulsion" was recorded using an interval recording system. Under this system, continuous 10-second interval periods were divided into a 7.5-second observation period and a 2.5-second scoring period. Observers watched the subject during the 7.5-second observation period. If either "tongue out" or "food expulsion" occurred, a plus was recorded during the scoring period. Only one plus per interval was recorded regardless of the number of those behaviors that may have occurred during that interval. "Tongue out" and "food expulsion" were then expressed as a percent of the intervals in which they occurred compared to the total number of intervals observed. Assessment of the two feeding-related behaviors provided the authors with an empirical measure of the rate of the behaviors and the observation that these two behaviors did not always occur simultaneously.

One aspect of the Thompson et al. (1979) report bears special emphasis. There was a need to determine what might be a realistic level of tongue thrust and food expulsion in a population of individuals comparable to their subject but not known to be tongue thrusters. This type of normative data, of course, did not exist, so they obtained an estimate by using their assessment system to record the target behaviors in nine individuals (seven retarded children, two normal adults). This social validation allowed a realistic estimate of the severity of the problem prior to treatment and a much more realistic expectancy of treatment success. As a side note, the behavioral treatment employed resulted in a reduction in the rate of tongue out and food expulsion to a level comparable to the mentally retarded controls but not to the two normal adults.

To digress for a moment, it should be kept in mind that the purpose of pretreatment assessment is not only to provide a baseline for comparison later in treatment. A major reason for assessment is to provide information on the current status of the problem so that a decision can be made as to whether there is a need for treatment at all and, if so, what a realistic goal would be in light of the child's developmental status and the parent's or caregiver's value system.

Other behaviors that interfere with eating (e.g., crying, leaving the table, etc.) have been assessed. In two studies, crying during the feeding session was assessed by simply recording the duration of crying and then transforming this to a percent of crying per session by dividing the actual time spent crying by the total length of the feeding session (Thompson & Palmer, 1974; Thompson, 1977). Riordan et al. (1980) measured crying using a partial interval procedure. In this study, crying was defined as one of a set of six disruptive behaviors. Use of this system allowed for the assessment of the percent of intervals in which any one of the behaviors occurred and a measure of the extent of overall disruptive behavior by looking at the percent of intervals in which at least one of the six behaviors occurred.

O'Brien and Azrin (1972) defined inappropriate responses as any response or behavior that would be deemed improper if performed by a customer in a restaurant. Several specific inappropriate behaviors were defined (i.e., drooling, licking, oversized bites, and touching food). Other possible behaviors were defined by example: throwing utensils, putting feet on table, etc. These behaviors were then recorded by frequency counts. A somewhat similar system was used by Barton et al. (1970). Of their seven behavioral categories, four described descriptive behaviors that interfered with proper eating. These were: "stealing," "fingers—using fingers to eat foods which were appropriately eaten by utensil," "messy utensil—spilling from utensil, loading utensil with fingers, and so forth," "pigging— eating of food spilled on table or chair or eating food without use of fingers or utensil." Assessment was accomplished by observing each child in turn until one of the defined behaviors occurred or until ten seconds had elapsed. Data was then presented on a group basis by percent of observations of each behavior category.

When the presenting problem is lack of self-feeding, it is still necessary to assess the pretreatment behavior. This is done by carefully defining what the appropriate behavior should be and then observing the child in an eating setting in which it is possible to perform the correct eating behavior. No assistance is given to the child during this time. This allows the clinician or therapist to observe what the child will do when entirely on his or her own. He or she may be able to initiate movement toward a spoon, for example, but may grasp it incorrectly, thus preventing the possibility of successful spoon use. An example of a well-defined, appropriate self-feeding behavior is presented by O'Brien and Azrin (1972) in the definition of correct feeding responses.

Fork response: moving appropriate food from the container (e.g., meat, beets) with the fork held in one hand, by the handle, right side up and without spilling, except back into the container from which the food was taken. (p. 391)

Assessment of Child-Feeder Behaviors

As discussed earlier in this chapter, an individual's behavior in any situation is determined not so much by the individual but by his or her interaction with his or her present environment, especially other individuals in that environment. In any behavioral assessment, it is crucial to observe the child in the eating situation with the individual or individuals who are responsible for that child's feeding. Few published studies have reported data on the behavior of the feeder or on the interaction between feeder and child. In a series of reports by Thompson and his colleagues (Thompson & Linscheid, 1976; Thompson, Palmer, & Linscheid, 1977), they described the adaptation of the mother-child interaction scale procedure originally developed by Moustakas, Segel, and Schalock (1956). Their adaptation was designed to incorporate concepts of operant conditioning and to make the scale applicable to the feeding situation. The scale, as a measure of interaction, did not attempt only to allow for the recording of each individual's behavior but attempted to permit the direct analysis of the behavior of one of the parties to the behavior of the other. The scale did yield useful data on the nature of the mother-child interaction. It was cumbersome to use, however, and required more time than was realistically possible (or would be available) in the average clinical setting. It is my belief that some type of interaction assessment needs to be developed for use in the assessment of eating problems. Mash, Terdal, and Anderson (1973) published a response class matrix system for recording parent-child interaction. This system has been used effectively (cf. Cunningham & Barkley, 1979) in record-

ing other types of parent-child interaction but as yet has not been used, to my knowledge, in the assessment of eating disorders.

TREATMENT OF CHILDREN'S EATING PROBLEMS

There is very little in the literature on the treatment of eating problems in normal children. Most recent literature is behavioral in nature and has addressed itself to the eating problem of the mentally retarded population or the problem of childhood obesity from the viewpoint of a weight reduction strategy.

The traditional psychoanalytically oriented literature, while not containing well-controlled studies of childhood eating problems, does contain an occasional report of a child with an eating problem, but such reports usually describe older children and often contain a great deal of speculation. Bruch (1957) has written extensively on the topic of childhood obesity, the nature of families in which it may occur, and more traditional psychotherapeutic approaches to its treatment.

The treatment strategies to be outlined in the remainder of this chapter will be direct intervention approaches calling for specific actions or behaviors on the part of the parent, therapist, or child. The issue of the uncooperative parent is often raised when the direct approach is suggested. It is true that parental cooperation, support, and follow-through are needed if feeding treatments are to be successful, and it is the responsibility of the child clinician to help to foster a cooperative working relationship. However, if the parent or parents are unable to accept the advice and recommendation of the therapist because of problems of their own, then those problems should become the focus of intervention. This may often require referral to an adult-oriented or family-oriented clinician. It is common practice at the Georgetown University Child Development Center to have parents seen by a psychologist or social worker before, during, and after any feeding treatment that may be conducted with their child. Most parents find this helpful; some find it essential.

The treatment of eating disorders will be looked at in two main categories. The first category of eating problems and their treatment contains those that are best treated within the feeding situation itself. These are most often problems for which quantity of intake is not a major component. The second category contains those eating problems for which direct treatment during eating may take place but for which treatment outside of the actual feeding situation is a more major component of the overall treatment plan. Quantity of intake, either excessive or insufficient, is a major component of this type of problem.

Direct Treatment of Non-Quantity-Related Eating Problems

Non-quantity-related eating problems are those in which the child continues to ingest sufficient quantities of food to maintain growth within normal limits. The problem arises because of food type, texture or variety, or because of specific mealtime conduct problems. In the classification scheme proposed in Table 25.1, non-quantity-related problems include mealtime conduct problems, prolonged subsistence on pureed foods, bizarre food habits, multiple food dislikes, and delays in self-feeding.

Despite adequate intake for weight maintenance, these problems are potentially very serious. For example, children with multiple food dislikes or bizarre food habits may be lacking in, or receiving excessive quantities of, certain essential vitamins or minerals that could cause serious and irreversible physical complications if allowed to continue. Prolonged subsistence on pureed food can cause abnormalities in gums and teeth and delays in self-feeding can lead to problems in socialization and independence, despite a nutritionally adequate diet.

The feeding situation is especially amenable to the use of behavior modification procedures to remedy this category of eating problems (Linschied, 1978). The eating process itself is made up of objectively definable and quantifiable behaviors, and it is relatively easy to spell out specific procedures and con-

tingencies. Hunger is a natural source of motivation that can be increased, if necessary, by withholding food (within limits) prior to a treatment session.

Planning for a behaviorally based feeding treatment program should include the following elements. First, a specification in the treatment goals in behavioral and nutritional terms should be made. For example, in an article reporting the treatment of a child who ate only cookies and milk, Thompson et al. (1977) stated treatment goals as follows:

M's intake was to be changed so that it was appropriately balanced in terms of food groups (meats, cereals, vegetables, and fruits) and adequate in nutrients (100% RDA). M's cooperation with requests to eat nonpreferred food was to be increased and his non-cooperation was to be decreased. M's mother's verbal and physical assaultiveness in response to non-cooperation was to be decreased and her timely praise in response to cooperation increased. (p. 46)

It is important to note that treatment goals for the feeder (in this case M's mother) were included as well. A more specific definition of terms such as cooperation and noncooperation is found elsewhere in the article.

A second requirement in planning a behavioral treatment is to establish a measurement system designed to accurately reflect progress toward treatment goals. The reliability of this measurement system must be empirically determined. (See Hersen & Bellack, 1976 for a description of observational measurement strategies and reliability determinations.) If the therapist has done a good job of pretreatment assessment, these measures have most probably been developed by the time treatment is to begin and often the pretreatment behavioral assessment may serve as the baseline against which to compare treatment effects.

A third requirement is that behavioral treatment procedures must be spelled out. This is the treatment plan and involves the specification of exact procedures to be used in the treatment. The procedures will include a description of what the feeder will do in response to the child's behavior. It is assumed that those procedures that are chosen are ones that have proven successful in similar situations and are based on operant or respondent conditioning principles.

Review of Common Behavioral Treatment Procedures

POSITIVE REINFORCEMENT. The use of a positive reinforcement procedure involves the delivery of a desired stimulus, contingent upon the occurrence of a predetermined behavior. Several studies have reported the use of positive reinforcement to increase the consumption of foods that were previously refused (Bernal, 1972; Palmer et al., 1975; Riordan et al., 1980; Thompson & Palmer, 1974; Berkowitz, Sherry, & Davis, 1971). The procedure typically involves the identification of a preferred food, a small portion of which is delivered to the child, along with social praise contingent upon the child consuming a bite of a nonpreferred food. Often, the treatment will begin with positive reinforcement delivered for each bite of nonpreferred food, and then the number of bites required before reinforcement is given will be increased (Riordan et al., 1980). Social praise and attention can be a strong reinforcer, especially if it is only available to the child contingent on the eating of nonpreferred food. It is not at all uncommon for foods that are classified as nonpreferred initially to become preferred foods after treatment has begun (Thompson et al., 1977) and hence become positive reinforcers themselves.

TIME-OUT FROM POSITIVE REINFORCEMENT. Time-out is a punishment technique designed to reduce the probability of a specific behavior or set of behaviors. Punishment as a behavioral term should not be interpreted to mean a procedure or event that is physically painful. Punishment in behavioral terminology refers to the reduction in the probabliity of a response because of a contingent stimulus event. Time-out from positive reinforcement is just what it suggests—a time period during which no positive reinforcement is delivered. If time-out is made contingent upon a specific behavior and that behavior decreases in frequency,

then time-out is a punisher. In feeding treatment, time-out has been used in a variety of ways. Barton et al. (1970) used two variations of time-out to reduce disruptive and inappropriate eating behaviors in a group of mentally retarded individuals. Upon the occurrence of certain behaviors thought to be serious in nature (stealing food, using fingers to eat), the offending individual was removed from the table and placed in a small room for the duration of the meal. Contingent upon the occurrence of other less serious behaviors (messiness, pigging), the individual's food tray was removed for a 15-second period. During the 15-second tray removal, no social interaction with the individual was allowed. Linscheid et al. (1978) described a time-out procedure in which the feeder physically turns away from the child and does not interact in any way until a preset time period has expired or until the child is quiet.

Time-out can be a very effective procedure, especially if it is revealed during the assessment phase that the child uses food refusal to increase social interaction with the feeder. In one case that was treated at the Georgetown Child Development Center, it was observed prior to treatment that the child's food refusals induced increased verbalizations from his mother. Quantitative analysis revealed that the rate of verbalization during the feeding session was 2.6 words per second. It was easy to see that treatment should include the withdrawal of social interaction (time-out) for food refusal and the contingent delivery of social praise and verbal interaction (positive reinforcement) based on acceptance of nonpreferred foods. The case was successfully treated in a very short time.

Christophersen and Hall (1978) suggest the use of time-out during meals in their advice to parents of normal children and suggest termination of the meal altogether if two shorter time-outs are not effective at any one meal.

EXTINCTION. Extinction is defined behaviorally as the reduction in the probability of a response when that response is no longer reinforced. In the feeding situation, it may be used to decrease the probability of an undesirable response if pretreatment analysis makes it possible to identify the source of reinforcement for that response. For example, a child who is dawdling over his or her food may be doing so to induce his or her mother to interact with him or her. Extinction, in the form of ignoring, might be used to treat such a problem.

Specifically, the parent would be instructed to pay no attention to the child when he or she was not actively eating (dawdling). If the child's dawdling had been reinforced by his or her mother's attention, we would expect dawdling to decrease when it is no longer reinforced. Extinction (ignoring), in this case, may sound very similar to a time-out procedure. Extinction and time-out, however, are really quite different procedures. Time-out requires an overt act such as turning away from the child, removing the child's food, or removing the child from the feeding situation itself. Time-out also imposes a time period during which the child can receive no positive reinforcement, regardless of his or her behavior. With the use of extinction, no specific behavior on the part of the feeder is required. The only requirement is that the feeder pay no attention to a specific behavior; that is, the feeder acts totally unaware that the child is engaged in the behavior. Extinction is not based on time and does not rule out the possibility of providing reinforcement for desirable responses.

While extinction seems on the surface to be a simple and straightforward concept, it is often ineffective in the treatment of feeding disorders. Two major difficulties are encountered when ignoring is used. First, it is usually impossible for a parent or feeder to ignore a behavior completely. The slightest bit of annoyance or distress shown on a parent's face while attempting to ignore a feeding behavior may be enough reinforcement for the child to insure that the behavior continues. Second, if ignoring is chosen as a treatment procedure, the parent or feeder must be willing to go all the way with the ignoring and not attend to the behavior even though it may increase in frequency or intensity (Drabman & Jarvie, 1977). A good example of this point is the child who gags when he or she eats foods that he or she does not like. Gagging may serve to increase attention from his or her mother and result in his or her being excused from eating any more of the nonpreferred food. It would be a logical treatment to suggest that this mother tell her child to eat the nonpreferred food and then to totally ignore his or her subsequent gagging. It is likely that the child will increase his or her gagging in response to his or her mother's ignoring and may even do so to the extent that he or she induces vomiting, a response which would be very difficult for his or her mother to ignore. The danger is that the child will learn that vomiting, not gagging, serves to increase mother's attention and remove the demand to eat nonpreferred foods.

In summary, while ignoring is a simple procedure conceptually, it is a very difficult procedure to conduct and should be used only in limited situations. Kanner (1957) warns against the use of ignoring, reasoning that the mother's (parent) underlying inability to ignore her child's behavior may be a major contributor to the problem in the first place. In my experience, this certainly is true, and it is much better to recommend a more active rather than passive treatment role for parents, especially if the treatment is to be conducted in the home and will not be directly supervised by a professional.

SHAPING. Shaping, or the method of successive approximations, is used to teach new behaviors that are not presently in the child's repertoire of responses. In a shaping procedure, the behavior to be taught is broken down into its components. The frequency or probability of each of the components is then increased through contingent reinforcement in a sequential manner, beginning with the component most removed from the final behavior and ending with the component that is the final stage of the total behavior.

The first task when planning to use a shaping procedure is to define the specific behavior to be taught and then specify the various components of that behavior. As an example, if spoon feeding pudding is the behavior to be taught, it would be composed of the following components. The child must be seated at the table with pudding and spoon placed in front of him or her. Then the child's hand must come in contact with the spoon, pick up the spoon, place the spoon into the pudding, elevate the spoon with pudding, and bring to the mouth. Then the child must open his or her mouth and insert the pudding, remove the pudding, remove the spoon from his or her mouth, chew and swallow the pudding. Treatment would proceed as follows. The child would be reinforced for sitting at the table only; then reinforcement would be withheld until he or she is at the table and touching the spoon. When he or she is consistently sitting at the table and touching the spoon, reinforcement is withheld until he or she picks up the spoon, and so on, until reinforcement is given only for the successful completion of the entire behavior resulting in the pudding being swallowed.

My colleagues and I used a modification of the shaping procedure to teach the acceptance of spoon feeding to a severely retarded 3-year-old (Linscheid et al., 1978). Prior to treatment, the child ate only from a bottle. Attempts to place anything other than a bottle with nipple near his mouth resulted in screaming, kicking, and the placing of his hands within his mouth. A procedure was developed in which the child was reinforced by brief access to the bottle for not tantrumming or placing his fingers in his mouth. The spoon was gradually brought closer to the child's mouth as a series of preplanned steps until he was required to allow it to touch his lips before reinforcement was delivered. Leibowitz and Holcer (1974) had previously used a similar procedure to teach spoon acceptance to a 5-year-old child.

FADING OF MANUAL GUIDANCE. With children, this procedure, often called fading, has been used most frequently to train proper self-feeding skills (Azrin & Armstrong, 1973; Berkowitz, et al., 1971; O'Brien, Bugle, & Azrin, 1972). The procedure involves the feeder manually guiding the child through the entire and complete behavior to be learned

and then gradually withdrawing his or her physical control. The withdrawal of control begins at the end of the behavior and is removed in a backward manner until only a slight physical prompt is needed to initiate the entire behavioral response.

Berkowitz et al. (1971) used this procedure to teach spoon feeding to seven retarded boys. The steps to be followed in conducting the procedure were spelled out as follows:

1. Aide, holding child's hand with spoon in child's hand, makes entire feeding cycle, from plate (scooping food) to mouth and back to plate.

2. Aide makes entire feeding cycle but partially releases child's hand (still holding spoon with food on it) 2–3 inches below the child's mouth. Child lifts spoon the last few inches by himself.

3. Aide releases child's hand approximately six inches from child's mouth. Child lifts spoon about six inches.

4. Aide scoops food, releases child's hand at plate level. Child lifts spoon from plate to mouth.

5. Aide brings child's hand to plate, releasing hand. Child scoops food and lifts spoon to mouth.

6. Aide releases hand after child has emptied spoon. Child brings spoon down to plate, scoops food, and lifts to mouth.

7. Child executes entire self-feeding cycle by himself. (p. 64)

The progress through the steps is determined by the child's response and is usually based on a preset number of correct responses at each level. It is often necessary to backtrack if the child is unable or unwilling to carry out the requirements of the next level. The procedure does require skill in the systematic withdrawal of control by the trainer and unless this is carefully monitored the results can be that the child effectively trains the trainer to do it for him or her (i.e., feed him or her).

An integrated procedure using fading and a mini-meal concept was developed by Azrin and Armstrong (1973). They proposed the use of the fading procedures conducted during short but frequent meals. The mini-meal was developed to provide more opportunities for training and to insure that motivation to eat remains high since the child is never allowed to eat a large quantity at any one meal. Azrin and Armstrong reported that retarded individuals were taught to self-feed in five days.

While fading is a useful and effective procedure for teaching self-feeding skills, it does not guarantee that the child will self-feed properly after training has been accomplished. O'Brien et al. (1972) described the case of a 6-year-old retarded girl who, despite successfully learning to use a spoon, reverted to finger feeding. They found that a motivational system was needed in addition to the manual guidance to insure that the girl continued to use the spoon. This is an important point to be considered in the original plan for teaching self-feeding skills.

Considerations in Selecting Behavioral Procedures

It can be seen that there is a variety of behavioral techniques that have been applied to the direct treatment of eating problems in the feeding situation. The problem, of course, is to select the proper technique for the specific problem in question. It is almost always the case that modifications in the basic procedures will have to be made to accommodate the unique requirements of the individual child's problem. In general, when teaching a new skill (e.g., spoon use), fading and shaping are the most frequently used procedures. When an existing behavior needs to be modified in rate or topography, then positive reinforcement and time-out procedures are often more appropriate.

It is important to consider who will be conducting the treatment, where it will be conducted, and what procedures will be introduced to insure follow-up and maintenance.

Problems Related to Intake

Childhood Obesity

The incidence of obesity in childhood is not well established because of lack of agreement on operational definitions and cut-off points used in weight or weight-to-height comparisons. Bakwin and Bakwin (1972) avoid the issue by simply stating that obesity is common, while Brownell and Stunnkard (1978) estimate the incidence to be as high as 25 percent. In an excellent review, Coates and Thoresen (1978) conclude that childhood obesity is a serious problem for three reasons. First, obese children are more likely to be obese adults. Second, there are increased medical risks associated with obesity. And, third, obese children and adolescents suffer from psychological and social problems in the areas of peer acceptance, discrimination from adults, disturbed body image and self-concept, and have a greater incidence of personality and character disorders than do normal weight peers.

There can be many causes of obesity in children. While no clear genetic relationship has been established, it has been shown that if one parent is obese the incidence of obesity in children increases to 40–50 percent and, if both parents are obese, the incidence of obesity in their children has been estimated to be as high as 70–80 percent. Obesity has been associated with developmental disorders such as Prader-Willi syndrome, Klinefelter's syndrome, cretinism, spina bifida, and some forms of cerebral palsy (Heins, 1978).

A more recent theory maintains that overfeeding in infancy leads to an increase in the number of and sizes of fat cells, leading to obesity later due to the increased need to eat more to feed the excess number of cells (Hirsch, 1975). Coates and Thoresen (1978) warn that as yet this theory of obesity is still theory and needs much more substantiation before it can be accepted as fact. They suggest that to accept this theory before it has been proven would naturally lead one to give up attempting to treat obesity since the fate of the obese individual would have been sealed in infancy.

A leading exponent of a psychogenic cause for some forms of obesity is Bruch (1957). She describes three groups of obese children. The first includes those children who are just large as a result of the normal variation in weight in the population. The second group contains those children whose obesity occurs in reaction to upsetting or traumatic events such as death of a close relative, school failure, or a serious medical condition. The third group of obese children are described as having a disturbed way of life that involves the whole family as well as the child. Bruch characterizes these families as having domineering, hard-driving mothers and quiet, acquiescent fathers. These mothers overfeed and overprotect their children in an effort to win their allegiance within a family structure that is characterized by discord and quarreling. The children come to regard eating as synonomous with nurturance and protection and increase their feeling of security through food. Bruch hypothesizes that many obese children are unwanted and that the mother's emphasis on feeding is an aspect of her guilt feelings, trying to make up for withheld affection by giving affection through food.

More recently, behaviorally oriented therapists have become involved in the treatment of obesity, initially with adults but most recently with children. While behavior therapists are not as concerned with the underlying reasons for obesity as psychodynamically oriented therapists would be, they reason that the two most direct causes of obesity, overintake of food and lack of exercise, do have a habit component to them, and thus can be modified by using behavioral procedures (Coates & Thoresen, 1978).

Treatment of obesity in children can best be described in two categories: direct and indirect. Indirect treatments are those that address underlying factors thought to be causes of obesity. It is assumed that if the underlying causes of obesity are alleviated, then weight loss will naturally occur.

INDIRECT TREATMENT.   Using Bruch's (1957) groupings of obese children, let us first consider the child whose obesity is reactive. If it is the case that the child's obesity is a reaction to a traumatic event or condition, then therapy may be directed toward the alleviation of the effects of the traumatic event or situation. (For a comparison, see Friedman & Russ, chap. 41, "Psyhcotherapy with Children," in this book.) For example, a play ther-apy approach may be used to assist a child in resolving and expressing his or her feelings about the death of a sibling or parent. Likewise, a reassessment of educational placement with a subsequent change of placement may make it possible for a child to experience academic and social success. Parental counseling aimed at increasing the parents' ability to help a child deal with the normal stresses of childhood may be helpful as well.

For Bruch's third group, those children who are overweight because of a disturbed family situation, a family therapy model would seem most appropriate. There are really no data, however, to suggest which specific form of traditional psychotherapy may be most effective in attempting to treat childhood obesity through the approach of therapeutic intervention for the child's disturbed family situation.

There are two major drawbacks to the indirect approach to childhood obesity. First, it is not always clear that emotional problems seen in children are the cause or the effect of the obsesity. One author (Mayer, 1966) believes that psychopathology is often the effect of obesity rather than the cause. It is certainly as logical to view a child's loss of peer relationships as a response to his or her obesity as it is to view the loss of friends as the cause of his or her obesity. The cause-effect question should be carefully thought out before the decision to treat the obesity indirectly is made. Second, there is no guarantee that the child will automatically lose weight, even if an indirect treatment is successful. Habits and food preferences learned while the child is obese are not easily changed, even if the desire to lose weight is strong and genuine.

DIRECT TREATMENT.   At present, the most promising direct approach to the reduction of weight in obese children is through behavior modification procedures originally developed for use with adults (cf. Rickard & Elkins, chap. 40, "Behavior Therapy," in this book). While there are now a significant number of studies documenting weight loss in obese children using behavior modification procedures (Brownell & Stunkard, 1978), the amount of weight loss has been small and the long term maintenance of weight reduction has not been demonstrated (Foreyt & Goodrick, 1981).

The major components of the behavioral approach have been described by Brownell and Stunkard (1978) and will be summarized below. Many of the procedures used in behavioral weight loss programs are the same as or similar to those used with adults.

SELF-MONITORING.   The child is required to write down or in some other way record daily his or her food intake and its caloric value and weight, his or her activity level and any occurrences that are felt to affect his or her moods or intake. Often the child would be asked to record other factors such as time of day that each food was eaten, who was present, where the food was eaten, and how the child felt at the time.

STIMULUS CONTROL.   One result of self-monitoring is the documentation of where the child eats, with whom he or she eats, and how he or she is feeling. The assumption is that if he or she frequently eats in a specific location (eg. in front of the TV), then that location will come to acquire the property of eliciting the desire to eat. With the knowledge gained from self-monitoring, stimulus situations that lead the child to eat can be identified and then avoided or changed so that they no longer elicit the desire to eat.

FAMILY INTERVENTION.   There is some evidence to suggest that parental involvement in a child's weight loss program is beneficial (Epstein et al., 1980). This certainly is a logical conclusion, and the participation and support of one or both parents seem of utmost importance when treating an obese child.

SLOWING THE ACT OF EATING.   Most obese adults eat faster than nonobese adults. This pattern has recently been documented in children as well (Drabman, Hammer, & Jarvie, 1977). Drabman et al. (1977) also observed that obese children chewed less than nonobese children. In order to slow the speed of eating, several techniques have been employed. One such technique involves having the child set

his or her utensils down between bites. Another technique requires the counting of each bite. A third technique introduces a delay of a set amount of time between helpings. Slower eating allows the initial absorption of food to send physiological messages of fullness before all the food is eaten.

REINFORCEMENT.   Reinforcement for weight loss or for behaviors incompatible with overeating constitutes a major component of most programs. This is easily accomplished with children because it is usually easy to identify and deliver reinforcers. Older children should be included in designing their own reinforcement system.

COGNITIVE RESTRUCTURING.   This is a form of self-control in which more productive thoughts or feelings are controlled through supplying the child with legitimate counterarguments. For example, a child who relates that he or she often says to himself or herself "I'll never be able to lose 20 pounds" may be instructed to say "My goal this week is only one pound. I can make that." Cognitive restructuring requires that the child be able to identify his or her own internal statements and be able to verbalize them accurately. For this reason, this technique may be more useful with the older child.

It can be seen that in order to use the behavioral approach to obesity effectively in children, the therapist must learn a great deal about the child's eating patterns and cognitive style. Two instruments have been developed to assist in assessing the situational control of eating. They are the Eating Analysis and Treatment Schedule (EATS), developed by Coates and Thoresen (1980), and the Food Intake Record (FIR), developed by Wheeler and Hess (1976). In addition to these instruments, which are used by the child himself or herself, direct observation of the child's eating skills and patterns is necessary. Substantial interviewing to determine the child's knowledge of calorie-exercise relationships and his or her cognitive control style is also important.

A recent article (Cohen et al., 1980) reported that maintaining weight loss is directly related to degree of self-regulation and amount of exercise. Those children who regained weight had more parental involvement (less self-regulation) in weight management than did normal children. These results suggest that self-regulation via self-monitoring and cognitive restructuring and the increase of physical exercise are significant factors to be stressed in treatment of obesity in children.

Failure to Thrive

Failure to thrive (FTT) is a syndrome of infants and children defined as physical growth failure in the absence of known medical causes. Diagnosis is made by ruling out medical causes of growth retardation and by verifying that the infant falls substantially (usually defined as two standard deviations) below the average weight and height for his or her age. Failure to thrive can extend into childhood. However, it is usually considered a syndrome of infancy and is described more extensively in Phyllis R. Magrab and Anita M. Sostek, "Clinical Problems of Birth, The Neonate and Infant" (chap. 12 of this book).

In children, the failure to gain weight in the absence of medical causes is usually ascribed to a disturbed parent-child interaction process or to a form of childhood depression (Bakwin & Bakwin, 1972). Palmer and Kim (1978) feel that an interdisciplinary team made up of a nutritionist, physician, social worker, psychologist, and public health nurse is essential to the successful treatment of FTT and should be involved from the very beginning of treatment. In light of the medical, social, and psychological components of this syndrome, their suggestion of the team approach seems highly justified.

Rumination

Rumination is the voluntary regurgitation of food or liquid. The food or liquid is either allowed to run from the mouth or is rechewed and reswallowed. It can occur in individuals at any age but seems to be found most often in two separate groups: normal infants between 4 months and 1 year and mentally retarded children and adults. There are reports of normal adult ruminators but these are extremely rare (Kanner, 1957). The incidence of rumina-

tion in infants is extremely low. Flanagan (1977), in reviewing the literature during the 20 years prior to his paper, found only 23 reported cases. The incidence for the mentally retarded population is much higher. For example, Hendricksen and Clayton (1974) found the incidence of ruminative vomiting in California State Hospitals to be 9.3 percent.

Rumination, especially in infants, is a potentially fatal behavior. Kanner (1957) found that, of 53 cases reviewed, 11 had died as a result of malnutrition and other complications directly attributable to rumination.

The diagnosis of rumination is made only after all potential medical explanations for the vomiting have been ruled out. Observation of the child while he or she is ruminating is very important when initially considering the diagnosis. One component of rumination mentioned by several authors is the observable pleasure or self-satisfaction that the infant appears to derive from rumination. Bakwin and Bakwin (1972) observed that the infant "seems to derive considerable pleasure from the activity" (p. 528) and Kanner (1957) states that rumination is "taken up as a pleasurable habit practiced voluntarily" (p. 468). For this reason, observation of the child can help to establish the diagnosis and can differentiate rumination from other sources of psychogenic vomiting that may be caused by stress, desire for attention, or spite (Bakwin & Bakwin, 1972).

Several explanations have been advanced for the cause of rumination in infants. Psychodynamic explanations centered in a disturbed mother-child interaction have been suggested. Lourie (1955) proposed that both overstimulation and increased tension or understimulation in the form of neglect by the mother are associated with rumination. The rumination is caused by the infant's turning to his or her own body for the satisfaction that has not been provided by his or her mother. Richmond, Eddy, and Green (1958) also felt that the cause of rumination is faulty mothering. They describe the mothers of ruminating infants as unable to relate to their babies; fearful of their infant's death; and immature, with an accompanying incapacity to want, accept, and give to their baby. Mental conflicts were often present in the parents of infant ruminators studied by Richmond et al. (1958) as well. A note of caution should be stated at this point. One must be careful when analyzing the interaction between mother and infant not to confuse cause and effect. It is important to keep in mind that the interaction between mother and infant can be significantly changed due to the prolonged occurrence of ruminating with resulting hospitalization. What would be the normal response of a mother whose infant is in a serious medical condition due to excessive self-initiated vomiting of unknown cause? It can not be assumed that a pattern of reaction to a highly stressful situation is evidence of the cause of that situation.

Behaviorally oriented authors have suggested that the basic causes of rumination for both infants and the mentally retarded are pleasurable self-stimulation and the attention that the behavior may elicit from others (Linscheid & Cunningham, 1977; Sheinbein, 1975). With this explanation, the crucial variable is not psychopathology itself but the resultant lack of attention that may be given to the infant as a result. Any situation leading to reduced stimulation or attention can lead to the development of rumination. In one case that I treated (Cunningham & Linscheid, 1976), rumination began during a one-week period when the infant's family was moving to a new location. The infant's mother reported that the infant was left alone more often than usual during that week because the mother was busy assisting with the move. Once the act of ruminating begins, it may be maintained by its pleasant, self-stimulatory properties and become a habit. Kanner (1957) recognized this possible etiology when he stated: "Whatever the primary occasion may have been, the habit nature of the act can hardly be questioned" (p. 468).

The behavioral explanation is applicable to rumination in the mentally retarded population as well. Certainly the incidence of self-stimulatory behavior is higher in this population and the sufficient condition of decreased stimulation is present in institutional setttings

Treatment based on the psychodynamic view of rumination involves providing the infant with a warm, caring, and stimulating environment, often requiring a mother substitute. In addition, psychotherapy for the mother or parents is often recommended. Richmond et al. (1958) and Berlin et al. (1957) both report successful treatment using this approach. Berlin et al. (1957) treated a 4-year-old child over an eight-month period of hospitalization with concommitant psychotherapy for his parents.

Behavioral treatment of rumination has employed aversive procedures with a great deal of success. Lang and Melamed (1969) were the first to use electric shock as an aversive stimulus and were successful in eliminating rumination in an infant within nine days of treatment. Subsequently, other authors have reported comparable success with infants over short periods using mild electric shock as the aversive stimulus (Cunningham & Linscheid, 1976; Linscheid & Cunningham, 1977; Toister et al., 1975). The procedure has been used with mentally retarded ruminators as well (Luckey, Watson, Musick, 1968).

As an alternative to electric shock, Sajwaj, Libet, and Agras (1974) successfully used lemon juice squirted into the child's mouth contingent upon rumination. Recently, working with retarded adolescents, Rast et al. (1981) experimentally demonstrated that there was a relationship between quantity of food consumed at a meal and the frequency of rumination. When his subjects were allowed to eat as much as they pleased, the rate of rumination decreased. This is a promising avenue of investigation.

To this point, there is no adequate follow-up data in the literature to provide or disprove any long term effects of aversive therapy procedures for the treatment of rumination. Short term follow-up suggests that there are no harmful carryover effects and that infants did not develop new symptoms (Linscheid & Cunningham, 1977). In the absence of successful treatment by less restrictive procedures, the possibility of aversive procedures should be considered, especially when rumination becomes life threatening.

Pica

Pica is the name given to the ingestion of inedible substances. Mouthing and occasional swallowing of nonfood items are common in all children before they begin to walk but usually disappear spontaneously. In children who engage in pica after they begin walking, the habit is especially difficult to break (Bakwin & Bakwin, 1972). The dangers from pica do not derive from the act itself but from the type of substances consumed. Common substances ingested are paint, soot, chalk, dirt, plaster, and cloth. In certain parts of the country, it is not uncommon for individuals to ingest substantial quantities of various types of clay. One study found that 16 percent of the children in a rural area in Georgia engaged in eating clay or soil (Vermeer & Frate, 1979).

The most serious result of pica is the potential for lead poisoning, which occurs when substances such as paint or plaster are consumed. Lead poisoning can lead to neurological impairment and mental retardation. The incidence of pica-related lead poisoning is much higher in children from lower socioeconomic levels who are more likely to be living in older homes where lead-based paint is readily available (de la Burde & Reames, 1973).

Two approaches to the reduction of pica-related lead poisoning are possible. The first approach is the elimination of the potential for lead ingestion by removing the sources of lead in the child's environment. Most urban communities do have programs to warn parents of these dangers; however, it will be some time before most, if not all, sources of environmental lead are removed.

The second approach is to eliminate or reduce pica, with the result of eliminating or reducing lead ingestion. Some authors feel that this is best accomplished by enriching the child's physical and emotional environment and report successful treatment of pica resulting from amelioration of social and emotional deprivation (Milligan & Lourie, 1970). Madden, Russo, and Cataldo (1980) point out that there is little research data to support the effectiveness of the empirical approach. They report the results of a study designed to investigate experimentally the relationship between pica, environmental objects, and amount of stimulation. They report that pica occurred significantly more often in impoverished environments and that the child's involvement with materials (play time) was negatively correlated with pica. This is the first objective data relating pica to impoverished environments and suggests that enrichment of environments may indeed be an appropriate treatment for pica. Much more research is needed in this area.

REFERENCES

AAP Committee on Nutrition. Commentary on breast-feeding and infant formulas, including proposed standards for formulas. *Pediatrics,* 1976, **57**(2), 278–285.

Azrin, N.H., & Armstrong, P.M. The "mini-meal"—a method for teaching eating skills to the profoundly retarded. *Mental Retardation,* 1973, **11**(1), 9–13.

Bakwin, H., & Bakwin, R.M. *Behavior disorder in children.* Philadelphia: Saunders, 1972.

Ball, T.S., Hendricksen, H., & Clayton, J. A special feeding for chronic regurgitation. *American Journal of Mental Deficiency,* 1974, **74**(4), 486–493.

Barton, E.S., Guess, D., Garcia, E., & Baer, D.M. Improvement of retardates' mealtime behaviors by time-out procedures using multiple baseline techniques. *Journal of Applied Behavior Analysis,* 1970, **3,** 77–84.

Berkowitz, S., Sherry, P.J., & Davis, B.A. Teaching self-feeding skills to profound retardates using reinforcement and fading procedures. *Behavior Therapy,* 1971, **2,** 62–67.

Berlin, I.N., McCullough, G., Lisha, E.S., & Szurek, S. Intractable episodic vomiting in a three year old child. *Psychiatric Quarterly,* 1957, **31,** 228–249.

Bernal, M.E. Behavioral treatment of a child's eating problem. *Journal of Behavior Therapy and Experimental Psychiatry,* 1972, **3,** 43–50.

Bernick, S.M. What the pediatrician should know about children's teeth. *Clinical Pediatrics,* 1971, **10,** 243–244.

Birch, L.L. Dimensions of preschool children's food preferences. *Journal of Nutrition Education,* 1979, **11**(2), 77–80.

Birch, L.L. The relationship between children's

food preferences and those of their parents. *Journal of Nutrition Education,* 1980, **12**(1), 14–18.

Brazelton, T.B. *Infants and mothers.* New York: Dell, 1969.

Brownell, K.D., & Stunkard, A.J. Behavioral treatment of obesity in children. *American Journal of Diseases in Children,* 1978, **132,** 403–412.

Bruch, H. *The importance of overweight.* New York: Norton, 1957.

Christophersen, E.R., & Hall, C.L. Eating patterns and associated problems encountered in normal children. *Issues in Comprehensive Pediatric Nursing,* 1978, **3,** 1–16.

Coates, T.J., & Thoresen, C.E. Treating obesity in children and adolescents: A review. *American Journal of Public Health,* 1978, **68,** 143–151.

Coates, T.J., & Thoresen, C.E. Treating obesity in children and adolescents: Is there any hope? In J.M. Ferguson & C.B. Taylor (Eds.), *Advances in behavioral medicine.* Englewood, N.J.: Spectrum, 1980.

Cohen, E.A., Gelfand, D.M., Dodd, D.K., Jensen, J., & Turner, C. Self-control practices associated with weight loss maintenance in children and adolescents. *Behavior Therapy,* 1980, **11,** 26–37.

Cunningham, C.E., & Barkley, R.A. The interaction of hyperactive and normal children with their mothers in free play and structured task. *Child Development,* 1979, **50,** 217–224.

Cunningham, C.E., & Linscheid, T.R. Elimination of chronic infant ruminating by electric shock. *Behavior Therapy,* 1976, **7,** 231–234.

de la Burde, B., & Reames, B. Prevention of pica, the major cause of lead poisoning in children. *American Journal of Public Health,* 1973, **63,** 737–743.

Drabman, R.S., & Jarvie, G. Counseling parents of children with behavior problems: The use of extinction and time-out techniques. *Pediatrics,* 1977, **59**(1), 78–85.

Drabman, R.S., Hammer, D., & Jarvie, G.J. Eating styles of obese and nonobese black and white children in a naturalistic setting. *Addictive Behaviors,* 1977, **2,** 83–86.

Ekvall, S. Assessment of nutrition status. In Palmer, S. & Edvall, S. (Eds.), *Pediatric nutrition in developmental disorders.* Springfield, Ill.: Thomas, 1978.

Epstein, L.H., Wing, R.R., Steranchak, L., Dick-son, B., & Michelson, J. Comparison of family-based behavior modification and nutrition education for childhood obesity. *Journal of Pediatric Psychology,* 1980, **5**(1), 25–35.

Flanagan, C.H. Rumination in infancy—Past and present. *American Academy of Psychiatric Services for Children,* 1977, **38,** 140–149.

Foreyt, J.P., & Goodrick, G.K. Childhood obesity. In E.J. Mash & L.G. Terdal (Eds.), *Behavioral assessment of childhood disorders.* New York: Guilford, 1981.

Freud, A. *The psychoanalytical treatment of children: Lectures and essays.* New York: Schochen, 1964. (Originally published, 1946.)

Heins, J.N. Obesity in children. In Palmer, S. & Ekvall, S. (Eds.), *Pediatric nutrition in developmental disorders.* Springfield, Ill.: Thomas, 1978.

Hersen, M., & Bellack, A.S. (Eds.). *Behavioral assessment: A practical handbook.* New York: Pergamon, 1976.

Hirsch, J. Cell number and size as a determinant of subsequent obesity. In M. Winick (Ed.), *Childhood obesity.* New York: Wiley, 1975.

Hoekelman, R.A., Blatman, S., Brunell, P.A., Friedman, S.B., & Seidel, H.M. (Eds.), *Principles of pediatrics: Health care of the young.* New York: McGraw-Hill, 1978.

Illingworth, R.S., & Lister, J. The critical or sensitive period, with special reference to certain feeding problems in infants and children. *Journal of Pediatrics,* 1964, **65,** 834–851.

Jackson, R.L., Westerfield, R., Flynn, M., Kimbal, E.R., & Lewis, R.B. Growth of "well-born" human infants fed human and cow's milk. *Pediatrics,* 1964, **33,** 642–652.

Kanner, L. *Child psychiatry* (3rd ed.). Springfield, Ill.: Thomas, 1957.

Kessler, J.W. *Psychopathology of childhood.* Engelwood Cliffs, N.J.: Prentice-Hall, Inc., 1966.

Kohlenberg, R.J. The punishment of persistent vomiting: A case study. *Journal of Applied Behavior Analysis,* 1970, **3,** 241–245.

Lang, P.J., & Melamed, B.G. Avoidance conditioning therapy of an infant with chronic ruminative vomiting. *Journal of Abnormal Psychology,* 1969, **74,** 139–142.

Leibowitz, J.M., & Holcer, P. Increasing food variety and texture. *The American Journal of Occupational Therapy,* 1974, **28,** 545–548.

Linscheid, T.R. Disturbances in eating and feeding. In P. Magrab (Ed.), *Psychological management of pediatric problems.* Baltimore: University Park Press, 1978.

Linscheid, T.R., & Cunningham, C.E. A controlled demonstration of the effectiveness of electric shock in the elimination of chronic infant rumination. *Journal of Applied Behavior Analysis,* 1977, **10**, 500.

Linscheid, T.R., Oliver, J., Blyler, E., & Palmer, S. Brief hospitalization for the behavioral treatment of feeding problems in the developmentally disabled. *Journal of Pediatric Psychology,* 1978, **3**, 72–76.

Lourie, R.S. Treatment of psychosomatic problems in infants. *Clinical Procedures in Children's Hospitals,* 1955, **2**, 142–151.

Luckey, R.E., Watson, C.M., & Musick, J.N. Aversive conditioning as a means of inhibiting vomiting and rumination. *American Journal of Mental Deficiency,* 1968, **73**, 139–142.

Madden, N., Russo, D.C., & Cataldo, M.F. Environmental influences on mouthing in children with lead intoxication. *Journal of Pediatric Psychology,* 1980, **5**, 207–216.

Magrab, P.R. (Ed.). *Psychological management of pediatric problems* (Vols. I & II.). Baltimore: University Park Press, 1978.

Martin, D., & McLaughlin, T.F. Contingency contracting at home by parents to increase weight and eating behavior of a child. *Psychological Reports,* 1975, **36**, 622.

Mash, E., Terdal, L., & Anderson, K. The response class matrix: A procedure for recording parent-child interactions. *Journal of Consulting and Clinical Psychology,* 1973, **40**, 163.

Mayer, J. Some aspects of the problem of regulation of food intake and obesity. *New England Journal of Medicine,* 1966, **274**, 610–616.

McNett, I. Psychologists in medical settings. *American Psychological Association Monitor,* 1981. **12**(8, 9), 12–13, 66–68.

Milligan, F.K. & Lourie, R.S. The child with pica and his family. In E. Anthony & E. Koupernik (Eds.), *The child in the family.* New York: Wiley, 1970.

Moss, A.J., & Moss, T.J. *The essentials of pediatrics: The clinical core in outline.* Philadelphia: Lippincott, 1980.

Moss, H.A. Sex, age and state as determinants of mother-infant interaction. *Merrill-Palmer Quarterly,* 1967, **13**, 19–36.

Moustakas, C.E., Segel, I.E., & Schalock, H.D. An objective method for the measurement and analysis of adult-child interaction. *Child Development,* 1956, **27**, 109–134.

O'Brien, F., & Azrin, N.H. Developing proper mealtime behaviors of the institutionalized retarded. *Journal of Applied Behavior Analysis,* 1972, **5**, 389–399.

O'Brien, F., Bugle, C., & Azrin, N.H. Training and maintaining a retarded child's proper eating. *Journal of Applied Behavior Analysis,* 1972, **5**, 67–72.

Palmer, S., & Horn, S. Feeding problems in children. In S. Palmer & S. Ekvall (Eds.), *Pediatric nutrition in developmental disorders.* Springfield, Ill.: Thomas, 1978.

Palmer, S., & Kim, M. Failure to thrive. In S. Palmer & S. Ekvall (Eds.) *Pediatric nutrition in developmental disorders.* Springfield, Ill.: Thomas, 1978.

Palmer, S., Thompson, R.J., Jr., & Linscheid, T.R. Applied behavior analysis in the treatment of childhood feeding problems. *Developmental Medicine and Child Neurology,* 1975, **17**, 333–339.

Rast, J., Johnston, J.M., Drum, C., & Conrin, J. The relation of food quantity to rumination behavior. *Journal of Applied Behavior Analysis,* 1981, **14**, 121–130.

Richmond, J.B., Eddy, E., & Green, M. Rumination: A psychosomatic syndrome of infancy. *Pediatrics,* 1958, **22**, 49–55.

Riordan, M.M., Iwata, B.A., Wohl, M.K., & Finney, J.W. Behavioral treatment of food refusal and selectivity in developmentally disabled children. *Applied Research in Mental Retardation,* 1980, **1**, 95–112.

Rothbart, M.K., & Maccoby, E.E. Parent's differential reaction to sons and daughters. *Journal of Personality and Social Psychology,* 1966, **4**, 237–243.

Sajwaj, T., Libet, J., & Agras, S. Lemon juice therapy: The control of life threatening rumination in a six month old infant. *Journal of Applied Behavior Analysis,* 1974, **7**(4), 557–563.

Schwartz, A.S. Eating problems. *Pediatric Clinics of North America,* 1958, **5**, 595–611.

Sheinbein, M. Treatment for the hospitalized infant ruminator. *Clinical Pediatrics,* 1975, **14**(8), 719–724.

Smith, D.W. *Introduction to clinical pediatrics.* Philadelphia: Saunders, 1977.

Thomas, A., Chess, S., & Birch, H. *Temperament*

and behavior disorders in children. New York: New York University Press, 1968.

Thompson, G.A., Jr., Iwata, B.A., & Poynter, H. Operant control of pathological tongue thrust in spastic cerebral palsy. *Journal of Applied Behavior Analysis,* 1979, **12,** 325–333.

Thompson, R.J., Jr. Applied behavior analysis in the treatment of mealtime tantrums and delay in self-feeding in a multi-handicapped child. *Journal of Clinical Child Psychology,* 1977, **6,** 52–54.

Thompson, R.J., Jr., & Linscheid, T.R. Adult child interaction analysis: Methodology and case application. *Child Psychiatry and Human Development,* 1976, 7(1), 719–724.

Thompson, R.J., Jr., & Palmer, S. Treatment of feeding problems—A behavioral approach. *Journal of Nutrition Education,* 1974, **6,** 63–66.

Thompson, R.J., Jr., Palmer, S., & Linscheid, T.R. Single subject design and interaction analysis in the behavioral treatment of a child with a feeding problem. *Child Psychiatry and Human Development,* 1977, **8,** 43–53.

Toister, R.P., Colin, J., Worley, L.M., & Arthur, D. Farodic therapy of chronic vomiting in infancy. A case study. *Journal of Behavior Therapy and Experimental Psychiatry,* 1975, 6(1), 55–59.

Vermeer, D.E., Frate, D.A. Geophagia in rural Mississippi: Environmental and cultural contexts and nutritional implications. *The American Journal of Clinical Nutrition,* 1979, **32,** 2129–2135.

Wheeler, M.E., & Hess, K.W. Treatment of juvenile obesity by successive approximation control of eating. *Journal of Behavior Therapy and Psychiatry,* 1976, **7,** 235–241.

CHAPTER 26

Mental Retardation

CHARLES CARR CLELAND

A continuum of reproductive failure exists, and, depending on the magnitude as well as the time of occurrence, various things happen to the developing human (Knobloch & Lilienfeld, 1956). If defects in egg and sperm are notable, life ends during the germinal stage. At lesser levels of trauma or insult, the pregnancy may terminate during the embryonic or fetal stage. A still lesser degree of reproductive failure may occasion a live birth, but the person will expire within minutes or hours. In this latter instance, some are what are termed medical monstrosities (anencephalics, cyclops, etc.). These are the mentally retarded that few individuals ever see, but specimens do exist in certain medical museums. Since the estimated ratio at conception is 125–135 males to 100 females and at birth has declined to between 120:100 or 100:100, it is obvious that most of the unborn or stillborn are males (Masland, 1958). For the retarded who do survive, males will outnumber females (Cleland, 1978, 1979).

MENTAL RETARDATION: CURRENT DEFINITION

Although many who succumb in prenatal life or at birth would undoubtedly be mentally retarded, our focal interest is with the living population of the retarded. As we note later in this chapter, there are many causes of mental retardation that occur pre-, peri-, or postnatally. Before examining the historical roots of mental retardation, a definition of the subject of this chapter is in order. "Mental retardation refers to significantly subaverge general intellectual functioning existing concurrently with deficits in adaptive behavior, and manifested during the developmental period" (Grossman, 1977, p. 11).

In the above definition, *adaptive behavior* refers to "the effectiveness or degree with which the individual meets the standards of personal independence and social responsibility expected of his age and cultural group," and the *developmental period* encompasses conception to age 18. In this latest definition provided by the American Association on Mental Deficiency's Committee on Classification and Terminology, both criteria of significantly subaverage general intellectual functioning and significantly subaverage adaptive behavior must be met in order to classify a person as mentally retarded. Psychometrically speaking, significantly subaverage means two or more standard deviations below the population mean of 100 as revealed through individually administered, standardized intelligence tests.

ANTIQUITY TO THE PRESENT

Let us examine certain aspects of the history of mental retardation and the retarded person's status in today's society. Mental retardation undoubtedly has existed since prehistoric times but our earliest *evidence* dates only to pre-Dynastic Egypt. In their x-ray examinations of ancient Egyptian mummies, Harris and Weeks (1973) found certain skeletal anom-

640

alies that are frequently, though not always, associated with mental retardation. The ubiquity of mental retardation across temporal and cultural periods is also noted in the pre-Columbian civilizations of the Mayas, Incas, and Aztecs (Guerra, 1971). These early writings mentioned epilepsy, which is sometimes associated with mental retardation. Polsky, Lippman, and Overton (1965) examined a variety of clay figures dating into the pre-Columbian era and their pooled medical judgment of these vessels in the form of humans yielded syphillis and von Recklinghausen's disease—both often associated etiologically with mental retardation. These vessels in the form of human anomalies suggested to these physicians that they were employed in teaching medicine or that they were of religious import.

In ancient Mediterranean civilizations, the Greek city-state of Sparta practiced infanticide on their unfit, and this practice persisted into Roman times. However, as Baumeister and Butterfield (1970) note, certain of the dull were kept by wealthy Romans for amusement—a practice that occurred in Europe for centuries.

Medieval times witnessed no better times for the retarded since a number of influential churchmen considered them possessed by evil spirits. Various "remedies," mainly beatings, were tried in an effort to exorcise the devils within them (Baumeister & Butterfield, 1970). By the advent of the medieval period, prisons and institutions for the mentally ill were in evidence, and many of Europe's retarded persons were placed in these facilities along with prostitutes, the mentally ill, and convicts. Little distinction between the mentally ill and the retarded was made, and it was not until John Locke (1632–1704) that a serious effort to differentiate these two conditions was made.

The utilization of the retarded as court jesters, fools, and pets by the Romans extended, albeit in slightly different form, well into the twentieth century. Until about 1945, the parallels with Roman practices were seen in the United States in circus sideshows or carnival midways where certain clinical types of the retarded were exhibited for others' amusement. The unique physical characteristics of cretins, hydrocephalics, or gargoyles motivated circus and carnival owners to satisfy public curiosity.

Superstitious thinking, exorcism, and fears of the public toward the retarded began to dissolve with the advent of the Renaissance. However, it is not until the nineteenth century that we see a really systematic attempt to teach a retarded person. The feral child, Victor, was discovered by hunters in the forest of Aveyron in 1799, and the French physician, Jean Itard, undertook the education of this wild, inarticulate 10- or 11-year-old boy. Pinel, the noted French psychiatrist, considered Victor an incurable idiot and warned Itard that education would be an impossibility.

Despite such cautions, Itard proceeded in a five-year project to attempt the mental and moral education of Victor employing what today would be termed behavior modification and other ingenious methods—methods that still retain their currency. The culmination of this five-year experiment resulted in Itard's classic, *The Wild Boy of Aveyron,* which, although only 100 pages in length, has been translated into numerous languages (Itard, 1932).

Itard's pioneering educational strategies, although failing to educate Victor to Itard's original goal of normalcy, did serve to generate a great acceleration of interest in the retarded throughout Europe. It also won him recognition from the French Academy of Science. Equally important was the continuation of Itard's work by his foremost student, Edouard Seguin (1812–1880), whose *Idiocy, Its Treatment by the Physiological Method* won instant acclaim. In this classic, Seguin employed Itard's principles of sensory training and added motor coordination training. Madame Montessori, the famous Italian physician-educator, then added further refinements, and her methods are still widely employed. As Crissy (1975) and Murphy (1949) indicate, Seguin was the greatest figure in the nineteenth century in the training of the mentally retarded, and his work with those considered untrainable earned him the title of "The Apostle of the Idiot." Seguin clearly recognized the importance of nonverbal communications such as eye contact and aversion, olfactory processes, and gestures that were accorded importance in diagnosis and treatment as well. Subsequent to his migration to the United States, he gained notoriety by his espousal of educational methods for the retarded in contrast to the custodial model then in vogue. In 1876, Seguin was elected the first President of the Association of Medical Officers of American Institutions for Idiotic and Feebleminded Persons, which evolved into the American Association on Mental Deficiency—today the foremost professional organization relating to the mentally retarded. Currently there are over 11,000 members of this organization and a major function is dissemination of knowledge through its two journals and monograph series.

The influence of Darwin (1809–1882) was felt in nearly every quarter of the scientific community and his *Origin of Species* (1859) and *The Expression of Emotion in Man and Animals* (1872) also influenced the study of mental retardation. His works led to the development of modern ethological theorizing, a major force in our understanding of nonverbal retarded persons (Paluck & Esser, 1971; Hereford, Cleland, & Fellner, 1973; Tinbergen, 1974). Darwin also attended to imitative processes in monkeys, microcephalic humans, and the exaggerated imitative tendency seen in certain morbid brain states. Imitation learning or modeling is currently employed to a considerable extent in teaching the retarded (McGavern, 1969; Cleland, 1973).

The next luminary that contributed to the assessment and training of the retarded was the father of intelligence testing, Alfred Binet (1857–1911). While his intelligence test (with Theodore Simon) overshadowed his other contributions, his development of mental orthopedics, experimentation with ink blots as projective techniques 20 years before H. Rorschach, research into hypnotism, and the study of children's fears were important in creating renewed interest in teaching the retarded. Binet also contributed a definition of intelligence—"the tendency to take and maintain a definite direction; the capacity to make adaptations for the purpose of attaining a desired end; and the power of auto-criticism" (Terman, 1916, p. 45). Interestingly, nearly every definition of intelligence advanced since Binet's includes adaptiveness as one critical component. Readers interested in Binet's many-faceted interests should consult Silverman and Krenzel (1964) or the very readable *The Experimental Psychology of Alfred Binet* by Pollack and Brenner (1969).

Insofar as the welfare of the mentally retarded is concerned, the first half of the twentieth century was characterized by a relative lack of interest. The two World Wars plus the Great Depression channeled monies into higher priority causes. However, in 1950 the National Association for Retarded Children (now NAR *Citizens*) was founded in Minneapolis, Minnesota. From its founding by a small group of parents of the retarded, the Association has grown to nearly 300,000, and their collective influence on legislation affecting the welfare of the retarded has fostered dramatic improvements in the retarded citizens' quality of life.

From the foregoing, it is evident that the route of the retarded to a quality life has been long and arduous. The culmination of efforts in the United States to provide the retarded with the rights and privileges of other citizens is seen in the passage of Public Law 94–142. This landmark law, called the Education for All Handicapped Children Act, insures a free and appropriate education to all, regardless of the degree and magnitude of the handicap.

This discussion of the historial aspects of the field of mental retardation, although brief, gives some of the more significant events and a glimpse into the fortunes of the retarded. Current authorities on the United States scene in mental retardation include, to mention only a few, William Sloan (now retired), Edward Zigler of Yale University, Norman Ellis of the University of Alabama, George Tarjan of UCLA, Herbert Grossman of UCLA, Gershon Berkson of Chicago, Illinois, and Nancy and Halbert Robinson of The University of Washington.

While the retarded have attained many rights and greatly improved treatment in our society, the enactment of laws will not substitute for basic knowledge. It is necessary at this point in history to have intensified research, especially with the profoundly retarded, so that teachers and other practitioners can know what and how to teach the retarded.

LEVELS, CHARACTERISTICS, AND INCIDENCE OF MENTAL RETARDATION

The latest *Manual on Terminology and Classification in Mental Retardation* (Grossman, 1977) lists four levels of retardation—mild, moderate, severe, and profound. Table 26.1 provides a comparison of several classification systems, ranging from the old American Clinical system to the latest American Association on Mental Deficiency (AAMD) system.

It should be noted that in the latest AAMD revision, the category of borderline has been eliminated. Thus the excision of the IQ range of 69–80 results in a 13.6 percent reduction in the prevalence of retardation when IQ alone is considered (Polloway & Payne, 1975). Psychometrically viewed, most authorities agree with this decision of the AAMD committee on classification, that is, exclusion of the borderlines as retarded.

The measurement of intelligence is, of course, approached by a variety of tests that are well-known to psychologists. The measurement of adaptive behavior is more complex, and psychologists cannot administer measures of adaptive behavior in their offices since the information is what a person routinely does in various settings. The most commonly employed measures of adaptive behavior include the *Vineland Social Maturity Scale* (Doll, 1953); the American Association on Mental Deficiency (AAMD) *Adaptive Behavior Scales* (Nihira et al., 1974); and the *Balthazar Scales of Adaptive Behavior* (Balthazar, 1971). A recent article by Arndt (1981) gives more detailed information on developments in the measurement of adaptive behavior, and an excellent and detailed discussion of the adaptive behavior construct is provided by Meyers, Nihira, and Zetlin (1979). The assessment of social functioning has been aided considerably by Lake, Miles, and Earle's (1973) *Measuring Human Behavior: Tools for the Assessment of Social Functioning,* which systematically reviews 84 different social-functioning measures.

Within the range of intelligence that depicts mental retardation, adaptive behaviors can be illustrated by the *highest* levels of functioning for 3-year-olds at four different intellectual levels—profound, severe, moderate, and mild.

Table 26.1   Comparative Classification Methods

American Clinical Classification*	Educational Classification	AAMD Intellectual Levels	IQ Range**	Mental Age Expectancy	AAMA Levels of Adaptive Behavior
Borderline retardation	Slow learner	Borderline intelligence	69–80	13	
Moron	Educable	Mild	52–68	8–12	I
Imbecile	Trainable	Moderate	36–51	3– 7	II
		Severe	20–35	0– 3	III
Idiot	Life support	Profound	Below 19		IV

Table 26.1 adapted from Cleland, *Mental Retardation: A Develpmental Approach.* Copyright © 1978 by Prentice-Hall. Used with permission of Prentice-Hall.

  *Now obsolete.
 **Stanford-Binet & Cattell.

The 3-year-old *profoundly* retarded may drink from a cup with help, sit unsupported, imitate sounds, and know and nonverbally interact with familiar persons (Grossman, 1977). A *severely* retarded 3-year-old will attempt finger feeding, stand alone or walk unsteadily, utter one or two words, and communicate simple needs. The *moderately* retarded 3-year-old will try to spoon feed self, walk steadily, use four to six words, and play with others for short periods. The *mildly* retarded person of CA 3 can self-feed with spoon, climb stairs but without alternating feet, speak in two- or three-word sentences, and interact with others in simple play activities (Grossman, 1977).

This brief discussion on adaptive behavior and its measurement is intended merely to indicate its importance in the diagnosis of mental retardation. Readers interested in a more in-depth treatment should consult Grossman (1977).

In the medical classification or the etiological approach to retardation, over 200 known causes have been isolated. Time of occurrence is one way of looking at the problem of etiology, i.e., did it occur pre-, peri-, or postnatally? However, the medical classifications in the latest revision of the *Manual* go beyond temporal factors and have grouped the over 200 causes into 10 major categories. These categories and specific illustrative causes within categories are as follows:

1. *Category 0:* mental retardation due to *infections and intoxications.* Included here are congenital syphillis, congenital toxoplasmosis, postnatal cerebral infections (such as bacterial or viral), and other conditions like toxemia of pregnancy, lead poisoning, or other maternal intoxications.

2. *Category I:* MR due to *trauma or physical agent;* encompasses prenatal injuries, mechanical injury at birth, postnatal hypoxia, or postnatal injuries.

3. *Category II:* MR due to *metabolism or nutrition;* includes neuronal lipid storage diseases, carbohydrate disorders (galactosemia, etc.), amino acid disorders (phenylketonuria), nucleotide disorders and mineral disorders, endocrine disorders, and nutritional disorders.

4. *Category III:* MR due to *gross brain disease* (postnatal); includes neurofibromatosis or von Recklinghausen's disease, tuberous sclerosis, Huntington's chorea, and other specific diseases.

5. *Category IV:* MR due to *unknown prenatal influence;* includes anencephaly, Cornelia de Lange syndrome, microcephaly, and hydrocephalus.

6. *Category V:* MR due to *chromosomal abnormality;* includes a variety of syndromes such as Down's syndrome (mongolism), *cri-du-chat,* Klinefelter's, Turner's, etc. Causes of such conditions include mutant genes, radiation, aged gametes, drugs or other chemicals, viruses, etc.

7. *Category VI:* MR due to *gestational disorders;* involves prematurity and postmaturity.

8. *Category VII* MR following *psychiatric disorder.*

9. *Category VIII:* MR due to *environmental influences* such as psychosocial disadvantage or sensory deprivation.

10. *Category IX:* MR due to *other conditions,* including defects of the special senses or other unspecified conditions.

In regard to etiologies, Hutt and Gibby (1965) noted that only about 50 percent of the institutionalized retarded had any specific etiological diagnosis recorded. That diagnosis is a complex problem is underscored by the fact that in a recent study of over 20,000 institutionalized cases, no change had occurred—over 50 percent still have no etiology assigned (Cleland, Manaster, & Case, 1980). However, with the recent advances in genetics, the incidence of unknown etiologies should decrease. As evidence, Down's syndrome, *cri-du-chat* syndrome, and Apert's syndrome have all been pinned down as mental retardation due to chromosomal involvement.

Further complications in assigning a specific etiology arise due to the fact that other conditions display similarities in cognitive or affective behaviors and thus mimic mental retardation. Among these mimics are severely autistic children and the sensorially handicapped deaf, blind, or multiply sensorially handicapped people. It should be recalled from the definition given earlier that bona fide retardation must occur during the developmental period (birth to 18 years), and adults suffering massive brain damage, even though they may be rendered totally vegetative, are not diagnosable as mentally retarded.

For convenience and to assist in diagnosis, two types of retarded individuals have been identified. One category is classified as *clinical types* or those who can be identified as retarded on the basis of appearance alone. Some examples of the clinical types are Down's syndrome, cretins, pronounced cases of hydrocephaly, and the rare Hurler's syndrome or gargoylism—the latter being possessed of "broad bridge of the nose, open mouth with protruding large tongue, thickened lips, corneal clouding, and coarse facial features" (Grossman, 1977, p. 142). The *aclinical* retarded persons constitute by far the largest number of the retarded population. These individuals manifest no physical stigmata to indicate their retardation, their intelligence quotients range generally between 50–69, and they account for over 70 percent of the total retarded population (Cleland, 1978). From an educational perspective, most of the aclinical types fall into the educable category.

INCIDENCE, PREVALENCE, AND LOCATION

Incidence refers to the number of new cases per 100,000 over a given period of time, while prevalence refers to all cases, new and old, that exist in a population at a given point in time (Mercer, 1973). Prevalence figures vary substantially as Wallin's (1958) survey revealed. He surveyed prevalence figures reported over a 60-year span and found a range from .05 to a whopping 13 percent! More recently, and more probable, the President's Committee on Mental Retardation reported a prevalence of 3 percent which would yield, based on the current U.S. population, about 7,000,000 retarded persons (President's Commission on Mental Retardation, 1972). Mercer (1973) challenges the 3 percent prevalence estimate as being too high—she holds with a 1 percent figure, which would mean that only about 2,400,000 retarded persons live in the United States. Either estimate indicates that mental retardation is a substantial problem.

For many years, authorities in mental retardation thought intelligence was normally distributed and generalized from the normal distribution curve to arrive at a 3 percent prevalence figure. In reality, and in recognition of the necessity of meeting the *dual* criteria for defining mental retardation, Mercer (1973) found in her eight-year study an actual rate of prevalence of only 1 percent. She also found an excess of individuals whose scores fell more than 3 standard deviations from the mean intelligence test score. Thus, rather than a symmetrical normal curve, there is a hump at the bottom of the bell (IQs below 50). Zigler (1967) had earlier postulated the existence of two groups of the retarded—those whose IQs were above 50 and displayed no discernible organicity and those whose IQs generally fell below 40 and suffered physiological or organic damage. Mercer's (1973) study is thus supportive of Zigler's two-group approach. For an excellent and extended discussion, readers should consult Zigler (1967).

Where are the mentally retarded? It is estimated that less than 5 percent are in public and private institutions. The vast majority are in the mainstream of society, and estimates range as high as 90–95 percent of the retarded are living in the community. Some of the retarded are in locations where we ordinarily do not expect them to be. For example, a study conducted over a quarter century ago by Levinson addressed a group of homeless males (then called hobos or tramps). An interesting finding was that fully 12 percent were mentally retarded—four times the prevalence rate of 3 percent (Levinson, 1955). In an unpublished study by the author, the Texas Prison System was surveyed for prisoners who were mentally retarded. Sixteen percent of the

State's prisoners had intelligence quotients below 70 (Cleland, 1963). It is also not too uncommon to find some mentally retarded living in state or private mental hospitals even in the 1980s. While the percentage of retarded who are prisoners, hobos, or inmates of mental hospitals would currently be reduced, there are still some retarded persons in settings considered inappropriate to their needs.

NATURE-NURTURE: THE PENDULUM STABILIZES

Persons with a *mild* level of retardation, the largest of all retarded groups, have been called in years past *garden variety* mental defectives, *cultural-familials,* and currently are termed *mentally retarded due to environmental influences*— due to presumed psychosocial disadvantage. *Garden variety* was a term employed to convey the fact that this aclinical and almost always mildly retarded subgroup was the most common. Later, the term *cultural-familial* was used to suggest that an hereditary component appeared to have etiological priority. To be labeled *familial,* the individual had to meet certain criteria. Namely, one or both parents of the retarded person were also retarded, and, if there were siblings, one or more were retarded, as well.

The influence of the hereditarian school was dominant in the early part of this century—feeblemindedness was thought to be transmitted along hereditary lines. One of the leading authorities of the early 1900s was Henry H. Goddard, and he strongly upheld the hereditarian banner. In 1912, his book *The Kallikak Family* was published. Its effect was dramatic, and segregation of the retarded in institutions was widely endorsed. Numerous eugenicists also advocated sterilization. Neither sterilization nor segregation has solved the problem of retardation, and currently the majority of workers in the field advocate deinstitutionalization of the retarded, and almost all states have abolished their laws on sterilization.

Although the hereditarian movement was the dominant force in retardation circles, the environmentalists got a "shot in the arm" from the work of the Russian physiologist Pavlov. This basic work of Pavlov was further extended by John B. Watson and formed the basis for the behavioristic movement in psychology. Both the hereditarians and environmentalists made extravagant claims—hereditarians claimed the ability to control man's future via eugenics, and the environmentalist, Watson, claimed, "Give me a child at birth and I can make it whatever I choose."

Currently, the most defensible position on causation in retardation would be an interactionist point of view. Both hereditary and environmental forces interact dynamically to contribute to the expression of intelligence. Dobzhansky (1955) provides a norm-of-reaction concept relative to nature-nurture that Gottesman (1963) has articulated in diagrammatic form. Figure 26.1 illustrates the norm-of-reaction.

Given genetic endowment, A, we see that the reaction range under even the most favorable environmental conditions is quite limited. As we ascend the genetic alphabet, the reaction range is seen to increase with each increment in genetic endowment if the environment is enriched. The reaction range (RR) signifies the range in phenotypic IQ. From the foregoing, it is evident that the nature-nurture controversy has abated somewhat, and even the staunchest supporters of an hereditarian position give some prominence to environmental contributions.

CURIOUS OMISSIONS IN MENTAL RETARDATION RESEARCH

Historically, the mentally retarded have failed to capture the research interests of the psychological and medical communities to the extent that the mentally ill have. In part, the overriding focus on mental illness was anchored in the belief that the retarded were generally possessed of a more dismal prognosis. During the early 1960s, interest in research on the retarded accelerated, and the propellant was, in a word,

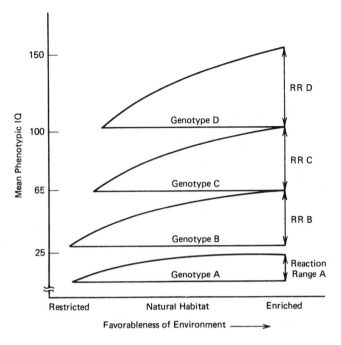

*By permission of Professor I. I. Gottesman.

Figure 26.1   Effect of environment on four genotypes. RR signifies reaction range in phenotypic IQ. From "Genetic Aspects of Intelligent Behavior" by I.I. Gottesman, in *Handbook of Mental Deficiency,* edited by N.R. Ellis. Copyright © 1963 by McGraw-Hill. Used with the permission of McGraw-Hill Book Company and Professor I.I. Gottesman.

money. As hospital improvement grants and funds for research on mental retardation were allocated by the government, interest in the retarded broadened. Coupled with the monetary incentive was the parent movement on behalf of their retarded children, which made legislators sensitive to the needs of the retarded in both institutional and community settings.

For neary a decade we have witnessed the adoption of the normalization principle, the deinstitutionalization movement and the advocation of the placement of the retarded in the least restrictive environment. The normalization principle, a Scandanavian import, "means making available to the mentally retarded patterns and conditions of everyday life which are as close as possible to the norms and patterns of the mainstream of society" (Nirje, 1969, p. 181). Deinstitutionalization and least restrictive environment are self-explanatory. With all these efforts to cease infantilization of the retarded, we still find many textbooks carrying the title *The Men-*

tally Retarded Child. Most of the retarded grow up and become adults, but the stigma of "perpetual child" lingers. There are other curious omissions or misconceptions, as evidenced by research or its absence.

Despite the general rise in crime in the nation and the reduction of segregation of the retarded in institutions, research on crime and delinquency among the retarded is substantially lacking. While in the first two decades of this century there was widespread belief that the retarded were almost always immoral, antisocial, vicious, and criminal, and several family-tree type studies focused on this supposed aspect of their nature, today the pendulum has swung to the "angel unaware" notion. Perhaps it is reaction formation against the early part of this century's overemphasis on the retarded person's presumed criminal nature. Or it may be that emotional blinders erect an unwillingness to see the retarded as *only,* but essentially human. They, like all others, are humans, not deities. *Acceptance* and objectivity would argue that the retarded be viewed as others are—some virtuous, some less so.

Another curious fact in research on mental retardation is the neglect of research on psychosomatic disorders, since many authorities indicate the retarded are more frustration prone, have higher anxiety levels than normals, and have histories of greater failure (Cromwell, 1963; Turnure & Zigler, 1964; Cleland, 1978). Like all other humans, the retarded experience the full range of emotions, and individual differences are notable even at the level of profound retardation (Cleland, 1979). With all the foregoing predispositions for psychosomatic disorders among the retarded, it is almost as though we accept the old dictum: "They're too dumb to be psychotic."

Another lacuna in the research literature on mental retardation is on aging. The retarded person will, in most cases, live into old age. However, there is a relativity in longevity among the retarded; for the profoundly retarded, the average age at death is about 38 years or about half the normal life expectancy (Cleland & Patton, 1965). Although half or more of the profoundly retarded are institutionalized, the same pattern prevails as in the larger U.S. society—females outlive the males. Thus the profoundly retarded age precociously, and by age 35 one could validly indicate they are into late old age. From a standpoint of gerontological research, the profoundly retarded could prove to be subjects of choice. Hypothetically, or speculatively, their unusual and even bizarre habits could lead to studies on precocity or resistances to the aging process. For example, almost all the profoundly retarded exhibit pica and about 9 percent manifest coprophagy (Cleland, Rago, & Jones, 1978). This means that their diets contain the customary and acceptable food *plus* a range of nonedibles such as dirt, tobacco, strings, and even human excrement. Among normal humans, taste buds are known to decrease with advance age (Pfaffman, 1963). To the extent the profoundly retarded engage in a very differnt fare, which includes literally everything they can swallow, while the normal old people have socialized appetites, one might ask if the profoundly retarded lose their taste buds, or if they resist this degeneration as a function of a more stimulating, albeit bizarre, dietary intake?

In an equally speculative view, a number of profoundly retarded and some at the severe level engage in self-biting (Butterworth & Bower, 1959). In those cases where the habit continues over a long time period in the same location (arm or hand), hair growth is greatly accelerated and keloid tumors often form at these sites. One is reminded of limb regeneration studies in biology or zoology wherein the wound at the site of amputation on a newt or frog is allowed to heal very slowly because experimenters continue to irritate the wound. Irritating the wound fosters regeneration. (In the social and behavioral sciences, we speak of growth (cognitive) as being promoted by *stimulation*—the hard sciences talk of *irritation*.) In any event, excessive and continued irritation or stimulation is seen in the profoundly retarded to foster hair growth plus tumors. Could we possibly learn more of the secrets of growth by looking more closely at the bizarre habits of the rarest subgroup of the retarded, the profound level?

The profoundly retarded also reflect a different cause of death than in the U.S. society at large. In one study of 660 deaths of the profoundly retarded, cancer as the cause of death was notable by its absence (Cleland, Powell, & Talkington, 1971). A later study by a California physician of 600 autopsied cases also failed to note a single case of cancer as the cause of death in profoundly retarded subjects (Chaney, 1978). Obviously, their abbreviated lifespans would allow scant opportunity to develop certain types of cancer, but cancer is not unknown in children.

At every level of retardation, research is minimal, indeed almost nonexistent, on a state in which nearly one-third of life is passed—sleep. In one of the few studies on sleep behaviors of the profoundly retarded, Case (1978) found that movements during sleep for the profoundly retarded (CA range 22–29; $\bar{X}$ SQ = 12) were only 6.48 per night in contrast to normal infants' 24 and normal adults' 33. Case suggested less movement could indicate more dream activity. In an earlier study, it was suggested that sleep-dream percent time could be employed to distinguish varied developmental levels in this compressed intellectual range (1–19 IQ). Sleep research with the nonverbal retarded person is discussed more fully elsewhere (Cleland, 1979).

In the few studies wherein retarded persons have been studied by polygraph recording of EEGs, the most commonly used subjects were Down's syndrome (DS) children. In some studies, normal REM-state-sleep percentages in Down's syndrome subjects were reported, while other studies employing DS subjects report a lower than normal amount of REM sleep (Clausen, 1978). In the studies of DS subjects, Clausen indicates "there is no variable on which all studies agree" (Clausen, 1978, p. 95). The most robust findings include less REM sleep, more awakenings, and more body movements. These findings are in contrast to Case's (1978) study of profoundly retarded subjects mentioned earlier, but the Down's syndrome subjects were all of a higher intellectual level.

Findings to date from investigations of aberrant neurophysiological mechanisms in relation to sleep records of the retarded are equivocal at best. As Clausen (1978) points out, a critical need exists for more information about sleep characteristics in retarded individuals at every intellectual level and Hawkins (1970) earlier indicated the potential of sleep patterns for diagnosing the integrity of CNS functioning. There is much to be learned yet about the sleep behaviors of the retarded.

Another area of research that could prove of benefit would be an intensive look at the emotions and their nonverbal expressions. As an example, blushing is an involuntary expression of shame, guilt, or awareness of committing a faux pas. McDougall, the early social psychologist, claimed that shame was incapable of being experienced until a self-sentiment had developed. Blushing, in turn, has been described as "the most peculiar and the most human of all expressions" (Darwin, 1872/1965 p. 309). So attuned are many to the massive cognitive deficit of the profoundly retarded or

severely autistic that to think of blushing as being in the repertoire of either seems ludicrous. Can the profoundly retarded possess even the dimmest hint of modesty, shame, or shyness? The author asked 10 physicans if they had ever noted a profoundly retarded person blush during a strip-down physical. What were their responses? "You're the only person who ever asked," or "No, I never have looked." A number of attendants experienced with this type of resident were also questioned, and after the initial surprise wore off I got, "I have two or three good blushers." Blushing does exist at even this level of intellect, and this, as well as other involuntary expressions of the emotions, could help establish functional subgroups in this narrow psychometric range of profound retardation or in severe autism. For the autistic blusher, it could mean some movement toward other humans from a group who have been described as "species avoiders" (Moore & Shiek, 1971). The reader interested in emotions and in hypotheses generated in this area will find Darwin (1872/1965) still provocative.

The foregoing discussion dwells primarily on the profoundly mentally retarded in order to alert readers to the most underresearched of all retarded subgroups. Unfortunately, as Goldstein and Simonson (1971) point out, the rejected client in psychotherapy is likely to be the HOUND patient (homely, old, ugly, nonverbal, and dumb). The preferred client is the YAVIS (young, attractive, verbal, intelligent, and successful) (Schofield, 1964). Perhaps knowledge could be advanced more rapidly by doing more research on the HOUND of the retarded ranks, the profoundly retarded. As I have attempted to point out, their many unique or exaggerated behaviors may yield knowledge of value to every level of intelligence and to every age group.

"COMMON SENSE" AND MYTHS ABOUT THE FIELD OF MENTAL RETARDATION

"The retarded person enjoys routine, monotonous, or tedious work in contrast to normals whose tolerance for monotony in work is very little" (Mayer-Gross, Slater, & Roth, 1960). "The profoundly retarded are impervious to gustatory or olfactory sensations"(Deb, 1958). In a similar vein, the "wisdom" of many in the field of mental retardation held that the retarded amputee was incapable of experiencing the phantom limb sensation (Simmel, 1959). "Big institutions are bad institutions." "Retarded children, as a group, are certainly not as happy as they might be"(Hutt & Gibby, 1965, p. 208). As Zigler (1975) has pointed out, many individuals in the field of mental retardation continue to hold the conviction that retarded persons are characterized by a behavioral rigidity that is reflected in their enjoyment of monotonous and repetitive tasks. Such a conviction in the behavioral rigidity of the retarded arose out of observations of their stereotyped and repetitive behaviors and was manifested theoretically in Lewin's (1935) dynamic theory of feeblemindedness. Another die-hard piece of "common sense" about the retarded is especially notable in institutional settings and in an exploration into the folklore of institutions as revealed through clichés. Dingman, Cleland, and Swartz (1970) found the moon is still "responsible" for increases in activity levels of residents. "The kids are high—must be a full moon" is illustrative of the moon's "influence." That Paracelsus (1493–1541) attributed insanity not to demons but to the lunar influence nearly five centuries ago and some, even today, believe that the moon influences behavior is one of the most tenacious myths extant. Such persistence of lunar influences on behavior is most notable in both institutions for the mentally ill and the retarded. What, then, does the research evidence say about these doggedly held notions?

The retarded person's supposed love of routine and monotonous work was tested with mildly retarded adult males ($\overline{M}$ IQ = 58). Subsequent to touring a greenhouse, a city garbage dump, an air base, an extract manufacturing plant, and a large library, these men were interviewed to ascertain preferences. Their overwhelming choice was the city library, and the reasons were "lots of girls

there," "it was air conditioned," "you could play records there,"etc. Least favored was the city dump because "it's too hot," "no girls," and "it stinks" (Dickerson & Cleland, 1967). This field study, although limited to the mild level, hardly upholds the conviction that the retarded thrive on monotonous jobs. In addressing the idea that the retarded manifest rigidity in thought processes, Zigler (1975) summarizes the work of 20 years that has largely disproven the conviction that the retarded are characterized by a cognitive rigidity.

Mayer-Gross et al. (1960) and Deb (1958) maintained that the profoundly retarded were impervious to gustatory or olfactory sensations, but Leath, Lawrence, and Cleland (1977) established that even at this level of cognitive deficit, taste preferences are manifest. In relation to the assumed anosmia among the profoundly retarded, it is true that many suffer from brain damage and the likelihood of an inability to smell would be magnified (Kalmus, 1952). However, that many profoundly retarded do have an ability to smell appears substantiated through Nueva-España and Fish's (1976) longitudinal study of olfactory acuity in the profoundly retarded. These investigators, employing an Olfactory Assessment Test, found that a loss of ability to smell was diagnostic of lowered viability and an early death. The failure to study the chemical senses, despite their importance in diagnosis and treatment, has been discussed elsewhere, and interested readers can refer to that source (Cleland, 1979).

"Big institutions are bad institutions" is common knowledge. However, what is the actual state of affairs? In practice, it is true that state institutions for the retarded have dramatically reduced their resident populations, thus consensually subscribing to the "big is bad" concept. In a review of the evidence on the size issue published nearly two decades ago, there were no hard data to support this belief (Cleland, 1965). More recently, Balla (1976) examined the relationship of institutional size to quality of care. He concluded by citing Zigler (1976) to the effect that "we have little knowledge about what is the best type of classroom or the optimal institutional setting for the retarded" (p. 6). For individuals interested in the size–quality-of-care issue in institutions, Cleland (1965) and Balla (1976) are recommended.

In regard to the idea that "retarded children, as a group, are certainly not as happy as they might be" (Hutt & Gibby, 1965), this writer has found no empirical work on happiness per se among the retarded. On the surface, the indirect evidence does suggest that the retarded are more anxious, frustration-prone, and have encountered more failure (Mac-Millan, 1977). As such, Hutt and Gibby may be correct although overall happiness is subject to variability and possibly to one's ability to know of his or her limitations.

Among things discussed occasionally by normal individuals are issues such as "Is there life after death?" In the writer's three decades of work with the retarded, such an issue has not spontaneously been voiced even by the mildly retarded. Despite the intellectual limitations that preclude philosophical discussions and perhaps much introspection about death, the retarded of the mild level do, in most instances, come to realize the inevitability and finality of death. In the mild level of retardation, mental age expectancies at adulthood range approximately from 8 to about 12 and Nagy's (1948) study of 3- to 10-year-old normals revealed that at around 9 the child manifests an adult conception of death. To the extent that adults are concerned or worried over dying, we would anticipate a lesser degree of worry as one descends the intellectual ladder.

Another line of evidence on the happiness issue would be a comparison of suicide rates among retarded and nonretarded individuals, for, as Peck (1975) indicates, the modal pattern observed in suicides is great sensitivity, loneliness, and unhappiness. Suicide is the ultimate escape behavior. If the retarded are more anxious, have poorer self-concepts, are frustration prone as most literature suggests, we would anticipate an above-average suicide rate, especially among the higher level retarded persons. Despite the magnitude of the problem of suicide in society at large, the writer unearthed only two studies that involved

retarded samples. Sternlicht, Pustel, and Deutsch (1970) studied attempted suicides at the Willowbrook State School (at the time, the world's largest) and found an incidence of suicidal attempts to be .9 percent of the total institutional population. This figure is slightly lower than the incidence of attempted suicides in the general population. In Cerbus' 1970 study, he addressed the issue of seasonal variations in suicides in mentally ill and mentally retarded institutionalized subjects. Unlike Sternlicht et al.'s (1970) study, which revealed no successful suicide attempt, Cerbus reported some suicides by the retarded did occur over a five-year timespan, but an incidence figure was not given. He did find a significant seasonal variation in both suicides and homicides, with April and May being peak months and February lowest. This seasonal aspect of suicide corresponds to that of the United States' general population (Stengel, 1964). From the minimal evidence available, suicides appear to be less common among the retarded than normals. However, since these studies involved only institutionalized individuals, whose available means of suicide are few and whose supervision is greater, one could not reasonably conclude that the retarded have a lower suicide rate.

In regard to the issue of retarded persons' overall happiness, it may be of some indirect help to compare the incidence of mental disorders among the retarded with normals. As Goldenson indicates, there does appear to be a higher incidence of mental disorder among the retarded. Some authorities have suggested that as high as 15 percent of the retarded have a severe mental disorder. From the foregoing indirect evidence, the happiness of the retarded as compared to nonretarded persons remains somewhat equivocal, but the existing studies would lend mild support to Hutt and Gibby's (1965) contention that the retarded may be less happy than they might be.

The notion that lunar influences tend to generate higher activity levels in both retarded and mentally ill persons has received no empirical support (Shapiro et al., 1970; Weiskott, 1974). Increases in activity levels have, however, been linked to barometric pressure changes (Watson et al., 1957) among individuals undergoing psychotherapy, and Lawrence's (1977) study of institutionalized, profoundly retarded males ($\bar{M}$ SQ = 13.4) also supports the view that barometric pressure change is related to activity level change. As such, there is some evidence that climatological variables can influence behavior. Lawrence (1977) suggested that biometeorological studies, especially the barometric, humidity, and temperature variables, warrant further study as to their effects on human behavior.

Phantom limb sensations, a term coined by Mitchell in 1871, refers to the experiencing of sensations albeit the limb is missing. It was widely believed that mentally retarded amputees failed to experience such sensations, but Simmel (1959) exploded this myth. In a study of 26 amputees who were mentally retarded, Simmel reported 11 subjects described definite phantoms. Twelve of the subjects were severely or profoundly retarded and too inarticulate to respond to Simmel's interview (Simmel, 1959), and three were excluded for medical reasons.

MOTIVATIONAL CONSIDERATIONS

The same motives that guide and energize behavior of the nonretarded are also seen at every level of retardation. When a motive is superstrong, as in addiction, one is often surprised at the accomplishments even a profoundly retarded person can achieve.

For example, one 34-year-old retarded woman whose Social Quotient was 16 was addicted to coffee in either liquid or solid form. Her dormitory kitchen was always locked when not in use but above the door was an open transom. Outside the kitchen were several large, wooden boxes. On noting this happy circumstance our subject immediately shoved one box into proximity of the locked door, stacked another on top, and climbed through the transom and fell to the floor. Some ten minutes elapsed before the cook returned and found her mouth was ringed with coffee.

Another 34-year-old male whose Social Quotient was 15 was addicted to tobacco. Above the doorway leading to the play-yard, an attendant had placed a cigarette (unlit). When the subject's atten-

tion was directed to the cigarette which was some four feet beyond his reach, he immediately ran to fetch a heavy steel bench and placed it under the cigarette. The use of the bench as a tool credits, incidentally, at the VIII to IX year level on the Vineland Social Maturity Scale (Doll, 1953)!

The above examples of spontaneous tool use in profoundly retarded individuals reflect an effort to delineate functional subgroups within the narrow psychometric range of 1–19 IQ (Cleland, Rago, & Mukherjee, 1978). Clearly, incentive strength is related to the subject's capability and reveals tool usage in some individuals—an ability few would expect to exist below IQ 19.

Reaction times of retarded individuals have consistently been demonstrated to be slower than normals, and RT speed is positively related to intelligence within the retarded range (Berkson, 1960). Here again, incentive strength is an important consideration, and the subject in the above case whose addiction to tobacco was notable is so fast in stealing a visitor's pack of cigarettes as to be termed incredible.

At the highest level of retardation, motivation also enters critically into educational and performance expectancies. Knowing that a large percentage of the mildly retarded come from disadvantaged homes and that a sizable number have one or both parents who are also mentally retarded equates to minimal motivation to attend school. The dropout rate for the mildly retarded is notoriously high. What can generate a greater desire to attend regularly? If we assume their homes are characterized by an absence of mirrors, cameras, tape recorders, and books and that their parents have already taught them not to expect anything good from schools, then schools can jar preestablished expectancies via cognitive dissonance. Knowing that the first day of school is critical and that each child has some curiosity about himself or herself good feedback is essential. On day one when classes begin, take photos of each child and the class as a whole and give each child one of each to take home. At recess, videotape the class at play and replay after recess to augment the novelty effect and to allow the class to quiet down. By personalizing a mass setting (the school), by showing parents their pictures, and so forth, the first day of school can become a magnet for the child to want to return the next day. These gimmicks and those the teacher develops are of primary importance in the early part of the school year, and, once regular attendance develops, such incentives would be faded (Cleland, 1977).

Can deprivation result in heightened motivation for mildly retarded adults to want to work? When 25- to 45-year-olds whose mental age average is on the order of 9½ years are confronted with the choice of work or play, which do they choose? Ordinarily, rehabilitation personnel assume that the mildly retarded have a similar desire to work that is manifested by normal adults, but empirical verification is lacking. In a field study, a plan was devised whereby institutionalized retarded males could have a free choice between work or play. The subjects were all employed as helper patients and had over five years on their jobs—8–5, five days per week. Using a reference population of mildly retarded adults from another state school, a "hedonic diet" was developed that established "favorite activities, foods, games, TV programs, etc.," and the subjects were abruptly placed on the play (hedonic) diet in lieu of work. The facility superintendent, on the first test day, announced that they were excused from work and to have a good time. Meals were professionally catered and this novelty greatly augmented the subjects' enthusiasm for the entire venture. When the subjects attempted to police-up after meals, the experimenters would do this for them—in brief, they were totally deprived of anything that approximated work. What happened? By the fourteenth day of the study, one of the 30 subjects became withdrawn and when asked why, he replied, "I'm sick of this play stuff—wanta go back to work." Another bolder subject simply walked off and returned to his former work station. Within a day or two, all were complaining openly and requesting permission to return to work. What occurred was a strike against "pleasure-play" and, interestingly, it occurred

the second week. As such, the subjects confessed that a two-week vacation was plenty, and that the meaning of work paralleled the importance of work so well documented for normals (de Grazia, 1964; Friedmann, 1961). Clearly, at least for an institutionalized sample of retarded adults, the deprivation of work greatly augmented their desire to work (Cleland & Swartz, 1969b). This study of work motivation, although covering a longer timespan, is reminiscent of the interrupted task paradigm employed by Zeigarnik (1927) and Ovsiankina (1928).

In perceptual-motor tasks, when verbal reinforcement is provided to educable (mild) level retarded persons, it has often been noted that response decrements occur as a function of stimulus satiation. To circumvent the loss of effectiveness of verbal reinforcement, a novel mode of presentation (via a recessed speaker with the experimenter not visible) significantly improved performance of a group of male retarded subjects (Altman, Talkington, & Cleland, 1971). Even the voice of the experimenter or teacher may be differentially reinforcing depending on the age and intellectual level of the subjects. In a study of profoundly retarded males having a mean Social Quotient of 11.7 that employed an operant strategy, Uno, Seitel, and Cleland (1975) found their preference to be for female voices. Stevenson (1961) had earlier established such a preference for 3- and 4-year-old normal children.

When reinforcers with the retarded are manually given, (e.g., handing a child an M&M or giving a handshake) it should be recalled that the prevalence of left-handedness among the retarded of mild level is higher than in normals (Doll, 1939) and at the profound level over 25 percent are southpaws (Cleland, 1979).

In one of the few studies wherein sex motivation was employed, favorable consequences ensued. Edgerton and Dingman (1964) studied the effects of reduced supervision over resident dating behavior and found that their subjects manifested improved control over time and space, better control over sexual impulses, and enhanced communication strategies. Appropriately, these investigators titled their study "Good Reasons for Bad Supervision: Dating in a Hospital for the Mentally Retarded."

These aforementioned motivational considerations in working with the retarded are representative although far from exhaustive. Additional concerns on motivation with various clinical problems can be found elsewhere in this book.

FRIENDSHIP AND ALTRUISM IN MENTAL RETARDATION

When working with the profoundly retarded, chance discoveries are occasionally encountered. Rago and Cleland (1978) were conducting a study involving territorial behaviors in the profoundly retarded and during preparatory arrangements noted an instance of altruistic behavior on the part of a man whose Social Quotient was 17. The following case outlines this event:

The residents were in their recreation room which was ringed with plastic benches. John was sitting on a bench against the wall and Reuben was sitting on a bench opposite John. An attendant appeared and distributed 4 magazines to 4 of the 14 residents. John received a magazine; Reuben did not. Another resident who failed to get a magazine walked over to John, snatched his magazine and returned to his seat. Reuben, noting these events, got up, walked across the room, and took the magazine from the "robber" and returned it to John. The most striking aspect of this behavior was its simplicity and spontaneity. (Rago & Cleland, 1978)

MacAndrew and Edgerton (1966), in an earlier account, described in detail the friendship between two severely retarded adults. The friendship was of long duration, was one of mutual help (one was blind, one crippled), and was totally devoid of any exploiting on the part of either. As both examples demonstrate, friendships, altruism, and the full range of the more tender emotions exist among the retarded—even extending to the profound level.

THERAPEUTIC CONSIDERATIONS

I have alluded to the retarded as failure prone, susceptible to frustrations of various sorts, and subject to more emotional disturbance than normal individuals. Is psychotherapy of any value in treatment of the retarded person having superimposed emotional problems? For a number of years, workers in the field held that average or above-average intelligence was essential for psychotherapeutic benefit. However, during the mid-fifties, psychologists and psychiatrists started systematic efforts to improve retarded clients' self-concepts, to promote fuller acceptance of their limitations, and to reduce acting-out behaviors on the part of selected clients (Goldenson, 1970). Art therapy and play therapy have been used to a considerable extent with the severe and moderate level retarded person since verbal communicative skills are minimized. Other therapeutic approaches include role playing or psychodrama, catharsis, group psychotherapy, and, more recently, assertion training has been employed.

Other considerations force our attention to parents of the retarded since one common problem is that of parental overprotection. Not infrequently, parents will be in conflict over their retarded child, and, in the child's earliest years, denial that their child is retarded is common. Again, as Blodgett (1971) points out, many parents are unable or unwilling to talk about their retarded child and their feelings about their problem. Professional assistance can help parents to a better understanding of retardation and, by helping them resolve conflicts and relieve stress, will indirectly benefit their retarded child. When parents who have only recently received the diagnosis that their child is retarded seek professional help, a rule of thumb is always to see both parents at least during the earliest visits. This helps insure that communication breakdowns don't occur and that the advice, answers to questions, and so forth, the therapist provides can be clarified or interpreted to both parents. For an interesting and informative way to gain insight into parental feelings, attitudes, and complaints, the Turnbulls' book (Turn-bull & Turnbull, 1978) is highly recommended. The 14 selections included are written by professionals who themselves are also parents of children having a variety of handicaps. Their stories are certain to provide psychotherapists with a greater understanding of the panorama of parental feelings.

For individuals who are profoundly or severely retarded, behavior modification has much to offer. Perhaps the earliest effort to utilize operant conditioning principles with the retarded dates to the late eighteenth century when Itard (1932) trained the Wild Boy of Aveyron in word recognition and rewarded correct responses with milk. Fuller (1949) trained a "vegetative idiot" to make a simple response by use of operant principles, but it was not until about 1960 that behavior modification really caught on in mental retardation circles. Currently, its use with the profoundly and severely retarded is the therapy of choice in modifying stereotypies, acting-out disorders, eating disorders, and other maladaptive behaviors. This therapeutic strategy and the variety of problems it has been employed to minimize in retarded clients has been given extended coverage in Thompson and Grabowski (1977).

SUMMARY

A chapter cannot a textbook be, and, as a consequence, a number of topics traditionally covered in the standard texts on mental retardation have been excluded. The areas of learning and academic skills, as well as those of sensory and perceptual processes, are perhaps the most notable omissions. However, readers interested in these topics will find MacMillan (1977), Cleland (1978), Cleland and Swartz (in press), or the Ellis' 11-volume series covering research in mental retardation to cover these areas. The aim of this chapter was primarily to whet readers' appetites to delve further into the field of mental retardation. The mention of areas of research neglect, the discussion of some myths about retardation, etiological

aspects, and motivation in mentally retarded individuals hopefully may be of heuristic value to readers. Finally, by indicating the retarded of every intellectual level share in and express every human emotion, it is apparent that our efforts should now concentrate on Maslow's (1954) higher order needs and how these might be augmented more fully through research and programs.

REFERENCES

Altman, R., Talkington, L.W., & Cleland, C.C. Effects of novelty on verbal reinforcement effectiveness with retardates. *The Psychological Record,* 1971, **21,** 529–532.

Arndt, S. A general measure of adaptive behavior. *American Journal of Mental Deficiency,* 1981, **85,** 554–556.

Balla, D. Relationship of institution size to quality of care: A review of the literature. *American Journal of Mental Deficiency,* 1976, **81,** 117–124.

Balthazar, E.E. *Balthazar scales of adaptive behavior, part one: Handbook for the professional supervisor.* Champaign, Ill.: Research Press, 1971.

Baumeister, A.A., & Butterfield, E. *Residential facilities for the mentally retarded.* Chicago: Aldine, 1970.

Berkson, G. An analysis of reaction time in normal and mentally deficient young men. I. Duration threshold experiment. *Journal of Mental Deficiency Research,* 1960, **4,** 51–58.

Blodgett, H. *Mentally retarded children.* Minneapolis: University of Minnesota Press, 1970.

Butterworth, T., & Bower, J.R. Self-biting among feebleminded persons. *Pennsylvania Medical Journal,* 1959, **63,** 201–204.

Case, J.C. Sleep postures and pre-sleep activity of the PMR. In J.D. Swartz, R.K. Eyman, C.C. Cleland, & R. O'Grady (Eds.), *The profoundly mentally retarded* (Vol. IV). Austin: Western Research Conference, 1978.

Cerbus, G. Seasonal variation in some mental health statistics. *Journal of Clinical Psychology,* 1970, **26,** 61–63.

Chaney, R.H. Respiratory complications in the profoundly mentally retarded. In J.D. Swartz,

R.K. Eyman, C.C. Cleland, & R. O'Grady (Eds.), *The profoundly mentally retarded* (Vol. IV). Austin: Western Research Conference, 1978.

Clausen, J. Psychophysiology in mental retardation. In N.R. Ellis (Ed.), *International Review of Research in Mental Retardation* (Vol. 9). New York: Academic Press, 1978.

Cleland, C.C. *Prisoners' intelligence in the Texas Prison System.* Unpublished manuscript, University of Texas at Austin, 1963.

Cleland, C.C. Evidence on the relationship between size and institutional effectiveness: A review and analysis. *American Journal of Mental Deficiency,* 1965, **70,** 423–431.

Cleland, C.C. Possibilities for social research among profoundly retarded? In R. Eyman, C. Meyers, & G. Tarjan (Eds.), *Sociobehavioral studies in mental retardation.* Washington, D.C.: American Association on Mental Deficiency, 1973.

Cleland, C.C. The first day of school for the educable retarded child. *Handicapsules for teachers: A brief programmed text on students with handicaps.* Austin: Project PREM, 1977.

Cleland, C.C. *Mental retardation: A developmental approach.* Englewood Cliffs, N.J.: Prentice-Hall, 1978.

Cleland, C.C. *The profoundly mentally retarded.* Englewood Cliffs, N.J.: Prentice-Hall, 1979.

Cleland, C.C., & Patton, W.F. Idiocy and longevity: A brief note. *Psychological Reports,* 1965, **17,** 649–650.

Cleland, C.C., & Swartz, J.D. *Mental retardation: Approaches to institutional change.* New York: Grune & Stratton, 1969. (a)

Cleland, C.C., & Swartz, J.D. Work deprivation as motivation to work. *American Journal of Mental Deficiency,* 1969, **73,** 703–712. (b)

Cleland, C.C., & Swartz, J. *Exceptionalities through the lifespan: An introduction.* New York: Macmillan Co., in press.

Cleland, C.C., Powell, H., & Talkington, L.W. Death in the profoundly retarded. *Mental Retardation,* 1971, **9,** 36–37.

Cleland, C.C., Rago, W., & Jones, J. Coprophagy in profoundly retarded persons. In J.D. Swartz, R.K. Eyman, C.C. Cleland, & R. O'Grady (Eds.), *The profoundly mentally retarded* (Vol. IV). Austin: Western Research Conference, 1978.

Cleland, C.C., Rago, W.V., & Mukherjee, A.K. Tool use in profoundly retarded persons: An approach to sub-group differentiation. *Bulletin of the Psychonomic Society,* 1978, **12,** 86–88.

Cleland, C.C., Manaster, G.J., & Case, J.C. IQs and etiologies: The two group approach to mental retardation. *Bulletin of the Psychonomic Society,* 1980, **15,** 413–415.

Crissy, M.S. Mental retardation: Past, present, and future. *The American Psychologist,* 1975, **30,** 800–808.

Cromwell, R.L. A social learning approach to mental retardation. In N.R. Ellis (Ed.), *Handbook of mental deficiency.* New York: McGraw-Hill, 1963.

Darwin, C. *The origin of species and the descent of man.* New York: Modern Library, Random House, 1859.

Darwin, C. *The expression of emotion in man and animals.* Chicago: University of Chicago Press, 1965. (Originally published 1872.)

Deb, S. Gustatory perceptions of the mentally retarded. *Indian Journal of Psychology,* 1958, **n.v.** 33.

de Grazia, S. *Of time, work, and leisure.* Garden City, N.Y.: Doubleday, 1964.

Dickerson, W.L., & Cleland, C.C. Note on experience in ability to predict retardates' job choice. *Psychological Reports,* 1967, **21,** 606–608.

Dingham, H.R., Cleland, C.C., & Swartz, J.D. Institutional "wisdom" as expressed through folklore. *Mental Retardation,* 1970, **6,** 2–8.

Dobzhansky, T. *Evolution, genetics and man.* New York: Wiley, 1955.

Doll, E.A. Growth studies in social competence. *American Journal of Mental Deficiency,* 1939, **44,** 90–96.

Doll, E.A. *The measurement of social competence: A manual for the Vineland social maturity scale.* Minneapolis: Educational Testing Bureau, 1953.

Edgerton, R.B., & Dingman, H.F. Good reasons for bad supervision: Dating in a hospital for the mentally retarded. *Psychiatric Quarterly Supplement,* 1964, **2,** 1–13.

Friedmann, N.G. *The anatomy of work.* New York: The Free Press, 1961.

Fuller, P. Operant conditioning of a vegetative

human organism. *American Journal of Psychology,* 1949, **62,** 587–590.

Goddard, H.H. *The Kallikak family.* New York: Macmillan, 1912.

Goldenson, R.M. *The encyclopedia of human behavior* (Vols. I & II). Garden City, N.Y.: Doubleday, 1970.

Goldstein, A.P., & Simonson, N.R. Social psychological approaches to psychotherapy research. In A.E. Bergin & S.L. Garfield (Eds.), *Handbook of psychotherapy and behavior change.* New York: Wiley, 1971.

Gottesman, I.I. Genetic aspects of intelligent behavior. In N.R. Ellis (Ed.), *Handbook of mental deficiency.* New York: McGraw-Hill, 1963.

Grossman, H.J. (Ed.). *Manual on terminology and classification in mental retardation.* Washington, D.C.: American Association on Mental Deficiency, 1977.

Guerra, F. *The pre-Columbian mind.* New York: Seminar Press, 1971.

Harris, J.E., & Weeks, K.R. *X-raying the pharaohs.* New York: Scribner's, 1973.

Hawkins, D.R. Implications of knowledge of sleep patterns in psychiatric conditions. *International Psychiatry Clinics,* 1970, **7,** 85–92.

Hereford, S.M., Cleland, C.C., & Fellner, M.J. Territoriality and scent-marking: A study of profoundly retarded enuretics and encopretics. *American Journal of Mental Deficiency,* 1973, **77,** 426–430.

Hutt, M., & Gibby, R.G. *The mentally retarded child.* Boston: Allyn & Bacon, 1965.

Itard, J.M. *The wild boy of Aveyron* (trans. by G. Humphrey & M. Humphrey). Englewood Cliffs, N.J.: Prentice-Hall, 1932.

Kalmus, H. Inherited sense defects. *Scientific American,* Reprint No. 406. San Francisco: W.H. Freeman & Co., 1952.

Knobloch, H., & Lilienfeld, A.M. Neuropsychiatric sequelae of prematurity: A longitudinal study. *Journal of The American Medical Association,* 1956, **161,** 581–585.

Lake, D.G., Miles, M.B., & Earle, R.B. *Measuring human behavior.* New York: Teachers College Press, Columbia University, 1973.

Lawrence, W. Profoundly mentally retarded: Relationship of behavior and climatological variables. In L.W. Talkington, C.C. Cleland, & R. O'Grady (Eds.), *Research with the profoundly*

retarded (Vol. III). Austin: Western Research Conference, 1977.

Leath, J., Lawrence, W., & Cleland, C.C. Taste preferences in profoundly retarded males. *Review of Sensory Disability,* 1977 (No. 29), 8–11.

Levinson, B.M. The intelligence of middle-aged white homeless men in receipt of public assistance. *Psychological Reports,* 1955, **1,** 35–46.

Lewin, K. *A dynamic theory of personality.* New York: McGraw-Hill, 1935.

MacAndrew, C., & Edgerton, R.B. On the possibility of friendship. *American Journal of Mental Deficiency,* 1966, **70,** 612–621.

MacMillan, D.L. *Mental retardation in school and society.* Boston: Little, Brown, 1977.

Masland, R.L. The prevention of mental subnormality. In R.L. Masland, S.B. Sarason, & T. Gladwin (Eds.), *Mental subnormality.* New York: Basic Books, 1958.

Maslow, A.H. *Motivation and personality.* New York: Harper & Row, 1954.

Mayer-Gross, W., Slater, E., & Roth, M. *Clinical psychiatry.* Baltimore: Williams & Wilkins, 1960.

McGavern, M.L. *Imitative learning in echophraxic, profoundly retarded.* Unpublished master's thesis, University of Texas at Austin, 1969.

Mercer, J. The myth of 3% prevalence. In Tarjan et al. (Eds.), *Sociobehavioral studies in mental retardation.* Washington, D.C.: Monographs of The American Association on Mental Deficiency, 1973 (No. 1) 1–18.

Meyers, C.E., Nihira, K., & Zetlin, A. The measurement of adaptive behavior. In N.R. Ellis (Ed.), *Handbook of mental deficiency* (2nd ed.). Hillsdale, N.J.: Lawrence Erlbaum, 1979.

Moore, D.J., & Shiek, D.A. Toward a theory of early infantile autism. *Psychological Review,* 1971, **78,** 451–456.

Murphy, G. *Historical introduction to modern psychology.* New York: Harcourt Brace, 1949.

Nagy, M. The child's theories concerning death. *Journal of Genetic Psychology,* 1948, **73,** 3–27.

Nihira, K., Foster, R., Shellhaas, M., & Leland, H. *AAMD Adaptive behavior scale, 1974 revision.* Washington, D.C.: American Association on Mental Deficiency, 1974.

Nirje, B. The normalization principle and its human management implications. In R.B.

Kugel & W. Wolfensberger (Eds.), *Changing patterns in residential care.* Washington, D.C.: President's Commission on Mental Retardation, 1969.

Nueva-España, D.S., & Fish, C.H. Olfactory assessment related to diagnosis and prognosis of human viability. In C.C. Cleland, J.D. Swartz, & L.W. Talkington (Eds.), *The profoundly mentally retarded* (Vol. II). Austin: Western Research Conference, 1976.

Ovsiankina, M. Wiederaufnahme unterbrochener handlungen. *Psychologie Forschung,* 1928, **11,** 302–315.

Paluck, R.J., & Esser, A.H. Aggressive behavioral repertoire and use of space in institutionalized retarded and normal boys. *American Zoologist,* 1971, **11,** 51.

Peck, M.L. Research and training in prevention of suicide in adolescents and youths. *Bulletin of Suicidology,* 1970 (No. 6), 35–40.

Pfaffman, C. Taste and smell. In S.S. Stevens (Ed.), *Handbook of experimental psychology.* New York: Wiley, 1963.

Pollack, R.H., & Brenner, M.J. (Eds.). *The experimental psychology of Alfred Binet.* New York: Springer, 1969.

Polloway, E.Z., & Payne, J.S. Comparison of the AAMD Heber and Grossman manuals on terminology and classification in mental retardation. *Mental Retardation,* 1975, **13,** 12–14.

Polsky, M., Lippman, O., & Overton, P. Abnormality and disease in pre-Columbian art. *Texas State Journal on Medicine,* 1965, **61,** 1–4.

President's Commission on Mental Retardation, *MR 71: Entering the era of human ecology.* Washington, D.C.: Department of Health, Education and Welfare (No. 5), 1972.

Rago, W.V., & Cleland, C.C. Altruistic behavior in a profoundly retarded male. *Sensory World,* 1978, **3,** 16–17.

Sargent, F. A survey of human biometeorology. *International Journal of Biometeorology,* 1965, **9,** 1–3.

Schofield, W. Psychotherapy, the purchase of friendship. Englewood Cliffs, NJ: Prentice-Hall, 1964.

Seguin, E. *Idiocy: And its treatment by the physiological method.* New York: Columbia University Press, 1907, (Originally published 1866.)

Shapiro, J.L., Streiner, D., Gray, A., Williams, N.L., & Soble, C. The moon and mental illness: A failure to confirm the Transylvania effect. *Perceptual and Motor Skills,* 1970, **30,** 827–830.

Silverman, H.L., & Krenzel, K. Alfred Binet: Prolific pioneer in psychology. *Psychiatric Quarterly Supplement,* 1964, **38,** 323–335.

Simmel, M.L. Phantom experiences in mental defective amputees. *Journal of Abnormal and Social Psychology,* 1959, **59,** 128–130.

Stengel, E. *Suicide and attempted suicide.* Baltimore: Penguin, 1964.

Sternlicht, M., Pustel, G., & Deutsch, M. Suicidal tendencies among institutionalized retardates. *Journal of Mental Subnormality,* 1970, **16,** 93–102.

Stevenson, H.W. Social reinforcement with children as a function of CA, sex of E, and sex of S. *Journal of Abnormal and Social Psychology,* 1961, **63,** 147–154.

Terman, L.M. *The measurement of intelligence.* Boston: Houghton-Mifflin, 1916.

Thompson, T., & Grabowski, J. *Behavior modification of the mentally retarded* (2nd ed.). New York: Oxford University Press, 1977.

Tinbergen, N. Ethology and stress diseases. *Science,* 1974, **185,** 20–27.

Turnbull, A.P., & Turnbull, H.R. (Eds.), *Parents speak out: Views from the other side of the two-way mirror.* Columbus: Merrill, 1978.

Turnore, J. & Zigler, E. Outer-directedness in the problem solving of normal and retarded children. *Journal of Abnormal and Social Psychology,* 1964, **69,** 427–436.

Uno, T., Seitel, A.L., & Cleland, C.C. Operant preferences for male and female voices by profoundly retarded males. *Psychological Reports,* 1975, **36,** 891–894.

Wallin, J.E.W. Prevalence of mental retardation. *School and Society,* 1958, **86,** 55–56.

Watson, P.D., Damasco, A., Kanter, S.S., Suter, E., & Greenblatt, M. A note on the influence of climatic factors of psychophysiological investigations. *Psychosomatic Medicine,* 1957, **19,** 419–423.

Weiskott, G.N. Moon phases and telephone counseling calls. *Psychological Reports,* 1974, **35,** 752–754.

Zeigarnik, B.V. Über das Behalten von erledigten und unterledigten Handlungen. *Psychologie Forschung,* 1927, **9,** 1–85.

Zigler, E. Familial mental retardation: A continuing dilemma. *Science,* 1967, **155,** 292–298.

Zigler, E. Cognitive development and personality factors in behavior. In J.M. Kauffman & J.S. Payne (Eds.), *Mental retardation: Introduction and personal perspectives.* Columbus: Merrill, 1975.

Zigler, E. *NICHD appropriations for mental retardation.* Unpublished manuscript, Yale University, 1976.

CHAPTER 27

Providing Mental Health Services to Elementary School Children

JOSEPH A. DURLAK

Despite the fact that schools represent one of our most important and cherished cultural and social institutions, we have very little good information on the psychological aspects of schools. For example, there is no general agreement on how to define or measure children's school maladaptation, and even less consensus on how to conceptualize and assess adaptive or prosocial behaviors. We do not know the most effective teaching methods, the manner in which teachers' behaviors affect children's behavior and vice versa, or the effects of physical characteristics on school achievement and behavior. Also, we lack systematic information on the interactions among the above factors. Further, we have no clear view of how major sociopolitical issues such as integration, mainstreaming of handicapped children, and community-imposed budgetary restraints have affected the schools and children.

There are several factors that contribute to our inadequate knowledge. First are the difficulties inherent in conducting research in natural community settings such as the schools. Investigators frequently lack control over important experimental factors and must take advantage of naturally occurring situations rather than introduce variables in a controlled fashion. Proposed designs are often affected negatively by practical school exigencies so that resultant conclusions and interpretations must be offered on less than ideal experimental data.

Second, reaching definite conclusions in any area is complicated because of the divergency among competing theoretical orientations, the different populations studied, and the means of identifying and measuring independent and dependent variables. Third, and most important, our conceptions of mental health are changing, based upon the recognition that many of our clinical theories have been unnecessarily restricted and incomplete. Previously, causal interpretations of behaviors have focused primarily on individual pathological conditions and deficiencies. Currently, however, we are more aware that attention to prosocial and adaptive behavior can enhance our understanding of child development and that behavior cannot be treated apart from its situational context.

Newer research findings emphasizing environmental factors cannot be easily integrated with previous work that focused predominantly upon individual pathology. In effect, our knowledge of childhood growth and development is discontinuous and fluctuates over time as a function of the prevailing research and clinical *Zeitgeist*.

The purpose of this chapter is to provide an overview of mental health programs for elementary school children with a focus on treatment rather than diagnosis. The review offered here must be considered in the context of this chapter's opening comments. Our conceptions of school mental health and our knowledge base of causal and intervening variables are fragmented at best, and many important issues have yet to be explored satisfactorily. Nevertheless, the intent of this chapter is to focus on the cutting edge between current and future research and practice. Major attention is given to evaluating the effectiveness of existing treatment with an emphasis on prevention services and issues involved in implementation of mental health programs. This chapter begins with a brief discussion of the nature and extent of school maladaptation and the major problems involved in classifying children.

SCHOOL MALADAPTATION

Estimates of the prevalence of school maladjustment range from 2 percent to 30 percent, depending on classification criteria, possible variations in interpretation of adjustment status, and data collection methods. Lower figures in this range usually refer to the proportion of children who should receive special education services because of severe emotional disturbance or behavioral disorders (Wood & Zabel, 1978). Higher figures include children experiencing at least mild adjustment problems (Glidewell & Swallow, 1969). Despite the subjectivity involved, most professionals accept a 10-percent figure as reflecting those children whose adjustment difficulties interfere seriously with their academic and social development in school. There is usually more dysfunction noted in minorities and among the poor although it is difficult to distinguish possible cultural and social biases from these higher prevalence rates.

Achenbach and Edelbrock (1978) and Quay (1979) have provided an excellent perspective on the classification of childhood psychopathology. These reviewers point out that psychopathology has been studied much more intensively in adults than in children and numerous experimental problems characterize the current child literature. For example, the major clinical diagnostic systems developed by the American Psychiatric Association (1980) and the Group for Advancement of Psychiatry (1966) possess questionable reliability and validity, and more psychometrically refined rating scales and checklists are not necessarily clinically helpful with individual children.

Nevertheless, progress is being made. Several well-standardized measures have recently been developed to assess child behavior (Achenbach, 1978; Achenbach & Edelbrock, 1979; McDermott, 1980; Miller, 1972; Wirt et al., 1977). These measures represent a considerable advancement in assessment with respect to matters of reliability and validity, presence of normative data, and attempted differentiation of separate behavioral clusters or factors. Moreover, several of the above instruments have been developed exclusively for school settings and/or specifically assess prosocial behavior or adaptive functioning, an often neglected aspect of assessment. These measures should be consulted in addition to those that have always been popular in school studies such as the Behavior Problem Checklist and Conners' Scales (Peterson, 1961; Goyette, Conners, & Ulrich, 1978).

The most prevalent school adjustment problems fall into six major categories: aggressive/disruptive behavior; hyperactivity; learning difficulties including learning disabilities; social withdrawal/social isolation; school phobia and school refusal; and test and performance anxiety. Since these problems are treated in detail both in this volume (Kerasotes & Walker, "Hyperactive Behavior in Children," chap. 20 and Neeper & Lahey, "Learning Disabilities of Children," chap. 28) or elsewhere (Mash & Terdal, 1981; Quay & Werry, 1979; Wolman, Egan & Ross, 1978), these categories are not discussed here. A few comments can be made, however.

First, the above categories do not represent independent problem clusters; most maladaptive children's behavior overlaps into several categories. Second, there is little uniformity in the identification and description of school dysfunction. Since clinicians, educators, and researchers often adopt different theoretical viewpoints and practical orientations, the same child may receive different labels from different sources. The same child may be described as "behaviorally disordered" or "emotionally disturbed" by the school, "unsocialized aggressive" or "oppositionally disordered" by a clinician, and "non-self-controlled" or "acting-out" by researchers. Duncan (cited in Goldstein et al., 1975) reported that one child acquired 28 different labels during the course of successive professional evaluations.

Third, regardless of classification, children with excessive aggressive or disruptive behavior are the most troublesome and distressing for teachers and other school staff. In fact, difficulty in maintaining discipline or control is often cited as the most pressing problem in the schools (Costin, 1978; Clarizio & McCoy, 1976). Finally, test and performance anxiety may be the most prevalent and at the same time most ignored of all problems. Although estimates suggest that up to 20 percent or more of all school children suffer from test anxiety (Eysenck & Rachman, 1965), clinical interventions to resolve children's anxious reactions to school situations are rare (Barabasz, 1975; Mann, 1972).

By far the most common and economical way to assess children's school behavior is to depend on teachers' general evaluations or data from teacher rating scales or checklists. Most reviewers conclude that teachers can make fairly reliable and valid judgments of children's adjustment status when comparisons are made against various independent criteria (Green et al., 1980; Harris, Drummond, & Schultz, 1977).

Nevertheless, the evaluation of any individual teacher bears close examination for at least three reasons. First, there is considerable variability in the accuracy of teacher-provided data, suggesting that some teachers are better judges than others of children's behavior. Second, there is often much overlap in ratings given to well-adjusted and maladjusted children, indicating that the utility of teachers' data for individual children is not necessarily established. Third, teacher-provided data are seldom specific enough for planning individualized treatment programs for identified children. In effect, teachers' judgments are most

useful for initial screening purposes, but further systematic assessment is needed to confirm the accuracy of teachers' impressions and to detail the specific character of children's adjustment difficulties. For example, Allen et al. (1976) designed a program to increase social interaction in socially isolated and withdrawn children and solicited relevant referrals from teachers. However, these investigators eliminated over 30 percent of all referred children (16 of 52) from the proposed treatment when baseline observations indicated these children were interacting with peers over 90 percent of the time.

Dangers of Classification

The three-volume report of the Project on the Classification of Exceptional Children (Hobbs, 1975a, 1975b, 1975c) is must reading for anyone working with children. The federally sponsored project involved 93 contributors who attempted to survey current classification and labeling systems for children, assess the consequences resulting from currently employed policies and procedures, and offer recommendations for improving practices.

Project staff recognized the power and potential abuse in diagnostic systems:

Categories and labels are powerful instruments for social regulation and control, and they are often employed for obscure, covert or hurtful purposes: to degrade people, to deny them access to opportunity, to exclude undesirables whose presence in some way offends, disturbs familiar custom, or demands extraordinary effort. (p. 11)

Although it was acknowledged that some classification process is necessary to plan, organize, evaluate, and improve services, the final Project report was highly critical of current school practices. Problems were noted in five areas: (1) imprecision in the evaluation of school maladjustment, especially when conditions are mild or moderate in nature; such imprecision may lead to serious classification errors that have far-reaching negative implications for the child's school career; (2) discrimination against minorities and the poor due to the use of culturally biased assessment procedures; (3) overemphasis on pathologically oriented interpretations regarding the child's weaknesses at the expense of a broader view considering childhood strengths and potentials, and situational factors that cause or contribute to existing difficulties; (4) lack of educational relevance for most classification schemes; that is, formal diagnoses seldom identify specific teaching techniques that should be used to educate the child more effectively; and, finally, (5) too great a tendency to increase negative stereotyping among labelled children. It is impossible to do justice to the complexities of the Project report, but the five problems noted above are offered as a stimulus for the reader to consult the full report for more detail and explanation.

EVALUATING SCHOOL MENTAL HEALTH SERVICE

Levine and Graziano (1972) have traced the historical developments of mental health services for school children and shown how they have changed over time as a function of mental health professionals' disenchantment or enthusiasm for different helping procedures, consumer satisfaction with services, and manpower resources. Several major forms of service delivery can be identified.

The earliest school mental health services were provided by mental health professionals who received referrals from schools and diagnosed and treated children in the community as private practitioners or members of public service agencies. The child guidance movement of the 1920s and 1930s received many referrals from the schools. Gradually, schools began to develop their own pupil personnel services, and psychologists, social workers, and counselors employed by the school began to share the responsibility for assessment and treatment of school maladaptation. During the 1940s and 1950s, other service delivery techniques were developed. For instance, community-based professionals entered the schools and conducted school-based treatment programs. During the late 1950s and

early 1960s, a variety of consultation programs were offered by either community- or school-based professionals; the use of paraprofessionals to provide direct helping services also proliferated. A few attempts at primary and secondary prevention were also begun. In addition, special classes for children with serious emotional, behavioral, or learning problems were established by most school districts.

Presently, all the above-mentioned services may be available in any school district, but service priorities have changed somewhat. Treatment of maladapting children is still prominent, but significant advances have been made in the development and evaluation of primary and secondary prevention programs (see below). The use of paraprofessionals and teachers to implement school-based treatment programs has become strongly established. Accordingly, consultation has probably become the most popular method of service delivery on the part of professionals. A content analysis of the 1979 and 1980 volumes of the *Journal of School Psychology* indicates more articles devoted to consultation than to any other form of intervention. Moreover, a recent national survey indicated that school psychologists spend four times more of their time in consultation activities than in providing direct therapy to children (Lacayo, Sherwood, & Morris, 1981).

Nevertheless, the general picture in school mental health is discouraging. Although more attention is devoted to treatment than to prevention, most maladapting children do not receive the help they need. Meyers, Parsons, and Martin (1979) cite surveys indicating that only 2–4 percent of the school population is referred to pupil personnel staff or to outside agencies for evaluation (versus the up to 30 percent who are experiencing school difficulty). Moreover, the 2–4 percent figures refer only to evaluation, not treatment, which may or may not be undertaken, and, if offered, may not be sucessful. Unfortunately, there is little evidence regarding the effectiveness of many helping services routinely provided to maladapting school children. In summary, the same crisis that exists in the child mental health field as a whole (Joint Commission,

1969) affects the schools. Most school children in need of help are not receiving any; and many who do receive helping services receive attention that is relatively late in coming and of dubious effectiveness. This state of affairs dictates that current school mental health programs should be critically examined. The following discussion evaluates first the major treatment techniques and then the different methods of service delivery that have been used to address the mental health needs of school children.

Table 27.1 presents a summary evaluation of the effectiveness of different treatment approaches for school maladjustment. The four major therapeutic techniques most commonly used in the schools (psychodynamic, humanistic, behavioral, and drug treatment) are evaluated using 15 criteria. The evaluative criteria were adapted from Kazdin (1978a) and

Table 27.1   Evaluation of Major Treatments for School Adjustment Problems Using 15 Selected Criteria

Criteria	Treatments			
	Psychodynamic	Humanistic	Behavioral	Pharmacological
Evidence of treatment effectiveness[a]				
1. Short term effects	3	2	1	2
2. Generalization effects	3	3	2	2
3. Maintenance of change	3	3	2	3
4. Social validity of change	?	?	2	?
5. Minimal negative side effects	?	?	1	3
6. Majority of clients improve with treatment	?	?	1	2
Implementation of treatment[b]				
7. Administrative & professional coordination/cooperation needed	1	1	1	1
8. Applicability for diverse problems	4	3	1	4
9. Staff-child ratio	4	3	2	2
10. Use of paraprofessionals	4	2	1	4
11. Brevity of therapy	4	2	1	2
Costs of treatment[b]				
12. Financial cost	4	3	1	3
13. Stigmatizing effect of treatment	4	4	3	4
14. Overall cost effectiveness (are all gains greater than all costs?)	?	?	?	?
Consumer evaluation of treatment[b]				
15. Consumer reaction to treatment (acceptability of, satisfaction with treatment; ratio of continuers vs. dropouts, etc.)	3	3	3	3

Note. These criteria are modified from Kazdin (1978a) and Sajwaj et al. (1979). Evaluations were based, in large part, upon information from Abramowitz (1976), Atkeson & Forehand (1978, 1979), Ayllon & Rosenbaum (1977), Barrett, Hampe, & Miller (1978), Baskin & Hess (1980), Clarizio (1979), Cobb & Medway (1978), Craighead, Wilcoxon-Craighead, & Meyers (1978), Elardo & Elardo (1976), Kirschenbaum & Ordman (in press), Klein (1979), Levine & Graziano (1972), MacMillan & Morrison (1979), Medway & Smith (1978), Meyers et al., (1979), O'Dell (1974), O'Leary & O'Leary (1976), Phillips & Ray (1980), Robin & Wegenfeld (1981), Romanczyk, Kistner, & Crimmins (1980), and Sajwaj et al. (1979).

A "?" for any rating indicates there is insufficient data upon which to make a rating or that advantages/disadvantages are mixed.

[a]Ratings for this section are: 1 = usually demonstrated; 2 = sometimes demonstrated; 3 = infrequently demonstrated.

[b]Ratings for this section are: 1 = very strong advantage for intervention; 2 = slight to moderate advantage; 3 = slight to moderate disadvantage; 4 = strong disadvantage.

Sajwaj, McNees, and Schnelle (1979) and only a few merit explanation.

Criterion 4, social validity, refers to whether or not investigators have assessed the clinical or applied significance as opposed to the statistical significance of treatment effects. Customary research procedures do not necessarily demonstrate the practical importance of treatment outcomes. Statistical significance may be achieved with changes of small magnitude or clients may change over time or differ at posttreatment from initially comparable untreated controls without displaying a "meaningful" change in their functioning. Kadzin (1977) and Van Houten (1979) have discussed various methods that can be used in determining a treatment's social validity.

Similarly, criterion 6, examining the proportion of subjects who improve with treatment, is another important evaluative dimension. Reliance upon grouped data exclusively does not indicate whether significant results were obtained because a majority of the treatment group changed favorably or because dramatic changes occurred in only a few subjects and therefore most were unaffected by the treatment. Inspection of individual data also assists in assessing the nature and extent of negative side effects.

It can be seen that each treatment was evaluated along four dimensions that relate to: clinical effectiveness (criteria 1–6), manner of implementation (9–11), cost (12–14), and consumer satisfaction (15). These criteria interact to determine the value or relevancy of alternative treatments in specific situations. A treatment that is lengthy and financially costly but produces long term therapeutic changes may be preferable to an inexpensive, brief intervention that has only transitory effects.

Several caveats must be offered regarding the ratings in Table 27.1. Whenever possible, ratings were based on the results of evaluative research reviews or the consensus of different authors. Many of these references are listed at the bottom of Table 27.1. Nevertheless, some ratings had to be made on limited information. Furthermore, ratings were made collectively for all variations of each therapy as applied to all adjustment problems. Unfortunately, such

a procedure discriminates against certain interventions depending on the situation. Pharmacotherapy receives a poor rating for its applicability to diverse problems although this treatment is often cited as the treatment of choice for hyperactivity. Pharmacotherapy is included in Table 27.1 primarily for comparative purposes. Since this intervention is treated in depth in another chapter of this book (Campbell, Perry, & Green, "Organic and Drug Treatment," chap. 27), it is not discussed further here.

Explanations for some ratings are necessary. To illustrate the advantages and disadvantages of such an approach, ratings on criterion 7 were made as if treatments were administered by professionals although behavioral techniques are more frequently implemented by paraprofessionals in the schools. As professionally administered interventions, the four treatments generally receive high ratings on criterion 7 but low ratings on criterion 13. Professionals assume the responsibility for treatment so that little administrative coordination regarding others' duties and responsibilities is needed, but, at the same time, treatment tends to stigmatize participating children as "maladjusted" or "disturbed." However, it must be emphasized that procedural variations can affect a treatment's ratings on any criterion.

Notwithstanding the above qualifications, some general observations can be drawn from Table 27.1. Generally, both psychodynamic and humanistic therapy receive poor ratings on several important criteria such as 8, 9, and 12. The last approach fares better than the first concerning the use of paraprofessionals, brevity of treatment, applicability for diverse problems, and staff-child ratio. However, research has only infrequently demonstrated the durability and generality of treatment effects for either therapy, and there is insufficient data regarding each therapy's social validity, the existence of side effects and the treatment's impact upon individual children (criterion 6).

Compared to the other approaches, behavior therapy receives the most favorable ratings overall and receives the highest possible ratings on several important criteria, namely, 1, 8, 10, and 11. Relative to the other treatments, there is much more evidence regarding behavior therapy's short term clinical effectiveness (criterion 1) and somewhat more evidence regarding its generalization and maintenance effects. Moreover, behavior therapy has the comparative advantage of brevity and applicability to diverse problems. Researchers have also made the most progress in demonstrating behavior therapy's social validity compared to other treatments, and its impact on a high proportion of treated individuals. Because of the extent to which behavioral techniques can be and have been taught to paraprofessionals, behavior therapy has added advantages of staff-child ratio, financial cost, and, of course, use of paraprofessionals.

The above conclusions are generally congruent with the views of others. Clarizio (1979) cited 10 major advantages for behavioral techniques ranging from their economical approach toward working in the child's natural social environment (the classroom) to their emphasis on the development of healthy behaviors as well as the reduction of negative behavior. Even Ryan (1979) who has reservations concerning the use of behavior modification in the schools, has recently admitted that

"it is generally accepted that in some circumstances and for children with certain problems any effective teacher or school psychologist should be able to implement a behavioral program" (p. 131).

Nevertheless, the apparent superiority of behavior therapy is relative; many issues have yet to be resolved regarding the clinical impact, efficiency, and value of behavior change techniques. It should be noted that no ratings were offered for any treatment's overall cost effectiveness (criterion 14), primarily because none of the interventions has been examined in sufficient depth and breadth to make such a determination. Moreover, definite claims of the relative superiority of one treatment over another cannot be made because of the paucity of well-controlled comparative research studies.

Furthermore, evaluations cannot be limited to the type of treatment administered. Equally important is the method of service delivery that interacts with the characteristics of a treatment to determine the overall value of a mental health program. Different methods of service delivery have different advantages and disadvantages. This is illustrated in Table 27.2, in which nine of the same evaluative criteria are applied to 10 different methods of service

Table 27.2   Evaluation of Alternative Methods of Service Delivery

	Criteria								
	7	8	9	10	11	12	13	14	15
Intervention initiated through:									
I. Referral to community-based professionals	2	1	3	3	3	4	4	?	3
II. Family-oriented programs	4	2	2	1	2	2	1	?	4
III. Consultation	4	1	2	3	2	2	1	?	4
School-based interventions implemented by:									
IV. Professionals	2	1	2	N/A	3	3	3	?	2
V. Paraprofessionals	3	1	1	N/A	1	1	1	?	3
Specialized services delivered through:									
VI. Special class placement	4	4	4	3	4	4	4	?	3
VII. Hospital day school placement	3	4	4	3	4	4	4	?	3
VIII. Institutional placement	3	4	4	3	4	4	4	?	3
Preventive interventions implemented as:									
IX. Primary prevention	4	1	1	1	2	2	1	?	3
X. Secondary prevention	4	1	1	1	2	2	3	?	3

Note. See Table 27.1 for explanation of criteria and rating dimensions and references upon which ratings were based.

delivery. Among the approaches considered, consultation, primary and secondary prevention, and paraprofessionally implemented programs possess several inherent advantages compared to the other methods of service delivery. Their strongest advantages appear on such criteria as 8, 9, 10, and 13. These approaches, however, have at least two major disadvantages stemming from the complexities involved in their implementation (criterion 7) and the fact that consumers may not respond to proposed treatment procedures (criterion 15). For example, the preventively oriented interventions may require complex administrative and professional arrangements with the staff of host schools. The task of negotiating these hurdles is often fraught with problems (Mannarino & Durlak, 1980).

Many parent-oriented programs are unable to reach those most in need. The parents of many children with serious school problems may not participate in the service that is offered (Levine & Graziano, 1972). Consultation is another procedure that is difficult to implement effectively. Consultation is usually conceptualized as an intricate interpersonal process with several stages, such as entry into a system; negotiation of a contract between consultant and consultee; problem identification; and the development, monitoring, and evaluation of some intervention. In comparison, there are fewer complexities involved in paraprofessional therapy programs providing that schools accept the paraprofessional as a legitimate service provider. Nevertheless, professionals must spend time and energy selecting, training, and supervising paraprofessionals if the latter are to work effectively, and few professionals have the necessary background and training in this regard (Durlak, 1982).

Since Table 27.2 was designed to compare alternative service delivery systems, the six criteria related to treatment effectiveness were not included. With some exceptions, any of the four treatments presented in Table 27.1 could conceivably be expedited in any of the 10 service delivery formats in Table 27.2. Practically speaking, however, behavior therapy has tended to be the most flexibly implemented (i.e., adaptable to most of the service delivery modes), followed by humanistic treatment, then psychodynamic treatment, and lastly, as one might expect, pharmacotherapy. It is possible to comment only briefly here on the effectiveness of interventions offered according to the different service delivery modes.

Community-Based Treatment

The effects of community-based professional services upon children's school behavior are often indeterminable. Private practitioners and staffs of community agencies may interpret behavior indicative of school maladjustment as stemming from intrapsychic or familial factors. Hence, referrals for poor school adjustment may be relabeled by the treatment agent and therapy outcome data relative to school functioning may not be collected. Therefore, it is difficult to ascertain the representativeness of findings from community-based studies that have collected school-related outcome data (e.g., Love, Kaswan, & Bugental, 1972).

Family-Oriented Programs

There have been many studies in which parents have been trained or counseled on how to deal with their child's problems, but many of these studies do not distinguish clearly between problems at home and those at school. Although many programs have successfully reduced children's school difficulties, the results of many programs fail to demonstrate generalized and durable overt changes in the child's school functioning (Atkeson & Forehand, 1978, 1979; Cobb & Medway, 1978; O'Dell, 1974). Moreover, it is still not clear whether working through parents (or teachers for that matter) yields better results than direct treatment of the child, since too few direct comparisons of alternative approaches have been conducted.

Consultation

Conclusions regarding the effectiveness of school consultation programs must be guarded. Consultation has produced positive results and the majority of successful programs have used behavioral principles, but not many studies have been well controlled (Meyers et al., 1979). It is hoped that the increasing interest in consultation will encourage more careful study of the conditions under which this style of helping is most effective.

School-Based Treatment

The results of school-based interventions appear to vary as a function of the treatment technique used. Behaviorally oriented interventions are generally effective whether employed by professionals or paraprofessionals; results for humanistic or psychodynamic treatment have been inconsistent regardless of the training of the helping agent. Paraprofessionals rarely implement psychodynamically oriented procedures, however.

It should be noted that, as a rule, paraprofessionally implemented programs have been very successful and paraprofessionals have been used extensively in schools. Paraprofessionals include all those who do not have formal postbaccalaureate mental health training. The paraprofessionals most often used in school programs are high school and college students, parents, housewives, teachers' aides, and teachers. The latter are included only to maintain the distinction that their professional training is in education, not mental health. Indeed, most teachers do not receive the training in mental health or child development that they need for their educational roles (see below). Peers have also been used successfully as therapeutic agents, and the results of many of the programs indicate the strong influence that peers have upon each other's behavior and development (McGee, Kauffman, & Nussen, 1977).

Specialized Services

Outcome data for the effectiveness of specialized treatment services (8, 9, and 10) are not encouraging. Evidence is meager with respect to the positive impact of special classes for school children, hospital day schools, and residential treatment programs. Moreover, these service approaches have several disadvantages on such criteria as financial costs, staff-child ratio, and brevity and stigmatizing effects of treatment.

Notwithstanding the above comments, there are examples of successful programs in these areas. These programs are usually multifaceted efforts that include combinations of psychoeducational programming, individual psychotherapy, behavioral modification, parent involvement, and perhaps pharmacotherapy (MacMillan & Morrison, 1979; Romanczyk et al., 1980).

Preventive Interventions

Before primary and secondary prevention are discussed in detail, it is necessary to distinguish these approaches from each other and from tertiary prevention. The four treatments evaluated in Table 27.1 were considered forms of tertiary prevention, that is, treatment for maladapting individuals whose problems were of a relatively long-standing nature. In effect, tertiary prevention is preventive only in the sense of reducing the possibility that current problems will become worse and therefore more debilitating. By contrast, secondary prevention involves prompt intervention for early detected dysfunction that is discovered through some systematic screening or early case-finding approach.

Primary prevention represents a significant departure from both secondary and tertiary prevention. Whereas the latter two approaches attend to maladaptive behavior, primary prevention is primarily non-problem-oriented and seeks to promote competency and adaptive behavior in asymptomatic populations. The ultimate goal of primary prevention is to prevent maladjustment, but it is believed that this goal is best reached by promoting mental health through the development of personal competencies. There is considerable confusion regarding primary, secondary, and tertiary prevention, and how to categorize different programs. As Cowen (1980) has observed, there are many more claims of preventive work than are warranted when one considers the characteristics and outcomes of the intervention in question. The primary and secondary preventive programs discussed here are those that have achieved consensual validation regarding their preventive character (see also chap. 50 in this book, Peterson & Ridley-Johnson, "Prevention of Childhood Disorders").

School-based preventive interventions are discussed in detail here for two important reasons. First, research on preventive programs has increased dramatically in the past few years so that readers need to be updated regarding recent programs and findings. Second, it seems necessary to redress some of the imbalance that has always existed in the literature favoring treatment over prevention. Prevention has much greater epidemiological value than treatment. The only way substantially to affect the overall incidence and prevalence of maladjustment in target populations is through prevention, not treatment.

For example, some simple arithmetic recently presented by Clarizio (1979) indicates that there is a far greater need for primary prevention than for any other type of service. Clarizio (1979) offered the reasonable estimates that approximately 30 percent of the total population of troubled children will also have serious adjustment problems as adults and approximately 8 percent of well-adjusted children will experience a similar fate. Assume that in a population of 20 million youth aged 18 and under, 10 percent are experiencing serious adjustment problems (Population A = 2 million); and the remaining youth are relatively well adjusted (Population B = 18 million). Over time, Population A will yield 600,000 disturbed adults (a 30-percent continuance rate) whereas Population B will contribute about 1,440,000 (an 8-percent continuance rate). In effect, compared to the population of disturbed children, the population of normal children will contribute more than twice as many bodies to the population of maladjusted adults. Clarizio (1979) estimates that 70 per-cent of disturbed adults were once "normal" children.

Primary Prevention

Many primary prevention programs have recently been implemented in the schools. These programs have been labeled and described in various ways and are often identified as efforts at "affective education." Affective education includes such programs as the Human Development Program ("Magic Circle"), Developing Understanding of Self and Others (DUSO), Teacher Effectiveness Training, Ojemann's Causal Approach, Interpersonal Problem-Solving Training, Schools Without Failure, and various program modifications (see Baskin & Hess, 1980; Elardo & Elardo, 1976; Medway & Smith, 1978). Programs vary widely in rationale, complexity, and procedural applications, but, in general, interventions are implemented by the regular classroom teacher in daily 10- to 30-minute periods. The focus is upon promoting interpersonal development by helping children first understand their own and their peers' attitudes, values, and feelings, and then to use this increased knowledge to guide their behavior in social situations. In effect, many programs attempt to affect children's emotional and social-cognitive development, which, it is hoped, will then improve their overt behavioral adjustment.

Affective education programs have obtained mixed results. Although a majority of programs have produced significant improvement in target measures underlying the program's rationale (e.g., interpersonal problem-solving abilities, affective sensitivity, self-perception), fewer investigations reflect positive changes in self-concept, peer relations, or overt indices of adjustment. Moreover, there is no clear evidence that success in reaching a program's primary learning or training objectives is actually related to any concomitant clinical or behavioral gains manifested by participating children. For example, Spivack and Shure (Spivack & Shure, 1974; Spivack, Platt, & Shure, 1976) have maintained that children's ability to solve interpersonal problems is an important determinant of their school adjustment. Accordingly, they developed a systematic approach to teach preschool and primary grade children these skills, and their approach has been emulated by several other investigators.

However, recent data fail to confirm Spivack et al.'s theory regarding the central role of interpersonal problem-solving skills. Investigators have failed to find significant relationships between children's problem-solving skills and other indices of school adjustment (Gillespie Durlak, & Sherman, 1982; Weissberg et al., 1981). In their evaluative review, Kirschenbaum and Ordman (in press) offer this somber assessment:

In sum, it appears that despite the intuitive appeal of SPS [social problem-solving skills], making their acquisition the core element for prevention programs directed at children in primary grades or older is a gamble that is not paying off. (p. 215)

Similarly, other reviewers have noted that empirical rationale for training children in various social, cognitive, or affective competencies in other affective education programs has also yet to be convincingly demonstrated (Baskin & Hess, 1980; Elardo & Elardo, 1976; Medway & Smith, 1978).

Therefore, it appears that conceptual and theoretical refinements are needed in many current affective education programs. The success of affective education is predicated upon correctly identifying core skills that undergrid adjustment and whose enhancement improves mental health. Such core skills that could serve as the basis of school-based training programs still need more precise identification and explication.

Another approach toward primary prevention is ecological. Preventive ecological interventions attempt to identify and maximize an environment's positive effects or reduce its negative effects, and/or to determine the best person-environmental fit or match for different subject groups. It seems logical that pupils react differently to different teaching methods and classroom atmospheres, but documenting these ecological interactions is difficult. The development of an effective taxonomy of school environments is just beginning and person-environmental interactions are tremendously complex (Gump, 1980; Weinstein, 1979). Centra and Potter (1980) note that the effects of any one variable are small compared to the combined interactive effects of all other relevant variables. Yet the population of all relevant variables is unknown, so that the task of measuring all potentially causal and intervening variables in ecological research is formidable indeed.

One promising approach that has yielded early positive returns involves creating learning situations that capitalize upon interdependent, cooperative behaviors among students and focus upon active versus passive learning. Gump (1980) has reviewed several of these programs. As one example, in the Teams-Games-Tournament (TGT) format, small groups of students of roughly equal academic ability are rewarded for working cooperatively to prepare for different educational tournaments or games. TGT has produced significant gains in academic achievement and motivation, self-esteem, and peer liking and support.

Peer tutoring is also an educational technique with implications for primary prevention. Studies have demonstrated that a tutoring relationship is often mutually beneficial for the tutor as well as the tutee; both participants may show improvement not only in learning but also in self-esteem and attitudes toward school (Allen, 1976). Peer tutoring can also foster peer cooperation and support and reduce competition and performance pressures. As noted earlier, many children experience test or performance anxiety in school situations, and peer tutoring and other interdependent learning situations such as TGT are one way to reduce negative environmental school pressures.

Finally, programs aimed at the prevention of illicit drug use and nonhealthy behaviors such as smoking deserve comment. Traditionally, preventively oriented programs in these areas have often depended upon fear arousal techniques emphasizing the hazardous psychosocial and physiological effects of drug taking. There is general agreement that such preventive programs have not been successful

(Kinder, Pape, & Walfish, 1980; Schaps et al., 1980). Many of these unsuccessful programs have implicitly or explicitly assumed that personal deficiencies dispose individuals toward the use, and, eventually, the abuse of drugs.

By contrast, recent preventive programs have speculated that a variety of psychosocial factors contribute to youthful drug taking. Accordingly, many multicomponent programs have emphasized social skills training including self-control and assertiveness training, work on effective decision-making skills, and, in particular, practice in resisting peer pressure to take drugs. Results of these social-skills-oriented programs have been promising. Several recent programs have reported success in changing students' smoking and drug-taking behaviors and some have also improved students' attitudes toward school and self (Hurd et al., 1980; Kearney & Hines, 1980; Kim, 1981a; 1981b; Perry et al., 1980). The long term impact of these interventions has not been determined, however.

Secondary Prevention

Several exciting developments have occurred in the secondary prevention of school maladjustment. For many years, the Primary Mental Health Project (PMHP) in Rochester, New York, served as virtually the only workable demonstration of a secondary prevention program. PMHP identified four primary components in its program model: (1) a focus on young children; (2) systematic screening and detection of maladapting children; (3) use of paraprofessionals as direct helping agents for identified children; and (4) a changing role for mental health professionals to emphasize program development, consultation, and the selection, training, and supervision of paraprofessionals.

Beginning in 1972 and assisted by NIMH-funding, PMHP staff began a five-year systematic national and regional dissemination program to encourage the development of conceptually related programs in other school districts. This dissemination effort was highly successful. A 1977 survey indicated that there were at least 30 other school programs that

had been directly or indirectly influenced by the PMHP program model and dissemination effort. During the 1976–1977 school year, secondary prevention programs were operating in over 200 schools throughout the country and had delivered over 100,000 helping services to approximately 3,250 children (Cowen, Davidson, & Gesten, 1980). The PMHP survey by no means covers all secondary prevention programs. Other programs that have developed independently of PMHP nevertheless share several similar features (Butler et al., 1980; Camp et al., 1977; Kellam et al., 1975).

Although current programs are similar conceptually, there has been wide variation in program practices. Duration of treatment has ranged from a few weeks to a year or more; both behavioral and nonbehavioral therapy techniques have been used in individual and group contexts; and teachers, housewives, college students, school counselors and nurses, and community volunteers have functioned as the primary therapeutic agents.

Despite this diversity of procedural elements, there has been amazing consistency in the results of systematic program evaluations. Studies conducted in 12 different school districts have indicated that secondary prevention programs are effective in the treatment of school maladaptation (Allen et al., 1976; Butler et al., 1980; Camp et al., 1977; Cowen et al., 1975; Durlak, 1977, 1980; Kellam et al., 1975; Kirschenbaum, 1979; Mannarino et al., 1982; Rickel & Smith, 1979; Sandler, Duricko, & Grande, 1975; Durlak & Mannarino, 1981). This research evidence is far from definitive, but outcome data indicate that prompt school-based treatment is effective in improving the school adjustment of target children. Furthermore, short term follow-up data suggest that treatment gains are, by and large, maintained.

An important issue in secondary prevention programs, apart from the effectiveness of interventions, is the accurate identification of school maladjustment. Lacking consensus regarding the definition of mental health or psychopathology, workers must proceed cautiously when attempting to classify children's adjustment status. For example, programs run the risk of labeling some children as maladjusted, thus establishing or reinforcing negative stereotypes or expectations among school staff regarding the child's personality or behavior. On the other hand, one of the principal assumptions of secondary prevention programming is that intervention for early detected dysfunction is more likely to be successful compared to services offered for long-standing problems. Therefore, it is urgent to detect adjustment problems early in the child's school career.

Several researchers have investigated the utility of one of the two screening instruments used by PMHP, the AML. The AML is an 11-item, three-factor, quick-screening teacher rating scale designed to detect early school maladjustment (Cowen et al., 1973). Research indicates that AML ratings offer effective, although imperfect, discriminations between well adjusting and maladapting children.

For example, Carberry and Handal (1980) assessed the AML's screening efficiency by making comparisons to professionals' independent evaluations of children's school adjustment. They reported an 86-percent hit rate for the AML for true positives (children with high AML scores and independently confirmed by professional evaluations as having problems). The percentage of false negatives could not be determined; 87 percent of the true negatives were correctly identified and 13 percent were false positives (children with high AML scores but not considered as maladapting according to professional evaluations). Similarly, Durlak, Stein, and Mannarino (1980) found significant correlations between AML scores and data obtained through independent observations of children's classroom behavior. They reported that it was difficult to classify children with AML scores in the middle of the distribution correctly but that anywhere from 60–100 percent of the children with the lowest and highest AML ratings could be correctly identified depending on the cut-off score utilized.

Although current data indicate that the AML is a relatively efficient mass-screening instrument, there are several limitations in its use. First, data are lacking on the number of false negatives in AML screening studies (i.e.,

how many children with low AML ratings are actually experiencing school adjustment problems). Second, it is unknown how many problems identified by the AML are transitory. Third, the AML more effectively identifies more extreme maladjustment as compared to moderate dysfunction. Finally, investigators are unanimous in their caution that the AML should not be the sole criterion to identify school maladaptation. Various supplemental assessments should be accomplished, particularly those that can help plan treatment to remedy the child's specific difficulties.

For the most part, previous reviewers had to be content with concluding that the secondary prevention of school maladjustment was a promising possibility with many unknowns such as the feasibility of widescale implementation and therapeutic impact. Now there are fewer unknowns. At this point it can be concluded: (1) A general model of secondary prevention (as exemplified by PMHP) is a viable alternative to conceptualizing and delivering school mental health services; (2) Mental health professionals and educators agree on several important features of a secondary preventive approach and many schools are willing to sponsor such efforts; (3) A general program model can be flexibly adapted to suit the needs, interests, resources, and characteristics of different schools and communities, as witnessed by the diversity of existing program practices; (4) Most important, interventions yield positive results, at least in the short term.

Summary

The information in Table 27.1 and 27.2 indicates the complexities involved in evaluating school mental health programs and presents one perspective regarding the value of currently used approaches. Determining the value of current programs is difficult because both the treatment and the manner in which it is offered can be assessed using multiple criteria. These criteria include clinical impact, characteristics regarding implementation, financial costs, and consumer reaction. Each treatment modality and method of service delivery has some advantages and disadvantages. The value of applying a specific treatment to a child in a particular school setting is thereby affected by multiple interacting factors. It is no wonder that we are still struggling to assess the relative effects of different treatment approaches for different problems. Ultimately, a three-tiered service model that integrates elements of primary, secondary, and tertiary prevention is necessary to respond comprehensively to the mental health needs of school children. Unfortunately, we are a long way from identifying the characteristics of such a model that would provide services to children in the most efficient, effective, and economical manner.

PROGRAM IMPLEMENTATION

The most important information regarding school mental health programs is the most difficult to acquire, namely, how the program was implemented. As Sarason (1971) has indicated, there are many dimensions to the change process including: (1) the specific conditions that gave rise to the need or motivation for change and the individuals involved with these conditions: (2) the alternative actions considered and finally adopted and why; (3) the problems or obstacles which arose during the program, as well as their resolution, and, finally, (4) the program evaluation procedures introduced, modified, and eventually conducted. Data regarding these important elements of program implementation are not available in most clinical or research reports.

Implementation refers to the actual use of an innovation, or what the innovation consists of in practice. Evidence suggests that highly similar programs are actually implemented very differently across settings; many proposed programs are either never put into practice or, if initiated, are not completed; and, finally, those programs that are begun are not always used, adopted, or evaluated as planned (Berman & McLaughlin, 1976; Fullan & Pomfret, 1977). Berman and McLaughlin (1976) suggest that in some cases the implementation strategy is a more important factor affecting outcome than the characteristics of

the proposed program or the quantity and quality of available resources.

Implementation is not the simple application of a proposed technique but a complex interactive process involving the proposed program, host setting, and associated personnel. The most effective combination of factors related to effective implementation is unknown. At the risk of simplifying a complex subject, it is possible to highlight several characteristics of the proposed innovation and the working relationship between the change agent and the schools that increase the likelihood that a proposed program will be conducted as planned.

The explicitness, simplicity, flexibility, and problem-solving potential of an innovation favor implementation. Likewise, a working relationship characterized by open channels of communication that allows teachers meaningful input into the decision-making process is also favorable. The change agent should prepare a clear and highly specific explanation of the proposed innovation; teachers cannot commit themselves to procedures they do not understand. The simplicity of an innovation refers to how much time, energy, and new role demands are required on the part of teachers; simple innovations are more apt to be carried out than complex ones. Teachers are apt to be apprehensive about proposed changes, particularly if these changes involve new role demands for them. Efforts to relieve this apprehension by continual professional and personnel support are essential. Problem-solving potential refers to whether or not an innovation is perceived as a response to locally identified needs and problems. Schools implement changes more effectively when changes are potential solutions to important issues they believe they are facing.

During the implementation process, it is important to give teachers a voice regarding the when and how of program procedures and to maintain both informal and formal open lines of communication. Some conflicts, tensions, or disagreements are to be expected and should be dealt with openly rather than denied or ignored. Providing teachers meaningful input into how the innovation is to be introduced is important; teachers who have input at the initial stages of change are apt to be more cooperative once the program is begun. An innovation's flexibility is important during this period of negotiation and compromise; procedures that can accommodate the unique features of a setting and the preferences and reactions of relevant staff will be more successful. Flexibility also refers to the explicit offering of a program as one possible solution out of a universe of many alternatives. Indeed, the process of change is best approached by constantly emphasizing that there are a multitude of ways to conceptualize and resolve problems and the task is to evaluate a range of alternatives in some systematic fashion. Schools are likely to dichotomize research and service and usually express little value for the former program element. Therefore, it is important that the change agent make sure there is a practical research pay-off to the schools and that teachers perceive research and service as inseparable and mutually supportive program components. Finally, change agents must be aware of possible obstacles and resistances to change and how to overcome them; this knowledge must be based on characteristics of the setting and individuals with which one is to work. Sarason (1971) has observed that many proposed school innovations are not conceptualized or implemented with an adequate understanding of the "culture" of the school. The "culture" of a school involves, among other things, its social structure, traditions, and usual ways of accommodating itself to change. Therefore, effective implementation is a time-consuming process that requires careful planning; hastily developed and executed programs are doomed to failure. The change agent must become realistically acquainted with the goals, practices, values, and structures of the school. Unless a proposed program is consonant with or can accommodate these dimensions of the setting, acceptance and incorporation of change are unlikely.

PL 94-142

The Education for All Handicapped Children Act, passed by Congress in 1975, is an excel-

lent example of the importance of the implementation process. PL 94–142, as it is commonly identified, is a complex piece of legislation that describes the rights of handicapped children in obtaining a free public education and the procedures school districts must follow in assuring these rights are safeguarded (see Ingram, 1980). In brief, PL 94–142 is designed to assure that all handicapped children receive an education appropriate to their individual needs and was enacted in the light of discriminatory practices against the handicapped that were apparent in many school districts throughout the country. According to the law, "handicapped" children include the mentally retarded, emotionally disturbed, learning disabled, and physically and sensory handicapped, aged 3–21, approximately 12 percent of all school children.

Although there is no major quarrel with the spirit and intent of the law, serious reservations have been expressed regarding the ultimate quantity and quality of implementation that will be demonstrated by different school districts (*Journal of Special Education,* 1981). First of all, educators are severely hampered in providing services for the handicapped since there are no established criteria to identify these children, diagnose their specific strengths and weaknesses, and determine and evaluate the best placements for them. Moreover, circumstances surrounding PL 94–142 violate several of the important principles listed above that are deemed important for an effective implementation process or strategy.

The most important issue is that the public law is an externally imposed innovation that does not necessarily respond to locally perceived needs and problems and, as such, may have limited potential for effective implementation. Sabbatino (1981) has noted that no externally imposed or mandated program has ever been effectively incorporated into the American school system. Moreover, many elements of the law lack operational clarity; local schools may be unclear as to what is and is not expected of them and how flexibly they can act. The law also requires many added duties and responsibilities of both regular and specialty teachers without providing the resources or anticipating the extensive training and development programs. In summary, what started out as a legislative attempt to improve services for handicapped school children has become seriously hampered by insufficient attention to a successful implementation process. Improvement of services for target children will ultimately depend on how well the advocates of PL 94–142 can overcome the complicated problems involved in the practical application of proposed changes.

A KIND WORD FOR TEACHERS

This chapter concludes with an attempt to increase empathy toward teachers, who, it seems, are often unfairly criticized for failing to do all they can for children. The American school system frequently undergoes intense social and political pressure for its failure to meet community expectations regarding the education of youth. Articles in the lay press with eyecatching headlines like "Schoolhouse Blues" (*New Republic,* 1981) and "Why Public Schools Fail" (*Newsweek,* 1981) often dramatize schools' educational deficiencies. Teachers, in particular, bear the brunt of this community pressure. For example, parents often attribute their child's unsatisfactory school performance to the teacher's professional or personal inadequacy or insensitivity. Such criticisms directed at teachers are unjustified.

In fact, most of the limitations that teachers demonstrate primarily result from built-in job pressures and stress and the unrealistic character of the educational enterprise. Sarason (1971) has painted a compassionate portrait of the typical classroom teacher that illustrates this point. In effect, teachers face an impossible task. There is virtually no way a teacher can provide all classroom children with the quantity and quality of instruction and attention each child deserves and needs.

Many factors account for this situation. Invariably, new teachers experience a "baptism by fire" since their professional training programs do not adequately prepare them for the psychological demands of their job. The overwhelming majority of teachers contacted by Sarason (1971) felt that their college experiences were largely irrelevant to their work. Moreover, and most importantly, teachers are assigned too many children who are too varied in ability. The demands of individualizing instruction for each child in each subject are overwhelming. Even those teachers who muster the considerable ability, creativity, and energy it requires to achieve acceptable educational results, may eventually "burn out" as the continual demands and pressures of teaching take their toll. Most teachers must function with inadequate physical and pedagogical resources and, in addition, usually do not receive the administrative, personal, and professional support they need. Under such circumstances, it is not surprising that at one time or another every teacher seriously considers quitting teaching forever.

Unfortunately, this discussion does not end on a happy note. Extensive modifications are needed in our school systems and professional training programs to make teaching a more realistic and less stressful occupation. There are no assurances that such changes will ever be implemented to the degree that they are needed. In the meantime, those who propose and offer mental health services that are attuned to educators' built-in job pressures and conflicts are apt to experience the most success in establishing effective working relationships with school personnel.

REFERENCES

Abramowitz, C.V. The effectiveness of group psychotherapy with children. *Archives of General Psychiatry,* 1976, **33,** 320–326.

Achenbach, T.M. The Child behavior profile: I. Boys aged 6 through 11. *Journal of Consulting and Clinical Psychology,* 1978, **46,** 478–488.

Achenbach, T.M., & Edelbrock, C.S. The classification of child psychopathology: A review and analysis of empirical efforts. *Journal of Consulting and Clinical Psychology,* 1978, **85,** 1275–1301.

Achenbach, T.M., & Edelbrock, C.S. The Child behavior profile: II. Boys aged 12–16 and girls aged 6–11 and 12–16. *Journal of Consulting and Clinical Psychology,* 1979, **47,** 223–233.

Allen, C.J., Chinsky, J.M., Larcen, S.W., Lochman, J.E., & Selinger, H.V. *Community psychology and the schools: A behaviorally oriented multi-level preventive approach.* Hillsdale, N.J.: Erlbaum, 1976.

Allen, V.L. (Ed.). *Children as teachers: Theory and research on tutoring.* New York: Academic Press, 1976.

American Psychiatric Association. *Diagnostic and statistical manual of mental disorders* (3rd ed.). Washington, D.C.: Author, 1980.

Atkeson, B.M., & Forehand, R. Parent behavioral training for problem children: An examination of studies using multiple outcome. *Journal of Abnormal Child Psychology,* 1978, **6,** 449–460.

Atkeson, B.M., & Forehand, R. Home-based reinforcement programs designed to modify classroom behavior: A review and methodological evaluation. *Psychological Bulletin,* 1979, **86,** 1298–1308.

Ayllon, T., & Rosenbaum, M.S. The behavioral treatment of disruption and hyperactivity in school settings. In B.B. Lahey & A.E. Kazdin (Eds.), *Advances in clinical child psychology* (Vol. 1). New York: Plenum, 1977.

Barabasz, A.F. Classroom teachers as paraprofessional therapists in group systematic desensitization of test anxiety. *Psychiatry,* 1975, **38,** 388–392.

Barrett, C.L., Hampe, E., & Miller, L. Research on psychotherapy with children. In S.L. Garfield & A.E. Bergin (Eds.), *Handbook of psychotherapy and behavior change: An empirical analysis* (2nd ed.). New York: Wiley, 1978.

Baskin, E.J., & Hess, R.D. Does affective education work? A review of seven programs. *Journal of School Psychology,* 1980, **18,** 40–50.

Berman, P., & McLaughlin, M.W. Implementation of educational innovation. *Educational Forum,* 1976, **40,** 345–370.

Butler, L., Miezitis, S., Friedman, R., & Cole, E. The effect of two school-based intervention programs on depressive symptoms in preadolescents. *American Educational Research Journal,* 1980, **17,** 111–119.

Camp, B.W., Blom, G.E., Hebert, F., & van Doorninck, W.J. "Think aloud": A program for developing self-control in young aggressive boys. *Journal of Abnormal Child Psychology,* 1977, **5,** 157–169.

Carberry, A.T., & Handal, P.J. The use of the AML scale with a headstart population: Normative and validation studies. *American Journal of Community Psychology,* 1980, **8,** 353–363.

Centra, J.A., & Potter, D.A. School and teacher effects: An interrelational model. *Review of Educational Research,* 1980, **50,** 273–291.

Clarizio, H.F. School psychologists and the mental health needs of students. In G.D. Phye & D.J. Reschly, (Eds.), *School psychology: Perspectives and issues.* New York: Academic Press, 1979.

Clarizio, H.F., & McCoy, G.F. *Behavior disorders in children* (2nd ed.). New York: Crowell, 1976.

Cobb, D.E., & Medway, F.J. Determinants of effectiveness in parent consultation. *Journal of Community Psychology,* 1978, **6,** 229–240.

Costin, L.B. *Social work services in schools: Historical perspectives and current directions.* Washington, D.C.: National Association of Social Workers, 1978.

Cowen, E.L. The wooing of primary prevention. *American Journal of Community Psychology,* 1980, **8,** 258–284.

Cowen, E.L., Davidson, E.R., & Gesten, E.L. Program dissemination and the modification of delivery practices in school mental health. *Professional Psychology,* 1980, **11,** 36–47.

Cowen, E.L., Dorr, D., Clarfield, S.P., Kreling, B., McWilliams, S.A., Pokracki, F., Pratt, D.M., Terrell, D.L., & Wilson, A.B. The AML: A quick screening device for early identification of school maladaptation. *American Journal of Community Psychology,* 1973, **1,** 12–35.

Cowen, E.L., Trost, M.A., Dorr, D.A., Lorion, R.P., Izzo, L.D., & Isaacson, R.V. *New ways in school mental health: Early detection and prevention of school maladaptation.* New York: Human Sciences, 1975.

Craighead, W.E., Wilcoxon-Craighead, L., & Meyers, A.W. New directions in behavior modification with children. In M. Hersen, R.M. Eisler, & P.M. Miller, (Eds.), *Progress in behavior modification* (Vol. 6). New York: Academic Press, 1978.

Durlak, J.A. Description and evaluation of a behaviorally oriented school-based preventive mental health program. *Journal of Consulting and Clinical Psychology,* 1977, **45,** 27–33.

Durlak, J.A. Comparative effectiveness of behavioral and relationship group treatment in the secondary prevention of school maladjustment. *American Journal of Community Psychology,* 1980, **8,** 327–339.

Durlak, J.A. Training programs for paraprofessionals: Issues and guidelines. In A.M. Jeger & R.S. Slotnick (Eds.), *Community mental health: A behavioral-ecological perspective.* New York: Plenum, 1982.

Durlak, J.A., & Mannarino, A.P. Behavioral vs. relationship treatment in the secondary prevention of school maladjustment. Manuscript submitted for publication, 1981.

Durlak, J.A., Stein, M.A., & Mannarino, A.P. Behavioral validity of a brief teacher rating scale (the AML) in identifying high risk acting-out school children. *American Journal of Community Psychology,* 1980, **8**, 101–115.

Elardo, P.T., & Elardo, R. A critical analysis of social development programs in elementary education. *Journal of School Psychology,* 1976, **14**, 118–130.

Eysenck, H.J., & Rachman, S. *The causes and cures of neurosis.* San Diego: Knapp, 1965.

Fullan, M., & Pomfret, A. Research on curriculum and instruction implementation. *Review of Educational Research,* 1977, **47**, 335–397.

Gillespie, J.F., Durlak, J.A., & Sherman, D. Relationship between kindergarten children's interpersonal problem-solving skills and other indices of school adjustment: A cautionary note. *American Journal of Community Psychology,* 1982, **10**, 149–153.

Glidewell, J.C., & Swallow, C.S. *The prevalence of maladjustment in elementary schools.* Chicago: University of Chicago Press, 1969.

Goldstein, H., Arkell, C., Ashcroft, S.C., Hurley, O.L., & Lilly, M.S. Schools. In N. Hobbs (Ed.), *Issues in the classification of children* (Vol. 2). San Francisco: Jossey-Bass, 1975.

Goyette, C., Conners, C.K., & Ulrich, R. Normative data on revised Conners Parent and Teacher Rating Scales. *Journal of Abnormal Child Psychology,* 1978, **6**, 221–236.

Green, K.D., Beck, S.J., Forehand, R., & Vosk, B. Validity of teacher nominations of child behavior problems. *Journal of Abnormal Child Psychology,* 1980, **8**, 397–404.

Group for Advancement of Psychiatry. *Psychopathological disorders in childhood: Theoretical considerations and a proposed classification.* New York: Author, 1966.

Gump, P.V. The school as a social situation. *Annual Review of Psychology,* 1980, **31**, 553–582.

Harris, W.J., Drummond, R.J., & Schultz, E.W. An investigation of relationships between teachers' ratings of behavior and children's personality traits. *Journal of Abnormal Child Psychology,* 1977, **5**, 43–52.

Hobbs, N. (Ed.). *Issues in the classification of children* (Vol. 1). San Francisco: Jossey-Bass, 1975. (a)

Hobbs, N. (Ed.). *Issues in the classification of children* (Vol. 2). San Francisco: Jossey-Bass, 1975. (b)

Hobbs, N. (Ed.). *The futures of children.* San Francisco: Jossey-Bass, 1975. (c)

Huba, G.J., Wingard, J.A., & Bentler, P.M. Applications of a theory of drug use to prevention programs. *Journal of Drug Education,* 1980, **10**, 25–38.

Hurd, P.D., Johnson, C.A., Peechacek, T., Bast, L.P., Jacobs, D.R., & Luepker, R.V. Prevention of cigarette smoking in seventh grade students. *Journal of Behavioral Medicine,* 1980, **3**, 15–28.

Ingram, C.F. *Fundamentals of educational assessment.* New York: Van Nostrand, 1980.

The Joint Commission on Mental Health of Children. *Crisis in child mental health: Challenge for the 1970s.* New York: Harper & Row, 1969.

Journal of Special Education. Symposium on Public Law 94–142. *Journal of Special Education,* 1981, **15**, 7–54.

Kazdin, A.E. Assessing the clinical or applied importance of behavior change through social validation. *Behavior Modification,* 1977, **1**, 427–452.

Kazdin, A.E. Criteria for evaluating psychotherapy. *Archives of General Psychiatry,* 1978, **35**, 407–416. (a)

Kazdin, A.E. The applications of operant techniques in treatment, rehabilitation and education. In S.L. Garfield & A.E. Bergin (Eds.), *Handbook of psychotherapy and behavior change: An empirical analysis* (2nd ed.). New York: Wiley, 1978. (b)

Kearney, A.L., & Hines, M.H. Evaluation of the effectiveness of a drug prevention education program. *Journal of Drug Education,* 1980, **10**, 127–134.

Kellam, S.G., Branch, J.D., Agrawal, K.C., & Ensminger, M.E. *Mental health and going to school: The Woodlawn program of assessment, early intervention, and evaluation.* Chicago: University of Chicago Press, 1975.

Kim, S. How do we know whether a primary prevention program on drug abuse works or does not work? *International Journal of the*

Addictions, 1981, **16**, 179–185. (a)

Kim, S. An evaluation of ombudsman primary prevention program on student drug abuse. *Journal of Drug Education*, 1981, **11**, 27–36. (b)

Kinder, B.N., Pape, N.E., & Walfish, S. Drug and alcohol education programs: A review of outcome studies. *International Journal of the Addictions*, 1980, **15**, 1035–1054.

Kirschenbaum, D.S. Social competence intervention and evaluation in the inner city: Cincinnati's social skills development program. *Journal of Consulting and Clinical Psychology*, 1979, **47**, 778–780.

Kirschenbaum, D.S., & Ordman, A.M. Preventive interventions for children: Cognitive behavioral perspectives. In A.W. Meyers & W.E. Craighead (Eds.), *Cognitive behavior therapy for children.* New York: Plenum, in press.

Klein, R.D. Modifying academic performance in the grade school classroom. In M. Hersen, R.M. Eisler, & P.M. Miller (Eds.), *Progress in behavior modification* (Vol. 8). New York: Academic Press, 1979.

Lacayo, N., Sherwood, G., & Morris, J. Daily activities of school psychologists: A national survey. *Psychology in the Schools*, 1981, **18**, 184–190.

Levine, M., & Graziano, A.M. Intervention programs in elementary schools. In S.E. Golann & C. Eisdorfer (Eds.), *Handbook of community mental health.* New York: Appleton-Century-Crofts, 1972.

Love, L.R., Kaswan, J., & Bugental, D.E. Differential effectiveness of three clinical interventions for different socioeconomic groupings. *Journal of Consulting and Clinical Psychology*, 1972, **39**, 347–360.

MacMillan, D.L., & Morrison, G.M. Educational programming. In H.C. Quay & J.S. Werry (Eds.), *Psychopathological disorders of childhood* (2nd ed.). New York: Wiley, 1979.

Mann, J. Vicarious densensitization of test anxiety through observation of videotaped treatment. *Journal of Counseling Psychology*, 1972, **19**, 1–7.

Mannarino, A.P., & Durlak, J.A. Implementation and evaluation of service programs in community settings. *Professional Psychology*, 1980, **11**, 220–227.

Mannarino, A.P., Durlak, J.A., Christy, M., & Magnussen, M.G. Evaluation of social compe-

tence training in the schools. *Journal of School Psychology*, 1982, **20**, 11–19.

Mash, E.J., & Terdal, L.G. (Eds.). *Behavioral assessment of childhood disorders.* New York: Guilford, 1981.

McDermott, P.A. Prevalence and constituency of behavioral disturbance taxonomies in the regular school population. *Journal of Abnormal Child Psychology*, 1980, **8**, 523–536.

McDonald, J.E., & Sheperd, G. School phobia: An overview. *Journal of School Psychology*, 1976, **14**, 291–306.

McGee, C.S., Kauffman, J.M., & Nussen, J.L. Children as therapeutic change agents: Reinforcement intervention paradigms. *Review of Educational Research*, 1977, **47**, 451–477.

Medway, F.J., & Smith, Jr., R.C. An examination of contemporary elementary school affective education programs. *Psychology in the Schools*, 1978, **15**, 260–269.

Meyers, J., Parsons, R.D., & Martin, R. *Mental health consultation in the schools.* San Francisco: Jossey-Bass, 1979.

Miller, L.C. School behavior check list: An inventory of deviant behavior for elementary school children. *Journal of Consulting and Clinical Psychology*, 1972, **38**, 134–144.

O'Dell, S. Training parents in behavior modification: A review. *Psychological Bulletin*, 1974, **81**, 418–433.

O'Leary, S.G., & O'Leary, K.D. Behavior modification in the school. In H. Leitenberg (Ed.), *Handbook of behavior modification and behavior therapy.* Englewood Cliffs, N.J.: Prentice-Hall, 1976.

Perry, C.L., Killen, J., Slinkard, L.A., & McAlister, A.L. Peer teaching and smoking prevention among junior high students. *Adolescence*, 1980, **40**, 277–281.

Peterson, D.R. Behavior problems of middle childhood. *Journal of Consulting Psychology*, 1961, **25**, 205–209.

Phillips, J.S., & Ray, R.S. Behavioral approaches to childhood disorders. *Behavior Modification*, 1980, **4**, 3–34.

Quay, H.C. Classification. In H.C. Quay & J.S. Werry (Eds.), *Psychopathological disorders of childhood* (2nd ed.). New York: Wiley, 1979.

Quay, H.C., & Werry, J.S. (Ed.). *Psychopathologi-*

cal disorders of childhood (2nd ed.). New York: Wiley, 1979.

Rickel, A.U., & Smith, R.L. Maladapting preschool children: Identification, diagnosis, and remediation. *American Journal of Community Psychology,* 1979, **7,** 197–208.

Robin, S.S., & Wagenfeld, M.O. (Eds.). *Paraprofessionals in the human services.* New York: Human Sciences Press, 1981.

Romanczyk, R.G., Kistner, J.A., & Crimmins, D.B. Institutional treatment of severely disturbed children: Fact, possibility, or nonsequitur? In B.B. Lahey & A.E. Kazdin (Eds.), *Advances in clinical child psychology* (Vol. 3). New York: Plenum, 1980.

Ryan, B.A. A case against behavior modification in the "ordinary" classroom. *Journal of School Psychology,* 1979, **17,** 131–136.

Sabbatino, D.A. Are appropriate educational programs operationally achievable under mandated promises of P.L. 94-142? *Journal of Special Education,* 1981, **15,** 9–23.

Sajwaj, T., McNees, M.P., & Schnelle, J.F. Clinical and community interventions with children: A comparison of treatment strategies. In B.B. Lahey & A.E. Kazdin, (Eds.), *Advances in clinical child psychology* (Vol. 2). New York: Plenum, 1979.

Sandler, I.N., Duricko, A., & Grande, L. Effectiveness of an early secondary prevention program in an inner-city elementary school. *American Journal of Community Psychology,* 1975, **3,** 23–32.

Sarason, S.B. *The future of the school and the problem of change.* Boston: Allyn & Bacon, 1971.

Schaps, E., Churgin, S., Palley, C.S., Takata, B., & Cohen, A.Y. Primary prevention research: A preliminary review of program outcome studies. *International Journal of the Addictions,* 1980, **15,** 657–676.

Schoolhouse blues. *The New Republic,* April 18, 1981, pp. 7–8.

Spivack, G., & Shure, M.B. *Social adjustment of young children: A cognitive approach to solving real-life problems.* San Francisco: Jossey-Bass, 1974.

Spivack, G., Platt, J.J., & Shure, M.B. *The problem-solving approach to adjustment.* San Francisco: Jossey-Bass, 1976.

Van Houten, R. Social validation: The evolution of standards of competency for target behaviors. *Journal of Applied Behavior Analysis,* 1979, **12,** 581–591.

Weinstein, C.S. The physical environment of the school: A review of the research. *Review of Educational Research,* 1979, **49,** 577–610.

Weissberg, R.P., Gesten, E.L., Rapkin, B.D., Cowen, E.L., Davidson, E., de Apodaca, R.F., & McKim, B.J. The evaluation of a social problem-solving training program for suburban and inner-city third grade children. *Journal of Consulting and Clinical Psychology,* 1981, **49,** 251–261.

Why public schools fail. *Newsweek,* April 20, 1981, pp. 62–65.

Wirt, R.D., Lachar, D., Klinedinst, J.K., & Seat, P.D. *Multidimensional description of child personality: A manual for the Personality inventory for children.* Los Angeles: Western Psychological Services, 1977.

Wolman, B.B., Egan, J., & Ross, A.O. (Eds.). *Handbook of treatment of mental disorders in childhood and adolescence.* Englewood Cliffs, N.J.: Prentice-Hall, 1978.

Wood, F.H., & Zabel, R.H. Making sense of reports on the incidence of behavior disorders/emotional disturbance in school aged populations. *Psychology in the Schools,* 1978, **15,** 45–51.

CHAPTER 28

Learning Disabilities of Children

RONALD NEEPER AND BENJAMIN B. LAHEY

Children who experience difficulties in academic learning have undoubtedly existed throughout the history of formal education. It has only been recently, however, that children who appear to have average intellectual abilities but fail to learn have been assigned diagnostic labels (Kauffman & Hallahan, 1978; Sattler, 1981). Among these labels are learning disability, minimal brain dysfunction, and dyslexia. Recent estimates propose that as many as 10 percent of the general population in the United States experience significant deficiency in reading (Meir, 1971). Yule (in press) presents data suggesting that as many as 8 percent of the children who participated in the Isle of Wight studies showed a deficit in reading. More boys experience reading problems than girls; Yule (in press) estimates that the sex ratio may be as high as two or three to one. It is evident, then, that learning disabilities constitute a significant problem. Children with learning deficits often develop poor self-images, become a source of concern for their families, and place a heavy burden on their teachers.

DEFINITIONS OF LEARNING DISABILITY

Learning disabilities have been viewed in both a broad sense, as implied by use of terms such as minimal brain dysfunction, and in a more specific (operational) sense, where the emphasis is on identifying specific skills deficits in reading, math, and so on (Sattler, 1982). Early definitions of learning disabilities tended to be based on inferred etiology and were conceptually broadly based (Kauffman & Hallahan, 1978; Lahey et al., 1978). These early conceptual definitions of learning disability offered little utility in direct efforts at successful remediation (Lahey, Vosk, & Habif, 1981).

Legal/administrative definitions of learning disability have been based more on what learning disability is *not* than what it is (Delamater, Lahey, & Drake, 1981; Ross, 1976). A child is considered learning disabled if he or she is of average intelligence but behind grade level in achievement and not mentally retarded, physically impaired, or disadvantaged (Ross, 1976, 1977). Ross (1977) notes the circularity of this definition by pointing out that when one removes the "not" qualifications attached to this definition of learning disability, one is left defining the learning-disabled child as an individual who is not learning. One result of the lack of an operational definition of learning disability is a confusing literature replete with heterogeneous and ill-defined populations (Ross, 1976), making it next to impossible to make comparisons across studies (Lahey et al., 1981).

Lahey et al. (1981) have conceptualized learning disabilities as a dimension of behavior composed of related learning difficulties. Using a dimensional conceptualization of learning disabilities, children can be viewed as lying at a particular point along a continuum that ranges from least to most disabled. The different levels of disability along the continuum may be behaviorally defined and measured accordingly. A final tenet of a dimensional approach to defining learning disabilities is that they exist independently of other dimensions of maladaptive behavior but are not entirely uncorrelated with them. Lahey et al. (1978) and Miller (1972) have provided some support for this approach in their factor analytic studies.

Adherence to a dimensional approach to learning disabilities would seem to promote more precise assessment with respect to defining clinical and research populations. Implicit in the dimensional conceptualization of learning disabilities is the assumption that all children given the label learning disabled are experiencing academic problems. They are, however, probably heterogeneous in the extent to which they are deviant on other dimensions of behavior. Therefore, within the dimensional diagnostic category of learning disability exists a number of different combinations of different dimensions of maladaptive behavior. To date, research on learning disabilities has used populations of children defined according to traditional diagnostic categories that explicitly have assumed a "syndrome" of behavior due to an underlying cause (Lahey et al., 1978). This approach has limited progress in the area and is in need of critical review. The remainder of this chapter will focus on a critical review of the "syndrome" or traditional approach to defining learning disabilities in children and will offer a behavioral alternative. Recent advances in the behavioral treatment of learning disabilities will also be presented.

THEORIES OF ETIOLOGY: A HISTORICAL PERSPECTIVE

Neuropsychological Theories

The earliest theories of learning disabilities conceptualized them as syndromes of brain damage. The neuropsychological theories arose out of Kurt Goldstein's work with World War I veterans who had sustained head injuries. Among the behavioral symptoms that learning-disabled children show that are similar to brain-damaged veterans are distractibility, memory problems, and short attention span. It was assumed, based on this conception, that learning-disabled children suffer from some form of "minimal" brain damage (Strauss & Lehtinen, 1947). Early remedial efforts for learning-disabled children based on the assumption of minimal brain damage resembled the sensory deprivation procedures developed for use wth head injury victims. As much as possible, all extraneous stimuli were removed from the classrooms. Teachers wore plain clothing, windows were partially covered to prevent a view of the outdoors, and the pupils were isolated from one another in cubicles. It was assumed that this reduction in distracting stimuli would aid in attending to school work.

Because no definite relationship between learning disabilities and actual brain damage was found, the term "minimal brain dysfunction" replaced "minimal brain damage" (Cruickshanck, 1967; Johnson & Mykelbust, 1967). Along with the change in terminology came a change in the conceptualization of learning disabilities. Emphasis was placed on presumed functional disorders of the brain rather than anatomical damage.

Perceptual and Perceptual-Motor Theories

A group of theories that emphasized the role of perception in learning disabilities was proposed. Although each of these theories proposed specific treatment methods to remedy the presumed perceptual deficits of learning-disabled children, the Gestaltlike definitions of perception that were put forth were so broad as to be synonymous with the term intelligence itself (Lahey et al., 1978).

Delacato (1966) and Kephart (1971) proposed developmental theories that emphasized a series of invariant stages of perceptual development that paralleled Piagetian theory. According to these theories, if early perceptual-motor learning experiences were deficient, normal intellectual development would not occur. In efforts to remedy the deficient perceptual-motor processes, extensive programs of physical exercise were prescribed.

The goal of Kephart's remedial program was to enable children accurately to perceive their own body's spatial orientation, and it was assumed improved spatial perception of letters and numbers would follow. Delacato speculated that the treatment methods he prescribed (e.g., forced crawling, restricted positions during sleep) would actually reorganize the neural structures of the brain.

Getman (Getman & Kane, 1964), a developmental optometrist, proposed that learning problems may be due to dysfunctional or uncoordinated eye muscles. The remedial program based on Getman's theory consists of a series of visual exercises designed to train the muscles of the eyes. One of the most widely used remedial programs is that of Frostig and Horne. Frostig and Horne developed the popular "Frostig Kits," which were designed to remedy problems in visual perception by having the children complete exercises such as copying geometric shapes. A program similar to Frostig's is that of Fernald (1943). Fernald's program emphasizes the integration of the visual, auditory, kinesthetic, and tactile sensory modalities while Frostig was concerned exclusively with visual perception.

Psycholinguistic Theories

Some researchers have conceptualized learning disabilities as resulting from developmental delays in the "psycholinguistic processes" (Kirk et al., 1968). Like perceptual theorists, these theorists define psycholinguistic skills in broad terms, making them nearly identical to the term intelligence. Kirk, McCarthy, and Kirk (1968) have based their theory on Osgood's (1957) model of psycholinguistic processing, developing a remedial program complete with an assessment device designed to specify particular areas of deficit (the Illinois Test of Psycholinguistic Abilities, or ITPA). A training program has also been developed that includes exercise designed to remedy deficits identified by the ITPA.

Genetics

Several studies have implicated genetic factors in the development of learning disability (Finucci et al., 1976; Hallgren, 1950; Ingram, Mason, & Blackburn, 1970). Owen (1978), in a review of this literature, has suggested that there may be a polygenetic factor that, in combination with environmental influences, predisposes an individual to learning disabilities.

Social-Learning Factors

Little research on the possible role of environmental factors in learning disability has been conducted. This is surprising in view of the positive results obtained using social-learning techniques in the remediation of learning disabilities. Barkley (1981) attributes this apparent lack of research interest to the inability of social-learning theories to explain how children may manifest disabilities in specific areas of achievement and still be at grade level in others.

Theories of Etiology: A Critical Evaluation

Of all the theories of learning disabilities, the neuropsychological theories have received the most research attention. Although neuropsychological assessment batteries have been shown reliably to detect frank brain damage, the results have been inconsistent with respect to finding minimal brain dysfunction in learning-disabled children. Psychophysiological studies have shown more consistent results, but the evidence for physiological differences between learning-disabled and normal children is still far from conclusive (Feuerstein et al., 1979). Until more homogeneous populations of learning-disabled children are used in research and more reliable results are found, neuropsychological hypotheses of learning disabilities can only be viewed as tentative.

The empirical evidence supporting the use of remedial programs based on perceptual-motor and psycholinguistic theories is also weak. The majority of studies investigating the effectiveness of these methods of treatment suffer from serious methodological flaws. Moreover, the few methodologically sound studies have failed to demonstrate significant treatment effects (Goodman & Hammill, 1973;

Hammill & Larsen, 1974; Hallahan & Kauffman, 1976; Lahey, 1976; Ross, 1976). Unfortunately, in spite of this lack of empirical support, perceptual training and psycholinguistic training are still the dominant remedial methods used in treating learning-disabled children.

DIAGNOSTIC CLASSIFICATION

Several authors have attempted to classify learning-disabled children into more homogeneous subgroups. Typically these attempts have been based on clinical impressions rather than empirical research (Boder, 1973). The apparent goal of the traditional classification approach has been to identify specific "syndromes" of learning disability. This chapter will not attempt to provide an exhaustive review of the numerous proposed subtypes of learning disability. Benton and Pearl (1978), Boder (1973), and Lyon and Watson (1981) have provided more complete discussions of this issue.

Specific Reading Disorders

In his review of the literature, Barkley (1981) concluded that three types of reading disorder are typically reported. Boder's (1973) classification is representative of these types of disorder and will be the focus of review here. The most common reading disorder is *dysphonetic disorder* (Boder, 1973). Children given this label show problems predominantly in vocabulary and articulation. They possess a small vocabulary of words that they can recognize on sight. Typically they read words as whole units and are seemingly unable to separate words into component parts. This is evidenced by their tendency to guess at words based on the first few letters and substitute similarly spelled words for others. Their spelling ability is at a level even lower than their reading level.

The least frequently encountered type of reading disability according to Boder (1973) is the *dyseidetic disorder*. Although children given this label possess adequate auditory memory, they experience difficulty in remem-

bering what letters look like. These children read in a slow and choppy fashion, sounding out each word phonetically. The most difficult words for them to read are irregular ones that cannot be read phonetically. The spelling errors made by these children are most frequently phonetic in nature.

The reading disability that occurs at a frequency intermediate to the dysphonetic and dyseidetic appears to be a combination of these two disorders. Boder (1973) has labeled this third reading disorder the *mixed dysphonetic-dyseidetic disorder*. These children are the most severely impaired, showing the letter reversals and sequencing problems that led researchers to develop the perceptual-motor theories of learning disability discussed earlier.

Specific Arithmetic Disorders

Arithmetic disorders often occur along with reading and spelling difficulties (Barkley, 1981). Based on his review of the research, Barkley (1981) has proposed the existence of two types of arithmetic disorders. The first type is characterized by children who do poorly in math yet have fewer problems in reading. These children are presumed by Barkley (1981) to have deficits in visuospatial skills, as they typically encounter problems on the performance subscales of the WISC (Rourke, Young, & Flewelling, 1971). The second group of math-disordered children show deficits in reading and language to a degree equal to their math problems. Little research has been done to identify characteristics of this second subgroup of math-disordered children (Barkley, 1981).

Writing Disorders

Disorders in writing appear to parallel the three previously identified categories of reading disorder (Barkley, 1981). The first type of writing disorder is related to the dysphonetic reading disorder, in that the writing deficit is theorized to be due to a lack of phonetic-analytic skills (Barkley, 1981; Maidoo, 1972). These children typically are more deficient in spelling than writing. Often their misspellings are unsystematic and their writing is not readable.

A second type of writing disorder is characterized by deficient visuospatial and word construction skills (Barkley, 1981). This disorder occurs more frequently with math and spelling difficulties than with reading problems. The spelling difficulties in this second category appear to parallel the dyseidetic pattern in that the errors in spelling are often phonetically correct. The third category of writing disorder, the apraxic writers (Heilman & Valenstein, 1979), appear to be deficient only in the motor coordination skills necessary for writing, as their reading and mathematical skills are often at grade level.

Diagnostic Classification: A Critical Evaluation

In order for a diagnostic category to be useful it must have differential meaning with respect to the etiology, prognosis, and/or response to treatment of the behavior pattern that it labels (Lahey et al., 1981). To date, very little evidence exists supporting the use of the diagnostic categories described above. Until more is known about the differential etiological and prognostic implications of the various diagnostic subtypes their use cannot be recommended except for research purposes. In particular, the diagnostic subtypes have not demonstrated their utility in the selection of treatment methods. Behavioral treatments have been shown to be effective across a wide variety of learning deficits (Kirby & Shields, 1972; Lahey et al., 1977; Novy et al., 1973; Stromer, 1977). This lack of differential implications for treatment strongly argues against the use of the traditional diagnostic subtype classifications.

This is not to argue that research should not be conducted on these and other proposed subtypes; clearly it should. But until it can be demonstrated that a classification system conveys differential information about etiology, prognosis, and, most importantly, response to treatment, the subtypes have no clinical utility.

RELATED BEHAVIOR PROBLEMS

Although children labeled learning disabled are homogeneous in the sense that they are all experiencing difficulties in academic achievement, they appear to be heterogeneous with respect to other dimensions of behavior problems (Lahey et al., 1981). Several behavior problems have been found to occur in learning-disabled children with a higher frequency than in normal populations, however.

The label most often applied concurrently with the diagnosis of learning disability is hyperactivity. Overlap between the two diagnoses is estimated as being from 50 percent (Lambert & Sandoval, 1980) to 80 percent (Safer & Allen, 1976). Recent research (Delamater et al., 1981) has attempted to determine what differences exist between hyperactive and nonhyperactive learning-disabled children. Hyperactive learning-disabled children were found to have a higher probability of being firstborn, were more often from stressed families, and were more easily distracted by external stimuli. No differences were found on several physiological measures of arousal, however. The lack of physiological differences between the hyperactive and nonhyperactive learning-disabled children has important etiological implications and merits further research (Delamater et al., 1981).

Aggression, social withdrawal, depression, phobias, and decreased self-confidence have also been shown to be related to learning disabilities (Boder, 1973; Peter & Spreen, 1979; Rutter et al., 1976; Sattler, 1982). In view of these associated difficulties, it is not surprising to find that learning-disabled children are not viewed positively by peers. Several studies, in fact, have shown that learning-disabled children are rejected by their peers on sociometric measures (Bryan, 1974, 1976; Horowitz, 1981). Since learning disabilities often remain stable over time (Boder, 1973; Gattesman, 1979; Satz et al., 1978), it appears that learning-disabled children are at risk for suffering the consequences of long term peer rejection. Included in these possible consequences are juvenile delinquency (Roff, Sells,

& Goblen, 1972), dropping out of school (Ullman, 1957), and psychiatric disturbance (Cowen et al., 1973).

It is usually unclear as to which causal relationships may result in the correlations between learning disabilities and other behavior problems. Sattler (1982) has outlined three plausible causal relationships. The first of these postulates the behavior problems as being a cause of the learning difficulties. Indeed, a hyperactive or conduct-disordered child who is frequently disruptive and inattentive is not likely to be doing well academically. The opposite relationship between learning disabilities and behavior problems may be in operation also. Cunningham and Barkley (1978) have proposed a causal model that suggests that frustration due to academic failure may lead to inappropriate behaviors and interpersonal difficulties. A final possible explanation is the existence of a third factor such as an autonomic abnormality that is causally related to both the learning disability and the conduct problem.

It is obvious, then, that assessing academic achievement alone is an incomplete approach in the assessment of learning-disabled children. Since any combination of these causal relationships may be operating in any individual case, it becomes imperative to assess completely the various dimensions of behavior.

PSYCHOMETRIC ASSESSMENT OF LEARNING DISABILITIES

Psychometric instruments are the most often-used tools in the assessment of learning disabilities. Indeed, all legal definitions of learning disabilities are based in part on scores from standardized psychometric instruments. Although the many cognitive tests that have been developed to assess general and specific abilities (e.g., reading achievement) appear to have face validity, they have contributed little to the development of effective remedial programs. We will provide a brief overview of a few of the most well-known psychometric instruments. The reader is referred to Sattler (chap. 7 of this book) for a more complete review.

Intelligence Tests

Several measures of general intelligence have been developed and standardized. The most widely used of these measures include the Stanford-Binet Intelligence Scale (1973); the Wechsler Intelligence Scale for Children—Revised (WISC-R) (1974); and the McCarthy Scale of Children's Abilities (McCarthy, 1972). Most often, learning-disabled children are defined by discrepancies between intelligence test and academic achievement test scores.

In addition to using intelligence tests in the identification of learning-disabled children, many researchers have attempted to identify specific patterns of subscale scores within the intelligence tests that might prove useful in differentiating learning-disabled from normal children (Ackerman, Peters, & Dykman, 1971; Rourke, 1978). The ACID profile on the WISC-R is one of the most frequently used of these score patterns. The ACID acronym refers to the presumed tendency of many children with reading disorders to score relatively lower on the arithmetic, coding, information, and digit span subtests of the WISC-R. Many researchers also view large differences between the verbal and performance subscales on the WISC-R as being associated with learning disabilities (cf. Barkley, 1981).

Dudley-Marling, Kaufman, and Tarver (1981) reviewed 24 studies that have compared performances of learning-disabled and normal children on the WISC and WISC-R. Based on their review, they drew the following conclusions: (1) no consistent verbal-performance differences may be considered characteristic of learning-disabled children. Kaufman (1981) also cautions against the use of verbal-performance differences as clear diagnostic indicators, since 25 percent of the standardization sample for the WISC-R showed verbal-performance differences that were statistically significant; (2) learning-disabled children show no more variation within subtests than normal children; (3) no reliable subtest score pattern on the WISC-R may be considered as being characteristic of learning-disabled children. In light of these conclusions, the use of intellectual tests as anything other than general predictors of future academic success is cautioned against.

Achievement Tests

Achievement tests have been devised to assess specific academic abilities, (e.g., reading, comprehension, oral reading), as opposed to the general information that is provided by tests of intelligence. Barkley (1981) provides a list of the published achievement tests most frequently used. Typically a battery of achievement tests is administered in order to assess a wide variety of academic behavior. Achievement tests should be used that closely resemble the behavior required in the classroom, but they should not be the sole measure by which treatment effects are assessed. Actual academic behavior should be assessed through classroom observations and the inspection of written products.

Analogue Laboratory Tasks

Several investigators have assessed the relationship between analogue tasks and actual academic performance (Bryden, 1972; Cohen & Netley, 1978; Koppitz, 1975; Torgesen & Goldman, 1977; Vellutino et al., 1975; Wiig & Roach, 1975). Much of this research has been done with reading disorders, which have been shown to be related to impulsivity, poor short term memory, poor visual discrimination, and a lack of sustained selective attention during the analogue tasks (Torgesen & Goldman, 1977). Results such as these may lead to effective remedial procedures as they provide a means of assessing "information-processing deficits" in poor readers.

Unfortunately, the relationships between performance on the analogue tasks and measures such as achievement tests are not strong enough to be considered clinically useful. Velluntino et al. (1975) propose that:

In both evaluating and remediating a learning problem, it would be more effective to conceptualize the learner's task and performance on units that most closely approximate the skill we ultimately wish to teach him, rather than subdivide these variables into basic sensory and intersensory processes involved in learning that skill but not unique to it. (p. 381)

This view is perhaps best supported by the failure of the earlier remedial programs that were based on assumed perceptual-motor and psycholinguistic processes (Lahey et al., 1981).

Additionally, despite the demonstrated ability of the analogue measures to differentiate learning-disabled children from normals across several factors of behaviors (e.g., short term memory, visual discrimination ability, impulsivity), these measures have yet to demonstrate an ability to differentiate learning-disabled children from children who have been given other diagnostic labels such as conduct disorders or hyperactivity (Lahey et al., 1981). Although a dimensional perspective of learning disabilities explicitly assumes heterogeneity of other behavioral dimensions within the group of children labeled, we do not yet know the extent to which performance on the analogue tasks is affected by the academic deficits or the other behavior problems (Lahey et al., 1981).

BEHAVIORAL ASSESSMENT OF LEARNING DISABILITIES

Instead of viewing learning disabilities as symptoms of underlying neurological or mental dysfunctions, behavioral conceptions treat learning disabilities simply as patterns of maladaptive behavior. As such, these maladaptive behaviors are considered to be modifiable by the same techniques found to be successful with other behavior problems. These remedial efforts are directed to the maladaptive behavior itself rather than the inferred perceptual-motor, neurological, or psycholinguistic processes (Lahey et al., 1978).

A behavior therapy approach to the remediation of learning disabilities depends on behavioral assessment. Target behaviors must be identified and measured before, during, and after treatment. In the brief history of behavioral approaches to learning disabilities, a number of different target behaviors have been proposed. Not all of these proposed targets are appropriate ones, however.

Inappropriate Targets for Assessment and Intervention—Attention Deficits

As suggested earlier, one view of learning disabilities is that some children have difficulties in maintaining selective attention to the academic task at hand. At first glance, this would appear to be an important target for remediation. However, several reasons may be proposed against focusing on attention deficits. First, several early studies of behavioral programs in school settings used attending to academic tasks as the focus of treatment (e.g., Wolfe, Giles, & Hall, 1968). However, this research indicated that increases in attending usually were not accompanied by improvements in academic performance (Ferritor et al., 1972; Kirby & Shields, 1972). A second argument against the direct modification of attention deficits comes from the fact that several attempts to identify more subtle aspects of attending behavior that distinguish learning-disabled from normal children have been unsuccessful (e.g., Lahey, et al., 1982).

Impulsivity

Kagan (1966) has demonstrated that children with academic problems tend to respond to academic tasks faster and with more errors than normal chldren. Kagan suggests that they respond before they have had time to think through their responses. Based on this theory it has been assumed that attempts to slow the response rates of the children with learning problems would be followed by increases in academic performance. Williams and Lahey (1977) tested this assumption by independently reinforcing response accuracy and longer response latency. The results did not support Kagan's hypothesis: reinforcing children for longer response latencies did not

result in concurrent increases in response accuracy. Conversely, those children reinforced for accurate responding improved in accuracy but did not increase their response latencies. Furthermore, reinforcing children for both longer response latencies and response accuracy did not prove to be any more effective than reinforcement for accuracy alone. Taken together, these findings suggest that targeting impulsive responding may not be a fruitful approach to the assessment and remediation of learning disabilities. It does not appear to be necessary to modify response latencies to improve academic accuracy.

Hyperactivity

As noted earlier, there is much overlap between the diagnoses of hyperactivity and learning disability. Several of the behaviors that tend to be associated with the diagnosis of hyperactivity (e.g., high rates of motor activity, distractibility, attention deficits, impulsivity) have been implicated as causes for learning problems (Lahey et al., 1981). Behavior therapists have treated hyperactivity by directly targeting "hyperacitve" behaviors in their remedial programs (Kent & O'Leary, 1976; O'Leary, Rosenbaum, & Price, 1977). Although decreases in these maladaptive behaviors may be desirable, it is not necessary to focus one's attention directly on the hyperactivity to be able to modify academic performance. For example, Ayllon, Layman, and Kandel (1975) have demonstrated that directly targeting academic performance in a token reinforcement program developed for hyperactive learning-disabled children both led to decreases in the "hyperactive" behaviors and improved academic performance.

Appropriate Targets for Assessments and Intervention—Academic

Although the etiological theories on which most conceptualizations of learning disabilities are based are extremely broad in scope (Lahey et al., 1978), the assessment of learning disabilities in educational settings tends to be "molecular" in its focus (Lahey et al., 1981).

That is, great emphasis is placed on identifying specific problems (poor letter discrimination skills, poor phonics skills, etc.). Different remedial programs are prescribed depending on the specific deficits that the child is believed to possess. Current research, however, suggests that it is possible to change more complex or "molar" units of academic performance without attending to more molecular or process components of academic performance (Ayllon et al., 1975; Lahey, 1979). For example, many studies of oral reading ability have demonstrated reliable increment in the molar response of "orally reading sentences" using contingent reinforcement for correct reading of entire sentences. This result appears to be consistent regardless of the specific errors (e.g., visual-perceptual, phonic) that the children had previously made (Lahey, 1976). Other molar academic behaviors that have been successfully modified using this same approach include reading comprehension (Lahey, McNees, & Brown, 1973), handwriting (Lahey et al., 1977), and sight-word vocabulary (Lahey & Drabman, 1974).

The following is a recommended protocol in the behavioral assessment of learning disabilities (Lahey et al., 1981).

1. *Achievement tests.* Standardized achievement tests can be useful as estimates of typical academic performance. However, in selecting a particular achievement test for use in assessment, one should be careful to select the test that most closely approximates the tasks required in the classroom itself. Some achievement tests that meet this criterion are the Arithmetic and Spelling subtests of the Wide Range Achievement Test (Jastak & Jastak, 1965) and the Spache Diagnostic Reading Scales (Spache, 1963).

2. *Samples of written academic work.* One of the hallmarks of a behavioral approach to education is its emphasis on repeated assessment (Lahey & Johnson, 1977). The collection of daily samples of the student's written work provides an unobtrusive means of collecting data in a continuous fashion. If possible, all academic work (not examples of the best or worst) should be included in the assessment.

3. *Direct observation in the classroom.* Direct observation provides a useful adjunct to achievement tests and work samples, particularly as it provides data on verbal academic tasks such as oral reading. Additionally, it provides a means of assessing environmental conditions (e.g., disruptive peers, inadvertent reinforcement from the teacher for not attending) that may be contributing to the academic deficits and/or the failure of remedial efforts (Lovitt, 1967; Lahey et al., 1981). A functional analysis of the environmental contingencies surrounding the targeted behaviors is then possible.

Since parents and teachers are often recruited to administer the treatment and monitor its effectiveness, they should be encouraged to be active participants in the selection of the goals to be achieved (Lahey et al., 1981). Selecting achievable goals, along with a flexible timetable for reaching them, provides an objective means of assessing treatment gains. Difficulties in achieving goals indicate a need for a repeated analysis of the environmental factors that may be impeding treatment progress. Variable performance after the initiation of treatment may be indicative of the operation of factors external to the treatment (e.g., peer influences). Setting unobtainable goals or using weak reinforcement, in contrast, tends to produce fairly stable low performance levels. Procedures designed to produce generalization and maintenance of treatment gains should be incorporated into every remedial program for obvious reasons. Such procedures include extending the treatment to all classroom situations, with the teachers applying the treatment across different subject areas. Until such generalization is demonstrated, one should not progress to more difficult tasks.

However, assessing only problems in academic achievement experienced by learning-disabled children is an insufficient approach, for they typically experience other behavioral problems as well (Rutter et al., 1976; Barkley, 1981). A complete assessment would include all problems across the various dimensions of behavior (Lahey et al., 1981).

BEHAVIORAL TREATMENT OF LEARNING DISABILITIES

As noted earlier, traditional methods of treatment for learning disabilities have yielded unfavorable results (Goodman & Hammill, 1973; Hammill & Larsen, 1974). However, behavioral techniques have been consistently demonstrated to be useful in the remediation of learning problems (Lahey, 1976; Lahey et al., 1978). The first applications of behavioral principles to learning problems focused more on the associated difficulties such as poor attention span, conduct problems, and hyperactivity in hopes that improved academic performance would follow the reduction of these incompatible behaviors (Madsen, Becker, & Thomas, 1968; O'Leary et al., 1969). However, neither decreasing disruptive behavior nor increasing the rate of attending behaviors has consistently been shown to result in increased academic performance (Ayllon et al., 1975; Ferritor et al, 1972).

Other researchers have investigated the effects of directly reinforcing correct responding (e.g., correct answers in math or reading workbooks) on academic performance (Ayllon & Roberts, 1974; Ayllon et al., 1975; Broughton & Lahey, 1978; Kirby & Shields, 1972). These investigators have proposed that correct responding is the last (terminal) behavior in the complex chain of behaviors that constitute academic performance. Examples of behaviors that occur earlier in the academic response chain include being in seat and attending to the work. By reinforcing the terminal academic response, behaviors that are incompatible with accurate academic performance (e.g., daydreaming, leaving one's seat) drop out of the response chain.

Reinforcement of Terminal Behavior: An Indirect Approach

Kirby and Shields (1972) found that attending to tasks increased when correct academic responses were reinforced. These investigators increased the math performance of a seventh-grade boy who was rated by his teacher as having difficulty in attending to his school work. Broughton and Lahey (1978) extended this approach using several different reinforcement contingencies. In their study, the effects of continuous positive reinforcement, response cost, and the combination of the two, were compared to a control condition. As in the Kirby and Shields (1972) study, math performance was directly targeted while both accurate math performance and the frequency of attending served as the dependent measures. All three treatments were equally effective in directly increasing academic performance and indirectly decreasing off-task behavior in comparison to a control group. Additionally, the effects were maintained even after the termination of the treatment.

Disruptive behavior may also be brought under control while directly targeting academic performance. Ayllon and Roberts (1974) established a token economy in a highly disruptive fifth-grade class. Correct performance in the reading workbook earned points that were later exchangeable for prizes. As treatment progressed, an increasing number of items were required to be completed before the student was able to turn in his paper for feedback. In addition to monitoring the amount of correct work completed, Ayllon and Roberts (1974) also recorded the percentage of time in which the children were engaged in disruptive behavior. Reliability decreases in disruption and increases in reading performance were observed during the treatment phases. However, gains made by the class during the reading period did not generalize to other classes, paralleling the results of Kirby and Shields (1972) and indicating the need to target each academic subject independently.

Ayllon et al. (1975) selected three children who had been diagnosed as both learning disabled and hyperactive to participate in a similar remedial program. Each of these children had been taking Ritalin to control their hyperactive behavior for periods ranging from one to four years. As in the Ayllon and Roberts (1974) study, a token economy targeting correct academic responses in workbooks comprised the treatment program. Treatment was conducted in a multiple baseline design across the reading and math classes in which all three children were enrolled. Initial baseline data indicated that although the Ritalin was maintaining control over the childrens' hyperactive behavior, their academic performance was consistently low. Following the initial baseline phase and a drug wash-out period, a second baseline was conducted with the children off medication. Each child showed marked increases in hyperactive behavior during this second baseline period; however, no concurrent change in academic performance was noted. The third phase of the treatment design consisted of token reinforcement of correct responding in a basic level math workbook. Reinforcement consisted of the teacher placing a check on a daily report card. The checks were exchangeable for prizes of various token values.

The effects of the token program in the math class were immediate and dramatic. Concurrently, performance in the math workbooks increased, and the amount of hyperactive behavior decreased to levels comparable to when the children were on Ritalin. Performance in the reading class remained unaffected. Additionally, the level of hyperactive behavior displayed by the children in the reading class remained at the high post-medication levels. In the fourth treatment phase accurate responding was reinforced in both the reading and math class. During this last phase, the effects of the token program parallelled those of the previous one in that increases in reading performance were accompanied by concurrent decreases in hyperactive behavior to levels comparable to those during medicated periods.

Several important implications arise out of the Ayllon et al. (1975) study and others reviewed earlier in this section. Reinforcement of terminal academic performance (such as correct answers to problems) can effectively control inattentive and disruptive behavior. Previous studies that have taken a direct approach to eliminating disruptive behavior either with behavioral techniques (Ferritor et al., 1972) or medication (Rie et al., 1976) have shown no beneficial effects on academic performance. Since directly targeting academic responding improves both disruptive behavior and academic performance, it would seem to

be the treatment of choice. Finally, a major concern directed toward the direct behavior modification of disruptive behavior is the resultant regimentation of the classroom (Winett & Winkler, 1972). Targeting academic performance rather than disruptive behavior enables the children to have the personal freedom to make the final decision as to which behaviors actually are incompatible with learning (Lahey et al., 1981).

Behavioral Interventions with Other Academic Problems

Children with severe handwriting problems (e.g., letter reversals) have in the past been assumed to be suffering from perceptual-motor disorders. Based on this assumption, training on perceptual-motor tasks has been conducted as remediation for those particular learning disorders. Traditional methods of remediation have shown little promise (Goodman & Hammill, 1973). On the other hand, behavioral techniques have been successful (Lahey et al., 1977).

Lahey et al. (1977) treated four children with extreme "perceptual-motor disorders" in two separate experimental programs. The first two children treated by these authors were placed in a learning disabilities classroom due to poor handwriting and a high frequency of letter reversals. Feedback and monetary reward (pennies) were given for correct responses, with correct responses defined as: (1) readable, (2) of proper spatial orientation, and (3) letters in correct sequence. The children were individually tutored and each day were asked to write their name five times, write five four-letter words, and draw five geometric figures. Additionally, generalization probes were interspersed throughout the baseline and treatment phases. The treatment produced marked effects in the legibility and proper sequencing of the children's handwriting. Figure 28.1 shows a sample of work before and after treatment from the first subject (Lahey, 1976; Lahey et al., 1977).

The subjects in the second experiment (students C and D) displayed handwriting difficulties that were more severe than the first

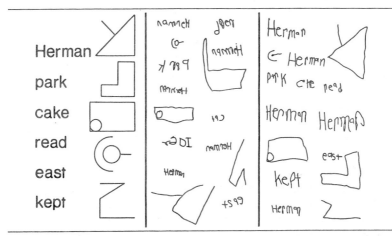

Figure 28-1.   Work sample from student A. The standard pattern appears on the left. The second segment contains the child's reproduction from the last baseline assessment. The final segment was taken from the eighth remedial session.

Note. Reprinted with permission of Academic Press. Copyright © by Academic Press, 1976. From B.B. Lahey, "Behavior with Learning Disabilities and Related Problems," in M. Hersen, R. Eisler, and P. Miller (Eds.), *Progress in Behavior Modification.* New York: Academic Press, 1976.

two subjects. As in Experiment I, reinforcement of correct responses produced clear effects in the handwriting of both students C and D. Although the treatment effects were reliably demonstrated for student C in the remedial sessions, little improvement was noted in his classroom work. This suggests the need to extend treatment contingencies to the classroom as well for some students. Figure 2

shows a sample of student C's handwriting. The improvement in writing behavior was maintained even after the reinforcement was discontinued, and both behaviors generalized to the classroom for student D.

Behavioral treatment programs have also been used successfully in the remediation of several other aspects of reading behavior (Lahey, 1977). Lahey and Drabman (1974)

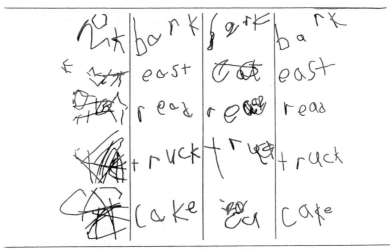

Figure 28-2.   Work samples for student C. Samples proceeding from left to right include: initial baseline, first treatment, reversal, and final treatment phases.

Note. Reprinted with permission of Academic Press. Copyright © by Academic Press, 1976. From B.B. Lahey, "Behavior with Learning Disabilities and Related Problems," in M. Hersen, R. Eisler, and P. Miller (Eds.), *Progress in Behavior Modification.* New York: Academic Press, 1976.

compared simple performance feedback to performance feedback plus token reinforcement in the acquisition and retention of sight-vocabulary words. Children in the no-token group required twice as many learning trials to acquire their new vocabulary words. Additionally, they did not retain their newly acquired vocabulary words as well as the children who had been reinforced for learning the words.

Lahey et al. (1973) modified a more molar reading behavior, reading comprehension. Treatment consisted of praise and monetary reinforcement contingent on correct answers to questions drawn from short passages that the children had just read aloud. The treatment produced reliable effects on the reading comprehension of the children. During treatment phases the number of correctly answered questions rose to levels comparable to those of children whose reading comprehension was two grade levels above the target children.

PHARMACOLOGICAL TREATMENT OF LEARNING DISABILITIES

Stimulant medications reliably produce decreases in the disruptive behaviors of children labeled hyperactive (Barkley & Cunningham, 1978; Gittelman et al., 1980). It has frequently been assumed that collateral improvements in academic performance would also occur (Ayllon et al., 1975; Barkley & Cunningham, 1978; Rie et al., 1976). Most research testing this hypothesis has looked at medications' effects on laboratory tasks that are assumed to be related to academic performance (Rie et al., 1976). For example, stimulant medications have been shown to have positive effects on paired-associate learning and the Porteus Mazes (Conners, Eisenberg, & Sharpe, 1964), picture recognition tasks (Sprague & Werry, 1974), and discrimination learning (Sprague, Barnes, & Werry, 1970). The results of studies that have directly assessed the effects of drugs on academic performance in the classroom, however, have not yielded positive results with learning disabled children, whether they exhibit hyperactivity or not (Barkley & Cunningham, 1978;

Rie et al., 1976). If used at all, stimulant medications should be used only when the primary objective of an intervention is to reduce high rates of disruptive and off-task behavior not for the enhancement of academic performance.

GENERAL CONCLUSIONS

Since its inception as a diagnostic term, learning disabilities have resulted in what is perhaps the most confusing literature in clinical child psychology. To date, many theories exist as to the etiology of learning disabilities. However, little can be concluded based on the research that these theories have spawned. Further research on the etiology of learning disabilities based on sound methodology should be given top priority. In addition to the lack of knowledge in regard to specific etiological factors, little is known about specific learning (processing) deficits that distinguish learning-disabled from normal children. Continued research in this area, with particular attention paid to operationally defining these processing deficits, is also greatly needed.

At this time, behavioral treatment programs appear to be the only consistently effective interventions for treating children with learning disabilities. This effectiveness seems to be consistent regardless of the specific traditional diagnosis applied to the child. Still, current experimental evaluations of the effectiveness of behavioral treatment methods cannot be viewed as conclusive. In the preparation of this chapter a large number of behavioral treatment studies were reviewed by the authors. No study was found that included a follow-up, and no studies comparing traditional treatment methods with behavioral treatment were found. These two serious flaws in the research literature must be corrected. The main conclusion that may be drawn from the existing literature is that extensive, well-controlled research is needed to investigate the specific etiological factors, identify the distinguishing characteristics, and develop effective treatment procedures for specific learning disabilities in children. For the time being, however, behavior interventions that focus directly on academic behavior are clearly the treatment of choice for practicing clinicians and educators.

REFERENCES

Ackerman, P., Peters, J.E., & Dykman, R.A. Children with specific learning disabilities: WISC profiles. *Journal of Learning Disabilities*, 1971, **4**, 150–166.

Ayllon, T., Layman, D., & Kandel, H.J. A behavioral-educational alternative drug control hyperactive children. *Journal of Applied Behavior Analysis*, 1975, **8**, 137–146.

Ayllon, T., & Roberts, M.D. Eliminating discipline problems by strengthening academic performance. *Journal of Applied Behavior Analysis*, 1974, **7**, 71–76.

Barkley, R.A. Learning disabilities. In E.J. Mash & L.G. Terdal (Eds.), *Behavioral assessment of childhood disorders*. New York: Guilford, 1981.

Barkley, R.A., & Cunningham, C.E. Do stimulant drugs improve the academic performance of hyperactive children? A review of outcome research. *Clinical Pediatrics*, 1978, **17**, 85–92.

Benton, A., & Pearl, D. (Eds.), *Dyslexia: An appraisal of current knowledge*. New York: Oxford University Press, 1978.

Black, F.W. WISC verbal-performance discrepancies as indicators of neurological dysfunction in pediatric patients. *Journal of Clinical Psychology*, 1974, **30**, 165–167.

Boder, E. Developmental dyslexia: A diagnostic approach based on three atypical reading-spelling patterns. *Developmental Medicine and Child Neurology*, 1973, **15**, 663–687.

Broughton, S.F., & Lahey, B.B. Direct and collateral effects of positive reinforcement, response cost, and mixed contingencies for academic performance. *Journal of School Psychology*, 1978, **16**, 126–136.

Bryan, T. Peer popularity of learning disabled children. *Journal of Learning Disabilities*, 1974, **1**, 621–626.

Bryan, T. Peer popularity of learning disabled children: A replication. *Journal of Learning Disabilities*, 1976, **9**, 49–53.

Bryden, M.P. Auditory-visual and sequential-spatial matching in relation to reading ability. *Child Development*, 1972, **43**, 824.832.

Cohen, R.L., & Netley, C. Cognitive deficits, learning disabilities, and WISC verbal-performance consistency. *Developmental Psychology*, 1978, **14**, 624–634.

Conners, C.K., Eisenberg, L., & Sharpe, L. Effects of methylphenidate (Ritalin) on paired-associated learning and Porteus maze performance in emotionally disturbed children. *Journal of Consulting Psychology*, 1973, **41**, 438–446.

Cruickshanck, W. *The brain-injured child in the home, school, and community*. New York: Syracuse University Press, 1967.

Cunningham, C.E., & Barkley, R.A. The role of academic failure in hyperactive behavior. *Journal of Learning Disabilities*, 1978, **11**, 15–21.

Delacato, C. *Neurological organization and reading*. Springfield, Ill.: Thomas, 1966.

Delamater, A., Lahey, B.B., & Drake, L. Toward an empirical subclassification of "learning disabilities": A psychophysiological comparison of "hyperactive" and "nonhyperactive" subgroups. *Journal of Abnormal Child Psychology*, 1981, **9**, 65–77.

Dudley-Marling, C.C., Kaufman, N.J., & Tarver, S.G. WISC and WISC-R profiles of learning disabled children: A review. *Learning Disability Quarterly*, 1981, **4**, 307–319.

Fernald, G. *Remedial techniques in basic school subjects*. New York: McGraw-Hill, 1943.

Ferritor, D.E., Buckholdt, D., Hamblin, R.L., & Smith, L. The noneffects of contingent reinforcement for attending behavior on work accomplished. *Journal of Applied Behavior Analysis*, 1972, **5**, 7–17.

Feuerstein, M., Ward, M.M., & LeBaron, S.W. Neuropsychological and neurophysiological assessment of children with learning and behavior problems: A critical appraisal. In B.B. Lahey & A.E. Kazdin (Eds.), *Advances in clinical child psychology* (Vol. 2). New York: Plenum, 1979.

Finucci, J.M., Guthrie, J.T., Childs, A.L., Abbey, H., & Childs, B. The genetics of specific reading disability. *Annals of Human Genetics*, 1976, **40**, 1–23.

Frostig, M., & Horne, D. *The Frostig program for the development of visual perception*. Chicago: Follett Educational Corporation, 1964.

Gattesman, R.L. Follow-up of learning disabled children. *Learning Disability Quarterly*, 1979, **2**, 60–69.

Getman, G.N., & Kane, E.R. *The physiology of readiness: An action program for the development of perception for children.* Minneapolis, Minn.: Programs to Accelerate School Success, 1964.

Gittelman, R., Klein, D.F., Abikoff, H., Katz, S., Pollock, E., & Maltes, J. A controlled trial of behavior modification and methylphenidate in hyperactive children. In C. Whalen & B. Henker (Eds.), *Hyperactive: The social ecology of identification and treatment.* New York: Academic Press, 1980.

Goodman, L., & Hammill, D. The effectiveness of Kephart-Getman activities in developing perceptual-motor and cognitive skills. *Focus on Exceptional Children,* 1973, **4**, 1–9.

Hallahan, D.P., & Kaufman, J.M. *Introduction to learning disabilities: A psychobehavioral approach.* Englewood Cliffs, N.J.: Prentice-Hall, 1976.

Hallgren, B. Specific dyslexia ("congenital word blindness"): A clinical and genetic study. *Acta Psychiatrica et Neurologica Scandinovica,* 1950, (Supplement 65).

Hammill, D.D., & Larsen, S. The effectiveness of psycholinguistic training. *Exceptional Children,* 1974, **41**, 5–15.

Harris, L.A. Attention and learning disordered children: A review of theory and remediation. *Journal of Learning Disabilities,* 1976, **9**, 100–111.

Heilman, K.M., & Valenstein, E. (Eds.). *Clinical neuropsychology.* New York: Oxford University Press, 1979.

Horowitz, E.C. Popularity, decentering ability, and role-taking skills in learning disabled and normal children. *Learning Disability Quarterly,* 1981, **4**, 23–30.

Ingram, T.T.S., Mason, A.W., & Blackburn, I. A retrospective study of 82 children with reading disability. *Developmental Medicine and Child Neurology,* 1970, **12**, 271–281.

Jastak, J.F., & Jastak, S.R. *The Wide range achievement test.* (Rev. ed.) Wilmington, Del.: Guidance Association of Delaware, 1965.

Johnson, D., & Myklebust, H. *Learning disabilities: Educational principles and practices.* New York: Grune & Stratton, 1967.

Kagan, J. Developmental studies in reflection and analysis. In A.H. Kidd & J.H. Rivoire (Eds.), *Perceptual development in children.* New York: International Universities Press, 1966.

Kauffman, J.J., & Hallahan, D.P. Learning disability and hyperactivity (with comments on minimal brain dysfunction). In B.B. Lahey & A.E. Kazdin (Eds.), *Advances in clinical child psychology.* (Vol. 2). New York: Plenum, 1978.

Kaufman, A.S. *Intelligent testing with the WISC-R.* New York: Wiley, 1981.

Kent, R.M., & O'Leary, K.D. A controlled evaluation of behavior modification with conduct problem children. *Journal of Consulting and Clinical Psychology,* 1976, **44**, 586–596.

Kephart, N. *The slow learner in the classroom.* Columbus, Oh.: Merrill, 1971.

Kirby, F.D., & Shields, F. Modification of arithmetic response rate and attending behavior in a seventh grade student. *Journal of Applied Behavior Analysis,* 1972, **5**, 79–84.

Kirk, S.A., McCarthy, J.J., & Kirk, W.D. *Illinois test of psycholinguistic abilities.* Urbana: University of Illinois Press, 1968.

Koppitz, E.M. Bender Gestalt test, Visual digit span test, and Reading achievement. *Journal of Learning Disabilities,* 1975, **8**, 132, 157.

Knights, R.M., & Bakker, D.J. (Eds.). *The neuropsychology of learning disorders.* Baltimore: University Park Press, 1976.

Lahey, B.B. Behavior modification with learning disabilities and related problems. In M. Hersen, R. Eisler, & P. Miller (Eds.), *Progress in behavior modification* (Vol. 3). New York: Academic Press, 1976.

Lahey, B.B. *Behavior therapy with hyperactive and learning disabled children.* New York: Oxford University Press, 1979.

Lahey, B.B., Busemeyer, M., O'Hara, C., & Beggs, V.E. Treatment of severe perceptual-motor disorders in children diagnosed as learning disabled. *Behavior Modification,* 1977, **1**, 123–140.

Lahey, B.B., Delameter, A., Kupfer, D.L., & Hobbs, S.A. Behavioral aspects of learning disabilities and hyperactivity. *Education and Urban Society,* 1978, **10**, 477–499.

Lahey, B.B., & Drabman, R.S. Facilitation of the acquisition and retention of sight-word vocabulary through token-reinforcement. *Journal of Applied Behavior Analysis,* 1974, **7**, 307–312.

Lahey, B.B., & Johnson, M.S. *Psychology and instruction.* Glenview, Ill.: Scott, Foresman, 1977.

Lahey, B.B., Kupfer, D.K., Beggs, V.E., & Landon, D. Do learning-disabled children exhibit peripheral deficits in selective attention? An analysis of eye movements during reading. *Journal of Abnormal Child Psychology,* 1982, **10,** 1–10.

Lahey, B.B., McNees, M.P., & Brown, C.C. Modifications of deficits in reading for comprehension. *Journal of Applied Behavior Analysis,* 1973, **6,** 475–480.

Lahey, B.B., Stempniak, M., Robinson, E.J., & Tyroler, M.H. Hyperactivity and learning disabilities in independent dimensions of child behavior problems. *Journal of Abnormal Psychology,* 1978, **87,** 330–340.

Lahey, B.B., Vosk, B.N., & Habif, V.L. Behavioral assessment of learning disabled children: A rationale and strategy. *Behavioral Assessment,* 1981, **3,** 3–14.

Lambert, N., & Sandoval, J. The prevalence of learning disabilities in a sample of children considered hyperactive. *Journal of Abnormal Child Psychology,* 1980, **8,** 33–50.

Lovitt, T.C. Assessment of children with learning disabilities. *Exceptional Children,* 1967, **34,** 233–239.

Lyon, R., & Watson, W. Empirically derived subgroups of learning disabled readers: Diagnostic characteristics. *Journal of Learning Disabilities,* 1981, **14,** 256–261.

McCarthy, D. *McCarthy scales of children's abilities.* New York: The Psychological Corporation, 1972.

Madsen, C.H., Becker, W.C., & Thomas, D.R. Rules, praise, and ignoring: Elements of elementary classroom control. *Journal of Applied Behavior Analysis,* 1968, **1,** 139–150.

Meir, J.H. Prevalence and characteristics of learning disabilities found in second grade children. *Journal of Learning Disabilities,* 1971, **4,** 7–18.

Miller, L.C. School behavior checklist: An inventory of deviant behavior for elementary school children. *Journal of Consulting and Clinical Psychology,* 1972, **38,** 134–144.

Maidoo, S. *Specific dyslexia.* New York: Wiley, 1972.

Novy, P., Burnett, J., Powers, M., & Sulzer-Azaroff, B. Modifying attending-to-work behavior of a learning disabled child. *Journal of Learning Disabilities,* 1973, **6,** 217–221.

O'Leary, K.D., Becker, W.C., Evans, M.B., & Saudargas, R.A. A token reinforcement program in a public school: A replication and systematic analysis. *Journal of Applied Behavior Analysis,* 1969, **2,** 2–13.

O'Leary, S.G., Rosenbaum, A., & Price, G.H. Behavioral treatment of hyperactive children: An experimental evaluation of its usefulness. *Clinical Pediatrics,* 1977, **15,** 274–279.

Osgood, C. *"A behavioral analysis" in contemporary approaches to cognition.* Cambridge: Harvard University Press, 1957.

Owen, F.W. Dyslexia—Genetic aspects. In A. Benton & D. Pearl (Eds.), *Dyslexia: An appraisal of current knowledge.* New York: Oxford University Press, 1978.

Peter, B.M., & Spreen, O. Behavior rating and personal adjustment scales of neurologically and learning handicapped children during adolescence and early adulthood: Results of a follow-up study. *Journal of Clinical Neuropsychology,* 1979, **1,** 75–92.

Rie, H.E., Rie, E.D., Stewart, S., & Ambuel, J.P. Effects of methylphenidate on underachieving children. *Journal of Consulting and Clinical Psychology,* 1976, **44,** 250–260.

Roff, M., Sells, S.B., & Golden, M.M. *Social adjustment and personality development in children.* Minneapolis, Minn.: The University of Minnesota, 1972.

Ross, A.O. *Psychological aspects of learning disabilities and reading disorders.* New York: McGraw-Hill, 1976.

Ross, A.O. *Learning disability: The unrealized potential.* New York: McGraw-Hill, 1977.

Rourke, B.P. Neuropsychological research in reading retardation: A review. In A. Benton & D. Pearl (Eds.), *Dyslexia: An appraisal of current knowledge.* New York: Oxford University Press, 1978.

Rourke, B.P., Young, G.C., & Flewelling, R.W. The relationships between WISC verbal-performance discrepancies and selected verbal, auditory-perceptual, visual-perceptual, and problem solving abilities in children with learning disabilities. *Journal of Clinical Psychology,* 1971, **27,** 475, 479.

Rutter, M., Tizard, J., Yule, W., Graham, P., & Whitmore, K. Research report: Isle of Wight studies. *Psychological Medicine,* 1976, **6,** 313–332.

Safer, D.J., & Allen, R.P. *Hyperactive children: Diagnosis and management.* Baltimore: University Park Press, 1976.

Sattler, J.M. *Assessment of children's intelligence and special abilities.* (2nd ed.). Boston: Allyn & Bacon, 1982.

Satz, P., Taylor, H.G., Friel, J., & Fletcher, J. Some developmental and predictive procursors of reading disabilities: A six year follow-up. In A. Benton & D. Pearl (Eds.), *Dyslexia: An appraisal of current knowledge.* New York: Oxford University Press, 1978.

Spache, G.D. *Diagnostic reading scales.* Monterey, Calif.: CTB/McGraw-Hill, 1963.

Sprague, R.L., Barnes, K.R., & Werry, J.S. Methylphenidate and thioridazine: Learning, reaction time, activity, and classroom behavior in disturbed children. *American Journal of Orthopsychiatry,* 1970, **40,** 615–628.

Sprague, R.L., & Werry, J.S. Psychotropic drugs and handicapped children. In L. Mann & D.A. Sabatino (Eds.), *The second review of special education.* Philadelphia: J.S.E. Press, 1974.

Stanford-Binet Intelligence Scale. Boston: Houghton Mifflin Co., 1973.

Strauss, A., & Lehtinen, L. *Psychopathology and education of the brain-injured child.* New York: Grune & Stratton, 1947.

Stromer, R. Remediating academic deficiencies in learning disabled children. *Exceptional Children,* 1977, **43,** 432–440.

Torgesen, J., & Goldman, T. Verbal rehearsal and short-term memory in reading-disabled child-ren. *Child Development,* 1977, **48,** 56–60.

Ullman, C.A. Teachers, peers, and tests as predictors of adjustment. *Journal of Educational Psychology,* 1957, **48,** 257–267.

Vellutino, F.R., Steger, J.A., Harding, C.J., & Phillips, F. Verbal vs. nonverbal paired-associates learning in poor and normal readers. *Neuropsychologia,* 1975, **13,** 75–82.

Wechsler, D. *Manual for the Wechsler intelligence scale for children—revised.* New York: The Psychological Corporation, 1974.

Wiig, E.H., & Roach, M.A. Immediate recall of semantically varied "sentences" by learning-disabled adolescents. *Perceptual and Motor Skills,* 1975, **40,** 119–125.

Williams, M., & Lahey, B.B. The functional independence of response latency and accuracy: Implications for the concept of conceptual tempo. *Journal of Abnormal Child Psychology,* 1977, **5,** 371–378.

Winett, R.A., & Winkler, R.C. Current behavior modification in the classroom: Be still, be quiet, be docile. *Journal of Applied Behavior Analysis,* 1972, **5,** 499–504.

Wolf, M.M., Giles, D.K., & Hall, R.V. Experiments with token reinforcement in a remedial classroom. *Behavior Research and Therapy,* 1968, **6,** 51–64.

Yule, W. The epidemiology of child psychopathology. In B.B. Lahey & A.E. Kazdin (Eds.), *Advances in clinical child psychology,* Volume 4. New York: Plenum, 1981.

CHAPTER 29

Communication Disorders of Children

LYNN C. RICHMAN AND MICHELE ELIASON

The psychological aspects of communication disorders in children are relatively new considerations for many clinical child psychologists. There are few child psychologists who specialize in communication disorders, and much of the clinical information available is frequently found in the speech and hearing literature. Speech problems in children are typically remedied by speech and language clinicians, especially those involving developmental articulation errors, primary stuttering, and voice disorders. However, with the recent influence from neuropsychology, research in language-related learning disabilities, and pediatric psychology, there are increasing demands on the clinical child psychologist to diagnose and treat children with language or communication disorders.

Psychology graduate training programs frequently are remiss in providing education or training in evaluation and treatment of children with communication disorders. The practicing child psychologist is, therefore, frequently ill prepared when presented with such a child. A hearing-impaired child who has not been previously diagnosed may be considered mentally retarded on the basis of a standardized test of intelligence, while a language-disordered child may be diagnosed as unmotivated when learning problems are identified or as emotionally disturbed when unusual language associations are observed. The obvious speech disorders mentioned are not typically brought to the child psychologist's attention; however, there are several areas of communication disorder that do require expertise from a psychological per-

spective. In the childhood range 6–12, many behavioral problems are related to subtle language disorders; some thought disorders are more appropriately considered language disorders; anxiety-based inhibition may be related to peripheral speech problems; and fluctuating hearing loss may lead to learning disability.

The purpose of this chapter is to review evidence from empirical investigation on communication disorder to provide a clinical perspective to assist the child psychologist in appropriate diagnosis and treatment of such children. Examination of three general groups of communication-disordered children will be undertaken; we will consider language-disordered, hearing-impaired, and cleft-palate children. Language-disordered children comprise an extremely high frequency of children with learning problems, behavior problems, and emotional problems. Hearing-impaired and deaf children require specialized assessment techniques and have special needs in education communication. Cleft-palate children represent one of the most frequently occurring congenital anomalies in children and represent a group of children with primary peripheral speech problems.

LANGUAGE DISORDERS

A developmental language disorder exists when there is a deficiency in expressing or understanding verbal communication that is not primarily due to mental retardation, hearing loss, or defect in peripheral oral mechanism. The term "language" will be used to refer to the symbolic system used for human communication purposes. Speech is the product of oral movement resulting in articulation of language expression, and verbal mediation is the use of the symbolic language system in thinking. This section will be concerned with disorders of language expression or reception as well as deficiency in verbal mediation. While these disorders may be accompanied by articulation deficiency, defective speech and articulation without language disorder will not be considered.

There is minimal objective evidence regarding the etiology of developmental language disorders. Diagnostic considerations rule out ostensible causative factors such as impoverished environment, hearing loss, and peripheral oral mechanism difficulties. Most hypotheses regarding etiology are derived from the adult aphasia literature or findings from neurological damage in children. It is not the intent of this chapter to examine in detail the neurology or neuropsychology of childhood aphasia or developmental language disorders, and the reader is referred to more complete information in this area (Eisenson, 1972; Gaddes, 1980; Ludlow, 1980).

Suggestive etiology of childhood language disorder ranges from genetic possibilities due to reported high familial incidence (Finucci, 1978) to atypical cerebral lateralization of language functions (Kinsbourne & Hiscock, 1978). There are also more specific hypotheses related to impairment of left hemisphere functions (Heilman, 1978). While the child clinician needs to be aware of the possibility of involved siblings of language-disordered children and etiology of neurologically involved patients, most children with developmental language disorders must be assessed and treated without etiological confirmation.

Language disorders have been reported in approximately 8 percent of white middle class children (Ludlow, 1980). Furthermore, there is even a higher incidence reported in lower socioeconomic and black children (Ludlow, 1980). Although learning disability is addressed in another chapter and will not be elaborated here, it is interesting to note that a high proportion of adolescents with learning disabilities displayed early signs of language disorder (Wiig & Semel, 1976). A comprehensive review of research in dyslexia (Vellutino, 1979) points out the pervasive nature of language-based learning disabilities. The relatively high incidence of language-based learning disability is exemplified by the findings of several studies that report the frequency of language disorders in general learning disability populations to be from 50 percent to 60 percent (Mattis, 1978). Rabinovitch (1959) noted that reading-disabled children frequently displayed difficulty in expressive language, word finding and verbal concept formation. Furthermore, Rabinovitch (1959) and others have found a high incidence of the low Verbal/high Performance WISC profile in groups of disabled readers (Belmont & Birch, 1966; Huelsman, 1970; Velluntino, 1979). Reading-disabled children were also found to display a high frequency of general speech and language problems (Fry, John, & Muehl, 1970; Ingram, Mason, & Blackburn, 1970; Warrington, 1967). A number of more specific aspects of linquistic functioning have also been found in reading-disabled populations, including verbal labeling (Denkla & Rudel, 1976), verbal encoding (Vellutino et al., 1975), and auditory-phonetic discrimination (Shankweiler & Liberman, 1976). Thus there is increasing evidence that many different types of language deficits should be considered when assessing the child with a reading disability. Furthermore, it has been shown that reading disability may be only one symptom of a more specific underlying language disorder that requires appropriate diagnosis and treatment (Richman, 1978; Richman & Lindgren, 1980).

Intellectual and Cognitive Symptoms

Research on intellectual development of language-disordered children suffers from the lack of an empirically derived classification system of identifying subgroups of language-disordered children (Ludlow, 1980). Since most studies of language-delayed or disordered children include heterogeneous groups, specific intellectual characteristics of language-impaired children have not been substantiated. Intelligence is usually quantified by scores on an intelligence test that consists of items requiring many different intellectual functions. For the language-disordered child there is disagreement regarding what constitutes an appropriate measure of intelligence. Johnson and Myklebust (1967) recommend use of both Verbal IQ and Performance IQ on the WISC, although it is suggested that the Full Scale should not be used in determining intellectual level if there is a significant discrepancy between the two. These authors state that the typical language-disordered child may have a low Verbal IQ, but a Performance IQ of 90 or above is felt to be indicative of average intelligence. Eisenson (1972) recommends the use of intelligence tests that do not require oral language or verbal mediation. He suggests using the Leiter International Performance Scale and Raven's Progressive Matrices to eliminate verbal mediation and the Peabody Picture Vocabulary Test to eliminate oral response. Subject selection based on only a nonverbal IQ to indicate average intelligence, along with some indication of language delay, has been reported to eliminate over 50 percent of children in classes for the language impaired (Ludlow, 1980). Therefore, it appears that evaluation of language functions beyond that provided on a standard intelligence test is needed.

Most language evaluation and treatment prior to the age of 5 is based on informal and formal procedures of the speech and language clinician. However, the child psychologist is frequently asked to assist in diagnostic assessment after school entrance since educational placement and treatment decisions are based on laws and guidelines that require some assessment of intellectual ability. Numerous questions may arise after the psychologist has administered a standard intelligence test such as the WISC-R to a language-disordered child. Some possible results and questions that might arise are listed below.

1. All three IQ scores (VS,PS,FS) are significantly below average:

   a. Is the child more generally mentally retarded than language-disordered?

   b. What if the child has a receptive language problem that results in confusion of directions even on the Performance section?

2. Verbal Scale is significantly below Performance Scale by 15 points or more, and Performance Scale is 90 or above:

   a. Does the lower VS indicate a language disorder?

   b. If a above is correct, is the language disorder general or specific?

3. Both Verbal Scale and Performance Scale are greater than 90 and are not significantly different:

   a. Does this suggest that the child does not have a language disability?

   b. What other tests should be administered to answer a above?

A review of the research on commonly occurring cognitive deficits of language-disordered children provides some direction related to psychological assessment of the language-disordered child. Since there is very little knowledge regarding specific subtypes of language-disordered children, specific language symptoms will be reviewed within the context of developmental aphasia. Although children with language disorders do not usually present a clear picture of etiology like some adult aphasics with localized brain damage, the terms "childhood aphasia" (Myklebust, 1971) and "developmental aphasia" (Eisenson, 1972) have been used to refer to children with delayed or disordered language development even though definitive neurological evidence is lacking. It is suggested by both authors that this condition might be suggestive of delay or dysfunction of the central nervous system. The reader is referred to these two sources for a more complete discussion of etiological theory. A recent discussion of developmental aphasia can also be found in Gaddes (1980). Some of the language symptoms identified by these authors are also discussed by Wiig and Semel (1976).

Some of the most frequently reported

symptoms of the developmental aphasic or language-disordered child include the following:

1. *Auditory perception deficit.* This includes the ability to discriminate phonetic sounds and to synthesize phonetic units into words (Shankweiler & Liberman, 1976).

2. *Naming and labeling deficits.* This includes naming common objects or pictures (Denkla & Rudel, 1976).

3. *Auditory memory deficit.* This includes both memory for isolated content as well as memory for more meaningful material (e.g., sentences). It also includes verbally mediated memory even when stimulus and response are nonaural (Blank, 1968; Senf & Freundl, 1972).

4. *Serial-order processing deficit.* This is separated from #3 above by errors in sequence or order rather than in memory span per se (Bakker, 1972; Corkin, 1974).

5. *Verbal concept formation and language association deficit.* This includes categorization of words and verbal association (Richman & Lindgren, 1980; Vellutino, 1979).

Asessment

There are comprehensive language test batteries developed or normed specifically for children, such as the Illinois Test of Psycholinguistic Abilities (McCarthy & Kirk, 1961) and the Neurosensory Center Comprehensive Examination for Aphasia (Crockett, 1974; Spreen & Benton, 1969). However, further work is needed in development and standardization of language assessment batteries for language-impaired children (Ludlow, 1980). At the present time the child psychologist must rely on a combination of intellectual, neuropsychological, and language assessment techniques in assessing the language-disordered child.

During the evaluation, the psychologist should be alert to symptoms that might suggest a language disorder. When articulation errors are noted, it should not necessarily be assumed that these are only evidence of peripheral speech problems. It has been demonstrated that some speech articulation errors may be associated with underlying language disorders (Leonard, Bolders, & Miller, 1976). The child clinician should also note other signs of language disorder that may be detected during administration of the WISC-R. Word-finding or naming problems frequently occur on the Picture Completion subtest when the child points to the appropriate missing part but may not be able to name it. Telegraphic speech (omission of articles, connectives, and prepositions, yet maintaining good meaning) may be elicited on the Comprehension and Vocabulary subtests. Other symptoms that should be noted include circumlocutions (roundabout explanations that do not quite answer the question) and delayed verbal response (answering a question that was previously asked during the response to a later question). While these symptoms should be recorded and alert the examiner to the possibility of a language disorder, they may not be reflected in the actual test scores.

After administration of the WISC-R, further assessment of specific language functions should proceed. The following tests have proven useful in our research and clinical evaluation of language-disordered children. The Hiskey-Nebraska Test of Learning Aptitude has assisted in identifying three separate subgroups of children who have language-based learning disability, no identifiable emotional or neurological disorders, and a low Verbal/high Performance WISC profile (Richman & Lindgren, 1980). Since the Hiskey allows evaluation of verbal mediation skills even though stimulus and response can be nonvocal, it is well suited for language-disordered children. A combination of WISC and Hiskey patterns was identified through factor analysis procedures, suggesting that these children have deficits in sequencing-memory, associative reasoning, or both. For a more extensive report on this procedure the reader is referred to the above reference.

The following selected tasks assist in evaluating differential language functions:

1. Associative language—expressive
   Similarities (WISC-R)
   Auditory Association (Illinois Test of Psycholinguistic Ability—ITPA)
   Word Fluency (Neurosensory Center Examination for Aphasia—NCCEA)

2. Associative language—receptive or mediational
   Picture Association (Hiskey-Nebraska Test of Learning Aptitude—Hiskey)
   Visual Association (ITPA)
   Token test (Multilingual Aphasia Battery—MLAB)

3. Naming and Word finding
   Visual Naming (MLAB)
   Boston Naming Test

4. Sequencing—memory (auditory—vocal)
   Digit Span (WISC-R)
   Rey Auditory Verbal Learning Test
   Sentence Repetition (NCCEA)

5. Sequencing—memory (verbally mediated, nonvocal)
   Memory for Color (Hiskey)
   Visual Attention Span (Hiskey)

Based on this battery of selected tests, several patterns of language strengths and weaknesses usually emerge. If there are no demonstrated weaknesses in any of the areas assessed, it is frequently found that other factors have been missed, and a primary language disorder is not diagnosed. Emotional or environmental problems are the most frequent factors that might produce symptoms similar to a primary language disorder. Thus if a language disorder is suspected, yet the child performs relatively well on the language battery, this should suggest caution and a reexamination of environmental conditions or emotional status that might have been previously ruled out.

Educational Considerations

Some children will demonstrate deficits on all of the subtests of the language battery. When this occurs, the child is most likely diagnosed as having a general language deficit. These children will also usually show deficits in all areas of academic achievement. Since there is deficiency in both memory and associative language functions and in both receptive and expressive modalities, the child will likely require some type of self-contained small group learning program such as classes for the communication disabled or self-contained learning disabled.

Many of the language-disordered children assessed in our center display differential strengths and weaknesses in associative language and memory functions. When this occurs, the next step is to relate the language strength or weakness to differential achievement levels and learning styles to provide a comprehensive treatment program.

Language Disorder I (Good Associative Reasoning/Poor Sequencing—Memory)

These children typically do well on language tasks that require verbal associations in reasoning and do poorly on sequencing and memory tasks. They may be identified by a typical WISC and Hiskey pattern that includes low Verbal/high Performance, along with higher scores on Similarities and Block Design on the WISC as well as Picture Association and Block Patterns on the Hiskey. These children also typically have lower scores on Arithmetic and Picture Arrangement on the WISC and several memory tasks on the Hiskey. Further information on objective identification is elaborated in a previous study (Richman & Lindgren, 1980).

The primary educational problems of these children relate to memory and sequencing difficulties. They have difficulty remembering words by sight and may show similar symptoms of impaired word recall in conversation (e.g., word recall, verbal labeling, increased latency in verbal response). Math problems are frequently identified, especially when they are required to provide automatic, rapid recall of math facts. The sequencing and memory deficiency is also expressed in poor spelling skills. Most teachers and parents consider these children to be bright due to their good associative reasoning skills. However, they are often considered to be lazy or unmotivated when the memory problem is not diagnosed.

Remedial procedures with this type of language-disordered child should focus on procedures that emphasize their good associative language skills and deemphasize rote recall. The use of phonetic strategies in reading is usually beneficial, and teaching "rules of reading" to use in word attack strategies capitalizes on their cognitive strengths. While children with language-based memory deficiency have difficulty with automatic recall of math facts, they are typically proficient in learning the principles of mathematical computation. Memory functions may be more efficient when the child learns to use visual and auditory associations to enhance recall of isolated content.

Language Disorder II (Good Sequencing—Memory/Poor Associative Reasoning)

Children with this disorder have a primary language deficiency in their ability to form verbal abstractions and in verbal logical processing. They are not usually identified in early elementary grades because of an isolated ability in automatic rote recall. The intellectual-cognitive pattern for these children has been demonstrated as a low Verbal/high Performance WISC profile with relatively better scores on Arithmetic, Picture Arrangement, and Coding, with low scores on Similarities and Block Design (Richman & Lindgren, 1980). Hiskey scores also reveal lower scores on associative tasks (Similarities and Block Patterns), with higher scores on memory subtests.

The educational problems of children with associative language disorder are more pervasive and severe than those of language-disordered children with only an auditory memory deficiency. Reading assessment of these children should not rely on simple word recognition skills such as the reading section of the Wide Range Achievement Test. It is important to evaluate oral reading in context and reading comprehension, which are usually deficient in this type of child. Reading symptoms are usually identified in deficient phonetic segmentation and synthesis. Boder's (1973) description of the dysphonetic reader is consistent with the reading pattern of this type of language-disordered child.

The primary educational remediation for these children consists of language therapy focusing on assistance with language categorization and concept formation as outlined by Eisenson (1972) for children with aphasia. Reading assistance should stress comprehension assistance by having children read a short passage and retell the passage in their own words. The clinician should be alert to the superficial word-calling ability of these children even though understanding may be deficient. In fact, a unique subgroup of these children who are hyperlexic have a superior word-calling ability with deficient language comprehension (Richman & Kitchell, 1981).

Behavior and Personality

There are few unique characteristic behaviors or personality traits of language-disordered children. Luria (1966) provides a comprehensive examination of the relationship between language mediation and self-regulation of behavior. Luria suggests that deficiency in higher cortical language functions such as associative logic may impair the development of internalized self-control of behavior. There is some research evidence to support the contention that language-deficient children display excessive aggression and impulsivity (Camp, 1977). Although it is likely that deficient verbal mediation ability may be related to excessive expression of impulse, it has been shown that this may be the case for only those language-disordered children with deficiency in language association (Richman & Lindgren, 1981).

Clinical evaluation of hyperactive, impulsive, or behaviorally disordered children should consider the possibility that lack of self-control of behavior may be related to undiagnosed associative language disorders in some of these children. Behavioral diagnosis should be placed within a context of language mediation skills. Meichenbaum (1975) has developed a treatment program for such children which focuses on cognitive behavior modification. This procedure attempts to provide assistance in developing verbal mediation strategies to self-guide and control behavior. With younger children who display excessive impulsivity secondary to language mediation deficiency, verbally mediated self-control may be increased through use of modeling of adults through vocalized reflective problem-solving strategies (Kagan, 1966).

CLEFT PALATE

It has been said of cleft palate: "Few congenital deformities can lead to such a great variety of disability—pitiable looks, dental caries, poor dental occlusion, poor speech, middle ear infections, psychological aberrations, economic burdens, and fear of hereditary patterns. Few congenital anomalies have challenged resources of more specialties and subspecialties" (Cook et al., 1979, p. 3).

Cleft palate is one of the most frequently occurring congenital anomalies. The incidence of cleft palate is 1/600–700 live births (Spriestersbach, 1973). Clefts can be complete or incomplete, bilateral or unilateral, and involve the lip, hard palate, and/or soft palate (Drillien, Ingram, & Wilkinson, 1966). Approximately 50 percent of all cleft cases involve lip and palate, 25 percent palate only and 25 percent lip only (Massengill & Phillips, 1975). There are over 50 recognized syndromes of which cleft palate is one feature, but these comprise a small proportion of the cleft population (Fraser, 1970). Seventy-one per-

cent of lip-and-palate and 85 percent of palate-only children are reported to have other physical anomalies in addition to their clefts, with females more likely than males to show other defects (Cook et al., 1979).

The incidence of cleft palate varies somewhat according to race and sex. American blacks have a relatively low incidence (1/2,000), and Orientals have a relatively high rate of occurrence (1.5–2/1,000). Clefts are reported to occur more frequently in males by a 6:4 ratio (Massengill & Phillips, 1975). More males exhibit cleft of both lip and palate, and, in general, males have more severe defects than females. Females are more likely to have isolated clefts of the palate than males. Cook et al. (1979) propose a difference in developmental time sequences for the sexes to account for this difference.

The cause of any individual case of cleft palate is largely speculative. About one-third of the cases have a family history of clefts, and these children do not usually have other congenital anomalies (Drillien et al., 1966). Nonfamilial clefts have many hypothesized causes including the presence during pregnancy of viral infections, toxic substances, metabolic deficiencies, endocrine imbalances, exposure to radiation, and hypoxia. Cook et al. (1979) report a significant correlation between the presence of a nonfamilial cleft and impaired reproductive capacity of the mother (including severe menstrual disturbances, abnormal outcome of other conceptions, and difficulty conceiving). There are more reports of other congenital anomalies for nonfamilial cleft children than for those with familial cleft.

Cleft children have a higher incidence of hearing disorders—hearing loss and middle ear disorders—than the general population. Cook et al. (1979) estimate that one-half of all cleft children have hearing problems, compared to about 5 percent of the general school age population. The hearing loss is frequently bilateral and conductive in nature (Spriestersbach & Sherman, 1968). The incidence of hearing loss does not seem to vary with type or severity of the cleft, sex, or time surgical management is initiated; however, there is reported to be a higher incidence of hearing loss in elementary-school-age cleft children than in other age groups. Cleft children frequently have fluctuating hearing losses that are difficult to identify without close monitoring and treatment. Yules (1970) found that 50 percent of a cleft sample sustained some degree of chronic conductive hearing loss.

Much has been written about the specific speech characteristics of cleft children. However, for general purposes these can be incorporated into two major areas: nasal voice quality and articulation errors. The incidence of speech problems in cleft populations has not been well established since studies vary in criteria used for normal speech, type and severity of clefts, and age of treatment. Spriestersbach and Sherman (1968) estimate that 40–60 percent achieve normal speech after primary surgical repair (closure of the defect), while another 30–40 percent have normal speech after secondary repair (pharyngeal flaps) or orthodontic intervention. These authors found that more palate-only children achieve normal speech than do lip and palate, although some conflicting data exist. Generally, children with cleft of only the soft palate have better speech than those with complete cleft of the hard and soft palate.

Speech difficulties can result from faulty anatomical and/or physiological apparatus as well as faulty learning. An open palate may allow air to escape through the nasal passage, causing difficulty pronouncing the nasal consonants. There may also be difficulty in forming consonants that require a build-up of air pressure, such as *p, b, d,* and so on. Faulty speech may also be related to compensatory effort in learning to speak before the defect is closed. The child often needs extensive speech therapy to relearn speech sounds. Massengill and Phillips (1975) report that many of these children are not aware that their speech is defective until it is pointed out to them.

Many investigators have found increased incidence of language delay in cleft children. Spriestersbach and Sherman (1968) found that, while cleft children were advanced in word recognition skills, they were delayed in

the ability to define words. Cleft children also produce less verbal output (fewer words per sentence and fewer total words per exchange) and less complex grammatical structure than noncleft children. However, Pannbacker (1975) found that adult cleft palate speakers use the same syntax and vocabulary as a group of matched controls, although cleft speakers had lower mean length of verbal responses.

Intellectual and Cognitive Symptoms

Although early studies reported that the average IQ of cleft samples was below that of the general population, most of these studies failed to use control groups and frequently used several different measures of intelligence within one study (Billig, 1951; Means & Irwin, 1954; Munson & May, 1955; Lewis, 1961; Estes & Morris, 1970). However, even when control groups have been utilized and a standard intellectual assessment used, the finding of slightly lower IQs in cleft children has been supported (Goodstein, 1968). One exception is a 1965 study by Ruess where no significant difference between cleft children and their siblings was found. These children had received intensive follow-up and habilitation, leading Ruess to suggest that with proper treatment the cleft child can be expected to approximate the population IQ mean. Lencione (1980) reviewed numerous studies that reported intellectual functioning of cleft children and concluded that, while the mean IQs were slightly lower than controls or the population norm, they were within the average range.

There is increasing evidence to suggest that the slightly lower Full Scale IQ reported for samples of cleft children may be primarily due to decreased verbal intelligence only. Goodstein (1961) found that a group of 105 cleft children exhibited a greater deficit on the Verbal Scale of the WISC than on the Performance Scale. Ruess (1965) also found a significant difference between cleft and control groups on Verbal IQ, with no significant difference between the groups on Performance Scale. Cleft children were also found to have significantly lower Verbal Scale IQ than their siblings, while there was no significant difference in Performance Scale IQ (Lamb, Wilson, & Leeper, 1973).

There have been several hypotheses proposed to explain the lower Verbal IQ found in cleft samples. Estes and Morris (1970) suggest that the deficit may be developmental or the result of a lack of language stimulation at home. Another possible cause is the high incidence of hearing disorder in cleft children. For example, Means and Irwin (1954) found a greater number of cleft children without hearing loss to have IQs over 100 than those with hearing loss. McWilliams and Musgrave (1972) considered the quality of speech as a factor related to intelligence and found that cleft children with normal speech had significantly higher IQs (mean of 109) than those with hypernasal speech (mean of 97). Morris (1962) reported a significant correlation between articulation scores and WISC scale scores.

Few studies have attempted to delineate specific cognitive abilities of cleft children. Brantly and Clifford (1979) found no significant differences among cleft adolescents, normal controls, and diabetic adolescents on several cognitive measures including visual perception, impulsivity-reflectivity, receptive language, spatial abilities, and isolated short term memory. Brennan and Cullinan (1974) found cleft children lower than controls on object naming and word recognition tasks. Richman (1980) identified two subgroups of cleft children with different language deficiencies. One group displayed only a verbal expressive deficit, while the other group showed a more general language deficit with problems in associative reasoning and categorization skills.

Several factors seem to confound the relationship between cleft palate and intelligence, such as type and severity of cleft, age, and sex. Goodstein (1961) found that palate-only children tended to have lower IQs than lip-and-palate cases, citing the higher incidence of other congenital anomalies as a contributing factor. Lewis (1961) also found children with multiple anomalies to have IQs about 10 points lower than those with cleft defects only. Estes and Morris (1970), however, did not find a significant difference in IQs between three types of clefts, although lip-only children tended to have slightly higher scores than lip-and-palate or palate-only groups. McWilliams and Matthews (1979) found that palate-only plus other anomalies had significantly lower IQs (mean of 84) than other groups. Lamb, Wilson, and Leeper (1973) found a sex x cleft-type difference in IQ levels. Female lip-and-palate and male palate-only children (which comprise the lowest type of frequency by sex) were considered more "language deficient" than were other groups. The results of Lamb et al. support Fraser's (1970) hypothesis that cleft lip and palate and palate alone are only one manifestation of a whole range of possible malformations due to a genetic developmental instability. They recommend a study of sex and cleft-type differences using a neuropsychological test battery to assess CNS functioning. A longitudinal study by Musgrave, McWilliams, and Matthews (1975) suggests some age differences. Mean IQs for two palate-only groups in their preschool years on the Stanford-Binet were 96 and 97. Ten years later, those means were 107 and 111 respectively. These data support the contention that some cleft children may be language delayed in the early years but improve in language functioning over time.

Assessment and Treatment

Research data suggest that in general the cleft palate population approximates the normal curve in general intellectual ability, but there is an increased incidence of specific verbal expressive deficit or a more general language delay. Therefore, assessment of the cleft child should focus on verbal cognitive skills. Particular attention should be given to differentiation of verbal expression versus symbolic language mediation abilities. Evaluation of cleft children should use an intelligence measure such as the Wechsler tests that have both verbal and nonverbal components. If a significant verbal deficit is present, a nonverbal test that assesses associative reasoning, categorization, and memory skills should be utilized. The Hiskey-Nebraska Test of Learning Aptitude has been useful in this respect and has norms for both hearing-impaired children and normal-hearing children (Richman, 1980).

The Peabody Picture Vocabulary Test (PPVT), although frequently used, has not been particularly useful in assessing language skills in cleft (McWilliams, 1974) or language-impaired children (Richman, 1979). McWilliams found poor predictive validity among the PPVT, the Stanford-Binet, and the Illinois Test of Psycholinguistic Ability (ITPA). Richman (1979) suggests that the PPVT does not necessarily assess the symbolic component of language but may be only a simple paired-associate learning test and tends to overestimate reading and cognitive abilities. The Hiskey assesses sequential memory and abstract reasoning skills that are important variables in reading and language development.

Lamb et al. (1973) recommend the use of neuropsychological testing to identify effects of past or present hearing loss and to determine if central nervous system impairment is present. While there are several standardized neuropsychological batteries available for children, those such as the Spreen-Benton NCCEA (1969) that focus on language functions are especially useful.

If a verbal-deficit—whether specific or general—is discovered, the child will probably benefit from language therapy. Those cleft children with general language deficits need extensive language therapy focusing on abstract reasoning and categorization. Children with more specific deficits in verbal expression, along with intact verbal mediation skills, will usually need only traditional speech therapy. Early language stimulation should be encouraged with home programs and parent training to avoid the reported tendency of decreased verbal interaction. The cleft child may not be reinforced for vocalizations as much as the normal child. Parents should be encouraged to reward early vocalization even though articulation errors and/or hypernasality may make utterances unintelligible.

Educational Considerations

There is less documentation of the academic achievement of cleft children than of intellectual or personality characteristics. One might expect that the speech and hearing problems, language delay, and altered physical appearance could have serious consequences on school achievement. Richman (1978a) found that teachers rate children with more noticeable facial disfigurement as having lower intelligence than measured by individual intelligence tests, while they are more accurate in estimating intelligence of cleft children with relatively normal appearance. Teachers also rate cleft children as more inhibited and withdrawn in the classroom than parents view them at home (Richman, 1978b). It was suggested that teachers' perceptions of a cleft child may have a detrimental influence on school achievement.

Cleft children, in spite of average intelligence, have been found to score lower than controls on standard group achievement tests (Richman, 1976; Richman & Harper, 1978). Richman (1980) also reported that over 50 percent of a sample of cleft children with average IQs exhibited significantly below average reading and math skills on the Wide Range Achievement Test. Kommers and Sullivan (1979) studied the written expression of a small group of cleft children with average to very superior IQs and found below average performance on total words, words per sentence, and syntax. Percentiles tended to decline as age increased, suggesting that the verbal deficit may not be only a developmental delay.

Inspection of questionnaire data reported by Spriestersbach (1973) indicates that twice as many cleft children are delayed in starting school than controls; twice as many cleft children were considered nine or more months delayed in school achievement by their parents; and twice as many repeat one or more grades in school. Spriestersbach also found that mothers of cleft children have a slightly lower expectation that their children will attend college (35 percent) compared to control mothers (45 percent).

Demb and Ruess (from McWilliams & Smith, 1973) report that the base rate for high school dropout is less for cleft children than their siblings. However, when cleft children do drop out, it is at an earlier age. Kapp (1979) found that females with clefts feel they are less successful in school than controls. Peter and Chinsky (1974) surveyed the level of educational attainment in cleft populations and found that slightly more siblings and random controls attend college than cleft groups. The cleft group also had lower aspirations for themselves than the control group.

Evaluation and Treatment

The clinician should be alert to the possibility that cleft children may have lower achievement levels than one would expect, based on parent interview. Research suggests that parents may have lower expectations for their children and thus not report lower achievement. Teachers may also underestimate the child's ability and expect less. Thus it is important to evaluate individual levels of reading and arithmetic in particular.

One would also expect that cleft children with verbal deficits or general language disability would have reading disabilities. A major problem in testing reading is that many of the available tests are based on oral reading errors. For the cleft child one must determine whether the errors are due to faulty articulation, the cleft child's language disorder, or reading disability. Tests of sight-word recognition may overestimate the cleft child's reading ability due to the emphasis on rote sight recall to avoid phonetic approaches. This emphasis may inflate word recognition beyond comprehension ability. Therefore, a reading comprehension test should always be included. An analysis of reading errors in cleft children may be fruitful; one might expect cleft children with more severe speech problems to have difficulty with a phonics approach. They have difficulty with sound-symbol articulation that may transfer to reading. These children may benefit more from a sight-word approach. A sample of written language should also be obtained—spelling patterns may reveal something about their phonics skills or lack of skills and may aid in determining an underlying language impairment.

Also related to evaluation and treatment of achievement in cleft children, one should determine the educational expectations of the parents and teacher and whether they are realistic based on the child's abilities. Many cleft children may not be encouraged to achieve at a level commensurate with their intellectual ability. Another issue related to the achievement of cleft children is that of their behavioral characteristic of inhibition. Their lack of competitiveness may interfere with classroom work. For example, cleft children who do not hear all of the directions may avoid asking the teacher to repeat them because they fear calling attention to themselves. Treatment of educational problems in cleft children must frequently focus on low self-esteem and anxiety that may result in neurotic learning inhibition.

Behavior and Personality

Attempts to document a "syndrome specific" personality type for cleft children have failed to identify unique personality traits related to the cleft condition. Tisza et al. (1958), using observations of preschool cleft children at play, found higher levels of muscular rigidity, bodily tensions, and distortions on psychomotor tasks. Gluck et al. (1965) compared clinical records of cleft children with records of children seen at a child guidance center and reported that cleft children had more somatic concerns, were more often regarded as shy, and had a higher incidence of enuresis than the child guidance cases. Spriestersbach (1973), using a parent interview format, found that parents perceive their cleft child as less confident, less aggressive, and less independent than other children. Other studies using paper-and-pencil personality tests and drawing tests have failed to uncover a unique "cleft palate personality" (Barker, 1951; Sidney & Matthews, 1956; Palmer & Adams, 1962;

Ruess, 1965; Watson, 1964). In general, use of projective techniques and tests designed to differentiate normal from psychopathological groups has failed to uncover differences in cleft populations. More recently, investigators have used measures that allow for more subtle differences to appear—tests that allow for measurement of variations of normal behavior.

Richman (1976) used teacher ratings of cleft and matched control groups on the Quay-Peterson Behavior Problem Checklist and found cleft children to score high on the internalizing factor, showing an excessive inhibition of impulse. Richman and Harper (1979), using a nonverbal personality test, the Missouri Child's Picture Series, also found greater inhibition in cleft children. A later study (Harper, Richman, & Snider, 1980) found a difference in behavior according to severity of impairment. Children with mild facial disfigurement displayed greater inhibition than more severely impaired children. In this study, children wtih clefts displayed more acting-out behavior than noted in earlier studies. However, this was an older group (mean age 14.1). The authors suggest that there may be a developmental trend of excessive behavioral inhibition in early childhood, changing to an increase in excessive expression of impulses in adolescence, especially for the more severely involved. The finding of greater inhibition in young cleft children may be a function of the children's desire to avoid situations that may call attention to themselves. However, in social situations or in a classroom, where some degree of independence and competitiveness is necessary for success, the inhibited child is at a disadvantage.

The adolescent with a cleft palate tends to show behavioral inhibition, self-concern, and ruminative self-doubts over interpersonal interactions on an MMPI profile analysis (Harper and Richman, 1978). Cleft females showed a greater dissatisfaction with their life situation than did males, possibly related to a greater emphasis on physical appearance in females. These MMPI profiles did not suggest emotional maladjustment but rather variations of normal behavior.

Evaluation and Treatment

Research evidence suggests that as a group cleft children do not display a unique personality trait related to their condition, nor is there indication of a high incidence of overt psychopathology. However, there is a consistent finding that cleft children are more likely to be inhibited, shy, and less independent than noncleft peers. Since it has been shown that cleft children are viewed differently by teachers than by parents, independent behavior ratings may be helpful in assessing adjustment in different environments. The cleft child is more likely to be characterized as independent and outgoing by the parents although this may not be the case in the classroom or peer social situations. Since there is evidence of a tendency for parents of cleft children to be overly protective, encouragement of earlier social interaction with peers and reinforcement of independence by the parents may be beneficial.

Adolescents with clefts frequently continue a pattern of excessive inhibition, along with feelings of anxiety in social situations and increased self-consciousness. Excessive inhibition may create increased feelings of social alienation for the cleft male since adolescent males more typically tend to display increased levels of impulsive behavior. Females with a cleft frequently experience low self-esteem and feelings of alienation due to increased concern regarding physical appearance. The clinician working with cleft adolescents should be alert to these concerns and provide supportive counseling in this regard.

HEARING IMPAIRMENT

Several centuries ago, Aristotle wrote, "The ear is the organ of education." Although that point may be disputed today, one cannot deny the importance of hearing in developing verbal communication and general language competence. From the moment of birth, the child begins a process of adaptation to the environment by means of sensory experiences. Hearing and vision constitute the most crucial senses for acquiring information about the world. Later, during the school years, one-half to two-thirds of the child's day is spent listening (Giangreco & Giangreco, 1970). In 1975, the Conference of Executives of American Schools for the Deaf adopted the following definitions:

Hearing impairment is a generic term indicating disability which may range in severity from mild to profound. It includes the subsets of deaf and hard-of-hearing. A deaf person is one whose hearing disability precludes successful processing of linguistic information through audition with or without a hearing aid. A hard-of-hearing person is one who, generally with the use of a hearing aid, has residual hearing sufficient to enable successful linguistic processing through audition. (Bess & McConnell, 1981)

This definition describes only one way to classify the hearing impaired and does not provide specific information about the individual child.

Some authors have classified hearing-impaired individuals on a continuum of degree of loss, with normal hearing at one end and profound hearing loss at the other extreme; still others classify hearing impairment based on location of the defect—middle ear (conductive), inner ear (sensorineural), eighth cranial nerve (neural), or higher cortical (central auditory). In most classifications, "deafness" implies a lack of opportunity to learn normal, spontaneous spoken language. This hearing loss is frequently present at birth or is frequently identified within the first two years. The term hard-of-hearing covers the other degrees of hearing loss. There are three well-accepted types and a fourth more controversial type of auditory impairment in children. A conductive loss results from blockage or damage to the middle ear, causing a reduction of the loudness of sound. A sensorineural loss affects the inner structures or nerve pathway and results in a reduced clarity of sound reception. A mixed loss involves some degree of both conductive and sensorineural loss. The fourth type is termed a "central auditory impairment" and does not involve an actual loss of hearing acuity but is hypothesized to arise from brain pathway dysfunction. This type of impairment is largely speculative and will not be discussed in this chapter.

The measurement of prevalence of hearing impairment is plagued by differences in criteria. What degree of hearing loss constitutes a potentially handicapping condition? Traditionally, the degree of loss had to exceed 26 dB in the speech frequencies to constitute a significant hearing loss (Northern & Downs, 1978). Many authors suggest that even a criterion of 15 dB would miss 50 percent of the children with otitis media and 40 percent of those with perforated ear drums (Jordan & Eagles, 1961; Melnick, Eagles, & Levine, 1964). Lewis (1976) felt that a 10 dB loss was educationally significant. Northern and Downs (1978) report that, if a multiple criterion of 15 dB loss, presence of middle ear pathology before 18 months, and fluctuating hearing loss is used, 10 percent of the school-age population could be considered hearing-impaired. Congenital deafness (present at birth) occurs at a rate of 1/2,000 live births and affects more males than females (Bess & McConnell, 1981). The presence of middle ear disturbance in children is very high. Bess and McConnell (1981) estimate that 76–95 percent of all children have at least one episode of otitis media before the age of 6 and that one child in 20 has recurrent ear infections with fluctuating hearing loss. Otitis media is very common in the young child, peaks at about age 6, then begins to decline in occurrence with increasing age.

Hearing loss can be due to endogenous causes (genetic factors, maternal insult during pregnancy) or exogenous (trauma, disease, ototoxicity to the child). A genetic etiology is indicated in approximately 50 percent of the deaf population. There are over 50 types of genetically transmitted causes of deafness that can be autosomal dominant, autosomal recessive, or sex linked (Bess & McConnell, 1981). Most forms of genetic transmission involve a severe degree of hearing impairment. Approximately two-thirds of the nongenetic causes are the result of prenatal factors such as Rh incompatibility, rubella, trauma, or medication during labor. These factors are more frequently associated with other anomalies, including brain damage, than other causes of hearing impairment. Postnatal causes of hearing loss include infectious disease (primarily otitis media, meningitis, measles, mumps), fever, high intensity noise, and ototoxic drugs (certain antibiotics). Otitis media is frequently related to a conductive hearing loss but may damage structures of the ear that allow infection into the inner ear to cause sensorineural damage (Northern & Downs, 1978).

Intellectual and Language Development

Language is learned through listening and practicing in the normal hearing child. It is reported that mothers of deaf children have less daily verbal communication with their children and tend to overprotect and isolate them (Fundudis, Kolvin, & Garside, 1979). This may lead to exacerbation of the language delay. There is a major controversy over the relationship between language and intelligence in the hearing impaired. Lewis (1976) states that the two are highly related and that language is the most important source of intellectual stimluation. The other view (Furth & Youniss, 1969) is that language and intelligence are more separate functions and develop somewhat independently. While hearing impairment most likely affects verbal intelligence more than nonverbal intelligence, it is likely that many tasks that appear to be nonverbal may be mediated by language-based strategies.

Most authors agree that the first three to four years of life constitute a critical period of language acquisition (Fundudis et al., 1979). The problems of acquiring language for the profoundly hearing impaired are obvious, but what of the child with a fluctuating hearing loss during the critical period? This hearing loss might not be detected when the child hears most vowel sounds adequately yet cannot detect high frequency consonants such as *s, f, t, th* (Roach & Rosecraus, 1972). This child may appear to hear but does not understand the complete message. The adult speaker may have learned to use context clues to fill in missing sounds, while the child may not have that strategy. It is not uncommon for the young child who has a mild high frequency hearing loss to appear intellectually slow due to deficient speech production and inattentive due to difficulty in understanding oral communication (Northern & Downs, 1978).

Based on an extensive review of intelligence of the hearing impaired, Vernon (1968) concluded that when nonverbal performance tests are used, hearing-impaired children approximate the normal distribution of intelligence. However, certain etiological factors (maternal rubella, prematurity, early meningitis) were more often associated with mental retardation. In general, Vernon found no significant relationship between IQ and degree of hearing loss or age of onset. The author offers support for the contention that language and intelligence are somewhat independent factors, since even severely language-disabled deaf children displayed average IQs on performance measures. Although Vernon considers performance tests as measuring academic potential, not all researchers do (Furth, 1966; Graham & Shapiro, 1953). Furth (1971) identified several areas of intellectual deficiency in hearing-impaired children even when no vocal response was required. Areas of deficiency included rule learning, categorization, and language-mediated memory.

There is considerable controversy over which ability tests to use with the hearing impaired. Only one well-known test, the Hiskey-Nebraska Test of Learning Aptitude has standardized pantomine directions and norms for both hearing-impaired and non-hearing-impaired children. The most commonly used tests, the Wechsler Intelligence Scale for Children—Revised (WISC-R) Performance Scale and the Leiter International Scale have verbal directions with no standardized modifications for the hearing impaired. However, there is data to suggest that different levels of functioning may be obtained on the WISC-R when deaf children receive a modified administration (Sullivan, 1978). Another issue is the training and experience of the examiner; Vernon (1968) found that examiners experienced with hearing-impaired children obtained IQs nearer to the national norm than did inexperienced examiners. Verbal scores are not used or rarely cited in most studies but are sometimes used as an indication of degree of speech and language impairment in children without severe hearing loss. However, Vernon warns us not to consider a Verbal IQ score as representative of the level of the child's learning potential.

While Vernon (1968) found no significant relationship between degree of hearing loss and IQ, Roach and Rosecraus (1972) did find a relationship. In children with mild hearing loss, IQ decreased as the frequency of the loss increased. Verbal scores of the WISC correlated negatively to the hearing loss in 1,500–4,000 cycles per second range. They concluded that a high frequency hearing loss has a significant impact on verbal-language facility in the mildly impaired child.

Evaluation and Treatment

Assessment of intellectual functioning of the hearing-impaired child should include specific tests of language-mediated skills that do not require vocal directions or responses. If a child has some degree of oral communication, the use of the complete WISC-R is recommended although the results must be interpreted with caution. Quite frequently, a low Verbal/high Performance WISC-R profile is identified, and several interpretations of this profile are possible. It might be suggested that the lower Verbal IQ reflects the child's "true potential." However, further assessment may provide more specific information regarding the type of language or intellectual deficiency.

If the hearing-impaired child receives a score on the Hiskey-Nebraska Test of Learning Aptitude that approximates the level of Performance Scale IQ, it is likely that verbal mediation and symbolic language skills are intact, and the deficiency is related only to verbal expressive difficulty. In this case, individual or small group assistance in oral communication improvement is warranted. It is likely that the child will benefit by remaining in a regular classroom with outside assistance from the language clinician.

If the hearing-impaired child's scores on the Hiskey are generally at a level of the lower Verbal Scale IQ on the WISC-R, it is likely that a self-contained classroom for hearing-impaired children is appropriate. This child is likely to have a general symbolic language or verbal medition deficiency. Hearing-impaired children with a low Verbal IQ and consistently low subtest scores on the Hiskey are not likely to progress adequately when educational emphasis is on oral langauge communication. Therefore, these children may benefit from instruction in sign language and instruction at a level consistent with intellectual expectations based on the Learning Age Equivalent of the Hiskey.

There are many hearing-impaired children with more specific cognitive deficits than verbal expression deficiency or general language disorder. Selected tests of associative language functions and memory skills are of assistance in identifying individual differences in these children. A battery of such tests has been previously identified in the Language Disorders section of this chapter, and the reader is referred there for further information. This battery of tests, which assess both verbal and visual modalities of associative and memory functions, is frequently beneficial in identifying specific cognitive strengths and weaknesses that may indicate a learning disability that warrants specialized intervention beyond general consideration of the hearing impairment per se.

Educational Functioning

Although some hearing-impaired children have the potential for average or above average achievement, it is more likely that such children will have significant educational problems. Vernon and Koh (1971) feel that this may represent a failure of education due to the methods and materials used. The controversy over the best method of teaching hearing-impaired children can be reviewed elsewhere (Ling, 1975). It is likely that there is no "best method" and that hearing-impaired children require the same individual evaluation and teaching methods as language-impaired or learning-disabled children.

Kodman (1963) surveyed 100 hearing-impaired public school children who had average intellectual functioning. This group was 1–2.24 years below intellectual expectation in achievement. These children had mild-to-moderate degrees of hearing loss, suggesting that even this level of hearing impairment may lead to considerable academic deficiency. Goetzinger, Harrison, and Baer (1964) found that school age children with a mild hearing loss acquired prior to age 1 were significantly below average on a test of auditory discrimination and received more teacher ratings of emotional problems. School adjustment difficulties may exacerbate academic deficiency. Furthermore, a mild hearing loss may not be considered to be educationally significant, yet auditory discrimination difficulty may interfere with learning. Boyd (1974) found that even children with normal hearing in one ear and hearing loss in the other have a mean achievement lag of 1.2 years.

Children with severe hearing loss have even greater academic problems. Wrightstone, Aronow, and Moskowitz (1963) found that between the ages of 10 and 16, deaf children gain less than one year in reading achievement. Only 3–5 percent of deaf children achieve a tenth-grade education, with the majority not reaching a fifth-grade level (Vernon & Koh, 1971).

Some researchers have attempted to delineate specific cognitive disabilities in hearing-impaired children. Wilson and associates (1975) evaluated neuropsychological functions of a group of hearing-impaired children and found deficits in visual-motor integration, visual memory, sequencing, categorization, and stereognosis. These children have average scores on the WISC Performance Scale and lower Hiskey scores. Conrad (1973) found deficient short term memory, and several authors (Withrow, 1968; McCarthy & Marshall, 1969; Blair, 1957; Furth, 1961) found specific visual memory deficits in children with significant hearing loss. Stress et al. (1978), on the other hand, identified no visual-perceptual or visual memory problems in the sample; however, they used young adults enrolled in a postsecondary institute for the deaf, a rather select population.

Katz and Illmer (1972) surveyed a population of learning-disabled children and found a high incidence of conductive hearing loss.

These hearing-impaired LD children were deficient in auditory perception (phonemic segmentation) compared to normal hearing LD children. Hoemann et al. (1976) suggest that deaf children have average or superior spelling ability. They state that deaf children have intact linguistic capabilities and are able spontaneously to acquire the rules of spelling. An alternative interpretation is that these children acquired proficient spelling through visual memory functions similar to the unique reading and spelling of hyperlexic children with language disorders (Richman & Kitchell, 1980).

Achievement of Children with History of Otitis Media

The most common hearing impairment of concern in the public schools is the mild, fluctuating variety seen in children with recurrent otitis media. Needleman (1977) compared 20 elementary school children with a two-year history of otitis media to matched controls. All children were in regular classes. The otitis media group had significantly lower scores on all tasks of comprehension and production of language. In this sample, the differences in performance decreased as age increased, suggesting that these children may be able to "catch up." Needleman points out that during the age range when reading is first introduced, children with hearing loss may not have achieved the phonological development necessary for reading. However, with maturation and improved hearing, this may not produce a long term reading disability.

Kaplan, Fleshman, and Bender (1973) studied a large number of Eskimo children with a history of otitis media over several years. Those with mild conductive hearing loss had lower mean Verbal scores than those with no hearing loss, and 56 percent of these children were behind their expected grade placement. There was a significant relationship between degree of hearing loss and achievement, with greater achievement deficiency at higher grade levels. These authors propose (in direct opposition to Needleman) that a past history of otitis media may have permanent deleterious effects on educational attainment. Lewis (1976), in a study of Australian and European children, supports Kaplan et al.'s findings, stating, "Certain types of middle ear disease may tend to encourage inefficient listening strategies that can persist well beyond the episodes of active ear disease" (p. 390). Brookhouser, Hixson, and Matkin (1979) examined a group of language-disordered children and found a significant incidence of early otitis media and fluctuating hearing loss. Holm and Kunze (1969) found that children with middle ear disease before age 2 scored lower than controls on all tasks requiring auditory input but had no differences on visual tasks. Battin (in Northern & Downs, 1978) found deficient verbal skills and auditory discrimination in children with otitis media.

There is increasing awareness that early hearing loss, even to a mild degree, may have a detrimental influence on educational functioning. The primary difficulty appears to be related to subtle language-learning problems, which are frequently undetected. It is important to consider such possibilities in obtaining a history of the child and in assessing language-learning abilities of children with overt hearing impairment or a history of otitis media.

Educational Placement

Karchmer, Milone, and Wolk (1979) point out that degree of hearing loss is the major factor in most educational placement decisions. Integrated programs typically include children with less severe losses but very few with severe-profound losses. Although the children with severe hearing losses are generally in special programs, the mildly hearing-impaired child is largely unserved by special education. Meyen (1978) points out that the child with a mild hearing loss (25–40 dB) will need favorable seating and some speech services. The child with a 41–55 dB loss understands only a limited amount of conversational speech and will need considerable educational intervention, including speech and language remediation, as well as a resource room for the hearing impaired for most academic subjects.

Unfortunately, educational placement for hearing-impaired children is not usually based on specific considerations of learning efficiency or cognitive strengths and weaknesses but is based on degree of hearing loss. Another consideration that is frequently not considered is auditory discrimination ability. Some children with only a mild degree of loss in hearing acuity may experience significant auditory discrimination deficiency that may be related to reading disability. Educational placement considerations for hearing-impaired children should be made on the basis of language and learning patterns similar to procedures used for developmentally delayed, language-disordered, or learning-disabled children.

Behavior/Personality

Vernon (1969) reports that emotional immaturity and denial are common features of the deaf child, possibly based on frustration related to speech and language difficulties. Fundudis et al. (1979) found a higher incidence of "psychiatric disorders," generally of an antisocial nature, than present in controls. The hearing impaired in this sample had fewer peer contacts, were more often teased by others, and were more moody in temperament. Teachers reported more behavioral disturbances than did parents. Vernon (1969) found a considerable amount of behavioral variance in deaf children that he relates to etiological factors. Conditions such as rubella, Rh incompatibility, and prematurity are also associated with higher incidence of brain damage, mental retardation, and mental illness. Vernon also found that the incidence of schizophrenia, paranoia, alcoholism, and depressive psychoses is no higher than in the general population. Schlesinger and Meadow (1972) compared students of a residential school for the deaf to the general school population and found that more deaf children were considered severely emotionally disturbed or seen as requiring a disproportionate share of the teacher's time when compared to controls. Deaf adults showed more "adjustment to living" difficulties, characterized by impulsive behavior, isolation, personality disorders, and immaturity. Jensema and Trybus (1975) found an incidence of 9.8 percent boys and 5.6 percent girls who were considered significant behavior problems among hearing impaired in special education programs.

Behavioral characteristics of children with milder hearing impairment include the following: lack of attention to casual conversation, withdrawal from social situations, restlessness, constant visual scanning of speaker's face, ignoring of verbal directions, turning head to one side when listening, reading disability with numerous spelling errors, and so on (Phillips, 1975). These characteristics may lead to a diagnosis of the student as having an attention problem or being a slow learner. However, these characteristics may be related to a primary hearing impairment that is not diagnosed. Studies using behavior-rating scales have found hearing-impaired children to be somewhat more withdrawn (Fischer, 1965) but to have the same major factors of conduct and personality disorders as the normally hearing population, with a third factor of immaturity and inadequacy (Reivich & Rothrock, 1972).

Evaluation and Treatment

One of the most common behavioral concerns for the young hearing-impaired child is distractibility and/or overactivity. Differential diagnostic considerations include hyperkinesis (motor drivenness) versus conduct type behavior problems. While typical diagnostic procedures such as assessment of parenting behaviors and behavioral management procedures of the teacher are indicated, specific observations during individual assessment of the child are important. If the child's distractibility and/or overactivity are related to difficulty in speech reception, the child may not be tractable to verbal directions. If the child becomes more attentive, and a decrease in motoric behavior is noted when pantomime procedures are used by the examiner, this may suggest that the behaviors of concern are related primarily to the hearing loss and not to other disorders. In this instance, nonverbal communication should be emphasized to parents and teachers to enhance behavioral control. If the child remains quite distractible and overactive during pantomime directions, this

should alert the examiner to the possibility of an attention deficit or hyperactivity that may require treatment beyond typical procedures indicated only for the hearing impairment.

Careful reexamination of intellectual functioning and specific cognitive skills should be considered when a hearing-impaired child demonstrates behavior problems in the educational setting. Since educational placement is frequently based on hearing impairment, specific learning disabilities or intellectual retardation may not have been identified. The behavior problems may be related to frustration in the learning situation even though procedures for hearing impaired are being used. A related behavioral concern may occur when an undiagnosed hearing-impaired child is placed in classes for the mentally retarded on the basis of a low IQ score. It is not unusual to see such children who have significant verbal expression deficiencies yet have adequate inner language skills become frustrated and act out as a response to misplacement. Here again, nonverbal intellectual assessment procedures such as the Hiskey, along with specific language assessment using neuropsychological tests mentioned previously, may be beneficial in differential diagnosis of primary versus secondary behavior problems.

There is support for the contention that hearing-impaired children present significant difficulty to parents related to behavioral controls (Schlesinger & Meadow, 1972). The goal of physical control procedures with children should be the association of physical control with external verbal admonishment and later development of self-control through self-regulation via verbal mediation. However, hearing-impaired children present a difficulty in this developmental sequence since it is usually difficult for parents to provide effective verbal communication and interpretation of disciplinary action. Therefore, the parents may maintain physical behavioral control procedures at a later age in the absence of associated verbal cues or explanations. A complicating factor is the problem of the hearing-impaired child in developing verbal outlets for frustration, anger, and response to parental restrictions and disapproval. Thus aggression or anger is more likely to be demonstrated physically than verbally and therefore is more likely to be punished (Hefferman, 1955; Altshuler, 1964). It is important for the clinician to recognize these communication barriers to traditional forms of behavioral control and expression of frustration by the hearing-impaired child and provide appropriate counseling to parents to assure adequate communication of disciplinary tactics to the child as well as assisting the child to develop socially acceptable means of communicating frustration.

Counseling intervention with the deaf or severely hard-of-hearing child will need to be undertaken by individuals with skills and experience in nonverbal communication and will not usually be provided by the typical clinical child psychologist. (For further information on emotional problems and treatment for the deaf, see Schlesinger & Meadow, 1972). However, the child with mild-to-moderate hearing impairment may be referred to the child psychologist for intervention concerning emotional problems. Standard behavioral ratings and personality tests can usually be used in the diagnostic evaluation of these children. Since social and emotional immaturity is a common finding reported in the literature, it should be determined whether this characteristic is related primarily to decreased peer contact and hypersensitivity regarding hearing loss before attributing these symptoms to an underlying emotional disturbance. Given early diagnosis and treatment, appropriate educational programming, and adequate parenting, it is likely that the child with a mild-to-moderate hearing loss will display a range of behaviors and emotional responsivity characteristic of non-hearing-impaired children. Therefore, if behavior or emotional problems do arise for such children, standard evaluation and treatment procedures should be used.

OTHER COMMUNICATION DISORDER SYMPTOMS

Although it has not been the intent of this chapter to examine all types of communication disorders in children, there are some communication disorder symptoms that may occur in language-disordered children and mimic symptoms of other psychological disorders. Children with symptoms of elective mutism, stuttering, or echolalia may be referred to the child psychologist when these symptoms are not considered to be either learned faulty speech patterns or organically based problems. Although any of these symptoms may be only one sign of a language disorder that is covered more extensively in this chapter, there may be a question regarding a possible psychogenic etiology.

Elective Mutism

Elective mutism refers to the withholding of speech in a child who has no speech or language disorder, adequate intelligence to develop adequate speech, and no physical defect of the speech mechanism. The term was first used by Tramer (1934) to describe children who spoke only to certain people such as immediate family members. Although other forms of mutism are common in children with childhood schizophrenia, autism, hearing loss, and aphasia, elective mutism unrelated to these conditions is usually given a behavioral or emotional interpretation. Frequently, there is manipulative control of the environment or excessive anxiety in situations where the symptom occurs. Reed (1963) identifies two clinical types of elective mutes: (1) those who display the symptoms as an attention-seeking or manipulative behavior and are not timid or anxious and (2) those with excessive tension, anxiety, and low self-esteem. Reed recommends behavioral treatment approaches for the first type and counseling regarding sources of anxiety and fear in the second type. For more information regarding behavioral and emotional treatment approaches to elective mutism, the reader is referred to the following references: Adams and Glasner (1954), Browne, Wilson, and Laybourne (1963), Reed (1963), and Reid et al. (1967).

Several considerations are important in distinguishing elective mutism from the mutism of the child with a language disorder. The chronicity of the symptom and premorbid verbal facility are important in the differential diagnosis. The child with a developmental language disorder or congenital organic condition is more likely to have a history of atypical speech and language development, while the elective mute child frequently has normal speech and language development during preschool years. It is common for the elective mute to remain undetected until school entrance, since the symptom does not usually occur at home. A rare instance of mutism with earlier normal speech and language that may be mistaken for elective mutism is found in some children with petit mal epilepsy (Lennox & Lennox, 1960).

Stuttering and Stammering

Stuttering and stammering are usually used to refer to excessive dysfluencies of phonemes, syllables, or words. There may be unusual lengthening or excessive repetitions of speech. Although these types of dysfluencies are not uncommon in young children (up to age 5), they are usually considered atypical after this age. Stuttering has been considered to be related to numerous factors including faulty learning, anxiety, and neurological dysfunction. There is considerable controversy regarding etiology and treatment of stuttering, and the reader is referred to more comprehensive reviews of the various theories and treatments (Johnson, 1955; Sheehan, 1970; and Van Riper, 1971). Approximately 1 percent of the population are considered stutterers beyond the age of 5 (Van Riper, 1963; Young, 1975). Stuttering is more frequent in males (Williams, Silverman, & Kools, 1968), and the symptom rarely has an onset after age 10. There are few consistent findings to suggest any generalizations regarding intellectual, behavioral, or personality characteristics of children who stutter. Furthermore, there is not consistent evidence of atypical parental characteristics related to childhood stuttering (Block & Goodstein, 1971).

Stuttering as an isolated symptom does not usually warrant psychological intevention, and treatment is typically provided by speech and language clinicians. However, onset after age 10 or sudden onset at a younger age without prior symptoms may suggest that the symptom is related to other emotional problems, and other signs of anxiety will usually be present. In this case, psychological evaluation may be indicated and the stuttering should not be the focus of treatment; rather, the focus should be on the possible sources of anxiety.

Some children who exhibit mild symptoms of stuttering, stammering, hesitations, or halting of speech may have developed this symptom secondary to an underlying language disorder. Children who display developmental language disorders may have anomia, word-finding problems, or auditory memory problems (see previous section on language disorders) and the symptom may be providing them time to retrieve a word or idea. In this case, the clinician should consider examination of language skills according to the guidelines presented in the section on language disorders.

Echolalia

Echolalia or the chronic repeating of words or phrases in imitation of another speaker is a symptom most often associated with autism or mental retardation. These latter conditions are not included in this chapter since the communication disorder associated with these disorders is only one aspect of the overall problem and each disorder requires extensive review beyond the scope of a chapter on communication disorder. However, the symptom of echolalia is occasionally identified in children without mental retardation or autism who demonstrate other symptoms of language disorder, and the reader is referred to the section on language disorder in this chapter for other diagnostic and treatment considerations. Furthermore, there is increasing support for the suggestion that autism may be related to a severe and global language disorder having many features of global aphasia (Churchill, 1972; Rutter, 1974).

When autism or mental retardation are not considered to be primary diagnoses and echolalia is present in school age children, consideration of a language disorder is warranted. The symptom of echolalia and "parrot-like" speech imitation has been identified in children who display hyperlexia (Richman & Kitchell, 1981). These children frequently have language disorders characterized by poor associative language skills and superior isolated memory ability. Specific assessment of these skills is presented in the section of this chapter on language disorders. Direct treatment of echolalia is not usually indicated, and evaluation and treatment of the underlying language-learning disorder are more appropriate.

CONCLUSION

This chapter has focused on research and clinical considerations in three areas of communication disorders of children: developmental language disorders, cleft palate, and hearing impairment. It is apparent from the conflicting research findings that many clinical considerations must be made without an extensive or consistent data base. There is promise, however, in the increased attention to children with communication disorders brought about by the Education for All Handicapped Children Act. Since this law emphasized educational placement in the least restrictive environment, many language-disordered and hearing-impaired children are receiving more careful diagnostic scrutiny. This places increased responsibility on the clinical child psychologist to make accurate diagnoses of children with communication disorders. The child psychologist evaluating and/or treating the language-impaired child should have knowledge of the aphasia literature and be able to employ procedures adopted from neuropsychology. Evaluation and treatment of the hearing-impaired child require close consultation with speech and hearing professionals and use of nonverbal procedures in assessment. The cleft-palate child may be the most neglected of the three groups in terms of psychological involvement. However, the research findings suggest that while this child may "get by," there is a need to overcome the subtle influences which may result in less than optimal academic progress and self-esteem.

There has been an emphasis in this chapter on diagnostic considerations due to the fact that many of the psychological problems of children with communication disorders are often ignored. This is most often the case when the disability is mild rather than severe. The child who sustains brain injury or disease and related aphasic symptoms comes to the attention of many professionals and is likely to receive extensive evaluation and rehabilitation treatment and benefits. However, the child with a developmental language disorder may not be identified as such and be considered as "slow" or emotionally disturbed. The deaf child will usually be identified and receive appropriate intervention, while the child with a mild-to-moderate hearing loss may be identified as mentally retarded or hyperactive. These children are also frequently attempting to compete in regular classrooms without adequate support services. Children with cleft palate rarely receive the consideration necessary to identify reading problems related to their condition or supportive guidance in responding to peer reaction to unusual speech problems and facial disfigurement.

While there is increasing research documentation of some of the unique intellectual, cognitive, and educational problems of children with communication disorders, there is a dearth of information regarding the behavioral and emotional adjustment of these children. This chapter has attempted to provide some of the more frequently identified adjustment concerns of these children. The child psychologist must usually proceed with standard behavior and personality assessment and treatment approaches when dealing with communication-disordered children, although some modification may be warranted. The need for further research in this area is apparent.

REFERENCES

Adams, H., & Glasner, P. Emotional involvement in some forms of mutism. *Journal of Speech and Hearing Disorders,* 1954, **19,** 59–69.

Altshuler, K.Z. Personality traits and depressive

symptoms in the deaf. In J. Wortis (Ed.), *Recent advances in biological psychiatry* (Vol. VI). New York: Plenum, 1964.

Bakker, D.J. *Temporal order in disturbed reading.* Rotterdam: Rotterdam University Press, 1972.

Barker, E.I. *A study of certain aspects of personality in given individuals having cleft palate.* MS thesis, Ann Arbor: University of Michigan, 1951.

Belmont, L., & Birch, H.G. The intellectual profile of retarded readers. *Perceptual and Motor Skills,* 1966, **22**, 787–816.

Bess, F.H., & McConnell, F.E. *Audiology, education, and the hearing-impaired child.* St. Louis: Mosby, 1981.

Billig, A.L. A psychological appraisal of cleft palate patients. *Proceedings of the Pennsylvania Academy of Sciences,* 1951, **29**, 31.

Blair, F.X. A study of the visual memory of deaf and hearing children. *American Annals of the Deaf,* 1957, **102**, 254–263.

Blank, M. Cognitive processes in auditory discrimination in normal and retarded readers. *Child Development,* 1968, **39**, 1091–1101.

Block, E.L., & Goodstein, L.D. Functional speech disorders and personality: A decade of research. *Journal of Speech and Hearing Disorders,* 1971, **36**, 295–314.

Boder, E. Developmental dyslexia: A diagnostic approach based on three atypical reading patterns. *Developmental Medicine and Child Neurology,* 1973, **15**, 663–687.

Boyd, S.F. *Hearing loss: Its educationally measurable effects on achievement.* M.S. thesis, Carbondale: Southern Illinois University, 1974.

Brantley, H., & Clifford, E. Cognitive, self-concept, and body image measures of normal, cleft, and obese adolescents. *Cleft Palate Journal,* 1979, **16**, 177–182.

Brennan, D., & Cullinan, W. Object identification and naming in cleft palate children. *Cleft Palate Journal,* 1974, **11**, 188–195.

Brookhouser, P., Hixson, P., & Matkin, N. Early childhood language delay: The otolaryngologist's perspective. *The Laryngoscope,* 1979, **89**, 1898–1913.

Brown, E., Wilson, V., & Laybourne, P. Diagnosis and treatment of elective mutism in children. *Journal of the American Academy of Child Psychiatry,* 1963, **2**, 605–617.

Camp, B.W. Verbal mediation in young aggressive boys. *Journal of Abnormal Psychology,* 1977, **86**, 145–153.

Churchill, D.W. The relation of infantile autism and early childhood schizophrenia to developmental language disorders of childhood. *Journal of Autism and Childhood Schizophrenia,* 1972, **2**, 182–197.

Cook, H., Harding, R., Krogman, W., Mazaheri, M., & Millard, R. *Cleft palate and cleft lip: A team approach to clinical management and rehabilitation of the patient.* Philadelphia: Saunders, 1979.

Conrad, R. Some correlates of speech coding in the short-term memory of the deaf. *Journal of Speech and Hearing Research,* 1973, **16**, 375–384.

Corkin, S. Serial-ordering deficits in inferior readers. *Neuropsychologia,* 1974, **12**, 347–354.

Crockett, D.J. Component analysis of within correlations of language-skills tests in normal children. *Journal of Special Education,* 1974, **8**, 361–375.

Denkla, M., & Rudel, R. Rapid automatized naming (RAN): Dyslexia differential from other learning disabilities. *Neuropsychologia,* 1976, **14**, 471–479.

Drillien, C., Ingram, T., & Wilkinson, E. *The causes and natural history of cleft lip and palate.* Baltimore: Williams & Wilkins, 1966.

Eisenson, J. *Aphasia in children.* New York: Harper & Row, 1972.

Estes, R., & Morris, H. Relationship among intelligence, speech proficiency, and hearing sensitivity in children with cleft palates. *Cleft Palate Journal,* 1970, **7**, 763–773.

Finucci, J. Genetic considerations in dyslexia. In H. Myklebust (Ed.), *Progress in learning disabilities* (Vol. IV). New York: Grune & Stratton, 1978.

Fischer, B. The social and emotional adjustment of children with impaired hearing attending ordinary classes. Unpublished M.Ed. thesis, University of Manchester, 1965 (Reported in Fundudis, et al.).

Fraser, F.C. The genetics of cleft lip and palate. *American Journal of Human Genetics,* 1970, **22**, 336–352.

Fry, M.A., John, C.S., & Meuhl, S. Oral language production in relation to reading achievement among selected second graders. In D.J. Bakker & P. Satz (Eds.), *Specific reading disability:*

Advances in theory and method. Rotterdam: Rotterdam University Press, 1970.

Fundudis, T., Kolvin, I., & Garside, R. *Speech retarded and deaf children: Their psychological development.* New York: Academic Press, 1979.

Furth, H.G. Visual paired associates task with deaf and hearing children. *Journal of Speech and Hearing Research,* 1961, **41,** 172–177.

Furth, H.G. A comparison of reading test norms of deaf and hearing children. *American Annals of the Deaf,* 1966, **111,** 461–462.

Furth, H.G. Linguistic deficiency and thinking: Research with deaf subjects. *Psychological Bulletin,* 1971, **76,** 58–72.

Furth, H.G., & Youniss, J. Thinking in deaf adolescents: Language and formal operations. *Journal of Communication Disorders,* 1969, **2,** 195–202.

Gaddes, W. *Learning disabilities and brain function: A neuropsychological approach.* New York: Springer-Verlag, 1980.

Giangreco, C.J., & Giangreco, M.R. *The education of the hearing impaired.* Springfield, Ill.: Thomas, 1970.

Gluck, M., Wylie, H., McWilliams, B.J., & Conkwright, E. Comparison of clinical characteristics of children with cleft palates and children in a child guidance clinic. *Perceptual and Motor Skills,* 1965, **21,** 806–808.

Goetzinger, C.P., Harrison, C., & Baer, C. Small perceptive hearing loss: Its effect in school age children. *Volta Review,* 1964, **66,** 124–132.

Goodstein, L. Intellectual impairment of children with cleft palates. *Journal of Speech and Hearing Research,* 1961, **4,** 287–294.

Goodstein, L. Psychological aspects of cleft palate. In D.C. Spriestersbach & D. Sherman (Eds.), *Cleft palate and communication.* New York: Academic Press, 1968.

Graham, E., & Shapiro, E. Use of the performance scale of the WISC and the deaf child. *Journal of Consulting Psychology,* 1953, **17,** 396–398.

Harper, D.C., & Richman, L.C. Personality profiles of physically impaired adolescents. *Journal of Clinical Psychology,* 1978, **34,** 636–642.

Harper, D.C., Richman, L.C., & Snider, B.C. School adjustment and degree of physical impairment. *Journal of Pediatric Psychology,* 1980, **5,** 377–383.

Hefferman, A. A psychiatric study of fifty preschool children referred to hospital for suspected deafness. In G. Caplan (Ed.), *Emotional problems of early childhood.* New York: Basic Books, 1955.

Heilman, K.M. Language and the brain: Relationship of localization of language function to the acquisition and loss of various aspects of language. In J. Chall & A. Mirsky (Eds.), *Education and the brain.* Chicago: University of Chicago Press, 1978.

Hoemann, H.W., Andrews, C.E., Florian, V.A., Hoemann, S.A., & Jensema, C.J. The spelling proficiency of deaf children. *American Annals of the Deaf,* 1976, **121,** 489–493.

Holm, V.A., & Kunze, L.V.H. Effect of chronic otitis media on language and speech development. *Pediatrics,* 1969, **43,** 833–839.

Huelsman, C.R. The WISC subtest syndrome for disabled readers. *Perceptual and Motor Skills,* 1970, **30,** 535–550.

Ingram, T.T.S., Mason, A.W., & Blackburn, I.A. A retrospective study of 82 children with reading disability. *Developmental Medicine and Child Neurology,* 1970, **12,** 271–281.

Jensema, C., & Trybus, R. *Reported emotional behavioral problems among hearing impaired children in special education programs: U.S. 1972–1973.* Washington, D.C.: Gallaudet College, 1975.

Johnson, D.J., & Myklebust, H.R. *Learning disabilities: Educational principles and practices.* New York: Grune & Stratton, 1967.

Johnson, W. *Stuttering in children and adults.* Minneapolis: University of Minnesota Press, 1955.

Jordan, R.E., & Eagles, E.L. The relation of air conduction audiometry to otologic abnormalities. *Annals of Oto Rhino Laryngology,* 1961, **70,** 819–827.

Kagan, J. Reflection-impulsivity: The generality and dynamics of conceptual tempo. *Journal of Abnormal Psychology,* 1966, **71,** 17–24.

Kaplan, G.K., Fleschman, J.K., & Bender, T.R. Long term effects of otitis media: A 10-year cohort study of Alaska Eskimo children. *Pediatrics,* 1973, **52,** 577–585.

Kapp, K. Self-concept of the cleft lip and/or palate child. *Cleft Palate Journal,* 1979, **16,** 171–176.

Karchmer, M.A., Milone, M.N., & Wolk, S. Educational significance of hearing loss at three levels of severity. *American Annals of the Deaf,* 1979, **124,** 97–109.

Katz, J., & Illmer, R. Auditory perception in children with learning disabilities. In J. Katz (Ed.), *Handbook of clinical audiology.* Baltimore: Williams & Wilkins, 1972.

Kinsbourne, M., & Hiscock, M. Cerebral lateralization and cognitive development. In J. Chall & A. Mirsky (Eds.), *Education and the brain.* Chicago: University of Chicago Press, 1978.

Kodman, F., Jr. Educational status of hard-of-hearing children in the classroom. *Journal of Speech and Hearing Disorders,* 1963, **28,** 297–299.

Kommers, M., & Sullivan, M. Written language skills of children with cleft palate. *Cleft Palate Journal,* 1979, **6,** 81–85.

Lamb, M., Wilson, F., & Leeper, H. The intellectual function of cleft palate children compared on the basis of cleft type and sex. *Cleft Palate Journal,* 1973, **10,** 367–377.

Lencione, R.M. Psychosocial aspects of cleft lip and palate. In M. Edwards & A. Watson (Eds.), *Advances in the management of cleft palate.* New York: Churchill Livingstone, 1980.

Lennox, W.G., & Lennox, M.A. *Epilepsy and related disorders* (Vol. 1). Boston: Little Brown, 1960.

Leonard, L.B., Bolders, J.G., & Miller, J.A. An examination of the semantic relations reflected in the language usage of normal and language-disordered children. *Journal of Speech and Hearing Research,* 1976, **19,** 371–392.

Lewis, N. Otitis media and linguistic competence. *Archives of Otolaryngology,* 1976, **102,** 387–390.

Lewis, R. A survey of the intelligence of cleft palate children in Ontario. *Cleft Palate Bulletin,* 1961, **11,** 83–85.

Ling, D. Recent developments affecting the education of hearing impaired children. *Public Health Reviews,* 1975, **4,** 117–152.

Ludlow, C. Children's language disorders; Recent research advances. *Annals of Neurology,* 1980, **7,** 497–507.

Luria, A.R. *Higher cortical functions in man.* New York: Basic Books, 1966.

Massengill, R., & Phillips, P. *Cleft palate and associated speech characteristics.* Cliffs Speech and Hearing Series. Lincoln, Neb.: Cliff Notes, 1975.

Mattis, S. Dyslexia syndromes: A working hypothesis that works. In A. Benton & D. Pearl (Eds.), *Dyslexia: An appraisal of current knowledge.* New York: Oxford University Press, 1978.

McCarthy, J.J., & Kirk, S.A. *Illinois test of psycholinguistic ability.* Urbana: University of Illinois, 1961.

McCarthy, R., & Marshall, H. Memory of deaf and hearing children. *Journal of Genetic Psychology,* 1969, **114,** 19–24.

McWilliams, B.J. Clinical use of the Peabody picture vocabulary test with cleft palate preschoolers. *Cleft Palate Journal,* 1974, **11,** 439–442.

McWilliams, B.J., & Matthews, H.P. A comparison of intelligence and social maturity in children with unilateral complete clefts and those with isolated cleft palates. *Cleft Palate Journal,* 1979, **16,** 363–372.

McWilliams, B.J., & Musgrave, R. Psychological implications of articulation disorders in cleft palate children. *Cleft Palate Journal,* 1972, **9,** 294–303.

McWilliams, B.J., & Smith, R.M. Psychosocial considerations. In ASHA report, *Speech, language, and psychosocial aspects of cleft lip and cleft palate: The state of the art.* New York, 1973.

Means, B., & Irwin, J. An analysis of certain measures of intelligence and hearing in a sample of the Wisconsin cleft palate population. *Cleft Palate Newsletter,* 1954, **4,** 2–4.

Meichenbaum, D. Toward a cognitive theory of self-control. In G. Schwartz & D. Shapiro (Eds.), *Consciousness and self-regulation: Advances in research.* New York: Plenum, 1975.

Melnick, W., Eagles, E.L., & Levine, H.S. Evaluation of a recommended program of identification audiometry with school age children. *Journal of Hearing Disorders,* 1964, **29,** 3–13.

Meyen, E. *Exception children and youth.* Denver: Love, 1978.

Morris, H. Communication skills of children with cleft lip and palates. *Journal of Speech and Hearing Research,* 1962, **5,** 79–90.

Munson, S., & May, A. Are cleft palate persons of subnormal intelligence? *Education Research Journal,* 1955, **48,** 617–622.

Musgrave, R., McWilliams, B.J., & Matthews, H. A review of the results of two different surgical procedures for the repair of clefts on the soft palate only. *Cleft Palate Journal,* 1975, **12,** 281–290.

Myklebust, H.R. (Ed.) *Progress in learning disabilities* (Vol. II). New York: Grune & Stratton, 1971.

Needleman, H. Effects of hearing loss from early recurrent otitis media on speech and language development. In B. Jaffe (Ed.), *Hearing loss in children.* Baltimore: University Park Press, 1977.

Northern, J., & Downs, M. *Hearing in children,* (2nd ed.). Baltimore: Williams & Wilkins, 1978.

Palmer, J.M., & Adams, M.R. The oral image of children with cleft lip and palate. *Cleft Palate Bulletin,* 1962, **12,** 72–76.

Pannbacker, M. Oral language skills of adult cleft palate speakers. *Cleft Palate Journal,* 1975, **12,** 95–106.

Peter, J.P., & Chinsky, R.R. Sociological aspects of cleft palate adults: Education. *Cleft Palate Journal,* 1974, **11,** 443–449.

Phillips, D. *Speech and hearing problems in the classroom.* Lincoln, Neb.: Cliff Notes, 1975.

Rabinovitch, R.D. Reading and learning disabilities. In S. Areti (Ed.), *American handbook of psychiatry.* New York: Basic Books, 1959.

Reed, G. Elective mutism in children: A reappraisal. *Journal of Child Psychiatry,* 1963, **4,** 99–107.

Reid, J., Hawkins, N., Keutzer, C., McNeal, S., Phelps, R., Reid, K., & Hayden, M. A marathon behavior modification of a selectively mute child. *Journal of Child Psychology and Psychiatry,* 1967, **8,** 27–30.

Reivich, R.S., & Rothrock, I.A. Behavior problems of deaf children and adolescents: A factor analytic study. *Journal of Speech and Hearing Research,* 1972, **15,** 93–104.

Richman, L.C. Behavior and achievement of the cleft palate child. *Cleft Palate Journal,* 1976, **13,** 4–10.

Richman, L.C. The effects of facial disfigurement on teachers' perceptions of ability in cleft palate children. *Cleft Palate Journal,* 1978, **15,** 155–160.

Richman, L.C. Parents and teachers: Differing views of behavior of cleft palate children. *Cleft Palate Journal,* 1978, **15,** 360–364.

Richman, L.C. Language mediation hypothesis:

Implications of verbal/performance discrepancy and reading ability. *Perceptual and Motor Skills,* 1978, **47,** 391–398.

Richman, L.C. Language variables related to reading ability of children with verbal deficits. *Psychology in the Schools,* 1979, **16,** 299–305.

Richman, L.C. Cognitive patterns and learning disabilities in cleft palate children with verbal deficits. *Journal of Speech and Hearing Research,* 1980, **23,** 447–456.

Richman, L.C., & Harper, D.C. School adjustment of children with observable disabilities. *Journal of Abnormal Child Psychology,* 1978, **6,** 11–18.

Richman, L.C., & Harper, D.C. Self-identified personality patterns of children with facial or orthopedic disfigurement. *Cleft Palate Journal,* 1979, **16,** 257–261.

Richman, L.C., & Kitchell, M. Hyperlexia as a variant of developmental language disorder. *Brain and Language,* 1981, **12,** 203–212.

Richman, L.C., & Lindgren, S.D. Patterns of intellectual ability in children with verbal deficits. *Journal of Abnormal Child Psychology,* 1980, **8,** 65–81.

Richman, L.C., & Lindgren, S.D. Verbal mediation deficits: Relation to behavior and achievement in children. *Journal of Abnormal Child Psychology,* 1981, **90,** 99–104.

Roach, R., & Rosecraus, C.J. Relation between verbal ability and reduced auditory acuity. *Exceptional Children,* 1972, **40,** 395–399.

Ruess, A. A comparative study of cleft palate children and their siblings. *Journal of Clinical Psychology,* 1965, **21,** 354–360.

Rutter, M. The development of infantile autism. *Psychological Medicine,* 1974, **4,** 147–163.

Schlesinger, H.S., & Meadow, K. *Sound and sign: Childhood deafness and mental health.* Berkeley: University of California Press, 1972.

Senf, G.M., & Freundl, P.C. Sequential auditory and visual memory in learning disabled children. *Proceedings of the Annual Convention of the American Psychological Association,* 1972, **7,** 511–512.

Shankweiler, D., & Liberman, I.Y. Exploring the relations between reading and speech. In R.M. Knights & D.J. Bakker (Eds.), *The neuropsychology of learning disorders: Theoretical approaches.* Baltimore: University Park Press, 1976.

Sheehan, J.G. *Stuttering: Research and therapy.* New York: Harper & Row, 1970.

Sidney, R., & Matthews, J. An evaluation of the social adjustment of a group of cleft palate children. *Cleft Palate Bulletin,* 1956, **6,** 10.

Spreen, D., & Benton, A. *Neurosensory center comprehensive examination of aphasia.* Victoria: University of Victoria, 1969.

Spriestersbach, D.C. *Psychosocial aspects of the "cleft palate problem"* (Vols. 1 & 2). Iowa City: University of Iowa Press, 1973.

Spriestersbach, D.C., & Sherman, D. *Cleft palate and communication.* New York: Academic Press, 1968.

Streff, M., Barefoot, S., Walter, G., & Crandall, K. A comparative study of hearing-impaired and normal hearing young adults—Verbal and nonverbal abilities. *Journal of Communication Disorders,* 1978, **11,** 489–498.

Sullivan, M. A comparison of administration modification on the WISC-R Performance scale with different categories of deaf children. Unpublished dissertation. Iowa City: University of Iowa, 1978.

Tisza, V., Silvertone, B., Rosenblum, O., & Hanlon, N. Psychiatric observations of children with cleft palates. *American Journal of Orthopsychiatry,* 1958, **28,** 416–423.

Tramer, J. Elekitiver Mutism bei Kindern. *Zeitschrift fur Kinderpsychiatrie,* 1934, **1,** 30–35.

Van Riper, C. *Speech correction.* (4th ed.). Englewood Cliffs, N.J.: Prentice-Hall, 1963.

Van Riper, C. *The nature of stuttering.* Englewood Cliffs, N.J.: Prentice-Hall, 1971.

Vellutino, F.R. *Dyslexia: Theory and research.* Cambridge: MIT Press, 1979.

Vellutino, F.R., Smith, H., Steger, J.A., & Kaman, M. Reading disability: Age difference and the perceptual deficit hypothesis. *Child Development,* 1975, **46,** 487–493.

Vernon, M. Fifty years of research on the intelligence of the deaf and hard of hearing. *Journal of the Rehabilitation of the Deaf,* 1968, **1,** 1–12.

Vernon, M. Sociological and pyschological factors associated with hearing loss. *Journal of Speech and Hearing Research,* 1969, **12,** 541–563.

Vernon, M., & Koh, S. Effects of oral preschool compared to early manual communication on education and communication in deaf children. *American Annals of the Deaf,* 1971, **116,** 569–574.

Warrington, E.K. The incidence of verbal disability associated with reading retardation. *Neuropsychologia,* 1967, **5,** 175–179.

Watson, G.G. Personality maladjustment in boys with cleft lip and palate. *Cleft Palate Journal,* 1964, **1,** 130–138.

Wiig, E., & Semel, E. *Language disabilities in children and adolescents.* Columbis, Oh.: Merrill, 1976.

Williams, D.E., Silverman, F.H., & Kools, J.A. Disfluency behavior of elementary school stutterers and nonstutterers: The adaptation effect. *Journal of Speech and Hearing Research,* 1968, **11,** 622–630.

Wilson, J., Rapin, I., Wilson, B., & Van Denburg, F. Neuropsychologic function of children with severe hearing impairment. *Journal of Speech and Hearing Research,* 1975, **18,** 643–651.

Withrow, F.B. Immediate memory span of deaf and normally hearing children. *Exceptional Children,* 1968, **35,** 33–41.

Wrightstone, J., Aronow, M., & Moskowitz, S. Developing reading test norms for deaf children. *American Annals of the Deaf,* 1963, **108,** 311–316.

Young, M.A. Onset, prevalence and recovery from stuttering. *Journal of Speech and Hearing Disorders,* 1975, **40,** 49–58.

Yules, R. Hearing in cleft palate patients. *Archives of Otolaryngology,* 1970, **91,** 319–323.

Problems of Adolescence

CHAPTER 30

Teen-Parent Problems

WILLIAM A. RAE

Adolescence is regarded by developmental theorists as being characterized by intense intrapsychic changes and interpersonal struggles. The adolescent, in a desire to be autonomous from the family, often separates from them in an awkward manner. This maladroit separation often takes the form of overt rebellion and acting out against authority figures, overidentification with peers, extreme changes in affect and mood, and unpredictable behaviors. Although not all adolescents go through a period of storm and stress, this developmental period often forces parents to deal with a revolutionary change in their child's behavior as well as to accept the reality that their adolescent is psychologically separating from them; they are no longer the primary source of protection and support for their child.

Given the fact that adolescent behavior is often unpredictable and changeable and that the adolescent's family is often upset, it is understandable that many clinical child psychologists may avoid treating the adolescent and his or her family. Adolescents in therapy are often mistrustful of the therapist and resistant to any intervention. In addition, they may be rebellious and act out in ways that are distressing to the therapist. In the same way, the adolescent's family can be in considerable distress and may have difficulty dealing with the adolescent or the therapist in a psychologically healthy manner. The prospect of altering the adolescent's behavior under these circumstances would appear dismal.

The purpose of this chapter is to describe some common problem areas between adolescents and their families. The emphasis will not be with adolescents or their families who have psychopathological problems but rather with normal adolescents and families who have complaints about each other. Although the presenting problems may range from adolescent acting-out or withdrawal behaviors to complaints that parents are too restrictive, most teen-parent conflicts appear to center around separation-individuation issues.

NORMAL ADOLESCENT DEVELOPMENT

Characteristics of Adolescents

Separation

The major task of adolescence is separation from the family in order to assume the role of an adult in society. The adolescent who has previously been physically and emotionally dependent on the family now must endure the trauma of separation. The adolescent risks leaving the security and stability of the structure within the family where the expectations of behavior are known. The exploration into the adult world can be threatening. The adolescent often has fears regarding his or her adequacy to master the developmental tasks of adolescence. If the adolescent becomes too anxious, he or she may retreat into the comfort of a dependent relationship with his or her parents. Often this situation results in a reemergence of the adolescent's dependency with accompanying feelings of being threatened and anxious. The danger of these fears is that the adolescent may be compelled to develop attachments outside the family at an early age. When this pseudomaturation occurs, the adolescent will often not be prepared truly to develop proper separation and individuation from his or her parents (Williams, 1973).

The ebb and flow that occurs between separation and individuation is also linked to the quality of the relationship between the adolescent and his or her parents. If the parents encourage a relationship that is too close, the teenager may have trouble separating. This may lead to social withdrawal in a form such as a school phobia or a depressed mood. Adolescents must have guidance available to them regarding what adulthood means. In a distant relationship with the parents, the teenager is left without the direction of an adult role model. If the parents encourage a relationship that is too distant, the teenager may participate in negative behaviors merely to attract the parents' attention.

Each teenager must pursue an independent, idiosyncratic method of separation. Unfortunately, parents often complicate this natural process because of confusion about their own value systems and their ambivalence about their teenager becoming truly independent. In addition, parents often mistakenly view their adolescent as already being completely autonomous from them. Parents have difficulty understanding why their adolescent does not seem to want a relationship with them. Parents will often withdraw their much needed emotional support in this situation because they feel exploited by their own teenager (Friedman & Sarles, 1980). Thus they will further confound the natural separation process. It is clear that when separation occurs naturally and at the proper time, the parental-adolescent relationship can be significantly improved (Sullivan & Sullivan, 1980).

Negative Affect and Rebellion

Rebellion and negative affect appear to be a necessary part of the adolescent developmental stage and the logical result of separation from parents. These behaviors aid the teenager by helping to test limits, search for

competency and autonomy, separate from parental standards, and develop an independent value system. Erikson (1968) states that during this stage the adolescent develops an identity of his or her own through having assimilated past experiences and seeing if they apply to new situations. Erikson maintains that the manifestation of behavior such as mood swings, acting-out behavior, and social alienation results from the role diffusion that accompanies this testing of the world. Unlike the adult, the adolescent must engage in these excessive behaviors since he or she has no other way to assimilate and put them in order (Brenton, 1979; Freud, 1958).

The adolescent's behavior is often characterized by an overt or covert expression of hostility or anger which can be very distressing to the parents. This anger may be the result of the adolescent feeling that he or she has been exploited because of the unrealistic, overdemanding expectations placed on him or her in order to feed parent's narcissistic wishes (Friedman & Sarles, 1980). As has been mentioned previously, the separation from parents is often accompanied by intense anxiety that can be translated into aggression. Adolescents are also frightened by their internal rage that accompanies the inner struggle for autonomy. These negative feelings are often projected on the parents (Williams, 1973). It should be noted that an adolescent's anger may also be the result of a diffuse anxiety that the adolescent is unable to identify adequately (Call, 1979).

Adolescents often have strong feelings of depression and withdrawal. Many adolescents have difficulty discussing their inner feelings of depression with a psychologist. Once their feelings have been clearly identified and a good relationship established, however, most adolescents can openly discuss their inner feelings of unhappiness, hopelessness, and depression. Unfortunately, many adolescents have difficulty identifying their feelings as depression (Friedman & Sarles, 1980). Depression in adolescence is often manifested by masked symptoms such as delinquency, sexual promiscuity, drug and alcohol abuse, and self-destructive behaviors. This depression can be indicative of anger turned inward and poor self-esteem (Malmquist, 1979).

Some adolescents remain relatively free of negative affect and rebellion without any deleterious effects. The adolescent stage is characterized by both revolt and, at the same time, conformity. The degree of the negative affect and rebellion is often a measure of the amount of force that is necessary to overcome the adolescent's ties to his or her parents and separate from them rather than any indication of true hostility toward the parents or the sign of underlying psychopathology.

Identity and Intimacy

In order truly to separate from his or her parents, the adolescent must develop a support system apart from the family. This usually takes the form of identification with a peer group (Erikson, 1963). If the teenager gets too little peer support, the adolescent will have difficulty breaking away from his or her parents. On the other hand, if the adolescent is too dependent on peer acceptance, he or she may develop undesirable behavior patterns merely to win approval from friends. This need for approval is strongly influenced by the adolescent's need to perceive himself or herself as normal. The adolescent's capacity for intimacy with his or her peer group has been shown to be affected by his or her parents' attitude toward the adolescent's need for independence. Unfortunately, the adolescent may, out of an intense need to separate from parents, develop a false intimacy characterized by a lack of significant intimacy. This can lead to problems in later relationships where the teenager remains inappropriately attached emotionally to his or her family (Williams, 1973).

Normal versus Abnormal Adolescent Psychosocial Development

Although numerous authors have described adolescence as conflict filled, little empirical support can be found for this idea (Coleman, 1978). In the same way, the notion of the existence of a generation gap between parents and teenagers appears to be exaggerated. Although it is acknowledged that the majority of adults have little interest in teenage fads, tastes, and cultural heroes (Oldham, 1978), conflict generated between parent and teenager by this disharmony is not sufficiently disruptive to create discord within the family (Hamid & Wyllie, 1980). Even though the adolescent may appear to rebel against the parental value system, the adolescent's value system closely correlates with that of the parents (Bakwin & Bakwin, 1972; Offer, 1969).

Coleman (1978) has developed a theory that correlates highly with the empirical evidence concerning teen-parent conflicts. He states that during adolescence the teenager experiences numerous minor stresses. Although a proportion of adolescents will experience serious psychological disturbance and disruption, this emotional turmoil occurs with only certain adolescents at specific times. Coleman posited a focal theory of adolescent development that states that at different ages particular relationship patterns become more or less prominent to the teenager. These patterns overlap and come into focus at different times for each person in a manner unique to the individual. This theory takes into account the vast individual differences that occur during the adolescent period.

Differentiating between normal and abnormal adolescent adjustment and development and determining when professional intervention appears warranted is often difficult. In fact, many professionals tend to attribute adolescent symptoms that are indicative of abnormality to temporary, developmental turmoil rather than to a psychological disorder. Often greater psychopathology results from this delay of psychotherapeutic intervention (Masterson, 1968). In addition, the therapist may either overinterpret or underinterpret the significance of the adolescent's symptoms because of the therapist's own value system, which may also impede treatment (Oldham, 1978). Although no clear-cut standard can be determined within the scope of this chapter for identifying pathology in adolescence, in most cases, when a psychologist is dealing with teen-parent problems, the necessity of professional intervention is directly proportional to the degree of intrapsychic distress or interpersonal conflict between the adolescent and the parents.

PARENTAL REACTIONS TO ADOLESCENCE

In order fully to understand the problems that occur between parents and teenagers, one must understand how parents react to their adolescent sons and daughters. In most cases, their interactions are characterized by poor interpersonal communication and negative emotionality, which result in ineffective behavioral management techniques (Lantz, 1975). Often parents react to teenagers in a manner consistent with stereotypes of teenagers that may or may not bear any resemblance to reality. These stereotypes can range from viewing the adolescent as a victimizer (a powerful, violent, and sexual being) or as the victim (a passive, impotent, and powerless being). These stereotypes promote significant barriers to communication and will force the adolescent to exclude the adult from his or her world by a conspiracy of silence or subcultural peer identification (Anthony, 1969).

Some characteristics have been identified in the adolescent-parent relationship which could account for positive interpersonal communication and an absence of conflict. Poor parenting appears closely associated with an adult environment that is indifferent and/or hostile to the adolescent's needs. When teens are confronted with this atmosphere, they will have an increased wish to lash out or escape, an increased rejection of parental values (such as scholastic achievement), and a disregard for positive personal attributes (Harris & Howard, 1979; Robinson, 1978). This adolescent response will often cause the adults to become more angry at and hostile to the teen. In contrast to the poor teen-parent relationship, families who have good relationships are characterized by honest and direct communication where parents and teenagers both have a capacity to listen. In addition to feeling that their parents are warm, interested, and caring adults, these adolescents are respected in their right to privacy and the pursuit of their own

interests (Berger, 1978). The competence of the family in these areas appears to have a substantial influence on the level of teen-parent conflict (Lewis, 1978).

Although good communication is a necessity in facilitating teen-parent interactions, parents are often not able to listen to and understand their adolescent, nor are they able to express and communicate their feelings to the adolescent. Many times parents create roadblocks for further communication. Parents give confused and double messages that only create further confusion and anger. In addition, the teenager might be made the scapegoat, as if he or she were the source of conflict within the family when, in fact, other problems may exist (such as a dysfunctional marital relationship). Although it is not effective, parents will lecture their adolescents or punish them for their misdeeds. Lectures only end up symbolizing the parents' reluctance to respect the adolescent's point of view, and punishments only serve to escalate hostility and interpersonal conflict (Brenton, 1979).

Many times parents find it difficult to relinquish the authority of being a parent; they have trouble permitting their adolescent to have greater latitude of action and responsibility. Although not relinquishing authority gradually during childhood can contribute to maladjustment and personality upheavals (Benedict, 1949), many parents are resistant to giving up their protective roles (Lidz, 1969). The cultural discontinuity of not allowing greater freedom and responsibility for the teenager can contribute to the continuation of a teen-parent conflict. In the same way, some parents give their tacit consent to their adolescent's acting-out because they are afraid of a negative confrontation. It can also reflect the parent's insecurity in being able to take a strong stand. Unfortunately, this situation allows the adolescent to manipulate, which will later lead to a maladaptive behavior pattern as an adult. Parents may also unconsciously encourage their adolescent to act out. For example, parents may indirectly foster teenage shoplifting in order to feel that their teen is not a "sissy." In addition, the parents may be vicariously participating in experiences they missed as youngsters.

If parents and teens are to reduce conflicts, open communication must take place with a minimum of conscious and unconscious roadblocks. If the parents are perceived as hostile, inconsistent, and uncaring, resolution of problem areas will be nearly impossible. Because parents often become extremely anxious about adolescent acting-out, they react with irrational and emotionally laden responses. Parents must be encouraged to listen to their adolescents, to understand them from their point of view, and to respect them unconditionally.

TYPICAL AREAS OF TEEN-PARENT CONFLICT

All adolescents overtly or covertly act out in some fashion. As a result, parents often complain that they have little control over the adolescent's behavior. Even though the parents perceive a loss of control over their teen, the adolescent is usually somewhat susceptible to their requests and demands. This struggle for power and control between the parent and adolescent is usually what precipitates intervention by a clinical child psychologist. The psychologist must determine if the current adolescent behavior represents a true loss of control or just a minor behavior transgression. In order to determine the extent of the problems, the psychologist should obtain a history of the degree, duration, and multiplicity of behavior problems. Certain kinds of behaviors, such as delinquent or criminal acts, suicide attempts, or sexual promiscuity, are indicators of severe problems and require immediate intervention. On the following pages, typical areas of teen-parent conflict that are often referred to a child psychologist will be discussed.

Rebellion against Parental Authority and Values

Parents frequently complain that their adolescent does not comply with parental discipline and rules. A simple request to empty the garbage is often met by disinterest, a tirade of anger, or passive noncompliance. Parents are confronted with the fact that they can no longer physically or psychologically compel their adolescent to do what they request. This resistance to their authority causes parents to attribute negative personal qualities to their adolescents; parents will often describe their teenagers as being rude or lazy. Although this rebellion provides a way to separate and individuate from the parents, parents still become confused at their teen's behavioral inconsistency. They do not understand why their teen, who is generally compliant and good natured, may suddenly become overtly uncompromising, rude, and rebellious. Because they feel that they have lost control of the adolescent, parents may feel that somewhere along the line they have abdicated their responsibility. As parents try to regain discipline and control, the adolescent will feel intruded upon. These teenagers with their new sense of independence and individuality will often resent being treated like children. This rebellion pattern is fueled by both the parent and the adolescent and can be the source of ongoing conflict during the teenage years.

No less important is the covert rebellion that surrounds the teenager's lifestyle. Parents complain that their adolescent's taste in music, dress, or hair style is unacceptable within the family. In the same way, teenagers and parents often have substantial philosophical and value disagreements surrounding contemporary issues on topics such as sex, politics, drugs, and religion. This quiet rebellion serves the same function as the overt rebellion described above in that it helps facilitate the separation of the adolescent from his or her parents.

School Difficulties

Many adolescents experience poor academic performance at some point in their teen years, which precipitates conflict in the family. In addition, rebellion and acting-out behavior may be manifested in school by not obeying school rules, getting into fights, or being truant. It has been shown that many adolescents experience considerable stress within secondary school settings (Bakwin & Bakwin, 1972). In addition, the transition between the elementary school to junior or senior high school can be especially stressful because of increased academic competition and heightened social consciousness. Parents often place a greater demand for above-average academic performance on their teenager since college is not far off. The secondary schools are often stressful environments, characterized by violence, overcrowding, and racial problems. Even the adolescent peer group may be very rejecting of teenagers who are regarded as being different.

Parents are often in conflict with their teenagers because the teens are perceived to lack motivation or to be preoccupied with only social matters. The psychologist must determine if the adolescent's behavior pattern is consistent with the teen's need for rebellion and separation from parents or if that behavior might indicate impairments in learning or emotional functioning. School failure can stem from learning and/or emotional problems. With early identification by the psychologist, the prognosis is good for remediation (Cannon & Compton, 1980). (For more complete description of the difficulties teenagers experience in academic settings, see Phillips, chap. 34 of this book, on school problems in adolescence.)

Adolescent Sexuality

Adolescence is a period of experimentation and trying out of new roles. Sexual behavior is often learned through experimentation. It is likely that the adolescent will express his sexuality in some fashion. In fact, approximately 50 percent of all teenagers will have engaged in coital intercourse sometime during their adolescent years (Katchadourian, 1980).

Although the teenager must explore both the physical and social aspects of a sexual relationship, conflicts between adolescents and parents surrounding sexual values and expression are common. In spite of a purported new openness about sex, parents have difficulty frankly discussing sexual matters with their teens. In addition, many parents fear a negative confrontation might occur when the divergent teen-parent values about sex collide.

Teenagers themselves have many fears and anxieties surrounding their developing sexuality. Every adolescent must make decisions in regard to the expression of sexuality, ranging from total suppression to indiscriminate acting on sexual urges. Indiscriminate sexual activity can be an indicator of poor self-concept and/or feelings of worthlessness. In the same way, sexual acting-out can be a way of getting revenge at parents or of luring and holding on to friends. Sexual acting-out is often performed without regard to potential negative ramifications, such as venereal disease or pregnancy (Wagner, 1980). (For a more complete description of some of the problems of puberty and sex roles in adolescence, see Reekers, chap. 33 of this book.)

Drug Use

Although it is clear that parents have knowledge concerning the medical, psychological, and legal issues of drug use (DeForest & Hays, 1975), any illicit use of a drug by an adolescent usually precipitates an intense teen-parent conflict. Many adolescents will use drugs such as alcohol and marijuana on a casual and intermittent basis in much the same way as adults use drugs. In addition, teens will often use drugs as a way of experimenting with life as well as a way of separating from parents by identification with a drug-oriented peer culture. Adolescents who are emotionally troubled and use dangerous drugs in an indiscriminate, frequent, and impulsive fashion clearly require immediate psychotherapeutic intervention.

In a comprehensive study of teenage marijuana and alcohol abuse, numerous psychosocial correlates were discovered to discriminate drug users from nonusers. Greater involvement with drug use was associated with a greater value on independence than on academic achievement, lower expectations for academic achievement, lesser religiousity, greater tolerance of deviance, less compatibility between friends and parents, greater models and support for problem behavior, and a greater influence of friends relative to parents (Jessor, Chase & Donovan, 1980). In addition, a negative parent-teen relationship and a low degree of supportive interaction with parents were found to be associated with drug use (Kandel, Kessler, & Margulies, 1978). If the relationship between the adolescent and the parents is close or if the teenager's dependence on the parents is high, the adolescent will probably not use drugs (Tudor, Petersen, & Elifson, 1980). A high correlation was also found between parental drug abuse and teen drug abuse. Finally, adolescent drug abusers tend to have a low self-esteem that may play a causal role in the abuse rather than be simply a consequence of personal dysfunction (Ahlgren, 1979). Therefore, it appears that any therapeutic intervention with an adolescent drug abuser should focus on the issues of both the teenager's self-esteem and the teen-parent relationship.

Drug abuse has been defined as falling into one of three categories (Wright, Schaefer, & Solomons, 1979). The first deals with the use of any drug that interferes with physical health or personality/social development and functioning. The second involves the use of a drug to the point of tolerance, habituation, dependency, or addiction. Finally, drug abuse involves the use of any controlled drug procured through illicit channels and used without medical supervision. Therefore, all adolescent drug users, even if they are moderate, casual users of drugs, would fall into the last category of drug abuse. For the casual teenage drug user or experimenter, the use of drugs can still create significant conflicts. Parents are concerned that their teen is using a drug that is illegal or that may be dangerous. Parents often have strong feelings about the adolescent's association with the drug culture as well as strong philosophical disagreements against any drug usage. (Further explication of the areas of substance abuse is delineated by Krug in chap. 36 of this book).

Withdrawal Gestures

Adolescents can become depressed, which often goes unnoticed by parents. Conflicts between teenagers and parents usually involve the active expression of their unhappiness and depression. These actions may take the form of simple social withdrawals like wanting to remain isolated with an accompanying suspension of interpersonal contacts, or may take the form of more noticeable "acting-out." Two very common ways that a teenager can act out his or her unhappiness through a withdrawal mechanism are by running away from home and by threatening suicide.

Although running away from home has been historically defined as a behavioral manifestation of psychopathology, the current literature suggests that runaways have equivalent psychosocial aptitudes and abilities to those of nonrunaway peers. When a teenager decides to run away, he or she is expressing unhappiness and dissatisfaction with his or her current life situation. Regardless of whether the teenager is a true runaway or a "pseudorunaway" where the parents know the teen's whereabouts, the threat, gesture, or completion of running away is an indication of stress and should be regarded as a cry for help of a distressed adolescent (Adams & Munro, 1979; Johnson & Carter, 1980).

In a similar way, an adolescent may threaten, gesture, or attempt suicide as a cry for help and as an expression of his or her depression and negative self-concept. Suicidal acting-out during adolescence is extremely frequent, with estimates ranging from 50 to 120 suicide attempts for every successful completion (Wright et al., 1979). Therefore, suicidal threats and gestures appear to be a method used by some adolescents to control their parents while at the same time attempting to escape from a situation that is felt to be unbearable. Many teens will spontaneously say that they want "to die" or "to kill" themselves, which is more of an expression of dissatisfaction with their life situation rather than true suicidal ideation. Regardless of the adolescent's intention, a suicide attempt, gesture, or threat should be regarded as a bonafide reflection of the teenager's distress, representing a clear cry for help. (For further information concerning adolescent suicide see Sheras, chap. 32 of this book.)

Antisocial Behavior

Most adolescents appear to hold social and moral values that are very different from those of society or of the adolescents' families. Although behaviorally the adolescent may appear to have little regard for rules and social customs, not all these behaviors should be regarded as true antisocial or delinquent acts. Petty stealing is an example of an antisocial-like act whose inappropriateness is influenced by social and cultural factors. Influencing factors might include cultural attitudes toward personal property. Many adolescent thefts can be regarded as acts of bravado rather than the result of a character disorder. Stealing may also serve as an initiating ritual through which the teenager proves that he or she is "one of the gang." This apparent antisocial act can also aid the teen in struggling with the concept of proper moral conduct (Meeks, 1979).

Lying is another area of conflict between parents and teenagers that is highly influenced by subcultural norms. In most situations, the adolescent will lie in order to protect himself or herself from further conflict within the family or with other authority figures. In this way, lying becomes a method whereby the teenager can truly become independent of parental influences by deescalating his or her parents' ability to intrude. Lying under these circumstances should not be regarded as an indication of a lack of moral values but, rather, as an act to insure the adolescent's survival.

Vandalism can be a manner in which an adolescent can express his power, fearlessness, anger, and hostility. In addition, vandalism can be a vindictive act directed at his or her parents. When an adolescent destroys his or her own property, this act can be an expression of a negative self-concept. Vandalism can also be a vehicle for the expression of aggression. When aggression goes beyond acceptable limits, adolescents have been known to harm their parents physically (Harbin & Madden, 1979). In most cases, teen violence is manifested by such things as slamming doors and yelling. Many antisocial acts by adolescents are the result of poor judgment. In addition, teenagers often do not appreciate the negative consequences of their behaviors at the time they engage in those behaviors. (Further antisocial adolescent behaviors that are more severe than the nonpathological forms found in the typical teen-parent conflicts are addressed by Shaw in chap. 37 of this book, concerning delinquency and criminal behavior.)

GUIDELINES FOR THERAPEUTIC INTERVENTION

Intervention Approaches

In dealing with teen-parent conflicts, both the adolescent and the parents must be involved if any intervention is to be successful (Kaplan, 1969; Rosenstock & Vincent, 1979). An inverse relationship appears to exist between the age of the adolescent and the necessity and importance of parental involvement. For example, younger adolescents who will be dependent on parents for guidance and support for a number of years have a much greater need to resolve teen-parent conflicts than many older adolescents who will be living away from their parents in a few years. In any involvement with parents, the therapist must be sensitive to the parent's needs as well as being careful not to compromise the therapeutic alliance that has been established with the teenager. Most teen-parent problems can be resolved with a short term intervention that will not greatly intrude upon or disrupt the family structure. Only in rare instances is separation of the adolescent from his or her family necessary in order to give both sides a chance to resolve the problems between them. If the tension in the family becomes unbearable, boarding schools, residential treatment centers, or a friend's or relative's home can be used as alternative living arrangements so that the conflicts can be resolved. Although the adolescent may have extreme conflicts with his or her parents, many teens can still have an exceedingly good relationship with the therapist as well as with other adults.

Although many intervention approaches have been effective in resolving teen-parent problems, the therapist must have a thorough knowledge of the dynamic processes of adolescent growth and development (Slaff, 1979). The therapist must understand teenage life stresses in order to establish a close working relationship with adolescent patients. In addition, the therapist must be able to understand the realities of the adolescent's environment, including the impact of the teenager's family and friends on his or her behavior. These basic principles apply to all intervention approaches, including individual psychotherapy, group psychotherapy, and family therapy.

Unless the adolescent appears to have severe ego deficits or intense intrapsychic emotional problems, individual psychotherapy would not be the most helpful intervention approach. On the other hand, if the cause appears to be the individual psychopathology of either parent or the adolescent, it must be dealt with directly. Parents often attribute the source of teen-parent conflicts to psychological maladjustment of the teen, but this is rarely the case. Although the therapist must always be sensitive to individual psychodynamic factors, individual psychotherapy alone is not usually sufficient to resolve teen-parent conflicts.

The adolescent's peer group has been recognized to be an important factor that must be taken into account in the treatment of adolescents. Although group therapy may appear to be the treatment of choice, traditional group therapy formats have not met the needs of many adolescents (Fluet, Holmes, & Gordon, 1980). A group approach has the advantage of providing a forum where significant confrontation and introspection can take place (Slaff, 1979). An adolescent group allows the teenager to escape the control of the adult world and provide a vehicle for socially acceptable self-assertion against parental authority. As in the case with individual psychotherapy intervention, group therapy alone neglects the importance of parental involvement. A group therapy approach would be especially useful for adolescents whose teen-parents problems are primarily the result of peer relationships or influences.

Although a family therapy intervention can be useful in understanding the characteristic interaction/dynamic patterns between family members, it has been criticized for its relative ineffectiveness in dealing with adolescent problems (Schimel, 1979; Williams, 1973). Most family therapists believe that no individual family member is the only source of problems within a family system. Rather, the pathology exists within the family as a whole. The patterns of family communication are understood as essential to the maintenance of equilibrium within the family (Lewis, 1978). Family therapy is especially useful in the resolution of teen-parent problems when the source of conflict centers around a family system dysfunction, such as with a failing marital relationship.

Intervention approaches such as individual psychotherapy, group therapy, and family therapy all make unique contributions to the treatment of teen-parent conflicts, although no single approach will work in all cases for the typical teen-parent problem areas in which the therapist is often confronted. The majority of teen-parent problems usually center around dysfunctional communication between the adolescent and his or her parent. At the same time, a breakdown takes place in their ability to resolve conflicts that arise normally on a day-to-day basis. A more direct approach to dealing with teen-parent problems involves a multimodal approach to conflict resolution that will be outlined later in this chapter.

The Adolescent as a Patient

The ability to communicate with adolescents who do not have significant conflicts with their parents requires special skills. Even these normal adolescents may appear hostile, uncommunicative, or aloof to any adult who might approach them. Teenagers very much appreciate the warm, sincere interest of an adult who is nonjudgmental and who respects the teen for who he or she is or what he or she does, not what he or she is supposed to be or to do. An adult must be interested in listening to the adolescent and be concerned about his or her feelings. Brusqueness, flippant advice, a hurried approach, or a moralizing attitude tends to inhibit communication (Hammar, 1973). Any adult who wants to facilitate communication should try to be honest and straightforward with the teenager.

The adolescent who does have significant conflicts with his or her parents presents even greater challenges. The adolescent who is a patient is often unpredictable and rebellious, which makes it difficult for the therapist to plan a treatment strategy. Adolescents in treatment are usually defensive, and their coping style appears to change from week to week. Psychologists who choose to treat adolescents should anticipate resistance to continuing treatment as adolescents have a great frequency of missed sessions, tardiness, and dropping out of treatment. As the therapist gets closer to sensitive areas of internal conflict, anxiety can be aroused for either the adolescent or his or her parents. This increased anxiety might contribute to the termination of treatment by the adolescent and/or the parents.

When a therapeutic relationship has been established, adolescents reveal themselves to be vulnerable, sensitive, and helpless. They are often plagued by self-doubts. Although they are angry about being compelled to see a psychologist and concerned that they may be viewed as "crazy," many teenage patients do come to their appointments even while they continue to protest. By seeing a psychologist, the teenager is overtly admitting that he might have a problem; acknowledging this can be upsetting to his or her sensitive self-esteem. The therapist should be aware of this possibility and be responsive to the adolescent's feelings. Even after some degree of rapport has been established, the adolescent will often use therapy as a way of expressing negative feelings. This ventilation should be viewed by the therapist as a useful, socially accepted way

for the teenager to express these feelings. Although adolescents often show unpredictable, rebellious behavior, many adolescents appreciate the chance to discuss their concerns with a sensitive, concerned adult who really listens to what they are saying.

The Therapeutic Alliance

Even though parents may try to compel a teenager to see a psychologist, the adolescent usually has the power to sabotage the psychotherapeutic intervention. Unlike the preadolescent child, the teenager will often oppose the parent's authority in attending therapy sessions. With this in mind, the psychologist should have as a primary goal promoting a positive therapeutic alliance during these initial stages of contact. The psychologist must communicate to the teenager that they both will be involved in a shared undertaking in order to improve the teenager's life. The adolescent should be helped to identify his or her problems. At this point, most teenagers will not admit that they have a problem although they will admit to distress or unhappiness either about their parents or about the trouble they get into. Using the adolescent's admitted unhappiness and distress is a good starting point to persuade the teenager to work with a psychologist so that these problems can be remedied.

At times, no matter how convincing the therapist is, the adolescent may still refuse to participate in therapy. In this situation, a certain amount of coercion may be called for during the first few appointments in order for rapport to be given an opportunity to develop. Although an adolescent may be compelled to attend therapy, in most cases the teen will eventually react to it favorably. Many of these resistant teenagers may actually want to attend but cannot overtly admit their need for psychological help. By attending under protest, the teenager can get the help needed and save face too. The psychologist must convince the adolescent of his or her concern for the adolescent's welfare, of his or her interest in the adolescent's point of view, and of his or her unconditional positive regard for the teenager. If the therapist projects a neutral, uncommitted relationship, he or she will be perceived as being indifferent or unconcerned. The teenager must believe that the psychologist will be his or her advocate in working to make things better. The therapist who is dealing with this developing therapeutic alliance must be prepared to show great flexibility when working with adolescents. The therapist must be actively involved in the relationship and must constantly adapt to the changeableness of the adolescent. The adolescent will often challenge the therapist's level of commitment to him or her. In this way, the teenager is testing the limits of the relationship with the therapist in much the same way that the teenager tests his or her parents. The therapist must also allow the adolescent an opportunity to ventilate feelings and provide an accepting, noncritical forum for his or her concerns. It is only when the therapist has not emotionally abandoned the teenager and not rejected the teenager's viewpoint that the teenager will trust the relationship and the therapeutic alliance will be strengthened.

The therapist's involvement with the adolescent's family can have a great influence on the therapeutic alliance. If the adolescent is to be convinced that an adult conspiracy has not been started against him or her, the adolescent should be treated with respect. In most cases, the adolescent should be able to make his or her own decisions concerning the therapy contract without undue interference from the parents. If the adolescent protests treatment, this could be indicative of adolescent rebellion or a true refusal to pursue therapy. Differentiating the reasons for protesting treatment is extremely important because the adolescent's true feelings must be understood. In all cases with teen-parent problems, the psychologist must work with both the adolescent and the parents from the beginning if the problems are to be addressed directly.

The initial contact is a time for the teenager and the parents to evaluate the psychologist critically. They should be given the opportunity while in the waitingroom to decide who will be seen first. In this way, neither the parents nor the teenager will feel slighted during this important first encounter. It will also allow the therapist to observe how such a choice is handled between them. If it is impossible that they be given a choice because of an overly crowded waitingroom or other constraints, the adolescent should be seen first since this will communicate an interest in and respect for the adolescent. In addition, it allows the teenager to tell his or her side of the story first.

It is only by treating the adolescent as a competent, responsible adult that the adolescent can assume that role. It should be explained to the adolescent that although he or she may be seen first, any workable solution to the problems would necessitate the involvement of other family members. It should be pointed out that this initial meeting has the purpose of allowing the adolescent to state his or her concerns confidentially. This is a good time to delineate some of the issues surrounding confidentiality, which are outlined in the next section. From this initial contact the adolescent must be reassured that he or she is not thought to be "crazy" nor is he or she seen as the only person with a problem in the family. If the adolescent refuses to acknowledge distress or unhappiness (as mentioned previously), the teenager will probably admit to a problem because his or her parents feel that he or she needs to see a psychologist. Although the adolescent may protest the appointment with a psychologist, the initial appointment can turn out to be a pleasant, relieving experience that will promote future attendance.

After the initial interview, the adolescent can be asked to fill out a sentence completion test or another paper-and-pencil questionnaire in which the adolescent can be allowed to express his or her feelings in written form. Teenagers will often write things on paper that they are not able to express verbally to a psychologist on a face-to-face basis. Of course, the psychologist should only request, rather than demand, that the teenager complete the forms, in keeping with the respect for the adolescent's wishes.

As with the teenager, the parents must feel respected and must be given a forum in order to discuss their feelings, complaints, and concerns. The psychologist must clearly indicate the factors that promote a positive outcome while at the same time being careful not to guarantee changing the adolescent's behavior pattern. It should be reiterated that if any meaningful change is to take place, it must be from the mutual efforts of the therapist, the adolescent, and the parents. This is an excellent time for the therapist to assess family dynamics that may be contributing to the teen-parent problems as well as any fears the parents may have concerning their adolescent. The psychologist must communicate his or her concern for the adolescent's well being. The parents should be warned that although the psychologist may appear to take sides against the parents, this approach will help facilitate communication and resolution of conflicts. The parents must be reassured that many of the adolescent's problems are the result of normal developmental issues. The psychologist must be sensitive that many parents are apprehensive about seeking help from a psychologist. They fear that they are responsible for the problems their adolescent is experiencing. The parents must be reassured in this respect and helped to understand that their distress is understandable. The therapist should point out common areas of concern between the adolescent and the parents. This commonality of goals (i.e., getting rid of the conflict, distress, and interpersonal problems) will support the mutual goal of solving the teen-parent problem.

Before terminating the initial session, the adolescent and the parents should be seen together. The psychologist should recap the issues discussed, being careful not to breach any confidences that were established during the individual interviews. Joint therapy goals can be discussed as well as a tentative treatment plan. Most adolescents will be able to see the utility of a therapeutic contract in which he or she feels that the psychologist will be an active advocate for the teen's interests.

Confidentiality

Confidentiality with the adolescent and his or her parents is an exceptionally sensitive issue.

Even the American Psychological Association, who spent nine years trying to revise the *Ethical Standards of Psychologists* (1979), were unable substantially to revise the confidentiality principles. The adolescent often mistrusts adults and is untrusting of therapy. Attempting to promote the therapeutic alliance as well as to provide adequate communication with the parents often complicates the maintenance of confidentiality.

Confidentiality is crucial when working with teenagers. The adolescent should feel from the beginning that the psychologist is his private confidant and vigorous advocate. It should be noted that no legal basis for confidentiality exists in most states when treating an adolescent minor since the parent or guardian is legally entitled to all information pertaining to minors. However, most therapists make an agreement with the parents in which the adolescent's confidentiality will be maintained as a condition of treating the teenager. When the therapist does communicate with the adolescent's parents, the teenager must not only consent to the discussion, but he or she must also be kept informed about the content and purpose of the meetings. In most cases, the adolescent should be given the choice of either attending the session with the parents or at least having veto power over the content discussed. This approach should defuse much of the adolescent's defensiveness and reinforce the trust in the therapist. The therapist must be careful not to pledge complete, blind confidentiality with the adolescent since circumstances may require divulging confidential information. For example, if the teenager appears to be a danger to himself or others, the therapist has a moral and legal obligation to disclose that information. These limits to confidentiality should be explained to the teenager. In the majority of cases, the adolescent will understand the reasons for not guaranteeing absolute confidentiality, and the therapeutic alliance will not be weakened (Slaff, 1979).

Although a double standard has been proposed where the adolescent's sessions are confidential while the parent's sessions are not (Schimel, 1979), the parents may end up feeling neglected during the process of therapy, which would complicate the therapy progress. The parents must be encouraged to discuss their concerns with the adolescent and the psychologist in a joint interview format. These joint interviews often help the teenager to understand and appreciate that his or her parent's concerns are sincere and, from their point of view, reality oriented rather than just punitive and meddling. Although the therapist may frequently be asked for advice during these joint interviews about how the adolescent should be handled, the therapist should try to avoid taking sides in the conflict resolution but should try instead to facilitate open communication between parents and teenagers while respecting their rights of privacy.

A Multimodal Approach to Conflict Resolution

In approaching the resolution of teen-parent conflicts, the use of a variety of therapeutic techniques can be extremely effective. A three-part approach to dealing with parent-child conflicts and problems has been described in an article by Rae and Riley (1975). When dealing with teen-parent problems, a similar multimodal approach would involve an attempt to help the parents understand their adolescent's psychosocial development, an attempt to help the adolescent and the parents communicate better, and an attempt to help the parents and their teenager agree to a viable behavioral contract in order to facilitate conflict resolution. The following components of the multimodal approach that are described below should take place concurrently since an interrelationship exists between components. For example, in order to have an agreeable behavioral contract, good communication must occur between the parent and the teenager. In the same way, in order to have good communication, it is often helpful to have the adolescent's acting-out behavior under control through the use of a contract.

Parent groups are often a useful format in which to teach many of the basic principles of the multimodal approach. Parents can discuss some of the problems they experience with their adolescent within a supportive forum. Many parents are relieved to discover that they are not alone in their distress of trying to raise a teenager. During these groups, the therapist can also help the parents talk about their own teenage years, which will aid them in becoming more sensitive to their teen. Parents often will realize during this recollection of their own past that their adolescent's behavioral pattern is not dissimilar to their own behavior as a teenager.

Understanding Adolescent Development

In order to promote the parents' positive response to their teenager, the parents must possess an understanding of the developmental stresses and problems that plague adolescence. Parents can, in this manner, anticipate potential areas of conflict, unhappiness, and distress. This sensitivity to their teenager will help avoid the common parental reaction of hostility to or rejection of the teen. The psychologist can counsel the parents so they will be able to recognize the adolescent's need for psychological and physical separation from them. For example, when the teenager desires to remain secluded in his room or when he or she attempts to reject parental values, the parents will be able to recognize this as an awkward attempt to separate from them. In addition, the parents will understand the teen's negative affect and rebellion as a similar developmental manifestation. The adolescent's intense identification with his or her peer group (which the parents may feel is a problem) can be recognized as a necessary developmental prerequisite for engaging in intimate relationships later in life. The parents must have a thorough understanding of normal adolescent development and behavior in order to facilitate resolution of teen-parent problems.

Communications Training

Open and positive communication is a necessity for dealing with teen-parent problems. Although both adolescents and their parents purport to listen to each other, in reality neither truly hears the other. The psychologist must teach communication skills to adolescents and parents through role playing or didactic instruction. The psychologist, in the course of therapy, can simply ask either the adolescent or the parent to repeat what he or she has heard the other person say. At this point, it is useful to point out the distortions that occur. After adequate basic listening skills have been developed, both the teenager and his other parents must be able to understand one another empathetically. Understanding his or her parents from their point of view will help the adolescent acknowledge parental support and concern. In the same way, when the parents empathetically understand the teenager, parents can better appreciate some of their son's or daughter's "trivial, unimportant" concerns (Gordon, 1970). The psychologist should encourage the parents and their teenager to have unconditional, positive regard for each other's feelings, which will promote and encourage future communications of feelings. When both parents and teenager have regard and respect for each other's feelings, constructive interpersonal exchanges will be facilitated.

Behavioral Contracting

In developing a behavioral contract between parents and the adolescent, the psychologist will most often serve as a mediator. Mediation has been shown to produce substantial concessions in positions and to aid in face saving in the negotiating process (Pruitt & Johnson, 1970). Behavioral contracting has been used in a wide variety of settings with adolescents. It has been used to manage predelinquent youth (Kifer et al., 1974; Stuart, et al., 1976), and delinquent youth (Alexander & Parsons, 1973; Douds, Engelsgjerd, & Collingwood, 1977; Stuart, 1971); to control behavioral problems in school (Davis & Borgen, 1978); and to reduce acting-out behaviors in an adolescent residential treatment program (Bardill, 1977). In the process of behavioral contracting, the psychologist helps both the parents and the teenager to reach a negotiated settlement between their conflicts. Since the parents are responsible for the teenager, the limits of their flexibility in the negotiation process must be ascertained. For example, if a teenager wants to stay out all night, this desire may be beyond the parents' limits although the parents may be willing to negotiate a later curfew with the help of the therapist.

The psychologist must actively arbitrate between the parents and adolescent in the resolution of teen-parent conflicts. It must be pointed out to both the parents and the adolescent that neither will get exactly what he or she wants; both will most likely have to settle for less than the ideal. It must be pointed out to the parents that most adolescents are independent enough to sabotage any parental limit setting. Therefore, it is in their best self-interest to negotiate a settlement that their teenager will find agreeable. For example, the parents might impose an unreasonably early curfew that the adolescent can sabotage easily by noncompliance. Greater flexibility on the parents' curfew limits can result in more compliance. A formal written contract is often helpful by making the terms of the agreement explicit. This procedure will eliminate future misunderstandings about what was stated. It is useful to make explicit both positive and negative consequences for compliance or noncompliance with the contract (Kifer et al., 1974). For example, if the teenager goes along with the parents' curfew, he or she should be given privileges, but if the teen does not fulfill the contract, he or she should face restriction or other negative consequences.

REFERENCES

Adams, G.R., & Munro, G. Portrait of the North American runaway: A critical review. *Journal of Youth and Adolescence,* 1979, **8**(3), 359–372.

Ahlgren, A. Self-esteem patterns distinctive of groups of drug abusing and other dysfunctional adolescents. *International Journal of Addiction,* 1979, **14**(6), 759–777.

Alexander, J.F., & Parsons, B.V. Short-term behavioral intervention with delinquent families: Impact on family process and recidivism. *Journal of Abnormal Psychology,* 1973, **81,** 219–225.

Anthony, J. The reactions of adults to adolescents and their behavior. In G. Caplan & S. Lebouici (Eds.), *Adolescence: Psychosocial perspectives.* New York: Basic Books, 1969.

Bakwin, H., & Bakwin, R.M. *Behavior disorders in children.* Philadelphia: Saunders, 1972.

Bardill, D.R. A behavior-contracting program of group treatment for early adolescents in a residential treatment setting. *International Journal of Group Psychotherapy*, 1977, **27**(3), 389–400.

Benedict, R. Continuities and discontinuities in cultural conditioning. In P. Mullahy (Ed.), *A study of interpersonal relations*. New York: Hermitage, 1949.

Berger, M.M. The point of view of reasonably healthy adolescents about their family life. *Psychiatric Quarterly*, 1978, **50**(1), 28–29.

Brenton, M. *How to survive your child's rebellious teens*. New York: Lippincott, 1979.

Call, J.D. Sources of anxiety and intrapsychic change during adolescence. In J.D. Call, J.D. Noshpitz, R.L. Cohen, & I.N. Berlin (Eds.), *Basic handbook of child psychiatry* (Vol. 1). New York: Basic Books, 1979.

Cannon, I.P., & Compton, C.L. School dysfunction in the adolescent. *Pediatric Clinics of North America*, 1980, **27**(1), 79–96.

Coleman, J.D. Current contraindicators in adolescent theory. *Journal of Youth and Adolescence*, 1978, **7**(1), 1–11.

Davis, W.L, & Borgen, W.A. Contracting: An entry point and a process. *Canadian Counsellor*, 1978, **12**(4), 242–245.

DeForest, J.W., & Hays, J.R. Drug knowledge and attitudes of parents of adolescents. *Drug Forum*, 1975, **5**(1), 89–93.

Douds, A.F., Engelsgjerd, M., & Collingwood, T.R. Behavior contracting with youthful offenders and their parents. *Child Welfare*, 1977, **56**(6), 409–417.

Erikson, E.H. *Childhood and society* (2nd ed.). New York: Norton, 1963.

Erikson, E.H. *Identity: Youth and crisis*. New York: Norton, 1968.

Ethical standards of psychologists. Washington, D.C.: American Psychological Association, Inc., 1979.

Fluet, N.R., Holmes, G.R., & Gordon, L.D. Adolescent psychotherapy: A modifed fishbowl format. *Adolescence*, 1980, **15**(57), 75–82.

Freidman, S.B., & Sarles, R.M. Out of control: Behavior in adolescents. *Pediatric Clinics of North America*, 1980, **27**(1), 97–107.

Freud, A. Adolescence. In R.S. Eissler (Ed.), *The psychoanalytic study of the child* (Vol. 16). New York: International Universities Press, 1958.

Gordon, T. *Parent effectiveness training*. New York: Peter Wyden, 1970.

Hamid, P.N., & Wyllie, A.J. What generation gap? *Adolescence*, 1980, **15**(58), 385–391.

Hammar, S.L. The approach to the adolescent patient. *Pediatric Clinics of North America* 1973, **20**(4), 778–779.

Harbin, H.T., & Madden, D.J. Battered parents: A new syndrome. *American Journal of Psychiatry*, 1979, **136**(10), 1288–1291.

Harris, I.D., & Howard, K.I. Phenomenological correlates of perceived quality of parenting: A questionnaire study of high school students. *Journal of Youth and Adolescence*, 1979, **8**(2), 171–180.

Jessor, R., Chase, J.A., & Donovan, J.E. Psychosocial correlates of marijuana use and problem drinking in a national sample of adolescents. *American Journal of Public Health*, 1980, **70**(6), 604–613.

Johnson, R., & Carter, M.M. Flight of the young: Why children run away from their homes. *Adolescence*, 1980, **15**(58), 482–489.

Kandel, D.B., Kessler, R.C., & Marguelies, R.Z. Antecedents of adolescent initiation into stages of drug use: A developmental analysis. *Journal of Youth & Adolescence*, 1978, **7**(1), 13–40.

Kaplan, A.H. Doing parent-adolescent interviews in the psychotherapy of the younger adolescent. In G. Caplan & S. Lebovici (Eds.), *Adolescence: Psychosocial perspectives*. New York: Basic Books, 1969.

Katchadourian, H. Adolescent sexuality. *Pediatric Clinics of North America*, 1980, **27**(1), 17–28.

Kifer, R.E., Lewis, M.A., Green, D.R., & Phillips, E.L. Training predelinquent youth and their parents to negotiate conflict situations. *Journal of Applied Behavior Analysis*, 1974, **7**, 357–364.

Lantz, J.E. The rational treatment of parental adjustment reaction to adolescence. *Clinical Social Work Journal*, 1975, **3**(2), 100–108.

Lewis, J.M. The adolescent and the healthy family. In S.C. Feinstein & P.L. Giovacchini (Eds.), *Adolescent psychiatry: Developmental and clinical studies* (Vol. 7). Chicago: University of Chicago Press, 1978.

Lidz, T. The adolescent and his family. In G. Caplin & S. Lebouici (Eds.), *Adolescence: Psychosocial perspectives*. New York: Basic Books, 1969.

Malmquist, C.P. Development from thirteen to sixteen years. In J.D. Call, J.D. Noshpitz,

R.L. Cohen, & I.N. Berlin (Eds.), *Basic handbook of child psychiatry* (Vol. 1). New York: Basic Books, 1979.

Masterson, J.F., Jr. The psychiatric significance of adolescent turmoil. *American Journal of Psychiatry,* 1968, **124**(11), 107–112.

Meeks, J.E. Behavioral and antisocial disorder. In J.D. Noshpitz (Ed.), *Basic handbook of child psychiatry.* New York: Basic Books, 1979.

Offer, D. *The psychological world of the teenager.* New York: Basic Books, 1969.

Oldham, D.G. Adolescent turmoil: A myth revisited. In S.C. Feinstein & P.L. Giovacchini (Eds.), *Adolescent psychiatry: Developmental and clinical studies* (Vol. 6). Chicago, Ill.: University of Chicago Press, 1978.

Pruitt, D.G., & Johnson, D.F. Mediation as an aid to face-saving in negotiation. *Journal of Personality and Social Psychology,* 1970, **14**, 239–246.

Rae, W.A., & Riley, H.D. Learning how to be a better parent. *American Baby,* 1975, **38**(1), 44–45.

Robinson, P.A. Parents of "beyond control" adolescents. *Adolescence,* 1978, **13**(49), 109–119.

Rosenstock, H.A., & Vincent, K.R. Parental involvement as a requisite for successful adolescent therapy. *Journal of Clinical Psychiatry,* 1979, **40**(3), 132–143.

Schimel, J.L. Adolescents and families: An overview. In S.C. Feinstein & P.L. Giovacchini (Eds.), *Adolescent psychiatry: Developmental and clinical studies* (Vol. 7). Chicago: University of Chicago Press, 1979.

Slaff, B. Adolescents. In S.I. Hanison (Ed), *Basic handbook of child psychiatry* (Vol. 3). New York: Basic Books, 1979.

Stuart, R.B., Tripodi, T., Jayaratne, S., & Camburn, D. An experiment in social engineering in serving the families of predelinquents. *Journal of Abnormal Child Psyehology,* 1976, **4**(3), 243–261.

Sullivan, K., & Sullivan, A. Adolescent-parent separation. *Developmental Psychology,* 1980, **16**(2), 93–99.

Tudor, C.G., Petersen, D.M., & Elifson, K.W. An examination of the relationship between peer and parental influences and adolescent drug use. *Adolescence,* 1980, **15**(60), 783–798.

Wagner, C.A. Sexuality of American adolescents. *Adolescence,* 1980, **15**(59), 567–577.

Williams, F.S. Family therapy: Its role in adolescent psychiatry. In S.C. Feinstein & P.L. Giovacchini (Eds.), *Adolescent psychiatry: Developmental and clinical studies* (Vol. 2). New York: Basic Books, 1973.

Wright, L., Schaefer, A.B., & Solomons, G. *Encylopedia of pediatric psychology.* Baltimore: University Park Press, 1979.

CHAPTER 31

Emotional Problems of Adolescence: A Review of Affective Disorders and Schizophrenia

ALAN S. WEINER

THE NATURE OF ADOLESCENCE

Previous reviews of the literature on adolescent functioning found it necessary to demonstrate that some adolescents can indeed have emotional disorders (e.g., Weiner, 1977). Studies of normal adolescents (Offer & Offer, 1975) and those with psychiatric disorders (e.g., Masterson, 1967; Weiner & DelGaudio, 1976) have indicated that not all adolescents experience emotional turmoil and that those who are experiencing difficulty do not automatically outgrow it. Such studies have led to a modification of the view that adolescence is by nature a period of emotional and behavioral lability, a view that has been attributed to a number of factors. These include psychoanalytic interpretations that suggested that greater difficulties were in store for the adolescent demonstrating a seemingly smooth adjustment to the period than for those experiencing some turmoil (A. Freud, 1958). It may well be that the intrapsychic changes described by psychoanalysts for adolescents (e.g., Blos, 1967) can involve wrenching conflicts and adjustments, but it is also clear that large numbers of adolescents readily adjust to the developmental tasks of this age without demonstrating or expressing behavioral or emotional problems (Offer & Offer, 1975). The more literary, quasi-scientific view of adolescence as a period of "Sturm und Drang" (Hall, 1904) has attractive, romantic elements that may induce a longing that clouds the perception of researchers and clinicians alike.

Many characteristics attributed to adolescents, upon closer empirical evaluation, turn out to be optimal at best, but certainly not normative (Weiner, 1977).

This traditional view is not easily altered. Offer, Ostrow, and Howard (1981) recently had 62 mental health professionals complete the Offer Self-Image Questionnaire with answers they thought would be given by "mentally healthy/well adjusted" adolescents. The form was also completed by normal, psychiatrically disturbed, and delinquent adolescents. The professionals not only attributed more problems to a normal adolescent than these adolescents themselves indicated, but conceptualized them as having even more problems than were demonstrated by the emotionally disturbed and delinquent groups. This was especially so with questions of mood, social and family relationships, and self-image.

Such a finding not only indicates that attitudes and beliefs are slowly changed by data, perhaps not surprising, but also raises methodological concern because so many of the findings to be reported in this chapter are based on ratings and interviews obtained by such mental health professionals and those who trained them. Statistical checks (such as interrater reliabilities) do not account for shared, but possibly inaccurate, perceptions.

Methodological and Conceptual Issues

Current reviews, while now able to acknowledge that adolescents have problems that go beyond normative adjustment issues, face the task of knowing what to call these problems. Adolescents remain difficult to diagnose. Several factors, methodological and conceptual, contribute to this difficulty.

The value of a developmental perspective in clinical work with children and adolescents is generally acknowledged. This typically means an acceptance that adolescents are different from adults. The question is: How?

One major difference is that they have not lived as long, so there is less of a history upon which a clinician can base a judgment. For example, in one follow-up study of adolescents, 42 percent were undiagnosed upon hospital admission at mean age of 16.2 years. Only 10 percent were so diagnosed upon reinterviewing (at mean age 25.6 years) (Welner, Welner, & Fishman, 1979). As the authors indicated, part of the problem may be that the research criteria they used (Feighner et al., 1972) may be less appropriate for adolescents than adults. That is an empirical question. Also, more data became available during the intervening nine years. For example, four subjects were reclassified from unipolar to bipolar affective disorders as manic features were now more obvious. Weiner and DelGaudio (1976) report that in their important, comprehensive study of a cumulative case register of adolescents between 12 and 18 years, the diagnosis of schizophrenia showed the highest agreement across time, but they also note that these patients had the highest rate of subsequent contact. Therefore, in comparison to other groups, more data were available on which to base the diagnoses.

Second, adolescents may not be as articulate or willing to talk to adult interviewers to provide information needed for a diagnosis. This may, in part, be related to features of cognitive development during adolescence. Early adolescence, coinciding with the onset of formal operational thinking (Inhelder & Piaget, 1958), brings with it certain features of egocentrism (Elkind, 1974). Also, the consolidation of formal operational thinking may need to take place before an adolescent can clearly reflect on his or her experience of the world and associated affects in order to be

able to put into words what is needed to aid in a diagnosis. Of course, not all adults can do this. However, the increased prevalence of depressive symptomatology and mood in later adolescence may be partially dependent on an increased capacity to express it.

There is an additional factor that can be implicit within a developmental perspective. Assumptions of continuity and stability are often taken as "givens" by developmentalists, and their task then becomes to find the earlier correlates of later behaviors. Kagan (1980) has asserted that these assumptions need not be automatic and discussed the problems and issues attendant in demonstrating if the same underlying structure is being expressed in different ways at varying points in development. For the clinician, this means judging not only if an adolescent's problem is beyond what would be considered normative but also if it is reflective of a disorder that would take a more typical, stable form in adulthood.

The above factors may be more of an issue in some areas of adolescent functioning than others. Adolescent psychological disorders have been identified in the three central domains for studying human functioning— affect, thought, and behavior. Conduct disorders, corresponding to the last domain, probably cause adults the most alarm and are easiest to identify. The signs of the disorder are observable—they can even be seen in childhood—and, therefore, the longitudinal course of children and adolescents with such a disorder can be followed. Indeed, there is impressive stability in conduct disorders from about age 10 onward (Robins, 1979). The important aspects of conduct disorders, delinquency, and antisocial personality are reviewed in chapters 19 and 37 in this volume.

The disorders of thought and affect will be the primary focus of the present chapter. There seem to be two major pathways for study and classification of these disorders. One approach has been to view children and adolescents as so different from adults that independent criteria would be needed for the two former groups. Indeed, one might even question, on theoretical grounds, whether certain disorders can even be found in early adolescents. An alternative approach, such as that embodied in the most recent edition of the *Diagnostic and Statistical Manual* of the American Psychiatric Association (DSM-III, 1980), uses major classifications for affective disorders, character disorders, schizophrenia, and situational disorders to cover the entire developmental range. Some classifications particular to adolescence are available (e.g., Identity Disorder). The issue then becomes the ability adequately to diagnose adolescents with such a schema, still illustrate those features within the disorder, if any, that are particular to adolescents, and be able to demonstrate changes, if any, in the form of the disorder as development proceeds. Factors such as these will serve as a guide for reviewing research on adolescent emotional problems. This perspective on adolescent, as well as child and adult, psychopathology is reflective of more recent research that has used clearly defined research criteria (e.g., Feighner et al., 1972; Spitzer, Endicott, & Robins, 1978) and those embodied in DSM-III. While one can readily argue the strengths and weaknesses of a system such as DSM-III, using such criteria allows for more desirable comparability of studies, replication, and further modification of criteria than was previously possible. It should also be noted that carefully constructed interview formats, relying on clearly stated criteria, are also necessary and may help to surmount the possibility that younger subjects can be poorer informants (Strober, Green, & Carlson, 1981).

Another caveat is that, despite great care, initial diagnosis will be especially unreliable or vague with adolescents. For example, Haslam (1978) reported that initial diagnosis was changed in 48 percent of his adolescent patients. Weiner and DelGaudio (1976) found fluctuating diagnoses in 45.9 percent of their population while 54.1 percent showed reasonable diagnostic agreement. The latter figure compares with 76.7 percent reported for adults. Ford, Hudgens, and Wilner (1978) report that 25 percent of the hospitalized adolescents they studied did not fit into traditional syndromes. They recommend using the category Undiagnosed Psychiatric Disorder

for such patients. On follow-up, approximately seven years later, 71 percent of those who could be contacted had been psychiatrically ill during the intervening period, and 80 percent of them could now be diagnosed as belonging to clear syndromes. Welner et al. (1979), with a sample of 265 hospitalized patients between 12 and 19 years of age, reported that 42 percent were undiagnosed at admission and 10 percent were undiagnosed approximately nine years later. While Strober et al. (1981) indicate that acceptable interrater agreement can be achieved by employing structured interviews, records, and DSM-III criteria, success here still varies with diagnosis. They employed the Kappa statistic and found that interrater agreement was inadequate for anxiety disorder and undiagnosed patients but was at a similar level to that found with adults for conduct disorders, personality disorders, major affective disorders, and schizophrenia.

The format of this review is as follows. To provide a picture of the range of adolescent psychopathology, the findings on the distribution of adolescent emotional disorders obtained from large samples will be presented first. These include British epidemiological studies reviewed by Rutter (1980) and a survey of adolescent psychopathology among those having contact with mental health professionals (Weiner & DelGaudio, 1976). These will be followed by a presentation of findings obtained in various studies of hospitalized adolescent patients. These generally include much smaller samples but also convey the diagnostic issues and methodological factors faced by clinicians and researchers. This will be followed by a review of affective and schizophrenic disorders in adolescents.

Nature and Distribution of Adolescent Emotional Disorders

Available data on the distribution of adolescent psychopathology should be viewed as tentative, primarily because of emerging changes in the manner in which adolescents are diagnosed (as reviewed in the previous section). Perhaps as an example of this trend and as a demonstration that empirical findings can have an impact, transient situational disorder had been the most common diagnosis given to adolescents—it was even ascribed to one-fourth of psychiatric inpatients (U.S. HEW, 1966). Situational disorder was reported for 27.1 percent of the 1,334 adolescents surveyed in the cumulative psychiatric case register by Weiner and DelGaudio (1976) for Monroe County, New York. This magnitude would be consistent with a view of adolescent problems and turmoil as being expectable and generally benign. Recent research with hospitalized patients has not included a situational or adjustment reaction component among the diagnostic spectrum (e.g., Strober et al., 1981; Welner et al., 1979).

Surveys

Rutter (1980), generally reviewing carefully prepared British epidemiological surveys, reported that psychiatric disorders increase during adolescence and may be slightly higher than in midadulthood. Prevalence can be a function of how it is measured. Disorders are found in 10–15 percent of 14–15-year-olds, but these figures jump to 21 percent when including those who are experiencing stress but who are not noticed by parents or teachers. The higher figure follows from self-report and psychiatric interview ratings. Referrals to clinics increased during adolescence for girls but remained stable for boys between 10 and 15 years of age. The following disorders increased during adolescence: suicide and suicide attempts; alcohol and drug abuse; schizophrenia, which is uncommon until the midteens, followed by a steep increase during the latter half of the teen years; and anorexia nervosa and depression, both of which are associated more with late than early adolescence.

Employing categories equivalent to disorders of affect, behavior, and thought for those with psychiatric conditions, Rutter (1980) reports the following: (1) 40 percent had emotional disorders. This primarily includes depression, anxiety states, and affective disorders. Obsessive-compulsive disorders, hysteria, phobic states, and tics also

occurred; (2) 40 percent had conduct disorders; (3) less than 20 percent displayed a mixture of antisocial and emotional problems; and (4) psychosis occurred only in about 1/1000 cases. Amongst inpatients, psychosis occurred in 15 percent of those who were under 14.5 years of age and in 25 percent of the older adolescents.

Weiner and DelGaudio (1976) reported the following distribution of disorders among a sample of 1,334 psychiatric patients between 12 and 18 years of age: personality disorder (31.4 percent), situational disorder (27.1 percent), neurosis (13.3 percent), schizophrenia (8.5 percent), suicide attempts (2.8 percent), organic brain syndrome (1.8 percent), and other disorders (14.8 percent). Two alcoholic patients and one with an affective psychosis are also reported. The last finding is remarkable, and it will be seen that recent studies report a significantly greater incidence of affective disorders. It is felt that this shift reflects a number of factors. Basically, the *Zeitgeist* has changed to the extent that affective disorders have become an area attracting greater attention, diagnostic criteria have been sharpened, a wider array of psychopharmacological agents are currently available for treatment, etiological models based on biological functioning have been offered, and theorists now allow for the possibility of affective disorders in children and adolescents.

There are consistently reported differences in adolescent psychopathology between boys and girls. After puberty, more emotional disorders are found in females than males (Rutter, 1980). This includes depression, hysteria, and neuroticism. Similarly, Weiner and DelGaudio (1976) report that, among those with disorders, neuroses and suicide attempts are more prevalent among females, but that personality disorders occur with greater frequency in males. The corresponding percentages for each disorder are as follows: neurosis (15.4 percent vs. 11.7 percent), suicide attempts (4.5 percent vs. 1.5 percent), and personality disorders (33.7 percent vs. 28.5 percent).

Rutter also reported a relationship between social class and adolescent psychopathology.

Neurosis and situational disorders are more frequent among higher than lower social classes while personality disorders and schizophrenia show the opposite relationship. These parallel the findings for adults.

Hospitalized Adolescents

The findings with hospitalized adolescents reported by various investigators at different clinical centers will follow. There is some difficulty in comparing studies because different diagnostic criteria are often used and there is a disparate range of ages observed. However, these studies are of interest because they do not always employ broad clinical categories (such as those used in surveys) and therefore provide a finer picture of the range of adolescent dysfunction.

Hospitalized adolescents need not be viewed as a fairly homogeneous group. Strober et al. (1981) based their diagnoses on DSM-III criteria and employed 13 different diagnoses when classifying 95 patients between 12 and 17 years of age. The majority of the adolescents, based on the opinion of at least one of two raters using records and structured interview data, were placed in the following diagnostic categories: conduct disorders (22.1 percent), personality disorders (20 percent), major affective disorders (17.8 percent), schizophrenia (15.7 percent), and undiagnosed (14.7 percent).

Research diagnostic criteria (e.g., Feighner et al., 1972), which had some influence on the development of DSM-III, also allow for a picture of the diversity of adolescent psychopathology. Hudgens (1974) employed such diagnostic criteria in a three-year study at Washington University in St. Louis. His group interviewed 110 adolescents 48 hours after admission. Their mean age was 16.5 years (SD = 2.04 years) and 60 percent of the population was female. Their diagnoses and frequency, in parenthesis, follow: depression (19), mania (11), schizophrenia (6), antisocial personality (7), and one patient each for mental deficiency, organic brain syndrome, alcoholism, and anorexia nervosa. Twenty-nine patients were unclassified, one had no psychiatric illness, and the remainder were undiagnosed

although it was possible to state which disorders their conditions most resembled.

A somewhat different picture emerges when broader diagnostic categories are used. Table 31.1 presents the distribution of adolescents diagnosed as neurotic, behavior disordered, personality disordered, psychotic, and schizophrenic in three follow-up studies of hospitalized patients. These categories generally include a wider range of pathology than represented in DSM-III groupings. The diversity of symptoms that can be found among patients so classified is indicated by Haslam (1978). Fifty-eight percent had phobic symptoms. Patients also demonstrated the following symptoms: anxiety (n = 30), serious depression (n = 36), thought disorder (n = 8), ideas of reference (n = 2), depersonalization phenomena (n = 9), pathological moodiness (n = 16), and marked aggression (n = 8). It does not appear that the classification system represented in Table 31.1 reflects these symptoms in a therapeutically useful manner. Most noteworthy is the frequency of affective symptoms (perhaps, in part, treatable pharmacologically) not captured by these diagnoses. To a certain extent, one must wonder if the doubt about the presence of affective disorders in adolescents was nurtured by a classificatory scheme that did not foster such diagnoses despite the presence of relevant symptomatology.

King and Pittman (1971) indicated that the broad diagnostic categories did not adequately predict the course of psychiatric disorders. When they used syndromes, their diagnoses tended to be more stable and they could accurately predict recovery or remission in 84 percent of subjects so classified. Syndromes included chronic brain syndrome, schizophrenia, sociopathy, acute brain syndrome, schizoaffective disorders, and affective disorders.

Several studies have examined the relation between various symptoms and the course of psychiatric illnesses. While these findings can be of some interest, a symptom approach may have its own shortcomings. Gossett et al. (1977) rated former patients on their current level of functioning more than one year after hospital discharge (range: 20 months–4 years). Several variables, such as severity of diagno-

Table 31.1   Distribution of Adolescent Psychiatric Disorders

Study	N	Ages	Neurotic	Behavior Disorder	Personality Disorder	Psychotic	Schizophrenia
Gossett et al. (1977)	55	13–19	10(18)[a]	31(56)	N/A[b]	14(25)	N/A
King and Pittman (1971)	65	17–19	10(15)	13(25)	N/A	10(15)	19(29)
Haslam (1978)	50	14–19	21(42)	N/A	15(30)	10(20)	N/A

Note. Data taken among hospitalized patients using broad diagnostic categories.
[a]Number in parentheses reflects percent of total sample.
[b]Indicates investigators did not employ this category.

sis, completeness of treatment termination, process or reactive onset, continuation of psychotherapy following hospitalization, and others, correlated with level of functioning. With all variables included, severity of onset accounted for most of the variance (.19). It could also be stated that a good outcome was found among one-third of the psychotic patients. Haslam (1978) was able to report correlations between symptoms and outcome. For example, phobic symptoms were significantly correlated with positive outcome ($r = .26$); depressive and aggressive symptoms were related to the appearance of residual symptoms; and thought disorder correlated with hospital readmission. Haslam (1978) points to some shortcomings of this type of approach. Fifty-four percent of matched, nonpsychiatric controls showed phobic symptoms. Therefore, the meaningfulness of a single symptom is unclear, the amount of variance accounted for is small, and there is considerable overlap between symptom clusters of the different diagnostic groups employed.

If adolescent psychopathology is looked at within a developmental perspective, it would be expected that the broad category approach, along with symptom correlations, would yield disappointing results. Further, it would be expected that its clinical usefulness would be limited because the patient, the possessor of the symptoms, is nowhere to be found. In effect, what is required is a method for studying individual differences over time. General issues of continuity and stability in development need to be considered (cf. Brim & Kagan, 1980).

During periods of relatively rapid change in development (e.g., infancy, adolescence), it is to be expected that different behaviors will be shown at different points in time, the frequency of behaviors that continue to occur will change in relation to the total behavioral matrix, and the meaning of a behavior can change as a function of age. Therefore, what may remain stable is a person described by an underlying psychological organization that can characterize the individual in relation to others at a particular point in development. The organization or structure can be described according to one's theoretical preference, or even atheoretically, but there is a recognition here that the emphasis may have to be placed on the meaning and organization of particular behaviors, perhaps including accompanying affect, rather than individual behaviors themselves. If one wants to see how adolescents change as they develop, regardless of questions about emotional disorders, it may be necessary to turn from seeking behavioral identities, or even from trying to specify how one form of a behavior may be replaced by a different one at a later time (e.g. Oldham, Looney, & Bloteky, 1980), to studying continuities in other ways. Recent work with young children (Block & Block, 1980) and infants

(Sroufe, 1979), which examines stability in styles of adaptation over time, may offer some guidelines.

Ford et al. (1978) did a follow-up study with adolescents whose disorders were classified as Undiagnosed Psychiatric Illness during their first hospitalization. They represented 22 percent of the patients from a larger sample being studied by those at Washington University in St. Louis (Hudgens, 1974; Welner et al., 1979). After an average of 7.2 years, 24 of 31 patients were contacted. Seventy-one percent (n = 15) had psychiatric illness during the interval and 11 of them were still symptomatic. Eighty percent of those still with problems could now be diagnosed. Regarding this change in ease of diagnosis it remains to be determined if certain individuals with certain disorders do not show characteristic symptomatology until after adolescence or if the earlier organizations of certain syndromes remain to be identified.

For example, for these undiagnosed adolescents, variables such as sex, race, age of onset, duration, birth order, length of hospitalization, history of suicide attempts, and family illness did not differentiate the 15 patients who continued to have problems after hospitalization from those who functioned well (Ford et al., 1978). However, psychotic symptoms such as delusions, hallucinations, thought disorder, and bizarre behavior did not occur among those who were well after hospitalization. They did occur in 11 of the 15 patients who remained ill, and these 11 patients appeared in all diagnostic groups.

King and Pittman (1971) interviewed 19 adolescents six years after they were hospitalized. All had been diagnosed as schizophrenic. Sixty-three percent did not have remissions. None of these subjects showed psychotic symptomatology until a few days prior to admission. All but one of those who had remained ill were severely ill prior to admission. Thus this study and the previous one indicate the importance of psychotic symptomatology but had different findings regarding the predictive value of the duration of the disorder. Among other possibilities, it may be

that the predictive value of a particular variable is a function of the diagnostic group being studied (e.g., Undiagnosed vs. Schizophrenic), that is, a function of the organization in which it is embedded.

Welner et al. (1979) provide information about the stability of diagnosis when strict criteria are used. They interviewed 77 of 110 patients nine years after index hospitalization. Seventeen percent were schizophrenic. Seven of the 13 subjects in this group had a different initial diagnosis. Twelve adolescents (16 percent) met the criteria for bipolar affective disorder. Eleven of them had a chronic course, including three males who committed suicide. This occurred despite the use of lithium. Sixteen (12 percent) were diagnosed as antisocial personalities, but seven of them were originally hospitalized for depressive symptomatology. Nine (12 percent) were diagnosed as having secondary depression. The Undiagnosed Disorder and No Illness groups each constituted 10 percent of the follow-up sample. The approach taken by this St. Louis group indicates the value of using clearly defined criteria that can result in reliably diagnosed groups. In addition to presenting the frequency of various disorders found in hospitalized patients, this approach provides the opportunity for following patients longitudinally with a degree of detail not possible with broad band categories. Also, this empirical approach can allow for modification. Welner et al. (1979) suggest that the research criteria for schizophrenia may lead to underdiagnosis or misdiagnosis in adolescents. This suggests that the schizophrenic organization may differ at various developmental points and should be indexed accordingly. Final note should be made of the frequency of affective disorders found in adolescents when diagnostic criteria allow for them.

It seems that approaches that have tried to emphasize careful diagnostic criteria, using signs and symptoms of syndromes when possible, have provided the clearest picture available thus far of the diversity and prevalence of psychiatric disorders among those adolescents demonstrating emotional problems. It is clear, though, that such approaches do not offer automatic solutions to all problems. For example, Mattison et al. (1979) found an average interrater reliability of 54 percent for Axis I syndromes for children on DSM-III—not at all satisfactory. However, Strober et al. (1981) have shown that reliable diagnoses can occur with DSM-III criteria when data are carefully gathered. A careful training in the deployment of the criteria is necessary to insure reliability of diagnoses. This may be especially important with adolescents.

Affective Disorders

Depressive Disorders

As already indicated, it has been shown that adolescents meeting clearly stated criteria for affective disorders can be identified among adolescent psychiatric populations. Further, the incidence of adolescent affective disorders may be substantially higher than previously thought. It is important to distinguish, though, between the presence of depressive symptomatology and a true depressive disorder.

Rutter (1980) reported that depressive disorders increase in frequency during adolescence. He used self-report and interview procedures with prepubescent ($n = 19$), pubescent ($n = 45$), and postpubertal boys ($n = 19$). Signs of depression included interview ratings of Misery and Self-Deprecation and self-report indications of being Miserable. Approximately 30 percent of the postpubertal boys showed signs of depression on all three measures and the pubescent boys were at an intermediate level among the three groups. Other interviews with those 14–15 years of age found that more than 40 percent said they felt miserable and depressed, 20 percent had feelings of self-deprecation, 7–8 percent had suicidal ideas, and 25 percent felt people were looking at them. More than 20 percent indicated on self-ratings that they felt depressed and had trouble sleeping. Rutter notes that these feelings may be fairly common in this age group but at a marked level in a minority of them. He also points out that developmental changes in self-expression coincide with these increased reports of depressive symptomatology.

Albert and Beck (1975) administered a 3-part questionnaire to 31 seventh- and 31 eighth-grade boys and girls. The questionnaire included 13 items constituting a short form of the Beck Depression Inventory (BDI). Using a cut-off point determined for adult populations, they found that there was a trend toward more depression among eighth-graders, especially girls, and that 33 percent of the entire sample was in the range of moderate-to-severe depressive symptomatology. The authors noted that these BDI scores were higher than those found in adulthood. It is not possible at the time to know how to interpret this finding. Klerman (1976) has noted an increase in nonpsychotic, reactive-looking depression among late adolescents. Their symptoms involve self-pitying, irritable, and depersonalized types of depression. He suggests that political-social factors contribute here. A direction for future work would seem to involve coordinating lifespan factors that could include generational adjustment demands, phase specific psychological issues, and phase specific biological features, in order to establish age appropriate diagnostic criteria indicating core features of a depressive disorder as well as those features which may systematically vary between different ages.

The points raised by Lefkowitz and Burton (1978) about childhood depression are relevant here. They note that the incidence of depressive symptoms in the Albert and Beck study, and in several other studies with younger children, is so high that such subjects could not be viewed as deviant from a statistical, epidemiological standpoint. Their work indicates the importance of longitudinal research to follow the natural course of these symptoms to determine which might be considered phase specific features of adolescence that diminish with age. It is also clear that well-defined criteria are needed so that the adolescent with a depressive disorder can be distinguished from those showing nonpathological depressive symptoms. Carlson and Cantwell (1980b) were able to show that

DSM-III criteria for a depressive disorder can be useful here. Of 102 adolescent patients, 28 percent met DSM-III criteria for a depressive disorder. This included 36 percent of their inpatient population and 16 percent of those attending an outpatient clinic. Of this same group, these authors indicated that 49 percent displayed a depressive syndrome based on scores on the Short Children's Depression Inventory, and 60 percent showed depressive symptoms on initial screening. Thus distinctions between depressive symptoms and affective disorders can be made with adolescents.

Many current investigators have turned to DSM-III, thereby using the same diagnostic criteria for identifying depressive disorders at all points in the lifespan. This should perhaps be viewed as a statement of a null hypothesis rather than a definitive statement about the nature of adolescent depression. Modifications in criteria can be based on empirical findings. It must also be noted that methods of gathering data relevant to this position are simultaneously being developed and the reliability and validity of questionnaires completed by parents and patients and of interviews performed by professionals remain to be clearly demonstrated.

Cytryn, McKnew, and Bunney (1980) recently compared the diagnostic criteria for depression detailed in DSM-III with criteria used by several investigators working with children. They concluded that child and adult criteria for affective disorders are similar and DSM-III seems valid for diagnosing childhood depression. This statement can be extrapolated to adolescents. However, construct validity remains to be demonstrated. Among the common features in the systems they reviewed are dysphoria, sadness, hopelessness, loss of appetite, sleep disturbance, loss of pleasure, decreased concentration, low self-esteem, aggression, suicidal thoughts, and psychomotor retardation. Disturbance in school, family, and other social settings is included.

Acceptance of the existence of depressive disorders in children and adolescents has solved another problem. It is no longer necessary to assume that an underlying depression in the child is masked (Cytryn & McKnew, 1972; Cytryn et al., 1980) or that certain behaviors reflect depressive equivalents (Bemporad & Wilson, 1978) and are appearing in situations when depression would be expected (e.g., following loss). Carlson and Cantwell (1980a) have shown that depressive disorders can coexist with hyperactivity, aggressive behaviors, and antisocial behaviors and that what had been suggested as signs of masked depression may just be symptoms of depression in children and adolescents (Kovacs & Beck, 1977). Carlson and Strober (1979) also suggest that the distinction between primary and secondary depression is useful and, for the latter, indicates that an affective component can exist along with other disorders. Again, Carlson and Cantwell's work stresses methodology in that their conclusions could only follow from their use of a highly structured interview format that elucidates relevant symptomatology in a reliable way. Others have also found little empirical support for the concept of depressive equivalents among adolescents with diagnosed depressive disorders (Hudgens, 1974; Inamdar et al., 1979).

Carlson and Strober (1979) identified 28 adolescents from a hospitalized population of 130 who met DSM-III criteria for unipolar affective disorder. Thirty-three symptoms were detailed; 17 of them occurred in half the patients. They point out that a similar symptom picture is found with adolescents and adults. Hudgens (1974) identified 25 adolescents with a definite unipolar affective disorder and also concluded that these patients resembled adults. These patients ranged in age from 14–19 years with a mean age of onset of 15.9 years (range: 10–19 years). Twenty-six percent had made at least one suicide attempt. Almost half had recurrent affective symptoms. Hallucinations were rare, but 50 percent had disturbed memory and 84 percent had difficulty concentrating. Gallemore and Wilson (1972) used DSM-II criteria to identify adolescents with affective disorders. They also concluded that the basic disorder is similar to that found in adults. More than half showed a decrease in sleep and appetite and had suicidal thoughts. They also had problems in concentrating.

Hudgens (1974) reported a high incidence of psychiatric disorders among his patients' parents and Carlson and Strober (1979) found that 43 percent of their unipolar patients had a family history of affective disorders.

Inamdar et al. (1979) used a structured interview in the process of identifying 30 depressed patients between 12 and 18 years of age. These investigators also compared the adolescent symptom picture with that reported for adults but did not find as much overlap as reported by Hudgens (1974) and Carlson and Strober (1979). The adult symptoms that they did not find in adolescents included restlessness, pacing and hand wringing, agitation, motor retardation, feelings of persecution, delusions of guilt, and hopelessness. Sexuality and libido could not be reliably measured, but Gallemore and Wilson (1972) found that, unlike adults, libido and sexual potential were unaffected in their adolescent patients. Symptoms reported by Inamdar et al. (1979) in at least 70 percent of their subjects included depressed mood associated with boredom, loss of interest and pleasure in activities, difficulty concentrating, decreased school performance, and suicidal ideation. Half their patients also had episodic intense moods, socially withdrew when depressed, felt lonely, unloved, and were self-deprecating. In addition, Gallemore and Wilson (1972) also reported finding anger in more than half their subjects.

Some investigators report an acute onset in their depressed adolescent patients (Gallemore & Wilson, 1972) while others find it can be gradual or acute (Hudgens, 1974; Inamdar et al., 1979). Clear precipitants may not be found in more than half (Gallemore & Wilson, 1974; Inamdar et al., 1979).

Several conclusions emerge thus far: (1) depression can be reliably diagnosed in adolescents; (2) similar criteria can be used to identify adults and adolescents with affective disorders; and (3) there is an appreciable degree of similarity between adult and adolescent depressive symptomatology but notable

distinctions as well. It can be expected that the use of standardized diagnostic criteria based on observable phenomena will contribute toward clearer comparisons between findings obtained by different groups of investigators because it will allow for a more confident assumption that the subject populations being compared indeed have the same disorder. However, it is also clear that diagnostic reliability is not an automatic byproduct with DSM-III or other research criteria (Mattison et al., 1979). Carefully devised data-gathering procedures are essential (Strober et al., 1981).

While it is felt that recent diagnostic approaches and accompanying findings have offered exciting additions to our understanding of adolescent depression, additions that should enhance therapeutic effectiveness as it relates to pharmacological treatment approaches, there is also a rich clinical literature that should not be lost because it, too, has psychotherapeutic usefulness. Further, this literature can be useful for generating research hypotheses because it suggests that depressed adolescents are not a unitary group.

Anthony (1970), basing his formulation on psychodynamic theory, has posited two types of clinical depression. He distinguishes these from normative adolescent depression, which is attributed to the loosening of object ties as the adolescent continues the process of separation-individuation (Blos, 1967). Malmquist (1971b) also attributes normative adolescent mood swings to this process. Also, Anthony believes that normative depression has a reactive component while the clinical form has its roots in childhood.

Those with a psychodynamic viewpoint have espoused a developmental orientation in which the form and symptoms of depression are thought to vary with the stage of development (Bemporad & Wilson, 1978; Malmquist, 1971a, 1971b). Anthony (1970) has taken such an approach and has contrasted adolescent depressions that have preoedipal and oedipal roots. The former is based on intrapsychic ties to an omnipotent mother who is sadistic, disparaging, and reproachful to the child. These adolescents have not adequately separated themselves physically or psychologically from their mothers. They experience a sense of help-lessness along with feelings of shame and humiliation. Those whose depression stems from the oedipal level have a more well-articulated sense of self and are able to experience guilt. They feel hostility towards parents who are not what they were idealized to be. The anger at the parents, or for the idealized parent by whom the adolescent has felt betrayed, is turned back onto the self. Suicide can be viewed as punishment for the wish to kill them.

Psychometric approaches have also been taken. These include attempts to develop a MMPI depression scale (Mezzich & Mezzich, 1979b) and cluster analysis of depressive symptomatology (Mezzich & Mezzich, 1979a). Using the latter approach, Mezzich and Mezzich (1979a) have identified three groups of depressed adolescents: restless, socially frustrated, and endogenous. The endogenous were so named because their self-blame and vegetative signs are similar to those found in adults with endogenous depression.

Bipolar Disorders

The findings of several investigators indicate that bipolar affective disorders are not restricted to adults. Loranger and Levine (1978) selected for review the hospital charts of 100 males and 100 females who met research diagnostic criteria for bipolar affective illness. These would be similar to DSM-III criteria. It was necessary to review 178 male and 215 female charts to reach the desired sample size. Early twenties was the peak period of age of onset; one-third were hospitalized before age 25; and 20 percent of the sample showed signs of the illness as adolescents. One-third of the manic-depressive patients seen by Winokur, Clayton, and Reich (1969) had their onset before age 20 and 40 percent of those studied by Perris (1968) were between 15 and 25 years of age. An increasing number of case reports of adolescent bipolar illness (Berg et al., 1974; Engstrom, Robbins, & May, 1978; Horowitz, 1977; Weizman et al., 1979; White & O'Shanick, 1977) and controlled investigations of this disorder (Carlson, Davenport, & Jamison, 1977; Carlson & Strober, 1978a; Carlson &

Strober, 1979; Hudgens, 1974) have been appearing in the literature.

Several authors have suggested that the incidence of manic-depressive illness among adolescents has been underestimated (Bowden & Sarabia, 1980; Carlson & Strober, 1978a; Preador & Wolpert, 1979). Reasons generally offered for this are as follows. Mistaken expectations about normative adolescent turmoil or the belief that bipolar disorders do not occur in adolescents may lead some not to think of this diagnosis. More likely, perhaps, is the misdiagnosis of the disorder because of the distracting effect of these patients' hyperactivity (Bowden & Sarabia, 1980), its confusion with schizophrenia (Bowden & Sarabia, 1980; Carlson & Strober, 1978a, 1978b), or a reluctance to give the adolescent a diagnosis that could potentially hurt his or her reputation (Bowden & Sarabia, 1980). Bowden and Sarabia (1980) point out that when the Research Diagnostic Criteria are used, the incidence of schizophrenia and manic-depressive disorder is similar.

The diagnostic picture is also confusing because the range of symptoms shown by adolescents receiving a bipolar diagnosis based on usual signs (e.g., DSM-III) can be considerable. This can include clinical syndromes such as alcoholism, delinquency, stupor, and excitement (Puig-Antich, 1980), anorexia (Berg et al., 1974), as well as school refusal, learning problems (Berg et al., 1974; Bowden & Sarabia, 1980), and antisocial behavior. Hudgens (1974) suggests that differential diagnosis involves encephalitis, neurological conditions, drug reactions, and schizophrenia.

It seems, though, that the major factor contributing to diagnostic difficulty here is the incidence of psychotic features among manic adolescents. Five of 11 hospitalized manic patients studied by Hudgens (1974) had psychotic symptoms such as hallucinations and delusions. Carlson and Strober (1978) report on the hospital chart review and subsequent follow-up of six patients initially diagnosed as schizophrenic but who displayed manic-depressive illness in later hospitalization. Their average age was almost 15 years at first hospitalization and 19 years at follow-up. Of the 23 reported episodes of mania (17) and depression (6), psychotic symptoms were present in 10 of them. At some point during the illness, all patients experienced psychotic symptoms and three patients showed recurrent psychotic symptomatology. Three of these patients had paranoid ideation.

In another series with nine patients identified by DSM-III criteria, paranoid delusions and confusion were found in 66 percent and hallucination in 50 percent (Carlson & Strober, 1979). This compares with a frequency of 33 percent, 19 percent, and 6 percent, respectively, in adults with bipolar affective disorders. Carlson and Strober (1979) indicated that only one of these nine patients had been accurately diagnosed. Carlson and Strober (1978a) argue that with research diagnostic criteria, manic-depressive adolescents can be distinguished from schizophrenics and that the characteristics of the affective disorder are recognizable at an early point. Further, they indicate that follow-up work shows that schizophrenics with a favorable outcome had manic-depressive symptoms. Consistent with this view, Horowitz (1977) described eight patients between 15 and 18 years who were diagnosed as having acute schizophrenic reaction upon hospital admission but later rediagnosed as having an affective disorder [using Feighner et al. (1972) criteria]. Auditory hallucinations were present in five of these patients, six demonstrated delusions of grandiosity, and four had persecutory delusions.

Carlson and Strober (1979) present data that allow for a comparison of symptomatology in adolescent and adult bipolar patients. The letter following each symptom indicates if it was observed during a depressive (D) or manic (M) phase of the illness. The adolescent data is derived from nine patients classified by DSM-III criteria. The following symptoms were demonstrated with somewhat similar frequency by adolescents and adults: dysphoric mood (D), irritability (M), hyperactivity (M), poor concentration (D), suicidal thought (D), and euphoria (M). Symptoms only or more frequently present in adolescents included: anhedonia (D), paranoid delusions (D), auditory hallucinations (D), confusion (D), insomnia (M), and paranoid grandiosity (M). Those found with greater frequency in adults include low self-esteem (D), fatigue (D), insomnia (D), anorexia (D), somatic complaints (D), and agitation (M). In general, adolescent-adult differences were more apparent during depressive than manic phases. It seems, too, that those features found more frequently in adolescents were disorders of thinking or ego functioning while the more frequent adult features related to vegetative signs or possible concomitants of superego functioning. This could be taken as consistent with psychodynamic theorizing reflecting the ongoing development of the ego and relatively weak superego (A. Freud, 1958) of the adolescent contrasted with the more solidified character structure of the adult.

Also consistent with this is Puig-Antich's (1980) report that state alterations during bipolar illness are more frequent in youngsters than adults. It may well be that these age differences in features of the disorder are related to developmental differences in physiology or are features of the disorder itself. However, at a different level of analysis, and for clinical purposes because treatment for these adolescents requires psychotherapy along with pharmacotherapy, a model—be it psychodynamic or otherwise—reflecting the psychological organization and the manner in which these adolescents construct their world, is useful.

The clinical characteristics described by Horowitz (1977) in his eight patients included disorders of mood [disturbance ($n = 8$); elevation ($n = 7$); lability ($n = 8$); depression ($n = 3$)], thought [flight of ideas ($n = 7$); ideas of reference ($n = 7$); delusions ($n = 6$); hallucinations ($n = 5$)], and behavior [pressured speech ($n = 8$); hyperactivity ($n = 6$); distractibility ($n = 6$); hypersexuality ($n = 4$); aggression ($n = 5$)]. Bowden and Sarabia (1980) suggest that the antisocial behavior of manic adolescents is more episodic, less influenced by peers, and less likely to show disorders of conscience than that shown by true antisocial personalities.

The description of the premorbid personalities of adolescent manic patients has varied.

They have been described as energetic, outgoing, with some mild mood swings or hyperactivity (Bowden & Sarabia, 1980), diagnosed as hyperactive and treated with stimulants (White & O'Shanick, 1977) or passive, dependent, and shy (Horowitz, 1977). Some have reported finding no clear precipitants (Bowden & Sarabia, 1980); others point to lethargy, depression, and accompanying stress, such as graduation or going to college, prior to symptom onset (Horowitz, 1977). Carlson and Strober (1978a) found psychosocial precipitants in four of their six subjects, and five of them had onset of symptoms just before school started. None of their patients had a prior psychiatric illness.

The incidence of psychiatric disorders in relatives of manic adolescents is elevated. Forty-six percent of Hudgens' (1974) patients had at least one ill parent, half of the eight cases described by Horowitz (1977) had alcoholism or affective disorder in their family, and 54 percent of early-onset and 35 percent of late onset patients described by Carlson et al. (1977) had disturbed first-degree relatives. Psychiatric disturbance in relatives, typically an affective disorder, has often been reported in single case descriptions as well (e.g., Berg et al., 1974; White & O'Shanick, 1977). Puig-Antich (1980) points to the need for systematic family data gathered with standard procedures.

Hudgens (1974) reported that the course of the disorder involves a decline in hyperactivity and pressured speech before the mood returns to normal. Carlson and Strober (1978b) describe a case, first seen when the child was 12 years old, who over the course of six years presented as nonpsychotic depressed and was diagnosed as adjustment reaction, psychotic depression diagnosed as undifferentiated schizophrenia, and mild depression and hypomania. Their position (Carlson & Strober, 1978a, 1978b) is to view such variations in symptoms as reflecting phase specific changes in episodes or varying intensities of recurrent attacks of the illness.

Regarding outcome, Hudgens (1974) reported that eight of his 13 patients needed rehospitalization. Carlson et al. (1977), reporting no statistically significant differences on a variety of measures between adolescent (mean age = 15.8 years) and adult (mean age = 50.6 years) onset patients with bipolar affective disorders, also found no differences between them in outcome functioning. Sixty percent were well functioning, 20 percent functioned but with significant impairment, and 20 percent were chronically incapacitated. Call and Bland (1972), in their review, point to a poor outcome in 17–47 percent of adolescents with manic-depressive illness but caution that the latter figure reflects conditions before the use of lithium.

Carlson and Strober (1978a) report that three of their six patients had dramatic improvements with lithium. These patients were also responsive to psychotherapy. White and O'Shanick (1977) detail their patient's improvement with lithium, and all eight of Horowitz's (1977) patients had a complete remission of psychotic features when therapeutic blood levels of lithium were reached. Adolescents appear to require higher doses of lithium than do adults (Berg et al., 1974; Engstrom et al. 1978). Youngerman and Canino (1978) present a careful review of the literature on the use of lithium carbonate with children and adolescents. Lithium was most effective in the 20 cases (18 adolescents) that met classic criteria for bipolar affective disorder. Many of these cases had a positive family history for bipolar disorder. They note that some cases had neurological dysfunction but could safely take lithium. A second group of patients had atypical major affective disorders with no clear alternating manic-depressive pattern. Lithium was least effective in a third group of severely disturbed patients who did not show clear affective symptoms. Only three of the 28 cases here showed some improvement with lithium.

Schizophrenia

Studies indicating the frequency of schizophrenia among disturbed adolescents were presented earlier in this chapter. It is clearly a disorder that occurs in youth. The incidence of schizophrenia was highest in the 15–24 year age group in the psychiatric case register of Monroe County, New York. At that age, it was shown by 2.57 white and 3.58 nonwhite males per 1,000 population. The peak age for women was in the 25–34 year age range. Forty-five percent of all cases of schizophrenia were in the 15–24 year old group (Babigian, 1975).

The features of the disorder and the psychological and psychosocial demands of adolescence are thought by Holzman and Grinker (1974) to account for this relationship between adolescence and schizophrenia. They delineated five features of schizophrenia: (1) difficulty in maintaining smooth, ordered thinking and perception; (2) lack of pleasure; (3) excessive dependency on family, teachers, or psychiatric staff; (4) an absence of general competence; and (5) a loss of self-esteem, which typically precipitated hospitalization. These are thought to reflect long-standing difficulties, perhaps with a physiological basis, that when coupled with the tasks of separation-individuation, school and vocational choices, and the interpersonal demands of adolescence, promote schizophrenia. They account for the gender difference in age of onset by suggesting that women experiencing difficulties can be sheltered by their families a bit longer. If so, one might expect the women's movement to contribute to changes in this statistic in the future.

Schizophrenia has often served as a focus for studying issues of diagnosis. The diagnostic problems here are not restricted to this disorder though, and may pose special difficulties with adolescents because so little is known about using the current descriptive nosologies with them.

The difficulty in diagnosing schizophrenic adolescents was previously alluded to when illustrating that many with a major affective disorder were misdiagnosed as schizophrenic. Hudgens (1974) suggested that psychosis is not a useful sign for identifying schizophrenics. The review of affective disorders demonstrated that psychotic symptomatology was found in a high number of these patients. However, the difficulty in diagnosing schizo-

phrenics is not restricted to the adolescent age group.

Spitzer and Fleiss (1974) reviewed several reliability studies of adult schizophrenia and found that the average reliability, reflected by the kappa statistic, was .57. Greater reliability can be achieved in at least two ways. First, clearly delineated criteria such as those reflected by the Feighner, Research Diagnostic Criteria, and DSM-III systems help. Second, the more information that is shared by raters, the higher their agreement with one another. It is noteworthy that a recent study demonstrating impressive reliability with DSM-III criteria with hospitalized adolescents (e.g., kappa for schizophrenia = .82), employed an interview-observer procedure in which both raters were present while patients were interviewed. The raters alternated as primary interviewers (Strober et al., 1981). Strober et al. (1981) also indicate the contribution of shared perspective and training to diagnostic reliability. It is important to be able to obtain this level of reliability, without which attempts to assess the validity of the diagnoses would be in vain.

While it is not unreasonable to anticipate that DSM-III can contribute to gains in diagnostic precision with all age groups, there must also be reservations. It is necessary to determine procedures with which greater reliability can be obtained by independent raters. Fenton, Mosher, and Matthews (1981) recently provided a detailed review of findings with current diagnostic systems as applied to schizophrenia. Included were the Feighner, Research Diagnostic Criteria, and DSM-III systems. They indicated that there is agreement on basic behaviors that can be called schizophrenia but that inclusion criteria will vary between systems. It was seen earlier that Feighner criteria, for example, may be likely to exclude many adolescent schizophrenics. Most importantly, they indicate that construct validity has not been demonstrated for any diagnostic system.

There seem to be at least two reproducible findings from the research completed thus far. First, there are several paths to adolescent schizophrenia. Second, there is a relationship between childhood adjustment and later adjustment following the onset of schizophrenia.

Ricks and Berry (1970) used case records to compare males who later developed schizophrenia with those cases having a more favorable outcome. The schizophrenic group contained some who showed a course marked by aggressive acting-out toward family members and others who showed a more withdrawn pattern of preschizophrenic behavior. Lewis and Shanok (1978) also posited a relationship between aggression and schizophrenia and reported a greater incidence of schizophrenia in the parents of adolescents seen in court than in parents of control adolescents. The withdrawn preschizophrenic pattern seems to characterize those who will have a less favorable adjustment in later life. Goldstein (1980) makes an important point about sampling. If schizophrenics with a poor premorbid adjustment are selected for study, then withdrawing behavior will appear to be the precursor of adolescent onset schizophrenia.

Masterson (1956) did a follow-up study of 153 hospitalized adolescents, 83 percent of whom were diagnosed schizophrenic. Fifty-six of these schizophrenic patients had a poor subsequent adjustment. Roff (1976) reported an unfavorable, chronic outcome in 61 percent of 33 adolescent onset schizophrenics and Annesley (cited in Robins, 1977) indicated that among hospitalized adolescent schizophrenics, 19 percent recover and 23 percent improve.

Masterson (1956) found that poor prior adjustment was associated with a poorer outcome, as was hospital admission prior to age 15. Aorkrog (1975), in a study of 100 adolescents diagnosed as psychotic or borderline (30 of whom were schizophrenic), reported that those with healthy childhoods were not admitted to the hospital before age 16. He also found that adolescent and childhood conditions were similar but the former was more intense, with additional symptomatology. A frequent finding is that those diagnosed as having single psychotic episodes or schizophrenia with affective features have better outcomes (e.g., Masterson, 1956; Roff, 1974, 1976). It was seen that some investigators regard this latter finding as suggestive of misdiagnosis.

Regarding psychotic symptomatology, Easson (1979) suggests that there is a critical period in adolescence, perhaps of one to two months, beyond which a thought disorder could result in chronic personality distortion. A thought disorder would be multiply determined and early signs could include: disorganization of thought integration shown by difficulty with abstract reasoning; distractibility; difficulty relaxing and fantasizing; difficulty controlling feelings and impulses; disturbed language, mood, and interpersonal relations.

CONCLUSION

A number of conclusions, compared with previous reports, follow from the research that has been reviewed. Recent findings indicate a higher incidence of affective disorders and a smaller incidence of situational disorders among adolescents with serious psychopathology. This includes a higher frequency of depressive and bipolar disorders. The latter had often been confused with schizophrenia. Psychotic symptomatology is not restricted to the latter diagnostic group and this has contributed to diagnostic difficulties. Investigators have begun to distinguish between depressive symptoms and depressive disorders and suggest that concepts such as masked depression and depressive equivalents are unnecessary. Bipolar disorders at the adolescent level typically involve thought processes and ego functions and the outcome is poor in approximately 20–45 percent of adolescents receiving this diagnosis.

A final comment about the difficulty of working with and diagnosing adolescents. There is truth to this but it is also necessary to guard against displacement onto patients who are not helping us with a difficult task. The disorders discussed here require the clinician and researcher to measure and distinguish between affects. They are not clearly observable, countable, or easily stated in our own words to colleagues. Why should adolescents be able to do it? It may be hard for patient and professional alike to distinguish between features such as blunted or depressed affect, apathy and psychomotor retardation. Until recently, affect, emotion, metacognition— areas basic to clinical work—have been given relatively less attention than other areas throughout psychology. Perhaps it is because they are hard for everyone to describe.

REFERENCES

Albert, N., & Beck, A. Incidence of depression in early adolescence: A preliminary study. *Journal of Youth and Adolescence,* 1975, **4,** 301–307.

Andreason, N., & Wasck, P. Adjustment disorders in adolescents and adults. *Archives of General Psychiatry,* 1980, **37,** 1166–1170.

Anthony, E.J. Two contrasting types of adolescent depression and their treatment. *Journal of the American Psychoanalytic Association,* 1970, **18,** 841–859.

Aorkrog, T. Psychotic and borderline psychotic adolescents. *Acta Psychiatrica Scandinavica,* 1975, **52,** 58–68.

Babigian, H. Schizophrenia: Epidemiology. In A. Freedman, H. Kaplan, & B. Sadock (Eds.), *Comprehensive textbook of psychiatry II.* (Vol. 1). Baltimore: Williams & Wilkins, 1975.

Bemporad, J., & Wilson, A. A developmental approach to depression in childhood and adolescence. *Journal of the American Academy of Psychoanalysis,* 1978, **6,** 325–352.

Berg, I., Hullin, R., Allsopp, M., O'Brien, P., & McDonald, R. Bipolar manic-depressive psychosis in early adolescence: A case report. *British Journal of Psychiatry,* 1974, **125,** 416–417.

Block, J., & Block, J. The role of ego-control and ego-resiliency in the organization of behavior. In A. Collins (Ed.), *Development of cognition, affect, and social relations. The Minnesota symposia on child psychology* (Vol. 13). Hillsdale, N.J.: Erlbaum, 1980.

Blos, P. The second individuation process of adolescence. *The Psychoanalytic Study of the Child,* 1967, **22,** 162–186.

Bowden, C., & Sarabia, F. Diagnosing manic-depressive illness in adolescents. *Comprehensive Psychiatry,* 1980, **21,** 263–269.

Brim, O., & Kagan, J. (Eds.). *Constancy and change in human development.* Cambridge: Harvard University Press, 1980.

Call, P., & Bland, R. Manic-depressive illness in adolescence and childhood. *American Journal of Psychiatry,* 1972, **24,** 255–263.

Carlson, G., & Cantwell, D. Unmasking masked depression in children and adolescents. *American Journal of Psychiatry,* 1980, **137,** 445–449. (a)

Carlson, G., & Cantwell, D. A survey of depressive symptoms, syndrome and disorder in a child psychiatric population. *Journal of Child Psychology and Psychiatry,* 1980, **21,** 19–25. (b)

Carlson, G., Davenport, Y., & Jamison, K. A comparison of outcome in adolescent- and late-onset bipolar manic-depressive illness. *American Journal of Psychiatry,* 1977, **134,** 919–922.

Carlson, G., & Strober, M. Manic-depressive illness in early adolescence. *Journal of the American Academy of Child Psychiatry,* 1978, **17,** 138–153. (a)

Carlson, G., & Strober, M. Affective disorder in adolescence: Issues in misdiagnosis. *Journal of Clinical Psychiatry,* 1978, **39,** 59–66. (b)

Carlson, G., & Strober, M. Affective disorders in adolescence. *Psychiatric Clinics of North America,* 1979, **2,** 511–526.

Cytryn, L., & McKnew, D. Proposed classification of childhood depression. *American Journal of Psychiatry,* 1972, **129,** 149–155.

Cytryn, L., McKnew, D., & Bunney, W. Diagnosis of depression in children: A reassessment. *American Journal of Psychiatry,* 1980, **137,** 22–25.

Diagnostic and statistical manual of mental disorders (3rd ed.). Washington: American Psychiatric Association, 1980.

Easson, W. The early manifestations of adolescent thought disorder. *Journal of Clinical Psychiatry,* 1979, **40,** 467–475.

Elkind, D. *Children and adolescents.* New York: Oxford University Press, 1974.

Engstrom, F., Robbins, D., & May, J. Manic-depressive illness in adolescence. *Journal of the American Academy of Child Psychiatry,* 1978, **17,** 514–520.

Feighner, J., Robins, E., Guze, S., Woodruff, R., Winokur, G., & Munoz, R. Diagnostic criteria for use in psychiatric research. *Archives of*

General Psychiatry, 1972, **26,** 57-63.

Fenton, W., Mosher, L., & Matthews, S. Diagnosis of schizophrenia: A critical review of current diagnostic systems. *Schizophrenia Bulletin,* 1981, **7,** 452-475.

Ford, K., Hudgens, R., & Wilner, A. Undiagnosed psychiatric illness in adolescents. *Archives of General Psychiatry,* 1978, **35,** 279-282.

Freud, A. Adolescence. *Psychoanalytic Study of the Child,* 1958, **13,** 255-278.

Gallemore, J., & Wilson, W. Adolescent maladjustment or affective disorder. *American Journal of Psychiatry,* 1972, **129,** 608-612.

Goldstein, M. The course of schizophrenic psychosis. In O. Brim & J. Kagan (Eds.), *Constancy and change in human development.* Cambridge: Harvard University Press, 1980.

Gossett, J., Barnhart, D., Lewis, J., & Phillips, V. Follow-up of adolescents treated in a psychiatric hospital. *Archives of General Psychiatry,* 1977, **34,** 1037-1042.

Hall, G.S. *Adolescence.* New York: Appleton, 1904.

Haslam, M. A study of psychiatric illness in adolescence. Psychiatric breakdown in adolescence: Diagnosis and prognosis. *International Journal of Social Psychiatry,* 1978, **24,** 287-294.

Holzman, P., & Grinker, R. Schizophrenia in adolescence. *Journal of Youth and Adolescence,* 1974, **3,** 167-279.

Horowitz, H. Lithium and the treatment of adolescent manic-depressive illness. *Diseases of the Nervous System,* 1977, **38,** 480-483.

Hudgens, R. *Psychiatric disorders in adolescents.* Baltimore: Williams & Wilkins, 1974.

Inamdar, S., Scoriopoulous, G., Osborn, M., & Bianchi, E. Phenomenology associated with depressed mood in adolescents. *American Journal of Psychiatry,* 1979, **136,** 156-159.

Inhelder, B., & Piaget, J. *The growth of logical thinking.* New York: Basic Books, 1958.

Kagan, J. Perspectives on continuity. In O. Brim & J. Kagan (Eds.), *Constancy and change in human development.* Cambridge: Harvard University Press, 1980.

Kashani, J., Husain, A., Shekeni, W., Hodges, K., Cytryn, L., & McKnew, D. Current perspectives on childhood depression. *American Journal of Psychiatry,* 1981, **138,** 143-153.

King, L., & Pittman, G. A follow-up of 65 adolescent schizophrenia patients. *Diseases of the Nervous System,* 1971, **32,** 328-334.

Klerman, G. Age and clinical depression: Today's youth in the 21st century. *Journal of Gerontology,* 1976, **31,** 318-323.

Kovacs, M., & Beck, A. An empirical-clinical approach towards a definition of childhood depression. In J. Schulterbrandt & A. Raskin (Eds.), *Depression in childhood.* New York: Raven, 1977.

Lefkowitz, M., & Burton, N. Childhood depression: A critique of the concept. *Psychological Bulletin,* 1978, **85,** 716-726.

Lewis, D., & Shanok, S. Delinquency and the schizophrenic spectrum of disorders. *Journal of the American Academy of Child Psychiatry,* 1978, **17,** 263-276.

Loranger, A., & Levine, P. Age at onset of bipolar affective illness. *Archives of General Psychiatry,* 1978, **35,** 1345-1348.

Malmquist, C. Depressions in childhood and adolescence. *New England Journal of Medicine,* 1971, **284,** 884-893. (a)

Malmquist, C. Depression in childhood and adolescence. *New England Journal of Medicine,* 1971, **284,** 955-961. (b)

Masterson, J. Prognosis in adolescent disorders. *Journal of Nervous and Mental Disease,* 1956, **124,** 219-231.

Masterson, J. *The psychiatric dilemma of adolescence.* London: Churchill, 1967.

Mattison, R., Cantwell, D., Russell, A. & Will, L. A comparison of DSM-II and DSM-III in the diagnosis of childhood psychiatric disorders: II. *Archives of General Psychiatry,* 1979, **36,** 1217-1228.

Mezzich, A. & Mezzich, J. A data-based typology of depressed adolescence. *Journal of Personality Assessment,* 1979, **43,** 238-246. (a)

Mezzich, A., & Mezzich, J. Symptomatology of depression in adolescence. *Journal of Personality Assessment,* 1979, **43,** 267-275. (b)

Offer, D., & Offer, J. *From teenage to young manhood: A psychological study.* New York: Basic Books, 1975.

Offer, D., Ostrow, E., & Howard, K. The mental health professional's concept of the normal adolescent. *Archives of General Psychiatry,* 1981, **38,** 149-152.

Oldham, D., Looney, J., & Bloteky, M. Clinical assessment of symptoms in adolescents. *American Journal of Orthopsychiatry,* 1980, **50,** 697-703.

Perris, C. The course of depressive psychosis. *Acta Psychiatrica Scandinavica,* 1968, **44,** 238-248.

Preador, D., & Wolpert, E. Manic-depressive illness in adolescence. *Journal of Youth and Adolescence,* 1979, **8,** 111–130.

Puig-Antich, J. Affective disorders in childhood: A review and perspective. *The Psychiatric Clinics of North America,* 1980, **3,** 403–424.

Ricks, D., & Berry, J. Family and symptom patterns that precede schizophrenia. In M. Roff & D. Ricks (Eds.), *Life history research in psychopathology.* Minneapolis: University of Minnesota Press, 1970.

Robins, L. Follow-up studies. In H. Quay & J. Werry (Eds.), *Psychopathological disorders of childhood* (2nd ed.). New York: Wiley, 1979.

Roff, J. Adolescent schizophrenia: Variables related to differences in long-term adult outcome. *Journal of Consulting and Clinical Psychology,* 1974, **42,** 180–183.

Roff, J. Adolescent development and family characteristics associated with a diagnosis of schizophrenia. *Journal of Consulting and Clinical Psychology,* 1976, **44,** 933–939.

Rutter, M. *Changing youth in a changing society.* Cambridge: Harvard University Press, 1980.

Spitzer, R., Endicott, J., & Robins, E. Research diagnostic criteria. *Archives of General Psychiatry,* 1978, **35,** 773–782.

Spitzer, R. & Fleiss, J. A reanalysis of the reliability of psychiatric diagnosis. *British Journal of Psychology,* 1974, **125,** 341–347.

Sroufe, A. Affective development in infancy. In J. Osofsky (Ed.), *Handbook of infant development.* New York: Wiley, 1979.

Strober, M. Green, J., & Carlson, G. Reliability of psychiatric diagnosis in hospitalized adolescents. *Archives of General Psychiatry,* 1981, **38,** 141–145.

U.S. Department of Health, Education and Welfare. *Patients in mental hospitals.* Chevy Chase, Md.: Public Service Publication no. 1818, 1966.

Weiner, A. Cognitive and social-emotional development in adolescence. *Journal of Pediatric Psychology,* 1977, **2,** 87–92.

Weiner, I., & DelGaudio, A. Psychopathology in adolescence. *Archives of General Psychiatry,* 1976, **33,** 187–193.

Weizman, A., Weizman, R., Tyano, S., & Wijsenbeck, H. Bipolar depression in early adolescence. *Adolescence,* 1979, **14,** 617–620.

Welner, A., Welner, Z., & Fishman, R. Psychiatric adolescent inpatients: 8-10 year follow-up. *Archives of General Psychiatry,* 1979, **36,** 698–700.

White, J.H., & O'Shanick, G. Juvenile manic-depressive illness. *American Journal of Psychiatry,* 1977, **134,** 1035–1036.

Winokur, G., Clayton, P., & Reich, T. *Manic depressive illness.* St. Louis: Mosby, 1969.

Youngerman, J., & Canino, I. Lithium carbonate use in children and adolescents. *Archives of General Psychiatry,* 1978, **35,** 216–224.

CHAPTER 32

Suicide in Adolescence

PETER L. SHERAS

This chapter is designed to present the issue of suicidal behavior among adolescents from a number of perspectives. It is obviously not within the scope of so short a work to explore adequately all aspects of the causes, occurrence, and treatment of this problem. However, it is assumed that some overview and review of the subject area will be valuable to those who may be working with a population of adolescents, some of whom may be prone to this type of self-destructive behavior. The following pages will describe the occurrence of suicide among adolescents in the United States population, the typical clinical picture presented by those attempting suicide (as well as those succeeding in it), and some current thinking on the etiology of adolescent suicide. Finally, issues related to treatment of suicidal individuals and notions of prevention will be discussed.

It is important at the outset to state, as some authors have, (Haim, 1974) that our knowledge and understanding of why some adolescents choose to kill themselves, or attempt to do so, and others do not, is still quite limited. It is hoped that presenting the prevailing thought by researchers and clinicians in this area will encourage those working with adolescents to examine carefully their own experiences with this group and encourage them to contribute further to the literature in order to alleviate what is rapidly becoming a catastrophically large problem in our society.

The author gratefully acknowledges the assistance of Ms. Ruth Ball in the preparation of this chapter.

The material presented here is designed more to orient the reader to the field than to prescribe appropriate action in clinical situations. The reader is invited to follow up on the information presented herein, especially in the area of clinical application. The author is sharing knowledge gained from his own experience with suicidal adolescents in the hope that this will stimulate the thoughts of researchers and practitioners not to accept what is said but to continue to look for relevant information on this topic.

THE OCCURRENCE OF ADOLESCENT SUICIDE

General Rates

In terms of reported occurrence, suicide among adolescents represents one of the major causes of death in this country for people ages 10–24. It has been estimated that suicide is currently the third leading killer of adolescents (Parker, 1974; Holinger, 1979, 1980; Eisenberg, 1980) behind only accidents and homicide. In addition, the suicide rate has been rapidly increasing over the last two decades. In the most general estimates, it appears that suicides have increased more than 100–150 percent during that period. Table 32.1 presents the most recent statistics, divided by sex, as the suicide rates are significantly different for males and females, a point to be discussed later. Table 32.2 presents the increase during

Table 32.1   Suicide Rates/100,000 U.S. Population (for sample years by age group and sex)

Year	Sex	Age Group 10–14	Age Group 15–19	Age Group 20–24
1960	Males	0.9	5.6	11.5
	Females	0.2	1.6	2.9
1965	Males	0.9	6.1	13.8
	Females	0.2	1.9	4.3
1970	Males	0.9	8.8	19.3
	Females	0.3	2.9	5.7
1975	Males	1.2	12.2	26.4
	Females	0.4	2.9	6.8
1977	Males	1.6	14.2	29.9
	Females	0.3	3.4	7.3

Note. Data from the Mortality Statistics Branch, National Center for Health Statistics, U.S. Department of Health, Education, and Welfare.

the period 1960–1977. The three age groups depicted in the tables were chosen to reflect the categories in the U.S. mortality statistics.

Underreporting

Underreporting of suicides, especially for adolescents, may occur for a number of reasons. As some authors have suggested (Marks & Haller, 1977; Holinger, 1979; Seiden, 1969), suicides may be covered up by families or physicians attempting to avoid the stigma of a suicide in the family. In addition, as Toolan (1975), Miller (1975), and others have indicated, it is often difficult to distinguish between a suicide and an accident. This distinction may purposely be blurred by those wanting to avoid the stigma, but it is also true that in many cases it is impossible to determine whether an accident or a suicide has occurred. This is particularly evident in the case of automobile accidents where suicidal intention may be present but cannot be established. Farberow (1974) defined two of the criteria for suicide as its intentional nature and its self-inflicted quality. In the case of accidents, each of these criteria may be impossible to establish. It must be remembered that the leading cause of death in adolescents is accidents. Given this sort of circumstance, Schrut (1964) believed that as many as 50 percent of all suicides might not be reported as such.

Table 32.2   Percentage Change in Suicide Rates by Sex and Age

Year		Age Group 10–14	Age Group 15–19	Age Group 20–24
1960–1977	Males	+78%	+154%	+160%
	Females	+50%	+112%	+152%
1975–1977	Males	+33%	+ 16%	+ 13%
	Females	−25%	+ 17%	+ 7%

Note. Compiled from data from the Mortality Statistics Branch, National Center for Health Statistics, U.S. Department of Health, Education, and Welfare.

Table 32.3   Ratio of Male to Female Suicides by Age Group

Year	10–14	15–19	20–24
1961	3.75:1	3.50:1	3.35:1
1975	3.05:1	4.22:1	3.88:1

Note. Compiled from data from the Mortality Statistics Branch, National Center for Health Statistics, U.S. Department of Health, Education, and Welfare.

Sex Differences

The statistics presented in Tables 32.1 and 32.2 are divided by sex. Most studies of adolescent suicide distinguish between males and females, both in regard to suicide and parasuicide, as the picture presented is often quite different. As indicated above, a significantly larger number of males than females in all three adolescent age groups (10–14, 15–19, and 20–24) commit suicide. Some authors (Frederick, 1978; Seiden, 1969) approximate the ratio of males to females at 3:1. Table 32.3 summarizes the mortality statistics for 1961 and 1975 and demonstrates ratios from 3:1 to more than 4:1.

Race Differences

Many studies of suicide have examined the variable of race. Both Seiden (1969) and Holinger (1978) demonstrate that whites in this age group generally have higher suicide rates than nonwhites. Nonwhite males in the 20–24 age range are the closest to whites of the same age in the most recent statistics and actually had higher rates in the 1961 tables. This trend seems to indicate that the rate of increase in suicide recently has been greater for white than for nonwhite adolescents.

Methods of Suicide

The methods of suicide seem to vary with age as well as with sex. Table 32.4 presents the percentages of suicides owing to particular methods for males and females as reported in a sample year (1975). This table indicates a number of important trends. It indicates, first, that firearms and explosives are by far the main instruments of adolescent suicide; second, that males are more likely to use firearms or hanging to kill themselves, while females will choose poisoning as a major method; third, that younger adolescents are more likely to use hanging and suffocation as a method than older adolescents. It must be remembered in these data that explosives and firearms are much more likely to succeed in killing the individuals involved than poisonings (frequently drug overdoses). This type of

Table 32.4   Methods of Suicide by Sex for Three Age Groups (1975)

Method	Age 10–14 Males	Age 10–14 Females	Age 15–19 Males	Age 15–19 Females	Age 20–24 Males	Age 20–24 Females
Poisoning	0	19%	5%	24%	9%	29%
Gases	1%	0	7%	3%	8%	8%
Hanging/Strangulation/Suffocation	47%	22%	22%	12%	17%	8%
Firearms/Explosives	51%	52%	62%	54%	60%	44%
Other Methods	1%	7%	4%	7%	6%	11%
	100%	100%	100%	100%	100%	100%

Note. Data from the Mortality Statistics Branch, National Center for Health Statistics, U.S. Department of Health, Education, and Welfare.

specific information is not available for attempted suicides, where it would be expected that poisonings would be a more frequent choice of method.

PARASUICIDE (ATTEMPTED SUICIDE)

General Rates

Many authors have attempted to draw a clear distinction between those who attempt suicide and those who succeed (Schneidman & Farberow, 1961, pp. 19–47; Seiden, 1969). Stengel (1964) points out that less than 10 percent of those who attempt suicide actually succeed at some later time. It also appears that many suicides are committed on first attempts. Although there will be some overlap (in the sense that some attempters may inadvertently succeed in killing themselves and that some potential suicide victims may survive their best efforts to die), the picture presented by these two groups is often quite different. Jacobziner (1965) estimated that the ratio of suicide attempters to succeeders may be as high as 100:1. Other authors have fixed the ratio a bit lower (e.g., Dublin, 1963, at 7:1). The distinction between suicides who may survive and parasuicides has obvious ramifications for treatment, most notably in the area of intentionality. This area will be discussed at a later point in this chapter.

Reporting Errors

As with the statistics on suicide, the parasuicide statistics are of questionable accuracy. Eisenberg (1980) points out that most reports of suicide attempts come from hospital emergency rooms. Since many attempts may be dealt with outside of the hospital—at home or in other places in the community—the hospital statistics would understate the occurrence of such attempts significantly. Access to mortality records makes studies of the occurrence of suicide a bit easier than studies of the frequency of attempted suicides in the general population or for adolescents. As no definitive records are available, it is small wonder that estimates of the ratio of attempted to successful suicides are so varied.

Sex Differences

The statistics in tables 32.1, 32.2, and 32.3 clearly demonstrate that males are much more likely to commit suicide than females. In the case of attempted suicide, however, the ratios are nearly reversed (Mintz, 1964). Balser and Masterson (1959), for example, estimated that 12 percent of suicide attempts were made by adolescents and that adolescent girls represented as many as 90 percent of this group. As the profile of adolescent attempters and adolescent committers of suicide cannot be seen as necessarily similar (Seiden, 1969), the fact that more females than males attempt suicide can shed some light on the difference in patterns of attempters and committers. Seiden (1969) states that one cannot conclude from any of the data that all suicidal behaviors could be placed on a continuum with all self-destructive behaviors. If this were the case, successful suicides would merely be the end point with all other self-destructive behaviors being, in essence, milder forms of suicidal actions. Rather, it appears that the pattern of attempters (parasuicides) is much different. This pattern will be further discussed below. It does, however, seem unequivocally clear that the pattern for suicide attempters most frequently fits that of females as opposed to males.

Methods in Parasuicide

It is difficult to separate the methods of attempted suicides from other factors of age and development in adolescents. In general, parasuicides will use more passive methods than suicides as a function of their desire to be discovered or rescued. These more passive methods (e.g., poisoning rather than the use of explosives or firearms) are also, as has been seen earlier, more common to female than to male suicide committers. By and large, suicide attempts involve most frequently slower forms of death or methods that leave time and/or opportunity to be discovered. Wrist cutting and drug overdoses are the two most common examples of this category.

The sex of the attempter may have something to do with the method chosen. It may also be true that age is a contributing factor. Suicide attempters as a group, in addition to being females, are also more likely to be younger than suicide committers. The reason for this may be related to the desires of younger adolescents to dramatize their situation, to communicate rather than to give up. It may also be related to changing concepts of death or ambivalence regarding decision making most characteristic of adolescents. It is important to be clear that, despite the seeming similarity in the methods and profiles of adolescent attempters, each case is somewhat unique and in a clinical setting needs to be considered in the overall context in which that person is functioning. This notion of context will also be discussed a bit later.

THE CLINICAL PICTURE

In describing the clinical picture of adolescent parasuicides or suicides, it is often difficult to separate an understanding of the causes of suicidal behavior from the dynamics or process of that behavior. This section will present some notions of the antecedents of suicidal behavior and taxonomies for understanding types of such behavior. The discussion of etiology of adolescent behavior will be covered in a later section of this chapter. An attempt will be made here to examine various authors' ideas of suicidal types, predispositions for suicide, antecedent events, stages in the development of suicidal behavior, and, finally, common symptomatology manifested by an adolescent likely to be involved in a suicidal gesture or act.

Types of Suicide

Some authors have attempted to differentiate between patterns of suicidal behavior by classifying suicides by types. Schneidman (1968), for instance, suggests that all committed suicides fall into one of three categories. He characterizes these types as: (1) egotic, (2) dyadic, or (3) ageneratic.

Egotic suicides are described as being a result of an intrapsychic struggle, a dialogue within the mind of the individual. In such cases, internal conflict becomes more important than the surroundings, the presence of supportive friends or peers, or other ties to a community. These types of suicide represent a desire for the destruction of the ego or the self. Such suicides occur without regard for the impact or effect upon significant others but rather are indicative of the internal struggle within the individual, often an existential conflict. These suicides are primarily psychological in that they occur almost entirely within the person, and the internal process of such a person may often include extreme instances of withdrawal, psychotic ideation, or severely neurotic thought. Such suicides can be seen as basically nihilistic and often magical, frequently filled with symbolism and metaphor.

The second type of suicide described by Schneidman is dyadic. These types of suicides are a function of the presence of a deep and unfulfilled need for relationship with a significant other. This form of dyadic suicide, although undertaken by the individual, can be considered interpersonal in nature. The contents of a suicide note often addressed to or referring to the significant other, often make it clear that this sort of suicide has occurred. In adolescence, as will be demonstrated, an interpersonal event, such as a rejection by a partner in a relationship, can be the event which precipitates the suicide or the attempted suicide.

The third type of suicide described by Schneidman he labels ageneratic. Ageneratic suicides are committed by those who "fall out" of their place in generations. These individuals lose the sense of generativity, of their place in the procession of generations. Often such people lose their general sense of belonging and may feel aliented, isolated, empty, or disengaged. Schneidman considers this type of suicide to be sociological, relating to group, cultural, national, or familial ties.

Adolescents surely may fall into any of the three categories. It is reasonable to assume that, in the case of ageneratic suicides, although their sense of generations may not be as strong as for adults, their alienation from parents or their group identification with peers may be quite cogent. It may be useful to consider these types in examining the etiology

of suicidal behavior. Circumstances or antecedents may be quite different and still lead to
a suicide. The above types demonstrate how
different these predispositions or precipitating
events might be to produce an identical
outcome.

Other authors have tried to characterize
types of adolescent suicide by categories relating to symptomatology (Finch & Poznanski,
1971). These taxonomies will be discussed in
the section on symptomatology below.

Predispositions

As with many other behaviors, there is frequently an attempt made to find some predisposing variables, some personality factors, for
instance, that might help to distinguish those
who commit or attempt suicide from those
who do not. Finch and Poznanski (1971)
discuss the role that certain types of character
disorders might play in a predisposition for
suicidal behavior. They use the examples of
impulsive character disorder to describe the
largest single group of adolescents who exhibited suicidal behavior. They also identify
adolescents with depressive symptomatology
as being likely to be more predisposed to
suicide. However, as they and others point out
(Otto, 1964; Mattsson, Seese, & Hawkins,
1969), the classic clinical picture of depression
in adults does not always hold for adolescents.
Adolescents are more likely to demonstrate
mood swings, social withdrawal, decreased
motivation, and poor appetite than adult
depressives. These signs of depression may be
more easily missed when observing adolescents as these behaviors occur to some extent
at some time during the normal developmental
course for a healthy adolescent. When depression does in reality exist for the adolescent, it
may also be manifest as school skipping,
rebelliousness, social isolation, or other self-
destructive behaviors such as substance abuse
or reckless behavior. In some adolescents,
according to Finch and Poznanski, depression
may be an extended expression of grief stemming from the loss of a loved one. This grief
may be accompanied by a feeling of loneliness

and isolation. Some adolescents become extremely self-deprecating, while others become
hostile to significant others. Some of these
depressive symptoms may be characterological in nature, creating a personality predisposition for suicide.

Another personality predisposition for suicide in adolescents may occur as a result of a
borderline syndrome. Gunderson (1977, pp.
173–192) describes borderlines as more likely
than either of his comparison groups of
depressives or schizophrenics to attempt suicide. These suicidal behaviors are often extremely manipulative in nature, including
wrist cutting, a syndrome reported by Finch
and Poznanski to be prevalent in adolescents
who attempt suicide. According to Gunderson, borderlines frequently overdose, mutilate
themselves, or attempt suicide not only by
wrist cutting but also by such behaviors as
head banging. Borderline adolescents might
seem more prone, then, to suicidal gestures or
attempts than actual suicides. This seems
most especially true for adolescent females.

Finally, the presence of psychosis (or
thought disorder) may create a predisposition
for suicide in adolescents. Finch and Poznanski present information that 16 percent of all
suicidal adolescents are diagnosed psychotic
while a small proportion are diagnosed as
manic depressives. This psychotic diagnosis is
twice as prevalent for males as for females.
Some of these individuals may undergo a
personality change during the three-month
period prior to the attempt, with suicide
potential being greatest during the first year of
the mental illness or during an acute psychotic
episode. This type of suicide may actually
represent the struggle between the healthy and
psychotic aspects of the person's functioning.
Suicide may be the integrating event or the
last effort of the intact part of the adolescent
to overcome the psychosis.

In addition to personality predispositions
as discussed above, it is necessary to examine
the relationship between a suicidal act or
attempt and the turmoil related to the developmental stage known as adolescence. It is
during this developmental period that there is

an acceleration in the rate of growth of the organism not experienced since early childhood. The changes that occur are not just physiological in nature but represent a quantum leap in cognitive and moral development, an expansion of social relationships, and a change in the emotional needs of the individual. As emotional and affiliation needs become greater, for example, the impact of social rejection may be much more severe and lead to more profound behavior changes in the individual. The intensity of these experiences cannot be underestimated. The interaction of physiological, psychological, and social development during adolescence creates a multitude of confusing and ambivalent feelings. The sense of the orderliness of the world, which is common in latency age children, begins to deteriorate rapidly with the onset of adolescence. Identity confusion and confused behaviors become commonplace.

Many adolescents desire to respond in a way that deals with the turmoil and confusion. This may be accomplished by arbitrarily making decisions for the sake of order, a notion similar to that which Marcia (1966) describes as "foreclosure." This can be done by escaping from reality (or distorting it significantly) or by attempting to impose order through a significant external act. Such an act may be a suicidal gesture designed to regain control over a world perceived to be confusing and out of control. Whether or not such an act may be necessary for an adolescent may depend upon the many areas of functioning in which the person finds himself or herself. In other words, a person may feel relatively more in control in some contexts than in others. These contexts may range from the family, school, peers, or subculture, to an internal perception of self, such as self-esteem or self-worth. If none of these areas are places where adolescents can feel effective and, therefore, at least somewhat in control, they may more easily experience alienation or anomie. As most adolescents will experience this type of ambivalence and confusion to some degree, it may be useful to look at their individual ability to tolerate such ambiguity as a factor

affecting their need to assert their control and, perhaps, their predisposition for acting out against themselves in the form of suicidal behavior.

The developmental considerations mentioned above clearly interact with events in the individual's life and not only represent predispositions but also help to create a background of personality and environmental variables that may determine a potential for suicide. The environmental factors will be discussed below and in the section on etiology. Hafen (1972), for instance, stated that adolescence magnified many suicidal elements, such as guilt, rage, impulsivity, feelings of inadequacy, desire for revenge, fear, loneliness, suggestibility, and hypersensitivity. As mentioned above, it is believed that the intensity of almost any emotion may be increased as a function of the developmental quality of the adolescent experience.

Antecedent Events

It is difficult to discriminate between antecedent events for suicide and suicide attempts in adolescents and factors related to their etiology. A number of antecedent occurences are, however, extant in the literature and will be mentioned here and elaborated upon later.

Finch and Poznanski (1971) noted that in females, suicide is often associated with menstruation. This may be as a result of physiological factors. In addition, suicide is in some cases associated with pregnancy. Whitlock and Edwards (1968) state that pregnancy is an associated factor in 5 percent of female suicides and that 7 percent of female suicides are pregnant.

Jacobs (1971) observed that frequency of residential moves and school changes, severe discipline at home, and living with stepparents helped to differentiate normals from suicide attempters. He also cites parental loss as a significant antecedent event. Barter, Swaback, and Todd (1969) see this loss as critical when it occurs before the age of 12. Crook and Raskin (1975) further elaborate the notion of parental loss to mean separation, desertion, or divorce of a parent as opposed to a parental death. This type of loss through separation also seems to be more significant for attempters than for suicide committers.

Finally, those who attempt suicide frequently have a history of previous suicide attempts. Also, a history of a relative committing suicide is frequently present (Teicher & Jacobs, 1966).

Stages of Development in Suicide Attempts

Teicher and Jacobs (1966), Jacobs (1971), and Teicher (1973) have presented a stage theory for understanding the preconditions and sequence of events in adolescent suicide *attempts*. Based upon a number of case studies, Jacobs (1971) hypothesizes that suicide attempts result from a feeling of progressive isolation from meaningful social relationships. Adolescent suicide attempters will have experienced five stages in sequence.

The first stage is a long standing *history of problems*. These problems usually exist throughout childhood until the onset of adolescence. Teicher (1973) lists some of these problems as:

1. Parents who have committed suicide
2. Parent ôr close relative who attempted suicide
3. One or both natural parents missing from the home
4. Feeling of contending with unwanted stepparent
5. Parent married more than once
6. All parents (one or two) working
7. An average of ten serious, problem-causing environmental changes (e.g., juvenile hall, foster home placement, death in family, hospitalization of members of the family, remarriage of parents, siblings departing, etc.)
8. Problem with alcoholic parent
9. Living with people other than parents (e.g., left with relatives)
10. A great deal of residential mobility and a large number of school changes

As a group, the suicide-attempting adolescents are more likely to have suffered prior separation from meaningful social relationships and more unpredictable than normals.

The second stage is a marked *escalation of problems* with the onset of adolescence. It is assumed that these problems are more frequent or severe than those that would ordinarily crop up at this time even in normal adolescents. Teicher (1973) elaborates this stage by characterizing the problems as a function of parents trying to cope with their newly developing adolescents. Specifically, these developments may include behavior problems. These problems can run the gamut from withdrawal into self, gloominess, and minor resistance to the wishes of parents, to lying, rebelling, withdrawing, or running away from home. Often these sorts of behaviors are designed to bring the problems to the attention of the parents. In addition to behavioral problems, escalations are frequently a result of changes due to the illness of a family member, not necessarily the adolescent. Adolescents may need to drop out of school, assume the role of caretaker for ill parents, and the like. By the end of this stage, such adolescents frequently feel out of control. They have often isolated themselves and alienated their parents, making it difficult to share their problems with anyone.

According to Jacobs (1971), the third stage is the progressive *failure of coping skills* of the adolescent. This will, in turn, lead to more isolation from meaningful social relationships.

Failures in the third stage lead to a chain reaction of failures in any meaningful social relationships in the short period of time prior to the attempt. This produces a fourth stage of *loss of hope* by the adolescent.

Finally, according to Jacobs (1971), the fifth stage is the internal process of *justification* of the suicide. During this stage, the adolescent bridges the gap between the thought of suicide and the action itself by constructing an argument for suicide.

Teicher (1973) combines these last three stages into one final stage. He characterizes this period as including difficulties in three areas: romance, school, and peer relationships. Romance is often the last attempt of the adolescent described above to reestablish a meaningful social tie with another person. By this time, friends and parents have been alienated and the failure of this romance and its perceived rejection leave the person feeling abandoned.

Over a third of adolescent suicide attempters are not enrolled in school at the time of their attempts (Teicher, 1973). Many of these believe that nonattendance at school was a contributing factor to their attempted suicide. Leaving school, then, is often a component of this final stage.

As implied above, the failure of peer relations during this time is a large contributing factor in this final stage. Adolescents feel that they, uniquely, have problems without solutions. They have nowhere to turn for support. As Teicher (1973) puts it, "Life is a chronic problem. There appears no way out. Solutions previously tried have failed. To end the chronic problem, death appears to be the only way left" (p. 137).

To summarize, the adolescent proceeds through a sequence of events that serves to isolate him or her from social relationships. This is usually based upon a history of problems (escalating recently) and often culminates in pressures from a ruined romance, an illness or death in the family, or a perception that there is no solution to the chronic problems of life. It is important to note that this final stage is often erroneously seen as the reason for the suicide. It seems clear from the above research that it is only the final phase in a more protracted process.

Symptoms

Aside from the behaviors that may appear as part of the stages leading up to a suicide attempt, many authors and researchers have attempted to describe the symptomatology of not only the adolescent suicide attempter, but the *committer* as well. The major symptom groups described in the literature are those associated with depression, impulsivity, psychosis, and interpersonal difficulty (Toolan, 1962, 1975; Hafen, 1972; Barter, Swaback, & Todd, 1969; Finch & Poznanski, 1971).

Depression

As discussed earlier, it is generally believed that one of the major symptoms manifested by suicidal adolescents is depression. Many researchers, however, have noted that there is a significant difference in the symptoms of depression for adolescents and for adults (Toolan, 1975; Finch & Poznanski, 1971; Weiner, 1970). The depressive symptoms may, in fact, be masked by more acting-out behaviors that appear as delinquent acts, for example, rather than depressed behaviors. Adolescents demonstrate fluctuating moods and energy swings that frequently mislead observers.

Sometimes, however, the classic signs of adult depression may also be present. These include the loss of interest in family and friends, low motivation, feelings of loneliness and sadness, eating and sleeping disturbances, as well as acknowledged suicidal ideation. In addition, the more frequent (and often misleading) symptoms of severe depression, especially in young adolescents, have been characterized by Glaser (1967) and Toolan (1962) as boredom and restlessness, fatigue and body preoccupations, difficulty in concentrating, flight to or from people, and acting out. Often, the acting-out behaviors of aggressiveness, promiscuity, delinquency, defiance, and running away, to name a few, may serve to defend the adolescent from thinking about his or her underlying feelings of worthlessness. It is easy to see, for instance, that trouble in school or difficulties with the law may, indeed, be symptoms of depression and indicate a potential for suicidal behavior.

Depression in later adolescence often looks similar to the same disorder in adults. There is, however, more of a tendency for rumination and the appearance of hopelessness. These signs may make it easier to diagnose the difficulty and to suspect suicidal potential.

It is believed that an underlying theme in depression is the experience of loss. The loss can be of a family member, of a friendship, of personal esteem or effectiveness, or the loss of bodily integrity through illness or disfigurement. These losses can be especially acute for an adolescent who is experiencing, as a function of development, almost daily changes in appearance. Adolescents are also extremely sensitive to issues related to social acceptability and fears of rejection that may enhance their perceptions of the loss of love or of low self-esteem.

Impulsivity

As mentioned earlier, impulsive character disorders represent a large number of adolescent suicides (Finch & Poznanski, 1971; Barter, 1969). Behaviors often characterized as angry or vengeful are examples of this sort of impulsive action. It is frequently the case that suicide attempts appear to be hastily planned and not well executed—signs of impulsivity. Again, the impulsiveness that, in general, becomes more evident as a characteristic in normal adolescent development may produce a greater likelihood of a suicidal gesture.

Despite this notion of impulsivity, some adolescents commit suicide with great premeditation and care. This may often be a function of the fifth stage described by Jacobs (1971). This stage of self-justification may develop over a period of time as the person comes to see death as the logical solution to life's problems. To the extent that such a solution seems reasonable, the suicide act may not be impulsive per se. It may be the case that many parasuicides are a result of impulsivity and that successful suicides may be more a result of logical justification constructed through forethought.

Psychosis

According to Finch and Poznanski (1971), roughly 16 percent of adolescents who attempt suicide are diagnosed as being psychotic. Most of these are considered to be schizophrenic. Suicides and parasuicides, as a result of this disorder, may occur as a function of delusions, hallucinations, or other distortions of reality. Since many of these individuals may be severely withdrawn or functioning primarily in fantasy, it is difficult to determine the process that may lead to the suicidal act. It does seem clear, however, that psychotic adolescents are prone to suicide, especially during the first year of their mental illness.

Interpersonal Difficulty

It seems frequently the case that suicidal adolescents manifest great interpersonal difficulties. As mentioned earlier, these may take the form of family problems, deteriorating peer relationships, or an inability to form good relationships with compeers. A broken romance or an acute perceived personal rejection often functions as the precipitating event or the "last straw" prior to a suicide attempt, underscoring the notion that it is the interpersonal difficulty that is central to the suicidal behavior. It would appear, then, that adolescents with good interpersonal experiences will be less likely to indulge in this type of self-destructive behavior. It is, unfortunately, characteristic of adolescent struggles for autonomy and identity that interpersonal conflicts occur with great regularity. For many people, however, it is either the family relationships or the peer relationships that at any point in time may be problematic. When only one of these difficulties is present, the other relationships (e.g., parents or peers) may serve as an interpersonal support for the adolescents. When both of these contexts are unsatisfying, there may be more of a possibility for suicidal behavior.

Summary

The clinical picture of an adolescent suicide or suicide attempter is quite complex. It may include contributing factors related to predispositions of character and specific antecedent events. Adolescent suicide attempts usually fall into a pattern that includes a sequence of stages related to a history of the problem, an escalation of the difficulties, a failure to cope, a loss of hope and, finally, an internal justification for the act. Various symptomatologies may be present in the adolescent suicide committer including depression, impulsivity, psychosis, or interpersonal difficulty.

ETIOLOGY

Attempting a full explication of the current understanding of the etiology of adolescent suicide is, again, beyond the scope of this chapter. There are, however, a number of important etiological factors that are found repeatedly in studies of adolescent suicidal behavior. These factors in etiology are the contributions of (1) individual development, (2) family dynamics, and (3) peer and social relations. In addition, some authors (e.g., Seiden, 1969) speak of sociocultural factors. Although it is obvious and important that there are interactions between all of these factors, each can be elucidated briefly to indicate some of the influences of these factors and, finally, the significance of their interaction.

Individual Development

Seiden (1969), in his review of studies in adolescent suicide, describes a number of individual determinants of suicide in adolescents. Other authors, including Finch and Poznanski (1971) support many of these determinants and provide some additional categories. The picture is not unclouded, but, in general, the categories below reflect these authors' notions and my own clinical experience.

Familial Tendencies

It was often the observation of those studying adolescents that suicidal behavior "runs in the family." Some early studies tend to demonstrate that there might, indeed, be a link between genetics and suicide (Shapiro, 1935; Swanson, 1960). Kallman and others, however, in their studies of twins (Kallman & Anastasio, 1946; Kallman et al., 1949) concluded that there is no special, inherited trait

for suicidal behavior. It is difficult to separate the environmental and mental factors from those that might be strictly genetic. Although there may indeed be a link, it is extremely difficult to substantiate.

Mental Illness

As mentioned above in the clinical picture section, clinical depression and schizophrenia are individual determinants that have been linked to adolescent suicide. It is interesting that some authors (Schneidman & Farberow, 1957) note that threats of suicide frequently represent greater psychological disturbance than actual attempts. Sanborn, Sanborn, and Cimbolic (1973) report, for instance, that threats of suicide are more significantly related to completed suicides than to attempts.

Impulsivity

Impulsivity as a personality characteristic has been discussed above and also relates to suicidal behaviors. Impulsivity and poor impulse control have been cited by numerous authors as a prominent feature in child and adolescent suicides (Winn & Halla, 1966; Lourie, 1966; Jacobziner, 1960). There is not, however, universal agreement on this point. Teicher and Jacobs (1966) have argued that their stages of development represent a progression of thoughts and events leading up to a suicide or an attempt. It is rarely an isolated impulsive act.

Concepts of Death

Studies of children's and adolescents' concepts of death have shown a number of things. It is often the case that the significance of death as a present circumstance may not be as cogent to an adolescent, especially a young adolescent, as it may be to an adult. Sometimes the act of killing oneself is seen as a form of running away, where there is little concept of mortality (Winn & Halla, 1966). The picture is complicated by the fact that many adolescents fantasize about death without necessarily understanding the finality of such a state. In general, it appears that suicidal adolescents fear death less than their normal counterparts (Lester, 1967a) and that death, largely denied in earlier adolescence, achieves an emotional significance in later adolescence (Alexander & Alderstein, 1958; Kastenbaum, 1959, pp. 99–113). How these concepts of death may influence a particular adolescent depends upon his or her own personality, the characteristics of the particular situation, and his or her motivation to act. There is little doubt but that some adolescents kill themselves to explore or experience death, and that some inadvertently kill themselves not realizing the biological significance of death.

Aggression and Revenge

Aggression and revenge are being considered together here since the notion of suicide as an aggressive act often, for children and adolescents, includes the idea of aggression turned inward. It is often the case that adolescents in their self-destructive acts try to show someone else something for spite or revenge. A broken romance or an argument with parents may lead to an attempt to get back at them by making them sorry (Moss & Hamilton, 1956). In some sense, the desire to make *others* grieve may motivate adolescent suicides. Stengel (1964), however, argues that aggressive acts toward others, not toward themselves, are more characteristic of suicide attempters than of those who succeed.

Another related aspect to this aggression and revenge pattern is manipulation. Especially in the case of suicide attempts, there is a motive to manipulate others, to get them to suffer, respond, or be sorry for the adolescent. Frequently, according to Bender and Schilder (1937), suicidal threats are used by children to assert their independence from their parents. This can also be seen as a possible theme for the adolescent's struggle with identity and desire to differentiate from parents. Suicidal behavior can represent an attempt to act out against the parents to gain autonomy. These acts of manipulation are also attempts to assert control over the behaviors of others and to have impact on the interpersonal environment when everything in the world may seem out of control.

Imitation

Seiden (1969) describes determining factors contributing to suicidal behavior in adolescents as identification, imitation, and suggestion. Although probably more true of children and younger adolescents, it is clear that adolescents are quite prone to responding to models. In a time when, for instance, parents are not considered to be useful models from the adolescent's perspective, more violent, rebellious, or self-destructive models may be chosen. Social pressure also plays a role in determining behavior patterns and coping skills in a particular segment of the peer population. For instance, epidemics of suicides in schools have been recorded (Seiden, 1969). If suicide is validated in a peer population or seen as a reasonable response to crises characteristic of adolescence, suicidal behavior may become more prevalent. An adolescent's suggestibility, then, given a particular type of peer surroundings, may be a determining factor in suicide. The media, TV, and records may glorify suicide as in past generations, poetry, plays, and art have documented and explored the inner conflicts of suicides.

Sexual Development

A number of authors have examined the effect of puberty and a growing sexuality upon suicidal behavior. Clashes between sexual development and environmental expectations may create problems for the individual (Goreix, cited in Seiden, 1969). Difficulties may arise over sanctions imposed by parents and the culture and the rising desire for autonomy. These conflicts may then be acted out in suicidal behavior.

A second and perhaps more important aspect of sexual development in puberty has to do with sexual identification. Confusions in sexual identification, fears of homosexuality, and fears of rejection by peers for being sexually inadequate may facilitate suicidal responses related to depression, rejection, or spite. Failure to establish a sexual identity (creating a sexual identity crisis) has been cited by a number of authors as leading to serious suicide attempts (Bigras et al., 1966; Schneer & Kay, 1962, pp. 180–201; Zilboorg, 1937).

Other developmental characteristics of puberty, such as mood swings, energy fluctuations, and concern about bodily changes may also contribute to problems where the perceived solution may be suicide. At the very least, puberty exacerbates feelings of isolation, anxiety, and depression, characteristic of suicidal adolescents. Also, the timing and sequence of the events of puberty may create stress in terms of self-perception and social acceptance. "Late bloomers," for instance, may feel especially isolated or alienated from family and peers.

Drugs

With the advent of psychedelic drugs into the youth culture and the increased use of illicit medication by a large percentage of the overall population, it is impossible to ignore the role such drugs play in suicidal behavior in adolescence. According to Cohen (cited in Seiden, 1969), for instance, LSD can be related to suicide in at least five ways: (1) accidental overuse, (2) exacerbation of suicide proneness, (3) intrusion of suicidal ideas while "tripping," (4) suicide from LSD-induced fantasy, and (5) flashback suicide to escape further reoccurrences.

In addition to psychedelic drugs, heavy use of popular drugs may enhance the likelihood of suicidal acts when suicidal ideation may already be present. It may also be true that some adolescents, taking drugs to escape the difficulties of their everyday lives, may overdose on drugs (or on the synergistic combination of drugs and alcohol) and kill themselves. Whether this sort of act can best be described as an accident or an actual suicide is not easy to decide. A similar dilemma relating to intent may also be present in the case of adolescents who abuse alcohol extensively and then get into their automobiles or onto their motorcycles and die in traffic accidents. In one sense, these may all be viewed as drug-related suicides.

Family Dynamics

In addition to individual determinants of adolescent suicidal behavior, a great deal has been written about the relation of family dynamics to an adolescent's propensity for self-destructive acts. These family dynamics are often viewed as interacting with individual determinants and peer/cultural pressures to potentiate the suicidal behaviors. The family factors listed below are those put together from the literature and the author's clinical experience as being most likely related to suicidal behavior. The presence of any one of these factors does not necessarily predispose a person to suicide, but some or many of these elements appear to be extant for suicidal adolescents.

Broken Homes

Jacobs (1971), in his study of adolescent suicide, cites a great deal of literature that attempts to relate broken homes to adolescent suicide. He concludes that this relationship may not be as strong as previously thought. Although a large percentage of adolescent suicide attempters did come from broken homes, many nonattempters did as well. The relationship was more significant between broken homes and the onset of depression in adult life, however. Perhaps a more meaningful way to speak of the type of broken home that relates to suicide is to examine family disorganization.

Recent Family Disorganization

Corder, Page, and Corder (1974), in their study of communication in families with adolescent suicides, cite recent family disorganization as a factor present significantly more in families with suicidal as opposed to nonsuicidal patients. This disorganization was usually a change in family structure due to illness, loss of job, or the like during the preceding year. The impact of this sort of loss of a family love object is a common theme in the study of adolescent suicides. Kerfoot (1980) cites parental loss as an important correlate of suicidal behavior. Seiden (1969) cites a number of frequent motivations that characterize such a disorganized family setting. These include (1) frequent moves of neighborhood and/or school; (2) active conflict between parents, producing estrangement (also cited by Corder, Shorr, & Corder, 1974); (3) financial difficulties; (4) sibling conflict; (5) illegitimate children; (6) parental absence; (7) conflict with stepparents; (8) rejection by parents or a negative attitude toward adolescent children; (9) institutionalization of a family member (jail or hospital); and (10) alcoholic parent or parents.

Sibling Order

There have also been some studies that indicate that sibling order may play a role in suicidal behavior (Cantor, 1972). In one such study, Toolan (1962), indicates a significantly higher adolescent suicide rate among first-born than later-born children. Lester (1967b) reasons that higher affiliative tendencies in firstborn and only-born children might seek expression through this type of suicidal behavior.

Child-Parent Role Reversal

Meeks (1971), in his review of motivations for suicidal behavior, refers to child-parent role reversals. It is sometimes the case that children are asked to take on the roles and responsibilities of parents as a result of a disorganized family structure or, more frequently, as a result of a loss or separation in the family. An oldest child, for instance, must replace or perform the role of a missing parent. This new and more responsible role often places pressure upon the individual adolescent to which it is difficult to respond maturely or appropriately. This pressure may then produce a feeling of hopelessness and loss of control, characteristic of adolescent suicide attempters. Role reversals, especially between mother and child, were cited as common by Kreider and Motto (1974) and Kerfoot (1979) characterized the adolescents' attempts to meet a number of developmental tasks from a confused or distorted frame of reference.

Communication Patterns

There is some research which seems to indicate that patterns of communication among family members and within family systems may be different for families with suicidal adolescents. Corder, Page and Corder (1974) found that the lack of communication between parents and adolescent children was present in significantly more families where patients were suicidal. It has also been discussed above

that one of the major issues for the suicidal adolescent is that there is no one with whom to communicate, most especially the parents. Such individuals often feel that their parents are not interested in speaking with them or hearing what they, the adolescents, have to say.

Discipline

Strict parental discipline and control, more rigid than is normal for a particular community, is also demonstrated by Corder, Page, and Corder (1974) to be present significantly more frequently in families with suicidal adolescents. This factor may also combine with a perception of loss of control over the environment that may in turn lead to the feeling of helplessness discussed above. Overly strict parents may also serve to eliminate communication with the children and create more of a pattern of alienation between parents and offspring.

Family Experience with Suicide

Exposure to suicides of family members, acquaintances, or relatives may also be correlated with suicidal behaviors (Corder, Page, & Corder, 1974). The fact that suicide has been used as a way to resolve problems in the immediate or extended family network may serve in some way to demonstrate that such behavior may be effective as a method of coping with difficulties. In the case of suicide attempters, discussions of such behaviors may demonstrate to the suicidal individual that attention may be focused upon a person who takes such action, assuring that it will have more impact on the family system if undertaken.

All of the above family factors are related in some parts of the literature to adolescent suicide or parasuicide. The picture of family etiology is obviously complex. It does seem clear, however, that family structure and functioning must be considered when looking for the causes of suicidal acts among adolescents.

Social and Cultural Dynamics

In addition to family and individual determinants of suicidal behavior, a number of authors have examined the role that peers and sociocultural influences play in adolescent suicide. Cultural mores and values as well as social influence by peers may serve to shape the strategies individuals use to resolve the perceived problems they face.

Social Relationships

As mentioned in a number of studies cited earlier in this chapter, *social isolation* often precedes a suicidal act. This process may be a withdrawal from a peer group with whom the adolescent has had meaningful ties or a long-standing fear of peer evaluation, which makes it difficult for an adolescent ever adequately to establish meaningful relationships with peers. Developmentally, social relationships are important during adolescence in establishing a reference for appropriate social behavior and in gaining support for such behaviors. Desires to conform and fears of rejection often heighten the sense of differentness which a person feels. This quality makes it easier for the adolescent to believe that his or her problems are uniquely unsolvable and, therefore, that a more radical or drastic solution may be in order. It may also be the case that an adolescent may choose to perform a suicidal act as a method to gain acceptance from peers. A good example of such a situation is with drug use. An adolescent, feeling hopeless and rejected, may, for instance, take a great quantity of drugs, perhaps as a way of becoming acceptable to a particular peer group. This act serves to tempt fate in the sense that the suicide attempt may be successful and death ensue, resolving the unsolvable problems, or the attempt may be survived and some kind of status as a drug user may be attained. A similar circumstance is present in adolescents who seemingly "live near the edge" in their everyday behavior.

According to Seiden (1969) and Reese (1972, pp. 220–224), social isolation is one of the attributes most frequently associated with adolescent suicidal behavior. This isolation may be a function of a feeling of alienation from people in general, or it may be based upon the perception that the individual is rejected by peers. In any event, this isolation leads to the development of yet another major determining factor for adolescent suicides, *lack of communication*. The desire to communicate ebbs as the person feels that it is useless to share problems with others, that such sharing will produce, at best, lack of interest and, at worst, scorn by friends and peers. Once this pattern is established, there is often no way to break it. Peers may perceive the withdrawn or withdrawing individual as aloof or condescending and make no attempt to reach out to him or her. This behavior is then constructed by the suicidal individual as indicative of lack of interest. One of the few successful ways to break this vicious cycle, ironically, is by attempting suicide, surviving, and becoming aware of the caring demonstrated by others. This may be why some suicide attempters describe their attempt as the turning point in their lives that allowed them to renew their commitment to living.

Cultural Factors

It is also important to examine the *cultural factors* that may contribute to suicidal behaviors. It seems clear to most students of adolescence that our Western culture engenders stress in the teenager. Adolescence is a period of transition when there is a great deal of ambiguity. Not only are adolescents confused about what is happening to them physiologically, the culture in many ways is confused about how to treat these in-between people. Adolescence represents not just a physical change but a change in status with respect to the culture. In general, the culture derogates teenagers and alternately expects them to act as children and then as adults. Lewin (1948) describes the adolescent as being a "marginal man," not belonging to either the group of adults or children within the culture. This marginality creates some confusion about how to respond and how to feel about oneself. In a time when reference information about attitudes, beliefs, and behaviors is most desperately needed by the adolescent, the culture is least able to provide it. Another useful notion to describe the stress the culture places upon the adolescent is that of cultural discontinuity (Benedict, 1938). The culture does not encourage the gradual taking of responsibility by its adolescents but, rather, expects that leaps be accomplished at specific times. For instance, a person goes from the irresponsible status of a minor at age 17 to the responsible role of adult at age 18, a transition expected to occur on or around the person's eighteenth birthday. This sort of expectation creates a great deal of stress within the adolescent. The inability to deal with this large amount of stress may contribute to the feeling suicidal adolescents may have that their problems are unsolvable. How could the culture possibly change to allow them to feel that they can effectively deal with their difficulties?

In addition to the inherent cultural stresses placed upon our transitional people, there are the added pressures from the *educational system*. This system, often representing the accepted values of the culture, demands a certain level of performance from students. As education is mandatory until the age of sixteen in most states, the structure of an educational setting may place demands upon the individual in terms of achievement and then overlay these demands with an evaluation orientation that often forces the adolescent to see the world in terms of success or failure. Individuals are not routinely allowed to opt out of the system without being labeled as significantly deviant. The result of such an experience for adolescents who may not regularly succeed according to the standard set up by the scholastic institutions is failure, often leading to reduced self-esteem and feelings of powerlessness and helplessness. These feelings set the stage for acting-out behaviors or withdrawal as ways of defending against continued negative interactions with the environment. The adolescent's behavior in the educational arena is a function of many factors. Suffice it to say here, however, that the school experience itself affects the adolescent greatly, creating a greater likelihood of self-destructive behavior in some cases.

A final area of cultural influence that might be considered is that of the *mass media*. A number of authors, including Seiden (1969), have looked at the effect of literature and media on suicidal behavior. Although there is at least some evidence to link popular media

stories related to suicide to subsequent suicides by adolescents, this causal connection has never been firmly established (Motto, 1967). It seems clear that the modern media, while not influencing nonsuicidal adolescents to commit suicide, may have a great impact upon those individuals who may have considered such action. Given this circumstance, the media, by glorifying such actions or examining the impact that such actions may have upon families or friends of victims, may actually allow the adolescent to make that crucial link of justification that changes the suicidal ideation into the suicidal act. In that sense, the influence of the media may be quite significant for some potential adolescent suicides.

Metadeterminants

An examination of the etiology of adolescent suicide on the basis of individual, family, and sociocultural determinants reveals, I believe, a common thread that can be considered a metadeterminant of suicidal behaviors. The quality that these three categories of etiological factors have in common is that they create a circumstance wherein individuals perceive themselves as having little impact upon the world around them. They have no means of gaining acknowledgement for their very existence. In short, they feel *invisible*. This lack of acknowledgement and its relationship to development, especially as it relates to family dynamics, is discussed by Satir (1972). She asserts that acknowledgement is necessary for any healthy growth.

In the case of the factors presented above, most of the individual determinants are efforts to have impact, to be noticed by those around one, or a resignation that such acknowledgement will not occur unless drastic action is taken. Individual factors may produce altered perceptions of reality to such an extent that impact is not accurately identified. Such may be the case with mentally ill adolescents or adolescents for whom suicidal histories in the family may be an obvious way to have an impact upon the surroundings. Suicide becomes the coin of the realm for acknowledgement in the environment. In the case of family, peers or the culture, the more invisible people feel the more likely they are to feel that they have little control of their lives and may, as a last desperate act, assert control by the highly visible act of suicide. It is interesting, for instance, that many suicidal adolescents imagine what it will be like for others when they are dead (e.g., imagining the funeral, reactions of others, etc.). Social withdrawal and isolation may represent the feeling that no one really cares anymore (or even sees them anymore) and the suicidal act is the last effort to be seen or leave a mark. It is this lack of acknowledgement that may be at the root of many self-destructive acts.

TREATMENT

There are many aspects to the treatment of suicidal adolescents. This section will deal with a number of those most frequently mentioned in the large body of literature on treatment. Treatments will vary with the particular clinical picture presented by an adolescent client or patient, so those aspects of treatment listed below may not and, indeed, should not apply in all cases. They merely represent the range of orientations used to deal with a self-destructive adolescent.

General Considerations

There are at least three general considerations in treating suicidal adolescents that are common threads throughout the literature. The first of these is that *all suicide attempts must be taken seriously.* There is no such thing as a trivial or meaningless gesture. All attempts, even the most innocuous, are cries for help that, if not heeded, may lead to more destructive behaviors. It is important that response to such gestures on the part of adults be considered carefully, as an impulsive counter act by a significant adult (parent, teacher, or the like) may merely confirm the adolescents' notion that they cannot control the environment in which they live.

A second common theme sounded by many authors and echoed by Weiner (1970) is that the suicide attempt is a communication from a person who has no other way of communicating except through this sort of desperate or radical act. It is essential, therefore, that treatment of such an individual must involve *reestablishing communication* with the person or taking up the slack left between the adolescent and significant adults. This communication must be cultivated if the individual is to improve.

The third general consideration, according to Durkheim (1897/1951) and as expressed by Eisenberg (1980), is that suicide is the ultimate expression of alienation. It, therefore, represents a lack of social connections or is a deficiency disease. Treatment of such a deficiency of social connection involves methods that will provide the client or patient with emotional support or sustenance needed to relieve the alienation and to provide continuing social connections.

Crisis Intervention

A number of authors have emphasized the suicidal act as occurring as part of a crisis situation (Peck, 1977, pp. 165–175; Richman, 1978; Rosenkrantz, 1978). Crisis intervention techniques by family members and helping professionals may be necessary to avoid the suicide from becoming successful. Active intervention is needed at this point. As Peck (1977, pp. 165–175) points out, a therapist may need to abandon a more nondirective or long term therapy to intervene actively at the time of the crisis. It may be the case that the adolescent has started a suicidal scenario that continues toward climax unless action is taken to stop it. This type of intervention requires the therapist to take charge and in some cases completely orchestrate the steps required to remove the person from the life-threatening situation. The short term crisis intervention should not be confused with the more protracted goals of psychotherapy.

Often friends or family members can be effective crisis intervention agents if they understand the need to provide the adolescent with alternatives for action while establishing a structure within which these alternatives can be carried out. Trained professionals with crisis intervention experience often employ such techniques as those that will reestablish contact with the desperate and withdrawing adolescent. Drye, Goulding, and Goulding (1973), for instance, discuss the use, in some cases, of "no suicide contracts." These contracts, according to them, must include a number of elements requiring the patient or client to take responsibility for his or her own actions. For instance, they suggest that the patient make the statement: "No matter what happens, I will not kill myself, accidently or on purpose, at any time." If the person does not report confidence in the statement, the authors suggest a qualified contract be established, setting a particular time period for the contract (e.g., "I will not kill myself for six months, 3 days," etc.). An essential element in the contract is that the person says "I *will not* kill myself." "I will try not to" or "I promise not to" are not as strong statements and need to be challenged. It is also important that "no matter what" is used so that the patient is not able to place responsibility for the act of suicide on an external person or circumstance. Drye et al. (1973) explicate this procedure, and it has been this author's experience that contracts that are explicit and almost legalistic in terms of qualification and conditions are most effective. In addition to contracts, techniques that are designed to promote communication with other people (including the therapist) can be quite useful. A large part of the problem in crisis situations is recognizing the crisis and acting decisively, but not rigidly, as soon as possible.

A second important consideration in dealing with the adolescent suicide attempt as a crisis is the understanding of that which needs to happen when the immediate crisis has passed. Too often, after the immediate crisis has dissipated, there is a tendency to believe that the problem that produced such a response is also over. It is essential to recognize that the crisis intervention is only the first step in a treatment process that must be followed up by psychotherapy or counseling of some sort, whether it be inpatient or outpatient.

Hospitalization

Seiden (1969) characterizes hospitalization as the most effective precautionary measure for the adolescent at risk for suicide. Hospitalization can occur following a suicide attempt or at such time as it appears that a self-destructive act is likely to occur. The effects of the hospitalization can be at least sixfold: (1) to provide a time to be away from the parents and vice versa, a breathing spell, according to Seiden (1969); (2) to remove the person from the stress-producing situation or environment; (3) to provide a time for observation of the person by professionals; (4) to communicate to the person that there are those who are interested in helping him or her and, more important, in making contact with the person in a caring way; (5) to help establish a relationship with a therapist or a significant other; and (6) to demonstrate to the adolescent the seriousness of his or her action in the eyes of those around him or her, to acknowledge the impact that the person has upon them, the larger interpersonal environment.

Even brief periods of hospitalization can be important in precluding future attempts and, more important, in addressing the issues that precipitated the self-destructive act. If the attempt (or feared attempt) was a result of more serious or chronic psychological problems, the hospitalization will serve as the entry point for the adolescent to receive treatment on a longer term basis.

The determination of when to hospitalize a potentially or actively suicidal adolescent is an important clinical judgement. Eisenberg (1980) believes that it is important not only to assess the potential lethality of an attempt from a scientific standpoint, but to understand that it is the adolescent's *perception* of that lethality that is crucial. The risk-rescue ratio must be examined, the method chosen, and the precipitating events as well as historical facts considered when making a determination about hospitalization. It is wise, in general, to take a conservative approach and hospitalize that adolescent if there is any doubt as to his or her self-destructive potential out of the hospital. At the very least, the hospitalization will demonstrate the concern of others and the impact upon the environment that the adolescent often desires consciously or unconsciously. The negative effects of the brief, perhaps unnecessary (by later determination), experience on a locked ward or on a suicide alert ward may also provide needed information to the person about how he or she may be unlike more disturbed individuals.

In general, hospitalization should be weighed carefully, but those who work with adolescent populations must not be afraid to put people in the hospital. They must know the procedure intimately so as not to hesitate for fear of looking foolish to other professionals. It is better to risk appearing absurd to one's colleagues than to risk the life of a suicidal adolescent.

Psychotherapy (Individual)

Individual psychotherapy is often a treatment used with suicidal adolescents. Regardless of the therapist's orientation to therapy or the setting in which the treatment takes place, there appears to be a number of important considerations for the therapist. Depending upon the notion one has of the causes of suicidal behavior, strategies used to deal with issues of (1) affect, (2) control, and (3) self-image have been widely discussed in the literature.

Affect

Weiner (1970) believes that the therapist must attempt to communicate with the adolescent to fill the gap to develop a relationship with another human being. This must take place in a setting that conveys warmth and support for an emotional exchange with the therapist and through this process to identify the motives that led the individual to the suicidal behavior. Learning to communicate the feelings clearly to the therapist will serve to reduce the risk of a further attempt made out of frustration. It is often the case that adolescents feel ignored or misunderstood as a function of their own inability to communicate to others the nature and the magnitude of their feelings.

Control

Bratter (1975) believes that another function of therapy is to help the adolescent learn to control his or her own self-destructive impulses. This can be best accomplished by the therapist exerting some degree of control in the therapeutic setting. The need for firmness and external control has been addressed by Leventhal and Sills (1963), Cohen and Grinspoon (1963), and Millar (1968) to name a few. In general, it is thought that the psychotherapist must deal humanely with the individual but firmly with those behaviors designed to have negative impact on the surrounding environment. Impact needs to be acknowledged by the therapist, but structure must be provided to influence appropriate behaviors. The control provides the structure for suicidal adolescents until such time as they can reestablish less self-destructive and more appropriate control for themselves. It is frequently the fear of not having control or the hopelessness the person feels about not being in control which precipitates the suicidal behavior. Alternative methods of control must be learned, often with the therapist modeling or suggesting them. Firmness, not rigidity, on the part of the therapist appears to be most helpful in this regard. Limits can be set in an atmosphere of communication and caring.

Self-Image

It is believed by some that the depression of adolescence is clearly related to poor self-image. Distortions of self-image can be seen as leading to destructive behaviors in some cases (Glaser, 1978). One of the goals in therapy, then, becomes helping the individual to examine his or her own characteristics, determine which are good and which could be changed, and set about the task of changing those characteristics. In addition to the identification of positive characteristics that enhance self-image, the act of problem solving leading to successful change can be extremely important in aiding the adolescent to a new feeling about his or her ability to take control by solving problems and a new perception of his or her ability to succeed at a given task.

It is difficult to determine at this time what sort of psychotherapy is most effective in dealing with adolescents with suicidal tendencies. It does seem clear, however, that validation of impact, ability to communicate feelings, feelings of being in control, and the concomitant increase in positive self-image are essential components to the psychotherapy process with an individual adolescent.

Psychotherapy (Group)

The usefulness of group psychotherapy has been addressed by a large number of authors. A few have specifically attempted to evaluate its effectiveness with a suicidal adolescent population (Frederick, 1978; Frederick & Farberow, 1970; Billings, 1974). In the most general sense, group situations can be effective for alienated adolescents if they can facilitate interaction between group members and produce some social cohesion. This process may be difficult to accomplish, but Frederick (1978) believes that such a form of treatment is advisable because it can (1) help to focus upon practical issues in reconstructing the person's life, (2) reduce the projection of blame by widening the transference, (3) help to eliminate resistance to treatment, (4) enhance the impact of catharsis, and (5) provide support from others with similar experiences. All of these are important features of group psychotherapy.

In addition, group therapy helps individuals to take responsibility for their own actions, both during and subsequent to their suicidal period, and to reassert control in their own lives. As part of this process, they can use others in the group as referents to reduce their distortion of the impact they have upon others and to receive suggestions for, and support in, finding new ways to solve what were previously seen to be unsolvable problems. A therapy can also produce a positive, caring atmosphere for adolescents who believed that they were not worth liking by anyone in their past. All of these factors can help to allow that adolescent to recover (and even grow) from his or her self-destructive experience in a group setting.

Psychotherapy (System)

As mentioned in the section on etiology, families play a central role in the understanding of adolescent self-destructive behavior. It is reasonable to assume, then, that effective treatment for a suicidal adolescent must at some point deal with the family system and the effects of being in such a system (e.g., a symbiotic relationship with a parent, an enmeshed family system). Families become important in treatment not only as they provide information of the causes of the adolescent's difficulty, but they often are the setting to which the person returns and, therefore, become the place where new problems and old ones must be confronted. A family systems type of therapy may help the family and the adolescent develop a process of communication that will facilitate the person's recovery and the maintenance of any therapeutic gains. In addition, families that can, as a result of family therapy, function in a more normal way will decrease the likelihood that other family members may subsequently be at risk for suicide or other psychological problems. The scope of this chapter does not allow for a full discussion of family intervention theories and techniques. Suffice it to say, however, that family forms of intervention are likely among the most effective in the long run for some of the above-stated reasons.

It may also be the case that the system of the adolescent who has become suicidal may include other significant units beside the family. Peer groups and schools may also be parts of the person's system and may have great impact on the suicidal adolescent and, therefore, contribute to his or her difficulties and their treatment. It is important to acknowledge the significance of these system parts and to address them in the treatment of the adolescent by working with the schools or even in some cases with friends of the patient or client in order to achieve a more significant and lasting change in the person.

Electroconvulsive Therapy (ECT)

Electroconvulsive therapy, although quite controversial, has been shown to be of benefit to some severely depressed individuals, leading to reduction in suicide attempts as well (Moss & Hamilton, 1956). Toolan (1966), however, asserts that children and adolescents do not seem to benefit from such treatment. Schechter (1957, pp. 131–142) also believes that such a type of treatment may make it even more difficult for the personal therapeutic relationship to develop, thereby making the long term effects of treatment much less positive. Seiden (1969) also reviews studies that may indicate that ECT is not the treatment of choice for suicidal adolescents.

Medication

The issue of medication as a treatment for suicidal behaviors in adolescence is quite large. To some extent, it would be irresponsibile to attempt to examine the role of chemotherapy as treatment in so brief a fashion. Research in this area is ongoing, and a practitioner who deals with medications must attempt to keep current. To review the effects of medication here, in any but the most general way, would be to oversimplify and date this discussion. I believe, instead, that the practitioner must know that medications are sometimes relevant to the treatment of depression and mental disorders, which are often present in adolescents who become suicidal.

Most generally, medications used in the treatment of adult depression, such as mood-elevating drugs, although often ineffective with younger children may be useful for older adolescents (Shaw & Schelkun, 1965). Tricyclic antidepressants and MAO inhibitors have been used on this population, but there are currently few critically evaluated efficacy studies of such treatments. Furthermore, there is little evidence the drug treatments have been effective by themselves in the treatment of psychotic adolescents, except as part of a total treatment plan (Campbell & Small, 1978, pp. 9–27). Most important, the individual adolescent and his or her developmental history and family structure must be taken into account before any chemotherapy is undertaken. The effects of psychiatric treatment in an inpatient or outpatient setting need to be assessed for a number of weeks before trials of medications are initiated (Campbell & Small, 1978). Adolescents frequently fall between the adult and child categories in drug treatment, and their developmental status, therefore, needs to be carefully examined. Once this determination has been made, a course of treatment, usually involving psychotherapy as well as the indicated medications, may be pursued.

Other Treatment Methods

A number of authors have addressed how the family physician can be of great value in some cases where immediate hospitalization may not be needed (Powers, 1954, 1956; Teicher & Jacobs, 1966). Often, taking time to listen to the person in treatment can be of great utility. Likewise, other significant people in the life of the adolescent, such as a family friend, a teacher, a public health nurse, or a clergyman, can serve to make the individual feel more connected and accepted.

Perhaps the most effective nonpsychiatric method in treatment of the suicidal adolescent would be the family. In some cases, therapy for the family and the adolescent is indicated, but it may also be true that the family, on its own, can be supportive of the suicidal adolescent, accept the adolescent as a family member, and take more time to listen. More frequent family activities and discussions may also function to reduce the alienation of the young person. There is no set prescription for this method except for the family to become more aware of the adolescent's situation and to react in a caring and giving manner. It is, however, often the case that the families most capable of such communication with their children would be less likely to have a suicidal adolescent. Sometimes the constraints of time or financial pressures cause a family to lose sight of the experience of the adolescent and even a slight shift toward more open communication can make a difference.

PREVENTION

It is difficult to document the effectiveness of
suicide prevention techniques. Little evaluative research has been done in this area, and
little can be reported here. There are a number
of considerations that seem obvious, however,
in attempting to stem the rising tide of adolescent suicidal behavior. Seiden (1969) discusses
prevention at three levels: (1) primary—the
recognition of the warning signs of potentially
suicidal adolescents; (2) secondary—the treatment of adolescents after the suicidal tendencies have been noticed; and (3) tertiary—
the efforts undertaken after a suicide has
occurred or an attempt has taken place.
Warning signs have, to a great extent, been
discussed in the clinical picture section of this
chapter and dealing with actively suicidal
adolescents has been addressed in the treatment section. Postsuicide procedures, that is,
the suicide in a family, is something that needs
to be dealt with in the context of that family.
As has been indicated above, whenever a
suicide or attempt has taken place, it is
essential to deal with as large a context of the
people involved as possible, to help them
understand what has happened, and to acknowledge the importance of the suicidal
person to them.

There is, however, another aspect of prevention that must be discussed. That aspect is
how, as a culture and society, we can reduce
the stresses placed upon adolescents that
precipitate the selection of suicide as a viable
solution to insurmountable problems. This
type of prevention must involve at least three
spheres of the adolescents' life—the family
sphere, the school sphere, and the social/
cultural sphere.

Family Sphere

It seems that families and family dynamics
play a large role in adolescent suicidal behavior. Prevention programs might, logically,
concentrate on family and parent education.
Family physicians, religious leaders, and even
work environments could encourage the training of parents to deal with their children. If
such education through the above auspices,
school parents' organizations, or community
health centers could be widely available and
used by community leaders, it could be de-
stigmatized for much of the population. Parent and family education could then teach and
demonstrate communication skills, personal
acknowledgement techniques, and even family
crisis management and problem solving. These
skills could serve to alleviate the loss of
contact and alienation most adolescents feel
prior to suicidal acts.

In addition to family dynamics, more work
must be done to help families stay together or
function more positively. Stress and conflict
at home, especially between parents, is one of
the major sources of alienation and isolation
for adolescent children. It is difficult to be
acknowledged positively by parents who are
not receiving acknowledgement themselves
from their spouses. It has been my experience,
in many cases, that a most effective intervention for a self-destructive adolescent can be
couples therapy for the parents.

School Sphere

The schools can aid in prevention of adolescent suicide in at least two ways. The first is to
realize that teachers are often the front line
adults to be dealing with the adolescent contemplating suicide. Training programs for
teachers might serve to be effective in identifying adolescents at risk and getting them
some help. Ross (1980) presents one such
program that might be feasible for schools to
undertake.

A second important prevention measure
involving schools is to create programs for the
education of adolescents themselves. Courses
or exercises that can validate the common
experience of young people, acquainting them
with the experiences of others and with
normative notions of physical and social
development, might serve to reduce stress and
break down the common feeling of alienation
and aloneness that many have. These types of
life education programs would not just be sex

education, but comprehensive attempts to have the adolescents learn about themselves and communicate how they feel to others.

Social Sphere

More adequate prevention methods must also focus upon how, as a culture, we make adolescence a stressful time. Although pragmatically it is difficult to suggest how changes might occur, as professionals we must continue to make the culture aware of how, by media and stereotype, we create stress by forcing adolescents to be adults too soon in some ways and by treating them as children in other ways. Social policy needs to be a force toward the creation of a more accepting and flexible social fabric. Money for prevention programs and the acknowledgement that there is a culturewide problem for adolescents that leads them more than ever toward self-destructive solutions must be sought. In the long term, these sorts of solutions will be the most meaningful.

General Considerations

To conclude, there are three components in the prevention process that can lead to the reduction of suicidal behavior. The first is the creation of as many *contact points* as possible between the adolescent and significant others, peers, and especially adults. This contact needs to be fostered in families, schools, or any other social settings.

The second component is *outreach* programs. Programs in schools, religious settings, and community settings that encourage participation by adolescents on any level must be encouraged.

Finally, *routine counseling* experiences are essential for adolescents, in school or at home, with family physicians or clergy, where they can, learn to communicate how they feel and what they are experiencing.

The prevention of suicidal behavior, as well as its treatment, is still an area where more research is necessary. It is clear that without research and intervention, the problem of adolescent suicide will become much worse.

REFERENCES

Alexander, I.E., & Alderstein, A.M. Affective responses to the concept of death in a population of children and early adolescents. *Journal of Genetic Psychology,* 1958, **93**, 167–177.

Balser, B.H. & Masterson, J.F. Suicide in adolescents. *American Journal of Psychiatry,* 1959, **116**, 400–404.

Barter, J.T. *Suicide among American Indians,* U.S. Public Health Service Publication No. 1903, 1969 (Also in B.Q. Hafen, *Self destructive behavior.* Minneapolis: Burgess, 1972, pp. 113–118.)

Barter, J.T., Swaback, D.O., & Todd, D. Adolescent suicide attempts: A follow-up study of hospitalized patients. *Archives of General Psychiatry,* 1969, **19**, 523–527.

Bender, L.L., & Schilder, P. Suicidal preoccupations and attempts in children. *American Journal of Orthopsychiatry,* 1937, **7,** 225–243.

Benedict, R. Continuities and discontinuities in cultural conditioning. *Psychiatry,* 1938, **1,** 161–167.

Bigras, J., Gauther, Y., Bouchard, C., & Tasse, Y. Suicidal attempts in adolescent girls: A preliminary study. *Canadian Psychiatric Association Journal,* (Supplement), 1966, 275–282.

Billings, J.H. Observations on long-term group therapy with suicidal and depressed persons. *Life-Threatening Behavior,* 1974, **4,** 160.

Bratter, T.E. Responsible therapeutic eros: The psychotherapist who cares enough to define and enforce behavior limits with potentially suicidal adolescents. *The Counseling Psychologist,* 1975, **5**(4), 97–104.

Campbell, M., & Small, A.M. Chemotherapy. In B. Wolman, (Ed.), *Handbook of treatment of mental disorders in childhood and adolescence.* Englewood Cliffs: Prentice-Hall, 1978.

Cantor, P. The adolescent attempter: Sex, sibling position and family constellation. *Life-Threatening Behavior,* 1972, **2**(4), 252–261.

Cohen, A.Y. LSD and the student: Approaches to education strategies. Unpublished manuscript, University of California Counseling Center, Berkeley, 1967. (Cited in Seiden, R.H., Suicide among youth. *Bulletin of Suicidology,* Supplement, 1969.)

Cohen, R., and Grinspoon, L. Limit setting as a corrective ego experience. *Archives of General Psychiatry,* 1963, **8**(1), 74–79.

Corder, B.F., Page, P.V., & Corder, R.F. Parental history, family communication interaction patterns in adolescent suicide. *Family Therapy,* 1974, **1**(13), 285–290.

Corder, B.F., Shorr, W., & Corder, R.F. A study of social and psychological characteristics of adolescent suicide attempters in an urban disadvantages area. *Adolescence,* 1974, **9**(33), 1–6.

Crook, T., & Raskin, A. Association of childhood parental loss with attempted suicide and depression. *Journal of Consulting and Clinical Psychology,* 1975, **43**, 277–282.

Drye, R.C., Goulding, R.L., & Goulding, M.E. No suicide decisions, patient monitoring of suicidal risks. *American Journal of Psychiatry,* 1973, **130**(2), 171–174.

Dublin, L.I. *Suicide: A sociological and statistical study.* New York: Ronald, 1963.

Durkheim, E. *Suicide.* Glencoe, Ill.: Free Press, 1951. (Originally published, 1897).

Eisenberg, L. Adolescent suicide: On taking arms against a sea of troubles. *Pediatrics,* 1980, **66**(2), 315–320.

Farberow, N.L. Suicide. In J.T. Spence, R.C. Carson, & J. Thibant (Eds.), *University programs modular studies.* Morristown, N.J.: General Learning Press, 1974.

Finch, S.M., & Poznanski, E.O. *Adolescent suicide.* Springfield, Ill.: Thomas, 1971.

Frederick, C.J. Current trends in suicidal behavior in the United States. *American Journal of Psychotherapy,* 1978, **32**(2), 172–200.

Frederick, C.J., & Farberow, N.L. Group psychotherapy with suicidal persons: A comparison with standard group methods. *International Journal of Social Psychiatry,* 1970, **26**, 103.

Glaser, K. Masked depression in children and adolescent. *American Journal of Psychotherapy,* 1967, **21**, 565.

Glaser, K. The treatment of depressed and suicidal adolescents. *American Journal of Psychotherapy,* 1978, **32**(2), 252–269.

Goreix, A. Le Suicide, l'adolescence et le poison, *Semaine eles Hospitaux de Paris,* 1963, **39**(50), 2371–2374. (Cited in Seiden, R.H., Suicide

among youth. *Bulletin of Suicidology,* Supplement, 1969.)

Gunderson, J.G. Characteristics of borderlines. In P. Hartocollis (Ed.), *Borderline personality disorders.* New York: International Universities Press, 1977.

Hafen, B.Q. (Ed.). *Self destructive behavior.* Minneapolis: Burgess, 1972.

Haim, A. *Adolescent suicide.* New York: International Universities Press, 1974.

Holinger, P.C. Adolescent suicide: An epidemiological study of recent trends. *American Journal of Psychiatry,* 1978, **135**(7), 754–756.

Holinger, P.C. Violent deaths among the young: Recent trends in suicide, homicide, and accidents. *American Journal of Psychiatry,* 1979, **136**(9), 1144–1147.

Holinger, P.C. Violent deaths as a leading cause of mortality: An epidemiological study of suicide, homicide, and accidents. *American Journal of Psychiatry,* 1980, **137**(4), 472–476.

Jacobs, J. *Adolescent suicide.* New York: Wiley-Interscience, 1971.

Jacobziner, H. Attempted suicides in children. *Journal of Pediatrics,* 1960, **56**(4), 519–525.

Jacobziner, H. Attempted suicides in adolescence. *Journal of the American Medical Association,* 1965, **191**, 7–11.

Kallman, F.J., & Anastasio, M.M. Twin studies on the psychopathology of suicide. *Journal of Heredity,* 1946, **37**, 171–180.

Kallman, F.J., Deporte, J., Deporte, E., & Feingold, L. Suicide in twins and only children. *American Journal of Human Genetics,* 1949, **1**, 113–126.

Kastenbaum, R. Time and death in adolescence. In Feifel (Ed.), *The meaning of death.* New York: McGraw-Hill, 1959.

Kerfoot, M. Parent-child role reversal and adolescent suicidal behavior. *Journal of Adolescence,* 1979, **2**, 337–343.

Kerfoot, M. The family context of adolescent suicidal behavior. *Journal of Adolescence,* 1980, **3**, 335–346.

Kreider, D.G., & Motto, J. Parent-child role reversal and suicide states in adolescents. *Adolescence,* 1974, **9**(35), 365–370.

Lester, D. Fear of death of suicidal persons. *Psychological Reports,* 1967, **20**(3, Part 2), 1077–1078. (a)

Lester, D. Sibling position and suicidal behavior.

Journal of Individual Psychology, 1967, **22,** 204–207. (b)

Leventhal, T., & Sills, M. The issue of control in therapy with character problem adolescents. *Psychiatry,* 1963, **26**(2), 149–167.

Lewin, K. *Resolving social conflict.* New York: Harper, 1948.

Lourie, R.S. Clinical studies of attempted suicide in childhood. *Clinical Proceedings of Children's Hospital of the District of Columbia,* 1966, **22,** 163–173.

Marcia, J.E. Development and validation of ego identity status. *Journal of Personality and Social Psychology,* 1966, **3,** 551–558.

Marks, P.A., & Haller, D.L. Now I lay me down for keeps: A study of adolescent suicide attempts. *Journal of Clinical Psychology,* 1977, **33**(2), 390–400.

Mattsson, A., Seese, L.R., & Hawkins, J.W. Suicidal behavior as a child psychiatric emergency. *Archives of General Psychiatry,* 1969, **20,** 100–109.

Meeks, J.E. *The fragile alliance: An orientation to the outpatient psychotherapy of the adolescent.* Baltimore: Williams & Wilkins, 1971.

Millar, T.P. Limit setting and psychological maturation. *Archives of General Psychiatry,* 1968, **18**(2), 214–221.

Miller, J.P. Suicide in adolescence. *Adolescence,* 1975, **10**(37), 11–24.

Mintz, R.S. A pilot study of the prevalence of persons in the city of Los Angeles who have attempted suicide. Unpublished ms (presented in abbreviated form at American Psychiatric Association meetings, L.A., May, 1964) UCLA Neuropsychiatric Institute, Los Angeles, 1964.

Mortality Statistics Branch, National Center for Health Statistics, *Vital Statistics of the United States,* Volume II, General Mortality, 1960–1970, 1972–1973, 1974–1975 and 1976–1977.

Moss, L.M., Hamilton, D.C. The psychotherapy of the suicidal patient. *American Journal of Psychiatry,* 1956, **112,** 814–820.

Motto, J. Suicide and suggestibility—the role of the press. *American Journal os Psychiatry,* 1967, **124**(2), 252–256.

Otto, V. Changes in the behavior of children and adolescents preceding suicide attempts. *Acta Psychiatrica Scandinavica,* 1964, **49**(4), 386–400.

Parker, A.M. *Suicide among young adults.* New York: Exposition Press, 1974.

Peck, M.L. Adolescent suicide. In C.L. Hatton, S.M. Valents, & A. Rink (Eds.), *Suicide: Assessment and intervention.* New York: Appleton-Century-Crofts, 1977.

Powers, D. Youthful suicide attempts. *Northwest Medicine,* 1954, **53**(10), 1001–1002; Part 2, 1231–1232.

Powers, D. Suicide threats and attempts in the young. *American Practitioner,* 1956, **7**(7), 1140–1143.

Reese, F.D. School age suicide and the educational environment. In B.Q. Hafen (Ed.), *Self destructive behavior,* Minneapolis: Burgess, 1972.

Richman, J. Symbiosis, empathy, suicidal behavior and the family. *Suicide and Life-Threatening Behavior,* 1978, **8**(3), 139–147.

Rosenkrantz, A.L. A note on adolescent suicide: Incidence, dynamics and some suggestions for treatment. *Adolescence,* 1978, **13**(50), 209–214.

Ross, C.P. Mobilizing schools for suicide prevention. *Suicide and Life-Threatening Behavior,* 1980, **10**(4), 239–243.

Sanborn, D.E., Sanborn, C.J., & Cimbolic, P. Two years of suicide: A study of adolescent suicide in New Hampshire. *Child Psychiatry and Human Development,* 1973, **3**(4).

Satir, V. *Peoplemaking.* Palo Alto: Science and Behavior Books, 1972.

Schechter, M.D. The recognition and treatment of suicide in children. In E.S. Schneidman & N.L. Farberow (Eds.), *Clues to suicide,* New York: McGraw-Hill, 1957.

Schneer, H.I., & Kay, P. *The suicidal adolescent.* In S. Lorand & H. Schneer (Eds.), *Adolescents.* New York: Paul Hosbar, 1962.

Schneidman, E.S. Orientation toward cessation: A reexamination of current modes of death. *Journal of Forensic Sciences,* 1968, **13**(1), 33–45.

Schneidman, E.S., & Farberow, N.L. (Eds.). *Clues to suicide.* New York: McGraw-Hill, 1957.

Schneidman, E.S., & Farberow, N.L. Statistical comparison between attempted and committed suicides. In N.L. Farberow & E.S. Schneidman (Eds.), *The cry for help.* New York: McGraw-Hill, 1961.

Schrut, A. Suicidal adolescents and children. *Journal of the American Medical Association,* 1964, **188**(13), 1103–1107.

Seiden, R.H. Suicide among youth: A review of the

literature 1900–1967. *Bulletin of Suicidology,* Supplement, 1969.

Shapiro, L.B. Suicide: Psychology and family tendency. *Journal of Nervous and Mental Disease,* 1935, **81,** 547–553.

Shaw, C.R., & Schelkun, R.F. Suicidal behavior in children. *Psychiatry,* 1965, **28**(2), 157–169.

Stengel, E. *Suicide and attempted suicide.* Baltimore: Penguin, 1964.

Swanson, D.W. Suicide in identical twins. *American Journal of Psychiatry,* 1960, **116**(1), 934–935.

Teicher, J.D. A solution to the chronic problem of living: Adolescent attempted suicide. In J.C. Schoolar (Ed.), *Current issues in adolescent psychiatry,* New York: Brunner/Mazel, 1973, 129–147.

Teicher, J.D., & Jacobs, J. Adolescents who attempt suicide: Preliminary findings. *American Journal of Psychiatry,* 1966, **122**(11), 1248–1257.

Toolan, J.M. Suicide and suicidal attempts in children and adolescents. *American Journal of Psychiatry,* 1962, **119,** 228–232.

Toolan, J.M. Suicide in children. In Lenore McNeer (Ed.), *Proceedings of Conference on Depression and Suicide in Adolescents and Young Adults.* Fairlee, Vermont: June 1966, pp. 9–13. Cited in Seiden, R.H., Suicide among youth. *Bulletin of Suicidology,* (Supplement, 1969.)

Toolan, J.M. Suicide in children and adolescents. *American Journal of Psychotherapy,* 1975, **29**(3), 339–344.

Weiner, I.B. *Psychological disturbance in adolescence.* New York: Wiley-Interscience, 1970.

Whitlock, F.A., & Edwards, J.E. Pregnancy and attempted suicide. *Comprehensive Psychiatry,* 1968, **9,** 1–12.

Winn, D., & Halla, R. Observations of children who threaten to kill themselves. *Canadian Psychiatric Association Journal,* 1966, **11** (Supplement), 283–294.

Zilboorg, G. Considerations on suicide, with particular reference to that of the young. *American Journal of Orthopsychiatry,* 1937, **7,** 15–31.

CHAPTER 33

Development of Problems of Puberty and Sex Roles in Adolescence

GEORGE A. REKERS AND ANTHONY P. JURICH

Knowledge regarding normal sex role development and the psychological and physiological impact of puberty provides the clinical psychologist a context for diagnostically differentiating normal needs for sex education and guidance in heterosocial development from special needs for therapeutic intervention for adjustment problems in adolescents (Rekers & Milner, 1978). This task of differentiating normal adjustment phases in psychosexual development from psychological disturbances is complicated by the fact that normal adolescents must make a wide range of developmental adjustments pertaining to their socially ascribed sex roles and their rate of sexual maturation across the years just before and during puberty.

ADJUSTMENT PROBLEMS ASSOCIATED WITH PUBERTAL CHANGES

Puberty is the period during which the child becomes fully mature sexually and able to reproduce (Marshall, 1972). The child undergoes a maturing of the reproductive organs, growth of the genitals, development of the secondary sex characteristics, changes in the quantity and distribution of fat and muscle tissue, and passage through the adolescent growth spurt (Barnes, 1975; Cheek, 1974; Faust, 1977; Grumbach, 1975; Marshall, 1972; Marshall, 1978; Marshall & Tanner,

1969, 1970; Nelson, 1978; Tanner, 1962). These changes are brought about by changes in the gonadotropin and sex steroid secretion (Faiman & Winter, 1974; Grumbach, 1975; Grumbach et al., 1974, chap. 6; Marshall & Tanner, 1968, 1969, 1970; Root & Russ, 1972; Sizonenko & Lewin, 1972; Visser, 1973; Zacharias & Wurtman, 1969).

Although pubertal changes are dramatic because of their suddenness and velocity (Faust, 1977; Logan, 1980), the sexual maturation process begins prenatally and reaches fruition in completely developed adults (Goldfarb, 1977; Money & Ehrhardt, 1972; Styne & Grumbach, 1978; Styne & Kaplan, 1979). Moreover, pubertal development is a multifaceted process, drawing not only from the human body, biology, and chemistry but also from environmental inputs (Goldfarb, 1977; Protinsky & Farrier, 1980).

Heightened Energy Level

Martin (1972) points out that the most obvious characteristic of the pubescent adolescent is a general "twitchiness." Many adolescents are often in "perpetual motion," with fingers tapping, heads turning, bodies squirming, and feet wiggling in a display of seemingly uncontrolled physical confusion (Blair & Burton, 1951; Martin, 1972; Petersen & Taylor, 1980). In general, this heightened energy level results from rapid changes within the adolescent's endocrine system (Hays, 1978). This "bundle of energy" may place the pubescent adolescent at risk for conflict with parental standards for behavior. The highly active adolescent may find it difficult to take time to keep neat and clean as he or she is frequently hurrying off somewhere (Blair & Burton, 1951). Even when clean and neat, the adolescent's physical activity level renders it difficult to remain in that condition for long. This enhanced energy level, coupled with a spurt in muscular development, accounts for the difficulty many adolescents have in trying to remain quiet or walk orderly. Active adolescent behavior often distracts and annoys adults, particularly the teenager's parents.

The heightened energy level accompanying puberty also influences the adolescent's emotional life, lowering the threshold for emotion-producing stimuli (Ausubel, Montemayor, & Svajian, 1977). Emotional reactions become more intense and occur more frequently to a wider range of stimuli. This makes the adolescent's emotional response unpredictable. It leads to a disparity between the adolescent's emotional reactions and the expectations of those around him or her, thus creating emotional problems (Frisk, 1975; Harrison, 1975). The adolescent may experience a moodiness characterized by strong feelings of guilt, anxiety, irritability, shame, erotic arousability, happiness, pleasure, pride, intolerance, and depression (Gallagher & Harris, 1976; Gustin, 1961; Hurlock & Sender, 1930; Nixon, 1966; Petersen & Taylor, 1980; Tryon, 1939). Because pubescent adolescents can feel so strongly, they are particularly vulnerable to depression and depressive cycles (Anyan, 1978). If an adolescent retreats into a shell of withdrawn silence, those around him or her, particularly his or her parents, may misinterpret this as anger or annoyance. Even if they correctly recognize the depression, the significant others in the adolescent's life may become frustrated in their attempts to draw the adolescent out of the depression. In response, they themselves may withdraw from the adolescent, contributing to further depression.

The Adolescent Growth Spurt

The increase in size during adolescence is one of the most socially salient aspects of the period of pubescence (Anyan, 1978; Faust, 1977; Frisch, 1974; McCammon, 1970; Nelson, 1978; Styne & Kaplan, 1979; Tanner, 1974; Tuddenham & Snyder, 1954). This growth involves both size and weight and is due to both skeletal maturation (Anyan, 1978; Bayer & Bayler, 1959; Faust, 1977; Marshall, 1978; Nelson, 1978; Stolz & Stolz, 1951; Tanner, 1974) and the development of skeletal muscles (Anyan, 1978; Cheek, 1968; Faust, 1977; Graystone, 1968; Marshall, 1978; McComas, Sica, & Petito, 1973; Nelson, 1978; Tanner, 1974). The increase in weight and strength is especially noticeable in boys, who gain 50 percent more muscle tissue during their growth spurt than do girls (Anyan, 1978; Faust, 1977; Jones, 1944). In girls, the growth spurt starts between 9.5 and 9.6 years, while the corresponding growth spurt for males starts between 11.6 and 11.7 years (Anyan, 1978; Faust, 1977; Frisch & Revelle, 1971; Tanner, Whitehouse, & Takaishi, 1966). The same studies found the peak of the growth spurt to occur between 11.8 and 12.1 years for girls and 14 and 14.1 years for boys. Because the boys' growth spurt lags on an average of two years behind the girls', the early adolescent girl is often taller than her male counterpart (Faust, 1977). Because of the discrepancy between the cultural ideal of a taller, stronger male and the reality of an earlier maturing female, many pubescent adolescent males resent their female counterparts and begin to act out in an effort to achieve equality. Theoretically, this phenomenon may constitute a source for some later male hostility toward women.

Especially in males, the discrepancy between the adolescent's physical capabilities and the performance demands placed upon him by others may contribute to serious emotional problems (Langen, 1977). Adolescent boys who demonstrated high levels of physical strength were rated by their peers as being more popular, having more emotional buoyancy, being better adjusted socially, and having better family adjustment (Jones, 1946). Boys with lower levels of physical strength had more generalized tensions and physical symptoms and rated themselves as being personally inferior. The adolescent male, who is relatively inferior in his physical development, is at risk for a compounding problem (Jones, 1944). His poor physical abilities lead to low levels of social prestige. Because of this, the adolescent shuns further physical and group activities. This causes even further isolation and a potential retardation of physical skill acquisition.

Perhaps the most outstanding characteristic of the adolescent growth spurt is the increase in velocity or rate of growth (Anyan, 1978; Blair & Burton, 1951; Faust, 1977; Gordon, 1972; Nelson, 1978; Roche & Davila, 1972; Styne & Kaplan, 1979; Tanner, 1974; Tuddenham & Snyder, 1954). An adolescent boy may grow 10.9 centimeters and 8.4 kilograms a year, while his female counterpart may grow 10.1 centimeters and 7.2 kilograms in a year (Tuddenham & Snyder, 1954). The adolescent's body is literally changing at a faster rate than his or her mind may be able to modify its body image. This can contribute to an unstable self-concept and to more self-consciousness (Protinsky & Farrier, 1980). Related to this, the adolescent may be inept at managing first impressions and feel particularly awkward in heterosocial contacts (Gordon, 1972). Many pubescent adolescents experience an increase of subjective anticipatory fears (Bamber, 1979). In these ways, the adolescent's rapid growth rate may contribute to restlessness, disciplinary problems, lack of initiative, and the temporary emergence of less agreeable personality traits (Blair & Burton, 1951).

Primary Sex Organ Changes

Shortly after the beginning of the growth spurt, the same hormonal trigger spurs the release of male and female sex hormones (androgens and estrogens), bringing about primary sex and reproductive organ changes

(Anyan, 1978; Faiman & Winter, 1974; Faust, 1977; Frisch & Revelle, 1971; Grumbach et al., 1974; Hafez, 1976; Highham, 1980; Marshall & Tanner, 1970; Nelson, 1978; Petersen & Taylor, 1980; Tanner, 1962; 1975; Tepperman, 1968; Zacharias & Wurtmen, 1969). In males, the most obvious changes are the enlargement and growth of the penis, the full descent and enlargement of the testicles, and the production of motile sperm (Anyan, 1978; Hafez, 1976; Higham, 1980; Lloyd, 1964; Marshall & Tanner, 1970; Parkes, 1970; Petersen & Taylor, 1980; Tanner, 1965). There is a corresponding growth in the internal reproductive organs, such as the seminal vesicles (Hafez, 1976; Higham, 1980; Lloyd, 1964; Tanner, 1975). There is an episodic secretion of luteinizing hormone during sleep (Petersen & Taylor, 1980), leading to a first ejaculation, typically between the ages of 12 and 13 (Levin, 1976), and to the occurrence of nocturnal emissions in males between the ages of 12 and 16 (Hafez, 1976; Lloyd, 1964; Ramsey, 1943; Tanner, 1965).

There is also noticeable growth in both the external and internal genitalia of the pubescent female, beginning at about 11–12 years old (Goldfarb, 1977; Petersen & Taylor, 1980). This coincides with the first appearance of vaginal secretions (Goldfarb, 1977; Styne & Kaplan, 1979) and a widening of the pelvic diameter (Hafez, 1976). The menstrual cycle of hormone production leading to menstrual flow of blood begins to take place (Higham, 1980; Petersen & Taylor, 1980). Menarche, the first menstrual cycle, occurs relatively late in the pubescent female's growth spurt (Faut, 1977), typically after the peak growth spurt (Anyan, 1978) and after the beginning of breast development (Hafez, 1976). The average of menarche ranges from 12 to 13.5, with the age ranges within studies fluctuating from 10 to 16.5 years (Goldfarb, 1977; Levin, 1976; Marshall & Tanner, 1969; Tanner, 1962; Zacharias, Wurtman, & Schatzoff, 1970). Despite the occurence of menarche, the typical adolescent girl does not achieve full reproductive capacity until a few years after menarche, when follicular maturation, ovulation, and the development of the corpus luteum have been completed (Hafez, 1976).

If the young adolescent is not prepared ahead of time for the occurrence of the changes, the above developmental events can be extremely traumatic. The boy, experiencing his first nocturnal emission, may believe that he is enuretic or abnormal in some way. The girl may believe she is physically wounded or sick (Logan, 1980). These first negative associations may be carried as developmental liabilities far into adulthood. Even if the adolescent has been fully prepared for the changes in primary sex organs, the changes are so dramatic and so sudden that he or she may, indeed, be overwhelmed by his or her own sexual blossoming.

Secondary Sex Characteristics

The first sign of secondary sex characteristics usually occurs between 8 and 13 in girls and a year or two later in boys (Marshall & Tanner, 1969; 1970). For specific developmental charts and graphs, the reader is referred to Tanner (1962). In the female, the most obvious secondary sex characteristic is the development of her breasts (Anyan, 1978; Faust, 1977; Styne & Kaplan, 1979; Tanner, 1962; 1975). Breasts may begin to bud as early as age 9 and usually take two to three years to complete. Development usually takes place in five stages (Marshall & Tanner, 1969):

1. There is elevation of the papilla only (Goldfarb, 1977).
2. In the "breast bud" stage, there is an elevation of the breast and the papilla as a small mound (Goldfarb, 1977; Gordon, 1972; Tanner, 1965).
3. Breast and areola both enlarge and are elevated as pigmentation begins to show (Goldfarb, 1977; Tanner, 1965).
4. The areola and papilla form a secondary mound projecting above the contour of the breast (Marshall & Tanner, 1969).
5. The papilla only projects, with the areola recessed to the general contour of the breast (Marshall & Tanner, 1969).

With most adolescent girls, their breast development is important as a symbol of sexual maturity and sex appropriateness (Ausubel et al., 1977). In fact, because the breasts are only slightly affected by clothing, they are most often the most important secondary sex characteristic for the adolescent girl. Because it is so crucial and because the young female has little or no control over her breast development, breast size is often a common cause for concern among adolescent girls (Nelson, 1978). Because of the emphasis placed upon breasts by American culture, few women are satisfied with their breast size. The pubescent girl must come to grips with the fact that these are the breasts she has developed and there is little she can do to alter them. This may cause a great discrepancy between reality and her ideal body image. She may withdraw from sports or stop wearing bathing suits or tight-fitting clothes because she feels self-conscious about her breasts (Anyan, 1978).

Pubescent boys may also become self-conscious about their breasts (Hafez, 1976). If the right amount of deactivation of estrogens fails to take place, as in some diseases of the liver, the male may find an embarrassing amount of breast development takng place during his puberty (Ausubel et ai., 1977).

The growth of body hair goes through similar stages of development (Marshall & Tanner, 1969, 1970). There is development in the pubic area, from a light vellus over the pubes, to long, slightly pigmented, tawny hair, to darker hair (which begins to cover the genitals), to sparsely spread adult pubic hair, to fully spread adult pubic hair (Goldfarb, 1977; Marshall & Tanner, 1969, 1970; Tanner, 1965). In most adolescents, pubic hair is the first secondary sex characteristic (Faust, 1977). Axillary and facial hair typically begin to grow and darken one to two years after the first appearance of pubic hair (Lloyd, 1964). Because of the inconspicuousness of external genitalia in women, pubic hair growth may be an important social criterion of pubescense in adolescent girls (Ausubel et al., 1977). However, for the adolescent boys, the appearance of facial hair is the most significant badge of sexual maturity (Ausubel et al., 1977). In women, hirsutism—the growth of dark, coarse terminal hairs on the face (especially those women who are dark-skinned)—may constitute a major problem, causing a large amount of self-concept difficulty (Anyan, 1978).

Although there is pubescent larynx growth in both sexes, the testosterone in the male stimulates a greatly accelerated rate of growth in the adolescent boy's larynx (Hafez, 1976; Petersen & Taylor, 1980). The rapidity of the growth is faster than the boy's ability to gain the skill to control his "voicebox" (Ausubel et al., 1977). It is not unusual for a pubescent boy's voice to crack during this period, causing him embarrassment.

The secondary sex characteristics are important to the adolescent because they serve as the prime indices of masculinity and femininity, as well as maturity (Ausubel et al., 1977). They are more readily available and socially accessible as criteria of maturity than are the primary sex organ changes. They also play a major part in the adolescent's peer group's definition of social attractiveness. Most adolescents view their secondary sex characteristics as a source of pride.

Sex Education in Adolescence

The adolescent will be potentially better adjusted to the transitions of puberty if he or she is provided accurate sex education information regarding the adolescent growth spurt, primary sex organ changes, and the development of secondary sex characteristics prior to their occurrence in his or her own life experience (Miles, 1971; Scanzoni, 1973; Shatin & Southworth, 1961). This education on the biology of sexual development and change is often introduced into the health education curricula in schools for the preadolescent and adolescent (Dearth, 1974; Haims, 1973). In addition to this information on physical

sexual development, adolescents benefit from knowledge about venereal disease (Fodor, 1973), society's laws regulating sexual behavior and marriage contracts (duMas, 1979; MacNamara & Segrin, 1977; Ploscowe, 1962), courtship relationships (Grant, 1973; Miles, 1971), and the ethical and moral dimensions of sexuality (Babbage, 1965; Braun & Rekers, 1981; Hefley, 1971; Olford & Lawes, 1963) given to them by their parents, church, school, and/or their clinical psychologist (Dickinson, 1971; Thornburg, 1972). When an adolescent is referred to a clinical psychologist for assessment or treatment of any of a variety of presenting problems, it often becomes appropriate to assess the adolescent's sex information over this range of issues. If the adolescent is lacking the basic information concerning sex, then it should be provided directly through counseling or assigned readings, or after consulting with the adolescent's parent, church, and/or physician, an appropriate referral should be made so that the adolescent receives the needed sex education elsewhere.

PROBLEMS SECONDARY TO PUBERTY RELATED TO SOCIAL APPEARANCE

If the adolescent should, in any way, feel abnormal or different, he or she can experience shame and embarrassment (Gallagher & Harris, 1976; Gordon, 1972; Stolz & Stolz, 1944). This is especially true for girls, because of society's emphasis on the physical attributes as criteria for social attractiveness. This physical "deviance" can be a tremendous disadvantage to the adolescent because of the peer group emphasis on physical attractiveness and can lead to self-concept problems and eventually even to behavior disorders (Gallagher & Harris, 1976; Jones, 1965).

Acne

Acne and the facial blemishes associated with it are the most frequently voiced concerns of adolescents (Anyan, 1978). Goldfarb (1977) found evidence for acne conditions in 75–90 percent of the adolescent population. The sudden increase in the production of testosterone causes an enlargement and increased activity of the sebaceous (oil-producing) glands (Anyan, 1978). Although the glands enlarge and increase activity, the excretory ducts do not, causing poor drainage that may lead to pimples, blackheads, and, if infection sets in, acne (Strauss & Pochi, 1976). This may cause great concern over cosmetic appearance among adolescents whose social and heterosocial adjustment may, in large part, be dependent upon this physical appearance (Ausubel, et al., 1977). This may cause the adolescent to withdraw from social activities, thereby contributing to self-concept problems. This situation is exacerbated by adults, such as parents and teachers, if they minimize the importance of acne and fail to understand the level of adolescent concern.

Aside from early dermatological treatment by a physician, little is known about how specific interventions might ameliorate the psychosocial problems associated wth acne. While the biological etiology of acne falls outside the realm of the psychological practitioner, psychotherapeutic assistance can best be directed toward working with the adolescent on self-acceptance and the development of social skills to minimize the potential self-esteem problems (Hops, Walker, & Greenwood, 1979). Medical treatment of the acne can have a beneficial psychological effect. In the absence of effective medical treatment, the adolescent may feel a powerlessness over his complexion. If this sense of powerlessness is generalized, an assessment should be conducted to ascertain whether the adolescent is at risk for acting-out disorders (Atkeson & Forehand, 1981) on one end of a continuum, or depression (Costello, 1981) on the other. Psychological assessment in the individual case can help to determine what kind of psychological treatment may be indicated for the potential problems in self-esteem, social adjustment, or mood state as a reaction to uncontrolled acne.

Obesity

Obesity is often clinically defined as 20 percent more than the expected body weight for the individual's height (Anyan, 1978). Shortly after the maximum growth spurt for the adolescent, it is common for the pubescent boy or girl to gain an accumulation of fat tissue (Faust, 1977; Nelson, 1978). For the obese adolescent, this gain in fat tissue may be neither temporary nor slight. It is a product of hereditary factors, nutrition, and sociocultural factors (Anyan, 1978; Heald & Khan, 1975). The obese adolescent typically suffers from a disturbed body image in which he or she feels unattractive and expects rejection from social relationships (Anyan, 1978; Kirkpatrick & Sanders, 1978). Therefore, he or she may withdraw from social interactions to dwell in a world of psychological and social distress (Heald & Khan, 1975; Mayer, 1972). As a result, obesity is a common problem for which adolescents seek both medical (Morgenthan, 1975) and mental health care (Mayer, 1972).

The psychological case management of the obese adolescent depends, in large part, upon the clinician's diagnosis of the genesis and maintenance of the obesity (Foreyt & Goodrick, 1981). If the obesity is physically or glandularly induced, the clinician may need to help the adolescent work on self-acceptance, develop social skills, and/or cope with the social and personal adjustment to a physical ailment (Hartz, Giefer, & Rimm, 1977). However, if the adolescent's obesity is diagnosed as psychogenic in etiology, the clinician must explore the factors that contribute to this physical condition in the individual. A multitude of treatment modalities may be appropriate, depending upon the specific nature of the psychosocial deficiency diagnosed. For example, client-centered approaches may assist the client to build self-acceptance. Psychodynamic approaches may explore the intrapersonal dynamics that result in obesity. Behavior modification techniques can aid in the management of a proper dietary and exercise regimen for weight reduction (Christakis et al., 1966; Coates & Thoreson, 1978, 1980; Jeffery, Wing, & Stundard, 1978; Moody et al., 1972; Stunkard & Mahoney, 1976; Wheeler & Hess, 1976).

Anorexia Nervosa

At puberty, some adolescents experience a weight loss that may be accompanied by a state of malnutrition (Styne & Kaplan, 1979). Such a weight loss may be consciously sought by the adolescent as a reaction to the gain in fat tissue during puberty. Although it occurs in males (Beumont & Beardwood, 1972), the occurrence of anorexia is more frequent in females. Particularly in females, when the weight loss is severe and is accompanied by food avoidance, a distorted body image, considerable physical activity, and amenorrhea, the condition of anorexia nervosa may exist (Styne & Kaplan, 1979). The adolescent may become obsessed with weight control or reduction. Anorexia may develop at a time of great change for the adolescent, such as menarche or other pubertal changes (Anyan, 1978). Although the adolescent remains physically active, he or she often isolates himself or herself from social contact in order to avoid peer or parental criticism. Physical health and survival can be threatened by this condition.

The psychological treatment of the anorexic adolescent focuses, for the most part, upon the underlying dimensions of the symptomatic behavior (Bruch, 1970). The clinician must assess the motivations maintaining the adolescent's anorexic behavior. Intervention may consist of individual psychotherapeutic or behavioral techniques, including readjustment of expectations and modified behavioral patterns. Family therapy is frequently recommended to deal with the social system involved in the etiology and maintenance of the problem (Chapman, 1974). (See other chapters in this book for specific clinical management of anorexia nervosa in adolescence.)

The Timing of Puberty

Adolescents vary greatly in the age of the onset of puberty and in the duration of time from onset to completion of the pubertal changes (Faust, 1977; Marshall, 1978). Although it is widely recognized that girls reach puberty earlier than boys, there is often greater variation among the girls' duration of puberty than there is between the girls' and boys' durations (Faust, 1977). Part of this variance in both onset and duration is due to the fact puberty is under the control of both endogenous and exogenous factors such as genetics, heredity, nutrition, geographical location, illness, socioeconomic status, social environment, physical environment, and family milieu (Hafez, 1976; Langen, 1977; Steger, 1976; Styne & Kaplan, 1979; Zacharias & Wurtman, 1969). Therefore, puberty is not a single event but a series of developmental cycles varying considerably in the age at which they occur and the age at which they end (Marshall, 1978).

Although there is a large group of adolescents that develop approximately on the norm of pubertal development, there are also two large groups whose puberty, when compared to that of their age mates, is either early or late (Anyan, 1978; Faust, 1977; Jones, 1965; Livson & Peskin, 1980; Marshall & Tanner, 1969; Nelson, 1978; Tanner, 1962). In many ways, both the early- and the late-maturing adolescents can feel at psychological disadvantage with respect to their peers. During adolescence, despite the reality of the lack of uniformity in pubertal development, there is a "tyranny of the norm" (Ausubel et al., 1977; Stolz & Stolz, 1944). Because of the increased importance of the body upon the adolescent's self-concept, the adolescent is very body conscious, and physical appearance becomes a major source of status in the peer group. Any deviation from the norm can become a source of psychosocial hardship for the adolescent (Langen, 1977). The seriousness of the problem depends upon the conspicuousness of the deviation. Therefore, the number of years of acceleration or retardation of puberty is relevant for determining the degree of stress upon the adolescent.

Early maturers tend to be taller, heavier, and more stout than their later maturing counterparts (Anyan, 1978; Frisch & Revelle, 1971). They grow faster during their growth spurts (Faust, 1977). Early-maturing boys get a better reception from the adult world because they are most often treated with reference to their physical, not chronological, age (Jones, 1965; Livson & Peskin, 1980). They are also superior to their peers in athletics. These advantages enable them to have a higher level of self-esteem, more behavioral confidence, and social maturity. Frequently, they marry at an earlier age and become fathers sooner than their later-maturing cohorts (Kiernan, 1977). The early-maturing girl is more "out of step" with her peers (Jones, 1949; Livson & Peskin, 1980; Peskin, 1973). Because her development is so rapid and different from that of her peers, the early-maturing girl can become self-conscious about her own body, preoccupied with her own sexual image, and socially vulnerable to her peers. She might tend to withdraw and become less expressive and more submissive. Ultimately, she is usually rated as less popular by her peers.

Late maturers finally achieve the same height as their earlier-maturing age mates, but they tend to be thinner (Anyan, 1978; Firsch & Revelle, 1971). Because he typically cannot perform up to the capabilities of his age mates, especially in sports, the late-maturing male must overcome his feelings of physical inferiority, shyness, inadequacy, and low self-concept (Jones, 1965; Livson & Peskin, 1980; Stolz & Stolz, 1951). He often accomplishes this by engaging in behavioral styles of bravado, such as being boisterous or bossy. This may lead to some behavioral problems and even delinquency, but it can also lead to a more flexible style of functioning as an older adolescent or adult (Stolz & Stolz, 1951). The late-maturing girl is usually perceived to be more in step than her early-maturing counterpart. Her growth is less abrupt, her stature can be considered petite, and she is more in synchrony with the development of the boys her age (Jones, 1949; Livson & Peskin, 1980; Peskin, 1973). She is typically rated by her peers as being good looking in appearance, attractive, expressive,

sociable, prestigious, gregarious, poised, socially aware, assertive, and active.

Consequently, early-maturing boys and late-maturing girls seem to have the fewest liabilities. Early-maturing girls and late-maturing boys often have the poorest adjustment because they stand out as the most socially conspicuous (Ausubel et al., 1977).

In some cases, because of pathological physical conditions, the adolescent either has an extremely early or an extremely late puberty (Goldrath & Sherman, 1976). Cases of precocious puberty are rare but do exist (Bain & Howard, 1976; Nelson, 1978; Styne & Kaplan, 1979; Winter, Faiman, & Reyes, 1978). Most often, these cases begin puberty before the age of 8 in females and 9.5 in males (Higham, 1980). These children typically have severe body-image problems, stemming from teasing about such things as breasts and menses or penis size and scrotal hair (Higham, 1980). This may lead to a poor self-concept, strained peer relationships, and a delay in dating behavior. In addition, many parents fear that the precocious pubertal child may become sexually promiscuous and run wild. Even though the data would indicate that promiscuity is not the result of precocious puberty, the fearful parent often overreacts to the child and adds to the difficulty of the pubertal transition.

If the boy's testes have not begun to enlarge by 13.5 or the girl's breast development has not started by age 13, the adolescent may be experiencing delayed puberty (Bain & Howard, 1976; Higham, 1980; Shenker, Nussbaum, & Kaplan, 1978; Styne & Kaplan, 1979; Winter et al., 1978). Such an extreme delay in puberty causes severe distress in the adolescent (Higham, 1980). The adolescent may feel embarrassment, shame, anxiety, and a lack of self-confidence. This may cause him or her to separate from his or her peers and withdraw from normal social interactions. Boys with delayed puberty have a difficult time competing in athletics, while the delayed-puberty girls may find themselves at social disadvantage in the dating market. In either case, the greater the delay in their physical development, the greater their potential psychological distress.

In the clinical management of cases of late or early puberty, the clinician must help the client cope with the fact that the cause of the pubertal timing (in the vast majority of cases) is beyond the control of the client, his or her physician, and the psychologist (Kaplan, 1975). The temptation of parents is to offer one of two pieces of superficial advice: (1) "Wait until you grow up," or (2) "Just wait until your friends catch up to you." Although ultimately and realistically the only factor that will physically alter the situation is time, the adolescent typically receives little benefit from such advice by itself. The clinician should attempt to ease the discomfort associated with coping with an advanced or retarded puberty. Assisting the adolescent in identity formation and self-acceptance can help. Group work, whether educative or rehabilitative, with early or late maturers and their peers can focus on social skills and empathy for peers at different levels of pubertal development. Family therapy, with both parents and siblings, can diffuse potential secondary problems and promote family cohesiveness as a mutual support system. These examples of potential interventions underline the need for assessing the emotional needs of the individual adolescent rather than reiterating the simplistic prescription to wait that is often offered by well-meaning parents (Thomas, 1973).

PSYCHOLOGICAL REORGANIZATION

A major task of the adolescent is to develop an adult personal identity by the end of the adolescent years (Erikson, 1950; Frisk, 1975; Haft, 1973). During puberty, elements of the adolescent's identity are examined and restructured (Frist, 1975; Haft, 1973; Harrison, 1975; Kagan, 1972). Because puberty is such a major change in physical characteristics, it often may contribute to a crisis experienced by the adolescent (Brigham et al., 1981; Frank & Cohen, 1979; Frist, 1975; Langen, 1975; 1977; Meilman, 1979). The changes in physi-

cal appearance prompt the adolescent to change his or her body image (Koff, Rierdan, & Silverstone, 1978; Peterson & Taylor, 1980; Rituo, 1977). This makes coping with a new body image a major task in early adolescence (Ausubel et al., 1977; Koff et al., 1978; Rituo, 1977; Sugar, 1979).

This process can result in stress for the pubescent adolescent for several reasons. The physical changes are so comprehensive and rapid that the adolescent may become confused (Ausubel et al., 1977). His or her body may change more quickly than he or she can adequately modify his or her body image (Stolz & Stolz, 1944). For the first time since infancy, the adolescent must cope with strong new drives that are biologically induced (Blos, 1972). The pubertal adolescent is faced with the emerging biological drives of an adult at a time when psychological adaptation skills are at an advanced childhood developmental level (Blos, 1972; Josselson, 1980; Kagan, 1972; Petersen & Taylor, 1980). Some pubescent adolescents attempt to cope by regression in adjustment (Josselson, 1980). If the adolescent is unable to progress from childhood coping strategies to a more adult adjustment, he may become fixated at an immature stage of development (Kagan, 1972).

The adolescent attempts to cope by scrutinizing thoughts, attitudes, and feelings about his or her body, the discrepancy between ideal and actual body characteristics, and the pubertal process (Frisk, 1975; Harrison, 1975; McCoy, 1974; Petersen & Taylor, 1980; Salzman, 1974; Sugar, 1979). This leads the adolescent to explore his or her attitudes about growing up, about gender role, and identifying with his or her parents (Barlow et al., 1977; Brown, 1972; Petersen & Taylor, 1980; Rekers et al., in press). The adolescent's family may play a key role in helping the adolescent with his or her psychological reorganization (Rituo, 1977; Schenfeld, 1966; Sugar, 1979). Particularly in the absence of a supportive family, peers play a crucial role in helping the adolescent affirm his or her newly reorganized self (Higham, 1980; Protinsky & Farrier, 1980; Koff et al., 1978).

SEXUAL ADJUSTMENT IN ADOLESCENCE

In the adjustment to a new body image, the pubescent adolescent must transform his or her self-image from that of a boy or girl to a sexual being (Higham, 1980; Langen, 1977; Meilman, 1979). The physiological changes in puberty prompt increased sexual thoughts, feelings, and actions in the adolescent (Bell, 1969; Johnson, 1973; Kagan, 1972; Martinson, 1972; Renshaw, 1975; Sigust & Schmidt, 1973; Sorensen, 1973). Frequency of masturbation increases, particularly in boys, and the exploration of heterosexual and homosexual behaviors increases (Ferguson & Rekers, 1979; Gagnen, 1972; Kinsey, Pomeroy, & Martin, 1948; Rekers, 1980; Stirt, 1940). Sexual thoughts, fantasies, and actions may produce considerable guilt and fear of parental discovery (Higham, 1980; Kagan, 1972; Koff et al., 1978; Protinsky & Farrier, 1980; Szasz, 1971; Vener, 1974). The problems stemming from these conditions often persist far into adulthood.

The etiology of many cases of sexual deviation has been traced to the adolescent period of development. The problems of transsexualism, transvestism, fetishism, and homosexuality will be reviewed below in the section on sex role development. A more extensive review of the treatment of sexual problems in adolescence is offered by Rekers (1978b). Here it is only briefly noted that clinical psychological treatment procedures have been reported for a variety of adolescent sexual adjustment problems, including exhibitionism (Callahan & Leitenberg, 1973; Lowenstein, 1973; MacCulloch, Williams, & Birtles, 1971), sadistic sexual fantasies (Mees, 1966), and promiscuous sexual behavior (Anant, 1968).

Other sexual problems in adolescence that have been reported in the clinical literature include excessive or public masturbation (Levine & Bell, 1956; Stirt, 1940), sexual asphyxias (Coe, 1974; Edmondson, 1972; Resnik, 1972; Shankel & Carr, 1956; Stearns, 1953), prostitution (Craft, 1966; Deisher, 1970; Deisher, Eisner, & Sulzbacher, 1969; Gandy & Deisher, 1970; Ginsburg, 1967;

Pittman, 1971; Raven, 1963; Reiss, 1963; Rosenblum, 1975; Russell, 1971), and sex offenses (Atcheson & Williams, 1954; Hackett, 1971; Nadler, 1968; Roberts, McBee, & Bettis, 1969; Shoor, Speed, & Bartelt, 1966).

Clinical psychologists also encounter adolescents who have been victims of various forms of sexual abuse (Brunold, 1964; Mangus, 1932; Schultz, 1972, 1973; Weiss et al., 1955). Adjustment problems have been reported in cases where the minor is exposed to the observation of certain adult sexual behavior or pornography (Bender & Grugett, 1952; Katzman, 1972; Mangus, 1953) and where minors have been victims of sexual seduction (Bender & Blau, 1937; Breen, Greenwald, & Gregori, 1972; Capraro, 1967; Langsley, Schwartz, & Fairbairn, 1968; Litin, Giffin, & Johnson, 1956). Treatment is often required for the adolescent victims of sexual abuse (Eaton & Vastbinder, 1969; Hogan, 1974; Kiefer, 1973; Roth, 1972; Schultz, 1972) as well as for their parents (Weeks, 1976). Various treatment approaches have been reported for adolescents and their families who are involved in incest (Cormier, Kennedy, & Sangowics, 1962; Eist & Mandel, 1968; Harbart et al., 1974; Hersko et al., 1961; Kennedy & Cormier, 1969; Langsley et al., 1968; Pittman, 1976).

PROBLEMS IN SEX ROLE DEVELOPMENT

Sex roles in adolescence are defined by the dimensions of masculine and feminine behavior and personality characteristics. While early psychological tests conceptualized masculinity/femininity as a unidimensional, bipolar phenomenon, more recent psychological research (see Rosen & Rekers, 1980) has involved the measurements of two separate continua—namely, the degree of masculinity (ranging from low to high) and, separately, the degree of femininity (also ranging from low to high). An adolescent scoring high on masculine behavior and low on feminine behavior (in some area of sex role development) would be designated as masculine. The adolescent scoring high on femininity and low on masculinity would be designated feminine for that aspect of sex role development. An individual measuring low in frequency of feminine behavior *and* masculine behavior would be designated undifferentiated in sex role. And a person scoring high on both masculinity *and* femininity is termed androgynous (Bem, 1974; 1975).

Sex role behaviors receive their definition from a variety of sources. There are four main categories for defining sex role characteristics (Rekers, 1981b):

1. Some masculine and feminine sex role characteristics are purely biologically defined. Breast-feeding is an example of feminine sex role, while impregnating a female is a masculine sex role behavior.

2. Other masculine and feminine sex role behaviors are socially defined but based on some physical sex differences. For example, modesty associated with the upper torso is a socially defined, feminine sex role behavior based upon anatomical sex differences while participation in aggressive athletic activity (such as boxing) appears to be a socially defined masculine sex role characteristic based upon a sex difference in aggression and physical strength. Sex-typed body gestures may have some basis in anatomical sex differences, even though they may be further differentiated by socialization processes (Rekers, Amaro-Plotkin, & Low, 1977; Rekers & Mead, 1979b; Rekers & Rudy, 1978; Rekers, Sanders, & Strauss, 1981; Rekers et al., 1976).

3. Some socially designated masculine and feminine behaviors are legitimate but arbitrary assignments with no direct biological basis, often acquired in adolescent development. In North American society, the wearing of lipstick is a feminine sex role behavior and the wearing of certain kinds of shirts with neckties is a masculine-assigned sex role behavior.

4. A number of masculine and feminine sex role stereotypes are both arbitrary and harmful to individual development in our culture. The role of a doctor has been stereotyped as masculine while the role of nurse has been stereotyped as feminine. This is the kind of destructive sex role stereotype that interferes with the optimal vocational achievement of individuals in our society. It is this last category that has become the target of enlightened criticism in recent decades (Rekers et al., 1978).

Sex Role Problems in Adolescent Boys

Problems in sex role development may occur as early as 3 and 4 years (Rekers, 1977a, 1982b). However, as children move toward adolescence, they become more and more aware of the socially defined components of sex roles and learn to make finer discriminations between masculine and feminine sex type behaviors in themselves and others (Rosen, Rekers, & Friar, 1977). This poses a particular diagnostic problem for the clinical child psychologist because the adolescent, unlike the young child, may rarely admit to deviant patterns of sex typing or to sexual identity problems (Rekers & Milner, 1981). If a parent or other social agent has referred the adolescent to the clinician, the self-conscious patient may not be initially cooperative with an assessment of potential problems in sex role development.

Hypermasculinity

One type of sex role problem in adolescent boys is a syndrome of excessive hypermasculinity. This pattern is seen in teenage boys who are destructive, interpersonally violent, belligerent, and uncontrolled and who lack gentle and socially sensitive behaviors (Harrington, 1970). These exaggeratedly "supermasculine" boys have adopted a "macho" caricature of the masculine social role and they require therapeutic intervention. Some cases of unsocialized aggressive behavior disorders have their etiology in a sex role development problem (Rekers et al., 1977).

A careful psychological assessment of the adolescent boy is necessary to ascertain the functional characteristics of the conduct disorder (Atkeson & Forehand, 1981) and its potential relationship to a psychosexual disorder (Rekers, 1981b). Based upon this individual assessment, treatment may be required for the conduct disorder itself (MacFarlane, Allen, & Honzik, 1954; Patterson et al., 1975; Phillips et al., 1972; Robins, 1966) and/or for the gender disturbance (Rekers, 1977a, 1978a, 1981b, 1982b).

Cross-Sex Identification

Another example of a sex role problem in adolescence is the case of the gender-identity-disturbed young man who insisted not only upon cross-dressing but also upon rigidly adhering to arbitrarily defined feminine sex role stereotypes (Stoller, 1968). It is often the case that the gender-identity-disturbed adolescent is the most rigidly involved in arbitrary sex role stereotypic behavior (George & Beumont, 1972).

A cross-sex identity is manifested in adolescent boys if their behavior pattern includes either: (1) labeling themselves as female, as evidenced by the stated desire to be a girl or woman or by excessive female role taking, sometimes including fantasies of bearing children and of breast feeding infants; or (2) a request by the adolescent boy to have his penis removed to have other sex reassignment medical procedures performed (Barlow, Reynolds, & Agras, 1973; Barlow, Abel, & Blanchard, 1979; Bentler, 1976; Greenson, 1966; Rekers, 1977a, 1977b; Stoller, 1964, 1965, 1968a). Such boys with cross-sex identification are typically normal physically (Rekers et al., 1979).

In the case of an adolescent boy referred for a potential cross-sex identification problem, a complete psychological assessment of the major dimensions of sex and gender should be conducted (see Rekers, 1981b). In the past, many clinicians speculated that radical surgical and hormonal sex reassignment procedures would eventually be required for the adolescent in the pretranssexual or transsexual condition. However, a longitudinal follow-up study of operated and unoperated adult transsexuals found no significant change in the adjustment scores of the operated transsexuals but did find significant improve-

ment in the adjustment scores of unoperated transsexuals (Meyer & Reter, 1979). Barlow, Reynolds, and Agras (1973) demonstrated with intrasubject replication design procedures that a combination of behavioral treatment procedures were effective in normalizing the gender identity and sexual arousal patterns of the adolescent transsexual boy. Because all other approaches to the treatment of cross-sex identification have failed, the behavioral treatment and procedures developed by Barlow and his colleagues constitute the only ethically responsible approach to the clinical management of adolescent cases of cross-sex identification. (See the discussion by Rekers, 1981b.) The only other form of intervention that has resulted in a demonstrated change in sexual identification has been religious conversion (Barlow, Abel, & Blanchard, 1977).

Cross-Gender Behavior Disorder

Without manifesting a complete cross-sex identity, some adolescents have a history of cross-sex stereotypic behavior that can be traced back to as young an age as 4 or 5 years (Bentler, Rekers, & Rosen, 1979; Rekers & Varni 1977a, 1977b). The earlier childhood behavioral history of such an adolescent boy includes (1) aversion toward or avoidance of peer activities with other boys or preoccupation with feminine sex-typed activities and games; (2) actual or improvised cross-dressing in feminine clothing; (3) use of feminine-appearing mannerisms, behavioral gestures, or gaits; (4) actual use or play-acting use of feminine cosmetic articles; (5) the use of a high femininelike vocal inflection and/or predominantly feminine speech content; and (6) taking a feminine role in play on frequent occasions (Bentler, 1968; Rekers, 1977a, 1979, 1981b; Rekers & Lovaas, 1974; Rekers, Lovaas, & Low, 1974; Rekers, 1975; Rekers et al., 1977; Rekers & Yates, 1976; Bentler, Rekers, & Rosen, 1979). For some adolescent males, cross-sex role behavior patterns take the form of sexual relations with other boys

(Barlow et al., 1975; Bentler, 1968; Canton-Dutari, 1974; Cox, 1962; Davenport, 1972; Fraiberg, 1961; Gadpaille, 1969, 1973; Gold & Neufeld, 1965; Gundlach, 1969; Herman, Barlow, & Agras, 1974; Huff, 1970; Kestenbaum, 1975; McConaghy, 1975; Roesler & Deisher, 1972; Sprince, 1964; Symonds, 1969).

The psychological assessment of cross-gender behavior disorders should be designed to include procedures that measure all the relevant psychosexual dimensions, including social sex assignment, sexual identification, sex role self-labeling, sex role behavioral adjustment, sexual arousal patterns, and genital behavior. (See Rekers, 1981b, for an overview of diagnostic procedures.) The treatment of cross-gender behavior disorders in adolescence (see review by Rekers, 1978b), may involve the procedures developed for transvestic behavior (Bentler, 1968), fetishistic patterns (Bond & Evans, 1967; McGuire, Carlisle, & Young, 1965; Mees, 1966; Strzyewsky & Zierhoffer, 1967), or problems with homosexual behavior (Barlow et al., 1975; Bentler, 1968; Callahan & Leitenberg, 1973; Canton-Dutari, 1974; Davison, Brierly, & Smith, 1971; Gold & Neufeld, 1965; Herman, Barlow, & Agras, 1974; Huff, 1980; Larson, 1970; MacCulloch & Feldman, 1967; McConaghy, 1969, 1970, 1975; McConaghy & Barr, 1973).

DEVELOPMENTAL COURSE OF SEX ROLE PROBLEMS

Sex role development problems in adolescence as well as the related sexual adjustment problems occur more frequently in male adolescents than in females (Green & Money, 1969; Kinsey et al., 1948; Mead & Rekers, 1979; Money & Ehrhardt, 1972; Rekers et al., in press; Stoller, 1968b).

In adolescents with sex role behavior disturbances and/or cross-sex identification problems, heterosocial dating deficits can serve to reinforce the development of a sexual dysphoria. Deviance in sex role behavior patterns predisposes the adolescent away from

heterosexual development and toward homosexual or other sexual behavior problems (Rekers, 1977b, 1982a). For example, the adolescent boy's peers are highly likely to label his feminine behavior as homosexual ("sissy," "queer," or "fag"), and adult men or other adolescent boys may make sexual advances toward the adolescent boy with sex role deviance. Such social experiences, in turn, have an impact upon the adolescent boy's identification and upon his overt sex role behavioral development (Rekers, 1978a; Rosen, Rekers, & Bentler, 1978).

The available evidence indicates that sex role deviations in males during childhood and adolescence are strongly predictive of transsexualism, transvestism, and homosexuality in adulthood (Bender & Pastor, 1941; Green, 1974, 1979; Green & Money, 1961, 1969; Pauly, 1969; Qualls, 1978; Rekers, 1977b; Stoller, 1967, 1968a, 1968b, 1970–1971). Unfortunately, the differential etiology of these conditions is not fully understood (Money, 1970a, 1970b; Money & Ehrhardt, 1972; Rosen, 1969; Zuger, 1970a, 1970b), although plausible developmental theories have been postulated (Bentler, 1976; Bradley et al., 1978). Although biological abnormalities may theoretically serve as potential contributing factors, (e.g., Hutt, 1978) social learning variables have been considered to be the main source of sex role deviance in childhood and adolescence (e.g., Meyer-Bahlburg, 1977). The available prospective longitudinal data indicate that effeminate behavior in boys and young adolescents is fairly predictive of adult male homosexuality (Bakwin, 1968; Green, 1974, 1979; Lebovitz, 1972; Zuger, 1966, 1970a, 1978; Zuger & Taylor, 1969; Money & Russo, 1978, note 1) and is retrospectively reported by adult male homosexuals (Bieber et al., 1962; Evans, 1969; Holemon & Winokur, 1965; Whitam, 1977), adult male transvestites (Prince & Bentler, 1972) and adult male transsexuals (Benjamin, 1966; Bentler, 1976; Bentler & Prince, 1970; Green & Money, 1969). Cross-sex behavior and cross-dressing begins in early boyhood and persists into the adolescent years for the majority of adult transsexuals and transvestites (Green, 1974; Money & Primrose, 1968; Prince & Bentler, 1972; Walinder, 1967; Zuger, 1966).

The various prospective studies of gender-disturbed boys predict a deviant sexual outcome in from 40–75 percent of the cases. For example, Zuger's (1978) long term prospective follow-up of a small sample of untreated gender-disturbed boys found that twenty years later, 65 percent of them were homosexual, 6 percent were transvestite, 6 percent were transsexual, and 12 percent were heterosexual; 25 percent had attempted suicide, and 6 percent had committed suicide. Considering all the available literature, therefore, the best scientific prediction is that a sex-role-disturbed boy will progress into adolescence with a high risk for transsexualism, transvestism, or homosexuality as contrasted to normal heterosexual development.

SEX ROLE PROBLEMS IN ADOLESCENT GIRLS

The detection of sex role behavior problems in adolescent girls is a much more complex task because of the relatively greater sex role flexibility allowed for girls in childhood and early adolescent development. Also, there is greater social acceptance of masculine clothing and behavior in girls as contrasted with the acute social concerns in our society over boys wearing dresses, for example (Rekers & Mead, 1980). Approximately 16–19 percent of normal adolescent girls express a preference for masculine sex role activities (Brown, 1956; Saghir & Robins, 1973). Therefore, the clinical child psychologist's task of diagnosing sex role deviance in girls poses even more complex issues than the parallel assessment for boys (Rekers & Mead, 1979a).

Tomboyism is often a normal, healthy part of feminine development. However, there are rare cases in which an excessive, rigid, and compulsive masculine behavior pattern develops in an adolescent girl as a chronic instead of phasic pattern. Prior to discussing the diagnostic variables involved in differen-

tiating a normal tomboy phase from a pattern of sex role develoment problems in an adolescent girl, an actual clinical illustration is presented here to orient the clinical child psychologist to one salient clinical syndrome.

Joan was a 14-year-old white female from a rural background whose home life included two divorces, fifteen moves in the past six years, and little affection from an adult male figure. When she first appeared in our clinic, she was wearing a masculine shirt, a black leather jacket, blue jeans, and cowboy boots. She claimed that no could force her to wear a dress. Joan reported feeling like and wanting to be a boy all her life, and she had made repeated requests for sex reassignment surgery. Her manner of speech, gestures, and mannerisms were hypermasculine. She reported a strong sexual interest in the same sex. Her social interactions were limited largely to boys, and she indicated her cross-sex identification by referring to this male group and herself as "we." An attitude of sexual interest was often conveyed whenever Joan discussed her few female friends. At school, she repeatedly received "F"s in physical education for refusing to participate since the coach would not allow her to play on the boys' team. She preferred to be called "Paul" and strongly identified with Paul Stanley, a male rock star with a group called "KISS." She frequently cross-dressed so that she resembled Paul Stanley, with white shoe polish on her face, a black star on her right eye, and red lipstick on her lips. Joan reacted negatively to her physical maturation as a woman. She wore a jacket or an overshirt to hide her developing breasts, refused to wear a bra, and would not tell her mother when she needed feminine hygiene articles. Joan was rejected by the majority of her peers. Her small circle of friends was noted for their social maladjustment and their tendencies to act out. Joan was very unhappy with her situation, experiencing frequent depressive episodes accompanied by suicidal ideation. She stated that she sometimes felt that she would rather be dead than to remain a female. (Rekers & Mead, 1980, p. 199)

Normal Tomboy Behavior Pattern

Many adolescent girls, such as Joan, have a childhood history including the following masculine sex role behaviors at high frequency rates: (1) avoidance of female peer activities and preoccupation with playing exclusively with boys, often with the expressed desire to be considered one of the boys; (2) rigid insistence upon wearing masculine sex-typed clothing, coupled with chronic rejection of dresses, skirts, cosmetic articles, and feminine jewelry; (3) the use of masculine-appearing behavioral gestures, postures, and gait, to the exclusion of feminine mannerisms; (4) the use of an artificially induced low voice inflection and/or predominantly masculine topics in speech content; and (5) the request be called by a boy's name or nickname.

While the transient phase of taking on the tomboy role appears to be part of adaptive behavioral development in many girls, a small percentage of such tomboys are genuinely unhappy about being females (Green, 1978). For this small minority, masculine sex role behavior patterns are frequently linked to cross-sex identification. Tomboyism in girls is much more prevalent and more likely to be a transient phenomenon than is effeminate behavior in boys. The vast majority of girls who prefer masculine activities in childhood will eventually accept their basic female identity, shift to more feminine interests at the onset of adolescence, and develop a heterosexual adjustment in adulthood.

Deviant Tomboy Behavior Pattern

In contrast to the normal progression of the tomboy phase, the gender-disturbed adolescent girl persists with predominantly masculine activities and interests from the childhood period continuing into adolescence. This chronicity of a predominantly masculine behavior pattern, coupled with indices of a cross-sex identification, is predictive of adult transsexualism or homosexuality in the female (Green, 1975b; Saghir & Robins, 1973). Stoller (1975) has reported a distinction between "masculine females" who progress from a period of normal feminine psychological development to a period of "secondary masculinity" and the development of female transsexuals, who are more typically masculine in

their development from an early age, often as early as 3–4 years old.

Nearly all female transsexuals retrospectively report that they desired to be a member of the opposite sex from their earliest recollected childhood (Benjamin, 1964; Green, 1974; Pauly, 1974a; Walinder, 1967). In the sample of 13 female adult transsexuals reported by Walinder, for example, 92 percent were tomboys in childhood and adolescence, and 100 percent felt prior to the onset of puberty as though they belonged to the opposite sex. In the majority of cases of female transsexualism in adolescence and adulthood, the cross-gender behavior began before the age of 3, and the process of cross-sex identification appears to be completed by age 7 or 8. (See Pauly's, 1974b, review of the literature.) Money and Brennan (1969) reported that as children, female transsexuals were not only very active but often displayed physical aggression, particularly against boys. By late adolescence and early adulthood, virtually all of them reported that they had preferred male playmates in childhood (Money & Brennan, 1969; Vogt, 1968; Walinder, 1967), and preferred masculine attire (Green, 1974; Money & Brennan, 1969; Vogt, 1968). Most of the adolescent and adult female transsexuals reported that they had avoided doll play as children (Money & Brennan, 1969) and they preferred boys' toys (Green, 1974; Pauly, 1974a; Vogt, 1968). During their childhood and adolescent years, the majority of them identified with their fathers rather than with their mothers (Pauly, 1974a). Benjamin (1964) found that the parents of female transsexuals reported an awareness that something was wrong with their girls in the first few years of their lives.

Trauma of Puberty in Gender-Disturbed Girls

The experience of puberty is reported to be very traumatic for female transsexuals. During adolescence, virtually all of them were repulsed by their own breast development (Benjamin, 1964; Money & Brennan, 1969; Pauly, 1974a; Walinder, 1967) and many of them reacted by binding their breasts with clothing in order to appear like a male (Money & Brennan, 1969; Pauly, 1974a). Similarly, these girls in adolescence were repulsed by menstruation (Benjamin, 1964; Money & Brennan, 1969), disliked their own sexual anatomy (Pauly, 1974a; Walinder, 1967), and typically requested sex reassignment surgery (Walinder, 1967). In early adolescence, most of these girls experience sexual attraction to very feminine females (Pauly, 1974a).

Differential Diagnosis of Normal Tomboyism from Prehomosexuals & Pretranssexuals

Not all gender-disturbed adolescent girls develop adulthood transsexualism. The eventual adulthood outcome may be transvestism, homosexuality, or even a normal heterosexual adjustment, instead of transsexualism. There are insufficient prospective studies to differentiate pretransexual from prehomosexual girls or from girls with other outcomes in their sex role development. (See the review by Rekers & Mead, 1980.) However, the retrospective reports of adult female homosexuals and adult female transsexuals suggest some similarities and some differences in the developmental course of female homosexuality as compared to female transsexualism.

The majority of adolescent and adult female homosexuals report that they desired to be a boy during their childhood and that they had a preference for male playmates and masculine activities (Saghir & Robins, 1973). As a group, female homosexuals typically identify with their fathers, and a majority of them report an awareness of their homosexual orientation before the age of 14 years. One difference between adolescent female transsexuals and adolescent female homosexuals is that the homosexuals rarely report the desire for surgical sex change.

Another difference in the developmental course of adolescent female homosexuality as contrasted to adolescent female transsexualism is the pattern of tomboyism. While nearly all of the female transsexuals reported being tomboys in their childhood and youth, ap-

proximately two-thirds of adult female homosexuals and 16 percent of the heterosexual control group report having been tomboys as children (Saghir & Robins, 1973). The pattern of tomboyism persisted into adolescence (and even into adulthood) for about one-half of the homosexual females but for none of the heterosexual females. Another difference reported by Saghir and Robins (1973) was that female homosexuals who reported a tomboy phase also reported definite disliking and avoidance of doll play, while the female heterosexual control subjects who were tomboys showed no such aversion to doll play.

Adolescent and adult female homosexuals (Kenyon, 1968) and adolescent and adult female transsexuals (Pauly, 1974b; Roback et al., 1976; Rosen, 1974; Walinder, 1967) are significantly more likely to report having had unhappy childhoods as well as current psychological distress, as compared to heterosexual controls. (A few studies, such as Thompson, McCandless, & Strickland, 1971, found no differences between nonpatient homosexuals and heterosexuals.) Saghir and Robins (1973) found that nonpatient female homosexuals were more susceptible than heterosexual comparisons to depression, suicide attempts, alcohol and drug abuse, and dropping out of college.

Because approximately 16–19 percent of normal adolescent girls have had a childhood history in which they expressed a preference for masculine activities (Brown, 1956; Saghir & Robins, 1973), the presence or existence of a given pattern of masculine and feminine activities in a girl at any particular point in time cannot be taken alone to define a sex role development problem. Instead, the intensity, the clustering, the chronicity, and the cultural context of a sex role behavior pattern must all be considered together in making a clinical diagnosis of female gender disturbance in adolescents. (See the extended discussion by Rekers & Mead, 1980.)

The psychological assessment of an adolescent girl with potential gender behavior disturbance or a cross-gender identity should include measures of all the major dimensions of sex and gender, as reviewed by Rekers (1981b) and Rekers and Mead (1980). Very little has been published on psychological treatment for gender disturbances in adolescent girls, even though early identification and early intervention to prevent adulthood transvestism and transsexualism are preferred clinical strategy (Benjamin, 1967; Green, 1974, 1975; Pauly, 1974a,b).

REFERENCES

Anant, S.S. Verbal aversion therapy with a promiscuous girl: Case report. *Psychological Reports*, 1968, **22**, 795–796.

Anyan, W.R. *Adolescent medicine in primary care.* New York: Wiley, 1978.

Atcheson, J.D., & Williams, D.C. A study of juvenile sex offenders. *American Journal of Psychiatry*, 1954, **111**, 366–370.

Atkeson, B.M., & Forehand, R. Conduct disorders. In E.J. Mash & L.G. Terdal (Eds.), *Behavioral assessment of childhood disorders.* New York: Guilford Press, 1981.

Ausubel, D.P., Montemayor, R., & Svajian, P.N. *Theory and problems of adolescent development.* New York: Grune & Stratton, 1977.

Babbage, S.B. *Sex and sanity.* Philadelphia: Westminster Press, 1965.

Bain, J., & Howard, N.J. Gonadal disorders in young males: Hyposonadism and precocious puberty. In E.S.E. Hafez & J.J. Peluso (Eds.), *Sexual maturity: Physiological and clinical parameters.* Ann Arbor: Ann Arbor Science Publishers, 1976.

Bakwin, H. Deviant gender-role behavior in children: Relation to homosexuality. *Pediatrics*, 1968, **41**, 620–629.

Bamber, J.H. *The fears of adolescents.* London: Academic Press, 1979.

Barlow, D.H., Abel, G.G., & Blanchard, E.B. Gender identity change in transsexuals: An exorcism. *Archives of Sexual Behavior*, 1977, **6**, 387–395.

Barlow, D.H., Abel, G.G., Blanchard, E.B. Gender identity change in transsexuals. *Archives of General Psychiatry*, 1979, **36**, 1001–1007.

Barlow, D.H., Abel, G.G., Blanchard, E.B., Bris-tow, A.R., & Young, L.D. A heterosocial skills behavior checklist for males. *Behavior Therapy*, 1977, **8**, 229–239.

Barlow, D.H., Agras, W.S., Abel, G.G., Blanchard, E.G., & Young, L.D. Biofeedback and reinforcement to increase heterosexual arousal in homosexual arousal in homosexuals. *Behavior Research and Therapy*, 1975, **13**, 45–50.

Barlow, D.H., Reynolds, E.J., & Agras, W.S. Gender identity change in a transsexual. *Archives of General Psychiatry*, 1973, **28**, 569–576.

Barnes, H.V. Physical growth and development during puberty. *Medical Clinics of North America*, 1975, **59**, 1305–1311.

Bayley, L.M., & Bayler, N. *Growth diagnosis.* Chicago: University of Chicago Press, 1959.

Bell, A.P. Adolescent sexuality and the schools. *North Central Association Quarterly*, 1969, **43**, 342–347.

Bem, S.L. The measurement of psychological androgyny. *Journal of Consulting and Clinical Psychology*, 1974, **42**, 155–162.

Bem, S.L. Sex role adaptability: One consequence of psychological androgyny. *Journal of Personality and Social Psychology*, 1975, **31**, 634–643.

Bender, L., & Blau, A. The reaction of children to sexual relations with adults. *American Journal of Orthopsychiatry*, 1937, **7**, 500–518.

Bender, L., & Grugett, A.E. Follow-up report on children who had atypical sexual experience. *American Journal of Orthopsychiatry*, 1937, **7**, 500–518.

Bender, L., & Grugeet, A.E. Follow-up report on children who had atypical sexual experience. *American Journal of Orthopsychiatry*, 1952, **22**, 825–837.

Bender, L., & Paster, S. Homosexual trends in children. *American Journal of Orthopsychiatry*, 1941, **11**, 730–743.

Benjamin, H. Clinical aspects of transsexualism in male and female. *American Journal of Psychotherapy*, 1964, **18**, 458–469.

Benjamin, H. *The transsexual phenomenon.* New York: The Julian Press, 1966.

Benjamin, H. Transvestism and transsexualism in the male and female. *Journal of Sex Research*, 1967, **3**, 107–127.

Bentler, P.M. Heterosexual behavior assessment—

1. Males. *Behavior Research and Therapy,* 1968, **6,** 21–25.

Bentler, P.M. A typology of transsexualism: Gender identity theory and data. *Archives of Sexual Behavior,* 1976, **5,** 576–584.

Bentler, P.M., & Prince, C. Psychiatric symptomatology in transvestites. *Journal of Clinical Psychology,* 1970, **26,** 434–435.

Bentler, P.M., Rekers, G.A., & Rosen, A.C. Congruence of childhood sex–role identity and behavior disturbances. *Child: Care, Health and Development,* 1979, **5,** 267–284.

Beumont, P.J.V., & Beardwood, C.F. The occurrence of the syndrome of anorexia nervosa in male subjects. *Psychological Medicine,* 1972, **2,** 216–231.

Bieber, I., Dain, H.J., Dince, P.R., Drellich, M.G., Grand, H.G., Gundlach, R.H., Kremer, M.W., Rifkin, A.H., Wilbur, C.B., & Bieber, T.B. *Homosexuality: A psychoanalytic study.* New York: Basic Books, 1962.

Blair, A.W., & Burton, W.H. *Growth and development of the preadolescent.* New York: Appleton-Century-Crofts, 1951.

Blos, P. The child analyst looks at the young adolescent. In J. Kagan & R. Coles (Eds.), *12 to 16: Early adolescence.* New York: Norton, 1972.

Bond, I., & Evans, D. Avoidance therapy: Its uses in two cases of underwear fetishism. *Canadian Medical Association Journal,* 1967, **96,** 1160–1162.

Bradley, S.J., Steiner, B., Zucker, K., Doering, R.W., Sullivan, J., Finegan, J.D., & Richardson, M. Gender identity problems of children and adolescents. *Canadian Psychiatric Association Journal,* 1978, **23,** 175–183.

Braun, M., & Rekers, G.A. *The Christian in an age of sexual eclipse.* Wheaton, Ill.: Tyndale, 1981.

Breen, J.L., Greenwald, E., & Gregori, C.A. The molested young female: Evaluation and therapy of alleged rape. *Pediatric Clinics of North America,* 1972, **19,** 717–725.

Brigham, S.L., Rekers, G.A., Rosen, A.C., Swihart, J.J., Pfrimmer, G., & Ferguson, L.N. Contingency management in the treatment of adolescent alcohol drinking problems. *Journal of Psychology,* 1981, **109,** 73–85.

Brown, D.G. Sex-role preference in young children. *Psychological Monographs,* 1956, **70** (14, Whole No. 421), 1–19.

Brown, F. Sexual problems of the adolescent girl. *Pediatric Clinics of North America,* 1972, **19,** 759–764.

Bruch, H. Eating disorders in adolescence. In J. Zubin & A.M. Freedman (Eds.), *The psychopathology of adolescence.* New York: Grune & Stratton, 1970.

Brunold, H. Observations after sexual traumata suffered in childhood. *Excerpta Criminologica* (Netherlands), 1964, **4**(1), 5–8.

Callahan, E.J., & Leitenberg, H. Aversion therapy for sexual deviation: Contingent shock and covert sensitization. *Journal of Abnormal Psychology,* 1973, **81,** 60–73.

Canton-Dutari, A. Combined intervention for controlling unwanted homosexual behavior. *Archives of Sexual Behavior,* 1974, **3,** 367–371.

Capraro, V.J. Sexual assault of female children. *Annals of the New York Academy of Sciences,* 1967, **142,** 817–819.

Chapman, A.H. *Management of emotional problems of children and adolescents* (2nd ed.). Philadelphia: Lippincott, 1974.

Cheek, D.B. Muscle cell growth in normal children. In D.B. Cheek (Ed.), *Human growth: Body composition, cell growth, energy, and intelligence.* Philadelphia: Lea & Febiger, 1968.

Cheek, D.B. Body composition, hormones, nutrition, and adolescent growth. In M.M. Grumbach, D.G. Grave, & F.E. Mayer (Eds.), *Control of the onset of puberty.* New York: Wiley, 1974.

Christakis, G., Sajeckie, G., Hillman, R.W., Miller, E., Blumenthal, S., & Archer, M. Effect of a combined nutrition education-physical fitness program on weight status of obese high school boys. *Federation Proceedings,* 1966, **25,** 15–19.

Coates, T.J., & Thoreson, C.E. Treating obesity in children and adolescents: A review. *American Journal of Public Health,* 1978, **68,** 143–151.

Coates, T.J., & Thoreson, C.E. Treating obesity in children and adolescents: Is there any hope? In J.M. Ferguson & C.B. Taylor, (Eds.), *Advances in behavioral medicine.* Englewood Cliffs, N.J.: Spectrum, 1980.

Coe, J.L. Sexual asphyxias. *Life-threatening Behavior,* 1974, **4,** 171–175.

Cormier, M., Kennedy, M., & Sangowics, J. Psychodynamics of father–daughter incest.

Canadian Psychiatric Association Journal, 1962, **7**, 203–217.

Costello, C.G. Childhood depression. In E.J. Marsh & L.G. Terdal (Eds.), *Behavioral assessment of childhood disorders.* New York: Guilford Press, 1981.

Cox, W. Panel on "Homosexuality in the male adolescent." *International Mental Health Research Newsletter,* 1962, **4**(1/2), pp. 7, 10.

Craft, M. Boy prostitutes and their fate. *British Journal of Psychiatry,* 1966, **112**, 1111–1114.

Davenport, C.W. Homosexuality—Its origins, early recognition and prevention. *Clinical Pediatrics,* 1972, **11**, 7–10.

Davison, K., Brierley, H., & Smith, C. A male monozygotic twinship discordant for homosexuality. *British Journal of Psychiatry,* 1971, **118**, 675–682.

Dearth, P.B. Viable sex education in the schools: Expectations of students, parents, and experts. *The Journal of School Health,* 1974, **44**, 190–193.

Deisher, R.W. The young male prostitute. *Pediatrics,* 1970, **45**, 153–154.

Deisher, R.W., Eisner, V., & Sulzbacher, S.I. The young male prostitute. *Pediatrics,* 1969, **43**, 936–941.

Dickinson, G.E. Sex information sources of black and white adolescents in a Southern community. *Sociological Symposium,* 1971, **6**, 19–22.

duMas, F.M. *Gay is not good.* Nashville: 1979.

Eaton, A.P., & Vastbinder, E. The sexually molested child: A plan of management. *Clinical Pediatrics,* 1969, **8**, 438–441.

Edmondson, J.S. A case of sexual asphyxia without fatal termination. *British Journal of Psychiatry,* 1972, **121**, 437–438.

Eist, H.I., & Mandel, A. Family treatment of ongoing incest behavior. *Family Process,* 1968, **7**, 216–232.

Erikson, E.H. *Childhood and society.* New York: Norton, 1950.

Evans, R.B. Childhood parental relationships of homosexual men. *Journal of Consulting and Clinical Psychology,* 1969, **33**, 129–135.

Faiman, C., & Winter, J.S.D. Gonadotropins and sex hormone patterns in puberty, clinical data. In M.M. Grumbach, G.D. Grave, & F.E. Mater (Eds.), *Control of the onset of puberty.* New York: Wiley, 1974.

Faust, M.S. Somatic development of adolescent girls. *Monographs of the Society for Research in Child Development,* 1977, **42**, 1.

Ferguson, L.M., & Rekers, G.A. Non-aversive intervention for public childhood masturbation. *The Journal of Sex Research,* 1979, **15**, 213–223.

Fodor, J.T. A conceptual approach to curriculum development in venereal disease education. *Journal of School Health,* 1973, **43**, 303–306.

Foreyt, J.P., & Goodrick, G.K. Childhood obesity. In E.J. Mash, L.G. Terdal (Eds.), *Behavioral assessment of childhood disorders.* New York: Guilford, 1981.

Fraiberg, S. Homosexual conflicts. In S. Lorand & H.I. Schneer (Eds.), *Adolescents: Psychoanalytic approach to problems and therapy.* New York: Hoeber, 1961.

Frank, R.A., & Cohen, D.J. Psychosocial concomitants of biological maturation in preadolescence. *American Journal of Psychiatry,* 1979, **136**, 1518–1524.

Frisch, R.E. Critical weight at menarche, initiation of the adolescent growth spurt, and control of puberty. In M.M. Grumbach, G.D. Grave, & F.E. Mayer (Eds.), *Control of the onset of puberty.* New York: Wiley, 1974.

Frisch, R.E., & Revelle, R. The height and weight of girls and boys at the time of initiation of the adolescent growth spurt in height and weight and the relationship to menarche. *Human Biology,* 1971, **43**, 140.

Frisk, M. Puberty: Emotional maturation and behavior. In S.R. Berenberg (Ed.), *Puberty: Biological and psychosocial components.* Leiden: Stenfert Kroese, 1975.

Gadpaille, W.J. Could that youngster become a homosexual? *Medical Economics,* November 24, 1969.

Gadpaille, W.J. Brief guide to office counseling: Adolescent concerns about homosexuality. *Medical Aspects of Human Sexuality,* 1973, **7** (11), 105–106.

Gagnen, J.H. The creation of the sexual in early adolescence. In J. Kagen & R. Coles (Eds.), *12 to 16: Early adolescence.* New York: Norton, 1972.

Gallagher, J.R., & Harris, J. *Emotional problems of adolescents* (3rd ed.). New York: Oxford, 1976.

Gandy, P., & Deisher, R. Young male prostitutes: The physician's role in social rehabilitation. *Journal of the American Medical Association,*

1970, **212,** 1661–1666.

George, G.C.W., & Beumont, P.J.V. Transsexualism in a fourteen-year-old male. *South African Medical Journal,* 1972, **46,** 1947–1948.

Ginsburg, K.N. The "meat-rack": A study of the male homosexual prostitute. *American Journal of Psychotherapy,* 1967, **21,** 170–185.

Gold, S., & Neufeld, I.L. A learning approach to the treatment of homosexuality. *Behavior Research and Therapy,* 1965, **2,** 201–204.

Goldfarb, A.F. Puberty and menarche. *Clinical Obstetrics and Gynecology,* 1977, **20,** 625–631.

Goldrath, M.H., & Sherman, A.I. Precocious puberty in the female. In E.S.E. Hafez & J.J. Peluso (Eds.), *Sexual maturity: Physiological and clinical parameters.* Ann Arbor: Ann Arbor Science Publishers, 1976.

Gordon, C. Social characteristics of early adolescence. In J. Kagan & R. Coles (Eds.), *12 to 16: Early adolescence.* New York: Norton, 1972.

Grant, W.W. *From parent to child about sex.* Grand Rapids: Zondervan Publishing House, 1973.

Graystone, J.E. Creatinine excretion during growth. In D.B. Cheek (Ed.), *Human growth: Body composition, cell growth, energy, and intelligence.* Philadelphia: Lea & Febiger, 1968.

Green, R. *Sexual identity conflict in children and adults.* New York: Basic Books, 1974.

Green, R. Sexual identity: Research strategies. *Archives of Sexual Behavior,* 1975, **4,** 337–352. (a)

Green, R. Adults who want to change sex; adolescents who cross-dress; and children called "sissy" and "tomboy." In R. Green (Ed.), *Human sexuality: A health practitioner's text.* Baltimore: Williams & Wilkins, 1975. (b)

Green, R. Intervention and prevention: The child with cross-sex identity. In C.B. Qualls, J.P. Wincze, & D.H. Barlow (Eds.), *The prevention of sexual disorders: Issues and approaches.* New York: Plenum, 1978.

Green, R. Childhood cross-gender behavior and subsequent sexual preference. *American Journal of Psychiatry,* 1979, **136,** 106–108.

Green, R., & Money, J. Effeminacy in prepubertal boys: Summary of eleven cases and recommendations for case management. *Pediatrics,* 1961, **27,** 286–291.

Green, R., & Money, J. (Eds.), *Transsexualism and sex reassignment.* Baltimore: Johns Hopkins University Press, 1969.

Greenson, R.R. A transvestite boy and a hypothesis. *International Journal of Psychoanalysis,* 1966, **47,** 396–403.

Grumbach, M.M. Onset of puberty. In S.R. Berenberg (Ed.), *Puberty: Biological and psychosocial components.* Leiden: Stenfert Kroese, 1975.

Grumbach, M.M., Roth, J.C., Kaplan, S.L., & Kelch, R.P. Hypothalamic pituitary regulation of puberty: Evidence and concepts derived from clinical research. In M.M. Grumbach, G.D. Grave, & F.E. Mayer (Eds.), *Control of the onset of puberty.* New York: Wiley, 1974.

Gundlach, R.H. Childhood parental relationships and the establishment of gender roles of homosexuals. *Journal of Consulting and Clinical Psychology,* 1969, **33,** 136–139.

Gustin, J.C. The revolt of youth. *Psychoanalysis and Psychoanalytic Review,* 1961, **98,** 78–90.

Hackett, T.P. The psychotherapy of exhibitionists in a court clinic setting. *Seminars in Psychiatry,* 1971, **3,** 297–306.

Hafez, E.S.E. Parameters of sexual maturity in man. In E.S.E. Hafez & J.J. Peluso (Eds.), *Sexual maturity: Physiological and clinical parameters.* Ann Arbor: Ann Arbor Science Publishers, 1976.

Haft, M.S. *An exploratory study of early adolescent girls: Body image, self-acceptance, acceptance of "traditional female role," and response to menstruation.* New York: Columbia University, 1973.

Haims, L.J. *Sex education and the public schools: A multidimensional study for the 1970s.* Lexington, Mass.: Lexington Books, 1973.

Harbert, I.L., et al. Measurement and modification of incestuous behavior: A case study. *Psychological Reports,* 1974, **34,** 79–86.

Harrington, C.C. *Errors in sex-role behavior in teenage boys.* New York: Teachers College Press, 1970.

Harrison, S. *The body experience of prepubescent, pubescent, and postpubescent girls and boys.* New York: Yeshiva University, 1975.

Hartz, A., Giefer, E., & Rimm, A.A. Relative importance of the effect of family environment and heredity on obesity. *Annals of Human Genetics,* 1977, **41,** 185–193.

Hays, S.E. Strategies for psychoendocrine studies of puberty. *Psychoneuroendocrinology*, 1978, **3**, 1-15.

Heald, F.P., & Khan, M.A. Obesity. In S.R. Berenberg (Ed.), *Puberty: Biological and psychosocial components.* Leiden: Stenfert Kroese, 1975.

Hefley, J.C. *Sex sense and nonsense.* Elgin, Ill.: 1971.

Herman, S.H., Barlow, D.H., & Agras, W.S. An experimental analysis of classical conditioning as a method of increasing heterosexual arousal in homosexuals. *Behavior Therapy*, 1974, **5**, 33-47.

Hersko, M., et al., Incest: A three-way process. *Corrective Psychiatry*, 1961, **7**, 22-31.

Higham, E. Variations in adolescent psychohormonal development. In J. Adelson (Ed.), *Handbook of adolescent psychology.* New York: Wiley, 1980.

Hogan, W.L. Brief guide to office counseling: The raped child. *Medical Aspects of Human Sexuality*, 1974, **8**, 129-130.

Holeman, E.R., & Winokur, G. Effeminate homosexuality: A disease of childhood. *American Journal of Orthopsychiatry*, 1965, **35**, 48-56.

Hops, H., & Greenwood, C.R. Social skills deficits. In E.J. Mash & L.G. Terdal (Eds.), *Behavioral assessment of childhood disorders.* New York: Gulford, 1981.

Hops, H., Walker, H.M., & Greenwood, C.R. PEERS: A program for remediating social withdrawal in the school setting: Aspects of a research and development process. In L.A. Hammerlynck (Ed.), *The history and future of the developmentally disabled: Problematic and methodological issues.* New York: Brunner/Mazel, 1979.

Huff, F.W. The desensitization of a homosexual. *Behavior Research and Therapy*, 1970, **8**, 99-102.

Hurlock, E.B., & Sender, S. The "negative phase" in relation to the behavior of pubescent girls. *Child Development*, 1930, **1**, 325-340.

Hutt, C. Biological bases of psychologicl sex difference. *American Journal of Diseases in Childhood*, 1978, **132**, 170-177.

Jeffrey, R.W., Wing, R.R., & Stunkard, A.J. Behavioral treatment of obesity: The state of the art 1976. *Behavior Therapy*, 1978, **9**, 189-199.

Johnson, W.R. Awakening sexuality of girls. *Sexual Behavior*, 1973, **3**(3), 3-6.

Jones, H.E. The development of physical abilities. In *National Society for the Study of Education* (Ed.), *Adolescence, the forty-third yearbook.* Chicago: University of Chicago Press, 1944.

Jones, H.E. Physical ability as a factor in social adjustment in adolescence. *Journal of Educational Research*, 1946, **40**, 287-301.

Jones, H.E. Adolescence in our society. In *The family in a democratic society.* Anniversary papers of the Community Service Society of New York. New York: Columbia University Press, 1949.

Jones, M.C. Psychological correlates of somatic development. *Child Development*, 1965, **36**, 899-911.

Josselson, R. Ego development in adolescence. In J. Adelson (Ed.), *Handbook of adolescent psychology.* New York: Wiley, 1980.

Kagan, J. A conception of early adolescence. In J. Kagan & R. Colse (Eds.), *12 to 16: Early adolescence.* New York: Norton, 1972.

Kaplan, J.G. Brief guide to office counseling: Retarded sexual development in adolescence. *Medical Aspects of Human Sexuality*, 1975, **9**, 47-48.

Katzman, M. Early sexual trauma. *Sexual Behavior*, 1972, **2**(2), 13-17.

Kennedy, M., & Cormier, B.M. Father-daughter incest—Treatment of the family. *Laval Medical*, 1969, **40**, 946-950.

Kenyon, F.E. Studies in female homosexuality: IV. Social and psychiatric aspects. *British Journal of Psychiatry*, 1968, **114**, 1337-1350.

Kestenbaum, C.J. Brief guide to office counseling: Adolescent homosexual experiences. *Medical Aspects of Human Sexuality*, 1975, **9**(1), 99-100.

Kiefer, C.R. Brief guide to office counseling: Sexual molestation of a child. *Medical Aspects of Human Sexuality*, 1973, **7**, 127-128.

Kiernan, K.E. Age at puberty in relation to age at marriage and parenthood: A national longitudinal study. *Annals of Human Biology*, 1977, **4**, 301-308.

Kinsey, A.C., Pomeroy, W.B., & Martin, C.E. *Sexual behavior in the human male.* Philadelphia: Saunders, 1948.

Kirkpatrick, S.W., & Sanders, D.M. Body image

stereotypes: A developmental comparison. *Journal of Genetic Psychology,* 1978, **132,** 87–95.

Koff, E., Rierdan, J., & Silverstone, E. Changes in representation of body image as a function of menarcheal status. *Developmental Psychology,* 1978, **14,** 635–642.

Langen, D. The later development of critical episodes during puberty. *Nervenarzt,* 1975, **46,** 581–585.

Langen, D. Initial and long-term evaluation of crisis during puberty. *Zeitschrift fur Kinder- und Jugendpsychiatric,* 1977, **5,** 138–140.

Langsley, D.G., Schwartz, M.N., & Fairbairn, R.H. Father-son incest. *Comprehensive Psychiatry,* 1968, **9,** 218–226.

Larson, D.E. An adaptation of the Feldman and MacCulloch approach to the treatment of homosexuality and the application of anticipatory avoidance learning. *Behaviour Research and Therapy,* 1970, **8,** 209–210.

Lebovitz, P.S. Feminine behavior in boys: Aspects of its outcome. *American Journal of Psychiatry,* 1972, **128,** 1283–1289.

Levin, J.T. A seasonal influence but no secular trend. *Journal of Sex Research,* 1976, **12,** 173–179.

Levine, M.I., & Bell, A.I. Psychological aspects of pediatric practice. II. Masturbation. *Pediatrics,* 1956, **18,** 803–808.

Litin, E.M., Giffin, M.E., & Johnson, A.M. Parental influence in unusual sexual behavior in children. *Psychoanalytic Quarterly,* 1956, **25,** 37–55.

Livson, N., & Peskin, H. Perspectives on adolescence from longitudinal research. In J. Adelson (Ed.), *Handbook of adolescent psychology.* New York: Wiley, 1980.

Lloyd, C.W. Problems associated with sexual maturation and abnormalities of differentiation. In C.W. Lloyd (Ed.), *Human reproduction and sexual behavior.* Philadelphia: Lea & Febiger, 1964.

Logan, D.D. The menarche experience in twenty-three foreign countries. *Adolescence,* 1980, **15,** 253–256.

Lowenstein, L.F. A case of exhibitionism treated by counter-conditioning. *Adolescence,* 1973, **8,** 213–218.

MacCulloch, M.J. & Feldman, M.P. Aversion therapy in management of 43 homosexuals. *British Medical Journal,* 1967, **2,** 594–597.

MacCulloch, M.J., Williams, C., & Birtles, C.J. The successful application of aversion therapy to an adolescent exhibitionist. *Journal of Behavior Therapy and Experimental Psychiatry,* 1971, **2,** 61–66.

MacFarlane, J.W., Allen, L., & Honzik, M.P. *A developmental study of the behavior problems of normal children between twenty-one months and fourteen years.* Berkeley, Calif.: University of California Press, 1954.

MacNamara, D.E.J., & Segrin, E. *Sex, crime, and the law.* New York: Free Press, 1977.

Mangus, A.R. Sex crimes against children. In K.M. Bournen, *Sexual deviation research.* Sacramento: Assembly of the State of California, March, 1932.

Mangus, A.R. Sexual deviation and the family. *Marriage and Family Living,* 1953, **15,** 325–331.

Marshall, S. *The physiology of reproduction.* London: Longmans, 1972.

Marshall, W.A. The relationship of puberty to other maturity indicators and body composition in man. *Journal of Reproduction and Fertility,* 1978, **52,** 437–443.

Marshall, W.A., & Tanner, J.M. Growth and physiological development during adolescence. *Annual Review of Medicine,* 1968, **19,** 283–301.

Marshall, W., & Tanner, J.M. Variations in the pattern of pubertal changes in girls. *Archives of Disease in Childhood,* 1970, **45,** 13–23.

Martin, E.C. Reflections on the early adolescent in school. In J. Kagan & R. Coles (Eds.), *12 to 16: Early adolescence.* New York: Norton, 1972.

Martinson, F.M. Sexual knowledge, values, and behavior patterns of adolescents. In H.L. Gochros & L.G. Schultz (Eds.), *Human sexuality and social work.* New York: Association Press, 1972.

Mayer, J. Obesity. *Postgraduate Medicine,* 1972, **51,** 66–69.

McCammon, R.W. *Human growth and development.* Springfield, Ill.: Thomas, 1970.

McComas, A.J., Sica, R.E.P., & Petito, F. Muscle strength in boys of different ages. *Journal of Neurological Psychiatry,* 1973, **36,** 171.

McConaghy, N. Subjective and penile plethysmograph responses following aversion-relief and apomorphine aversion therapy for homosexual impulses. *British Journal of Psychiatry,*

1969, **115**, 723–730.

McConaghy, N. Penile response conditioning and its relationship to aversion therapy in homosexuals. *Behavior Therapy,* 1970, **1**, 213–221.

McConaghy, N. Aversive and positive conditioning treatments of homosexuality. *Behavior Research and Therapy,* 1975, **13**, 309–319.

McConaghy, N., & Barr, R.F. Classical, avoidance and backward conditioning treatments of homosexuality. *British Journal of Psychiatry,* 1973, **122**, 151–162.

McCoy, K. Adolescent sexuality: A national concern. Report on the Wingspread Conference on adolescent sexuality and health care. *Journal of Clinical Child Psychology,* 1974, **3**(3), 18–22.

McGuire, R.J., Carlisle, J.M., & Young, B.G. Sexual deviations as conditioned behavior: A hypothesis. *Behavior Research and Therapy,* 1965, **2**, 185–190.

Mead, S.L., & Rekers, G.A. The role of the father in normal psychosexual development. *Psychological Reports,* 1979, **45**, 923–931.

Mees, H.L. Sadistic fantasies modified by aversive conditioning and substitution: A case study. *Behavior Research and Therapy,* 1966, **4**, 317–320.

Meilman, P.W. Cross-sectional age changes in ego identity status during adolescence. *Developmental Psychology,* 1979, **15**, 230–231.

Meyer, J.K., & Reter, D.J. Sex reassignment: Follow-up. *Archives of General Psychiatry,* 1979, **36**, 1010–1015.

Meyer-Bahlburg, H.F.L. Sex hormones and male homosexuality in comparative perspective. *Archives of Sexual Behavior,* 1977, **6**, 297–325.

Miles, H.J. *Sexual understanding before marriage.* Grand Rapids: Zondervan, 1971.

Money, J. Critique of Dr. Zuger's manuscript. *Psychosomatic Medicine,* 1970, **32**, 463–465. (a)

Money, J. Sexual dimorphism and homosexual gender identity. *Psychological Bulletin,* 1970, **74**, 425–440. (b)

Money, J., & Brennan, J.G. Sexual dimorphism in the psychology of female transsexuals. In R. Green & J. Money (Eds.), *Transsexualism and sex reassignment.* Baltimore: Johns Hopkins Press, 1969.

Money, J., & Ehrhardt, A.A. *Man and woman, boy and girl.* Baltimore: Johns Hopkins Press, 1972.

Money, J., & Primrose, C., Sexual dimorphism and dissociation in the psychology of male transsexuals. *Journal of Nervous and Mental Disease,* 1968, **147**, 472–486.

Money, J., & Russo, A. *Establishment of homosexual gender identity/role: Longitudinal follow-up of discordant gender identity/role in childhood.* Paper presented at the meeting of the American Psychological Association, Toronto, August 28–September 1, 1978. Note 1.

Moody, D.L., Wilmore, J.H., Girandola, R.N., & Royce, J.P. The effects of a jogging program on the body composition of normal and obese high school girls. *Medicine and Science in Sports,* 1972, **4**, 210–213.

Morgenthan, J.E. Adolescent obesity: A clinical perspective. In S.R. Berenberg (Ed.), *Puberty: Biological and psychosocial components.* Leiden : Stenfert Kroese, 1975.

Nadler, R.P. Approach to psychodynamics of obscene telephone calls. *New York State Journal of Medicine,* 1968, **68**, 521–526.

Nelson, R.M. Physiologic correlates of puberty. *Clinical Obstetrics and Gynecology,* 1978, **21**, 1137–1149.

Nixon, R.E. Psychological normality in adolescence. *Adolescence,* 1966, **1**, 211–223.

Olford, S.F., & Lawes, F.A. *The sanctity of sex.* Old Tappan: Revell, 1963.

Parkes, A.S. The reproductive life cycle. *Science Journal,* 1970, January, p. 26.

Patterson, G.R., Reid, J.B., Jones, R.R., & Conger, R.E. *A social learning approach to family intervention: Families with aggressive children* (Vol. 1). Eugene, Ore.: Castalia, 1975.

Pauly, I.B. Adult manifestations of male transsexualism. In R. Green & J. Money (Eds.), *Transsexualism and sex reassignment.* Baltimore: Johns Hopkins University Press, 1969.

Pauly, I.B. Female transsexualism: Part I. *Archives of Sexual Behavior,* 1974, **3**, 487–507. (a)

Pauly, I.B. Female transsexualism: Part II. *Archives of Sexual Behavior,* 1974, **3**, 509–526. (b)

Peskin, H. Influence of the developmental schedule of puberty on learning and ego functioning. *Journal of Youth and Adolescence,* 1973, **2**, 273–290.

Petersen, A.C., & Taylor, B. The biological approach to adolescence: Biological change and psychological adaptation. In J. Adelson

(Ed.), *Handbook of adolescent psychology.* New York: Wiley, 1980.

Phillips, E.L., Phillips, E.A., Fixsen, D.L., & Wolf, M.M. *The teaching-family handbook.* Lawrence, Kan.: University of Kansas Printing Service, 1972.

Pittman, D.J. The male house of prostitution. *Trans-Actions,* 1971, **8**(5, 6), 21–27.

Pittman, F.S. Brief guides to office counseling: Counseling incestuous families. *Medical Aspects of Human Sexuality,* 1976, **10**, 54–58.

Ploscowe, M. *Sex and the law* (Rev. ed.). New York: Ace, 1962.

Prince, C.V., & Bentler, P.M. A survey of 504 cases of transvestism. *Psychological Reports,* 1972, **31**, 903–917.

Protinsky, H., & Farrier, S. Self-image changes in pre-adolescents and adolescents. *Adolescence,* 1980, **15**, 890–892.

Qualls, C.B. The prevention of sexual disorders: An overview. In C.B. Qualls, J.P. Wincze, & D.H. Barlow (Eds.), *The prevention of sexual disorders: Issues and approaches.* New York: Plenum, 1978.

Ramsey, C. The sexual development of boys. *American Journal of Psychology,* 1943, **56**, 217–234.

Raven, S. Boys will be boys: The male prostitute in London. In H.M. Ruitenbeek (Ed.), *Problem of homosexuality in modern society.* New York: Dutton, 1963.

Reiss, A.J. Social integration of queers and peers. In H.M. Ruitenbeek (Ed.), *Problem of homosexuality in modern society.* New York: Dutton, 1963.

Rekers, G.A. Stimulus control over sex-typed play in cross-gender identified boys. *Journal of Experimental Child Psychology,* 1975, **20**, 136–148.

Rekers, G.A. Assessment and treatment of childhood gender problems. In B.B. Kahey & A.E. Kazdin (Eds.), *Advances in clinical child psychology* (Vol. 1). New York: Plenum, 1977. (a)

Rekers, G.A. Atypical gender development and psychosocial adjustment. *Journal of Applied Behavior Analysis,* 1977, **10**, 559–571. (b)

Rekers, G.A. A priori values and research on homosexuality. *American Psychologist,* 1978, **33**, 510–512. (a)

Rekers, G.A. Sexual problems: Behavior modification. Chapter 17 in B.B. Wolman (Ed.), *Handbook of treatment of mental disorders in childhood and adolescence.* Englewood Cliffs, N.J: Prentice-Hall, 1978. (b)

Rekers, G.A. Sex-role behavior change: Intrasubject studies of boyhood gender disturbance. *Journal of Psychology,* 1979, **103**, 255–269.

Rekers, G.A. Therapies dealing with the child's sexual difficulties. In Jean-Marc Samson (Ed.), *Enfance et sexualite/Childhood and sexuality.* Montreal & Paris: Les Editions Etudes Vivantes, Inc., 1980.

Rekers, G.A. Childhood sexual identity disorders. *Medical Aspects of Human Sexuality,* 1981, **15**(3), 141–142. (a)

Rekers, G.A. Psychosexual and gender problems. In E.J. Mash & L.G. Terdal (Eds.), *Behavioral assessment of childhood disorders.* New York: Guilford, 1981. (b)

Rekers, G.A. *Growing up straight: What families need to know about homosexuality.* Chicago: Moody, 1982. (a)

Rekers, G.A. *Shaping your child's sexual identity.* Grand Rapids: Baker, 1982. (b)

Rekers, G.A., Amaro-Plotkin, H., & Low, B.P. Sex-typed mannerisms in normal boys and girls as a function of sex and age. *Child Development,* 1977, **48**, 275–278.

Rekers, G.A., Bentler, P.M., Rosen, A.C., & Lovaas, O.I. Child gender disturbances: A clinical rationale for intervention. *Psychotherapy: Theory, Research and Practice,* 1977, **14**, 2–11.

Rekers, G.A., Crandall, B.F., Rosen, A.C., & Bentler, P.M. Genetic physical studies of male children with psychological gender disturbances. *Psychological Medicine,* 1979, **9**, 373–375.

Rekers, G.A., & Lovaas, O.I. Behavioral treatment of deviant sex-role behaviors in a male child. *Journal of Applied Behavior Analysis,* 1974, **7**, 173–190.

Rekers, G.A., Lovaas, O.I., & Low, B.P. The behavioral treatment of a "transsexual" pre-adolescent boy. *Journal of Abnormal Child Psychology,* 1974, **2**, 99–116.

Rekers, G.A., & Mead, S.L. Early intervention for female sexual identity disturbances: Self-monitoring of play behavior. *Journal of Abnormal Child Psychology,* 1979, **7**, 405–423. (a)

Rekers, G.A., & Mead, S.L. Human sex differences in carrying behaviors: A replication and extension. *Perceptual and Motor Skills,* 1979, **48,** 625–626. (b)

Rekers, G.A., & Mead, S.L. Female sex-role deviance: Early identification and developmental intervention. *Journal of Clinical Child Psychology,* 1980, **8,** 199–203.

Rekers, G.A., Mead, S.L., Rosen, A.C., & Brigham, S.L. Family correlates of male childhood gender disturbance. *The Journal of Genetic Psychology,* in press.

Rekers, G.A., & Milner, G.C. Sexual identity disorders in childhood and adolescence. *Journal of the Florida Medical Association,* 1978, **65,** 962–964.

Rekers, G.A., & Milner, G.C., III. How to diagnose and manage childhood sexual disorders. *Behavioral Medicine,* 1979, **6,** 18–21.

Rekers, G.A., & Milner, G.C. Early detection of sexual identity disorders. *Medical Aspects of Human Sexuality,* 1981, **15**(11), 32EE–32FF.

Rekers, G.A., Rosen, A.C., Lovaas, O.I., & Bentler, P.M. Sex-role stereotypy and professional intervention for childhood gender disturbances. *Professional Psychology,* 1978, **9,** 127–136.

Rekers, G.A., & Rudy, J.P. Differentiation of childhood body gestures. *Perceptual and Motor Skills,* 1978, **46,** 839–845.

Rekers, G.A., Sanders, J.A., & Strauss, C.C. Developmental differentiation of adolescent body gestures. *Journal of Genetic Psychology,* 1981, **138** (1), 123–131.

Rekers, G.A., Sanders, J.A., Strauss, C.C., Rasbury, W.C., & Mead, S.L. Differentiation of adolescent activity participation. *The Journal of Genetic Psychology,* in press.

Rekers, G.A., & Varni, J.W. Self-monitoring and self-reinforcement processes in a pretranssexual boy. *Behaviour Research and Therapy,* 1977, **15,** 177–180. (a)

Rekers, G.A., & Varni, J.W. Self-regulation of gender-role behaviors: A case study. *Journal of Behavior Therapy and Experimental Psychiatry,* 1977, **8,** 427–432. (b)

Rekers, G.A., Willis, R.J., Yates, C.E., Rosen, A.C., & Low, B.P. Assessment of childhood gender behavior change. *Journal of Child Psychology and Psychiatry,* 1977, **18,** 53–65.

Rekers, G.A., & Yates, C.E. Sex-typed play in feminoid boys vs. normal boys and girls. *Journal of Abnormal Child Psychology,* 1976, **4,** 1–8.

Rekers, G.A., Yates, C.E., Willis, T.J., Rosen, A.C., & Taubman, M. Childhood gender identity change: Operant control over sex-typed play mannerisms. *Journal of Behavior Therapy and Experimental Psychiatry,* 1976, **7,** 51–57.

Renshaw, D.C. Sexuality and depression in infancy, childhood, and adolescence. *Medical Aspects of Human Sexuality,* 1975, **9** (June), 24, 29–45.

Resnik, H.L.P. Erotized repetitive hangings: A form of self-destructive behavior. *American Journal of Psychotherapy,* 1972, **26,** 4–21.

Rituo, S. Adolescent to woman. In H.P. Blum (Ed.), *Female psychology: Contemporary psychoanalytic views.* New York: International Universities Press, 1977.

Roback, H.B., McKee, E., Webb, W., Abramowitz, C.V., & Abramowitz, S.I. Psychopathology in female sex-change applicants and two help-seeking controls. *Journal of Abnormal Psychology,* 1976, **85,** 430–432.

Roberts, R., McBee, G.W., and Bettis, M.C. Youthful sex offenders: An epidemiologic comparison of types. *Journal of Sex Research,* 1969, **5,** 29–40.

Robins, L.N. *Deviant children grown up: A sociological and psychiatric study of sociopathic personality.* Baltimore: Williams & Wilkins, 1966.

Roche, A.F., & Davila, G.H. Late adolescent growth in stature. *Pediatrics,* 1972, **50,** 874.

Roelser, T., & Deisher, R.W. Youthful male homosexuality: Homosexual experience and the process of developing homosexual identity in males aged 16 to 22 years. *Journal of the American Medical Association,* 1972, **219,** 1018–1023.

Root, A., & Russ, R.D. Effect of L-dihydroxyphenylalanine upon serum growth hormone concentrations in children and adolescents. *Journal of Pediatrics,* 1972, **81,** 808–813.

Rosen, A.C. The intersex: Gender identity, genetics, and mental health. In S. Plog & R. Edgerton (Eds.), *Changing perspectives in mental illness.* New York: Holt, 1969.

Rosen, A.C. Brief report of MMPI characteristics of sexual deviation. *Psychological Reports,* 1974, **35,** 73–74.

Rosen, A.C., & Rekers, G.A. toward a taxonomic framework for variables of sex and gender. *Genetic Psychology Monographs,* 1980, **102,** 191–218.

Rosen, A.C., Rekers, G.A., & Bentler, P.M. Ethical issues in the treatment of children. *Journal of Social Issues,* 1978, **34,** 122–136.

Rosen, A.C., Rekers, G.A., & Friar, L.R. Theoretical and diagnostic issues in child gender disturbances. *Journal of Sex Research,* 1977, **13,** 83–103.

Rosenblum, K.E. Female deviance and the female sex role: a preliminary investigation. *British Journal of Sociology,* 1975, **26,** 169–185.

Roth, E.I. Emergency treatment of raped children. *Medical Aspects of Human Sexuality,* 1972, **6,** 85.

Russell, D.H. On the psychopathology of boy prostitutes. *International Journal of Offender Therapy,* 1971, **15**(1), 49–52.

Saghir, M.T., & Robins, E. *Male and female homosexuality: A comprehensive investigation.* Baltimore: Williams & Wilkins Co., 1973.

Slazman, L. Sexual problems in adolescence. *Contemporary Psychoanalysis,* 1974, **10,** 198–207.

Scanzoni, L. *Sex is a parent affair.* Glendale, Cal.: Regal, 1973.

Schenfeld, W. Body-image disturbances in adolescents: Influence of family attitudes and psychopathology. *Archives of General Psychiatry,* 1966, **15,** 16–21.

Schultz, L.G. Psychotherapeutic and legal approaches to the sexually victimized child. *International Journal of Child Psychotherapy,* 1972, **1,** 115–128.

Schultz, L.G. The child sex victim: Social, psychological and legal perspectives. *Child Welfare,* 1973, **52,** 147–157.

Shankel, L.W., & Carr, A.C. Transvestism and hanging episodes in a male adolescent. *Psychiatric Quarterly,* 1956, **30,** 478–493.

Shatin, L., & Southworth, J.A. Sex knowledge intelligence and sexual adjustment. *The Journal of Social Psychology,* 1961, **54,** 219–233.

Shenker, I.R., Nussbaum, M., & Kaplan, E. Delayed puberty and short stature in adolescence. *Pediatric Annals,* 1978, **7,** 605–613.

Shoor, M., Speed, M.H., & Bartelt, C. Syndrome of the adolescent child molester. *American Journal of Psychiatry,* 1966, **122,** 783–789.

Sigusch, V., & Schmidt, G. Teenage boys and girls in West Germany. *Journal of Sex Research,* 1973, **9,** 107–123.

Sizonenko, P.C., & Lewin, M. Problemes physio-logiques de la puberté. *Archives of French Psychiatry,* 1972, **29,** 169–183.

Sorenson, R.C. *Adolescent sexuality in contemporary America: Personal values and sexual behavior, ages thirteen to nineteen.* New York: World, 1973.

Sprince, M.P. A contribution to the study of homosexuality in adolescence. *Journal of Child Psychology and Psychiatry,* 1964, **5**(2), 103–117.

Stearns, A.W. Cases of probable suicide in young persons without obvious motivation. *Journal of Child Psychology and Psychiatry,* 1964, **5**(2), 103–117.

Stearns, A.W. Cases of probable suicide in young persons without obvious motivation. *Journal of the Maine Medical Association,* 1953, **44**(1), 16–23.

Steger, R.W. Extrahypothalamic neural influences affecting the onset of puberty in the female. In E.S.E. Hafez & J.J. Peluso (Eds.), *Sexual maturity: Physiological and clinical parameters.* Ann Arbor: Ann Arbor Science Publishers, 1976.

Stirt, S.S. Overt mass masturbation in the classroom. *American Journal of Orthopsychiatry,* 1940, **10,** 801–804.

Stoller, R.J. A contribution to the study of gender identity. *International Journal of Psychoanalysis,* 1964, **45,** 220–226.

Stoller, R.J. Passing in the continuum of gender identity. In J. Marmer (Ed.), *Sexual inversion.* New York: Basic Books, 1965.

Stoller, R.J. It's only a phase. *Journal of the American Medical Association,* 1967, **201,** 98–99.

Stoller, R.J. Male childhood transsexualism. *Journal of the American Academy of Child Psychiatry,* 1968, **7,** 193–209. (a)

Stoller, R.J. *Sex and gender: The development of masculinity and femininity.* New York: Science House, 1968. (b)

Stoller, R.J. Psychotherapy of extremely feminine boys. *International Journal of Psychiatry,* 1970–1971, **9,** 278–280.

Stoller, R.J. *Sex and gender: The transsexual experiment.* New York: Aronson, 1975.

Stolz, H.R., & Stolz, L.M. Adolescent problems related to somatic variation. In *The National Society for the Study of Education* (Ed.) *Adolescence: the forty-third yearbook.* Chicago: University of Chicago Press, 1944.

Stolz, H.R., & Stolz, L.M. *Somatic development of adolescent boys.* New York: Macmillan, 1951.

Strauss, J.S., & Pochi, P.E. Acne and some other skin disorders. In J.R. Gallagher, F.P. Heald, & D.C. Garell (Eds.), *Medical care of the adolescent* (3rd ed.). New York: Appleton-Century, 1976.

Strzyewsky, J., & Zierhoffer, M. Aversion therapy in a case fetishism with transvestistic component. *The Journal of Sex Research,* 1967, **3**, 614–618.

Stunkard, A.J., & Mahoney, M.J. Behavioral treatment of the eating disorders. In H. Leitenberg (Ed.), *Handbook of behavior modification and behavior therapy.* Englewood Cliffs, N.J.: Prentice-Hall, 1976.

Styne, D.M., & Grumbach, M.M. Puberty in the male and female: Its physiology and disorders. In R. Jaffe & S. Yen (Eds.), *Reproductive endocrinology: Physical and clinical aspects.* Philadelphia: Saunders, 1978.

Styne, D.M., & Kaplan, S.L. Normal and abnormal puberty in the female. *Pediatric Clinics of North America,* 1979, **26**, 123–148.

Sugar, M. *Female adolescent development.* New York: Brunner/Mazal, 1979.

Symonds, M. Homosexuality in adolescence. *Pennsylvania Psychiatric Quarterly,* 1969, **9**(2), 15–24.

Szasz, G. Adolescent sexual activity. *Canadian Nurse,* 1971, **67**, (October), 39–43.

Tanner, J.M. *Growth at adolescence* (2nd ed.). Oxford: Blackwell, 1962.

Tanner, J.M. *Biological aspects of social problems.* Edinburgh: Oliver & Boyd, 1965.

Tanner, J.M., Whitehouse, R.H., & Takaishi, M. Standards from birth to maturity for height, weight, height velocity, and weight velocity: British children, 1965. Part II. *Archives of Disease in Childhood,* 1966, **41**, 613.

Tanner, J.M. Sequence and tempo in the somatic changes in puberty. In M.M. Grumbach, G.D. Grave, & F.E. Mayer (Eds.), *Control of the onset of puberty.* New York: Wiley, 1974.

Tanner, J.M. Growth and endocrinology of the adolescent. In L. Gardner (Ed.), *Endocrine and genetic diseases of childhood and adolescence* (2nd ed.). Philadelphia: Saunders, 1975.

Tepperman, J. *Metabolic and endocrine physiology.* Chicago: Year Book Medical Publishers, 1968.

Thomas, J.K. Adolescent endocrinology for counselors of adolescents. *Adolescence,* 1973, **8**, 395–406.

Thompson, J.L., McCandless, B.R., & Strickland, B.R. Personal adjustment of male and female homosexuals and heterosexuals. *Journal of Abnormal Psychology,* 1971, **78**, 237–240.

Thornburg, H.D. A comparative study of sex information sources. *Journal of School Health,* 1972, **42**, 88–91.

Tryon, C.M. Evaluations of adolescent personality by adolescents. *Monographs of the Society for Research in Child Development,* 1939, **4**, 4.

Tuddenham, R.D., & Snyder, M.M. Physical growth of California boys and girls from birth to eighteen years. *University of California Publications in Child Development,* 1954, **1**, 183.

Vener, A.M. Adolescent sexual behavior in middle America revisited: 1970–1973. *Journal of Marriage and the Family,* 1974, **36**, 728–735.

Visser, H.K.A. Some physiological and clinical aspects of puberty. *Archives of Disease in Childhood,* 1973, **48**, 169–183.

Vogt, J.H. Five cases of transsexualism in females. *Acta Psychiatria Scandinavia,* 1968, **44**, 62–88.

Walinder, J. *Transsexualism: A study of forty-three cases.* Goteborg: Scandinavian University Books, 1967.

Weeks, R.B. Brief guide to office counseling: Counseling parents of sexually abused children. *Medical Aspects of Human Sexuality,* 1976, **10**, 43–44.

Weiss, J., Rogers, E., Darwin, M.R., & Dutton, C.E. A study of girl sex victims. *Psychiatric Quarterly,* 1955, **29**, 1–27.

Wheeler, M.E. & Hess, K.W. Treatment of juvenile obesity by successive approximation control of eating. *Journal of Behavior Therapy and Experimental Psychiatry,* 1976, **7**, 235–241.

Whitam, F.L. Childhood indicators of male homosexuality. *Archives of Sexual Behavior,* 1977, **6**, 89–96.

Winter, J.S.D., Faiman, C., & Reyes, F.I. Normal and abnormal pubertal development. *Clinical Obstetrics and Gynecology,* 1978, **21**, 67–86.

Zacharias, L., & Wurtman, R.J. Age at menarche, genetic and environmental influences. *New England Journal of Medicine,* 1969, **280**, 868–876.

Zacharias, L., Wurtman, R.J., & Schatzoff, M. Sexual maturation in contemporary American girls. *American Journal of Obstetric Gynecology,* 1970, **108,** 833.

Zuger, B. Effeminate behavior present in boys from early childhood: I. The clinical syndrome and follow-up studies. *Journal of Pediatrics,* 1966, **69,** 1098–1107.

Zuger, B. Gender role determination: A critical review of the evidence from hermaphroditism. *Psychosomatic Medicine,* 1970, **32,** 449–467. (a)

Zuger, B. The role of familial factors in persistent effeminate behavior in boys. *American Journal of Psychiatry,* 1970, **126,** 1167–1170. (b)

Zuger, B. Effeminate behavior present in boys from childhood. Ten additional years of follow-up. *Comprehensive Psychiatry,* 1978, **19,** 363–369.

Zuger, B., & Taylor, P. Effeminate behavior present in boys from early childhood. II. Comparison with similar symptoms in non-effeminate boys. *Pediatrics,* 1969, **44,** 375–380.

CHAPTER 34

School Problems of Adolescence

BEEMAN N. PHILLIPS

This chapter reviews school problems of adolescence, focusing on a developmental and ecological perspective. Current evidence about different types of school problems is summarized, and basic approaches to school intervention are surveyed. Overall, the chapter takes a conceptual and descriptive rather than prescriptive view of the school problems of adolescence.

A CONCEPTUAL PERSPECTIVE ON ADOLESCENCE

Adolescence is not an isolated phenomenon. For example, Blos (1979) would argue that the adolescent must rework certain intrapsychic tensions initially faced in childhood if healthy adulthood is to follow. As further evidence, it has been found that childhood and adolescent behavior disorders influence later adjustment. A recent study of Cass and Thomas (1979) is a case in point. They followed 200 children seen in a child guidance center during the early 1960s who were then interviewed at 18 and 27 years of age. At the time that they were seen in the clinic, they averaged 9 years of age, and the vast majority were boys. One of the best predictors of adult psychopathology was poor *school* adjustment although a number of childhood indices were significant predictors. Of special interest is the finding that problems in early adolescence had special utility in predicting adult status.

There is also the need to reflect on one's purpose in isolating such phenomena for special consideration. Presumably, such a focus facilitates a clear understanding of the unique aspects of school problems that are not generalizable to other students in other developmental periods. For example, the consideration of "adolescent" drug use or "adolescent" pregnancy suggests that there is something unique about adolescence in relation to these problems. While it is in adolescence that sexual activity is first likely to occur and drug use to intensify, if one focuses too narrowly on that period, one is not apt fully to realize the similarities and differences in such behaviors across developmental periods.

One also can view adolescence from a social psychological, psychodynamic, evolutionary, cognitive, or normative perspective. Examining adolescence in different cultures adds still another perspective and leads to the realization that there are different paths from childhood to adulthood. Further, within the period of adolescence, one can postulate subperiods corresponding to early adolescence (12–15 years) and late adolescence (15–18 years). While such a breakdown has some arbitrariness, it is a useful distinction because one can posit important developmental and secondary school events on such a scale of time. For example, early adolescence is a crucial period of cognitive, psychosexual, and affective development (see Block, 1971; Blos, 1979). Sex differences are also important in this early phase of adolescence because girls mature earlier than boys.

In essence, the perspective that is taken in this chapter sees the adolescent as moving

813

through a *cumulative set* of determining experiences. There is a series of chained options through which the adolescent passes that give direction to outcomes. At many points, new experiences, feedback, or exposure to new role models may redirect the development of the adolescent. Secondary school experiences are important in this general developmental model, as, for example, when the adolescent who establishes a pattern of high achievement in secondary school then has the option of continuing his or her education. This further schooling, in turn, allows for the possibility of certain careers that then have personal, economic, lifestyle, and cultural implications.

SCHOOL PROBLEMS OF ADOLESCENCE: A PROBLEM OF PERCEPTION?

To some extent, labeling certain behaviors as "school problems" is a perennial problem in itself. To what extent, for example, is there an objective reality to school problems? Or is a label a value choice of the teacher or school? Focusing on the primary school diagnostic agent (i.e., the classroom teacher) one could argue that identification of certain behaviors as school problems reflects only deviation from the dominant values of the school. For example, there is a greater tendency to associate school problems with black or lower socioeconomic status adolescents. This general situation may support the idea that the judgments of school professionals are influenced by their own backgrounds, educational values, assumptions about schooling, and expectations for certain groups.

A second level of reality in school problem identification focuses on whether the school's perception of the student parallels perceptions in other ecological contexts such as the family and peer group. The attitudes of teachers, for example, may be divergent from those of peers, and this raises the question of whether there is less of a tendency to label behavior as deviant where there is congruence. Furthermore, if we focus on objective manifestations,

a school problem may be manifested differently among different groups of adolescents. In the middle class, for example, there is a tendency toward passive as opposed to the more active manifestation of developmental disorders in the lower class.

In addition, schools must deal with adolescents in a variety of confrontational situations, and in such situations it is important to distinguish between normal adolescent behavior and behavior that may indicate serious psychological difficulties. However, as Rubin and Balow (1978) point out, definitions of mental disorders are far from standardized, and the same behavior may be accepted in one environmental setting and rejected in another. Therefore, although adequate classifications of deviant behavior and development need to be available to school professionals, there is some danger inherent in the use of such classification.

The most widely known classification system is the *Diagnostic and Statistical Manual for Mental Disorders* (American Psychiatric Association, 1978). One problem with this and similar systems is that their classification categories are not as well developed for adolescents as for adults. These systems also depend on narrative rather than empirical descriptions of disorders, which makes it difficult to determine how school problems differ in etiology, prognosis, and responses to treatment.

An alternative is an empirically derived taxonomy although such efforts have concentrated on children rather than adolescents. One example is Peterson's Problem Checklist, which has been used by researchers with adolescents. Quay and Quay (1965) used it with seventh- and eighth-graders, and through factor analysis found three main factors. One, conduct problems, included disruptive behaviors such as disobedience, hyperactivity, and fighting. Another, personality problems, involved feelings of insecurity, anxiety, and social withdrawal. A third factor, immaturity, consisted of characteristics like laziness in school, short attention span, and preoccupation.

One of the most empirically derived classification systems applicable to adolescents is that developed by Achenbach and Edelbrock (1979). Their checklist consists of both behavior problems and social competence items, and separate profiles have been developed taking into account age and sex differences. The factors for boys, ages 12–16, were: aggressive, delinquent, hyperactive, hostile withdrawal, obsessive-compulsive, immature, uncommunicative, schizoid, and somatic complaints. For girls, ages 12–16, the factors were: aggressive, delinquent, immature-hyperactive, cruel, anxious-obsessive, depressed-withdrawal, schizoid, and somatic complaints.

Edelbrock (1979) points out some of the limitations of such instrumentation. When parents are used as raters, for example, analyses typically yield a broader band of factors than when teachers are used. As he notes, this may be because teachers observe only a limited portion of an adolescent's behavior. But a more important reason may be differences in behavioral expectations.

The issue is even more complicated when adolescents are evaluated in terms of their educational needs. Here we are dealing with a classification scheme that is really a placement system for special education purposes. A standard nomenclature used in special education programs in many states includes: (1) educable mentally retarded, (2) trainable mentally retarded, (3) health or physically impaired, (4) learning disabled, and (5) emotionally disturbed. These or similar labels are widely utilized, but the problem of such a construct system is that its definitions are too broad. To arrive at a more adequate definition of terms, one might, in the beginning, look at behaviors commonly referred to as learning disabilities, mental retardation, etc. But comparative study is likely to bring out important similarities and differences that will clarify the forms of behavioral and learning problems. In due course, more useful definitions might evolve that will keep psychologists and educators from straying from the basic purpose of classification, which is appropriate intervention. But that is an achievement that must await further research and application efforts.

EFFECTS OF SECONDARY SCHOOL ON SCHOOL PROBLEMS OF ADOLESCENTS: A PROBLEM IN ETIOLOGY

School adjustment, broadly defined, is the interplay between the student and the school environment although in this chapter we are preoccupied with school problems where there is a lack of adjustment. In both cases, however, there is a need to assess relationships between the school environment and student outcomes. However, until recently such relationships remained tangled, and few school effects were shown, in spite of extensive research. Best known among these studies is that by Coleman et al. (1966). This large scale survey indicated that schools had little effect on the students although the appropriateness of this and similar studies has been questioned, partly because of the limited variables used to evaluate school impact.

More recently, research has focused more directly on school process and ecological influence. Rutter et al. (1979), for example, considered not only achievement outcomes but student behaviors as well. The total pattern of their findings suggests that students' behaviors in secondary schools are influenced by experiences they have in school. Among their specific findings, they found that delinquency rates are predictable, as is variation in school attendance—two school problems of considerable concern in relation to adolescence. Many other indications of the potential of schools to influence student outcomes are reported by Walberg, Schiller, and Haertel (1979). They examined hundreds of studies and concluded that certain school conditions consistently produce positive effects on student outcomes.

In the light of such results, one might argue that an epidemiological approach to school problems of adolescence that would not only deal with the incidence and distribution of school problems but also with their control would be justified. But this is not possible because the etiology of school problems of adolescence is very complex. The secondary school may serve as an antecedent in the sense that something that happens there precedes the onset of a school problem; it may function as a determinant that shapes the nature of a school problem; or events in the secondary school may be the occasions in which underlying causes are activated or manifested. But the secondary school is not usually *the* cause of a school problem, in the sense of providing the conditions or circumstances that effectively and inevitably call forth the problem.

SECONDARY SCHOOL EXPERIENCES OF ADOLESCENTS VIEWED FROM AN ECOLOGICAL PERSPECTIVE

One of Bronfenbrenner's (1979) more interesting ideas is that of developmental contexts. He believes that typical analyses of environmental influences on development do little more than identify the environments from which students come. For example, studies regularly show that family background is an important factor in school achievement. But such studies tell us little about the processes involved, even where there is a focus on interpersonal factors, as in studies of parent-child relationships, because they lack generalizability across settings and contexts. What are needed, he maintains, are concepts and data that go beyond the dyadic level and relate to transcontextual factors.

To apply Bronfenbrenner's general thesis, the environments in which adolescents live and the processes through which these environments affect the course of development are crucial to an understanding of their school problems. In developing his general thesis, Bronfenbrenner has specified four properties of ecological environments that foster development, including:

1. Primary developmental contexts, where the adolescent engages in ongoing activity with or under the guidance of a person(s) knowledgeable in those activities, and with whom the adolescent has a positive relationship.
2. Secondary developmental contexts, where there are opportunities and re-

sources to engage in these activities without the active involvement and guidance of the aforementioned knowledgeable person(s).
3. The development potential of settings, which depends on the extent to which third parties in such settings support or undermine the activities of those persons engaged in interaction with adolescents.
4. The developmental potential of settings, which increases as a function of supportive links between settings in the form of shared activities, communication, and information.

If these concepts are applied to the secondary school, the classroom could be considered a key primary developmental context. On the other hand, many extracurricular activities fit the concept of a secondary developmental context. Furthermore, the extent to which a principal supports his or her teachers is illustrative of the role of third parties, and supportive links between the family and secondary school are examples of the last principle.

Carrying this ecological perspective further, *changes* in school developmental contexts may be critical. For example, in terms of secondary school students' classroom experiences, according to a preliminary report on Goodlad's "A Study of Schooling" (Benham, Giesen, & Oakes, 1980), by the senior-high-school level the frequency of encouraging behaviors and positive interaction by teachers has dropped to 50 percent of what is reported in elementary school. But whether such changes are related to organizational factors, instructional factors, or other school differences has yet to be determined.

Moreover, the linkage between peer groups and the school is an equally important consideration. For example, when secondary students in the same study were asked to respond to the "one best thing about their school," 35 percent chose their friends. Sports and good student activities were the next most popular type of response. The classes they were taking, the variety of course offerings, and teachers were less often mentioned. Adding to the significance of these results, students with lower self-concepts didn't participate as much in extracurricular aspects of secondary schooling and tended to have less satisfactory relations with peers. That this is a reciprocal relationship is indicated by other research suggesting that the self-concept also is influenced by participation in extracurricular activities in secondary schools (see, e.g., Gump, 1980).

As another illustration of the need for an ecological perspective, in many secondary schools there are various forms of academic tracking, the most common tracks being vocational and college bound. Such segregation probably influences the character of both in-class and out-of-class experiences. Further, when individual high schools were ranked according to student perceptions, schools consistently filled in particular positions across the various dimensions of ranking, suggesting that the nature and quality of the developmental contexts varied from high school to high school (Benham et al., 1980).

SCHOOL CONDUCT AND ACHIEVEMENT PROBLEMS OF ADOLESCENCE

A wide array of school problem behaviors occur in the classroom, including tantrums, verbal abuse, aggression, disruptive or inattentive behavior, and so forth. While in some instances these can be serious, they more often are only bothersome to teachers and other students. Other school conduct and achievement problems are more serious, and these are discussed below although some might be considered as school/community problems rather than strictly as school problems.

Violence in Secondary Schools

In discussing violence in secondary schools, there is an initial problem of agreeing on what should be called violence. It certainly is not a unidimensional problem. Acts against students and teachers are different from such "victimless" crimes as vandalism.

As to the incidence of violence and vandalism, in Partland and McDill (1977) there is a vivid firsthand account of what happened during a 10-month period in the Los Angeles Unified School District. There were 232 recorded assaults against teachers and other school personnel, 338 against students, and 60 against security agents. It is further estimated that loss and damage to school buildings and other property amounted to more than 4 million dollars during the 1975–76 school year.

At this point, social scientists have not contributed much substantive knowledge about the "whys" of various kinds of violence in secondary schools. However, for adolescents having aggression problems, Bandura (1973) does provide a general theoretical perspective that can be the basis of a variety of intervention strategies. Beyond this, theories of delinquency imply that major changes in secondary schools would be a necessary step to reduce violence significantly, and restructuring the family, work settings, and the stratification system of society would be ultimately required.

In-School Truancy

A problem that particularly plagues urban high schools is in-school truancy (Teachman, 1979). Teachman reports, for example, that absence from classes in which students are enrolled in the Detroit Public Schools during 1977–79 was nearly 20 percent. But this was only the official rate. Teachers' attendance figures suggest that the percentage was actually closer to 30 percent.

While this is an in-class problem, students in the building but not in class are the source of other problems. For example, most of the violence in high schools occurs outside the classroom. Interestingly, in the Detroit high schools, in-school truancy was highest in the ninth grade, during the first and second hours of the school day, and for all classes after lunch (Teachman, 1979).

These data suggest that it is not just whether classes are relevant and interesting that determine the incidence of in-school truancy. Student characteristics, as well as teaching effectiveness, attendance policies, and other school factors enter in as well. As an indication of the importance of both student and school factors, Teachman (1979) points out that official in-school truancy rates varied from 33.5 percent at one high school to a low of 6.9 percent at another that had a selected student body.

Drug Use and Abuse

In the past decade or more, public concern about nonmedical drug use has stimulated much research. As to the prevalence of drug use in the adolescent age range, in a 1972 household survey conducted by the National Commission on Marihuana and Drug Abuse (1973), it was reported that .6 percent of those aged 12–17 reported one or more uses of heroin. The prevalence of other drug use among adolescents is reflected in other statistics of the commission. For example, about 15 percent of the same age group reported use of marihuana, about 5 percent use of various hallucinogens, and about the same percentage reported use of amphetamines and barbiturates.

In examining the etiology of drug use and abuse, one sees the involvement of school factors. For example, B.D. Johnson (1973) reports on a longitudinal survey of 2,000 male tenth-graders during the late 1960s. He found that those who became users were more dissatisfied with school, studied less, and made poorer grades. Studies of young adults add other characteristics to this pattern that, however, may not be equally applicable to adolescents. They receive more traffic violation citations, belong to fewer organizations, have sexual relations at an earlier age, have less respect for authority, and are more likely to be more alienated from society (L. Johnson, 1973).

Treatment procedures reported in Kendall and Hallon (1979) would be useful in treating the drug problem itself. To deal with related academic deficiencies, cognitive instruction approaches such as those presented in Lesgold et al. (1978) would be more appropriate.

Therapeutic techniques discussed by Millman, Schaefer, and Cohen (1980) would also have value, especially in helping such adolescents with emotional problems.

Delinquency

Juvenile delinquency is a pervasive phenomenon in many areas of the country. The FBI's *Uniform Crime Reports* show that 50 percent of all arrests for property offenses involve persons under 18. More than 1 million youngsters are accused of delinquent and/or criminal behavior annually and appear in the juvenile court system. In terms of the expectations that the public has for its schools, one can assume that the school has some responsibility for the out-of-school life of its students so that there is a broad relationship between the schools and delinquency. Further, since delinquency is a legal concept, the point of contact between the adolescent and delinquency is the juvenile justice system. Juvenile justice is intrinsically linked, therefore, to the schools.

Most directly related to the purpose of this chapter, however, is the school-related delinquent. This refers to children and adolescents who demonstrate serious antisocial behavior only in school. They not only have a history of academic failure but exhibit serious uncooperative classroom conduct, including a contempt for authority figures in the school. When such behaviors reach a certain level, they enter the juvenile justice system on the basis of incorrigibility and/or truancy.

For an excellent discussion of intervention strategies that can be used with delinquents, the reader should consult Kendall and Hallon (1979). One approach advocated, which focuses on problem-solving, role-taking, and self-control strategies, is particularly useful.

Suicide among Adolescents

Between 1950 and 1975, the suicide rate of white adolescents between the ages of 15 and 19 increased from 2.8 deaths per 100,000 to 7.6, an increase of 170 percent (U.S. Department of Health, Education, and Welfare,

1975). While the absolute number of suicides is small in this age group, the rate of increase was larger than for any other age group during that period. In addition, for each successful suicide there are many more attempted suicides among this age group.

Although theories of suicide point to both psychic as well as societal factors as etiological influences, poor school performance, truancy, and other school problems occur frequently among adolescents who *attempt* suicide. The school is further involved because suicides and suicide attempts rarely occur without warning and teachers are in a position to be aware of behavioral and verbal signals of distress. The possibility of suicide is enhanced, for example, where quality of school work deteriorates dramatically, when excessive use of alcohol and drugs occurs, or when there are other major changes in behavior. In addition to recognizing the potentially serious problem, teachers can take steps to put the adolescent in contact with appropriate agencies and specialists.

Pregnant Adolescents

Millions of 15–19-year-old females are sexually active, and a considerable number get pregnant. Some estimates are as high as 1 million, and 600,000 give birth each year (Guttmacher Institute, 1976). This is a very serious problem for many reasons, one being that pregnancy is the most frequent reason that females drop out of school. Many school districts, however, have developed special programs for such students, and one index of the success that such programs can have is that pregnant adolescents more often stay in school. In addition, disciplinary and other school problems tend to decrease. The problem is extremely complex, however, and schools can only ameliorate some aspects. Coordinated community, governmental, and broad societal efforts are needed.

Single-Parent Families

The number of adolescents in school who live with a lone parent is increasing due to deser-

tion by fathers (and mothers), death of spouses, increasing number of divorces, and the birth of children to unmarried women. Research for 1979–80 by the Kettering Foundation (Brown, 1980) shows important school behavioral differences between two-parent and one-parent families. Results for absenteeism, suspensions, truancy, expulsions, dropouts, tardiness, and discipline problems all show an advantage to the two-parent family. Of course, one-parent families are more often in the low income category, but the disparities still exist when this and related background factors are controlled.

The seriousness of the single-parent family as an influence on school problems is further indicated by U.S. Census Bureau projections that almost 50 percent of the children born in 1980 will live a considerable time with only one parent before they reach 18 (Brown, 1980). This obviously has implications for the elementary and secondary schools of this country beyond the school problems focus of this chapter.

Developmental Crises of Parents

Adolescence coincides with certain types of parental crises, including concerns about mid-life transitions, aging, marital deficiencies, and anticipation of the empty nest. The point is made by Blow (1979), who presents a psychoanalytic theory of development, that intrapsychic changes associated with the adolescent passage require systematic external influence, mainly by parents. This puts additional strains on the family that may already be in crisis. He further argues that the developmental tasks that are commonly recognized as important to adolescence can't be achieved without significant conflict with parents. For example, the sense of autonomy is important to adolescence, and the adolescent must give up the dependency characteristic of preadolescence to make the passage to adolescence successfully.

But there is much in the situation that makes parents want to hang on to, or even increase, the controls, and much ambivalence about the adolescent's growing sense of independence occurs. Such conflicts can add to the parents' own developmental crises, and their reactions can be counterproductive. The adolescent's need for understanding and guidance as well as autonomy and parental confidence, therefore, is not met, with the result that the adolescent's school adjustment often suffers.

There are a number of interesting parent education programs described in Fine (1980), although credible evidence is lacking on their success, despite the fact that some programs, such as the very popular PET program, have reached thousands of parents. This program, and others like Parents Anonymous described in Fine's book, are appropriate for parents with teenagers.

Test Anxiety

Although many aspects of test anxiety have been studied, its school ecology is the least understood. Testing situations are common to adolescents in school and are the focus of much anxiety. Moreover, the secondary school environment is highly evaluation oriented, and test anxiety permeates a wide range of school situations and activities (Phillips et al., 1980). In addition, the effects of test anxiety seem to be pervasive and readily generalized. It is negatively related to a large number of behavioral, personal, and school performance measures. To name a few, test anxiety is related to academic achievement, attentional behavior, utilization of instructional cues, physiological states, memory processes, attributions of reasons for success or failure, interpersonal behavior, self-concept, responses to role models, problem-solving strategies, and self-control mechanisms (Phillips, Martin, & Meyers, 1972, pp. 409–464; Sarason, I., 1980).

The test anxiety literature, however, tells us much more about the person with high test anxiety than it does about the person with low test anxiety. Further, we know less about the *processes* involved than we know about the products of test anxiety. Beyond this, as Phillips et al. (1980) point out, we need to know more about the behaviors of teachers and how they are implicated in the development of test anxiety and students' reaction to it.

Nevertheless, research on adapting classroom instruction to test-anxious students' problems is making significant progress (Tobias, 1980), and there is an abundance of conceptual models for the treatment of test anxiety (Denney, 1980, pp. 209–243; Meichenbaum & Butler, 1980, pp. 187–208; Rosenthal, 1980). But, surprisingly, there is almost no research on the developmental aspects of test anxiety, even after a promising beginning by Sarason and his colleagues (Sarason et al., 1960). They related the development of test anxiety to early parent-child relationships that are reinforced by initial encounters with teachers. The past research emphasis on elementary school and college age subjects, at the expense of the adolescent age group, may have contributed to this developmental gap that future research needs to fill.

Test Bias and Misuse

The issues of test bias and misuse in public schools is a major concern of minorities and other groups. They not only point to abuses of tests in the early years of the testing movement, but, for them, test bias and misuse are painfully obvious today. Objections that have been raised (Reynolds, 1982) to the use of educational and psychological tests include: (1) inappropriate content, (2) inappropriate standardization samples, (3) examiner and language bias, (4) inequitable educational and social consequences, (5) measurement of different constructs, and (6) differential predictive validity. Of these, the most pertinent to this chapter's focus is inequitable educational and social consequences, because inappropriate diagnostic and intervention activities are likely to have a disproportionate impact on minority students. Such deleterious outcomes are compounded, of course, by the concomitant effects of labeling, teacher expectancy effects, and special class placement.

Such effects are not always unidirectional, however, and reversals in the function of such biasing factors sometimes occur. For example, Meyers, MacMillan, and Yoshida (1978) found that there was a tendency *not* to place black children in special education classes even when they were failing in the regular classroom. This tendency extends into non-school settings as well, as in the case of black adolescents seen in mental health centers whose behavior disorders are dismissed as aberrations appropriate to coping in a disadvantaged environment, while white adolescents with similar behavioral problems are diagnosed as disturbed and referred for treatment (Lewis, Balla, & Shanok, 1979).

At an empirical level, the problem of test bias is ultimately a question of validity while in test use it becomes an issue involving values and fairness. For example, differences in mean performance between two racial/ethnic groups does not necessarily mean that the test is invalid. Nor does this necessarily tell us anything about the fairness of the test (Thorndike, 1971). One can assume, of course, that a test producing a mean difference between groups is discriminatory if one can demonstrate that there is no valid reason for the difference. In the same vein, teacher-made tests have not been scrutinized in terms of test bias. Yet this area of testing may have an even greater impact on the adolescent in school.

Reading Problems

Adolescents who present reading problems show a pattern of early reading failure that is highly resistant to remediation (Kraus, 1973). In Kraus's longitudinal study, one of the most intensive longitudinal studies of children in the school setting, 50 percent of 165 children studied initially in kindergarten were followed through high school. In the study, children who were good readers in the second grade continued to be superior readers in the sixth and ninth grades. Careful following of those children who had early reading problems showed that those problems continued through later school years. The pattern of reading failure was only broken in those situations where children were able to attend reading clinics or received intensive help from remedial reading specialists. Thus the course reading problems follow is developmental and cumulative, and, unless major intervention occurs, they usually continue through high school. Changing reading problems, therefore, is a formidable task, and, while Gibson and Levin (1975) weren't directly concerned with curricular intervention, their program of basic research and general theoretical framework forms the basis for many curricular intervention possibilities.

Mathematics Problems of Girls

Attitudes toward mathematics influence achievement in the subject, and both attitudes and achievement favors boys over girls, especially in high school and beyond (Aiken, 1976). Mathematics anxiety is similarly sex related (Richardson & Woolfolk, 1980).

To explain sex differences in attitudes, anxiety, and achievement, sociocultural expectations are commonly used although a variety of views can be found in the literature (Aiken, 1976; Richardson & Woolfolk, 1980). Some emphasize the role of the school, especially curricular materials in the elementary school, where boys are more often portrayed as participating in mathematics and science activities. Still others look to the mathematics curriculum and the way mathematics is taught as a source of the problem. Others point out the fact that boys take more mathematics and science courses in high school. Further, the sex role socialization process stereotypes mathematics as a male domain. There also appear to be certain biological differences between the sexes that emerge during adolescence, including differences in spatial visualization skills.

Programs to increase the participation of females in mathematics and related courses of study have been implemented, especially at the college level (Richardson & Woolfolk, 1980). As they further note, the evaluative form of mathematics content seems to be a source of strong apprehensions. For this reason, programs usually include efforts to remedy these fears and apprehensions as well as to teach a better understanding of the subject.

Science Underachievement

Based on Piaget's theory, only a small percentage of adolescents reach the level of formal operations that is presumably critical in scientific reasoning and achievement. Dulit (1972), for example, found that only 25–33 percent of adolescents aged 14–17 exhibited formal operations although the percentage of gifted 16–17-year-olds reached 60 percent. Generally, there is increasing success with age, but the level of logical thinking varies between schools (e.g., Beard, 1962) although student background and the effects of schooling probably enter into such variations.

As to training of scientific reasoning among adolescents, Levine and Linn (1977) report evidence that programmed instruction, inductive instructional principles, and experiential programs are helpful. Concrete experience is an especially valuable aid in high schools that have a large percentage of low income students. As DeCarcer, Gabel, and Staver (1978) point out, however, one cannot be overly optimistic that school experiences can directly influence scientific reasoning and achievement, at least in terms of formal operations. Nevertheless, they review a series of studies of special training procedures that seemed to enhance scientific reasoning abilities of adolescents.

Decline in General Achievement in the Secondary School

From the middle 1960s, there has been a steady decline in subject matter and basic skills achievement among secondary school students (Copperman, 1979). This decline shows up in scores on college aptitude tests like the SAT and ACT, on academic achievement tests like the MAT, and in the number of students who graduate from high school with achievement levels below the typical eighth-grade student. To put the matter concretely, the average high school student today func-tions about as well as his or her counterparts in the early 1950s. To illustrate the point further, this effect is equivalent to replacing the top quarter of a typical class in 1965, when high school achievement may have peaked, with students somewhat below average by 1965 standards.

The educational significance of such a drop in achievement is enormous, and states have responded to this situation by enacting legislation to insure minimum standards and acting to reduce or eliminate social promotion. Some states are also approving minimum competency for graduation from high school. We can anticipate that educators will further respond by developing guidelines that will improve professional practice. In addition to developing recommendations concerning teachers in practice, there needs to be an effort to insure that preservice education standards are tightened up.

Equally clear, to the extent that the formal part of the learning process cannot be isolated from changes in society, such educational interventions may be viewed as simplistic solutions. For example, a major part of the decline probably reflects a change in the composition of the student body, created largely by the expansion of the proportion of students staying on in high school. In addition, the shift from courses in the traditional disciplines to newer electives, the decline in standards that is reflected in grade inflation and the diminution in students' learning motivation cannot be separated from the broader learning and societal context that includes the changing role of the family in the educational process, the impact of television, and major disruptive national events. It is pervasively evident, therefore, that *comprehensive* educational interventions offer the best chance of success in raising general achievement in the secondary school.

Career and Vocational Indecision

Making wise career decisions is one of the critical school problems of late adolescence although knowledge of how people make career decisions is inadequate. Nevertheless, the area is receiving increased attention, and progress in recent years has been impressive. For example, one general inference that can be made is that adolescents who are good at making such decisions probably know more about occupations. Another is that there is likely to be more congruence between such knowledge and their own vocational aspirations. Jepsen (1975) studied how adolescents organize information about themselves and their strategies for relating this to occupations and found that discrepancies are associated with career indecision. A lower grade point average (GPA) (Lunneborg, 1975) and self-concept (Barrett & Tinsley, 1977), and a higher anxiety (Hawkins, Bradley, & White, 1977) are also related to poorly developed career plans.

Vocational indecision is not necessarily a unitary trait, however, and it is likely that different factors are associated with such difficulties. For example, Noeth, Roth, and Prediger (1975) studied a large national sample of high school students and found that even eleventh-graders couldn't answer most of the items on the occupational knowledge test that was used. In the same survey, more than half of the eleventh-graders also reported that they received little help from their high schools with career plans and problems. Overall, career maturity tends to show developmental progress over the adolescent years. Those higher in career maturity, for example, have been more successful in resolving crises represented in the first six psychological stages of Erikson's theory (Munley, 1975).

Female adolescents of course have special problems in career choices and decisions, especially when they are inclined toward nontraditional occupations. Sex role stereotypes are but one of the factors that complicate the issue because there are also conflicts between a career orientation and marriage and family responsibilities to deal with. Further, since the origin of career choices relates back to parents and family, the career development options of female adolescents may be compromised early in life so that males are more likely than females to prefer high prestige occupations (Barnett, 1975). Another developmental factor

is the degree of realism in career aspirations. Adolescents generally tend to have unrealistic aspirations, although they do distinguish between their expectations and aspirations (Thomas, 1976).

INTERVENING IN THE SCHOOL PROBLEMS OF ADOLESCENTS

A fair reading of the literature suggests that no single intervention technique succeeds for the majority of students with a particular school problem. On the other hand, one cannot find an intervention technique that does not work with at least one school problem and one student. The focus of this section lies between these poles.

There are other possible approaches that might be adopted in attempting to represent the diverse areas of intervention. At one extreme, they could be viewed simply as an aggregation of unrelated techniques whose only commonality is their relevance to the issue of remediation of school problems of adolescents. At the other extreme, they might be construed as integrated parts of an overarching theory of interventions applied to school problems.

At the present time, however, educational and psychological intervention appears to be more than an assortment of loosely defined techniques but less than a comprehensive, coherent paradigm. One might, in fact, characterize interventions as an array of techniques loosely organized around theoretical systems, and one might similarly characterize school problems as sets of learning and behavior syndromes without a firm grounding in a coherent theory relating etiology, prognosis, and treatment.

For these reasons, we take a conceptual and descriptive rather than a prescriptive approach to intervention in the school problems of adolescence. In Figure 34.1, for example, we identify a conceptual perspective on school intervention that ranges from models of the nature and causes of school dysfunction to models related to the appropriate time to initiate intervention. In addition, conditions of intervention range from aims, to targets, to systems of intervention having a common framework of theorizing, research, and derivative practice. Moreover, there is a correspondence between these systems and intervention strategies that are, in turn, linked to particular techniques.

In Figure 34.2, we carry this process a step further. Each year, schools put thousands of adolescents into diverse school surroundings through differential placement and treatment based on the nature and severity of their school problems, and Figure 34.2 develops a clarifying set of descriptors that encompass this metastrategy of school intervention. While everyone knows that the results of such intervention vary enormously, it is not known

to what extent these variations result from the types of students placed as distinguished from setting influence after placement. One other possibility may be crucial, however, although there are no measures of it. Most of the students placed in such settings are there *involuntarily,* with minimal expectations of reassignment to the regular school program.

However, in addition to global, holistic relations between school problems and interventions, there are particularistic features of *specific* problems and intervention techniques that are important. Thus there are concrete or first-order functional relations between school problems and school intervention techniques. Table 34.1 has been prepared to help answer questions about which techniques to use with

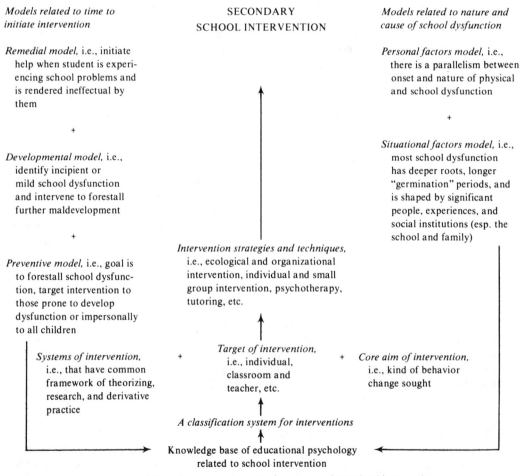

Figure 34.1.   A conceptual perspective on secondary school intervention.

Move the adolescent into a residential
school environment outside of the school
system. This of course further ruptures
the adolescent's contact with his/her
natural school environment.

Shift the adolescent with more severe
school problems to special classrooms,
including alternative high schools, classes
for the emotionally disturbed, etc. This
separates adolescents from their normal
peers and therefore is a critical decision.

Decreasing
restrictiveness
of school
environment

Increasing
severity of
school problems,
and separation
from normal
peers and
natural school
environment

Provide supportive services for the
classroom teacher to assist adolescents
with school problems. Examples of this
would be consultation with teachers, and
the use of paraprofessionals like teacher
aides.

Enable teachers to deal more effectively
with school problems of adolescents in
the regular classroom. Inservice programs
and use of affective education programs
(e.g., Magic Circle, Reality Therapy) are
examples of relevant interventions.

Figure 34.2. A metastrategy for secondary school intervention: engineering environments that optimize adaptation and development in relation to school problems of adolescence.

Table 34.1 Types of Interventions That Can Be Used with School Problems of Adolescence

1. Mental health consultation (Meyers, Parsons, & Martin, 1979)
2. Use of tutors (Allen, 1976)
3. Parent conferences as school intervention (Losen & Diament, 1978)
4. Behavioral consultation (Bergan, 1977)
5. Family intervention (Goldenberg & Goldenberg, 1980; Mash, Hammerlynck, & Handy, 1976)
6. Therapeutic strategies in the classroom (Millman, Schaefer, & Cohen, 1980)
7. Personalized systems of instruction (Kulik, Kulik, & Cohen, 1979)
8. Cognitive instruction (Anderson, Spiro, & Montague, 1977; Klahr, 1976; Lesgold et al., 1978)
9. Teaching as treatment (Carkhuff & Berenson, 1976)
10. Microskills training for helpers (Cormier & Cormier, 1979)
11. Cognitive-behavioral interventions (Kendall & Hallon, 1979)
12. Skill building (Goldstein et al., 1980)
13. Education for cognitive development (Wadsworth, 1978)
14. Behavioral strategies (Haynes & Wilson, 1979)
15. Helping people change strategies (Kanfer & Goldstein, 1975)

which school problems. In this table, a number of references have been accumulated that report research and practical results of particular relevance to intervening in school problems of adolescents. But the literature represented is so vast, and the number of available techniques so large, that the contents of the table can serve only to exemplify the process.

SCHOOL ECOLOGICAL PROBLEMS OF ADOLESCENTS

As previously noted, what happens to adolescents in secondary schools occurs in one behavior setting or another. In a recent review, by Gump (1980), of the school as a social situation, it was pointed out that physical milieu, participants, and program factors are the basic components of school settings. Barker and his colleagues (1978), in their ground-breaking efforts, examined these features of behavior settings in a variety of environments and have traced the ways that settings have consequences for participants. This establishes the framework for this section, which will review aspects of secondary school settings that can be sources of school problems.

Size of Secondary Schools

Barker and Gump (1964) and, later, Wicker (1968) and Baird (1969) have traced the consequences of undermanning and overmanning in secondary schools. This theory states that as high schools become larger, the number of students rises faster than the number of settings, resulting in more students per setting in larger high schools. With more students available, there are fewer pressures and opportunities to become actively involved in setting operations. When applied to extracurricular activities, for example, students in smaller high schools experience more opportunities to participate and take responsibility and are more likely to perform leadership and other supportive roles.

A consequence of this increased involve-

ment is more satisfaction with such activities, which is important to school satisfaction generally. Such satisfactions are related to feelings of gains in competence and to feelings of success (Barker & Gump, 1964). In addition, there is a "promotion effect" in that participants are more often pushed into leadership roles (Gump, 1980). Of special interest, it has been found that these effects may be greater for academically marginal students (Willems, 1967).

In summary, analyses of overmanning and undermanning have indicated some of the disadvantages of large high schools, which are typical of urban areas. To adolescents enrolled in such schools, there is less likelihood that they will experience feelings of responsibility and importance. This lack of needs/environment fit can influence behavioral and other school problems.

Crowding

Large high schools tend to be more crowded, in the sense of having more students per class. Although this refers to density rather than crowding, they are related concepts, and substantial progress has been made in analyses of the experience of crowding (Stokols, 1978). This research shows that high density is a factor in feeling crowded and that such feelings relate to perceptions of personal control. In general, there is a reduction in beliefs of personal control over environments that have high density or crowded conditions. Such feelings are more salient in primary settings than in settings that are less important, and they tend to be more intense and difficult to cope with in psychologically important settings (Stokols, 1975).

The negative effects of prolonged exposure to high density and crowding are important in considerations of school problems of adolescence since these and other factors, like high noise levels, serve as environmental stressors. Although the impact of such stressors is mediated by various psychological factors, impaired school behavior is a potentially frequent outcome.

Desegregation

Social relationships in secondary schools often involve different racial and ethnic groups, and, when desegregation occurs, school problems of a social nature frequently increase, at least temporarily (Stephan, 1978). To combat this, vigorous attempts are sometimes made to improve students' racial attitudes. Weigel, Wiser, and Cook (1975) provide an example of such an effort, utilizing an interdependent format in several newly desegregated junior and senior high schools. The results were mixed, however, and no overall reduction in prejudice for the cooperating groups occurred.

But what have the results of desegregation generally been? Although some reviewers are more optimistic, the weight of the evidence offers little basis for a positive view (Stephan, 1978). Anyone hoping for a straightforward assessment will be disappointed, however, because many of the studies manifest research and design problems that raise doubts about specific findings. Nevertheless, there is little to support the early hopes that there would be a reduction in school problems in desegregated school settings after the initial hurdles were overcome.

Obviously, however, a comprehensive assessment of the effects of desegregation has not been made. The Stephan (1978) review, for example, focused only on hypotheses concerning the effects of desegregation on prejudice, self-esteem, and achievement that were derived from testimony provided by social scientists in early U.S. Supreme Court decisions on segregation in public schools. Although the review by St. John (1975) takes a broader perspective, it does not deal with long term effects of desegregation, such as effects on dropout rates and the number of students who attend college, or on the quality of education offered in a community.

Mainstreaming

The Education for All Handicapped Children Act (PL 94–142) mandates a "free appropriate public education" in the "least restrictive environment" for all handicapped children from 3 to 21 years of age. In addition to expanding public education beyond the ages for which it is normally provided, the usual definition of education is expanded to include basic child care and socialization activities that normally are the responsibility of parents. A broad range of support services, including full time residential care if needed, is included in provisions for "related services." But parent participation in developing and implementing an "individualized educational plan" is perhaps the most revolutionary aspect of the act.

If successful, the law would create a social and educational revolution in the schools. One effect would be many more handicapped children in regular classrooms, with support services provided as needed in the form of resource classrooms, special teachers, school psychologists, etc. Another would be a broad spectrum of related services ranging from psychological services to families with handicapped children, to special medical services, to keeping public schools open the whole year for handicapped children who need it.

To sum up the research on mainstreaming, the evidence is very mixed. Mainstreamed children seem to be no better off academically than nonmainstreamed children (Budoff & Gottlieb, 1976). The same thing can be said for the effects of mainstreaming on self-concept and school expectations (Gruen, Ottinger, & Ollendick, 1974). The evidence that mainstreamed children would be less stigmatized is not there either (Iano et al., 1974). However, this research and other studies of the issues have been conducted almost exclusively at the elementary level where the initial impact of mainstreaming has been most felt. The results are further complicated by difficulties in research design and variations in the implementation of mainstreaming across school systems.

The ecological significance of mainstreaming is of special interest because the idea of interdependency is central to relations between handicapped students and other students. The cooperative intragroup arrangements reviewed by Gump (1980) are particularly noteworthy in relation to classroom learning activities involving normal and handicapped students. Although this research was not directed specifically at handicapped students, the emphasis being on minorities, some of the educational and social relationships are similar. Interestingly, some of this research has involved junior and senior high school students, and substantial achievement benefits have been noted (DeVries & Slavin, 1978). Its applicability to handicapped adolescents is therefore within the realm of reason. Peer tutoring, which involves another type of interdependency, yields similar achievement gains and has special relevance to mainstreaming involving adolescents (Devin-Sheen, Feldman, & Allen, 1976). The DeVries and Slavin study, as well as others referred to, produced social and personal benefits that might be considered even more important than academic behaviors although such results were less consistently positive.

SCHOOL PROBLEMS OF ADOLESCENCE IN A RETROSPECTIVE FRAMEWORK

A distinctive approach to school problems is to examine them from the perspective of young adults, and Project TALENT makes this possible. In a recent report by Flanagan (1978) of life history interviews acquired in 1975 from 1,000 30-year-old participants in this longitudinal project, a high degree of satisfaction with the quality of life in general was found although this was not true of memories of their high school experience.

Five types of factors were identified as educational factors having a lasting impact, including personal support and counseling, individualization, vocational guidance, quality of teaching, and curriculum. The overall results clearly indicated that memories were overwhelmingly negative for all areas except quality of teaching. The most common theme of dissatisfaction with high school was its lack of relevance to later life. This was followed by lack of concern for the individual and his or her mental health. Training for leisure time also is reported to be inadequate, and evidently

the curriculum contributed little to later employment possibilities.

As to suggestions for educational change in the high school, a need for greater concern for positive human relationships and mental health is evident. A variety of other suggestions were offered by the authors, including more emphasis on definition of goals and task analysis and the need for strong educational leadership.

ALIENATION AS A UNIFYING THEME IN THE SCHOOL PROBLEMS OF ADOLESCENCE

There is a great deal of data that support the view not only that school problems of adolescence are on the increase, but that much adolescent school conduct, attitudes, and achievement can be characterized as symptomatic of societal problems. The data, therefore, raise important questions about the continuing vitality of American society since that vitality ultimately depends on the effectiveness of secondary schools in helping adolescents to mature into competent adults.

In an eloquent response to this situation, Bronfenbrenner (1974, 1978) has described the school as an increasingly insular setting, isolated from the home and community. To some extent, the size of secondary schools, their resultant distance from the neighborhood, and the concomitant size of staffs are factors in this process. This insularity is further magnified by segregation into academic, vocational, and other tracks and by a curriculum that is highly compartmentalized, with students moving from class to class during the school day. There is the additional age grading of students so that they are thrown together primarily with their own peers, which contributes to the disruptive forces at work in the secondary school environment. In many communities, crosstown busing has added to these disintegrative pressures.

Although there is an absence of hard data, Bronfenbrenner hypothesizes that the escalation of school problems of adolescence in the last two decades is the result of these converging trends and that school problems of adolescence are reflections of the alienation of adolescents. He further argues that such alienation has led to the decline in academic achievement and, in its more acute forms, is the source of rising delinquency, drug use, suicide, and other serious behavioral problems. Another indication of alienation is rising school violence and vandalism, which is a pattern of destructive behavior that is no longer confined to urban, innercity areas.

With such a perspective, the interrelated concepts that point to the systemic character of secondary schools become important. Schools have their own cultures, as Sarason (1971) notes, and the idea of culture turns our attention to the total pattern of behavior in secondary school settings. The things to be examined and understood and, if necessary, changed therefore, are those found in the *context* of secondary schools. Ecological theory, which is necessarily grounded in contextual data, then becomes increasingly appealing to those who see major reform of secondary schools as a critical factor in coping with school problems of adolescence.

Building on this broad ecological thesis, there is an obvious need to begin with the basic environmental unit, which is the behavior setting. In the secondary school, the classroom is the major behavior setting, and, in this setting, the behaviors of the students and teachers and the arrangements of the physical space within the boundaries of this setting are highly coordinated. However, the classroom is linked to other school and nonschool behavior settings, and the ways in which these behavior settings are linked to one another needs extensive exploration.

Apart from the need to understand both school and nonschool behavior settings of adolescents and their linkages, there is the need for a wide range of ecologically oriented intervention strategies to improve setting functioning and to increase the well being and satisfaction of the adolescents who occupy them. To achieve such benefits, Wicker (1979) advocates deliberate use of behavior setting technology and gives several examples of such interventions. Although not specifically applied to school settings, the illustrations show the importance of behavior-setting analysis and the need for continuous monitoring of the effects of interventions. In addition, in the development of such a technology, it is important to include key strategic components of the community since they are part of the total ecological matrix of the adolescent.

REFERENCES

Achenbach, T.M., & Edelbrock, C.S. The Child behavior profile: II. Boys aged 12–16 and girls aged 6–11 and 12–16. *Journal of Consulting and Clinical Psychology,* 1979, **47**, 223–233

Aiken, L.R. Update on attitudes and other affective variables in learning mathematics. *Review of Educational Research,* 1976, **46**, 293–311.

Allen, V.L. *Children as teachers: Theory and research on tutoring.* New York: Academic Press, 1976.

American Psychiatric Association. *Diagnostic and statistical manual of mental disorders* (3rd ed.). Washington, D.C.: Author, 1978.

Anderson, R.C., Spiro, R.J., & Montague, W.E. (Eds.). *Schooling and the acquisition of knowledge.* Hillsdale, N.J.: Erlbaum, 1977.

Baird, L.L. Big school, small school: A critical examination of the hypothesis. *Journal of Educational Psychology,* 1969, **60**, 253–260.

Bandura, A. *Aggression: A social learning analysis.* Englewood Cliffs, N.J.: Prentice Hall, 1973.

Barker, R.G., & Associates. *Habitats, environments and human behavior.* San Francisco: Jossey-Bass, 1978.

Barker, R.G., & Gump, P.V. *Big school, small school.* Palo Alto, Calif.: Stanford University Press, 1964.

Barnett, R.C. Sex differences and age trends in occupational preferences and occupational prestige. *Journal of Counseling Psychology,* 1975, **22**, 35–38.

Barrett, T.C., & Tinsely, H.A. Vocational self-concept crystallization and vocational indecision. *Journal of Counseling Psychology,* 1977, **24**, 301–307.

Beard, R.M. Children's reasoning. *Mathematics Teaching,* 1962, **21**, 33–39.

Benham, B.J., Giesen, P., & Oakes, J. A study of

schooling: Students' experiences in schools. *Phi Delta Kappan,* 1980, **61,** 337–340.

Bergan, J.R. *Behavioral consultation.* Columbus, Oh.: Merrill, 1977.

Block, J. *Lives through time.* Berkeley, Calif.: Bancroft, 1971.

Blos, P. *The adolescent passage.* New York: International Universities Press, 1979.

Bronfenbrenner, U. The origins of alienation. *Scientific American,* 1974, **231,** 53–61.

Bronfenbrenner, U. Who needs parent education? *Teachers College Record,* 1978, **79,** 767–787.

Bronfenbrenner, U. Contexts of child rearing: Problems and prospects. *American Psychologist,* 1979, **34,** 844–850.

Brown, B.F. A study of the school needs of children from one-parent families. *Phi Delta Kappan,* 1980, **61,** 537–540.

Budoff, M., & Gottlieb, J. Special class students mainstreamed: A study of an aptitude (learning potential) x treatment interaction. *American Journal of Mental Deficiency,* 1976, **81,** 1–11.

Carkhuff, R., & Berenson, B. *Teaching as treatment: An introduction to counseling and psychotherapy.* Amherst, Mass.: Human Resources Development Press, 1976.

Cass, L.K., & Thomas, C.B. *Childhood pathology and later adjustment: The question of prediction.* New York: Wiley-Interscience, 1979.

Coleman, J.S., Campbell, E.Q., Hobson, C.J., McPartland, J., Mood, A.M., Weinfeld, F.D., & York, R.L. *Equality of educational opportunity.* Washington, D.C.: U.S. Government Printing Office, 1966.

Copperman, P. The achievement decline of the 1970s. *Phi Delta Kappan,* 1979, **60,** 736–739.

Cormier, W.H., & Cormier, L.S. *Interviewing strategies for helpers: A guide to assessment, treatment, and evaluation.* Monterey, Calif.: Brooks/Cole, 1979.

DeCarcer, I.A., Gabel, D.L., & Staver, J.R. Implications of Piagetian research for high school science teaching: A review of the literature. *Science Education,* 1978, **62,** 571–583.

Denney, D.R. Self-control approaches to the treatment of anxiety. In I. Sarason (Ed.), *Test anxiety: Theory, research, and applications.* Hillsdale, N.J.: Erlbaum, 1980.

Devin-Sheen, L., Feldman, R.S., & Allen, V.L.

Research on children tutoring children. *Review of Educational Research,* 1976, **46,** 355–385.

DeVries, D.L., & Slavin, R.E. Teams-games-tournaments (TGT): Review of ten classroom experiments. *Journal of Research and Development in Education,* 1978, **12,** 28–38.

Dulit, D. Adolescent thinking à la Piaget: The formal stage. *Journal of Youth and Adolescence,* 1972, **1,** 281–301.

Edelbrock, C.S. Empirical classification of children's behavior disorders: Progress based on parent and teacher ratings. *School Psychology Digest,* 1979, **8,** 355–369.

Fine, M.J. (Ed.), *Handbook on parent education.* New York: Academic Press, 1980.

Flanagan, J.C. (Ed.), *Perspectives on improving education: Project TALENTS's young adults look back.* New York: Praeger, 1978.

Gibson, E.J., & Levin, H. *The psychology of reading.* Cambridge, Mass.: 1975.

Goldenberg, I., & Goldenberg, H. *Family therapy: An overview.* Monterey, Calif.: Brooks/Cole, 1980.

Goldstein, A.B., Sprafkin, R.P., Gershaw, N.J., & Klein, P. *Skill-streaming the adolescent: A structured learning approach to teaching prosocial skills.* Champaign, Ill.: Research Press, 1980.

Gruen, G., Ottinger, D., & Ollendick, T. Probability learning in retarded children with differing histories of success and failure in school. *American Journal of Mental Deficiency,* 1974, **79,** 417–423.

Gump, P.V. The school as a social situation. *Annual Review of Psychology,* 1980, **31,** 553–582.

Guttmacher Institute. *11 million teenagers: What can be done about the epidemic of adolescent pregnancies in the United States.* New York: Alan Guttmacher Institute, 1976.

Hawkins, J.G., Bradley, R.W., & White, G.W. Anxiety and the process of deciding about a major and vocation. *Journal of Counseling Psychology,* 1977, **24,** 398–403.

Haynes, S.N., & Wilson, C.C. *Behavioral assessment: Recent advances in methods, concepts, and applications.* San Francisco: Jossey-Bass, 1979.

Iano, R.P., Ayers, D., Heller, H.B., McGettigan, J.F., & Walker, V.S. Sociometric status of retarded children in an integrative program. *Exceptional Children,* 1974, **40,** 267–271.

Jepsen, D.A. Occupational decision development over the high school years. *Journal of Vocational Behavior,* 1975, **7,** 225–237.

Johnson, B.D. *Marihuana users and drug subculture.* New York: Wiley, 1973.

Johnson, L. *Drugs and American youth.* Ann Arbor: University of Michigan, 1973.

Kanfer, F.H., & Goldstein, A.P. (Eds.). *Learning foundations of behavior therapy.* New York: Wiley, 1975.

Kendall, P.C., & Hallon, S.D. (Eds.). *Cognitive-behavioral interventions: Theory, research, and procedure.* New York: Academic Press, 1979.

Klahr, D. (Ed.). *Cognition and instruction: Tenth annual Carnegie symposium on cognition.* Pittsburgh: Department of Psychology, Carnegie-Mellon University, 1976.

Kraus, P.E. *Yesterday's children: A longitudinal study of children from kindergarten into the adult years.* New York: Wiley-Interscience, 1973.

Kulik, J.A., Kulik, C.C., & Cohen, P.A. A meta-analysis of outcome studies of Keller's personalized system of instruction. *American Psychologist,* 1979, **34,** 307–318.

Lesgold, A., Pellegrino, J.W., Fokkema, S.D., & Glasser, R. (Eds.). *Cognitive psychology and instruction. NATO International Conference on Cognition and Instruction.* New York: Plenum, 1978.

Levine, D.I., & Linn, M.C. Scientific reasoning ability in adolescence: Theoretical viewpoint and educational implications. *Journal of Research in Scientific Teaching,* 1977, **14,** 371–384.

Lewis, D.O., Balla, D.A., & Shanok, S.S. Some evidence of race bias in the diagnosis and treatment of the juvenile offender. *American Journal of Orthopsychiatry,* 1979, **49,** 53–61.

Losen, S.M., & Diament, B. *Parent conferences in the schools: Procedures for developing effective partnership.* Boston: Allyn & Bacon, 1978.

Lunneborg, P.W. Interest differentiation in high school and vocational indecision in college. *Journal of Vocational Behavior,* 1975, **7,** 297–303.

Mash, E.J., Hamerlynck, L.A., & Handy, L.C. (Eds.). *Behavior modification and families.*

New York: Brunner/Mazel, 1976.

Meichenbaum, D., & Butler, L. Toward a conceptual model for the treatment of test anxiety: Implications for research and treatment. In I. Sarason (Ed.), *Test anxiety: Theory, research, and applications.* Hillsdale, N.J.: Erlbaum, 1980.

Meyers, C.E., MacMillan, D.L., & Yoshida, R.K. Validity of psychologists' identification of EMR students in the perspective of the California decertification experience. *Journal of School Psychology,* 1978, **16,** 3–15.

Meyers, J., Parsons, R.D., & Martin, R. *Mental health consultation in the schools.* San Francisco: Jossey-Bass, 1979.

Millman, H.L., Schaefer, C.E., & Cohen, J.J. *Therapies for school behavior problems: A handbook of practical interventions.* San Francisco: Jossey-Bass, 1980.

Munley, P.H. Erik Erikson's theory of psychosocial development and vocational behavior. *Journal of Counseling Psychology,* 1975, **22,** 314–319.

National Commission on Marihuana and Drug Abuse. *Drug use in America: Problem in perspective.* Washington, DC: U.S. Government Printing Office, 1973.

Noeth, R.J., Roth, J.D., & Prediger, D.J. Student career development: Where do we stand? *Quarterly of Vocational Guidance,* 1975, **25,** 210–218.

Partland, J.M., & McDill, E.L. (Eds.). *Violence in schools: Perspectives, programs, and positions.* Lexington, Mass.: Lexington Books, 1977.

Phillips, B.N. *School stress and anxiety: Theory, research, and intervention.* New York: Human Sciences Press, 1978.

Phillips, B.N., Martin, R.P., & Meyers, J. Interventions in relation to anxiety in school. In C.D. Spielberger (Ed.), *Anxiety: Current trends in theory and research.* New York: Academic Press, 1972.

Phillips, B.N., Pitcher, G.D., Worsham, M.E., & Miller, S.C. Test anxiety and the school environment. In I. Sarason (Ed.), *Test anxiety: Theory, research, and applications.* Hillsdale, N.J.: Erlbaum, 1980.

P.L. 94–142. *Education for All Handicapped Children Act,* November 29, 1975. Washington, DC: United States Congress.

Quay, H.C., & Quay, L.C. Behavior problems in

early adolescence. *Child Development*, 1965, **36**, 215–220.

Reynolds, C.R. The problem of bias in psychological assessment. In C.R. Reynolds & T.B. Gutkin (Eds.), *A handbook for school psychology*. New York: Wiley, 1982.

Richardson, F.C., & Woolfolk, R.L. Mathematics anxiety. In I. Sarason (Ed.), *Test anxiety: Theory, research, and applications*. Hillsdale, N.J.: Erlbaum, 1980.

Rosenthal, T.L. Modeling approaches to test anxiety and related performance problems. In I. Sarason (Ed.), *Test anxiety: Theory, research, and applications*. Hillsdale, N.J.: Erlbaum, 1980.

Rubin, R.A., & Balow, B. Prevalence of teacher identified behavior problems: A longitudinal study. *Exceptional Children*, 1978, **45**, 102–113.

Rutter, M., Maughan, B., Mortimore, P., & Ouston, J. (with Smith, A.). *Fifteen thousand hours: Secondary schools and their effects on children*. Cambridge, Mass.: Harvard University Press, 1979.

Sarason, I. (Ed.), *Test anxiety: Theory, research, and applications*. Hillsdale, N.J.: Erlbaum, 1980.

Sarason, S.B. *The culture of the school and the problem of change*. Boston: Allyn & Bacon, 1971.

Sarason, S.B., Davidson, K.S., Lighthall, F.F., Waite, R.R., & Ruebush, B.K. *Anxiety in elementary school children*. New York: Wiley, 1960.

St. John, N.H. *School desegregation: Outcomes for children*. New York: Wiley, 1975.

Stephan, W.G. School desegregation: An evaluation of prediction made in Brown vs. the Board of Education. *Psychological Bulletin*, 1978, **85**, 217–238.

Stokols, D. Toward a psychological theory of alienation. *Psychological Review*, 1975, **82**, 26–44.

Stokols, D. Environmental psychology. *Annual Review of Psychology*, 1978, **29**, 253–295.

Teachman, G.W. In-school truancy in urban schools: The problem and a solution. *Phi Delta Kappan*, 1979, **61**, 203–205.

Thomas, M.J. Realism and socioeconomic status (SES) of occupational plans of low SES black and white male adolescents. *Journal of Counseling Psychology*, 1976, **23**, 46–49.

Thorndike, R.L. Concepts of culture-fairness. *Journal of Educational Measurement*, 1971, **8**, 63–70.

Tobias, S. Anxiety and instruction. In I. Sarason (Ed.), *Test anxiety: Theory, research, and applications*. Hillsdale, N.J.: Erlbaum, 1980.

U.S. Department of Health, Education, and Welfare, (HEW). *Suicide in the United States: 1950–1975*. Washington, D.C.: U.S. Government Printing Office, 1975.

Wadsworth, B.J. *Piaget for the classroom teacher*. New York: Longman, 1978.

Walburg, H.J., Schiller, D., & Haertel, G.D. The quiet revolution in educational research. *Phi Delta Kappan*, 1979, **61**, 179–183.

Weigel, R.H., Wiser, P.L., & Cook, S.W. The impact of cooperative learning experiences on cross ethnic relations and attitudes. *Journal of Social Issues*, 1975, **31**, 219–244.

Wicker, A.W. Undermanning, performances, and students' subjective experiences in behavior settings of large and small high schools. *Journal of Personality and Social Psychology*, 1968, **10**, 255–261.

Wicker, A.W. Ecological psychology: Some recent and prospective developments. *American Psychologist*, 1979, **34**, 755–765.

Willems, E.P. Sense of obligation to high school activities as related to school size and marginality of student. *Child Development*, 1967, **38**, 1247–1260.

CHAPTER 35

Career Choice: Problems and Issues

PAUL G. BANIKIOTES AND WILLIS E. BARTLETT

Career problems had originally been thought to involve simply making an occupational choice and were viewed to be unrelated to other areas of life functioning. The career decision was to be made at one particular point in life (often, the earlier the better) and once resolved was no longer a matter of concern. More recently, career development has come to be viewed as a lifelong process that is integrally related to one's overall mental health adjustment. Osipow (1979) has suggested that psychologists, and especially counseling psychologists, combine their interests in mental health and vocational development and focus their efforts on "occupational mental health." He noted:

Occupational mental health deals with questions of mental health related to the quality of life experienced by people associated with work settings. Recognizing that work occupies a substantial portion of the time that people spend in their working lives, and recognizing that in any context work is a major source of personal status or satisfaction, it is clear that attention to occupational mental health provides a significant opportunity both to identify potential resources that people can use to enhance their life satisfaction and effectiveness, as well as a significant source of difficulty that either has to be addressed through intervention or which can be prevented or minimized by appropriate programmatic interventions at earlier stages. (p. 65)

Problems and issues related to the career development of children and young adolescents often do not involve making a firm choice relative to the occupation that the individual will eventually attain. Rather, the problems and issues relate to the development of particular attitudes, the acquisition of specific knowledge about oneself and the world around one, and the development of particular skills to make choices and to present oneself effectively.

Selecting an occupation is a developmental process that occurs over a period of time and is affected, directly or indirectly, by a variety of factors. Super (1957) and Ginzberg et al. (1951) were pioneers in the field of vocational psychology who presented theories accounting for the various developmental stages within the career choice process. Within this process, individuals experience various developmental phenomena that are systematically related to time. Such developmental tasks have been presented by Havighurst (1953), Erikson (1963), Super (1957), Tiedman and O'Hara (1963), and Gribbons and Lohnes (1968). Herr and Cramer (1979, pp. 110–113) compared various theoretical conceptualizations of the development of vocationally related behavior by providing specific examples of specific behaviors appropriate at various life stages.

During the ages of 10–18, specific vocational attitudes can be helpful to individuals developing their self-concept and experiencing the translation of this self-concept into vocational terms, which leads to implementation of self-concept through the selection of an occupation. Studies completed by Super and Overstreet (1960) and Gribbons and Lohnes (1968) have documented the importance of such vocational attitudes and identified them as being able to plan, to develop alternative plans, and to learn how to evaluate consequences of decision making. Bartlett (1968) found that adolescents with high vocational maturity were more assertive, persistent, goal oriented, forceful, and independent than their peers who had low vocational maturity. Gribbons and Lohnes (1968) concluded that it was important for an individual to have self-knowledge, knowledge of the world of work, and access to feedback as to the accuracy of such knowledge in order to validate one's own self-assessment. A major finding, supported by their longitudinal research, indicated that as people experience success with earlier developmental tasks, the chances for their experiencing success with tasks at later stages is greatly enhanced. Past vocational behavior is indeed a strong indicator of future vocational choice behavior. Munley (1975) used Erikson's theory of psychosocial development and compared it with the individual's career maturity. His results also supported the above assumption. Thus there appear to be changing demands on individuals as they progress through life stages and encounter various developmental tasks. These change from stage to stage, requiring a certain level of success in order for individuals to meet the next series of tasks in a successful manner.

The ultimate culmination of career development is for people to be prepared to achieve successful career adjustment. When people encounter serious vocational choice problems, the attainment of vocational adjustment becomes more difficult. Successful management of adolescents' cultural, sociological, psychological, and personal variables during the Exploratory Stage (ages 14–21) enhances their opportunity to be successful during the subsequent stages—Establishment, Maintenance, and Retirement. Due to the importance of these various stages, more research and attention is currently being given to a lifespan or ontogenetic conceptualization of career development, with particular emphasis on the importance of career adjustment, its antecedents, reinforcers and nonreinforcers, and the outcomes of successful and unsuccessful adjustment.

Based on the previous comments, it would appear that career development is deterministic in nature and irreversible. It is believed that career development's major thrust is deterministic, yet not irreversible, because it can be modified through the use of various intervention strategies (Crites, 1976). These interventions are now available to those individuals who experience inappropriate or maladaptive vocational behavior.

The first major part of this chapter focuses on the types of vocational problems that adolescents often experience and deals primarily with counseling efforts aimed at remedying the problems they may present. The second major part of this chapter focuses on programmatic efforts directed at preventive and developmental interventions through the school and the family. Additionally, attention is given to coping with restrictive situations resulting from stereotypical perceptions of occupational appropriateness.

INDIVIDUAL CHOICE PROBLEMS

The primary focus of this part of the chapter will be on the types of vocational choice problems adolescents experience. During the Exploratory Stage (ages 14–24), adolescents become involved in a series of decision-making experiences. Important components of the decision-making process are: (1) those skills and prior experiences they bring to the choice point, such as previous successful experience with prior developmental tasks, as indicated by Herr and Cramer (1979) and presented in Table 35.1; (2) vocational maturity factors, such as accurate self-knowledge, accurate knowledge of the world of work, and a sense of planfulness, with possible contingency plans included for the present and immediate future as well as long range plans; (3) specific developmental tasks that need to be mastered and the acquisition of decision-making skills; and (4) the mediating factors influencing adolescents' occupational choice in terms of specific occupational field and entry level to be selected, in other words, cultural, sociological, psychological, and personal factors. The interaction of these four components leads to an eventual occupational choice, and, if an appropriate choice is made and the individual experiences no other choice problems, then

Table 35.1 Super's Conception of Life Stages and Developmental Tasks

Growth	Exploration	Establishment	Maintenance
Birth	*14 years*	*24 years*	*44 years*
Self-concept develops through identification with key figures in family and school; needs and fantasy are dominant early in this stage; interest and capacity become more important with increasing social participation and reality testing; learn behaviors associated with self-help, social interaction, self-direction, industrialness, goal setting, persistence.	Self-examination, role try-outs and occupational exploration take place in school, leisure activities, and parttime work.	Having found an appropriate field, an effort is made to establish a permanent place in it. Thereafter changes which occur are changes of position, job, or employer, not of occupation.	Having made a place in the world of work, the concern is how to hold on to it. Little new ground is broken, continuation of established pattern. Concerned about maintaining present status while being forced by competition from younger workers in the advancement stage.

Growth	Exploration	Establishment	Maintenance
Substages:	Substages:	Substages:	Tasks:
Fantasy (4–10 years) Needs are dominant; role playing in fantasy is important.	*Tentative* (15–17) Needs, interests, capacities, values, and opportunities are all considered, tentative choices are made and tried out in fantasy, discussion, courses, work, etc. Possible appropriate fields and levels of work are identified.	*Trial-Commitment and Stabilization* (25–30) Settling down. Securing a permanent place in the chosen occupation. May prove unsatisfactory resulting in one or two changes before the life work is found or before it becomes clear that the life work will be a succession of unrelated jobs.	Preservation of achieved status and gains.
Interest (11–12 years) Likes are the major determinant of aspirations and activities.	Task—Crystallizing a vocational preference		
Capacity (13–14 years) Abilities are given more weight and job requirements (including training) are considered.	*Transition* (18–21) Reality considerations are given more weight as the person enters the labor market or professional training and attempts to implement a self-concept. Generalized choice is converted to specific choice.	*Advancement* (31–44) Effort is put forth to stabilize, to make a secure place in the world of work. For most persons these are the creative years. Seniority is acquired; clientele are developed; superior performance is demonstrated; qualifications are improved.	

Decline

			Decline
			64 years

Growth	Exploration	Establishment	Decline
Tasks:	Task—Specifying a vocational preference		As physical and mental powers decline, work activity changes and in due course ceases. New roles must be developed: first, selective participant and then observer. Individual must find other sources of satisfaction to replace those lost through retirement.
Developing a picture of the kind of person one is. Developing an orientation to the world of work and an understanding of the meaning of work.	*Trial-Little Commitment* (22–24) A seemingly appropriate occupation having been found, a first job is located and is tried out as a potential life work. Commitment is still provisional and if the job is not appropriate, the person may reinstitute the process of crystallizing, specifying, and implementing a preference.	Tasks: Consolidation and advancement	Substages: *Deceleration* (65–70) The pace of work slackens, duties are shifted, or the nature of work is changed to suit declining capacities. Many men find parttime jobs to replace their fulltime occupations.
	Task—Implementing a vocational preference		*Retirement* (71 on) Variation on complete cessation of work or shift to parttime, volunteer, or leisure activities.
			Tasks: Deceleration, disengagement, retirement

Note. From Edwin L. Herr and Stanley H. Cramer, *Career Guidance Through the Life Span: Systematic Approaches,* Table 4.1. Copyright © 1979 by Edwin L. Herr and Stanley H. Cramer. Reprinted by permission of the publisher, Little, Brown and Company.

successful career adjustment is accomplished. For those individuals who experience choice problems, their opportunity of attaining career adjustment is greatly decreased.

Vocational Choice Problem Categories

The basic vocational choice problem paradigm used in this chapter was developed by Crites (1969). (The reader interested in the historical development of earlier vocational choice problem systems used in vocational psychology and also for more detail of supporting research of Crites's system is referred to chapter 7, "Problems in Vocational Choice," of his text.) Some definitions are appropriate in discussing the particular problem categories.

The *adjusted* individual's choice is congruent with his or her interests and aptitudes. It is also assumed that people with an adjusted choice have a supply of choices, are motivated to make a choice, and have the freedom to choose. Hence, there is no problem with the choice as such although some individuals will seek feedback to determine if their self-knowledge and knowledge of the world of work is reasonably accurate. Sometimes people in this category need reassurance that their choice is "on track."

Individuals who are labelled as *maladjusted* make a choice that does not agree with their interests and aptitudes or any combination of these two choice components. There are two broad categories of vocational choice problems: indecision and unrealism. The indecision category includes the following subcategories: multipotential, undecided, and uninterested. The unrealism category includes these subcategories: unrealistic, unfulfilled, and coerced. Each of these choice problem areas will be discussed in terms of: (1) description of the category, (2) typical problematic concerns and their possible causes, and (3) appropriate intervention strategies that can be used.

Indecision

This general category of vocational choice problems includes three separate subgroups: multipotential, undecided, and uninterested. Individuals in this general category have vocational choice problems because they are unable to select an occupation for several reasons.

MULTIPOTENTIAL.   *Description*—To be included in this category, individuals select two or more occupations that are congruent with their interest and aptitude level, yet cannot make a specific choice. *Typical concerns*—These individuals have difficulties because they have made too many choices and cannot specify one occupation of the many that have been selected. There are several possible causes of this dilemma. One possibility is that individuals refuse or lack the ability to make negative decisions and therefore specification cannot occur. Another suggestion has been the fear that if a choice is made, those experiences that were associated with those occupations not selected would be forfeited. Another interpretation of causality for multipotential vocational choice problems is that individuals are unwilling, or even fear, making a commitment. The implementation of stated career choice would imply such a commitment. *Intervention strategies*—Discussing the relationship among the various choices of the individual can be helpful. Are the choices based in a similar or related occupational field or job family? This can help these people realize that specification may not eliminate as many of the experiences they thought it might. Sometimes it is helpful to have these individuals list the advantages and disadvantages of each choice and then attempt to determine priorities related to job attractiveness. Another suggestion would be to encourage them to evaluate their problem in terms of realizing that not making a choice *is* a choice, and that they need to evaluate the results of such a nonchoice. Sometimes the consequences of a nonchoice are more severe than the presumed consequences of making a choice.

It can also be helpful if individuals in this choice problem category evaluate what types of anticipated vocational experiences can be gained avocationally. By making a commitment, these people still are not completely eliminating some of the experiences that were thought to be gained only through their occupation.

Lastly, it is important to realize that in some instances individuals may have selected two occupations that are not related to each other, even though equally attractive. It is helpful for these individuals to realize that they may experience some conflict after a choice is made. The more prepared these individuals are to deal with this conflict, the more successful will be their career adjustment experiences.

UNDECIDED. *Description*—The major characteristic of individuals in this category is that they have no stated choice. They may have clear and specific interest patterns as well as the aptitude necessary to be successful in several occupations, so the major difficulty becomes the lack of a stated choice. *Typical concerns*—Three major clusters of individuals are included in this category and have been described by Holland and Holland (1977). The first group of undecided people are at a particular point in their lives when it is not important for them to make such a choice. When the time comes for them to make such a choice, they indeed do and seem to experience little or no difficulty because of the apparent delay in specifying their choice. Kelso (1975) conducted a study of Australian high school students and found that the awareness of making an occupational choice was related to how soon a high school student went to work. Although cautious generalization is warranted in applying these results to American youth, it would appear that such a cluster of individuals does exist.

A second cluster of undecided people includes those individuals experiencing career immaturity, anxiety, interpersonal difficulties, and lack of the work value. Osipow, Carney, and Barak (1976) developed a scale to measure educational-vocational undecidedness and completed a factor analysis of the 16 indecision items. They found four factors that accounted for 81.3 percent of the total variance. Factor I involved the lack of structure and confidence of the student in approaching decision making, which was accompanied with anxiety leading to avoidance of a choice. Factor II indicated the presence of some external barriers to a preferred choice, along with questions about appropriate alternatives. Factor III involved student difficulty in deciding from several choices, which was described as an "approach-approach" problem. And Factor IV indicated a personal conflict related to decision making.

Munley (1975) applied Erikson's theory of psychosocial development to vocational behavior of college students and concluded that undecided students had not successfully resolved earlier stage crises and had not positively resolved their identity crises while decided students had resolved earlier stage crises and developed better identity. It appears that there are both external and internal factors that influence those individuals who are undecided.

The third cluster of undecided individuals is similar to the group above except that they experience more severe immaturity, alienation, and interpersonal conflict. Crites (1969) has combined these two groups of individuals and described them as being indecisive. There are several possible reasons for this condition and the specific causes need to be examined in order to develop a specific intervention strategy. Holland and Holland (1977) suggested relabeling this type of vocational maladaptive behavior as the "indecisive disposition." These individuals have a life history of failures with regard to learning to develop self-confidence and acquiring adequate cultural involvement and knowledge of self and environment in order to experience vocational adjustment. Several studies have attempted to determine the extent to which these variables influence levels of decidedness (Hawkins, Bradley, & White, 1977; McGowan, 1977; Greenhaus & Simon, 1977; Barrett & Tinsley, 1977). *Intervention Strategies*—The undecided individuals in the first group listed above need little or no intervention. They do what many intelligent adults do by delaying the choice until it needs to be made. The differential nature of the individuals in the second and third groups warrants intervention that varies from individual to individual, depending upon the specific causality and its severity. For those individuals who do have some idea of their interest, it is helpful to encourage them to translate their general interests into vocational interests and activities. The most difficult individuals to work with are those who have weak or no interest patterns. Many times this is an indication of a more severe interpersonal conflict or environmental barrier. The professional who might be inexperienced in working with these types of individuals either needs to refer them to a competent counselor or obtain consultation if help is needed.

Holland and Holland (1977) stated that those students who do not respond to various types of treatment, such as assessment, workshops, decision-making training, and occupational information are more likely to have the personal characteristics associated with the "indecisive disposition." Some individuals may need help in learning decision-making skills. Others may need more occupational information and/or self-information in order to obtain more knowledge on which to base a decision. Also, it seems important to determine if the three essential elements of making an occupational choice are present: the individual has several (at least two) choices, is motivated to make a choice, and is free to choose. If any of these are lacking, the individual will probably remain undecided.

UNINTERESTED. *Description*—Persons in this category have at least one stated choice and the appropriate aptitude level necessary for that occupation. The major source of difficulty is the lack of an interest pattern. *Typical concerns*—These individuals appear to be in a quandary regarding an occupational choice. When asked about their interests, they tend to respond, "I don't know." For many, this is an honest and sincere response rather than an attempt to avoid dealing with the issue. Several possible causes for this include:

1. Lack of socialization and cultural experiences, which minimizes the person's repertoire of life experiences, and, if there is sufficient deprivation of cultural experiences, provides undecided individuals with no basis on which to develop vocational choice behaviors.

2. Anxiety related to the consequences of implementing a stated choice, as a result of which these individuals allow themselves little opportunity to develop or become more aware of any interests they might have.

3. Identification with and use of someone else's identity and the consequent failure to develop their own interests because they have not experienced the need to do so. These individuals have not developed a clear picture of the kind of people they are, which indicates lack of successful completion of vocational tasks listed in the previous Growth Stage—(see Table 35.1).

4. Pseudo-crystallization (Ginzberg et al., 1951), or the experience of stating a choice which hopefully relieves some of the pressure they perceived being placed on them generally by family, peers, or significant others to make a choice.

5. A rather "bland" personality that interferes with any type of interest development.

Intervention strategies—Many of the intervention strategies suggested for use with undecided individuals would be applicable to individuals in this category. It is important to attempt to understand individual differences and to develop an intervention strategy accordingly, which includes the following:

1. Suggesting various types of enrichment experiences that will provide these individuals more cultural and life experiences on which to develop more vocational maturity and the development of the ability to discriminate their likes and dislikes.

2. Recommending some type of anxiety management program in order to help reduce their anxiety level and thus their inhibitions in exploring possible interest areas.

3. Encouraging these individuals in becoming differentiated from other members of their family.

4. Helping individuals realize the importance of their own future happiness by being responsible for obtaining that happiness and in not allowing parents or others to make the choice for them. They should also realize the necessity of experiencing freedom during the decision-making process in order to achieve the personal satisfaction of making the choice and experiencing future success in career adjustment.

5. Determining if the seriousness of the personality inadequacies preempts any possible vocational focus and, if such is the case, referring these individuals for psychotherapy (Bordin & Kopplin, 1973).

Unrealism

This general category, according to Crites's (1969) paradigm, has three subcategories: unrealistic, unfulfilled, and coerced. The focus of this category is on the individuals' accurate self-appraisal of their abilities. The major issue or problem experienced by persons in the unrealistic and unfulfilled categories is one of selecting an occupation appropriate to their aptitude level. An accurate appraisal of interests of individuals is a key element for those in the coerced group.

UNREALISTIC. *Description*—Individuals state a choice that may agree with their interest pattern, or individuals may not have an interest pattern, but their stated choice does not agree with measured aptitude level. In this case, the selected occupation requires an aptitude level higher than the individual's measured level. *Typical concerns*—Typically, people in this category do not have a clear sense of their own ability, or if they do have some understanding of their aptitude level they may be denying such an understanding. If these individuals do not have an understanding of the range of their abilities, they encounter difficulty in implementing their self-concept and remain fixated at an earlier developmental stage in which choices are primarily based on fantasy. There is a great deal of discrepancy between their real self-concept and their ideal self-concept. These

individuals will focus and base their decision on the latter. *Intervention strategies*—A strategy that can be used with individuals who are unaware of or deny their ability range (strengths and limitations) is to observe and evaluate how they process their own self-information. It is important to determine at what point their processing of data procedure breaks down, followed by suggested remediation and development of alternative processes. A second strategy would be to help individuals focus on dimensions of the Tentative substage (see Table 35.1), especially on their needs, interests, capabilities, values, and opportunities. One method of doing this is through the use of various assessment procedures. Results can be used in an attempt to increase individuals' self-awareness and develop a more accurate self-concept. If this is accomplished, then this information can be used by individuals to identify possible occupational fields and entry levels of work congruent with their self-concept. Some individuals in this category refuse help, and, therefore, intervention becomes difficult. Some need to experience the ineptitude of their choice before they may be willing to assume the responsibility for obtaining a clearer and more accurate picture of the kind of people they may be.

UNFULFILLED. *Description*—As with the unrealistic individual, unfulfilled people have interest patterns that agree with their stated choice. The major source of difficulty stems from their stating a choice that has an aptitude level requirement lower than their measured aptitude level. *Typical concerns*—Some individuals in this category do not express any concerns. They either may be fully aware that they are underselecting and are satisfied with their choices, or they do not have any idea that they are underselecting. Women tend to experience this problem more than men, and it appears to be present during the early high school years, if not earlier. Vondracek and Kirchner (1974) investigated young children's ability to project themselves into the future as being an adult. They found that the girls underwent occupational foreclosure earlier than their male peers. Neeley (1980) found in her study that ninth-grade girls experienced premature closure of career opportunities while the boys did not although she found that the boys tended to experience greater precareer anxiety than did the girls. Barnett (1975) concluded that women learn to avoid pursuing high prestige occupations and possibly do exhibit a "fear of success."

Betz (1977) reviewed the literature on vocational behavior published during the previous year and concluded that many people restrict their career alternatives because of inaccurate perceptions of their possibilities. This was especially true for blacks (Thomas, 1976), lower income groups (Burlin, 1976b; Goodale & Hall, 1976), and women (Burlin, 1976a). Nelson (1978), in an investigation of age and sex differences in the thinking process that underlies children's occupational choice, used nursery school children (age range 2–4) and third-graders and found that the range of occupations selected increased with age for both boys and girls. Both sexes expressed a broader range of choices for themselves than they did for the opposite sex. She concluded that the process of vocational development is related to cognitive development and that children's choices reflected their changing modes of understanding the world. Her results support the need for developing intervention programs and implementing such programs at the elementary school level. In summary, the major difficulty experienced by people in this category (related to their eventual career adjustment) is that they will not be able to achieve much success in their efforts because they will continually allow themselves to be underemployed. *Intervention strategies*—The major approach would be to encourage people to keep their options open until they need to make a specific choice. By doing this, they minimize the potential of premature closure. Encourage individuals to obtain an accurate estimation of their capabilities and focus on what choices are possible and what choices are not possible for them to implement. Several group intervention programs are helpful, especially programs like Born Free (Hansen & Keierleber, 1978). This program and other developmental programs are described in more detail in the second part of this chapter.

COERCED. *Description*—Individuals' stated choice is at the level of their measured aptitude. The major difficulty is that individuals have no interests related to the stated choice. *Typical concerns*—The most frequent concern expressed by members of this group is that the stated choice is made as a result of outside pressure, generally from parents or spouses. Goodale and Hall (1976) examined the relationship of work values and parental influence between social origin and college plans of 437 male and female high school sophomores. They used path analysis, which revealed that student perceptions of parents' interest in students' school work and parents' hopes that their child will attend college were mediating factors between social class origin and plans for college and career. Girls received less overall parental interest and pressure regarding their school work than did boys in this study. Parental interest can be supportive, yet too much interest could be perceived as pressure. Evidently, there still remains the tendency for some parents to place more emphasis on their sons' school work, which may reflect the belief that boys will be the major supporters and, therefore, that it is more important for them to be successful. There are some people in this category who have made an occupational choice based on its glamor or some other type of attractor. Unlike their counterparts in the two preceding categories who either did or did not have the appropriate aptitude levels for their selected occupations, persons in this category have no related interests and may decide to enter an occupation for the financial advantages it may offer, the prestige it may impart, or some other reason. If these individuals are aware of these reasons and have decided to endure the possible disadvantages of the position, such as being bored, their chances for successful vocational adjustment may be temporarily increased. *Intervention strategies*—In most instances, parents do have the best interests of their children's welfare and future occupation role in mind yet need to realize the importance of how they can facilitate their children's vocational development rather than erect barriers to their children's vocational choice and adjustment process. Herr and Cramer (1979, pp. 262–263) included specific ways parents can contribute to and share in the career guidance responsibility of their children. Of special note to parents who have children in this situation is the importance of their role in encouraging their children to explore and consider a wide variety of alternatives, without stereotyping these alternatives in order to discourage or pressure their children to eliminate a particular choice. Parents' major role in career guidance is the type of example or role model they present their children. If parents are not experiencing career adjustment, the likelihood of their children having similar experience is increased. An important role for parents is to provide the necessary example and also develop open communication with their children in order to help them establish and maintain a positive self-concept. Parents can also help their children become differentiated by giving them feedback in terms of the characteristics the child has that are similar to the father's and mother's and those characteristics that are unique to that child. It is helpful if children have access to a support system while experiencing critical developmental periods of their life. (A more detailed discussion of parental involvement follows in the second part of this chapter. Specific references are included for parents who choose to be active partners in their children's career choice experience.)

Special Populations

The categories presented have included the more frequent or typical types of vocational choice problems experienced by adolescents. Due to the limited scope of this chapter, the inclusion of a detailed discussion of all of the complexities of the vocational choice process becomes difficult, especially in terms of special populations, that is, career adjustment problems of middle-aged and older women (Bartlett & Oldham, 1978). Mention needs to be made, however, of the career choice problems of a group to which little attention has been given: handicapped persons. Little is mentioned in the literature in terms of research,

but, with the advent of Public Law 94–142, there is an effort being made to start meeting the counseling needs of these individuals. Often professionals feel they are unprepared to deal with this special population. The counselor does not realize that, even with their handicaps, these students go through a similar type of vocational choice process as nonhandicapped individuals. These individuals may not experience the same process in terms of time lines because it might take them longer and they also may encounter different types of barriers to their choice. Crites (1981) compares the differing assumptions of career development under ideal conditions versus disability conditions. Laramore (1981a, 1981b) has described procedures the counselor can use in working with handicapped individuals. The first step that he describes is the use of vocational assessment that appropriately measures the aptitudes and interest of handicapped students. He includes various types and examples of such instruments and assessment procedures. An evaluation summary is then developed that summarizes the assessment results, with specific emphasis on the original characteristics or capabilities the individual has: the handling of large materials, using small tools, sorting by touch, and other similar areas. These types of skills are then related to the typical high school curriculum, the eventual related jobs that can be attained from training, and the specific skills learned in the various programs.

Obviously, the success of such a program requires other professionals and community members becoming involved. Again, as with other nonhandicapped students, the goal is to help individuals achieve successful vocational adjustment. Thus self-knowledge and knowledge of the work become extremely important to handicapped individuals so that they do not make unrealistic choices or become perpetually indecisive.

Conclusion

In conclusion, the major thrust of this section has been to illustrate: (1) how making an occupational choice is part of a lifespan developmental process; (2) how the successful achievement of the vocational tasks of one stage enhances continued success during later stages; (3) the importance of conceptualizing vocational-choice problem disorders into different categories (each with its own unique characteristics), typical problems the individual experiences, and specific intervention strategies; (4) the need to emphasize the importance of achieving career adjustment. Heath (1976), in a longitudinal study of professional and managerial men, found that psychological maturity—whether measured when one is an adolescent or an adult—consistently predicted vocational adaptation. Professionals can become more involved in sharing the responsibility of facilitating individuals' career adjustment, especially for those experiencing low self-esteem, immature vocational behavior, anxiety, and other types of maladaptive behavior.

Osipow (1979) presented the concept of occupational mental health, which is also developmental and does not occur accidentally. It becomes important for the health care provider to become more aware of the mental health problems stemming from work. Osipow identified external causes, internal causes, and special problem populations that cause occupational mental health problems. The external causes included role overload, dealing with hostile consumers, job role discrepancy, supervisor stress, and organizational variables. Internal causes were based upon what the person brings to the work setting, such as a Type A personality, displacement of nonwork problems to the work setting, and job role discrepancies in terms of the extent to which one experiences fulfilled expectations of the occupation. The special work-related problems included specific populations such as women who experience anxiety, depression, alcohol problems (as a result of working outside the home), or of the housewife who may have similar problems working at home.

Various intervention strategies are being developed to help people cope with work-related problems. An important role the professional working with adolescents can provide would include individual and/or group programs preparing young people for career

adjustment and occupational mental health. For example, an issue such as "burn out" or role overload can be discussed during the Exploration Stage so that adolescents are prepared to develop strategies to minimize the likelihood of this, recognize symptoms they are experiencing in the process of becoming "burned out," and learn remedial or corrective activities by which they can overcome the negative consequences of "burn out." Successful and healthy career adjustment, then, is based on the types of skills and resources the person brings to each stage of career development, accompanied with the ability and experience to cope successfully with the various thwarting conditions one encounters during this process. Members of special populations experience similar stages of career development, yet can encounter thwarting conditions unique to them. This warrants special professional efforts in attempting to help these individuals experience successful career adjustment. The more knowledgeable we become of the characteristics and dynamics of those conditions that limit their chances of occupational mental health, the better equipped we will be to develop preventive programs that can be implemented at an early age.

PROGRAMMATIC INTERVENTIONS

Rather than waiting for individual problems to develop, some psychologists and counselors have developed programs directed at assisting effective career development and maturation. In this consultant-trainer role (Banikiotes, 1973), schools and families are frequently the target institutions through which the programmatic interventions are offered. This second part of the chapter focuses attention on preventive and developmental programs operating within the family and school framework and additionally gives attention to restrictive conditions that may hamper career development.

Family

Parents play a particularly important role in influencing the career planning and decision making of their children. Amatea and Cross

(1980) have noted that high school students and graduates consistently rank their parents ahead of teachers and counselors as important career resources. Parents, however, in spite of viewing assistance in career planning as part of the responsibilities of their parental role, often feel uncertain and ill equipped to help their children in this domain (Bartz, 1978). Numerous efforts have been developed to aid parents in becoming more effective in assisting their childrens' career development. One approach has involved the presentation of information about their childrens' career-planning needs and opportunities through booklets (Knapp & Bedford, 1967), presentations, such as college or career nights (Hoppock, 1976), or individual conferences (Gilmore, 1971). More recent efforts have focused on more extensive and elaborate programs for groups of parents discussing occupational opportunities, career guidance resources, and the nature of the vocational decision-making process (Harvey & Roper, 1973; Lea, 1976).

In summarizing an examination of the different modes of parental involvement, Amatea and Cross (1980) have noted four emerging trends in such programs. First, there is movement toward involving parents in the total career-planning process rather than providing them information about one facet (such as job trend information). Second, parents are encourged to learn the skills involved in career planning and decision making themselves. Third, there has been a substantial shift toward viewing skill acquisition as an active and experientially based process that involves tryout and skill rehearsal rather than as an exclusively didactic, information-giving process. Fourth, the career-planning process is increasingly becoming perceived as a joint and supportive endeavor in which student and parent are equally involved. These new trends and directions have been incorporated into a new career guidance program for teenagers and their parents, entitled "Going Places" (Amatea & Cross, 1980). This program is designed for ninth- through twelfth-grade students and their parents. Six central components of career planning are included: (1) compiling self-information including values, interests, and competencies, (2) exploring occupations in a systematic way, (3) developing information-getting strategies, (4) relating self-information to occupational alternatives, (5) exploring educational/training options, and (6) developing self-management skills in goal setting and decision making. These components are presented through a process of discussion, small group activities, reading materials, skill rehearsal, and at-home tryout and application. The program is designed for groups of 16–20 (8–10 student/parent pairs). The structured-group process format is used to personalize information, model interaction skills, and build a supportive environment for self-exploration and disclosure. Amatea and Cross (1980, pp. 278–280) present a more elaborate description of the six two-hour weekly sessions.

Laramore (1978, 1979, 1980) has also written concerning career counseling for families. His model is also applicable to other multiage groups. He perceives career problems as existing for most members of the family and describes an occasional American family pattern as "a father who is fed up with his job, a mother who wants to reenter the labor market or who wants a job change, and two teenagers who do not know where they are going." (Laramore, 1978, p. 555). His program has been developed for family counseling and normally requires 8–10 weekly three-hour sessions. Initial efforts are made to dispel myths related to career choice. It is contended that career choice is not a magical phenomenon that occurs in adolescence but rather a lifelong process in which people change jobs and occupations as they develop and the labor market changes. Additionally, focus is placed on self-awareness and career awareness, with involvement in a variety of activities aimed at sharing mutual perceptions about each other and the world of work. Career options are discussed and steps for decision making are introduced and practiced. Finally, information on effective job-seeking skills is presented and role playing of interviews takes place.

One of the most extensive and effective sources of information for parents interested in assisting their children in career planning is a book by Hummel and McDaniels (1979) entitled *How to Help Your Child Plan a*

Career. A wide range of areas covered includes assisting parents to develop the child's feeling of worthiness, reinforce the child's success in work and in play, teach the child to make career decisions, and explore the world of work in terms of data, places, and things. Additionally, information is provided regarding forecasting the labor market and the use of standardized tests, resource people, and other information sources. There is a variety of games, activities, checklists, and tests that makes implementing suggestions from the book a valuable, interesting, and enjoyable experience.

Also recognizing the enormous impact of the family on the child's career development, Birk (1980) has described a number of activities for elementary school children (primarily grades one and two) and their parents. The program presupposes teacher awareness of the delimiting effect of sex role stereotyping and a commitment to create a sex fair climate in the school. The activities are aimed at maximizing the parents' potential to influence their child's career development in such a manner that a full range of options are considered, regardless of family social status, race, sex, or other traditional determinants of occupational choice. Activities suggested include: (1) a PTA meeting that contains a slide show depicting media impact on children's career development and a children's skit where role reversals would be portrayed; (2) informal newsletters sent home to parents heightening their awareness of the influences of sex role stereotypes on the children's daily lives and further career planning and also indicating how school-related activities are being used to reinforce nonstereotypic as well as traditional behaviors; and (3) homework assignments designed to encourage parents and children to consider wider ramifications of sex role stereotyping. Overall, the primary focus of this program is to increase awareness of the negative impact of the influence of certain aspects of society on career development. Specifics involved with regard to actual planning are left to other programs that students might encounter in their later development. Other issues and programs related to enhanc-

ing opportunities for females are presented later.

It is important for parents to be brought into the career development process with their children in a manner that makes this task a collaborative and cooperative effort. Parents who take this facilitative rather than dictatorial role are less likely to experience strife with their children regarding career choices and directions. On occasions when the child may be following a direction that is inappropriate, and the parents are aware of this, it may be desirable to take a more positive rather than negative stance. The child might be assisted to seek additional relevant information or to gain experiences that would allow a more appropriate career direction to be taken. Negative perspectives and dictatorial commands will rarely have a positive impact and may cause the child to strengthen a viewpoint that had previously been only tentative. As in a wide variety of other arenas of personal growth, it is important for the children to perceive their parents as respecting their points of view and as allies rather than adversaries in this overall process.

School

The school is one of the primary institutions that can have an important effect on the vocational development of our children. A variety of programs have been implemented within the school setting in order to assist and foster the development of students in the vocational domain. The programs have taken a wide variety of forms, and it is the purpose of this section of the chapter to review a representative sample of such programs.

A fairly traditional intervention that is brief and often narrow in range is providing students an opportunity to take vocational tests and to receive feedback about the tests they have taken (Banikiotes & McCabe, 1972). A primary focus of this approach is to elevate the awareness of students regarding the relationship of their interests and values to the world of work. Zener and Schnuelle (1976) evaluated the effect of vocational testing on high school students. Students completing vocational testing, compared to a control group, reported being more satisfied with their current occupational choice, were considering more occupational alternatives, and had selected occupations more consistent with their personality traits.

Programs have also been developed and implemented that focus on providing information to students. A comprehensive vocations week program has been described by Zeller (1975). Although it may be unusual for all facets of this program to be implemented in one school, some aspects of this program are usually found to exist in most schools. Following are some of the most significant parts of the program:

1. Filmstrips on specific careers, career values, and career selection.
2. Occupational booths representing a variety of careers, with a focus on sharing information, conducting demonstrations, and displaying equipment.
3. Resource persons invited into classrooms to discuss their occupations and to share information about work roles, attitudes, and salaries.
4. College night, where representatives of post-high-school training programs (colleges, technical and trade schools, and the armed services) were available to discuss educational opportunities with students and their parents.
5. Career seminars in which members of the Rotary Club presented information about five general career interest areas (health, business, human services, technical/scientific, and communications).
6. A demonstration for students and faculty regarding the use of computer data relating to both careers and post-high-school training. Informal assessment of the effect of this program showed it to be quite positive.

Some programs that have been developed are broader and make an effort to have an effect on a wider range of behaviors and planning rather than simply provide information. These programs may focus on teaching skills such as seeking information (Fisher, Reardon, & Burck, 1976) or making decisions (Egner & Jackson, 1978). Some programs have also focused on intervention programs conducted through courses within the curriculum (Hamdani, 1977; Stillwell & Collison, 1974). Other extensive programs involve a life-planning workshop directed toward high school students (Brown, 1980) and a life experiences model for considering career education (Munson, 1978). Both these types of programs consider career development within a broader perspective and perceive it as interrelated with other aspects of life development.

Brown (1980) has noted the interrelationships existing among the life roles individuals fill as workers, family members, leisure participants, and citizens. He bemoans the infrequency with which the professional literature and practice consider these roles simultaneously. Drawing upon content of previous workshops (Thomas, 1972; Knickerbocker & Chesney, 1975) that focused on developing self-control and decision-making skills with college students, Brown (1980) developed a structured group experience for high school students that is conducted in six to eight one-hour meetings. Following is a brief description of the seven components of this workshop. (1) "Why people behave as they do"—focusing on the two major ideas that behavior is goal directed and that one is responsible for one's own behavior. (2) "Winners and losers" —delineating description of winners as individuals who accept responsibilities for their own behavior, make good decisions, and plan ahead and losers as those who do not do this but can learn to. (3) "Fantasy life"—encouragement of fantasy, with a focus on planning that could derive from it, especially with regard to education, career, close relationships, leisure, and community involvement. (4) "Your real life"—outlining a set of realistic life expectations and comparing them to fantasy experience. (5) "Setting life goals"—focuses on decision-making processes and planning by using a forcefield analysis approach that examines forces that contribute to goal attainment and those that retard it. (6) "Short term life planning"—focus is on high school graduation and on giving students the experience in using the decision-making skills they have learned. (7) "Long term life planning"—both short term and long term planning in the areas of education, career, close relationships, leisure, and community involvement, with an effort at looking at the interrelationship among these various facets and the potential of each as a source of personal fulfillment. Following the workshop, especially after the long term planning portion, additional individual experiences may be necessary (i.e., assertiveness training, finding sources of financial support).

In his life experiences model, Munson (1978) conceives of work as a significant aspect of everyday school, home, and community life. These life experiences are viewed as a structure for the introduction of concepts about work, work roles, and work functions as an integral part of the teaching-learning process. This life experiences model emphasizes the importance of classroom exposure and the involvement of classroom teachers in the creation and presentation of career education activities. Work functions are categorized as being associated with data, people, and things. Valuable illustrative examples are provided in tabular form that show how work functions can be translated into small work tasks, how work functions can be integrated with classroom activities, and how home and community activities can be integrated with courses of study in the school. This overall approach of making career education highly related to everyday life experiences appears to have much potential in assisting individuals in their continuing search for their self-identity and ways of sharing this identity with their world of work.

One of the underlying assumptions of many of these types of programs is to provide individuals access to career information and other resources that would be of benefit to them. Many schools provide various simulated career information systems such as IBM's DISCOVER or CVIS—Computerized Vocational Information System (Harris, 1968). Such computerized programs provide indi-

viduals instruction and simulated exercises in values clarification, decision making, and occupational information. There are other career information sources that are more available than the computerized programs. The most popular and traditional source has been printed material such as *Dictionary of Occupational Titles* and *The Occupational Outlook Handbook* published by the U.S. Office of Printing. Many private firms publish career literature and resources. Some materials are expensive while others can be inexpensive or free. An excellent source for reviewing such literature is published in each issue of the *Vocational Guidance Quarterly*.

Herr and Cramer (1979) also include a list of bibliographic sources and samples of such information. The chapter, "Information in Career Guidance", in their book, is also an excellent resource. Hummel and McDaniels (1979) also provide bibliographic sources as well as a chapter on forecasting trends and predictions about the labor market. Other resources available outside the school include regional career centers, which generally have excellent career literature libraries as well as access to computerized programs at some locations. Other excellent strategies suggested by Herr and Cramer (1979) include the use of field trips, direct work experience, and simulated approaches. Having accurate information about the world of work and specific occupations is as important to the process as accurate self-information. Both are needed to enhance career choice adjustment.

Overall, programmatic efforts to assist career development of students within the schools are likely to have the strongest impact. It is incumbent upon educators and counselors to provide programs to assist all children and to give special attention to populations that in the past have been restricted with regard to career development opportunities. Following is a discussion of issues and programs related to restricted opportunities of career exploration.

Gender and Other Restrictive Conditions

The expansion of career options for individuals has received increasing attention in the

1970s. Societal, parental, and personal pressure to conform to occupational choices traditionally viewed as being appropriate for one's gender has an effect on both boys and girls. Although this limitation is detrimental to each, its greatest impact is likely to be on females because occupations traditionally held by females are normally at lower socioeconomic levels than those held by males. Barnett (1975) investigated the relationship of occupational preferences and aversions and occupational prestige for males and females, ages 9 through 17. Relationships between prestige and preference were positive and stronger for the males than for the females, while the relationships between prestige and aversion were positive and stronger for females than for males. Schlossberg and Goodman (1972) observed no significant differences in the occupational stereotyping of kindergarten and sixth-grade students. The children perceived women to be appropriate as waitresses, nurses, or librarians but clearly not appropriate for fixing autos or television sets or designing buildings. Men, however, were not similarly limited. They were able to fix automobiles, teach children, or even be nurses. Content analyses of career materials (Helshusius-Gilsdorf & Gilsdorf, 1975) have also demonstrated differential depiction of males and females in the world of work.

There appears to be general agreement among vocational psychologists that our current situation, which restricts career opportunities for women, needs to be remedied. Efforts have been made to investigate women who have made nontraditional choices (Krumboltz, Becker-Haven, & Burnett, 1979) and to understand some of the reasons for the restrictions that females experience (Burkhart, 1975). Such information might be of some assistance in the development of intervention programs that focus on expanding career perspectives and opportunities. Women who have made the nontraditional choice of entering the male-dominated occupations have been characterized as being higher in internal locus of control (Burlin, 1976a), mathematical ability (Goldman & Hewitt, 1976), and self-esteem (Richardson, 1974) as well as having more interest in verbal-linguistic occupations

(Tipton, 1976), greater cognitive complexity (Lawlis & Crawford, 1975), and closer identification with the father despite a perception of the father as less accepting (Oliver, 1975).

Burkhart (1975) has reviewed literature related to the scope of the problem and the major underlying reasons for some of the observed gender differences. These include aspects of the early childhood socialization process (Harmon, 1970), religious doctrine supporting the notion that women are subservient or inferior to men (Bem & Bem, 1974), female focus of energy on and vicarious achievement through relationships with boyfriend or husband (Madison, 1969), fear of success, especially with regard to perception that intelligent women threaten men (Matthews & Tiedman, 1964; Horner, 1969), and concerns about successful careers being incompatible with successful marriage and family life (Horner, 1969; Hawley, 1971).

Different aspects of the problem seem to emerge at different developmental levels. This has had some influence on the types of interventions that have been developed and the age level of the target population. Harmon (1970) observed differences between 2-year-old boys and girls. Little girls were less likely to be involved in independent exploration and were more likely to call for their mothers. Herr and Cramer (1979) observed that the junior high school years were a time when differences in gender exerted important influences in curriculum choice and choice considerations operated differently in males and females. Osipow (1973) has compared the vocational decision making of males and females at different stages by using Super's developmental scheme. During the Tentative period (ages 11–15), he found similarity between the behavior of girls and boys. Noticeable gender differences emerged in the Capacity stage. Seventeen-year-old females exhibited a strong orientation toward marriage and homemaking while boys' concerns centered on making choices on the basis of their interests, abilities, and ideas about work.

Intervention programs directed at minimizing occupational stereotypes and at expanding career opportunities for females have been directed at a range of age levels and have had a variety of different effects. Little and Roach (1974) observed a significant increase of interest in nontraditional occupations by college women who viewed a videotape where interest in such occupations were modeled by a female and positively reinforced by a male counselor. The presentation of nontraditional models and curriculum materials, however, was not observed to have any significant effects on kindergarten children. Vincenzi (1977) was able to reduce successfully the number of occupations perceived to be sex typed through an intervention that involved two 30-minute sessions a week during a 10-week period. During the experimental treatment, the subjects participated in the following:

1. Reviewing and discussing magazine articles related to women working in traditionally masculine, sex-typed jobs.
2. Examining through discussion the definitions of a stereotype and the identification of other than occupational stereotypes.
3. Meeting seven women who work in traditionally masculine occupations, with each speaking for 30 minutes, giving a short demonstration, and explaining her job and why she chose it.

The occupations discussed were doctor, lawyer, chemist, television reporter, architect, telephone linesperson, and auto mechanic.

One of the most extensive programs aimed at assisting more effective career development through eliminating the influence of sex role stereotyping is project Born Free (Hansen & Keierleber, 1978). The specific goals and strategies utilized in the project are depicted by its title: Build Options, Reassess Norms, and Free Roles through Educational Equity (BORN FREE). The project is a major attempt to bring about educational change in the area of career development. A collaborative consultation approach (Kurpius & Brubaker, 1976) is applied at a variety of levels in order to have maximum impact upon students. At one level, university-based staff serve as external consultants to the staff (consultees) in the project institution. These consultants

provide expertise related to the effects of sex role stereotyping on student career development; the types of institutional policies, practices, and patterns of educator behavior and communication that could reflect stereotypic perspectives; method for identifying these types of practices within the institutional setting; and alternative strategies for bringing about change. The consultees, on the other hand, provide specific expertise on the characteristics of their institutions and staffs; the structure and climate of their organization; staff attitude and morale; institutional priorities; goal alternatives; and possible points of entry for intervention. At another level, members of the project field staff function as internal consultants to assist interested colleagues, the consultees, in defining areas of need and developing change strategies for the improvement of the delivery of services to a second client system—the students themselves. The collaborative approach to consultation encourages the identification of problem and solution in consultee relevant terms: institutions, work setting, professional responsibilities, students, colleagues, and personal goals. Of particular importance is the mutual collaboration and cooperation between consultant and consultee regarding the development of methods and materials (videotapes and training activities) to be used as part of the intervention strategy. Although extensive evaluation of this project has not yet been completed, it appears that this type of multipronged intervention activity is likely to have a good chance of bringing about positive changes.

In an effort to expand options available to individuals of lower social class and women, Farmer (1978) has discussed reasons for limitations in options and possible methods by which this type of problem can be remedied. On the basis of her previous writing (Farmer, 1976) and that of Phares (1976), Farmer (1978) identified several factors related to perceived helplessness in career decision making. Differences were observed between individuals of internal orientation and high self-esteem and those of external orientation and low self-esteem. The former choose more career goals that promise intrinsic satisfaction, seek more complete information relevant to problem solving and career decision making, identify problem-solving rules more rapidly, engage in moderate risk taking rather than high risk behavior, and are more likely to try out new behaviors and persist at them even when faced with initial failure.

Interventions directed at changing such perceived feelings of helplessness have also been developed. McClelland and Winter (1969) have had considerable success with a structured group program aimed at increasing the control that lower class adults feel over their own destiny. The six-month program, which meets weekly, focuses on developing in clients a clear understanding of themselves; their strengths and weaknesses; their ideal and their real selves; their values, fears, aspirations, and even daydreams. It was easier to help adults change their sense of control over their lives than to change their values about the nature of work and careers. Some aspects of the McClelland and Winter (1969) program have been incorporated into a program for lower class black adolescents by deCharms (1972). His goal was to enable these students to behave like an "origin" rather than a "pawn" by providing experiences to help them identify realistic goals, to know their own strengths and weaknesses, to determine concrete actions that can help movement toward goal achievements, and to consider how to evaluate good progress. This program has been primarily employed by teachers in the classroom.

As disadvantaged youths have been observed to lag two years behind their middle class counterparts in vocational development (Ansell & Hansen, 1971), Hamdani (1977) evaluated the impact of a program of curricular experiences on the vocational development of disadvantaged innercity adolescents. The experimental curriculum was implemented for a class period each day during a semester (100 hours) and was designed to facilitate career and self-exploration. Significant increases in vocational maturity (as measured by planning orientation, familiarity with and use of resources for career exploration, and occupational information and decision mak-

ing) were observed to occur immediately as well as last for a four-month follow-up.

Kleinberg (1976), in an effort to take into account differing economic circumstances, has developed a vocational contingency planning (VCP) program to be used in recessionary times. The primary goal of this workshop is for individuals eventually to implement their occupational preference by taking detours that will be helpful in attaining the ultimate goal. Focus is on building up a positive work history, making relevant contacts, pursuing advanced training, developing a rich repertoire of competencies, and attending conferences sponsored by professional organizations.

Conclusion

Overall, the programmatic efforts discussed are focused on assisting in the facilitation of vocational adjustment. These programs may be aimed at individuals at a particular developmental stage or at certain individuals who may be at risk with regard to the occurrence of some problems. Programs operating through the family or the school seem to have the greatest possibility of having positive impact and preventing problems. It is especially important in these times of increasing accountability to maximize the helping human resources that we have available. The types of preventive programs discussed are likely to limit the number of individuals who will require remedial attention.

REFERENCES

Amatea, E.S., & Cross, E.G. Going Places: A career guidance program for high school students and their parents. *Vocational Guidance Quarterly* 1980, **28**, 274–282.

Ansell, E.M., & Hansen, J.C. Patterns in vocational development of urban youth. *Journal of Counseling Psychology,* 1971, **18**, 505–508.

Banikiotes, P.G. A preventive approach to mental health in the schools. *Counseling and Values,* 1973, **17**, 112–117.

Banikiotes, P.G., & McCabe, S.P. A sophomore vocational counseling and testing program.

Journal of College Student Personnel, 1972, **13,** 273.

Barnett, R.C. Sex differences and age trends in occupational preference and occupational prestige. *Journal of Counseling Psychology,* 1975, **22,** 35–38.

Barrett, T.C., & Tinsley, H.E. A vocational self-concept crystallization and vocational indecision. *Journal of Counseling Psychology,* 1977, **24,** 301–307.

Bartlett, W.E. Vocational maturity and personality variables of manpower trainees. *Vocational Guidance Quarterly,* 1968, **17,** 104–108.

Bartlett, W.E., & Oldham, D. Career adjustment counseling of young-old women. *Vocational Guidance Quarterly,* 1978, **27,** 156–164.

Bartz, K. Selected child-rearing tasks and problems of mothers and fathers. *Family Coordinator,* 1978, **27,** 209–214.

Bem, S.L., & Bem, D.J. *Training the woman to know her place: The social antecedents of woman in the world of work.* Harrisburg: Pennsylvania Department of Education, 1974.

Betz, E.L. Vocational behavior and career development, 1976: A review. *Journal of Vocational Behavior,* 1977, **11,** 129–152.

Birk, J.M. Helping parents to help their children: A step toward resocialized career development. *Sex roles: A guide for educators.* Washington, D.C.: National Vocational Guidance Association, 1980.

Bordin, E.S., & Kopplin, D.A. Motivational conflict and vocational development. *Journal of Counseling Psychology,* 1973, **20,** 154–161.

Brown, D. A life-planning workshop for high school students. *Vocational Guidance Quarterly,* 1980, **29,** 77–83.

Burkhart, M.Q. Career development for women. In R.C Reardon & H.D. Burck (Eds.), *Facilitating career development.* Springfield: Thomas, 1975.

Burlin, F.D. Locus of control and female occupational aspiration. *Journal of Counseling Psychology,* 1976, **23,** 126–129. (a)

Burlin, F.D. The relationship of parental education and maternal work and occupational status to occupational aspiration in adolescent females. *Journal of Vocational Behavior,* 1976, **9,** 99–104. (b)

Crites, J.O. *Vocational psychology.* New York: McGraw-Hill, 1969.

Crites, J.O. A comprehensive model of career development in early adulthood. *Journal of Vocational Behavior,* 1976, **9,** 105–118.

Crites, J.O. *Career counseling: Models, methods, and materials.* New York: McGraw-Hill, 1981.

deCharms, R. Personal causation training in the schools. *Journal of Applied Social Psychology,* 1972, **2,** 95–113.

Dictionary of occupational titles (Vols. I & II). Washington, D.C.: Government Printing Office, 1978.

Egner, J.R., & Jackson, D.R. Effectiveness of a counseling intervention program for teaching career decision-making skills. *Journal of Counseling Psychology,* 1978, **25,** 45–52.

Erikson, E.H. *Childhood and society* (2nd. ed.). New York: Norton, 1963.

Farmer, H. Inquiry project: Computer assisted counseling centers for adults. *Counseling Psychologist,* 1976, **6,** 50–54.

Farmer, H. Career counseling implications for lower social class and women. *Personnel and Guidance Journal,* 1978, **56,** 467–471.

Fisher, T.J., Reardon, R.C., & Burck, H.D. Increasing information seeking behavior with a model reinforced videotape. *Journal of Counseling Psychology,* 1976, **23,** 234–238.

Gilmore, J. Parent counseling and the productive personality. *Journal of Education,* 1971, **154,** 5–37.

Ginzberg, E., Ginsburg, S.W., Axelrad, S., & Herma, J.R. *Occupational choice: An approach to a general theory.* New York: Teachers College Press, Columbia University, 1951.

Goldman, R.D., & Hewitt, B.N. The Scholastic aptitude test "explains" why college men major in science more often than college women. *Journal of Counseling Psychology,* 1976, **23,** 50–54.

Goodale, J.G., & Hall, D.T. Inheriting a career: The influence of sex, values, and parents. *Journal of Vocational Behavior,* 1976, **8,** 19–30.

Greenhaus, J.H., & Simon, W.E. Career salience, work values, and vocational indecision. *Journal of Vocational Behavior,* 1977, **10,** 104–110.

Gribbons, W.D., & Lohnes, P.R. *Emerging careers.* New York: Teachers College Press, Columbia University, 1968.

Hamdani, A. Facilitating vocational development among disadvantaged inner-city adolescents.

Vocational Guidance Quarterly, 1977, **26,** 60–68.

Hansen, L.S., & Keierleber, D.L. Born Free: A collaborative consultation model for career development and sex-role stereotyping. *Personnel and Guidance Journal,* 1978, **56,** 395–399.

Harmon, L.W. *The childhood and adolescent career plans of college women.* Milwaukee: University of Wisconsin Press, 1970.

Harris, J. The computerization of vocational information. *Vocational Guidance Quarterly,* 1968, **17,** 12–20.

Harvey, D., & Roper, E. The parent's role in career development: A continuing education project in support of the vocation of parenthood. *Journal of Continuing Education and Training,* 1973, **2,** 293–298.

Havighurst, R.J. *Human development and education.* New York: Longmons, Green, 1953.

Hawkins, J.G., Bradley, R.W., & White, G.W. Anxiety and the process of deciding about a major and vocation. *Journal of Counseling Psychology,* 1977, **24,** 398–403.

Hawley, P. What women think men think: Does it affect their career choice? *Journal of Counseling Psychology,* 1971, **18,** 195–199.

Heath, D.H. Adolescent and adult predictors of vocational adaptation. *Journal of Vocational Behavior,* 1976, **9,** 1–9.

Helshusius-Gilsdorf, L.T., & Gilsdorf, D.L. Girls are females, boys are males: A content analysis of career materials. *Personnel and Guidance Journal,* 1975, **54,** 206–211.

Herr, E.L., & Cramer, S.H. *Career guidance through the life span.* Boston: Little, Brown, 1979.

Holland, J.L., & Holland, J.E. Vocational indecision: More evidence and speculation. *Journal of Counseling Psychology,* 1977, **24,** 404–414.

Hoppock, R. *Occupational information.* New York: McGraw-Hill, 1976.

Horner, M. Fail, bright women. *Psychology Today,* 1969, **3,** 36.

Hummel, D.L., & McDaniels, C. *How to help your child plan a career.* Washington, D.C.: Acropolis, 1979.

Kelso, G.I. The influences of stage of leaving school on vocational maturity and realism of vocational choice. *Journal of Vocational Behavior,* 1975, **7,** 29–39.

Kleinberg, J.L. Vocational contingency planning in a recession. *Vocational Guidance Quarterly,* 1976, **24,** 366–368.

Knapp, J.L., & Bedford, J.H. *The parent's role in career development.* Washington, D.C.: National Vocational Guidance Association, 1967.

Knickerbocker, B., & Chesney, M. *Life planning workshop* (Rev. ed.). University Counseling Center, Colorado State University, Fort Collins, 1975.

Krumboltz, J.D., Becker-Haven, J.F., & Burnett, K.F. Counseling Psychology. *Annual Review of Psychology,* 1979, **30,** 555–602.

Kurpius, D., & Brubaker, J.C. *Psychoeducational consultation.* Bloomington: Indiana University Press, 1976.

Laramore, D.L. *Careers: A guide for parents and counselors.* Provo, Utah: Brigham University Press, 1978.

Laramore, D.L. Career counseling for families (and other multi-age groups). *Personnel and Guidance Journal,* 1979, **57,** 55–56.

Laramore, D.L. The family's role in career development. *Inform,* 1980, **9**(2), 1–3.

Laramore, D.L. Career counseling students with special needs: Part I. *Inform,* 1981, **9**(6), 1–5. (a)

Laramore, D.L. Career counseling of special needs students: Part II. *Inform,* 1981, **9**(7), 1–7. (b)

Lawlis, G.F., & Crawford, J.D. Cognitive differentiation in women and pioneer-traditional vocational choices. *Journal of Vocational Behavior,* 1975, **6,** 263–267.

Lea, H.D. A personalized parents' workshop on vocational choice. *Vocational Guidance Quarterly,* 1976, **24,** 373–375.

Little, D.M., & Roach, A.J. Videotape modeling of interest in nontraditional occupations for women. *Journal of Vocational Behavior,* 1974, **5,** 133–138.

Madison, P. *Personality development in college.* Reading, Mass.: Addison Wesley, 1969.

Matthews, E., & Tiedeman, D.E. Attitudes toward career and marriage and the development of life style in young women. *Journal of Counseling Psychology,* 1964, **11,** 375–384.

McClelland, D., & Winter, D. *Motivating economic achievement.* New York: Free Press, 1969.

McGowan, A.S. Vocational maturity and anxiety among vocationally undecided and indecisive students: The effectiveness of Holland's self-directed search. *Journal of Vocational Behavior,* 1977, **10,** 196–204.

Munley, P.H. Erik Erikson's theory of psychological development and vocational behavior. *Journal of Counseling Psychology,* 1975, **22,** 314–319.

Munley, P.H. Erikson's theory of psychosocial development and career dvelopment. *Journal of Vocational Behavior,* 1977, **10,** 261–269.

Munson, H.L. Career education reconsidered: A life experiences model. *Personnel and Guidance Journal,* 1978, **57,** 136–139.

Neeley, M.A. Career maturity inventory interpretations for grade 9 boys and girls. *Vocational Guidance Quarterly,* 1980, **29,** 113–123.

Nelson, J.A.N. Age and sex differences in the development of children's occupational reasoning. *Journal of Vocational Behavior,* 1978, **13,** 287–297.

Occupational outlook handbook. Washington, D.C.: Government Printing Office, 1978–79.

Oliver, L.W. The relationship of parental attitudes and parent identification to career and homemaking orientation in college women. *Journal of Vocational Behavior,* 1975, **7,** 1–12.

Osipow, S.H. *Theories of career development* (2nd ed.). New York: Prentice-Hall, 1973.

Osipow, S.H. Occupational mental health: Another role for counseling psychologists. *The Counseling Psychologist,* 1979, **8,** 65–70.

Osipow, S.H., Carney, C.G., & Barak, A. A scale of educational-vocational undecidedness: A typological approach. *Journal of Vocational Behavior,* 1976, **9,** 233–243.

Phares, J.E. *Locus of control: Current trends in theory and research.* New York: Wiley, 1976.

Richardson, M.S. The dimensions of career and vocational orientation in college women. *Journal of Vocational Behavior,* 1974, **5,** 161–172.

Schlossberg, N.K., & Goodman, J. A woman's place: Children's sex stereotyping of occupations. *Vocational Guidance Quarterly,* 1972, **20,** 266–270.

Stillwell, L., & Collison, B.B. A career development program for a small school. *Vocational Guidance Quarterly,* 1974, **23,** 174–177.

Super, D.E. *The psychology of careers.* New York: Harper & Row, 1957.

Super, D.E., & Overstreet, P.L. *The vocational maturity of ninth grade boys.* New York: Teachers College Press, Columbia University, 1960.

Thomas, J.J. Realism and socioeconomic status (SES) of occupational plans of low SES black and white male adolescents. *Journal of Counseling Psychology,* 1976, **23,** 46–49.

Thomas, L.E. *Leader's manual: Life planning workshop.* University Counseling Center, Colorado State University, Fort Collins, 1972.

Tiedeman, D.V., & O'Hara, R.P. *Career development: Choice and adjustment.* New York: College Entrance Examination Board, 1963.

Tipton, R.M. Attitudes toward women's roles in society and vocational interests. *Journal of Vocational Behavior,* 1976, **8,** 155–165.

Vincenzi, H. Minimizing occupational stereotyping. *Vocational Guidance Quarterly,* 1977, **25,** 265–268.

Vondracek, S.H., & Kirchner, E.P. Vocational development in early childhood: An examination of young children's expressions of vocational aspiration. *Journal of Vocational Behavior,* 1974, **5,** 251–260.

Zeller, B.J. A vocations week program. *Personnel and Guidance Journal,* 1975, **54,** 107–108.

Zener, T.B., & Schnuelle, L. Effects of the self-directed search on high school students. *Journal of Counseling Psychology,* 1976, **23,** 353–359.

CHAPTER 36

Substance Abuse

RONALD S. KRUG

INTRODUCTION

In the early-to-mid-1960s psychoactive drug use in youth apparently began to increase significantly. This apparent increase precipitated a public reaction that resulted in hundreds of thousands of research articles, books and other publications that focused on the etiologic, maintenance, and intervention variables associated with chemical consumptive behaviors. The issue of positive or nonproblematic use of drugs has been adequately covered by other authors (Marin & Cohen, 1971). The focus of this chapter is problematic chemical consumption or substance abuse.

"Substance abuse" is a general phrase that conveys a minimum of useful information and a maximum of cognitive confusion, emotional arousal, and attitudinal-prejudicial reaction, particularly when applied to youth. Because it is a general phrase found in both professional literature and public media, its specific meaning has become compromised. Consequently, when the phrase is employed to describe the many varieties of chemical consumptive behavior patterns, confusion results.

Patterns of Chemical Consumption

If one is describing the category "fish" and includes whales, seals, and walruses because they swim in water, a somewhat less than useful definition will be forthcoming. So it is with the term "substance abuse."

The major discrimination that must be made regarding substance abuse is the pattern of drug consumption. Typically the different patterns are conceptualized as a continuum with five points: nonusers, experimenters, recreational users, problem users, and addicts. Each point represents multiple coalescing variables that are progressively different at each point on the continuum. The variables include frequency of use, dose used, type of drug used, amount of money expended on drugs, method of procurement of the drugs and the money for same, and, most important, the personal consequences of the drug use. The reason this major discrimination must be made, particularly for young persons involved in chemical consumption is the implication correct classification has for the intervention strategy planned. An unconscionable disservice is rendered if a 12-year-old person in rural America is found to be experimenting with a relatively innocuous chemical and he or she is placed in a protracted-care inpatient facility designed for 16–18-year-old chronic narcotic addicts from metropolitan innercity locations.

The Use/Abuse Concept

A great deal of controversy, rhetoric, and ambivalence is marshalled around whether an individual's chemical consumption pattern is "use or abuse." In America this dialogue can be traced to the pilgrim fathers of the country and the puritan ministers who served them. Sermons of the time extolled alcohol as a gift from God and condoned its use; however, drunken behavior was proscribed (National Center for Alcohol Education, 1977). The distinction clearly was then and is now on the behavioral consequences of chemical consumption not the consumption itself. The question is, can use suddenly and unavoidably become abuse; and the answer conceivably is yes. On a given occasion a person may consume his or her characteristic amount of a given chemical; but, due to an anaphylactic reaction to the chemical, onset of sudden illness in interaction with the chemical, etc., that individual is rendered impaired while driving a car and a traffic fatality ensues. Based on the consequences of drug involvement, the term abuse certainly can be applied and the fatality registered as drug related. If the person had not used the chemical, the fatality would not have occurred.

An additional dimension of the use/abuse discussion is that of legality. In America no one can consume heroin legally; therefore, all use of the chemical no matter how minimal is abuse. For youth below the age of 16 all nonprescriptive use of all mind-altering chemicals is illegal and therefore abuse.

Other factors are involved in the use versus abuse discussion; however, as one explores these, a quote attributed to Gertrude Stein is relevant: "A difference, to be a difference, must make a difference."

Conceptual Models of Substance Abuse

Different conceptual presentations have been posited to explain the phenomenon of substance abuse (Lattieri, Sayers, & Pearson, 1980). Two models will be briefly presented below because of their relevance for treatment and/or intervention. However, the reader should be reminded that a model is a small imitation of the real thing, and imitations frequently are not true to the reference situation. What appears to be developing in the substance use/abuse literature is the reality that initiator variables, maintenance variables, and intervention variables are quite distinct and perhaps unrelated. For example, a 15-year-old youth may initiate heroin use because of peer pressure, but, because of heroin's intense physiological addicting properties may maintain its use to avoid painful withdrawal symptoms. Intervention strategies

may involve aversive conditioning and, therefore, be totally unrelated to either peers or fleeing from withdrawal.

The Mental Illness Model

In brief this model considers substance use-abuse as the individual's response to underlying dynamic conflicts. Consumption of mind-altering chemicals represents the conflicted-stressed person's attempt to cope with his or her internal emotional and external social and physical environment through self-medication (Khantzian, 1980). This model is the partial basis for the frequently quoted formula that People + Stress → Drug-Seeking Behavior.

The Medical Model

The medical model for substance abuse was first presented by Jellinek (1960) and was confined to alcoholism. Today the Public Health Model of infectious diseases is the most accepted representation (Noble, 1978). This model states that a *host* with given unique constellations of factors (e.g., age, health, predispositions, etc.) and an *agent* (alcohol, heroin, amphetamines, etc.) interact in an *environment* to produce the disease of substance abuse.

Most successful intervention strategies are a skillful admixture of both models reflecting the necessity first to withdraw or detoxify the person from the chemical and maintain abstinence and, second, to begin the examination and correction of the etiological and maintenance variables of the chemical dependence that well may be psychological or behavioral problems. In some instances it well may be found that after detoxification no further intervention is necessary.

THE DRUGS OF ABUSE

The following is a brief discussion of the major drugs of abuse arranged primarily by their effects on the central nervous system (CNS). The major categories will be: depressants, stimulants, hallucinogens, and marijuana. Additionally phencyclidine (PCP) and volatile inhalants will be discussed briefly because of their special use/abuse status. Persons interested in a more detailed discussion of these drugs of abuse are referred to the Medical Monograph Series (NIDA, 1979a, 1979b, 1980) or Gilman, Goodman, and Gilman's (1980) text on pharmacotherapeutics. Two terms must be defined before proceeding to discuss the separate drugs. First, the word *addicting* applied to a chemical means that a drug has three properties:

1. *Tolerance.* Due to physiological adaptation factors, increased amounts of the drug are required to produce the desired effect. Tolerance is usually an interactive effect between dose, length of time used, and frequency of administration.

2. *Dependence.* Again this phenomenon is due to physiological factors and means the addicted person's body has accommodated to the chemical ingested in such a manner that if the use of the chemical is abruptly interrupted a characteristic "withdrawal syndrome" appears that is uncomfortable and in some instances fatal (NIDA, 1979a).

3. *Habituation.* This term means the person has a need (perhaps from habit) to experience the psychological effect of the drug.

This definition of the term *addicting* emphasizes that all three properties must be present to label the drug addicting. A drug may produce habituation, but, if it does not produce tolerance and dependence, it should not be labeled "addicting." Also simply because a person ingests an addicting drug does not mean that person is addicted. Unfortunately the substance abuse literature is replete with misapplications of these words (e.g., "psychologically addicting" probably means habituation), and the problem that evolves is one of impaired communication.

The second term requiring definition is *synergism.* Synergism in drug consumption is the phenomenon in which the addition of one standard dose of a particular drug to an equivalent dose of another drug does not produce an additive "two-standard-dose" response. Rather, the effect is an enhanced multiplicative one (Dorland, 1965). Due to synergistic effects, frequent "accidental" deaths from drug overdose are encountered.

While most drugs of abuse have specific effects a *common dose dependent psychological effect* has been suggested. That effect is the continuum of (1) euphoria, (2) dysphoria, and, for the non-CNS-depressant drugs, (3) hallucinations, and (4) paranoid psychotic symptomatology (Jeri et al., 1978). This is probably a CNS reaction and represents a common psychological manifestation of an acute Organic Brain Syndrome (OBS). This point is raised because sometimes toxic patients will confuse the dysphoric stage with the discomfort of withdrawal and ingest more drugs, resulting in overdose and/or more pronounced psychological symptomatology.

The major routes of introducing drugs into the bloodstream for conduction to the brain include the following. (Street terms are given in parentheses.)

1. Oral ("dropping"): taken by mouth and absorbed through the gut.

2. Respiratory ("smoking"): taken through smoking and absorbed through the alveoli of the lungs.

3. Nasal ("snorting"): taken through the nose and absorbed across the mucosal lining into the vascular system.

4. Subcutaneous ("skin popping"): injected under the dermis and absorbed into surrounding blood vessels.

5. Intravenous ("mainlining"): injected into a vein and absorbed directly.

6. Cutaneous (no street term): rubbed on the skin and absorbed into subcutaneous vessels.

In the discussion that follows, common drugs of abuse are listed and their expected effects presented. The reader would do well to keep in mind that behavioral effects of drugs are extremely variable both between and within individuals. Factors such as health, emotional state, age, length of drug use, dose, polydrug states, environmental surround—to name a few—will result in different clinical pictures between two different persons taking the same drug or the same person taking the drug on two different occasions.

A glossary of street terms and street names for given drugs of abuse is included in the appendix.

Depressants

The major CNS depressant drugs of abuse are alcohol, sedative-hypnotics, and narcotics. Their depressant effects tend to be dose related, and most are fatal in doses that exceed the individual's established tolerance level. Their perceived euphoric effects are due to depression of the action of certain CNS structures. All of the chemicals in these categories are addicting with some being cross-tolerant (higher doses of one will be necessary if the individual has tolerance to another) and/or cross-dependent (one drug can be substituted for another to prevent the withdrawal syndrome) (NIDA, 1979b). Alcohol and sedative-hypnotics are synergistic so that relatively small doses of both chemicals ingested simultaneously can produce life-threatening conditions.

Alcohol and other sedative hypnotics also interfere with various portions of the sleep cycle that do not return to normal until after protracted periods of abstinence.

The withdrawal syndrome from alcohol and sedative-hypnotics is similar and can become complicated by convulsions for the person addicted to these substances. If the person is addicted, then medically graduated decreases of a cross-dependent medication is indicated because convulsions and death are a possibility. While the abrupt withdrawal from narcotics is painful, it is rarely fatal or as complicated as the other CNS depressant drugs (NIDA, 1979b).

Alcohol

This drug, while classified by itself, should probably be included as a special type of sedative-hypnotic since its behavioral effects, both in toxicity and withdrawal from addic-

tion, are virtually identical to those of other sedative hypnotics.

The major physical effects (proportional to concentrations in the blood) of acute doses of alcohol are: CNS depression that results in ataxia, slowed brain waves, impaired coordination, delayed reaction time, detachment, analgesia, anesthesia, and respiratory depression. Also, vasodilation resulting in a flushing of the skin, gastric stimulation, and inhibition of the sex response cycle are observed. Common physical pathologic findings in chronic, excessive alcohol use include: liver pathology; peripheral nerve degeneration; CNS deterioration; dietary deficiencies leading to malnutrition; reproductive-gonadal abnormalities; increased susceptability to infections; and cancer of the mouth, pharnyx, esophagus and stomach. The latter appears to be synergistic with tobacco consumption (Noble, 1978).

The psychological effects are euphoria, a sense of self-confidence, disinhibition, verbosity, and mood swings. While some individuals report that the use of alcohol is an aphrodisiac, this is probably a part of the disinhibition effect. This disinhibition, coupled with the inhibition of the sexual response cycle, can produce a condition in which sexual contact is sought but once found cannot be acted upon. Shakespeare's famous quote from Macbeth, Act II, Sc. 3, is worth repeating at this point: "[Drink] provokes the desire, but it takes away the performance" (Ward, 1980). With chronic, excessive use the characteristic findings of psychological dysfunction are irritability, impulsiveness, impaired memory, short attention span, grossly maladjusted sexuality (including testicular atrophy and gynecomastia in males, amenorrhea in females, loss of pubic hair in both sexes, etc.), and dementia.

The major withdrawal syndrome from alcohol addiction is called delerium tremens (DTs) (Ward, 1980) and is characterized by progressive tremor that can result in grand-mal-like seizures and hallucinations in which there is distortion of size (usually very large or small animals) and color (pastels) leading to the proverbial "pink elephants." Usually hand tremor, irritability, and impaired concentration are the signs of less severe withdrawal.

Sedative-Hypnotics

These chemicals are those that produce a somnolent state. They include all of the various barbiturates, doridan, methaqualone, and the benzodiazepines (Valium, Librium, Atavan, and Dalmane). It is important to note that Valium and Librium are sedative-hypnotics (Gilman et al., 1980). The term "minor tranquilizer" applied to these preparations has been misleading since it intimates a "safe" drug. In reality the benzodiazipines are addicting, and the dependence can be profound. Since Valium is the number one prescription drug in America (Hollister, 1980), it is readily available to youth via the family medicine cabinet. In some countries the benzodiazepines are an over-the-counter (OTC) preparation.

In low doses, these preparations mildly depress CNS action and decrease the activity of both skeletal and smooth muscles. They slow cardiac and respiratory rates and lower the blood pressure. They produce sedation (which is dose dependent) and euphoria. They also have anticonvulsant properties. In moderate doses, which are the commonly sought toxic levels of abuse, the resultant behavior is virtually indistinguishable from alcohol toxicity and includes disinhibition, euphoria, mental confusion, slurred speech, ataxia, impaired thought processes, and memory dysfunction. Persons who abuse sedative-hypnotics tend to prefer those with shorter action since the effects have a more rapid onset (NIDA, 1979a).

Very large doses of sedative-hypnotics (with the exception of benzodiazapines) can produce deep sleep, convulsions, coma, and death. Death is usually due to either respiratory depression or cardiovascular collapse. The ingestion of very large doses is usually accidental and due to the individual being in a moderate dose state where there is impairment of the thought process, memory dysfunction, and mental confusion, resulting in the ingestion of more drugs to recapture the euphoric feelings. Irreversible physiological dysfunctions solely associated with chronic sedative-hypnotic medication use/abuse are not noted in reference texts (Goodman & Gilman, 1975).

The withdrawal syndrome from sedative-hypnotics varies in intensity to the amount of tolerance the individual has. It can be as mild as a fine tremor, restlessness, and impaired sleep patterns or as severe as psychotic proportion hallucinations and convulsions.

It would appear then that for youth who are involved in sedative-hypnotic use there are four major concerns from a physiological standpoint. First, there is the potential of overdose with individuals exceeding their tolerance limit and subsequently dying. Second, there are synergistic effects between sedative-hypnotics and alcohol, and accidental overdose can occur by mixing sedative-hypnotics and alcohol, which produces the multiplicative effect. Third, abrupt cessation of the use of the medication after the person has become physiologically dependent can produce an abstinence syndrome (similar to delirium tremens) in which the individual can become convulsive and die. Fourth, the mental confusion and coordination (ataxia) produced by these chemicals can make operation of complex machinery (e.g. cars or airplanes) hazardous and result in severe accidents and death.

Narcotics

The general term "narcotic" encompasses those chemical preparations that are derived from the opium poppy as well as synthetic analogues. Those that are derived from the opium poppy include opium, heroin, morphine, and codeine. Other forms of morphine that are abused include dilaudid and percodan. The major synthetic narcotics are methadone (Dolophine), meperidine (Demerol), and pentazocine (Talwin).

All narcotic drugs are used medically for their analgesic (pain-relieving) properties and/or reduction of gastrointestinal activity. Narcotics apparently depress virtually all activities of the human body (Gilman et al., 1980). In addition to this depressant effect, psychologically these drugs produce an intense experience of euphoria. This euphoria is intensified if the drug is injected intravenously, after which the person experiences a "rush" described as a full body orgasm. Shortly after the onset of this intense, euphoric feeling, there is a period that is called "being on the nod" or "kissing the table." During this state the individual feels dozy, dreamy, and in an intensely relaxed condition. Sometimes these individuals will enter light sleep ("nod out"); however, they can be easily aroused simply by calling their name (Freedman, Kaplan, & Sadock, 1976). With the exception of methadone, all of the narcotics tend to be short acting in their duration (1–5 hours) (Gilman et al., 1980). The most common and untoward situation for the narcotics is that they are all addicting. That is, they produce tolerance, dependence, and habituation. If one exceeds physiological tolerance, then overdose with respiratory depression and cardiac arrest can occur, which can be fatal.

Narcotic overdose can be rapidly reversed (within 1–2 minutes) by the intravenous injection of a narcotic antagonist. The major antagonist used today is naloxone hydrochloride (Narcan). Narcan is preferred over other narcotic antagonists because it has low agonistic properties and is almost purely antagonistic to the effects of narcotics. This is important since, typically persons who abuse depressant drugs use many different types, and, if sedative-hypnotics have been ingested, agonistic properties of antagonists may further depress CNS activity and precipitate crisis.

Antagonists do not neutralize the narcotic or remove it from the body, they simply compete for the narcotic receptor site. This fact is important because the antagonist may have a shorter half-life than the narcotic used, and upon the antagonist's metabolization the person can re-enter the overdose state. Withdrawal from narcotics is usually extremely painful but not fatal. The major signs and symptoms of the abstinence syndrome are: yawning; sweating; lacrimation (tearing); rhinorrhea (runny nose); dilation of pupils; intense muscle spasms; gooseflesh; vomiting; diarrhea; and increased respiration, blood pressure, body temperature, and metabolic rate.

The major complications with narcotic addiction are physical and social. Physically, besides overdose death, people who inject narcotics frequently do so with an apparatus ("rig") that is usually not sterile, constructed at home or borrowed from a confederate. This can produce medical complications such as blood poisoning, infection at injection sites, tetanus, serum hepatitis, malaria, endocarditis, and osteomyelitis (NIDA, 1979a). The social complications are associated with the expense of narcotics and their highly controlled distribution. From the expense standpoint persons with a narcotic addiction usually must spend approximately $200 per day. The majority of this money is derived from illegal sources such as breaking and entering, prostitution, illicit drug sales, etc. (Smith & Gay, 1972). If the individual is not supplying money for addiction through the above activities he or she in fact may commit armed robbery at pharmacies. This involvement in illegal activities to supply narcotics typically results in an interface with the criminal justice system and complications with a police record for the remainder of the individual's life.

Stimulants

The major stimulant chemicals are amphetamines, cocaine, and caffeine. All of these drugs are similar in their stimulant activity of the CNS, producing a state of euphoria and physical activation. Also, many of the stimulant drugs produce anorexia (loss of appetite).

Amphetamines

Amphetamine ("speed") is the generic chemical structure for Benzedrine, Dexedrine, and other related preparations. It does appear that these preparations may have some addictive properties (Gilman et al., 1980). The major effects of the amphetamines in low-to-moderate doses are a burst of energy, elevated blood pressure, pupil dilation, dry mouth, sweating, headache, anorexia, nausea and vomiting (infrequently), bronchial dilation, and urinary retention. Higher doses produce agitation, anxiety, talkativeness, confusion, dizziness, irritability, bruxism (tooth grinding), and hypertension. The psychological effects are also dose dependent with lower doses producing euphoria, alertness, self-confidence, and a sense of well being. Larger doses produce an inability to organize thoughts and prolonged high dose use can precipitate a condition that is similar in appearance to paranoid schizophrenia.

Withdrawal from these preparations is usually uncomplicated physically; however, a refractory depression can frequently be observed shortly after the individual begins to withdraw (3–5 days) that may last for 2–3 weeks. It is believed that this depressive state is on a neurochemical basis; however, at this time that has not been established. Permanent physiological dysfunction as a result of use of these chemicals is not reported at this time although some evidence now exists that chronic use of amphetamines may cause microvascular damage in some brain areas (Gilman et al., 1980).

Cocaine

Cocaine is obtained from the leaves of the cocoa plant indigenous to Peru and Bolivia. It is usually "snorted" and the effects are similar to those of amphetamine with euphoria and an intense feeling of well being comprising the psychological effects that persons seek.

A new form of cocaine ("freebase") has recently become popular. The freebase form can be smoked as opposed to being "snorted" and appears to be more potent than regular cocaine (Cohen, 1980a).

Street cocaine is chemically cocaine hydrochloride, and "freebasing" is a process that converts the street cocaine hydrochloride into alkaloidal cocaine or basic cocaine. Freebase melts at body temperature and passes into smoke quite readily (Cohen, 1980a). Its effects are reported to be more intense and of more rapid onset.

Irreversible physiological dysfunction as a result of either acute or chronic administration of the drug is not documented. In the past, cocaine has been regarded as a relatively safe recreational drug, but it is now clear that persons can overdose with cocaine, leading to convulsions and death.

Cocaine is an expensive drug because of supply and demand. A small amount of cocaine is available due to its limited production, and there is a high demand for the drug.

Caffeine

Caffeine is the powerful CNS stimulant found in coffee, tea, and some other natural plants. It has complicated effects on the cardiovascular system with relaxation of smooth muscles and increased strength in the contraction of skeletal muscles. It has diuretic properties, causes increased gastric secretion and an increase in the basal metabolic rate.

Caffeine is mentioned as a drug of abuse in this chapter on adolescent substance abuse because not only do coffee and tea contain caffeine but significant amounts are also found in cocoa and most of the cola "soft drinks." A standard 12-ounce bottle of a cola drink contains approximately 45–50 percent of the caffeine of a standard cup of coffee or tea. Therefore, most youth are accustomed to ingesting large quantitites of this particular drug.

Common untoward reactions to very high doses of caffeine include insomnia, restlessness, and excitement in early symptoms progressing to mild delirium as a late stage symptom. Sensory disturbances such as tinnitus (ringing in the ears) and flashes of light are common, muscles frequently become tense and tremulous, and tachycardia and increased respiration are also noted (Gilman et al., 1980).

While there are certainly physiological effects of caffeine ingestion, until recently there has been no evidence that "the morning cup of coffee" is in any way harmful (Gilman et al., 1980). Presently research linking regular amounts of caffeine to pancreatic cancer has been reported (MacMahan et al., 1981). While the pharmacokinetics of caffeine have not been extensively studied in the past, recent research has begun to document the effects of caffeine in various doses and administration formats (Modrow et al., 1981).

Tobacco

Nicotine found in tobacco is a very strong stimulant chemical that apparently produces tolerance, habituation, and dependence (i.e., it is addictive). It is an extremely common drug of abuse, and the physical dysfunctions that are attendant on chronic tobacco use are well known (Jarvik et al., 1977). Due to the increase of tobacco use by females, and particularly females at a younger age, it is important in this chapter to make brief mention of neonatal effects of nicotine. Women who are pregnant and who smoke heavily during pregnancy have an increased chance of delivering an infant of less than normal birth weight (Postotinik, 1978). Infants who are of less than normal birth weight may in fact have a compromised survival rate due to the undevelopment.

Psychedelics

The psychedelics include such chemicals as lysergic acid diethylamide (LSD), mescaline, psilocybin, DMT, and STP. The physical effects of psychedelic chemicals that are usually ingested orally include an increased heart rate and increased blood pressure. There are dilation of the pupils, tremors of the extremities, cold sweaty palms, flushing, chills, gooseflesh, dry mouth, some reported nausea, anorexia, urgency of urination, hyperactive reflexes, and increased body temperature. That is, ingestion of these preparations produces physiological activation.

The psychological effects of psychedelic drugs are somewhat misleading from their label. That is, the psychedelic drugs are also called hallucinogens with the implication that the chemical provides an integrated perceptual experience that mimics a psychotic hallucinatory state. This is not the case. The psychological effects of psychedelic preparations include changes in perception, with sharpened and/or heightened sense of taste, vision, smell, touch, and hearing. Some persons ingesting these chemicals have reported synesthesia, in which the psychological experience of sensory stimulation is crossed (i.e.,

hearing colors and seeing sounds). Some persons under the influence of psychedelics also report the concurrent experience of two strong opposing emotions such as love and hate towards the same objects. Frequently there is a rapid shift of emotions with extreme mood swings and distortions in the sense of time. Individuals under the influence of these chemicals also report a loss of boundaries between body and space.

Idiosyncratic and toxic reactions including panic and paranoia have been reported in a few individuals. The phenomenon of "flashbacks" has been reported by some individuals. Flashbacks vary in intensity from a complete re-experience of a previous toxic episode to small and transient "feeling states." While "flashbacks" are poorly understood, they appear to be learned anxiety responses to situations in which individuals are stressed or anxious (Cohen, 1977). Usually flashbacks are self-limiting after two years if the person terminates all psychedelic and marijuana use.

Clinicians can assist the person with flashbacks by following a few basic guidelines.

1. Assume a nonjudgmental stance.
2. Reassure the patient of the time-limited nature of dysfunction.
3. Advise the patient that smoking marijuana has been observed to trigger flashbacks; therefore, marijuana use should be suspended.
4. Explain the association between anxiety/stress states and appearance of a flashback.
5. Teach anxiety/stress control procedures: e.g., meditation, Jacksonian Relaxation, etc.

If a flashback occurs in the clinician's presence, he or she can best assist the individual by assuming a nonjudgmental stance; reassuring the patient of the nonfatal nature of the experience; establishing comforting physical contact (e.g., an arm around the shoulder); focusing on "centering" the patient's attention to one object; slowly, through suggestion, changing negative aspects of the flashback to positive attitudes (e.g., suggesting that a threatening, vicious dog is becoming playful and friendly); and allowing the person to live through the trip in a safe environment with the clinician.

Accidental deaths following psychedelic ingestion have been reported, but these are not usually due to suicidal ideation. Rather, typically the individual has a delusional belief of being impervious and walks in front of a truck to try to prove his or her immortality. Other delusional individuals have reportedly believed themselves to be birds capable of flight and leaped off high places in an attempt to test their delusional system. There have also been a few reported instances in which individuals have ingested a psychedelic substance and subsequently become chronically psychotic (NIDA, 1979a). They probably represent individuals who had a premorbid borderline adjustment to reality, and the drug use tipped their adjustment into emotional disruption. Any other intense experience could probably have done the same.

There also have been numerous reports of chromosomal alterations and malformed offspring resulting from psychedelic chemical use. However, most of these studies have serious research flaws with inadequate control of other substances ingested, such as tobacco and alcohol, which are known teratogens, and nutritional status of the pregnant women was not reported. At this time, teratogenetic effects of psychedelic substances remain to be proven; however, they are unlikely since the members of the Native American Church use psychedelic drugs regularly and have no higher rate of birth defects reported than the general population of Native Americans.

Marijuana

The effects of marijuana have been thought to be innocuous and transient. However, as research has continued it is clear that there may be some chronic, irreversible effects from marijuana use as well as important acute effects that may prove to be significant for persons who use the drug (Cohen, 1979).

The physical effects of marijuana include reddened conjuntiva, mild tachycardia, insig-

nificant fluctuations in blood pressure, some infrequent nausea, decreased salivation, lacrimation, mild unsteadiness, impaired coordination, hunger (particularly for sweets), drowsiness, occasionally some slowed speech, respiratory difficulties (bronchitis, rhinitis, nasal pharyngitis) and, *extremely rarely,* anaphylactic allergic reactions. There is also a documented decrease in the immune response and a suppression of testosterone production in males (Cohen, 1979).

The psychological effects for which persons usually ingest the drug include a sense of contentment, inner satisfaction, tranquilization/relaxation, heightened awareness of sounds and colors, giddiness, alteration in time and space perception, euphoria, disinhibition, and sometimes occasional anxiety and suspiciousness. Most important is the impairment of immediate memory recall. There have been recorded some adverse psychological effects of infrequent high dose that include some delusions (usually of a paranoid nature), hallucinations, and severely impaired memory.

An adverse psychological effect of chronic use, called the amotivational syndrome, was suggested by McGlothlin and West (1968). The amotivational syndrome as described includes a passive attitude, withdrawal, apathy, loss of goal-oriented drive, an inability to think and speak clearly, and preoccupation with acquiring additional marijuana. While there has been refutation of the amotivational syndrome by many large scale studies, Cohen (1980b, 1981) reviewed the literature and documented some support for its possible existence. The question still to be resolved is whether the "amotivational syndrome" is only found in certain persons and represents the exaggeration of pre-existent personality variables. The high prevalence of marijuana use and the relatively low rate of report of the amotivational syndrome would support this interpretation.

Over the last five years, the THC content of street marijuana has increased at about the rate of 1 percent per year (Cohen, 1979). Obviously, marijuana available five years ago with THC content of about 1 percent would not have had as intense an effect as marijuana today. The effects listed above established on 1 percent THC should be expected to be intensified as the THC content increases in the standard dose that people ingest.

There have been significant recent developments in research with marijuana that underscores this drug's potential problem for individuals who chronically use it. For example, the decrease in testosterone production is well documented and for adult males is clinically nonsignificant. However, for the pubescent male, suppression of testosterone production may have serious implications for development of secondary sex characteristics, etc. Additionally, it has been documented that there are significant amounts of carcinogens in marijuana (Cohen, 1979). Due to the method in which marijuana is ingested (deep inhalation and retention of smoke) the lungs are significantly exposed to adverse factors. With regard to respiratory vital capacity decrease the ratio has been established that one marijuana cigarette is equivalent to sixteen standard tobacco cigarettes in their adverse effect (Tashkin, Calverese, & Simmons, 1978).

Because marijuana is lipophilic it is retained in the body for considerable periods of time. With the documented effects of marijuana ingestion on mental functioning (Peterson, 1980), there is concern that young persons who use marijuana either daily or even on alternate days may compromise their ability to acquire new knowledge and skills information.

While there are some claims for the teratogenicity of marijuana the Director of the National Institute of Drug Abuse in his report to Congress indicated there are no sound data at this time that would support teratogenic properties of this drug. However, it is clear that the possibility of fetal effects from maternal ingestion of marijuana is strong enough to discourage its use by pregnant females (Pollin, 1980).

It has now been established that marijuana use produces a very mild addiction (Jones & Benowitz, 1976). That is, while physical dependence, tolerance, and psychological habituation can be demonstrated in the laboratory, the clinical effects are so slight that individuals can go through withdrawal with no awareness of an abstinence syndrome.

The question "Does marijuana use lead to use of 'harder' drugs?" is a concern. There is nothing in the chemical structure of marijuana that demands an individual who uses it to progress to the utilization of any other chemical (NIDA, 1979b). However, on the basis that individuals who distribute marijuana have other drugs to sell, there is the reality that individuals who use the drug may be at risk to experiment with other chemicals. By analogy, if only one grocery is allowed to sell coffee, the sales of all other items in the store will increase. Retention of the sale of marijuana to persons who have other drugs to sell potentiates the sale of the other drugs.

Inhalants

The inhalants include industrial use substances such as glue, lacquer thinner, paint, and gasoline, and also freon (the propellant found in certain types of aerosol dispensers of food), butyl nitrite ("Locker Room," "Rush," "Jac Aroma," etc.) and nitrous oxide ("laughing gas" used by dentists as an anesthesia and also found as a propellant in aerosol-packaged whipped cream and rocket fuel and as a detector for gas leaks).

Inhalants are typically abused by young adolescents. One nationwide study of high school students reported that 12 percent of the graduating class in 1978 had a lifetime prevalence of inhalant use. About 2 percent were current users. During the same time period more than 150 people died as a result of inhaling volatile substances with approximately 1,800 additional individuals requiring emergency room treatment (Hect, 1980). There are documented acute and chronic physiological effects of the utilization of inhalants including immediate loss of consciousness, heart irregularities, or death. An OBS may develop that is characterized by loss of muscle coordination, lethargy, irritability, confusion, and/or disorientation. Inhaling volatile substances can also lead to peripheral nerve injury and liver and kidney disease. Long range effects that may not appear for 10–30 years include an increased risk of developing cancer as well as genetic changes (Hect, 1980). Many of the significant detrimental effects of inhalants appear to reverse if the person terminates use. Death from inhalant abuse has been largely due to heart irregularities brought on when sniffing was followed by vigorous exercise. Deaths in this instance usually were associated with the inhalation of various aerosols from packaged foods and commercial/industrial solvents. The abuse pattern as well as death from butyl nitrite and nitrous oxide is different. Usually deaths are due to nitrous oxide overdose in which too much dinitrous (N_2) has been ingested and, because oxygen has not been available, the person becomes anoxic (Hect, 1980).

The psychological effect of inhalant use is a transient euphoric feeling with an accompanying heightened awareness of the senses. Time is frequently distorted, so the subjective experience of elapsed time is lengthened. Some users of inhalants (particularly butyl nitrite) report that inhalation of the substance at the point of sexual orgasm produces a subjective experience of an extended orgasm (Cohen, 1978a).

Since these substances are not addicting, withdrawal from them poses no significant problem. However, the psychological reinforcement from them is intense and termination of use is difficult.

Phencyclidine (PCP)

Phencyclidine is a dissociative anesthesia. Historically it was developed for humans; however, experimental use demonstrated significant untoward side effects and it is presently confined to veterinary applications. Ketamine is the human analog of phencyclidine and at present is being used in a nonmedicinal manner by a number of individuals.

PCP apparently works at a central as well as peripheral level to block the experience of pain and dissociate body experiences from mental awareness. The public media have given a great deal of publicity to the use/abuse of PCP; however, most experiences are judged to be pleasant and devoid of catastrophic reactions (Cohen, 1978b).

The reported psychological effects of the use of phencyclidine include euphoria, relaxation, "out-of-body" experiences, and heightened perceptual experiences. Psychomotor activity is also affected. Initially there is hyperactivity followed shortly by ataxia and incoordination. Persons who routinely use the drug for recreational purposes also report a heightened ability to "get inside oneself" and explore the "inner resources of the mind."

Death from phencyclidine ingestion is usually attributed to one of two causes. First, if the individual overdoses, vital functions of the body are impaired. Second, and more important, is the problem of youth who use the substance in a recreational manner and attempt to engage in a somewhat complicated and dangerous activity such as swimming, water skiing, or driving a car and the ataxic effects of the toxicity results in compromised functioning and death.

Other untoward circumstances that occur with the ingestion of PCP (and ketamine) include "the four Cs" (Smith et al., 1978), which are dose dependent. The first "C" is *combative* in which the individual may assault others in the immediate environment particularly if a threat is perceived. Along with this combativeness the individual has an increased pain threshold so normal deterrents may be ineffective. The second "C" is *catatonia* in which the individual has decreased movements of the extremities and may sit for protracted periods of time in one position with minimal activity. The third "C" is *convulsions.* Moderate-to-high doses of this chemical can lead to a hyperexcitable CNS and consequently convulsions will occur. The fourth "C" is *coma,* and in this state the individual frequently must have external life support systems. This comatose state can be expected to last between 12 hours and many days (Aronow & Done, 1978). As the person emerges from the comatose condition, the clinical picture is episodic and similar to psychedelic or stimulant toxicity interspersed with stuperous or comatose conditions.

Addiction and physical pathology secondary to chemical use of this drug is unverified at this time. The major physiological problems are the problems of overdose and difficulty with coordination.

EPIDEMIOLOGY

Caveats need to be offered about the interpretations of epidemiological data in substance abuse. First, data are usually based on cross-sectional research that samples different age groups at the same time. This yields data that reflect current trends of who reports use of drugs *at the present time.* However, the generalization of those data to indicate future report patterns of these same persons at a later age is unwarranted. The second caution is that data are usually either derived indices (e.g., arrest rates) or self-report. Derived indices such as arrest rates are notorious for their lack of representativeness. That is, frequently ethnic subgroups have different arrest rates, and, consequently, a very distorted view of who is using what substances can occur. Self-report data is exactly that. It is what individuals are willing to say they are doing and may be a correct report, a low report, or a fallaciously high report. The only conclusion one can draw from self-report data is that this is what

people say they are doing. It may or may not be reality. A third caution is how subjects are identified for inclusion in a survey. The temptation when reading an epidemiological study is to examine for stratification, geographic representation, etc. However, one should also look at other heuristic parameters. For example, the National Survey on Drug Abuse (NIDA, 1977) is a household survey. While it is well stratified and representative of geographic areas, etc., one of the limiting parameters is that to be included in the study a subject had to be living in a household. This automatically eliminated two very large groups of individuals known to be high rate users of drugs: persons in the military and persons who are in institutions such as universities and colleges.

Table 36.1 presents the data on graduating high school seniors for four consecutive periods of time for various drugs of abuse (ADAMHA, 1981).

From 1975 through 1980 there has been a trend of stabilization of the report of use of most drugs that were investigated. Alcohol is reported as the drug that has most experimentation (ever used) and the highest rate of current use, but it is third behind cigarettes and marijuana in daily use. With regard to cigarette smoking, there is a trend toward decrease in reported experimentation, current use, and daily use. The data on marijuana reflect the report of experimentation has

Table 36.1   High School Seniors' Use of 9 Drugs, 1975–1980 (Percentages)

	Ever Used				Currently Using				Daily Users			
	Class of				Class of				Class of			
	'75	'77	'79	'80	'75	'77	'79	'80	'75	'77	'79	'80
Marijuana	47	56	60	60	27	35	37	34	6	9	10.3	9.1
Inhalants	—[a]	11	13	12	—	1	2	1	—	0	0	0.1
PCP	—	—	13	10	—	—	2	1	—	—	0.1	0.1
Cocaine	9	11	15	16	2	3	6	5	0.1	0.1	0.2	0.2
Heroin	2	2	1	1	0.4	0.3	0.2	0.2	0.1	0	0	0
Stimulants	22	23	24	26	9	9	10	12	0.5	0.5	0.6	0.7
Methaqualone	8	9	8	10	2	2	2	3	0	0	0	0.1
Alcohol	90	93	93	93	68	71	72	72	6	6	7	6
Cigarettes	74	76	74	71	37	38	34	31	27	29	25	21

[a]—— - not asked

Table 36.2   Substance Use Prevalence Rates (Percent) by Age Group, 1977

	Age	Lifetime Prevalence (Ever Used)	Last Month
Marijuana	12–17	28.2	16.1
	18–25	60.1	27.2
	26+	15.4	3.2
	18+	24.5	8.2
Inhalants	12–17	9.0	.7
	18–25	11.2	.5
	26+	1.8	.5
	18+	3.7	.5
Hallucinogens	12–17	4.6	1.6
	18–25	19.8	2.0
	26+	2.6	.5
	18+	6.1	.5
Cocaine	12–17	4.0	.8
	18–25	19.1	3.7
	26+	2.6	.5
	18+	6.0	1.0
Heroin	12–17	1.1	.5
	18–25	3.6	.5
	26+	.8	.5
	18+	1.4	.5
Opiates-nonopiates	12–17	6.1	.6
	18–25	13.5	1.0
	26+	2.8	.5
	18+	5.0	.5
Stimulants	12–17	5.2	1.3
	18–25	21.2	2.5
	26+	4.7	.6
	18+	8.1	1.0
Sedatives	12–17	3.1	.8
	18–25	18.4	2.8
	26+	2.8	.5
	18+	6.0	.6
Tranquilizers	12–17	3.8	.7
	18–25	13.4	2.4
	26+	2.6	.5
	18+	4.8	.8
Alcohol	12–17	52.6	31.2
	18–25	84.2	70.0
	26+	77.9	54.9
	18+	79.2	58.0
Cigarettes	12–17	47.3	22.3
	18–25	67.6	47.3
	26+	67.0	38.7
	18+	67.1	40.5

From National Survey on NIDA Publication, 1977

leveled at approximately 60 percent, 34–37 percent report current use, and a stable figure of 9–10 percent report daily use. The individuals who report using marijuana, alcohol, and tobacco are not necessarily independent. That is, one student may be reporting use of alcohol, marijuana, and other substances.

The data that are presented in Table 36.2 have been abstracted from the National Survey on Drug Abuse (NIDA, 1977). In this cross-sectional study it appears that the group of persons in 1977 who were most likely to report use of chemicals last month is the age group of 18–25. Whether this represents a cross-sectional finding, a stable characteristic, or a longitudinal fact cannot be determined by these data.

However, there is one 27-year longitudinal study that suggests many individuals do tend to decrease their drug consumption after the peak period of time at the young adult (18–25) level (Filmore, Bacon, & Hyman, 1979).

ETIOLOGIES

Research into causes of substance abuse have centered in three domains: the physiological, the psychological, and the sociological. While research has tended to focus on each area singly, most students of substance abuse clearly indicate the belief that these three interact to cause the phenomenon.

Physiological Etiologies

Physiological research on the etiology of substance abuse has two major components: genetic and induced mechanisms.

Genetics

Most genetic studies have focused specifically on alcoholism (Goodwin, 1976). Goodwin's studies of twins separated shortly after birth from their parents support the proposition that for some persons alcoholism is an inherited disorder. Schuckit and Ralyses (1979) presented data on the relatives of alcoholics that demonstrate that alcoholics' relatives produce higher blood acetaldehyde concen-

trations when they consume alcohol than do matched controls. Since it is believed that blood acetaldehyde is one of the significant variables in alcoholism, Schuckit's support of Goodwin's data is noteworthy. Most theoreticians who consider the inherited aspects of substance abuse (specifically alcoholism) believe there is a physiological abnormality in either structure or function of the central nervous system or metabolism that is normalized by substances of abuse. In this view it would not be substance abuse per se that is inherited; rather, it would be the underlying anatomical/physiological dysfunction that is passed from generation to generation. The resultant use of substances of abuse is simply viewed as self-medication.

Acquired Physiological Aspects

While genetic data focus on that with which the person is born, the proponents of acquired physiological causes of substance abuse suggest that certain drugs create physiological/biochemical dependence and tolerance that may be permanent. Dependence implies a strong physiological craving for a substance, and, depending upon the strength of the craving, various levels of drug-seeking behavior will be noted. Davis (1973) presented data regarding enzymatic changes attendant to chronic ingestion of alcohol. Her findings suggest that when alcohol is consumed for protracted periods of time (years) an enzyme shift is noted that converts consumed alcohol to alkaloids that have opiatelike properties. This suggests that with a long history of exposure to the chemical there is a (permanent?) change in enzymatic systems that forces the individual to seek a drug to palliate opiatelike cravings, which are known to be extremely intense.

While most individuals believe a few days of detoxification from the various drugs of abuse will eliminate the physiological craving for the drug, there are data from research with opiates (Martin & Jasinski, 1969) and alcohol withdrawal studies (Kissin, 1977) that suggest a protracted episodic abstinence syndrome that will spontaneously occur and create drug craving that is unrelated to environmental or personal events. Data have been collected on amphetamine dependence that indicate that persons dependent on these chemicals frequently will have two to three weeks of reaction to abstinence from the drugs (NIDA, 1979a).

It is clear that certain drugs that have their inception of use under given parameters (e.g., recreational) can create a physiological/biochemical condition in the body so that the individual must have the drug or risk severe discomfort and in some instances death from withdrawal. Physiological aspects cannot be overlooked as significant contributors to substance abuse.

Youth who have not acquired other coping mechanisms or have limited ability to postpone gratification or endure discomfort may in fact be responding more to physiological dependence than other attributes of etiological variables. Likewise, there is suspicion at this time that physiological alterations secondary to drug ingestion may occur at an accelerated rate for youth as opposed to adults.

Psychological Etiologies

Classical Conditioning

Frequently youth ingest drugs (UCR) because of anticipation of positive effects. This usually takes place in a context of environment, time, and persons (CS). The context frequently becomes substituted for the anticipation of positive effects resulting in drug ingestion (CR) being cued by the context (CS). Clinically, addicts report they can be free of drugs for years while imprisoned; however, when they leave prison and return to the environment in which they used drugs, the substance craving reappears as they encounter the skyline of the city, their old neighborhood, friends with whom they used drugs, etc. That is, external events have become conditioned stimuli that produce conditioned responses of drug-seeking behavior.

Operant Conditioning

Under operant-conditioning paradigms, the individual ingests drugs that produce a fairly specific response that is intrinsically reward-ing (Wikler, 1973). Not only do youth take drugs for the hedonistic pleasure, but apparently some consume drugs in response to family, peer, school, developmental stress (e.g., sexual tension), etc., in an attempt either to decrease the felt stress or to escape the realities of unpleasant situations. This is the basic premise behind the phrase "People plus stress leads to drug-seeking behavior." Drug-seeking behavior generally leads to drug-taking behavior, and the issue is compounded by the possibility that the individual will become physiologically addicted. With physiological addiction present, discontinuing use of the drugs would precipitate an unpleasant abstinence syndrome. A situation has developed in which, for psychological (familial, peer, etc.) reasons, the individual may seek drugs to decrease a particular felt stress condition. However, because of the addicting properties of some drugs, what was a search for pleasure or relief from a psychological state is converted into an avoidance of a physiological withdrawal discomfort. This operant model is most specifically associated with stress reduction and is probably one of the major etiologies for youthful drug involvement. It also has implications for intervention strategies, which will be discussed below.

Social Learning

Social-learning (modeling) explanations of substance abuse focus on youth acquiring substance use/abuse behavior from significant other models (Barnes, 1977). In this framework, significant others demonstrate chemical use/abuse to children and model consumption of drugs as a mechanism for coping with stressful situations (Cotten, 1979). Also parents may set a social model for the *nonuse* of drugs that is particularly effective until the youth enters high school (Margules, Kessler, & Kandel, 1977). As young persons mature peers appear to become more important as role models for substance use than are parents as role models of abstinence. In adolescence, youths have the developmental task of establishing independence from parents. The need for affection and approval is still present; however, due to the developmental task (independence) it is no longer feasible to receive that approval and affection from parents; therefore, adolescents will search for approval from peers. If the price of peer approval, affection, and acceptance is the utilization of various chemicals, adolescents will have little compunction about consuming these substances.

Addictive Personality

The erroneous belief that there is an "addictive personality" is widely held. To date there has been no scientific support of an addictive personality whose existence has been defined prior to the actual substance abuse (Ewing, 1977). Studies of the addictive personality appear to be commonly flawed in their focus on the individual who is known to have complete addiction. It is not possible under these postdiction research conditions to ascertain whether substance abuse is the result of a particular set of personality variables or whether distinguishing personality variables associated with substance abuse are the result of chemical consumption (Platt, 1975). The most common psychological variables associated with the use/abuse of psychoactive chemicals are "low self-esteem" (Roman, 1978), external locus of control (Jacobson, Van Dyke, & Steinbach, 1976), alienation (Steyton & Diener, 1979), and a poor self-concept (Cutter, Jones, & Maloof, 1979). The realistic conclusion at this time is that there have been studies that associated selected personality variables with complete substance abuse problems (Gross & Carpenter, 1980); however, a predictive longitudinal study of all individuals with a given premorbid personality variable and their relative outcome regarding development of chemical dependence has not been done. Until such a study is effected no valid statements can be made regarding "addictive personality."

Developmental Variables

Considerable evidence has accumulated that regards substance use/abuse as a "normal" developmental reality. That is, authors have noted the high prevalence rate of substance use/abuse in youth and young adults and suggest that data reflect a "natural" stage through which young people develop as they mature. Mandell and Ginzberg (1976) reported that drug use is an orderly, evolving behavior pattern, and Brisbane (1976) suggested that at least for black youth it is a portion of the transition from childhood to adulthood. Ingestion of mind-altering drugs appears to have become a fixed part of the adolescent environment (Braxton, 1978).

In summary, it is helpful to understand that there is an interaction between psychological and physiological factors with regard to substance use/abuse by young people. There may be multiple psychological reasons that any one individual may initiate substance use (i.e., classical conditioning, operant conditioning, social learning, personality variables, and/or developmental progressions). However, either because of pharmacological characteristics of some psychoactive substances or genetic predispositions, the individual may trigger an addictive process. Once the individual becomes physiologically/biochemically dependent upon the chemical, he or she can no longer easily avoid chemical use. Because of the protracted abstinence syndrome of some drugs, the young person is vulnerable to reintroduction of chemical use as a way to avoid the discomfort of withdrawal. A circular, interdependent psychological/physiological etiological combination to substance use and/or abuse is usually found.

Sociological Variables

Sociological aspects include data regarding ethnic and religious considerations as well as environmental correlates of substance abuse.

Ethnic and Religious Variables

There are clear ethnic differences in prevalence rates of substance use/abuse. With regard to alcohol consumption, Native Americans have the highest rate of problems, persons of Spanish surname are second, whites are third, followed by blacks, with Orientals experiencing the fewest problems associated with alcohol consumption (Noble, 1978). However, these data assume all racial and ethnic groups have a common composition, which is not true. Within the category "white" are persons of Jewish religion who experience low rates of problems associated with alcohol consumption. While alcohol consumption is a part of the Jewish culture, it is used in an integrated, ritual-ceremonial fashion and with meals, and there are few social models (parents or peers) for abusive consumption of alcohol. Likewise with other ethnic groups within the category of "white," there are high rates of other drugs of abuse besides alcohol. Other religious correlates to drug use exist as well. Data indicate that Catholics have high proportions of drinkers and heavy drinkers, liberal Protestants show few heavy drinkers, and conservative Protestants have the largest proportion of abstainers and a small proportion of heavy drinkers (Byrne & Price, 1979).

Special Environments

Certain environmental settings promote substance use and abuse. Environments in which (1) the individual feels isolated and unaccepted by the predominant population of that environment, (2) the individual does not have a personal support system for nondrug consumption, and (3) the individual's limited alternatives to drug consumption tend to promote an abusive pattern of psychoactive drug use/abuse. Predictably young persons who are members of highly transient families (e.g., military), who are frequently disrupted in their interpersonal relations with peers, who encounter educational systems that are widely variant, and who are faced with socioeconomic deprivation are at high risk for chemical use/abuse, particularly if parents and peers set a social model for drug consumption as a coping mechanism.

Other environmental data regarding substance abuse indicate that drug consumption is regionally distributed with the Northeast, West, and North Central United States having the highest rates of use and the South the lowest. Drug-of-choice report varies by national region and time suggesting some "faddishness" in drug consumption behavior (NIDA, 1977), and there is a positive correlation between the amount of urbanism of a city and drug consumption (Peck, 1977).

IDENTIFICATION AND RECOGNITION OF SUBSTANCE ABUSE IN YOUTH

Simply observing young people's behavior and concluding correctly that a given set of behavioral attributes indicates that the young person is using a specific chemical is at best risky. Because of normal maturational developmental behavioral changes, illness, environmental stresses, etc., different behavioral patterns can be observed and are not necessarily the result of ingestion of chemicals.

Likewise, experienced drug users are usually aware of the behaviors and physiological signs that identify given types of drug use/abuse, and they circumvent the signs. For instance, with marijuana use one of the only reliable signs of toxicity is a reddened conjunctiva; however, certain types of eyedrops will "take the red out." Other signs such as dilated or constricted pupils can be covered with sunglasses, and the phenomenon of behavioral tolerance to drug effects is well documented (Krasnegor, 1978).

The only reliable method of ascertaining whether someone has used chemicals in the very recent past is through laboratory toxicology. However, few parents and/or school authorities would condone routine surveillance of their children through a urine-screening program. As an adjunct to treatment, medically supervised toxicology studies can be a useful tool to assist young people in staying free of the drugs. If a young person has routinely used psychoactive chemicals that can be isolated in clinical laboratory analysis and the youth has motivation to terminate use of the drugs and accepts a urine-screening program, then the urine analysis can be of significant assistance if used appropriately. If urine screening is employed as an indicator of life stress–conflict or as a positive reinforcer of self-esteem (ability to remain drug free), it can be extremely useful. However, utilization of toxicology as a punitive "detective" measure should be avoided since this philosophical stance precipitates a game of "cops and robbers" in which the goal of assisting the young person to stay drug free is lost and the refocus is how much or how many drugs the young person can use without getting caught.

The most viable index one has of substance abuse is a nonjudgmental high index of concern for the youngster whose traditional behavior pattern (family, school, extracurricula, peer relations, etc.) suddenly shifts. For example, if a student has been achieving and suddenly grades drop precipitously, the youngster becomes isolated from the usual peer group, becomes excessively irritable at home and perhaps develops some physiological signs of dysfunction (e.g., chronic gastrointestinal distress), then responsible adults should consider the possibility that the youth is using/abusing psychoactive chemicals. However, a great injustice, disservice, and perhaps irreparable distrust can be created if the concerned adult erroneously accuses a young person of having used/abused drugs when perhaps in fact the child is struggling with naturally evolving intense sexual drives.

SIGNIFICANT PROBLEMS TO BE CONSIDERED

Physiological Problems

The major concerns for youth with regard to the physiological aspects of substance abuse have to do with both the acute and chronic effects of some drugs. First, the addictive quality of selected drugs can create significant financial, physical, legal, etc., problems for young people. Second, certain drugs can attenuate reaction time and severely impair coordination. If a young person ingests such a chemical and attempts to engage in complex activities such as driving, swimming, etc., the effect of the drug can significantly impair responsivity and coordination. Third, most of the drugs of use/abuse have "overdose" po-

tential, and a number have withdrawal syndromes that can be fatal if not medically managed. Fourth, with regard to certain types of physiological properties of various drugs, the individuals may in fact create physical conditions that may be permanent. For example, it is unknown what large amount of alcohol, marijuana, etc., may do to impair given physiological systems in the young developing body that may never return to normal.

Psychological Problems

There are two major concerns about psychological functioning that arise with drug use/abuse. The first is interference in psychological processes such as cognition, memory, perception, and motivation. It is known that certain chemicals impair these so that young persons are either not fully attendant to or capable of comprehending educational processes necessary for full adult functioning.

The second is that youth will rely upon chemical coping mechanisms in dealing with the ordinary demands and stresses of life. That is, if a young person relies on chemicals for stress and conflict management, that youth is deprived of learning behavioral coping strategies for dealing with the world and, as an adult, is incapable of managing stress in an independent adaptive dynamic manner.

Sociologic Problems

Problems in sociological functioning include restricting the young person to a given group of individuals that eventually will be maladaptive. That is, if a young person associates at a young age with peers who are substance users/abusers, primary social identity is linked to drug use. Further, if the young person has become physiologically addicted to an expensive chemical (e.g., heroin) and relies upon it as a coping mechanism, that young person must identify with a basically criminal subculture to procure money to satisfy the physiological addiction and/or psychological dependence on the chemical. This subculture is usually an antisocial group of individuals that integrates the young person into criminal behavior patterns that eventually will involve that youngster in legal difficulties.

Progeny

One of the significant problems attendant on substance abuse is the reality that many substances that are used/abused have significant effects on offspring. Two major points with regard to the high rate of youthful sexual experimentation, pregnancy, and drug use need to be considered.

Fetal Alcohol Effects

At this time there is no question that alcohol is a teratogen that, when used prior to conception and during pregnancy, can have significant morphological effects upon the fetus, particularly in the first trimester (Noble, 1978). The fetal alcohol effects are distributed on a continuum with a wide range from minimal or negligible on one end through the full Fetal Alcohol Syndrome on the other.

The Fetal Alcohol Syndrome is characterized by morphological abnormalities of the head (including cleft palate, hare lip, microcephaly, hirsutism, etc.), cardiac and respiratory system fistulas, retarded development for gestational age, and mental retardation (Finnegan, 1979).

Addicted Newborns

Women who are pregnant and ingest psychoactive chemicals supply the fetus with that drug *in utero*. The placenta is not a barrier but a sieve. Drugs that are in the mother's system pass directly to the fetus, and when the fetus is born it is abruptly separated from its source of chemicals. Because the newborn is physiologically dependent, it will usually experience the general withdrawal syndrome (Desmond et al., 1972), which can be fatal. That is, in the adult, withdrawal from certain drugs can be minimal or simply painful; however, in the neonate a condition of hyperactivity can be created that leads to dehydration and possible convulsions if it is not medically managed. At this time, there are few data that indicate these addicted neonates either do or do not have significant problems as adults.

INTERVENTION

Intervention is complicated by the young person's motivation for assistance in termination or attenuation of drug use. Frequently, (as with adults) drug use is perceived by the user as no problem until a significant untoward or traumatic consequence is personally experienced. At that time assistance is often reluctantly accepted. Intervention into substance abuse patterns with the poorly motivated youth can be done if the concerned others are committed to the task (Manatt, 1979).

In considering intervention strategies with youth involved in substance use/abuse the initial question should be "Intervention into what?" That is, youth who are discovered to be using chemicals may be experimenting, using drugs for recreational purposes, self-medicating an intolerable home situation, or suffering from physiological addiction. Intervention strategies will vary depending upon the type of drug-taking pattern the young person manifests.

If a young person is experimenting with chemicals or using them for recreational purposes but is not self-medicating or addicted, *intelligent* education and viable alternatives that are less self-destructive and provide more positive reinforcement than drug use are probably the most efficacious methods of intervention available today. Intelligent education is stressed because what is truly known and unknown about the various substances of abuse need to be placed before the young person for his or her consideration. The generalization to youth of information derived from adults may be very inappropriate. For example, the physical effects of one standard dose of a drug (e.g., alcohol) may be quite different between adults and children, simply because of body size alone. Scare tactics should be avoided because they are unsuccessful in preventing persons from involving themselves in risk-taking behaviors and have been a dismal failure with youth. Young persons do not conceive of themselves as mortal but rather have a self-concept of permanence and invulnerability. Because youth have not developed highly abstract cognitive abilities, they are unable to conceive of long term negative drug effects applying to them personally. Likewise they have many peers involved in various aspects of drug use/abuse without turning into "stupid and/or raving monsters." If scare tactics are attempted one can generally anticipate that youth will discount that particular message and all others associated with it.

For the young person who is significantly involved in substance abuse through self-medication or addiction more organized/structured intervention measures may need to be employed.

The general orientation to intervention in chemical abuse for the addicted person usually follows a 4-phase treatment strategy. In phase 1, the individual is detoxified from the chemical to which addiction has occurred. This is typically a medical management issue and is a short-lived portion of intervention, usually 1–2 weeks. However, the protracted abstinence syndrome mentioned above should be remembered.

The second major rehabilitation phase is the abstinence period during which the major focus is to assist individuals in maintaining abstinence from the chemical upon which they have become dependent. During this abstinence phase, other elements of habilitation and rehabilitation may be addressed, but the major focus is towards assisting the person to structure life to avoid use of chemicals of abuse. For youth who may have minimal internal controls and/or lack a supportive environment that encourages abstinence, an inpatient program may be necessary.

The third major therapeutic stage is that of developing alternative coping skills. If a young person has become dependent on a particular mind-altering substance, then that individual must learn or relearn nonchemical ways of dealing with stressful conditions. After the person has progressed through the detoxification and abstinence stage, this development of

alternative coping skills is the major focus. During this phase, a significant task of "parenting" (education and effective disciplining for internalization of socially appropriate behavior and responses to social conditions) must be part of the intervention process.

The fourth and last stage of the habilitation/rehabilitation process focuses on interpersonal relations. If a youngster has become addicted to a given substance, parents and nonaddicted peers may have been alienated by either the antisocial behaviors mandatory for financial support of the addiction or the behavioral effects of the drugs. Consequently significant repair of those disrupted relationships needs to be effected. It is during this interpersonal relations phase that family therapy can be useful to identify cause-effect stress points in the home environment.

Treatment Strategies

The major mechanisms for achieving these four stages of the therapeutic habilitation/rehabilitation process are contained in Figure 36.1

Figure 36.1 demonstrates nine different intervention strategies that are useful in substance-abusing persons. The combination of three columns of Crisis Intervention, Therapeutic Community, and Pharmacological Intervention in combination with the three lines of Inpatient, Intermediate, and Outpatient constitute the nine strategies. Each will be discussed below.

Inpatient Crisis Intervention

Inpatient crisis intervention indicates that the individual will be in a facility for more than 24 hours to alleviate the crisis he or she has encountered with chemical use. If the youth has physically overdosed or is experiencing a severe, untoward psychological reaction to chemical use this inpatient crisis intervention strategy is best represented by a hospital emergency room or medical intensive care unit. Typically the inpatient crisis intervention is short term and oriented toward medical detoxification of the individual to eliminate the effects of the responsible chemical.

	Crisis Intervention	Therapeutic Community	Pharmacologic Intervention
Inpatient			
Intermediate			
Outpatient			

Figure 36.1. Intervention strategies in substance abuse.

Intermediate Care Crisis Intervention

This modality implies that the individual will be in a crisis intervention facility less than 24 hours. The individual is typically detoxifying from the acute effects of low or moderate doses of the chemical he or she has ingested and needs to "sleep it off." Medically supervised social detoxification facilities have been established in most metropolitan areas, so that persons have an alternative to expensive inpatient medical treatment or being housed in a criminal facility (e.g., "drunk tank").

Outpatient Crisis Intervention

This strategy suggests that the individual can be seen for a short period of time (typically 1–2 hours) while a negative reaction to a particular chemical is being resolved. This implies that the local physician or other health care professional can manage the untoward reaction in a brief period of time either through administration of a given antagonist or palliative medication or that the crisis is a panic reaction to substance use and the individual is simply "talked down" in a short period of time.

Inpatient Therapeutic Community

For young persons who are seriously addicted to or dependent upon various chemicals, it may be necessary to spend considerable time in some highly structured community setting in which availability of chemicals is controlled. Typically, youth who have developed only chemical-coping mechanisms are unable to remain abstinent from substances of abuse (perhaps due to the protracted abstinence syndrome) without a great deal of external structure. Usually, with inpatient therapeutic community settings, after the individual is detoxified she or he is placed in various therapeutic activities to rehabilitate and/or habilitate given physical and psychological aspects of his or her life. Usually in these facilities there are highly confrontive activities or therapies that are designed to circumvent denial defense mechanisms, promote verbal (rather than behavioral) catharsis of emotional states, and allow the young person to accept full personal responsibility for maladaptive behavior. Also, in inpatient therapeutic communities, there are other ancillary therapies that involve the nuclear family and the spouse if the person is married. Usually there are educational activities and facilities available. The thrust of therapeutic communities is to help the individual develop the internal ability to say "no" to the use of chemicals and begin exploration and development of other less self-destructive coping skills to deal with stress.

Intermediate Care Therapeutic Communities

Intermediate care therapeutic community settings are those in which the person spends either the day or night in a structured environment that provides support for non-drug-taking behavior and other more adaptive alternative behavioral mechanisms. For example, the youth may be able to attend school and abstain from drug consumptive behaviors, but in the evening that young person may use chemicals to "make it through the night" because peer pressure for drug use is intense or familial problems are overwhelming. The reverse may also be true. The young person may not be able to avoid drugs at school but can in the evening when in the support system of the family. The intermediate care therapeutic community is designed to address those vulnerable periods of a youngster's 24-hour life and to provide support for that vulnerable time.

Outpatient Therapeutic Community

In the outpatient therapeutic community, essentially a supportive environment is made available to the youngster whenever it is necessary. Typically, this is on a structured basis (e.g., Alcoholics Anonymous) where the youngster for a short period of time is surrounded by a non-drug-taking support environment. Usually coupled with this supportive environment is a "safety valve" mechanism by which the youngster at any time he or she feels the need for support can call a sponsor who will meet with the youth and offer assistance through a particular "at-risk" time.

Inpatient Chemical Blockade Programs

While most youth do not have chemical blockade programs available to them in the form of Antabuse programs for young alcoholics or methadone maintenance programs for narcotic addicts there are exceptions to that rule. Basically Antabuse is a chemical which prevents the breakdown of acetaldehyde (the first step in the metabolization of alcohol within the body). Consequently the individual suffers acetaldehyde reaction, which is uncomfortable. Signs of the reaction include flushing, perspiration, nausea, vomiting, chills, and other uncomfortable physiological events. An individual takes Antabuse until there is an effective blood Antabuse level (usually five days), and then, at any time in the future, if the person ingests alcohol that

person will suffer the negative consequences. Antabuse is not a cure for alcoholiosm; however, it does serve as a significant aid to allow the person to maintain abstinence.

Methadone is a synthetic narcotic addicting drug; however, it is long acting so that the individual need only ingest one dose of methadone a day and then be free from narcotic craving and dangers of narcotic withdrawal. Treatment programs which provide methadone maintenance for persons under the age of 18 must have special permission from appropriate federal authorities. For certain young persons who may be 15 years old and have a five-year history of narcotic addiction, methadone maintenance may be an appropriate treatment modality. Generally, methadone as well as Antabuse is administered on an inpatient basis for only enough time to insure there are no untoward reactions to the drug and there is an appropriate blood level obtained. At that point the person is transferred to one of the following programs.

Intermediate Care Chemical Blockade

If chemical blockade is used, it is most efficacious to combine it with either an inpatient therapeutic community or intermediate care therapeutic community so the youngster begins to develop other more adaptive mechanisms for dealing with stresses and maturation phases than consumption of illegal chemicals.

Outpatient Chemical Blockade

In outpatient chemical blockade programs individuals who are on some chemical blockade program typically see a counselor weekly to alter the patients' maladaptive behavior patterns while maintaining abstinence from drugs of abuse.

It should be noted that on chemical blockade programs there is nothing curative in the chemicals used; however, they provide significant assurance of abstinence from substances of abuse during the initial phases of treatment.

Intervention References

In each of the 50 states, there is a Single State Authority (SSA) for alcohol and drug use.

Sometimes this is one office of substance abuse and in some states there are two separate structures. The SSA is responsible for certification of adequacy and, therefore, can be consulted about effective treatment programs.

A new publication on Guidelines to Effective Youth Alcoholism Treatment Programs should be available from the National Center for Alcohol Education (NCAE, 1981) in 1983.

APPENDIX

Definitions of Words and Terms Related to Drugs

Abscess Infection from needle

Acid LSD, purple double domes, orange swirls, wedges, quicksilver, white lightning

Acid head One who takes acid (LSD)

Angel dust Phencyclidine

Bad trip An unpleasant experience, usually used in the context of an unpleasant psychedelic experience

Bag A packet of a drug, as a nickel bag ($5); a special ability or lifestyle, as, "That's his bag"

Beans Benzedrine tablets—an amphetamine

Benny Benzedrine tablet

Blast, blasted A sudden strong reaction to injected drugs; to be drugged

Blotter Type of LSD on blotter paper. Also known as paper acid

Blow your mind Frenzied or excited state of mind, sometimes caused by drugs

Bong A smoking device to concentrate effects of marijuana

Bread Money

Bring down To cause loss of intoxicated, drugged state; also to cause depression

Bummer Bad trip

Burn, burned To cheat or to be cheated in a drug transaction

Bust Arrest. It is the act of being apprehended, arrested, or discovered by authorities

Cap A capsule containing a drug

Cat A man

Chick A girl

Chipping Occasional using of drugs

Clean Not having drugs on person. Also to remove seeds and stems from marijuana

Clip A device to hold a marijuana cigarette butt

Coke Cocaine

Cold turkey To stop using drugs abruptly without the aid of any medication

Color trip LSD experience where major psychedelic effect is distortion of colors

Come down Slowly to lose effects of drugs

Connection Person from whom drugs are obtained

Contact A drug peddler, a connection

Contact high An altered state of consciousness obtained by being in contact with someone who is high or something that reminds one of the drugged state, e.g. an addict's personal injection paraphernalia

Cook, cooker To heat drug powder with water; the device for doing so, as a bent-handled spoon or a bottle cap

Cool Good, okay

Cop To buy drugs

Crash Sometimes to come down off a drug, usually to go to sleep

Crash pad Place; apartment

Crosses Amphetamine drug, a benzedrine tablet

Crystal Methamphetamine

Cut Any drug that has been adulterated with any substance, such as marijuana with alfalfa

Dealing Selling drugs

Dig Listen, understand

Dime $10 quantity of a drug

DMT Sometimes called the businessman's psychedelic because its effects last only fifteen to thirty minutes. Its effects are similar to those of LSD, being perhaps a little more intense. A relatively rare drug

Doing Using, as in "doing grass"; also, "doing your own thing"

Dope Any drug

Doper Any user

Downers Central nervous system depressants. (e.g. barbiturates)

Drop To take a drug by swallowing it

Dynamite Good quality, as in "dynamite grass"

Establishment Any form of organization, government, or ordered way of life at which "users" aim frustration

Far out Extraordinary

Fat Having a good supply of drugs

Fit   A hypo syringe. A kit for giving an injection

Fix   To inject narcotics; also a single injection of heroin

Flash   The sudden onset of euphoria just after injecting a drug; also, to throw up after injecting drugs

Flying   Under the influence of drugs

Freak, to freak (verb)   To become frightened, frenzied, paranoid or insecure

Freak (noun)   A person—a long-haired person or a drug user obsessed with a drug or scene

Free trip   A recurrence of a drug reaction without using the drug again

Fucked up   Very high or very stoned

Funky   Weird, good weird or bad weird

Fuzz   Police

Ganja   A high grade of marijuana

Goof balls   Mixture of barbiturates and amphetamines

Grass   Marijuana

Groovy   A good thing

Guide   One who stays nontoxic in order to supervise the LSD trip of another

H   Heroin

Habit   Addiction; also, amount of addiction, as, "an eight-bag habit"

Hang loose   Relax

Hash   Hashish, a concentrated derivative of marijuana

Hash oil   A marijuana extract with very high THC content

Hassle   A difficult situation, trouble

Head   A drug user

Heat   Police (cf. fuzz)

Heavy   A serious or intellectual conversation, situation

High   Drug-induced exhilaration

Hit   The act of injecting a drug, or to take a puff of marijuana

Hog   PCP

Holding   Having drugs on person

Hustling   Stealing, prostitution, or using other illicit means to obtain money for drugs

Hype   One who injects drugs intravenously

Into   Using, as to be into pot; also, involved, as, into music

Joint   A marijuana cigarette

Juice, juicer   Alcoholic beverage; a drinker

Junk   Heroin

Kick (the habit)   To stop using drugs

Kilo (kee, key)   A kilogram (2.2 pounds) of a drug sold in bulk lots

Krystal   Phencyclidine (note: must distinguish from *crystal* which is methamphetamine)

Lid   A 10–15 dollar quantity of marijuana, usually about an ounce or less

Loaded   Full of drugs

Ludes   Methaqualone

Magic mushroom   The Mexican mushroom containing psilocybin

Mainline   To inject drugs I.V.

Man, the   Person in authority. Also a drug dealer

Manicure   To prepare marijuana for use in cigarettes by removing stems and seeds

Marijuana   Grass, pot, weed, stick, reefers, Mary Jane

Mellow yellow   Dried banana skins for smoking labeled "The Great Banana Hoax" by California medical researchers, as the substance has no hallucinogenic properties

Methedrine, meth   An amphetamine, speed

Mike   A microgram

Narc, narco, nark   A narcotics law enforcement agent. The word is sometimes used to belittle in a most uncomplimentary way

Nickle bag   A 5-dollar quantity of drug

Nod, nodding, on the nod   The stuporous, lethargic state with lolling head following opiates injection

O.D.   Overdose

Orange sunshine   LSD which produces a color trip

"Out of sight"   Extraordinary, really great

Outfit   Paraphernalia for injecting drugs, including a needle, syringe, cooker, etc.

Pacalolo   A very expensive, high-THC-content marijuana cultured in Hawaii

PDR   Physician's Desk Reference

Pep   Amphetamines

Point   A needle for giving injections

Pop   To inject subcutaneously (cf. skin pop); also, to swallow, as pop a pill

Pot   Marijuana

Purple haze   Type of LSD

Pusher   Person who sells drugs, dope peddler

Rapping, rapping down   Helping a person off a bad trip by talking him down. *Rapping* means to talk

Reds   Also *Redbirds*: Seconal (a barbiturate)

Reefer Marijuana cigarette

Rig A kit for injecting drugs

Roach The butt of a marijuana cigarette, said to contain a high concentration of the drug

Roach holder A device (often alligator clip or hemostat) used to hold marijuana cigarette butt. A roach clip

Rush The sensation of becoming progressively more stoned, of feeling the drug effects mounting noticeably. Usually rapid onset

Score To get drugs

Script A drug prescription

Sherman A cigarette (marijuana or otherwise) sprayed with PCP

Shoot up To inject a drug into one's veins

Sinsemilla A high-THC-content marijuana from Northern California

Skin pop To inject drugs subcutaneously

Smack Heroin

Snow Cocaine

Sopers Methaqualone

Spaced Stoned, high

Spaced out In a mind-altered state; high; also, extended to mean dazed, sick from excessive drug use

Speed An amphetamine

Speed freak One who regularly takes speed

Speedball A mixture of an upper and a downer, such as methadrine and heroin

Spike A hypodermic needle

Split To leave, go, as, "let's split"

Square A nonuser of drugs

Straight A person who doesn't use drugs or is establishment, also not under influence of, honest

Stash A place to conceal dope

Stoned Under the influence of drugs

Strawberries LSD + strychnine

Strung out To be out of drugs and craving them; also, to be sick from excessive use of a drug (cf. *spaced out*)

Talking down The act of helping a person off a bummer by talking to him

Toke Draw on a joint, puff

Toke up To smoke marijuana; to light a marijuana cigarette

Tracks Needle scars

Trip Experiencing the effects of a psychedelic, or to take a psychedelic. (also a way or philosophy of life)

Turn on To use drugs; also, to be under the influence of drugs, turned on; also, to produce any pleasure, as, "that song turns me on"

Uppers Speed, amphetamines

Uptight Hyper, angry, or agitated person

Vibes Vibrations; feeling one gets from any situation, place, person, karma

Weed Marijuana

Weekend habit An occasional use of drugs

Windowpane Type of LSD

Wired This word usually means speeding or a user who has taken a stimulant

Works The paraphernalia for injecting drugs (cf. outfit)

Yellows Nembutal. A barbiturate. Also called yellow jackets

Zonked Highly intoxicated by a drug

REFERENCES

ADAMHA. High school seniors' use of 9 drugs, 1975–1980. *ADAMHA NEWS,* 1981, **7**(5), p. 5.

Aronow, R., & Done, A.K. Phencyclidine overdose: An emerging concept of management. *Journal of the American College of Emergency Physicians,* 1978, **7**(2), 56–59.

Barnes, G.M. Development of adolescent drinking behavior: An evaluative review of the impact of the socialization process within the family. *Adolescence,* 1977, **12**(48), 571–591.

Braxton, E.R. *Alcohol and delinquency: Is there a bond?* Brookline, Me.: Brookline Health Department, Alcohol and Drug Program, 1978.

Brisbane, F. Causes and consequences of alcohol use among black youth. *Journal of Afro-American Issues,* 1976, **4**(2), 241–254.

Byrne, J.T., & Price, J.H. In sickness and in health: The effects of religion. *Health Education,* 1979, **10**(1), 6–10.

Cohen, S. Flashbacks. *Drug Abuse and Alcoholism Newsletter,* Vista Hill Foundation, 1977, **6**(9).

Cohen, S. Amyl nitrite rediscovered. *Drug Abuse and Alcoholism Newsletter,* Vista Hill Foundation, 1978, **7**(1). (a)

Cohen, S. PCP (Angeldust): New trends in treatment. *Drug Abuse and Alcoholism Newsletter,* Vista Hill Foundation, 1978, **7**(6). (b)

Cohen, S. Marijuana: A new ballgame: *Drug Abuse and Alcoholism Newsletter,* Vista Hill Foundation, 1979, **8**(4).

Cohen, S. Coca paste and freebase: New fashion in cocaine use. *Drug Abuse and Alcoholism Newsletter,* Vista Hill Foundation, 1980, **9**(3). (a)

Cohen, S. Cannabis: Impact on motivation, Part I. *Drug Abuse and Alcoholism Newsletter,* Vista Hill Foundation, 1980, **9**(10). (b)

Cohen, S. Cannabis: Impact on motivation, Part I. *Drug Abuse and Alcoholism Newsletter,* Vista Hill Foundation, 1981, **10**(1).

Cotten, N.S. Familial incidence of alcoholism: A review. *Journal of Studies on Alcohol,* 1979, **40,** 89–116.

Cutter, H.S.G., Jones, W.C., & Maloof, B.A. Pain is a joint function of alcohol intake and customary reasons for drinking. *International Journal of the Addictions,* 1979, **14,** 173–182.

Davis, V.E. Neuroamine-derived alkaloids: A possible common denominator in alcoholism and related drug dependencies. *Annals of the New York Academy of Science,* 1973, **215,** 111–115.

Desmond, M.M., Schwanecke, R.P., Wilson, G.S., Yasunga, S., & Burgdorff, I. Maternal barbiturate utilization and neonatal withdrawal symptomatology. *Journal of Pediatrics,* 1972, **80**(2), 190–197.

Dorland's illustrated medical dictionary. Philadelphia: Saunders, 1965.

Ewing, J.A. Biopsychosocial look at drinking and alcoholism. *Journal of the American College Health Association,* 1977, **25**(3), 204–208.

Filmore, K.M., Bacon, S.O., & Hyman, M. *The 27-year-longitudinal panel study of drinking by students in college, 1949–1976. Final report to NIAAA, 1979* [Contract no. (ADM) 281-76-0015].

Finnegan, L. (Ed.). *Drug dependence in pregnancy: Clinical management of mother and child* [NIDA Services Research Monograph Series, DHEW Publication No. (ADM) 79-678], 1979.

Freedman, A.M., Kaplan, H.I., & Sadlock, B.J. *Modern synopsis of the comprehensive textbook of psychiatry* (Vol. II). Baltimore: Williams & Wilkins, 1976.

Gilman, A.G., Goodman, L.S., & Gilman, A. *Goodman and Gilman's: The pharmacological basis of therapeutics* (6th ed.). New York: Macmillan, 1980.

Goodman, L.S., & Gilman, A. *The pharmacological basis of therapeutics* (5th ed.). New York: Macmillan, 1975.

Goodwin, D. *Is alcoholism hereditary?* New York: Oxford University Press, 1976.

Gross, W.F., & Carpenter, L.L. Alcoholic personality: Reality or fiction? In D.A. Ward (Ed.), *Alcoholism introduction to theory and treatment.* Dubuque, Iowa: Kendall/Hunt, 1980.

Hect, A. Inhalants: Quick route to danger. *FDA Consumer* (Order No. 1980-311-254/72). Washington, D.C.: U.S. Government Printing Office, May, 1980.

Hollister, L.E. Benzodiazepines 1980: Current update. A look at the issues. *Psychosomatics,* 1980, Supplement to Vol. **21**(10).

Jacobson, G.R., VanDyke, A., & Steinbach, T.G. Field dependence among male and female alcoholics: II norms for the rod-and-frame test. *Journal of Perceptual Motor Skills,* 1976, **43,** 399–402.

Jarvik, M.E., Cullen, J.W., Gritz, E.R., Vogt, T.M., & West, L.J. *Research on smoking behavior* (NIDA Research Monograph Series No. 17, No. 017-024-00694-7), 1977.

Jellinek, E.M. *The disease concept of alcoholism.* New Brunswick, N.J.: Hillhouse, 1960.

Jeri, F.R., Sanchez, C.C., del Pozo, T., Fernandez, M., & Carbajal, C. Further experience with the syndrome provided by coca paste smoking. *Bulletin on Narcotics,* 1978, **30**(3), 1–11.

Jones, R.T., & Benowitz, N. The 30-day trip—Clinical studies of cannabis tolerance and dependence. In Baude, M.C. & Szara, S. (Eds.), *Pharmacology of marijuana.* New York: Raven, 1976, pp. 627–642.

Khantzian, E.J. An ego/self theory of substance dependence. A contemporary psychoanalytic perspective. In D.J. Lettier, M. Sayers, & H.W. Pearson (Eds.), *Theories on drug abuse* (NIDA Research Monograph 30, No. ADM 80-967), 1980, pp. 29–33.

Kissin, B. Alcoholism and drug dependence. In R.L. Simons & H. Pardes (Eds.), *Understanding human behavior in health and illness.* Baltimore: Williams & Wilkins, 1977.

Krasnegor, N.A. *Behavioral tolerance: Research and treatment implications* (NIDA Research Monograph 18, No. 017-024-00699-8), 1978.

Lettieri, D.J., Sayers, M., & Pearson, H.W. *Theories on drug abuse.* (NIDA Research Monograph 30, No. ADM 80-967), 1980.

MacMahon, B., Yen, S., Trichopoulos, D., Warren, K., & Nardi, G. Coffee and cancer of the pancreas. *The New England Journal of*

Medicine, 1981, **304**(11), 630–633.

Manatt, M. *Parents, peers and pot.* [DHEW Publication No. (ADM) 79–812]. 1979.

Mandell, W., & Ginzberg, A. Youthful alcohol use, abuse and alcoholism. In B. Kissin & H. Begleiter (Eds.), *Social Aspects of Alcoholism.* New York: Plenum, 1976.

Margules, R., Kessler, R.C., & Kandel, D.B. Longitudinal study of onset of drinking among high school students. *Journal of Studies on Alcohol,* 1977, **38**(5), 897–912.

Marin, P., & Cohen, A.Y. *Understanding drug use: An adults' guide to drugs and the young.* New York: Harper & Row, 1971.

Martin, W.R., & Jasinski, D.R. Physiological parameters of morphine dependence in man— tolerance, early abstinence, protracted abstinence, *Journal of Psychiatric Research,* 1969, **7**, 9–17.

McGlothin, W.H., & West, L.J. The marijuana problem: An overview. *American Journal of Psychiatry,* 1968, **125**, 1126–1134.

Modrow, H.E., Holloway, F.A., Christensen, H.D., & Carney, J.M. Relationship between caffeine discrimination and caffeine plasma levels. Submitted to *Pharmacology, Biochemistry and Behavior,* 1981.

National Center for Alcohol Education. *Spirits of America.* Westfield, Ma.: Film Tech., Inc., 1977. (Film)

National survey on drug abuse: 1977. Volume I, main findings. (DHEW Publication No. (ADM) 78–618), 1977.

NIDA, *Pharmacological and toxicological perspectives of commonly abused drugs* [Medical Monograph Series, **1**(5)]. 1979. (a)

NIDA, *The primary physician's guide to drug abuse treatment* [Medical Monograph Series, **1** (7)]. 1979. (b)

NIDA, *Frequently prescribed and abused drugs* [Medical Monograph Series, **2**, (1)]. 1980.

Noble, E.P. *Third special report to the U.S. Congress on alcohol and health.* (No. 017-024-00892-3). 1978.

Peck, C.W. Wirth, Whiskey and WASP's: Some consequences of community size for alcohol use. *Sociology Quarterly,* 1977, **18**, 209–222.

Peterson, R.C. (Ed.), *Marijuana research findings 1980* (NIDA Research Monograph No. 31). 1980.

Platt, J.J. "Addiction proneness" and personality in heroin addicts. *Journal of Abnormal Psychology,* 1975, **84**(3), 303–306.

Pollin, W. *Marijuana and health* (Eighth annual report to the U.S. Congress). DHEW No. ADM 80-945. 1980.

Postotinik, P. Drugs and pregnancy. *FDA Consumer,* (No. 1979-281-27216). 1978.

Roman, P.M. Possible effects of using alcohol to control distress: A reanalysis of Pearlin and Radabaugh's data. *American Journal of Sociology,* 1978, **83**, 987–991.

Schuckit, M.A., & Ralyses, V. Ethanol ingestion: Differences in blood acetaldehyde concentrations in relatives of alcoholics and controls. *Science,* 1979, **203**, 54–55.

Smith, D.E., & Gay, G. *"It's so good, don't even try it once": Heroin in perspective.* Englewood Cliffs, N.J.: Prentice-Hall, 1972.

Smith, D.E., Wesson, D.R., Buxton, M.E., Seymour, R., & Kramer, H.M. The diagnosis and treatment of the PCP abuse syndrome. In R.C. Peterson & R.C. Stillman (Eds.), *Phencyclidine (PCP) abuse: An appraisal.* (Research Monograph No. 21). 1978, 229–240.

Steyton, S.E., & Diener, R.G. Personality characteristics of juvenile heroin users. *International Journal of the Addictions,* 1979, **14**(4), 585–587.

Tashkin, D.P., Calverese, B., & Simmons, M. Respiratory status of 75 chronic marijuana smokers: Comparison with matched controls. *American Review of Respiratory Disease,* 1978, **117** (No. 4-Part 2), 261.

Ward, D.A. *Alcoholism: Introduction to theory and treatment.* Dubuque, Iowa: Kendall Hunt, 1980.

Wikler, A. Dynamics of drug dependence. *Archive of General Psychiatry,* 1973, **28**, 611.

CHAPTER 37

Delinquency and Criminal Behavior

WILLIAM JAMES SHAW

Juvenile delinquency is defined as illegal behavior committed by a minor. Although this definition is a rather simple one, the tremendous volume of literature that exists on delinquency and the many disciplines that have contributed to this body of literature, including criminology, law, sociology, and psychology, indicate that the issue itself is complex.

Delinquent behavior is a relative concept: it has meaning only in relation to the laws that apply to a given population at a specific point in time. This makes discussion of the incidence of delinquency virtually meaningless since those things that define a behavior as delinquent can vary from time to time, culture to culture, and even state to state (Lunden, 1964). The most accurate statistics are compiled by agencies that can control for the variations in legislation and criminal justice practices. Therefore, the reader wishing such data is referred to the annual reports published by the United States Department of Justice and state and local law enforcement agencies.

As Cressey (1960) pointed out, the most precise study of delinquency and criminal behavior is drawn from the psychological and sociological literature. The President's Commission on Law Enforcement and Administration of Justice (1967) correctly noted that the complexities of human psychology are such that any attempt to find the cause of crime in human motivation alone is pointless. Sobel (1979) expressed a similar view relative to the inadequacies of traditional theories of personality development and the understanding of the delinquent offender. The sociolog-

ical literature on delinquency is vast but lacks sufficient depth by itself to explain the etiology of particular delinquent patterns or to spell out the steps necessary to control or correct these patterns.

So, to provide as complete a report as possible of the contemporary views on delinquency, this chapter will review some of the significant work in both the sociological and psychological fields. In addition, the efforts of scholars and clinicians to integrate the most promising work will be presented.

THEORIES OF DELINQUENCY

A vast amount of research and writing has been done on the subject of juvenile delinquency. Much of the work has attempted to locate a single factor that would account for delinquency. However, today most experts in the field believe in multiple causation, that is, the probability that, in any particular case, a combination of factors is responsible for delinquent behavior. Furthermore, three spheres of influence are seen as playing a major part in the development of personality and behavioral patterns, including delinquency. These spheres of influence are home and family, peer group and community, and psychological and biological factors.

The Influence of Home and Family

Glueck and Glueck (1950) reported that the influence of the home and the family far outweigh cultural or socioeconomic influences in the development of delinquent behavior. These respected investigators felt that an inadequate home life was a major contributor to delinquency, increasing the chances that a child would become delinquent to 98 out of 100. They believed that a child in a good home had only 3 chances in 100 of becoming delinquent. Homes judged as inadequate were those where separation and/or divorce had occurred; those where parents demonstrated a consistent avoidance of responsibility; those in which criminal history, significant health problems, or alcohol abuse were noted. The parents were seen as hostile or, at best, indifferent to their children. Discipline was erratic, ranging from none at all to extreme physical punishment. Clearly, Glueck and Glueck were focusing on the poor modeling that failed to provide the children with correct social discrimination.

The influence of the family was also examined in reports by Powers and Witmer (1951) and McCord and McCord (1958). Reporting on the longitudinal Cambridge-Somerville Youth Study, these authors identified a dual process of rejection of the child by one parent (usually the mother) in the presence of criminal modeling by the other parent (usually the father). This process was seen as facilitating the development by the child of aggressive behavior that is directed into criminal activity during adolescence and young adulthood.

An especially sobering realization drawn from this work is that delinquency and criminal behavior do not begin suddenly in adolescence. They are acquired at an early age and maintained through the pervasive and substantial influence of the parents.

Further evidence of parental influence in the development of delinquency has been reported by Shaw and McKay (1929), Merrill (1947), Johnson and Szurek (1952), and Bandura and Walters (1959). These authors have given special attention to the tendency of children to imitate undesirable, dissocial behavior of the parents. The work by Johnson and Szurek is interesting because it points to the evolution of delinquent behavior in a child who may, in fact, be acting out the hidden antisocial tendencies of the parent. This proc-

ess will be discussed later in conjunction with psychodynamic theories of delinquency.

Toman (1969) reported several studies that showed a relatively high percentage of delinquents who have experienced the early loss of a close family member or who grew up in fatherless homes. In the studies reported, it was found that more severe crimes were committed by persons whose early loss was more severe, as judged by criteria such as recency, age, family size, availability of a substitute for the lost member, the ratio of male to female family members and the number and severity of all losses sustained. Other studies have also discussed the relationship between family loss and delinquency (Bowlby, 1951; Earle & Earle, 1961).

Toby (1967) reported on two separate mechanisms that have been suggested to account for the relationship between parental inadequacy and juvenile delinquency. First, the developing personality of the child is impaired by parental rejection and neglect. The child becomes poorly socialized and lacks impulse control. As a result, the child reacts violently to trivial provocation and the behavior of the child lacks purpose. The second mechanism also begins with parental inadequacy and neglect. The parents absolve themselves of control of the family and direct the child away from the family, toward the peer group. Then the family and the peer group become competitors for the allegiance of the child. If the peer group is delinquent, the child's need for acceptance forces him or her also to engage in delinquent activities.

Many of the psychological theores are also concerned with the influence of the family. Consequently, more about these families interactions will be discussed in the section on psychological theories of delinquency.

The Influence of the Community

There is, indeed, quite a volume of literature dealing with the impact of the community on a child or adolescent. As one might expect, sociology and social psychology have been the disciplines from which most of the work has emerged.

The school is an important community influence in the etiology and maintenance of delinquency (Hunt & Hardt, 1965; Silverberg & Silverberg, 1971). Truancy is probably the most obvious and common school-related behavior demonstrated by delinquents. A disproportionately high number of delinquents are poor readers, inattentive, impulsive, and concrete in their thinking. Although these conditions correlate with delinquency, they do not seem to play a causative role.

Many experts believe that negative experiences in school may lead youth to follow delinquent styles. School is seen as a source of frustration, a constant embarrassment to children or adolescents who are unable or unwilling to succeed (Schafer & Polk, 1967, pp. 222–227). Yochelson and Samenow (1976) identified a significant role played by the school in the evolution of delinquent and criminal patterns. They noted a tendency for the delinquent child to develop deviant behavior patterns at approximately 10 years of age although these behaviors may not be serious violations of school rules. The child is seen as sneaky, attention seeking, disobedient, and, at best, marginal in his or her adjustment to school. The adjustment deteriorates through junior and senior high school. The description by Yochelson and Samenow offers a view of a child who is self-centered, uninterested in scholastic activities, sensation seeking, and resistant to external authority. For such children, school is merely the arena and their friends the facilitators for their adventures. Both of these elements, school and friends, are important in the evolution of the criminal patterns.

The community influence on the evolution of delinquency most often involves the neighborhood, specifically the role of socioeconomic class and the relative impact of the slum and inner city. In fact, for years, the standard explanations and discussions of delinquency focused on the impact of overcrowding, poverty, and substandard housing (Shaw, 1938; Block & Flynn, 1956). Dilapidated settings where employment is low and crime is high provide settings in which a variety of delinquent activities can occur. Shaw pointed out the importance of the social disorganization that pervades slum areas. The diversity leads to variations in social norms and codes of conduct. Little control exists, and expediency is the norm. The sociological theories of human ecology are based on the study of the spatial relations that exist between organisms and their environment, thus illustrating that this particular influence represents an important subject of study by itself.

Law enforcement agents are an important community influence. Their role in the prevention and control of criminal activity is obvious. However, some authorities in the field of criminology believe that criminal and delinquent behavior may actually be reinforced by apprehension, arrest, and confinement. It has been further suggested that the criminal justice process actually serves as a catalyst for budding delinquent careers (Tannenbaum, 1938; Cloward & Ohlin, 1960; Becker, 1963). Little has been done fully to study these hypotheses relative to the juvenile offender. The need for research in this area is significant. Perhaps the most obvious should be stressed. A child or adolescent comes to see himself or herself as delinquent because someone has determined his or her behavior to be criminal. Such an identification almost always begins with apprehension by the police. It is possible that such encounters, if frequent, may not only increase the youth's hostility toward the police but may desensitize him or her to the sanctions of the criminal justice system (Piliavin & Briar, 1964).

Crime and delinquency are not limited to one class in society. Miller (1958) reported on gang delinquency as a function of the lower class. Miller sees certain realities existing in the lower classes that contribute to the violation of legal and social standards. First, certain basic, common practices found in lower classes are automatically violations of certain laws. These practices often allow a person to achieve or acquire something desirable quicker and more easily than more lawful means, even when the lawful means are readily available. Finally, some situations occur regularly in lower class neighborhoods. There are specific ways of responding to such situations that are not merely accepted—they are required. Since the law does not address solutions to such situations in ways that are accepted by the lower class, these required responses are usually illegal.

While the presence of crime and delinquency in the lower class is clear, Vaz (1967) specifically addressed the problem of delinquency in the middle class. A fundamental point is stressed: as long as delinquency remains faithful to the values of a particular class, it will tend to advance the social status of the child or adolescent and will become more firmly rooted in the individual and in that level of society. Similar theories have been offered by Clark and Wenninger (1962), Erickson and Empey (1965), and Polk (1967, Appendix R, pp. 343–347). Of particular note is the work by Erickson and Empey.

Erickson and Empey found strong indications that the degree of commitment to peers may vary from class to class and may be more predictive of delinquency than social class alone. The evidence in their study pointed to middle class youth as having the strongest commitment to peers followed by the lower class and, finally, by the upper class, which is the least committed to peer groups. The question of whether this peer group influence is more critical than social class certainly warrants further study.

Delinquents are often thought to have adopted deviant standards of a nondominant portion of society and not to have learned the rules or values of the dominant society. Sykes and Matza (1957) have proposed an alternative process whereby the person becomes delinquent by first learning the moral implications of a particular act according to the standards of the dominant society. However, the delinquent learns to neutralize the moral implications of the act. While social class may play a role, the key in this explanation is that no moral imperative at all is felt, rather than a moral imperative of a deviant culture.

A significant sociological concept dealing with the norms, or lack of norms, in the prevailing culture is called "anomie" (Durkheim, 1951; Merton, 1957; Cloward, 1959; Cohen, 1965). The theory is based on the interaction between the norms that exist in a society and the goals to which the society encourages its youth to aspire. The key element is the opportunity that the society offers its youth to accomplish these goals. A basic issue in the theory is that some social systems exert pressure on certain members to engage in deviant behavior. This occurs when the society prescribes certain goals or aspirations for its members but fails to support the prescribed means for reaching these goals. Those aspiring to the goals, generally the youth of the society, will identify the most efficient means of reaching these goals and, whether legal or not, these means will be followed. The social structure becomes unsteady as a result of the failure by society to provide its members with legal means to achieve the goals that the society itself values. This basic flaw in a society encourages and maintains delinquent and criminal behavior.

Finally, a theory advanced by Sutherland (1939) has received a great deal of attention and support. His differential association theory is essentially a learning model which incorporates genetic and sociological elements. Sutherland believed it would explain all criminal patterns of behavior. Subsequent work has yielded mixed results. Essentially, Sutherland believed that delinquency developed as a result of an excess of attitudes and definitions favoring violation of the law over attitudes and definitions favoring compliance with the law (Sutherland & Cressey, 1966). The basic theory has been revised by a variety of students in sociology and criminology including Glaser (1956) and Burgess and Akers (1966). These revisions were intended to focus more on the process by which delinquent models are selected and to incorporate established learning principles. In many ways these attempts have helped sociology use the theory of differential association to clarify how individual delinquent patterns emerge as well as those patterns that are descriptive of group behavior. Furthermore, this theory has helped pull the sociological and psychological perspectives more closely together, especially in those formulations based on learning theory.

To help the reader understand Sutherland's theory of differential association and its application by modern writers, the nine basic propositions that Sutherland used to express his theory will be presented, each followed by the reformulation of his theory as offered by Burgess and Akers (1966). Sutherland's first proposition can be best understood by combining it with his eighth proposition. Sutherland stated that, first, criminal behavior is a learned behavior. He then stated that the process through which criminal behavior is learned involves association with criminal and noncriminal patterns of behavior and that it involves all of the mechanisms that are involved in any other learning. Burgess and Akers incorporated these two propositions into their reformulated statement that "criminal behavior is learned according to the principles of operant conditioning" (p. 137).

Sutherland's second proposition essentially stated that criminal behavior is learned through interactions and communication with other persons. Burgess and Akers reformulated this position to state that "criminal behavior is learned both in non-social situations that are reinforcing or discriminative and through that social interaction in which the behavior of other persons is reinforcing or discriminative for criminal behavior" (p. 139).

Sutherland's third proposition emphasized the importance of intimate personal groups as the vehicle through which the principle part of the learning of criminal behavior occurs. In the reformulation, Burgess and Akers stated that "the principal part of the learning of criminal behavior occurs within those groups which comprise the individual's major source of reinforcements" (p. 140).

Sutherland noted, through his fourth proposition, that the learning of criminal behavior requires that the individual learn, first, the techniques of committing the crime, which may be complicated or simple and, second, the specific direction of criminal motives, drives, rationalizations, and attitudes. The reformulation of this proposition according to reinforcement theory is as follows: "The learning of criminal behavior, including specific techniques, attitudes, and avoidance procedures, is a function of the effective and available reinforcers, and the existing reinforcement contingencies" (p. 141).

In his fifth proposition, Sutherland stated that the direction of motives and drives was learned as a result of legal codes being defined as favorable or unfavorable to the individual or group. Burgess and Akers restated the proposition: "The specific class of behaviors which are learned and their frequency of occurrence are a function of the reinforcers which are effective and available, and the rules or norms to which these reinforcers are applied" (p. 142).

Proposition six is generally seen as the crux of Sutherland's differential association theory. It reads: "A person becomes delinquent because of an excess of definitions favorable to violation of the law over definitions unfavorable to violation of the law" (Sutherland & Cressey, 1966, p. 78). In their reformulation of this statement, Burgess and Akers state: "Criminal behavior is a function of norms which are discriminative for criminal behavior, the learning of which takes place when such behavior is more highly reinforced than non-criminal behavior" (pp. 143–144).

Proposition seven stated that these differential associations may vary considerably in their frequency, duration, priority, and intensity. Burgess and Akers apply reinforcement theory to reformulate the proposition as: "The strength of criminal behavior is a direct function of the amount, frequency, and probability of its reinforcement" (p. 144).

Sutherland's last proposition acknowledged that criminal behavior may be an expression of general needs and values. However, Sutherland stated that criminal behavior cannot be explained by those general needs and values since the same needs and values can be expressed through noncriminal behavior. Since this proposition deals essentially with the contingencies of reinforcement for criminal behavior that have been handled throughout their reformulations, Burgess and Akers omitted this final proposition from their reformulation of Sutherland's theory.

In their reformulation, Burgess and Akers intended to apply current reinforcement theory to the important ideas advanced by Sutherland in a sociological context. Burgess and Akers felt that it was important to operationalize Sutherland's theory so that it could be subjected to research and examination. Furthermore, they felt that Sutherland addressed two important questions: first, how an individual becomes delinquent, and, second, what sustains the delinquent. Burgess and Akers hoped to emphasize the importance of a third question, namely, what sustains the pattern of delinquent behavior and what contingencies serve as reinforcement.

Biological and Psychological Influences

During the middle ages, demonic possession was the explanation offered most frequently for delinquent and criminal behavior (Lowry, 1944). In the early twentieth century, hereditary "moral insanity" was held forth as the most widely accepted theory (Tredgold, 1915). Lombroso (1911) advanced a theory that criminals had certain physical characteristics that distinguished them from noncriminals. It was believed that these physical characteristics were indicative of a criminal predisposition. The notion of inherited predisposition as indicated by physical appearance has been considered by many to be firmly established (Sheldon, 1949; Glueck & Glueck, 1956; Bandura & Walters, 1963; Gibbens, 1963). The classic studies of the Jukes (Dugdale, 1877) and Kallikaks (Goddard, 1912) also had a profound impact on the possibility of a link between heredity and crime. Another major authority in the field of delinquent behavior, William Healy (1934), studied 1,000 delinquents and found no relation between inheritance and delinquency. Many other studies have examined this question and have concluded that criminality is not inherited. However, if a person's behavior appears to be consistently deviant and poorly controlled,

the disposition to engage in delinquent and criminal activities seems to be greater than among those individuals whose behavior is more controlled and in conformity with social standards (Healy, 1915; Glueck, 1918; Healy & Bronner, 1926, 1939).

Lange (1931) conducted twin studies to examine the question of heredity. As might be expected, Lange found that of thirteen identical twins who had been imprisoned, ten of their identical siblings also had been in prison, although the children had been raised apart.

Burt (1925) studied groups of delinquents and nondelinquents and concluded that heredity had little to do with the genesis of criminal behavior. The most significant developments were, in his view, rooted in the family.

A good summary of the work in this area is provided by Scott (1971). Scott's conclusion is notable. It is relatively simple to exaggerate the importance of certain physical conditions once delinquency has developed. The cause-and-effect relationship, however, is not evident.

A well-known theory of criminality is that of the XYY chromosomal structure (Stock, 1968). Although the theory of an extra Y chromosome generated a good deal of speculation and controversy, research has thus far not been able to establish a significant causative relationship between the extra Y chromosome and the criminal behavior.

Research into possible connections between biological-physiological development and delinquency has continued. Extreme variations in rates of maturation have been found, with delinquents developing more rapidly (Healy & Bronner, 1936; MacFarlane, Allen, & Honzik, 1954) as well as less rapidly (Neumeyer, 1949) than nondelinquents.

Studies have also shown evidence of EEG abnormalities (Hill & Watterson, 1942; Grey, 1953). Other researchers (East, 1942; Levy, 1959; McCord & McCord, 1959; Pygott & Street, 1960; Prechtl, 1961) have found significant impairment of the central nervous system in delinquents. To put the issue in balance, however, many authorities have focused on the possibility that central nervous system or other organic impairment may only be significant insofar as it underscores or exacerbates other negative influences such as psychological impairment, unstable homes, or cultural influences (Bender, 1953; Grunberg & Pond, 1957; Harrington & Letemendia, 1958; Pond, 1961).

Several studies have examined birth trauma and perinatal influences (Pasamanick, Rogers, & Lilienfeld, 1956; McCord & McCord, 1959; Brandon, 1960). Although some work has been suggestive of a relationship, no conclusive findings have emerged.

A rather recent line of research is interesting and possibly promising. It deals with the apparent relationship between left-handedness and delinquency. Several studies have examined this relationship (Fitzhugh, 1973; Andrew, 1978; Krynicki, 1978). Although the factors involved in any such relationship are not clear, Gabrielli and Mednick (1980) reported interesting research into the matter and discussed their findings in terms of left hemisphere deficiencies. They believe that these deficiencies limit the ability to use verbal skills in understanding or resolving problems. These authors conclude that cerebral dominance may play an important, but as yet unclear, role in the evolution of delinquent patterns.

The biological approach has failed to provide definitive conclusions regarding the etiology of delinquency. Most of the data suggest that biological factors, if involved, play an interactive role with environmental, cultural, and psychological factors.

Sociology and psychology have, thus far, played the most pivotal roles in the study of delinquency. Although no one discipline has been able fully to analyze this complex area, the contributions of psychology have been significant.

Juvenile delinquency was a proper area of interest for the early psychoanalysts. A fine summary of their position can be found in Feldman (1964). The psychoanalytic explanation is that delinquency and criminal behavior are used to maintain psychic equilibrium. In the early analytic thinking, criminality was

viewed as a form of neurosis that, rather than taking the symbolic form of symptoms, took the form of overt acting-out against others (Ilg & Ames, 1955; Blos, 1961). The criminal is seen as wishing to be punished so as to relieve the guilt arising from poorly sublimated sexual drives.

A second analytic position describes the criminal as an antisocial personality unwilling or unable to conduct himself or herself in a socially accepted way, to endure frustration, or to delay gratification.

A third view regards the criminal as one striving to compensate for needs and wishes that are unfulfilled in the family (Healy & Bronner, 1936).

A fourth analytic theory is that the delinquent is acting out unconscious wishes of the parents and thus vicariously reinforcing pathological strivings (Greenacre, 1945; Johnson & Szurek, 1952).

A fifth position is similar to the sociological theory of anomie in which society blocks or limits legal access to valued goals. Thus the person is forced to pursue these goals through illegal means. Erickson's concepts of delinquency, as explained by Maier (1969), focus on the adolescent need to establish identity and to gain mastery in situations where positive, socially accepted conduct is ineffective.

Blos (1962) and others, (Aichhorn, 1949; Schmideberg, 1956) thought delinquency in girls to be unique. It is a defense against the regressive pull to the pre-Oedipal mother, to homosexuality. Though regression does not occur, it is a conflict that goes unresolved. This conflict is crucial in the development of delinquency and it outweighs the influence of environmental factors. Female delinquency is pseudosexuality, sexual acting-out, a symptom of the unresolved conflict described.

Healy and Bronner (1926) described delinquency as a symptom of disturbance that reflects a need to escape, to compensate, to gain recognition, to seek punishment, etc. Delinquency was thus defined as being a meaningful experience for the individual in terms of his or her personal drives and needs being acted out in the environment. The position has also been reflected in the work of

Aichhorn (1935) and Lindner (1944). Blos pointed out that the exclusive use of antisocial solutions directed against the environment is an element of criminal behavior and juvenile delinquency that set them apart from other failures to adjust and adapt.

Ego development plays a key role in psychodynamic formulations of delinquency. Aichhorn (1935) felt that delinquents are unable to integrate the reality principle, that is, to postpone gratification and accurately to evaluate the world around them. Superego deficiencies result, leading to an absence of guilt regarding their behavior (Ilg & Ames, 1955; Blos, 1961; Vaz, 1967).

Because of the nature and consequences of delinquent behavior, it was logical for behavior therapists and learning theorists to investigate delinquency from their theoretical positions.

One of the major psychodynamic notions that the behavior therapists have investigated is the paradoxical idea that guilt, often seen as an agent of self-control, is seen as causing antisocial behavior. Research reported by Bandura and Walters (1963) fails to support the assertion that antisocial personalities are either guilt free or guilt ridden. Bandura and Walters take the position that the intermittent reinforcement of criminal activity is substantial and far outweighs the inhibitory effects of punishment or the possibility of punishment. These punishments generally are some form of social sanction: suspension from school, arrest and criminal charges, fines, jail sentences, etc. When delinquent behavior occurs in spite of these sanctions, it is not necessarily true that the delinquent is unsocialized if unsocialized is taken to mean that he or she does not understand the norms of society and is unable to anticipate the consequences of his or her behavior. An alternative explanation, in light of the work of Bandura and Walters, is that, regardless of the delinquent's level of understanding of social norms, the habitual delinquent's learning or reinforcement history is such that the incentive to secure rewards through delinquent behavior is stronger than the incentive to comply with social codes. For example, a delinquent may be fully aware that it is a violation of state law to steal a car. He or she may also be aware that such a crime is punishable by a stiff sentence. However, the thrill of the act itself, the admiration of friends for being able to "pull it off," the freedom gained through the possession and use of the car all may provide incentive to commit the crime regardless of the possible sanction. The punishment may have little inhibitory effect since he or she may believe any of the following to be true: (1) car thieves are seldom caught; (2) even if caught, it will take time for him or her to be apprehended and he or she will have use of the car for quite a while; (3) he or she is unlikely to be convicted, and the prestige to be drawn from "beating the rap" may be considerable; (4) even if convicted, the punishment is not severe and represents only an "occupational hazard."

The theory of socialization (Mowrer, 1950; Eysenck, 1957, 1964; Trasler, 1962) examines how conformity to social rules is learned. This theory states that there is a difference between the way skilled forms of behavior, such as walking, and values are learned. The child is taught skilled forms of behavior that are rewarded and approved by society. However, the values of society usually pertain to behaviors that are exhibited by children but that society requires be inhibited. These rules often conflict with the child's natural urges and impulses. Society must train the child to conform to certain rules seen as necessary for the preservation of society. This training, or socialization, is thought to occur through passive avoidance training, a process through which fear is conditioned to, and, as a result, anxiety is aroused as the child approaches the undesirable act. This conditioned fear then inhibits the act as soon as it begins to occur. Physical punishment and withdrawal of parental approval are the means by which the anxiety and fear are conditioned to the early stages of the behavior. For the behavior to be fully self-regulated, the values must be internalized; that is, the child must develop a conscience. The major contribution of this theory is its consideration of individual differences in degrees of socialization and how they are produced. Conformity is a function of the interaction between conditionability and the amount and severity of training. The conditionability is seen as dependent on constitutional resources. Socialization occurs when fear responses are conditioned that inhibit the tendency to perform delinquent behaviors. The delinquent has poor constitutional capacity for socialization in the presence of below average training in social skills. Those given better socialization training in the presence of poor constitutional capacity will be nondelinquent but not strongly so. Those individuals who have satisfactory constitutional capacity to be socialized but who receive inadequate training will become solitary delinquents or, if subjected to strong delinquent peer influences, will become members of delinquent gangs.

Several studies have been conducted on delinquents using this theory (Quay, Peterson, & Consalvi, 1960; Peterson, Quay, & Tiffany, 1961; Randolph, Richardson, & Johnson, 1961; Quay & Blumen, 1963; Quay, 1964; Quay & Quay, 1965; Quay, 1966). Based on these studies, three types of delinquent seem to have been identified: the unsocialized, psychopathic delinquent; the neurotic delinquent with acting-out tendencies; the socialized, subcultural adolescent.

In the context of social-learning theory, modeling and reinforcement are important in the acquisition and maintenance of aggressive, antisocial behavior patterns (Bandura, Ross, & Ross, 1961, 1963; Bandura, 1969, 1973; Hayes, Rincover, & Volosin, 1980). It has been shown in the latter study that modeling influences are significant in the acquisition of aggressive behaviors while sensory reinforcement determines the maintenance of the behaviors. It is likely that acquisition of delinquent patterns can be explained in similar ways through the influence of modeling with continuous or frequent reinforcement and the maintenance of delinquent patterns through intermittent reinforcement, thus making the behaviors more resistant to extinction (Bandura & Walters, 1963; Bandura, 1969). The behavioral and social-learning approaches have made significant contributions to the study of delinquency. They deal with concepts that are based on the same observations as other theories but these concepts are trans-lated into behavior that can be identified and measured more readily. The conceptualizations also allow for prevention and treatment to be designed based on the empirical data and for these programs to be further tested as to their effectiveness.

Proponents of social-learning and behavior theories also believe that these approaches allow more resources within the community to be involved in solving the problem of juvenile delinquency. They believe that these theories reduce dependence on the traditional clinical approaches and increase the ability of resources such as law enforcement agencies, schools, and residential facilities to play a part in resolving the problems associated with juvenile delinquency on an individual as well as communitywide basis.

IDENTIFICATION AND ASSESSMENT OF JUVENILE DELINQUENCY

The psychologist seeking to identify the presence of juvenile delinquency and to assess the severity of these tendencies must be aware that a high percentage of delinquent behaviors and juvenile crimes are committed by nondelinquents, that is, youngsters for whom there is no persistent, serious pattern of unlawful activity. McCandless and Evans (1973, p. 475) refer to this as the distinction between true delinquency and pseudodelinquency. A persistent, regular pattern of illegal activity is the most critical difference between the true delinquent, the one-time offender and the nonoffender. For this reason, anyone evaluating juvenile delinquents should not rely upon court records. Court records report the most serious offenses committed but, by their nature, cannot address the pattern, either in its regularity or its severity (Erickson & Empey, 1963).

An evaluation of a juvenile delinquent must start with a complete history. This history should be drawn from various sources for the purpose of verification. The complete history is extremely important when an assessment is being conducted at the request of a court or in conjunction with court proceedings. One of the major concerns of juvenile courts is the living situation of the delinquent: how it contributes to the criminal pattern and what resources may be available to correct this pattern. The other major concern of a court requesting psychological evaluation is an assessment of the character structure of the delinquent (Piliavin & Briar, 1964).

In reference to an assessment of the character structure of the delinquent, courts are not looking for elaborate descriptions of the learning history or psychodynamic patterns of the delinquent. Instead, the courts are concerned with the degree to which the delinquent is a threat to the safety of the community. Potential for rehabilitation is, of course, an important concern, but satisfactory psychological evaluation of a delinquent will always weigh the potential for rehabilitation against the risks that are incurred by society in order to provide rehabilitation opportunities. For example, Miller (1958) identified six basic concerns of juveniles, particularly those from lower classes. In assessing the delinquent potential of a juvenile, Miller urges careful evaluation of the positive or negative valence that a youngster displays in each of these areas. Miller contends that such an evaluation will greatly improve the understanding of the juvenile's motivations and his or her orientation toward society and its values.

According to Miller, the first concern to be evaluated as part of any assessment is the relative importance of staying out of trouble versus the degree to which trouble is welcomed as an opportunity to prove oneself. The definition of trouble is not absolute. It may refer to conflicts with peers or with family. However. in its most extreme form, trouble would be defined as conflict with the law and other recognized social authorities.

The second concern of lower class juveniles that requires evaluation is the importance that the youngster places on being tough. In its most extreme form, being tough is seen as a sign of bravery and accomplishment. Anything that indicates weakness or gullibility is to be avoided at all costs and at anyone's expense.

Intelligence is a concern of lower class juveniles but not in the traditional sense. A great deal about the youth can be learned by understanding the degree to which intelligence is believed to be the ability to outsmart people, to "run games."

Sensation seeking is a fourth common concern of lower class juveniles. Many incidents of pseudodelinquency are, in fact, done for the excitement and thrill. However, it certainly is possible for this to evolve into a pattern, and a comprehensive evaluation should attempt to determine the youth's need for excitement in the form of danger and risks. A basic point to be examined is the willingness of the youngster to pursue such activities beyond the limits of the law.

Lower class juveniles often see life as beyond their control. They see themselves as victims of fate with little or no sense of responsibility for what they do or what happens to them.

Finally, authority is a basic concern of the lower class juvenile. A juvenile's tendency to rebel against authority is common and is often pointed out in evaluation reports. However, it is important for an evaluation to assess the degree to which the youth rejects external authority as something that stands in the way of "getting what's coming to me."

Earlier it was discussed how some theorists feel that delinquents are able to neutralize the moral imperatives of a society and thus avoid any sense of responsibility for their actions. Rationalization is a psychological parallel to this process and was described by Schwendinger and Schwendinger (1967) and Yochelson and Samenow (1976). Delinquent and adult criminals judge their actions as being justified by moral indignation. The victim may be an individual or it may be society. The delinquent and the criminal see the victim as deviant or representative of deviant norms against which they have the moral right, or even obligation, to act.

Many studies have noted a wide range of factors more likely to be found in the history of psychological evaluation of a delinquent than a nondelinquent. Jersild (1963) noted several factors. These include lower intelligence; impulsivity and restlessness; poor self-control; social assertiveness; suspicious, defiant, and hostile attitudes; destructiveness; suggestibility. Jersild proceeded to stress an important but often misunderstood point. "[These factors] tell very little about the individual or how he came to be a delinquent.... A history that is constructed in retrospect cannot adequately reveal the experiences in the past which had a critical or crucial bearing on an individual's present condition .... which of these, if any, had an important influence on his delinquent tendencies.... [or] how this or that personality trait or character trait came into being" (pp. 310–311). In other words, the factors have historical significance that tell very little about an individual adolescent. Not all of the factors would be present or absent to the same degree, nor would they be of equal importance in the evolution of a specific individual's delinquent patterns. To some extent, they beg the question and add little to our understanding of the delinquent or delinquency since hostility, destructiveness, impulsivity, etc., may constitute part of a definition of delinquency and thus add nothing to the understanding of a particular delinquent. Finally, one cannot know for certain if such descriptions precede or follow the identification of the adolescent as delinquent, so it is debatable whether they are causative or descriptive and whether modification of these factors will alter delinquent patterns of behavior.

One must be careful not to "diagnose delinquency." Blos (1961) noted that delinquency is a phenomenological term. Since it does not clarify a "pathological condition" it is not a diagnostic term. Time and experience will judge whether DSM III's designation of conduct disorder, socialized-unsocialized, aggressive-nonaggressive are improvements over previous diagnostic categories.

Ilg and Ames (1955) suggested the need for comprehensive psychological evaluation of young children to identify potential delinquents. However, there is little evidence that the data from such evaluations are sufficiently reliable to permit accurate identification of those most at risk for later delinquent behavior. Furthermore, on traditional psychological evaluations, there are few indicators directly correlated with delinquent behavior. Rapaport, Gill, and Schafer (1968) suggested

that the Rorschach will often show impaired ability to deal with the entire stimulus and a tendency toward content that is poorly grounded in reality. They reported a tendency for delinquents to give fabulized responses on the Rorschach that are likely to be illustrations of tendencies to excessive lying, even to the point where youngsters are unable to distinguish their own lies from the truth. The same authors also suggested that the Rorschach would reflect relatively low intelligence and poor ideational development. In general, they believed that indicators on projective testing would be those commonly associated with the psychopathic or sociopathic personality. The reader may note an apparent conflict between the suggestion that the indicators on psychological testing will be essentially those of personality or character disorders while several psychoanalytic and psychodynamic theories described delinquency as essentially a neurotic process. Although these contradictions should not be surprising in view of the wide diversity of theories regarding delinquency, it does suggest that the psychoanalytic and psychodynamic formulations of delinquency should be carefully reexamined.

Cattell, Eber, and Tatsuoka (1970) divided antisocial and maladaptive behavior into two large groups. The first group consisted of those adolescents whose profile on the High School Personality Questionnaire was suggestive of a personality disorder, a profile that is similar to that found in adult neurotics who have been tested using the 16PF. The second group of adolescents identified by the High School Personality Questionnaire consisted of those giving evidence of behavior problems such as conduct disorders, delinquency, and acting out. Thus, socially maladapted adolescents may present clinical pictures more in line with classic personality disorders while the neurotic conflicts may be more frequently found in adult deviance. Cattell, Eber, and Tatsuoka stressed the importance of motivation in the psychological testing of delinquents. One must always be aware of attempts to distort test findings to present an erroneously good or bad impression.

Cressey and Schuessler (1950) and Schuessler (1954) pointed out that traditional measures of personality and personality deviation are not valid relative to criminology. They pointed out that criminal tendencies are often assumed to be measured by scales designed to assess psychopathy. Unfortunately, psychopathy is often defined as criminallike behavior. Thus, when such measures are correlated with criminality, the same construct is being measured twice. Cattell, Eber, and Tatsuoka (1970) gave a summary of their findings regarding delinquency using the High School Personality Questionnaire 16PF (pp. 277–284). These tests, however, were designed using the factor-analytic approach. Measures of delinquency are determined by a combination of personality traits. The test against which most of the criticism offered by persons such as Cressey and Schuessler has been directed is the Minnesota Multiphasic Personality Inventory.

The Psychopathic Deviate Scale (Pd) of the MMPI had as its criterion group cases that had come to the attention of courts because of delinquent behaviors and that had been referred by the courts to psychiatric settings. Therefore, correlations between the Pd Scale and criminal activity should not be surprising. Furthermore, serious questions can be raised regarding its utility in the psychological evaluation of persons with known criminal histories (Dahlstrom, Welsh, & Dahlstrom, 1972). Megargee and Bohn (1979) have done considerable work in this field recently and reported promising results.

It would seem important that the entire issue of psychological evaluation of delinquents be reexamined. Although he was speaking of risk assessment in corrections, a specific application of psychological evaluation in the criminal justice system, Eber presented a framework that would be useful in applying principles of psychological testing to the evaluation of the delinquent (Eber, 1976).

First, the outcome of the evaluation should be uncontaminated by subjective data or by any data other than that which is necessary to determine which tests should be used and how the results should be analyzed and reported.

Additional information known to be useful should be determined such as age at first arrest, number of prior arrests, disposition of previous cases, severity of offenses, and social-family support systems.

Second, the evaluation should focus on those personal characteristics that are changeable as a function of maturity or intervention. To the degree possible, the evaluation should lead to recommendations based on the amount of change needed, the probability of such change occurring, the means by which such change can be brought about, and the risk involved to society.

The psychologist should have a systematic approach to the assessment of delinquents, making alterations in the procedure only when necessary. As much as possible, objective, empirically derived tests should be used. The procedures should be clear and easily explained to appropriate lay persons. The research supporting the procedures should also be understandable by those not necessarily familiar with psychological terminology. The recommendations should be clearly linked to the procedures used and the findings reported. Recommendations should be clear, observable, and measurable. As much as possible, the use of available resources should be stressed rather than scarce professional resources.

A fourth need is for some of the techniques of assessment, if not all, to be available when necessary and not be contingent upon the availability of experts. There is often need for these techniques in rural areas, county jails, and other settings in which psychologists are not readily available. This need could be addressed through the use of paraprofessionals trained in the administration of psychological tests or by making certain screening tools available. Of course, the psychologist would have the ethical obligation to insure that these tools and techniques were used with appropriate consultation and supervision.

Finally, the adequacy of a procedure should be continuously evaluated in terms of its accuracy and its errors. It is especially important to analyze the errors, that is, inaccurate assessments or inappropriate recommendations. This would allow for the identification of systematic bias or other errors of measurement.

Certainly, there is a place for traditional clinical instruments in the evaluation of delinquents. These must be used with due regard for their limitations. There is not evidence that traditional instruments can clearly predict violent or dangerous behavior. Inaccurate statements in these types of evaluations at best call into question the competence of the one conducting the evaluation. At worst, the constitutional rights of the youngster can be seriously jeopardized.

A potentially useful approach may be the development of a multiaxial approach based on DSM-III. This would allow for the evaluation of traditional clinical pathology as well as a comprehensive examination of other factors.

The Psychological Screening Inventory (Lanyon, 1970) is an objective instrument that may have utility as a screening instrument with adolescents. This inventory was found to be useful in the differentiation of groups of juveniles on probation as compared to those more or less likely to appear in court (Kantor, Walker, & Hays, 1976).

The Jesness Inventory (Jesness, 1962, 1963) has been shown to have promise in the identification and classification of delinquents. Martin (1981) reported a cross-validation of the instrument. He determined this inventory to be a valid tool in the differentiation of delinquents from nondelinquents. The potential usefulness of this inventory can be verified by the attention that it has gotten in the professional literature in recent years (Kelly & Baer, 1969; Vallance & Forrest, 1971; Shark & Handal, 1977).

In evaluation of children below the age of 6 years, Glueck and Glueck (1956) suggested a social prediction score. In addition to the child's personality, this prediction score is computed from factors such as family cohesiveness, parental discipline, and parental attitudes. Glueck and Glueck report an accuracy rate in excess of 90 percent in the prediction of delinquency by this method.

As was noted earlier, there appears to be some link between delinquency and the functioning of the central nervous system. Although it may simply be that it is easier for a child to become delinquent if the functioning of the central nervous system is impaired, such findings would represent important information in the understanding and remediation of juvenile delinquency. The field of neuropsychology may have reached a level of sophistication where the examination of such issues is within reach.

Finally, a method of assessment often used in controlled settings such as schools, penal institutions, and residential facilities is applied behavioral analysis (Bassett, Blanchard, & Koshland, 1975; Cohen & Filipczak, 1971; Winett & Winkler, 1972). Types of observations carried out in applied behavioral analysis can most easily be done in controlled settings. However, psychological evaluation of delinquents can include applied behavior analysis. In fact, this method should be strongly encouraged in any setting where the target behaviors can be clearly specified and where reliable measurement of these behaviors can be obtained.

Monahan (1981) provided an outline for the clinical examination of potentially violent persons. Since acting-out behavior, both violent and nonviolent, is a primary concern in such an evaluation, Monahan's outline is appropriate as a model for the psychological evaluation of juvenile delinquents. The procedure is essentially a multimethod, multisource approach, that is, an approach that uses a variety of psychological techniques and draws data from a variety of sources.

Since the best evaluations are those that break down complex problems into simpler questions, the psychologist must clarify the reason for the referral, the questions to be answered, and the purposes to which the report will be put. Before beginning the evaluation, the psychologist must determine if he or she is being asked to evaluate the adolescent with an emphasis on overall personality functioning, psychopathology, specific delinquent patterns, or a combination of all three. The emphasis may vary depending on the source of the referral and the use to which the report will be put.

Any evaluation must include a comprehensive interview and history. The multimethod, multisource approach suggests that the interview could consist of a standard interview as well as one or more self-report or behavioral checklists. These provide a more objective, standardized framework for gathering data. Also, significant people could be interviewed to give a complete description of the adolescent in a variety of experiences and settings. In the process of gathering this data, the psychologist should pay special attention to the circumstance and settings in which the delinquent or other behavior in question has occurred. Also, the psychologist should attempt to understand the stresses to which the adolescent is subject and the characteristic behaviors, especially delinquent behaviors, that are exhibited in response to that stress. Also, the gains that maintain the behavior should be clarified.

Leaving the selection of individual tests to the psychologist, a sound battery would consist of the following: an interview with the adolescent and significant others from whom data could be obtained; self-report measures for the adolescent and behavioral checklists to be completed by the adolescent and by significant others; a sound, standardized intelligence test; an empirically derived measure of psychopathology with norms appropriate for the individual being tested; an empirically derived test of personality that focuses on the assessment of dimensions of normal personality functioning rather than emphasizing psychopathology; observation of the adolescent's behavior in the natural environment; miscellaneous screening instruments or tests to address questions specific to an individual case. The reader may note that no mention is made of projective techniques. Such instruments can, of course, be used and may contribute valuable information to the full assessment. However, an evaluation of a delinquent may often be used in court or as part of another legal proceeding. In such cases, it is best to use projective techniques as part of the interview process and to refer to them as means of conducting a structured interview rather than as tests. Projective devices have an apparent subjectivity that is inconsistent with the common notion of a test and that may make their acceptability in a legal forum doubtful.

The MMPI is a popular test and, as such, as likely to be often used in the assessment of a juvenile delinquent. Some of the current work being done with this test has been reported by Fowler (1981), and several points should be noted by a psychologist using this instrument in the evaluation of adolescent delinquents.

Of primary importance is the set of norms that are used. Several groups do not fit the typical adult norms (ethnic minorities; persons who speak no English or who have English as a second language; persons from lower socioeconomic levels, etc.). Adolescents and criminal offenders are also groups for whom the adult norms are inappropriate. A valid, reliable psychological evaluation requires, therefore, that adolescent norms be used. Exceptions can be made but should be limited to older adolescents (17–18 years of age) whose history indicates they have clearly begun to experience responsibilities consistent with an adult population (marriage, childbearing, divorce, entry into the work force, etc.). In the latter cases, adult norms may more accurately measure the individual.

A second point concerns the prediction of violence. Essentially, psychological tests are not good predictors of violence, a reality that must be stressed since assessment of the potential for violence is often the reason for referral. Although several scales on the MMPI may aid in assessing the presence or absence of pathology that may contribute to violent acting-out, sole reliance on these scales will lead to drastic overprediction of violence. This not only risks clinical error but may lead to unnecessary legal restraints and sanctions being imposed, possibly to the point of violation of due process rights. History and situational factors must be given consideration. To illustrate, the Psychopathic Deviate (Pd) scale is often elevated in offenders and in adolescents. Therefore, its ability to discriminate the violent versus nonviolent is weak. When Psychasthenia (Pa), Schizophrenia (Sc), and Mania (Ma) are high, they suggest a tendency toward irrational thinking and behavior in a generally tense person. Generally, when adolescent norms are applied, the elevations on the right side, or psychotic side, tend to decrease, again reducing the ability to discriminate violent from nonviolent acting-out.

The T-score of 70 is less significant as a cut-off with adolescents than with adults. For example, using the T-score of 70 as the cut-off, juvenile delinquents, as a group, tend to have lower psychotic indicators than normal adolescents.

In summary, the MMPI can be important in the evaluation of juvenile delinquents. It must be viewed, however, as one component of evaluation and proper weight must be given to other data. Where a very brief screening is needed, the MMPI can be used alone, but it should be interpreted in light of the other available evidence. In scoring and interpretation, adolescent norms such as those developed by Marks, Seeman, and Haller, (1974) should always be used. In the case of older adolescents, as was mentioned, the usual adult norms can be used in addition to the adolescent norms.

TREATMENT AND REHABILITATION OF THE DELINQUENT

Blos (1961) reported that insight is inaccessible to the delinquent since his or her acting-out is ego syntonic. If the delinquent behaviors start in adolescence following a period of latency, Blos believes the prognosis is favorable. The goal in this psychoanalytic approach is to make the delinquent behavior a neurotic symptom rather than a symptom equivalent. As the resulting conflicts emerge, they can be treated through psychoanalysis.

One way to bring about the change from symptom equivalent to a neurotic symptom is to set firm limits on the child's behavior. The effectiveness of these limits depends on the strength of the relationship between the therapist and the child (Engel, 1972). This setting of limits reduces the capacity of the ego to tolerate the misbehavior and increases the neurotic conflict.

In such a process, progress will be slow. Delinquents often have difficulty handling tension. Distrust of adults in general, including the therapist, leads the youth to provoke the adult, to force limits and punishment. When the positive relationship with the therapist is formed, it is formed because the therapist has "passed the test." The delinquent tends to present regressed demands for gratification, demands that can threaten the relationship and the therapy if not fully understood.

Scott (1971) outlined the appropriate role of the clinician. The most basic responsibility is to determine if there is an identifiable clinical syndrome. If an identifiable clinical syndrome exists, the clinician should focus attention on the symptomatology that results from the syndrome. It is important to avoid focusing on the offense. The therapist should focus attention on the anxiety that precipitates the deviant behavior and should do so through exploration of the delinquent's fantasy life. Scott believed that by following this procedure psychoanalysis could be effective in correcting delinquent behavior. Scott believed that psychoanalysis was generally ineffective with antisocial children since analysts often focus on the offensive behavior and, therefore, that psychoanalysts should avoid treating such children unless some psychiatric syndrome was present that could be treated apart from the delinquent behavior.

Friedlander (1945) described many features of delinquent behavior as they are conceptualized by the psychoanalyst. Friedlander noted the difficulty that delinquents have in delaying gratification and in planning for the future. This inability or unwillingness to delay gratification has been reported many times in the literature and is accepted as a primary characteristic of juvenile delinquency. A critical factor in the success of therapy is the ability of the therapist to establish a sound relationship as a means through which to improve the adolescent's ability to tolerate frustration, delay gratification, and control aggression.

Since the family influences are important in the evolution of juvenile delinquency, family therapy is an important tool in the rehabilitative process (Alexander, et al., 1976). Bell (1975) offered four reasons to support the value of family therapy in the rehabilitation of the delinquent. First of all, the family is the smallest, most important social group of which the delinquent is a member. Second, the family plays a basic role in the etiology of delinquent patterns of behavior and provides a vehicle through which the problem can be addressed at one of its sources. Third, family therapy provides the opportunity to reduce the pressure within the family that elicits criminal responses on the part of the adolescent. Finally, the family can help supply the delinquent with the motivation and strength necessary successfully to change behaviors. An important contribution found in Bell's work is his discussion of the role of family therapy in the rehabilitation of the institutionalized offender, a situation that is common but unfortunately often overlooked.

Family therapy can provide a means of prevention as well as rehabilitation. Klein, Alexander, and Parsons (1977) offered a model of prevention using family therapy that was intended to reduce recidivism and sibling delinquency. Delinquency was explained as a function of the disintegration of the family system in which the delinquent resides. This disintegration is likely to facilitate the development of a criminal pattern in several of the children particularly in those families where one child has already engaged in extensive delinquent activity. The goal of therapy in these cases is to improve the disrupted patterns of communication that are seen as contributing to the disintegration of the family. By improving the clarity of communication within the family, it is anticipated that the tensions and conflicts can be reduced and that the family will be more effective in communicating the values of society and in reinforcing compliance with these values.

At this point, it is useful to note that, even in poorly socialized families, few authorities categorically advocate breaking ties between the delinquent and the family. Intervention is favored since dissolution of the family is seen as having serious consequences even in the most pathological circumstances. Schwitzgebel (1967) and Phillips (1967) both noted the advantages of a natural environment over an institution. The family, of course, is the most natural environment. However, in those instances where it becomes totally impossible to keep the delinquent with his or her family, halfway houses or group-living homes are thought to be more capable of providing supportive and therapeutic environments than the more traditional large institutions.

The halfway houses and group-living homes represent attempts to emphasize a family model of interdependence and mutual support in a clearly defined program. Such programs often follow a token economy model that stresses that bad behavior has bad consequences (i.e., punishment) and does not necessarily require an assumption of pathology requiring clinical intervention (Fersch, 1979).

Residential treatment is not new. It represented one of the first extensions of psychoanalysis following World War I. Aichhorn (1935) based this model on the belief that delinquents failed to learn delayed gratification (a common psychoanalytic theory, as was noted earlier) and that deficiencies in superego controls resulted. The goal of treatment was to allow the delinquents to gratify impulses with no restrictions and to allow them to suffer the consequences of their own actions.

The current approaches, stressing the token economy (Ayllon & Milan, 1979; Phillips et al., 1973) and social skills training (Freedman et al., 1978) are well known. These programs are based on social learning and behavior therapy approaches. Just as modeling is thought to facilitate the acquisition of deviant behavior, so too these influences with appropriate reinforcement and punishment, are thought to be capable of modifying the deviant patterns of behavior.

Apart from group-living homes, a wide variety of behavior modification approaches exist for altering deviant patterns of behavior.

In many cases, such approaches are extremely necessary since the deviant behaviors represent serious problems to the delinquent and to society. These problems must be quickly and efficiently controlled. Methods have been developed to control impulsive behavior such as having the child delay before responding (Kagan, Pearson, and Welsh, 1966); modeling (Debus, 1970); and making reinforcement contingent on controlled, planned responses (Briggs, 1968; Finney, 1970; Heider, 1971).

Cognitive behavioral approaches have also been used including self-instruction (Meichenbaum, 1975); self-control, in which clients manage their own contingencies in order to modify their own behaviors (Bandura, 1969); and cognitive self-instruction (Snyder & White, 1979; Novaco, 1975).

While the behavioral and social-learning models appear promising, the major difficulty appears to rest in questions regarding the degree to which these interventions can improve more than simple, discrete behaviors. It remains unclear whether such methods are effective in bringing about the wholesale changes in delinquent patterns that are seen as necessary. Furthermore, behavioral approaches have often suffered from exaggerated hopes and poorly controlled applications. The principles of behavioral and social-learning approaches are more complex than is first apparent. Continued extensive research under careful conditions and by qualified professionals is necessary to understand fully the strengths and limitations of these approaches in treating the juvenile delinquent.

R.K. Schwitzgebel and R.L. Schwitzgebel have been two of the prominent proponents of learning theory or behavioral approaches to the treatment of the offender. In 1971, R.K. Schwitzgebel said that the introduction of treatment programs was being handicapped by vague definitions, inconsistent classification, and inadequacies of the criminal justice system. Schwitzgebel stated that the most promising approach may be through the use of treatment programs based on learning theory. He was of the opinion that the greatest potential rested in the methodology and success that had already been noted in clinical and laboratory applications. Schwitzgebel pointed out that new legal and ethical standards may have to be developed by the legal and psychological communities working together to permit the application of learning theory to the rehabilitation of juvenile offenders. Schwitzgebel has supported his position with research into basic problems in the rehabilitation of the delinquent. In 1964, Schwitzgebel reported the ability of behavior techniques to shape the behavior of delinquents to carry out tasks that they are reluctant at first to execute. In 1964, Schwitzgebel and Kolb reported being able significantly to improve the promptness of delinquents through contingency management. Although the importance of improving this particular behavior may not appear to be great, what is significant is the fact that the delinquents with whom the authors worked were drawn from the streets, from the natural environment of the delinquent subculture. Rather than approaching the modification of delinquent behaviors in a rigid, mechanistic fashion, Schwitzgebel and Kolb (1964) stressed the importance of the therapist's attitude in contributing to modification of delinquent behavior. They reported the positive effect that the friendliness and enthusiasm of the therapist toward the delinquent can have on the outcome of any therapeutic effort. The importance of the therapist maintaining this posture toward the adolescent is even more critical when one notes the negative reaction that adolescent juvenile delinquents often draw from persons with whom they come in contact. R.L. Schwitzgebel (1967) emphasized a basic but often overlooked point. In any effort to rehabilitate the juvenile delinquent, it is important to emphasize the learning of prosocial behaviors as well as the elimination of deviant behaviors.

Yochelson and Samenow (1976) advanced a theory that is similar in principle to many of the cognitive behavioral therapies. However, it incorporates principles of learning theory, behavior therapy, and psychodynamic formulations. Essentially, Yochelson and Samenow viewed delinquency as a type of thinking disorder. They saw certain critical errors in thinking and judgment as fundamental in the evolution of delinquent patterns of behavior. Their therapy emphasizes that crime is a free choice made by the offender. They focus extensively on the erroneous thinking of the offender that includes seeing himself or herself as a victim of circumstances who should not be held responsible for his or her behavior. Their therapy forces the offender to become more self-critical and to develop a compassion for the victim by making the offender sensitive to the consequences of criminal behavior. It forces the criminal to see himself or herself as a criminal, as a person whose behavior is unacceptable and without justification.

Yochelson and Samenow wrote that criminal patterns are deeply embedded and well integrated into the personality of the individual. They stressed that any program would have to be intensive and long term, possibly going as long as four years or more. The criminal or delinquent would have to be closely supervised and carefully directed in many facets of life by the therapist.

Finally, the work of Yochelson and Samenow can possibly be summed up by citing their emphasis on habilitation rather than rehabilitation. A basic premise of their approach is that the delinquent and the adult offender have not been socialized and have not learned or endorsed the appropriate norms for social conduct. Rather than relearning of these norms, the therapist is responsible for helping the delinquent or criminal learn these norms for the first time.

Finally, the question of delay in moral development and how it may contribute to juvenile delinquency has been raised. Based on the work of Kohlberg (1969, pp. 347–480) a group therapy format has been developed and has been reported in the literature (Fleetwood & Parish, 1976; Copeland & Parish, 1979). Essentially, this treatment technique utilized the group as a means through which moral dilemmas are presented and are discussed. Through techniques such as role playing, the delinquents are required to solve the dilemma and to justify their solution to other members of the group. The main advantage is the opportunity that the more morally mature adolescents have to challenge the delinquent and to "teach" more effective problem solving based on more age appropriate moral reasoning.

A great deal of work remains to be done in the development of effective treatment programs for juvenile delinquents. A variety of techniques exist. At the present time, however, it seems that the most profitable research will focus on attempting to match the delinquents according to variables such as age, sex and offense, as well as with types of therapies, settings, qualifications of therapists, and length of treatment. Although we have far to go in the study of juvenile delinquency and criminal behavior, it does appear that we have made a start.

CONCLUSION

It may be idealistic ever to hope for a society free of crime and delinquency. One wonders if some degree of deviation in the form of crime and delinquency is not inevitable and part of the natural order of things in a free and democratic society. Furthermore, for the most part, crime and delinquency are not absolutes. They are highly determined by factors that change over time as a result of modifications in the law and changes in social customs. Only time will yield the truth, if any truth exists, and history will have to be the ultimate judge of how well we, in the twentieth century, studied, understood, and effectively responded to crime and delinquency.

In all probability, no one discipline has all the answers. We may find that delinquency and crime result from causes and determinants that are quite broad and varied, including significant social problems such as poverty and psychological and learning factors as well as physiological and biological causes. A final basic point must be stressed. While the pressure to provide services, to "counsel" or "rehabilitate" is great, the need for continuing research, thought, and study is paramount. Our present methods of assessment and intervention are inadequate. A basic reason for the inadequacy is that we do not yet fully understand the problem. The answers cannot be found either in extreme permissiveness or in a punitive vigilante mentality. The simplicity of these options makes them very attractive to a population frustrated by rising crime rates and perceived disruption in the social system. It is necessary that a society insure that its responses to crime and delinquency are based on reason and this reason must be drawn from careful, thoughtful analysis of the problem in its fullest dimensions apart from political considerations and considerations born out of vested, "turf" issues.

REFERENCES

Aichhorn, A. *Wayward youth.* New York: Viking, 1935.

Aichhorn, A. Notes on the psychic structure and social care of a certain type of female juvenile delinquent. In A. Freud, H. Hartmann & E. Kris (Eds.). *Psychoanalytic study of the child* (Vols. 3–4). New York: International Universities Press, 1949.

Alexander, J.F., Barton, C., Schiavo, R.S., & Parsons, B.V. Systems-behavioral intervention with families of delinquents. Therapist characteristics, family behavior and outcome. *Journal of Consulting and Clinical Psychology,* 1976, **44**(4), 656–664.

American Psychiatric Association, *Diagnostic and statistical manual of mental disorders* (Vol. III). Washington, D.C.: Author, 1980.

Andrew, J.M. Laterality on the Tapping test among legal offenders. *Journal of Clinical Child Psychology,* 1978, **7**, 149–150.

Ayllon, T., & Milan, M.A. *Correctional rehabilitation and management: A psychological approach.* New York: Wiley, 1979.

Bandura, A. *Principles of behavior modification.* New York: Holt, Rinehart & Winston, 1969.

Bandura, A. *Aggression: A social learning analysis.* Englewood Cliffs, N.J.: Prentice-Hall, 1973.

Bandura, A., Ross, D., & Ross, S.A. Transmission of aggression through imitation of aggressive models. *Journal of Abnormal and Social Psychology,* 1961, **63**, 575–582.

Bandura, A., Ross, D., & Ross, S.A. Imitation of film-mediated aggressive models. *Journal of Abnormal and Social Psychology,* 1963, **66**, 3–11.

Bandura, A., & Walters, R.H. *Adolescent aggression.* New York: Ronald, 1959.

Bandura, A., & Walters, R.H. *Social learning and personality development.* New York: Holt, Rinehart, & Winston, 1963.

Bassett, J.E., Blanchard, E.B., & Koshland, E. Applied behavior analysis in a penal setting: Targeting "free world" behaviors. *Behavior Therapy,* 1975, **6**(5), 639–648.

Becker, H.S. *Outsiders: Studies in the sociology of deviance.* New York: Free Press of Glencoe, 1963.

Bell, J.E. *Family therapy.* New York: Aronson, 1975.

Bender, L. *Aggression, hostility and anxiety in children.* Springfield, Ill.: Thomas, 1953.

Block, H.A., & Flynn, F.T. *Delinquency.* New York: Random House, 1956.

Blos, P. Delinquency. In S. Lorand & H.I. Schneer (Eds.), *Adolescents: Psychoanalytic approach to problems and therapy.* New York: Dale, 1961.

Blos, P. *On adolescence: A psychoanalytic interpretation.* New York: Free Press, 1962.

Bowlby, J. *Maternal care and mental health.* Geneva: World Health Organization Monograph, 1951.

Brandon, S. *An epidemiological study of male adjustment in childhood.* Unpublished thesis for the degree of Doctor of Medicine, University of Durham, 1960.

Briggs, C.H. An experimental study of reflection impulse severity in children (Doctoral dissertation, University of Minnesota, 1966). *Dissertation Abstracts International,* 1968, **28**, 3891B–3892B. (University Microfilms No. 68-1610).

Burgess, R.L., & Akers, R.L. A differential association-reinforcement theory of criminal behavior. *Social Problems,* 1966, **14** (2), 128–147.

Burt, C. *The young delinquent.* New York: Appleton, 1925.

Cattell, R.B., Eber, H.W., & Tatsuoka, M.M. *Handbook for the Sixteen personality factor questionnaire.* Champaign, Ill.: Institute for Personality and Ability Testing, 1970.

Clark, J.P., & Wenninger, E.P. Socioeconomic class and area as correlates of illegal behavior among juveniles. *American Sociological Review,* 1962, **27**, 826–834.

Cloward, R.A. Illegitimate means, anomie, and

deviant behavior. *American Sociological Review*, 1959, **24,** 164–176.

Cloward, R.A., & Ohlin, L.E. *Delinquency and opportunity: A theory of delinquent gangs.* Glencoe, Ill.: Free Press, 1960.

Cohen, A.K. The sociology of the deviant act: Anomie theory and beyond. *American Sociological Review*, 1965, **30,** 5–14.

Cohen, H.L., & Filipczak, J. *A new learning environment.* San Francisco: Jossey Bass. 1971.

Copeland, T.F., & Parish, T.S. An attempt to enhance moral judgment of offenders. *Psychological Reports,* 1979, **45**(3), 831–834.

Cressey, D.R. Epidemiology and individual conduct: A case from criminology. *Pacific Sociological Review,* 1960, **3,** 47–58.

Cressey, D.R., & Schuessler, K.F. Personality characteristics of criminals. *American Journal of Sociology,* 1950, **55,** 476–484.

Dahlstrom, W.G., Welsh, G.S., & Dahlstrom, L.E. *An MMPI handbook* (Vol. I). Minneapolis: University of Minnesota Press, 1972.

Debus, R.L. Effects of brief observation of model behavior on conceptual tempo of impulsive children. *Developmental Psychology,* 1970, **2,** 22–32.

Dugdale, R. *The Jukes: A study in crime, pauperism, disease and heredity.* New York: Putnam, 1877.

Durkheim, E. [*Suicide*] (J.A. Spaulding & G. Simpson, trans.). Glencoe, Ill.: Free Press, 1951. (originally published 1930, 2nd edition)

Earle, A.M., & Earle, B.V. Early maternal deprivation and later psychiatric illness. *American Journal of Orthopsychiatry,* 1961, **31,** 181–186.

East, N. *The adolescent criminal: A medico-sociological study of 4000 male adolescents.* London: Churchill, 1942.

Eber, H. *Some psychometric correlates of inmate behavior.* Unpublished manuscript, 1976. (Available from H. Eber, Ph.D., Psychological Resources, 74 14th St., N.W., Atlanta, Ga., 30309).

Engel, M. *Psychopathology in childhood: Social, diagnostic and therapeutic aspects.* New York: Harcourt, Brace Jovanovich, 1972.

Erickson, M.L., & Empey, L.T. Court records, undetected delinquency, and decision-making. *The Journal of Criminal Law, Criminology and Police Science,* 1963, **54**(4), 456–469.

Erickson, M.L., & Empey, L.T. Class position, peers and delinquency. *Sociology and Social Research,* 1965, **49,** 268–282.

Eysenck, H.J. *The dynamics of anxiety and hysteria.* London: Routledge & Kegan Paul, 1957.

Eysenck, H.J. *Crime and personality.* London: Routledge & Kegan Paul, 1964.

Feldman, D. Psychoanalysis and crime. In B. Rosenberg, I. Gerver & F.W. Howton (Eds.) *Mass society in crisis.* New York: Macmillan, 1964.

Fersch, E.A. *Law, psychology and the courts.* Springfield, Ill.: Thomas, 1979.

Finney, B.J. The modifiction of conceptual tempo in disadvantaged boys (Doctoral dissertation, Case Western Reserve University, 1968). *Dissertation Abstracts International,* 1970, **30,** 3782 A. (University Microfilms No. 70–5016).

Fitzhugh, K.B. Some neuropsychological features of delinquent subjects. *Perceptual and Motor Skills,* 1973, **36,** 494.

Fleetwood, R.S., & Parish, T.S. Relationship between moral development test scores of juvenile delinquents and their inclusion in a moral dilemma discussion group. *Psychological Reports,* 1976, **39**(3, pt. 2) 1075–1080.

Fowler, R.D. Personal communication, July 1981.

Freedman, B.J., Rosenthal, L., Donahoe, C.P., Schlundt, D.G., & McFall, R.M. A social-behavioral analysis of skill deficits in delinquent and nondelinquent adolescent boys. *Journal of Consulting and Clinical Psychology,* 1978, **46**(6), 1448–1462.

Friedlander, K. *The psychoanalytical approach to juvenile delinquency.* New York: International Universities Press, 1945.

Gabrielli, W.F., & Mednick, S.A. Sinistrality and delinquency. *Journal of Abnormal Psychology,* 1980, **89**(5), 654–661.

Gibbens, T.C.N. *Psychiatric studies of Borstal boys.* London: Oxford University Press, 1963.

Glaser, D. Criminality theories and behavioral images. *American Journal of Sociology,* 1956, **61,** 433–444.

Glueck, B. A study of 608 admissions to Sing Sing Prison. *Mental Hygiene,* 1918, **2**(1), 85–151.

Glueck, S., & Glueck, E. *Unraveling juvenile delinquency.* Cambridge: Commonwealth Fund, 1950.

Glueck, S., & Glueck, E. *Physique and delinquency.* New York: Harper, 1956.

Goddard, H. *The Kallikak family: A study of the heredity of feeblemindedness.* New York: Macmillan, 1912.

Greenacre, P. Conscience in the psychopath. *American Journal of Orthopsychiatry,* 1945, **15,** 495–509.

Grey, W. In J.M. Tanner & B. Inhelder (Eds.), *Discussions on child development.* New York: International Universities Press, 1953.

Grunberg, F., & Pond, D.A. Conduct disorders in epileptic children. *Journal of Neurosurgery and Psychiatry,* 1957, **20,** 65–68.

Harrington, J.A., & Letemendia, F.J.J. Persistent psychiatric disorders after head injuries in children. *Journal of Mental Science,* 1958, **104,** 1205–1218.

Hayes, S.C., Rincover, A., & Volosin, D. Variables influencing the acquisition and maintenance of aggressive behavior: Modeling versus sensory reinforcement. *Journal of Abnormal Psychology,* 1980, **89**(2), 254–262.

Healy, W. *The individual delinquent.* Boston: Little, Brown, 1915.

Healy, W. *One thousand juvenile delinquents.* Cambridge: Harvard University Press, 1934.

Healy, W., & Bronner, A. *Delinquents and criminals: Their making and unmaking.* New York: Macmillan, 1926.

Healy, W., & Bronner, A. *New light on delinquency and its treatment.* New Haven: Yale University Press, 1936.

Healy, W., & Bronner, A. *Treatment and what happened after.* Boston: Judge Baker Foundation Guidance Center, 1939.

Heider, E.R. Information processing and the modification of an impulsive conceptual tempo. *Child Development,* 1971, **42,** 1276–1281.

Hill, D., & Watterson, D. Electroencephalographic studies of the psychopathic personality. *Journal of Neurology and Psychiatry,* 1942, **5,** 47–64.

Hunt, D.E., & Hardt, R.H. Developmental stage, delinquency, and differential treatment. *Journal of Research in Crime and Delinquency,* 1965, **2,** 20–31.

Ilg, F.L., & Ames, L.B. *Child behavior.* New York: Harper & Row, 1955.

Jersild, A.T. *The psychology of adolescence.* New York: Macmillan, 1963.

Jesness, C.F. The Jesness inventory: Development and validation (Research Report No. 29). Sacramento, Calif.: California Youth Authority, 1962.

Jesness, C.F. Redevelopment and revalidation of the Jesness Inventory. (Research Report No. 35). Sacramento, Calif.: California Youth Authority, 1963.

Johnson, A.M., & Szurek, S.A. The genesis of anti-social acting out in children and adults. *Psychoanalytic Quarterly,* 1952, **21,** 323–343.

Kagan, J., Pearson, L., & Welsh, L. Modifiability of an impulsive tempo. *Journal of Educational Psychology,* 1966, **57,** 359–594.

Kantor, J.E., Walker, C.E., & Hays, L. A study of the usefulness of Lanyon's Psychological screening inventory with adolescents. *Journal of Consulting and Clinical Psychology,* 1976, **44**(3), 313–316.

Kelly, F.J., & Baer, D.J. Jesness inventory and self-concept measures for delinquents before and after participation in Outward Bound. *Psychological Reports,* 1969, **25,** 719–724.

Klein, N.C., Alexander, J.F., & Parsons, B.V. Impact of family systems intervention on recidivism and sibling delinquency: A model of primary prevention and program evaluation. *Journal of Consulting and Clinical Psychology,* 1977, **45**(3), 469–474.

Kohlberg, L. Stage and sequence: The cognitive developmental approach to socialization. In D.A. Goslin (Ed.), *Handbook of socialization theory and research.* Chicago: Rand McNally, 1969.

Krynicki, V.E. Cerebral dysfunction in repetitively assaultive adolescents. *Journal of Nervous and Mental Disease,* 1978, **166,** 59–67.

Lange, J. *Crime as destiny.* London: Allen & Unwin, 1931.

Lanyon, R.E. Development and validation of a Psychological Screening Inventory. *Journal of Consulting and Clinical Psychology Monograph,* 1970, **35**(I, Pt. 2), 1–24.

Levy, S. Post-encephalitic behavior disorder—A forgotten entity. *American Journal of Psychiatry,* 1959, **115,** 1062–1067.

Lindner, R.M. *Rebel without a cause.* New York: Grune & Stratton, 1944.

Lombroso, C. [*Crime: Its causes and remedies*] (H.P. Herton, trans.). Boston: Little, Brown, 1911.

Lowry, L.G. Delinquent and criminal personalities. In J. McV. Hunt (Ed.), *Personality and the behavior disorders* (Vol. 2). New York: Ronald, 1944.

Lunden, W.A. *Statistics on delinquents and delinquency.* Springfield, Ill.: Thomas, 1964.

MacFarlane, J.W., Allen, L., & Honzik, M.P. *A developmental study of the behavior problems of normal children.* Berkeley, Calif.: University of California Press, 1954.

Maier, H.W. *Three theories of child development.* New York: Harper & Row, 1969.

Marks, P., Seeman, W., & Haller, D. *The actuarial use of the MMPI with adolescents and adults.* Baltimore: Williams & Wilkins, 1974.

Martin, R.D. Cross-validation of the Jesness inventory with delinquents and nondelinquents. *Journal of Consulting and Clinical Psychology,* 1981, **49**(1), 10–14.

McCandless, B.R., & Evans, E.D. *Children and youth: Psychosocial development.* Hinsdale, Ill.: Dryden, 1973.

McCord, W., & McCord, J. Effects of parental role models on criminality. *Journal of Social Issues,* 1958, **14**, 66–74.

McCord, J., & McCord, W. *The origins of crime.* New York: Columbia University Press, 1959.

Megargee, E.I., & Bohn, M.J. *Classifying criminal offenders: A new system based on the MMPI.* Beverly Hills, Calif.: Sage, 1979.

Meichenbaum, D.H. Self-instructional methods. In F. Kanfer & A. Goldstein (Eds.), *Helping people change.* New York: Pergamon, 1975.

Merrill, M.A. *Problems of child delinquency.* Boston: Houghton Mifflin Company, 1947.

Merton, R.K. *Social theory and social structure.* Glencoe, Ill.: Free Press, 1957.

Miller, W.B. Lower class culture as a generating milieu of gang delinquency. *Journal of Social Issues,* 1958, **14**(3), 5–19.

Monahan, J. *Predicting violent behavior: An assessment of clinical techniques.* Beverly Hills, Calif.: Sage, 1981.

Mowrer, O.H. *Learning theory and personality dynamics.* New York: Ronald, 1950.

Neumeyer, M.H. *Juvenile delinquency in modern society.* New York: Van Nostrand, 1949.

Novaco, R. *Anger control: The development and evaluation of an experimental treatment.* Lexington, Ma.: Heath, 1975.

Pasamanick, B., Rogers, M.E., & Lilienfeld, A.M. Pregnancy experience and the development of behavior disorders in children. *American Journal of Psychiatry,* 1956, **112**, 613–618.

Peterson, D.R., Quay, H.C., & Tiffany, T.L. Personality factors related to juvenile delinquency. *Child Development,* 1961, **32** 355–372.

Phillips, E.L. *Youth Home: The application of token reinforcement procedures in a "halfway house" for boys.* Unpublished manuscript, University of Kansas, 1967.

Phillips, E.L., Phillips, E.A., Fixsen, P.L., & Wolf, M.M. Behavior-shaping for delinquents. *Psychology Today,* 1973, **7**, 74–108.

Piliavin, I., & Briar, S. Police encounters with juveniles. *American Journal of Sociology,* 1964, **70**, 206–214.

Polk, K. *Delinquency and community action in nonmetropolitan areas.* (In Task Force report: Juvenile delinquency and youth crime, report on juvenile justice and consultant's papers, Task Force on Juvenile Delinquency—The President's Commission on Law Enforcement and Administration of Justice). Washington: Government Printing Office, 1967.

Pond, D.A. Psychiatric aspects of epileptic and brain-damaged children. *British Medical Journal,* 1961, **2**, 1377–1382, 1454–1459.

Powers, E., & Witmer, H. *An experiment in the prevention of delinquency.* New York: Columbia University Press, 1951.

Prechtl, H.F.R. *Children with minimal brain damage.* Address to the Association for Child Psychology and Psychiatry, London, June 1961.

President's Commission on Law Enforcement and Administration of Justice. *Crime in America: The challenge of crime in a free society.* Washington: Government Printing Office, 1967.

Pygott, F., & Street, D.F. Unsuspected, treatable organic dementia. *Lancet,* 1960, **1**, 1371.

Quay, H.C. Dimensions of personality in delinquent boys as inferred from the factor analysis of case history data. *Child Development,* 1964, **35**, 479–484.

Quay, H.C. Personality dimensions in preadolescent delinquent boys. *Educational Psychology and Measurement,* 1966, **26**, 99–110.

Quay, H.C., & Blumen, L. Dimensions of delinquent behavior. *Journal of Social Psychology,* 1963, **61**, 273–277.

Quay, H.C., Peterson, D.R., & Consalvi, C. The interpretation of three personality factors in juvenile delinquency. *Journal of Consulting Psychology,* 1960, **24**, 555.

Quay, H.C., and Quay, L.C. Behavior problems in early adolescence. *Child Development,* 1965, **36**, 215–220.

Randolph, M.H., Richardson, H., & Johnson, R.C. A comparison of social and solitary male delinquents. *Journal of Consulting Psychology,* 1961, **25,** 293–295.

Rapaport, D., Gill, M.M., & Schafer, R. (R. Holt, Ed.). *Diagnostic psychological testing* (Rev. ed.). New York: International Universities Press, 1968.

Schafer, W.E., & Polk, K. *Delinquency and the schools.* (In Task Force report: Juvenile delinquency and youth crime.) Washington, D.C.: U.S. Government Printing Office, 1967.

Schmideberg, M. Delinquent acts as perversions and fetishes. *International Journal of Psychoanalysis,* 1956, **37,** 422–424.

Schuessler, K.F. Analyzing and predicting juvenile delinquency with the MMPI. *American Journal of Sociology,* 1954, **60,** 321–322.

Schwendinger, H., & Schwendinger, J. Delinquent stereotypes of probable victims. In M.W. Klein (Ed.), *Juvenile gangs in context.* Englewood Cliffs, N.J.: Prentice-Hall, 1967.

Schwitzgebel, R.K. Development and legal regulation of coercive behavior modification techniques. (*Crime and Delinquency Monograph Series,* DHEW, Public Health Services Publication No. 2067), Washington, D.C.: U.S. Government Printing Office, 1971 (reprint 1972), pp. 50–54.

Schwitzgebel, R.L. *Streetcorner research: An experimental approach to the juvenile delinquent.* Cambridge, Mass.: Harvard University Press, 1964.

Schwitzgebel, R.L. Short-term operant conditioning of adolescent offenders on socially relevant variables. *Journal of Abnormal Psychology,* 1967, **72,** 134–142.

Schwitzgebel, R., & Kolb, D.A. Inducing behavior change in adolescent delinquents. *Behavior Research and Therapy,* 1964, **1,** 297–304.

Scott, P.D. Delinquency. In J.G. Howells (Ed.), *Modern perspectives in child psychiatry.* New York: Brunner/Mazel, 1971.

Shark, M.L., & Handal, P.J. Reliability and validity of the Jesness inventory: A caution. *Journal of Consulting and Clinical Psychology,* 1977, **45,** 692–695.

Shaw, C.B. *Brothers in crime.* Chicago: University of Chicago, 1938.

Shaw, C.B. & McKay, H.D. *Delinquency areas.* Chicago: Univeristy of Chicago, 1929.

Sheldon, W.H. *Varieties of delinquent youth.* New York: Harper & Row, 1949.

Silverberg, N.E., & Silverberg, M.C. School achievement and delinquency. *Review of Educational Research,* 1971, **41,** 17–34.

Snyder, J.H., & White, M.J. The use of cognitive self-instruction in the treatment of behaviorally disturbed adolescents. *Behavior Therapy,* 1979, **10,** 227–235.

Sobel, S. Psychology and the juvenile justice system. *American Psychologist,* 1979, **34**(10), 1020–1023.

Stock, R.W. The XYZ and the criminal. *The New York Times Magazine,* October 20, 1968.

Sutherland, E.H. *Principles of criminology.* Philadelphia: Lippincott, 1939.

Sutherland, E.H., & Cressey, D.R. *Principles of criminology.* Philadelphia: Lippincott, 1966.

Sykes, G.M., & Matza, D. Techniques of neutralization: A theory of delinquency. *American Sociological Review,* 1957, **22,** 664–670.

Tannenbaum, F. *Crime and the community.* New York: Ginn, 1938.

Toby, J. Affluence and adolescent crime. (In Task Force report: Juvenile delinquency and youth crime, report on juvenile justice and consultants papers, task force on juvenile delinquency—The President's Commission on Law Enforcement and Administration of Justice). Washington, D.C.: U.S. Government Printing Office, 1967.

Toman, W. *Family constellation: Its effects on personality and social behavior.* New York: Springer, 1969.

Trasler, G. *The explanation of criminality.* London: Routledge & Kegan Paul, 1962.

Tredgold, A.F. *Mental deficiency.* Boston: Wood, 1915.

Vallance, R.C., & Forrest, A.R. A study of the Jesness personality inventory with Scottish children. *British Journal of Educational Psychology,* 1971, **41,** 338–344.

Vaz, E.W. Juvenile delinquency in the middle-class youth culture. In E.W. Vaz (Ed.), *Middle class juvenile delinquency.* New York: Harper & Row, 1967.

Winett, R.A., & Winkler, R.C. Current behavior modification in the classroom: Be still, be quiet, be docile. *Journal of Applied Behavior Analysis,* 1972 **5,** 449–504.

Yochelson, S., & Samenow, S.E. *The criminal personality* (Vol. I & II). New York: Aronson, 1976.

Intervention Strategies

CHAPTER 38

Parenting: The Child in the Context of the Family

RUSSELL H. JACKSON

There is no other event that parents look forward to with greater anticipation or experience with more elation, no event that produces more satisfaction than the arrival of a new healthy infant. With the arrival of the first infant (Hoffman & Manis, 1978) also comes adulthood, new responsibilities, and the "birth of a new family." Even if the child is welcome and wanted, intense mixed feeings may develop on the part of the parents as they try to meet the demands of the new infant and the realities of guiding this dependent and relatively helpless baby on the path to independence. The changing infant progressing through all of the developmental stages insures a continued challenge to the parents and many new decisions each day. In addition, no matter what the commitment of the parents or the advantages of the social context in which the child arrives, there is *no guarantee* that loving and nurturing a child will lead to a reciprocal loving and caring response. Perhaps this is the most disheartening thought of all to parents, that a child may not pursue a course of behavior that meets with their expectations. Once this possibility is recognized, however, it can be a powerful insight to help traverse numerous inexplicable childrearing realities (Greenberg, 1978).

On the other hand, the arrival of an unwanted infant, particularly outside the context of the family, can set in motion a scenario that brings many harsh realities and frustrations into the lives of those involved (David & Baldwin, 1979). The social context of poverty and/or minority status serves further to create significant doubt in a parent's confidence and ability to be successful in childrearing.

This chapter will focus on the intact two-parent family—a group that represents 80 percent of the U.S. households with children under 2 years of age (Glick & Norton, 1977). "All the evidence we have suggests that child-rearing is most enjoyable, most enriching, and most successful when it is performed jointly by two parents in the context of a secure marital relationship" (Lamb, 1976, p. 33).

This chapter will present some of the factors that professionals should be aware of in helping parents assume their rightful responsibility to make decisions concerning their children and to help promote more positive functioning within families.

The central thesis of this chapter is that to intervene or to advise parents on rearing their children apart from the total context of the familial, social, and cultural realities and without accepting "normal" parents as capable individuals who are doing the best they can for their children is to invite failure.

PARENTHOOD

Parenthood is only one of several essential roles that an adult in our society must assume, and even though a parent may be willing to give *all* for a child, there must be a balance

The preparation of this chapter was supported in part by the Bureau of Community Health Services, Maternal and Child Health Services Project 920. The author is indebted to his colleagues Ann Garner and Leif Terdal for reading this chapter and sharing their helpful comments.

with other roles (e.g., the person as a unique individual in his or her own right and the role of a friend and companion to another adult peer). When other roles are being effectively performed, the likelihood of an individual becoming an effective parent is dramatically increased. Thus, as much as we hear about parenting being a fulltime job, it must be considered only a parttime one (Rapoport et al., 1977). Joy in the parenthood role (Rapoport et al., 1977) comes about when the other roles are satisfying and a state of harmony exists among many diverse forces within the parenting role, including the biological and emotional needs of the child, the needs and expectations of the parents, and the expectations and demands of society.

There are many reasons for having children. A woman may want children because "that is what she was meant for." Children are in a sense the "poor man's" capital. There may be familial reasons for having children such as extending the family name. But the most significant reason is that "parenthood is a unique experience. It is a part of life, of personal growth, that simply cannot be experienced in any other way, and hence is a literally indispensable element of the 'full life'" (Berelson, 1976, p. 19). As children have lost their economic value, the move is from quantity to the quality of the child.

Whether parents become too intensely involved with the child or assume too few of the responsibilities of parenting, there is a relative absence of social support to help parents establish and sustain an appropriate balance of roles. This is one function the professional can play. The task for parents today is no longer one of fitting into the traditional pattern of parenting but one of working out new patterns that will suit them in their situation as they take into account changing economic times, changing sex roles, and other current concerns. Once parents have established an appropriate parental pattern it becomes easier to make the myriad of daily decisions with greater confidence and competence.

Many individuals have entered into parenthood without realizing what demands would be made on them. Perhaps the "crisis of parenthood" point of view (LeMasters, 1957) reflects this lack of preparation. The author has heard a number of parents make the comment: "If I had known what I was getting in for, I would have never become a parent." The present parenting literature emphasizes clearly informing potential parents of the realities of parenthood including both the frustrations and demands of parenthood as well as the joys and satisfactions that are likely to arise. Refer to Russell (1974) for an example of the "transition to parenthood" point of view.

Peck and Granzig (1978) have developed the "Parent Test" to help individuals assess how they might measure up as parents. This is particularly important in light of a more positive trend in one group of young people's attitudes and expectations toward marriage and having children. In a survey of 17,000 high school seniors in the 1980 graduating class, nearly three-quarters stated that a happy marriage and good family life were extremely important to them, and almost 90 percent indicated that they wanted to have children ("Youth on the Move," 1980). However, it is not known how well these youth are prepared to become parents.

Although parents are continually told that there is not one "best" or "right" way to raise a child, if there are problems they usually ask themselves: "What did I do wrong?" Professionals have not helped the matter. When deficiencies may be traced to either the environment or the parents we have too easily assumed it is the incapacity of the parents (Comer & Schraft, 1980; Doherty & Ryder, 1980; Rapoport et al., 1977).

There is no simple formula on how to rear an individual child to reach the parents' expectations. Certainly parenting skills are more than the kind of consequences provided for deviant and prosocial behavior. What about the parents' ability to work together, to negotiate compromises among family members, or to implement long range plans for the children. Parents, in addition, must realize there are many factors over which they have only some control (for example the influence of the peer group). At any point in time a specific problem that appears to be simple may not have a right answer—merely choice. During the era of the "social mold" theories the assumed direction of influence was from parent to child. Thus parents were responsible for shaping the personality of their children. This led to considerable stress on the parents as is illustrated by the following quote from the 1950's by Millicent MacIntosh, the President of Barnard College (cited in Richmond & Janis, 1980): "Even the most innocent appearing act or carefully spoken word may harm a child or damage his future happiness. You hurt them by comparing them to other children, you hurt them by not comparing them and praising them for being special, you hurt them by being too affectionate to them and by not being affectionate enough" (p. 5). Under these conditions parents find it difficult to make parenting decisions regarding their children. Professionals are available to help, but parents often do not seek out and use advice from these professionals.

Clarke-Stewart (1978) found consultation with a professional (most often a doctor) to be equally likely from the 1940s to the present based upon reports of parents at various ages. However, just because parents are most likely to consult a physician does not mean that our health care system fosters the type of relationship between parent and physician that is most desirable. Guerney and Drake (1973), in an exploratory survey undertaken with stable middle class families, found that this highly educated and relatively wealthy sample of mothers did not go to anyone for help with many of their childrearing concerns. When they did seek help, they frequently found the answers to their questions unsatisfactory.

THE FAMILY IN OUR SOCIETY

There is some evidence that the nuclear family (Glick & Kessler, 1980; Wernick, 1974) has always existed and is not something that has evolved. The family has served as the principal means of accomplishing two functions: (1) the psychosocial protection of its members and (2) accommodation to the culture (Minuchin, 1974). As society's smallest unit, the family has served as a focus for adapting to change while at the same time providing sufficient continuity for children to establish some roots. Because of their dependence upon adults, children are the first to suffer (or benefit) from changes affecting the family (Glick & Kessler, 1980).

In traditional society children had only to emulate their parents' behavior in order to function successfully as adults. Occupational skills were acquired largely by apprenticeship. The family often worked as a unit, with parents and children laboring side by side. The parents were the "experts," with their knowledge accumulated through experience (Eisenberg, 1976). With the transition from an agrarian to an industrialized society, the family's role as the economic unit was eroded. Work roles of men and women were differentiated, and there were demands for specialized skills. A more mobile work force brought multiple moves and the loss of the extended family although some suggest (Uzoka, 1979) that the extended family is present psychologically and in some ways functionally (e.g., mutual financial support, assistance in daycare and old age, and support during special events such as weddings and deaths).

Beginning with Bronfenbrenner and now confirmed by many social scientists there is some agreement that the traditional family is in danger of joining the extended family as a thing of the past. The American family is clearly depicted in the popular press as in transition. Some describe the family as emotionally unstable, economically weak, and not up to the task of raising children ("Saving the Family," 1978). Others feel (Kagan, 1978) that the very forces that initially weakened the family are going full cycle and now producing conditions likely to strengthen the family. Bernardo (1980) feels in the next decade we will be studying how families manage or even thrive on life's hardships.

Only one family in four (25 percent) now fits the stereotype of breadwinning dad, homemaking mom, and dependent children. The average American family has shrunk from 4.8

children in 1900 (Glick & Kesler, 1980) to 2.3 children at present (Lewis & Feiring, 1978). However, in spite of the many changes, 98 percent of all American children are raised in families, and, in 1977, 79 percent of these were living with two parents ("Saving the Family," 1978).

Bronfenbrenner (1977) notes that the two most potent influences on the family—work and neighborhood—no longer provide the support that is essential for the family. More and more families require both parents to work. Of married mothers with school age children, the number who work has now soared to 51 percent (Lamb, Chase-Lansdale, & Tresh Owen, 1978). The work hours make it difficult for parents to be parents. Mobility makes neighborhood attachments difficult. The average American moves 14 times during a lifetime, and 20 percent of the American population moves each year (Califano, cited in Calhoun, 1980). Many families may not know their next door neighbor. As an example, the neighbor may call the police when his window is broken rather than approach the child's parents and discuss the matter with them.

In the early history of the U.S., the government played little or no role in the upbringing of children. In fact it was seen as the duty of parents to assume the responsibility for the support and discipline of their children, often in a very authoritarian way. The complexity of parenting has increased because of the shift in our society from autocratic to more democratic procedures for rearing children (Dinkmeyer & McKay, 1973; Dreikurs, Gould, & Corsini, 1974). However, a totally "democratic" family in which all members have an equal voice seems unrealistic (Glick & Kessler, 1980).

In recent years there has been a move to specify the rights of children in our society (White House Conference on Children, 1970). The present concept of parental responsibility implies that parents must fulfill these obligations to their children and, if they do not, it is the responsibility of society then to protect children's rights (Calhoun, 1980). With the focus on children's rights, some children have attempted to obtain damages from their parents for inadequate parenting. Thus far none have been successful in their endeavor (Sussman & Guggenheim, 1980).

Governmental intrusion is usually rejected in favor of family autonomy at the abstract level. However, the behavior of a specific family may be so unacceptable as to lead to unquestioned intervention by the state. There is a need for empirical evidence about what happens to the parent-child relationship and/or the family unit when an outside agency makes decisions that allow youth to obtain abortions without parental approval, to request to be removed from the home, and to be granted permission to marry (Walters & Walters, 1980).

With the growth of social services and governmental programs to help chidren, parents have been relieved of much of the responsibility in the fundamental areas of family life: school, work, and health.

The mode of government operation has been to provide services, primarily to children. The catalog of federal domestic assistance lists over 268 programs to provide direct financial assistance or services to individuals and families (Family Impact Seminar, cited in Calhoun, 1980).

In spite of the belief that the best way to help children is by helping their families (Edelman, 1981), there are many examples of how present policies do not. Families can literally disintegrate before the state intervenes. When intervention does occur it usually focuses its attention on the child as the victim. Thus the family context in which the child lives may not be taken into account. In fact, the further the child is from the home, the more society is willing to pay for care and treatment, which means keeping child away from natural support mechanisms (Calhoun, 1980; Edelman, 1981). For example, funds for inpatient care are paid in full, but funds for less restrictive care such as day treatment are paid only in part. Overall, the message for parents becomes: "You are not competent to decide how to live your life" (Kellerman, 1981).

The trend of the last two decades is toward society having a more pervasive influence at an earlier age in children's lives (e.g., influence of TV, schools, and peer groups). However, when the adolescent is leaving the family unit there is not a support system available in the community (Minuchin, 1974).

Bronfenbrenner (1977) points out that many of the problems that have arisen come because of our haste in establishing untried social programs. Our country does not send astronauts into space without careful testing of the *whole* mission. In social programs, there is often no pretesting of the parts, let alone the whole program. The program may be sent out to people with little knowledge of the complex effects it may have.

With government now wanting to strengthen the family, it is clear we must proceed with some caution. Calhoun (1980) suggests that parents must learn the skills that will allow them to gain the support services that are available. In a sense, parents are becoming service brokers whose role is to make sure that their children receive the best goods and services. Ford (1979) has begun teaching parents how and when to consult providers of services in an effective way.

On the other hand, there is increasing pressure to make a statement of goals regarding the socialization of children. The plea comes in part because there are so many who share in socialization. For the middle class family, there is often minimal discrepancy between what the family teaches and what society is able to support. In poorer families, on the other hand, auxiliary services have often been concerned with sustaining a family seen as unstable and incompetent. Recent federal programs have attempted to involve parents in advisory roles. Headstart has the largest organized group of parents in the country—some 900,000—but they are ineffectively organized so that they wield little clout (White, 1976).

Most social scientists have avoided specifying the outcome of the socialization of the child and focused on how it occurs. Kohlberg (1976), on the other hand, strongly emphasizes that we must face the issues of what the end result of socialization is to be. Individuals with vastly different interests and goals may

be equally socialized in terms of their own social group. The basic issue for parents becomes: "What do we teach our children so they can succeed in our society?"

Kagan (1976) emphasizes that the organism's requirements can never be separated from the environment in which it is living. He then suggests what our society demands:

1. The child believes he or she is valued by parents and a few special people in the community.
2. The child attains competence in academic subjects.
3. The child develops autonomy.
4. The child attains loyalty to the self rather than to the institution.
5. The child learns that the young adult needs to be heterosexually successful.

Parents and professionals alike should take note that Kagan feels there is "insufficient emphasis on intimacy and too much on self-interest; insufficient emphasis on cooperation and too much on competitiveness; insufficient emphasis on altruism and too much on narcissism" (p. 166).

RESEARCH IN CHILDREARING

In the past, researchers assumed that the mother fulfilled the infant's needs, which in turn led to the infant trusting the mother, which led to attachment, which led to identification and, finally, to the socialization of the child through the incorporation of the goals and values of the mother. Early psychoanalytic and behavioral views stressed the importance of early experience. The mother-infant relationship was usually chosen for the focus of research because: (1) the mother gives birth to the infant; (2) the mother is the one who nurses the baby; (3) when taking the developmental stance you begin at the beginning; and (4) the mother-infant interaction was viewed as the basis for other social interactions (Vietze & Hopkins, 1980).

Lamb (1978a) suggests three basic assumptions of relatively recent origin that affect how the social scientist now tends to view the study of childrearing.

1. *Early development occurs in the context of a complex family system rather than in the context of the mother-infant dyad.* There is now evidence that the infant is an active organism capable of adapting to its environment and developing a "synchrony" with its caretakers often differentiating mother from father in the first days of life (Brazelton et al., 1978). As researchers have attempted to include the father in the study of the interaction with the infant, a new unit of analysis has come into focus (Lerner & Spanier, 1978): *The child within a family system.* We must now relinquish our notions of universal laws and instead conceptualize development as a probabilistic phenomenon. That is, the nature and extent of developmental change become relative to the boundaries imposed by the changing context within which the child lives. The focus becomes the interpersonal interaction in the context of overlapping circles of family, neighborhood, and community (Bell, 1979). A four-element system (the number of individuals in the average American family) has the possibility of four triadic interactions that can be bidirectional with both direct and indirect effects. The challenge we now face is how to develop a methodology for this complex system.

2. *Children have an influence on the "socializers" and are not simply the target of socializing forces.* The theoretical basis for this change in conceptualization comes from papers by Bell (1971, 1974) and Bell and Harper (1977) who argue that results might well be viewed in terms of the child's "impact on the caregiver." Korner (1971) found that four of five interactive responses were initiated by infants rather than parents. There are indications that caregiving in the first two months is largely guided by signals from the infant (Bell, 1979). The compelling nature of an infant's behavior is suggested by how an infant can induce abuse by a larger individual even when the adult behavior is against the sanctions of society. Infants have an ability to resist and divert the socialization efforts of parents. One of the most potent ways of

helping parents is to point out how the infant is an individual personality right from the start. Whereas parents used to be sensitized to how their childrearing could traumatize children, it may now be time to focus on the guidance required from parents (Bell, 1979).

3. *Social and psychological development is not confined to infancy and childhood but is a process that continues from birth to death.* With the view that infants possess varying temperamental characteristics and have the beginning of their own personality, parents are no longer viewed as being solely responsible for the child's emotional development. Yarrow (1973) reports how research on reinforcement and the influence of modeling has unmistakenly demonstrated the modifiability of older children. Patterson (1979a, 1980) clearly demonstrates the potent effect of antecedent and consequent responses from the environment in eliciting and maintaining aggressive behavior. Thus, even in the first mother-infant interaction, we are now aware that it is not necessarily the content of the interactions that is so critical (e.g., feeding) but the social context in which it occurs. Zigler (cited in Richmond & Janis, 1980, p. 5) concludes that "every segment of the life cycle from conception through maturity is of crucial importance and requires certain environmental nutrients" as there is a "growth toward health" (Kagan, 1979b). In a natural interaction, it appears that it is not so much the stimuli presented by each of the participants that matter as the extent to which the recipient of the stimuli believes himself or herself to have been affected by them.

Over the last decade the psychological abstracts alone contain more than 5,000 entries relating to parent-child relationships (Walters & Walters, 1980). But these studies have not yielded the new information we would like. In large part this result comes because we have not accepted Mussen's (1977) declaration that the ultimate criterion for the evaluation of behavioral science research must be its social relevance and usefulness. During the 1950s child development research had moved away from considerations of social relevance to more of a laboratory model. The simple summary variables previously used have had little predictive power because childrearing practices cannot be understood without some knowledge of the environments in which children are living. For example, in the maternal deprivation literature (Rutter, 1972), infants were deprived of much more than mother love (e.g., fathers, toys, and social stimulation), and this literature has recently been reinterpreted (Rutter, 1979). After reviewing some 500 studies on fathering, Lamb concluded that little new information had been gained because most of the studies were extensions of previous research (Lamb, 1977).

In addition, past research is relatively unstable, using differing subjects, differing social contexts, and differing methods of gathering data in a changing society. Other problems include waiting for longitudinal results over a generation and trying to study the family in the clinic. When the social context is manipulated by the experimenter, it can no longer be assumed to represent the naturally occurring system of the family. By artificially reducing the freedom of the individuals observed (e.g., Johnson's or Patteron's rules for the home observations), the experimenters may create conditions to fulfill their own expectancy. Baumrind (1980) maintains: "Few, if any, experimental strategies are sufficiently valid ecologically to apply to in situ family relationships and few, if any, nonexperimental studies control the independent variables sufficiently to disentangle cause and effect relations" (p. 649). The organismic model (Overton & Reese, 1973) suggests use of naturalistic and longitudinal investigations that treat persons or the family as the unit of study. Baumrind (1980) proposed that future research should take advantage of naturally occurring social experiments to help parents.

CURRENT PRACTICE

The Birthing Process

As there are better preparations for parenthood, the probability increases that the pregnancy and delivery will be a positive experience. As inadequate as the preparation for parenthood might have been, it is unlikely that expectant parents do not make some anticipatory adjustments prior to childbirth that soften its impact. The duration of the pregnancy allows not only for biological growth but for the associated psychological and social adjustment of the parents (Rapoport et al., 1977). As all professionals become more sensitized to the needs of parents and look for ways to be supportive, there will be many more opportunities for parents to have a positive experience with the professional. For example, the obstetrician may no longer assume that, because a woman is married, she will only have positive feelings about the pregnancy when coming in for her first visit and may take time to discuss how she feels about the pregnancy.

The way we talk about the experience of childbirth is changing. Whereas the arrival of an infant might have been labeled as a "crisis" in the past (Hobbs, 1965; LeMasters, 1957), investigators have talked about "the transition to parenthood." Klaus and Kennell (1976a) hypothesize that the heightened emotions during this time prepare the parents for the changes that are assured by the arrival of the child. The birth of an infant is a profoundly moving experience for both parents.

In retrospect, our society appears to have done better in providing for individual health care than in making the birth of an infant a family affair. As we take the family perspective, many procedures and practices are being altered to be more supportive of parents.

Mothers are more conscious of the important role of appropriate nutrition and are using wisdom in choosing and preparing nutritionally sound foods (Sugarman, 1977) and using professional advice to determine strategies for weight control.

There is increased involvement of fathers throughout the pregnancy, including attending the prenatal classes and visits to the obstetrician. Many fathers are now present during and after birth (Klaus & Kennell, 1976a, 1976b).

There are many types of prenatal courses for parents to help them prepare for parenthood. The prenatal courses offered in hospitals become unique when they are taught by the nurses working in the hospital who will be following the couple from admission to dismissal (Davis, A.J., 1979). Many supplementary home study type reference programs are available (Perkins, 1979). However, there is not clear evidence that attending these classes is associated with any differences in the degree of difficulty encountered during the adjustment to parenthood (Parke & O'Leary, 1975; Wente & Crockenberg, 1976). The chances of the mother feeling more in control during labor and delivery are significantly increased (Snyder 1980). This comes in part from attention to the physical and emotional support of the mother during labor and delivery by the hospital staff and the more homelike atmosphere of the birthing room: less direct intervention, such as artificial rupture of the membranes, internal fetal monitoring, and the use of medications (Sugarman, 1977), has had a positive response from parents. The more aggressive procedures have been called into question as home births attended to by midwives result in a better outcome in terms of perinatal mortality than overall U.S. hospital births of comparable years—a difference not accounted for by the type of patient population. Scaer and Korte (1978) note that the most important concern of a mother during labor and delivery is the attitude of the staff.

Presently there is less separation of mothers and babies during hospitalization. Instead of immediately removing the infant, many hospitals examine the baby in front of the parents (Klaus & Kennell, 1976a; Sniderman, 1980). Some hospitals leave the parents and infant alone for 30 minutes of uninterrupted time shortly after birth (Klaus & Kennell, 1976a).

In the past the mother was often sent home from the hospital without the infant because of hyperbilirubinemia in the child. Sniderman (1980) encourages the mother to stay with the infant and have the phototherapy done in the mother's room. Other technological advances such as remote control screens for parents to monitor their child or free long distance phones to check on a hospitalized infant may help parents maintain contact with infants. The attitude of the professional is more and more one of flexibility, allowing for the modification of procedures that do not put the infant or mother at risk.

Physicians are now developing a two-track system, with some parents using a birthing room and those at risk using the regular delivery room. To date, the data showing the effectiveness of the screening procedure for use of the birthing room are impressive. Sniderman (1980) reports that of 1,000 deliveries scheduled for the birthing room, 77 percent were delivered there. Klaus and Kennell (1976b) refer to a study of 2,100 ifants delivered in a maternity clinic in Denmark. Only 25 were premature, and none of them died.

The pattern of behavior seen in home deliveries (still a rather select population in the U.S.) differs in some respects from the behavior pattern observed in hospital deliveries. Lang (1972) describes how the mother is an active participant who picks up the infant immediately after delivery to begin an interaction and then breastfeeds the infant shortly thereafter. Lang reports that those who watch the delivery become more closely attached to the new baby than close friends who did not watch the delivery (cited in Klaus & Kennell, 1976b).

As home deliveries increase, birth is becoming once again more of a family affair. Some parents have siblings present for the birth so that the older children will feel less left out for having participated in the process. Anderson (1979) reports that in 22 of 25 cases of home delivery the reaction of the children present at labor and birth was overwhelmingly positive. Anderson suggests guidelines for having siblings present at birth and for care of children during the birthing process.

As the knowledge concerning the importance of bonding becomes more general and is stressed in the popular press, any necessary hospitalization of children may leave parents overly distressed. Professionals can anticipate this and help parents understand what effects such a separation may or may not have.

There has been much comment on the time, expertise, and team effort that goes into seeing that a new infant leaves the hospital healthy, but few have looked at what the infant goes home to. In the past, the mother's six-week postpartum physical examination may have been the lone intervention offered to the family during this period.

Physicians, more sensitive to the needs of parents, try to prevent postpartum blues through more frequent visits. Pediatricians may call the parents at home to see how the mother and infant are doing and to allow the mother to talk about her positive experience and/or ask questions of concern. Many of the birthing units that release mother and infant early have follow-up nursing visits to the home (Sniderman, 1980).

Sweeny and Davis (1979) developed a group program that extends to three months postpartum. The unique aspect of their group is that the infants were brought to the sessions, which led to seating in family groups and a focused discussion of the needs of the new family.

More ambitious parent education programs (DeSocio & Hollen, 1978) have developed workshops for parents with children in various age groups (e.g., infant, toddler, preschooler, school age, and adolescent). The content of the groups resulted from the parents' expressed needs (e.g., sleeping problems, feeding schedules, etc.). It is of interest that the topics brought up were ones parents did not bother the pediatrician with or were ones for which they had not received support when they did consult the physician. When listened to, parents will become more able and willing to express their concerns.

Professionals are now looking for more effective ways of meeting parents in the situations where the parent is on familiar ground. For example, in some public health clinics ("Parents Help Children Learn and Play," 1979) where parents are waiting for their doctor's appointment, materials and help are available so they can spend time making toys and playing games with their children. Jackson and Terdal (1978) developed a parent group format in conjunction with a pediatric practice. This program attempted to demonstrate meaningful collaboration between the pediatrician and psychologist, easy entry for parents into a health care system aimed as much at prevention as problem solving, and a program that responded to the whole child in the context of the family. The program was unique because of the easy access to the group and the long term follow-up by the pediatricians.

Other professionals have developed community service programs such as telephone answering services for parents (Schroeder, 1979). Others such as Ford (1979) have begun teaching parents better skills to decide how and when to consult an appropriate health provider. Such strategies should make parents more effective not only in seeking out professionals but in providing more adequate information about their family.

Mother-Infant Interactions

If all has gone well, the newborn infant arrives as an active, alert organism who is ready from the beginning to begin interacting with the environment (cf. Lang, 1972). The very young infant is able to differentiate inanimate from animate interactions (Brazelton et al., 1978). With an object, the goal is visual exploration. With the adult, the goal appears to be "affective synchrony," and the infant responds to feedback within the reciprocal interaction. The synchrony may represent the condition by which a nurturing adult shapes the infant— affectively and physiologically (Brazelton et al., 1978).

Sugarman (1977) reports that, in the newborn nursery with multiple caretakers, night-day rhythms were not established before 10 days of age, while infants with a single caretaker could establish the routine in a few days. By the third month of age (and as early as the first), infants have developed the expectation that adults will behave in a contingent fashion and are distressed when expectations are not met (Lamb, 1978a). Having the environment respond to the infant's initiations is a greater source of satisfaction than passively experiencing such changes (Martin, 1975). The various interactional games between parents and infant meet the temporal requirements proposed by Watson (1967) and are critical to the development of social interaction. But most importantly, Goldberg (1977) proposes that the reciprocity in early social relationships is mediated by the mutual enhancement of feelings of competence between the infant and parent. Dickie and Gerber (1980) provide empirical evidence for this point of view.

An important change in hospital procedure has been suggested by Klaus and Kennell (1976a) who leave parents alone with the infant after delivery so they can become better acquainted. As important as the time together is for the development of positive interaction, the more important message conveyed to the parents by those making the delivery is: "You are the important ones to the baby's survival, not we" (p. 90). Thus, from the beginning, it is important to give the healthy mother responsibility for the care of the infant.

With contact and responsibility there is a system to ensure the proximity of the mother and infant. Crying is the potent stimulus that initially maintains the parent's proximity. Later it is the positive interactions promoted by parental attempts to elicit smiling that keep the parent near.

To continue to be successful, the parents must stay attuned to individual difference factors such as gender, temperament, and developmental level. Korn, Chess, and Fernandez (1978) point out that not all infants have the same "temperament" and have described the "difficult child syndrome." This is an infant who presents the following behaviors:

1. Irregularity or nonpredictability of repetitive functions such as sleep-wake cycles.
2. Withdrawal or negative responses to new situations, foods, and people.
3. Difficulty and slowness in changing an initial pattern of reactions to a socially desirable response.
4. Unpleasant behavior and crying.
5. High energy level of response regardless of its quality.

Parents who perceive their baby's temperament as difficult fail to respond to changes in infant's signals. These parents may have spe-cial difficulty "reading" their child or may come to regard infant cues as not requiring immediate attention (Donovan & Leavitt, 1977; Donovan, Leavitt, & Balling, 1978). In effect these parents are less sensitive.

There is evidence to show that other stimuli such as labeling a baby "premature" led parents to believe it to be more unattractive than the same baby described as normal (Frodi et al., 1978).

However, additional information that provides a label for a previously unlabeled child may have positive implications as, for example, when parents find that a difficult child has a genetic label such as Klinefelter's Syndrome (Jackson, 1981).

In the longitudinal study by Thomas, Chess, and Birch (1968), temperament alone did not predict later adjustment. It appears that it is the interactions between a difficult infant and an insensitive parent that most frequently were associated with later pathology. With ongoing development, an infant may not necessarily remain "difficult" but may keep the label. Goodman Campbell (1979) found difficult infants received less responsive mothering at 3 months, and the pattern was still evident at an 8-month follow-up. However, maternal ratings and observations of infant behavior suggested that the infants were not very different from controls at the later time. The results clearly reflect the reciprocal nature of parent-child interaction. As professionals become more aware of the intricate nature of parent-child interaction and the influence of parental perceptions (Broussard & Hartner, 1970; Broussard, 1976), steps can be taken to prevent some of the problems that arise between parents and children.

Individual differences may determine how parents react to some behaviors. Thus a high level of motoric activity may delight some parents and distress others. Contextual variables are heavily relied on to help parents understand what is happening. The normally competent infant is capable of providing the kind of experiences that give rise to the feelings of competence on the part of the parents. However, no matter how efficient in the age appropriate sense the infant's behavior is, it can be totally ineffective when paired with an unresponsive caretaker. Even the earliest task—feeding—is a cooperative effort.

Although it is possible to specify extremes of interaction styles that are detrimental to children, *we have not been able to come to any agreement regarding what the optimal mother-infant interaction is* (Vietze & Hopkins, 1980). The ideal is not a 100-percent contingency ratio, which would lead to boredom. Parents are aware of this and use variations in timing and quality of behavior to maintain infant behavior (Goldberg, 1977). For the parents, the course of ordinary development guarantees the emergence of novel infant behaviors.

One of the most useful techniques for relieving new parents of their anxiety about their own adequacy with a new infant is to show them the strengths of the infant as a potent individual. When the parents see the child has a personality of his or her own, they no longer feel entirely responsible and are then able to focus on the interaction (Klaus & Kennell, 1976a).

Goldberg (1977) suggests working with an incompetent parent-child dyad by facilitating infant development, developing parental skills in predicting and reading infant behavior, and fostering sensitivity to the contingency experiences provided by the infant.

Any stimulation to the infant must be appropriate to the stage of development. For example, stimulation of a 6-day-old normal infant with bright objects may be upsetting, but the same stimulus to a 2.5-month-old infant may be pleasurable.

The parent's perception of infant characteristics and behavior is probably a more powerful determinant of interactions than any other assessment of the infant (Broussard, 1976; Broussard & Hartner, 1970; Goldberg, 1977).

Role of Fathers

Whereas the mother of a child is biologically obvious because of the pregnancy and often nursing, the biological definition of father tells us little about the father's behavioral relationship to the child. The consequence of our ignorance about the role of fathers is that we are unable to offer the kind of guidance that parents would like (Lewis & Weinraub, 1974).

In many societies the role of the father is minimal during the first year of life. Some investigators (Biller, 1971, 1974) indicate that there is no evidence that father deprivation in the first year of life has an adverse effect on the infant. The literature on the effects of father absence has been generally vague without specifying type, length, or beginning age of father absence. Lynn (1974) suggests that until recently fathers were most often seen as being in a support role to their wife. Despite the low amount of interaction that infants engage in with their fathers there is good evidence that most infants raised in traditional two-parent families do develop attachment to their fathers (Lamb, 1976; 1978b; Lewis & Weinraub, 1974).

In early studies of father-infant interaction (cf. Pedersen & Robson, 1969) the investigators collected the data by interviewing mothers. In more recent times observational studies have been the method of choice. The focus has been on parental behavior in the home setting or a comparison of the infant's behaviors wih the mother and father utilizing the presence or absence of differences as a basis for making inferences about the nature of the infant's relationship (Pedersen et al., 1978). Virtually every investigation has found more similarities than differences in the interaction of mothers and fathers with their infant.

As we have become aware of an infant's social competence, it has become clearer that it is not the content (e.g., feeding) but the quality and quantity of interaction that is important. Thus Parke and Sawin (1976, 1977a) compared maternal and paternal sensitivity during feeding sessions with infants up to 4 months of age. They found that there were differences in interactional styles but that both mothers and fathers responded appropriately, contingently, and nurturantly to their infants' cues. These authors note that by 3 months of age there tends to be some convergence in parental behavior as they share the care of the infant. To date most research has demonstrated that the father's main role is that of playmate to the infant. The fathers may spend four to five times as much time playing with their infants as taking care of them.

Although the research indicates that fathers do have skills for interacting with their children, in the typical family, there may need to be some adjustments to include the father in a *more regular* interaction pattern. For example, if the father works until late in the evening, the child can take naps and spend time with him when he comes home or have a regularly scheduled time in the morning (Biller, 1976).

Gresh (1980) suggests some things that a woman can do to help her husband be actively involved: (1) share what she has seen and learned about the infant each day in a positive way; (2) encourage the husband to have a special activity that occurs regularly (e.g., bathing); and (3) encourage the husband to play with the child in prime time such as the mornings. It should be noted that in some families increased participation by the father may cause conflicts and disrupt the family pattern by threatening well-established and satisfying roles (Parke & Sawin, 1977b).

Pedersen et al. (1978) present clear evidence that the father's influence in the home must be understood within the family context.

First of all, distributions of time may be an important factor in how parents interact with infants. For example, Pedersen et al. (1978) found that the father might be with the infant approximately 30 minutes a day when the mother was not around, while the mother might be with infant up to six hours a day when the father was not present. These authors draw the following implications from these data:

1. The father is frequently a "back up," and this may help explain the degree to which fathers play with infants.

2. There is more time spent in three-person interactions and less time in purely dyadic interaction with the infant. The father may divide his time between the infant and spouse while the mother has a more focused interaction with the infant.

3. Fathers experience relatively long periods of time away from the baby. This may increase the potency to the infant of behavior emitted by the father. Lewis and Weinraub (1974) suggest father may thus facilitate more abstract conceptualization in the infant than the mother. If this hypothesis proves correct it would account for the findings of Jakobson (1962) that "daddy" precedes "mommy" in children's first speech. Also it is consistent with the findings of Brooks and Lewis (1975) that infants label pictures of their fathers prior to those of their mothers.

Pedersen et al. (1978) break down the influence of the father into direct effects, in which the influences of the father upon the infant are a product of direct interaction, and indirect effects or mediated effects, in which the influences of the mother on the child are mediated through the father's relationship with the mother (e.g., being a source of positive support to the mother so that she is more effective in her parenting).

With the explosion of studies about fathers interacting with their children and their role in the family, we have begun to understand the contribution they make as well as begin to realize the complexity in the family interaction.

From the child's point of view, the father's salience in the child's life rather than the particular technique used seems to be the significant factor (Mussen & Distler, 1959). It is clear that children need both adequate amounts of parental availability and parental nurturance/sensitivity. For example, Biller (1974) points out that a child with a highly nurturant father who is seldom at home may be frustrated that his or her father is not home more often. In fact, an infant's positive reaction to the returning father may be a beginning of his or her reactions to the entry of other people into his or her life, especially if already valued by those he or she is attached to (Biller & Meredith, 1975). The father-absent child may not be paternally deprived if there is an adequate father surrogate or if the child develops a more flexible image of adult men and is seeking out male relationships (Biller, 1970, 1971, 1974). The child with an ineffectual or rejecting father may avoid interaction with adult males (Biller, 1971).

Pedersen et al. (1978) develop a rationale using the personal construct theory of Kelly (1955) to suggest how there may be some real potential benefits from the two parents interacting with the infant. Kelly maintains that, to develop a construct, three elements must be present and the individual (in this case the infant) must differentiate how two of the three elements differ from a third. Thus, if the infant has a construct of "me" versus "not me" that subsumes two people (mother and father), then the child is on the way to developing a construct needed for more complex social exchanges. Kelly would indicate that this process is a more abstract one than making a discrimination between two objects. Pedersen, from this rationale, poses three hypotheses regarding paternal influence on the infant:

1. The father's interaction provides a basis for an enlarged range of sensory discrimination.

2. The differences in the behavioral repertoire of father and mother add to the variety and novelty of the infant's life and increase the richness of experience.

3. The father may have an influence on the infant's attachment to the mother even if it is only to emphasize the mother's responsiveness by his own ineptitude.

Siblings in the Family

About 13 percent of the completed American families contain an only child (U.S. Bureau of Census, 1970). In a 1972 survey, 80 percent of the repondents chose "disadvantaged" to describe only children (Blake, 1974). Only children are often stereotyped as selfish, lonely, and maladjusted (Thompson, 1974). One of the major reasons cited for having a second child is to prevent the first from becoming an only (Solomon, Clare, & Westoff, 1956). On the other hand, Falbo (1978) concludes that only children may be prone to greater cooperativeness, autonomy, and leadership than those who grow up with siblings.

Kagan (1976) notes that the presence of a second sibling acts as an incentive for change. The first child is pushed to differentiate himself or herself from the other, usually toward the values of the parents, in order to retain the favored position. His or her growth toward adulthood may be accelerated. The youngest child is likely to see his or her role as adaptive and retain it for longer than needed. Thus the birth of a second child seems to elicit demands for attention from the mother of the firstborn. It may also exert a more powerful pull toward involving the father in the interaction (Lamb, 1978a). If there is increased attention by the father, the older child may still be special when another child is born (Legg, Sherick, & Wadland, 1975). If there is a positive interest by the first child in entertaining and showing things to the new baby, there is a higher proportion of positive interaction between siblings later (Dunn & Kendrick, 1978). Jacobs and Moss (1976) indicate a mother may spend less time in social, affectionate, and caretaking interaction with the firstborn after the birth of the second child. The problem may be compounded if there are continual verbal comments about the new child. For example, Dunn and Kendrick (1978) found one family where 25 percent of the mother's utterances to the older child were direct references to the second born. If there is a negative response to the birth of a sibling, Dunn and Kendrick (1978) found the firstborn child may become more demanding and negative with increased sleeping, toileting, and feeding difficulties. Positive behavior on the part of the older sibling usually includes taking greater responsibility for initiating joint play and conversational episodes. Lamb, Chase-Lansdale, and Tresh Owen (1978) suggest that, when the older child is in a daycare or preschool, the birth of an infant may be far less traumatic.

As siblings become older, their interaction is often marked by its affective quality—either being very warm and affectionate with both siblings enjoying the contact or having many disputes. Some authors (Gilberg, 1975) feel that sibling rivalry has become more intense because of the change in family structure. In the past, children knew the concept of family as a team that worked, played, and lived together; thus competitive feelings were submerged because they were not tolerated. For example, a child several generations ago might have spent more time worrying whether his or her father was going to work that day than in fighting with a sibling over a toy.

Growing up in a family context that includes brothers and sisters is an experience that 80 percent of American children share (Mussen, Conger, & Kagan, 1974). Evidence suggests that, as the number of siblings increases, the impact of parents on the siblings decreases (Schvaneveldt & Ihinger, 1979). There are many functions that siblings perform for each other such as negotiating with parents, being a friend, and helping provide differentiation from other siblings. In addition, there may be considerable overlap between the patterns of interaction of an infant with his or her mother and those of the father and siblings (e.g., an elder sister mothering the infant). With many families, a variety of coalitions are formed that may be constructive or destructive (Schvaneveldt & Ihinger, 1979). Greenbaum and Landau (1978) found that siblings provided more verbal stimulation to the other children than the father in most cases.

Siblings form the first peer group, and the child tends to build peer relationships along the lines of the model provided in the sibling structure of his or her own family (Campbell, 1964). Since it is through interactions with mixed age groups rather than same age groups (Konner, 1975) that children have the greatest impact on the socialization of one another, siblings can be a potent socializing force. There is some evidence that children more frequently prefer to play with those of the opposite sex when there is a sibling of the opposite sex in the family than when there is only a same sex sibling.

Some evidence is accumulating that there are times when siblings may be the key pathogenes in the deviancy process (Patterson, 1979a). The potent effect of an older delinquent brother is demonstrated in the 67-percent likelihood of delinquency in the younger target child (West & Farrington, 1973).

Finally, it should be noted that children may serve as major socializing agents for parents in that children lead their parents through a number of activities outside of the family context such as the neighborhood and school (Hill & Aldous, 1969).

In summary, there are minimal data for understanding the role of siblings in the family. There are still many methodological problems including marked disparities between observations made on young siblings at home and studies of age mates in the laboratory (Dunn & Kendrick, 1978). Some evidence is available that adult and peer interactional systems comprise relatively independent sources of influence on the development of infants and toddlers (Lewis et al., 1975; Lamb, Chase-Lansdale, & Tresh Owen, 1978). Only now are we beginning to understand the complexity of the interaction patterns present when there are siblings in the family.

INTERVENTION WITH PARENTS

Parenthood in the Popular Media

Whereas there is comparatively little attention paid to preparing individuals for parenthood, giving advice to individuals once they become parents is big business. The most widespread means of disseminating advice about childrearing is through the popular literature. Clarke-Stewart (1978) reveals some interesting facts in her research. For example, *Ladies Home Journal, Redbook, Good Housekeeping,* and *McCall's* have a combined circulation of some 26 million and always have an article or column written by a child specialist. The 1975 *Books in Print* lists over 200 books on popular child care. Some magazines are devoted in their entirety to parents (e.g., Parents Magazine). Bookstores may carry anywhere from 50 to 175 titles on parenting in regular stock. Books sell best with such titles as "How to Cope as a Parent"—rather than "How to Raise a Creative Child."

In a survey undertaken by Clarke-Stewart

(1978) taking random names from the phone book, 94 percent of the parents claimed to have read at least one child care article, and 25 percent had read more than five books. There appears to have been an increasing trend to read child care books from the 1940s to the present. In the same survey, Clarke-Stewart found that books were not sought for advice regarding specific problems of childrearing but usually to know about child development in general. Those parents most likely to read the child care books were mothers with first-born children. Forty-two percent of the mothers surveyed had not had any child care experiences outside of their own family. Parents who were reported to do the most reading were younger, more highly educated, and more worried about being good parents. Our society's increased focus on the parent-child relationship serves to heighten the parents' felt responsibility for the way the child turns out at a time when the parent has less overall control over the direction of the child's development (Gadlin, 1978) and less experience and time with children (Clarke-Stewart, 1978).

There are many factors influencing parents to seek out information about childrearing. As times change more rapidly from one generation to the next, childrearing methods are felt to be outmoded by the time the next generation begins to raise children. At times, conflicting goals (e.g., to raise the publicly successful adult versus the personally happy adult) lead to parental uncertainties. Finally, parents may have a sense of what not to be doing with their children without any firm sense of what they should be doing. Caldwell (1976) is confident that many parents would talk more to their children if they were convinced that it was really important.

The authors of the popular child care books address all parents, but the underlying assumption on which their advice is based is that the readers lead a model middle class life (Clarke-Stewart, 1978). Parents were reported to feel that most books were too permissive, impractical, and not specific enough. From the professional's viewpoint, the popular childrearing books lack an empirical basis for many of the recommendations made, and they

generally disregard individual differences in both children's development and family circumstances.

Self-Help Books

To date, there are no data regarding the general knowledge of behavioral skills that parents of normal children might have (O'Dell, Tarler-Benlolo, & Flynn, 1979), let alone a demonstrated relationship beween parents' level of knowledge and their skill in managing child behavior (Eastman & Eyberg, 1981).

It therefore becomes understandable why the evidence supporting the general use of self-help books written for parents is weak or nonexistent (Glasgow & Rosen, 1978). These self-help books for parents are written with the idea of their changing someone's behavior. They attempt to teach parents to apply behavioral methods that have been tested and found to be effective only under therapist-directed conditions. For example, Butler (1976) and Matson and Ollendick (1977) report that numerous parents failed to toilet train their children when using, on a self-administered basis, the written program by Azrin and Foxx (1974) for toilet training children. It appears that in most clinical situations the therapist still has an important contribution to make to the successful therapeutic outcome.

The more circumscribed the child's behavior problem, the more useful a manual for the parent. Ideally, the problem should be specific and confined to a given time and place. (See Greene, Clark, & Risley, 1977, for specific advice to parents regarding shopping with children.) At this level of specificity, there should be considerable success with parents reading the manual on their own.

Another variable that may be important to consider in increasing the success of written material is matching the readability of the book with the parents' level of school. Arkell, Kubo, and Meunier (1976) sampled nine different behavior modification books for parents and found that reading level varied from grade 6 to college. Bernal and North (1978) present a review of 26 parent-training manuals along the dimensions of target population, readability, evaluation of method, and references to follow-up studies. Another excellent review of various books for parents and professionals is found in Abidin (1980).

Preparation for Parenting in the Context of the Schools

It is of note that such an important and universal career as parenting has received so little attention within the curriculum of our schools. As early as 1925 the Parent-Teacher Association emphasized the need for teaching potential parents about parenting (Parke & Sawin, 1977a). This movement was slow getting started, and information was usually given to students through lectures. Hawkins (1972) proposed that students be given practical child experiences in daycare centers or nursery schools affiliated with the high school. McIntire (1973) proposed a course that would teach a variety of topics such as nutrition, health, child development, and behavior management skills. The proposed result was to require a license for parents just as society requires a license to drive a car. Although the licensing of parents has not yet become a reality, the Office of Education did undertake a training program within 500 school districts beginning in the 1973–74 school year (Marland, 1973). This program was undertaken with the assumption that parenting is a universal and demanding career. The multiple goals included: (1) to prepare teenagers for parenthood by giving them opportunities to learn about child development and work with children, (2) to encourage students to consider careers in working with children, and (3) to learn about the development of children with the idea of helping teenagers learn more about themselves (Jones, 1973).

More recently, education for parenthood has moved onto the college campus (Shoop, 1979). In this "living laboratory," students worked as partners throughout the course. In addition to the direct experience with children, "partners" in the course were able to explore in depth such issues as whether to have children themselves, their relationship with their own parents, and child development in general.

At present there is no systematic or comprehensive program available to students across the U.S. to help them prepare for parenthood. Individual schools or districts make the decision about whether there will be preparation for parenthood courses and their content. But, even when such courses are taught, they may not be highly valued by the students, teachers, or the community and often have a small enrollment. In fact, generally speaking, the less something has to do with human development and behavior (Grams, 1973) the higher its ranks in academia, (e.g., the hard sciences rank above the humanities).

Parent Education

Prior to 1960, parent education was thought to be a panacea for most of the problems related to parenting (Abidin & Carter, 1980). The group parent education movement initially centered on the lecture-discussion model, with the goal of helping parents to develop a philosophy of parenthood that would guide them in rearing their children (Kawin, 1963). Group leaders found from experience that there was a need for more specificity in the instructions that parents received. The transition to a more skill-oriented approach began with Auerbach (1968) who stated the goals of parent education to be: (1) familiarizing parents with the basic concepts of child growth and development; (2) clarifying the parents' role and that of their children; and (3) helping parents to make better management decisions. Today parent education programs are conducted for more and more specific target populations such as parents of hyperactive children, learning-disabled children, and aggressive children (Abidin & Carter, 1980; Arnold, 1978).

In addition, there are many popular parent education groups (Brown, 1976) that follow a specific theory or point of view, such as Parent Effectiveness Training (Gordon, T., 1970; Gordon, T. & Sands, 1976), Behavioral Management Groups (Becker, 1971; Patterson, 1971; Patterson, & Gullion, 1971; Smith, & Smith, 1976), Dreikurs type groups (Dinkmeyer, & McKay, 1973; Dreikurs, & Stolz, 1964) and groups based on Reality Therapy (Glasser, 1965). The focus of most parent groups is on education rather than therapy. It should be noted that the vast majority of problems faced by parents in these groups would be trivial if they weren't so chronic: e.g., messiness, neglect of chores, sibling fights, homework, general disobedience, and lack of communication.

Abidin and Carter (1980) summarize the guidelines for conducting parent groups and suggest the basic requirements for the group leader. This approach is limited due to the difficulty in tracking the complex interaction of the group and the fact that the group itself is not the locus of the problem.

More specific criticisms can be raised against parent groups that operate from a particular frame of reference. For example, Doherty and Ryder (1980) present a number of cogent arguments about the limitations of Parent Effectiveness Training (PET), one of the most popular and widespread parent education programs. They note that any set of techniques becomes tedious, at best, if used regularly and suggest that emphasis on technique may keep the parent from being spontaneous. By using active listening as a single technique, the parent is in danger of becoming a "counselor" rather than the "parent." PET states that all parents are in need of training and then applies its few principles indiscriminately to every age level. PET assumes that causality goes essentially in one direction from parent to child and offers a theory and skill for dyadic relationships and not for the more complex relationships within families. Thus, in spite of whatever beneficial effects might accrue from its use, there are many limitations or perhaps even dangers.

In addition, caution should be exercised in how we use parent education groups in general. Guirguis (1978) suggests that education for parenthood may help basically good parents become better parents, but it may make disturbed parents feel more inadequate and more guilty so that they may actually become more violent toward their children. Abidin and Carter (1980) also caution that parents may come away from a parent group feeling more depressed and inadequate than before entering. They proposed that this is not due to ineffective concepts and methods but to the group leaders' failure to recognize the general goal of enhanced parental self-respect and confidence. Whatever else happens in the group, it must not increase the disparity between what the parent feels needs to be done and his or her adequacy to cope with it but in reality must increase the parent's sense of self-respect and confidence in the childrearing role (Abidin & Carter, 1980). The motivation for seeking help in the first place is not so much a specific problem confronting a parent in rearing a child but rather the parent's feelings of inadequacy to handle the problem.

The group parent education approach has not met the needs of low income families. The stress of poverty is such that: "Good parenting is in a sense a luxury that can be engaged in only when the self is psychologically and physically secure" (Chilman, 1973, pp. 406–407). Comer and Schraft (1980) point out that undereducated and poor families lack access to the most basic support systems all parents need to raise healthy children. In the past, the basic strategies for reaching this population have operated on the assumption that the problem faced by the children was the result of their parents' inadequacies rather than a need to change the environment.

Although programs with major ecological intervention such as the Milwaukee project (Heber & Garber, 1975) have been attempted without parents' being actively involved, some authors (Vietze & Hopkins, 1980) feel such programs should be implemented only when parental rights have been terminated. It is clear that programs involving one or both parents as the targets of intervention have been the most effective in insuring enduring change in the developmental competence of children as measured by IQ tests (Bronfenbrenner, 1974).

More recent trends have been to alleviate

family stresses rather than to attempt only to change individual parents. The strategy has been to help parents participate within their environment as more effective members of social action groups (e.g., as employees, as community members, and as parents of school children).

Another trend is to develop programs that try to provide direct services to parents that may include assistance in managing the total family situation. Out of this philosophy, the home visitation model was developed (Boyd, 1979; Forrester, 1972; Gordon, I.J., 1971; Gray, 1971). Home visitation as a model has the advantage of being able to be tailored to the circumstances unique to each family. The Child and Family Resource Program (Honig, 1980) is one of the latest efforts in enhancing the environment in which the child lives. The key feature is flexibility and thoroughness in meeting the family's and child's needs. An assessment of the needs and strengths of the family is undertaken, and then there is mutual development of a plan of action between the parent and resource person to meet the identified needs. If intervention is warranted, it should begin as early as possible and should focus on the parent as the agent of change until the child is ready for a group experience (Vietze & Hopkins, 1980). Even when going to the family's home, the program will fail unless the parent receives emotional support, trust is built between the family and the resource person coming to the home, and the program addresses the parent's felt needs. The overwhelming need at the present time is to begin parent education programs early before adults become parents.

Behavioral Intervention

While the medical and mental health professions have suggested the significance of the family in child development and child pathology, many treatment procedures have emphasized the separation of the child from his or her family (Minuchin & Minuchin, 1976). The advent of behavioral strategies and the assumption that maladaptive behavior is acquired within the child's natural environment

focused considerable attention on the family for treatment (Patterson, 1979b). With the focus on the family came the realization that parents may not only be the cause of many child-related problems but that they could also be provided with the techniques and skills to deal with and prevent future problems. Berkowitz and Graziano (1972), representing this point of view, assume that parents: (1) have the major moral, ethical, and legal responsibility for children; (2) have the greatest contact with and control of children; and (3) are willing to assume and carry out detailed and direct therapeutic measures.

The first study teaching parents the principles of behavior modificiation (Pumroy & Pumroy, 1965) was undertaken in 1965. As early as 1968, Franks and Susskind (1968) suggested that parents could become active behavioral cotherapists and not merely recipients of therapy. However, a review of studies shows that parental involvement varies from simply carrying out the therapist's instructions to participation as cotherapist (Berkowitz & Graziano, 1972). When parents do implement behavioral programs largely designed by the therapist (Tharp & Wetzel, 1969), parents can change children's behavior. The child is seen as the target of behavioral change, and the selection of target behaviors is based on the nuisance value of the presenting problem to the parents. The therapist does not necessarily see the child. Professionals have attempted to train parents using a variety of models (Hawkins et al., 1966; Russo, 1964; Wahler et al., 1965).

Parents, as well as the general public, have often seen behaviorism as manipulative, mechanistic, and rigid, and they may be hesitant to implement behavioral programs. In part, this may come from the way in which therapists have presented parents the behavioral program to be followed and the parents' lack of involvement in the program's development.

Problems also arise when therapists apply existing treatment packages to new, broadly defined problems without knowing what the specific effective ingredients of a given technique are (Barlow, 1980). For example, the use of social approval or differential attention is found in almost every packaged treatment. Herbert et al. (1973) found that differential attention was ineffective in some cases and actually made children worse in terms of disruptive behavior in other cases. Although there is no lack of behavioral data as reflected in the growth from two journals in 1969 to approximately 21 at present (Barlow, 1980), there is a large gap between clinical reality and the production and use of scientifically reasonable data (Barlow, 1981).

The direct observation of behavior and the advent of general coding systems have made possible the collection of normative observation data. However, there is little of this type of data available (e.g., Eyberg & Ross, 1978). As an example, Wahl et al. (1974) found that "normal" parents provided positive consequences to 59 percent of their children's nondeviant behavior; however, 40 percent of the children's deviant behavior also received positive consequences. Forehand and King (1977) taught mothers of noncompliant children to use positive reinforcement. After treatment, these parents emitted more reinforcement to children than did a sample of mothers of nonclincial, normal children.

In addition, there are many difficulties associated with the use of independent observers (Roberts & Forehand, 1978), such as loss of information with the use of the coding system, the assessment and calculation of reliability, observer error, the subjective reactivity to being observed, and the effect of instructions upon the individual. Even the home observation has sufficient guidelines for the family that Terdal, Jackson, and Garner (1976) raise the quesion of whether this is a "naturalistic" observation *or* a structured observation in the home.

Tailored programs that emphasize actual behavioral learning have produced the desired results in the widest range of parents (O'Dell, 1974). See Bernal (1969), Eyberg (1979), and Hanf and Kling (1973) for examples of effective treatment programs for mother-child dyads. However, one must remember that dropout rates are still relatively high: 22 percent in Patterson (1979b), 29 percent in Eyberg and Johnson (1974), and 38 percent in

Bernal (cited in Patterson, 1979b). Dropout rates for traditional therapies have been in the 40–60 percent range (Graziano & Fink, 1973). As often as not, cases who drop out during treatment are not included when estimating success rates. Patterson (1979b) discusses in some detail a rationale for determining whether there is success or failure in a treatment program. The success rate increases as one moves from molecular measures (39–78 percent), to parents' attitudes (81–89 percent) to parents' global ratings (90–100 percent). In the carefully designed methodology used by Patterson (Patterson et al., 1975) criteria for success include reduction from baseline to "normal limits" of two or more "hard" behavioral measures (usually observational) and *changes in the family system* (which includes changes in variables measuring family process, parent attitudes and perception).

The question becomes: How much should the parent be brought into our science to insure that our pursuits are of social relevance? Wolf (1976) proposes three questions: (1) Are the specific behavior goals we are talking about what society really wants? (2) Do the parents and care givers consider the treatment procedures acceptable? and (3) Are parents satisfied with the results including unpredictable ones?

Caution must be used in giving the same weight to the parents' subjective judgment as to the objective observations of the experimenter because discrepancies do exist between parent-reported data and observer-reported data. The discrepancy may exist because of situational variables or because parents are responding to changes in behavior that are not being recorded. Also some parents may not be accurate reporters. Most researchers use multiple measures (Johnson & Eyberg, 1975; Patterson, 1979b) including both parent and observational data and treat each of them as valid in their own right. Terdal, Jackson, and Garner (1976) suggest that to assume the observed behavior is right and the parent report wrong may be to ignore the cues of parental readiness for intervention and thus to prejudice the therapeutic outcome.

Eyberg and Matarazzo (1980) made a

comparison between individual mother-child training and parent group treatment. They found that parents may experience greater satisfaction from relatively short periods of exclusive personal attention to themselves and their children than from longer contact in the group.

The above discussion suggests that care must be used in determining which intervention is selected for use with parents as well as what criterion is used to measure success.

Parents of Developmentally Disabled Children

No parents are exempt from the possibility of having a developmentally disabled child. With the arrival of a disabled child, "parents are suddenly cast in a role that they never expected, one they do not want, and one for which they had never been psychologically prepared" (Heifetz, 1980, p. 353).

Jackson and Seitz (1977) point out that professionals often describe the resulting parental reactions using such terms as guilt, depression, and chronic sorrow. On the other hand, parents who write about their experience of having a disabled child are likely to use the terms fear, helplessness, and frustration to describe their situation. Jackson and Seitz conclude that there may be basic differences between how the professional and the parent view the situation and what needs to be done.

When parents do seek information and help from professionals in the community, they often come away dissatisfied, feeling that they did not get what they went for. For example, the message the physician may communicate to the parent is that "this child is not my business" (Gorham et al., 1975, p. 157). Anderson and Garner (1973) present data showing that mothers of retarded children were satisfied only half of the time with interviews they had with psychologists.

Part of the apparent difficulty arises because professionals are uncertain about the best way to help parents coming to them. After reviewing the relevant research data, Warren (1974) states:

There are many ways to help, some more effective than others, some more suitable than others. However, in view of the current contradiction of findings concerning techniques of helping parents of disabled children, it may well be that the best technique for a given professional to use is the one with which s/he feels most familiar and confident. (p. 147)

The present author feels that the focus of intervention must remain on the family's needs and not the professional's comfort with a particular therapeutic strategy. The professional must be very aware of the frame of reference within which he or she is operating.

Heifetz (1980) suggests that the impairment mode of the retarded child led to the assumption that we are dealing with an impaired parent. Parents are assumed to employ various defense mechanisms of neurotic proportions when confronted with a situation too painful to be completely accepted. Thus professionals offering "therapeutic programming" instead of responding to parents' request for limited and realistic service may arouse resentment on the part of the parent. With the present trend to seek ways enabling parents of retarded children to maintain the child within the family, parents have come to be considered as providers of service rather than only consumers.

As the normally developing child grows he or she provides parents with relatively clear cues as to needs, feelings, and level of understanding. Age, size, and cognitive and motor skills may change in a relatively congruent and predictable pattern. When parents are accommodative to their infants and young children, the usual finding is that children are responsive to and compliant with their parents (Lytton & Zwirner, 1975). In the case of the disabled child, however, there are a number of potential problems in the parent-child interaction. For example, Fraiberg (1974) has found that parents of blind infants are frequently emotionally indifferent to their child because of his or her lack of facial expression and contingent smiling. With deaf infants, there may be limited or atypical participation in social exchange with parents, and problems may develop before appropriate diagnosis is made (Korn et al., 1978). The young cerebral-palsied child is more likely to experience a diminishing amount of maternal warmth during the second and third year, especially if the child is not walking (Kogan & Tyler, 1973). Parents with these types of interactional difficulties often find consultation with professionals helpful.

THE FAMILY AS A MEANS OF INTERVENTION

Bronfenbrenner (1979) points out that we know more about children than about the environments in which they live or the processes through which these environments affect the course of development. He goes on to conceptualize a "primary developmental context" for childrearing defined as: "One in which the child can observe and engage in ongoing patterns of progressively more complex activity jointly with or under the direct guidance of persons who possess knowledge and skill not yet acquired by the child and with whom the child has developed a positive emotional relationship" (p. 845).

Bronfenbrenner also suggests the need for a "secondary developmental context" for childrearing defined as: "One in which the child is given opportunity, resources and encouragement to engage in the activities he or she has learned in primary developmental contexts, but now without the active involvement or direct guidance of another person possessing knowledge and skill beyond the levels acquired by the child" (p. 845).

The above processes most usually occur within the intact two-parent family. The necessary conditions may be mutually exclusive in time but can take place within the same setting (family) or from one setting to the next (family and daycare). However, Bronfenbrenner suggests that many settings fall short of meeting the requirements he proposes. Thus children spend many hours in situations where they do not have available to them valued adults who engage in progressively more complex joint activities (primary developmental context) nor in a situation likely to be one that provides resources and incentives for children to engage in complex activities previously learned (a secondary developmental context). He further proposes that the developmental potential of a setting depends on whether third parties support or undermine the activities of those interacting with the child. Bronfenbrenner finally proposes that the developmental potential of a setting is increased as the number of supportive links between settings increases. His point here is that alienation of children develops when there are no links between settings (e.g., home and school). He concludes that most families are functioning the best they can under difficult circumstances and that it is the circumstances that need to be changed and not the families. It is because the environment may be unsupportive of parents that they often turn to professionals for help.

The impact of the family context can be seen when children are adopted into a family. Becoming a parent is a biological act, but research suggests that it is not necessary for the biological parents to do the parenting. A review of some 2,616 adoptive placements from 1924 to 1970 (Mech, 1973) shows that approximately 75 percent were judged as satisfactory. Scarr and Weinberg (1976), in a study of black children adopted by white families who were highly educated and above average in occupational status and income, found a significant change in IQ score. The child's score was more similar to the mean of the white reference group than the black reference group. Interracial children adopted at an early age performed at an even higher level. Results such as these strongly suggest that parenting is a psychological endeavor that takes a commitment to the child and does best in a stable family context where the general environment is supportive of the family. Through adoption, a child's whole rearing setting of parents, siblings, home, peers, school, neighborhood, and community may be drastically transformed.

The current flood of information regarding preterm infants and parent-child relationships is of interest to us in the present discussion. Longitudinal studies of high risk infants that have recently been reported (Caputo, Goldstein, & Taub, 1981; Sigman et al., 1981; Sigman & Parmelee, 1979) have emerged with a rather consistent finding. The early medical factors associated with preterm infants, although they cannot be overlooked, have the least impact on the child's development. Competence at 2 years of age is more likely to be related to demographic factors such as the language background and socioeconomic status of the family. Sigman and Parmelee (1979) found that a firstborn English-speaking child of a family with substantial economic and educational resources was likely to show skills at age 2 that even a later-born normal sibling might not have. There is presently considerable interest in early intervention programs that strengthen the family's caretaking resources to prevent some of the disabilities associated with preterm birth (Sigman et al., 1981).

Based on the belief that early intervention is beneficial to the infant, adoption agencies no longer feel obliged to hold infants until their potential can be assessed but now ask the adoptive parents to assume some of the same risks that are faced by natural parents, namely, to accept an infant whose characteristics are not known with any certainty at placement. Now infants are often placed right from the hospital into the adoptive home. In addition to the satisfaction that may come to these adoptive parents, there can be a great financial saving to the state by adoption placement over maintaining the same child in a foster home for 18 years.

In 1980, the Adoption Assistance and Child Welfare Act provided increased federal funds for promoting child permanence in some families through federal adoption subsidies (Edelman, 1981). This type of program is an attempt to insure that some hard-to-place children will not only be able to grow up in the "least restrictive environment"—but to have a most potent intervention—the family.

Parents have asked professionals to inform them of the critical behaviors they must use in childrearing in order to be successful. (See Arnold, 1973, and Grams, 1973, for a list of some general guidelines for parents.) However, many theorists feel that to make such a list is presumptuous. Kagan (1976) makes the following statement about what children need: "When food and protection from excessive disease and physical discomfort are guaranteed, CHILDREN DO NOT REQUIRE ANY SPECIFIC ACTIONS FROM ADULTS IN ORDER TO DEVELOP OPTIMALLY" (p. 165).

This conclusion is based, in part, on cross-cultural studies (Kagan, 1976) of American, Japanese, and Guatemalan children who were all found to be equally adapted to their societies in spite of much different conceptions of children. There is a remarkable similarity among the 10-year-olds in each of these settings.

Many differing lines of research (Rollins & Thomas, 1979) converge to suggest parental "responsiveness," "sensitivity," and/or "support" as the important variables in the development of synchrony of behavior between parents and children. For some infants, obedience and internalization seem to develop naturally without any special effort on the part of the parent.

There is some evidence that parental "sensitivity" for older children is reflected in the authoritative parenting style described by Baumrind (1971, 1975). The pattern of authoritative parenting involves a willingness on the part of parents to "meet their children as persons and maintain sufficient flexibility in the face of their children's individuality that they can learn from the latter the kind of parenting to which they will best respond" (Lamb & Baumrind, 1978, p. 54). Thus parents appear to encourage individual growth instead of imposing alien standards. These parents are able to make age appropriate demands and to grant the child the degree of independence (and support) that he or she is ready to assume.

Some parents are reluctant to share the role of parenting with others outside of the family context. Kagan (1979a) suggests that the major consequences of an undiluted and close parent-child relationship is to promote child receptivity to the values of the family. When the form of childrearing in the family is significantly different from that of the majority of society, considerable stress may be placed on the family. In addition to trying to provide a responsive environment for children within the family, committed and devoted parents feel obligated to take over and orchestrate the overall caretaking if the support system outside the family fails.

As much as parents would like to make a child's life totally stable and predictable, particularly within the family, this is not a real possibility. Baumrind (1980) points out that, within the family, the child is also faced with: (1) scarcity of resources (even the best of parents are not 100 percent responsive), (2) reciprocity as a pattern of exchange through which the mutual dependence of individuals is brought about, and (3) imperfect justice that demands that children develop sufficient resiliency to enable them to respond flexibly to change. The realities of the family interaction can help children prepare for the realities of life outside the family.

THE PROFESSIONAL-PARENT RELATIONSHIP

The question most frequently asked the author in consultation with professionals cross a wide range of disciplines and settings is: "How do I engage parents in an appropriate therapeutic relationship?" At the present time, the professionals' interaction with parents is the most difficult and elusive ingredient of a successful therapeutic outcome to achieve. Other ingredients for a successfully therapeutic outcome are generally present:

1. Parents who are asking for help
2. Appropriate information about child development
3. Behavioral and group techniques for implementing behavioral change
4. Dedicated and trained professionals to work with parents

If the professional takes on the responsibility of making the treatment plan *for* the parents, they are more likely to refuse the treatment program offered, to ostensibly accept the program but drop out before it is completed, and/or to have more difficulty developing an effective generalized strategy. The magnitude of the problem is suggested by the huge dropout rates that continue to plague us in the outcome research literature as discussed in a previous section.

When the needs and feelings of the parents are not discussed, the message to the parents may become, "What you see and feel doesn't matter." Some empirical evidence exists to suggest that direct observation of behavior is more effective when the professional elicits the parents' perception (Jackson & Seitz, 1977) and attitude (Parke & Sawin, 1977b) about what is occurring in the situation.

Kelly (1955) makes the basic assumption that scientists (professionals) are trying to anticipate events in order to predict and control their environment. The present author, in agreement with Kelly, suggests that parents are in a sense "scientists" as they try to anticipate events in order to predict and control the behavior of their children. If accepted, this assumption emphasizes the similarity of the goal of both parents and professionals and provides a rationale for including the parent as a *colleague* from the first contact.

As a general strategy, the professional must assume that parents are much more capable than many of us thought they were. If we can facilitate their requests for help by providing support and appropriate structure, they can not only tell us much about themselves but become active colleagues who are "the best experts on themselves and are eminently qualified to participate in the development of descriptions and predictions about themselves—not to mention decisions about themselves" (Mischel, 1977, p. 249). Much of the professional's task is to help parents in the search for their own personal constructs rather than to force the professional's favorite dispositional label on them.

The experimental evidence suggests that once an individual has developed an orientation or point of view (Lazarus, 1971, p. xi; Rosenthal, 1966; Johnson & Bolstad, 1973), the information he or she seeks or receives usually is construed to fit his or her assumption or theoretical orientation. Thus, the hypotheses or decisions we make may literally affect how we see the problem and its outcome. In fact, our decisions may reveal more about ourselves than the parents we are working with (Kelly, 1955).

If two professionals are working on a common problem and find that they have differing hypotheses, they work out a means of gathering more data to find out which hypothesis might be most appropriate. In the same manner, the professional and parent may need to work together to compile sufficient data to make hypotheses about the basis of the parental concerns. The parent-professional team must pay attention to: (1) the cues the child presents, (2) the needs and behavior of the parents, (3) the interaction between parents and child, (4) the context of the family, (5) the stresses and forces impinging from the social environment at large, and (6) the relationship between parent and professional. The central issue is to see if it is possible to have parents involved every step of the way (Gorham et al., 1975).

If the parent is seen as the one responsible for making decisions about the child, the goal becomes one of finding a way to have the parents and professional jointly gather data, compare perceptions and feelings, and formulate a plan of action in which the professional can provide ongoing feedback and support. The professional also brings to the parent a knowledge of human behavior and development, knowledge of community resources, and strategies for influencing society (e.g., schools, employer). The goal is to help the parent develop competence so that he or she can in turn foster competence in the child.

Part of the problem in dealing with parents in the past has been that psychology has focused on pathology. There is now a need to sort out "normal" parents seeking information and/or help from those who have seriously maladaptive behavior. In an earlier section, we reviewed how successful the medical profession has become in screening out "normal" expectant mothers from those who are at risk for problems during childbirth.

Many professionals have suggested the idea of parents becoming cotherapists. Thus the suggestion made here may not appear new. However, it is the author's opinion that professionals have often tried to teach parents their language and their role (i.e., to make therapists out of parents). We do not have empirical evidence that "therapist behavior" on the part of parents leads to the most successful childrearing. The more important issue is for the professional to understand the parents' frame of reference and fit into their construction of the parental role to be a helpful consultant. Perhaps one of the reasons parents find the early childhood education literature helpful is that it presents the adult as the teacher of children.

Davis, W.D. (1974) suggests that, in any therapeutic relationship, the elements of listening, empathy, and relationship building, together with active prescriptions, need to be present with varying balance, depending on the problem being treated. It is only through the joint gathering of data and an ongoing dialogue that it will be clear to the professional the direct action to be taken.

Although every parent who comes in contact with a professional may have an expectation for change, the parents are not always aware of which behavior they would like changed. To speak of a patient as unready to change is to point up an essential need: mutually to arrive at an understanding of those behaviors that need to be changed.

REFERENCES

Abidin, R.R. (Ed.), *Parent education and intervention handbook*. Springfield, Ill.: Thomas, 1980.

Abidin, R.R., & Carter, B.D. Workshops and parent groups. In R.R. Abidin (Ed.), *Parent education and intervention handbook*. Springfield, Ill.: Thomas, 1980.

Anderson, K.A., & Garner, A.M. Mothers of retarded children: Satisfaction with visits to professional people. *Mental Retardation,* 1973, **2,** 36–39.

Anderson, S.V. Siblings at birth: A survey and study. *Birth and the Family Journal,* 1979, **6,** 80–87.

Arkell, R.N., Kubo, H.R., & Meunier, C.P. Readability and parental behavior modification literature. *Behavior Therapy,* 1976, **7,** 265–266.

Arnold, A. Are you a perfect parent? The Association for Childhood Education International Parenting: Washington, D.C., 1973.

Arnold, L.E. (Ed.). *Helping parents help their children.* New York: Brunner/Mazel, 1978.

Auerbach, A.B. *Parents learn through discussion: Principles and practices of parent group education.* New York: Wiley, 1968.

Azrin, N.H., & Foxx, R.M. *Toilet training in less than a day.* New York: Simon & Schuster, 1974.

Barlow, D.H. Behavior therapy: The next decade. *Behavior Therapy,* 1980, **11,** 315–328.

Barlow, D.H. On the relation of clinical research to clinical practices: Current issues, new directions. *Journal of Consulting and Clinical Psychology,* 1981, **49,** 147–155.

Baumrind, D. Current patterns of parental authority. *Developmental Psychology Monographs,* 1971, **4,** 1–102.

Baumrind, D. *Early socialization and the discipline controversy.* Morristown, N.J.: General Learning Press, 1975.

Baumrind, D. New directions in socialization research. *American Psychologist,* 1980, **35,** 639–652.

Becker, W.C. *Parents are teachers.* Champaign, Ill.: Research Press, 1971.

Bell, R.Q. Stimulus control of parent or caretaker behavior by offspring. *Developmental Psychology,* 1971, **4,** 63–72.

Bell, R.Q. Contributions of human infants to caregiving and social interaction. In M. Lewis, & L.A. Rosenblum (Eds.), *The effect of the infant on its caregiver.* New York: Wiley, 1974.

Bell, R.Q. Parent, child and reciprocal influence. *American Psychologist,* 1979, **34,** 821–826.

Bell, R.Q., & Harper, L.V. *The effect of children on parents.* Hillsdale, N.J.: Erlbaum, 1977.

Berelson, B. The value of children: A taxonomical essay. In N.B. Talbott (Ed.), *Raising children in modern America: Problems and prospective solutions.* Boston: Little, Brown, 1976.

Berkowitz, B.P., & Graziano, A.M. Training parents as behavior therapists: A review. *Behavior Research and Therapy,* 1972, **10,** 297–317.

Bernal, M.E. Behavioral feedback in the modification of brat behaviors. *Journal of Nervous and Mental Disorders,* 1969, **148,** 375–385.

Bernal, M.E., & North, J.A. A survey of parent training manuals. *Journal of Applied Behavior Analysis,* 1978, **11,** 533–541.

Bernardo, F.M. Decade preview: Some trends and directions for family research and theory in the 1980s. *Journal of Marriage and the Family,* 1980, **42,** 723–728.

Biller, H.B. Father absence and the personality development of the male child. *Developmental Psychology,* 1970, **2,** 181.

Biller, H.B. *Father, child and sex role.* Lexington, Mass.: Lexington Books, D.C. Heath, 1971.

Biller, H.B. *Paternal deprivation.* Lexington, Mass.: Lexington Books, D.C. Heath, 1974.

Biller, H.B. The father-child relationship: Some crucial issues. In V.C. Vaughn, & T.B. Brazelton (Eds.), *The family—Can it be saved?* Chicago: Year Book Medical Publishers, 1976.

Biller, H.B., & Meredith, D.L. *Father power.* New York: David McKay, 1975.

Blake, J. Can we believe recent data on birth expectations in the United States? *Demography,* 1974, **11,** 25–44.

Boyd, R.D. Systematic parent training through a home based model. *Exceptional Children,* 1979, **45,** 647–648.

Brazelton, T.B., Yogman, M.W., Als, H., & Tronick, E. The infant as a focus for family reciprocity. In M. Lewis, & L.A. Rosenblum (Eds.), *The child and its family.* New York: Plenum, 1978.

Bronfenbrenner, U. *Is early intervention effective? A report on longitudinal evaluations of preschool programs* (Vol. 2). Washington, D.C.: DHEW Office of Child Development, 1974.

Bronfenbrenner, U. Nobody home: The erosion of the American family. *Psychology Today,* 1977, **10,** 41–47.

Bronfenbrenner, U. Contexts of child rearing. *American Psychologist,* 1979, **34,** 844–850.

Brooks, J., & Lewis, M. Mirror-image stimulation and self-recognition in infancy. Paper presented at the Society for Research in Child Development meetings, Denver, April, 1975.

Broussard, E.R. Neonatal prediction and outcome at 10–11 years. *Child Psychiatry and Human Development,* 1976, **7,** 85–93.

Broussard, E.R., & Hartner, M.S. Maternal perception of the neonate as related to development. *Child Psychiatry and Human Development,* 1970, **1,** 16–25.

Brown, C.C. It changed my life. *Psychology Today,* 1976, **10,** 47–57, 108–112.

Butler, J.F. The toilet training success of parents after reading Toilet training in less than a day. *Behavior Therapy,* 1976, **7,** 185–191.

Caldwell, B.M. Arbitration between the child and the family. In V.C. Vaughn, & T.B. Brazelton (Eds.), *The family—Can it be saved?* Chicago: Year Book Medical Publishers, 1976.

Calhoun, J.A. Developing a family perspective. *Children Today,* 1980, **9,** 2–8.

Campbell, J.D. Peer relations in childhood. In M.L. Hoffman, & L.W. Hoffman (Eds.), *Review of child development research.* New York: Russell Sage Foundation, 1964.

Caputo, D.U., Goldstein, K.M., & Taub, H.B. Neonatal compromise and later psychological development: A ten-year longitudinal study. In S.H. Friedman, & M. Sigman (Eds.), *Preterm birth and psychological development.* New York: Academic Press, 1981.

Chilman, C.S. Programs for disadvantaged parents: Some major trends and related research. In B.M. Caldwell, & H.N. Ricciuti (Eds.), *Review of child development research.* Chicago: The University of Chicago Press, 1973.

Clarke-Stewart, K.A. Popular primers for parents. *American Psychologist,* 1978, **33,** 359–369.

Comer, J.P., & Schraft, C.M. Working with black parents. In R.R. Abidin (Ed.), *Parent education and intervention handbook.* Springfield, Ill.: Thomas, 1980.

David, H.P., & Baldwin, W.P. Childbearing and child development: Demographic and psychosocial trends. *American Psychologist,* 1979, **34,** 866–871.

Davis, A.J. Prenatal classes: The baby business. *Supervisor Nurse,* 1979, **10,** 57–58, 61.

Davis, W.D. The patient unready for behavior therapy. In W.G. Klopfer, & M.R. Reed (Eds.), *Problems in psychotherapy: An eclectic approach.* Washington: Hemisphere, 1974.

DeSocio, C.A., & Hollen, P. What is a PEDS program? *Pediatric Nursing,* 1978, **4,** 16–19.

Dickie, J.R., & Gerber, S.C. Training in social competence: The effects on mothers, fathers and infants. *Child Development,* 1980, **51,** 1248–1251.

Dinkmeyer, D., & McKay, G.D. *Raising a responsible child: Practical steps to successful family relationships.* New York: Simon & Schuster, 1973.

Doherty, W.J., & Ryder, R.G. Parent effectiveness training (P.E.T.): Criticisms and caveats. *Journal of Marital and Family Therapy,* 1980, **6,** 409–419.

Donovan, W.L., & Leavitt, L.A. Early cognitive development and its relation to maternal physiologic and behavioral responsiveness. Paper presented to the Society for Research in Child Development, New Orleans, 1977.

Donovan, W.L., Leavitt, L.A., & Balling, J.D. Maternal physiological responses to infant signals. *Psychophysiology,* 1978, **15,** 68–74.

Dreikurs, R., Gould, S., & Corsini, R. *Family Council.* Chicago: Regnery, 1974.

Dreikurs, R., & Soltz, V. *Children: The challenge.* New York: Hawthorn Books, 1964.

Dunn, J., & Kendrick, C. Interaction between young siblings in the context of family relationships. In M. Lewis, & L.A. Rosenblum (Eds.), *The child and its family.* New York: Plenum, 1978.

Eastman, A.M., & Eyberg, S.M. The relationship between behavior problems and parent knowledge of behavior management skills. Paper presented at the 13th Banff International Conference on Behavior Modification, Banff, Alberta, March, 1981.

Edelman, M.W. Who is for children? *American Psychologist,* 1981, **36,** 109–116.

Eisenberg, L. Youth in a changing society. In V.C. Vaughn, & T.B. Brazelton (Eds.), *The family—Can it be saved?* Chicago: Year Book Medical Publications, 1976.

Eyberg, S.M. A Parent-child interaction model for the treatment of psychological disorders in early childhood. Paper presented at the annual meeting of the Western Psychological Association, San Diego, California, April, 1979.

Eyberg, S.M., & Johnson, S.M. Multiple assessment of behavior modification with families: Effects of contracting and order of treated problems. *Journal of Consulting and Clinical Psychology,* 1974, **42,** 151–156.

Eyberg, S.M., & Matarazzo, R.G. Training parents as therapists: A comparison between individual parent-child interaction training and parent group didactic training. *Journal of Clinical Psychology,* 1980, **36,** 492–499.

Eyberg, S.M., & Ross, A.W. Assessment of children's behavior problems: The validation of a new inventory. *Journal of Clinical Psychology,* 1978, **7,** 113–116.

Falbo, T. Only children, stereotypes, and research. In M. Lewis, & L.A. Rosenblum (Eds.), *The child and its family.* New York: Plenum, 1978.

Ford, J.D. An interpersonal-effectiveness approach to consumer health education. *Medical Care,* 1979, **17,** 1061–1067.

Forehand, R., & King, H.E. Noncompliant children: Effects of parent training on behavior and attitude change. *Behavior Modification,* 1977, **1,** 93–108.

Forrester, B.J. Parents as educational change agents for infants: Competencies not credentials. Paper presented at the meeting of the Council on Exceptional Children, Washington, D.C., March, 1972.

Fraiberg, S. Blind infants and their mothers: An examination of the sign system. In M. Lewis, & L.A. Rosenblum (Eds.), *The effect of the infant on its caregiver.* New York: Wiley, 1974.

Franks, C.M., & Susskind, D.J. Behavior modification with children: Rationale and technique. *Journal of School Psychology,* 1968, **6,** 75–88.

Frodi, A.M., Lamb, M.E., Leavitt, L.A., & Donovan, W.L. Father's and mother's responses to infant smiles and cries. *Infant Behavior and Development,* 1978, **1,** 187–198.

Gadlin, H. Child discipline and the pursuit of self: An historical interpretation. In H.W. Reese, & L.P. Lipsitt (Eds.), *Advances in child development and behavior* (Vol. 12). New York: Academic Press, 1978.

Gilberg, A.L. The stress of parenting. *Child Psychiatry and Human Development,* 1975, **6,** 59–67.

Glasgow, R.E., & Rosen, G.M. Behavioral bibliotherapy: A review of self-help behavior therapy manuals. *Psychological Bulletin,* 1978, **85,** 1–23.

Glasser, W. *Reality therapy: A new approach to psychiatry.* New York: Harper & Row, 1965.

Glick, I.D., & Kessler, D.R. *Marital and family therapy.* New York: Grune & Stratton, 1980.

Glick, P.C., & Norton, A.J. Marrying, divorcing and living together in the U.S. today. *Population Bulletin,* 1977, **32**(No. 5), 3–39.

Goldberg, S. Social competence in infancy: A model of parent-infant interaction. *Merrill-Palmer Quarterly,* 1977, **23,** 163–175.

Goodman Campbell, S.B. Mother-infant interaction as a function of maternal ratings of temperament. *Child Psychiatry and Human Development,* 1979, **10,** 67–77.

Gordon, I.J. *Early child stimulation through parent education.* Final report (Project No. PHS-R-306). Washington, D.C.: DHEW Children's Bureau, Social and Rehabilitation Service, 1971.

Gordon, T. *Parent effectiveness training: The tested new way to raise responsible children.* New York: Wyden, 1970.

Gordon, T., & Sands, J.G. *P.E.T. in action.* New York: Wyden, 1976.

Gorham, K.A., Des Jardins, C., Page, R., Pettis, E., & Scheiber, B. Effect on parents. In N. Hobbs (Ed.), *Issues in the classification of children* (Vol. 2). San Francisco: Jossey-Bass, 1975.

Grams, A. Parenting: Concept and process. The Association for Childhood Education International Parenting. Washington, D.C., 1973.

Gray, S. Home visiting programs for parents of young children. *DARCEE Papers and Reports,* 1971, **5**(4).

Graziano, A.M., & Fink, R.S. Secondary effects in mental health treatment. *Journal of Consulting and Clinical Psychology,* 1973, **40,** 356–364.

Greenbaum, C.W., & Landau, R. The infant's exposure to talk by familiar people: Mothers, fathers and siblings in different environments. In M. Lewis, & L.A. Rosenblum (Eds.), *The child and its family.* New York: Plenum, 1978.

Greenberg, S. *Right from the start: A guide to nonsexist child rearing.* Boston: Houghton Mifflin, 1978.

Greene, B.F., Clark, H.B., & Risley, T.R. *Shopping with children: Advice for parents.* San Rafael, Calif.: Academic Therapy, 1977.

Gresh, S. Fathers and babies: A brand new closeness. *Glamour,* 1980, **78,** 155–156.

Guerney, B.G., & Drake, A. An exploratory survey on maternal child-rearing concerns and help seeking. *Child Psychiatry and Human Development,* 1973, **3,** 165–178.

Guirguis, W.R. Is parenthood teachable? *British Journal of Psychiatry,* 1978, **133,** 283–284.

Hanf, C., & Kling, J. Facilitating parent-child interaction: a two-stage training model. Unpublished manuscript, Oregon Health Sciences University, 1973.

Hawkins, R.P. It's time we taught the young how to be good parents (And don't you wish we'd started a long time ago?). *Psychology Today,* 1972, **6,** 28–40.

Hawkins, R.P., Peterson, R.F., Schweid, E., & Bijou, S.W. Behavior therapy in the home: Amelioration of problem parent-child relations with the parent in a therapeutic role. *Journal of Experimental Child Psychology,* 1966, **4,** 99–107.

Heber, R., & Garber, H. The Milwaukee project: A study of the use of family intervention to prevent cultural-familial mental retardation. In B.Z. Friedlander, G.M. Sterritt, & G.E. Kirk (Eds.), *Assessment and intervention: Exceptional infant* (Vol. 3). New York: Brunner/Mazel, 1975.

Heifetz, L.J. From consumer to middleman: Emerging roles for parents in the network of services for retarded children. In R.R. Abidin (Ed.), *Parent education and intervention handbook.* Springfield, Ill.: Thomas, 1980.

Herbert, E.W., Pinkston, E.M., Hayden, M.L., Sajwaj, T.E., Pinkston, S., Cordua, G., & Jackson, C. Adverse effects of differential parental attention. *Journal of Applied Behavior Analysis,* 1973, **6,** 15–30.

Hill, R., & Aldous, J. Socialization for marriage and parenthood. In D.A. Goslin (Ed.), *Handbook of socialization theory and research.* Chicago: Rand McNally, 1969.

Hobbs, D.F. Parenthood as crisis: A third study. *Journal of Marriage and the Family,* 1965, **27,** 367–372.

Hoffman, L.W., & Manis, J.D. Influences of children on marital interaction and parental satisfactions and dissatisfactions. In R.M. Lerner, & G.B. Spanier, (Eds.), *Child influences on marital and family interaction: A life-span perspective.* New York: Academic Press, 1978.

Honig, A.S. Working with parents of preschool children. In R.R. Abidin (Ed.), *Parent educa-*

tion and intervention handbook. Springfield, Ill.: Thomas, 1980.

Jackson, R.H. Other genetic disorders. In J. Lindemann, *The psychological and behavioral aspects of physical disability: A manual for health practioners.* New York: Plenum, 1981.

Jackson, R.H., & Seitz, S. When parents ask for help. Unpublished manuscript, Oregon Health Sciences University, 1977.

Jackson, R.H., & Terdal, L. Parent education within a pediatric practice. *Journal of Pediatric Psychology,* 1978, **3,** 2–5.

Jacobs, B.S., & Moss, H.A. Birth order and sex of sibling as determinants of mother-infant interaction. *Child Development,* 1976, **47,** 315–322.

Jakobson, R. Why "mama" and "papa"? *Selected writings of Roman Jakobson.* The Hague: Mouton, 1962.

Johnson, S.M., & Bolstad, O.D. Methodological issues in naturalistic observation: Some problems and solutions for field research. In L.A. Hamerlynck, L.C. Handy, & E.J. Mash (Eds.), *Behavior change: Methodology, concepts, and practice.* Champaign, Ill.: Research Press, 1973.

Johnson, S.M., & Eyberg, S.M. Evaluating outcome data: A reply to Gordon. *Journal of Consulting and Clinical Psychology,* 1975, **43,** 917–919.

Jones, P.A. High school programs for future parents. The Association for Childhood Education International Parenting. Washington, D.C., 1973.

Kagan, J. The role of family during the first half decade. In V.C. Vaughan, & T.B. Brazelton (Eds.), *The family—Can it be saved?* Chicago: Year Book Medical Publishers, 1976.

Kagan, J. The child in the family. In A.S. Rossi, J. Kagan, & T.K. Hareven (Eds.), *The family.* New York: Norton, 1978.

Kagan, J. Family experience and the child's development. *American Psychologist,* 1979, **34,** 886–891. (a)

Kagan, J. Overview: Perspectives on human infancy. In J. Osofsky (Ed.), *Handbook of infant development.* New York: Wiley, 1979. (b)

Kawin, E. *Parenthood in a free nation* (3 vols.). New York: Macmillan, 1963.

Kellerman, J. Big brother and big mother. *Newsweek,* January 12, 1981, 15.

Kelly, G.A. *The psychology of personal constructs* (Vols. 1 & 2). New York: Norton, 1955.

Klaus, M.H., & Kennell, J.H. *Maternal-infant bonding*. St. Louis: Mosby, 1976. (a)

Klaus, M.H., & Kennell, J.H. Parent-to-infant attachment. In V.C. Vaughn, & T.B. Brazelton (Eds.), *The family—Can it be saved?* Chicago: Year Book Medical Publishers, 1976. (b)

Kogan, K.L., & Tyler, N. Mother-child interaction in young physically handicapped children. *American Journal of Mental Deficiency*, 1973, **77**, 492–497.

Kohlberg, L. Children's perceptions of contemporary value systems. In N.B. Talbot (Ed.), *Raising children in modern America: Problems and prospective solutions*. Boston: Little, Brown, 1976.

Konner, M. Relations among infants and juveniles in comparative perspective. In M. Lewis, & L.A. Rosenblum (Eds.), *Friendship and peer relations*. New York: Wiley, 1975.

Korn, S.J., Chess, S., & Fernandez, P. The impact of children's physical handicaps on marital quality and family interaction. In R.M. Lerner, & G.B. Spanier (Eds.), *Child influences on marital and family interaction: A life-span perspective*. New York: Academic Press, 1978.

Korner, A.F. Individual differences at birth: Implications for early experience and later development. *American Journal of Orthopsychiatry*, 1971, **41**, 608–619.

Lamb, M.E. The role of the father: An overview. In M.E. Lamb (Ed.), *The role of the father in child development*. New York: Wiley, 1976.

Lamb, M.E. Father-infant and mother-infant interaction in the first year of life. *Child Development*, 1977, **48**, 167–181.

Lamb, M.E. Influence of the child on marital quality and family interaction during the prenatal, perinatal and infancy periods. In R.M. Lerner & G.B. Spanier (Eds.), *Child influences on marital and family interaction: A life-span perspective*. New York: Academic Press, 1978. (a)

Lamb, M.E. The father's role in the infant's social world. In J.H. Stevens & M. Mathews (Eds.), *Mother/child, father/child relationships*. Washington, D.C.: National Association for the Education of Young Children, 1978. (b)

Lamb, M.E., & Baumrind, D. Socialization and personality development in the preschool years. In M.E. Lamb (Ed.), *Social and personality development*. New York: Holt, Rinehart & Winston, 1978.

Lamb, M.E., Chase-Lansdale, L., & Tresch Owen, M. The changing American family and its implications for infant social development: The sample case of maternal employment. In M. Lewis, & L.A. Rosenblum (Eds.), *The child and its family*. New York: Plenum, 1978.

Lang, R. *Birth book*. Cupertino, Calif.: Genesis, 1972.

Lazarus, A.A. *Behavior therapy and beyond*. New York: McGraw-Hill, 1971.

Legg, C., Sherick, I., & Wadland, W. Reactions of preschool children to the birth of a sibling. *Child Psychiatry and Human Development*, 1975, **5**, 5–39.

LeMasters, E.E. Parenthood as crisis. *Marriage and Family Living*, 1957, **19**, 352–355.

Lerner, R.M., & Spanier, G.B. A dynamic interactional view of child and family development. In R.M. Lerner, & G.B. Spanier (Eds.), *Child influence on marital and family interaction: A life-span perspective*. New York: Academic Press, 1978.

Lewis, M., & Feiring, C. The child's social world. In R.M. Lerner & G.B. Spanier (Eds.), *Child influences on marital and family interaction: A life-span perspective*. New York: Academic Press, 1978.

Lewis, M., & Weinraub, M. Sex of parent x sex of child; socioemotional development. In R. Richart, R. Friedman, & R. Vande Wiele (Eds.), *Sex differences in behavior*. New York: Wiley, 1974.

Lewis, M., Young, G, Brooks, J., & Michalson, L. The beginning of friendship. In M. Lewis & L. Rosenblum (Eds.), *Friendship and peer relations: The origins of behavior* (Vol. 4). New York: Wiley, 1975.

Lynn, D.B. *The father: His role in child development*. Monterey, Calif.: Brooks/Cole, 1974.

Lytton, H., & Zwirner, W. Compliance and its controlling stimuli observed in a natural setting. *Developmental Psychology*, 1975, **11**, 780–787.

Marland, S.P. Education for parenthood. *Children Today*, 1973, **2**, 3.

Martin, B. Parent-child relations. In F.D. Horowitz (Ed.), *The Development of behavioral competency in infancy*. Chicago: University of Chicago Press, 1975.

Matson, J.L., & Ollendick, T.H. Issues in toilet training normal children. *Behavior Therapy*, 1977, **8**, 549–553.

McIntire, R.W. Parenthood training or mandatory

birth control: Take your choice. *Psychology Today,* 1973, **7,** 34–39, 132–133, 143.

Mech, E.V. Adoption: A policy perspective. In B.M. Caldwell & H.N. Ricciuti (Eds.), *Review of child development research.* Chicago: The University of Chicago Press, 1973.

Minuchin, S. *Families and family therapy.* Cambridge: Harvard University Press, 1974.

Minuchin, S., & Minuchin, P. The child in context: A systems approach to growth and treatment. In N.B. Talbot (Ed.), *Raising children in modern America: Problems and prospective solutions.* Boston: Little, Brown, 1976.

Mischel, W. On the future of personality measurement. *American Psychologist,* 1977, **32,** 246–254.

Mussen, P.H. Choices, regrets and lousy models (with reference to prosocial development). Presidential address to the Division of Developmental Psychology, presented at the meeting of the American Psychological Association, San Francisco, August, 1977.

Mussen, P.H., Conger, J.J., & Kagan, J. *Child development and personality.* New York: Harper & Row, 1974.

Mussen, P.H., & Distler, L. Masculinity, identification and father-son relationships. *Journal of Abnormal and Social Psychology,* 1959, **59,** 350–356.

O'Dell, S.L. Training parents in behavior modification: A review. *Psychological Bulletin,* 1974, **81,** 418–433.

O'Dell, S.L., Tarler-Benlolo, L., & Flynn, J.M. An instrument to measure knowledge of behavioral principles as applied to children. *Journal of Behavior Therapy and Experimental Psychiatry,* 1979, **10,** 29–34.

Overton, W.F., & Reese, H.W. Models of development: Methodological implications. In J.R. Nesselroade, & H.W. Reese (Eds.), *Life-span developmental psychology: Methodological issues.* New York: Academic Press, 1973.

Parents help children learn and play in public health clinics and hospital-based schools. *Hospitals,* 1979, **53,** 14–15.

Parke, R.D., & O'Leary, S. Father-mother-infant interaction in the newborn period: Some findings, some observations and some unresolved issues. In K.R. Riegel & J. Meacham (Eds.), *The developing individual in a changing world: Social and environmental issues* (Vol. 2). The Hague: Mouton, 1975.

Parke, R.D., & Sawin, D.B. The father's role in infancy: A reevaluation. *Family Co-ordinator,* 1976, **25**(4).

Parke, R.D., & Sawin, D.B. Fathering: It's a major role. *Psychology Today,* 1977, **11,** 109–112. (a)

Parke, R.D., & Sawin, D.B. The family in early infancy: Social interactional and attitudinal analyses. Paper presented to the Society for Research in Child Development, New Orleans, March, 1977. (b)

Patterson, G.R. *Families.* Champaign, Ill.: Research Press, 1971.

Patterson, G.R. Siblings: Fellow travelers in coercive family processes. Paper presented at the Eleventh Annual Banff International Conference on Behavior Modification, Banff, Alberta, March 1979. (a)

Patterson, G.R. Treatment for children with conduct problems: A review of outcome studies. In S. Feshbach & A. Fraczek (Eds.), *Aggression and behavior change: Biological and social processes.* New York: Praeger, 1979. (b)

Patterson, G.R. Mothers: The unacknowledged victims. *Monographs of the Society for Research in Child Development,* 1980, **45,** 1–54.

Patterson, G.R., & Gullion, M.E. *Living with children: New methods for parents and children.* Champaign, Ill.: Research Press, 1971.

Patterson, G.R., Reid, J.B., Jones, R.R., & Conger, R.E. *A social learning approach to family intervention: Families with aggressive children* (Vol. 1). Eugene, Ore.: Castalia, 1975.

Peck, E., & Granzig, W. *The parent test: How to measure and develop your talent for parenthood.* New York: Putnam, 1978.

Pedersen, F.A., & Robson, K.S. Father participation in infancy. *American Journal of Orthopsychiatry,* 1969, **39,** 466–472.

Pedersen, F.A., Yarrow, L.J., Anderson, B.J., & Cain, R.L. Conceptualization of father influences in the infancy period. In M. Lewis, & L.A. Rosenblum (Eds.), *The child and its family.* New York: Plenum, 1978.

Perkins, E.R. A look at the open university parenthood courses. *Midwife, Health Visitor and Community Nurse,* 1979, **15,** 223–227.

Pumroy, D.K., & Pumroy, S.S. Systematic observation and reinforcement technique in toilet training. *Psychological Reports,* 1965, **16,** 467–478.

Rapoport, R., Rapoport, R.N., Strelitz, Z., &

Kew, S. *Fathers, mothers and society: Towards new alliances.* New York: Basic Books, 1977.

Richmond, J.B., & Janis, J. A perspective on primary prevention in the earliest years. *Children Today,* 1980, 9, 2–6.

Roberts, M.W., & Forehand, R. The assessment of maladaptive parent-child interactions by direct observation: An analysis of methods. *Journal of Abnormal Child Psychology,* 1978, **6,** 257–270.

Rollins, B.C., & Thomas, D.L. Parental support, power and control techniques in the socialization of children. In W.R. Burr, R. Hill, F.I. Nye, & I.L. Reiss (Eds.), *Contemporary theories about the family* (Vol. I). New York: Free Press, 1979.

Rosenthal, R. *Experimenter effects in behavioral research.* New York: Appleton-Century-Croft, 1966.

Russell, C.S. Transition to parenthood: Problems and gratifications. *Journal of Marriage and the Family,* 1974, **30,** 294.

Russo, S. Adaptations in behavioral therapy with children. *Behaviour Research and Therapy,* 1964, **2,** 43–47.

Rutter, M. *Maternal deprivation reassessed.* Harmondsworth, England: Penguin, 1972.

Rutter, M. Maternal deprivation, 1972–1978: New findings, new concepts, new approaches. *Child Development,* 1979, **50,** 283–305.

Saving the family. *Newsweek,* May 15, 1978, 63–90.

Scaer, R., & Korte, D. MOM Survey: Maternity options for mothers—What do women want in maternity care? *Birth and the Family Journal,* 1978, **5,** 20–26.

Scarr, S., & Weinberg, R.A. IQ test performance of black children adopted by white families. *American Psychologist,* 1976, **31,** 726–739.

Schroeder, C.S. Psychologists in a private pediatric practice. *Journal of Pediatric Psychology,* 1979, **4,** 5–18.

Schvaneveldt, J.D., & Ihinger, M. Sibling relationships in the family. In W.R. Burr, R. Hill, F.I. Nye, & I.L. Reiss (Eds.), *Contemporary theories about the family* (Vol. I). New York: Free Press, 1979.

Shoop, L.L. Education for parenthood. *Children Today,* 1979, **8,** 23–26.

Sigman, M., Cohen, S.E., Beckwith, L., & Parmelee, A.H. Social and familial influences on the development of preterm infants. *Journal of Pediatric Psychology,* 1981, **6,** 1–13.

Sigman, M., & Parmelee, A.H. Longitudinal evaluation of the preterm infant. In T.M. Field, A.M. Sostek, S. Goldberg, & H.H. Shuman (Eds.), *Infants born at risk: Behavior and development.* New York: SP Medical and Scientific Books, 1979.

Smith, J.M., & Smith, D.E.P. *Child management: A program for parents and teachers.* Champaign, Ill.: Research Press, 1976.

Sniderman, S. Modifying practices to promote family-centered care in the neonatal intensive care nursery. *Birth and the Family Journal,* 1980, **7,** 255–259.

Snyder, D.M. Future directions in the care of the full-term newborn. *Birth and the Family Journal,* 1980, **7,** 264–267.

Solomon, E.S., Clare, J.E., & Westoff, C.F. Social and psychological factors affecting fertility. *The Millbank Memorial Fund Quarterly,* 1956, **34,** 160–177.

Sugarman, M. Paranatal influences on maternal-infant attachment. *American Journal of Orthopsychiatry,* 1977, **47,** 407–421.

Sussman, A., & Guggenheim, M. *The basic ACLU guide to the rights of parents.* New York: Avon, 1980.

Sweeny, S.L., & Davis, F.B. Transition to parenthood: A group experience. *Maternal-Child Nursing Journal,* 1979, **8,** 59–64.

Terdal, L., Jackson, R.H., & Garner, A.M. Mother-child interactions: A comparison between normal and developmentally delayed groups. In E.J. Mash, L.A. Hamerlynck, & L.C. Handy (Eds.), *Behavior modification and families.* New York: Brunner/Mazel, 1976.

Tharp, R.G., & Wetzel, R.J. *Behavior modification in the natural environment.* New York: Academic Press, 1969.

Thomas, A., Chess, S., & Birch, H.G. *Temperament and behavior disorders in children.* New York: New York University Press, 1968.

Thompson, V.D. Family size: Implicit policies and assumed psychological outcomes. *Journal of Social Issues,* 1974, **30,** 93–124.

U.S. Bureau of the Census, Census of population: 1970, Subject reports: Final report PC(2)-3A. *Women by number of children ever born.*

Uzoka, A.F. The myth of the nuclear family: Historical background and clinical implications. *American Psychologist,* 1979, **34,** 1095–1106.

Vietze, P.M., & Hopkins, J.B. Mother-infant interaction: The arena of early learning. In R.R. Abidin (Ed.), *Parent education and intervention handbook.* Springfield, Ill.: Thomas, 1980.

Wahl, G., Johnson, S.M., Johansson, S., & Martin, S. An operant analysis of parent-child interaction. *Behavior Therapy,* 1974, **5,** 64–78.

Wahler, R.G., Winkel, G.H., Peterson, R.F., & Morrison, D.C. Mothers as behavior therapists for their own children. *Behaviour Research and Therapy,* 1965, **3,** 113–124.

Walters, J., & Walters, L.H. Parent-child relationships: A review, 1970–1979. *Journal of Marriage and the Family,* 1980, **42,** 807–822.

Warren, S.A. The distressed parent of the disabled child. In W.G. Klopfer & M.R. Reed (Eds.), *Problems in psychotherapy: An eclectic approach.* Washington: Wiley, 1974.

Watson, J.S. Memory and "contingency analysis" in infant learning. *Merrill-Palmer Quarterly,* 1967, **13,** 55–76.

Wente, A.S., & Crockenberg, S.B. Transition to fatherhood: Lamaze preparation, adjustment difficulty and the husband-wife relationship. *The Family Coordinator,* 1976, **25,** 351–357.

Wernick, R. *The family.* New York: Time-Life Books, 1974.

West, D.J., & Farrington, D.T. *Who becomes delinquent: Second report of the Cambridge study in delinquent development.* New York: Crane, Russak, 1973.

White House conference on children: Report to the president. Washington, D.C.: United States Government Printing Office, 1970.

White, S.H. Socialization and education—For what and by what means? In N.B.Talbot (Ed.), *Raising children in modern America: Problems and prospective solutions.* Boston: Little, Brown, 1976.

Wolf, M.W. Social validity: The case for subjective measurement or how applied behavior analysis is finding its heart. Invited address to the Division of the Experimental Analysis of Behavior, American Psychological Association, Washington, D.C., September, 1976.

Yarrow, M.R. Research on child rearing as a basis for practice. *Child Welfare,* 1973, **52,** 209–219.

Youth on the move. *U.S. News and World Report,* December 29, 1980, 72–80.

CHAPTER 39

The Development of Moral Values and Behavior: Implications for Clinical Practice

GERALD E. GRUEN AND JULIE LARRIEU

Research and theory in the area of the development of moral values and moral conduct has been confined largely to the laboratory and the ivory tower of academia. Some attempts have been made to apply knowledge about moral development in educational settings (Blatt & Kohlberg, 1974; Mosher & Sprinthall, 1970, 1971; Selman & Lieberman, 1975; Sullivan, 1975), but little effort has been directed toward possible applications of this knowledge in the clinic. The purpose of this chapter is to make a first step in that direction.

The need for bringing these two rather diverse enterprises—basic research on moral development and clinical practice—into some kind of amalgamation may not readily be apparent. Both the traditional psychotherapies and the newer behavioral (or cognitive-behavioral) approaches to working with children in the clinic have paid little attention to the accumulating body of knowledge in this area. There may be several reasons for this. First of all, the contributions that this body of literature could make to clinical practice have not been made evident. We hope to begin to remedy this state of affairs. Second, many clinicians have not had the time nor the inclination to keep up with the latest findings in an area that they may view as rather esoteric and tangential to their more practical aims. And, third, it is very likely that for many clinicians the whole area of "morality" has acquired negative connotations. The first thing that clinicians, even behaviorally oriented ones, are taught is the importance of being warm and accepting and, above all, not to make moral judgments concerning their clients. While this is generally a reasonable and helpful dictum, ignoring knowledge about moral development on this basis could only be due to confusion about who is making the moral judgments—the clinician or the child. The theory and research in this area, of course, deal with the child's judgments vis-a-vis their own, or others', behaviors, in situations where perceptions of what one "ought" to do is the issue. We are persuaded that knowledge concerning children's changing concepts of right and wrong, as well as related behavioral changes, is knowledge that could be useful to the clinician.

This is particularly true in instances where antisocial or delinquent acts are the problem for which children are referred to the clinic or, in a not necessarily reciprocal instance, where a low frequency of prosocial behavior or a relative absence of concern for others may be the problem. The exact percentage of clients referred to the clinic for these kinds of problems is not known, but it is probable that they make up a significant proportion of referrals. There are, of course, many children referred to clinics for social behavior problems that are not uniquely "moral" in any sense—e.g., inappropriate or bizarre interpersonal behavior or a lack of social skills—but these are not the focus of this chapter. We will attempt only to review theory and research dealing with the development of behavior and concepts that might in some sense fall under the rubric of "moral."

Our orientation in this review will be decidedly developmental. That is, we will emphasize studies that have explored age-related changes in moral conduct as well as those that have focused on specific cognitive and affective developmental processes related to moral development. The relationship between moral judgment and conduct will also be addressed. We will not be concerned with studies that deal with the acquisition of "values" (in the broad sense) that simply reflect the core cultural pattern of society. Such studies (e.g., Beech & Schoeppe, 1974) typically report a relative stability of the ranking of different values—such as Rokeach's (1968) 18 "terminal" and 18 "instrumental" values—across age levels. Rather, we will direct our attention to those studies that deal with developmental changes in the level of organization of judgments of right and wrong and those that deal specifically with prosocial or antisocial acts.

The chapter will be divided into three major divisions: (1) contrasting views of moral development, (2) review of research on factors influencing moral development, and (3) implications of theory and research for practicing clinicians.

CONTRASTING VIEWS OF MORAL DEVELOPMENT

As might be expected, representatives of the three major theoretical perspectives in developmental psychology have approached moral development in distinctly different ways. In this section we will briefly discuss the differing approaches derived from the psychoanalytic, the social-learning, and the cognitive-developmental theories. Following that, we will attempt to extract that which is agreed upon by all three theories and to suggest some ways in which the theories complement each other.

The Psychoanalytic Approach

The central thrust of the psychoanalytic approach to moral development has been reconstructed very succinctly by Hoffman (1970).

He correctly pointed out that, from his point of view, parental intervention and control subject the young child to many frustrations that become the source of hostility toward the parent. However, the child represses this hostility due to anxiety over anticipated punishment, especially loss of the parents' love:

To help maintain the repression, as well as elicit continuing expressions of affection, the child adopts in relatively unmodified form the rules and prohibitions emanating from the parent. He also develops a generalized motive to emulate the behavior and adopt the inner states of the parent. In addition he adopts the parent's capacity to punish himself when he violates a prohibition or is tempted to do so... This self-punishment is experienced as guilt feelings, which are dreaded because of their intensity and their resemblance to the earlier anxieties about punishment and abandonment. The child therefore tries to avoid guilt by acting always in accordance with incorporated parental prohibitions and erecting various mechanisms of defense against the conscious awareness of impulses to act the contrary. (Hoffman, 1970, p. 282)

From this point of view, it is assumed that the basic processes of conscience formation are accomplished by about 5 or 6 years of age. Anxiety over physical retribution or loss of parental love is seen as the largely irrational and unconscious motive upon which moral standards are based, and these moral standards, in turn, serve the function of keeping antisocial impulses from conscious awareness. In order to reduce anxiety, "the child tries to be like the parent—to adopt the parent's behavioral mannerisms, thoughts, feelings, and even the capacity to punish oneself and experience guilt over violating a moral standard" (Hoffman, 1979, p. 959).

With this theoretical orientation, it is not surprising that research deriving from psychoanalytic theory has emphasized either (1) guilt that results when these standards are violated, (2) identification processes in which moral standards and values that were originally external to the child become part of the child's own set of values, and (3) the enduring effects of parental discipline techniques, or, more broadly, parent-child interaction styles, on the child's moral development. With its emphasis on the self-gratifying aspects of children's behavior, psychoanalytic theory has been relatively more fruitful in raising hypotheses germane to antisocial than prosocial behavior development.

The Social-Learning Approach

Social-learning theorists are in some ways consistent with psychoanalytic theorists in their approach to conceptualizing moral development. For example, "conscience" may be seen as a conditioned reflex (Eysenck, 1976), an anxiety-based avoidance of acts that have been punished by society or, society's representatives, parents. From this theoretical perspective, morality has been defined in terms of specific acts (or avoidance of acts) that are learned on the basis of rewards, punishments, or vicarious reinforcements through modeling. Inevitably, this leads to "right" and "wrong" being defined solely in terms of culturally shared standards of conduct; for example, Berkowitz (1964, p. 44) defined moral values as "'evaluations' of action believed by members of a given society to be right."

Like psychoanalytic theory, learning-theory approaches to morality also have been concerned with the ways in which the individual comes to administer his or her own rewards and punishments, that is, how he or she "internalizes" controls that were originally external and thus becomes capable of behavior that is independent of external sanctions. Although the specific mechanism or mechanisms for accomplishing this important feat of internalization have never been explicitly articulated, the impetus for the development of internal moral standards is clearly the direct or indirect rewards and punishments present in the external environment. These standards are usually mediated by socialization agents such as parents or teachers. Observational learning (cf. Bandura, Ross, & Ross, 1961; Bandura & McDonald, 1963) has been widely accepted by investigators utilizing this approach as an effective means of modifying both aggressive and prosocial behaviors in children.

Unlike psychoanalytic or cognitive-developmental theories, social-learning theories generally do not view moral development as a unitary process. Rather, it is seen as but one more example of discrimination learning. Certain responses are elicited or inhibited in the presence of specific stimuli as a result of reinforcement contingencies. Social-learning theories appear equally able to "explain" the acquisition of prosocial and antisocial behaviors. These theories are not "developmental" in that the same principles of behavior acquisition are assumed to operate with any aged child or adult. Nevertheless, some investigators with a social-learning point of view have been interested in behavior changes associated with age; this approach has been very fruitful and heuristic in generating studies with children and adolescents.

The Cognitive-Developmental Approach

The primary proponents of the cognitive-developmental approach to studying moral development have been Piaget (1932) and Kohlberg (1969). From this point of view, children are not seen as passive masses of protoplasm who are either driven by instinctive impulses or totally shaped by environmental forces. Rather, they act on their environment and, in turn, are acted upon by it. The child actively perceives, interprets, and organizes stimuli in his or her environment in such a way as to further adaptation.

The thought structures underlying moral concepts are believed to change with development and bring about related changes in the network of moral concepts that characterize a child's evaluations of right and wrong. It is assumed that there is an invariant sequence, or series of stages, through which all individuals develop. In its pure form this means that each stage is seen as an integrated whole that is qualitatively different from all other stages. Thus, there should be a consistency in level of response among an individual's acts and thoughts that reflects the defining characteristics of his or her current stage of development.

Further, there is thought to be a general direction of movement from relatively global, undifferentiated ways of viewing the world to increasingly differentiated and integrated forms of reasoning. In the course of development, an emerging stage develops out of its predecessor and a synthesis between the old and the new is formed. This synthesis cannot be forced on the individual readymade but must be constructed by the individual alone. The order of succession of stages is constant and universal although the environment and level of cognitive development can advance or retard the appearance of the stage.

For Piaget, the natural direction of moral development is simply characterized by a number of shifts: from absolutism to relativism of moral perspective; from heteronomous (reliance on adult authority) to autonomous respect for rules; from "objective responsibility" (exclusive concern with the consequences of acts) to "subjective" concern with intentions; and from ideas of immanent justice to more reality-based views of punishment. For Kohlberg, moral development proceeds more specifically through three general levels of moral orientation composed of two stages each. Briefly, the first level is a hedonistic, premoral level in which rules are imposed from external sources. The only motive for compliance is to obtain rewards, to avoid punishment, or to have favors returned (reminiscent of the social-learning position). The second level is characterized by conventional conformity in which rules are obeyed simply to secure approval, to meet others' expectations, not to disappoint "significant others," or to maintain the conventional social order. Finally, the highest level is characterized by conformity to rationally derived principles and standards that can be negotiated or shared with others. These principles can acquire the status of rights or duties. The cognitive-developmental approach can be viewed as providing a structure that describes the cognitive constraints, or the limits, of the moral judgments that are possible for the child at the various developmental levels.

Some Points of Agreement

In a very real sense, the various theoretical points of view address differing domains of moral development: psychoanalytic theory stresses motives and affect, social-learning theory stresses behavior or observable acts, and cognitive-developmental theory stresses the judgment process or cognitions. Thus, they can be viewed as complementary. It is also clear that none of these theories can handle all aspects of moral development.

However, there are several points at which these theories meet. For example, Mussen and Eisenberg-Berg (1977) have pointed out three areas of agreement among these theories:

1. Children are initially self-centered;
2. Children become more oriented toward others as they achieve greater cognitive maturity and experience; and
3. With development the control of moral behavior shifts from external rewards and punishments to internalized motives or individualized principles. (p. 34)

Points one and three are obvious given the review of the theories above. However, point two deserves some elaboration. Increasingly, investigators in this area (cf. Lickona, 1975; Aronfreed, 1968, p. 265) agree that there is a strong cognitive component to moral development. Mischel and Mischel (1976) have pointed out that cognitive competencies were among the best predictors of "honesty" in conduct in the classic study of morality by Hartshorne and May (1928). And the Mischels themselves, in their development of a "cognitive social-learning approach" to moral development, have given a prominent role to "cognitive competencies."

Increasing cognitive competence, in turn, has been associated with greater ability to take the perspectives of others (Flavell, 1968; Piaget & Inhelder, 1956; Selman, 1971). Competence in perspective taking makes it possible for the developing child to orient more fully to the covert feelings, thoughts, and intentions of others (Shantz, 1975)—an orientation that many believe is a prerequisite for reaching higher levels of moral development.

Lickona (1975) has suggested another point at which the theories are beginning to converge. This juncture centers on the role of affect in moral development, namely, the idea that some form of optimal conflict, arousal, or disequilibrium facilitates growth of moral development:

Social learning theory (e.g., Burton, 1976) talks about moderate levels of anxiety as optimally motivating states for learning new moral behaviors or performing old ones. Hoffman asserts that the child needs "the normal run of distress experience" to develop sympathy and requires a certain amount of social conflict to allow him to learn that differences among people can be worked out... Cognitive-developmental theories like Piaget's and Kohlberg's hold that disequilibrium is necessary to stimulate reorganization of thinking into higher state forms. (Lickona, 1975, p. 6)

We do not wish to overemphasize the commonalities among these theories because they do focus on very different aspects of moral development. They also are based on discrepant philosophical assumptions about the nature of human beings and cannot, therefore, easily be integrated into one common point of view. Nevertheless, it is instructive to find that there are some points of agreement even among theories as diverse as these.

Recent Attempts to Integrate the Theories

Some recent attempts have been made to develop what Zigler (1969) has called "middle range" theories of moral development. Mischel and Mischel (1976), for example, have made a valiant effort to integrate social-learning and cognitive-developmental theory in arriving at their "cognitive social-learning approach" to morality and self-regulation. And Hoffman (1976) has developed a theory of altruism that highlights a close relationship between cognition and affect. Space does not permit a detailed review of these middle range theories here, but a few observations inspired by these attempts may be helpful.

One of the thorniest issues in the area of moral development has been the relationship between moral judgment and moral conduct. The Mischels have offered a key concept that they believe may help to establish the rela-

tionship between judgment and conduct, namely, self-regulation. For them, maturing morally means learning to regulate one's own behavior to achieve self-chosen goals. They believe that we need to study not only what people endorse "in principle," as the cognitive-developmentalists do, but also what people do in the face of difficult conditions. The ability to regulate one's own behavior in the face of strong temptations and situational pressures without the aid of obvious external rewards or supports derives from what they call "self-imposed goals (standards) and self-produced consequences." Presumably, these goals and the ability to reward or punish oneself come directly from the child's socialization history and indirectly from the observed standards of salient models (such as parents). Self-regulation involves not only setting one's own goals but also considering alternative "plans" or routes to them. It also involves considering the consequences of each plan and requires formulating rules to guide one's choices, selectively attending and mentally transforming distracting situations into innocuous ones, and executing lengthy, interlocking sequences of thought and behavior. As Lickona (1975) remarked in reviewing this approach, that is a "tall cognitive order." However, this approach is consistent with social-learning theory (Rotter, 1954) in that even the noblest altruism or behavior consistent with the highest of Kohlberg's moral stages still depends on expected consequences. These consequences are more temporally distant; they are not in the immediate environment, they are not easily identified, they reside in the actor himself, and they hinge on self-evaluations and self-administered outcomes.

While the Mischels have offered a promising approach for conceptualizing the relationship between moral judgment and moral conduct, Hoffman's (1976) recent theory of the development of altruism emphasizes the close relationship between cognition and affect. Hoffman has given a central role to empathy in describing the development of altruism in young children. Empathy is defined as an internal response to cues about the affective states of someone else. Thus, the child's empathic reaction depends heavily on the actor's cognitive sense of the other as distinct from the self. Hoffman sees this distinction as the basis for altruistic motivation.

He described four levels (Hoffman, 1979) in the development of empathic distress: (1) at the first level, the infant's empathic response lacks an awareness of who is actually in distress. This is because the response occurs before the infant can differentiate himself or herself from others. For example, an 11-month-old girl, on seeing a child fall and cry, looked like she was about to cry herself; she then put her thumb in her mouth and buried her head in her mother's lap, which is what she does when she is hurt. (2) At 11–12 months, "person permanence," or awareness of others as distinct physical entities, occurs. However, the other's inner states are unknown and may be assumed to be the same as one's own. Thus, an 18-month-old boy reportedly fetched his own mother to comfort a crying friend, although the friend's mother was also present. The boy did recognize that the other person, and not the self, was in distress. The child at this level is still egocentric, though, as illustrated again by the toddler who offered her own favorite doll to cheer up an adult who looked sad. (3) With the beginning of the capacity for role taking, children can consider others as distinct individuals with their own inner states—feelings, thoughts, and emotions. At first, empathic responses may still be restricted to another's immediate, transitory, and situation specific distress. Gradually, empathy becomes an increasingly veridical response to the other's feelings in the situation. (4) By late childhood, the child can mentally represent another's general level of distress or deprivation and is not limited to empathic responses for the immediate situation. With further cognitive development, the child can comprehend the plight of a whole class of people (the poor, oppressed, etc.).

Thus Hoffman sees empathic distress as a prosocial motive that is intimately tied up with cognitive development. As the individual's cognitive capacity changes, the nature of the sympathetic distress he or she feels for a victim changes.

INFLUENCES ON MORAL DEVELOPMENT

Thus far, we have devoted much time and space to providing a conceptual overview and a developmental framework for understanding moral development. In this section we will review selected research that deals with influences on moral development. Our purpose in focusing on these areas of research is that we believe it may be most relevant to the clinician. We will review parental and other socializing influences first and then summarize various kinds of training procedures. Our intent is not to provide an exhaustive review of this literature but to provide a representative sampling of current research that has implications for the clinician.

Socialization Influences on Moral Development

As we saw in the theoretical portion of this chapter, the parent plays a prominent role in the child's life just by virtue of providing a model with which he or she can identify. Fry (1975) addressed the issue of the relationship between moral judgment and parental identification in 9.5–11.5-year-old children. He presented evidence that indicated a clear, positive relationship between high level parental identification and a higher stage of moral judgment in the child. While this positive association existed for identification with both parents, father identification was more prominent and significantly correlated with the girls' stage of moral development than was maternal identification.

Hoffman (1971) measured parent identification in middle and lower class seventh-grade children in terms of their admiration, desire to emulate, and perception of similarity. Several significant relationships between these kinds of identification and various indexes of moral orientation were obtained. Father identification was related to rule conformity in middle class boys and girls, internal moral judgment in middle and lower class boys, and moral values in middle class boys. However, guilt, confession, and acceptance of blame did not relate to identification in any of the groups. Hoffman (1971) concluded that identification seems to be important in the child's internalization of *visible* moral attributes. The child used internalized principles, not external sanctions, as the criteria for right and wrong, as in judging the behavior of others. However, these internalized moral standards apparently were not used by the seventh-grade children to evaluate their own behavior in the absence of authority.

Parents are not only models with whom children identify but may stimulate or retard children's moral development by the way they treat them. Denney and Duffy (1974) interviewed 6-, 10-, and 14-year-old children and their mothers to determine if an association could be established between the child's level of moral reasoning and the moral reasoning implied by the mother's behavior in discipline and nondiscipline encounters (e.g., what she would say and do if she found out her child had stolen something). The results indicated a developmental trend: the older the child, the higher the level of moral reasoning he or she employed. Likewise, the older the child, the higher the level of the mother's moral reasoning and what her behavior implied to her child. This positive relationship between the level of moral reasoning implied by the mother's behavior and the level used by the child remained significant even when age of the child was partialed out. Of course, these data are correlational, so causation cannot be inferred; nevertheless, the authors suggest the direction of effect was from mother to child.

Another way parents affect their children's moral development is through the style of discipline they employ. Hoffman (1963) consistently has found that parental *power assertion,* defined as including physical punishment, deprivation of material objects or privileges, the direct application of force, or the threat of any of these, leads children to develop a moral orientation based on the fear of external detection and reprisal. On the other hand, non-power-assertive discipline, called psychological, indirect, or love-oriented discipline, typically leads to a moral orientation characterized by independence of external sanctions and high guilt. In addition, Hoffman (Hoffman, 1963; Hoffman & Saltzstein, 1967) has suggested and provided some evidence to show that the effectiveness of non-power-assertive techniques might lie more in their "empathy-arousing" capacity rather than their love-withdrawing properties. Hoffman and Saltzstein (1967) made a distinction, therefore, between two kinds of non-power-assertive parenting techniques: *induction* and *love withdrawal.*

Induction refers to techniques in which the parent points out the painful consequences of the child's act for either the parent or others. This includes, generally, a reference to the covert feelings or thoughts of the other, i.e., the hurt, disappointment, etc. of the other individual(s). Love withdrawal refers to the parent's openly withdrawing love by ignoring the child, turning his or her back on the child, refusing to speak to him or her, explicitly stating that she or he dislikes the child or isolating him or her. Hoffman and Saltzstein (1960, 1967) have hypothesized that induction, and not love withdrawal, relates most strongly to various measures of moral development. In their view, induction capitalizes on the child's capacity for empathy, which, they believe, provides a powerful emotional and cognitive support for the development of moral controls. Indeed, their research has indicated that moral maturity is associated with infrequent use of power assertion and with frequent use of induction. It is, furthermore, infrequently associated with love withdrawal.

In support of Hoffman and Saltzstein's (1967) position, Dlugokinski and Firestone (1974) have recently found that children (grades 5 and 8) who perceived their parents as "inductive" reported greater importance of "other-centered" values and more mature understanding of the meaning of kindness and were rated by their peers as kind and considerate. Power assertiveness, on the other hand, had little value in predicting other-centeredness.

However, the effects of more sophisticated childrearing techniques, such as inductive techniques, depend upon child attributes.

Hoffman and Saltzstein (1967) and Nevius (1977), for example, found no consistent differential effects of various childrearing techniques on lower class children. And Borgman (1972) found inductive techniques related to the child's level of moral development only in children with mental ages (MAs) greater than 6 years. With MAs less than 6, the relationship was reversed. That is, maternal directedness was negatively related to levels of moral development with MAs greater than 6 and positively related with MAs less than 6.

The literature also suggests that childrearing techniques have an impact on very young children's orientation toward others and on their moral development. This has been demonstrated recently with children 1.5–2.5 years old by Zahn-Waxler, Radke-Yarrow, and King (1979). These investigators assumed that the core of moral behavior is the child's sense of concern and responsibility for the welfare of others and that altruism and reparation share this core. They investigated the relationship between the ways mothers handle children's transgressions against persons, the ways children make reparation for transgressions, and children's altruism as bystanders to distress in others. Empathic caregiving by mothers was found to be positively associated with children's reparation and altruism. Affectively delivered explanations ("You made Doug cry. It's not nice to bite." "You must *never* poke anyone's eyes." "When you hurt me, I don't want to be near you.") also were associated with children's reparations for transgressions and with children's altruism when they were bystanders to another's distress. The authors hypothesized that what is being taught by mothers is a basic orientation toward others. It would be interesting to speculate about how this basic orientation may form the roots of later cognitive role-taking abilities of children.

These studies all suggest a possible link between patterns of parent-child interaction and social-cognitive development. The notion that parental focusing on covert, psychological events, as occurs more frequently in inductive, and person-oriented childrearing practices, should be related to the development in children of empathy, role taking, intentionality, and moral development has strong face validity.

Socialization and Delinquency

Clinical investigators may have a special interest in the relationship between parental morality and the development of moral judgment and delinquent behavior in the child. In an attempt to determine the nature of this relationship, Hudgins and Prentice (1973) utilized Kohlberg's structured moral dilemmas to assess the level of moral judgment of adolescent delinquents and their mothers, as well as that between nondelinquent adolescents and their mothers. Results revealed that mothers in both groups used a higher, more sophisticated stage of moral reasoning than their sons. Nondelinquent adolescents used higher stage reasoning than did delinquents. In addition, mothers of nondelinquents exhibited more mature moral judgments than did mothers of delinquents.

In a similar investigation, Jurkovic and Prentice (1974) established the level of moral maturity for delinquent adolescents and their mothers as well as that for nondelinquent-mother pairs using Kohlberg's moral dilemmas; they then presented each mother-son dyad with additional moral dilemmas and instructed them to reach mutual agreement on their solution. The analysis of moral discussion revealed that delinquent family interactions were significantly higher on dominance, hostility, and conflict. Nondelinquent mother-son interactions were significantly warmer, and mothers of nondelinquents tended to be more encouraging. Mother-child interaction involving hostility, dominance, and conflict may limit role-taking opportunities as well as discourage family relationships based on affection, loyalty, and trust. These factors appear to be important in the child's attainment of more advanced levels of moral judgment.

Campagna and Harter (1975) examined the moral reasoning of sociopathic and normal children matched on mental age and IQ using Kohlberg's moral development interview. The records of the sociopathic children indicated that, in dealing with their offspring, parents were frequently described as inconsistent, at times being totally permissive and in other instances showing harsh restrictiveness. Some of the histories indicated that the sociopath's needs were ignored, frustrated, or arbitrarily overindulged. There also were indications that the children were often the target of the parents' displaced hostility. Therefore, there is some evidence to suggest that the familial and environmental conditions of the sociopaths may have restricted role-taking opportunities and discouraged identification, both of which have been associated with lower levels of moral development.

In order to define more clearly the differences that may exist between deviant and normal children, Deitz (1972) surveyed the values considered important by both delinquent and nondelinquent adolescents. Males and females were asked to write down personal qualities they regarded as important for people to have. The delinquent group seemed concerned about making a favorable social impression in that they listed more traits such as attractiveness, neatness, good personality, and being well-dressed than did the nondelinquents. Within the delinquent group's hierarchy of values, those integral to social responsibility such as kindness, trustworthiness, respect for others, and getting along with others were omitted. This finding suggests that delinquents deem the advancement of self and the gratification of personal needs as preferable to the acceptance of social responsibility. Similarly, Thompson and Gardner (1969) found that delinquents more heavily weigh behaviors associated with the need strivings of dominance, aggression, exhibition, and succorance while nondelinquents give greater emphasis to nurturant, deferent, and affiliative behaviors, as well as to achievement-related actions including endurance and order.

In order to elucidate the relationship between behavioral norms, moral norms, and behavior displayed, Buffalo and Rodgers (1971) presented institutionalized delinquents with dilemmas that portrayed realistic problems of adjustment for a teenage boy. Each was asked to indicate what he thought most boys his age would do (his perception of peer behavioral norms), what he would do (his behavioral attachment), and what he thought he should do (his moral norms). The findings led the investigators to conclude that the delinquent recognizes that his behavior does not conform to the dominant moral and legal norms of society. As indicated by his perception of behavioral norms, however, he believes that most people do not conform to these societal norms. Buffalo and Rodgers (1971) state that the delinquent expresses concern over failure or "getting caught," yet delinquents believe most people do deviate from acceptable norms and are not detected. Therefore, according to these researchers, expression of concern over moral conflict on the part of the delinquent is not expected because his or her behavior is interpreted to be either conforming or positively deviant, based on his or her perception of behavioral norms.

TRAINING INFLUENCES DESIGNED TO MODIFY MORAL CONDUCT OR JUDGMENT

A number of interventions have been developed as attempts to change children's moral behavior and moral concepts. In this section we will review some of these interventions with the expectation that they might suggest possible interventions for use in the clinic. The techniques summarized here primarily include those derived from the social-learning and cognitive-developmental theories. This reflects the current research literature. The studies deriving from social-learning theory involve reinforcement and modeling techniques designed either to modify delinquent behavior or to increase prosocial behavior. Therefore, these topics will be considered separately. Following that, the studies deriving from the cognitive-developmental viewpoint that are designed to effect changes in moral reasoning will be presented.

Effects of Modeling and Reinforcement on Antisocial Behavior

Very few investigations have been done utilizing modeling and reinforcement principles to effect a change in those who display antisocial behavior. Those that have been conducted report varying degrees of success in the treatment of juvenile delinquents.

Prentice (1972) demonstrated that live and symbolic modeling of intentionality judgments concerning moral stories significantly increased the use of intentionality judgments of adolescent delinquent males. However, on a test of moral relativism given to assess the generalizability of the effect, no differences were obtained between experimental and control groups. Moreover, a postexperimental follow-up occurring nine months later revealed no differences between groups in the number, type, or severity of delinquent offenses committed in the intervening period. However, this finding should be viewed in light of the evidence suggesting that the relationship between moral judgment and moral behavior is also not isomorphic for nondelinquents.

Thelen et al. (1976) report that male delinquents received significantly better home adjustment ratings after viewing a series of videotapes depicting a model who gradually mastered a problematic interpersonal situation in a home environment. The adolescents also role played the model's part as a component of these training sessions. Individual behavior ratings became significantly more positive over those given during baseline. However, this improvement was not maintained during additional training, which included observing an exemplar and role playing his behavior in a school setting. This lack of maintenance was evidenced during two-week posttests. The investigators suggest that this methodology may benefit from the inclusion of staff members in the treatment who display appropriate reactions to improved interpersonal behavior.

Jesness (1975) conducted an extended project that incorporated the services of the personnel of two juvenile rehabilitation institutions. Two treatment approaches were implemented. One school's intervention strategy was based on the methods of transactional analysis. The other program was derived from the principles of behavior modification. In this behavioral program, the subjects earned reinforcers for manifesting appropriate behavior change. To be recommended for parole, each boy had to accumulate a predetermined number of these behavior change units. Results indicated that improvement on various psychological measures (e.g., increased positive feelings toward self and others) favored the transactional analysis group, while behavior ratings favored those in the behavior modification treatment condition. However, the data suggested that the adolescents at both institutions experienced positive attitudinal and behavioral changes. For example, violation rates for project subjects were significantly lower than those for age mates released from other youth authority institutions.

Effects of Modeling and Reinforcement on Prosocial Behavior

Researchers of prosocial behavior have consistently reported that exposing a child to an altruistic exemplar will enhance the child's subsequent generosity and sharing behavior (Bryan & Walbek, 1970a, 1970b; Elliott & Vasta, 1970; Grusec, 1971; Grusec & Skubiski, 1970; Rice & Grusec, 1975; Rosenhan & White, 1967; Rushton, 1975; Rushton & Owen, 1975; Staub, 1971). The effectiveness of behavioral example in eliciting altruism in children was demonstrated in an early investigation by Rosenhan and White (1967). Fourth- and fifth-graders were exposed to a model who enlisted each child's participation in a game. The model donated half of his or her gift certificates to a charity every time he or she made a winning play. Of the subjects who observed the model's generous behavior 63 percent donated while playing with the exemplar. Moreover, witnessing the donating model significantly increased the number of children who behaved charitably in his absence. Nearly half of these children contributed while none in the control condition gave.

In a naturalistic setting, Yarrow, Scott, and Waxler (1973) created various kinds of socialization environments for preschool children, all of which included the modeling of altruism by an adult. Both modeling in symbolic and behavioral form were found to be highly effective in developing children's helping responses to others in distress. During a two-week retest with personnel quite different from those present in training, children who were given extensive interaction with a nurturant model showed dramatic transfer effects by helping in "real life" behavioral opportunities that were provided.

Additional evidence of the modeling of altruism is provided by first-grade children who were invited to share marbles with a same-age recipient who attended another school (Presbie & Coiteux, 1971). The exemplar was given the option of sharing or keeping as many marbles as he wished. The charitable model consistently donated three times as many marbles to the recipient as he kept for himself. The stingy model reversed this procedure. Praise was administered to both models for their actions. Subjects who watched the behavior of the generous model shared significantly more on every trial than did those who saw the stingy model. Praise of the charitable model's behavior accentuated sharing while praise of the model's selfishness decreased sharing.

Thus, modeling processes do have an impact on the amount, direction, specificity, durability, and generalizability of prosocial behavior. Reinforcement, or rewards, have also been found to be effective in increasing helping behavior in children. Fischer (1963), for example, demonstrated that material reinforcement was effective in eliciting sharing behavior in preschool children. In addition, an adult's praise of preschool children who shared pictures with a peer was found to increase amounts of giving to age mates (Doland & Adelber, 1967). Likewise, social reinforcement (i.e., approval) given by an adult for the sharing behavior of children resulted in increased donating to a charity in later trials (Midlarsky, Bryan, & Brickman, 1973). If the adult had previously exhibited selfish behavior, his or her approval led to decreases in sharing when additional opportunities to donate were provided. Therefore, expectations concerning the effectiveness of reinforcement should be established in light of the evaluation the reinforcing agent receives from the recipients of the reward.

Although praise appears to produce increments in sharing behavior in many immediate tests, the durability of the reinforced behavior is questionable. Kindergarten and first-grade children who displayed low rates of donating to a needy peer were given instructional prompts to share and were then praised for each donation (Gelfand et al., 1975). Even though the children gave numerous pennies when rewarded verbally for their generosity, the majority discontinued sharing when the praise was no longer given. Therefore, the administration of reinforcement appears to raise the level of children's prosocial behavior under various conditions, but the durability and generalizability of these responses are uncertain.

Effects of Cognitive Stimulation on Moral Development

It will be recalled that from the cognitive-developmental point of view children develop through successive stages of moral reasoning. The later, more complicated and differentiated stages grow out of simpler ones. Change is assumed to result from experiences that bring about internal conflict. Rest (1974) explained this process beautifully with a computer analogy, likening the "program" by which inputs (experience) are processed and outputs (behavior) generated to the person's cognitive structures. From the cognitive-developmental, interactionistic position, these programs are neither "wired in" biologically nor simply reflections of environmental contingencies:

Instead, the interactionist view is that the human-computer...is a *self-programming* computer such that new programs are developed to more adequately organize experience and give clearer directions for action...As the child encounters new and different experiences which cannot be understood adequately or reacted to in terms of established structures, the child seeks to revamp his way of thinking. The new experience interacts with previously established cognitive structures to prompt the search for more adequate structures. Once a new "program" is found which can successfully "compute" the new situation, the program becomes part of the person's repertoire. Therefore, the essential condition for the cumulative elaboration for cognitive structure is the presentation of experiences which "stretch" one's existing thinking and set into motion the search-and-discovery process for more adequate ways to organize experience and action. (Rest, 1974, p. 245)

The role of the clinician faced with a child or adolescent whose moral reasoning is deemed to be underdeveloped, deficient, or arrested, then, would be to stimulate this "stretching and searching" process. Kohlberg (1971) argues that the best way to stimulate moral reasoning is to provide models of thinking that are one stage above the individual's current level of reasoning.

Turiel (1966) attempted a laboratory test of this hypothesis. He provided seventh-grade boys who had been assigned stage levels based on their responses to Kohlberg's moral dilemmas with arguments either above or below their own stage position—one or two stages above (+1 or +2) or one stage below (–1). The boys were retested a week later on moral dilemmas, some of which were the same and some different from those on which they were pretested. As would be predicted from cognitive-developmental theory, Turiel reported that the boys were better able to assimilate moral reasoning one stage, rather than two stages, above their current level. However, Hoffman (1970) has pointed out that in actuality the –1 group and the control group (for some unknown reason) both shifted slightly more in the –1 direction than the +1 group shifted in the +1 direction. Thus this evidence does not clearly support the notion that when children are presented with arguments at different levels they tend to prefer those above, rather than those below, their own level.

An often-cited study by Bandura and McDonald (1963) also has raised doubts about this latter hypothesis. Boys from 5 to 11 years of age were just as likely to shift their own moral judgments to a less advanced as to a more advanced level after being exposed to a model being reinforced for expressing moral judgments. These findings were replicated by Cowan et al., (1969) and LeFurgy and Woloshin (1969). These findings call into question the cognitive-developmental assumptions "that the stages occur in an invariant and irreversible sequence and that movement through the stages involves a process of successive synthesis" (Hoffman, 1970, p. 273). However, Hoffman (1970) has pointed out that these latter studies are also inconclusive because: (1) the items in the posttest dealt with the same moral dimension and were similar to those used in the preexposure test—thus the changes could reflect changes in surface responses rather than changes in children's underlying moral conceptualizations; (2) in two of the studies the model and the experimenter were adults and one of them was always present; thus the children may have reported new judgments to meet adult expectations communicated by the model and not because they had actually changed their views.

Although Kohlberg does not specifically address the point of whether +1 modeling is necessary for change or is just catalytic to change, Rest (1974) clearly believes that +1 modeling is not essential. He points out that Piaget himself usually describes the acquisition of new structures in terms of the single individual trying to reorganize his or her thoughts, not learning from a model, and new cognitive structures can be evolved in the absence of higher stage models. Rest asks "Who was +1 for Socrates?" (Rest, 1974, p. 246).

Nevertheless, the hypothesis that exposure to reasoning one stage above one's own level facilitates the development of moral reasoning gains some support from studies in educational settings and in prisons. Blatt and Kohlberg (1974) were among the first to use a dilemma discussion approach with small groups of junior high school students over a 12-week period. They reported stage gains for most subjects involved in these discussions, and these gains were still observable one year later.

Gains in stage of moral reasoning have similarly been reported as a result of peer discussion (Colby, Fritz, & Kohlberg, 1974), the use of filmstrips combined with teacher-led classroom discussions (Selman & Lieberman, 1975), a moral education program based on discussion of hypothetical moral dilemmas (Sullivan, 1975), and the use of dilemmas in moral discussions that included the children's mothers (Grimes, 1974). Mosher and Sprinthall (1970, 1971; Sprinthall, 1971) recently have deemphasized dilemma discussion and have developed a "Deliberate Psychological Education" program for adolescents that reportedly results in gains on Kohlberg's moral stage measure. Their approach combines a practicum experience that involves high school students in some practical work in which they are forced to change their social role (counseling other teenagers, serving as teacher aids in elementary school, working in a nursery school, etc.) and a seminar in which the students reflect on the meaning of their new social experience. The goal of the program is consistent with cognitive-developmental principles in that the aim is to foster "structural development," that is, to help the students acquire new ways of organizing their activities that are enhancing cumulatively and in a long term way.

Finally, Hickey (1974), Scharf (1974), and others in Kohlberg's group at Harvard have brought the approach of discussion of moral dilemmas into prison settings. Hickey found it necessary to develop new dilemmas consisting of issues relating to prison life to deal with the prisoners' real concerns. And Scharf developed an interview and classification system to indicate the way in which the "moral atmosphere" of the prison was viewed by the prisoners. The major findings were summarized by Rest (1974):

Prisoners tend to view the practicing morality in a prison at a low state (perceiving the justice practices of the institution as governed by power and obedience morality or an instrumental exchange morality) and that prisoners conceptualize prison life at a lower stage than their moral judgments of hypothetical dilemmas. Hence prison life gives the inmate little impetus for developing a higher stage understanding of the moral basis for law, society, and cooperation. (Rest, 1974, p. 249)

It should be mentioned before closing this section that there are many problems with these studies conducted in educational and prison settings. Problems include those of experimental design, nonrandom sample selection, poor reliability and validity of measuring instruments, absence of appropriate controls, and others (cf. Lockwood, 1978, for a thorough evaluation of these studies). Rest (1974) has added his criticisms of:

half-hearted application of the principle of optimum curriculum match and programmatic sequencing of curriculum; restriction of curriculum resources to those inside the participants' heads; and the unrealistic expectation that the discussion leader can compose +1 verbalizations on the spot. (Rest, 1974, p. 250)

IMPLICATIONS FOR CLINICAL PRACTICE

We will present the practical implications of the literature just reviewed in the order of their developmental relevance. That is, suggestions most appropriate for preschool children will be presented first; then those that are appropriate for elementary-school-aged children will be presented. One general implication of the literature that led us to adopt this approach is the repeatedly reinforced notion that the experiences encountered by children, whatever they might be, are likely to have their greatest impact when they are appropriate to the developmental level of the child. Thus, reasoning with a 4-year-old on the basis of principles of fairness, reciprocity, or "the greatest good for the greatest number" might be expected to have little impact on the child.

Implications for Preschool Children

Principles of learning, and social-learning theory in general, that rely on reinforcement appear to us to be most helpful for working with very young and preschool-aged children. Perhaps all the theories could agree on this to some extent—psychoanalytic theory emphasizes the "pleasure principle" as governing the behavior of young children, and cognitive-developmentalists refer to young children as "hedonists." Thus, direct and indirect rewards and punishments would be expected to be important factors in controlling the behavior of young children from the viewpoint of all three theories. Since learning theorists have been the most explicit about the manipulation of reinforcement contingencies to control behavior, they have provided the most specific information for shaping the behavior of young children. Thus, problems that might be broadly considered to involve either "antisocial" (aggressive hitting, fighting, disobeying rules) or "prosocial" (sharing, helping, cooperating) behaviors probably can best be dealt with by behavioral management techniques (Bandura, 1969; Patterson & Gullion, 1976; O'Leary, 1975).

Since these techniques are relatively well known and readily available, we will not devote much time or space to discussing them here. It might be useful, however, to give one example of a behavioral management technique that has proven useful and is also consistent with the moral development research literature. Hill (1960) has stressed the importance of the timing of punishment and reward for their effectiveness in conscience development. For example, physical punishment may not be effective in reducing the frequency of undesirable behavior because it is likely to terminate at the time of the deviant act and, in itself, gives no clue as to the corrective act. The "time-out" procedure, on the other hand, in which the child is physically removed from those people and things in his or her environment that might be maintaining an "undesirable" behavior (such as a temper tantrum), utilizes this knowledge in an effective way. In this procedure, the child remains in a relatively nonrewarding room or other space until ready to emit the "desirable" response or responses (such as interacting with others calmly). According to Hill, this

kind of procedure should aid moral development. Many other examples could be given, including the research on behavioral management techniques themselves, that demonstrate the effectiveness of applying learning principles in shaping young children's behavior.

However, the literature suggests that reinforcement contingencies are not the only factors nor the most important factors affecting moral development in preschool children. Models are also important in their influence on children's moral development. The literature suggests that, at the preschool level, the ways in which parents and other models handle anger and affection, engage in comforting distressed persons, demonstrate concern for others, model fairness, and show concern with the child's or others' reasons (intentions) for doing things, can all have significant impact on the child's moral development. Observing other children in either natural or contrived settings who are punished for transgressions or rewarded for prosocial behavior can also have effects on the observing child's behavior. With older preschool children, the use of videotapes, acting out dioramas with dolls or puppets, or simple role playing of various interpersonal problems in the home can all be effective. Generosity, sympathetic helping behavior, rescue behavior, and attending to intentions behind acts have all been increased through exposure to models and through role playing. However, the generalizability and endurance of these effects has been questioned because of a lack of evidence for them.

The importance of arousing the young child's "capacity for empathy" has also been suggested (Hoffman, 1979; Zahn-Waxler et al., 1979) as important for moral development. Although much more hard evidence is needed to confirm this, there is at least anecdotal evidence that young children do respond to others' distress. Empathic caregiving, the use of affectively delivered explanations for why children should not hurt others, and "inductive" discipline techniques appear to capitalize on the preschool child's ability to empathize; and they are related to altruism and reparative behavior on the child's part.

Treatment

The preceding summary suggests a number of general approaches the clinician might take in working with parents whose children are described as "undersocialized," overly aggressive, lacking in concern for others, or lacking in altruistic behavior. The approaches suggested here all are directed primarily at working with parents, who have the most opportunity to observe and intervene in their child's activities. In our view, working with the parents rather than the child is both more effective and more economical than working with the child alone in the clinic at this age. Since the parents are the most influential people in the child's environment, changing their behavior in appropriate directions is the most powerful way of influencing the child. Both the father and the mother must be involved in these activities since the literature on moral development has shown that both are critically important.

Therefore, parent groups should be set up to:

1. Teach parents behavior management techniques, especially including effective ways to set limits on behavior, ways to become more consistent in reactions to the child's behaviors, how to reward prosocial behaviors effectively, etc.;
2. Teach parents the importance of delivering developmentally appropriate verbalizations in explaining the reasons for rules and limits on behavior;
3. Teach parents what are the expected developmental milestones for preschool children with respect to aggressive or prosocial behaviors—for example, that toddlers probably will not often share with others and will not understand pleadings or explanations based on ideas of fairness or reciprocity;
4. Demonstrate to parents the importance of their example as models—not only for specific behaviors, but for values and for general orientation of concern for others;
5. Teach parents to provide many opportunities for their children to cooperate, share, or help others—and then reward them for it.

Implications for Elementary-School-Aged Children

Most of the suggestions made for preschool children would also hold for school-aged children. However, with increased affective and cognitive development, the emphasis in parenting should shift from the heavy reliance on behavioral principles and external reinforcements to a utilization of these emerging capacities. The "inductive" and "person-oriented" parenting styles referred to in the literature review should be particularly effective at this age. Role-taking ability shows dramatic improvement across these middle childhood years and permits increasingly complex understanding of other persons' feelings, thoughts, and views.

In the clinic, the determination of the child's role-taking ability as a diagnostic procedure could be useful. Selman (1976) and Jurkovic and Selman (1980) have provided some specific ways of measuring level of role taking in children and have provided some examples of the usefulness of this knowledge for clinical practice. Knowledge of the child's level of role-taking ability could enable the clinician to communicate more effectively with him or her and to understand the child's view of the world. It could also suggest treatment approaches.

For example, Selman (1976) reported a case of an extremely aggressive, egocentric 8-year-old who was at the lowest level of role taking and moral judgment. Although individual therapy with this boy was not productive, being placed in a summer camp that provided an environment where reasons behind rules and actions were consistently pointed out resulted in progress. He not only advanced to higher stages of moral development—e.g., he understood intentions behind acts—but he also began to form friendships. The articles by Jurkovic and Selman (1980) and a book by Selman (1980) provide more specifics about this developmental approach to clinical problems.

With respect to prosocial behavior, there is again good evidence that modeling plays an important role in moral development during this age period. In addition, there is increasing evidence that modeling is a very effective tool in teaching children of this age social skills (Gottman, Gonso, & Rasmussen, 1975; Oden & Asher, 1977). Potentially, these social skills training programs could be used both to show children how to respond appropriately to empathic feelings in order to be most helpful in a given situation and how to inhibit immediate, aggressive responses and substitute more acceptable ones.

Treatment

Parent groups of the sort described in the previous section and individual or group treatment approaches could all be used at this age level:

1. Parent groups of the type described above would still be useful but would include parents with children in this age range. More emphasis would be given to teaching parents aspects of the inductive and person-oriented parenting styles. Teaching them to listen to the child and, in so doing, show respect for the child as a person may be the most important ingredient in these approaches. Directing children's attention to the effects of their actions on others' covert feelings and giving them many opportunities for role taking also could be stressed.

2. In the clinic, the practitioner could use measures of role taking as part of the diagnostic battery. Teaching the child to role play and to develop better role-taking skills would be an important part of therapy. Videotapes, dolls, puppets, or even pictures might be used to demonstrate appropriate behavior when someone is distressed or aggressive. This could be done individually or in a group; if it were done in

a group, the child could profit not only from his or her own direct experiences but from watching others as well.

3. Social skills training that was directed at inhibiting inappropriate aggressive or otherwise antisocial behavior could also be conducted either individually or in a group. In fact, this kind of training has already been developed to some extent.

4. Modeling, either live or on videotapes, would be a part of the latter two approaches.

Implications for Adolescents

With increasing cognitive competencies and a wider range of behavioral possibilities, adolescents apparently need to be more involved in experiences designed to change their behavior. The lack of success with juvenile delinquents in traditional forms of therapy indicates that dramatic new approaches need to be tried. The work of Hickey (1974) and the Harvard group with adult prisoners as well as that of Mosher and Sprinthall (1971) with high school students are, therefore, very intriguing. Setting limits, giving appropriate level explanations, being an empathic parent who is consistent in setting rules are still important at this age, but additional inputs may be needed.

Treatment

The literature suggests that working with adolescents' parents in combination with several forms of group therapy may be most effective:

1. The social-learning literature suggests that parents need to be impressed with the importance of their example in influencing their adolescents. Parents may conclude from the popularized literature that peers have taken over as influences on their offspring and that they have little effect. The literature reviewed here suggests that they have powerful effects on adolescents, especially in the realm of values. As far as

juvenile delinquency is concerned, the most detrimental values that adolescents may pick up from their parents are the overimportance of making a good impression and concern with self-gratification, domination, and aggressiveness. What delinquents appear to lack in their value structure are values like kindness, trustworthiness, respect for others, and social responsibility. Parents need to be made aware of the importance of modeling these values.

2. The cognitive-developmental literature suggests that discussion of moral issues in groups, particularly if the issues are from real life experiences, can be instrumental in advancing moral judgment. Exposure to slightly higher forms of reasoning than one's own is thought to be especially beneficial.

3. Giving adolescents opportunities to change their social roles and then to reflect on their experiences with peers may also be helpful. Although this has mainly been tried in educational settings, it might work well as a form of group therapy.

4. Helping adolescents verbally relate their actual behavior to their highest level of moral reflection may enhance consistency between thought and action. Kohlberg and Turiel (1971) have suggested that this works best when the person has done something positive and then is encouraged to reflect on it.

CONCLUSIONS

The facilitation of moral development is a complex enterprise that requires knowledge of behavioral, affective, and cognitive trends in development. Although clinicians often tend to gravitate to one particular school of thought—such as behavioral, psychoanalytic, Rogerian, etc.—and then feel the need to systematize their clinical work within that framework, the literature dealing with moral development suggests that no one school is capable of dealing with all aspects of it. For a behavior to be considered moral it must be informed by cognition (decision making); affective factors play an important role in determining the consistency between moral judgment and moral conduct. While eclecticism runs the risk of being unsystematic, it appears to be necessary within this area of behavior.

Ordering moral judgment, conduct, and affect along a developmental continuum may help to provide some systematic basis for integrating these diverse threads into at least a loosely woven tapestry. If nothing else, it may help to provide perspective on a very complex problem. However, it must be acknowledged that merely describing moral development is not sufficient for explaining it. The clinician who wants concrete, specific, "nuts-and-bolts" direction on how to intervene to facilitate moral development may feel a sense of frustration at the state of the art in this area because the scientific basis for such direction does not exist. On the other hand, the scientist-practitioner may find many intriguing problems that are susceptible to exploration and invite improved efforts toward their resolution.

Finally, we conclude that no single clinical procedure is sufficient for ensuring positive growth in developing morally. The need for situational supports or supports from the sociocultural context in which the child lives is obvious. The studies with prisoners indicated that they did not raise their level of moral reasoning as long as the issues debated were set in the context of the prison community. Moral development apparently requires exposure to a just community.

REFERENCES

Aronfreed, J. *Conduct and conscience: The socialization of internalized control over behavior.* New York: Academic Press, 1968.

Bandura, A. *Principles of behavior modification.* New York: Holt, 1969.

Bandura, A., & McDonald, F.J. Influence of social reinforcement and the behavior of models in shaping children's moral judgments. *Journal of Abnormal and Social Psychology,* 1963, **67,** 274–281.

Bandura, A., Ross, D., & Ross, S. Transmission of aggression through imitation of aggressive models. *Journal of Abnormal and Social Psychology,* 1961, **63,** 575–582.

Beech, R.P., & Schoeppe, A. Development of value systems in adolescents. *Developmental Psychology,* 1974, **10,** 589–778.

Berkowitz, L. *Development of motives and values in a child.* New York: Basic Books, 1964.

Blatt, M., & Kohlberg, L. The effects of classroom moral discussion upon children's level of moral judgment. M.L. Kohlberg & E. Turiel (Eds.), *Moralization: The cognitive developmental approach.* New York: Holt, Rinehart, & Winston, 1974.

Borgman, R.D. (North Carolina State U.) Maternal influences upon development of moral reasoning in retarded children. *Dissertation Abstracts International,* 1972, **33,** Sep., (2-B), 72-24,072, 1280–1281.

Bryan, J.H., & Walbek, N. Preaching and practicing generosity: Children's actions and reactions. *Child Development,* 1970, **41,** 329–353. (a)

Bryan, J.H., & Walbek, N. The impact of words and deeds concerning altruism on children. *Child Development,* 1970, **41,** 747–757. (b)

Buffalo, M.D., & Rodgers, J.W. Behavioral norms, moral norms, and attachment: Problems of deviance and conformity. *Social Problems,* 1971, **19,** 101–113.

Burton, R. Honesty and dishonesty. In T. Lickona (Ed.), *Moral development and behavior: Theory, research, and social issues.* New York: Holt, Rinehart, & Winston, 1976.

Campagna, A., & Harter, S. Moral judgment in sociopathic and normal children. *Journal of Personality and Social Psychology,* 1975, **31,** 199–205.

Colby, A., Fritz, B., & Kohlberg, L. The relation of logical and moral development stages. Unpublished manuscript. Harvard University, 1974.

Cowan, P.A., Langer, J., Heavenrich, J., & Nathanson, M. Social learning and Piaget's theory of moral development. *Journal of Personality and Social Psychology,* 1969, **11,** 261–274.

Deitz, G.E. The influence of social class, sex, and delinquency-nondelinquency on adolescent values. *Journal of Genetic Psychology,* 1972, **121,** 119–126.

Denney, N.W., & Duffy, D.M. Possible environmental causes of stages in moral reasoning. *Journal of Genetic Psychology,* 1974, **125,** 277–283.

Dlugokinski, E., & Firestone, I.J. Other centeredness and susceptibility to charitable appeals: Effects of perceived discipline. *Developmental Psychology,* 1974, **10,** 21–28.

Doland, D.J., & Adelberg, K. The learning of sharing behavior. *Child Development,* 1967, **38,** 695–700.

Elliott, R., & Vasta, R. The modeling of sharing: Effects associated with vicarious reinforcement, symbolization, age, and generalization. *Journal of Experimental Child Psychology,* 1970, **10,** 8–15.

Eysenck, H.J. The biology of morality. In T. Lickona (Ed.), *Moral development and behavior.* New York: Holt, Rinehart, & Winston, 1976.

Fischer, W.F. Sharing in preschool children as a function of amount and type of reinforcement. *Genetic Psychology Monographs,* 1963, **68,** 215–245.

Flavell, J.H. *The development of role-taking and communication skills in children.* New York: Wiley, 1968.

Fry, P.S. Moral judgment and parental identification among children. *Journal of Clinical Psychology,* 1975, **31,** 476–483.

Gelfand, P.M., Hartmann, D.P., Cromer, C.C., Smith, C.L., & Page, B.C. The effects of instructional prompts and praise on children's donation rates. *Child Development,* 1975, **46,** 980–983.

Gottman, J., Gonso, J., & Rasmussen, B. Social interaction, social competence, and friendship in children. *Child Development,* 1975, **46,** 709–718.

Grimes, P. *Teaching moral reasoning to 11-year-olds and their mothers: A means of promoting moral development.* Unpublished doctoral dissertation. Boston University (School of Education), 1974.

Grusec, J.E. Power and the internalization of self-denial. *Child Development,* 1971, **42,** 93–105.

Grusec, J.E., & Skubiski, S.L. Model nurturance demand characteristics of the modeling experiment, and altruism. *Journal of Personality and Social Psychology,* 1970, **14,** 352–359.

Hartshorne, H., & May, M.A. *Studies in the nature of character. Studies in deceit* (Vol. I). New York: Macmillan, 1928.

Hickey, J. Designing and implementing a correctional program based on moral development theory. In L. Kohlberg & E. Turiel (Eds.), *Moralization: The cognitive developmental approach*. New York: Holt, Rinehart, & Winston, 1974.

Hill, W.F. Learning theory and the acquisition of values. *Psychological Review*, 1960, **67**, 317–331.

Hoffman, M. Parent discipline and the child's consideration of others. *Child Development*, 1963, **34**, 573–588.

Hoffman, M. Moral development. In P.H. Mussen (Ed.), *Carmichael's manual of child psychology*. (3rd ed.) (Vol. 2). New York: Wiley, 1970.

Hoffman, M. Identification and conscience development. *Child Development*, 1971, **42**, 1071–1082.

Hoffman, M. Empathy, role-taking, guilt, and development of altruistic motives. In T. Lickona (Ed.), *Moral development: Current theory and research*. New York: Holt, Rinehart, & Winston, 1976.

Hoffman, M. Development of moral thought, feeling, and behavior. *American Psychologist*, 1979, **34**, 958–966.

Hoffman, M., & Saltzstein, H.D. Parent practices and the development of children's moral orientations. In W.E. Martin (Chair), *Parent behavior and children's personality development: Current project research*. Symposium presented at the meetings of the American Psychological Association, Chicago, September, 1960.

Hoffman, M., & Saltzstein, H.D. Parent discipline, and the child's moral development. *Journal of Personality and Social Psychology*, 1967, **5**, 45–57.

Hudgins, W., & Prentice, N.M. Moral judgment in delinquent and nondelinquent adolescents and their mothers. *Journal of Abnormal Psychology*, 1973, **82**, 145–152.

Jesness, C.F. Comparative effectiveness of behavior modification and transactional analysis programs for delinquents. *Journal of Consulting and Clinical Psychology*, 1975, **43**, 758–779.

Jurkovic, G., & Prentice, N. Dimensions of moral interaction and moral judgment in delinquent and nondelinquent families. *Journal of Consulting and Clinical Psychology*, 1974, **42**, 256–262.

Jurkovic, G., & Selman, R.L. A developmental analysis of intrapsychic understanding: Treating emotional disturbances in children. In R.L. Selman & R. Yando (Eds.), *New directions for child development* (Vol. 7). San Francisco: Jossey-Bass, 1980.

Kohlberg, L. Stage and sequence: The cognitive-developmental approach to socialization. In D.A. Goslin (Ed.), *Handbook of socialization theory and research*. Chicago: Rand McNally, 1969.

Kohlberg, L. Stages of moral development as a basis for moral educaiton. In C.M. Beck, B.S. Crittenden, & E.V. Sullivan (Eds.), *Moral education: Interdisciplinary approaches*. Toronto: University of Toronto Press, 1971.

Kohlberg, L., & Turiel, E. Moral development and moral education. In G. Lesser (Ed.), *Psychology and educational practice*. Chicago: Scott, Foresman, 1971.

LeFurgy, W.G., & Woloshin, G.W. Immediate and long-term effects of experimentally induced social influence in the modification of adolescents' moral judgments. *Journal of Abnormal and Social Psychology*, 1969, **12**, 104–110.

Lickona, T. What optimizes moral development and behavior? Where the theories converge. Paper presented as part of a symposium on New directions and enduring issues in the study of moral development and behavior. Society for Research in Child Development, Denver, 1975.

Lockwood, A.L. The effects of values clarification and moral development curricula on school-age subjects: A critical review of recent research. *Review of Educational Research*, 1978, **48**, 325–364.

Midlarsky, E., Bryan, J.H., & Brickman, P. Aversive approval: Interactive effects of modeling and reinforcement on altruistic behavior. *Child Development*, 1973, **44**, 321–328.

Mischel, W., & Mischel, H. A cognitive social-learning approach to morality and self-regulation. In T. Lickona (Ed.), *Moral development: Theory, research and social issues*. New York: Holt, Rinehart, & Winston, 1976.

Mosher, R.L., & Sprinthall, N.A. Psychological education in secondary schools: A program to promote individual and human development. *American Psychologist*, 1970, **25**, 911–924.

Mosher, R.L., & Sprinthall, N.A. Psychological education: A means to promote personal development during adolescence. *The Coun-*

seling Psychologist, 1971, **2**, 3–83.

Mussen, P., & Eisenberg-Berg, N. *Roots of caring, sharing, and helping.* San Francisco: Freeman, 1977.

Nevius, J.R. Level of moral judgment as a function of inductive discipline. *Journal of Social Psychology,* 1977, **103**, 155–156.

Oden, S., & Asher, S. Coaching children in social skills for friendship making. *Child Development,* 1977, **48**, 495–506.

O'Leary, K.D. *Behavior therapy: Application and outcome.* Englewood Cliffs, N.J.: Prentice-Hall, 1975.

Patterson, G.R., & Gullion, M.E. *Living with children.* Champaign, Ill.: Research Press, 1976.

Piaget, J. *The moral judgment of the child.* New York: Free Press, 1932.

Piaget, J., & Inhelder, B. *The child's conception of space.* London: Routledge & Kegan Paul, 1956.

Prentice, N.M. The influence of live and symbolic modeling on promoting moral judgment of adolescent delinquents. *Journal of Abnormal Psychology,* 1972, **80**, 157–161.

Presbie, R.J., & Coiteux, P.F. Learning to be generous or stingy: Imitation of sharing behavior as a function of generosity and vicarious reinforcment. *Child Development,* 1971, **42**, 1033–1038.

Rest, J.R. Developmental psychology as a guide to value education: A review of "Kohlbergian" programs. *Review of Educational Research,* 1974, **44**, 241–259.

Rice, M.E., & Grusec, J.E. Saying and doing: Effects on observer performance. *Journal of Personality and Social Psychology,* 1975, **32**, 584–593.

Rokeach, M.A. A theory of organization and change within value-attitude systems. *Journal of Social Issues,* 1968, **24**, 13–33.

Rosenhan, D.L., & White, G.M. Observation and rehearsal as determinants of prosocial behavior. *Journal of Personality and Social Psychology,* 1967, **5**, 425–431.

Rotter, J.B. *Social learning and clinical psychology.* Englewood Cliffs, N.J.: Prentice-Hall, 1954.

Rushton, J.P. Generosity in children: Immediate and long term effects of modeling, preaching, and moral judgment. *Journal of Personality and Social Psychology,* 1975, **31**, 459–466.

Rushton, J.P., & Owen, D. Immediate and delayed effects of TV modeling and preaching on children's generosity. *British Journal of Social and Clinical Psychology,* 1975, **14**, 309–310.

Scharf, P. The effects of the justice structures of penal institutions upon the moral judgments of inmates. In L. Kohlberg & E. Turiel (Eds.), *Moralization: The cognitive developmental approach.* New York: Holt, Rinehart, & Winston, 1974.

Selman, R.L. Taking another's perspective: Role-taking development in early childhood. *Child Development,* 1971, **42**, 1721–1734.

Selman, R.L. Toward a structural analysis of developing interpersonal relations concepts: Research with normal and disturbed preadolescents. In A.D. Pick (Ed.), *Minnesota symposia on child psychology* (Vol. 10). Minneapolis: University of Minnesota Press, 1976.

Selman, R.L. *The growth of interpersonal understanding: Developmental and clinical analyses.* New York: Academic Press, 1980.

Selman, R.L., & Lieberman, M. Moral education in the primary grades: An evaluation of a developmental curriculum. *Journal of Educational Psychology,* 1975, **67**, 712–716.

Shantz, C.U. The development of social cognition. In E.M. Hetherington (Ed.), *Review of child development research* (Vol. 5). Chicago: University of Chicago, 1975.

Sprinthall, N.A. A program for psychological education: Some preliminary issues. *Journal of School Psychology,* 1971, **9**, 373–382.

Staub, E. A child in distress: The influence of nurturance and modeling on children's attempts to help. *Developmental Psychology,* 1971, **5**, 124–133.

Sullivan, E. *Moral learning.* New York: Paulist Press, 1975.

Thelen, M.H., Fry, R.A., Dollinger, S.J., & Paul, S.C. Use of videotaped models to improve the interpersonal adjustment of delinquents. *Journal of Consulting and Clinical Psychology,* 1976, **44**, 492.

Thompson, G.G., & Gardner, E.F. Adolescents' perceptions of happy-successful living. *Journal of Genetic Psychology,* 1969, **115**, 107–120.

Turiel, E. An experimental test of the sequentiality of developmental stages in the child's moral judgments. *Journal of Personality and Social Psychology,* 1966, **3**, 611–618.

Yarrow, M.R., Scott, P.M., & Waxler, C.Z. Learning concern for others. *Developmental Psychology,* 1973, **8,** 240–260.

Zahn-Waxler, C., Radke-Yarrow, M., & King, R. Child rearing and children's prosocial initiations toward victims of distress. *Child Development,* 1979, **50,** 319–330.

Zigler, E. Metatheoretical issues in developmental psychology. In M.H. Marx (Ed.), *Theories in contemporary psychology,* N.Y.: Macmillan, 1969.

CHAPTER 40

Behavior Therapy with Children

HENRY C. RICKARD AND PAULINE D. ELKINS

Interventions that attempt to change behavior through the application of psychological principles are variously referred to as behavior modification, applied behavior analysis, and behavior therapy. Behavior modification is a broad term that has come to incorporate, particularly in the view of the public, a wide array of influence and control techniques. The term applied behavior analysis is more circumscribed and appeals to those who are primarily concerned with the demonstration of a functional relationship between observable events. The term behavior therapy suggests a focus upon clinical problems as opposed to educational, industrial, social systems, and other nonclinical applications. The fit is not perfect but appears to describe best the contents of this chapter.

The history of behavior therapy is available in a number sources (Craighead, Kazdin, & Mahoney, 1981; Kazdin, 1978a; Ullmann & Krasner, 1965) and will not be reviewed here. However, it should be noted that, except for a few barely noticed experiments and demonstrations, the data base of the movement was extremely low prior to the early 1960s. Since that time the development of the field has been astonishing to say the least. Hersen (1981) reviewed the growth of behavior therapy and noted that there are now almost two dozen journals devoted to the subject. Part of the upsurge in publications reflects an interest in the treatment of children. Behavior therapy journals have always included such studies, but increasing numbers are now appearing. At least one journal, *Child and Family Behavior Therapy,* publishes exclusively in that area.

An orientation to child behavior therapy can best be accomplished by a brief analysis of behavior therapy in general. The same principles apply to clients of all ages although, as we shall see, in some instances modifications must be made for young children and the developmentally retarded. The term *behavior therapy* refers to a large number of procedures and techniques. There are obvious differences in approaches based upon operant methodology, classical conditioning, observational learning, and cognitive theory—to mention a few of the more common paradigms associated with specific behavior therapies. It seems only fair to admit that, as the boundaries of behavior therapy are extended, particularly to include cognitive techniques, it becomes increasingly difficult to abstract common denominators binding the therapies together.

Principles of learning have been central to the development of behavior therapy (Eysenck, 1960; Skinner, 1953; Wolpe, 1958) although it is now apparent that other core areas—for instance perception, social, and developmental psychology—increasingly guide behavior therapy research and application (Ross, 1981). In general, behavior therapists concentrate on the events of the present as opposed to the past; few seek client insight into the relationship between current maladaptive behavior and childhood experiences. Basic to behavior therapy is a supposition that the same principles of learning govern the acquisition and extinction of both adaptive and maladaptive behaviors. Behavior therapists are empiricists and adapt their treatment to the client's problem rather than offer a uniform therapeutic approach. More complete discussions for the assumptions underlying behavior therapy are available elsewhere (Craighead et al., 1981; Redd, Porterfield, & Anderson, 1979; Rimm & Masters, 1979).

Behavior therapy may be considered both a treatment technique and an experimental method. Ideally, each behavior therapy case yields results beneficial to the client and at the same time provides data that can be used by other behavior therapists. This emphasis upon adding to the data base suggests that the core of behavior therapy is a methodology that permits replication of findings. Unlike most systems of psychotherapy, behavior therapy is expected to include a detailed description of treatment procedures and measures used to reflect that treatment; the design of the study should permit data collection, analysis, and interpretation. Both single-case and group designs are employed. The methodology of behavior therapy has been discussed fully in numerous behavioral publications, and several books devoted to the subject are available (e.g., Hersen & Barlow, 1976; Kratochwill, 1978).

A chapter on behavior therapy could be organized in a variety of ways; we have chosen to order our discussion by well-established treatment procedures. The first section will describe operant-based approaches with different populations of children in a variety of settings. Modeling procedures, relaxation training, systematic desensitization, and cognitive behavior therapy will provide a framework for further illustrations of behavior therapy.

OPERANT-BASED TREATMENT

The principles of operant conditioning (Skinner, 1938, 1953), which focus upon the relationship between observable events, have exerted a powerful influence upon the development of behavior therapy. An excellent overview of this descriptive approach to behavior change has been presented by Craighead et al. (1981). The following hypothetical example is presented to illustrate how a behaviorally oriented classroom teacher might be guided by operant conditioning principles in his or her attempts to modify a selected behavior pattern.

A child in a classroom "talks out" on 15 occasions during a school day at times when the students have been told to study quietly. Rather than speculate as to why the disruptive behavior occurs—conflicted home environment, hyperactivity, antisocial personality, etc.—an operant approach would require that the target behavior be operationally defined and that independent observers observe and record the events preceding "talking out," the occurrence of the behavior itself, and the consequences following the behavior.

Operant extinction is said to take place when a reduction in response frequency is observed following removal of reinforcement. Thus the teacher might ignore the child's behavior, turning his or her back to the class and becoming busy with paperwork. *Punishment* decreases the probability of a response through the presentation of an aversive event or the removal of a positive event contingent upon a response. Since in this example the child is not engaging in behavior immediately harmful to self or others, e.g., self-injury, there seems little likelihood that the teacher would consider the application of strong, aversive events to decrease the frequency of the target behavior. However, a response-cost technique might be used in which points, exchangeable for backup prizes, would be removed following "talking out."

In the establishment of control over a target behavior, it is frequently desirable to identify and define behavior incompatible with the unwanted response. In this case, a response incompatible with "talking out" might consist of not talking and raising one's hand in response to a question. This behavior would be defined, observed, and recorded by independent judges. Since the aim would be to increase hand-raising behavior, either *positive reinforcement* or *negative reinforcement* could be applied following the behavior. Positive reinforcement is defined as the presentation of a stimulus contingent on a response to increase the frequency of that response. Points, exchangeable for backup reinforcers (perhaps camping equipment) might be applied with the expectation that hand-raising behavior would increase in frequency. The target behavior might be increased also by removing an aversive stimulus, for example a noxious noise or uncomfortable temperature contingent upon the response. This strategy would illustrate the use of negative reinforcement to increase the frequency of a response. In the situation described, it appears that positive reinforcement would be more easily engineered.

It is probable that the new response would be weak, incomplete, and in need of *shaping*. Initially, the teacher would award points for slight movements and abortive lifting of the hand; later, a more fully developed response would be required before the administration of positive reinforcement. Since newly acquired responses are weak, the teacher would choose a near continuous *schedule of reinforcement* to build in the desired response rapidly, administering attention and points for each response. Later, intermittent reinforcement would be applied since it is known that such a schedule of reinforcement is associated with response maintenance. Should the child fail to respond to instructions, training procedures might be initiated in special sessions outside the classroom. Perhaps early in the training sequence it would be necessary for the teacher to stand next to the child, guiding his or her hand to make the behavior more probable. Instruction paired with guiding, followed by touching, then gestures, and later instructions alone, illustrates the use of *prompts,* and the systematic *fading* of those prompts. As the training progresses the teacher might move further and further from the child until he or she is standing behind a desk, much as in the actual classroom situation. Engineering a similarity between training and classroom cues should enhance the probability that *stimulus generalization* will occur and that the child will transfer the target behavior from the training room to the classroom setting. In implementing training outside the classroom

setting, it is clear that the stimulus control gained, helpful in the prompting, shaping, and reinforcement of the target behavior, is a trade-off against the problems likely to be encountered in promoting generalization to the classroom. The newly learned behavior emitted in the classroom will be weak and will likely undergo extinction unless reinforced by the teacher. It has been noted repeatedly that generalization of a target behavior must be programmed, not left to chance.

Adult attention has been identified as an unintended reinforcer for a variety of inappropriate behaviors. In a frequently quoted study, Williams (1959) reported the successful treatment of tantrum behavior in a 21-month-old male child by the removal of reinforcement. After being put to bed the child would scream and fuss if the parents left the room; one of the parents was spending up to two hours in the bedroom waiting until the child went to sleep. An extinction procedure was initiated in which the child was put to bed and left screaming and raging. The amount of time spent in tantrum behavior decreased rapidly after the first session, and by the tenth occasion the child no longer fussed when the parent left the room, smiling instead. An aunt reinstated the tantrum behavior by returning to the child's bedroom; similar procedures were instituted and the behavior was extinguished a second time. No undesirable side effects were observed, and the child upon follow-up was described as friendly and outgoing. An analysis of stomach pain complaints in a 10-year-old girl was presented by Miller and Kratochwill (1979) who found that the mother emitted a number of attentive behaviors contingent upon the complaints. Treatment consisted of removing adult attention for verbal pain complaint episodes. The frequency of pain complaints were rapidly reduced both in the home and school settings; follow-up indicated no additional problems with stomach pain episodes.

The principle of positive reinforcement to help a child achieve and maintain play relationships with her peers was employed by Allen et al. (1964). The 4-year-old girl was observed to interact freely with adults but seldom with children. The positive reinforcement procedure consisted of teacher attention to the child for all play with other children, no attention when alone, and minimum attention when she contacted adults only. At the end of the treatment period she was interacting frequently with peers and was described as a confident, happy member of the group.

Magrab and Papadopoulou (1977) report the effect of a token reinforcement program upon the maintenance of dietary control for four children on hemodialysis. A prize list was constructed based on the children's personal choices. Points were earned, exchangeable for the prizes, for maintaining acceptable levels of weight, protein breakdown, and potassium level—measures important to the child on dialysis treatment. The program resulted in significant improvements in the dietary patterns of each of the four children.

Forehand and his associates (see Forehand & Peed, 1979, for a comprehensive review) have conducted a series of investigations to examine the effectiveness of a parent-training program designed specifically for the modification of child noncompliance. The high quality of research design and methodology providing data to support the efficacy of their program make it an excellent model for teaching parents to use operant procedures in an outpatient clinic setting. A parental interview followed by clinic observations of parent-child interactions provides a baseline for determination of treatment efficacy. Phase I of the training program focuses on teaching the parent to increase the frequency and range of social rewards and to eliminate negative verbal behaviors. The goal is to have the parent give contingent positive attention for child behavior that he or she considers desirable. Although training emphasizes the use of verbal praise statements that label the desirable behavior (e.g., "What a good girl you are to put the toys away!"), alternative rewards such as television time, social outings, and tangible treats are also discussed. Phase II involves training the parent to use a brief time-out procedure. Compliance initiated within five seconds of a parental command is rewarded with positive attention. If not, the parent gives a verbal warning of the specific time-out consequences for continued noncompliance. If the child does not comply within five seconds after the warning, the parent places the child in a chair in the corner of the room. Two quick spanks is the consequence for leaving the chair; this procedure is repeated until the child sits quietly in the chair for two to three minutes. The initial parental command is then restated, and compliance is rewarded with positive attention. The training program also requires that parents, with the therapist's assistance, select target behaviors and develop a home program for practice of their newly acquired skills between clinic training sessions.

The highly structured nature of the parent training program just described has made it particularly amenable to laboratory as well as clinical investigations to establish empirical support for treatment efficacy. Feedback from ongoing research has also led to some modifications of training parameters. For example, laboratory studies with nonclinic children have demonstrated that limiting the number of parental commands, labeling verbal rewards, and consequating the *initiation* of compliance are most effective in modifying child noncompliance (Bernhardt & Forehand, 1975; Forehand & Scarboro, 1975).

Some children exhibit behavior so disordered that home care is extremely difficult and, in some cases, impossible. These children exhibit behavior deficits (little or no language development; failure to acquire ordinary self-help skills including dressing, toileting, and appropriate eating skills; and a lack of social behaviors) as well as behavior excesses (e.g., self-stimulatory behaviors, self-destructive behaviors, and aggressive behaviors) that are highly resistant to modification.

In the training of severely behaviorally disturbed children, the control of destructive behavior, both self-injury and aggression toward others, must be given high priority. Serious injuries have been sustained by children banging their heads against walls and other objects; irreversible brain damage or even death can result. Variables related to the administration and effectiveness of contingent punishment, a procedure appliable to self-injurious behavior, have been summarized by Rimm and Masters (1979). The punishing stimulus should have a clear onset and offset and be introducd and maintained at a high intensity. Punishment should follow the problem behavior immediately and occur on a continuous schedule. Since punishment suppresses behavior rather than teaching a new response, alternate appropriate behaviors should be programmed. Also, there are possible negative outcomes of punishment that indicate caution in its use. Some behaviors, such as tantrums, may be exacerbated by punishment, and anxiety responses may be conditioned both to the stimuli present during the event and the stimulus characteristics of the person administering the punishment. But in the control of severely disordered, self-injurious behavior, punishment is effective and may be considered far kinder than less intrusive techniques that prove ineffective or lead only to slow behavior change. A wide range of aversive stimuli have been used as punishers for inappropriate behaviors in children: e.g., mild mouthwash for biting behavior (Matson & Ollendick, 1976), a bright light for nocturnal rocking (Martin & Conway, 1976), and a loud noise for teeth grinding (Heller & Strang, 1973).

The effective use of punishment to control self-injurious behavior is illustrated by the following case report. Tate and Baroff (1966) treated a 9-year-old blind, psychotic child who, since the age of 4, had engaged in frequent self-injurious behavior (e.g., head banging, hitting his shoulder with his chin, and slapping his face with his hands). The child was calm when restrained in bed, but, "when left alone and free, he would cry, scream, flail his arms about, and hit himself or bang his head" (p. 282). One treatment procedure consisted of response contingent electric shock. Self-injurious behavior decreased rapidly in frequency and was eliminated by the one-hundred-forty-seventh day. Time in bed and restraints decreased, and time engag-

ing in physical therapy and play activities increased. Interestingly, firm commands, paired with the click of the shock apparatus (without shock delivery) was effective in decreasing other inappropriate behavior—e.g., retaining saliva in his mouth, posturing, and refusal to swallow food and liquids.

There were several treatment components in the program for severely behaviorally retarded children described by Lovaas et al. (1973). Generally, the children displayed little social and self-help behavior, responded minimally to simple commands, were mute or displayed echolalic speech, and exhibited self-stimulatory behavior. They were not affectionate or socially responsive; when required to respond to rules of social conduct the children exhibited scratching, biting, and other aggressive behaviors. The authors described their treatment procedures, in part, as follows:

> The procedures employed to extinguish and suppress pathological behavior (including biting and scratching of self and others, feces smearing, etc.) rely heavily on several operations: (1) contingent reinforcement withdrawal, that is the adult simply looked away from the child when he was engaged in undesirable behavior, left the child in his room, or placed the child in an isolation room (separate from the treatment room); (2) contingent aversive stimulation, for example, slap or painful electric shock; or (3) reinforcement of incompatible behavior such as sitting quietly on a chair. (p. 134)

The children were taught to respond to simple directions, for instance, to look at the therapist or be seated without displaying tantrums or other inappropriate behavior. In addition to language acquisition training, the children were taught self-help skills (dressing, table manners, toothbrushing, etc.) and social skills including friendly greetings and affectionate behaviors. During treatment, appropriate behaviors increased and inappropriate behaviors decreased in all children. There were large individual differences; some children improved dramatically while others made only modest changes. Follow-up data indicated that those children who were hospitalized showed decreases in appropriate behavior while those returning to trained parents showed further improvement.

MODELING PROCEDURES

Bandura (1969) observes that "virtually all learning phenomena resulting from direct experiences can occur on a vicarious basis through observation of other persons' behavior and its consequences for them" (p. 118). In a discussion of this ubiquitous behavior change procedure, he identifies separate components: (1) attentional processes that are influenced by both modeling stimuli and characteristics of the observer, (2) retention processes such as symbolic coding and motor rehearsal, (3) motor reproduction processes to include feedback as to accuracy and physical capabilities of the observer, and (4) motivational processes that have to do with external, vicarious, and self-reinforcement. The reader who is interested in a thorough overview of the theoretical and research aspects of modeling is referred to an excellent summary chapter by Bandura (1969).

There are relatively few studies reported in which modeling procedures alone have been used to modify problem behaviors in children. Both in institutions and outpatient settings modeling procedures tend to be used as part of a treatment package. As a treatment component, modeling has frequently served to evoke an adaptive response. Once emitted, many of those responses have reinforcing environmental consequences that do not need to be programmed by the therapist. For other behaviors, the therapist must provide the reinforcing consequences for an initially weak response not under control of the natural environment. The studies summarized below are included to illustrate the use of modeling in the acquisiton of a new response (learning how to imitate), overcoming a behavioral deficit (low socialization), reducing a behavioral excess (aggressiveness), and making an adaptive response (entering a hospital for treatment) more comfortable through fear reduction. Other examples of modeling as part of a multicomponent treatment package

will be discussed in the section on cognitive behavior therapies.

A first step in the use of modeling procedures is to assure that the child has available the imitative response itself. As noted earlier, Lovaas and his associates found it necessary to teach imitative responses to some autistic children before an operant-based training program could be effective. Baer, Peterson, and Sherman (1967) have demonstrated that severely retarded children who apparently have no imitative responses in their repertoire can be taught to acquire new behavior patterns through modeling. This was accomplished by modeling a simple response, prompting the child to respond imitatively when necessary, and following the response with a food reinforcer. After a series of training trials, the children imitated new behaviors demonstrated by the experimenter.

A study by O'Conner (1969) illustrates the modification of a problem behavior, social withdrawal, through modeling techniques. Nursery school children, exhibiting marked social withdrawal, were assigned to two conditions. One group was shown a film depicting social interactions between children that resulted in reinforcing consequences; the other group viewed a film in which social interactions were not shown. The experimental group showed an increase in social responsiveness, but the control group did not.

Modeling procedures may be used to teach a new pattern of behavior consisting of responses already in the individual's repertoire. The behavior pattern, making an appropriate request of a teacher, consists of many component responses, e.g., making eye contact, facing the teacher, speaking fluently, etc. Most children are capable of exhibiting separately each of these responses, but they may not occur in this particular "request" pattern. As Bandura (1969) has pointed out, using other examples, it would be highly uneconomical of time and effort to select out and shape through operant procedures each individual behavior in a pattern.

Melamed and Siegel (1975) used filmed modeling to reduce anxiety in children, ages 4–12, who were being hospitalized for surgery.

The experimental group viewed a film in which a 7-year-old peer model, while initially showing some anxiety, coped with each of 15 common hospital scenes in a nonanxious manner. Control group subjects saw a film similar in interest value but not related to hospitalization. Self-report, behavioral, and physiological measures all favored the experimental as compared to the control group.

Bandura and Walters (1963) have summarized an important early study by Chittenden (1942) who used symbolic models to modify aggressive behaviors in preschool children. The children observed dolls exhibit both aggressive and prosocial reactions, after which they reached an agreement with the experimenter as to the appropriateness of the response as compared to a control group. The children showed a decrease in aggressiveness and also appropriate gains in social behaviors.

Masters and Driscoll (1971) note that models shown on film are comparable in effectiveness to live models. However, in certain cases special steps might need to be taken to enhance learning, including the presence of a live model. Imitative responses exist at a very low level in a repertoire of some children, especially those labeled severely retarded and autistic. As mentioned above, in those cases the child must be trained to imitate (Baer et al., 1967; Lovaas et al., 1973), and further direct training would probably be required before the child could be expected to imitate a filmed model. In general, children with attentional problems should respond better to a live model offering individualized prompts. Before their treatment equivalence can be stated with confidence, comparisons must be made between symbolic and live models with special populations of children.

However, filmed and taped models offer both convenience and experimental control. Examples of clinical problems that have been treated successfully, in part through the use of filmed modeling, include social withdrawal (O'Conner, 1972), snake phobia (Bandura, Blanchard, & Ritter, 1969), dental fears (Melamed et al., 1975), and hospitalization fears (Melamed & Siegel, 1975). A recent imaginative use of filmed modeling has been presented by Dowrick (1979). A socially withdrawn 5-year-old boy whose behavior included a low frequency of verbal interaction with other children was given a single 5-mg dose of diazepam. A short while later the child was filmed talking fluently with a peer; this film was later replayed to the child in a series of treatment sessions. Immediately after treatment, and in later telephone contacts, the parents reported increased talkativeness in the home environment. Filmed modeling procedures lend themselves particularly well to the treatment of populations of children with problem behaviors that are not extremely pathological in kind or degree—moderate behavioral excesses and deficits, fears, anxieties, etc. Some children in almost every educational setting exhibit such behaviors. For example, Roberts et al. (1981) developed a slide-audiotape package featuring two children who shared their experience of being hospitalized for minor surgery. Elementary school children who viewed the slide show reported a reduction in general medical fears as well as greater medical knowledge when compared to an attention control group. Conceivably, in the future, more of these carefully developed "modeling education" films could be shown as part of the elementary school curriculum.

Of course films are not the only possible form of symbolic modeling. The Chittenden study noted above successfully used doll play to model classes of appropriate behavior. It is reasonable to suppose that another form of symbolism, one in which the subject imagines a model performing the goal behavior, would also prove effective. In fact, this use of symbolism, known as covert modeling, has been reported by a number of investigators with adult subjects (Cautela, Flannery, & Hanley, 1974; Kazdin, 1974a, 1974b). Recently Chertock and Bornstein (1979) explored the effects of covert modeling in the treatment of children's dental fears. The covert modeling groups and the control group were not significantly different. The authors indicate that almost one-third of the subjects had difficulty visualizing scenes; signs of restlessness and efforts to terminate the treatment were noted.

Perhaps the live or filmed model, as opposed to the covert one, better captures and holds the child's attention. This hypothesis seems reasonable since in another study of dental fears (Melamed et al., 1975) a reduction in inappropriate behaviors was obtained with a filmed model.

RELAXATION TRAINING

Jacobson (1911) introduced a procedure for reducing muscle contractions, assumed to be associated with arousal, by successively tensing and relaxing specific muscle groups. Wolpe (1958) developed a brief procedure for progressive relaxation training that can be accomplished in five to seven sessions, about 20 minutes in length, plus two home practice sessions each day. In this procedure, counterconditioning is said to occur in which the relaxation response is substituted for the anxiety response. Relaxation and other responses, such as assertive and sexual behavior, which are associated with high levels of parasympathetic activity should be capable of inhibiting sympathetic activity and arousal, thus reducing states of anxiety. Alternative theoretical explanations for the effects of relaxation in the presence of imagined or in vivo stimuli have been advanced (Rimm & Masters, 1979).

In contrast to the equivocal state of the theoretical basis of relaxation training, there is empirical evidence for beneficial effects, both in terms of physiological measures (Beiman, Israel, & Johnson, 1978; Jacobson, 1970; Paul 1969a, 1969b) and control of client presented problems (Redd et al., 1979). Generalization of the relaxation response is promoted through cue-controlled and differential relaxation. In cue-controlled relaxation the client achieves relaxation in response to self-produced cues. Paul (1966) describes a procedure in which the relaxed client focuses attention on his or her own breathing, subvocalizing a cue word, e.g., "calm" each time he or she exhales. The client adequately trained in this technique presumably would be able to evoke relaxation responses in the presence of stress-

ful stimuli by cuing with the world "calm." In differential relaxation, the client learns to relax these muscle groups not involved in the performance of an activity. Many children in classroom situations and elsewhere operate under high tension levels, but the effects of general, cue-controlled, and differential relaxation upon those conditions, and the extent to which they generalize, have barely been explored.

Brief progressive relaxation training, as currently practiced, is far from standardized. Usually subjects are seen in an area free of noise and distraction and asked to close their eyes and rest comfortably in a reclined position. After that, variability is marked. Summary tables identifying leading proponents of relaxation training and the procedures that they advocate are presented by O'Bannon (1981). While no one procedure can be described as standard and universally accepted, a manual for the helping professions written by Bernstein and Borkovec (1973) illustrates an easily learned training procedure that may serve as the basis for relaxation training for children. A recent review and critique of abbreviated progressive relaxation is available for the interested reader (King, 1980).

In a discussion of relaxation training for the mentally retarded, Harvey (1979) suggests a number of modifications including (1) rewarding initial compliance with social or consumable incentives, (2) simplifying the training procedure through the use of plain language and appropriate imagery, (3) nonverbal communication including gestures and demonstrations, (4) rewarding successive approximations to the desired relaxation response, and (5) beginning training with easily controlled and discriminated parts of the body such as arms and legs. Cautela and Groden (1978) have produced a manual on relaxation, in a programmed learning format, that includes suggestions for working with children with physical disabilities and severe behavior problems. Readiness exercises are emphasized, including sitting still for five seconds, maintaining eye contact for three seconds, and following simple instructions.

The authors suggest the use of concrete as well as social reinforcers, touching, and the use of reinforcers tailored to the needs of a particular child.

Koeppen (1974) developed a clever relaxation training script for use with elementary school age children that capitalizes upon the child's willingness to engage in imagery and fantasy. In her script, the child squeezes a lemon rather than merely making a fist. In stretching and pulling the shoulders the child is instructed to pretend to be a furry, lazy cat. The following excerpt illustrates tension-release cycles for the shoulder and neck:

Now pretend you are a turtle. You're sitting out on a rock by a nice, peaceful pond, just relaxing in the warm sun. It feels nice and warm and safe here. Oh—oh! You sense danger. Pull your head into your house. Try to pull your shoulders up to your ears and push your head down into your shoulders. Hold it tight. It isn't easy to be a turtle in a shell. The danger is passed now. You can come out into the warm sunshine, and, once again, you can relax and feel the warm sunshine. (p. 18)

Two or three sessions per week, about 15 minutes in length, are recommended. Children are described as variable in their responses, thus timing, pacing, and repetition of scenes should be fashioned to their needs.

In a review of the treatment of children's disorders by relaxation training, Walker (1979) reports success with a diversity of stress-related children's disorders ranging from fears to psychosomatic disorders. Weil and Goldfried (1973) treated insomnia in an 11-year-old child through self-relaxation procedures. The quality of handwriting in children diagnosed as minimally brain damaged has been improved through relaxation training (Carter & Synolds, 1974). Other problem behaviors treated include hyperkinesis (Lupin et al., 1976), acting-out behavior (Elitzer, 1976), asthma (Alexander, Miklich, & Hershkoff, 1972), psychotic behavior (Graziano & Kean, 1971), and toilet phobia (Walker, 1979). A general impression of relaxation as a treatment procedure can be gained from the two case studies that follow.

Shaw and Walker (1979) employed relaxation training in the short term treatment of fetishistic behavior in an 8-year-old moderately retarded boy. The boy exhibited inappropriate and excessive sexual responses in the presence of barefoot women. This had apparently resulted from sexual stimulation experienced at a younger age when his mother massaged his stomach with her bare feet. Relaxation was proposed as a self-control response that was incompatible with the inappropriate behavior. The boy was taught to use relaxation in specific situations during which he became sexually aroused *without* eliminating the ability to respond sexually in other situations where such behavior is appropriate.

Commercial audiotapes (Lupin, 1976) provided basic relaxation techniques that were also modeled by the therapist. Assessment of learning relaxation was determined by the following three criteria: (1) decrease in time to reach relaxation, (2) increase in time spent voluntarily in relaxation after instructions, and (3) self-report of relaxation. Four sessions were devoted to relaxation training, followed by six sessions with a female assistant who remained barefoot while playing games and socially interacting with the boy. She cued the boy to take a deep breath and relax when he attended to her feet and rewarded him with praise and candy for successful attempts. All of the sessions were conducted during one week of hospitalization at a clinical research center. At the time of discharge, the boy was able to be continually in the presence of the barefoot female assistant without becoming sexually aroused or engaging in inappropriate behavior. The parents were trained in the relaxation procedures, provided with audiotapes, and instructed to make relaxation a part of the evening routine at home. Follow-ups at 6-, 12-, and 18-month intervals indicated no recurrence of the inappropriate sexual behavior. Parents and teachers also reported that the boy functioned much better at school and that his previous hyperactive behavior was greatly reduced.

In another example of relaxation training with children, Weil and Goldfried (1973) reported the successful use of relaxation training to treat insomnia in an 11-year-old girl.

The child presented two major problems: (1) difficulty in falling asleep at night, and (2) reluctance to remain at home when her parents went out. The therapist decided to focus on insomnia first because of its detrimental effect on school performance as well as the assumption that the other problem would be minimized if the child could get to sleep without difficulty. The first session involved a home visit by the therapist to provide progressive muscle relaxation at bedtime. After this initial session of live instruction, the child listened to a 30-minute tape of relaxation instructions nightly for two weeks. She fell asleep either halfway through or immediately after the instructions and consequently appeared to be more rested and relaxed during the day. At two-week intervals, the external directions were gradually faded by first eliminating the tension cycle of progressive relaxation, then reducing instruction time to 15 minutes, and finally reducing the time to five minutes. After one week of using the five-minute tape, the child was instructed to self-relax without the tape and was able to get to sleep almost immediately. Confirming the therapist's assumption, the parents were also able to go out regularly without protest from their daughter. Follow-ups at three- and six-month intervals showed maintenance of treatment gains.

It should be noted that relaxation training is frequently used in combination with other treatment procedures. As part of a classroom strategy to control impulsive behavior, relaxation was combined with problem solving; rewards were forthcoming for those who used the techniques or cued their peers to do so (Schneider & Robin, 1976). Anxiety in hospitalized children was controlled by a treatment package that included imaginal distraction, comforting self-talk, and relaxation training (Peterson & Shigetomi, 1982). A combination of relaxation training and contingency management procedures has been used to control hyperactivity in the classroom (McMahon & Sulzbacher, 1980). Systematic desensitization, the best known treatment package in which relaxation training is a major component, will be discussed in the next section.

Although one might receive the impression that relaxation training is a simple procedure, in fact it is very complex. First, as noted earlier (O'Bannon, 1981), there is a lack of uniformity in relaxation instructions. And, while the training procedures described by Bernstein and Borkovec (1973) are increasingly used in experimental studies, there is little evidence to support the comparative efficacy of their particular set of instructions. To complicate matters further, tape recordings of relaxation instructions have been developed by a number of therapist-researchers (e.g., Budzinski, 1974; Lazarus, 1970). Tape recordings offer uniformity in delivering instructions, a convenient mechanism for home practice, and, for the trainer, relief from the tedium of a repetitious task. Unfortunately, there is little evidence for the comparative effectiveness of the various tapes. Further, Paul and Trimble (1970) report that the live trainer produces better results. We hypothesize that whether the instructions are live or taped may be less important than the presence or absence of the therapist during training; the presence of the therapist may communicate a state of "caring" that is independent of the mode of instruction delivery. However, the live trainer, or at least the trainer present while the tape is played, may be especially important for children whose attention may require prompting.

DESENSITIZATION THERAPY

In a pioneer study Jones (1924) explored a number of procedures for the elimination of children's fears. One of these, which she referred to as the method of direct conditioning, associated positive stimuli with fear provoking stimuli. In one instance, a child almost 3 years old, exhibited fear of a white rabbit. The child was placed in a high chair and given food in the presence of the rabbit, placed at a distance that did not elicit fear. During successive sessions the rabbit was moved closer at a rate the child could tolerate without exhibiting overt signs of emotional arousal. After about two months of treatment the child played with the rabbit and allowed it to nibble at his fingers.

Similar techniques in which the individual's actual environment is manipulated to reduce fear and anxiety are now referred to as in vivo desensitization. Operations differ across studies, but the goal is to control arousal and anxiety in the presence of stimuli that heretofore have intefered with adequate performance and/or subjective comfort. In vivo desensitization has been employed as a component in the treatment of school phobia (Tahmisian & McReynolds, 1971; Lazarus, Davison, & Polefka, 1965), fear of dogs and public buses (Obler & Terwilliger, 1970), fear of water (Lewis, 1974), fear of darkness (Leitenberg & Callahan, 1973), elective mutism (Rasbury, 1974), and avoidance of reading (Word & Rozynko, 1974).

Wolpe (1958, 1973) developed and provided clinical support for the widely adopted desensitization treatment procedure known as systematic desensitization. As opposed to in vivo desensitization, this treatment typically occurs in an office situation rather than the environment in which the client experiences discomfort. While in a state of relaxation the client is asked to imagine clearly and vividly anxiety-evoking stimuli with the expectation that relaxation will inhibit anxiety. In the Jones study, the eating response could be said to have inhibited the effects of the feared stimulus, brought closer by small steps. Wolpe has observed that assertive and sexual responses as well as eating and relaxation responses are capable of inhibiting anxiety, but, of these responses, relaxation is most frequently used as a component of systematic desensitization.

Wolpe advocates the use of a hierarchy of scenes beginning with those that the client identifies as producing no emotional discomfort, progressing by small steps to those that describe scenes evoking strong emotional reactions. The procedure is viewed as counterconditioning, in which the relaxation response "reciprocally inhibits" the anxiety response so long as each step in the hierarchy engenders little or no increment in arousal. Empirically, the results of systematic desensitization therapy, which to this point has been practiced primarily on adult outpatient populations, have been good (Kazdin & Wilcoxon, 1976). It should be noted, however, that the contributions of the various components of the desensitization package (e.g., hierarchical presentation of stimuli) and the conceptualization of systematic desensitization as a counterconditioning process remain in question (Rimm & Masters, 1979, p. 58).

The treatment of test anxiety in children provides an example of the systematic desensitization approach most frequently employed with adults, in which arousal is countered by relaxation. Mann and Rosenthal (1969) found that both individual and group desensitization successfully reduced test anxiety in junior high school students. However, their most effective treatment was a vicarious desensitization procedure in which subjects viewed a peer model undergoing desensitization and gaining control over the fear. Barabasz (1973) demonstrated the effectiveness of group desensitization in reducing test anxiety among highly anxious fifth- and sixth-grade children, although a less anxious group of students receiving the same treatment were not significantly different from a control group on measures of test anxiety. Deffenbacher and Kemper (1974) used desensitization as a counseling procedure for a group of test anxious sixth-graders and found a significant increase in grade point average.

Multiple phobias in a 10-year-old boy were treated by both imaginal and in vivo systematic desensitization (Miller, 1972). The boy's fear concerning separation from his mother, his own death, and the school situation were treated separately using Wolpe's systematic desensitization procedure. As the boy reported gradual decreases in anxiety to the imagined scenes, his pattern of telephoning his mother at work four to five times each week declined; by the ninth week of treatment, the calls had ceased. Imaginal systematic desensitization was not successful for the death phobia, but a procedure in which the therapist induced relaxation by telephone proved effective; by the sixth week of treatment he was able to get to sleep without difficulty, and his reported fears of death were eliminated. The final treatment phase involved establishing a hierarchy asociated with the school situation. After imaginal desensitization, he agreed to reenter gradually by means of an in vivo desensitization procedure. Follow-ups at 3 and 18 months revealed maintenance of all treatment gains and reports that the boy's anxiety level was low.

An additional example of a multiple component treatment procedure has been presented by Wish, Hasazi, and Jurgela (1973). The client was an 11-year-old boy who had a nine-year fear of explosives that had generalized to other loud noises. The fears had resulted in much avoidance behavior that interfered with his daily functioning. In vivo systematic desensitization was ruled out because of the wide range of noises, difficulty in controlling these stimuli, and, in particular, the danger in handling explosives. Imaginal systematic desensitization was considered to be too difficult to administer, perhaps because the problem seemed to warrant a considerable amount of treatment. The treatment decided upon was a combination of direct deconditioning, systematic desensitization, and reinforced practice. First, a hierarchy of feared noises was established. Next, the child received training in progressive muscle relaxation for two half-hour sessions with daily practice. The third phase of treatment involved automation and self-administration of the deconditioning procedure. One of the boy's favorite record albums was tape-recorded with feared stimuli superimposed at 30-second intervals. The boy was instructed to turn off the tape if he was unable to maintain relaxation, but he never exercised this option. Practice was reinforced by having the parents reward him with verbal praise and a baseball card after each session. To test the generalization of treatment gains to other conditions, the child was directly exposed to a selected group of sounds from the hierarchy without evidence of fear. A nine-month follow-up revealed maintenance of treatment gains over time. The authors suggest the use of automated deconditioning was more efficient and required less therapist time than traditional deconditioning procedures. As mentioned earlier, the approach seems especially appropriate where in vivo procedures are impractical or where imaginal procedures are difficult to employ (e.g., young or nonverbal children). The authors further suggest that phobic stimuli of a visual nature might be automated by videotape or audio-taped verbal description.

Miklich (1973) treated a 6½-year-old boy who had a long history of panic during asthma attacks that interfered with medical treatment. Traditional systematic desensitization procedures were ruled out because of hyperkinesis and denial of fear or anxiety associated with the attacks. The first task was to teach the boy "relaxed sitting." Treatment sessions were conducted daily after school. The therapist told him that he could begin playing a game to earn points that could be traded for toys when he was able to sit relaxed for five minutes. The game involved biweekly sessions of imaginal systematic desensitization. Each session began with a three-minute period of relaxation followed by the therapist describing various frightening scenes (e.g., wild animals in the room, ceiling falling in). The boy could earn points by maintaining relaxation during the descriptions. After the boy became successfully desensitized to other fears, the asthma panic was introduced. Elimination of the asthma panic as well as considerable improvement in general behavior, particularly hyperkinesis, were noted at the end of treatment. At an eight-month follow-up, the treatment gains for asthma panic were maintained; however, hyperkinesis had returned to pretherapy rates. The success of this treatment is especially noteworthy because it eliminated the need for sedatives or tranquilizers previously ordered by attending physicians to control the child's asthma attack panic.

The desensitization literature indicates that the progress made with the adult population since Jones's early contributions has not translated with equal sophistication to reduction of fears and anxieties in children. The relatively few studies available tend not to rely upon the relaxation response to counter emotional arousal. Part of the problem appears to relate to a concern about the effectiveness of "standard" relaxation procedures for children. As noted in the earlier discussion of relaxation training procedures, therapists go to great lengths to modify those procedures so that they will be palliative to the child. It appears that most therapist-researchers have assumed that children cannot profit from relaxation instructions of the usual variety. While this is undoubtedly true in the extreme case, there is little experimental evidence bearing on that point (Hatzenbuehler & Schroeder, 1978). Hatzenbuehler and Schroeder have presented an excellent review of the current status of desensitization therapy for children 18 years and under.

COGNITIVE-BEHAVIORAL THERAPY

Cognitive-behavioral therapy represents an attempt by psychologists to integrate two opposing perspectives of behavioral causality, that is, the strict behaviorist position of external determinants and the more traditional position of internal determinants (Rimm & Masters, 1979). Although some have questioned the theoretical consistency of combining the two perspectives (see Bandura, 1976; Catania, 1975), there is little doubt that many behavior therapists do use cognitive techniques. Mahoney (1977) has traced the development of this contemporary psychotherapeutic trend in terms of fundamental assertions, issues, and practical implications. Meichenbaum (1977) and Kendall and Hollon (1979) have provided basic guides for the clinician who wishes to learn about cognitive-behavioral strategies.

An early cognitive-behavioral approach with children can be found in Luria's (1961) work in the use of verbal mediators to control overt speech. Vygotsky (1962) later proposed that the ability to internalize verbal commands is crucial for the child's progression from external control to voluntary self-control of behavior. Meichenbaum and Goodman (1971) expanded this basic theoretical model in their development of a cognitive self-instructional training procedure for impulsive

children. Over a series of four training sessions, the therapist modeled appropriate on-task behavior accompanied by overt self-instruction (thinking aloud) for a variety of tasks ranging from simple sensorimotor skills to more complex problem-solving situations. Task variety was programmed to ensure that the child did not develop task specific response sets. The self-instruction emphasized four basic performance relevant skills for each task: (1) defining the problem, (2) focusing attention and response guidance, (3) self-reinforcement, and (4) self-evaluative coping skills and error-correcting options (Meichenbaum, 1979). These skills are illustrated by the following training protocol for a task that required copying line patterns:

Okay, what is it I have to do? You want me to copy the picture with the different lines. I have to go slowly and carefully. Okay, draw the line down, down, good; then to the right, that's it; now down some more and to the left. Good, I'm doing fine so far. Remember, go slowly. Now back up again, No, I was supposed to go down. That's okay. Just erase the line carefully... Good. Even if I make an error I can go on slowly and carefully. I have to go down now. Finished. I did it! (Meichenbaum & Goodman, 1971, p. 117)

Each session also involved having the child rehearse the modeled behavior according to the following sequence of task performance instructions: (1) external instruction from therapist, (2) overt self-instruction, (3) faded (whispered) overt self-instruction, and (4) covert self-instruction. The results indicated that self-instructional training was effective in modifying impulsive behavior on a variety of psychometric tests (e.g., WISC Performance IQ, Matching Familiar Figures Test); however, training effects did not generalize to teacher ratings of classroom behavior. Douglas et al. (1976) also failed to find significant generalization of training effects to classroom behavior in their use of a similar self-instructional procedure with hyperactive boys. They suggested that combining self-instructional training with contingency management techniques might be a possible solution to the generalization dilemma. Kendall and Finch (1979) responded by developing a training program for impulsive children that combined self-instructions with social praise and a response-cost contingency. The effectiveness of this program, particularly in terms of generalization to the classroom setting, has been demonstrated in the context of a case study (Kendall & Finch, 1976) as well as a group comparison study (Kendall & Finch, 1978).

Several variations of the basic self-instructional training paradigm (Meichenbaum & Goodman, 1971) have used modeling videotapes to present the cognitive strategies. For example, Gottman, Gonso, and Shuler (1976) developed a treatment program to increase the social interaction of isolated children. The modeling component consisted of four videotaped vignettes featuring children who want to join a group of peers. Each vignette was narrated by a female who verbalized the children's thoughts and provided coping self-statements to facilitate social interaction. Other treatment components included teaching the children basic social skills (e.g., giving positive reinforcement, effective listening) via role playing, instructions, and classroom practice. Treatment resulted in greater peer acceptance as measured by sociometric ratings; however, there was no change in the total frequency of social interaction. Goodwin and Mahoney (1975) used a similar modeling videotape in their cognitive-behavioral treatment of three aggressive boys. The boys were shown a 3-minute videotape of a child being taunted by five peers. Covert self-instructions of the child model were dubbed in on the tape (e.g., "I'm not going to let them bug me"). The first viewing of the tape resulted in no observable treatment effects; however, a second viewing followed by therapist coaching and rehearsal of the cognitive strategy for coping with verbal assault resulted in behavioral improvements that were maintained at a one-week follow-up.

The examples of cognitive-behavioral strategies described thus far have been applied to rather broad and/or complex classes of behavior (i.e., impulsivity, hyperactivity, social isolation, and aggression). The strategies are also applicable to more specific problem behaviors. For example, Kanfer, Karoly, and Newman (1975) reported the effectiveness of teaching children simple self-instructional statements to reduce kindergarten children's fear of the dark. Teaching the children sentences which emphasized their active control or competence in the fearful situation (e.g., "I'm a brave boy [girl]") was more effective than teaching sentences that reduced the aversive quality of the situation (e.g., "The dark is a fun place to be") or neutral sentences (e.g., "Mary had a little lamb").

We have presented several examples of self-instructional strategies that have been used successfully in the treatment of a variety of child behavior problems. Another basic cognitive-behavioral intervention is problem-solving training. Spivac, Platt, and Shure (1976) found that emotionally disturbed and behaviorally disruptive children tend to show problem-solving deficits relative to matched controls. They developed a training program in social reasoning skills (Spivack & Shure, 1974) that had significant positive effects on the peer relations of preschool children that were maintained at a one-year follow-up. The program consisted of 30 lessons (presented as "games") for teaching the children problem-solving skills (e.g., identifying emotions, learning to gather information about other people, finding alternative solutions). A number of similar training programs have been developed for other populations including acting-out preadolescents in a residential treatment setting (Russell & Thoresen, 1976) and normal school age children (e.g., Poitras-Martin & Stone, 1977; Stone, Hinds, & Schmidt, 1975).

Clearly, cognitive-behavioral strategies represent an important move toward helping children learn the skills to use in determining their own behavior. Research supporting the therapeutic effectiveness of these strategies is encouraging but sometimes equivocal. The interested reader should note that a recent review (O'Leary & Dubey, 1979) has critically examined the research literature on self-control procedures for children (primarily cognitive-behavioral) in terms of basic effectiveness, comparisons with other interventions, maintenance of treatment effects, and problems for future research. Urbain and Kendall (1980) have also reviewed the more specific area of social-cognitive problem-solving interventions with children.

CONCLUSIONS

Operant-based studies, barely sampled in this chapter, have been applied to a very wide range of disorders and problems compared to the other approaches discussed. These studies tend to be conceptually clear and couched in designs that permit interpretation of the results reported. The variables manipulated are public, and trained observers can agree as to their occurrence. Cognitive behavior therapy with children presents the most marked contrast to operant-based procedures. Cognitions are not observable, leading some researchers to question their utility (Rachlin, 1977; Wolpe, 1977). Labeling certain forms of cognitive therapy as behavioral has led to problems as to what strategies should be included under that umbrella. Rational emotive therapy (Ellis, 1962), rational restructuring (Goldfried & Goldfried, 1975), stress innoculation (Meichenbaum, 1975), and thought stopping (Wolpe, 1973) are examples of widely adopted procedures with adult clients that may also be applied to children. We are now beginning to see an expanded list of cognitive behavior therapies (Rimm & Masters, 1979), including, for instance, learned helplessness (Seligman & Maier, 1967) and self-efficacy (Bandura, 1977), both complex theoretical positions based on laboratory experimentation that attempts to take into account a wide range of variables and their interactions. While the conceptualization and development of cognitive behavior therapy techniques is needed, one wonders about the temptation to further expand the list when the existing research data base, particularly in respect to children, is so limited. The use of behavior therapy modeling procedures is still in a comparatively early stage of development although a recent upsurge in research has been noted (Rimm & Masters, 1979). Frequently, modeling studies

that do, indeed, modify important behaviors (e.g., fear of animals) are intended primarily to develop the theory of observational learning. Many modeling procedures evoke a particular behavior already in the repertoire of the individual so that it may then be modified through consequences controlled by the experimenter. Thus modeling and operant-based components are frequently combined. At this time, the treatment of children through relaxation and systematic desensitization procedures is based primarily on case studies. As is true of modeling, these procedures frequently contain operant-based treatment components.

Redd et al. (1979, p. 10), after reviewing the common approaches to behavior modification, note that the largest group of behavioral clinicians cannot be identified with a particular theoretical position. Rather, they select from the techniques available and do not feel the necessity of remaining within the boundaries of a particular approach. The underachieving child may be placed on a point system to increase homework accuracy and productivity; concurrently cognitive restructuring techniques may be useful in controlling intrusive thoughts that interfere with studying. As we have seen, behavior therapy procedures concentrating upon punishment or modeling approaches typically include reinforcing consequences for competing behaviors. So long as the therapist is concerned about outcome only a behavioral eclecticism can be defended. The therapist must be aware, however, that some aspects of the treatment may be contributing nothing to the effect; long range research efforts should be directed at a determination of the relative contribution of the components.

Behavioral therapies lend themselves readily to a description of operations that can be taught to paraprofessionals, parents, and other caretakers in a variety of settings. These procedures can be adapted to the individual needs of clients and frequently can be implemented in the environment in which the problem behavior occurs. In the use of these procedures, the responsible therapist will take into account their impact upon the total well being of the client. Teaching a child an assertive response that may evoke physical abuse from a parent would be counterproductive unless the behavior of the parent is also modified. Goldfried and Davison (1976, p. 55) have described problems experienced by the technically skilled therapist who fails to deal adequately with context and interpersonal variables.

At this time, sufficient data are available to justify the continued application of behavior therapies to the problems of children. As this brief overview has indicated, some procedures are based on extensive research findings while the data base for others is quite limited. However, research efforts are continuing at a rapid pace; the clinician-researcher can anticipate an accelerating fund of research data to support the use of behavior therapy procedures with children.

REFERENCES

Alexander, A.B., Miklich, D.R., & Hershkoff, H. The immediate effects of systematic relaxation training on peak expiratory flow rates in asthmatic children. *Psychosomatic Medicine,* 1972, **34**, 388–394.

Allen, K.E., Hart, B.M., Buell, J.S., Harris, F.R., & Wolf, M.M. Effects of social reinforcement on isolate behavior of a nursery school child. *Child Development,* 1964, **35**, 511–518.

Baer, D.M., Peterson, R.F., & Sherman, J.A. The development of imitation by reinforcing behavioral similarity to a model. *Journal of the Experimental Analysis of Behavior, 1967,* **10**, 405–416.

Bandura, A. *Principles of behavior modification.* New York: Holt, Rinehart, & Winston, Inc., 1969.

Bandura, A. Self-reinforcement: Theoretical and methodological considerations. *Behaviorism,* 1976, **4**, 135–155.

Bandura, A. *Social learning theory.* Englewood Cliffs, N.J.: Prentice-Hall, 1977.

Bandura, A., Blanchard, E.B., & Ritter, R. The relative efficacy of desensitization and modeling approaches for inducing behavioral, affective, and attitudinal changes. *Journal of Personality and Social Psychology,* 1969, **13**, 173–199.

Bandura, A., & Walters, R.H. *Social learning and personality development.* New York: Holt, Rinehart, & Winston, 1963.

Barabasz, A.F. Group desensitization of test anxiety in elementary school. *The Journal of Psychology,* 1973, **83**, 295–301.

Beiman, I., Israel, E., & Johnson, S.A. During training and posttraining effects of live and taped extended progressive relaxation, self-relaxation, and electromyogram biofeedback. *Journal of Consulting and Clinical Psychology,* 1978, **46**, 314–321.

Bernhardt, A., & Forehand, R. The effects of labeled and unlabeled praise upon lower and middle class children. *Journal of Experimental Child Psychology,* 1975, **19**, 536–543.

Bernstein, D.A., & Borkovec, T.D. *Progressive relaxation training: A manual for the helping professions.* Champaign, Ill.: Research Press, 1973.

Budzyndski, T.H. *Tense-slo-relax.* New York: Biofeedback Systems, 1974. (Tape)

Carter, J.L., & Synolds, D. Effects of relaxation training upon handwriting quality. *Journal of Learning Disabilities,* 1974, **7**, 236–238.

Catania, C.A. The myth of self-reinforcement. *Behaviorism,* 1975, **3**, 192–199.

Cautela, J.R., Flannery, R., Jr., & Hanley, S. Covert modeling: An experimental test. *Behavior Therapy,* 1974, **5**, 494–502.

Cautela, J.R., & Groden, J. *Relaxation: A comprehensive manual for adults, children, and children wth special needs.* Champaign, Ill.: Research Press, 1978.

Chertock, S.L., & Bornstein, P.H. Covert modeling treatment of children's dental fears. *Child Behavior Therapy,* 1979, **1**(3), 249–255.

Chittenden, G.E. An experimental study in measuring and modifying assertive behavior in young children. *Monographs of the Society for Research in Child Development,* 1942, **7**(1, Serial No. 31).

Craighead, W.E., Kazdin, A.E., & Mahoney, M.J. *Behavior modification: Principles, issues, and applications* (2nd ed.). Boston: Houghton Mifflin, 1981.

Deffenbacher, J.L., & Kemper, C.C. Counseling test-anxious sixth graders. *Elementary School Guidance and Counseling,* 1974, **9**, 22–29.

Douglas, V.I., Parry, P., & Garson, C. Assessment of a cognitive training program for hyperactive children. *Journal of Abnormal Child Psychology,* 1976, **4,** 389–410.

Dowrick, P.W. Single dose medication to create a self model film. *Child Behavior Therapy,* 1979, **1**(2), 193–198.

Elitzer, B. Self-relaxation programs for acting out adolescents. *Adolescence,* 1976, **11,** 570–572.

Ellis, A. *Reason and emotion in psychotherapy.* New York: Lyle Stuart, 1962.

Eysenck, H.J. (Ed.). *Behavior therapy and the neuroses.* New York: Macmillan, 1960.

Forehand, R., & Peed, S. Training parents to modify the noncompliant behavior of their children. In A.J. Finch, Jr., & P.C. Kendall (Eds.), *Clinical treatment and research in child psychopathology.* New York: Spectrum, 1979.

Forehand, R., & Scarboro, M.E. An analysis of children's oppositional behavior. *Journal of Abnormal Child Psychology,* 1975, **3,** 27–31.

Goldfried, M.R., & Davison, G.C. *Clinical behavior therapy.* New York: Holt, Rinehart, & Winston, 1976.

Goldfried, M.R., & Goldfried, A.P. Cognitive change methods. In F. Kanfer & A. Goldstein (Eds.), *Helping people change.* Oxford: Pergamon, 1975.

Goodwin, S.E. & Mahoney, M.J. Modification of aggression through modeling: An experimental probe. *Journal of Abnormal Child Psychology,* 1976, **4,** 179–197.

Graziano, A.M., & Kean, J.E. Programmed relaxation and reciprocal inhibition with psychotic children. In A.M. Graziano (Ed.), *Behavior therapy with children.* Chicago: Aldin, 1971.

Harvey, J.R. The potential of relaxation training for the mentally retarded. *Mental Retardation,* 1979, **17,** 71–76.

Hatzenbuehler, L.C., & Schroeder, H.E. Desensitization procedures in the treatment of childhood disorders. *Psychological Bulletin,* 1978, **85,** 831–844.

Heller, R.F., & Strang, H.R. Controlling bruxism through automated aversive conditioning. *Behavior Research and Therapy,* 1973, **11,** 327–329.

Hersen, M. Complex problems require complex solutions. *Behavior Therapy,* 1981, **12,** 15–29.

Hersen, M., & Barlow, D.H. *Single-case experimental designs: Strategies for studying behavior change.* New York: Pergamon, 1976.

Jacobson, E. The technic of progressive relaxation. *Psychological Review,* 1911, **18,** 568–578.

Jacobson, E. *Modern treatment of tense patients.* Springfield, Ill.: Thomas, 1970.

Jones, M.C. The elimination of children's fears. *Journal of Experimental Psychology,* 1924, **7,** 382–390.

Kanfer, F.H., Karoly, P., & Newman, A. Reduction of children's fear of the dark by competence-related and situational threat-related verbal cues. *Journal of Consulting and Clinical Psychology,* 1975, **43,** 251–258.

Kazdin, A.E. Covert modeling, model similarity, and reduction of avoidance behavior. *Behavior Therapy,* 1974, **5,** 325–340. (a)

Kazdin, A.E. Effects of covert modeling and model reinforcement on assertive behavior. *Journal of Abnormal Psychology,* 1974, **83,** 240–252. (b)

Kazdin, A.E. *History of behavior modification: Experimental foundations of contemporary research.* Baltimore: University Park Press, 1978. (a)

Kazdin, A.E. Methodological and interpretive problems of single-case experimental designs. *Journal of Consulting and Clinical Psychology,* 1978, **46**(4), 629–642. (b)

Kazdin, A.E., & Wilcoxon, L.A. Systematic desensitization and nonspecific treatment effects: A methodological evaluation. *Psychological Bulletin,* 1976, **83,** 729–758.

Kendall, P.C., & Finch, A.J., Jr. A cognitive behavioral treatment for impulse control: A case study. *Journal of Consulting and Clinical Psychology,* 1976, **44,** 852–857.

Kendall, P.C., & Finch, A.J., Jr. A cognitive-behavioral treatment for impulsivity: A group comparison study. *Journal of Consulting and Clinical Psychology,* 1976, **44,** 852–857.

Kendall, P.C., & Finch, A.J., Jr. A cognitive-behavioral treatment for impulsivity: A group comparison study. *Journal of Consulting and Clinical Psychology,* 1978, **46,** 110–118.

Kendall, P.C., & Finch, A.J., Jr. Developing nonimpulsive behavior in children: Cognitive-behavioral strategies for self-control. In P.C. Kendall & S.D. Hollon (Eds.), *Cognitive-behavioral interventions: Theory, research, and procedures.* New York: Academic Press, 1979.

Kendall, P.C., & Hollon, S.D. (Eds.). *Cognitive-behavioral interventions: Theory, research, and procedures.* New York: Academic Press, 1979.

King, N.J. The therapeutic utility of abbreviated

progressive relaxation: A critical review with implications for clinical practice. In M. Hersen, R.M. Eisler, & P.M. Miler (Eds.), *Progress in behavior modification* (Vol. 10). New York: Academic Press, 1980.

Koeppen, A.S. Relaxation training for children. *Elementary School Guidance and Counseling,* 1974, **9**, 14–21.

Kratochwill, T.R. (Ed.), *Single subject research: Strategies for evaluating change.* New York: Academic Press, 1978.

Lazarus, A.A. *Relaxation exercises I.* Chicago: Instructional Dynamics, 1970. (Tape)

Lazarus, A.A., Davison, G.C., & Polefka, D.A. Classical and operant factors in the treatment of school phobia. *Journal of Abnormal Psychology,* 1965, **70**, 225–229.

Leitenberg, H., & Callahan, E.J. Reinforced practice and reduction of different kinds of fears in adults and children. *Behaviour Research and Therapy,* 1973, **11**, 19–30.

Lewis, S. A comparison of behavior therapy techniques in the reduction of fearful avoidance behavior. *Behavior Therapy,* 1974, **5**, 648–655.

Lovaas, O.I., Koegel, R., Simmons, J.Q., & Long, J.S. Some generalization and follow-up measures on autistic children in behavior therapy. *Journal of Applied Behavior Analysis,* 1973, **6**, 131–166.

Lupin, M. The family relaxation and self-control program. A therapeutic cassette for both adults and children. Houston: Biobehavioral Publishers & Distributors, 1976.

Lupin, M., Braud, L.W., Braud, W., & Duer, W.F. Children, parents, and relaxation tapes. *Academic Therapy,* 1976, **12**, 105–113.

Luria, A. *The role of speech in the regulation of normal and abnormal children.* New York: Liveright, 1961.

Magrab, P., & Papadopoulou, Z. The effect of a token economy on dietary compliance for children on hemodialysis. *Journal of Applied Behavior Analysis,* 1977, **10**, 573–579.

Mahoney, M.J. Reflections on the cognitive-learning trend in psychotherapy. *American Psychologist,* 1977, **32**, 5–13.

Mann, J., & Rosenthal, T. Vicarious and direct counterconditioning of test anxiety through individual and group desensitization. *Behavior Research and Therapy,* 1969, **7**, 359–367.

Martin, R.D., & Conway, J.B. Aversive stimulation to eliminate infant nocturnal rocking.

Journal of Behavior Therapy and Experimental Psychiatry, 1976, **7**, 200–238.

Masters, J.C., & Driscoll, S.A. Children's "imitation" as a function of the presence or absence of a model and the description of his instrumental behaviors. *Child Development,* 1971, **42**, 161–170.

Matson, J.L. & Ollendick, T.H. Elimination of low frequency biting. *Behavior Therapy,* 1976, 410–412.

McMahon, R.J., & Sulzbacher, S.I. Relaxation training as an adjunct to treatment in a hyperactive boy. *Clinical Pediatrics,* 1980, **19**, 497–498.

Meichenbaum, D.H. Self-instructional methods. In F.H. Kanfer & A.P. Goldstein (Eds.), *Helping people change.* New York: Pergamon, 1975.

Meichenbaum, D.H. *Cognitive-behavior modification: An integrative approach.* New York: Plenum, 1977.

Meichenbaum, D.H. Teaching children self-control. In B.B. Lahey & A.E. Kazdin (Eds.), *Advance in clinical child psychology* (Vol. 2). New York: Plenum, 1979.

Meichenbaum, D.H., and Goodman, J. Training impulsive children to talk to themselves: A means of developing self-control. *Journal of Abnormal Psychology,* 1971, **77**, 115–126.

Meichenbaum, D.H., & Goodman, J. Training impulsive children to talk to themselves: A means of developing self-control. *Journal of Abnormal Psychology,* 1971, **77**, 115–126.

Melamed, B.G., Hawes, R., Heiby, E., & Glick, J. The use of film modeling to reduce uncooperative behavior of children during dental treatment. *Journal of Dental Research,* 1975, **54**, 797–801.

Melamed, B.G., & Siegel, L.J. Reduction of anxiety in children facing hospitalization and surgery by use of filmed modeling. *Journal of Consulting and Clinical Psychology,* 1975, **43**, 511–521.

Miklich, D.R. Operant conditioning procedures with systematic desensitization in a hyperkinetic asthmatic boy. *Journal of Behavior Therapy and Experimental Psychiatry,* 1973, **4**, 177–182.

Miller, A.J., & Kratochwill, T.R. Reduction of frequent stomachache complaints by time out. *Behavior Therapy,* 1979, **10**, 211–218.

Miller, P.M. The use of visual imagery and muscle relaxation in the counterconditioning of a phobic child: A case study. *Journal of Nervous and Mental Disease,* 1972, **154,** 457–460.

O'Bannon, R.M. *The effectiveness of brief progressive relaxation training as a function of procedural variation and anxiety level.* Unpublished doctoral dissertation, University of Alabama, 1981.

Obler, M., & Terwilliger, R.F. Pilot study on the effectiveness of systematic desensitization with neurologically impaired children with phobic disorders. *Journal of Consulting and Clinical Psychology,* 1970, **34,** 314–318.

O'Conner, R.D. Modification of social withdrawal through symbolic modeling. *Journal of Applied Behavior Analysis,* 1969, **2,** 15–22.

O'Connor, R.D. Relative efficacy of modeling, shaping, and the combined procedures for modification of social withdrawal. *Journal of Abnormal Psychology,* 1972, **79,** 327–334.

O'Leary, S.G., & Dubey, D.R. Applications of self-control procedures by children: A review. *Journal of Applied Behavior Analysis,* 1979, **12,** 449–465.

Paul, G.L. *Insight vs. desensitization in psychotherapy: An experiment in anxiety reduction.* Stanford: Stanford University Press, 1966.

Paul, G.L. Outcome of systematic desensitization. II. Controlled investigations of individual treatment, technique variations, and current status. In C.M. Franks (Ed.), *Behavior therapy: Appraisal and status.* New York: McGraw-Hill, 1969. (a)

Paul, G.L. Physiological effects of relaxation training and hypnotic suggestion. *Journal of Abnormal Psychology,* 1969, **74,** 425–437. (b)

Paul, G.L., & Trimble, R.W. Recorded vs. "live" relaxation training and hypnotic suggestion: Comparative effectiveness for reducing physiological arousal and inhibiting stress response. *Behavior Therapy,* 1970, **1,** 285–302.

Peterson, L., & Shigetomi, C. The use of coping techniques to minimize anxiety in hospitalized children. *Behavior Therapy,* 1982, **12,** 1–14.

Poitras-Martin, D., & Stone, G. Psychological education: A skills-oriented approach. *Journal of Counseling,* 1977, **24,** 153–157.

Rachlin, H. Reinforcing and punishing thoughts. *Behavior Therapy,* 1977, **8,** 659–665.

Rasbury, W.C. Behavioral treatment of selective mutism: A case report. *Journal of Behavior Therapy and Experimental Psychiatry,* 1974, **5,** 103–104.

Redd, W.H., Porterfield, A.L., & Anderson, B.L. *Behavior modification: Behavioral approaches to human problems.* New York: Random House, 1979.

Rimm, D.C., & Masters, J.C. *Behavior therapy: Techniques and empirical findings* (2nd ed.). New York: Academic Press, 1979.

Roberts, M.C., Wurtele, S.K., Boone, R.R., Ginther, L.J., & Elkins, P.D. Reduction of medical fears by use of modeling: A preventive application in a general population of children. *Journal of Pediatric Psychology,* 1981, **6**(3), 293–300.

Ross, A.O. *Child behavior therapy: Principles, procedures, and empirical basis.* New York: Wiley, 1981.

Russell, M., & Thoreson, C. Teaching decision-making skills to children. In J.D. Krumboltz & C.E. Thoreson (Eds.), *Counseling methods.* New York: Holt, Rinehart, & Winston, 1976.

Schneider, M., & Robin, A. The turtle technique: A method for the self-control of impulsive behavior. In J.D. Krumboltz & C.E. Thoresen (Eds.), *Counseling methods.* New York: Holt, Rinehart, & Winston, 1976.

Seligman, M.E.P., & Maier, S.F. Failure to escape traumatic shock. *Journal of Experimental Psychology,* 1967, **74,** 1–9.

Shaw, W.J., & Walker, C.E. Use of relaxation in the short-term treatment of fetishistic behavior: An exploratory case study. *Journal of Pediatric Psychology,* 1979, **4**(4), 403–407.

Skinner, B.F. *The behavior of organisms: An experimental analysis.* New York: Appleton, 1938.

Skinner, B.F. *Science and human behavior.* New York: Macmillan, 1953.

Spivack, G., Platt, J., & Shure, M. *The problem solving approach to adjustment.* San Francisco: Jossey-Bass, 1976.

Spivack, G., & Shure, M. *Social adjustment of young children: A cognitive approach to solving real life problems.* San Francisco: Jossey-Bass, 1974.

Stone, G., Hinds, W., & Schmidt, G. Teaching mental health behaviors to elementary school children. *Professional Psychology,* 1975, **6,** 34–40.

Tahmisian, J.A., & McReynolds, W.T. Use of parents as behavioral engineers in the treatment of a school-phobic girl. *Journal of Counseling Psychology,* 1971, **18,** 225–228.

Tate, B.G., & Baroff, G.S. Aversive control of self-injurious behavior in a psychotic boy. *Behavior Research and Therapy,* 1966, **4,** 281–287.

Ullmann, L.P., & Krasner, L. (Eds.). *Case studies in behavior modifications.* New York: Holt, 1965.

Urbain, E., & Kendall, P.C. A review of social-cognitive problem-solving approaches to therapy with children. *Psychological Bulletin,* 1980, **88,** 109–143.

Vygotsky, L. *Thought and language.* New York: Wiley, 1962.

Walker, C.E. Treatment of children's disorders by relaxation training: The poor man's biofeedback. *Journal of Clinical Child Psychology,* 1979, **8,** 22–25.

Weil, G., & Goldfried, M.R. Treatment of insomnia in an eleven-year-old child through self-relaxation. *Behavior Therapy,* 1973, **4,** 282–284.

Williams, C.D. The elimination of tantrum behavior by extinction procedures. *Journal of Abnormal and Social Psychology,* 1959, **59,** 269.

Wish, P.A., Hasazi, J.E., & Jurgela, A.R. Automated direct deconditioning of a childhood phobia. *Journal of Behavior Therapy and Experimental Psychiatry,* 1973, **4,** 279–283.

Wolpe, J. *Psychotherapy by reciprocal inhibition.* Stanford, Calif.: Stanford University Press, 1958.

Wolpe, J. *The practice of behavior therapy* (2nd ed.). Oxford: Pergamon, 1973.

Wolpe, J. Inadequate behavior analysis: The Achilles heel of outcome research in behavior therapy. *Journal of Behavior Therapy and Experimental Psychiatry,* 1977, **8**(1), 1–3.

Word, P., & Rozynko, V. Behavior therapy of an eleven-year-old girl with reading problems. *Journal of Learning Disabilities,* 1974, **7,** 551–554.

CHAPTER 41

Psychotherapy with Children

DONALD K. FREEDHEIM AND SANDRA R. RUSS

DEVELOPMENT OF CHILD PSYCHOTHERAPY

Historical Perspectives

The treatment of behavior disorders in children has changed greatly over time, partly as a function of social and humanistic concerns and partly as a function of the frames of reference in which the behavior has been viewed.

The very terms mental illness and behavior disorder denote different perceptions of the individual so identified. The fact that children were essentially ignored as individuals, with notable exceptions, until the past century makes it impossible to differentiate early treatment of children from adults. Because children were seen as "little adults," the perception of individuals who were seen as "different" no doubt pertained to all individuals.

In primitive times the "disturbed" individual was alternatively revered as an inspired being or tortured as one possessed of evil spirits (Cattell, 1938). The treatment, if it can be called by that name, of individuals viewed as "lunatic" was in the domain of the priesthood. With the exception of Hippocrates, the Greek, who believed that physicians should care for mental conditions, the church alone took responsibility for curing the mentally ill until the time of the Renaissance. During the earlier periods, treatment took the form of "undoing" the problem. For example, since it was supposed that shock precipitated mental disorder, sufferers were hurled aloft, spun around, or dropped unexpectedly into ice water in order to shock the illness out. The same underlying philosophy inspired bleeding and trepanning of the skull, which were accepted treatments of the late Middle Ages.

During the reforms of the nineteenth century, the differentiation of mental illness from mental retardation and attempts to understand the underlying causes of behavioral deviance began to emerge. At the end of the nineteenth century, three basic forces—the education movement, increasing humanitarian concerns, and scholarly efforts toward understanding individual behavior—merged to form the groundwork of child psychology as we know it today. Coincidental with the origins of the field of child psychology, the roots of psychological treatment of children began to emerge as the foundations for modern day psychotherapy with children.

The classic first "case" for clinical psychology was a child who came to Lightner Witmer's Clinic at the University of Pennsylvania in 1896 (Witmer, 1909). The child was a poor speller, the prototype for learning problems of today. Witmer published his treatment of the child in his journal *The Psychological Clinic* the same year that Sigmund Freud described his treatment of Little Hans (S. Freud, 1909/1955), which also has implications for modern day treatments. Freud treated Little Hans via his parent (father), which is now a popular treatment of choice with children under 6 years of age (Furman, 1957). Also, around this time in 1908, Clifford Beers founded the mental hygiene movement, which led to the establishment of child guidance clinics throughout the nation (Rie, 1974).

However, all was not complete harmony within the burgeoning ranks of psychotherapists. William James discussed the work of Freud in his lectures at Harvard University and was criticized by Lightner Witmer who wrote an article entitled, "Is Psychology Taught at Harvard a National Peril?" (Postman, 1962).

During the 1920s and 1930s, the behavioral experiments of psychologists was paralleled by behavioral treatments of problems in children (Wolman, Egan, & Ross, 1978). During this time, behavioral and educational approaches to childhood problems seemed to hold sway although there was some understanding that parent-child communication problems formed the basis of many difficulties (Chadwick, 1928; Wickes, 1927). The book, notable for its title alone, *Crooked Personalities in Childhood and After* (Cattell, 1938), described the treatment of children through child guidance clinics, stressing the importance of early home environment in the formation of personality and potentials for treatment.

The psychodynamic or analytic movement's influence on child treatment began to emerge in the early 1930s and came into its own with the first publication of *The Psychoanalytic Study of the Child* in 1945. The work of Klein (1932/1960) with very young children and Aichorn (1935), particularly with adolescent youth, described various psychoanalytic techniques with children. A treatment emphasizing emotional release to undo depression was stressed by Levy (1938). Applications of the theories of S. Freud, Adler, and Jung to children were made by Baker and Traphagen (1935).

Through the 1940s, the child analytic movement grew rapidly, with various authors stressing the active participation of the child in treatment (Allen, 1942), the need for emotional support of children (Ribble, 1943), abnormally strong mother-child relationships (Mahler, 1945), the role of child defenses (A.

Freud, 1946), and the importance of milieu treatment for severely disturbed children (Bettelheim, 1950).

In the midst of the strong psychodynamic movement of the 40s, Grace (1946) promulgated the potentials of tutoring as a device in therapy. An alternative to treatments that emphasized verbal exchanges with children was offered by Axline (1947) who described the use of play in therapy in a more nondirective approach. A review of child therapies in the 1940s can be found in Haworth (1947). However, the treatment of children was not entirely through communication and in relationship with a therapist. More severely disturbed children were not amenable to such approaches and—reminiscent of the Middle Ages?—electric shock was attempted, albeit with questionable results (Bender, 1947).

Recent Developments

Beginning in the 1960s, a dichotomy in the philosophy toward the treatment of children began to emerge, with one view emphasizing drug-related treatments (mainly prescribed and supervised by pediatricians and psychiatrists) and the other view emphasizing behavioral approaches (Routh, 1981). Despite the growing movement to relegate childhood problems to the faults of biology, with the inevitable search for the right drug combination to correct the imbalance or deficit, other observers of child behavior focused on normal developmental stages and the stressors during these periods for cues as to pathological behavior (Blos, 1962; A. Freud, 1965). Through the careful analysis of normal development, therapeutic approaches were recommended to deal with delays and deviations from the expected pattern of mature development. At the same time, therapeutic endeavors utilizing the group as a medium through which children could learn better ways of handling feelings and behavior emerged (Gratten, 1962). Glasser's (1965) reality therapy approach has been particularly successful in school settings. Comprehensive reviews of psychotherapy through the mid-

1960s can be found in the works of Esman (1965) and Kessler (1966).

The field of child psychotherapy expanded rapidly in the late 1960s and through the 70s. No one approach dominated the scene, with the exception of the work with the severely and moderately retarded for whom the advancements in behavior modification therapy were most beneficial (Finch & Kendall, 1979). For children with learning difficulties, neurotic or behavior disturbances, and for those reacting to traumatic experiences, a whole array of specific techniques has been derived. Among the most popular is the mutual storytelling technique, described by R. Gardner (1975b). The technique is viewed as applicable to a wide range of problems (Gardner, 1974, 1975a). The technique calls upon the therapist to initiate, intervene in, or complete stories with themes analogous to or symbolic of the child's problem. A radio station format engages the child's interest and allows the stories to be taped for later review by the patients or their parents. Other techniques utilizing storybooks (Berg-Cross, 1976), the telephone (Spero, 1980), fantasy and metaphor (Brooks, 1981), and active group interaction (Schacter, 1974) represent variations on earlier themes.

Another approach to child therapy that has been found indispensable is treatment via the parents (Furman, 1957). Recent examples of specific guides to parents in treating the problems of their children are found in the work of Wright (1978) and Finch and Kendall (1979). And there are brave souls who treat both parents and children together in family treatment and view the family as a systematic, organic unit (German & Kniskern, 1981). In dealing with particularly difficult children with autistic behavior (Ross, 1981a) or subtle learning problems (Kenny & Burka, 1980), therapists have stressed the need for multiple and flexible interventions that utilize various approaches at different times with the same child.

The current practices in child psychotherapy vary widely (Koocher & Pedulla, 1977), from traditional analytic principles (Sours, 1978) to the use of toys and games in therapy (Adams, 1974). In general, individual child psychotherapy is viewed as being most effective in the mild to moderate problems of childhood (Reisman, 1973). However, there is still lack of significant progress in determining the efficacy of therapeutic approaches (Phillips & Bierman, 1981). No specific remedies for specific problems have been reliably found. There is a need for large scale clinical trials with appropriate research techniques to determine the effects of various treatments. With all of the current research, there is still little confidence that can be put in current findings due to poor sampling and even poorer definitions of symptomatology (Phillips & Bierman, 1981).

One of the more disturbing signs of the times is the finding that the presence or absence of insurance coverage probably plays a role in determining the length of therapeutic sessions offered to a child (Koss, 1980).

Given the vast array of intervention techniques, the remaining sections of this chapter will focus on individual psychotherapy approaches with children.

Current Practice of Child Psychotherapy

In most forms of individual child psychotherapy, the child and the therapist meet individually once or twice a week for 45-minute to one-hour sessions. The mutual agreement between the child and therapist is that the therapist is there to help the child understand feelings, thoughts, and behaviors. For some children, a specific problem that the child is concerned about, such as failing in school, or feeling unhappy, can be identified. For others, who feel they have no problems and resent seeing a therapist, no agreed upon reason for therapy can be reached, at least initially.

The therapeutic relationship is a professional one, with the therapist there to help the child express feelings and thoughts, understand causes of behavior, and form a relationship with the therapist. The therapist does not take over the parental role. Play is a major tool in therapy. The child communicates with the therapist both verbally and through play. Usually, the child structures the therapeutic hour by choosing the topics, forms of play, etc. In this way, the child determines the pace of the therapy. The therapist tries to be sensitive to the material that is being expressed at a number of different levels. Therapists differ in how much they guide the therapy through comments and interpretations.

Goals of therapy and therapeutic techniques depend upon the type of problem and personality development of the child, which are elaborated later in this chapter. What occurs in therapy also depends upon the theoretical approach and personal style of the therapist. However, Reisman (1973) defines seven principles to which most child therapists would adhere: (1) the therapist assesses the child as a precondition to psychotherapy and as an integral part of the therapy process; (2) the therapist listens to the child and allows opportunities for feelings and beliefs to be expressed; (3) the therapist communicates understanding of the child, respect, and the wish to be of help; (4) the therapist negotiates with the child a goal for their meeting; (5) the therapist makes clear what is unusual or inconsistent in the child's behavior, feelings, and beliefs; (6) when dealing with behaviors that are supported within a system (family, school, etc.), the therapist may modify that behavior by negotiating with the system; (7) the therapist negotiates termination with the child when the advantages of ending the therapy outweigh those of continuing.

It is important to point out that, in most cases, individual work with the child is only one part of a larger treatment program. Parent guidance, family therapy, remediation, school consultation, and/or group therapy frequently occur simultaneously with individual child therapy. In fact, as Koocher and Broskowski (1977) point out, a number of different types of interventions are necessary for optimal treatment of multiproblem families. Thus it is actually a disservice in many cases to treat only the child.

There is a host of practical issues that come up in working with children such as setting reasonable limits, maintaining confidentiality, helping the child separate from mother in the waiting room, choosing appropriate toys, taking the child to the bathroom (or not), and

dealing with vacations. This chapter will not go into the "how to's" of child psychotherapy. For suggestions on how to deal with these issues, Axline (1947), Bruch (1974), Haworth (1964), Kessler (1966), and Reisman (1973) are good sources.

An oft-raised question both by clients and by beginning therapists is "How does talking (or playing) help?" How does change occur by two people meeting and spending a limited amount of time together? What are the mechanisms of change within child psychotherapy?

MECHANISMS OF CHANGE IN INDIVIDUAL CHILD PSYCHOTHERAPY

Variables Within the Therapy Process that Effect Change

The basic premise of many forms of individual psychotherapy with children is that if certain events occur between two people and specific techniques are utilized, specific therapeutic processes will unfold. These therapeutic processes result in changes within the child. Identifying these techniques and therapeutic processes has been the focus of much clinical writing and many therapy outcome studies.

A central question is, "How does change occur within the child as a result of psychotherapy?" Applebaum (1978) and Garfield (1980) have identified major ways in which change occurs in psychotherapy with adults. Many of these therapeutic variables are also important in child psychotherapy. The following emerge as major hypothesized mechanisms of change within the child as a result of individual psychotherapy.

1. *Catharsis and labeling of feelings.* The release of emotion and expression of feelings is thought to be therapeutic by a number of different schools of child therapy (Axline, 1947; A. Freud, 1965; Moustakas, 1953). Expression of negative feelings, in particular, is important for many children (Moustakas, 1953). Helping children to feel safe to express feelings is a major task of the therapist.

The therapist also labels and reflects the

feelings that are being expressed. Dorfman (1951) and Ginott (1965) both stress the importance of reflecting the feeling tone rather than the content of the material. By saying to the child that he or she (or the puppet, doll, etc.) seems to be feeling angry, a label is connected to a feeling state. Words help to put feelings into a context for the child, thus making feelings less overwhelming.

2.   *Insight and working through.* The child develops cognitive insight into problems. Verbal labeling and cognitive mediation permit understanding of behavior and symptoms. Higher order reasoning processes can be applied to problem solving (Dollard & Miller, 1950). To develop insight, behavior is linked to feelings and thoughts by interpretations by the therapist. The behavior then becomes understandable to the child. For example, the interpretive statement by the therapist, "You seem to take things from your mother's purse when you are feeling uncared for and alone," puts the behavior into a framework. If this interpretation is well timed (the child is ready to hear it) and accurate, it also helps the child feel understood. Lowenstein (1956) has a good discussion of the role of speech in psychotherapy.

Equally important to the development of cognitive insight through therapy is the emotional resolution of conflicts or the "working through" process. That is, the emotional re-experiencing of major developmental conflicts is an important aspect of therapy. Ambivalent emotions and conflictual material is expressed, thought about, talked about, played out, and, consequently, worked through. Play is particularly important in providing a vehicle for conflicts to be expressed and resolved.

3.   *Corrective emotional experience.* The child's learned expectations are not met. The relationship between the therapist and child is especially important for a corrective emotional experience to occur. For example, a child expresses angry thoughts and feelings about mother. The therapist, contrary to the child's expectations, is not angry or punishing. Rather, the therapist is accepting of the feelings and works with the child to help understand the reasons for the anger. After a number of these

therapeutic events, a corrective emotional experience occurs. The automatic connection between angry thoughts and guilt or anxiety gradually decreases (or extinguishes). The child no longer reacts so immediately to angry thoughts with guilt or anxiety and a variety of defensive maneuvers and symptoms. A different attitude is developing. Instead of asking the question, "How can I be so angry—what's wrong with me?", the child is now asking, "Why am I so angry?" The child is then more comfortable with feelings and impulses.

4.   *Learning alternate problem-solving techniques and coping strategies.* Many forms of individual therapy do directly help the child think about alternate ways of handling a problem. The therapist may, in a more directive approach, help the child think of different solutions or may directly suggest another solution to a problem. The therapist might also suggest a different way of viewing a situation.

5.   *Development of internal structure.* Children with structural deficits need to develop structure that permits self/object differentiation, self-esteem regulation, impulse control, object constancy, reality testing, etc. (Kohut, 1977; Mahler, 1968). These children are suffering from early developmental problems. They have not developed the necessary cognitive and affective functions to help them differentiate fantasy from reality, inside from outside, self from other. The therapist serves as a stable figure who helps the child develop these ego functions as much as possible (Gilpin, 1976).

6.   *A variety of nonspecific variables.* Nonspecific variables are being increasingly recognized as important in their own right. Possible nonspecific variables in child therapy might be that the child no longer feels alone, sees that the problem is being attended to, has expectations of change, or is aware of family involvement.

Similarities and Differences in Types of Individual Child Psychotherapy

Different types of individual psychotherapy *emphasize* different mechanisms of change within the child. Thus, different mechanisms of change and different techniques would be emphasized in different forms of individual psychotherapy.

All forms of individual therapy with children have, as a broad goal, to help the child progress along developmental paths. The growth process has been disrupted and the goal of therapy is to get the child moving again (A. Freud, 1965; Palmer, 1970). Individual therapy is recommended when there are disturbances in emotional and personality development. Psychological assessment is especially important in determining in which specific areas development has been interfered with and how severe and pervasive the problems are. Based upon this assessment, decisions are made about how to focus the therapy. Increasingly, when individual therapy is recommended, it is in conjunction with a number of other interventions with the family, school, and community.

Kessler (1966) identifies what many forms of therapy with children have in common. They all involve the release of emotion, the use of play, and the attempt "to re-educate the child through corrective experiences and verbal explanations" (p. 372).

The importance of a warm, accepting, and trusting relationship between the child and the therapist has been repeatedly stressed (Axline, 1947; Moustakas, 1953; Reisman, 1973). It is through this relationship that corrective emotional experiences can occur, that emotions and fantasies can be explored, that risks can be taken, and that the child can internalize the acceptance and understanding offered by the therapist. A good relationship is a basic requirement of all forms of individual therapy with children.

Also of major importance in many forms of individual therapy is the use of play. Play is a major vehicle for change in psychotherapy. Over the years, play has been discussed from a variety of different theoretical approaches as being an important function in child development (Axline, 1947; Erikson, 1950; A. Freud, 1956; Gould, 1972; Piaget, 1951; Schaefer, 1979; Singer, 1973). Schaefer (1979) points out that both Freud and Piaget thought of play as an adaptive function "to help a young child gradually assimilate and gain mastery over unpleasant experiences" (p. 15). Through play, the child expresses affect, calls forth "forbidden" fantasy and feelings, works through and masters developmental problems, and resolves conflicts. Individual therapy provides a safe atmosphere in which the child can use play experiences to resolve conflicts.

The therapy experience adds several elements to the normal play situation. In therapy, an adult is present to provide a permissive and accepting environment for the child. This permissive environment is particularly emphasized by the nondirective play therapists (Axline, 1947) and the more relationship-oriented therapists (Moustakas, 1959). Also, the therapist labels and interprets the play content. Interpretation is utilized more frequently in psychodynamic approaches (Klein, 1932) to different degrees by different therapists. Labeling and interpretation by the therapist facilitates the child's own work.

Classifying different types of individual psychotherapy with children is a difficult task. Mendelsohn (1975) offers a sophisticated synthesis of major types of individual psychodynamic therapy with children that is consistent with Dewald's (1964) and Weiner's (1975) classification systems with adults. In considering individual psychotherapy with children, three broad classifications of treatment emerge. Each type has different treatment goals and emphasizes different techniques and mechanisms of change within the child. These are not "pure" categories in that a mix of techniques is used with each child.

Although these broad types of therapy apply mainly to psychodynamic approaches, it is likely that nondirective play and relationship approaches also emphasize different techniques and mechanisms of change, depending upon the needs of the child.

The first major type of individual therapy for children is insight-oriented therapy. The goals of this type of therapy are conflict resolution and the mastering of developmental crises. Interpretation is an important therapeutic technique as is helping the child deal with forbidden material in fantasy and play so that this material can be thought about, worked through, and mastered. Verbal labeling of unconscious impulses, conflicts, and causes of behavior helps lend higher order reasoning skills to understanding problems. Forbidden material, as it is expressed and released, is then available to be worked through in play and fantasy and integrated into the personality. Important mechanisms of change for this type of therapy would be insight and working through, catharsis, and corrective emotional experiences.

Insight-oriented therapy is appropriate for children who have good overall ego development, can tolerate anxiety, are struggling with internal conflicts, trust adults, and are able to think about their behavior and what it means. The 9-year-old boy, Mark, who, in the intake interview, said that his main problem was that "I have trouble with my vocabulary words because when I get nervous I can't concentrate," was demonstrating a good ability to think about himself and causes of behavior—a good "observing ego." He was a good candidate for insight-oriented therapy. Therapy with this boy focused on the expression and understanding of unconscious underlying conflicts that were causing the anxiety and, in turn, school achievement problems.

A central conflict concerned his aggressive impulses and associated guilt. Mark was unaware of these feelings and thoughts. The therapist helped Mark to permit this material to surface and be expressed in the therapy. Angry feelings towards his father and guilt about these feelings were expressed verbally and in play. He was also afraid of punishment by his father for his aggressive impulses. His conflict regarding aggression resulted in inhibitions in a learning situation—a kind of fear of success. The therapist helped Mark to accept these feelings and have access to this material so that it could be worked through. Mark used the therapy well, expressed angry feelings, did a lot of verbalizing, and worked through the conflict to a large degree. There was no longer a need for the inhibition. He was a bright child (IQ of 135) and began doing well in school once his anxiety decreased. At the end of that school year, the school felt that Mark was ready for a class for gifted children

in a different school. Mark again dealt with a conflict about that issue. He wanted to go but felt bad about leaving his siblings and his friends. He also felt some guilt. Mark was the youngest of seven children in an innercity neighborhood with an unemployed father. Success for him raised a number of real life issues. He was, however, now able to talk about his feelings and explore all sides of the issue. Because the material was mainly conscious, he was able to talk about it and make his decision during one therapy session. He decided to go to the gifted program, and, at a six-month follow-up, was doing well.

A second major type of individual therapy with children is supportive psychotherapy. Supportive psychotherapy focuses on helping the child develop problem-solving techniques and coping strategies. Dewald (1964) and Weiner (1975) both have excellent descriptions of the differences between insight-oriented and supportive therapy. The focus in supportive therapy is on everyday problems and "here-and-now" conflicts. There is less uncovering of anxiety-producing material. The therapist may help the child think of steps in planning a project rather than focusing on what underlying conflicts were making it difficult to plan in the first place. A major goal in supportive therapy is to improve the child's day-to-day functioning and general adjustment in an immediate fashion. Mechanisms of change that are emphasized are learning alternative problem-solving strategies, learning alternative ways of viewing a situation or oneself, corrective emotional experience, catharsis, and feeling that someone is there to help and attend.

Children for whom supportive therapy is appropriate are children who have major developmental problems, have a less well-developed ego and sense of self, and who are not "psychologically minded." Many of these children also have difficulty trusting an adult. Therefore, developing a trusting relationship with the therapist becomes a major goal of therapy.

For example, James, a 16-year-old boy, got into frequent fights in school that were triggered by other boys staring at him. At these times, he would become frightened. He interpreted their staring as meaning that they were going to pick on him and start a fight (he was "beating them to the punch"). At a deeper level, James had fears of homosexual assault. Granted that James was utilizing the defense of projection of his own aggressive and sexual impulses onto others a great deal. Much of this material was untouchable in the therapy. In a supportive approach, the therapist suggested another way of viewing the situation. The therapist said that many times, when other boys stared at James, it might be for different reasons than wanting to start a fight. It might simply be that they were feeling friendly or curious about him. Or it might not mean anything at all. This statement made by the therapist was one of the most therapeutic events of the therapy. It helped James to view the situation differently and to lessen the intensity of his own projection. Fighting decreased considerably and, in time, he began to feel safer with others. It was only within the context of a trusting relationship with the therapist that James was able to hear alternative ways of viewing the situation and truly to consider other possibilities. If this statement had been made early in the therapy, it would have been ineffective. The other major mechanism of change for James was his development of trust in the therapist. Trust in the therapist generalized to trust in other people.

A third major form of child therapy focuses on developing structure in children who have structural deficits. Borderline psychotic children and children with narcissistic disorders are thought to suffer from structural deficits which result in self/other boundary disturbances and the impairment of object relations (Blatt & Wild, 1976; Eckstein, 1966; Kohut, 1977; Leichtman & Shapiro, 1980; Mahler, 1968; Masterson, 1972; Pine, 1974). Borderline psychotic children have difficulty distinguishing fantasy from reality, especially in unstructured situations and during times of stress. They also have difficulty integrating positive and negative feelings about one individual. This is a difficult combination of problems. One 10-year-old girl, Donna, became furious with the therapist and threatened to kill her. Since the wish is often equal to the act for these children, Donna needed to

hear that wishing someone were dead was not the same as killing and that wishing would not cause the therapist to die. In this way, the therapist was helping Donna distinguish inside from outside, fantasy from reality. She also needed reassurance that the therapist would not let Donna hurt her, nor would the therapist hurt Donna. Donna also needed to hear that she could be angry with the therapist sometimes and feel affection at other times, that it was possible to feel conflicting feelings toward one person. And it was important that the therapist empathize with the anger and attempt to understand and help Donna verbalize the reasons for the anger.

Borderline psychotic children also show the need/fear dilemma (Blatt & Wild, 1976; Cass & Thomas, 1979). Because they have difficulty differentiating themselves from others, getting too close to the therapist or becoming too attached results in a fear of merging or engulfment. If they are too distant from others, there is a fear of annihilation, loss of identity, and personality disorganization.

One 12-year-old boy attempted to describe this state as he neared the end of three years of therapy. He drew a picture of a boy on the blackboard. He then said, "I used to be afraid that this would happen to me" and then erased the picture. He was attempting to describe the state of loss of self—complete annihilation. He also said that he still got those feelings sometimes but now knew that he would be all right.

The primary role of the therapist with these children is to be a stable object that the child can slowly take in (Gilpin, 1976). The therapist's consistency, predictability, empathy, help with self/other differentiation, and help with separating fantasy from reality all help to develop internal structure in the child. This is a slow process, usually taking at least two years of therapy. The major mechanism of change in these children is the development of psychological structure, that is, cognitive and affective functions necessary for adaptive interaction in the world.

It is important to point out that, to some degree, all mechanisms of change occur in all types of individual therapy. What differs is which techniques are emphasized in the treatment. With some children, different types of therapy are used in different phases of the treatment. For example, a borderline psychotic child may move into insight-oriented treatment after several years of intensive therapy in which certain internal structures have developed. Although there are clinical guidelines about when to use which type of therapy, we need more empirical guidelines about what the optimal interventions are with specific populations of children.

A few words about contraindications for individual psychotherapy with children. Individual therapy on an outpatient basis should not be recommended if the parents will not support the treatment. If the parents will not be able to bring the child for the therapy sessions or will probably drop out quickly, individual therapy should not be started. Other more short term treatment approaches would be more appropriate.

If altering situational factors will eliminate the problem, there is no need to work individually with the child. Working with the parents, family, school, and community would be the appropriate treatment strategies. This often is the case with children under 6 who have not yet internalized conflicts and who are very responsive to environmental changes. It is true for many other children as well.

Often, personality and emotional problems are secondary to problems in other areas of development, such as neurologically based learning disabilities, chronic illness, etc. Although individual psychotherapy might prove helpful, it should be a supplement to the major intervention in the primary problem area.

Individual outpatient psychotherapy should not be recommended if, in all probability, it will not make a significant difference for the child. This may be because of the severity of the problems within the child, such as in the case of a psychotic child. It may also be because of the pathology of the home environment. Other treatment approaches are called for.

Finally, when individual psychotherapy might be helpful but is not the "optimal" intervention, it should not be recommended.

This last point is where the field of child psychotherapy runs into trouble. The ultimate purpose of the assessment process is to make optimal treatment decisions (Cole & Magnussen, 1966). When evaluating a child and family, the clinician must ask, "What is the probability that individual therapy will make a difference in this child's development? Is individual psychotherapy the most optimal treatment approach? If so, what therapeutic techniques and mechanisms of change should be emphasized in the therapy. What other interventions should be carried out in conjunction with individual therapy?" There are few empirically based guidelines for answers to any of these questions.

RESEARCH IN CHILD PSYCHOTHERAPY

The major current reviews of the literature in child psychotherapy research are those of Hartmann, Roper, and Gelfand (1977) and Barrett, Hampe, and Miller (1978). Both reviews conclude that the effectiveness of individual psychotherapy with children is still to be demonstrated. Hartmann et al. (1977) state that "mental-health practices with children rest on a rather tenuous empirical base" (p. 4). This tenuous empirical base is partly due to the kinds of questions asked in previous outcome research and to methodological problems that arise in carrying out psychotherapy research with children.

One of the classic pieces of child therapy outcome research is that of Levitt (1957). He found, after reviewing 18 child psychotherapy studies, that the mean improvement rate for children in treatment was not significantly better than the baseline improvement rate of 72.5 percent. The 72.5 percent improvement rate for untreated controls was obtained from studies by Witmer and Keller (1942) and Lehrman et al. (1949). In his later work, based on 47 reports of child therapy outcome, Levitt (1963, 1971) concluded that approximately two-thirds of treated children are improved at the close of treatment. About 80 percent are improved at follow-up. The crucial point is that untreated controls, "defectors," showed as much improvement as children who received treatment. Levitt's analysis raised a challenge to the field of child psychotherapy.

A number of authors wrestled with Levitt's conclusions (Halpern, 1968; Heinicke & Goldman, 1960; Hood-Williams, 1960). One of the major issues in this controversy was the adequacy of the use of defectors as the untreated control group. Defectors are children who were evaluated and recommended for treatment but who did not enter into treatment. A number of confounding variables may be operating here that make the defector groups not comparable to the treated groups. Finding adequate control groups has been a difficult task in child therapy research (Hartmann, et al., 1977; Meltzoff & Kornreich, 1970; Strupp & Bergin, 1969).

A major recent longitudinal retrospective study by Cass and Thomas (1979) offers a number of results that are consistent with previous outcome research. They followed 200 children seen from 1961 to 1965 at the Washington University Child Guidance Clinic and interviewed them as adults, from 17 to 27 years of age. Cass and Thomas (1979) conclude that there is little continuity between child and adult disturbances, except for extreme personality deviations. Looking at the effect of treatment, children who received outpatient psychotherapy did not show better adjustment at follow-up than untreated children. In fact, untreated children received significantly better social adjustment ratings than treated children. In further analysis of the data, these differences disappeared when only the children seen by staff therapists (as opposed to trainee therapists) were included in the treatment group. In general, these results are consistent with those of studies reviewed by Levitt (1957). Cass and Thomas (1979) discuss the possible confounding variables in the untreated control group. For example, the parents of these children, for whom treatment was recommended, may have been better copers than parents of children who were treated and/or may have learned as a result of the evaluation process how to intervene in the home.

Directions for Future Research

In reviewing the literature on psychotherapy outcome research, several methodological directions emerge as necessary for future research.

First, the need for research to become specific is increasingly stressed. Bergin and Strupp (1972) convincingly argue that research should focus on specific mechanisms in psychotherapy that affect specific variables in the individual. They call for an end to global outcome studies with adults. They point out that outcome studies of behavioral approaches have usually investigated specific processes. Research with other forms of psychotherapy must move in this direction even though the concepts involved may be more difficult to operationalize. Frank (1979) also emphasized the importance of focusing on specific forms of therapy and specific therapist-patient interactions. Kiesler (1966) stated that discrete bits of knowledge must be worked on separately in psychotherapy research. Bergin and Lambert (1978) also stressed the importance of investigating specific kinds of change.

In the child area, the same call for specificity is made by Barrett et al. (1978) and Heinicke and Strassman (1975). Barrett et al. (1978) take a close look at Levitt's (1957, 1963) work and the research literature in general and conclude that one of the major problems in these studies is that of their global nature. Barrett et al. (1978) conclude:

If we resort to macrovariable research (e.g., combining all kinds of diagnostic categories, patients being seen by therapists with a wide variety of personal styles, each making all kinds of interventions, and then assessing outcome in some gross fashion like improved, partially improved, unimproved) we will continue to demonstrate that 70 percent of disturbed children improve with psychotherapy or with time alone. (p. 430)

They go on to say that the question in psychotherapy research should not be "Does psychotherapy work?" but rather "Which set of procedures is effective when applied to what kinds of patients with which sets of problems and practiced by which sorts of therapists?" (p. 428).

One might become even more specific and ask "Which specific interventions affect which specific cognitive, personality, and affective processes? How are these processes related to behavior and practical clinical criteria?" Asking these kinds of questions would enable us to identify the developing processes in children that are involved in particular clinical problems. They would also enable us to investigate which interventions facilitate the development of these processes and which do not. Many of the past outcome studies in the child area have either ignored these underlying processes, used inadequate measures, or not made distinctions among them.

A second guideline that emerges from the literature is the need to use multiple outcome criteria (Barrett et al., 1978; Heinicke & Strassman, 1975; O'Leary & Turkewitz, 1978; Waskow & Parloff, 1975). As Bergin and Lambert (1978) put it, "Divergent methods of criterion measurement must be used to match the divergency of human beings" (p. 171). Hogan, DeSoto, and Solano (1977) point out that many theoretical conceptualizations of the personality are multidimensional in nature. The personality consists of a number of complex dimensions rather than one unitary dimension. The complexity of the person can not be handled by a few concepts nor, one might extrapolate, by a few measures. Kiesler (1966), in the same vein, speaks of the myth of the one-process dimension in psychotherapy. He speculates that patient change occurs along a number of different dimensions. These dimensions may respond in different ways to different aspects of the therapy process. Stollack, Gershowitz, and Rief (1978) suggest that measures of inner experience as well as behavioral measures be used.

Strupp and Hadley (1977) have stressed the need for multiple perspectives in evaluation of therapy. In their tripartite model, they suggest using three vantage points in evaluation: that of the society, of the individual, and of the mental health professional. The vantage point of society would be reflected in measures of adaptive behavior. For children, that would include measures of school achievement, behavioral adjustment, peer relations, coping strategies, etc. The point of view of the individual would be reflected in the child's sense of well being. The vantage point of the mental health professional would be reflected in measures of cognitive and personality structure. Strupp and Hadley call for comprehensive evaluations that would use a variety of measures that reflect multiple values in judging therapy outcome.

Measures of general behavior, such as behavior rating scales, have frequently been used in outcome research but there are a number of problems involved in using *only* these measures with children. First, as Achenbach (1978a) has stated, few measures of children's behavior have been adequately standardized and validated for studying psychopathology. Second, similar behaviors may reflect different underlying problems in different children. For example, hyperactivity may reflect organicity, anxiety, need for attention, etc. Third, similar behaviors have different meanings at different ages. Bedwetting at 6 has a different meaning from bedwetting at 14. Fourth, behavioral measures are rarely tightly linked to underlying cognitive and personality processes. Therefore, changes in these behaviors as a result of intervention tell us little about what specific variables are being influenced, and how. For example, improvements in school achievement as a result of psychotherapy might be due to improved self-esteem, increased motivation, improved impulse control, greater flexibility in problem solving, or any combination of the above (as well as a host of other factors). Different interventions may be optimal for dealing with problems in each of these areas. To tease out what types of therapeutic interactions are most helpful to problems in self-esteem as opposed to problems in emotional integration, and how these, in turn, are related to school achievement, we have to formulate very specific empirical questions and use multiple measures that tap different levels of functioning.

This brings us to the third methodological guideline, the need for theoretical validity (Mahoney, 1978). Theoretical validity is the logical bearing an experiment has on a hypothesis. The experimental procedure is relevant to the theoretical model. Thus the measures that are used in outcome studies should be theoretically relevant to the intervention. The measures should "make sense" theoretically and be conceptually linked to the intervention. Heinicke and Strassman (1975) and Bergin and Lambert (1978) stress that the measures should also be theoretically linked to the clinical problem and to the group being investigated. Thus, if we want to improve reading achievement in a group of children with emotionally based learning disorders, we must measure underlying cognitive and personality processes that are components of reading achievement. In this way, we begin to develop a conceptual framework that links the type of intervention to specific cognitive and personality processes, which, in turn, are related to practical clinical criteria. Heinicke and Strassman's (1969) study of children with reading disorders in psychodynamic psychotherapy is a good example of a study that chose measures of variables such as ego flexibility and ego integration which would be expected to be altered by psychodynamic therapy and would in turn effect the reading process. This study made theoretical sense.

Our knowledge of child development and our knowledge of how therapy works should guide us in designing theoretically valid studies (see Simeonsson, "Theories of Child Development," chap. 2 of this book). There needs to be a greater synthesis of the research and ideas in child development and in clinical child psychology. Frequently, the left hand does not know what the right hand is doing and is not particularly interested.

Heinicke and Strassman (1975) cover a number of other methodological issues important for research in the child area, such as the importance of classification according to developmental level. Controlling for maturational effects is a problem unique to the child therapy area (Koocher & Broskowski, 1977). The need for homogenous treatment groups has been stressed by many (Achenbach, 1978b; Hartmann et al., 1977; Kiesler, 1966). Cass and Thomas (1979) point out the importance of controlling for sex and age variables.

The Hartmann et al. (1977) review covers a multitude of methodological issues in child psychotherapy research.

Waskow and Parloff (1975) have suggested using a standard core battery of outcome measures with adults. The child area would benefit from standard measures, as well. For research with children, developing specific core batteries for different developmental processes would be more in keeping with a developmental approach. Also, a number of specific core batteries rather than one core battery is consistent with the principles of specificity and theoretical relevance. Specific core batteries of tests that tap different levels of functioning need to be developed for different child populations and for different research areas.

These specific batteries could be used to match groups before intervention, an issue Kiesler (1966) feels is very important. Also, matching groups prior to intervention provides the opportunity to use statistical alternatives that are preferable to using unreliable change scores (Achenbach, 1978b).

The focus in this discussion of research in child psychotherapy has been on therapy outcome research that permits inferences about cause and effect. The area of program evaluation research for children's programs is a broad area with somewhat different goals. Koocher and Broskowski (1977) point out that the primary goal in program evaluation research is to assess program effectiveness and improve service delivery. The primary question in program evaluation research is, "Is the program effective?" Specific questions about why and how the program is effective are secondary. The Leventhal and Weinberger (1975) study is a good example of a comprehensive program evaluation study that demonstrates the effectiveness of a multimodal program of brief psychotherapy for children.

In designing research studies, one must be clear about the type of research one is doing and the primary purpose of the research—to determine if the program is effective, to investigate specific mechanisms of change, or both.

In summary, a number of psychotherapy researchers in both the adult and child areas are calling for (1) specific processes to be investigated and specific questions to be asked, (2) the use of multiple outcome criteria, and (3) the need for theoretical validity. Many of the past studies in child psychotherapy have not followed these guidelines. A large number of studies have been global in nature using only a few crude outcome measures. This type of approach has not given much empirical support for the success of child psychotherapy when compared with base rates, (Levitt, 1971) nor has it contributed to the knowledge of how psychotherapy effects change.

For the field of child psychotherapy to progress, we must identify specific interventions that effect specific changes in cognitive and personality functioning and development. Basic questions that relate developmental processes to clinical problems need to be tested before or simultaneously with intervention manipulations. Doing systematic, specific studies is a time-consuming endeavor but necessary if we are going to discover which of the myriad of interventions that occur in the therapy process affect which specific cognitive and personality variables. We need to refine our interventions and our measures.

Ultimately, child psychotherapy research cannot be separated from basic research in child personality and cognitive development.

IMPLICATIONS FOR THE FUTURE OF INDIVIDUAL CHILD PSYCHOTHERAPY

We can only speculate about the future of the field of individual therapy for children. Based upon the history of the field, the current trends in outcome research, and new developments in the child area in general, what can we predict about the next 50 years? What will child therapy be like in the year 2020? Here are a few predictions and suggestions.

The field is realizing and will continue to realize the necessity for obtaining empirical support for therapy practices. A dedication to systematic research programs is beginning to develop, and this is encouraging. It is crucial that we focus on why and how specific inter-

ventions effect change. This type of step-by-step research is very time consuming. It often means validating measures and answering some basic questions empirically before investigating interventions. Ross (1981b), in an appropriately titled paper, "On Rigor and Relevance," has stressed the importance of developing a programmatic series of "interrelated consecutive and simultaneous" studies that are both methodologically rigorous and clinically relevant. He states that it is especially important to have a closer relationship between the clinic and the laboratory. There should be a reciprocal relationship between the clinical case study and the experiment. In this way, we can achieve a systematic accumulation of knowledge.

Also, a more concerted effort could be made in large scale program evaluation studies to include measures that would permit inferences about why and how change occurred.

If we do not build a sounder empirical base, the field of child psychotherapy will become obsolete. It is important that graduate programs prepare students to carry out evaluation studies that contribute to the field of scientific knowledge. Perhaps one goal of graduate training should be that the student be able to design a methodologically sound psychotherapy outcome study.

As child psychotherapy research becomes more specific, so will child psychotherapy practice become more specific. As we gain knowledge about particular interventions effecting specific variables with specific groups of children, psychotherapy practice should become more focused. Thus, there may be more specific goals and more deliberate use of specific techniques within the therapy. Schaefer and Millman (1977) also see child therapists moving away from one "all-purpose" therapeutic mold to more specific approaches.

The danger involved in becoming more focused is that of losing sight of the "whole" child. Working with the whole child, focusing on different conflicts as they come up, and different developmental levels as the child is ready, has always been a strong advantage of individual therapy with children. It will be a challenge to the therapist to be "optimally" focused, emphasizing specific goals and techniques, and yet remain sensitive to all dimensions of the child.

The developing knowledge about the interaction between cognitive and affective processes will affect what therapists do (Brooks, 1979; Russ, 1980, 1982; Santostefano, 1980). Research investigating the effect of play on cognitive functioning (Dansky & Silverman, 1973; Smith & Dutton, 1979) and the manner in which play in psychotherapy affects children (Singer, 1973; Singer & Singer, 1976; Stollack et al., 1978) should have direct implications for child therapy. Incorporating evolving research-based techniques into clinical practice is important. On the other hand, child therapists have a great deal of knowledge about the interaction of cognitive-affective processes that needs to be shared with and listened to by child developmental researchers. There needs to be a closer, more reciprocal relationship between the child therapist and the child researcher, for the benefit of both. Harter's (1977) work on a cognitive-developmental approach to children's expression of conflicting feelings is a good example of the integration of child development theory and child psychotherapy practice.

Individual psychotherapy will be increasingly carried out within a situational context. From the beginning of the child guidance movement there has been an emphasis on working with the child's environment in conjunction with individual therapy. Working with parents and the school has always been a part of the treatment plan. New conceptualizations of the reciprocal relationships between systems has been discussed by Bronfenbrenner (1979). The transactional perspective stresses the interactional nature of different systems. Each affects the other. These new conceptualizations will affect how the therapist thinks about the child in relation to situational factors. The child therapist will be increasingly involved as a consultant to the school and the community and will need to be knowledgeable in consultation theory and practice.

In general, the next few decades should bring a refinement of interventions, greater use of specific therapy techniques for specific problems and child populations, and more empirical support for therapy practice. Individual child psychotherapy has always been both an art and a science. Hopefully, the next 50 years will strengthen child psychotherapy as a science while maintaining the art.

REFERENCES

Achenbach, T. Psychopathology of childhood: Research problems and issues. *Journal of Consulting and Clinical Psychology,* 1978, **46,** 759–776. (a)

Achenbach, T. *Research in developmental psychology.* New York: Free Preess, 1978. (b)

Adams, P.L. *A primer of child psychotherapy.* Boston: Little, Brown, 1976.

Aichorn, A. *Wayward youth.* New York: Viking, 1935.

Allen, F. *Psychotherapy with children.* New York: Norton, 1942.

Applebaum, S. Pathways to change in psychoanalytic therapy. *Bulletin of the Menninger Clinic,* 1978, **42,** 239–251.

Axline, V. *Play therapy.* Boston: Houghton Mifflin, 1947.

Baker, H.J., & Traphagen, V. *The diagnosis and treatment of behavior problem children.* New York: Macmillan, 1935.

Barrett, C., Hampe, T.E., & Miller, L. Research on child psychotherapy. In S. Garfield & A. Bergin (Eds.), *Handbook of psychotherapy and behavior change.* New York: Wiley, 1978.

Bender, L. One hundred cases of childhood schizophrenia tested with electric shock. *Transcriptions of the American Neurological Association,* 1947, 165–169.

Berg-Cross, G., & Berg-Cross, L. Bibliotherapy for young children. *Journal of Clinical Child Psychology,* 1976, **5,** 35–38.

Bergin, A., & Lambert, M. The evaluation of therapeutic outcome. In S. Garfield & A. Bergin (Eds.), *Handbook of psychotherapy and behavior change.* New York: Wiley, 1978.

Bergin, A., & Strupp, H. *Changing frontiers in the science of psychotherapy.* Chicago: Aldine-Atherton, 1972.

Bettelheim, B. *Love is not enough.* New York: Free Press, 1950.

Blatt, S., & Wild, C. *Schizophrenia: A developmental analysis.* New York: Academic Press, 1976.

Blos, P. *On adolescence.* New York: Basic Books, 1962.

Bronfenbrenner, U. *The ecology of human development.* Cambridge: Harvard University Press, 1979.

Brooks, R. Psychoeducational assessment: A broader perspective. *Professional Psychology,* 1979, **10,** 708–722.

Brooks, R. Creative characters: A technique in child therapy. *Psychotherapy: Theory, Research, and Practice,* 1981, **18,** 131–139.

Bruch, H. *Learning psychotherapy.* Cambridge: Harvard University Press, 1974.

Cass, L., & Thomas, C. *Childhood pathology and later adjustment.* New York: Wiley, 1979.

Cattell, R.B. *Crooked personalities in childhood and after.* New York: Appleton-Century-Crofts, 1938.

Chadwick, M. *Difficulties in child development.* New York: John Day, 1928.

Cole, J., & Magnussen, M. Where the action is. *Journal of Consulting Psychology,* 1966, **30,** 539–543.

Dansky, J., & Silverman, I. Effects of play on associative fluency in preschool-aged children. *Developmental Psychology,* 1973, **9,** 38–43.

Dewald, P. *Psychotherapy: A dynamic approach.* New York: Basic Books, 1964.

Dollard, J., & Miller, W.E. *Personality and psychotherapy.* New York: McGraw-Hill, 1950.

Dorfman, E. Play therapy. In C. Rogers (Ed.), *Client-centered therapy.* Boston: Houghton Mifflin, 1951.

Eckstein, R. *Children of time and space, of action and impulse.* New York: Appleton-Century-Crofts, 1966.

Erikson, E.N. *Childhood and society.* New York: Norton, 1950.

Esman, A. Treatment of personality disorders in children. In B.B. Wolman (Ed.), *Handbook of clinical psychology.* New York: McGraw-Hill, 1965.

Finch, A.J., & Kendall, P.C. (Eds.). *Clinical treatment and research in child psychopathology.* New York: Spectrum, 1979.

Frank, J. The present status of outcome studies. *Journal of Consulting and Clinical Psychology,* 1979, **47,** 310–316.

Freud, A. *The psychoanalytic treatment of children.* London: Imago, 1946.

Freud, A. *Normality and pathology in childhood: Assessments of development.* New York: International Universities Press, 1965.

Freud, S. Analysis of a phobia in a five-year-old boy (2nd ed., Vol. 10). London: Hogarth, 1955. (Originally published, 1909).

Furman, E. Treatment of under-5's by way of parents. In the *Psychoanalytic study of the child* (Vol. 12). New York: International Universities Press, 1957.

Gardner, R. The mutual storytelling technique in the treatment of psychogenic problems secondary to minimal brain dysfunction. *Journal of Learning Disabilities,* 1974, **7,** 135–143.

Gardner, R. *Psychotherapeutic approaches to the resistant child.* New York: Aronson, 1975. (a)

Gardner, R. *Therapeutic communication with children: The mutual storytelling technique.* New York: Aronson, 1975. (b)

Garfield, S. *Psychotherapy: An eclectic approach.* New York: Wiley, 1980.

German, A.S., & Kniskern, D.P. (Eds.). *Handbook of family therapy.* New York: Brunner/Mazel, 1981.

Gilpin, D. Psychotherapy of borderline psychotic children. *American Journal of Psychotherapy,* 1976, **30,** 483–496.

Ginott, H.G. *Between parent and child.* New York: Macmillan, 1965.

Glasser, W. *Reality therapy.* New York: Harper & Row, 1965.

Gould, R. *Child studies through fantasy.* New York: Quadrangle, 1972.

Grace, A. *Tutoring as therapy.* New York: Commonwealth Fund, 1946.

Gratten, L. Psychoanalytic group therapy for preschool children. *Canadian Psychiatry Association Journal,* 1962, **7,** 90–96.

Halpern, W.I. Do children benefit from psychotherapy? A review of the literature on follow-up studies. *Bulletin of the Rochester Mental Health Center,* 1968, **1,** 4–12.

Harter, S. A cognitive-developmental approach to children's expression of conflicting feelings and a technique to facilitate such expression in play therapy. *Journal of Consulting and Clinical Psychology,* 1977, **45,** 417–432.

Hartmann, D.P., Roper, B.L., & Gelfand, D.M. An evaluation of alternative modes of child pyshotherapy. In B. Lahey & A.E. Kazden (Eds.), *Advances in clinical child psychology* (Vol. 1). New York: Plenum, 1977.

Haworth, M.R. (Ed.). *Child psychotherapy.* New York: Basic Books, 1947.

Haworth, M.R. (Ed.). *Child psychotherapy.* (2nd ed.) New York: Basic Books, 1964.

Heinicke, C. Frequency of psychotherapeutic session as a factor affecting outcome: Analysis of clinical ratings and test results. *Journal of Abnormal Psychology,* 1969, **74,** 533–560.

Heinicke, C., & Goldman, A. Research on psychotherapy with children: A review and suggestions for further study. *American Journal of Orthopsychiatry,* 1960, **30,** 483–494.

Heinicke, C., & Strassman, L. Toward more effective research on child psychotherapy. *Journal of Child Psychiatry,* 1975, **14,** 561–588.

Hogan, R., DeSoto, C., & Solano, C. Traits, tests and personality research. *American Psychologist,* 1977, **32,** 255–264.

Hood-Williams, J. The results of psychotherapy with children. *Journal of Consulting Psychology,* 1960, **24,** 84–88.

Kenny, T.J., & Burka, A. Coordinating multiple interventions. In H.E. Rie & E.D. Rie (Eds.), *Handbook of minimal brain dysfunction: A critical review.* New York: Wiley, 1980.

Kessler, J. *Psychopathology of childhood.* New Jersey: Prentice-Hall, 1966.

Kiesler, D. Some myths of psychotherapy research and the search for a paradigm. *Psychological Bulletin,* 1966, **65,** 110–136.

Klein, M. *The psychoanalysis of children.* New York: Grove, 1960. (Originally published, 1932.)

Kohut, H. *The restoration of the self.* New York: International Universities Press, 1977.

Koocher, G., & Broskowski, A. Issues in the evaluation of mental health services for children. *Professional Psychology,* 1977, **8,** 583–592.

Koocher, G., & Pedulla, B. Current practices in child psychotherapy. *Professional Psychology,* 1977, **8,** 275–287.

Koss, M.P. Descriptive characteristics and length of psychotherapy of child and adult clients seen in private practice. *Psychotherapy: Theory, Research and Practice,* 1980, **17,** 268–271.

Lehrman, L.J., Sirluck, H., Black, B.J., & Glick, S.J. Success and failure of treatment of children in the Child Guidance Clinics of the Jewish Board of Guardians. *Research Monographs,* 1949, No. 1.

Leichtman, M., & Shapiro, S. An introduction to the psychological assessment of borderline conditions in children: Borderline children and the test process. In J. Kwawer, H. Lerner, P. Lerner, & A. Sugarman (Eds.), *Borderline phenomena and the Rorschach test.* New York: International Universities Press, 1980.

Leventhal, T., & Weinberger, G. Evaluation of a large-scale brief therapy program for children. *American Journal of Orthopsychiatry,* 1975, **45,** 119–130.

Levitt, E.E. The results of psychotherapy with children: An evaluation. *Journal of Consulting Psychology,* 1957, **21,** 189–196.

Levitt, E.E. Psychotherapy with children: A further evaluation. *Behavior Research and Therapy,* 1963, **1,** 45–51.

Levitt, E.E. Research in psychotherapy with children. In A.E. Bergin & S.L. Garfield (Eds.), *Handbook of psychotherapy and behavior change: An empirical analysis.* New York: Wiley, 1971.

Levy, D. Release therapy in young children. *Psychiatry,* 1938, **1,** 387–390.

Lowenstein, R.M. Some remarks on the role of speech in psychoanalytic techniques. *International Journal of Psychoanalysis,* 1956, **37,** 460–468.

Mahler, M.S. Child analysis. In N. Lewis & D. Pacella (Eds.), *Modern trends in child psychiatry.* New York: International Universities Press, 1945.

Mahler, M.S. *On human symbiosis and the vicissitudes of individuation.* New York: International Universities Press, 1968.

Mahoney, M. Experimental methods and outcome evaluation. *Journal of Consulting and Clinical Psychology,* 1978, **46,** 660–672.

Masterson, J. *Treatment of the borderline adolescent.* New York: Wiley-Interscience, 1972.

Meltzoff, J., & Kornreich, M. *Research in psychotherapy.* New York: Atherton Press, 1970.

Mendelsohn, R. A manual for the seminar on psychotherapeutic process. *Collected seminar notes at Washington University Child Guidance Center,* 1975.

Moustakas, C. *Children in play therapy.* New York: McGraw-Hill, 1953.

Moustakas, C. *Psychotherapy with children: The living relationship.* New York: Ballantine, 1959.

O'Leary, D., & Turkewitz, N. Methodological errors in marital and child treatment research. *Journal of Consulting and Clinical Psychology,* 1978, **46**, 747–758.

Palmer, J. *The psychological assessment of children.* New York: Wiley, 1970.

Phillips, J.S., & Bierman, K.L. Clinical psychology: Individual methods. In *Annual Review of Psychology,* 1981, **32**, 405–438.

Piaget, J. *Play, dreams and imitation in childhood.* New York: Norton, 1951.

Pine, F. On the concept of "borderline" in children. *The psychoanalytic study of the child.* 1974, **29**, 341–368.

Postman, L. (Ed.). *Psychology in the making.* New York: Knopf, 1962.

Reisman, J. *Principles of psychotherapy with children.* New York: Wiley, 1973.

Ribble, M. *The right of infants.* New York: Columbia University Press, 1943.

Rie, H. (Ed.), *Perspectives in child psychopathology* (Vol. 3). Minneapolis: University of Minneapolis Press, 1974.

Ross, A.O. Child psychopathology. *Annual Review of Psychology,* 1981, **32**, 243–278. (a)

Ross, A.O. On rigor and relevance. *Professional Psychology,* 1981, **12**, 318–327. (b)

Routh, D. Child treatment citation classics. *Professional Psychology,* 1981, **11**, 901–906.

Russ, S. Primary process integration on the Rorschach and achievement in children. *Journal of Personality Assessment,* 1980, **44**, 338–344.

Russ, S. Sex differences in primary process thinking and flexibility in problem solving in children. *Journal of Personality Assessment,* 1982, **46,** in press.

Santostefano, S. Cognition in personality and the treatment process: A psychoanalytic view. *Psychoanalytic Study of the Child,* 1980, **35**, 41–66.

Schacter, R. Kinetic psychotherapy in the treatment of children. *American Journal of Psychotherapy,* 1974, **28**, 430–437.

Schaefer, C. (Ed.). *Therapeutic use of child's play.* New York: Aronson, 1979.

Schaefer, C., & Millman, H. *Therapies for children.* San Francisco: Jossey-Bass, 1977.

Singer, J. *The child's world of make-believe.* New York: Academic Press, 1973.

Singer, J., & Singer, D. Imaginative play and pretending in early childhood: Some experimental approaches. In A. Davids (Ed.), *Child personality and psychopathology: Current topics* (Vol. 3). New York: Wiley, 1976.

Smith, P., & Dutton, S. Play and training in direct and innovative problem solving. *Child Development,* 1979, **50**, 830–836.

Sours, J. The application of child analytic principles to forms of child psychotherapy. In J. Glenn (Ed.), *Child analysis and therapy.* New York: Aronson, 1978.

Spero, M.H. Use of the telephone in child play therapy. *Social Work,* 1980, **25**, 57–60.

Stollack, G., Gershowitz, M., & Rief, T. Fantasy play in child psychotherapy. Paper presentd at the American Psychological Association Meeting, Toronto, 1978.

Strupp, H.H., & Bergin, E. Some empirical and conceptual bases for coordinated research in psychotherapy: ·A critical review of issues, trends, and evidence. *International Journal of Psychiatry,* 1969, **7**, 18–90.

Strupp, H., & Bergin, E. Some empirical and conceptual bases for coordinated research in psychotherapy: A critical review of issues, trends, and evidence. *International Journal of Psychiatry,* 1969, **7**, 18–90.

Waskow, I.E., & Parloff, M.B. (Eds.), *Psychotherapy change measures.* DHEW Publication No. (ADM) 74–120 (Supt. Doc. Stock No. 1724–00397), 1975.

Weiner, I.B. *Principles of psychotherapy.* New York: Wiley, 1975.

Wickes, F.G. *The inner world of childhood.* New York: Appleton, 1927.

Witmer, H.L., & Keller, J. Outgrowing childhood problems: A study of the value of child guidance treatment. *Smith College Studies in Social Work,* 1942, **13**, 74–90.

Witmer, L. Clinical psychology. *Psychological Clinic,* 1909, **1**, 1–9.

Wolman, B.B., Egan, T., & Ross, A. (Eds.). *Handbook of treatment of mental disorders in childhood and adolescence.* New Jersey: Prentice-Hall, 1978.

Wright, L. *Parent power: A guide to responsible childrearing.* New York: Psychological Dimensions, 1978.

CHAPTER 42

Family Therapy

JEFFREY ZIMMERMAN AND DIANA SIMS

As a separate and distinct form of therapy, family therapy has grown rapidly, especially over the last ten years. Indeed, there have been a great number of books recently published as well as several new journals devoted to family and marital therapy (Kaslow, 1980). This chapter will not attempt to review this voluminous amount of material but will try to provide the reader with the basic concepts in the field. The first hope is that the reader will be spurred on to pursue areas that stimulate interest. The second hope is that the ideas in the chapter will help beginning clinicians look at clinical material in other than purely individualistic ways.

Prior to the early 1950s, only individual models of psychotherapy were in vogue. When a child was referred for psychological or behavioral difficulties, he or she was typically given a battery of tests and then seen in individual therapy by a psychiatrist. If the parent was involved, it was typically the mother working with a social worker (Kaslow, 1980). A frequent outcome to this "child guidance" approach was that the child was often removed from therapy just as improvements and changes were beginning to take place. Beginning in the early 1950s, individuals from various mental health fields began seeing and evaluating families as a unit (Haley, 1971). When these professionals began viewing the family as whole, it became evident that children's problems were often indicative of family difficulties, especially of difficulties in the marital relationship (Bowen, 1965). Furthermore, problems in the marital relationship seem to influence the kind of relationships the parents form with the children and also the kind of relationships the children form with each other. Children's problems thus took on a new meaning for family therapists. As Haley (1976) stated, "A problem is defined as a type of behavior that is part of a sequence of acts between several people.... A symptom is a label for such a sequence. Thinking of such symptoms...as a contract between people...leads to a new way of thinking about therapy" (p. 2).

Regardless of one's theoretical approach to individual therapy (i.e. behavioral, psychodynamic, etc.) family interaction variables are involved in that they contribute either to the development and/or maintenance of the child's problems. This chapter will attempt to present an outline of how a family perspective can be applied in different settings no matter what one's favored method of psychotherapeutic intervention. Included also will be the topics of assessment, types of treatment, and outcome and process research.

APPLICATION

When a child is brought into an outpatient mental health setting, "who" is expected to accompany the child varies depending on the setting; sometimes this is left vague, sometimes one or both parents are requested to attend the session. Typically, it is satisfactory for one parent to bring the child in order to provide a report of the current concerns about the child's behavior. If a family perspective is taken, however, the person making the appointment needs to make it understood that the entire family is to come in for the initial session, whether it be for assessment or treatment purposes. A rationale must be offered to make this request understandable—this typically includes some statement about needing the whole family's help in understanding the problems. Expecting the entire family to attend means that the appointment must be flexible so that all members can attend. Often, appointments must be made late in the day so that the father is able to come to the session. Fathers are usually the most reluctant to attend, so it is suggested that every effort be made to accommodate them to insure their presence. Including the father is likely to increase chances for a positive outcome (Gurman & Kniskern, 1981).

The child's behavior can be viewed from many different levels. Analytically oriented therapists tend to consider the intrapsychic or internal makeup of the child. This could be considered an object-relations-level perspective, for the focus is centered on the individual. Moving along the hierarchy, behaviorally oriented therapists tend to look at how the child's behaviors are reinforced and maintained by factors in the environment. This could be considered a behavioral level perspective in that another dimension is added to the focus on the individual, that of the influence of the environment. Neither of these views is incompatible with each other, nor is either in conflict with a family perspective. Each way of viewing a child's problems represents a different level of conceptualizing the behavior. Taking a family perspective is comparable to a structural level view in that the focus is on the way interactions in the family are organized.

A family systems view of behavior looks at the function of the child's symptom in maintaining the balance of relationships or equilibrium of the family. How this process works will be discussed in the next section. This balance is pathological in that a symptomatic member is needed. Taking a family perspective, then, means recognizing the family issues that exist to keep the child symptomatic and realizing that family "rules" will need to be

restructured if the child's symptoms are to be removed (Haley, 1962). More times than not, the child's symptomatic behavior serves a primary function in the marital relationship. Madanes' (1980) work characterizes the symptom as a protective function for the marital relationship in that it attracts attention to the child and thus distracts the family from the marital problem. In this situation, the symptom also offers a degree of control for the spouse who is "one-down" in the relationship over the more overtly controlling spouse. The present authors believe this level of analysis to be critical in understanding the home environment if individual treatment of the child is attempted, as the marital hierarchy will need to be "rebalanced" or at least coped with by the child. While therapists generally advocate working with whole or parts of families, it is possible to work with children in individual therapy models as long as some understanding of how the child's behavior fits into the family is achieved.

For those who are oriented toward individual analytic therapy, making a family assessment can be very helpful in understanding the internal makeup of the child. Skynner (1976) suggests that seeing the family in operation can help the therapist understand the projective systems developed by individual family members. This understanding can be more directly achieved through family assessment techniques. Thus working through the child's intrapsychic conflicts can be facilitated by direct observation and understanding of how those conflicts have been produced.

If a behavioral approach is taken, one generally investigates how the child's symptomatic behavior is maintained by his or her environment. A behavioral program is then designed to involve the parents and child in an effort to reinforce more desirable behaviors and decrease maladaptive, symptomatic behaviors. Through a family assessment, the therapist can understand why the presence of the symptom is, at some level, reinforcing to the parents. While they are troubled by the problem behavior, the function the behavior serves in the marital relationship makes the response cost of the symptom more costly if *not* maintained. Having this understanding enables the therapist to design a behavioral program in such a way that it will not be ultimately sabotaged by one or both parents who may have ulterior motives for the presence of the symptom. A good example here would the parent who subtly reinforces the child's bad behavior in such a way that the other parent is hurt by it, or who makes "alliances" with the child against the other parent. Understanding this process allows the behavior therapist to manipulate the reinforcement parameters so that this family pattern is circumvented.

In taking a family approach, the family assessment is a natural way to begin getting the entire family involved in sessions and in being part of the intervention. This is not to say that every session has to include every family member. In fact, family therapists now (Bowen, 1976b) seem to be moving more toward working with different parts of the family on different occasions. Another model being used involves breaking the session into parts and doing family work, marital work, behavior management, or individual psychotherapy as needed. Nevertheless, getting the entire family involved at the begining often makes it easier to bring in other family members later on. The absolute refusal of one parent (or other family member) to attend even one session at least provides some important data on the way relationships are maintained in the family. When there is only a single parent, typically as a result of divorce, it is the authors' experience that the behavior of the single parent and/or the child is often related to unresolved issues involving the absent parent. Thus, in a family assessment, it is useful to consider the absent parent as "part" of the current family picture. When possible, the absent parent should be seen at least for the assessment and sometimes even in certain phases of the treatment.

Considerations of family involvements are slightly different when working with children on an inpatient unit. Children are usually placed on inpatient psychiatric units because they are evidencing problems that are more serious in nature than can be managed in outpatient therapy. The child is often treated on the unit in a manner that only peripherally involves the family. Clearly, from the previous discussions about outpatient work, these symptoms can serve a function in the family makeup as well. Given that the child will probably someday return home, family interventions are a useful part of the inpatient work. This can be accomplished indirectly by working with the child on family issues or directly through regular, ongoing family sessions. One helpful way of differentiating the type of family considerations that need to be addressed is to keep in mind the age of the child. With a younger child, the family can be involved in a way that facilitates the transfer of the child from the inpatient setting back into the family unit. Again, an understanding of the function of the child's symptoms as it pertains to the family functioning is helpful. Even in the instances where the child's main problem has an organic basis, the child's resultant behavior either has a tremendous effect on, or is affected by, family functioning. The child's behavior may be used in family struggles and/or may affect the everyday functioning of the family. With older children or adolescents (i.e., those at the point of beginning to seek independence from the family), working with the family can help facilitate the adolescent's transition from a family member to an independent young adult. Haley (1980) introduced strategies for using the family as an aid rather than encountering them as sabotaging agents when the adolescent attempts to make this transition.

Working with the family or parents when a child has been initially diagnosed as having a medical problem seems to be particularly helpful as a preventive measure. The initial diagnosis of a handicapped infant presents the parents with a number of stresses with which to cope (McCollum & Gibson, 1970). Interventions, at diagnosis, to help the parents appropriately manage both the child's needs and their own needs can help prevent the development of problems in these areas in the future. When an older child is diagnosed with a medical problem that will become chronic (e.g., diabetes) or when the child has suffered an injury that will have lasting effects (e.g., spinal cord damage), problems often arise that seem to be the result of family interaction styles that adversely affect the child's psychosocial growth and/or affect the child's compliance with a required medical regime. Present interaction styles that may presently be resulting in minor problems may become magnified and more rigid by the stress of meeting the demands created by the medical problem. For example, parents who tend to be somewhat overprotective may become even more so because of *their* anxiety about the medical problem and/or problematic issues in their own relationship. In addition, controlling, angry parents (who are like that in their own relationship) may adversely push the child towards compliance. The child may then develop resentful attitudes toward being "made" to follow a required medical regime and become noncompliant when she or he becomes an adolescent and has achieved enough autonomy to say "no." Overprotection can result in a child's becoming overly dependent on the parents and have great difficulty in accepting responsibility for managing his or her own illness when she or he becomes of age. One area where pediatric psychologists commonly encounter the results of both of the above interactional styles is in work with diabetic children. Parents, frightened by the long term medical implications of the disease, often approach the illness in maladaptive ways that result in adolescents' developing resentful attitudes and/or not developing necessary self-help for independent functioning. Minuchin and colleagues (Minuchin et al., 1975) reported great success using structural family therapy working with troubled families with diabetic, anorectic, or asthmatic children.

From a different perspective, the medical symptoms may become tactics for the child or adolescent to use in efforts to control parents or may serve a function in maintaining the relationship. We see many cases at the Oklahoma Children's Memorial Hospital in which medical symptoms seem to arise in response to parental conflict. For example, one adolescent's stress-related medical disorder (i.e. hereditary angioedema) flaired regularly to protect her from facing the demands of growing up and to protect her parents from facing conflict in their own relationship. The deflection of the conflict to the child may serve to exacerbate the medical symptoms in ways that are ultimately harmful to the child. In the preceding discussion of parent interaction styles and medical problems, the "overprotective" or "controlling" behaviors from the parents in response to the child's social or medical needs may serve to maintain the family equilibrium in the same way that parents' inappropriate response to a child's behavioral problems and needs serves to maintain pathological equilibrium in that situation. The most important variable is the way the family is organized rather than the type of symptom the child has (i.e., medical, behavioral).

ASSESSMENT

In assessing the status of an individual client, information can be gathered in several ways. The therapist conducts an interview, completes psychological testing, and notes how the client interacts with the therapist. Family therapists follow these procedures, but their task is more complicated because there are more than two in the room. In addition to the above-mentioned information-gathering tasks, included in family assessment is close observation of the interactions in the group. Interpreting family assessment data is a huge task for the therapist given the large amount of material involved.

There seem to be two guiding principles that cut across all forms of family work (Wynne, 1981). First, the focus in family therapy tends to be more on observable behaviors than on intrapsychic functioning. The second principle involves a systems framework that most family therapists use despite their theoretical orientation. This section will first present a brief description of systems theory as it pertains to families and then describe more structured assessment techniques.

A problem in presenting this material is the lack of adequate terminology to describe sets of interactions in a systems framework. Haley (1963) alluded to this problem and commented that common descriptions, such as a person being "infantile," a wife being "dominating," or a husband being "passive," used when describing individual behaviors, are not of much value when it comes to describing different types of relationships. Haley goes on to point out that these individual dichotomies are not adequate because they do not take into account systems of interactions.

An organizational framework developed by Waters (personal communication, May 1977) will be used to present the different components of systems theory as it relates to families. Waters's four tenets or facets will serve as starting points for each aspect of the theory.

According to Waters, the beginning facet of systems theory as related to families points out that the family is a complex of interrelated parts. As Bodin (1981) notes, this interrelated complex has both a history of interaction and an expectation of future interaction and interdependence. Furthermore, this process is both continuous and ongoing. Accordingly, any attempt to punctuate the process by selectively viewing one or more interactions has to be considered an arbitrary punctuation. Discrete behavioral interactions typically have meaning in a much larger context; that is, they have a place and serve a function in the continuous set of interactions of the family. An illustration of this point involves the difference between looking at a movie as opposed to single snapshots. Obviously, the snapshot would not contain the valuable process information that would be included in the entire movie. Considering the above, then, the view of causality as an arbitrary phenomenon also begins to emerge. In point of fact, we can find causality wherever we begin to view the system from, but the most adequate description of causality is in a description of the interaction of the system. Thus, factors such as a mother or father "reinforcing attention-getting behavior," or a child having "poor ego control" may be components of the problem situation, *but may not reflect direct causality.* Symptomatic behavior is viewed in

a similar manner. Symptoms are seen as contracts between members of a system—contracts that have message qualities for the entire system as well as a function in the entire interpersonal network (Stanton, 1981). The symptoms can be viewed as a metaphor of the problem in the system of which they are a part (Madanes, 1980). It follows, then, that symptoms cannot be viewed apart from their interpersonal context. What this indicates, as Haley (1963) pointed out, is that the cause of any particular behavior in any sequence can only be determined after evaluating and describing the entire system. Conceptualizations of children's problem behaviors are most useful when they include each individual involved in the system of ongoing behavior. A focus on changing the individual's symptomatic behavior will not produce a change in the entire system that is producing and maintaining the pathological behavior. This brings us to the second component of a family as a system.

As previously mentioned, the family is a complex of interrelated parts, to the extent that a change in any one part will lead to changes in all parts. Clearly, if the system is interrelated and the behavior of one member affects and is affected by the behaviors of others, then in order for the system to maintain itself a change in one component must correspond to changes in other components of the system. If this were not characteristic of a system, then the system and the way it is maintained would be threatened. In clinical practice, this problem is often encountered when a therapist works individually with a child, not in a family context. The child begins to improve and the parents typically come back reporting symptoms from a different child. In order for the system to maintain itself and its current way of operating, somebody in the system must have symptoms. Only changes in the rules of the entire system itself would allow for changes in an individual member without requiring new symptoms from another member. For this reason, it is difficult to work with a child out of the context of the family. This appears to be one reason why parents take children out of therapy when they began to get better. Improvement in the child threatens the balance in the system itself.

One clinical problem area that typically involves the above concept is in work with adolescents. Adolescence is, in and of itself, a threat to the family system, especially when the adolescent child is attempting to become more independent and so change in some manner or, eventually, when it is time for him or her to leave home. If the family system is dependent on that adolescent in some way, then the rest of the system will try to prevent the adolescent from making any changes. In the medical center where the authors presently work, we frequently encounter psychosomatic and psychogenic symptoms (e.g., stomachaches, headaches, hysterical symptoms, anorexia) from adolescents who are attempting to free themselves from rigid systems and are prevented from doing so by other family members (see also Minuchin, 1977). These adolescents seem to be using their symptoms to gain some control over a system that is threatened by their changing.

An appropriate case example involves a boy with a congenital endocrine disease (i.e., adrenogenital hyperplasia). This boy had early onset of puberty and was making precocious sexual advances to other young children. He was also throwing temper tantrums, especially in relation to efforts of control by his father. The young boy was involved in an overly close, dependent relationship with his mother. The parents had labeled him as the problem child or the "black sheep" and his sister as the perfect child or "white knight." From observing the family, it was obvious that the parents' struggle regarding the boy mirrored some covert problems in their own marriage. When the boy and the father fought, the mother would get in the middle and begin arguing with the father about how he was treating the boy. A family approach was not taken at first. The boy was seen separately from his parents and worked with on ways to develop self-control. The parents were trained in behavior management principles and taught to stop reinforcing his tantrums. Their marital issues were not worked on in therapy, and they appeared very threatened by attempts to

move in that direction. As soon as the boy began to show improvement, the parents stated that they were now concerned that their "perfect" teenage daughter had begun having sexual relations with a boyfriend. This case is a good illustration of how problems will continue when a child's behavior is treated separately from the family system. It also illustrates how changes from one member will lead to changes in other members. For things to change in this family, the way the family members as a group dealt with conflict, particularly the conflict between the parents, needed to be the focus.

The third important facet in viewing the family as a system is that a system seeks to maintain a homeostatic balance. All biological systems are characterized by homeostasis. If homeostasis does not exist, the result is chaos. Though it is difficult to explain how homeostasis works, one can easily observe it in operation by examining the stability of roles in all relationships. It is not just coincidence that the observer will see one child being a scholar and another child being an athlete or one person being the joker and another being the listener. Roles between people tend to be very stable although people can take different (but stable) roles vis-á-vis other people. While the role one takes with different people may vary, once established, the role tends to be consistent. Built-in styles of relating and interacting often develop because of these adopted, set roles. Kaplan and Kaplan (1978) use the Gestalt term *confluent* to describe the rigid, patterned ways of interaction that develop as "a ritual playing-out of roles rather than a 'contact' between humans." These patterns of behavior often become redundant. In discussing Don Jackson's works, Greenberg (1977), points out that the family has rules to govern this redundant system. The roles, then, can be thought of as a function of the rules that govern the family relationships. There are even rules about rules, and these may be either implicit or explicit. Furthermore, if one exceeds a certain implicit limit in relation to another person, the other person will generally react in a such a way that these limits are again restored and maintained.

Homeostatis is often described using the analogy of a thermostat. A thermostat is set at a certain point and designed so that, when the temperature deviates from the fixed point, the thermostat reacts to bring the room temperature back to the set limit. The only way for permanent change to occur is to change the setting on the thermostat. If limits are deviated from in a family or group of people, pressure is exerted by the system to bring back the original limits. As Haley (1963) pointed out, no single element (i.e., in the family) can be blamed in this process. The limits remain firm because they are maintained by rules that govern the entire system. Only by changing the rules of the system can change occur. Using systems theory language, this process is described as a negative feedback loop. Negative feedback operates in a system to maintain the status quo (Maruyama, 1968). Families have a range of functioning, but, when events go beyond certain set points, negative feedback operates to bring the system back to status quo. If events occur that far exceed the boundaries of the system, then a "runaway" could be produced and the existence of the system would be threatened (Hoffman, 1971). We have all had the experience of fighting with another person up to a certain point and then backing off.

Positive feedback is also present in a system. Positive feedback functions to allow for change (Maruyama, 1968). Ideally, a system will have a balance of both positive and negative feedback. Olson, Sprenkle, and Russell (1979) discuss the dimensions of cohesion and adaptability in relation to systemic balance. Adaptability is characterized by morphogenesis (change) and morphostasis (stability). Cohesion refers to the balance between emotion bonding and autonomy in the family. The family is better able to cope with stress when these two dimensions are balanced. For example, if there is an extremely high level of cohesion, the family is said to be enmeshed; a low level of cohesion signifies disengagement. In these types of families, or in other words in families whose boundaries and rules are too rigid or too diffuse, the system is easily threatened by any sort of change. This includes even normative changes, such as an adolescent's leaving home.

In a well-functioning system, there are rules that allow for change as well as rules that maintain order. These rules govern the range in which a family functions. In a healthy family, these rules are flexible, and there are rules that exist to allow some changes in rules (metarules). In families with symptomatic members, metarules that normally allow for change do not seem to exist. One label that has been given to this process is pathological equilibrium. Pathological equilibrium is an equilibrium that is maintained at the expense of one member. If the "sick" label is removed from the symptomatic member, then the family will recalibrate around a different member in order to maintain the pathological equilibrium. Only a change in rules of the system will allow for a different process to occur.

Homeostasis is often maintained by a process labeled triangulation (Bowen, 1965). Triangulation with a third member by two individuals occurs as a way of reducing tension between these individuals. For people who have difficulty with intimacy, triangulation on a third person is a way to keep distance between them. Dyads seem to be the most important and effective relationships but are also the most fragile. They require constant work. If work at maintaining the dyad stops, triangulation around a third person or around issues (the boss at work, etc.) will most probably occur. In the case example given above, the boy served a function by being triangulated into the parents' relationship. Instead of working together on intimacy and closeness with each other and fighting the battles that had gotten in the way of this closeness, they used the boy as the focus of their conflict. Rigid roles and triangulation are often diagnostic signs in a family assessment session.

It may then seem to the novice reader that the task is clear. The therapist simply brings the whole family together and works on changing the rules so that members can change and establish more effective relationships within and outside of the family. However, the fourth component in viewing the family as a system illuminates the difficulties in this process. This fourth component is that systems resist change. Pressure on a system to change will often result in counterpressure by the system to resist change. People are caught in their roles and are threatened by the thought of abandoning them. The strategic family therapy approaches are based on the use of this resistance in the change process. The reader is referred to Watzlawick, Weakland, and Fisch's book, *Change,* published in 1974.

Apart from using general systems theory to make inferences about families, there exist only limited approaches for organizing data in a more structured manner. Haley (1976) suggested items that the therapist can observe in the first interview that will give clues about the function the symptom serves. These include, among others, observing how the parents and children interact, how the problem is presented, the family seating arrangement, who interrupts whom and how often, reactions of family member to what is being said, and who does the talking. Minuchin (1974) suggested that, as the therapist is exploring different areas, guidelines of what qualities are found in effectively functioning families should be kept in mind. The therapist looks for ineffective interactions and relationships but also looks for ways in which boundaries are maintained. (Boundaries will be discussed in a later section.) Satir (1967) advocates use of a family life chronology or "history-taking process" (p. 112). From this process, the therapist can gain knowledge about the marital relationship, the individual members of the family, how the family unit deals with disagreement, parental expectations, and a host of other valuable pieces of information. Satir has outlined 52 suggestions for the therapist in conducting this interview so that the interview can take place in a nonthreatening manner.

While suggestions from Satir, Haley, and Minuchin are valuable in gaining information about how families work, these suggestions still do not provide the interviewer with a structured, standardized assessment process. An attempt to develop such a standardized interview has been made by Watzlawick (1966).

Watzlawick developed what is known as the structured family interview. This interview can be quite useful to the therapist in defining the mechanics of a family and facilitating conversation among family members so that important family styles of relating can be observed. Scapegoating, blaming, and "symptoms-producing" features are often exposed in these structured interactions. Watzlawick suggests that the therapist working with the family observe the interview from behind a one-way mirror so as best to view the way the family functions. While this is often not practical in many clinical settings, the structured family interview can still be used by a clinician to gather data. The interview consists of the following parts:

1. Main problem. The interviewer asks each family member, either privately or as a group, what he or she sees as the main problems in the family. Asking each family member this question individually gives each the message that what he or she has to say is important and that his or her point of view is of value. This question also deflects attention from the identified patient by implying that the interviewer senses several conflicts in the family unit and does not necessarily accept the presenting complaint or symptom as *the* problem.

After each member has had a turn at stating his views, the interviewer then states that it is obvious they have not discussed these issues as a group and should do so now. By facilitating group discussion the interviewer can then observe how the members interact.

2. Plan something together. The interviewer next instructs the family to plan an activity that they can all do together. They have about five minutes to do this. Watzlawick stressed that the intent of the family's final decision may be of interest, but is not so important as how the decision is reached, if it is reached within the time limit, who is involved in offering suggestions, etc. Observing this decision-making process can provide valuable insight into family mechanics.

3. How did you meet? The interviewer asks the parents how they met and got together. The children may or may not be

asked to wait outside for this. As the parents relay information and experiences about this question, patterns of marital interaction are often exposed. Not only are past interactions revealed, but, more often than not, present patterns also come into focus. Again, the process and style of relating to each other in the interview are of more concern than the actual content of the discussion.

4.   Proverb. While the children wait outside, the interviewer instructs the parents to discuss the meaning of a proverb given to them. They have five minutes in which to do this and then are to teach the meaning of the proverb to their children.

The proverb always used is "A rolling stone gathers no moss" because it has several interesting characteristics. It can be discussed at either the literal or metaphorical level, and there is no positive or negative value assigned to its content. This makes for interesting conversation, and the reader is encouraged to read Watzlawick's discussion of the "content and mode of marital communication" regarding this section of the interview. The manner in which the parents teach the meaning of the proverb to their children gives the therapist an idea as to how the parents go about setting up other learning situations and opportunities.

5.   Blame. The interviewer arranges the family's seating arrangements so that the father is at his left, followed by the mother, followed by the oldest child, next oldest, and so on until the youngest child is on the interviewer's right side. Each are given a pencil and slip of paper. The interviewer instructs them to write the main fault of the person on their left (with the youngest child writing about the father rather than the interviewer). They are to be brief and to use no identifying names or features. The interviewer collects the papers and tells the family that he will add two statements of his own (these are always "too good" and "too weak") and that they may pertain to any two family members. The therapist then shuffles the papers, reads the first one, and asks each family member in turn to whom they think the statement applies. This format is followed until each slip of paper has been read and discussed. This is the section where the "scapegoating," favoritism,

and self-blame in the family are revealed. The patterns of incorrectly attributing blame to self or other or deflecting blame away from a member are readily exposed in this task.

It is apparent that using the structured family interview can yield an abundance of valuable information for the therapist to work with. The dynamics of the family are readily exposed, and the therapist can begin the intervention process. Bodin (1981) has an excellent discussion of the structured family interview itself, along with some variations and suggestions for use. A potentially very useful but difficult task would be to research the structured family interview and gather normative data on each of the tasks.

Attempts at developing typologies of families have occurred over the past few years. These typologies use a "multidimensional approach that provides a more comprehensive and realistic picture of the complexity of these systems" (Olson et al., 1979, p. 15). Lewis et al. (1976) attempted empirically to validate their description of families ranging from dysfunctional, to midrange, to healthy, but methodological weaknesses impeded any clear results. Wertheim (1973, 1975), and Reiss (1971a, 1971b) have also developed family typologies, but little has been done to see how these relate to family diagnosis or treatments. As discussed earlier, the Circumplex Model of Olson et al. (1979), identifies sixteen types of family systems based on the two dimensions of adaptability and cohesion. This model provides a useful framework for clinicians, both for systematic diagnosis and the establishment of treatment goals.

Several paper-and-pencil instruments have been developed to aid in the family assessment process. The reader is referred to Cromwell, Olson, and Fournier (1976) for a listing of these. Also, there have been several fine reviews on family interaction research (Framo, 1965; Jacob, 1975; Riskin & Faunce, 1972) that would be of value to the interested reader.

Again, while these techniques are useful and helpful, much research is needed in developing a way of measuring the systems level functioning of the family. To accomplish this, new methodologies need to be developed that would allow for the measurement of the complexities of interactions in a group of people over time.

MODELS OF FAMILY THERAPY

The development of different models of family therapy parallels the development of family therapy itself and can be traced to the different geographic locations where family therapy began. For two comprehensive reviews of this process, the reader is referred to Guerin's (1976) chapter entitled "Family Therapy, the First Twenty-Five Years" and Kaslow (1980) "History of Family Therapy in the United States." In this chapter we will take up the models of family therapy as they exist now.

Kaslow (1980) expanded a schema devised by Gurman (1979) and extended it from his dyadic analysis to apply to larger family systems. Gurman divided the various schools of family therapy into three different groups: (1) psychoanalytically oriented family therapy; (2) systems models of family therapy, divided into Bowenian family therapy and communications-oriented family therapy; and (3) behavioral models of family therapy. To this categorization, Kaslow (1980) suggested several additions: first, that the communications theorists be broken into those who posit structural family therapy methods and those who posit strategic family therapy. In addition, she mentions the intergenerational or contextual family therapy of Boszormenyi-Nagy and Spark (1973). Kaslow suggested that this type of family therapy be placed somewhere between psychoanalytic therapy and Bowenian therapy within the Gurman categorization. Finally, in Guerin's (1976) classification, he placed group-oriented family therapy and experientially oriented family therapy among the analytic therapies. For the purpose of discussion in this chapter, we will combine Kaslow and Guerin's models and discuss each type of therapy on a continuum of analytically oriented therapy on one end and behaviorally oriented therapy on the other end.

Dynamic Models

Early analytically oriented family therapists considered the family environment as it was related to the individual pathology and to the psychosocial development of the child. Guerin (1976) pointed out that Nathan Ackerman was one of the early analytically oriented family therapists who used common analytical theoretical threads, such as dependency, sex, and aggression. Ackerman (1970) believed in the need to resolve "pathogenic conflicts" and attempted to induce change and growth by means of a dynamic depth approach to the affective currents of family life. He believed in looking at the behavior of each family member separately as well as considering them as individuals in a group. Analytically oriented family therapists often use both individual- and family-oriented techniques (Guerin, 1976). Gurman (1979) pointed out that ana-

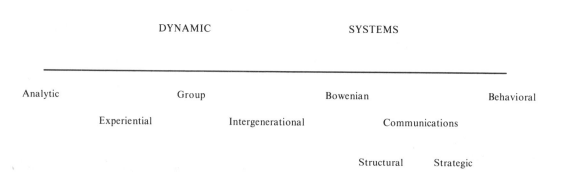

Figure 42.1.   A continuum of family therapy.

lytically oriented family therapists still could consider the establishment of a therapeutic alliance and the resolution of the transference issue as being paramount in therapy. Furthermore, the therapist is concerned about unconscious dynamics in the marital relationship and how this relates to choice of mate. More current work also focuses more intensively on the family as a series of interlocking dyads (Guerin, 1976). These interlocking dyads can be viewed in terms of their interlocking, interpsychic processes. Skynner's work (1976, 1981) illustrates a modern psychoanalytic model of family therapy and will be discussed in some detail.

Skynner believes that families evolve over generations having met or not met important developmental milestones akin to developmental levels of the Freudian schema. If a family or couple has not developed important relationship skills, these "blind spots" will be transmitted to the children, and developmental failures will occur over generations. These failures occur primarily due to the lack of learning of important social insights or to the faulty learning of certain expectations about the social behavior of others. Skynner labeled these expectations "projective systems" and suggested that people with relationship difficulties are "stuck" with expectations that are appropriate in childhood only. These projective systems "seek to preserve in unchanging form some past state of relationships, real or fantasized, and to manipulate others into behavior which will confirm this rigidly-held view of the world" (Skynner, 1981, p. 43).

It follows, then that Skynner's focus is on the projective systems that men and women bring to their marital relationship and the part that these projective systems play in the marital choice. Involved in the selection of this mate is the mutual "fit" of the projective system of both members as a couple. While this fit seems to provide for initial attraction, Skynner suggests that soon both partners begin making similar demands and each projective system will begin to fight for control of the other to the point where the relationship becomes endangered. The control battle involves the effort of each partner to get the other to function in a parent role despite the impossibility of each partner's being a parent to the other. More simply, one cannot provide parenting and at the same time seek parenting from the other.[1]

One usual concomitant of the type of relationship described above involves the use of a child to provide a partial resolution of the relationship problem by "loading" some aspects of the projection onto the child. Skynner suggested that this is the process by which "pathology" is "transmitted" to the next generation in an effort to save the marriage. It follows, then, that psychotherapy involves the identification of these projective systems and the attempt to take the projection off the identified child patient and return it to the marriage where a more adaptive resolution can be attempted.

Like most family therapists, Skynner discusses the importance of understanding and changing the family structure, of clarifying communication, and of teaching new skills. Nevertheless, Skynner believes that, while these types of interventions may result in new patterns for the family, these new patterns remain as problematic as the old. He believes that other efforts need to be made to facilitate differentiation and provide more growth in a general sense than a mere change in the system will provide. Skynner pointed out that this process might involve longer term therapy of a more analytic nature with concomitant periods of greater conflicts, and pain and suffering in an effort to differentiate themselves as "separate, independent persons, enjoying, but no longer simply needing each other" (Skynner, 1981, p. 55). Be that as it may, Skynner did state that couples must desire this type of growth before that type of therapy is attempted.

In Skynner's model, the therapist engages "with the family system through a semipermeable interface permitting mutual exchange of personal information. The therapist and family interact to facilitate a process of growth and development on *both* sides" (Skynner, 1981, p. 57). Through a process of first being receptive and responsive to family (and individual) issues and then becoming aware of the emotional attitudes that are absent in the family, the therapist can begin to introduce the emotions being denied based on the family's projective system and defensive structure.

Obviously this is a simplistic reduction of Skynner's work, and interested readers are referred to his original writings for a more complete discussion (Skynner, 1976, 1981). Skynner is flexible in that he does not suggest growth-oriented techniques for all types of families. Nevertheless, he believes in an insight-oriented, growth-producing model for those families than can manage this level of interaction. We will see that other schools of thought do not posit this type of change in their work.

The next form of family therapy within the dynamic group is experientially oriented family therapy. Experientially oriented family therapists consider therapy sessions as an "experiential happening." The focus is on "process" issues that occur during the session, and an attempt is made to produce a feeling-level focus for the family. Changes theoretically occur in this model as family members experience changes in feelings toward each other and the therapist. One name associated with this school of thought is Carl Whitaker (Whitaker & Malone, 1953; Whitaker & Keith, 1981). Whitaker believes that intimacy and separateness are related processes, stating: "One can only be as close as one can be separate, and one can only be as separate as one can be close" (Whitaker et al., 1981, p. 193). Whitaker also believes that the roots of conflicts related to dependency and autonomy can be found in relationships that can be traced back to each member of the couple's family of origin. It is not surprising, then, that some of Whitaker's goals in therapy include both getting the family to function better as a unit and getting each family member to develop more of a sense of himself as an individual. In addition, separation of the generations and from the family of origin is considered critical. Whitaker suggests that the curative factors in therapy include "interactional insight" an increase in here-and-now awareness, and the development of a

sense of the family as an integrated whole (p. 217). Whitaker also believes that family members must learn to play and that therapists sometimes need to be "crazy and inconsistent" in an effort to get change (p. 218). Indeed, Guerin (1976) pointed out that Whitaker has since changed his focus to attempting to set up experiences for himself (the therapist) rather than the family.

The next school of thought involves those therapists who consider family therapy to be a particular mode of group therapy. Families are seen as natural groups in this model, and so therapists attempt to promote interaction, clarify processes, and interpret interpersonal dynamics, somewhat akin to a T-group model (Guerin, 1976). Bell (1976), who is most associated with this model, stated that he sees himself as a leader involved with group process. In this role, Bell focuses on what goes on between family members instead of within members as individuals. Bell's comments on what he sees going on among the family members include comments on their specific interactions and statements made in an effort to characterize total group interactions. As a group leader, Bell also attempts to monitor listening and to distribute opportunities for different family members to speak. In placing the burden of resolution on the family members, he attempts to put the responsibility on them for growth and change. While Bell assists them in exploring what will work and encourages attempts at new interactions, in the end the family members are the ones to determine that they have solved the problems that they have come into therapy for. Bell points out that these tasks are very similar to tasks that leaders have in small task-oriented groups and attempts to study these groups in an effort to devise new techniques in family therapy.

The final model we will go into in the dynamic school involves the work of Boszormenyi-Nagy (1965, Boszormenyi-Nagy & Spark, 1973, Boszormenyi-Nagy & Ulrich, 1981). Contextual family therapy began in the 1960s with its focus on the involvements of transgenerational relationships in the family structure. This type of therapy considers dynamic concepts as they are linked across generations. More recently, this view has been broadened to include a contextual view, considering the family as a social institution with its linkages into the organization of society.

A multigenerational perspective commonly includes a framework of at least three generations that are considered to overlap into the present generation. Several concepts have been introduced by Boszormenyi-Nagy to explain how this process works. The term "legacy" was coined to introduce the set of expectations that originate from "rootiveness" in past generations and that affect present offsprings. The term "split loyalty" points out the problem that occurs when parents set up conflicting claims so that the child is forced to offer loyalty to one parent at the cost of loyalty to the other. These legacies and loyalties are "invisible" in the sense that they are not overtly recognized but influence the behavior of the individuals in the family. When a person grows in a family with an abundance of split loyalties and maladaptive legacies, the end result is often what this school of therapy calls a "revolving slate of loyalties" in that a person's relationship to his or her present spouse and children is colored by the invisible loyalties from the past. The difference between this type of thinking and a more traditional analytic approach is that the traditional approach uses the patient-therapist relationship as a therapeutic tool, where as contextual therapy "seeks to work within the context of the original relationships" (Boszormenyi-Nagy & Ulrich, 1981, p. 172). The main aim of the therapy is to "loosen the chains of invisible loyalty and legacy so that each person can give up symptomatic behaviors and explore new options" (Boszormenyi-Nagy & Ulrich, 1981, p. 174).

What characterizes all these dynamic approaches seems to be the use of insight to achieve growth of the family members. Whether insight is based on current interactions, affective needs, or resolution with the past, this insight is considered the method of change in the therapy. This is in sharp contrast to methods of change implied in other schools of thought.

Systems Models

Murray Bowen's work appears to represent a bridge between analytically oriented therapies and systems-oriented therapies. Bowen (1976a) pointed out that the first part of this theory was developed between 1957 and 1963 and included concepts (to be defined later in the text) about the "nuclear family emotional system," the "family projection process," the concept of "differentiation of self," the concept of "triangles," the concept of "multigenerational transmission process," and the concept of "sibling position." Bowen (1966) published these six concepts as a theory that represented the culmination of his efforts (Bowen, 1960, 1961, 1965). Furthermore, Bowen (1976a) went on to point out that in 1975 he added two new concepts, the "emotional cutoff" and the concept of "societal regression." Also, at that time, the name "Family Systems Theory" was changed to "Bowen's Theory." Bowen's family systems theory is a theory about emotional functioning and in this sense differs from general systems theory (Bowen, 1976a). Bowen claims that he uses the term systems theory because conventional thinking or analytically oriented theories focus on the why of behavior, whereas systems theory avoids these explanations and the difficulties that Bowen feels they lead to in therapy. Bowen is concerned with the how, when, and what of emotional functioning and not, "the content of these intense emotions" (Bowen, 1976a, p. 63). In other words, Bowen focuses on the functional facts of a relationship system, especially its affective structure. Bowen's focus on affective issues represents his ties to the analytic school while an effort to focus on functional roles in a system represented one of the first uses of a system theory.

Bowen's concept of differentiation of the self is critical to his theory. Bowen suggests that people can be placed on a continuum, with one end representing "ego fusion" and little self-differentiation and the other end representing the self-actualized person who is flexible and has inner direction. Bowen (1976a) stated: "A more differentiated person can participate freely in the emotional sphere without the fear of becoming too fused with others" (p. 67). In therapy, Bowen makes an effort to get individual family members to differentiate himself or herself and thus "rise up out of the emotional togetherness" (p. 73) characteristic of their family functioning. Bowen believes that the level of differentiation of any person is related to the level of differentiation from his or her family of origin. Another important concept in Bowen's theory is the concept of "triangles." Triangles represent the most stable relationship system. When a two-person system encounters stress, often the system is stabilized through forming a triangle with (usually) another person. Bowen's concept of the "nuclear family emotional system" describes the pattern of emotional functioning in the family, which he feels are replications of patterns of past generations. Bowen believes that people pick spouses who have similar levels of differentiation, with the lower levels of differentiation making for more emotional fusion in marriage. He also seems to believe that this emotional fusion usually results in emotional distance as well as marital conflict and/or dysfunction in one's spouse. In other words, being "too close" is as artificial and distant as being too separate. Another problematic area that occurs in these marriages results in a "family projection process." This process results in a father-mother-child triangle, especially in regard to the projection that occurs from the couple to the child. Finally, Bowen's other concepts involve a description of how the family projection process continues through multiple generations ("multigenerational transmission process"), the use of Toman's (1961) work on personality profiles of each child's position in the family ("sibling position"), the idea that societal emotional problems are similar to emotional problems in the family (societal regression), and the importance of the way people handle and separate from their attachment to their parents ("emotional cutoff"). For a more complete description of his latest theory, the interested reader is referred to Bowen's works (1978) as well as his previous work (1960, 1961, 1965, 1966, 1976a, & 1976b).

We now turn to the more purely systems-oriented therapies. The first example will be that of "structural" family therapy. The name most associated with this model is Minuchin (Minuchin et al., 1967; Minuchin, 1974; Minuchin et al., 1975; Minuchin, Rosman, & Baker, 1978). Other works associated with Minuchin's include Liebman's (Liebman, Minuchin, & Baker, 1974; Liebman, Honig, & Berger, 1976), Baker's (Baker & Barcai, 1970; Baker et al., 1975) work with psychosomatic difficulties, and Aponte's work (1976, 1979, 1980) in community areas. Three important concepts in this area are the concepts of boundaries, alignments, and balance of forces. There are three types of boundaries. The first type, generational boundaries, involves the boundary around the parents as the executives of the family as separate from the children. Other generational boundaries include boundaries around both the siblings' and grandparents' subsystems. Clinical examples of a lack of good boundaries include the "parenting" child and interfering grandparents. The second type of boundary is the sexual boundary. This does not involve sex stereotypes but certain behaviors that belong in each sex group. This is especially important when older children are trying to develop roles. One extreme instance of the crossing of both sexual and generational boundaries is the problem of incest. The third type of boundary is the individual boundary. Each person is entitled to some rights of his or her own, and each person in the family needs to have this right. Work with anorexic children (Liebman et al., 1974) often uncovers a lack of individual boundaries for the symptomatic child in the family.

The second major concept in structural therapy is that of alignments. Alignments involve the positive, negative, and neutral connections between people in the family. It is important to determine what type of connection people have to each other and if certain people have more or less than their share of connections. Sometimes, alignments are not what they initially seem to be. One extreme case of no positive alignments involves the family scapegoat. In this situation, the scapegoat cannot negotiate for himself because he is not connected to anyone in a positive sense. It is also important to consider which family members may be overaligned with others and which may be underaligned. If alignments do not function properly, the individuals in the family will cross generational boundaries to get emotional needs met. Minuchin's third concept involves the balance of forces in the family. Clearly, whom one is connected to in the family has to do with that person's relative importance. Some family members may have overt power while some family members have covert power. For example, family members may make it seem as if "mom rules the roost" in the family (thus she has overt power), but all the kids go to dad on the sly (covert power). In this situation, the father most definitely has the balance of forces operating in his direction although not openly so.

Aponte (1981) pointed to the three major techniques of structural family therapy. They are: "creation of the transaction"; "joining with the transaction"; and "restructuring the transaction." Aponte states that there are three ways to create the transaction. The first way is "structuralization," which involves the therapist's interacting with family members in a manner that influences the patterns of their interaction. For example, someone who assumes an attitude of inferiority with respect to other family members is related to by the therapist as if the individual were in a position of status and power. The therapist constantly puts the person in the position where his or her judgments are valued. The second type of process in creating transaction involves "enactment inducement." This procedure involves the therapist's giving the family tasks through which he or she can promote the family members' typical patterns of relating. For example, the therapist may ask the husband and wife to have a discussion over something that is likely to result in the same kind of discussion that the spouses have at home. Finally, the process of "task setting" within the family involves giving assignments to family members to carry out (usually) when they are at home. Three different procedures are also employed in "joining with the transaction." "Tracking" involves the therapist's use of the symbols of family life (e.g., language, life themes, history) to communi-

cate with the family. In "accommodation," the therapist relates to the family by accepting the family rules and their ways of relating. The third process is labeled "mimesis," and here the therapist joins with the family members by adopting some of that family member's mannerisms, body language, or other modes of communication. All of these techniques are ways to get the therapist involved with the family in a way the family readily accepts.

The third area where structural techniques are applied is in the area of "restructuring" the family. This involves "system recomposition," which is a technique that attempts structural change by adding or taking away some subsystems from the systems that are involved in the problem. An example here is the removal of inlaws from the home of a newlywed couple or attempting to add a spouse to a system. "Symptom-focusing" techniques are techniques that borrow from the strategic school, and these will be described in a later section. And last, structural modification is attempted through techniques that "disassemble, construct, reinforce and reorganize" the structure of the family. These are all techniques "that are employed to directly affect the alignment, boundary and power structure within and among the system" (Aponte, p. 334, 1981). The preceding descriptions have been taken from Aponte (1981), and the interested reader is referred to that and other works in the area. Minuchin (1974) is also a particularly good source.

Finally, structural family therapists are one of the few groups that have attempted to attach outcome research to their work. Their research involves problems of delinquency, psychosomatic problems, and problems with drug and alcohol addiction (see outcome section). The efficacy of their procedures and the quality of their work was pointed to by Gurman and Kniskern (1981) when they stated that structural family therapy seems to be the therapy of choice for those particular problems mentioned.

Strategic approaches to family therapy (as well as structural approaches) presently occupy the center stage in the family therapy field (Stanton, 1981). Erickson (1954, Erickson & Rossi, 1979) is considered the master of strategic therapy, and Haley (1967, 1973), who described Erickson's work, laid the groundwork for this type of approach with families. Milton Erickson's "uncommon" techniques were aimed at getting people to produce shifts in their typical transactional patterns in a way that did not engender the kind of resistance that direct comment often produces (Haley, 1973). Much of the other original work in the strategic area was done with schizophrenics, but in recent years strategic techniques have been applied to a wide variety of problems. For a comprehensive review of the types of problems and references on their management, see Stanton (1981).

Strategic therapists tend not to use conventional diagnostic systems because they believe that diagnostic labels or labels that present the problem in individualistic terms do nothing more than hamper therapy and present the problem in terms that make treatment more difficult. For example, pointing to a problem as evidence of "deeper unconscious problems" presents the situation in terms that make it difficult for the person to change (Watzlawick et al., 1974). Furthermore, strategic therapists structure their therapy along brief therapy models. The goal of therapy is to get change in transactional patterns with the idea that the family will reorganize in a different manner and thus be able to go on with the process of living their lives. Strategic therapists are behaviorally oriented in that their focus is on symptoms and their approach is one in which insight is not considered necessary for change to occur (Stanton, 1981). Nevertheless, problems are conceptualized in a systems framework, and the behavioral strategies are designed to change the way the system operates without necessarily commenting directly to the family about the system. The cornerstone, then, of the strategic approach is the use of directives (Stanton, 1981). These directives are designed to "go with the resistance" and thus avoid power struggles with the family. These strategies take into account the family's conception of the problem and are often aimed at making covert control games more overt, thus eliminating their usefulness.

Stanton (1981, p. 365) summarizes this strategic view of dysfunction as follows:

1. Symptoms are types of behavior which serve a function in the homeostatic mechanism of the family (Jackson, 1957, 1965);

2. Symptoms are not conceived as problems in/or of a particular identified patient, but must be considerd in the context in which they occur with the function for which they serve in the relationships of the family. Symptoms are regarded as communicative acts which send messages to various members in the family and which serve as a contract between the members as a means of stabilizing the system (Haley, 1976);

3. Individual change is related to family system change (Haley, 1962);

4. Change occurs without necessarily involving insight on the part of the family. (Haley, 1969)

The work of Watzlawick et al. (1974) has been very influential in the development of the strategic approach. Watzlawick sees problems or symptoms occurring from wrong attempts at changing ordinary difficulties. Watzlawick goes on to suggest that the typical tactic of therapists, as well as people in distress, is to apply the idea of change through application of the opposite: for example, trying to cheer up a depressed person, trying to force oneself to fall asleep, or trying to get a withdrawing member to come closer through encouragement of lack of withdrawal. The application of the opposite, however, feeds into negative feedback loops in the family and tends to produce what Watzlawick calls only first-order change. First-order change is change which does not involve change of the system structure itself. As discussed earlier, a typical example of a negative feedback system is a thermostat that regulates room temperature—when the temperature gets too hot, the system acts to cool things down. This involves the application of the opposite. In order to get a real change in the system, one has to change the setting of the temperature itself, which will make the system operate in a completely different way. Watzlawick calls this type of change "second order change," in that there are changes in the basic structure of the system. What typically happens, Watzlawick suggests, is that the application of the opposite results in a game without end and turns what are ordinary difficulties into bigger problems.

There are three ways in which solutions are attempted that lead to bigger problems. (1) Solutions are attempted by denying problems. In other words, action is necessary and not taken. Watzlawick sees avoidance as a typical example of this and does not consider this an unconscious defense but interpersonal and often conscious. The solution "not to see" creates a problem and greatly compounds the original difficulty because people go to extremes not to see what is going on. (2) Solutions are attempted for something unchangeable or nonexistent. In other words, action is taken when it is not necessary. Watzlawick suggests that people often believe that things should be better than they are, and the belief in this causes distress and causes change in the way people operate to the point where problems occur. This may involve the setting of utopian goals for oneself or others. For example, when newlyweds expect that their married life will be totally happy and it turns out not to be so, they begin to develop all sorts of problem-engendering solutions to cope with a difficulty they really do not have. (3) The third type involves what Watzlawick calls an error in logical typing, wherein solutions or action is taken at the wrong level (i.e. first-order change rather than second-order change). For a more complete description of the theory behind these ideas, see *Change* (1974).

Watzlawick points out that, in human relations, one can find many examples in which this type of confusion (action taken on the wrong level) arises in trying to overcome difficulties. For example, if a couple is having some difficulties and attempts to change these difficulties without a renegotiation of the rules of the relationship, any solution that the couple comes up with will be dependent upon the rules of the original contract and so will represent no change at all. Second-order change occurs when the contract itself is changed. The couple that has a covert rule that states: "We will never be angry with each other or comment on each other's shortcomings" has involved itself in a dilemma because any attempt to negotiate anger issues is a violation of the contract itself and usually ends up producing more problems. Action must be taken at the next level and the relationship rule of never commenting on anger must be renegotiated. As noted earlier, however, these rules have a homeostatic quality and are often seen as unchangeable. The original marital contract—what Jackson (1966) called the marital *quid pro quo* (something for something)—is considered to be "the reality" and not something that has been behaviorally negotiated based on definitions of the self *at that time.* These self-definitions can change, and so can the contract.

One kind of "solution" the couple mentioned above might employ, is to avoid dealing with their anger directly, since they have a rule prohibiting this and may not see that they need to negotiate on this level, and instead express their anger through their child. This solution creates the problem, as it makes it difficult for the couple to resolve their differences and also contributes to producing symptoms in the child. Therefore, when considering second-order change, one must apply action to the attempted solutions, not to the difficulty itself. Confronting the couple on their own difficulties and asking them to resolve them would probably produce denial, resistance, and more of the same: a typical first-order change effort involving the application of opposite. Common sense, however, suggests this type of tactic. In contrast, second-order change tactics, which would be applied to the "solutions" in this and the preceeding two paragraphs, often seem unexpected and paradoxical. Some of these techniques, which are applied to effects and not causes, will be described in the following paragraphs.

Strategic therapists use a number of techniques or strategies to effect this system level change. One technique commonly used is the technique of reframing (Watzlawick et al., 1974). Reframing involves changing the conceptual and/or emotional setting of the situation and placing it in a different frame. This new frame fits "the facts" of the concrete situation just as well and thereby changes the entire meaning for the person. What has changed is not the situation but the meaning attributed to the situation and, so, its consequences. This attribution is what people and sometimes therapists refer to as "reality," which is nothing more than what the people or family have agreed to call real. A classic example of reframing involves Tom Sawyer's reframing the drudgery of painting the fence into some kind of pleasure for which one has to pay (Watzlawick et al., 1974, pp. 92–93). Once people decide that a situation has a particular value or meaning, they often find it difficult to see in terms of something else. This creates what they see as a lack of alternatives. Once a situation is reframed and an alternative attribution is produced, people generally find it difficult to go back to the "trap and anguish of a former view of reality" (Watzlawick et al., 1974); they are thus forced to think about it in a different way. Reframing lifts the situation out of the symptom frame and into another frame that does not imply unchangeability. Not just any frame is used, but one that fits with the person's way of thinking and of categorizing reality. For example, a therapist might relabel hostility from a mother to a child into the mother's way of expressing her concern and care for the child. Reframing in this manner takes away the need to use blaming and criticism in therapy and makes for more positive feedback. If behavior is viewed as concern rather than hostility, then people's reaction to it will obviously be different and thus produce changes.

Another technique that has been widely used is that of paradoxical intervention or "prescribing the symptom." As stated earlier, if a person is encouraged to perform the symptom, it becomes evident that the symptomatic behavior is under the person's control. The therapist utilizes the person's resistance in an effort to defeat his or her prescripton, thus removing the symptom. For example, a parent and a child encouraged to have a fight on a regular basis will soon find that they "can't do it" and begin to interact in a different manner.

This is in sharp contrast to the idea of encouraging people to do the opposite of what they are doing, which often results in patients' returning and stating, "Well, we tried to stop, but we just couldn't do it." Paradoxical methods should not be attempted without the therapist's being trained in their use and having a full understanding of the theory and method of application. Watzlawick et al., (1974) presents theoretical ideas about why paradoxes work, and the technique has been described by several other writers (e.g. Haley, 1976; Weakland et al., 1974). Madanes (1981) also suggests other strategies such as providing an ordeal to occur for the person when the symptom is presented or instructing people to "pretend" to have the symptom. These techniques are used to make covert control maneuvers more overt. Interested readers are referred to Madanes and others' works listed above.

One final technique that bears mention involves "restraining" change. In this, the therapist may tell the patient to go slow or even emphasize the dangers of improvement. For resistant patients who are ambivalent about change, this is a particularly useful technique in that it allows the patient to push for change rather than to fight it. The author has found this type of technique particularly useful with young adults who are attempting to grow up and take responsibility but are frightened to do so. Young adults are asked whether or not they are ready to change, and it is suggested that perhaps "we need to go slow enough until you are ready to make some moves." The effect is often that the young person moves ahead more quickly. Again, this is in contrast to applying the opposite, where one pushes for more responsibility and finds that the patient fights by being less responsible. For a more full description, see Haley (1976). For a good discussion of what techniques are useful in particular situations see Fisher, Anderson, and Jones (1981).

Before attempting any of these techniques, supervision by someone experienced in them is necessary. Given that the outcome literature supports brief therapy models as being as effective as longer term models, strategic therapy seems to be a way of helping people with their difficulties and not involving them in long term or in-depth therapy. Theoretically, achieving change will have a snowball effect in that the family or patient will return to his or her normal life situation, do things differently, and continue to "grow" through natural processes. This is in sharp contrast to the schools of therapy that emphasize growth within therapy itself as important.

Behavior School

Behavioral methods of family therapy attempt to apply principles of human learning in an effort to change the maladaptive behavior that family members are engaging in. The focus in this model is on assessment and behavioral analysis from which treatment strategies to change behaviors evolve. Behavior therapists do not consider the history of the family or unconscious dynamics to be of importance in their model (Gurman, 1979). Behavior therapists often use operant methods to increase positive interaction and use more structured methods and goals to facilitate the development of skills that are needed to increase the family's ability to maintain more positive types of interpersonal behavior. As examples of this work, we will briefly consider issues involved in parent training and then discuss Patterson's model of family therapy, the Oregon Marital Studies Program, and Richard Stewart's model of therapy for marital problems.

Behavioral parent training involves the use of parents as agents to maintain generalized behavior changes (Tavormina, 1974). Gordon and Davidson (1981) point out that behavioral parent training is often not thought of as family therapy in and of itself although many types of family therapy make some use of it. Gordon and Davidson further state that this type of therapy suggests a dyadic model, in that there is an assumption that some type of faulty interaction between parent and child is at the root of the child's problem. As we have mentioned earlier, parents may resist or sabotage the training program because of their own difficulties, and, when this occurs, Gordon and Davidson suggest that the model needs to be expanded. Even Gordon and

Davidson point to the need for therapists also to use traditional and systems techniques to work on these "interferences." Clearly, as discussed earlier, nonbehavioral approaches suggest that deviant child behavior represents conflicts elsewhere in the family, especially in the marriage. Behaviorists tend to see the issue as complex, because it is difficult to determine whether marital discord contributes to the development of child problems or child problems add strain to the marriage. This issue needs to be investigated in future research. Nevertheless, parent-training methods appear to be at least a useful adjunct in therapy for families when the child is referred as the problem. Interested readers are referred to Gordon and Davidson (1981) for a review of this area and a description of their particular model. In addition, readers are referred to the chapter in this book on parent training.

Patterson (1976) questioned the notion that changes in deviant child behavior can be brought about only by resolving underlying family difficulties. Patterson et al. (1975) presented what they call a social-learning approach to family intervention. This group has done a number of research projects with families focusing on chldren who are socially aggressive. The model involves at least one month of training and consists of several components. One component involves studying the programmed text on social-learning-based management techniques, which includes Living With Children (Patterson & Harris, 1968) or Families (Patterson, 1971). Parents are also taught to track and record deviant and/or prosocial child behaviors. Parents are then assigned to parent-training groups where modeling and role-playing techniques are used to teach child management techniques. Parents are also taught the technique of behavioral contracts in which parents and children develop a contract that specifies particular contingencies for certain problem behaviors occurring at home.

Analysis of the data obtained by Patterson (e.g., Patterson, 1974) indicates that there was a change in these child behaviors that were targeted during the training and that these effects remained during the twelve-month follow-up. Furthermore, in his analysis, Patterson (1975, pp. 299–322) determined that not only were these targeted children more aggressive than their peers but that all members of the children's families were more aggressive. Additionally, Patterson's (1975, pp. 299–322) research suggested that these parents tended to provide positive consequences for deviant behavior and aversive consequences for prosocial behavior. It follows, then, that modification of the way that these families go about managing each other's behavior would result in more positive interaction with each other. Moreover, Patterson (1976) pointed out that these changes in behavioral interaction seemed to instigate a chain of reactions that resulted in alterations in the entire family structure. These changes seemed to be of the type that resulted in family members being more "giving" toward each other. He hypothesized that these types of changes would also result in concomitant changes in the way the targeted children feel about themselves. In this model, changes in behavior theroretically result in changes in attitudes of the various family members. Other researchers and clinicians have used similar methods with good results. Barton and Alexander (1981) incorporate social-learning theory and systems interventions in their "functional family therapy." Alexander (Alexander & Parsons, 1973; Alexander et al., 1976), whose work had been mostly with delinquent youths, also offers empirical evidence for success in what he used to call "short term behavioral family systems intervention."

The behavior therapists have focused more on marital relationships than they have on family unit variables. While we are trying to keep to an orientation of children and families for this chapter, we will briefly discuss the theory behind behavioral approaches to marital therapy. The works of Jacobson (Jacobson & Martin, 1976; Jacobson, 1977) and Stuart (1975, 1976, 1980) among others represent significant contributions to the treatment of marital problems with good empirical outcomes. We will first describe what a social-learning view of marital conflict is and then briefly describe the Oregon Marital Studies Program.

Jacobson (1981) pointed out that both individuals entering into a marital relationship have a learning history that predisposes him or her to finding certain behaviors on the part of the partner reinforcing. The maintenance of the relationship is dependent on the degree to which couples provide each other with reinforcing benefits and that these benefits must be higher than the cost of being in the relationship. The research behind these ideas comes primarily from Thibaut and Kelley's (1959) exchange theory model of social psychological interaction. This model suggested that a given relationship is maintained by a comparison level of the rewards and costs in the relationship versus what they would be in other relationships. Jacobson's social-learning model borrowed these ideas and went on to hypothesize that the rate of reinforcers received from the partner helps to determine both the subjective satisfaction in the relationship and the rate of rewards directed in return for the partner. The "reciprocity" in a marital relationship between rewards given and received, then, is critical to the success of the relationship. This concept has been investigated by Gottman, Markman, and Notarius (1977).

A complementary process, called "coercion," describes the interaction between two people that is based on the use of aversive stimuli to control the behavior of the other person. Successful marriages, according to behavioral marital therapists, involve the use of reciprocity of positive reinforcers and less reliance on coercive and aversive tactics to control the behavior of the other person. There has been some empirical support for this idea, but the results have been inconsistent. In addition, Jacobson (1981) claimed that social-learning models have considered skill at conflict resolution critical for successful marriages. Based on these notions, treatment programs have been developed to increase the rate of positive rewarding behaviors among couples, decrease the rate of aversive control methods, and teach specific conflict resolution and communication skills.

These same principles are used by Stuart (1976, 1980) in what he calls an "operant interpersonal approach" towards working on changes in maladaptive behavior between spouses. These operant methods are used to increase positive interaction and develop interpersonal skills. Several techniques are suggested by Stuart to increase the rate at which couples exchange positive behaviors, which Stuart points out are incompatible with many of the negative behaviors that the spouses are engaged in. Stuart's model involves a number of techniques, which will be briefly summarized. One technique used by Stuart is the institution of what he calls "caring days." Spouses are asked to list things that they like in each other's behavior and to label the occurrence of each of these behaviors as evidence that the one spouse cares for the other. Stuart suggests that each spouse engage in 8–20 of these caring behaviors per day and that these behaviors should be engaged in independent of what the other spouse does. If spouses' behaviors are overly linked to what the other spouse does, then the negative cycle that the spouses have been engaged in will persist.

Stuart also suggests the use of skill instruction to enhance the spouses' ability to communicate with each other. The outcome literature in family therapy provides consistent positive empirical support for therapies that employ instruction and methods for increasing the couple's communication skills (Gurman & Kniskern, 1981). Given this result, including communication skills training seems to be an important aspect of family and marital therapy. Like Patterson and Jacobson, Stuart suggests the use of contracts that state responsibilities for each spouse and rewards based on the completion of these responsibilities. Again, contracts are not drawn up based on a "you-do-this-and-I-do-that" method (at least in behavioral marital therapy models) but are constructed so that if either spouse completes some of his responsibilities, he or she is allowed to ask for certain privileges. Other aspects of Stuart's model involve helping the couple divide responsibilities between them, and setting some rules for the couple to use that provide for maintenance of the changes that occur in therapy. For more complete review, readers are referred to Stuart (1980) and the tapes Stuart has made to illustrate his approach.

In their discussion of behavioral marital therapy Gurman and his colleagues (Gurman, Knudson, & Kniskern, 1978) pointed out that behavioral marital therapy's focus on overt behaviors is not complete enough to take into account covert control issues and other aspects of the marital relationship that could maintain past behavior despite the couple's willingness to change. They also claim that behavioral marital therapy does not take into account such concepts as resistance to change. For a complete review of their arguments and a reply to them (Jacobson & Weiss, 1978), the reader is referred to the June, 1978, edition of *Family Process*. While behavioral marital therapy has some limitations, the techniques used in behavior therapy are useful adjuncts to therapy. One helpful combination involves using systems- and strategic-oriented techniques to get changes in basic interactions and then using behavioral techniques to shape up more positive interactions and provide specific skill instruction (Madanes & Maley, 1980).

FAMILY THERAPY PROCESS AND OUTCOME RESEARCH

The development of new methods for working with people's problems always brings with it a need to evaluate the effectiveness of these methods. For example, the effectiveness of individual psychotherapy has been under scrutiny for a number of years. Eysenck's (1952) proclamation regarding its ineffectiveness spawned study after study by researchers trying to disprove his claim. While researchers (e.g., Meltzoff & Kornreich, 1970; Glass & Smith, 1976) have gone on to demonstrate that individual psychotherapy does have positive effects, Eysenck's conclusions resulted in researchers upgrading their own studies on psychotherapy outcome in order to provide results that contradict Eysenck's findings. These new research efforts led psychotherapy researchers to clarify, operationalize, and measure the process and outcome variables involved in individual psychotherapy.

With the birth of family therapy, it was only a matter of time before the question of its effectivenss was raised. As efforts were made to measure empirically both process variables and outcome in family therapy, it became increasingly evident that this was going to be a difficult task.

Ackerman (1970) identified a difficulty that family therapy process investigators need to overcome. He pointed out that the results of research are more precise when aimed at a single, particular factor, such as the therapist's or patient's verbal behavior. The nature of family therapy, however, demands that the researcher look at broader, more complex results. As the focus broadens, the precision of the results is decreased. The problem, then, arises in deciding what behaviors to study at what level (individual, interpersonal, global) and being satisfied that the obtained results are representative of the total event.

In attempts to begin family therapy process research, several coding systems were developed to measure an individual family member's behavior (e.g. Alexander & Barton, Schiavo & Parsons, 1976; DeChenne, 1973; Guttman et al., 1972; Winer, 1971; Zuk, Boszormenyi-Nagi, & Heiman, 1963), the therapist's behavior (e.g. Alexander et al., 1976; Chagoya, Presser, & Sigal, 1974; Pinsof, 1979a, 1979b; Sigal et al., 1973; Sigal et al., 1977; Sigal et al., 1979; Dowling, 1979) and family member–therapist interactions and behaviors (e.g. Allred & Kersey, 1977; Benjamin, 1977; and Scheflen, 1973). The majority of these coding scales focus on verbal communications during the sessions. These coding system instruments are used by trained observers in direct observation of the session, in taping of the session applied to tapes (audio or video), or in verbatim transcripts. There have been several techniques and games developed (e.g. Haley, 1962; Santa-Barbara & Epstein, 1974; Straus & Tallman, 1971; Gerber, 1973) that stimulate family discussion and involvement. Not only can verbal behaviors be observed, but the nonverbal, physical behaviors of the family can be viewed as well.

One final type of measure used by some investigators (e.g. Hollis, 1967a, 1967b, 1968a, 1968b; Shapiro & Budman, 1973; Rice, Fey, & Kepecs, 1972; Rice, Gurman, & Razin, 1974; Rice, Gurman, & Razin, 1976) has been the attempt to tap into the "experiential or phenomenological" aspects of the therapeutic process (Pinsof, 1981).

Mixed results have been obtained from these various systems. Many of these coding systems are still in a developmental stage and so are questionable in terms of normative, reliability, and validity data. Pinsof (1981, p. 720) characterizes these studies as "exploratory" and as "pilot studies." Replication studies have not been attempted. In their review article, Riskin and Faunce (1972) comment about the topic of replication as being dull work in such a young, exciting, growing field. Though they made these observations ten years ago, they still seem quite appropriate today. Young pioneers in the field seem to be more interested in "doing family therapy" than they are in repeating someone else's study to see if they get similar results. The only clear, consistent findings in this line of research have been in the area of therapist variables, as further discussed in the outcome research section.

The lack of consistent process research results could be due to several factors. First, process research in family therapy is still in an infancy stage of development. There is a multitude of complex factors and interactions to be studied such as nonverbal and verbal behaviors, system level interactions, as well as dealings with problems in obtaining measurements in these areas. The language used to describe these processes is not yet adequately developed, and so barriers in communication may impede development. Theoretical constructs need to be defined operationally, but it seems that their abstract, complex nature makes this a difficult task.

Another hindrance to the study of family therapy process variables is that there is no single "family therapy"; there are influential theoretical orientations and many different therapists who ascribe to the different approaches. Haley (1962) implies that therapists who work with families hesitate to publish their findings because they are uncertain of their techniques and results. Haley (1971) has also suggested that therapists had been hesitant to have their therapy sessions videotaped, possibly due to the discrepancy between theory and what was being taught versus what was being practiced. This, too, could have slowed down the research on process variables. Therapists believe that their techniques work, but empirically measuring them is a difficult task. Thus the lack of empirical family therapy process research data is not surprising. One possible solution to the problem of comparibility of different approaches would be for therapists to tighten their theoretical base and work solely from it so that deviations could be easily spotted.

One further research effort bears particular mention. The work of Beavers and Lewis at the Timberlawn Foundation (Lewis et al., 1976; Beavers, 1977) was an effort to divide families into a continuum of functioning based on their effectiveness. The authors trained raters to measure system variables that included structure (overt power, parental coalition, and family closeness), mythology (view of themselves), goal-directed negotiation (problem solving), system tolerance for autonomy (differentiation of boundaries), and affective or feeling issues. Based on these variables, 103 white middle and upper-middle-class families were divided into those which were "severely dysfunctional," "midrange," and "healthy families." This work is notable because it was an attempt to provide information on what compromises "healthy" family functioning. Readers may wish to consult the above-mentioned work for more detailed information, as well as the several reviews of family process research that exist (Framo, 1965; Riskin, & Faunce, 1972; Jacob, 1975; Cromwell et al., 1976; Pinsof, 1981).

Much more research has been done in the area of family therapy outcome. Gurman and Kniskern (1981) commented on the number of literature reviews suggesting that there is no justification or need for any further extensive reviews of the literature because most probably they would not add anything significant to what has already been said. Researchers need to focus on pertinent questions that need answers and on what needs to be studied in the future. Since the authors are in agreement

with this view, the following discussion on family therapy outcome research will not be a review of the literature. Rather, it will offer an overview of the research and cite pertinent references that the reader may consult before conducting further research.

Family therapy outcome research, though in a more developed stage than process research, seems to have many obstacles to overcome before clinically sound results can be obtained. Outcome researchers must deal with a gamut of variables such as the experience level of the therapist, type of symptoms or referral concerns, severity of family disturbance, length of treatment, what improvement criteria to use for each unit of assessment, and in which unit to assess change. In an article by Lebow (1981) several issues in family therapy outcome research are discussed. Some of these include treatment and population variables, treatment goals and values and their influence on research, the problems in operationalizing family therapy concepts, considering reliability, validity, and experimental control in research design, considering the generalizability of findings, and others. These are difficult variables to control, and it is no wonder that many of the outcome studies previously done have had methodological flaws. However, these results can still be of use, especially toward the development of more improved methods. Controlled studies in the literature seem to be scarce, but when one stops to consider the complexity involved it is not surprising. Gurman and Kniskern (1978a) reported an 86 percent increase in the number of controlled studies of nonbehavioral family therapy since 1970, so that it appears that research in the field is increasing. Hopefully, as research increases, the methodological approach will become more refined.

In the same article, Gurman and Kniskern (1978a) discuss an uncontrolled investigation of 41 cases reporting huge improvements as a result of family therapy. In half of the families there was a child or adolescent presented as the identified patient, and the identified patient in the remaining half was an adult. They reported the following results: "child-adolescent improved, 71 percent; not improved, 29 percent; adult improved, 65 percent; and not improved, 35 percent" (p. 823). The cases included covered a wide range of family therapy techniques, but the results do show a more favorable outcome with family treatment. Though no controlled outcome studies have been done, it seems that outcome is more favorable when the identified patient is a child or adolescent rather than an adult (Gurman & Kniskern, 1978a). Gurman and Kniskern (1981) maintain their position, after reviewing controlled studies of nonbehavioral family therapy outcomes, that family therapy interventions are effective at above the chance level. In fact, they found that "every study to date that has compared family therapy with other types of treatment has shown family therapy to be equal or superior" (p. 835).

Encouraging comments are made by Gurman and Kniskern (1981) regarding behavioral family therapy versus no treatment. They, however, pointed to the studies (Cole & Morrow, 1976; Karoly & Rosenthal, 1977; Reisinger, Frangia, & Hoffman, 1976) that demonstrated the inefficiency of focal operant strategies when used with families involving both serious marital problems and extreme child difficulties.

Wells and Dezen (1978) comment on the behavioral and nonbehavioral methods in their review of the nonbehavioral approaches. They apparently had difficulty in making sharp distinctions between these two methods. Given the eclectic set of notions that seem to be dominating family therapies, distinguishing between behavioral and nonbehavioral approaches may be a difficult task. Wells, Dilkes, and Burkhart (1976) refer to the fact that there is no form of family therapy whose theoretical principles, methods, and techniques are accepted by all the therapists in the profession. In considering the effectiveness of family therapy, researchers need to delineate carefully the type of family treatment used and include a complete description of the population upon which its efficacy has been tested. This seems to be one of the present shortcomings of outcome studies.

Minuchin (1974) reported great success in treating childhood and adolescent psychosomatic problems with structural family therapy. Treatment of anorexia, asthma, diabetes, and other psychosomatic symptoms (Minuchin et al., 1975) by intervening in the family at a systems level is gaining more and more popularity and rapidly becoming the treatment of choice for many of these presenting problems. Kaplan (1977) has obtained positive results in using structural family therapy for treating families with parental divorce in which a child is symptomatic. Studies of structural family therapy with heroine addicts (Stanton & Todd, 1978) "are among the very best controlled outcome studies in the entire research literature on family therapy" (Gurman & Kniskern, 1981, p. 750). A positive factor in these studies using structural family therapy is that improvement is measured by objective criteria (e.g. weight gain, blood sugar levels, decrease in number of asthma episodes. etc.). Though this is beneficial for outcome studies, defining the process by which this occurs at a systems level remains an obstacle. Nevertheless, Gurman and Kniskern (1981) concluded that for these types of problems (e.g., adolescent psychosomatic problems, drug and alcohol abuse) as well as for certain childhood behavior problems, (e.g., "soft" delinquency) and sexual dysfunction, marital and family therapies appear to lead to "good to excellent therapeutic outcomes" (p. 750).

Wellisch, Vincent, and Ro-Trock (1976) did a comparative study of family therapy versus individual therapy in the treatment of adolescent inpatients. They reported that 43 percent of the individually treated adolescents had been rehospitalized before the three-month follow-up but none of the adolescents receiving family therapy had returned for a hospital stay. Hunter, Hackney, and Kingdom (1978), Madanes (1980), Minuchin (1974), Minuchin et al. (1975), among others, are developing useful family intervention techniques for child and adolescent inpatients in hopes of preventing rehospitalization.

The topic of deterioration, or negative effects, in family therapy has been addressed by Gurman and Kniskern (1978a, 1978b, 1981).

Though little controlled research has been done in this area, Gurman and Kniskern report that "5 to 10 percent of patients of marital or family relationships worsen as the result of marital-family therapy"(1978b, p. 5). Keeping in mind the notion of the identified patient as symptomatic of family pathology, some investigators wondered if other family members would "worsen" as a result of family therapy restructuring the family system. Studies by Arnold, Levine, and Patterson (1975), Jackson and Weakland (1961), and Klein, Alexander, and Parsons (1975) have demonstrated that parents or siblings of the identified patient may, in fact, be "worse" at the end of treatment.

Deterioration effects have not been pinpointed to any one family therapy technique or method, but there is evidence indicating that therapist variables play an important role in treatment outcome, particularly those involving relationship-building skills (e.g. Alexander et al., 1976; Klein et al., 1975). Certain family therapist styles also seem to have a negative therapeutic effect. Gurman and Kniskern (1978b) sum the "deterioration-inducing" (Gurman & Kniskern, 1981, p. 748) therapist as being:

[An individual with] poor relationship skills who directly attacks "loaded issues" and family members' defenses very early in treatment, fails to intervene in or interpret intra-family confrontation in ongoing treatment, and does little to structure and guide the opening of therapy or to support family members. Such a style is even more likely to be counter-therapeutic with patients who have weak ego-defenses or feel threatened by the nature or very fact of being in treatment. (p. 14)

More investigation of deterioration in family therapy is needed. Several guidelines are proposed by Gurman and Kniskern (1978b) for future studies and those readers interested are certainly encouraged to read their views regarding this concept.

Another important issue involves the duration of therapy, with comparisons made between short term therapy and therapy of longer duration. Gurman and Kniskern (1981) conclude that with all factors considered (types of outcome, generalizability, and duration of effects), "briefer therapies should be judged superior to longer-term methods" (p. 771).

Suffice it to say, after one has read and synthesized the outcome literature, that the use of family therapy generally yields positive results. As previously mentioned, however, there are still many methodological issues to struggle with in doing family therapy outcome research. Lebow (1981) points out that as one attempts to combat the complexities, more methodological problems tend to arise.

In beginning to work toward resolving these issues, Lebow suggests "broad multivariate studies and highly controlled considerations of single techniques are needed" (p. 185). Using a nonfactorial design with families who have been both randomly selected and assigned to experimental and control groups is suggested by Wells, Dilkes, and Burkhart (1976). With this design, they recommend obtaining multiple outcome measurements at appropriate time intervals. Many researchers (e.g., Bergin & Strupp, 1972; Leitenberg, 1973; Wells & Dezen, 1978) are emphasizing the use of single-case experimental designs. This may be difficult, especially for nonbehavioral approaches, as it will require specificity of techniques and goals. As previously mentioned, the problem of operationalizing constructs and goals already poses a problem in family therapy outcome research. Thus it seems that, before sound results can be expected, efforts first need to be focused on providing groundwork on which proper methodology can be built. The outcome literature identifies and discusses these issues, and the reader is referred to several excellent reviews in this area (Gurman & Kniskern, 1981; Lebow, 1981; Wells & Dezen, 1978).

NOTE

1. This point of view can be considered as an object relations level view of behavior. A more systems-oriented therapist, while considering the interlocking systems of the parent, would attempt to effect that system from a here-and-now structural level as opposed to a projective level.

REFERENCES

Ackerman, N.W. Family psychotherapy and psychoanalysis—implications of difference. In N.W. Ackerman (Ed.), *Family process.* New York: Basic Books, 1970.

Alexander, J., Barton, C., Schiavo, R.S., & Parsons, B.V. Systems—Behavioral intervention with families of delinquents: Therapist characteristics, family behavior and outcome. *Journal of Consulting and Clinical Psychology,* 1976, **44,** 656–664.

Alexander, J.F., & Parsons, B. Short term behavioral intervention with delinquent families: Impact on family process and recidivism. *Journal of Abnormal Psychology,* 1973, **81,** 219–225.

Allred, G.H., & Kersey, F.L. The AIAC, a design for systematically analyzing marriage and family counseling: A progress report. *Journal of Marriage and Family Counseling,* 1977, **3,** 17–25.

Aponte, M.J. Under organization in the poor family. In P.J. Guerin, (Ed.), *Family therapy: Theory and practice.* New York: Gardner, 1976.

Aponte, M.J. Diagnosis in family therapy. In C.B. Germain (Ed.), *Social work practice.* New York: Columbia University Press, 1979.

Aponte, M.J. Family therapy and the community. I.M. Gibbs, J.R. Lachenmeyer, & J. Sigel (Eds.), *Community psychology: Theoretical and empirical approaches.* New York: Gardner, 1980.

Aponte, M.J., & VanDeusen, J.M. Structural family therapy. In A.S. Gurman & D.D. Kniskern (Eds.), *Handbook of family therapy.* New York: Brunner/Mazel, 1981.

Arnold, J.E., Levine, A.G., & Patterson, G.R. Changes in sibling behavior following family intervention. *Journal of Consulting and Clinical Psychology,* 1975, **43,** 683–688.

Baker, L., & Barcai, A. Psychosomatic aspects of diabetes mellitus. In O.W. Hill (Ed.), *Modern trends in psychosomatic medicine* (Vol. 2). London: Butterworths, 1970.

Baker, L., Minuchin, S., Milman, L., Liebman, R., & Todd, T. Psychosomatic aspects of juvenile diabetes mellitus: A progress report. In *Modern Problems in Pediatrics* (Vol. 12). Basel: Karger, 1975.

Barton, C., & Alexander, J.F. Functional family therapy. In A.S. Gurman & D.P. Kniskern (Eds.), *Handbook of family therapy.* New York: Brunner/Mazel, 1981.

Beavers, W.R. *Psychotherapy and growth: A family systems perspective.* New York: Brunner/Mazel, 1977.

Bell, J.E. A theoretical framework for family group therapy. In P.J. Guerin (Ed.), *Family therapy: Theory and practice.* New York: Gardner, 1976.

Benjamin, L.S. Structural analysis of a family in therapy. *Journal of Consulting and Clinical Psychology,* 1977, **45,** 391–406.

Bergin, A.E., & Strupp, H.H. *Changing frontiers in the science of psychotherapy.* Chicago: Aldine-Atherton, 1972.

Bodin, A.M. The interactional view: Family therapy approaches of the Mental Research Institute. In A.S. Gurman & D.P. Kniskern (Eds.), *Handbook of family therapy.* New York: Brunner/Mazel, 1981.

Boszormenyi-Nagy, I. A theory of relationships: Experience and transaction. In I. Boszormenyi-Nagyt & J. Framo (Eds.), *Intensive family therapy: Theoretical and practice aspects.* New York: Harper & Row, 1965.

Boszormenyi-Nagy, I., & Spark, G.M. *Invisible loyalties: Reciprocity in intergenerational family therapy.* New York: Harper & Row, 1973.

Boszormenyi-Nagy, I., & Ulrich, D.N. Contextual family therapy. In A.S. Gurman & D.P. Kriskern (Eds.), *Handbook of family therapy.* New York: Brunner/Mazel, 1981.

Bowen, M. A family concept of schizophrenia. In D. Jackson (Ed.), *The etiology of schizophrenia.* New York: Basic Books, 1960.

Bowen, M. Family psychotherapy. *American Journal of Orthopsychiatry,* 1961, **30,** 346.

Bowen, M. Family psychotherapy with schizophrenia in the hospital and in private practice. In I. Boszormenyi-Nagy & J.L. Framo (Eds.), *Intensive family therapy: Theoretical and practical aspects.* New York: Harper & Row, 1965.

Bowen, M. The use of family theory in clinical practice. *Comparative Psychiatry,* 1966, **7,** 345.

Bowen, M. Theory in the practice of psychotherapy. In P.J. Guerin (Ed.), *Family therapy: Theory & practice.* New York: Garner, 1976. (a)

Bowen, M. Family therapy and family group

therapy. In D. Olson (Ed.), *Treating relationships*. Lake Mills, Ia: Graphic, 1976. (b)

Bowen, M. *Family therapy in clinical practice*. New York: Aronson, 1978.

Chagoya, L., Presser, B., & Sigal, J.J. *Family therapists intervention scale-I*. Unpublished manuscript. Institute of Community and Family Psychiatry, Jewish General Hospital, Montreal, 1974.

Cole, C., & Morrow, W.R. Refractory parent behaviors in behavior modification training groups. *Psychotherapy*, 1976, **13**, 162–169.

Cromwell, R., Olson, D., & Fournier, D. Diagnosis and evaluation in marital and family counseling. In D.H.L. Olson (Ed.), *Treating relationships*. Lake Mills, Ia: Graphic, 1976.

DeChenne, T.K. Experiential facilitation in conjoint marriage counseling. *Psychotherapy: Theory, Research, & Practice*, 1973, **10**, 212–214.

Dowling, E. Co-therapy: A clinical researcher's view. In S. Walrand-Skinner (Ed.), *Family and marital therapy*. London: Routledge & Kegan Paul, 1979.

Duhl, B.S., & Duhl, F.J. Integrative family therapy. In A.S. Gurman & D.P. Kniskern (Eds.), *Handbook of family therapy*. New York: Brunner/Mazel, 1981.

Erickson, M.N. Indirect hypnotic of a bedwetting couple. *Journal of clinical and Experimental Hypnosis*, 1954, **2**, 171–174.

Erickson, M.N., & Rossi, E.L. *Hypnotherapy: An exploratory casebook*. New York: Irvington, 1979.

Eysenck, H. The effects of psychotherapy, an evaluation. *Journal of Consulting Psychology*, 1952, **16**, 319–324.

Fisher, L., Anderson, A., & Jones, J.E., Types of paradoxical intervention and indications/contraindications for use in clinical practice. *Family Process*, 1981, **20**(1) 25–35.

Framo, J.L. Systematic research on family dynamics. In I. Boszormenyi-Nagy & Framo (Eds.), *Intensive family therapy*. New York: Harper & Row, 1965.

Gerber, G.L. Psychological distance in the family as schematized by families of normal, disturbed, and learning-problem children. *Journal of Consulting and Clinical Psychology*, 1973, **40**(1), 139–147.

Glass, G.V., & Smith, M.L. Meta-analysis of psychotherapy outcome studies. Paper presented at the Society for Psychotherapy Research, San Diego, 1976.

Gordon, S.B. & Davidson, N. Behavioral parent training. In A.S. Gurmant & D.P. Krniskern (Eds.), *Handbook of family therapy*. New York: Brunner/Mazel, 1981.

Gottman, J., Markman, M., & Notarius, C. The topography of marital conflict: A sequential analysis of verbal and nonverbal behavior. *Journal of Marriage and the Family*, 1977, **39**, 461–477.

Greenberg, G.S. The family interactional perspective: A study and examination of the work of Don D. Jackson. *Family Process*, 1977, **16**, 385–412.

Guerin, P.J. Family therapy: The first twenty-five years. In P.J. Guerin (Ed.), *Family therapy: Theory and practice*. New York: Gardner, 1976.

Gurman, A.S. Dimensions of marital therapy: A comparative analyis. *Journal of Marriage and Family Counseling*, 1978, **4**(1), 127–132.

Gurman, A.S. Dimensions of marital therapy: A comparative analysis. *Journal of Marital and Family Therapy*, 1979, **5**, 5–18.

Gurman, A.S., & Kniskern, D.P. Research on marital and family therapy: Progress, perspective, and prospect. In S.L. Garfield & A.E. Bergin (Eds.), *Handbook of psychotherapy and behavior change*. New York: Wiley, 1978. (a)

Gurman, A.S., & Kniskern, D.P. Deterioration in marital and family therapy: Empirical, clinical, and conceptual issues. *Family Process*, 1978, **17**, 3–20. (b)

Gurman, A.S., & Kniskern, D.P. Behavioral marriage therapy: Empirical perspective. *Family Process*, 1978, **17**(2), 139–148. (c)

Gurman, A.S., & Kniskern, D.P. Family therapy outcome research: Knowns and unknowns. In A.S. Gurman & D.P. Kniskern (Eds.)., *Handbook of family therapy*. New York: Brunner/Mazel, 1981.

Gurman, A.S., & Knudson, R.M. Behavioral marriage therapy: A psychodynamic-systems analysis and critique. *Family Process*, 1978, **17**(2), 121–138.

Gurman, A.S., Knudson, R.M., & Kniskern, D.P. Behavioral marriage therapy: Reply: Take two aspirin and call us in the morning. *Family Process*, 1978, **17**(2), 165–180.

Guttman, H.A., Spector, R.M., Sigal, J.J., Epstein, N.B., & Rakoff, V. Coding of affective expression in conjoint family therapy. *American Journal of Psychotherapy,* 1972, **26,** 185–194.

Haley, J. Family experiments: A new type of experimentation. *Family Process* 1962, **1,** 265–293.

Haley, J. *Strategies of psychotherapy.* New York: Grune & Stratton, 1963.

Haley, J. (Ed.). *Advanced techniques of hypnosis and therapy: Selected papers of Milton H. Erickson.* New York: Grune & Stratton, 1967.

Haley, J. A review of the family therapy field. In J. Haley, *Changing families.* New York: Grune & Stratton, 1971.

Haley, J. *Uncommon therapy.* New York: Norton, 1973.

Haley, J. *Problem solving therapy.* San Francisco: Jossey-Bass, 1976.

Haley, J. *Leaving home.* New York: McGraw-Hill, 1980.

Heckel, R.V. Predicting role flexibility in group therapy by means of a screening scale. *Journal of Clinical Psychology,* 1972, **28,** 570–573.

Hoffman, L. Deviation-amplifying processes in natural groups. In J. Haley (Ed.), *Changing families.* New York: Grune & Stratton, 1971.

Hollis, F. Explorations in the develoment of a typology of casework treatment. *Social Casework,* 1967, **48,** 489–497. (b)

Hollis, F. A profile of early interviews in marital counseling. *Social Casework,* 1968, **49,** 35–43. (a)

Hollis, F. Continuance and discontinuance in marital counseling and some observations on joint interviews. *Social Casework,* 1968, **49,** 167–174. (b)

Hunter, W.B., Hackney, N., & Kingdom, M.L. Family intervention in a treatment program for the hospitalized adolescent. *International Journal of Family Counseling,* 1978, **6**(1), 45–51.

Jacob, T. Family interaction in disturbed and normal families: A methodological and substantive review. *Psychological Bulletin,* 1975, **82,** 33–65.

Jacobson, N.S. Problem-solving and contingency contracting in the treatment of marital discord. *Journal of Consulting and Clinical Psychology,* 1977, **45,** 92–100.

Jacobson, N.S. Behavioral marital therapy. In A.S. Gurman & D.P. Kniskern (Eds.), *Handbook of family therapy.* New York: Brunner/Mazel, 1981.

Jacobson, N.S. & Martin, B. Behavioral marriage therapy: Current status. *Psychological Bulletin,* 1976, **83,** 540–556.

Jacobson, N.S. & Weiss, R.L. Behavioral marriage therapy: Critique: The contents of Gurman et al. may be hazardous to our health. *Family Process,* 1978, **17**(2), 149–164.

Jackson, D.D. The question of family homeostasis. *Psychiatric Quarterly Supplement,* 1957, **31,** 79–90.

Jackson D.D. The study of the family. *Family Process,* 1965, **4,** 1–20.

Jackson, D.D. The marital quid pro quo. In G. Zok & I. Boszormenyi-Nagy (Eds.), *Family therapy for disturbed families.* Palo Alto, Calif.: Science & Behavior Books, 1966.

Jackson, D.D., & Weakland, J.H. Conjoint family therapy. *Psychiatry.* 1961, **24,** 30–45.

Kaplan, S.L. Structural family therapy for children of divorce: Case reports. *Family Process,* 1977, **16**(1), 75–83.

Kaplan, M.L., & Kaplan, N.R. Individual and family growth: A Gestalt approach. *Family Process,* 1978, **17**(2), 195–206.

Karoly, P., & Rosenthal, M. Training parents in behavior modification: Effects on perceptions of family interactions and deviant child behaviors. *Behavior Therapy,* 1977, **8,** 406–410.

Kaslow, F.W. History of family therapy in the United States: A kaleidoscopic overview. *Marriage & Family Review,* 1980, **3,**(1/2), 77–111.

Klein, N., Alexander, J., & Parsons, B. Impact of family stems intervention on recidivism and sibling delinquency: A study of primary prevention. Paper read at Western Psychological Association, Sacramento, 1975.

Lebow, J. Issues in the assessment of outcome in family therapy. *Family Process,* 1981, **20,** 167–188.

Leitenberg, H. The use of single-case methodology in psychotherapy research. *Journal of Abnormal Psychology,* 1973, **82,** 87–101.

Lewis, J.M., Beavers, W.R., Gossett, J.T., & Phillips, V.A. No single thread: Psychological dearth in family systems. New York: Brunner/Mazel, 1976.

Liebman, R., Honig, P., & Berger, M. An integrated treatment program for psychogenic pain. *Family Process,* 1976, **15,** 397–405.

Liebman, R., Minuchin, S., & Baker, L. An integrated treatment program for anorexia nervosa. *American Journal of Psychiatry,* 1974, **131,** 432–436.

Madanes, C. Protection, paradox, and pretending. *Family Process,* 1980, **19,** 73–85.

Madanes, C. *Strategic family therapy.* San Francisco, Calif.: Jossey-Bass, 1981.

Madanes, C., & Maley, J. Strategic marital therapy. Workshop, 1980, Montreal, Canada.

Maruyama, M. The second cybernetics: Deviation amplifying mutual causal processes. In W. Buckley (Ed.), *Modern systems research for the behavioral scientist.* Chicago: Aldine, 1968.

Masten, A.S. Family therapy as a treatment for children: A critical review of outcome research. *Family Process,* 1979, **18,** 323–336.

McCollum, A.T., & Gibson, L.E. Family adaptation to the child with cystic fibrosis. *Journal of Pediatrics,* 1970, **77**(4), 571–578.

Meltzoff, J.E., & Kornreich, M. *Research in psychotherapy.* New York: Atherton, 1970.

Minuchin, S. *Families and family therapy.* Boston: Harvard University Press, 1974.

Minuchin, S. A conceptual model of psychosomatic illness in children: Family organization and family therapy. In E.D. Wittkowen & M. Warnes (Eds.), *Psychosomatic medicine.* Hagerstown, Md. Harper & Row, 1977.

Minuchin, S., Baker, L., Rosman, B.L., Liebman, R., Milman, L., & Todd, T.C. A conceptual model of psychosomatic illness in children: Family organization and family therapy. *Archives of General Psychiatry,* 1975, **32,** 1031–1038.

Minuchin, S., Baker, L., Rosman, B.L., Liebman, R., Milman, L., & Todd, T.C. A conceptual model of psychosomatic illness in children: Family organization and family therapy. *Archives of General Psychiatry,* 1975, **32,** 1031–1038.

Minuchin, S., Montalvo, B., Gverney, B., Rosman, B., & Schumer, F. *Families of the slums.* New York: Basic Books, 1967.

Minuchin, S., Rosman, B., & Baker, L. *Psycho somatic Families.* Cambridge: Harvard University Press, 1978.

Moos, R., & Moos, B. A typology of family social environments. *Family Process.* 1976, **15,** 357–371.

Olson, D.H., Sprenkle, D.H., & Russell, C.S. Circumplex model of marital and family systems: I. Cohesion and adaptability dimensions, family types, and clinical applicants. *Family Process,* 1979, **18,** 3–28.

Patterson, G.R. Families: Applications of social learning to family life. Champaign, Ill.: Research Press, 1971.

Patterson, G.R. Interventions for boys with conduct problems: Multiple settings, treatments, and criteria. *Journal of Consulting and Clinical Psychology,* 1974, **42,** 471–481.

Patterson, G.R. Multiple evaluations of a parent training program. In T. Thompson & W.S. Dockens III (Eds.), in *Applications of behavior modification.* New York: Academic Press, 1975. (b)

Patterson, G.R. Parents and teachers as change agents: A social learning approach systems. In D.M.L. Olson (Ed.), *Treating relationships.* Lake Mills, Iowa: Graphic Publishing, 1976.

Patterson, G.R., & Gullion, M.E. Living with children: New methods for parents and teachers. Champaign, Ill.: Research Press, 1968.

Patterson, G.R., Reid, J.B., Jones, R.R., & Conger, R.E. A social learning approach to family intervention (Vol. 1). The socially aggressive child. Eugene, Ore.: Castalia Press, 1975.

Pinsof, W.M. The family therapist behavior scale (FTBS): Development and evaluation of a coding system. *Family Process* 1979, **18,** 451–461. (a)

Pinsof, W.M. The family therapist coding system (FTCS) coding manual. Center for family studies, Department of Psychiatry, Northwestern University Medical School, Chicago, 1979. (b)

Pinsof, W.M. Family therapy process research. In A.S. Gurman & D.P. Kniskern (Eds.), *Handbook of family therapy.* New York: Brunner/Mazel, 1981.

Postner, R.S., Guttman, H., Sigal, J., Epstein, N.B., & Rakoff, V. Process and outcome in conjoint family therapy. *Family Process,* 1971, **10,** 451–474.

Reisinger, J.J., Frangia, G.W., & Hoffman, E.H. Toddler management training: Generalization and marital status. *Journal of Behavior Therapy and Experimental Psychiatry,* 1976, **7,** 333–340.

Reiss, D. Varieties of consensual experience I: A theory for relating family interaction to individual thinking. *Family Process,* 1971, **10,** 1–27. (a)

Reiss, D. Varieties of consensual experience II: Dimensions of a family's experience of its environment. *Family Process,* 1971, **10,** 28–35. (b)

Rice, D.G., Fey, W.F., & Kepecs, J.G. Therapist experience and "style" in co-therapy. *Family Process,* 1972, **11,** 1–12.

Rice, D.G., Gurman, A.S., & Razin, A.M. Therapist matching. *Journal of Marriage and Family Counseling,* 1976, **2,** 55–63.

Riskin, J.M., & Faunce, E.E. An evaluative review of family interactions research. *Family Process,* 1972, **11,** 365–466.

Santa-Barbara, J., & Epstein, N.B. Conflict behavior in clinical families: Preasymototic interactions and stable outcomes. *Behavioral Science,* 1974, **19,** 100–110.

Satir, V. *Conjoint family therapy: A guide to theory and technique* (Rev. ed.), Palo Alto, Calif.: Science and Behavior Books, 1967.

Scheflen, A.E. *Communicational structure: Analysis of a psychotherapy transaction.* Bloomington & London: Indiana University Press, 1973.

Shapiro, R., & Budman, S. Defection, termination, continuation in family and individual therapy. *Family Process,* 1973, **12,** 55–67.

Sigal, J.J., Guttman, H.A., Chagoya, L., & Lasry, J.C. Predictability of family therapists' behavior. *Journal of Consulting and Clinical Psychology,* 1973, **18,** 199–202.

Sigal, J.J., Lasry, J.C., Guttman, H.A., Chagoya, L., & Pilon, R. Some stable characteristics of family therapists; interventions in real and simulated therapy sessions. *Journal of Consulting and Clinical Psychology.* 1977, **45,** 23–26.

Sigal, J.J., Presser, B.G., Woodward, C.W., Santa-Barbara, J., Epstein, N.B., & Levin, S. *Therapists' interventions in a simulated family as predictors of outcome in family therapy.* Unpublished manuscript. Institute of Community and Family Psychiatry, Jewish General Hospital, Montreal, 1979.

Skynner, A.C.R. *Systems of family and marital psychotherapy.* New York: Brunner/Mazel, 1976.

Skynner, A.C.R. An open-systems, group analytic approach to family therapy. In A.S. Gurman & D.P. Kniskern (Eds.), *Handbook of family therapy.* New York: Brunner/Mazel, 1981.

Stanton, M.D. Strategic approaches to family therapy. In A.S. Gurman & D.P. Kniskern (Eds.), *Handbook of family therapy.* New York: Brunner/Mazel, 1981.

Stanton, M.D., & Todd, T.C. Some outcome results and aspects of structural family therapy with drug addicts. J.D. Smith, S. Anderson, M. Buxton, T. Chung, N. Gottlies, & W. Maruey (Eds.), *A multicultural view of drug abuse.* Cambridge, Mass.: Schenkman, 1978.

Straus, M.A., & Tallman, I. SIMFAM: A technique for observational measurement and experimental study of families. In J. Aldous et al. (Ed.), *Family problem solving.* Hinsdale, Ill. Dryden press, 1971.

Stuart, R.B. Behavioral remedies for marital ills: A guide to the use of operant interpersonal techniques. In A. Gurman & D. Rise (Eds.), *Couples in conflict: New directions in marital therapy.* New York: Aronson, 1975.

Stuart, R.B. An operant interpersonal program for couples. In D.M.L. Olson (Ed.), *Treating relationships.* Lake Mills, Ia.: Graphic, 1976.

Stuart, R.B. *Helping couples change.* New York: Guilford, 1980.

Tavormina, J.B. Basic models of parent counseling: A review. *Psychological Bulletin,* 1974, **81,** 827–835.

Thibaut, J.W. & Kelley, M.M. *The social psychology of groups.* New York: Wiley, 1959.

Toman, W. *Family constellation.* New York: Springer Verlag, 1961.

Waters, D. Personal communication. May, 1977.

Watzlawick, P. A structural family interview. *Family Process,* 1966, **5,** 256–271.

Watzlawick, P., Beavin, J.M., & Jackson, D. *Pragmatics of human communication: A study of international patterns, pathologies & paradoxes.* New York: Norton, 1967.

Watzlawick, P., Weakland, J., & Fisch, R. *Change: Principles of problem formation and problem resolution.* New York: Norton, 1974.

Weakland, J., Fisch, R., Watzlawick, P., & Bodin,

A.M. Brief therapy: Focused problem resolution. *Family Process,* 1974, **13,** 141–168.

Wellisch, D., Vincent, J., & Ro-Trock, G. Family therapy versus individual therapy: A study of adolescents and their parents. In D.H.L. Olson (Ed.), *Treating relationships.* Lake Mills, Ia.: Graphic, 1976.

Wells, R.A., & Dezen, A.E. The results of family therapy revisited: The nonbehavioral methods. *Family Process,* 1978, **17,** 251–274.

Wells, R.A., Dilkes, T.C., & Burkhart, N.T. The results of family therapy: A critical review of the literature. In D.H.L. Olson (Ed.), *Treating relationships.* Lake Mills, Ia.: Graphic, 1976.

Wertheim, E. Family unit therapy and the science and typology of family systems. *Family Process,* 1973, **12,** 361–376.

Wertheim, E. The science and typology of family systems II: Further theoretical and practical considerations. *Family Process,* 1975, **14,** 285–308.

Whitaker, C., & Malone, T. *The roots of psychotherapy.* London: Blakiston, 1953.

Whitaker, C.A., & Keith, D.V. Symbolic-experimental family therapy. In A.S. Gurman, & D.P. Kniskern (Eds.), *Handbook of family therapy.* New York: Brunner/Mazel, 1981.

Winer, L.R. The qualified pronoun count as a measure of change in family psychotherapy. *Family Process,* 1971, **10,** 243–248.

Wynne, L.C. Foreward. In A.S. Gurman & D.P. Kniskern (Eds.), *Handbook of therapy.* New York: Brunner/Mazel, 1981.

Zuk, G., Boszormenyi-Nagy, I., & Heiman, E. Some dynamics of laughter during family therapy. *Family Process,* 1963, **2,** 302–314.

CHAPTER 43

Use of Imagery and Imagination in Treatment of Children

CHARLES ELLIOTT AND MICKEY OZOLINS

Over 15 years ago Holt (1964) hailed the resurging interest in the investigation of imagery in both academic and clinical circles. Indeed, during the years following Holt's report, there has been a tremendous increase in therapy techniques that employ imagery and imagination as major tools. For the purposes of this chapter, imagery and imagination will be considered as a type of sensory (or quasisensory) experience that frequently occurs or is created "in the absence of directly relevant external stimulation" (Tower & Singer, 1981). Generally, the experience has some degree of visual quality, although imagery can be more of an auditory, tactile, or olfactory experience. The term *imagination* usually has less of a visual and more of a verbal connotation than the term *imagery*. Singer (1974) reviewed many of the uses that have been made of imagery in a wide spectrum of therapeutic frameworks, although Strosahl and Ascough (1981) recently noted that behavior therapy has undoubtedly generated the greatest proliferation of imagery-based techniques.

Several excellent reviews have been made of imagery in the treatment of adult disorders (e.g., Strosahl & Ascough, 1981; Singer, 1974). These reviews, as well as a number of recent theoretical critiques of imagery and its measurement (e.g. Pylyshyn, 1973; Anderson, M.P., 1981; Tower & Singer, 1981; Tower, 1981), have delineated a number of important weaknesses in past conceptualizations and uses of imagery. Some of these issues will be reviewed briefly here.

A notable gap exists in the literature with respect to reviews of the use of imagery and imagination in the treatment of children. This gap is rather puzzling, given that applications of imagery to children's clinical problems have been increasing at a rapid rate and may provide particularly effective methods for treatment, rapport building, and diagnosis. Therefore, the present chapter will largely represent an attempt to review the burgeoning clinical use of imagery with children. In addition, some of the major conceptual, functional, developmental, and measurement issues involving imagery will be discussed, especially as they may relate to clinical applications with children.

A brief word concerning the state of the art is probably in order. As we will note, the clinical use of imagery with adults is currently poorly understood, with important issues regarding conceptualization and measurement/ assessment being revised and worked out. In the area of children, these issues, as well as important developmental factors, have been addressed only at a rudimentary level to date. In spite of these problems, however, there does exist an exciting array of imagery-based clinical tools for the treatment of children. These will be reviewed and directions for further research will be noted.

CONCEPTUAL AND DEFINITIONAL ISSUES

Most psychological theories and discussions of imagery have at least informally referred to the notion that the term imagery can be largely described by the metaphor of a picture (Pylyshyn, 1973). However, recent critiques have clearly demonstrated the inadequacy and possibly misleading effects of this metaphor (Pylyshyn, 1973; Strosahl & Ascough, 1981).

These critiques have noted that the brain storage capacity would have to be virtually unlimited in order to store intact sensory data directly without prior interpretation. In addition, it is apparent that the retrieval of images does not operate in a manner analogous to retrieving photographs. For example, missing elements from an image cannot be explained in the same way that missing parts of a photograph can be (i.e., a torn piece, fading, etc.). Rather, missing elements of an image generally involve information about a perceptual attribute or relation, such as colors, spatial relations, particular events, etc. In some ways, imagery representations have been noted to be more like descriptions of scenes than pictures of them (Pylyshyn, 1973). Pylyshyn also noted the possibility that "while picture-like entities are not stored in memory, they can be constructed during processing, used for making new interpretations (i.e. propositional representations) and then discarded" (p. 19). Recent reviews, then, have generally concurred that the concept "mental image," is certainly not adequate to describe a particular type of visual memory representation. Rather, propositional network theory (Lang, 1977), data structuring, representations, and procedure representations may have more value in explaining the nature of memory representations derived from visual-sensory information, although substantial controversies in this area remain (Strosahl & Ascough, 1981).

A number of investigators have suggested that images are something like incomplete pictures or analogues that carry various types of multiply represented information of an affective, verbal, and visual as well as abstract nature (Kosslyn, 1976; Anderson, J.R., 1978; Strosahl & Ascough, 1981). Clearly, this information is far more than that contained in a simple photograph. It appears that substantial evidence exists to support the idea that there is some independence between the visual and verbal processing systems, but that the systems corepresent and share processing of new information (Strosahl & Ascough, 1981; Paivio, 1971).

Clinical relevance of such a multiple representational view of imagery can be seen by noting the limitations created by the contrasting, functional equivalence doctrine, which is related to the photograph metaphor of imagery. Strosahl and Ascough (1981) provide a thorough review of these positions, and only a few of the crucial points will be noted here. The functional equivalence assumption suggests that covert and overt behaviors are essentially equivalent, and that the same laws of learning operate in the same direct ways to modify them. This assumption has generally been used to provide the rationale for imagery-based behavior therapies and has been formally detailed by Cautela (Cautela, 1976; Cautela & Baron, 1977). Unfortunately, the empirical support for the functional equivalence assumption is mixed at best. For example, several studies have shown that covert techniques, which violate basic learning principles, have demonstrated clinical efficacy (e.g., Foreyt & Hagen, 1973; Goldfried, 1971).

If one accepts the possible limitations of the functional equivalence assumption and the related picture metaphor, then a number of other corollaries that frequently follow can also be challenged. For example, behavior therapists (Lazarus, 1976, 1977) have frequently recommended training in imagery prior to treatment. However, most studies have shown that pretreatment imagery ability has little relationship to treatment outcome, suggesting that image *content* may be as or more important than image *quality* (Strosahl & Ascough, 1981). Along this same vein, Kazdin (1979) has noted that idiosyncratic elaborations of imagery may be a crucial factor in the success of covert modeling procedures. Overall, Strosahl and Ascough (1981) have concluded that basic reproductive imagery, as well as the functional equivalence assumption, have some explanatory value, but the more important determinant of therapeutic outcome is "how the individual transforms and re-evaluates the image" (p. 435).

This discussion suggests that a number of

considerations be taken into account in the clinical use of imagery with children. First, it cannot be assumed that children are necessarily creating images in the manner they are instructed to without elaboration. Furthermore, that elaboration itself may have invaluable therapeutic significance and needs greater investigation. For example, research by Spanos (1971) and Kazdin (1979) has clearly suggested that better responses to imagery can be obtained when subjects actively elaborate suggested scenes on their own.

In addition to elaboration, children may form images that are quite different from what the therapist intended, simply because of the child's limited understanding of the words used to describe a given scene or situation. For example, Whitt et al. (1979) noted that a preoperational child might easily become focused on the concept of "death" when told that the doctor will inject some "dye." Careful attention to the young child's limited ability to deal with such double meanings is advised.

Finally, even if we have a good understanding of the actual image employed by a child, it may be more important to understand the *meaning* that the child attaches to the image and the conditions under which that meaning (not just the image) might change. For example, two children could have an image of a teacher standing over them. The first child might attach a meaning to that image that would relate to an expected positive encounter, while the second child might attach a meaning to the image involving an expected unpleasant consequence, such as criticism. This notion is virtually the same argument that Meichenbaum and Butler (1979) have advanced in recent discussions on cognitive assessments.

Function of Imagery

Some of the early studies on the function of imagery were aimed at distinguishing between verbal and imaginal processes in learning. Generally, this early learning research has indicated that imagery is highly related to concreteness, while words are related to abstractness. Further, imagery does facilitate some forms of learning, possibly because it allows for a faster readout than sequential word processing.

These early studies laid groundwork for later research in both associative and prose learning with children, which Levin and his colleagues (Levin, 1976) carried out in an effort to identify teaching strategies suited to learner's ability. Of importance here is that children's learning may be enhanced when learning strategies are matched to both the materials to be learned and the learner's specific abilities (e.g., verbal versus visualizer styles discussed in the section on assessment). This suggests that two significant modes of information processing occur, probably with a great deal of overlap. It also seems clear that imagery functions to enhance learning, at least with more concrete materials. Exciting implications for tailored teaching warrant further investigation into the differences between these two processes and clarification about the ways in which development affects imagery ability.

Singer (1971) approached the function of imagery at a more macro level. He also described imagery as an information-coding mechanism, whose function is to process sensorimotor input, but went on to suggest that "a complex series of well-established images" (p. 83) are ingrained, so that a cognitive map of greater and greater complexity is built up. In this way, automatic behaviors can be emitted without conscious effort while simultaneously processing new information on a more thoughtful level. For example, one can drive a car along a familiar route while simultaneously carrying on a conversation and perhaps engaging in a series of daydreams.

By contrast, Freud discussed imagery as a predominately negative phenomenon. He contended that only unhappy people fantasize and that fantasy is often used maladaptively. According to this view, it may be that when children overuse fantasy life as a refuge, they miss out on opportunities to develop social skills and feelings of confidence in mastering new situations. In addition, Zimbardo (1979) pointed out that while fantasy is adaptively used for wish fulfillment, when it becomes the primary avenue of thinking, this can be considered a schizophrenic thought disorder. In such cases, the person uses his or her internal perception as a validation of external reality and does not operate under normal, reality-based constraints.

Other literature suggests that the simple use of imagery and imagination by itself is not necessarily negative or positive. For example, studies on imaginary companions found no correlation with emotional disturbances (Manosevitz, Prentice, & Wilson, 1973). In fact, the only consistent finding in this body of literature is that imaginary companions occur more often in firstborn or only children (Ames & Learned, 1946; Svendsen, 1934; Singer, 1961; Manosevitz et al, 1973). These authors suggest that imaginary companions function as substitute peers or, in some cases, as outlets for otherwise unacceptable behaviors.

Developmental Issues

For Piaget, the basis for the development of conceptual thinking is "the mental image and symbolic schemas that are involved in play" (Baldwin, 1968, p. 230). In this view, the initial function of imagery is assimilation. Imagery is thought to occur first in late infancy (Piaget's stage 6) when "deferred imitation" takes place. "Deferred imitation" requires that the child distinguish the mental image from the actual act or event it represents. Until the infant is capable of making this distinction, mental imagery presumably cannot occur. At this point in development, the image is considered to be "an internalized imitation of an overt sensory motor action" (p. 231). Piaget suggests that it is very specific to the event it is imitating and, while it may be more a stereotype than a point to point representation, it is concrete rather than conceptual. In the same way, "pretend" also requires a mental representation to stand for the real event and cannot occur until the child can distinguish the pretense from the action.

The development of imagery has been further broken down into two classes: *reproductive imagery,* referring to the above-described type of concrete image, and *antici-patory imagery,* which presumably first occurs at about 7–8 years of age. Anticipatory imagery involves manipulation of the mental representation (image) to the extent that it can be moved about in space and changed in form (Piaget & Inhelder, 1971).

In support of this notion of two classes of imagery, Wolff and Levin (1972) and Levin (1976) found significant differences between kindergartners' and third-graders' performance on associative learning tasks using an induced imagery strategy. Subjects were told to "make up a picture in your head of the two things (toys) in each pair doing something together" (p. 116). The third-grade imagery group outperformed the no-imagery control group while no such effect was found for the kindergartners. It was presumed that they were unable to manipulate their images. A third condition was also studied in which kindergartners were told to physically make the actual toys interact. It was expected that the motor behavior, in keeping with Piaget's thinking, would generate a mental image of the interaction. Recall performance of the kindergartners in this condition did exceed control levels.

It seems likely from Levin's research that older children, beginning at about 7 or 8, can conjure up and manipulate appropriate images when told to do so and thereby improve associative learning. Younger children do not profit from such instructions unless they can also manipulate the actual toys to be remembered. Levin found, however, that with "motor imagery training" (prolonged practice in physically manipulating the toys) kindergartners could effectively use an imagery strategy (Levin, 1976, p. 116).

While the ability to manipulate one's images is undoubtedly a very important variable in learning, Bruner (1969) also suggested that *the number of attributes* of the stimulus to which the child can attend is limited according to his or her developmental stage (p. 321). Therefore, the scope of the child's ability to attend to stimulus complexity, as well as his or her ability to manipulate imagery, may contribute to task performance.

Singer (1961) suggested an additional developmental aspect of imagery in the area of self-regulation. He specifically addressed fantasy or daydreaming, which were described as integrated forms of imagery. The child, as his or her imaginative abilities begin to develop, can rely on daydreaming as a means of filling time and delaying gratification. This hypothesis was tested by comparing waiting ability of children assessed with either "high" or "low" ability to fantasize, with instruction to subjects to imagine that they were involved in an astronaut candidacy selection procedure. The "high fantasy" children were able to sit or stand in one place for longer periods than the "low fantasy" group.

Mischel and Moore (1973) carried out a related study where children (mean age of 4.5) were told they could earn a previously chosen reward if they waited or worked ten minutes, or they could terminate the condition sooner and earn a less preferred reward. Subjects who were shown a slide of the relevant rewards were able to wait longer than those viewing slides of similar, but irrelevant objects and the no slide controls. Interestingly, previous studies found that attention to the actual rewards resulted in shorter waiting time than when rewards were absent (Mischel & Ebbesin, 1970) and that instruction to think about the reward resulted in shorter waiting time than "thinking about fun things," both with the reward present and absent (Mischel, Ebbesin, & Zeiss, 1972). Mischel et al. (1972) began this research expecting that attending to the actual rewards or internal representations of the rewards would help children engage in "self-persuasion and anticipatory gratification" (p. 205), and enhance delay of gratification. Instead, they found that both internally and externally presented rewards resulted in over-arousal of the child and a reduction in his or her ability to delay, *unless* the reward was presented as a slide. Thus, they asked a similar group of subjects to cognitively transform the actual rewards either into pictures of the rewards or into actual objects, i.e., "make them real." Subjects who were asked to construe rewards as "real" obtained the shortest waiting times (Moore, Mischel, & Zeiss, 1976).

These studies clearly demonstrate that the way in which children cognitively represent rewards partially determines the degree of frustration they must cope with. Without intervention, children at this stage of development tend to respond to concrete elements of the stimulus, therefore arousing so-called consumatory impulses. However, when rewards are more abstractly represented as "pictures in the mind" or presented in slide form, children are able to distance themselves and respond instead to informational cues of the stimulus. In this way, they can remind themselves of the contingencies, distract themselves, and, in general, cognitively enhance delay ability (Moore et al., 1976).

In contrasting Singer's study of fantasy and waiting ability with Mischel's work, the importance of developmental effects is further revealed. While both studies found that imagery can, at times, enhance ability to delay, Singer's subjects (ages 6–9 with a mean age of 7.5) represent a different developmental stage with presumably more sophisticated and abstract imagery ability. In fact, it may be that his low fantasy group possessed less mature imagery ability and were consequently less able to profit from the fantasy suggestions. Bruner (1969) addressed this point, suggesting that through about 5 years of age the child's mental representation has properties of a picture and the developmental shift occurs as the picture is translated into a "code or set of rules" (p. 319). He found that 5-year-olds could perform conservation operations, but, when faced with a contradictory visual display, this "perceptual or sense information" (p. 319) overwhelmed the child's tenuous grasp of the rules of conservation and his performance regressed. Six-year-olds had less trouble with this task, and 7-year-olds were completely undistracted from their original correct judgment.

While Piaget, Levin, and other learning researchers have dealt with imagery development as an evolution toward more effective information processing, Singer (1961) has also looked at how the child's *environment* interacts with the development of imagination. He suggests that children are more likely to develop fantasy skills when: (1) they have either few siblings or little involvement with siblings, and (2) when they have regular posi-tive contact with a parent and, consequently, greater identification with that parent. His hypothesis is that children with little peer con-tact rely more on fantasy because they have more opportunity to do so and because they are more dependent on this form to pass time. He also points out that creative interactions with parents, such as storytelling, are more conducive to fantasy development than struc-tured games of skill and chance.

Singer's assessment of the high and low fantasy subjects along the above dimensions revealed the following: (1) there were more only children among the high fantasy group; (2) there was greater parental contact reported by the high fantasy group; (3) there was a greater propensity among high fantasy chil-dren to single out a preferred parent upon request. While Singer's subject pool provided too narrow a range to assess the effects of intelligence, Wallach (1970) pointed out that the above variables construed to be conducive to richer fantasizing are also likely to be con-ducive to higher levels of intelligence. In elab-orating this point, Wallach (1970) described a study by Helsen where preference for imagin-ative activities in childhood was highly corre-lated with verbal aptitude tests and grade point averages in college students.

Although two investigations of "imaginary companions" (Jersild, Markey, & Jersild, 1933; Svendsen, 1934), which were based on a similar hypothesis, found a positive correla-tion between the utilization of imaginary companions and intelligence, two others did not (Bairdain, 1959; Manosivitz, Fling, & Prentice, 1977). Finally, Schaefer (1969) found creativity to be related to imaginary compan-ions. However, this area of research is replete with methodological weaknesses, and these questions have not yet been adequately resolved.

Overall, the literature on the functional and developmental aspects of imagery and imagination has important implications for the use of such strategies in the treatment of children. In viewing the research by Mischel and his colleagues, as well as by Singer, one is struck by the possible role of imagery in the related areas of impulse control, self-

regulation, and attention span. Although di-rect evidence is lacking, these problems may very well be caused, in part, by developmental delays in the ability to use more abstract and possibly less emotionally arousing forms of imagery. Treatment possibilities are obvious if this hypothesis is found to be valid.

Another treatment consideration suggested by this literature is that young children (below about 7 or 8) may use concrete images, which have an especially high degree of affect asso-ciated with them. If so, the therapist should be quite careful in the use of any imaginal stimuli of an aversive nature. One should also keep in mind the potential for the child to create unin-tended aversive stimuli whether through mis-understanding or spontaneous elaborations. This problem might be avoided by carefully choosing the words used to describe imagined scenes and situations, asking the child to report what he or she "sees," and by checking his or her apparent affective responses as indi-cated by breathing patterns, facial expres-sions, etc.

Finally, one should be careful not to make imagined scenes, pretend situations, etc., too complex for the younger child. If manipula-tion of the image is needed with a younger child, it might be preferable to manipulate an acted-out, pretend situation rather than a totally covert scene or to use the related tech-niques of modeling where the manipulations are carried out by someone else.

ASSESSMENT

In a recent review, Tower and Singer (1981) noted that the measurement of imagery may have value in answering clinical questions in the area of diagnosis, intervention, and eval-uation. Unfortunately, most formal tech-niques for the assessment of imagery have been designed either exclusively to answer laboratory-based questions or to assess var-ious properties of images that at times appear to have tenuous relationships to these clinical questions.

Recent reviews have summarized a number of particularly important and somewhat over-lapping issues to be considered in the assessment of imagery, including: *passive versus active nature of imagery, imagery abilities, relationship to perception, subjectivity versus objectivity, consciousness, individual differences,* and *imagery as a learned ability* (Strosahl & Ascough, 1981; Anderson, M.P., 1981; Tower & Singer, 1981; Tower, 1981). Because of the recency and completeness of these reviews, only a few highlights will be presented here.

With respect to the issue of the *passive versus active nature of imagery,* we have already noted that imagery is currently considered to be an active process of construction and reconstruction rather than merely a product that is passively reviewed. M.P. Anderson (1981) has noted the ease of lapsing into considering imagery from the more passive view, as well as the problems in choosing the appropriate assessment tools if the distinction is not maintained.

The issue of assessing *imagery abilities* (such as vividness, controllability, involvement, and clarity) has received considerable attention in the literature, which may be particularly explained by the previously noted functional equivalence assumption. Unfortunately, most of the terms used to describe imagery ability have been rather loosely defined. For example, vividness has usually been assumed to be equivalent to imagery ability in spite of other possible referents for the term, including clarity, sharpness, sensory richness, and involvement in the imaginal activity (Anderson, M.P., 1981). In addition, evidence is accumulating that suggests that the emphasis in image quality as opposed to image content and meaning may have been a mistake (e.g., Stroshal & Ascough, 1981; Meichenbaum & Butler, 1979; Kazdin, 1976). It is difficult to question the notion that at least some dimensions of image quality have clinical relevance, but it certainly appears that greater attention to image content and meaning would result in significant payoffs. An examination of the conditions under which image quality changes would also appear to have value. For example, a person's affective state is likely to not only be affected by the type of ongoing cognitive and imagery processes, but imagery qual-

ity itself may also be substantially altered by various affective states (Euse & Haney, 1975; Michenbaum & Butler, 1979).

The *relationship of imagery to perception* may have particular clinical relevance in the treatment of children. Tower and Singer (1981) have noted that children's "learning disabilities are examples in which the continuum between perception and imagination is of primary psychological interest" (p. 6). The authors noted the particular relevance of behavioral and possibly psychological measures in this area. The interaction between imaginal and perceptual processes represents an intriguing area of investigation. Along this line, one cannot help but be struck by the implications of the previously noted potential impact of affective states on imagery quality. Thus a child who has become conditioned to fear certain types of learning material or learning situations might find that his or her imagery encoding, processing, and/or recall functions are fundamentally disrupted by the negative arousal engendered by either the material or the situation.

Subjectivity versus objectivity of imagery is an issue related to the relationship of imagery to perception and has clinical implications as well. Objective imagery essentially refers to the ability to perform cognitive tasks that presumably require the presence of vivid imagery. Such performance clearly has relevance for work in areas such as those we discussed in regard to learning disabilities. However, performance on such objective measures has generally failed to demonstrate a significant relationship with more subjective rating of imagery quality (Tower & Singer, 1981). In fact, Neisser (1970) has noted the possibility that subjectively experienced imagery may be quite different from imagery that functions for the purpose of information processing.

In many clinical areas, subjective imagery is the primary area of concern. For example, children may be plagued by intrusive, fear-provoking images, uncontrolled obsessional images, images of unresolved conflicts, and so on, in which the distress is largely subjective and dependent on numerous idiosyncratic variables. All in all, it does not seem especially surprising that a child's or an adult's ability to perform on tasks, such as picture memory tests, would fail to demonstrate a reliable relationship with his or her images of a distressing nature, such as being attacked by spiders or ridiculed by peers. Along this line, Guy and McCarter (1978) recently obtained evidence in support of the notion that ability to form "sensory images" is related to, but also separate from, the ability to form "emotive imagery" and developed the only scale to date designed to assess the quality of emotive imagery.

Consciousness of imagery is another issue relevant to the assessment as well as the definition of imagery. Considerable data reviewed by Singer (1974) and Tower and Singer (1981) suggest that one need not assume awareness of imagery for imagery itself to exist. The data indicate that imagery (and cognition in general) is constantly generated and processed and that in certain conditions people can become more aware of this process. Singer (1974) has further suggested that an essential learning task that takes place early in life consists of learning to ignore much of our task-irrelevant imagery in the same way that it is essential to block out or ignore subtle muscle twitchings, kinesthetic feedback, minor stomach gurglings, etc. The notion of ongoing, but not necessarily fully conscious imaginal processes, is quite similar to Beck's (e.g., Beck et al., 1979) discussion of "automatic thoughts" that also presumably are constantly ongoing but so habitual as to have become essentially automatic and outside of immediate awareness.

Individual differences in imagery style have also received attention for their potential clinical, as well as research, applicability. Probably the most researched area of individual differences in imaginal styles is the verbalizer-visualizer dimension. Richardson (1977) has argued that this construct represents a stable difference in processing style. Numerous differences between these two groups have been cited in areas such as alpha rhythms, breathing patterns, vocational choices, and possibly therapeutic implications (Tower & Singer, 1981). By contrast, McKellar (1965) found

that the true verbalizer is quite rare and Strosahl and Ascough (1981) argued that not many adult subjects can even be considered as "poor imagers" according to most self-report instruments. The issue of processing style may be somewhat different, and possibly more important when viewed from a developmental perspective, however. For example, Tower et al. (1979) and Friedrich and Stein (1975) found differential processing of visual and auditory information presented via television to preschool boys and girls. Levin, McCabe, and Bender (1974) also found differential learning styles in children, with some chidren learning equally well with pictures and words, some learning much more efficiently from pictures, and some learning poorly from both words and pictures. Thus, with respect to the verbalizer-visualizer dimension, the more important issue for children may be *when* good imaging skills develop and whether *delays* in such development have clinical and/or academic significance. Unfortunately, little research has as yet been conducted although the results from such studies could have substantial impact on the use of imagery treatments with children.

One partial exception to this trend can be found in research by London and Cooper (1969) who found that at least in the area of response to a hypnotic suggestability scale (London, 1963), which appears largely based on certain kinds of imagery creation abilities, children demonstrate good susceptibilities by age 5 that increase until around age 9. They also noted some decrease in susceptibility in adults, which probably is due more to the development of interfering attitudes than any decrease in imaging skills. Still, we have not discovered any research to date that addresses the question of the child who lags behind his or her peers in development of sophisticated imagery abilities.

Finally, the notion of *imagery as a learned ability* has been discussed by Strosahl and Ascough (1981). They have noted that, in spite of the abundant interest in pretreatment imagery assessment, research investigating the possible learning effects on imagery ability are apparently nonexistent. Imagery training strategies have been proposed (e.g., Lazarus, 1977), but assessment of improvement following such training or even following repeated imagery-based treatment does not seem to exist. Extrapolating from London and Cooper's (1969) research, one might speculate that imagery training might function predominantly to eliminate interferences with imagery abilities that would presumably develop naturally unless some combination of events caused them to be suppressed. This would suggest that most young children (after the age of 4 or 5) would readily be able to use some form of imagery-based treatments unless specific experiences had exerted deleterious effects on their visual capacities.

Measurement Techniques

A number of excellent reviews have recently surveyed the various instruments and strategies that have been developed for the measurement of imagery and its effects, and the reader is referred to these for a detailed accounting, including information on reliability, validity, and limitations (Tower & Singer, 1981; Tower, 1981; Anderson, M.P., 1980; Strosahl & Ascough, 1981). These reviews have noted that there are essentially the following four types of such measures: (1) self-report; (2) behavioral; (3) physiological; (4) projectives, and that the type of measures selected obviously affects the nature of the information that will be obtained. Self-report measures stress the attainment of consciously available information of a subjective nature; behavioral measures assess performance on tasks that presumably require some degree of imagery to solve and yield information, such as matching perceptions to memories; physiological measures assess one's reactions to imagery and have shown promise in helping to clarify the actual functions and processes of imagery; and projective measures provide information, possibly of an unconscious nature, as well as various theme associations and affects (Tower, 1981).

Unfortunately, very few of the wide variety of instruments currently available were developed for use with children, and the few that should be used for that purpose generally have not been used in any systematic fashion. Thus, with the exception of some work in the area of visual and verbal recall, we have relatively little information concerning the *clinical* relevance of children's imagery and the function of their imagery with respect to psychopathology. Some indirect information concerning the nature and frequency of some types of children's imagery can be found in recent children's fear surveys (e.g., Student Attitude Survey, Walker, 1979) if one assumes that most children's fears have an imaginal component. In addition, the Children's Hypnotic Susceptibility Scale developed by London (1963) does provide preliminary norms for the degrees to which children respond to hypnotic suggestions of an imaginal nature. Also, a few projective instruments, such as the Children's Apperception Test, the Rorschach, House-Tree-Person, and the Draw-a-Person utilize imagery heavily for diagnostic purposes. The Imaginative Child Interview form developed by Walker (1977) is another instrument that uses imagery and imagination for diagnostic as well as rapport-building purposes. Our clinical experience with this instrument has found it to be quite useful. However, objective scoring criteria and norms on these types of instruments are not available.

As we will note later, the relative paucity of imaginal assessment strategies for children has certainly not slowed down the development of new imagery-based therapies for children. With a few notable exceptions, these treatments have been virtually carbon copies of treatments used for adults with little or no consideration given to developmental factors that might suggest needed alterations or age dependent limitations. Clinicians are largely left to "shoot in the dark" with respect to this issue until research provides the needed data on imagery as it relates to the developmental sequence.

TREATMENT APPROACHES

The diversity of imagery- and imagination-based treatment procedures available to the child clinician is indeed impressive. Some of these strategies are creative as well as exciting, given the wide variety of problems to which they have been applied. It appears that for many children imagery and imagination may be a highly effective means of gaining rapport, obtaining important diagnostic information, and designing interesting treatment strategies. On the other hand, very little has been done to systematize and empirically validate these applications.

In spite of the wide variety of techniques (as well as theoretical bases for them) a number of commonalities in procedures, function, and rationale have been cited by various authors (e.g., Wilkins, 1974). One of these common issues concerns the use of imagery to utilize and enhance the affective component of experience, which is often accompanied by distortion of reality. Thus the full affective meaning behind children's statements such as, "I am afraid of dogs," or "I am afraid of my teacher" may be lost without the accompanying images of gnarling teeth, being yelled at, being overwhelmed, etc. Indeed, it appears that the patient's affect and behavior are much more congruent with the images than other objectively defined reality (Beck, 1970; Horowitz, 1968; Singer, 1974; Brown, 1969). Some imagery treatments explicitly and directly attempt to modify these distortions, but it has also been noted that the patient, on his or her own, may quite readily engage in *self-correction simply with practice in the use of imagery* (Jellinik, 1953; Brown, 1969; Singer, 1974). In many respects, such uses of imagery can be thought of as a process of developing an important cognitive skill. In a sense, most imagery-based therapies provide training for patients to increase their awareness of their imaginal processes, to learn to value their imagery, and to "accept, control and even enjoy their new fantasies rather than having to plunge into some type of excessive motor activity, rapid cognitive shifting or focusing upon their physical condition in order to avoid confronting recurrent fears, doubts, suspicions or memories of embarassing moments" (Singer, 1974, p. 40).

A number of investigators have noted that developing imagery skills frequently results in "desensitization" or, perhaps more accurately, an extinction effect (e.g., Singer, 1971, 1974; Wilkins, 1974). A rather wide variety of strategies involve having the patient confront, deal with, or work through unpleasant images, whether directly related to the target problems or not. For example, Chethik and Fast (1970) suggested that borderline children engage in an overuse of pleasure fantasies to deny and ward off their image of the real world, which is distorted in overly unpleasant and painful terms. They utilize a psychoanalytically based imagery treatment that involves the therapist in gradually encouraging elaborations and changes in the child's fantasies in such a way as to expose underlying fears and anxieties, as well as to increase acceptance of reality as not entirely painful. Regardless of the author's psychoanalytic assumptions, the process of extinction is clear in the gradual exposure to unpleasant stimuli without unpleasant consequences.

One should note that a cognitive decision-making process may also account for some of the effects of imagery-based therapies. For example, Singer (1974) has pointed out that even with some aversive covert behavior therapies, presumably based on conditioning principles, the patient is actively engaged in his or her own thought processes, which could include the realization of the absurdity of delivering unpleasant consequences, such as a shock to himself or herself, while engaging in certain thoughts or images. That realization alone could lead to significant behavior change independent of specific conditioning effects.

Although the balance of this chapter will focus on children's imagery- and imagination-based therapies, it is also useful to realize that imagery may be a significant mediator in other therapies that do not involve any specific, intentional use of imaginal processes. For example, Kanfer, Karoly, and Newman (1975) described a verbal cue procedure for reducing children's fear of the dark. Competence-related verbal cues were found to be particularly effective in reducing the children's fears. The competence group cues included self-statements, such as, "I am a brave boy (girl)," and the stimulus cues included statements like, "There are many good things in the dark." One can readily imagine a rich array of both beneficial and deleterious imagery that might be elicited by such self-statements, which, unfortunately, were not assessed or considered by the authors. Imagery induced by such procedures would seem to be a worthwhile area of investigation. Once again, this possibility highlights the importance of the patient's elaborations of imagery described by the therapist. We have already discussed the possible importance of such elaborations and feel that they may represent a crucial commonality amongst the various treatment strategies discussed below.

Play Therapy

Play therapy relies heavily upon a child's imaginative abilities and has been loosely defined as "the treatment of a child through play, in order that he or she might attain a better understanding of behaviors, or gain a safe outlet for antisocial impulses" (Rogers, 1977, p. 473). This therapy is not a single technique although its earliest applications were grounded in psychoanalytic theory and chiefly used the technique of interpretation.

Play has been used as a medium for therapy by theorists of several schools and has been variously labeled as psychoanalytic, nondirective, and directive play therapy and, less frequently, play fantasy, according to the particular underlying theoretical assumptions. Nondirective play therapy, as per Axline (1947, pp. 15–30; 1948), has probably been the most widely used and investigated approach. This technique involves provision of appropriate play materials and an unrestricted and totally accepting atmosphere in which the child can achieve "emotional relaxation" and then "self-actualization" (p. 15).

More directive approaches developed by learning theorists have utilized a variety of behavioral techniques in play situations with children. Those techniques included stimulus substitution and generalization, counterconditioning, and social reinforcement (Schaefer

& Millman, 1978). Behavioral techniques have also been applied in play settings with groups of children; for example, Doubros and Daniels (1966) used differential reinforcement to teach retarded children, and Carlin and Armstrong (1968) combined token reinforcement, cost response, and time-out to reduce hostility in socially acting-out children.

In a review of therapies for children, Schaefer and Millman (1978) described a number of case studies where play therapy was used to treat a variety of children's disorders, such as neurotic behaviors, including obsessive-compulsive, hysterical, fearful, and social withdrawal behavior; habit disorders, including refusal to eat, hair pulling, and encopresis; and antisocial behavior. Although play therapy seems to be a fruitful instrument for change in children, little systematic investigation has been carried out. Many of these studies used small Ns and/or very inadequate controls.

A few outcome studies have been carried out (e.g., Fleming & Snyder, 1947; Cox, 1953; Dorfman, 1958; Seeman, Barry, & Ellinwood, 1964), suggesting that nondirective play therapy is an effective mode of therapy. However, with the exception of the Cox study, methodological weakness rendered the conclusions tentative at best. There has also been a virtual dearth of investigations using behavioral techniques in play therapy, with a notable exception by Clement and Milne (1967). They compared the use of tangible and verbal reinforcers with socially withdrawn boys in play situations. After 14 sessions, tangibly reinforced subjects demonstrated increased social approach behavior and decreased problem behavior compared to the verbally reinforced and the control groups.

Due to the number of approaches used, the multitude of target symptoms successfully treated and methodological weaknesses of existing research, the effective elements of play therapy are difficult to sort out. According to Bruner (1969), play itself, regardless of structure or direction, is an essential tool to the developing child. He described the function of play as the means for trying out behaviors that could not otherwise be practiced, with minimal consequences. Viewed in this light, any modality of play therapy could be effective. However, given the function of play, behavioral approaches employing deliberate modeling and shaping of appropriate behaviors seem ideally suited to play therapy. Within this context, excellent use can be made of the child's existing capacities for fantasy and imagination. Based upon the previously noted research by Levin (1976), it may be that acting out a young child's fantasies and imagination through play therapy would be more efficacious than purely covert strategies, which would require a greater ability to manipulate complex imagery than that of which the child is capable.

Psychodrama

Psychodrama was introduced by J.L. Moreno in the 1940s and is another imaginal treatment method that holds promise for use with children although it has usually been applied to adolescents and adults. This method employs a variety of roleplay techniques designed to facilitate expression of feelings and resolution of conflicts. It typically requires a group of participants to serve both as actors in the life dramas of those involved and as an audience that provides feedback (Moreno, 1972, 1975).

Moreno reported this treatment method to be effective with both children and adults. In fact, he described psychodrama "experiments" that he and his wife carried out with their 2-year-old son. Nevertheless, formal reports of the use of psychodrama with children are rare and have most frequently been published in the non-English literature.

Psychodrama has been used to teach primary and secondary grade children problem-solving and decision-making skills (Mathis, Fairchild, & Cannon, 1980) and to measure understanding of responsibility of delinquent behaviors in so-called feebleminded boys (Matsumato, 1978). There is also an interesting report by Dallas (1978) where psychodrama was used with 50 elementary school children who demonstrated symptomatic behavior after witnessing a particularly gruesome homicide. For a detailed description of age appropriate psychodrama techniques and their application, see Shearon (1980).

Hypnosis

Without reviewing the controversies regarding the nature of "specialness" of the so-called trance states, hypnosis in many ways can be thought of as "a self-generated extension of a normal state of profound relaxation and *imagery control*" (Singer, 1974) (emphasis added). Although some types of hypnotic suggestions rely only minimally on imagery, its use with children generally includes a substantial use of imagery for both induction and suggestion purposes. There is a wide diversity of induction and suggestion procedures that can be used with children, and there is no clear way of defining what factors specifically are responsible for the effects obtained. For that matter, there also are not clear guidelines for what factors are crucial for a given procedure to be called hypnosis; many of the procedures described in the hypnosis literature could almost as easily have been given labels such as covert modeling, covert assertion, imagery rehearsal, and so on.

Nevertheless, we will briefly review a few of the major, so-called hypnotic induction and suggestion strategies for children as well as review some of the varied applications of them. As we previously discussed, evidence does suggest that children make excellent hypnotic subjects. Most investigators have found that children, in fact, make better hypnotic subjects than adults (Gardner, 1974; Cooper & London, 1971; Morgan & Hilgard, 1973), with clear abilities being demonstrated by age 4 or 5 and improvement occurring over the next several years of development. Gardner (1974) has speculated that children's marked responsiveness to hypnosis is due to a number of factors such as their relatively concrete thinking, greater willingness to engage in fantasy, openness to new experiences, intensity of their feelings, among others. In spite of this presumed effectiveness, Gardner has noted that the actual use of hypnosis with children has been relatively limited.

Maximizing children's response to hypnosis has been discussed by a number of investigators (e.g., Gardner, 1974; Williams & Singh, 1976). Although research is lacking regarding this issue, one might assume from the literature on developmental factors that the preoperational child under hypnosis would show decreased responsiveness as either stimulus complexity of the imagery or the amount that he or she is expected to manipulate or alter presented images increases. Gardner (1974) has further suggested that inductions and suggestions should be as concrete as possible although realism per se is not as essential. Thus when trying to get a child to eat, it has been suggested that images of the sight, smell, and taste of specific foods be used in addition to suggested feelings of hunger (Gardner, 1974). Sleep inductions are considered somewhat inadvisable since many children tend to resist sleep. An especially popular induction strategy is the "television technique," which has been described by Ambrose (1968) and Kroger (1963) in detail and has also been used as a strategy for delivering treatment suggestions. Basically, the child is instructed to imagine a television screen in his or her mind. The television is then "turned on" to a favorite program to initiate involvement in the imagery. Clinically relevant imagery, either for the purpose of assessment or treatment, can then be described. Other excellent descriptions of induction procedures have been provided by Ambrose (1968), Illovsky and Freeman (1976), and Spiegel (1972), among others.

In a general sense, hypnotism with children is often considered to increase the child's sense of mastery or control (e.g., Gardner & Tarnow, 1980; Gardner, 1974; Williams & Singh, 1976). Thus it is often recommended that the child be taught self-hypnosis, which is sometimes augmented by the use of cassette tapes that can be listened to at home. More specifically, hypnotism, usually with rich imagery content, has been applied to an amazing variety of children's problems although generally it is not the sole treatment employed (e.g., Kaffman, 1968). A partial list of these problems includes hyperactivity (Illovsky & Freeman, 1976), enuresis, tics, sleep disturbances (Ambrose, 1961, 1968), thumbsucking (Tilton, 1980), asthma (Rose, 1967), autism (Gardner & Tarnow, 1980), coping with pain related to cancer and burn treatment (Keane & Pillemer, 1980), persistent attacks of vomiting (Kaffman, 1968), taking oral medications, and presurgical anxiety (Gardner 1974). Rather distressingly, outcome studies on these applications are virtually nonexistent. Such studies will, of course, not be easy to conduct for a variety of reasons, especially including the limited subject populations available for these problems and the fact that hypnosis is usually employed as one part of an overall treatment package. At this point, it appears that hypnosis is a promising technique for children, partially because of their willingness and ability to engage in vivid fantasy. However, controlled-outcome studies, including single-case experimental designs as recently reviewed by Hayes (1981) would be highly desirable.

Miscellaneous Techniques

There is also a variety of loosely structured and defined imagery techniques that have been applied to a wide range of childhood problems. Some of these methods have much in common with hypnosis and are rooted in European psychoanalytic theory. The European techniques rely heavily on the symbolic, interpretive value of imagery and in some cases also use the patient's fantasy productions as diagnostic indicators of progress.

One of the earliest techniques of this type was first described by Desoille (Schoettle, 1980) who used "Guided Daydreaming" to suggest symbolic scenes to relaxed adult patients, eliciting and guiding their productions toward confrontation with Jungian archtypical figures and Oedipal issues. Leuner (1969) later provided more formal structure to this technique, labeling it "Guided Affective Imagery" (GAI). He described 10 standard imaginary situations to be suggested to patients, some of which are highly structured and designed to explore specific behavioral areas while others are loosely structured and are expected to evoke almost any projection. Leuner also suggested five methods for "evoking and interpreting imagery" (p. 6), which included techniques to facilitate imagery training, diagnosis, associative imagery, six specific techniques to direct the course of images, and psychoanalysis.

Schoettle (1980) successfully utilized "Guided Imagery" with an 11-year-old anorectic boy who had not responded to several therapies. However, he pointed out drawbacks he had encountered in using this technique with children. He found that middle-aged children tended to open their eyes and initiate unrelated conversation, a problem that might be partially solved by shorter sessions. In addition, some children as old as 8 years were too afraid of their menacing imagery to carry on, presumably because they confused their fantasy with reality. This point has been indirectly made by several authors mentioned previously and suggests that such procedures be used very cautiously and gradually with children in order to avoid sensitization. One last drawback Schoettle found was the tendency in young children to describe movie plots rather than those suggested by the therapist.

Guided imagery was also used with children in conjunction with group process (Scheidler, 1972). The author hypothesized that symbolic revelation, via imagery description, facilitated consequent interpersonal sharing. The contraindications of guided imagery with children reported by Schoettle (1980) would seem to be partially compensated for by two alternative techniques, "fantasy enactment" and "story making." "Fantasy enactment" requires that the child literally act out either *his or her own* fantasy, as reported by MacDonald and Allan (1975) in a case study with an autistic child, or a fantasy suggested by the therapist (Fino, 1979). This technique would be particularly effective with younger children, who seemingly have difficulty in manipulating images and in remaining still and attending for long periods.

"Story making" procedures with children are more frequently reported in the literature and are often used in conjunction with drawings. Gardner (1971) is largely responsible for publicizing the use of stories in treating children. His "Mutual-Story-Telling" technique is described to the child as "Make-up-a-story-television," with rules that their story must be original, rather than about movies seen or real events and it must have a beginning, middle, and end. After the child tells his or her story, the therapist makes up a story with the same characters and general plot but modifies the character's behaviors toward more appropriate resolutions.

Although Gardner's use of this technique is grounded in psychoanalytic theory, his case descriptions occasionally rely on behavioral terminology, such as token reinforcement and desensitization. In fact, the efficacy of this technique could easily be attributed to such behavioral and cognitive-behavioral concepts as desensitization and cognitive restructuring while tearing down irrational thoughts rather than to the resolution of Oedipal or other unconscious conflicts or drives. For that matter, all of the fantasy techniques described might be just as effective without interpretations and inferences about psychosexual processes.

A few other interesting uses of stories in pediatric treatment have been reported. Robertson and Barford (1970), for example, described a case study where stories were written for a respirator dependent boy. The boy's fantasy hero was used as the pretend provider of real gifts that served as rewards for time off the respirator. Porter (1975) introduced another modification of the storytelling technique in his treatment of childhood insomnia. In this method only the parents are interviewed, and the child's interests and fantasy topics are ascertained, as well as his or her sleep patterns and any fears or traumatic events relating to sleep. The therapist uses this material to develop a story in which the child helps some other person, animal, or object to sleep. The story is tape recorded and sent home to be played as a bedtime story when the child first goes to bed, and again one hour after sleep onset. According to Porter, this technique lends a sense of control to the child and avoids the self-perception that he or she is a patient with a problem.

In one other case, the therapist enlisted the aid of an artist to facilitate the therapeutic process with a noncommunicative child (Remotigue-Ano, 1980). The artist met with the child prior to each therapy session and apparently illustrated the child's fantasy characters and stories. This method reportedly improved the child's self-concept and her ability to communicate with others.

Several of the above authors found that adolescents were less appropriate candidates for these treatments than children and generally credited their reluctance to embarrassment. Perhaps instructions could be modified so that the procedures are relabeled in such a way as to render them more palatable to adolescents. However, it is apparent that further research needs to be carried out in order to clarify the teenager's presumed difficulties with imagery and fantasy.

Virtually all of these loosely defined imagery techniques were case studies, and the true degree of their efficacy can only be speculated. Further, little is known about their applicability with adolescents. Clearly, the utility of these techniques would be greatly enhanced by more structured guidelines, operationally defined terminology, and investigation of age effects.

Imagery-Based Behavior Therapies

Imagery-based behavior therapies have been increasing at a rapid rate, and several excellent sources are available that describe these procedures as well as empirical validations (e.g., Rimm & Masters, 1979; Walker et al., 1981; Keat, 1979). Most of the literature to date has strongly emphasized applications to adults. In fact, many investigators have applied these techniques to children with very little modification from their original design. We will not discuss any of the operant strategies covered in chapter 40 of this book although it is interesting to consider the degree to which some of these may be mediated by imagery. For example, a child who has been reinforced repeatedly with candy (or whatever) for making appropriate verbalizations may actually be getting indirect training in the formation of positive images. The previously noted literature by Mischel and his colleagues would also suggest that operant strategies might tend to work less effectively with some problems if they evoked strong, concrete images of the actual reward in a young child. Finally, we have already discussed the possibility that strategies, presumably based only on the manipulation of covert verbalizations, may also involve unintended changes in imagery.

We will briefly note some of the imagery-based behavior therapies as they have been applied to children at this time. Clearly, systematic desensitization and several similar techniques have gained widespread acceptance and utilization in clinical practice as anxiety and fear-reducing strategies. Although systematic desensitization probably has more tests of its efficacy with children than most other strategies, Firestone, Waters, and Goodman (1978), as well as Graziano, DeGiovanni, and Garcia (1979), concluded in reviews that there has not been anything even approximating an adequate examination of the procedure with children, especially in the area of clinically significant problems. In fact, Firestone et al. (1978) found only three controlled studies of systematic desensitization with clinical populations. All of these investigations used additional therapeutic strategies such as reinforcement schedules, assertiveness training, and breathing strategies, thus rendering the specific contribution made by systematic desensitization indeterminable. In addition, they found that most investigations used the theoretically related technique of modeling with younger children aged approximately 4–7. No rationale for this procedural variation has been presented to date although Firestone et al. suggest it may be due to the immaturity of the subjects who presumably might have greater difficulty manipulating and using imagery.

This question would appear to be a particularly interesting and important one for future research. Modeling procedures are certainly more elaborate and difficult to arrange, which suggests that systematic desensitization type procedures would be preferable *if younger children can use them.* The evidence supports the idea that 4- and 5-year-olds can use imagery, but whether they can manipulate and use it in the ways required for systematic desensitization is an unanswered question. The previously noted intensity of children's affective responses to imagery at younger ages, coupled with possibly uncontrolled elaborations and deviations of the presented images could lead to substantial differences in applying the technique to children. Some of the specific children's problem areas that systematic desensitization has been used for include: asthma (Moore, N., 1965) and a wide variety of phobias (e.g. Obler & Terwilliger, 1970; Miller et al., 1972; Hampe et al., 1973). Most of the effective outcomes have been with older children, and methodological problems have been substantial (Firestone et al., 1978). By contrast, modeling has been found to be the most consistently effective strategy for reducing children's fears and has been evaluated with relatively sound research (Graziano et al., 1979).

Lazarus and Abramovitz (1962) developed the technique of "emotive imagery," which is an especially interesting variation of systematic desensitization originally intended specifically for use with children. The technique was developed due to difficulties in training some children in the use of relaxation, which was originally presumed to serve as an anxiety-inhibiting response to the standard desensitization procedure. As a solution to this difficulty, Lazarus attempted to use so-called "emotive" images as the anxiety-inhibiting response. Essentially, this type of imagery is designed to "arouse feelings of self-assertion, pride, affection, mirth and similar anxiety-inhibiting responses" (Lazarus & Abramovitz, 1962, p. 191). Essentially, the following steps were outlined for the basic imagery technique: (1) develop a graduated hierarchy of the patient's fears, starting with the least fearful situation to the most fearful; (2) ascertain the child's hero image such as Batman, Superman, etc.; (3) have the child imagine a series of credible events within

which is woven a story about his or her favorite hero; (4) carefully arouse the child's affective reactions with the story; and (5) when the positive emotions have been aroused, the therapist introduces the lowest rated item from the hierarchy as a part of the ongoing narrative. The child is also instructed to raise a finger if he or she feels afraid, at which time the therapist removes the feared item from the narrative and reestablishes the child's anxiety-inhibiting emotions. The procedure is repeated until the entire hierarchy has been covered without distress, just as in typical systematic desensitization (Lazarus & Abramovitz, 1962).

In this initial article, Lazarus reported that the procedure was successful in seven out of nine phobic children, aged 7–14 years, *in a mean of only 3.3 sessions.* One of the failures was a child who was highly disturbed in other ways and refused to cooperate, while the other failure had a history of encephalitis and was unable to concentrate on the images. Of the seven successful patients, four had undergone unsuccessful treatment previously, and informal follow-up contacts indicated no symptom substitutions, no remissions, and some cases of positive generalization.

Since this initial report, Lazarus (1977) has claimed to have treated dozens of children with the technique with no negative side effects and no problems with children failing to differentiate fantasy from reality. Other investigators have also advocated the use of emotive imagery with children (e.g., Ayer, 1973; Keat, 1972, 1979). Incredibly, we have been unable to find any controlled outcome studies designed to test the efficacy of the procedure with children in almost 20 years since its initial introduction! Reports have been limited to case studies and have often included a number of procedural variations as well as other concomitantly administered treatments.

Clearly, this treatment appears to have tremendous potential for the amelioration of children's phobias. As described by Lazarus (1977), we speculate that the success of the strategy would largely depend upon the creativity and detail included in the scene descriptions. For example, note the following portion of a scene utilized by Lazarus (1977) for a problem of school phobia:

Imagine that Batman and Robin have asked you to assist them in catching a criminal. They lend you a special wrist radio so that they can contact you whenever necessary. Nobody must know the secret, that you are actually helping Batman and Robin to solve a crime right in your own school. Batman says to you 'Peter, I have placed a secret message in your school locker. When you get to school tomorrow morning, go to your locker as soon as possible and read the message. Then destroy it! Of course you don't want to tell Batman and Robin about your fears, so you go to school the next morning and head straight for your locker. Picture yourself going to school. As you ride toward the school in the bus, you are wondering what the message will say. You get into the school yard, get out of the bus, and you walk slowly to your locker. You don't want to rush there because you don't want to make anyone suspicious. (p. 101)

The effectiveness of the treatment may also rely upon the ability of the narratives to elicit what Meichenbaum and Butler (1979) have called a different set of "current concerns." Thus, with emotive imagery, a child might have current concerns of a heroic nature rather than have concerns of being overwhelmed by a mean teacher.

This same notion has struck the current authors and our colleagues in our clinical work with children undergoing repeated painful medical treatments for burn injuries and cancer. It has appeared clear to us that children who cope poorly are dominated by concerns of obtaining nurturance, sympathy, and possibly avoidance while children who cope well have concerns such as being "a big boy or girl." We have also found a sharp developmental change with children age 6 and above being treated for cancer tending to cope much better than younger children, as measured on a Behavioral Observation Scale for anxiety and fear (Jay, Ozolins, & Elliott, study in progress). We are now in the process of attempting to teach the poor copers with a treatment that heavily emphasizes the elicitation of a new set of current concerns through imagery transformations of context, a strategy highly related

to emotive imagery but without systematic hierarchies, and it occurs in vivo. For example, burned children are taught to imagine situations such as the hydrotherapy tank as a beach with waves lapping over them or to imagine that they are an agent of Superman or some other favored hero during their painful treatments. Initial data have been highly encouraging, but there is a profound need for more controlled tests of the efficacy of these types of procedures.

Kelley (1976) has noted other variants of the traditional desensitization strategies for use with children. These deviations have included using pictures, drawings, and play instead of imagery, as well as other anxiety-inhibiting responses such as eating. Positive reinforcement of various types have also been included rather frequently. Virtually nothing is known about the relative efficacy of these variants.

Relaxation training is often (though, as noted, not always) a part of systematic desensitization and has received considerable attention as a potential treatment for children in and of itself (e.g., MacDonald, 1975; Matthews, 1979; Walton, 1979; Braud, 1975; Walker et al., 1981). The basic procedures of teaching muscle relaxation, as well as numerous variations, have been reviewed in detail by Walker, who also noted promising applications to children, such as for hyperactivity (Lupin, Braud, & Duer, 1974) and the improvement of handwriting (Carter & Synolds, 1974) among others. Of interest here is the possibility that imagery may be used to increase the ability of young children to obtain effective levels of relaxation as has been suggested by Koeppen (1974). For example, rather than simply telling a child to tense his or her stomach muscles, an image of an elephant about ready to step on their stomachs could be added. We have found this approach to be quite effective in some cases.

The senior author has developed another imagery technique for inducing relaxation and controlled breathing in young children. In this strategy, the children are taught to inhale by "pumping their bodies up like a tire" and then to exhale very slowly by imagining that their body ("tire") has been punctured and is slowly relaxing and "deflating." They are further taught to make a "hissing" sound while exhaling in order to add realism to the image and facilitate control over the exhalation rate. Unfortunately, we are once again beset with a highly promising and intriguing, albeit untested, strategy.

Another type of imagery-based behavior therapy that has been applied to children involves the use of aversive images as in the related strategies of implosive therapy and flooding. Even a cursory review of the literature in this area suggests that considerable inconsistencies exist in the terminology used to refer to these treatments (for that matter, the same can be said of the other strategies reviewed above). A tentative definition of flooding, as suggested by Marshall, Gauthier, and Gordon (1979) is as follows: "Flooding is a generic term for procedures that have as their goal the extinction of classes of maladaptive responses to aversive stimuli by exposure to high-intensity subsets of these aversive stimuli for prolonged periods in the absence of actual physically injurious consequences" (p. 215). The stimuli may be presented imaginally or in vivo. Implosive therapy is quite similar although numerous differences have been described at various times. Of prime importance appears to be the inclusion, within implosion, of a maximization of anxiety through the use of imagined physically injurious or adverse consequences as well as psychodynamic cues.

It is quite important to note, however, that the use of these terms in the literature at times differs radically from these definitions. For example, Handler (1972) described the use of so-called implosive therapy to eliminate nightmares in children. However, the technique described would appear to be much more akin to covert assertion than implosion since no adverse consequences, psychodynamic cues, or heightening of anxiety were included. In this application, Handler had the child, through imagery, confront the monster that had been intruding into his dreams. In a series of scenes, after the child had formed an image of the monster, he was taught to "chase the monster away," both within his images as well as through overt yelling and pounding. A considerable variation of the standard implosive therapy technique was also reported by Hersen (1968) in the successful treatment of a 12-year-old male with a compulsive and phobic disorder. In this case, a hierarchy was employed, apparently in order to insure that the anxiety elicited by the scenes was controlled rather than risk a sensitization effect. Essentially, the child was instructed to visualize scenes of not performing ritualistic behaviors. These scenes engendered anxiety on their own but were not elaborated to maximize the child's anxiety as would be the case with standard implosive therapy.

One of the few relatively standard applications of implosive therapy with children was presented by Smith and Sharpe (1970) in the successful treatment of a 13-year-old school phobic child. The scenes in this application were presented in a flowing sequence rather than on a hierarchical basis. In addition, anxiety was maximized by having the boy imagine unpleasant outcomes, such as the entire student body laughing at him and teachers jeering him. A total of six daily sessions resulted in greatly reduced anxiety in school and improved attendance.

Another use of aversive imagery involves its use as a means of reducing the frequency of target behaviors presumably through either an operant or a classical conditioning process. Davison (1976), for example, discussed the use of and imagined aversive contingency to control an 11.5-year-old boy's disobedience. The boy was simply instructed to use the imagined aversive consequence of his father's anger in situations where he might normally be disobedient. Furthermore, Kolvin (1967) presented procedures for using aversive imagery to eliminate a fetish in a 14-year-old male and a petrol addiction in a 15-year-old male. The aversive stimulus in both of these cases consisted of imagined scenes of falling from a great height. Treatment successfully controlled the habits within ten hours of treatment sessions spread over two to three weeks.

As usual, these accounts are exclusively of a case study nature and are also fewer in number than the desensitization and relaxation strategies. Recent reviews of flooding and implosion (Marshall, Gauthier, & Gordon, 1979) have concluded that maximizing anxiety does not appear to be an essential aspect of treatment and that flooding without implosive content appears at least as effective as desensitization procedures. Rimm and Masters (1979) have noted that sensitization effects from imagined scenes with aversive content are rather rare, although, as Elliott and Denny (1975) found, they can occur. However, these conclusions were based almost exclusively on application to adults.

We would urge extreme caution in extrapolating these conclusions to applications with children, and especially to the preadolescent. We have already noted the probability that young children experience more intense affect in response to imagery. This possibility, combined with the fact that children might be expected to deviate or escape from the therapist's described scenes more readily than adults, would suggest that the risk of sensitization or maladaptive increases in anxiety responses could be increased with young children. This may account for the relative paucity of such applications to young children in the literature.

A number of other imagery-based behavior therapy techniques either have been, or theoretically could be, applied to children. At best, these are isolated case reports and do not seem to merit review here. However, an exciting array of strategies, such as covert assertion, covert positive reinforcement, cognitive rehearsal, cognitive modeling, stress innoculation, and coping imagery, among others reviewed by Rimm and Masters (1979), only await systematic application and evaluation with children.

CONCLUSIONS

Imagery and imagination appear to be potentially rich tools for the treatment of a variety of children's problems. In addition, imagery-based strategies may be useful for the purposes of rapport building and diagnosis.

Numerous caveats are in order, however. Literature to date has been replete with enthusiastic endorsements of imagery- and imagination-based therapies but amazingly deficient in empirical validations. Just because a technique has been empirically supported in use with adults, it cannot be assumed that equivalent efficacy will be found in use with children. Additionally, "children" do not represent a homogeneous group. Important differences in terms of age, sex, and development level will have to be considered. It will also be important for future research to include assessments of the precise content of what children actually imagine in response to instructions as opposed to what is in the instructions themselves.

Finally, significant issues in the areas of conceptualization, measurement, and assessment remain. These will not be easily resolved but could greatly facilitate the implementation of sophisticated treatment outcome studies that have been lacking to date.

REFERENCES

Ambrose, G. *Hypnotherapy with children* (2nd ed.). London: Staples, 1961.

Ambrose, G. Hypnosis in the treatment of children. *American Journal of Clinical Hypnosis,* 1968, **11**(1), 1–5.

Ames, C.B., & Learned, J. Imagery companions and related phenomena. *Journal of Genetic Psychology,* 1946, **69**, 147–167.

Anderson, J.R. Arguments concerning representation for mental imagery. *Psychological Review,* 1978, **85**, 249–277.

Anderson, J.R. Further arguments concerning representations for mental imagery: A response to Hayes, Roth, & Pylyshyn. *Psychological Review,* 1979, **86**(4), 395–406.

Anderson, M.P. Imaginal processes: Therapeutic applications and theoretical models. M.J. Mahoney (Ed.), *Psychotherapy process: Current issues and future directions.* New York: Plenum, 1980.

Anderson, M.P. *Assessment of imaginal processes: Approaches and issues.* Unpublished manuscript. Houston Cardiovascular Rehabilitation Center, Houston, 1981.

Axline, V. *Play therapy: The inner dynamics of childhood.* Boston: Houghton Mifflin, 1947.

Axline, V. Some observations on play therapy. *Journal of Consulting Psychology,* 1948, **12,** 209–216.

Ayer, W.A. Use of imagery in needle phobic children. *Journal of Dentistry for Children,* March-April 1973, 41–43.

Bairdain, E.F. Psychological characteristics of adolescents who have had imaginary companions. *Dissertations Abstracts International,* 1959, **29,** 747.

Baldwin, A.L. *Theories of child development.* New York: Wiley, 1968.

Beck, A.T. Role of fantasies in psychotherapy and psychology. *The Journal of Nervous and Mental Disease,* 1970, **150,** 3–17.

Beck, A.T., Rush, A.J., Shaw, B.F., & Emery, G. *Cognitive therapy of depression.* New York: Guilford, 1979.

Braud, L.W. The effects of EMG biofeedback and progressive relaxation upon hyperactivity and its behavioral concomitants. *Dissertaion Abstracts International,* 1975, **36**(1-B), 433, 75–10,584.

Brown, B. The use of induced imagery in psychotherapy. *Psychotherapy: Theory, Research and Practice,* 1969, **6**(2), 120–121.

Bruner, J. Image and symbol in development of magnitude and order. In J.F. Rosenblitz & W. Allinsmith (Eds.), *The causes of behavior: Readings in child development and educational psychology.* Boston: Allyn & Bacon, 1969.

Carlin, A.S., & Armstrong, H.E. Rewarding social responsibility in disturbed children: A group play technique. *Psychotherapy: Theory, Research and Practice,* 1968, **5,** 169–174.

Carter, J.L., & Synolds, D. Effects of relaxation training upon handwriting quality. *Journal of Learning Disabilities,* 1974, **7,** 53–55.

Cautela, J. Covert sensitization. *Psychological Reports,* 1967, **20,** 459–468.

Cautela, J. The present status of covert modeling. *Journal of Behavior Therapy and Experimental Psychiatry,* 1976, **6,** 323–326.

Cautela, J., & Baron, M.G. Covert conditioning: A theoretical analysis. *Behavior Modification,* 1977, **1,** 351–368.

Chethik, M., & Fast, I. A function of fantasy in the borderline child. *American Journal of Orthopsychiatry,* 1970, **40**(5), 756–765.

Clement, P.W., & Milne, D.C. Group play therapy and tangible reinforcers used to modify the behavior of eight-year-old boys. *Behavior Research and Therapy,* 1967, **5,** 301–312.

Cooper, L., & London, P. The development of hypnotic susceptibility. *Child Development,* 1971, **42,** 487–503.

Cox, P.M. Sociometric standards and individual adjustment before and after play therapy. *The Journal of Abnormal and Social Psychology,* 1953, **48,** 354–356.

Dallas, D. Psychology in action: Savagery, show and tell. *American Psychologist,* 1978, **33**(4), 388–390.

Davison, G.C. Self-control through "imaginal aversive contigency" and "onedownmanship": Enabling the powerless to accommodate unreasonableness. In J.D. Krumboltz & C.E. Thorensen (Eds.), *Behavioral counseling: Cases and techniques.* New York: Holt, Rinehart & Winston, 1976.

Dorfman, E. Personality outcomes of client-centered child therapy. *Psychological Monographs: General and Applied,* 1958, **72,** (3, Whole No. 456).

Doubros, S.G., & Daniels, G.I. An experimental approach to the reduction of overactive behavior. *Behavior Research and Therapy,* 1966, **4,** 251–258.

Elliott, C.H., & Denney, D.R. Weight control through covert sensitization and false feedback. *Journal of Consulting and Clinical Psychology,* 1975. **43,** 842–850.

Euse, F., & Haney, J. Image clarity, controllability, and emotional intensity: Correlations with introversion, neuroticisms and anxiety. *Perceptual and Motor Skills,* 1975, **40,** 443–447.

Fino, J. Guided imagery and movement as a means to help disturbed children draw together. *American Journal of Art Therapy,* 1979, **18,** 61–62.

Firestone, P., Waters, B.C.H., & Goodman, J.T. Desensitization in children and adolescents: A review. *Journal of Clinical Child Psychology,* 1978 **7**(2), 142–148.

Fleming, L. & Snyder, W.V. Social and personal changes following nondirective group play therapy. *American Journal of Orthopsychiatry,* 1947, **17,** 101–116.

Foreyt, J.P., & Hagen, R.L. Covert sensitization: Conditioning or suggestion? *Journal of Abnormal Psychology,* 1973, **82**(1), 17–23.

Friedrich, L., & Stein, A. Prosocial television and young children: The effects of verbal labeling and role playing on learning behavior. *Child Development,* 1975, **46**, 27–38.

Gardner, G.G. *Therapeutic communication with children-mutual story telling techniques.* New York: Aronson, 1971.

Gardner, G.G. Hypnosis with children. *The International Journal of Clinical and Experimental Hypnosis,* 1974, **22**, 20–38.

Gardner, G.G., & Tarnow, J.D. Adjunctive hypnotherapy with an autistic boy. *The American Journal of Clinical Hypnosis,* 1980, **22**(3), 173–179.

Goldfried, M. Systematic desensitization as training in self-control. *Journal of Consulting and Clinical Psychology,* 1971, **37**. 228–234.

Graziano, A.M., DeGiovanni, I.S., & Garcia, K.A. Behavioral treatment of children's fears: A review. *Psychological Bulletin,* 1979, **86**(9), 804–830.

Guy, M.E., & McCarter, R.E. A scale to measure emotive imagery. *Perceptual and Motor Skills,* 1978, **46**, 1267–1274.

Hampe, E., Noble, H., Miller, C., & Barrett, C.L. Phobic children one and two years posttreatment. *Journal of Abnormal Psychology,* 1973, **83**, 446–453.

Handler, L. The amelioration of nightmares in children. *Psychotherapy: Theory, Research and Practice,* 1972, **9**, 54–56.

Hayes, S.C. Single case experimental design and empirical practice. *Journal of Consulting and Clinical Psychology,* 1981, **49**(2), 193–211.

Hersen, M. Treatment of a compulsive and phobic disorder through a total behavior therapy program: A case study. *Psychotherapy: Theory, Research and Practice,* 1968, **5**(4), 220–225.

Holt, R. Imagery: The return of the ostracized. *American Psychologist,* 1964, **19**, 254–264.

Horowitz, M. Visual thought images in psychotherapy. *American Journal of Psychotherapy,* 1968, **22**, 55–59.

Illovsky, J., & Freeman, N. Group suggestion in learning disabilities of primary grade children: A feasibility study. *The International Journal of Clinical and Experimental Hypnosis,* 1976, **24**(2), 87–97.

Jay, S.M., Ozolins, M., & Elliott, C.H. *Anxiety and behavioral stress of pediatric cancer patients and their parents concerning bone marrow aspiration procedures.* Study in progress.

Jellinik, A. Spontaneous imagery and its psychodiagnostic uses. *Revue de Psychologie Appliqué,* 1953, **3**, 320–325.

Jersild, A.T., Markey, F.V., & Jersild, C.L. Children's fears, dreams, wishes, daydreams, likes, dislikes, pleasant and unpleasant memories. *Child Development Monograph,* No. 12, New York: Bureau of Publications, Teachers College, Columbia University, 1933.

Kaffman, M. Hypnosis as an adjunct to psychotherapy in child psychiatry. *Archives of General Psychiatry,* 1968, **18**, 725–738.

Kanfer, F.H., Karoly, P., & Newman, A. Reduction of children's fears of the dark by competence-related and situational threat-related verbal cues. *Journal of Consulting and Clinical Psychology,* 1975, **43**, 251–258.

Kazdin, A. Assessment of imagery during covert modeling of assertive behavior. *Journal of Behavior Therapy and Experimental Psychiatry,* 1976, **7**, 213–219.

Kazdin, A. Imagery and self efficacy in the covert modeling treatment of unassertive behavior. *Journal of Consulting and Clinical Psychology,* 1979, **47**, 725–733.

Keane, W.M., & Pillemer, E.M.G. *Hypnosis with pediatric cancer patients: Giving control in an uncontrolled situation.* Paper presented at the annual meeting of the American Psychological Association, Montreal, September, 1980.

Keat, D.B. Broad spectrum behavior therapy with children: A case presentation. *Behavior Therapy,* 1972, **3**, 454–459.

Keat, D.B. *Multimodal therapy with children.* New York: Pergamon, 1979.

Kelley, C.K. Play desensitization of fear of darkness in preschool children. *Behavior Research and Therapy,* 1976, **14**, 79–81.

Koeppen, A.S. Relaxation training for children. *Elementary School Guidance and Counseling,* 1974, **2**, 14–21.

Kolvin, I. Case histories and shorter communications: Aversive imagery treatment in adolescents. *Behavior Research and Therapy,* 1967, **5**, 245–258.

Kosslyn, S. Can imagery be distinguished from other forms of internal representation? Evidence from studies of information retrieval time. *Memory and Cognition,* 1976, **4,** 291–297.

Kroger, W.S. *Clinical experimental hypnosis in medicine, dentistry and psychology.* Philadelphia: Lippincott, 1963.

Lang, P. Imagery in therapy: An information processing analysis of fear modification using an automated desensitization procedure. *Journal of Abnormal Psychology,* 1977, **76,** 220–234.

Lazarus, A.A. *Multimodal behavior therapy.* New York: Springer, 1976.

Lazarus, A.A. *In the mind's eye.* New York: Rawson, 1977.

Lazarus, A.A., & Abramovitz, A. The use of "emotive imagery" in the treatment of children's phobias. *Journal of Mental Science,* 1962, **108,** 191–195.

Leuner, H. Guided affective imagery (GAI). *American Journal of Psychotherapy,* 1969, **23,** 4–22.

Levin, J.R. What have we learned about minimizing what children learn? In J.R. Levin & V.L. Allen (Eds.), *Cognitive learning in children: Theories and strategies.* New York, Academic Press, 1976.

Levin, J.R., McCabe, A.E., & Bender, B.G. *Imagery induction in the preimagery child.* Technical Report No. 292. Wisconsin Research and Development Center for Cognitive Learning, University of Wisconsin, 1974.

London, P. *The children's hypnotic susceptibility scale.* Palo Alto, Calif.: Consulting Psychologists Press, 1963.

London, P., & Cooper, L.M. Norms of hypnotic susceptibility in children. *Developmental Psychology,* 1969, **1,** 113–124.

Lupin, M., Braud, W.G., & Duer, W.F. *Effects of relaxation upon hyperactivity using relaxation tapes for children and parents.* Presented at the 11th Annual International Convention for Learning Disabilities, Houston, February, 1974.

MacDonald, M.L. Multiple impact behavior therapy in a child's dog phobia. *Journal of Behavior Therapy and Experimental Psychiatry,* 1975, **6,** 317–322.

MacDonald, R.T., & Allen, J.A.B. The use of fantasy enactment in the treatment of an emerging autistic child. *Journal of Analytic Psychology,* 1975, **20,** 57–68.

Manosevitz, M., Prentice, N.M., & Wilson, F. Individual and family correlates of imaginary companions in preschool children. *Developmental Psychology,* 1973, **8,** 72–79.

Manosevitz, M., Fling, S., & Prentice, N.M. Imaginary companions in young children: Relationships with intelligence, creativity, and waiting ability. *Journal of Child Psychology and Psychiatry,* 1977, **18,** 73–78.

Marshall, W.L., Gauthier, J., & Gordon, A. The current status of flooding therapy. In M. Hersen, R.M. Eisler, & P.M. Miller (Eds.), *Progress in behavior modification.* New York: Academic Press, 1979.

Mathis, J., Fairchild, L., & Cannon, T. Psychodrama and sociodrama in primary and secondary education. *Psychology in the Schools,* 1980, **17**(1), 96–101.

Matsumato, Y. The recognition of feeble-minded boys on their delinquent behaviors expressed in psychodrama. *Acta Criminologiae et Medicinae Legalis Japonica* (Tokyo), 1978.

Matthews, L.H. *Intervention techniques with preschoolers in a medical setting.* In E.M. Schwartz (chair), *Innovative techniques in clinical child psychology.* Symposium presented at American Psychological Association convention, New York, 1979.

McKellar, P. The investigation of mental images. *Penguin Science Survey* (Biological Sciences), 1965.

Meichenbaum, D., & Butler, L. Cognitive ethology: Assessing the streams of cognition and emotion. In K. Blankstein, P. Pliner, & J. Polivy (Eds.), *Advances in the study of communication and affect. Assessment and modification of emotional behavior.* New York: Plenum, 1979.

Midcentury White House Conference on Children and Youth. A healthy personality for every child. 1951. Reprinted in J.F. Rosenblitz & W. Allinsmith (Eds.), *The causes of behavior.* Boston: Allyn & Bacon, 1969.

Miller, L.C., Barrett, L., Hampe, E., & Noble, H. Comparison of reciprocal inhibition, psychotherapy and waiting list control of phobic children. *Journal of Abnormal Psychology,* 1972, **79,** 269–279.

Mischel, W., & Ebbesin, E.B. Attention in delay of gratification. *Journal of Personality and Social Psychology,* 1970, **16,** 329–337.

Mischel, W., Ebbesin, E.B., & Zeiss, A. Cognitive and attentional mechanisms in delay of gratification. *Journal of Personality and Social Psychology,* 1972, **21,** 204–218.

Mischel, W., & Moore, B. Effects of attention and symbolically presented rewards on self-control. *Journal of Personality and Social Psychology.* 1973, **28**(2), 172–179.

Moore, B., Mischel, W., & Zeiss, A. Comparative effects of the reward stimulus and its cognitive representation in voluntary delay. *Journal of Personality and Social Psychology,* 1976, **34,** 419–424.

Moore, N. Behavior therapy in bronchial asthma: A controlled study. *Journal of Psychosomatic Research,* 1965, **9,** 257–276.

Moreno, J.L. *Psychodrama.* (Vol. 6). New York: Beacon, 1972.

Moreno, J.L. *Psychodrama.* (Vol. 7). New York: Beacon, 1975.

Morgan, A., & Hilgard, E. Age differences in susceptibility to hypnosis. *International Journal of Clinical and Experimental Hypnosis,* 1973, **21,** 78–85.

Moustakas, C.E., & Schlalock, H.D. An analysis of therapist child interaction in play therapy. *Child Development,* 1955, **26**(2), 143–157.

Neisser, U. Visual imagery as process and as experience. In J. Antrobus (Eds.), *Cognitive and affect.* Boston: Little, Brown, 1970.

Obler, M., & Terwilliger, R.F. Pilot study on the effectiveness of systematic desensitization with neurologically impaired children with phobic disorders. *Journal of Consulting and Clinical Psychology,* 1970, **34,** 314–318.

Paivio, A. *Imagery and verbal processes.* New York: Holt, Rinehart, & Winston, 1971.

Piaget, J., & Inhelder, B. *Mental imagery in the child.* New York: Basic Books, 1971.

Porter, J. Guided fantasy as a treatment for childhood insomnia. *Australian and New Zealand Journal of Psychiatry,* 1975, **9,** 169.

Pylyshyn, Z. What the mind's eye tells the mind's brain: A critique of mental imagery. *Psychological Bulletin,* 1973, **80,** 1–22.

Remotigue-Ano, N. The hidden agenda of story-making therapy. *American Journal of Psychotherapy,* 1980, **34,** 261–268.

Richardson, A. Verbalizer-visualizer: A cognitive style dimension. *Journal of Mental Imagery,* 1977, **1,** 109–126.

Rimm, D.C., & Masters, J.C. (Eds.). *Behavior therapy.* New York: Academic Press, 1979.

Robertson, M., & Barford, F. Story-making psychotherapy with a chronically ill child. *Psycho-*

therapy: Theory, Research, and Practice, 1970, **7,** 104–107.

Rogers, D. *Child psychology* (2nd ed.). Monterey, California: Brooks/Cole, 1977.

Rose, S. A general practitioner approach to the asthmatic patient. *American Journal of Clinical Hypnosis,* 1967, **10,** 30–32.

Schaefer, C.E. Imaginary companions and creative adolescents. *Developmental Psychology,* 1969, **8,** 72–79.

Schaefer, C.E., & Millman, H.L. *Therapies for children.* San Francisco: Jossey-Bass, 1978.

Scheidler, T. Use of fantasy as a therapeutic agent in latency age groups. *Psychotherapy: Theory, Research, and Practice,* 1972, **9,** 299–302.

Schoettle, U. Guided imagery-A tool in child psychotherapy. *American Journal of Psychotherapy,* 1980, **34,** 220–227.

Seeman, J., Barry, E., & Ellinwood, C. Interpersonal assessment of play therapy outcome. *Psychotherapy: Theory, Research and Practice,* 1964, **1,** 64–66.

Shearon, E. Psychodrama with children. *Group Psychotherapy, Psychodrama and Sociometry,* 1980, **33,** 142–155.

Singer, J.L. Imagination and waiting ability in young children. *Journal of Personality,* 1961, **29,** 396–413.

Singer, J.L. Theoretical imlications of imagery and fantasy techniques. *Contemporary Psychoanalysis,* 1971, **8,** 82–96.

Singer, J.L. *Imagery and daydreaming methods in psychotherapy and behavior modification.* New York: Academic Press, 1974.

Smith, R.E., & Sharpe, T.M. Treatment of a school phobia with implosive therapy. *Journal of Consulting and Clinical Psychology,* 1970, **35**(2), 239–243.

Spanos, N.P. Goal-directed fantasy and the performance of hypnotic test suggestions. *Psychiatry,* 1971, **34,** 86–96.

Spiegel, H. An eye-roll test for hypnotizability. *American Journal of Clinical Hypnosis,* 1972, **15,** 25–28.

Strosahl, K.D., & Ascough, J.C. Clinical uses of mental imagery: Experimental foundations, theoretical misconceptions, and research issues. *Psychological Bulletin,* 1981, **89**(3), 422–438.

Svendsen, M. Children's imaginary companions. *Archives of Neurological Psychiatry,* 1934, **32,** 985–999.

Tilton, P. Hypnotic treatment of a child with thumbsucking, enuresis, and encopresis. *The American Journal of Clinical Hypnosis,* 1980, **22,** 238–240.

Tower, R.B. Imagery measurement in clinical settings: Matching the method to the question. In E. Klinger (Ed.), *Imagery: Concepts, results, and applications.* New York: Plenum, 1981.

Tower, R.B., & Singer, J.L. The measurement of imagery: How can it be clinically useful? In P.C. Kendall & S. Hollon (Eds.), *Assessment methods for cognitive-behavioral interventions.* New York: Academic Press, 1981.

Tower, R.B., Singer, D.G., Singer, J.L., & Biggs, A. Differential effects of television programming on preschoolers' cognition, imagination, and social play. *American Journal of Orthopsychiatry,* 1979, **49,** 265–281.

Walker, C.E. *The imaginative child interview.* Unpublished document, University of Oklahoma Health Sciences Center, Oklahoma City, Oklahoma, 1977.

Walker, C.E. Behavioral intervention in a pediatric setting. In J. Regis McNamara (Ed.), *Behavioral approaches to medicine: Application and analysis.* New York: Plenum, 1979.

Walker, C.E., Heberg, A., Clement, P.W., & Wright, L. *Clinical procedures for behavior therapy.* Englewood Cliffs, N.J.: Prentice-Hall, 1981.

Wallach, M. Creativity. In P. Mussen (Ed.), *Carmichael's manual of child psychology* (Vol. I). (3rd ed.). New York: Wiley, 1970.

Walton, W.T. The use of relaxation curriculum and biofeedback training in the classroom to reduce inappropriate behaviors of emotionally handicapped children. *Behavioral Disorders: Journal of the Council for Children with Behavioral Disorders,* 1979, **1,** 10–18.

Whitt, K., Dykstra, W., & Taylor, C.A. Children's conceptions of illness and cognitive development. *Clinical Pediatrics,* 1979, **18,** 327–334.

Wilkins, W. Parameters of therapeutic imagery: Directions from case studies. *Psychotherapy: Theory, Research, and Practice,* 1974, **11**(2), 163–171.

Williams, D., & Singh, M. Hypnosis as a facilitating therapeutic adjunct in child psychiatry. *Journal of American Academy of Child Psychiatry,* 1976, **15,** 326–342.

Wolff, P., & Levin, J.R. The role of overt activity in children's imagery production. *Child Development,* 1972, **43,** 537–647.

Wright, L., Truax, C.B., & Mitchell, K.M. Reliability of process ratings of psychotherapy with children. *Journal of Clinical Psychology,* 1972, **28,** 232–234.

Zimbardo, P. *Psychology and life* (10th ed.). Glenview, Ill: Scott Foresman, 1979.

CHAPTER 44

Biofeedback with Children

WILLIAM W. FINLEY

There is an unwritten, and therefore largely untested assumption that children are probably more amenable than adults to biofeedback procedures. The assumption is strengthened by the widely held belief of greater neuronal plasticity of children relative to adults. In addition, there is the recognition that children are subject to most of the same stress-related ills to which adults fall victim. Finally, children seem to have their own special class of stressors centered in the educational system. Hence, there is a strong impetus to make biofeedback available to children, not only to treat stress-related or stress-aggravated problems of childhood but to heighten their level of self-awareness as to their own mind-body integration.

Although there is considerable interest in pediatric biofeedback, an examination of the history of biofeedback development reveals that children have been largely bypassed by emerging biofeedback technology and procedures. Initially, feedback of physiology not normally under volitional control was supplemented by procedures of instrumental conditioning. Later investigators, all of whom were working with adult subjects, found that explicit, physical reinforcement could be eliminated as knowledge of results was sufficiently rewarding to encourage continued responding to the physiology being displayed. Despite the eventual elimination of physical reinforcers, biofeedback, as it evolved in the 1960s retained its roots in operant conditioning since it has generally been realized that the act of learning to self-regulate bodily function is inherently rewarding for most adults. The reinforcing aspect of clinical biofeedback is most apparent in patients who are attempting to acquire mastery over physiology associated with their clinical symptomatology. But what about children? Can we assume they too will respond to long term, abstract goals? Specifically, can we reasonably expect an asthmatic child to understand that if only he or she learns to relax frontal electromyographic (EMG) activity, that over a period of weeks and months this will affect the bronchiole of the lungs and decrease airway resistance? Some exceptional children will comprehend and act upon this understanding. Many others will not but, with considerable supervision from therapists, parents, and teachers, may learn enough to experience therapeutic impact. In recognition of the difficulties inherent in pediatric biofeedback, significant modifications in the biofeedback treatment protocol have been introduced, and a number of pediatric symptoms have been successfully treated. Childhood problems for which therapeutic efficacy of biofeedback have been investigated include asthma, cerebral palsy, epilepsy, headache, hyperkinesis, and associated learning disabilities.

ELECTROPHYSIOLOGIC BEHAVIOR MODIFICATION

Because patient motivation is a serious consideration in biofeedback therapy (Schwartz, 1973), particularly with children, investigation of the effects of incentives on EMG feedback training of children has been urgently needed. A study by Finley et al., (1977) on cerebral-palsied (CP) children demonstrated that instrumental conditioning could be successfully applied to neurologically impaired children who would not be reachable through routine biofeedback procedures. Finley et al., (1981) described the construction and operation of a simple reward system to be used in the biofeedback training of children. Data showing efficacy of the approach was presented. On-line reinforcement was achieved through an automated reward system designed for use with commercially available EMG biofeedback instrumentation. Rewards (toys, tokens, money, candy, etc.) were automatically dispensed from a universal feeder (UF) contingent on tonic and/or phasic EMG reductions. Ten children were assigned to the on-line group and five to the off-line reward group. All children were trained for EMG reductions from combined frontal EMG and forearm flexor EMG recording sites.

An analysis of variance showed a significant group main effect, with the UF-trained on-line reinforcement group achieving lower EMG levels than the off-line non-UF-trained group. However, a definite learning curve (see Figure 44.1) was evident for the off-line reward group, indicating that children can acquire biofeedback skills without special reinforcement equipment. Virtually all of the published biofeedback research on children has been conducted under conditions similar to those seen in the off-line reinforcement group. However, when reinforcements are immediately available, as in the on-line group, learning proceeds more efficiently and rapidly, allowing the child to reach deeper levels of muscle relaxation.

One of the major advantages of Electrophysiologic Behavior Modification (EBM) is that it is essentially a nonverbal treatment procedure. For this reason, it can be successfully applied to infants as well as severely handicapped children who lack receptive language skills. The EBM procedure was recently used with a severely disabled 2-year-old blind CP child who manifested extreme body rigidity to the point that normal respiration was compromised. Since the child was not only young but retarded intellectually, the usual reinforcers such as toys or tokens were without value to the child. Consequently, food rewards were made contingent on brief sup-

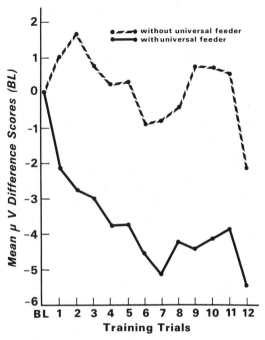

Figure 44.1 Mean microvolt (Average Integral Value) difference scores from baseline and 12 training trials for two groups of cerebral-palsied children. The solid line represents EMG difference scores for those who received rewards from the universal feeder on-line for EMG reductions. The broken line shows EMG reductions for those who trained in a standard biofeedback situation but were given rewards at the end of each 20–30 minute training session. From "A Simple EMG Reward System," by W.W. Finley, M.D. Etherton, D. Dickman, D. Karimian, and R.W. Simpson. In *Biofeedback and Self-Regulation,* 1981. Used by permission of Plenum Publishing Corp. Copyright © by Plenum Publishing Corp., 1981.

pression of audio (click) feedback from combined frontal EMG and forearm EMG sites. Whenever the clicks (which varied in proportion to the muscle tension) slowed and briefly stopped (initially in between brief spasms), the UF was triggered, which served as a cue to the mother to place in her child's mouth a small spoonful of chocolate pudding. Within 30 minutes of training onset, the child was able to keep the clicks (muscle tension) at very reduced levels for sustained periods of time in order to obtain the food reward. When the UF triggered, rewards were not automatically dispensed from the machine; rather, the sound of the machine advancing to the next empty tray served as a discriminative stimulus to the child who responded by tongue thrusting in anticipation of the forthcoming reward. The desired therapeutic impact of general body relaxation was achieved quickly, and the child made a number of gains including improved respiratory function.

When working with children 4–10 years of age, toys, tokens, money, candy, coupons, etc., are employed as reinforcers. The nature of the reward is unimportant. What is important is that the reinforcer is desired by the child. When toys are used as reinforcers, the usual procedure is for the parents to take the child to a toy store and allow the child to purchase whatever is desired with the alloted amount of money, usually around $50.00. The items selected by the child cannot be played with and must remain in the original packaging. Those items too large to fit in the UF are placed in the training room in full view of the child during biofeedback training. Toys that will fit in the trays of the UF are placed there with the least-desired items in the lowest trays, which will be "earned" first. The most-desired toys are placed in the upper trays so that the child will have to perform consistently well in order to reach the desired level in the UF. Interlaced throughout the UF are tokens, worth from one cent to one dollar. These tokens serve as house money to be accumulated and ultimately applied toward the purchase of toys too large to be dispensed from the UF. Also, tokens can be used to purchase a highly desired item within the UF. Tokens can be saved across training sessions. As with toys, the more highly valued tokens are placed toward the upper trays of the UF. Trays can also be stocked with candy or gum or can be left empty. Initially during the first week or two of EBM training, all trays contain a reward. Later, more and more trays are left empty, hence constituting variable-ratio (VR) intermittent reinforcement. A VR intermittent schedule is useful in reducing the likelihood of relapse of the acquired relaxation. In learning-theory terms, relapse is viewed as extinction of the acquired response. Shaping of low EMG levels toward ever-deepening relaxation can also be easily achieved both within and across sessions. Shaping is achieved (1) by requiring deeper levels of EMG relaxation in order to

obtain a reward, and (2) by requiring the child to sustain for longer periods of time a reduced level of EMG activity in order to earn a reward.

With children 10 years of age or older, use of the UF becomes optional as the child can be treated more like an adult. Even so, coupons for privileges are often used as rewards, as are also candy and even cash.

The primary disadvantage of the EBM approach is the cost of stocking the instrument with toys and other rewards for which the child is willing to work. However, in cases involving serious disability, financial concerns are small in comparison to other (often overwhelming) costs of care for these children.

Overtraining is routinely employed to promote generalization of the relaxation beyond the confines of the clinic. In addition, children are encouraged to practice their newly acquired biofeedback skills both at home and at school without relying on biofeedback instrumentation. Relaxation test sessions without feedback are scheduled once every two or three weeks to assess ability to relax. Training usually is conducted three times a week, 30-minute sessions, over 6–8 weeks. Children who are hyperactive or have short attention spans are initially given shorter training sessions but are shaped across sessions to train for the full 30 minutes.

Assessment of therapeutic impact depends on the nature of the problem for which the child was referred (i.e., asthma, cerebral palsy, epilepsy, hyperkinesis, etc.). Usually a battery of assessment procedures are administered prior to onset of biofeedback training. Parents and/or teachers then keep daily and weekly records of the relevant behaviors during the course of treatment. Finally, a post-treatment assessment battery is administered towards the end of treatment. Biofeedback training is not abruptly terminated; rather the patient is weaned off of feedback, cutting back from three sessions per week to two, then one, and finally once a month. If no relapse is evident, treatment is then terminated after one or two months at one session per month. Booster sessions are recommended once or twice a year, or as needed.

TREATMENT APPLICATIONS

Beyond the more obvious problems of making biofeedback suitable for children, it is important to note that, as yet, efficacy of biofeedback treatment for adult patients remains an incompletely resolved issue. Experimental problems notwithstanding, the use of clinical biofeedback has grown enormously over the past decade. Although only 11 percent of the published research on biofeedback has been based on children, a survey of the membership directory of the Biofeedback Society of America, 1980, shows that of 852 biofeedback providers, 222 (26 percent) offer clinical biofeedback to children in at least one diagnostic category.

Asthma

Childhood asthma is one of the most widespread and potentially devastating disorders encountered by the pediatric medical community. Estimates of the prevalence of childhood asthma range as high as 23 percent. The somatic component of the disorder is an inherent instability of the bronchial system causing overreaction both to constricting and dilating influences. Long term drug therapies include oral sympathomimetics (xanthines, antihistamines, corticosteroids, etc.), and aerosol bronchodilators. The child's self-attitudes, as well as those of his or her family, his or her emotional reactivity, and emotional adjustment are all considered prime contributing factors to asthma. Specific stimuli that sensitize the inherently labile bronchioles include inhaled allergens; unsuspected bronchial infection; psychological and/or physical stress; prolonged exercise; and normal emotions of excitement, anger, and fear. Conditioning, both classical and instrumental (Dekker, Pelser, & Groen, 1957; Khan, 1977; Turnbull, 1962), has been implicated in the etiology of asthma.

Two biofeedback approaches have been investigated for the control of asthma. These include (1) electromyographic (EMG) training to promote general relaxation not only of the external striate musculature but of the bronchial pathways as well, and (2) airway resistance (AR) feedback studies to improve airflow into and out of the lungs. Both biofeedback approaches obtain airway resistance measures since airway resistance represents a subclinical manifestation of asthma. Indeed, asthma is a product of heightened AR. Physiological factors that increase AR include edema of bronchial mucosa, blockage of the airway by secretions, and changes in tone of the bronchial musculature. Because AR is so important to the evaluation and treatment of asthma, a number of different but related measures have been devised to assess AR. These include peak expiratory flow rate (PEFR), forced expiratory volume in one second (FEV1), total respiratory resistance (TRR), and maximum midexpiratory flow rate (MMEF). These various measures of AR are relied on extensively in the biofeedback studies for treatment of asthma.

Frontal EMG Studies

Because emotional factors and anxiety have long been recognized as precipitators of asthmatic attacks, clinicians often advise their patients to sit quietly at the onset or during an episode. Frequently such quiescence will alleviate the wheezing and other respiratory symptoms. Clinical observations showing the beneficial effects of relaxation suggested to Alexander, Miklich, and Hershkoff (1972) that Jacobson relaxation procedures might be of therapeutic benefit during attacks. Forty-four children, 10–15 years of age, were divided into experimental and control groups, matched closely for severity. Experimental subjects received 3–6 modified Jacobsonian relaxation sessions. Controls were simply asked to sit quietly. The primary dependent variable of interest was peak expiratory flow rate (PEFR), defined as the maximum airflow rate during the first .1 second of a forced expiration. Difference score PEFR measures pre- and postsession showed that Jacobsonian relaxation training led to significantly improved airflow rates in asthmatic children while simply sitting still did not.

Davis et al. (1973) may be credited with the

first biofeedback study on asthma in children. They assigned 24 asthmatic children to one of three groups: modified Jacobsonian procedure plus biofeedback; modified Jacobsonian procedure only; and no treatment. Pre- and post-PEFR readings were obtained for each child at each 30-minute treatment session. Three weeks were required to run each child through the research protocol, and medication schedules were held constant during the study. Biofeedback was a continuous, proportional audio signal from the frontal EMG.

Airflow measures were significantly improved for the less severe asthmatics in the relaxation plus biofeedback group, and older children improved more than younger children. The PEFR measures for the other groups were not significant. Also, the PEFR gains made during training did not sustain during the posttreatment assessment. The absence of generalization at follow-up is not unexpected since the total treatment time was quite short. Also, Davis et al. (1973) did not assess clinical impact in terms of actual asthma attack parameters. Because two different treatments were simultaneously provided, the therapeutic impact of biofeedback alone on PEFR measures was not fully assessed.

Kotses et al. (1976) evaluated the effects of frontal EMG alone on respiratory behaviors associated with bronchial asthma. The study was conducted at a summer camp for asthmatic children (Camp Bronco Junction, Charleston, West Virginia). Children were assigned to three groups: contingent feedback; noncontingent (yoked control) feedback; and no treatment. Nine training sessions over three weeks were given, including test periods for the maintenance of control in the absence of feedback. Measures of PEFR were "blindly" obtained three times daily from all campers regardless of whether a child was in the study. The contingent feedback group showed a significant reduction in frontal EMG and a corresponding increase in PEFR. The two control groups did not show similar changes, leading the investigators to conclude that frontal EMG relaxation training caused the improvements in airflow measures. Again, clinical measures of therapeutic impact were not obtained. Scherr et al. (1975) conducted a

clinical study at Camp Bronco Junction very similar to the Kotses et al. (1976) investigation. In addition to PEFR, number of infirmary visits and asthma attacks were evaluated in an EMG-biofeedback-trained group of 22 asthmatic children and 22 control asthmatics who did not receive biofeedback. Following biofeedback training, airflow measures approximated normal for the biofeedback-trained group, particularly during the late afternoon. Perhaps more important than airflow measures, number of infirmary visits decreased significantly for the biofeedback-trained campers, supporting the conclusion that frontal EMG biofeedback training does reduce asthma attack frequency.

Kotses and Glaus (1978) attempted to show that frontal EMG is indeed related to improved PEFR measures by comparing training of frontal EMG with brachioradialis EMG training. Changes in frontal EMG were inversely related to changes in PEFR; however, reliable increases and decreases in brachioradialis tension did not result in differential PEFR behavior. The results applied to both asthmatic children and adults.

Collectively, all of the published studies investigating the effects of frontal EMG biofeedback training on childhood asthma are very supportive. However, the available studies fail to demonstrate long term treatment impact either on airflow measures or clinical attack frequency, duration, or severity. Until such data becomes available, long term efficacy of the biofeedback frontal EMG treatment approach remains undemonstrated.

Airway Resistance Studies

Another promising line of biofeedback application to childhood asthma was introduced by Khan, Staerk, and Bonk (1973), in which direct feedback of forced expiratory volume in one second ($FEV1$, measured in ml/sec) was provided. The $FEV1$ is a readily obtainable measure of the amount of air that, after a maximal inspiration, can be exhaled in one second. As such, an almost direct measure of bronchodilation or constriction was fed back to asthmatic children with a binary visual feedback signal (with criterion $FEV1$ a light came on). Prior to biofeedback training of

FEV1, Khan et al. (1973) first subjected asthmatic children to a neutral saline vapor they were instructed to inhale along with the suggestion that they were inhaling a potent allergen. Those who developed bronchospasms, wheezing, and a 20 percent or greater reduction in FEV1 were grouped as "reactors." Those who did not respond were "nonreactors."

Ten asthmatic children were assigned to each group. Half underwent FEV1 biofeedback training while the remainder served as controls. Training was conducted in two phases: phase 1 consisted of five sessions in which children attempted to increase FEV1; phase 2 consisted of 10 sessions in which bronchospasms were deliberately induced either through suggestion or medication, after which the child attempted to use his or her feedback training to abort the attack. The children were coached through verbal praise. Retraining was offered at six-month intervals and follow-up was conducted at one year. The Khan et al. (1973) study is unique in a number of ways, but perhaps its greatest attribute was that it assessed the effects of FEV1 challenge training on number of emergency room visits, hospitalizations, amount of medication, and number of attacks. Pre- and postdifferences on all of the clinical dependent variables were statistically signficant, favoring the FEV1 biofeedback-trained group. There were no significant differences in any of the clinical measures between treated reactors and nonreactors. Learned self-regulation of FEV1 was not reported, therefore allowing alternative explanations for the observed therapeutic impact on the asthma.

Feldman (1976), building on the procedures introduced by Khan et al. (1973), attempted to lower respiratory resistance by directly feeding back continuously monitored total respiratory resistance (TRR). Biofeedback of TRR was achieved using a "forced oscillation technique" in which a low amplitude 3 Hz pressure variation was continuously introduced into the airflow each child was breathing. The resulting airflow signal was fed back to four severely asthmatic children with instruction that a lower tone meant they were breathing better. In addition to the audio feedback signal, respiration was paced, assuring that all children put forth the same amount of effort. Pretraining baseline measures showed that all four children had abnormal pulmonary function indicative of reversible obstructive lung disease. The measures of pulmonary function included the maximum midexpiratory flow rate (MMEF), PEFR, TRR. Children were given 3–10 training sessions each lasting 5–10 minutes. After biofeedback of TRR, measures of TRR, PEFR, MMEF were again taken. The results showed statistically significant improvements for all children in TRR and MMEF but not for PEFR. The observed improvements in pulmonary function were approximately equal to that achieved by a therapeutic dose of Isoproterenol, a drug used to induce bronchodilation. A single 30-minute rest period without biofeedback did not produce significant changes in any of the pulmonary measures. Feldman points out that neither biofeedback or Isoproterenol therapy returned any of the pulmonary function indices to normal values. In view of the pulmonary changes obtained, Feldman concluded that severely asthmatic children can learn to lower airway resistance in brief biofeedback sessions. He speculates that the technique might be used to control airway reactivity completely while other asthmatics might use biofeedback for symptomatic relief. Feldman, like his predecessors Khan et al. (1973), presents no evidence that actually demonstrates learned self-regulation of airway resistance measures. Further, no efforts were made to assess therapeutic impact on frequency, duration, or severity of asthmatic attacks, nor was long term follow-up data collected.

Finally, Khan (1977), in an attempt to replicate and extend the findings of the Khan et al. (1973) study, divided 80 children, 8–15 years, into biofeedback and control groups. The two groups were further divided into reactors and nonreactors using the same neutral vapor inhalation suggestion procedure as described by Khan et al. (1973). Biofeedback of FEV1 was provided for 5–8 sessions. The controls were recorded for "basal readings" for 5 sessions each. All children in the biofeedback group showed significant decreases in airway resistance. Following the preliminary FEV1 biofeedback training, each child was subjected to a variety of bronchial constriction stimulation, both emotional and environmental, and, in the presence of the constrictions, the child practiced the previously learned dilation assisted by biofeedback, i.e., a counterconditioning paradigm. The children were followed for one year, examining the number and duration of asthma attacks, amount of medication used, and frequency of emergency room hospital admissions. Overall, the results indicated significant improvement for both reactor and nonreactor asthmatics who received FEV1 biofeedback treatment. However, significant improvement by the nontreatment reactor group also occurred, making it apparent that asthmatics who are most reactive to environmental and/or emotional stimuli will improve with attention and time, regardless of airway resistance biofeedback training.

Regarding the efficacy of biofeedback for asthma, the verdict is not yet in; however, the collective results support biofeedback as a viable nonmedication treatment alternative. With improved research methodology and additional clinical trials, biofeedback will probably become the major therapeutic tool of behavioral medicine in the treatment of childhood asthma.

Cerebral Palsy

Reduction of abnormal muscle tone, reduced spasticity, and improved head control usually constitute the major therapeutic goals in the habilitation of the cerebral-palsied (CP) child. Attainment of these goals serves the patient as a necessary foundation or base from which training of speech and fine and gross motor skills can commence. Unfortunately, moderately and severely involved CP children too often prove refractory to the best combined therapeutic efforts of physical and occupational therapists and of parents. By normalizing muscle tone, the CP child is more readily able to achieve normal motor patterns. Medication frequently is employed to bring relief to hypertonic muscles in spastic and athetoid CP

children. However, drug effectiveness in relieving spasm and hypertonicity is sometimes compromised by serious side effects. When physical and occupational therapies fail, and when skeletal-motor relaxants and other drugs do not work or cannot be used, numerous surgical techniques are available. Surgical, orthopedic intervention is sometimes used to correct or prevent various deformities due to hypertonic muscle conditions and, occasionally, neurectomy of the peripheral nervous system is required.

With older CP children and adults, Jacobson's relaxation training techniques have been employed to aid in reduction of muscle tone (Keats, 1965). Once relaxation is achieved, specific motion from the relaxed position may start. Unfortunately, far too many CP children are unable to attain the degree of relaxation necessary for training of purposeful movements; hence habilitative efforts are thwarted by an inability to achieve initial relaxation.

Finley et al. (1977) evaluated the therapeutic impact of electrophysiologic behavior modification (EBM) of frontal–forearm flexor EMG on speech and fine and gross motor skills in four cerebral-palsied children, age 6–10 years, manifesting primarily a spastic component. Prior to onset of six weeks of EBM, each child was evaluated for speech function and for fine and gross motor skills. The EBM procedure consisted of combined audiovisual feedback from frontal and forearm flexor electrode sites with rewards automatically delivered, contingent upon criterion EMG reductions, through automated equipment. During the first six weeks of training, all four children reduced their frontal EMG level across trials to a statistically significant degree. Posttraining evaluation showed that all children experienced significant improvements in speech and motor skills. After six weeks without therapy of any kind, a third evalution of speech and motor function was performed that revealed significant (marked) deterioration of gains noted at the second assessment. Retraining with EBM was instituted for three of the four children, leading to further reductions in frontal-forearm EMG, accompanied by improvements in speech and motor skills.

Collectively, the results showed that CP children manifesting primarily a spastic component were amenable to learned biofeedback EMG reductions when coupled with behavior modification techniques.

Currently the status of biofeedback as a palliative treatment for cerebral-palsied children and adults is that these procedures hold considerable promise. Unfortunately, a paucity of research in this area exists, and good controlled-outcome investigations have not yet been conducted.

Epilepsy

Most of the original work on biofeedback control of epilepsy came from the work of Sterman (Sterman & Friar, 1972; Sterman, Macdonald, & Stone, 1974), Finley (Finley, Smith, & Etherton, 1975), and Lubar (Seifert & Lubar, 1975; Lubar & Bahler, 1976). The epilepsy work of these three investigators has centered on the training of an electroencephalographic (EEG) frequency called the sensorimotor rhythm (SMR). The SMR was first recognized as a distinct EEG rhythm by Sterman and Wyrwicka (1967). Working with the cat, Sterman found a 12–14 cycle per second rhythm over the sensorimotor cortex. The impetus for biofeedback training of the SMR in epileptics came from an EEG and behavioral study conducted by Sterman, LoPresti, and Fairchild (1969) on monomethylhydrazine toxicity in the cat. In the cat, monomethylhydrazine cause dose-related epileptic seizures. Somewhat serendipitously, Sterman observed that animals pretrained to produce SMR through operant-conditioning procedures were protected from the convulsant effects of monomethylhydrazine. To explore further the possiblity that SMR training had anticonvulsant properties, Sterman and Friar (1972) trained a 23-year-old epileptic female to produce the SMR. Dramatically, her seizures improved. Shortly thereafter, Sterman's pioneering efforts were replicated by Finley and Lubar.

Sterman, Finley, and Lubar have worked primarily with adult epileptics. However, some training of children has been reported from each of these investigators. The earliest detailed report on biofeedback control of epilepsy in a child (Finley et al., 1975) described the treatment of a 13-year-old male with a history of a convulsive disorder dating back to febrile convulsions noted at 2 years of age. When he was first seen for baseline recording of EEG prior to sensorimotor (SMR) biofeedback training he was experiencing approximately 70 seizures per day and was taking Valium, 30 mg tid, and Phenobarbital, 60 mg tid. The parents kept a log of his seizure frequency for one hour each day. Biofeedback training of EEG was initially restricted to 12 Hz activity signaled to the patient by illumination of a blue light and onset of a tone. In order to motivate the patient, a "beat-the-clock" game format was introduced in which, for every 5 seconds the child accumulated of the blue light and tone, he was rewarded one point on a digital counter located beneath the blue light. If he accumulated or exceeded an assigned number of points before time was called (shown by an elapsed timeclock in his view), he could win between $1.00 and $3.00 cash. Beyond the more obvious problems manifested by this child, he was also mildly retarded intellectually, was definitely learning disabled, and could not read, count, or tell time on a clock. In addition, he had no concept of money. These problems notwithstanding, after only a few sessions it became obvious that the patient was very motivated to win the cash rewards and he quickly learned to read the elapsed timeclock and to count points on the counter. Also he learned to alter his 12 Hz EEG activity as evidenced by a sixfold increase in proportion of 12 Hz activity. Along with the marked increase in 12 Hz EEG, a corresponding decrease occurred in seizure frequency. After three months of 12 Hz EEG training, his seizure rate had decreased to approximately one attack per hour. Beginning at about the third month into the training program, the patient was provided feedback not only of 12 Hz activity, but also of 4–7 Hz epileptiform activity, signaled to him by the illumination of a red light. Occurrence of the red light overrode the blue light if it was on; hence he could not earn points and win money so long as the red light was illuminated. Whenever the red light came on, his usual response was to order loudly, "Red light off!" Invariably it would, allowing him to return his attention to the blue light. The introduction of the red light, which was electronically driven by the presence of serious EEG abnormalities, had an immediate and marked impact on his EEG. Specifically, his grossly abnormal EEG showed signs of normalization, indicated by a reduction in amplitude of abnormal slow wave frequencies, reduction of paroxysms, and a marked reduction in the overall variance of his EEG in terms of day-to-day appearance. Introduction of seven weeks of noncontingent EEG feedback led to an exacerbation of his seizure condition. Seizure improvement occurred with a return to reinforcement of normal EEG parameters (Finley, 1976).

Sterman et al. (1974) presented research data on biofeedback training of three adults and one child, age 6 years. The boy was diagnosed as a mixed seizure disorder, manifesting both generalized and multifocal EEG abnormalities. The patient was maintained throughout biofeedback training on Dilantin (100 mg) and Phenobarbital (100 mg). The biofeedback display was tailored to achieve optimal performance from the child in learning to augment 12–14 Hz EEG activity called the sensorimotor rhythm (SMR). During the first six months of training, abnormal high voltage 4–7 Hz activity gradually declined and power spectral analysis of the child's EEG revealed continued progress in the direction of EEG normalization, particularly in the trained hemisphere. Cessation of biofeedback training led to an exacerbation of the seizure disorder occurring four weeks after the withdrawal. With reinstitution of SMR training, the child's EEG improved and the frequency of seizures diminished.

Lubar and Bahler (1976) presented clinical case studies of long term SMR biofeedback training of eight severe epileptics, seven of whom were under 20 years of age. In addition to SMR feedback, signaled by illumination of a series of lights, epileptiform presence was indicated by the turning off of a green lamp. Some of Lubar and Bahler's patients were intellectually retarded and/or had serious emotional disorders that complicated their successful epilepsy treatment not only with biofeedback but with anticonvulsant medications. One 14-year-old female patient routinely experienced an exacerbation of the seizure disorder with return to school. Her school-related problems may have been further complicated by the fact that she was grossly overweight, which contributed to her school adjustment problems, and in addition, she was behaviorally hyperkinetic. Despite her many problems, she evidenced an ability to learn to augment the occurrence of the SMR EEG and experienced a corresponding improvement in her EEG and a decrease in her seizure rate.

The youngest patient trained by Lubar and Bahler was a mildly retarded 12-year-old male. Although he experienced some improvement in seizure frequency over seven months of training, his overall improvement was the poorest in the series of cases reported by Lubar and Bahler. The investigators speculate that age may have been a factor since he was the youngest in the study. Also he might have learned to alter his EEG to a much greater degree had the feedback display been individually tailored for his motivational needs.

Although it is generally acknowledged that the published research on biofeedback control for epilepsy is technically among the most advanced in terms of bioelectronics, all of the published studies amount to no more than a series of interesting single-case studies lacking rigorous experimental controls.

Normalization of the EEG is a constant feature found and reported in those patients who respond to biofeedback therapy for epilepsy. However, power spectral analyses have, with distressing regularity, shown that even in epileptics trained with SMR, there is no increased abundance of the trained frequency in the computerized EEG analysis. What does appear is a frequency shift away from the slower frequencies toward the faster frequencies. The power spectral findings are forcing a revision in our thinking, with deemphasis of SMR and emphasis on EEG normalization. Biofeedback training for EEG normalization would include suppression of abnormal high voltage, slow wave frequencies and augmentation of all fast frequencies for which the untrained epileptic EEG is abnormally deficient. Such training is particularly suitable for epileptic children in view of the current notions about plasticity of the central nervous system in the young. Future biofeedback studies will be directed toward the reshaping of the EEG power spectral distribution with deemphasis of SMR. It is likely that biofeedback studies on improved epilepsy control will utilize children more frequently as research subjects, along with improved experimental designs.

Migraine Headaches

Although clinical biofeedback has found its widest range of application in the treatment of headaches, both of the muscle contraction and migraine varieties, virtually all of the available published research is based on adults. There are no published guidelines for the clinician in the form of controlled-outcome investigations on biofeedback therapy for children's headaches. Some scant literature on childhood migraine is available largely in abstract form and is anecdotal rather than experimental.

Headache in children is a common symptom, with the reported incidence between 1.4–4 percent in school children 7–15 years of age. As children grow older, the incidence increases. According to Congdon and Forsythe (1979), most childhood migraine starts between 6 and 10 years of age, with males leading females in age of onset by about three years. Children's attacks are often incomplete, with all of the typical migraine symptoms present but with no headache. When pain occurs, it is focused mainly in the frontal, temporal, or retro-orbital regions of the scalp. Hemicrania is more frequently encountered in older children; however, it is suspected that this may in part be due to an inability of younger children to describe their symptoms accurately.

Standard treatment for acute attacks includes mild analgesics, but the most effective form of treatment to end an attack is ergotamine tartrate (Congdon & Forsythe, 1979). Methysergide is the recommended preventive therapy for childhood migraine. However, Congdon and Forsythe advocate judicious use in children as methysergide treatment can cause retroperitoneal fibrosis. Other drug therapies include clonidine, propranolol, and anticonvulsants. The therapeutic results for clonidine and anticonvulsants (Phenobarbital and Dilantin) are generally regarded as equivocal. Many of the newer drugs found therapeutic for adults have not been approved for use with children.

The earliest application of biofeedback to childhood migraine (Diamond & Franklin, 1976) reports that 32 patients between the ages of 9 and 18 years were treated with temperature hometrainers leased to the family in conjunction with twice weekly EMG training. In addition, progressive relaxation exercises and autogenic phrases were part of the treatment protocol. Poor results were obtained in only two of the patients, both of whom were described as suffering from an underlying depression. Diamond and Franklin add that, in their clinical experience, biofeedback has consistently been an excellent tool in treating childhood migraine. Diamond (1979) indicates that the best therapeutic outcomes seen in the Diamond and Franklin (1976) study were obtained in children under 12 years of age. Details pertaining to methodology are not available in the Diamond studies on biofeedback for childhood migraine. Hence, it is not possible to assess the potential value of the described biofeedback procedures for treatment of migraine in children.

Werder (1978) trained four migrainous children, age 10–17 years, to increase hand temperature through thermal biofeedback, relaxation techniques, and autogenic phrases. All learned self-regulation of hand temperature within four weeks and were able to abort migraine attacks by the end of training. Follow-up at four months posttraining revealed all children to be headache free and off all medication. Werder comments that the children made excellent biofeedback trainees, were not as skeptical as adults about the possible outcome of therapy, and the relaxation response was easier to elicit in them than with adults. The only disadvantage she noted in working with children was that they did not keep good symptom-medication records.

Two related studies, both conducted on nonmigrainous children, attempted to demonstrate that children are indeed able to learn peripheral temperature biofeedback skills. Loughry-Machado and Suter (1979) studied hand warming and cooling in 38 children, age 6–10. Each child was paired with one parent. Parent and child were given two sessions of audio biofeedback training of skin temperature from the web dorsum of each hand, one hand at a time. Children were significantly superior to their parents in self-regulating skin temperature. Dikel and Olness (1980) divided 48 children, ages 5–15 years, into three groups: self-hypnosis; self-hypnosis plus peripheral temperature (warming and cooling) biofeedback; and peripheral temperature biofeedback. Results showed that all children were able to control skin temperature with and without biofeedback of skin temperature. However, self-regulation of skin temperature was best in the biofeedback only group. Interviews revealed that the biofeedback children used imagery to mediate the warming or cooling of skin temperature.

Collectively, currently available studies on learned temperature control through biofeedback and the impact of this on migraine headaches suggests that children can indeed benefit from these procedures. Whether the effect is specific or nonspecific remains in question. Presently available results are largely anecdotal. However, the studies on learned temperature control in normal children indicate that children may be able to acquire self-regulation skills better than adults and that they are able to achieve these skills through use of vivid mental imagery. Clearly, no firm conclusions can be drawn at this time as to efficacy of biofeedback for migraine headaches either in children or in adults. The necessary research simply has not been done, and, until such results become available, application of biofeedback training to migrainous children remains uncharted territory

Hyperkinesis

There are at least three major theories of hyperkinesis. These include the overarousal theory, the underarousal theory, and the hypoinhibitory theory.

Overarousal Theory

The oldest theory of hyperkinesis was founded on the premise that hyperkinesis is a known result of an organic brain lesion, a lesson learned from clinical observations on postencephalitic cases (Strauss & Lehtinen, 1947). Strauss further added that perceptual problems arise from brain injury and become manifest through an inability to filter out irrelevant information. Borrowing openly from classic stimulus-response (SR) psychology, Strauss reasoned that, because a flood of sensory input leads to a flood of motor response, hyperactivity and distractibility are predictable behaviors occurring in response to overstimulation. Further, because the child cannot organize sensory input, the resulting behavior is also disorganized. The Strauss and Lehtinen (1947) theory was tested by Cruickshank (Zentall, 1975), who reasoned that if a classroom was stripped of all possible distracting stimuli, then academic performance of the hyperkinetic child should improve. The academic performance of children educated in a stimulus-deprived classroom was compared with the academic performance of hyperkinetic children receiving instruction in a normal classroom. Although Cruickshank felt that the results supported Strauss's theory, the results were equivocal.

Underarousal Theory

The leading proponents of the low arousal or underarousal theory of hyperkinesis have been Satterfield and Dawson (1971) and Zentall (1975). They both indicate that hyperactive behavior is secondary to lowered levels of reticular activating system (RAS) excitation. Hyperkinesis represents an attempt on the part of the child to increase proprioceptive and interoceptive input. In support of their argument, Satterfield and Dawson presented autonomic data showing that hyperkinetic children differ from normal controls in a number of galvanic skin resistance measures. Their results were interpreted as reflecting reduced levels of arousal in the hyperactive children. Behaviorally, the hyperkinetic children also showed signs of low arousal since two hyperactive children, when requested to sit quietly during the recording sessions, fell asleep. None of the normal children fell asleep under similar circumstances. Their observation is consistent with the hypothesis that increased amounts of spontaneous motor activity are secondary to lowered levels of RAS excitation, and, when deprived of this proprioceptive and interoceptive input, hyperactive children are no longer able to maintain a sufficient level of arousal to sustain consciousness and, therefore, fall asleep.

The low arousal hypothesis not only has considerable face validity, but accounts for some observations that were formerly without explanation—notably, the so-called "paradoxical effect" of the stimulant drugs Ritalin and Dexedrine. In view of the low arousal hypothesis, the effect of these drugs on hyperactives is exactly the same as in normal active children and adults; it raises everyone's level of arousal. In the case of low-arousal-syndrome children, they are functioning at such an abnormally low level of arousal in terms of the arousal continuum, that administration of a stimulant raises their arousal to a more optimal level, obviating the need for hypermotility. Only one major piece of clinical evidence stands in conflict with the low arousal hypothesis, and that is the common clinical observation that hyperactive children are very poor sleepers (Shouse & Lubar, 1978).

Hypoinhibitory Theory

An alternative to the low arousal theory is the theory that limbic and forebrain structures involved in behavioral inhibition have been compromised. Animal models with lesions of the septal area manifest behavior quite similar to that manifested by hyperkinetic children: shortened attention span, behavioral impulsivity, subtle learning disability, and emotional lability. According to Rosenthal and Allen (1978), immaturity would be expected

to arise as a result of deficient forebrain inhibition. There are no specific therapies that have been spawned by the hypoinhibitory theory, although numerous behavior modification techniques directed towards improved impulse control and reduced motor activity have been available for the past decade. Also, there is an increased interest among biofeedback providers to offer biofeedback treatment to hyperkinetic children. Biofeedback training for hyperkinesis seems to best fit, at least at a superficial level, the hypoinhibitory model: specifically, the training is designed to strengthen the child's defective inhibitory mechanisms and improve impulse control through learned self-regulation.

Frontal EMG Biofeedback Studies

Braud, Lupin, and Braud (1975) are credited as being the first to apply biofeedback procedures to the treatment of hyperkinesis. They gave 11 training sessions of frontal EMG relaxation training to a 6.5-year-old boy. Behavioral improvements were noted by the child's teacher and parents. Test scores on the Illinois Test of Psycholinguistic Abilities improved following the training sessions. Methodological weaknesses of the Braud, Lupin, and Braud study included a failure to specify the criteria by which hyperactivity was defined, an absence of behavioral indices, and a lack of control procedures.

Encouraged by the results of the Braud et al. (1975) study, Haight, Jampolsky, and Irvine (1976) assigned eight children, ages 11–15 years, to two treatment groups. Group 1 received nine EMG relaxation training sessions over three weeks and group 2 was left essentially untreated. Four children were assigned to each treatment group. Pretraining EMG baseline levels for the children were not unusually high. The investigators did not observe significant decrements in frontal EMG for the biofeedback group although children in both groups showed improvements in their hyperactivity and, in addition, experienced an increase in auditory attention span for sentences. It is apparent that nonspecific effects led to improvement in both conditions.

Negative results were also reported by Baldwin et al. (1978). Unlike the Haight et al., (1976) study, these investigators were successful in training four hyperkinetic boys to reduce frontal EMG activity. However, no changes were noted by parents and teachers following successful biofeedback training.

Jeffrey and Hayes (1978) divided 27 hyperactive children into two groups. Group 1 received operant conditioning to relax and group 2 received biofeedback EMG training. Both groups learned to relax to about the same degree; however, follow-up 10 months later showed long term gain by the biofeedback group in terms of significant reductions in amphetamine usage.

Braud (1978) compared the effects of frontal EMG biofeedback with progressive relaxation upon hyperactivity in a sample of 15 hyperactive children, ages 6–13 years. The children were assigned in groups of five to one of three treatment conditions: frontal EMG biofeedback; progressive relaxation; and no treatment control. In addition, 15 nonhyperactive controls were evaluated. Pre- and post-intervention behavioral and psychological test measures were obtained. Children assigned to biofeedback training received 12 training sessions over six weeks. No special incentives were provided to the children during biofeedback training; however, shaping procedures were employed. Those children assigned to relaxation training without biofeedback listened to relaxation tapes and followed a modified Jacobsonian relaxation procedure. Periodically, all children were seen for physiological monitoring that included frontal EMG and finger-forehead skin temperature. Results for frontal EMG showed that the hyperactive children had significantly higher frontal EMG levels than the nonhyperactive controls. Both EMG biofeedback and progressive relaxation training significantly reduced EMG levels. Also, measures for hyperactivity, distractibility, irritability, impulsivity, explosiveness, aggressivity, and emotionality were improved in the hyperkinetic children. No differences were seen in the EMG improvement of children receiving drug therapy at the time of the study versus those who were off of medica-

tion. However, nonmedicated children did achieve higher marks in terms of their behavioral ratings. Most of the physiological, behavioral, and psychological measures used to evaluate the children were quite close, but there were some statistically significant exceptions favoring biofeedback over progressive relaxation. Nevertheless, Braud concludes that given the expense and relative difficulty associated with biofeedback therapy, progressive relaxation exercises would do just as well in the treatment of the hyperkinetic child.

Hampstead (1979) provided frontal EMG biofeedback training to six hyperkinetic children, ages 6–9 years. The children were assigned to one of two study conditions: study 1 consisted of an A—B—A—B—A treatment sequence; study 2 used an A—B—A—BC—A sequence. Condition A was defined as resting level recordings of frontal EMG; condition B was frontal EMG biofeedback using rate-proportional clicks; and condition BC was combined EMG feedback plus verbal feedback from the experimenter. Parents and teachers rated each child's behavior using the Hyperkinetic Index, a behavioral tracking tool. No special shaping or reinforcement procedures were employed. In addition to feedback of frontal EMG, the children were asked to practice their biofeedback relaxation skills both at home and at school. Significant EMG reductions on B and BC sessions relative to A sessions occurred. Verbal plus EMG feedback (BC) did not lead to further improvements in self-regulation of frontal EMG activity. Behavioral improvements noted by parents and teachers closely reflected the changes shown by the children in their EMG levels. Most importantly, self-regulatory skills were maintained in five of the six children at a six-month follow-up assessment, and those requiring stimulant medication at the start of the study no longer needed it as judged by parents and teachers.

Hughes, Henry, and Hughes (1980) provided biofeedback over 2.5 months, to three children, ages 6, 9, and 10 years. Each child was reinforced for frontal EMG increments and decrements using verbal praise and tokens exchangeable for candy or toys at the end of each session. An actometer (a modified wrist-watch) was used to monitor activity level during each training session. During the latter part of each session, each child was given the additional task of working arithmetic problems while maintaining EMG control. The results showed that pretraining EMG levels were generally high; however, all three achieved EMG reduction under biofeedback conditions. Tension induction was easily achieved by the three children without resorting to gross facial distortions. Activity level readings closely followed the frontal EMG alterations. Performance on the arithmetic measures during training improved during the frontal EMG reduction phases. The only effect of muscle tension induction was to negate the desirable effects of EMG reductions. Parental ratings of problem behaviors improved for all children by the close of the study. In a similar study, Loux and Ascher (1980) also noted improvements in behavior (Conners Behavior Rating Scale) following frontal EMG and finger temperature training of hyperactive children. Further, Linn and Hodge (1980) reported that EMG training of hyperactives led to improved internalization as measured by the Locus of Control for Children.

SMR Biofeedback Studies

The rationale for SMR training of hyperkinesis is that SMR has been associated with behavioral (motoric) immobility in cats (Chase & Harper, 1971). There is no firm evidence to support the observed relationship; rather, existing support is of an incidental observation nature. Nevertheless, the hypothesized relationship between SMR and motor inhibition received some unexpected support in an SMR-training study for control of epilepsy (Lubar & Bahler, 1976). Specifically, they noted that improvement in motor control did occur following SMR training of a 14-year-old child who was both epileptic and hyperactive. Subsequently, Luber and Shouse (1976) reported preliminary data for one 11-year-old hyperactive boy. The child was maintained on methylphenidate therapy throughout the course of biofeedback training. Monetary reward was used to maintain the child's

interest in the training task. The training schedule may best be described as an ABA sequence with condition A consisting of 12–14 Hz EEG augment and 4–7 Hz suppress. Condition B amounted to a contingency reversal so that 12–14 Hz was suppressed while augmenting 4–7 Hz. Prior to and during the course of biofeedback training, two independent raters observed and rated the child on 13 behavioral categories that served as indices of overactivity and short attention span. Production of SMR followed the ABA sequence perfectly. Moreover, chin EMG measures were found to be inversely related to SMR to a high degree. Classroom observation measures showed that 8 of the 13 measures followed the ABA sequence to a reasonable degree with greatest therapeutic impact seen in terms of decrements in undirected activities, time out of their seat, and increments in cooperation and school work. Because chin EMG varied inversely with SMR production, the investigators interpreted this as support for the motor inhibition hypothesis. Unfortunately, the investigators overlooked the fact that SMR detection is confounded by the logic of their feedback system, which requires almost total relaxation of head and neck before responding to EEG activity. It is probable that the observed SMR changes were mediated through muscle artifact.

In an attempt to replicate and extend their findings based on their single case study, Shouse and Lubar (1979) trained SMR in four additional hyperkinetic children under six conditions: no drug baseline; drug baseline; drug plus SMR training I; drug plus SMR reversal training; drug and SMR training II; and no drug but SMR training. The EEG contingency was a dual one requiring production of 12–14 Hz and suppression of 4–7 Hz. The four children selected for participation were judged most severe in terms of classroom conduct, and all were judged deficient in resting SMR EEG activity. Further, all were Ritalin responders to some degree. Behavior was assessed by two independent raters observing classroom activity. Contingent increases and decreases in SMR occurred in 3 of 4 children and were associated with similar changes in classroom assessments of motor activity. Combining medication and SMR training resulted in substantial improvements that exceeded drug effects alone. Moreover, improved activity level ratings were sustained after medication withdrawal, except in one child who failed to acquire the SMR task. Pretraining levels of SMR reflected the severity of original motor deficits and the susceptibility of hyperkinetic children to both treatments. Although the procedure clearly reduced hyperkinetic behavior, a salient, specific therapeutic factor could not be identified due to the dual EEG contingency imposed, combined with associated changes in scalp EMG. Also, the therapeutic results could be due to training of the EEG toward cortical arousal (Lubar and Shouse, 1979). Nevertheless, they conclude that SMR training is a meaningful treatment for hyperkinesis when overactivity is the prominent symptom.

The biofeedback approaches seem to best fit the hypoinhibitory model for hyperkinesis. Hence frontal EMG relaxation training may be interpreted as strengthening deficient inhibitory mechanisms by rewarding deep muscle relaxation and motor stillness. Training of the SMR has been related by Lubar and Shouse to inhibition of motor activity. Yet, Gargiuio and Kuna (1979) caution that EMG biofeedback training may not strengthen, but weaken, whatever inhibitory mechanisms the child may possess. Exactly how biofeedback training might exacerbate an already weakened inhibitory system is not made clear, but their cautionary note does raise another issue. If some hyperkinetic children do suffer from a low arousal syndrome as many authors indicate (Satterfield & Dawson, 1971; Zentall, 1975; Hastings & Barkley, 1978; Shouse & Lubar, 1978), then relaxation training, which lowers arousal further (Stoyva & Budzynski, 1974), would seemingly be contraindicated for the low arousal hyperkinetic child.

It is probable that 33–66 percent of the hyperkinetic children who served as subjects in the EMG biofeedback studies manifested the low arousal syndrome. Moreover, the majority benefited from EMG biofeedback training, a procedure that has the general effect of lowering arousal level. How can such results be reconciled? Indeed, should not the goal for biofeedback training be to raise the level of arousal in low arousal hyperkinetics rather than to lower it further? Clearly, the consensus of results is that low arousal training is therapeutic for most hyperactives. The proposed mechanism of therapeutic impact can be interpreted in terms of a modified overarousal hypothesis. Specifically, in some children, hyperactivity, an unconditioned response to low arousal, occurs (mostly by day), because the child is overaroused at night. In other words, low arousal hyperkinetic children seem to have a sleep disorder (Hastings & Barkley, 1978). Because their sleep is disturbed at night, they are naturally sleepy by day and therefore hyperactive. The proposed mechanism of therapeutic impact for frontal EMG relaxation training is that low arousal training directly affects the poor sleep caused by the overarousal (Coursey et al., 1980). Once the child begins to experience improved sleep, both qualitatively and quantitatively, then the drowsiness by day (reflected in the low arousal physiological profiles, and by clinical examination of the child, i.e., dark circles under red eyes, yawning, falling asleep when physically confined) and hyperactivity disappear.

Although the proposed mechanism of therapeutic impact for SMR training of hyperkinetic children is strengthening of deficient (motor) inhibition, EMG is confounded with SMR since the patient must first relax scalp EMG before SMR EEG can be passed to the biofeedback filters. Hence, the mechanism for therapeutic impact of SMR on hyperkinesis (and even epilepsy) may be through EMG relaxation, a necessary prerequisite for SMR training. Another possible avenue is that SMR training has been shown to affect the EEG sleep pattern directly (Hauri, 1978). Shouse and Lubar (1979) have proposed that by training the EEG away from slow wave activity and towards faster frequencies, as in SMR training, one would be shaping the EEG spectrum in a direction compatible with a higher arousal level. Their data could be interpreted in this way, but again EMG relaxation training precludes acceptance of this hypothesis as well. Indeed, all EEG biofeedback training (including EEG biofeedback for epilepsy) demands EMG reductions prior to feedback of the EEG signal.

Learning Disabilities

Many of the children who served as subjects in the hyperkinesis studies (reviewed above) were also learning disabled yet were able to learn the necessary biofeedback skills required to normalize their activity levels. However, there is very little information available that demonstrates therapeutic impact of biofeedback training on learning disability (LD) directly.

Guralnick and Mott (1976) presented a single-case study of an 11-year-old LD boy who, in addition to his learning disability problems, suffered from an unaccountable breathing difficulty that prevented him from exercising voluntary control over his breathing, hence affecting his speech. Respiration feedback was provided, and the child responded with improved voluntary control over his breathing within eight biofeedback sessions. Possible impact on his other problems, including speech, was not assessed, but Guralnick and Mott believe their results demonstrate that even the learning disabled can learn and benefit from psychophysiological self-regulation.

Hunter et al., (1976) hypothesized that optimal learning is achieved in the presence of a fully attentive, attuned, and stable internal state, with psychophysiological noise reduced to a minimum. They reasoned that finger temperature biofeedback training of LD children would lead to a stable, internal, noise free state and have a positive impact on learning. A variable-intensity lamp signaled finger temperature changes, and power to an electric train was controlled by criterion temperature increments. Results showed LD children were able to increase finger temperature with biofeedback training and were more successful in doing so than normal controls. Younger children acquired temperature control better than older children, and girls did better than boys. However, there was no detectable impact on a number of psychometric test measures purporting to assess factors reflecting learning disability.

Encouraged by the Hunter et al. (1976) results, Russell and Carter (1978) report a pilot study conducted on four LD boys who received forearm EMG feedback. Possible impact of forearm EMG relaxation training was assessed by pre- and posttreatment administration of the Wide Range Achievement Test (WRAT). After 10 feedback sessions, improvements in reading, spelling, and arithmetic were shown on the WRAT. Further, parents and teachers noted behavioral improvements in terms of greater self-control, reduced impulsivity, less distractibility, fewer errors in homework, and more conscientiousness at school.

Russell and Carter (1978) attempted to replicate their findings with a larger group of children (16 LD children assigned to an experimental group and 14 assigned to a control groups). Over 12 sessions, forearm EMG decreased significantly and impact on seven of nine test score measures was noted. The results were interpreted as indicating that, as the LD children became more relaxed, they could learn more effectively. The investigators further speculate that, through relaxation training with biofeedback, the LD children may have achieved more effective access to previously learned material without excessive interference generated by their fluctuating musculoskeletal and autonomic responses. In this regard, it is apparent that Russell and Carter assume an overarousal model for learning disability children.

REFERENCES

Alexander, A.B., Miklich, D.R., & Hershkoff, H. The immediate effects of systematic relaxation training on peak expiratory flow rates in asthmatic children. *Psychosomatic Medicine,* 1972, **34,** 388–394.

Baldwin, B.G., Benjamins, J.K., Meyers, R.M., &

Grant, C.W. EMG biofeedback with hyperkinetic children: A time-series analysis. *Biofeedback and Self-Regulation*, 1978, **3**, 204–205.

Braud, L.W. The effects of frontal EMG Biofeedback and progressive relaxation upon hyperactivity and its behavioral concomitants. *Biofeedback and Self-Regulation*, 1978, **3**, 69–87.

Braud, L.W., Lupin, M.N., & Braud, W.G. The use of electromyographic biofeedback in the control of hyperactivity. *Journal of Learning Disabilities*, 1975, **8**, 420–425.

Chase, M.H., & Harper, R.M. Somatomotor and visceromotor correlates of operantly conditioned 12–14 c/sec sensorimotor cortical activity. *Electroencephalography and Clinical Neurophysiology*, 1971, **31**, 85–92.

Congdon, P.J., & Forsythe, W.I. Migraine in childhood. *Clinical Pediatrics*, 1979, **18**, 353–359.

Coursey, R.D., Frankel, B.L., Gaardner, K.R., & Mott, D.E. A comparison of relaxation techniques with electrosleep therapy for chronic sleep-onset insomnia: A sleep-EEG study. *Biofeedback and Self-Regulation*, 1980, **5**, 57–73.

Davis, M.H., Saunders, D.R., Creer, T.L., & Chai, H. Relaxation training facilitated by biofeedback apparatus as a supplemental treatment in bronchial asthma. *Journal of Psychosomatic Research*, 1973, **17**, 121–128.

Dekker, E., Pelser, H.E., & Groen, J. Conditioning as a cause of asthmatic attacks. *Journal of Psychosomatic Research*, 1957, **2**, 97–108.

Diamond, S. Biofeedback and headache. *Headache*, 1979, **19**, 180–184.

Diamond, S., & Franklin, M. Biofeedback-choice of treatment in childhood migraine. *Biofeedback and Self-Regulation*, 1976, **1**, 349.

Dikel, W., & Olness, K. Self-hypnosis, biofeedback, and voluntary peripheral temperature control in children. *Pediatrics*, 1980, **66**, 335–340.

Feldman, G.M. The effect of biofeedback training on respiratory resistance of asthmatic children. *Psychosomatic Medicine*, 1976, **38**, 27–34.

Finley, W.W. Effects of sham feedback following successful SMR training in an epileptic: Follow-up study. *Biofeedback and Self-Regulation*, 1976, **1**, 227–235.

Finley, W.W., Etherton, M.D., Dickman, D.,

Karimian, D., & Simpson, R.W. A simple EMG-reward system for biofeedback training of children. *Biofeedback and Self-Regulation*, 1981, **6**, 169–180.

Finley, W.W., Niman, C.A., Standley, J.G,. & Ender, P. Frontal EMG biofeedback training of athetoid cerebral palsy patients: A report of six cases. *Biofeedback and Self-Regulation*, 1976, **1**, 169–182.

Finley, W.W., Niman, C.A., Standley, J.G., & Wansley, R.A. Electrophysiologic behavior modification of frontal EMG in cerebral-palsied children. *Biofeedback and Self-Regulation*, 1977, **2**, 59–79.

Finley, W.W., Smith, H.A., & Etherton, M.D. Reduction of seizures and normalization of the EEG in a severe epileptic following sensorimotor biofeedback training: Preliminary study. *Biological Psychology*, 1975, **2**, 189–203.

Gargiuio, R.M., & Kuna, D.J. Arousal level and hyperkinesis: Implications for biofeedback. *Journal of Learning Disabilities*, 1979, **12**, 4–5.

Guralnick, M.J., & Mott, D.E.W. Biofeedback training with a learning disabled child. *Perceptual and Motor Skills*, 1976, **42**, 27–30.

Haight, M., Jampolsky, G., & Irvine, A. The response of hyperkinesis to EMG biofeedback. *Biofeedback and Self-Regulation*, 1976, **1**, 326.

Hampstead, W.J. The effects of EMG assisted relaxation training with hyperkinetic children: A behavioral alternative. *Biofeedback and Self-Regulation*, 1979, **4**, 113–125.

Hastings, J.E., & Barkley, R.A. A review of psychophysiological research with hyperkinetic children. *Journal of Abnormal Child Psychology*, 1978, **6**, 413–447.

Hauri, P. Biofeedback techniques in the treatment of serious chronic insomniacs. *Biofeedback and Self-Regulation*, 1978, **3**, 209.

Hughes, H., Henry, D., & Hughes, A. The effect of frontal EMG biofeedback training on the behavior of children with activity-level problems. *Biofeedback and Self-Regulation*, 1980, **5**, 207–219.

Hunter, S.H., Russell, H.L., Russell, E.D., & Zimmerman, R.L. Control of fingertip temperature increases via biofeedback in learning-disabled and normal children. *Perceptual and Motor Skills*, 1976, **43**, 743–755.

Jeffrey, T.B., & Hayes, S.B. The effects of operant conditioning and electromyographic biofeedback on the relaxed behavior of hyperkinetic children. *Biofeedback and Self-Regulation,* 1978, **3**, 205.

Keats, S. *Cerebral palsy.* Springfield, Ill.: Thomas, 1965.

Khan, A.U. Effectiveness of biofeedback and counter-conditioning in the treatment of bronchial asthma. *Journal of Psychosomatic Research,* 1977, **21**, 97–104.

Khan, A.U., Staerk, M., & Bonk, C. Role of counter-conditioning in the treatment of asthma. *Journal of Psychosomatic Research,* 1973, **18**, 89–92.

Kotses, H., & Glaus, K.D. Facial muscle tension influences peak expiratory flow rate in normals and in asthmatic children. *Biofeedback and Self-Regulation,* 1978, **3**, 233.

Kotses, H., Glaus, K.D., & Bricel, S.K. Muscle relaxation effects on peak expiratory flow rate in asthmatic children. *Biofeedback and Self-Regulation,* 1977, **2**, 314.

Kotses, H., Glaus, K.D., Crawford, P.L., Edwards, J.E., & Scherr, M.S. Operant reduction of frontalis EMG activity in the treatment of asthma in children. *Journal of Psychosomatic Research,* 1976, **20**, 453–459.

Linn, R.T, & Hodge, G.K. Use of EMG biofeedback training in increasing attention span and internalizing locus of control in hyperactive children. *Biofeedback and Self-Regulation,* 1980, **5**, 373.

Loughry-Machado, G, & Suter, S. Skin temperature biofeedback in children and their parents. *Biofeedback and Self-Regulation,* 1979, **4**, 281.

Loux, D.R., & Ascher, L.M. Effect of biofeedback-assisted relaxation upon the classroom behavior of hyperkinetic children. *Biofeedback and Self-Regulation,* 1980, **5**, 374.

Lubar, J.F., & Bahler, W.W. Behavioral management of epileptic seizures following EEG biofeedback training of the sensorimotor rhythm. *Biofeedback and Self-Regulation,* 1976, **1**, 77–104.

Lubar, J.F., & Shouse, M.N. EEG and behavioral changes in a hyperkinetic child concurrent with training of the sensorimotor rhythm (SMR): A preliminary report. *Biofeedback and Self-Regulation,* 1976, **1**, 293–306.

Rosenthal, R.H., & Allen, T.W. An examination of attention, arousal, and learning dysfunctions of hyperkinetic children. *Psychological Bulletin,* 1978, **85**, 689–715.

Russell, H.L., & Carter, J.L. Biofeedback training with children: Consultation, questions, applications and alternatives. *Journal of Clinical Child Psychology,* 1978, **7**, 23–25.

Satterfield, J.H., & Dawson, M.E. Electrodermal correlates of hyperactivity in children. *Psychophysiology,* 1971, **8**, 191–197.

Scherr, M.S., Crawford, P.L., Sergent, C.B., & Scherr, C.A. Effect of biofeedback techniques on chronic asthma in a summer camp environment. *Annals of Allergy,* 1975, **35**, 289–295.

Schwartz, G.E. Biofeedback as therapy: Some theoretical and practical issues. *American Psychologist,* 1973, **28**, 666–673.

Seifert, A.R., & Lubar, J.F. Reduction of epileptic seizures through EEG biofeedback training. *Biological Psychology,* 1975, **3**, 157–184.

Shouse, M.N., & Lubar, J.F. Physiological basis of hyperkinesis treated with methylphenidate. *Pediatrics,* 1978, **62**, 343–351.

Shouse, M.N., & Lubar, J.F. Operant conditioning of EEG rhythms and Ritalin in the treatment of hyperkinesis. *Biofeedback and Self-Regulation,* 1979, **4**, 299–312.

Sterman, M.B., & Friar, L. Suppression of seizures in an epileptic following sensorimotor EEG feedback training. *Electroencephalography and Clinical Neurophysiology,* 1972, **33**, 89–95.

Sterman, M.B., LoPresti, R.W., & Fairchild, M.D. *Electroencephalographic and behavioral studies of monomethylhydrazine toxicity in the cat.* Technical Report AMRL-TR-69-3, Air Force Systems Command, Wright-Patterson Air Force Base, Ohio, 1969.

Sterman, M.B., Macdonald, L.R., & Stone, R.K. Biofeedback training of the sensorimotor electroencephalogram rhythm in man: Effects on epilepsy. *Epilepsia,* 1974, **15**, 395–416.

Sterman, M.B., & Wyricka, W. EEG correlates of sleep: Evidence for separate forebrain substrates. *Brain Research,* 1967, **6**, 143–163.

Stoyva, J., & Budzynski, T. Cultivated low arousal—an anti-stress response? In L. DiCara (Ed.), *Limbic and autonomic nervous system research.* New York: Plenum, 1974.

Strauss, A., & Lehtinen, L. *Psychopathology and*

education of the brain-injured child (Vol. 1). New York: Grune & Stratton, 1947.

Turnbull, J.W. Asthma conceived as a learned response. *Journal of Psychosomatic Research,* 1962, **6,** 59–70.

Werder, D.S. An exploratory study of childhood migraine using thermal biofeedback as a treatment alternative. *Biofeedback and Self-Regulation,* 1978, **3,** 242–243.

Zentall, S. Optimal stimulation as theoretical basis of hyperactivity. *American Journal of Orthopsychiatry,* 1975, **45,** 549–563.

CHAPTER 45

Residential Treatment of Emotionally Disturbed Children

DAVID R. WILSON AND ROBERT D. LYMAN

Generating an accurate estimate of the number of emotionally disturbed children receiving residential treatment services is difficult due to the range of programs and the lack of a central reporting agency concerned with this area. In 1970, there were estimated to be 26,792 children in mental hospitals and residential treatment centers in the United States (U.S. Census, 1970, pp. 5–20). These children's problems cover the range of childhood disturbances, from schizophrenia to social maladjustment, and the duration of their treatment may be as brief as one night or as long as a lifetime. The settings in which these children are housed also vary considerably, from group homes for six or eight children located in suburban neighborhoods to institutional programs for 100 or more, isolated from the community. Almost the only characteristic shared by these children is the fact that their treatment requires them to reside away from their natural homes. This tremendous diversity makes it difficult to adequately review the field of residential treatment for disturbed children, but such treatment is important both in numbers of children served and as one component of a comprehensive service delivery system. This chapter will discuss the historical development of residential treatment and the position residential treatment occupies in a continuum of mental health services for emotionally disturbed children. The major approaches to residential treatment will be reviewed and critical dimensions delineated. The final section of this

chapter will include detailed discussion of research and evaluation issues and components, with a review of the current state of knowledge and suggestions for future development.

HISTORICAL DEVELOPMENT

Residential programs for disturbed children are a relatively recent development. Prior to the sixteenth century, virtually all care of children with emotional or behavioral problems was provided by their immediate families or, in the case of parental absence or abandonment, by relatives, neighbors, or friends. The church provided the only alternative to this informal system of child care by offering limited housing, education, and spiritual training to a few abandoned children without other resources.

The first public, non-church-related system of residential care for children began in England with the establishment of alms houses for destitute children in the 1600s (Mayer, Richman, & Balcerzak, 1977). From that time until today there have existed in Western Europe and the United States two parallel systems of residential care for children. One system is predominantly church related and privately funded and serves mostly dependent children. The other system is largely publicly funded and serves disturbed, handicapped, and delinquent as well as dependent children. During the same period that public alms

1069

houses were established in England, the practice of indenturing children to private individuals provided formal legal recognition to the informal process of foster home placement that had existed for centuries (Mayer et al., 1977). The incentive (free labor) remained the same, but the process now became part of the public child care network.

For the next several hundred years, this system of institutional child care flourished in Europe and in America. Social and political upheaval increased the number of dislocated and homeless children even as it destroyed many of the informal family and community care networks that had existed for centuries. Private and public institutions grew to accommodate this need, and abuses became widespread.

Public awareness of conditions in children's institutions as well as a growing recognition of children's rights in general, led in the late 1800s and early 1900s to a sentiment against large institutional programs for children and in favor of foster care placement or more homelike residential care (Hopkirk, 1944). In response to this sentiment, many institutions adopted a decentralized or "cottage" model while others endeavored to reduce their overall size. Many children were discharged to foster care, often inappropriately. A further result of this focus on deinstitutionalization was the emergence of interest in reuniting children with their natural parents. Historically, child care institutions had viewed their purpose as raising children to adulthood. Now, efforts were made to identify changes in conditions of children's natural families that might allow successful return to that environment.

At the same time as these tremendous changes were affecting institutional child care, Freud's psychoanalytic theories were sweeping the mental health world. These theories provided the first systematic rationale for mental health treatment and their influence was soon felt in the area of child care. Beginning with Aichorn (1935) in the 1930s and continuing with the work of Bettelheim (1950) and Redl and Wineman (1957) in the 1940s and 50s, psychoanalytic practitioners postulated a model of residential treatment specifically for children with emotional disturbances. This "milieu therapy" model caused further differentiation in residential child care as emotionally disturbed children were separated from dependent children for the purpose of providing more appropriate treatment even though, in many cases, the differentiation of the two groups was arbitrary. Thus, for the first time, specific residential treatment centers for disturbed children were identified. Since then there has been a further refinement of the residential treatment model and incorporation of such divergent treatment philosophies as behavior therapy, positive peer culture, and the psychoeducational model. Residential treatment has developed into a unique component in the continuum of treatment alternatives, but, to understand it, it must be viewed in perspective of other kinds of mental health intervention.

CONTINUUM OF TREATMENT ALTERNATIVES

Residential care occupies one position in a continuum of treatment alternatives for emotionally disturbed children. It is imperative, because of the disruptive effects of removing children from their homes and the dangers of institutionalization and stigmatization, that the full range of alternatives be evaluated and a specific rationale for residential treatment be formulated before such treatment is considered. In order of increasing disruption of the child's natural environment, the following constitute the major categories of mental health intervention available to the child mental health practitioner.

Outpatient Treatment

Outpatient mental health treatment with emotionally disturbed children may range from verbal psychotherapy (Levitt, 1971) and play therapy (Axline, 1947) to behavior therapy (Ross, 1964). It may continue for years or for as few as three sessions, and in most cases there is minimal disruption of the child's environment. Seldom does treatment involve a time commitment of more than five hours per week and a child's school and community relationships are usually unaffected. Treatment may involve only the child or the entire family and may involve somatic treatments such as medication or environmental changes instituted through the parents or by actual entry of a mental health practitioner into the child's environment.

Day Treatment or Special Education Programming

The provision of mental health services for some, all, or most of the day involves the removal of children from school and enrollment in an identified therapeutic or remedial milieu. The child's residential environment is unaffected, and parental involvement is usually maintained.

Shelter or Respite Care

Residential care provided for short periods of time (12 hours to three weeks) is usually termed respite care if the need is defined by parents or caretakers, and shelter care if the need is defined by external agents (i.e., police or welfare workers). Such care is typically provided in response to emergencies such as abuse, abandonment, or parental drunkenness or in response to parental requests for relief from the strain of living with a disturbed child. Shelter and respite care programs may offer formal therapeutic interventions, including educational programs, or provide only temporary housing for the child.

Foster Care

Voluntary or involuntary removal of a child from home and placement in a foster home with adults who may or may not have received training in working with the emotionally disturbed constitutes a major disruption of the child's environment, but some factors remain unaffected. Public school or other external schools are still attended and the residential environment is still homelike with "parents" and usually no more than four natural or foster children. The duration of foster care may range from one month to several years.

Group Home Care

Group home care is differentiated from foster home care by the number of children placed in one home (up to 10 or 12 at once) and by the characteristics of the residential environment. In many cases, foster parents act as free agents while group homes are agencies which employ houseparents, child care workers, or other staff. Thus group homes tend to be less homelike and more regimented. Although the residence will frequently have the appearance of a family house, other aspects reveal its agency characteristics. A formal treatment program or philosophy is usually evident in contrast with the informal provision of treatment by foster parents. Case records are maintained and agency personnel think of themselves as treatment staff. In most cases, children in group home care attend external schools although in-house programs are not unknown. As in foster care, duration of treatment may range from one month to several years.

Residential Treatment Centers

These programs are characterized by stronger agency identification than group homes and less similarity to children's natural environment. Often programs are somewhat isolated from the community and provide activities within the facility rather than through community resources. Schooling for at least some children is provided at the center. There is usually a well-defined treatment program or philosophy and staff other than houseparents to implement it. Some programs utilize child care workers or nursing staff in addition to, or instead of, houseparents. Case workers or clinical staff are usually given treatment responsibility. Although the size of such programs may range up to 100 children or more, usually functional units of no more than 25 children are identified and frequently housed separately. Duration of treatment may range from three months to a number of years.

Inpatient Hospitalization

Although the duration of treatment in clearly identified hospital or medically oriented settings is usually shorter (1 week to 1 year) than in residential treatment centers, the extreme dissimilarity to the natural environment can be more disruptive. Usually, nursing staff are utilized rather than child care workers or houseparents, and there is much more regimentation and formality in daily routine. There is often little opportunity for children to engage in such normal activities as room cleaning, snacking, or going outside. Frequently schooling is temporarily suspended or offered only on the ward. Typically, group or individual therapy is considered primary treatment intervention.

Institutional Treatment

The primary definitional characteristic of institutional programs is the absence of normalizing or natural environmental experiences and the deemphasis of reentry into the natural environment. Institutional programs are frequently isolated from the community and extremely regimented and impersonal in daily routine. Few if any opportunities are offered for residents to leave the facility. Generally, duration of treatment is measured in years, with a common expectation being that the resident will be at the facility for life. There is frequently little personal freedom given residents in such areas as dress and room decor, and personal possessions are minimal or discouraged. Schooling is invariably provided in the institution. Although historically many state hospitals have been in this category, many are currently shedding their institutional characteristics. A program of any size, under private or public jurisdiction, may be described as institutional if it fails to provide normalizing life experiences for children and does not actively pursue the goal of reentry into the natural environment.

The above constitutes a brief description of the treatment care options available for disturbed children and youth. The next issue to be addressed is the determination of need for residential care and the choice of a setting in which this care can be most effectively delivered.

DECISION MAKING AND THE PLACEMENT PROCESS

Four guiding principles should govern the decision-making process in residential care placement. The first of these principles is that care should be provided in the setting that is least disruptive of the child's natural environment. Thus outpatient interventions should be considered and tried prior to day treatment while day treatment should be considered prior to implementation of residential treatment. The appropriate exceptions to this principle are those involving immediate placement in shelter or respite care because of danger to the child or parental collapse and immediate placement in inpatient care because of a clear need for intensive medical diagnosis and/or treatment. It is also possible that individual clinical characteristics, such as severe thought disorder or self-destructive behavior, may suggest consideration of more disruptive treatment alternatives without prior implementation of less disruptive options. However, recent work suggesting that outpatient management of severe disorders may be effective (e.g., Johnson, Whitman, & Barloon-Noble, 1978) indicates that caution in such cases is advised.

The second guiding principle is that treatment be provided in the setting that allows for maximum therapeutic effectiveness. It is extremely difficult to modify school behavior problems on an inpatient ward without a school program. Similarly, communication problems between parents and child cannot be effectively treated if residential treatment precludes their interaction. Of central importance is the issue of maximizing generalization of treatment effects. One approach to insuring that treatment effects generalize is to minimize dissimilarities between the treatment environment and the environment to which the child will return (Conway & Bucher, 1976).

The third guiding principle is that the child's behavior and clinical condition should be matched to the structure and capabilities of the treatment environment. Some children require placement in programs with more resources, such as nighttime staff or locked facilities, while other children require only houseparent supervision. Placement of children in a program with inadequate resources to treat their condition effectively may lead to staff burnout, creation of a nontherapeutic environment, and dangerously uncontrolled circumstances. Placement of a child in a program with more resources than necessary may result in a loss of treatment effectiveness through decreased generalization as well as a squandering of limited treatment resources.

The fourth guiding principle is that treatment should be implemented in as cost effective a way as possible. Clearly, residential care is far more expensive than outpatient treatment, with some residential or inpatient program charges exceeding $200.00 per day (American Association of Childrens' Residential Centers, 1981). However, an adequate appraisal of cost effectiveness must include consideration of treatment efficacy, treatment duration, and the social cost of recidivism or treatment failure in its determinations. Five years of weekly outpatient therapy may prove far more costly than six months of residential treatment if the above factors are adequately considered.

Cost effectiveness also needs to be considered in comparing different types of residential care. For example, if a therapeutic camp can effectively treat a child for $30.00 a day, there is no justification for employing $100.00 per day residential care in a more traditional setting (Lyman, 1981). The question of cost effectiveness is becoming increasingly important in an era of decreasing governmental support for human services. Limited resources will require maximum utilization of funds, staff, and physical facilities.

Subsumed under these four guiding principles are a number of considerations that are unique to each case. For example, can the parents implement follow-up treatment at home? Are siblings suffering from neglect because of one child's needs? Will parents' insurance pay for hospitalization but not day treatment? These and many other factors must be considered in any individual case; however, the general decision-making process in considering residential care should be in accordance with the four principles discussed above.

MODELS OF RESIDENTIAL TREATMENT

In order to provide a context for understanding our discussion of the essential ingredients of residential treatment, we will present a brief overview of selected contributors to the literature on residential treatment. This is intended to introduce some of the theoretical frameworks that have been important to the area. Those who are interested should refer to the original sources cited, or to Whittaker's (1979) discussion of the major approaches.

Psychoanalytic Models

As previously mentioned, Aichorn, Bettelheim, and Redl, among others, were instrumental in applying the concepts of psychoanalysis to residential treatment for disturbed children. Basic elements of the psychoanalytical model of residential treatment as expressed by Bettelheim (1950, 1974) include the isolation of children from their natural parents and the use of an analytical framework for all treatment interventions. Bettelheim presents numerous examples of ways in which the residential environment could be utilized to affect children therapeutically and allow exploration and resolution of their dynamic conflicts, but little of this information is applicable in other settings. In contrast, Redl (1966) formulates a practical, flexible, and broadly applicable model of residential treatment. He emphasizes the treatment of children by child care workers in the residential environment through the "life space inter-view," a set of verbal interventions initiated in response to events in the child's daily life. These techniques are analytically based but expressed in practical terms and intended for use by paraprofessionals.

Redl's work, however, conflicts with the child guidance model that represents the main-stream of analytically based residential treatment (Whittaker, 1979). This model empha-sizes the therapeutic importance of a treat-ment team consisting of psychiatrist, psychol-ogist, and social worker, while deemphasizing the importance of the on-line child care work-er. Individual psychotherapy is considered the primary focus of treatment. The child guid-ance model remained the standard for resi-dential treatment programs until the advent of behaviorally oriented programs in the 1960s.

Behavioral Models

Residential treatment programs based on the principles of behavior therapy began as part of a more general questioning of psychoana-lytic concepts in mental health. While the analytical model had been the dominant force throughout the first half of the twentieth century, its limited applicability to some client populations (e.g., retarded, psychotic, or eco-nomically deprived) and the lack of empirical demonstrations of effectiveness encouraged a search for alternative treatment approaches.

This search led to the application of labor-atory-derived learning principles to the treat-ment of human problems. Although Jones (1924), Gesell (1938), and Mowrer and Mowrer (1938), among others, had described learning-based treatment approaches, it was not until later that this alternative gained much support. Wolpe (1958) produced the first widely distributed work in support of behavior therapy while Lazarus (1960), Ross (1964), and Lovaas et al. (1967), among others, ex-tended the use of this technique into the area of child therapy. With Ferster's (1961) work, operant-conditioning techniques were utilized with children in institutional care, and the next two decades marked increasing acceptance of behaviorally based residential treatment.

Behaviorally oriented residential treatment programs have in common a focus on the child's overt behavior rather than on such factors as inner personality states or dynamic conflicts. Problematic behaviors are viewed as largely resulting from past learning experi-ences. Remediation of those behaviors con-sists of systematic regulation of positive and negative consequences or control of stimulus-response pairings in accordance with estab-lished learning principles. On-line child care staff are viewed as the primary intervention agents as opposed to the child guidance model's view of the psychiatric team as central in importance. In addition, treatment is viewed primarily as a learning process rather than a healing one. Comprehensive models for behav-iorally based residential treatment have been developed at Achievement Place (Phillips et al., 1973), at the National Training School (Cohen & Filipczak, 1971), and at the Chil-dren's Center of Wisconsin (Browning & Stover, 1971).

Psychoeducational Models

Psychoeducational models are perhaps best represented by Project Re-Ed (Hobbs, 1966), a model for residential treatment that stresses the teaching of more appropriate behaviors and coping skills to children. The Re-Ed program emphasizes community involvement and short term treatment that allows for continued contact between a child and his or her parents if at all possible. The staff consists of specially trained teachers, and the philo-sophical and attitudinal focus of the program is on reeducation rather than treatment. Many behavioral principles are incorporated in Re-Ed programming, and in many ways the two models are complementary. Both emphasize the importance of on-line staff and the struc-turing of daily activities and natural conse-quences for therapeutic effectiveness.

Peer Culture Models

Another recently developed model of residen-tial treatment stresses the importance of inter-personal factors in therapeutic programming. Raush, Dittman, and Taylor (1959) and Polsky (1962) were among the first to recognize the importance of peer interaction in residential treatment of children. Flackett and Flackett (1970) and Vorrath and Brendtro (1974), among others, offer more complete treatment approaches intended to enlist peer support for positive behavior changes in residential treatment.

Most peer culture programs rely on formal or informal group discussions as well as group control of privileges or rewards. The effectiveness of the treatment derives from both the confrontation and feedback of the group discussions and the reinforcement of appropriate behavior with positive consequences. Staff are significantly involved as participants in the treatment process with much of the effectiveness of these programs attributed to interactions between residents.

Although there are major theoretical and philosophical differences among these residential models, there are also identifiable dimensions about which decisions must be made within any program. Differences along these dimensions are reflected in program priorities, structures, and operations.

CRITICAL DIMENSIONS IN RESIDENTIAL TREATMENT

The interposing of the concepts "residential" and "treatment" creates problems of definition and clarity in terms of what elements of residential treatment are therapeutic. Virtually every residential treatment center operates with the assumption that "the events of daily living are used as formats for teaching competence in basic life skills. The living environment becomes both a means and a context for growth and change informed by a culture that stresses learning through living" (Whittaker, 1979, p. 36). Ideas of what constitutes treatment have evolved to the point where this "learning through life" is considered central. We will present some critical dimensions of residential treatment about which explicit choices should be made in order to increase the likelihood that a given milieu is indeed therapeutic.

Physical Location and Facilities

A program's location and physical characteristics are determined to a degree by theoretical beliefs but even more by practical considerations such as money available, community acceptance, and zoning laws. Attention to physical detail varies, with Bettelheim, for example, discussing the importance of the appearance of bathrooms in assisting children in working through problems occurring in the anal stage of psychosexual development (Bettelheim & Sanders, 1979). There is general agreement that programs should have rather low visibility so that differences with the community are not emphasized (Whittaker, 1979). Some programs use converted homes with few modifications; others use specially constructed buildings with such features as childproof windows and secure time-out rooms. There are also differences in the degree that children are free or restricted in their range of movement and in the amount of personal space and privacy allowed. Some programs permit a great deal of personalizing; others are stark and devoid of this personal touch. A special type of residential treatment program, the therapeutic camp, is based on the assumed advantages of the facility being located in the wilderness, with benefits accruing from the isolation, the beauty, and the inherent challenges of nature (Loughmiller, 1965; Redl, 1966; Rickard & Dinoff, 1974).

Staffing—Who Provides the Treatment?

The staff is considered critical in every program, but there are significant differences in what type of staff is considered essential. The traditional idea of the psychotherapist as the central figure with the other staff considered secondary and a part of the "other 23 hours" (Trieschman, Whittaker, & Brendtro, 1969), has largely given way to the recognition that each member of the milieu is important. This may be due, in part, to a theoretical recognition of the effectiveness of a milieu approach, but even more to the practical reality that few programs can afford to have highly trained doctoral or masters level staff provide a large percentage of the treatment that occurs. Programs vary according to whether or not they operate from an egalitarian position, with all staff considered roughly equal in therapeutic potential, as suggested by Bettelheim (Bettelheim & Sanders, 1979), or from a more hierarchical position with greater therapeutic potential and responsibility residing with particular staff. Most programs recognize that those who have the most direct contact with the children, the child care workers and classroom staff, are critical (Trieschman et al., 1969), but programs vary in how much attention is given to procedures such as training, supervision, and assigned case responsibility to insure that this contact is therapeutic. There has been increasing support for consideration of child care as a profession, with certification and training requirements. There are training materials, such as those developed by Group Child Care Consultant Services (1977) to be used for child care workers and supervisors, and the Achievement Place materials, which are oriented toward house- or teaching-parents (Phillips et al., 1972). The major distinction that is made regarding direct care staff is that some programs employ child care staff who work shifts, while others utilize house- or teaching-parents in a more family-oriented setting.

Characteristics of Children Served

Most residential programs have stated acceptance criteria, with particular behavioral or psychological problems that are assumed to be most responsive to the treatment offered by the program. These tend to be rather vague (e.g., "school behavior problems," or "peer relationship difficulties"), and programs can typically be much more specific regarding exclusion criteria, i.e., the children or kinds of problems that are considered inappropriate for the programs (such as homicidal behavior, arson, or suicidal behavior).

It is misleading to focus entirely on the behavior of the child as the only or even major criterion for admission to residential treatment. There are many children who are never referred to such programs whose behavior is more severe or problematic than those who are admitted. It is important to examine other factors, such as community tolerance for particular behaviors, range of alternative services available, and the willingness or ability of parents or school personnel to work with and manage the child. In looking at why children are in residential treatment, it is useful to take an ecological perspective that extends the analysis beyond the particular child's behavior (Hobbs, 1966). Residential treatment is necessitated because of an inadequate fit between the particular needs of the child and the resources available in the environment in which he or she is expected to live. Residential treatment programs, while necessarily focusing on the child, should also explicitly attend to these other factors, for example, by conducting parent training and various forms of community programming.

Involvement of the Child in Treatment

Most residential treatment staff would agree that children should be involved in their own treatment, but there is much variation in how much or in what form this involvement actually occurs. Explicit attention is given to this dimension in the Positive Peer Culture approach, with its emphasis on the group's functioning and each member's contribution to it (Vorrath & Brendtro, 1974). The behaviorally oriented approaches have also provided useful detail, with techniques including self-monitoring of progress, contracting, goal setting, and self-control training. Token, point, and levels systems may also be used in ways that either encourage or undermine personal responsibility (Kazdin, 1977). Participation in treatment meetings is another form of involvement (Dinoff et al., 1978).

The Role of Formal Individual Psychotherapy

Ideas about what constitutes treatment evolved from theories developed for individual applications. In the past, psychotherapy was often seen as the main instrument of change, with the rest of the residential program serving to house and insulate the child from countertherapeutic influences. Today, programs in which formal psychotherapy is considered the prime ingredient of residential treatment are in the minority: "A truly therapeutic milieu cannot be organized around the concept of individual psychotherapy as the central mode of treatment" (Whittaker, 1979, p. 56).

If therapy is not central, what should its role be? Results of research in child psychotherapy are disappointing (Barrett, Hampe, & Miller, 1978; Leavitt, 1971) and indicate that verbal psychotherapy is not the treatment of choice for many childhood problems and for many of the children in residential treatment. Psychotherapy in the context of residential treatment is subject to very different parameters and influences from those of outpatient therapy, such as the client's concerns and conflicts over removal from home and the more active role of the therapist in the child's life (Brodie, 1972). In the authors' experience, staff frequently request more psychotherapy when things are going particularly badly for a child or for the group as a whole. This often represents a misconception regarding what can be accomplished in therapy and may be seen as a search for a magical solution. This reveals the need for education of staff regarding the role of therapy.

In any milieu, there may be informal but potentially helpful "therapy" occurring throughout the child's day. Redl and others have discussed the use of the life space interview as appropriate for this kind of emergent therapy (Morse & Small, 1959; Redl, 1966). Programs differ widely in how much child care workers are expected or permitted to engage in such interactions. Issues of importance here include what is communicated to staff regarding their role, how supervision and training are provided, and what steps are taken to insure that every child has access to someone with whom he or she can discuss private and sensitive matters. Access to a formal psychotherapist is no guarantee that this will actually occur, and a child care worker responding sensitively and empathetically to a child's thoughts and concerns at an opportune moment may be very therapeutic. Behaviorally oriented programs tend to downplay formal therapy as well as these informal counseling interactions even though most behavioral practitioners probably recognize their importance. Those using the Achievement Place model have attempted to structure this area by specifying components of the "teaching interaction" (Phillips et al., 1972).

Role and Involvement of the Group

No matter what the stated theory of treatment, much of what actually occurs in residential treatment will be determined by group factors and influences. Much power resides in the peer subculture that develops in residential treatment (Polsky, 1962; Polsky & Claster, 1968), and peers frequently reinforce undesirable behaviors (Buehler, Patterson, & Furniss, 1966). The literature on the Positive Peer Culture discusses using the group as a therapeutic tool (Vorrath & Brendtro, 1974). The Achievement Place model also attends to these influences through techniques such as the use of peer managers and peer monitoring (Phillips et al., 1973).

There is a great deal of therapeutic potential in the group, but negative aspects must also be considered, as in the fictional example offered by *The Lord of the Flies* (Golding, 1955). Regarding Positive Peer Culture approaches, there are concerns that they are not appropriate for many children, are too dependent on staff personality, and are unclear about what should happen outside of formal group meetings (Whittaker, 1979). Specific ways to harness positive group potential include use of group problem-solving methods (Loughmiller, 1965), the use of group contingencies and reinforcement (Herman & Tramontana, 1971), and reliance on formal group meetings and group therapy. The literature on group therapy for children suggests that group composition is important (Rose, 1972); the role of group composition within the residential treatment center has been discussed by Redl (1966).

Daily Living

A milieu approach assumes there is much potential for "learning through living," and useful sources on realizing this potential are available (Group Child Care Consultant Services, 1977; Redl, 1966; Trieschman et al., 1969). These training materials discuss what child care workers may do to reap therapeutic benefit from day-to-day activities. Involved is the recognition that learning may come as a part of any activity in which the child participates. Particularly important are setting goals and priorities, supervision and monitoring, and detailing in individual treatment plans how goals are to be achieved in the context of activities. Life space interviews and group problem solving may be useful techniques when activities are not going well. Incentive systems may be helpful in detailing activities and reinforcers. A problem is that if everything is potentially therapeutic, a child may become tired of and therefore resistant to the constant scrutiny, so there should be some areas of the child's life that are not always subject to treatment or feedback.

How Specific Skills are Taught

The learning of adaptive behaviors, such as self-help, social, and academic skills, is critical to any treatment program for disturbed children. Project Re-Ed, an example of a program with an explicit educational focus, "was designed to create a total living and learning environment for the troubled child and stresses the teaching of competence across the total spectrum of the child's development as the fundamental purpose of the helping environment" (Whittaker, 1979, p. 71). The Achievement Place programs also take note of the importance of specific skills training, with attention to the teaching interaction and the targeted adaptive behaviors that are built into a highly structured incentive system. A different context is the therapeutic camp, with the potential for learning in a wilderness environment, and the challenges therein.

Specific intervention techniques that have been used to provide skills training include social skills training (Clark, Caldwell, & Christian, 1979), modeling by staff and other group members (Rogers-Warren & Baer, 1976), and the learning of group interaction skills via

participation in Positive Peer Culture approaches (Vorrath & Brendtro, 1974). The opportunity to teach a wide range of skills may be one of the major advantages and challenges of residential treatment.

Behavior Management and Control

Even if programs emphasize a positive, adaptive skills focus, children's behaviors often require attention to management and control. Approaches to behavioral control vary, ranging from the permissive tolerance at The Orthogenic School (Bettelheim, 1974), to the control residing with the members of the group in a Positive Peer Culture approach, to the extreme attention to detail in some behaviorally oriented programs. The writings of Redl may be considered a melding of analytic wisdom and behavioral practicalities. He offers excellent suggestions for dealing with problem behaviors (Redl, 1966). *The Other 23 Hours* (Trieschman et al., 1969) contains a number of chapters on managing problem behaviors at various points throughout a program.

The behaviorally oriented approaches have attended most explicitly to issues of and techniques for behavioral management and control. A wealth of behavioral research has documented the effectiveness of numerous techniques that are directly applicable in residential treatment, such as points and levels systems (Kazdin, 1977), overcorrection (Azrin & Wesolowski, 1974), contracting (Stuart, 1971), self-control training (Drabman, Spitalnik, & O'Leary, 1973), and time-out and related procedures (Wilson & Lyman, in press). Because of the nature of residential settings, there may be problems in effectively applying these techniques due to factors such as administrative constraints and limited resources (Repucci & Saunders, 1974). Browning and Stover (1971) and Monkman (1972) provide descriptions of the application of behavioral techniques in residential treatment centers.

Behavior management and control techniques should be recognized as a means to an end, for behavior control is not the ultimate goal. These techniques are only effective when they are part of a total program for teaching children more adaptive skills to enable them to live in the less restrictive environment of their homes and communities.

Parent Involvement in Residential Treatment

Involving parents in residential treatment is problematic, in that the child is removed from the home, with the treatment staff assuming some of what are usually considered parental functions. Most providers of residential treatment would agree that treatment success is dependent on meaningful and sustained involvement of parents in the treatment process and that the child and his or her family should be jointly considered as clients. Meaningful parental involvement may be precluded by geographical factors due to the wide area served by many centers and economic problems both for programs and parents. Parents' personal problems, feelings of guilt and failure, or the lack of encouragement and innovative programming on the part of the residential facility may inhibit parental involvement. Many programs have also stifled involvement by endorsing the "family etiology hypothesis" (Whittaker, 1979) and blaming the parents for the child's problems. Many children lack parents of any kind or may be in agency custody, rendering family involvement unlikely.

Formats for parental involvement include parent support groups, parent education groups, and specific skills training, such as in communication skills (Gordon, 1971) or in behavior management skills (Patterson, Cobb, & Ray, 1972), as well as individual or family therapy.

Whatever treatment model is used, research indicates that if the child is ever to live outside of residential treatment, much of the effort that is put into that treatment is wasted if changes do not occur in the environment in which he or she is expected to survive after treatment (Taylor & Alpert, 1973). For this reason, parents as well as community agencies should be involved in the treatment process before, during, and after residential treatment.

Community Linkages

Although residential care, by definition, involves some disruption of a child's life, it is imperative that continuity and communication be maintained between the residential treatment environment and the child's home community. Programming for generalization should be a continuing concern throughout the course of the intervention (Conway & Bucher, 1976).

These linkages must be functional on two levels. Clinically, there should be provisions for maximum interaction of a child with the home community while in residential care. The interaction may take the form of regular home visits, placement in community schools, or parent involvement in family therapy. Only in rare instances is a residential treatment program justified in severing all contacts between a child and the home environment. On some occasions it may be necessary for the residential program to create community linkages for a particular child who otherwise lacks such interactions. The use of visiting resources such as short term foster homes can create a level of community integration that otherwise would not exist.

There should also be linkages between the residential treatment environment and the home environment after a child is discharged from treatment. Allerhand, Weber, and Haug (1966) maintain that the most significant factor in determining the success of residential treatment is the posttreatment environment. This environment can be considerably enhanced through the support and intervention of residential treatment staff (Cavior, Schmidt, & Karacki, 1972; Mayer et al., 1977).

Community linkages must also be effective at the organizational level. In order to insure community receptivity to the residential program's mission and to guarantee access to community resources, a high level of community integration and contact must be maintained. Coates and Miller (1973) describe some of the community interface problems that confront residential treatment programs. These problems range from fear of residents' behavior to concern that property values near the facility will suffer. The most effective weapon in combating such attitudes is information sharing and open communication between residential program staff and community residents.

Provisions for Individualized Treatment and Goal Setting

Residential treatment should be a goal-directed process, and each child should have personalized goals. A problem relevant to most residential centers is the tendency to apply approaches across all types of children and situations, with inadequate attention to individual differences that should warrant differential programming. Most programs claim to have such programming, and there are legal mandates for the individual's right to treatment (Wyatt v. Stickney, 1971) and statutory requirements for individualized education plans. Such requirements, although a step in the right direction, can easily be circumvented, with individualized treatment plans consisting of stock phrases and standardized interventions. Because residential programs are treating children, who as a class are somewhat powerless in our society, special care needs to be taken to insure that goals relevant to the individual's needs are selected and appropriate treatment is provided.

Reliance on Data and Objective Indicators of Progress

If programs are to utilize individual goals and treatment procedures, some means of measuring behavior, monitoring progress, and evaluating treatment effectiveness are important. As will be seen in the research and evaluation section, most residential treatment centers are at a primitive stage in terms of utilization of evaluation data. The development of some means of monitoring each child's behavioral functioning on relevant dimensions will serve clinical as well as research and evaluation purposes. The behaviorally oriented programs have led the way here, with their emphasis on the use of objective data. *Behavior Modifica-*

tion in Child Treatment (Browning & Stover, 1971) is a particularly relevant source with a section on the use of single-subject research designs in assessing the effectiveness of interventions. In a less "behavioral" vein, Redl (1966) and Whittaker (1969) both offer excellent suggestions on observing behavior in the context of residential treatment. With increasing pressure for treatment programs to demonstrate their effectiveness in order to receive funding, this area should be a top priority.

RESEARCH AND EVALUATION IN RESIDENTIAL TREATMENT

A commentary on the state of the art in residential treatment is the fact that it is necessary to organize this chapter with a separate section on research and evaluation issues and findings. It would be preferable to discuss what is known about treatment dimensions and approaches in light of sound research findings, but this is not currently possible.

Evaluative research and program evaluation are often presented as being distinct endeavors. In discussing the evaluation of children's mental health services, Koocher and Broskowski (1979) make this distinction, saying that research is guided by the "standards of science" while the primary concern of program evaluation is "to improve ongoing service programs" (p. 583). This is a questionable distinction because, if information is to be useful to program planners, it must also be reliable and valid. Clinical and administrative decision makers require sound data as much as do journal editors interested in advancing the cause of science. Research and evaluation may be conducted with different concerns and for different reasons, but each would benefit from a mutual blending—to make research more relevant, and to make program evaluations methodologically more refined. The research to be reviewed selectively here is by its nature evaluative. This section is not concerned with demonstrations of the effects of behavioral or psychological techniques in isolation but rather with the outcomes of programs that are composed of a multitude of specified and unspecified treatment components. Knowledge of the effectiveness of programs and, more importantly, why they have these effects will depend upon the increased adoption of applicable research strategies.

Five critical aspects of evaluative research will be identified, based on the authors' experience in evaluating programs and on suggestions from three reviews of residential treatment research (Durkin & Durkin, 1975; Quay, 1979; Whittaker, 1979). These three reviews all conclude that there is a dearth of methodologically adequate research in this area. The statement that "within child/family agencies the current state of the art or science of program evaluation...is primitive or nonexistent" (Koocher & Broskowski, 1979, p. 585) is especially true for residential treatment programs. In presenting these basic components, a research model will be detailed that is applicable across the continuum of care collectively known as residential treatment.

Components of Research

Measurement of Outcome

The primary concern in evaluating residential treatment is to determine what outcomes are experienced by children during and after treatment although the position of those who recommend a systems approach (Durkin & Durkin, 1975) is somewhat at variance with this. There are two distinct types of outcome that may be measured: (1) in-program and (2) follow-up. Few studies have adequately examined both of these. In discussing the range of measures that have been used, some of the higher quality research that has been done will be reviewed.

Two frequently cited studies relate in-program functioning to follow-up status (Allerhand et al., 1966; Taylor & Alpert, 1973). In the former, program records were used to generate five indices of adaptability and role fulfillment during and after treatment, as well as to measure situational stress after treatment, but the reliability data were inadequate. Taylor and Alpert (1973) used a revision of the

Community Adaptation Scale to measure postdischarge adaptation and adaptability while in-program data consisted of ratings of self-worth and behavioral improvement. Another measure that was used and found to be significantly related to adjustment was a child's perception of support in the postdischarge environment. Reliability data were also lacking in this study. Other measures that have been used include systematic ratings of posthospital adjustment, with the ratings based on developmental tasks and garnered from a clinical interview (Garber, 1972), judgments of improvement (Silver, 1961), psychological measures at entry and at discharge, and number of criminal offenses (Craft, Stephenson, & Granger, 1964). One of the best studies included in-program behavioral and attitude measures and related these to work attendance and number of days spent in jail (Goldenberg, 1971).

Behaviorally oriented programs have generated much in-program data based on rating scales, behavioral observations, and records of response to behavioral interventions (Browning & Stover, 1971; Monkman, 1972; Phillips et al., 1973). An excellent evaluation was carried out on Project Re-Ed (Weinstein, 1974) with attention to methodology as well as social relevance. This study compared treatment and two control groups on variables such as internal stress, behavioral improvement, and attitude ratings by Re-Ed staff and referring agencies. Also considered were psychological measures including ideal and perceived self, locus of control, and impulsivity, as well as family relationships, sociometric ratings, a rating of postschool adjustment, and measures of academic achievement.

A wide range of measures has been used, but many are virtually worthless due to their unreliability. Increased use of a research perspective would modify the tendency to make clinical use of measures that have questionable reliability and validity. Points for future consideration include:

1. Outcome should be conceptualized and measured as multidimensional and multidirectional, allowing for both posi-

tive and negative changes in a variety of behavioral areas.

2. More programs should use standardized measures recommended by Achenbach and Edelbrock (1978). Unfortunately, there is also a need for more relevant measures (Wilson & Prentice-Dunn, 1981).

3. Most programs are not even gathering simple outcome data due in part to overreliance on narrative reports, as discussed by Glaser (1973). Programs should adopt quantifiable measures, such as behavioral ratings, to replace some of the narrative information. Other possibilities include Goal Attainment Scaling approaches (Kiresuk & Sherman, 1968).

4. All programs should attend to the ideas raised by Emery and Marholin (1977) regarding the social irrelevance of many measures selected by intervention programs. This is particularly true in regard to residential treatment centers, which may focus on particularly troublesome in-house behaviors with questionable relevance in the outside world.

5. Programs should also include measures of consumer satisfaction in their outcome assessment (Margolis, Sorensen, & Galano, 1977).

6. The child's perceptions should be considered, but this often is not the case.

There are many problems faced by anyone who is attempting to measure outcome of child treatment, such as how to deal with maturation and developmental changes (O'Leary & Turkewitz, 1978). Also of particular relevance to evaluating residential treatment are problems in defining success and failure and the possible nonlinearity of change. Most strategies for evaluation are based on assumptions that change will occur in a linear fashion.

Defining and Measuring Treatment

In regard to intervention programs for children, it has been suggested that the actual components of treatment (i.e., the independent variable) have neither been specified nor independently verified (Wodarski, Feldman, & Pedi, 1974, p. 240). There has been some recent improvement in relation to child treatment programs in general, but this is not so for residential treatment. There are only a few examples (Jesness, 1975) that report a quantified estimate of the degree to which the treatment program was actually implemented.

There are significant problems in even conceptualizing what is included in treatment, but in order to evaluate residential treatment "the treatment itself must be specified in enough detail to be replicable, and judgments about the adequacy of the implementation of a treatment should be possible" (Quay, 1979, p. 387). Berg (1979) discussed the problems inherent in evaluating treatment in therapeutic communities and residential treatment programs, with a focus on developing procedures to determine the consistency between proposed treatment and actual operating procedures. Such efforts in children's residential treatment would be helpful although Berg suggests that the evaluation of such complex programs is unique and nonreplicable. This may be true, but more effort to evaluate and document what is actually occurring should aid in replications and cross-program generalization of research findings. Research such as that conducted by Moos (1974) in evaluating treatment environments should also be applied to residential treatment as, for example, in assessing social climate within a particular program and relating that to outcome.

There will always be problems in trying to yield clear causal pathways between an entire program consisting of numerous elements and behavioral outcomes, which are multidimensional and multidirectional. One strategy is to examine particular elements of treatment that are considered critical and therefore assumed to result in fairly specific outcomes. Browning and Stover (1971) and the Achievement Place literature (Phillips et al., 1973) are replete with examples of such microevaluations. Carefully examining such interventions within the context of specific programs will yield useful evaluation information and add to our knowledge regarding the application of techniques in specific programs. Such individual intervention studies are a step toward determining what elements are contributing to the overall outcome of the program.

Research Design

A research design provides the framework for interpreting, understanding, and using outcome data and determining possible relationships with treatment. Many purported evaluations of residential treatment have no recognizable design beyond the reporting of some measure taken after treatment has terminated. It is rare to see anything approximating classical experimental designs with random assignment and control groups. Research that has actually approached this standard includes Goldenberg's (1971) evaluation of a residential treatment center for delinquents. He used experimental and control groups, but with nonrandom assignment, because he was required to place the 25 most serious cases in the treatment group and the other 25 in a control group. Project Re-Ed (Weinstein, 1974) provides an excellent example of research design. This study did not have random assignment because the project accepted children that no other program could or would work with. There were different controls—a "normal" group and an untreated disturbed group—with analyses demonstrating this group's similarity to the experimental group. Utilizing data gathered at four points in time, comparisons were made across the three groups, with results demonstrating positive treatment effects.

Research designs have also been used in studies of institutionalized delinquents in which there were very large samples and enough administrative control to allow random assignment. Jesness (1971) randomly assigned 655 youths to an experimental treatment and 518 to the control group. Jesness (1975) compared the effects of a behavior modification and a transaction analysis treatment, with 400 subjects assigned randomly to the two different experimental treatments. Such research approaches are not possible for most residential treatment programs, which have a limited number of subjects and no opportunity for random or differential assignment.

Almost all of the work in this area suffers from serious design flaws ranging from comparison on different measures (Allerhand et al., 1966) to the use of only posttreatment measures (Silver, 1961; Garber, 1972; Taylor & Alpert, 1973). Typical research has been based on unreliable data and on judgments of improvement made at discharge or at some time during follow-up with minimal or no comparisons to any baseline data.

Even though there are numerous problems in conducting controlled research in residential treatment settings, there are also possibilities within these limitations. One reason for the past dearth of research may be the tendency to do nothing if traditional experimental designs cannot be used. But there are strategies that are applicable. Especially useful in evaluating particular treatment techniques and their effect on either groups or individuals are the single-subject type designs. Browning and Stover (1971) discussed the use of these designs as part of their experimental-clinical approach to residential treatment. More detail is also provided by Hersen and Barlow (1976).

There is also a need to investigate the applicability of the quasi-experimental designs discussed by Campbell and Stanley (1963). For example, such designs as the time series or interrupted time series, and the nonequivalent control (comparison) group approach should all be applicable. A starting point for any program is to use pre-, post-, and follow-up measures with demonstrated reliability. If these measures are representative of the changes that take place during residential treatment, improvement should be revealed if the program has been effective. If such positive changes are found, further higher level analyses should be used. If not, there is no need for more complex analysis.

Multivariate statistical models (Kerlinger & Pedhazur, 1973) are also useful in evaluating residential treatment. For individual programs, these may be used as a number of cases accumulate over time in order to determine if certain variables, such as child characteristics, are predictive of outcome. The use of such a model would also be facilitated if programs were able to combine resources and samples, with evaluations occurring across a number of programs using the same variables and outcome measures.

Child Characteristics

In addition to outcome, treatment, and design consideration, it would also be helpful if more analyses included child characteristics. This would help identify what kinds of children respond in what ways to what treatments. Very few studies differentiate among children treated although there are certainly interactions between child and treatment characteristics. Jesness (1975) examined nine delinquent subtypes, and Davids, Ryan, and Salvatore (1968) looked at a variety of classification variables. Clients in Project Re-Ed were classified as "acting out" or "withdrawn," by Weinstein (1974) and Prentice-Dunn, Wilson, and Lyman (1981) demonstrated that certain child characteristics were predictive of outcome in a residential treatment center. More of such studies would be helpful if programs utilized existing demographic and classification data. An alternative to the typically unreliable diagnostic categories (Spitzer & Fleiss, 1974) would be the use of behavioral rating scales that allow children to be quantified on a variety of dimensions or subscales. Other possibilities include translating clinical judgments contained in narrative reports into quantifiable data (Glaser, 1973) and use of other ratings, such as overall severity of disorder ratings and ratings of family stressors and support. Research should include data regarding the child's perceptions of himself or herself and of the support that is present in the environment (Taylor & Alpert, 1973). Such information can be readily analyzed and utilized with a multivariate statistical model and can be especially useful in the initial stages of inquiry into linking child, treatment, and program characteristics with outcome.

Systems Considerations

A systems perspective is another approach to evaluating residential treatment. Durkin and Durkin (1975) provide an extensive discussion of this model and the importance of considering the network of interacting influences in residential treatment. Although it is conceptually and theoretically useful as well as important for clinical decision making and placement planning to consider these influences, there is a danger of being lost in a web of complexity. Such an evaluation model is beyond the capabilities of most residential treatment programs. Durkin and Durkin discuss a statewide project conducted in Georgia to determine the community orientation of programs, as well as to gather data to assess program impact on 1,800 children. Such evaluation approaches are most relevant to decision makers at higher levels. For example, statewide funding agencies, who provide the funds for hundreds of children in a variety of treatment programs in a state, may thereby be in a position to conduct large scale evaluations.

RESULTS: WHAT WE KNOW ABOUT RESIDENTIAL TREATMENT

Making any definitive statement about the effectiveness of residential treatment is about as helpful as a similar comment about the effectiveness of psychotherapy (Barrett et al., 1978; Levitt, 1971). It is more useful to examine what kinds of children in what kinds of setting with what specific interventions have what kinds of outcomes measured at which points in time. The literature reviewed does not approach this level of specificity, but there have been some studies pointing the way. Being aware of the methodological limitations involved, what do studies of residential treatment find? Most report some improvement while the child is in the residential program, with this assessment typically based on a global judgment made at or after discharge. Few studies, however, demonstrate improvement compared to any control or comparison group, with Goldenberg (1971) and Weinstein (1974) notable exceptions. Follow-up evaluations have been less positive. For example, Achievement Place programs have provided a wealth of information regarding in-program changes, but comparisons with nontreated delinquents in terms of post-program recidivism have been disappointing (Braukmann, Kirigin, & Wolf, 1976). A number of studies have found little or no relationship between in-program behavior and behavior following discharge (Allerhand et al., 1966; Davids et al., 1968; Taylor & Alpert, 1973). A few studies have demonstrated relationships between child variables and outcomes; for instance, IQ, age, parental involvement, and living situation were shown to be predictive of improvement on behavioral ratings (Prentice-Dunn et al., 1981).

To summarize, the investigation of residential treatment has not been such that there is anything approaching a science or a clear model of what works. If work proceeds on the dimensions noted, future reviews can be more definitive. Current indications are that societal influences and more competition for scarce funds will force programs to be more accountable. An unfortunate effect of this process will be the curtailing of some needed services. Hopefully, those programs that are indeed effective and accomplishing what they claim will be in a position to have their claims substantiated by sound evaluation data and thereby continue to provide services to those children who need them.

REFERENCES

Achenbach, T.M., & Edelbrock, C.S. The classification of child psychopathology: A review and analysis of empirical efforts. *Psychological Bulletin,* 1978, **85,** 1275–1301.

Aichorn, A. *Wayward youth.* New York: Viking, 1935.

Allerhand, M.E., Weber, R., & Haug, M. *Adaptation and adaptability: The Bellefaire follow-up study.* New York: Child Welfare League, 1966.

American Association of Children's Residential Centers. *1981 directory of organizational members.* Washington, D.C.: 1981.

Axline, V.M. *Play therapy.* Houghton Mifflin, 1947.

Azrin, N.H., & Wesolowski, M.D. Theft reversal: An overcorrection procedure for eliminating stealing by retarded persons. *Journal of Applied Behavior Analysis,* 1974, **7,** 577–581.

Barrett, C.L., Hampe, I.E., & Miller, L.C. Research on child psychotherapy. In S.L. Garfield & A.E. Bergin (Eds.), *Handbook of psychotherapy and behavior change* (2nd ed.). New York: Wiley, 1978.

Berg, W.E. The evaluation of treatment in therapeutic communities: Problems of design and implementation. *Evaluation and Program Planning,* 1979, **2,** 41–48.

Bettelheim, B. *Love is not enough.* New York: Free Press, 1950.

Bettelheim, B. *A home for the heart.* New York: Knopf, 1974.

Bettelheim, B., & Sanders, J. Milieu therapy: The orthogenic school model. In J.D. Noshpitz (Ed.), *Basic handbook of child psychiatry* (Vol. 3). New York: Basic Books, 1979.

Braukmann, C.J., Kirigin, K.A., & Wolf, M.M. *Achievement Place: The researcher's perspective.* Paper presented at the annual meeting of the American Psychological Association, Washington, D.C., 1976.

Brodie, R.D. Some aspects of psychotherapy in a residential treatment center. In G.H. Weber & B.J. Haberlein (Eds.), *Residential treatment of emotionally disturbed children.* New York: Behavioral Publications, 1972.

Browning, R.M., & Stover, D.O. *Behavior modification in child treatment.* Chicago: Aldine, 1971.

Buehler, R.E., Patterson, G.R., & Furniss, J.M. The reinforcement of behavior in institutional settings. *Behavior Research and Therapy,* 1966, **4,** 157–167.

Campbell, D.T., & Stanley, J.C. *Experimental and quasi-experimental designs for research.* Chicago: Rand McNally, 1963.

Cavior, E.C., Schmidt, A., & Karacki, L. *An evaluation of the Kennedy Youth Center differential treatment program.* Washington: U.S. Bureau of Prisons, 1972.

Clark, H.B., Caldwell, C.P., & Christian, W.P. Classroom training of conversational skills and remote programming for the practice of these skills in another setting. *Child Behavior Therapy.* 1979, **1,** 139–160.

Coates, R.B., & Miller, A.D. Neutralization of community resistance to group homes. In Y. Bakal (Ed.), *Closing correctional institutions.* Lexington, Mass.: Heath, 1972.

Cohen, H.L., & Filipczak, J. *A new learning environment: A case for learning.* San Francisco: Jossey-Bass, 1971.

Conway, J.B., & Bucher, B.D. Transfer and maintenance of behavior change in children: A review and suggestions. In J. Mash, L.A. Hamenlynck, & L.C. Handy (Eds.), *Behavior modification and families.* New York: Brunner/Mazel, 1976.

Craft, M., Stephenson, G., & Granger, C.A. A controlled trial of authorization and self-governing regimen with adolescent psychopaths. *American Journal of Orthopsychiatry,* 1964, **34,** 543–554.

Davids, A., Ryan, R., & Salvatore, P. Effectiveness of residential treatment. *American Journal of Orthopsychiatry,* 1968, **38,** 469–475.

Dinoff, M., Rickard, H.C., Love, W., & Elder, I. A patient writes his own report. *Adolescence,* 1978, **13,** 135–141.

Drabman, R.S., Spitalnik, R., & O'Leary, K.D. Teaching self-control to disruptive children. *Journal of Abnormal Psychology,* 1973, **82,** 10–16.

Durkin, R.P., & Durkin, A.B. Evaluating residential treatment programs for disturbed children. In M. Guttentag & E.L. Struening (Eds.), *Handbook of evaluation research* (Vol. 2). Beverly Hills, Calif.: Sage, 1975.

Emery, R.E., & Marholin, D., II. An applied behavior analysis of delinquency: The irrelevancy of relevant behavior. *American Psychologist,* 1977, **32,** 860–873.

Ferster, C.B. Positive reinforcement and behavioral deficits of autistic children. *Child Development,* 1961, **32,** 437–456.

Flackett, J.M., & Flackett, G. Criswell House: An alternative to institutional treatment for juvenile offenders. *Federal Probation,* 1970, **34,** 30–37.

Garber, B. *Follow-up study of hospitalized adolescents.* New York: Brunner/Mazel, 1972.

Gesell, A. The conditioned reflex and the psychiatry of infancy. *American Journal of Orthopsychiatry,* 1938, **8,** 19–29.

Glaser, D. *Routinizing evaluation: Getting feedback on effectiveness of crime and delinquency programs.* Rockville, Md.: National Institute of Mental Health, 1973.

Goldenberg, I. *Build me a mountain: Youth, poverty and the creation of new settings.* Cambridge, Mass.: MIT Press, 1971.

Golding, W. *The lord of the flies.* New York: Cowand-McCann, 1955.

Gordon, T. *Parent effectiveness training.* New York: Wyden, 1971.

Group Child Care Consultant Services. *Basic course for residential child care workers.* Chapel Hill, N.C.: School of Social Work, 1977.

Herman, S.H., & Tramontana, J. Instructions and group versus individual reinforcement in modifying disruptive group behavior. *Journal of Applied Behavior Analysis,* 1971, **4,** 113–120.

Hersen, M., & Barlow, D.H. *Single-case experimental designs: Strategies for studying behavior change.* New York: Pergamon, 1976.

Hobbs, N. Helping disturbed children: Psychological and ecological strategies. *American Psychologist,* 1966, **21,** 1105–1151.

Hopkirk, H.W. *Institutions serving children.* New York: Russell Sage Foundation, 1944.

Jesness, C.F. The Preston typology study: An experiment with differential treatment in an institution. *Journal of Research in Crime and Delinquency,* 1971, **8,** 38–52.

Jesness, C.F. Comparative effectiveness of behavior modification and transactional analysis programs for delinquents. *Journal of Consulting and Clinical Psychology,* 1975, **43,** 758–799.

Johnson, M.R., Whitman, T.L., & Barloon-Noble, R. A home-based program for a preschool, behaviorally disturbed child with parents as therapists. *Journal of Behavior Therapy and Experimental Psychiatry,* 1978, **9,** 65–70.

Jones, M.C. A laboratory study of fear: The case of Peter. *Journal of Genetic Psychology,* 1924, **31,** 308–315.

Kazdin, A. *The token economy.* New York: Plenum, 1977.

Kerlinger, F.N., & Pedhazur, E.J. *Multiple regression in behavioral research.* New York: Holt, Rinehart, & Winston, 1973.

Kiresuk, T.J., & Sherman, R. Goal attainment scaling: A general method for evaluating community mental health programs. *Community Mental Health Journal,* 1968, **4,** 443–453.

Koocher, G.P., & Broskowski, A. Issues in the evaluation of mental health services for children. *Professional Psychology,* 1979, **8,** 583–592.

Lazarus, A. The elimination of children's phobias by deconditioning. In H.J. Eysenck (Ed.),

Behavior therapy and the neuroses. New York: Pergamon, 1960.

Levitt, E.E. Research on psychotherapy with children. In A.E. Bergin & S. Garfield (Eds.), *Handbook of psychotherapy and behavior change.* New York: Wiley, 1971.

Loughmiller, C. *Wilderness road.* Austin: University of Texas, 1965.

Lovaas, O.O., Freitag, L., Nelson, K., & Whalen, C. The establishment of imitation and its use for the development of complex behavior in schizophrenic children. *Behavior Research and Therapy,* 1967, **5**, 171–181.

Lyman, R.D. Non-institutional residential facilities for children and adolescents. In M. Dinoff & D.L. Jacobson (Eds.), *Neglected problems in community mental health.* Alabama: University of Alabama Press, 1981.

Margolis, R.B., Sorensen, J.L., & Galano, J. Consumer satisfaction in mental health delivery services. *Professional Psychology,* 1977, **8**, 11–16.

Mayer, M.F., Richman, L.H., & Balcerzak, E.A. *Group care of children: Crossroads and transitions.* New York: Child Welfare League, 1977.

Monkman, M. *A milieu therapy program for behaviorally disturbed children.* Springfield, Ill.: Thomas, 1972.

Moos, R.H. *Evaluating treatment environments: A social ecological approach.* New York: Wiley, 1974.

Morse, W.C., & Small, E.R. Group life space interviewing in a therapeutic camp. *American Journal of Orthopsychiatry,* 1959, **29**, 27–45.

Mowrer, O.H., & Mowrer, W.M. Enuresis—A method for its study and treatment. *American Journal of Orthopsychiatry,* 1938, **8**, 436–459.

O'Leary, K.D., & Turkewitz, H. Methodological errors in marital and child treatment research. *Journal of Consulting and Clinical Psychology,* 1978, **46**, 747–758.

Patterson, G.R., Cobb, J.A., & Ray, R.A. A social engineering technology for retraining the families of aggressive boys. In H.E. Adams & I.P. Unikel (Eds.), *Issues and trends in behavior therapy.* Springfield, Ill.: Thomas, 1972.

Phillips, E.L., Phillips, E.A., Fixsen, D.L., & Wolf, M.M. *The teaching family handbook.* Lawrence, Kansas: University of Kansas Printing Service, 1972.

Phillips, E.L., Phillips, E.A., Wolf, M.M., &

Fixsen, D.L. Achievement Place: Development of the elected manager system. *Journal of Applied Behavior Analysis,* 1973, **6**, 541–563.

Polsky, H.W. *Cottage six: The social system of delinquent boys in residential treatment.* New York: Russell Sage Foundation, 1962.

Polsky, H.W., & Claster, D.S. *The dynamics of residential treatment: A social system analysis.* Chapel Hill, N.C.: University of North Carolina Press, 1968.

Prentice-Dunn, S., Wilson, D.R., & Lyman, R.D. Client factors related to outcome in a residential and day treatment program for children. *Journal of Clinical Child Psychology,* 1981, **10**, 188–191.

Quay, H.C. Residential treatment. In H.C. Quay & J.S. Werry (Eds.), *Psychopathological disorders of childhood* (2nd ed.). New York: Wiley, 1979.

Raush, H.L., Dittman, A.T., & Taylor, J.J. The interpersonal behavior of children in residential treatment. *Journal of Abnormal and Social Psychology,* 1959, **58**, 9–26.

Redl, F. *When we deal with children.* New York: Free Press, 1966.

Redl, F., & Wineman, D. *The aggressive child.* New York: Free Press, 1957.

Repucci, N.D., & Sanders, J.T. Social psychology of behavior modification: Problems of implementation in natural settings. *American Psychologist,* 1974, **29**, 649–660.

Rickard, H.C., & Dinoff, M. (Eds.). *Behavior modification in children: Case studies and illustrations from a summer camp.* University, Al.: University of Alabama Press, 1974.

Rogers-Warren, A., & Baer, D.M. Correspondence between saying and doing: Teaching children to share and praise. *Journal of Applied Behavior Analysis,* 1976, **9**, 335–354.

Rose, S.D. *Treating children in groups: A behavioral approach.* San Francisco: Jossey-Bass, 1972.

Ross, A.O. Learning theory and therapy with children. *Psychotherapy: Theory, Research and Practice,* 1964, **1**, 102–108.

Silver, H. The residential treatment of emotionally disturbed children: An evaluation of 15 years' experience. *Journal of Jewish Communal Service,* 1961, **38**(2).

Spitzer, R.L., & Fleiss, J.L. A reanalysis of the reliability of psychiatric diagnosis. *British*

Journal of Psychiatry, 1974, **125,** 341–347.

Stuart, R.B. Behavioral contracting within the families of delinquents. *Journal of Behavior Therapy and Experimental Psychiatry,* 1971, **2,** 1–11.

Taylor, D.A., & Alpert, S.W. *Continuity and support following residential treatment.* New York: Child Welfare League, 1973.

Trieschman, A.E., Whittaker, J.K., & Brendtro, L.K. *The other 23 hours.* Chicago: Aldine, 1969.

U.S. Bureau of the Census. Persons in institutions and other group quarters. *U.S. Census of Population, Subject Reports,* PC(2)–4E, Tables 3–10, 1970.

Vorrath, H.H., & Brendtro, L.K. *Positive peer culture.* Chicago: Aldine, 1974.

Weinstein, L. *Evaluation of a program for re-educating disturbed children: A follow-up comparison with untreated children.* Final Report to the Bureau of Education of the Handicapped, OE, USDHEW. Project Nos. 6–2974 and 552023, December 1974.

Whittaker, J.K. Observing and recording children's behavior. In A.E. Trieschman, J.K.

Whittaker, & Brendtro, L.K. (Eds.), *The other 23 hours.* Chicago: Aldine, 1969.

Whittaker, J.K. *Caring for troubled children.* San Francisco: Jossey-Bass, 1979.

Wilson, D.R., & Lyman, R.D. Time-out in the treatment of childhood behavior problems: Implementation and research issues. *Child Behavior Therapy,* in press.

Wilson, D.R., & Prentice-Dunn, S. Rating scales in the assessment of child behavior. *Journal of Clinical Child Psychology,* 1981, **10,** 121–126.

Wodarski, J.S., Feldman, R.A., & Pedi, S.J. Objective measurement of the independent variable: A neglected methodological aspect in community-based behavioral research. *Journal of Abnormal Child Psychology,* 1974, **2,** 239–244.

Wolpe, J. *Psychotherapy by reciprocal inhibition.* Stanford, Calif.: Stanford University Press, 1958.

Wyatt *v.* Stickney, 325 F. Supp. 781 (M.D. Ala. 1971), enforced in 334 F. Supp. 1341 (M.D. Ala. 1971), 344 F. Supp. 373, 379 (M.D. Ala. 1972, aff'd sub nom Wyatt *v.* Aderholt, 503 F. 2d 1305 (51 Cir. 1974).

CHAPTER 46

Hospitalization and Medical Care of Children

LAWRENCE J. SIEGEL

Each year more than five million children are hospitalized for diagnostic and treatment procedures or surgery (American Academy of Pediatrics, 1970). An estimated 45 percent of children have been admitted to the hospital for various medical reasons by the time they have reached the age of 7 (Davies, Butler, & Goldstein, 1972). While many children remain in the hospital for a brief time, often for only one day, they encounter numerous aversive experiences. Petrillo and Sanger (1972) state that:

Illness and hospitalization constitute a major stress in early development. They effect a profound change in the child's early life style; he faces separation from his parents and from the security of home routines. He also finds himself at the mercy of a hostile environment—a world of unfamiliar sights, sounds, and smells and of strange people who inflict pain. (p. 99)

This chapter addresses the psychosocial aspects of the medical care of children in the hospital, including the effects of hospitalization on children and approaches for facilitating their adjustment to the hospital experience. While the issues discussed in this chapter are generally applicable to all children who enter the hospital, the primary focus is on children who are hospitalized for elective diagnostic medical procedures and surgery. Typically, these situations involve planned

The author would like to thank Nancy P. Davidson for her helpful comments on this manuscript.

hospitalizations in which there is an opportunity to prepare the child in advance for the events that he or she will experience. Some cases, such as acute appendicitis, burns, or meningitis, require emergency admission to the hospital. Because emergency admissions are unpredictable, they do not permit the child to be prepared in advance for the hospitalization. The special challenges presented by the child who is hospitalized on an emergency basis also will be briefly discussed in this chapter.

Finally, there are the children with chronic illnesses such as kidney disease, cystic fibrosis, sickle cell anemia, or leukemia who require numerous hospitalizations for treatment and/or surgery. For many of these children, extended periods of hospitalization occur throughout their entire lifetime. In addition, some chronic disorders such as leukemia or cystic fibrosis are highly life threatening, and, as a result, admission to the hospital may have a considerably different meaning for these children and their families compared to children who are hospitalized for elective surgery such as tonsillectomy. Therefore, while chronically ill children encounter many experiences in the hospital similar to those of acutely ill children or children admitted for elective treatment, the stresses of a chronic illness present special problems and challenges in adjustment that are beyond the scope of this chapter. The interested reader is referred to Abram (1972), Debuskey (1970), Fomuford (1980), Frederick (1977), Mattson (1972), and Pless (1973) for a more comprehensive discussion of the psychosocial problems of chronically ill children.

HISTORICAL DEVELOPMENTS IN THE CARE OF HOSPITALIZED CHILDREN

Systematic concern with the psychosocial needs of the physically ill and hospitalized child has been a relatively recent phenomenon. Advances in the medical treatment of children have, until recently, far surpassed the changes that have occurred in hospital procedures to promote the emotional well being of the child and his or her family. Kenny (1975) presents a vivid picture of the conditions that children typically encountered in the hospital prior to the early 1950s.

The earliest concern in hospital care for children was mainly disease oriented or custodial. The predominant emphasis in the management of the child was the facilitation of medical treatment plans. Even worse, the management routine was usually an adaptation of the procedures used with adults. This approach totally ignored the children's developmental status and the complications that would result from restructuring the child's psychosocial development while treating his physical illness. Indeed when rules and procedures were modified for children, they were more limited and discriminatory than sensitive and beneficial. Rules for visiting, bed confinement and feeding were all more restrictive for children than adults. The child was separated from his family, and parents were usually allowed to visit him only once a week for an hour. The child was seldom treated as a person, least of all a person whose major needs centered on close, personal, loving support to help him deal with his world. In the hospital the child was handled and prodded by efficient, but unknown persons. It is a wonder any child coped successfully with the psychological trauma that hospitalization added to the trauma of physical illness. (p. 583)

The pioneering work of James Robertson at the Tavistock Clinic in London was instrumental in changing the practices in hospitals toward the treatment and medical care of children. Robertson made two films in the 1950s, one clearly portraying the intense emotional distress of a young child who was separated from his parents for a week while undergoing minor surgery in the hospital and the other demonstrating, in sharp contrast, the positive adjustment of a young child who was permitted to remain with his mother while he was hospitalized for surgery. These films provided the impetus for changing the restrictive policies of many hospitals that denied parents the opportunity to remain with their children during their hospitalization. As Shore and Goldston (1978) have noted, during the decade portrayed in these films, only 28 out of 5,500 general hospitals permitted parents to remain with their children overnight in the hospital.

Another significant event that helped to call attention to the importance of providing an environment in the hospital that was responsive to the emotional needs of children was the publication by the National Institute of Mental Health in 1965 of a collection of papers entitled *Red Is the Color of Hurting: Planning for Children in the Hospital* (United States Department of Health, Education, and Welfare, 1965). This document presented an interdisciplinary perspective on the impact of hospitalization on children and resulted in specific recommendations for reducing the unnecessary stress typically encountered by hospitalized children.

At the present time, the primary advocacy group for the comprehensive care of hospitalized children is the Association for the Care of Children's Health (ACCH). This multidisciplinary organization was founded in 1965 to promote the psychosocial welfare of children and their families in health care settings. In addition to publishing its own journal, *Children's Health Care,* this organization has established guidelines for developing hospital programs that are consistent with children's emotional and developmental needs (Association for the Care of Children's Health, 1980). Among other things, ACCH advocates the participation of parents in their children's health care, unlimited visiting rights of parents of hospitalized children, the establishment of alternative medical care to avoid hospitalization wherever possible, and the availability of facilities for parents who desire to remain with their children in the hospital overnight. Guidelines for developing Child Life Programs in hospitals have also been established (Association for the Care of Children's Health, 1980). Child Life Programs provide activities for the hospitalized child that attempt to facilitate coping with stressful experiences and to maintain patterns of living that closely approximate the child's normal environment. Currently, Child Life Programs are more typically found in pediatric hospitals that serve only children rather than in general hospitals that have only one or several wards for pediatric patients.

Considerable progress has been made in the overall care that children receive in hospitals since Robertson called attention to the needs of hospitalized children three decades ago. However, as Shore and Goldston (1978) have indicated, many hospital policies affecting the care of children continue to be perpetuated more by tradition than by the influence of our knowledge of children's physical and emotional growth. These authors (Shore & Goldston, 1976) have also pointed out that this country lags considerably behind the hospital care provided to children and their families in many European countries. For example, in some countries parents can take official paid leave from work to remain with their children during the duration of the hospitalization. Furthermore, special facilities are provided to permit the parents to stay overnight in the hospital, and the parents are regarded as an integral part of the health care team rather than as intruders into the domain of the hospital staff.

PSYCHOLOGICAL EFFECTS OF HOSPITALIZATION AND MEDICAL CARE

Many potential sources of stress for the hospitalized child undergoing medical procedures have been identified in the literature. Among the factors that have been suggested as contributing to children's emotional distress in the hospital are separation from family members; pain and discomfort from illness, injury, or medical treatment; unfamiliarity with the hospital environment and its personnel; immobility; disruption of typical routines and loss of control over daily events; greater dependency on others; concerns about bodily harm and embarrassment; and distortions and misconceptions about the purpose of hospitalization and medical procedures (cf. Belmont, 1970; Gellert, 1958; Goslin, 1978; Kenny, 1975; Rae, 1981).

Different children are obviously affected by these factors to a greater or lesser degree. There has been considerable speculation about which variables will influence whether a child perceives the above factors as stressful and, therefore, determine the child's actual response to the hospital experience. These moderator variables have included the age, sex, and cognitive-developmental level of the child; medical diagnosis; length of hospitalization; previous experience with medical procedures and the hospital; nature and timing of preparation for the hospital experience; prehospital psychological adjustment; and parental ability to function as a supportive resource for the child (cf. Menke, 1981; Petrillo & Sanger, 1972; Vernon et al., 1965).

Even a cursory review of the literature on the psychological sequelae of hospitalized children indicates that there are few methodologically sound studies in this area. Most of the early work on the effects of hospitalization and medical treatment on children were case studies or presented descriptive or anecdotal evidence with little objective data (Chapman, Loeb, & Gibbons, 1956; Deutsch, 1942; Freud, A., 1962; Jackson et al., 1953; Jessner, Blom, & Woldfogel, 1952; Jessner & Kaplan, 1949; Levy, 1945; Prugh et al., 1953). Evidence from these early reports suggested that the incidence of children's stress reactions during and following hospitalization varied from 10–30 percent for severe psychological disturbances to as much as 90 percent for mild emotional reactions in children hospitalized for surgery (Jessner et al., 1952; Prugh et al., 1953; Schaffer & Callender, 1959). These stress reactions have been reported to manifest themselves as a variety of behavior problems including sleep and appetite disturbances, regressive or compulsive behaviors, anger and aggression, enuresis or encopresis, phobias and social withdrawal (Prugh, 1965; Prugh & Eckhardt, 1980).

In a comprehensive review of over 200 articles and books on the psychological reactions of children to hospitalization and illness, Vernon et al. (1965) delineated four variables that were most often cited as major determinants of psychological upset: (1) unfamiliarity of the hospital setting, (2) separation from parents, (3) age, and (4) prehospital personality. They concluded that there was sufficient evidence that unfamiliarity and separation were clearly associated with behavioral disturbances *following* hospitalization. Separation and age were judged to be most important to the child's emotional response *during* the hospital experience. There was a curvilinear relationship between the age of the child and the extent of his or her stress reaction with the younger children (6 months to 4 years old) appearing to be the most likely to become psychologically upset. While there was no consistent relationship between the child's prehospital personality and response to the hospital experience, there was some suggestive evidence that poor adjustment prior to hospitalization was more likely to result in more frequent and extreme behavior problems both during and after hospitalization. Evidence for consistent relationships between children's psychological response to hospitalization and several other variables examined by Vernon et al. (1965) (i.e., previous hospitalization, sex of the child, and nature of the child's illness and treatment) was either insufficient or equivocal.

In addressing themselves to the question "Is hospitalization upsetting?" Vernon and his colleagues concluded that this question is difficult to answer because the studies reviewed have numerous methodological problems limiting the meaning and generalizability of their findings. Among some of the methodological problems noted by these authors are the failure of investigators clearly to operationalize and describe the psychological variables that they were attempting to measure

during and after hospitalization, failure to demonstrate acceptable reliability and validity of the measures used, failure to use raters or observers who are "blind" to the purpose of the study or the subjects' experimental condition, and failure to use multiple observers to obtain data on observer reliability. In addition, differences between studies on a number of important dimensions such as the measures used to assess the child's response to the hospital experience, the time at which the child's behavior was measured, variability in hospital procedures, and differences in a number of patient variables prohibits a comparison of results from one study to the next. Finally, the absence of appropriate norms for the incidence of stress reactions in children who have not been hospitalized precludes an accurate assessment of the impact of hospitalization-induced stress in the development of behavior problems in children (Davenport & Werry, 1970).

Vernon and his colleagues (Vernon, Schulman, & Foley, 1966; Vernon, Foley, & Schulman, 1967), have attempted a more systematic investigation of the effects of hospitalization and medical procedures on children's behavior. They developed the Post-Hospital Behavior Rating Scale composed of 28 problem behaviors most frequently cited in the literature as occurring in children following their hospitalization. They mailed the questionnaire to 800 parents of children between the ages of 1 month to 16 years who had been hospitalized for various reasons. Approximately 48 percent of the questionnaires were returned, allowing for an analysis of data from 387 children. A factor analysis of the questionnaire responses yielded six factors: (1) general anxiety and regression, (2) separation anxiety, (3) anxiety about sleep, (4) eating disturbance, (5) aggression toward authority, and (6) apathy withdrawal. They found that children in the age range of 6 months to 4 years were the most adversely affected by the hospitalization, showing significantly higher scores than other age groups on all six factors, particularly separation anxiety. Length of hospitalization was also an important variable, with children hospitalized for more than two weeks manifesting psychological upset on three of the factors. No systematic effects of prior hospital experience, sex, or birth order were observed on any of the factors.

A particularly interesting finding was that approximately 25 percent of the children were reported by their parents to have improved in their behavior or remained relatively unchanged. Therefore, for these children, most of whom were from lower socioeconomic families, the hospital experience actually appeared to have a positive psychological effect.

This latter finding is consistent with some of the literature that indicates that hospitalization does not uniformly produce psychological distress in children and, in fact, can be a highly positive experience resulting in psychological and emotional benefits for children (cf. Oremland & Oremland, 1973; Rae, 1981; Shore, Geiser, & Wolman, 1965; Solnit, 1960). It has been suggested, for example, that the hospital experience can provide an opportunity for children to learn to master internal states such as anxiety and external stresses in their environment such as separation and pain and, thereby, increase their self-confidence and coping self-efficacy (Menke, 1981; Rae, 1981). Furthermore, with children from home environments that are particularly stressful or who have been deprived of normal developmental opportunities, hospitalization can provide the child with physical, social, and emotional experiences that are therapeutically beneficial (Oremland & Oremland, 1973; Rae, 1981; Solnit, 1960; Vernon et al., 1965). For example, for some children, the hospital may provide access to more nutritional, recreational, and educational opportunities than are typical in their home environment. Corrective emotional and social experiences can also result from the attention and supportive care provided by the hospital staff and from the opportunity for social experiences with other hospitalized children. Goslin (1978) has suggested that many of these positive effects from hospitalization can be attributed to recent changes in hospital policies and an increased awareness of the psychosocial needs of hospitalized children.

A final study by Davenport and Werry (1970) is relevant to this area. They investigated 145 children 1–15 years old using the Post-Hospital Behavior Rating Scale (Vernon et al., 1966) to measure children's behavioral adjustment two weeks after hospitalization. Children undergoing general anesthesia for tonsillectomies or dental surgery were compared to a control group of children composed of either siblings of the patients or children from an outpatient pediatric clinic. Most children tended to show slight overall improvement on the questionnaire with specific improvements noted on four of the six factors. No differences were found between the hospitalized and nonhospitalized groups. While the investigators conclude that these results do not support the generally held assumption that many children experience problems in behavioral adjustment following discharge from the hospital, there are several methodological problems with this study that make interpretations of these findings difficult. For example, there was no attempt to control for the child's diagnosis or length of stay in the hospital or to evaluate the possible effects of these factors in the data analysis. In addition, the hospital and control groups were not matched on important variables such as age, sex, socioeconomic status, or prior history of hospitalization.

In summary, the literature does not consistently support the notion that hospitalization adversely affects most children. It would appear that some children can encounter the hospital experience with no appreciable effects on their behavior or can even improve in their behavioral adjustment following the experience. While there is some empirical support for the widely held view that hospitalization for surgery and associated medical procedures such as anesthesia can result in psychological upset in many children both during and after hospitalization, the evidence is far from unanimous.

As noted earlier, the child's cognitive level of development has been considered an important factor in influencing the manner in which the child will respond to his or her illness, the hospital experience, or the medical procedures. Various writers have proposed that the effects of hospitalization on children can best be understood within a developmental framework (cf. Goslin, 1978; Rae, 1981; Shore & Goldston, 1978) since a child's perceptions of an event as threatening or stressful will be influenced, to a large extent, by his or her conceptual understanding of the experience. Information about the developmental progression of children's concepts regarding the etiology and treatment of illness and reasons for hospitalization should enable health care workers to predict better how a particular child will respond to the hospital experience and to communicate more effectively with children about the medical procedures they will undergo.

Recently several investigators have explored children's concepts of health and illness as a function of developmental level. Campbell (1975) asked 264 hospitalized children, 6–12 years old, for their definition of illness. The children's responses were categorized by two independent raters into 11 categories pertaining to somatic feeling states, objective detectable indicators, and psychosocial indicators. Consistent developmental trends were observed in the children's definitions of illness ranging from undifferentiated feeling states (e.g., feeling sick) to specified and localized somatic states (e.g., stomach aches), visible external signs (e.g., swollen arm), objective signs not clearly visible (e.g., hot forehead) and finally specific disease concepts (e.g., diabetes, appendicitis). Thus, the children's developmental level of cognitive sophistication is consistent with their progression in sophistication of their definitional concepts of illness.

Three stages in the development of a concept of illness were identified in 60 hospitalized children 5–9 years of age by Simeonsson, Buckley, and Monson (1979). In the first stage, the child's thought process involved magical thinking and circular logic with illness being viewed as the result of some specific human action (e.g., becoming ill after eating someone else's food). In the second stage, children viewed illness as caused by one specific external factor related to illness or health (e.g., illness caused by germs or a cut finger).

Finally, illness in the third stage was viewed in terms of generalized or abstract notions of physical susceptibility (e.g., illness caused by getting a virus from another person or because the pancreas is not producing sufficient insulin to use the sugar in the blood).

Bibace and Walsh (1980) interviewed 72 children, 4, 7, and 11 years old, asking them 12 questions pertaining to the causes and cures of illness. The children's responses were classified according to Piaget's three broad stages of cognitive development. Each of these stages was further subdivided into two subcategories as follows: (1) preoperational stage—phenomenism and contagion, (2) concrete operational stage—contamination and internalization, and (3) formal operational stage—physiological and psychophysiological. Approximately 70 percent of 4-year-olds gave phenomenistic explanations, 75 percent of 7-year-olds provided contaministic explanations, and 70 percent of 11-year-olds gave physiological explanations.

In a related investigation, Pidgeon (1981) studied the coping functions of the questions asked by young hospitalized children. Question asking was viewed as a means of helping children to manage novelty and incongruity in their environment, to establish supportive social contacts with adults in a stressful situation, to influence the actions of others, and to achieve cognitive clarity or reality testing. The spontaneous questions of 3–5-year-old children were sampled in structured and unstructured situations during the first two days after admission to the hospital. Using Piaget's functional classification system, the largest number of children's questions (53 percent) were about the actions and intentions of hospital personnel regarding therapeutic activities, play and social activities, and routine care. The second largest category of children's questions were about the names of objects and persons in the hospital environment. These findings suggest that the preschool-aged child maintains a vigilant orientation in the hospital and that preparation procedures should include information about the actions and intentions of hospital personnel and the identification of familiar and unfamiliar objects.

Siegel (1981a, 1981b) conducted an ecological assessment of self-generated coping strategies used by hospitalized children to determine if children who make an optimal adjustment to hospitalization for illness or surgery use different coping strategies from those of children who make a less satisfactory adjustment to the experience. This investigation was particularly interested in assessing the cognitive and behavioral coping responses in which children engaged during stressful and painful medical procedures. A multidimensional assessment approach was used to evaluate the anxiety level and response to pain of 80 children, 8–14 years old, who were hospitalized for minor elective surgery. In addition, that evening before surgery and following several stress points (e.g., blood test, diagnostic procedures, preoperative injection) a structured interview was conducted with the children to evaluate, among other things, their typical coping responses to painful and anxiety-provoking experiences both in and out of the hospital. An example of one of the interview questions was:

Pretend your best friend has to go to the doctor for a blood test like you just had. What advice would you give him or her so that they wouldn't be worried about it or so it wouldn't bother them? Did you do any of those things or think about any of those things when you had your blood test?

Children were classified as successful copers if they were consistently rated by a nurse and physician as being cooperative with the procedures, showing low anxiety, and manifesting high thresholds for physical discomfort. On the other hand, unsuccessful copers were defined as being uncooperative, showing high anxiety, and manifesting low tolerance for discomfort. The results indicated that successful copers had more accurate information about why they were in the hospital and asked more questions about the hospital than unsuccessful copers. Successful copers also reported using more different strategies for managing stressful and painful experiences than unsuccessful copers such as imagery-based rehearsal in which they planned how

they might confront a stressful or painful event prior to its occurrence. Unsuccessful copers, on the other hand, reported using significantly more negative self-statements regarding their ability to tolerate discomfort, such as thinking about how much the needle was hurting, and reported thinking more often about past experiences where they were unable effectively to tolerate painful procedures similar to those encountered in the hospital. A multiple regression analysis revealed that the number of different coping strategies used by the children accounted for most of the variance of successful coping followed by the extent of accuracy of their knowledge regarding the reason for their hospitalization, with 23 percent and 18 percent of the variance respectively.

Taken together, these studies indicate that it is important to identify those factors that influence coping responses in children to enable health care workers to understand better the transient or long term behavioral problems that are sometimes observed during or following the hospitalization of a child. Such factors must also be considered when developing intervention programs to facilitate children's coping with the hospital experience. Children's conceptual abilities and typical modes of responding to stressful situations will most certainly affect their ability to manage their hospitalization effectively and their ability to benefit from preparation programs. Mastery of the hospital experience is dependent, to a large extent, on the cognitive, affective, and behavioral resources that are available in the child's repertoire.

PREPARATION OF CHILDREN FOR HOSPITALIZATION AND MEDICAL PROCEDURES

While there is some disagreement about the ideal timing for preparation of children for the hospital experience, particularly when this is accompanied by surgery or other medical procedures, there is almost universal agreement in the literature about the necessity for some form of preparation to reduce the stress often associated with hospitalization (Siegel, 1976). Most of the work in this area has been in the preparation of children for surgery or invasive diagnostic procedures.

A survey of the prehospital preparation programs offered at 62 nonchronic pediatric hospitals in the United States was recently conducted by Peterson and Ridley-Johnson (1980). While 74 percent of the hospitals reported using some prehospital preparation procedure, only 42 percent provided such preparation to all children who entered the hospital. Thirty-seven percent reported that all children undergoing surgery received some form of preparation while only 19 percent provided preparation for children receiving special diagnostic procedures such as cardiac catheterization. Finally, 86 percent of the respondents (e.g., nurses, hospital administrators, child life workers) rated hospital preparation as "essential" while the remaining 14 percent rated preparation as "helpful but nonessential." Although there are no comparable data on the prehospital preparation programs provided to children in general hospitals, it is likely that there are considerably fewer systematic preparation programs offered to children in such settings.

Even where preparation programs are available, patients may not take advantage of them. Hunnisett and Knowles (1970), for example, report that only 15 percent of parents and their children who were invited to a preadmission preparation tour of the hospital actually attended the program. These children had been scheduled to enter the hospital for various medical problems.

Vernon et al. (1965) have delineated three variables that are the focus of most preparation programs with children: (1) giving information to the child, (2) encouraging emotional expression, and (3) establishing a trusting relationship between the child and the hospital staff. Several methods have been used to prepare children for the stressful events associated with hospitalization and surgery by incorporating one or more of these variables into the preparation procedure.

At the present time, the most frequently used method of preparing children for the hospital and surgery is preoperative instruction (Heller, 1967; Mellish, 1969; Peterson & Ridley-Johnson, 1980). It is typically assumed that the emotional stress that the child often experiences during hospitalization is the result of the child's exposure to a setting, procedures, and people with which he or she is unfamiliar and which the child does not understand. In addition, it has been suggested that children about to be hospitalized for surgery who do not have accurate information about the hospital are likely to develop distorted ideas that may contribute to their anxiety and emotional upset. These views are supported by a study by Gofman, Buckman, and Schade (1957) in which 100 children were asked what their parents had told them about the reason for their hospitalization. They found that 26 percent of the children had been told nothing, 22 percent were given vague or unclear explanations, and 27 percent had obtained information from overhearing the conversation of others. Only 25 percent of the children had received adequate information about the reasons for their hospitalization. The primary purpose of the preoperative instruction is, therefore, to impart information to the child that will correct any misinformation that he or she might have and to help the child to master the experience by anticipating events and procedures and understanding their meaning and purpose. It is presumed by this reasoning that unexpected stress is more anxiety producing for the child than is anticipated or predictable stress (Siegel, 1976).

Various methods have been used to provide the child with information about the hospital and surgery. A nurse or child life worker may visit the child at home or in the hospital and show him or her pictures of the hospital and its personnel and answer any questions that the child may have. A storybook, pamphlet, or coloring book explaining the forthcoming hospitalization and surgery may be sent to the parents that they read to the child before he or she comes to the hospital. In some instances the child and his or her parents may visit the hospital prior to the day of admission to become familiar with the setting and staff. In addition, the surgeon and/or anesthesiologist will frequently visit the child in the hospital room prior to surgery to explain the nature of the operation and the events the child will experience.

The nature of the information given to the child varies from one hospital to the next and is determined in part by the child's age and reason for hospitalization. In general, most authors have proposed that the hospitalized child who is about to experience some medical procedure should be told what will happen and why and what he or she will experience. It is suggested that this be done in a way that is both candid and reassuring and that takes into account both the child's age and general level of emotional and cognitive development.

Cohen and Lazarus (1980) have identified four specific types of information that can be provided in the context of medical treatment. Information can be provided to the patient regarding: (1) the nature of the disease or reasons for medical treatment, (2) the actual medical procedures that will be used, (3) the sensations that will be experienced and possible side effects of treatment, and (4) specific coping strategies that the patient might utilize to manage the forthcoming procedures. These authors note that several types of information are typically presented to the patient in the context of a supportive relationship with the hospital staff. As a result, it is difficult to determine the relative efficacy of the relationship or information factors in facilitating the patient's adjustment to the experience.

Play therapy programs have also been described in the literature as preoperative preparation techniques with children (Azarnoff & Flegal, 1975; Dimock, 1960; Impallaria, 1955; Knudsen, 1975; Tisza, Hurwitz, & Angoff, 1970). The child is given the opportunity to act out, through doll or puppet play or through drawing, the events that he or she will experience in the hospital. It is felt that such activities permit the child to express fears and concerns and, with the assistance of a supportive adult, to control and reduce them. Knudsen (1975) notes that "play is an effective method for both decreasing anxiety and providing concrete information. Play is the nat-

ural world of children. It is an excellent resource readily available to the staff for helping the child master unfamiliar or foreign experiences" (p. 682). Finally, Impallaria (1955) observes that, through active play, children encourage each other to express and act out their fears and concerns about the hospital and that reassurance provided by a child may be more beneficial than reassurance given by an adult. In regard to this latter point, peer support groups have also been used to facilitate the child's adjustment to the hospital experience (Cofer & Nir, 1975; Frank, 1978; Sheridan, 1975).

Most of the literature on the preparation of children for hospitalization and medical procedures consists of descriptive reports of the preparation program or anecdotal evidence for its effectiveness. There were several early attempts to evaluate the effects of a preparation procedure (primarily the presentation of factual information concerning the hospital experience) on children's adjustment both during and following hospitalization (e.g., Cassell, 1965; Jackson et al., 1953; Jessner et al., 1952; Prugh et al., 1953; Vaughn, 1957). These studies have numerous methodological problems that seriously limit the conclusions that can be drawn from them (cf. Siegel, 1976; Vernon et al., 1965). Comprehensive discussions of methodological issues in research on the preparation of children for hospitalization and medical treatment have been discussed in detail elsewhere (cf. Melamed, 1977; Melamed & Siegel, 1980; Siegel, 1976).

During the last decade, there has been an increase in the number of adequately designed studies that have investigated various procedures for preparing children for hospitalization and surgery.

Vernon (1973) and Vernon and Bailey (1974) found that children 4–9 years old who observed a film depicting several children responding in a calm and cooperative manner to anesthesia induction exhibited significantly less disruptive and fearful behaviors during induction of anesthesia than a control group who did not observe the modeling film. There were no differences between the groups on posthospital adjustment.

In a more elaborate study, Melamed and Siegel (1975) investigated the efficacy of filmed modeling in reducing the anxiety of 4–12-year-old children who were admitted to the hospital for elective surgery. The study also evaluated the effects of the modeling preparation film on the children's emotional adjustment during the posthospitalization period. In order to avoid the methodological problems of earlier research, this study controlled for the age, sex, prior hospitalization, and type of surgery. A multidimensional approach to assessing the child's response to the hospital experience was used, which included self-report, and physiological and behavioral observation measures of anxiety. In addition, the measures were further selected to differentiate between the state and trait dimensions of anxiety (Spielberger, 1966).

The effectiveness of the hospital preparation film in reducing the preoperative anxiety of experimental children was compared with that of a film with content unrelated to the hospitalization shown to a control group. The experimental film depicted a peer model coping with a wide range of experiences typically encountered by children hospitalized for elective surgery. In addition to the explanations of the hospital procedures provided by the medical staff, various scenes were narrated by the child, who described his feelings and concerns at each stage of the hospital experience.

State measures of anxiety revealed a significant reduction of preoperative (night before surgery) and postoperative (3–4 weeks postsurgery examination) fear arousal in the experimental as compared to the control film group. That is, experimental subjects showed lower sweat gland activity, fewer self-reported medical fears, and fewer exhibited anxiety-related behaviors than children in the control group. Furthermore, parents reported a significant increase in the number of behavior problems in the children who did not see the modeling film. As predicted, the trait measures of anxiety did not demonstrate an effect of the treatment conditions.

A related study by Siegel (1977) investigated the effects of prior history of hospitalization and exposure to a peer-modeling film on anxiety-related behaviors in children under-going elective surgery. The procedure was the same as Melamed and Siegel (1975) had used with the exception that history of hospitalization was included as an independent variable. Children admitted to the hospital for elective surgery were assigned to treatment groups based on whether this was their first or second hospital experience. In general, the results of the Melamed and Siegel (1975) study were replicated in that the film was effective in reducing the emotional distress of children were who hospitalized for the first time. However, the film tended to have no significant effect on children seeing it immediately prior to their second hospitalization for surgery. Children who were hospitalized for the second time had significantly higher prefilm levels of anxiety on the self-report and physiological indices of anxiety, suggesting that the second hospitalization may be more anxiety producing for some children. In addition, children with previous hospital experience tended to be significantly more anxious the evening prior to surgery than were children in the hospital for the first time, regardless of the film intervention. These findings demonstrate that not all children may benefit from exposure to the same preparation program and are contrary to the generally held assumption that underlies most of the prehospital preparation literature. Although several authors have discussed time of preparation and its possible influence on the effectiveness of the preparation of children of various ages, there has been little systematic investigation of this variable. Most authors seem to agree that older children may need a longer interval between the preparation and surgery than younger children. Mellish (1969) suggests that younger children need only a few days of preparation since a longer period of time may serve to intensify anxiety about the impending hospitalization and surgery. Similarly, Heller (1967) comments that "the older children will need a more detailed and lengthy preparation. The younger child, because of a shorter attention can be prepared much closer to the actual time of hospitalization.... A few days of preparation for the younger child and several days to weeks for the older child would seem reasonable" (p. 13). Dimock (1960) has recommended that preparation begin 1–3 weeks prior to hospitalization, while Robertson (1958) and Pillsbury (1951) suggest that preparation begin not earlier than one week prior to admission.

A recent study by Melamed et al. (1976) investigated the effects of time of preparation on children's response to hospitalization. The subjects and procedures were similar to that used by Melamed and Siegel (1975). Children were divided into two groups, one which viewed the peer-modeling film 6–9 days prior to their admission to the hospital. The results indicated that time of preparation was not a major factor influencing the children's overall response to the hospital. The age of the child, however, was found to be an important factor in evaluating the optimal time for film preparation. Younger children did not benefit from advanced preparation but did exhibit reduced stress reactions when they were prepared immediately before admission. Older children, on the other hand, appeared to benefit from the film regardless of whether they viewed it several days prior to admission or the day they came to the hospital.

Using a nonpatient population of children, 7–12 years old, Roberts et al. (1981) investigated a preventive program for reducing children's fears of hospitals and medical procedures. One group of school children viewed a 30-minute slide and audiotape show depicting two children in the hospital for tonsillectomies. Various medical procedures, personnel, and equipment were shown and described. The audiotape was narrated by the child models. Another group of children saw a slide show that was unrelated to the hospital. The results indicated that children who observed the hospital relevant slide and audiotape package exhibited a significant reduction in self-reported medical fears compared to the control group. These group differences were maintained at a two-week follow-up assessment. Although such a prevention program remains to be validated in terms of children's actual behavior in medical settings, these findings do suggest that children's concerns about hospitalization and medical treatment can be reduced even when there is no impending admission to the hospital. Furthermore, as the investigators note, such a preventive program has potential applicability for children who require admission to the hospital on an emergency basis where prehospital preparation may not be possible at the time of admission.

PREPARATION OF PARENTS

Some investigators have focused on the parents of hospitalized children, particularly the mother, as the primary point of intervention in facilitating the child's adjustment to the hospital. As McCue (1980) has noted parents are usually

> the primary support system for most children and with proper information and education, they can do more for their child emotionally, than even the best trained staff. When parents attend the actual preparation, not only do they receive detailed medical information, but they can observe and model the calm, mastery-oriented approach of the preparation therapist. (pp. 250–251)

It has also been suggested that parents who are anxious about their child's hospitalization will transmit their anxiety to the child and, therefore, increase the child's stress reaction rather than facilitate coping behavior (Vander-Veer, 1949). While there are some data to suggest that the mother's presence during stressful medical procedures can reduce the emotional impact of the experience for the child and increase cooperative behavior (Schulman et al., 1967), there are also data that indicate that the mother's presence may increase the child's emotional behavior during the procedure (Shaw & Routh, 1980). These discrepant findings may be the result of individual differences in the mother's ability to moderate the child's stress response. The mother's coping behavior, however, was not assessed in these studies. In addition, the mothers did not receive any formal preparation or anticipatory counseling prior to their child's undergoing the medical procedures.

In a series of studies by Skipper and Leonard (1968) and Skipper, Leonard, and Rhymes (1968), the effects of an intervention program with mothers on their child's response to hospitalization for minor elective surgery were investigated. The results indicated that mothers who received the experimental intervention either at the time of their child's admission to the hospital or at several stressful periods, such as the child's return from the recovery room, rated themselves as being considerably less anxious, more satisfied with the medical and nursing care, and more helpful to their child than control group mothers who did not receive any special intervention program. In these studies the experimental intervention consisted of a supportive and reassuring nurse who provided the mothers with information about the hospital routines and medical procedures and informed the mothers of their role in caring for their child in the hospital. The most significant finding was the effect of this intervention program on the children. Numerous physiological and behavioral measures indicated that experimental group children exhibited less emotional distress, more rapid physical recovery in the hospital, and fewer behavioral disturbances following hospitalization than children in the control group. Similar results are reported by Mahaffy (1965) in which mothers of hospitalized children were the primary focus of the preparation program. These studies suggest that parent-focused intervention can have a considerable impact not only on the parent's adjustment to the hospital experience but, more importantly, on the child's ability to cope effectively with the stresses of hospitalization.

Taking a different approach to parental preparation, Roskies, Mongeon, and Gagnon-Lefebvre (1978) were interested in increasing mothers' participation in the care of their young children in the hospital. In a preliminary study, these investigators found that few mothers were taking advantage of the extended visiting hours in the hospital. They were primarily concerned with reducing the stresses of parental separation for young children 1–5 years old. Mothers in the experimental group met with a nurse for one-half hour prior to their child's admission to the hospital. The mother was provided information about the hospital routine, the medical treatment that the child would receive, and

typical psychological reactions of children to hospitalization. The mother's role in providing routine physical care and emotional support to her child was also emphasized and encouraged. The results indicated that mothers in the experimental group spent significantly more time with their children in the hospital than mothers in the control group who did not receive any intervention. Fathers in the experimental group also visited their children more often than control fathers despite the fact that mothers were the primary focus of the intervention program. In addition to spending more time with their children, experimental group parents also spent significantly more time actively providing both routine physical care and psychological support. Unfortunately, the study did not assess whether increased parental involvement had any effect on the child's adjustment to the hospitalization.

JOINT PARENT-CHILD PREPARATION

Several programs have been developed in which both the child and parents have received some form of preparation intervention in the hospital. A comprehensive parent-child preparation program was evaluated by Wolfer and Visintainer (1975). In the experimental condition, the mother and child received extensive preparation and supportive care at six "stress points" throughout the hospitalization, including time of admission, before the blood test, in the afternoon before surgery, before the preoperative medications, before transport to the operating room, and upon return from the recovery room. The child component of the preparation included information about the sequence of events, sensory expectations, identification of appropriate roles and expected behaviors, rehearsal of upcoming events, and emotional support. A nurse provided mothers in the experimental group with individual attention at the stress points, an opportunity to clarify their feelings and thoughts, accurate information and reassurance, and an explanation regarding ways in which the mother could help care for her child. Parents and children in the control group received regular hospital care and had no contact with the special nurse. Children in the experimental group were significantly less upset and more cooperative in the hospital and exhibited fewer posthospital adjustment problems than the control children. Parents in the experimental group rated themselves as considerably less anxious, more informed, and more satisfied with the hospital experience than parents in the control group.

In a second study, Visintainer and Wolfer (1975) attempted to evaluate the specific contribution of a supportive relationship or information in combination with a supportive relationship. Parents and their children were assigned to receive either stress point preparation, single-session preparation, consistent supportive care, or no specific preparation.

The results indicated that children in the stress point preparation and single-session preparation conditions tended to be less upset, more cooperative, and to have greater ease of fluid intake than children receiving supportive care or no preparation. The single-session preparation was found to be more effective than the supportive care and control groups on ratings of cooperation during the blood test and preoperative medication injection. The consistent supportive care group also was significantly more cooperative than the control group during the blood test and injection of the preoperative medication. Thus, on these behavioral ratings, only the stress point preparation was consistently superior to the other conditions except when compared to the single-session preparation. This would support the role of information in stress reduction.

Parents in the stress point preparation group were less anxious, more adequately informed, and more satisfied with the care they received than were parents in the other three conditions. Thus the benefit of combining information with the opportunity of a supportive relationship with a nurse at stressful periods during the hospitalization was demonstrated. Additional research is needed to examine more clearly the role played by parental preparation. In order to assess more accurately the contributions of individual and joint preparation, however, one must compare parent preparation alone, child preparation alone, and concurrent parent and child preparation. Such a study has yet to be conducted.

In a study by Peterson and Shigetomi (1981), children 2–10 years old and their parents were treated together in small groups. In addition to receiving a tour of the hospital by a nurse, children and their parents received one of the following interventions: (1) preoperative information provided through a puppet show, (2) cognitive and behavioral coping procedures introduced by puppets, (3) filmed modeling using the film investigated by Melamed and Siegel (1975), or (4) coping plus the filmed modeling procedure. The coping techniques condition included instruction in cue-controlled relaxation, distracting mental imagery, and comforting self-talk. Parents actively assisted their children in practicing these techniques. Results from this study indicated that children receiving the coping plus modeling techniques were less distressed and more cooperative during the hospital experience than children receiving coping techniques or filmed modeling alone. In addition, the coping procedures were found to be more effective than the modeling-only condition on some of the observational measures. The parents' ratings of their own anxiety, feelings of competence, and view of their hospital experience indicated the superiority of the coping condition over the information and modeling-only groups. In situations in which the child confronted a painful stimulus, such as the blood test or preoperative medication injection, the modeling plus coping procedures were found to be the most effective in reducing distress and enhancing the child's cooperative behavior. The investigators suggest that such medical procedures require the child to perform some adaptive coping behavior in addition to merely inhibiting some maladaptive behaviors. As a result, observing another child coping with specific anxiety-provoking situations in addition to practicing some specific coping strategies may have resulted in more positive behaviors than either procedure alone.

Finally, a study by Ferguson (1979) investigated the comparative effectiveness of filmed modeling and a preadmission home visit by a nurse on the anxiety level of children and their mothers. Children and their parents were assigned to one of four conditions: (1) non-hospital-related film, (2) hospital peer-modeling film depicting children experiencing various events when hospitalized for tonsillectomies, (3) a preadmission visit from a nurse in their home in which information was provided to the mother and child regarding hospital routines, medical procedures, and the sensations that the child would encounter following surgery, and viewing of a non-hospital-related film, (4) a preadmission home visit from a nurse and viewing of the hospital peer-modeling film. Children's responses to the hospitalization were measured by self-report measures of anxiety, electromyographic recordings of muscle tension, and ratings of behavioral distress. Measures of parental satisfaction with the hospital experience, information received, as well as self-reported anxiety, were also obtained.

The results suggested that a preadmission visit by the nurse was effective in reducing the mother's anxiety both during and following her child's hospitalization and resulted in significantly greater satisfaction with the care and information she and her child received. Children in the peer-modeling film condition exhibited a significant decrease in physiological indices of anxiety at all measurement periods. In addition, children who viewed the modeling film had a lower incidence of behavioral adjustment problems following their hospitalization.

MAXIMIZING ADJUSTMENT TO SPECIAL HOSPITAL ENVIRONMENTS

Some children require medical care that is inherently more traumatic than that encountered during routine elective admission to the hospital. Recently, several investigators have examined the psychosocial problems encountered by children who are exposed to unusually stressful environments within the hospi-

tal, including the emergency room, intensive care units, and isolated or protected environments. Several intervention programs have also been studied to evaluate their effectiveness in reducing children's adverse reactions to the highly aversive experiences to which they are exposed within these special environments.

An emergency admission to the hospital represents a crisis situation for the child and his family (Axlerod, 1976). The child's illness or injury may be life threatening and, therefore, necessitate immediate diagnosis, treatment, or surgery. This situation requires that efforts be directed toward a rapid adjustment of the child and family to a frightening series of events. The emergency room staff is also under considerable pressure to attend quickly to the medical needs of the child, making it difficult to attend concurrently to the child's emotional reactions. Under such circumstances, it is difficult, at best, to prepare the child adequately for these stressful experiences.

Despite the inherent stresses of an emergency admission, there has been little research on children's behavior under these conditions. An interesting study by Roskies et al. (1975) compared extensive observations of the behavior of eight children admitted on an emergency basis with the behavior of eight children having elective admissions. They were also interested in the effects that the parents' and staff's behavior had on the child's reaction to the hospital. Subjects were included in the study if they were 4–8 years old, accompanied by at least one parent, conscious so that they could be observed, had come directly to the hospital, and were eventually admitted to the pediatric ward. At least six hours of observations of the natural sequence of events in the admissions process were obtained for each child, including at least one hour of observation on the ward. The number and type of people present during the emergency and elective admission and the nature of the interactions that occurred with the parents and child were also recorded. The observations were later categorized into the number of painful events that the child experienced and the number of positive, negative, and neutral interactions that occurred between the parent and child. The results indicated that on all the dimensions that were measured, the emergency admission was considerably more stressful for the parents and children than were elective admissions. For example, children in the emergency group experienced an average of eight painful procedures during the first six hours in the hospital compared to an average of three for the elective group. Emergency group children were also found to have more contact with strangers, were moved to more different locations in the hospital, and were separated from their parents much earlier than were children in the elective group. While parent-child interactions in the elective group were characterized by an equal number of positive and neutral interactions, the majority of the interactions in the emergency group were either neutral or negative. A particularly interesting finding was that children in the elective group were no better informed about the reasons for their hospitalization than children in the emergency group where preparation for admission is clearly more difficult. However, even when it was possible to provide an explanation or a warning that a painful procedure was going to occur to children in the emergency group, only 7 percent of the time were such communications provided.

These investigators conclude that given the preeminent medical concerns with the child, "it is possible that during the period of emergency admissions itself, little psychological intervention is possible" (p. 580). However, in most cases, it is still possible to provide the child with information about a procedure as it is occurring and to assure him or her that every effort will be made to make a painful procedure as brief as possible (Axelrod, 1976). For example, emergency room personnel might use the tell-show-do technique in which the child is told what is about to be done, shown how it will be done, and informed about what sensations he or she can expect to occur and when the procedure will be completed. In addition, reinforcing the child with praise for specific cooperative be-

haviors and encouraging the use of various coping strategies such as relaxing imagery or calming self-talk might also be used with children in the emergency room. It also has been suggested that such children may require extended support throughout their hospitalization as well as during a follow-up period after discharge from the hospital to assist them in understanding their experiences in the hospital (Petrillo & Sanger, 1972).

Another particularly stressful environment for the hospitalized child is the intensive care unit where children with a life-threatening condition must receive medical care. The child is typically immobilized, subjected to numerous painful medical procedures, and exposed to an unfamiliar and highly threatening setting. Two studies of children on a Pediatric Intensive Care Unit (PICU) are reported by Cataldo et al. (1979). In the first study, behavioral observations were conducted on 99 children on the PICU during a two-month period. These children were admitted for injuries, surgery, or illness. The average length of stay in the PICU was approximately five days. Six categories of child behavior were observed: waking state, position, verbalization, eye contact, activity, and affective state. The behavior of caregivers was also observed, including verbalizations to the child and the number and type of persons at his or her bedside. The observations indicated that approximately one-third of the children were conscious and alert in the PICU but were not responsive to their environment, frequently "staring into space" and "not attending to anything specific." In addition, there was a low rate of verbalizations by the children and a high level of neutral or unresponsive affective behaviors.

In the second study, Cataldo et al. (1979) provided 11 children, who were judged to be sufficiently alert, with an experimental intervention to improve their overall psychosocial status in the PICU. Children were exposed to several treatment conditions, including the opportunity to interact with a child life worker while playing with age appropriate toys or the opportunity to play with the toys alone. Behavior observations of the child's behavior were recorded during each session, which lasted approximately five minutes. These brief and relatively simple interventions were found to increase the child's interaction, attention to activities, and positive affect and considerably to reduce inappropriate and nonadaptive behaviors.

Finally, Kellerman and his colleagues (Kellerman et al., 1976; Kellerman, Rigler, & Siegel, 1979) have discussed the effects of protected environments or reverse isolation on pediatric patients. Where the risk of infections must be minimized, some children need to be confined, often for extended periods of time, to a room where the air is continually cleaned. The use of such environments is particularly common with children undergoing chemotherapy for cancer in which the medication significantly increases the risk of infection by affecting the child's immunological system. Prolonged isolation can have a potentially deleterious effect on the child's psychological adjustment because of potential sensory deprivation as a result of confinement to a limited area and to a limited number of persons.

These investigators studied 14 children with cancer who were hospitalized in a protected environmental unit while undergoing chemotherapy. The children ranged in age from 3 to 17 years old and had an average stay in the isolation unit of 92 days. Ratings of the children were conducted three times each day using 36 behavioral categories related to physical discomfort, affect, perceptual-motor functioning, activity level, management problems, appetite and sleep patterns, and social-interpersonal functioning. Based on these data, no significant or prolonged psychological effects were noted in the children. While some children evidenced transitory periods of depression, this problem was effectively reduced by providing the children with stimulating activities. The authors stress that these positive findings can be attributed to the comprehensive psychosocial program that is provided on a daily basis, including recreational and stimulating activities. In addition, the deleterious effects of prolonged isolation are reduced by providing access to windows and clocks, a daily routine, regular visits from family members, a school teacher, and counseling for the family.

CONCLUSION

Much progress has been made in the last several decades in our understanding of the psychosocial needs of hospitalized children. However, in spite of a growing awareness of the importance of special preparation of children for hospitalization and the research evidence for the effectiveness of various preparation programs in facilitating the child's adjustment to this stressful experience, the actual implementation of such programs on a *systematic* basis has yet to be achieved in most pediatric and general hospitals. Mechanisms for affecting changes in hospital policies that determine routine medical practices with children need to be investigated. A more consistent use of prehospital preparation programs with a greater number of children is likely to occur with the development of preparation procedures that can be easily implemented within a typical hospital routine and that require little investment of professional time.

There are several factors in the area of preparation for hospitalization that warrant further study. While time of preparation has been suggested as an important factor as it relates to the possible differential effectiveness for children of various ages, this variable has received little research attention. In addition, the same type of preparation procedure may not be equally effective for children with a previous history of hospitalization as compared to children who have never been in the hospital. Few studies even have investigated whether children actually understand and recall the information that has been presented to them. Little research has been devoted to the variables that indicate which children will respond the most favorably to a particular preparation strategy. The investigation of these and other variables relevant to the preparation of children for hospitalization and surgery will permit a refinement of the various preparation procedures so as to provide an intervention program that yields a maximum therapeutic benefit for children.

Finally, research efforts also need to be directed at identifying the effective cognitive and behavioral coping strategies that children use to modulate and control their response to the stressful experiences in the hospital. At the present time, we know little about self-generated strategies used by hospitalized children to cope with stressful and painful medical procedures. Identifying the coping strategies that are utilized by children who make a satisfactory adjustment to the hospital experience would permit those who work with hospitalized children to develop more effective preparation programs by building upon the coping skills that children already have in their repertoires. Another reason for identifying the coping styles that children use is evidence from the adult literature that indicates that patients often prefer to use their own coping strategies in the hospital rather than rely on those provided in a standard preparation program. In addition, it is possible that a preparation procedure might conflict with the child's own effective coping style that he or she uses when confronting a stressful situation. It is not unreasonable to assume that different types of preparation may be indicated for children with different coping styles.

REFERENCES

Abram, H. Psychology of chronic illness. *Journal of Chronic Diseases,* 1972, **25,** 659–664.

American Academy of Pediatrics. *Care of children in hospitals.* Evanston, Ill.: Author, 1970.

Association for the Care of Children in Hospitals. *Child life activity study section position paper.* Washington, D.C.: Author, 1979.

Association for the Care of Children's Health. *Psychosocial policy guidelines for administration of pediatric health care facilities.* Washington, D.C.: Author, 1980.

Axlerod, B.H. Mental health considerations in the pediatric emergency room. *Journal of Pediatric Psychology,* 1976, **1,** 14–17.

Azarnoff, P., & Flegal, S. *A pediatric play pro-gram.* Springfield, Ill.: Thomas, 1975.

Belmont, H.S. Hospitalization and its effects upon the total child. *Clinical Pediatrics,* 1970, **22,** 590–600.

Bibace, R., & Walsh, M.E. Developmental stages in children's concepts of illness. In G.C. Stone, F. Cohen, & N.E. Adler (Eds.), *Health psychology—A handbook.* San Francisco: Jossey-Bass, 1980.

Campbell, J. Illness is a point of view: The development of children's concepts of illness. *Child Development,* 1975, **46,** 92–100.

Cassell, S. Effects of brief puppet therapy upon the emotional responses of children undergoing cardiac catheterization. *Journal of Consulting Psychology,* 1965, **29,** 1–8.

Cataldo, M.F., Bessman, C.A., Parker, L.H., Pearson, J.E., & Rogers, M.C. Behavioral assessment for pediatric intensive care units. *Journal of Applied Behavior Analysis,* 1979, **12,** 83–97.

Chapman, A.H., Loeb, D.G., & Gibbons, M.J. Psychiatric aspects of hospitalization of children. *Archives of Pediatrics,* 1956, **73,** 77–88.

Cofer, D.H., & Nir, Y. Theme-focused group therapy on a pediatric ward. *International Journal of Psychiatry in Medicine,* 1975, **6,** 541–550.

Cohen, F., & Lazarus, R.S. Coping with the stress of illness. In G.C. Stone, F. Cohen, & N.E. Adler (Eds.), *Health psychology—A handbook.* San Francisco: Jossey-Bass, 1980.

Davenport, H.T., & Werry, J.S. The effects of general anesthesia, surgery, and hospitalization upon the behavior of children. *American Journal of Orthopsychiatry,* 1970, **40,** 806–824.

Davies, R., Butler, N., & Goldstein, H. *From birth to seven: The second report of the National Child Development Study (1958 cohort).* London: National Children's Bureau, 1972.

Debuskey, M. The *The chronically ill child and his family.* Springfield, Ill.: Thomas, 1970.

Deutsch, H. Some psychoanalytic observations in surgery. *Psychosomatic Medicine,* 1942, **4,** 105–115.

Dimock, H.G. *The child in the hospital: A study of his emotional well-being.* Philadelphia: Davis, 1960.

Ferguson, B.F. Preparing young children for hospitalization: A comparison of two methods. *Pediatrics,* 1979, **64,** 656–664.

Fomuford, A.K. Chronically ill institutionalized children: Psychosocial effects of prolonged hospitalization on the terminally sick child. *Social Science and Medicine,* 1980, **14,** 239–242.

Frank, J.L. A weekly group meeting for children on a pediatric ward: Therapeutic and practical functions. *International Journal of Psychiatry in Medicine,* 1978, **8,** 267–283.

Frederick, W.N. Ameliorating the psychological impact of chronic physical disease on the child and family. *Journal of Pediatric Psychology,* 1977, **2,** 26–31.

Freud, A. The role of bodily illness in the mental life of children. *The psychoanalytic study of the child* (Vol. 7). New York: International Universities Press, 1962.

Gellert, E. Reducing the emotional stress of hospitalization for children. *American Journal of Occupational Therapy,* 1958, **12,** 125–129.

Gofman, H., Buckman, W., & Schade, G.H. Parents' emotional response to child's hospitalization. *American Journal of Diseases of Children,* 1957, **93,** 629–637.

Goslin, E.R. Hospitalization as a life crisis for the preschool child: A critical review. *Journal of Community Health,* 1978, **3,** 321–326.

Heller, J.A. *The hospitalized child and his family.* Baltimore: The Johns Hopkins Press, 1967.

Hunnisett, F.W., & Knowles, D.J. Orienting prospective patients. *Journal of the American Hospital Association,* 1970, **44,** 51–54.

Impallaria, C. The contribution of social group, the hospitalized child. *American Journal of Orthopsychiatry,* 1955, **25,** 293–318.

Jackson, K., Winkley, R., Faust, O.A., Cermack, E.G., & Brutt, M.M. Behavior changes indicating emotional trauma in tonsillectomized children. *Pediatrics,* 1953, **12,** 23–27.

Jessner, L., Blom, G.E., & Woldfogel, S. Emotional implications of tonsillectomy and adenoidectomy in children. In R.S. Eisler (Ed.), *The psychoanalytic study of the child* (Vol. 7). New York: International Universities Press, 1952.

Jessner, L., & Kaplan, S. Observations of the emotional reactions of children to tonsillectomy and adenoidectomy. In M.J. Senn & J. Macy (Eds.), *Problems of infancy and childhood.* New York: Foundation, 1949.

Kellerman, J., Rigler, D., & Siegel, S.E. Psycho-logical responses of children to isolation in a protected environment. *Journal of Behavioral Medicine,* 1979, **2,** 263–274.

Kellerman, J., Rigler, D., Siegel, S.E., McCue, K., Pospisil, J., & Uno, R. Pediatric cancer patients in reverse isolation utilizing protected environments. *Journal of Pediatric Psychology,* 1976, **1,** 21–25.

Kenny, T.J. The hospitalized child. *Pediatric Clinics of North America,* 1975, **22,** 583–593.

Knudsen, K. Play therapy: Preparing the young child for surgery. *Nursing Clinics of North America,* 1975, **10,** 679–686.

Levy, D.M. Psychic trauma of operations in children. *American Journal of Diseases of Children,* 1945, **69,** 7–25.

Mahaffy, P.R. Effects of hospitalization on children admitted for tonsillectomy and adenoidectomy. *Nursing Research,* 1965, **13,** 12–19.

Mattson, A. Long-term physical illness in childhood: A challenge to psychosocial adaptation. *Pediatrics,* 1972, **50,** 801–811.

McCue, K. Preparing children for medical procedures. In J. Kellerman (Ed.), *Psychological aspects of childhood cancer.* Springfield, Ill.: Thomas, 1980.

Melamed, B.G. Psychological preparation for hospitalization. In S. Rachman (Ed.), *Contributions to medical psychology* (Vol. 1). New York: Pergamon, 1977.

Melamed, B.G., Meyer, R., Gee, C., & Soule, L. The influence of time and type of preparation on children's adjustment to the hospital. *Journal of Pediatric Psychology,* 1976, **1,** 31–37.

Melamed, B.G., & Siegel, L.J. Reduction of anxiety in children facing hospitalization and surgery by use of filmed modeling. *Journal of Consulting and Clinical Psychology,* 1975, **43,** 511–521.

Melamed, B.G., & Siegel, L.J. *Behavioral medicine: Practical applications in health care.* New York: Springer, 1980.

Mellish, R.W. Preparation of children for hospitalization and surgery. *Pediatric Clinics of North America,* 1969, **16,** 543–553.

Menke, E.M. School-aged children's perceptions of stress in the hospital. *Children's Health Care,* 1981, **9,** 80–86.

Oremland, E.R., & Oremland, J.D. (Eds.). *The effects of hospitalization on children: Models for their care.* Springfield, Ill.: Thomas, 1973.

Peterson, L., & Ridley-Johnson, R. Pediatric hospital response to survey on prehospital preparation for children. *Journal of Pediatric Psychology,* 1980, **5,** 1–7.

Peterson, L., & Shigetomi, C. The use of coping techniques to minimize anxiety in hospitalized children. *Behavior Therapy,* 1981, **12,** 1–14.

Petrillo, M., & Sanger, S. *Emotional care of hospitalized children.* Philadelphia: Lippincott, 1972.

Pidgeon, V. Functions of preschool children's questions in coping with hospitalization. *Research in Nursing and Health,* 1981, **4,** 229–235.

Pillsbury, R.M. Children can be helped to face surgery. *Children,* 1951, **7,** 122–124.

Pless, I.B. The challenge of chronic illness. *American Journal of Diseases of Children,* 1973, **126,** 741–742.

Prugh, D.G. Emotional aspects of the hospitalization of children. In *Red is the color of hurting: Planning for children in the hospital.* Washington, D.C.: United States Department of Health, Education, and Welfare, Public Health Service. National Clearinghouse for Mental Health Information, 1965.

Prugh, D.G., & Eckhardt, L.O. Stages and phases in the responses of children and adolescents to illness and injury. In B.W. Camp (Ed.), *Advances in behavioral pediatrics* (Vol. 1). New York: JAI Press, 1980.

Prugh, D.G., Staub, E.M., Sands, H.H., Kirschbaum, R.M., & Lenihan, E.A. A study of the emotional reactions of children and families to hospitalization and illness. *American Journal of Orthopsychiatry,* 1953, **23,** 70–106.

Rae, W.A. Hospitalized latency-age children: Implications for psychosocial care. *Children's Health Care,* 1981, **9,** 59–63.

Roberts, M.C., Wurtele, S.K., Boone, R.R., Ginther, L., & Elkins, P.D. Reduction of medical and psychological fears by use of modeling: A preventive application in a general population of children. *Journal of Pediatric Psychology,* 1981, **6,** 293–300.

Robertson, J. *Young children in hospitals.* New York: Basic Books, 1958.

Roskies, E., Bedard, P., Gauvreau-Guilbault, H., & Lafortune, D. Emergency hospitalization of young children: Some neglected psychological considerations. *Medical Care,* 1975, **13,** 570–581.

Roskies, E., Mongeon, M., & Gagnon-Lefebvre, B. Increasing maternal participation in the hospitalization of young children. *Medical Care,* 1978, **16,** 765–777.

Schaffer, H.R., & Callender, W.H. Psychological effects of hospitalization in infancy. *Pediatrics,* 1959, **24,** 528–539.

Schulman, J.L., Foley, J.M., Vernon, D.T.A., & Allan, D. A study of the effects of the mother's presence during anesthesia induction. *Pediatrics,* 1967, **39,** 111–114.

Shaw, E.G., & Routh, D.K. *Pain, protest, and parenting: Children receiving injections cry more when mother is there.* Paper presented at the meeting of the Psychonomic Society, St. Louis, November, 1980.

Sheridan, M.S. Talk time for hospitalized children. *Social Work,* 1975, **20,** 40–44.

Shore, M.F., Geiser, R.L., & Wolman, H.M. Constructive uses of a hospital experience. *Children,* 1965, **12,** 3–8.

Shore, M.F., & Goldston, S.E. Guest editorial. *Journal of Pediatric Psychology,* 1976, **1,** 2.

Shore, M.F., & Goldston, S.E. Mental health aspects of pediatric care: Historical review and current status. In P.R. Magrab (Ed.), *Psychological management of pediatric problems* (Vol. 1). Baltimore: University Park Press, 1978.

Siegel, L.J. Preparation of children for hospitalization: A selected review of the research literature. *Journal of Pediatric Psychology,* 1976, **1,** 26–30.

Siegel, L.J. *Therapeutic modeling as a procedure to reduce the stress associated with medical and dental procedures.* Paper presented at the Association for Advancement of Behavior Therapy, Atlanta, December, 1977.

Siegel, L.J. *An ecological assessment of children coping in the hospital.* Paper presented at the American Psychological Association, Los Angeles, August, 1981. (a)

Siegel, L.J. *Naturalistic study of coping strategies in children facing medical procedures.* Paper presented at the Southeastern Psychological Association, Atlanta, April, 1981. (b)

Simeonsson, R.J., Buckley, L., & Monson, L. Conceptions of illness causality in hospitalized children. *Journal of Pediatric Psychology,* 1979, **4,** 77–84.

Skipper, J.K., & Leonard, R.C. Children, stress,

and hospitalization: A field experiment. *Journal of Health and Social Behavior*, 1968, **9**, 275–287.

Skipper, J.K., Leonard, R.C., & Rhymes, J. Child hospitalization and social interaction: An experimental study of mothers' feelings of stress, adaptation and satisfaction. *Medical Care*, 1968, **6**, 496–506.

Solnit, A.J. Hospitalization: An aid to physical and psychological health in childhood. *American Journal of the Diseases of Children*, 1960, **99**, 155–163.

Spielberger, C.D. Theory and research on anxiety. In C.D. Spielberger (Ed.), *Anxiety and behavior*. New York: Academic Press, 1966.

Tisza, V., Hurwitz, I., & Angoff, K. The use of a play program by hospitalized children. *Journal of the American Academy of Child Psychiatry*, 1970, **9**, 515–531.

United States Department of Health, Education, and Welfare. *Red is the color of hurting: Planning for children in the hospital*. Washington, D.C.: National Clearinghouse for Mental Health Information, 1965.

VanderVeer, A.H. The psychopathology of physical illness and hospital residence. *Quarterly Journal of Child Behavior*, 1949, **1**, 55–71.

Vaughn, G.F. Children in hospital. *Lancet*, 1957, **272**, 1117–1120.

Vernon, D.T.A. Use of modeling to modify children's responses to a natural, potentially stressful situation. *Journal of Applied Psychology*, 1973, **59**, 351–356.

Vernon, D.T.A., & Bailey, W.C. The use of motion pictures in the psychological preparation of children for induction of anesthesia. *Anesthesiology*, 1974, **40**, 68–72.

Vernon, D.T.A., Foley, J.M., & Schulman, J.L. Effect of mother-child separation and birth order on young children's response to two potentially stressful experiences. *Journal of Personality and Social Psychology*, 1967, **5**, 162–174.

Vernon, D.T.A., Foley, J.M., Sipowicz, R.R., & Schulman, J.L. *The psychological responses of children to hospitalization and illness*. Springfield, Ill.: Thomas, 1965.

Vernon, D.T.A., Schulman, J.L., & Foley, J.M. Changes in children's behavior after hospitalization: Some dimensions of responses and their correlates. *American Journal of Diseases of Children*, 1966, **111**, 581–593.

Visintainer, M.A., & Wolfer, J.A. Psychological preparation for surgical pediatric patients: The effects on children's and parent's stress responses and adjustment. *Pediatrics*, 1975, **56**, 187–202.

Wolfer, J.A., & Visintainer, M.A. Pediatric surgical patients' and parents' stress responses and adjustment. *Nursing Research*, 1975, **24**, 244–255.

CHAPTER 47

Pharmacotherapy

MAGDA CAMPBELL, WAYNE H. GREEN, RICHARD PERRY, AND LOWELL T. ANDERSON

This chapter represents an overview of pharmacotherapy in children. Children's psychopharmacology is still trailing behind its adult counterpart; much less is known about the outcome of chronic pharmacotherapy and its consequences in children than in adults. While critical assessments of psychomotor stimulants using well-designed studies already existed in the 1960s and in the early 70s, until recently, there has been a paucity of such research conducted with neuroleptics, antidepressants, and lithium. And still there is little information about the role, if any, of anticonvulsants and anxiolytics even though the anxiolytics are widely used in children.

In the last decade, there has been an increasing concern about the effects of psychoactive drugs on cognition and learning and about the short and long term safety of these agents in children. This is a welcome trend since it meant a more critical assessment of drugs not only on behavioral symptoms but also on other crucial parameters. Some investigators raised the question whether one can arrive at a dosage that is therapeutically effective for the individual child without yielding serious untoward effects on cognition, learning, central nervous system, neuroendocrine system, and growth.

The following classes of drugs will be covered: psychomotor stimulants, food additives, antidepressants, neuroleptics, lithium carbonate, anticonvulsants, and anxiolytics.

Whenever appropriate in each class, the following issues will be addressed:

1. Indication
2. Dosage
3. Short term efficacy
   Behavioral
   Cognitive
4. Long term treatment
5. Untoward effects
   Immediate
   Behavioral
   Cognitive
   Central nervous system
   Laboratory
   Other
   Long term
   Growth
   Central nervous system

METHODOLOGICAL ISSUES

When to use a psychoactive drug in addition to psychosocial treatments in a child with behavioral disorder and which type of drug is to be chosen should be based upon the findings of well-conducted research. Such research utilizes well defined and diagnostically homogeneous patient samples of reasonable size, adequate controls under double-blind conditions, random assignments to treatments, standardized assessment instruments sensitive to treatment effects with emphasis on ecology, and appropriate experimental designs. The literature is abundant with reports of investigators who failed to meet these basic

This work was supported in part by Public Health Service Grant MH-32212. The authors wish to thank Dr. George Gardos for advice.

requirements and, above all, lack critical assessments. Therefore, the reader should carefully evaluate and interpret the results of such clinical trials. Methodological considerations were recently reviewed elsewhere (Campbell, Cohen, & Perry, 1982). In addition, readings by Sprague and Baxley (1978), Werry (1978), Conners and Werry (1979) and Klein et al. (1980) are recommended.

PSYCHOMOTOR STIMULANTS

This group of drugs consists of the central nervous system (CNS) sympathomimetic amines (amphetamines), the CNS stimulants (methylphenidate, magnesium pemoline, and caffeine), and a putative precursor of the CNS neurotransmitter acetylcholine, deanol.

Indications

The psychomotor stimulants are clinically accepted by child psychiatrists as the drugs of choice in treating children with DSM-III (1980) diagnosis of attention deficit disorder (ADD) with associated symptoms of hyperactivity and impulsivity. In the earlier literature, these children have been typically labeled as having minimal brain dysfunction (MBD) or minimal cerebral dysfunction.

Though it is estimated that about 5–20 percent of school age children suffer from ADD (Wender, 1971), there is still a controversy over its existence (Shaffer & Greenhill, 1979). Clearly, only about 20 percent of youngsters with this behavioral syndrome display the symptoms in the doctor's office (Sleator & Ullmann, 1981); it is for that reason that rating scales for teachers (Conners, 1969) and parents (Conners, 1970) were developed. Normative data are available documenting that there are substantial differences in the behaviors of normal and hyperactive children on the basis of teachers' ratings in the classroom (Sprague, Christensen, & Werry, 1974).

Stimulants may also be helpful in treating narcolepsy—a disorder characterized by paroxysmal and recurrent attacks of irresistible

sleep (Yoss & Daly, 1960). Because of its rarity in childhood, it will not be further discussed.

Contraindications

Stimulants frequently cause increased disorganization in psychotic youngsters (Campbell, Fish, David, Shapiro, Collins, & Koh, 1972; Campbell et al., 1976; Fish, 1971; Janowsky et al., 1973); they also appear to precipitate psychotic symptoms in some vulnerable children with borderline personality organizations.

Dosage

Dosage is shown in Table 47.1

Table 47.1   Psychomotor Stimulants

	Dosage
Dextroamphetamine (Dexedrine)	5–25 mg/day
Methylphenidate (Ritalin)	10–60 mg/day (0.3 mg/kg/day)
Magnesium Pemoline (Cylert)	37.5–112.5 mg/day (1.9–2.7 mg/kg/day)

Short Term Efficacy

Behavioral

The stimulants were introduced into child psychiatry by Bradley (1937). He administered amphetamine sulfate to 30 children in a residential setting with various behavioral problems: half of the children showed remarkable improvement, the drug having a calming effect on them.

Since that time, a large literature on the use of stimulants in children has appeared. The superiority of dextroamphetamine, methylphenidate, and magnesium pemoline (Conners & Taylor, 1980) over placebo unquestionably has been demonstrated in many well-designed, adequately controlled studies. These drugs repeatedly yield significant decreases in hyperactivity, impulsivity, and distractibility and increase in attention span. The effects of these drugs were compared to behavior modification, and their interaction has been explored

(Sprague et al., 1974; Conners & Wells, 1977; Firestone et al., 1981; Gittelman et al., 1979). In reviewing the literature, Klein and associates (1980) conclude that behavior therapy alone is inferior to methylphenidate treatment. The combination of both therapies may produce clinically a greater reduction of symptoms than methylphenidate alone though this may not reach statistical significance.

In studies comparing stimulants with the antidepressant imipramine (Rapoport et al., 1974) or with neuroleptics (Gittelman-Klein et al., 1976) in treating hyperkinetic children, the stimulants are the more effective drugs.

Cognitive

In addition to decreases in behavioral symptoms in the classroom and at home, administration of dextroamphetamine, methylphenidate, or pemoline results in improvement on various performance and cognitive tasks in the laboratory. It should be noted that Sprague and Sleator's (1975, 1977) work indicates that, while methylphenidate is effective in reducing behavioral symptoms in doses between 0.3–1.0 mg/kg/day, the optimal effects on performance are in evidence only at lower doses (0.3 mg/kg/day); others do not concur (Klein et al., 1980).

Whereas psychomotor stimulants enhance cognitive performance, this has not been shown to be accompanied by improvement in academic achievement in children with pure learning disabilities without ADD (Gittelman, 1980).

The following critical reviews on psychomotor stimulants are recommended: Cantwell and Carlson (1978); Conners (1972, 1974); Conners and Werry (1979); Gittelman-Klein (1975); and Klein et al. (1980). Rapoport et al. (1978; Rapoport, Buchsbaum, Weingartner, Zahn, Ludlow, & Mikkelsen, 1980) have explored and compared the effects of dextroamphetamine in normal and hyperactive children and young adult volunteers.

Concerning deanol, an article by Conners (1973) is particularly recommended. Klein et al. (1980) have recently reviewed the available literature on deanol and concluded that this drug has a weak effect at best and does not deserve inclusion in the armamentarium used to treat hyperkinetic children.

A similar conclusion has been reached concerning the therapeutic efficacy of caffeine (for review, see Klein et al., 1980).

Long Term Treatment

Psychomotor stimulants are used almost exclusively in children diagnosed as having an attention deficit disorder with hyperactivity. Because this is a chronic disorder, the question arises as to how long the stimulants are effective and how long it is necessary to administer the drug to the hyperactive child. Sprague is the only investigator who addresses himself to this issue (Sleator, von Neumann, & Sprague, 1974). In a sample of 42 hyperactive children who were receiving methylphenidate continuously for two years, 26 percent functioned well without the drug after a one-month placebo period. Only 40 percent showed worsening on placebo. A clinical trial by Gittelman-Klein et al. (1976) showed that 5 percent of hyperactive children no longer required medication after three months. Since remissions can develop and on the basis of these findings periodic drug free periods are recommended.

There is some evidence that the psychomotor stimulants are superior to other drugs in the treatment of hyperactive children not only in terms of short term efficacy but also in terms of long term efficacy. In a study by Gittelman-Klein et al. (1976), thioridazine was more effective at four weeks than at 12 weeks, when mild worsening of behavior was observed on several measures. Similarly, while early in treatment imipramine was as effective as methylphenidate, subsequently its effects weakened (Gittelman-Klein, 1974; Quinn & Rapoport, 1975; Rapoport et al., 1974). In Rapoport et al.'s (1974) study imipramine (mean dose 80 mg/day, maximum dose 150 mg/day) was compared to methylphenidate and to placebo in a double-blind trial of six-weeks duration; while both drugs were rated to be more effective, after about 10 weeks of treatment there seemed to be a "wear-off" with imipramine.

In the study of Quinn and Rapoport (1975) 73 of 76 hyperactive boys were seen on one-year follow-up after an initial six-week drug trial. Of the 38 boys who were receiving methylphenidate (mean daily dose 20.65 mg ± 8.56), 29 remained on methylphenidate with good clinical results. However, these boys were still hyperactive in comparison to available norms.

Magnesium pemoline too was investigated in a long term study as part of a large collaborative multiclinic investigation (Page et al., 1974). After the completion of a nine-week, double-blind, placebo-controlled trial, pemoline was given on an open basis for 18 months to 288 children, ages 6–13 years (256 males and 32 females) in doses of 1.91–2.51 mg/kg/day. Both on physicians' global ratings and on parents' ratings, the initial improvements were maintained throughout the 18-month period.

However, the long term outcome of attention deficit disorder with hyperactivity may not be altered by the use of drugs. In recent years, several reports have emerged on the long term outcome of this syndrome; all of these studies are retrospective (Weiss & Hechtman, 1979). Weiss et al. (1975) conducted a five-year follow-up in which 3 groups were compared: 24 children were treated with methylphenidate, 22 with chlorpromazine, and 20 received no medication. While initially there were marked differences between the 3 groups on ratings of hyperactivity and family diagnosis, at five years, hyperactivity decreased in all, and family diagnosis remained unchanged. The authors concluded that "no doubt the stimulants are effective drugs for many hyperactive children, but as the sole method of management their value is limited" (p. 164). A pertinent finding in this study is that only among those taking methylphenidate did initial ratings on family diagnosis predict final outcome by almost every measure of outcome. Only this group showed a significant correlation between family diagnosis and school achievement, delinquency and emotional adjustment. This suggests that there is an interaction between a useful drug and a healthy family and that this influences prognosis. Similarly, one can postulate that, to change the outcome, a useful drug will interact with other treatment variables such as behavior modification, family counseling, optimal classroom situations, tutoring, and skilled, supportive teachers. While at five years, delinquent behavior was more frequent in follow-up patients than in controls, a 10–12-year follow-up of 75 subjects indicated that delinquent behavior decreased at this point in time (Weiss et al., 1979). However, between the ages of 17 and 24 years, these individuals continued to have problems when compared to controls: they had impulsive personality traits, impaired self-esteem, and were found to be one year behind their matched controls in the level of education attained. There was no difference between the two groups as to court appearances, drug use ("hash" or "grass"), and performance on job. Of the 75 subjects, 17 were receiving chlorpromazine in doses of 25–200 mg/day for 18–48 months; there was no difference on outcome measures between these patients and 21 matched subjects who received medication for less than six months.

It is wishful thinking to expect that a useful drug alone will change the outcome of a fairly serious condition such as severe chronic hyperactivity, which is often associated with learning disorders and has a variety of etiologies.

However, Satterfield, Satterfield, and Cantwell (1980), based on their two-year assessment of hyperactive boys, suggest that a combination of stimulant drug and psychological treatments resulted in behavioral and academic improvement in these children. It is difficult to evaluate the results of this study since the sample of 61 hyperactive boys represents those subjects who were available for follow-up; the 31 patients who dropped out in the first year of treatment represent the controls.

Untoward Effects

It is only in the past few years that attention has been paid to untoward effects of stimulants.

Immediate Untoward Effects

According to the studies of Sprague and Werry (1973), immediate side effects increase with dosage of methylphenidate until at 1.0 mg/kg/day over one-half of the children have untoward effects. Insomnia, anorexia, and weight loss are most commonly observed with these drugs. Irritability, increased depression, crying, sadness, and drowsiness are the most frequent behavioral untoward effects. Pain, particularly abdominal pain, pallor, and headaches have been reported, as well as tics and hallucinosis. The occurrence of Tourette's disorder with magnesium pemoline (Mitchell & Matthews, 1980) and methylphenidate (Golden, 1974) was also reported. Both heart rate and blood pressure may increase. Elevation of serum glutamic oxaloacetic transaminase (SGOT) and serum glutamic pyruvic transaminase (SGPT) has been reported with magnesium pemoline (Page et al., 1974).

Long Term Untoward Effects

GROWTH. There has been a concern about the adverse effect of stimulants on height and weight since the report of Safer, Allen, and Barr (1972). This study was retrospective and suffered from methodological flaws. In a prospective long term follow-up of hyperactive children who were receiving 0.3–1.86 mg/kg/-day of methylphenidate (mean, 0.59 mg/kg/-day) for a period of two years, body weight and height did not significantly differ from controls (McNutt et al., 1976). This study of Sprague and his co-workers is a methodologically fine study; it was criticized by some because the doses used are relatively low (mean dose 0.59 mg/kg/day).

In a partially retrospective study Gross (1976) reported on 60 children who were treated with methylphenidate up to eight years. After the first year, there was a significant decrease in weight but not in height. In the 15 children who were receiving the drug for seven years, gains in both height and weight were significantly greater than expected.

Magnesium pemoline failed to produce significant adverse effects on growth when given to 288 hyperactive children over a period of up to 77 weeks, in doses of 1.91–2.51 mg/kg/day (Page et al., 1974). Satterfield and associates (1979) found a spurt of growth at year two, after an initial suppression of growth at year one. This represented a study of the growth of 72 hyperactive boys, ages 6–12 years who were receiving methylphenidate in mean doses of 0.47 mg/kg/day in the first year and 0.52 mg/kg/day in the second year. The temporary growth rate reduction was less than 1 percent deficit in full height. Discontinuation of methylphenidate during summer may have helped weight gain but had no effect on height gain. Satterfield's study was criticized by Klein et al. (1980) and by Roche and colleagues (1979) since it used the Iowa growth charts, which are no longer valid.

The possible adverse effect of stimulants on growth was explored in a prospective study by Puig-Antich, Greenhill, Sassin, and Sachar (1978). It involved seven hyperactive boys, 6–9.5 years of age. They were receiving dextroamphetamine continuously in doses of 10–30 mg/day (mean dose 22.8 mg/day, or 0.82 mg/kg/day). The control group matched for a variety of variables consisted of nine boys; four were receiving chlorpromazine (mean dose 115 mg/day), and four were treated with thioridazine (mean dose 156 mg/day). The children receiving dextroamphetamine showed decrease in height and weight percentile after the first year, but those receiving phenothiazines made gains in both height and weight; these differences were statistically significant. While there were only insignificant decreases in growth hormone secretion during dextroamphetamine administration, mean plasma concentration of prolactin during sleep showed significant depression after one month and an even more significant drop after six months of treatment with the stimulant. The authors speculated that growth inhibition was mediated by inhibition of prolactin secretion.

A panel appointed by the FDA carefully and critically reviewed the available evidence and concluded that stimulants may yield minor suppression in linear growth when administered in average-to-high doses (Roche et al., 1979).

OTHER. Behavioral withdrawal effects were also reported with stimulants. Klein et al. (1980) report that, in their experience, about 20 percent of children suffer from withdrawal effects when moderate-to-high doses of stimulants are discontinued. These phenomena are transient; they may last from 12 hours up to a week, and they represent a rebound effect. They are usually manifested as worsening of preexisting symptoms. Rapoport et al. (1978) reported such phenomena in normal prepubertal boys after the administration of dextroamphetamine in a single dose.

Apparently, there is no increase in drug abuse in adolescents to whom stimulants were medically prescribed in childhood (Weiss et al., 1979; Freedman, 1971).

FOOD ADDITIVES

There has been a great concern in recent years about possible behavioral and cognitive toxicity of food additives (Feingold, 1974). A few well-controlled studies have not entirely clarified this issue though it appears that only less than 5 percent of hyperactive ADD children are behaviorally sensitive to additives (Conners, 1980; Brunner, Vorhees, & Butcher, 1981).

ANTIDEPRESSANTS

Two classes of drugs comprise this category: the tricyclics (e.g., imipramine, amitriptyline, nortriptyline) and the monoamine oxidase (MAO) inhibitors.

Indications

In adults, these drugs are primarily indicated in the treatment of depressive disorders; studies are available on the efficacy of tricyclics in certain phobias (Klein et al., 1980).

In prepubertal children, only recently has major depressive illness been defined by using the same operationally defined criteria as in adults (Puig-Antich, Blau, Marx, Greenhill, & Chambers, 1978; Weinberg et al., 1973).

Earlier reports indicating the efficacy of tricyclics (Frommer, 1967) and MAO inhibitors (Frommer, 1967) in depressed children failed to define the diagnostic criteria of depression. In addition, little is known about the safety of MAO inhibitors in children. Currently, knowledge is accumulating about the effectiveness of imipramine in the treatment of depression in children (Puig-Antich, Blau, Marx, Greenhill, & Chambers, 1978).

At the present time, imipramine is most frequently used in enuresis. Its efficacy has been well demonstrated in well-controlled studies (Poussaint & Ditman, 1965); however, we wish to emphasize that psychological causes underlying enuresis should be investigated and, whenever feasible, treated with nonpharmacological methods. There is supportive evidence that relapse is more frequent after drug withdrawal than after conditioning (for review, see Campbell, 1979; Mikkelsen et al., 1980; Rapoport, Mikkelsen, Zavadil, Nee, Gruenau, Mendelson, & Gillin, 1980; Shaffer, 1977).

Dosage

Dosage is shown in Table 47.2. The Food and Drug Administration recommends that doses of imipramine not exceed 5 mg/kg/day (Hayes, Logan Panitch, & Barker, 1975).

Table 47.2 Representative Antidepressant

	Dosage
Imipramine hydrochloride (Tofranil)	25–225 mg/day[a] (1–5 mg/kg/day)

[a]Dosage for enuresis: For children under 12 years of age, 25–50 mg 1 hour before bedtime; for patients over 12 years of age, 75 mg.

Short Term Efficacy

Behavioral

The antienuretic effects of tricyclics were recently studied and reported (Rapoport, Mikkelsen, Zavadil, Nee, Gruenau, Mendelson, & Gillin, 1980); data failed to support the concept that enuresis is a disorder of arousal (Mikkelsen et al., 1980).

The superiority of imipramine with conjoint psychosocial treatments over placebo has been demonstrated in children with school phobia (Gittelman-Klein & Klein, 1971). In this double-blind, placebo-controlled study, most of the children were depressed; depression and separation anxiety, but not anticipatory anxiety decreased significantly with imipramine. Drug response was delayed as in depression in adults.

Rapoport et al. (1974) found imipramine superior to placebo in the treatment of ADD with hyperactivity as measured by several raters and a variety of rating scales. However, when compared to methylphenidate, imipramine was less effective on all measures. This is a well designed and controlled study involving a large sample (*N* = 76) of boys, ages 6–12 years, with IQs of 80 and above (mean, 98). In a small sample of hyperactive children who failed to respond to methylphenidate, imipramine too was shown to be ineffective (Winsberg et al., 1980).

At the present time, the psychomotor stimulants remain the treatment of choice in ADD with hyperactivity.

As for the efficacy of tricyclics in depressed children, both imipramine and amitriptyline were effective in a sample of 19 prepubertal outpatients (Weinberg et al., 1973). Diagnosis was made on the basis of a 10-item scale; improvements were seen in areas of self-deprecation, social withdrawal, and school performance. Another pilot study, involving eight children who met the Research Diagnostic Criteria (Spitzer, Endicott, & Robins, 1975) for major depressive illness of adults, too has shown that imipramine yields therapeutic changes in children who failed to respond to psychiatric hospitalization (Puig-Antich, Blau, Marx, Greenhill, & Chambers, 1978).

Cognitive

The above-mentioned study of Rapoport et al. (1974) showed only a weak positive effect of imipramine on cognitive performance. In only a few studies were effects of imipramine on cognition investigated (Waizer et al., 1974; Winsberg et al., 1972).

Long Term Treatment

Data indicate that the initial efficacy of imipramine diminishes after about 10 weeks of maintenance (Rapoport et al., 1974). Of the 76 hyperactive ADD boys randomly assigned to imipramine, methylphenidate, or placebo over a period of six weeks, only 23 were receiving imipramine six months later "because of clinical complaints." Forty-nine children were receiving methylphenidate, one dextroamphetamine, and in three medication was discontinued. It should be noted that the investigators wished to keep all responders on their initial drug condition at the time when the code was broken. Of these 76 boys, 73 were seen after one year for follow-up (Quinn & Rapoport, 1975). Of the 29 boys who were initially on imipramine, 13 were still on it at this time. Significantly, more children discontinued imipramine than methylphenidate: including seven for unchanged behavior and seven for irritability and temper tantrums. Even those who were maintained on drug showed behavioral problems. The authors suggest that this resulted from decreasing clinical efficacy of imipramine, a conclusion that is supported by other studies (Gittelman-Klein, 1974; Waizer et al., 1974).

Untoward Effects

Immediate

Drowsiness, dryness of mouth, constipation, and increased blood pressure are the most commonly reported untoward effects. Increase in diastolic blood pressure too was observed (Rapoport et al., 1974; Saraf et al., 1974). Winsberg et al. (1975) also reported electrocardiographic abnormalities and reviewed critically the pertinent literature. Possible epileptogenic properties of imipramine have been also reported (Petti & Campbell, 1975; Brown et al., 1973). Saraf et al. (1974) and Klein et al. (1980) are recommended for more detailed information.

Long Term

GROWTH. In the one-year follow-up study of Quinn and Rapoport (1975), the children who were maintained on imipramine (or on methylphenidate) have shown a significant decrease in growth rate for weight when compared to those who had discontinued drug; this was not true for height.

OTHER.   Anorexia was the most common untoward effect after one year of maintenance (39 percent of children); a few children complained occasionally of irritability, but no seizures were reported (Quinn & Rapoport, 1975). Three children discontinued imipramine because of the development of hypertension. No adverse effects were revealed on psychological testing.

NEUROLEPTICS

There are five major categories of neuroleptics, known as major tranquilizers or antipsychotic drugs: phenothiazines, thioxanthenes, butyrophenones, dihydroindolones, and dibenzoxazepines, as listed in Table 47.3.

Indications

In adults, these drugs have proved effective in the most severe psychopathologies: they are

Table 47.3   Representative Neuroleptics

	Dosage
Phenothiazines	
Chlorpromazine (Thorazine)	10–200 mg/day
Fluphenazine (Prolixin)	.25–16 mg/day
Trifluoperazine (Stelazine)	1–20 mg/day
Thioridazine (Mellaril)	10–200 mg/day
Thioxanthenes	
Thiothixene (Navane)	1–40 mg/day
Butyrophenones	
Haloperidol (Haldol)	.5–16 mg/day
Dihydroindolones	
Molindone hydrochloride (Moban)	1–155 mg/day
Dibenzoxazepines	
Loxapine succinate (Loxitane)	10–75 mg/day (only for adolescents 16 years of age and over)

almost exclusively used in the treatment of psychoses. In children, the neuroleptics are used in psychoses but also in some nonpsychotic conditions such as conduct disorder, aggressive type, and ADD with hyperactivity. Moreover, children with Tourette's disorder have benefited from haloperidol. Though neuroleptics are widely used in retarded individuals with behavioral problems such as aggressiveness directed against self or others, in the majority of cases there is no evidence that the administration of these drugs yields therapeutic changes (Lipman et al., 1978; Breuning, 1981).

Dosage

Dosage is shown in Table 47.3.

Short Term Efficacy

Behavioral

In most reports involving psychotic children, the samples are diagnostically heterogeneous, combining children with early infantile autism and those with psychoses that clinically appear much more similar to schizophrenia. In addition, the methodology is poor, which makes it difficult to interpret the results (Campbell, 1978).

Fish (1970) observed that prepubertal children were excessively sedated by chlorpromazine at dosages necessary to control the psychotic symptoms. Clinically, sedation appeared to interfere with learning and functioning. This prompted Fish to study the effect of trifluoperazine, a potent neuroleptic. In a double-blind, controlled study, the most impaired nonverbal autistic children showed a significant improvement (Fish, Shapiro, & Campbell, 1966). Positive clinical changes were not accompanied by excessive sedation. The efficacy of other low dose, high potency neuroleptics has been explored in similar populations. Englehardt et al. (1973) compared fluphenazine to haloperidol in 30 outpatient autistic children, ages 6–12 years: 93 percent improved on fluphenazine and 87 percent on haloperidol on the Clinical Global Impressions Scale (CGI). As rated on the

Children's Psychiatric Rating Scale (developed by the authors), fluphenazine yielded among other improvements significant decrease in compulsive acts and self-mutilation while, with haloperidol, increases in affect, self-care, exploratory behavior, and language communication were observed. However, no placebo control was employed in this trial.

Because development of communicative language is the single most important predictor for outcome in infantile autism, and because no treatment yields dramatic therapeutic changes in this syndrome, the efficacy of haloperidol was compared to behavior modification (with emphasis on language acquisition), and the interaction of both was critically assessed (Campbell, Anderson, Meier, Cohen, Small, Samit, & Sachar, 1978). Both therapies had placebo counterparts yielding a 2 × 2 between-groups factorial blind study, the 40 children were randomly assigned to one of the four treatment conditions; ratings were carried out by multiple, independent raters on five types of rating scales, under different conditions and using videotapes. Haloperidol (at doses of .5–4.0 mg/day, mean, 1.65 mg/day) was significantly superior to placebo in reducing the symptoms of stereotypies and withdrawal; this effect was statistically significant ($p < .05$) only in children between ages of 4.5–7 years but not in those who were younger. The combination of haloperidol and language training was significantly more effective than these treatments alone in facilitating the acquisition of imitative speech.

The effects of haloperidol on behavioral symptoms were replicated in a subsequent placebo-controlled, double-blind trial employing an ABAB design and objective rating scales (Cohen et al., 1980). A study was designed in order to answer the question: How does haloperidol facilitate learning—by directly affecting attentional mechanisms or by reducing stereotypies and withdrawal?

This double-blind, placebo-controlled clinical trial of haloperidol in autistic children is in progress. The study comprises two components: a trial of the efficacy of haloperidol on (1) behavioral symptoms and (2) learning (Campbell, Anderson, Small, Perry, Green, & Caplan, 1982). A total of 33 subjects age 2.3–7.9 years (mean, 4.7) have thus far completed the first part of the study. The children's intellectual functioning ranged from mildly to profoundly retarded. Children were initially maintained for two weeks on placebo for baseline evaluation; those suitable were randomly assigned to one of two treatment sequences: placebo-haloperidol-placebo or haloperidol-placebo-haloperidol. Each treatment period lasted four weeks. Five rating scales were used, including objective rating scales taken in four different situations. The results are as follows: haloperidol, in doses of .5–3.0 mg/day (mean, 1.12 mg/day) was found to be significantly superior to placebo on Clinical Global Impressions (GCI) and on the Children's Psychiatric Rating Scale CPRS); specifically, stereotypies, withdrawal, hyperactivity, abnormal objective relations, and fidgetiness were lower on drug ($p < .001$). The placebo scores were significantly higher than haloperiodol scores on the Conners' Parent Teacher Questionnaire (PTQ) ($p < .01$). The Timed Behavioral Rating Sheet revealed that the effects on stereotypy were a function of the structure of the rating conditions.

The effects of haloperidol on attentional learning were also investigated in the same patient sample; the results will be discussed below in the section on cognitive effects.

To the best of our knowledge there is no double-blind, placebo-controlled study on the efficacy of neuroleptics in schizophrenic prepubertal children, and there is only one published on adolescents. In this trial, 75 patients with acute schizophrenia or chronic schizophrenia with acute exacerbation were randomly assigned to loxapine succinate, haloperidol, or placebo (Pool et al., 1976). Ratings were carried out on the Brief Psychiatric Rating Scale (BPRS), the Nurses' Observation Scale for Inpatient Evaluation (NOSIE), and Clinical Global Impressions (CGI). All three groups showed marked improvement over the four-week period as measured by the BPRS and NOSIE. Loxapine, however, was significantly better than placebo on Hallucinatory

Behavior, Disorientation, and Thinking Disorder factors for the BPRS and on Manifest Psychosis for the NOSIE. Haloperidol showed no significant differences from loxapine as rated by the BPRS. However, on the NOSIE, at week two loxapine was significantly better than haloperidol on Social Interest and Manifest Psychosis factors, and there was a trend favoring loxapine for Total Patient Assets. Of those patients who were rated as "severely ill" or "very severely ill" at baseline on the CGI, 87.5 percent of those receiving loxapine and 70 percent receiving haloperidol showed improvement while only 36.4 percent of those on placebo improved at week four.

The efficacy of neuroleptics was also explored and assessed in the treatment of nonpsychotic psychiatric outpatients and inpatients. Haloperidol was effective in reducing aggressive and hyperactive behavior in children with conduct disorder and ADD (Werry & Aman, 1975; Campbell, Cohen, & Small, 1982).

Preliminary results of a pilot study indicated that molindone hydrochloride is a promising agent in the treatment of hospitalized children with conduct disorder associated with aggressivity (Greenhill et al., 1981).

In a well-controlled and well-designed trial of a large number of ADD children with hyperkinesis, thioridazine was less effective than methylphenidate alone or methylphenidate in combination with thioridazine (Gittelman-Klein et al., 1976).

Haloperidol is beneficial in tics (Connell et al., 1967) and Tourette's disorder (Cohen et al., 1979; Shapiro, Shapiro, & Wayne, 1973; Shapiro et al., 1978).

Cognitive

There is some suggestion that the effects of neuroleptics on cognition in children may be dose related (Werry & Aman, 1975; Campbell, Anderson, Meier, Cohen, Small, Samit, & Sachar, 1978; Greenhill et al., 1981). Werry and Aman (1975) have investigated this issue in children of normal intelligence using sophisticated laboratory measures. On .025 mg/kg/day of haloperidol, performance was facilitated, while on .05 mg/kg/day there was no

effect with the exception of a short term memory task where deterioration was observed. This seemed to be the result of an interaction between haloperidol and level of task difficulty. As noted above, in two well-controlled studies involving retarded autistic children, haloperidol facilitated learning (Campbell, Anderson, Meier, Cohen, Small, Samit, & Sachar, 1978; Campbell, Anderson, Small, Perry, Green, & Caplan, 1982). The design and behavioral results of the second study were described above; here the effects of haloperidol on attentional learning in 22 autistic children who completed this part of the study will be given. A computer-controlled, operant-conditioning apparatus, was used to present stimuli, record responses and durations of stereotypic behavior, and present reinforcers according to a specified schedule (Campbell, Anderson, Small, Perry, Green, & Caplan, 1982). Motor activity levels were recorded from pressure sensors mounted under carpeting. Children were required to learn that reinforcement was available if the level was pressed during the presentation of an auditory-visual stimulus pattern (SD) and was not available when the stimulus pattern was off (SΔ). Discrimination indices were computed for each child and the mean across children plotted as a function of sessions and treatments. The results indicate that children receiving haloperidol learned the discrimination while those on placebo did not. This was by virtue of the haloperidol group displaying fewer responses to the SΔ. Children who acquired the discrimination of the haloperidol retained it when placed on placebo. Thus the effects appear to be associative. Children shifted from placebo to haloperidol showed continued improvements in performance and decelerations in inappropriate responding that were comparable to the children who acquired the discrimination on haloperidol. Developmental level per se did not interact with drug to determine performance. The lack of significant effect of the medication on stereotypy in the laboratory suggests that reduction in this behavior is not responsible for the improvement in learning. The fact that haloperidol was associated with a reduced tendency to respond inappropriately suggests that it directly affects the child's ability to withhold inappropriate behavior. Further studies are suggested.

Long Term Treatment

Although neuroleptics are administered over a prolonged period to many children with psychiatric disorders and to the mentally retarded who have behavioral problems (Lipman et al., 1978), there is little systematic research as to the long term efficacy of these drugs.

In a prospective 10-year follow-up study of 75 hyperactive children, 17 subjects were receiving chlorpromazine in doses of 25–200 mg/day for 18–48 months (Weiss et al., 1979). They did not differ on any of the outcome measures from the matched controls who were receiving medication for less than six months.

As noted earlier, Gittelman-Klein et al. (1976) made the observation that, in hyperactive children, thioridazine is less effective after 12 weeks of treatment than it was at 4 weeks as reflected by psychiatrists' and teachers' ratings. Moreover, this drug yielded untoward effects at 12 weeks so that the mean dose was dropped from the initial 193 mg/day (6.0 mg/kg/day) to 160 mg/day (4.54 mg/kg/day). The mothers' and psychologists' evaluations failed to show this shift over time.

The long term therapeutic efficacy and safety of haloperidol is currently being investigated in a prospective study; the sample and the results of the short term effects were described above (Campbell, Anderson, Cohen, Perry, Small, Green, Anderson, & McCandless, 1982). Eleven of the 33 children completed their six-month evaluations on haloperidol and six were evaluated after being 12 months on this drug. There was a four-week placebo period after the first six months of haloperidol maintenance in order to assess the efficacy of the drug and to establish whether continuation of drug treatment was required. During the first week of placebo, on the CPRS ratings of fidgetiness, hyperactivity, abnormal object relations, withdrawal, stereotypies, and

the CGI ratings showed significant increase in mean scores; during the second week of placebo, abnormal object relations increased. These changes plateaued; resumption of drug treatment was required at the end of the fourth week. The same effects in terms of increase of symptoms were obtained following discontinuation of haloperidol at 12 months.

Thus our results indicate that haloperidol in doses of .5–3.0 mg/day remains therapeutically effective up to one year in those autistic children who were responders in the initial 12-week trial utilizing an ABA design.

Untoward Effects

Immediate

The immediate untoward effects of neuroleptics in children were recently reviewed (Engelhardt & Polizos, 1978; Simeon, 1976; Campbell, 1979; Winsberg & Yepes, 1978).

BEHAVIORAL.   Of the immediate untoward effects, behavioral toxicity is most common in children, particularly in the younger age group. In order to assess behavioral toxicity, a stable baseline observation and evaluation of the child prior to drug treatment is required. This is because most behavioral toxicity is manifested as worsening of preexisting symptoms, such as hyperactivity, irritability, and apathy, to name a few. Other signs are symptoms *de novo:* a child who was previously hyperactive may become hypoactive, or "like in a daze." To look for behavioral toxicity is very important, particularly in the young age group, since they are often unable or unwilling to complain about their subjective feelings such as headaches, dryness of mouth, or a sensation of being slowed down.

In the older age group, subjective response to drug may be important: dysphoric responders may experience more side effects and refuse further drug treatment (Van Putten et al., 1981).

COGNITIVE.   Results of most studies indicate that neuroleptics have no effect or an adverse effect on cognitive performance (for review, see Hersh et al., submitted for publication 1982; Campbell, 1979; Klein et al., 1980). Werry and Aman (1975) have given evidence that such effects of haloperidol in children of normal intelligence are dose related. In retarded autistic children, there was no change from baseline to posttreatment on a cognitive battery on optimal doses of haloperidol (.5–4.0 mg/day, mean, 1.65) while above these doses all children were sedated (Campbell, Anderson, Meier, Cohen, Small, Samit, & Sachar, 1978). In another sample of autistic children, by using objective methods, it was demonstrated that haloperidol facilities learning at doses (mean, 1.12 mg/day) that yield significant reduction of behavioral symptoms while the bioavailability of the drug is evidenced by detectable plasma levels (Poland et al., 1982).

Thus it is possible to elicit behavioral improvement in a severely disturbed child with a potent neuroleptic such as haloperidol and to enhance learning at the same time. This is of crucial importance when we deal with children, particularly if they are mentally retarded.

Shapiro et al. (1978) treating children of normal intelligence with Tourette's disorder also made the clinical observation that haloperidol, at doses that control the tics, is associated with sedation. This results in deterioration of academic performance. At lower doses (1–3 mg/day) the suppression of tics is not complete, but an A student will not become a C student.

CENTRAL NERVOUS SYSTEM. These are the extrapyramidal side effects: acute dystonic reactions, parkinsonian signs, and akathisia. This group of untoward effects is usually seen early in treatment: in the first few days, as acute dystonic reactions or, in the first few weeks, as the parkinsonian side effects. However, they can occur late in drug treatment (Gardos, 1981). The "rabbit syndrome" is a rare subcategory of the extrapyramidal untoward effects, of late onset and characterized by perioral muscular movements resembling the rapid, chewinglike movements of the rabbit's mouth (Villeneuve, 1972). The likelihood of acute dystonic reaction may be diminished by starting with a very low dose; in the case of haloperidol, with .25 or .5 mg/day with very gradual increments. Such reaction is readily relieved by 25 mg of Benadryl orally or intramuscularly. The younger the child, the less frequent the parkinsonian side effects (Campbell, Anderson, Meier, Cohen, Small, Samit, & Sachar, 1978). They can be relieved by decreasing dosage. There is some, though inconclusive, evidence that antiparkinsonian agents can product significant decrease of neuroleptic levels in plasma and worsening of preexisting psychotic symptoms (Rivera-Calimlim et al., 1976; Cooper, Simpson, & Lee, 1976).

Onset of grand mal seizures or increase in their frequency in individuals with preexisting seizure disorders was reported with chlorpromazine (Tarjan, Lowery, & Wright, 1957).

LABORATORY. Neuroleptic-induced blood dyscrasias and hepatotoxicity are rare in children according to the literature (for review, Campbell, 1979; Engelhardt & Polizos, 1978; Simeon, 1976; and DiMascio, Soltys, & Shader, 1970, are recommended). However, baseline laboratory assessment is required.

Long Term Untoward Effects

GROWTH. There has not been any systematic investigation concerning the long term effects of neuroleptics on growth in children.

Chlorpromazine is known to decrease growth hormone secretion in adults (Sherman et al., 1971); such studies are not available in psychiatric populations of children. The question remains as to what the relationship, if any, is between neuroleptic-induced drop of growth hormone levels and the linear growth of the child. When mentally retarded and autistic children are under consideration, it has to be remembered that, as a group, they are of shorter stature than children of normal intellect (Campbell et al., 1980; Simon & Gillies, 1964; Dutton, 1964).

Linear growth on neuroleptic maintenance was studied in a small sample of hyperactive school age children ($N = 8$) under rigorous conditions; however, growth hormone studies were not carried out (Greenhill et al., 1981). Four children were maintained on chlorpromazine (mean dose 115 mg/day), and four were receiving thioridazine (mean, 156 mg/day). After one year of drug maintenance, children showed nonsignificant increases in height and weight percentiles.

In a sample of 13 psychotic children, ages 5–12 years (mean, 9.8 years) receiving neuroleptics, acceleration of growth was related to length of drug administration (Simeon, Gross, & Mueller, 1977). Acceleration of linear growth occurred in six boys, receiving pharmacotherapy for a mean of 71 weeks, whereas heights remained in the same percentile range for the five boys who were on medication for only 39 weeks. For the two boys who received medication for less than 11 weeks, there were no significant changes. Weight gain was also observed in these children.

Engelhardt and Polizos (1978) followed 20 autistic boys ages 4–11 years who were receiving neuroleptics over a period of 1–6 years (mean, 4 years). Their mean heights and weights did not deviate significantly from the fiftieth percentile when first placed on neuroleptics. One to 6 years later, they "moved even closer to the 50th percentile" on these measures, according to the authors.

CENTRAL NERVOUS SYSTEM. Neuroleptic-induced movement disorders are long term untoward effects that are of great concern. These are tardive dyskinesia and the neuroleptic withdrawal emergent dyskinesias (Gardos, Cole, & Tarsy, 1978). The "rabbit syndrome" described above is perhaps a separate group, a late onset extrapyramidal untoward effect (Villeneuve, 1972). While a vast amount of literature and some systematic research exist in adult psychiatric populations (for review, see Berger & Rexroth, 1980; Gardos & Cole, 1980), including the mentally retarded, (Breuning, Ferguson, & Cullari, in press), the information on children is limited to a few case reports and to retrospective, uncontrolled clinical surveys (for review see Gualtieri et al., 1980). The assessment measures of these movements disorders, their validity, and their reliability still present a problem even in adults, and prevalence figures range from .5–56 percent (Gardos, Cole, & LaBrie, 1977; Gardos & Cole, 1980). In children, the methodology has

yet to be developed. Moreover, there are at least two additional problems: (1) many children who are on chronic neuroleptic maintenance had no stable baseline assessment; (2) various abnormal movements exist prior to initiation of neuroleptic administration in Tourette's disorder and in many autistic and retarded children. These include various stereotypies, posturings, tics, movements, and chewing of the tongue, to name a few. In studies that employed objective rating scales and an intensive ABAB design with placebo control, it was demonstrated that these movements, which are part of the clinical pathology, are significantly reduced by neuroleptic administration, specifically by haloperidol (Cohen et al., 1980; Campbell, Anderson, Cohen, Perry, Small, Green, Anderson, & McCandless; Anderson, Small, Perry, Green, & Perry, 1982). Thus reports on the frequency of occurrence of neuroleptic-induced abnormal movements, particularly of those referred to as withdrawal emergent symptoms (Engelhardt & Polizos, 1978) have to be interpreted with caution.

In a prospective study of autistic children, using multiple independent raters and rating scales, 12 percent (4 children) developed abnormal movements after 3–11 months of haloperidol maintenance; their duration ranged from less than 1–11 months (Campbell, Anderson, Cohen, Perry, Small, Green, Anderson, & McCandless, 1982).

OTHER. Behavioral "neuroleptic withdrawal symptoms" were reported and included insomnia, agitation, and worsening of preexisting psychotic symptoms in adult patients (Berger & Rexroth, 1980). Vomiting, weight loss, anorexia, sweating, and diarrhea were reported within four weeks after discontinuation of neuroleptics (Breuning et al., 1980; Gardos et al., 1978).

Significant increases in IQ scores were obtained in mentally retarded adults after discontinuation of chronic neuroleptic administration (mean number of years on medication was 1.05–2.06; mean daily dosages in chlorpromazine equivalents were 567–933 mgs), suggesting that neuroleptics have adverse effects on intellectual functioning when given in these doses (Breuning & Davidson, 1981). Very little has been published regarding the untoward effects of neuroleptics on the endocrine system in children (for review in adults, Shader & DiMascio, 1970, is recommended). Englehardt and Polizos (1978) reported gynecomastia developing in one child who was receiving thioridazine in daily doses of 300 mgs.

LITHIUM

Indications

In adults, lithium is mainly used in the treatment of manic depressive illness and as a prophylactic agent of affective disorders (Prien, 1979). It appears to be also effective in patients with schizoaffective or cyclothymic disorders who show maniclike symptoms (Klein et al., 1980). The antiaggressive properties of lithium, demonstrated in animals and humans have been recently reviewed by Schou (1979).

In children, the indications for lithium have not been established yet (Campbell, Schulman, & Rapoport, 1978).

Dosage

Dosage and therapeutic range of lithium levels in plasma are shown in Table 47.4.

Table 47.4   Lithium

	Dosage
Lithium carbonate	450–2,000 mg/day and/or .25–1.2 mEq/l (in serum)

Short Term Efficacy

Behavioral

Lithium yielded significant decrease of mood swings in young people diagnosed as having an emotionally unstable character disorder as compared to placebo under double-blind con-

ditions (Rifkin et al., 1972). This effect was achieved at lithium levels of .6–1.5 mEq/l in blood. In an open study (Dostal, 1972, p. 491) retarded youngsters with severe disruptive and aggressive behavior were administered lithium; these children failed to respond previously to treatment with neuroleptics. Only in those individuals who exhibited aggressiveness associated with explosiveness, a marked decrease of these symptoms was observed.

Some uncontrolled studies have been reported in which children described as manic or depressed have benefited from lithium (for review, see Campbell, Shulman, & Rapoport, 1978). The samples in these studies have been poorly described and stringent diagnostic criteria are lacking. Only a few controlled studies have been done and are reviewed by Campbell, Shulman, and Rapoport, 1978; Youngerman and Canino, 1978; and Lena, 1979, 1980.

Lithium's use in explosive and aggressive or self-mutilating children who failed to respond to other types of treatments, including pharmacotherapy and behavior modification, has drawn some interest (Campbell, Cohen & Small, 1982). Its efficacy in a well-defined sample of explosive and aggressive conduct-disordered children of normal IQ has been demonstrated (Campbell, Small, Green, Jennings, Perry, Bennett, Padron-Gayol, & Anderson, 1982).

In a double-blind trial involving a small sample of hyperactive children, lithium failed to show therapeutic efficacy (Greenhill et al., 1973).

Cognitive

Information on the effects of lithium on cognition is limited to adults (for review, see Platt et al., 1981). Only three reports exist in children, and the patient samples are small. In a pilot study (Campbell, Cohen, & Small, 1982) and then in a placebo-controlled study (Platt et al., 1981), lithium was shown markedly to reduce aggression without significantly impairing cognition. In a third study, there were no significant changes in trials of reaction time (Greenhill et al., 1973).

Long Term Treatment

Only four reports were found in the literature where lithium was administered to children or to young retarded adults over a period of time exceeding four months. It appears that the behavioral efficacy of lithium can be maintained over a prolonged time. DeLong (1978) administered lithium to 12 aggressive children of normal intelligence, over a period of 6–33 months; 9 of these children had mood swings "suggesting manic-depressive illness." Of the 15 aggressive retarded patients treated with lithium for three months up to five years, a few were adolescents (Dale, 1980). Dostal (1972) treated 14 retarded aggressive adolescents for eight months. Ziring and Teitelbaum (1980) have been treating seven severely aggressive and/or self-mutilating retarded institutionalized adults for up to two years with lithium. Self-mutilating behavior ceased completely in an adolescent autistic child who has been receiving this drug for over five years (Shopsin, personal communication).

Untoward Effects

Lithium administration requires careful clinical and laboratory monitoring; this includes keeping plasma or saliva levels within an acceptable and safe limit (Reisberg & Gershon, 1979). Untoward effects, including those due to prolonged treatment, have been extensively reviewed recently (Reisberg & Gershon, 1979; Schou, 1981). In both reviews, the interactions of lithium with other drugs, including neuroleptics, were discussed. Untoward effects of lithium in retarded and autistic children were reported by Dostal (1972) and Campbell, Fish, Korein, Shapiro, Collins, and Koh (1972).

ANXIOLYTICS

Only two benzodiazepines (diazepam and chlordiazepoxide) will be referred to here. Though diazepam is perhaps the most frequently prescribed drug in the United States, it is unclear how many children and adolescents receive this drug.

At the present time there is still a lack of evidence of the usefulness of benzodiazepines in the treatment of behavioral disorders in children. There is a paucity of controlled studies, and these suggest either no significant therapeutic effect or a somewhat detrimental effect. Petti et al. (1982) note that children who are impulsive or psychotic tend to deteriorate on chlordiazepoxide. Most positive reports have been based on an open clinical administration of the drugs.

For review, Greenblatt and Shader (1974), and Klein et al. (1980) are recommended.

ANTICONVULSANTS

Since the early 1940s, drugs of this class have been used for the management of children with behavior problems; the rationale was that many of these children had abnormal electroencephalograms (Lindsley & Henry, 1941). The most commonly used drugs were diphenylhydantoin and phenobarbital. However, the few well-controlled studies failed to demonstrate the superiority of these drugs over placebo (e.g., Looker & Conners, 1970).

MacLeod, Dekaban, and Hunt (1978) reported that, in adult epileptic patients, phenobarbital adversely affected speed of access to information in short term memory and that short term memory was highly sensitive to increased phenobarbital levels. Speed of access to long term memory was not so affected at the two blood levels most comonly prescribed in epilepsy. These authors note that impairment of short term memory may critically affect a child's ability to maintain attention, a crucial ability for school age epileptic children trying to acquire new information.

In view of the above, anticonvulsants should not be prescribed to children in the absence of seizure disorders even though the behavioral problems may be associated with abnormal electroencephalograms.

For review, chapters by Conners and Werry (1979) and Stores (1978) are suggested.

CONCLUSION

At our present state of knowledge, the role of psychoactive drugs in the treatment of children is viewed only as an adjunct to other treatment modalities. For those children who require pharmacotherapy, careful clinical and laboratory monitoring is recommended.

Above all, before initiating pharmacotherapy, alternate treatment modalities should be considered and explored. Systematic and thoughtful research is needed regarding the effects of drugs on the child's cognition and academic work and the long term adverse effects on the neuroendocrine and central nervous systems.

REFERENCES

Berger, P.A., & Rexroth, K. Tardive dyskinesia: Clinical, biological, and pharmacological perspectives. *Schizophrenia Bulletin,* 1980, **6,** 102–116.

Bradley, C. The behavior of children receiving benzedrine. *American Journal of Psychiatry,* 1937, **94,** 577–585.

Breuning, S.E. Assessing drug effects in mentally retarded individuals. Council for Exceptional Children Convention, New York, N.Y., April 15–18, 1981.

Breuning, S.E., & Davidson, N.A. Effects of psychotropic drugs on intelligence test performance of institutionalized mentally retarded adults. *American Journal of Mental Deficiency,* 1981, **85,** 575–579.

Breuning, S.E., Ferguson, D.G., & Cullari, S. Analysis of single-double blind procedures, maintenance of placebo effects, and drug-induced dyskinesia with mentally retarded persons. *Applied Research in Mental Retardation,* 1980, **1,** 175–192.

Brown, D., Winsberg, B., Bialer, I., & Press, M. Imipramine therapy and seizures. *American Journal of Psychiatry,* 1973, **130,** 210–212.

Brunner, R.L., Vorhees, C.V., & Butcher, R.E. Food colors and behavior. *Science,* 1981, **212,** 578–579.

Campbell, M. The use of drug treatment in infantile autism and childhood schizophrenia: A review. In M.A. Lipton, A. DeMascio, & K. Killam

(Eds.), *Psychopharmacology: A generation of progress.* New York: Raven, 1978.

Campbell, M. Psychopharmacology. In J.D. Noshpitz (Ed.), *Basic handbook of child psychiatry* (Vol. 3). New York: Basic Books, 1979.

Campbell, M., Anderson, L.T., Cohen, I.L., Perry, R., Small, A.M., Green, W.H., Anderson, L., & McCandless, W. Haloperidol in autistic children: Effects on learning, behavior and abnormal involuntary movements. *Psychopharmacology Bulletin,* 1982, **18**(1), 110–112.

Campbell, M., Anderson, L.T., Meier, M., Cohen, I.L., Small, A.M., Samit, C., & Sachar, E.J. A comparison of haloperidol and behavior therapy and their interaction in autistic children. *Journal of the American Academy of Child Psychiatry,* 1978, **17,** 640–655.

Campbell, M., Anderson, L.T., Small, A.M., Perry, R., Green, W.H., & Caplan, R. The effects of haloperidol on learning and behavior in autistic children. *Journal of Autism and Developmental Disorders,* 1982, **12,** 167–175.

Campbell, M., Cohen, I.L., & Perry, R. Psychopharmacological treatment. In T.H. Ollendick & M. Hersen (Eds.), *Handbook of child psychopathology.* New York, Plenum, 1982.

Campbell, M., Cohen, I.L., & Small, A.M. Drugs in aggressive behavior. *Journal of the American Academy of Child Psychiatry,* 1982, **21,** 107–117.

Campbell, M., Fish, B., David, R., Shapiro, T., Collins, P., & Koh, C. Response to triiodothyronine and dextroamphetamine: A study of preschool schizophrenic children. *Journal of Autism and Childhood Schizophrenia,* 1972, **2,** 343–358.

Campbell, M., Fish, B., Korein, J., Shapiro, T., Collins, P., & Koh, C. Lithium and chlorpromazine: A controlled crossover study of hyperactive severely disturbed young children. *Journal of Autism and Childhood Schizophrenia,* 1972, **2,** 234–263.

Campbell, M., Petti, T.A., Green, W.H., Cohen, I.L., Genieser, N.B., & David, R. Some physical parameters of young autistic children. *Journal of the American Academy of Child Psychiatry,* 1980, **19,** 193–212.

Campbell, M., Schulman, D., & Rapoport, J.L. The current status of lithium therapy in child and adolescent psychiatry. *Journal of the*

American Academy of Child Psychiatry, 1978, **17,** 717–720.

Campbell, M., Small, A.M., Collins, P.J., Friedman, E., David, R., & Genieser, N.B. Levodopa and levoamphetamine: A crossover study in schizophrenic children. *Current Therapeutic Research,* 1976, **18,** 70–86.

Campbell, M., Small, A.M., Green, W.H., Jennings, S.J., Perry, R., Bennett, W.G., Padron-Gayol, M., and Anderson, L. Lithium and haloperidol in hospitalized aggressive children. *Psychopharmacology Bulletin,* 1982, **18**(3), 126–129.

Cantwell, D.P., & Carlson, G.A. Stimulants. In J.S. Werry (Ed.), *Pediatric psychopharmacology: The use of behavior modifying drugs in children.* New York: Brunner/Mazel, 1978.

Cohen, D.J., Shaywitz, B.A., Young, J.G., Carbonari, C.M., Nathanson, J.A., Lieberman, D., Bowers, M.B., & Maas, J.W. Central biogenic amine metabolism in children with the syndrome of chronic multiple tics of Gilles de la Tourette. *Journal of the American Academy of Child Psychiatry,* 1979, **18,** 320–341.

Cohen, I.L., Campbell, M., Posner, D., Small, A.M., Triebel, D., & Anderson, L.T. Behavioral effects of haloperidol in young autistic children: An objective analysis using a within-subjects reversal design. *Journal of the American Academy of Child Psychiatry,* 1980, **19,** 665–677.

Connell, P.H., Corbett, J.A., Horne, D.J., & Mathews, A.M. Drug treatment of adolescent tiquers: A double-blind trial of diazepam and haloperidol. *British Journal of Psychiatry,* 1967, **113,** 375–381.

Conners, C.K. A teacher rating scale for use in drug studies with children. *American Journal of Psychiatry,* 1969, **126,** 152–156.

Conners, C.K. Symptom patterns in hyperkinetic, neurotic, and normal children. *Child Development,* 1970, **41,** 667–682.

Conners, C.K. Pharmacotherapy of psychopathology in children. In H.C. Quay & J.S. Werry (Eds.), *Psychopathological disorders of childhood.* New York: Wiley, 1972.

Conners, C.K. Deanol and behavior disorders in children: A critical review of the literature and recommended future studies for determining efficacy. *Psychopharmacology Bulletin,* Special issue: Pharmacotherapy of children, 1973.

Conners, C.K. (Ed.). *Clinical use of stimulant drugs in children.* Amsterdam: Excerpta Medica, 1974.

Conners, C.K. *Food additives and hyperactive children.* New York: Plenum, 1980.

Conners, C.K., & Taylor, E. Pemoline, methylphenidate and placebo in children with minimal brain dysfunction. *Archives of General Psychiatry,* 1980, **37,** 922–930.

Conners, C.K., & Wells, K.C. Behavioral and physiological measurement of psychopharmacological effects in children. Read at the annual meeting of the American College of Neuropsychopharmacology, San Juan, Puerto Rico, 1977.

Conners, C.K., & Werry, J.S. Pharmacotherapy, In H.C. Quay & J.S. Werry (Eds.), *Psychopathological disorders of childhood* (2nd ed.). New York: Wiley, 1979.

Cooper, T.B., Simpson, G.M., & Lee, J.H. Thymoleptic and neuroleptic drug plasma levels in psychiatry: Current status. *International Review of Neurobiology,* 1976, **19,** 269–309.

Dale, P.G. Lithium therapy in aggressive mentally subnormal patients. *British Journal of Psychiatry,* 1980, **137,** 469–474.

DeLong, G.R. Lithium carbonate treatment of select behavior disorders in children suggesting manic-depressive illness. *Journal of Pediatrics,* 1978, **93,** 689–694.

Diagnostic and statistical manual of mental disorders (DSM-III) (3rd ed.). Washington, D.C.: The American Psychiatric Association, 1980.

DiMascio, A., Soltys, J.J., & Shader, R.I. Psychotropic drug side effects in children. In: R.I. Shader & A. DiMascio (Eds.), *Psychotropic drug side effects,* Baltimore: Williams & Wilkins, 1970.

Dostal, T. Antiaggressive effects of lithium salts in mentally retarded adolescents. In A.L. Annell (Ed.), *Depressive states in childhood and adolescence.* Stockholm: Almquist & Wiksell, 1972.

Dutton, G. The growth pattern of psychotic boys. *British Journal of Psychiatry,* 1964, **110,** 101–103.

Engelhardt, D.M., & Polizos, P. Adverse effects of pharmacotherapy in childhood psychosis. In M.A. Lipton, A. DiMascio, & K.F. Killam (Eds.), *Psychopharmacology: A generation of progress.* New York: Raven, 1978.

Engelhardt, D.M., Polizos, P., Waizer, J., & Hoffman, S.P. A double-blind comparison of fluphenazine and haloperidol. *Journal of Autism and Childhood Schizophrenia,* 1973, **3,** 128–137.

Feingold, B.F. *Hyperkinesis and learning difficulties (H-LD) linked to the ingestion of artificial colors and flavors.* Paper presented at the annual meeting of the American Medical Association, Section on Allergy, Chicago, June 24, 1974.

Firestone, P., Kelly, M.J., Goodman, J.T., & Davey, J. Differential effects of parent training and stimulant medication with hyperactives: A progress report. *Journal of the American Academy of Child Psychiatry,* 1981, **20,** 135–147.

Fish, B. Psychopharmacologic response of chronic schizophrenic adults as predictors of responses in young schizophrenic children. *Psychopharmacology Bulletin,* 1970, **6,** 12–15.

Fish, B. The "one child, one drug" myth of stimulants in hyperkinesis: Importance of diagnostic categories in evaluating treatment. *Archives of General Psychiatry,* 1971, **25,** 193–203.

Fish, B., Shapiro, T., & Campbell, M. Long-term prognosis and the response of schizophrenic children to drug therapy: A controlled study of trifluoperazine. *American Journal of Psychiatry,* 1966, **123,** 32–39.

Freedman, D.X. *Report of the conference on the use of stimulant drugs in the treatment of behaviorally disturbed young school children.* Office of Child Development and the Office of the Assistant Secretary for Health and Scientific Affairs, U.S. Department of Health, Education, and Welfare, Washington, D.C., 1971.

Frommer, E.A. Treatment of childhood depression with antidepressant drugs. *British Medical Journal,* 1967, **1,** 729–732.

Gardos, G. Dystonic reaction during maintenance antipsychotic therapy. *American Journal of Psychiatry,* 1981, **138,** 114–115.

Gardos, G., & Cole, J.O. Overview: Public health issues in tardive dyskinesia. *American Journal of Psychiatry,* 1980, **137,** 776–781.

Gardos, G., Cole, J.O., & LaBrie, R. The assessment of tardive dyskinesia. *Archives of General Psychiatry,* 1977, **34,** 1206–1212.

Gardos, G., Cole, J.O., & Tarsy, D. Withdrawal syndromes associated with antipsychotic drugs. *American Journal of Psychiatry,* 1978, **135,** 1321–1324.

Gittelman, R. Indications for the use of stimulant treatment in learning disorders. *Journal of the American Academy of Child Psychiatry,* 1980, **19,** 623–636.

Gittelman, R., Klein, D.F., Abikoff, H., Katz, S., Pollack, E., & Mattes, J. A controlled trial of behavior modification and methylphenidate in hyperactive children. In C. Whalen & B. Henker (Eds.), *Hyperactive children: The social ecology of identification and treatment.* New York: Academic Press, 1979.

Gittelman-Klein, R. A pilot clinical trial of imipramine in hyperkinetic children. In C.K. Conners (Ed.), *Clinical use of stimulant drugs in children.* Amsterdam: Excerpta Medica, 1974, 192–201.

Gittelman-Klein, R. Review of clinical psychopharmacological treatment of hyperkinesis. In D.F. Klein & R. Gittelman-Klein (Eds.), *Progress in psychiatric drug treatment.* New York: Brunner/Mazel, 1975.

Gittelman-Klein, R., & Klein, D.F. Controlled imipramine treatment of school phobia. *Archives of General Psychiatry,* 1971, **25,** 204–207.

Gittelman-Klein, R., Klein, D.F., Katz, S., Saraf, K.R., & Pollack, E. Comparative effects of methylphenidate and thioridazine in hyperkinetic children: I. Clinical results. *Archives of General Psychiatry,* 1976, **33,** 1217–1231.

Golden, G.S. Case report—Gilles de la Tourette's syndrome following methylphenidate administration. *Developmental Medicine and Child Neurology,* 1974, **16,** 76.

Greenblatt, D.J., & Shader, R.I. *Benzodiazepines in clinical practice.* New York: Raven, 1974.

Greenhill, L.L., Puig-Antich, J., Chambers, W., Rubinstein, B., Halpern, F., & Sachar, E.J. Growth hormone, prolactin and growth responses in hyperkinetic males treated with d-amphetamine. *Journal of the American Academy of Child Psychiatry,* 1981, **20,** 84–103.

Greenhill, L., Rieder, O., Wender, H., Buchsbaum, M., & Zahn, P. Lithium carbonate in the treatment of hyperactive children. *Archives of General Psychiatry,* 1973, **28,** 636–640.

Gross, M.D. Growth of hyperkinetic children taking methylphenidate, dextroamphetamine or imipramine/desipramine. *Pediatrics,* 1976, **58,** 423–431.

Gualtieri, C.T., Barnhill, J., McGimsey, J., & Schell, D. Tardive dyskinesia and other movement disorders in children treated with psychotropic drugs. *Journal of the American Academy of Child Psychiatry,* 1980, **19,** 491–510.

Hayes, T.A., Logan Panitch, M., & Barker, E. Imipramine dosage in children: A comment on "Imipramine and electrocardiographic abnormalities in hyperactive children." *American Journal of Psychiatry,* 1975, **132,** 546–547.

Hersh, S.P., Platt, J.E., Fish, B., Shapiro, T., & Campbell, M. *The effects of amphetamine sulfate and chlorpromazine on cognition and behavior: A placebo-controlled, double-blind trial.* Manuscript submitted for publication, 1982.

Janowsky, D.S., El-Yousef, M.K., Davis, J.M., & Sekerke, H.J. Provocation of schizophrenic symptoms by intravenous administration of methylphenidate. *Archives of General Psychiatry,* 1973, **28,** 185–191.

Klein, D.F., Gittelman, R., Quitkin, F., & Rifkin, A. Diagnosis and drug treatment of childhood disorders. In D.F. Klein, R. Gittelman, F. Quitkin, & A. Rifkin (Eds.), *Diagnosis and drug treatment of psychiatric disorders: Adults and children* (2nd ed.). Baltimore: Williams & Wilkins, 1980.

Lena, B. Lithium in child and adolescent psychiatry. *Archives of General Psychiatry,* 1979, **36,** 854–855.

Lena, B. Lithium treatment of children and adolescents. In F.N. Johnson (Ed.), *Handbook of lithium therapy.* Baltimore: University Park Press, 1980.

Lindsley, D., & Henry, C. The effect of drugs on behavior and the electroencephalograms of children with behavior disorder. *Psychosomatic Medicine,* 1941, **4,** 140–149.

Lipman, R.S., DiMascio, A., Reatig, N., & Kirson, T. Psychotropic drugs and mentally retarded children. In M.A. Lipton, A. DiMascio, & K. Killam (Eds.), *Psychopharmacology: A generation of progress.* New York: Raven, 1978.

Looker, A., & Conners, C.K. Diphenylhydantoin in children with severe temper tantrums. *Archives of General Psychiatry,* 1970, **23,** 80–89.

MacLeod, C.M., Dekaban, A.S., & Hunt, E. Memory impairment in epileptic patients: Selective effects of phenobarbital concentration. *Science,* 1978, **202,** 1102–1104.

McNutt, B.A., Boileau, R.A., Cohen, M.N., Sprague, R.L., & von Neumann, A. *The effects of long-term stimulant medication on the growth and body composition of hyperactive children. II: Report on 2 years.* Paper presented at the annual Early Clinical Drug Evaluation Unit meeting, Psychopharmacology Research Branch, National Institute of Mental Health, Key Biscayne, Florida, May 20–22, 1976.

Mikkelsen, E.J., Rapoport, J.L., Nee, L., Gruenau, C., Mendelson, W., & Gillin, J.C. Childhood enuresis. I: Sleep patterns and psychopathology. *Archives of General Psychiatry,* 1980, **37,** 1139–1144.

Mitchell, E., & Matthews, K.L. Gilles de la Tourette's disorder associated with pemoline. *American Journal of Psychiatry,* 1980, **137,** 1618–1619.

Page, J.G., Bernstein, J.E., Janicki, R.S., & Michelli, F.A. A multiclinic trial of pemoline in childhood hyperkinesis. In C.K. Conners (Ed.), *Clinical uses of stimulant drugs in children.* Amsterdam: Excerpta Medica, 1974, 98–124.

Petti, T.A., and Campbell, M. Imipramine and seizures. *American Journal of Psychiatry,* 1975, **132,** 538–540.

Petti, T.A., Fish, B., Shapiro, T., Cohen, I.L., & Campbell, M. Chlordiazepoxide treatment of disturbed children, *Journal of Clinical Psychopharmacology,* 1982, **2**(4), 270–273.

Platt, J.E., Campbell, M., Green, W.H., Perry, R., & Cohen, I.L. Effects of lithium carbonate and haloperidol on cognition in aggressive hospitalized school-age children. *Journal of Clinical Psychopharmacology,* 1981, **1,** 8–13.

Poland, R.E., Campbell, M., Rubin, R.T., Perry, R., and Anderson, L. Relationship of serum haloperidol levels and clinical response in autistic children. *Collegium Internationale Neuro-Psychopharmacologicum 13th C.I.N.P. Congress, Abstracts,* (Vol. 2), 1982, p. 591.

Pool, D., Bloom, W, Mielke, D.H., Roniger, J.J., & Gallant, D.M. A controlled evaluation of loxitane in seventy-five adolescent schizophrenic patients. *Current Therapeutic Research,* 1976, **19,** 99–104.

Poussaint, A.F., & Ditman, K.S. A controlled study of imipramine (Tofranil) in the treatment of childhood enuresis. *Journal of Pedi-*

atrics, 1965, **67,** 283–290.

Prien, R.J. Lithium in the prophylactic treatment of affective disorders. *Archives of General Psychiatry,* 1979, **36,** 847–848.

Puig-Antich, J., Blau, S., Marx, N., Greenhill, L.L., & Chambers, W. Prepubertal major depressive disorder. A pilot study. *Journal of the American Academy of Child Psychiatry,* 1978, **17,** 695–707.

Puig-Antich, J., Greenhill, L.L. Sassin, J., & Sachar, E.J. Growth hormone, prolactin and cortisol responses and growth patterns in hyperkinetic children treated with dextroamphetamine: Preliminary findings. *Journal of the American Academy of Child Psychiatry,* 1978, **17,** 457–475.

Quinn, P.O., & Rapoport, J.L. One year follow-up of hyperactive boys treated with imipramine or methylphenidate. *American Journal of Psychiatry,* 1975, **132,** 241–245.

Rapoport, J.L., Buchsbaum, M.S., Weingartner, H., Zahn, T.P., Ludlow, C., & Mikkelsen, E.J. Dextroamphetamine: Its cognitive and behavioral effects in normal and hyperactive boys and normal men. *Archives of General Psychiatry,* 1980, **37,** 933–943.

Rapoport, J.L., Buchsbaum, M.S., Zahn, T.P., Weingartner, H., Ludlow, C., & Mikkelsen, E.J. Dextroamphetamine: Cognitive and behavioral effects in normal prepubertal boys. *Science,* 1978, **199,** 560–563.

Rapoport, J.L., Mikkelsen, E.J., Zavadil, A., Nee, L., Gruenau, C., Mendelson, W., & Gillin, J.C. Childhood enuresis, II. Psychopathology, tricyclic concentration in plasma and antienuretic effect. *Archives of General Psychiatry,* 1980, **37,** 1146–1152.

Rapoport, J.L., Quinn, P., Bradbard, G., Riddle, D., & Brooks, E. Imipramine and methylphenidate treatments of hyperactive boys. *Archives of General Psychiatry,* 1974, **30,** 789–793.

Reisberg, B., & Gershon, S. Side effects associated with lithium therapy. *Archives of General Psychiatry,* 1979, **36,** 879–887.

Rifkin, A., Quitkin, F., Carillo, C., Blumberg, A., & Klein, D. Lithium carbonate in emotionally unstable character disorders. *Archives of General Psychiatry,* 1972, **27,** 519–523.

Rivera-Calimlim, L., Nasrallah, H., Strauss, J., & Lasagna, L. Clinical response and plasma levels: Effect of dose, dosage schedules, and drug interactions on plasma chlorpromazine levels. *American Journal of Psychiatry,* 1976, **133,** 646–652.

Roche, A.F., Lipman, R.S., Overall, J.E., & Hung, W. The effects of stimulant medication on the growth of hyperkinetic children. *Pediatrics,* 1979, **63,** 847–850.

Safer, D., Allen, R., & Barr, E. Depression of growth in hyperactive children on stimulant drugs. *New England Journal of Medicine,* 1972, **287,** 217–220.

Saraf, K.R., Klein, D.F., Gittelman-Klein, R., & Groff, S. Imipramine side effects in children. *Psychopharmacologia,* 1974, **37,** 265–274.

Satterfield, J.H., Cantwell, D.P., Schell, A., & Blaschke, T. Growth of hyperactive children treated with methylphenidate. *Archives of General Psychiatry,* 1979, **36,** 212–217.

Satterfield, J.H., Satterfield, B.T., & Cantwell, D.P. Multimodality treatment. A two-year evaluation of 61 hyperactive boys. *Archives of General Psychiatry,* 1980, **37,** 915–918.

Schou, M. Lithium in the treatment of other psychiatric and nonpsychiatric disorders. *Archives of General Psychiatry,* 1979, **36,** 856–859.

Schou, M. Lithium. Paper presented at the 7th Annual International Symposium on Psychopharmacology. Psychopharmacology update: Chronic treatment, drug interactions and side effects. Louisville, Kentucky, February 27–28, 1981.

Shader, R.I., & DiMascio, A. (Eds.). *Psychotropic drug side effects.* Baltimore: Williams & Wilkins, 1970.

Shaffer, D. Enuresis. In M. Rutter & L. Hersov (Eds.), *Child psychiatry, modern approaches.* London: Blackwell Scientific Publications, 1977.

Shaffer, D., & Greenhill, L. A critical note on the predictive validity of "the hyperkinetic syndrome." *Journal of Child Psychology and Psychiatry,* 1979, **20,** 61–72.

Shapiro, A.K., Shapiro, E.S., Brunn, R.D., & Sweet, R.C.: *Gilles de la Tourette Syndrome.* New York: Raven, 1978.

Shapiro, A.K., Shapiro, E., & Wayne, H. Treatment of Tourette's syndrome. *Archives of General Psychiatry,* 1973, **28,** 92–97.

Sherman, L., Kim, S., Benjamin, F., & Kolodny, H.D. Effect of chlorpromazine on serum growth-hormone in man. *New England Jour-*

nal of Medicine, 1971, **284**, 72–74.

Shopsin, B. Personal communication.

Simeon, J. Pediatric psychopharmacology: A review of our findings and experience. In D.V.S. Sankar (Ed.), *Psychopharmacology of Childhood*. Westbury, N.Y.: PJD Publications, 1976.

Simeon, J., Gross, M., & Mueller, J. Neuroleptic drug effects on children's body weight and height. *Psychopharmacology Bulletin*, 1977, **13**(2), 50–53.

Simon, G.B., & Gillies, S.M. Some physical characteristics of a group of psychotic children. *British Journal of Psychiatry*, 1964, **110**, 104–107.

Sleator, E.K., & Ullmann, R.K. Can the physician diagnose hyperactivity in the office? *Pediatrics*, 1981, **67**, 13–17.

Sleator, E.K., von Neumann, A., & Sprague, R.L. Hyperactive children: A continuous long-term placebo-controlled follow-up. *Journal of the American Medical Association*, 1974, **229**, 316–317.

Spitzer, R.L., Endicott, J., & Robins, E. *Research diagnostic criteria* (2nd ed.). Biometrics Research, New York State Psychiatric Institute, New York, 1975.

Sprague, R.L., & Baxley, G.B. Drugs used for the management of behavior in mental retardation. In J. Wortis (Ed.), *Mental retardation* (Vol. 10). New York: Grune & Stratton, 1978.

Sprague, R.L., Christensen, D.E., & Werry, J.S. Experimental psychology and stimulant drugs. In C.K. Conners (Ed.), *Clinical use of stimulant drugs in children*. Amsterdam: Excerpta Medica, 1974, 141–164.

Sprague, R.L., & Sleator, E.K. What is the proper dose of stimulant drugs in children? In R. Gittelman-Klein (Guest ed.), Recent advances in child psychopharmacology. *International Journal of Mental Health*, 1975, **4**, 75–104.

Sprague, R.L., & Sleator, E.K. Methylphenidate in hyperkinetic children: Differences in dose effects on learning and social behavior. *Science*, 1977, **198**, 1274–1276.

Sprague, R.L., & Werry, J.S. Pediatric psychopharmacology. *Psychopharmacology Bulletin* (DHEW Pub. No. 73-9002, 1973, Pharmacotherapy in children) (Special Issue). 1973, 21–23.

Stores, G. Antiepileptics (anticonvulsants). In J.S. Werry (Ed.), *Pediatric psychopharmacology:*

The use of behavior modifying drugs in children. New York: Brunner/Mazel, 1978.

Tarjan, G., Lowery, V.E., & Wright, S.W. Use of chlorpromazine in two hundred seventy-eight mentally deficient patients. *Journal of Diseases of Childhood*, 1957, **94**, 294–300.

Van Putten, T., May, P.R.A., Marder, S.R., & Wittmann, L.A. Subjective response to antipsychotic drugs. *Archives of General Psychiatry*, 1981, **38**, 187–190.

Villeneuve, A. The rabbit syndrome: A peculiar extrapyramidal reaction. *Canadian Psychiatric Association Journal*, 1972, **17**, 69–72.

Waizer, J., Hoffman, S.P., Polizos, P., & Engelhardt, D.M. Outpatient treatment of hyperactive school children with imipramine. *American Journal of Psychiatry*, 1974, **131**, 587–591.

Weinberg, W.A., Rutman, J., Sullivan, L., Penick, E.C., & Dietz, S.G. Depression in children referred to an educational diagnostic center: Diagnosis and treatment—Preliminary report. *Journal of Pediatrics*, 1973, **83**, 1065–1072.

Weiss, G., & Hechtman, L. The hyperactive child syndrome. *Science*, 1979, **205**, 1348–1354.

Weiss, G., Hechtman, L., Perlman, T., Hopkins, J. & Wener, A. Hyperactives as young adults: A controlled prospective ten-year follow-up of 75 children. *Archives of General Psychiatry*, 1979, **36**, 675–681.

Weiss, G., Kruger, E., Danielson, V., & Elman, M. Effect of long-term treatment of hyperactive children with methylphenidate. *Canadian Medical Association Journal*, 1975, **112**, 159–165.

Wender, P.H. *Minimal brain dysfunction in children*. New York: Wiley-Interscience, 1971.

Werry, J.S. Measures in pediatric psychopharmacology. In J.S. Werry (Ed.), *Pediatric psychopharmacology: The use of behavior modifying drugs in children*. New York: Brunner/Mazel, 1978.

Werry, J.S., & Aman, M.G. Methylphenidate and haloperidol in children: Effects on attention, memory and activity. *Archives of General Psychiatry*, 1975, **32**, 790–795.

Winsberg, B.G., Bialer, I., Kupietz, S., & Tobias, J. Effects of imipramine and dextroamphetamine on behavior of neuropsychiatrically impaired children. *American Journal of Psychiatry*, 1972, **128**, 1425–1431.

Winsberg, B.G., Goldstein, S., Yepes, L.E., & Perel, J.M. Imipramine and electrocardiographic abnormalities in hyperactive children. *American Journal of Psychiatry,* 1975, **132,** 542-545.

Winsberg, B.G., Kupietz, S.S., Yepes, L.E., & Goldstein, S. Ineffectiveness of imipramine in children who fail to respond to methylphenidate. *Journal of Autism and Developmental Disorders,* 1980, **10,** 129-137.

Winsberg, B.G., & Yepes, L.E. Antipsychotics. In J.S. Werry (Ed.), *Pediatric psychopharmacology. The use of behavior modifying drugs in children.* New York: Brunner/Mazel, 1978.

Yoss, R.E., & Daly, D.D. Narcolepsy in children. *Pediatrics,* 1960, **25,** 1025-1033.

Youngerman, J., & Canino, I. Lithium carbonate use in children and adolescents. *Archives of General Psychiatry,* 1978, **35,** 216-224.

Ziring, P.R., & Teitelbaum, L. *Affiliation with a university department of psychiatry: Impact on the use of psychoactive medication in a large public residential facility for mentally retarded persons.* Paper presented at conference on the use of medications in controlling the behavior of the mentally retarded. September 22-24, 1980, University of Minnesota, Minneapolis, Minnesota.

SECTION SEVEN

Special Topics

CHAPTER 48

Education and Enrichment Approaches

PAUL WEISBERG

In our highly verbal, technological society, it is not difficult to imagine the severity of adjustment problems encountered daily by the more than 2.5 million children who, during the decade of the 1960s, dropped out of school with less than eight years of formal education, barely literate and barely employable. These youths were likely to be retained for several grades or placed in special classes for children in emotional conflict; they were most certainly to have negative school attitudes and low self-esteem and to be rated by teachers as low in achievement motivation (U.S. Commission on Civil Rights, 1967; Zigler & Butterfield, 1968). Individuals with academic skill deficiencies are likely to be one and the same population associated with high delinquency, unemployment, and imprisonment. Interviewing and consulting the records of 150 institutionalized delinquent males, Burke and Simon (1965) found that 92 percent had a history of truancy and poor school adjustment, 75 percent failed two or more grades, 75 percent left school before the legal age of 16, and 67 percent read below a sixth-grade level. Nearly 60 percent of the group, however, had IQs between 90 and 110, meaning that they were certainly capable of school learning. When asked what could have been

Support was furnished in part by the University of Alabama Office of Contracts and Grants, under the direction of Dr. Robert L. Wells. The author is extremely grateful to Roberta Weisberg of the Tuscaloosa City Board of Education for reading an early draft of this chapter and to Connie Sulentic for her excellent typing and proofing skills. Both they and Margaret Stark lent much support and encouragement.

done to keep them in school, 76 percent indicated the need for more teacher encouragement and counseling on the importance of education. These facts are known to clinicians, and it is no wonder that many effective treatment conditions for troubled children and those with personality maladjustments have had at their core an educational intervention approach (Hewett, 1968; Hobbs, 1969; Meichenbaum & Asarnow, 1979; Swift & Spivack, 1974).

To lessen the economic discord and psychological shame attached to a history of incomplete and low quality schooling, a large number of federally and privately supported intervention projects were begun in the 1960s. Most were directed at preventing extreme academic failure and low self-esteem from occurring in the first place. Many projects focused on the preschool years; a few started intervention even earlier, during infancy; and some concentrated on the early elementary grades. That early intervention can have a profoundly favorable influence on a person's later life has recently been documented by Schweinhart and Weikert (1980). High risk children who attended an experimental preschool were later found, at age 15, relative to those not receiving the preschool treatment, to have: (1) a stronger commitment to schooling, (2) higher academic achievement scores at all grade levels, (3) a 50-percent reduction in the need for special education services through the end of high school, and (4) a lower tendency to display antisocial or delinquent behavior outside of school. In addition, the savings to taxpayers of the costs of short term schooling compared to the much higher costs of long term remediation for the nonattending controls was substantial.

A large segment of this chapter deals with a description of the various educational philosophies and approaches to early intervention as well as failures and successes of some of the more renowned projects. Where data indicate that certain preconceived notions about early intervention were naive or inadequate, these faulty conceptions will be highlighted in the hope that we do not commit the same mistakes again. Although attention to the preschool and early public school years is emphasized and the primary place of intervention is a school setting, this should not be taken to mean that other forms of intervention in different environments are of any less value. Intervention work beginning in infancy that uses the mother as an important change agent and trains her in the home, clinic, or elsewhere is acknowledged. Limited space prevents coverage of this promising research dimension (Lally & Honig, 1977; Palmer & Anderson, 1979).

It is further recognized that amelioration of educational handicaps is far from the sole answer to treating disturbed and maladapted children, nor will literate individuals from economically disadvantaged backgrounds necessarily make it in our technological society without unified and sustained effort from other institutions in the community besides the schools. Nevertheless, the successful implementation of a program that consistently trains basic and vital academic skills for many individuals not otherwise helped is still critical for adjustment. The final segment of this chapter considers the ramifications of poor academic achievement and what can be done by the clinical child psychologist.

INTERVENTION PROJECTS

Head Start and the Westinghouse Report

The largest and most ambitious government project aimed at overcoming the academic handicaps of the poor and the indigent focused on the preschool years. Four years after Head Start was launched in 1965, the Office of Economic Opportunity (OEO) contracted with the Westinghouse Learning Corporation to study the impact of Head Start (HS) in areas of school readiness. From a list of about 13,000 HS centers existing in 1966–1967, 104 centers were randomly selected. To preserve the 7:3 ratio of summer to full year HS programs during that period, of the 104 sampled centers, 75 were summer based and 29 were full year programs. Instead of the more suitable "before-after" design, an "after-only" design was employed (White, 1971). About 4,000 former HS children who were attending the first three grades were identified and matched on several variables with about the same number of non-HS controls who were in the same grade levels.

The conclusions of the Westinghouse Report, released in 1970, are well known: (1) "summer programs are ineffective in producing lasting gains in affective and cognitive development," and (2) "full-year programs are ineffective in aiding affective development and only marginally effective in producing lasting cognitive gains" (Westinghouse, 1969, summary page). The evidence for declining academic performance in absolute terms was equally dismal (Datta, 1979). According to White (1971), full year HS children were at the forty-fourth percentile on the first-grade Metropolitan Readiness Test, at the twentieth percentile on the second-grade Stanford Achievement Test, and on the Illinois Test of Psycholinguistic Ability, an instrument designed to measure comprehension and expression of symbolic material, they were eight months below national norms across all grades. (The absolute scores were low at grade 3, but a shortage of full year participants did not permit an adequate evaluation.)

As was the case for government-sponsored projects that followed it, Head Start's scope and rate of growth was dictated significantly by the political realities and practicalities of the day. Shriver (1979), the OEO Director, was advised first to field test HS and limit its size to 2,500 children due to the lack of qualified teachers to handle any more than that number. However, to satisfy political and other pressures, Shriver reasoned that HS could begin immediately on a more massive scale if a six-to-eight-week summer project became the major intervention model. School buildings were available as were hundreds of dedicated teachers. Crash one-week-long teacher sessions, sometimes assembling 300–500 teachers in one place, were instantly instituted. The flood of HS applications from community action groups was incredible. Sixty-five percent of the nation's counties applied for summer support and, ultimately, 40 percent were funded (White, 1971). When all was said and done, 560,000 preschoolers, instead of the originally contemplated 2,500, participated in the first summer 1965 project. In the fall, a full year program with 20,000 children began. Including local and federal funding, the cost for summer intervention alone was $95 million (Richmond, Stipek, & Zigler, 1979).

Scores of compensatory-minded educators accepted the naive and oversimplified notion that a little bit of "summer magic" would somehow turn the economically disadvantaged into good learners (Becker, 1977). True, large IQ and other achievement gains had been reported within a short "intervention" period (Weikert, 1967). However, these were likely spurious improvements due to unfavorable motivational conditions such as test shyness, which can grossly suppress the preintervention test score (Bereiter & Engelmann, 1966), or the gains were due to very low initial IQs of children from extremely deprived environments (Jensen, 1968). Almost all educators would now agree with Becker (1981) that "the building of language and reasoning processes which underlie major aspects of intelligent behavior requires long-term, sustained, and cumulative effort" (p. 182). But, given the wave of enthusiasm and optimism in the mid-1960s, few dared publicly to protest the unrealistic goals of the HS summer program (Caldwell, 1974). If the Westinghouse Report findings had a single redeeming feature, it was the demise of the myth of brief intervention claims. Decision makers seemed to have learned that lesson well: a year after the Report in 1970, the number of summer enrollees fell to 230,000; by 1977, it plummeted to 15,000; and, in recognition of the necessity for a more intensive, sustained effort, the number of full year participants increased from 20,000 in 1965 to 300,000 in 1977 (Richmond et al., 1979).

Another half-truth dispelled was that the period from conception to preschool was one in which intellectual activity was most rapid so that if learning and enrichment began during this critical period it would somehow innoculate the child against failure later on. This notion stemmed partly from popularization of Bloom's (1964) data showing that the correlation of IQ at preschool and at maturity (age 17) was .70. By squaring this coefficient to determine the percentage of IQ variation at maturity "explainable" by IQ variation at preschool, Bloom (1964) was led to say "about 50% of the development (in measured intelligence) takes place between conception and age 4" (p. 88). The popular press unfortunately took this to mean that half of all we ever learn we know before we are 5. Zigler and Anderson (1979) are critical of the logic behind this notion. They note the equally fallacious conclusion that half of a child's learning occurs *before* birth since the correlation between average parental IQ and the child's mature IQ is similarly .70. Rather than searching for mythical critical periods where some didactic magic can occur, the current emphasis is on continuity in intellectual and social development (Stipek, Valentine, & Zigler, 1979), supporting the view that whatever gains are made at one school period must be recognized and built upon by those responsible for teaching the child at the next period. Viewed in this light, it was wholly unfair to judge the effectiveness of Head Start or any other preschool program by how its graduates did several years later when placed in a different learning setting. As Bereiter (1972) asks, would we want to judge the effectiveness of a weight reduction pill taken at age 10 by how well it prevented people from getting fat at age 50?

Permissive-Enrichment: The Dominant Model for Early Intervention

Before the advent of HS, preschools were places primarily for advantaged middle and upperclass children. Preschools existed to give them experiences and opportunities not normally found or allowed in the advantaged child's home. Whatever facilities existed for children of the working class were largely for custodial care. According to Bereiter and Engelmann (1966), the middle class preschool stressed "seeing and doing" activities and an emphasis on active, daring physical routines in contrast to more sedentary homebound activities; the preschool encouraged greater freedom and independence, more opportunity to engage in messy activities and fantasy play normally prohibited in the highly reality-oriented lifestyle of the overprotective home; it encouraged child-determined standards and decisions that commonly ended in coopera-tive, socially adjustive peer group encounters rather than parent- or adult-determined goals that sought high achievement standards through competitive comparisons with other advantaged children. Finally, the preschool stressed enjoyment of the present while the middle class home was future oriented.

In keeping with the psychodynamic and mental hygiene movement prior to 1960, the major goals of these preschools was to pro-mote the child's social adjustment (Sears & Dowley, 1963). In these settings, "language and intellectual development are placed last in a list of desired attributes to be developed" (Blank & Solomon, 1969, p. 60). Not surpris-ingly, preschool graduates, at least before the 1960s, were not substantially different on intellectual or achievement tasks from middle class children not attending preschools, either in their early or later public school grades (Mussen, Conger, & Kagan, 1969; Zigler as cited in Brophy et al., 1975). Strodbeck (1964) pointed to the hidden curriculum of the middle class home as responsible for early academic achievement. Here, mothers typi-cally view themselves as teachers of their children (Smilansky, 1968), and they freely enter into numerous didactic interchanges with them.

Reviewing studies that related parental influences to aspects of high childhood achievement, Freeberg and Payne (1967) pointed to a home environment "evidenced by pressures to succeed and (giving) assistance in doing so, particularly in the development of the child's verbal skills" (p. 71). Laboratory studies of the communication pattern of mid-dle class mothers (Hess & Shipman, 1965) revealed that it is one that teaches the same verbal skills and language concepts typically used by middle class teachers to impart infor-mation (Jensen, 1968). The language pattern also corresponded to the one adopted by authors of preschool readiness tests to assess the child's receptiveness, understanding, and application of verbal and school-related skills (Milner, 1951). In short, middle class parents teach the "language of instruction" and, if a preschool teacher happened to elaborate upon that language, so much the better will be the child's academic and cognitive achievement.

It is generally agreed that the early HS programs were adaptations of the then pre-dominant traditional preschools for the mid-dle class. Although OEO administrators and HS curricula descriptions at the time expressed the rhetoric of overcoming learning handicaps, the attitude of HS directors consistently re-vealed "preference for a supportive, unstruc-tured socialization program rather than a structured, informational program" (Boyd, 1966, p. 38). Descriptions of these preschools as applied to disadvantaged children are found in several sources (Bissell, 1973; Maccoby & Zellner, 1970; Miller & Dyer, 1975; Stone, 1979). These preschools have been classified as permissive-enrichment (Bissell, 1973), normative-developmental (Cowles, 1971), and vintage or regular HS (Branche & Overly, 1971).

The disadvantaged child was said to be insecure and more in need of affection, so in these regular HS programs everyday preschool experiences were to provide warmth, support, and trust yet still maintain the order of a predictable environment. The classroom atmosphere was to be one of happy freedom within limits. A flexible curriculum was advised, with no one activity conceived of as more vital than any other. Emphasis was on the relatedness of information in all areas—physical, socioemotional, intellectual, verbal—and it was to include all sense modalities. Like that environment provided for the advantaged child, an object rich environment prevailed and included all sorts of toys, building materials, and games. Appropriate "teaching" techniques consisted of conversation, role playing, exercise, songs, dances, fragrant boxes, field trips, movies, and whatever else it took to broaden the disadvantaged child's experience, arouse curiosity, and encourage imagination—in short, "enrichment of the whole child."

In these traditional programs, the teacher was not to take a strong role in guiding the child. Rather, he or she was to watch and wait for emerging behavior patterns that belied some underlying need and to be responsive to and facilitative of these different childhood styles and interests. Free play periods, sometimes called work periods, predominated, and it was assumed that incidental forms of learning provided the freely engaging child much in the way of planning and organizing thoughts and developing skills. Rather than being committed to a predetermined sequence, the teacher was to provide opportunities for learning and follow whatever direction the child's interests seemed to lead. The teacher, however, could introduce activities and plan events, but his or her teaching was to be concerned mainly with pointing out and elaborating on what the child brought to the situation. In keeping with the philosophy and tradition of Dewey, planned classroom themes on units (see Weikert, 1972) such as farm animals, modes of transportation, occupations, and traffic signs were permissible. It is from these themes that a variety of academic concepts and skills were assumed to be learned because they were presented in a context that was relevant and made the child an active participant.

It is important to note that, although pre-Head Start intervention projects with pre-

school children were few in number, those that were undertaken appeared to endorse the philosophy and practice of the permissive-enrichment approach. The classic study by Skeels and Dye (1939) is one such illustration. One group of 13 orphanage-reared infants, when about 18 months of age, was placed in a state institution for the mentally retarded and was raised by the female inmates for approximately 15 months. Intellectual improvement was substantial and dramatic—the median IQ gain was about 23 points! Although the intervention environment was not described in any detail, the wards to which the different children were assigned contained surrogate mothers who were said to offer love and affection and opportunities to play with materials in an ample space.

This intervention environment was, curiously enough, far from ideal for the promotion of intellectual endeavors—the "mothers," after all, were mentally retarded. This milieu did, however, contrast sharply with that of the orphanage where care was custodial, relatively affection free, and the children were generally described as apathetic and poor in motor attainments. Supporting evidence for this extremely unfavorable cognitive and socially adaptive atmosphere was that the IQs for another group of 12 infants who remained in the orphanage fell by 32 points. It is fair to say that the orphanage environment and the nature of the caregiving routine was hardly typical of that found in the disadvantaged child's home. Moreoever, the description of the depressingly inadequate social and motor behaviors displayed by the orphanage children suggests that the intervention settings acted chiefly to overcome the extremely nonadaptive emotional handicaps that interfered with the child's ability to profit from learning. No matter how true the findings of Skeels and Dye (1939), the study gave credence to the oversimplified notion that creating an environment that was trusting and unstructured but rich in concrete objects was the key to early intervention with disadvantaged children.

While Head Start was being implemented, a number of experimental preschool projects, smaller in scope, were funded to design curricula and independently test the soundness of their particular brand of early compensatory intervention. These newer programs questioned whether the goal of making small and marginal gains in many different areas, most notably socially adjustive behaviors, was worth the effort if gains in the major areas of cognitive and language deficiencies were not highlighted.

Special Preschool Programs

The placing of preschool curricula and approaches into tight groupings is difficult because of the many different ways one program can be similar to or different from another. Often the correspondence between a model's philosophy and its stated goals may vary considerably from what actually occurs in the classroom implementation of the program. Weikert (1972) classified preschools by the degree to which the teacher or child "initiates" or "responds" in the classroom. Models were characterized as "programmed"(teacher initiates, child responds), "open framework" (teacher initiates, child initiates), "child centered" (child initiates, teacher responds), and "custodial" (teacher responds, child responds). Bissell (1973) used a threefold criterion system as a basis for classification that leads to the same approximate groupings of early compensatory programs as Weikert's and others (Miller & Dyer, 1975; Parker, 1972). Bissell's criteria are: (1) the program's *objectives,* (2) the preschool *strategy* or the plans of action through which classroom activities are conducted (i.e., teacher directive or teacher nondirective where children determine their own activities), and; (3) classroom *structure* or the degree to which the sequence of activities or experiences are already organized and laid out for the child. In practice, strategy and structure are highly correlated. Four major types of preschool programs emanate from the mix of Bissell's criteria.

1. *Permissive-Enrichment* programs have already been described in detail. They have multiple objectives oriented toward the development of the "whole child." The strategy involves letting the children's emerging needs determine activities, with the teacher capitalizing on informal teaching experiences as they arise. The degree of structure given to sequenced activities is low or moderate. A leading preschool model fitting these descriptions is the Bank Street Program (Biber, 1977; Minuchin & Biber, 1968). Another is the Education Development Center (see Abt Associates, 1976, 1977) that derives much of its philosophy from the British Infant School Movement where learning occurs in open classrooms. Emphasis is on self-development and allowing children to assume responsibility for their own learning.

2. *Structured-Cognitive* programs place greater stress on linguistic and conceptual attainments. Rather than teaching mastery of specific academic skills, however, these programs assume that a performance, like reading, can be facilitated by focusing first on the processes or abilities that underlie learning. Reading or arithmetic skills are treated as inevitable outcomes of basic cognitive abilities involving spatial relations, auditory discriminations, memory, and so forth. The objectives are then to develop aptitudes related to learning processes, especially language development.

The teacher is to be friendly and warm but firm when necessary and not forget that his or her major role is teaching, not providing emotional support or being a surrogate mother. The teacher selects and directs activities, even those during play, and although the child has some choice in the matter, the teacher must see to it that some conceptual and language learning is occurring. Classroom structure ranges from moderate to high. The teacher determines what activities will take place, their order, and when they will occur. He or she directs activities that are thought to provide the greatest amount of learning.

Concepts are taught in a sequential pattern and the teacher is guided by several recommendations; for example, he or she might move from the concrete to the abstract, as in starting from the motor levels of object expression and representation, then moving to the verbal object labeling level, and, finally, to the symbolic level for abstract thinking. Another illustration is in guiding auditory discriminations with gross sound recognition (loud-quiet) introduced first, then refined to comparatives (louder-quieter), and, finally, containing superlative distinctions (the loudest, the quietest).

Classroom activities, like the Permissive-Enrichment programs, are frequently organized around units with the content intended to promote basic abilities such as classification, sequencing, verbal communication, and so forth. Table games are frequently employed involving matching tasks, design copying, picture cards, recognition of numerals and letters, and school readiness activities. Multidimensional materials, such as beads, blocks, puzzles, pegboards, and counting cubes, provide a wide range of stimuli for perceptual discriminations and the practicing of manipulatory skills.

Language development is an ongoing process that receives major emphasis. Verbalizations are encouraged during manipulation of concrete objects, specially designed group game formats, mealtime, and any structured or unstructured activity where appropriate language expression is a possibility. The teacher is present to correct, modify, and expand verbal and other modes of communication.

Developing attitudes that are related to academic tasks and school routines (for instance, following directions, self-discipline, achievement motivation, using verbal rather than physical forms of persuasion) is a key component, as is the necessity of including parents in the program. With proper school attitudes instilled and with parent participation, these programs assume that long term, cumulative gains will be made.

Many preschool models subscribe to the Structured-Cognitive tenets. Among the best known are the Cognitively Oriented Approach of Weikert (1972), which emphasizes a Piagetian curriculum for conceptual development, the Ameliorative Programs of Karnes (Karnes, Zehrbach, & Teska, 1972; Karnes, Zehrbach, & Teska, 1977), and the Demonstration and Research Center for Early Education (or Darcee model) of Gray and Klaus (Gray & Klaus, 1965; Gray et al., 1966; Klaus & Gray, 1968).

3. *Structured-Informational* programs have highly focused objectives directed toward the teaching of those academic skills and concepts needed for elementary school success. These skills include, for example, reading, spelling, writing, math computation, and mastery of those behaviors needed for learning the language of instruction. The content is carefully programmed and presented in a prescribed manner in a highly structured classroom setting.

In the Direct Instruction model of Bereiter and Engelmann's (1966) academic preschool, and later in the elaboration of this model by Becker and Engelmann (1978) for use in public school, the children are taught daily in small groups. Each teaching session lasts about 30 minutes, and the contents covered are language, reading, and arithmetic. The teacher follows prepared scripts and signals the children to respond together, much as a choir director leads a group. The group members are taught to a high mastery level on a series of skills before they are advanced to a related task that specifies these low order skills as prerequisite behaviors. The classroom atmosphere is decidedly task oriented and the pacing is fast to maximize on-target responding and to provide lots of practice. The teacher is encouraged to conduct the class in a lively, enthusiastic, and animated manner and to provide many successful experiences of what it means to "think big," "be smart," and "try and work hard." Many friendly competitive games are played. For instance, a teacher will make a deliberate but unannounced mistake on material for which the children should know the answer and thus should be able to catch and correct him or her. Such activities are intended to teach the children that accident or luck had nothing to do with detecting errors of an authoritative figure such as the teacher. Increased self-confidence in one's ability to succeed in school is not the primary focus; it is, however, expected as a byproduct of success in academic and related work.

Two other programs that rely on programmed instruction are Bushell's Behavioral Analysis Model (Bushell & Brigham, 1971) and Resnick's Primary Education Project (1977). Both emphasize individual prescribed, self-paced instruction rather than teacher-directed group instruction. Complex behaviors are broken down into the necessary component skills, and the error rates of the learner are continually evaluated and the tasks revised accordingly. Both programs make heavy use of token economies to develop academic and socially appropriate school behaviors not normally controlled by natural contingencies. Teachers are trained in the analysis and modification of behavior.

4. *Structured-Environment* programs feature many of the same learning process goals as Structured-Cognitive models, but the former, as the name implies, offer a highly structured, orderly, and "prepared" classroom. These programs allow self-selection and self-direction of activities through intensive interaction with didactic teaching devices and materials that are constructed to contain self-correcting feedback mechanisms and to be intrinsically reinforcing to the children who manipulate them. The built-in "steps" and autocorrective nature of these devices are also intended to let the child learn inductively at his or her own rate and to work independently.

Traditional Montessori programs (Montessori, 1964, 1965) exemplify this kind of preschool. Montessori classrooms provide didactic materials and routines to develop competence in daily activities (housekeeping and personal care), perceptual discrimination, conceptual learning, and character development (respecting property and the rights of others and self-discipline). There are, for example, formboards and frames to teach buttoning and tying, sensorial materials and apparatus to teach the properties of objects (loudness, color, roughness, smell, etc.), as well as the labels for the different sensations. Other auto-educational devices, such as graded cylinder blocks, teach concepts about relative size, thickness, and serialization. Learning to read and write letters is taught by having the letters traced on sandpaper and sounded out. A movable alphabet is used to help construct words. Mathematical concepts and operations are taught through various counting frames.

Although the teacher, called a "directress," can demonstrate the initial use of the didactic instrument and can encourage that it be used in a standard way, he or she is cautioned not to engage in direct instruction. The directress is considered a resource person, tactfully present at the sidelines, ready to help the child and promote self-reliance and independence. The children are expected to develop self-control by working independently and continually in tasks suited for them and to show respect for the materials and the rights of others.

Kohlberg (1968) has suggested that the Montessori method could greatly benefit the disadvantaged in terms of self-discipline and conceptual progress. He has recommended that it include more traditional goals such as a greater emphasis on fantasy play and peer cooperation. Nevertheless, the problem with the Montessori method is that it does not encourage enough language expression.

In the Responsive Education Model of Nimnicht (Nimnicht & Barnes, 1971; Nimnicht, Arango, & Cheever, 1977), the environment consists of learning centers containing different multisensory, self-instructional devices (such as O.K. Moore's "talking typewriter") that are to teach concepts and tasks in a self-rewarding or "autotelic" manner. By actively experimenting with a responsive environment, the child is said to learn a number of higher order concepts without distraction or extrinsic reinforcement and in a way that fosters self-mastery and a positive self-concept.

General Intervention Outcomes

Each of these experimental preschools has participated in intervention studies, with data sometimes collected by the program designers themselves for one or two preschool years. Each has also reported marked improvements in those areas in which the disadvantaged have been cited by the particular model designers as being weak or deficient. For example, Karnes et al. (1977) found that their structured-cognitive (Ameliorative) approach produced large initial gains in verbal expression subtests of the ITPA and in Stanford-

Binet IQs. Engelmann (1971) similarly found very large IQ gains, as much as a mean of 21 points, and was able to attain beyond first-grade achievement scores in reading, math, and spelling on the Wide Range Achievement Test for disadvantaged children attending the Bereiter-Engelmann academic preschool for two years. Reviewing studies on Montessori preschools, Miezitis (1973) concluded that they have their most marked impact for the disadvantaged on learner style characteristics (i.e., task persistence, decreased distractability, and task orientation). Montessori preschoolers were also rated high on measures of effectiveness and curiosity (Miller & Dyer, 1975).

Reviewers of intervention research (Bereiter, 1972; Miller, 1979; Weikert, 1967) have generally found that, relative to models with a strong instructional base, traditional enrichment preschools for the disadvantaged have ended up on the bottom rung of the ladder of immediate effectiveness in cognitive and academic measures. Moreover, on a variety of motivation and adjustment indicators, where program input is claimed strongest by traditional philosophy, children in these programs are not better off than those in instructional-based programs (Miller & Dyer, 1975), and sometimes they are worse off (Erickson et al., 1969) although they are superior to non-preschool controls. Reviews of studies including Montessori classes as a treatment (Di-Lorenzo, Salter, & Brady, 1969; Karnes, 1977; Miezitis, 1973; Miller & Dyer, 1975) have found results similar to those of traditional classes; that is, they do significantly poorer on cognitive measures than structured-cognitive and structured-information models. Bereiter (1972) notes that one-year Montessori programs, by focusing on lower level preschool activities (housekeeping and sense training), never let the children work their way up to more complex skills. Moreover, the higher level activities have been tied to a few concrete representations of concepts and are not the kind expected to produce abstract reasoning in young children (Mussen et al., 1969). The lack of any provision for the remediation of linguistic deficits and expressive skills in the disadvantaged also contraindicates expecting higher order behavior from Montessori preschools.

Most well-implemented structured programs have produced immediate gains in measures that assess a wide range of skills, such as those tested in the Stanford-Binet and in Caldwell's Preschool Inventory (Miller, 1979). However, no consistent differences have been found among the various experimental models of these general cognitive meaures. As previously mentioned, where model differences appear they are limited to specific types of immediate behavioral outcomes that are mainly those that the models emphasize and teach in their curriculum. For example, the children in the Karnes' Ameliorative preschool were taught readiness skills, and they did somewhat better on the Metropolitan Readiness Test than those in the Bereiter-Engelmann preschools who were instead directly taught first-grade academic skills (Karnes et al., 1977). Not surprisingly, the Bereiter-Engelmann children did well on the Wide Range Achievement Test and were able to pass many items reserved for first and second graders (Engelmann, 1971). In the 1970–1971 evaluation year of the Head Start Planned Variation Project, in which 11 experimental preschools participated, the Behavior Analysis model was most successful in the achievement subtest measuring numeral recognition, letter knowledge, and shape names (Smith, 1973). In the 1971–1972 evaluation year, the three didactic models (Direct Instruction, Behavior Analysis, and Individually Prescribed Instruction) accounted for 12 of the 17 positive effects, all but three of which comprised academic skills such as letter and numeral recognition.

Boosting IQ: Temporary or Permanent Effects?

As the lackluster public school follow-up data of graduates from the newer compensatory preschools began to surface, the optimistic picture sketched from the short term gains turned to one of pessimism and caution (Caldwell, 1974). Most of the elevated IQ scores achieved during preschool from successful programs, such as those designed by

Bereiter-Engelmann, Karnes, Gray and Klaus, and Weikert, all began to plummet with increasing public school experience, and the scores finally converged with those of children in traditional preschool and other control conditions.

The reason for the fade-out effects rests with the overemphasis on the IQ test as the bastion for assessing long term intervention effects. A successful program is commonly judged in one or both of two ways: by gains in IQ and in academic achievement (e.g., improved scores in reading, math, language usage, etc.). Of the two, Jensen (1969) noted that IQ can be more efficiently "measured" than academic achievement, particularly if there is no "achievement" to begin with. That is, the IQ test can be administered prior to preschool intervention and any time thereafter, and so one can seemingly discover fairly soon whether the intervention effort is working by getting periodic readouts on IQ changes. Academic achievement, on the other hand, is a long term affair, and it is risky business to think that improvement in performances tapped by assessment procedures limited to the preschool year, like readiness tests, will prove worthwhile in the long run. Because of this possibility, a working hypothesis by some interventionists was to assume that the IQ was indicative of a more fundamental intellectual ability than the acquisition of specific academic skills and concepts. Since early IQ predicted later achievement in academic skills better than any other single preschool measure, it was further assumed that, if the IQ can be elevated, later academic achievement would more or less take care of itself, given proper school attitude and motivation. These assumptions seem to be those of the Structured-Cognitive group. Those advocating programmed instruction, on the other hand, do not take for granted generalized improvement in academic skills because of IQ gains. They prefer instead to teach directly the operations necessary for the various skills, starting in the preschool and encouraging the public schools to build on them just as intensively.

Why the IQ gain and then the eventual loss? Some of the acceleration in preschool IQ, according to Jensen (1969), can be attributed to "easy" gains: the program works because it allows the child to overcome the unfavorable testing conditions at the preintervention evaluation; the initial selection of young children at the low end of the IQ distribution who, upon retesting, make gains because of statistical regression upwards to the group mean on the retest; and the correspondence of materials traditionally found in nursery schools (blocks, puzzles, bead stringing, pictures of common objects, etc.) and those found on the Stanford-Binet as well as the actual teaching of some of the simple items (e.g., names of body parts, names of familiar objects, etc.). Jensen (1969) notes that "the effort required to boost IQ from 80 to 90 at 4 to 5 years of age is miniscule compared to the effort that would be required by age 9 or 10" (p. 102). He estimates the possibility of a 5 or 6 IQ point gain in disadvantaged preschoolers in nursery schools presenting a rather diffuse enrichment program but no real focus at acquisition of specific cognitive skills. A more substantial increase of about 10 IQ points is possible by adding on special cognitive training, especially in verbal skills. Average gains rarely exceed this value unless intensive preschool instruction in specific skills is given and the program is extended to the home. Then, about a third of the children can gain as much as 20 IQ points.

Jensen (1969) has questioned the unidimensional concept of intelligence as an adequate model for understanding social class differences in ability. He has proposed that two kinds of abilities are sampled from items in the IQ test. Those items or components that sample concept learning or problem solving are called Level II abilities. They require a general ability to transform or manipulate incoming information before a response output is produced. These are apparently synonymous with Cattell's fluid intelligence. In contrast, Level I abilities require associative learning, that is, a high correspondence between information on the stimulus input and response output sides. Learning and recalling simple information in a paired associative or sequential task are examples. Possession of

Level I abilities is a necessary, but not a sufficient, condition for the possession of Level II abilities. Middle and lower SES classes are not differentiated by Level I functions. Since these abilities are largely tapped by the IQ items in the preschool years, it is possible to boost IQ by concentration of instruction in these abilities. It is in Level II functioning that SES differences matter. The growth of Level II abilities is assumed by Jensen to be much lower in low SES children and it does not attain the same absolute levels as in high SES children. Since IQ tests began to assess more of Level II abilities, beginning at and continuing through public school, deficiency or a delay in these abilities is a major reason for the relative decline in (boosted) IQ among the disadvantaged during formal schooling.

Part of the decline further stems from the requirement to pass a greater number of subtests with increasing age (until the teens) just to maintain the same improvement in IQ. Since two-months of credit is given for each subtest passed, a 4-year-old must get two extra subtests correct to improve from an IQ of 91 to 100. To sustain the 9-IQ-point advantage, that same youngster must, at ages 8 and 12 respectively, pass five and six extra subtests. Also supporting a decline is Thorndike's (1975) finding that when the 4-year-old norming group of the Stanford-Binet was followed longitudinally, there was about a 1-IQ-point loss per year between ages 4 and 9. With the traditional age norming of the Binet by a cross-sectional method, a "decline" cannot occur and the phenomenon is unnoticed.

Interventionists (e.g., Deutsch, 1969; Hunt, 1969) have rejected Jensen's contentions about the temporary boosts in IQ and the poor prognosis of educational efforts to maintain IQ gains. Seriously questioned was his hypothesis that lower class minority groups were deficient or delayed in Level II abilities and his emphasis on teaching basic academic skills with techniques that rely exclusively on the learning of Level I abilities. The decrement in IQ was claimed to be due to the discontinuance of effective programs and return to the same poor quality of general environmental input

that prevailed prior to implementation of the special preschool programs. If, as Campbell and Frey (1970) argued, the postpreschool IQ differences between intervention and control groups were due to differences in powerful learning variables, one should predict a "wash-out" simply because the controlling variables favoring the intervention group were no longer present.

Blame was placed on the public schools, including public kindergarten, for not following through on earlier effective models. Not only were basic cognitive processes involving reasoning, thinking, and other general abilities tapped on IQ tests not carried forth, but specific and impressive academic achievements made in preschool were not advanced in the elementary school. As a case in point, once the children in the Bereiter-Engelmann preschool who had made great strides in reading decoding skills and math computations (Engelmann, 1971) began to attend public school (and the intensive compensatory efforts had terminated), they slipped further and further behind normative levels on higher grade achievement tests (Karnes, 1977). What was badly needed was a planned, systematic variation of major educational models that would continue into kindergarten and the early school grades. The nature of this longitudinal venture was the Follow Through project.

The Follow-Through Project

Although originally conceived as a nationwide educational and comprehensive program like Head Start, a restriction of government funds established the Follow-Through (FT) project as a large scale educational experiment. There were actually two planned variation projects that overlapped each other. The Head Start Planned Variation (HSPV) Project, under the auspices of the newly created Office of Child Development, was adopted in 1968. It contained 11 different preschool models, encompassing many of the diverse models already described using Bissell's (1973) four categories. The models were located in 28 Head Start school districts or sites, geographically distributed across the country and encompassed about 135 classrooms. The evaluation of HSPV (Weisberg, 1973) included a sample of 750 intervention children. Another 850 regular Head Start children from 12 sites and 140 non-preschool-attending children from three sites acted as control groups.

The other planned variation project was Follow-Through (FT). It covered the first three grade levels and, in the majority of cases, the program started in kindergarten, making it a four-year program. The project was administered by the Office of Education. The hope was to make HSPV and FT an interlocking cooperative venture: children trained with a particular preschool model under HSPV were to enter a nearby FT public school using that same model, obviously, for program continuity's sake and to lessen the effect of confounding variables. That ideal arrangement was infrequently satisfied for a variety of reasons; instead, the HSPV and the public school FT projects might best be viewed as separate evaluations.

As many as 20 different sponsors, serving 75,000 low income children yearly, from 170 communities, participated in FT at one time or another. The models were to have educational foundations, but they could also (and many did) provide supporting services in child health and nutrition and involved the participation of the communities being served. Becker and Engelmann (1978) identified nine "major" sponsors who were independently evaluated by Abt Associates (1976, 1977) in each of four to eight sites that contained a kindergarten-starting program. The nine accounted for about 80 percent of the sites evaluated. For children on whom there were complete data, over 9,000 FT and 6,400 NFT comparison children were included in the sample. At an annual budget of $59 million, the FT project was clearly the largest and most expensive educational experiment of its kind.

Becker and Carnine (1980) divided the nine major models into three categories. First, there were those that derived their philosophy from the nonbehavioral theories of Piaget, Freud, and Dewey. These programs focused on improving basic cognitive processes and the whole person through a host of eclectic activities that permitted individualized, self-motivated and self-discovery ways of adapting to the environment. This grouping essentially combined Bissell's (1973) Permissive-Enrichment, Structured-Cognitive, and Structured-Environment approaches. Five models were included, four of which were previously described: Bank Street, Education Development Center (Open Education), Cognitively Oriented Curriculum, and Responsive Education Model. The fifth was the Tucson Early Education Model (TEEM) first developed by Hughes with Spanish-speaking children and expanded by Henderson (1972). Like the Structured-Cognitive approach, its goal was to teach basic processes, such as comparing, recalling, attending, and spatial relationships. The TEEM program used a language experience approach to teach reading. Like Permissive-Enrichment and Structured-Environment approaches, children were assumed to have different styles of learning and interests. "Teaching elaborates on and explores what is already salient for the children—their environment and their current interests" (Maccoby & Zellner, 1970, pp. 15–16).

Becker's second group contained models based on the behavioral principles of Skinner and other advocates of small step, carefully structured instructional sequences of relevant school-life concepts and operations that are established and maintained by deliberate reinforcement contingencies. The two models representative of this philosophy were Direct Instruction and Behavior Analysis. (The Primary Education Project participated in FT, but it served only a few sites.)

The third group contained two models that shared common features with the previous ones and yet had specialized goals and unique practices. The Parent Education Model (Gordon, Guinagh, & Jester, 1977) assumed that relatively long-lasting stable gains were possible by working through the parents of disadvantaged youngsters and educating these parents in "developmentally beneficial" ways of interacting with their children. Parent educators served as links between home and school and spent part of their time in both settings. This model did not prescribe any particular classroom curriculum or organization although it did try to present tasks in the home based on Piagetian educational philosophy. The last model is the Southwest Educational Development Laboratory (SEDL). It served a high percentage of non-English-speaking children (Spanish, French) and used a bilingual approach where appropriate. It assumed that children would want to learn English and develop competencies in two languages if primary instruction were first given in their native language. Programmed materials formed a strong part of the curricula; reading was based on a sequential presentation of oral subject matter followed by the same subject in written form.

The differences in the two major educational philosophies represented in FT are summarized by Becker and Carnine (1980): The philosophies include:

Those concerned with rules or principles of *natural growth* processes, and those concerned with rules or principles for *changing behavior* in desired ways. Those from the first line concern themselves with issues that supposedly relate to long-lasting effects of particular experiences. Those from the second line are most concerned with the immediate, and measurable. While the first group discusses internal processes, the second deals with objective aspects of learned behavior. While the first group stresses "process" and depreciates the value of content, the second group emphasizes the importance of specific content and specific behaviors. (pp. 12–13)

The formal evaluation of FT included a number of norm-referenced instruments given to children at the end of third grade. The data were collected by Stanford Research Institute and analyzed by Abt Associates, which prepared the final report (individual sponsors were free to collect data on measures of their own choice). The test battery included measures of basic academic skills, and measures relating to affect or self-concept. The FT models were evaluated in two major ways. The first way was based on relative comparisons. For each measure, a covariance-adjusted comparison was made with a local non-follow-through (NFT) group and also with a pooled national comparison group. Positive effects occurred when FT was statistically better than NFT and negative effects when FT was statistically poorer. With positive and negative outcomes, a spread of at least one-fourth standard deviation (.25 SD) had to separate the FT-NFT comparison. To summarize model effects, Becker and Carnine (1980) adopted a measure called the Index of Significant Outcomes (ISO). For each sponsor, the number of negative outcomes for a particular measure was subtracted from the number of positive outcomes and the difference divided by the total number of comparisons, which also included null (no effect) outcomes. The ISOs thus permit a relative comparison of models and of skill differences within models. The second kind of evaluation was based on the model's absolute standing on a number of norm-referenced tests for total and subtest scores.[1]

Listed in part of Table 48.1 is each model's absolute score in terms of percentiles (derived by median grade-equivalent scores) on the Metropolitan Achievement Test (MAT).

The twentieth percentile is a fair representation of the place where economically disadvantaged fall on third-grade achievement tests (U.S. Office of Education, 1976). The set of percentile points on a normal distribution that are equidistant from each other in terms of .25 SD are (starting with the fiftieth percentile and moving downward): fiftieth, fortieth, thirty-first, twenty-third, sixteenth, and eleventh percentile. Thus, on MAT language, the difference between Direct Instruction, which is at the fiftieth percentile, and many of the models at or close to the twenty-third percentile is .75 SD. The U.S. Office of Education has taken an increase of .25 SD as an educationally significant finding for compensatory models.

Direct Instruction was clearly the highest in normative performance attaining close to or at national norms on all MAT subtests. In MAT Reading, it is better by almost .5 SD than the next closest model (Behavior Analysis) and in MAT Math, it is at least .5 SD ahead of all the others. In MAT Spelling, Direct Instruction, and Behavior Analysis

Table 48.1 Outcomes of Third-Grade Achievement and Affective Measures for Nine Follow-Through Models

Model	Sponsor(s)/Designer(s)	Metropolitan Achievement Test (percentiles)				Ranks for Average ISOs[a]		
		Total Reading	Total Math	Spelling	Language	Basic Skills	Cognitive	Affective
Direct Instruction University of Oregon	Engelmann & Becker	41	48	51	50	1	1	1
Southwest Education Development Laboratory (SEDL)	Nedler & Caudle	15	15	19	18	2	2	4
Parent Education Model University of Florida	Gordon	24	14	32	20	3	3	3
Behavior Analysis University of Kansas	Bushell	34	28	49	22	4	6	2
Bank Street College Model	Gilkeson & Zimiles	30	19	32	23	5	4	7
Responsive Education Model Far West Laboratory	Nimnicht	28	17	28	18	7	5	6
Tucson Early Education Model (TEEM) University of Arizona	Hughes & Henderson	26	18	27	22	6	7	9
Cognitively Oriented Curriculum -High/Scope Educational Research Foundation	Weikert	21	11	22	12	9	8	5
Open Education Educational Development Center	Armington	18	14	18	19	8	9	8

Note. Adapted from data compiled by Becker and Engelmann (1978).

[a] ISO is the Index of Significant Outcomes. It is derived for each FT model by subtracting the number of statistically significant negative outcomes (non-FT Comparison group better than that FT model) from the number of positive outcomes (FT model better than non-FT) and dividing the difference by the total number of comparisons, null outcomes included.

scores approach national norms, and both are about .5 SD higher than the rest. In MAT Language (usage, punctuation, and sentence type), Direct Instruction is .75 SD ahead of the other programs. For Language, Behavior Analysis is a distant second to Direct Instruction and most of the other models have not advanced the economically disadvantaged beyond the twentieth-percentile baseline.

Direct Instruction also ranked first not only across a number of MAT subtests that measured basic skills (Word Knowledge, Spelling, Language, and Math Computation) but also on another set that measured cognitive-conceptual skills (Reading Comprehension, Math Concepts, and Math Problem-Solving). The ISO values for Direct Instruction were uniformly positive and substantial for both the basic skill and cognitive measures (Becker & Engelmann, 1978). On the basics, Parent Education, Behavior Analysis, and SEDL produced an average ISO effect near zero. The other models produced substantial negative ISOs. On the cognitive measures, SEDL also yielded positive ISOs, albeit of much lower value than Direct Instruction. The cognitive ISOs for the remaining seven models were negative. The rankings of the various models based on the mean ISO values for the basic and cognitive measures are provided in Table 48.1.[2]

The oft-heard but unsubstantiated claim that, although Direct Instruction can possibly help children overcome handicaps in the basic skills area, it will falter in the realm of more complex, cognitive concepts and operations, was found to be untrue by the MAT data. In contrast, those models stressing the early development of basic cognitive-conceptual processes were evidently unsuccessful in these endeavors and in the attainment of basic skills as well. It cannot be said that Direct Instruction's relative success in higher level academic performance is due to its systematic use of reinforcement procedures. Behavior Analysis also employed a great deal of extrinsic reinforcement to raise academic achievement, but this model's relatively poor standing on the cognitive measures in comparison to basic skills suggests it will take something more to teach the more complex skills. That something more, suggest Becker and Carnine (1980), may lie in the instructional design principles of Direct Instruction's unique curriculum material and in its special mode of instruction—matters that will be discussed later.

The Raven's Coloured Progressive Matrices Test was used to evaluate novel problem-solving abilities. The test presents colored matrix patterns with a part missing and the child is to select the missing part from six choices. It was expected that children in programs emphasizing the manipulation of objects and self-discovering activities in a responsive environment would do well on the Raven's. It turned out that, regardless of whether programs espoused a behavioral or a cognitive approach to education, performance on the Raven's test was less than adequate. Negative ISOs were found for Direct Instruction and Behavior Analysis, as well as for the Cognitively Oriented Curriculum, Responsive Education, and Open Education. The highest average ISO, which was slightly positive, was found for Parent Education, a model that employed traditional curriculum material in the classroom. Since six of the nine FT models produced negative ISO and one (Bank Street) had an ISO of zero, it is possible that the kind of abilities measured by the Raven's test is less sensitive to the kind of instruction offered by the FT models.

To evaluate the children's impression of their abilities and feelings, Coopersmith's (1967) Self-Esteem Inventory and the Intellectual Achievement Responsibility Scale (IARS: Crandall, Katkowsky, Crandall, 1965) were used. The Coopersmith test is designed to measure the children's feelings about themselves, feelings about school, and how they think others feel about them. The IARS attempts to measure the extent to which children attribute their successes (+) or failures (–) to themselves (inner locus of control) or to outside forces (external locus of control). Abt Associates' (1977) determination of the internal reliability coefficient for the Coopersmith found it to be respectable (.80); however, the low coefficients for IARS + (.59) and IARS – (.65) are just above the threshold for trustworthiness for group comparisons.

The rankings for the nine models based on ISO comparisons averaged for the Coopersmith and the IARS (Becker & Carnine, 1980) are reported in Table 48.1. Again, Direct Instruction ranked first. Its ISOs were highest in positive value, with Behavior Analysis, Parent Education, and SEDL being the only other models to produce positive ISOs, in that order. To some researchers, the high standing of Direct Instruction on the affective measures was unexpected. Its practice of tightly controlling the instructional setting was thought by critics to discourage children from freely expressing themselves and would thus inhibit the development of self-esteem and other affective attitudes. Even before FT, the designers of Direct Instruction (Becker, Engelmann, & Thomas, 1975) suggested that children's positive attitudes about learning and themselves will be reflected as byproducts of effective teaching. As Direct Instruction children were provided with the academic tools and strategies to produce mastery of academic content, with which many of their peers and older siblings had encountered failure, and as they were awarded well-deserved teacher and possible parental-peer approval for their academic efforts, the children began to develop realistic impressions about their academic abilities in relation to others. Those who emphasized self-esteem as a primary goal in education, claim Becker et al. (1975), probably have the cart before the horse. It is interesting to note that the second-ranking model on affective measures (Behavior Analysis) also provided instances of reinforced accomplishments, whereas programs that concentrated on building self-esteem without first guaranteeing academic success (e.g., Responsive Education, Open Education) fared poorly on the ISO rankings. Weisberg (1981) found that measured achievement motivation and self-esteem of disadvantaged preschool children taught advanced academic skills on the level of second grade were markedly higher than a comparable group functioning at the normal preschool level on academic readiness skills.

Shifting to the question of why Direct Instruction children did not reach the fiftieth percentile on Total Reading, which was the stated goal of this model, raises questions on the much larger issue of the future school success of these children (and the success of any disadvantaged child) if certain aspects of reading comprehension are not improved. The below norm reading performance lies not with Direct Instruction's design or training in phonic strategies to teach functional decoding or word attack skills. Direct Instruction's track record for decoding training is very good and, on the third-grade WRAT Reading section, which mainly assesses decoding, the children in Direct Instruction placed at the eighty-second percentile (Becker & Engelmann, 1978).

Disadvantaged third-graders are not as successful in reading because they have not been taught the necessary language concepts and vocabulary that third- and upper-grade-achievement tests begin to stress in items related to word knowledge and comprehension. Until third grade, the introduction of new words and their referents is fairly well controlled, and reading comprehension does not suffer. But after that, the amount of new vocabulary introduced is greatly accelerated and moves in an uncontrolled manner to a sizeable adult vocabulary. Without knowing what key words mean, sentence and paragraph comprehension becomes arduous and frustrating. For many disadvantaged third-graders, the vocabulary-concept load of items in many achievement tests and textbooks is beyond their experience (Becker, 1977). Words such as *exterminator, penicillin, Egyptians of old, huge, obviously, probably,* and *country* (meaning nation) are not likely to be understood. Added to the problem is the increased variation and sophistication of the different kinds of syntax and semantics the third-grader is expected to know. Faced with "Dawn crept into the tent," many will offer a literal translation of the metaphor, and they will also probably misinterpret "He did everything under the sun."

Advantaged children from middle class backgrounds are relatively more adept at vocabulary and Standard English phraseology because their home-peer environments normally provide and/or supplement whatever syntactical and semantical skills are essential for school and achievement test performance. The disadvantaged, denied these language accomplishments in nonschool settings, must depend increasingly on the schools for this kind of learning. According to Becker (1977), schools are not currently teaching vocabulary knowledge systematically, and, until that is done, children with weak home training will begin to flounder on comprehension and word knowledge items starting in the fourth grade, if not before. The upshot of all of this is that the absolute reading performance of *all* FT children, including those in Direct Instruction, will begin to slip even further under current educational circumstances.

To understand the magnitude of the teaching effort, consider that the average high school senior knows about 7,000 basic words, which matches the average adult competency. On the average, 5,000 of these basic words are learned after third grade, and almost all contain at least two divergent meanings. Add on another 1,000 words that are proper nouns and, not counting derivates, inflections, and compounds, there are probably 11,000 words to learn between fourth and twelfth grade. Assuming a 35-week school year, a child in nine years would need to master about 35 new words per week just to maintain an average vocabulary. When viewed in this light, it becomes understandable why the disadvantaged will continue to exhibit academic difficulties, especially when the sprawling and unique vocabulary found in books about science, history, and literature enter into the equation. This analysis should further reinforce the axiom that effective instruction needs to be thought of as a continuous and intensive process and that, for many, achievement gains produced in one period will not magically sustain themselves throughout the remaining school years.

IMPLICATIONS FOR THE CHILD CLINICIAN

School-aged children spend a major portion of their waking hours engaged in academic and related activities. It is during this time in school that many children will experience difficulty in learning basic academic concepts and operations. The byproducts of academic failure will, of course, be reflected directly in the classroom itself, with many children avoiding academic work, acting out, getting into trouble, and developing negative attitudes about school and the authority figures found there. Some of these same avoidance behaviors will manifest themselves outside of school in peer and parent interactions. An antischool attitude and its inappropriate behavioral manifestations may become so severe that the child is eventually referred to a clinic for help.

The clinical child psychologist must be careful to discern whether the child is a "won't do" or a "can't do" learner. The first type of learner is one who has the necessary conceptual and response repertoires for attending to and completing academic tasks but, for some reason, fails to do so. The second type lacks the necessary academic skills or does not yet have the conceptual understanding to master or complete the tasks set for him or her. The clinical child psychologist has had great success with the "won't do" child through the adoption of contingency contracts and other motivational measures within the school setting and between the teacher and parent. However, for the "can't do" learner, no amount of reinforcement or special contingencies will rectify the problem if its origin stems from inadequate learning due to poor or insufficient instruction. Adding to the difficulty in diagnosis is that a "can't do" child may have already turned into a noncaring "won't do" child and the clinician may falsely think that the basis for the difficulty is a motivational one when that is only part of a larger academic problem.

Looking at the child's failing grades or giving personality tests will not get at the heart of the problem, which is: How does one successfully present and sequence tasks so that the child will learn and generalize? Simply talking to the teacher may not help much either, especially when actual classroom observation reveals that it is the teacher who presents tasks in a confusing and incomplete manner. Giving norm-referenced achievement tests may help to isolate some of the academic difficulty although these tests are only samples of many different programs and textbooks and do not necessarily tap the content taught to the target child at the present time. Also, these tests certainly do not reveal the manner in which the teacher imparts knowledge. If the goal is to find out what the current academic problems are, it is a far better practice to have the child read, write, or work problems directly from the textbooks in use at the time. The clinician, finding that the child is placed at an inappropriate grade level, must call the teacher's attention to this fact and both parties must seek academic remediation. Unable to make a judgment about whether the current academic program is in step with the child's achievement level, the clinician, in conjunction with the parent and the school authorities, should seek the advice of an educational specialist.

NOTES

1. Because the NFT comparison children were more advantaged than the FT children on a number of pre-Follow-Through measures related to school success, covariance adjusted scores were derived to determine ISO outcomes. These adjusted scores tend to provide conservative estimates of real outcomes. The upshot is that the standings of a few of the models on the relative measures (ISOs) in Table 48.1 do not consistently match their absolute standings on the MAT. The discrepancy is most serious for the SEDL model and, to a lesser extent, for the Behavior Analysis model.

2. House, Glass, McLean, and Walker (1978) have questioned whether the various Follow Through models differed from one another or from Non-Follow-Through programs. For a rebuttal to House et al., see Becker and Carnine (1980) and Bereiter and Kirkland (1981).

REFERENCES

Abt Associates. *Education as experimentation: A planned variation model* (Vol. III). Cambridge, Mass.: Abt Associates, 1976.

Abt Associates. *Education as experimentation: A planned variation model* (Vol. IV). Cambridge, Mass.: Abt Associates, 1977.

Becker, W.C. Teaching reading and language to the disadvantaged: What we have learned from field research. *Harvard Education Review*, 1977, **47**, 518–543.

Becker, W.C. It is just not that easy. Review of Project Head Start: A legacy of the war on poverty by E. Zigler & J. Valentine in *Developmental Review*, 1981, **1**, 181–185.

Becker, W.C., & Carnine, D.W. Direct instruction: An effective approach to educational intervention with the disadvantaged and low performers. In B.B. Lahey, & A.E. Kazdin (Eds.), *Advances in clinical child psychology* (Vol. 3). New York: Plenum, 1980.

Becker, W.C., & Engelmann, S. *Analysis of achievement data on six cohorts of low-income children from 20 school districts in the University of Oregon Direct Instruction Follow Through Model* (Technical Report, 78–1). Eugene, Ore.: University of Oregon, College of Education Follow Through Project, December, 1978.

Becker, W.C., Engelmann, S., & Thomas, D.R. *Teaching 2 -Cognitive learning and instruction.* Chicago: Science Research Associates, 1975.

Bereiter, C. An academic preschool for disadvantaged children: Conclusions from evaluation studies. In J.C. Stanley (Ed.), *Preschool programs for the disadvantaged: Five experimental approaches to early childhood education.* Baltimore: Johns Hopkins University Press, 1972.

Bereiter, C, & Engelmann, S. *Teaching disadvantaged children in the preschool.* Englewood Cliffs, N.J.: Prentice-Hall, 1966.

Bereiter, C., & Kirkland, M.A. A constructive look at Follow Through results. *Interchange,* 1981–82, **12**, 1–22.

Biber, B. A developmental-interaction approach: Bank Street College of Education. In M.C. Day, & R.K. Parker (Eds.), *The preschool in action: Exploring early childhood programs.* Boston: Allyn & Bacon, 1977.

Bissell, J.S. The cognitive effects of preschool programs for disadvantaged children. In J.L. Frost (Ed.), *Revisiting early childhood education: Readings.* New York: Holt, Rinehart & Winston, 1973.

Blank, M., & Solomon, F. How shall the disadvantaged child be taught? *Child Development,* 1969, **40,** 47–61.

Bloom, B.S. *Stability and change in human characteristics.* New York: Wiley, 1964.

Boyd, J. *Project Head Start: An evaluation of the effects of Head Start centers.* Princeton, N.J.: Education Testing Service, 1966.

Branche, C.F., & Overly, N.V. Illustrative descriptions of two early childhood programs. *Educational Leadership,* 1971, **28,** 821–826.

Burke, N.S., & Simon, H.E. Factors which precipitate dropouts and delinquency. *Federal Probation,* 1965, **29,** 28–32.

Bushell, D., Jr., & Brigham. T. Classroom token systems as technology. *Educational Technology,* 1971, **11,** 14–17.

Caldwell, B.M. A decade of early intervention programs: What we have learned. *American Journal of Orthopsychiatry,* 1974, **44,** 491–496.

Campbell, D.T., & Frey, P.W. The implications of learning theory for the fade-out of gains from compensatory education. In J. Hellmuth (Ed.), *Disadvantaged child* (Vol. 3). New York: Brunner/Mazel, 1970.

Coopersmith, S. *The antecedents of self-esteem.* San Francisco: Freeman, 1967.

Cowles, M. Four views of learning and development. *Educational Leadership,* 1971, **28,** 790–795.

Crandall, V.C., Katkowsky, W., & Crandall, V.J. Children's beliefs in their own control of reinforcements in intellectual-academic achievement situations. *Child Development,* 1965, **36,** 91–109.

Datta, Lois-ellin. Another Spring and other hopes: Some findings from national evaluations of Project Head Start. In E. Zigler, & J. Valentine (Eds.), *Project Head Start: A legacy of the war on poverty.* New York: Free Press, 1979.

Deutsch, M. Happenings on the way back to the forum. *Harvard Educational Review,* 1969, **3,** 523–557.

Di Lorenzo, L.T., Salter, R., & Brady, J.J. *Prekindergarten programs for educationally disadvantaged children* (Final Report). Albany, N.Y.: University of the State of New York, State Education Department, Office of Research and Evaluation, 1969.

Engelmann, S. The effectiveness of direct instruction on IQ performance and achievement in reading and arithmetic. In J. Hellmuth (Ed.), *Disadvantaged child* (Vol. 3). New York: Brunner/Mazel, 1971.

Erickson, E.L., McMillan, J., Bennell, J., & Callahan, O.D. *Experiments in Head Start and early education: Curriculum structures and teacher attitudes.* Washington, D.C.: Office of Economic Opportunity, Project Head Start, 1969.

Freeburg, N.E., & Payne, D.T. Parental influence on cognitive development in early childhood: A review. *Child Development,* 1967, **38,** 65–87.

Gordon, I.J., Guinagh, B., & Jester, R.E. The Florida parent education infant and toddler programs. In M.C. Day, & R.K. Parker (Eds.), *The preschool in action: Exploring early childhood programs.* Boston: Allyn & Bacon, 1977.

Gray, S.W., & Klaus, R.A. An experimental preschool program for culturally deprived children. *Child Development,* 1965, **36,** 887–898.

Gray S.W., Klaus, R.A., Miller, J.O., & Forrester, B.J. *Before first grade.* New York: Teachers College Press, 1966.

Henderson, R.W. *Arizona center for early childhood education* (Final Report). St. Ann, Mo.: National Coordination Center for Early Childhood Education, 1972.

Hess, R.D., & Shipman, V.C. Early experience and the socialization of cognitive modes in children. *Child Development,* 1965, **36,** 869–886.

Hewett, F. *The emotionally disturbed child in the classroom.* Boston: Allyn & Bacon, 1968.

Hobbs, N. Helping disturbed children: Psychological and ecological strategies. In H. Dupont (Ed.), *Educating emotionally disturbed children.* New York: Holt, Rinehart & Winston, 1969.

House, E.R., Glass, G.V., McLean, L.D., & Walker, D.E. No simple answer: Critique of the Follow Through evaluation. *Harvard Educational Review,* 1978, **48,** 128–160.

Hunt, J.M. *Intelligence and experience.* New York: Ronald, 1961.

Hunt, J.M. The psychological basis for using preschool enrichment as an antidote for cultural deprivation. *Merrill-Palmer Quarterly,* 1964, **10,** 209–248.

Hunt, J.M. Has compensatory education failed? Has it been attempted? *Harvard Educational Review,* 1969, **39,** 278–300.

Jensen, A.R. The culturally disadvantaged and the heredity-environment uncertainty. In J. Hellmuth (Ed.), *Disadvantaged child* (Vol. 2). New York: Brunner/Mazel, 1968.

Jensen, A.R. How much can we boost IQ and scholastic achievement? *Harvard Educational Review*, 1969, **39**, 1–123.

Karnes, M.B. *The University of Illinois study on the differential effects of five preschool problems.* Paper presented at the annual meeting of the American Educational Research Association, New York, April 1977.

Karnes, M.B., Zehrbach, R.R., & Teska, J.A. An ameliorative approach in the development of curriculum. In R.K. Parker (Ed.), *The preschool in action: Exploring early childhood programs.* Boston: Allyn & Bacon, 1972.

Karnes, M.B., Zehrbach, R.R., & Teska, J.A. Conceptualization of the GOAL (Game-Oriented Activities for Learning) curriculum. In M.C. Day, & R.K. Parker (Eds.), *The preschool in action: Exploring early childhood programs.* Boston: Allyn & Bacon, 1977.

Klaus, R.A., & Gray, S.W. The early training project for disadvantaged children: A report after five years. *Monographs of the Society for Research in Child Development*, 1968, **33**, (4, Serial No. 120), 1–66.

Kohlberg, L. Montessori with the culturally disadvantaged: A cognitive developmental interpretation and some research findings. In R.D. Hess, & R.M. Bear (Eds.), *Early education.* Chicago: Aldine, 1968.

Lally, J.R., & Honig, A.S. The family development research program. In M.C. Day, & R.K. Parker (Eds.), *The preschool in action: Exploring early childhood programs.* Boston: Allyn & Bacon, 1977.

Maccoby, E.E., & Zellner, M. *Experiments in primary education.* New York: Harcourt, Brace, Jovanovich, 1970.

Meichenbaum, D., & Asarnow, J. Cognitive-behavior modification and metacognitive development: Implications for the classrooms. In P.C. Kendall, & S.D. Hollon (Eds.), *Cognitive-behavioral interventions.* New York: Academic Press, 1979.

Miezitis, S. The Montessori method: Some recent research. In J.L. Frost (Ed.), *Revisiting early childhood education: Readings.* New York: Holt, Rinehart & Winston, 1973.

Miller, L.B. Development of curriculum models in Head Start. In E. Zigler, & J. Valentine (Eds.), *Project Head Start: A legacy of the war on poverty.* New York: Free Press, 1979.

Miller, L.B., & Dyer, J.L. Four preschool programs: Their dimensions and effects. *Monographs of the Society for Research in Child Development*, 1975, **40** (5–6, Serial No. 162), 1–164.

Milner, E. A study of the relationship between readiness in grade one school children and patterns of parent-child interactions. *Child Development*, 1951, **22**, 95–112.

Minuchin, P., & Biber, B. A child development approach to language in the preschool disadvantaged child. *Monographs of the Society for Research in Child Development*, 1968, **33** (8, Serial No. 124), 10–18.

Montessori, M. *The Montessori method.* New York: Bentley, 1964.

Montessori, M. *Dr. Montessori's own handbook.* New York: Schocken, 1965.

Mussen, P.H., Conger, J.J., & Kagan, J. *Child development and personality* (3rd Ed.). New York: Harper & Row, 1969.

Nimnicht, G., & Barnes, B. *Objectives of the responsive Head Start and Follow Through program.* San Francisco: Far West Laboratory for Educational Research and Development, 1971.

Nimnicht, G.P., Arango, M., & Cheever, J. The responsive educational program. In M.C. Day, & R.K. Parker (Eds.), *The preschool in action: Exploring early childhood programs.* Boston: Allyn & Bacon, 1977.

Palmer, F.H., & Anderson, L.W. Long-term gains from early intervention: Findings from longitudinal studies. In E. Zigler, & J. Valentine (Eds.), *Project Head Start: A legacy of the war on poverty.* New York: Free Press, 1979.

Parker, W.K. (Ed.). *The preschool in action: Exploring early childhood programs.* Boston: Allyn & Bacon, 1972.

Resnick, L.B., Wang, M.C., & Rosner, J. Adaptive education for young children: The Primary Education Project. In M.C. Day, & R.K. Parker (Eds.), *The preschool in action: Exploring early childhood programs.* Boston: Allyn & Bacon, 1977.

Richmond, J.B., Stipek, D.J., & Zigler, E. A decade of Head Start. In E. Zigler, & J.

Valentine (Eds.), *Project Head Start: A legacy of the war on poverty.* New York: Free Press, 1979.

Sears, P., & Dowley, E. Research on teaching in the nursery school. In N. Gage (Ed.), *Handbook of research on teaching.* Chicago: Rand McNally, 1963.

Schweinhart, L.J., & Weikert, D.P. *Young children grow up: The effects of the Perry preschool program on youths through age 15.* Ypsilanti, Mich.: The High/Scope Press, 1980.

Shriver, S. Head Start, a retrospective view: The founders. In E. Zigler, & J. Valentine (Eds.), *Project Head Start: A legacy of the war on poverty.* New York: Free Press, 1979.

Skeels, H.M., & Dye, H.B. A study of the effects of differential stimulation on mentally retarded children. *Proceedings and Addresses of the American Association on Mental Deficiency,* 1939, **44**, 114–136.

Smith, M.S. *Some short-term effects of Project Head Start: A preliminary report on the second year of planned variation—1970-71.* Cambridge, Mass.: Huron Institute, 1973.

Stipek, D.J., Valentine, J., & Zigler, E. Project Head Start: A critique of theory and practice. In E. Zigler, & J. Valentine (Eds.), *Project Head Start: A legacy of the war on poverty.* New York: Free Press, 1979.

Stone, J.G. General philosophy: Preschool education within Head Start. In E. Zigler & J. Valentine (Eds.), *Project Head Start: A legacy of the war on poverty.* New York: The Free Press, 1979.

Strodbeck, F.L. The hidden curriculum of the middle class home. In C.W. Hunnicutt (Ed.), *Urban education and cultural deprivation.* Syracuse, N.Y.: Syracuse University Press, 1964.

Swift, M., & Spivack, G. Therapeutic teaching: A review of teaching methods in behaviorally troubled children. *Journal of Special Education,* 1974, **8**, 259–289.

Thorndike, R.I. Mr. Binet's test 70 years later. *Educational Researcher,* 1975, **4**, 3–7.

U.S. Commission on Civil Rights. *Racial isolation in the public schools* (Vol. 1). Washington, D.C.: U.S. Government Printing Office, 1967.

U.S. Office of Education. *Annual evaluation: Report on programs administered by the U.S. Office of Education.* Washington, D.C.: Capital Publication, Educational Resources Division, 1976.

Weikert, D.P. Preschool programs: Preliminary findings. *Journal of Special Education,* 1967, **1**, 163–181.

Weikert, D.P. Relationship of curriculum, teaching, and learning in preschool education. In J.C. Stanley (Ed.), *Preschool programs for the disadvantaged: Five experimental approaches to early childhood education.* Baltimore: Johns Hopkins University Press, 1972.

Weisberg, H.I. *Short-term cognitive effects of Head Start programs: A report on the third year of planned variation—1971-72.* Cambridge, Mass.: Huron Institute, 1973.

Weisberg, P. *Direct instruction in the preschool—logical and empirical validation.* Paper presented at the meeting of the Association for Behavior Analysis, Milwaukee, May 1981.

Westinghouse Learning Corp. *The impact of Head Start: An evaluation of the effects of Head Start on children's cognitive and affective development* (Executive Summary). Washington, D.C.: Ohio University report to the Office of Economic Opportunity, 1969.

White, S.H. The national impact study of Head Start. In J. Hellmuth (Ed.), *Disadvantaged child* (Vol. 3). New York: Brunner/Mazel, 1971.

Zigler, E., & Anderson, K. An idea whose time has come: The intellectual and political climate. In E. Zigler, & J. Valentine (Eds.), *Project Head Start: A legacy of the war on poverty.* New York: Free Press, 1979.

Zigler, E.F., & Butterfield, E.O. Motivational aspects of changes in IQ performance of culturally deprived nursery school children. *Child Development,* 1968, **39**, 1–14.

CHAPTER 49

Sex Education

SOL GORDON AND SUSAN UNTENER SNYDER

While the specific intent of this chapter is to support and promote the clinical psychologist in his or her role of facilitating parents as the primary sex educators of their own children, the actual approach to the topic is far more ambitious.

Professionals frequently address questions of patient treatment in their clinical endeavors without the concomitant realization that they must often deal with similar or identical issues in their own lives. Most are themselves parents and therefore need to consider first how to come to terms with their own sexuality and subsequently with the emerging sexuality of their children.

For this reason, the present work will focus not only upon specific interventions recommended for use with parents, but will supplement professionals' working knowledge of the field by reviewing current research and scholarly thinking. It is hoped that such "demythologizing" of this sometimes volatile and often controversial area will assist professionals in examining their attitudes about sexuality for the purpose of assessing how askable (approachable) they might appear to clients.

The senior author shall not forget an incident which occurred after lecturing to a county medical society regarding the role of the physician as sex educator. A doctor in the audience angrily arose, contending that, "I've been in practice for 35 years, and I think that everything you've said is nonsense. In all that time, not a single patient asked me a question about sex." It did not require a complicated diagnosis for virtually everyone present to recognize that this physician was simply not askable.

Not unlike the old dictum, "Physician, heal thyself," the concerned professional should be sensitive to personal values, beliefs, and attitudes about sexuality and willing to adjust those that might interfere with delivering effective therapy *prior to* ministering to and educating his or her clientele. This process is facilitated by an examination of personal feelings and beliefs about such issues as masturbation, homosexuality, birth control, abortion, and pre- and extramarital sex, with a complementary awareness of the impact that individual religious and/or philosophical ideologies have. Social and political factors that impinge upon personal values also play a role in determining professional effectiveness: the psychologist is simultaneously a member of a family and a network of friends, a colleague and often an employee.

A PHILOSOPHY OF SEX EDUCATION

Parents *are* the primary sex educators of their own children, whether they fulfill this role well or badly. Basic sex education begins in the home, and, indeed, much of what children learn in this area occurs during the preschool years before they enter the formal educational system.

We concur with Passmore's (1980, pp. 27–32) contention that sex education is, in essence, a form of moral education. We also agree that the definition of what constitutes moral education is a cause for concern and has been the focus of much opposition (albeit misinformed) to the field.

A crucial distinction must be made, there-

1154

fore, between moral and moralistic teaching. Our underlying assumption is that sex education cannot, and should not, be value free. The "point" of such instruction, whether at home or at school, extends beyond mere dissemination of biological (reproductive) information. It entails suggesting ways for individuals to modify uninformed sexual attitudes and behaviors by providing them with a foundation for responsible choices and decision making. Sex education in this perspective is best conceptualized in terms of *preparation for loving relationships.*

Optimally, moral instruction in this area conveys and reinforces our society's highest ideals: e.g., it is simply wrong to exploit another human being, for whatever reason. Moralistic teaching, on the other hand, involves the imposition of one's own idiosyncratic views in a dogmatic fashion: e.g., "If you engage in premarital sex, you'll go to hell." Opponents of the sex education process are often oblivious of this critical difference and ironically argue against sex education in their own decidedly moralistic fashion (Szasz, 1980; Willke & Willke, 1978).

Especially insidious in this regard are the so-called "profamily" and "moral majority" special interest groups that paint woeful pictures of society's demise at the hands of "secular humanists": e.g., sex educators, family planners, and most public school teachers. Following are some representative extremist statements cited from the Spring 1981 *Sex Education and Mental Health Report,* published by Christian Family Renewal and Valley Christian University.

Murray Norris, publisher of the *Report* and president of CFR, maintains in his editorial entitled, "Let's Get it Straight," that "our children are being taught Humanistic sex education, death education, and values clarification. All with one aim in mind—to destroy belief in God, the Judeo-Christian values, and the family." In the same *Report,* "Shocking Story on Sex Ed Teacher Training" asserts:

How are sex ed teachers trained?

Instructors who teach many sex ed teachers feel it is absolutely necessary that they get sensitivity training. This notorious activity frequently leaves the teacher filled with frustrations, anxieties and confusions. It is no wonder that they will disrobe before their students or perform other "kinky" acts after these sessions.

In 1981, a successful attempt to legislate morality was embodied in the so-called "profamily" chastity bill sponsored by Senators Jeremiah Denton and Orrin Hatch.[1] The senators' bill provides for the expenditure of $30 million for each of the next three years to remedy "adolescent premarital sexual relations." Additionally, the bill calls for a form of sexuality counseling that would discourage pregnant teens from having abortions and encourage them to choose adoption as the best option.

Moralistic ideologies, then, operate under the assumption that only one belief system is acceptable and that it is permissible to enforce that system via the necessary social sanctions and legislation. Moral education, conversely, advances the idea that individuals who feel good about themselves and who view life as worthwhile and as an opportunity are not candidates for exploitation. Love, caring, and consideration for oneself and for others are the backbone of responsible sexuality. As Passmore (1980) indicates, a "course of action is responsibly chosen when the agent takes account of other people, of their 'right to choose,' of their feelings, and of the broader, social consequences of what he is doing" (p. 30).

We subscribe to the World Health Organization's (1975) directive that sex education address not only reproductive anatomy and physiology but ethical issues in interpersonal relationships and questions of reproductive responsibility. Furthermore, as described and interpreted by one of the world's most distinguished pioneers in the field, Dr. Mary Calderone (founder of the Sex Education and Information Council of the United States), the intent of sexuality education is the development of mature individuals capable of making wise and responsible decisions in the fulfillment of their sexual lives.

Finally, in line with the foregoing discussion, it behooves educators (and, by definition, parents) to teach *against* sexism, sex role rigidity, and the double standard. While these issues will be discussed in more detail shortly, a recent study by Adler (1981) has supported what sex educators have continually encountered: "Sex role socialization of both males and females works against the effectiveness of sex education" (p. 57).

Demythologizing Sex Education

We wish at this time to address two of the most common myths that serve as rationales for opposition to sex education by some parents and some professionals as well. The first myth is best expressed by the statement that "today's youth already know everything there is to know about sex."

The research evidence, however, indicates that the opposite is true: the earlier a child has sexual intercourse, the *less* he or she usually knows about it. Early sexual experience actually fosters an unwillingness to learn about sex, partly because the individual feels that he or she is already knowledgeable and partly because there is a fear of appearing naive if one seeks information. In addition, there is a strong correlation between ignorance and risking pregnancy and sexually transmitted disease (STD) (Gordon, Scales, & Everly, 1979).

Teenagers are engaging in sexual intercourse at earlier ages, and the proportion of teenagers who have had intercourse is increasing. In their 1979 national survey dealing with sexual activity, contraceptive use, and premarital pregnancy and its resolution among 15–19-year-old women living in metropolitan areas, Zelnik and Kantner found that the proportion of teenage women engaging in premarital sexual activity had increased substantially: from 30 percent in 1971, to 43 percent in 1976, and to 50 percent in 1979.[2] Race, socioeconomic status, residence, and religious affiliation have little bearing on these increases, as premarital sexual activity is increasing among all elements of the teenage population (Alan Guttmacher Institute, 1981).[3] Each year 1.3 million 10–19-year-olds become pregnant, with one-third of all girls pregnant before reaching their twentieth birth-

day (Kirby, Alter, & Scales, 1979). Unless current trends are reversed, four out of every 10 girls aged 14 will become pregnant at least once during their teenage years (Alan Guttmacher Institute, 1981). The proportion of premaritally pregnant teen women has nearly doubled in less than 10 years: from 9 percent in 1971, to 13 percent in 1976, to 16 percent in 1979. Most of the increase is directly attributable to the rise in the proportion of teenagers with premarital sexual experience (Zelnik & Kantner, 1980, p. 223). While teens comprise only 18 percent of all sexually active women capable of becoming pregnant, they account for nearly half (46 percent) of all out-of-wedlock births, and just under one-third (31 percent) of all abortions (Alan Guttmacher Institute, 1981). Despite evidence of increased and more consistent contraceptive use, teens who never used contraception comprised fully one-half of all teenagers who had had a premarital pregnancy. The data additionally suggest that teens were using *less* effective methods of contraception in 1979 than in the period just three years previous. The use of the pill and IUD declined by 41 percent from 1976 to 1979, while use of withdrawal and the rhythm method increased by 86 percent (Zelnik & Kantner, 1980, p. 236). Teens who practice contraception, however, tend to wait until they have been sexually active for approximately nine months before doing so. This delay accounts for more than half of the pregnancies conceived within six months of the first act of intercourse, and a fifth of the pregnancies conceived during the first month (Alan Guttmacher Institute, 1981).

Admittedly, not all of these findings are the result of simple ignorance on the part of young people, and the researchers themselves caution against too facile interpretations (Zelnik & Kantner, 1980). However, this should not obscure the fact that nearly two-thirds of teenage girls questioned said that they either never used contraception or did so only erratically, and 51 percent said they did not think they could get pregnant (Alan Guttmacher Institute, 1981). Some of the responses offered include, "I didn't think I could get pregnant standing up"; "He said he'd pull out in time"; "I didn't think I could get pregnant the first time" (Gordon et al., 1979; Shah, Zelnik, & Kantner, 1975).

These findings directly concern the family and specifically the role of parents as sex educators. Studies have indicated that poor relationships with parents are linked to the incidence of teen sexual intercourse (Chilman, 1978/1980; Jessor & Jessor, 1975; Zelnik & Kantner, 1972): as the number of sexual topics discussed by the parents increases, the likelihood that adolescents will engage in sexual intercourse decreases (Lewis, 1973; Scales, 1976).

These findings dramatically contradict the second myth impeding the provision of sex education: the belief that knowledge is harmful. Virtually all opposition to sex education is based upon this assumption—that children who are knowledgeable about sexuality will participate in sexual intercourse. Once again, the research evidence supports the opposite conclusion. As previously detailed, ignorance promotes risk taking. in terms of more frequent intercourse and the failure to use contraceptives and protect oneself against possible exposure to STDs. Discussion of sexuality—and specifically discussion of sexuality *in the home*—is related to the postponement of sexual activity and to more responsible use of contraception when engaging in sex (Fox & Inazu, 1978; Goldfarb et al., 1977; Gordon et al., 1979; Jessor & Jessor, 1975; Miller, 1976).

Parents and Children—Teach Us What We Want to Know

A recent important study of 1,400 Cleveland parents which sought to illuminate the role that parents play in their children's sexual learning revealed that only 25 percent of all parents felt that they were doing "very well" in educating their children about sexuality. The study concluded that while parents considered the topics of sexual intercourse, premarital sex, contraception, and sexually transmitted disease important for their children to know about prior to reaching adolescence, the majority provided little or no direct information

regarding these issues. Between 85 and 95 percent of all parents interviewed said that they had never mentioned any aspect of erotic behavior or its social consequences to their children (Roberts et al., 1978, p. 56).

Another study conducted in England in the mid-70s for similar purposes uncovered much the same pattern. Of the nearly 350 parents interviewed, the vast majority said that parents should be involved in discussing reproduction (90 percent) and sexual intercourse (79 percent) with their children, yet less than half had discussed the former and just over a quarter had discussed the latter (Farrell, 1978, p. 89).

It is significant that both of the aforementioned studies indicate that parents have particular difficulty discussing certain aspects of sexuality with their children. Parents and children typically avoid discussion of issues where value disagreement and the potential for conflict are greatest—issues that tend to be of particular concern to the child and most problematic for the parents (Scales, 1976; Scales & Everly, 1977; Sorensen, 1973). The Cleveland study discovered that while 75 percent of the mothers and 50 percent of the fathers had discussed pregnancy with their child, only 15 percent of the mothers and less than 8 percent of the fathers had discussed sexual intercourse. Further, less than 2 percent of all fathers and 8 percent of all mothers had ever mentioned contraception (Roberts et al., 1978, p. 55). Farrell's (1978) findings coincide quite closely: with respect to contraception, few parents felt that they should. be the first ones to discuss birth control with their children. Though 71 percent of the parents believed that they should be the children's first sources for reproductory information, only 41 percent felt this way about discussing contraception. Additionally, there was a strong sentiment that this area was best handled outside of the family setting altogether (Farrell, 1978, p. 94).

Results are similar regarding parental discussion of STDs, with 97 percent supporting discussion with young people but only 33 percent feeling that one or both parents should be involved in the process. Nearly one-half of the parents believed that the teacher should assume a role in this area, providing information either autonomously or in conjunction with the parents. In practice, parents were more likely to acknowledge that they had talked about STDs than birth control with their children: 35 percent as compared to 27 percent (Farrell, 1978, pp. 95–96). Roberts et al. (1978, p. 62) report similarly low rates of parental discussion of these areas, with between 6 and 10 percent having ever mentioned STDs, and only 2–6 percent having discussed contraception.

These findings point to the probable negative effects on children when parents speak only about pregnancy and birth *outside of the context* of sexual intercourse, contraception, and sexually transmitted diseases. In light of this, it is possible to imagine that at least some young people fail to make the "connection" between the processes—with obviously disastrous consequences. Roberts et al. (1978, p. 56) hypothesize that, at minimum, failure to obtain complete information from parents may well affect the child's willingness to request additional information as he or she matures. The parent has previously demonstrated himself or herself to be an unreliable or resistant source of information in this area—in a nutshell, appears *unaskable* to the child.

Why *don't* parents talk to their children about sex? Many simply do not know what to say. They find it difficult to broach the subject and feel ill equipped to deal with the sexual issues of concern to their children. Ambiguity about their own sexual attitudes and the applicability of these for the lives of their sons and daughters may further serve to "paralyze" parents and to prevent them from entering into dialogue. As children mature, parents typically find it increasingly difficult to discuss sexual topics (Lewis & Lewis, 1980; Rothenberg, 1978; Rubin & Calderwood, 1973) and may feel even more uncertain that they are doing so in a satisfactory manner. Many are repeating the past patterns of noncommunication about sexual matters that they experienced with their own parents. Numerous studies have indicated that the majority of parents surveyed expressed dis-

satisfaction regarding the lack of quality sex education they received as children (Abelson et al., 1970; Gordon et al., 1979; Libby & Nass, 1971; Scales, 1976; Schofield, 1965, 1973; Sorensen, 1973).

Most parents want to be the sex educators of their own children and, according to a recent Gallup poll,[4] favor the teaching of sex education in school. Most would also like help from professionals and the community in fulfilling their roles as primary sex educators (Institute for Family Research and Education, 1977). Specifically in regard to talking with older children about sex, parents have identified the areas of value clarification, value conflict, embarrassment, and communications difficulties as problematic and as targets for outside assistance (Roberts et al., 1978).

Parent-child communications difficulties are of particular concern. As Scales and Everly (1977) indicate, "Family sexual communication is generally characterized by silence, rulemaking, and the exercise of authority more than by the exploration of values in a verbal atmosphere of cooperative disagreement and influencing" (p. 37). Furthermore, a random telephone survey of 904 Syracuse adults conducted by the Institute for Family Research and Education (1977) revealed that while 87 percent agreed that parents should answer children's questions about sex—regardless of their age—a full 41 percent felt that children do not *want* their parents to talk to them about sex.

The majority of young people, however, *prefer* their parents to be the primary sources of advice and information in the area of sexuality (Gordon et al., 1979; Lewis & Lewis, 1980; Scales, 1976; Scales & Everly, 1977; U.S. Commission on Obscenity and Pornography, 1970). Despite this preference, most young people concur that parents have not been functioning adequately in their roles as counselors and sex educators. Most do not talk to their parents about sexual matters. Sorensen's (1973) study of 411 adolescents aged 13–19 revealed that 72 percent of the boys and 70 percent of the girls responded that they did not talk freely about sex with their parents and that most are unsure of what their parents want them to know in this regard. Our own ongoing research at Syracuse University supports these findings, with less than 25 percent of the thousands of undergraduates surveyed reporting their parents as adequate sex educators (Institute for Family Research and Education, 1976–1982).

Studies conducted during the past 35 years indicate that between 75 and 90 percent of all young people report having learned most of what they know about sex from friends (Gordon & Dickman, 1977). Farrell's (1978) findings additionally suggest that boys and girls who first learned about sex from friends were more likely to be sexually experienced and more likely to say they were dissatisfied with the way they had learned about sex. When asked what they thought was the best way to learn about sex, many named an authoritative source such as school or parent, with *subsequent* discussion with friends or "someone who knows" (Farrell, 1978).

Rogers and Strover's (1980) discussion of the influence of peer communications about sexuality within a developmental framework convincingly demonstrates the saliency of the peer group for the adolescent in particular. In attempting to account for the vast amount of sexual misinformation that is communicated among young people, the researchers consider the nature of teen peer networks—noting the high degree of homogeneity and restrictiveness of alliances: "Hence, adolescents with relatively low levels of knowledge talk with highly similar peers. Such horizontal patterns of interpersonal communication amount to sharing limited knowledge, misinformation, and ignorance.... One's peers only know what one already knows" (Rogers & Strover, 1980, p. 173). The researchers conclude their assessment on somewhat of a hopeful note, however —indicating the potential effectiveness of peer counseling programs in sexuality by near peers: individuals slightly older than the teen clients but perceived as "optimally similar for communication purposes" (p. 177).

Before concluding this section, it is important to note the contributions of the media and printed material to the sex education of children. In the Cleveland study, more than half of all parents reported that, other than from themselves, they believed their children learned the most about sexuality from television. Parents who reported watching the most TV indicated that television viewing precipitated sexual discussions within the family (Roberts et al., 1978). The majority, however, were uncertain and/or displeased about the messages television is imparting to children about sexuality. Content analyses of programming indicate that these misgivings are not ill founded. There is a decided lack of intimacy (physical/verbal expressions of tenderness) portrayed on television, with only a fraction of close relationships on prime time between women (10 percent); the rest are between men (47 percent), or between women and men (43 percent). Marriage and family life are primarily "women's concerns," with most women (70 percent) depicted in or around the home, and few (less than 20 percent) of all male interactions pertaining to these areas. (Fewer than one in ten married TV mothers has a job.) Finally, when verbal references to sexual behaviors on dramatic/ action-adventure programs occur, they primarily result from discussion of sex crimes (Roberts et al., 1978, pp. 83–84).

Himmelweit and Bell (1980) alert us to the ramifications of such findings for role modeling and sex role stereotyping. Comstock (1978) has noted that it is not uncommon for children in our society to view up to six and seven hours of television per day. Television functions as an important source of sexual information—particularly for the very young, who have typically been viewed and responded to as essentially asexual, and for whom alternate role models remain limited:

We would expect that television would exert a strong impact. Children, though aware of their own sexual identity at an early age, have little direct experience with a variety of adult male and female models. Television provides them with many models. The ingredients for a strong impact are: an interest in the subject matter, an absence of well-established attitudes, the possibility of identifying with models of the same sex through fictional programs, and the perception of such fiction as real. Such factors apply particularly to the young and (within each age group) to those with fewest alternative role models or least access to alternative information. (Himmelweit & Bell, 1980, p. 123)

Regarding the impact of printed media, Sorensen's (1973) study indicated that nearly 40 percent of the more than 400 teens in his sample had never read a serious article about sex, with fewer than 50 percent having read an educational book on the subject. Although the results of Farrell's (1978) study were a bit more optimistic in this regard (i.e., nearly two-thirds (62 percent) had read books or articles about sexual matters), one must question the quality of the materials consulted. The most frequently cited sources of information were women's magazines (15 percent), sex magazines (15 percent), novels and other magazines (10 percent), psychology books (9 percent), biology books (8 percent), pamphlets (on STDs, birth control, etc.) (4 percent). Less than a quarter (21 percent) of the teens indicated that such reading had been very helpful[5] (Farrell, 1978, pp. 68–69).

An analysis of more than 30 of the most widely used books for the sexual instruction of adolescents documents probable explanations for such teen dissatisfaction. Harvard researchers recently determined that 20 percent of the books failed even to mention sexual intercourse and over 90 percent of those materials that did address it did so in a deficient (unacceptable) manner. Fully one-quarter failed to discuss pregnancy, 30 percent did not mention love, 40–50 percent ignored the topics of sexually transmitted diseases, birth control, abortion, and possible guilt resulting from sexual activity, and 55 percent made no mention of the enjoyment derived from sex or of the issue of prostitution. The researchers concluded that only 20 percent of all of the books considered were "impartial" (nonjudgmental) in their discussions of sexuality (Rubenstein, Watson, & Rubenstein, 1977).

The Role(s) of the Clinical Psychologist

In the normal course of performing his or her professional duties, the clinician typically functions as role model, educator, communications facilitator, and counselor. Each of these "roles" is undeniably overlapping and interrelated, yet each also requires a specific repertoire of skills—skills that uniquely equip the practicing clinical psychologist working with children and families with the resources necessary to mediate and enhance the sex education process between parent and child.

The evidence is convincing that parents want to educate their children about sex but, for the various reasons identified, are unable to do so. One of the most significant deterrents to honest and open communication about sexuality is the absence of adequate role modeling: the parents themselves were unable to talk to *their* parents about sexual matters of concern. This cycle of silence thus repeats itself from generation to generation.

The clinical psychologist has the opportunity to serve as role model for parents in the sex education process. The professional's quality of approachability—his or her responsiveness to sexual communication—could prove helpful to clients in their marital interactions and in discussions about sexuality with their children. Such responsiveness additionally facilitates parental examination of attitudes about particular sexual issues. Conceivably, clinical interventions in this area might nevertheless be met with some resistance. The authors maintain, however, that parents who are reasonably comfortable with their own sexuality and with their marital relationship not only appear more askable to their children but are better role models as well. We specifically find it helpful to encourage parental consideration of personal feelings, values, and beliefs about sexuality, involving both individual and *couple* awareness of how each feels about sexual matters.

Husbands and wives could be encouraged to talk to each other, to ask each other questions: "Am I/are you satisfied with our sexual relations?"; "Are we able to express the affection we feel for each other?"; "How has our marriage affected our sexual relationship?" It is in asking—and in answering—these types of questions that couples will become more in touch with their feelings and sexuality. The professional might also want to encourage couples to discover the pleasures of various forms of physical expression: simple touching and holding, kissing and caressing. The emphasis on sexual performance prevalent in some of the new sex therapies and popularized in the media and "sex manuals" can be restrictive and pressuring, often inhibiting couples from expressing their authentic feelings of love and caring for each other. Husbands and wives must be "given permission," so to speak, to experience their sexuality in its myriad aspects, both for their own enjoyment and for the sake of conveying healthy attitudes about sexuality to their children. For example, a child who does not see physical affection expressed between his or her parents may come to believe that physical affection is altogether inappropriate or limited to the bedroom and to sexual intercourse. Parents, and by association children, need awareness training in *sensuality:* the ability to express and enjoy sexuality in the broadest possible sense and not just exclusively in genital ways.

The clinician should also be sensitive to the fact that after centuries of silence and secrecy about sexual concerns, parents are suddenly being asked to "liberate" themselves and speak freely with their children. Without a solid foundation and rationale, however, this is an unreasonable expectation. The professional is now able to function as educator: to reassure and provide parents with the guidance and information necessary for effective sex education. Following are some basic concepts that the senior author in 30 years of clinical experience has found to be crucial in helping parents. Clinicians will find that questions pertaining to these concepts very often arise quite naturally in conversations with parents about their own and their children's sexuality. Such concerns are best responded to in an easy and matter-of-fact manner by providing the relevant information and atmosphere conducive to attitude consideration and change.

1. *Normal and abnormal.* All thoughts, wishes, dreams, and fantasies are normal: behavior can be wrong/abnormal but not ideas. Guilt is the energy for the involuntary repetition of unacceptable ideas. Normal sexual behavior among adults is characterized as voluntary, nonexploitative, and consensual. Generally, this behavior is pleasurable and guilt free. Abnormal sexual behavior among adults is characterized as compulsive (involuntary), exploitative, often nonconsensual, guilt ridden, and rarely pleasurable.

2. *Masturbation.* Masturbation is a normal expression of sexuality at any age, for child or adult. In early childhood, it is a natural outgrowth of the child's healthy curiosity and exploration of his or her body. Later it may become a normal release for sexual tension and a healthy alternative to sexual intercourse. No physical or mental harm results from masturbation per se (that is, if it is guilt free), regardless of how frequently it occurs. One cannot masturbate "too much"; masturbating *once* is too much if the individual does not enjoy it or if it is accompanied by guilt and self-condemnation. Masturbation is best when voluntary (as opposed to compulsive), guilt free, and accompanied by a wide range of fantasies.

3. *Size.* The size of one's sexual organs has nothing to do with the giving or receiving of sexual pleasure.

Penis Size. Males needlessly worry about penis size. However, it is not possible to determine the size of a penis by observing its nonerect state.

Vagina. Similarly, women needlessly worry that their partners' penises are either too small for sexual satisfaction or too big for their vaginas. Regarding the latter concern in particular, it is well to remember that the vagina accommodates the birth of a baby, which is many times larger than the male penis. Tension or anxiety can cause a tightening of the vagina (vaginismus) that makes intercourse painful or impossible, but this is unrelated to the size of the penis or the vagina's ability to accommodate it.

Breasts. Breast size or shape has nothing to do with sexual or personal adequacy. There is a wide range of perfectly normal and healthy breast sizes and shapes and worry about "uneven" or "late" development is unnecessary.

4. *Nocturnal emissions (wet dreams) and menstruation.* Both girl and boy children need to be informed about these normal maturational events. There is no excuse for any child to be unprepared for these experiences.

5. *Homosexuality.* Many young people are needlessly concerned because they feel, or have felt, attracted to someone of the same sex. Our definition of a homosexual is an adult who has and prefers sexual relationships with partners of the same sex. Little is known about why a person becomes a homosexual as an adult. However, it is important for parents to know that a homosexual experience—even a few of them—does not "make" a child homosexual. No one can "predict" if an individual will be homosexual in his or her adult life. Regardless of parental desires, however, at least 5 or 6 percent of children growing up today will be homosexual: some estimates indicate that as much as 10 percent of the adult population is exclusively homosexual in orientation. It is almost certain that individuals do not deliberately *choose* to be homosexual (or heterosexual), and there is no evidence to support the popular myths that young people grow up to be homosexual because they had strong mothers and weak fathers or came from single-parent families. Homosexuals come from every type of family (primarily from two-parent heterosexual families). In addition, parents themselves needlessly worry that they will "make" their child homosexual, with respect to expressions of affection toward boy children in particular— specifically by allowing the child to play and behave in non-sex-stereotyped ways. There is no evidence to justify either fear, and, concerning the latter, we are not aware of a single documented case of a young man's becoming homosexual because of his father's openly affectionate behavior.

The majority of mental health professionals are in agreement that homosexuality as a lifestyle/orientation is not inherently unhealthful.

6. *A balanced perspective.* Parents have a crucial role in helping to put sexuality into perspective for their children. Despite the preponderance of sexual messages in the media, sex is not the most important aspect of life and should never be a test of love. The senior author has found it useful to suggest that of the 10 most important components of a relationship, sex is number 9. Love and caring for another person, a sense of humor, and communication (numbers 1, 2, and 3 respectively) are far more significant.[6]

7. *Nudity in the home.* Parents often wonder if they should shower with their young children (i.e., aged 2–5) or undress in front of them. These are good opportunities for children to raise questions, and their developing sense of privacy will dictate when these activities are no longer appropriate, usually at about ages 5–6. If children have not asked any questions pertaining to sexuality by age 5, it is the responsibility of parents to initiate discussions.

8. *Child molestation.* Even young children need to understand the difference between public and private places and parts of the body. In the great majority of cases, girl children are the victims of sexual abuse by an adult male. In 1979, of the total reported incidents of maltreatment (physical and emotional abuse and neglect), 11,306 were incidents of sexual maltreatment.[7] Additionally, 96 percent of these reported incidents were perpetrated by someone the child knew, usually a close family member: 55 percent occurred between the child and a natural parent, 39 percent between the child and a foster or stepparent, and nearly 2 percent by another relative (American Humane Association, 1981). These statistics are particularly alarming in view of the fact that they are indicative of *reported* cases only. Children should be encouraged to reveal the identity of the individual who has sexually abused them even though they may have been admonished not to tell anyone. Parents need to be loving and supportive and not make comments such as, "Why did you let him or her do it?" Children are never at fault in such situations: responsibility always rests with the adult molester. The

guilt and shame generated by these experiences can become more devastating than the sexual violation itself.

Parents have many other questions and concerns about their children's emerging sexuality, and, although not all will be detailed here,[8] it is important for the professional to be aware of some of those most commonly and repeatedly expressed.

First and foremost, parents wonder if children should really know "such things." Fearful of "overstimulating" their children and convinced that they are not really appropriate sources of sexual information because they are neither totally comfortable with talking about sex nor "experts," parents abdicate their responsibilities. The clinical psychologist can literally "work miracles" in this respect by providing good, solid factual information. It is a good idea to begin by divesting parents of the two most prevalent myths discussed at the beginning of this chapter. Parents need to understand that today's youth do *not* know everything there is to know about sex and that knowledge is not harmful. One cannot "overstimulate" a child with too much information. If you tell a child more than he or she really wants to know or offer information that is too advanced he or she will simply "tune out" what is perceived as irrelevant: become bored, stop listening, or change the subject. The Child Study Association of America, in its publication, *When Children Ask About Sex* (1974), notes that when children's curiosity is satisfied by providing them with answers to their questions, they demonstrate reduced need to engage in sexual experimentation. Conversely, children who continue to wonder about sexual differences are more likely to indulge in experimentation to satisfy their unanswered queries.

We believe that much can be accomplished in the areas of empathy development and improved family communication through the encouragement of parent-child dialogue about sex and sexuality. For example, the simple recognition during a family therapy session that parents and children have sexual concerns may introduce some change in family consciousness. Family interaction may consequently be expected to alter in some way, and some open discussion around the issue(s) may be advantageously fostered in the therapy sessions. The psychologist may now act as communications facilitator, aiding family members in exploring some of their unspoken assumptions and questions about sexuality. Parents and children often experience a substantial amount of difficulty in accepting each other as sexual beings, with nonacceptance particularly acute at specific stages of the life course. In childhood, masturbation may be an issue fraught with misunderstanding and embarrassment for parents and guilt and shame for the child. In adolescence, the young person may feel confused about the normalcy of physiological and emotional changes accompanying puberty while parents are frequently fearful of what they perceive may be premature sexual involvement for their child. Similarly, as parents themselves age, children may feel that it is no longer "appropriate" for older people (i.e., their own mothers and fathers) to be sexual.

Engaging in sexual communication with children will enhance parents' askability. One of the ways in which comfort can be facilitated in these areas is by learning and *saying* the correct sexual terminology, beginning when the children are infants. This position is convincingly advocated in the recent Rocky Mountain Planned Parenthood (1979) publication, *Starting Early Xperience*, a guide for parents that discusses the "Bathing Baby" routine in which the parents bathe children and simultaneously indicate, "This is your little elbow, the nice little hinge that lets you bend your little arm. This is your little mouth, to eat with, and kiss Mommy with. This is your little penis (if the baby is a boy) to pee with and make love with when you grow up to be a man" (p. 7). Parents (*both* mothers and fathers, ideally) may also talk to children about the opposite sex in this context as well. For example, "Little girls don't have a penis like little boys do. Little girls have a vulva, instead, and a vagina. That's a nice place for the penis to fit when men and women make love, and up inside is the nice, warm place for babies to be started when the man and woman decide they want some" (p. 9).

The point of the foregoing is to maximize parental comfort in educating their children about sex *while the children are still young.* An infant will not understand much of what the parent is conveying, but the establishment of such a foundation of askability—*in infancy*—will enable the parent to engage in more open and effective dialogue with the child when he or she *is* able to understand.

But what about talking with older children? Or what happens if the parent is simply unable to feel at ease talking about sex, despite sincere efforts? The clinical psychologist needs to reassure parents that it is okay to feel uncomfortable, to feel nervous, or even upset or frightened. However, the professional must also convey to parents that these feelings should not paralyze them, prevent them from discussing sexuality with their children. Husband-wife role playing (i.e., where one spouse is the parent and the other the child), and joint "practicing" of correct sexual terminology may be recommended to reduce discomfort to manageable levels.

Also, parents might be encouraged to *admit* their discomfort to their children, saying that their parents never discussed sexuality with them if this was the case. It is amazing how readily many children will respond with reassurance and understanding: "It's OK, Mom (or Dad)."

As regards the parental belief (myth) that one needs to be an "expert" to be an adequate sex educator, the professional is advised to indicate to parents, first, that they *are* experts in many ways: as parents, they already know a great deal. In addition, parents often overestimate what it is that the child really wants to know. Calderone and Johnson (1981) in *The Family Book About Sexuality*—probably the best and most comprehensive book for parents available to date—indicate:

When a child, especially an adolescent, asks a question, it is sometimes most fruitful to use the question as an opener for what may become a long and serious exchange of knowledge, ideas, and attitudes. At other times, it may be better to try to answer a factual question plainly, briefly, and factually, not going beyond the question but not hedging either. When you *tell children what they want to know* (emphasis ours), you open the way to further questions and conversation. (p. 145)

Bernstein (1978) provides parents with sound "clues" as to what their child is *really* asking by discussing the importance of the awareness of the child's *developmental stage.* Before the child is 3, according to Bernstein, he or she is concerned with the actual *physical location* of the baby, with the "geography" of reproduction. From 3 to 7 (approximately), the child's interest extends beyond mere geography (i.e., the awareness that the baby is inside the mother in the uterus, *not* stomach) to the growing awareness that babies are "manufactured." He or she is beginning to attain the capacity to understand that babies have a beginning and that people must take action to start a baby. From about 4 to 8, the child is capable of comprehending that three major ingredients go into making babies—social relationships (love and marriage), sexual intercourse, and union of sperm and ovum—yet is still unable to combine these into a coherent whole. Parents at this stage may function in clearing up the child's misconceptions about how these "ingredients" combine to "manufacture" a baby. Children aged 5–10 are eager for facts: e.g., *how* does the sperm arrive at its destination? This is also a good time for parents to discuss values about sexuality in order to correct lingering inaccuracies in the child's thinking: e.g., by making explicit such beliefs (values) as the love and deep commitment that parents should feel for each other before they decide to have a baby. Children 7–12 hunger for accuracy, for concrete information about sexual processes, and for reassurance from parents that they can ask questions freely. Appropriate topics for discussion at this level include menstruation and nocturnal emissions and the other bodily changes that will accompany maturation. From 10 to 13, the child is able and willing to speculate about *why* sperm and ovum must unite to form new life. Rather complex genetic information can be provided at this stage, with the contributions of the genes from sperm and ovum discussed. Finally, as a child enters adolescence, parents will want to discuss dating and sexual decision making, being honest and clear about their own standards of sexual morality:

Young people are more likely to adopt their parents' values when they understand that those values come from careful consideration of the issue and real concern for their children's growth and happiness, rather than fear and the arbitrary exercise of parental power. Only values which the adolescents have made their own, internalizing their parents' respect for them as self-respect, will have a lasting effect on their actions. (Bernstein, 1978, p. 148)

Parents are particularly concerned at adolescence about providing their children with birth control information and about the issue of premarital sex. Armed with the awareness that knowledge is not harmful and that children who have talked to their parents about sexuality are more likely to delay first intercourse and to have sexual responsibility when they do so, parents should be advised to instruct their children in these areas AND to state their values. For example, there are many valid reasons—medical, moral, and psychological—why a teenager should not have intercourse. Talking about intercourse and contraception does not imply tacit parental approval but rather acknowledges the reality of sexuality. This is why conveying parental values along with factual information is so crucial for the formation of responsible attitudes and behaviors.

Parents may also benefit from an awareness of some of the questions that have been identified as "typical" of particular age groups of children:

Questions most asked by preschoolers.
Will I have breasts (or a penis) like yours?
How did I get into Mommy's stomach?
Why do you have breasts (or a penis) and I don't?
What does the word "fuck" mean?
What is a tampon for?

Does intercourse hurt?
Where do babies come from?
How do babies get out of their Mommy's tummy?
Does it hurt to have a baby?
Questions most asked by preteens.
How does a baby stay alive inside the mother?
What does "have sexual intercourse" mean?
What happens when girls menstruate?
Why do kids say "dirty" words?
What is a wet dream?
Do boys have periods?
Do girls have wet dreams?
When will I develop like my friends?
What are men's balls for?
Why are some children adopted?
What's a rubber (condom) for?
Questions most asked by teens.
Is it normal to masturbate?
Am I masturbating too much?
Do I have homosexual tendencies?
Am I abnormal if I have thoughts involving sex with people I know, even members of my own family?
What is a homosexual?
Are my breasts/penis/vagina too small?
How can you tell if you have VD (STD)?
How can I tell if I'm really in love?
Is there something wrong with me if I remain a virgin?
How can you avoid pregnancy?
How can I say "no?"
How can I tell if I have an orgasm?
Is sexual intercourse painful?
Is oral sex normal?
What about having sex with someone you're not in love with?

The clinical psychologist may well discover that improved communications about sexuality will affect family communication in other areas as well. Indeed, therapeutic interest in sexual issues may constitute only a facet of the overall objectives of therapy. However, a family's difficulty in addressing and discussing sexual concerns is frequently symptomatic of more general communications difficulties, difficulties that may become more readily apparent to family members in the course of dealing with sexuality. Another benefit of exploring sexual matters is the increased sense of comfort and accomplishment that clients may experience as a result of talking about "embarrassing" topics. Parents may leave therapy with the sense that if they can exchange ideas with their children about sex, they can talk to them about anything!

Clinicians are also in an extraordinary position to contribute to research on both the process of sex education (i.e., the provision and acquisition of sexual information) and recommended sexual counseling interventions. We have offered a number of issues in sexuality that the clinical psychologist may expect to encounter in his or her work with parents and children. There is a pronounced void in the research literature regarding how family members change, adjust to, cope with the vicissitudes of sexuality and sexual development over the course of the lifespan. Through the imparting of sexual information ("demythologizing"), and in actual sexual counseling, the psychologist is an integral part of this process of growth and change. For this reason, the field would profit tremendously from data gathered within the clinical setting.

Sex Education Is a Family Experience

Many researchers and other professionals recommend the adoption of a social-learning-theory perspective for a comprehensive understanding of childhood sexual learning.[9] As Roberts (1980c) indicates:

Understanding sexuality involves understanding our feelings and beliefs about masculinity and femininity; it means coming to terms with how we want to express our affection or love for another person; it encompasses our notions about the erotic and our ease with emotional intimacy. Human sexuality is multidimensional, and sexual learning is a lifelong developmental process, not limited to formal, compartmentalized curricula. (p. 262)

Gender role learning has a significant impact upon a child's development of sexual attitudes, values, and behaviors. For example, Adler (1981) reports that "among adolescents, lack of self-esteem and passivity with regard to one's partner appear to play roles in relation to both engaging in intercourse and using contraception" (p. 57) (e.g., Goldsmith et al., 1972; Steinhoff, 1978). Additionally, "several studies that have specifically examined the link between sex roles and contraceptive use provide direct evidence that traditionally 'feminine' women are less effective contraceptors than are women who are less conventional in their sex role orientation (Adler, 1974; Chilman, 1978/1980)" (Adler, 1981, p. 57).

An essential element of the child's gender role learning is parental beliefs about who men and women are and consequently about what their respective roles in society should be. Substantial research documents that children are, from the moment of birth, treated differently by their parents, according to whether they are boy children or girl children. Such differences in treatment, from simple physical handling and parent-to-child verbalizations to the toys boys and girls play with and the manner in which they are either encouraged or discouraged to explore the world around them, convey very strong messages to the child about "appropriate" gender role attitudes and behaviors.

Differential friendship patterns and expressions of emotionality and intimacy are readily identifiable among boys and girls. Not only do the intensity and type of friendships vary with gender, but play styles and the kind of games played differ as well. As Rogers and Strover (1980) note,

Boys' play fosters strategic thinking, skill development, competition, face-to-face confrontation, and the ability to work for team goals; girls' play fosters an indirect style of competition, inexperience with leadership roles and strategizing, and a preference for small groups. In fact, girls more often prefer to be around one good friend, while boys prefer to be in groups. (p. 163)

Lever (1978) has interpreted such differences in play as facilitating empathy skills in girls and competition, organization, and teamwork in boys. Also, as other social scientists have discussed, game playing is actually a form of role rehearsal and reinforces "appropriate" (i.e., traditional) gender role standards.

The Cleveland study again indicates many inconsistencies between parental attitudes and behaviors regarding gender role appropriateness (Roberts et al., 1978). While nearly half of the 1,400 parents interviewed (fathers as well as mothers) believed that men and women should not have different roles in life, many, particularly fathers, were uncertain about the degree to which gender roles could or should be restructured. Some evidence exists that apprehension may cause parents to discourage their sons from forming close and often intimate friendships while they stimultaneously encourage similar ties for their girl children—despite parental desires that their sons be more emotionally expressive:

Feelings of anxiety on the part of parents, teachers, friends, and relatives regarding "male sexuality" may contribute to the discouragement of close intimate friendships between two boys. Such intimate dyadic friendships between boys may trigger fears of either "unmanly behavior" or potential homosexuality. (Roberts, 1980b, p. 8)

In many cases, then, the necessary modeling of non-sex-stereotyped behaviors is simply not occurring.

Parental attitudes about choice of lifestyle and family roles have also been surveyed. While their own, often high, level of commitment to marriage and family does not automatically translate into the belief that their children should follow similar life courses, it is nevertheless difficult for many parents to endorse "options" or "alternatives" (e.g., cohabitation, single parenthood, etc.). With respect to division of labor, the vast majority of all two-parent families report that the wife does all or most of the household chores—again, a strong modeling message to children about appropriate male and female roles.

In general, research indicates that fathers participate minimally in child care and household responsibilities, a situation that could conceivably foster the children's perception that father is less accessible to them in many areas and less askable about sexuality in particular. In contrast, more *equalitarian* homes, households characterized by more equal sharing of tasks and child care responsibilities, are also homes in which the father is more frequently asked about matters related to sexuality by the child.

Paternal attitudes with respect to acceptable sexual behaviors also vary with gender of the child, particularly regarding masturbation and premarital sexual activity. The double standard, while waning in some areas, is nevertheless still operative: these behaviors are consistently viewed as more acceptable for a male child to engage in than for a female child. Even those parents indicating accepting attitudes toward premarital sexual activity for their daughters maintain that a girl should engage in sex "less frequently" in order to protect her "reputation" (Roberts et al., 1978, p. 60). Women's participation in the labor force and more liberal gender role attitudes tend to mitigate such sex role stereotypic convictions to some degree.

The research data again indicate an overwhelming lack of the father's participation in the sex education (learning) process (Inman, 1974; Kirkendall, 1968; Potter & Smith, 1976; Roberts et al., 1978): sexual information conveyed by the father tends to be verbalized in a cautionary or corrective fashion (e.g., admonitions against acting like a "sissy" or "tomboy"). This is exemplary of what Libby and Nass (1971) have described as "proscriptive" rather than "discussion-oriented" communication.

Roberts et al. (1978) discuss several of the reasons why sexuality and the sex education process are perceived to be the woman's responsibility. These are readily identifiable as gender-role-specific rationales, and may be briefly discussed as follows:

1. The mother has traditionally been the primary caretaker of the child. Therefore, more opportunities have existed for the child to pose questions about sexuality within the context of dyadic (mother-child) interaction.

2. The mother has also traditionally been viewed as the more affectionate and emotion-

ally expressive parent, and, therefore, she is likely to be perceived by the child as more approachable (askable) with regard to questions of a sexual nature.

3.   If the father is primarily perceived in the role of disciplinarian by the child, it may be hypothesized that he therefore will be viewed as less approachable about sexual issues.

4.   The "usual" aspects of sexuality discussed pertain specifically to reproduction: a "female" process.

Gender role constraints inhibiting the father from taking a more active role in the sex education of his children are likely to foster an image of the father as "unaskable" in the child's eyes and serve to perpetuate the dichotomy of the entire area of sexuality as discrete men's and women's issues.

We agree with Ross' (1979) contention that "The social, emotional and sexual development of sons and daughters should command equal interest, attention and concern from both father and mother" (p. 13). Specifically, our position is that a child's sexual questions should be answered by the parent who is present; there is no reason why sexual discussion must be restricted to same sex parent-child interaction. We also concur with Uslander, Weiss, and Telman (1977), who maintain that:

In order to fully appreciate his or her own sexuality, a child should be able to approach either or both parents for sex information whenever necessary, because each parent has much to contribute in preparing a child for adult relationships with the other sex. Sex education, then, becomes an integral part of education toward family living, helping in the development of understanding and appreciation of individual family roles. (p. 47)

In addition, we advocate inclusion of brothers and sisters in the process, as the older siblings especially often serve as complementary sources of sexual information. In this context, sex education is truly a family experience.

RECOMMENDATIONS

We would like to conclude by suggesting several general principles for psychologists to adopt in their communications with parents about sexuality. They form a sound starting point from which to begin the facilitation of the parent-child sex education process:

1.   Compile a listing of parent-serving agencies in your community for further referral. Agencies and other helping professionals often offer many worthwhile workshops and seminars for parents that provide both solid factual information (e.g., parenting skills) and support groups for mothers and fathers.

2.   Compile a recommended reading list that includes general parenting information and information specifically pertaining to sexuality and the role of parents as sex educators. Include names and addresses of additional sources of information. See the list at the end of this chapter.

3.   Leave booklets, leaflets, and other readings on sex education in your waiting-room.

4.   When talking to parents, do not use much jargon. Adopt a straightforward, non-condescending approach.

5.   Listen to what the parent is saying and to what he or she is *not* saying. Bear in mind that discomfort in discussing sexual issues can extend beyond the familial context to impede communication with a professional as well. Empathy is crucial.

6.   Do not hesitate to "demythologize" false beliefs about the effects of sex education or notions that parents need to be expert or totally comfortable in order to communicate with their children.

7.   Give parents "permission" to impart their values about sexual issues to their children—along with the facts.

8.   Gallup and other pollsters indicate that parents and communities would support professionals in the role of sex educators. Clinical psychologists are in a special position to work effectively with parents and children in this regard. The clinician's positive role modeling, provision of sound information,

and empathy will serve to generally facilitate all aspects of the sex education process.

9.   Psychologists might also serve as leaders in sex education programs for parents as well as in the actual training of social service and mental health professionals.[10]

10.   Support and help organize the numerous programs created annually in observance of National Family Sexuality Education Week, held early in October each year.[11]

APPENDIX

A Selected Bibliography for Professionals

A Personal Library

Blum, G., & Blum, B. *Feeling good about yourself.* Available from Feeling Good Associates, 507 Palma Way, Mill Valley, CA 94941, 1981.

Briggs, D. *Your child's self-esteem.* New York: Dolphin, 1975.

Calderone, M.S., & Johnson, E.W. *The family book about sexuality.* New York: Harper & Row, 1981.

Carrera, M.A. *Sex: The facts, the act and your feelings.* New York: Crown, 1981.

Gordon, S., Scales, P., & Everly, K. *The sexual adolescent* (2nd ed.). North Scituate, Mass.: Duxbury Press, 1979.

Haeberle, E.J. *The sex atlas.* New York: Seabury, 1978.

Kosnick, A., Carroll, W., Cunningham, A., Modras, R., & Schulte, J. *Human sexuality: New directions in American Catholic thought.* New York: Paulist Press, 1977.

Marmor, J. (Ed.). *Homosexual behavior: A modern reappraisal.* New York: Basic Books, 1980.

Nass, G.D., Libby, R., & Fisher, M.P. *Sexual choices.* Belmont, Calif.: Wadsworth, 1981.

Nelson, J.B. *Embodiment: An approach to sexuality and Christian theology.* Minneapolis: Augsburg Publishing House, 1978.

Pocs, O. (Ed.). *Human sexuality 81/82.* (Annual edition). Guilford: Dushkin, 1981.

Talese, G. *Thy neighbor's wife.* New York: Dell, 1980.

Coping with the Opposition

Dickman, I.R. *Winning the battle for sex education.* New York: SIECUS, 1982.

Children under 7—(Books for professionals to suggest to parents to read to, or with, their children and to use in the classroom. Recommended for school libraries.)

Andry, A.C., & Schepp, S. *How babies are made.* New York: Time-Life, 1974.

Gordon, S., & Gordon, J. *Did the sun shine before you were born?* (2nd ed.). Fayetteville, N.Y.: Ed-U Press, 1979.

Knudsen, P.H. *The true story of how babies are made.* Chicago: Children's Press, 1973.

Stein, S.B. *Making babies: An open family book.* New York: Walker, 1974.

Children 7–11

Gordon, S. *Girls are girls and boys are boys—So what's the difference?* (2nd ed.). Fayetteville, N.Y.: Ed-U Press, 1979.

Gruenberg, S.M. *The wonderful story of how you were born.* New York: Doubleday, 1973.

Levine, M.I., & Seligman, H.J. *A baby is born.* New York: Golden Press, 1978.

Rushnell, E.E. *My mom's having a baby.* New York: Grosset & Dunlap, 1978.

Adolescents and Young Adults

Bell, R., et al. *Changing bodies, changing lives. A book for teens on sex and relationships.* New York: Random House, 1980.

Gardner-Loulan, J.A., Lopez, B., & Quackenbush, M. *Period—A book about menstruation.* San Francisco: New Glide, 1979.

Gordon, S. *Facts about sex for today's youth* (Rev. ed.). Fayetteville, N.Y.: Ed-U Press, 1983.

Gordon, S. *Facts about VD for today's youth* (Rev. ed.). Fayetteville, N.Y.: Ed-U Press, 1979.

Gordon, S. *The teenage survival book* (formerly entitled *YOU*). New York: Times Books, 1981.

Gordon, S. *You would if you loved me.* New York: Bantam, 1978.

Hamilton, E. *Sex, with love. A guide for young people.* Boston: Beacon, 1978.

Johnson, E.W. *Love and sex in plain language* (3rd rev. ed.). Philadelphia: Lippincott, 1977.

Johnson, E.W. *Sex: Telling it straight* (Rev. ed.). New York: Bantam, 1979.

Johnson, C.B., & Johnson, E.W. *Love and sex and growing up* (Rev. ed.). New York: Bantam, 1979.

Kelly, G. *Learning about sex: A contemporary guide for young adults.* New York: Barron's Educational Services, 1977.

Mayle, P. What's happening to me? Secaucus, N.J.: Stuart, 1975.

Pomeroy, W.B. *Boys and sex.* (2nd rev. ed.) New York: Delacorte, 1981.

Pomeroy, W.B. *Girls and sex.* (2nd rev. ed.) New York: Delacorte, 1981.

Pamphlets

National Education Association (NEA) catalogue of publications and audiovisual materials. Available from NEA Distribution Center, The Academic Building, Saw Mill Road, West Haven, CT 06516.

NEA and the American Medical Association (AMA) five-part sex education series. Developed by Marion O. Lerrigo & Helen Southard. It may be ordered from either the NEA, 1201 16th St., N.W., Washington, D.C. 20036 or the AMA, 535 North Dearborn St., Chicago, IL 60610:

Parents' responsibility.

A story about you. For children in Grades 4, 5, & 6.

Finding yourself. For junior high students.

Approaching adulthood. For youth 15–20.

Facts aren't enough. For adults with responsibilities for children and youth.

Especially for Parents

Gochros, J.S. *What to say after you clear your throat. A parents guide to sex education.* Kailua, Hawaii: Press Pacifica, 1980.

Gordon, S., & Dickman, I.R. *Sex education: The parent's role.* (Pamphlet no. 549). New York: Public Affairs Committee, 1977.

Lewis, H.R., & Lewis, M.E. *The parent's guide to teenage sex and pregnancy.* New York: St. Martin's Press, 1980.

Lyman, M. *Sex education at home—A guide for parents.* Available from Planned Parenthood of Syracuse, Inc., 1120 E. Genesee St., Syracuse, N.Y. 13210.

Pogrebin, L.C. *Growing up free: Raising your child in the 80s.* New York: McGraw-Hill, 1980.

Rocky Mountain Planned Parenthood. *Starting Early Xperience.* 1979. Available from Rocky Mountain Planned Parenthood Publications, 1852 Vine St., Denver, CO 80206.

Ross, S.S. *What is sex-education all about? A guide for parents.* Chicago: Adams Press, 1979.

Uslander, A.S., Weiss, C., & Telman, J. *Sex education for today's child. A guide for modern parents.* New York: Association Press, 1977.

Sources for Additional Information

Alan Guttmacher Institute, 360 Park Avenue South, New York, N.Y. 10010.

American Association of Sex Educators, Counselors and Therapists, 2000 N. St., N.W., Suite 110, Washington, D.C. 20036.

Institute for Family Research and Education, 760 Ostrom Avenue, Syracuse, N.Y. 13210.

National Clearinghouse for Family Planning Information, PO Box 2225, Rockville, MD 20852.

Planned Parenthood Federation of America, Inc., 810 Seventh Avenue, New York, N.Y. 10019.

Sex Information and Education Council of the United States, 80 Fifth Avenue, New York, N.Y. 10011.

Sex education and the library: A basic bibliography for the general public with special resources for the librarian. Compiled by Sol Gordon and available from the ERIC Clearinghouse on Information Resources, Syracuse University, School of Education, Syracuse, N.Y. 13210.

Distributors

Ed-U Press, Inc., Box 583, Fayetteville, N.Y. 13066. Sex education books, pamphlets, and audiovisuals.

Perennial Education, Inc., 477 Roger Williams, P.O. Box 855 Ravinia, Highland Park, IL 60035. Sex education films and filmstrips.

NOTES

1. S. 1090. Signed into law, 1981.
2. Moreover, 70 percent of 17–21-year-old young men reported having had sexual intercourse prior to marriage for the year 1979: 83 percent of those ever married and 69 percent

of those never married (Zelnik and Kantner, 1980, pp. 231–233).

3. Professionals in particular will find the latest Alan Guttmacher Institute publication, *Teen Pregnancy: The Problem that Hasn't Gone Away* (New York: Planned Parenthood Federation of America, 1981), to be a valuable resource.

4. "American Families—1980," a public opinion poll of nearly 1,600 adults nationwide conducted by the Gallup Organization for The White House Conference on Families, revealed that 87 percent of those surveyed support public school instruction in marriage and family life, 79 percent support school sex education with parental permission, and 34 percent support sex education even *without* parental consent.

5. Excellent reading materials for parents and children in the areas of sexuality and sex education are contained in the authors' recommended reading list at the end of this chapter.

6. As detailed in the book for teenagers, *You Would If You Loved Me,* by Sol Gordon. Copyright © 1978 by Bantam Books, New York. The book also lists seductive "lines" boys use to obtain sex from girls, along with possible responses.

7. Although 296, 321 reports were filed, a full 114, 172 either did not respond at all to the item on sexual maltreatment or responded that incidence was unknown. American Humane Association, 1981.

8. For a thorough discussion and treatment of specific issues parents raise, refer to *Sex Education: The Parent's Role* (1977) by Sol Gordon and Irving R. Dickman. See also *Let's Make Sex a Household Word,* by Sol Gordon (New York: John Day, 1975).

9. See *Childhood Sexual Learning: The Unwritten Curriculum,* edited by E. Roberts. Cambridge, Mass.: Ballinger, 1980. (a)

10. Refer to *Community Family Life Education Programs for Parents—A Training Manual for Organizers,* by the Institute for Family Research and Education. Available from Ed-U Press, PO Box 583, Fayetteville, N.Y. 13066.

11. See the *Guidebook for National Family Sexuality Education Week,* published jointly by the Department of Education, Planned Parenthood Federation of America, Inc., and the Institute for Family Research and Education. Available from PPFA, 810 Seventh Avenue, New York, N.Y. 10019.

REFERENCES

Abelson, H., Cohen, R., Heaton, E., & Slider, C. Public attitudes toward and experience with erotic materials. In U.S. Commission on Obscenity and Pornography, *Technical Reports of the Commission.* Washington, D.C.: U.S. Government Printing Office, 1970, **6**.

Adler, N.E. *Factors affecting contraceptive use.* Paper presented at the 82nd annual convention of the American Psychological Association, New Orleans, September, 1974.

Adler, N.E. Sex roles and unwanted pregnancy in adolescent and adult women. *Professional Psychology,* 1981, **12**(1), 56–66.

Alan Guttmacher Institute. *Teenage pregnancy: The problem that hasn't gone away.* New York: Planned Parenthood Federation of America, 1981.

American Families—1980: A summary of findings. Princeton, N.J.: Gallup Organization, 1980.

American Humane Association. *National analysis of official child neglect and abuse reporting (1979).* Denver: American Humane Association, 1981.

Bernstein, A. *The flight of the stork.* New York: Delacorte, 1978.

Calderone, M.S., & Johnson, E.W. *The family book about sexuality.* New York: Harper & Row, 1981.

Child Study Association of America. *When children ask about sex* (Rev. ed.). New York: Child Study Press, 1974.

Chilman, C.S. *Adolescent sexuality in a changing American society* (NIH Publication No. 80–1426). Washington, D.C. U.S. Department of Health, Education and Welfare, 1980. (Originally published, 1978.)

Comstock, G. Television's four highly attracted audiences. *New York University Education Quarterly,* 1978, **10**(2), 23–28.

Farrell, C. (with Kellaher, L.). *My mother said... The way young people learned about sex and birth control.* Boston: Routledge & Kegan Paul, 1978.

Fox, G.L., & Inazu, J.K. *Talking about sex: Patterns of mother-daughter communication.* Paper presented at the annual meeting of the Michigan Sociological Association, Detroit, November, 1978.

Goldfarb, J.L., Mumford, D.M., Schum, D.A., Smith, P.B., Howers, C., & Schum, C. An attempt to detect 'pregnancy susceptibility' in indigent adolescent girls. *Journal of Youth and Adolescence,* 1977, **6**(2), 127–144.

Goldsmith, S., Gabrielson, M., Gabrielson, I., Mathews, V., & Potts, L. Teenagers, sex and contraception. *Family Planning Perspectives,* 1972, **4**(11), 32–38.

Gordon, S. *Let's make sex a household word.* New York: Day, 1975 (out of print; available in libraries).

Gordon, S., & Dickman, I.R. *Sex education: The parent's role* (Pamphlet no. 549). New York: Public Affairs Committee, 1977.

Gordon, S., Scales, P., & Everly, K. *The sexual adolescent* (2nd ed.). North Scituate, Mass.: Duxbury, 1979.

Himmelweit, H.T., & Bell, N. Television as a sphere of influence on the child's learning about sexuality. In E.J. Roberts (Ed.), *Childhood sexual learning: The unwritten curriculum.* Cambridge, Mass.: Ballinger, 1980.

Inman, M. What teenagers want in sex education. *American Journal of Nursing,* October 1974, 1866–1867.

Institute for Family Research and Education. *Community family life education programs for parents.* Fayetteville, N.Y.: Ed-U Press, 1977.

Institute for Family Research and Education. *Human sexuality survey.* Unpublished research, 1976–1982. Institute for Family Research and Education, 760 Ostrom Avenue, Syracuse, N.Y. 13210.

Jessor, S.L., & Jessor, R. Transition from virginity to nonvirginity among youth: A social-psychological study over time. *Developmental Psychology,* 1975, **11**(4), 473–484.

Kirby, D., Alter, J., & Scales, P. *An analysis of U.S. sex education programs* (Vol. I). Center for Disease Control Report No. CDC–2021–79–DK–FR. Atlanta: Center for Disease Control, July 1979.

Kirkendall, L.A. How premarital sex may hurt girls. In I. Rubin & L.A. Kirkendall (Eds.), *Sex in the adolescent years.* New York: Association Press, 1968.

Lever, J. Sex differences in the complexity of children's play. *American Sociological Review,* 1978, **43**, 471–482.

Lewis, H.R., & Lewis, M.E. *The parents' guide to teenage sex and pregnancy.* New York: St. Martin's Press, 1980.

Lewis, R.A. Parents and peers: Socialization agents in the coital behavior of young adults. *Journal of Sex Research,* 1973, **9**(2), 156–170.

Libby, R.W., & Nass, G. Parental views on teenage sexual behavior. *Journal of Sex Research,* 1971, **7**, 226–237.

Miller, W.B. Sexual and contraceptive behavior of young unmarried women. *Primary Care,* 1976, **4**, 427–453.

Norris, M. From the publisher…Let's get it straight. *Sex Education and Mental Health Report,* Winter 1980.

Passmore, J. Sex education. *The New Republic,* October 1980, pp. 27–32.

Planned Parenthood Federation of America, Inc. *Guidebook for National Family Sexuality Education Week Oct. 5–11.* New York: Planned Parenthood, 1981.

Potter, S.J., & Smith, H.L. Sex education as viewed by teenage unwed mothers. *Intellect,* April 1976, 515–516.

Roberts, E.J. (Ed.). *Childhood sexual learning: The unwritten curriculum.* Cambridge, Mass.: Ballinger, 1980. (a)

Roberts, E.J. Dimensions of sexual learning in childhood. In E.J. Roberts (Ed.), *Childhood sexual learning: The unwritten curriculum.* Cambridge, Mass.: Ballinger, 1980. (b)

Roberts, E.J. Sexuality and social policy: The unwritten curriculum. In E.J. Roberts (Ed.), *Childhood sexual learning: The unwritten curriculum.* Cambridge, Mass.: Ballinger, 1980. (c)

Roberts, E.J., Kline, D., & Gagnon, J. *Family life and sexual learning: A study of the role of parents in the sexual learning of children* (Vol. I). Cambridge, Mass.: Population Education, October 1978 (Summary Report).

Rocky Mountain Planned Parenthood. *Starting Early Xperience.* Denver: Rocky Mountain Planned Parenthood Publication, 1979.

Rogers, E.M., & Strover, S.L. Peer communication and sexuality. In E.J. Roberts (Ed.),

Childhood sexual learning: The unwritten curriculum. Cambridge, Mass.: Ballinger, 1980.

Ross, S.S. *What is sex education all about?* Chicago: Adams Press, 1979.

Rothenberg, P.B. *Mother-child communication about sex and birth control.* Paper presented at the annual meetings of the Population Association of America, Atlanta, April, 1978.

Rubenstein, J.S., Watson, F.G., & Rubenstein, H.S. An analysis of sex education books for adolescents by means of adolescents' sexual interests. *Adolescence,* 1977, **12,** 293–311.

Rubin, I., & Calderwood, D. *A family guide to sex.* New York: New American Library, 1973.

Scales, P.C. A quasi-experimental evaluation of sex education programs for parents (Doctoral dissertation, Syracuse University, 1976). *Dissertation Abstracts International,* 1976, **37** (11), 7352A. (University Microfilms No. DCJ77-09903)

Scales, P., & Everly, K. A community sex education for parents. *Family Coordinator,* 1977, **26,** 37–45.

Schofield, M. *The sexual behavior of young people.* Boston: Little, Brown, 1965.

Schofield, M. *The sexual behavior of young adults.* London: Allen Lane, 1973.

Shah, F., Zelnik, M., & Kantner, J.F. Unprotected intercourse among unwed teenagers. *Family Planning Perspectives,* 1975, 7(1), 39–44.

Shocking story on sex ed teacher training. *Sex Education and Mental Health Report,* Winter 1980.

Sorensen, R.C. *Adolescent sexuality in contemporary America.* New York: World, 1973.

Steinhoff, P.G. Premarital pregnancy and the first birth. In W.B. Miller & L.F. Newman (Eds.), *The first child and family formation.* Chapel Hill, N.C.: Carolina Population Center, 1978.

Szasz, T. *Sex by prescription.* New York: Anchor Press/Doubleday, 1980.

U.S. Commission on Obscenity and Pornography. *Technical report of the commission* (Vol. VI). Washington, D.C.: U.S. Government Printing Office, 1970.

Uslander, A., Weiss, C., & Telman, J. *Sex education for today's child.* New York: Association Press, 1977.

Willke, J.C., & Willke, Mrs. *Sex education—in the classroom?.* Cincinnati, Oh.: 1978.

World Health Organization. *Education and treatment in human sexuality: The training of health professionals* (Technical Report No. 572). Washington, D.C.: WHO Publications, 1975.

Zelnik, M., & Kantner, J.F. Sexuality, contraception and pregnancy among young unwed females in the U.S. In C.F. Westoff & R. Parke, Jr. (Eds.), *Demographic and social aspects of population growth* (Vol. I). (Commission on Population Growth and the American Future Research Reports). Washington, D.C.: U.S. Government Printing Office, 1972.

Zelnik, M., & Kantner, J.F. Sexual activity, contraceptive use and pregnancy among metropolitan-area teenagers: 1971-1979. *Family Planning Perspectives,* 1980, **12**(5): 230–237.

CHAPTER 50

Prevention of Disorders in Children

LIZETTE PETERSON AND ROBYN RIDLEY-JOHNSON

The concept of prevention is not new to psychology. Since the 1920s, the popularity of prevention and community intervention has waxed and waned (Lamb & Zusman, 1979) and an orientation toward prevention rather than remediation of disorders has intermittently been urged (e.g., Caplan, 1964; Klein & Goldston, 1977). In the last five years, psychologists have demonstrated an actively renewed interest in the concept of prevention. This interest has resulted in a burgeoning of prevention research, in the use of "prevention" as an index term for *Psychological Abstracts* (begun in 1973), and in the formation of new journals such as the *Journal of Prevention* and *Prevention,* dedicated to the dissemination of information on prevention. This new emphasis on prevention has not occurred in isolation but has been accompanied by psychologists' increasing involvement with communitywide intervention and with cross-disciplinary interests involving psychology, medicine, and law.

If past behavior is an accurate predictor of future behavior in the case of prevention research, the current enthusiasm for prevention, especially prevention in children, should yield a large proportion of discursive articles and a smaller overall proportion of actual empirical reports on prevention, followed by a general disappointment in the results and a turning away from future preventive attempts. Currently, there are many more advocates for prevention than there are investigators of prevention (Cowen, 1973). However, because current psychological techniques such as behavior therapy may result in improvements in prevention over more traditional methods of psychotherapy (Peterson, Hartmann, & Gelfand, 1980) and because joint involvement in other disciplines may extend the parameters of prevention in psychology (Stachnik, 1980), there is reason to hope that current interest in prevention may be matched by innovative, empirical demonstrations of prevention. The literature reviewed here should thus best be regarded with cautious optimism. Prevention in many areas currently under investigation by psychologists has yet to be demonstrated to be successful, feasible, and cost effective. However, if reasonable expectations concerning what prevention *might* do are maintained and empirical demonstrations of what prevention *can* do are continued in line with the research reviewed here, the hopes of the cautious optimist may be rewarded.

Many mental health workers regard prevention as vitally important, exceeded in importance only by the need for better child therapy programs (Lamb & Zusman, 1979). The areas of child therapy and of prevention would seem to be closely related. If a disorder is to be prevented entirely or damage from a disorder minimized, the ideal target population would seem to be young individuals who have not yet experienced severe damage from those threats they have contacted. In fact, the largest recent increase in preventive research may have been with children. So many areas of threats to children's physical and mental health have been addressed by recent research that compiling a comprehensive review of prevention and treatment programs for children is prohibitive if not impossible. This discussion will instead describe illustrations of prevention attempts in several areas, some traditionally identified as within the domain of the psychologist (such as screening children for early signs of learning problems), some more traditionally considered in other domains (such as increasing immunization levels in children).

Specifically, threats to children's physical health as well as their psychological well being will be considered here as appropriate for psychological research. Many physicians acknowledge that future improvements in general health will not come from improvements in medical technology but will instead be a function of changes in habitual lifestyles (e.g., Knowles, 1977). The most serious threats to physical health in this country are actually lifestyle behavior problems. Alleviation of these problems can be achieved through behavior changes (Matarazzo, 1980), changes perhaps most important to children who have not yet acquired health-threatening habits (Stachnik, 1980) and who may not yet have acquired positive health habits like physical exercise (Folkins & Sime, 1981). Furthermore, many threats to children's health are outside of the realm of medical intervention. Home accidents involving children are a major health hazard (e.g., Pearn et al., 1979) and industry has created many devices for child safety, including items such as child safety caps and child seat belts (e.g., Allen & Bergman, 1976). The appropriate use of these items requires behavioral changes in the children's caretakers, and, to a large extent, these changes have not been forthcoming (e.g., Christophersen & Rapoff, 1980). Interventions for children that depend on successful behavior changes to avoid or reduce negative influences on their psychological or physical well being may most appropriately be undertaken by psychologists trained in methods of behavior change.

Such attempts at behavior change may occur at a variety of levels. Caplan (1964) described three levels of prevention, including primary, secondary, and tertiary prevention. Primary prevention refers to preventing a disorder before it occurs, secondary prevention refers to minimizing the impact of a disorder by early detection and treatment, and

tertiary prevention involves preventing long term disability resulting from a disorder. It should be noted that prevention may take place on a variety of levels and depending on the immediate goal of treatment, may constitute either primary, secondary, or tertiary prevention. Take, for example, problems with children's reading. A program organized to deal with possible deficits before any reading handicap appears might deal with preschool children who have not experienced problems but who are at risk for later reading handicaps. This would constitute primary prevention. A program oriented toward identifying children showing the first signs of reading difficulty and correcting these problems before the child falls behind in his or her studies would be regarded as secondary prevention. Finally, a program focused on remedying serious reading difficulties already experienced in order to prevent further academic deficits would exemplify tertiary prevention. Thus the difference between primary, secondary, and tertiary prevention is determined by the goal of intervention and is more than a semantic distinction. However, tertiary prevention is most often regarded as remediation or treatment rather than prevention per se. Most research that purports to offer preventive interventions has either primary or secondary prevention as a goal. This discussion, while recognizing the possible overlap in the two terms, will first describe attempts at primary prevention in children and will then discuss areas of secondary prevention. Finally, conclusions and suggestions for future intervention will be advanced.

PRIMARY PREVENTION

Threats to Physical Well Being

Primary prevention of threats to children's health may be conceptualized as utilizing one of three kinds of interventions. First, prevention may involve avoiding contact with the health-threatening stimulus, second, modifying contact to reduce the threat, and third, increasing contact with stimuli that reduce threat.

In the first case, prevention involves avoiding the onset of health-threatening behaviors such as smoking, drinking, and drug abuse. Despite warnings concerning the ill effects of cigarette smoking, over 3,000 youngsters start smoking per day (Garell, 1976). Since research with adults suggests that therapeutic interventions to help individuals stop smoking have been largely unsuccessful (McFall, 1978), this would seem to be an important area for prevention. Evans (1976) described a longitudinal program in which videotaped presentations were used to model how pressures to smoke from peers, parents who smoke, and media can be successfully overcome. Prompts in the form of posters representing scenes from the videotapes were displayed in the classroom. Early findings suggest that this program has some promise in preventing smoking (Evans, 1978). Workshops focusing on increasing assertive responses to resist peer pressure to smoke and allowing students to role play difficult behavioral sequences also has reduced the number of children who begin smoking (Spitzzeri & Jason, 1979).

Similar projects are suggested for prevention of alcohol abuse, as children are drinking at progressively younger ages and alcohol abuse continues to be a national health problem (Lee, 1976). However, although many states have mandated education about alcohol abuse in elementary school, few attempts have been made to evaluate the success of these programs. Indeed, projects aimed at the reduction of both alcohol and drug abuse have rarely been evaluated (Richards, 1971), and, when evaluations have been done, the results of those studies have been contradictory (Berberian et al., 1976). In one well-controlled study, Stuart (1974) examined the utility of a 10-session drug education program run by either a student or a teacher. As compared with no treatment controls, subjects receiving drug education showed significant *increases* in the reported use of alcohol, marijuana, and LSD, as well as reported increases in selling these substances. While it is possible that the increased leader contact in the experimental groups resulted in simply more accurate reporting than in the control group, these results

are very disquieting. More typical findings from such studies have either not examined actual drug use or have found no decrease in drug use (e.g., Lewis, Gossett, & Phillips, 1972; Swisher, Warner, & Herr, 1972). Programs utilizing group therapy (Coleman, S.B., 1978) or focusing on parents as therapeutic agents for their children (e.g., Thomas, Friscone, & Lipson, 1971) have reported similar results. Finally, those studies that report successful prevention of drug use in the majority of children treated have typically relied entirely on self-reported intentions for use (e.g., McCune, 1970). Berberian et al. (1976) argued cogently that no drug education or drug prevention program should be utilized without detailed evaluation of both short and long term results. Thus, while some psychological techniques such as role playing and problem solving might be useful for preventing alcohol and drug abuse in children and adolescents, there is little empirical evidence to support the use of past programs at this time and some evidence to militate against their use.

Similar problems have been reported from sex education programs aimed at young adolescents. In light of the growing rates of adolescent pregnancy, some professionals (e.g., McAnarney, 1978) have opted to provide information on family planning and contraception to adolescents, thereby reducing the risk of pregnancy rather than attempting to alter sexual behavior (e.g., Gordis et al., 1970). This is an example of the previously mentioned tactic of modifying rather than preventing contact with the threat. Recently, Litt, Cuskey, and Rudd (1980) described a variety of characteristics of adolescent noncompliers to contraception and suggested that pediatricians should identify and provide special help to these individuals. However, few studies concerning a method for providing this special help in improving compliance to contraception have been reported. This is, then, another area in which the use of psychological techniques such as problem solving or interpersonal skill training would seem to have some promise (Schinke & Gilchrist, 1977), but more data are needed before definitive conclusions as to their effectiveness can be made. Further discussion of these problems is presented by Gordon and Untener in chapter 49 of this book.

Finally, there are a variety of disorders in which the prevention program may entirely avoid physical illness or trauma by increasing contact with procedures that can remove or reduce the threat to the child. Using alternatives to lead-based paints (Hunt, 1978), using toothbrushes and mouthwash to prevent dental disease (Kegeles, Lund, & Weisenberg, 1978), checking cribs for safety (Smialek, Smialek, & Spitz, 1977), teaching children self-protection behaviors toward potential child molesters (Poche, Brouwer, & Swearingen, 1981), and preventing bathtub drownings by adequate supervision (Pearn et al., 1979) are examples of such behaviors. Limited success has been noted by prevention programs that have attempted to increase parental compliance to immunization schedules for prevention of childhood diseases such as diphtheria, polio, rubella, measles, and mumps. Some states have achieved success in immunizing school age children by legally mandating immunization prior to school entry (Roberts, 1981). However, such programs do not affect the children who may be most at risk for preventable childhood diseases—preschool children (Marcuse, 1975). Peterson (1981) noted that while public service media announcements had relatively little impact on children's immunization status, direct experimenter contact with the children's caretakers did result in increased immunization obtaining for high risk preschoolers. In this study, prompts were delivered either by mail or by telephone contact. No impact on parents' behavior was noted for written prompts, but telephone contact resulted in substantial increases in parents' seeking out immunizations for their children. Yokley et al. (1980) similarly reported that the use of written prompts alone had little impact on parents' behavior but the use of written prompts plus a reinforcer (the opportunity to earn a lottery ticket) resulted in significant increases in children's immunizations. Finally, Minear and Guyer (1979) noted that contact at home by a nurse was

effective in increasing immunization obtaining although the cost of such contact was relatively high, with a 32 percent improvement in immunization in children from a neighborhood clinic at a cost of $2,460. Combinations of the techniques described above may produce further improvements in cost effective ways to promote immunization obtaining in both high risk and communitywide prevention programs.

The use of prompts and reinforcements has also been demonstrated to influence the use of automobile infant restraint devices, which may prevent the leading cause of death among preadolescent children—highway deaths (Shelness & Charles, 1975). Allen and Bergman (1976), for example, reported that families receiving information about infant restraint devices either in the form of written or filmed informational prompts reported increased purchases and use of infant restraint devices. The use of written instructions alone has also shown some success in encouraging parents to employ carseats for children (Christophersen & Rapoff, 1980). The promise that behavioral technology has to offer for prevention of physical illness and injury in children has just begun to be realized. The possibilities for future investigation are extensive and include any physical disorder that might be avoided by behavior change, either in the child or the child's caretaker.

Threats to Psychological Well Being

Traditionally, the psychologist's involvement with children has been solely as a treatment agent, and the psychologist has been charged with altering behavior and emotional problems in the child upon referral by a concerned parent, teacher, or physician. In a later section of this discussion, advances in early problem recognition and reporting by parents and by other professionals will be described. The present discussion will focus on the role of the psychologist in providing psychological interventions that may enable parents and other child care agents to prevent rather than to recognize and subsequently ameliorate child problems. Many of the tools that may be used to effect such primary prevention will be familiar techniques originally developed for remediation of child problems (Gelfand, 1977). Other techniques that emphasize initially training appropriate child behaviors may avoid later problems through early increases in adaptive responding.

Primary Prevention and the Parent

There is a variety of parenting techniques that show promise for successful primary prevention. For example, methods for toilet training (Azrin & Foxx, 1974), dealing with bedtime problems and temper tantrums (Rainey & Christopher, 1976), and correcting inappropriate mealtime behavior (McMahon & Forehand, 1978) may avoid serious problems in these areas in the future. Clark et al. (1977) outlined areas in which parents commonly report experiencing problems with their children and described a treatment plan for children in one selected problem area. Taking a child shopping is described as a common source of negative child-parent interactions. Clark et al. (1977) reported using a contingency management approach with children, whereby the parents explained some basic rules (e.g., no demanding that parents buy something, no running through the store) and child adherence to the rules was reinforced with portions of the child's financial allowance. Such an approach resulted in diminished negative child behaviors and concomitant negative parental-child interactions. Barnard, Christophersen, and Wolf (1977) demonstrated similar success with this problem behavior. Such a training approach could be used effectively in any area in which problematic parent-child interactions were routinely noted, such as during long automobile trips, rainy afternoons with many children in close quarters, and preparation for bath or bedtime. Furthermore, such training could be instituted prior to the occurrence of problematic responding.

Special help may be given to both children and parents when the parental relationship is altered by separation and divorce (Felner, Farber, & Primavera, 1980). Specific parental interventions directed toward eliminating in-creased depression and fear (Kelly & Wallerstein, 1976) and aggression (Hetherington, Cox, & Cox, 1978) may be routinely planned for children whose parents are divorcing. The Children of Divorce Project (Wallerstein & Kelly, 1977) may offer such help although this program of time-limited psychotherapy and parental training has not been systematically evaluated.

A number of parent-training techniques suitable for both separated and intact parents have been combined into formal treatment packages that attempt to train parents to use such techniques as contingency management and contract negotiation with their children (e.g., Mash, Handy, & Hamerlynck, 1976). Some of these programs are now available in commercial training manuals (e.g., Barker, Heifetz, & Brightman, 1972; McMahon & Forehand, 1979; Patterson et al., 1975) that may provide low cost preventive intervention to families. Although the efficacy of the sole use of such manuals has not been demonstrated, written instruction in combination with minimal therapist contact may be a promising avenue for future parental training (Glasgow & Rosen, 1978).

Some researchers have suggested that the consequence of adequately preparing parents to deal with their child's behavior problems may ultimately be the prevention of the most tragic outcome of parental inadequacy—child abuse (Davidson, 1977). Most of the research that has been directed toward preventing child abuse has utilized secondary prevention through early identification of abused children; this research will be discussed later. There have been some attempts, however, to outline variables that might make the primary prevention of child abuse possible. While it has been customary to attempt to locate the cause for abuse in the abusing parent (e.g., Spinetta & Rigler, 1972), many studies suggest that abusing parents may be indistinguishable from any randomly selected group of parents (e.g., Kempe & Helfer, 1972; Steele & Pollock, 1974). It may be more fruitful to identify high risk children by isolating characteristics of the child that may provoke abuse. Some researchers have found a large proportion of abused children to be of low birth weight (e.g., Fomufod, Sinkford, & Lony, 1975), to have an IQ of less than 80 (e.g., Elmer, 1967), and to have particularly "irritating" behavioral characteristics such as tantrums and shrill and continuous crying (e.g., Friedrich & Boriskin, 1978). Early identification of such children might lead to special visits from health care agents, enrollment in daycare programs, and early intervention from psychologists and physicians (Friedrich & Boriskin, 1978). Even earlier intervention by promoting community-oriented, family-centered childbirth may ultimately be the answer for at-risk children and their families (Garbarino, 1980a).

The early identification of faulty parent-child interactions might also serve as impetus for prevention (Garbarino, 1980b). For example, Leiderman (1974) notes that mothers of premature infants are more likely to have negative or hostile feelings about their babies than mothers of full term infants. Leiderman has subsequently developed a screening device to measure maternal attitudes that may later lead to abuse or neglect. Monitoring visits to the hospital nursery may also prove useful; Fanaroff, Kennell, and Klaus (1972) found that nearly 25 percent of the mothers who visited their infants less than twice a week were subsequently involved in failure-to-thrive or in child abuse cases.

There has been a variety of governmental programs that have attempted to prevent child abuse. The education for parenthood program sponsored by the Office of Child Development has attempted to prepare teenagers for effective parenthood by providing both information and actual experience with young children in daycare settings. The Home Start Program, (Davidson, 1977) which developed out of the Head Start Program from the Office of Child Development, has provided specially trained agents to meet in the homes of economically disadvantaged families with preschool children. These agents provide supportive counseling. Projects such as PACER (Parent and Child Effective Relations) have attempted to begin with observations on maternity wards and to follow through with special services for families at risk for abuse. Finally, Parents

Anonymous serves as a volunteer self-help program for abusing parents and for parents who feel themselves at risk for abuse. However, in spite of the many attempts at primary prevention currently in operation, there is little empirical evidence for the actual prevention of abuse by these programs. This is an area of unsurpassed importance in the prevention of disorders in children. Large contributions to this area could be made by providing empirical evidence of the effectiveness of programs aimed at preventing child abuse. Approaches to the prevention and treatment of child abuse are described in more detail by Williams in chapter 52 of this book.

Primary Prevention and the School

Just as intervention with parents offers a promising avenue for primary prevention, working through the school systems may also offer a means for early intervention and prevention (Vogelsong, Most, & Yenchka, 1979). Programs attempting primary prevention in the schools have typically relied either on treating entire classes of children or on treating high risk groups of children. Much work has recently been done on identification of children who are likely to experience social or academic dysfunction in school. Numerous behavior checklists (e.g., Quay, 1977; Spivack & Swift, 1977a) and structured interviews (e.g., Herjanic & Campbell, 1977) have been utilized successfully to discriminate children at risk for school-based behavioral problems from children not at risk. Academic inconsistency has also been shown to predict children at risk (Blechman, Kotanchik, & Taylor, 1981). Identification of life stresses (moving, marital problems of parents, illness) affecting the child in the previous year has been demonstrated to provide identification for children at risk for school problems (Sandler & Black, 1979). The behavioral results of such stresses, including withdrawn, fearful, or aggressive responding may be likely targets for early remediation, before the behavior becomes identified as a problem. Interestingly, recent research suggests that fear and withdrawing in combination with lack of self-confidence and a dependency upon adults for problem solving are the best early predictors of later problems in the schoolchild (Spivack & Swift, 1977b). Although the more salient behaviors such as being disruptive, aggressive, and uncooperative may indicate risk when they appear later in childhood, the passive and confused kindergarten child is more likely to show poor academic achievement and classroom adjustment later in school. Such problems may be prevented by exposing the at-risk kindergarten child to programs that will enhance involvement at school both through improving the home-school relationship (Mussen & Kuhlman, 1966) and through increasing the child's ability to participate verbally (e.g., Friedman, 1973) and to solve problems independently (e.g., Lovitt, 1973).

Shure and Spivack (1979) have successfully employed such procedures to prevent inhibited and impulsive behavior in 4- or 5-year-old high risk subjects. These children received intensive interpersonal cognitive problem-solving training over a two-year period. Children were asked to generate options to difficult interpersonal situations and were given training in evaluating these options. Improvements seen in decreased inhibited and impulsive behavior lasted at least one year as assessed by follow-up intervention. Shure and Spivack (1979) suggest that, although kindergarten children can benefit from such a program, intervention at a preschool age may be most desirable as this will enable subjects to begin elementary school with the requisite social behaviors for later success. However, Kendall and Zupan (1981) have utilized cognitive behavioral self-control training with children up to 10 years of age and have noted changes in a variety of forms of child self-control. They echo the suggestions of Shure and Spivack for intensive cognitive training.

Intensive cognitive skill training would appear to be an effective preventive mode, but unfortunately a very expensive one. Even if such programs can be shown to be cost effective in the long run, educators and legislators may be reluctant to fund as many of these programs as might be needed. Frangia and Reisinger (1979) note an alternative model for preschool intervention. Their model, the

Early Intervention Program (EIP), combines assessment and treatment for both the child and the parent. Parents receive thorough training in behavior management and specifically learn how to help a child acquire and maintain self-help skills; how to decrease tantrums, noncooperation, and other "unmanageable" behaviors; and how to increase appropriate prosocial responding. Parents track their child's behavior by graphing both the child's behavior and the parent's response to that behavior. If such exhaustive training was done by professionals, the cost would be very high. However, training is done by previously trained parents at the repayment rate of five hours of service due for every hour of treatment received. Thus, with a small professional resource staff to supervise volunteers, the training can be accomplished at very low cost. Data collection and follow-up, as well as outreach community efforts are also possible using this model. Later benefits in appropriate classroom behavior also testify to the cost effectiveness of the program. Chapter 27 by Durlak in this book discusses other programs that focus on school-based intervention.

In addition to treatment that focuses on high risk children in the schools, a few innovative researchers have attempted to apply preventive treatment to entire school populations. For example, Glidewell, Gildea, and Kaufman (1973) examined 426 families for a period of 30 months following their children's entry into third grade. Families either received no special mental health services, an educational program operated by the parents, or a dual educational parent program in combination with an in-school program. Both of the latter programs significantly reduced behavioral problems in boys but not in girls, with immediate effects in upper-middle-class families and delayed effects in lower class families. Similarly, Hartman (1979) describes a social skills training program for high school students which utilizes RET principles, systematic desensitization, problem solving, and role playing. Difficult and anxiety-provoking situations were rehearsed, both problematic internal and external responses noted, and adaptive alternatives practiced. Trained subjects demonstrated increased coping and performance skills in a variety of social and school situations.

Since the preschool, elementary, and intermediate level school systems have been shown to be successful avenues for primary prevention in a variety of endeavors (Lemle, 1976), future research might examine the feasibility of combining behavioral self-control procedures with typical classroom curriculum. While it may be true that teachers currently have little free time to deal with additional curricular demands, clever engineering of behavioral techniques might necessitate little extra effort on the part of the teacher or teacher's aide. Relaxation techniques to be used in stressful situations could be taught for a few moments as the children begin their "naptime" in early school grades. Selective reinforcement throughout the day could increase prosocial and adaptive responding (Friedman, 1973). Teaching cognitive management techniques along with other components of successful public speaking may decrease public-speaking anxiety (Cradock, Cotler, & Jason, 1978). Physical education in schools could be oriented toward teaching physical fitness and resultant improvements in self-concept and mood (Folkins & Sime, 1981). Children may even acquire social management skills economically by serving as tutors to improve responding in younger children (Douglas & Jason, 1979). Finally, parent training might also be utilized to prevent school-based problems in children from preschool to high school. The possibilities for primary prevention in the schools are just beginning to be explored.

Primary Prevention in Medical Settings

The area of primary prevention in child medical patients received some of the earliest attention from researchers who wished to prevent psychological distress during a variety of medical procedures. Currently, interventions in the schools and in medical settings have interfaced with programs that may attempt to prevent medical fears prior to the child's actual exposure to a medical setting. Roberts et al. (1981) have exposed local

school children to a 30-minute slide show that describes the local hospital procedures during a child model's elective surgery. Such exposure resulted in diminished self-reported fear of medical personnel and procedures by schoolchildren. While these authors note that it is not clear that this approach would lower children's fears during actual hospitalization, the lowered general medical fear might make emergency medical procedures less frightening and might make the child amenable to additional preparation for elective medical procedures.

Siegel and Peterson (1980; 1981) prepared low income children in a preschool setting prior to their second visit to a dentist. Some of these children received experimenter contact only with no discussion of dental treatment; these children heard a story from "Winnie-the-Pooh." A second group received sensory information concerning the entire procedure for the use of topical anesthetic, injection of local anesthetic, drilling, and placement of an amalgam restoration filling, and this information was narrated with rich sensory detail. Threatening experiences were described with accurate but positive sensory information. For example, the injection of a local anesthetic was described as the dentist putting "sleepy water" around the tooth. The child was told that there would be a pinch and then some tingling, and, after that, the child's mouth might feel "big and heavy." A third group received training in comforting self-instruction (e.g., "I'm going to be alright"; "Everything will be over soon"), distracting imagery (e.g., "I'm eating my favorite ice cream in a sunny meadow"), and cue-controlled relaxation.

Children in the two treatment groups were more cooperative, less anxious, and less physiologically aroused than were children in the control group during the second dental session immediately following psychological preparation. Furthermore, these gains were maintained in a third dental session even though no further psychological treatment was given.

Preparation of subjects within the actual dental treatment situation has demonstrated the effectiveness of systematic desensitization (Machen & Johnson, 1974), reinforcement and information (e.g., Stokes & Kennedy, 1980), and filmed modeling (e.g., Melamed et al., 1975) in preventing undue anxiety during dental treatment although the maintenance of these treatments has not yet been established. Since children tend to become increasingly sensitized to sequential dental visits (Venham, Bengston, & Cipes, 1977), the problem of maintenance is of both theoretical and pragmatic importance. Future research in this area should attempt to compare cost effective methods that would be likely to be employed by dentists and dental assistants to decrease distress in young dental patients.

Prevention of distress in young surgical patients has successfully utilized all of the techniques described above to decrease pre- and postoperative distress. Because Siegel (in chap. 46 of this book) discusses prevention of child problems in medical settings, this topic will be dealt with very briefly here. A recent survey of pediatric hospitals noted that nearly three-quarters of the hospitals in the United States employ some form of formal psychological preparation (Peterson & Ridley-Johnson, 1980). The hospitals appear to utilize techniques that have been shown to be effective in past research. For example, 37 percent of the hospitals utilized a filmed model, 21 percent used a puppet show, and 16 percent used behavioral coping techniques; all of these techniques have been established as successful in past investigations (e.g., Cassell, 1965; Melamed & Siegel, 1975; Peterson & Shigetomi, 1981, respectively). Peterson et al. (1981) contrasted two of these methods with a minimal preparation control. Preparation from the physician and nurse plus experimenter contact was compared with a program that used a hospital tour and either an in vivo puppet model, a child actor model in a locally produced videotape, or a commercial modeling film. Results from blind observers, parents, and nurses indicated that all three modeling programs were equally effective and all were more effective in reducing anxiety and maladaptive behaviors than was informal preparation. Thus it might appear that hospitals may be able to select the modeling technique that is most appropriate to their own

setting and budget. Prior to the use of any preparation technique in a new setting with a new population, however, empirical validation of that technique should take place.

Peterson and Shigetomi (1981) examined in vivo coping techniques in combination with modeling techniques. They found that child surgery patients who viewed an in vivo puppet show or a film *and* received in vivo training in self-instruction, distracting imagery, and cue-controlled relaxation were better prepared than children receiving either treatment alone. Thus, teaching coping responses would seem to be a useful addition to modeling techniques. However, it is not clear whether training of coping techniques could be effectively accomplished with a prepackaged film or videotape. If such preparation is not sufficiently flexible to promote coping skills training, then hospitals wishing to utilize this technology will need to rely on personnel skilled in administering such training. As is the case with distress in dental settings, future research with children in medical settings must attempt to define the most cost effectve primary prevention treatment for each child patient. This will demand both additional component and comparative research to identify optimal treatment combinations and also may involve assessing children's unique responses to medical stress in order to select the optimal treatment combination for each child.

SECONDARY PREVENTION

As has been noted previously, the designated goal of prevention determines whether primary or secondary prevention will take place. Whereas primary prevention may attempt to isolate a group at risk for, but not yet experiencing, distress from a problem, secondary prevention may attempt to define the at-risk group by noting those individuals already in early stages of distress from the problem. There are some commonly occurring types of screening for secondary prevention, including: (1) the routine measurement of certain observable physical characteristics (e.g., low birthweight infants); (2) referral by self or parent (e.g., parent-training groups) or (3) the routine screening by state or federal agencies (e.g., high risk preschoolers assigned to Head Start; predelinquent behavior noted in court), concerned teachers (e.g., hyperactivity), or physicians (e.g., obesity). However, for other kinds of disorders there is no regular screening source or clear behavioral definition and these disorders are the most difficult to affect with secondary prevention. Pragmatically, one of the difficulties associated with any form of secondary prevention is the necessity for definition and identification of the at-risk group. Some frequently occurring disorders are complex and difficult to define and identify. For example, efforts to develop and employ screening instruments for child abuse have not had notable success (e.g., Newberger & Daniel, 1979) and authors have noted that it is "nearly impossible" to identify children at risk for juvenile delinquency (VandenBos & Miller, 1980, p. 136). Disorders with a low base rate of occurrence in the general population may be even more difficult to identify with a cost effective screening device. The following sections will consider both the readily identified and more difficult-to-screen-for disorders that may be appropriate targets for secondary intervention.

Screening of Infants

During the first days of life, some infants may present a complicated set of symptoms that have not been readily identified as risk indicators in past research. Since 1972, Thoman (cited in Trotter, 1980) and her colleagues have been studying early infant development and methods of early screening. In one study, normal full term infants were observed in various behavioral states (waking active, quiet alert, fuss or cry, drowse, active sleep, and quiet sleep). Healthy infants demonstrated a consistent individual pattern of these behavioral states from day to day. This consistency was known as the State Stability Index (SSI). Inconsistent behavior from day to day (a low SSI), rather than the time spent in each state per se, was found to be associated with various infant problems, including sudden crib death,

mental retardation, and severe anemia. Thoman's study suggests that the infant's State Stability Index may be used to facilitate early diagnosis. In one case, two infants were determined to be at risk for sleep apnea and were put on special monitoring devices. Both of the infants later experienced prolonged periods in which they required prompts to begin breathing regularly again. Screening using the State Stability Index might be useful for screening all neonates but would be particularly useful for premature infants.

Premature infants are considered at risk for virtually every aspect of their development. Retardation in physical growth and physical defects, impairment of cognitive functioning as measured by IQ scores, academic and school problems, and the occurrence of behavior problems have all been reported to occur with greater frequency in children who were born prematurely than in their full term counterparts. Alarmingly, such effects have been reported even into adolescence. (See Caputo & Mandell, 1970, for a review of the consequences of prematurity.) The psychological literature is just beginning to report intervention attempts with low birthweight infants aimed at reducing effects of their early difficulties and facilitating optimal conditions for their subsequent development. Efforts at secondary prevention for the preterm infants have focused on two likely sources contributing to the unfortunate sequelae outlined above, including sensory deprivation due to the isolation of the baby at birth (Rothschild, 1967) and the separation of these infants from their mothers at birth for days, if not weeks (Leifer et al., 1972; Seashore et al., 1973).

Some researchers have noted that sensory stimulation may be facilitative for preterm infants who are frequently placed in isolettes, an environment that deprives them of tactile, visual, and kinesthetic stimulation normally present in the infant's environment (Powell, 1974; Rice, 1977; Scarr-Salapetek & Williams, 1973; Solkoff et al., 1969). For example, Rice (1977) arranged for mothers to provide tactile-kinesthetic stimulation for their infants for one month following their arrival home from the hospital, by stroking and massaging their babies four times a day for fifteen minutes. Infants in the stimulation program showed significant gains over control infants in weight gain, neurological development, and higher scores on the Mental Development Index of the Bayley Scales at 4 months of age.

Scarr-Salapetek and Williams (1973) instituted a stimulation program for low birth-weight infants of low socioeconomic status parents. Increased visual, tactile, and kinesthetic stimulation for these infants was accomplished in the hospital nursery by introducing human voices and faces, handling, and patterned visual stimuli as soon as possible after birth. Unlike the usual hospital regimen for the control infants, who were handled minimally and kept in their isolettes virtually continuously, experimental infants were handled, rocked, cuddled, talked to, and played with by nurses during eight daily feeding sessions, and infants were removed from their isolettes into bassinets as soon as possible. After the infants went home, social workers paid weekly visits to the home until 1 year of age, bringing mobiles, toys, rattles, books, and infants seats and, importantly, instructing mothers in methods of stimulating child care such as game playing. When tested at 4 weeks of age using the Brazelton scales, experimental infants showed slight to significant advantages over control infants on all scales; additionally, weight gain was significantly greater for this group. At 1 year of age, experimental infants averaged 10 IQ points higher than control infants on Cattell's intelligence scales. The mean IQ for the experimental group was 95.3, close to normal for the population, while controls lagged one standard deviation below the mean with an average IQ of 85.7.

While Rice (1977) and Scarr-Salapetek and Williams (1973) demonstrated that such programs facilitated normal development, it is not clear whether the quantity of stimulation alone or increased maternal involvement as well produced such encouraging results. Regardless of the source of the improvement, such programs are also likely to be cost effective in the reduction of services that may be necessary as the infant gets older.

Most psychologists agree that the separation of the premature infant and mother at birth may have adverse effects upon later mother-child interaction and on the infant's development (see Beckwith et al., 1976; Cohen & Beckwith, 1979; Leifer et al., 1972; Seashore et al., 1973). Furthermore, there is evidence that the cry and appearance of a premature infant is perceived as more aversive than that of full term babies (Frodi et al., 1978). Results from studies attempting to increase maternal involvement with their premature infants have been inconsistent (Brown et al., 1980; Leifer et al., 1972; Maisto & German, 1979; Minde et al., 1980; Widmayer & Field, 1980). For example, in the Leifer et al. (1972) study, where maternal behavior was observed over a two-year period, mothers who had been in a "contact" group and had been allowed to handle their infants in the incubator and to participate in child care procedures did not differ in observed maternal attachment behaviors from control mothers who had no such opportunity to interact with their infants. However, the finding of no differences could be due to the fact that contact mothers only visited their infants, on the average, once every six days! The practical difficulties such as child care for other siblings, transportation, etc. encountered by mothers, particularly lower SES mothers, must be taken into account in designing pragmatically feasible interventions.

More positive findings for attempts to improve mother-child interactions were reported by Widmayer and Field (1980). This program trained parents to assess their own infants, with the goal of increasing maternal sensitivity to infants' interactive skills and ultimately enabling mothers to facilitate positive interactions with their babies. When mothers administered the mother's version of the Brazelton scales, (the Mother's Assessment of the Behavior of her Infant) to their infants at birth and weekly for the first month of life, their infants received more optimal interactive process scores on the Brazelton at 1 month in comparison to controls, and mothers were rated as having more optimal feeding interactions with their infants. Mothers who observed the administration of the Brazelton in addition to their own assessments had the highest-scoring infants and mother-infant interactions, suggesting that modeling of optimal interaction benefited these mothers.

Summarizing and evaluating prevention efforts for premature infants, the results of interventions are encouraging. Providing extra stimulation and/or improving the quality of mother-child interactions has been demonstrated to have significant positive effects (both statistically and practically) on these infants' development. Especially encouraging are the gains possible in later cognitive development. There have been very few attempts at prevention with premature infants, yet the available evidence supports its efficacy. Future research may yield additional information concerning optimal methods of implementing such prevention. Additional information on the clinical problems of infants is presented in chapter 12 by Magrab and Sostek.

Screening and Secondary Prevention with Parents

The use of parents as change agents for their own children has a relatively long history (Cone & Sloop, 1973). Tertiary prevention or treatment for a wide range of clearly maladaptive behavior has been effected by parents of children who were aggressive (Zeilberger, Sampen, & Sloane, 1968), uncooperative (Wahler, 1969), obese (Aragona, Cassady, & Drabman, 1975), or experiencing problems in school (Schumaker, Hovell, & Sherman, 1977). Currently, numerous suggestions are being made concerning ways in which child problems can be identified very early in their formation and secondary prevention can be implemented. A variety of screening devices have been created. Some, like the Children's Behavioral Classification Project (Dreger, 1977), are focused at the early identification of maladaptive responding in children. The Children's Behavioral Classification Project consists of 274 behavioral items, which are rated as problematic or nonproblematic by the

parent. Scores on this inventory suggest early sources of parent-child problems, and, because discrete behaviors are listed, the scores on this device may also suggest a precise behavioral target for early intervention.

Identification of a child's problems is only the first step to remediation, however, and often, although the problems are well known, solutions seem elusive. Academic deficits in low socioeconomic youngsters may be easily recognized by preschool age, but often intervention to alter these deficits has been disappointing (Karnes et al., 1970). An early attempt at successful secondary prevention of school dysfunction was made by the Mother-Child Home Program (Levenstein, Kochman, & Roth, 1973). In this program, mothers were given suggestions for new methods of interacting with their preschool children, with the goal of creating a stimulating, mutually supporting dyad of mother and child. The program utilized specific toys and books as tools for flexible, programmed verbal interaction techniques. Following two years in this program, children treated by their mothers demonstrated significant IQ gains as compared with control children. Later follow-up indicated that children retained these gains as well as demonstrating improved performance in reading achievement and arithmetic ability when compared to untreated controls.

More recently, behavioral programs that instruct the parents to identify and react flexibly to a variety of recognized child problems have manifested good potential for secondary prevention. For example, Gordon, Lerner, and Keefe (1979) have reported on a project in which parents received training in responsive parenting to deal with both currently identified and future behavior problems. Parents for 8–10 weeks were taught to observe, measure, and modify the maladaptive behavior of their children. Parents were able to react differently and effectively to a wide variety of child behavior problems. In a similar project, Jason (1977) reported training parents through home-based programs of modeling and instruction to deal with behavior problems in their economically disadvantaged toddlers. A wide range of specific behavioral excesses (e.g., aggression, tantrumming) and deficits (e.g, eye contact, imitation, vocalizing) were targeted as the parents continued to identify the need for changes during three months of both home and health care facility visits. Treated children demonstrated significant increases in appropriate learning behavior following treatment as compared to a control group, and these gains were maintained during a three-month follow-up. Parental involvement was cited as a major factor in maintenance of positive change. Similarly, Blechman et al. (1981) utilized parental reinforcement cued by teacher reports of improved academic performance to increase academic performance in at-risk children, and increased generality was anticipated due to the home-based program.

Although the majority of programs aimed at secondary prevention in children have involved young children, older children can benefit from parental intervention with problem behavior as well. For example, Rodick and Henggeler (1980) utilized seventh-grade students with academic skill deficits to contrast the Reverend Jesse Jackson's home-based parent-administered "PUSH for Excellence" program with the school-based standard remedial reading, or SMART (Staats Motivation Activating Reading Technique) program, which utilized advanced undergraduate tutors. Interestingly, immediately after the termination of the programs, students receiving SMART procedures demonstrated greater increases in academic skills and achievement motivation than students in other groups. At a six-month follow-up, however, both students receiving PUSH and SMART procedures showed maintained gains in achievement motivation and academic ability. This delayed effect from the home-based treatment is very similar to that seen in the home-based primary prevention program for low income families that was discussed earlier (Glidewell et al., 1973). This may suggest that, even when immediate change is not forthcoming, parental involvement can lead to long range, maintained change.

Involvement of the family has also been shown to be useful for secondary prevention of interactional difficulties like physical abuse. Grodner (1977) describes a systems approach to child abuse in which the causes of abuse can be understood in terms of interactions between various family members and early intervention can be effected by systems level changes. Similarly, Rosenstein (1978) described a family outreach program that through the use of trained volunteers working as family consultants, attempted to offer preventive services to families in which early signs of abuse or neglect appear. This program utilized training in problem solving and in the application of alternative response patterns to family members. Finally, McCaffrey and Tewey (1978) outlined a community study that focused on the combined role of educators and families in the early identification and treatment of child abuse and neglect.

While the above articles contain careful descriptions of program construction, training of treatment agents and family members, and of goals and aspirations of the programs, it is unfortunate that they do not as yet contain empirical proof that child abuse can be diminished through early intervention. Such proof may be difficult to obtain, but the challenge remains to future research to demonstrate that either primary or secondary prevention of child abuse is not only a worthwhile and well-approached goal, but also an attainable goal.

In general, parent-based secondary prevention programs have shown most success in areas in which parents are motivated to intervene, in which behavioral technologies are appropriate, and in which the problem behaviors can be clearly defined. Future research may examine methods to extend these findings to more complex behavior patterns and different populations.

Screening and Secondary Prevention in the Schools

Numerous investigators have commented on the high proportion of children who experience school maladjustment either in the form of disruptive or withdrawn behavior or in the form of severe learning problems. Surveys report that from 30 to 70 percent of school age children experience significant problems in adjusting to the demands of school (Glidewell & Swallow, 1969). These early problems are predictive of later, more severe problems in school (Zax & Cowen, 1969) and in later adult adjustment (Roff, 1969). Thus early identification and treatment of maladaptive emotional and academic responses would seem to warrant the large number of studies that have attempted secondary prevention in the schools in the last two decades (e.g., Cowen et al., 1972; Durlak, 1977; Durlak & Mannarino, 1977).

A typical approach to secondary prevention in the school population can be illustrated by a study reported in Sandler, Duricko, and Grande (1975). Children's behaviors were rated by teachers and nonprofessional child therapist volunteers on several behavioral inventories that sampled social (acting out vs. prosocial), emotional (moody, etc.), and academic (specific problems in learning) responses. Children judged to be at risk for school problems were placed into control and experimental groups. Experimental children were seen biweekly by the volunteers who were in turn supervised weekly by the program psychologists. Volunteers did specific tutoring, discussed difficulties in peer relationships, and attempted to increase children's feelings of competence and leadership. Experimental subjects were rated as improved by the child worker volunteers and the teachers on all of the inventories used. Improvements in GPA and academic skills were noted but were not statistically significant. While this study and the many others like it report promising results, there are many problems with the way in which such studies are designed and reported. The target behaviors are typically referred to as mean scores on the behavioral inventories, the interventions are described in general and nonbehavioral terms, and the blindness to condition of individuals rating the children is not insured. Finally, the lack of

significant impact on academic performance is problematic since, at least ostensibly, maintained improvements in academic performance were the primary goal for treatment. This issue is further discussed by Weisberg in chapter 48 of this book.

Recently reported work in a preschool setting that utilized the same behavioral inventories as reported above (Rickel & Smith, 1979; Rickel, Smith, & Sharp, 1979) have adopted a prescriptive intervention approach in which the specific behavioral deficits and excesses of individual children are noted and selected behavioral interventions are programmed. This method allows analysis of the differential success of the various interventions that are employed. However, neither of these studies utilized measures of academic achievement, and thus it remains unclear whether improvements in the target behaviors will yield the sought-after improvements in academic responses. This would appear to be another fruitful area for investigation of both the sought-after and the actual effects of such secondary prevention.

Currently, a variety of articles strongly urge the use of school-based secondary prevention of problems ranging from social isolation (Hartup, 1979), learning disabilities (Lansdown, 1978) and hyperactivity (Arnold, 1976), to child abuse (Poppen & Broadhurst, 1976) and emotional problems stemming from physical handicaps (Mason, 1978) or early school failure (Clarfield, 1974). In summation, there are many fine attempts to accomplish school-based secondary prevention described in the literature. However, too few of these attempts have been designed to yield empirical demonstrations of efficacy, and such demonstrations in future research may be necessary before schools will adopt and routinely utilize secondary preventive methods.

Screening and Secondary Prevention by Physicians

Interestingly, the pediatrician is not only sought out for consultation concerning the child's physical health, but the pediatrician is also more likely to be the first to be consulted concerning the developmental and psychological problems of the preschool child than any other professional (Task Force on Pediatric Education, 1978). Many of the behavior problems presented to the physician are not linked to any physical or developmental disability (Sumpter, 1975), and the opportunity for the physician to engage in secondary prevention of psychological as well as physical problems has recently been emphasized (e.g., Reisinger & Lavigne, 1980). Psychologists in concert with pediatric physicians may make continued contributions to this important area.

Pediatricians have for years been trained to utilize psychodiagnostic instruments such as the Denver Development Screening test or the Bayley Scales of Infant Development (Wright, 1979). However, recent data suggest that, although most pediatricians agree that routine screening is valuable in identifying at-risk children or in implementing early intervention, typically such screening occurs only with a small percentage of children already identified as having problems (Smith, 1978). The use of paraprofessional assessors in combination with more efficient screening instruments may make screening by physicians more likely in the future. Metz et al. (1976) describe an addition to the Pediatric Multiphasic Examination, which can successfully screen children for a variety of psychological problems. Similarly, Jellinek, Evans, and Knight (1979) report on a pediatric patient behavior checklist, which is as accurate as a psychiatric interview in determining which children require early psychological intervention. Shaywitz, Cohen, and Shaywitz (1979) also note a checklist method to establish diagnostic criteria for specific psychological problems in pediatric patients. Finally, Roberts and Wright (in press) describe a variety of screening devices that could be used by pediatricians, including the use of flow charts with branching questions to indicate specifically the nature of common behavioral problems.

Physicians must often ascertain the psychological contribution to physical complaints. Early examination of recurrent abdominal pains, stomach pains, and headaches may

reveal that anxiety preceded the experience of pain and that social reinforcers follow it (Roberts & Wright, in press). By altering both the preceding anxiety and the reinforcing consequences for pain, a chronic, debilitating condition could be prevented.

Similarly, in many cases, the physician depends on the parents or the child's compliance to the medical regimen. Later medical complications can be prevented if the patient is educated to the need for compliance, if the behaviors necessary for total compliance are successfully shaped, and if these methods fit into the patient's daily routine (e.g., Dunbar & Stunkard, 1977). Special psychological programs have successfully affected medical compliance for a variety of physical problems, including diabetic management (e.g., Lowe & Lutzker, 1979), renal dialysis (Magrab, 1975), and seizure disorders (Zlutnick, Mayville, & Moffat, 1975). Increased cooperation and decreased anxiety in response to injections, stitches, and cast removals might also result from techniques used in other medical settings, including sensory information (e.g., Johnson, 1975), filmed modeling (e.g., Melamed & Siegel, 1975), and coping techniques (e.g., Peterson & Shigetomi, 1981). Siegel's chapter 46 in this book discusses such issues further.

Reisinger and Lavigne (1980) suggested that there are four groups of children who can benefit from early intervention in pediatric settings: (1) those with developmental disabilities, (2) those with illnesses or handicaps, (3) those with temperamental traits that could lead to parent-child interaction problems, and (4) those with behavior problems. Johnson (1979) also describes a number of psychological interventions that could limit distress in pediatric patients suffering from the stress of being ill, personality problems secondary to illness, psychological preparation for medical experiences, behavior management problems, rehabilitation from illness, and the need to cope with impending death. Finally, Roberts and Wright (in press) describe a variety of roles the pediatric psychologist might assume in consultation with pediatricians. Future research in this area could identify additional areas in which psychological technology could employ secondary prevention in pediatric patients.

CONCLUSION AND RECOMMENDATIONS

The preceding descriptions of the many areas in which primary and secondary prevention are being attempted with children merely provide illustration of the current possibilities for psychological intervention at these two levels. There are many other areas not mentioned here, such as interventions in the ecological structure of the child's community, classroom, or play materials (e.g., Gelfand & Hartmann, 1977; Peterson et al., 1980). These illustrations can be used to gauge the current state of the art and can allow the reader to judge the extent to which the "cautious optimism" described earlier is warranted. Certainly, psychology has demonstrated that there is a wide variety of problems that would seem to be good targets for preventive intervention. In a limited number of cases, psychological research has demonstrated that such intervention does actually prevent disorders in children. However, in relatively few cases has there been careful empirical demonstration of the cost effectiveness of intervention, of the maintenance of preventive treatment, and of the actual routine implementation of preventive interventions after the research portions of the projects are discontinued. In addition, little is known about the ethical limits of prevention in children when parents or other caretakers are not involved in the intervention. Similarly, little is known about how to deliver prevention programs to those who wish such programs without infringing on those who do not.

It will be difficult to evaluate such problems with implementation using current methodology. Methodological problems in preventive research are in some cases similar to those noted for ordinary treatment studies, and such inadequacies in design and reporting have been briefly noted throughout this discussion. Too often the goals for prevention have not been defined in concrete terms, dependent variables have been global and nonspecific, treatment descriptions have included vague references to "consultation" or "support," and the outcomes of the studies have not supported the efficacy of preventive interventions. It is sometimes unclear who the actual "client" is. Future research faces a challenge implicit in attempts at preventing rather than treating a disorder. Treating entire groups may not be cost effective, yet the alternative—attempts at clearly defining the at-risk population—are relatively new and are not yet clearly effective in discriminating risk. Intervention strategies that may seem to have face validity often prove to be ineffective, and some even backfire, making the disorder worse than before (e.g., McCord, 1978; Stuart, 1974). Assessing the absence of a problem following intervention requires special planning, persistence, and technology. Demonstrating cost effectiveness is difficult when the treatment cost is high and the benefit or savings may not be realized for several years. Too many authors have merely avoided such problems by using case history data (e.g., Fish, 1976) or broad generalizations (e.g., Apolito, 1978).

Fortunately, other investigators have found innovative ways to deal with some of the problems in preventive research. Treating children in captive groups (for example, in churches or classrooms) has been attempted (Roberts et al., in press). Epidemiological tools may enable the researcher to track behavior of an entire community (e.g., Peterson, 1981). Increasing improvements have been made in isolating at-risk groups both by treating children in special settings (e.g., Melamed & Siegel, 1975) or by using clear behavioral measures to define risk in traditional settings (e.g., Trotter, 1980). The use of new interventions and treatment agents shows much promise (e.g., Jason, 1977) and, in rare cases, follow-up has demonstrated the long term efficacy of prevention (e.g., Levenstein et al., 1973). We conclude that the cautious optimist has a chance to see the promise of prevention fulfilled—in limited studies dealing with special disorders conducted by energetic, talented, and "lucky" investigators.

The 1980s may be the era of prevention but only if hard-fought gains continue to be made. Prevention research in psychology would appear to have evolved from infancy to toddlerhood, but there is a great deal more to be accomplished before psychologists can take the demonstrated efficacy of prevention for granted. Unfortunately, the 1980s may not support preventive efforts at the level required for such progress to take place. Individuals in the general community do not recognize the need for prevention as readily as they do for treatment (Gelfand & Hartmann, 1977), and the resulting absence of problematic responding following effective prevention is unlikely to be reinforced by the general population (Peterson et al., 1980). Furthermore, other investigators express concern about the diverting of funds from first-line treatment programs to support "utopian" preventive programs serving individuals currently in far less need of treatment (Brill, 1977). Such arguments often explicitly ask if the role of the psychologist is to prevent unhappiness and social incompetence in the entire population or to attempt to reach those few individuals who are experiencing severe distress (Lamb & Zusman, 1979). If professionals working in the area of child disorders hold such beliefs, it should not be surprising if the lay community echos such sentiments. With multiple demands on the scarce funding available for children who are already suffering from severe physical, behavioral, and emotional disorders, it is difficult to see which community members will lobby for and demand preventive intervention. Indeed, the most powerful barrier to prevention may be the lack of support for preventive endeavors by a powerful constituency (Broskowski & Baker, 1974).

Psychologists are unlikely to receive such support unless they can demonstrate benefits accruing from prevention both in terms of diminished distress and in terms of financial savings. Increased attention directed toward the feasibility of program implementation by the appropriate professionals or community members is required. Regardless of how effective a treatment might be, if it cannot be readily utilized by those in need, its actual effectiveness is very low indeed. In contrast, a moderately effective treatment that can be readily implemented is exceedingly valuable. Theoretically, the implementation of tertiary prevention or treatment is less costly to the community than no treatment at all, secondary prevention is less costly than tertiary prevention, and primary prevention is the most cost effective strategy of all. Deciding when this abstraction is true, mustering hard empirical data to support this viewpoint, and insuring that politically appropriate individuals have access to such data could be the challenge to the preventionist in the 80s. The promise of preventive intervention for children is already at hand; the fulfillment remains in the future.

REFERENCES

Allen, D.G., & Bergman, A.G. Social learning approaches to health education: Utilization of infant auto restraint devices. *Pediatrics,* 1976, **58,** 323–328.

Apolito, A. Primary prevention: A breakthrough in sight. *The American Journal of Psychoanalysis,* 1978, **38,** 121–127.

Aragona, J., Cassady, J., & Drabman, R.S. Treating overweight children through parental training and contingency contracting. *Journal of Applied Behavior Analysis,* 1975, **8,** 269–278.

Arnold, L.E. Causes of hyperactivity and implications for prevention. *School Psychology Digest,* 1976, **5,** 10–22.

Azrin, N.H., & Foxx, R.M. *Toilet training in less than a day.* New York: Simon & Schuster, 1974.

Barker, B.L., Heifetz, L.J., & Brightman, A.J. *Parents as teachers: Manuals for behavior modification of the retarded child: Studies in family training.* Cambridge, Mass.: Behavioral Educator Projects, 1972.

Barnard, J.D., Christophersen, E.R., & Wolf, M.M. Teaching children appropriate shopping behavior through parent training in the supermarket setting. *Journal of Applied Behavior Analysis,* 1977, **10,** 49–59.

Beckwith, L., Cohen, S.E., Kopp, C.B., Parmalee, A.H., & Marcy, T.G. Caregiver-infant interaction and early cognitive development in preterm infants. *Child Development,* 1976, **47,** 579–587.

Berberian, R.M., Gross, C., Lovejoy, J., & Paparella, S. The effectiveness of drug education programs: A critical review. *Health Education Monographs,* 1976, **4,** 377–398.

Blechman, E.A., Kotanchik, N.L., & Taylor, C.J. Families and schools together: Early behavioral intervention with high risk children. *Behavior Therapy,* 1981, **12,** 308–319.

Brill, N.Q. Preventive psychiatry. *Psychiatric Opinion,* 1977, **14,** 30–34.

Broskowski, A., & Baker, F. Professional, organizational, and social barriers to primary prevention. *American Journal of Orthopsychiatry,* 1974, **44,** 707–719.

Brown, J.V., LaRossa, M.M., Aylward, G.P., Davis, D.J., Rutherford, P.K., & Bakeman, R. Nursery-based intervention with prematurely born babies and their mothers: Are there effects? *The Journal of Pediatrics,* 1980, **97,** 487–491.

Caplan, G. *Principles of preventive psychiatry.* New York: Basic Books, 1964.

Caputo, D.V., & Mandell, W. Consequences of low birth weight. *Developmental Psychology,* 1970, **3,** 363–383.

Cassell, S. Effect of brief puppet therapy upon the emotional responses of children undergoing cardiac catheterization. *Journal of Consulting and Clinical Psychology,* 1965, **29,** 1–8.

Christophersen, E.R., & Rapoff, M.A. Pediatric psychology: An appraisal. In B. Lahey & A. Kazdin (Eds.), *Advances in clinical child psychology* (Vol. 3). New York: Plenum, 1980.

Clarfield, S. The development of a teacher referral form for identifying early school maladaption. *American Journal of Community Psychology,* 1974, **2,** 199–203.

Clark, H.B., Greene, B.F., Macrae, J.W., McNees, M.P., Davis, J.L., & Risley, T.R. A parent advice package for family shopping trips: Development and evaluation. *Journal of Applied Behavior Analysis,* 1977, **10,** 605–624.

Cohen, S.E., & Beckwith, L. Preterm infant interaction with the caregiver in the first year of life and competence at age two. *Child Development,* 1979, **50,** 767–776.

Coleman, L. Problem kids and preventive medicine: The making of an odd couple. *American Journal of Orthopsychiatry,* 1978, **48,** 56–70.

Coleman, S.B. Sib group therapy: A prevention program for siblings from drug addicted families. *The International Journal of Addictions,* 1978, **13,** 115–127.

Cone, J.D., & Sloop, E.W. Parents as agents of change. In A. Jacobs & W. Spradlin (Eds.), *Group as agent of change.* New York: Behavioral Publications, 1973.

Cowen, E.L. Social and community interventions. *Annual Review of Psychology,* 1973, **24,** 423–472.

Cowen, E.L. Dorr, D.A., Trost, M.A., & Izzo, L.D. Follow-up study of maladapting school children seen by nonprofessionals. *Journal of Consulting and Clinical Psychology,* 1972, **39,** 235–238.

Cradock, C., Cotler, S., & Jason, L.A. Primary prevention: Immunization of children for speech anxiety. *Cognitive Therapy and Research,* 1978, **2,** 389–396.

Davidson, A.T. Child abuse: Causes and prevention. *Journal of the National Medical Association,* 1977, **69,** 817–820.

Douglas, J.A., & Jason, L.A. Transitions: Utilizing behavioral technology to facilitate entry into a school and an occupation. *Crisis Intervention,* 1979, **10,** 68–79.

Dreger, R.M. The children's behavioral classification project: An interim report. *Journal of Abnormal Child Psychology,* 1977, **5,** 289–297.

Dunbar, J., & Stunkard, A.J. Adherence to diet and drug regimen. In R. Levey, B. Rifkind, B. Dennis, & N. Ernst (Eds.), *Nutrition, lipids, and coronary heart disease.* New York: Raven, 1977.

Durlak, J.A. Description and evaluation of a behaviorally oriented school-based preventive mental health program. *Journal of Consulting and Clinical Psychology,* 1977, **45,** 27–33.

Durlak, J.A., & Mannarino, A.P. Social skills development program: Description of a school-based preventive mental health program for high-risk children. *Journal of Clinical Child Psychology,* 1977, **6,** 48–52.

Elmer, E. *Children in jeopardy: A study of abused minors and their families.* Pittsburgh: University of Pittsburgh, 1967.

Evans, R.I. Smoking in children: Developing a social psychological strategy of deterrence. *Preventive Medicine,* 1976, **5,** 122–127.

Evans, R.I. Deterring the onset of smoking in children: Knowledge of immediate physiological effects and coping with peer pressure, media pressure, and parent modeling. *Journal of Applied Psychology,* 1978, **8**, 126–135.

Fanaroff, A., Kennell, J., & Klaus, M. Follow-up of low birth weight infants: The predictive value of maternal visiting patterns. *Pediatrics,* 1972, **49**, 287–290.

Felner, R.D., Farber, S.S., & Primavera, J. Children of divorce, stressful life events, and transitions. In R.H. Price, R.H. Ketterer, B.C. Bader, & J. Monahan (Eds.), *Prevention in mental health.* Beverly Hills: Sage, 1980.

Fish, B. An approach to prevention in infants at risk for schizophrenia. *Journal of the American Academy of Child Psychiatry,* 1976, **15**, 62–82.

Folkins, C.H., & Sime, W.E. Physical fitness training and mental health. *American Psychologist,* 1981, **36**, 373–389.

Fomufod, A.K., Sinkford, S., & Lony, V. Mother-child separation at birth: A contributing factor in child abuse. *Lancet,* 1975, **7934**, 549–550.

Frangia, G.W., & Reisinger, J.J. Parent implementation of a preschool intervention system. *Journal of Clinical Child Psychology,* 1979, **8**, 64–68.

Friedman, P. Relationship of teacher reinforcement to spontaneous verbalization within the classroom. *Journal of Educational Psychology,* 1973, **65**, 59–64.

Friedrich, W.N., & Boriskin, J.A. Primary prevention of child abuse: Focus on the special child. *Hospital and Community Psychiatry,* 1978, **29**, 248–251.

Frodi, A.M., Lamb, M.E., Leavitt, L.A., Donovan, W.L., Neff, C., & Sherry, D. Fathers' and mothers' responses to the faces and cries of normal and premature infants. *Developmental Psychology,* 1978, **14**, 490–498.

Garbarino, J. An ecological perspective on child maltreatment. In L. Pelton (Ed.), *The social context of child abuse and neglect.* New York: Human Sciences Press, 1980. (a)

Garbarino, J. Preventing child maltreatment. In R.H. Price, R.F. Ketterer, B.C. Bader, & J. Monahan (Eds.), *Prevention in mental health,* Beverly Hills: Sage, 1980. (b)

Garell, D.C. A new approach to teen-age smoking. *Pediatrics,* 1976, **57**, 465–466.

Gelfand, D.M. *Prevention: Why we must change our priorities.* Invited paper presented at the annual meeting of the Association for the Advancement of Behavior Therapy, Atlanta, December, 1977.

Gelfand, D.M., & Hartmann, D.P. The prevention of childhood behavior disorders. In B.B. Lahey & A.E. Kazdin (Eds.), *Advances in clinical child psychology* (Vol. 1). New York: Plenum, 1977.

Glasgow, R.E., & Rosen, G.M. Behavioral bibliotherapy: A review of self-help behavior therapy manuals. *Psychological Bulletin,* 1978, **85**, 1–23.

Glidewell, J.C., Gildea, M.C.L., & Kaufman, M.K. The preventive and therapeutic effects of two school mental health programs. *American Journal of Community Psychology,* 1973, **1**, 295–329.

Glidewell, J.C., & Swallow, C.S. *The prevalence of maladjustment in elementary schools.* Chicago: University of Chicago Press, 1969.

Goldston, I.E. Primary prevention programming from the federal perspective: A progress report. *Journal of Clinical Child Psychology,* 1979, **8**, 80–83.

Gordis, L., Finkelstein, R., Fassett, J.D., & Wright, B. Evaluation of a program for preventing adolescent pregnancy. *New England Journal of Medicine,* 1970, **282**, 1078–1084.

Gordon, S.B., Lerner, L.L., & Keefe, F.J. Responsive parenting: An approach to training parents of problem children. *American Journal of Community Psychology,* 1979, **7**, 45–46.

Grodner, B.A. A family-systems approach to child-abuse: Etiology and intervention. *Journal of Clinical Child Psychology,* 1977, **6**, 32–35.

Hartman, L.M. The preventive reduction of psychological risk in asymptomatic adolescents. *American Journal of Orthopsychiatry,* 1979, **49**, 121–135.

Hartup, W.W. Peer relations and the growth of social competence. In M.W. Kent & J.E. Rolf (Eds.), *Primary prevention of psychopathology: Social competence in children.* Hanover, N.H.: University Press of New England, 1979.

Herjanic, B., & Campbell, W. Differentiating psychiatrically disturbed children on the basis of a structured interview. *Journal of Abnormal Psychology,* 1977, **5**, 127–133.

Hetherington, E.M., Cox, M., & Cox, R. The aftermath of divorce. In J.H. Stevens, Jr., & M. Mathews (Eds.), *Mother/child Father/child relationships.* Washington, D.C.: National Association for the Education of Young Children, 1978.

Hunt, T.J. Caretaker attitude as related to pica and lead poisoning. University of Maryland *Dissertation Abstracts International,* 1978, **38** (10–B), 4988.

Jason, L.A. Early secondary prevention with disadvantaged preschool children. *American Journal of Community Psychology,* 1975, **3**, 33–45.

Jason, L.A. A behavioral approach in enhancing disadvantaged children's academic abilities. *American Journal of Community Psychology,* 1977, **5**, 413–421.

Jellinek, M., Evans, N., & Knight, R.B. Use of a behavior checklist on a pediatric inpatient unit. *The Journal of Pediatrics,* 1979, **94**, 156–158.

Johnson, J.E. Stress reduction through sensation information. In I.G. Sarason & C.C. Spielberger (Eds.), *Stress and anxiety* (Vol. 2). Washington, D.C.: Hemisphere, 1975.

Johnson, M.R. Mental health interventions with medically ill children: A review of the literature. *Journal of Pediatric Psychology,* 1979, **4**, 147–164.

Karnes, M.B., Teska, J.A., Hodgins, A.S., & Badger, E.D. Educational intervention at home by mothers of disadvantaged infants. *Child Development,* 1970, **41**, 925–935.

Kegeles, S.S., Lund, A.K., & Weisenberg, M. Acceptance by children of a daily home mouth rinse program. *Social Science and Medicine,* 1978, **12**, 199–210.

Kelly, J.B., & Wallerstein, J.S. The effects of parental divorce: Experiences of the child in early latency. *American Journal of Orthopsychiatry,* 1976, **47**, 40–51.

Kempe, C.H., & Helfer, R.E. *Helping the battered child and his family.* Philadelphia: Lippincott, 1972.

Kendall, P.C., & Zupan, B.A. Individual versus group application of cognitive-behavioral self-control procedures with children. *Behavior Therapy,* 1981, **12**, 344–359.

Klein, D.C., & Goldston, S.E. *Primary prevention: An idea whose time has come.* Klein (DHEW PHS Pub No. ADM 77-447). Rockville, Maryland: Department of Health, Education and Welfare, 1977.

Knowles, J. The responsibility of the individual. In J. Knowles (Ed.), *Doing better and feeling worse: Health in the United States.* New York: Norton, 1977.

Lamb, H.R., & Zusman, J. Primary prevention in perspective. *American Journal of Psychiatry,* 1979, **136**, 12–17.

Lansdown, R. The learning-disabled child: Early detection and prevention. *Developmental Medicine and Child Neurology,* 1978, **20**, 496–497.

Lee, E.E. Alcohol education and the elementary school teacher. *The Journal of School Health,* 1976, **46**, 271–272.

Leiderman, P.H. Mothers at risk: A potential consequence of the hospital care of the premature infant. In E.J. Anthony & C. Koupernik (Eds.), *The child in his family: Children of psychiatric risk.* New York: Wiley, 1974.

Leifer, A.D., Leiderman, P.H., Barnett, C.R., & Williams, J.A. Effects of mother-infant separation on maternal attachment behavior. *Child Development,* 1972, **43**, 1203–1218.

Lemle, R. Primary prevention of psychological disorders in elementary and intermediate schools. *Journal of Clinical Child Psychology,* 1976, **5**, 26–32.

Levenstein, P., Kochman, A., & Roth, H.A. From laboratory to real world: Service delivery of the Mother-Child Home Program. *American Journal of Orthopsychiatry,* 1973, **43**, 72–78.

Levine, M., & Graziano, A.M. Intervention programs in elementary schools. In S.E. Golann and C. Eisdorfer (Eds.), *Handbook of community mental health.* New York: Appleton-Century-Crofts, 1972.

Lewis, J.H., Gossett, J.T., & Phillips, V.A. Evaluation of a drug prevention program. *Hospital Community Psychiatry,* 1972, **23**, 124–126.

Litt, I.F., Cuskey, W.R., & Rudd, S. Identifying adolescents at risk for noncompliance with contraceptive therapy. *The Journal of Pediatrics,* 1980, **96**, 742–745.

Lovitt, T.C. Self-management projects with children with behavioral difficulties. *Journal of Learning Disabilities,* 1973, **6**, 138–150.

Lowe, K., & Lutzker, J.R. Increasing compliance to a medical regimen with a juvenile diabetic. *Behavior Therapy,* 1979, **10**, 57–64.

Machen, J.B., & Johnson, R. Desensitization, model learning and the dental behavior of children. *Journal of Dental Research,* 1974, **53**, 83–87.

Magrab, P.R. Psychological management and renal dialysis. *Journal of Clinical Child Psychology,* 1975, **4,** 38–40.

Maisto, A.A., & German, M.L. Variables related to progress in a parent infant training program for high-risk infants. *Journal of Pediatric Psychology,* 1979, **4,** 409–419.

Marcuse, E.K. Immunization: An embarrassing failure. *Pediatrics,* 1975, **56,** 493–494.

Martin, H.P., & Beezley, P. Prevention and the consequences of child abuse. *Journal of Operational Psychiatry,* 1974, **6,** 68–77.

Mash, E.J., Handy, L.C., & Hammerlynck, L.A. (Eds.). *Behavior modification approaches to parenting.* New York: Brunner/Mazel, 1976.

Mason, H. The role of audiologists and speech pathologists in the mental health of the hearing impaired. *Hearing Rehabilitation Quarterly,* 1978, **13,** 8–9.

Matarazzo, J.D. Behavioral health and behavioral medicine: Frontiers for a new health psychology. *American Psychologist,* 1980, **35,** 779–789.

McAnarney, E.R. Adolescent pregnancy—A national priority. *American Journal of Diseases of Children,* 1978, **132,** 125.

McCaffrey, M., & Tewey, S. Preparing educators to participate in the community response to child abuse and neglect. *Exceptional Children,* 1978, **45,** 114–122.

McCord, J. A thirty-year follow-up of treatment effects. *American Psychologist,* 1978, **33,** 284–289.

McCune, D.A. *A study of more effective education relative to narcotics, other harmful drugs, and hallucinogenic substances.* Progress report submitted to the California Legislature, California State Department of Education, 1970.

McFall, R.M. Smoking-cessation research. *Journal of Consulting and Clinical Psychology,* 1978, **46,** 703–712.

McMahon, R.J., & Forehand, R. Nonprescription behavior therapy: Effectiveness of a brochure in teaching mothers to correct their children's inappropriate mealtime behaviors. *Behavior Therapy,* 1978, **9,** 814–820.

McMahon, R.J., & Forehand, R. Self-help behavior therapies and parent training. In B.B. Lahey & A.E. Kazdin (Eds.), *Advances in clinical child psychology* (Vol. 2). New York: Plenum, 1979.

Melamed, B.G., Hawes, R.R., Heiby, E., & Glick, J. The use of filmed modeling to reduce uncooperative behavior of children during dental treatment. *Journal of Dental Research,* 1975, **54,** 797–801.

Melamed, B.G., & Siegel, L.J. Reduction of anxiety in children facing hospitalization and surgery by use of filmed modeling. *Journal of Consulting and Clinical Psychology,* 1975, **43,** 511–521.

Metz, J.R., Allen, C.M., Barr, G., & Shinefied, H. A pediatric screening examination for psychosocial problems. *Pediatrics,* 1976, **58,** 595–606.

Minde, K., Shosenberg, N., Marton, P., Thompson, J. Ripley, J., & Burns, S. Self-help groups in a premature nursery—A controlled evaluation. *The Journal of Pediatrics,* 1980, **96,** 933–940.

Minear, R.E., & Guyer, B. Assessing immunization services at a neighborhood health center. *Pediatrics,* 1979, **63,** 416–419.

Mussen, P., & Kuhlman, C. Initiating responses. In J. Bruner (Ed.), *Learning about learning.* USDHEW Cooperative Research Monograph No. 15, 1966.

Newberger, E., & Daniel, J. Knowledge and epidemiology of child abuse: A critical review of concepts. In R. Bourne & E. Newberger (Eds.), *Critical perspectives on child abuse.* Lexington, Mass.: D.C. Health, 1979.

Patterson, G.R., Reid, J.B., Jones, R.R., & Conger, R.E. *A social learning approach to family interaction* (Vol. 1). Eugene, Ore.: Castalia Publishing, 1975.

Pearn, J.H., Brown, J., Wong, R., & Bart, R. Bathtub drownings: Report of seven cases. *Pediatrics,* 1979, **64,** 68–70.

Peterson, L. *Prevention and community compliance to immunization schedules.* Paper presented at the meeting of the Midwestern Psychological Association, St. Louis, 1981.

Peterson, L., Hartmann, D.P., & Gelfand, D.M. Prevention of child behavior disorders: A lifestyle change for child psychologists. In P.O. Davidson & S.M. Davidson (Eds.), *Behavioral medicine: Changing health lifestyles.* New York: Brunner/Mazel, 1980.

Peterson, L., & Ridley-Johnson, R. Pediatric hospital response to survey on prehospital preparation for children. *Journal of Pediatric Psychology,* 1980, **5,** 1–7.

Peterson, L., Schultheis, K., Ridley-Johnson, R., Miller, D.J., & Tracy, K. *Comparison of three modeling procedures in the preparation of child surgery patients.* Manuscript submitted for publication, 1981.

Peterson, L., & Shigetomi, C. The use of coping techniques to minimize anxiety in hospitalized children. *Behavior Therapy*, 1981, **12**, 1–14.

Poche, C., Brouwer, R., & Swearingen, M. Teaching self-protection to young children. *Journal of Applied Behavior Analysis*, 1981, **14**, 169–175.

Poppen, W.H., & Broadhurst, D.D. Idea exchange column. *Elementary School Guidance and Counseling*, 1976, **10**, 222–226.

Powell, L.F. The effect of extra stimulation and maternal involvement on the development of low-birth-weight infants and on maternal behavior. *Child Development*, 1974, **45**, 106–113.

Prugh, D.G., Staub, E.M., Sands, H.H., Kirschbaum, R.M., & Lenihan, E.A. A study of the emotional reactions of children and families to hospitalization and illness. *American Journal of Orthopsychiatry*, 1953, **23**, 70–106.

Quay, H.C. Measuring dimensions of deviant behavior: The Behavior problem checklist. *Journal of Abnormal Child Psychology*, 1977, **5**, 277–287.

Rainey, S.K., & Christopher, E.R. Behavioral pediatrics: The role of the nurse clinician. *Comprehensive Issues in Pediatric Nursing*, 1976, **1**(4), 19–28.

Reisinger, J.J., & Lavigne, J.V. An early intervention model for pediatric settings. *Professional Psychology*, 1980, **11**, 582–590.

Rice, R.D. Neurophysiological development in premature infants following stimulation. *Developmental Psychology*, 1977, **13**, 69–76.

Richards, L. Evaluation in drug education. *School Health Review*, 1971, **2**, 22–27.

Rickel, A.U., & Smith, R.L. Maladapting preschool children: Identification, diagnosis, and remediation. *American Journal of Community Psychology*, 1979, **7**, 197–208.

Rickel, A.U., Smith, R.L., & Sharp, K.C. Description and evaluation of a preventive mental health program for preschoolers. *Journal of Abnormal Child Psychology*, 1979, **7**, 101–112.

Roberts, M.C. Personal communication, June 11, 1981.

Roberts, M.C., & Wright, L. The role of the pediatric psychologist as consultant to pediatricians. In J. Tuma (Ed.), *The practice of pediatric psychology*. New York: Wiley, in press.

Roberts, M.C., Wurtele, S.K., Boone, R.R., Ginther, L.V., & Elkins, P.D. Reduction of medical fears by use of modeling: A preventive application in a general population of children. *Journal of Pediatric Psychology*, 1981, **6**, 293–300.

Rodick, J.D., & Henggeler, S.W. The short-term and long-term amelioration of academic and motivational deficiencies among low-achieving inner-city adolescents. *Child Development*, 1980, **51**, 1126–1132.

Roff, M. Some life history factors in relation to various types of adult adjustment. In M. Roff & D.F. Ricks (Eds.), *Life history studies in psychopathology*. Minneapolis: University of Minnesota Press, 1969.

Rosenstein, P.J. Family outreach: A program for the prevention of child neglect and abuse. *Child Welfare*, 1978, **57**, 519–525.

Rothschild, B.F. Incubator isolation as a possible contributing factor to the high incidence of emotional disturbance among prematurely born persons. *The Journal of Genetic Psychology*, 1967, **110**, 287–304.

Sandler, I.N., & Black, M. Life stress and maladaptation of children. *American Journal of Community Psychology*, 1979, **7**, 425–440.

Sandler, I.N., Duricko, A., & Grande, L. Effectiveness of an early secondary prevention program in an inner-city elementary school. *American Journal of Community Psychology*, 1975, **3**, 23–32.

Scarr-Salapetek, S., & Williams, M.L. The effects of early stimulation on low-birth-weight infants. *Child Development*, 1973, **44**, 94–101.

Schinke, S.P., & Gilchrist, L.D. Adolescent pregnancy: An interpersonal skill training approach to prevention. *Social Work in Health Care*, 1977, **3**, 159–167.

Schumaker, J.B., Hovell, M.F., & Sherman, J.A. An analysis of daily report cards and parent-managed privileges in the improvement of adolescents' classroom performance. *Journal of Applied Behavior Analysis*, 1977, **10**, 449–464.

Seashore, M.J., Leifer, A.D., Barnett, C.R., & Leiderman, P.H. The effects of denial of early mother-infant interaction on maternal self-confidence. *Journal of Personality and Social Psychology,* 1973, **26,** 369–378.

Shaywitz, B.A., Cohen, D.J., & Shaywitz, S.E. Editors Column. *The Journal of Pediatrics,* 1979, **95,** 734–736.

Shelness, A., & Charles, S. Children as passengers in automobiles: The neglected minority on the nation's highways. *Pediatrics,* 1975, **56,** 271–275.

Shure, M.B., & Spivack, G. Interpersonal problem solving and primary prevention: Programming for preschool and kindergarten children. *Journal of Clinical Child Psychology,* 1979, **8,** 89–94.

Siegel, L.J., & Peterson, L. Stress reduction in young dental patients through coping skills and sensory information. *Journal of Consulting and Clinical Psychology,* 1980, **48,** 785–787.

Siegel, L.J., & Peterson, L. Effects of coping skills and sensory information on the maintenance of children's response to repeated dental procedures. *Behavior Therapy,* 1981, **12,** 530–535.

Smialek, J.E., Smialek, P.Z., & Spitz, W.U. Accidental bed deaths in infants due to unsafe sleeping situations. *Clinical Pediatrics,* 1977, **16,** 1031–1036.

Smith, R.D. The use of developmental screening tests by primary-care pediatricians. *The Journal of Pediatrics,* 1978, **93,** 524–527.

Solkoff, N., Yaffe, S., Weintraub, D., & Blase, B. Effects of handling on the subsequent developments of premature infants. *Developmental Psychology,* 1969, **1,** 765–768.

Spinetta, J.J., & Rigler, D. The child-abusing parent: A psychological review. *Psychological Bulletin,* 1972, **77,** 296–304.

Spitzzeri, A., & Jason, L.A. Prevention and treatment of smoking in school age children. *Journal of Drug Education,* 1979, **9,** 285–296.

Spivack, G., & Swift, M. The Hahnemann high school behavior (HHSB) rating scale. *Journal of Abnormal Child Psychology,* 1977, **5,** 299–307. (a)

Spivack, G., & Swift, M. "High risk" classroom behaviors in kindergarten and first grade. *American Journal of Community Psychology,* 1977, **5,** 385–397. (b)

Stachnik, T.J. Priorities for psychology in medical education and health care delivery. *American Psychologist,* 1980, **35,** 8–15.

Steele, B.F., & Pollock, C.B. A psychiatric study of parents who abuse infants and small children. In R.E. Helfer & C.H. Kempe (Eds.), *The battered child.* Chicago: University of Chicago Press, 1974.

Stokes, T.F., & Kennedy, S.H. Reducing child uncooperative behavior during dental treatment through modeling and reinforcement. *Journal of Applied Behavior Analysis,* 1980, **13,** 41–50.

Stuart, R.B. Teaching facts about drugs: Pushing or preventing. *Journal of Educational Psychology,* 1974, **66,** 189–201.

Sumpter, E. Behavior problems in early childhood. *Pediatric Clinics of North America,* 1975, **22,** (2), 663–672.

Swisher, J.D., Warner, R.W., & Herr, E. Experimental comparison of four approaches to drug abuse prevention among 9th and 11th graders. *Journal of Counseling Psychology,* 1972, **19,** 328–332.

Task Force on Pediatric Education. *The future of pediatric education.* Evanston, Ill.: Author, 1978.

Thomas, P., Frisone, G., & Lipson, D. An evaluation of parent drug education. *Mental Hygiene,* 1971, **55,** 456–460.

Trotter, R.J. Born too soon. *Science News,* 1980, **118**(15), 234–235.

VandenBos, E.R., & Miller, M.O. Delinquency prevention programs. In R.H. Price, R.F. Ketterer, B.C. Bader, & J. Monahan (Eds.), *Prevention in mental health.* Beverly Hills: Sage, 1980.

Venham, L., Bengston, D., & Cipes, M. Children's response to sequential dental visits. *Journal of Dental Research,* 1977, **56,** 454–459.

Vogelsong, E.L., Most, R.K., & Yenchka, A. Relationship enhancement training for preadolescents in public schools. *Journal of Clinical Child Psychology,* 1979, **8,** 97–100.

Wahler, R.C. Setting generality: Some specific and general effects of child behavior therapy. *Journal of Applied Behavior Analysis,* 1969, **2,** 239–246.

Wallerstein, J.S., & Kelly, J.B. Divorce counseling: A community service for families in the midst of divorce. *American Journal of Orthopsychiatry,* 1977, **47,** 4–22.

Widmayer, S.M., & Field, T.M. Effects of Brazelton demonstrations on early interactions of preterm infants and their teenage mothers. *Infant Behavior and Development,* 1980, **3,** 79–89.

Wright, L. A comprehensive program for mental health and behavioral medicine in a large children's hospital. *Professional Psychology,* 1979, **10,** 458–466.

Yokley, J.M., Glenwick, D.S., Hedrick, T.E., & Page, N.D. *Increasing the immunization of high risk preschoolers: An evaluation of applied community interventions.* Paper presented at the meeting of the Association for Advancement of Behavior Therapy, New York, November, 1980.

Zax, M., & Cowen, E.L. Research on early detection and prevention of emotional dysfunction in young school children. In C.D. Spielberger (Ed.), *Current topics in clinical and community psychology* (Vol. 1). New York: Academic Press, 1969.

Zeilberger, J., Sampen, S.E., & Sloane, H.M. Modification of a child's problem behaviors in the home with the mother as therapist. *Journal of Applied Behavior Analysis,* 1968, **1,** 47–53.

Zlutnick, S., Mayville, W.J., & Moffat, S. Modification of seizure disorders: The interruption of behavioral chains. *Journal of Applied Behavior Analysis,* 1975, **8,** 1–12.

CHAPTER 51

Television Viewing in Children

STEPHEN NOWICKI, JR. AND TERESA BOLICK

The twentieth century can be characterized as a time of rapid technological advancement. Tremendous progress in the field of electronics has had profound effects on the day-to-day life of all of us.

Escalating sales of television sets in the late 1940s and early 1950s were matched by increasing fears regarding effects of the new medium upon children and adolescents. Over the years, the nature of these fears evolved from concerns over the impact upon the child's physical well being to questions about the effects of television upon the child's behavior. For example, in the early 1950s a major concern was that television might damage eyesight (Himmelweit, Oppenheim, & Vince, 1958), lower intelligence, and decrease academic achievement (e.g., Clark, 1951; Ridder, 1963; Witty, 1951). With the advent of the 1960s, researchers focused on the effects of television upon the child's personality and behavior, culminating in congressional hearings and an investigation commissioned by the Surgeon General of the United States. While TV violence has been of particular interest to researchers (e.g., Comstock & Rubinstein, 1972; Liebert, Neale, & Davidson, 1973), television has also been examined in terms of its impact upon prosocial behavior (Stein & Friedrich, 1975) and stereotyped attitudes (McArthur & Eisen, 1976). Even "Sesame Street" and cereal commercials have been scrutinized (e.g., Goldberg, Gorn, & Gibson, 1978).

The authors' goal in this chapter is to discuss the theory and research regarding the interaction between television and the modern child. While not exhaustive, the present compilation allows us to point out both the advantages and the disadvantages of this electronic wonder that has "forced" its way into our lives.

TELEVISION VIEWING IN CHILDREN

The importance of research concerning TV becomes clearer when the pervasiveness of the medium is understood. In 1948, there were approximately 100,000 television sets in American homes; within one decade that number had grown to 50 million (Schramm, Lyle, & Parker, 1961).

Today, television is almost universally available to Americans from a very early age. Some researchers suggest that children begin to watch TV actively before they are 3. By the age of 5, 82 percent of American children view TV regularly, and that figure increases to 94 percent in 7-year-olds (Stevenson, 1972).

Various attempts have been made to quantify the amount of time a child spends in front of a television. These attempts have encountered methodological problems in measuring viewing. For instance, parental reports of their children's viewing range from 1 to 4.5 hours per day while children themselves estimate their viewing time at 5.88 hours a day (Friedrich & Stein, 1973; Rossiter & Robertson, 1975; Woodrick, Chissom, & Smith, 1977). According to some investigators, children spend over one-third of their waking hours in front of the television screen (Friedrich & Stein, 1973). Viewing time seems to

1198

peak in sixth or seventh grade and to decline in high school (Bogart, 1958; Schramm et al., 1961). Sex differences in viewing time have been reported for preschoolers, with boys watching more television than girls (Stevenson, 1972). When all the time spent watching television is totaled, one author, Lesser (1970, pp. 208–214), stated that, by the age of 18, a child had spent more time watching television than in any activity other than sleeping.

Viewing preferences also appear to be related to age and sex of the viewer. Preschool and primary school children show marked preferences for children's programs and cartoons, followed by situation comedies. With this age group, educational, dramatic, and violent programs are significantly less popular (Friedrich & Stein, 1973; Woodrick et al., 1977). Preferences for children's programs begin to decline by age 10 (Bogart, 1958). These age changes in program preferences seem to be affected by sex of subject, however. Sex differences appear as early as first grade when girls begin to choose programs that relate to later sex-related roles while boys maintain their preferences for programs involving adventure, excitement, and physical contact well into adolescence (Schramm et al., 1961).

Socioeconomic status and race also seem to be important mediators of the amount of viewing and program preference, at least among adolescents. Lower class adolescents watch significantly more television than their middle class white counterparts, and, among lower class respondents, blacks spent more time viewing than whites (Dominick & Greenberg, 1970). Lower class tenth-graders were more likely to watch programs that meet their need for fantasy while middle class students prefer reality-oriented programs (Schramm et al., 1961). While adventure and "spy" shows are favorites across racial and socioeconomic lines, black students seem to prefer programs that idealize family life, in contrast to the white students' orientation toward variety shows (Dominick & Greenberg, 1970). There are indications that children prefer programs that portray characters of like ethnicity (Greenberg, 1972; Lyle, 1972) and that black children are more likely than white children to use television as a source of social information (Gerson, 1966; Surlin & Dominick, 1970).

In summary, while the amount and preferences of television viewing may vary according to demographic characteristics of the child and as a function of measurement techniques, there is ample evidence that TV viewing comprises a significant portion of the child's day. As Schramm et al. (1961) concluded 20 years ago, in words still appropriate today: "Television is probably the greatest source of common experience in the lives of children, and, along with the home and school, it has come to play a major part in socializing the child" (p. 12).

FOUNDATIONS FOR RELATING PSYCHOLOGICAL THEORIES TO EFFECTS OF TELEVISION VIEWING

Television has a pervasive influence upon the life of the American child. The mass communications theorists have provided ideas emanating from research related to mass media and attitude and behavior change. These variables also have been explained in terms of theories of observational learning or cognitive development.

Mass communications researchers emphasize that the term "communication" implies the transmission of information (Liebert & Schwartzberg, 1977). This information may be transmitted at different cognitive and emotional levels, and the effects of transmission may be immediate or delayed, overt or covert (Halloran, 1963). Early critics have warned that the mass media may be used to insure the political and social status quo to dull the viewer's capacity for creative and critical thinking, and to promote escapism and passivity (Lazarsfeld & Merton, 1960). Early studies of pre- and posttelevision communities have revealed that the amount of time spent reading magazines and books decreased significantly after the introduction of TV (Bogart, 1958). This suggestion of increased passivity has been explained on the premise that television can satisfy needs for information and entertainment and may communicate that the individual is not required to meet these needs in a more active manner (Glynn, 1956). There are also indications that frequent viewing is associated with belief in the social and political stereotypes portrayed on television (Gerbner & Gross, 1976). Thus mass communications theorists have proposed and begun to demonstrate that the information transmitted via television has both specific and general effects upon the beliefs and behavior of the viewer. Himmelweit et al. (1958) suggested that the effects of such transmission of information are greatest when the viewpoints are presented repeatedly and in a dramatic or emotional form. Susceptibility also is increased if the values presented are congruent with the viewer's current interests or desires. The lack of internal or environmental standards with which to evaluate the information presented also increases the likelihood that the viewer will endorse televised values. Thus attractive and dramatic format of programs coupled with the relative lack of experiences against which to gauge the validity of televised ideas make the child viewer more likely to be influenced by the medium.

The manner in which these factors may influence the viewer can be explained in terms of *observational learning* of behaviors and attitudes. In a less industrialized society, a child could learn about roles and expectations merely by observing neighbors and family members. As society became more diverse and complex, the child was less likely to observe directly all of the attitudes and behavior that he or she might assume in life. Television has come to provide information for the child's conceptualizaton of modern society by providing representations of expectations and experience (Noble, 1975). Bandura's theory of modeling proposes that learning occurs when the observer acquires symbolic representations of experiences or expectations and incorporates them into his or her own repertoire. Implicit in this theory is the assumption that vicarious exposure to an activity may have an impact similar to that of the actual experience. Observational learning, or modeling, includes

three phases: exposure, acquisition, and acceptance. The exposure phase of observational learning is a function of the actual content portrayed as well as the attitudinal and physical surroundings of the viewer. Of course, this exposure can have no impact unless the viewer understands and stores the information presented. This second stage, called the acquisition phase, and the initial exposure stage are both greatly affected by such factors as the viewer's attention and motivation and the information's affective valence and distinctiveness (Bandura, 1965, 1977). Television's attractive, entertaining, and fast-paced mode of presentation should maximize the attentional and motivational factors affecting the exposure and acquisition phases of observational learning.

While modeling theory was originally proposed to explain observational learning of overt behaviors, the theory has been extended to include the acquisition of attitudes and emotional responses. After observation models respond consistently to diverse situations, the viewer is able to abstract the common features and formulate general attitudes (Bandura, 1973). As Glynn (1956) suggested:

The customary repeated experience of television structures the viewer's whole idea of the world and his relations to it. It is here that permanent responses to television lie; it is here that character is formed, for these attitudes are what the viewer then takes into the rest of his experience. (p. 177)

Thus television can act as an agent of socialization to instill values, reinforce habits, and create expectations, just as parents and other persons in the child's life can do (Schramm et al., 1961). By portraying rewards and punishments that follow certain behaviors, television aids in the formulation of expectations that underlie behavior change (Bandura, 1973).

Before enumerating the specific behavioral, attitudinal, and emotional correlates of television viewing in children, it is important to consider a possible mediating variable. Himmelweit et al. (1958) suggested that the viewer is more likely to endorse televised ideas if he or she has neither the experience nor the critical thinking capacities to evaluate the validity of those ideas. Young children may be particularly "gullible" as a function of their level of cognitive development. In the Piagetian stage of preoperational thought, extending roughly from the age of 18 months to 7 years, the child has difficulty distinguishing between reality and fantasy (Noble, 1975). Preoperational children may focus on one dimension of the stimulus and, as a result, fail to understand other dimensions or interrelationships. Children under the age of 6 are also less likely to employ verbal mediators that might facilitate their comprehension of TV events (Wackman & Wartella, 1977). In addition, understanding of televised sequences is limited by a child's ability to attend to a stimulus or to delay a response (McCall, Parke, & Kavanaugh, 1977). However, the semiabstract and fable-like characters of children's programs are very attractive to the target viewers, and the children are also likely to believe in and identify with the characters and events. Thus the level of perceived reality is fairly high in children (Winick & Winick, 1979). This "all-or-none" mode of conceptualizing both life and television presumably is replaced by a growing skepticism as the child moves toward and through the concrete-operational phase of cognitive development. In fact, both the understanding of commercials and a "healthy skepticism" toward advertised messages are correlated highly with maturation (Rossiter & Robertson, 1976). By the age of 12 or 13, the viewer is willing to admit that less than half of what is shown on television is "true-to-life" (Greenberg & Dominick, 1970). More recent research has suggested that the age-related decrease in perceived reality may not be as clear cut as originally reported, since even 12-year-olds demonstrate high levels of believability and identification with fantasy programs (Winick & Winick, 1979). Reexamination of the "perceived reality" construct has permitted an interpretation that is still consistent with a stage theory of cognitive development. It seems that a child's belief that TV is a "magic window" does decrease linearly with age and cognitive development. For example, nursery school and first-grade students were

more likely than third- and fifth-graders to agree that "if you went to Hawaii, you might meet Detective McGarrett..." (a character from a police show taking place in Hawaii). While such a literal belief in televised characters and events decreases with greater cognitive sophistication, older children were as likely as their younger counterparts to employ TV as a basis for expectations about the world (Hawkins, 1977). The use of these expectations in play and spontaneous conversation also has been described (Bolick, 1980). The use of television as a source of expectations may vary as a function of the subjects' real life experience as well as level of cognitive development. It has been reported that children in the 8–16-year-old range are more likely to view television as an accurate representation of occupational and racial groups if they have little actual experience or knowledge to use as a standard of critical evaluation (Donohue & Donohue, 1977).

Not only does comprehension increase with age (and, presumably, experience), but children seem to understand programs better if the content is similar to that common to their own family and environment (Newcomb & Collins, 1979). Apart from maturation, one of the few reliable predictors of children's understanding of and attitude toward commercials is their socialization history (Rossiter & Robertson, 1976). Thus it is apparent that both maturation and experience are important determinants of a child's reaction to television, whether that reaction is behavioral, attitudinal, cognitive, or emotional. As Greenberg and Reeves (1976) suggest:

To the extent that television content is the sole or principal source of information for a child on some particular issue or social situation, that information is more likely to be judged by the child as realistic and to be accepted. To the extent that television content is perceived to be real-to-life, the child's attitudes and behaviors are more likely to be consistent with the content of that exposure. (p. 87)

In summary, researchers in mass communications and psychological disciplines concur in suggesting that the interactions between child and television maximize the conditions for observational learning to take place. Television's impact on the child varies as a function of (1) the recurrence of values or attitudes from one program to another; (2) the dramatic presentation of events; (3) the presentation of material relevant to the viewer's current environment and needs; (4) the viewer's lack of previous knowledge against which to evaluate the values and events portrayed (Halloran, 1963).

TELEVISION AND AGGRESSION

American history can be characterized as being a history of violence. To quote Eron (1963):

It requires only perfunctory analysis to demonstrate that aggression has been an integral component of nearly every major endeavor, institution, and function of the United States as well as of most other "civilized" countries. For example, it is almost banal to say that the founding of this country comprised a series of violent acts from the Boston Tea Party through the battles of the American Revolution to the Declaration of Independence and the virtual extinction of the native American Indian. (p. 7)

Of course there are innumerable other instances of violence in American history: the bloody Civil War; the victimization of various minority groups by violent subgroups such as the Klu Klux Klan, Black Panthers, etc.; and the various assassinations of our country's leaders such as John Kennedy, Robert Kennedy, and Martin Luther King, Jr. At the time that we are writing this chapter, the city of Atlanta is under a virtual siege of fear because of a seemingly unending rash of murders of young black adolescents. Violence seems to surround us and seems to have the power to dictate the quality of life that we enjoy. Television has become the medium of the masses and as such seems to be a very significant link in a circle of violence from the general community to TV and back to the general community. If a person watches an average amount of television he or she will be

a witness to well over 400 violent murders, beatings, or violent disruptions in a month (Duke & Nowicki, 1978). The effect of this constant barrage of violence on the developing human organism has been a matter of intensive debate since the inception of television. Some investigations have focused on the impact of televised scenes of physical cartoon violence and verbal violence on the preschool youngster. While we do not know the long-lasting effects of such intensive portrayals of violence, we do know that, for example, these scenes of physical violence produce fear and worry in the youngsters that view such stimulation (Lagerspetzs et al., 1978).

Generally, there have been three theoretical attempts to predict the effects of steady diets of violence on children and adolescents. The first of these theories, the psychoanalytic theory, states that each person is generally endowed with a certain amount of energy directed to destructiveness and that this energy must be expressed in one form or another (Freud, 1925). If this energy toward destructiveness is blocked or inhibited from a direct external expression, then it will be turned back on the individual and expressed indirectly (Feshbach & Singer, 1971). In this view, the biological nature of aggressive impulses and actions is emphasized, and experiential factors, while not completely ignored, are underplayed. In psychoanalytic theory, the concepts of fantasy and catharsis play major roles in explaining or predicting the effect of viewing violent stimuli on the behavior of children and adolescents. Within this framework, fantasies are seen as substitutes for desired but relatively unobtainable goal states, and they serve to lower tension or drive states. Consistent with this view, then, aggressive fantasies are seen as substitutes for injuring someone when such an action is inhibited by fear of either external or internal punishment. The degree of reward or satisfaction from such substitute fantasy activity is less than the amount that could be obtained from overt aggressive behavior and, therefore, only partially reduces the aggressive drive. According to Feshbach, a leading proponent of the catharsis theory, televised violence operates through fantasy functions to decrease the possibility or probability of aggressive behavior (Feshbach & Singer, 1971). Feshbach argues that fantasy injury partially substitutes for the actual inflicting of injury as a way of discharging the aggressive drive. This drive reduction reinforces violent thoughts, which are posited to be incompatible with overt aggression. Violent television, then, is seen as providing rewarding substitutes for aggressive action.

As an example of the kind of study that has been done to support this view, Feshbach and Singer (1971) showed either aggressive or mostly nonaggressive television programs to boys enrolled in residential private schools and in homes for the underprivileged. During this time, supervisory personnel rated the boys' verbal and physical aggression, and the boys were given a number of personality tests. The authors report that their findings provide evidence that exposure to televised violence reduces aggressive behavior. However, they came to their conclusion even though, when the boys were statistically equated for initial differences in aggressiveness, those in the private schools did not differ on any of the measures of overt aggression.

Patterson and Neustadter (1978) have reviewed the evidence for and against the catharsis hypothesis. Generally, they conclude that results regarding the theory are somewhat equivocal. There does not seem to be the hardcore scientific evidence that would be telling in support of this theoretical explanation of the effect of viewed violence on the expression of violence in children and adolescents. However, this does not stop the appearance of much literature, especially within the psychoanalytic area, in support of this hypothesized relationship presented in catharsis theory.

In contrast to psychoanalytic theory, desensitivity theory posits that the viewing of violence blunts children's sensitivity to violence. Generally this theory suggests that viewers become used to high levels of violence viewed on TV. Consistent with this theory, it is also posited that, in order to protect themselves, children become somewhat cool and distant to the numbers of smashings, beatings, murders, and monsters they are viewing. Wertham (1964) points out that, as well as blunting their usual emotional responses to aggression, television may serve as an effective "school for violence."

Whether crime and violence programs arouse a lust for violence, reinforce it when it is present, show a way to carry it out, teach the best way to get away with it or merely blunt the child's (and adult's) awareness of its wrongness, television has become a school for violence.

In this school young people are never, literally never, taught that in itself violence is reprehensible. The lesson they do get is that violence is the great adventure and a sure solution, and he who is best at it wins. (p. xii)

Drabman and his colleagues have presented a number of studies whose results support the desensitization theory. For example, in one study (Drabman & Thomas, 1974), third-graders first were exposed to a 15-minute violent or nonviolent television segment. When they witnessed the fight between two younger children, it was found that those in the group that had watched the televised violence were less ready to summon appropriate adult help than those who had witnessed the baseball segment. Likewise, these subjects in the violent condition were less likely to intervene at all after viewing the violent film as compared to the other group. Using somewhat the same experimental procedure, Thomas and Drabman (1975) showed that third-grade subjects who viewed the violent film were slower to report real violence than third-graders who had seen the film on baseball. From these as well as other studies (e.g., Drabman, Thomas, & Jarvie, 1977) Drabman concluded that TV violence teaches children to increase levels of acceptable aggression. Thus Drabman's conclusion is consistent with the idea that children see so much violence on television that it desensitizes them to violence occurring in real life and diminishes the likelihood that they will make a prosocial response to observed violence.

In support of the concept that there is a lowered arousal state in those who see violence, Thomas (1977) tested the hypothesis that exposure to violence decreases emotional responsivity to portrayals of real life aggression. Subjects viewed either a violent TV show or an exciting but nonviolent sport event. They were then shown a videotape scene of real aggression. When emotion was measured by changes in skin resistance, it was found that subjects who had viewed the aggressive stimuli were less aroused by the scenes of real aggression than those who had not seen the aggressive stimuli. Moreover, Thomas found that the amount of television violence normally viewed was negatively related to responsivity while viewing any kind of aggressive stimuli on TV. That is, heavy TV viewers were less responsive to viewing aggression in this experimental situation. These results held for 8- and 10-year-olds and college students and reflect the significance television viewing can have on the real life behavior of a wide age range of subjects.

The last group of theoretical approaches can be subsumed under the general heading of learning theories. While learning theorists do not deny the possible biological underpinnings of aggression suggested by psychoanalytic theorists, they assume that the effects of experience are most important in the causation and expression of aggression.

Some of these learning theorists have suggested that aggression is a byproduct of frustration. Important in determining the nature and extent of future aggressive behavior are the learning conditions associated with the initial responses to frustration and the further reinforcement history of those responses. Reinforcing factors are, therefore, given an important role in the development of aggression. Reinforcement and modeling have been offered as alternatives to the idea that aggression results from frustration. Indeed, the most prevalent learning-theory approach at present is that developed by Bandura and his colleagues who espouse an observational learning model. As mentioned earlier, observational learning involves three steps. First, the observer is exposed to modeling cues. Second, after this exposure he or she must acquire and recall what he or she has seen before the third

step, which is his or her acceptance of the model's behavior as a guide for his or her own. Beginning with his now famous series of experiments with a "Bobo" doll, Bandura and his associates demonstrated the principles and factors involved in observational learning (Bandura, Ross, & Ross, 1961, 1963). Two critical factors affecting the modeling process have been uncovered: vicarious consequences and status of the model. That is, if a television character is rewarded for his aggression, then certainly it will have a proactive effect on the observer. And further, should this model who is rewarded for the aggressive behavior have some status, then the impact on future aggressive behavior of the child will be increased significantly. Usually this impact on the child occurs despite the child's self-statements that aggression may be undesirable and morally reprehensible. That is, although a child says he or she does not endorse aggressive behavior, should the model be rewarded for aggression and the model be of some high status, the child will show increased aggressive behavior in spite of self-statements to the contrary. The frightening consequences implied in this theoretical reasoning are delineated by Liebert and Schwatzberg (1977). They had participants view either a 3.5-minute sequence from a violent show or an exciting sports event. (As you can see, this is much like the research approach used by Drabman and his associates.) Each child was then escorted to a room and given the opportunity to push two buttons each time a light came on. One of the buttons was labeled "hurt" and the other "help." Using a total duration of pushing the "hurt" button as their measure of aggression, these investigators found that regardless of sex, children who viewed the aggressive program were significantly more willing to hurt another child than those who had watched the sports sequences.

Learning theorists have helped others to realize the potential effect of the situation on the generalization and impact of watched TV violence. Others have pointed out that factors such as disadvantaged background, amount of TV viewing, presence or absence of adults, and type of family climate all have an effect on the impact of televised violence (e.g., Mc-Carthy, 1975; Charlton, Liebelt, & Sultz Jetta Tausch, 1974).

When one looks back over the long history of violent television programming and its effects on the lives of United States citizens, there could be some cause for pessimism concerning the future. The same reservations regarding the quality of television programming, especially in regard to that concerned with violent behavior, that were offered two decades ago are being offered today. With some exceptions (e.g., the attempt to reduce violent programming during a family viewing hour from 8–9 p.m.) television programming of violence has continued without much change. There is some choice for the viewing public in that the public broadcasting networks offer much less violence than that shown on the commercial stations (Poulos, Harvey, & Liebert, 1976). However, the ability of community agencies such as the PTA to change the types of programs shown on commercial television has been relatively unsuccessful. Only the theoretical framework involving cartharsis gives us any reason to believe that the violence shown on TV may have positive impact on the developing attitudes of children. Unfortunately, of the three theoretical approaches offered, this one has the least amount of empirical support. Seemingly, as long as violence seems to satisfy the viewing public and is related to selling products, commercial television will continue to show violence, in spite of the fact that research evidence suggests televised violence has a significant potential for negative impact on the developing child.

TV AND PROSOCIAL BEHAVIOR

The amount of attention devoted to investigations of the effect of television on prosocial behavior in children is second only to examinations of the impact of TV violence. Laboratory and field studies have demonstrated that television is a powerful agent for observational learning not only of aggression but also of prosocial behavior. As early as 3 years of age, a child can imitate adaptive play behavior that he or she watched on television (McCall, Parke, & Kavanaugh, 1977). Exposure to specially produced TV sequences has been associated with increased adherence to rules (Stein & Bryan, 1972; Wolfe & Cheyne, 1972) and delay of gratification in elementary school students (Yates, 1974). Similar increases in tolerance for delay, rule obedience, and task persistence were demonstrated in preschoolers exposed to "Mister Rogers' Neighborhood" (Friedrich & Stein, 1973). Children who watched only four 15-minute episodes of "Mister Rogers" displayed increased social contacting and expression of approval toward peers (Coates, Pusser, & Goodman, 1976). First-graders who watched a prosocial episode of "Lassie" were more willing to engage in helpful behavior than students who watched a neutral "Lassie" segment or an episode of "Brady Bunch" (Sprafkin, Liebert, & Poulos, 1975). Helping behavior was also more frequent among students who watched a program in which intense conflict was resolved in a constructive manner than among children who watched a violent resolution of conflict (Collins & Getz, 1976). There are also indications that prosocial programs such as "Sesame Street" may produce short term reduction of aggressive behavior (Bankart & Anderson, 1979).

However, as with exposure to violence, exposure to prosocial television may have differential impacts for different socioeconomic groups. During a four-week period of exposure to "Mister Rogers Neighborhood," low socioeconomic preschoolers displayed significant increases in prosocial classroom behavior while higher socioeconomic children showed little change. Children who showed the greatest increases in cooperative behavior during the exposure period were those who typically watched more violent programs at home and who tended to be from low income families (Friedrich & Stein, 1973). Project Head Start children did not show increases in social interaction, self-regulation, or imaginative play as a function of exposure to "Mister Rogers" unless the classroom setting included toys or specific training designed to reinforce the televised values (Friedrich-Cofer et al., 1979). It is likely that socioeconomic status is an important mediator in the acquisition of prosocial behaviors, but systematic investigation is necessary for specification of the relationships between SES, viewing, and prosocial behavior.

While prosocial programs seem to have positive effects upon the behavior of some children, the durability of these effects over time may be negligible. Friedrich and Stein (1973) reported that increases in prosocial behavior were maintained during the four-week viewing period but did not extend to the two-week posttest. Similarly, Bankart and Anderson (1979) found that their preschool subjects returned to preexposure levels of aggression on the day after viewing. Researchers who found changes after brief exposure cautioned that these changes were short lived and very specific (Sprafkin et al., 1975). It seems that increases in prosocial behavior are maintained most effectively when viewing occurs in a naturalistic setting over a longer period of time (Friedrich & Stein, 1975) and when televised behaviors and attitudes are supported by environmental reinforcement (Friedrich & Stein, 1973).

TV AND ATTITUDES

Besides aggressive and prosocial behavior, investigators have focused on the relationship between TV viewing and racial and sex role attitudes by examining program content, viewer ideas, and manipulations designed to change attitudes. For example, content analyses of network entertainment programming revealed that male characters occupied 66–75 percent of all scripted parts and that 70–90 percent of the characters were white. White males were powerful, persistent, relatively nonaltruistic, and involved in occupational roles that were highly professional, prestigious, and powerful. While black males were persistent and helpful, they were not portrayed as powerful or forceful in the traditional senses of the words. Both black and white females were unlikely to display persis-

tence, delay of gratification, or power. White females were portrayed as the unemployed "gatekeepers" of societal rules, while black females were engaged in attempts to resolve conflict and reassure others (Donagher et al., 1975).

Characters in Saturday morning children's programs were equally role stereotyped. Males demonstrated expertise and problem solving more frequently than females, who were often in search of guidance. Females were highly compliant, in contrast to the autonomy displayed by male characters (McArthur & Eisen, 1976; Nolan, Galst, & White, 1977). The power and independence of televised male characters (especially white males) is relevant since viewers are more likely to identify with and imitate characters who are considered powerful (Bandura, Ross, & Ross, 1961; Zimmer & Sheposh, 1975). As might be predicted on the basis of theories of observational learning and mass communications, kindergarten and second-grade students who watched more than 25 hours of television per week were more likely to endorse television's traditional sex role stereotypes than children who watched less than 10 hours per week (Frueh & McGhee, 1975). The association between amount of viewing and sex role stereotyping was not, however, demonstrated in a sample of older children, but the researchers suggested that their results were a function of the abstract and difficult nature of the questionnaire rather than a refutation of previous findings (Perloff, 1977).

Although the association between television viewing and stereotyped values typically has been regarded in a negative light, there are suggestions that nontraditional programs and commercials can change racial and sex role stereotypes. Even though the program was not designed expressly to change racial attitudes, children who watched "Sesame Street" for two years displayed more favorable attitudes toward blacks than they had previously (Bogatz & Ball, 1972). White preschoolers who watched specially produced program segments portraying an integrated play setting were more likely to voice a preference for Oriental and Indian playmates than children exposed to segments with only white children (Gorn, Goldberg, & Kanungo, 1976). Similar changes in sex role behavior and attitudes have been demonstrated. Nursery school children showed an increased frequency of "like sex" play activities after viewing a "traditional" nine-minute program. After watching a male model play with "feminine" toys, nursery school boys were more likely to play with these than with "masculine" toys (McArthur & Eisen, 1976). Five- and six-year-old girls who watched a "reversed stereotyped" children's program were significantly less traditional in sex role attitudes than viewers of "traditional stereotyped" Saturday morning shows (Davidson, Yasuna, & Tower, 1979). After watching nonstereotyped commercials, low income black, white, and Mexican-American girls showed increased preferences for traditionally male jobs (O'Bryant & Corder-Bolz, 1978a, 1978b; Pingree, 1978). While there are reports of attitude or behavior changes as a function of viewing nontraditional programs, there are no reliable indications that such changes are enduring or generalizable across sex and age and may be confounded by the child's tendency to endorse ideas or actions that are novel (Krugman, & Hartley, 1960; Zajonc, 1968). At present, then, the questions of the impact of television upon racial and sex role attitudes warrants further investigation.

TELEVISION AND COGNITIVE VARIABLES

The examination of the associations of television viewing with variables such as intelligence, achievement, attention, concept learning, and information processing must include an emphasis on educational television. Investigation of impact of educational television has focused on two areas: the acquisition of skills and knowledge, and attention. Generally, the developers and viewers of programs such as "Sesame Street," "The Electric Company," "Mister Rogers' Neighborhood," and the like, assume that these programs do have

positive effects on the development of various cognitive skills. However, conclusive support for these assumptions is somewhat elusive. As we will see, subjects in some studies show increases in certain cognitive areas while subjects in other studies do not. For example, in a study by Diaz-Guerrero et al. (1976) 3-, 4- and 5-year-olds from lower class daycare centers in Mexico City viewed a culturally adapted version of "Sesame Street." The experimental subjects watched 50 minutes a day for six months while the controls watched noneducational material. Pre-/posttesting showed that the experimental group made significant gains in four of nine cognitive and perceptual areas. However, a follow-up study that included three socioeconomic levels found no differences between the experimental and control groups. Other studies have shown that educational programs have some significant, though small, effects on cognitive functioning. Salomon (1976) studied 5-, 7-, and 8-year-old Israeli children who watched "Sesame Street." Subjects who were pre- and posttested demonstrated new knowledge in direct relation to the amount of viewing that they did. However, only the 7- and 8-year-olds showed improved cognitive skill mastery, and the skill mastery was only found in heavy viewers. Those children with already developed cognitive skills gained very little as compared to those whose skills were not so well developed.

While there are indications that children can learn from educational TV, there have not been studies to substantiate that children can transfer problem-solving abilities learned from TV to real life. Hodapp (1977) had 52 5.5–6.5-year-olds see a television segment where a problem was presented and solved. A smaller number of children were shown a television scene of the same length. When these children were asked to perform an identical or transfer problem task, it was found that young children could imitate but could not learn to transfer the problem-solving strategies that they saw on the TV to the solving of a real life problem.

In the related area of attention, Levin and Anderson (1976) investigated the relationship between preschool children's visual attention to a TV program and the program content itself. The subjects were 12- to 14-month-old white middle class children who were videotaped while watching "Sesame Street." Using various procedures, the observers recorded the offset and onset of each child's visual attention. They found that increased attention to TV was age related with a sharp increase occurring at about 2.5 years. Various attributes (sex of actors, activity level, etc.) of the program were also found to have significant effects on attention.

Some investigators have studied attention and information acquisition as a function of the manner of program presentation. Zillman et al. (1980) studied kindergarten and first-grade students ($n = 70$) under various conditions of humor and pacing. On the basis of information acquisition as measured pre and post, both humor conditions produced more effective information acquisition than any of the no-humor groups. Likewise, fast pacing of these humorous inserts produced a significant facilitative effect on information acquisition more rapidly than did slow pacing. Others have suggested that fast pacing may be detrimental. Tower et al. (1979) studied preschoolers who watched two weeks of either "Mister Rogers' Neighborhood" or "Sesame Street" or a control condition of films about animals and nature. It was found that "Sesame Street" watchers showed more variability and superior performance on inferential questions while "Mister Rogers' Neighborhood" viewers did better on factual and recognition kinds of questions. As with all other studies in this area, these effects interacted in a complex manner with age, sex, imaginativeness, and IQ. However, the authors suggested that slow-paced format such as that found in "Mister Rogers' Neighborhood" yielded positive changes especially for less imaginative subjects. The finding that "Mister Rogers' Neighborhood" had these prosocial effects on preschool children is consistent with the belief of some critics who assert that television in general, and educational TV's "Sesame Street" in particular, produce hyperactivity, impulsivity, and reduced or shortened attention spans in the young viewers. These critics believed

that the fast pace of a program like "Sesame Street" teaches the children to desire and expect that intensive pace in other areas of their life, too. To study this problem, Anderson, Levin, and Lorch, (1977) had 4-year-olds view a slowly paced or rapidly paced "Sesame Street" program or had them listen to stories read by a parent and then observed these children in testing and play conditions. Using a number of measures to assess the differences between the groups, these investigators found no evidence that rapid TV pacing has any immediate negative effect on the behavior of preschool children.

Certainly, while television seems to be having some effect on the cognitive processing abilities of children, the exact effects are difficult to ascertain and appear to be related to a complex array of subjects and situational factors. It seems clear that, while educational programs such as "Sesame Street," "Mister Rogers' Neighborhood," and the like, do not have negative effects on children, there is a surprising lack of substantial support that they have a positive effect on the cognitive processing abilities of their viewers. Certainly, in this of all areas, more research is crucially needed with complex designs that include subject and situational variables.

Although educational programs have been the focus of a great deal of research, they account for only a fraction of the typical child's viewing time, especially in the older child. Unfortunately, our understanding of the relationship between entertainment television programming and intelligence and achievement is much less firm. As stated above, early critics of television focused on the effects of viewing upon IQ and achievement. The assumption that time taken away from reading, homework, or active exploration of the environment led to the expectation that heavy viewing would hinder intellectual and academic development. However, the results of published research examining this issue have been equivocal. In some schools, the intelligence test scores of fifth-graders (IQ range = 85–130) were not associated significantly with the time devoted to TV, although IQs were related to time spent reading (Long & Henderson, 1973). Others have suggested that "high" IQ (above 123) fifth- and sixth-graders watched less TV than their "low" IQ (below 108) peers (Bailyn, 1959). Yet another proposal is there is no relationship between IQ and viewing in the lower grades but that from eighth grade on lower IQ children watch more television (Schramm et al., 1961). The findings relating TV viewing to achievement are equally confusing. Examination of the English, social studies, and mathematics grades of seventh- and eighth-grade viewers revealed no significant relationship between academic achievement and total number of hours spent watching television (Ridder, 1963). This finding is consistent with the results for "normal achieving" fifth- and sixth-graders. Yet underachieving fifth- and sixth-grade girls watch more TV than their overachieving counterparts (Bailyn, 1959).

It is apparent that the question of the associations between TV viewing, IQ, and achievement is far from resolved, but a search of the recent literature suggests that the investigations have been relegated primarily to doctoral dissertations. The absence of continuing research is not surprising considering the large number of variables that may confound IQ-achievement-TV relationships (e.g., sex of child, family income, parental education). The authors propose that a more relevant focus is on the differential functions of TV for children of differing abilities. For example, it has been shown that mentally retarded children watch TV for extended periods of time but that they learn little from the activity (Ahrens & Singh, 1977). After observing that both low and high IQ children learn more from televised instruction than from live conventional instruction, researchers suggest that children with differential intellectual sophistication may vary not so much in the amount of TV exposure as in the way they process what they view. It was suggested that low IQ viewers benefited from televised instruction because it focused their attention on relevant information. On the other hand, for high IQ children, television presented information at a faster rate, which was more consistent with their preferred rate of learning (Schramm,

1962; Snow & Salomon, 1968; Westley & Barrow, 1959). There are some indications that higher IQ children (at least males) have program preferences which differ from those of lower IQ children (Bailyn, 1959). In conclusion, it seems that more intelligent children may "use" television for different purposes and may be affected by TV programs in a way that is qualitatively different from the functions the medium serves for less intelligent children. Thus our research efforts should focus on the specifics of the interactions between TV, intelligence, and achievement and the means by which these interactions can be optimized.

TV AND PERSONALITY VARIABLES

There are relatively few recent studies that describe relationships between television viewing and the child's personality. Early in the era of television, negative personality changes, such as "reactive apathy," were linked with television viewing (Meerloo, 1954). Some researchers suggested that TV viewing was a passive activity that interfered with play (Bogart, 1958) and reinforced the idea in viewers that they could rely on others as sources of satisfaction and security (Glynn, 1956). Heavy viewers (defined as those who watched TV for more than half of the time between school and bedtime) were described by teachers as submissive, shy, and retiring. Compared to light viewers, heavy viewers provided personality test responses that reflected more anxiety and peer difficulties (Himmelweit et al., 1958), "personal problems" (Bailyn, 1959), or unsatisfactory peer relationships (Riley & Riley, 1954).

More recent investigations of TV viewing have also provided some support for an association between viewing and personality. Japanese boys who watched "humanity-type" programs were more moralistic and sympathetic than boys who watched "masculinity-type" shows (Ogura, 1979). One investigator reported that television violence may lead to anxiety, rather than aggressive behavior, in children (Kniveton, 1978) while others suggested that some programs may permit the child viewer to overcome his or her fears (Hayes & Schauble, 1978; Salje, 1978). Boys rated as "low adjusted" in the classroom and their fathers spent significantly more time watching television than "high adjusted" boys (Hume, O'Connor, & Lowery, 1977). However, other researchers failed to find television viewing to be associated with more global self-report measures of personality (Bolick, 1980; Satterfield, 1972).

Thus amount of television viewing has shown positive, negative, or negligible correlations with desirable personality characteristics in child viewers. The confused (and confusing) nature of these results suggest several interpretations. First current behavioral and paper-and-pencil measures of personality may not be sophisticated enough to reveal consistent associations with viewing. Second, while television may act as an agent of socialization, other environmental influences (such as family and teachers) may play an even greater role in personality formation and these influences are difficult, if not impossible, to control experimentally.

TV COMMERCIALS AND THEIR EFFECT ON CHILDREN

Children spend the greatest portion of their television viewing time watching the commercial networks. On these networks, programs are placed on the air and remain on the air only because people in business have something they want to sell and believe that they can sell enough of that product through advertising to make up for the cost of putting that show on television. Therefore, it is crucially important for advertisers to persuade others to buy the product they are trying to sell. It became apparent in the late 1950s and 60s that some television advertising was having negative effects on various groups of television watchers. More recently, those television advertisers who have focused their appeals on young children have come under intensive attack by various community groups. These community groups have

pointed out that young children have few defenses to deal with the onslaught of sophisticated advertising techniques that persuades them to want candy, other sugar-flavored food stuffs, and toys. For these reasons, various community groups like the national Parent Teacher Association and Catholic League of Decency have attempted to put pressure on the networks to cut back and/or change the kind of TV advertising that is done with young children, especially during the hours when young children probably will be watching television.

Research on television advertising has generally been done by two camps of people. The first camp is made up of those scientists who are attempting to find out what kinds of children are most susceptible to intensive advertising, with the implicit belief that certain sets of advertisements could have negative effects on the lives of these children. In contrast, the second camp of researchers are those advertisers who are looking for more effective ways of getting people in general and children in particular to buy their products. Both of these groups have come to a similar conclusion that, indeed, there are groups of children that are more susceptible to certain types of TV advertising. For example, Ward, Wackman, and Wartella (1977) studied the effects of TV advertising on children whose mothers were either blue collar or middle class. They found that there were differences among the three age groups and the attention they paid to TV commericals. The older children more often used information-processing strategies that are fundamental to their choosing the products that they really need. However, these researchers found that younger children have more difficulty than their older peers in being able to decipher and delineate what is appropriate for themselves. In fact, Gorn and Goldberg (1977) found that in low income children even a single exposure to a commercial produced favorable attitudes toward that product. In this same vein, Robertson and Rossiter (1977) examined the effects of exposure to TV advertising as a function of age, peer integration, and parental education. The dependent measure in their study was the number of requests children made for advertised items. As expected, those subjects who were heavy TV viewers requested significantly more toys and games than did low exposure subjects. However, even more interesting was the fact that younger subjects made significantly more requests than older subjects. Furthermore, when heavy TV viewing was combined with low social integration, these subjects made the most requests for the advertised products. The results of this study suggest the importance of taking other factors into consideration when attempting to determine the impact of TV advertising.

There seems little doubt that intensive advertising in the short term can have a significant impact on children's behavioral choices. What is more surprising is that some advertising affects all ages similarly. For example, Robertson and Rossiter (1976) studied first-, third-, and fifth-graders' choices of certain toys and games during Christmas time. Surveys made between one and five weeks before Christmas of children's choices showed significant increases (of 5 percent) in toys and games targeted as a function of the ad campaign.

What may be less obvious but most important is the effect of persuasive commercials on the behavior of the children in their relationship with their parents. Sheikh and Moleski (1977) studied the effects of TV commercials on children from the first, third, and fifth grades. Generally, they found that commercials have a strong effect on children's behavior by the time they reach the third grade. In fact, not only do children make more purchase requests, but they also seem less prone to accept parental refusal and more likely to react aggressively when faced with frustration. One can only imagine how these behaviors create a climate of tension within a family. The potentially damaging effects of such parent-child interactions within the family were also pointed out by Galst and White (1976).

Researchers have also become aware that advertising can have differential impact on boys and girls (Rust & Watkins, 1975). For example, boys seem to respond more to purely physical kinds of advertisements whereas girls are more apt to be persuaded by social and interpersonal kinds of commercials. However, all children seemed to pay more attention when there is physical action in the commercial as opposed to static kinds of presentations.

There have been some attempts to study the relationship between commercials and the production of prosocial behaviors and attitudes. Some commercials are presented to help the child to discriminate between what is real and unreal. Pingree (1978) studied the possibility that TV content commercials can teach either traditional or nontraditional sex-typed attitudes in regard to women. She found that the subject's perceptions of reality can be successfully manipulated and that attitude change can take place although there were other complex relationships she uncovered. These complexities may have prevented O'Bryant (1978a,b) from finding a relation between commercials showing counterstereotypic situations portrayed by TV actresses and changes in subjects' stereotypic views of women. However, she did find that the subject's knowledge of occupations increased through the use of these commercials. It seems apparent that TV commercials could be very helpful in providing prosocial and counterstereotypic messages that could have significant prosocial effects on the children viewing them. Likewise, it would be very helpful if advertisers would be more attuned to the knowledge base of the children they are focusing on. In one study (Liebert et al., 1977) investigators found that subjects exposed to commercials with the disclaimer "some assembly required" did not understand the need for putting the object together. However, when the subjects were exposed to this commercial with the modified disclaimer "you have to put it together" they understood the need more clearly and this affected their ability to make a choice as to whether they wanted the object or not.

Some researchers have criticized advertisers for giving the viewers, especially children, the view of a world where everything is in order and all wishes are fulfilled. The contrast between this kind of world and the realities of the present and foreseeable future in which there are shortages of fundamental commodities potentially creates a great deal of tension in the children. Friedlander (1977) suggests that the values of consumerism and fulfillment through consumerism can be gradually removed if those in charge focus on the effects they are having on the social and familial life. Parents also have been concerned about commercials that are directed at their children (Feldman, Wolf, & Warmouth, 1977). It has been pointed out that 65 percent of parents surveyed preferred some sort of regulation of child-directed commercials. While there has been some impact of consumer groups on the manner in which advertising is done with younger children, recent reviews of the empirical research on television advertising to children suggests that little movement has been made (Chestnut, 1979).

NEW DIRECTIONS

While TV may act as a powerful influence in the life of the child, it is likely that its impact is affected by mediating variables. Mediators such as sex, age, and socioeconomic status were discussed above. However, examinations that focus on associations between viewing and characteristics of the child himself or herself ignore potentially the most powerful mediating variable: the family. When child-rearing practices were examined in relation to television viewing in middle class families, researchers found that preschool children of punitive parents watched more television than other preschoolers (Maccoby, 1954). Others have suggested that mothers who demonstrate independent, thoughtful, or internally oriented values tended to take a more active role in monitoring the viewing of their children and to emphasize programs low in aggression or violence. Children of such mothers also tended to be more imaginative in play than offspring of mothers who defined their roles primarily in terms of other people (Singer & Singer, 1976).

It seems that the family may influence the quantity of viewing, the choice of programs,

and the viewer's reactions to television. Communications theorists have provided a framework for interpreting the mediating effect of family communications upon the observational learning process. The framework is based upon two assumptions: (1) a child's viewing is determined in part by interpersonal factors; (2) a child's interpretation of TV content affects subsequent interpersonal relationships. In assessing the validity of these assumptions, Chaffee and Tims (1976) identified two dimensions of family communication: idea oriented and socio-oriented. Families high in idea-oriented communication encourage the child to express ideas openly, but socio-oriented families "teach" their children to avoid familial conflict even if it requires suppression of individual viewpoints (Abel, 1976). Investigations of the relationship between family communication and TV viewing have revealed that modeling effects are strongest in high socio-oriented families (Chaffee, McLeod, & Atkin, 1971) and that the children in such families express viewing preferences similar to their perceptions of parental preferences (Abel, 1976). Socio-oriented children who watch a powerful TV character might be expected to endorse behaviors and attitudes similar to those of the character since they have learned that children should not question the authority of powerful others. In contrast, the idea-oriented child might be more likely to question the ideas presented by television (Chaffee, 1978). One unanswered question is that of the net result of conflict between televised and familial values, especially in socio-oriented families. Another question concerns the associations between family communications and acquisition of specific behaviors and attitudes. The family communications framework appears to be a promising means of controlling a portion of the variance contributed by differing environmental conditions. This framework may allow us to change our questions from "How does TV affect children?" to "Which types of programs produce which effects in what type of family?"

In general, there are more questions than answers about how to deal with the interactions among children, families, and television. Even as scientists have attempted to answer these important questions, the mass media have expressed the concerns of parents and educators just as vocally and frequently. Scarcely a month passes without an article on TV and children being published in a popular magazine. Just as the scientific literature has moved from opinion and speculation to empirical investigation of TV-related issues, so have the popular media. At this writing, *TV Guide* (May 23, 1981) has initiated a monthly feature concerning television and family life, written by two active and respected TV researchers, Jerome and Dorothy Singer (Singer & Singer, 1981).

What advice might we, as scientist-practioners, offer to parents and teachers? First and foremost, we suggest that the television set should not be allowed to become a battleground. Particularly in families with young children, parents should not hesitate to set a limit on amount of viewing nor to veto inappropriate programs. Second, parents should transform television viewing into an "active" activity. This process may range from choosing specific programs to watch (rather than watching whatever comes on) to encouraging children to read about the people, places, or ideas presented on television. Our third recommendation for parents is in the same vein: parents should watch TV with their children as often as possible. After the program ends, the family can discuss the program and the ways in which it conforms to or diverges from the family or community values. This is especially important when TV programs present violence or controversial ideas. Parents should be ready to turn off a program that they find objectionable, but this act can be used as a forum for discussion. Parents should provide an abundance of alternatives to television: reading material; arts and crafts supplies; family activities. Finally, parents themselves should act as models for active viewing instead of passive observation. At this point, our advice to parents may be summed up in the words used by Shayon (1951) 30 years ago: "It would seem, then, that what television can do to your child will depend upon what your child is, what you are educat-ing and guiding him to be, before he looks at television" (p. 23). We could not offer a better conclusion or guide for researchers, clinicians, or parents.

REFERENCES

Abel, J.D. The family and child television viewing. *Journal of Marriage and the Family,* 1976, **38,** 331–335.

Ahrens, M.G., & Singh, N.N. Television viewing habits of mentally retarded children. *Australian Journal of Mental Retardation,* 1977, **4,** 1–3.

Anderson, D.R., Levin, S.R., & Lorch, E.P. The effects of TV program pacing on the behavior of preschool children. *AV Communication Review,* 1977, **25,** 159–166.

Bailyn, L. Mass media and children: A study of exposure habits and cognitive effects. *Psychological Monographs,* 1959, **73,** (Whole No. 4.), 41–48.

Bandura, A. Vicarious processes: A case of no-trial learning. In L. Berkowitz (Ed.), *Advances in experimental social psychology* (Vol. 20). New York: Academic Press, 1965.

Bandura, A. *Aggression: A social learning analysis.* Englewood Cliffs, N.J.: Prentice-Hall, 1973.

Bandura, A. *Social learning theory.* Englewood Cliffs, N.J.: Prentice-Hall, 1977.

Bandura, A., Ross, D., & Ross, S.A. Transmission of aggression through imitation of aggressive models. *Journal of Abnormal and Social Psychology,* 1961, **63,** 575–582.

Bandura, A., Ross, D., & Ross, S.A. Imitation of film-mediated aggressive models. *Journal of Abnormal and Social Psychology,* 1961, **63,** 575–582.

Bandura, A., Ross, D., & Ross, S.A. Imitation of film-mediated aggressive models. *Journal of Abnormal and Social Psychology,* 1963, **66,** 3–11.

Bankart, C.P., & Anderson, C.C. Short-term effects prosocial television viewing on play of preschool boys and girls. *Psychological Reports,* 1979, **44,** 935–941.

Bogart, L. *The age of television.* New York: Ungar, 1958.

Bogatz, G.A., & Ball, S. *The second year of Sesame Street: A continuing evaluation.* Princeton, N.J.: Educational Testing Service, 1972.

Bolick, T.L. *Relationships between Saturday morning television viewing and expectancies of young boys.* Unpublished doctoral dissertation, Emory University, 1980.

Burr, P. & Burr, R.M. Product recognition and premium appeal. *Journal of Communication,* 1977, **27**, 115–117.

Chaffee, S.H. Communication patterns in the family: Implications for adaptibility and change. Presented at the 64th annual meeting of the Speech Communication Association, Minneapolis, Minnesota, 1978.

Chaffee, S.H., McLeod, J.M., & Atkin, C.K. Parental influences on adolescent television use. *Journal of Social Issues,* 1976, **32**, 98–115.

Charlton, M., Liebelt, E., & Sultz Jetta Tausch, A.M. Influence of models in a TV Western on group work and aggression latency of 3rd graders. *Psychologie in Erziehung und Unterricht,* 1974, **21**, 164–175.

Chesnut, Robert W. Comparing facts with findings: Empirical research on television advertising to children. *Catalog of Selected Documents in Psychology,* 1979, **9**, 57.

Clark, W.J. *Of children and television.* Cincinnati: Xavier University, 1951.

Coates, B., Pusser, H.E., & Goodman, I. The influence of "Sesame Street" and "Mister Rogers' Neighborhood" on children's social behavior in the classroom. *Child Development,* 1976, **47**, 138–144.

Collins, W.A., & Getz, S.R. Children's social responses following modeled reactions to provocation: Prosocial effects of a television drama. *Journal of Personality,* 1976, **44**, 488–500.

Comstock, G.A., & Rubinstein, E.A. (Eds.). *Television and social behavior.* (Vol. 1). *Media content and control.* Washington, D.C.: U.S. Government Printing office, 1972.

Davidson, E.S., Yasuna, A., & Tower, A. The effects of television cartoons on sex-role stereotyping in young girls. *Child Development,* 1979, **50**, 597–600.

Desmond, R.J. Cognitive development and television comprehension. *Communication Research,* 1978, **5**, 202–220.

Diaz-Guerrero, R., Reyes-Lagunes, I., Witzke, D.B., & Holtzman, W.H. Plaza Sesamo in Mexico: An evaluation. *Journal of Communication,* 1976, **26**, 145–154.

Dominick, J.R., & Greenberg, B.S. Mass media functions among low-income adolescents. In B.S. Greenberg (Ed.), *Use of the mass media by the urban poor.* New York: Praeger, 1970.

Donagher, P.C., Poulos, R.W., Liebert, R.M., & Davidson, E.S. Race, sex, and social example: An analysis of character portrayals on interracial television entertainment. *Psychological Reports,* 1975, **37**, 1023–1034.

Donohue, T.R. Effect of commercials on black children. *Journal of Advertising Research,* 1975, **15**, 41–47.

Donohue, W.A., & Donahue, T.R. Black, white, white gifted, and emotionally disturbed children's perceptions of the reality in television programming. *Human Relations,* 1977, **30**, 609–621.

Drabman, R.S., & Thomas, M.H. Exposure to filmed violence and children's tolerance of real life aggression. *Personality & Social Psychology Bulletin,* 1974, **1**, 198–199.

Drabman, R.S., Thomas, M.H., & Jarvie, G. Will our children care? New evidence concerning the effects of televised violence on our children. *Journal of Clinical Child Psychology,* 1977, **6**, 44–46.

Duke, M.P., & Nowicki, S. *Abnormal psychology: The experience of being different.* Monterey, California, Brooks/Cole, 1978.

Eron, L.D. Relationship of television viewing habits and aggressive behavior in children. *Journal of Abnormal and Social Psychology,* 1963, **67**, 193–196.

Feldman, S., Wolf, A., & Warmouth, D. Parental concern about child-directed commercials. *Journal of Communication,* 1977, **27**, 125–137.

Feshbach, S., & Singer, R.D. *Television and aggression: An experimental field study.* San Francisco: Jossey-Bass, 1971.

Freud, S. *Collected papers.* London: Hogarth, 1925.

Friedlander, B.Z. Against the effect of advertising. *Fernsehen und Bildung,* 1977, **11**, 186–191.

Friedrich, L.K., & Stein, A.H. Aggressive and prosocial television programs and the natural of preschool children. *Monographs of the Society for Research in Child Development,* 1973, **38**,(4, Serial No. 151).

Friedrich, L.R., & Stein, A.H. Prosocial television and young children: The effect of verbal labeling and role playing on learning and behavior. *Child Development,* 1975, **46,** 27–38.

Friedrich-Cofer, L.K., Huston-Stein, A., Kipnis, C.M., Susman, E.J., & Clewett, A.S. Environmental enhancement of prosocial television content: Effects of interpersonal behavior, imaginative play, and self-regulation in a natural setting. *Developmental Psychology,* 1979, **15,** 637–646.

Frueh, T., & McGhee, P.E. Traditional sex role development and amount of time spent watching television. *Developmental Psychology,* 1975, **11,** 109.

Galst, J.P., & White, M.A. The unhealthy persuader: The reinforcing value of television and children's purchase-influencing attempts at the supermarket. *Child Development,* 1976, **47,** 1089–1096.

Gerbner, B., & Gross, L. Living with television: The violence profile. *Journal of Communication,* 1976, **26,** 173–199.

Gerson, W.M. Mass media socialization behavior: Negro-white differences. *Social Forces,* 1966, **45,** 40–50.

Glynn, E.D. Television and the American character: A psychiatrist looks at television. In W.Y. Elliott (Ed.), *Television's impact on American culture.* Lansing, Mich.: Michigan State University Press, 1956.

Goldberg, M.E., Gorn, G.J., & Gibson, W. TV messages for snack and breakfast foods: Do they influence children's preferences? *Journal of Consumer Research,* 1978, **5,** 73–81.

Gorn, G.J., & Goldberg, M.E. The impact of television advertising on children from low income families. *Journal of Consumer Research,* 1977, **4,** 86–88.

Greenberg, B.S., & Dominick, J. Television behavior among disadvantaged children. In B.S. Greenberg & B. Dervin (Eds.), *Use of the mass media by the urban poor.* New York: Praeger, 1970.

Hayes, L., & Schauble, L. Nothing to fear but fear itself: Experiences from Sesame Street. *Fernsehen und Bildung,* 1978, **12,** 58–71.

Heslop, L.A. An experimental study of the effects of premium advertising on cereal choices by parent and children. University of Western Ontario, *Dissertation Abstracts International,* 1978, **38,** 5675.

Himmelweit, H.T., Oppenheim, A.N., & Vince, P. *Television and the child: An empirical study of the effect of television on the young.* London: Oxford University Press, 1958.

Hodapp, T.V. Children's ability to learn problem-solving strategies from television. *Alberta Journal of Educational Research,* 1977, **23,** 171–177.

Hume, N., O'Conner, W.A., & Lowery, C.R. Family, adjustment, and the psychosocial ecosystem. *Psychiatric Annals,* 1977, **7,** 32–49.

Kniveton, B.H. Anxiety instead of aggression: An effect of violent films? *Fernsehen und Bildung,* 1978, **12,** 41–47.

Lagerspetz, K.M., & Engblom, P. Immediate reactions to TV violence by Finnish preschool children of different personality types. *Scandinavian Journal of Psychology,* 1979, **20,** 43–53.

Lagerspetz, K.M., Wahlroos, C., Wendelin, C., & Akademi. Facial expressions of preschool children while watching televised violence. *Scandinavian Journal of Psychology,* 1978, **19,** 213–222.

Lazarsfeld, P.F., & Merton, R.K. Mass communication, popular taste, and organized social action. In W. Schramm (Ed.), *Mass communications.* Urbana: University of Illinois Press, 1960.

Lesser, G.S. Designing a program for broadcast television. In F.F. Korten, S.W. Cook, & G.L. Lacey (Eds.), *Psychology and the problems of society.* Washington, D.C.: American Psychological Association, 1970.

Levin, S.R., & Anderson, D.R. The development of attention. *Journal of Communication,* 1976, **26,** 126–135.

Liebert, R.M., Neale, J.M., & Davidson, E.S. *The early window: Effects of television on children and youth.* New York: Pergamon, 1973.

Liebert, D.E., Sprafkin, J.N., Liebert, R.M., & Rubinstein, E.A. Effects of television commercial disclaimers on the product expectations of children. *Journal of Communication,* 1977, **27,** 118–124.

Liebert, R.M., & Schwartzberg, N. Effects of mass media. *Annual Review of Psychology,* 1977, **28,** 141–173.

Long, B.H., & Henderson, E.H. Children's use of time. Some personal and social correlates.

Elementary School Journal, 1973, **73**, 193–199.

Lowenstein, L.F. Television violence and its effect on the young mind. *New & View*, 1978, **3**, 25–27.

Lyle, J. Television in daily life: Patterns of use overview. In E.A. Rubinstein, G.A. Comstock, & J.P. Murray (Eds.), *Television and social behavior* (Vol. 4). *Television in day-to-day life: Patterns of use.* Washington, D.C.: U.S. Government Printing Office, 1972.

Maccoby, E. Why do children watch television? *Public Opinion Quarterly*, 1954, **18**, 239–244.

McArthur, L.Z., & Eisen, S.V. Television and sex-role stereotyping. *Journal of Applied Social Psychology*, 1976, **6**, 329–351.

McCall, R.B., Parke, R.D., & Kavanaugh, R.D. Imitation of live and televised models by children one to three years of age. *Monographs of the Society for Research in Child Development*, 1977, **42**(5).

McCarthy, E.D. Violence and behavior disorders. *Journal of Communication*, 1975, **25**, 71–85.

Meerloo, J.A.M. Television addiction and reactive apathy. *Journal of Nervous and Mental Disease*, 1954, **120**, 290–291.

Meringoff, L.K. Influence of the medium on children's story apprehension. Journal of Educational Psychology, 1980, **72**, 240–249.

Newcomb, A.F., & Collins, W.A. Children's comprehension of family role portrayals in televised dramas: Effects of socioeconomic status, ethnicity, and age. *Developmental Psychology*, 1979, **15**, 417–423.

Noble, G. *Children in front of the small screen.* Beverly Hills, Calif.: Sage, 1975.

Nolan, J.D., Galst, J.P., & White, M.A. Sex bias on children's television programs. *Journal of Psychology*, 1977, **96**, 197–204.

O'Bryant, S.L., & Corder-Bolz, C.R. Black children's learning of work roles from television commercials. *Psychological Reports*, 1978, **42**, 227–230. (a)

O'Bryant, S.L., & Corder-Bolz, C.R. The effects of television on children's stereotyping of women's work roles. *Journal of Vocational Behavior*, 1978, **12**, 233–244. (b)

Ogura, C. Effects of TV heroes on sex-related personality formation in preschool children. *Journal of Child Development*, 1979, **15**, 1–7.

Patterson, A.C., & Neustadter, C. How to cope with violence on the tube. *Audiovisual Instruction*, 1978, **23**, 40–42.

Perloff, R.M. Some antecedents of children's sex-role stereotypes. *Psychological Reports*, 1977, **40**, 463–466.

Pingree, S. The effects of nonsexist television commercials and perceptions of reality on children's attitudes about women. *Psychology of Women Quarterly*, 1978, **2**, 262–277.

Poulos, R.W., Harvey, S.E., & Liebert, R.M. Saturday morning television: A profile of the 1974–75 children's season. *Psychological Reports*, 1976, **39**, 1047–1057.

Quisenberry, N.I., & Klasek, C.B. *Audiovisual Instruction*, 1977, **22**, 56–57.

Ridder, J. Pupil opinions and the relationship of television to academic achievement. *Journal of Educational Research*, 1963, **57**, 200–206.

Riley, M.W., & Riley, J.W. A sociological approach to communication research. In W. Schramm (Ed.), *The process and effects of mass communication.* Urbana: University of Illinois Press, 1954.

Robertson, T.S., & Rossiter, J.R. Short-run advertising effects on children: A field study. *Journal of Marketing Research*, 1976, **13**, 68–70.

Robertson, T.S., & Rossiter, J.R. Children's responsiveness to commercials. *Journal of Communication*, 1977, **27**, 101–106.

Rossiter, J.R. Reliability of a short test measuring children's attitudes toward TV commercials. *Journal of Consumer Research*, 1977, **3**, 179–184.

Rossiter, J.R., & Robertson, T.S. Children's television viewing: An examination of parent-child consensus. *Sociometry*, 1975, **38**, 308–326.

Rossiter, J.R., & Robertson, T.S. Canonical analysis of developmental, social, and experiential factors in children's comprehension of television advertising. *Journal of Genetic Psychology*, 1976, **129**, 317–327.

Rust, L., & Watkins, T.A. Children's commercials: Creative development. *Journal of Advertising Research*, 1975, **15**, 21–69.

Salje, G. Transformation of anxiety through children's phantasies about animals: Some comments on a favoured category of children's television programmes. *Fernsehen und Bildung*, 1978, **12**, 71–79.

Salomon, G. Cognitive skill learning across cultures. *Journal of Communication*, 1976, **26**, 138–144.

Satterfield, J.R. *Televiewing practices as a function of certain personality variables variables and reading achievement levels of middle socioeconomic status, fourth-grade children.* Unpublished doctoral dissertation, University of Oklahoma, 1972.

Schramm, W. What do we know about learning from educational television? In W. Schramm (Ed.), *Educational television: The next ten years.* Stanford: Institute for Communication Research, 1962.

Schramm, W., Lyle, J., & Parker, E.B. *Television in the lives of our children.* Stanford: Stanford University Press, 1961.

Sheikh, A.A., & Moleski, L.M. Conflict in the family over commercials. *Journal of Communication*, 1977, **27**, 152–157.

Singer, D.B., & Singer, J.L. Family television viewing habits and the spontaneous play of preschool children. *American Journal of Orthopsychiatry*, 1976, **46**, 496–502.

Singer, D., & Singer, J. Stop feeling guilty when TV's baby-sitting. *TV Guide*, May 23, 1981, 6–7.

Snow, R.E., & Salomon, G. Aptitudes and instructional medial. *Audiovisual Communication Review*, 1968, **16**, 341–357.

Squire, L.R., Chace, P.M., & Slater, P.C. Assessment of memory for remote events. *Psychological Reports*, 1975, **37**, 223–234.

Stein, A.H., & Friedrich, L.K. Impact of television on children and youth. In E.M. Hetherington (Ed.), *Review of child development research.* Chicago: University of Chicago Press, 1975.

Stevenson, H.W. Television and the behavior of preschool children. In J.P. Murray, E.A. Rubinstein, & G.A. Comstock, (Eds.), *Television and social behavior* (Vol. 2). *Television and social learning.* Washington, D.C.: U.S. Government Printing Office, 1972.

Surlin, S.H., & Dominick, J.R. Television's function as a "third parent" for black and white teenagers. *Journal of Broadcasting*, 1970, **15**, 55–64.

Swanson, R.A., & Henderson, R.W. Effects of televised modeling and active participation on rule-governed question production among Native American preschool children. *Contemporary Educational Psychology*, 1977, **2**, 345–352.

Thomas, M.H., & Drabman, R.S. Toleration of real life aggression as a function of exposure to televised violence and age of subject. *Merrill-Palmer Quarterly*, 1975, **21**, 227–232.

Thomas, M.H. et al. Desensitization to portrayals of real-life aggression as a function of television violence. *Journal of Personality & Social Psychology*, 1977, **35**, 450–458.

Tower, R.B., Singer, D.G., Singer, J.L., & Jerome, A. Differential effects of television programming on preschoolers' cognition, imagination, and social play. *American Journal of Orthopsychiatry*, 1979, **49**, 265–281.

Wackman, D.B., & Wartella, E. A review of cognitive development theory and research and the implication for research on children's responses to television. *Communication Research*, 1977, **4**, 203–224.

Ward, S., Wackman, D.B., & Wartella, E. *How children learn to buy: The development of consumer information-processing skills.* Beverly Hills, Calif.: Sage, 1977.

Wertham, F. School for violence. In O.N. Larsen (Ed.), *Violence and the mass media.* New York: Harper & Row, 1964.

Westley, B.M., & Barrow, Jr., L.C. Exploring the news: A comparative study of the teaching effectiveness of radio and television. *Audiovisual Communication Review*, 1959, **7**, 14–23.

Witty, P. Interest in TV and success in school. *Educational Administration and Supervision*, 1951, **37**, 193–210.

Winick, M.P., & Winick, C. *The television experience: What children see.* Beverly Hills, Calif.: Sage, 1979.

Wolfe, J., & Cheyne, J.A. Persistence of effects of live behavioral, televised behavioral, and live verbal models on resistance to deviation. *Child Development*, 1972, **43**, 1429–1436.

Woodrick, C., Chissom, B., & Smith, D. Television-viewing habits and parent-observed behaviors of third-grade children. *Psychological Reports*, 1977, **40**, 830.

Yates, G.C.R. Influence of televised modeling and verbalization on children's delay of gratification. *Journal of Experimental Child Psychology*, 1974, **18**, 333–339.

Zajonc, R.B. Attitudinal effects of mere exposure. *Journal of Personality and Social Psychology*,

1968, **9,** (Monograph Supplement), 1027.

Zillman, D., Williams, B.R., Bryant, J., Boynton, K.R., & Wolf, M.A. Acquisition of information from educational television programs as a function of differently paced humorous inserts. *Journal of Educational Psychology,* 1980, **72,** 170–180.

Zimmer, J.L., & Sheposh, J.P. Effects of high status and low status actor's performance on observers' attributions of causality and behavioral intentions. *Sociometry,* 1975, **38,** 395–407.

CHAPTER 52

Child Abuse

GERTRUDE J. RUBIN WILLIAMS

Estimates of the incidence of child abuse vary widely because of variations in definitions and modes of data collection. Most investigators agree that official reports are gross underestimates. There is no single cause or simple set of causes of child abuse. The causes of child abuse are many, varied, and interactive. They include poverty, stress, social sanctions for violence within the family and for corporal punishment of children, unwanted pregnancy, sexist and pronatalist ideologies, predisposing characteristics in abuse parents and children. Although certain psychosocial traits characterize actively abusing parents, these are neither necessary nor sufficient to produce abuse. Although the experience of abuse in childhood increases the probability of becoming an abusive parent, it is not an inevitable result. Indeed, many adults abused as children do not abuse their children. Predisposing characteristics include teenage parenthood, egocentricity, intense dependence yet resistance to seeking help, emotional isolation, manipulativeness, unrealistic expectations of their children, fear of "spoiling" them, and a righteous belief in the use of corporal punishment. Alcohol and/or drug addiction may serve as a releaser for child abuse.

Infants and young children are more frequently abused than older children. Certain vulnerabilities, such as mental retardation, physical handicaps, developmental deviation, and prematurity are risk factors for abuse. These characteristics heighten stress in the family and threaten the fragile self-concept of immature, abuse prone parents.

Child abuse has profound effects on the psychobiological, psychosocial, and developmental processes of children. These include death, brain damage, neuromotor dysfunction, intellectual and cognitive impairment, endocrinological dysfunction manifested in hyposomatotropinism or abuse dwarfism, and emotional and social problems. The more prolonged the maltreatment, the less likely it is that the damaging effects will be reversible. An increasing number of studies indicate that some of the effects of abuse are reversible if the child is removed early enough from the abusive parental home. Information on indicators of child abuse is being circulated to schools and other child-related agencies so that early identification and intervention can occur.

Another type of child abuse, sexual abuse, is a form of exploitation of children and adolescents in sexual activities that they do not fully understand, that are appropriate to a psychosexual stage beyond their developmental level, to which they are unable to give informed consent, and that violate social taboos regarding roles and relationships within the family (Kempe & Kempe, 1978; Johnston, 1979). It includes molestation as well as rape and incest, whether forcible or not. Ordinarily, incest involves fondling, masturbation, or oral-genital sex; because of the incest victim's immaturity, genital penetration is rare in childhood.

The major goal of most current child abuse programs is to keep the family intact, a focus that has discouraged development and research on new strategies directed toward creating alternatives to keeping the child in the abusive home and based on the goals of protection and enhancement of the child's well being. The major treatment focus has been on the abusive parents rather than the abused child. Such treatment of abusive parents includes individual and group therapy, homemaker services, parent aides, and parent education. Another treatment component is Parents Anonymous and other self-help groups that may be helpful in curbing child abuse only in combination with highly skilled professional services. Abused children rarely receive treatment for their manifold psychosocial problems. Typically, their treatment is focused on psychoeducational and cognitive development in addition to their medical problems.

Evaluation of treatment effectiveness, including model child abuse programs offering a supermarket of professional and paraprofessional services, indicates that recidivism rates range from 40–85 percent. These research findings clearly challenge the parent- and family-oriented philosophy undergirding current child abuse programs. A child advocacy orientation directed toward protecting children from further abuse and enhancing their development appears to be a promising alternative. In light of research findings demonstrating the therapeutic effects of removal from the abusive parents, earlier termination of parental rights and freeing abused children for adoption are viewed as the wave of the future by many experts in child abuse. Only radical transformations in destructive social institutions and practices cited above as the causes of child abuse can lead to the primary prevention of this serious symptom of social, family, and individual pathology.

HISTORICAL BACKGROUND

At first glance, child abuse appears to be a repugnant, unnatural act alien to daily life. Yet, viewed from a historical perspective, it loses its anomalous appearance; for, since the beginning of time, children have been treated with incredible cruelty and have had little recourse to the law, which regarded them as chattel of their parents or the state. DeMause (1975), founder of the new discipline of psychohistory, characterizes the history of childhood as "a nightmare from which we have only recently begun to awaken" (p. 85). He reports that child care has gradually evolved over the past two millenia from an infanticidal mode in antiquity to the current beginnings of a helping mode.

The protection of children against abuse by their parents is usually viewed as a product of the past two decades because of extensive media coverage and legislation during that era. As far back as 1735, however, Massachusetts had passed a law providing for the removal of children from neglectful parents and their placement with good families (Folks, 1902). Williams (1980a) documents that history has indeed repeated itself, for over a century ago there was furor over parental abuse of children, sensational newspaper accounts of abuse, and strong child protective legislation. But these reforms in the 1870s were followed by waning concern about child abuse, a concern that was not revived until the 1960s.

DEFINITION AND INCIDENCE

Child abuse consists of a multitude of nonaccidental physical and psychological traumas to children, in the vast majority of cases, over an extended period of time. Acts of abuse include such bodily violence as beating, squeezing, lacerating, binding, burning, suffocating, poisoning, or exposing to excess heat or cold. Abuse also includes such psychological traumas as sensory overload with light, sound, stench, aversive taste, itching, pain, or prevention of sleep and verbal overload with insults, accusations, and indoctrination. Neglect is also a form of abuse and is frequently more damaging than assault. Neglected children are deprived of such physiological necessities as nourishment, drink, clothing, shelter, and sanitation and of such psychological requirements as sensory stimulation, affection, supervision, social communication, and schooling.

The definition of emotional abuse and neglect is beginning to receive attention. Garbarino (1978) defines emotional abuse as obstructing the development of competence in children by punishing such positive behaviors as exploration, attachment, self-esteem, and social relationships beyond the home.

Abusive acts appears to be so distinct that defining them would seem to present no problems. Yet medical, psychological, and sociological definitions abound, and the law is no more consistent than the sciences. Legal definitions of abuse vary from state to state. Some states define it narrowly as physical assault, whereas others include physical and emotional neglect and/or abuse in their statutes. Some states do not even subsume sexual abuse under child abuse.

In light of these definitional problems, it is not surprising that estimates of child abuse range from 580,000 (National Council of Organizations for Children and Youth, 1976, p. 83) to over 4,000,000 (Gil, 1970). Inconsistencies in the definitions of child abuse are but one reason for the wide range of estimates of incidence. The information on which estimates are based comes from many sources, including social agencies, hospitals, police reports, and national surveys, all of which are based on different kinds of samples and reporting criteria. Moreover, many estimates are inferential or speculative. There is general agreement, however, that cases of child abuse are significantly underreported. The U.S. Department of Health, Education, and Welfare (HEW, vol. 1, 1975, p. 4) concludes that "reported cases account for the visible tip of the iceberg...Estimates suggest a problem of staggering proportions."

The use of the term "child abuse" in this chapter refers to the physical assault of a child by parents, by far the most investigated form of child abuse. Other forms of abuse, such as neglect or parental incest, are specified as such if distinctions are made in the investigations reviewed.

CAUSES OF CHILD ABUSE

Child abuse is not caused by a single factor or set of factors. Even staunch proponents of the view that poverty and other social factors contribute significantly to child abuse, such as Gil (1970) and Pelton (1981), do not deny the role of individual psychological factors. Likewise, Kempe (1979) and his associates at the National Center for the Prevention and Treatment of Child Abuse and Neglect (NCPTCAN), who conceptualize child abuse within a medical or psychodynamic model, also emphasize the role of socioeconomic and cultural factors. Many investigators (Alvy, 1975; Williams, 1976; Williams & Money, 1980) take a comprehensive view of child abuse that encompasses both individual abuse and the abuse of children by social institutions. Garbarino (1981) applies Bronfenbrenner's (1977) ecological approach to child abuse by examining the interaction between personal and social variables.

Thus the causes of child abuse are many, varied, multiplicative, and interacting. Some combinations of predisposing factors are more potent than others in generating abuse, but weights cannot be accurately assigned to them. Indeed, even the variables associated with child abuse are neither necessary nor sufficient to produce it. For example, while poverty and a parent's experience of abuse in childhood are frequent correlates of child abuse, they do not explain child abuse either singly or in combination. Many poverty-stricken parents who had been abused as children do not abuse their children. Some parents who had not been abused as children and who are now affluent do abuse their children. While certain characteristics of parents and children combine with stress to predispose a family to abuse, this constellation may occur in families in which child abuse is absent. The factors that inhibit child abuse in such families and the differential impact of predisposing conditions on different families is still unknown. Furthermore, the constellation of adversities that produce child abuse in one family may lead to parental overprotection, other types of crimes, or aggression at work in other families, and coping and competence in childrearing in still others.

Keeping in mind the tremendous complexity of the problem, we will now examine the causes of child abuse.

Poverty

One contributor to child abuse is poverty with its aversive accompaniments of crime-ridden neighborhoods, poor education, unemployment, health and safety hazards, and inadequate health services, transportation, housing, and recreation. Proponents of social pathology, rather than psychopathology, as the preeminent cause of child abuse (Gil, 1970; Pelton, 1981) agree with Besharov and Besharov (1977), Fraser (1976–1977), and Steele (1975) that child abuse is found in all social classes but contend that it is unevenly distributed and correlates highly with poverty. Pelton (1981) concludes that the vast majority of abuse families live in poverty or near poverty, a conclusion supported by the American Humane Association (1978) and Young (1977).

Some investigators explain such findings as artifacts of underreporting of child abuse among middle and upper class physicians. Social agencies have much more access to the poor and are more likely to report cases of child abuse than private physicians. Light (1973) states that, if every low income abuse family were given a higher income as a means of reducing child abuse, the incidence of abuse would appear to decrease as a function of improved economic resources. In reality, however, the apparent decrease would be an artifact because "the child abuser will have purchased the private pediatrician's lower reporting rates" (p. 238).

According to Pelton (1981), the "public scrutiny argument" cannot explain findings on lower class child abusers, all of whom are more open to public scrutiny than members of other economic classes. For example, Gil (1970) found that the most serious or fatal abuse of children occurred in the poorest families. Wolock and Horowitz (1977) reported that the highest incidence of abuse was found among those living in the most extreme poverty. Pelton (1978) concludes that poverty, not public scrutiny, can account for these findings on child abuse *within* the lower class.

Spinetta and Rigler (1972) contend that citing poverty as the primary cause of child

abuse does not explain the occurrence of middle and upper class abuse or the fact that the vast majority of poor parents do not abuse their children. Nor can it explain, Kempe (1979) asserts, "the high incidence and serious nature of child abuse among a group of individuals who do have a job, housing, cheap food, free comprehensive health care, are married, and live surrounded by potentially helpful people" (p. xiii); namely, military families.

Social Sanctions for Violence

The normative acceptance of violence in the American home and the belief that violence against children is a right of adults have been cited as major causes of child abuse. In the 1960s, an era of increasing public awareness of violence in American society, a knowledge base on the extent of domestic violence began to develop and burgeoned in the 1970s. The Federal Bureau of Investigation (1966) reported that violence in the home was the major source of violence in the United States and that 25 percent of all homicides occurred in the family. Between 1960 and 1965, more policemen were killed responding to domestic disturbances than to any other calls. The National Commission on the Causes and Prevention of Violence (1969) reported that one-third of American adults had been hit frequently during childhood and that one-fifth of the males approved of slapping their wives' faces. Using representative samples of American families, Levinger (1966) found that physical assault against a spouse was an important factor in divorce.

More recent research corroborates and heightens the findings on the acceptance of violence against children (Gelles, 1979, 1980; Steinmetz, 1977; Straus, 1979; Straus, Gelles, & Steinmetz, 1980). Straus found that 14 percent of children in a normative sample were abused each year, a finding more than 26 times greater than estimates of child abuse from the National Center for Child Abuse and Neglect. Gelles (1979) interprets these results as indicating that "violence against children is an extensive and patterned phenomenon in parent-child relations." He concludes that this violence goes far beyond ordinary physical punishment and is promoted by social sanctions for hitting one's children.

The view that corporal punishment is a euphemism for violence against children and that it is a significant contributor to child abuse is endorsed by numerous professionals, who also call attention to the schools's participation in violence against children (Feshbach & Feshbach, 1973; Gil, 1970; Hyman & Wise, 1979; Maurer, 1974; Welsh, 1976; Williams, 1975, 1976). In the case of Ingraham v. Wright (1977) the United States Supreme Court ruled in favor of school personnel who had beaten two students so severely that they could not attend school for two weeks. Thus the highest court in the nation and a major social structure, the schools, serve as models to parents of socially sanctioned violence against children.

Circumstances of the Conception and the Pregnancy

Unwanted conception and pregnancy are significant contributors to child abuse. Steele and Pollock (1968) state: "An infant born as the result of a premaritally conceived pregnancy or who comes as an accident too soon after the birth of a previous child, may be quite unwelcome to the parents and start life under a cloud of being unwanted and unsatisfying to the parents. Such infants may be perceived as public reminders of sexual transgression or as extra, unwanted burdens rather than need-satisfying objects" (pp. 128–129). Wasserman (1967) contends that a child conceived out of wedlock often becomes a "hostility sponge" for an unwanted marriage, or reminds the mother of the man who deserted her during pregnancy, or reminds the stepfather of his wife's transgressions.

Bishop (1971); Gaddis et al. (1979); Gil (1970); Green (1976); MacCarthy (1977); Prescott (1976); Scott (1980); and Spinetta and Rigler (1972), all refer to a significant relationship between child abuse and unwanted pregnancy, pregnancy occurring shortly after the birth of a previous child, and/or large families with four or more children. Oates et al., (1979) in England and West and West (1979) in Australia found a significantly higher frequency of unplanned, unwanted, and illegitimate pregnancies among abusive parents compared to control samples. Ferguson, Fleming, and O'Neill (1972) report that child abuse and neglect rates in New Zealand are higher for illegitimate children and in larger families.

Resnick (1970) reviewed the world literature on the murder of the newborn and found that the majority of mothers attributed the murder simply to not wanting the infant. Passivity was a prominent characteristic of these young women who planned neither the pregnancy nor the murder. However, "when reality is thrust upon them by the infants' first cry, they respond by permanently silencing the intruder" (p. 1416). Resnick contrasts neonaticidal women with those who seek abortions: the latter recognize the reality of the unwanted pregnancy early and cope actively with the problem. Rohner and Rohner (1980) point to a worldwide relationship between severity of punishment for abortions and child abuse, which they attribute to the higher incidence of unwanted children. Kempe (1976) states that rejection of the newborn, which can be observed in the delivery room, is a high risk factor for abuse.

While not wanting the pregnancy or the child is a parental attitude related to child abuse, wanting the pregnancy and the child is insufficient to prevent abuse. Lenoski (1974) describes a group of mothers who intensely wanted the children they subsequently abused, who were more likely than a control group to name the children after a parent and who had even worn maternity clothes earlier. Martin and Beezley (1974) explain the seemingly contradictory findings of abusive parents who wanted the child or adoptive parents who abuse their wanted adoptive children by referring to the findings of Steele and Pollack (1968) that abusive parents typically expect the child to meet their own intense emotional needs. This egocentric expectation is the basis for wanting the child, who is incapable of meeting it. Consequently, the parent lashes out at the child, who is irrationally viewed as withholding love. Walsh (1977) drew a similar conclusion for a group of abusive adolescent mothers who viewed pregnancy and motherhood as ways of defining their identity and social role and of providing the security absent during their own childhoods. When the babies they wanted so intensely failed to meet these unrealistic expectations, the adolescent mothers expressed their rage and frustration by abusing their children. Steele and Pollack (1968) refer to a "splitting" in abusive parents between compassion for the child and a sense of righteousness about beating a disobedient, frustrating child. These two contradictory systems, walled off from each other and existing concurrently, are manifested in the abuse of the child who is also wanted and loved by its abusive parents.

Helfer (1975) describes a group of abusive young women with such strong desires to become pregnant that they had refused contraception and abortion and with whom "family planning and birth control measures must be pursued even though frequently resisted" (p. 29). These women had experienced the "World of Abnormal Rearing," a pattern of abusive, rejecting, emotionally damaging relationships with their own parents. Their motivations for the pregnancy were "to free themselves from their unhappy home, prove to their parents and themselves they can indeed be good parents, provide them with someone to keep them company, or (they expect) the baby to role reverse and begin to parent the parents" (p. 34). The infants, incapable of granting these egocentric wishes, became the targets of their mothers' desperation.

Predisposing Characteristics of Abusive Parents

The vast majority of studies focus on characteristics of actively abusive parents. Little attention has been paid to the passive abuser, the parent who fails to protect the child against the violent parent or who, by subtle encouragement, covertly participates in the abuse. Little is known about neglectful parents. Polansky, DeSaix, and Sharlin (1973)

report that abusive parents are more emotionally invested in their children than neglectful parents, but Scott (1980) found no differences between them.

Certain psychosocial factors characterize actively abusive parents, but these are neither necessary nor sufficient to produce abuse. The childhood abuse of later abusive parents has been found by a multitude of investigators (Gelles, 1974; Owens & Straus, 1975; Parke & Collmer, 1975; Scott, 1980; Straus, 1979; Steinmetz, 1977). Steele and Pollack (1968) describe the recurrence of child abuse in four successive generations. Steinmetz (1977) indicates that even less serious forms of abuse are transmitted from generation to generation. Straus, et al. (1980) report that the probability of becoming an abusive parent or spouse increases with the frequency of family violence during childhood. Bovelek, et al. (1979) found similarities between the childrearing practices of abused adolescents and those of abusive parents.

Nevertheless, childhood abuse is not an inevitable precursor of abusive parenting. Many adults who had been abused do not abuse their children. Novelist Charles Dickens transformed the memory of his childhood neglect into a commitment to child advocacy (Gardner, 1977). Cameronchild (1978), in a first-person account, was similarly able to "use" the experience of childhood abuse by contributing to the helping professions. In the author's experience, psychotherapy with adults abused as children indicated that some of them refrain entirely from physical punishment of their children because of their intense empathy with those in pain.

Egeland (1979); Oates et al. (1979); and West and West (1979) found that the youth of the parents, especially the mother, is a high risk factor in abuse. DeLissovoy (1973) found that teenage parents were impatient, irritable, unfamiliar with developmental expectations and prone to use physical punishment, all factors characteristic of abusive parents. Smith, Hanson, and Nobel (1975) found that the average age of abusive mothers in their sample was 19 years old at the birth of the first child and that they were ignorant of childrearing principles. Adolescent childbearing is associated with many variables related to child abuse (Green & Potteiger, 1977; Friedrich & Boriskin, 1976; Lynch & Roberts, 1977). These variables include a high risk of complications during pregnancy, labor, and delivery; high incidence of low birth weight and prematurity; and high risk of mental retardation and cerebral palsy among infants of adolescent mothers.

According to reviews of the literature by Spinetta and Rigler (1972) and Shorkey (1978), many child-abusing parents are emotionally immature; impulsive; egocentric; intensely dependent yet resistant to seeking help; socially isolated; low in self-confidence, empathy and warmth; have difficulty in enjoying themselves and their children; lack reasonableness and flexibility; have distorted perceptions and unrealistic expectations of their children; fear "spoiling" them; and righteously believe in the use of corporal punishment. Young (1977) found that abusive parents were significantly higher on powerlessness and social isolation, measured by Rotter's Internal-External Locus of Control Scale and the Fundamental Interpersonal Relations Scale. Using the Adolescent Parenting Scale, Bavolek and Keene (1980) found that both adult abusers and adolescent parents were significantly higher than controls on inappropriate expectations of their children, inability to empathize, strong belief in physical punishment, and role reversal. Role reversal, a term introduced by Morris and Gould (1963), is described by Steele and Pollack (1968) as a pattern in which "the parent acts like a frightened, unloved child, looking to his own children as if they were an adult capable of providing comfort and love" (p. 109).

Few abusive parents are psychotic, but many have severe personality disorders. Money and Needleman (1976) and Money and Werlwas (1980) describe the *folie à deux* or pathological collusion of abusive parents who, by evasion and cover-up, present a picture of a happy family concurrent with their abuse of the child. Wright (1976), using psychological tests, described a constellation of psychopathology and manipulativeness in abusive parents whom he characterized as "sick but slick." The findings of Billing et al. (in press) and Carr (1975) indicate a relationship between alcohol or drug addiction and child abuse. Perinatal addiction is a serious early warning signal for subsequent abuse.

Predisposing Characteristics of Abused Children

Although children of all ages are abused, infants and young children are abused more frequently. The higher incidence of nonaccidental injuries among infants contrasts significantly with incidence rates for accidental injuries, which are minimal below 9 months (Elmer, 1967), a finding helpful to clinicians seeking the etiology of injuries in young infants.

An array of vulnerabilities that predispose children to abuse have been observed by numerous investigators (Martin & Beezley, 1974; Ounstead, Oppenheimer, & Lindsay, 1974). These vulnerable or "different" or "difficult" infants are often described as being more irritable and demanding, crying frequently, tending to be more unresponsive and unrewarding to their parents than other children, requiring more care, and generally threatening their parents' self-esteem because of their failure to respond to care. Martin and Beezley (1974) view the parent as vulnerable in that it is the parent who has a low threshold for tolerating the child's deviancy.

In their review of the literature, Friedrich and Boriskin (1976) report that mental retardation, physical handicaps, and prematurity are other vulnerabilities that intensify parental stress and increase the risk for abuse. Klein and Stern (1971) report a range of low birth weight for abused children from 19–30 percent, significantly greater than the expected incidence of low birth weight in the general population, which ranges from 7–9 percent. Low birth weight and prematurity may also be the result of maternal malnutrition, which may reflect inadequate prenatal care because of poverty and/or maternal rejection of the pregnancy.

Kennell, Voos, and Klaus (1978) and Klaus

and Kennell (1976) suggest that the common hospital practice of placing premature and low birth weight infants in intensive care nurseries and thus separating them from their mothers over an extended period of time may seriously interfere with mother-neonate attachment. Klein and Stern (1971) contend that the length of separation between mother and infant, rather than prematurity or low birth weight per se, is the crucial variable that predisposes the infant to abuse. Klaus and Kennell (1976) theorize that there is a "maternal sensitive" period during which separation of mother from neonate interferes with bonding between mother and infant and her subsequent care of the infant and sets the stage for abuse.

Various adverse conditions during the prenatal period and neonatorium of abused children that may contribute to bonding failure between mother and child are reported by Lynch (1976) and Money and Needleman (1976). These include infant's or mother's illness during the infant's first year, other early separations from the mother, and abnormal pregnancy, labor, and delivery.

Findings that the most abuse is directed toward infants, that they suffer from special vulnerabilities, and that there is a subtle, intricate interaction between these vulnerabilities and early adversities should lay to rest, once and for all, the scientifically unfounded, absurd, "blaming the victim" hypothesis that abused children solicit abuse from their parents.

Asynchronous Family Interaction

A promising approach to dynamic understanding of the causes of child abuse is the observation of the interaction between abusive parents and their children. Burgess and Conger (1977) and Redlener (1979) describe the inappropriateness, intrusiveness, and lack of reciprocity among family members. Hyman, Parr, and Browne (1979) report on the similarity between the interactive behavior of their sample of abused infants and that of a group of insecurely attached children of inconsistent, insensitive mothers observed by Ainsworth, Bell, and Stayton (1971). In his examination of the origins of child abuse in the mother-infant dyad, Schwarzbeck (1980) posits a subtle interplay of asynchronous signals between mother and infant that sets the stage for abuse.

Chronic Stress

Many investigators refer to an association between child abuse and stress (Gil, 1970; Parke & Collmer, 1975; Straus et al., 1980). Kempe and Kempe (1978) report that when other predisposing factors are present, a crisis may trigger an abuse incident. Naturalistic observation of animals suggests that stress may trigger violence by animal mothers against their offspring. Lorenz (1967) refers to the role of stress in deactivating aggression-inhibiting mechanisms. Williams (1976) hypothesizes that ferocity is a component of mothering that has survival value in that it is elicited by attackers of the offspring; it becomes misdirected, however, when the mother is under stress.

The existence of chronic stress in a family may partially account for the repetitive nature of child abuse. Justice and Duncan (1978) found that such continued life crises as unemployment, overwork, and job-related moves predisposed parents to child abuse. Justice and Justice (1978) found that abusive parents had high scores on the Social Readjustment Rating Scale (Holmes & Rahe, 1967). They concluded that a chronic bombardment of unpredictable changes increases the probability of violence toward the child by decreasing parents' ability to adapt.

Despite these findings, Straus (1980) emphasizes that stress cannot be considered a direct cause of child abuse, for violence is but one of many responses to stress. For example, in a study of British women, Brown and Harris (1978) found that their response to stress was not child abuse but depression. Using a normative sample of American families, Straus (1980) reported that, although the rate of child abuse was directly correlated with the number of stresses in a given year, the rate of abuse did not increase with increased stress as much for mothers as for fathers. Furthermore, the relationship between stress and child abuse was minimal or absent unless one or more of the following conditions were also present: growing up in violent families; low emotional involvement in the marriage; dominance of the husband in the marriage; a combination of low income, education, and occupation; approval of physical punishment of children and of slapping a spouse; and social isolation. Straus concluded that stress is a mediating variable between these family variables and child abuse, not a direct cause of child abuse.

EFFECTS OF ABUSE ON CHILDREN

Parental abuse of children is a pathological pattern of childrearing that has profound physical, psychobiological, developmental, and psychosocial effects on children. The abused child is exposed to chronic trauma; abuse is rarely a one-time occurrence. The more prolonged the abuse, the less likely the damage is to be reversible. Physical effects include fractures, neurological damage, orthopedic and sensory handicaps, gastrointestinal and manifold other medical problems.

Death

All too often abuse results in death. Leavitt (1974) states that more children under 5 years old die of injuries inflicted by their parents than a combination of deaths from whooping cough, tuberculosis, polio, measles, diabetes, rheumatic fever, and appendicitis. The reported number of deaths from child abuse is 6,000 annually, but the Center for the Improvement of Child Caring (1977) and Roberts (1974) estimate that the actual number is closer to 50,000. U.S. Dept. of Health, Education and Welfare (1975) indicates that heavy case loads, inconsistency of criteria, and other complex factors contribute to the underestimates of deaths due to child abuse. For example, U.S. Dept. of Health, Education and Welfare reports that the Los Angeles Police Department Child Abuse Unit listed

the cause of death as "natural" of a 16-month-old extremely undernourished baby who had been treated for anemia one month earlier and for burns on both legs at 4 months of age.

Brain Damage, Neuromotor Dysfunction, Intellectual and Cognitive Impairment

Martin and Rodeheffer (1976) estimate that 25–30 percent of surviving abused children "have brain damage or neurological dysfunction resulting directly from physical trauma about the head" (p. 13). They are especially vulnerable to reabuse because the damage decreases their general ability to function and to cope with their parents' irrational expectations. According to Mitchell (1977), "nonaccidental injury is probably responsible for a substantial number of cases of mental handicap, cerebral palsy and other chronic neurological disorders" (p. 9). Elmer and Gregg (1967) studied the longitudinal effects of abuse over a 10-year period, using pediatric, audiometric, and psychological assessments. Only 10 percent of their sample fell within normal limits on the measures. The authors conclude that abused children have a 6–10 percent chance of death and a 90 percent chance of developmental retardation. Buchanan and Oliver (1977) found that 3–11 percent of children in a British institution for the retarded had been rendered profoundly intellectually retarded as a result of abuse.

Kent (1976) and Reidy et al. (1980) found intellectual and psychosocial impairment in both abused and neglected children. Applebaum (1980) reports developmental delays in cognitive, motor, language, and social areas in abused children as young as 2–39 months. Inasmuch as infants with severe head trauma had been excluded from the research, such early impairment appears to reflect inadequate parent-infant bonding and other deficits in parenting.

Birch (1974), Cravioto (1966), and Martin (1979) report that abused children had a high incidence of undernutrition, a condition associated with poor physical growth, failure to thrive, sensory and motor dysfunction, intellectual retardation, and impaired learning, attention, and social responsiveness. Although child neglect is less lurid than abuse, its effects are likely to be equally or more damaging. Martin (1976) found that undernourished children have a significantly poorer prognosis for neurological integrity and mental functioning than abused, well-nourished children. Elmer (1967, 1981) found no differences between lower class abused and nonabused children on frequency of chronic illness and speech, learning, and emotional problems. Inasmuch as the effects of poverty are at least as devastating to children as the effects of abuse, poverty may be viewed as societal abuse and neglect of children.

Impaired Endocrinological Functioning

Reversible hyposomatotropinism is an effect of abuse described by MacCarthy (1977), Money (1980), Money and Needleman (1976), and Powell, Brasel, and Blizzard (1967). The syndrome, also termed abuse dwarfism or psychosocial dwarfism, is an effect of abuse and neglect leading to failure of growth hormone secretion, impaired statural growth, delayed puberty, and often failure of adrenocorticotropin (ACTH) secretion. Psychological effects accompanying the syndrome include retarded intellectual and motor development, pain agnosia, temper outbursts, and unusual eating and drinking behavior. Removal from the abusive parental home results in reversibility of hyposomatotropinism.

Emotional and Social Problems

Emotional problems in abused children range from hyperaggressiveness to passivity. Findings that abused children are significantly more aggressive than nonabused children is consistent with the social-learning theory formulation that aggressive parents serve as models of aggression to their children. In their classic study, Sears, Maccoby, and Levin (1957) concluded:

The unhappy effects of punishment have run like a dismal thread through our findings...Mothers who punished aggressive behavior severely had more aggressive children than mothers who punished lightly...Harsh physical punishment was associated with high childhood aggressiveness. (p. 57)

Much empirical support has been given to the hypothesis that violence breeds violence. Bandura (1973), Gelles (1974), Glueck and Glueck (1950), and Welsh (1976) report positive relationships between severe parental punishment and delinquency, aggression, and antisocial values in children. Reidy (1977) and Reidy et al. (1980) found that abused children showed significantly greater frequencies of hyperaggressiveness, behavior problems at school, and lower self-esteem than neglected or nonabused children.

Abused children are also described as withdrawn, passive, anxious, ingratiating, and nonaggressive and compliant in action and fantasy (Rolston, 1971). Gray and Kempe (1976) found compliance as a personality characteristic in 75 percent of abused children at NCPTCAN; the remainder were described as having hyperactive or aggressive personalities. In a clinical study, Morrison and Brubakken (1980) report on a syndrome of autism associated with severe maternal neglect. It differed from classical autism in that symptoms were reversed after removal from the neglectful home and treatment.

The traumatic interpersonal environments to which abused children are forced to adapt and the manifold effects on their personality development and emotional-social behavior have been reported by Martin, a pioneer in this line of investigation, and his associates at the NCPTCAN. Personality characteristics include hypervigilance, joylessness, low self-esteem, and chameleonlike behavior in which the abused child rapidly changes behavior in response to the erratic family environment (Martin, 1976; Martin & Rodehoffer, 1976).

Herzberger, Potts, and Dillon (in press) found that a large percentage of abused children whom they interviewed regarded their parents' treatment of them as unusual and unique. The ambivalence of abused children is revealed in their reports of also feeling loved and cared for by their parents. This double-bind response exemplifies one of the ways the abused child is forced to adapt to the "schizophrenogenic world" described by Martin (1976) and others. The results of the study by Herzberger et al. (in press) were not corroborated by Kempe and Kempe (1978) who report that abused children view their harsh punishment as rightful and normative. Obviously, cross-validational research is in order to clarify these discrepant findings.

Recent research is demonstrating an array of psychologically damaging effects of parent-child incest that include neurotic symptoms such as guilt, shame, and anxiety; sexual malfunctioning such as frigidity and promiscuity; long-lasting antisocial behavior; suicide attempts; truancy; school difficulties; juvenile and adult prostitution; mistrust and misinterpretation of others' behavior; revulsion at being touched; and marital, interpersonal, and identity problems (Anderson, 1979; Densen-Gerber, 1979; Geiser, 1979; Herjanic & Bryan, 1980; Johnston, 1979; Jorné, 1979; Kempe, 1978; Rush, 1980; Williams, in press). The 1977 U.S. Senate Subcommittee on Juvenile Delinquency found that many of the more than one million American children who run away from home are victims of physical and sexual abuse. Both males and females are victims of incest, usually by the father. Johnston (1979) states:

It is difficult to understand the characterization of the child as the initiator or seductress since the child is frequently involved in sexual activity which she does not understand, to which she has not given informed consent and which is characteristic of a psychosexual stage beyond her developmental level. (p. 943)

Yorukoglu and Kemph (1966) report two cases of father-daughter and mother-son incest in which the children did not appear to be severely damaged. They attribute the children's "ability to withstand this trauma...[to] their having developed healthy ego functioning prior to the incestuous experience" (p. 124). Jorné (1979) concluded that the effects of incest may be less damaging if it has been of short duration, has not been accompanied by brutality, if the incestuous parent is ambivalent about the practice, and if the family receives treatment.

Reversibility of the Effects of Abuse

Progress is being made in determining the variables associated with the reversibility of the psychophysiological effects of abuse. Kent (1976) found that intellectual and psychosocial impairment was partially reversible following foster-home placement of abused children. A trend toward lesser impairment among younger abused children suggests the importance of early intervention. Dennis (1973) described a group of institutionalized children deprived of psychological stimulation during infancy and early childhood. Those adopted after 2 years old showed irreversible intellectual impairment, in many cases as much as 50 percent for each year of deprivation. The importance of early intervention was also highlighted by the finding that those adopted before 2 years of age overcame their retardation and showed subsequent average intelligence.

The syndrome of abuse dwarfism is characterized by reversibility after removal of the abused child from the parental home. Money and Annecillo (1976) found that progressive IQ elevation by as much as 50–60 points may follow placement of abuse dwarfs in a domicile away from the abusive parents. These changes were accompanied by increases in statural growth. Morrison and Brubakken (1980) demonstrated the reversibility of autism induced by parental neglect by means of an intensive, multidisciplinary, psychoeducational, residential treatment program.

Such studies indicate that the whole quality of life in the domicile to which abused children are transferred, rather than separation from the parents, is a crucial variable in reversibility of the effects of abuse. Longitudinal studies by Koluchová (1972, 1976) highlight this point. She describes the remarkable development of twins who suffered extreme deprivation and abuse until they were rescued at the age of seven years. A poor prognosis would certainly have been appropriate. Yet their placement in the stable, nurturing home of two sisters and special education resulted in significant advances in all psychobiological spheres and an absence of psychopathology and average intelligence on follow-up eight years later. In discussing Koluchová's first report, Clarke (1972) emphasizes that "the results underline the inadequacy of theories stressing the overriding importance of early experiences for later growth" (p. 106). He adds:

The relatively late age of rescue (7 years) from 5½ years of almost unprecedentedly bad conditions, as well as the responsiveness to remediation, underlines the resilience of these children, and has a bearing on such concepts as critical periods of development. Where studies stress the permanency of the effects of early deprivation, one should examine carefully the new situation in which the child finds himself and ask whether it continues to reinforce earlier experiences. Indeed, the pessimism with which the whole area has been surrounded may have itself contributed to a passivity in the subsequent treatment of deprived children. (p. 106)

Indicators of Child Abuse

Early identification of child abuse is a crucial first step in protecting children against further assaults and treating the families. A composite of indicators of the effects of abuse reported in various brochures and studies is presented to help the clinical child psychologist recognize child abuse.

Regarding physical indicators, abused children may have cheek bruises or unusual body marks such as oval scars formed by burning cigarettes or the distinctive mark of an electric cord. The child may wear a long-sleeved shirt or long pants in warm weather or other inappropriate clothing that hides injuries. Child neglect does not necessarily accompany child abuse: abused children may be well-groomed and well-nourished.

Behavioral-psychological characteristics of abused children may include frequent fatigue, excessive fear, compliance, passivity, and ingratiation in many abused children; hyperaggressiveness and temper outbursts in some of them; erratic expressions of regressive behavior, such as thumbsucking, bedwetting, whining, and disruptiveness; academic performance well below intelligence; preference for remaining at school after class rather than returning home; secretiveness or paucity of spontaneous communication about happenings at home.

Behavioral characteristics of abusive parents may include delay in seeking medical attention for the child's illness or injuries; seeking treatment for the child outside the neighborhood, which may indicate "hospital shopping"; conflicting or inappropriate explanations of a child's bruises, injuries, or illness; unexplained death of a sibling; few or no complimentary references to or about the child; expressions of intense hostility or inordinate blaming of the child; unrealistic expectations of the child; intense fear of "spoiling" the child; social isolation of the family; rejection of friendly overtures; a righteous belief in harsh corporal punishment rigidly supported by Biblical reference. Redlener (1979) describes the following punishment practices as indicators of abuse: any form of physical punishment of an infant under 18 months old; hitting a child with any object or fist other than upon the hand or buttocks; striking a child when the parent is extremely angry.

Difficulty in disciplining or making the child "mind," sometimes given as a parent's ostensible reason for referral to a psychologist, may veil concern over losing control during corporal punishment of the child. It should be noted that most abusive parents do not start out to abuse; their intention is to punish the child corporally. A thorough exploration of the parent's punishment practices, their frequency, intensity, and basis, often makes the difference between the continuation of abuse and prevention of further abuse by provision of the therapeutic help the parent is tacitly seeking.

Inappropriate interactions of the abused child with others, especially the parents, lend support to suspicions of child abuse. Some abused children are wary of physical contact with adults or cringe in response to admonitions or even a glance from the parent. Others fail to exhibit comfort-seeking responses from parents but express excessive affection to strangers. The fact that the child sits on a parent's lap in the hospital or clinic waiting-room, however, does not rule out abuse; it may reflect the child's fear of the violent consequences of noncompliance with the parent's expectation of unconditional affection. Some psychologists may be put off by the seeming social precocity of role reversal behavior of an abused child; caring for an infant sibling or comforting a distraught mother by a three-year-old does not constitute healthy development.

Indications of sexual abuse in children under 5 years include intense fears, night terrors, clinging, and developmental regressions; in school age children, there may be sudden drops in school performance, running away, and sudden onset of anxiety, and weight loss or gain (Kempe, 1978). A combination of dysfunctional family relationships, a sexualized home environment, and the child's insecurity and unmet needs for affection and attention predispose a child to sexual abuse by a parent or nonrelative. According to Johnston (1979), so-called seductiveness in sexually abused children is actually affection-seeking behavior patterned on the sexualized family environment.

Hospitalized abused infants behave differently from children hospitalized for accidental injury. Morris, Gould, and Matthews' (1964) report that nonabused infants cling to their parents when they enter a hospital, turn to them for comfort and reassurance, and demonstrate by their actions that they want to go home. In contrast, abused children cry very little, are apprehensive when adults approach other crying children, and watch them curiously. They are less afraid when first admitted to the ward, tend to settle in quickly, are wary of physical contact with their parents or other adults, seem to have no expectation of being comforted by them, and do not look to parents for reassurance. Abused hospitalized children between 3 and 42 months are extremely frightened of all contact, withdraw from tactile stimulation, whimper, and attempt to hide under the sheets. Others are apathetic to the point of stupor, show profound emotional blunting, and appear shell shocked. They differ from autistic children in that "it appears not so much that their psychic life is distorted or idiosyncratic, but rather that it has been completely suspended" (Galdston, 1965, p. 4).

Lenoski (1974) introduced the term "postural compliance" to describe catatoniclike posturing elicited by elevating one or more limbs into an awkward position. A child between 10 months and 5 years who retains the position for at least fifteen seconds is demonstrating an indicator of abuse. Most children this age will resist attempts to place their limbs in such uncomfortable positions. Redlener (1979) refers to abused children's "frozen watchfulness" and states that "they are so fearful of violent consequences for disobeying an adult that they will make every effort to comply with the demands of the stranger" (p. 94). Postural compliance disappears in the hospital and in other safe, predictable environments.

TREATMENT OF CHILD ABUSE

In order to protect and provide advocacy for abused children, the clinical child psychologist must become closely acquainted with the myriad problems related to remedial intervention. Failure to intervene, careless action, or irresponsible decision making at any point in this intricate process can result in the reabuse or death of the child. Before treatment per se can be implemented, numerous steps must be taken.

Problems of Intervention in Child Abuse

The first step, identification of child abuse, at times is not taken because of a psychologist's inadequate training or unconscious denial. If abuse is identified, it may not be reported, despite legal mandates, because of a psychologist's concern over jeopardizing a professional practice, fear of becoming involved, or rationalizations about confidentiality. If a report is made, the child protection agency or police may erroneously dismiss the charge or delay protective action on the child's behalf.

Even if the psychologist follows through by repeated reports so that the child protective and legal systems are activated, the abused child's life and physical and mental health may be jeopardized by a multitude of professional and bureaucratic incompetencies, delays, apathy, burnout, nitpicking, goofs, and computer errors.

A case in point is the careful examination of the role of the "helping system" in the needless death of a 5-year-old boy repeatedly beaten and starved by his mother and her paramour (Slater, 1981; Orso & Schechter, 1981). Shortly after his birth, his parents accused each other during divorce proceedings of beating him and his 2-year-old sister, but the judge did not act to protect them. Shortly afterwards, the mother voluntarily surrendered her rights to the child she subsequently murdered so that he could be adopted. The judge refused to terminate parental rights because of a legal technicality and on his opinion that the agency had not provided "proper guidance" to the mother. Several years later the child was removed from her home because of abuse. Still another judge ordered his return five months before his murder, later alleging that the court had received no evidence of child abuse. After the child's return, the school principal called a child abuse hotline once but did not pursue the matter, even though the child continued to arrive at school so severely and visibly injured that he was not included in a kindergarten photograph. Other reports had not been relayed to the Central Registry from which information on previous abuse had not been retrieved. Police did respond to another anonymous call by referring the case to a child protective agency. The social worker accepted the explanation of the abusive mother that the serious, extensive injuries, including two black eyes, broken ribs, and malnutrition, were the result of a fall from a jungle gym followed by a fight with his 7-year-old sister. The night before his murder, the agency failed to follow up a teacher's report that the child had not returned to school.

The scenario of the child-wrecking helping system is not rare. A two-year, in-depth study by Terr and Watson (1967) revealed the "rebrutalization" of ten abused children as a result of bungling by numerous professionals in hospitals, courts, and social agencies. As will be amplified later, recidivism rates among abusive parents are high, so that, even if an agency does intervene, child abuse has a high probability of continuing during and after a supermarket of treatment services, including psychotherapy, are provided to the parents. Furthermore, it is highly unlikely that the abused child will receive more than medical treatment for physical injuries.

There are a number of reasons for these problems. A root problem is the overriding mission of all child abuse programs: namely, that of keeping the child with the parents and placement of the child as a last resort. Termination of parental rights and freeing the child for adoption rarely occur, even when the parents are not capable of becoming rehabilitated, even using minimal standards of child care. This philosophy has deep roots in the belief in the absolute sanctity of the home, expressed in the old Anglo-Saxon adage that "a man's home is his castle." Regardless of what brutal practices have occurred there, the home has been off-limits to protective intervention. The privacy of the home, coupled with vestiges of a legal heritage that decrees children to be chattel of their parents and continues to deny them legal rights, have led to social sanctions for manifold abuses against children and, ironically, continue to influence social structures purporting to help children. Williams (1980b) examined reappraisals of Bowlby's (1951) studies that support the conclusion that, in many cases, the least damaging alternative for a child is removal from the parental home and placement elsewhere. Current child protection philosophy is a misapplication of Bowlby's work, Kempe (1971) indicates, for "it does not have to be the biological mother who mothers the baby, though there has to be a mothering person for every child" (p. 36).

Nevertheless, a legacy of ancient law is the transcendence of parental rights over those of children, and clinical child psychologists in the child abuse arena must continually grapple with legal tenets frequently antithetical to the welfare of children. They must also make every effort to convey their specialized knowledge to legal personnel who have little if any knowledge of psychology, children, families, or mental health. Indeed, in some areas, juvenile judges do not even have law degrees.

Some progress is being made toward solving legal problems obstructing child protection. One advance made in 26 states is the appointment of a guardian *ad litum,* a court-appointed guardian, usually an attorney, whose sole purpose is to represent the child's interests and who should be requested by the child abuse staff (Fraser, 1979). All too often, however, the guardian *ad litum* is too busy to participate in the case.

Several states have defined more clearly the legal requirements for involuntary termination of parental rights, thus removing abused children from legal limbo. These new laws can spare them from innumerable foster-home placements and free them for adoption. The National Council of Jewish Women (undated) provides court-appointed, well-trained, volunteer special advocates to expedite permanent placement of abused and other children in foster care in Dallas, Texas; Jacksonville, Florida; and St. Louis, Missouri. Efforts are also being made to improve communication between lawyers and helping professionals. For example, the Schools of Law, Medicine, and Social Work at the University of Michigan are involved in an interdisciplinary project to enhance collaboration in child abuse matters (Duquette & Jones, 1979). An organization to improve legal representation of children, The National Association of Counsel for Children (1205 Oneida St., Denver, Colorado 80220), was founded in 1977 (Bross, 1980).

Another contributor to problems of intervention is the field of child protection itself. There is often large turnover in the field, low job satisfaction, large case loads, and burnout, so that the abuse family rarely sees the same worker throughout treatment. Furthermore, primary care workers, who are expected to help these most difficult, multiproblem families, usually have little training in carrying out tasks that would tax the most expertly trained professionals. For example, many workers have only an undergraduate degree in any discipline. Despite recommendations by national child welfare groups of no more than twenty abuse cases per worker, the average is often twice that much. Referring to burnout in child protection workers, Kempe (1979) contends that 'they are the only public servants willing to constantly stretch their case load to meet any demands. They do so because they are not a militant profession with defined duties" (p. x). Reposa (1979) stresses the importance of self-care for those working with abuse families and suggests using cotherapy as a means of coping with burnout. Armstrong (1979) describes symptoms of burnout in the child abuse field and offers guidelines on avoiding it. In addition to myriad human factors, there are management problems in monitoring and guiding child abuse treatment because of agencies' failure to apply scientific and technological advances in using central registers (Olson & Besharov, 1979).

Management

In view of the manifold problems in working in child abuse, it is not surprising that interdisciplinary cooperation and coordination are stressed. Although social work and medicine pioneered in the treatment of child abuse, no single discipline merits a special authoritative role on the team (U.S. Dept. HEW, vols. 1 and 2, 1975; Helfer, 1975).

Management refers to numerous practical arrangements and actions, including identifying and reporting suspected abuse, diagnosis, crisis intervention, short and long term treatment planning, and follow-up. Hospitals, institutions, physicians, and nurses are legally mandated to report abuse in most states. Other mandated reporters include psychologists, social workers, clergy, and dentists. Some states penalize mandated persons for failing to report child abuse and have made provisions for anonymous reporting in order to overcome reluctance to report. If abuse is not found, reporters are exempt from legal action. A 24-hour-a-day toll-free hotline receives reports in most areas.

The National Center on Child Abuse and Neglect has established a number of federally funded demonstration projects throughout the United States (Cohn, Ridge, & Collignon, 1975) based on the multidisciplinary, coordinated, community team approach developed by Helfer (1975). One guideline for the child protection team offered by Carroll and Schmitt (1978) is a psychological examination of the abused child, who is almost certain to have behavioral problems and developmental delays, especially in speech and communication. Even if siblings have not been abused, they should also receive psychological examinations because living with a dysfunctional, abusive family is likely to result in behavioral and developmental problems. According to Fraser (1979), abusive parents are routinely examined psychologically and psychiatrically in many states.

Carroll and Schmitt (1978) strongly urge rapid adjudication when the abused child's injuries are severe, when termination of parental rights has been considered since initial contact with the case, and when parents refuse to participate in treatment. In all cases, request for a guardian *ad litum* should be made.

Parent- and Family-Oriented Treatment

According to U.S. Dept. of HEW (vol. 3, 1975), "Of the three components of the community-team program—identification and diagnosis, treatment, and education—treatment tends to be most notably lacking. It is not uncommon for a community to develop extensive identification and diagnostic resources and then find itself ill-equipped to help identified families" (p. 65). Even when a community has remedial resources, agencies may be reluctant to modify services to meet the unique needs of abuse families. Cohn and Miller (1977) indicate that treatment is often equated with casework, psychotherapy, or

medical care, rather than the wide range of services required for such multiproblem families.

Ideally, treatment of child abuse involves a variety of services, in addition to psychotherapy, that include parent aides, self-help groups, homemakers, crisis nurseries, casework, hotlines, and other remedial resources characterizing such programs as NCPTCAN (Helfer & Kempe, 1976; Kempe & Kempe, 1978) and other federally funded child abuse projects (Cohn, Ridge, & Collignon, 1975). Spinetta (1977) refers to the reality that "very little encouragement is given to the therapist who does not have easy access to the new interdisciplinary treatment programs and who, in many instances, remains the sole agent for a particular set of families" (p. 2). Treatment is given to abusive parents, rather than abused children, an expression of the family-oriented philosophy of child protection programs. Cohn and Miller (1977) state that only adult members are receiving treatment services in the 85 percent of abuse families in federally funded programs.

Currently, psychological treatment of abusive parents is based mainly on trial-and-error efforts by the child abuse staff and therapists to develop an approach acceptable to these resistant parents. The selection of the therapist and therapy modality are usually dependent on the availability of psychotherapists or on a number of other practical or extraneous considerations that lack a theoretical or empirical foundation. Individual, group, marital, and family therapy and casework have been used with abusive parents.

Cohn (1979) found that providing abusive parents with a combination of individual psychotherapy by skilled professionals and lay services, including parent aides and Parents Anonymous, was more effective in helping them cope with their problems than individual or group therapy without lay services. Parent aides were well-trained and received ongoing supervision by a professional in providing abusive parents with friendship, support, and/or social contact; met with the family several times a week; and were available to them daily if necessary. Lower reincidence rates were found in programs where the most highly qualified professional conducted intake interviews and treatment planning and where the length of treatment was at least six months. Other variables related to effective treatment of abusive parents included smaller case loads of about twenty families; same-day crisis intervention; multidisciplinary intake and treatment planning; continuous use of consultants from various disciplines; weekly contacts between case managers and abusive parents regarding treatment progress; and 4–6 week follow-up to make sure termination of treatment was appropriate.

Individual therapy, however, has many drawbacks. Abusive parents are often too erratic to submit to regularly scheduled 50-minute sessions; insufficiently psychologically minded to avail themselves of psychotherapy; and/or so emotionally demanding or insatiable that treatment by one therapist is grossly inadequate. It is not surprising that group therapy is widely used in the treatment of abusive parents. Interpretations are usually accepted more readily from other abusive parents than from a professional, and confrontation can occur earlier. Moreover, a greater number of parents can be reached.

Controlled regression of abusive parents is a primary feature of group therapy applied by Paulson and Chaleff (1973). They demonstrate that interaction with empathic, nonjudgmental male and female cotherapists increases abusive parents' trust and fosters identification with and modeling of these parent surrogates. Justice and Justice (1976) describe a multifaceted approach to group therapy for abusive parents that includes behavior modification, transactional analysis, relaxation training, and parent education regarding appropriate responses to children at each developmental stage.

Family therapy for abuse families is the least applied modality because the abused child may be reexposed to the traumatizing rage of parents who are unable to tolerate the child's expression of anger. Beezley, Martin, and Alexander (1976) stress that such tolerance must be thoroughly assessed before family therapy is implemented and that concurrent individual sessions may need to take place.

Ounstead et al. (1974) in England and McBogg, McQuiston, and Alexander (1979) in the U.S. describe residential treatment programs for the entire abuse family. This strategy has the advantage of protecting the child from reabuse while keeping the family together. The regression-enhancing environment offers nurturance to the affect-hungry parents and provides the abused child with a safe, predictable, trust-promoting environment.

Wolfe et al. (1980) found that parents who were court-ordered to complete a treatment program emphasizing child management skills as a requirement for return of child custody were five times more likely to complete it than voluntarily treated parents. Thus the court can play a crucial role in influencing abusive parents to improve child-caring skills. Oates (1979) devised a classification of child abuse related to prognosis for treatment. The best prognoses for adequate child care were for normal mothers with high stress who had not abused siblings. Poor prognoses included adolescent, psychopathic, or multiply handicapped parents.

Parents Anonymous and similar self-help groups are another component of the multifaceted treatment services to abusive parents. Chapters across the nation provide telephone hotlines for parents who feel they are in danger of losing control and abusing their children. Lieber and Baker (1977) concluded that the program improved parents' attitudes, knowledge, and behavior regarding their children. A number of serious flaws in the research, however, casts doubts on this conclusion. Findings were based on self-reports to a questionnaire in which social desirability and other pertinent test variables were not controlled. Furthermore, positive findings are probably spurious because other forms of treatment probably occurred concurrently with participation in Parents Anonymous but such variables were not taken into account.

As cited earlier (Cohn, 1979), a combination of professional and professionally supervised lay therapy appears to be the most effective treatment for abusive parents. Despite wide media coverage, the effectiveness of self-help groups is doubtful in the absence of the many and varied services needed by abuse families. Although many abusive parents express gratification with these programs, there is no evidence that membership improves parent-child relations, increases positive feelings toward the child, or curbs abuse. A major shortcoming is that these groups lack models of healthy parenting for abusive parents to try to emulate. The fact that Parents Anonymous groups have failed to sponsor affiliated groups for their abused children, analogous to Al-Teen for children of members of Alcoholics Anonymous, reflects their purely parent-centered philosophy.

Education in child development and management and home-based practical behavior modification procedures, including anger control, are described as helpful adjuncts (Ambrose & Hazzard, 1980; Christophersen et al., 1976). Another component of services to abuse families is the homemaker, who helps organize the often chaotic home, serves as a model of good child care and home management, and contributes to breaking up the abuse family's isolation from the community.

Treatment of Abused Children

Progress in the psychological treatment of abused children has been considerably slower than that of abusive parents. Cohn and Miller (1977) state that

While we must continue to test out innovative strategies working with abusive parents, we clearly must spend more time implementing and testing methods for treating children who have been injured. We must more consciously learn ways of allowing these children to develop to their fullest potential, thereby breaking into the intergenerational pattern of abuse. (p. 49)

One obstruction is the medical and social-legal models of child abuse (Beezley et al.,

1976). The first model views the child as suffering from physical injuries requiring medical treatment. The second model deflects attention from the child to the abusive parents, who are viewed as criminals deserving punishment or needing rehabilitation. Psychological treatment of the abused child is bypassed by these models, which are too simplistic to encompass the intense psychological trauma to the abused child or the extent of family dysfunction of which the abuse is a manifestation.

Abusive parents, even those in the process of rehabilitation, are another obstruction to psychological treatment of abused children. Although the children require psychotherapy for their extensive personality problems, abusive parents often feel too threatened to permit any but medical treatment and special education for the children they have abused. Although parents' refusal to permit child psychotherapy constitutes the continuation of abuse in more passive or subtle forms or the substitution of emotional abuse and neglect for physical abuse and neglect, agencies often compromise their recommendations by adhering to the parents' egocentric wishes.

Flanzraich and Steiner (1980) describe a psychotherapeutic approach geared to the level of ego development of abused children. Several clinical studies of therapy with abused children have been reported by Boston (1972, 1979), D'Ambrosio (1970), Morrison and Brubakken (1980), and Weinberg (1980). Drotar, Malone, and Negray (1980) discuss the importance of psychological assessment in determining therapeutic effectiveness for infants and young children who fail to thrive. Davoren (1979) describes innovative low budget play therapy for abused young children that was unthreatening to their parents. Kempe (1979) states:

It has been very encouraging to us to see how relatively quickly (abused) children can be reconstituted emotionally, provided only that they receive appropriate emotional support of a skilled, reliable kind and at once. Individual and group treatment must be tailor-made to each child's needs. To fail to address the emotional needs of the abused child effectively and from the first should nowadays have to be regarded as malpractice. (p. xii)

Martin (1976) and Kempe and Kempe (1978) describe various other therapeutic interventions. These include therapeutic play schools, daycare centers, or public schools where emotionally sensitive teachers engender trust and confidence in abused children and help them overcome handicapping personality traits; opportunities for socialization to counteract the effects of poor parental models of interpersonal interaction; developmental stimulation and remediation of lags and deficits at special schools; and group therapy for preadolescent and adolescent children.

Recidivism and the Effects of Treatment in Abuse Families

In the past, the effectiveness of treatment was informally reported in pessimistic or optimistic impressions by pioneers in the child abuse field. For example, Polansky and Polansky (cited in Gil, 1970) asserted that "most hardheaded observers report *little success* with the methods of aggressive casework (or unaggressive psychiatry) now being practiced" (p. 44). Steele (1975) contended that "even in the face of rather haphazard selection mechanisms, remarkably good results have come from parents who have been treated by many different methods" (p. 21). Today, however, programs purporting to treat child abuse are under increasing pressure to demonstrate accountability by achievement rather than merely by subjective anecdotal appraisals of efficacy or good intentions.

Studies of treatment effectiveness have measured mainly parent variables because treatment has been based on what Kempe (1979) calls the "trickle down" theory by which "giving nurturing help to the mother was thought to improve her total life and marriage, and would then permit her to be a more competent mother and wife. It was the credo of protective services for one hundred years" (p. xi). Measures have been clinical

evaluations of abusive parents' progress in psychotherapy or overall assessments of family-oriented projects (Comptroller General of the U.S., 1976; Seaberg, 1975). Empirical research on the effects of psychotherapy on abused children is lacking. The only study found on the effects of family-oriented treatment on child variables was that of Taitz (1980) in England who reported that, of 38 infants and children whose families had received casework during a five-year period, only 12 were classified as satisfactory on mental development, speech attainment, and growth outcome.

The crucial parent variable in studies of treatment effectiveness is recidivism of abuse. Admittedly, a number of thorny problems are associated with this measure. First, recidivism is likely to be underestimated. Cohn and Miller (1977) contend:

(1) It may not be detected by treatment providers; (2) the child may have been removed from the home making reincidence impossible; or (3) reincidence may not occur until long after treatment (or the study) is over. The supportive treatment environment may serve to delay or inhibit abusive/ neglectful behavior. Thus, while the presence of reincidence may give us clues about what is happening in the family, the absence may tell us nothing. (p. 455)

Furthermore, treatment followed by low recidivism would, by definition, be viewed as effective even though the child may continue to suffer from untreated, severe emotional problems resulting from the earlier parental abuse. Nevertheless, despite its narrowness and the probability of underestimation of abuse, the criterion of recidivism has the merits of objectivity, specifiability, quantifiability, and appropriateness as a dependent variable in investigations of the effects of treatment.

Early studies of recidivism reported ranges from 20–60 percent (Friedman, 1972; Skinner & Castle, 1969). Higher recidivism rates are found in recent, more methodologically sophisticated studies. In a follow-up study of 328 families who had received services for child abuse, Herrenkohl et al. (1979) found 66.8 percent of verified incidents of reabuse compared to 25.4 percent in official reports. Depending on the number of perpetrators, targets, and types of abuse in a family, recidivism ranged from 44–85 percent. Even after cases had been closed, presumably because abuse was no longer believed to be present, recidivism was found in 18.5 percent of the cases, 25 percent of whom had received over 36 months of treatment. Combs et al. (1980) devised a Protection Index that estimates the proximity of danger to abused children, measures changes in their condition during ongoing protective services, and evaluates the impact of various treatments on the family.

Perhaps the most significant investigation of the effects of treatment is Cohn's (1979) 40-month evaluation of 11 federally funded child abuse demonstration projects. A combination of highly skilled professional counseling and lay services was more effective than professional and group treatment without lay services in alleviating problems that trigger abuse and in reducing the propensity for reabuse, which remained high in all treatment groups, however, and ranged from 47–62 percent of abusive parents. Reincidence of severe abuse occurred in 56 percent of cases considered serious at intake, regardless of treatment used. Of the entire sample, 30 percent seriously reabused their children while the parents were being treated. Inasmuch as the measures of reincidence excluded mild physical abuse or neglect and emotional abuse and neglect, the findings are an underestimate of reincidence had a broader definition of child abuse been used. Furthermore, it can be assumed that recidivism rates are even higher in abuse families who do not receive the benefits of funding, consultation, and other support provided by these demonstration projects.

Butterfield, Jackson, and Nangle (1979) corroborate these dismal findings in England. In a 2.5-year follow-up of extensive services to abusive parents, they report that 46 of 69 children remained at risk, were reabused, or had a sibling who was abused.

Separation of Children from Abusive Parents

The high recidivism rate among abusive parents during and after long term, comprehensive treatment services indicates that, for their own protection, more children should be removed from the parental home and fewer should be returned. Numerous studies (Dennis, 1973; Kent, 1976; Koluchová, 1972, 1976; Money & Annecillo, 1976) demonstrate that abused children placed in even moderately supportive environments show at least partial reversiblity of some of the psychological, developmental, hormonal, and statural effects of abuse. Further support for removal from the parental home for the best interests of the child comes from Browder (1975), Moss and Moss (1975), and Tizard (1974) who demonstrate the therapeutic contributions of some foster homes to children. Kadushin (1970) and Tizard (1979) describe positive outcomes of adoption of abused or unwanted children. Polansky and Polansky (cited in Gil, 1970) make the following recommendations "some of which may seem rather shocking to people accustomed to viewing with genial detachment the sufferings of children outside their own families" (p. 44): immediate removal and long term placement of abandoned children or those neglected to the point of starvation; permanent removal of children abused before the age of 3 years; legally requiring parents of failure-to-thrive children to bring their children to clinics for regular medical check-ups; imprisonment rather than probation for child abusers because of the known instances in which a parent has murdered a child while on probation.

Much resistance to removing children from the parental home is based on a romanticization of mother-child attachment rather than on empirical findings. For example, Douglas and Blomfield (1958) found that damaging effects on a child followed separation from the mother only when separation was accompanied by environmental change. Williams (1980b) concludes that separation of abused children from their parents would be less damaging if the parents left home and moved to a therapeutic foster-home while the child remained at home with another adequate caretaker.

Even when abusive parents are rehabilitated, return of the abused child to the home may be damaging. As Solnit (1978) contends:

The younger the child the more vulnerable they are to the threat of feeling unprotected and unwanted by the parent who has attempted to destroy him or her. Although such a parent may make a full recovery, our inability to make long-term predictions about recurrences and the child's inability to overcome and reduce the felt risk of being exposed to the full care of such a parent will tend to produce an atmosphere deleterious to the child's basic needs for a daily, hourly, sense of safety, feeling loved, wanted and well-guided. (p. 200)

In short, in many instances, the community's resources will be more profitably spent on facilitating adoption and developing other child care facilities than on the manifold services required to bring the parental home up to even marginal standards of child care, where the prized goal of all these efforts is not adequate care but stopping parents from abusing their children. Referring to the work of the National Society for the Prevention of Cruelty to Children in England, Jones (1977) states: "With the benefit of hindsight, we now realize that in several of our cases the child's interest might have been better served if the focus of our intervention had been on helping the parents to relinquish the child rather than on working toward rehabilitation" (p. 116).

Kempe and Kempe (1978) emphasize that recommendations for termination of parental rights does not mean the parents are not deserving of treatment but that "the child should not be used as the instrument of treatment." They maintain:

Quite commonly, a professional who is treating a parent and who has overidentified with the needs of his patient will say that losing custody of the child will harm the parent and set back his progress in treatment. But we firmly believe that a child's rights must be independently recognized. A child's devel-

opmental timetable simply does not allow undue delay. A parent may require three or four years of treatment before he can safely look after a child, but the child cannot wait that long in "temporary placement." There must be a more civilized way of dealing with incurable failures than providing a martyred child. (p. 10)

Inasmuch as the guiding philosophy of child protection, keeping the family together at all costs, is contradicted by many findings that this guideline does not protect and may indeed harm abused children, alternative child advocacy strategies are being devised. The Model State Subsidized Adoption Act (Katz & Gallagher, 1976) provides subsidies for eligible, low income adoptive parents. A Model Act to Free Children for Permanent Placement, devised by Katz (1979) at the request of the U.S. government, provides guidelines for meeting the child's needs for permanency, whether or not parental rights are terminated. National Center for the Prevention and Treatment of Child Abuse and Neglect (1978) describes a model Parent-Child Legal Relationship Termination Act that assumes that:

Parents and children are equal in their right to the satisfaction of a permanent and sustaining family life, and that they are also equal in their rights to life, liberty and the pursuit of happiness. No room is left for the presumption that children are the property of their parents. This Act further states that the court shall give primary consideration to the needs of the child. (p. 1)

Kempe (1979) forecasts that "early termination of parental rights to make the child available for adoption will, in years to come, be seen as a key element in the chain of progress for abused children" (p. xiii).

Preventive Treatment

Studies indicate that families with a high potential for child abuse can be identified during the prenatal and perinatal periods and the neonatorium and that early outreach can prevent abuse potential from being expressed

(Gray et al., 1976; Kempe, 1976; Schneider, Hoffmeister, & Helfer, 1976; Schmitt, 1980). Signs of potential abuse during the prenatal period include denial or depression regarding the pregnancy, not following through on a desired abortion, lack of family support, and concern that the baby will not meet parental standards. Signs during postpartum and pediatric checkups include negative verbalizations about the baby, disappointment in the baby's sex, repulsion at the baby's messiness, and jealousy by the husband.

Cost-effective outreach programs have already resulted in prevention of abuse in high risk families provided with total-push services including parenting classes that discourage physical punishment, counseling and parent aid services, crisis nurseries, supportive phone calls, and visits from the clinic or hospital staff, in addition to conventional instruction in infant care. A nationwide health visitor system, which would involve early detection of abuse potential and preventive strategies, has been endorsed by Justice and Justice (1976), Kempe (1976), and Schmitt (1980) and is similar to that used in the United Kingdom and Scandinavia. Additional discussion on the topic will be found in chapter on the prevention of childhood disorders, by Peterson and Ridley-Johnson (chap. 50 of this book).

TOWARD THE PRIMARY PREVENTION OF CHILD ABUSE

If parental abuse of children is ever to be prevented, radical transformations must occur in attitudes, practices, and programs. Yet primary prevention receives scant attention because these transformations are so controversial. It is less threatening for professionals and politicians to focus on the treatment of child abuse with its evocation of the graphic images and rescue fantasies that inspire public support.

The elimination of child abuse can occur only when its root causes are eliminated. One cause of child abuse, corporal punishment of children, is a deeply engrained practice in the U.S. The family and school are the only social institutions, other than the police and the military, that sanction physical force as a means of social control and against children, who are least able to defend themselves physically or legally. As Feshbach (1980) states: "The case against the use of physical or corporal punishment as a socializing practice has been made so often and so convincingly and in so many contexts...that its continuation gives us some indication of the irrational forces that maintain this practice" (p. 111). Nonviolent alternatives to disciplining and instructing children have been described by Feshbach and Feshbach (1973), Hyman and Wise (1979), and Valusek (1974).

That corporal punishment is unnecessary in the rearing and teaching of children is indicated by its abolition in the schools of Denmark, Finland, Holland, Israel, Japan, Norway, the Soviet Union, and Sweden. It is practiced in such English-speaking countries as Australia and Britain, as well as the U.S. Feshbach (1980) reports on a Swedish law explicitly forbidding parents from striking or humiliating their children, a law that "recognizes the integrity of the child and the child's right (not privilege) to be trained by more positive modes of discipline" (p. 111).

The relationship between unwanted or egocentrically motivated pregnancy and child abuse highlights the necessity of contraceptive and abortion counseling for all ages and segments of society if child abuse is to be prevented. Competent, ethical, nonpropagandistic counseling for women, especially adolescents, with unplanned pregnancies is essential. Antiabortion agencies, which violate ethical standards when they exhort conflict-ridden women with problem pregnancies to carry their children to term, often emphasize the ease with which these women discover that they really want their children. Inasmuch as few women place their children for adoption, antiabortion agencies may be inadvertently contributing to child abuse, for as Helfer (1975) and others have shown, wanting a child in no way rules out parental abuse of that "wanted" child after its birth.

The finding that some women abuse the

child they want underscores the importance of transforming attitudes toward women's roles, childbearing, and the definition of the family. The abysmal failure of these women in a role they sought with joyous expectations poignantly depicts the destructiveness of sexist and pronatalist childrearing. In all likelihood, they learned to accept without question the major tenets of sexism and pronatalism: namely, sex role stereotyping and the beliefs that anatomy is destiny, that the only fulfilling lifestyle for women is motherhood, and that a woman becomes validated as a person only when she becomes a mother. Despite their background in the "World of Abnormal Rearing" (Helfer, 1975), these women need not have become child abusers. Had the culture offered them a variety of socially sanctioned options, in addition to motherhood, they might have become contributors to society rather than a drain on its resources.

Adoption of the tenets of the Women's Movement and the National Alliance for Optional Parenthood would significantly contribute to the eradication of child abuse. These tenets include the facts that anatomy is not destiny for either women or men, that many lifestyles can be fulfilling, that the family is a unit that may or may not include children, and that childfree marriage and singlehood merit social sanctions equal to marriage and parenthood.

Pronatalist and sexist ideologies promoted in textbooks, advertising, and sex education courses contribute indirectly but powerfully to child abuse because they assume that the ability to bear children equips women, in some mysterious way, with the ability to rear them adequately. Not only must textbooks depict Dick and Jane as equally proficient in social and occupational roles, but they must also include stories about families in which neither Dick, Jane, nor any other children are part of the household. Beach et al. (1976) have constructed a test to measure attitudes toward becoming a parent that can be used to aid couples in examining the consequences of a decision to have a (another) child.

The distorted, sentimental view of children as always cute, clean, and quiet, a pronatalist depiction devised by the media to sell products, contributes to child abuse. Unrealistic expectations of children, a major characteristic of abusive parents, are continuously reinforced by commercials that portray children as adorable, ever-fulfilling cherubs whose disposable diapers are never soiled, who gurgle quietly, and who never utter the shrill, ear-piercing wails that often trigger parental violence against the infant.

A massive campaign, including persuasive contacts with advertisers by child advocates, will be required to correct the damaging distortions of children inflicted on the public. Such a campaign would also need to include unsentimentalized courses in family life education that realistically present the sometimes ugly, dirty, unrewarding, unfulfilling, frustrating aspects of children and parenthood. Parenting courses would need to give equal time to nonparenting lifestyles. Indeed, the substitution of courses on lifestyles for the much-touted parenting courses would present youth with the varied range of their relational options, teach them realistic expectations of children, and help them make an informed choice rather than one determined by social pressures if parenthood is eventually selected.

These are but a few of the changes that must take place if child abuse is to be eradicated. Current programs are grossly insufficient stopgap measures that cannot solve this enormous problem. As Helfer (1978) states:

Every year 1½–2 percent of our children are reported as suspected victims of child abuse. While social agencies are working to help this year's 2 percent, they are still trying to figure out what to do with last year's 2 percent and are pleading with legislators for more money to deal with next year's 2 percent. The problems of abuse and neglect accumulate at the rate of 1½–2 percent children each year. (p. 1)

Tragically, the meager funds allotted to stem child abuse are being used to treat rather than prevent it, and the knowledge we already possess to prevent child abuse is not being implemented. Unless priorities are changed, parental abuse of children will continue indefinitely. As Fraser (1979) concludes:

The current child abuse system in America is destined to failure. As the identification process becomes more efficient and more thorough, the system will overload and short. Treatment services which are already functioning at capacity will sink. Slowly at first then rapidly. If America is to be successful in dealing with the problems of child abuse, it must develop a new and different perspective. The perspective is prevention. To do anything less is to worship at the altar of futility. (p. 42)

REFERENCES

Ainsworth, M.S. Further research into the adverse effects of maternal deprivation. In J. Bowlby, (Ed.), *Child care and the growth of love* (2nd ed.). Baltimore: Penguin, 1965.

Ainsworth, M.S., Bell, S., & Stayton, D. In R. Schaeffer (Ed.), *Origin of human social relations.* London: Academic Press, 1971.

Alvy, K.T. On child abuse: Values and analytic approaches. *Journal of Clinical Child Psychology,* 1975, **4,** 36–37.

Ambrose, S., & Hazzard, A. Cognitive-behavioral parenting groups for abusive families. *Child Abuse and Neglect,* 1980, **4,** 119–125.

American Humane Association. National analyses of official child neglect and abuse reporting. Denver: American Humane Association, 1978.

Anderson, D. Touching: When is it caring and nurturing and/ or when is it exploitative and damaging? *Child abuse and neglect,* 1979, **3,** 793–794.

Appelbaum, A.S. Developmental retardation in infants as a concomitant of physical child abuse. In G.J. Williams & J. Money (Eds.), *Traumatic abuse and neglect of children at home.* Baltimore: Johns Hopkins Press, 1980.

Armstrong, K.L. How to avoid burnout: A study of the relationship between burnout and worker, organizational and management characteristics in eleven child abuse and neglect projects. *Child Abuse and Neglect,* 1979, **3,** 145–149.

Bandura, A. *Aggression: A social learning analysis.* Englewood Cliffs, N.J.: Prentice-Hall, 1973.

Beach, L.R., Townes, B.D., Campbell, F.L., & Keating, G.W. Developing and testing a decision aid for birth planning decisions. *Organizational Behavior and Human Performance,* 1976, **15,** 99–116.

Beezley, P., Martin, H., & Alexander, H. Comprehensive family oriented therapy. In R.E. Helfer & C.H. Kempe (Eds.), *Child abuse and neglect: The family and the community.* Cambridge, Mass.: Ballinger, 1976.

Besharov, D., & Besharov, S. Why do parents harm their children? *National Council of Jewish Women,* Winter 1977, 6–8.

Billing, L., Eriksson, M., Larsson, G., & Zetterstrom, R. Amphetamine addiction and pregnancy III. *Acta Paedopsychiatrica,* in press.

Birch, H.G. Health and the education of socially disadvantaged children. In G.J. Williams & S. Gordon (Eds.), *Clinical child psychology: Current practices and future perspectives.* New York: Human Sciences Press, 1974.

Bishop, F.I. Children at risk. *Medical Journal of Australia,* 1971, **1,** 623.

Boston, M. Psychotherapy with a boy from a children's home. *Journal of Child Psychotherapy,* 1972, **2,** 53.

Boston, M. Interim notes on a study of psychotherapy with severely deprived children. *Child Abuse and Neglect,* 1979, **3,** 539–546.

Bovelek, S., & Keene, R. *Primary prevention of child abuse: Identification of high risk parents.* Eau Claire: University of Wisconsin, 1980.

Bovelek, S., Kline, D.F., McLaughlin, J.A., & Publicover, P.R. Primary prevention of child abuse and neglect: Identification of high risk adolescents. *Child Abuse and Neglect,* 1979, **3,** 1071–1080.

Bowlby, J. *Maternal care and mental health.* Geneva: World Health Organization, 1951.

Bronfenbrenner, U. Toward an experimental ecology of human development. *American Psychologist,* 1977, **32,** 513–531.

Bross, D.C. An organization to improve legal representation of children—The National Association of Counsel for Children. *Child Abuse and Neglect,* 1980, **4,** 115–117.

Browder, J.A. Adoption and foster care of handicapped children in the United States. *Developmental Medicine and Child Neurology,* 1975, **17,** 614–619.

Brown, G.W., & Harris, T. *Social origins of depression: A study of psychiatric disorders in women.* London: Tavistock, 1978.

Buchanan, A., & Oliver, J.E. Abuse and neglect as a cause of mental retardation: A study of 140 children admitted to subnormality hospitals in Wiltshire. *British Journal of Psychiatry,* 1977, **131,** 458–467.

Burgess, R.L., & Conger, R.D. Family interaction patterns related to child abuse and neglect. *Child Abuse and Neglect,* 1977, **1**, 2–4.

Butterfield, A.M., Jackson, A.D.M., & Nangle, D. Child abuse—A two-year follow-up. *Child Abuse and Neglect,* 1979, **3**, 985–989.

Cameronchild, J. An autobiography of violence. *Child Abuse and Neglect,* 1978, **2**, 139–149.

Carr, J.N. Drug patterns among drug-addicted mothers: Incidence variance in use and effects on children. *Paediatric Annals,* 1975, **4**, 65.

Carroll, C.A., & Schmitt, B.D. Guidelines for the protection and treatment of the abused child. *Child Abuse and Neglect,* 1978, **2**, 2109–116.

Center for the Improvement of Child Caring. *Save the children.* Los Angeles: Author, 1977.

Christophersen, E.R., Kuehn, B.S., Grinstead, J.D., Barnard, J.D., Rainey, S., & Kuehn, F.E. A family training program for abuse and neglect families. *Journal of Pediatric Psychology,* 1976, **1**, 90–94.

Clarke, A.D.B. Commentary on Koluchová's "Severe deprivation in twins: A case study." *Journal of Psychology and Psychiatry,* 1972, **13**, 103–106.

Cohn, A.H. Essential elements of successful child abuse and neglect treatment. *Child Abuse and Neglect,* 1979, **3**, 491–496.

Cohn, A.H., & Miller, M.K. Evaluating new modes of treatment for child abusers and neglectors: The experience of federally funded demonstration projects in the USA. *Child Abuse and Neglect,* 1977, **1**, 453–458.

Cohn, A.H., Ridge, S.S., & Collignon, F.C. Evaluating innovative treatment programs. *Children Today,* 1975, **4**, 10–12.

Comptroller General of the U.S. *More can be learned and done about the well-being of children.* Washington, D.C.: General Accounting Office, 1976.

Coombes, P., McCormack, M., Chipley, M., & Archer, B. Are we protecting children? An approach to measuring impact in protective services. *Child Abuse and Neglect,* 1980, **4**, 105–113.

Cravioto, J. Nutrition, growth, and neurointegrative development: An experimental and ecologic study. *Journal of Pediatrics,* 1966, **38**, 319–372.

D'Ambrosio, R. *No language but a cry.* Garden City, N.Y.: Doubleday, 1970.

Davoren, E. Low budget play therapy for very young children. *Child Abuse and Neglect,* 1979, **3**, 199–204.

DeLissovoy, V. Child care by adolescent parents. *Children Today,* 1973, **2**, 22–25.

DeMause, L. Our forebears made childhood a nightmare. *Psychology Today,* April, 1975, 85–88.

Dennis, W. *Children of the creche.* New York: Appleton-Century-Crofts, 1973.

Densen-Gerber, J. Sexual and commercial exploitation of children: Legislative responses and treatment challenges. *Child Abuse and Neglect,* 1979, **3**, 61–66.

Douglas, J.W.B., & Blomfield, J.M. *Children under five.* New York: Allen & Unwin, 1958.

Drotar, D., Malone, C., & Negray, J. Intellectual assessment of young children with environmentally based failure to thrive. *Child Abuse and Neglect,* 1980, **4**, 23–31.

Duquette, D.N., & Jones, C.O. Interdisciplinary education of lawyers and social workers as advocates for abused children and their families. *Child Abuse and Neglect,* 1979, **3**, 137–143.

Egeland, B. Preliminary report of a prospective study of the antecedents of child abuse. *Child Abuse and Neglect,* 1979, **3**, 269–278.

Elmer, E. *Children in jeopardy.* Pittsburgh: University of Pittsburgh Press, 1967.

Elmer, E. Traumatized children, chronic illness and poverty. In L.H. Pelton (Ed.), *The social context of child abuse and neglect,* New York: Human Sciences Press, 1981.

Elmer, E., & Gregg, G.S. Developmental characteristics of abused children. *Pediatrics,* 1967, **40**, 596–602.

Federal Bureau of Investigation. *Uniform crime reports.* Washington, D.C.: U.S. Government Printing Office, 1966.

Ferguson, D.M., Fleming, J., & O'Neill, D.P. *Child abuse in New Zealand.* Wellington, N.Z.: Department of Social Welfare, 1972.

Feshbach, N. Tomorrow is here today in Sweden. *Journal of clinical child psychology,* 1980, **9**, 109–112.

Feshbach, S., & Feshbach, N. Alternatives to corporal punishment: Implications for training and controls. *Journal of Clinical Child Psychology,* 1973, **2**, 46–49.

Flanzraich, M., & Steiner, G.L. Therapeutic interventions that foster ego development in abused/neglected children. In G.J. Williams

& J. Money (Eds.), *Traumatic abuse and neglect of children at home.* Baltimore: Johns Hopkins Press, 1980.

Folks, H. *The care of destitute, neglected and delinquent children.* New York: Macmillan, 1902.

Fraser, B. Independent representation for the abused and neglected child: The guardian ad litum. *California Law Review,* 1976–1977, **13,** 10.

Fraser, B. Child abuse in America: A de facto legislative system. *Child Abuse and Neglect,* 1979, **3,** 35–43.

Friedman, S.B. The need for intensive follow-up of abused children. In C.H. Kempe & R.E. Helfer (Eds.), *Helping the battered child and his family.* Philadelphia: Lippincott, 1972.

Friedrich, W.N., & Boriskin, J.A. The role of the child in abuse: A review of the literature. *American Journal of Orthopsychiatry,* 1976, **46,** 580–590.

Gaddis, D.C., Monaghan, S.M., Muir, R.C., & Jones, C.J. Early prediction in the maternity hospital. *Child Abuse and Neglect,* 1979, **3,** 757–766.

Galdston, R. Observations on children who have been abused by their parents. *American Journal of Psychiatry,* 1965, **122,** 440–443.

Garbarino, J. The elusive "crime" of emotional abuse. *Child Abuse and Neglect,* 1978, **2,** 89–99.

Garbarino, J. An ecological approach to child maltreatment. In L.H. Pelton (Ed.), *The social context of child abuse and neglect.* New York: Human Sciences Press, 1981.

Gardner, L.I. The endocrinology of abuse dwarfism: With a note on Charles Dickens as child advocate. *American Journal of Diseases of Children,* 1977, **131,** 505–507.

Geiser, R.L. *Hidden victims: The sexual abuse of children.* Boston: Beacon Press, 1979.

Gelles, R.J. *The violent home.* Beverly Hills, Calif.: Sage, 1974.

Gelles, R.J. Violence toward children in the United States. In R. Bourne & E.H. Newberger (Eds.), *Critical perspectives on child abuse.* Lexington, Mass.: Heath, 1979.

Gelles, R.J. Violence in the family: A review of research in the seventies. *Journal of Marriage and the Family,* November 1980, 873–885.

Gil, D.G. *Violence against children.* Cambridge: Harvard University Press, 1970.

Glueck, S., & Glueck, E. *Unraveling juvenile delinquency.* Cambridge: Harvard University Press, 1950.

Gray, J., Cutler, C., Dean, J., & Kempe, C.H. Perinatal assessment of mother-baby interaction. In R.E. Helfer & C.H. Kempe (Eds.), *Child abuse and neglect: The family and the community.* Cambridge, Mass.: Ballinger, 1976.

Gray, J., & Kempe, R. The abused child at time of injury. In H. Martin (Ed.), *The abused child.* Cambridge, Mass.: Ballinger, 1976.

Green, A. A psychodynamic approach to the study and treatment of child abusing parents. *Journal of Child Psychiatry,* 1976, **15,** 213–224.

Green, C.P., & Potteiger, K. *Teenage pregnancy: A major problem for minors.* Washington, D.C.: Zero Population Growth, 1977.

Helfer, R.E. Child abuse and neglect: The diagnostic process and treatment programs. Washington, D.C.: U.S. Government Printing Office, Publication No. OHD 75–69, 1975.

Helfer, R.E. *Prevention of serious breakdowns in parent child interaction.* Paper presented at the National Committee for Prevention of Child Abuse, 1978.

Helfer, R.E., & Kempe, C.H. *Child abuse and neglect: The family and the community.* Cambridge, Mass.: Ballinger, 1976.

Herjanic, B., & Bryan, B. Sexual abuse of children. *Human Sexuality,* 1980, **April,** 92–99.

Herrenkohl, R.C., Herrenkohl, E.C., Egolf, B., & Seech, M. The repetition of child abuse: How frequently does it occur? *Child Abuse and Neglect,* 1979, **3,** 67–72.

Herzberger, S.D., Potts, D.A., & Dillon, M. Abusive and nonabusive parental treatment from the child's perspective. *Journal of Consulting and Clinical Psychology,* in press.

Holmes, T.H., & Rahe, R.H. The social readjustment rating scale. *Journal of Psychosomatic Research,* 1967, **11,** 213–218.

Hyman, C.A., Parr, R., & Browne, K. An observational study of mother-infant interaction in abusing families. *Child Abuse and Neglect,* 1979, **3,** 241–246.

Hyman, I., & Wise, J. (Eds.). *Corporal punishment in American education: Readings in history, practice, alternatives.* Philadelphia: Temple University Press, 1979.

Ingraham *v.* Wright. 498 F. 2d 248 (5th Cir. 1977).

Johnston, M.S.K. The sexually mistreated child:

Diagnostic evaluation. *Child Abuse and Neglect*, 1979, **3**, 943–951.

Jones, C.O. A critical evaluation of the work of the NSPCC's battered child research department. *Child Abuse and Neglect*, 1977, **1**, 111–118.

Jorné, P.S. Treating sexually abused children. *Child Abuse and Neglect*, 1979, **3**, 285–290.

Justice, B., & Duncan, D.F. How do job-related problems contribute to child abuse? *Occupational Health and Safety*, July-August 1978, 42–45.

Justice, B., & Justice, R. *The abusing family.* New York: Human Sciences Press, 1976.

Kadushin, A. *Adopting older children.* New York: Columbia University Press, 1970.

Katz, S.N. Proposed legislation for freeing children for permanent placement. *Child Abuse and Neglect*, 1979, **3**, 31–34.

Katz, S.N., & Gallagher, U.M. Subsidized adoption in America. *Family Law Quarterly*, 1976, **10**, 3–54.

Kempe, C.H. Pediatric implications of the battered baby syndrome. *Archives of Diseases in Childhood*, 1971, **46**, 28–37.

Kempe, C.H. Approaches to preventing child abuse: The health visitors concept. *American Journal of Diseases of Children*, 1976, **130**, 941–947.

Kempe, C.H. Sexual abuse, another hidden pediatric problem. *Pediatrics*, 1978, **62**, 382–389.

Kempe, C.H. Recent developments in the field of child abuse. *Child Abuse and Neglect*, 1979, **3**, ix–xv.

Kempe, R.S., & Kempe, C.H. *Child abuse.* Cambridge, Mass.: Harvard University Press, 1978.

Kennel, J., Voos, D., & Klaus, M. Parent-infant bonding. In R.E. Helfer & C.H. Kempe (Eds.), *Child abuse and neglect: The family and the community.* Cambridge, Mass.: Ballinger, 1976.

Kent, J.T. A follow-up study of abused children. *Journal of Pediatric Psychology*, 1976, **1**, 25–31.

Klaus, M.H., & Kennell, J.H. (Eds.). *Maternal-infant bonding.* St. Louis: Mosby, 1976.

Klein, M., & Stern, L. Low birthweight and the battered child syndrome. *American Journal of Diseases of Children*, 1971, **122**, 15–18.

Koluchová, J. Severe deprivation in twins: A case study. *Journal of Child Psychology and Psychiatry*, 1972, **13**, 107–114.

Koluchová, J. The further development of twins after severe and prolonged deprivation: A second report. *Journal of Child Psychology and Psychiatry*, 1976, **17**, 181–188.

Leavitt, J.E. *The battered child.* Morristown, N.J.: General Learning Press, 1974.

Lenoski, E.F. Paper presented at Seminar on Child Abuse, Denver, September, 1974.

Levinger, G. Sources of marital satisfaction among applicants for divorce. *American Journal of Orthopsychiatry*, 1966, **36**, 804–806.

Lieber, L.L., and Baker, J.M. Parents Anonymous —Self-help treatment for child abusing parents: A review and an evaluation. *Child Abuse and Neglect*, 1977, **1**, 133–148.

Light, R.J. Abused and neglected children in America: A study of alternative policies. *Harvard Educational Review*, 1973, **43**, 556–598.

Lorenz, K. *On aggression.* New York: Bantam, 1967.

Lynch, M.A. Ill-health and child abuse. *Lancet*, August 16, 1976, 317–319.

Lynch, M.A., & Roberts, J. Predicting child abuse: Signs of bonding failure in the maternity hospital. *British Medical Journal*, 1977, **1**, 624.

MacCarthy, D. Deprivation dwarfism viewed as a form of child abuse. In A.W. Franklin (Ed.), *The challenge of child abuse.* London: Academic Press, 1977.

Martin, H.P. *The abused child.* Cambridge, Mass.: Ballinger, 1976.

Martin, H.P. Child abuse and child development. *Child Abuse and Neglect*, 1979, **3**, 415–421.

Martin, H.P., & Beezley, P. Prevention and the consequences of child abuse. *Journal of Operational Psychiatry*, 1974, **6**, 68–77.

Martin, H.P., & Rodeheffer, M.A. The psychological impact of abuse on children. *Journal of Pediatric Psychology*, 1976, **1**, 12–15.

Maurer, A. Corporal punishment. *American Psychologist*, 1974, **29**, 614–626.

McBogg, P., McQuiston, M., & Alexander, H. Circle House residential treatment center. *Child Abuse and Neglect*, 1979, **3**, 863–867.

Mitchell, R.G. *Child health in the community.* Edinburgh: Churchill Livingstone, 1977.

Money, J. Dwarfism and growth responses. In G.J. Williams & J. Money (Eds.), *Traumatic abuse and neglect of children at home.* Baltimore: Johns Hopkins Press, 1980.

Money, J., & Annecillo, C. IQ changes following change of domicile in the syndrome of reversible hyposomatotropinism (psychosocial drawf-ism). *Psychoneuroendocrinology*, 1976, **1**, 427–429.

Money, J., & Needleman, A. Child abuse in the syndrome of reversible hyposomatotropic dwarfism (psychosocial dwarfism). *Journal of Pediatric Psychology*, 1976, **1**, 20–23.

Money, J., & Werlwas, J. Folie á deux in the parents of psychosocial dwarfs: Two cases. *Bulletin of the American Academy of Psychiatry and the Law*, 1976, **4**, 351–362.

Morris, M.G., & Gould, R.W. Role reversal: A concept in dealing with the neglected/battered child syndrome. *Child Welfare League of America*, 1963, 28.

Morris, M.G., Gould, R.W., & Matthews, P.J. Toward prevention of child abuse. *Children*, 1964, **2**, 55–60.

Morrison, H.L., & Brubakken, D.M. Social isolation and deprivation: An environment of rehabilitation. In G.J. Williams & J. Money (Eds.), *Traumatic abuse and neglect of children at home*. Baltimore: Johns Hopkins Press, 1980.

Moss, S.Z., & Moss, M.S. Surrogate mother relationships. *American Journal of Orthopsychiatry*, 1975, **45**, 382–390.

National Center for the Prevention and Treatment of Child Abuse and Neglect. Legislation to terminate parent-child legal relationships. *National Child Protection Newsletter*, 1978, **6**, 1–3.

National Commission on the Causes and Prevention of Violence. Washington, D.C., author, 1969.

National Council of Jewish Women. *What is a court appointed special advocate?* St. Louis: Author, undated.

National Council of Organizations for Children and Youth. *America's Children*. Washington, D.C.: Author, 1976.

Oates, M.R. A classification of child abuse and its relation to treatment and prognosis. *Child Abuse and Neglect*, 1979, **3**, 907–915.

Oates, R.K., Davis, A.A., Ryan, M.G., & Stewart, L.F. Risk factors associated with child abuse. *Child Abuse and Neglect*, 1979, **3**, 547–553.

Olson, J., & Besharov, D.J. Using central registers to monitor and guide child abuse treatment activities. *Child Abuse and Neglect* 1979, **3**, 151–156.

Orso, J., & Schechter, B. Abused children: Victims of the system. *St. Louis Globe Democrat*, February 7–8, 1981, 1, 6A.

Ounstead, C., Oppenheimer, R., & Lindsay, J. Aspects of bonding failure: The psychopathology and psychotherapeutic treatment of families of battered children. *Developmental Medicine and Child Neurology*, 1974, **16**, 447–456.

Owens, D., & Straus, M.A. Childhood violence and adult approval of violence. *Aggressive Behavior*, 1975, **2**, 193–211.

Parke, R.D., & Collmer, C.W. Child abuse: An interdisciplinary analysis. In M. Hetherington (Ed.), *Review of Child Development Research* (Vol. 5). University of Chicago Press, 1975.

Paulson, M.J., & Chaleff, A. Parent surrogate roles: A dynamic concept in understanding and treating abusive parents. *Journal of Clinical Child Psychology*, 1973, **2**, 38–40.

Pelton, L.H. *The social context of child abuse and neglect*. New York: Human Sciences Press, 1981.

Polansky, N., DeSaix, C., & Sharlin, S.A. *Child neglect: Understanding and reaching the child*. New York: Child Welfare League of America, 1973.

Polansky, N., & Polansky, N. The current status on child abuse and child neglect in this country: Report to the Joint Commission on Mental Health of Children, February, 1968, In D.G. Gil (Ed.), *Violence against children*. Cambridge: Harvard University Press, 1970.

Powell, G.F., Brasel, J.A., & Blizzard, R. Emotional deprivation and growth retardation simulating idiopathic hypopituitarism: I. Clinical evaluation of the syndrome. *New England Journal of Medicine*, 1967, **267**, 1279–1283.

Prescott, J. Abortion or the unwanted child: A choice for a humanistic society. *Journal of Pediatric Psychology*, 1976, **1**, 62–67.

Redlener, I.E. Children's rights and parents' rights in child abuse: New diagnostic problems. *Child Abuse and Neglect*, 1979, **3**, 93–97.

Reidy, T.J. The aggressive characteristics of abused and neglected children. *Journal of Clinical Psychology*, 1977, **4**, 1140–1145.

Reidy, T.J., Anderegg, T.R., Tracy, R.J., & Cotler, S. Abused and neglected children: The cognitive, social and behavioral correlates. In G.J. Williams & J. Money (Eds.), *Traumatic abuse and neglect of children at home.* Baltimore: Johns Hopkins Press, 1980.

Reposa, R.E. Mental health team training and treatment tools with abusing families. *Child Abuse and Neglect,* 1979, **3,** 741–747.

Resnick, P.J. Murder of the newborn: A psychiatric review of neonaticide. *American Journal of Psychiatry,* 1970, **126,** 1414–1420.

Roberts, A.R. *Childhood deprivation.* Springfield, Ill.: Thomas, 1974.

Rohner, R.P., & Rohner, E.C. Antecedents and consequences of parental rejection: A theory of emotional abuse. *Child Abuse and Neglect,* 1980, **4,** 189–198.

Rolston, R. *The effect of prior physical abuse on the expression of overt and fantasy aggressive behavior in children.* Unpublished doctoral dissertation, Louisiana State University, 1971.

Rush, F. *The best kept secret: sexual abuse of children.* New Jersey: Prentice Hall, 1980.

Schmitt, B.D. The prevention of child abuse and neglect: A review of the literature with recommendations for application. *Child Abuse and Neglect,* 1980, **4,** 171–177.

Schneider, C., Hoffmeister, J., & Helfer, R.E. The predictive screening questionnaire for potential problems in mother-child interactions. In R.E. Helfer & C.H. Kempe (Eds.), *Child abuse and neglect: The family and the community.* Cambridge, Mass.: Ballinger, 1976.

Schwarzbeck, C. Identification of infants at risk for child abuse: Observations and inferences in the examination of the mother-infant dyad. In G.J. Williams & J. Money (Eds.), *Traumatic abuse and neglect of children at home.* Baltimore: Johns Hopkins Press, 1980.

Scott, W.J. Attachment and child abuse: A study of social history indicators among mothers of abused children. In G.J. Williams & J. Money (Eds.), *Traumatic abuse and neglect of children at home.* Baltimore: Johns Hopkins Press, 1980.

Seaberg, J. *Survey of measures available for evaluation of child abuse and neglect demonstration project.* Seattle: University of Washington, School of Social Work, 1975.

Sears, R.E., Maccoby, E.E., & Levin, H. *Patterns of childrearing.* New York: Harper & Row, 1957.

Shorkey, C.T. Psychological characteristics of child abusers: Speculation and the need for research. *Child Abuse and Neglect,* 1978, **2,** 69–76.

Skinner, A.E., & Castle, R.L. *78 battered children: A retrospective study.* London: National Society for the Prevention of Cruelty to Children, 1969.

Slater, W. Everyone did his job, yet Alan died. *St. Louis Globe Democrat,* January 24–25, 1981.

Smith, S.M., Hanson, R., & Noble, S. Parents of better children: A controlled study. In A.W. Franklin (Ed.), *Concerning child abuse.* New York: Churchill Livingston, 1975.

Solnit, A.J. The rights of the child in a changing society. *Child Abuse and Neglect,* 1978, **2,** 193–201.

Spinetta, J.J. *Parental personality factors in child abuse.* Paper presented at the annual convention of the American Psychological Association, San Francisco, 1977.

Spinetta, J.J., & Rigler, D. The child-abusing parent: A psychological review. *Psychological Bulletin,* 1972, **77,** 296–304.

Steele, B.F. *Working with abusive parents from a psychiatric point of view.* Publication No. OHD 75-70. Washington, D.C.: U.S. Government Printing Office, 1975.

Steele, B.F., & Pollock, C.B. A psychiatric study of parents who abuse infants and small children. In R.E. Helfer & C.H. Kempe (Eds.), *The battered child.* University of Chicago Press, 1968.

Steinmetz, S.K. *The cycle of violence: Assertive, aggressive and abusive family interaction.* New York: Praeger, 1977.

Straus, M.A. Family patterns and child abuse in a nationally representative American sample. *Child Abuse and Neglect,* 1979, **3,** 213–225.

Straus, M.A. Stress and physical child abuse. *Child Abuse and Neglect,* 1980, **4,** 75–88.

Straus, M.A., Gelles, R.J., & Steinmetz, S.K. *Behind closed doors: Violence in the American family.* Garden City, N.Y.: Doubleday, 1980.

Taitz, L.S. Effects on growth and development of social, psychological and environmental factors. *Child Abuse and Neglect,* 1980, **4,** 55–65.

Terr, L.C., & Watson, A.S. The battered child rebrutalized: Ten cases of medical-legal confusion. *American Journal of Psychiatry,* 1967, **124,** 1432–1439.

Tizard, B. Adopting older children from institutions. *Child Abuse and Neglect,* 1979, **3,** 535–538.

U.S. Department of Health, Education and Welfare. *Child abuse and neglect: An overview of the problem* (Vol. 1). Publication No. (OHD) 75–30073. National Center on Child Abuse and Neglect. Washington, D.C.: U.S. Government Printing Office, 1975.

U.S. Department of Health, Education and Welfare. *Child abuse and neglect: The roles and responsibilities of professionals* (Vol. 2). Publication No. (OHD) 75–30074. National Center on Child Abuse and Neglect. Washington, D.C.: U.S. Government Printing Office, 1975.

U.S. Department of Health, Education and Welfare. *Child abuse and neglect: The problem and its management* (Vol. 3). Publication No. (OHD) 75–30075. National Center on Child Abuse and Neglect. Washington, D.C.: U.S. Government Printing Office, 1975.

Valusek, J.E. *People are not for hitting.* Wichita: Valusek, 1974.

Walsh, T. *Premature parenting and child abuse.* Paper presented at the Workshop on Teen Parenthood, March 8, 1977, Onondaga Community College, New York.

Wasserman, S. The abused parent of the abused child. *Children,* 1967, **14,** 175–179.

Weinberg, S.J. The transmission of psychopathology through four generations of a family. In G.J. Williams & J. Money (Eds.), *Traumatic abuse and neglect of children at home.* Baltimore: Johns Hopkins Press, 1980.

Welsh, R.S. Severe parental punishment and delinquency: A developmental approach. *Journal of Clinical Child Psychology,* 1976, **5,** 17–23.

West, J.E., & West, E.D. Child abuse treated in a psychiatric hospital. *Child Abuse and Neglect,* 1979, **3,** 699–707.

Williams, G.J.R. An editor's reflections on pain: Legalized child battering in U.S. public schools. *Journal of Clinical Child Psychology,* 1975, **4,** 56–57.

Williams, G.J.R. Origins of filicidal impulses in the American way of life. *Journal of Clinical Child Psychology,* 1976, **5,** 2–11.

Williams, G.J.R. Cruelty and kindness to children: Documentary of a century, 1874–1974. In G.J.R. Williams & J. Money (Eds.), *Traumatic abuse and neglect of children at home.* Baltimore: Johns Hopkins Press, 1980. (a)

Williams, G.J.R. Toward the eradication of child abuse and neglect at home. In G.J.R. Williams & J. Money (Eds.), *Traumatic abuse and neglect of children at home.* Baltimore: Johns Hopkins Press, 1980. (b)

Williams, G.J.R. Responsible sexuality and the primary prevention of child abuse. In G. Albee, S. Gordon & H. Leitenberg (Eds.), *Promoting sexual responsibility and preventing sexual problems.* Vermont: University Press of New England, in press.

Williams, G.J.R., & Money, J. *Traumatic abuse and neglect of children at home.* Baltimore: Johns Hopkins Press, 1980.

Wolfe, D.A., Aragona, J., Kaufman, K., & Sandler, J. The importance of adjudication in the treatment of child abusers: Some preliminary findings. *Child Abuse and Neglect,* 1980, **4,** 127–135.

Wolock, I., & Horowitz, B. Factors relating to levels of child care among families receiving public assistance in New Jersey. Final report (Vol. 1) (Grant No. 90–C–418). Submitted to the National Center on Child Abuse and Neglect, Department of Health, Education and Welfare, 1977.

Wright, L. The "sick but slick" syndrome as a personality component of parents of battered children. *Journal of Clinical Psychology,* 1976, **32,** 41–45.

Young, L. *Wednesday's children: A study of child neglect and abuse.* New York: McGraw-Hill, 1964.

Young, M. Lonely parents: Observations by public health nurses of alienation in child abuse. *Research in Education,* 1977, July, 11.

Yorukoglu, A., & Kemph, J.P. Children not severely damaged by incest with a parent. *Journal of the American Academy of Child Psychiatry,* 1966, **5,** 111–124.

CHAPTER 53

The Effect of Divorce on Parents and Children

H. ELIZABETH KING AND CAROL P. KLEEMEIER

DIVORCE

Any discussion of the problems of the single parent or the effects of divorce upon children must take into account the process of divorce itself. Divorce specifically refers to the legal action that dissolves a marriage and, when appropriate, determines custody of children, visiting rights of the noncustodial parent, division of property, and child support. Even this obviously complex procedure fails to reflect the more intricate emotional and psychological process that accompany the dissolution of a marriage.

Long before a couple decides to separate, a period of emotional disengagement and/or conflict occurs. This conflict or detachment may occur over a period of weeks, months, or years. The role of the child during this time may vary from being an onlooker, a scapegoat, a go-between, a referee, or an active participant. There is little disagreement that interparent hostility in divorcing families can adversely affect a child's psychological adjustment (Berg & Kelly, 1979; Hetherington, Cox, & Cox, 1979a; Hetherington, 1980). Thus it is imperative to consider the amount of preseparation conflict and aggression in a marriage when attempting to understand a parent's or child's postdivorce adjustment.

Divorce as a Stress

The physical separation of the marital partners is often the period of most intense emotional distress for parents and children. The extent to which a separation or divorce is a crisis for the individual may vary; however, there is much data to suggest that a divorce should be considered a major life stress. Goode (1949) and Chiriboga and Cutler (1977) noted an increase in behavioral indices such as sleep disturbances, declining work efficiency, and increased drinking and smoking.

The findings of these studies as well as numerous clinical reports leave no doubt that divorce is a stress that jeopardizes the physical and emotional health of the individuals involved. The extent of the stress associated with separation and divorce is best described by Bloom, Asher, and White (1978) in an excellent review article noting many correlates of marital disruption. Psychopathology has been consistently associated with marital status, with the separated and divorced overrepresented among psychiatric patients. The admission rates for psychiatric hospitals are highest among the divorced and separated. Bloom et al. also concluded that the relationship between psychopathology and marital disruption is stronger for men than women. Thus, in spite of the relatively greater number of practical or daily-living problems facing the separated woman, especially one with custody of a young child, the emotional difficulties faced by the man cannot be minimized.

In addition to psychopathology, lethal behaviors such as automobile accidents and suicide are also more frequent in separated or divorced people. The National Center for Health Statistics (1970) reports that automobile fatality rates are three times higher for the divorced man or woman than for the married. Their data also reflects higher suicide rates for the divorced.

Marital disruption can be a significant stress in the life of an individual, and the consequences of this stress can be quite severe. For the majority of people, however, divorce is more successfully managed, and neither psychiatric hospitalization nor lethal behaviors occur. For these people the stress may be reflected in less severe emotional distress and problem behaviors.

Emotional Reactions During Separation and Divorce

Although reactions are individual, there appear to be common emotional reactions at various points of the divorce process. Hackney and Ribordy (1980) evaluated men and women who were in marriages they described as good; were in marriage counseling; had filed for divorce but had not yet been to court; or had been divorced for 6–12 months. Their results suggest that the decision to separate and file for divorce may significantly increase depression, anxiety, and hostility in both men and women; however, the postdivorce (or adjustment) phase is accompanied by less intense depression, anxiety, and hostility.

Hetherington, Cox, and Cox (1977) noted a longer (two-year), more difficult course of emotional adjustment. At 2–3 months postdivorce, many men and women reported elation alternating with depression; however, after the 12-month period, the elation had been replaced by depression, anxiety, or apathy. More striking, at one year after divorce, most fathers and mothers reported that they thought the divorce might have been a mistake.

The Process of Divorce

Spanier and Casto (1979) found that two distinct adjustments were involved in the process of divorce: dissolution of the marriage and setting up a new lifestyle. Dissolution of the marriage involved the legal procedures and the individual's emotional reactions and

problems related to divorce. The setting up of a new lifestyle included social and economic changes. Social involvement and the ability to form heterosexual relationships were positively related to postdivorce adjustment. Emotional difficulties such as loneliness, depression, and lowered self-esteem were reported by those individuals who had the most difficulty in adjusting to their new life. Additionally, these people were the most likely to regret the separation.

Wiseman (1975) found that the adjustment of the individual to a divorce required a reworking of identity in many areas: personal, vocational, sexual, and social. The impact of divorce on a person's identity or self-definition was discussed by Pais and White (1979). How one is perceived by others determines, to some extent, one's self-definition. Divorce from an important person, one who has helped shape or determine an individual's self-definition, precipitates a redefinition of the self. Further, the impact of the divorce on other relationships may also effect a redefinition of self. Thus the postdivorce involves the processes of individual redefinition and family redefinition.

Factors Associated with Postdivorce Adjustment

Divorce confronts all women with a reassessment or redefinition of themselves; however, this is not necessarily a threat to all women and may even be perceived by some as an opportunity. Brown and Manela (1978) hypothesized that the more nontraditional a woman's sex role attitudes, the more positive the psychological outcomes she will experience following a divorce. Conversely, those women who cannot or do not redefine their investment in the traditional roles of wife, homemaker, and mother will have less positive psychological outcomes. After a study of 253 women confirmed their hypothesis, the authors concluded that cognitive restructuring of a woman's attitudes, especially concerning her sex role, is adaptive. To the extent that a woman's sex role attitude gives meaning to the events in her life, and her beliefs are congruent with her actual life situation, she will experience lower distress, increased self-esteem, and an increased sense of personal effectiveness.

Granvold, Pedler, and Schellie (1979) also studied the postdivorce adjustment of women and found that women with more equalitarian sex role expectations were better adjusted than women who were less equalitarian. A significant positive relationship between a woman's social support system and her postdivorce adjustment were also noted.

The importance of socialization in postdivorce adjustment has been documented (Raschke, 1977; Hackney & Ribordy, 1980). Higher levels of social participation are related to lower stress. Raschke (1977) found men were significantly more involved in activities outside the home and they reported less stress than did women. The majority of the women studied had custody of their children; therefore, they had less available time for socializing.

These studies suggest several factors that may be helpful in understanding postdivorce adjustment. The loss of the spouse will affect many significant areas. For most people a grieflike reaction involving depression, anxiety, and hostility will occur initially. This emotional reaction may recede after the individual begins an emotional and functional redefinition of self. The return of the woman to the working world, often necessitated by economic factors, may be accompanied by a redefinition of sex role attitudes or expectancies. A liberal or nontraditional sex role is associated with less distress and more positive postdivorce psychological adjustment. Other factors that are positively associated with postdivorce adjustment are active social participation and the existence of a social support system.

PROBLEMS OF THE SINGLE PARENT

Custodial Mothers

The complexity of postdivorce adjustment is increased if children are involved. The major stress for the custodial mother is economic, and the downward mobility of custodial mothers following a divorce has been extensively documented (Spanier & Casto, 1979; Goode, 1949; Kriesberg, 1970; Brandwein, Brown, & Fox, 1974). An inadequate level of child support or alimony, failure of the ex-husband to make those payments, the woman's lack of marketable skills, and economic discrimination in the job market due to sex are responsible for the downward economic mobility.

The role adjustment to single parenthood is difficult and often requires the acquisition of new identities: those of single parent and of single person (Loge, 1977). The role adjustment from housewife and mother to employee is an additional stress for many women. Changes in self-perception and self-definition are necessary and difficult, but external problems allow little time for self-reflection. Although school may provide much of the daily child care, transportation and child care arrangements before and after school are often necessary. Dinner preparations, assistance with homework, and preparation for the next day leave little time for the relationship she and her children once enjoyed. Lack of time and energy adversely affects the single mother's relationship with her children, and she may long for the easy and gratifying relationship of the past (Hetherington et al., 1977).

The extent to which economic stress affects the mother and her children has not been adequately documented. The data that does exist suggests that one-parent families whose income is below poverty level experience the most serious detrimental effects, both physically and emotionally. Those families whose incomes are within the middle class range experience few difficulties (Tcheng-Laroche & Prince, 1979; Hetherington et al., 1977), although the economic stress following a divorce often precipitates negative changes in less affluent families. There may be a drop in consumption, a change in housing accommodations, and a decrease in the quality of care and supervision provided children.

In most families, the power and authority attributed to the male by society are reflected in the family power structure. It is to the father that children attribute authority and power, and he is often the source of discipline and structure. Mothers, on the other hand, most often assume the more affectionate or nurturant role, sometimes serving as a buffer against the anger and aggression of the father. When she becomes a single parent, the mother faces the formidable task of redefining her role with regard to the children. Hetherington et al. (1977) found that fathers obtained greater compliance from children, whether in intact or divorced families. They also noted that divorced mothers gave significantly more commands than divorced fathers or mothers, or fathers in intact families. Further, during the first year of divorce, mothers responded ineffectually or inappropriately to their children's behaviors: they failed to reinforce compliance and ignored noncompliance. This response pattern improved over the second year, and the children's compliance increased; however, the compliance rates of children from divorced families never equalled that of children from intact families.

It appears that a major role of the mother is to become a disciplinarian and to learn to respond appropriately to the behaviors of her children. The importance of this role is clearly reflected in the findings of Santrock and Warshak (1979) regarding laissez-faire parenting strategies in single-parent mothers. Mothers who interacted in this manner had children who were rated as showing little warmth, higher anger, high demandingness, and little social conformity. Finally, Brandewein et al. (1974) found mother's supervision was more important in predicting delinquency than father's absence.

Perhaps the most emotionally demanding role of the divorced mother is to redefine the relationship with the ex-spouse. Visitation is particularly stressful during the first year. The mother may feel threatened and frustrated because of her difficulties as a provider and disciplinarian, and her relationship with her children is at its lowest. In contrast, the father may appear to have successfully adapted to his new roles, and his arrival for a "weekend" is often perceived by the mother and children as a vacation. The contrast in lifestyles and apparent differences in adjustment may engender feelings of anger and jealousy in the mother.

Visitation can be a vehicle for continuing the conflict and animosity between the ex-spouses. Limiting access to the children, discouraging their relationship to the visiting father, or open conflict with the ex-spouse are common. However, the psychological well-being of the child is enhanced by a truce or resolution that allows a reduction in overt conflict and permits extensive contact with the visiting parent. Both Hetherington et al. (1977) and Wallerstein (1981) found that support and agreement between divorced parents were correlated to less disruption in the family functioning.

Custodial Fathers

Gasser and Taylor (1976) studied the role adjustment of single-parent fathers and found that single fathers, like single mothers, have to adjust to new roles and role responsibilities. Single fathers reported difficulties in their social lives and their employment situations; however, economic problems were not prevalent. For fathers, the major changes appear to be in the assumption of the housekeeping and child care roles.

The effects of parenting style may differ dramatically in mother-custody and father-custody homes. Santrock and Warshak (1979) found that a parenting strategy of warmth, clear setting of rules and regulations, and extensive verbal give-and-take were significantly correlated with higher warmth, self-esteem, maturity, sociability, and social conformity in children in both types of custodial arrangements.

However, in father-custody homes, a significant positive correlation between the use of an authoritarian style and anger and lack of independence in children was found. Use of an authoritarian style in mother-custody homes was not correlated to the child's social competence. The use of a laissez-faire style by mothers resulted in children who were rated as showing little social conformity, little warmth, high anger, and high demandingness; however, there were no correlations between the use of a laissez-faire style by fathers and the child's social competence.

Few studies have focused on the special strengths or weaknesses of the fathers. The paucity of literature is no doubt related to the relative infrequency of fathers obtaining custody of their children. Typically, fathers who obtain custody do so only after desertion by the mother, the mother's having been proven unfit, or the mother's decision that the father would provide a better home for the children. Thus the sample of custodial fathers is unique, and caution must be used in making generalizations regarding the effects of living with single-parent fathers.

Lowenstein and Koopman (1978) found no differences between boys (ages 9–14 years) with single-parent mothers versus boys living with single-parent fathers. Stephens and Day (1979) reached the same conclusion studying adolescent girls. However, methodological problems, the narrow scope of variables examined, and the findings of Hetherington et al. (1977), Whitehead (1979), Rutter (1980), and Schoettle and Cantwell (1980) make these conclusions questionable.

Santrock and Warshak (1979) noted differences between boys who lived in single-parent mother, single-parent father, and intact homes. Their data suggest that children living with the opposite sex parent (father-custody girls and mother-custody boys) are less well-adjusted than children living with the same sex parent. Whether theoretically conceptualized in terms of modeling, identification, or the facilitation of the appropriate resolution of the Oedipal situation, the authors argue that living with the same sex parent may be the most beneficial custody arrangement for the child. Santrock and Warshak also noted differences in father-custody and mother-custody homes: father-custody homes were economically superior, more frequently utilized social supports, and had more visitations with the noncustodial parent.

The Visiting Parent

There is no literature regarding the role of the mother as a visiting parent; however, several recent studies have examined the feelings, attitudes, and problems of noncustodial fathers. Keshet (1977) described a three-stage process in becoming a parttime single parent. During "Transition," the fathers separated from the original family unit and experienced emotional and physical upheavals. During "Development," the fathers established stable living and child care arrangements. Separate lifestyles, often involving dating, emerged, and these men developed new self-images (as fathers, lovers, and workers). In the final stage, "Routinization," patterns combining social activities, homemaking, and parenting emerged. During this stage, fathers viewed themselves positively and expressed self-confidence and competence as parents and individuals.

Hetherington et al. (1976) conducted a two-year longitudinal study of divorced fathers. The pervasive concern for all fathers was the loss of their children. Loss of contact did occur in some cases, and almost 20 percent of the fathers decreased their visits over time. In contrast, almost 25 percent reported a positive change in their relationship with their children; these men had been in marriages with a great deal of conflict. Changes in the style or manner of relating of most fathers were noted over the two-year period. Divorced fathers never became as restrictive as the fathers from intact families.

Problem areas most frequently identified by visiting fathers were occupational, interpersonal, and economic. The economic problems, the most frequent cause of conflict between ex-spouses, were often mitigated by increased working time by the fathers. No relationship between problems in the children and real or perceived economic stress was noted, probably because the sample was relatively affluent.

Feelings of loss, guilt, anxiety, and dependency were predominant at the time of separation. They were greatest in older men and men who had been married longer. At two months postdivorce, a sense of freedom emerged and alternated with feelings of depression, anxiety, and apathy. At the end of the two-year period, the depression, anxiety, and apathy had decreased.

Changes in self-concept were also noted. Feelings of competency decreased over the first year. The fathers viewed themselves as failures as husbands and fathers. The most important factor related to a positive change in self-concept was involvement in an intimate relationship. Happiness, self-esteem, and feelings of competence in heterosexual relationships increased over the two-year period of the study but were never as high as those feelings of the married fathers. Fathers who had remarried during the study had similar ratings in terms of happiness, but their ratings were not as high as married fathers on self-esteem or competence.

The findings of a study by Greif (1978) suggested that lack of contact with his child produces problems for the separated and divorced father. The absence of the child led to feelings of dissatisfaction, devaluation, and loss of the parental role. The degree of child absence, as defined by the custody arrangement, was associated with significant differences in these fathers' perceptions of parenting. Fathers who had greater contact with their children were the most satisfied.

Daniel (1977), utilizing data from the population studied by Kelly and Wallerstein (1976), evaluated father-child intimacy in divorced families. Intimacy was defined as open communication; mutual satisfaction with visits; the father's sensitivity to the child's needs; the child's feeling supported by the father and the child having trust, empathy, and respect for the father. Data was gathered at the time of filing for marital dissolution and during a follow-up 12–18 months later. Daniel (1977) drew several major conclusions. Interactional patterns are more important determinants of father-child intimacy than the specific personality traits or characteristics of the father. Divorced fathers who had intimate relationships with their children had former spouses who felt positively toward them and facilitated visitation. Although fathers who were nurturant and empathetic often had intimate relationships with their children, father characteristics were less important than factors related to the child or situation. Fathers were more intimate with the less angry children, who were most often preschool or early latency age. For children 8 years old or

younger the quality of the relationship prior to the separation carried over into the post-divorce relationship. However, this was not true of older children, perhaps because of the inhibiting effects of the child's anger. Children 4–6 years of age at the time of the separation were the most intimate with the father, whereas children who were 9 and 10 at the time of the separation were the least intimate with their fathers.

The studies involving the visiting parent are largely retrospective and lack quantification. Nevertheless, some findings with significant implications appear to be consistent. Divorced fathers face many physical, social, and emotional adjustments during and immediately following the separation. A sense of loss, feelings of dependency and incompetency, and concern regarding the loss of his children are predominant. Over time, the father adjusts to a new identity, a new social life, and a new role with regard to his children. Some fathers will decrease their involvement with their children during the two years following the separation; however, others will maintain previously positive relationships. Fathers whose marriages were filled with conflict may establish for the first time a positive relationship with their children. The most salient factors in predicting the father's postdivorce relationship with his child are amount of contact with the child, relationship with the ex-spouse, age of the child, and personality variables of the father such as openness and warmth.

EMOTIONAL REACTIONS OF THE CHILD TO DIVORCE

Two studies based on parental perceptions of their children's adjustment postdivorce have been conducted. Kurdek and Siesky (1978) found that parents' greatest concerns were behavior problems due to the separation, behavior problems due to the ex-spouse's visit, discipline, and the availability of a same sex model. Specific problems exhibited by children include decreases in school performance, discipline problems, excessive demands for attention, psychophysiological problems, and peer problems (Kurdek & Siesky, 1979).

To date, the majority of literature consists of clinical work with individual children or observations of groups of children. The longitudinal study by Wallerstein and Kelly (1980) is flawed by the lack of systematic observations or behavioral coding. Nevertheless, there is dramatic consistency throughout the literature regarding three facts: (1) Children exhibit different short term and long term reactions to divorce. (2) Age or developmental stage is a significant factor in children's initial and short term (one year) reaction to divorce. (3) Interparent conflict and hostility are more detrimental to children than divorce itself.

Immediate and Short Term Reactions

The Preschool Child

McDermott's (1968) clinical observations of children whose parents were in the process of separation and divorce were the beginning of research and study in this area. The children he observed were 3–5 years of age at the time of the separation and had no known psychiatric problems. Acute behavioral changes were noted in over half the children, and they were management problems at school. Four groups of children emerged over time: (1) Children in whom no change was noticed. These children were previously viewed as well adjusted and well liked. Their continued good adjustment may have been related to their positive relationships with both parents. (2) Children who experienced acute grief and exhibited denial and regression. Their behavior at school was characterized by diffuse anger and grief. Improvement was noted 6–8 weeks after the separation. (3) Children who became extremely detached and confused. They exhibited extreme regression and disorganization and required psychiatric treatment. (4) The final group consisted of children viewed as having hidden problems. These were pseudo-adult girls who exhibited personality constriction, quarrelsome attitudes, bossiness, and pseudomature mannerisms before the separation; however, an increase in their previous problem behaviors was noted. Four factors appeared to be significantly affecting the children's postdivorce adjustment: the direct impact of the strife and conflict, the loss of a parent, the impact of the divorce on the remaining parent, and the loss of a parental model.

Wallerstein and Kelly (1975), who also studied the reactions of preschool children, noted three distinct age groupings. The youngest (2.5–3.25-year-olds) demonstrated regression in toilet training, increased irritability, disturbances in sleep, and increased aggressiveness. Generalized anxiety and acute separation anxiety were also noted. There was a noticeable decrease in symptoms in 66 percent of the children after one year; however, all children showed a general neediness in relationships. This was exhibited by behaviors such as climbing into adults' laps. No relationship was noted between the initial response and functioning of the child at follow-up. The quality of the caretaking the child received was critical. Continued discord between the parents and/or a breakdown in the parenting capacity of the caretaking adult appeared to contribute significantly to the problems in the children.

The second group had an age range of 3.75–4.75 years. During the divorce process, these children were irritable, whiney, and tearful. An increase in aggression or fear of aggression was noted. Twelve months later, 63 percent of these children were worse. Lowered self-esteem and constriction in play or fantasy were noted. All children exhibited a need for physical contact, individual attention, and adult approval. All of their fathers had been harsh, erratic disciplinarians with unrealistic expectations; therefore, these divorces entailed not only the loss of a parent but a decrease in limits and controls. Further, the majority of the fathers had psychiatric disorders; thus these children may have experienced much conflict, including aggression, in the home. The majority of the mothers had experienced a year of high tension and frenetic activity, and their relationship with the children had changed dramatically. They were less available, less supportive, and were no longer protecting the children from the fathers; rather, they were now functioning as the disciplinarians.

Children aged 5–6 years composed the third group. These children initially showed increased anxiety and aggression. They were restless and moody and exhibited separation problems and temper tantrums. Unlike the younger children, they had a reasonable understanding of the divorce process, more diverse responses to the divorce, and greater consistency in terms of their immediate and short term reactions. Those children (approximately 35 percent) who were worse 12 months later exhibited childhood depression. Their school reports reflected decreased academic performance and difficulties with peers.

Wallerstein and Kelly (1975) noted no sex differences in the initial reactions of the preschoolers; however, 63 percent of the girls as contrasted with 27 percent of the boys were experiencing difficulties 12 months later. The unusual difficulties of the parents of the middle group have already been noted; therefore, it is unclear whether these findings are the result of sex differences or because of the sample.

Hodges, Wechsler, and Ballantine (1979) studied preschool children from intact and divorced homes. Contrary to predictions, there was not greater aggression, withdrawal, dependency, or other signs of emotional immaturity and stress in the children from divorced homes. Although both parents and teachers reported that divorce had had a profound effect on the children's behaviors, they noted few differences in behavioral ratings. Children from intact homes were rated as more cooperative by their parents than the children from divorced homes.

A second hypothesis, that the longer the time since separation the lower the degree of maladjustment, was not supported. There was no relationship between time since separation and behavioral problems. A third hypothesis, that frequent contact with a noncustodial parent would alleviate the negative effects of divorce, was not supported. In fact, the more visits made by the noncustodial parent the lower the child's score on mother-related

cooperation and the higher the amounts of teacher-rated and parent-rated aggression. Factors such as relative youth of divorced parents, lower income of father, and frequency of moving were found to affect adversely the children from the divorced homes.

Several methodological problems should be noted concerning the Hodges et al. (1979) study. Only parental reports were utilized to evaluate behaviors at home, and the amount of conflict in the intact families was not controlled. Although the quality of the marriage was found to be significantly related to the pathology of the children, the authors did not separate the intact families into high and low conflict groups. Hetherington et al. (1979a) found significant differences between preschoolers from divorced versus intact families when marital conflict was taken into account. During the first year, children in divorced families functioned less well than those in nuclear families with either high or low discord. The children of divorced parents were more oppositional, aggressive, lacking in self-control, distractible, and demanding of help and attention at home and at school. However, by the second year, the difference between children from the high discord and divorced families were reversed.

The lack of significant findings on the first two hypotheses of the Hodges et al. (1979) study may be related to the complexity of the interactions. Changes in the children from divorced families may not be observable unless sex of child, type of aggression, method of evaluation, and the amount of conflict in the comparison nuclear families are taken into account. Finally, Hodges et al. (1979) interpret the positive relationship of increased aggression to frequency and duration of father's visits as a failure to support their third hypothesis (frequent contact with the noncustodial parent would alleviate the effects of divorce). However, given their overall findings that boys from intact homes were more aggressive than boys from mother-custody homes, the noted increase in aggression after contacts with father could be interpreted as a positive change in boys. Indirect support for this interpretation comes from Hetherington et al. (1979c) who found that boys from homes where mothers encouraged aggression had more appropriate sex role identities.

The Latency-Aged Child

A subsequent study by Kelly and Wallerstein (1976) involved children who were 7 or 8 years of age at the time of the separation. The immediate reaction of these children was intense grief and sadness. The children were so overwhelmed by their feelings that they appeared immobilized and unable to function autonomously. They were also extremely fearful about the unstable family situation and often expressed feelings of deprivation with regard to food and toys. Fantasies of reconciliation were prevalent, with all but one of the children hoping for a reconciliation.

Most children expressed acute feelings of loss with regard to their fathers. This was especially true of the younger boys and was not related to the quality of the father-child relationship before the separation. The children complained that visitation (every other weekend) was not adequate, and they wished for more frequent contact. For many children, the need for a father was so intense that they asked their mothers to remarry. This need for a father appeared multidetermined, with issues of discipline, control, masculine identification, and the unresolved Oedipal situation all contributing to it.

Feelings toward the custodial mother were less positive than those toward the visiting father. Boys, often profoundly hurt and extremely anxious because of the loss of the father, sometimes expressed anger toward the mother. Most children, however, displaced their anger about the divorce to siblings, friends, or teachers.

Although one-fourth of these children described specific pulls from a parent to form an allegiance, they remained loyal to both parents. Those children who formed an alliance with the mother experienced much conflict over their disloyalty to the father.

Twelve months later, most children had a sad, resigned acceptance regarding the divorce although one-third of the boys continued to hope for reconciliation. Strong loyalty to the father remained, and more visitation was desired. This wish occurred regardless of the mother's derogation of the father or the lack of visits by the father. Children resolved loyalty conflicts by psychologically distancing the parent making the demands. Overall, 50 percent of the children remained the same; 15 percent improved; 23 percent had fewer difficulties; and 12 percent were not reevaluated.

Thirty-one older, latency-aged children (9- and 10-year-olds), were described by Wallerstein and Kelly (1976). These children appeared sad but composed, having some understanding of the divorce. They appeared partially successful in their efforts at coping and mastery; however, they would sometimes succumb to the emotional pain they experienced. Fifty percent were angry at their mothers, 50 percent were angry with their fathers, and some were angry with both parents. The anger was expressed via tantrums, scolding, demanding, or dictatorial attitudes and behaviors. In spite of their difficulties, these children continued to progress developmentally. Unlike the younger latency children, the 9- and 10-year-olds experienced intense anger that was organized and object directed.

Hess and Camara (1979) studied the reactions to divorce of children 9–11 years of age. They evaluated these children two years after the parents separated. Children of divorced families showed greater stress and less productive work styles than a comparison group of children in intact families. Consistent with the findings of Hetherington et al. (1979), differences between the divorced and intact groups were greater for boys than for girls on stress and aggression.

Adolescence

Wallerstein and Kelly (1980) were surprised by the extent of the distress exhibited by the adolescents they studied. Divorce seemed to be a particularly distressing event for the adolescent, and the major developmental task, detaching from the family, suffered, at least temporarily, from the disruption of the family unit. The sometimes adolescent behavior of the parent not only deprived the adolescent of a stable, consistent parent during a developmental stage fraught with turbulence, but the sexual activities of the parents were often quite threatening to the adolescents.

With few exceptions, the adolescents experienced a great deal of pain regarding the divorce. The effects of anger and sadness were most frequent as the adolescent grieved the loss of the family. Distress was often communicated in terms of lack of money, loyalty conflicts, a deidealization or devaluation of parents, or difficulties regarding the sexuality of the parents.

Many of these problems were successfully dealt with in the 12–18-month period between the initial evaluation and follow-up. Most adolescents became more realistic about money and learned to tolerate delays in gratifications. Loyalty conflicts were often resolved by a withdrawal from the parent imposing the demand of loyalty. Devaluation was often replaced by realistic perceptions of each parent as an individual. Sexuality was the most problematic issue, and many of the difficulties noted at follow-up involved premature or promiscuous sexual behavior. Other difficulties noted at follow-up included prolonged or disrupted entry into adolescence. Those adolescents who appeared to be coping best seemed, from the beginning of the crisis, to have detached themselves from the parental conflict. Although they initially appeared self-centered and insensitive, these were the youngsters who exhibited the highest levels of functioning. They also appeared to have a realistic but compassionate understanding of their parents.

Long Term Reactions

In the most long range study yet conducted about children of divorce, Wallerstein and Kelly (1980) followed 131 children between the ages of 3–18 for five years. The immediate and short term reactions were strongly related to age and developmental level; however, the long term outcome was most affected by the overall quality of life in the postdivorce family and relationships of the child with the custodial mother (Wallerstein, 1981).

One-third of the children were functioning well at the five-year mark. Both parents of these children had retained their commitment to the child and provided good parenting. Those children who were functioning better five years after the divorce were those who had escaped from a relationship with a psychologically disturbed, physically abusive, or inappropriately erotic parent. Thirty-seven of the children and adolescents suffered moderate-to-severe depressions. These distressed and troubled children often felt rejected or neglected by the absent father. Poor father-child relationships, marked by infrequent or irregular visits and/or the insensitivity or the father, were linked with depression in the children.

FACTORS RELATED TO CHILDREN'S POSTDIVORCE ADJUSTMENT

Jacobson (1978a, 1978b, 1978c) conducted a longitudinal study of families who had experienced a parental separation within 12 months prior to the research. A wide variety of measures were utilized: the Louisville Behavior Checklist, child and parent interviews, and interviewer ratings. The first Jacobson study (1978a) addressed children's adjustment following a separation ($\bar{x} = 140$ days). For children 3–13 years of age, significant relationships between the loss of time in father's presence and maladjustment of the child in terms of aggression, inhibition, and learning problems were noted. The loss of time spent in activities with the mother was not related to adjustment; however, a significant association was found for the loss of activities with father and irritability. Trends were noted with hyperactivity and aggression.

For the 3–6-year-olds, the time loss with father was inversely related to the overall severity of problems, immaturity, irritability, and unusual problems. No significant relationships between mother presence, mother activity, father activity, or any child problems were noted.

For 7–13-year-olds, time lost with father

was inversely related to aggression, inhibition, learning difficulties, and overall problems. No relationship was found with the loss of activities with father. Time lost with mother was not significantly related to any problems; however, antisocial behaviors and academic problems were significantly related to the loss of activities with mother.

The second Jacobson (1978b) article examined the relationship between the interparent hostility and adjustment of the child. For children 3–13, the greater the amount of interparent hostility experienced prior to the marital separation, the greater the aggression and inhibition and the overall severity of problems. As expected, the findings were stronger for children aged 7–13 than for children 3–6. A significant association between hostility expressed by parents and maladjustment in the child was found. The single interparental behavior most likely to be associated with maladjustment was physical aggression by one or both parents. These findings confirm the adverse effects of parental conflict before and after separation. They further suggest that physical aggression between parents has especially serious consequences for children who observe its occurrence. Separation, in some situations, not only appeared to lead to a reduction in conflict between parents, but it reduced the chance that the conflict would occur in the child's presence.

Parent-child communciation, especially regarding the separation or divorce, and its relationship to child adjustment was the focus of the third Jacobson article (1978c). The results indicated that the more attention given to the child in dealing with the separation, the less the cognitive or learning difficulties, the lower the aggression, and the lower the overall severity of problems. The more discussion about the separation was encouraged, the less the cognitive or learning disabilities. Contrary to expectation, differences between the adjustment of children with whom the separation had been discussed in advance and those with whom no such discussion was reported were minimal. Jacobson (1978c) found that the parent most likely to discuss the separation

was the mother. This finding was replicated by Kurdek and Siesky (1979), who found that mothers were more likely to explain the separation than fathers, even custodial fathers.

Desimore-Louis, O'Mahoney, and Hunt (1979) obtained data on children between the ages of 7–13. Of the 30 demographic factors studied, only one emerged as significant: all children classified as deviant or severely maladjusted lived with a single parent who reported an income drop of 50 percent or more after the separation.

Whitehead (1979) studied sex differences in children's responses to family discord and separation. She evaluated 2,775 firstborns who were 7 years of age. Assessment included a parental questionnaire, teacher and health visitor assessments, and a medical examination. Some information with regard to family discord was available.

A strong association was found in boys, but not in girls, between discord in the family and ratings of hostility by the health visitor and teacher. Mother reports, however, indicated a strong relationship between family discord and fighting with other children for boys and girls. Additionally, girls were rated by their mothers as being sensitive or "high strung" if family discord was frequent. Girls from homes with tension or discord had an increased likelihood to be rated as maladjusted emotionally by the physician. The data suggest that marital discord is strongly associated with maladjustment in boys and girls, and these problems do not appear to be exclusively antisocial behavior. Parental separation revealed a lesser but statistically significant trend toward antisocial behavior in boys, and a slight but significant tendency toward withdrawn behavior in girls. These results suggest that discord is more detrimental than separation and that antisocial behavior associated with marital tension is more likely to be exhibited at school by boys.

Schoettle and Cantwell (1980) examined demographic variables, symptoms, and diagnoses of 2,351 child psychiatry patients. Comparisons of children from divorced and intact families were made. The results indicate that non-firstborns and children from larger families are less vulnerable to psychiatric problems after a divorce. Physically aggressive behavior was more frequent in boys (0–11 years of age) with divorced parents, but verbally aggressive behavior was significantly more common for all children of divorce. However, when age and sex were considered independently, verbal aggression was only significant for adolescent females. Overall, children of divorce were more likely to have problems with behavior, social relationships, family problems, academic and school problems, and affective difficulties than were children from intact families.

Hess and Camara (1979) explored the relationships between family members following a divorce. They, like Wallerstein (1981), found that the level of parental harmony was as closely related to the child outcomes as was the divorce. Further, they found that relationships between the family members had a larger contribution to child outcomes than did family type. Level of parental harmony, mother-child and father-child relations were better predictors of aggressive behavior than divorce. Parental harmony was strongly related to measures of stress but was less important on most variables than was the affective postdivorce relationships between the parent and child. Children who had positive relationships with both parents had lower scores on measures of stress and aggression. Their relationships with peers and ability to work were also better. Those children who maintained a positive relationship with one parent showed less severe effects than those whose relationships with both parents were unsatisfactory.

The frequency of visits with father was not highly related to a child outcome; rather, the duration or length of time spent on visits was related to the quality of the father-child relationship.

Children's perceptions of the adverse effects of divorce vary as a function of intelligence, locus of control, age, and interpersonal knowledge. Kurdek and Siesky (1980), studying children whose ages ranged from 5–19 years, found that children high on these variables reported loss of contact with the noncustodial parent and increased stress upon the custodial parent. Children low on these variables were more likely to report no adverse effects and more child-oriented bad feelings. Older children and children with high levels of interpersonal knowledge were more likely to report the absence of fighting as a beneficial outcome than were younger children or children low on interpersonal knowledge. Older children and children whose parents were recently separated were likely to report improved relations with the custodial parent. The discrepancy between this finding and Hetherington et al.'s (1979) finding of a worsening in parent-child relationships is probably due to the age differences. Unlike Hetherington's preschoolers, Kurden and Siesky's (1980) latency-aged subjects were capable of being supportive of the custodial parent, which could improve the relationship.

In summary, age, especially in combination with high levels of locus of control and interpersonal knowledge, appears to be a critical variable in a child's understanding of divorce as an emotional or psychological separation based on parental personalities. Older children are better able to comprehend the conflict and stress preceding the separation, to appreciate its absence, and to experience improved relations with the custodial parent.

The results of these studies suggest that the factors that are most influential in the child's short term adjustment to divorce appear to be amount of parental conflict, postdivorce relationship with custodial parent, postdivorce relationship with noncustodial parent, economic situation of the single-parent family, and sex and age of the child.

THE IMPACT OF DIVORCE ON THE CHILD'S DEVELOPMENT

Personality Factors

Self-Esteem/Self-Concept

Despite the generally accepted belief that a child's self-esteem can be greatly affected by parental divorce, little systematic research has been conducted to explore the actual consequences of divorce in terms of the child's view of himself or herself. Wallerstein and Kelly (1976, 1980) observed that latency-aged children often experienced a shaken self-image, confusion, and anxiety. The father's role in affecting the child's self-esteem was noted as particularly important. Fathers who did not visit regularly, who disappointed their children by breaking commitments, or who had entirely abandoned their children, had the greatest negative impact on the child's self-esteem and feelings of rejection.

The few empirical studies that have been done suggest that there is not a simple, inevitable relationship between the experience of divorce and lowered self-esteem in children. Berg and Kelly (1979) compared the self-concept of children from divorced homes with children from intact homes who viewed their families as satisfactory (intact-accepted), and those who view their families as unsatisfactory (intact-rejected). The divorced and intact-accepted family groups did not differ, but the intact-rejected family group had significantly lower self-esteem than the other two groups. The authors conclude that divorce itself does not automatically result in decreased self-esteem. Unfortunately, the design of this study does not control for age of child, time since divorce, or degree of rejection or acceptance of their families by the children in the divorce group. A much more accurate picture of the relationships between family acceptance, self-esteem, and parental divorce could have been obtained if these factors had been analyzed.

Raschke and Raschke (1979) hypothesized that children's self-concepts would be affected not by the family structure, but by their perception of family conflict. Self-esteem, as measured by the Piers-Harris, was lower for those children reporting family fighting, adult fighting, and unhappiness among adults in the family. No significant relationship was found for self-concept scores and parental marital status; number of siblings; or the age, sex, or race of the child.

The relationship between the child's self-esteem, the parent's self-esteem, and the sex of the parent with whom the child resides was investigated by Lowenstein and Koopman (1978). No significant differences in self-

esteem of the boys, regardless of the parent with whom they lived or the amount of time they had lived in a single-parent home were found. Surprisingly, no correlation was found between the child's and parent's self-esteem, and there were no significant differences in levels of self-esteem between the mothers and fathers. Those boys, however, who saw the noncustodial parent once a month or more had higher self-esteem. Parental conflict, as perceived by the custodial parent, was not significantly related to the child's self-esteem although there was a trend toward lowered self-esteem when conflict was greater. The inconsistency with the Raschke and Raschke (1979) findings suggests that lower self-esteem in a child may be related to the child's rather than the parent's perceptions of conflict.

Another study looked at the effects of divorce and sex of the custodial parent on the self-concepts of older girls (Stephens & Day, 1979). As in the Lowenstein and Koopman study (1978), no differences in self-concept were found among father-absent, mother-absent, or intact families. Sex role identification with the mother was greater for girls in intact families than in father-absent families.

In summary, the few empirical studies of the relationship between the child's self-esteem and divorce do not verify the frequently reported clinical observations of the negative impact of divorce on self-esteem. Degree of family conflict and frequency of contact with noncustodial parent appear to be the most relevant variables affecting the child's self-esteem, not the family structure itself. Further exploration is needed to investigate more systematically the short term versus long term effects of divorce on a child's self-esteem, and the consistency of the trends noted thus far for both sexes and across a range of ages. If replicated, they may suggest that visitation contacts should be frequent (at least once a month).

Sex/Role Identity

Father absence has long been considered to be a major influence on the development of appropriate sex role identity in males, but only in the last decade has the impact on females been documented. Recent studies have explored the differential effects of father absence due to divorce versus death, as well as the age of the child at onset of father absence, and maternal influences.

Biller and Bahm (1971) predicted that a boy's masculine identity in a father-absent household would be stronger if the boy perceived his mother as encouraging masculine behavior (i.e., aggression and independence). They found that boys who had lost fathers prior to age 5 viewed themselves as less masculine than the father-present or later father-absent boys, and had more masculine self-concepts if they perceived their mothers as encouraging aggression. Perceptions of maternal encouragement of independence were not related to any differences in masculinity among the father-absent or father-present groups. Reasons for father absence were also found to be unrelated to the boy's perception of his masculinity.

Hetherington (1972) has done the most comprehensive investigation of the impact of divorce on a girl's sex role identity and behavior. Adolescent girls from intact homes were compared with girls whose fathers were absent due to divorce and girls whose fathers had died. Both father-absent groups were more dependent on female adults, and girls from divorced homes maintained closer proximity to male peers and adults and sought more attention and physical contact from them. The divorced group was also more verbal, smiled more, and had higher rates of other nonverbal behaviors indicating more responsiveness to males.

When rated on sex role identity, feminine interests, attitudes toward the female role, or similarity to parents, no differences were found. Girls from divorced homes indicated more negative attitudes and more conflicts with their fathers but also more heterosexual activity than did the other groups.

As expected, divorced mothers had a more negative attitude toward their ex-spouses. They were also more inconsistent in discipline after their daughters reached adolescence and more punitive regarding sexual activity. Both father-absence groups of mothers were more protective of their daughters when younger,

particularly when the father's absence occurred earlier. No differences were noted in patterns of affection, control, discipline, reinforcement of feminine behaviors, or attitudes toward men among the three groups of mothers.

Despite the lack of differences on traditional measures of sex role identity, Hetherington's study quite consistently demonstrates that the impact of father absence on observed interactions with males varies dramatically depending on the reason for the father absence. Girls from divorced homes are much more likely to exhibit increased attention seeking and responsiveness to males, while girls whose fathers have died will exhibit a pattern of withdrawal and avoidance.

In a follow-up study of the same girls (Hetherington & Parke, 1975), the daughters of divorcees were found to marry younger, to have a higher incidence of pregnancy at the time of marriage, and to have a higher rate of divorce than daughters of widows or daughters from intact families. In contrast, daughters whose fathers had died were found to have a much lower frequency of marriage than girls from intact families. Girls from divorced homes also had more negative perceptions of their fathers, husbands, and males in general, while girls whose fathers had died had more idealized views of men, in comparison to girls from intact homes. Both father-absent groups perceived their fathers and husbands to be more similar than did girls from intact homes. The impact of father absence, while not detectable until adolescence, appeared to have a long term impact on the girls' attitude towards males, their decision to marry, their eventual choice of a marriage partner, and satisfaction with the relationship.

In the Hetherington et al. (1979a) longitudinal study of preschool boys and girls post-divorce, no differences were noted for girls in sex role preference, sex role orientation, or overall sex role adoption, with the exception of a temporary increase in aggressive behavior at the one-year period. By two years post-divorce, boys from divorced homes had more feminine sex role preferences and sex role orientation, and play activities more frequently involved girls. The boys also showed a temporary increase in physical aggression but, by the end of two years, shifted to a pattern of high verbal aggression and continued dependency.

In intact families, fathers had a greater impact on sex role typing than mothers. For boys, parental warmth, dominance, maturity demands and participation in decision making were associated with more masculine sex role preferences, orientation, and adoption. Fathers in intact families who had masculine sex role preferences, positive attitudes towards women, and who were warm and restrictive, but who reinforced their daughter's femininity, had daughters who were extremely feminine. In contrast, maternal warmth was the only factor influencing femininity in girls in intact families.

In the divorced families, the father's influence on the child's sex role identity was initially similar to that of fathers in the intact families, but it greatly diminished over time. By two years postdivorce, the only paternal factor associated with increased sex role stereotyping is the father's availability. Maternal variables such as reinforcement for independence and sex-typed behavior and a positive attitude toward the father increase the son's masculinity, while overprotectiveness and reinforcement for dependency result in more feminine behaviors in boys.

The results of the more recent studies of children of divorced parents clearly demonstrate the strong influence of both parents in the development of the child's sex role identity. In these studies, the child resides with the mother, and the father is the visiting parent. Maternal and paternal influences are inversely related, with father characteristics being more crucial in intact or newly divorced families, while maternal variables increase in importance in the years after divorce.

Locus of Control

Locus of control has also been examined in terms of the child's ability to cope with the stress of divorce. It has been found to be a significant predictor of a child's postdivorce adjustment. Kurdek and Siesky (1980) found

that age and locus of control were the best predictors of the child's reactions to the divorce, with internals reporting less negative feelings about the divorce.

Parish and Copeland (1980) found that there were no differences in locus of control for college students from intact families or those families with father absence due to divorce. Only males whose fathers had died were subsequently found to be more external than males from the intact or divorced groups. This difference did not hold true for females in their sample. Grossman, Shen, and Adams (1980) replicated these findings and concluded that effects of father absence do not negatively affect the children by the time they are of college age.

Hetherington (1972) also found no differences in locus of control for adolescent girls from intact homes or homes where fathers were absent due to death or divorce. Both father-absent groups were, however, more external for the factor pertaining to personal control over one's life.

Cognitive Factors

Although the effects of father absence on children's cognitive development have frequently been studied, few researchers have examined these effects in terms of age of child at time of initial father absence and type of father absence (death versus divorce or separation). Santrock's (1972) review of the literature reflects the many negative effects on a child's intellectual functioning and academic achievement that may or may not be specific to children of divorce. Santrock investigated the intellectual performance and achievement scores of boys and girls with respect to age at time of father absence and type of father absence. Absence of the father due to divorce in the first two years of a child's life had the most negative effect on achievement and IQ for boys. Both the 0–2 and 3–5 age periods for parental divorce were significantly detrimental for girls. The age period of 12–13 was also a critical age for both boys and girls with respect to father absence due to divorce, with significant decreases in IQ and/or achievement noted at that time. Although achievement and IQ were negatively affected by father absence, regardless of reason, it is striking that both boys and girls whose fathers were absent due to divorce showed significantly greater cognitive deficits than those children whose fathers had died.

In the most comprehensive study of the impact of divorce on cognitive development to date, Hetherington et al. (1979a) assessed cognitive development at two months, one year, and two years following divorce. Two years postdivorce, when the mean age of the subjects was almost 6, children from intact families were found to have significantly higher WISC-R Full Scale IQs, with no significant sex differences. Parental variables that were associated with concurrent measures of IQ were observed to shift over time in their importance. Immediately following the divorce, parental factors were strongly related to Full-Scale and Performance IQs, especially for boys. By two years postdivorce paternal variables had decreased in their importance, with the maternal variables increasing in their significance. The declining impact of paternal factors was most noticeable for girls, with no significant paternal variable at the two-year retest period. Hetherington et al. (1979a) concluded that, while paternal influences on both boys' and girls' intellectual functioning diminished over time, paternal availability, which may affect male identification, continues to be an important factor in a boy's cognitive development.

The data also indicated that children who are impulsive, inattentive, and distractible at the two-month period have mothers who are inconsistent, disorganized, and have little control over their children. Two years postdivorce, these same children show decreases in Performance IQ, particularly with respect to tasks requiring sustained attention.

In a study of children's cognitive style with respect to field dependence-independence, Gershansky, Hainline, and Goldstein (1978) found that correlations of maternal and child field dependence were lower for children in father-absent homes, particularly for boys. The strength of the relations between mater-

nal and child scores varied depending on the sex of the child, age at onset of father absence, and reason for absence, with no differences occurring solely on the basis of father death versus divorce.

Moral Development

The relationship between paternal divorce and a child's moral development has for the most part been ignored despite frequent documentation of higher rates of delinquency for children from divorced homes (Offord, Allen, & Abrams, 1978; Offord et al., 1979; Rutter, 1980). Santrock (1975), however, did compare boys from father-absent and father-present homes on several behavioral measures of moral development, perceived maternal discipline, and teacher ratings of moral behavior. Although no differences were found on the behavioral measures, teachers rated father-absent boys as significantly lower in their moral behavior, regardless of reason for father absence, and rated boys from divorced homes higher on social deviation (stealing, lying, cheating). Boys whose parents were divorced perceived their mothers as using more power assertive discipline than boys whose mothers were widowed. The results of this study suggest that situational factors may be more important than general moral development in predicting specific behavior.

Social Interactions

The long term effects of divorce on the social interactions of children have seldom been explored, despite considerable evidence of at least temporary disruptions in peer relationships for children following divorce. Hetherington et al. (1979b) have provided the only longitudinal data regarding the social interactions of preschool children over a two-year period. In free play settings, both boys and girls whose parents had divorced two months earlier showed less imaginative play and more functional, less associative and cooperative play, and more onlooker behavior. Although girls from divorced families showed only a few differences in play patterns after one year, and none at two years, the play of boys from divorced homes showed more disruption. They had more solitary and parallel play and decreased cooperative, constructive, imaginative, and game play over the two-year period than males from intact homes.

At two months postdivorce, both boys and girls were more angry, hostile, and threatening than children from intact homes. Negative affect was still present two years later for boys but not for girls.

Children from divorced homes sought more help, attention, and proximity, and expressed greater fantasy, aggression, and opposition. They had less sharing, helping, or positive nonverbal behaviors than their peers, more negative verbal and nonverbal behaviors, and more frequent activity changes. Two years later, boys with divorced parents still demonstrated more negative behaviors and were becoming more socially isolated, although some of their negative behaviors had diminished. A pattern of high verbal aggression and low physical aggression was also characteristic of the boys from divorced homes at the two-year period.

Initial reactions of male peers to the negative behavior of boys with divorced parents included ignoring, opposition, physical and verbal aggression, negative nonverbal responses, and negative termination of interactions, with a higher rate of ignoring still evident two years later. Few differences in interactions were noted between boys of divorce and female peers. Since the boys from divorced families were more accepted by younger children and girls when initiating play, the authors suggest that this could explain the more feminine play patterns of father-absent boys noted in earlier studies.

In contrast to the boys, girls from divorced homes received fewer negative responses from peers. Although female peers were initially more verbally hostile and made more frequent negative terminations, they also showed more positive behaviors such as sympathy, helping, and sharing. By two years postdivorce, there were no differences in responses from female peers.

Boys from divorced homes were viewed by peers as more aggressive and less socially constructive at two months and at one year. Despite the boys' decrease in negative behaviors, they were still rated as aggressive and less popular after two years. It was concluded that the persistence in negative peer ratings for boys from divorced homes was a reaction to the earlier behavior problems. Boys who transferred to a new school during the second year received more positive peer and teacher ratings.

Girls from divorced homes were rated by peers as more aggressive at two months and more withdrawn, anxious, and dependent throughout the two-year period. No differences in popularity were noted for the girls at any point.

In the Hodges et al. (1979) study cited earlier, negative social behaviors were expected to occur more frequently for children from divorced homes, but in fact few differences were found. There was also no relationship between time since divorce and the number or degree of behavior problems. These findings, which are in striking contrast to the authors' own predictions as well as Hetherington's findings, may be due to the length of time since separation, which averaged over two years for Hodges' subjects. Since Hetherington had found all of the differences for females and some of the differences for males to dissipate by two years, it is not surprising that the Hodges study, with its higher proportion of females, did not show marked differences between children from divorced and intact homes.

Santrock and Warshak (1979) compared the social development of children from father-custody, mother-custody, and intact homes. Observations of parent-child interactions, nearly three years postdivorce, revealed that father-custody boys were more socially competent than boys from intact homes. The former group was more mature, sociable, warm, independent, and less demanding. Girls in father-custody homes, however, were less warm, mature, sociable, or independent and were more demanding as compared to girls from intact homes. Mother custody was associated with higher ratings on self-esteem for boys by the observers; however, this finding may reflect the tendency for boys in mother-custody homes to see themselves as the "man of the house," rather than reflecting an actual increase in self-esteem. Mother-custody girls, in contrast, had lower self-esteem than intact-family girls. Boys in father custody were less demanding, more mature, sociable, and independent than girls in father custody. In mother-custody homes, however, the relationships were reversed with girls being less demanding, more mature, sociable, and independent than boys. The authors conclude that custody by the same sex parent is related to more positive social behaviors for children.

In summary, the findings of these studies indicate that in the year following divorce there is a negative impact on play and social relationships. The behavior of children experiencing parental divorce was more stable across situations in the first year than for children from intact homes. During the initial stress of divorce, the child's internal state, rather than situational factors, may control the child's behaviors. By two years post-divorce these children seem less preoccupied with their internal state and are more responsive to situational factors. Although there is a significant improvement after two years, there is still evidence of an adverse effect on boys from divorced families, living with a single-parent mother. Custody with the same sex parent is associated with more positive social behaviors for both males and females.

Delinquency

One of the most frequently documented findings regarding the impact of divorce upon children is the higher rate of delinquency or antisocial behavior associated with parental divorce. Rutter (1980) has conducted a number of epidemiological studies to determine what aspects of parent-child separations most crucially affect the child's psychological development and behavior. Antisocial behavior was not higher for children from single-parent homes but was more prevalent for children whose parents had "poor" marriages. Delinquency rates were repeatedly found to be nearly twice as high for boys with divorced or separated parents, as compared to boys who had a parental death or who were from intact families. Rutter concludes that it is the parental discord associated with divorce rather than the actual separation from the parent that results in more frequent delinquent or antisocial behavior. He also concludes that the negative effects of parental discord are greater for boys than girls.

Offord et al. (1978) compared delinquent and nondelinquent boys to determine what family variables were associated with court involvement. The delinquent group had much greater frequency of parental divorce or separation and parental disability. Higher rates of antisocial symptoms, particularly severe ones, were also more frequent in delinquents from nonintact homes.

In a parallel study, (Offord et al., 1979) delinquent girls were much more likely to have parents who were divorced or separated. Maternal mental illness, paternal criminality, and a welfare history were also more frequent in the delinquent population. The researchers agree with Rutter's conclusion that parental discord is a significant factor in delinquency.

They found the prevalence of parental divorce much higher for female delinquents than male delinquents and conclude that the negative impact of parental divorce is greater for females. This is in opposition to Rutter's conclusion that divorce is more detrimental for boys. No explanation of the discrepancy in findings is given by Offord et al. (1979). It may be that the incidence of female delinquency is so low that significant differences will not show up when groups of girls from divorced and intact homes are compared. The association may become apparent only in studies that begin with samples of delinquent girls and then examine the history of parental divorce.

The use of legal and illegal drugs has also been examined in the context of delinquency and parental divorce. Drug use was found to be more frequent for those whose parents were divorced and separated (Bell & Champion, 1979). Separation from the father before age 10 was associated with a higher usage of drugs by males and females. In contrast, separation from the mother before the age 10 was correlated with a greater use of drugs by females but not males.

Despite the diverse methodologies and populations of the studies cited above, there is considerable consistency in the finding that parental divorce is associated with later delinquency for both males and females. Furthermore, researchers who have more closely examined the role of parental conflict rather than only the divorce variables are finding that the former may be the most crucial factor influencing the child's later antisocial or delinquent behavior.

THE EFFECT OF DIVORCE ON ADULT ADJUSTMENT

In an effort to control for the methodological problems of early studies regarding the impact of parental divorce on adult adjustment, Kulka and Weingarten (1979) used data from two national cross-sectional surveys done 20 years apart. Respondents were compared on a variety of self-report indicators of psychological adjustment. Their findings indicated that adults from divorced homes viewed childhood as the most unhappy time of their lives, reported more psychological distress and poorer physical health, and more frequently sought psychiatric help. Higher rates of anxiety, but not depression, were related to parental divorce, and the negative impact of divorce was slightly greater for males than females. Adults who had a history of parental divorce more frequently reported marital problems in their own marriage and had a slightly higher divorce rate but surprisingly did not differ from controls in their evaluations of marital unhappiness. The authors note that, although this may reflect a greater openness in acknowledging marital conflict rather than an actual difference in the amount of conflict, the higher divorce rate for this group suggests more frequent marital difficulties.

In assessing the respondents' view of the marital and parental roles, there was evidence that men from divorced homes had a weaker investment in the parental role while values towards marriage differed very little. Women from divorced homes, however, seemed less invested in the marital role but more invested in the parental role. No differences were found in perceived problems of raising children or feelings of inadequacy as a parent for either men or women. Since the surveys revealed relatively few differences between adults from divorced and intact homes when such factors as socioeconomic level were controlled, Kulka and Weingarten conclude that parental divorce has few long term effects on adult adjustment. They also conclude that males tend to be more negatively affected than females, supporting the findings of previous studies (Hetherington, 1979a; Rutter, 1980; Whitehead, 1979).

These conclusions would appear premature, however, in view of the study's inherent methodological limitations. The self-report format used, while important in ascertaining subjective perceptions of adults from divorced homes, does not address more objective or reliable measures of adult adjustment. For example, the Hetherington & Parke (1975) longitudinal study of girls of divorce found that parental divorce resulted in earlier marriage, higher rates of premarital pregnancies, more negative attitudes toward males, and higher divorce rates.

Using paper-and-pencil measures of ego development, locus of control, and ego identity achievement, Grossman et al. (1980) did not find that parental divorce had a negative impact on college students. In fact, males from divorced homes had higher achievement identity levels than their peers from intact homes.

Neither the Kulka and Weingarten (1979) study nor the Grossman et al. (1980) investigation take into account the degree of marital conflict in the divorce and intact family groups. Since there is strong evidence that degree of marital conflict, rather than divorce itself, is a crucial factor in a child's adjustment, this may be a key variable in predicting the long term effect of divorce on adult adjustment.

In summary, while self-report measures do

not reveal many contrasts between adults from intact or divorced homes, they do indicate differences in attitudes toward the opposite sex and marital and parental roles as well as a trend for adults from divorced homes to report more marital conflict. Behavioral indices of the long term effect of a parental divorce on adjustment show higher divorce rates for adults from divorced homes as well as earlier marriages and premarital pregnancies.

PSYCHOLOGICAL INTERVENTIONS

Several types of interventions are available and have been utilized with children whose parents were divorcing (Benedek & Benedek, 1979). Advice to the separating parent, individual psychotherapy with the child (Gardner, 1976; Tessman, 1978), and children's groups (Wilkinson & Bleck, 1977) are among the most popular. Some therapists have tried the alternative strategy of family therapy with divorced parents. The clinician's choice of intervention strategy will be a function of the particular family situation, the child's age and level of functioning, and the parents' openness to therapy for themselves or their child. Indirect intervention in the form of bibliotherapy may be useful in some cases.

Interventions with Parents

The focus of intervention with the separating parent will be twofold. The clinician must be supportive and helpful to the parent regarding personal difficulties and must provide constructive and helpful guidance regarding the child. Thus education about divorce from the child's perspective and normal reactions of children to stress is a major component. Personal difficulties such as a depressive reaction on the part of a parent can have an adverse effect on any child, and the situation is more harmful for a child who is also experiencing a physical separation from the other parent. The initial focus of therapy may be oriented toward providing support to the depressed parent in the hope of enhancing his or her level of functioning during the separation and postdivorce adjustment period.

Conflict between the parents is common, even normal, during the separation and immediately postdivorce; however, it can have very detrimental effects on the child. Intervention can assist the parents in insulating the child from much of the conflict and avoiding use of the child as a weapon against the other parent.

The decision to separate is a difficult one, and many parents need assistance in communicating the news of divorce to the child. The person most likely to inform the child is the mother, who is very upset herself. Depending upon the age of the child, discussions regarding separation are probably best held shortly before the separation takes place. A young child, unlike an adult, will not necessarily benefit from this knowledge weeks or months before the separation occurs. Knowledge of the separation could increase the child's anxiety during each parental argument or conflict, and the child may attempt to prevent the separation. Given the child's lack of power, or lack of input in what is appropriately a parental decision, informing the child of the decision shortly before it is implemented may be best for all concerned. Additionally, it may be best to discourage lengthy conversations between the parents and child regarding the impending separation. The parents are unlikely to be able to provide the safe, supportive atmosphere necessary for the child to react to and discuss the news. Each parent's feelings of hurt and anger toward the other are likely to be communicated and to increase the confusion and anxiety of the child. Unless the child is in therapy or has a relatively neutral adult available with whom to discuss the family dissolution, extensive anticipatory preparation is contraindicated.

Avoidance of additional stress on the new single-parent family is important. Changes such as moving into a new home, going to a different school, obtaining a new housekeeper or different child care arrangements should be avoided when possible. Divorce, like any other crisis, is best dealt with in a situation that maximizes the person's coping skills. This is most likely when children are in familiar surroundings and can utilize their familiar social support systems.

Changes in the relationships between parent and child are inevitable; however, many adverse changes should be avoided. Loyalty conflicts can be minimized if both parents actively support the child's relationship with each. The custodial parent may also benefit from learning that accessibility to and a positive relationship with the noncustodial parent is very important in the child's future functioning. Comments that convey envy or jealousy of the child's relationship with the ex-spouse must be avoided as they place the child in a very conflictual situation. Even the parent who cannot support the child's relationship with the ex-spouse can avoid criticizing or condemning it. On the other hand, the custodial parent should not provide excuses for the noncustodial parent who visits infrequently or is unreliable. Failures of the noncustodial parent to visit or call will be very disappointing to the child, and he or she should be allowed to react with anger or sadness. The custodial parent should be encouraged to minimize his or her reactions so that the child does not feel that he or she must console the parent or that he or she is "taking sides" by reacting to the parent's disappointment. The child should be reassured that it is the problem of the noncustodial parent and does not reflect the unworthiness of the child.

Some parents react to the loss of the spouse by forming an intense attachment to the child. This type of overly involved relationship is harmful to the child. Independence and autonomy suffer greatly, and peer relationships may be minimal. Future relationships are likely to be fraught with problems since the child is isolated from social interactions. A sense of specialness, unrealistic expectations of others, or an overinflated concern with self may be the long term result of such alliances. For these reasons, it is helpful to encourage the custodial parent to utilize his or her social support system and to obtain child care in order to participate in adult activities.

The therapist may find articles or books regarding divorce useful in terms of educating the parent about the divorce process. *Surviving the Breakup* (Wallerstein & Kelly, 1980), *The Parents Book About Divorce* (Gardner, 1979), and *Divorced Dads* (Shepard & Goldman, 1980) are three which may be helpful.

Interventions with Children

The initial focus of therapy with a child whose parents are divorcing is to provide a safe and supportive atmosphere for grieving over the loss of the intact family. Typically, the child is overwhelmed by feelings of sadness, loss, and bewilderment but is not free to express these in the tense and angry atmosphere of the home. Freedom to grieve openly and express anger and rage at both parents is a major goal of therapy.

Often the child will alternate between rage and a fear of abandonment. After clarifying that abandonment by the noncustodial parent is not a possibility, the clinician can provide reassurance and realistic expectations for the child. The task is not easy since children must understand why the adults who stopped loving each other will not stop loving him or her. If one or both parents have the psychological resources, it may be very helpful to see the parent and child together. This neutral setting, with a supportive adult, often provides an atmosphere of safety for the child who can then verbalize his or her fears. The process of expressing intense feelings of anger to a parent who does not leave or react with anger can be very therapeutic for both family members.

Reality testing about the permanence of the changes in the family unit will be a continual theme of therapy, as will the reassurance that children don't have to choose between parents. One of the benefits of divorce can be that the child forms a relationship with each of the parents rather than the parental unit. Thus the child may receive more attention from each parent and learn that his or her mother and father are different, neither is better or worse, and each can provide an important relationship.

Children whose parents are divorcing often respond with feelings of embarrassment and humiliation as well as disrupted behaviors. The feelings they experience are often overwhelming and immobilizing; thus their self-esteem and/or self-concept may suffer. Reassurance from the therapist regarding the child's intrinsic goodness and worth is very helpful. Additionally, the therapist can help the child in acknowledging and accepting the relative powerlessness of his or her position with regard to the separation. Learning that the helplessness is due to the situation, not to the child's inadequacy, can be a relief. The therapist can also point out those areas in which the child can have input. For example, latency-aged children may respond well if they actively plan and prepare a meal with a parent. For the preschooler, having the power to choose the dessert at a meal or to pick between two play activities can assist in restoring a sense of control and autonomy.

Play therapy is the most appropriate intervention for preschoolers and the young latency-aged child. Older latency-aged children and adolescents may respond to the chance to verbalize their feelings; however, some may feel more comfortable when engaged in activities or games. Older children may respond well in short term groups, but screening the children individually to determine their level of impairment is essential. Finally, books such as *The Boys and Girls Book About Divorce* (Gardner, 1970) and *What Every Child Wants His Parents to Know* (Salk, 1973) have proven to be very successful with latency-aged and adolescent children.

In summary, successful intervention will depend upon the therapist's knowledge of the short and long term effects of divorce upon parents and children and upon his or her responsiveness to the individual family situation. The type of strategy is less important than the therapist's ability to provide emotional support and guidance to both the parent and child. Clinicians will find *Children of Parting Parents* (Tessman, 1978) and *Psychotherapy with the Children of Divorce* (Gardner, 1976) excellent resources.

REFERENCES

Baidance, S.M., Hill, H.A., & Serritilla, D.A. Conjoint family therapy following a divorce: An alternative strategy. *American Journal of Family Therapy,* 1978, **6,** 55–59.

Bell, D.S., & Champion, R.A. Deviancy, delinquency and drug use. *British Journal of Psychiatry,* 1979, **134,** 269–76.

Benedek, R., & Benedek, E. Children of divorce: Can we meet our needs? *Journal of Social Issues,* 1979, **35,** 155–169.

Berg, B., & Kelly, R. The measured self-esteem of children from broken, rejected, and accepted families. *Journal of Divorce,* 1979, **2,** 363–369.

Biller, H., & Bahm, R. Father-absence, perceived maternal behavior, and masculinity of self-concept among junior high school boys. *Developmental Psychology,* 1971, **4,** 178–181.

Bloom, B., Asher, S., & White, S. Marital disruption as a stressor: A review and analysis. *Psychological Bulletin,* 1978, **85,** 867–894.

Bohannan, P. The six stations of divorce. In P. Bohannon (Ed.), *Divorce and after.* Garden City, N.Y.: Doubleday, 1971.

Brandwein, R., Brown, C., & Fox, E. Women and children last: The social situation of divorced mothers and their families. *Journal of Marriage and the Family,* 1974, **36,** 498–514.

Brown, P., & Manela, R. Changing family roles: Women and divorce. *Journal of Divorce,* 1978, **1,** 315–328.

Chiriboga, D.A., & Cutler, L. Stress responses among divorcing men and women. *Journal of Divorce,* 1977, **1,** 95–106.

Daniel, R.M. Father-child intimacy in divorced families. (Doctoral dissertation, California School of Professional Psychology, 1977). *Dissertation Abstracts International,* 1977, **38** (6-B), 2854. (University Microfilms No. 73-29, 395).

Desimore-Luis, J., O'Mahoney, & Hunt, D. Children of separation and divorce: Factors influencing adjustment. *Journal of Divorce,* 1979, **3,** 37–41.

Gardner, R. *The boys and girls book about divorce.* New York: Aronson, 1970.

Gardner, R. *Psychotherapy with children of divorce.* New York: Aronson, 1976.

Gardner, R. *The parents book about divorce.* New York: Bantam, 1979.

Gasser, R.D., & Taylor, C.M. Role adjustment of single parent fathers with dependent children. *The Family Coordinator,* 1976, **25,** 397–401.

Gershansky, I., Hainline, L., & Goldstein, H. Maternal differentiation, onset and type of father's absence and psychological differentiation in children. *Perceptual and Motor Skills,* 1978, **46,** 1147–1152.

Goode, W.J. Problems in post-divorce adjustment. *American Sociological Review,* 1949, **14,** 394–401.

Granwold, D.K., Pedler, L.M., & Schellie, S.G. A study of sex role expectancy and female post-divorce adjustment. *Journal of Divorce*, 1979, **2**, 383–393.

Greif, J.B. Child absence: Fathers' perceptions of their relationship to their children subsequent to divorce. (Doctoral dissertation, Adelphi University, 1977). *Dissertation Abstracts International*, 1978, **38** (9-A), 5714–5715. (University Microfilm No. 7800328).

Grossman, S., Shen, J., & Adams, G. Effects of parental divorce during early childhood on ego development and identity formation of college students, *Journal of Divorce*, 1980, **3**, 263–272.

Hackney, G.R., & Ribordy, S.C. An empirical investigation of emotional reactions to divorce. *Journal of Clinical Psychology*, 1980, **36**, 105–110.

Hess, R., & Camera, K. Post-divorce family relationships as mediating factors in the consequences of divorce for children. *Journal of Social Issues*, 1979, **35**, 79–97.

Hetherington, E.M. Effects of father absence on personality development in adolescent daughters. *Developmental Psychology*, 1972, **7**, 313–326.

Hetherington, E.M. Children and divorce. In R. Henderson (Ed.), *Parent-child interaction: Theory research and prospect*. New York: Academic Press, 1980.

Hetherington, E.M., Cox, M., & Cox, R. Divorced fathers. *The Family Coordinator*, 1976, **25**, 417–428.

Hetherington, E.M., Cox, M., & Cox, R. The aftermath of divorce. In J.H. Stevens, Jr., & M. Matthews (Eds.), *Mother-child, father-child relations*. Washington, D.C.: NAEYC, 1977.

Hetherington, E.M., Cox, M., & Cox, R. Family interaction and the social, emotional and cognitive development of children following divorce. In V. Vaughn & T. Brazelton (Eds.), *The family: Setting priorities*. New York: Science & Medicine, 1979. (a)

Hetherington, E.M., Cox, M., & Cox, R. Play and social interaction in children following divorce. *Journal of Social Issues*, 1979, **35**, 26–49. (b)

Hetherington, E.M., & Parke, R. Socialization and the development of sex role. In E.M. Hetherington & R. Parke (Eds.), *Child psychology: A contemporary viewpoint*. New York: McGraw-Hill, 1975.

Hodges, W., Wechsler, R., Ballantine, C. Divorce and the preschool child: Cumulative stress. *Journal of Divorce*, 1979, **3**, 55–67.

Jacobson, D. The impact of marital separation/divorce on children: I. Parent-child separation and child adjustment. *Journal of Divorce*, 1978, **1**, 341–360. (a)

Jacobson, D. The impact of marital separation/divorce on children: II. Interparent hostility and child adjustment. *Journal of Divorce*, 1978, **2**, 3–19. (b)

Jacobson, D. The impact of marital separation/divorce on children: III. Parent-child communication and child adjustment, and regression analysis of findings from overall study. *Journal of Divorce*, 1978, **2**, 175–193. (c)

Kelly, J.B., & Wallerstein, J.S. The effects of parental divorce: Experiences of the child in early latency. *American Journal of Orthopsychiatry*, 1976, **46**, 20–32.

Keshet, H.F. Part-time fathers: A study of separated and divorced men. (Doctoral dissertation, University of Michigan, 1977). *Dissertation Abstracts International*, 1977, **38** (3-A), 1686–1687.

Kriesberg, L. *Mothers in poverty: A study of fatherless families*. Chicago: Aldine, 1970.

Kulka, R., & Weingarten, H. The long-term effects of parental divorce in childhood on adult adjustment. *Journal of Social Issues*, 1979, **35**, 50–78.

Kurdek, L., & Siesky, Jr., A. Divorced single parents' perceptions of child-related problems. *Journal of Divorce*, 1978, **1**, 361–369.

Kurdek, L., & Siesky, Jr., A. An interview study of parents' perceptions of their children's reactions and adjustments to divorce. *Journal of Divorce*, 1979, **3**, 5–17.

Kurdek, L., & Siesky, Jr., A. Sex role self-concepts of single divorced parents and their children. *Journal of Divorce*, 1980, **3**, 249–261.

Loge, B.J. Role adjustments to single parenthood: A study of divorced and widowed men and women. (Doctoral dissertation, University of Washington, 1976). *Dissertation Abstracts International*, 1977, **37**(7-A), 4647. (University Microfilm No. 77-602).

Lowenstein, J., & Koopman, E. A comparison of the self-esteem between boys living with single-parent mothers and single-parent fathers. *Journal of Divorce*, 1978, **2**, 195–207.

McDermott, J. Parental divorce in early childhood. *American Journal of Psychiatry*, 1968, **124**, 1424–1432.

National Center for Health Statistics. *Mortality from selected causes by marital status.* (Series 20, Nos. 8A & 8B, USDHEW). Washington, D.C.: U.S. Government Printing Office, 1970.

Offord, D., Abrams, N., Allen, N., & Porshinsky, M. Broken homes, parental psychiatric illness, and female delinquency. *American Journal of Orthopsychiatry*, 1979, **49**, 252–264.

Offord, D., Allen, N., & Abrams, N. Parental psychiatric illness, broken homes, and delinquency. *Journal of American Academy of Child Psychiatry*, 1978, **17**, 224–238.

Pais, J., & White, P. Family redefinition: A review of the literature toward a model of divorce adjustment. *Journal of Divorce*, 1979, **2**, 271–281.

Parish, T., & Copeland, T. Locus of control and father loss. *Journal of Genetic Psychology*, 1980, **136**, 147–148.

Raschke, H.J. The role of social participation in postseparation and postdivorce adjustment. *Journal of Divorce*, 1977, **1**, 129–140.

Raschke, H.J., & Raschke, V. Family conflict and children's self-concepts: A comparison of intact and single-parent families. *Journal of Marriage and the Family*, 1979, **41**, 367–374.

Rutter, M. Parent-child separation: Psychological effects on the child. In S. Harrison & J. McDermott, Jr. (Eds.), *New directions in childhood psychopathology*. New York: International University Press, 1980.

Salk, L. *What every child wants his parents to know*. New York: Warner, 1973.

Santrock, J. Relation of type and onset of father absence to cognitive development. *Child Development*, 1972, **43**, 455–469.

Santrock, J. Father absence, perceived maternal behavior, and moral development in boys. *Child Development*, 1975, **46**, 753–757.

Santrock, J., & Warshak, R. Father custody and social development in boys and girls. *Journal of Social Issues*, 1979, **35**, 112–125.

Schoettle, N.C., & Cantwell, D.P. Children of divorce: Demographic variables, symptoms, and diagnoses. *Journal of American Academy of Child Psychiatry*, 1980, **19**, 453–457.

Shepard, M., & Goldman, G. *Divorced dads*. New York: Berkley, 1980.

Spanier, G.B., & Casto, R.F. Adjustment to separation and divorce: An analysis of 50 case studies. *Journal of Divorce*, 1979, **2**, 241–253.

Stephens, N., & Day, H.D. Sex-role identity, parental identification, and self-concept of adolescent daughters from mother-absent, father-absent, and intact families. *Journal of Psychology*, 1979, **103**, 193–202.

Tcheng-Laroche, F., & Prince, R. Middle income, divorced female heads of families: Their lifestyles, health and stress levels. *Canadian Journal of Psychiatry*, 1979, **24**, 35–42.

Tessman, L.H. *Children of parting parents*. New York: Aronson, 1978.

Tooley, K. Antisocial behavior and social alienation post-divorce: the "man of the house" and his mother. *American Journal of Orthopsychiatry*, 1976, **46**, 33–42.

Waller, W. *The old love and the new: Divorce and readjustment*. London: Feffer & Simons, 1967.

Wallerstein, J.S. Children of divorce: The long-term impact. *Human Sexuality*, 1981, **15**, 36–47.

Wallerstein, J.S., & Kelly, J.B. The effects of parental divorce: The adolescent experience. In J. Anthony & C. Koupernik (Eds.), *The child in his family: Children at psychiatric risk*. New York: Wiley, 1974.

Wallerstein, J.S., & Kelly, J.B. The effects of parental divorce: Experiences of the preschool child. *Journal of American Academy of Child Psychiatry*, 1975, **14**, 600–616.

Wallerstein, J.S., & Kelly, J.B. The effects of parental divorce: Experiences of the child in later latency. *American Journal of Orthopsychiatry*, 1976, **46**, 256–269.

Wallerstein, J.S., & Kelly, J.B. *Surviving the breakup*. New York: Basic Books, 1980.

Weisfeld, D., & Laser, M.S. Divorced parents in family therapy in a residential treatment setting. *Family Process*, 1977, **16**, 229–236.

Whitehead, L. Sex differences in children's responses to family stress: A reevaluation. *Journal of Child Psychology and Psychiatry*, 1979, **20**, 247–254.

Wilkinson, G.S., & Bleck, R.T. Children's divorce groups. *Elementary School Guidance and Counseling*, 1977, **11**, 205–213.

Wiseman, R. Crisis theory and the process of divorce. *Social Casework*, 1975, **56**, 205–212.

CHAPTER 54

Grief and Loss in Childhood

GERALD P. KOOCHER

Dealing with issues of grief and loss in childhood is no easy task. From the adult's standpoint, there is concern about helping the child to cope or at least not become too upset. At the same time most adults have acquired a personal history of loss experiences and cannot help but draw on these when asked to share in another's loss. In addition to these potential transference relationship difficulties, adults may sometimes fail to recognize that the salience or emphasis of loss-related events may differ markedly given the developmental level of the child. From the child's standpoint, losses may generate anger, feelings of insecurity, or fearfulness in the face of events that are difficult to comprehend if not totally new experiences altogether. The clinician who would work with children on such issues will need some special knowledge of developmental trends and a high degree of comfort with personal loss experiences.

As this chapter continues, discussion of clinical issues and intervention strategies will focus on three subgroups of children, each with a different context for confronting death. First the author will discuss the "normal child" who thinks about death in connection with a dead animal in the road, a story seen on television, or hearsay from a peer. This will include questions of how death and loss are conceptualized in the least threatening of circumstances, so that the reader may develop a foundation for considering both healthy and pathological reactions in other circumstances. Second, the author will address the matter of the child with a life-threatening illness. In such instances, there is a variety of special factors

including the child's awareness of his or her own condition, that demand special consideration. The third subgroup of children are those who are bereaved by the loss of a parent, sibling, or other significant person in their lives. Although common developmental threads will flow through consideration of children in each of these subgroups, the thrust of clinical work and nature of the interventions attempted will necessarily differ.

RESEARCH LITERATURE

Conceptions of Death in Normal Children

In their review of psychological perspectives on death, Kastenbaum and Costa (1977) note three oft-held assumptions about children's perceptions of death. First is the assumption that children do not comprehend death. Second is the assumption that adults do comprehend death. Finally, there is an assumption that even if children were able to understand death, it would be harmful for them to be concerned about it. These assumptions are clearly superficial and reflect defensiveness on the part of their proponents rather than any valid view of actual circumstances.

Two early classics in what has become a substantial body of literature on children's conceptions of death are the studies by Anthony (1940) and Nagy (1948). Both represented initial attempts to study the child's conception of death from a systematic developmental perspective, and both also provide validation evidence to support the theory that these conceptions follow a developmental progression. While neither study is a paragon of scientific rigor, they represented nearly the whole body of material on the topic for two decades. One result was that many writers simply accepted and repeated their findings without question or additional investigation (e.g., Kübler-Ross, 1969, pp. 178–79).

Anthony's study (1940) described a developmental sequence in understanding the word "dead," with a progression from initial ignorance, through personal associations, to an ultimate biological understanding of the concept. Nagy (1948) described three biodevelopmental stages along a similar continuum. She noted that children under age 5 tended to regard death as a reversible process associated with separation. Her second state involved an alleged tendency by children to "personify" death as a kind of "boogy man" or "black coachman." Finally, Nagy concludes that children begin to regard death as a lawful universal process at about age 9.

More recent research has provided firm empirical documentation of the manner in which the death concept develops. A Piagetian framework has been applied to demonstrate how children's responses to questions about death reflect their levels of cognitive development (Koocher, 1973, 1974). Other developmental studies have documented acquisition of the universality and irrevocability of death concepts (White, Elsom, & Prawat, 1978), as well as highlighting children's own awareness of their potential death (Spinetta, 1974).

These studies suggest that the egocentrism and magical thinking that are a part of preoperational thought in young children dominate concerns about death in early childhood. With the arrival of concrete operations at about age 6 or 7, the child becomes capable of taking the role of another person in the cognitive sense and thereby begins to sense the permanence of death. At this stage, however, the child may still think of death as something that occurs as a specific consequence of illness or injury rather than the outcome of a biological process. When adolescence arrives with accompanying abstract reasoning capability and formal operational thought a fuller com-

prehension of death as a concept becomes possible. It will come as no surprise that the specific concerns and fantasies expressed by children of different ages with respect to death are reflective of their cognitive understanding about it.

Bowlby's writings (1973) on the theme of separation demonstrate the importance of social relationships and consequences of their disruption, especially during the early years of development. It is the interaction of these social relationships and the cognitive accommodation capacities that determine coping abilities in concert with other individual factors. A brief review of these elements from a child development standpoint may be found in a forthcoming volume on children's conceptions of health and illness (Koocher, 1981). A detailed and well-integrated review is already in print in an outstanding volume by Lonetto (1980), which synthesizes the literature on children's conceptions of death with heretofore unparalleled clarity and scholarship. Carrying all of this research to a logical conclusion, the reader may wish to examine a detailed analysis leading to a "death education curriculum." This scholarly work by Duncan (1979) draws the existing research literature into a detailed curriculum for teaching children about death in a nonthreatening context from kindergarten through high school.

In summary, there are distinctly developmental trends in the normal process of acquiring a concept of death. These trends will influence the style and substance of adaptive reactions in the face of a loss and the grief reaction that follows. It will be important for the reader to become familiar with one of the brief (Koocher, 1974) or more detailed (Lonetto, 1980) accounts of these trends prior to beginning therapeutic work on this topic with children.

During early childhood, when preoperational thinking is the rule, it is not possible to take on the "role of the other." As a result, children's conceptualizations are limited by their own experience. Death is therefore considered solely in terms of the child's own experiences by analogy with sleep, separation, and injury. The preoperational child cannot truly consider, "Who do I know who has died? What generalizations can I draw from that with respect to myself?" These children are not yet able to regard death as an irreversible process, and they are most worried about the duration of separation from loved ones that death implies.

When children become capable of concrete operations, they are able to use information gleaned in the media, from friends, and from parents in forming their impressions. Facts become more usable, but not in the abstract sense. The child's predictions become more accurate although this occurs by means of a gradual testing process over several years. At this point, youngsters are most concerned with issues of pain and inflicted injury although separation remains an issue as well.

The onset of adolescence brings formal operational reasoning and the ability to make use of abstract reasoning. For the first time the child is able truly to realize that "that which is" may differ from "that which might be." Conceptions of death begin to involve more issues of uncertainty, and abstract reasoning including theological elements may enter the child's considerations of issues. Clearly, the adolescent's approach to conceptualizing (and hence reacting to) death will be quite different from that of younger children.

The Child with Life-Threatening Illness

The dying child's awareness of death has long been a topic of concern to health care providers, at least partially because of their own intense discomfort in working with children who are so gravely ill. If there is a single paper that sums the issues up best, it is the classic by Vernick and Karon (1965) titled: "Who's Afraid of Death on a Leukemia Ward?" Through the use of life space interviews, they documented the fact that children clearly knew the seriousness of their illnesses and were quite eager to have someone to talk with about it. They described the communication barriers often erected by adults to "protect the child" and noted that when a child is passive with respect to discussing these concerns it is often a reflection of the environment. A

number of empirical studies have yielded supportive data (Binger et al., 1969; Waechter, 1971; Spinetta, Rigler, & Karon, 1973, 1974; Spinetta & Maloney, 1975).

Reviews of professional opinion and research data have consistently stressed that children as young as 5 or 6 have a very real understanding of the seriousness of their illness, and still younger children show definite reactions to increased parental stress and other concomitants of a terminal diagnosis on the family (Spinetta, 1974; Gogan, O'Malley, & Foster, 1977; Slavin, 1981). Despite this recognition by children of their serious illness, conceptualizations of death and loss issues do not really differ from the general developmental trends noted above. The predominant modes of response tend to reflect age-related concerns about separation, pain, and disruption of usual life activities (Bowlby, 1973; Koocher, 1980a).

Just as Kübler-Ross's (1969) groundbreaking work emphasized the importance of systematic psychological intervention for the adult with terminal illness, the parallel needs of children are also being recognized. Even among normal children, there are substantial elements of death anxiety (Koocher et al., 1976). It is not surprising, therefore, to find a variety of adverse psychological symptoms and behavior problems among dying children and members of their families (Slavin, 1981). Indeed, the need for psychological interventions predicated on the awareness of such children has been recognized as routine (Adams, 1979; Kellerman, 1980; Koocher & O'Malley, 1981).

Chronic life-threatening illness presents an additional subset of emotional issues requiring special attention. Advances in modern medical diagnosis and therapeutics have altered the natural histories of many diseases, and this has proved to be a mixed blessing. Diseases that were acutely fatal just 2–3 decades ago have been converted into conditions that still threaten death but are much more chronic than acute in their course. Childhood cancer and cystic fibrosis are good examples. Children diagnosed as having acute lymphoblastic leukemia 30 years ago usually died within six months. Today such children have a 50-percent chance of surviving five or more years in a disease free state, and very few fail to achieve a remission of at least 18–24 months (Koocher & O'Malley, 1981). Half of the patients diagnosed in infancy as having cystic fibrosis during the 1950s died within a year, while the median survival point today is at least 18 years with many patients living into their 20s and 30s (Cystic Fibrosis Foundation, 1980).

These new survival statistics have generated a whole host of psychological stress issues. Not the least of these is the matter of long term uncertainty and the stresses of the chronic helplessness this induces (Seligman, 1975; Koocher & O'Malley, 1981). What of the families of such patients? Should they attempt to anticipate the child's death and accommodate to the loss, or should they attempt to deny and repress their anxieties about a potential loss while hoping for the best? Either course may lead to long term psychological sequelae (Kemler, 1981). The uncertainty component clearly cannot be overlooked when considering the psychological adaptation of the child patient, siblings, parents, or extended family members.

The Bereaved Child

Loss and separation issues in childhood have been well represented in the literature of child development, psychology, and psychiatry. Three works probably deserve mention as "classics" whenever one writes of coping with death and loss from a developmental perspective. Certainly, the work of Bowlby (1973) is one, as discussed earlier in this chapter. Another is Rochlin's (1953) study of children's play representations of fears associated with death. The third is Lindemann's (1944) detailed discussion of the acute grief reaction, with special focus on the survivors of a disastrous nightclub fire. Although Lindemann's work does not focus on children per se, it is one of the most insightful discussions of the grief process available.

A number of studies have focused specifically on patterns of mourning and bereave-

ment in children. Some have reported descriptions of bereavement in children as young as 3 years of age although most tend to make only rather gross age distinctions tending instead to focus on middle childhood and adolescence. In general, the pattern of bereavement is described as including regression, denial, hopelessness, and occasionally animistic fantasies as a child struggles to cope with the loss of a grandparent, parent, or sibling (Brown, 1961; Fleming, 1980, pp. 178–187; Moriarty, 1967; Sharl, 1961). Other retrospective studies have attempted to link losses in childhood to adult depression (Brown, 1961; Munro, 1966) or other late psychological sequelae. An excellent summary of these studies compiled by Fleming (1980) concludes that the course and outcome of childhood bereavement experiences may well influence adult affective disturbance years later, but the nature of the relationship is certainly not clear.

The role of the family in the whole context of grief and loss is critical for children. The literature has consistently documented the fact that children can manifest both cognitive and emotional disruption in the aftermath of a family member's death almost without regard for the specific circumstances of the loss (Cain, Cain, & Erickson, 1964; Furman, 1974; Hollingsworth & Pasnau, 1977). In some circumstances, as in the case of a parent's suicide, the reactions may be unusually intense and prolonged (Cain, Cain, & Fast, 1966). Even the death of a public figure with parent surrogate qualities can evoke a significant mourning response in both children and adults. This was well illustrated by the authors of an interdisciplinary volume written to discuss children's reactions to the Kennedy assassination (Wolfenstein & Kliman, 1965). For many children and adults, the public assassination and funeral were akin to losing our country's father figure, and the interviews with the children reported in that volume underscore the point.

At least one author has suggested that the only way to do away with the debilitating consequences of the death of a family member is to do away with death itself (Rosenblatt, 1967). This tongue-in-cheek observation is a rather telling comment with respect to cultural values. The antithesis is well represented in a thoughtful paper on the Amish way of death by Bryer (1979) that underscores the importance of the family as a support system in the face of death. Bryer demonstrates how community orientation, family structure, and cultural attitudes toward life and death can facilitate bereavement within a supportive atmosphere that tends to minimize emotional trauma associated with the loss. Death is prepared for throughout life, and, though the time of actual passing is certainly a sad one, the coping of survivors seems somehow less trying.

The importance of the funeral as a family ceremony has been well documented in a variety of cultures (Feifel, 1977; Kalish & Reynolds, 1976), and the welfare of survivors is regarded as of paramount importance to most ethnic groups. At the same time, many families are not well prepared to integrate children into this ceremony, asserting that it is for the children's own protection. It is generally difficult enough for adults to bear their own brief and confrontation with mortality, and the thought of dealing with a child's worries in addition is frightening to many. It is not always clear just who is being protected from what, although most writers on bereavement in childhood stress the importance of openness, communication, and family support in helping children to cope with loss (see especially Furman, 1974; Schoenberg et al., 1975; Slavin, 1981).

ASSESSMENT ISSUES

Death and Loss Concerns of the Normal Child

Spontaneous questions about death and loss are certainly not symptoms of psychopathology in childhood. All children think about death, encounter dead animals, and experience separations from loved ones during their preschool years. Their thoughts and fantasies are acted out in play and translated into many questions that often make adults quite nervous. The usual difficulty adults encounter in assessing the extent and nature of the child's concerns stems from the fact that the adults' loss experiences and attendant "emotional baggage" may color their reactions to the naive questioning of the child. It is crucial that adults who work with youngsters on these issues have accommodated and successfully integrated loss experiences into their own lives (Koocher, 1980b).

Assessment of what is normal or pathological will generally be matters of gauging the intensity and duration of the grief reaction and the degree to which psychological defense mechanisms are successful in protecting the child from anxiety (Lindemann, 1944; Rochlin, 1953; Fleming, 1980). Separation and loss syndromes with detailed accounts of childhood grief reactions (Rochlin, 1953; Bowlby, 1973) sketch the templates through which patterns of normal adaptation and exaggerated grief reactions may manifest themselves.

Descriptions of potential pathological reactions follow in the next section of this chapter, while modes of addressing the normal concerns of children with respect to death and loss are also detailed below. The key point to be underscored, prior to discussions of pathology and intervention plans, is that such concerns are a normal part of growing up and should be treated as such by both parents and clinicians.

Pathological Bereavement in Children

Symptoms associated with grief reactions in childhood may include tearfulness; social and emotional withdrawal; loss of interest in favorite toys or pastimes; decreased attention span; development of tics; loss of appetite; persistent insomnia or nightmares; decreased effectiveness in school; increases in unfocused activity level; and expressions of guilt over past activities, especially in relation to the deceased (Lindemann, 1944; Rochlin, 1953; Brown, 1961; Cain et al., 1964, 1966; Bowlby, 1973). The natural dependency of childhood, along with the potential for animistic and magical thinking (Koocher, 1973, 1974; Lonetto,

1980), make children particularly vulnerable to prolonged adverse psychological sequelae following an important loss. At the same time, the absence of any symptoms of acute grief or a sharply truncated reaction may herald premature application of denial or avoidance defenses with the potential for emergence of symptoms at a much later point in time.

One key to diagnostic assessment of childhood grief reactions is the presence or absence of anxiety. The child or adolescent who is in the process of adapting to the loss should be able to verbalize some sadness and related feelings in the course of a psychodiagnostic evaluation. Inability to discuss the loss, denial of affect, or anxiety and guilt themes in relation to the deceased or surviving family members would all be indicators that some additional evaluation or psychotherapeutic intervention may be warranted.

Time can also be an important factor in assessing adaptation to loss, but there are no uniform guidelines to apply. While the intensity of the depressive symptoms will often abate substantially over a period of several weeks, so-called "anniversary phenomena" may trigger renewed symptoms. Arrival of a birthday, holiday, or other family event, for example, may induce a return of sadness, tension, or stress along with thoughts of the deceased person. Usually, these recurrences are much less intense than the acute mourning experience. If they persist more than several days following the stimulus event or evoke a heretofore unseen intensity, a diagnostic evaluation is certainly warranted.

The clinician must also be especially sensitive to the principle that the bereaved child cannot accurately be evaluated outside of the family context. Grief reactions in children are subject to both amelioration and exacerbation based on the presence or absence of emotional supports within the surviving family. Behavioral contagion and social learning also play roles in determining a child's response. Religious rituals and family behavior patterns provide opportunities for observational learning and imitation that may be either facilitative or inhibitory with respect to the child's adaptation (Kalish & Reynolds, 1976; Bryer, 1979).

Children may also react to mourning, depression, or anxiety in their parents or caretakers even though they have had no personal contact with the deceased individual.

Psychopathology in the Child at Risk for Death

Children who are terminally ill or who face an uncertain but potentially fatal outcome from some chronic illness are at substantial risk for emotional disturbance as a function of stress. A host of papers (e.g., Binger et al., 1969; Vernick & Karon, 1965), review articles (Spinetta, 1974; Gogan et al., 1977; Slavin, 1981), and books (e.g., Adams, 1979; Kellerman, 1980; Koocher & O'Malley, 1981) have documented and detailed the core stresses and common symptoms. Depending on the course and trajectory of the disease process, even children who were quite "normal" prior to becoming ill may develop increased anxiety, loss of appetite, insomnia, social isolation, emotional withdrawal, depression and apathy, and marked ambivalence toward those adults who are providing primary care.

The groundbreaking work of Kübler-Ross (1969) must be considered whenever one thinks of reactions to the possibility of impending death. She described five "stages" of adaptation to death in adults: denial, rage and anger, bargaining, depression, and acceptance. It is important to note that these stages were an outgrowth of her work with adults and are to be regarded as flexible rather than absolute. Unfortunately, in child psychology one often thinks of "stages" as a cumulative sequence or developmental progression and this leads to some confusion with Kübler-Ross's intent from time to time. Her listing should actually be considered a roster of potential reactions that may occur in any sequence, remit and reappear, or never occur at all. In the case of children, the reactions will often be acted out or expressed via play. The reactions are also characteristic of family members who anticipate the loss of one of their number.

The nature of these reactions are generally best regarded as responses to acute or chronic stress rather than as functional psychopathology. It is predictable, however, that children or families with preexisting emotional pathology will experience an exacerbation. The primary model for how this occurs is best described in the work of Seligman (1975) and other writers on the topic of learned helplessness. When people come to believe that the outcome they will confront (i.e., death) is independent of their own behavior, the helplessness syndrome and accompanying emotional stress is dramatic (Seligman, 1975).

Much research has focused on the child's awareness of his or her own fatal illness (Vernick & Karon, 1965; Waechter, 1971; Spinetta, 1974). It is clear that even young children are very aware of their medical conditions. Empirical data exist, for example, that demonstrate that anxiety levels of childhood leukemia patients increase parallel to increases in the frequency of outpatient clinic visits (Spinetta & Maloney, 1975). This is the opposite of what one would find in youngsters with chronic non-life-threatening illnesses. Other data demonstrate the increasing sense of isolation that dying children may tend to experience (Spinetta et al., 1974). It is clear that one cannot shield sick children from anxiety about their conditions.

Even children who otherwise seem to be coping quite well through a prolonged illness course may develop specific problems such as conditioned-reflex vomiting, anxiety linked to specific medical procedures, depressive reactions to progressive loss of physical capacities, or family communication inhibitions (Koocher & Sallan, 1978; Kellerman, 1980). Sometimes children and their families cope quite well during periods of active treatment, even when noxious procedures are involved, only to become overwhelmed when the need for continued treatment is over (Koocher & Sallan, 1978; Koocher & O'Malley, 1981). Although this type of reaction may seem a paradoxical reaction to the cessation of a noxious experience, hospitalizations and even harsh treatment regimens may come to be imbued with some protective value along the lines of functional autonomy. A variety of ameliorative strategies are discussed in the pages that follow.

MODES OF INTERVENTION

Addressing Everyday Fears

The best strategy for helping the normal child to cope with death and grief issues is advance preparation. Death education curricula in schools (Duncan, 1979) and family discussions of these matters at prime *teaching moments* are both important. One should not wait until the death of an important person in the child's life to begin thinking about how to communicate on the matter. During the course of normal developments from story telling, to television watching, to family outings there will be encounters with death. A dead animal on the highway or a story on the evening news might be an appropriate everyday type of occurrence from which to begin a discussion with the child who has noticed and inquired about it (Koocher, 1979).

When assessing the reactions and concerns of young children, it is important to avoid adult metaphors. One adult may talk to another about the neighbors who "lost their child last week," but imagine the anxiety and confusion this might induce in a 4-year-old who wonders, "Why couldn't they find him?" It is important to understand the concepts and vocabulary from the child's perspective. This will require special attentiveness to the questions children are asking and the issues of prime concern to them.

Unarticulated concerns often include questions such as: "Could that happen to me (or my parents)?"; "Who will take care of me?"; "What will be expected of me?" It is sometimes helpful to have an adult note that these are things all people worry about, as the questions are answered in a thoughtful and supportive manner (Koocher, 1979). Discussions of how people cope wtih sadness, the purpose of memorial services, what cemeteries and funeral directors are for, and so forth, can all be a part of answering children's questions.

Rituals and religious services can also be important to children of all ages but only if they are well integrated with family values. A religious funeral service, for example, will probably be of little value to the child whose family has seldom participated in religious services previously, and it may actually be more frightening than reassuring. Fables or similar religious stories raise many potential problems for children whose developmental level makes them prone to literal interpretation in concretistic fashion. On the other hand, a child may gain considerable comfort and support from participating in rituals or services involving well known and liked people and contexts. One must carefully assess whether the child's participation in the funeral, for example, meets the child's needs or is being dictated for the vicarious benefit of adults.

The best suggestion would be to describe anticipated events to the child objectively and encourage him or her to express a preference free of guilt. For example, in discussing an upcoming funeral one might tell a child, "There will be a minister (priest or rabbi) talking about the person who died. The body will be in a casket in the room. A lot of people may be crying because they are so sad that the person died. Some people like to go to funerals so they can be with other people when they feel sad, but others would rather not go. What do you want to do?"

A final suggestion for consideration whenever a discussion about death is held with a child, especially a young child, would be a debriefing session. That is to say, one should ask the child to restate key elements of the explanation or talk about feelings relative to the discussion or events just passed. Only in this way can one immediately become aware of misconceptions and potentially anxiety-arousing communication errors.

Psychotherapy for the Child at Risk for Death

Not all children with fatal or life-threatening illnesses are in need of psychotherapy or mental health services. For those who do require such services, there are two basic need paradigms. First, there is the child or family for whom psychological intervention would have been needed even without the illness by virtue of preexisting difficulties. Second is the child and family struggling with acute stress as a function of the illness affecting a heretofore well-adapted psychosocial system. Both

groups will be in need of supportive and crisis intervention treatment services at various points in the treatment of the child's illness (Adams, 1979; Kellerman, 1980; Koocher & O'Malley, 1981).

Most children with chronic life-threatening illnesses will require relatively sophisticated medical care and will probably be treated at or in consultation with major medical centers. In the ideal circumstance, mental health services will be available at these centers through the primary treatment team (Koocher et al., 1979). Even in the best of circumstances there will be powerful stresses on all concerned with treating such patients (Koocher, 1980b) and many opportunities for needless irritations among children, parents, and the treatment staff (O'Malley & Koocher, 1977). The potential difficulties are magnified when the mental health service providers and the medical staff do not know and trust each other's judgment. At the same time, the mental health personnel must become familiar with the natural history of and treatments for the illnesses their patients are struggling with. While mental health centers and practitioners in the community often quite justifiably feel inadequate to the task of serving such families, a variety of models for providing such care have been well described in the literature (Adams, 1979; Kellerman, 1980; Koocher et al., 1979; Koocher & O'Malley, 1981).

The precise nature of actual intervention strategies and techniques will certainly vary as a function of the individual patient's needs. In addition to the writings cited above, Burton's (1974) fine volume as well as recent books by the Spinettas (Spinetta & Spinetta, 1981) and Sourkes (1982) provide substantial detail about both programmatic and individual treatment approaches. Sourkes's (1982) volume is particularly rich in detail with inclusion of extensive, well-edited interview material. A solid background in psychotherapy is necessary, but not sufficient, for the role of the clinician with such children and their families may include those of communication facilitator, information provider, advocate, and at times even a comourner.

The basic intervention approach should

include consideration of the following clinical questions: What does the child know about the illness? What surface concerns does the child have? What sources of support are available? What sources of stress are anticipated?

Knowing exactly what information has been communicated to the child and family is very important, but it is also critical to recognize that what has been comprehended may differ substantially from what information was allegedly offered. While the nature of the anxieties a child may face is quite complex, some facets are more easily verbalized than others, and these surface concerns should be addressed first. This strategy will establish a climate within which the child will later be able to verbalize more complex worries. Sources of support include the child's own personality and coping abilities as well as the emotional support available from family members. There will be considerable variability across individuals and families with respect to such supports, and the clinician must be sensitive to this. While it is not always possible to predict the timing of stress events associated with the treatment of life-threatening illnesses, the events themselves are well known to those who treat such children (e.g., alopecia among cancer patients, infections, or unexpected hospitalizations). It is often possible to lessen the psychological stress of such events by preparing the child for them in advance with anticipatory discussions. The clinician who explores all of these issues with the child will have begun the most important parts of a constructive intervention program.

Telling a child that he or she is dying is probably the most burdensome act an adult can undertake. Still, opening the door to supportive communication in the face of death can be very rewarding and intensely meaningful. If one waits, however, until it is evident that death is near to initiate such discussions, a tragic error has been made. Even young children can be told at diagnosis if their illness is "a very serious disease: people can die from it." This can be followed by other information about how the medical staff plans to "fight the disease," including eliciting the

support of the child in the battle. The critical point is that from the very beginning the child be engaged in an emotional climate that encourages supportive discussions of even the most stressful issues.

During the course of treatment for the illness one might routinely ask what the child is worried about, even mentioning, "Do you ever worry about dying?" specifically. If the child answers in the affirmative, one can proceed to discuss the matter. If such fears are denied, one can note, "Well, I'm glad you're not, but if you do get worried I hope you'll let me (or your parents) know so we can talk about it and help."

When it becomes clear that a child is indeed entering a terminal trajectory, it is best to meet with the parents and explore the best ways to handle communications on the matter. At times, a child will be open and direct. In that case, most of the clinician's work may focus on helping the family and staff deal with their own concerns about discussing death. In other cases, the child will deny any concern but show obvious separation anxiety or other symptoms of similar concern. In such cases, it may be wisest to treat the symptoms by helping to see that the child is not alone or provide similar interventions without confronting the issue of death directly. There are times when one can best facilitate coping by leaving defenses intact. Careful consideration of family values and the level of adaptation operating at any point in time are important. A good rule of thumb is not to disturb a homeostasis unless there is a real problem confronting the parties involved and pressing the issue will facilitate adaptation.

Psychotherapeutic Care of the Bereaved Child

The central concern in the psychotherapeutic care of the bereaved child has two focal points. The first is the need to help the child differentiate his or her fate from that of the deceased. Second is the need of the child to arrive at an acceptable sense of closure with regard to the loss. This may involve feelings of guilt or responsibility for the death as well as magical fears about what actually transpired.

Both foci are important issues for any child who experiences a loss, although the need is more acute in the case of pathological bereavement, described earlier in this chapter.

The need to differentiate between the recently deceased and the living is a common cognitive adaptation mechanism among both children and adults. Adults are not immune to magical thinking, especially in times of emotional stress, but children have a particular need to distinguish between real and imagined causes of death. Investigators of cognitive development have long documented the difficulties children of different ages may have in coping with abstractions, and since death is a one-time-only final experience for each of us, it certainly qualifies as an abstract experience when it comes to individual mastery issues.

Lonetto (1980) discusses the cognitive issues quite well, noting that the same phenomena that make abstractions difficult for young children to grasp also make them more tolerant of ambiguities in learning about death. He also illustrates the use of play and drawings as a means of reducing abstraction and ambiguity to a meaningful level for children in various age groups. Writings from a quite different frame of reference, Rochlin (1953) uses the psychoanalytic model to arrive at similar conclusions. He notes that the child's play is organized to protect the self against fears associated with her or his understanding of death.

Involvement in funerary rituals may be quite helpful and supportive in a family context if such involvement is well explained and consistent with the child's wishes. Vicarious satisfaction of adults is not a proper basis for making the decision whether to involve a child in such activities or not. Introduction of philosophical or religious concepts may tend to confuse and frighten young children, especially in the absence of close family supports (Furman, 1974).

The questions a child may be presumed to worry about in the aftermath of a salient death would include the following: Why (i.e., by what means) did that person die? Will that happen to me (or someone else I care about)? Did I have anything to do with it? Who will take care of me (if the deceased was one of the child's caretakers) now? While these questions may not be specifically articulated by the child, they are almost always a part of the underlying anxiety that accompanies a prolonged grief reaction. The psychotherapeutic remedy must involve both informational or cognitive and affective components.

Whether one is considering the needs of the bereaved child, the child with life-threatening illness, or simply children in general, emotional climate is the paramount guarantor of security and adaptation. When the social and emotional context provides a sense of trust and empathic understanding, coping is greatly facilitated. Establishing such a context within the family and in psychotherapy, along with a recognition of salient issues from the child's standpoint, is the most effective base on which to begin dealing with grief and loss in childhood.

REFERENCES

Adams, D.W. *Childhood malignancy: The psychosocial care of the child and his family.* Springfield, Ill.: Thomas, 1979.

Anthony, S. *The child's discovery of death.* New York: Harcourt, Brace, 1940.

Binger, C.M., Ablin, A.R., Feverstein, R.C., Kushner, J.H., Zoger, S., & Mikkelsen, C. Childhood leukemia: Emotional impact on patient and family. *New England Journal of Medicine,* 1969, **280**(8), 414–418.

Bowlby, J. *Separation: Anxiety and anger.* New York: Basic Books, 1973.

Brown, F. Depression and childhood bereavement. *British Journal of Psychiatry,* 1961, **107**, 754–777.

Bryer, K. The Amish way of death: A study of family support systems. *American Psychologist,* 1979, **34**(3), 255–261.

Burton, L. (Ed.). *Care of the child facing death.* London: Routledge & Kegan Paul, 1974.

Cain, A.C., Cain, B.S., & Erikson, M.E. Children's disturbed reactions to the death of a sibling. *American Journal of Orthopsychiatry,* 1964, **34**, 741–752.

Cain, A.C., Cain, B.S., & Fast, I. Children's disturbed reactions to parent suicide. *Ameri-*

can *Journal of Orthopsychiatry*, 1966, **36**, 873–880.

Cystic Fibrosis Foundation. *Patient registry report.* Rockville, Md: Author, 1980.

Duncan, C. Teaching children about death: A rationale and model for curriculum. (Doctoral dissertation, Boston College, 1979).

Feifel, H. *New meanings of death.* New York: McGraw-Hill, 1977.

Fleming, S. Childhood bereavement. In R. Lonetto (Ed.), *Children's conceptions of death.* New York: Springer, 1980.

Furman, E. *A child's parent dies.* New Haven: Yale University Press, 1974.

Gogan, J.L., O'Malley, J.E., & Foster, D.J. Treating the pediatric cancer patient: A review. *Journal of Pediatric Psychology*, 1977, **2**(2), 42–48.

Hollingsworth, E.E., & Pasnau, R.O. *The family in mourning.* New York: Grune & Stratton, 1977.

Kalish, R.A., & Reynolds, D.K. *Death and ethnicity: A psychocultural investigation.* Los Angeles: University of Southern California Press, 1976.

Kastenbaum, R., & Costa, P.T. Psychological perspectives on death. *Annual Review of Psychology*, 1977, **28**, 225–249.

Kellerman, J. (Ed.). *Psychological aspects of childhood cancer.* Springfield, Ill.: Thomas, 1980.

Kemler, B. Anticipatory grief and survivorship. In G.P. Koocher & J.E. O'Malley (Eds.), *The Damocles syndrome: Psychosocial consequences of surviving childhood cancer.* New York: McGraw-Hill, 1981.

Koocher, B.P. Childhood, death, and cognitive development. *Developmental Psychology*, 1973, **9**, 369–374.

Koocher, G.P. Talking with children about death. *American Journal of Orthopsychiatry*, 1974, 404–411.

Koocher, G.P. Why isn't the gerbil moving any more? Discussing death in the classroom and at home. *Children Today*, 1979, **4**(1), 18–21.

Koocher, G.P. Initial consultations with pediatric cancer patients. In J. Kellerman (Ed.), *Psychological aspects of childhood cancer.* Springfield, Ill.: Thomas, 1980. (a)

Koocher, G.P. Pediatric cancer: Psychosocial problems and the high costs of helping. *Journal of Clinical Child Psychology*, 1980, **9**, 2–5. (b)

Koocher, G.P. Children's developmental conceptions of death. In R. Bibace & M.E. Walsh (Eds.), *Children's conceptions of health, illness, and bodily functions.* San Francisco: Jossey-Bass, 1981.

Koocher, G.P., & O'Malley, J.E. *The Damocles syndrome: Psychosocial consequences of surviving childhood cancer.* New York: McGraw-Hill, 1981.

Koocher, G.P., O'Malley, J.E., Foster, D.J., & Gogan, J.L. Death anxiety in normal children and adolescents. *Psychiatria Clinica*, 1976, **9**, 220–229.

Koocher, G.P., & Sallan, S.E. Psychological issues in pediatric oncology. In P. Magrab (Ed.), *Psychological management of pediatric problems.* College Park, Md.: University Park Press, 1978.

Koocher, G.P., Sourkes, B.M., & Keane, W.M. Pediatric oncology consultations: A generalizable model for medical settings. *Professional Psychology*, 1979, **10**, 467–474.

Kübler-Ross, E. *On death and dying.* New York: Macmillan, 1969.

Lindemann, E. Symptomatology and management of acute grief. *American Journal of Psychiatry*, 1944, **101**, 141–148.

Lonetto, R. *Children's conceptions of death.* New York: Springer, 1980.

Moriarty, D. *The loss of loved ones.* Springfield, Ill.: Thomas, 1967.

Munro, A. Parental deprivation in depressive patients. *British Journal of Psychiatry*, 1966, **115**, 305–311.

Nagy, M. The child's theories concerning death. *Journal of Genetic Psychology*, 1948, **73**, 3–27.

O'Malley, J.E., & Koocher, G.P. Psychological consultations to a pediatric oncology ward. *Journal of Pediatric Psychology*, 1977, **2**(2), 54–57.

Rochlin, G. Loss and restitution. *Psychoanalytic Study of the Child*, 1953, **8**, 288–309.

Rosenblatt, B. Relations of children to the death of loved ones: Some notes based on psychoanalytic theory. In D. Moriarty (Ed.), *The loss of loved ones.* Springfield, Ill.: Thomas, 1967.

Schoenberg, B., Gerber, I., Wiener, A., Kutscher, A.H., Peretz, D., & Carr, A.C. *Bereavement: Its psychosocial aspects.* New York: Columbia University Press, 1975.

Seligman, M.E.P. *Helplessness.* San Francisco: Freeman, 1975.

Sharl, A. Regression and restitution in object loss. *Psychoanalytic Study of the Child,* 1961, **16,** 471–480.

Slavin, L.A. Evolving psychosocial issues in the treatment of childhood cancer: A review. In G.P. Koocher & J.E. O'Malley (Eds.), *The Damocles syndrome: Psychosocial consequences of surviving childhood cancer.* New York: McGraw-Hill, 1981.

Sourkes, B.M. *The deepening shade: Psychological aspects of life-threatening illness.* Pittsburgh: University of Pittsburgh Press, 1982.

Spinetta, J.J. The dying child's awareness of death: A review. *Psychological Bulletin,* 1974, **81**(4), 256–260.

Spinetta, J.J., & Maloney, L.J. Death anxiety in the outpatient leukemic child. *Pediatrics,* 1975, **65**(6), 1034–1037.

Spinetta, J.J., Rigler, D., & Karon, M. Anxiety in the dying child. *Pediatrics,* 1973, **52**(6), 841–845.

Spinetta, J.J., Rigler, D., & Karon, M. Personal space as a measure of a dying child's sense of isolation. *Journal of Consulting and Clinical Psychology,* 1974, **42**(6), 751–756.

Spinetta, J.J., & Spinetta, P.D. (Eds.). *Living with childhood cancer.* St. Louis: Mosby, 1981.

Waechter, E.H. The child's awareness of fatal illness. *American Journal of Nursing,* 1971, **7,** 1168–1172.

Vernick, J., & Karon, M. Who's afraid of death on a leukemia ward? *American Journal of Diseases of Children,* 1965, **109,** 393–397.

White, E., Elsom, B., & Prawat, R. Children's conceptions of death. *Child Development,* 1978, **49,** 307–310.

Wolfenstein, M., & Kliman, G. (Eds.). *Children and the death of a president.* Garden City, New York: Doubleday, 1965.

CHAPTER 55

Ethical and Legal Issues in the Treatment of Children

NANCY S. EHRENREICH AND GARY B. MELTON

Whether treating a psychotic adolescent in a state hospital, counseling a runaway at a storefront clinic, or running a therapy group for abused children, the child clinician confronts special legal and ethical issues. The clinician is treating an individual who is doubly disadvantaged (i.e., both by age and by disability) and arguably in need of special protections. Furthermore, both ethically and legally, the clinician is required to consider the impact of his or her actions not only upon the child client but also upon the rights, responsibilities, and relationships that tie the child to his or her parents. The purpose of this chapter is to explore these special issues of clinical child practice and the related policy concerns.

TRENDS IN LAW ON CHILDREN'S RIGHTS

The law concerning the relationship between children and their parents has become significantly more complex over the last 15 years, primarily because the general legal status of children has been in flux. Prior to *In re Gault*[1] in 1967 and *Tinker v. Des Moines Independent School District*[2] in 1969, it was not clear that minors were to be considered "persons" under the Fourteenth Amendment, which applies the Bill of Rights to the states. In *Gault,* however, the Supreme Court held that basic procedural protections under the Fifth and Sixth Amendments belonged to juvenile respondents in delinquency proceedings and, in *Tinker,* that minors had First Amendment rights to freedom of expression. This trend toward recognition of minors' constitutional rights and toward increased self-determination for children has been further supported by a line of Supreme Court cases recognizing that minors have a constitutional right to privacy. Initially articulated in cases dealing with adults' rights to purchase contraceptives,[3] the right to privacy now encompasses a broader right to be free from unwanted violations of bodily integrity and has been cited by the Supreme Court as the basis for granting both children[4] and adults[5] a limited right to obtain abortions.

Despite these developments, however, the limits of autonomy for minors remain unclear. First, there may be constraints placed upon that autonomy by the child's level of competence to make a particular decision. The abortion decisions, for example, have been predicated upon a right to privacy for *mature* minors.[6] Furthermore, in *denying* minors due process rights when they are being "voluntarily" admitted to mental hospitals by their parents, the Court has assumed that "most children, even in adolescence, simply are not able to make sound judgments concerning many decisions, including their need for medical care or treatment. Parents can and must make those judgments."[7]

Second, the autonomy of even a mature child may be limited to a certain extent by the state's deference to parental decisions about what is best for him or her (see, generally, Melton, 1982). Historically, children were viewed essentially as the property of their biological parents, whose right (and responsibility) it was to control and provide for them.[8]

To a large extent, this view has persisted in notions about parents' liberty to rear children as they see fit, short of gross threats to the children's health and safety.[9] In recent years, this stance has been articulated in terms of the importance of preserving family integrity and parental authority in order to meet the psychological needs of immature minors (see, e.g., Goldstein, Freud, A., & Solnit, 1979).[10]

Nevertheless, despite the prevalence of this assumption of an identity of interest between parent and child, the courts have never viewed parental control over offspring as unlimited. Rather, they have held that the state has the authority (and the duty) to protect children from serious harm when their parents cannot or will not do so. This authority, known as the *parens patriae* power, derives from the legitimate state interest in protecting members of society who cannot protect themselves and in assuring that children grow up to be productive, responsible citizens. It has been used, for example, to uphold compulsory education[11] and child labor laws,[12] to support the termination of parental rights based on abuse or neglect,[13] and to override parental refusals to consent to life-saving medical treatment, even when those refusals were based on religious grounds.[14]

The assumption that parents can be depended upon always to act in their children's best interests in the treatment context is belied by both clinical literature and litigated cases. Simmonds (1976), for example, has suggested that children are particularly vulnerable to labeling as the "identified patient" in the face of family strife. Interestingly, there is also some evidence that children are more likely than their parents to identify presenting problems in psychotherapy as problems of the whole family (Small & Teagno, 1979).

Several cases that have reached the courts demonstrate the fact that, despite good intentions, parents may overestimate their children's need for psychiatric treatment and try to hospitalize them because of what really amounts to a difference in lifestyle.[15] In addition, a parent's perceptions may sometimes be slanted by his or her own emotional problems,[16] while at other times the parent may actually be motivated more by self-interest than by sincere concern for the child.[17] Hospital records regarding juvenile patients also indicate that the child's best interest is not always promoted by his or her parents (Ferleger, 1973).

Finally, the "true" allocation of decision-making power is further obfuscated by controversies concerning the proper limits of state authority in shaping the lives of children. The child advocacy movement itself is split on this point (Mnookin, 1978; Rogers & Wrightsman, 1978). While some commentators argue for further extension of self-determination rights to minors, others believe strongly in the appropriateness and effectiveness of state intervention in the lives of children and families even where neither the child nor the parents desire such "help." The child-helping professions have, in fact, grown up with such an ideology (see Bakan, 1971, and Levine & Levine, 1970, for historical reviews). For example, early child guidance clinics developed around the juvenile court system, in which due process and concern for the respondents' personal liberty were sacrificed in the name of "treatment," often for noncriminal behavior that was, though perhaps bothersome, arguably a product of "normal" adolescent group norms.

Such conflicts among child, family, and state are ubiquitous in the practice of clinical child psychology (see Szasz, 1979, for one analysis of these conflicts). Children rarely come to a therapist on a purely voluntary basis, and, if they do, it may well be without parental knowledge or consent. Is the therapist's primary allegiance to the child, the parent, or the state as *parens patriae?* Under what conditions does the allegiance shift?[18] Because the law is not clear, standards for clinicians' decision making on this point may also be unclear. Furthermore, child clinicians can find little guidance in professional ethical standards (but see Koocher, 1983, for a sensitive discussion of the issues); the American Psychological Association's (1981) Ethical Principles, for example, require only that "psychologists take special care to protect the minors' best interests" (Principle 5d). Recognizing that the conflicting interests and ambiguous case law in this area preclude simple answers, we will nevertheless attempt in this chapter to clarify the ethical issues and identify the prevailing legal trends affecting clinical child practice, particularly with regard to consent, refusal of consent, treatment in institutions, and confidentiality.

ACCESS TO TREATMENT

Minors and Informed Consent

The legal principles relating to juveniles' access to treatment stem primarily from the "common law"—a set of general rules developed by courts through case-by-case decision making. However, many of these principles have also been enacted into statutory law by state legislatures. While we will focus on the general trends in minors' consent to treatment, it should be noted that states vary widely in the extent to which they follow those trends. Thus it is important for individual clinicians to consult the applicable statutes and relevant case law in their states in order to determine the specific rules governing mental health practice there.

The most important principle applying to the treatment of adult patients is the doctrine of informed consent. That doctrine provides that a physician or mental health professional can be held liable for battery or negligence if treatment is provided to an individual without appropriately informing that person of the risks and benefits attendant to that treatment and obtaining the patient's voluntary consent to receive it. It is important to note that an individual cannot give such consent unless he or she is mentally competent to do so. That is, he or she must have the actual ability to understand and appreciate the nature, risks, and benefits of and the alternatives to the proposed treatment. If the individual is not competent, a substitute decision maker, such as a legal guardian, must be consulted. There are two exceptions to the informed consent requirement: (1) Emergencies: The treatment provider need not obtain consent if faced with

an emergency situation where the time necessary to obtain such consent could result in loss of life or serious bodily injury. (2) Therapeutic privilege: Disclosure of information need not include very severe and unlikely consequences of the treatment when disclosure of such consequences would prevent the patient from reaching a rational decision about the treatment. This privilege is eroding, however, largely because it might have the effect of negating the very purpose of the informed consent doctrine—"humanizing" the clinician-patient patient relationship by discouraging unilateral decisions by the clinician and supporting individual liberty and privacy.

Beyond these general exceptions, several special issues affect the application of the informed consent doctrine to minors' access to treatment. In most jurisdictions, minors are considered to be per se incompetent. That is, they are assumed, by virtue of their age alone, to lack the ability to make treatment decisions. Parents have traditionally been authorized to make such decisions not only because of the original natural philosophy concept of the parents' right to control their children's lives but also because of the more recent belief that parents could protect their children from unnecessary or harmful treatment. Where a parent is not available, a guardian or other person or agency acting *in loco parentis* (in place of the parent) is authorized to provide consent.

Thus, when applied to the treatment of children, the informed consent doctrine has been held to give parents, not the child, the right to be informed and consulted. The consent or refusal of the child himself or herself is considered to be not only insufficient but irrelevant, for once the parent has consented, treatment can be provided even over the child's objection.

However, as will be described in more detail later, there are several situations in which the per se incompetence rule will not apply and the child will be authorized to consent to or refuse treatment on his or her own. Under such circumstances, however, the clinician should not assume that he or she is now free to treat the consenting child. Rather, the clinician should refer to and follow the general requirements for adult consent, for if the child is mentally incompetent to give consent or does not consent voluntarily, the clinician may still be liable. Nonetheless, the exceptions to the per se rule at least raise the possibility of minors' consenting to treatment independently of their parents. Those exceptions are thus worthy of some discussion.

Exceptions

Emancipation

Under certain circumstances, courts will hold that a minor is sufficiently independent of and separate from his or her parents to justify treating him or her as an adult for certain purposes. Thus, for example, an emancipated minor, as such a child is called, might be able to enter into valid contracts, make a will, or consent to a blood test. The evidence that establishes emancipation varies from state to state and, although some states statutorily define this term, most leave its application to case-by-case judicial determinations. Factors commonly cited as indicative of emancipation include: financial independence, living separate from the parents, enlistment in the armed forces, marriage, and parental acquiescence in such assertions of independence. If a child is found to be emancipated, a court will usually hold that he or she is legally competent to consent to psychological treatment, and the child will probably be mentally competent as well.

Mature Minors

Apparently responding either to social welfare concerns that a parental consent requirement might prevent minors from obtaining treatment or to libertarian concerns that minors' privacy in health-related matters should be respected, the courts have created a specific exception to the parental consent rule, known as the mature minor exception.[19] One author has summarized the common elements of cases in which that exception is applied as follows: (1) the child is of a relatively mature age; (2) the treatment is beneficial to the child

(as opposed to being for the benefit of another person[20]); (3) the child has the capacity to understand the nature of the procedure to which he or she consented; and (4) the treatment is not considered to be major (Wadlington, 1973).

Although a few states have adopted statutory versions of the mature minor rule,[21] in most it is purely a judicially created doctrine. In federal case law, it has been adopted most clearly in cases involving minors' access to abortions.[22] Unfortunately, the courts rarely provide a definitive articulation of the factors relevant to a finding of "maturity"[23] to which a psychologist can refer in deciding whether to provide treatment to a given minor. Thus, while judicial decisions in which a physician is held liable for nonnegligent treatment of a child over age 15 are extremely unlikely (see Pilpel, 1972), the variable definition and retrospective application of this rule will no doubt still deter some mental health professionals (as well as physicians in general) from providing treatment to minors whom they are not certain the law will view as mature.

Minor Consent Statutes

In recent years, the vast majority of the states have enacted one or more statutes specifically authorizing children to consent to certain types of treatment. Concluding that the societal interest in assuring that such treatment will be received by the child outweighs both the latter's parents' interest in controlling his or her conduct and any danger that the child will receive unneeded services, many states have statutorily authorized children to consent to the provision of pregnancy-related services, treatment for venereal disease, and drug and alcohol abuse treatment. A smaller number have also passed such a law allowing minors to consent to mental health services.[24] In addition, some have adopted a more general approach, authorizing children to consent to all medical treatment.[25] (However, these latter statutes by their language—e.g., "treatment by a qualified physician"—might sometimes exclude psychologists). Some minor consent statutes include a minimum age at which children can consent—and the age may vary with the treatment—while others provide no floor.[26]

Although these laws provide helpful guidance to many professionals who deal with children, they often tend to raise as many questions as they answer. For example, they frequently fail to address the role that the parent should play, if any, in the treatment process: Can treatment under such a law be based on parental consent alone, or does the child have the right to refuse treatment as well as consent to it? Can the provider inform the parents of the fact that he or she is treating their child? Can the provider inform the parents of the details of such treatment? Is the parent liable for necessary medical treatment provided under such statutes? In addition, such laws may authorize consent to pregnancy-related services without specifying whether such services should be interpreted to encompass abortion or authorize consent to mental health treatment without specifying which specific professionals and which specific treatments are included. Finally, these statutes do not remove the fact that the psychologist probably has an ethical obligation to determine whether his or her patient does in fact have the capacity to consent to the treatment being rendered (American Psychological Association, 1981, Principle 5d).

Another impediment to the effectiveness of minor consent statutes is that they are not always effectively disseminated to the people whom they will affect. Thus, over one year after the passage by one state legislature of a broad statute authorizing juveniles to consent to psychotherapy, 39 percent of a sample of community mental health clinics surveyed by one researcher were unaware of the existence of the law (Melton, 1981b). Furthermore, virtually none of the clinics that did know the law disseminated information concerning it to minors themselves. Not surprisingly, no substantial change in the number of children seeking treatment was reported by the clinics, although the one agency that had established an outreach program to inform minors of their right to consent to mental health treatment experienced a 3 percent increase in its total caseload.

State Authority to Order Treatment over Parental Objections

The *parens patriae* power of the state authorizes a court to override parental preferences where the matter at issue is sufficiently important to the state's interest in the welfare of the child. In the area of consent to medical or mental health treatment, the state intervention usually takes place under the rubric of the neglect laws. Since parents have a legal obligation to provide necessary medical treatment to their children, a parent's refusal to consent to such treatment can result in a finding that the child is neglected and a court order mandating treatment. In such a situation, the child's preferences may be considered by the court, but he or she has no independent right to consent to or refuse the treatment. "Necessary" medical treatment has traditionally been interpreted to mean only treatment necessary to save the life of the child.[27] However, in recent years, the courts have become more willing to order desirable, but not life-preserving, medical procedures over parental objection.[28] Nevertheless, cases holding that mental health services constitute necessary medical treatment are very rare.[29]

Financial Liability for Treatment

Even if the child is able to give valid consent and has done so, he or she may be precluded from obtaining treatment because of an absence of funds to pay for it. Although parents generally are liable for their children's necessary medical expenses, they probably would not be required to pay for nonemergency treatment to which they had refused consent or about which they had not been consulted. Thus it is unlikely that parents would be required to pay for routine psychological services provided to their child without their consent unless they were considered to be "necessaries." Similarly, courts usually refuse to require the parents of an emancipated child to pay his or her medical bills.

It should be noted, however, that statutes have been proposed for making insurance companies liable, under certain circumstances, for treatment of children to which the parents (and policy holders) did not consent.[31] Nevertheless, such statutes might not fully solve the problem, for the fact that it would be difficult for a child to contact an insurance company and for the latter to provide coverage for the claim without the parents' discovering that treatment was being obtained might deter the child from seeking coverage.

Where the parents are not liable as a result of their child's emancipation, the minor will clearly be legally responsible for the cost of treatment although practically speaking he or she may simply not have the funds to pay. Where the minor is not emancipated, however, his or her liability depends upon whether the minor was competent to enter into a binding contract for services (i.e., treatment). Minors are generally considered competent to enter into (and are bound by) contracts only if they are for the purchase of "necessaries." In other words, a child cannot use his or her minor status as a basis for disaffirming (backing out of) such a contract. Once an agreement has been made to purchase necessaries, the minor is legally obligated to pay for them. (Note, however, that the same problem of penniless purchasers can occur here also.) Both medical and dental care are generally considered to be necessaries. Psychiatric treatment, especially for a severe emotional disturbance, would probably be included as well. Mental health services provided by psychologists and nonmedical professionals, however, are less likely to be viewed by the courts as "necessaries"; therefore, it is conceivable that in some circumstances neither the child nor the parent would be liable for such treatment.

Current Practices

Despite the formidable legal impediments to the provision of mental health services to minors without parental consent, the general practice among American clinicians seems to be to provide those services anyway. A recent survey of mental health professionals and other counselors in Massachusetts found that 75 percent of them treated children under age 16 without parental consent, apparently contrary to state law (study by Apsler, cited in Wilson, 1978). In another investigation, in which questionnaires were sent to 30 private agencies in Maryland, 10 of the 12 agencies that responded reported counseling minors without parental consent, one said that such treatment had occurred once only, and one answered that children were not counseled there without parental consent (Note, 1971). And a third study, in a state that had recently enacted a minor consent statute covering psychiatric services, found that many of the public mental health clinics in the state had had a policy of accepting minors as patients without parental consent even before the enactment of the law (Melton, 1981b). It is not clear whether these practices, in violation of implicit or explicit per se rules in state statutes, are based on ignorance of the law or on ethical, or perhaps constitutional, objections to the law.

TREATMENT IN INSTITUTIONS

Institutional settings present special issues in terms of rights of minors to access to treatment. The right of juveniles residing involuntarily in state institutions to receive treatment while confined is well established in the law. Although the Supreme Court has never addressed this issue, several federal courts have held that institutionalized minors have a right to adequate treatment.[32] The right has been granted to children who are temporarily detained,[33] to adjudicated delinquents,[34] to status offenders (e.g., children found to be "in need of supervision"),[35] to neglected children who have been removed from their homes,[36] and to children "voluntarily" admitted into institutions by their parents.[37] Probably because a variety of such juveniles is often found in one institution, the courts have usually not distinguished among them and, when they have, have still found that the same rights apply to all.

Courts have based the finding of a right to treatment on several constitutional arguments, each of which derives from a line of cases involving the right to treatment of adults who are institutionalized in hospitals for the mentally ill. First, some courts have noted that the state justifies the fact that a juvenile is *not* granted procedural protections equivalent to those accorded criminal defendants on the grounds that his or her confinement will confer a benefit (rehabilitation) on him or her.[38] If this justification for fewer protections is used, they conclude, then the state should be obligated to provide that benefit.[39] Another, and possibly more persuasive, argument suggests that, if the state's purpose in institutionalizing minors (whether or not they are delinquents) is to help or rehabilitate them, then it is constitutionally required to provide treatment aimed at accomplishing that goal. This rehabilitative purpose is not only found in the history and original purpose of the juvenile court but also is specifically articulated in many state statutes establishing juvenile institutions or juvenile court systems. Thus, if the state fails to provide rehabilitative services to children it confines, it has violated the fundamental principle of constitutional law that states that the nature and duration of involuntary confinement must be reasonably related to its purpose.[40] Finally, some courts have taken the position that a denial of treatment to those held in noncriminal custody may violate the Eighth Amendment's prohibition against cruel and unusual punishment or the equal protection clause of the Fourteenth Amendment.[41] Employing various combinations of the above arguments, as well as relying upon applicable state statutes, the courts have declared several juvenile facilities to be in violation of the law. In doing so, they have invoked the right to treatment doctrine not only to mandate the development of treatment programs but also to order major changes in the conditions of confinement imposed upon minors.

Adequate Treatment Defined

Judicial opinions have articulated the treatment requirements in the context of the adult mentally ill with great specificity. In the landmark case of *Wyatt v. Stickney*,[42] for example, the judge listed three essential components of adequate treatment—a humane physical and psychological environment, individualized treatment plans, and professional staff in adequate numbers to implement those plans. He also outlined specific and detailed quantitative and qualitative standards, ranging from staff-patient ratios to the number of toilets required.[43] Recognizing that psychiatry and psychology are imprecise sciences, the courts have not required doctors to prove that the treatment provided will actually cure the patients but only that it constitutes a bona fide and professionally accepted effort to help them.[44]

The courts have defined adequate treatment of children to include all of the conditions required for adults.[45] In addition, they have cited several characteristics of young people that justify the imposition of further requirements in juvenile facilities. Most obvious and important of these characteristics is the child's need for education[46]; thus it has been held that institutionalized juveniles are entitled not only to traditional schooling but also to special education classes and bilingual instruction.[47] In addition, children should be provided with recreation and play opportunities[48] and regular and frequent access to mental health professionals.[49] Furthermore, the minor's individualized treatment program must be specifically tailored to his or her developmental and maturational level.[50] *Morales v. Turman*,[51] the broadest federal case in this area, has even required vocational education, as well as individual or group psychotherapy for each child for whom it is indicated.

The special vulnerability of children has also been cited by the courts as justifying the imposition of additional constraints upon the staffs of juvenile facilities, especially regarding the use of seclusion or isolation rooms. In *Lollis v. N.Y. State Department of Social Services*,[52] the first federal case to address this issue, the court held that seclusion of a PINS girl (status offender) for two weeks without anything to do violated the Eighth Amendment's proscription against cruel and unusual punishment. The defendant, a state institution, was ordered to develop standards for the use of seclusion to prevent further violation.[53] One court has even ruled that, after a minor has been solitarily confined for five days, he or she is entitled to a hearing.[54] Durational limits below five days have not, however, been imposed. Thus one court refused to prohibit either (1) seclusion for over two hours without a psychiatric certification of dangerousness or (2) seclusion for over 24 hours in one week, stating that it lacked sufficient evidence to know exactly when isolation becomes harmful to a child.[55] The use of physical restraints on juveniles is likely to be similarly scrutinized by the courts. In *Lollis,* for example, the court was receptive to the plaintiff's argument that she had been unconstitutionally handcuffed and bound but refused to rule on this issue because it lacked sufficient evidence regarding how long such restraint had lasted.[56]

Corporal punishment and drug treatment are also subject to restriction. Thus, in *Nelson v. Hyne,*[57] a federal circuit court of appeals concluded that the beating of children housed in an Indiana boys' school, as punishment for escapes or assaults, constituted cruel and unusual punishment. The court also ruled unconstitutional the boys' school's practice of allowing nurses to administer injections of major tranquilizers under standing orders from physicians, without trying less extreme medications first and without guidance from the physicians.[58] Finally, judicial decisions declaring the unconsented use of aversive conditioning programs for adults to be a violation of the Eighth Amendment's prohibition against cruel and unusual punishment[59] are likely to be extended to the treatment of children when such cases arise. In addition, the use of aversive conditioning in the treatment of mentally ill or mentally retarded adults has been strictly regulated by statute or regulation in many states, and such restrictions may be applicable to children as well. Right-to-treatment decisions, also, implicitly limit the range of acceptable reinforcement to a significant extent; for instance, any item essential to a humane and healthy environment (e.g., food) probably cannot be used

(Wexler, 1973). Furthermore, some states require external review of the use of such treatment in addition to the obtaining of personal—or, in the case of a minor, parental —consent.[60]

A third argument, besides those regarding the special needs and vulnerabilities of children, has been suggested as the basis for a higher standard of care for minors in institutions. Citing the *parens patriae* purposes behind the state's confinement of children, this position maintains that, once the state removes the child from the home, it is obligated to provide to him or her, "so far as can reasonably be required...what proper parental care would provide."[61] In other words, the state must provide all that is necessary to assure the normal growth and development of the child. If taken to its logical extreme, this position would prohibit any antitherapeutic conditions and any failure to provide a service that could help the juvenile to attain his or her full potential. However, no court has imposed such a demanding standard on a state institution, probably because judges recognize that many parents would have difficulty meeting it themselves. Nevertheless, this argument raises the important point that the state should consider carefully the alternatives it has to offer before it removes a child from the home. Furthermore, federal statutory requirements for meeting all of a child's special educational needs, including needs for "related services" such as psychotherapy,[61] may come close to mandating this higher standard, regardless of whether it is constitutionally required.

REFUSAL OF TREATMENT

As the discussion thus far has revealed, the children's rights movement in general and the right to consent to treatment in particular have been supported by two very different lines of reasoning, one advocating child protection, the other child autonomy. It is important to note, however, that these two strains of analysis necessarily lead to diametrically opposed positions on the question of whether a mentally competent child who has been given the right to consent to treatment is also entitled to refuse it.

Briefly, the *parens patriae* approach, sometimes referred to as "child saving," approves of minor consent in order to encourage beneficial treatment and thereby protect the child from harm. Thus this view is not only inconsistent with, but arguably even prohibits, the granting of a right to refuse treatment to children, because such a right could prevent minors from receiving needed help.

The child autonomy, or "kiddie lib" position, on the other hand, supports right to consent to treatment, because: (1) basic respect for children as human beings requires that they be allowed to participate in decisions regarding their lives to the maximum extent that they are capable; and (2) neither parents nor state can be relied upon to act in the child's best interests anyway. This approach, of course, logically implies that a child who is legally and mentally competent to consent to a given treatment should also be allowed to refuse that treatment if he or she wishes to do so.

Minor Consent Statutes

Courts have generally applied this second line of reasoning in interpreting minor consent statues. Thus, for example, in *In re Smith*,[63] the Maryland Supreme Court was asked to construe a state law that provided that, for pregnancy-related treatment, "a minor shall have the same capacity to consent as an adult." The case involved a pregnant 16-year-old girl who had been ordered by a juvenile court to obey her mother's direction to get an abortion; the girl preferred to marry her boyfriend and have her child, and the physician to whom her mother brought her refused to perform the operation without the girl's consent. The Maryland high court had no trouble interpreting the statute as implying a right to refuse the abortion, possibly because of the law's explicit presumption of competency. In a similar case,[64] the Connecticut Supreme Court held that a statute authorizing

children aged 16 or older to admit themselves to mental hospitals necessarily implied that a 17-year-old boy who had been "voluntarily" admitted to a hospital by his parents two years earlier could sign himself out against their wishes.

Limited Right to Resist Certain Treatments

Even where a right to consent to treatment has not been provided, however, there may be reason to grant the child a limited right to refuse. Particularly where a significant deprivation of rights could result, such as when hospitalization or an instrusive or aversive therapy is proposed, reliance on the parent's judgment alone might not be warranted. In such situations, it has been argued, the child's objection to his or her parent's decision should trigger an external review of the need for treatment.

Hospitalization of Adults

Adults enter mental hospitals in two ways. First, an individual may be the subject of a petition for involuntary commitment. In such situations, the due process clause of the Constitution mandates that he or she be given a judicial hearing, at which he or she is represented by counsel and has a right to offer evidence.[65] The judge hearing the petition can order hospitalization only if he or she finds the individual to be both mentally ill and either (1) dangerous to himself or herself, (2) dangerous to others, or (3) unable to care for himself or herself. Furthermore, institutionalization can only be used if no less restrictive alternative forms of treatment are available, and its appropriateness must be periodically reviewed.[66]

Second, an individual can enter the hospital voluntarily. If mentally competent to make such a decision, he or she can simply request admission to the facility, which can admit the person even if he or she does not meet the above criteria for civil commitment. Whenever the voluntary patient decides to leave, the hospital must discharge him or her although it can be required that notice of an intention to leave be given one or two days beforehand. In addition, in some states, the voluntary patient is allowed to refuse medication or other treatments to which he or she objects.[67]

Hospitalization of Children

Like adults, children can enter mental institutions either as voluntary or as involuntary patients. In most states, however, it is the parent rather than the child who is authorized to request the latter's "voluntary" admission, which will be granted as long as the hospital staff agrees that the child needs treatment (Ellis, 1974). The parent is also authorized to exercise on behalf of the child the other rights that accrue to a voluntary patient—the right to petition (and receive) discharge and to consent to or refuse medication.

The Supreme Court upheld the "voluntary" admission of juveniles by their parents in the 1979 case of *Parham* v. *J. R.*[68] That case was an appeal from a three-judge federal court's decision declaring unconstitutional a Georgia statute that allowed parents to admit their children to mental hospitals "voluntarily" and provided no judicial review of the need for inpatient treatment.[69] Rejecting the lower court's conclusion that parents should not be assumed to act in their children's best interests, the Court held that a minor can be constitutionally confined in a mental hospital without a hearing of any kind.

In reaching this result, Chief Justice Burger, writing for the majority, emphasized that a formal hearing could disrupt the parent/child relationship and further upset an already emotionally unstable child. It could also deter parents from seeking needed treatment for their offspring. Furthermore, approval of the parents' request by a staff physician from the institution to which commitment was sought was sufficient protection against parents who might try to use hospitalization to abandon a healthy child. Even where the minor was in the custody of a state agency, the Court held, the agency could act in the same way that a parent could, and no further safeguards were warranted.

This faith in parental decision making and

medical restraint was reiterated in *Secretary of Public Welfare v. Institutionalized Juveniles,*[70] a companion case to *Parham* decided the same day. In that case, the Supreme Court overturned a federal court in Pennsylvania, which had ruled that children in that state were constitutionally entitled to a full adversary hearing prior to hospitalization.[71] Quoting language in *Parham* requiring a "neutral factfinder" who interviews the prospective patient,[72] the Court held that a psychiatric examination conducted on admission by the hospital treatment team satisfied this requirement. The Court also emphasized that periodic reassessment of a child's condition is necessary to insure that the initial admission decision is made correctly and ruled that state regulations requiring review of a patient's condition every 30 days constituted sufficient periodic review.

The Supreme Court's decisions in *Parham* and *Institutionalized Juveniles* do not, however, prohibit a state from providing additional procedural protections for minors who may be hospitalized. These decisions merely state that such protections are not constitutionally required. Thus several states have at least partially adopted the approach taken by the lower federal courts in these cases, mandating more adversarial procedures for the hospitalization of certain juveniles.

The Pennsylvania statute at issue in *Institutionalized Juveniles,* for example, applied only to children less than 14 years old.[73] Older minors could not be hospitalized against their will without a full hearing. Similarly, Michigan has a law that permits children aged 13 or older to object to "voluntary" admission and thereby trigger a formal commitment hearing.[74] And Tennessee has adopted a statute authorizing all juveniles aged 16 or over to consent to their own voluntary admission and allowing all other minors admitted "voluntarily" to request and obtain a discharge unless the hospital petitions for and wins an order of involuntary commitment.[75]

There are a number of reasons to support these developments on the state level.[76] First, they acknowledge that parents do not always recognize or act in their children's best interests, especially when seeking mental health treatment. Despite the best of intentions, parents might fail to recognize personal or family pathologies that contribute to a child's behavior (see Ellis, 1974) or might misperceive lifestyle differences as mental illness (see Holder, 1977).

Second, it is unrealistic to assume that the hospital psychiatrist or psychologist who admits the child will provide a check to the danger of overhospitalization by parents. To begin with, clinicians often differ on individual diagnoses, partly because they are forced to rely on potentially unreliable sources such as family and friends of the child for much of the information on which they base those diagnoses. Furthermore, a clinician is likely to err on the side of finding severe mental illness and recommending hospitalization. His or her humanistic concern for the prospective patient, orientation towards helping and healing, and understandable concerns about malpractice liability, all cause the mental health professional to overdiagnose. In addition, he or she may be influenced (perhaps unconsciously) by institutional pressures, such as those stemming from over- or undercrowding or high level preferences for certain types of patients. Finally, the fact that the psychiatrist or psychologist is asked to admit the child by the parent (an adult with whom he or she will probably be able to communicate easily) might cause the clinician to overidentify with the latter and prevent him or her from conducting a completely objective evaluation.

A third reason for prohibiting parental admission of a child without a hearing is that such a procedure provides no assurance that the parent, physician, or anyone else will pursue the possibility of less extreme forms of treatment before hospitalizing the child and review such alternatives as soon as his or her condition improves. The right to be confined in a manner that restricts one's freedom as little as possible and to receive periodic review of the appropriateness of such confinement are fundamental elements of due process for adults who are civilly committed.[77] In order to prevent unnecessary removal from the home and harmful prolongation of institutional con-

finement, such rights should be provided to children as well.

CONFIDENTIALITY

Adults

Confidentiality involves an individual's right to prohibit his or her therapist from disclosing to others information that the individual communicates during the course of treatment. It is related to, but different from, testimonial privileges, which will be addressed below. The mental health professional has both an ethical (e.g., American Psychological Association, 1981, Principle 5) and, in many states, a legal duty to preserve the confidences of his or her clients. This duty has been imposed not only out of concern for the client's personal feelings and rights but also for two more practical, policy-oriented reasons. First, the knowlege that their communications will be confidential encourages people to seek needed treatment in the first place. Second, that knowledge facilitates the development of a trusting relationship and a willingness to be completely honest with the therapist, thereby increasing the chances that the treatment will be successful.

Also, for reasons of social policy, the confidentiality of therapist/patient communications is not absolute. Thus, for instance, in order to protect the general welfare, a professional whose patient has a contagious disease is often legally required to inform anyone who might come in contact with that person, and all states either authorize or require a professional who suspects that a child has been abused to report that suspicion to a social services agency. Some courts have even required psychiatrists with dangerous clients either to warn the known potential victims of such violence or to take other actions to prevent it.[78]

Children

While the legal rules regarding confidentiality of adults' records and communications are currently in a state of flux, those regarding children are even less clear. It should be noted, however, before exploring these issues in detail, that, in certain areas of confidentiality, the legal rules are spelled out in meticulous detail. The most important example of such a detailed articulation of confidentiality rules is the federal regulations on substance abuse treatment that govern any state agency that receives federal funds.[79] Those regulations have produced their own set of problems, which there is insufficient space to discuss here, but the regulations should certainly be read closely by any clinician who deals with drug- or alcohol-abusing children.

Where Parents Have Consented to Treatment

In general, parents are authorized to have access to their children's records, whether they are in the custody of a mental health professional, a school, or a juvenile court.[80] However, parents do not necessarily have the right to control the disclosure of such records. For instance, many states allow attorneys, welfare departments, and insurance companies to obtain a child's mental hospital records, and some even have a catchall provision authorizing disclosure whenever it would be in the minor's best interest (see Wilson, 1978, p. 261). Similarly, while juvenile court records, often containing reports of psychological evaluations and social history material, are generally confidential, special exceptions for school officials and others are frequently found (Wilson, 1978, pp. 263–265).

Children are rarely statutorily granted a personal right of access, as opposed to a right that is exercised by parents or guardians. Only three states specifically authorize children themselves to see their hospital records, and only eight allow personal viewing of juvenile court records (Wilson, 1978). Thus, where the minor has not been treated as competent to consent to treatment on his or her own, his or her confidentiality rights are usually exercised by the parents only.

It could be argued, of course, that even a child who has not consented to his or her own treatment might still be capable of appreciating the importance and meaning of confi-

dentiality and resent disclosure to parents or others of information that he or she has conveyed to a therapist. Nevertheless, parental access is probably appropriate in such situations if for no other reason than that the parent is responsible for consenting to third-party access and needs to be familiar with the records to make such decisions. At a minimum, however, the child should be informed by the mental health professional of the limited confidentiality that will be accorded to his or her communications (American Psychological Association, 1981, Principle 5). In addition, the clinician can attempt to obtain the parents' permission to delete extremely sensitive material before giving the records to them.

Where the Child Has Consented to Treatment

The confidentiality rights of a child who has consented to treatment are far less clear than those of an adult who has so consented. Statutes in this area frequently fail to address the issue of confidentiality at all and, when they do address it, often do so inadequately or inconsistently. Some minor consent statutes, for example, are silent on the question of whether the minor not only has a right to consent to treatment but also has a concomitant right to control access to the records of that treatment.[81] Others specifically authorize the service provider to inform the parents that the child is receiving treatment[82] but may still be unclear as to whether he or she can also disclose the details of such treatment to them. In the absence of a minor consent statute, the situation is murkier still. There is no case law, for example, on whether a mature minor has confidentiality rights during the course of treatment to which he or she provided valid consent. A recent Supreme Court opinion could be read as implying that a mature minor seeking an abortion might have a right to prohibit disclosure of her plans to her parents, but the Court did not address that question directly.[83]

In support of full disclosure to the parents whose child has independently consented to treatment, it can be argued that mental health treatment is rarely effective if the family is not included and that the parents cannot effectively fulfill their duty to care for and protect their offspring unless they are aware of all significant factors in the latter's life. On the other hand, mandatory disclosure arguably vitiates the primary purpose of minor consent statues and the mature minor rule—the encouragement of treatment that the minor would be unlikely to seek if parental consent were required. In other words, merely the knowledge that his or her parents would be informed of the treatment, even where the parent could not prohibit it, might be sufficient to dissuade a youth from seeking such treatment to begin with. In addition, respect for the mature child's autonomy, privacy, and judgment dictate that his or her confidentiality rights should be recognized.

This is not to imply, however, that the clinician's duty to preserve confidences is or should be exactly the same for juvenile clients as for adult clients. For example, as mentioned above, it has been held that a clinician has a duty to warn the potential victim of an adult client's threats to harm him or her,[84] and that duty can logically be extended to clinicians who treat juveniles.[85] Nonetheless, while it has also been held that there is no corresponding duty to warn the family of an adult client's suicidal tendencies,[86] the fact that both the parents and the state are legally obligated to protect dependent minors from harm might constitute sufficient reason to impose such a duty when the therapist is treating a minor. In fact, it could even be argued that the parents' duty to care for and control their children entitles them to be informed of self-destructive or violent behavior that does not reach suicidal or homicidal proportions. There is, however, little case law on this question. Therefore, the clinician is well advised to establish a policy regarding disclosures to parents, discuss that policy with his or her client when beginning treatment, and carefully document both the policy itself and the reasons for any exceptions that he or she makes to it.

One interesting approach to reconciling the competing concerns in this area has been suggested by the Institute of Judicial Administration/American Bar Association Juvenile Justice Standards Project (1980, Standards Relating to the Rights of Minors, Std. 4.2, Commentary). In its proposal, the Project distinguishes between drug treatment and pregnancy-related treatment (including abortions and treatment for venereal disease) on the one hand and treatment for emotional or mental disorders on the other. It allows a child of any age to consent to the former (if competent to do so) and prohibits disclosure of such treatment to parents without the child's consent unless failure to notify them could seriously jeopardize the child's health. However, the Standards require notification of parents whose child is receiving mental health treatment (which can be consented to only by children over 14), after three therapy sessions and prohibit further treatment without parental consent. The Project justifies these restrictions on the grounds that such treatment has a potential impact on familial relationships, requires family involvement to be effective, and could continue for a prolonged period of time.

Where a Court Has Ordered Treatment

Confidentiality questions also arise when the child is receiving treatment under a court order. Such treatment is often imposed as a condition of probation, in which case the child's failure to comply with the court's order could result in a revocation of the probation and confinement in a juvenile institution. Thus a mental health professional treating a minor pursuant to a court order may be asked to inform the probation officer or the judge if the client stops treatment or misses an appointment. In states where the juvenile court is authorized to order state agencies to provide services to a child, the therapist may even be ordered to report any absence to the court. However, if no such order exists, the clinician is left to his or her own judgment as to the appropriate action to take. If he or she decides to notify the court in such situations, the therapist should at least inform all patients beforehand that he or she will report any willful failure to comply with a court order mandating treatment (see Juvenile Justice Standards Project, Standards Relating to Dispositions, 1980: Standard 5.4). Even where operating under a court order mandating notification of the judge, however, the clinician should first attempt to determine whether the client had a legitimate reason for missing an appointment in order to insure that the judge's subsequent action is based upon a full understanding of the situation.

In general, many of the problems regarding court-ordered treatment can be avoided by clearly working out with the judge ahead of time the terms of disclosure of confidential information. Such discussions with court personnel will not only prevent conflict or confusion on individual cases but might also lead to increased understanding on the part of the judge of the importance of confidentiality in treatment and encourage him or her to agree to more limited disclosure in such situations.

Testimonial Privileges

Adults

The physician/patient privilege provides that a doctor can be prohibited from testifying in court regarding a confidential communication that related to the treatment sought and was made by his or her patient in the course of receiving treatment. Over two-thirds of the states have adopted this rule by statute (see generally, Wilson, 1978). Unfortunately, however, the privilege is sometimes interpreted as covering only treatment for physical illness, so that not only psychologists (who are excluded because they are not medically trained) but also psychiatrists may have to testify in court.

The purpose of the privilege is to assure the confidentiality necessary to encourage people to seek, and facilitate the successfulness of, necessary medical treatment. For similar reasons, most states protect other relationships such as the attorney/client relationship and the priest/penitent relationship through privileges as well. The doctor/patient privilege can be asserted only by the patient; in other words, the physician cannot refuse to testify if his or her patient has no objection. Also, it may be

eliminated for compelling policy reasons, such as preventing epidemics or a need for more information, which the judge in his or her own discretion can decide are sufficiently crucial to override the patient's confidentiality rights. Finally, the privilege cannot be asserted where the very condition for which the patient sought treatment has been put at issue by the patient.

In addition to physician/patient privilege statutes, many jurisdictions have passed specific psychotherapist/patient privilege statutes as well. These laws, however, usually list the particular professionals included (and whether certification is required) and courts often refuse to extend coverage to types of clinicians not specifically mentioned. Thus, not only are psychiatric social workers often excluded, but also psychologists and even psychiatrists may find themselves covered by neither the physician/patient nor the psychotherapist/patient statute in their state (Wilson, 1978).

Children

It is possible that, where parents have consented to the treatment of their child, the assertion or waiver of the therapist/patient privilege will be held to be up to them. Privilege laws rarely address this question directly, but conclusions can sometimes be drawn from the statutory language. For example, if the term "patient" is defined to include minors and the patient is specifically given the power to assert the privilege, then the parent is less likely to be able to do so for his or her child.[87] However, statutes usually provide little guidance, and the courts have not addressed the issue. Therefore, in the absence of a statutory provision to the contrary, a clinician should probably inform minor patients, where such a possibility is likely, that the clinician could be required to testify in court as to their confidential communications if their parents consent to such disclosures.

Where the child himself or herself has consented to treatment, the arguments in favor of allowing him or her to assert the testimonial privilege are the same as those concerning the confidentiality of records: personal dignity, autonomy, promotion of full disclosure during therapy, and potential for parents to fail to act in the child's best interest. Here, as in the confidentiality area, there is little case law concerning how these considerations should be balanced against parental rights and obligations. Thus, until this issue has been resolved by the courts, the best that a clinician can do is to inform his or her child client, where appropriate, that waiver of the privilege by his or her parents, while unlikely, might be allowed by a court.

CHILDREN'S COMPETENCY

Implicit in many of the statutes and judicial opinions regarding children's rights in the treatment context are assumptions regarding whether minors are capable of appreciating, or at least of benefiting from, the right to make their own treatment choices. While developmental research and theory are obviously relevant to these determinations, the courts have virtually ignored the psychological literature.[88] It is beyond the scope of this chapter to review in detail the expanding literature on the capacity of minors to make various decisions and the effects of decisional autonomy on them and their families (for extensive reviews, see Grisso & Vierling, 1978; Koocher, 1983; Melton, 1981a, 1983; Weithorn, 1982, 1983). Nonetheless, a brief overview of the current state of knowledge on those subjects provides a useful empirical basis for consideration of the difficult legal and ethical questions facing legislators, judges, and clinicians who deal with the treatment of children.

In their seminal review of research relevant to children's competence to consent to therapy, Grisso and Vierling (1978) analyzed the cognitive capacity to give "knowing and intelligent" consent, by drawing inferences from research on minors' abilities to assimilate and analyze complex information at different developmental stages. They also speculated on developmental trends in the "voluntariness" of children's treatment decisions, based on social-developmental research on children's

deference to authority (cf. Saks, 1978). Grisso and Vierling (1978) reached the following conclusions on the basis of their review of these two lines of developmental research:

1. There may be no circumstances that would justify sanctioning independent consent by minors under 11 years of age given the developmental psychological evidence for their diminished psychological capacities.

2. There appear to be no psychological grounds for maintaining the general assumption that minors at age 15 and above cannot provide competent consent.

3. Ages 11–14 appear to be a transition period in the development of important cognitive abilities and perceptions of social expectations, but there may be some circumstances that would justify allowing independent consent by these minors for limited purposes, especially when competence can be demonstrated in individual cases. (p. 424)

While Grisso and Vierling's review was generally well reasoned, there were two important weaknesses in the article, reflecting the state of the literature at the time. First, the review was largely devoid of studies dealing dirctly with treatment decisions. Second, the samples used in most of the studies cited were not clinical samples and may have been unrepresentative of children actually involved in treatment decisions.

There are now several studies directly on point, however. These investigations have generally found strong developmental trends of the sort predicted by Grisso and Vierling, as might be expected given the complexity of the social-causality notions necessary to an adequate understanding of psychotherapy and emotional disturbance. Thus it has been found that accurate perception of professional help givers (Dollinger & Thelen, 1978) and understanding of social factors in childhood disturbances (e.g., Coie & Pennington, 1976; Dollinger, Thelen, & Walsh, 1980; Novak, 1974, 1975) increase developmentally. As to the child's ability affirmatively to assert the right to consent to treatment, the evidence suggests that there are developmental factors in children's ability to conceptualize a right as an entitlement that can be claimed rather than as a privilege that is passively accepted (Melton, 1980).

Even where immature minors are involved, however, at least for therapies entailing minimal risk or aversiveness, the dangers of allowing them to make their own treatment decisions may not be as great as one would expect. A particularly persuasive study on this point, conducted recently by Weithorn (1980), involved the administering of a series of vignettes about both medical and psychological problems to normal 9-, 14-, 18-, and 21-year-olds. Consistent with previous research, Weithorn found the 14-year-olds to be as adept as the adult groups in understanding relevant information and reasoning about treatment decisions. Of particular import here, however, is that the 9-year-olds, while using immature reasoning, reached the same decisions as the older groups. While definitive conclusions cannot be drawn until this laboratory study is confirmed by evaluations of real life treatment decision making by children, its results suggest that, at least for "routine" treatment decisions, even young children would often meet "reasonable person" tests in their treatment decisions. That conclusion is further suggested by studies of children's decision making in "open" health care (Lewis, C.E., 1983) and education settings (Rosen, 1978), which show not only that children rarely make outrageous decisions but also that, when given some responsibility for routine decisions, they experience a heightened sense of efficacy as a result. These findings are consistent with predictions based on the moral development and legal socialization literatures (cf. Melton, 1983).

On the other hand, autonomy may have detrimental effects as well. It may provide too much power to immature children, producing stress and anxiety rather than augmenting the minor's sense of control. Furthermore, it will necessarily effect a redistribution of power within the child's world and may produce or increase conflicts between the child and his or her parents or other authority figures such as teachers, "setting up" the child for punishment. Thus minors might not benefit from the

power to make their own treatment decisions unless both they and the significant adults in their lives are able to accept this allocation of increased independence. Nonetheless, it is important to note that there is essentially no empirical basis for the assertion of some clinical theorists, most notably Goldstein, Freud, A., and Solnit (1973, 1979) that children generally *need* seemingly omnipotent parents (for a similar view not based on psychoanalytic theory, see Baumrind, 1980). Evidence is also lacking to support the idea, suggested by the Supreme Court in *Parham,*[89] that instituting formal due process procedures in instances of potential parent-child conflict over treatment alternatives will result in psychological harm to the child. Indeed, there is some reason to predict psychological *benefits* from such procedures (Melton & Lind, 1982). Careful evaluation research on programs in which minors have been given some decision-making authority is needed to identify more specifically the circumstances under which autonomy is beneficial to children and the factors related to individual differences in response to increased autonomy.

In summary, there is a growing body of data to support the conclusion that older adolescents (beginning about age 14) can make treatment decisions as well as adults and can appreciate and benefit from increased decisional authority. Furthermore, elementary school children can frequently respond appropriately when given the opportunity to make routine treatment decisions. Additional research is needed, however, with clinical samples in actual treatment contexts, in order to produce data that can be generalized more confidently to similar groups and settings.

CONCLUSIONS

As has been noted throughout this chapter, the *ultimate* distribution of authority among child, parents, and state is unclear legally. Nonetheless, there appears to be no reason legally why children should not be encouraged at least to *participate* in decision making about their treatment (or lack of it), even if they do not actually possess the power of consent or refusal. The empirical evidence suggests that even elementary school children can handle some of this responsibility. We would argue that, except where they will be harmed by exercising such autonomy, respect for children as persons requires attention to their views and concerns.

Beyond the ethical imperative involved, such participation by children in their treatment planning is, pragmatically, simply good clinical practice. Holmes and Urie (1975) found that pretherapy interviews with children, to review their expectations and to establish a truly mutual treatment contract between therapist and child client, reduced premature terminations. Similarly, Day and Reznikoff (1980) found that inaccurate expectations of therapy by children were related to treatment dropout.

Finally, there are also both ethical and pragmatic reasons for protecting minors' privacy in treatment relationships insofar as possible. (In this regard, clinicians should, however, be sensitive to prevailing law in their jurisdictions, which may limit this prerogative.) Respect for privacy is grounded ethically in respect for personal dignity, for the integrity of the self. Assuming again that one views children as "persons," such respect would logically accrue to them ethically, barring a demonstrable harm.

There are some indications that adolescents may even avoid treatment without a guarantee of privacy (see Melton, 1983, for review). In addition, in adolescence, privacy tends increasingly to be conceptualized as information management (i.e., protection of confidences) rather than as physical privacy (Wolfe, 1979). One of us has discussed the potential impact of this line of research and theory elsewhere (Melton, 1983):

Wolfe (1979) has hypothesized more generalized personality effects of maintenance of privacy. She and her colleagues have argued that experiences of privacy are important in development of sense of self. Specifically, in the present context, successful information management by adolescents might be important in keeping a close relationship with peers byeond the limits of the family and in developing intimacy and sense of oneself as an independent person. One might add that respect for information management might increase sense of interpersonal trust and self-esteem (as a respected person). While these possible personality effects are important ones, they are at this point essentially intuitive hypotheses based to a large extent on clinical theory. They might be researched through interventions designed to increase privacy of thought in home or school situations. (p. 34)

In general, research in natural settings is needed on what in fact *does* happen when minors' privacy and autonomy are increased. Nonetheless, the few such investigations available (see Lewis, C.C., 1980, on abortion decisions; Lewis, C.E., 1983, on a pediatric "card-care" system; Melton, in press-c, on the effects of a mental health consent statute), combined with interview studies reviewed elsewhere in this chapter, give ample reason to treat most minors as partners in the treatment process.

NOTES

1. 387 U.S. 1 (1967).
2. 393 U.S. 503 (1969).
3. Eisenstadt v. Baird, 405 U.S. 438 (1972); Griswold v. Connecticut, 381 U.S. 479 (1965).
4. Planned Parenthood of Central Missouri v. Danforth, 428 U.S. 52 (1976).
5. Roe v. Wade, 410 U.S. 113 (1973).
6. Planned Parenthood of Central Missouri v. Danforth, *supra* note 4.
7. Parham v. J.R., 442 U.S. 584, 603 (1979).
8. *See, e.g.,* Pierce v. Society of Sisters, 268 U.S. 510 (1925).
9. *See, e.g.,* Wisconsin v. Yoder, 406 U.S. 205 (1972).
10. *Cf.* Parham v. J.R., *supra* note 7, at 610 (1979) (possibility of disruption of parent/ child relationship cited as reason for denying right to hearing before mental hospitalization).
11. Pierce v. Society of Sisters, *supra* note 8.
12. United States v. Darby, 312 U.S. 100 (1940).
13. *E.g.,* Roe v. Connecticut, 417 F. Supp. 769, 779 (M.D. Ala. 1976) (dicta).

14. *E.g.,* State v. Perricone, 37 N.J. 463 (1962); *In re* Seiferth, 309 N.Y. 80 (1955); *In re* Hudson, 13 Wash.2d 673 (1942); *cf. In re* Sampson, 65 Misc. 2d 658 (N.Y. 1970) (overriding parents' decision where no threat of death existed).

15. *See, e.g., In re* Sealy, 218 So.2d 765 (Dist. Ct. App. 1969).

16. *See, e.g., In re* Sippy, 97 A.2d 455 (D.C. 1953).

17. *See, e.g., In re* Anonymous, 42 Misc. 2d 572 (N.Y. 1964).

18. For a medical case raising such issues, see *In re* Green, 448 Pa. 338 (1972).

19. *See* Younts v. St. Francis Hospital and School of Nursing, Inc., 205 Kan. 292 (1970); Lacey v. Laird, 166 Ohio St. 12 (Sup. Ct. 1956).

20. *E.g.,* Bonner v. Moran, 126 F.2d 121 (D.C. Cir. 1941) (minor not allowed to consent to skin graft to help burned cousin).

21. *E.g.,* MISS. CODE ANN. § 41-43-3(h) (1972).

22. Planned Parenthood of Central Missouri v. Danforth, *supra* note 4.

23. *See, e.g.,* H.L. v. Matheson, 450 U.S. 398 (1981).

24. *E.g.,* VA. CODE ANN. § 54-325.2(d)(4) (Cum. Supp. 1979).

25. *E.g.,* ARK. STAT. ANN. § 82-363 (1973).

26. *Compare* DEL. CODE ANN. tit. 13 § 708 (1953), as amended *and* ARK. STAT. ANN., *supra* note 25.

27. *See, e.g., In re* Seiferth, 309 N.Y. 80 (1955); *In re* Hudson, 13 Wash. 2d 763 (1942).

28. *See, e.g., In re* Karwath, 199 N.W.2d 147 (Iowa 1972); *In re* Sampson, 65 Misc. 2d 658 (N.Y. 1970).

29. *But see In re* Carstairs, 115 N.Y.S. 2d 314 (1952).

30. *E.g.,* Poudre Valley Hospital District v. Heckert, 491 P.2d 984 (Colo. 1971); Ison v. Fla. Sanitorium and Benevolent Ass'n., 302 So. 2d 200 (Fla. 1974).

31. *But see* 1979 Cal. Legis. Serv., ch. 832, § 1(b) (parents not liable for therapy to which minor consents).

32. *E.g.,* Nelson v. Hyne, 491 F.2d 351 (7th Cir. 1974), *cert. denied,* 417 U.S. 976 (1974); Morales v. Turman, 383 F. Supp. 52 (E.D. Tex. 1974), *rev'd on other grounds,* 535 F.2d 864 (5th Cir. 1976), *rev'd per curiam,* 430 U.S. 322 (1977); Martarella v. Kelley, 349 F. Supp. 575 (S.D. N.Y. 1972); Inmates of Boys' Training School v. Affleck, 346 F. Supp. 3154 (D.C. R.I. 1972).

33. Martarella v. Kelley, *supra* note 32.

34. Morales v. Turman, *supra* note 32.

35. Nelson v. Hyne, *supra* note 32; Martarella v. Kelley, *supra* note 32.

36. Inmates of Boys' Training School v. Affleck, *supra* note 32.

37. Id.

38. *See, e.g.,* McKeiver v. Pennsylvania, 403 U.S. 528 (1971) (juveniles denied the right to a jury trial in delinquency proceedings).

39. Morales v. Turman, *supra* note 32.

40. Nelson v. Hyne, *supra* note 32, at 358-59; Morales v. Turman, *supra* note 32, at 71.

41. *E.g.,* Martarella v. Kelley, *supra* note 32, at 599. It is important to note, however, that the Fourteenth Amendment applies only to governmental action. Thus, courts are unlikely to find private facilities in violation of the Constitution under any of the three theories just described.

42. 344 F. Supp. 373, 375 (M.D. Ala. 1972).

43. *Id.* at Appendix A.

44. *E.g.,* Rouse v. Cameron, 373 F.2d 451 (D.C. Cir. 1961).

45. *E.g.,* Morales v. Turman, *supra* note 32, at 88; Wyatt v. Stickney, *supra* note 42, at 385.

46. Morales v. Turman, *supra* note 32, at 89-92; Wyatt v. Stickney, *supra* note 52, at 385-86; Inmates of Boys' Training School v. Afflect, *supra* note 32, at 1369-70.

47. Morales v. Turman, *supra* note 32, at 88.

48. Wyatt v. Stickney, *supra* note 42, at 386.

49. Morales v. Turman, *supra* note 32, at 88.

50. Nelson v. Hyne, *supra* note 32, at 360; Wyatt v. Stickney, *supra* note 42, at 386.

51. *Supra* note 32 at 105.

52. 322 F. Supp. 473 (S.D.N.Y. 1970); *accord* Inmates of Boys' Training School v. Affleck, *supra* note 32, at 1366-67.

53. Lollis v. N.Y., *supra* note 52 at 482-83.

54. Morales v. Turman, *supra* note 32, at 84.

55. Inmates of Boys' Training School v. Afflect, *supra* note 32, at 1372.

56. Lollis v. N.Y., *supra* note 52, at 484.

57. *Supra* note 32 at 355.

58. *Id.* at 356-57; *cf.* U.S. ex rel. Wilson v. Coughlin, 472 F.2d 100 (7th Cir. 1973) (tranquilizers cannot be used for control or punishment).

59. *E.g.,* Knecht v. Ġillman, 488 F.2d 1136 (8th Cir. 1973).

60. *E.g.,* VA DEPT. OF MENTAL HEALTH AND MENTAL RETARDATION, RULES AND REGULATIONS TO ASSURE THE RIGHTS OF PATIENTS AND RESIDENTS OF HOSPITALS AND OTHER FACILITIES, § VI F(2) (1978).

61. Nelson v. Hyne, *supra* note 32, at 360; *see also* INST. OF JUDICIAL ADMINISTRATION - AM. BAR ASS'N., JUVENILE JUSTICE STANDARDS PROJECT, Standards Relating to Dispositions, Standard 4.1 and Commentary (1980).

62. Pub. L. 94-142, 20 U.S.C. §§ 1401-1461.

63. 16 Md. App. 209 (1973).

64. Melville v. Sabbatino, 30 Conn. 320 (1972).

65. *See, e.g.,* Lessard v. Schmidt, 349 F. Supp. 1078, (E.D. Wis. 1972), *vacated on other grounds,* 414 U.S. 473 (1974), *reheard,* 379 F. Supp. 1376 (E.D. Wis. 1974), *vacated,* 421 U.S. 957 (1975), *prior judgment reinstated,* 413 F. Sup. 1318 (E.D. Wis. 1976); Heryford v. Parker, 396 F.2d 393 (10th Cir. 1967); Hawks v. Lazaro, 157 W. Va. 417 (1974).

66. *See, e.g.,* Lessard v. Schmidt, *supra* note 65; Welsh v. Likins, 373 F. Supp. 487 (D. Minn. 1974); Hawks v. Lazaro, *supra* note 65.

67. *E.g.,* Rennie v. Klein, 476 F. Supp. 1294 (D.N.J. 1979).

68. 442 U.S. 584 (1979).

69. J.L. v. Parham, 412 F. Supp. 112 (M.D. Ga. 1976), *reversed and remanded sub nom.* Parham v. J.R., 442 U.S. 584 (1979); *cf.* Saville v. Treadway, 404 F. Supp. 430 (M.D. Tenn. 1974) (absence of procedural safeguards in "voluntary" commitment of mentally retarded juveniles violates the Due Process Clause of the Constitution).

70. 442 U.S. 640 (1979).

71. 459 F. Supp. 30 (E.D. Pa. 1978), *reversed and remanded,* 442 U.S. 640 (1979).

72. Institutionalized Juveniles, *supra* note 70, at 646.

73. *Id.* at 643, nn. 2-5.

74. MICH. STAT. ANN. § 330-1417 (1974).

75. TENN. CODE ANN. § 33-601 (1975), as amended.

76. *See generally* Parham v. J.R., *supra* note 68 (concurring and dissenting opinion).

77. Lessard v. Schmidt, *supra* note 65; Hawks v. Lazaro, *supra* note 65.

78. *See, e.g.,* Tarasoff v. Bd. of Regents, 17 Cal. 3d 425 (1976).

79. DEPT. OF HEALTH, EDUCATION AND WELFARE, CONFIDENTIALITY OF ALCOHOL AND DRUG PATIENT RECORDS, 42 C.F.R. 2 (1975).

80. Family Educational and Privacy Rights Act (Buckley Amendment), 20 U.S.C.A § 1232g (1974).

81. *E.g.,* VA. CODE ANN. § 54-325.2(d)(4) (Cum. Supp. 1979).

82. *E.g.,* ILL. STAT. ANN. c. 111 § 4504 (1980).

83. H.L. v. Matheson, *supra* note 23.

84. Tarasoff v. Bd. of Regents, *supra* note 78.

85. *See* McIntosh v. Milano, 168 N.J. Super. 466 (1979).

86. *E.g.,* Bellah v. Greenson, 81 Cal. App. 3d 614 (1978).

87. *E.g.,* CONN. GEN. STAT. ANN. §§ 52-14(c)(f) (1981).

88. The single exception was Justice Douglas's dissent in Wisconsin v. Yoder, *supra* note 9, at 245-46, n.3.

89. *Supra* note 71 at 610.

REFERENCES

American Psychological Association. *Ethical standards of psychologists.* Adopted by the Council of Representatives in January, 1981.

Bakan, D. Adolescence in America: From idea to social fact. In J. Kagan & R. Coles (Eds.), *Twelve to sixteen: Early adolescence.* New York: Norton, 1971.

Baumrind, D. Reciprocity: Development of prosocial behavior in children. *Educational Perspectives,* 1980, **19**(4), 3-9.

Coie, J.D., & Pennington, B.F. Children's perception of deviance and disorder. *Child Development,* 1976, **47**, 407-413.

Day, L., & Reznikoff, M. Social class, the treatment process, and parent's and children's expectations about child psychotherapy. *Journal of Clinical Child Psychology*, 1980, **9**, 195–198.

Dollinger, S.J., & Thelen, M.H. Children's perceptions of psychology. *Professional Psychology*, 1978, **9**, 117–126.

Dollinger, S.J., Thelen, M.H., & Walsh, M.L. Children's conceptions of psychological problems. *Journal of Clinical Child Psychology*, 1980, **9**, 191–194.

Ellis, J.W. Volunteering children: Commitment of minors to mental institutions. *California Law Review*, 1974, **62**, 840–916.

Ferleger, D. *Incarcerated juveniles—Why? An analysis of partial data submitted by defendants in response to interrogatories by plaintiffs.* In *Bartley v. Kremens*, Civil Action No. 72–2272 (U.S.D.C., E.D. Pa., September 17, 1973).

Goldstein, J., Freud, A., & Solnit, A.J. *Beyond the best interests of the child.* New York: Free Press, 1973.

Goldstein, J., Freud, A., & Solnit, A.J. *Before the best interests of the child.* New York: Free Press, 1979.

Grisso, T., & Vierling, L. Minors' consent to treatment: A developmental perspective. *Professional Psychology*, 1978, **9**, 412–427.

Holder, A.R. *Legal issues in pediatrics and adolescent medicine.* New York: Wiley, 1977.

Holmes, D.S., & Urie, R.G. Effects of preparing children for psychotherapy. *Journal of Consulting and Clinical Psychology*, 1975, **43**, 311–318.

Institute of Judicial Administration/ American Bar Association Juvenile Justice Standards Project. *Standards relating to dispositions.* Cambridge, Mass.: Ballinger, 1980.

Institute of Judicial Administration/ American Bar Association Juvenile Justice Standards Project. *Standards relating to juvenile records and information.* Cambridge, Mass.: Ballinger, 1980.

Koocher, G.P. Competence to consent: Psychotherapy. In G.B. Melton, G.P. Koocher, & M.J. Saks (Eds.), *Children's competence to consent,* New York: Plenum, 1983.

Levine, M., & Levine, A. *A social history of helping services: Court, clinic, school, and community.* New York: Appleton-Century-Crofts, 1970.

Lewis, C.C. A comparison of minors' and adults' pregnancy decisions. *American Journal of Orthopsychiatry*, 1980, **50**, 446–453.

Lewis, C.E. Decision-making related to health: When could/should children act responsibly? In G.B. Melton, G.P. Koocher, & M.J. Saks (Eds.), *Children's competence to consent.* New York: Plenum, 1983.

Melton, G.B. Children's participation in treatment planning: Psychological and legal issues. *Professional Psychology*, 1981, **12**, 246–252. (a)

Melton, G.B. Effects of a state law permitting minors to consent to psychotherapy. *Professional Psychology*, 1981, **12**, 647–654. (b)

Melton, G.B. Children's rights: Where are the children? *American Journal of Orthopsychiatry*, 1982, **52**, 530–538.

Melton, G.B. Decision-making by children: Psychological risks and benefits. In G.B. Melton, G.P. Koocher, & M.J. Saks (Eds.), *Children's competence to consent.* New York: Plenum, 1983.

Melton, G.B., & Lind, E.A. Procedural justice in family court: Does the adversary model make sense? In G.B. Melton (Ed.), *Legal reforms affecting child and youth services.* New York: Haworth, 1982.

Mnookin, R.H. Beyond kiddie libbers and child savers. *Journal of Clinical Child Psychology*, 1978, **7**, 163–167.

Note. Counseling the counselors: Legal implications of counseling minors without parental consent. *Maryland Law Review*, 1971, **31**, 332–354.

Novak, D.W. Children's reactions to emotional disturbance in imaginary peers. *Journal of Consulting and Clinical Psychology*, 1974, **42**, 462.

Novak, D.W. Children's responses to imaginary peers labeled as emotionally disturbed. *Psychology in the Schools*, 1975, **12**, 103–106.

Pilpel, H.F. Minors' rights to medical care. *Albany Law Review*, 1972, **36**, 462–487.

Rogers, C.M., & Wrightsman, L.S. Attitudes toward children's rights: Nurturance or self-determination. *Journal of Social Issues*, 1978, **34**(2), 59–68.

Rosen, C.E. The impact of an Open Campus program upon high school students' sense of control over their environment. *Psychology in the Schools*, 1977, **14**, 216–219.

Simmonds, D.W. Children's rights and family

dysfunction: "Daddy, why do I have to be the crazy one?" In G.P. Koocher (Ed.), *Children's rights and the mental health professions.* New York: Wiley, 1976.

Small, A.C., & Teagno, L. *A comparative study of children's and their parents' expectations of psychotherapy.* Paper presented at the meeting of the American Association of Psychiatric Services for Children, Chicago, November 1979.

Szasz, T.S. Critical reflections on child psychiatry. *Children and Youth Services Review,* 1979, **1,** 7–29.

Wadlington, W.L. Minors and health care: The age of consent. *Osgoode Hall Law Journal,* 1973, **11,** 115–125.

Weithorn, L.A. *Competency to render informed treatment decisions: A comparison of certain minors and adults.* Unpublished doctoral dissertation, University of Pittsburgh, 1980.

Weithorn, L.A. Developmental factors and competence to make informed treatment decisions. In G.B. Melton (Ed.), *Legal reforms affecting child and youth services.* New York: Haworth, 1982.

Weithorn, L.A. Involving children in decisions affecting their own welfare: Guidelines for professionals. In G.B. Melton, G.P. Koocher, & M.J. Saks (Eds.), *Children's competence to consent.* New York: Plenum, 1983.

Wexler, D.B. Token and taboo: Behavior modification, token economies, and the law. *California Law Review,* 1973, **61,** 81–109.

Wilson, J.P. *The rights of adolescents in the mental health system.* Lexington, Mass.: Lexington Books, 1978.

Wolfe, M. Childhood and privacy. In I. Altman & J.F. Wohlwill (Eds.), *Human behavior and environment: Advances in theory and research* (Vol. 3). New York: Plenum, 1979.

CHAPTER 56

The Forensic Connection

ROBERT GORDON, JEFFREY SIEGEL, AND JOY BENGFORT

The state of the art in contemporary psychology requires the health service provider to develop an awareness of his or her forensic responsibilities in order to develop the skills necessary to discharge them. This continuing education prescription is mandatory because few psychologists can constructively contribute to the administration of justice. This was not always the case. Until the second half of this century, the relationship between psychologists and the judicial system was replete with misunderstanding and conflict. Nor could psychologists agree among themselves whether forensic applications were either necessary or desirable.

In 1879, Professor Wilhelm Wundt set out to train the first psychologist in Leipzig, Germany. His orientation was experimental, purist, and rigid. In his laboratory, young Hugo Munsterberg sought to apply rudimentary concepts of empirical analysis of conscious experience to the resolution of legal issues (Boring, 1957). An example of this was his study of the perception of children as witnesses to various crimes in an effort to assess their accuracy. He discovered the testimony of children was generally honest though, not surprisingly, inaccurate.

The application of experimental psychology to the resolution of evidentiary issues was considered pseudophilosophical and even bizarre by Wundt. He summarily banished Munsterberg from his program. The brilliant psychologist, William James, learned of Munsterberg's plight and invited him to Harvard where together they founded one of the first psychological laboratories in America and one that specialized in child clinical issues.

If Wundt's attitude toward Munsterberg typified the reaction of early psychology to forensic application, then Judge Moore's (1908) attitude toward Munsterberg at the turn of the century typified the reaction of lawyers. "I would rather have Sherlock Holmes in the courtroom, than a psychologist," he penned. In part, he was angry about psychological impact in particular cases. Munsterberg had examined a teenager in Chicago who was charged with the crime of capital murder. The boy had signed a confession in a highly publicized trial. Munsterberg (1908) took the stand in the boy's defense and stated that his examination revealed that the boy's confession was false—it was motivated by an unconscious compulsion to confess (Reik, 1945). The community was outraged by the use of psychological testimony to attempt to free a defendent that the popular media had portrayed as guilty. Munsterberg was accused of practicing "yellow psychology."

The psychologists who followed Munsterberg to the witness stand in the following three decades did not fare better. They were viewed with suspicion and distrust. Their methods and language seemed strange and the validity of their clinical procedures were challenged. Not surprisingly, Dean Wigmore's classical multivolume treatise on the law of evidence relegates the psychologist's contribution to the resolution of legal issues to a footnote.

During the 1950s, American psychologists with forensic interests emerged from their hibernation of research and practice created by Munsterberg's debacle, only to be obscured once again by a seemingly significant piece of research. In 1954, a distinguished group of psychologists and attorneys at the University of Chicago (Committee on Judiciary, 1955) determined that seasoned trial lawyers were uninformed as to why and how a jury reaches a verdict. With the Court's permission, they surreptitiously bugged a jury room in Wichita, Kansas. Their rigorous analysis of the psychological process of small group decision making was presented at the Tenth Judicial Conference held in Estes Park, Colorado. It was heralded by the conferees as a breakthrough in forensic science. Back in Washington, the House on Unamerican Activities Committee took a different view. They issued subpoenas to the researchers to investigate their apparent attempt to subvert the American jury process (Gordon, 1968).

During the 1970s, a generation of psychologists and attorneys were trained by American Universities who were socialized in interdisciplinary strategies. Their painstaking, quiet, yet persistent effort at initiating forensic psychology seminars and forensic internships were successful. Their pioneering efforts were given official recognition by the American Psychological Association in 1980 when the Psychology-Law Division was established. At the same time, legal scholars introduced into traditional legal education innovative interdisciplinary courses, especially in the areas of family law, juvenile law, criminal law, and trusts and estates. Practicing lawyers not only encouraged psychologists to contribute to the resolution of legal issues through evaluation, reports, and testimony, they demanded it (Gordon, 1975). Psychological practitioners who chose not to work with legal cases discovered that the subpoena was indeed a most compelling invitation.

The purpose of this chapter is to define the forensic responsibilities of child psychologists, to describe the state of the art with regard to clinical forensic techniques, and to survey areas of jurisprudence where child psychologists may contribute to the administration of justice. Future developments and trends will also be anticipated. Finally, it is hoped that this chapter will serve as a springboard for future research in this emerging subspecialty for psychology (Gordon, 1976).

FORENSIC TECHNIQUES

What transforms a clinical case into a forensic challenge? It is legal issues accompanying the referral and the translation of clinical results (diagnosis and treatment) into practical terms so that a judge or jury can use them to achieve a just result. The clinical diagnosis of children and adolescents proceeds along well-established lines. The publication of DSM III provides psychologists with what seasoned trial attorneys believe is a nationally recognized standard for disagreement.

The well-prepared attorney understands nosology and will exploit its strengths and weaknesses in describing behavior to persuade the jury and court. The prudent psychologist presumes that the attorneys are as conversant with differential diagnosis as he or she is. Some clinicians expend great effort in formulating a dynamically precise diagnosis that would awe interns but that makes absolutely no sense to a court or jury. More perplexing than the sophist is the overly cautious courtroom psychologist who avoids entrapment by concluding that everything causes everything else, more or less, depending on your frame of reference. He or she, too, speaks to an empty jury box and peripherally observes the judge to be reading unrelated materials. Because judges, attorneys, and jurors are skeptical of psychological information based on clinical inference, the psychologist should present his or her findings in a clear, direct, and precise manner, even at the risk of oversimplification. Since clinical records are subject to a subpoena *duces tecum,* psychologists are sometimes embarrassed to discover that imaginative clinical insights may only please themselves. The casual notation can serve as a basis to impeach our credibility. Since interpretations are raw meat for the hungry attorney during cross-examination, every health service provider should review his note-taking system to adapt it to ultimate revelation in the courtroom drama.

Psychological testing, especially projective techniques, present severe problems for the psychologist on the witness stand. The Rorschach, TAT, Bender-Gestalt, and the Draw-a-Person tests are easily discredited by a socratic examiner. The psychologist who delights in the analysis of rich clinical data will appear foolish as he explains to the jury that a tree without leaves is a sign of depression rather than winter and that clapping clowns are evidence of homoeroticism rather than a wholesome, childhood fantasy. Even the MMPI and Weschler Intelligence Scales are problematic—the MMPI, because of the sampling group on which it was normed, and the Weschler, because its recipe for construction omits the essential ingredients for an effective life: motivation and creativity. The skillful attorney voraciously reads the Mental Measurement Yearbook (Buros, 1965) in order to raise pointed questions regarding test validity and reliability.

Like diagnostics and psychometrics, describing psychological treatment in court offers the clinician a unique challenge. For most lay persons simply do not understand when it's indicated, why it's indicated, and how one determines whether it's successful. The clinician must distinguish between long and short term intervention and also between different therapeutic styles and regimens, such as explaining the difference between dynamically oriented treatment and behavioral therapy. He or she must articulate the nexus between the diagnosis and the treatment of choice; the projected length of treatment and its cost effectiveness. Accountability and the balancing of risks are seminal concerns. The psychologist who recommends and runs will find his or her credibility diminished. Also, it is better for the psychologist to describe the limitations of psychological treatment on direct examination than to have them discovered during cross-examination.

Forensic clinical report writing is a separate skill wherein substance and form are treated differently than in writing generic clinical reports. As clinicians love their insights, attorneys adore words. Words have special and precise meaning and connotations in the law.

Insights can be brilliant but never precise. Yet each word of a clinical report is scrutinized as if psychological words also have precise meanings. Even the careful use of psychological terms can give way to psychobabble in the uncharted waters of legal applications. Our prescription is a report that is clear, informative, issue oriented, and conclusionary, written in lay terms.

The prudent psychologist learns the rudimentary principles of legal research, sufficient to address reports on testimony to the legal issues involved in the case. It is only then that the psychologist can contribute to the administration of justice. The most useful report is one that supports negotiation and settlement in civil cases and plea bargaining in delinquency matters. The most useful testimony is that which makes workable alternatives clear to the court. In this way, psychological participation is efficient and cost effective. The adversary system itself was designed to protect liberty, not necessarily to be efficient. Only kangaroo courts and firing squads are efficient.

Psychological reports and testimony, though subject to attack, can constructively and positively contribute to the administration of justice by presenting a different perspective, a clinical perspective. This perspective becomes an element of judgment for the court and jury along with the facts of the case and the applicable law and, therefore, enhances the likelihood of justice prevailing. This is the only social policy justification for the psychologist's participation. The following are principles of effective testimony prepared by Gordon (1980):

1. Understand and respect the Adversary System. The basis of the legal system is the search for truth via the discovery and explanation and understanding of relevant facts.

2. Effective testimony begins at the time of referral, not at the time of taking the stand. From the moment of referral, facts are being accumulated by the psychologist. Just as the Mental Status Examination starts with the patient's response to the clinician's "hello," so

the Forensic evaluation (and preparation for courtroom testimony) begins at the time of the psychologist's entry into the case.

3. Know and understand the legal issues involved in the case. Consult with the client's attorney to understand the questions at issue. Remember, the court is interested in testimony that is relevant to the specific case. All cases are different, just as all patients are different.

4. Be an advocate for justice, not for the person who is paying your fee. The psychologist, just as the lawyer and the judge, should be interested in the acquisition of fact and equitable resolution of conflict. The psychologist is in the court to shed light on the facts, the judge or jury is charged with decision making. The psychologist's honest testimony on the facts is the best way to aid in the administration of justice.

5. Develop a mental set for the courtroom atmosphere and its unique physical, interpersonal dimensions. Visit a courtroom while in session or vacant, and become familiar with physical spacing and placement of the judge, jury, attorneys, witness area and spectator areas. Remember that, in a jury trial, the psychologist will field questions from the attorneys but should direct his responses to the jury.

6. Be certain the subpoena which you have received is valid. The psychologist should be familiar with the rules of civil procedure of the state where he practices. These rules contain the proper information that should be included in a valid subpoena and subpoena duces tecum (a request by the court for records pertaining to a specific case).

7. Insist that the rules of protocol for calling expert witnesses are observed. Again, The Rules of Civil Procedure and consultation with the psychologist's attorney will be helpful. As an expert witness, the psychologist has certain rights and privileges. To ease the strain of testimony, understanding and clarification of these rules with the attorney that has requested your evaluation is heartily recommended.

8. Be thoroughly prepared. Preparation before testimony makes a courtroom appearance a positive, rewarding experience. The psychologist who understands his material, the reasons for testimony and the dynamics of the court contributes not only to justice, but to the field of psychology.

9. Don't overqualify your assessment or employ psychobabble. The information the psychologist offers is time limited on its scope. Only what he has observed or heard described can be dealt with. Everyone has their limitations, even psychologists and psychological assessment/evaluation methods. Simply and succinctly state the answer to the questions. Provide information that is requested; if more is needed or desired, the attorney will ask.

10. Understand the rules of courtroom procedure. Again, as in #5 and #7, the statutes regarding Rules of Civil Procedure and consultation with a competent attorney are the best learning aids.

11. Understand the Court's role in the proceedings. The court and the judge are impartial triers of fact, seeking only the truth. The court will not intervene on the psychologist's behalf (while a witness) unless it is felt that she/he is being inappropriately treated. Legal consultation again is helpful.

12. Anticipate the cross-examination. Cross-examination can be anxiety provoking. Remember that your statements, test protocols, conclusions, and recommendations are opinion-based testimony. Cross-examination seeks to rectify unclear or disputed points and to challenge opinions that the attorney feels are not in the best interest of his client.

Although effective courtroom testimony implies the acquisition of special skills, ultimately, the psychologist's credibility, honesty, and concern are more important.

AREAS OF CONTRIBUTION

1979 was designated as the International Year of the Child. This designation reflected a heightened state of awareness of and concern for children's rights. This awareness and concern promises to become a social policy periscope to the 1980s (Shore, 1979). Laws dealing with children are typically included in a family code or juvenile code promulgated by stae legislatures. Most states pattern their codes on uniform acts developed by working committees of the American Bar Association and various law reform commissions appointed by the President (4 American Law Reports 331, 1981). Family and juvenile codes are classified as civil law. However, the growing appreciation of children's rights has led to the evolution of constitutional guarantees for children, such as are typically reserved for criminal defendents (Gamson, 1978; Schel, 1979).

For more than a decade, psychologists have participated in court evaluations that are presented as evidence in child custody litigation. For an excellent review of a child's perception of divorce, consult Hetherington (1979). Readers are also encouraged to familiarize themselves with the Uniform Marriage and Divorce Act (1979), the Uniform Enforcement of Support Act (1980), and the Uniform Child Custody Jurisdiction Act (1979). Despite the adoption of no-fault divorce in most states, the issues of child conservatorship are hotly contested. Moreover, the question of what visitation regimen the noncustodial parent should have is frequently contested.

Prior to the 1970s, it was extraordinarily difficult for a father successfully to pursue a suit for custody. With precedent couched in Biblical law, conventional wisdom stated that a child, especially a young child, belonged with its mother. Only if a mother was retarded, a drug addict, or lascivious, would justification exist for custody being awarded to the father. The changing roles of men and women in society gave birth to the concept of father's rights, and organizations to support that cause are flourishing in most metropolitan areas (Hetherington, 1979; Salk, 1977). Even those parents who believe that their children would be better cared for by the other spouse are motivated by social and familial pressure and by guilt to pursue such litigation. Once the floodgates of litigation opened and the attorneys squared off, parental attitudes became polarized, Not surprisingly, hostility becomes exacerbated by formbook petitions that allege the most outrageous behaviors by the respondant. Both Mom and Dad fell victim in the crossfire of discrediting one another. In a study conducted in 1974, it was not surprising to learn that over 90 percent of the litigants in a family court considered themselves to be defendants even though half of them were clearly plaintiffs.

The superordinate concept guiding the disposition of all custody cases in all jurisdictions is the "best interest of the child." But what is the best interest, and who determines what that interest is (Mnookin, 1978)? Unable to apply Solomon's sword to a technological world in continuous flux, the courts turned to psychologists who, by conducting diagnostic examinations of the parents and children, would inform the court about compelling and relevant factors such as lifestyles; economic, social, and moral strengths; parenting skills; and parent-child rapport (Derdeyn, 1978; Duquette, 1978; Gardner, 1977; Henning & Oldham, 1977). It was the assessment of qualities such as these rather than evidence of psychopathology that the courts and jury would inquire about.

It is said that there is nothing new under the sun. However a variation of custodial arrangement called joint custody has been developed over the past few years with some success. The joint custody proposition elaborates a fundamental principle—each parent has equal access to and responsibility for the children. Given an opportunity and sufficient trust, each parent is expected to develop their own living style comparable with the care, residence, and needs of the child. Such arrangements, which still constitute a social experiment, vary from a child spending nine months with one parent and three months with the other, to dividing the week between residences. Although some of these arrangements seem unstable, children, as most psychologists will agree, are unusually adaptive and resilient. The joint custody arrangement clearly is superior to the traditional managing-possessory conservator arrangement in some cases.

It is always discouraging for the psychologist to learn that a parent has sought custody only in an effort to soften up the other spouse with regard to disposition of property. Nevertheless, this occurs. So it is more likely that each will insist on his or her day in court. Ironically, the child psychologist's success in assisting the court in litigated cases has contributed to litigation (Mnookin, 1978; Swerdlow, 1978). Consider the common scenario of mother with her psychologist, opposed by father and his psychologist. In a state of puzzlement, the court orders all parties to go to a third psychologist who everybody believes will be more objective. The battle of the experts highlights the limitations of our knowledge and the borders of our ethical principles.

A recent innovation is the single-parent conservatorship or adoption, which is recognized as a possible alternative to the traditional family unit. Today, social policy, rather than clinical diagnosis, determines the outcome of child custody suits. Most judges of district courts with jurisdictions over family matters are elected so that the passions and pressures of their constituencies must be recognized as well as their clients. Another recent innovation is the efforts by one parent to terminate all of the rights of the noncustodial parent. The reasons for such efforts vary, but mistreatment and abuse are prominent causes. A review of such cases can be found in a penetrating article by Judge Coleman writing in Wayne State Law Review (1980).

All family codes treat the issues of juvenile offenders. Typically, a juvenile is defined as a child, under the legal age of majority. This implies that the child is unable to care for his own best interests. In many juvenile cases, the psychologist will be requested to perform an evaluation and advise the court as to what disciplinary treatment strategies would work with reasonable psychological probability. The psychologist can also explain how children differ developmentally from adults and thus warrant special treatment.

During the first phase, the adjudication phase, the psychologist is asked by the courts, by the family, or by the district attorney, to perform a psychological study (Melton, 1978b). In more affluent counties, such studies are routine. During the adjudication phase, the study is conducted as soon as the competency question is raised. In juvenile law, competency may become an issue at three different times during the proceeding. First, is the juvenile competent to stand trial? In most states, this is defined as whether the juvenile has the mental capacity to understand the nature of the charges against him or her, the nature of the proceedings, and whether the juvenile can advise and consult with his or her attorney in preparation of his or her case. This is called *competency to proceed.*

The second time the competency question may be raised is when the court considers the act itself. In most states, competency under this condition is defined as whether the child suffered from a mental disease or defect so that the child was unable to distinguish right from wrong or was unable to conform his or her behavior to the requirements of the law.

A psychologist may also be asked to evaluate a child who has committed multiple minor, delinquent acts, and the court has determined that the child is in need of supervision. This is a recently evolved concept that describes the youngster who is uncontrollable by his parents or by basic institutions within the community such as school and church. Yet, such children have committed only minor delinquent acts, per se. Readers are encouraged to familiarize themselves with their own state's Family and Juvenile Codes, as well as the Uniform Juvenile Law Sections of Corpus Juris Secundum and the American Law Reports. All such codes are located in university and county law libraries.

In most jurisdictions, a delinquent act can range from capital murder, aggravated assault and robbery, to truancy and runaway. The juvenile process is generally bifurcated. This means that the judgment of whether the child engaged in a delinquent act is considered first. Then, if delinquent behavior is found, a disposition phase ensues. The second phase or disposition phase is circumscribed by the concern for how best to help the child and yet protect society. Most states ascribe to the juvenile the rights of a criminal defendant (see Gamson, 1978) such as the right to trial, the right to counsel, and the right to cross-examine witnesses. The child psychologist can meaningfully contribute to the administration of juvenile justice as an advocate of the child (Sobel, 1979).

The child adjudicated to be unfit to proceed is typically committed to a state or private mental hospital by reference to the procedures of the state's civil commitment statutes. Most states define civil commitment in terms of whether the youngster is suffering from a mental disease or defect such that he or she is a danger to self or others. Typically, temporary insanity produced by drugs or alcohol will not support a competency defense. Nor will delinquent acts that are solely the result of a psychopathic personality. As one alert youngster exclaimed at the end of his examination, "I told you I was remorseful, didn't I?" Nor can a young person be sentenced to a state youth council or reformatory when he or she is found incompetent. He or she must first be civilly committed. Such incompetency is also referred for treatment.

As noted earlier, the second phase of juvenile law is called the disposition phase. It is here that the psychologist will make recommendations to the court either for incarceration, probation with treatment, family counseling, referral to community services, or any other treatment-discipline-rehabilitation program available. Unhappily, finances often play a determining role in fulfilling such recommendations. For particularly heinous offenses, the youngster may be certified as an adult and therefore subject to the adult criminal process. Typically, the crimes of rape, arson, and murder will lead to a certification proceeding. But crimes against property except arson generally will not. During the certification proceeding, the court will consider the maturity of the child, the nature of the offense, and the child's capacity for rehabilitation. If certified and found guilty, the child may be incarcerated as are adult felons in a state penitentiary. Often, youngsters who abuse drugs become involved in the felony type offenses that lead to certification despite a lack of premeditation. The Court again must attempt to balance society's needs with the best interest of the child.

Psychologists also participate in the legal system because we treat kids who are victims

of crime. Other than treason, few categories of crime evoke as much distress and community ire as crimes against children (Starr, 1979). Unhappily, the most common crime is abuse. Child abuse is multifaceted. It can range from breaking bones and inflicting cigarette burns to creating subtle personality imbalances through the intentional elitication of mental distress by a neurotic or schizophrenic parent. All states have adopted statutes that protect the child against physical and mental abuse. Some jurisdictions provide a central registry for the storing of complaints that some complain is an invasion of privacy because of state open records laws. Prior to the adoption of modern child abuse statutes, the physician and teacher were the front line of defense against child abuse, but they often were afraid to report because of the fear of suit. Today, most statutes provide immunity from civil liability for violating confidentiality by reporting child abuse (4 American Law Reports 802).

The emergency room physician may discover on x-ray differential healing of fractures and breaks. The teacher may discover marks or welts. The psychologist may observe depression or learn of suicidal ideation. Since many disturbed families send a representative for treatment, the psychologist has an excellent vantage point. As one abused preadolescent girl said in a psychologist's office when asked how she felt about her mother, "If it weren't for my mother, I wouldn't be here. Then again, if it weren't for my mother I wouldn't be here."

Recently, civil libertarians have raised a note of alarm about welfare departments that take children away from parents who are maliciously or mistakenly reported by neighbors for child abuse. Such parents undergo fretful ordeals involving thousands of dollars of legal expenses and sleepless nights until their children are finally returned. Not only are false accusations commonplace against parents and babysitters but also against brothers and sisters. The battered child syndrome is well recognized but not so the battered sibling syndrome. The latter includes tragic cases where a jealous sibling has abused or murdered a brother or sister, a melancholy phenomenon that explains at least some crib deaths.

Childnapping is a crime of passionate community concern as best dramatized by the Lindberg kidnapping. Childnapping's mildest form is the taking of a child by a noncustodial parent without the conservator's permission (66 Virginia Law Review 256, 1978). Nevertheless, childnapping by a parent elicits irreversible trauma for the child, yet the crime is seldom prosecuted because the aggrieved parent must ultimately face the child with an explanation as to his or her role in the incarceration of the other parent. In one case, a child was surreptitiously taken from his mother and hidden for over three years by his father, who, by changing his social security number, driver's license, job, and domicile, was able to disappear. The child was finally discovered and returned. But three years of intense programming left the child emotionally scarred and hostile toward his aggrieved mother. In such cases, as well as those involving teenagers drawn into cult groups, a lay therapist called a "deprogrammer" is often thought to be skilled in reversing the damage of the brainwashed youngster.

The authors do not wish to imply that "deprogramming" is the only treatment choice. Those persons involved in such a situation should consult an attorney regarding the specific legal situation and a competent mental health professional. Those persons who have experience in the needed area can often be located via local area psychological or psychiatric societies.

Sexual abuse of a child is one of the few universal taboos in both modern and primitive societies. Typically, the sexual abuse of a female child is at the hand of a disturbed father or stepfather. However, older brothers, uncles, friends of the family can also invade a child's physical privacy. Analysts have claimed that a passive and inadequate mother plays a significant role in creating the circumstances that allow the abuse. Frequently, disclosure of the crimes comes years after the fact and only then when the female child wishes to receive help over feelings of irrational guilt. Unhappily, malicious claims of sexual abuse presented to courts during child custody issues typically involve children 3–5 years of age who are inarticulate and subject to suggestion. Related to this are the child pornography cases where both parents may abuse the child through the incentive of economic gain (66 Virginia Law Review 253, 1978).

The psychologist who treats children who are victims of crime is faced with a legal and ethical dilemma. He or she is charged with the affirmative duty to report such crimes and yet may be sued for malpractice for the violation of confidentiality (Gordon, 1980; Paulson, 1978). Many clinicians argue that to report a crime is to lose the opportunity for treatment. So psychologists are increasingly concerned that Miranda type warnings should be given to certain patients at the time of the first interview to inform them of their rights despite its untoward implications for trust and rapport. These rights may include, in criminal cases, that information the client provides during the evaluation can be reported to the court, via the psychologist's report or testimony. In other dealings with juveniles, statements regarding confidentiality of communication and potential danger to others should be made clear to the client and his or her parents or guardian.

Other important areas of contribution for the clinician are delineated. There are issues regarding whether an impartial jury can be found to sit in judgment of emotionally ladened events; and the capacity of a youngster to contract, to hold or convey land, and to marry. Most states recognize legal majority to begin at 17 years of age. However, many states will permit a minor to enter into a binding contract as long as the contract is reaffirmed when the young person becomes a legal adult. In the case of marriages, most states permit marriages with parental consent to occur from the age of 14. A voidable marriage is one in which marriage is legally binding providing no one contests it. Trust instruments often hold real property for children until they are of legal majority. However, adults may still be subject to such trusts where concern about their maturity is raised. Such trusts are called spendthrift trusts. Parents or grandparents may create such trusts to insulate the trusts' corpus from legal separations and divorces of their beneficiaries. Psychological testimony is probative on all these points.

When a child is found to be irresponsible or retarded, a guardianship proceeding may ensue. The purpose of the guardianship is to place the legal responsiblity for the child in the hands of someone other than a parent or to administer an estate of an adult person believed to be retarded or mentally ill. In one case, the senior author examined a patient who was placed in guardianship by her brother after a deep depression following an unrequited love affair. After the brother died, the lady asserted her competency only to discover that her brother had become guardian over a fortune that she had inherited.

Other civil cases are resolved through psychological participation. A tort is a civil wrong, usually the result of negligence, such as an automobile or industrial accident. The elements of a tort are: that an act occurred; that an act constituted negligence; that the negligence produced an injury, and, but for the negligence of the defendant, the injury would not have occurred (Prosser, 1941). In such cases, the psychologist is asked to examine an injured child or teen in order to describe his injury in psychological terms, to explain its etiology, and to project a prognosis for treatment and rehabilitation. In one case, an 8-year-old girl fell down an elevator shaft and miraculously survived by clinging to conveyor ropes. In addition to severe dominant hand injuries, the child developed phobias with regard to elevator use that generalized to escalators and other vehicles. In another case, a young girl was scalded when a hot water pipe burst near the apartment complex where she lived. The pipes had been in need of repair for some time, and, as a result, the girl received third-degree burns over 75 percent of her body. Psychological examination documented the injuries, prognosis, and treatment of choice and played a significant role in the jury's determination of damages. For gross negligence, punitive damages may be awarded.

A controversy persists since the time of common law as to whether a plaintiff ought to recover damage for mental distress where there is no physical injury. The tort of mental distress relies entirely on psychic injury and is best explained in court by properly trained mental health professionals (Capital Law Review 281, 1980; Gordon, 1970a, 1970b). In one case, a child successfully sued for the tort of mental distress when she observed her mother struck down by a hit-and-run driver. The symptoms described by the senior author in court were nightmares and phobia, and a final diagnosis of posttraumatic syndrome was made. The court gave the child a substantial award. Nevertheless, other jurists have voiced the opinion that to permit a recovery from mental distress where no physical impact occurred is to open the floodgates to litigation.

Related to this tort is a suit for wrongful death. A psychological autopsy may be requested in which it is important to reconstruct the life of a child or teenager in order to determine whether the death was by accident or suicide. This forensic function is performed by a psychologist in those cases in which insurance precludes recovery when death results within two years of the issuance of the policy and when the young person is designated as the insured. The autopsy is performed by interviewing parents, extended family, friends, teachers, ministers, and others, as well as analyzing behavior samples, such as writing, in an effort to reconstruct the deceased's personality profile. This type of evaluation is based on the clinician's knowledge of child and adolescent personality development. The understanding of these areas is essential to perform the psychological autopsy of a child.

An emerging area of concern of constitutional experts is the issue of the child's right to treatment (Melton, 1978a; Mnookin, 1978). In the course of a custody determination or personal injury case, the psychologist may discover emotional problems requiring treatment. The child's parents or guardian may refuse to seek professional help. Cases are common in which a teenager desires treatment for an unwanted pregnancy or a conflict with parents but parents refuse to respond. When the parents refuse, the psychologist must determine if the child's emotional or cognitive state is such that deprivation of treatment would have an irreversibly harmful effect. Even then, the psychologist risks being sued when he conducts a preliminary interview with a child without parental consent. More problematic is determining whether a noncustodial parent has the right to present a child for treatment without the consent of the managing conservator. In most states' Family Codes, the specific rights and duties of the managing conservator (parent with custody,) and possessory conservator (parent without custody, who has specified visitation) are elaborated. The clinician should consult these codes in order to provide the parent (guardian) with the proper information so that the requested examination is legal and appropriate.

The psychologist can play an important role in today's expanding judicial system. To be effective in contributing to the administration of justice, the competent mental health professional should insist on meeting with the attorney who refers a case so that he has an understanding of his specific functions. He must understand, first, the reason for the referral, the nature of the presenting problem, and, second, the nature of the specific legal questions of the case. The psychologist should then consult the statutes of the state so that if there are questions they can be discussed before court.

The court welcomes those that are informed and knowledgeable regarding the issues at hand. Succinct, plain-spoken, truthful answers will not only serve the intent of the court to seek the truth but also further the judicial system's respect for psychology.

CARTOGRAPHY

If constitutional scholars determine that a child has the right to treatment (Birnbaum, 1960), then it can also be argued that a child has the right not to be treated (Melton, 1978a). Thousands of children are coerced by their parents each year into an unwanted therapeutic relationship. In determining whether

there shall be a right to be left alone, the courts must evaluate the role of the psychologist in society. Is the psychologist a helping agent whose primary responsibility is to his or her patient, or is the psychologist a social police officer who treats those who are troublesome and poorly adjusted? And, if the latter is true, does not the reflection of psychology in America frighteningly resemble that of Soviet psychology in which young people with antistate views are treated with psychotherapy?

Additional concerns for the future of forensic child psychology involve the evolution of international law, including space travel, and genetic engineering and research (Gordon, 1970). What will be the legal status of conservatorship during space travel? What state or federal court or international forum will have jurisdiction over crimes committed by children and against children in space? Currently, there is a lack of uniform cooperation between states and countries with regard to such issues. International tribunals such as the United Nations and the World Court at The Hague have competent judges but no capacity for enforcing orders. Who will monitor psychological research involving children? Can the principles developed at Nuremberg and APA. guidelines insure respect for human subjects? How will the paternity of testtube babies be determined, and what will be the relationship of such children to hereditary mothers, to carrier mothers, and to nurturing mothers? What names will the babies carry? What laws will evolve to protect them and their legitimacy? The authors believe that psychologists have a responsibility and opportunity to share their knowledge that will assist the courts, legislatures, and Congress in resolving these vital issues and thereby contribute to the administration of justice.

Everyone who has
exchanged glances
with a child
cares about
the future
of our world.

The glance
defines
a silent trust.

REFERENCES

1 American Law Reports 4th 38 (1980)

4 American Law Reports 4th 331 (1981)

Birnbaum, M. The right to treatment. *American Bar Association Journal*, 1960, **46**, 499–503.

Boring, E. *A history of experimental psychology*. New York: Appleton-Century-Crofts, 1957.

Buros, O.K. *The mental measurement yearbook*. New Jersey: Gryphon, 1965.

Capital Law Review 281 (1980)

Cincinnati Law Review 615 (1980)

Committee on Judiciary. Recording on Jury deliberations. *Pursuant to S. Res*, 1955, **58**, 1–127.

35 Corpus Juris Secundum 935

43 Corpus Juris Secundum 63

Derdeyn, A.P. Child custody: A reflection of cultural change. *Journal of Clinical Child Psychology*, 1978, **3**, 169–172.

Diagnostic statistical manual of mental disorders (3rd ed.). The American Psychiatric Association, 1981.

Duquette, D.N. Child custody decision-making: The lawyer-behavioral scientist interface. *Journal of Clinical Child Psychology*, 1978, **3**, 192–195.

Gamson, M.A. A delinquent's dilemma: Child advocacy versus appropriate treatment. *Journal of Clinical Child Psychology*, 1978, **3**, 168.

Gardner, R.A. Children of divorce: Some legal and psychological considerations. *Journal of Clinical Child Psychology*, 1977, **2**, 3–6.

Gibson, G.G., & Risher, M.J. *By her own admission*. New York: Doubleday, 1977.

Gordon, R. A study in forensic psychology: Petit jury verdicts as a function of the number of jury members. *Dissertation Abstracts*, 1968, **26**(3), 1161-B.

Gordon, R. Superordinate goals in space law. *Baylor Law Review*, 1970, **21**, 520–527.

Gordon, R. Tort liability of the research psychologist. *American Psychologist*, 1970, **25**, 90–191. (a)

Gordon, R. Mental distress in psychological research. *Baylor Law Review*, 1970, **21**, 520–527. (b)

Gordon, R. *Forensic psychology*. Tucson: Lawyers & Judges Publishing, 1975.

Gordon, R. Applications of psychology to law. *Psychology and Law Review*, 1976, **2**.

Gordon, R. The psychologist's role in the juvenile process. In W. Steele (Ed.), *Criminal law*. Austin: The Texas Bar Association Press, 1976.

Gordon, R. *Changing channels*. Dallas: Wilmington, 1979.

Gordon, R. *How to avoid malpractice*. An Audio Publication. Dallas: Wilmington, 1980.

Gordon, R. *How to present courtroom testimony*. An Audio Publication. Dallas: Wilmington, 1980.

Gordon, R., & Temerlin, M.K. Forensic psychology: The judge and jury. *Judicature*, 1969, **52**, 328–333.

Henning, J.S., & Oldham, J.T. Children of divorce: Legal and psychological crises. *Journal of Clinical Child Psychology*, 1977, **2**, 55–58.

Hetherington, E.M. Divorce: A child's perspective. *American Psychologist*, 1979, **10**, 851–858.

Kaplan, H., Freedman, A., & Sadlock, B. (Eds.). *Comprehensive textbook of psychiatry III*. Baltimore: Williams & Wilkins, 1980.

Melton, G.B. Children's right to treatment. *Journal of Clinical Child Psychology*, 1978, **3**, 200–202. (a)

Melton, G.B. The psychologist's role in juvenile and family law. *Journal of Clinical Child Psychology*, 1978, **3**, 189–191. (b)

Mnookin, R. Children's rights: Beyond kiddie libbers and child savers. *Journal of Clinical Child Psychology*, 1978, **3**, 163–167.

Moore, C. Yellow psychology. *Law Notes*, 1908, **11**, 125.

Munsterberg, H. *On the witness stand*. New York: McClure, 1908.

Paulson, M.J. Incest and sexual molestation: Clinical and legal issues. *Journal of Clinical Child Psychology*, 1978, **3**, 177–180.

Prosser, W.L. *Handbook of the law of torts*. St. Paul: West, 1941.

Reik, T. *The compulsion to confess*. New York: Farrar, Straus, & Udahy, 1945.

Salk, L. On the custody rights of fathers in divorce. *Journal of Clinical Child Psychology*, 1977, **2**, 49–50.

Shore, M.F. Legislation, advocacy, and the rights of children and youth. *American Psychologist*, 1979, **34**, 1017–1019.

Sobel, S.B. Psychology and the juvenile justice system. *American Psychologist*, **34**, 1029–1023.

Starr, R.H. Child abuse. *American Psychologist,* 1979, **34,** 872-878.

Swerdlow, E.L. Mental health services available to the bench and bar to assist in resolving problems relating to custody and visitation in family law cases. *Journal of Clinical Child Psychology,* 1978, **3,** 174–176.

Uniform Child Custody Jurisdiction Act. 4328 (1979)

Uniform Interstate Compact on Juveniles. 113

Uniform Marriage and Divorce Act. 1 (1979)

Uniform Reciprocal Enforcement of Support Act. 100 (1980)

66 Virginia Law Review 253 (1978)

66 Virginia Law Review 256 (1978)

26 Wayne Law Review 315 (1980)

Author Index

Subject Index

Psychology and Psychiatry in Courts and Corrections: Controversy and Change
  by Ellsworth A. Fersch, Jr.

Restricted Environmental Stimulation: Research and Clinical Applications
  by Peter Suedfeld

Personal Construct Psychology: Psychotherapy and Personality
  edited by Alvin W. Landfield and Larry M. Leitner

Mothers, Grandmothers, and Daughters: Personality and Child Care in
Three-Generation Families
  by Bertram J. Cohler and Henry U. Grunebaum

Further Explorations in Personality
  edited by A. I. Rabin, Joel Aronoff, Andrew M. Barclay, and Robert A. Zucker

Hypnosis and Relaxation: Modern Verification of an Old Equation
  by William E. Edmonston, Jr.

Handbook of Clinical Behavior Therapy
  edited by Samuel M. Turner, Karen S. Calhoun, and Henry E. Adams

Handbook of Clinical Neuropsychology
  edited by Susan B. Filskov and Thomas J. Boll

The Course of Alcoholism: Four Years After Treatment
  by J. Michael Polich, David J. Armor, and Harriet B. Braiker

Handbook of Innovative Psychotherapies
  edited by Raymond J. Corsini

The Role of the Father in Child Development (Second Edition)
  edited by Michael E. Lamb

Behavioral Medicine: Clinical Applications
  by Susan S. Pinkerton, Howard Hughes, and W. W. Wenrich

Handbook for the Practice of Pediatric Psychology
  edited by June M. Tuma

Change Through Interaction: Social Psychological Processes of Counseling and
Psychotherapy
  by Stanley R. Strong and Charles D. Claiborn

Drugs and Behavior (Second Edition)
  by Fred Leavitt

Handbook of Research Methods in Clinical Psychology
  edited by Philip C. Kendall and James N. Butcher

A Social Psychology of Developing Adults
  by Thomas O. Blank

Women in the Middle Years: Current Knowledge and Directions for Research and Policy
  edited by Janet Zollinger Giele

Loneliness: A Sourcebook of Current Theory, Research and Therapy
  edited by Letitia Anne Peplau and Daniel Perlman

Hyperactivity: Current Issues, Research, and Theory (Second Edition)
  by Dorothea M. Ross and Sheila A. Ross

Review of Human Development
  *edited by Tiffany M. Field, Aletha Huston, Herbert C. Quay, Lillian Troll,
  and Gordon E. Finley*

Agoraphobia: Multiple Perspectives on Theory and Treatment
  edited by Dianne L. Chambless and Alan J. Goldstein

The Rorschach: A Comprehensive System, Volume III: Assessment of Children and Adolescents
  by John E. Exner, Jr. and Irving B. Weiner

Handbook of Play Therapy
  edited by Charles E. Schaefer and Kevin J. O'Connor

Adolescent Sexuality in a Changing American Society: Social and Psychological Perspectives
for the Human Service Professions (Second Edition)
  by Catherine S. Chilman

Failures in Behavior Therapy
  edited by Edna B. Foa and Paul M.G. Emmelkamp